SYMBOLS AND UNITS OF PHYSICAL QUANTITIE

QUANTITY	SYMBOL*	UNITS	QUANTITY	SYMBOL	UNITS
Acceleration	$\mathbf{a}$	m/s^2	Entropy	S	J/K
Angle	θ, ϕ	rad	Force	$\mathbf{F}$	N
Angular acceleration	$\boldsymbol{\alpha}$	$rad/s^2, s^{-2}$	Frequency	f	Hz
Angular frequency, angular			Heat	Q	J
speed, angular velocity	$\omega, \boldsymbol{\omega}$	$rad/s, s^{-1}$	Heat flow	H	J/s
Angular momentum	$\mathbf{L}$	$kg \cdot m^2/s$	Inductance	L	H
Atomic number	Z		Intensity	$I, S, \mathbf{S}$	W/m^2
Capacitance	C	F	Magnetic field	$\mathbf{B}$	T
Charge	q, Q, e	C	Magnetic flux	ϕ_B	$T \cdot m^2$
Charge density			Mass	m, M	kg
Line	λ	C/m	Mass number	A	
Surface	σ	C/m^2	Molar specific heat	C_V, C_P	$J/mol \cdot K$
Volume	ρ	C/m^3	Momentum	$\mathbf{p}$	$kg \cdot m/s$
Conductivity	σ	$\Omega^{-1} \cdot m^{-1}$	Period	T	s
Current	I	A	Power	P	W
Current density	$\mathbf{J}$	A/m^2	Pressure	P	Pa
Density	ρ	kg/m^3	Resistance	R	Ω
Dielectric constant	κ		Resistivity	ρ	$\Omega \cdot m$
Dipole moment, electric	$\mathbf{p}$	$C \cdot m$	Rotational inertia	I	$kg \cdot m^2$
Dipole moment, magnetic	$\boldsymbol{\mu}$	$A \cdot m^2$	Temperature	T	K
Distance, displacement,	$x, y, z, s, d,$		Time	t	s
length, position	$\ell, w, h, \mathbf{r}$	m	Torque	$\boldsymbol{\tau}$	$N \cdot m$
Electric field	$\mathbf{E}$	N/C, V/m	Specific heat	c	$J/kg \cdot k$
Electric flux	ϕ, ϕ_E	$N \cdot m^2/C$	Speed, velocity	$v, \mathbf{v}$	m/s
Electric potential	V	V	Volume	V	m^3
Electromotive force	$\mathscr{E}$	V	Wavelength	λ	m
Energy	E, U, K	J	Wavenumber	k	m^{-1}
			Work	W	J

*Boldface indicates vector quantities.

TRIGONOMETRY

Definition of angle (in radians): $\theta = \frac{s}{r}$

2π radians in complete circle
1 radian $\simeq 57.3° = 2.06$ arc sec

TRIGONOMETRIC FUNCTIONS

$\sin\theta = \frac{y}{r}$

$\cos\theta = \frac{x}{r}$

$\tan\theta = \frac{\sin\theta}{\cos\theta} = \frac{y}{x}$

THE GREEK ALPHABET

	UPPERCASE	LOWERCASE
Alpha	A	α
Beta	B	β
Gamma	Γ	γ
Delta	Δ	δ
Epsilon	E	ε
Zeta	Z	ζ
Eta	H	η
Theta	Θ	θ
Iota	I	ι
Kappa	K	κ
Lambda	Λ	λ
Mu	M	μ
Nu	N	ν
Xi	Ξ	ξ
Omicron	O	o
Pi	Π	π
Rho	P	ρ
Sigma	Σ	σ
Tau	T	τ
Upsilon	Y	υ
Phi	Φ	ϕ
Chi	X	χ
Psi	Ψ	ψ
Omega	Ω	ω

248

20788-8AR

Physics

A marvelous blend of readability and fact, of insight and history, of graphs and pictures, of physics-physics and of physics in the world around. A tremendous piece of work, well done.

John Archibald Wheeler
Princeton University

Physics

For Scientists and Engineers

Third Edition

Richard Wolfson

Middlebury College

Jay M. Pasachoff

Williams College

ADDISON-WESLEY

An imprint of Addison Wesley Longman, Inc.

Reading, Massachusetts · Menlo Park, California · New York · Harlow, England
Don Mills, Ontario · Sydney · Mexico City · Madrid · Amsterdam

On the cover: Optical fibers transmit information in the form of light.

The fiber optics story—told in more detail on page 926—is one of growth of an enabling technology connecting the peoples of the world in a global information system. Fiber optics form the backbone of the global Internet, intercontinental telephone, and, increasingly, local communications. Fiber-optic links are the superhighways that carry the deluge of data, voice, and images that are the currency of the information revolution.

Fiber-optic technology calls on many areas of physics. A solid understanding of electromagnetism and optics has been critical in the field of optic development. Materials science challenges include the fabrication of glass fiber so clear that a kilometer-long piece is as transparent as a window pane. Electrical engineering and solid-state physics are essential in the opto-electronic devices—miniature lasers and high-speed, light-sensitive diodes—that translate fiber-optic signals to and from the world of conventional electronics.

Acquisitions Editor	Sami Iwata
Publisher	Robin J. Heyden
Market Developer	Andy Fisher
Director of Marketing	Stacy Treco
Channel Marketing Manager	Gay Meixel
Publishing Associate	Bridget Biscotti Bradley
Developmental Editor	Catherine Flack
Production Editor	Joan Marsh
Manufacturing Supervisor	Holly Bisso
Photo Researcher	Kathleen Cameron
Design and Production Coordination	Elm Street Publishing Services, Inc.
Illustrators	Precision Graphics
Cover Photograph	© Image Bank
Composition and Film	Interactive Composition Corporation
Cover Printer	Lehigh Press
Printer and Binder	World Color Corporation

Library of Congress Cataloging-in-Publication Data

Wolfson, Richard.
    Physics for scientists and engineers / Richard Wolfson, Jay M.
  Pasachoff. — 3rd ed.
        p.   cm.
  Includes index.
  ISBN 0-0321-3571-2
  1. Physics.   I. Pasachoff, Jay M.   II. Title.
QC21.2.W653   1999   98-45265
530—dc21   CIP
        7 8 9 10 QWV 03

Brief Contents

Part 5

Optics   915

Part 6

Modern Physics   1007

Appendixes

Contents

Preface

PHYSICS: CHALLENGE AND SIMPLICITY

Physics is fundamental. To understand physics is to understand how the world works, both at the everyday level and on scales of time and space so small and large that they defy intuition.

To the student, physics can be at once fascinating, challenging, subtle, and yet simple. Physics fascinates with its applications throughout science and engineering and in its revelation of unexpected phenomena like superconductivity, black holes, and chaos. It challenges with the need for precise thinking and skillful application of mathematics. Physics can be subtle, especially in describing phenomena at odds with everyday intuition. Most importantly, physics is simple. Its few fundamental laws are succinct, yet they encompass a universe of natural phenomena and technological devices.

GOALS OF THIS BOOK

This text is for science and engineering students. Its main goals are:

- to help students develop an understanding of the physical universe at its most fundamental level
- to explore a wide range of physics applications in science, technology, and everyday life
- to develop students' analytical and quantitative skills as applied to problems in science and engineering

The standard version of this text covers the full sequence of calculus-based university physics, and the extended version adds seven chapters on modern physics.

ORGANIZATION

The book is organized into six parts. Part 1 (Chapters 2 through 14) develops the basics of mechanics. Part 2 (Chapters 15 through 18) applies mechanics to the study of oscillations, waves, and fluids. Part 3 (Chapters 19 through 22) covers thermodynamics. Part 4 (Chapters 23–34) deals with electricity and magnetism. Part 5 (Chapters 35 through 37) treats optics. Part 6 (Chapters 38 and 39) briefly introduces relativity and quantum physics. Part 6 of the extended version (Chapters 38 through 45) expands the coverage of modern physics and its applications to atoms, molecules, and the solid state; nuclear physics and its applications; and particle physics and cosmology. Each part ends with a set of Cumulative Problems that synthesize concepts from the chapters in that part.

Distinguishing Features of the Third Edition

This third edition continues to hone the text and illustrations for clarity and precision, and to ensure that physics is tied closely with the latest in applications that are scientifically exciting and relevant to the student's everyday experience or future professional activities. Below we detail the many changes we've made, as well as describing new and continuing features designed to help students learn.

Improvements in Content This revision includes many substantial changes and improvements, most of which were suggested by instructors who have used the text or reviewed the manuscript. We've also added new pedagogical features to help develop both conceptual and quantitative understanding, and to test students' understanding of subtle concepts. Here are some of the more significant changes we've implemented in this edition.

- We extensively rewrote Chapters 5 (Force and Motion) and 6 (Using Newton's Laws) to account for the results of new research in physics education, especially the Force Concept Inventory.
- We substantially reorganized a number of other chapters to enhance the clarity and logical structure. For example, readers will find the presentations of magnetism and of physical optics much clearer due to chapter reorganization in this new edition. In all chapters, significant rewriting and art revisions improve clarity and provide tie-ins with preceding material.
- We revised the problem sets to include more "real-world" problems and a better balance of easy, multi-step, and challenging problems. In each chapter, up to 20 percent of the problems are new.
- A new category of "annotated figures" links text and art, using captions within the figure to guide students through complex concepts.
- A new feature, **Got It!** boxes, provide conceptual and largely non-quantitative reinforcement of students' understanding.
- The new **Math Toolbox** feature presents important mathematical tools separately from the main text.
- We have integrated *ActivPhysics*—the comprehensive simulation and visualization software—throughout the book, to provide a valuable option for both instructors and students. *ActivPhysics* helps students explore the major concepts from all parts of physics. Students can make predictions and test assumptions by changing variables and running the simulations. *ActivPhysics* references in the text, and icons in the margin, are strategically placed at common student trouble spots. Used in the classroom, lab, or for self-study, *ActivPhysics* will help the student develop imagery and intuition, and will reinforce the student's understanding of basic physics.
- We've updated for new scientific discoveries and technological developments, including the finding that neutrinos have mass, advances in superconductivity, and fiber optic technology, and many others.

Other features carry over from the second edition with significant revisions and improvements. These include

Applications and Examples A rich array of practical and up-to-date applications illustrates the use of physics principles in both technology and in natural phenomena. Applications range from the life sciences through the frontiers of technology, and include biomedical technology, antilock brakes, global warming, microelectronics, lasers, and much more. Some new applications and examples in this third edition include hybrid cars with flywheel energy storage; the digital video disc; kayaking; electrical models for the cell membrane; gel electrophoresis for protein separation; capacitive transducers; medical defibrillators, and many others. As in previous editions, we integrate many applications with the text and problem sets, rather than presenting just a few applications as guest essays.

Questions These follow the chapter synopsis and can be used for class discussion, in peer-based learning strategies, or to get students thinking about concepts before they begin work on quantitative problems.

Problems Science and engineering students learn physics best by working physics problems. This third edition contains nearly 3,000 end-of-chapter problems, with significant revision of the problem sets, especially in the early chapters. Problems range from simple confidence builders, to more complex and realistic multi-problems, to difficult **Supplementary Problems** that will challenge the best students. A section of unique **Paired Problems** for each chapter lets students practice problem-solving techniques on a pair of problems whose solutions involve closely related physical concepts or mathematical approaches. **Cumulative Problems** integrate material from the chapters of each major part of the text. Frequent text references to specific problems link text and problems in the common purpose of enhancing the student's understanding of physics.

Worked Examples These reinforce basic concepts, illustrate problem-solving strategies, and often serve to introduce "real-world" applications of physics. Most examples are followed by an exercise that further reinforces concepts and strategies. A **Similar Problems** line after each example points out related end-of-chapter problems.

Tip Boxes Tip boxes appear throughout the text and warn against common pitfalls or give helpful problem-solving hints.

Pedagogical Use of Color The book's design is an essential pedagogical feature. The carefully planned use of color in figures and in highlighting important equations and definitions, as well as the selection of photographs, all reinforce the text and enhance communication of concepts to the student. Specific colors are used consistently for different physical elements in the figures; for example, velocity vectors and graphs of velocity use the same color, while force vectors and graphs consistently use a different color. A list of elements and their colors follows this preface.

Chapter Synopses Chapter summaries emphasize key concepts and remind students of new terms and mathematical symbols. Each summary ends with a reminder of limitations and approximations used in the theories, models, and equations developed in the chapter.

Appendices and Endpapers The book's appendices and endpapers contain a mathematical review and a wealth of up-to-date physical data, conversion factors, and information on measurements systems.

PHYSICS AND MATHEMATICS

For many students, the university physics course is their first contact with practical applications of calculus. We recognize that students have a range of mathematical abilities, from those taking their first calculus course concurrently with physics to those fluent in both differential and integral calculus. The former will find our new Math Toolboxes, along with many of the Tip boxes and figures, helpful in building confidence in their mathematical skills; the latter will find a selection of challenging calculus-based problems.

In this book mathematics is a tool, not an end in itself. Therefore we always relate mathematical solutions and derivations back to the underlying physics. After deriving an equation or solving a sample problem, we frequently ask: "Does this result make sense?" We show that it does by examining easily understood special cases, thus building physical intuition along with mathematical confidence. We explore the meaning of equations verbally and through figures, ensuring that concepts are clear before students begin to use the material quantitatively.

SUPPLEMENTS

Professors and students alike find it useful to have supplements designed to complement their text. For the third edition, we offer a new expanded supplements package.

For the Instructor

Instructor's Solutions Manual (0-321-03578-X), prepared by Edw. S. Ginsberg, University of Massachusetts-Boston, includes worked solutions to all problems in the text. The solutions manual is now available on CD-ROM in TeX, techexplorer, and Microsoft Word, for easy editing and posting of homework solutions in documents or on the web (0-321-05149-1).

TestGen-EQ Computerized Test Bank is an expanded testbank that allows instructors to edit and change the order of questions, add entirely new questions in six different formats and print different versions of a test. The testbank is available for Windows (0-321-03579-8) and Macintosh (0-321-03580-1). A print version is also available (0-321-03590-9).

Transparency Acetates (0-321-03577-1) contain over 150 color acetates of figures from the text, useful in lectures and classroom discussions.

For the Student

Student Solutions Manual (0-321-03575-5), by Edw. S. Ginsberg, University of Massachusetts-Boston, includes detailed solutions to all the odd-numbered problems in the text.

Study Guide with ActivPhysics, is a book and CD package. The study guide, by Jeffrey J. Braun, University of Evansville, provides an overview of each chapter of *Physics for Scientists and Engineers* and summarizes definitions and key equations. The *ActivPhysics* worksheets and CD-ROM by Alan Van Heuvelen, The Ohio State University, and Paul D'Alessandris help students develop imagery and intuition by changing variables and running the simulations. *ActivPhysics* prompts students with questions that help develop a more thorough understanding, step by step. The *ActivPhysics* CD-ROM is dual platform, for both Macintosh and Windows. *Study Guide with ActivPhysics* is available in two volumes.

- *Volume 1 (covering Wolfson/Pasachoff—Physics for Scientists and Engineers Chapters 1–22) 0-321-05148-3*
- *Volume 2 (covering Wolfson/Pasachoff—Physics for Scientists and Engineers Chapters 23–45) 0-321-05147-5.*

Preparing for General Physics: Math Skill Drills and Other Useful Help, by Arnold D. Pickar of Portland State University, is a self-study workbook that reviews algebra and trigonometry topics for university physics (0-201-53802-4).

ACKNOWLEDGMENTS

A project of this magnitude is not the work of its author alone. Here we acknowledge the many people whose contributions made the book possible. Colleagues using the second edition at universities and colleges throughout the world have volunteered suggestions, and will find most of those incorporated here. Students in Middlebury's Physics 109–110 courses have made significant contributions to the book's accuracy and readability. RW's Middlebury colleagues Ann Broughton, Cris Butler, Jeff Dunham, Bob Prigo, Steve Ratcliff, Susan Watson, and Frank Winkler all provided substantial suggestions or help on this project. We are especially grateful to a group of "on call" reviewers who provided instant feedback to questions from author and editors during the revision: Jerry Hosken, *City College of San Francisco;* Andy Odel, *Northern Arizona University;* James Rohlf, *Boston University;* Gurbax Singh, *University of Maryland;* Robert Weidman, *Michigan Technological University.*

It is frustrating to find numerical errors in a textbook, especially in answers to problems. We have gone to great lengths to make this book as free from error as possible, and we credit the people who helped achieved this goal. Edw. S. Ginsberg, *University of Massachusetts-Boston,* meticulously checked all numerical results in examples, exercises, and end-of-chapter problems. Mark Coffey of the *University of Colorado at Boulder,* and John Bartelt of the *Stanford Linear Accelerator Center* provided valuable accuracy checks.

Prior to this revision, every chapter of the book was thoroughly reviewed by users of both this and competing texts. Reviewers made general as well as more detailed suggestions, nearly all of which we have been able to incorporate in the third edition. We are grateful to these reviewers, and to reviewers of the second edition:

Edward Adelson, *Ohio State University*
Vijendra Agarwal, *Moorhead State University*
William Anderson, *Phoenix College*
Gordon J. Aubrecht, *Ohio State University—Marion*
Paul Avery, *University of Florida*
Douglas Bennett, *University of California, Los Angeles*
Marvin Blecher, *Virginia Polytechnic Institute and State University*
Gary Bowman, *Northern Arizona University*
John Brient, *University of Texas at El Paso*
James H. Burgess, *Washington University*
Bernard Chasan, *Boston University*
Roger Clapp, *University of South Florida*
Claire D. Dewberry, *Florida Community College at Jacksonville*
Jeffrey Dunne, *Purdue University*
Robert J. Endorf, *University of Cincinnati*
Heidi Fearn, *California State University—Fullerton*
Shechao Feng, *University of California, Los Angeles*
Albert L. Ford, *Texas A & M University*
Ian Gatland, *Georgia Institute of Technology*
Edw. S. Ginsberg, *University of Massachusetts—Boston*
James Goff, *Pima Community College*
Alan I. Goldman, *Iowa State University*
Philip Goode, *New Jersey Institute of Technology*
Denise S. Graves, *Clark Atlanta University*
Donald Greenberg, *University of Alaska*
Phillip Gutierrez, *University of Oklahoma*
Stephen Hanzely, *Youngstown State University*
Kenneth Hardy, *Florida International University*
Gerald Harmon, *University of Maine at Orono*
Randy Harris, *University of California, Davis*
Warren Hein, *American Association of Physics Teachers*
Roger Herman, *The Pennsylvania State University*
P. G. Hjorth, *Technical University of Denmark*
Francis L. Howell, *University of North Dakota*
J. N. Huffaker, *University of Oklahoma*
Quinton Hurst, *Arizona State University*
Javed Iqbal, *University of British Columbia*
Wayne James, *University of South Dakota*
Karen Johnston, *North Carolina State University*
Evan Jones, *Sierra College*
Randy Knight, *California Polytechnic State University*
Dean Langely, *St. John's University*
Chew-Lean Lee, *Florida Community College*
Brian Logan, *University of Ottawa*

Peter Loly, *University of Manitoba*
Hilliard K. Macomber, *University of Northern Iowa*
David Markowitz, *University of Connecticut*
Daniel Marlow, *Princeton University*
Nolan Massey, *University of Texas at Arlington*
Ralph McGrew, *Broome Community College*
Victor Michalk, *Southwest Texas State University*
Allen Mincer, *New York University*
P. James Moser, *Bloomsburg University*
Vinod Nangia, *University of Minnesota*
Andrew Odell, *Northern Arizona University*
Robert Osborne, *Yakima Valley Community College*
Michael O'Shea, *Kansas State University*
George Parker, *North Carolina State University*
Graham Pearson, *Novia Scotia Agricultural College*
R. J. Peterson, *University of Colorado*
Slawomir Piatek, *New Jersey Institute of Technology*
Gerald Pogatshnik, *Southern Illinois University*
Joseph F. Polen, *Shasta College*
Talat Rahman, *Kansas State University*
Dennis Roark, *The King's College*
James Rohlf, *Boston University*
Alfons Schulte, *University of Central Florida*
Neil Shafer-Ray, *University of Oklahoma*
Gurbax Singh, *University of Maryland*
Roger F. Sipson, *Moorhead State University*
John Sperry, *Sierra College*
Lon D. Spight, *University of Nevada at Las Vegas*

Robert Sprague, *Foothill College*
Julien. C. Sprott, *University of Wisconsin-Madison*
Konrad M. Stein, *Golden West College*
Bryan H. Suits, *Michigan Technological University*
Leo Takahashi, *The Pennsylvania State University— Beaver Campus*
Frank Tanherlini, *College of the Holy Cross*
Karl Trappe, *University of Texas*
Michael Trinkala, *Hudson Valley Community College*
Loren Vian, *Centralia College*
Clarence Wagener, *Creighton University*
Robert Weidman, *Michigan Technological University*
George Williams, *University of Utah*
Robert J. Wilson, *Colorado State University*
Arthur Winston, *Gordon Institute*
David Yee, *City College of San Francisco*
John Yelton, *University of Florida*
Dale Yoder-Short, *Michigan Technological University*

We also thank editors Catherine Flack, Sami Iwata, Joan Marsh, and publisher Robin Heyden at Addison Wesley for their vigorous support of and collaboration on this project, and Ingrid Mount of Elm Street Publishing Services for her skillful efforts in bringing it to fruition. Finally, RW thanks his family, colleagues, and students for their patience during the intense process of revising this book.

Richard Wolfson
Jay M. Pasachoff

A Visual Guide to the Book

Tip

How Does the Battery Know? How does the battery in Fig. 28-5 "know" how much current to supply? How does it even "know" there are two resistors, and what their values are? For the brief instant when the circuit is first connected, the battery doesn't "know," and some rather complicated action occurs as charge moves from the battery, encounters resistance, and accumulates to establish the potential differences across the resistors. During that brief time the current is not the same everywhere. But very soon the circuit reaches a steady state, with the same current throughout. Later in this chapter, when we consider circuits with capacitors, we'll look in more detail at the approach to the steady state; for now, our analyses assume that circuits have already reached that state.

> **Tip** boxes appear throughout the text to help a student with difficult concepts, warn against common pitfalls, and give problem-solving hints.

EXAMPLE 28-1 | *Designing a Voltage Divider*

A light bulb with a resistance (when on) of 5.0 Ω is designed to operate at a current of 600 mA. To operate this lamp from a 12-V battery, what resistance should you place in series with it?

Solution

Let R_2 be the lamp and R_1 the unknown series resistor. Since resistors in series add, the current through both resistors is $I = \mathcal{E}/(R_1 + R_2)$, which is supposed to be 600 mA or 0.60 A. Solving for R_1 gives

$$R_1 = \frac{\mathcal{E} - IR_2}{I} = \frac{12\,V - (0.60\,A)(5.0\,\Omega)}{0.60\,A} = 15\,\Omega.$$

You can also get this result by noting that the light bulb's proper operating voltage is $V = IR_2 = (0.60\,A)(5.0\,\Omega) = 3.0\,V$. This is one-fourth of the battery voltage, so the light bulb's 5-Ω resistance should be one-fourth of the total. That makes the total 20 Ω, leaving 15 Ω for R_1.

EXERCISE Suppose that in Fig. 28-5 $R_1 = 470\,\Omega$. If the voltage across R_2 is 59% of the battery voltage, find R_2.

Answer: 676 Ω

Some problems similar to Example 28-1: 23–25

Got It!

What is the voltage across the resistor R at the top of each circuit shown in Fig. 28-7? In (a) the second resistor has the same resistance R, and in (b) the g is an open circuit (infinite resistance). Think about it first, then verify y answers using Equations 28-2.

(a)   (b)   (c)

FIGURE 28-7 What's the voltage across the upper resistor in each circuit?

> **Got It!** boxes provide conceptual reinforcement of a student's understanding.
>
> Here the student is asked to stop and think about three simple circuits, to probe their understanding before moving on to the next topic. They are asked to apply what they have learned in a qualitative way, and then asked to verify using the equations.

If I is the current in the circuit of Fig. 28-5, then there must be a voltage $V_1 = IR_1$ across R_1 to drive the current through this resistor. Similarly, the voltage across R_2 is $V_2 = IR_2$. Thus, the voltage across the two resistors together is $V_1 + V_2 = IR_1 + IR_2$. But the battery is connected directly across this series combination, so we have

$$IR_1 + IR_2 = \mathcal{E},$$

or

$$I = \frac{\mathcal{E}}{R_1 + R_2}.$$

Comparison with Ohm's law in the form $I = V/R$ shows that the two resistors in series behave like an equivalent resistance equal to the sum of their resistances. In an obvious generalization to more resistors in series, we have

$$R_{series} = R_1 + R_2 + R_3 + \cdots \qquad (28\text{-}1)$$

In other words, resistors in series add.

Given the current, we can use Ohm's law in the form $V = IR$ to solve for the voltage across each resistor:

$$V_1 = \frac{R_1}{R_1 + R_2}\mathcal{E} \qquad (28\text{-}2a)$$

and

$$V_2 = \frac{R_2}{R_1 + R_2}\mathcal{E}. \qquad (28\text{-}2b)$$

These expressions show that the battery voltage divides between the two resistors in proportion to their resistance. For this reason a series combination of resistors is called a **voltage divider**. Figure 28-6 depicts the voltages throughout the circuit of Fig. 28-5, and shows explicitly that the resistors divide the battery voltage.

FIGURE 28-6 Voltages in the circuit of Fig. 28-5, with $V = 0$ at the negative battery terminal. Note that there is no potential difference across the wires, since they have negligible resistance, and that potential increases across the battery and decreases across the resistors. Can you tell from the graph which resistance is greater? (Here we've ™unrolled⌋ the circuit so we can clearly show the voltage as a function of position around the circuit. But remember that the circuit is a closed loop, so the left and right ends of the graph represent the same physical point, namely the negative battery terminal.)

Charge doesn't lose any energy flowing through the wires, since they're assumed to be perfect conductors.

Voltage—energy per charge—increases by the battery voltage $\mathcal{E}$ as the battery does work on charges, "lifting" them against its internal electric field.

Charge loses energy through collisions within the resistors. The energy loss per unit charge is IR.

In the steady state, charge has lost all the energy it gained from the battery by the time it gets through the entire circuit.

> **Annotated figures** guide a student through complex concepts.
>
> Here we see potential difference in a simple circuit explained step-by-step. Leading the student through the graphical representation of this important, but tricky, concept can lead to a more thorough understanding of the phenomena of voltage.

A rich array of **applications** reinforces
understanding of underlying physics in both
technology and natural phenomena.
Applications range from the life sciences
through the latest technology. They bring the
subject alive by providing relevance of the
theory to a student's everyday world.

Here DVDs are compared to CDs to
give the student knowledge of this topical
development.

Throughout the book, icons in the margins
and references in the text link to the
powerful simulation package **ActivPhysics.**
The simulations in **ActivPhysics** provide
an opportunity for students to make
predictions and test those predictions. The
student becomes an active participant
through manipulation and visualization of
hard-to-grasp concepts.

---

998 Chapter 37 Interference and Diffraction

EXAMPLE 37-8   Asteroid Alert!

An asteroid appears on a collision course with Earth, at a distance of 20×10^6 km. What is the minimum size asteroid that the 2.4-m-diameter diffraction-limited Hubble Space Telescope could resolve at this distance, using 550-nm reflected sunlight?

Solution
Resolving the asteroid means being able to distinguish its opposite edges in the telescope image and therefore to assess its size. Suppose the asteroid's long dimension (it might not be spherical) is ℓ. Then at a distance $L \gg \ell$ it subtends an angle given very nearly by $\theta = \ell/L$. Using this result in Equation 37-13b with the mirror diameter and wavelength given, we have

$$\frac{\ell}{L} = \frac{1.22\lambda}{D},$$

or

$$\ell = \frac{1.22\lambda L}{D} = \frac{(1.22)(550\times10^{-9}\text{ m})(20\times10^9\text{ m})}{2.4\text{ m}} = 5.6\text{ km}.$$

This is a potentially dangerous object, comparable in size to the asteroid that scientists believe caused the extinction of the dinosaurs, and somewhat larger than the comet fragments that slammed into Jupiter in 1994, causing Earth-sized disturbances on the giant planet.

EXERCISE Two ants stand 1 cm apart. Assuming diffraction limited vision, at what distance could a human eye, with an iris aperture of 4 mm, tell that two are indeed separate creatures? Assume a wavelength of 550 nm, near the middle of the visible spectrum. (Other limitations of the human eye prevent its realizing this diffraction limit.)

Answer: 60 m

Some problems similar to Example 37-8: 55–59

APPLICATION   Movies on Disc: From CD to DVD

Standard audio CDs have a maximum playing time of 74 minutes—a value that's set by the optical diffraction limit. In the Application "CD Music, Continued" earlier in this chapter, we showed how a CD encodes information in "pits" 1.6 μm apart and as short as 0.83 μm in length. Standard CDs are read with 780-nm infrared laser light and the pit size and separation are chosen to ensure that diffraction effects at this wavelength don't cause the CD player's optical system to confuse adjacent pits. Ultimately, therefore, the 74-minute playing time is limited by the laser wavelength.

When CDs were first developed, inexpensive semiconductor lasers were available only in the infrared. But today's semiconductor lasers produce light well into the visible—with significantly shorter wavelengths than the infrared light used in CD players and CD-ROM drives. The new DVDs introduced in the late 1990s (read either "digital video disc" or "digital versatile disc") exploit these shorter-wavelength lasers.

Using laser wavelengths of 635 and 650 nm, DVDs can function with significantly lower pit sizes and spacings because of the lower diffraction limit at these shorter wavelengths (Fig. 37-39). Coupled with a two-layer structure (as opposed to the standard CD's single information layer) and more sophisticated data-compression schemes, the smaller pits and pit spacing give DVDs more than 12 times the information-storage capacity of standard CDs. That translates into more than two hours of high quality video and audio, as opposed to the CD's 74 minutes of audio alone. In computer use, it means a DVD can hold some 8.5 gigabytes of information as opposed to a CD's 680 megabytes (by comparison, a 3.5″ floppy disc holds only 1.44 MB). And DVDs can be made in two-sided versions, providing another doubling in capacity. Despite their high capacity, DVDs are physically the same size as CDs, and DVD players are compatible with standard CDs as well.

FIGURE 37-39 A comparison of a standard CD and a DVD. The smaller pit size and closer pit spacing of the DVD result in a much higher information storage capacity, and are made possible by the lower diffraction limit associated with the DVD player's shorter wavelength laser light. Both images are microphotographs of the same size region, about 8 μm on a side. The pits lie on a single spiral track that covers most of the disc.

(a) *(b)*

---

946 Chapter 36 Image Formation and Optical Instruments

last step in this equality follows from Equation for ℓ' and using the result in the equatio

$$f = \frac{R}{2}$$

Thus the focal length of a spherical mirror
We emphasize that the results derived based on the assumption that the spherical parabola. Equivalent ways of describing curvature radius is large compared with Fig. 36-12c and (2) that all rays reflecti nearly parallel to the mirror axis (the para ings can't accurately reflect these conditi clearly the ray paths.

15.7
Spherical Mirror Problems

EXAMPLE 36-2   Sizing Up Hubble: A Concave Mirror

During assembly of the Hubble Space Telescope, a technician stood 3.85 m in front of the telescope's concave mirror and viewed his image (Fig. 36-13). Given the telescope's focal length of 5.52 m, find (a) the location and (b) the magnification of the technician's image. (c) Repeat for the case when the technician stands 15.0 m from the mirror.

Solution
Since the mirror is *concave*, the focal length f is *positive*.
(a) We can solve the mirror equation (Equation 36-2) to get

$$\frac{1}{\ell'} = \frac{1}{f} - \frac{1}{\ell} = \frac{\ell - f}{f\ell},$$

or

$$\ell' = \frac{f\ell}{\ell - f} = \frac{(5.52\text{ m})(3.85\text{ m})}{3.85\text{ m} - 5.52\text{ m}} = -12.7\text{ m}.$$

Why the *negative* answer? Because the technician is closer to the mirror than the focal point, so this is a *virtual* image located *behind* the mirror.
(b) Equation 36-1 gives the magnification:

$$M = -\frac{\ell'}{\ell} = -\frac{(-12.7\text{ m})}{3.85\text{ m}} = 3.30.$$

This *positive* answer indicates an *upright* image, enlarged about three times as shown in Fig. 36-13.
(c) If the technician stands 15.0 m from the mirror, similar calculations give

$$\ell' = \frac{f\ell}{\ell - f} = \frac{(5.52\text{ m})(15.0\text{ m})}{15.0\text{ m} - 5.52\text{ m}} = 8.73\text{ m}$$

and

$$M = -\frac{\ell'}{\ell} = -\frac{8.73\text{ m}}{15.0\text{ m}} = -0.582.$$

FIGURE 36-13 A technician standing in front of the Hubble Space Telescope mirror. Where and how big is the technician's image?

Now ℓ' is *positive*, so the image is *real* and in *front* of the mirror; the *negative* magnification shows that it's *inverted*, and it's reduced in size.

EXERCISE You're scrutinizing your nose using a handheld concave mirror with curvature radius 2.2 m. How far from your face should you hold the mirror to see your nose doubled in size?

Answer: 55 cm

Some problems similar to Example 36-2: 3–9, 11–14

Worked examples are an integral part of the text and reinforce basic concepts. Real world applications are interwoven to give relevance to a student's experience. Many worked examples are followed by **Exercises. Similar Problems** from the end-of-chapter problems are indicated for students who want to work more problems on the topic.

In principle, we could imagine making the interval Δt as close to zero as we like, and getting ever better approximations to the instantaneous velocity. In practice, given a graph of position versus time, an easy approach is to "eyeball" the tangent line to the graph at the point we're interested in; the slope of the tangent line is the slope of the graph at that point, and is therefore the instantaneous velocity. Figure 2-5 shows this approach. Note that the slope of the tangent line, and therefore the velocity, varies from place to place on the graph. That's the whole point of the instantaneous velocity–it's a quantity that can vary continually.

Got It!

Figure 2-6 shows position-versus-time graphs for several objects. Which object is moving with constant speed? Which reverses direction? Which starts slowly and then speeds up?

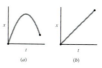

Often, we're given the position as a mathematical function of time. We could draw a graph and measure the slopes of tangent lines to find the velocity at different points. But calculus provides a quicker way. In calculus, the result of the limiting process described in Equation 2-2a is called the **derivative** of x with respect to t, and is given the special symbol dx/dt:

$$\frac{dx}{dt} = \lim_{\Delta t \to 0} \frac{\Delta x}{\Delta t}.$$

The quantities dx and dt are called **infinitesimals**; they represent vanishingly small quantities that result from the limiting process. We can then write Equation 2-2a as

$$v = \frac{dx}{dt}. \qquad (2\text{-}2b)$$

When we're given the position x as a function of time t, calculus provid[es a] simple way to calculate the velocity $v = dx/dt$. Consult the Math Toolbox i[f you] haven't yet seen derivatives in your calculus class, or if you need a refres[her.]

FIGURE 2-5 The instantaneous velocity at a given time is the slope of the tangent line at the point on the position-versus-time graph corresponding to that time. If the position-versus-time graph is not a straight line, then the instantaneous velocity varies with time.

Math Toolbox

Derivatives Do we need to go through an elaborate limiting process every [time] we want an instantaneous velocity? No! In calculus you either have or will d[erive] formulas for the derivatives of common functions. For example, any functi[on of] the form

$$x = bt^n,$$

where b and n are constants, has the derivative

$$\frac{dx}{dt} = bnt^{n-1}.$$

Derivatives of other common functions, including trig functions, exponen[tials] and logarithms, are listed in Appendix A. If a function is made up of a su[m of] terms, its derivative is just the sum of the derivatives of the individual te[rms.]

Math Toolboxes help a student through the math necessary for a full understanding of the physics. They emphasize math as a tool, in context with the physics.

Chapter Synopses emphasize key concepts and remind students of new terms and mathematical symbols. **Limitations to Keep in Mind** remind students of approximations, idealizations, and limited applications of physical concepts and equations. The **Problems You Should Be Able To Solve** section allows a student to evaluate their comprehension of the material in the chapter.

CHAPTER SYNOPSIS

Summary

1. Newton's **first law of motion** states that a body continues in uniform motion unless acted on by a nonzero net force. Uniform motion is a natural state; the study of motion then emphasizes not the cause of motion itself, but the cause of *changes* in motion.

2. Newton's **second law of motion** quantifies the change in motion brought about by a force. The law states that the rate of change of a body's momentum (product of mass and velocity; symbol **p**) is equal to the net force on the body:

$$\mathbf{F}_{net} = \frac{d\mathbf{p}}{dt}$$

As long as the mass of the body does not change, Newton's second law can also be written in the form

$$\mathbf{F}_{net} = m\mathbf{a}.$$

Here $\mathbf{F}_{net}$ is the **net force** on a body—that is, the vector sum of all the individual interaction forces acting on the body. The SI unit of force is the **newton**, defined as the force that gives a 1-kg mass an acceleration of 1 m/s².

3. **Weight** is the force of gravity on an object: $\mathbf{W} = m\mathbf{g}$. In an accelerated frame of reference, the **apparent weight** differs from the gravitational force; in particular, the apparent weight of an object in free fall is zero.

4. Newton's **third law of motion** states that forces always come in pairs. When one object exerts a force on another, the second object exerts an oppositely directed force of equal magnitude back on the first. Newton's second and third laws together permit a consistent description of the motions of interacting objects.

5. Elastic objects such as springs provide a practical way of measuring forces. When the force exerted by a spring is directly proportional to the amount of stretch or compression, the spring is said to obey **Hooke's law**; the force is then given by

$$F = -kx, \quad \text{(Hooke's law)}$$

where k is the **spring constant**, with SI units of N/m.

Terms You Should Understand

(Pairs are closely related terms whose distinction is important; number in parentheses is chapter section where term first appears.)

dynamics (introduction)
Aristotle, Galileo, Newton (5-1)
force, net force, interaction force (5-2)
momentum (5-2)
Newton's laws of motion (5-2, 5-7)
inertia (5-2)
gravitational, electroweak, color forces (5-3)
mass, weight (5-5)
apparent weight (5-5, 5-8), weightlessness (5-5)
third-law pair (5-7)
normal force (5-4)
tension force, compression force (5-8)
Hooke's law (5-8)
spring constant (5-8)

Symbols You Should Recognize

F (5-2)
p (5-2)
N (5-4)
g (5-5)
W (5-5)
k (5-8)

Problems You Should Be Able to Solve

calculating force, mass, or acceleration from the other two quantities (5-4)
calculating weight or mass given the other (5-5)
solving for forces or accelerations in one-dimensional situations (5-6)
applying Newton's second and third laws together in one-dimensional situations (5-7)
determining spring force, extension/compression, or spring constant given the other two quantities (5-8)
determining apparent weight (5-8)

Limitations to Keep in Mind

Newton's laws apply only when relative velocities are much less than the speed of light; aside from that restriction, the basic material of this chapter is universally applicable.
Newton's laws are valid in inertial reference frames.
Newton's second law in the form $\mathbf{F} = m\mathbf{a}$ is valid only when mass remains constant; the form $\mathbf{F} = d\mathbf{p}/dt$ is more general.
Real springs deviate from ideal Hooke's law behavior when stretched or compressed substantially.

Questions will prompt a student to think about concepts in a chapter before they start on the problems.

QUESTIONS

1. Why can a bird perch on a high-voltage power line without getting electrocuted?
2. One proton is accelerated from rest by a uniform electric field, the other by a nonuniform electric field. If they move through the same potential difference, how do their final speeds compare?
3. Would a free electron move toward higher or lower potential?
4. The potential difference from A to B in Fig. 25-33 is zero since the two points are equidistant from the charge Q. How can this be, when a charge moving along the path shown clearly experiences an electric force not perpendicular to the path?

DANGER
ELECTROCUTION HAZARD
KEEP CLEAR
DEATH OR SERIOUS INJURY CAN RESULT FROM CONTACT WITH LOAD, MACHINE OR VEHICLE IF THEY BECOME ELECTRICALLY CHARGED

FIGURE 25-34 Question 12.

how this hazard a...
to someone on th...

Paired Problems let a student practice problem-solving on a pair of problems whose solutions involve closely related physical concepts or mathematical approaches.

Section 25-5 Potentials of Charged Conductors

52. (a) What is the maximum potential (measured from infinity) for the sphere of Example 25-3 before dielectric breakdown of air occurs at the sphere's surface? (Breakdown of air occurs at a field strength of 3 MVm.) (b) What is the charge on the sphere when it's at this potential?
53. The spark plug in an automobile engine has a center electrode made from wire 2.0 mm in diameter. The electrode is worn to a hemispherical shape, so it behaves approximately like a charged sphere. What is the minimum potential on this electrode that will ensure the plug sparks in air? Neglect the presence of the second electrode.
54. A large metal sphere has three times the diameter of a smaller sphere and carries three times as much charge. Both spheres are isolated, so their surface charge densities ... form. Com...

...re far apart. One
...other -10 nC.
...the spheres are
...potential on each
...ach charge must
...ve equilibrium?
...s for the isolated,

...in diameter and
...part. Determine
...ld strength at the
...midway between
...e between the

Paired Problems

(Both problems in a pair involve the same principles and techniques. If you can get the first problem, you should be able to solve the second one.)

59. Three 50-pC charges sit at the vertices of an equilateral triangle 1.5 mm on a side. How much work would it take to bring a proton from very far away to the midpoint of one of the triangle's sides?
60. Repeat the preceding problem for the case when one of the charges is -50 pC and the proton is brought to the midpoint of the side between the two positive charges.
61. A pair of equal charges q lies on the x axis at $x = \pm a$. (a) Find expressions for the potential at points on the x axis for which $x > a$ and (b) show that your result reduces to a point-charge potential for $x \gg a$.
62. (a) For the charge distribution of the preceding problem, find an expression for the potential at *all* points on the y axis. (b) Show that your result reduces to a point-charge potential for $y \gg a$.
63. A 2.0-cm-radius metal sphere carries 75 nC and is surrounded by a concentric spherical conducting shell of radius 10 cm carrying -75 nC. (a) Find the potential difference between the shell and the sphere. (b) How would your answer change if the shell charge were changed to $+150$ nC?
64. A coaxial cable consists of a 2.0-mm-radius central wire carrying 75 nC/m, and a concentric outer conductor of radius 10 mm carrying -75 nC/m. (a) Find the potential

Almost 3000 **end-of-chapter problems,** ranging from confidence builders to realistic multi-problems, will help a student understand concepts and develop problem-solving skills. The problems are thought provoking and encourage critical thinking, and are relevant to a student's everyday life.

PROBLEMS

ActivPhysics can help with these problems:
Activities 11.9, 11.10.

Section 25-2 Potential Difference

1. How much work does it take to move a 50-μC charge against a 12-V potential difference?
2. The potential difference between the two sides of an ordinary electrical outlet is 120 V. How much energy can an electron gain when it moves from one side to the other?
3. It takes 45 J to move a 15-mC charge from point A to point B. What is the potential difference ΔV_{AB}?
4. Show that 1 V/m is the same as 1 N/C.
5. Find the magnitude of the potential difference between two points located 1.4 m apart in a uniform 650 N/C electric field, if a line between the points is parallel to the field.
6. A charge of 3.1 C moves from the positive to the negative terminal of a 9.0-V battery. How much energy does the battery impart to the charge?
7. Two points A and B lie 15 cm apart in a uniform electric field, with the path AB parallel to the field. If the potential difference ΔV_{AB} is 840 V, what is the field strength?
8. Figure 25-37 shows a uniform electric field of magnitude E. Find expressions for (a) the potential difference ΔV_{AB} and (b) ΔV_{BC}. (c) Use your result to determine ΔV_{AC}.

FIGURE 25-37 Problem 8.

9. A proton, an alpha particle (a bare helium nucleus), and a singly ionized helium atom are accelerated through a potential difference of 100 V. Find the energy each gains.
10. The electric field within the membrane separating the inside and outside of a biological cell is approximately 8.0 MV/m, and is essentially uniform. If the membrane is 10 nm thick, what is the potential difference across the membrane?
11. What is the potential difference between the terminals of a battery that can impart 7.2×10^{-19} J to each electron that moves between the terminals?
12. Electrons in a TV tube are accelerated from rest through a 25-kV potential difference. With what speed do they hit the TV screen?
13. A 12-V car battery stores 2.8 MJ of energy. How much charge can move between the battery terminals before it is totally discharged? Assume the potential difference remains at 12 V, an assumption that is not realistic.
14. What is the charge on an ion that gains 1.6×10^{-15} J when it moves through a potential difference of 2500 V?
15. Two large, flat metal plates are a distance d apart, where d is small compared with the plate size. If the plates carry surface charge densities $\pm\sigma$, show that the magnitude of the potential difference between them is $V = \sigma d/\varepsilon_0$.
16. An electron passes point A moving at 6.5 Mm/s. At point B the electron has come to a complete stop. Find the potential difference ΔV_{AB}.
17. A 5.0-g ob... carr... ...arge of 3.8... ...It acqu...
a speed v w...
difference V...
the same c...

Most of the problems are **referenced by section** to allow a student to refer easily to the relevant text.

Supplementary Problems drawn from throughout the chapter are more difficult problems that will challenge the best students.

Supplementary Problems

69. A conducting sphere 5.0 cm in radius carries 60 nC. It is surrounded by a concentric spherical conducting shell of radius 15 cm carrying -60 nC. (a) Find the potential at the sphere's surface, taking the zero of potential at infinity. (b) Repeat for the case when the shell also carries $+60$ nC.
70. Show that the result of Example 25-9 approaches the field of a point charge for $x \gg a$. *Hint:* You will need to apply the binomial theorem to the quantity $1/\sqrt{x^2 + a^2}$.
71. The potential on the axis of a uniformly charged disk at ... V; the potential 10 cm ... the disk radius and its ...

76. Repeat the preceding problem for the case $\lambda = \lambda_0(x/\ell)$. Why is your answer for $x \gg \ell$ different? *Hint:* What does this charge distribution resemble at large distances?
77. For the situation of Example 25-10, find an equation for the equipotential with $V = 0$ in the x-y plane. Plot the equipotential, and show that it passes through the points described in Example 25-10 and its exercise.
78. A disk of radius a carries a nonuniform surface charge density given by $\sigma = \sigma_0(r/a)$, where σ_0 is a constant. (a) Find the potential at an arbitrary point on the disk axis, a distance x from the disk center. (b) Use the result of (a) to find the electric field on the disk axis, and (c) show that the field reduces to an expected form for $x \gg a$.
79. An open-ended cylinder of radius a and length $2a$ carries charge q spread uniformly over its surface. Find the potential on the cylinder axis at its center. *Hint:* Treat the cylinder as a stack of charged rings, and integrate.

PART 4 *Cumulative Problems*

These problems combine material from chapters throughout the entire part or, in addition, from chapters in earlier parts, or they present special challenges.

1. An air-insulated parallel-plate capacitor has plate area 100 cm^2 and spacing 0.50 cm. The capacitor is charged and then disconnected from the charging battery. A thin-walled, nonconducting box of the same dimensions as the capacitor is filled with water at 20.00°C. The box is released at the edge of the capacitor and moves without friction into the capacitor (Fig. 1). When it reaches equilibrium the water temperature is 21.50°. What was the original voltage on the capacitor?

50 T/s while that in the right-hand solenoid is decreasing at 30 T/s. Find the current in the resistance wire shared by both triangles. Which way does the current flow?

FIGURE 3 Cumulative Problem 3.

4. A long solenoid of length ℓ and radius R has a total of N

The student is asked to integrate knowledge from previous chapters to solve the **Cumulative Problems.** They test a student's understanding of a range of topics, and accumulation of knowledge.

The Authors

Richard Wolfson is Professor of Physics and George Adams Ellis Professor of the Liberal Arts at Middlebury College, where he has taught since 1976. He did undergraduate work at the Massachusetts Institute of Technology and Swarthmore College and holds the M.S. degree from the University of Michigan and Ph.D. from Dartmouth. He has published widely in scientific journals, including works ranging from medical physics research to experimental plasma physics, electronic circuit design, solar energy engineering, and theoretical astrophysics. He is also an interpreter of science for the nonspecialist, as a contributor to *Scientific American* and author of the book *Nuclear Choices: A Citizen's Guide to Nuclear Technology*. His videotaped course "Einstein's Relativity and the Quantum Revolution," produced by The Teaching Company, brings the key ideas of modern physics to nonscientists. Professor Wolfson has spent sabbatical years as Visiting Scientist at the National Center for Atmospheric Research in Boulder, Colorado, at St. Andrews University in Scotland, and at Stanford University.

Jay M. Pasachoff is Field Memorial Professor of Astronomy and Director of the Hopkins Observatory at Williams College. He was born and brought up in New York City. After attending the Bronx High School of Science, he received his A.B. degree from Harvard College and his A.M. and Ph.D. from Harvard University. He then held postdoctoral fellowships at Harvard and at the California Institute of Technology before going to Williams in 1972. His research has dealt mainly with solar physics, most recently the solar corona as studied at total eclipses, and with nuclear astrophysics, namely, the abundances of the light elements and their formation in the first minutes of the universe. Professor Pasachoff has spent sabbatical leaves at the University of Hawaii, at l'Institut d'Astrophysique in Paris, at the Institute for Advanced Study in Princeton, and at the Harvard-Smithsonian Center for Astrophysics. He is also author or co-author of major texts in physics, calculus, physical science, and astronomy.

Color Key for Figures

The artwork for this third edition is carefully designed to make effective use of color printing as a learning aid. In particular, we have assigned colors to the vector quantities that are so important in physics, and we have used those colors consistently throughout the book. The table below lists some important physical quantities, along with their text and graphic symbols and color assignments. We also include electric circuit symbols, which, to be consistent with usage in engineering, are printed in black.

Vector	Text Symbol	Graphic Symbol
Displacement	$\mathbf{r}, \boldsymbol{\ell}$	
Velocity	$\mathbf{v}$	
Acceleration	$\mathbf{a}$	
Force	$\mathbf{F}$	
Linear momentum	$\mathbf{p}$	
Angular velocity	ω	
Torque	τ	
Angular momentum	$\mathbf{L}$	
Electric field	$\mathbf{E}$	
Magnetic field	$\mathbf{B}$	
Electric dipole moment	$\mathbf{p}$	
Magnetic dipole moment	μ	
Electric charge		
Positive charge	q, Q	
Negative charge	q, Q	
Circuit symbols		
Battery, emf	$\mathcal{E}$	
Resistor	R	
Capacitor	C	
Inductor	L	
Switch	S	

Credits

Page abbreviations are as follows: (T) top, (C) center, (B) bottom, (L) left, (R) right.

429BR Courtesy of T.D. Rossing/Northern Illinois University

430 Courtesy of Fox Products, South Whitley, IN

431 From PSSC Physcis, 2nd ed., 1965 D.C. Heath and Co. with Education Development Center

432 ©Camerique/H. Armstrong Roberts

435L Courtesy of Dr. Gary Settles

435C ©The Harold E. Edgerton 1992 Trust/Palm Press

435R ©H. Armstrong Roberts

437 ©David R. Frazier Photolibrary

439L ©Greg Cranna/Stock Boston

439R ©Philippe Plailly/SPL/Photo Researchers, Inc.

441 ©Peter Rauter/Tony Stone Images

447 ©Bill Gallery/Stock Boston

448CL ©J.Cochin//Explorer/Photo Researchers, Inc.

448CR ©Fred McConnaughey/Photo Researchers, Inc.

448B Courtesy of Lawrence Livermore National Laboratory

449L ©Fredrik D. Bodin/Stock Boston

449R ©W.Eastep/The Stock Market

450 ©Wolfgang Kaehler

452TR Courtesy of Mercedes Benz

452TL ©Diane Schiumo/Fundamental Photographs

452C Courtesy of NASA

454 ©Dan McCoy/Rainbow

458T ©Tod Planck/Tony Stone Images

458B ©Larry Mulvehill/Photo Researchers, Inc.

459T ©J. Toers/George Hall Photos

459B ©Globus Brothers

460 ©Peter Menzel/Stock Boston

461 ONERA photo, H. Werle 1974, from Milton van Dyke, An Atlas of Fluid Motion

464B ©Bruce Thomas/The Stock Market

471 ©Ray Ellis/Photo Researchers, Inc.

472 ©NASA/SS/Photo Researchers, Inc.

474C ©Jay M. Pasachoff

474B ©1998 PhotoDisc, Inc.

477 ©G.R. Roberts

478 ©Robert Fried/Stock Boston

483 ©John Wilson White/Addison Wesley Longman

484 ©Manuel G. Velarde

485T ©Keith Wood/Tony Stone Images

485B ©Camerique/H. Armstrong Roberts

496 ©Paolo Koch/Photo Researchers, Inc.

505 ©Alexander Tsiaras/Photo Researchers, Inc.

507C ©Paul Silverman/Fundamental Photographs

507B ©Richard Megna/Fundamental Photographs

511T Courtesy of the Hartford Steam Boiler and Insurance Company

511C ©AP/Wide World

516 ©Bruce M. Wellman/Stock Boston

517 ©Jim Richardson/H. Armstrong Roberts

519 ©Jan Halaska/Photo Researchers, Inc.

523 ©David R. Austen/Stock Boston

527 Courtesy of Price Weber

529T ©Geoff Juckes/The Stock Market

529B ©Thomas Ives/The Stock Market

543 ©Sinclair Stammers/SPL/Photo Researchers, Inc.

546L ©David R. Frazier Photolibrary/Photo Researchers, Inc.

546R Courtesy of the Environmental Protection Agency

550 ©Rick Browne/Stock Boston

551 ©Martin Bond/SPL/Photo Researchers, Inc.

552T Courtesy of Lockheed

552B ©Hank Morgan/Photo Researchers, Inc.

569 ©Astrid and Hans Frieder Michler/SPL/Photo Researchers, Inc.

570 ©Gary Ladd

571L ©Richard Megna/Fundamental Photographs

571R Courtesy of Intel

573T ©Lawrence Berkeley Laboratory/SPL/Photo Researchers, Inc.

573C ©Richard Megna/Fundamental Photographs

763   ©Lawrence Berkeley Laboratory/SPL/Photo Researchers, Inc.

770   ©Ray Pfortner/Peter Arnold, Inc.

771   Courtesy of the American Association of Physics Teachers

774   ©1990 Richard Megna/Fundamental Photographs

775   ©NASA/SPL/Photo Researchers, Inc.

776   ©1990 Richard Megna/Fundamental Photographs

777   Courtesy of Boebinger, AT&T Bell Labs

779   Courtesy of the National Center for Atmospheric Research

785   ©1990 Richard Megna/Fundamental Photographs

787   ©Will and Deni McIntyre/Photo Researchers, Inc.

789   ©John Wilson White/Addison Wesley Longman

790   ©1990 Richard Megna/Fundamental Photographs

803   ©1998 PhotoDisc, Inc.

813T ©Milt and Joan Mann/Cameramann International, Ltd.

813B ©David R. Frazier Photolibrary

814   ©Erik Borg/Addison Wesley Longman

815   ©1998 PhotoDisc, Inc.

816   ©Erik Borg/Addison Wesley Longman

818   Courtesy of NASA

822   Courtesy of General Electric

824   Courtesy of IBM

826   Courtesy of Jay M. Pasachoff

833   ©Milt and Joan Mann/Cameramann International, Ltd.

835   Courtesy of Jay M. Pasachoff

843   Courtesy of NASA

845   Courtesy of American Superconductor

852   ©Werner H. Muller/Peter Arnold, Inc.

865   ©Erik Borg/Addison Wesley Longman

873   ©H. Abernathy/H. Armstrong Roberts

873   ©Chris Rogers/The Stock Market

873   ©G. Fritz/H. Armstrong Roberts

873   ©Coco McCoy/Rainbow

873   ©Camerique/H. Armstrong Roberts

873   ©Coco McCoy/Rainbow

873   ©Michael Mathers/Peter Arnold, Inc.

882   ©Dale Boyers/Photo Researchers, Inc.

894   Courtesy of NASA

896T ©P. Degginger/H. Armstrong Roberts

896C ©Mike Devlin/SPL/Photo Researchers, Inc.

897TL ©J. Amos/H. Armstrong Roberts

897TR Courtesy of the National Radio Astronomy Observatory

897CL Courtesy of JPL/NASA

897CR ©NRSC Ltd/SPL/Photo Researchers, Inc.

898   ©1992 Diane Hirsch/Fundamental Photographs

899R ©Sepp Geitz/Woodfin Camp and Associates

904   ©1998 PhotoDisc, Inc.

905   ©Bruce M. Wellman/Stock Boston

907L Courtesy of AT&T, Bell Laboratories

907R Courtesy of Hughes Research Laboratory

912L Courtesy of NASA

912R ©David R. Frazier Photolibrary

915   ©Pete Saloutos/The Stock Market

916   Courtesy of Schott Corporation

918   ©Richard Megna/Fundamental Photographs

919   Courtesy of NASA

920   ©Richard Megna/Fundamental Photographs

924T ©John W. Dunay IV/Fundamental Photographs

924B ©Richard Megna/Fundamental Photographs

926B ©Luettge/ZEFA/H. Armstrong Roberts

926T ©Foto Forum

927T ©Alfred Pasieka/Peter Arnold, Inc.

927C Courtesy of Alfred Letiner/Rensselaer Polytechnic Institute

927B Courtesy of R. Giovanelli and H.R. Gillett/ CSIRO National Measurement Laboratory, Australia

1053L   Courtesy of AT&T Bell Laboratories

1054   Courtesy of the Meggers Gallery, AIP

1057T   Courtesy of the Institute of Theoretical Physics, Lund, Sweden

1057B   Courtesy of Carl D. Anderson/California Institute of Technology

1058   ©AP/Wide World

1060T   ©U.S. Navy/SPL/Photo Researchers, Inc.

1060B   Courtesy of Ullstein Bilderdienst

1061   Courtesy of Ullstein Bilderdienst

1062   Courtesy of the Stein Collection, AIP

1064L   Courtesy of Fermilab Visual Media Services

1064R   Courtesy of CERN

1065T   Courtesy of Ralph Crane

1065B   ©Patrice Loiez/CERN/SPL/Photo Researchers, Inc.

1067   ©Joe Stancampiano and Karl Luttrell/National Geographic Society

1071   ©Dan McCoy/Rainbow

1072R   ©Mark Marten/Los Alamos National Laboratory/Photo Researchers, Inc.

Extended

1044   ©Wexler/Burgess/SPL/Photo Researchers, Inc.

1046   Courtesy of The Exploratorium

1057T   Courtesy of R. Giovanelli and H.R. Gillett/ CSIRO National Measurement Laboratory, Australia

1057B   Courtesy of Alfred Leitner/Rensselaer Polytechnic Institute

1058   Courtesy of the AIP Niels Bohr Library, photo by Paul Ehrenfest

1063L   ©Prof. P.M. Motta/SPL/Photo Researchers, Inc.

1063R   ©CNRI/SPL/Photo Researchers, Inc.

1064   Courtesy of AT&T Bell Laboratories

1068   Courtesy of the AIP Niels Bohr Library

1074   Courtesy of the Lawrence Livermore National Laboratory

1076   Courtesy of Elisha Huggins, Dartmouth

1077T   From C. Jonsson, Zeitscrift fer Physik, Springer-Verlag, Berlin, Heidelberg, New York

1077B   Courtesy of the AIP, Meggers Gallery

1079   Courtesy of Paul Ehrenfest

1088   Courtesy of Don Eigler, IBM Almaden

1089L   Courtesy of IBM

1089R   Courtesy of IBM

1090L   Courtesy of Don Eigler, IBM Almaden

1090R   Courtesy of R.M. Penner, University of California, Irvine

1094   Courtesy of Fermilab Visual Media Services

1100   ©Ken Eward/Photo Researchers, Inc.

1113   Courtesy of the National Radio Astronomy Observatory

1115T   Courtesy of Mike Matthews/JILA

1115B   ©Richard Megna/Fundamental Photographs

1121T   Courtesy of the Astronomical Data Center (ADC) catalog A6016, by Reader J., Corliss Ch.H.:1981, 'Line Spectra of the Elements', CRC Handbook of Chemistry and Physics; NSRDS-NBS 68

1121B   Courtesy of Osram/Sylvania, Inc.

1124   ©SPL/Photo Researchers, Inc.

1126   Courtesy of D.A. Calvert/Royal Greenwich Observatory

1127TL ©Skelton Photography

1127TC ©Dan McCoy/Rainbow

1127TR ©Paul Shambroom/Photo Researchers, Inc.

1127C   ©Dagmar Schilling/Peter Arnold, Inc.

1127B   ©Dan McCoy/Rainbow

1133   ©Science Source/Photo Researchers, Inc.

1136   ©Geoff Tomplinson/SPL/Photo Researchers, Inc.

1150T   ©1998 PhotoDisc, Inc.

1150B   ©John Mead/SPL/Photo Researchers, Inc.

1152L   ©IBM Research/Peter Arnold, Inc.

1152C   Courtesy of Brookhaven National Laboratory and NYU Medi-Cal Center

1153T   Courtesy of Conductus

1153B   Courtesy of the American Superconductor Corp.

Doing Physics

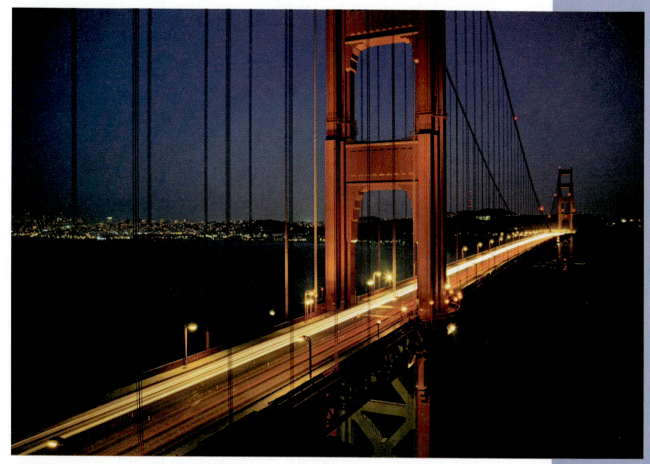

The laws of physics determine whether the Golden Gate Bridge stands or falls, the fuel efficiency of the cars crossing the bridge, the brightness of the cars' headlights, and the dynamics of the ocean currents that flow beneath the bridge.

When you ride a bicycle, fly in a jet plane, or watch a thunderstorm, you experience physical laws. **Physics** is the science that tells us how and why things work. Knowledge of physics will help you understand both natural phenomena and the technologies that increasingly pervade our lives. In this book, we set out the basic laws of physics and show how they apply to a myriad of phenomena from atoms and molecules to cars and airplanes, rockets and computers, stars and galaxies.

Why study physics? If you are going on in a field such as chemistry, geology, engineering, materials science, or physics itself, you'll find the principles of physics at the foundation of all that you do. Students of biological and premedical sciences will find physics at work not only in the phenomena of living systems but also in instrumentation used for everything from probing individual cells to restarting fibrillating hearts. Although this book is written primarily for students of science and engineering, many others will find the insights physics gives into the workings of the natural world and contemporary technology both useful and philosophically enriching.

1-1 FIELDS OF PHYSICS

Physics has evolved into a discipline with many subfields. Some, such as planetary motion, have long histories and are now solidly understood. Others have taken great leaps in recent years; today's electronic technology, for example, could not have existed fifty years ago due to the limits of our physical knowledge. Unanswered fundamental questions, such as the nature of matter and the origin of the universe, spur vigorous research and lively debate in the fields of particle physics and cosmology. Even fields where the basic physics is long established continue to surprise with new applications in the natural world and in technology.

This book introduces you to the great progress that has been made in our comprehension of the physical universe, and shows where we still have more to learn. For our purposes, we divide physics into six major branches, as shown in Fig. 1-1. Each of these has many subfields, and each of those is the subject of specialized books and research areas. Furthermore, many contemporary fields—such as biophysics and astrophysics—straddle our six general branches. You should view Fig. 1-1 not as a rigorous division of physics but as a convenient organizational scheme.

The branch of physics governing motion is called **mechanics**. You use the laws of mechanics when you drive a car, ride a skateboard, or build a skyscraper. Through most of this book, we deal with **classical mechanics**, which applies to objects from molecules to galaxies that are moving at speeds small compared with the speed of light. In later chapters, we will see that classical mechanics is but an approximation to a more comprehensive set of physical laws that includes quantum mechanics and Einstein's relativity.

In the first nine chapters we deal with the motion of single objects, often called particles. Then, in Chapters 10 to 15, we generalize to the motion of many-particle systems. The wave of standing spectators that sweeps through a football stadium, ocean waves that pound the coastlines, and the sound waves by which we communicate are examples of a special kind of many-particle motion called **wave motion**, which we examine in Chapters 16 and 17.

Our Earth is five-eighths covered by liquid water and is surrounded entirely by a gaseous atmosphere. Even the continents on which we live float on an underlying fluid layer. The cells of our bodies are nurtured by the motion of fluid through our circulatory systems. And the bulk of the matter in the universe—stars and interstellar gas—is in the fluid state. In Chapter 18, we apply the laws of mechanics to fluids.

FIGURE 1-1 In this book physics has been divided into six branches, providing an organizational structure to the subject. Divisions among the branches are not rigid, and the same fundamental principles apply in several branches.

Nearly all life on Earth thrives on a constant supply of energy from the Sun, and a delicate balance of energy-transfer processes keeps our planet at a habitable temperature; we worry increasingly that human activity will upset that balance and bring severe climatic changes. We have developed nuclear power plants, gasoline engines, solar collectors, oil and gas furnaces, and a host of other energy sources. Worries about our planet's energy balance and the operation of our energy technologies are both concerns of **thermodynamics**—the study of heat and its interaction with matter. We follow our study of mechanics with four chapters on thermodynamics.

We deal extensively with another major branch of physics: **electromagnetism**. The Greeks knew something of the electric and magnetic properties of matter; the words *electricity* and *magnetism* themselves originate in Greek words for natural materials displaying electric and magnetic effects. The Chinese invention of the magnetic compass resulted by the twelfth century A.D. in widespread use of Earth's natural magnetism to aid navigation. In 1800, Alessandro Volta invented the electric battery, paving the way for experiments involving electric current and its magnetic effects. By the late 1800s, application of electromagnetism led to practical technologies including telegraph, telephone, and electric power distribution. In one of the most sweeping syntheses in the history of science, James Clerk Maxwell in the 1860s formulated a complete description of electromagnetism, showing that electricity and magnetism are intimately related. A startling prediction of Maxwell's theory was that light is an electromagnetic wave and that other electromagnetic waves should be possible as well. Radio and television follow directly from that prediction. Today, electromagnetic technology dominates our civilization, as evidenced by our digital watches, video recorders, microwave ovens, and especially computers (Fig. 1-2). We devote twelve chapters to electromagnetism.

The behavior of light is intimately tied to electromagnetism. Chapters 35 through 37 explore the branch of physics called **optics**, building an understanding of light and of optical devices such as lenses, prisms, diffraction gratings, and the instruments we build from them—microscopes, telescopes, spectrometers, and the like (Fig. 1-3).

Electromagnetic theory led directly to many practical technologies, but it also raised baffling, fundamental questions about the nature of light, motion, space, and time. With a radically simple statement whose implications seem to violate our common sense, Albert Einstein in 1905 confronted these questions (Fig. 1-4). His **special theory of relativity** gives a surprisingly simple picture of reality, in the context of radically altered notions of space and time. Although relativity provides a more correct description of physical reality than does classical mechanics, the two theories differ significantly only at speeds approaching that of light—seven times around the Earth in one second. In our everyday existence we need not worry about relativity. But in particle accelerators probing the basic structure of matter; in studies of exploding supernovas, neutron stars, and the early universe; and even in designing a color television, we must take account of relativity. We explore the theory of relativity in Chapter 38.

But what *is* light? This question leads to one of the major developments of twentieth-century thought: **quantum mechanics**. Dealing with the smallest objects in the universe, quantum mechanics blurs the distinction between light and matter, giving a description of matter on the atomic scale for which our macroscopic intuition is simply inadequate. We give a brief introduction to

FIGURE 1-2 This tiny silicon chip, containing over a million electronic components, forms the heart of a personal computer. The chip is small enough to fit through the eye of a needle.

FIGURE 1-3 The Hubble Space Telescope is an example of an optical system.

FIGURE 1-4 Albert Einstein was 26 and the father of a young child when he developed the special theory of relativity.

quantum mechanics and its philosophical implications in Chapter 39, where we also discuss our evolving knowledge of the elementary particles that are the fundamental constituents of matter and the implications of that knowledge for the origin of the universe. The extended version of this text explores quantum mechanics in four chapters, including quantum applications in atomic, molecular, and solid-state physics as well as technological devices such as lasers. Two chapters on nuclear physics and its applications follow, and the extended version ends with a look at elementary particle physics, cosmology, and future directions in physics.

1-2 THE SIMPLICITY OF PHYSICS

Physics is the fundamental science. Its laws and theories describe the workings of the universe at the most basic level. For that reason physics is immensely powerful; the same laws describe the behavior of molecules, of airplanes, and of galaxies. Although no one has done so, most scientists believe in principle that it would be possible to describe the operation of a living cell or organism using only the fundamental laws of physics.

Applying the laws of physics can give rise to challenging problems whose solutions call for clever insight and mathematical agility. The challenge of problem solving is what gives physics some of its intellectual interest and also its reputation as a difficult subject. But if you approach this course thinking that physics presents you with numerous difficult things to learn, you're missing the point. Because it is so fundamental, physics is inherently simple. There are only a few basic laws to learn; if you really understand those laws, you can apply them in a wide variety of situations. We wrote this book in a spirit that emphasizes the underlying simplicity of physics by reminding you how diverse examples are really manifestations of the *same* underlying physical laws. You should come to understand the basic laws thoroughly so you can apply them confidently in new situations. As you read the text and work the problems, remember the simplicity of the underlying physical principles. Ask yourself how each problem you approach is really similar to other problems and to the text examples. And you will find that similarity, because the many problems and examples really do involve only a few underlying laws. So physics is simple—challenging, too—but with an underlying simplicity that reflects the scope and power of this fundamental science.

1-3 MEASUREMENT SYSTEMS

"A long way" means different things to a sedentary person, to a marathon runner, to a pilot, and to an astronaut. We need to quantify our measurements. Today, nearly every country in the world uses the **metric system**, in which the fundamental quantities length, mass, and time are measured in meters, kilograms, and seconds, respectively. The United States remains the only industrialized country that has not "gone metric," although economic pressures and new legislation are gradually moving the United States toward adoption of the metric system. The modern version of the metric system is known as **SI**, for Système International d'Unités (International System of Units). The SI is a universal language for science, and it incorporates scientifically precise definitions of the fundamental quantities.

Length

The **meter** was first defined at the time of the French Revolution to be one ten-millionth of the distance from the equator to the north pole through Paris. This distance, of course, is not trivial to determine—surveyors sent out at the time to measure a portion of the path were nearly guillotined—and more readily accessible measuring standards proved necessary.

In 1889, a standard meter was carefully made; it is the distance between two lines on a certain bar made of a platinum-iridium alloy when examined at the temperature of the melting point of ice. It is kept in a temperature-controlled room at the Bureau International des Poids et Mesures in Sèvres, France, where the international treaty on measurement signed in 1875 is monitored. Thirty secondary standards were also made from the same ingot of alloy. (Comparisons over 15 years showed that the standard meters remained the same to within 2 ten-millionths of a meter.) But as new methods developed, even the standard meter was not sufficiently accurate. In 1960, the meter was redefined as 1,650,763.73 wavelengths of orange-red light emitted by the isotope krypton-86.

More recently, even this standard became insufficient. By the 1970s, the speed of light had become one of the most accurately determined quantities. As a result, in 1983 the meter was redefined in terms of the speed of light:

> *The meter is the length of the path traveled by light in vacuum during a time interval of 1/299,792,458 of a second.*

This definition is more useful than a meter stick kept in Paris, since anyone with an accurate clock can reproduce the standard meter (Fig. 1-5). The redefinition of the meter also means that the speed of light is now a defined quantity; its value is exactly 299,792,458 m/s.

Time

The division of time into hours, minutes, and seconds goes back to the Babylonians. The **second** used to be defined by the Earth's rotation, as $1/(24 \times 60 \times 60)$ of a mean solar day, until it was recognized that the Earth's rotation is slowing slightly. The second was then redefined as a specific fraction of the year 1900. In 1967 the second was again redefined, now in terms of the vibrations of a specific atom, to give our current definition:

> *The second is the duration of 9,192,631,770 periods of the radiation corresponding to the transition between the two hyperfine levels of the ground state of the cesium-133 atom.*

The device that implements this definition—which will seem a lot less obscure once you've studied some atomic physics—is called an atomic clock (Fig. 1-6). Like the definition of the meter, the atomic-clock definition of the second is reproducible in any laboratory with the appropriate equipment.

FIGURE 1-5 A surveyor using laser light for accurate distance determination. The standard measure of length—the meter—is defined in terms of the speed of light.

FIGURE 1-6 This cesium atomic clock at the National Institute of Standards and Technology (NIST) keeps time to an accuracy of about 3 μs/y. It is part of the NIST Atomic Time System, which established the United States' standard for time measurement.

FIGURE 1-7 The international prototype kilogram in its vault at the International Bureau of Weights and Measures
in Sèvres, France.

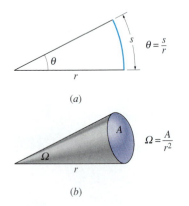

FIGURE 1-8 The SI units of angle. (a)
The radian measure of an angle is
defined as the ratio of the subtended arc
length to the radius. Since the circumference of a circle is $2\pi r$, there are 2π
radians in a complete circle. One radian
is then equal to $360°/2\pi$ or $57.3°$.
(b) The measure of a solid angle is
defined as the ratio of the subtended
area to the radius squared.

Recently, devices called hydrogen masers have been used as even more stable
time standards. And some scientists anticipate that even more accuracy will be
available using pulsars—celestial objects that emit radio signals at extremely
steady rates. So the definition of the second may someday change again.

It's a good thing that we have better standards of time than the rotation of the
Earth: Recent research shows that Earth's rotation rate changes slightly as the
wind blows! To keep atomic time and Earth-spin time in agreement, "leap
seconds" are added to our terrestrial clocks when necessary, usually about once
a year.

Mass

The standard of mass is now the least satisfactory. Unlike the standards of length
and time, which are based on measurement procedures that can be repeated by
scientists anywhere, the unit of mass is still defined in terms of a particular
object—the international prototype **kilogram** kept at the International Bureau
of Weights and Measures at Sèvres, France (Fig. 1-7):

> *The kilogram is the unit of mass; it is equal to the mass of the international
> prototype of the kilogram.*

The prototype kilogram is made out of a special platinum-iridium alloy that is
very hard, not subject to corrosion, and very dense. Nevertheless, it could
conceivably change, and in any event comparison with such a standard is less
convenient than a procedural standard that can be checked in a laboratory. So
scientists are now working on techniques to measure the spacing of atoms in a
crystal of silicon, essentially counting the atoms in a given volume, to scale up
from the mass of a single silicon atom to a new definition of the kilogram.

Other SI Units

SI includes seven independent base units: In addition to the three we've just
defined, there are the ampere (A) for electric current, the kelvin (K) for temperature, the mole (mol) for the amount of substance, and the candela (cd) for
luminosity. Two supplementary units are used to measure angle—the radian
(rad) for ordinary angles and the steradian (sr) for solid angles (Fig. 1-8). Units
for all other quantities are derived from these base units. In mechanics, we use
only the first three of the base units—meter, kilogram, and second—along with
measures of angle.

You could specify the length of a bacterium (e.g., 0.00001 m) or the distance
to the next city (e.g., 58,000 m) in meters, but the results are unwieldy; too small
in the first case and too large in the latter. So we use prefixes to indicate multiples
of the SI base units. For example, the prefix k (for "kilo") means 1000; 1 km is
1000 m, and the distance to the city is more easily expressed as 58 km. Similarly,
the prefix μ (the lowercase Greek "mu") means "micro", or 10^{-6}. So our
bacterium is 10 μm long. Table 1-1 lists the SI prefixes, and is repeated inside
the front cover of this text. We'll use the prefixes routinely in examples and
problems.

TABLE 1-1 *SI Prefixes*

PREFIX	SYMBOL	POWER	
yotta	Y	10^{24}	= 1 000 000 000 000 000 000 000 000
zetta	Z	10^{21}	= 1 000 000 000 000 000 000 000
exa	E	10^{18}	= 1 000 000 000 000 000 000
peta	P	10^{15}	= 1 000 000 000 000 000
tera	T	10^{12}	= 1 000 000 000 000
giga	G	10^{9}	= 1 000 000 000
mega	M	10^{6}	= 1 000 000
kilo	k	10^{3}	= 1 000
hecto	h	10^{2}	= 100
deca	da	10^{1}	= 10
—	—	10^{0}	= 1
deci	d	10^{-1}	= 0.1
centi	c	10^{-2}	= 0.01
milli	m	10^{-3}	= 0.001
micro	μ	10^{-6}	= 0.000 001
nano	n	10^{-9}	= 0.000 000 001
pico	p	10^{-12}	= 0.000 000 000 001
femto	f	10^{-15}	= 0.000 000 000 000 001
atto	a	10^{-18}	= 0.000 000 000 000 000 001
zepto	z	10^{-21}	= 0.000 000 000 000 000 000 001
yocto	y	10^{-24}	= 0.000 000 000 000 000 000 000 001

When two units are used together, a hyphen appears between them: newton-meter. Each unit has a symbol, such as m for meter or km for kilometer. Since these are symbols, rather than abbreviations, they are not followed by periods. Neither are the plural forms followed by an "s." Symbols are ordinarily lowercase; only those named after people are uppercase. Thus, the symbol for gram is a lowercase g; the unit "newton" is written with a small "n" but its symbol is a capital N. The only exception is for the volume unit, the liter, defined as the volume of a cube one-tenth of a meter on each side. Since the lowercase "l" is easily confused with the number one, the symbol for liter is written with a capital L. When two units are multiplied, their symbols are separated by a centered dot: N·m for newton-meter. Division of units is expressed using the slash (/) or by writing the symbol for the denominator unit raised to the -1 power. Thus the SI unit of speed is the meter per second, written m/s or m·s^{-1}. When four or more digits are used together, SI recommends the use of spaces to separate groups of three: 34 365.456 32. We tend to use commas instead of spaces in the United States, though some countries use a comma as we use a period to indicate a decimal point.

Other Unit Systems

The inches, feet, yards, miles, and pounds of the so-called English system still dominate measurement in the United States. Other non-SI units such as the hour for time are often mixed with English or SI units, as when speed limits are given in miles per hour or kilometers per hour. In some specialized fields of physics there are good reasons for using non-SI units. We'll discuss these as the need arises and will occasionally use non-SI units in examples and problems. We'll also often find it convenient to use degrees rather than radians in measuring angles. The vast majority of examples and problems in this book, however, use strictly SI units.

1-4 CHANGING UNITS

FIGURE 1-9 With a height of 553 m, Toronto's CN Tower is the world's tallest free-standing structure.

Sometimes we need to change from one unit system to another—for example, from English to SI units. Appendix C contains extensive tables for converting among unit systems; you should familiarize yourself with this and the other appendices and refer to them often.

For example, Appendix C shows that 1 ft = 0.3048 m. Since 1 ft and 0.3048 m represent the same physical distance, multiplying any distance by their ratio will change units but not the actual physical distance. Then the 1815-ft CN Tower in Toronto—the world's tallest free-standing structure—is

$$(1815 \text{ ft})\left(\frac{0.3048 \text{ m}}{1 \text{ ft}}\right) = 553.2 \text{ m}$$

high (Fig. 1-9). Had we wanted to convert meters to feet, we would have used the ratio 1 ft/0.3048 m.

Often, you'll need to change several units in the same expression. Keeping track of the units through a chain of multiplications helps prevent you from carelessly inverting any of the conversion factors.

EXAMPLE 1-1	*Changing Units*

Express a 65 mi/h speed limit in meters per second.

Solution

In Appendix C, we find that 1 mi = 1609 m, so we can multiply miles by the ratio 1609 m/mi to get meters. Similarly, we use the conversion factor 3600 s/h to convert hours to seconds. So we have

$$65 \text{ mi/h} = \left(\frac{65 \text{ mi}}{\text{h}}\right)\left(\frac{1609 \text{ m}}{\text{mi}}\right)\left(\frac{1 \text{ h}}{3600 \text{ s}}\right) = 29 \text{ m/s}.$$

EXERCISE Aeronautical engineers in the United States often express aircraft speeds in knots (nautical miles per hour). For a 767 jetliner, touchdown speed is 145 knots. Use information from Appendix C to express this speed in meters per second.

Answer: 74.6 m/s

Some problems similar to Example 1-1: 10, 15, 17, 20

1-5 DIMENSIONAL ANALYSIS

Whether we measure length in meters or feet, we're still talking about the same physical quantity—length. And meters per second, miles per hour, or furlongs per fortnight all measure the same thing—speed. No matter what the unit system, speed is always expressed in units of length per unit of time. We call these underlying terms the **dimensions** of a physical quantity. Symbolically, we use the letters L, T, and M to signify the dimensions length, time, and mass; thus, the dimensions of speed are L/T.

In **dimensional analysis**, we examine physical quantities and equations with regard to their dimensions only. For example, both sides of an equation must have the same dimensions for it to make sense. (You can't equate apples and oranges!) Thus a dimensional analysis of the familiar formula "distance equals speed times time" is

$$L = \left(\frac{L}{T}\right)T.$$

The T's cancel on the right-hand side, giving $L = L$ and showing that this equation makes dimensional sense. Dimensional analysis is an important check on the answer to a physics problem since an answer with the wrong dimensions can't be right.

Dimensional analysis also gives scientists and engineers hints as to the form equations must take. For example, you've probably heard of Einstein's famous formula $E = mc^2$ relating energy E, mass m, and the speed of light c. (You'll meet this equation in Chapter 8 and again in Chapter 38.) But why not $E = mc^3$ (Fig. 1-10)? It doesn't take an Einstein to see why not. The dimensions of the energy E are ML^2/T^2, as we will see later. So a dimensional analysis of $E = mc^3$ gives

FIGURE 1-10 Dimensional analysis could help Einstein with his problem.

$$M\left(\frac{L^2}{T^2}\right) = M\left(\frac{L}{T}\right)^3.$$

Dividing both sides by $M(L^2/T^2)$ and multiplying by T then yields $T = L$, which is *not* true. So $E = mc^3$ is dimensionally incorrect. Dimensional analysis of $E = mc^2$ shows that this equation *is* dimensionally correct. What dimensional analysis won't tell us is whether the right equation is $E = mc^2$, $E = \frac{1}{2}mc^2$, $E = 5mc^2$, or $E = \pi mc^2$. What it confirms is that an equation relating energy to mass and the speed of light must involve the term mc^2.

EXAMPLE 1-2	*Water Waves*

The speed of waves in shallow water depends only on the acceleration of gravity g, a quantity with dimensions L/T^2, and on the water depth h. Which of the following formulas for the wave speed v could be correct? (a) $v = \frac{1}{2}gh^2$; (b) $v = \sqrt{gh}$

Solution

Water depth clearly has the dimension L, and speed has the dimensions L/T, so a dimensional analysis of formula (a) gives $(L/T) = (L/T^2)(L^2) = L^3/T^2$. You can probably see that this can't be an identity, but if that isn't obvious, then a little algebra reduces it to $T = L^2$, which is patently false. Note that we ignore the factor $\frac{1}{2}$ since in dimensional analysis we're concerned only with dimensions and not with numerical size.

Analysis of formula (b), on the other hand, gives $L/T = \sqrt{(L/T^2)(L)} = \sqrt{L^2/T^2} = L/T$. This is an identity, so (b) could be the right formula.

Again, we know only that (b) has the right dimensions; it might be that $v = 2\sqrt{gh}$, for example. In this case, though, (b) is, in fact, the correct expression for the wave speed.

EXERCISE The frequency of a pendulum (number of back-and-forth swings it executes in a unit time) depends only on the length ℓ of the pendulum and on the acceleration of gravity g. Which of these formulas for the frequency f of a pendulum could be correct?

(a) $f = \dfrac{1}{2\pi}\sqrt{\dfrac{g}{\ell}}$; (b) $f = 2\pi\sqrt{g\ell^2}$

Answer: $f = \dfrac{1}{2\pi}\sqrt{\dfrac{g}{\ell}}$

Some problems similar to Example 1-2: 27, 28, 63

1-6 SCIENTIFIC NOTATION

The range of measured quantities in the universe is enormous; lengths alone range from about $1/1,000,000,000,000,000$ m for the radius of the proton to $10,000,000,000,000,000,000,000$ m for the size of a galaxy; our telescopes see 10,000 times farther still. Therefore, we frequently express numbers in **scientific notation**, with a number of reasonable size multiplying some power of ten. For example, 4,185 is 4.185×10^3, and 0.00012 is 1.2×10^{-4}. Tables 1-2 through 1-4 suggest the range of measurements we work with for the fundamental quantities of length, time, and mass. Take a minute (about 10^2 heartbeats, or 3×10^{-8} of a typical human lifespan) to peruse these tables along with Figs. 1-11 and 1-12.

TABLE 1-2 *Some Typical Distances*

Distance to farthest quasar detected	1×10^{26} m
Distance to nearest large galaxy (Andromeda)	2×10^{22} m
Diameter of our galaxy (Milky Way)	8×10^{20} m
Distance to nearest star (Proxima Centauri)	4×10^{16} m
Radius of Pluto's orbit	6×10^{12} m
Radius of Earth's orbit	1.5×10^{11} m
Diameter of Earth	1.3×10^{7} m
Deepest ocean trench (Marianas Trench)	1.1×10^{4} m
Skyscraper (Sears Tower, Chicago)	4.4×10^{2} m
Height of person	2 m
Smallest object visible to naked eye	1×10^{-4} m
Diameter of red blood cell	8×10^{-6} m
Diameter of virus	1×10^{-7} m
Atomic diameter (hydrogen)	1×10^{-10} m
Diameter of proton	2×10^{-15} m

TABLE 1-3 *Some Typical Times*

Time since Big Bang	5×10^{17} s
Age of Earth	1.5×10^{17} s
Time for Sun to orbit galactic center	8×10^{15} s
Existence of human species	6×10^{13} s
Half-life of plutonium	8×10^{11} s
Human lifespan	2×10^{9} s
Orbital period of Earth (1 year)	3×10^{7} s
Rotation period of Earth (1 day)	9×10^{4} s
Flight time of intercontinental missile	1×10^{3} s
Human heartbeat	1 s
Reaction time of human nervous system	1×10^{-1} s
Period of highest audible sound	5×10^{-5} s
Period of AM radio wave	1×10^{-6} s
Time for fast computer to add two numbers	1×10^{-9} s
Period of rotation of typical molecule	1×10^{-12} s
Shortest light pulse produced in laboratory	1×10^{-15} s
Half-life of neutral pion	6×10^{-17} s
Time for light to cross a proton	7×10^{-24} s
Earliest time after Big Bang to which known laws of physics apply	10^{-43} s

TABLE 1-4 *Some Typical Masses*

Galaxy (Milky Way)	4×10^{41} kg
Sun	2×10^{30} kg
Earth	6×10^{24} kg
Mountain	2×10^{18} kg
747 jetliner	4×10^{5} kg
Compact car	1×10^{3} kg
Human	65 kg
Raisin	1×10^{-3} kg
Raindrop	1×10^{-6} kg
Red blood cell	1×10^{-13} kg
DNA molecule	2×10^{-18} kg
Uranium atom	4×10^{-25} kg
Proton	1.7×10^{-27} kg
Electron	9.1×10^{-31} kg

FIGURE 1-11 A galaxy can be 10^{21} m across, with a mass of some 10^{42} kg.

0.74 μm spacing

0.4 μm minimum

FIGURE 1-12 Among the smallest commercially manufactured structures are the pits that encode information on compact discs (CDs). This photo shows a portion of a DVD (Digital Video Disc), a newer format that can hold over two hours of high-quality video on a disc the same physical size as a standard audio CD. The region shown is about 8 μm on a side, and the smallest pits measure only 400 nm in length.

Scientific calculators handle numbers in scientific notation. But straightforward rules allow you to manipulate scientific notation if you don't have such a calculator handy:

Math Toolbox

Addition/Subtraction To add (or subtract) numbers in scientific notation, first give them the same exponent, then add (or subtract):

$$3.75 \times 10^6 + 5.2 \times 10^5 = 3.75 \times 10^6 + 0.52 \times 10^6 = 4.27 \times 10^6.$$

Multiplication/Division To multiply (or divide) numbers in scientific notation, multiply (or divide) the digits and add (or subtract) the exponents:

$$(3.0 \times 10^8 \text{ m/s})(2.1 \times 10^{-10} \text{ s}) = (3.0)(2.1) \times 10^{8+(-10)} \text{ m}$$
$$= 6.3 \times 10^{-2} \text{ m}.$$

Powers/Roots To raise numbers in scientific notation to any power, raise the digits to the given power and multiply the exponent by the power:

$$\sqrt{(3.61 \times 10^4)^3} = \sqrt{3.61^3 \times 10^{(3)(4)}} = (47.04 \times 10^{12})^{1/2}$$
$$= \sqrt{47.04} \times 10^{(12)(1/2)} = 6.86 \times 10^6.$$

"Powers" include roots since these can be expressed as fractional powers. Example 1-3 illustrates the application of all these rules.

EXAMPLE 1-3	*Scientific Notation*

As we'll see in Chapter 9, the altitude necessary to put a satellite in geosynchronous orbit—where it appears fixed in the sky, like the satellites at which TV dish antennas are pointed—is given by

$$h = \sqrt[3]{\frac{GM_E T^2}{4\pi^2}} - R_E,$$

where $M_E = 5.97 \times 10^{24}$ kg is the mass of the Earth, T is the orbital period (24 hours or 8.64×10^4 s for a geosynchronous satellite), $R_E = 6.37 \times 10^6$ m is Earth's radius, and $G = 6.67 \times 10^{-11}$ m³/kg·s² is a constant. Find the value of h.

Solution

Writing the cube root as its argument to the one-third power, we have

$$h = \left[\frac{(6.67 \times 10^{-11} \text{ m}^3/\text{kg·s}^2)(5.97 \times 10^{24} \text{ kg})(8.64 \times 10^4 \text{ s})^2}{4\pi^2} \right]^{1/3}$$
$$- 6.37 \times 10^6 \text{ m}$$

$$= \left[\frac{(6.67)(5.97)(8.64)^2}{4\pi^2} \right]^{1/3} [(10^{-11})(10^{24})(10^4)^2]^{1/3}$$

$$\times \left[\left(\frac{\text{m}^3}{\text{kg·s}^2} \right)(\text{kg})(\text{s})^2 \right]^{1/3} - 6.37 \times 10^6 \text{ m}$$

$$= (75.30)^{1/3}(10^{-11+24+(2)(4)})^{1/3}(\text{m}^3)^{1/3} - 6.37 \times 10^6 \text{ m}$$

$$= (4.222)(10^{21})^{1/3} \text{ m} - 6.37 \times 10^6 \text{ m}$$

$$= 4.222 \times 10^7 \text{ m} - 0.637 \times 10^7 \text{ m} = 3.59 \times 10^7 \text{ m}.$$

This is about 36,000 km or 22,000 miles above Earth's surface. Note again how the units worked out. In this case, the exponent (21) turned out to be a multiple of three, so taking the one-third power was easy. Had this not been the case, we would have had to rewrite the exponential term with an appropriate exponent; for example, $(10^{20})^{1/3} = (100 \times 10^{18})^{1/3} = (100)^{1/3}(10^{18})^{1/3} = 4.64 \times 10^6$. A scientific calculator would handle all this automatically.

EXERCISE The speed of sound in air is given by $v = \sqrt{\gamma kT/m}$, where γ is a dimensionless constant equal to 1.4, $k = 1.38 \times 10^{-23}$ kg·m²/K·s² is another constant, T is the temperature in kelvins (K), and $m = 4.84 \times 10^{-26}$ kg is the mean mass of an air molecule. Find the speed of sound in air at room temperature (300 K).

Answer: 346 m/s

Some problems similar to Example 1-3: 30, 32, 35

1-7 ACCURACY AND SIGNIFICANT FIGURES

How accurate are the numbers we've just calculated? In Example 1-3, we were given the value 6.37×10^6 m for the radius of the Earth. The three **significant figures** in this number imply that the radius lies closer to this value than to 6.36×10^6 m or 6.38×10^6 m. The fewer significant figures, the less accurately we can claim to know a given quantity.

In Example 1-3 we were, in fact, given three significant figures for all quantities. The mere act of calculating cannot add accuracy, so we rounded our answer to three significant figures as well. Calculators and computers often give us numbers with many figures, but some or even most of those are usually meaningless.

What is the circumference of the Earth? It's $2\pi R_E$, of course. And π is approximately 3.14159. . . . But if you only know Earth's radius as 6.37×10^6 m, knowing π to more significant figures doesn't mean you can claim to know the diameter any more accurately. This example suggests a rule for handling calculations involving numbers with different accuracies:

> When multiplying or dividing, the answer should have the same number of significant figures as the least accurate of the quantities entering the calculation.

You're engineering an access ramp to a bridge whose main span is 1.248 km long. The ramp will be 65.4 m long. What will be the overall length of the structure? A simple calculation gives 1.248 km + 0.0654 km = 1.3134 km. How should you round this? Here, you know the bridge length to ± 0.001 km, so even the addition of an amount this small is significant. Thus, your answer should have three digits to the right of the decimal point, giving 1.313 km as the appropriate answer. This example suggests the rule for handling significant figures when adding or subtracting:

> When adding or subtracting, the number of digits to the right of the decimal point should equal that of the term in the sum or difference that has the smallest number of digits to the right of the decimal point.

FIGURE 1-13 Uranium fuel rods being lowered into a nuclear reactor.

When subtracting, this rule can quickly lead to loss of accuracy, as Example 1-4 illustrates.

EXAMPLE 1-4	*Nuclear Fuel*

A uranium fuel rod is 3.241 m long before insertion in a nuclear reactor (see Fig. 1-13). After insertion, heat from the nuclear reaction has raised its length to 3.249 m. What is the increase in its length?

Solution

Simple subtraction gives 3.249 m − 3.241 m = 0.008 m or 8 mm. Should this be 8 mm or 8.000 mm? Just 8 mm. Subtraction affected only the last digit of our four-significant-figure lengths, leaving only one significant figure in the answer.

EXERCISE Roof 1 measures 8.22 m by 6.51 m; roof 2 measures 8.46 m by 6.11 m. Find the area of each roof, and determine how much more area of roofing material is needed for the larger roof.

Answers: $A_1 = 53.5$ m²; $A_2 = 51.7$ m²; $A_1 - A_2 = 1.8$ m²

Some problems similar to Example 1-4: 36–39

Numbers with zeroes before the decimal point can be ambiguous. When we say the speed of a jetliner is 950 km/h, do we mean 9.50×10^2 km/h or 9.5×10^2 km/h? Strictly speaking, it is best to write the former if we really know the number to three significant figures. Sometimes, though, we will opt for the convenience of a number like 950 km/h; usually in such cases other numbers present will set the accuracy for the calculation.

Tip

Intermediate Results Although it's important that your final answer reflect the accuracy of the numbers that went into it, any intermediate results you get on the way to that answer should be expressed with at least one more significant figure. Otherwise rounding of intermediate results could alter the rightmost significant figure in your answer.

1-8 ESTIMATION

Some problems in physics and engineering call for precise numerical answers. We need to know exactly how long to fire a rocket to put a space probe on course for a distant planet, or exactly what size to cut the tiny quartz crystal whose vibrations set the pulse of a digital watch. But for many other purposes, we need only a rough idea of the size of a given physical effect. Often, a rough estimate will tell us that we can ignore a certain effect before we go to the trouble of calculating it exactly. In other cases, an estimate—even though it may be off by a factor of ten or more—may help decide among competing theories. And we can often make a rough estimate to check whether the results of more difficult calculations make sense.

EXAMPLE 1-5	*A Brainy Student*

Estimate the mass of your brain and the number of cells it contains.

Solution

My head is about 6″ or 15 cm wide, but there's a lot of skull bone in there, so maybe my brain is about 10 cm or 0.1 m

FIGURE 1-14 The typical human brain has a mass of 1.3 kg and contains at least 10^{11} cells. Image at right is a cross section through a live brain, produced by magnetic resonance imaging.

across. I don't know its exact shape, but for estimating, I'll just take it to be a cube. Then its volume is $(10 \text{ cm})^3 = 1000 \text{ cm}^3$, or 10^{-3} m^3. I'm mostly water, and water has a density of one gram per cubic centimeter (1 g/cm^3), so my 1000 cm^3 brain has a mass of about 1 kg.

How big is a brain cell? I don't know, but Table 1-2 lists a red blood cell at about 10^{-5} m in diameter. If brain cells are roughly the same size, then each cell has a volume of approximately $(10^{-5} \text{ m})^3 = 10^{-15}$ m^3. Then the number of cells in my 10^{-3} m^3 brain is roughly

$$N = \frac{10^{-3} \text{ m}^3/\text{brain}}{10^{-15} \text{ m}^3/\text{cell}} = 10^{12} \text{ cells/brain} .$$

Crude though they are, these estimates aren't bad. The average adult brain's mass is about 1.3 kg, and it contains at least 10^{11} cells, with some neuroscientists believing the number to be much higher (Fig. 1-14).

EXAMPLE 1-6	*Estimation: Nuclear-Electric Cars?*

(a) Estimate the annual consumption of gasoline by cars in the United States. (b) Burned in a car, a gallon of gasoline is roughly equivalent to 30 kilowatt-hours (kWh) of electricity. If a large nuclear power plant produces electricity at the rate of 10^6 kWh per hour, how many such plants would have to be built if the United States converted to electric cars recharged with nuclear-generated electricity?

Solution

How far is your car driven each year? Mine goes about 12,000 miles, or roughly 10^4 mi. A typical car might get 20 miles per gallon, so at 10^4 miles/year, it would use $(10^4 \text{ mi/y})/(20 \text{ mi/gal}) = 500$ gal/y. How many cars are there in the United States? There are over 200 million people, but certainly not everyone has a car. My family has four people and two cars, so perhaps there are about 100 million, or 10^8 cars. The annual gasoline consumption of all these cars is then $(500 \text{ gal/y/car}) \times (10^8 \text{ cars}) = 5 \times 10^{10}$ gal/y. (Figures from the U.S. Department of Energy show total gasoline consumption of somewhat over 10^{11} gal/y, so our estimate is low by only a factor of about 2.)

At 30 kWh/gal, our estimated gasoline consumption is equivalent to $(30 \text{ kWh/gal})(5 \times 10^{10} \text{ gal/y}) \sim 10^{12}$ kWh/y. How many power plants would this require if we converted to electric cars? Each plant produces electricity at the rate of 10^6 kWh/h. But there are 24×365 or about 10^4 hours in a year, so each plant produces $(10^6 \text{ kWh/h})(10^4 \text{ h/y})$ or 10^{10} kWh/y. We need 10^{12} kWh/y; this requires $(10^{12} \text{ kWh})/(10^{10} \text{ kWh/plant})$ or 100 new nuclear plants. Since there are about 100 nuclear power plants in the United States, this would represent substantial new construction.

EXERCISE Estimate the thickness of tread worn off in one revolution of an average car tire.

Possible Answer: 10^{-7} cm, with reasonable assumptions about tire diameter, total distance, and initial tread thickness. There's no single right answer to an estimation problem!

Some problems similar to Example 1-5 and 1-6: 41–50

1-9 ANALYTIC AND NUMERICAL ANALYSIS

Most of the examples and problems in this book—and in most introductory physics courses—involve so-called **analytic** calculations that you can do with pencil and paper and a simple calculator. Most of the mathematical techniques you need for physics you've already learned in algebra, geometry, and trigonometry. You'll also need calculus—either from a previous course or from a course you're taking concurrently with physics. We'll introduce some additional math in the text as needed. And to refresh your understanding of important math ideas you've probably seen before, we include **Math Toolboxes**, like the one on page 11.

Increasingly, though, working scientists and engineers resort to computers to handle their problems. That's not just because computers make calculations easier; more importantly, it's because they allow us to solve problems that would have been either unsolvable or would have taken literally lifetimes to solve. Learning the detailed techniques for such **numerical analysis** is beyond the scope of this book. However, sophisticated calculators now have built-in numerical analysis capabilities, and ever more powerful computer software allows almost automatic solution of problems requiring numerical analysis. Although the problems in this book do not require the use of computers or advanced calculators, you may nevertheless find these tools helpful.

1-10 PROBLEM SOLVING

Most physics problems are quantitative, and for many the answer is a number. That's why we've reviewed topics such as scientific notation and significant figures. But if you view physics as a quest for numerical answers, you're missing the point. The excitement of physics lies not in plugging numbers into formulas but in asking broad questions about how the natural world works and about how we forge the technologies at the heart of modern civilization. The power of physics lies in its answering those questions with quantitatively precise laws, and the challenge of physics—and of engineering based on physical principles—lies in applying those laws in specific situations.

The best way to learn physics is to work problems. Problem solving will give you a deeper understanding of the underlying physical principles and will sharpen your analytical skills. Problem-solving skills are emphasized through-out this text in several ways that are outlined below and in "A Visual Guide to the Book" located in the front of this book. Each chapter contains numerous **worked examples** that illustrate the application of specific principles and tech-niques. Most examples are followed by **exercises** that are similar, with answers supplied. If you really understand the example you should have no trouble working the exercise. After each example is a list of some **end-of-chapter problems** whose solutions are similar to that of the example. The end-of-chapter problems themselves range from simple "confidence builders" to multistep problems; some have **hints** to get you started. Most of the problems are grouped according to the text section to which they most directly relate; within a group, problems appear in order of increasing difficulty. A separate section contains **paired problems** that are about different situations but are the same in their mathematical essentials. An answer to the first problem in each pair is given in the back of the book; if you can get that one, you should also be able to solve the second problem of the pair. A **supplementary problems** section contains additional problems not linked to specific text sections; some of these relate material from different chapters, are especially challenging, or go beyond the text material. Each of the book's six major parts is also followed by a brief set of **cumulative problems** designed to draw on several chapters' material or to present special challenges. **Answers** to all odd-numbered problems are in the back of the book.

No matter how strong your mathematical and analytical skills, however, you'll have difficulty working problems if you don't understand the underlying physical concepts. Simpler problems, which you can solve by plugging numbers into equations, won't help you learn physics unless you know what the terms in your equations mean and how those equations embody fundamental physical principles. To ensure that you understand the underlying concepts, we've placed **"Got It!"** boxes at strategic points in the text. These include simple, mostly qualitative questions that you should be able to answer if you grasp the basic ideas of the section you're reading. Take a moment to consider these questions before proceeding. In addition, you may find it helpful to discuss them with a classmate.

At the end of each chapter, we give a **synopsis** including a brief summary of key concepts and lists of terms and symbols you should recognize. We also list the kinds of problems you should be able to solve after studying the chapter and

FIGURE 1-15 The *ActivPhysics*™ icon. Where you see this icon, a simulation on the *ActivPhysics*™ CD will help you with this material. Underneath the icon will be a reference to a specific *ActivPhysics*™ simulation.

state any limitations that apply to the material. Finally, within the text are numerous **tips**, set off from the main text, that will help your problem-solving efforts.

Several additional products are available to help you learn physics in conjunction with this book. The *ActivPhysics*™ *CD and Workbook* feature simulations of many phenomena, problems, and examples that this textbook can describe only with words or still pictures. To help you use *ActivPhysics*™, we've placed the *ActivPhysics*™ icon (Fig. 1-15) throughout the book to show where simulations in *ActivPhysics*™ can help you with the material.

> ### Tip
>
> *Read!* Before you start work on a problem, *read* the problem statement thoroughly. Be sure you understand what information is given, what's being asked for, and the meaning of the terms used in stating the problem. If you don't know what something means, reread the appropriate text sections or look in the index. If some information seems to be missing, check the appendices. Although physics has a reputation of being hard because it's so mathematical, experienced physics teachers agree that one of the greatest difficulties students have comes from not reading thoroughly!

CHAPTER SYNOPSIS

Summary

1. **Physics** is the fundamental science, dealing with the most basic laws governing the behavior of the universe. This book deals mainly with **classical physics**, an approximation to the more accurate description provided by **quantum mechanics** and **relativity**. Classical physics is a valid approximation for dealing with all but the smallest systems and the most rapid motion.

2. Physics is simple, in that a few fundamental principles describe a host of diverse phenomena.

3. Physics is a quantitative science. In this book and throughout the scientific community, we use the **SI** system of measurement units. Although SI includes seven base units, the three most central to mechanics are those of length, time, and mass.

   a. The SI unit of length is the **meter**, defined as the distance light travels in a specific time.

   b. The SI unit of time is the **second**, defined in terms of the vibration period of the cesium-133 atom.

   c. The SI unit of mass is the **kilogram**, defined by the international prototype kilogram in Paris.

4. **Dimensional analysis** is used to check that the units of a physical quantity are correct and can also help reveal the correct forms for equations.

5. Numbers are generally expressed in **scientific notation**, with a number typically between one and ten multiplying some power of ten. The simple rules for using scientific notation are described in the Math Toolbox on page 11.

6. **Significant figures** convey the precision of a number. Results of a calculation should not convey more precision than the precision of the numbers used in the calculation.

7. In some applications **estimation** may be all that is required to grasp the significance of a physical phenomenon.

8. Most problems in introductory physics involve **analytic analysis**—the use of simple algebra, trigonometry, and calculus. **Numerical analysis**, using computers or sophisticated calculators, extends the range of problems that scientists and engineers can tackle.

9. **Problem-solving skills** are crucial to your success in physics. This book provides many ways of building your problem-solving skills.

Terms You Should Understand

(Number in parentheses is the chapter section where term first appears.)

metric system (1-3)	dimensional analysis (1-5)
SI (1-3)	scientific notation (1-6)
meter, kilogram, second (1-3)	significant figures (1-7)
SI prefixes (Table 1-1)	estimation (1-8)

Symbols You Should Recognize

kg, m, s; other SI symbols as they arise (1-3)
M, L, T in dimensional analysis (1-5)
scientific notation (e.g., 4.85×10^6) (1-6)

Problems You Should Be Able to Solve

changing units (1-4)
checking answers and equations using dimensional analysis
(1-5)

adding, subtracting, multiplying, dividing, and raising to any
power numbers in scientific notation (1-6)
rounding answers to the appropriate number of significant
figures (1-7)
estimating answers (1-8)
using the features throughout this book to help with problem
solving (1-10)

QUESTIONS

1. Explain why measurement standards based on laboratory procedures are preferable to those based on specific objects such as the international prototype kilogram.
2. Which measurement standards are now defined procedurally? Which are not?
3. Given present-day definitions of the fundamental units, is it meaningful to attempt a more accurate measurement of the speed of light?
4. Why are "leap seconds" necessary?
5. When a computer carrying 7 significant figures adds 1.000000 and 2.5×10^{-15}, what answer does it display? Why?
6. In what way are the sciences of biology and chemistry based in physics?
7. Why does Earth's rotation not provide a suitable standard of time?
8. For which of the two coordinates—latitude or longitude—do navigators need a precise measure of time? Explain.

9. Astronomers distinguish two different measures of the length of a day—solar and sidereal. A solar day is the interval between times when the Sun is at its highest position in the sky. A sidereal day is the interval between times when any star other than the Sun is at its highest position in the sky. Why are they different? Which is longer?
10. To raise a power of ten to another power, you multiply the exponent by the power. Explain why this works.
11. A scientist and a creationist are arguing about the age of the Earth. What facts might the scientist use in estimating this age?
12. How would you determine the length of a curved line?
13. How would you measure the thickness of a sheet of paper?
14. Write $1/\sqrt{x}$ as x to some power.
15. How might you define the kilogram so that the standard kilogram could be reproduced anywhere?

PROBLEMS

Section 1-3 Measurement Systems

1. What is your mass in (a) kg; (b) g; (c) Gg; (d) fg?
2. The power output of a typical large power plant is 1,000 megawatts (MW). Express this result in (a) W, (b) kW, (c) GW.
3. The diameter of a hydrogen atom is about 0.1 nm, and the diameter of a proton is about 1 fm. How much bigger is a hydrogen atom than a proton?
4. Use the definition of the meter to determine how far light travels in 1 ns.
5. How long, in nanoseconds, is the period of the cesium radiation used to define the second?
6. Lake Baikal in Siberia holds the world's largest quantity of freshwater, about 14 Eg. How many kilograms is that?
7. A hydrogen atom is about 0.1 nm in diameter. How many hydrogen atoms lined up side-by-side would make a line 1 cm long?

8. How long a piece of wire would you need to form a circular arc subtending an angle of 1.4 rad, if the radius of the arc is 8.1 cm?
9. Making a turn, a jetliner flies 2.1 km on a circular path of radius 3.4 km. Through what angle does it turn?

Section 1-4 Changing Units

10. A car is moving at 35.0 mi/h. Express its speed in (a) m/s and (b) ft/s.
11. I have enough postage for a 1-oz letter but only a metric scale. What's the maximum mass for my letter, in grams?
12. A year is very nearly $\pi \times 10^7$ s. By what percentage is this figure in error?
13. How many cubic centimeters (cm^3) are there in a cubic meter (m^3)?
14. I need a 14-mm wrench to remove the spark plugs in my car, but I have only an English set with sizes that are

increments of one-sixteenth of an inch. What size should I use?

15. By what percentage do the 1500-m and 1-mile foot races differ?
16. A gallon of paint covers 350 ft². What is its coverage in m²/L?
17. Superhighways in Canada have speed limits of 100 km/h. How does this compare with the 65-mi/h speed limit common in the U.S.?
18. One m/s is how many km/h?
19. Express Neptune's distance from the Sun in astronomical units (see Fig. 1-16). *Hint:* Consult Appendices C and E.

Sun

Earth

Neptune

— 1 AU —

FIGURE 1-16 Problem 19 (sketch is not to scale).

20. The United States uses about 550 billion barrels of oil a year. Express this rate in (a) gallons/s and (b) L/s.
21. A 3.0-lb box of grass seed will seed 2100 ft² of lawn. Express this coverage in m²/kg.
22. A radian is how many degrees?
23. A degree is how many radians?
24. Engineers sometimes use an angular measure called the *grad*, defined as one one-hundredth of a right angle. What is one grad in (a) degrees and (b) radians? (Your calculator may have a switch labelled "DRG" to select degrees, radians, or grads as its angular measure.)

Section 1-5 Dimensional Analysis

25. An equation you'll encounter in the next chapter is $x = \frac{1}{2}at^2$, where x is distance and t is time. Use dimensional analysis to find the dimensions of a.
26. Show that the quantity $\sqrt{2GM/r}$ has the dimensions of speed (i.e., L/T), where M is mass, r a length, and where G has the dimensions given in Example 1-3.
27. The speed of waves in deep water depends only on the gravitational acceleration g, with dimensions L/T^2 and on the wavelength λ, with dimension L. Which of these formulas *could* be the right one for the wave speed? (a) $v = \sqrt{g/\lambda}$; (b) $v = \lambda g^2$; (c) $v = \sqrt{\lambda g}$.
28. Energy has the dimensions $M \cdot L^2/T^2$. The energy U stored in a stretched spring is given by an equation of the form $U = \frac{1}{2}kx^\alpha$, where k is a constant with the dimensions M/T^2, and x is the stretch. What should be the value of the exponent α?

Section 1-6 Scientific Notation

29. Add 3.6×10^5 m and 2.1×10^3 km.
30. The volume of the Sun is 1.4×10^{27} m³. What is its radius?
31. Divide 4.2×10^3 m/s by 0.57 ms, and express your answer in m/s².
32. Add 5.1×10^{-2} cm and 6.8×10^3 μm, and multiply the result by 1.8×10^4 N (1 N is the SI unit of force).
33. If there are 1 million electronic components on a semiconductor chip that measures 5.0 mm by 5.0 mm, (a) how much area does each component occupy? (b) If the individual components are square, how long is each on a side?
34. What is the cube root of 6.4×10^{19}? Do this without a calculator.
35. In Chapter 19, we will show that the average temperature of the Earth should be given roughly by $T = \sqrt[4]{S/4\sigma}$, where T is the temperature in kelvins, $S = 1.4 \times 10^3$ kg·s⁻³ is the intensity of sunlight, and $\sigma = 5.7 \times 10^{-8}$ kg·s⁻³·K⁻⁴ is a constant. Find the value of T.

Section 1-7 Accuracy and Significant Figures

36. Add 1.46 m and 2.3 cm.
37. A 3.6-cm-long radio antenna is added to the front of an airplane 41 m long (Fig. 1-17). What is the overall length?

3.6 cm

N28RA

— 41 m —

FIGURE 1-17 Problem 37.

38. Repeat the preceding problem, now given that the airplane's length is 41.05 m.
39. "Machine epsilon" is a computer term describing the minimum quantity that can be added to 1 to give a different number. If machine epsilon for a certain computer is 0.000001, roughly how many significant figures does the computer carry in its calculations?
40. To see that it is important to carry more digits in intermediate calculations, determine $(\sqrt{3})^3$ to three significant figures in two ways: (a) find $\sqrt{3}$ and round to three significant figures, then cube and again round. (b) find $\sqrt{3}$ to four significant figures, then cube and round to three significant figures.

Section 1-8 Estimation

41. Paper is made from wood pulp. Estimate the number of trees that must be cut to make one day's run of a big city's daily newspaper. Assume no recycling.
42. The average dairy cow produces about 10^4 kg of milk per year. Estimate the number of dairy cows needed to keep the United States supplied with milk.

43. How many Earths would fit inside the Sun?
44. Estimate the number of people, standing with outstretched arms touching, needed to form a line from New York to Los Angeles (see Fig. 1-18).

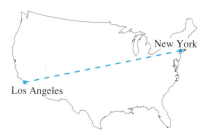

FIGURE 1-18 Problem 44.

45. The average American uses electrical energy at the rate of about 3 kilowatts (kW). Solar energy reaches Earth's surface at an average rate of about 300 watts on every square meter. What fraction of the United States' land area would have to be covered with solar cells to provide all our electrical energy? Assume the cells are 20% efficient at converting sunlight to electricity.
46. (a) Estimate the volume of water going over Niagara Falls each second. (b) The falls provides the outlet for Lake Erie; if the falls were shut off, estimate how long it would take Lake Erie to rise 1 m.
47. (a) Estimate the volume of water in Earth's oceans. (b) If scientists succeed in harnessing nuclear fusion as an energy source, each gallon of sea water will be equivalent to 340 gallons of gasoline. At our present rate of gasoline consumption (see Example 1-6), how long would the oceans supply our fuel needs?
48. Estimate the number of air molecules in your dormitory room.
49. The density of interstellar space is about 1 atom per cubic cm. Stars in our galaxy are typically a few light-years apart (one light-year is the distance light travels in one year) and have typical masses of 10^{30} kg. Estimate whether there is more matter in the stars or in the interstellar gas.
50. Solar power roughly equivalent to the light from ten 100-watt light bulbs falls on each square meter of Earth's surface. Using the fact that Earth is 150 million km from the Sun, and that the Sun radiates energy equally in all directions, estimate how many 100-watt light bulbs are equivalent to the Sun's total power output.

Supplementary Problems

51. A human hair is about 100 μm across. Estimate the number of hairs in a typical braid.

52. The density of bubble gum is about 1 g/cm^3. You blow an 8-g wad of gum into a bubble 10 cm in diameter. What is the thickness of the bubble? *Hint:* think about unrolling the bubble into a flat sheet. The surface area of a sphere is $4\pi r^2$.
53. The moon barely covers the Sun at a solar eclipse. Given that the moon is 4×10^5 km from Earth and that the Sun is 1.5×10^8 km from Earth, determine how much bigger the Sun's diameter is than the moon's. If the moon's radius is 1800 km, how big is the Sun?
54. The semiconductor chip at the heart of a personal computer is a square 4 mm on a side, and contains 10^6 electronic components. (a) If each component is a square, what is the distance across each component? (b) If a calculation requires that electrical impulses traverse 10^4 elements on the chip, each a million times, how many such calculations can the computer perform each second? The maximum speed of an electrical impulse is close to the speed of light, 3×10^8 m/s.
55. Estimate the number of (a) atoms and (b) cells in your body.
56. When we write the number 3.6 as typical of a number with two significant figures, we are saying that the actual value is closer to 3.6 than to 3.5 or 3.7. That is, the actual value lies between 3.55 and 3.65. Show that the percent uncertainty implied by two-significant-figure accuracy varies with the value of the number, being the least for numbers beginning with 9 and the most for numbers beginning with 1. In particular, what is the percent uncertainty implied by the numbers (a) 1.1, (b) 5.0, and (c) 9.9?
57. A good-sized nuclear weapon has an explosive yield equivalent to one million tons (1 megaton) of the chemical explosive TNT. Estimate the length of a train of boxcars needed to carry 1 megaton of TNT. (A 1-megaton nuclear weapon, in contrast, is on the order of 1 m long and may have a mass of a few hundred kg.)
58. Continental drift occurs at about the rate at which your fingernails grow. Estimate the age of the Atlantic Ocean, assuming eastern and western hemispheres have been drifting apart.
59. As you will see in Chapter 16, the speed of waves on a stretched string depends only on the tension, F_0, in the string and on the mass per unit length of string μ. Tension has the dimensions $M\cdot L/T^2$ and mass per unit length obviously has dimensions M/L. Find a combination of F_0 and μ that has the units of speed; this combination must play a prominent role in the expression for the speed of waves on the string.

Part One

Mechanics

Lava chunks spew from an erupting volcano. The laws of mechanics describe their graceful trajectories—as they do all other motion in the realm of classical physics.

I f all motion stopped, nothing whatsoever would happen; the universe would be "frozen." Motion is ultimately what makes everything happen. Motion occurs at all scales, from electrons streaming to the front of your TV or computer monitor to paint an image, to the intricate dance of molecules at the heart of life's cellular mechanisms, to the everyday motion of cars, baseballs, and our own bodies, and on to the stately procession of celestial bodies and the overall expansion of the universe itself. The study of motion is called **mechanics**. In the 13 chapters of Part 1 we introduce the physics of motion, first for individual bodies and then for complicated systems whose constituent parts move relative to one another. Concepts of motion developed here lay the groundwork for much of our subsequent study of physics.

2   Motion in a Straight Line

How fast? Faster than the speed of sound. In 1997 the British ThrustSSC jet-powered car became the first land vehicle to break the sound barrier. ThrustSSC was clocked at 1228 km/h (763 miles per hour) in the Nevada desert.

Electrons swarming around atomic nuclei, cars speeding along a highway, blood coursing through your arteries, galaxies rushing apart in the expanding universe—all these are examples of matter in motion. In physics, the study of motion itself, without regard to its cause, is called **kinematics** (from the Greek "kinema," or motion, as in motion pictures). This chapter deals with the simplest case of motion: A single particle moving along a straight line. This may sound overly restrictive, but we will in fact find important cases of one-dimensional motion—including objects falling under the influence of gravity. Later, we generalize to motion in more dimensions and with more complicated objects. But the basic concepts and mathematical techniques we develop here remain fundamental to these more complex situations.

A **particle** is an isolated point of mass whose size, structure, and internal motions are insignificant. Whether a real object counts as a particle depends on the circumstances. To an astronomer describing Earth's orbit, our planet is essentially a particle. To a geologist, it is a complex system with an array of internal motions. In later chapters, we will see how the behavior of such complex objects follows from the laws we develop for their constituent particles.

2-1 AVERAGE MOTION

"How fast?" is a basic question about motion. There are several ways to answer this question, and we need to be precise about exactly which way we mean.

Distance and Displacement, Speed and Velocity

Suppose you drive 15 minutes to a pizza place 10 miles away, grab your pizza, and return home in another 15 minutes. We call the total length of the path traveled—without regard to direction—the **distance**. Then the **average speed** over some time interval is the distance traveled divided by the travel time. In this example, you've gone a total of 20 miles in half an hour, so your average speed is 40 miles per hour.

On the other hand, you're back home with your pizza. Although you've traveled, the net effect is no change in your position: you were at home before you set out, and you're at home again. **Displacement** means overall change in position. In the pizza example, your displacement between the beginning and the end of the pizza expedition is zero. The **average velocity** is the displacement over some time interval divided by the time. Symbolically, we write

$$\bar{v} = \frac{\Delta x}{\Delta t}, \qquad (2\text{-}1)$$

where Δx is the displacement and Δt the time. The bar over the v indicates an average quantity (and is read "v bar"). The symbol Δ (capital Greek delta) stands for "the change in . . . ." If the value of Δx or Δt isn't given, you can calculate it as the difference between the values of x or t at the two ends of the interval; thus $\Delta x = x_2 - x_1$, where x_1 is the x value at the beginning of the interval and x_2 is the value at the end (see Fig. 2-1). In the pizza example, your overall displacement is zero and, therefore, your average velocity for the entire trip is zero.

If I set out from home, it matters whether I go north or south, east or west. Displacement—the change in position—includes not only how far but also in which direction. When motion is confined to one dimension, there are still two possible directions: forward or backward, north or south, up or down, left or right. We use negative and positive numbers to distinguish the two directions in one-dimensional motion. For vertical motion, we might call the upward direction positive and the downward negative; on Earth's surface, north might be positive and south negative. But the choice is entirely arbitrary. For convenience, we also choose an origin and mark coordinates representing positive and negative displacements. The choice of origin, like the choice of positive and negative directions, is ours to make.

$t_1 = 3$ PM $t_2 = 3:30$ PM

$x_1 = 10$ km $x_2 = 35$ km

(a)

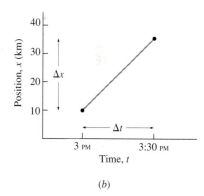

(b)

FIGURE 2-1 A car travels from position $x_1 = 10$ km to position $x_2 = 35$ km in the time interval from $t_1 = 3$ PM to $t_2 = 3:30$ PM. (Positions are measured with respect to an arbitrary origin, just as times are measured with respect to an arbitrary starting time for the day.) The displacement is $\Delta x = x_2 - x_1 = 25$ km, and the time interval is 30 min or 0.50 h. Thus, the average velocity is $\bar{v} = \Delta x/\Delta t = 50$ km/h. (a) shows the actual motion, while (b) is a position-versus-time graph that assumes a constant speed for the car.

FIGURE 2-2 Describing north-south motion in the central United States. Kansas City has been arbitrarily chosen as the origin and the northward direction as positive. Motion from Houston to Des Moines (red arrow) represents approximately a displacement of $+1,300$ km; from International Falls to Des Moines (blue arrow) an approximate displacement of -750 km. How would you describe the overall displacement for a trip from Kansas City to International Falls and then on to Houston?

Figure 2-2 shows some midwestern cities that happen to lie very nearly on a north-south line. We've marked their positions on a coordinate system with the northward direction positive and the origin at Kansas City. Arrows show displacements from Houston to Des Moines and from International Falls to Des Moines. The displacement from Houston to Des Moines is approximately $+1300$ km; from International Falls to Des Moines is approximately -750 km, with the minus sign indicating a southward direction. Suppose the Houston-to-Des Moines trip takes 2.6 hours by plane; then the average velocity is $(1300\ \text{km})/(2.6\ \text{h}) = 500$ km/h. If the International Falls-to-Des Moines trip takes 10 hours by car, then the average velocity is $(-750\ \text{km})/(10\ \text{h}) = -75$ km/h; again, the minus sign indicates a southward direction.

In calculating average velocity, all that matters is the overall displacement. Maybe that trip from Houston to Des Moines was a nonstop flight going 500 km/h. Or maybe it involved a faster plane that stopped for a while in Kansas City. Maybe the plane even went first to Minneapolis, then backtracked to Des Moines. No matter: the displacement remains 1300 km and, as long as the total time is 2.6 hours, the average velocity remains 500 km/h.

Got It!

We've just described three possible plane trips from Houston to Des Moines: one direct, one with a stop in Kansas City, and one that goes to Minneapolis and then backtracks. For which of these trips is the average speed the same as the average velocity? For which does it differ? Where the average speed and the average velocity differ, which is greater?

EXAMPLE 2-1	*Cheap Flight, Lousy Connection*

To get a cheap flight from Houston to Kansas City—a distance of 1000 km—you have to connect in Minneapolis, 700 km north of Kansas City. The flight to Minneapolis takes 2.2 h, then you have a 30-min layover, then a 1.3 h flight to Kansas City. What are (a) your average velocity and (b) your average speed on this trip? Express your average velocity in both km/h and m/s.

Solution
The total time is $\Delta t = 2.2\ \text{h} + 0.50\ \text{h} + 1.3\ \text{h} = 4.0\ \text{h}$. Since Kansas City is 1000 km north of Houston, your displacement is $\Delta x = 1000$ km and so your average velocity is

$$\bar{v} = \frac{\Delta x}{\Delta t} = \frac{1000\ \text{km}}{4.0\ \text{h}} = 250\ \text{km/h}$$

$$= \left(\frac{250\ \text{km}}{\text{h}}\right)\left(\frac{1000\ \text{m}}{\text{km}}\right)\left(\frac{\text{h}}{3600\ \text{s}}\right) = 69\ \text{m/s}.$$

On the other hand, you've traveled a total distance of 1000 km + 700 km, or 1700 km in the 4.0 h. Thus your average speed is $(1700\ \text{km})/(4.0\ \text{h}) = 425$ km/h, nearly twice your average velocity.

EXERCISE You get in your car at 7 PM and head toward a movie theater 5.0 km distant. Unfortunately, the theater's parking lot is full, so you continue an extra 1.0 km beyond the theater to a parking garage. You park and walk back to the theater, arriving at 7:30 PM. Find your average velocity and average speed for this trip.

Answer: $\bar{v} = 10$ km/h; average speed = 14 km/h

Some problems similar to Example 2-1: 1–7

Tip

Watch Your Units Note how, in calculating the average velocity in m/s, we canceled units just as we multiplied and divided numbers. Had our answer not come out with the correct units, we would have had a sure indication of an error. Checking the units of your answers is always good practice and is easier if you carry units along with numbers throughout your calculations.

2-2 INSTANTANEOUS VELOCITY

Average velocity tells us about the rate at which position has changed over an entire time interval, but it doesn't give us the details. Did the plane speed up and slow down, or did it maintain a constant speed? Does a falling object go faster as it falls? Did the marathoner run faster downhill than uphill? Clearly, velocity can change over time. To understand motion in all its detail, we need to know just what the velocity is at each instant.

Figure 2-3a shows a technique geologists use to measure the speed of lava flows. They drop a stick into the flowing lava and measure the time it takes the stick to go a known distance. Dividing the distance by the time then gives the average velocity—which, in this case where the motion is in a straight line from one point to another, is the same as the average speed.

But did the lava flow faster at the beginning of the interval? Was there a region where it slowed down? The geologists could answer those questions with a series of observations over smaller intervals of time and distance (Fig. 2-3b).

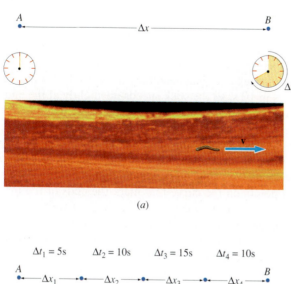

(a)

(b)

FIGURE 2-3 Determining the velocity of a lava flow. (a) Measuring the time Δt for a branch to go the distance Δx from A to B gives the average flow velocity $\bar{v} = \Delta x/\Delta t$. (b) A series of measurements over shorter intervals gives a more detailed picture of the flow, by providing values for the velocities $\bar{v}_1 = \Delta x_1/\Delta t_1$, $\bar{v}_2 = \Delta x_2/\Delta t_2$, etc. Can you tell from the clock readings when the flow is fastest and when it is slowest?

FIGURE 2-4 (a) Position-versus-time graph for the motion in Fig. 2-3. Steeper curve indicates higher velocity. Average velocity over the interval from t_1 to t_2 is the ratio $\Delta x/\Delta t$, or the slope of the blue line. With t_2 far from t_1, this is not a good approximation to the instantaneous velocity at t_1. (b) Enlargement showing a portion of the position-versus-time graph in the vicinity of t_1. As the point defining the end of the interval approaches t_1, the slope of the line joining the two points approaches the tangent to the curve, which is the instantaneous velocity at t_1.

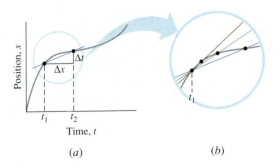

(a)   (b)

As the size of the intervals shrinks and the number of intervals grows, a more detailed picture of the motion emerges. Ultimately, we would like to know the velocity of an object at each instant of time. This quantity, which may vary from one instant to another, is called the **instantaneous velocity**, or, simply, the **velocity**. (Although we use the term "instantaneous" throughout the rest of this section, get used to "velocity" alone as meaning instantaneous velocity.) The magnitude of the instantaneous velocity is the **instantaneous speed**, or, simply, **speed**. We can get a good approximation to the instantaneous velocity by measuring the displacement over a very small time interval, and then calculating the average velocity over that interval. But we can do even better than that, as we now show.

Figure 2-4a graphs position versus time for the stick in the lava flow of Fig. 2-3. We've drawn the graph in the usual format for describing motion: position on the vertical axis and time on the horizontal axis. The gray curve thus represents position as a function of time. Where the position-versus-time curve is steep, the position changes rapidly in a short time—so the velocity is large. Where the curve is flatter, the position changes less rapidly with time, so the velocity is lower. To see that the curve in Fig. 2-4a corresponds to the motion in Fig. 2-3, note the clock showing that the stick takes only 5 s to undergo the first displacement Δx_1. But it takes 10 s for the equal displacement Δx_2, and 15 s for Δx_3. So it's slowing down. And that's just what Fig. 2-4a shows, with the curve starting out steep and then becoming more gradual. Finally, the displacement Δx_4 occurs in 10 s, so the stick speeds up slightly at the end; correspondingly, the curve in Fig. 2-4a has a slight upturn near its end.

Suppose we want to know the instantaneous velocity at the time marked t_1 in Fig. 2-4a. We can approximate this quantity by measuring the displacement Δx over the time interval Δt between t_1 and some later time t_2; the ratio $\Delta x/\Delta t$ is then average velocity over this interval. Note that this ratio is the slope of a line drawn through points on the curve that mark the ends of the interval.

Figure 2-4b shows an enlargement of the region we're interested in from Fig. 2-4a. It also shows what happens as we make the time interval Δt arbitrarily small: eventually, the line between the two points becomes indistinguishable from the tangent line to the curve. That tangent line is the slope of the curve right at the point we're interested in—that is, the ratio of displacement to time interval—and therefore it defines the instantaneous velocity at that point. We write this mathematically by saying that the instantaneous velocity is the limit, as the time interval Δt becomes arbitrarily close to zero, of the ratio of displacement Δx to Δt:

$$v = \lim_{\Delta t \to 0} \frac{\Delta x}{\Delta t}. \tag{2-2a}$$

In principle, we could imagine making the interval Δt as close to zero as we like, and getting ever better approximations to the instantaneous velocity. In practice, given a graph of position versus time, an easy approach is to "eyeball" the tangent line to the graph at the point we're interested in; the slope of the tangent line is the slope of the graph at that point, and is therefore the instantaneous velocity. Figure 2-5 shows this approach. Note that the slope of the tangent line, and therefore the velocity, varies from place to place on the graph. That's the whole point of the instantaneous velocity—it's a quantity that can vary continually.

Got It!

Figure 2-6 shows position-versus-time graphs for several objects. Which object is moving with constant speed? Which reverses direction? Which starts slowly and then speeds up?

Often, we're given the position as a mathematical function of time. We could draw a graph and measure the slopes of tangent lines to find the velocity at different points. But calculus provides a quicker way. In calculus, the result of the limiting process described in Equation 2-2a is called the **derivative** of x with respect to t, and is given the special symbol dx/dt:

$$\frac{dx}{dt} = \lim_{\Delta t \to 0} \frac{\Delta x}{\Delta t}.$$

The quantities dx and dt are called **infinitesimals**; they represent vanishingly small quantities that result from the limiting process. We can then write Equation 2-2a as

$$v = \frac{dx}{dt}. \tag{2-2b}$$

When we're given the position x as a function of time t, calculus provides a simple way to calculate the velocity $v = dx/dt$. Consult the Math Toolbox if you haven't yet seen derivatives in your calculus class, or if you need a refresher.

Math Toolbox

Derivatives Do we need to go through an elaborate limiting process every time we want an instantaneous velocity? No! In calculus you either have or will derive formulas for the derivatives of common functions. For example, any function of the form

$$x = bt^n,$$

where b and n are constants, has the derivative

$$\frac{dx}{dt} = bnt^{n-1}. \tag{2-3}$$

Derivatives of other common functions, including trig functions, exponentials, and logarithms, are listed in Appendix A. If a function is made up of a sum of terms, its derivative is just the sum of the derivatives of the individual terms.

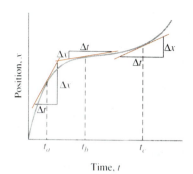

FIGURE 2-5 The instantaneous velocity at a given time is the slope of the tangent line at the point on the position-versus-time graph corresponding to that time. If the position-versus-time graph is not a straight line, then the instantaneous velocity varies with time.

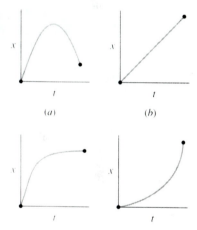

FIGURE 2-6 Can you read these graphs? (See the "Got It!" box.)

EXAMPLE 2-2	*A Space Shuttle Ascends*

The altitude of a space shuttle in the first half minute of its ascent is given by $x = bt^2$, where the constant b is 2.90 m/s², x is in meters, and t is in seconds. Find a general expression for the shuttle's velocity as a function of time and from it the instantaneous velocity at 20 seconds after liftoff. Determine also the average velocity for the first 20 seconds (Fig. 2-7).

Solution

The instantaneous velocity v is the derivative of position with respect to time. Applying Equations 2-2 and 2-3, we have

$$v = \frac{dx}{dt} = \frac{d(bt^2)}{dt} = 2bt \,.$$

This is our expression for the instantaneous velocity at any time t; evaluating it at $t = 20$ s gives $v = (2)(2.9 \text{ m/s}^2)(20 \text{ s}) = 116$ m/s. Note how the units work out; multiplying meters per

second squared (m/s²) by seconds gives meters per second (m/s), the correct unit for velocity.

What about the *average* velocity for the first 20 s? Here we need the total displacement—given by the expression for x itself: $x = bt^2$. So the average velocity from liftoff to some time t is given by

$$\bar{v} = \frac{\Delta x}{\Delta t} = \frac{x}{t} = \frac{bt^2}{t} = bt \,,$$

where we've used x for Δx and t for Δt since both position and time are taken to be zero at liftoff. Comparing with our result for the instantaneous velocity, we see that the average velocity from liftoff to any time is just half the instantaneous velocity at that time. For the first 20 s, then, the average velocity is 58 m/s.

Tip

Watch Your Language The language of physics often holds clues to the meaning and use of physical concepts. In this example, for instance, we speak of the *instantaneous* velocity *at* a particular time. That wording should remind you of the limiting process that focuses on a single instant. In contrast, we talk about the *average* velocity *over an interval* of time, since averaging explicitly involves more than one time.

FIGURE 2-7 As a space shuttle ascends, its velocity increases (Example 2-2).

EXERCISE At time $t = 0$ you slam on your car's brakes. From then until the car stops, your position is given by $x = ct - bt^2$, where $c = 20$ m/s, $b = 1.2$ m/s², and x is the displacement in meters from the point where you applied the brakes. (a) What is your speed 5.0 s after you start braking? (b) What is the car's average velocity during the first 5.0 s of braking? Remember that the derivative of a sum of terms is the sum of the derivatives of those terms.

Answers: (a) 8.0 m/s; (b) 14 m/s

Some problems similar to Example 2-2: 23, 24, 25, 87

2-3 ACCELERATION

In our space shuttle example, the velocity of the shuttle was changing. When velocity changes, an object is said to undergo **acceleration**. Quantitatively, we define acceleration as the rate of change of velocity, just as we defined velocity as the rate of change of position. The **average acceleration** over a time interval Δt is

$$\bar{a} = \frac{\Delta v}{\Delta t}, \tag{2-4}$$

where Δv is the change in velocity and where the bar over the a indicates that this is an average value. Just as we defined instantaneous velocity through a limiting procedure, so we define **instantaneous acceleration** as

$$a = \lim_{\Delta t \to 0} \frac{\Delta v}{\Delta t} = \frac{dv}{dt}. \tag{2-5}$$

As we did with velocity, we'll also use the term *acceleration* alone to mean instantaneous acceleration.

In one-dimensional motion, the acceleration must be either in the direction of the velocity or directly opposite it. In the latter case, the magnitude of the velocity decreases, and we sometimes use the term *deceleration*. In solving problems, though, it's easier to use only the term *acceleration* and let the algebra indicate whether the velocity change is a speeding up or a slowing down (Fig. 2-8). When we deal with two-dimensional motion, we'll find a much richer range of relationships between the directions of velocity and acceleration.

Since acceleration is the rate of change of velocity, the units of acceleration must be (unit of velocity) per (unit of time). Since the units of velocity are distance per time, the units of acceleration are (distance/time) per time, which can be written distance/time². For example, if you accelerate in such a way that your velocity changes by 5 m/s during each second, your acceleration is 5 (m/s)/s or 5 m/s². Sometimes acceleration is specified in mixed units; for example, a car going from 0 to 60 mi/h in 10 seconds has an average acceleration of 6 mi/h/s.

FIGURE 2-8 In one-dimensional motion, acceleration implies speeding up or slowing down. In (*a*), velocity and acceleration are both to the right, and the car speeds up. In (*b*), velocity and acceleration are in opposite directions, and the car slows down. Algebraically, the two quantities have the same sign in (*a*) and opposite signs in (*b*).

EXAMPLE 2-3	*Average Acceleration*

A jetliner rolls down the runway with constant acceleration. From rest, it reaches its takeoff speed of 250 km/h in 1 min. What is its acceleration? Express in km/h².

Solution

The plane undergoes a velocity change Δv of 250 km/h in time $\Delta t = 1$ min or 1/60 h. The average acceleration is therefore

$$\bar{a} = \frac{\Delta v}{\Delta t} = \frac{250 \text{ km/h}}{(1/60 \text{ h})} = 15{,}000 \text{ km/h}^2.$$

Does this huge result make sense? Yes—the jet reaches 250 km/h in only 1 min, so an increase of 15,000 km/h in 1 h is not unreasonable. Of course, the plane never reaches such a high speed because it does not accelerate for a full hour.

Tip

Is This Reasonable? After solving a problem, it's always a good idea to ask whether your answer makes sense. Getting 350 km/s for the speed of a basketball is totally unreasonable; so is 55 kg for the mass of an elementary particle, or 100 milliwatts for the power needed to run your car. In Example 2-3 the result at first seemed unreasonably large, but a little thought showed that it makes sense.

EXAMPLE 2-4	*Acceleration and Deceleration*

Two cars are moving eastward at 20 m/s. At time $t = 0$ both undergo accelerations of magnitude 2 m/s², with one car's acceleration eastward and the other westward. How fast is each car going 5 s later?

Solution

Each car's velocity changes at the rate of 2 m/s², or 2 (m/s)/s, so in 5 s, each velocity has changed by (2 m/s²)(5 s) = 10 m/s. (Note how the units work out.) Both cars are *moving* eastward. For the car that is also *accelerating* eastward, this change represents a speeding up to 30 m/s. But for the car that

is accelerating westward—opposite to the direction of its velocity—the change represents a slowing down, to 10 m/s.

EXERCISE A car moving at 90 km/h brakes and, 5.0 s later, is moving at 40 km/h. (a) Find the average acceleration. (b) Find the additional time it would take for the car to stop, assuming the same average acceleration.

Answers: (a) 2.78 m/s²; (b) 4.0 s

Some problems similar to Examples 2-3 and 2-4: 28–32

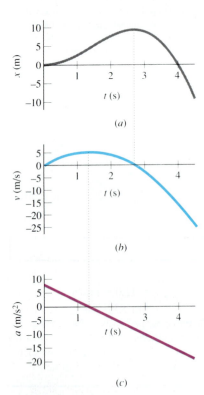

(a)

(b)

(c)

FIGURE 2-9 Position, velocity, and acceleration versus time for one-dimensional motion with position given by $x = bt^2 - ct^3$, where $b = 4$ m/s² and $c = 1$ m/s³. Note that zero velocity occurs where the *slope* of the position graph is zero, and zero acceleration where the *slope* of the velocity graph is zero. In general, each graph gives the *slope* of the one above it; there is no particular relation between the actual *values* on one graph and those on a lower graph. It is the rate of change of a quantity that relates one graph to the next.

Just as velocity is the slope of the position-versus-time graph at a given point, so acceleration is the slope of the velocity-versus-time graph. Figure 2-9 shows graphs of position, velocity, and acceleration versus time for a particle undergoing one-dimensional motion. The rise and then fall of the position-versus-time graph in Fig. 2-9a tells us that the object moves away from the origin ($x = 0$) in the positive x direction, then turns around, returns to the origin at time $t = 4$ s, and continues moving into the region $x < 0$. A closer look, concentrating on the slope of the position-versus-time graph, shows the object moving rather slowly at first (modest slope), speeding up for a while (steeper slope), coming momentarily to rest (zero slope, right at the peak of the curve), and then gaining speed in the negative x direction. Although not needed for this qualitative analysis, the position as a function of time in Fig. 2-9a is in fact given by $x = bt^2 - ct^3$, where $b = 4$ m/s² and $c = 1$ m/s³.

Figure 2-9b is a plot of velocity as a function of time—that is, of the *slope* of the position-versus-time curve. Note that where the curve of Fig. 2-9a is steep—where the position x changes rapidly—the magnitude of the velocity in Fig. 2-9b is large. When x is increasing with time, the velocity is positive; when x is decreasing, the velocity is negative. Where the position-versus-time curve is instantaneously level, the velocity is instantaneously zero. We could have produced Fig. 2-9b by carefully measuring slopes on Fig. 2-9a, but since we know the position as a function of time, we can obtain the velocity by differentiation:

$$v = \frac{dx}{dt} = \frac{d}{dt}(bt^2 - ct^3) = 2bt - 3ct^2 .$$

It is this function that we've plotted in Fig. 2-9b.

Similarly, we study the slope of the velocity-versus-time curve in Fig. 2-9b to learn about the acceleration, which we show in Fig. 2-9c. Where the velocity is increasing, the acceleration is positive; where the velocity is decreasing, the acceleration is negative. And where the velocity is instantaneously not changing—at the peak of the curve in Fig. 2-9b, where the slope is zero—the acceleration is zero. We can get a mathematical expression for the acceleration by differentiating the velocity:

$$a = \frac{dv}{dt} = \frac{d}{dt}(2bt - 3ct^2) = 2b - 6ct ;$$

this equation is plotted in Fig. 2-9c.

In Fig. 2-9, notice that the *value* of the velocity is unrelated to the *value* of the position. The velocity is the *slope* of the position curve—and the slope depends on how the position is *changing*, not on its actual value. Similarly, the value of the acceleration depends only on the rate of *change* of velocity, not on the velocity itself. In particular, we can have zero velocity and still be accelerating! You can see this in Fig. 2-9, where the point of zero velocity does not correspond to zero acceleration.

How can something be accelerating if it's not moving? Consider a ball thrown straight up (see Fig. 2-10). Just before it reaches the peak of its flight, it's moving upward. Just after, it's moving downward. Right at the peak, its velocity is instantaneously zero. No matter how small a time interval you consider about that peak, there's always a change in velocity—and therefore the ball is accelerating, even right at the instant its velocity is zero.

Acceleration is the rate of change—that is, the derivative with respect to time—of velocity, and velocity is the rate of change of position. That makes acceleration the rate of change of the rate of change of position. This sounds less awkward mathematically: as we say that the acceleration is the **second derivative** of the position with respect to time. Symbolically, we write the second derivative as d^2x/dt^2; this is just a symbol and doesn't mean that anything is actually squared. Then the relationship among acceleration, velocity, and position can be written

$$a = \frac{dv}{dt} = \frac{d}{dt}\left(\frac{dx}{dt}\right) = \frac{d^2x}{dt^2}. \qquad (2\text{-}6)$$

2-4 CONSTANT ACCELERATION

In many situations, acceleration is essentially constant. The description of motion then takes an especially simple form. Suppose an object starts at time $t = 0$ with some initial velocity v_0 and constant acceleration a. Later, at some time t, it has velocity v. We can write the average acceleration as the change in velocity divided by the time interval. But because the acceleration doesn't change, its average and instantaneous values are identical, so we have

$$a = \bar{a} = \frac{\Delta v}{\Delta t} = \frac{v - v_0}{t - 0},$$

or, rearranging,

$$v = v_0 + at. \qquad (2\text{-}7)$$

This equation says simply that the velocity changes from its initial value by an amount that is the product of acceleration and time.

1.2

Analyzing Motion Using Graphs

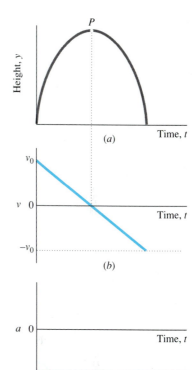

FIGURE 2-10 (*a*) Position, (*b*) velocity, and (*c*) acceleration versus time for a ball thrown straight up. At the greatest height, *P*, of its flight, the ball is instantaneously at rest ($v = 0$). But even at that point, the velocity is in the process of changing—here from upward to downward—so the acceleration is nonzero. In this case the acceleration is, in fact, constant and downward (i.e., negative).

Tip

Know Your Limits Many equations we develop are special cases of more general laws. Understanding how they are derived will help you to recognize their limitations and to know when it is appropriate to use them. Equation 2-7 is a case in point: It applies *only when acceleration is constant*. Only then are instantaneous and average accelerations identical, and it was by identifying a and $\bar{a}$ that we were led to Equation 2-7.

1.3

Predicting Motion from Graphs

Having determined velocity as a function of time under constant acceleration, we now consider position. Since the velocity is not constant, we can't simply multiply velocity by time to get the change in position. But with constant acceleration, the velocity increases at a steady rate—and thus the average velocity over an interval is just the average of the velocities at the beginning and end of that interval. So we can write

$$\bar{v} = \tfrac{1}{2}(v_0 + v) \tag{2-8}$$

for the average velocity over the interval from $t = 0$ to some later time when the velocity is v. We can also write the average velocity as the change in position divided by the time interval. Suppose that at time $t = 0$ our object was at some position x_0. Then its average velocity over a time interval from 0 to some time t is

$$\bar{v} = \frac{\Delta x}{\Delta t} = \frac{x - x_0}{t - 0},$$

where x is the object's position at time t. Equating this expression for $\bar{v}$ with that of Equation 2-8, and rearranging, gives

$$x = x_0 + \bar{v}t = x_0 + \tfrac{1}{2}(v_0 + v)t. \tag{2-9}$$

But we already found the instantaneous velocity v appearing in this expression; it's given by Equation 2-7. Substituting from that equation and simplifying the result then gives the position as a function of time:

$$x = x_0 + v_0 t + \tfrac{1}{2}at^2. \tag{2-10}$$

Does this equation make sense? In the absence of any acceleration ($a = 0$), the position would increase linearly with time, at a rate given by the initial velocity v_0. With constant acceleration, the additional term $\tfrac{1}{2}at^2$ describes the effect of the ever-changing velocity. That time is squared in this term makes sense, too: With constant acceleration, the longer an object travels, the faster it moves, so the more distance it covers in a given time. Figure 2-11 shows the meaning of the terms in Equation 2-10.

How much runway do I need to land a jetliner, given the touchdown speed and assuming constant deceleration? Sometimes we're interested in questions such as this, where we want to relate position, velocity, and acceleration directly without explicit mention of time. We can solve Equation 2-7 for time:

$$t = \frac{v - v_0}{a}.$$

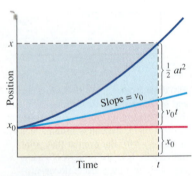

FIGURE 2-11 Meaning of the terms in Equation 2-10. An object starts at position x_0. Were there no velocity or acceleration, it would stay at x_0, and its position-versus-time curve would be the pink horizontal straight line. If it started with an initial velocity v_0 but no acceleration, its position would change linearly with time, as shown in the light blue slanted straight line. A constant acceleration increases the velocity, causing the actual position-versus-time to bend upward in a parabola (dark blue). How would the curves differ if the acceleration and velocity had opposite signs?

Substituting this expression for t in Equation 2-10, we can write

$$x - x_0 = \tfrac{1}{2}\frac{(v_0 + v)(v - v_0)}{a},$$

or, since $(a + b)(a - b) = a^2 - b^2$,

$$v^2 = v_0^2 + 2a(x - x_0). \tag{2-11}$$

Equations 2-7, 2-9, 2-10, and 2-11 link all possible combinations of position, velocity, and acceleration for motion with constant acceleration. We summarize these equations in Table 2-1.

TABLE 2-1 *Equations of Motion for Constant Acceleration*

EQUATION	CONTAINS	NUMBER
$v = v_0 + at$	v, a, t; no x	2-7
$x = x_0 + \frac{1}{2}(v_0 + v)t$	x, v, t; no a	2-9
$x = x_0 + v_0 t + \frac{1}{2}at^2$	x, a, t; no v	2-10
$v^2 = v_0^2 + 2a(x - x_0)$	x, v, a; no t	2-11

We derived the equations of Table 2-1 starting from the assumption of constant acceleration, and we emphasize that they apply *only* in that case. It's also possible to go backward, differentiating Equation 2-10 once to get Equation 2-7 and again to get the acceleration. Problem 38 explores this approach.

2-5 USING THE EQUATIONS OF MOTION

The equations in Table 2-1 provide a full description of motion under constant acceleration. Don't regard these equations as a set of separate laws, but instead recognize them as complementary descriptions of a single underlying phenomenon—one-dimensional motion with *constant acceleration*. The advantage in having several equations lies in their providing convenient starting points for problem solving. Don't memorize these equations; instead, you should grow familiar with them as you work problems.

1.4, 1.6, 1.8, 1.9
Predicting Motion from Equations
Problem-Solving Strategies for Kinematics

EXAMPLE 2-5	*Landing a Jetliner*

A jetliner touches down at a speed of 270 km/h (Fig. 2-12). On landing, the plane decelerates at 4.5 m/s^2. What is the minimum runway length on which the aircraft can land?

FIGURE 2-12 A 767 touches down. How much runway does it need to stop safely (Example 2-5)?

Solution
Here we're given an initial velocity and acceleration and asked for a distance. Equation 2-11 provides the link we need. Solving for x, we have

$$x = x_0 + \frac{v^2 - v_0^2}{2a}.$$

We can take $x_0 = 0$ at the beginning of the runway, where the speed is v_0; at the unknown position x, we want the plane to be stopped, so $v = 0$. Then we have

$$x = \frac{-v_0^2}{2a} = \frac{-[(270 \text{ km/h})(1{,}000 \text{ m/km})/(3{,}600 \text{ s/h})]^2}{(2)(-4.5 \text{ m/s}^2)}$$
$$= 625 \text{ m}.$$

Note that we used a negative value for the acceleration since the plane decelerates after landing. We also converted the touchdown speed to meters per second for compatibility with the units given for the acceleration. A required safety margin brings the minimum legal runway for this aircraft to about 800 m (one half mile).

Tip

Be Careful with Mixed Units Frequently problems are stated in units other than those of the SI system. Although it's sometimes possible to work consistently in other units, when in doubt it's always best to convert to SI units. In this problem, a sure indication of the need for conversion is the fact that the acceleration is expressed in SI (m/s^2), while the velocity is not.

EXERCISE On a dry road, a car with conventional brakes can achieve a maximum deceleration of 7.3 m/s^2. Assuming constant deceleration at this value, what is the stopping distance for a car moving initially at 100 km/h?

Answer: 53 m

Some problems similar to Example 2-5: 44, 47, 51

| EXAMPLE 2-6 | Escaping a Dog |

I am riding my bicycle at a leisurely 10 km/h, then speed up at a steady rate for 10 s to escape a dog. At the end of that time, I am going at 30 km/h. How far did I go during the 10-s interval?

Solution

We want to link v and t, which we know, with x, which we don't know. Equation 2-9 does this. Our answer is the distance $x - x_0$ traveled during the time t:

$$x - x_0 = \tfrac{1}{2}(v_0 + v)t$$
$$= \tfrac{1}{2}(10 \text{ km/h} + 30 \text{ km/h})(10 \text{ s})(1 \text{ h}/3600 \text{ s})$$
$$= 0.056 \text{ km} = 56 \text{ m} .$$

Again, with time in seconds and velocity in kilometers per hour, we had to convert seconds to hours for consistency of units.

EXERCISE Electrons in a particle accelerator are moving at 9.0×10^5 m/s when they enter a tube where they are accelerated to 6.5×10^6 m/s. If they spend 0.61 μs in the tube, what is the tube's length?

Answer: 2.26 m

Some problems similar to Example 2-6: 43, 45, 54

1.12–1.14

Solving Two-Vehicle Problems

Sometimes, we're interested in comparing the one-dimensional motions of two different objects, as the following example illustrates.

| EXAMPLE 2-7 | Speed Trap! |

A speeding motorist zooms through a 50 km/h zone at 75 km/h, without noticing a stationary police car by the roadside. The police officer immediately heads after the speeder, accelerating at 9.0 km/h/s. When the officer pulls alongside the speeder, how far down the road are they, and how fast is the police car going?

Solution

In this example, we deal with two different one-dimensional motions, both described by Equation 2-10. We want to know when the two cars are in the same place—that is, when equations for the positions of the two cars give the same value. In working such a problem, it's important to define the initial positions and times consistently for both motions; otherwise a comparison is meaningless.

Let $t = 0$ be the time the speeder first passes the police car, and let $x = 0$ be the position at which this occurs. Then $x_0 = 0$ for both cars. (We'll use subscripts s and p for quantities associated with the speeder and police, respectively.) For the speeder, we have $v_{s0} = 75$ km/h $= 21$ m/s and $a_s = 0$. For the police car, $v_{p0} = 0$ but $a_p = 9.0$ km/h/s $= 2.5$ m/s². Then for the two cars, Equation 2-10 becomes

$$x_s = v_{s0}t \quad \text{(speeder)}$$

and

$$x_p = \tfrac{1}{2}a_p t^2 \quad \text{(police)} .$$

Equating these expressions tells when the speeder and police car are at the same place:

$$v_{s0}t = \tfrac{1}{2}a_p t^2 .$$

This equation is satisfied when $t = 0$ or $t = 2v_{s0}/a_p$. Why two answers? We asked the equations for *any* times when the two cars were in the same place. Our first answer is just the initial encounter as the speeder passes the stationary police car. The second answer is the one we want—the time when the officer catches up with the speeder. *Where* does this occur? Using the time $2v_{s0}/a_p$ in the speeder equation, we have

$$x = v_{s0}t = v_{s0}\frac{2v_{s0}}{a_p} = \frac{2v_{s0}^2}{a_p} = \frac{(2)(21 \text{ m/s})^2}{2.5 \text{ m/s}^2} = 350 \text{ m} .$$

We can calculate the police car's speed at this time from Equation 2-7, with $v_{p0} = 0$:

$$v_p = a_p t = a_p \frac{2v_{s0}}{a_p} = 2v_{s0} = 150 \text{ km/h} .$$

Does this result make sense? Yes—the police car and the speeder cover the same distance in the same time. Therefore, their average velocities must be the same. The speeder maintains constant velocity, but the police car accelerates from rest. Since the average velocity with constant acceleration is half the sum of the initial and final velocities, the police car must be going twice as fast as the speeder when they meet again.

Figure 2-13 shows both motions plotted on the same graph. Sketching such a graph is often helpful in understanding problems involving two or more one-dimensional motions.

EXERCISE An astronaut making repairs on a space station accidentally lets go of a wrench, which drifts off at a speed of 1.1 m/s. The astronaut immediately fires a rocket-powered backpack and heads after the wrench with a constant acceleration of 0.64 m/s^2. (a) How far does the wrench travel before it's retrieved? (b) How fast is the astronaut going upon reaching the wrench?

Answers: (a) 3.8 m; (b) 2.2 m/s

Some problems similar to Example 2-7: 56–59, 92

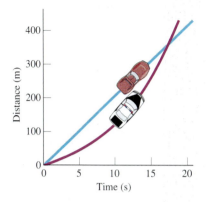

FIGURE 2-13 Position versus time for the speeder and police car of Example 2-7.

2-6 THE CONSTANT ACCELERATION OF GRAVITY

When you drop an object, it falls at an ever-increasing rate (Fig. 2-14), accelerating because of gravity—a phenomenon we will study further in Chapter 9. Experimentally, we find that the acceleration remains constant for objects falling near the surface of the Earth, and furthermore that this constant acceleration has the same value for all objects, independent of mass or other properties. The rate at which the speed of a falling object increases—the **acceleration of gravity**—is approximately 9.8 m/s^2 near Earth's surface. (A more exact value is given in Appendix E, along with values for the other planets.)

The acceleration of gravity applies strictly only to objects in **free fall**—that is, objects under the influence of gravity alone. The presence of other forces, in particular air resistance, may alter dramatically the statement that all objects fall with the same constant acceleration. Try dropping a flat piece of paper and a rock, for example. Their behavior is radically different. But if you crumple the paper, lessening its air resistance, it falls with an acceleration close to that of the rock. An experiment illustrating that all objects fall with the same acceleration was carried out by astronauts on the moon in 1971, when they showed that a feather and a hammer fell together at the airless lunar surface. The acceleration of gravity on the moon is different from that on Earth, but the crucial point is that all objects at the same location experience the same gravitational acceleration.

Galileo is reputed to have shown that all objects fall with the same acceleration by dropping objects off the Leaning Tower of Pisa in about 1600. There is no evidence that the Tower of Pisa played a role, but it is known that Galileo carried out careful experiments by rolling balls down inclined planes. The gradual inclines "diluted" the effect of gravity, allowing Galileo to make more precise measurements. We now study vertically falling bodies with strobe lights or video cameras.

That the acceleration of gravity near Earth's surface is a constant 9.8 m/s^2 means that objects moving in vertical paths change velocity at the rate of 9.8 m/s in each second. Moving upward, an object slows down until it stops and reverses direction; moving downward, its speed increases. These changes in velocity, for an object initially moving upward, were shown earlier in Fig. 2-10.

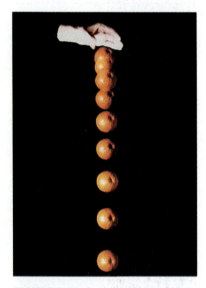

FIGURE 2-14 Strobe photo of a falling orange. Successive images are farther apart, showing that the orange is accelerating.

**1.7
Balloonist Drops
Lemonade**

We emphasize again that acceleration is independent of velocity; the gravitational acceleration of an object near Earth's surface is g, downward, regardless of whether the object is moving up, down, or sideways.

The magnitude of the gravitational acceleration is given the symbol g. Although g is approximately the same at all points near Earth's surface, it varies slightly with latitude and even with local geological structure. Variation of g with altitude becomes substantial even at the relatively low altitudes of Earth-orbiting spacecraft. Nevertheless, close to Earth's surface g can be considered uniform to a very good approximation. Then an object moving near Earth's surface under the influence of gravity alone undergoes constant acceleration, so the equations of Table 2-1 apply. In working gravitational problems, we usually replace x in those equations with the variable y, representing position in the vertical direction. If we take the upward direction as positive—an arbitrary but common choice—then the acceleration a becomes $-g$ since the gravitational acceleration is in the downward (i.e., negative) direction.

EXAMPLE 2-8	*Cliff Diver*

A diver drops from a 10-m-high cliff (Fig. 2-15). Assuming negligible air resistance, at what speed does he enter the water? Give the answer in both meters per second and miles per hour. How long is he in the air? If a photographer's motor drive can take three frames per second, how many frames cover the dive?

Solution

Given the distance and acceleration, we can use Equation 2-11 to find the speed. Since the diver starts from rest, $v_0 = 0$, and the equation becomes

$$v^2 = -2g(y - y_0),$$

where we've set $a = -g$ and we use y rather than x as the position variable. Setting $y = 0$ at the surface of the water, the initial height is $y_0 = 10$ m. Then we have

$$v^2 = (-2)(9.8 \text{ m/s}^2)(0 \text{ m} - 10 \text{ m}) = 196 \text{ m}^2/\text{s}^2.$$

Taking the square root, we find that the speed—the magnitude of the velocity—at impact with the water is 14 m/s. (The actual velocity is -14 m/s, with the negative sign indicating the diver's downward motion.) Converting this result to miles per hour gives

$$|v| = (14 \text{ m/s})(3600 \text{ s/h})(0.001 \text{ km/m})(0.62 \text{ mi/km})$$
$$= 31 \text{ mi/h},$$

where $|v|$ indicates the absolute value of v. Note how the units cancel. Appendix C is useful for conversions such as this one.

Knowing the initial and final velocities, we can use Equation 2-7 to find out how long the diver is in the air. Solving that equation for time t gives

$$t = \frac{v_0 - v}{g} = \frac{0 \text{ m/s} - (-14 \text{ m/s})}{9.8 \text{ m/s}^2} = 1.4 \text{ s}.$$

FIGURE 2-15 A cliff dive (Example 2-8).

(Note here that we were careful to use the negative sign with v, indicating a downward velocity.) Alternatively, we could have obtained the time from Equation 2-10, knowing the distance and acceleration. Solving for t^2 and setting $y_0 = 10$ m (top of cliff), $y = 0$ (water), and $v_0 = 0$, we have

$$t = \sqrt{\frac{2(y_0 - y)}{g}} = \sqrt{\frac{2(10 \text{ m} - 0 \text{ m})}{9.8 \text{ m/s}^2}} = 1.4 \text{ s}.$$

At three frames per second, the diver will appear on (1.4)(3), or four complete frames after the dive starts.

EXAMPLE 2-9	A Volcanic Eruption

The fountains of lava at the volcanic eruption shown in Fig. 2-16 are so hot that geologists can't get close. But they can watch chunks of lava that have been thrown upward, and time their fall. If lava chunks at the peak of the fountain take 5.0 s to fall, how high are the fountains?

Solution

Here we know the time and the acceleration, so we can calculate the distance from Equation 2-10. Let $y_0 = h$, our unknown height at the peak of the fountain, and take $y = 0$ at the ground. With $v_0 = 0$ at the peak, Equation 2-10 becomes

$$0 = h - \tfrac{1}{2}gt^2,$$

so

$$h = \tfrac{1}{2}gt^2 = \tfrac{1}{2}(9.8 \text{ m/s}^2)(5.0 \text{ s})^2 = 120 \text{ m}.$$

EXERCISE Dropped by a seagull, a clamshell crashes down on a seaside rock at 8.3 m/s. (a) From what height did the gull drop the clamshell? (b) How long was it falling?

Answers: (a) 3.5 m; (b) 0.85 s

FIGURE 2-16 A lava fountain at the 1983 eruption of Kilauea volcano in Hawaii (Example 2-9).

Some problems similar to Examples 2-8 and 2-9: 60, 65, 70, 89

So far, we've treated only examples of objects that are actually moving downward. In that case, the magnitude of the velocity increases because the acceleration is in the same direction as the velocity. But the acceleration of an object subject only to gravity is 9.8 m/s² *downward* no matter what the direction of its motion. When you throw a ball straight up, for example, it is accelerating *downward* even while moving *upward*. Why? Because its upward velocity is *decreasing*—that is, the *change* in velocity is negative.

EXAMPLE 2-10	Up and Down

You toss a ball straight up with an initial speed of 7.3 m/s. When it leaves your hand, it is 1.5 m above the floor. Use Equation 2-13 to determine when it hits the floor. Find also the maximum height it reaches and its speed when it passes your hand on the way down.

Solution

If we choose $y = 0$ at the floor, then $y_0 = 1.5$ m and $v_0 = +7.3$ m/s. To find out when the ball hits the floor, we must ask of Equation 2-10: At what time t is the ball at $y = 0$? That is, we want t such that

$$0 = y_0 + v_0 t - \tfrac{1}{2}gt^2.$$

Using the quadratic formula (see Appendix A), we have

$$t = \frac{v_0 \pm \sqrt{v_0^2 + 2y_0 g}}{g}.$$

The quantity under the square root is

$$v_0^2 + 2y_0 g = (7.3 \text{ m/s})^2 + 2(1.5 \text{ m})(9.8 \text{ m/s}^2)$$
$$= 82.7 \text{ m}^2/\text{s}^2,$$

so

$$t = \frac{7.3 \text{ m/s} \pm \sqrt{82.7 \text{ m}^2/\text{s}^2}}{9.8 \text{ m/s}^2} = 1.7 \text{ s or } -0.18 \text{ s}.$$

The first answer, 1.7 s, is reasonable, but what about the second answer, −0.18 s? Setting $a = -g$ in Equation 2-10 assumes that gravity alone provides the acceleration. The equations don't "know" anything about the upward acceleration of your hand or about the ball stopping when it hits the floor; they "think" the ball always undergoes a downward acceleration g. Our negative answer means simply this: had our hand not been involved, a ball traveling upward at 7.3 m/s when it was 1.5 m

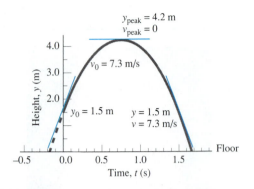

FIGURE 2-17 Height-versus-time curve for the ball of Example 2-11. The ball's trajectory in space is straight up and down; the curve shown is the ball's height as a function of time. Tangents to the curve give the instantaneous velocities: ± 7.3 m/s when the ball is at 1.5 m height and zero at the peak. The dashed curve to the left shows that the ball would have been at the floor at $t = -0.18$ s had it not been thrown at $t = 0$.

off the floor would have been on the floor 0.18 s *earlier*. The positive answer, the one we expected, says that the ball will again hit the floor 1.7 s *later*. Figure 2-17 shows both these answers.

At the peak of the ball's flight, its instantaneous velocity is zero since it is moving neither up nor down at that point. Setting $v^2 = 0$ in Equation 2-11, we can then solve for the peak height y:

$$0 = v_0^2 - 2g(y - y_0),$$

so

$$y = \frac{2gy_0 + v_0^2}{2g} = y_0 + \frac{v_0^2}{2g} = 1.5 \text{ m} + \frac{(7.3 \text{ m/s})^2}{(2)(9.8 \text{ m/s}^2)}$$

$$= 4.2 \text{ m}$$

above the floor.

To determine the speed when the ball reaches 1.5 m on the way down, we can set $y = 1.5$ m in Equation 2-11 and solve for v. Since $y_0 = 1.5$ m, the term $y - y_0 = 0$, and Equation 2-11 becomes simply $v^2 = v_0^2$. There are two possibilities: $v = v_0$ and $v = -v_0$. Again, our formulation of the problem does not really ask only about the downward flight; it simply asks for the velocity *whenever* the height is 1.5 m. The positive answer corresponds to the initial upward velocity and the negative answer to the velocity on the downward flight. In deriving this result, we have demonstrated the important point that an object thrown upward returns to its initial height with the same speed with which it left that height. (This result is exactly true only in the absence of air resistance.) Figure 2-17 is a plot of the motion in this example.

Tip

Think About Multiple Answers Frequently you'll encounter physics problems where the mathematics gives you more than one answer. Before you discard one of the answers, think about what each means. Sometimes an extraneous answer won't be consistent with assumptions you made in setting up the problem. But often, as in this example, both answers have physical meaning—even though both may not be what you're looking for. Often you'll gain more insight into the physics of your problem if you consider the meaning of multiple answers.

EXERCISE A student holds a book outside her dormitory window and tosses it straight up with an initial velocity of 3.1 m/s. How much time passes before she has to catch it? If she misses, how long after it was thrown will it hit the ground, 8.6 m below the window?

Answers: (a) 0.63 s; (b) 1.68 s

Some problems similar to Example 2-11: 70, 71, 81, 82, 88

CHAPTER SYNOPSIS

Summary

1. **Kinematics** is the study of motion. In this chapter we limit ourselves to the one-dimensional motion of **particles**—objects that have no extent and therefore cannot rotate or vibrate. Real objects approximate particles to the extent we can ignore their rotation, vibration, or other internal motions.

2. **Displacement** is the change in an object's position. In one dimension, displacement is characterized by a positive or negative number whose sign describes which of the two possible directions is involved.

3. **Velocity** is the rate of change of position. The **average velocity** $\bar{v}$ is the displacement Δx divided by the time interval Δt over which it occurred:

$$\bar{v} = \frac{\Delta x}{\Delta t}.$$

4. The **instantaneous velocity** is the limit of the average velocity as the time interval becomes arbitrarily small. Mathematically, this process defines the **derivative** dx/dt:

$$v = \lim_{\Delta t \to 0} \frac{\Delta x}{\Delta t} = \frac{dx}{dt}.$$

Graphically, the instantaneous velocity—the derivative of position with respect to time—is the slope of the position-versus-time curve.

5. **Acceleration** is the rate of change of velocity. If Δv is the change in velocity in a time interval Δt, then the **average acceleration** over that interval is

$$\overline{a} = \frac{\Delta v}{\Delta t}.$$

Like the instantaneous velocity, the **instantaneous acceleration** is defined as the average acceleration taken in the limit of arbitrarily small time intervals Δt:

$$a = \lim_{\Delta t \to 0} \frac{\Delta v}{\Delta t} = \frac{dv}{dt}.$$

The direction of the acceleration—indicated by algebraic sign—is the same as that of the velocity when speed is increasing and opposite when speed is decreasing.

6. For **constant acceleration**, position is a quadratic function of time. The following equations relate displacement, time, velocity, and acceleration in one-dimensional motion with constant acceleration:

$$v = v_0 + at$$
$$x = x_0 + v_0 t + \tfrac{1}{2}at^2$$
$$x - x_0 = \tfrac{1}{2}(v_0 + v)t$$
$$v^2 = v_0^2 + 2a(x - x_0).$$

7. The **acceleration of gravity** is the same for all objects at the same location. Near Earth's surface, the acceleration of gravity is directed downward and is essentially constant at 9.8 m/s².

Terms You Should Understand

(Pairs are closely related terms whose distinction is important; number in parentheses is chapter section where term first appears.)

kinematics (introduction)
particle (introduction)
distance, displacement (2-1)
speed, velocity (2-1)
average, instantaneous (2-2)
derivative (2-2)
acceleration (2-3)

Symbols You Should Recognize

$\overline{v}$ (2-1) Δv (2-3)

$\Delta, \Delta x, \Delta t$ (2-1) $\dfrac{dv}{dt}$ (2-3)

$\dfrac{dx}{dt}$ (2-2) g (2-6)

$\overline{a}$ (2-3)

Problems You Should Be Able to Solve

calculating time, displacement, or average velocity from the other two (2-1)
taking a derivative to get instantaneous velocity, given position as a function of time (2-2, possibly in consultation with Appendix A)
calculating time, velocity change, or average acceleration from the other two
taking derivatives to get instantaneous acceleration, given either position or velocity as a function of time (2-3, possibly in consultation with Appendix A)
constructing plots of velocity and acceleration versus from position-versus-time curves (2-3)
solving any problem involving the kinematics of one-dimensional motion (2-5)
solving problems involving vertical motion under the influence of uniform gravity (2-6)

Limitations to Keep in Mind

This chapter covers only motion in one dimension; changes of direction other than reversals along a single line have not yet been treated.
Many of the equations derived apply only to cases of constant acceleration.
Equations for motion under the influence of gravity apply only near Earth's surface (for heights much less than Earth's radius), and do not account for air resistance.

QUESTIONS

1. Why can we consider Earth to be a particle in some applications but not in others?
2. Give three common examples of velocity units.
3. What is the difference between your displacement and the total distance you travel between the time you wake up and the time you go back to bed on a typical day?
4. You are driving straight at a steady 80 km/h, but stop a while for a picnic lunch. How does the stop affect your average velocity?
5. Does a speedometer measure speed or velocity?
6. You check your odometer at the beginning of a day's driving, and again at the end. Under what conditions would the difference between the two readings represent your displacement?
7. In the previous question, under what conditions would the difference in odometer readings, divided by the total time, equal the magnitude of your average velocity?

8. Consider two possible definitions of average speed: (a) average speed is the average of the values of the instantaneous speed over a time interval; (b) average speed is the magnitude of the average velocity. Are these definitions equivalent? Give examples to demonstrate your conclusion.

9. Is it possible to be at the position $x = 0$ and still be moving?

10. Is it possible to have zero velocity and still be accelerating?

11. Is it possible to have zero average velocity over a 10-s interval and still be accelerating during the interval? If so, give an example. If not, why not?

12. Is it possible to have zero instantaneous velocity at all times in a 10-s interval and still be accelerating during the interval? If so, give an example. If not, why not?

13. Suppose your car's brakes provide nearly constant deceleration, independent of speed. If you double your initial speed, what does this do to the time it will take to stop your car? What does it do to the distance the car travels while stopping?

14. If you know the initial velocity v_0 and the initial and final heights y_0 and y, you can use Equation 2-10 to solve for the time t when the object will be at height y. But the equation is quadratic in t, so you'll get two answers. Physically, why is this?

15. Starting from rest, an object undergoes an acceleration given by $a = bt$, where t is time and b is a constant. Can you use the expression bt for a in Equation 2-10 to predict the object's position as a function of time? Why or why not?

16. In which of the velocity-versus-time graphs shown in Fig. 2-18 would the average velocity over the interval shown equal the average of the velocities at the ends of the interval?

17. What would the third derivative of position signify? (The third derivative is sometimes called the "jerk." It's what can make you sick on an amusement park ride.)

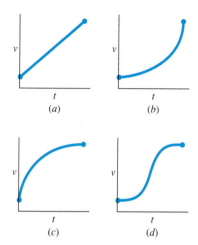

FIGURE 2-18 Question 16.

18. Standing on a roof, you simultaneously throw one ball straight up and drop another from rest. Which hits the ground first? Which hits the ground moving faster?

19. Can the height of the lava fountains in Fig. 2-16 be used to estimate the masses of the lava chunks? Why or why not?

20. If you travel in a straight line at 50 km/h for 1 h and at 100 km/h for another hour, is your average velocity 75 km/h? If not, is it more or less?

21. If you travel in a straight line at 50 km/h for 50 km, and then at 100 km/h for another 50 km, is your average velocity 75 km/h? If not, is it more or less?

22. If you drop one rock from rest, and throw another down with velocity v_0, is the difference in their velocities when they hit the ground more than, less than, or equal to v_0? Don't apply any equations here; just think about how long each rock experiences the acceleration of gravity.

PROBLEMS

ActivPhysics can help with these problems:
Activities 1.2–1.9

Section 2-1 Distance, Time, Speed, and Velocity

1. In 1996 Donovan Bailey of Canada set a world record in the 100-m dash, with a time of 9.84 s. What was his average speed?

2. When races in a track meet are timed manually, timers start their watches when they see smoke from the starting gun, rather than when they hear the gun. How much error is introduced in timing a 200-m dash over a straight track if the watch is started on the sound rather than the smoke? The speed of sound is about 340 m/s.

3. In 1996, Josia Thugwame of South Africa won the Olympic Marathon, completing the 26-mi, 385-yd course in 2 h 12 min 36 s. What was Thugwame's average speed, in meters per second?

4. Human nerve impulses travel at about 10^2 m/s. Estimate the minimum time that must elapse between the time you perceive a stalled car in front of you and the time you can activate the muscles in your leg to brake your car. (Your actual "reaction time" is much longer than this estimate.) Moving at 90 km/h, how far would your car travel in this time?

5. Starting from home, you bicycle 24 km north in 2.5 h, then turn around and pedal straight home in 1.5 h. What are

your (a) displacement at the end of the first 2.5 h, (b) average velocity over the first 2.5 h, (c) average velocity for the homeward leg of the trip, (d) displacement for the entire trip, and (e) average velocity for the entire trip?

6. The Pathfinder spacecraft landed on Mars on July 4, 1997, at which time Mars was approximately 190 million km from Earth. How long did it take Pathfinder's radio signals, traveling at the speed of light, to reach Earth?

7. Australian Chris McCormack won the 1997 world triathlon championship, completing the 1500-m swim, 40-km bicycle ride, and 10-km run in 1 h, 48 min, 29 s. What was McCormack's average speed?

8. (a) Find a value, good to one significant figure, for the speed of light in feet per nanosecond (ft/ns) (1 ns = 10^{-9} s). (b) Electrical signals in wires travel at about half the speed of light. What is the maximum possible separation between a computer's central processing unit and its memory if the central processor is to be able to get a signal to memory requesting data, and have the data return, all in 8 ns?

9. You allow yourself 40 min to drive 25 mi to the airport, but are caught in heavy traffic and average only 20 mi/h for the first 15 min. What must your average speed be on the rest of the trip if you are to get there on time?

10. Taking Earth's orbit to be a circle of radius 1.5×10^8 km, determine the speed of Earth's orbital motion in (a) meters per second and (b) miles per second.

11. What is the conversion factor from meters per second to miles per hour?

12. If the average American driver goes 5000 mi each year on interstate highways, how much less time did the average driver spend on interstate highways each year as a result of the 1995 increase in the speed limit from 55 mi/h to 65 mi/h?

13. A fast base runner can get from first to second base in 3.4 s. If he leaves first base as the pitcher throws a 90 mi/h fastball the 61-ft distance to the catcher, and if the catcher takes 0.45 s to catch and rethrow the ball, how fast does the catcher have to throw the ball to second base to make an out? Home plate to second base is the diagonal of a square 90 ft on a side.

14. Despite the fact that jet airplanes fly at about 1000 km/h, plane schedules and connections are such that the 4800-km trip from Burlington, Vermont, to San Francisco ends up taking about 11 h. (a) What is the average speed of such a trip? (b) How much time is spent on the ground, assuming that the actual distance covered by the several aircraft involved in connecting flights is 6700 km and that the planes maintain a steady 960 km/h in flight?

15. If you drove the 4600 km from coast to coast of the United States at 65 mi/h (105 km/h), stopping an average of 30 min for rest and refueling after every 2 h of driving, (a) What would be your average velocity for the entire trip? (b) How long would it take?

16. I can run 9.0 m/s, 20% faster than my kid brother. How much head start should I give him in order to have a tie race over 100 m?

17. A jetliner leaves San Francisco for New York, 4600 km away. With a strong tailwind, its speed is 1100 km/h. At the same time, a second jet leaves New York for San Francisco. Flying into the wind, it makes only 700 km/h. When and where do the two planes pass each other?

18. Figure 2-19 shows the position of an object as a function of time. Determine the average velocity for (a) the first 2 s; (b) the first 4 s; (c) the first 6 s; (d) the interval from 3 s to 4 s.

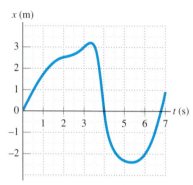

FIGURE 2-19 Problem 18.

Section 2-2 Motion in Short Time Intervals

19. On a single graph, plot distance versus time for the two trips from Houston to Des Moines described on page 24. For each trip, identify graphically the average velocity and, for each segment of the trip, the instantaneous velocity.

20. For the motion plotted in Fig. 2-20, estimate (a) the greatest velocity in the positive x direction; (b) the greatest velocity in the negative x direction; (c) any times when the object is instantaneously at rest; and (d) the average velocity over the interval shown.

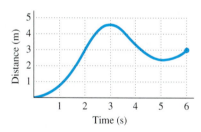

FIGURE 2-20 Problem 20.

21. Figure 2-21 shows the position of an object as a function of time. From the graph, determine the instantaneous velocity at (a) 1.0 s; (b) 2.0 s; (c) 3.0 s; and (d) 4.5 s. (e) What is the average velocity over the interval shown?

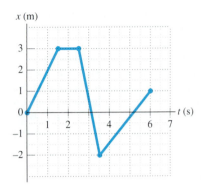

FIGURE 2-21 Problem 21.

22. The position of an object as a function of time is given by $x = bt + ct^3$, where $b = 1.50$ m/s and $c = 0.640$ m/s^3. To study the limiting process leading to the definition of instantaneous velocity, calculate the average velocity of the object over time intervals from (a) 1.00 s to 3.00 s; (b) 1.50 s to 2.50 s; (c) 1.95 s to 2.05 s. (d) Obtain the instantaneous velocity as a function of time by differentiating, and compare its value at 2 s with your average velocities.

23. A model rocket is launched straight upward; its altitude y as a function of time is given by $y = bt - ct^2$, where $b = 82$ m/s, $c = 4.9$ m/s^2, t is the time in seconds, and y is in meters. (a) Use differentiation to find a general expression for the rocket's velocity as a function of time. (b) When is the velocity zero?

24. The position of an object as a function of time is given by $x = bt^4$, where b is a constant. Find an expression for the instantaneous velocity as a function of time, and show that the average velocity over the interval from $t = 0$ to any time t is one-fourth of the instantaneous velocity at t.

25. The position of an object is given by $x = bt^3 - ct^2 + dt$, with x in meters and t in seconds. The constants b, c, and d are $b = 3.0$ m/s^3, $c = 8.0$ m/s^2, and $d = 1.0$ m/s. (a) Find all times when the object is at position $x = 0$. (b) Determine a general expression for the instantaneous velocity as a function of time, and from it find (c) the initial velocity and (d) all times when the object is instantaneously at rest. (e) Graph the object's position as a function of time, and identify on the graph the quantities you found in (a) to (d).

26. In a drag race, the position of a car as a function of time is given by $x = bt^2$, with $b = 2.000$ m/s^2. In an attempt to determine the car's velocity midway down a 400-m track, two observers stand 20 m on either side of the 200-m mark and note the time when the car passes them. (a) What value do the two observers compute for the car's velocity? Give your answer to four significant figures. (b) By what percentage does this observed value differ from the actual instantaneous value at $x = 200$ m?

Section 2-3 Acceleration

27. A giant eruption on the Sun propels solar material from rest to a final speed of 450 km/s over a period of 1 h. What is the average acceleration of this material, in m/s^2?

28. Starting from rest, a subway train first accelerates to 25 m/s, then begins to brake. Forty-eight seconds after starting, it is moving at 17 m/s. What is its average acceleration in this 48-s interval?

29. A space shuttle's main engines cut off 8.5 min after launch, at which time the shuttle's speed is 7.6 km/s. What is the shuttle's average acceleration during this interval?

30. An egg drops from a second-story window, taking 1.12 s to fall and reaching a speed of 11.0 m/s just before hitting the ground. On contact with the ground, the egg stops completely in 0.131 s. Calculate the average magnitudes of its acceleration while falling and of its deceleration while stopping.

31. An airplane's takeoff speed is 320 km/h. If its average acceleration is 2.9 m/s^2, how long is it on the runway after starting its takeoff roll?

32. ThrustSSC, the world's first supersonic car, accelerates from rest to 1000 km/h in 16 s. What is its acceleration, in m/s^2?

33. Your plane reaches its takeoff runway and then holds for 4.0 min because of air-traffic congestion. The plane then heads down the runway with an average acceleration of 3.6 m/s^2. It is airborne 35 s later. What are (a) its takeoff speed and (b) its average acceleration from the time it reaches the takeoff runway until it's airborne?

34. Under the influence of a radio wave, an electron in an antenna undergoes back-and-forth motion whose velocity as a function of time is described by Fig. 2-22. From the graph, estimate the electron's maximum acceleration.

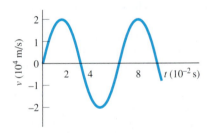

FIGURE 2-22 Problem 34.

35. Determine the instantaneous acceleration as a function of time for the motion in Problem 25.

36. The position of an object is given by $x = bt^3$, where x is in meters, t is in seconds, and where the constant b is 1.5 m/s^3. Determine (a) the instantaneous velocity and (b) the instantaneous acceleration at the end of 2.5 s. Find (c) the average velocity and (d) the average acceleration during the first 2.5 s.

Section 2-4 Constant Acceleration

37. A car accelerates from rest to 25 m/s in 8.0 s. Determine the distance it travels in two ways: (a) by multiplying the average velocity given in Equation 2-8 by the time and (b) by calculating the acceleration from Equation 2-7 and using the result in Equation 2-10.
38. Differentiate both sides of Equation 2-10, and show that you get Equation 2-7.
39. If you square Equation 2-7, you'll have an expression for v^2. Equation 2-11 also gives an expression for v^2. Equate the two expressions for v^2, and show that the resulting equation reduces to Equation 2-10.

Section 2-5 Using the Equations of Motion

40. Electrons that "paint" the picture in a TV tube undergo constant acceleration over a distance of 3.8 cm. If they reach a final speed of 1.2×10^7 m/s, what are (a) the electrons' acceleration and (b) the time spent accelerating?
41. A rocket rises with constant acceleration to an altitude of 85 km, at which point its speed is 2.8 km/s. (a) What is its acceleration? (b) How long does the ascent take?
42. On packed snow, use of computerized antilock brakes can reduce the stopping distance for a car by 55%. By what percentage is the stopping *time* reduced?
43. Starting from rest, a car accelerates at a constant rate, reaching 88 km/h in 12 s. (a) What is its acceleration? (b) How far does it go in this time?
44. A car moving initially at 50 mi/h begins decelerating at a constant rate 100 ft short of a stoplight. If the car comes to a full stop just at the light, what is the magnitude of its deceleration?
45. In an x-ray tube, electrons are accelerated to a velocity of 10^8 m/s, then slammed into a tungsten target. The electrons undergo rapid deceleration, producing X rays. If the stopping time for an electron is on the order of 10^{-19} s, approximately how far does an electron move while decelerating? Assume constant deceleration.
46. A particle leaves its initial position x_0 at time $t = 0$, moving in the positive x direction with speed v_0, but undergoing acceleration of magnitude a in the negative x direction. Find expressions for (a) the time when it returns to the position x_0 and (b) its speed when it passes that point.
47. The Barringer meteor crater in northern Arizona is 180 m deep and 1.2 km in diameter. The fragments of the meteor lie just below the bottom of the crater. If these fragments decelerated at a constant rate of 4×10^5 m/s^2 as they ploughed through the Earth in forming the crater, what was the speed of the meteor's impact at Earth's surface?
48. A gazelle accelerates from rest at 4.1 m/s^2 over a distance of 60 m to outrun a predator. What is its final speed?
49. A hockey puck moving at 32 m/s slams through a wall of snow 35 cm thick. It emerges moving at 18 m/s. (a) How much time does it spend in the snow? (b) How thick a wall of snow would be needed to stop the puck entirely?

50. Amtrak's 20th-Century Limited is en route from Chicago to New York at 110 km/h, when the engineer spots a cow on the track. The train brakes to a halt in 1.2 min with constant deceleration, stopping just in front of the cow. (a) What is the magnitude of the train's acceleration? (b) What is the direction of the acceleration? (c) How far was the train from the cow when the engineer first applied the brakes?
51. A jetliner touches down at 220 km/h, reverses its engines to provide braking, and comes to a halt 29 s later. What is the shortest runway on which this aircraft can land, assuming constant deceleration starting at touchdown?
52. A motorist suddenly notices a stalled car and slams on the brakes, decelerating at the rate of 6.3 m/s^2. Unfortunately this isn't good enough, and a collision ensues. From the damage sustained, police estimate that the car was moving at 18 km/h at the time of the collision. They also measure skid marks 34 m long. (a) How fast was the motorist going when the brakes were first applied? (b) How much time elapsed from the initial braking to the collision?
53. The maximum acceleration that a human being can survive even for a short time is about $200g$. In a highway accident, a car moving at 88 km/h slams into a stalled truck. The front end of the car is squashed by 80 cm on impact. If the deceleration during the collision is constant, will a passenger wearing a seatbelt survive?
54. A racing car undergoing constant acceleration covers 140 m in 3.6 s. (a) If it is moving at 53 m/s at the end of this interval, what was its speed at the beginning of the interval? (b) How far did it travel *from rest* to the end of the 140-m distance?
55. The maximum deceleration of a car on a dry road is about 8 m/s^2. If two cars are moving head-on toward each other at 88 km/h (55 mi/h), and their drivers apply their brakes when they are 85 m apart, will they collide? If so, at what relative speed? If not, how far apart will they be when they stop? On the same graph, plot distance versus time for both cars.
56. George, a physics student, leaves his dormitory at a speed of 1.2 m/s, heading for the physics building 95 m away. Just as he leaves his dorm, Amy, another physics student, leaves the physics building and heads toward George at a steady 1.6 m/s. George immediately spots her and begins accelerating at 0.075 m/s^2. Where and when do the two meet? Plot position-versus-time curves for both students on a single graph.
57. After 35 minutes of running, at the 9-km point in a 10-km race, you find yourself 100 m behind the leader and moving at the same speed. What should your acceleration be if you are to catch up by the finish line? Assume that the leader maintains constant speed throughout the entire race.
58. You're speeding at 85 km/h when you notice that you're only 10 m behind the car in front of you, which is moving at the legal speed limit of 60 km/h. You slam on your brakes, and your car decelerates at 4.2 m/s^2. Assuming the

car in front of you continues at constant speed, will you collide? If so, at what relative speed? If not, what will be the distance between the cars at their closest approach?

59. Repeat the preceding problem, now assuming your initial speed is 95 km/h.

Section 2-6 The Constant Acceleration of Gravity

60. You drop a rock into a deep well and 4.4 s later hear the splash. How far down is the water? Neglect the travel time of the sound.

61. Your friend is sitting 6.5 m above you in a tree branch. How fast should you throw an apple so that it just reaches her?

62. A model rocket leaves the ground, heading straight up at 49 m/s. (a) What is its maximum altitude? What are its speed and altitude at (b) 1 s; (c) 4 s; (d) 7 s?

63. A foul ball leaves the bat going straight upward at 23 m/s. (a) How high does it rise? (b) How long is it in the air? Neglect the distance between the bat and the ground.

64. A Frisbee is lodged in a tree branch, 6.5 m above the ground. A rock thrown from below must be going at least 3 m/s to dislodge the Frisbee. How fast must such a rock be thrown upward, if it leaves the thrower's hand 1.3 m above the ground?

65. Space pirates kidnap an earthling and hold him imprisoned on one of the planets of the solar system. With nothing else to do, the prisoner amuses himself by dropping his watch from eye level (170 cm) to the floor. He observes that the watch takes 0.95 s to fall. On what planet is he being held? *Hint:* Consult Appendix E.

66. The Mars Pathfinder spacecraft landed in 1997 and deployed a robot Rover that explored the Martian surface. Pathfinder's landing was cushioned by airbags, and the spacecraft bounced 12 m vertically after its first impact. Assuming no loss of speed at contact with the Martian surface, what was Pathfinder's impact speed?

67. A falling object travels one-fourth of its total distance in the last second of its fall. From what height was it dropped?

68. The defenders of a castle throw rocks down on their attackers from a 15-m-high wall. If the rocks are thrown with an initial speed of 10 m/s, how much faster are they moving when they hit the ground than if they were simply dropped?

69. A kingfisher is 30 m above a lake when it accidentally drops the fish it is carrying. A second kingfisher 5 m above the first dives toward the falling fish. What initial speed should it have if it is to reach the fish before the fish hits the water?

70. Two divers jump from a 3.00-m platform. One jumps upward at 1.80 m/s, and the second steps off the platform as the first passes it on the way down. (a) What are their speeds as they hit the water? (b) Which hits the water first and by how much?

71. A balloon is rising at 10 m/s when its passenger throws a ball straight up at 12 m/s. How much later does the passenger catch the ball?

72. A conveyor belt moves horizontally at 80 cm/s, carrying empty shoe boxes. Every 3 s, a pair of shoes is dropped from a chute 1.7 m above the belt. (a) How far apart should the boxes be spaced? (b) At the instant a pair of shoes drops, where should a box be in relation to a point directly below the chute?

Paired Problems

(Both problems in a pair involve the same principles and techniques. If you can get the first problem, you should be able to solve the second one.)

73. You drive 14 km to the next town, maintaining a speed of 50 km/h except for a stop lasting 4.1 min at a red light. You shop for 20 min, then head back toward your starting point at a steady 70 km/h. You stop at a gas station 4.4 km from the town. What are (a) your average speed and (b) the magnitude of your average velocity between your starting point and the gas station?

74. The itsy-bitsy spider climbed 3.7 m up the water spout, starting at the bottom, in 6.2 minutes. She paused at the top for a 5.0-min rest. Then down came the rain, and washed the spider out—all the way to the ground, 0.41 m below the bottom of the spout, in 2.8 s. What were the spider's (a) average speed and (b) magnitude of her average velocity for the entire adventure?

75. A skier starts from rest, and heads downslope with a constant acceleration of 1.9 m/s². How long does it take her to go 20 m, and what is her speed at that point?

76. Landing on the moon, a spacecraft fires its retrorockets and comes to a complete stop just 12 m above the lunar surface. It then drops freely to the surface. How long does it take to fall, and what is its impact speed? (Consult Appendix E.)

77. A frustrated student drops a book out of his dormitory window, releasing it from rest. After falling 2.3 m, it passes the top of a 1.5-m high window on a lower floor. How long does it take to cross the window?

78. Launched from the ground, a rocket accelerates vertically upward at 4.6 m/s². It passes through a band of clouds 5.3 km thick, extending upward from an altitude of 1.9 km. How long is it in the clouds?

79. A subway train is traveling at 80 km/h when it approaches a slower train 50 m ahead traveling in the same direction at 25 km/h. If the faster train begins decelerating at 2.1 m/s², while the slower train continues at constant speed, how soon and at what relative speed will they collide?

80. A parachutist is drifting vertically downward at a constant 11 m/s. An airplane passes a mere 8.4 m directly above the parachutist, and the pilot throws an orange straight downward at 2.2 m/s. How much later do the orange and parachutist meet, and what is their relative speed?

81. You toss a hammer over the 3.7-m high wall of a construction site, starting your throw at a height of 1.2 m above the sidewalk. On the other side of the wall, the hammer falls to the bottom of an excavation 7.9 m below the sidewalk (see

FIGURE 2-23 Problem 81.

Fig. 2-23). (a) What is the minimum speed at which you must throw the hammer for it to clear the wall? (b) Assuming it's thrown with the speed given in part (a), when will it hit the bottom of the excavation?

82. You toss a book into your dorm room, just clearing a windowsill 4.2 m above the ground. (a) If the book leaves your hand 1.5 m above the ground, how fast must it be going to clear the sill? (b) How long after it leaves your hand will it hit the floor, 0.87 m below the windowsill?

Supplementary Problems

83. A car accelerates away from a red light at 2.5 m/s² until its speed reaches 10 m/s. It travels at that speed for 8.0 s, then brakes to a stop at the next red light with deceleration 4.0 m/s². What is the distance between lights?

84. Consider an object traversing a distance ℓ, part of the way at speed v_1 and the rest of the way at speed v_2. Find expressions for the average speeds (a) when the object moves at each of the two speeds for half the total *time* and (b) when it moves at each of the two speeds for half the *distance*.

85. You see the traffic light ahead of you is about to turn from red to green, so you slow to a steady speed of 10 km/h and cruise to the light, reaching it just as it turns green. You accelerate to 60 km/h in the next 12 s, then maintain constant speed. At the light, you pass a Porsche that has stopped. Just as you pass (and the light turns green) the Porsche begins accelerating, reaching 65 km/h in 6.9 s, then maintaining constant speed. (a) Plot the motions of both cars on a graph showing the 10-s period after the light turns green. (b) How long after the light turns green does the Porsche pass you? (c) How far are you from the light when the Porsche passes you?

86. In the accident of Problem 53, calculate the relative speed with which a passenger not wearing a seatbelt collides with the dashboard. Assume the passenger undergoes no deceleration before striking the dashboard, and that the passenger is initially 1 m from the dashboard.

87. The position of a particle as a function of time is given by $x = x_0 \sin \omega t$, where x_0 and ω are constants. (a) Take derivatives to find expressions for the velocity and acceleration. (b) What are the maximum values of velocity and acceleration? *Hint:* Consult the table of derivatives in Appendix A.

88. Ice skaters, ballet dancers, and basketball players executing vertical leaps often give the illusion of "hanging" almost motionless near the top of the leap (see Fig. 2-24). To see why this is, consider a leap that takes an athlete up a vertical distance h. Of the total time spent in the air, what fraction is spent in the upper half (i.e., at $y > \frac{1}{2}h$)?

FIGURE 2-24 What fraction of the skater's jump is spent in the upper half of the jump height? (Problem 88)

89. A faucet leaks water at the rate of 15 drops per second. At the instant one drop leaves the faucet, another strikes the sink below, and two additional drops are in between on the way down. How far is it from the faucet to the sink bottom?

90. The depth of a well is such that an object dropped into the well hits the water going far slower than the speed of sound. Use the binomial theorem (see Appendix A) to show that, under these conditions, the depth of the well is given approximately by

$$d = \frac{1}{2}gt^2\left(1 - \frac{gt}{v_s}\right),$$

where t is the time from when you drop the object until you hear the splash, and v_s is the speed of sound.

91. A student is staring idly out her dormitory window when she sees a water balloon fall past. If the balloon takes 0.22 s to cross the 130-cm-high window, from what height above the top of the window was it dropped?

92. A police radar has an effective range of 1.0 km, while a motorist's radar detector has a range of 1.9 km. The motorist is going 110 km/h in a 70 km/h zone when the radar detector beeps. At what rate must the motorist decelerate to avoid a speeding ticket?

3 The Vector Description of Motion

Direction is an essential attribute of motion and of many other physical quantities, as suggested by this sign. The mathematical language of vectors helps characterize such directional quantities.

Motion is rarely limited to a single straight road, or a purely vertical flight. The motion of a football player around the football field, or balls on a billiard table, cannot be completely described by the use of positive and negative numbers that we used to define motion in a straight line in Chapter 2. We need to introduce another dimension to describe the *two-dimensional* motion of the footballer or the billiard ball. Some motion, such as scaling a mountain, flying from city to city, or throwing a ball across a basketball court, adds the vertical dimension to give *three-dimensional* motion. In this chapter we develop mathematical tools for the full description of motion.

3-1 VECTORS AND SCALARS

Motion in more than one dimension offers rich possibilities: I can head north, east, south, or west—or any direction in between. I can run in a circle or follow any other curved path. I can throw a ball at any angle. Think of a frog's leap, a hummingbird's flight, the casting of a fishing line. These motions beg questions not just of "how far?" and "how fast?" but also "which direction?"

In Chapter 2 we specified position along a straight line, with a single number giving the distance from some origin. We used a positive or negative sign to indicate either of the two directions possible in one dimension. In two or three dimensions we still can give the distance from the origin, but now we need to distinguish among many possible directions. A quantity like position, whose full specification requires both a size as well as a direction, is called a **vector**. We represent vectors using arrows; the length of the arrow represents the **magnitude**, or size, of the vector quantity, and the arrow's orientation gives the vector's direction. Position in two or three dimensions is clearly a vector, specified by giving the distance and direction from a chosen starting point, or **origin** (Fig. 3-1). Velocity, acceleration, and a number of other quantities we will encounter in physics are also vectors. Full specification of a vector in two dimensions requires two numbers, which could be the magnitude and direction; in three dimensions, specification of a vector requires three numbers.

In contrast, a **scalar** is a quantity that can be represented by a single number, such as time, mass, or temperature. In this text we distinguish vectors from scalars by using boldface type for vector symbols and italics for scalars. When handwriting vectors, it's common practice to use an arrow over the symbol for a vector quantity. As you work physics problems, it's important that you consistently distinguish vectors from scalars.

3-2 VECTOR ARITHMETIC

We can add, subtract, and multiply vectors; these operations expand the concepts of scalar addition, subtraction, and multiplication with which you're already familiar. Here, we illustrate vector arithmetic graphically so you can understand how it works; later we show how to handle vector arithmetic with analytic techniques. Grasping the techniques of vector arithmetic will help you to understand complex motion and other physical phenomena.

The most obvious vector quantity is **position**. Where is the next city? It's 45 km to the northwest. That specification of how far and in what direction amounts to giving the position vector for the next city, as measured from your city. We always specify position relative to some origin point. The choice of origin is yours to make and is completely arbitrary. We designate a position vector with the symbol **r**, represented as an arrow from the origin to the object's actual position. Figure 3-1 shows the position vector $\mathbf{r}_1$ for a rock located 2 m from an origin designated O.

Adding Vectors

Suppose we move the rock in Fig. 3-1 one m to the right, as suggested in Fig. 3-2. The rock's position has now changed. Generalizing our definition of displacement from the previous chapter, we define **displacement** as the change in position. Now, however, displacement isn't just a signed number but a vector.

FIGURE 3-1 The position vector $\mathbf{r}_1$ for a rock located 2 m from the origin at 30° to an arbitrarily chosen axis.

FIGURE 3-2 Vector addition. The rock's new position vector $\mathbf{r}_2$ defines the vector sum of the old position vector $\mathbf{r}_1$ and the displacement $\Delta\mathbf{r}$. Graphically, we sum the vectors by placing them head-to-tail.

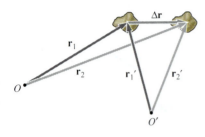

FIGURE 3-3 The moving rock, again. Its displacement Δr does not depend on the choice of origin. Here O is the origin introduced in Figs. 3-1 and 3-2, and O' is a new origin, with r_1' and r_2' the position vectors from the new origin. Mathematically, we can write $r_2 = r_1 + \Delta r$ and $r_2' = r_1' + \Delta r$; the same displacement Δr relates both pairs of position vectors.

So how do we find the rock's new position, designated r_2? From the original position at the head of position vector r_1, we simply add the displacement vector Δr by placing its tail at the tip of r_1. Since we moved the rock 1 m to the right, the displacement vector Δr is represented by a rightward-pointing arrow half as long as the position vector r_1 that represents a 2-m separation from the origin. The new position r_2 is then represented by a vector from the origin to the head of Δr, as shown in Fig. 3-2. This procedure defines vector addition, and we write

$$r_2 = r_1 + \Delta r$$

for the vectors of Fig. 3-2. Note that we've written the $+$ and $=$ signs in bold-face to emphasize that these are operations performed on vectors. We'll use this convention throughout the text to help remind you that vectors are different mathematical objects than scalars. For the same reason, we boldface the $\mathbf{0}$ that results when vectors sum to zero.

In Fig. 3-2 we formed the vector sum graphically; to specify the resultant vector, we could measure its length and angle on our graph. Or, we could use trigonometric relations such as the laws of sines and cosines, as explored in Problem 65. But we'll find it easiest and most elegant to handle vector arithmetic with the methods of analytic geometry, which we describe in Section 3-3.

We emphasize that the choice of origin is arbitrary. With the rock of Fig. 3-2, the important physical quantity is the rock's displacement Δr; that tells what actually happens to the rock, namely how far it moves and in what direction. We chose to specify the rock's position using position vectors r_1 and r_2 from the origin O shown in Fig. 3-2. With a different choice of origin, those vectors would be different—but, as Fig. 3-3 shows, the physically important quantity Δr remains the same.

Adding three or more vectors is a simple extension of the two-vector addition we've just described: to form the sum $A + B + C$, for example, first add the vectors A and B, then add C to the sum $A + B$. Figure 3-4 shows that vector addition is both commutative and associative.

Multiplying Vectors by Scalars

You and I both set out jogging toward the northeast, but you go twice as far as I do. Both our displacements are described by northeast-pointing vectors, and your displacement vector—call it B—is twice as long as mine, which we'll call A. Mathematically, $B = 2A$. That is, multiplying a vector by a scalar simply changes the magnitude of the vector. If the scalar is positive, the direction of the product vector is unchanged; if the scalar is negative, the direction reverses. Figure 3-5 shows the effects of multiplying a vector by different scalars.

Note in Fig. 3-5 that $-A$ is a vector with the same magnitude as A, but in the opposite direction. This makes sense: just as in ordinary arithmetic, $-A$ is the additive inverse of A—that is, the vector that, when added to A, gives zero. Think of displacement vectors: If you go 10 m to the northeast (call that vector A), then going 10 m to the southwest (vector $-A$) will get you right back where you started. Your net displacement is then zero, showing that $A + (-A) = \mathbf{0}$.

(a)

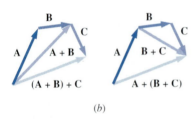

(b)

FIGURE 3-4 (a) Vector addition is commutative; whether we form the sum $A + B$ or the sum $B + A$, we get the same result. (b) Vector addition is also associative; that is, $(A + B) + C = A + (B + C)$.

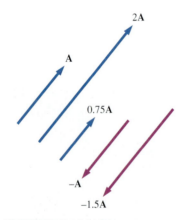

FIGURE 3-5 Multiplying a vector by a scalar. A positive scalar leaves the direction unchanged, while a negative scalar reverses the direction. Note that where a vector starts doesn't matter; its direction and magnitude fully characterize the vector.

Multiplication by a scalar obeys the familiar distributive property; that is, $c(\mathbf{A} + \mathbf{B}) = c\mathbf{A} + c\mathbf{B}$, as shown in Fig. 3-6.

Is it possible to multiply one vector by another? In fact, there are several types of vector multiplication. We will introduce them in later chapters as the need arises.

Subtracting Vectors

What if we had been given the rock's initial and final positions $\mathbf{r}_1$ and $\mathbf{r}_2$ in Fig. 3-2 and were asked to find its displacement $\Delta\mathbf{r}$? Since $\mathbf{r}_2 = \mathbf{r}_1 + \Delta\mathbf{r}$, we can write

$$\Delta\mathbf{r} = \mathbf{r}_2 - \mathbf{r}_1 .$$

What does this subtraction mean? As with real numbers, the difference $\mathbf{A} - \mathbf{B}$ is the sum of $\mathbf{A}$ and $-\mathbf{B}$, where $-\mathbf{B}$ has the same magnitude as $\mathbf{B}$ but the opposite direction, as we saw in Fig. 3-5. Thus, finding the displacement vector $\Delta\mathbf{r}$ of Fig. 3-2 means adding the vectors $\mathbf{r}_2$ and $-\mathbf{r}_1$, as shown in Fig. 3-7.

> ### Tip
> *The Starting Point Doesn't Matter* Does it bother you that Fig. 3-7 doesn't look much like Fig. 3-2? That's ok: The vector $-\mathbf{r}_1$ shown in Fig. 3-7 is the same length as $\mathbf{r}_1$, and it points in the opposite direction. Length and direction are all that matter; we've moved $-\mathbf{r}_1$ into the right position to add it to $\mathbf{r}_2$, and that's all right as long as we preserve length and direction. Similarly, the vector $\Delta\mathbf{r}$ is in different places in Figs. 3-2 and 3-7—but its magnitude and direction are the same, and that's all that matters. Get used to sliding vectors around as needed when you add them.

FIGURE 3-6 Multiplication of a vector by a scalar is distributive—that is, $1.5(\mathbf{A} + \mathbf{B}) = 1.5\mathbf{A} + 1.5\mathbf{B}$.

FIGURE 3-7 To perform the subtraction $\mathbf{r}_2 - \mathbf{r}_1$, we add to $\mathbf{r}_2$ the vector $-\mathbf{r}_1$—that is, a vector the same length as $\mathbf{r}_1$ but pointing in the opposite direction. The result is the vector difference $\Delta\mathbf{r}$.

3-3 COORDINATE SYSTEMS, VECTOR COMPONENTS, AND UNIT VECTORS

We'll be adding lots of vectors throughout this book, sometimes infinitely many in a single sum! Although the graphical methods used in the preceding section show conceptually what vector operations mean, we'll find it more convenient to do vector arithmetic using techniques of analytic geometry.

Coordinate Systems

A **coordinate system** is a framework for the quantitative description of positions in space. A familiar example in two dimensions is the grid of latitude and longitude that locates points on Earth's surface; the pair of numbers specifying a given position are its **coordinates** (Fig. 3-8). Think about how difficult it would be to specify the position of a boat, or an island in the Pacific Ocean, without those coordinates! Adding an altitude coordinate gives three-dimensional position information.

You're probably familiar with the **Cartesian**, or **rectangular coordinate system**, in which points in a plane are represented by pairs of numbers (x, y)

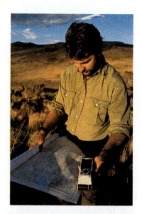

FIGURE 3-8 A GPS (Global Positioning System) receiver gives one's position on the latitude-longitude coordinate system used on Earth's surface.

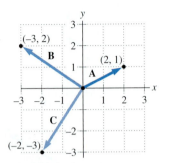

FIGURE 3-9 Several points, labeled by their coordinates on a rectangular coordinate system. We can describe the points equally well with position vectors. The components of the position vectors are the coordinates of the points, for example, $A_x = 2$ and $A_y = 1$.

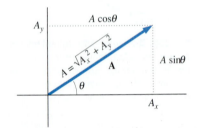

FIGURE 3-10 The Pythagorean theorem and simple trigonometry give the relation between the components and the magnitude and direction of a vector.

corresponding to distances along two perpendicular axes (Fig. 3-9). We might equally well think of these points as marking the heads of vectors—vectors that describe the position of each point relative to the origin. Then the coordinates x and y fully specify each vector. In this context, the coordinates are called the **components** of a vector. Although the points on our graph could represent actual positions, they might equally well be velocities, forces, or other vector quantities. Let's therefore consider an arbitrary vector **A**. We'll use the symbol A—the same letter as the vector symbol itself, but italic and not bold—for the magnitude of A, and for its x and y components we'll use the symbols A_x and A_y. If we're dealing with a position vector **r**, then the components r_x and r_y are simply the coordinates x and y.

Previously, we described a vector by its magnitude and direction; now we have the option of giving its components. How are these specifications of the same vector related? Figure 3-10 shows the relation. Using the Pythagorean theorem and the definition of the tangent function, we can relate the magnitude A and direction θ to the components:

$$A = \sqrt{A_x^2 + A_y^2} \tag{3-1}$$

and

$$\tan\theta = \frac{A_y}{A_x}. \tag{3-2}$$

Going the other way, we can use the definitions of sine and cosine to write

$$A_x = A\cos\theta \tag{3-3}$$

and

$$A_y = A\sin\theta. \tag{3-4}$$

We stress that giving a pair of x-y components or the magnitude A and direction θ are perfectly equivalent ways of describing the same vector.

Unit Vector Notation

It's cumbersome to say "a vector of magnitude 2 m at 30° to the x axis," or, equivalently, "a vector whose x component is 1.73 m and whose y component is 1.0 m." To express vectors in compact form, we define three **unit vectors**, $\hat{\mathbf{i}}$, $\hat{\mathbf{j}}$, and $\hat{\mathbf{k}}$, which have magnitude 1, no units, and which point in the x, y, and z directions, respectively. To make any vector pointing in the x direction, we multiply the unit vector $\hat{\mathbf{i}}$ by a positive or negative number whose absolute value is the vector's magnitude. Similarly, any vector pointing in the y direction can be written as a multiple of $\hat{\mathbf{j}}$. Suppose we have an arbitrary vector **A** in the x-y plane, with components A_x and A_y. As Fig. 3-11a shows, we can think of this

FIGURE 3-11 (a) Any vector in the x-y plane can be written as a combination of the two unit vectors $\hat{\mathbf{i}}$ and $\hat{\mathbf{j}}$, each multiplied by the appropriate components. (b) Similarly, any vector in space can be written in terms of the three unit vectors $\hat{\mathbf{i}}$, $\hat{\mathbf{j}}$, and $\hat{\mathbf{k}}$.

(a)

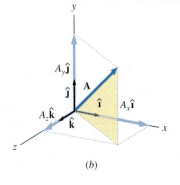

(b)

vector as the sum of two vectors, one of magnitude A_x pointing in the x direction and the other of magnitude A_y pointing in the y direction. In unit vector notation, those two vectors are $A_x\hat{\mathbf{i}}$ and $A_y\hat{\mathbf{j}}$, respectively. So the vector **A** itself is given by **A** = $A_x\hat{\mathbf{i}}$ + $A_y\hat{\mathbf{j}}$, as suggested in Fig. 3-11. In general, we can write *any* vector in the *x-y* plane as a sum of the unit vectors $\hat{\mathbf{i}}$ and $\hat{\mathbf{j}}$ with suitable values multiplying each. Analogously, any vector in space can be written in terms of the three unit vectors $\hat{\mathbf{i}}$, $\hat{\mathbf{j}}$, and $\hat{\mathbf{k}}$ (Fig. 3-11*b*).

Note that vector components themselves are just numbers; the directionality and therefore the vector character of the vector **A** is contained entirely in the unit vectors $\hat{\mathbf{i}}$ and $\hat{\mathbf{j}}$. On the other hand, the unit vectors themselves are dimensionless; the dimensions of the vector **A** are those of its components A_x and A_y.

EXAMPLE 3-1	*Unit Vectors*

You drive from home to a city 160 km distant, in a direction 35° north of east. Express your new position vector **r** in unit vector notation, using a coordinate system with the x direction eastward and the y direction northward. Figure 3-12 is a graphical depiction of this example.

Solution

Using Equations 3-3 and 3-4 we have

$$x = r\cos\theta = (160\ \text{km})(\cos 35°) = 131\ \text{km}$$

and

$$y = r\sin\theta = (160\ \text{km})(\sin 35°) = 92\ \text{km}\,.$$

Then your new position **r** is

$$\mathbf{r} = 131\hat{\mathbf{i}} + 92\hat{\mathbf{j}}\ \text{km}\,.$$

Note that we treat the entire $131\hat{\mathbf{i}} + 92\hat{\mathbf{j}}$ as a single vector quantity, labeling it at the end with the appropriate unit. It's just as important to keep track of units with vectors as it is with scalars.

Tip

Be Consistent with Vectors Vectors and scalars are different, so it's impossible for a scalar to equal a vector. That means any equation you write with a vector on one side *must* have a vector on the other side. In the answer to this example, for instance, the boldface **r** on the left tells you this is a vector equation, so the right-hand side must also be a vector. And it is, as shown by the presence of the unit vectors $\hat{\mathbf{i}}$ and $\hat{\mathbf{j}}$. On the other hand, the magnitude and the components of a vector are simply numbers, so they can appear in scalar equations.

FIGURE 3-12 The city's position is described by the vector $\mathbf{r} = 131\hat{\mathbf{i}} + 92\hat{\mathbf{j}}$ km.

Some problems similar to Example 3-2: 11–16

Vector Addition and Subtraction with Unit Vectors

Unit vector notation makes vector addition and subtraction straightforward extensions of their scalar counterparts. Suppose we have two vectors **A** and **B**, expressed in terms of unit vectors as **A** = $A_x\hat{\mathbf{i}}$ + $A_y\hat{\mathbf{j}}$ and **B** = $B_x\hat{\mathbf{i}}$ + $B_y\hat{\mathbf{j}}$. Their sum **A** + **B** is then

$$\mathbf{A} + \mathbf{B} = (A_x\hat{\mathbf{i}} + A_y\hat{\mathbf{j}}) + (B_x\hat{\mathbf{i}} + B_y\hat{\mathbf{j}}) = (A_x + B_x)\hat{\mathbf{i}} + (A_y + B_y)\hat{\mathbf{j}}\,.$$

In other words, the components of the sum are just the sums of the components of the individual vectors. Had we subtracted **B** from **A**, we would have subtracted the components. To find the magnitude and direction of the sum or difference vector, we can apply Equations 3-1 and 3-2.

EXAMPLE 3-2	*Vector Addition with Unit Vectors*

Do the vector addition of Fig. 3-2 using unit vector notation.

Solution
Referring to Fig. 3-13, we see that the components x_1 and y_1 of the vector $\mathbf{r}_1$ are given by

$$x_1 = r_1 \cos \theta_1 = (2.0 \text{ m}) \cos 30° = 1.73 \text{ m}$$

and

$$y_1 = r_1 \sin \theta_1 = (2.0 \text{ m}) \sin 30° = 1.00 \text{ m} .$$

Similarly, the 1.0-m-long horizontal vector $\Delta\mathbf{r}$ obviously has components $\Delta x = 1.0$ m and $\Delta y = 0$. Then $\mathbf{r}_1 = 1.73\hat{\mathbf{i}} + 1.00\hat{\mathbf{j}}$ m and $\Delta\mathbf{r} = 1.0\hat{\mathbf{i}}$ m, so their sum is

$$\mathbf{r}_2 = \mathbf{r}_1 + \Delta\mathbf{r} = (1.73\hat{\mathbf{i}} + 1.00\hat{\mathbf{j}} \text{ m}) + (1.0\hat{\mathbf{i}} \text{ m})$$

$$= 2.73\hat{\mathbf{i}} + 1.00\hat{\mathbf{j}} \text{ m} .$$

The final expression here is a complete answer for $\mathbf{r}_2$ expressed compactly in unit vector notation. If we want the magnitude and direction of $\mathbf{r}_2$, we apply Equations 3-1 and 3-2:

$$r_2 = \sqrt{x_2^2 + y_2^2} = \sqrt{(2.73 \text{ m})^2 + (1.00 \text{ m})^2} = 2.9 \text{ m}$$

and

$$\theta_2 = \tan^{-1}\left(\frac{y_2}{x_2}\right) = \tan^{-1}\left(\frac{1.00}{2.73}\right) = 20° .$$

FIGURE 3-13 Components x_1 and y_1 of the vector $\mathbf{r}_1$ are given by the magnitude of $\mathbf{r}_1$ (2.0 m) multiplied, respectively, by the cosine and sine of the 30° angle that $\mathbf{r}_1$ makes with the x axis. The vector $\Delta\mathbf{r}$ has only an x component, Δx, equal to $\Delta\mathbf{r}$'s 1.0-m magnitude. The vector sum $\mathbf{r}_2$ has components x_2, y_2 that are the sums of the components of $\mathbf{r}_1$ and $\Delta\mathbf{r}$.

EXERCISE An airplane takes off heading west, and goes 5.0 km before turning 25° northward. It proceeds 10 km in this direction. Express its position in unit vector notation, using a coordinate system with origin at the airport and with the x axis to the east and the y axis to the north.

Answer: $-14\hat{\mathbf{i}} + 4.2\hat{\mathbf{j}}$ km

Some problems similar to Example 3-2: 19–26

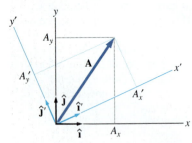

FIGURE 3-14 A vector A analyzed into components in two different coordinate systems. Although the components A_x and A_y depend on the choice of coordinates, the actual physical properties of the vector—its length and orientation in space—do not. Here, for example, $A_x^2 + A_y^2 = A_x'^2 + A_y'^2$, showing that the two different pairs of components do indeed represent a vector with the same length in both coordinate systems.

Got It!

Which of the following describes a displacement of 10 units in a direction 30° below the positive x axis? (a) $10\hat{\mathbf{i}} - 10\hat{\mathbf{j}}$; (b) $5.0\hat{\mathbf{i}} - 8.6\hat{\mathbf{j}}$; (c) $8.6\hat{\mathbf{i}} - 5.0\hat{\mathbf{j}}$; (d) $10(\hat{\mathbf{i}} + \hat{\mathbf{j}})$

Coordinate Systems and Reality

Vectors represent real physical quantities such as the displacement between two cities, the velocity of a hurricane, or the acceleration of a rocket. Coordinate systems, in contrast, are mathematical constructs we use for convenience in doing calculations. Coordinate systems have no intrinsic reality, and the choice of coordinate system is ours to make. Figure 3-14 shows two different coordinate systems for treating the same vector. Although its components are different in the two systems, the vector's overall length and its orientation in space are the same.

How do we choose a coordinate system? Usually the geometry suggests a choice. Often convention dictates: for example, coordinate systems describing motion on Earth's surface often use east-west and north-south oriented coordinate axes. But in a city with a rectangular grid of streets that don't coincide with the compass directions, it would be more convenient to use a coordinate system aligned to the street grid. In problems including vertical motion, the vertical and horizontal directions often provide the most convenient choice of coordinate axes. But not always; analyzing a skier's motion, for example, may be easier in a coordinate system with axes parallel and perpendicular to the ski slope.

We stress again that the choice of coordinate system is purely for convenience, with no physical content. You should get the right answer no matter what coordinate system you choose, but a sensible choice may make your work a lot easier (and less prone to error).

FIGURE 3-15 A climber climbs to the summit of a mountain on a path described by the displacement vectors **A**, **B**, and **C**. Describing this climb quantitatively would be easier in coordinate system x'-y' than in the horizontal-vertical system x-y, since the vectors **A** and **C** would then have only one nonzero component each.

Tip

Choose Your Coordinates Wisely Figure 3-15 shows the path a climber takes to the top of a mountain. Suppose you were asked to find the magnitude of the overall displacement on this trip. You could treat each of the three distinct segments as a separate vector, and sum them to get the overall vector displacement, then take its magnitude. But think before you automatically draw horizontal and vertical axes! Two of the vectors are in the same direction, so why not make that the direction of one coordinate axis? Then you'll have two fewer components to calculate and the problem becomes that much easier. Problem 27 explores the two coordinate systems suggested for Fig. 3-15.

3-4 VELOCITY AND ACCELERATION VECTORS

Velocity

If I'm in Boston and I want to go the 400 km to Montreal in 4 hours, it's not enough that I go at 100 km/h. I've also got to go in the right direction, namely toward the north-northwest. In other words, velocity is a vector; I must specify both magnitude and direction in order to give a full description of how I'm moving.

In one dimension, we defined velocity as the rate of change of position. Here we do the same, except that now the change of position—the displacement—is itself a vector. So we write

$$\bar{\mathbf{v}} = \frac{\Delta \mathbf{r}}{\Delta t} \tag{3-5}$$

for the average velocity, in analogy with Equation 2-1. Here, division of the vector $\Delta \mathbf{r}$ by the scalar Δt means multiplying $\Delta \mathbf{r}$ by the reciprocal of Δt; we defined such multiplication by a scalar in Section 3-2.

We can apply the limiting process defined in Chapter 2 to get the instantaneous velocity:

$$\mathbf{v} = \lim_{\Delta t \to 0} \frac{\Delta \mathbf{r}}{\Delta t} = \frac{d\mathbf{r}}{dt}. \tag{3-6}$$

What does this vector derivative, $d\mathbf{r}/dt$, mean? Again, it's just a shorthand way of expressing the result of the limiting process, taking ever smaller times and the associated displacements $\Delta\mathbf{r}$. Another way of looking at Equation 3-6 is in terms of components; if $\mathbf{r} = x\hat{\mathbf{i}} + y\hat{\mathbf{j}}$, then Equation 3-6 becomes

$$v_x\hat{\mathbf{i}} + v_y\hat{\mathbf{j}} = \frac{dx}{dt}\hat{\mathbf{i}} + \frac{dy}{dt}\hat{\mathbf{j}}. \tag{3-7}$$

In other words, the vector Equation 3-6 incorporates the two scalar equations $v_x = dx/dt$ and $v_y = dy/dt$. For instance, we found that the trip of Example 3-1 was described by a displacement vector $\Delta\mathbf{r} = 131\hat{\mathbf{i}} + 91.8\hat{\mathbf{j}}$ km. Suppose this displacement took place in 1.43 h; then the average velocity would be

$$\bar{\mathbf{v}} = \frac{\Delta\mathbf{r}}{\Delta t} = \frac{131\hat{\mathbf{i}} + 91.8\hat{\mathbf{j}} \text{ m}}{1.43 \text{ h}} = 91.6\hat{\mathbf{i}} + 64.2\hat{\mathbf{j}} \text{ km/h}.$$

EXAMPLE 3-3	*LA to Denver via Salt Lake City*

You leave Los Angeles on a flight to Denver, with a stop in Salt Lake City. Flying 55° north of east, the plane makes the 970-km trip to Salt Lake City in 72 min. After 40 min on the ground, the plane heads for Denver, which is 600 km away and in a direction 10° south of east. The plane reaches Denver 55 min after leaving Salt Lake City. Determine the average velocity of the plane between Los Angeles and Denver.

Solution
Figure 3-16 shows the situation graphically. The vector displacement $\Delta\mathbf{r}_{LD}$ from Los Angeles to Denver is the sum of the displacement $\Delta\mathbf{r}_{LS}$ from Los Angeles to Salt Lake City and the displacement $\Delta\mathbf{r}_{SD}$ from Salt Lake City to Denver. Choosing coordinate axes x and y running east-west and north-south, respectively, we can compute the components needed to write these vectors in unit vector notation:

$$\Delta\mathbf{r}_{LS} = (970 \text{ km})(\cos 55°)\hat{\mathbf{i}} + (970 \text{ km})(\sin 55°)\hat{\mathbf{j}}$$

$$= 556\hat{\mathbf{i}} + 795\hat{\mathbf{j}} \text{ km}$$

$$\Delta\mathbf{r}_{SD} = (600 \text{ km})[\cos(-10°)]\hat{\mathbf{i}} + (600 \text{ km})[\sin(-10°)]\hat{\mathbf{j}}$$

$$= 591\hat{\mathbf{i}} - 104\hat{\mathbf{j}} \text{ km}.$$

Note that the angle associated with the Salt Lake City to Denver displacement is negative since the direction is south of east. Adding these vectors gives the displacement vector $\Delta\mathbf{r}_{LD}$ from Los Angeles to Denver:

$$\Delta\mathbf{r}_{LD} = \Delta\mathbf{r}_{LS} + \Delta\mathbf{r}_{SD} = (556\hat{\mathbf{i}} + 795\hat{\mathbf{j}} \text{ km})$$

$$+ (591\hat{\mathbf{i}} - 104\hat{\mathbf{j}} \text{ km}) = 1147\hat{\mathbf{i}} + 691\hat{\mathbf{j}} \text{ km}.$$

The total elapsed time for this trip includes the two flight times and the 40-min ground time, so $\Delta t = 72$ min + 40 min + 55 min = 167 min or 2.78 h. The average velocity is then

$$\bar{\mathbf{v}} = \frac{\Delta\mathbf{r}_{LD}}{\Delta t} = \frac{1147\hat{\mathbf{i}} + 691\hat{\mathbf{j}} \text{ km}}{2.78 \text{ h}} = 413\hat{\mathbf{i}} + 249\hat{\mathbf{j}} \text{ km/h}.$$

FIGURE 3-16 Displacement vectors for a flight from Los Angeles to Denver via Salt Lake City.

The magnitude of this average velocity is given by Equation 3-1:

$$\bar{v} = \sqrt{\bar{v}_x^2 + \bar{v}_y^2} = \sqrt{(413 \text{ km/h})^2 + (249 \text{ km/h})^2}$$

$$= 482 \text{ km/h}.$$

Since the actual path is not straight and is therefore longer than the magnitude of the vector $\Delta\mathbf{r}_{LD}$, the average *speed* would be greater than this.

EXERCISE Oceanographers on a research voyage sail 340 km in a direction 10° east of north, at a steady 12 km/h. They pause for 5.2 h to take a sediment sample from beneath the ocean floor, then proceed 115 km directly east. The eastward leg takes 12.1 h. After a pause of 3.6 h, the ship heads southwest for 190 km; this takes 18.4 h. Determine the average velocity vector for this trip, and calculate its magnitude and compass direction. Use a coordinate system with the x direction eastward and the y direction northward.

Answers: $\bar{\mathbf{v}} = 0.587\hat{\mathbf{i}} + 2.96\hat{\mathbf{j}}$ km/h; $v = 3.02$ km/h; $\theta = 11.2°$ east of north

Some problems similar to Example 3-3: 28–34

Acceleration

Just as velocity is the rate of change of displacement, so is acceleration the rate of change of velocity. And just as where you end up depends on which direction you go, so the change in your velocity depends not only on the magnitude of your acceleration, but also on its direction. That is, acceleration is a vector quantity. Mathematically, we write

4.1

ActivPhysics

Determining Acceleration Direction Graphically

$$\bar{\mathbf{a}} = \frac{\Delta \mathbf{v}}{\Delta t} \qquad (3\text{-}8)$$

for the average acceleration and

$$\mathbf{a} = \lim_{\Delta t \to 0} \frac{\Delta \mathbf{v}}{\Delta t} = \frac{d\mathbf{v}}{dt} \qquad (3\text{-}9)$$

for the instantaneous acceleration. We could also write the vector equation 3-9 in terms of components, just as we did for velocity in Equation 3-7.

| **EXAMPLE 3-4** | *Close Call!* |

An asteroid is discovered heading straight toward Earth at 15 km/s. An international team manages to attach a giant rocket engine to the asteroid. The rocket fires for 10 min, after which the asteroid is moving at 28° to its original path, at a speed of 19 km/s. Find its average acceleration.

Solution

A convenient coordinate system has its x axis in the direction of the asteroid's initial motion, as shown in Fig. 3-17a. Then the asteroid's initial velocity is $\mathbf{v}_1 = 15\hat{\imath}$ km/s. Its final velocity has components in both x and y directions: $v_{2x} = (19 \text{ km/s}) \cos 28° = 16.8$ km/s and $v_{2y} = (19 \text{ km/s}) \sin 28° = 8.92$ km/s, so $\mathbf{v}_2 = 16.8\hat{\imath} + 8.92\hat{\jmath}$ km/s. Then the average acceleration is the change in velocity divided by the 10-min time interval:

$$\bar{\mathbf{a}} = \frac{\Delta \mathbf{v}}{\Delta t} = \frac{\mathbf{v}_2 - \mathbf{v}_1}{\Delta t} = \frac{(16.8\hat{\imath} + 8.92\hat{\jmath} \text{ km/s}) - 15\hat{\imath} \text{ km/s}}{(10 \text{ min})(60 \text{ s/min})}$$

$$= 3.0\hat{\imath} + 15\hat{\jmath} \text{ m/s}^2.$$

What about the direction of this average acceleration? The much larger size of the y component says that this vector's direction is only slightly different from the y direction. Figure 3-17b shows the change in velocity, $\Delta \mathbf{v}$, which has the same direction as the average acceleration.

(a)

(b)

FIGURE 3-17 (a) Asteroid velocities before and after rocket firing (Example 3-4). (b) The velocity change $\Delta \mathbf{v}$, which is in the same direction as the average acceleration.

EXERCISE A proton enters a particle accelerator moving in the x direction at 3.8×10^5 m/s. It emerges 0.94 μs later, moving at 7.6×10^6 m/s at an angle of 23° to the x axis. Determine the average acceleration vector, as well as its magnitude and direction.

Answers: $\bar{\mathbf{a}} = 7.0 \times 10^{12}\hat{\imath} + 3.2 \times 10^{12}\hat{\jmath}$ m/s², with the y axis in the plane defined by the initial and final velocities; $a = 7.7 \times 10^{12}$ m/s²; $\theta = 24°$

Some problems similar to Example 3-4: 36–38, 53, 54

Notice in Fig. 3-17b that the direction of the velocity change—and therefore of the average acceleration—is different from that of either the initial or the final velocity. In this case, in fact, the change is nearly perpendicular to the initial velocity. Although the acceleration results in a small speed increase (from 15 km/s to 19 km/s), it has a much more substantial effect on the direction of the asteroid's motion. This example makes an important point about motion in two or three dimensions: *Any* change in velocity (a vector quantity) means acceleration has occurred. That change may be in speed alone, or it may be in direction alone, or—as in Example 3-4—it may be a combination of the two.

Tip

Acceleration Does Not Necessarily Mean Speeding Up! You're probably used to thinking of "acceleration" as a synonym for "speeding up." But "acceleration" is a far richer term, and it's crucial that you understand its full meaning. *Acceleration* means the rate of change of velocity. Since velocity is a vector, acceleration occurs whenever velocity changes—in magnitude (speed), direction, or both. In some cases, acceleration implies a speed increase—but in other cases it does not. Step on your car's accelerator pedal, and you speed up; since your velocity changes in magnitude, you've accelerated. But turn the steering wheel while your speed remains constant, and you also accelerate. Why? Because your velocity has once again changed—this time in direction. Get used to thinking "change in velocity," not just "change in speed" when you hear the word "acceleration."

Example 3-4 dealt with average acceleration. We can also find instantaneous acceleration if we know the velocity as a function of time. Example 3-5 shows how.

EXAMPLE 3-5	*Differentiating Vectors*

The position of a particle as a function of time t is given by $\mathbf{r} = (bt^3 + ct)\hat{\mathbf{i}} + (ft^2 + g)\hat{\mathbf{j}}$, where b, c, f, and g are constants. Find expressions for the velocity and acceleration of the particle.

Solution

Velocity is the rate of change, or derivative, of position—as expressed in Equation 3-6. So:

$$\mathbf{v} = \frac{d\mathbf{r}}{dt} = \frac{d}{dt}[(bt^3 + ct)\hat{\mathbf{i}} + (ft^2 + g)\hat{\mathbf{j}}]$$

$$= \frac{d}{dt}(bt^3 + ct)\hat{\mathbf{i}} + \frac{d}{dt}(ft^2 + g)\hat{\mathbf{j}},$$

where we made use of the fact that the derivative of a sum is the sum of the derivatives. Now the unit vectors $\hat{\mathbf{i}}$ and $\hat{\mathbf{j}}$ are *constants;* they don't change with time. So, as with the constants b, c, f, and g, they aren't affected by differentiation. Then, applying Equation 2-3 to differentiate the various powers of t, we have

$$\mathbf{v} = \frac{d}{dt}(bt^3 + ct)\hat{\mathbf{i}} + \frac{d}{dt}(ft^2 + g)\hat{\mathbf{j}} = (3bt^2 + c)\hat{\mathbf{i}} + 2ft\hat{\mathbf{j}}.$$

We get the acceleration by differentiating once again:

$$\mathbf{a} = \frac{d\mathbf{v}}{dt} = \frac{d}{dt}[(3bt^2 + c)\hat{\mathbf{i}} + 2ft\hat{\mathbf{j}}] = 6bt\hat{\mathbf{i}} + 2f\hat{\mathbf{j}}.$$

Thus we have an acceleration that initially points in the y direction, with magnitude $2f$, but whose x component then grows linearly with time while the y component remains constant.

EXERCISE Find the acceleration as a function of time for an object whose position is given by $\mathbf{r} = (v_0 t + bt^2)\hat{\mathbf{i}} + (y_0 + ct^4)\hat{\mathbf{j}}$, where all quantities except $\mathbf{r}$ and t are constants.

Answer: $\mathbf{a} = 2b\hat{\mathbf{i}} + 12ct^2\hat{\mathbf{j}}$

Some problems similar to Example 3-5: 35, 42, 43

3-5 RELATIVE MOTION

What does it mean to say that a car is moving at 80 km/h? Usually, it means 80 km/h relative to Earth. But Earth is moving at 30 km/s relative to the Sun, so the car's speed relative to the Sun is much greater. Statements about velocity and speed are meaningful only when we have an answer to the question "velocity relative to what?" The object or system with respect to which velocity is measured is called a **frame of reference**; in most of the examples we have considered, Earth is our frame of reference. But playing tennis on the deck of a moving ship, you would find the ship's frame of reference more appropriate for describing the motion of the tennis ball. Similarly, the motion of a comet or interplanetary space probe is described most simply in the reference frame of the Sun. We'll designate different frames of reference using the symbols S and S'.

You're speeding down the road in your sports car at 80 km/h. A police officer behind you is moving at the legal speed limit of 50 km/h (see Fig. 3-18). The

(a)

(b)

FIGURE 3-18 (a) A police car and a sports car are moving in the same direction at $V = 50$ km/h and $v = 80$ km/h, respectively, as measured with respect to the road (reference frame S). (b) Looking at the situation from the police car's frame of reference (designated S'), the sports car is moving to the right with speed $v' = 30$ km/h and the road is moving leftward at 50 km/h.

officer clocks your speed with radar. What does the radar indicate? Your position is changing at the rate of 80 km every hour; the officer's at the rate of 50 km/h. So the distance between you is increasing at 30 km/h. That's your relative speed—and that's what the police radar reads. Since the police car has a known speed of 50 km/h relative to the road, the officer can easily determine that you're going at

$$50 \text{ km/h} + 30 \text{ km/h} = 80 \text{ km/h}$$

relative to the road. So you'll get a speeding ticket!

We can put this more abstractly but also more generally. Suppose some object (e.g., your car) has velocity **v** (e.g., $80\hat{\i}$ km/h) relative to some frame of reference designated S (e.g., the Earth). Suppose another reference frame S' (e.g., the police car) is moving with velocity **V** (e.g., $50\hat{\i}$ km/h) relative to S. Then the velocity **v′** of the object relative to frame S' is given by

$$\mathbf{v'} = \mathbf{v} - \mathbf{V}. \qquad (3\text{-}10)$$

In our speeding example, this means that your speed relative to the police car (i.e., your speed **v′** relative to frame S') is

$$\mathbf{v'} = 80\hat{\i} \text{ km/h} - 50\hat{\i} \text{ km/h} = 30\hat{\i} \text{ km/h}.$$

We used the full vector formalism in this one-dimensional example because Equation 3-10 holds regardless of the directions of motion of the object and the reference frames. Example 3-6 illustrates the power of the relative velocity concept applied to a practical problem in navigation.

EXAMPLE 3-6	*Navigating a Jetliner*

A jetliner has airspeed 960 km/h. It embarks on a flight from Houston to Omaha, a distance of 1290 km northward. In what direction should it fly if there is a steady 190 km/h wind from the west at its cruising altitude? What will be its groundspeed? How long will the trip take?

Solution

Let S be the frame of reference of the ground, and choose x and y axes pointing east and north, respectively. Let S' be the frame of reference of the air, so the velocity **V** of frame S' relative to S is $190\hat{\i}$ km/h. The velocity **v′** of the plane relative to the air has magnitude 960 km/h, but we don't know its direction. We can write this velocity as

$$\mathbf{v'} = v' \cos\theta \,\hat{\i} + v' \sin\theta \,\hat{\j},$$

where v' is 960 km/h and θ is the angle **v′** makes with the positive x axis (see Fig. 3-19). The velocity **v** points northward, so it can be expressed in the form

$$\mathbf{v} = v\hat{\j},$$

where we don't know the magnitude v. We can now write the

FIGURE 3-19 Vector diagram for Example 3-6. The plane's velocity **v′** with respect to the air sums with the wind velocity **V** to give the velocity **v** with respect to the ground.

two components of Equation 3-10:

$$v'_x = v_x - V_x$$
$$v'_y = v_y - V_y.$$

Using our expressions for the various velocities, these equations become

$$v' \cos \theta = 0 - V,$$

where $V = 190$ km/h is the magnitude of $\mathbf{V}$, and

$$v' \sin \theta = v - 0.$$

We can solve the first of these equations for θ:

$$\theta = \cos^{-1}\left(\frac{-V}{v'}\right) = \cos^{-1}\left(\frac{-190 \text{ km/h}}{960 \text{ km/h}}\right) = 101.4°.$$

Using this result in the second equation gives

$$v = v' \sin \theta = (960 \text{ km/h})(\sin 101.4°) = 941 \text{ km/h}.$$

So the plane should fly at 101° to the x axis, or 11° west of north, and its groundspeed will be 941 km/h. The 1290-km trip will then take $(1290 \text{ km})/(941 \text{ km/h}) = 1.37$ h. Figure 3-19 is a vector diagram relating the velocities $\mathbf{v'}$, $\mathbf{v}$, and $\mathbf{V}$. Before the advent of sophisticated navigation equipment, pilots routinely carried out such calculations, often using graphical techniques.

EXERCISE A boat sails at 14 km/h relative to the water. Its captain wants to sail from one island to another 83 km directly northward. However, a current flows at 3.6 km/h from west to east between the islands. In what direction should the captain head the boat, and how long will the trip take?

Answers: 15° west of north; 6.1 h

Some problems similar to Example 3-6: 46, 48, 50, 57, 58, 67

What about the acceleration of an object in two different reference frames? Suppose $\mathbf{a}$ is the acceleration in some frame S; that is, $\mathbf{a} = d\mathbf{v}/dt$, where $\mathbf{v}$ is the velocity relative to frame S. Equation 3-10 gives the velocity $\mathbf{v'}$ in a frame S' moving with velocity $\mathbf{V}$ relative to S. Differentiating this equation then gives the acceleration $\mathbf{a'}$:

$$\mathbf{a'} = \frac{d\mathbf{v'}}{dt} = \frac{d\mathbf{v}}{dt} - \frac{d\mathbf{V}}{dt}.$$

We generally consider only reference frames that are not themselves accelerating; such a frame is therefore in uniform motion and is called an **inertial reference frame** (more on the meaning of this term in Chapter 5). If the frames S and S' are not accelerating, then their relative velocity $\mathbf{V}$ is constant, and thus $d\mathbf{V}/dt = \mathbf{0}$. Furthermore, $d\mathbf{v}/dt$ is just the acceleration $\mathbf{a}$ in the frame S, so the equation above becomes simply

$$\mathbf{a'} = \mathbf{a}. \tag{3-11}$$

That is, the acceleration of an object is the same in all inertial frames of reference. This simple result is true because acceleration depends on *changes* in velocity, and the addition of any constant velocity does not alter those changes.

That acceleration has the same value in all inertial reference frames has a deep significance in physics. Consider the simple experiment of dropping a ball from rest. Do this on Earth's surface, and the ball falls straight downward with constant acceleration g. Do the same in an airplane moving with constant velocity in any direction—even upward or downward, it doesn't matter—and you'll get exactly the same result. Observers on Earth and in the plane will disagree about the *velocity* of the ball dropped on the plane, and therefore about the shape of the path it takes, but they both will agree that the ball's acceleration is downward and has magnitude g (Fig. 3-20). Further, both would agree that if they did truly identical experiments—each dropping a ball with zero initial velocity *with respect to their own frame*—they would have identical outcomes.

FIGURE 3-20 (a) Dropping a ball on an airplane results in a straight downward fall with acceleration g. As long as the plane is moving with constant velocity—no matter what direction—its motion is irrelevant. (b) The same situation viewed from the frame of reference of the ground. Here, the ball's velocity has a significant horizontal component, and its path is a parabolic arc. Observers on the ground and in the plane will disagree about the ball's velocity, but both will agree that it has acceleration g directly downward. Note that the initial direction of the ball's path is parallel to **V**. Why?

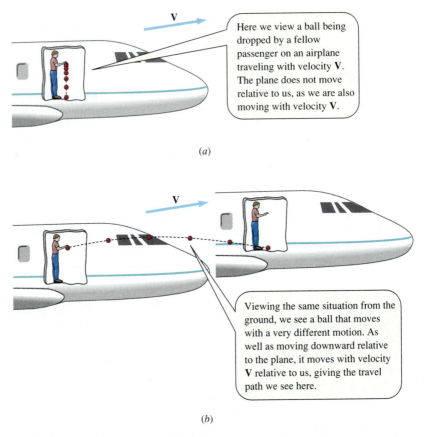

Here we view a ball being dropped by a fellow passenger on an airplane traveling with velocity **V**. The plane does not move relative to us, as we are also moving with velocity **V**.

(a)

Viewing the same situation from the ground, we see a ball that moves with a very different motion. As well as moving downward relative to the plane, it moves with velocity **V** relative to us, giving the travel path we see here.

(b)

If you were on a plane flying through perfectly smooth air, there is in fact no experiment involving motion that you could do to tell that the plane was moving. All experiments would come out exactly the same as they would on the ground. This fact is expressed in a simple statement, called the **principle of Galilean relativity**:

❙ The laws of motion are the same in all inertial frames of reference.

What this means is that there is no way of using the laws of motion—the only laws of physics we will consider until Chapter 23—to answer the question "am I moving?" With respect to the laws of motion, the question is meaningless; only *relative motion* matters.

Although our discussion of relative motion and the principle of Galilean relativity may seem almost obvious and straightforward, in fact that discussion rests on deep-seated notions about the nature of time and space. In Chapter 38, after we have completed our study of electromagnetism, we will see how Albert Einstein was able to extend the principle of Galilean relativity to all of physics; the result is Einstein's special theory of relativity. In the process, Einstein showed that our commonsense notions of space and time are not quite right. As a result, Equations 3-10 and 3-11—and indeed all the equations we develop in Chapters 1 through 22—are really only approximately correct; they work well for our everyday experience, and even for spacecraft probing the solar system, but they break down when relative speeds approach the speed of light.

CHAPTER SYNOPSIS

Summary

1. **Vectors** are used to describe motion in two or three dimensions. Vector quantities have magnitude and direction; we visualize vectors using arrows whose length represents magnitude and whose direction is that of the vector. A vector is described fully by giving its magnitude and direction or, equivalently, its components on a chosen set of coordinate axes.

2. **Unit vectors** are dimensionless vectors of magnitude 1 that lie along the coordinate axes. They allow vectors to be written in compact mathematical notation; if a vector **A** has components A_x and A_y, then $\mathbf{A} = A_x\hat{\imath} + A_y\hat{\jmath}$, where $\hat{\imath}$ and $\hat{\jmath}$ are the unit vectors in the x and y directions, respectively.

3. Vectors may be added: the vector sum **A** + **B** is formed by placing the tail of vector **B** at the head of **A**; the sum is then a vector from the tail of **A** to the head of **B**. Alternatively, vectors may be added by adding their components to get the components of the sum: the x component of the vector **A** + **B**, for example, is just $A_x + B_x$. Vector addition is commutative: **A** + **B** = **B** + **A**. It is also associative: (**A** + **B**) + **C** = **A** + (**B** + **C**).

4. A vector may be multiplied by a scalar. If c is a scalar and **A** a vector of magnitude A, the vector $c\mathbf{A}$ is a vector of magnitude cA having the same direction as **A**. Multiplication by a scalar is distributive: $c(\mathbf{A} + \mathbf{B}) = c\mathbf{A} + c\mathbf{B}$.

5. Vector subtraction **A** − **B** means adding to **A** the vector −**B**, whose magnitude is the same as **B**'s but which points in the opposite direction.

6. **Velocity** is a vector describing the rate of change of position. The average velocity over a time interval Δt is given by the change in position divided by the time interval:

$$\bar{\mathbf{v}} = \frac{\Delta \mathbf{r}}{\Delta t},$$

where $\Delta \mathbf{r} = \mathbf{r}_2 - \mathbf{r}_1$, with $\mathbf{r}_1$ and $\mathbf{r}_2$ the positions at the beginning and end of the time interval Δt. The **instantaneous velocity** is obtained by taking the limit of arbitrarily small time intervals:

$$\mathbf{v} = \lim_{\Delta t \to 0} \frac{\Delta \mathbf{r}}{\Delta t} = \frac{d\mathbf{r}}{dt}.$$

7. **Acceleration** is a vector describing the rate of change of velocity; the average acceleration over a time interval Δt is

$$\bar{\mathbf{a}} = \frac{\Delta \mathbf{v}}{\Delta t},$$

while the instantaneous acceleration is

$$\mathbf{a} = \lim_{\Delta t \to 0} \frac{\Delta \mathbf{v}}{\Delta t} = \frac{d\mathbf{v}}{dt}.$$

Since velocity is a vector, it can change in either magnitude or direction or both; any change in velocity represents an acceleration.

8. Statements about velocity are meaningful only in the context of a **reference frame**. Given the velocity **v** of an object relative to some reference frame, the object's velocity relative to another frame is given by

$$\mathbf{v'} = \mathbf{v} - \mathbf{V},$$

where **V** is the velocity of the second reference frame relative to the first.

9. An **inertial reference frame** is one that is not accelerated. The **principle of Galilean relativity** states that the laws of motion hold equally well in all inertial reference frames.

Terms You Should Understand

(Pairs are closely related terms whose distinction is important; number in parentheses is chapter section where term first appears.)

vector, scalar (3-1)	unit vector (3-3)
magnitude (3-1)	velocity vector (3-4)
coordinate system (3-3)	acceleration vector (3-4)
component (3-3)	inertial reference frame (3-5)

Symbols You Should Recognize

r (3-2)	$\mathbf{A} = A_x\hat{\imath} + A_y\hat{\jmath}$ (3-3)
A + **B** (3-2)	$\dfrac{d\mathbf{r}}{dt}$ (3-4)
A − **B** (3-2)	$\dfrac{d\mathbf{v}}{dt}$ (3-4)
$c\mathbf{A}$ (3-2)	
x, y, r, θ (3-3)	
$\hat{\imath}, \hat{\jmath}, \hat{k}$ (3-3)	

Problems You Should Be Able to Solve

adding and subtracting vectors graphically (3-2)
determining vector components (3-3)
writing vectors in unit vector notation (3-3)
doing vector arithmetic using unit vector notation (3-3)
determining average and instantaneous velocity vectors (3-4)
determining average and instantaneous acceleration vectors (3-4)
evaluating vectors in different frames of reference (3-5)

Limitations to Keep in Mind

Coordinate systems are artificial constructs established for convenience. When solving a problem, you are free to pick any coordinate system you choose. A wise choice may make your work much easier.

You yourself may have come to physics with a limited concept of the term "acceleration." *Acceleration* means the rate of change of velocity—and that may involve a change in speed, a change in direction, or both. "Acceleration" therefore need not mean the same thing as "change in speed."

The description of motion developed in the first half of this book is valid only for relative speeds much less than the speed of light.

QUESTIONS

1. Under what conditions is the magnitude of the vector sum **A** + **B** equal to the sum of the magnitudes of the two vectors?
2. Which of the following are valid expressions? Explain. (a) **C** = **A** − **B**; (b) a = **B** + c; (c) **B** = c**A**; (d) **B** = **A**/c; (e) **B** = c/**A**.
3. Can two vectors of equal magnitude sum to zero? Can two vectors of unequal magnitude?
4. Repeat the preceding question for three vectors.
5. One way of adding vectors is to place them tail-to-tail, and then form a parallelogram as shown in Fig. 3-21. The sum of the two vectors is then a vector along the diagonal of the parallelogram. Why is this method equivalent to the head-to-tail method described in the text?

FIGURE 3-21 Parallelogram method of adding vectors (Question 5).

6. Three vectors sum to zero. Placed head-to-tail, what geometrical figure must they form? Explain.

7. Is vector subtraction commutative?
8. Two vectors **A** and **B** have magnitude A and B, respectively. What is the maximum possible magnitude for the vector **A** + **B**? How must **A** and **B** be oriented for their sum to have this maximum possible magnitude?
9. A fly heads west 5 m, then north 3 m, then straight up 6 m. A mosquito starts from the same place, flies straight up 6 m, west 5 m, and north 3 m. Compare their final positions.
10. Is it possible to form the unit vector $\hat{\mathbf{k}}$ from a sum of $\hat{\mathbf{i}}$ and $\hat{\mathbf{j}}$, each multiplied by appropriate scalars? Explain.
11. Is it meaningful to talk about vectors without mention of coordinate systems or components?
12. Can an object have a southward acceleration while moving northward? A westward acceleration while moving northward?
13. Can an object move northward for 10 minutes, all the while having a southward acceleration?
14. Can an object move northward for 10 minutes, all the while having a westward acceleration?
15. Why can we usually use Cartesian coordinates on Earth's surface even though Earth is round?
16. A space shuttle completes one full orbit in 89 min. What are its average velocity and average acceleration over this interval? Is its average speed equal to its average velocity?
17. Why is the statement "I am moving" meaningless?

PROBLEMS

ActivPhysics can help with these problems:
Activity 4.1

Section 3-2 Vector Arithmetic

1. You walk west 220 m, then north 150 m. What are the magnitude and direction of your displacement vector?
2. An ion in a mass spectrometer (a device that sorts atomic-size particles) follows a semicircular path of radius 15.2 cm. What are (a) the distance it travels and (b) the magnitude of its displacement?
3. A migrating whale follows the west coast of Mexico and North America toward its summer home in Alaska. It first travels 360 km due northwest to just off the coast of Northern California and then turns due north and travels 400 km toward its destination. Determine graphically the magnitude and direction of its displacement vector.
4. A city's streets are laid out with its north-south blocks twice as long as its east-west blocks. You walk 8 blocks east and 3 blocks north. Determine (a) the total distance you've walked and (b) the magnitude of your displacement vector. Express in units of east-west blocks.
5. Vector **A** has magnitude 3.0 m and points to the right; vector **B** has magnitude 4.0 m and points vertically upward. Find the magnitude and direction of a vector **C** such that **A** + **B** + **C** = **0**.

6. Two vectors **A** and **B** have the same magnitude, A, and are at right angles. Find the magnitude of the vectors (a) **A** + 2**B**; (b) 3**A** − **B**.
7. Vectors **A** and **B** in Fig. 3-22 have the same magnitude, A. Find the magnitude and direction of (a) **A** − **B** and (b) **A** + **B**.

FIGURE 3-22 Problem 7.

8. Vector **A** has magnitude 1.0 m and points at 35° clockwise from the x axis. Vector **B** has magnitude 1.8 m. What angle should **B** make with the x axis in order that **A** + **B** be purely vertical?
9. Three vectors **A**, **B**, and **C** have the same magnitude L and form an equilateral triangle, as shown in Fig. 3-23. Find the magnitude and direction of the vectors (a) **A** + **B**, (b) **A** − **B**, (c) **A** + **B** + **C**, (d) **A** + **B** − **C**.

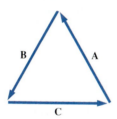

FIGURE 3-23 Problems 9, 16, and 22. (All vectors have magnitude L.)

10. A direct flight from Orlando, Florida, to Atlanta, Georgia, covers 660 km and heads at 29° west of north. Your flight, however, stops at Charleston, South Carolina, on the way to Atlanta. Charleston is 510 km from Orlando, in a direction 9.3° east of north. Use graphical techniques to find the magnitude and direction of the Charleston-to-Atlanta leg of your flight.

Section 3-3 Coordinate Systems, Vector Components, and Unit Vectors

11. Vector **V** represents a displacement of 120 km at 29° counterclockwise from the x axis. Write **V** in unit vector notation.
12. Find the magnitude of the vector $34\hat{\imath} + 13\hat{\jmath}$ m, and determine the angle it makes with the x axis.
13. Express each of the vectors of Fig. 3-24 in unit vector notation, with the x axis horizontally to the right and the y axis vertically upward.

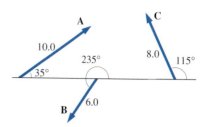

FIGURE 3-24 Vectors for Problems 13, 19, and 20. Lengths are in arbitrary units.

14. (a) What is the magnitude of $\hat{\imath} + \hat{\jmath}$? (b) What angle does it make with the x axis?
15. Repeat Problem 3, using unit vector notation.
16. Express the vectors of Fig. 3-23 in unit vector notation, taking the x axis horizontal and the y axis vertical. Each vector has length A.
17. Let **A** = $15\hat{\imath} − 40\hat{\jmath}$ and **B** = $31\hat{\jmath} + 18\hat{k}$. Find a vector **C** such that **A** + **B** + **C** = **0**.
18. A proton travels in a circular path around the 2.0-km-diameter accelerator at Fermilab, near Chicago. Write expressions for the proton's displacement vector from the center of the circle when it is at (a) 0°; (b) 30°; (c) 45°; (d) 60°; (e) 90°; (f) 180°, as measured counterclockwise from the x axis.
19. Use the result of Problem 13 to find the vectors (a) **A** + **B** + **C**, (b) **A** − **B** + **C**, and (c) **A** + 1.5**B** − 2.2**C**.
20. Find a vector **D** such that **A** + **B** + **C** + **D** = **0** for the vectors of Fig. 3-24.
21. You're trying to reach a pond that lies 3.5 km to the northeast of your starting point. You first follow a logging road that runs east for 0.80 km. Then you follow a deer trail heading northeast for 2.1 km. From there you bushwack straight to the pond. Describe your final displacement vector, (a) in unit vector notation; and (b) as a magnitude and compass direction.
22. For the vectors of Fig. 3-23, find 2 values for the scalar c such that **A** + c**B** has magnitude $2.18L$.
23. In Fig. 3-14 the angle between the x and x' axes is 21°, the angle between the vector **A** and the x axis is 54°, and **A**'s magnitude is 10 units. (a) Find the components of **A** in both coordinate systems shown. (b) Verify that the magnitude of **A**, computed using Equation 3-1, is the same in both coordinate systems.
24. A vector **A** is 10 units long and points 30° counterclockwise (CCW) from horizontal. What are the x and y components on a coordinate system (a) with the x axis horizontal and the y axis vertical; (b) with the x axis at 45° CCW from horizontal and the y axis 45° CCW from vertical; and (c) with the x axis at 30° CCW from horizontal and the y axis 90° CCW from the x axis?
25. Express the sum of the unit vectors $\hat{\imath}, \hat{\jmath}$, and $\hat{k}$ in unit vector notation, and determine its magnitude.

26. A mountain expedition starts a base camp at an altitude of 5500 m. Four climbers then establish an advance camp at an altitude of 7400 m; the advance camp is southeast of the base camp, at a horizontal distance of 8.2 km. From the advance camp, two climbers head directly north to a 8900-m summit, a horizontal distance of 2.1 km. Using a coordinate system with the x axis eastward, the y axis northward, and the z axis upward, and with origin at the base camp, express the positions of the advance camp and summit in unit vector notation, and determine the straight-line distance from base camp to summit.

27. In Fig. 3-15, suppose that vectors **A** and **C** both make 30° angles with the horizontal while **B** makes a 60° angle, and that $A = 2.3$ km, $B = 1.0$ km, and $C = 2.9$ km. (a) Express the displacement vector $\Delta\mathbf{r}$ from start to summit in each of the coordinate systems shown, and (b) determine its length.

Section 3-4 Velocity and Acceleration Vectors

28. An object is moving at 18 m/s at an angle of 220° counterclockwise from the x axis. What are the x and y components of its velocity?

29. A car drives north at 40 mi/h for 10 min, then turns east and goes 5.0 mi at 60 mi/h. Finally, it goes southwest at 30 mi/h for 6.0 min. Draw a vector diagram and determine (a) the car's displacement and (b) its average velocity for this trip.

30. A biologist studying the motion of bacteria notes a bacterium at position $\mathbf{r}_1 = 2.2\hat{\mathbf{i}} + 3.7\hat{\mathbf{j}} - 1.2\hat{\mathbf{k}}$ μm (1 μm = 10^{-6} m). After 6.2 s the bacterium is at $\mathbf{r}_2 = 4.6\hat{\mathbf{i}} + 1.9\hat{\mathbf{k}}$ μm. What is its average velocity? Express in unit vector notation, and calculate the magnitude.

31. The Orlando-to-Atlanta flight described in Problem 10 takes 2.5 h. What is the average velocity? Express (a) as a magnitude and direction, and (b) in unit vector notation with the x axis east and the y axis north.

32. The minute hand of a clock is 5.5 cm long. What is the average velocity vector for the tip of the hand during the interval from the hour to 20 minutes past the hour, expressed in a coordinate system with the y axis toward noon and the x axis toward 3 o'clock?

33. A hot-air balloon rises vertically 800 m over a period of 10 min, then drifts eastward 14 km in 27 min. Then the wind shifts, and the balloon moves northeastward for 15 min, at a speed of 24 km/h. Finally, it drops vertically in 5 min until it is 250 m above the ground. Express the balloon's average velocity in unit vector notation, using a coordinate system with the x axis eastward, the y axis northward, and the z axis upward.

34. Figure 3-25 shows the path of a bug as it crawls around a tabletop. Dots mark the position of the bug at each second. Determine the average velocity of the bug over the interval (a) from 1.0 s to 2.0 s; (b) from 2.0 s to 4.0 s; (c) 0 to 6.0 s.

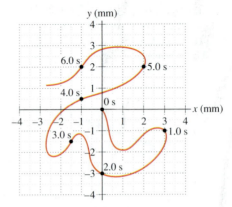

FIGURE 3-25 Problem 34.

35. An object's position as a function of time is given by $\mathbf{r} = 12t\hat{\mathbf{i}} + (15t - 5.0t^2)\hat{\mathbf{j}}$ m, where t is time in s. (a) What is the object's position at $t = 2.0$ s? (b) What is its average velocity in the interval from $t = 0$ to $t = 2.0$ s? (c) What is its instantaneous velocity at $t = 2.0$ s?

36. A supersonic aircraft is traveling east at 2100 km/h. It then begins to turn southward, emerging from the turn 2.5 min later heading due south at 1800 km/h. What are the magnitude and direction of its average acceleration during the turn?

37. A car, initially going eastward, rounds a 90° bend and ends up heading southward. If the speedometer reading remains constant, what is the direction of the car's average acceleration vector?

38. Earth moves in a nearly circular orbit about the Sun. What is the magnitude of its average acceleration over the intervals (a) from January 1 to July 1 and (b) from January 1 to April 1? (c) What is the angle between the two average acceleration vectors for the intervals given? Consult Appendix E for Earth's orbital speed.

39. What are (a) the average velocity and (b) the average acceleration of the tip of the 2.4-cm-long hour hand of a clock in the interval from 12 P.M. to 6 P.M.? Express in unit vector notation, with the x axis pointing toward 3 P.M. and the y axis toward 12 P.M.

40. Attempting to stop on a slippery road, a car moving at 80 km/h skids across the road at a 30° angle to its initial motion, coming to a stop in 3.9 s. Determine the average acceleration in m/s², using a coordinate system with the x axis in the direction of the car's original motion and the y axis toward the side of the road to which the car skids.

41. An object undergoes acceleration of $2.3\hat{\mathbf{i}} + 3.6\hat{\mathbf{j}}$ m/s² over a 10-s interval. At the end of this time, its velocity is $33\hat{\mathbf{i}} + 15\hat{\mathbf{j}}$ m/s. (a) What was its velocity at the beginning of the 10-s interval? (b) By how much did its speed change? (c) By how much did its direction change? (d) Show that the speed change is *not* given by the magnitude of the acceleration times the time. Why not?

42. An object's position as a function of time is given by $\mathbf{r} = (bt^3 + ct)\hat{\mathbf{i}} + dt^2\hat{\mathbf{j}} + (et + f)\hat{\mathbf{k}}$, where b, c, d, e, and f are constants. Determine the velocity and acceleration as functions of time.

43. The position of an object is given by $\mathbf{r} = (ct - bt^3)\hat{\mathbf{i}} + dt^2\hat{\mathbf{j}}$, with constants $c = 6.7$ m/s, $b = 0.81$ m/s^3, and $d = 4.5$ m/s^2. (a) Determine the object's velocity at time $t = 0$. (b) How long does it take for the direction of motion to change by $90°$? (c) By how much does the speed change during this time?

44. For the object of Problem 35, determine (a) the average acceleration in the interval from $t = 0$ to $t = 2.0$ s and (b) the instantaneous acceleration at $t = 2.0$ s.

Section 3-5 Relative Motion

45. A dog paces around the perimeter of a rectangular barge that is headed up a river at 14 km/h relative to the riverbank. The current in the water is at 3.0 km/h. If the dog walks at 4.0 km/h, what are its speeds relative to (a) the shore and (b) the water as it walks around the barge?

46. A jetliner with an airspeed of 1000 km/h sets out on a 1500-km flight due south. To maintain a southward direction, however, the plane must be pointed 15° west of south. If the flight takes 100 min, what is the wind velocity?

47. A spacecraft is launched toward Mars at the instant Earth is moving in the $+x$ direction at its orbital speed of 30 km/s, in the Sun's frame of reference. Initially the spacecraft is moving at 40 km/s relative to Earth, in the $+y$ direction. At the launch time, Mars is moving in the $-y$ direction at its orbital speed of 24 km/s. Find the spacecraft's velocity relative to Mars.

48. You wish to row straight across a 63-m-wide river. If you can row at a steady 1.3 m/s relative to the water, and the river flows at 0.57 m/s, (a) in what direction should you head? (b) How long will it take you to cross the river?

49. You're on an airport "people mover," a conveyor belt going at 2.2 m/s through a level section of the terminal. A button falls off your coat and drops freely 1.6 m, hitting the belt 0.57 s later. What are the magnitude and direction of the button's displacement and average velocity during its fall in (a) the frame of reference of the "people mover" and (b) the frame of reference of the airport terminal? (c) As it falls, what is its acceleration in each frame of reference?

50. An airplane with airspeed of 370 km/h flies perpendicularly across the jet stream. To achieve this flight, the plane must be pointed into the jet stream at an angle of 32° from the perpendicular direction of its flight. What is the speed of the jet stream?

Paired Problems

(Both problems in a pair involve the same principles and techniques. If you can get the first problem, you should be able to solve the second one.)

51. A rabbit scurries across a field, going eastward 21.0 m. It then turns and darts southwestward for 8.50 m. Then it pops down a rabbit hole, 1.10 m vertically downward. What is the magnitude of the displacement from its starting point?

52. A cosmic ray plows into Earth's upper atmosphere, liberating a shower of subatomic particles. One of these particles moves downward 3.2 km, then undergoes a collision after which it moves 1.6 km at 27° northward of the vertical. It then undergoes another collision that sends it moving horizontally eastward for 2.1 km before it annihilates with another particle. What is the magnitude of its overall displacement?

53. A car is heading into a turn at 85 km/h. It enters the turn, slows to 55 km/h, and emerges 28 s later at 35° to its original direction, still moving at 55 km/h. What are (a) the magnitude and (b) the direction of its average acceleration, the latter measured with respect to the car's original direction?

54. The Galileo space probe was originally to be launched directly toward its destination, Jupiter. But the 1986 explosion of the space shuttle Challenger led to a decision that Galileo's liquid-fueled booster rocket was unsafe to fly on the shuttle. As a result, Galileo's trajectory became a complicated path through the inner solar system, picking up speed through a so-called gravity assist maneuver involving close encounters with the planets Venus and Earth. The first Earth encounter occurred on December 8, 1990, when Galileo, outbound from Venus, passed 200 miles from Earth. Thirty days before the encounter, Galileo was approaching Earth at 2.99×10^4 m/s. Thirty days after the encounter, Galileo was moving at 54° to its preencounter direction, at a speed of 3.51×10^4 m/s. What were (a) the magnitude and (b) the direction of Galileo's average acceleration during this interval, the latter measured with respect to its pre-encounter direction?

55. The sweep-second hand of a clock is 3.1 cm long. What are the magnitude of (a) the average velocity and (b) the average acceleration of the hand's tip over a 5.0-s interval? (c) What is the angle between the average velocity and acceleration vectors?

56. A proton in a cyclotron follows a circular path 23 cm in diameter, completing one revolution in 0.17 μs. What are the magnitude of (a) the average velocity and (b) the average acceleration as the proton sweeps through one-twelfth of the full circle? (c) What is the angle between the average velocity and acceleration vectors?

57. A ferryboat sails between two towns directly opposite one another on a river. If the boat sails at 15 km/h relative to the water, and if the current flows at 6.3 km/h, at what angle should the boat head?

58. A flock of geese is attempting to migrate due south, but the wind is blowing from the west at 5.1 m/s. If the birds can fly at 7.5 m/s relative to the air, in what direction should they head?

Supplementary Problems

59. A satellite is in a circular orbit 240 km above Earth's surface, moving at a constant speed of 7.80 km/s. A tracking station picks up the satellite when it is 5.0° above the horizon, as shown in Fig. 3-26. The satellite is tracked until it is directly overhead. What are the magnitudes of (a) its displacement, (b) its average velocity, and (c) its average acceleration during the tracking interval? Is the value of the average acceleration approximately familiar?

FIGURE 3-26 Problem 59 (figure is not to scale).

60. The sum, **A** + **B**, of two vectors is perpendicular to the difference, **A** − **B**. How do the magnitudes of the two vectors compare?

61. Find two vectors in the x-y plane that are perpendicular to the vector $a\hat{\imath} + b\hat{\jmath}$.

62. Find the angle between the vectors $3.0\hat{\imath} + 1.7\hat{\jmath}$ and $6.1\hat{\imath} - 4.2\hat{\jmath}$.

63. Write an expression for a unit vector that lies at 45° between the positive x and y axes.

64. A vector **A** has components A_x and A_y in a coordinate system with axes x and y. Find its components A'_x and A'_y in a coordinate system whose axes x' and y' are rotated counterclockwise through an angle θ from the x and y axes. Test your result for the cases $\theta = 0$ and $\theta = 90°$.

65. Figure 3-27 shows two arbitrary vectors **A** and **B** that sum to a third vector **C**. By working with components, prove the law of cosines: $C^2 = A^2 + B^2 - 2AB\cos\gamma$.

66. You wish to paddle a canoe perpendicularly across a river of width w and back. If the river's flow speed is c, and you

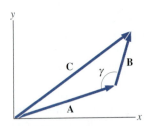

FIGURE 3-27 Problem 65.

can paddle at speed v relative to the water, show that your round-trip travel time is given by $\Delta t = 2w/\sqrt{v^2 - c^2}$.

67. Town B is located across the river from Town A and at a 40.0° angle upstream from A, as shown in Fig. 3-28. A ferryboat travels from A to B; it sails at 18.0 km/h relative to the water. If the current in the river flows at 5.60 km/h, at what angle should the boat head? What will be its speed relative to the ground? *Hint:* Set up Equation 3-10 for this situation. Each component of Equation 3-10 yields two equations in the unknowns v, the magnitude of the boat's velocity relative to the ground, and ϕ, the unknown angle. Solve the x equation for $\cos\phi$ and substitute into the second equation, using the relation $\sin\phi = \sqrt{1 - \cos^2\phi}$. You can then solve for v, then go back and get ϕ from your first equation.

FIGURE 3-28 Problem 67.

68. A space shuttle orbits the Earth at 27,000 km/h, while at the equator Earth rotates at 1300 km/h. The two motions are in roughly the same direction (west to east), but the shuttle orbit is inclined at 25° to the equator. What is the shuttle's velocity relative to scientists tracking it from the equator?

Motion in More Than One Dimension

Landing a jetliner involves a complex sequence of motions in three dimensions.

What is the speed of an orbiting satellite? How should I leap for best results in a long-jump competition? How much advance warning does my country have against a nuclear missile fired from a submarine offshore? How should I throw this ball so it gets over the roof? How should I engineer the curve in this road for safe driving? How wide a stage does a dancer need to execute a grand jeté? Chapter 3's introduction of the displacement, velocity, and acceleration vectors has prepared us to answer these and many other questions about motion in two and three dimensions.

4-1 VELOCITY AND ACCELERATION

Motion in a straight line may or may not involve acceleration. But motion in two or more dimensions *must* be accelerated motion. Why? Because moving in two dimensions requires changing direction—and that means at least the direction of the velocity vector must change. We emphasize again that *any* change in velocity—in magnitude, direction, or both—involves acceleration.

In Chapter 2 we stressed that the numerical values of velocity and acceleration in one dimension are completely unrelated; acceleration depends not on velocity but on *changes* in velocity. The same is true in two dimensions, where both velocity and acceleration are *vectors*. That means the acceleration vector can have not only any magnitude, but also any direction relative to the velocity vector. Mathematically, the relation between velocity and acceleration is described completely by Equations 3-8 and 3-9, which we repeat here:

average acceleration: $$\overline{\mathbf{a}} = \frac{\Delta \mathbf{v}}{\Delta t} \tag{4-1}$$

instantaneous acceleration: $$\mathbf{a} = \lim_{\Delta t \to 0} \frac{\Delta \mathbf{v}}{\Delta t} = \frac{d\mathbf{v}}{dt}. \tag{4-2}$$

If the acceleration is constant—in *both* magnitude and direction—then the average and instantaneous accelerations are the same. To understand further the relation between acceleration and velocity, it's helpful to consider several special cases.

Colinear Velocity and Acceleration

Suppose you're driving along a straight road at speed v_0, and you step on the gas to give a constant acceleration a for a time Δt. Then Equation 4-1 says that the magnitude of your change in velocity is $\Delta v = a\Delta t$. But what about direction? Stepping on the gas while driving on a straight road doesn't change your direction at all; it just makes you go faster. That is, the acceleration vector for this case is in the same direction as the velocity vector. So, too, is the velocity change $\Delta \mathbf{v}$, since it's just the acceleration vector $\mathbf{a}$ multiplied by Δt. Figure 4-1a shows the vector addition for this case.

What if you had stepped on the brake instead of the gas? Then you would have slowed while continuing to move forward. In that case the acceleration vector points opposite to the velocity vector, and the result is a decrease in the magnitude of the velocity but, again, no change in direction (Fig. 4-1b).

We summarize the situation when velocity and acceleration are colinear, either parallel or antiparallel:

> Acceleration colinear to velocity changes only the magnitude of the velocity, not its direction.

Use of vectors here is overkill; we could have handled this case using the one-dimensional methodology of Chapter 2. But we use the full vector description to emphasize both the similarities and differences between this and our next special case.

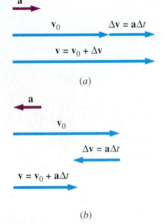

FIGURE 4-1 With acceleration and velocity in the same direction, the velocity vector changes in magnitude but not direction. (a) With velocity and acceleration parallel, the magnitude of the velocity increases. (b) With velocity and acceleration antiparallel, the magnitude of the velocity decreases.

Tip

Vectors Tell It All Are you thinking there should be a minus sign somewhere in Fig. 4-1*b*, because the magnitude of the velocity is decreasing? No, there shouldn't! The vector symbols stand for quantities with magnitude *and* direction. Full specification of **a** in Fig. 4-1*b* includes the fact that it's pointing to the left—and that's enough to show that this acceleration vector will decrease the magnitude of the right-pointing velocity. The vector addition $\mathbf{v} = \mathbf{v}_0 + \mathbf{a}\Delta t$ really tells it all. It's only when you write this in components that a negative sign will appear; in a coordinate system with its *x* axis to the right, for example, a_x of Fig. 4-1*b* is a negative number and the addition of the components v_{x0} and $\Delta v_x = a_x\Delta t$ becomes a subtraction. In general, you shouldn't worry about signs when adding vectors, even those in opposite directions; only when you write components in your chosen coordinate system do signs become important.

Perpendicular Velocity and Acceleration

A bird is flying eastward at speed v_0, when a gust of wind blows from the north, giving the bird a constant acceleration *a* for a short time Δt. Again, the magnitude of the change in velocity is $\Delta v = a\Delta t$, but now the acceleration is perpendicular to the initial velocity. Figure 4-2*a* shows the vector addition in this case. We could calculate the magnitude and direction of the new velocity vector, but the important point here is a qualitative one: the new velocity differs in direction from the initial velocity and is not much different in magnitude. Why? Because the acceleration vector is perpendicular to the initial velocity vector, so the dominant effect of the acceleration is to change the direction of the velocity. When it first acted, in fact, the acceleration changed *only* the direction; Fig 4-2*b* shows that for very short times, the initial and final velocities have essentially the same magnitude. As the velocity changed, it was no longer exactly perpendicular to the acceleration, and the magnitude began to change as well. Had the acceleration direction changed to keep it perpendicular to the velocity, only the direction would have changed (Fig. 4-2*c*). We conclude:

> **Acceleration that is always perpendicular to velocity changes only the direction of the velocity, not its magnitude.**

In a case like that of Fig. 4-2*a*, where the acceleration is perpendicular to the velocity and produces a change $\Delta \mathbf{v}$ considerably smaller in magnitude than the initial velocity, this statement is approximately true. When the acceleration and velocity are *always* perpendicular, as in Fig. 4-2*c*, it becomes exactly true.

The General Case

In general, velocity and acceleration vectors can be at any angle to each other. Then both the magnitude and direction of the velocity will change, as suggested in Fig. 4-3. Which changes most depends on the orientation of the vectors and on the magnitude of the change $\Delta \mathbf{v}$.

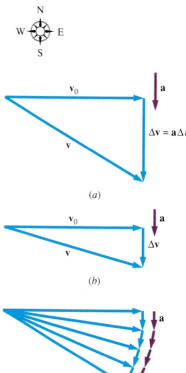

(a)

(b)

(c)

FIGURE 4-2 (*a*) A bird flying eastward accelerates southward during a brief wind gust. Its new velocity is changed considerably in direction but only slightly in magnitude. (*b*) If the perpendicular velocity change $\Delta \mathbf{v}$ is smaller, the initial and final velocities are closer in magnitude. (*c*) If the acceleration direction changes, so the velocity and acceleration are *always* perpendicular, then the velocity changes in direction only and its magnitude remains constant.

ActivPhysics

3.4
Projectile *x*- and *y*-Accelerations

FIGURE 4-3 In general, acceleration changes both the magnitude and direction of the velocity vector.

EXAMPLE 4-1	*Blown Off Course!*

A plane is flying eastward at 250 m/s when it encounters a crosswind that gives it a southward acceleration of 1.2 m/s². What are the magnitude and direction of its velocity at the end of 1 minute? Repeat for the case of an eastward acceleration.

Solution

Choosing a coordinate system with the x axis eastward and the y axis northward, the initial eastward velocity is $\mathbf{v}_0 = 250\hat{\imath}$ m/s. Similarly, the southward acceleration is $\mathbf{a} = -1.2\hat{\jmath}$ m/s². Using this acceleration in Equation 4-1 gives the change in velocity over the 1-min interval:

$$\Delta\mathbf{v} = \mathbf{a}\Delta t = (-1.2\hat{\jmath} \text{ m/s})(60 \text{ s}) = -72\hat{\jmath} \text{ m/s} .$$

Then the velocity at the end of 1 min is given by

$$\mathbf{v} = \mathbf{v}_0 + \Delta\mathbf{v} = 250\hat{\imath} \text{ m/s} - 72\hat{\jmath} \text{ m/s} .$$

The magnitude of the vector $\mathbf{v}$ can be calculated from its components, using Equation 3-1:

$$v = \sqrt{v_x^2 + v_y^2} = \sqrt{(250 \text{ m/s})^2 + (-72 \text{ m/s})^2} = 260 \text{ m/s} ,$$

while the tangent of the angle θ that $\mathbf{v}$ makes with the x-axis is the ratio of v_y to v_x:

$$\theta = \tan^{-1}\left(\frac{v_y}{v_x}\right) = \tan^{-1}\left(\frac{-72 \text{ m/s}}{250 \text{ m/s}}\right) = -16° ,$$

or 16° south of east. Note that this acceleration—directed initially at right angles to the velocity—has relatively little effect on the magnitude of the velocity. The latter increases by only 10 m/s, even though the acceleration produces a 72 m/s change in the southward component of the velocity. This is essentially the situation shown in Fig. 4-2a.

When the acceleration acts eastward, the situation is reduced to a one-dimensional problem. In vector notation, we still have $\mathbf{v}_0 = 250\hat{\imath}$ m/s, but now $\mathbf{a} = 1.2\hat{\imath}$ m/s², so $\Delta\mathbf{v} = 72\hat{\imath}$ m/s. Then the velocity after 1 min is

$$\mathbf{v} = \mathbf{v}_0 + \Delta\mathbf{v} = 250\hat{\imath} \text{ m/s} + 72\hat{\imath} \text{ m/s} = 322\hat{\imath} \text{ m/s} .$$

Here the acceleration—now in the same direction as the velocity—results in a substantial change in speed but no change in direction. This case is essentially that of Fig. 4-1a.

EXERCISE A hockey puck is gliding across the ice at 14 m/s, when a player's stick gives it an acceleration of 81 m/s² at an angle of 72° to its initial velocity. If the acceleration is applied for 0.23 s, what are the direction and magnitude of the final velocity?

Answer: 27 m/s at 42°

Some problems similar to Example 4-1 3, 4

Got It!

An object is subject to a downward acceleration. Which, if any, of the following is true?

(a) The object cannot be moving upward.
(b) The object cannot be moving in a straight line.
(c) If the object is moving horizontally before the acceleration begins, it will be moving directly downward as soon as the acceleration starts.

3.2
Two Balls Falling

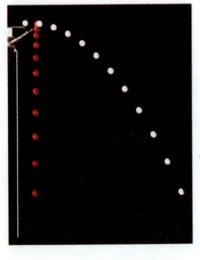

4-2 CONSTANT ACCELERATION

When acceleration is constant—no change in either magnitude or direction—then the individual components of the acceleration vector are themselves constant. Experimentally, we find that the component of acceleration in one direction has no effect on the motion in a perpendicular direction (Fig. 4-4; see also ActivPhysics Activity 3.2 for an animation of this experiment). Then with constant acceleration, the separate components of the motion must obey the constant-

FIGURE 4-4 Two marbles, one dropped and the other projected horizontally at the same time, are photographed with a strobe camera. At each instant their vertical positions are identical, showing that the vertical and horizontal motions are independent. Time interval between images is 0.025 s.

acceleration formulas we developed in Chapter 2 for one-dimensional motion. Using vector notation, we can then generalize Equations 2-7 and 2-10 to read

$$\mathbf{v} = \mathbf{v}_0 + \mathbf{a}t \tag{4-3}$$

$$\mathbf{r} = \mathbf{r}_0 + \mathbf{v}_0 t + \tfrac{1}{2}\mathbf{a}t^2, \tag{4-4}$$

where $\mathbf{r}$ is the position vector. In two dimensions, each of these vector equations represents a pair of scalar equations describing constant acceleration in two mutually perpendicular directions; Equation 4-4, for example, contains the pair $x = x_0 + v_{x0}t + \tfrac{1}{2}a_x t^2$ and $y = y_0 + v_{y0}t + \tfrac{1}{2}a_y t^2$. (Remember that the components of the displacement vector $\mathbf{r}$ are just the coordinates x and y.) In three dimensions there would be a third equation for the z component of the motion. The other one-dimensional equations of Table 2-1 also hold for the individual components of multidimensional motion with constant acceleration.

EXAMPLE 4-2	*Windsurfing*

A sailboard is sailing at 7.3 m/s when a gust of wind hits, causing it to accelerate at 0.82 m/s^2 at a 60° angle to its original direction of motion. If the acceleration lasts 8.7 s, what is the board's net displacement during the wind gust?

Solution

Equation 4-4 gives the position of an object undergoing constant acceleration. Since we're working in two dimensions, we need an x-y coordinate system. A reasonable choice is to take the x axis along the direction of the sailboard's initial velocity; then we have $\mathbf{v}_0 = 7.3\hat{\mathbf{i}}$ m/s and, as Fig. 4-5 shows, $\mathbf{a} = 0.41\hat{\mathbf{i}} + 0.71\hat{\mathbf{j}}$ m/s^2. (Another reasonable choice would be to take the x axis along the acceleration direction; then the acceleration would have only one nonzero component, while the initial velocity would have two.) If we choose the origin to be the point where the wind gust first hit, we have $x_0 = y_0 = 0$, and the two components of Equation 4-4 become

$$x = v_{x0}t + \tfrac{1}{2}a_x t^2 = (7.3 \text{ m/s})(8.7 \text{ s})$$
$$\quad + \tfrac{1}{2}(0.41 \text{ m/s}^2)(8.7 \text{ s})^2 = 79.0 \text{ m}$$
$$y = \tfrac{1}{2}a_y t^2 = \tfrac{1}{2}(0.71 \text{ m/s}^2)(8.7 \text{ s})^2 = 26.9 \text{ m} ,$$

where in writing the y equation, we used the fact that $v_{y0} = 0$. The new position vector is then given by $\mathbf{r} = x\hat{\mathbf{i}} + y\hat{\mathbf{j}} = 79.0\hat{\mathbf{i}} + 26.9\hat{\mathbf{j}}$ m, so the net displacement is

$$r = \sqrt{x^2 + y^2} = \sqrt{(79.0 \text{ m})^2 + (26.9 \text{ m})^2} = 83.5 \text{ m} .$$

Figure 4-6 shows the position vector $\mathbf{r}$ formed from the sum of component vectors $x\hat{\mathbf{i}}$ and $y\hat{\mathbf{j}}$. Although this vector gives the overall displacement of the sailboard during the wind gust, it is *not* the path of the board; rather, since the board's velocity is constantly changing, the actual path is the curve shown in Fig. 4-6.

EXERCISE A spaceship is traveling in a straight line at 6.2 km/s, when a rocket is fired that gives it an acceleration of

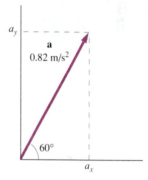

FIGURE 4-5 The components of the acceleration vector are $a_x = a \cos 60° = 0.41$ m/s^2 and $a_y = a \sin 60° = 0.71$ m/s^2, where $a = 0.82$ m/s^2 is the magnitude of the acceleration vector.

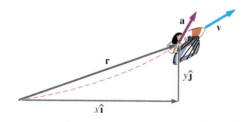

FIGURE 4-6 Displacement vector for the accelerating sailboard. Because the board's velocity is constantly changing, its actual trajectory is the curved path shown. Note that displacement, velocity, and acceleration vectors all point in different directions.

0.36 km/s^2 in a direction 75° to its initial velocity. If the rocket firing lasts 22 s, what is its net displacement during the firing?

Answer: 180 km

Some problems similar to Example 4-2: 7, 9, 10

As Example 4-2 shows, we handle problems of multidimensional motion by breaking them into two or three one-dimensional problems. We solve each of these using the methods of Chapter 2, then combine the solutions to give a full vector description of the motion.

4-3 PROJECTILE MOTION

A **projectile** is an object that is launched into the air and then moves predominantly under the influence of gravity. Examples are numerous: baseballs, jets of water, fireworks, missiles, ejecta from volcanoes, drops of ink in an ink-jet computer printer, and leaping dolphins are all projectiles (Fig. 4-7).

To treat projectile motion, we make two simplifying assumptions: (1) we neglect any variation in the direction or magnitude of the gravitational acceleration and (2) we neglect air resistance. Assumption 1 is equivalent to neglecting the curvature of the Earth, and is valid for projectiles whose displacements are small compared with Earth's radius. Air resistance has a more variable effect; for dense, compact objects it is often negligible, but for objects whose ratio of surface area to mass is large—like ping-pong balls and parachutes—air resistance may dramatically alter the motion. And the more subtle motions of a baseball—its curves and wobbles—can only be explained by invoking air resistance. We'll discuss air resistance later in this chapter and, more quantitatively, in Chapter 6. In the following, we assume air resistance is negligible unless explicitly stated otherwise.

To describe projectile motion, it is usually convenient to choose a coordinate system with the y axis vertically upward, and the x axis horizontal and in the direction of the horizontal component of the projectile's initial velocity. Then there is neither velocity nor acceleration in the z direction, and we have purely two-dimensional motion in the x-y plane (Fig. 4-8). Furthermore, with the only

FIGURE 4-7 Sparks fly in a welding operation. Note how the sparks follow paths—trajectories—of similar shape. For objects moving near Earth's surface, under the influence of gravity alone, that shape is parabolic.

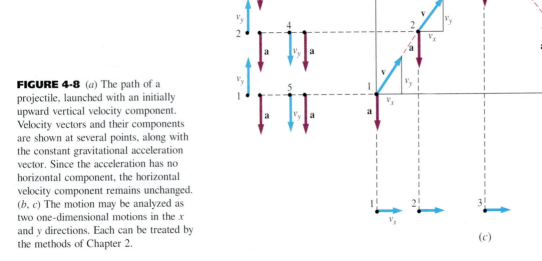

FIGURE 4-8 (*a*) The path of a projectile, launched with an initially upward vertical velocity component. Velocity vectors and their components are shown at several points, along with the constant gravitational acceleration vector. Since the acceleration has no horizontal component, the horizontal velocity component remains unchanged. (*b, c*) The motion may be analyzed as two one-dimensional motions in the x and y directions. Each can be treated by the methods of Chapter 2.

acceleration provided by gravity, $a_x = 0$ and $a_y = -g$, so the components of Equations 4-3 and 4-4 become

$$v_x = v_{x0} \tag{4-5}$$
$$v_y = v_{y0} - gt \tag{4-6}$$
$$x = x_0 + v_{x0}t \tag{4-7}$$
$$y = y_0 + v_{y0}t - \tfrac{1}{2}gt^2. \tag{4-8}$$

In writing these equations, we take g to be a positive number, as we did in Chapter 2, and account for the downward direction using minus signs. Equations 4-5 to 4-8 tell us mathematically what Fig. 4-8 tells us physically: that projectile motion can be broken down into two perpendicular and independent components: horizontal motion with constant velocity and vertical motion with constant acceleration.

We emphasize that there's nothing new in Equations 4-5 through 4-8; they're simply the constant-acceleration Equations 4-3 and 4-4, written in components for the case where the acceleration is that of gravity near Earth's surface. Although we presented them here, you should be able to go back to Equations 4-3 and 4-4 and specialize them as needed to this or any other constant-acceleration situation. Furthermore, there's nothing special about the choice of x axis horizontal and y axis upward. To remind you that the coordinate system is yours to choose, we'll occasionally work examples with other choices.

3.1
Solving Projectile Motion Problems

EXAMPLE 4-3	*Washout*

A raging flood has washed away a section of highway, creating a gash 1.7 m deep. A car moving at 31 m/s goes right over the edge, as shown in Fig. 4-9. How far from the edge of the washout does the car land?

Solution

The answer we seek is the distance the car moves horizontally after leaving the road. Since there's no horizontal acceleration, the car's horizontal velocity remains unchanged at 31 m/s. If we knew the time the car was airborne, we could figure out how far it went.

We can find the time by analyzing the vertical motion. Since the car leaves the road moving horizontally, $v_{y0} = 0$. If we choose our origin at the bottom of the washout, as shown in Fig. 4-9, then $y_0 = 1.7$ m. Then we want to find the time when $y = 0$. Setting $y = 0$ in Equation 4-8 and solving for t gives

$$t = \sqrt{\frac{2y_0}{g}} = \sqrt{\frac{(2)(1.7\text{ m})}{9.8\text{ m/s}^2}} = 0.589\text{ s}.$$

This is the time it takes the car to drop the 1.7-m distance to the bottom of the washout; during this time the car is moving horizontally at 31 m/s, so it goes a horizontal distance

$$x = v_{x0}t = (31\text{ m/s})(0.589\text{ s}) = 18\text{ m}.$$

Formally, we got this from Equation 4-7 with $x_0 = 0$, but it should be obvious to you from the definition of velocity.

FIGURE 4-9 Example 4-3.

Instead of evaluating t numerically in the first step of our solution, we could have kept $t = \sqrt{2y_0/g}$ in symbolic form until the end. Keeping expressions symbolic as long as possible is usually preferable: There's no roundoff error, so it's more accurate; there aren't a lot of numbers to keep writing; there are no units to keep track of; and often a little intuition will tell you if an algebraic expression "looks" right or wrong.

How hard does the car hit the ground? You can find out by doing the exercise below.

EXERCISE With what vertical speed does the car in this example hit the bottom of the washout?

Answer: 5.8 m/s

Tip

Multistep Problems In Example 4-3, we were asked for the horizontal position of the car. But to find that, we needed to know the time— which we weren't given. This is a common situation in all but the simplest "plug-in" physics problems: It isn't immediately obvious how to get from the given information to the final answer. In such cases it's often best to work backward, asking "What would I need to know to get the answer?" and then figuring out how to get that quantity from the given information. Here, the missing quantity was the time, which we got by analyzing the vertical motion. In essence, we had to formulate a second problem: "Given a vertical drop of 1.7 m, how long does it take an object to fall?" Solving that problem then gave the information we needed to solve the original problem.

When faced with a multistep problem, don't hesitate to assign a symbol to any unknown quantity you need—in this case the time, t—even if the problem doesn't mention it. That quantity will not appear in your final answer, but it may be essential in doing the intermediate calculations.

3.6, 3.7

Target Practice

ActivPhysics

EXAMPLE 4-4	*Fish Drop*

An osprey is flying at 18 m/s at an angle of 30° below the horizontal when it accidentally drops a fish. If the osprey is 16 m above a lake when the fish drops, (a) how long does it take the fish to fall, and (b) at what velocity does the fish hit the water?

Solution

This example is similar to the previous one, except that here the fish has an initial vertical velocity component. To remind you that the choice of coordinate system is arbitrary, we'll work this example in a coordinate system with the x axis horizontal and the y axis vertically *downward* (see Fig. 4-10).

Equations 4-5 through 4-8 were derived for a different coordinate system, so let's go back to the basic equations: 4-3 and 4-4. We'll need the y component of Equation 4-4 to get the time. With $y_0 = 0$ (the fish starts at the origin of our chosen coordinate system); $v_{y0} = v_0 \sin\theta$, as shown in Fig. 4-10; and with $a_y = +g$ since we're taking the positive y direction downward, the y component of Equation 4-4 becomes

$$y = (v_0 \sin\theta)t + \tfrac{1}{2}gt^2.$$

Writing this as a quadratic in t and solving for the positive root (to give a time *after* the fish was dropped), we have

$$t = \frac{-v_0 \sin\theta + \sqrt{v_0^2 \sin^2\theta - 4(\tfrac{1}{2}g)(-y)}}{g} = 1.11 \text{ s},$$

where we used $v_0 = 18$ m/s, $\theta = 30°$, and $y = 16$ m (here it's easier to carry the number rather than the complicated expression for t into subsequent calculations).

We can then find the velocity using Equation 4-3; we'll work directly with the vector form:

$$\mathbf{v} = \mathbf{v}_0 + \mathbf{a}t = (v_0 \cos\theta \,\hat{\mathbf{i}} + v_0 \sin\theta \,\hat{\mathbf{j}}) + g\hat{\mathbf{j}}\, t$$

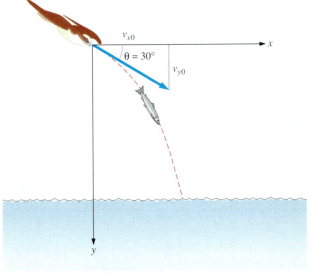

FIGURE 4-10 Example 4-4.

Using our computed value for t and grouping the terms for the x and y directions gives $\mathbf{v} = 16\hat{\mathbf{i}} + 20\hat{\mathbf{j}}$ m/s; the impact speed is the magnitude of this vector, or 25 m/s. Then the $\hat{\mathbf{j}}$ term is positive reflects our choice of coordinate system, with the downward direction positive.

EXERCISE Repeat Example 4-4 for the case when the osprey is flying upward at 30° above the horizontal; all other quantities remain unchanged.

Answer: $t = 2.9$ s; impact velocity is unchanged.

Some problems similar to Examples 4-3 and 4-4: 15–20

Projectile Trajectories

We're often interested in the path, or **trajectory**, of a projectile without the details of where it is at each instant of time. A look at Fig. 4-7 suggests that objects undergoing projectile motion have similarly shaped trajectories. What is that shape?

We can specify a projectile's trajectory by giving its height y as a function of horizontal position x. Consider a projectile launched from the origin $(x_0 = y_0 = 0)$ at some angle θ_0 to the horizontal, with initial speed v_0. As Fig. 4-11 suggests, the components of the initial velocity are $v_{x0} = v_0 \cos \theta_0$ and $v_{y0} = v_0 \sin \theta_0$. Then Equations 4-7 and 4-8 become

$$x = v_0 \cos \theta_0 t \quad \text{and} \quad y = v_0 \sin \theta_0 t - \tfrac{1}{2} g t^2 .$$

Solving the x equation for the time t gives

$$t = \frac{x}{v_0 \cos \theta_0} ;$$

using this result in the y equation, we have

$$y = v_0 \sin \theta_0 \left(\frac{x}{v_0 \cos \theta_0} \right) - \tfrac{1}{2} g \left(\frac{x}{v_0 \cos \theta_0} \right)^2 ,$$

or

$$y = x \tan \theta_0 - \frac{g}{2 v_0^2 \cos^2 \theta_0} x^2 . \quad \text{(projectile trajectory)} \quad (4\text{-}9)$$

In Equation 4-9 we have the mathematical description of the projectile's trajectory. Since y is a quadratic function of x, the trajectory is a parabola.

Equation 4-9 gives the trajectory of *any* particle moving under the influence of uniform gravity alone—i.e., neglecting air resistance and the effects of Earth's curvature. Every one of the sparks in Fig. 4-7, for example, describes a parabolic trajectory. Individual trajectories differ because the sparks have different initial speeds and directions, but they're all included in Equation 4-9. We emphasize, though, that this equation introduces no new physics; it follows directly from the constant acceleration Equations 4-3 and 4-4.

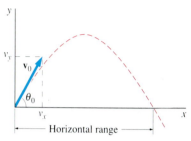

FIGURE 4-11 Parabolic trajectory of a projectile.

3.5
Initial Velocity Components

EXAMPLE 4-5	*Out of the Hole*

A construction worker is standing in a 2.6-m-deep hole, 3.1 m from the side of the hole. He tosses a hammer to a companion outside the hole. If the hammer leaves his hand 1.0 m above the bottom of the hole, at an angle of 35° to the horizontal, what is the minimum speed it must have to clear the edge of the hole, as shown in Fig. 4-12? How far from the edge of the hole does it land?

Solution

If it just clears the edge of the hole, the hammer must be on a trajectory that has $y = 1.6$ m when $x = 3.1$ m, where we take the origin at the point where the hammer leaves the construction worker's hand.

Solving Equation 4-9 for v_0 and using these x and y values along with $\theta_0 = 35°$ gives the required speed:

$$v_0 = \sqrt{\frac{g x^2}{2 \cos^2 \theta_0 (x \tan \theta_0 - y)}} = 11 \text{ m/s} .$$

FIGURE 4-12 Example 4-5.

To find where the hammer lands on the level ground 1.6 m above the throwing point, we need to know the horizontal position when $y = 1.6$ m. Rearranging Equation 4-9 into the standard form for a quadratic equation gives

$$\frac{g}{2 v_0^2 \cos^2 \theta_0} x^2 - (\tan \theta_0) x + y = 0 .$$

Applying the quadratic formula (Appendix A), we then have

$$x = \frac{\tan\theta_0 \pm \sqrt{\tan^2\theta_0 - 4y(g/2v_0^2\cos^2\theta_0)}}{(g/v_0^2\cos^2\theta_0)}$$

$$= 3.1 \text{ m or } 8.7 \text{ m}.$$

These answers are the horizontal positions where the hammer is at ground level. The first provides a useful check on our work: it's just the position when the hammer clears the edge of the hole. The second answer is the one we want; it shows that the hammer lands 8.7 m − 3.1 m = 5.6 m to the right of the hole's edge.

EXERCISE A daredevil motorcyclist attempts to leap a 48-m-wide gorge, as shown in Fig. 4-13. At the side where the cyclist starts, the ground slopes upward at 15° to the gorge rim, as shown in Fig. 4-13. Beyond the far rim the ground is level and is 5.9 m below the near rim, as shown. (a) What is the minimum speed necessary for the cyclist to clear the gorge? (b) If the cyclist

FIGURE 4-13 A daredevil cyclist.

exceeds that minimum by 50%, how far from the far rim will he land?

Answers: (a) 25 m/s; (b) 44 m

Some problems similar to Example 4-5: 29, 30, 38, 55, 56

3.9

Motorcycle Daredevil

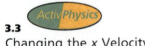

3.3

Changing the x Velocity

(a)

(b)

FIGURE 4-14 (a) Equation 4-10 gives the horizontal range of a particle that returns to its starting height. (b) It does *not* apply otherwise.

The Range of a Projectile

How far will a soccer ball go if I kick it at 12 m/s at 50° to the horizontal? If I can throw a rock at 15 m/s, can I get it across a 30-m-wide pond? At what angle should I throw it for maximum distance? How far off vertical can a rocket's trajectory be and still have it land within 50 km of its launch point? As in these examples, we're frequently interested in the **horizontal range** of a projectile—that is, in how far it moves horizontally over level ground.

Equation 4-9 describes the trajectory—height y versus horizontal position x—for a projectile. For a projectile launched on level ground, we can ask when the projectile will return to the ground by setting $y = 0$ in Equation 4-9:

$$0 = x\tan\theta_0 - \frac{g}{2v_0^2\cos^2\theta_0}x^2 = x\left(\tan\theta_0 - \frac{gx}{2v_0^2\cos^2\theta_0}\right),$$

where we factored to show that the two solutions are $x = 0$, corresponding to the launch point, or

$$x = \frac{2v_0^2}{g}\cos^2\theta_0\tan\theta_0 = \frac{2v_0^2}{g}\sin\theta_0\cos\theta_0.$$

Here we used $\tan\theta_0 = \sin\theta_0/\cos\theta_0$; recalling further that $\sin 2\theta_0 = 2\sin\theta_0\cos\theta_0$ (see Appendix A), we can write

$$x = \frac{v_0^2}{g}\sin 2\theta_0. \quad \text{(horizontal range)} \quad (4\text{-}10)$$

> **Tip**
>
> *Know Your Limits* We emphasize that Equation 4-10 gives the *horizontal* range—the distance a projectile travels horizontally before returning *to its starting height*. From the way it was derived—setting $y = 0$—you can see that it does *not* give the horizontal distance when the projectile returns to a different height (Fig. 4-14).

Does Equation 4-10 make sense? When $\theta_0 = 0$, the range is zero: a projectile launched horizontally on level ground immediately hits the ground. When $\theta_0 = 90°$, $\sin 2\theta_0 = \sin 180° = 0$, and again the range is zero. Here the projectile is launched vertically upward, so of course it returns to the same point. When is the range a maximum? The largest value of $\sin 2\theta_0$ is 1, which occurs when $\theta_0 = 45°$. For a given initial speed v_0, then, the maximum range is attained by launching at 45°. Note that you can also get this result using calculus (see Problem 72). Figure 4-15 shows the trajectories of projectiles launched at different angles with the same initial speed. At angles less than 45° the projectile has a greater horizontal component of velocity, but it doesn't get as high and therefore isn't in the air as long as the projectile launched at 45°; the net effect is a shorter range. At angles greater than 45°, the projectile rises higher and is therefore in the air longer, but its horizontal velocity is lower and the net effect is again a shorter range. In fact, as you can prove in Problem 39, the range is the same for angles equally spaced on either side of 45°.

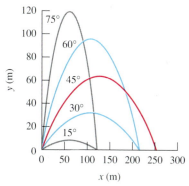

FIGURE 4-15 For a given initial speed, the range of a projectile is maximum at a launch angle of 45°. For launch angles equally spaced above and below 45°, the range is the same. Curves are for an initial speed of 50 m/s, with launch angles indicated.

Tip

Know the Fundamentals Equations 4-9 for the trajectory and 4-10 for the range of a projectile are certainly useful—but they're hardly fundamental equations of physics. Both are specialized results that follow directly from the constant-acceleration Equations 4-3 and 4-4. It's important that you understand fully what Equations 4-3 and 4-4 say and how special results such as Equations 4-9 and 4-10 follow from them. Otherwise, you're seeing physics as a hodgepodge of equations and missing the big picture of a science with a few underlying principles from which all else follows.

EXAMPLE 4-6	*Probing the Atmosphere*

A rocket is launched from a remote desert site to probe the upper atmosphere. With a short firing of its engine, the rocket quickly reaches a speed of 4.6 km/s. If the rocket is to land within 50 km of its launch site, what is the maximum allowable deviation from a vertical trajectory? Neglect air resistance.

Solution

Here we neglect the short distance over which the rocket accelerates, considering that it left the ground with its initial speed of 4.6 km/s. Then the answer to the problem is the angle θ_0 for which the range x is 50 km. Solving Equation 4-10 for $\sin 2\theta_0$ gives

$$\sin 2\theta_0 = \frac{gx}{v_0^2} = \frac{(9.8 \text{ m/s}^2)(50 \times 10^3 \text{ m})}{(4.6 \times 10^3 \text{ m/s})^2} = 0.0232 \,.$$

There are two solutions to this equation, corresponding to $2\theta_0 = \sin^{-1}(0.0232) = 1.33°$ and $2\theta_0 = 180° - 1.33°$. The

second solution is the one we want; it represents a nearly vertical launch angle $\theta_0 = 90° - 0.67°$, so the launch angle must be within 0.67° of vertical.

EXERCISE As an engineer, you're asked to design a fountain for a public park. Water droplets squirt from holes arranged around a circle of negligible size, and the water is supposed to land in a circular trough of radius 1.7 m. If the water emerges from the holes at 4.3 m/s, at what angle should the holes be oriented? Choose the answer that gives the maximum fountain height consistent with the given radius and initial speed.

Answer: 58°

Some problems similar to Example 4-6: 33, 35

EXAMPLE 4-7	*Lighting the Olympic Flame*

The Olympic Flame at the 1992 Barcelona Olympics was lit by a flaming arrow shot from a point 60 m horizontally and 24 m vertically from the flame (Fig. 4-16). Find the initial speed necessary for the arrow to reach the flame at the peak of its trajectory. Ignore aerodynamic effects (actually significant for an arrow).

Solution

Let $\ell = 60$ m and $h = 24$ m be the horizontal and vertical distances, respectively. If the trajectory is to peak at $x = \ell$, the range must be 2ℓ and Equation 4-10 then gives

$$2\ell = \frac{v_0^2}{g} \sin 2\theta_0 ,$$

or

$$v_0^2 = \frac{2g\ell}{\sin 2\theta_0} = \frac{g\ell}{\sin\theta_0 \cos\theta_0} .$$

The trajectory must have $y = h$ when $x = \ell$; using our expression for v_0^2 in the trajectory Equation 4-9 then gives

$$h = \ell \tan\theta_0 - \frac{g}{2\dfrac{g\ell}{\sin\theta_0 \cos\theta_0}\cos^2\theta_0}\ell^2$$

$$= \ell \tan\theta_0 - \tfrac{1}{2}\ell \tan\theta_0 = \tfrac{1}{2}\ell \tan\theta_0 .$$

Thus, the launch angle is

$$\theta_0 = \tan^{-1}\left(\frac{2h}{\ell}\right) = \tan^{-1}\left(\frac{(2)(24\text{ m})}{60\text{ m}}\right) = 38.66° ,$$

which then gives an initial speed of

$$v_0 = \sqrt{\frac{2g\ell}{\sin 2\theta_0}} = \sqrt{\frac{(2)(9.8\text{ m/s}^2)(60\text{ m})}{\sin[(2)(38.66°)]}} = 34.7\text{ m/s} .$$

FIGURE 4-16 Cross section of the Olympic stadium in Barcelona, Spain, showing trajectory of arrow used to light the Olympic flame (Example 4-7).

Tip

Trust Your Algebra This example was a bit more complicated, in that it wasn't at all obvious at first how to get the answer. But the two physical constraints—the given range and height—could be expressed by two independent algebraic equations, each containing the two unknowns θ_0 and v_0. And that's enough to ensure that if a solution exists, it can be found—usually by the methods of algebra.

EXERCISE A zany astronaut takes a golf ball and club to the moon and wants to hit the ball over a 380-m high hill on an otherwise level plain. If the astronaut is 870 m horizontally from the hilltop, at what speed and angle should the ball be hit so it just clears the hill at the peak of its trajectory?

Answer: 53 m/s at 41°

Some problems similar to Example 4-7: 34, 70, 71

The Effect of Air Resistance

We've been neglecting air resistance in our treatment of projectile motion. But air resistance can have a significant effect, especially at high speeds or for objects of large surface area and low mass. The more time spent in the air, the greater the effect. That means air resistance has less effect with lower launch angles; as a result, the launch angle for maximum range turns out to be less than 45°. Calculating trajectories with air resistance is not trivial; it generally requires a computer. Figure 4-17 compares the trajectories of a baseball with and without air resistance.

FIGURE 4-17 Computed trajectories of a baseball with (red) and without (blue) air resistance. The ball is launched at 45 m/s at a 60° angle. Note that the trajectory with air resistance is not symmetric; since the ball loses speed, it falls more steeply after reaching its peak. [Adapted from Brancazio, *Sport Science* (Simon & Schuster, 1984).]

| APPLICATION | *Ballistic Missile Defense* |

Since the development of nuclear-armed missiles in the late 1950s, it's been the case that the United States could be destroyed in half an hour—and there's nothing we can do to prevent it. Although the threat of nuclear attack from Russia has faded, the proliferation of missile technology raises the danger that others could launch a missile attack.

Is there a defense against ballistic missiles? That question is wrapped in technological and political controversy, but the general parameters of the answer are set by the physics of projectile motion. A ballistic missile is one that gets an initial rocket boost, then coasts under the influence of gravity alone; as soon as the rockets stop firing, the missile is simply a projectile. (So-called cruise missiles, in contrast, are like airplanes, using aerodynamic lift and engine power to get to their targets.)

The range of intercontinental missiles is so great that Earth's curvature becomes important, rendering invalid our simplifying assumption that the gravitational acceleration is constant. But for short- and intermediate-range missiles, treating the missile like a projectile is a good approximation. Consider a missile launched from a submarine 1,000 km off the coast (Fig. 4-18). How long does the defense have to deal with the attack?

For the optimum launch angle of 45°, Equation 4-10 shows that a 1,000-km range requires a launch speed of 3.1 km/s; the horizontal component of the velocity is then $v_x = (3.1 \text{ km/s})(\cos 45°) = 2.2$ km/s. At this rate, the missile flight lasts only $(1,000 \text{ km})/(2.2 \text{ km/s}) = 450$ s or 7.5 minutes! It might take a minute or so to detect the launch, determine the missile's trajectory, confirm that the attack was real, and notify defensive systems. That leaves very little time to intercept the incoming missile.

Since the early 1980s, the United States has spent billions of dollars on schemes for defense against ballistic missiles. Although many scientists and engineers are convinced that an effective defense is technologically impossible, the search continues. Some of the most exotic proposals involve high-power lasers and particle beams, which would function most effectively in the vacuum of space. For submarine-launched missiles, a simple

FIGURE 4-18 The flight time for a submarine-launched ballistic missile can be under 10 minutes.

expedient to foil such systems is to launch at less than the optimum angle. At 45°, for example, our 1,000-km-range missile reaches a peak altitude given by solving Equation 2-11 for y, with $v_y = 0$ at the peak:

$$ y = \frac{v_{y0}^2}{2g} = \frac{[(3100 \text{ m/s})(\sin 45°)]^2}{(2)(9.8 \text{ m/s}^2)} = 245 \text{ km}, $$

well above the atmosphere. But a launch angle of 15° gives a maximum altitude of 67 km, well within the atmosphere. There's a cost to the attacker: The launch speed now rises to 4.4 km/s, requiring a more powerful rocket. But there's also an advantage: the missile's flight time drops to just 3.9 minutes.

Problems 27 and 40 explore further the grim physics of ballistic missiles.

4-4 UNIFORM CIRCULAR MOTION

An important case of accelerated motion in two dimensions is **uniform circular motion**—the motion of an object describing a circular path at constant speed (see Fig. 4-19). Although the speed is constant, the motion is accelerated because the *direction* of the velocity is changing.

FIGURE 4-19 A satellite in a circular orbit undergoes uniform circular motion. Its speed is constant but its velocity is changing in direction—so it's accelerating.

FIGURE 4-20 Velocity vectors for an object in uniform circular motion are tangent to the circular path.

Examples of uniform circular motion are numerous. Many spacecraft are in circular orbits, and the orbits of the planets and their natural satellites are approximately circular. The Earth's daily rotation carries you around in uniform circular motion. Pieces of rotating machinery describe uniform circular motion. In laboratory apparatus and astrophysical objects, electrons undergo uniform circular motion when they encounter magnetic fields. Even with the atom itself, we can gain some insight by picturing electrons in uniform circular motion about the nucleus—although this view is not fully consistent with modern quantum mechanics. Other situations involve uniform circular motion over a limited path. Driving around a curve at constant speed, you are temporarily in uniform circular motion. As you swing a baseball bat, golf club, or hockey stick, you produce motion that is circular and that may be approximately uniform.

Here we derive an important relation among the acceleration, speed, and radius of uniform circular motion. Figure 4-20 shows several velocity vectors for an object moving with speed v around a circle of radius r. Note that the velocity vectors are tangent to the circle, indicating the instantaneous direction of motion. In Fig. 4-21a we focus on two nearby points described by position vectors $\mathbf{r}_1$ and $\mathbf{r}_2$, showing also the velocity vectors $\mathbf{v}_1$ and $\mathbf{v}_2$. Figure 4-21b shows the displacement $\Delta\mathbf{r}$ that represents the difference between $\mathbf{r}_1$ and $\mathbf{r}_2$; similarly, Fig. 4-21c shows the velocity difference $\Delta\mathbf{v}$.

Because $\mathbf{v}_1$ is perpendicular to $\mathbf{r}_1$, and $\mathbf{v}_2$ is perpendicular to $\mathbf{r}_2$, the angles θ shown in all three parts of Fig. 4-21 are the same angle. Therefore, the triangles in Fig. 4-21b and c are similar, and we can write

$$\frac{\Delta v}{v} = \frac{\Delta r}{r}.$$

Now suppose the angle θ is small, corresponding to a short time interval Δt for motion from position $\mathbf{r}_1$ to $\mathbf{r}_2$. Then the length of the vector $\Delta\mathbf{r}$ is approximately that of the circular arc joining the endpoints of the position vectors, as suggested in Fig. 4-21b. The length of this arc is just the distance traveled by the object in

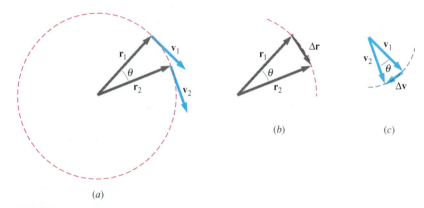

FIGURE 4-21 (*a*) Position and velocity vectors for two nearby points on the circular path. (*b*) The vectors $\mathbf{r}_1$ and $\mathbf{r}_2$ differ by $\Delta\mathbf{r}$. For small angles θ, the length of $\Delta\mathbf{r}$ is very nearly equal to the arc connecting the ends of $\mathbf{r}_1$ and $\mathbf{r}_2$. (*c*) Similarly, vectors $\mathbf{v}_1$ and $\mathbf{v}_2$ differ by $\Delta\mathbf{v}$. The triangles in (*b*) and (*c*) are similar, so the angles θ are the same.

the time Δt, or $v\Delta t$, so $\Delta r \simeq v\Delta t$. Then our relation between similar triangles becomes

$$\frac{\Delta v}{v} \simeq \frac{v\Delta t}{r}.$$

Rearranging this equation gives an approximate expression for the magnitude of the average acceleration:

$$\bar{a} = \frac{\Delta v}{\Delta t} \simeq \frac{v^2}{r}.$$

Taking the limit $\Delta t \to 0$ gives the instantaneous acceleration; in this limit the angle θ approaches 0, the circular arc and the vector $\Delta \mathbf{r}$ become indistinguishable, and the relation $\Delta r \simeq v\Delta t$ becomes exact. So we have

$$a = \frac{v^2}{r} \quad \text{(uniform circular motion)} \qquad (4\text{-}11)$$

for the magnitude of the instantaneous acceleration of an object moving in a circle of radius r at constant speed v. What about the direction? As Fig. 4-21c suggests, $\Delta \mathbf{v}$ is very nearly perpendicular to both velocity vectors; in the limit $\Delta t \to 0$, $\Delta \mathbf{v}$ and the acceleration $\Delta \mathbf{v}/\Delta t$ become exactly perpendicular to the velocity as Fig. 4-21a shows. The direction of the acceleration vector is therefore toward the center of the circle.

Clearly, our geometrical argument would have applied to any point on the circle, so we conclude that the acceleration in uniform circular motion has constant magnitude v^2/r, and that the acceleration vector always points toward the center of the circle. Isaac Newton coined the term *centripetal* to describe this center-pointing acceleration. However, we'll use that term sparingly because we want to emphasize that centripetal acceleration is fundamentally no different from any other acceleration: It's simply a vector describing the rate of change of velocity.

Does Equation 4-11 make sense? Yes. An increase in speed v means the time Δt for a given change in direction of the velocity becomes shorter. Not only that, but the associated change $\Delta \mathbf{v}$ in velocity is larger. These two effects combine to give an acceleration that depends on the *square* of the speed. On the other hand, an increase in radius with a fixed speed simply increases the time Δt associated with a given change in velocity, so the acceleration is inversely proportional to the radius.

Although we derived Equation 4-11 geometrically, we could have obtained the same result by writing the position in unit vector notation and then differentiating twice to get the acceleration. Problem 78 explores this approach.

Tip

Circular Motion and Constant Acceleration The direction toward the center changes as an object moves around a circular path, so the acceleration vector is *not constant*, even though its magnitude is. Uniform circular motion is *not* motion with constant acceleration, and our constant-acceleration equations *do not apply*. In fact, we know that constant acceleration in two dimensions implies a parabolic trajectory, not a circle. Figure 4-22 clarifies this difference.

4.3
Magnitude of Centripetal Acceleration

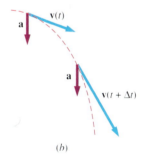

FIGURE 4-22 (*a*) In uniform circular motion, the acceleration vector is always perpendicular to the velocity, and only the direction of the velocity changes. Although the acceleration vector is constant in magnitude, its direction continually changes. (*b*) With truly constant acceleration, i.e., constant magnitude and direction, the velocity and acceleration cannot stay perpendicular, and the velocity generally changes in both direction and magnitude.

EXAMPLE 4-8	A Space Shuttle Orbit

A space shuttle is in a circular orbit at a height of 250 km, where the acceleration of Earth's gravity is 93% of its surface value. What is the period of its orbit? ("Period" means the time to complete one orbit.)

Solution

Here we are given the acceleration and radius and asked to find the period. Our equations for uniform circular motion relate acceleration, radius, and speed. But we can write the speed as the distance traveled in one orbit—the orbital circumference $2\pi r$—divided by the orbital period T:

$$v = \frac{2\pi r}{T}.$$

Using this result in Equation 4-11, we have

$$a = \frac{v^2}{r} = \frac{(2\pi r/T)^2}{r} = \frac{4\pi^2 r}{T^2}. \qquad (4\text{-}12)$$

This equation is equivalent to Equation 4-11, but relates a, r, and T rather than a, r, and v. Here we are given that $a = 0.93g$ and that the shuttle is 250 km above Earth's surface. But the r in Equation 4-12 is the distance to the center of the circular path—

that is, to the center of the Earth. So $r = R_{\text{Earth}} + 250 \text{ km} = 6.62 \times 10^6$ m, where we used $R_{\text{Earth}} = 6.37 \times 10^6$ m from Appendix E. Solving Equation 4-12 for the period T then gives

$$T = \sqrt{\frac{4\pi^2 r}{a}} = \sqrt{\frac{(4\pi^2)(6.62 \times 10^6 \text{ m})}{(0.93)(9.8 \text{ m/s}^2)}}$$

$$= 5355 \text{ s} = 89 \text{ min},$$

or about an hour and a half. This value is the approximate orbital period of objects orbiting Earth at altitudes small compared with Earth's radius. Scientists and engineers have no choice here; the orbital period is fixed by the size and mass of Earth. (At higher altitudes the decrease in the strength of gravity becomes more noticeable, and orbital periods lengthen. The moon, 390,000 km distant, orbits Earth with a period of 27 days. We will study gravity and orbits further in Chapter 9.)

EXERCISE An airplane on its landing approach executes a 180° turn by describing a semicircular path, at constant speed, with radius 5.3 km. An accelerometer in the cockpit reads 1.7 m/s² during the turn. How long will it take to complete the turn?

Answer: 2.92 min

Some problems similar to Example 4-8: 45, 48–50

EXAMPLE 4-9	Engineering a Road

A flat, horizontal road is being designed for an 80-km/h speed limit. If the maximum acceleration of a car traveling this road at the speed limit is to be 1.5 m/s², what is the minimum radius for curves in the road?

Solution

Here we are given speed and acceleration, so we can solve Equation 4-11 for the radius r:

$$r = \frac{v^2}{a} = \frac{[(80 \times 10^3 \text{ m/h})(1 \text{ h}/3600 \text{ s})]^2}{1.5 \text{ m/s}^2} = 330 \text{ m}.$$

A limit on acceleration is necessary to keep the car on the road, as we will see more clearly in Chapters 5 and 6.

EXERCISE An engineer is designing a circular saw blade. For cutting efficiency, the teeth of the blade are to move at 40 m/s. The bonds that hold the carbide cutting tips to the blade can withstand a maximum acceleration of 2.0×10^4 m/s². What is the maximum diameter of the blade?

Answer: 16 cm

Some problems similar to Example 4-9: 46, 48

FIGURE 4-23 (a) A ball whirled about on a string in a vertical circle undergoes circular motion with nonconstant speed; it moves faster near the bottom and more slowly near the top.

4-5 NONUNIFORM CIRCULAR MOTION

What about an object moving in a circle with variable speed, like a ball whirling around in a vertical circle (Fig. 4-23)? Since both the direction and magnitude of the velocity are changing, the acceleration cannot be strictly parallel or perpendicular to the velocity. But we can break the acceleration vector into two parts, one perpendicular to the velocity and one parallel. We call the former the **radial acceleration** a_r, since it points radially inward toward the center of the circular path; the latter is the **tangential acceleration** a_t, since it is tangent to the path. The radial acceleration changes only the direction of the velocity; it acts just like the acceleration in uniform circular motion, and therefore has magnitude

$a_r = v^2/r$. The tangential acceleration changes only the magnitude of the velocity; it acts just like one-dimensional acceleration, and therefore has magnitude $a_t = dv/dt$. The net acceleration vector can be found by combining these two components, as Example 4-10 illustrates.

4.2
Acceleration Direction of a Car

EXAMPLE 4-10	*Taking That Curve Too Fast*

A road makes a 90° bend with a radius of 190 m. A car enters the bend moving at 20 m/s. Finding this too fast, the driver decelerates at 0.92 m/s². Determine the acceleration of the car when its speed rounding the bend has dropped to 15 m/s.

Solution
Since it is rounding a curve, the car has a radial acceleration associated with its changing direction, in addition to the tangential deceleration that changes its speed. We are given that $a_t = 0.92$ m/s²; since the car is slowing down, the tangential acceleration is directed opposite the velocity. The radial acceleration is given by Equation 4-11:

$$a_r = \frac{v^2}{r} = \frac{(15 \text{ m/s})^2}{190 \text{ m}} = 1.2 \text{ m/s}^2.$$

Figure 4-24 shows both components of the acceleration and their vector sum, which is the net acceleration. From the figure, we see that this sum has magnitude

$$a = \sqrt{a_r^2 + a_t^2} = \sqrt{(1.2 \text{ m/s})^2 + (0.92 \text{ m/s})^2} = 1.5 \text{ m/s}^2$$

and points at an angle

$$\theta = \tan^{-1}\left(\frac{a_r}{a_t}\right) = \tan^{-1}\left(\frac{1.2 \text{ m/s}^2}{0.92 \text{ m/s}^2}\right) = 53°$$

from the tangent to the circle, as shown.

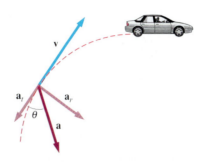

FIGURE 4-24 The radial and tangential accelerations add vectorially to give the net acceleration.

EXERCISE You slip a compact disc into a CD player, and the disc rapidly spins up toward its operating speed. During the spin-up, what are the direction and magnitude of the acceleration vector for a point on the rim of the 12.7-cm-diameter disc when the rim is moving at 31.2 cm/s, with its speed increasing at 91.4 cm/s²?

Answer: 178 cm/s² at 59.2° to the direction of motion

Some problems similar to Example 4-10: 54, 65, 66

Although we've discussed radial and tangential acceleration in the context of a circular path, those concepts apply even when the path has an arbitrary shape. At any point on the path, we can define a **radius of curvature** that describes how sharply the path is bending (Fig. 4-25). If a particle is moving at speed v at a point where the curvature radius is r, then its radial acceleration is still v^2/r; if its speed is also changing, then its tangential acceleration is still dv/dt. Now, however, both v and r may change as the particle moves along the path.

FIGURE 4-25 Each point on an arbitrary path can be characterized by the radius of curvature r at that point. An object moving with speed v has radial acceleration of magnitude v^2/r and tangential acceleration of magnitude dv/dt. In general, both v and r may change as the particle moves.

CHAPTER SYNOPSIS

Summary

1. The acceleration vector describes the rate of change of the velocity vector. In two or three dimensions, the acceleration can have any direction relative to the velocity vector. When the acceleration lies along the same line as the velocity, then only the magnitude of the velocity changes. When the acceleration is strictly perpendicular to the velocity, only the direction of the velocity changes. An acceleration at an arbitrary angle generally changes both the direction and magnitude of the velocity.

2. When an object undergoes **constant acceleration**, its motion is described by the vector equations

$$\mathbf{v} = \mathbf{v}_0 + \mathbf{a}t$$
$$\mathbf{r} = \mathbf{r}_0 + \mathbf{v}_0 t + \tfrac{1}{2}\mathbf{a}t^2.$$

These equations may be broken into components along any chosen coordinate axes; the result is a set of equations describing independently the components of the motion along the different axes.

3. An important case of constant acceleration is **projectile motion**, which occurs for objects experiencing the essentially constant acceleration of gravity near Earth's surface. The path of an object undergoing projectile motion is a parabola; this and other properties of projectile motion follow directly from the vector equations for constant acceleration.

4. An object moving around a circle of radius r at constant speed v is in **uniform circular motion**. Since the direction of its velocity is changing, it is accelerating. The magnitude of its acceleration is

$$a = \frac{v^2}{r}, \qquad \text{(uniform circular motion)}$$

and the acceleration vector always points toward the center of the circle.

5. When an object moves in a curved path with varying speed, the acceleration vector is the sum of the **radial acceleration** v^2/r, where r is the local radius of curvature, and the **tangential acceleration** dv/dt. The radial acceleration changes the direction of motion, while the tangential acceleration changes the speed.

Terms You Should Understand

constant acceleration (4-2)
projectile (4-3)
projectile motion (4-3)
trajectory, parabolic trajectory (4-3)
uniform circular motion (4-4)
radial acceleration (4-5)
tangential acceleration (4-5)
radius of curvature (4-5)

Symbols You Should Recognize

vector equations, e.g., $\mathbf{r} = \mathbf{r}_0 + \mathbf{v}_0 t + \tfrac{1}{2}\mathbf{a}t^2$ (4-2)
$\mathbf{a}_r$, $\mathbf{a}_t$ (4-5)

Problems You Should Be Able to Solve

Use vector analysis to show the effects of accelerations at different angles to the velocity. (4-1)
Given initial position and velocity for objects undergoing constant acceleration, determine position and velocity as functions of time. (4-2)
Determine the motion of projectiles, including position and velocity as functions of time, trajectories, ranges, and initial conditions needed for an object to follow a given trajectory. (4-3)
Relate velocity, radius, and acceleration in circular motion. (4-4)
Determine radial and tangential acceleration for objects moving on curved trajectories. (4-5)

Limitations to Keep in Mind

Equations for constant acceleration apply *only* when both the magnitude and direction of the acceleration are unchanged.
Our work in this chapter neglects air resistance, which can substantially affect projectile motion.
Uniform circular motion is *accelerated* motion since the direction of the velocity vector changes.
Uniform circular motion is *not* motion with *constant* acceleration since the direction of the acceleration vector changes.

QUESTIONS

1. Moving along a road with the wheels pointed straight ahead, you step on the brake of your car. Describe the direction of the resulting acceleration in relation to your car's velocity.
2. How is it possible for an object to be moving in one direction but accelerating in another?
3. Is there any way to negotiate a curved path without accelerating?
4. A satellite glides through space at a steady 29,000 km/h in a circular orbit around Earth. Is the satellite accelerating? If so, in what direction? If not, why not?
5. You're moving northward when you accelerate briefly toward the east. Is your subsequent motion strictly eastward? Explain.

6. Why is the case of Fig. 4-2a not strictly a case of acceleration always perpendicular to velocity? After all, the velocity and acceleration vectors shown are perpendicular.

7. An object is moving at some modest initial speed, when a large acceleration is applied perpendicular to the direction of the initial velocity. What can you say, approximately, about the relative directions of velocity and acceleration after the acceleration has been applied for a long time? Explain with a simple vector diagram.

8. In what sense is Equation 4-4 really two (or three) equations?

9. In a problem involving constant acceleration, why might it be sensible to choose a coordinate system with one axis along the direction of the acceleration?

10. Is the speed of a projectile constant throughout its parabolic trajectory?

11. Three objects are released from the same height, one from rest, one with horizontal velocity component v_x, the other with horizontal velocity component $2v_x$. Compare the times each is in the air. Compare the horizontal distances traveled by each.

12. A hunter's bullet emerges from a gun, moving horizontally above level ground. At the same instant, the hunter drops another bullet from the height of the gun muzzle. Which hits the ground first? Explain.

13. Can there be a true "line drive" in baseball? What is required for the ball to travel in a nearly straight, horizontal trajectory?

14. What is the vertical component of a projectile's velocity at the peak of its trajectory?

15. Is there any point on a projectile's trajectory where the velocity and acceleration are perpendicular?

16. Projectiles launched at 30° and 60° have the same range. Does this mean they stay in the air the same amount of time?

17. Earth's curvature renders Equation 4-10 inexact for projectiles with very long ranges. Do you expect the actual range of such a projectile to be longer or shorter than Equation 4-10 would imply? Explain.

18. A friend who's not taking physics insists that you can't be accelerating when you drive around a curve since the speedometer reading remains steady. Refute this argument.

19. You're driving around a curve. Is there any way of stepping on the gas or brake such that your tangential acceleration cancels your radial acceleration, giving a net acceleration of zero? How or why not?

20. An object starts from rest, accelerating with constant tangential acceleration on a circular path. Which is greater when it starts, its tangential or its radial acceleration? Which is greater after a long time? Explain.

21. An object moves outward along the spiral path shown in Fig. 4-26. Must its speed increase, decrease, or remain the same if the magnitude of its radial acceleration is to remain constant?

FIGURE 4-26 Question 21.

PROBLEMS

ActivPhysics can help with these problems: All Activities in Section 3, Projectile Motion

Section 4-1 Velocity and Acceleration

1. A skater is gliding along the ice at 2.4 m/s, when she undergoes an acceleration of magnitude 1.1 m/s² for 3.0 s. At the end of that time she is moving at 5.7 m/s. What must be the angle between the acceleration vector and the initial velocity vector?

2. In the preceding problem, what would have been the magnitude of the skater's final velocity if the acceleration had been perpendicular to her initial velocity?

3. An object is moving in the x direction at 1.3 m/s when it is subjected to an acceleration given by $\mathbf{a} = 0.52\,\hat{\mathbf{j}}$ m/s². What is its velocity vector after 4.4 s of acceleration?

4. An airliner is flying at a velocity of $260\hat{\mathbf{i}}$ m/s, when a wind gust gives it an acceleration of $0.38\hat{\mathbf{i}} + 0.72\,\hat{\mathbf{j}}$ m/s² for a period of 24 s. (a) What is its velocity at the end of that time? (b) By what angle has it been deflected from its original course?

Section 4-2 Constant Acceleration

5. The position of an object as a function of time is given by $\mathbf{r} = (3.2t + 1.8t^2)\hat{\mathbf{i}} + (1.7t - 2.4t^2)\hat{\mathbf{j}}$ m, where t is the time in seconds. What are the magnitude and direction of the acceleration?

6. An airplane heads northeastward down a runway, accelerating from rest at the rate of 2.1 m/s². Express the plane's velocity and position at $t = 30$ s in unit vector notation, using a coordinate system with x axis eastward and y axis northward, and with origin at the start of the plane's takeoff roll.

7. An asteroid is heading toward Earth at a steady 21 km/s. To save their planet, astronauts strap a giant rocket to the asteroid, giving it an acceleration of 0.035 km/s² at right angles to its original motion. If the rocket firing lasts 250 s, (a) by what angle does the direction of the asteroid's motion change? (b) How far does it move during the firing?

8. An object is moving initially in the x direction at 4.5 m/s, when an acceleration is applied in the y direction for a period of 18 s. If it moves equal distances in the x and y directions during this time, what is the magnitude of its acceleration?

9. A hockey puck is moving at 14.5 m/s when a stick imparts a constant acceleration of 78.2 m/s² at a 90.0° angle to the original direction of motion. If the acceleration lasts 0.120 s, what is the magnitude of the puck's displacement during this time?

10. Repeat the preceding problem, except that now the acceleration makes a 65.0° angle with the original direction of motion.

11. A particle leaves the origin with initial velocity $\mathbf{v}_0 = 11\hat{\mathbf{i}} + 14\hat{\mathbf{j}}$ m/s. It undergoes a constant acceleration given by $\mathbf{a} = -1.2\hat{\mathbf{i}} + 0.26\hat{\mathbf{j}}$ m/s². (a) When does the particle cross the y axis? (b) What is its y coordinate at the time? (c) How fast is it moving, and in what direction, at that time?

12. A particle starts from the origin with initial velocity $\mathbf{v}_0 = v_0\hat{\mathbf{i}}$ and constant acceleration $\mathbf{a} = a\hat{\mathbf{j}}$. Show that the particle's distance from the origin and its direction relative to the x axis are given by $d = t\sqrt{v_0^2 + \frac{1}{4}a^2t^2}$ and $\theta = \tan^{-1}(at/2v_0)$.

13. Figure 4-27 shows a cathode-ray tube, used to display electrical signals in oscilloscopes and other scientific instruments. Electrons are accelerated by the electron gun, then move down the center of the tube at 2.0×10^9 cm/s. In the 4.2-cm-long deflecting region they undergo an acceleration directed perpendicular to the long axis of the tube. The acceleration "steers" them to a particular spot on the screen, where they produce a visible glow. (a) What acceleration is needed to deflect the electrons through 15°, as shown in the figure? (b) What is the shape of an electron's path in the deflecting region?

FIGURE 4-27 A cathode-ray tube (Problem 13).

Section 4-3 Projectile Motion

14. You toss an apple horizontally at 8.7 m/s from a height of 2.6 m. Simultaneously, you drop a peach from the same height. How long does each take to reach the ground?

15. A carpenter tosses a shingle off a 8.8-m-high roof, giving it an initially horizontal velocity of 11 m/s. (a) How long does it take to reach the ground? (b) How far does it move horizontally in this time?

16. An arrow fired horizontally at 41 m/s travels 23 m horizontally before it hits the ground. From what height was it fired?

17. A kid fires water horizontally from a squirt gun held 1.6 m above the ground. It hits another kid 2.1 m away square in the back, at a point 0.93 m above the ground (see Fig. 4-28). What was the initial speed of the water?

FIGURE 4-28 Question 17.

18. In a chase scene, a movie stuntman is supposed to run right off the flat roof of one city building and land on another roof 1.9 m lower. If the gap between the buildings is 4.5 m wide, how fast must he run?

19. Ink droplets in an ink-jet printer are ejected horizontally at 12 m/s, and travel a horizontal distance of 1.0 mm to the paper. How far do they fall in this interval?

20. Protons in a particle accelerator drop 1.2 μm over the 1.7-km length of the accelerator. What is their approximate average speed?

21. Standing on the ground 3.0 m from the wall of a building, you want to throw a package from your 1.5-m shoulder level to someone in a second floor window 4.2 m above the ground. At what speed and angle should you throw it so it just barely reaches the window?

22. Derive a general formula for the horizontal distance covered by a projectile launched horizontally at speed v_0 from a height h.

23. A car moving at 40 km/h strikes a pedestrian a glancing blow, breaking both the car's front signal light lens and the pedestrian's hip. Pieces of the lens are found 4.0 m down the road from the center of a 1.2-m wide crosswalk, and a lawsuit hinges on whether the pedestrian was in the crosswalk at the time of the accident. Assuming that the lens was initially 63 cm off the ground, and that the lens pieces continued moving horizontally with the car's speed at the time of the impact, was the pedestrian in the crosswalk?

24. Repeat Problem 15 for the case when the shingle is thrown with a speed of 11 m/s at 14° below the horizontal.

25. In part (b) of the exercise following Example 4-5, what is the vertical component of the velocity with which the cyclist strikes the ground?

26. Compare the travel times for the projectiles launched at 30° and 60° in Fig. 4-15, both of which have the same starting and ending points.

27. A submarine-launched missile has a range of 4500 km. (a) What launch speed is needed for this range when the launch angle is 45°? (b) What is the total flight time? (c) What would be the minimum launch speed at a 20° launch angle, used to "depress" the trajectory so as to foil a space-based antimissile defense?

28. A rescue airplane is flying horizontally at speed v_0 at an altitude h above the ocean, attempting to drop a package of medical supplies to a shipwreck victim in a lifeboat. At what line-of-sight angle α (Fig. 4-29) should the pilot release the package?

FIGURE 4-29 Problem 28.

29. At a circus, a human cannonball is shot from a cannon at 35 km/h at an angle of 40°. If he leaves the cannon 1.0 m off the ground, and lands in a net 2.0 m off the ground, how long is he in the air?

30. Preparing to give an injection, a physician ejects a drop of medicine to ensure there's no air in the syringe. The syringe is pointing upward, at 20° to the vertical, with the tip of the needle 45.0 cm above a tabletop. The drop leaves the needle at 1.30 m/s. (a) What maximum height does it reach? (b) How long is it before the drop hits the tabletop? (c) How far does the drop travel horizontally?

31. If you can hit a golf ball 180 m on Earth, how far can you hit it on the moon? (Your answer is an underestimate, because the distance on Earth is restricted by air resistance as well as by a larger g.)

32. Prove that a projectile launched on level ground reaches its maximum height midway along its trajectory.

33. A projectile launched at an angle θ to the horizontal reaches a maximum height h. Show that its horizontal range is $4h/\tan\theta$.

34. You're 5.0 m from the left-hand wall of the house shown in Fig. 4-30, and you want to throw a ball to a friend 5.0 m from the right-hand wall. (a) What is the minimum speed that will allow the ball to clear the roof? (b) At what angle should it be thrown? Assume the throw and catch both occur 1.0 m above the ground.

FIGURE 4-30 Problem 34.

35. A circular fountain has jets of water directed from the circumference inward at an angle of 45°. Each jet reaches a maximum height of 2.2 m. (a) If all the jets converge in the center of the circle and at their initial height, what is the radius of the fountain? (b) If one of the jets is aimed at 10° too low, how far short of the center does it fall?

36. When the Olympics were held in Mexico City in 1968, many sports fans feared that the high altitude would result in poor performances due to reduced oxygen. To their surprise, new records were set in track and field events, probably as a result of lowered air resistance and a decrease in g to 9.786 m/s², both ultimately associated with the high altitude. In particular, Robert Beamon set a new world record of 8.90 m in the long jump. Photographs suggest that Beamon started his jump at a 25° angle to the horizontal. If he had jumped at sea level, where $g = 9.81$ m/s², at the same angle and initial speed as in Mexico City, how far would Beamon have gone? Neglect air resistance in both cases (although its effect is actually more significant than the change in g).

37. In 1991 Mike Powell shattered Bob Beamon's 1968 world long jump record with a leap of 8.95 m (Fig. 4-31). Studies show that Powell jumps at 22° to the vertical. Treating him as a projectile, at what speed did Powell begin his jump?

FIGURE 4-31 Problem 37.

38. A motorcyclist driving in a 60-km/h zone hits a stopped car on a level road. The cyclist is thrown from his bike and lands 39 m down the road. Was the cyclist speeding? To answer, find the minimum speed he could have been going just before the accident.

39. Show that, for a given initial speed, the horizontal range of a projectile is the same for launch angles $45° + \alpha$ and $45° - \alpha$, where α is between $0°$ and $45°$.

40. One model of the Scud missile used in the 1991 Persian Gulf war has a range of 630 km. (a) What is its launch speed, given a 40° launch angle? (b) What is the missile flight time?

41. A basketball player is 15 ft horizontally from the center of the basket, which is 10 ft off the ground. At what angle should the player aim the ball if it is thrown from a height of 8.2 ft with a speed of 26 ft/s?

Section 4-4 Uniform Circular Motion

42. How fast would a car have to round a turn 75 m in radius in order for its acceleration to be numerically equal to that of gravity?

43. Estimate the acceleration of the moon, which completes a nearly circular orbit of 385,000 km radius in 27 days.

44. An object is in uniform circular motion. Make a graph of its average acceleration, measured in units of v^2/r, versus angular separation for points on the circular path spaced 40°, 30°, 20°, and 10° apart. Your graph should show the average acceleration approaching the instantaneous value v^2/r as the angular separation decreases.

45. When Apollo astronauts landed on the moon, they left one astronaut behind in a circular orbit around the moon. For the half of the orbit spent over the far side of the moon, that individual was completely cut off from communication with the rest of humanity. How long did this lonely state last? Assume a sufficiently low orbit that you can use the moon's surface gravitational acceleration (see Appendix E) for the spacecraft.

46. A 12-in-diameter circular saw blade rotates at 3500 revolutions per minute. What is the acceleration of one of the saw teeth? Compare with the acceleration of gravity.

47. A jet is diving vertically downward at 1200 km/h (see Fig. 4-32). If the pilot can withstand a maximum acceleration of $5g$ (i.e., 5 times Earth's gravitational acceleration) before losing consciousness, at what height must the plane start a quarter turn to pull out of the dive? Assume the speed remains constant.

FIGURE 4-32 Problem 47.

48. Electrons in a TV tube are deflected through a 55° angle, as shown in Fig. 4-33. During the deflection they move at constant speed in a circular path of radius 4.30 cm. If they experience an acceleration of 3.35×10^{17} m/s^2, how long does the deflection take?

FIGURE 4-33 Problem 48.

49. How long would a day last if Earth were rotating so fast that the acceleration of an object on the equator were equal to g?

50. A runner rounds the semicircular end of a track whose curvature radius is 16 m. The runner moves at constant speed, with an acceleration of 0.94 m/s^2. How long does it take to complete the turn?

Section 4-5 Nonuniform Circular Motion

51. A space station 120 m in diameter is set rotating in order to give its occupants "artificial gravity." Over a period of 5.0 min, small rockets bring the station steadily to its final rotation rate of 1 revolution every 20 s. What are the radial and tangential accelerations of a point on the rim of the station 2.0 min after the rockets start firing?

52. A plane is heading northward when it begins to turn eastward on a circular path of radius 9.10 km. At the instant it begins to turn, its acceleration vector points 22.0° north of east and has magnitude 2.60 m/s^2. (a) What is the plane's speed? (b) At what rate is its speed increasing?

53. An object is set into motion on a circular path of radius r by giving it a constant tangential acceleration a_t. Derive an expression for the time t when the acceleration vector points at 45° to the direction of motion.

54. A car moving at 65 km/h enters a curve that describes a quarter turn of radius 120 m. The driver gently applies the brakes, giving a constant tangential deceleration of magnitude 0.65 m/s^2. Just before emerging from the turn, what are (a) the magnitude of the car's acceleration and (b) the angle between the acceleration vector and the direction of motion?

Paired Problems

(Both problems in a pair involve the same principles and techniques. If you can get the first problem, you should be able to solve the second one.)

55. An alpine rescue team is using a slingshot to send an emergency medical packet to climbers stranded on a ledge, as shown in Fig. 4-34. What should be the launch speed from the slingshot?

FIGURE 4-34 Problem 55.

56. A cat leaps onto a counter 90 cm off the floor, starting 65 cm from the edge of the counter. It leaps at an initial angle of 79° to the horizontal and lands on the counter 22 cm from the edge. What was its initial speed?

57. If you can throw a stone straight up to a height of 16 m, how far could you throw it horizontally over level ground? Assume the same throwing speed and optimum launch angle.

58. In a conversion from military to peacetime use, a missile with a maximum horizontal range of 180 km is being adapted for studying the upper atmosphere. What is the maximum altitude it can achieve, if launched vertically?

59. I can kick a soccer ball 28 m on level ground, giving it an initial velocity at 40° to the horizontal. At the same initial speed and angle to the horizontal, what horizontal distance can I kick the ball on a 15° upward slope?

60. A model rocket has a horizontal range of 280 m on level ground, when given a 45° launch angle. What horizontal distance will the rocket cover when launched at 45° to the horizontal from the top of a hill whose sides slope down at 21°?

61. A fireworks rocket is 73 m above the ground when it explodes. Immediately after the explosion, one piece is moving at 51 m/s at 23° to the upward vertical direction. A second piece is moving at 38 m/s at 11° below the horizontal direction. At what horizontal distance from the explosion site does each piece land?

62. A hose nozzle sprays water drops in a fan-shaped pattern as suggested in Fig. 4-35. The drops leave the nozzle moving at 4.6 m/s. With the hose aimed as shown, the directions of the emerging drops range from 10° below the horizontal to 25° above. If the nozzle is 1.7 m above the ground, how wide is the region (marked w in Fig. 4-35) that gets wet?

FIGURE 4-35 Problem 62.

63. You toss a chocolate bar to your hiking companion located 8.6 m up a 39° slope, as shown in Fig. 4-36. Determine the initial velocity vector so that the chocolate bar will reach your friend moving horizontally.

FIGURE 4-36 Problem 63.

64. A circus lion prepares to leap through a flaming hoop. A line from the lion to the hoop is 2.2 m long and makes a 26° angle with the floor. With what initial velocity should the lion leap so as to pass through the hoop moving horizontally?

65. After takeoff, a plane makes a three-quarter circle turn of radius 7.1 km, maintaining constant altitude but steadily increasing its speed from 390 to 740 km/h. Midway through the turn, what is the angle between the plane's velocity and acceleration vectors?

66. On its landing approach a plane makes a semicircular turn of radius 6.7 km, remaining at constant altitude while its speed drops steadily from 840 km/h to 290 km/h. At the midpoint of the turn, what is the angle between the plane's velocity and acceleration vectors?

67. Verify the maximum altitude and flight time for the 15° launch angle trajectory of the missile described at the end of the Application: Ballistic Missile Defense (page 79).

68. A juggler's hands are 80 cm apart, and the balls being juggled reach a maximum height of 100 cm above the juggler's hands. (a) At what velocity do the balls leave the juggler's hands? (b) If four balls are being juggled, how often must the juggler catch a ball?

69. A monkey is hanging from a branch a height h above the ground. A naturalist stands a horizontal distance d from a point directly below the monkey. The naturalist aims a tranquilizer dart directly at the monkey, but just as she fires the monkey lets go. Show that the dart will nevertheless hit the monkey, provided its initial speed exceeds $\sqrt{(d^2 + h^2)g/2h}$.

70. A child tosses a ball over a flat-roofed house 3.2 m high and 7.4 m wide, so it just clears the corners on both sides, as shown in Fig. 4-37. If the child sits 2.1 m from the wall, what are the ball's initial speed and launch angle? Assume the ball is launched essentially from ground level.

FIGURE 4-37 Problem 70.

71. A diver leaves a 3-m board on a trajectory that takes her 2.5 m above the board, and then into the water a horizontal distance of 2.8 m from the end of the board. At what speed and angle did she leave the board?

72. In your calculus class, you may have learned that you can find the maximum or minimum of a function by differentiating and setting the result to zero. Do this for Equation 4-10, differentiating with respect to θ, and thus verify that the maximum range occurs for $\theta = 45°$.

73. A projectile is launched with speed v_0 from the edge of a cliff of height h; the ground below the cliff is flat. Using the technique of the preceding problem, show that the maximum range occurs when the launch angle is

$$\theta = \tan^{-1}\left(\frac{v_0}{\sqrt{2gh + v_0^2}}\right).$$

74. Two projectiles are launched with the same speed v_0, at angles $45° + \alpha$ and $45° - \alpha$. As Fig. 4-15 shows, they have the same horizontal range. Derive an expression for the difference in their flight times.

75. A well-engineered ski jump is less dangerous than it looks because skiers hit the ground with very small velocity components perpendicular to the ground. Skiers leave the Olympic ski jump in Lake Placid, New York, at 28 m/s, at an angle of 9.5° below the horizontal. Their landing zone is a horizontal distance of 55 m from the end of the jump. The ground at that point is contoured so skiers' trajectories make an angle of only 3.0° with the ground on landing, as suggested in Fig. 4-38. What is the slope of the ground in the landing zone?

FIGURE 4-38 Problem 75.

76. A particle is moving along the x axis with velocity $\mathbf{v}_0$ in the positive x direction. As it passes the origin, it begins to experience a constant acceleration $\mathbf{a}$ in the y direction. Show that, at any subsequent time, the tangent of the angle its velocity makes with the x axis is twice the tangent of the angle its displacement vector makes with the x axis.

77. Derive a general expression for the flight time of a projectile launched on level ground with speed v_0 and launch angle θ_0.

78. An object moves at constant speed v in the x-y plane, describing a circle of radius r centered at the origin. It is on the positive x axis at time $t = 0$. Show that the position of the object as a function of time can be written $\mathbf{r} = r[\cos(vt/r)\hat{\mathbf{i}} + \sin(vt/r)\hat{\mathbf{j}}]$, where the argument of the sine and cosine is in radians. Differentiate this expression once to obtain an expression for the velocity and again for the acceleration. Show that the acceleration has magnitude v^2/r and is directed radially inward (that is, opposite to $\mathbf{r}$).

79. In the Olympic hammer throw, contestants whirl a 7.3-kg ball on the end of a 1.2-m-long steel wire before releasing it. In a particular throw, the hammer is released from a height of 1.3 m while moving in a direction 24° above the horizontal. If it travels 84 m horizontally, what is its radial acceleration just before release (see Fig. 4-39)?

FIGURE 4-39 The Olympic hammer throw (Problem 79).

80. A projectile is launched at an angle θ to the horizontal, with sufficient speed to give it a horizontal range x. Show that the radius of curvature at the top of its trajectory is given by $r = (x/2)\tan\theta$.

81. Two golfers stand equal distances on opposite sides of a hole, as shown in Fig. 4-40. Golfer A hits his ball at a 50° angle to the horizontal. At the instant she hears A's club hit the ball, Golfer B hits her ball at the same speed as A, but at a 40° angle. If the two balls reach the hole simultaneously, how far apart are the golfers? The speed of sound is 340 m/s.

FIGURE 4-40 How far apart are the golfers? (Problem 81).

82. A convertible is speeding down the highway at 130 km/h, when the driver spots a police airplane 600 m back at an altitude of 250 m. The driver decelerates at 2.0 km/h/s. (a) If the plane is flying horizontally at a steady 210 km/h, where should the plane be in relation to the car for the police officer to drop a speeding ticket into the car? Assume the ticket is dropped with no initial vertical motion, and it is in a heavy capsule that experiences negligible air resistance. (b) How fast will the car be moving when the ticket reaches it?

83. A projectile is launched with initial speed v_0 at an angle θ_0 to the horizontal. Find expressions for the angle the trajectory makes with the horizontal (a) as a function of time (b) as a function of position.

5 | Force and Motion

Forces of wind, water, gravity, and human muscle determine the motion of a sailboard.

An interplanetary spacecraft moves effortlessly through space; its rocket engines were shut down years ago. So why does it keep moving? A baseball heads toward the batter. The batter swings, connects, and suddenly the ball is heading toward left field. Why did its motion change?

Questions about the "why" of motion are the subject of the branch of physics called **dynamics**. In this chapter we develop the basic laws that answer "why" questions about motion. Isaac Newton first stated those laws over 300 years ago, yet they remain a vital part of physics and engineering today, helping astrophysicists to guide spacecraft to distant planets, engineers to develop better cars, and biologists to manipulate the components of individual cells. In the next chapter, we'll apply the laws of motion in a wide variety of practical situations.

5-1 THE WRONG QUESTION

We began this chapter with two questions—one about why a spacecraft *moved*, the other about why a baseball's motion *changed*. For nearly 2000 years following the work of Aristotle (384–322 B.C.), the first question—"Why do things move?"—was the crucial one. And the answer seemed obvious: it took a force—a push or a pull—to keep something moving. This idea made a lot of sense in Aristotle's time; when an ox stopped pulling an oxcart, for example, the cart stopped. It makes sense today, too: stop exerting yourself when jogging, and you stop moving; take your foot off the gas pedal, and your car soon stops. Everyday experience seems to suggest that Aristotle was right, and most of us carry in our heads the Aristotelian idea that motion requires a cause—in particular, something that pushes or pulls on a moving object to keep it going.

You might wonder about an object such as a baseball or an arrow that seems to have no continuous push or pull, and yet keeps moving. The Aristotelians thought up a way to include these cases under their general scheme: they believed that such objects keep moving because air rushes from the front to the back to push the object forward.

Actually, "What keeps things moving?" is the wrong question. In the early 1600s, Galileo Galilei did experiments that convinced him that a moving object has an intrinsic "quantity of motion" and needs no push to keep it moving (Fig. 5-1). Instead of answering "What keeps things moving?" Galileo declared that the question needs no answer. In so doing, he set the stage for centuries of progress in physics, beginning with the achievements of Issac Newton and culminating in the work of Albert Einstein.

The Right Question

The first question we asked in this chapter—about why the spacecraft keeps moving—is the wrong question. So what's the right question? It's the second one—about why the baseball's motion *changed*. The study of dynamics isn't about what causes motion itself—it's about what causes *changes* in motion. Changes include starting and stopping, speeding up and slowing down, and changing direction. Any *change* in motion begs an explanation, but motion itself does not. Get used to this important idea, even if it goes against your Aristotelian preconceptions, and you'll have a much easier time with physics. But if you remain a "closet Aristotelian," secretly looking for causes of motion itself, you'll find it difficult to understand, appreciate, and apply the simple laws that actually govern motion.

It was Galileo who identified the right question about motion. But it was Isaac Newton (Fig. 5-2) who formulated the quantitative laws describing exactly how motion changes. We use those laws today for everything from designing antilock braking systems, to building skyscrapers that don't fall down, to guiding the electrons that "paint" the pictures on TV screens and computer monitors.

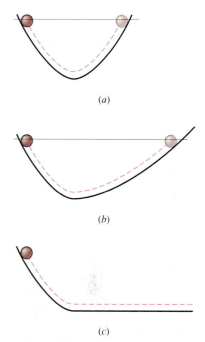

(a)

(b)

(c)

FIGURE 5-1 (*a*) Galileo recognized that a ball rolling down an incline would rise to nearly its starting height on a second incline. (*b*) Making the second incline more gradual would result in the ball's traveling farther in the horizontal direction. (*c*) If the second incline were reduced to a horizontal surface, Galileo reasoned, the ball's motion should continue forever.

FIGURE 5-2 Isaac Newton at age 59. When Newton was in his twenties the plague had swept across England, shutting down the universities. After two years' seclusion in the English countryside, Newton had laid the groundwork for his laws of motion and gravity and had begun the development of calculus.

(a)

(b)

FIGURE 5-3 The net force—the vector sum of individual interaction forces acting on an object—is what determines the change in its motion. (*a*) Here two people push a car, producing a net force in the forward direction. (*b*) The vector sum of the interaction forces acting on this plane is zero, so its motion is unchanging and the plane is cruising in a straight line at constant speed.

5-2 NEWTON'S FIRST AND SECOND LAWS

Let's again ask the right question: What caused the baseball's motion to change? Obviously, it was the bat pushing against the ball. Again, we use the term *force* to describe a push or a pull. And the essence of dynamics is simply this:

❚ Force causes change in motion.

We'll soon elaborate on and quantify this notion, writing equations and solving numerical problems. But the essential point is in the simple sentence above. If you want to change an object's motion, you need to apply a force. If you see an object's motion change, you know there's a force acting. Note the profound difference from the Aristotelian notion: contrary to Aristotle, and probably to your own intuitive sense as well, it does *not* take a force to keep something in unchanging motion; force is needed *only* to *change* an object's state of motion.

The Net Force

I can push a ball left or right, up or down. My car's tires can push the car forward or backward, or make it round a curve. Force has direction and is a vector quantity. Furthermore, more than one force can act on a single object (Fig. 5-3). We call the individual forces acting on an object **interaction forces**, because they always involve other objects interacting with the object in question. In Fig. 5-3*a*, for example, the interaction forces are the individual forces exerted by the people pushing the car; the term "interaction forces" is appropriate because these forces involve interaction between the people and the car. In Fig. 5-3*b* the interaction forces include the force that air exerts on the plane, the engine force caused by the hot exhaust gases, and the gravitational force exerted by Earth.

Our main point in this chapter is that force causes changes in motion, and we now explore in more detail the relation between force and change in motion. Experiment shows that what matters is the **net force**, meaning the vector sum of all individual interaction forces acting on an object. If the net force on an object is not zero, then the object's motion must be changing—in direction or speed or both. If the net force on an object is zero—no matter what individual interaction forces contribute to the vector sum that is the net force—then the object's motion is unchanging.

Newton's First Law

The last statement of the preceding paragraph—really just a rephrasing of our basic idea that force causes change in motion—is **Newton's first law**:

> *Newton's first law of motion:* A body in uniform motion remains in uniform motion, and a body at rest remains at rest, unless acted on by a nonzero net force.

Here we've paraphrased Newton's original wording to make it more consistent with modern usage. The word "uniform" is essential; **uniform motion** means unchanging motion—that is, motion in a straight line at constant speed. The phrase about "a body at rest" isn't really necessary because rest is just the special case of uniform motion with zero speed, but we include it for consistency with Newton's original statement.

The first law says that uniform motion is a perfectly natural state, requiring no further explanation. If an object is moving uniformly, the law says, then the net force on the object must be zero and it will continue in uniform motion until a nonzero net force acts on it. Again, the word "uniform" is crucial. The first law does *not* say that an object moving in a circle will continue to do so without a nonzero net force; in fact, it says that an object moving in a circle—or in any other curved path—*must* be subject to a nonzero net force. That's because any curved path involves changing direction, and a change in direction is a change in motion—and therefore requires a force. *Any* change in an object's motion—in speed, direction, or both—means that the motion is nonuniform, so a nonzero net force must be acting on the object.

Got It!

Figure 5-4 is a view looking down on a horizontal tabletop. On the tabletop is a curved barrier that exerts a force on a ball, guiding its motion in a circular path, as shown. After the ball ceases contact with the barrier, which of the dashed paths shown does it follow?

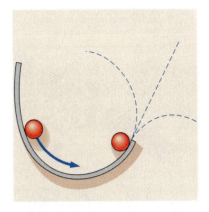

FIGURE 5-4 Top view of a horizontal tabletop. The barrier guides the ball in a curved path. How does the ball move once it leaves the barrier?

Newton's first law is simplicity itself—but it does seem to violate our Aristotelian preconceptions. Aristotle's oxcart really stopped when the ox stopped pulling, and your car soon stops when you take your foot off the gas. But because the motion changes, that just means—as the first law says—that there must be a nonzero net force acting. That force is often a "hidden" one, like friction or air resistance, that isn't as obvious as the push or pull of human or animal muscle. Go to an ice show or hockey game, or other situation where frictional forces are minimized, and the first law becomes a lot more obvious.

Newton's Second Law

Newton's second law quantifies the relation between force and change in motion. In formulating the second law, Newton reasoned that the product of mass and velocity was the best measure of an object's "quantity of motion." The modern term for Newton's "quantity of motion" is **momentum**. The momentum of an object of mass m moving with velocity $\mathbf{v}$ is the product $m\mathbf{v}$. We use the symbol $\mathbf{p}$ for momentum:

$$\mathbf{p} = m\mathbf{v}. \quad \text{(momentum)} \qquad (5\text{-}1)$$

As the product of a scalar (mass) with a vector (velocity), momentum is itself a vector quantity. Newton's second law relates the rate of change of an object's momentum to the net force acting on that object:

Newton's Second Law of Motion: The rate at which a body's momentum changes is equal to the net force acting on the body:

$$\mathbf{F}_{\text{net}} = \frac{d\mathbf{p}}{dt}. \quad \text{(Newton's 2nd law)} \qquad (5\text{-}2)$$

We emphasize again that it's the *net force*—the vector sum of all individual interaction forces that may be acting on an object—that is important in determining the change in the object's motion.

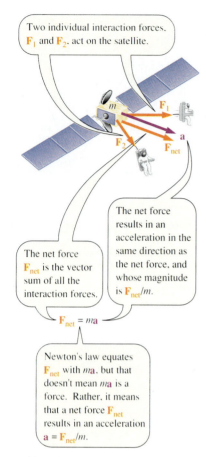

Two individual interaction forces, $\mathbf{F}_1$ and $\mathbf{F}_2$, act on the satellite.

The net force results in an acceleration in the same direction as the net force, and whose magnitude is $\mathbf{F}_{net}/m$.

The net force $\mathbf{F}_{net}$ is the vector sum of all the interaction forces.

$\mathbf{F}_{net} = m\mathbf{a}$

Newton's law equates $\mathbf{F}_{net}$ with $m\mathbf{a}$, but that doesn't mean $m\mathbf{a}$ is a force. Rather, it means that a net force $\mathbf{F}_{net}$ results in an acceleration $\mathbf{a} = \mathbf{F}_{net}/m$.

FIGURE 5-5 Meaning of the terms in Newton's second law. Here two astronauts pull on cables attached to a satellite of mass m, exerting individual interaction forces $\mathbf{F}_1$ and $\mathbf{F}_2$. The net force is their vector sum, and it results in the satellite's acceleration $\mathbf{a} = \mathbf{F}_{net}/m$. The satellite's velocity—both magnitude and direction—is irrelevant, since Newton's law is about *changes* in velocity, not velocity itself.

When a body's mass remains constant, we can use the definition of momentum, $\mathbf{p} = m\mathbf{v}$, to write

$$\mathbf{F}_{net} = \frac{d\mathbf{p}}{dt} = \frac{d(m\mathbf{v})}{dt} = m\frac{d\mathbf{v}}{dt}.$$

But $d\mathbf{v}/dt$ is the acceleration, $\mathbf{a}$, so

$$\mathbf{F}_{net} = m\mathbf{a}. \quad \text{(Newton's 2nd law, constant mass)} \qquad (5\text{-}3)$$

Although Newton originally wrote his second law in the form 5-2, which remains the most general form, the form 5-3 is more widely recognized.

Newton's second law includes the first law as the special case $\mathbf{F}_{net} = 0$. In this case the second law in the form 5-3 gives $\mathbf{a} = 0$, which simply means that the object's velocity does not change. So an object on which the net force is zero remains moving in a straight line at constant speed (speed zero if at rest), just as the first law says. Conversely, if an object is accelerating, then Newton's second law implies that there must be a nonzero net force acting on it. Once again, remember that *any* change in velocity—whether in magnitude (speed) or direction—implies acceleration.

Tip

Understand that Equation! You can't hope to apply Newton's second law successfully unless you understand the terms in the mathematical statement of this law. On the left side is the net force, $\mathbf{F}_{net}$, applied to an object. This net force is always the vector sum of all the real physical interaction forces—pushes and pulls—that act on the object. The term $m\mathbf{a}$ on the right-hand side of the equation, on the other hand, is not a force. The equals sign says that the two sides of the equation have the same value, not that they're physically the same thing. So when you consider the forces acting on an object, don't go adding an extra force $m\mathbf{a}$ to the physical interaction forces that are actually present! Figure 5-5 illustrates the meaning of Newton's second law.

Mass, Inertia, and the Units of Force

Because it takes a force to change an object's motion, one way of interpreting the first law is to say that objects naturally resist changes in motion. The term **inertia** describes this resistance to changes in motion, and for this reason the first law is also called the **law of inertia**. Just as in everyday life we might describe a sluggish person as having a lot of inertia, so an object that is hard to start moving—or hard to stop once started—has a lot of inertia (Fig. 5-6). If we solve the second law for the acceleration $\mathbf{a}$, we find that $\mathbf{a} = \mathbf{F}/m$—showing that a given force is *less* effective in changing the motion of a *more massive* object (Fig. 5-6). The mass m that appears in Newton's laws is thus a measure of an object's inertia, and determines the object's response to a given force.

FIGURE 5-6 Two identical trucks develop the same force as they start up from rest. The loaded truck has greater mass—more inertia—than the empty one, so its acceleration is smaller.

We can actually use Newton's second law to measure mass. By comparing the acceleration a certain force gives to a known and an unknown mass we can determine the unknown mass. From Newton's second law for a force of magnitude F,

$$F = m_{known}a_{known} \text{ and } F = m_{unknown}a_{unknown},$$

where for this purpose we're interested only in magnitudes so we don't use vectors. Equating these two expressions for the same force and using algebra to form ratios of masses and accelerations, we have

$$\frac{m_{unknown}}{m_{known}} = \frac{a_{known}}{a_{unknown}}. \tag{5-4}$$

Equation 5-4 can be considered an operational definition of mass; it shows how, given a known mass and a fixed force, we can apply the force to different unknown masses and use the resulting accelerations to determine those masses. With an accurately known mass, such as the standard kilogram defined in Chapter 1, Equation 5-4 provides a way of determining any other mass. This method is used routinely to measure the masses of astronauts in orbiting spacecraft; see Example 5-5.

The force required to accelerate a 1-kg mass at the rate of 1 m/s² is defined to be 1 **newton** (N). Equation 5-3 shows that 1 N is equivalent to 1 kg·m/s². Other common force units are the English pound (lb, equal to 4.448 N) and the dyne, a metric unit equal to 10^{-5} N. A 1-N force is rather small; you can readily exert forces measuring hundreds of newtons with your own body.

Inertial Reference Frames

Why don't flight attendants serve beverages when an airplane is accelerating down the runway? For one thing, their beverage cart wouldn't stay put; it would appear to the passengers to accelerate toward the back of the plane—even in the absence of a net force acting on it. So is Newton's first law wrong? No—it's just that Newton's laws don't apply in an accelerating airplane. With respect to the ground, in fact, the beverage cart is doing just what Newton says it should: it's remaining in its original state of motion (at rest), while all around it plane and passengers accelerate toward takeoff.

In Section 3-5 we defined a reference frame as a system (e.g., a laboratory, an airplane, Earth, or whatever) with respect to which we measure velocities. We further defined an inertial reference frame as an unaccelerated frame—that is, a frame in uniform motion. We can now see the reason for the name "inertial reference frame." It's only in such a frame that the law of inertia—Newton's first law—is valid. With respect to a noninertial frame such as the accelerating airplane, a car rounding a corner, or a whirling merry-go-round, an object at rest doesn't remain at rest, and an object in uniform motion doesn't remain in uniform motion, even when the net force on the objects is zero. In fact, the best test of whether we're in an inertial reference frame is to check whether the first law is obeyed.

We emphasize that Newton's laws are valid only when motion is described relative to an inertial reference frame. We saw in Section 3-5 that acceleration has the same value in all inertial frames. Since Newton's second law relates force and acceleration, that means the second law is valid in all inertial frames.

The same is true for Newton's third law, which we'll introduce shortly. Thus the laws of motion—Newton's laws—are valid in all inertial reference frames. This is the principle of Galilean relativity that we introduced in Chapter 3.

Strictly speaking, our rotating Earth is not an inertial frame, and therefore Newton's laws aren't quite valid in an Earth-based frame of reference. But Earth's rotation has an insignificant effect on most motions we're interested in, so we can usually treat the Earth frame as being inertial. An important exception involves the large-scale motions of the atmosphere and oceans; here, oceanographers and atmospheric scientists must take account of Earth's rotation.

If Earth isn't an inertial frame, what is? That's a surprisingly subtle question, and it pointed Einstein the way to his general theory of relativity. The law of inertia and the principle of relativity are intimately related, and both raise deep questions about the nature of space, time, and gravity—questions whose answers lie in Einstein's theory. We'll look briefly at that theory later in the book; for now, be content with the understanding that Newton's laws hold in any inertial frame of reference.

5-3 FORCES

The most familiar example of a force is a push or pull you apply with your own body. But it does not require an animate creature such as a human or an animal to produce a force. A car collides with a stopped truck and comes to a stop itself. Why? Because the truck exerts a force on it. The moon has been circling Earth for billions of years, rather than moving away in a straight line. Why? Because of the gravitational force that Earth exerts on it. You stand on the second floor of a building and don't fall through. Why? Because the floor exerts an upward force that counters the downward force of gravity. You take your foot off the gas, and your car coasts to a stop. Why? Because a frictional force acts on the car. An airplane flies. Why? Because the air exerts an upward force on its wings. You pull your clothes from the dryer and find socks clinging to the clothes. Why? Because an electric force acts on the socks.

Some forces, such as a particular force you choose to apply with your muscles or the force of gravity on a specific object, have fixed values. Other forces take on values determined by the situation. Consider the simple act of sitting, motionless, in a chair (Fig. 5-7). You're at rest, unaccelerated, so Newton's first law guarantees that the net force on you is zero. But you know there's a gravitational force downward; call it $\mathbf{F}_g$. So there must be another force, pointing upward, that sums with the gravitational force to give zero net force; that other force must be equal to $-\mathbf{F}_g$. And where does this upward force come from? From the one thing that keeps you from falling toward the floor, namely the chair. The chair compresses when you sit on it, and the resulting rearrangement of molecules results in an upward force—ultimately electric in origin—with the same magnitude as the downward gravitational force. Because the chair's force results from compression of the chair, it's called a **compression force**. Other examples of compression forces include the forces in building materials that support the overlying weight of a building, the force of a compressed spring in an automobile suspension system, or the force of a gas compressed under pressure, as in a car's tires.

FIGURE 5-7 When you sit in a chair, the chair compresses and exerts an upward force on you. As you sink deeper, the compression force increases until it's equal in magnitude to the gravitational force; then you're at rest and unaccelerated. The compression force is ultimately an electrical force that arises from interactions among the chair's molecules. We've shown a cushioned chair to emphasize the compression, but the same would happen in any chair—it's just that a harder chair would compress less to provide the same force.

How is the chair so smart as to provide just the right upward force to balance the gravitational force? It isn't. As you begin to sit down, the force from the chair at first isn't very large, and you still experience a net downward force. So you sink deeper into the chair, compressing it further and increasing the compression force. Eventually the compression force and the gravitational force have equal magnitudes, and then you're in an equilibrium situation at rest in the chair. If the chair isn't strong enough to support you, it will break and you'll continue accelerating downward until the floor provides a force that stops you.

The same thing happens with **tension forces** that result when objects are stretched—as in rubber bands, springs, ropes, and cables. A rope or cable supporting an unaccelerated object stretches just enough that it provides an upward tension force equal in magnitude to the downward gravitational force (Fig. 5-8).

Got It!

The words "unaccelerated" and "equal" in the preceding sentence go together. Why? How would the magnitudes of the gravitational force and the tension force compare if the load in Fig. 5-8 were accelerating upward? What if it were accelerating downward? Would the relative magnitudes of the forces be any different if it were moving upward at a constant speed rather than dangling at rest from the cable?

FIGURE 5-8 The cables stretch to provide an upward tension force that supports the load.

Forces such as the pull you exert on a wagon, the upward force of a chair on your body, the force a bat exerts on a baseball, the force the cable exerts in Fig. 5-8, or the force of friction between two objects are often called **contact forces** because one object exerts a force on another through direct contact. Other forces, such as the gravitational force, the electric force, and the magnetic force, are called **action-at-a-distance forces** because they seemingly act between distant objects—as with the gravitational force between Earth and moon. Actually, the distinction between these two types of forces is not clear-cut; at the microscopic level, what we call contact forces involve action-at-a-distance electric forces between the particles composing macroscopic objects such as chairs and human bodies. And the action-at-a-distance concept itself is troubling. How can an object such as Earth "reach out" across empty space and pull on the moon? Later we'll look at a more sophisticated approach to forces that helps resolve this quandary.

The Fundamental Forces

We've just mentioned a plethora of forces—gravitational forces, contact forces, frictional forces, electrical forces, tension and compression forces, magnetic forces. How many kinds of forces are there? Actually, physicists believe there is only one fundamental force, although we don't yet know how to describe it. At present, physicists identify three basic forces—the **gravitational force**, the **electroweak force**, and the **color force**. Each of these subsumes other forces once considered distinct. This **unification** of seemingly unrelated forces as

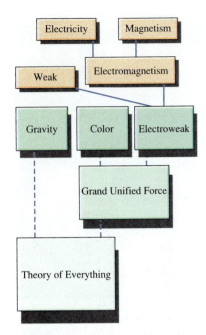

FIGURE 5-9 Unification of forces has been a major theme in the history of physics. Grand unification of the electroweak and color forces may be achieved soon, but a "theory of everything" that incorporates gravity and the other forces appears to be a more distant goal.

aspects of a common, more fundamental force has been a major theme in the history of physics, and is a central problem of contemporary physics (Fig. 5-9). Later, in Chapters 23–34, we'll explore the unification of electricity and magnetism. In the final chapter we consider in more detail the fundamental forces and the prospects for their unification; here we simply introduce each force and give a brief description.

The **gravitational force** is an attractive force that acts between all matter. You're intimately familiar with it through the gravitational force that Earth exerts on you. Yet familiar though it is, gravity is the weakest and perhaps the least understood of the fundamental forces. But as the gravitational force is always attractive, its effect is cumulative. That makes gravity the dominant force in determining the structure of large objects, from planets, to galaxies and the universe itself. We'll look at the force of Earth's gravity in the next chapter, and will explore gravity more generally in Chapter 9.

The **electroweak force** subsumes **electromagnetism** and the so-called **weak nuclear force**. Virtually all the nongravitational forces we encounter in everyday life are electromagnetic, including contact forces, friction, tension forces, the forces in your muscles, and the forces that hold ordinary matter together at the atomic and molecular level. The weak nuclear force is less obvious, but is important in helping determine which atomic nuclei are stable and which are radioactive. In particular, processes involving the weak force occur in the core of the Sun and help produce the solar energy that keeps us alive.

The theory that links electromagnetism and the weak force as aspects of the common electroweak force was developed in the 1970s and confirmed experimentally in the 1980s; before then physicists listed four fundamental forces. A century earlier, in the 1860s, a similar unification of electricity and magnetism had occurred; that unification is the overriding theme of Chapters 23–34.

The third basic force was proposed in the 1930s to explain how atomic nuclei stay together. It was originally called the **nuclear force** (or sometimes the strong nuclear force, to distinguish it from the weak nuclear force), and referred to the force between individual protons and neutrons. Today we know that protons and neutrons are themselves composites of simpler particles called **quarks** (Fig. 5-10). The force between quarks is called the **color force**, although it has nothing to do with the visual phenomenon of color. The force binding neutrons and protons into atomic nuclei is a residual manifestation of the extremely strong color force. Although the color force is not obvious in our everyday lives, it determines the structure of matter at the most fundamental level. If the strength of the color force were even slightly different, atoms more complex than helium would not be possible, and the universe would be an entirely different place—a place devoid of, among other things, life.

Although the three fundamental forces are at the heart of all that happens in the physical world, in our study of force and motion on the macroscopic scale we'll rarely consider forces at such a fundamental level—with the important exception of gravity. Instead, we'll deal with frictional forces on car tires, contact forces between skis and snow, the force of air on an airplane wing, the tension in a climbing rope, and so forth. Philosophically, it's good to remember that all these are manifestations of the three fundamental forces (almost always the electromagnetic aspect of the electroweak force), but it isn't necessary to use that knowledge to solve practical problems.

FIGURE 5-10 A proton consists of three quarks, held together by a 50,000-N (10,000 pound) color force. Although the color force is not obvious in everyday life, it is essential in determining the basic structure of matter.

5-4 APPLYING NEWTON'S SECOND LAW

Why are we so interested in forces? Because forces cause changes in motion, so if we know the net force on a body we can calculate its acceleration and thus determine its subsequent motion. In this section we'll get a practical feel for Newton's second law through some simple examples in which a single force acts on an object.

We introduced Newton's second law in Section 5-2; for an object of constant mass, the law takes the form

$$\mathbf{F}_{net} = m\mathbf{a}. \qquad (5\text{-}3)$$

Does this statement of the second law make sense? It sure does: it should take a larger force to produce a given acceleration in a more massive object (Fig. 5-11a). And that's just what Equation 5-3 says: with fixed $\mathbf{a}$, the force needed to accelerate an object is directly proportional to the object's mass. And with a given mass, a larger force should give a larger acceleration (Fig. 5-11b). Again, that's just what the equation says: with fixed m, the net force $\mathbf{F}_{net}$ and acceleration $\mathbf{a}$ are directly proportional.

Remember that Newton's law is a vector equation, because forces and accelerations are vector quantities. So the proportionality between force and acceleration expressed in Newton's law means two things: that the magnitude of the acceleration is proportional to the magnitude of the force, and that the acceleration is in the same direction as the force.

We now apply Newton's second law to some simple examples, showing how it can be used to determine unknown forces, to measure masses, and to predict an object's motion given the forces acting on it. In Chapter 6 we'll show how the same ideas can be extended to more complicated cases involving multiple interaction forces.

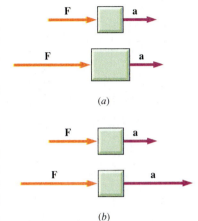

FIGURE 5-11 (a) For two objects to have the same acceleration, a greater force must be exerted on the more massive object. (b) When two objects have the same mass, the one with the greater force experiences the greater acceleration.

EXAMPLE 5-1	*Force, Mass, and Acceleration*

Solution

A 1200-kg car accelerates from rest to 20 m/s in 7.8 s, moving in a straight line with constant acceleration. What is the net force acting on it? If the car then rounds a bend 85 m in radius at a steady 20 m/s, what net force acts on it?

Solution

To calculate the net force from Newton's second law, we need to know the acceleration and the mass being accelerated. When the car accelerates from rest to 20 m/s in 7.8 s, it undergoes an acceleration of magnitude

$$a = \frac{\Delta v}{\Delta t} = \frac{20 \text{ m/s}}{7.8 \text{ s}} = 2.6 \text{ m/s}^2.$$

The magnitude of the force causing this acceleration is then

$$F_{net} = ma = (1200 \text{ kg})(2.6 \text{ m/s}^2) = 3100 \text{ kg}\cdot\text{m/s}^2$$
$$= 3100 \text{ N}.$$

Force is a vector, and the full vector form of Newton's second law—$\mathbf{F}_{net} = m\mathbf{a}$—shows that the force is in the same direction as the acceleration, which in this case also happens to be in the direction of motion. What is the physical origin of the force? Newton's law does not tell us that. *Any* physical mechanism providing the same net force on the car would produce the same acceleration. Here the force is provided by friction between tires and road. If the driver tried to accelerate on frictionless ice, the wheels would simply spin and the car would not accelerate.

When the car rounds a circular bend at constant speed, we know from Section 4-4 that it undergoes an acceleration of magnitude v^2/r directed toward the center of the circle. Newton's second law therefore requires a net force acting toward the center of the circle; the magnitude of this force is

$$F = ma = \frac{mv^2}{r} = \frac{(1200 \text{ kg})(20 \text{ m/s})^2}{85 \text{ m}} = 5600 \text{ N}.$$

Note that Newton's law does not distinguish between forces that result in a change in speed (accelerating in a straight line) and those that result in a change in direction (accelerating in a circular path at constant speed). Newton's second law relates force, mass, and acceleration in *all* instances.

What provides the accelerating force in the car's circular motion? Again, it's the force of friction between tires and road. On an icy road, the car may skid off the road in a straight line, since the frictional force is virtually absent. We'll study circular motion and frictional forces in detail in the next chapter.

Figure 5-12 shows the force vectors for the two cases in this example.

EXERCISE A 2.1×10^6-kg freight train takes 3.8 min to accelerate from rest to 75 km/h. What force does its locomotive exert?

Answer: 1.9×10^5 N

Some problems similar to Example 5-1: 4, 5, 8

(a)   (b)

FIGURE 5-12 Forces on the car of Example 5-1. (*a*) Accelerating in a straight line. (*b*) Rounding a curve. (Only forces in the horizontal plane are shown; there are also vertical forces from gravity and the road that sum to zero.)

Got It!

A nonzero net force acts on an object. Does that mean the object necessarily moves in the same direction as the force? Give an example.

EXAMPLE 5-2	*Electrons in a TV Tube*

Electrons in a TV tube are accelerated essentially from rest to a speed of 8.4×10^7 m/s in the "electron gun" at the back of the tube. If the electron gun is 8.2 cm long and if the acceleration in the gun is constant, what force is exerted on each electron?

Solution

To calculate the force, we need the acceleration and mass of the electron. Equation 2-11 relates acceleration, velocity, and distance in one-dimensional motion. With $v_0 = 0$, this equation becomes

$$v^2 = 2a(x - x_0),$$

so

$$a = \frac{v^2}{2(x - x_0)}.$$

Here $x - x_0$ is the 8.2-cm length of the electron gun and v is the 8.4×10^7 m/s velocity of electrons emerging from the gun. Then

Newton's second law gives

$$F = ma = \frac{mv^2}{2(x - x_0)} = \frac{(9.11\times10^{-31}\ \text{kg})(8.4\times10^7\ \text{m/s})^2}{(2)(0.082\ \text{m})}$$
$$= 3.9\times10^{-14}\ \text{N}.$$

That such a small force can accelerate electrons to such high speed in only a few centimeters is possible because of their minuscule mass. (Our answer in this case is only approximate because effects of relativity become important at this high speed.)

EXERCISE The merging lane on which cars enter a highway is 180 m long. A 1.2×10^3-kg car enters the merging lane moving at 40 km/h. What force must its drive wheels exert to get it safely to the 100 km/h speed limit before it merges with traffic on the main highway?

Answer: 2.2×10^3 N

Tip

Get to Know Your Book Example 5-2 didn't give the mass of the electron, which was needed to get the answer. Inside the front cover of the book is a table listing common physical constants, including the electron mass. The appendices contain much more detailed information. Get used to consulting the inside covers and the appendices!

2.13

Tension Change

We just used Newton's second law as a prescription for measuring forces. Conversely, given the force on an object, we can calculate the object's acceleration and thus predict its motion. It is this use of Newton's law that lets us send a spacecraft to Jupiter, design engines appropriate to a new aircraft, or determine the safe distance between cars on a highway. It also helps us analyze a skyscraper's response to gale-force winds, predict the positions of the planets and the timing of eclipses, and develop better tennis rackets. It is only a slight exaggeration to say that the equation $\mathbf{F}_{net} = m\mathbf{a}$ covers all of classical physics.

2.11

Pole Vaulter Vaults

EXAMPLE 5-3	An Airport Runway

Fully loaded, a 747 jetliner has a mass of 3.6×10^5 kg. Its four engines provide a total thrust (force) of 7.7×10^5 N. How long a runway is needed for a 747 to achieve takeoff speed of 310 km/h (86 m/s)?

Solution

We are given force and mass, from which we can calculate acceleration using Newton's second law:

$$a = \frac{F}{m}.$$

We need then to relate acceleration to speed and distance; Equation 2-11 provides this relation:

$$v^2 = 2a(x - x_0).$$

Solving for the runway length $x - x_0$ and using $a = F/m$,

we have

$$x - x_0 = \frac{v^2}{2a} = \frac{v^2}{2(F/m)} = \frac{mv^2}{2F}$$

$$= \frac{(3.6 \times 10^5 \text{ kg})(86 \text{ m/s})^2}{(2)(7.7 \times 10^5 \text{ N})} = 1700 \text{ m}.$$

EXERCISE A 50-kg skater can exert a horizontal force of 940 N against the ice. If she's gliding toward a wall of the rink at 6.7 m/s, how close can she get before attempting to stop and still avoid colliding with the wall?

Answer: 1.2 m

Some problems similar to Examples 5-2 and 5-3: 10, 11, 13, 14, 53, 54, 58

EXAMPLE 5-4	Predicting Motion Using Newton's Second Law

A force $\mathbf{F} = 2.4\hat{\mathbf{i}} + 1.7\hat{\mathbf{j}}$ N acts on a 1.2-kg object initially at rest at the origin. What is the object's acceleration? Where is the object and how fast is it moving 3.5 s after the force is first applied?

Solution

Solving Newton's second law for the acceleration gives

$$\mathbf{a} = \frac{\mathbf{F}}{m} = \frac{2.4\hat{\mathbf{i}} + 1.7\hat{\mathbf{j}} \text{ N}}{1.2 \text{ kg}} = 2.0\hat{\mathbf{i}} + 1.4\hat{\mathbf{j}} \text{ m/s}^2.$$

Given the acceleration, we use methods of the previous chapters to find the position and speed. Equation 4-4 gives the position of an object undergoing constant acceleration:

$$\mathbf{r} = \mathbf{r}_0 + \mathbf{v}_0 t + \tfrac{1}{2}\mathbf{a}t^2 = \tfrac{1}{2}(2.0\hat{\mathbf{i}} + 1.4\hat{\mathbf{j}} \text{ m/s}^2)(3.5 \text{ s})^2$$

$$= 12\hat{\mathbf{i}} + 8.7\hat{\mathbf{j}} \text{ m}.$$

Here we have set $\mathbf{r}_0$ and $\mathbf{v}_0$ to zero since the object is initially at rest at the origin. The velocity after 3.5 s is given by Equation 4-3:

$$\mathbf{v} = \mathbf{v}_0 + \mathbf{a}t = (2.0\hat{\mathbf{i}} + 1.4\hat{\mathbf{j}} \text{ m/s})(3.5 \text{ s}) = 7.0\hat{\mathbf{i}} + 5.0\hat{\mathbf{j}} \text{ m/s},$$

so the speed is

$$v = \sqrt{v_x^2 + v_y^2} = [(7.0 \text{ m/s})^2 + (5.0 \text{ m/s})^2]^{1/2} = 8.6 \text{ m/s}.$$

EXERCISE A 940-kg spacecraft is moving uniformly at 4.8 km/s when it fires a small rocket that exerts a 4.5×10^3-N

FIGURE 5-13 A rocket thrust.

force at 67° to the initial direction of motion, as suggested in Fig. 5-13. If the rocket fires for 120 s, (a) how far does the ship move during the rocket firing? (b) How fast and in what direction is it moving after the firing?

Answers: (a) 590 km; (b) 5.1 km/s, at 6.0° to its original direction

Some problems similar to Example 5-4: 15, 34

A third use of Newton's law is to determine unknown masses from measured forces and accelerations. This approach is actually used in spacecraft, where weightlessness (see Section 5-5) precludes more conventional mass measurements.

EXAMPLE 5-5	"Massing" an Astronaut

To study physiological effects of spaceflight, astronauts routinely measure their masses using a movable chair subject to the force exerted by a spring (Fig. 5-14). If the 15-kg chair undergoes an acceleration of 24 mm/s^2 when the spring force is 1.8 N, what is the astronaut's mass?

Solution

Solving Newton's second law for mass gives

$$m = \frac{F}{a} = \frac{1.8 \text{ N}}{24 \times 10^{-3} \text{ m/s}^2} = 75 \text{ kg}.$$

This is the combined mass of chair and astronaut; subtracting the 15-kg chair then gives 60 kg for the astronaut's mass.

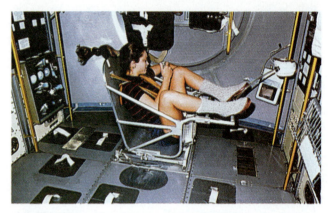

FIGURE 5-14 Astronaut Tamara Jernigan using a mass-measuring device aboard the space shuttle.

5-5 MASS AND WEIGHT: THE FORCE OF GRAVITY

Newton's second law shows that mass is a measure of a body's resistance to changes in motion—that is, of its inertia. A body's mass is an intrinsic property; it doesn't depend on location or any other circumstances. If my mass is 65 kg, it is 65 kg whether I am on Earth, in an orbiting spacecraft, on the moon, or in the remote reaches of intergalactic space. That means no matter where I am, a force of 65 N is needed to give me an acceleration of 1 m/s^2.

We commonly use the term "weight" to mean the same thing as mass. In physics, though, **weight** is the name for a force—the force that gravity exerts on a body. Near the surface of Earth, a body allowed to fall freely accelerates downward at 9.8 m/s^2; we designate this acceleration vector by **g**. Newton's second law, **F** = m**a**, then says that the force of gravity on a body of mass m is m**g**; this force is the body's weight:

$$\mathbf{W} = m\mathbf{g}. \quad \text{(weight)} \tag{5-5}$$

With my 65-kg mass, my weight near Earth's surface is then (65 kg)(9.8 m/s^2) or 640 N. On the moon, where the acceleration of gravity is only 1.6 m/s^2, I would weigh only 100 N. And in the remote reaches of intergalactic space, far from any gravitating object, my weight would be essentially zero.

| **EXAMPLE 5-6** | *Exploring Mars: Mass and Weight* |

The Pathfinder spacecraft that landed on Mars in 1997 had a weight of 2.70 kN on Earth. What was Pathfinder's mass on Earth and Mars, and its weight on Mars?

Solution

Weight is the force of gravity; Equation 5-5 shows that its magnitude is given by $W = mg$. Solving for m and using the weight and acceleration of gravity on Earth, we have

$$m = \frac{W}{g} = \frac{2700 \text{ N}}{9.8 \text{ m/s}^2} = 276 \text{ kg} .$$

The mass is the same everywhere; on Mars the weight is then given by

$$W = mg_{Mars} = (276 \text{ kg})(3.74 \text{ m/s}^2) = 1.03 \text{ kN} ,$$

where we obtained the acceleration of gravity on Mars from Appendix E.

EXERCISE A rope can support a maximum weight of 350 N. Could it support a 70-kg astronaut on (a) Earth and (b) Mercury? *Hint:* Consult Appendix E.

Answers: (a) no; (b) yes

Some problems similar to Example 5-6: 17–23

One reason we confuse mass and weight stems from the common use of the SI unit kilogram to describe "weight." At the doctor's office you may be told that you "weigh" 55 kg. You don't; you have a mass of 55 kg, so your weight is (55 kg)(9.8 m/s²) or 540 N. The unit of force in the English system is the pound, so giving your weight in pounds is correct. The English unit of mass is the slug, which is rarely used.

That we confuse mass and weight at all results from the remarkable fact that the gravitational acceleration of all objects at a given location is the same. This makes the *weight* of a body—a property defined in terms of gravity— proportional to its *mass*—a property that describes its inertia in terms that have nothing to do with gravity. First inferred by Galileo from his experiments with falling bodies, this relation between gravitation and inertia seemed a coincidence until the early twentieth century. Finally, in his general theory of relativity, Albert Einstein showed how that simple relation reflects the underlying geometry of space and time in a way that links intimately the phenomena of gravitation and acceleration.

Although we defined weight in terms of the acceleration of gravity, a body need not be accelerating to have weight. When you're sitting in a chair, for example, gravity is still exerting a downward force $m\mathbf{g}$ on you. That force $m\mathbf{g}$ is your weight; it's just that the chair is exerting an upward force that keeps you from accelerating. In fact, it's the forces acting between you and the chair, and the forces of your muscles supporting the rest of your body, that make you conscious of your weight.

Weightlessness

What about astronauts aboard a space shuttle? Aren't they "weightless?" Not according to our definition. At the shuttle's altitude, the acceleration of gravity has about 93% of its value at Earth's surface, so the gravitational forces $m\mathbf{g}$ on the shuttle and its occupants are almost as large as they would be on Earth. But the astronauts *seem* weightless, and indeed they *feel* weightless (Fig. 5-15). What's going on?

Imagine yourself in an elevator whose cable has broken and is dropping freely downward with the gravitational acceleration g. In other words, the elevator and its occupant are in **free fall**, with only the force of gravity acting. If you let go of

FIGURE 5-15 Astronauts Richard Truly and Guy Bluford floating about the cabin of a space shuttle.

FIGURE 5-16 Objects in free fall appear weightless because they experience the same acceleration as their reference frame. Weightlessness would occur in a freely falling elevator near Earth's surface just as it does in an orbiting spacecraft. In both cases, the person, book, and elevator or spaceship all have the same acceleration toward Earth so none accelerates relative to its surroundings.

Earth

(a)

Earth

(b)

a book you're holding, it too falls freely with acceleration g. But so does everything else around it—and therefore the book stays put relative to you (Fig. 5-16a). To you, the book seems "weightless," since it doesn't seem to fall when you let go of it. And you're "weightless" too; if you jump off the elevator's floor, you float to the ceiling rather than falling back down. Of course you, the book, and the elevator are *all* falling, but because all have the same acceleration that isn't obvious to you. The gravitational force is still acting; it's what's making you fall. So you really do have weight, and your condition is best termed **apparent weightlessness**.

A falling elevator is a dangerous place; your state of apparent weightlessness would end with a deadly smash caused by nongravitational contact forces when you hit the ground. But apparent weightlessness occurs permanently in a state of free fall that doesn't intersect Earth—as in an orbiting spacecraft (Fig. 5-16b). It's not that they're in outer space that makes astronauts seem weightless; it's just that they, like our hapless elevator occupant, are in free fall—moving under the influence of the gravitational force alone. The condition of apparent weightlessness in orbiting spacecraft is sometimes called "microgravity."

APPLICATION	*Hollywood Goes Weightless*

The film *Apollo 13* shows Tom Hanks and his fellow actors floating weightlessly around the cabin of their movie-set spacecraft. What special effects did Hollywood use here? None: the actors' apparent weightlessness was the real thing. But even Hollywood's budget wasn't enough to buy a space shuttle flight. So the film's producers did the next best thing: they rented NASA's weightlessness training aircraft, aptly dubbed the "vomit comet" (Fig. 5-17). This airplane executes parabolic trajectories that mimic projectile motion. While on such a trajectory the plane and its occupants are in free fall, so they experience apparent weightlessness. Normally the aircraft's cabin is an empty space with padded surfaces but the *Apollo 13* set crew constructed a mock-up of the ill-fated Apollo 13 spacecraft inside the NASA aircraft's cabin.

Accounts of the making of *Apollo 13* marveled at how the film "simulated the weightlessness of outer space." Nonsense! The actors in their movie set were in free fall just as much as the real astronauts on board the real Apollo 13, and they experienced exactly the same physical phenomenon—apparent weightlessness in a reference frame moving under the influence of gravity alone.

FIGURE 5-17 In *Apollo 13,* a mock-up of the Apollo 13 spacecraft rides in this NASA training aircraft, whose parabolic trajectory produces apparent weightlessness.

2.12
Skydiver

ActivPhysics

Got It!

A popular children's book explains the weightlessness astronauts experience by saying there's no gravity in space. Critique this statement. If there were no gravity in space, what would be the motion of a space shuttle, a satellite, or, for that matter, the moon?

5-6 ADDING FORCES

The simple examples we've done so far considered only a single force acting on an object. But often several forces act, and we've emphasized that it's the vector sum of those individual interaction forces—the net force $\mathbf{F}_{net}$—that determines the acceleration through Newton's second law. We've been careful to write $\mathbf{F}_{net}$ every time we use Newton's law, to emphasize that the net force is what matters. Some books write $\Sigma\mathbf{F} = m\mathbf{a}$ to remind readers that the net force is the vector sum of all the individual interaction forces.

Tip

Trust Newton Newton's second law says it all: an object's mass and the net force acting on it determine its acceleration. In particular, if you see an object that's not accelerating—either it's at rest, or it's moving with velocity that doesn't change in magnitude or direction—then you know the net force must be zero. If you think there's a nonzero net force, look again; there *must* be additional interaction forces such that all the interaction forces sum to zero (see Fig. 5-18).

FIGURE 5-18 A parachutist descends straight downward at constant speed; for simplicity we treat the 'chutist and 'chute as a single object (we'll justify this in Chapter 10). At first it may seem that gravity is the only force acting, but because the 'chutist is not accelerating, the net force must be zero. So there must be a second interaction force, in this case the upward force of the air on the parachute. Since the two interaction forces sum to give zero net force, they must have the same magnitude.

In this first chapter on Newton's laws, we'll consider the addition of forces in one dimension only. But forces are vectors, and finding the net force generally involves vector addition. In the next chapter we'll deal with Newton's laws in two and three dimensions.

| **EXAMPLE 5-7** | *An Elevator* |

Solution

A 740-kg elevator is accelerating upward at 1.1 m/s², pulled by a cable of negligible mass, as shown in Fig. 5-19. What is the tension force in the elevator cable?

Solution

This is an important example, and understanding it thoroughly will help you apply Newton's second law correctly in more complicated situations. We're given the acceleration and mass and asked for the force in the cable. Can't we just write $\mathbf{F} = m\mathbf{a}$ for that force? No! $\mathbf{F} = m\mathbf{a}$ is true only for the *net force,* and here the cable tension is *not* the only force acting. There is also the force of gravity, which has magnitude mg and points downward. We've shown both forces in Fig. 5-19*b*, where we indicate the elevator by a simple dot. Such a diagram, in which we isolate a single object and show all the forces acting on it, is called a **free-body** diagram. We'll make extensive use of free-body diagrams in the next chapter.

> **Tip**
>
> *Identify the Forces* A key step in solving any Newton's law problem is to identify the forces acting on the object or objects of interest. There's no sense proceeding unless you know the *net* force—and that requires identifying *all* the individual forces acting. Drawing a free-body diagram, as in Fig. 5-19*b*, is crucial in identifying all the forces.

Calling the tension force $\mathbf{T}$ and the gravitational force $\mathbf{F}_g$, Newton's second law becomes

$$\mathbf{F}_{net} = \mathbf{T} + \mathbf{F}_g = m\mathbf{a}. \tag{5-6}$$

> **Tip**
>
> *Vectors Tell It All* You might be tempted to put minus signs in Equation 5-6. But not yet! This is a *vector* equation, and information about signs is built into the directional nature of the vectors. Skipping the step of writing Newton's law in vector form will often get you into trouble. And in writing the vector equation, you never need to worry about signs.

Having written the vector form of Newton's second law, we next choose a coordinate system and write the components of Newton's law in that system. Here all the forces are vertical, so we choose our y axis pointing vertically upward. Now we write the components of our vector equation 5-6. In this one-dimensional problem only the y equation is interesting; formally,

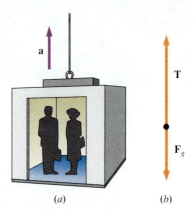

FIGURE 5-19 Forces on the elevator include the cable tension $\mathbf{T}$ and the gravitational force $\mathbf{F}_g$; the net force is their vector sum. Since the elevator is accelerating upward, this net force must be upward. (*b*) A free-body diagram showing both forces acting on the elevator, which is represented by the small black dot.

it reads

$$T_y + F_{gy} = ma_y. \tag{5-7}$$

Now the tension force $\mathbf{T}$ points upward, or in the $+y$ direction; its vertical component T_y is positive and is equal to the magnitude T of $\mathbf{T}$. The gravitational force $\mathbf{F}_g$ has magnitude mg and points vertically downward, in the $-y$ direction. Its vertical component F_{gy} is therefore $-mg$. Then Equation 5-7 is

$$T - mg = ma_y,$$

so

$$T = ma_y + mg = m(a_y + g). \tag{5-8}$$

Before putting in specific numbers, let's see if this result makes sense. Suppose the acceleration a_y were zero. Then the net force on the elevator would have to be zero. In this case, Equation 5-8 tells us that $T = mg$, showing that the tension force and gravity have the same magnitude. Since they point in opposite directions, they indeed sum to zero.

If, on the other hand, the elevator is accelerating upward, so a_y is positive, then Equation 5-8 requires that the magnitude of the tension force exceed that of the gravitational force by an amount ma_y. Why is this? Because in this case the cable not only supports the elevator against gravity, but also provides the upward acceleration. For the numbers of this example, we have

$$T = m(a_y + g) = (740 \text{ kg})(1.1 \text{ m/s}^2 + 9.8 \text{ m/s}^2)$$

$$= 8100 \text{ N}.$$

What if the elevator were accelerating downward? Then a_y is negative and Equation 5-8 shows that the tension force is less than mg. Does this make sense? Yes. For a downward acceleration, the net force must be downward so that the magnitude of the downward gravitational force exceeds that of the upward tension force. Were the elevator in free fall, so $a_y = -g$, the tension force would be exactly zero.

You probably could have reasoned out the answer to this problem in your head. But by applying the steps illustrated here—specifically, writing Newton's second law as a vector equation and then breaking it into components—you will be able to handle more complicated situations without confusion. We will outline the steps in solving a Newton's law problem more formally in the next chapter.

EXERCISE A 270-kg rocket accelerates straight upward from Earth at 51 m/s². What is the thrust (force) provided by the rocket's engine?

Answer: 1.6×10^4 N

Some problems similar to Example 5-7: 26–31

Got It!

In Example 5-7 we said the elevator was accelerating upward. Did that mean it was necessarily moving upward? Think about the difference between velocity and acceleration! In solving Example 5-7, we found that the cable tension exceeded the elevator's weight. In which of the following situations would that be true? (a) Elevator starts moving upward, accelerating from rest; (b) Elevator is moving upward, then decelerates to a stop; (c) Elevator starts moving downward, accelerating from rest; (d) Elevator is moving downward, then decelerates to a stop.

2.2
Raising a Crate

2.3
Lowering a Crate

5-7 NEWTON'S THIRD LAW

Push your book across your desk; you feel the book pushing back on your hand (Fig. 5-20). Kick a ball with bare feet, and your toes hurt. Why? You've exerted a force on the ball, and the ball has exerted a force back on you. Or imagine a rocket engine, exerting forces that expel hot gases out of its nozzle. Something else happens, too: the hot gases exert a force on the rocket, accelerating it forward (Fig. 5-21).

Experiment shows that whenever one object exerts a force on a second object, the second object also exerts a force on the first. The two forces are in opposite directions, but they have equal magnitudes. This fact constitutes **Newton's third law of motion**. The familiar expression that "for every action there is an equal and opposite reaction" is Newton's statement of the third law in seventeenth-century language. But there's really no distinction between "action" and "reaction"; both are always present. In modern language, we express the third law by stating

> *Newton's Third Law:* If object A exerts a force on object B, then object B exerts an oppositely directed force of equal magnitude on A.

Newton's third law is about forces between objects. It says that such forces always occur in pairs—that it's not possible for object A to exert a force on object B without B's exerting a force back on A. You can see now why we coined the term "interaction forces"—when there's force between two objects, it's always a true *inter*action, with both objects exerting forces and both experiencing forces. Neither object passively experiences a force from the other. We'll use the terms **interaction force pair** or **third-law pair** for the two forces described by Newton's third law.

FIGURE 5-20 When you push on a book, the book pushes back on you; otherwise you wouldn't feel its presence. The forces $\mathbf{F}_{AB}$ and $\mathbf{F}_{BA}$ have equal magnitudes and constitute an action-reaction pair.

FIGURE 5-21 The combustion chamber of a rocket engine exerts a force $\mathbf{F}_1$ on the hot gases, expelling them through the nozzle. In return, the gases exert a force $\mathbf{F}_2$ of equal magnitude on the rocket, accelerating it forward.

It's crucial to recognize that the forces of a third-law pair act on *different* objects; the force $\mathbf{F}_{AB}$ of object A acts on object B, and the force $\mathbf{F}_{BA}$ of B acts on A. The forces have equal magnitudes but opposite directions; therefore, $\mathbf{F}_{AB} = -\mathbf{F}_{BA}$. But they don't cancel to give zero net force, *because they don't act on the same object*. In Fig. 5-20, for example, $\mathbf{F}_{AB}$ is the force the hand exerts on the book. There's no other horizontal force shown acting on the book, so the net force on the book is nonzero and the book will accelerate. The hand, in contrast, experiences the force $\mathbf{F}_{BA}$ and also forces from the arm muscles that aren't shown in the figure, so it, too, accelerates to the right to push the book. Failure to recognize that the two forces of a third-law pair act on different objects leads to a contradiction, embodied in the famous horse-and-cart dilemma described in Fig. 5-22.

FIGURE 5-22 The horse exerts a force on the cart, and the cart exerts an equal but opposite force on the horse. So how can the two start moving? The answer comes from looking at the *net* force on the horse. This includes not only the backward-pointing force of the cart, but also a forward-pointing force that the road exerts on the horse in reaction to the horse's pushing against the road. Those two forces aren't part of a third-law pair, so they need not have equal magnitudes.

EXAMPLE 5-8	*Newton's Third Law*

On a surface with negligible friction, you push with force $\mathbf{F}$ on a book of mass m_1 that in turn pushes on a book of mass m_2 (Fig. 5-23). What is the force exerted by the second book on the first?

Solution

Newton's *third* law tells us that the force of the second book on the first is equal in magnitude to that of the first book on the second. But what is that force? We can find it by applying Newton's *second* law to the combination of two books, then individually to the second book. To help visualize what's going on, we draw in Fig. 5-23 not only the entire situation but also separate diagrams of the individual books and the forces acting on them. In working a problem involving more than one object, it's a good idea to draw separate force diagrams for each object.

The total mass m of the two books is $m_1 + m_2$, and the net force applied to this combination is $\mathbf{F}$. Then Newton's second law, $\mathbf{F}_{net} = m\mathbf{a}$, gives

$$\mathbf{a} = \frac{\mathbf{F}}{m} = \frac{\mathbf{F}}{m_1 + m_2}$$

FIGURE 5-23 Forces on the two books of Example 5-8. (*a*) The entire situation. (*b*) Book 1, showing the two forces that act on it. (*c*) Book 2, showing the single force acting on it.

for the acceleration of the two books as they move together. Now the only (horizontal) force on the second book is the force $\mathbf{F}_{12}$ exerted on it by the first book. So $\mathbf{F}_{12}$ is the net force on book 2, and we can apply Newton's second law to find this force:

$$\mathbf{F}_{12} = m_2\mathbf{a} = m_2 \frac{\mathbf{F}}{m_1 + m_2} = \frac{m_2}{m_1 + m_2}\mathbf{F}.$$

The answer we want is $\mathbf{F}_{21}$, the force book 2 exerts on book 1. Newton's third law tells us this force has the same magnitude as $\mathbf{F}_{12}$ we've just calculated, but points in the opposite direction:

$$\mathbf{F}_{21} = -\mathbf{F}_{12} = -\frac{m_2}{m_1 + m_2}\mathbf{F}.$$

Does all this make sense? We can see it does by considering the motion of the first book. It too undergoes an acceleration $\mathbf{a} = \mathbf{F}/(m_1 + m_2)$. And what is the *net* force on it? For the first book, there are *two* forces acting in the horizontal plane: the applied force $\mathbf{F}$ and the force $\mathbf{F}_{21}$ exerted by the second book. So the net force on the first book is

$$\mathbf{F}_1 = \mathbf{F} + \mathbf{F}_{21}.$$

Using our expression for $\mathbf{F}_{21}$ then gives

$$\mathbf{F}_1 = \mathbf{F} - \frac{m_2}{m_1 + m_2}\mathbf{F} = \frac{\mathbf{F}(m_1 + m_2) - m_2\mathbf{F}}{m_1 + m_2}$$

$$= \frac{m_1}{m_1 + m_2}\mathbf{F} = m_1\mathbf{a}.$$

This is consistent with Newton's second law: we know that both books have the same acceleration $\mathbf{a} = \mathbf{F}/(m_1 + m_2)$, and indeed we find that the force on the first book is the product of that acceleration with the book's mass. Our result shows how Newton's second and third laws are both necessary for a fully consistent description of the motion.

Understanding this example thoroughly will give you confidence in applying Newton's laws of motion correctly.

Tip

Forces and Objects Newton's second law relates the *net force* on an object to the mass and acceleration *of that object*. In this example, the force $\mathbf{F}$ acts on the first book, but the acceleration of the book is *not* $\mathbf{F}/m_1$, because $\mathbf{F}$ is not the *net* force on the book. The force $\mathbf{F}_{21}$ also acts on the first book, so its acceleration is $(\mathbf{F} + \mathbf{F}_{21})/m_1$, as we showed in this example.

EXERCISE A railroad switching engine with a mass of 7.2×10^4 kg exerts a force of 8.5×10^4 N against the tracks, while pulling a boxcar with a mass of 5.5×10^4 kg. What force does the boxcar exert on the engine?

Answer: 3.7×10^4 N

Some problems similar to Example 5-8: 38, 39, 43, 44

Got It!

Figure 5-24 shows two blocks with two forces acting on the pair. Are you justified in concluding that the net force on the larger block has magnitude 2 N?

A contact force such as the force between the books in Example 5-8 is called a **normal force** because it acts at right angles to the surfaces in contact. ("Normal" comes from the Latin for "according to the carpenter's square.") Other examples of normal forces include the upward force that a table or bridge exerts on objects it's supporting or the force perpendicular to a sloping surface supporting an object (Fig. 5-25). As we discussed in connection with Fig. 5-7, normal forces ultimately involve electrical interactions among atoms in the contacting surfaces.

FIGURE 5-24 Got It! Is the magnitude of the net force on the larger block equal to 2 N?

FIGURE 5-25 Normal forces. (*a*) The upward force of a table on a block. (*b*) The normal force of a sloping surface on a block. Also shown in each case is the gravitational force on the block; since both the normal force and the gravitational force act on the same object, they do not constitute a third-law pair. In (*a*) the two forces balance, but in (*b*) they add to give a net force that accelerates the block down the slope.

FIGURE 5-26 Standing on the ground involves two third-law pairs: gravitational forces that Earth exerts on you and that you exert on Earth, and normal forces between your feet and the ground. The net force on each object is zero and therefore neither accelerates.

FIGURE 5-27 Forces on you and on Earth as you fall freely toward one another. The forces constitute a third-law pair, but since each acts on a different object and is the only force acting on that object, both objects accelerate. By Newton's third law, the force on each object has the same magnitude, but Earth is so much more massive that its acceleration is negligibly small.

Newton's third law also applies to a force such as gravity that doesn't involve direct contact. Since Earth exerts a downward force on you, Newton's third law says you must exert an upward force on Earth. When you're standing on the ground, both those forces are cancelled by normal forces, as shown in Fig. 5-26. But if you're in free fall, then both you and Earth experience nonzero net forces. Following Newton's second law, you accelerate toward Earth—and Earth accelerates toward you (Fig. 5-27). Does this really happen? It does—but Newton's third law shows that the forces on you and on Earth have the same magnitude, and since Earth's mass is some 10^{23} times yours, Newton's second law implies its acceleration is negligibly small.

When we first listed Newton's laws in Section 5-2, we noted that Newton himself wrote the second law as a relation between force and the rate of change of "quantity of motion," or momentum, defined by $\mathbf{p} = m\mathbf{v}$. In Chapter 10, we'll see how Newton's second law in this form combines with the third law to make a powerful statement about the momentum of systems consisting of more than one particle.

5-8 MEASURING FORCE

We've talked a lot about force in this chapter, but have not said much about how to measure this important physical quantity. Newton's second law provides us a direct approach: apply an unknown force to a known mass and measure the resulting acceleration; the force is then the product of mass and acceleration.

Often, though, it's more convenient to use elastic objects such as springs to measure forces. A spring, when stretched or compressed, exerts forces on

FIGURE 5-28 (*a*) An unstretched spring attached to a wall. (*b*) When stretched, the spring exerts **tension forces** that oppose the stretching. (*c*) When compressed, it exerts **compression forces** that oppose the compression. The distance *x* in Equation 5-9 is measured from the unstretched position, here marked $x = 0$. Compression corresponds to a negative value of *x* and therefore a positive direction of force on the free end of the spring, and vice versa for stretching. In (*b*) and (*c*) the spring exerts a force not only on the hand but also on the wall.

whatever is deforming it (Fig. 5-28). In the case of a stretched spring, these are **tension forces**; for a compressed spring, they are **compression forces**. In either case, Newton's third law requires that the forces be oppositely directed but of equal magnitude to the external forces acting on the ends of the spring.

Over a limited range of stretching and compression, the force exerted by a spring is directly proportional to the distance stretched or compressed. When this direct proportionality holds, the spring is said to obey **Hooke's law**. We then write

$$F = -kx, \qquad \text{(Hooke's law; ideal spring)} \qquad (5\text{-}9)$$

where *x* is the amount by which the spring is stretched or compressed from its normal state, and where the minus sign indicates that the spring force is directed oppositely to the stretching or compression. The constant *k* is called the **spring constant**; its units are obviously N/m. A spring with $k = 200$ N/m (typical of a spring a few inches long that you might hold in your hand) would exert a force of 2 N when stretched or compressed 1 cm. If it were an **ideal spring**—one that obeyed Hooke's law (Equation 5-9) no matter how much it was deformed—it would exert a force of 200 N when stretched 1 m. A real spring a few inches long would break before reaching 1 m in length, and at any rate would cease to obey Hooke's law well before that point.

We can use a spring to make a **spring scale** by attaching an indicator and a scale calibrated in force units (Fig. 5-29). Common bathroom scales, hanging scales in supermarkets, and laboratory spring scales are all examples of such scales. Even electronic scales widely used at supermarket checkouts are spring scales, with their "spring" a material that produces an electrical signal when deformed by an applied force.

We can use a spring scale to weigh objects by attaching one end of the scale to a fixed point and hanging the unknown weight from the other end. When the object hangs at rest on the scale, the scale force balances the gravitational force *mg*, and is therefore equal in magnitude to the object's weight. Since mass and weight are proportional at a given location, the spring scale also provides a measure of the object's mass.

FIGURE 5-29 A simple spring scale, made from a spring of known spring constant *k*, an indicating needle, and a scale calibrated in force units.

EXAMPLE 5-9	*Weighing a Fish*

When a fish is suspended from a spring of spring constant $k = 320$ N/m, the spring stretches 15 cm. What are the weight and mass of the fish?

Solution
From Equation 5-9, a 15-cm stretch corresponds to a spring force of magnitude

$$F = kx = (320 \text{ N/m})(0.15 \text{ m}) = 48 \text{ N}.$$

Since the net force on the fish is zero, the magnitude of the fish's weight is also 48 N. But weight is given by $W = mg$, so $m = W/g = (48 \text{ N})/(9.8 \text{ m/s}^2) = 4.9$ kg.

Apparent Weight

When a spring scale is in an accelerating reference frame, its reading—called the **apparent weight**—differs from the gravitational force mg. Why? Because the object it's weighing is also accelerating, so Newton's laws require a net force on that object. If the only forces acting are gravity and the spring force of the scale, then those two forces can't balance. We've already seen a special case of apparent weight in Section 5-6, where we found that the apparent weight of an object in free fall is zero. In general, the scale reading will be more or less than the actual weight depending on whether the acceleration is upward or downward, as shown in Fig. 5-30 and Example 5-10.

FIGURE 5-30 In an elevator accelerating upward your apparent weight is more than your real weight!

EXAMPLE 5-10	*A Helicopter Ride*

A helicopter rises vertically, carrying a load of concrete to make the foundation for a ski lift. A 35-kg bag of concrete is resting on a scale in the helicopter. A construction worker in the copter notes that the scale reads 280 N. What is the helicopter's acceleration?

Solution

This problem is similar to Example 5-7. The two forces acting on the bag of concrete are the force of gravity $\mathbf{F}_g$ and the force of the scale $\mathbf{F}_s$ (Fig. 5-31). Newton's second law tells us that the net force is the product of mass and acceleration:

$$\mathbf{F}_{net} = \mathbf{F}_g + \mathbf{F}_s = m\mathbf{a}.$$

Since the motion is entirely vertical, we need work only with the vertical component of this equation. Choosing the positive y direction upward, the vertical component of the downward gravitational force is $-mg$; that of the scale force is positive and is equal to the magnitude F_s of the scale force. Then the y component of Newton's second law for this case becomes

$$-mg + F_s = ma_y,$$

so the vertical acceleration is

$$a_y = \frac{-mg + F_s}{m} = -g + \frac{F_s}{m} = -9.8 \text{ m/s}^2 + \frac{280 \text{ N}}{35 \text{ kg}}$$

$$= -1.8 \text{ m/s}^2.$$

What does this negative result mean? It means that the direction of the helicopter's *acceleration* is downward—even though the helicopter is *moving* upward. That is, its speed is decreasing at the rate of 1.8 m/s² even as it rises. The result of this example is consistent with that of Example 5-7. There, a downward acceleration would result in a cable tension lower than the weight mg. Here, a downward acceleration results in a scale reading lower than the weight, as suggested by the length of the force vectors in Fig. 5-31.

FIGURE 5-31 Forces on the concrete of Example 5-10.

Tip

Don't Confuse Acceleration and Velocity As early as Chapter 2 we emphasized that knowing the acceleration at some instant does not tell you anything about velocity at that instant, and vice versa. Rather, acceleration is the *rate of change* of velocity. It doesn't depend on the instantaneous magnitude of the velocity, nor on its direction. This example, with an upward velocity but downward acceleration, is a good case in point. The magnitude and direction of the helicopter's velocity are completely irrelevant.

EXERCISE A 65-kg person steps on a spring scale in the elevator of Example 5-7. Even though the scale measures force, it's calibrated in kilograms under the assumption that $g = 9.8$ m/s². What does it read?

Answer: 72 kg

Some problems similar to Example 5-10: 33, 57, 58, 66

CHAPTER SYNOPSIS

Summary

1. Newton's **first law of motion** states that a body continues in uniform motion unless acted on by a nonzero net force. Uniform motion is a natural state; the study of motion then emphasizes not the cause of motion itself, but the cause of *changes* in motion.

2. Newton's **second law of motion** quantifies the change in motion brought about by a force. The law states that the rate of change of a body's momentum (product of mass and velocity; symbol **p**) is equal to the net force on the body:

$$F_{net} = \frac{d\mathbf{p}}{dt}.$$

As long as the mass of the body does not change, Newton's second law can also be written in the form

$$F_{net} = m\mathbf{a}.$$

Here F_{net} is the **net force** on a body—that is, the vector sum of all the individual interaction forces acting on the body. The SI unit of force is the **newton**, defined as the force that gives a 1-kg mass an acceleration of 1 m/s^2.

3. **Weight** is the force of gravity on an object: $\mathbf{W} = m\mathbf{g}$. In an accelerated frame of reference, the **apparent weight** differs from the gravitational force; in particular, the apparent weight of an object in free fall is zero.

4. Newton's **third law of motion** states that forces always come in pairs. When one object exerts a force on another, the second object exerts an oppositely directed force of equal magnitude back on the first. Newton's second and third laws together permit a consistent description of the motions of interacting objects.

5. Elastic objects such as springs provide a practical way of measuring forces. When the force exerted by a spring is directly proportional to the amount of stretch or compression, the spring is said to obey **Hooke's law**; the force is then given by

$$F = -kx, \quad \text{(Hooke's law)}$$

where k is the **spring constant**, with SI units of N/m.

Terms You Should Understand

(Pairs are closely related terms whose distinction is important; number in parentheses is chapter section where term first appears.)

dynamics (introduction)
Aristotle, Galileo, Newton (5-1)
force, net force, interaction force (5-2)
momentum (5-2)
Newton's laws of motion (5-2, 5-7)
inertia (5-2)
gravitational, electroweak, color forces (5-3)
mass, weight (5-5)
apparent weight (5-5, 5-8), weightlessness (5-5)
third-law pair (5-7)
normal force (5-7)
tension force, compression force (5-8)
Hooke's law (5-8)
spring constant (5-8)

Symbols You Should Recognize

F (5-2)
p (5-2)
N (5-4)
g (5-5)
W (5-5)
k (5-8)

Problems You Should Be Able to Solve

calculating force, mass, or acceleration from the other two quantities (5-4)
calculating weight or mass given the other (5-5)
solving for forces or accelerations in one-dimensional situations (5-6)
applying Newton's second and third laws together in one-dimensional situations (5-7)
determining spring force, extension/compression, or spring constant given the other two quantities (5-8)
determining apparent weight (5-8)

Limitations to Keep in Mind

Newton's laws apply only when relative velocities are much less than the speed of light; aside from that restriction, the basic material of this chapter is universally applicable.
Newton's laws are valid in inertial reference frames.
Newton's second law in the form $\mathbf{F} = m\mathbf{a}$ is valid only when mass remains constant; the form $\mathbf{F} = d\mathbf{p}/dt$ is more general.
Real springs deviate from ideal Hooke's law behavior when stretched or compressed substantially.

QUESTIONS

1. Distinguish between the Aristotelian and Galilean/Newtonian view of the natural state of motion.
2. Use Newton's laws of motion to explain the function of a car airbag.
3. A ball bounces off a wall with the same speed it had before it hit the wall. Has its momentum changed? Has a force acted on the ball? Has a force acted on the wall? Relate your answers to Newton's laws of motion.
4. We often use the term "inertia" to describe human sluggishness. How is this usage related to the meaning of inertia in physics?
5. My high school physics teacher defined mass as "inverse pushability aroundness." Comment.
6. Which of the fundamental forces do you deal with in everyday life? Give several examples.
7. Does a body necessarily move in the direction of the net force on it?
8. A truck crashes into a stalled car. A student trying to explain the physics of this event claims that no forces are involved; the car was just "in the way" so it got hit. Comment.
9. Can a motorcycle and a truck have the same momentum? Explain.
10. A barefooted astronaut kicks a ball across the recreation area of a space station. Does the ball's apparent weightlessness mean the astronaut's toes don't get hurt? Explain.
11. Does the length of time that a force is applied to an object affect the change in the object's momentum? Explain.
12. Does the length of time that a force is applied to an object affect the object's acceleration? Explain.
13. An elevator in the physics building at the University of Colorado includes a built-in physics demonstration consisting of a 10-kg mass suspended from a spring scale. Is the scale reading more than, less than, or equal to 98 N when the elevator (a) is stationary; (b) first starts moving upward; (c) moves steadily upward; (d) slows down on its way up; (e) starts moving downward; (f) moves steadily downward; (g) slows down on its way down?
14. The surface gravity of Jupiter's moon Io is one-fifth that of Earth. What would happen to your weight and to your mass if you were to travel to Io?
15. What does it mean to say that someone "weighs" 50 kilograms?
16. Consider two teams in a tug-of-war (Fig. 5-32). Newton's third law says that the force team A exerts on team B is equal in magnitude to the force team B exerts on team A. How, then, can either team win?
17. In paddling a canoe, you push water backward with your paddle. What force actually propels the canoe forward?
18. Two objects of different mass fall freely. Since their acceleration is the same (namely, *g*), does this mean the force on each is the same? Comment.

A   B

FIGURE 5-32 A tug-of-war (Question 16).

19. Is it possible for a nonzero net force to act on an object, without the object's speed changing? Explain.
20. As you sit in your chair, the chair exerts an upward force on you. Why don't you accelerate upward?
21. As you sit in a car, what direction is the horizontal component of the force exerted on you by the car seat (a) when the car accelerates in the forward direction; (b) when the car brakes while moving in a straight line; (c) while the car rounds a corner at constant speed?
22. As your plane accelerates down the runway, you take your keys from your pocket and suspend them by a thread. Do they hang vertically? Explain.
23. You weigh 140 lbs, but you're standing on a scale in an elevator and the scale reads 175 lbs. (a) Can you tell whether the elevator is moving up or down? (b) Can you tell whether the direction of the elevator's acceleration is up or down?
24. A friend thinks that astronauts are weightless because there is no gravity in outer space. Criticize this statement, and supply your friend with a correct explanation for weightlessness.
25. Why does your stomach seem to head for your throat when a high-speed elevator stops its upward journey?
26. A tractor-trailer truck is stopped at a red light. How can it ever get started, given that Newton's third law requires that the force of the trailer on the tractor be equal and opposite that of the tractor on the trailer?
27. I tell passengers in my car to buckle their seatbelts, explaining that I believe in the law of inertia. What's that got to do with seatbelts?
28. You're eating dinner on an airplane when the plane encounters sudden turbulence and drops abruptly downward. You've got your seatbelt on, but to your amazement your dinner rises momentarily off the seatback tray. What can you conclude about the magnitude of the downward acceleration caused by the turbulence?

PROBLEMS

ActivPhysics can help with these problems: All activities in Section 2, Forces and Motion.

Section 5-4 Newton's Second Law

1. A subway train has a mass of 1.5×10^6 kg. What force is required to accelerate the train at 2.5 m/s²?

2. A railroad locomotive with a mass of 6.1×10^4 kg can exert a force of 1.2×10^5 N. At what rate can it accelerate (a) by itself and (b) when pulling a 1.4×10^6-kg train?

3. A small plane starts down the runway with acceleration 7.2 m/s². If the force provided by its engine is 1.1×10^4 N, what is the plane's mass?

4. A car leaves the road traveling at 110 km/h and hits a tree, coming to a complete stop in 0.14 s. What average force does a seatbelt exert on a 60-kg passenger during this collision?

5. In an x-ray tube, electrons are accelerated to speeds on the order of 10^8 m/s, then slammed into a target where they come to a stop in about 10^{-18} s. Estimate the average stopping force on each electron.

6. A 280-kg crate is secured in a truck with ropes running horizontally forward and backward, as shown in Fig. 5-33. What is the maximum tension force these ropes must be able to withstand if the most rapid deceleration anticipated is 6.5 m/s²? Assume the tension is initially zero.

FIGURE 5-33 Problem 6.

7. Object A accelerates at 8.1 m/s² when a 3.3-N force is applied. Object B accelerates at 2.7 m/s² when the same force is applied. (a) How do the masses of the two objects compare? (b) If A and B were stuck together and accelerated by the 3.3-N force, what would be the acceleration of the composite object?

8. A hockey player strikes a 170-g puck, accelerating it from rest to 50 m/s. If the hockey stick is in contact with the puck for 2.5 ms, what is the average force applied by the stick?

9. By how much does the force required to stop a car increase if the initial speed is doubled and the stopping distance remains the same?

10. A car moving at 70 km/h collides with a concrete bridge support. The bridge support is unaffected, but the front of the car is compressed by 0.94 m. What average force must a seatbelt exert in order to restrain a 75-kg passenger during this collision?

11. The maximum braking force of a 1400-kg car is about 8.0 kN. Estimate the stopping distance when the car is traveling (a) 40 km/h; (b) 60 km/h; (c) 80 km/h; (d) 55 mi/h.

12. As a function of time, the velocity of an object of mass m is given by $\mathbf{v} = bt^2\hat{\mathbf{i}} + (ct + d)\hat{\mathbf{j}}$, where b, c, and d are constants with appropriate units. What is the force acting on the object, as a function of time?

13. A car moving at 50 km/h collides with a truck, and the front of the car is crushed 1.1 m as it comes to a complete stop. The driver is wearing a seatbelt, but the passenger is not. The passenger, obeying Newton's first law, keeps moving and slams into the dashboard after the car has stopped. If the dashboard compresses 5.0 cm on impact, find and compare the forces exerted on the driver by the seatbelt and on the passenger by the dashboard. Assume the two have the same 65-kg mass.

14. A 3800-kg jet touches down at 240 km/h on the deck of an aircraft carrier, and immediately deploys a parachute to slow itself down. If the plane comes to a stop in 170 m, what is the average force of air on the parachute? Assume the parachute provides essentially all the stopping force.

15. A 1.25-kg object is moving in the x direction at 17.4 m/s. 3.41 s later, it is moving at 26.8 m/s at 34.0° to the x axis. What are the magnitude and direction of the force applied during this time?

Section 5-5 Mass and Weight: The Force of Gravity

16. Show that the units of acceleration can be written N/kg. Why would it make sense to state g as 9.8 N/kg when talking about mass and weight?

17. My spaceship crashes on one of the Sun's nine planets. Fortunately, the ship's scales are intact, and show that my weight is 532 N. If I know my mass to be 60 kg, where am I? *Hint:* Consult Appendix E.

18. If I can barely lift a 35-kg concrete block on Earth, how massive a block can I lift on the moon?

19. A cereal box says "net weight 340 grams." What is the actual weight (a) in SI units? (b) in ounces?

20. I weigh 735 N. What's my mass?

21. A bridge specifies a maximum load of 10 tons. What's the maximum mass, in kilograms, that the bridge can carry?

22. The gravitational acceleration at a typical space shuttle altitude is about 93 percent of its surface value. What is the weight of a 68-kg astronaut in a shuttle at this altitude?

23. A neutron star is a fantastically dense object with the mass of a star crushed into a region about 10 km in diameter. If my mass is 75 kg, and if I would weigh 5.8×10^{14} N on a certain neutron star, what is the acceleration of gravity on the neutron star?

Section 5-6 Adding Forces

24. A 50-kg parachute jumper descends at a steady 40 km/h. What is the force of air on the parachute?

25. A rope can withstand a maximum tension force of 450 N before breaking. The rope is used to pull a 32-kg bucket of water upward. What is the maximum upward acceleration if the rope is not to break?

26. A 930-kg motorboat accelerates away from a dock at 2.3 m/s². Its propeller provides a thrust force of 3.9 kN. What is the drag force exerted by the water on the boat?

27. An elevator accelerates downward at 2.4 m/s². What force does the floor of the elevator exert on a 52-kg passenger?

28. What is the vertical lifting force on a 747 jetliner when the plane is (a) flying at constant altitude and (b) accelerating upward at 1.1 m/s²? The aircraft's mass is 4.5×10^5 kg.

29. An airplane encounters sudden turbulence, and you feel momentarily lighter. If your apparent weight seems to be about 70% of your normal weight, what are the magnitude and direction of the plane's acceleration?

30. A 74-kg tree surgeon rides a "cherry picker" lift (Fig. 5-34) to reach the upper branches of a tree. What force does the bucket of the lift exert on the surgeon when the bucket is (a) at rest; (b) moving upward at a steady 2.4 m/s; (c) moving downward at a steady 2.4 m/s; (d) accelerating upward at 1.7 m/s²; (e) accelerating downward at 1.7 m/s²?

FIGURE 5-34 Problem 30.

31. At liftoff, a space shuttle with 2.0×10^6-kg total mass undergoes an upward acceleration of 0.60g. (a) What is the total thrust force developed by its engines? (b) What force does the seat exert on a 60-kg astronaut during liftoff?

32. A ballet dancer (Fig. 5-35) executes a vertical jump during which the floor pushes up on his feet with a force 50% greater than his weight. What is his upward acceleration?

33. An elevator moves upward at 5.2 m/s. What is the minimum stopping time it can have if the passengers are to remain on the floor?

FIGURE 5-35 Mikhail Baryshnikov jumping (Problem 32).

34. A 2.50-kg object is moving along the x axis at 1.60 m/s. As it passes the origin, two forces $\mathbf{F}_1$ and $\mathbf{F}_2$ are applied, both in the y direction (plus or minus). $\mathbf{F}_1 = 15\,\hat{\jmath}$ N. The forces are applied for 3.00 s, after which the object is at the point $x = 4.80$ m, $y = 10.8$ m. Find $\mathbf{F}_2$.

Section 5-7 Newton's Third Law

35. What upward force does a 5600-kg elephant exert on Earth?

36. Blocks of 1.0, 2.0, and 3.0 kg are lined up on a table, as shown in Fig. 5-36. A rightward-pointing 12-N force is applied to the leftmost block. What force does the middle block exert on the rightmost one?

FIGURE 5-36 Problem 36 (Reverse left-right order of blocks for Problem 37).

37. Repeat the preceding problem, now with the left-right order of the blocks reversed. (That is, find the force on the rightmost mass, now 1.0 kg.)

38. A 68-kg astronaut pushes off a 420-kg satellite, exerting a force of 120 N for the 0.89 s they're in contact. (a) Find the speed of each after they've separated. (b) How far apart are they after 1.0 min?

39. I have a mass of 65 kg. If I jump off a 120-cm-high table, how far toward me does Earth move during the time I fall?

40. A child pulls an 11-kg wagon with a horizontal handle whose mass is 1.8 kg, giving the wagon and handle an acceleration of 2.3 m/s². (a) The tension at each end of the handle is different. Why? (b) Find the tension at each end of the handle.

41. A 2200-kg airplane is pulling two gliders, the first of mass 310 kg and the second of mass 260 kg, down the runway with an acceleration of 1.9 m/s^2 (Fig. 5-37). Neglecting the mass of the two ropes and any frictional forces, determine (a) the horizontal thrust of the plane's propeller; (b) the tension force in the first rope; (c) the tension force in the second rope; and (d) the net force on the first glider.

FIGURE 5-37 Problem 41.

42. In a tractor pulling contest, a 2300-kg tractor pulls a 4900-kg sledge with an acceleration of 0.61 m/s^2. If the tractor exerts a horizontal force of 7700 N on the ground, determine the magnitudes of (a) the force of the tractor on the sledge, (b) the force of the sledge on the tractor, and (c) the frictional force exerted on the sledge by the ground.

Section 5-8 Measuring Force

43. What force is necessary to stretch a spring 48 cm, if the spring constant is 270 N/m?
44. A 35-N force is applied to a spring with spring constant $k = 220$ N/m. How much does the spring stretch?
45. A spring stretches 22 cm when a 40-N force is applied. If a 6.1-kg mass is suspended from the spring, how much will it stretch?
46. A spring with spring constant $k = 340$ N/m is used to weigh a 6.7-kg fish. How far does the spring stretch?
47. A father pulls his 27-kg daughter across frictionless ice, using a horizontal spring with spring constant 160 N/m. If the spring is stretched 32 cm from its equilibrium position, what is the child's acceleration?
48. You want to make a spring scale that reads directly in mass units. If a change of 1 cm in the position of the scale's indicating needle is to correspond to a mass difference of 100 g, what should the spring constant be?
49. A biologist is studying the growth of rats in an orbiting space station. To determine a rat's mass, she puts it in a 320-g cage, attaches a spring scale, and pulls so the scale reads 0.46 N. If the resulting acceleration of the rat and cage is 0.40 m/s^2, what is the rat's mass?
50. An elastic tow rope has a spring constant of 1300 N/m. It is connected between a truck and a 1900-kg car. As the truck tows the car, the rope stretches 55 cm. Starting from rest, how far do the truck and car move in 1 min? Assume the car experiences negligible friction.

51. A 7.2-kg mass is hanging from the ceiling of an elevator by a spring of spring constant 150 N/m whose unstretched length is 80 cm. What is the overall length of the spring when the elevator (a) starts moving upward with acceleration 0.95 m/s^2; (b) moves upward at a steady 14 m/s; (c) comes to a stop while moving upward at 14 m/s, taking 9.0 s to do so? (d) If the elevator measures 3.2 m from floor to ceiling, what is the maximum acceleration it could undergo without the 7.2-kg mass hitting the floor?
52. An accelerometer consists of a spring of spring constant $k = 1.25$ N/m and unstretched length $\ell_0 = 10.0$ cm fastened to a frictionless surface by a pivot that allows it to swivel in any direction in a horizontal plane. A 50.0-g mass is attached to the other end of the spring, as shown in Fig. 5-38. The whole system is mounted securely in an automobile. When the vehicle accelerates, the spring provides a force to keep the 50-g mass accelerating with the vehicle; by measuring the stretch of the spring, the acceleration can then be determined. To calibrate the accelerometer, circles marked with values of acceleration can be drawn on its frictionless surface. (a) How far apart should the circles be if each represents an acceleration of 0.250 m/s^2 larger than the next smaller circle? (b) What should be the radius of the circle marked 2.0 m/s^2? (c) How do you read the direction of the car's acceleration from this device?

FIGURE 5-38 Problem 52.

Paired Problems

(Both problems in a pair involve the same principles and techniques. If you can get the first problem, you should be able to solve the second one.)

53. Starting from rest, a 940-kg racing car covers 400 m in 4.95 s. What is the average force acting on the car?
54. Starting from rest, a 200-g hockey puck moves 1.1 m during the 75 ms it's in contact with the stick. What average force does the stick exert on the puck?

55. In an egg-dropping contest, a student encases an 85-g egg in a styrofoam block. If the force on the egg is not to exceed 1.5 N, and if the block hits the ground at 1.2 m/s, by how much must the styrofoam crush?

56. In a front-end collision, a 1300-kg car with shock-absorbing bumpers can withstand a maximum force of 65 kN before damage occurs. If the maximum speed for a nondamaging collision is 10 km/h, by how much must the bumper be able to move relative to the car?

57. You step into an elevator, and it accelerates to a downward speed of 9.2 m/s in 2.1 s. How does your apparent weight during this acceleration time compare with your actual weight?

58. A spacecraft blasts off from the moon's surface, achieving an upward speed of 2.5 km/s at the end of its rocket firing. During the firing, an astronaut on board feels she weighs exactly the same as she would on Earth. How long does the rocket firing last?

59. A 20-kg fish at the end of a fishing line is being yanked vertically into a boat. When its acceleration reaches 2.2 m/s², the line breaks and the fish goes free. What is the maximum tension the line can tolerate without breaking?

60. Tarzan (mass 73 kg) slides down a vine that can withstand a maximum tension of 620 N before breaking. What minimum acceleration must Tarzan have?

61. A 2.0-kg mass and a 3.0-kg mass are on a horizontal frictionless surface, connected by a massless spring with spring constant $k = 140$ N/m. A 15-N force is applied to the larger mass, as shown in Fig. 5-39. How much does the spring stretch from its equilibrium length?

FIGURE 5-39 Problem 61.

62. Two large crates, with masses 640 kg and 490 kg, are connected by a stiff, massless spring ($k = 8.1$ kN/m) and propelled along an essentially frictionless, level factory floor by a force applied horizontally to the more massive crate. If the spring compresses 5.1 cm from its equilibrium length, what is the applied force?

Supplementary Problems

63. In throwing a 200-g ball, your hand exerts a constant upward force of 9.4 N for 0.32 s. How high does the ball rise after leaving your hand?

64. What downward force is exerted on the air by the blades of a 4300-kg helicopter when it is (a) hovering at constant altitude; (b) dropping at 21 m/s with speed decreasing at 3.2 m/s²; (c) rising at 17 m/s with speed increasing at 3.2 m/s²; (d) rising at a steady 15 m/s; (e) rising at 15 m/s with speed decreasing at 3.2 m/s²?

65. What engine thrust (force) is needed to accelerate a rocket of mass m (a) downward at $1.40g$ near Earth's surface: (b) upward at $1.40g$ near Earth's surface; (c) at $1.40g$ in interstellar space far from any star or planet?

66. An elevator cable can withstand a maximum tension of 19,500 N before breaking. The elevator has a mass of 490 kg, and a maximum acceleration of 2.24 m/s². Engineering safety standards require that the cable tension never exceed two-thirds of the breaking tension. How many 65-kg people can the elevator safely accommodate?

67. You have a mass of 60 kg, and you jump from a 78-cm-high table onto a hard floor. (a) If you keep your legs rigid, you come to a stop in a distance of 2.9 cm, as your body tissues compress slightly. What force does the floor exert on you? (b) If you bend your knees when you land, the bulk of your body comes to a stop over a distance of 0.54 m. Now estimate the force exerted on you by the floor. Neglect the fact that your legs stop in a shorter distance than the rest of you.

68. An F-14 jet fighter has a mass of 1.6×10^4 kg and an engine thrust of 2.7×10^5 N. A 747 jumbo jet has a mass of 3.6×10^5 kg and a total engine thrust of 7.7×10^5 N. Is it possible for either plane to climb vertically, with no lift from its wings? If so, what vertical acceleration could it achieve?

69. A spider of mass m_s drapes a silk thread of negligible mass over a stick with its far end a distance h off the ground as shown in Fig. 5-40. The stick is lubricated by a drop of dew, so that there is essentially no friction between silk and stick. The spider waits on the ground until a fly of mass $m_f (m_f > m_s)$ lands on the other end of the silk and sticks to it. The spider immediately begins to climb her end of the silk. (a) With what acceleration must she climb to keep the fly from falling? (b) If she climbs with acceleration a_s, at what height y above the ground will she encounter the fly?

FIGURE 5-40 Problem 69.

70. As the Mars Pathfinder spacecraft fell toward its landing in 1997, a rocket fired for approximately 2.3 s to slow it from about 61 m/s to essentially zero speed, after which it dropped freely to the Martian surface. What force did the rocket engine exert on the 276-kg spacecraft? (Don't forget gravity, which has essentially its Martian surface value.)

71. Three identical massless springs of unstretched length ℓ and spring constant k are connected to three equal masses m as shown in Fig. 5-41. A force is applied at the top of the upper spring to give the whole system the same acceleration a. Determine the length of each spring.

FIGURE 5-41 Problem 71.

72. A 90-kg weightlifter is standing on a scale calibrated in newtons, holding a 140-kg barbell. (a) What does the scale read? (b) The lifter then gives the barbell a constant upward acceleration. If the scale reads 2400 N, what is the acceleration of the barbell? (c) Suppose the lifter were in an orbiting spaceship with his feet contacting an identical scale. If he gave the barbell the same acceleration as in (b), what would the scale read? Assume in (b) and (c) that the lifter keeps his body rigid, bending only his arms, and neglect the mass of the arms and any downward acceleration of the lifter.

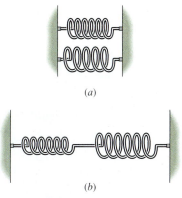

(a)

(b)

FIGURE 5-42 Problem 73.

73. Two springs have the same unstretched length but different spring constants k_1 and k_2. (a) If they are connected side-by-side and stretched a distance x, as shown in Fig. 5-42a, show that the force exerted by the combination is $(k_1 + k_2)x$. (b) If they are now connected end-to-end and the combination is stretched a distance x (Fig. 5-42b), show that they exert a force $k_1 k_2 x/(k_1 + k_2)$.

74. A tow truck exerts a 750-N force on a 54.4-kg tow chain. The other end of the chain is attached to a car, and the whole system accelerates at 0.436 m/s^2. Find (a) the force exerted on the truck by the cable, (b) the force exerted on the car by the cable, and (c) the mass of the car. Assume there are no horizontal forces acting on the car except for the cable. Why are your answers to (a) and (b) different?

75. Although we usually write Newton's law for one-dimensional motion in the form $F = ma$, the most basic version of the law reads $F = \dfrac{d(mv)}{dt}$. The simpler form holds only when the mass is constant. (a) Consider an object whose mass may be changing, and show that the rule for the derivative of a product (see Appendix A) can be used to write Newton's law in the form $F = ma + v\dfrac{dm}{dt}$. (b) A railroad car is being pulled beneath a grain elevator that dumps in grain at the rate of 450 kg/s. What force must be applied to keep the car moving at a constant 2.0 m/s?

6 Using Newton's Laws

This roller coaster's path is anything but a straight line at constant speed, and therefore it's subject to a net force. Can you identify the individual forces that sum to provide that net force?

The preceding chapter introduced Newton's three laws of motion and used them in simple one-dimensional applications. Now we apply those laws in a wide variety of physical situations, most involving two dimensions. The methods we develop are at the heart of all applications of Newton's laws, from textbook problems to the complicated systems that guide spacecraft to distant planets. Because this chapter emphasizes methods for applying Newton's laws, it consists largely of examples. We also introduce new material on frictional forces and air resistance, and elaborate further on circular motion.

Tip

Look for the Underlying Principles This chapter contains a wide variety of examples. As you study them, don't think of each as something new to learn; rather, try to understand how each is an application of the same underlying physical principles—namely, Newton's laws. That will build your confidence in applying those principles in new situations—always a challenge for a scientist or engineer.

6-1 USING NEWTON'S SECOND LAW

Newton's second law, $\mathbf{F}_{net} = m\mathbf{a}$, is the cornerstone of mechanics. Using it, we can develop faster skis, engineer structures that won't fall down, design safer roads, specify the properties of a climbing rope or the thrust of a rocket, determine how much space an airplane needs to turn, invent better running tracks, and solve a myriad of practical problems.

The first example we work in great detail, and from it we develop a general strategy for solving Newton's law problems. You should follow this example closely, and understand how the strategy we develop is grounded in Newton's simple statement that the vector sum of individual interaction forces acting on an object determines the object's acceleration. Further, you should recognize that our problem-solving strategy not only gives you numerical answers but also helps you to understand the underlying physics.

EXAMPLE 6-1	*Skiing*

A skier of mass $m = 65$ kg slides down a slope that makes an angle $\theta = 32°$ to the horizontal, as shown in Fig. 6-1. Find (a) the skier's acceleration and (b) the magnitude of the force the snow exerts on the skier. The snow is so slippery that you can neglect friction.

Solution

What's this problem all about? It's about the motion of the skier. So the skier is what we're interested in; it's the object to which we're going to apply Newton's law. So we've completed an important first step in solving our problem:

1. **Identify the object of interest.**
   Remember that Newton's law relates the net force *on an object* to the mass and acceleration *of that object*. So unless you've clearly identified the object or objects of interest, you won't be able to apply Newton's law correctly.

   Newton's law says that the net force on an object determines the object's acceleration. Here we're interested in the skier's acceleration, so we need the net force on the skier. The net force is the sum of the individual interaction forces acting on the skier. So our next step is . . .

2. **Identify the individual interaction forces acting on the object of interest.**
   How to do this? The best way is to *draw diagrams.* If a diagram of the physical situation isn't provided, draw one.

FIGURE 6-1 What's the skier's acceleration?

Then think about all the interaction forces that may be acting on the object of interest, and draw force vectors right on your diagram, as we've done in Fig. 6-1. What are the forces acting on the skier? Clearly there's the gravitational force $\mathbf{F}_g$, which points straight downward. If there were no other forces acting, the skier's acceleration would be straight downward. But that isn't the case; rather, the skier's motion is constrained to follow the slope, so there must be at least one other force acting. Skier and slope are in contact, so there's a contact force of the slope acting on the skier. As we saw in Chapter 5, this force is perpendicular, or **normal**, to the slope's surface; we call it the **normal force**, **N**. Of course Newton's third law also requires that the skier exert a normal force on the slope, and for that matter a gravitational force on Earth—but neither the slope nor Earth are the objects that interest us here, so those forces don't concern us, because they don't act *on* the object of interest.

Are there any other forces on the skier? We're told that friction is negligible; we assume the same is true of air resistance. (These are valid assumptions as long as those forces are much smaller than the normal and gravitational forces. Later in the chapter, we'll show how to deal with friction and air resistance when they aren't negligible.) There's nothing else in contact with the skier, and there are no other relevant action-at-a-distance forces, so it looks like the gravitational force and the normal force are the only interaction forces acting. Figure 6-1 is then a complete picture of the situation.

Pictures such as Fig. 6-1 can be cluttered and confusing. It's best to *redraw a simpler diagram* that shows only the object of interest and the forces acting on it. This is the **free-body diagram** that we introduced in Example 5-7. The term "free body" indicates that the diagram shows the object of interest in isolation from other objects. To make things even simpler, we represent the object in the free-body diagram by a dot, and start all the force vectors with their tails at that dot. Figure 6-2 is a free-body diagram for the skier.

Tip

Free-body Diagrams Drawing a free-body diagram helps isolate the object of interest, making it clear which forces are acting *on that object*. Only those forces go into the vector sum comprising the net force in Newton's law. Furthermore, with extended objects such as people or cars, the different forces may be acting at different points, or, with a force such as gravity, on the entire extended object. In later chapters we'll see cases where this issue is important; here, where we treat objects as point particles, it's clearer and physically valid to show the object as a single point with all forces acting at that point. In Fig. 6-2, we show a ghostly outline of the skier to remind you that the dot at the tail of the force vectors represents the skier. We'll eliminate this ghostly image in subsequent free-body diagrams.

Now we know all the interaction forces that sum to give the net force in Newton's law, so we're ready for the next step:

3. **Write Newton's law, $\mathbf{F}_{net} = m\mathbf{a}$, using for $\mathbf{F}_{net}$ the vector sum of the forces you've identified.**

Remember that forces are vectors, so Newton's law is a vector equation. For our skier the net force comprises the

gravitational force and the normal force, so $\mathbf{F}_{net} = m\mathbf{a}$ becomes

$$\mathbf{N} + \mathbf{F}_g = m\mathbf{a}.$$

At this point we've done all the physics; the rest is math.

Tip

Vectors Tell It All Did you think we should put a minus sign on $\mathbf{F}_g$, since the gravitational force is downward? **NOT YET!** A vector includes full information about direction; the words "positive" and "negative" don't apply to vectors. We've been careful to write Newton's law as a vector equation, expressing forces and acceleration as vector quantities. In doing this, we didn't need to worry at all about directions or signs; a vector symbol such as **N** or $\mathbf{F}_g$ tells it all. We really do want to *add* the normal force (a vector quantity) and the gravitational force (another vector quantity) to get the net force. We gave this same tip with Example 5-7, but it's so important that we repeat it here. By the way, it's crucial that you write vectors in a way that clearly distinguishes them from scalars; we use boldface in this text, but you probably put an arrow over a vector's symbol when writing by hand. Whatever you do, don't get sloppy and forget those vector signs!

Our vector equation is really two scalar equations, one for each of the two components on two perpendicular coordinate axes. What axes? That's entirely up to you. Again, coordinate systems aren't reality; they're mathematical constructs we use to solve problems. The vector quantities in our Newton's law equation are real, physical forces and accelerations; in contrast, how they break up into components depends on your choice of coordinate system.

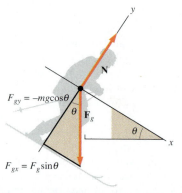

FIGURE 6-2 Forces on the skier are the gravitational force $\mathbf{F}_g$ and the normal force **N** exerted by the slope. A free-body diagram, representing the skier as a simple dot, shows all forces acting at the same point. The ghostly image of the skier reminds you what the dot represents; we'll eliminate it in subsequent free-body diagrams. We've added a suitable coordinate system and indicated similar triangles (shading) that help in finding the components of $\mathbf{F}_g$.

That said, a smart choice of a coordinate system can make the math much easier—although it can never alter the physical meaning of the answer. To move on with solving our equation, the next step is therefore to . . .

4. **Choose a convenient coordinate system, and draw the coordinate axes on your force diagrams.**
You might instinctively rush to draw a coordinate system with x axis horizontal and y axis vertical, like you've seen over and over in math and science courses. But it's your choice! In this problem a smarter choice is a coordinate system with one axis along the slope and the other axis perpendicular. Why? Because then the acceleration—a quantity we're asked to find—has a component along only one coordinate axis. So does one of the two forces (namely, **N**). So we'll go with this slightly odd-looking coordinate system, which we've indicated in the free-body diagram, Fig. 6-2. To show that the choice of coordinate system doesn't matter, we're going to rework this problem in Example 6-2 using a horizontal-vertical coordinate system.
Now we're ready for the next step:

5. **Write your equation for Newton's law in components along the chosen coordinate axes.**
Here our vector equation is $\mathbf{N} + \mathbf{F}_g = m\mathbf{a}$. Formally, its components are

x component: $\qquad\qquad N_x + F_{gx} = ma_x$

and

y component: $\qquad\qquad N_y + F_{gy} = ma_y$,

but this doesn't help much yet because we don't know the x and y components of the vectors **N**, $\mathbf{F}_g$, and **a**. But because the skier's motion is constrained to the straight line of the slope, the acceleration vector **a** must point downslope—which, by our choice of coordinate axes in Fig. 6-2, is the positive x direction. Thus a_x is just the magnitude, a, of the acceleration vector, and $a_y = 0$. The normal force is just as easy: it's perpendicular to the slope, entirely in the $+y$ direction. So $N_y = N$, the magnitude of the normal force, and $N_x = 0$.
Finally, there's the gravitational force. We've shaded two triangles in Fig. 6-2; they're similar triangles, and therefore the angle that $\mathbf{F}_g$ makes with the negative y axis (which, remember, is not vertical but perpendicular to the slope) is the same angle θ that the slope makes with the horizontal. The vector $\mathbf{F}_g$ in Fig. 6-2 forms the hypotenuse of a right triangle whose sides are the components of $\mathbf{F}_g$. Since the sine of an angle is the ratio of the side opposite the angle to the hypotenuse, we have $F_{gx} = F_g \sin\theta$. Is the sign right? Yes: because we've defined the positive x axis as pointing *down* the slope, the x component of the gravitational force is positive. But we've defined the y axis as *upward* from the slope, so the y component of the gravitational force is *negative;* the definition of cosine as the ratio of adjacent side to the hypotenuse shows that $F_{gy} = -F_g \cos\theta$. Finally, we

know from Chapter 5 that the magnitude of the gravitational force is $F_g = mg$, with g the acceleration due to gravity. Having worked out the components of the three relevant vectors, our component equations become

x component: $\qquad\qquad mg\sin\theta = ma$

and

y component: $\qquad\qquad N - mg\cos\theta = 0$.

Next, we can . . .

6. **Solve the equations for the quantities of interest.**
Here we were asked for the acceleration and the force the slope exerts on the skier. The x component equation immediately gives the first of these:

$$a = g\sin\theta.$$

This result shows that the skier's acceleration is constant and independent of mass, just as it would be in a vertical fall. But the magnitude of the acceleration is reduced by the factor $\sin\theta$ from the free-fall value g. This reduced gravitational acceleration on sloping surfaces helped Galileo study the behavior of falling bodies.
We also want the force the snow exerts on the skier; this is the normal force **N**. The y component equation solves to give

$$N = mg\cos\theta.$$

The equations give only the magnitudes of **a** and **N**, but the directions of these vectors are obvious from our diagrams: downslope for **a** and perpendicular to the slope for **N**.
Next is a really important step:

7. **Ask whether your answers make sense.**
In particular, *look at special cases* where the answer is more obvious. Not only will this help you catch mistakes, but it can greatly increase your understanding of physics. After all, the numerical value of a skier's acceleration on a 32° slope doesn't tell you a whole lot; understanding how that acceleration varies with angle is much more enlightening.
Two special cases for the situation in this example are the extreme values for θ: $\theta = 0$ and $\theta = 90°$. In the former case we have a horizontal surface, and our answer $a = g\sin\theta$ shows that the acceleration is zero. Of course: there's no component of the gravitational force on a horizontal slope, so no acceleration. Meanwhile our expression for N shows that, with $\theta = 0$ and therefore $\cos\theta = 1$, the magnitude N of the normal force is equal to the skier's weight mg. Of course: with a horizontal surface the normal force is vertical, opposite the direction of the gravitational force. With zero acceleration, the net force must be zero, so the gravitational and normal forces must have equal magnitudes and opposite directions. At the other extreme $\theta = 90°$ and the slope is vertical. Then $a = g$ and the hapless skier is in free fall. Since $\cos 90° = 0$, the result $N = mg\cos\theta$ becomes $N = 0$. Thus there's no force between slope and skier, and it doesn't matter whether the slope is there or not.

So the extreme cases make sense—as do the in-between cases, with acceleration varying from a small fraction of g at low angles to approaching g at steep angles, and the normal force being nearly the skier's weight at low angles but becoming less significant as the slope steepens.

We could also make some simple checks on our answers; for example, do they represent the right physical quantities? Since trig functions are dimensionless, our answer for a has the same units as g, which we know to be an acceleration. So that's OK. And our answer for N has the same units as mg, which we know to be the force called weight. So that's OK, too.

Finally, this problem asked for some numerical answers, so as our last step we . . .

8. Insert the given numerical values and do the arithmetic.

$$a = g \sin \theta = (9.8 \text{ m/s}^2)(\sin 32°) = 5.2 \text{ m/s}^2$$

and

$$N = mg \cos \theta = (65 \text{ kg})(9.8 \text{ m/s}^2)(\cos 32°) = 540 \text{ N}.$$

Although we could have put numbers in much earlier, there's far more insight to be gained by keeping problems in symbolic form until the very end. Furthermore, it's easier to write a compact symbol such as g than a number and its units, such as 9.8 m/s^2.

Although we checked the algebraic answers to see if they made sense, it's a good idea to check numerical answers, too. Here the units work out to give m/s^2 and N, respectively. Furthermore, the numerical answers make sense; 5.2 m/s^2 is less than g but not dramatically so; that seems reasonable for this significant slope. Had our acceleration come out either greater than g or extremely small, we should have been suspicious of a mistake in algebra or arithmetic.

Congratulations! You've now been through a Newton's law problem in great detail and should understand thoroughly the physics and mathematics leading to its solution.

EXERCISE At what angle should you tilt a surface so an object sliding down it without friction experiences an acceleration of $0.10g$?

Answer: 5.7°

Some problems similar to Example 6-1: 4–7

2.1.4

Sliding on an Incline, Question 1

We took a lot of time with Example 6-1, because the methods developed there work in all Newton's law problems. Below we summarize the basic strategy we developed in Example 6-1, which can be used for solving all such problems:

Strategy

Solving Newton's Law Problems

1. Identify the object of interest.
2. Identify all the individual interaction forces acting *on* the object, and draw them as force vectors on a free-body diagram that shows the object of interest in isolation as a simple dot.
3. Write Newton's second law, $\mathbf{F}_{net} = m\mathbf{a}$, using for $\mathbf{F}_{net}$ the vector sum of the forces you identified in step (2). Remember that you're dealing with *vector* quantities.
4. Choose a convenient coordinate system, and draw the coordinate axes on your free-body diagram.
5. Write the components of your vector equation in your chosen coordinate system. Be guided by the geometry of the free-body force diagram and by any constraints on the motion (like the constraint in Example 6-1 that the skier move along the slope).
6. Solve the equations symbolically for whatever quantities the problem asks for.
7. Ask whether your results make sense, in particular by checking special cases where the answers are obvious.
8. If the problem calls for numerical answers, insert numerical values and work the arithmetic.

Don't memorize these steps. Refer to them as you begin a problem and be sure to follow them thoroughly. You'll gradually come to see this problem-solving strategy as simply reflecting the full meaning of Newton's second law. Avoid the temptation to take shortcuts: following the full strategy will keep you out of trouble and help reinforce your sense that all problems involving Newton's law are essentially similar.

2.10
Pushing a Crate Up an Incline

EXAMPLE 6-2	*Another Coordinate System*

Rework Example 6-1 to find the acceleration of the skier at an arbitrary slope angle θ, this time in a coordinate system with x axis horizontal and y axis vertical.

Solution
This is the same physical problem as Example 6-1, so steps 1–3 of our strategy—steps that deal with physical reality independent of our arbitrary choice of coordinate system—remain the same.
1. The object of interest is the skier.
2. The forces on the skier are the gravitational force and the normal force. We've already drawn the physical situation in Figs. 6-1 and 6-2; here we redraw the free-body diagram as Fig. 6-3.
3. The vector forces don't depend on choice of coordinate system, so Newton's law remains as in Example 6-1: $\mathbf{N} + \mathbf{F}_g = m\mathbf{a}$.
4. We're told to use a horizontal-vertical coordinate system. We still have some choice here (up or down, left or right), and we've arbitrarily chosen the y axis upward and the x axis to the right. We show this coordinate system in Fig. 6-3.

5. Now we find the components. Formally, we still have

   x component: $N_x + F_{gx} = ma_x$

   and

   y component: $N_y + F_{gy} = ma_y$,

   but now things get different. In our new coordinate system, the gravitational force $\mathbf{F}_g$ is actually simpler: its vertically downward direction is now the negative y direction. So $F_{gy} = -F_g = -mg$ and $F_{gx} = 0$. But now the normal force and the acceleration each have components on both axes. Figure 6-3 shows that $N_x = N\sin\theta$ and $N_y = N\cos\theta$, while Fig. 6-4 shows that $a_x = a\cos\theta$ and $a_y = a\sin\theta$. Using these results in our component equations gives

   x component: $N\sin\theta = ma\cos\theta$

   and

   y component: $-mg + N\cos\theta = -ma\sin\theta$.

Tip

Getting Those Signs Right How do you know what signs to give terms in the component equations? Again, that depends on your coordinate system. In Fig. 6-4, for example, we've drawn the vector $\mathbf{a}$ on our chosen coordinates; perpendiculars from the tip of $\mathbf{a}$ to the axes intersect the *positive x* axis and the *negative y* axis, showing that a_x is positive while a_y is negative. We stress again that signs are only an issue with *components;* vectors themselves are neither positive nor negative.

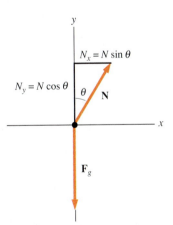

FIGURE 6-3 Free-body diagram for the skier, now with a horizontal-vertical coordinate system. Note that the forces—which are physically real—are exactly the same as in Fig. 6-2. Only their components depend on the arbitrary choice of coordinate system.

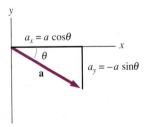

FIGURE 6-4 The acceleration vector points downslope, so its components are $a_x = a\cos\theta$ and $a_y = -a\sin\theta$.

6. Now we're supposed to solve for the magnitude a of the acceleration. With Example 6-1's more sensible coordinate system, the x equation gave that answer directly—reflecting the fact that we had chosen a coordinate system in which **a** had only one nonzero component. But here we need to solve both equations simultaneously. Since the quantity we're interested in is the acceleration, we can solve the x equation for N to eliminate one unknown:

$$N = \frac{ma\cos\theta}{\sin\theta}.$$

Using this result in the y equation leaves a single equation in the unknown a:

$$-mg + \frac{ma\cos^2\theta}{\sin\theta} = -ma\sin\theta.$$

The mass m cancels, and we can simplify the equation by multiplying through by $\sin\theta$ and rearranging to get

$$a(\cos^2\theta + \sin^2\theta) = g\sin\theta.$$

But $\cos^2\theta + \sin^2\theta = 1$, so we recover our previous result

$$a = g\sin\theta.$$

Of course we *had* to get the same result, because we described the same physical situation. But a poor choice of coordinate system made the algebra much more complicated.

Tip

Choose Your Coordinate System Wisely Comparison of Examples 6-1 and 6-2 shows that a little thought about coordinate systems can save a lot of mathematical effort!

Sometimes we're not so much interested in finding an object's acceleration as in finding conditions under which it won't accelerate. This includes engineering problems such as ensuring that bridges and buildings don't fall down, or physiology problems involving the strength of muscles and bones. Here we give a wilder example:

EXAMPLE 6-3	*Bear Precautions*

To protect her 17-kg pack from bears, a camper hangs it from ropes strung between two trees (Fig. 6-5). What is the tension force in each rope?

FIGURE 6-5 Bear precautions.

Solution

We follow our Newton's law strategy:

1. We're asked for the tension in each rope. But the ropes are supporting the pack; that's why they exert tension forces. We want to know what tension force will support the pack against gravity—i.e., keep it from accelerating downward. So the object of interest is the pack.

2. Forces on the pack include gravity and tension forces from the two ropes. We've added these to Fig. 6-5, and in Fig. 6-6 have drawn a free-body diagram for the pack.

3. Now we write Newton's second law. The net force, on the left side of Newton's law, is the sum of the two rope tension forces and the gravitational force. In this problem, we want the pack to hang from the ropes without accelerating, so **a = 0**. Then Newton's law reads

$$\mathbf{T}_1 + \mathbf{T}_2 + \mathbf{F}_g = m\mathbf{a} = \mathbf{0}.$$

4. Now we have to choose a coordinate system. Since the tension forces act in different directions, there's not much sense in orienting a coordinate system along either rope; instead, a horizontal-vertical system is a reasonable choice. We've

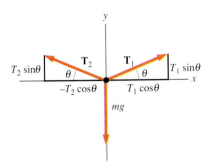

FIGURE 6-6 Free-body diagram for the pack, showing a coordinate system and components of the tension forces.

added such a coordinate system to our free-body diagram, Fig. 6-6.

5. Formally, the components of our Newton's law equation are

x component: $\quad\quad\quad\quad T_{1x} + T_{2x} + F_{gx} = 0$

y component: $\quad\quad\quad\quad T_{1y} + T_{2y} + F_{gy} = 0$.

You can probably see that, since the two ropes make the same angle with the horizontal, the two tension forces must have equal magnitudes. Utilizing that fact would save some work, but we'll pretend we didn't notice and just grind on with the math. Figure 6-6 shows that the components of the tension forces are $T_{1x} = T_1 \cos\theta$, $T_{2x} = -T_2 \cos\theta$, $T_{1y} = T_1 \sin\theta$, and $T_{2y} = T_2 \sin\theta$. With the y axis vertically upward, the gravitational force has no x component and its y component is just $-mg$. So our Newton's law components become:

x component: $\quad\quad\quad T_1 \cos\theta - T_2 \cos\theta = 0$

y component: $\quad\quad T_1 \sin\theta + T_2 \sin\theta - mg = 0$.

6. Now we solve the equations. Since the angle θ is the same for both ropes, $\cos\theta$ cancels from the x component equation, which then gives $T_1 = T_2$—i.e., the magnitudes of the two tension forces are the same, as we could have recognized from the symmetry of the situation. We'll call this common magnitude T. Then the y equation becomes

$$2T \sin\theta = mg,$$

giving

$$T = \frac{mg}{2\sin\theta}.$$

7. We've got our answer in symbolic form; does it make sense? Suppose θ were 90°, as shown in Fig. 6-7a. Then $\sin\theta = 1$ and our result gives $T = mg/2$. Of course: each piece of rope supports half the weight of the pack, and since the ropes are strictly vertical, there's no horizontal component

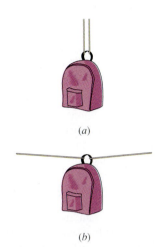

(a)

(b)

FIGURE 6-7 (a) When the ropes hang vertically, each supports half the pack's weight, so the tension in each is $mg/2$. (b) The tension is enormous when the ropes are nearly horizontal.

to contribute greater tension. If θ becomes very small, on the other hand, the tension grows enormously (Fig. 6-7b). That, too, makes sense: with the ropes nearly horizontal, the vertical component is only a tiny fraction of the overall tension. Since each rope's vertical tension component must equal half the pack's weight, that makes the overall tension vastly greater than the weight. In fact, you can see from this example that it's impossible to support a weight with perfectly horizontal ropes or cables; the required tension would be infinite!

8. The numerical answer, for a 17-kg pack and 22° angle, is

$$T = \frac{mg}{2\sin\theta} = \frac{(17\text{ kg})(9.8\text{ m/s}^2)}{(2)(\sin 22°)} = 220\text{ N}.$$

This is considerably more than the pack's weight, as our argument in step (7) suggests it should be.

EXERCISE You hang a wet blanket with mass 14 kg in the middle of a clothesline. The line sags until its two halves make 27° angles with the horizontal. (a) What is the tension in the clothesline? (b) You decide the blanket is too close to the ground, so you tighten up the clothesline. If the line can withstand a maximum tension of 250 N before breaking, what is the minimum angle the clothesline can make with the vertical?

Answers: (a) 150 N; (b) 16°

Some problems similar to Example 6-3: 9, 11, 13

EXAMPLE 6-4	*Ski Racer*

A 60-kg skier stands on a frictionless 30° slope at the start of a ski race. What magnitude of force, applied horizontally, is necessary to restrain the skier before the start of the race?

Solution

We apply our strategy:
1. The object of interest is obviously the skier.
2. Figure 6-8 shows the situation, which is similar to Examples 6-1 and 6-2 except that now there's a third interaction force—the horizontal force $\mathbf{F}_h$ restraining the skier. We've shown all three forces on Fig. 6-8 and drawn a free-body diagram in Fig. 6-9.
3. Here we're trying to restrain the skier, so we want her acceleration to be zero. In that sense, this example is like the preceding one. With three interaction forces and zero acceleration, Newton's second law becomes

$$\mathbf{F}_g + \mathbf{N} + \mathbf{F}_h = m\mathbf{a} = \mathbf{0}\,.$$

4. Choice of coordinate system? The situation looks deceptively like that of Example 6-1, but there are two important differences. First, the acceleration is zero, so there's no vector parallel to the slope. The normal force is still perpendicular to the slope, so it would be simplest in the tilted coordinate system of Example 6-1. But gravity is still vertically downward, and now there's a new force in the horizontal direction. So, with two of the three force vectors either horizontal or vertical, and with zero acceleration, a horizontal/vertical coordinate system is simplest. We've drawn such a coordinate system on Fig. 6-9.
5. As before, a formal writing of Newton's law in components gives

x component:	$F_{gx} + N_x + F_{hx} = 0$
y component:	$F_{gy} + N_y + F_{hy} = 0\,.$

For the coordinate system shown in Fig. 6-9, it's clear that $F_{gx} = 0$ and $F_{gy} = -F_g = -mg$. $\mathbf{F}_h$ points horizontally to the left, in the $-x$ direction, so its components are $F_{hx} = -F_h$ and $F_{hy} = 0$. Finally, trigonometry applied to the triangle in Fig. 6-9 shows that $N_x = N\sin\theta$ and $N_y = N\cos\theta$. So the component equations are

x component:	$N\sin\theta - F_h = 0$
y component:	$-mg + N\cos\theta = 0\,.$

6. Now we solve for the quantity we want, namely F_h. We'll need information from both equations; first solving the y equation for N gives

$$N = \frac{mg}{\cos\theta}\,.$$

N

$\mathbf{F}_h$

$\mathbf{F}_g$

30°

FIGURE 6-8 Restraining a skier.

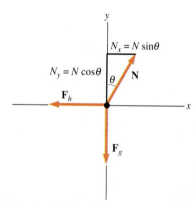

y

$N_x = N\sin\theta$

$N_y = N\cos\theta$

θ **N**

$\mathbf{F}_h$ x

$\mathbf{F}_g$

FIGURE 6-9 Free-body diagram for the restrained skier. Since there's no acceleration, and two of the three vectors are horizontal or vertical, a horizontal/vertical coordinate system makes most sense. Trigonometry gives the components of the normal force in this system.

Using this result in the x equation, we have

$$F_h = \frac{mg}{\cos\theta}\sin\theta = mg\tan\theta\,.$$

7. Does this result make sense? With $\theta = 0$ we have a horizontal surface and $F_h = 0$. Of course! It doesn't take any force to restrain a skier on flat ground. As the slope approaches vertical, however, $\tan\theta \to \infty$ and it becomes impossible for a purely horizontal force to restrain the skier.
8. Finally, we determine F_h from the numbers given:

$$F_h = mg\tan\theta = (60\text{ kg})(9.8\text{ m/s}^2)(\tan 30°) = 340\text{ N}\,.$$

EXERCISE A roofer secures a 28-kg toolbox while working on an essentially frictionless metal roof pitched at a 40° angle. He uses a rope running horizontally to the roof ridge, as shown in Fig. 6-10. What is the tension in the rope?

Answer: 230 N

Some problems similar to Example 6-8: 12, 20

FIGURE 6-10 Securing a toolbox.

Although Example 6-4 dealt with an object—the skier—held at rest, the same analysis would apply in any case of unaccelerated motion on a slope with a horizontal applied force; ActivPhysics Activity 2.10 provides a good example, and has the additional force of friction present; we'll explore friction in Section 6-4.

6-2 MULTIPLE OBJECTS

In each of the preceding examples there was a single object whose motion interested us. But often there are several objects whose motion is linked. The strategy developed in the preceding section still applies, but with several modifications as indicated below in italics:

Strategy

Solving Problems with Multiple Objects

1. Identify *all the objects* of interest, *and note how their motions are linked.*
2. Identify all the individual interaction forces acting *on each object, and draw separate free-body diagrams for each object.*
3. Write a version of Newton's second law, $\mathbf{F}_{net} = m\mathbf{a}$, *for each object,* using for $\mathbf{F}_{net}$ the vector sum of the forces you identified in step (2) *as acting on that object.*
4. Choose coordinate systems *appropriate to each object,* and draw the coordinate axes on your *separate* free-body diagrams. *The separate coordinate systems need not have the same orientations.*
5. Write the components of *your vector equations for each object in the associated coordinate systems.*
6. Solve the equations symbolically for whatever quantities the problem asks for. *Use the physical linkage between the objects to relate quantities appearing in the equations for the different objects.*
7. Ask whether your results make sense.
8. Insert numerical values and work the arithmetic.

EXAMPLE 6-5	*An Alpine Rescue*

An unfortunate climber of mass 70 kg finds himself dangling over the edge of an ice cliff, as shown in Fig. 6-11. Fortunately, he's roped to a 940-kg rock located 51 m from the edge and help is on the way. Unfortunately, the ice is frictionless, and the climber starts to accelerate downward. How long does he have before the rock goes over the edge? Neglect the rope's mass.

Solution

Following the strategy outlined above,
1. The objects of interest are the climber and the rock; the rope links their motions and requires that they have the same acceleration.
2. The forces on the climber are rope tension and the gravitational force; the forces on the rock are the gravitational force, the normal force from the ice, and rope tension. Figure 6-12 shows free-body diagrams for each object.
3. Referring to Fig. 6-12, we write Newton's law for each object:

climber: $$\mathbf{T}_c + \mathbf{F}_{gc} = m_c \mathbf{a}_c$$
rock: $$\mathbf{T}_r + \mathbf{F}_{gr} + \mathbf{N} = m_r \mathbf{a}_r,$$

where the subscripts c and r stand for climber and rock, respectively. We don't need to subscript $\mathbf{N}$ since only the rock experiences a normal force.
4. Now we need to choose coordinate systems. Since all the forces on both objects are either horizontal or vertical, we could just use the same horizontal/vertical coordinate system for both. On the other hand, the rope that links the two turns a right-angle corner, so the rock and climber have physically different acceleration directions. The math will turn out less confusing if we use different coordinate systems for each object, each with its x axis in the direction of the object's acceleration. Besides, that will give practice for cases in which different directions really help in a big way, as in the exercise at the end of this example.
   So let's use a normal y-axis-vertical, x-axis-to-the-right system for the rock, and a system with the positive x axis

(a)

(b)

FIGURE 6-12 Free-body diagrams for (a) the climber and (b) the rock of Example 6-5. Once again we include the ghostly images to remind you which diagram is which. Note the unusual choice of coordinate system in (a), with the x axis downward. That makes the x direction for each object the direction of its acceleration.

downward and the y axis to the right for the climber. We've drawn these on the free-body diagrams.
5. Now we need the component equations for each object. In the rock's case, the gravitational and normal forces are entirely vertical while the tension has no vertical component; thus $N_y = N$ and $F_{gry} = -m_r g$. Furthermore, the ice surface prevents the rock from accelerating in the vertical direction, so $a_{ry} = 0$. So the y component equation for the rock is

rock, y: $$N - m_r g = 0.$$

The only force acting on the rock in the x direction is the rope tension, which is entirely horizontal and pulls the rock to the right. So $T_{rx} = T_r$. The rock's acceleration is entirely horizontal and to the right, so $a_{rx} = a_r$, and the x component of Newton's law for the rock becomes

rock, x: $$T_r = m_r a_r.$$

On to the climber. There are no forces on the climber in the horizontal direction, which, in the climber's coordinate system, is designated the y direction. So the climber's y equation reads $0 = 0$, and is of no interest or usefulness.

FIGURE 6-11 A climber in trouble.

The climber's x equation (x being the *vertical* direction for the climber) involves both the rope tension and the gravitational force on the climber. With the positive x direction *downward*, we have $a_{cx} = a_c$, $F_{gc} = m_c g$, and $T_{cx} = -T_c$, where, as usual, a_c and T_c are the magnitudes of the acceleration and the tension force, and are thus positive quantities. So the climber's x equation is

climber, x: $\qquad -T_c + m_c g = m_c a_c$.

That completes step 5, writing the equations; given that the horizontal equation for the climber is trivial, we're left with three useful equations.

6. Now we solve the equations. However, there seem to be five unknown quantities—T_c, T_r, a_c, a_r, and N, but only three equations. Here's where we use the linkage between our two objects. Physically, that linkage is the rope. Since it's attached to both rock and climber, the accelerations of both must have the same magnitude. Thus $a_c = a_r$, and we'll just call this common acceleration magnitude a.

In addition, the tension forces on the rock and climber have the same magnitude. Why? Because the only forces on the rope are pulls at both ends from the rock and climber. We're assuming the rope's mass is negligible, so there's essentially no net force required to accelerate the rope (whose acceleration, obviously, has the same magnitude as that of the rock and climber). Thus the net force on the rope is essentially zero, and that means the forces pulling at opposite ends must be equal in magnitude. Those forces—from the rock and climber, respectively—form third-law pairs with the tension forces on the rock and climber, respectively. So the tension forces must also be equal in magnitude. Thus $T_c = T_r$, and we'll call this common tension magnitude T.

With these new relations, our three equations become

rock, y: $\qquad N - m_r g = 0$.

rock, x: $\qquad T = m_r a$.

climber, x: $\qquad -T + m_c g = m_c a$.

The first just tells us that the normal force from the ice balances the gravitational force on the rock; it doesn't give us any information about the tension or the acceleration. The rock's x equation gives an expression for T; substituting this into the climber equation and rearranging gives

$$(m_c + m_r)a = m_c g,$$

or $\qquad a = \dfrac{m_c g}{m_c + m_r}.$

7. Before proceeding, let's see if this result makes sense. Suppose there's no rock, or that the rock mass is negligible. Then we have $a = m_c g/m_c = g$ for the climber's acceleration and, from the rock's x equation, $T = 0$ for the rope tension. Of course: with no rock there's nothing for the rope to accelerate, so there's no rope tension. The only force on the climber is gravity, which gives the free-fall acceleration g. If the rock becomes much more massive than the climber, though, the acceleration gets arbitrarily small. With an infinitely massive rock, the climber would simply dangle without accelerating.

You can see what's going on in this problem and why the result makes sense. Basically, the gravitational force acting on the climber is transmitted, via the rope tension, to the rock. So that force—of magnitude $m_c g$—has to accelerate both the climber and the rock. The result is an acceleration of magnitude $m_c g/(m_c + m_r)$.

8. We're actually not quite done with the problem, since we're asked to find the time until the rock goes over the edge. But since we have the acceleration and the distance the rock has to go, that's a problem from Chapter 2 and we'll treat it as part of the arithmetic. Solving the Chapter 2 expression $x = \frac{1}{2}at^2$ for t, and using our result for the acceleration, we have

$$t = \sqrt{\frac{2x}{a}} = \sqrt{\frac{(2x)(m_c + m_r)}{m_c g}}$$

$$= \sqrt{\frac{(2)(51\ \text{m})(70\ \text{kg} + 940\ \text{kg})}{(70\ \text{kg})(9.8\ \text{m/s}^2)}} = 12\ \text{s}.$$

Help better come soon!

EXERCISE Suppose the climber in Example 6-5 was on a steep, frictionless slope rather than over a cliff, as shown in Fig. 6-13. Show that the magnitude of the climber's acceleration is now given by $a = \dfrac{m_c g \sin\theta}{m_c + m_r}$.

Some problems similar to Example 6-5: 15, 17–20
You can also simulate the physical situation in this example with ActivPhysics Activity 2.14, which allows you to adjust the two masses and to add friction.

2.14
Modified Atwood Machine

FIGURE 6-13 A climber in a little less trouble.

FIGURE 6-14 (*a*) Hands pull with 1-N forces on both ends of a rope. Is the rope tension 2 N or 1 N? (*b*) A section of the rope is highlighted. The section isn't accelerating, and the 1-N force of the hand acts at the left end. So there must be a 1-N force pulling to the right on the right end of the section. That force is provided by the rope tension, which is therefore 1 N. By Newton's third law, the left section of rope also exerts a 1-N force on the right section.

2.2, 2.3, 2.9, 2.12, 2.13, 2.14

FIGURE 6-15 Now what's the tension in the rope? And what force does the wall exert on the rope? Is this situation different from that of Fig. 6-14?

Tip

Tension Forces and Massless Ropes Tension forces can cause a lot of confusion. In this example, the rock pulls on one end of the rope and the climber on the other. So why isn't the rope tension the sum of these two forces? And why is it important that we neglect the rope's mass?

Figure 6-14*a* shows a simpler situation that raises the same questions. Two people pull on opposite ends of a rope (or a spring, or a rubber band, or any other object, for that matter), each with a force of 1 N. What's the tension in the rope? You might think it's 2 N, but it's not. To see why, consider just part of the rope, as highlighted in yellow in Fig. 6-14*b*. At the left end of this piece, the hand is pulling leftward with a 1-N force. The rope isn't accelerating, so there must be a 1-N force pulling on the right end of the piece. That force is provided by the remainder of the rope. You could imagine dividing the rope, as we did in Fig. 6-14b, at any point; no matter what point you considered, you would come to the conclusion that each part of the rope exerts a 1-N force on the adjacent part (and vice versa, by Newton's third law). That 1-N force, which exists throughout the rope, is what we mean by the rope tension. At the ends of the rope, that tension force has the same magnitude it does throughout, and it acts on whatever is connected to the rope. That's why the tension is the same at both ends.

The rope in Fig. 6-14 isn't accelerating, so Newton's second law assures us that the net force on it must be zero; that's why the forces at the opposite ends must have the same magnitude. Even if the rope were accelerating, but had negligible mass, the net force would still be negligible and the forces at the two ends would have essentially the same magnitude. That's why we often use the approximation of a "massless rope." Such a rope—whose mass must be negligible compared to the masses of objects attached to it—requires negligible force to accelerate it, and therefore the forces at its two ends are essentially equal in magnitude. A massless rope simply transmits the force applied at one end, via the tension within the rope, to the other end. If a rope's mass is not negligible and it's accelerating, then the tension forces at opposite ends will have different magnitudes; according to Newton's second law, the difference will just be the product of the rope's mass and its acceleration. You can also explore tension forces with ActivPhysics Activities 2.2, 2.3, 2.9, 2.12, 2.13, and 2.14.

Got It!

Once you're sure you understand Fig. 6-14, take a look at Fig. 6-15. Here we've replaced the hand pulling on the left side of the rope with a hook attaching the rope to a rigid wall. On the right end, a hand still pulls with a 1-N force. Now what are the rope tension and the force exerted on the rope by the wall?

6-3 CIRCULAR MOTION

A sports car rounds a curve. A satellite circles Earth. A proton whirls around the giant particle accelerator at Fermilab. Since they're not going in straight lines, Newton's first law tells us that a nonzero force acts on each (Fig. 6-16). Newton's second law gives us the magnitude of that force: $F = ma$. For an object moving with constant speed v in a circular path of radius r, we know from Section 4-4 that the object accelerates—because the direction of motion is changing—with acceleration of magnitude $a = v^2/r$ and direction toward the center of the circular path. So for an object of mass m in uniform circular motion, the net force acting on the object must have magnitude

$$F_{net} = ma = \frac{mv^2}{r} \quad \text{(force in uniform circular motion).} \qquad (6\text{-}1)$$

This force is in the same direction as the acceleration, toward the center of the circular path. For that reason it's sometimes called the **centripetal force**.

FIGURE 6-16 A car rounds a turn. Since the direction of its motion is changing, it's accelerating—and therefore a force must be acting on it.

Tip

Look for Real Forces "Centripetal force" is *not* some new kind of force. It's just the name for the net force that acts to keep an object in circular motion. Similarly, the quantity mv^2/r is nothing new; it's just the product ma for an object in circular motion. As always with Newton's law, this product is not itself a force but is numerically equal to the magnitude of the net force. That net force always results from real, physical interaction forces acting on the object. Common forces involved in circular motion include the gravitational force on a satellite, friction between tires and a road, the magnetic force, tension forces, normal forces, and combinations of these and other forces.

Newton's second law describes circular motion in exactly the same way that it does any other motion: by relating net force, mass, and acceleration. The examples below show that we can analyze circular motion using exactly the same steps outlined in Section 6-1, since we're dealing with exactly the same law of motion. ActivPhysics Activity 4.4 also explores general approaches to circular motion problems.

4.4

Circular Motion Problem Solving

EXAMPLE 6-6	*A Mass on a String*

A ball of mass m is whirled around in a horizontal circle at the end of a string of length ℓ. The string makes an angle θ with the horizontal. Determine (a) the speed of the ball and (b) the tension in the string.

Solution

This problem is just like any other involving a single object and Newton's second law, so we simply apply the strategy developed in Section 6-1:

1. The object of interest is the ball.
2. There are two forces acting on the ball, the gravitational force and the string tension. Figure 6-17 shows the physical situation, while Fig. 6-18 is a free-body diagram.

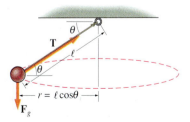

FIGURE 6-17 A ball being whirled about at the end of a string. Forces include the gravitational force and the string tension. Note that the radius of the ball's circular path is $r = \ell\cos\theta$.

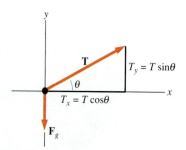

FIGURE 6-18 Free-body diagram for the ball of Example 6-6, showing a coordinate system and vector components.

Tip

Don't Introduce Forces That Aren't There! Were you tempted to draw a third force in Fig. 6-17, perhaps pointing outward to balance the other two? **DON'T!** The tension and gravitational forces **DO NOT BALANCE**. Why not? Because the ball is accelerating, so there must be a nonzero net force acting on it.

Or maybe you're tempted to draw a third force pointing inward, the force mv^2/r. **DON'T!** As we argued in the tip following Equation 6-1, the quantity mv^2/r is *not* another force; it's just the product of mass and acceleration that always appears on the right-hand side of Newton's law.

Students often complicate Newton's law problems by introducing forces that aren't there. That makes physics seem harder than it is. If an object is accelerating there's a net force on it. Here that force is provided by gravity and the string tension. No more forces. Period.

3. With the two forces we've identified, Newton's law $\mathbf{F}_{net} = m\mathbf{a}$ becomes

$$\mathbf{T} + \mathbf{F}_g = m\mathbf{a}.$$

4. With two forces at an arbitrary angle, you might think the choice of a coordinate system is a toss-up. But there's also the acceleration vector to consider. The ball is in circular motion, so **a** points toward the center of the circular path. That path lies in a horizontal plane, as Fig. 6-17 makes clear, so the acceleration vector is horizontal. With the gravitational force vertical and the acceleration horizontal, two of the three vectors in our statement of Newton's law are horizontal or vertical, so a horizontal/vertical coordinate system makes the most sense. We show this system on the free-body diagram, Fig. 6-18.

5. The downward-pointing gravitational force has no x component, and its y component is $F_{gy} = -F_g = -mg$. Figure 6-18 shows that the tension force has components $T_x = T\cos\theta$ and $T_y = T\sin\theta$. Finally, the acceleration points toward the center of the circle, which is the $+x$ direction in Fig. 6-18. So the acceleration vector has no y component, and, since the acceleration of an object in circular motion has magnitude v^2/r, the x component of the acceleration is $a_x = v^2/r$. Here r is the radius of the circle; Fig. 6-17 shows that, in terms of quantities given in the problem statement, this radius is $r = \ell\cos\theta$. So $a_x = v^2/\ell\cos\theta$, and the two components of Newton's law become

x component: $$T\cos\theta = \frac{mv^2}{\ell\cos\theta}$$

y component: $$T\sin\theta - mg = 0.$$

6. Now we can solve for the tension and the speed. The y equation gives the tension:

$$T = \frac{mg}{\sin\theta}.$$

Using this result in the x equation, we have

$$\frac{mg}{\sin\theta}\cos\theta = \frac{mv^2}{\ell\cos\theta}$$

or

$$v = \sqrt{\frac{g\ell\cos^2\theta}{\sin\theta}}.$$

7. Do these results make sense? When $\theta = 90°$, so the string hangs vertically, $\cos\theta = 0$ and thus $v = 0$. In this case there's no acceleration, and the string tension is just equal in magnitude to the ball's weight mg. But as $\theta \to 0$, $\sin\theta \to 0$ and the speed v becomes very large—and would be infinite at $\theta = 0$. This says that it's not possible to whirl the ball around with the string exactly horizontal. Why not? Because—just as in Example 6-3—there must be a vertical component of the tension force equal in magnitude to the ball's weight. As the angle shrinks, that component becomes an insignificant fraction of the overall tension. The latter becomes huge, and with it comes a huge speed v for the whirling ball.

8. There are no numerical values in this example.

EXERCISE A string of length 1.5 m can withstand a tension of 90 N before breaking. A 250-g rock is attached to the string and whirled in a horizontal circle. At what speed will the string break?

Answer: 23 m/s

EXAMPLE 6-7	*Engineering a Road*

Roads designed for safe, high-speed travel have banked curves to give the normal force that the road exerts on a car a component toward the center of the curve. This allows cars to turn without relying on any frictional force between tires and road. At what angle should a road with a 150-m curvature radius be banked for travel at a constant speed of 75 km/h (21 m/s)?

Solution

We apply our Newton's law strategy.

1. Although we're asked a question about the road, the object of interest—to which we're going to apply Newton's law—is a car on the road.
2. Figure 6-19 shows the situation. The two forces acting on the car are the gravitational force and the normal force due to the road. Figure 6-20 shows a free-body diagram for the car.
3. With the two forces we've identified, Newton's law becomes

$$\mathbf{F}_g + \mathbf{N} = m\mathbf{a}\,.$$

4. As in the preceding example, the car's acceleration is horizontal so a horizontal/vertical coordinate system makes the most sense. We've drawn this on Fig. 6-20, where we show the components of the normal force.
5. In our chosen coordinate system, the gravitational force has only a y component: $F_{gy} = -F_g = -mg$. As Fig. 6-20 shows, the normal force has components $N_x = N\sin\theta$ and $N_y = N\cos\theta$. The acceleration points toward the center of the curve, which we've taken as the $+x$ direction. So the acceleration has no y component. Since its magnitude is v^2/r, the acceleration's x component is $a_x = v^2/r$. Then the components of Newton's law become

x component: $$N\sin\theta = \frac{mv^2}{r}$$

y component: $$-mg + N\cos\theta = 0\,.$$

The y equation gives $N = mg/\cos\theta$; substituting this for N in the x equation, we have

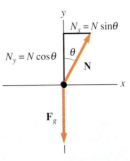

FIGURE 6-20 Free-body diagram, showing a coordinate system and force components.

$$\frac{mg}{\cos\theta}\sin\theta = \frac{mv^2}{r}$$

or $$\tan\theta = \frac{v^2}{gr}\,.$$

7. Does this result make sense? At very low speeds, $\tan\theta$ is small and so, therefore, is θ. Very little banking is needed. But at high speeds, the force needed to maintain circular motion increases, and so does the banking angle. Note that our result is independent of the car's mass. The larger the mass, the larger the force needed to accelerate the car—but that acceleration is provided by the normal force, which in turn is proportional to the gravitational force on the car. So a more massive car experiences a proportionally greater force, making the banking angle independent of mass.

8. For the numbers of this angle,

$$\theta = \tan^{-1}\!\left(\frac{v^2}{gr}\right) = \tan^{-1}\!\left[\frac{(21\text{ m/s})^2}{(9.8\text{ m/s}^2)(150\text{ m})}\right] = 17°\,.$$

EXERCISE When an airplane turns, it banks as shown in Fig. 6-21 to give the lifting force of the wings a horizontal component that turns the plane. If a plane is flying level at 950 km/h and the banking angle is not to exceed 40°, what is the minimum curvature radius for the turn?

Answer: 8.5 km

Some problems similar to Examples 6-6 and 6-7: 27, 30, 33–35

FIGURE 6-19 A car rounding a banked curve; center of the curvature is to the right. Forces acting on the car are the gravitational force and the normal force exerted by the road. The horizontal component of the normal force provides the acceleration.

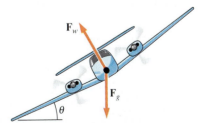

FIGURE 6-21 The horizontal component of the wing force $\mathbf{F}_w$ is what turns a plane. Which way is it turning?

EXAMPLE 6-8   *Loop-the-Loop*

The "Great American Revolution" roller coaster at Valencia, California, includes a loop-the-loop section whose radius is 6.3 m at the top (Fig. 6-22). What is the minimum speed for a roller coaster car at the top of the loop if it's to stay on the track?

FIGURE 6-22 A loop-the-loop roller coaster. At the top of the loop, the net force on a car and its passengers is directly downward; that force provides the acceleration that keeps them in their circular path. In general, the net force is the vector sum of the gravitational force and the normal force from the track, as shown.

Solution

What does it mean for the car to stay on the track? It means there must be a nonzero normal force between car and track; if the normal force becomes zero, car and track are no longer in contact. We'll work this problem for an arbitrary normal force **N**, then consider what happens when **N** becomes zero. We use our usual strategy:

1. The object of interest is the car.
2. Forces acting on the car are the gravitational force and the normal force of the track. Figure 6-23 shows these forces for two positions of the car; Fig. 6-24 is a free-body diagram for the car at the top of the track, where both forces point downward.
3. With the two forces identified, Newton's law becomes

$$\mathbf{F}_g + \mathbf{N} = m\mathbf{a}.$$

4. At the top of the loop, both forces point vertically downward. So a vertical/horizontal coordinate system makes the

most sense, and it's easiest if we take the downward direction as positive. We show this coordinate system on Fig. 6-24.

FIGURE 6-23 Forces on the car include the gravitational force and the normal force. At the top of the loop, both point downward.

FIGURE 6-24 Free-body diagram for the car at the top of the loop.

5. At the top of the loop, horizontal components of both forces and of the car's acceleration are zero, so only the vertical component of Newton's law is nontrivial. In our coordinate system with the downward direction positive, $F_{gy} = F_g = mg$, $N_y = N$, and $a_y = v^2/r$; the latter result follows since the car is in a circular path with its center downward from the top of the track. Then the vertical component of Newton's law is

$$mg + N = \frac{mv^2}{r}.$$

6. Now we can solve this one equation for the single unknown, v:

$$v = \sqrt{gr + \frac{N}{m}}.$$

We've argued that the minimum allowed speed occurs when N just becomes zero; in this case we have

$$v_{\min} = \sqrt{gr}.$$

7. Do these results make sense? The gravitational contribution to the force on the car is fixed at the value mg; if we increase the speed v and thus the acceleration v^2/r, the normal force of the track must contribute more. Our general equation for v shows just this: as v increases, so does N. As with so many

problems involving gravitation, our expression for the minimum speed shows it to be independent of the car's mass—a good thing, because it means the same criterion applies to the riders, no matter what their masses. If the car stays on the track, they'll stay in the car! Note also that the bigger the radius r, the larger the minimum speed. That makes sense, too: less force would be needed to keep the car in a larger circular path, and therefore it must be going faster before the normal force "kicks in."

For speeds lower than v_{min}, the normal force would become zero before the car reached the top, and the car with its hapless passengers would leave the track on the parabolic trajectory of a projectile (Fig. 6-25).

8. For the "Great American Revolution," $r = 6.3$ m so that $v_{min} = \sqrt{gr} = 7.9$ m/s. The actual speed of the car at the loop is 9.7 m/s to provide a margin of safety. Incidentally, the shape of the track provides another safety margin; its radius of curvature is slightly smaller at the top, resulting in a lower minimum speed.

EXERCISE A stunt plane executes a vertical loop-the-loop. If the loop radius is 320 m and the plane maintains a steady 270 km/h, what force does the seat exert on a 75-kg pilot (a) at the top of the loop and (b) at the bottom of the loop?

Answers: (a) 580 N; (b) 2.1 kN

FIGURE 6-25 If the car's speed were too low, the normal force would become zero and the car would leave the track on a parabolic trajectory, subject only to the gravitational force.

Some problems similar to Example 6-8: 28, 31, 36
ActivPhysics Activities 4.5 and 4.6 relate to this example.

4.5
Cart Goes over Circular Path

4.6
Ball Swings on a String

Got It!

Explain why the passengers don't fall out of the roller coaster in Fig. 6-22, even at the top of the loop and even if they forget to attach their seat belts.

6-4 FRICTION

Your everyday experience of motion seems inconsistent with Newton's first law. Slide a book across the floor, and it stops. Take your foot off the gas, and your car coasts to a stop. But Newton's law is right, so these examples show that some force must be acting. That force is **friction**.

On Earth, we can rarely ignore friction. As much as 20% of the gasoline burned in a car is used to overcome friction in the engine. Friction causes wear and tear whenever moving pieces of machinery are in contact. But friction is also useful: without frictional forces between tires and road, your car could not start, turn, or stop. Absent the frictional forces between the threads making up your clothing, your clothes would simply fall apart. And without friction between your feet and the ground, you couldn't walk.

Frictional Forces and Their Properties

Friction is a force that acts between two surfaces. It's ultimately an electrical force between molecules in the surfaces. Even the smoothest of surfaces is irregular on a microscopic scale (Fig. 6-26). When two surfaces contact,

FIGURE 6-26 Studies using a so-called friction-force microscope show that friction is associated not only with surface irregularities but also with defects in the underlying molecular order. Photo shows frictional force encountered in dragging a microscopic probe across a sample measuring 2 μm by 2 μm. Lighter regions represent higher frictional forces, and are associated largely with surface irregularities up to 24 nm high.

(a)

(b)

FIGURE 6-28 Frictional force acting on an initially stationary object also subject to an applied force. At first the frictional force increases to oppose the applied force, and the object remains at rest. At breakaway the applied force momentarily exceeds the maximum force of static friction, and the object accelerates. After that, the applied force needs only to counter the lower force of kinetic friction to keep the object moving with constant speed.

FIGURE 6-27 (a) When two surfaces contact, high points of their microscopic irregularities adhere, producing a force that opposes relative motion of the surfaces. (b) When the normal force between the surfaces increases, the irregularities compress and the actual contact area grows. This increases the frictional force.

microscopic irregularities adhere, as suggested in Fig. 6-27a. This makes it difficult for the surfaces to move across one another, and at the macroscopic level the effect of the microscopic irregularities manifests itself as a force that opposes any attempt to move the surfaces relative to one another.

Experiment shows that the magnitude of the frictional force between two surfaces does not depend on their area, but does depend on the normal force between them. Figure 6-27b shows why this makes sense: as normal forces push the surfaces together, the actual contact area increases. This causes more adherence between the surfaces, and thus increases the frictional force.

As Fig. 6-27 shows, friction is actually a complicated phenomenon involving microscopic processes. The simple equations we'll develop in this section to describe friction as a macroscopic force are but approximate descriptions of what happens as a result of the underlying microscopic processes. Friction is important, especially in situations we encounter in everyday life, but we emphasize that it's not a deep and fundamental aspect of physics.

Behavior of Frictional Forces

Imagine trying to push a heavy trunk across the floor. You begin by exerting a horizontal force on the trunk, but it's really heavy and nothing happens. You push harder. Still nothing. Finally, as you push even harder, the trunk begins to slide—and you may notice that once it gets going you don't have to push as hard as you did to get it started (Fig. 6-28).

What's going on here? Why is it harder to get the trunk started than to keep it moving? When the trunk is sitting at rest on the floor, the microscopic regions of contact between trunk and floor, as pictured in Fig. 6-27, have a chance to form relatively strong bonds. As you push on the trunk, at first you simply distort those bonds without breaking them; they respond with force that opposes your applied force. This is the force of **static friction**, F_s, so called because it arises when the two surfaces in question are at rest (i.e., static) relative to each other. As you increase the force you apply to the trunk, the opposing force of static friction increases to remain equal in magnitude to the applied force, and the trunk remains at rest.

Eventually, though, your push becomes strong enough to break the bonds between trunk and floor; this is the breakaway point shown in Fig. 6-28. The trunk begins to move. As it does so, microscopic bonds continually form and break, but they don't have time to strengthen, so the force required to overcome them is not as great as was required to get the trunk moving. The frictional force between surfaces in relative motion—in this case trunk and floor—is the force of **kinetic friction**, F_k.

Before you started pushing your trunk, it was sitting at rest with no net force on it. So the force of static friction must have been zero. Then, as you pushed harder, static friction pushed back with a force equal to your applied force. Eventually the applied force reached the maximum value that static friction could counter. Experimentally, we find that this maximum value is proportional to the normal force between the surfaces; we therefore write

$$F_s \le \mu_s N . \quad \text{(static friction)} \quad (6\text{-}2)$$

Here the proportionality constant, designated μ_s, is the **coefficient of static friction**, a quantity that depends on the nature of the two surfaces in contact. We use the sign $\leq$ rather than $=$ because the force of static friction ranges from zero up to the maximum value given in Equation 6-2.

Once surfaces are in relative motion, experiment shows that the force of kinetic friction is also approximately proportional to the normal force between the surfaces:

$$F_k = \mu_k N, \quad \text{(kinetic friction)} \tag{6-3}$$

where μ_k is the **coefficient of kinetic friction**. Unlike static friction, the force of kinetic friction is independent of the value of any applied force. We've marked both F_k and the maximum F_s on Fig. 6-28.

Equations 6-2 and 6-3 give only the magnitudes of the frictional forces. For kinetic friction, the frictional force between the surfaces is parallel to the surfaces and in a direction that opposes their relative motion (Fig. 6-29a). For static friction, where there is no relative motion, the frictional force opposes whatever force or sum of forces is applied in the direction parallel to the surfaces (Fig. 6-29b).

For a given pair of surfaces, the coefficient of static friction is larger than the coefficient of kinetic friction. This fact represents mathematically what we found in our trunk example: that it takes more force to get an object moving than to keep it moving. Since they describe a proportionality between two forces, coefficients of friction are dimensionless. Typical values of μ_k range from less than 0.01 for smooth or well-lubricated surfaces to about 1.5 for very rough ones. For metallic surfaces μ_k is about 0.5 and μ_s about 0.75; lubrication reduces these coefficients to roughly 0.05 and 0.15, respectively. Rubber on dry concrete—a vital interaction in driving an automobile—has μ_k about 0.8 and μ_s as high as 1. A properly waxed ski on dry snow has roughly the same frictional coefficient as teflon on teflon; $\mu_k \approx 0.04$, while the synovial fluid that lubricates joints in the human body reduces μ_k to a low 0.003—only one-hundredth the value for dry bone on bone.

If you push a moving object with a force just equal to the force of kinetic friction, the net force on the object will be zero and, according to Newton, it will move at constant speed. Since friction is nearly always present, but not as obvious as the push of a hand or pull of a rope, you can see why it's so easy to develop the preconception that force is needed to make things move—rather than, as Newton recognized, to make them accelerate.

We emphasize that friction, and Equations 6-2 and 6-3 that describe it, are not fundamental aspects of physics. The equations, in particular, are empirical expressions that describe the results of experiments and account in an approximate way for complicated but more basic interactions at the microscopic level. Our friction equations have neither the precision nor the fundamental, universal character of Newton's laws.

We now look at some examples where frictional forces are important—examples that we treat just like all other examples involving Newton's law.

Examples of Kinetic Friction

Problems involving kinetic friction are slightly more straightforward because Equation 6-3, unlike Equation 6-2, gives a definitive value for the frictional force.

(a)

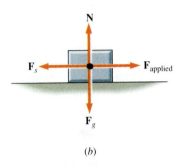

(b)

FIGURE 6-29 (a) The force of kinetic friction acts to oppose relative motion, and is therefore parallel to the contacting surfaces and perpendicular to the normal force. In the absence of an applied force to the right, the block shown here would decelerate. (b) The force of static friction acts to oppose an applied force.

EXAMPLE 6-9	*Pulling a Trunk*

You pull a trunk of mass m across a level floor using a massless rope that makes an angle θ with the horizontal (Fig. 6-30). The coefficient of friction between trunk and floor is μ_k. What rope tension is required to move the trunk at constant velocity?

Solution

We're asked to keep the trunk moving at constant velocity—meaning there's no net force on it. So this is a problem, like Example 6-3, about making sure the interaction forces on an object sum to zero. As with any Newton's law problem, we use our strategy:
1. The object of interest is the trunk.
2. Figure 6-30 shows the physical situation; there are the usual normal force and gravitational force in the vertical direction, the tension in the rope, and now the frictional force as well. The applied force in Fig. 6-30 moves the trunk toward the right, so the frictional force is to the left. Note that the frictional force is parallel to the contacting surfaces—i.e., horizontal—even though the applied force has an upward component. Figure 6-31 is a free-body diagram for the trunk.
3. With the forces identified in Fig. 6-30, Newton's law becomes

$$\mathbf{T} + \mathbf{F}_g + \mathbf{N} + \mathbf{F}_k = m\mathbf{a} = \mathbf{0},$$

where we set the right-hand side to zero because we want the trunk to move at constant velocity—i.e., with zero acceleration.
4. Three of the four forces are horizontal or vertical, so clearly we want a horizontal/vertical coordinate system. We've drawn this on Fig. 6-31, and also show the components of the tension force.
5. On our coordinate system, the normal force is vertically upward, so $N_x = 0$ and $N_y = N$. The gravitational force is downward, so $F_{gx} = 0$ and $F_{gy} = -mg$. The frictional force is in the negative x direction in Fig. 6-31, and from Equation 6-3 it has magnitude $\mu_k N$. So $F_{kx} = -\mu_k N$ and $F_{ky} = 0$. Finally, Fig. 6-31 shows that $T_x = T\cos\theta$ and $T_y = T\sin\theta$. So the components of Newton's law become

x component: $\qquad T\cos\theta - \mu_k N = 0$

y component: $\qquad T\sin\theta + N - mg = 0$.

6. Solving the y equation for N gives $N = mg - T\sin\theta$; using this result in the x equation, we have

$$T\cos\theta - \mu_k(mg - T\sin\theta) = 0,$$

or

$$T(\cos\theta + \mu_k\sin\theta) = \mu_k mg.$$

FIGURE 6-30 Forces on a trunk being pulled across a level floor include the rope tension **T**, the gravitational force $\mathbf{F}_g$, the normal force **N**, and the force of kinetic friction $\mathbf{F}_k$.

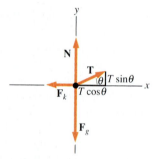

FIGURE 6-31 Free-body diagram for the trunk of Example 6-9, showing a coordinate system and components of the tension force.

Then the rope tension T is

$$T = \frac{\mu_k mg}{\cos\theta + \mu_k\sin\theta}.$$

7. Does this result make sense? As $\mu_k \to 0$, the frictional force vanishes and the force needed to pull the trunk with constant velocity becomes zero, in accordance with Newton's first law. Look also at extreme cases for the angle θ: for $\theta = 0$, $\cos\theta = 1$ and $\sin\theta = 0$, so $T = \mu_k mg$. Of course: pulling the trunk with a horizontal force requires overcoming a frictional force equal to μ_k times the object's weight mg. But with $\theta > 0$, the upward component of the tension force helps balance the gravitational force, reducing the normal force and therefore the required tension force. Finally, at $\theta = 90°$, $T = mg$, independent of μ_k. And this makes sense, too: here we're lifting the trunk vertically; with no acceleration, we must apply a force equal to the trunk's weight. Friction plays no role because the trunk is no longer sliding along a surface.

EXERCISE A logging vehicle pulls a 2.1×10^{6}-kg redwood log at constant speed, using a chain that angles downward at 15°, as shown in Fig. 6-32. The coefficient of friction between the log and ground is 1.3. What is the tension in the chain? Why is this not a sensible orientation for the towing chain?

Answer: 43 MN; downward pull increases the normal force, hence the frictional force.

Some problems similar to Example 6-9: 39–41
ActivPhysics Activity 2.5 provides a simulation of this example, in which you can adjust the coefficient of friction and other parameters.

FIGURE 6-32 Pulling a redwood log.

2.5
Truck Pulls Crate

EXAMPLE 6-10	*Sledding*

A child sleds down a 20° snow-covered slope. If the coefficient of kinetic friction is $\mu_k = 0.085$, what is the child's acceleration? At what angle would the child slide with constant speed?

Solution
1. The object of interest is the child/sled combination.
2. Forces on the child/sled include the gravitational force, the normal force, and the frictional force. We show these in Fig. 6-33 and again in a free-body diagram, Fig. 6-34.
3. With the forces shown, Newton's law becomes

$$\mathbf{F}_g + \mathbf{N} + \mathbf{F}_k = m\mathbf{a} .$$

4. Here the acceleration is down the slope, so, as in Example 6-1, the simplest coordinate system has axes parallel and perpendicular to the slope. We show this system in Fig. 6-34. The frictional force points upslope, or in the $-x$ direction, so $F_{kx} = -\mu_k N$ and $F_{ky} = 0$, while the normal force is entirely in the $+y$ direction. Figure 6-34 shows that the x and y components of the gravitational force are $mg \sin\theta$ and $-mg \cos\theta$, respectively. With acceleration downslope, $a_x = a$ and $a_y = 0$. Then the components of Newton's law become

x component: $\qquad mg \sin\theta - \mu_k N = ma$
y component: $\qquad N - mg \cos\theta = 0 .$

6. Solving the y equation gives $N = mg \cos\theta$; using this result in the x equation, we have

$$a = g \sin\theta - \mu_k g \cos\theta .$$

If the sled is to slide with constant velocity, its acceleration must be zero; then

$$g \sin\theta = \mu_k g \cos\theta ,$$

or

$$\mu_k = \frac{\sin\theta}{\cos\theta} = \tan\theta .$$

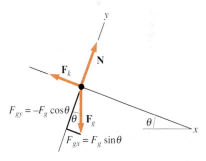

FIGURE 6-33 Forces on the child and sled.

FIGURE 6-34 Free-body diagram, showing components of the gravitational force on a tilted coordinate system.

7. Do these results make sense? When $\mu_k = 0$, our expression for the acceleration gives $a = g \sin\theta$—the result we found in Example 6-1 for a frictionless surface. And, as our expression for μ_k shows, a steep slope (large θ) requires a large coefficient of friction to prevent acceleration. For a horizontal slope, on the other hand, $\theta = 0$ and the sled slides with constant velocity only in the absence of friction ($\mu_k = 0$). Finally, note that mass plays no role in our final result; the

more massive the child and sled, the proportionately greater all the forces—gravitational, normal, and hence frictional—and therefore the acceleration remains the same.

8. For the numbers given, we have

$$a = g\sin\theta - \mu_k g\cos\theta = (9.8 \text{ m/s}^2)$$

$$\times [\sin 20° - (0.085)(\cos 20°)] = 2.6 \text{ m/s}^2$$

for the acceleration on a 20° slope, and

$$\theta = \tan^{-1}\mu_k = \tan^{-1}(0.085) = 4.9°$$

for the sled to undergo no acceleration.

Some problems similar to Example 6-10: 43, 53, 54, 71, 72, 83

ActivPhysics Activity 2.8 simulates this example.

2.8

Skier Goes down a Slope

Tip

Missing Information? This example doesn't give the mass of child and sled. Yet mass appears in Newton's law, so you might think some vital information is missing. It isn't—as the canceling of mass from the final results shows. In cases like this it's best to assign a symbol to the "missing" information and proceed to solve the problem. If the information really isn't necessary, the quantity in question—in this case the mass *m*—will eventually drop from the mathematics.

Got It!

In Examples 6-9 and 6-10, the magnitude of the frictional force was not simply the coefficient of friction multiplied by the weight of the object. Explain why not.

EXAMPLE 6-11	*Losing a Piano*

Workers are pulling a 210-kg piano up a building using a massless rope over a frictionless, massless pulley as shown in Fig. 6-35. At lunchtime they tie the rope to a 260-kg desk,

3.1 m

FIGURE 6-35 A piano at risk.

leaving the piano dangling 3.1 m above the ground. Unfortunately the desk begins to slide; the coefficient of kinetic friction is $\mu_k = 0.71$. What's the piano's acceleration? At what speed does it hit the ground?

Solution

This is a multiple-object problem, much like Example 6-5 except that now there's a frictional force involved. We apply our strategy:

1. The objects of interest are the piano and the desk.
2. Figure 6-36 shows free-body diagrams for both objects. Gravity and the rope tension act on the piano; gravity, normal force, rope tension, and the frictional force all act on the desk.
3. Having identified the forces, we write Newton's law for both objects:

piano: $$\mathbf{F}_{gp} + \mathbf{T}_p = m_p\mathbf{a}_p$$

desk: $$\mathbf{F}_{gd} + \mathbf{N} + \mathbf{T}_d + \mathbf{F}_k = m_d\mathbf{a}_d.$$

4. Given the geometry, we'll use horizontal/vertical coordinate systems for each object; as in Example 6-5, we'll take

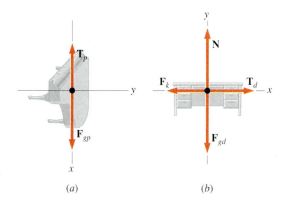

FIGURE 6-36 Free-body diagrams for piano and desk. Also shown are coordinate systems for each object, with the x axes chosen in the direction of the object's acceleration.

the x axis in each case to be in the direction of the object's acceleration. That means the piano's x axis is vertically downward, as shown in Fig. 6-36.

5. In our chosen coordinate systems, each vector has only one nonzero component, and the components of Newton's law become

piano, x: $$m_p g - T_p = m_p a_p$$

desk, x: $$T_d - \mu_k N = m_d a_d$$

desk, y: $$-m_d g + N = 0.$$

There's no y equation for the piano, since it's trivial (we've defined the y direction as horizontal for the piano's coordinate system, and that there are no horizontal forces on the piano). We've written the frictional force explicitly as $\mu_k N$; it enters the equations with a negative sign because it points in the $-x$ direction in the desk's coordinate system.

6. We have three equations in five unknowns—but just as we did in Example 6-5, we can argue that the accelerations have equal magnitude, and so do the tension forces at either end of the rope. (Check Example 6-5 if you're not clear on this.) Then our equations become

piano, x: $$m_p g - T = m_p a$$

desk, x: $$T - \mu_k N = m_d a$$

desk, y: $$-m_d g + N = 0.$$

Solving the desk's y equation for N and using the result in the desk's x equation gives

$$T - \mu_k m_d g = m_d a.$$

We solve this equation for T and substitute in the piano equation to get

$$m_p g - m_d a - \mu_k m_d g = m_p a.$$

Finally, we can solve for the unknown acceleration a:

$$a = \frac{(m_p - \mu_k m_d)g}{m_p + m_d}.$$

7. Does this result make sense? In the frictionless case $\mu_k = 0$ we recover the result of Example 6-5. If there's no desk ($m_d = 0$), there's no friction or tension and the piano falls freely with acceleration g. Finally, if $\mu_k m_d = m_p$, then the frictional force on the desk just balances the gravitational force on the piano, and the pair remain at rest. But what if $\mu_k m_d > m_p$? Then our equations seems to imply an upward acceleration for the piano! But that condition violates our assumption that the frictional force points to the left, so our equation does not apply.

Tip

Know Your Assumptions Sometimes you'll get a result that doesn't make sense under certain conditions. Check those conditions against the assumptions you made in setting up the problem; if they violate your assumptions, then the suspicious result can be rejected.

8. Finally, the numbers of this example give

$$a = \frac{(m_p - \mu_k m_d)g}{m_p + m_d}$$

$$= \frac{[210 \text{ kg} - (0.71)(260 \text{ kg})](9.8 \text{ m/s}^2)}{210 \text{ kg} + 260 \text{ kg}} = 0.530 \text{ m/s}^2.$$

The piano falls 3.1m; Equation 2-11 then shows that it hits the ground with speed

$$v = \sqrt{2a\,\Delta x} = \sqrt{(2)(0.530 \text{ m/s}^2)(3.1 \text{ m})} = 1.8 \text{ m/s}.$$

Smash!

EXERCISE The coefficient of kinetic friction between a 2.5-kg block and a tabletop is 0.57. The block is connected by massless ropes over massless pulleys to a 5.0-kg block and a 3.0-kg block, as shown in Fig. 6-37. Find the acceleration of the block on the table.

Answer: 0.54 m/s², to the right

Some problems similar to Example 6-11: 20, 45, 67, 68 ActivPhysics Activity 2.14 simulates this example.

2.14
Modified Atwood Machine

FIGURE 6-37 What's the acceleration?

FIGURE 6-38 Forces involved in walking. Foot in contact with the ground is momentarily at rest, and pushes back on the floor with the force F_1 of static friction. By Newton's third law, the ground exerts a frictional force F_2 of equal magnitude on the foot. Transmitted through muscle and bone, this is the force that accelerates your body forward.

Examples of Static Friction

Static friction determines the minimum force needed to start an object moving. But it also plays a vital role in everyday activities such as walking and driving. When you walk, the foot contacting the ground is temporarily at rest, pushing back against the ground. By Newton's third law, the ground pushes forward on the foot (Fig. 6-38), accelerating you forward. Both forces of the third-law pair—foot on ground and ground on foot—arise from static friction between foot and ground. On a nearly frictionless surface, walking becomes very difficult (Fig. 6-39). Note here that the static frictional force, far from opposing your walking motion, is what makes that motion possible.

Similarly, the tires of an accelerating car push back against the road. If they aren't slipping, the bottom of each tire is momentarily at rest (we'll have more to say about this counter-intuitive notion in Chapter 12, Section 5). Therefore the force a tire exerts on the road is that of static friction. The third law then requires a frictional force of the road pushing forward on the tires; that's what accelerates the car. When the car brakes, the tires now push forward and the road pushes backward to decelerate the car (Fig. 6-40). Note that the brakes stop only the wheels; it's friction that stops the car. You know this if you've ever applied your brakes on an icy road!

FIGURE 6-40 The frictional force between tires and road is what stops the car.

B.C.   by johnny hart

HI, MR. SNAIL !

WHAT ARE YOU DOING ON THE ICE ?

ABOUT THREE FEET A WEEK.

FIGURE 6-39 Walking is difficult on a nearly frictionless surface!

| **APPLICATION** | *Antilock Brakes* |

Most modern cars come with computer-controlled antilock braking systems (ABS). How do these work? Ultimately, they depend on the fact that the coefficient of static friction exceeds the coefficient of kinetic friction.

When you slam on the brakes of a non-ABS car so hard that the wheels lock and skid without turning, the force between tires and road is *kinetic* friction. But if you can manage to keep the wheels from skidding, then the bottoms of the tires are momentarily at rest, and then the force is the larger force of *static* friction (Fig. 6-41).

To maintain static friction, drivers of non-ABS cars are advised to "pump" their brakes when making emergency stops. Actually, a host of complicating factors limits the success of this strategy—including the fact that the driver can't know what each individual wheel is doing. But electronic sensors in

FIGURE 6-41 (*a*) In a locked, skidding wheel, all points move with the same velocity. Kinetic friction acts between wheel and road. (*b*) With the brakes pumped so the wheel keeps rolling, the bottom of the tire is momentarily at rest and the force is static friction. Because $\mu_s > \mu_k$, the stopping distance is shorter when the wheels don't skid.

FIGURE 6-42 Stopping distances for ABS braking systems (brown) and conventional brakes (green).

ABS brakes *can* tell what's happening at each wheel, and they feed that information to a computer that controls the brakes to keep each wheel just on the verge of slipping. Drivers of ABS-equipped cars should slam the brakes on hard in an emergency stop; the loud clattering sound that ensues reveals the ABS system at work. As Fig. 6-42 shows, ABS brakes achieve substantially reduced stopping distances.

Of course, no braking system will stop you very quickly on slippery snow or ice. But here ABS has another advantage: by preventing any one wheel from locking, the ABS system helps the car stay in control, moving in a straight line rather than going into an uncontrolled skid. A non-ABS car under similar circumstances will often skid off the road or, worse, into the oncoming lane.

EXAMPLE 6-12	*Stopping*

The kinetic and static coefficients of friction between a car's tires and a dry road are 0.61 and 0.89, respectively. If the car is traveling at 88 km/h (24 m/s) when the brakes are applied, determine (a) the minimum stopping distance and (b) the stopping distance with the wheels fully locked and the car skidding.

Solution

1. The object of interest is obviously the car (Fig. 6-43).
2. Forces on the car include the gravitational force, the normal force from the road, and a frictional force $\mathbf{F}_f$ of either static or kinetic friction. They're shown in the free-body diagram (Fig. 6-44).
3. With the forces shown, Newton's law becomes

$$\mathbf{F}_g + \mathbf{N} + \mathbf{F}_f = m\mathbf{a}.$$

4. The appropriate coordinate system is obviously a horizontal/vertical one, as shown on the free-body diagram.
5. Each of the three forces has only an x or a y component, and the acceleration is obviously in the x direction (actually, for this braking car, it's in the $-x$ direction, but we'll let the algebra tell us this). Then the components of Newton's law become

FIGURE 6-43 A braking car. The acceleration is in the direction opposite the car's motion.

FIGURE 6-44 Free-body diagram for the braking car.

x component:	$-\mu N = ma_x$
y component:	$-mg + N = 0.$

Here we've written F_f as μN, and left the subscript off μ because we're being asked to compare kinetic and static friction.

6. Solving the y equation for N and substituting in the x equation, we quickly find that

$$a_x = -\mu g.$$

7. Does this make sense? As with so many problems involving gravity, the car's mass doesn't matter. A more massive car needs a larger frictional force to stop—but it has more weight, and thus a greater normal force, and thus the frictional force is proportionately greater. The minus sign on a_x confirms what we expected; the acceleration is in the $-x$

direction, opposite the direction of the car's velocity, thus showing that the car is decelerating.

8. We still have a Chapter 2 type of problem to complete; Equation 2-11 gives $v^2 = v_0^2 + 2a\Delta x$. Putting $v = 0$ for the stopped car and using our $a_x = -\mu g$ for the acceleration gives the stopping distance:

$$\Delta x = \frac{v^2}{-2a_x} = \frac{v^2}{2\mu g}.$$

The minimum stopping distance occurs when the wheels don't skid; then static friction applies and we have

$$\Delta x_{\text{no skid}} = \frac{v_0^2}{2\mu_s g} = \frac{(24 \text{ m/s})^2}{(2)(0.89)(9.8 \text{ m/s}^2)} = 33 \text{ m}.$$

Repeating this calculation with $\mu_k = 0.61$ for the skidding car gives $\Delta x_{\text{skid}} = 48$ m. The 15-m difference could well be enough to prevent an accident.

Tip

Watch Your Speed! This tip isn't so much about physics, but about driving. Our result shows stopping distance increasing as the *square* of the car's speed. That's one thing that makes high speeds so dangerous: doubling your speed increases the distance needed to stop by a factor of four.

Static friction also plays a role in steering a car, as Example 6-13 shows:

EXAMPLE 6-13	*Steering*

A level road makes a 90° turn with a 73-m radius of curvature. What is the maximum speed for a car to negotiate this turn (a) when the road is dry and the coefficient of static friction is 0.88 and (b) when the road is snow-covered and $\mu_s = 0.21$?

Solution

1. Obviously, the object of interest is the car (Fig. 6-45).
2. The only force in the horizontal direction is that of static friction. Why *static* friction? Because the car is not moving in the radial direction, perpendicular to its curved path (Fig. 6-46). In addition, there are the gravitational force and the normal force. Figure 6-47 shows these forces on a free-body diagram.
3. Newton's law for the forces we've identified reads

$$\mathbf{F}_s + \mathbf{F}_g + \mathbf{N} = m\mathbf{a}.$$

4. The obvious choice is a horizontal/vertical coordinate system, shown on the free-body diagram.
5. With the gravitational and normal forces in the vertical direction, the frictional force in the horizontal direction,

FIGURE 6-46 Rounding a curve. The force of static friction acts on the bottom of the tire and is directed toward the center of curvature to keep the car accelerating in its circular path.

FIGURE 6-45 Forces on a car rounding a corner include gravity, the normal force, and the force of static friction between tires and road.

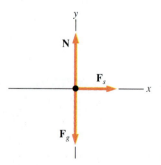

FIGURE 6-47 Free-body diagram for the cornering car. Center of its curved path is to the right.

and the acceleration horizontal and directed toward the center of the curve (which Fig. 6-47 shows we've chosen to be the $+x$ direction), the components of Newton's law become

x component:
$$\mu_s N = ma_x = m\frac{v^2}{r}$$

y component:
$$-mg + N = 0,$$

where we've written $\mu_s N$ for the force of static friction and v^2/r for the acceleration of the car in its curved path.

6. The y equation gives $N = mg$; using this result in the x equation and solving for v gives our answer:
$$v = \sqrt{\mu_s gr}.$$

7. Does this make sense? On a frictionless road, $v = 0$; you couldn't corner without the frictional force to deflect you from a straight-line path. With friction, the maximum safe speed increases as the curve becomes more gradual—that is, with increasing r.

8. For the numbers given, we have
$$v_{\text{dry road}} = \sqrt{(0.88)(9.8 \text{ m/s}^2)(73 \text{ m})} = 25 \text{ m/s} = 90 \text{ km/h}$$

and
$$v_{\text{snow}} = \sqrt{(0.21)(9.8 \text{ m/s}^2)(73 \text{ m})} = 12 \text{ m/s} = 44 \text{ km/h}.$$

Exceed these speeds, and your car must inevitably move in a path of greater radius—and that means going off the road!

EXERCISE A car moving at 75 km/h enters a turn on an icy road where the coefficient of static friction is 0.17. If the radius of the turn is 150 m, will the car stay on the road?

Answer: no

Some problems similar to Example 6-13: 51, 80
ActivPhysics Activity 4.7 simulates this example, allowing you to pick the car's speed and see if it stays on the road.

4.7
Car Circles a Track

Static friction is generally what keeps objects at rest on sloping surfaces; therefore, it plays an important role in such disparate fields as geology, landscape design, dam engineering, the selection of cross-country ski waxes, and avalanche safety.

EXAMPLE 6-14	*Avalanche!*

A storm dumps new snow on a ski resort. The coefficient of static friction between the new snow and the older layer underneath is 0.46. What is the maximum slope angle to which the new snow can adhere? For angles above this maximum, the new snow won't stick; just below the maximum angle, snow builds up and can result in dangerous avalanches.

Solution

We model the new snow as a block of mass m on a surface making angle θ with the horizontal (Fig. 6-48). On with our usual solution strategy:

1. The object of interest is the new snow layer.
2. Forces on the snow include the gravitational force, the normal force from the underlying layers, and the frictional force. We want the snow to remain at rest, so the latter is the force of static friction. We show these forces on Fig. 6-48 and on a free-body diagram (Fig. 6-49).
3. With the forces identified, Newton's law becomes
$$\mathbf{F}_g + \mathbf{N} + \mathbf{F}_s = m\mathbf{a} = 0,$$

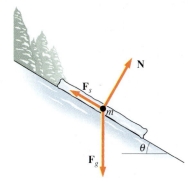

FIGURE 6-48 Avalanche danger! A layer of new snow is modeled as a slab at rest on a sloping surface.

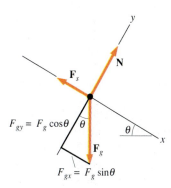

FIGURE 6-49 Free-body diagram for the snow slab. Compare with Fig. 6-33.

where we've set the right-hand side to zero because we want to find conditions under which the snow will not accelerate.

4. The geometry in this problem is identical to that of Example 6-10; in fact, the two examples are almost identical except that here we're dealing with static friction rather than kinetic friction. As in Example 6-10, a tilted coordinate system makes the most sense; we've shown it on the free-body diagram, where the components of the gravitational force are obviously the same as in Example 6-10.

5. In our coordinate system, the component equations become

x component: $\qquad mg\sin\theta - \mu_k N = 0$

y component: $\qquad N - mg\cos\theta = 0$.

(See Example 6-10 for details; these are identical to that example's equations except that we've changed μ_k to μ_s and set the acceleration explicitly to zero.)

6. Solving, we get the same result we did in Equation 6-10 when the acceleration there was zero:

$$u_s = \tan\theta.$$

7. Does this make sense? Yes, and for the same reasons it did in Example 6-10. A steeper slope requires a larger coefficient of friction—approaching infinitely large as the slope becomes vertical. This is partly because the downslope component of gravity increases, but more importantly because the normal force gets smaller, reducing the frictional force for a given μ_s.

8. For the numbers of this example, we have

$$\theta = \tan^{-1}(0.46) = 25°.$$

FIGURE 6-50 An avalanche thunders down a mountainside. Friction of snow on snow helps determine whether a potentially dangerous buildup of snow will occur.

At this slope and steeper, the new snow won't stick, or will slide off in small avalanches as soon as any significant amount accumulates. The real danger comes at slightly lower angles, where a thick snowpack can build up. Changes in composition of the snow with temperature, humidity, and pressure from the weight of the overlying snow may alter the coefficient of friction and trigger a sudden avalanche (Fig. 6-50).

EXERCISE Which Wax? A cross-country skier prepares to head up a trail whose steepest slope is 19°. What is the minimum coefficient of static friction that will allow the skier to stand on this trail without slipping backward?

Answer: 0.34

Some problems similar to Example 6-14: 46

6-5 DRAG FORCES

Friction is not the only "hidden" force that robs objects of their motion and obscures Newton's first law. When an object moves through a fluid such as air or water, it experiences a **drag force** that opposes the relative motion of object and fluid. Ultimately, the drag force arises from collisions between the object and individual molecules in the fluid.

For a limited but important range of objects and speeds, experiment shows that the drag force is approximately proportional to the fluid density ρ (mass per unit volume), the cross-sectional area A the object presents to the fluid, and the square of its speed v relative to the fluid. In this case we write

$$F_D = \tfrac{1}{2}C\rho A v^2 \qquad (6\text{-}4)$$

for the magnitude of the drag force; the direction is opposite the object's motion relative to the fluid. Here C is a constant called the **drag coefficient**, which depends on details such as the object's shape and the texture of its surface. Remarkably, C can be lower for rough surfaces; that's one reason tennis balls are fuzzy and golf balls are dimpled.

FIGURE 6-51 Forces on a falling body include the gravitational force $\mathbf{F}_g$ and drag force $\mathbf{F}_D$. (*a*) At the start of the fall, $v = 0$ and the drag force is zero. (*b*, *c*) As the object gains speed, the drag force increases. (*d*) Eventually the magnitude of the drag force is equal to the gravitational force. Then the net force is zero, and the object no longer accelerates; it's at its terminal speed.

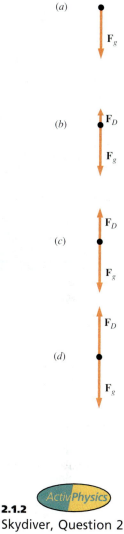

Equation 6-4 holds, approximately, for blunt objects such as a ball, a rock, or a human body, but not for streamlined objects such as a javelin or an airplane. For Equation 6-4 to hold, the object's speed must be great enough that the fluid flow behind the object becomes chaotic (also called turbulent flow). These conditions apply to typical objects with sizes measured in cm or larger, moving through air with speeds measured in m/s. (At much lower speeds, the drag force is proportional to the speed itself, rather than its square.)

You can verify that the quantity $\rho A v^2$ in Equation 6-4 has the units of force; thus C must be dimensionless. Typical values of C lie roughly in the range from 0.2 to 2. We emphasize that Equation 6-4, like Equations 6-2 and 6-3 for frictional forces, is *not* a fundamental equation of physics. Rather, it's an empirical result that captures approximately, over a limited range of parameters, the effect of many individual molecular collisions in producing a net drag force.

Falling Objects

When an object begins falling from rest, its speed v is at first small and therefore so is the velocity-dependent drag force. For a falling object, the net force is the sum of the downward gravitational force and the upward drag force. So at first, the drag force is negligible and the object accelerates downward with the gravitational acceleration g. But as the falling object gains speed, the drag force becomes significant. The magnitude of the net force is then less than mg, and the acceleration drops (Fig. 6-51). If it falls far enough, the object reaches a speed where the magnitude of the drag force equals that of the gravitational force. This is the **terminal speed**—so called because once this speed is reached, the net force on the object is zero and it falls thereafter with constant speed. Figure 6-52 graphs speed versus time for a falling object; ActivPhysics Activity 2.1.2 Question 2 provides animations of both Figs. 6-51 and 6-52.

ActivPhysics

2.1.2
Skydiver, Question 2

FIGURE 6-52 Speed versus time for a falling object. Thin diagonal line shows constant acceleration that would occur in the absence of a drag force; with drag the acceleration is approximately constant only early in the fall. Acceleration decreases toward zero as speed approaches the terminal speed.

Because the drag force depends on an object's area and the gravitational force depends on its mass, the terminal speed is lower for lighter objects with relatively large areas. A parachute, for example, is designed specifically to present a large surface area to the air; a typical terminal speed for a parachutist is around 5 m/s. A Ping-Pong ball and a golf ball have roughly the same physical size and therefore area, but because their masses differ, so do their terminal speeds v_t. For a Ping-Pong ball v_t is about 10 m/s; for a golf ball it's more like 50 m/s. For an irregularly shaped object, the drag coefficient and thus the terminal speed depend on how much surface area the object presents to the air as it falls (Fig. 6-53).

FIGURE 6-53 Skydivers assume a "spread-eagle" position to maximize surface area, thus maximizing drag and lowering terminal speed.

EXAMPLE 6-15	*Skydiving*

In a spread-eagled position, a 70-kg skydiver presents a cross-sectional area of about 0.7 m² to the air, and has a drag coefficient C of about 0.4. The density of air is about 1.2 kg/m³. Find the approximate terminal speed for such a skydiver.

Solution

This is a simple one-dimensional Newton's law problem, but we can still follow the numbered steps of our Newton's law strategy:
(1) The object of interest is the skydiver; (2) forces acting include gravity and the drag force, so (3) Newton's law becomes $\mathbf{F}_g + \mathbf{F}_D = m\mathbf{a} = \mathbf{0}$, where we set the acceleration to zero because we want the terminal speed. The lowest frame of Fig. 6-50 constitutes our free-body diagram. (4) Choosing a coordinate system with the positive y direction downward, we have $F_{gy} = mg$ and $F_{Dy} = -\frac{1}{2}C\rho Av_t^2$ from Equation 6-4. Here the minus sign arises because the drag force is upward, which we've taken to be the negative y direction, and we've labeled the speed with subscript t to indicate the terminal speed. Then (5) we have the single component equation

$$mg - \tfrac{1}{2}C\rho Av_t^2 = 0,$$

which (6) we solve to get

$$v_t = \sqrt{\frac{2mg}{C\rho A}}.$$

(7) Does this make sense? Yes: the larger the area A, the larger the drag force at a given speed, so the lower the terminal speed. The larger the mass, the larger the gravitational force and so the faster the object has to move before the drag force is equal in magnitude to the gravitational force. And the denser the air, the more molecular collisions contributing to the drag force, so the lower the terminal speed. (8) With the numbers of this example,

$$v_t = \sqrt{\frac{2mg}{C\rho A}} = \sqrt{\frac{(2)(70\text{ kg})(9.8\text{ m/s}^2)}{(0.4)(1.2\text{ kg/m}^3)(0.7\text{ m}^2)}} = 64\text{ m/s},$$

or a lethal 140 miles per hour. In a head-first position, the skydiver's terminal speed can be considerably greater. Opening the parachute drops the skydiver's terminal speed to several m/s.

EXERCISE Find the terminal speed of a 600-g basketball 24 cm in diameter for which $C \approx 0.5$.

Answer: 21 m/s

Some problems similar to Example 6-15: 63–66

How far would the skydiver of Example 6-15 have to fall to reach terminal speed? That's a difficult question, since the acceleration is not constant and we don't have an expression for speed or position as a function of time. Although it is possible to set up Newton's law and solve for the motion, the mathematics involves a differential equation beyond the scope of introductory calculus (see Problem 86 for this challenge). In practice, a skydiver falls roughly 500 m before reaching terminal speed.

Don't assume that terminal speed means maximum possible speed. When a parachutist first deploys her parachute, she's moving faster than terminal speed with the parachute. So what happens? The magnitude of the drag force exceeds that of the gravitational force, and thus the net force is upward. The skydiver experiences an upward acceleration that lowers her speed until she reaches the new terminal speed. Similarly, baseball pitches routinely leave the pitcher's hand going faster than the terminal speed; the drag force then acts to slow them down.

Got It!

You drop two spherical lumps made from the same clay, starting both from rest at the same height. Which reaches the ground first, the larger clump or the smaller one? Explain.

Drag and Projectile Motion

In Chapter 4 we consistently neglected air resistance—i.e., the drag force due to air—except when we showed the effect of drag in Fig. 4-17. Looking at Equation 6-4, you can see why calculation of drag effects on projectiles is not trivial. At each point the drag force depends on speed, which in turn depends on earlier effects of the drag force. Although it's possible to set up Newton's law as two simultaneous differential equations to be solved for the two components of the motion, it's generally not possible to obtain analytic solutions. So calculations of projectile motion with air resistance are generally done numerically, using a computer procedure that calculates the acceleration at one time from Newton's law and the speed at that time, then steps forward in time to obtain a new velocity and acceleration, and so forth. Despite the physicist's need for elaborate computer calculations to deal with drag forces, others—including birds, bats, basketball players, ping-pong players, baseball outfielders, and dogs leaping to catch a ball—all have a built-in feel for drag forces that lets them catch their prey or play their sports by judging correctly where a projectile under the influence of drag forces is going to go.

CHAPTER SYNOPSIS

Summary

1. Newton's second law provides a universal description of motion in the realm of classical physics. The following steps will help you apply Newton's law correctly:

1. Identify the object of interest.
2. Identify all forces acting on the object, and draw the force vectors on a free-body diagram that shows the object of interest as a simple dot.

3. Write Newton's law in vector form: $\mathbf{F}_{net} = m\mathbf{a}$, where $\mathbf{F}_{net}$, the net force, is the vector sum of the forces you have identified.
4. Choose a suitable coordinate system.
5. Write the components of Newton's law in your coordinate system.
6. Solve algebraically for the quantities of interest.
7. Check some special cases to see if your answers make sense.
8. Insert numerical values to obtain numerical answers.
2. When two or more objects are linked, it's necessary to write Newton's law for each object, then use the physical linkage to relate quantities appearing in the separate equations.
3. When an object undergoes circular motion at speed v in a circle of radius r, it accelerates at the rate v^2/r in the direction toward the center of the circle. Newton's second law shows that a net force of magnitude mv^2/r must then be acting in the same direction.
4. **Friction** is a force associated with microscopic bonds between two contacting surfaces. When the surfaces are in relative motion, **kinetic friction** occurs, with the force of kinetic friction $\mathbf{F}_k$ opposing the relative motion. When the surfaces are at rest, **static friction** occurs. As long as the surfaces remain at rest, the force of static friction $\mathbf{F}_s$ opposes any applied force that would otherwise set the surfaces in relative motion. Both frictional forces depend on the magnitude, N, of the normal force between the surfaces:

$$F_k = \mu_k N$$
and
$$F_s \leq \mu_s N.$$

Here μ_k and μ_s are the **coefficient of kinetic friction** and the **coefficient of static friction**, respectively. In general, $\mu_s > \mu_k$.

5. **Drag forces** act on objects moving through fluids; the magnitude of the drag force depends on the object's speed relative to the fluid. The presence of drag results in a **terminal speed** for an object falling through a fluid.

Terms You Should Understand

(Pairs are closely related terms whose distinction is important; number in parentheses is chapter section where term first appears.)

free-body diagram (6-1)
static friction, kinetic friction (6-4)
coefficient of (static, kinetic) friction (6-4)
drag force (6-5)
terminal speed (6-5)

Symbols You Should Recognize

mv^2/r (6-3)
μ_k, μ_s (6-4)

Problems You Should Be Able to Solve

Setting up Newton's second law for a single object and solving for any unknown quantities in two dimensions (6-1)
Newton's law problems for two or more linked objects (6-2)
Problems involving forces in circular motion (6-3)
Problems involving kinetic and static friction (6-4)
Calculating drag force and terminal speed (6-5)

Limitations to Keep in Mind

Newton's second law works only if you take into account *all* the forces acting on an object.
Newton's law does not apply in accelerated reference frames.

QUESTIONS

1. Compare the net force on a heavy trunk when it is (a) at rest on the floor; (b) being slid across the floor at constant speed; (c) being pulled upward in an elevator whose cable tension equals the combined weight of the elevator and trunk; (d) sliding down a frictionless ramp.
2. The force of static friction acts only between surfaces at rest. Yet that force is essential in walking and in accelerating or braking a car. Explain.
3. A jet plane flies at constant speed in a vertical circular loop (Fig. 6-54). At what point in the loop does the seat exert the greatest force on the pilot? The least force?
4. In cross-country skiing, skis should easily glide forward but should remain at rest when the skier pushes back against the snow. What frictional properties should the ski wax have to achieve this goal?

FIGURE 6-54 Question 3.

5. Why is it easier for a child to stand nearer the inside of a rotating merry-go-round?

6. Can a coefficient of friction exceed 1?

7. By pushing horizontally with your hand, you can hold a book at rest on a perfectly vertical wall (Fig. 6-55). How is this possible?

FIGURE 6-55 Question 7.

8. In general, a mass suspended from a string will not point exactly toward the center of Earth. Explain in terms of Earth's rotation. Are there places on Earth where the string will point toward the center?

9. Earth's gravity pulls a satellite toward the center of Earth. So why doesn't the satellite actually fall to Earth?

10. Why can front-wheel-drive cars corner better on slippery roads than do rear-wheel-drive cars? Explain in terms of the forces acting on the wheels.

11. Explain why ABS brakes result in a shorter stopping distance for a car.

12. A fishing line has a breaking strength of 20 lb. Is it possible to break the line while reeling in a 15-lb fish? Explain.

13. Two blocks rest on slopes of unequal angle, connected by a rope passing over a pulley (Fig. 6-56). If the blocks have equal masses, will they remain at rest? Why? Neglect friction.

FIGURE 6-56 Question 13, Problems 17, 19.

14. Why do a car's front brakes usually wear out before the rear brakes?

15. Why do airplanes bank when turning?

16. Someone once tried to describe the orbital motion of a satellite by saying that "the gravitational force balances the force mv^2/r." Criticize this statement.

17. In what sense is the force of friction between two surfaces independent of their contacting surface areas? In what sense does the force depend on surface area?

18. On landing, jet aircraft sometimes reverse their engine thrust to assist in stopping. Is this braking mechanism dependent on friction with the runway? Explain.

19. If surfaces are very highly polished, friction actually increases. Why might this be?

20. A car rounds a banked turn at a speed lower than the design speed. Which way does the frictional force point?

21. For safety, automobile racetracks are banked as shown in Fig. 6-57. Explain why this improves the safety of the track.

FIGURE 6-57 Banking of an automobile racetrack. Inside edge of turn is to left (Question 21).

22. In contrast to the automobile racetrack of the previous question, well-designed running tracks are sometimes banked as shown in Fig. 6-58. Explain why, neglecting safety considerations, this is a more appropriate banking scheme.

FIGURE 6-58 Banking of a running track. Inside edge of turn is to left (Question 22).

23. You're in a plane making a banked turn (see Fig. 6-21 and associated exercise). A drink is on your seatback tray, which is essentially frictionless. Will the drink slide toward the low side of the plane as it banks? Explain.

PROBLEMS

ActivPhysics can help with these problems:
Activities in Section 2 "Forces and Motion" and
Section 4 "Circular Motion."

Section 6-1 Using Newton's Second Law

1. Two forces, both in the x-y plane, act on a 1.5-kg mass, which accelerates at 7.3 m/s² in a direction 30° counterclockwise from the x axis. One force has magnitude 6.8 N and points in the $+x$ direction. Find the other force.

2. Two forces act on a 3.1-kg mass, which undergoes acceleration $\mathbf{a} = 0.91\hat{\mathbf{i}} - 0.27\hat{\mathbf{j}}$ m/s². If one of the forces is $\mathbf{F}_1 = -1.2\hat{\mathbf{i}} - 2.5\hat{\mathbf{j}}$ N, what is the other force?

3. A 3700-kg barge is being pulled along a canal by two mules, as shown in Fig. 6-59. The tension in each tow rope is 1100 N, and the ropes make 25° angles with the forward direction. What force does the water exert on the barge (a) if it moves with constant velocity and (b) if it accelerates forward at 0.16 m/s²?

FIGURE 6-59 Problem 3.

4. At what angle should you tilt an air table to simulate motion on the moon's surface, where $g = 1.6$ m/s²?

5. A block of mass m slides with acceleration a down a frictionless slope that makes an angle θ to the horizontal; the only forces acting on it are the force of gravity $\mathbf{F}_g$ and the normal force $\mathbf{N}$ of the slope. Show that the magnitude of the normal force is given by $N = m\sqrt{g^2 - a^2}$.

6. A skier starts from rest at the top of a 24° slope 1.3 km long. Neglecting friction, how long does it take to reach the bottom?

7. A block is launched up a frictionless ramp that makes an angle of 35° to the horizontal. If the block's initial speed is 2.2 m/s, how far up the ramp does it slide?

8. At the start of a race, a 70-kg swimmer pushes off the starting block with a force of 950 N directed at 15° below the horizontal. (a) What is the swimmer's horizontal acceleration? (b) If the swimmer is in contact with the starting block for 0.29 s, what is the horizontal component of his velocity when he hits the water?

9. A 15-kg monkey hangs from the middle of a massless rope as shown in Fig. 6-60. What is the tension in the rope? Compare with the monkey's weight.

FIGURE 6-60 Problem 9.

10. A tow truck is connected to a 1400-kg car by a cable that makes a 25° angle to the horizontal, as shown in Fig. 6-61. If the truck accelerates at 0.57 m/s², what is the magnitude of the cable tension? Neglect friction and the mass of the cable.

FIGURE 6-61 Problem 10.

11. A 10-kg mass is suspended at rest by two strings attached to walls, as shown in Fig. 6-62. Find the tension forces in the two strings.

FIGURE 6-62 Problem 11.

12. A 1,100-kg car goes off the road and plunges down a 23° embankment, coming to rest against a tree. The contact between tree and car is such that the force exerted on the car by the tree is purely horizontal, as suggested in Fig. 6-63. Find the magnitude of that force once the car is fully stopped.

FIGURE 6-63 Problem 12.

13. A camper hangs a 26-kg pack between two trees, using two separate pieces of rope of different lengths, as shown in Fig. 6-64. What is the tension in each rope?

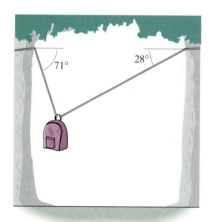

FIGURE 6-64 Problem 13.

14. A construction worker is lifting a 92-kg bundle of plywood onto an upper floor using the arrangement shown in Fig. 6-65. What force must the worker apply to lift the bundle at constant speed? Assume the pulley is massless and frictionless.

FIGURE 6-65 Problem 14.

Section 6-2 Multiple Objects

15. Your 12-kg baby sister is hanging on the bottom of the tablecloth with all her weight. In the middle of the table, 60 cm from each edge, is a 6.8-kg roast turkey. (a) What is the acceleration of the turkey? (b) From the time she starts pulling, how long do you have to intervene before the turkey goes over the edge of the table?

16. Find expressions for the acceleration of the blocks in Fig. 6-66, where the string is fastened securely to the ceiling. Neglect friction and assume that the masses of pulley and string are negligible.

FIGURE 6-66 Problem 16.

17. If the left-hand slope in Fig. 6-56 makes a 60° angle with the horizontal, and the right-hand slope makes a 20° angle, how should the masses compare if the objects are not to slide along the frictionless slopes?

18. In a setup like that shown in Fig. 6-37, but with different masses, a 4.34-kg block starts from rest on the left edge of a frictionless tabletop 1.25 m wide. It accelerates to the

right, and reaches the right edge in 2.84 s. If the mass of the block hanging from the left side is 3.56 kg, what is the mass hanging from the right side?

19. Suppose the angles shown in Fig. 6-56 are 60° and 20°. If the left-hand mass is 2.1 kg, what should be the right-hand mass in order that (a) it accelerates downslope at 0.64 m/s²; (b) it accelerates upslope at 0.76 m/s²?

20. Two unfortunate climbers, roped together, are sliding freely down an icy mountainside. The upper climber (mass 75 kg) is on a slope at 12° to the horizontal, but the lower climber (mass 63 kg) has gone over the edge to a steeper slope at 38°. (a) Assuming frictionless ice and a massless rope, what is the acceleration of the pair? (b) The upper climber manages to stop the slide with an ice ax. Once the climbers have come to a complete stop, what force must the ax exert against the ice?

21. In a florist's display, hanging plants of mass 3.85 kg and 9.28 kg are suspended from an essentially massless wire, as shown in Fig. 6-67. Find the tension in each section of the wire.

54.0°   68.0°

13.9°

3.85 kg

9.28 kg

FIGURE 6-67 Problem 21.

22. A rectangular block of mass m_1 rests on a wedge-shaped block of mass m_2, as shown in Fig. 6-68. All contact surfaces are frictionless. Find an expression for the magnitude of the horizontal force **F** that must be applied to the wedge in order that the rectangular block not slide along the wedge.

F

m_1

m_2

FIGURE 6-68 Problem 22.

Section 6-3 Circular Motion

23. A simplistic model for the hydrogen atom pictures its single electron in a circular orbit of radius 0.0529 nm about the fixed proton. If the electron's orbital speed is 2.18×10^6 m/s, what is the magnitude of the force between the electron and the proton?

24. Suppose the moon were held in its orbit not by gravity but by the tension in a massless cable. Estimate the magnitude of the cable tension. (See Appendix E for relevant data.)

25. Show that the force needed to keep a mass m in a circular path of radius r with period T is $4\pi^2 mr/T^2$.

26. A mass m_1 undergoes circular motion of radius R on a horizontal frictionless table, connected by a massless string through a hole in the table to a second mass m_2 (Fig. 6-69). If m_2 is stationary, find (a) the tension in the string and (b) the period of the circular motion.

R m_1

m_2

FIGURE 6-69 Problem 26.

27. A 940-g rock is whirled in a horizontal circle at the end of a 1.3-m-long string. (a) If the breaking strength of the string is 120 N, what is the maximum allowable speed of the rock? (b) At this maximum speed, what angle does the string make with the horizontal?

28. If the rock of the previous problem is whirled in a vertical circle, what is the minimum speed needed at the top of the circle in order that the string remain taut?

29. A subway train rounds an unbanked curve at 67 km/h. A passenger hanging onto a strap notices that an adjacent unused strap makes an angle of 15° to the vertical. What is the radius of the turn?

30. An Olympic hammer thrower whirls a 7.3-kg hammer on the end of a 120-cm chain. If the chain makes a 10° angle with the horizontal, what is the speed of the hammer?

31. Riders on the "Great American Revolution" loop-the-loop roller coaster of Example 6-8 wear seatbelts as the roller coaster negotiates its 6.3-m-radius loop with a speed of 9.7 m/s. At the top of the loop, what are the magnitude and direction of the force exerted on a 60-kg rider (a) by the roller-coaster seat and (b) by the seatbelt? (c) What would happen if the rider unbuckled at this point?

32. A 45-kg skater rounds a 5.0-m-radius turn at 6.3 m/s. (a) What are the horizontal and vertical components of the force the ice exerts on her skate blades? (b) At what angle can she lean without falling over?

33. An indoor running track is square-shaped with rounded corners; each corner has a radius of 6.5 m on its inside edge. The track includes six 1.0-m-wide lanes. What should be the banking angles on (a) the innermost and (b) the outermost lanes if the design speed of the track is 24 km/h?

34. A jetliner flying horizontally at 850 km/h banks at 32° to make a turn. What is the radius of the turn?

35. You're a passenger in a car rounding a turn with radius 180 m. You take your keys from your pocket and dangle them from the end of your keychain. They make an 18° angle with the vertical, as shown in Fig. 6-70. What is the car's speed?

= 18°

θ

FIGURE 6-70 Problem 35.

36. A bucket of water is whirled in a vertical circle of radius 85 cm. What is the minimum speed that will keep the water from falling out?

37. A 1200-kg car drives on the country road shown in Fig. 6-71. The radius of curvature of the crests and dips is 31 m. What is the maximum speed at which the car can maintain road contact at the crests?

FIGURE 6-71 Problem 37.

38. The Tethered Satellite System (TSS) is a NASA experiment consisting of a 500-kg satellite connected to the space shuttle by a 20-km-long cable of negligible mass. Suppose the shuttle is in a 250-km-high circular orbit, where the acceleration of gravity is 0.926 times its value at Earth's surface. The TSS hangs vertically on its tether (Fig. 6-72), and at its

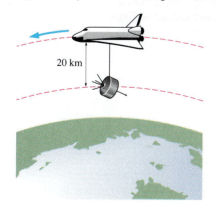

20 km

FIGURE 6-72 NASA's Tethered Satellite System (Problem 38).

230-km altitude the acceleration of gravity is 0.932 times its surface value. What is the tension in the cable?

Section 6-4 Friction

39. Movers slide a file cabinet along a floor. The mass of the cabinet is 73 kg, and the coefficient of kinetic friction between cabinet and floor is 0.81. What is the frictional force on the cabinet?

40. You make a huge snowball with a mass of 33 kg. If the coefficient of friction between the ball and an ice-covered pond is 0.16, with what force must you push the ball to move it (a) at constant velocity and (b) with an acceleration of 0.84 m/s²?

41. Eight 80-kg rugby players climb on a 70-kg "scrum machine," and their teammates proceed to push them with constant velocity across a field. If the coefficient of kinetic friction between scrum machine and field is 0.78, with what force must they push?

42. A hockey puck is given an initial speed of 14 m/s. If it comes to rest in 56 m, what is the coefficient of kinetic friction?

43. A child sleds down a 12° slope at constant speed. What is the coefficient of friction between slope and sled?

44. The handle of a 22-kg lawnmower makes a 35° angle with the horizontal. If the coefficient of friction between lawnmower and ground is 0.68, what magnitude of force is required to push the mower at constant velocity? Assume the force is applied in the direction of the handle. Compare with the mower's weight.

45. Repeat Example 6-5, now assuming that the coefficient of kinetic friction between rock and ice is 0.057.

46. During an ice storm, the coefficients of friction between car tires and road are reduced to $\mu_k = 0.088$ and $\mu_s = 0.14$. (a) What is the maximum slope on which a car can be parked without sliding? (b) On a slope just steeper than this maximum, with what acceleration will a car slide down the slope?

47. A bat crashes into the vertical front of an accelerating subway train. If the coefficient of friction between bat and train is 0.86, what is the minimum acceleration of the train that will allow the bat to remain in place?

48. In a factory, boxes drop vertically onto a conveyor belt moving horizontally at 1.7 m/s. If the coefficient of kinetic friction is 0.46, how long does it take each box to come to rest with respect to the belt?

49. The coefficient of static friction between steel train wheels and steel rails is 0.58. The engineer of a train moving at 140 km/h spots a stalled car on the tracks 150 m ahead. If he applies the brakes so that the wheels do not slip, will the train stop in time?

50. If you neglect to fasten your seatbelt, and if the coefficient of friction between you and your car seat is 0.42, what is the maximum deceleration for which you can remain in your

seat? Compare with the deceleration in an accident that brings a 60-km/h car to rest in a distance of 1.6 m.

51. A bug crawls outward from the center of a compact disc spinning at 200 revolutions per minute. The coefficient of static friction between the bug's sticky feet and the disc surface is 1.2. How far does the bug get from the center before slipping?

52. A 310-g paperback book rests on a 1.2-kg textbook. A force is applied to the textbook, and the two books accelerate together from rest to 96 cm/s in 0.42 s. The textbook is then brought to a stop in 0.33 s, during which time the paperback slides off. Within what range does the coefficient of static friction between the two books lie?

53. A 2.5-kg block and a 3.1-kg block slide down a 30° incline as shown in Fig. 6-73. The coefficient of kinetic friction between the 2.5-kg block and the slope is 0.23; between the 3.1-kg block and the slope it is 0.51. Determine the (a) acceleration of the pair and (b) force the lighter block exerts on the heavier one.

FIGURE 6-73 Problem 53.

54. Children sled down a 41-m-long hill inclined at 25°. At the bottom the slope levels out. If the coefficient of friction is 0.12, how far do the children slide on the level?

55. In a typical front-wheel-drive car, 70% of the car's weight rides on the front wheels. If the coefficient of friction between tires and road is 0.61, what is the maximum acceleration of the car?

56. Repeat the previous problem for a rear-wheel-drive car with the same portion of its weight over the front wheels.

57. A police officer investigating an accident estimates from the damage done that a moving car hit a stationary car at 25 km/h. If the moving car left skid marks 47 m long, and if the coefficient of kinetic friction is 0.71, what was the initial speed of the moving car?

58. A slide inclined at 35° takes bathers into a swimming pool. With water sprayed onto the slide to make it essentially frictionless, a bather spends only one-third as much time on the slide as when it is dry. What is the coefficient of friction on the dry slide?

FIGURE 6-74 Problem 59.

59. You try to push a heavy trunk, exerting a force at an angle of 50° below the horizontal (Fig. 6-74). Show that, no matter how hard you try to push, it is impossible to budge the trunk if the coefficient of static friction exceeds 0.84.

60. A block of mass m is being pulled at constant speed v down a slope that makes an angle θ with the horizontal. The pulling force is applied through a horizontal rope, as shown in Fig. 6-75. If the coefficient of kinetic friction is μ_k, find an expression for the rope tension.

FIGURE 6-75 Problem 60.

61. A block is shoved down a 22° slope with an initial speed of 1.4 m/s. If it slides 34 cm before stopping, what is the coefficient of friction?

62. If the block in the previous problem were shoved up the slope with the same initial speed, (a) how far would it go? (b) Once it stopped, would it slide back down?

Section 6-5 Drag Forces

63. Find the drag force on a 7.4-cm-diameter baseball moving through air (density 1.2 kg/m³) at 45 m/s. The drag coefficient is 0.50.

64. A football's terminal speed is 53 m/s when it's falling pointed end first and 32 m/s when it's falling with its long dimension horizontal. If the football is 28 cm long as its longest, what is the diameter on its short dimension? Assume the drag coefficient C is the same in both orientations.

65. Find the terminal speed of a 1.0-mm-diameter spherical raindrop in air. The densities of air and water are 1.2 kg/m³ and 1000 kg/m³, respectively, and the drag coefficient is 0.50.

66. Will a golf ball of mass 45 g and diameter 4.3 cm reach terminal speed when dropped from a height of 25 m? The drag coefficient is 0.35 and the density of air is 1.2 kg/m³.

Paired Problems

(Both problems in a pair involve the same principles and techniques. If you can get the first problem, you should be able to solve the second one.)

67. In Fig. 6-76, suppose $m_1 = 5.0$ kg and $m_2 = 2.0$ kg, and that the surface and pulley are frictionless. Determine the magnitude and direction of m_2's acceleration.

FIGURE 6-76 Problems 67, 68.

68. Repeat the preceding problem, now taking $m_1 = 3.0$ kg with m_2 still 2.0 kg.
69. A tetherball on a 1.7-m rope is struck so it goes into circular motion in a horizontal plane, with the rope making a 15° angle to the horizontal. What is the ball's speed?
70. An airplane goes into a turn 3.6 km in radius. If the banking angle required is 28° from the horizontal, what is the plane's speed?
71. Starting from rest, a skier slides 100 m down a 28° slope. How much longer does the run take if the coefficient of kinetic friction is 0.17 instead of 0?
72. At the end of a factory production line, boxes start from rest and slide down a 30° ramp 5.4 m long. If the slide is to take no more than 3.3 s, what is the maximum frictional coefficient that can be tolerated?
73. A car moving at 40 km/h negotiates a 130-m radius banked turn designed for 60 km/h. (a) What coefficient of friction is needed to keep the car on the road? (b) To which side of the curve would it move if it hit an essentially frictionless icy patch?
74. A passenger sets a coffee cup on the seatback tray of an airplane flying at 580 km/h. The plane goes into a 2.6-km-radius turn, getting part of its turning force from its rudder and part from banking at 25° (i.e., it's banking at a lower angle than required to give the full turning force). (a) What coefficient of friction is needed to keep the coffee cup on the tray? (b) If there were insufficient friction, which way would the cup slide?

Supplementary Problems

75. A space station is in the shape of a hollow ring, 450 m in diameter (Fig. 6-77). At how many revolutions per minute should it rotate in order to simulate Earth's gravity—that is, so that the normal force on an astronaut at the outer edge would be the astronaut's weight on Earth?

450 m

FIGURE 6-77 For what rotation rate will astronauts feel like they're on Earth? (Problem 75)

76. Figure 6-78 shows a 0.84-kg ball attached to a vertical post by strings of length 1.2 m and 1.6 m. If the ball is set whirling in a horizontal circle, find (a) the minimum speed necessary for the lower string to be taut and (b) the tension in each string if the ball's speed is 5.0 m/s.

1.6 m

1.2 m

FIGURE 6-78 Problem 76.

77. In the loop-the-loop track of Fig. 6-25, show that the car leaves the track at an angle ϕ given by $\cos \phi = v^2/rg$, where ϕ is the angle made by a vertical line through the center of the circular track and a line from the center to the point where the car leaves the track.
78. An astronaut is training in a centrifuge that consists of a small chamber whirled around horizontally at the end of a 5.1-m-long shaft. The astronaut places a notebook on the vertical wall of the chamber and it stays in place. If the coefficient of static friction is 0.62, what is the minimum rate at which the centrifuge must be revolving?

79. You stand on a spring scale at the north pole and again at the equator. (a) Which scale reading will be lower, and why? (b) By what percentage will the lower reading differ from the higher one? (Here you're neglecting variations in g due to geological factors.)

80. Driving in thick fog on a horizontal road, a driver spots a tractor-trailer truck jackknifed across the road, as in Fig. 6-79. To avert a collision, the driver could brake to a stop or swerve in a circular arc, as suggested in Fig. 6-79. Which offers the greater margin of safety? Assume that the same coefficient of static friction is operative in both cases, and that the car maintains constant speed if it swerves.

FIGURE 6-79 Problem 80.

81. A highway turn of radius R is banked for a design speed v_d. If a car enters the turn at speed $v = v_d + \Delta v$, where Δv can be positive or negative, show that the minimum coefficient of static friction needed to prevent slipping is

$$\mu_s = \frac{|\Delta v|}{gR} \frac{(2v_d + \Delta v)}{[1 + (v_d v/gR)^2]}.$$

82. Suppose the coefficient of friction between a block and a horizontal surface is proportional to the block's speed: $\mu = \mu_1 v/v_1$, where μ_1 and v_1 are constants. If the block is given an initial speed v_0, show that it comes to rest in a distance $x = v_0 v_1/\mu_1 g$.

83. A block is projected up an incline making an angle θ with the horizontal. It returns to its initial position with half its initial speed. Show that the coefficient of kinetic friction is $\mu_k = \frac{3}{5} \tan \theta$.

84. The victim of a political kidnapping is forced into a north-facing car and then blindfolded. The car pulls into traffic and, from the sound of the surrounding traffic, the victim knows that the car is moving at about the legal speed limit of 85 km/h. The car then turns to the right; the victim estimates that the force the seat exerts on him is one-fifth of his weight. The victim experiences this force for 28 s. At the end of that time, in what direction can the victim conclude that he is heading?

85. A 2.1-kg mass is connected to a spring of spring constant $k = 150$ N/m and unstretched length 18 cm. The pair are mounted on a frictionless air table, with the free end of the spring attached to a frictionless pivot. The mass is set into circular motion at 1.4 m/s. Find the radius of its path.

86. This problem is for those with unusually advanced math skills. Set up Newton's law for an object falling from rest, subject to the drag force of Equation 6-4. Use a coordinate system with the y axis vertically downward, and write the acceleration as $a_y = dv_y/dt$. Your Newton's law then becomes a differential equation. Integrate it to show that the speed as a function of time is given by

$$v(t) = \sqrt{\frac{2gm}{CA\rho}} \tanh\left(\sqrt{\frac{CАg\rho}{2m}} t\right),$$ where tanh is the hyperbolic tangent function $\tanh(x) = (e^x - e^{-x})/(e^x + e^{-x})$.

Work, Energy, and Power

Lifting a heavy object requires that work be done against the gravitational force **F**$_g$. Here the cable tension forces **T** do work on the object.

Figure 7-1*a* shows a skier starting from rest at the top of a uniform slope. What's the skier's speed at the bottom? You could easily solve this problem by applying Newton's second law to find the acceleration, then using the appropriate constant acceleration equation to find the speed. But what about the skier in Fig. 7-1*b*? Here the slope is continuously changing and so is the acceleration. Constant acceleration equations do not apply, so solving for the details of the skier's motion would be difficult.

(a)

(b)

FIGURE 7-1 Skier on (a) a uniform slope and (b) a nonuniform slope.

There are many cases, like that of Fig. 7-1b, where we need to analyze motion subject to changing forces and accelerations. In this chapter we introduce the important physical concepts of **work** and **energy**. These powerful concepts allow us to "shortcut" the detailed application of Newton's law and arrive easily at answers to these more complex problems. We begin with the concept of work.

7-1 WORK

We all have an intuitive sense of the term "work." Carrying a piece of furniture upstairs involves work. The heavier the furniture, or the higher the stairs, the greater the work. Pushing a stalled car involves work. The harder we push, or the farther we push, the more work we do. Our precise definition of work reflects this intuition:

For an object moving in one dimension, the work W done on the object by constant applied force F is

$$W = F_x \Delta x, \tag{7-1}$$

where F_x is the component of the force in the direction of the object's motion and Δx is the object's displacement.

In writing this definition, we've taken the x axis to point in the direction of the object's motion. The force **F** need not be the net force; if we are interested, for example, in how much work *we* must do to drag a heavy box across the floor, then **F** is the force *we apply* and W is the work *we do*.

Equation 7-1 shows that the SI unit of work is the newton-meter (N·m). One newton-meter is given the name **joule**, in honor of the nineteenth-century British physicist and brewer James Joule.

The SI unit of work is the joule (J), defined as 1 newton-meter (N·m).

Equation 7-1 shows that the person pushing the car in Fig. 7-2 does work equal to the force he applies times the distance the car moves. But the person pulling the suitcase in Fig. 7-3 does work equal only to the horizontal component of the force she applies times the distance the suitcase moves. Furthermore, by our definition, the waiter of Fig. 7-4 does no work on the tray. Why not? Because the direction of the force he applies is perpendicular to the horizontal motion of the tray; there is no component of force along the direction of motion. Similarly, the weightlifter

FIGURE 7-2 When pushing in the direction of the car's motion, the person does work equal to the force he applies times the distance the car moves.

FIGURE 7-3 The suitcase is moving horizontally, so only the horizontal component of the force, F_x, contributes to the work.

FIGURE 7-4 The waiter applies a vertical force $\mathbf{F}_{up}$ to the tray; since this is perpendicular to the tray's horizontal motion, the waiter does no work on the tray.

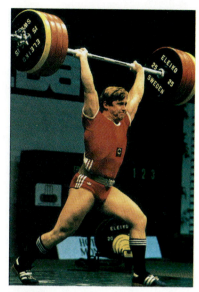

FIGURE 7-5 The weightlifter, strain though he may, is not doing work on the barbell while he holds it stationary.

of Fig. 7-5 does no work while he holds the barbell steady over his head, only while he lifts it.

EXAMPLE 7-1	*Pushing a Trunk*

You push a 75-kg trunk 6.4 m across a floor, exerting a horizontal force of 540 N. How much work do you do?

Solution

Since the force is in the direction of motion, Equation 7-1 gives simply

$$W = F\Delta x = (540\ \text{N})(6.4\ \text{m}) = 3.5\times10^3\ \text{N}\cdot\text{m} = 3.5\ \text{kJ}.$$

If you push the trunk at constant speed, this work is expended against the frictional force.

EXAMPLE 7-2	*A Garage Lift*

A garage lift raises a 1300-kg car a vertical distance of 2.3 m at constant speed. How much work does it do?

Solution

To find the work, we need the force the lift exerts on the car. Since the car is raised at constant speed, it is not accelerating and therefore the *net* force on it is zero. The two forces acting are the upward lift force and the downward force of gravity; with no acceleration, they have the same magnitude, *mg*. The lift force is in the same direction as the motion, so the work done by the lift is

$$W = F\Delta x = mg\,\Delta x = (1300\ \text{kg})(9.8\ \text{m/s}^2)(2.3\ \text{m})$$
$$= 2.9\times10^4\ \text{kg}\cdot\text{m}^2/\text{s}^2 = 2.9\times10^4\ \text{J}.$$

EXERCISE The total mass of an elevator and its passengers is 1400 kg. How much work does the lifting mechanism do on the elevator and passengers in raising them 90 m at constant speed?

Answer: 1.2 MJ

Some problems similar to Examples 7-1 and 7-2: 1–4

5.1
Work Calculations

In the previous two examples, the force we were interested in was in the same direction as the motion. When that is not the case, we must first determine the component of force along the direction of motion.

EXAMPLE 7-3	*Pulling a Suitcase*

The airline passenger of Fig. 7-3 pulls her wheeled suitcase, exerting a 60-N force at a 35° angle to the horizontal. How much work does she do on the suitcase in pulling it 45 m from a taxi to the check-in counter?

Solution

Figure 7-6 shows that the horizontal component of the force is $F_x = F \cos \theta$, so the work is

$$W = F_x \Delta x = F \cos \theta \Delta x = (60 \text{ N})(\cos 35°)(45 \text{ m})$$

$$= 2.2 \text{ kJ}.$$

EXERCISE You push a lawnmower, exerting a 95-N force along the handle, at 40° to the horizontal. How much work do you do on the mower while cutting a 22-m long stretch of grass?

Answer: 1.6 kJ

Some problems similar to Example 7-3: 8, 69, 70

FIGURE 7-6 Example 7-3.

Work can be positive or negative. When a force acts in the same general direction as the motion, the work it does is positive. Acting at 90° to the direction of motion, a force does no work. And when a force acts to oppose motion, it does negative work (Fig. 7-7).

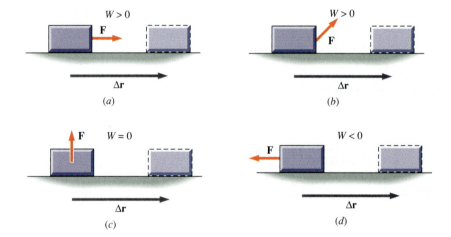

FIGURE 7-7 (*a*, *b*) A force applied in the same general direction as an object's motion does positive work on the object. (*c*) A force acting at right angles to the motion—like the normal force of the floor—does no work. (*d*) A force acting to oppose the motion—like the frictional force—does negative work. Here Δ**r** is the object's displacement vector.

EXAMPLE 7-4	*Stopping a Car*

The coefficient of kinetic friction between a wet, horizontal road and the wheels of a skidding car is 0.21. The mass of the car is 1500 kg. How much work does the frictional force do on the car if the car comes to a stop in 54 m?

Solution

To find the work, we need to know the frictional force. On a horizontal road, the normal force balances gravity, so $N = mg$. Then the magnitude of the frictional force is $\mu_k N = \mu_k mg$. The direction of this force is opposite the car's motion. If we take the positive x direction in the direction of motion, then the compo-

nent of force along this direction is negative: $F_x = -\mu_k mg$. So the work done by friction is

$$W = F_x \Delta x = (-\mu_k mg)(\Delta x)$$

$$= -(0.21)(1500 \text{ kg})(9.8 \text{ m/s}^2)(54 \text{ m})$$

$$= -1.7 \times 10^5 \text{ kg·m}^2/\text{s}^2 = -1.7 \times 10^5 \text{ J}.$$

The negative answer means the force acts to oppose the car's motion.

Some problems similar to Example 7-4: 6, 77, 78

7-2 WORK AND THE SCALAR PRODUCT

Work is a *scalar* quantity; it is specified completely by a single number and has no direction. But Fig. 7-7 shows clearly that work involves a relation between two *vectors*—the force **F** and the displacement Δ**r**. If θ is the angle between these two vectors, then the component of the force along the direction of motion is $F \cos \theta$, and the work is

$$W = (F \cos \theta)(\Delta r) = F \Delta r \cos \theta. \qquad (7\text{-}2)$$

This equation is a generalization of our definition 7-1; choose the *x* axis along Δ**r**; then $\Delta r = \Delta x$ and $F \cos \theta = F_x$, so we recover Equation 7-1.

Equation 7-2 shows that work is the product of the magnitudes of the vectors **F** and Δ**r** and the cosine of the angle between them. This combination—a product of vector magnitudes with the cosine of the angle between the vectors—occurs so often that it's given a special name: the **scalar product** of two vectors.

> The scalar product of any two vectors A and B is defined as
>
> $$\mathbf{A} \cdot \mathbf{B} = AB \cos \theta, \qquad (7\text{-}3)$$
>
> where A and B are the magnitudes of the vectors and θ the angle between them.

The term "scalar product" should remind you that $\mathbf{A} \cdot \mathbf{B}$ is itself a *scalar,* even though it's formed from two vectors. Note that a centered dot is used to designate the scalar product; for this reason, it's also called the **dot product**. Figure 7-8 shows a geometrical interpretation of the dot product, while the Math Toolbox lists several other mathematical properties, including its expression in unit vector notation.

$\mathbf{A} \cdot \mathbf{B} = A\,B\,\cos\theta$

FIGURE 7-8 The scalar product of two vectors is the product of the vector lengths and the cosine of the angle between them. Geometrically, it is the length of vector **A** multiplied by the component of vector **B** in the direction of **A**.

Math Toolbox

The Scalar Product Equation 7-3 defines the scalar product of two vectors:

$$\mathbf{A} \cdot \mathbf{B} = AB \cos \theta$$

Since the product of scalars is commutative, this defining equation shows that the scalar product is also commutative: $\mathbf{A} \cdot \mathbf{B} = \mathbf{B} \cdot \mathbf{A}$. Problem 11 asks you to confirm that the scalar product is also distributive:

$$\mathbf{A} \cdot (\mathbf{B} + \mathbf{C}) = \mathbf{A} \cdot \mathbf{B} + \mathbf{A} \cdot \mathbf{C}.$$

The defining Equation 7-3 is written in terms of vector magnitudes and the angle between two vectors. With vectors expressed in unit vector notation, Problem 12 shows how the distributive law gives a simple form for the scalar product; if $\mathbf{A} = A_x \hat{\mathbf{i}} + A_y \hat{\mathbf{j}} + A_z \hat{\mathbf{k}}$ and $\mathbf{B} = B_x \hat{\mathbf{i}} + B_y \hat{\mathbf{j}} + B_z \hat{\mathbf{k}}$, then

$$\mathbf{A} \cdot \mathbf{B} = A_x B_x + A_y B_y + A_z B_z. \qquad (7\text{-}4)$$

Comparing Equation 7-2 with Equation 7-3 shows that the work done by a constant force **F** moving an object through a straight-line displacement Δ**r** is just

$$W = \mathbf{F} \cdot \Delta \mathbf{r}. \qquad (7\text{-}5)$$

As the examples below show, either Equation 7-3 or Equation 7-4 can be used in evaluating the dot product in this expression for work. We emphasize what Equation 7-5 and the definition of the scalar (dot) product both show: the work W is itself a *scalar;* it has no direction.

EXAMPLE 7-5	Pig Push

The boy in Fig. 7-9 pushes on the pig with a force $\mathbf{F} = 490\hat{\imath} + 230\hat{\jmath}$ N, giving the pig a displacement $\Delta\mathbf{r} = 1.77\hat{\imath} + 1.90\hat{\jmath}$ m. How much work does the boy do?

Solution
We're given the force and displacement in unit-vector notation, so we use Equation 7-4 for the dot product in Equation 7-5:

$$W = \mathbf{F} \cdot \Delta\mathbf{r} = F_x \Delta x + F_y \Delta y$$

$$= (490 \text{ N})(1.77 \text{ m}) + (230 \text{ N})(1.90 \text{ m})$$

$$= 1.3 \text{ kJ}.$$

FIGURE 7-9 Pig Push. How much work does the boy do on the pig?

EXAMPLE 7-6	A Tugboat: Finding the Angle

A tugboat pushes an ocean liner with a force of 830 kN, moving it 0.38 km and doing 290 MJ of work. What is the angle between the direction of the tugboat's push and the motion of the ship?

Solution
Here we know the magnitudes of the force and displacement, and their dot product $W = \mathbf{F} \cdot \Delta\mathbf{r}$, so we can solve Equation 7-3 for the angle:

$$\theta = \cos^{-1}\left(\frac{\mathbf{F} \cdot \Delta\mathbf{r}}{F\Delta r}\right) = \left(\frac{290 \times 10^6 \text{ J}}{(830 \times 10^3 \text{ N})(380 \text{ m})}\right) = 23°.$$

Is this answer reasonable? Yes: 830 kN multiplied by 0.38 km is a little more than 290 MJ. We need a small but nonzero angle between force and displacement to make the actual work lower.

EXERCISE A force $\mathbf{F} = 34\hat{\imath} + 61\hat{\jmath}$ N acts to move an object along a straight path given by $\Delta\mathbf{r} = 4.6\hat{\imath} + 5.1\hat{\jmath}$ m. Find (a) the work done by the force and (b) the angle between force and displacement. *Hint:* This exercise combines the two preceding examples.

Answers: (a) 470 J; (b) 13°

Some problems similar to Examples 7-5 and 7-6: 16, 19–22

Tip

Don't Confuse Vectors and Scalars Vectors and scalars are different, and that means an equation must have either scalars on both sides or vectors on both sides; you can't equate a scalar to a vector. Be especially careful with this when you're working with dot products; the quantity $\mathbf{A} \cdot \mathbf{B}$, despite being written in terms of vectors, is itself a *scalar*. Thus the equation $c = \mathbf{A} \cdot \mathbf{B}$ makes mathematical sense, while $\mathbf{C} = \mathbf{A} \cdot \mathbf{B}$ does not. Later we'll encounter a way of multiplying two vectors to make another vector.

7-3 A VARYING FORCE

Often, the force applied to an object varies with position. Especially important examples include the fundamental forces of nature; the electrical and gravitational forces, for example, vary as the inverse square of the distance between interacting objects. The force of a spring that we encountered in Chapter 5 provides another example; as the spring stretches, the force increases.

How do we calculate the work done by a varying force? Consider first the case of one-dimensional motion. Figure 7-10 is a plot of a force F that varies with position x. We would like to find the work done by the force as an object moves from x_1 to x_2. We can't simply write $F(x_2 - x_1)$; since the force varies, there's no single value for F. What we can do, though, is divide the region into rectangles of width Δx, as shown in Fig. 7-11a. If we make Δx small enough, the force will be nearly constant over the width of each rectangle (Fig. 7-11b). Then the work ΔW done in moving the width Δx of one such rectangle is approximately $F(x)\Delta x$, where $F(x)$ is the force at the midpoint x of that rectangle; we write $F(x)$ to show explicitly that the force is a function of position. Note that the quantity $F(x)\Delta x$ is simply the area of the rectangle, expressed in the appropriate units (N·m, or J). Suppose there are N rectangles. Let x_i be the midpoint of the ith rectangle. Then the total work done in moving from x_1 to x_2 is given approximately by the sum of the individual amounts of work ΔW_i associated with each rectangle, or

$$W \simeq \sum_{i=1}^{N} W_i = \sum_{i=1}^{N} F(x_i)\Delta x. \tag{7-6}$$

How good is this approximation? That depends on how small we make the rectangles. Suppose we let them get arbitrarily small. Then the number of rectangles must grow arbitrarily large. In the limit of infinitely many infinitesimally small rectangles, the approximation in Equation 7-6 becomes exact (Fig. 7-11c). Then we have

$$W = \lim_{\Delta x \to 0} \sum_i F(x_i)\Delta x, \tag{7-7}$$

where the sum is over all the infinitesimal rectangles between x_1 and x_2. The sum of infinitely many infinitesimal quantities is a **definite integral**. The quantity on the right-hand side of Equation 7-7 is the definite integral of the function $F(x)$ over the interval from x_1 to x_2. We introduce a special symbolism for the limiting process of Equation 7-7, writing

$$W = \int_{x_1}^{x_2} F(x)\,dx. \quad \left(\begin{array}{c}\text{work done by a varying}\\ \text{force in one dimension}\end{array}\right) \tag{7-8}$$

What does expression 7-8 mean? It means, by definition, exactly the same thing as Equation 7-7: it tells us to break the interval from x_1 to x_2 into many small rectangles of width Δx, to multiply the value of the function $F(x)$ at each rectangle by the width Δx, and to sum those products. As we take arbitrarily many arbitrarily small rectangles, the result of this process gives us the value of the definite integral. You can think of the symbol $\int$ in Equation 7-8 as standing for "sum," and the symbol dx as a limiting case of arbitrarily small Δx. The definite integral has a simple geometrical interpretation: as the sum of the areas of the many rectangles, it is the area under the curve $F(x)$ between the limits x_1 and x_2.

How are we to evaluate the infinite sum implied in Equation 7-8? One way is to back off and take a sum over a large but finite number of small, but not infinitesimally small, rectangles. This method gives a good approximation if the rectangle width Δx is small enough. It is widely used in computer calculations and for integrals that cannot be handled in any other way. But in many cases we can use the methods developed in calculus (see Math Toolbox).

FIGURE 7-11 Work is the area under the force-versus-position curve. (a) It can be approximated by dividing the region into rectangles and summing their areas. (b) The more rectangles, the more accurate the approximation. (c) The limit of infinitely many infinitesimally small rectangles gives the exact area.

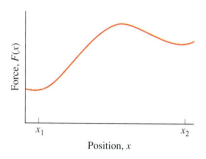

FIGURE 7-10 A force $F(x)$ that varies with position x.

(a)

(b)

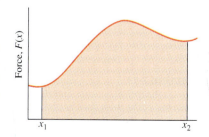

(c)

Math Toolbox

Integration In your calculus course you've either learned, or will soon learn, that integrals and derivatives are inverses of each other. In a Math Toolbox in Section 2.2 we saw that the derivative of x^n is nx^{n-1}; therefore, the integral of x^n involves the expression $(x^{n+1})/(n+1)$, as you can verify by differentiating. We determine the value of a definite integral by evaluating this expression at upper and lower limits and subtracting:

$$\int_{x_1}^{x_2} x^n \, dx = \frac{x^{n+1}}{n+1} \bigg|_{x_1}^{x_2} = \frac{x_2^{n+1}}{n+1} - \frac{x_1^{n+1}}{n+1}, \qquad (7\text{-}9)$$

where the middle term in this expression is a shorthand notation for the difference given in the rightmost term. A review of integration and a table of common integrals are given in Appendix A.

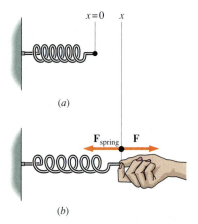

(a)

(b)

FIGURE 7-12 Stretching a spring. The left end of the spring is fixed, and in *(a)* the equilibrium position of the right end defines $x = 0$. *(b)* In stretching the spring, the hand applies a force **F** to oppose the spring force. The work done by the external agent is $\frac{1}{2}kx^2$, Equation 7-10.

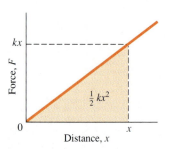

FIGURE 7-13 The force required to stretch the spring increases linearly with distance x. The work done in stretching the spring is the triangular area under the force-versus-distance curve, given by $W = (\frac{1}{2})(x)(kx) = \frac{1}{2}kx^2$.

Stretching a Spring

A spring provides an important example of a force that varies with position. We introduced springs in Section 5-8 and found that an ideal spring exerts a force proportional to its displacement from equilibrium

$$F = -kx,$$

where k is the spring constant and where the minus sign shows that the spring force is opposite to the direction of the displacement. It's not just coiled springs that we're interested in here; many physical systems, from molecules to skyscrapers to stars, behave as though they contain springs. The work and energy considerations we develop here and in subsequent chapters apply to those systems as well as to actual springs.

Suppose we stretch a spring from its equilibrium length. The force exerted *by* the spring is $-kx$, so the force exerted *on* the spring *by* the external stretching force is $+kx$. If we let $x = 0$ be one end of the spring at equilibrium and if we hold the other end fixed and pull the spring until its free end is at a new position x, as shown in Fig. 7-12, then Equation 7-8 shows that the work done on the spring by the external force is

$$W_{\text{done on spring}} = \int_0^x F(x) \, dx = \int_0^x kx \, dx = \tfrac{1}{2}kx^2 \bigg|_0^x = \tfrac{1}{2}kx^2 - \tfrac{1}{2}k(0)^2,$$

or

$$W_{\text{done on spring}} = \tfrac{1}{2}kx^2, \qquad (7\text{-}10)$$

where we've used Equation 7-9 to evaluate the integral. Does this result make sense? The more we stretch the spring, the greater the force we must apply— and that means we must do more work for a given amount of additional stretch. Figure 7-13 shows graphically why the work depends quadratically on the displacement. Although we used the word "stretch" in developing Equation 7-10, the result applies equally to compressing a spring a distance x from equilibrium.

| EXAMPLE 7-7 | Bungee Jumping |

An elastic cord used in bungee jumping (Fig. 7-14) is 20 m long and has spring constant $k = 11$ N/m. At the lowest point in the jump, the cord length has doubled. (a) How much work has been done on it? (b) Compare the amount of work involved in the first meter of stretch with that involved in the last meter.

Solution

(a) Equation 7-10 gives the work needed to stretch the cord from equilibrium:

$$W = \tfrac{1}{2}kx^2 = (\tfrac{1}{2})(11 \text{ N/m})(20 \text{ m})^2 = 2.2 \text{ kJ},$$

where we use $x = 20$ m since we're told that the amount of stretch is equal to the initial length of the cord.

(b) For the first meter of stretch, we repeat the calculation with $x = 1$ m: $W_1 = (\tfrac{1}{2})(11 \text{ N/m})(1 \text{ m})^2 = 5.5$ J. For the last meter, we want the work needed to go from $x = 19$ m to $x = 20$ m. We can repeat the calculation leading to Equation 7-10, this time using 19 m as the lower limit instead of zero. Then we have

$$W_{19-20} = (\tfrac{1}{2})(11 \text{ N/m})(20 \text{ m})^2 - (\tfrac{1}{2})(11 \text{ N/m})(19 \text{ m})^2 = 214 \text{ J}.$$

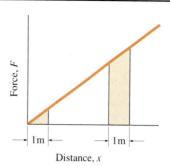

FIGURE 7-15 Work is the area under the force-distance curve. It takes a lot more work to stretch the last meter than it does the first meter.

Why is this number so much larger than the work required for the first meter? Because the bungee cord exerts a large force by the time it's been stretched 19 m, and stretching it further requires that a lot of work be done against that force (Fig. 7-15).

EXERCISE Uncompressed, the spring for an automobile suspension is 45 cm long. It needs to be fitted into a space 32 cm long. If the spring constant is 3.8 kN/m, how much work does a mechanic have to do to fit the spring?

Answer: 32 J

FIGURE 7-14 A bungee jumper leaps from a crane, suspended by a strong elastic cord. At its maximum extension, the cord length will double.

Tip

Don't Just Multiply Whenever a force depends on position, you can't just multiply force by distance to get work. You can see that because there's no unique value to use for the force—but it's still a common mistake. Instead you need to integrate, or use an equation resulting from integration, as with Equation 7-10. As you continue with physics, you'll find other times when you're essentially summing over a quantity that varies continuously. In all such cases you can't just multiply; rather, your answer must be the result of integration.

Some problems similar to Example 7-7: 26, 27, 75, 76

| EXAMPLE 7-8 | Rough Sliding |

Workers pushing a 180-kg trunk across a level floor encounter a 10-m-long region where the floor becomes increasingly rough; the coefficient of kinetic friction increases from 0.17 to 0.79 according to the expression

$$\mu_k = \mu_0 + ax^2,$$

where $\mu_0 = 0.17$, $a = 0.0062$ m^{-2}, and x is the distance in meters from the beginning of the rough region. How much work does it take to push the trunk at constant speed across the region?

Solution

Pushing at constant speed on a level floor requires a force equal in magnitude to the frictional force $\mu_k mg = (\mu_0 + ax^2)mg$. This force varies with position, so we must integrate—using Equation 7-8—to get the work:

$$W = \int_{x_1}^{x_2} F\,dx = \int_{0}^{10} (\mu_0 + ax^2)mg\,dx$$

$$= mg(\mu_0 x + \tfrac{1}{3}ax^3)\big|_{x=0}^{x=10\,\text{m}}$$

$$= (180 \text{ kg})(9.8 \text{ m/s}^2)[(0.17)(10 \text{ m})$$

$$+ (\tfrac{1}{3})(0.0062 \text{ m}^{-2})(10 \text{ m})^3 - 0] = 6.64 \text{ kJ}.$$

Does this result make sense? It is well above the 3.0 kJ we get by calculating $\mu_k mg\,\Delta x$, with μ_k equal to its value 0.17 at the beginning of the rough interval. But it's much less than the 14 kJ we get using the value $\mu_k = 0.79$ appropriate to the end of the interval. Since the actual coefficient varies between these limits, we expect the work to lie between these extremes.

Figure 7-16 shows the force $\mu_k mg$ as a function of position. Unlike the previous example, we can't calculate the work using a simple geometrical formula; to get the exact area under the curve we must integrate. However, we can approximate the work by estimating this area graphically; Problem 28 explores this approach.

FIGURE 7-16 Force versus position for Example 7-8.

EXERCISE As a 7.6-cm-long nail is driven into a block of wood, the frictional force on the nail increases according to $F = ax^2$, where $a = 16 \text{ N/cm}^2$. (a) Find the work needed to drive the entire nail into the wood. (b) What per cent of the total work is involved in driving the last centimeter?

Answers: (a) 23 J; (b) 35%

Some problems similar to Example 7-8: 25, 31, 32, 71, 72

Got It!

A rubber band is stretched 5 cm, at which point it exerts a force of 2 N. Is the work done in stretching the rubber band 10 J? Explain.

7-4 FORCE AND WORK IN THREE DIMENSIONS

What if a force varies not only in magnitude but also in direction? Or what if an object's path is not straight but curved? Then how do we calculate work? Our basic definition $W = \mathbf{F} \cdot \Delta \mathbf{r}$ provides the answer. Figure 7-16a shows the curved path of an object and several vectors of an applied force for which we would like to know the work. In this most general case, both the direction of the path and the direction and magnitude of the force vary. But if we magnify a small section $\Delta \mathbf{r}$ of the path (Fig. 7-17a), it will appear essentially straight and the force will not vary significantly over the segment. Over this short segment, with the force a

FIGURE 7-17 (a) An object moves on a curved path. We want to know the work done by a force that may vary in direction and/or magnitude along the path. (b) A very small segment $\Delta \mathbf{r}$ of the path appears straight and the force does not vary significantly over that segment. The work involved in traversing the short segment is $\Delta W = \mathbf{F} \cdot \Delta \mathbf{r}$.

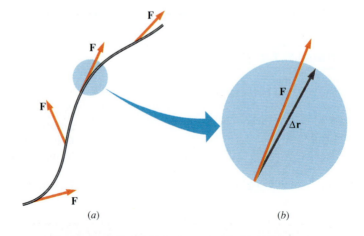

(a)   (b)

nearly constant quantity $\mathbf{F}$, the work ΔW is approximately

$$\Delta W = \mathbf{F} \cdot \Delta \mathbf{r}.$$

If we determine the work ΔW associated with each small segment of the path from some point $\mathbf{r}_1$ to another point $\mathbf{r}_2$, then the total work is given by summing all the ΔW's:

$$W \simeq \sum \Delta W = \sum \mathbf{F} \cdot \Delta \mathbf{r}.$$

If we let the size of the segments grow arbitrarily small and their number increase without bound, this approximation becomes increasingly accurate. In the limit $\Delta \mathbf{r} \to 0$, the sum becomes an integral and we write

$$W = \int_{\mathbf{r}_1}^{\mathbf{r}_2} \mathbf{F} \cdot d\mathbf{r}, \qquad (7\text{-}11)$$

where the limits $\mathbf{r}_1$ and $\mathbf{r}_2$ imply that the integral is taken over the specified path from point $\mathbf{r}_1$ to $\mathbf{r}_2$. An integral such as Equation 7-11, involving the dot product of a vector with a particular path, is called a **line integral**. You will encounter line integrals again when you study electromagnetism.

What does the line integral 7-11 mean? Its meaning comes from the procedure we used to arrive at it: form the many scalar quantities $\mathbf{F} \cdot \Delta \mathbf{r}$ over the path of interest and sum them, taking the limit as $\Delta \mathbf{r}$ becomes arbitrarily small. Example 7-9 illustrates the use of a line integral.

EXAMPLE 7-9	*Work and the Gravitational Force*

A car drives down the hill shown in Fig. 7-18a. How much work does the force of gravity do on the car as it drives from the top of the hill $(y = h)$ to the bottom $(y = 0)$?

Solution

Figure 7-18b shows a small segment $\Delta \mathbf{r}$ of the path, which can be written $\Delta \mathbf{r} = \Delta x \hat{\imath} + \Delta y \hat{\jmath}$ in a coordinate system with x axis horizontal and y axis vertically upward. The force of gravity is always downward: $\mathbf{F}_g = -mg \hat{\jmath}$. Then the amount of work ΔW done by gravity as the car undergoes the displacement $\Delta \mathbf{r}$ is

$$\Delta W = \mathbf{F} \cdot \Delta \mathbf{r} = (-mg \hat{\jmath}) \cdot (\Delta x \hat{\imath} + \Delta y \hat{\jmath}) = -mg \Delta y,$$

where $\hat{\jmath} \cdot \hat{\imath} = 0$ since the two unit vectors are perpendicular and $\hat{\jmath} \cdot \hat{\jmath} = 1$ since $\hat{\jmath}$ has magnitude 1 and is parallel to itself. Summing over the entire path and taking the limit as $\Delta y \to 0$ gives

$$W = \int_{y=h}^{y=0} (-mg\,dy) = -mgy \Big|_h^0$$
$$= -mg(0) - (-mgh) = mgh.$$

In this case the details of the path don't matter at all; the work depends only on the vertical distance h. This illustrates an important property of the gravitational force that we'll explore further in the next chapter.

EXERCISE The irregular hill shown in Fig. 7-1b has a vertical drop of 44 m. How much work does the gravitational force do on a 62-kg skier traversing this run?

Answer: 27 kJ

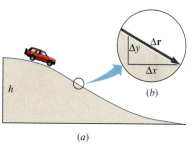

FIGURE 7-18 (a) Hill of Example 7-9; (b) shows a small portion of the hill where the car undergoes displacement $\Delta \mathbf{r} = \Delta x \hat{\imath} + \Delta y \hat{\jmath}$.

Some problems similar to Example 7-9: 35, 36, 39

Tip

Don't Leave Out d(something) An integral is a sum over infinitely many infinitesimally small quantities. It's the *d(something)* that makes the integrand—the quantity to the right of the integral sign—infinitesimally small. Any integral must include this infinitesimal, or its value is infinite! In this example, for instance, it would be incorrect to write $\int(-mg)$ for the work; not only would the value be infinite, but it would be dimensionally incorrect as well. The correct expression includes the infinitesimal dy: $W = \int(-mg)\,dy$.

An important case involving work as a line integral is provided by uniform circular motion. Here the force **F** is always perpendicular to the displacement vector $\Delta\mathbf{r}$; the product $\mathbf{F} \cdot \Delta\mathbf{r}$ is therefore always zero and no work is done, no matter how far the object moves in its circular path. Thus it takes no work to whirl a ball around on the end of a horizontal string; similarly, Earth's gravity does no work on a satellite in a circular orbit.

7-5 KINETIC ENERGY

Closely related to work is **energy**—one of the most important concepts in all of physics. Here we introduce the energy associated with motion, or **kinetic energy**. In the next chapter we develop the concept of **potential energy**; together, kinetic and potential energy provide powerful insights into the behavior of mechanical systems. Later we'll introduce still more forms of energy, associated with the phenomena of heat, electricity, and magnetism.

To develop the concept of kinetic energy and its relation to work, we'll evaluate the net work done on an object, and then apply Newton's second law. The net work is the work done by all the forces acting on the object, so we can find the net work by using the net force in our expression for work:

$$W_{\text{net}} = \int \mathbf{F}_{\text{net}} \cdot d\mathbf{r}. \tag{7-12}$$

For example, if you push a heavy crate across the floor at constant speed, you do work on the crate. But the frictional force does negative work of equal magnitude; the net force is zero and so is the total work done on the crate.

Here we consider the case of one-dimensional motion; the general case is readily treated by retaining all three terms that form the dot product in Equation 7-12. In one dimension, Equation 7-12 becomes

$$W_{\text{net}} = \int F_{\text{net}} \, dx.$$

But the net force can be written in terms of Newton's second law: $F_{\text{net}} = ma$, or $F_{\text{net}} = m \, dv/dt$, so

$$W_{\text{net}} = \int m \frac{dv}{dt} dx. \tag{7-13}$$

The quantities dv, dt, and dx arose as the limits of small numbers Δv, Δt, and Δx. In your calculus class, you will have shown that the limit of a product or quotient is just the product or quotient of the individual terms involved. For these reasons, we can rearrange the symbols dv, dt, and dx to rewrite Equation 7-13 in the form

$$W_{\text{net}} = \int m \, dv \, \frac{dx}{dt}.$$

But $dx/dt = v$, so we have

$$W_{\text{net}} = \int mv \, dv.$$

The integral is simple; it's just like the form $\int x \, dx$, which we integrate by raising the exponent and dividing by the new exponent. What about the limits? Suppose our object starts out at some speed v_1 and ends up at v_2. Then we have

$$W_{net} = \int_{v_1}^{v_2} mv\, dv = \tfrac{1}{2}mv^2 \Big|_{v_1}^{v_2} = \tfrac{1}{2}mv_2^2 - \tfrac{1}{2}mv_1^2. \qquad (7\text{-}14)$$

Equation 7-14 shows that an object has associated with it a quantity $\tfrac{1}{2}mv^2$ that changes when, and only when, net work is done on the object. This quantity plays a vital role in physics and is called the object's **kinetic energy**:

> The kinetic energy K of an object of mass m moving at speed v is
>
> $$K = \tfrac{1}{2}mv^2. \qquad (7\text{-}15)$$

Like velocity, kinetic energy is a relative term; its value depends on the reference frame in which it's measured. But unlike velocity, kinetic energy is a *scalar*. And since it depends on the *square* of the velocity, kinetic energy is never negative. All moving objects possess kinetic energy. Since the masses and speeds of objects vary enormously, so do their kinetic energies (see Table 7-1).

Equation 7-14 equates the change in an object's kinetic energy with the net work done on the object, a result known as the **work-energy theorem**:

> Work-energy theorem: The change in an object's kinetic energy is equal to the net work done on the object:
>
> $$\Delta K = W_{net}. \qquad (7\text{-}16)$$

Equations 7-14 and 7-16 are equivalent statements of the work-energy theorem.

We've already seen that work can be positive or negative; so, therefore, can *changes* in kinetic energy. If I stop a moving object, for example, I reduce its kinetic energy from $\tfrac{1}{2}mv^2$ to zero—a change $\Delta K = -\tfrac{1}{2}mv^2$. So I do negative work, by applying a force directed oppositely to the motion. By Newton's third law, the object exerts an equal but oppositely directed force on me, therefore doing positive work $\tfrac{1}{2}mv^2$ on me. So an object of mass m moving at speed v can do work equal to its initial kinetic energy, $\tfrac{1}{2}mv^2$, if it's brought to rest.

TABLE 7-1 *Typical Kinetic Energies, in Joules*

Earth's orbital motion	2.7×10^{33}
Orbiting space shuttle	6.1×10^{13}
747 jet	1.5×10^{10}
Car @ 100 km/h	5.8×10^{5}
World class sprinter	6.7×10^{3}
Person walking	2.3×10^{1}
Bumblebee	2.0×10^{-3}
Electron in TV tube	4.6×10^{-15}
Electron in hydrogen atom	2.2×10^{-18}
Air molecule, room temperature	2.8×10^{-21}

EXAMPLE 7-10 | *Passing Zone*

A 1400-kg car enters a passing zone and accelerates from 70 to 95 km/h to pass a slower car. How much work must be done on the car? If it then brakes to a stop, how much work is done on it?

Solution

The work-energy theorem tells us that the work is given by the change in kinetic energy. To accelerate the car, we have

$$W_{net} = \tfrac{1}{2}mv_2^2 - \tfrac{1}{2}mv_1^2 = \tfrac{1}{2}m(v_2^2 - v_1^2)$$
$$= (\tfrac{1}{2})(1400 \text{ kg})[(26.4 \text{ m/s})^2 - (19.4 \text{ m/s})^2]$$
$$= 2.2 \times 10^5 \text{ J},$$

where we converted speeds to meters per second (m/s) before doing the calculation.

The work-energy theorem applies equally to braking the car; now we have $v_1 = 26.4$ m/s and $v_2 = 0$, so

$$W_{net} = \tfrac{1}{2}m(v_2^2 - v_1^2) = -\tfrac{1}{2}mv_1^2$$
$$= -(\tfrac{1}{2})(1400 \text{ kg})(26.4 \text{ m/s})^2$$
$$= -4.9 \times 10^5 \text{ J}.$$

Here the work done *on* the car is negative, implying that the car does positive work on the external world. In both cases the forces that do the work—either positive or negative—are ultimately the frictional forces between tires and road.

EXERCISE A cyclotron accelerates protons from rest to a speed of 2.1×10^7 m/s. How much work does it do on each proton?

Answer: 3.7×10^{-13} J

Some problems similar to Example 7-10: 41, 44

EXAMPLE 7-11	*Rough Sliding, Again*

Movers are pushing a 78.0-kg trunk at 0.710 m/s when they encounter a 2.25-m-long stretch of floor where the coefficient of kinetic friction is 0.295. If they push with a steady force $F = 220$ N, determine the speed of the trunk at the end of the 2.25-m stretch (see Fig. 7-19).

Solution

The frictional force has magnitude $\mu_k mg$ and points opposite the trunk's motion. Taking the positive x direction in the direction of the trunk's motion, the x component of the net force becomes

$$F_{net} = F - \mu_k mg$$
$$= 220 \text{ N} - (0.295)(78.0 \text{ kg})(9.8 \text{ m/s}^2) = -5.498 \text{ N},$$

so the work done on the trunk is

$$W_{net} = F_{net}\Delta x = (-5.498 \text{ N})(2.25 \text{ m}) = -12.37 \text{ J}.$$

The work is negative because the frictional force opposing the motion is greater than the force F with which the movers push; thus, we expect the trunk will slow down. The work-energy theorem equates the work to the change in kinetic energy: $\Delta K = W_{net}$, or

$$\tfrac{1}{2}mv_2^2 - \tfrac{1}{2}mv_1^2 = W_{net}.$$

Solving for the final velocity v_2, we have

FIGURE 7-19 Rough sliding (Example 7-11).

$$v_2 = \sqrt{v_1^2 + \frac{2W_{net}}{m}} = \sqrt{(0.710 \text{ m/s})^2 + \frac{(2)(-12.65 \text{ J})}{78.0 \text{ kg}}}$$
$$= 0.432 \text{ m/s}.$$

As we expected, the trunk has slowed down since the net work done on it was negative.

EXERCISE A block is sliding on a horizontal surface at an initial speed of 2.8 m/s. The coefficient of kinetic friction is 0.56. Use the work-energy theorem to determine how far the block will slide before it stops.

Answer: 71 cm

Some problems similar to Example 7-11: 47, 49

Energy Units

Since work is equal to the change in kinetic energy, the units of energy are the same as those of work. In SI, the unit of energy is therefore the joule, equal to 1 newton-meter. In science, engineering, and everyday life, though, you will encounter other energy units. Scientific units include the **erg**, used in the centimeter-gram-second system of units and equal to 10^{-7} J; the **electron-volt** used in nuclear, atomic, and molecular physics; and the **calorie** used in thermodynamics and to describe the energies of chemical reactions. English units include the **foot-pound** and the **British thermal unit** (Btu); the latter is commonly used in engineering of heating and cooling systems. Your electric company charges you for energy use in **kilowatt-hours** (kW·h or kWh); we'll see in the next section how this unit relates to the SI joule. Appendix C contains an extensive table of energy units and conversion factors, as well as the energy contents of common fuels.

7-6 POWER

Climbing a flight of stairs requires the same amount of work no matter how fast you go. Why? As long as you maintain constant speed, the upward force you apply is equal to your weight—and you apply that force over a fixed displacement. Since work is the product of force and displacement, the work is independent of speed.

But it's harder to *run* up the stairs than to walk. Harder in what sense? In the sense that you do the same work in a shorter time; the *rate* at which you do work is greater. We define **power** as the rate of doing work:

If an amount of work ΔW is done in a time Δt, then the average power $\bar{P}$ is

$$\bar{P} = \frac{\Delta W}{\Delta t}.$$ (7-17)

Often the rate of doing work varies with time. Then we define the **instantaneous power** as the average power taken in the limit of arbitrarily small time interval Δt:

$$P = \lim_{\Delta t \to 0} \frac{\Delta W}{\Delta t} = \frac{dW}{dt}.$$ (7-18)

Equations 7-17 and 7-18 both show that the units of power are joules/second. One J/s is given the name **watt** (W) in honor of James Watt, a Scottish engineer and inventor who was instrumental in developing the steam engine as a practical power source.

The watt (W) is the SI unit of power: 1 watt is equal to 1 joule/second.

Watt himself defined another unit, the horsepower. One horsepower (hp) is about 746 J/s or 746 W.

EXAMPLE 7-12	*Climbing Mount Washington*

A 55-kg hiker ascends New Hampshire's Mount Washington, a vertical rise of 1300 m from the base elevation. The hike takes 2 hours. A 1500-kg car drives up the Mount Washington Auto Road, the same vertical rise, in half an hour. What is the average power output in each case? Assume the hiker and car maintain constant speed and neglect friction, so each does work only against the gravitational force.

Solution

In Example 7-9, we found that the work done by gravity depends only on the overall change in vertical position. Here the hiker and car do positive work $\Delta W = mgh$ to overcome the negative work $-mgh$ done by gravity. So the average power outputs are

$$\bar{P}_{\text{hiker}} = \frac{\Delta W}{\Delta t} = \frac{(55 \text{ kg})(9.8 \text{ m/s}^2)(1300 \text{ m})}{(2.0 \text{ h})(3600 \text{ s/h})} = 97 \text{ W}$$

and

$$\bar{P}_{\text{car}} = \frac{\Delta W}{\Delta t} = \frac{(1500 \text{ kg})(9.8 \text{ m/s}^2)(1300 \text{ m})}{(0.50 \text{ h})(3600 \text{ s/h})} = 1.1 \times 10^4 \text{ W}.$$

These values correspond to 0.13 hp and 14 hp, respectively. The figure of 97 W is typical of the sustained long-term power output of the human body. Remember that next time you leave a 100-W light bulb burning! The power plant supplying the electricity is doing work at about the rate your body can (actually, it's doing work at about three times this rate, for reasons we will examine in Chapter 22). You may be surprised at the low output of the car, given that it probably has an engine rated at several hundred horsepower. Actually, only a small fraction of a car engine's rated horsepower is available in mechanical power to the wheels. The rest is lost in friction and heating.

Some problems similar to Example 7-12: 52, 54, 56

Got It!

Two hikers of equal mass climb the same mountain. One takes 2 hours; the other 3 hours. Which, if either, does more work? Which, if either, produces greater power?

When power is constant, so the average and instantaneous power are the same, then Equation 7-17 shows that the amount of work W done in a time Δt is just

$$W = P\Delta t. \tag{7-19}$$

When the power is not constant, we can consider small amounts of work ΔW, each taken over so small a time interval Δt that the power is nearly constant. Adding all these amounts of work, and taking the limit as Δt becomes arbitrarily small, we have

$$W = \lim_{\Delta t \to 0} \sum P\Delta t = \int_{t_1}^{t_2} P\,dt, \tag{7-20}$$

where t_1 and t_2 are the beginning and end of the time interval over which we calculate the power.

EXAMPLE 7-13	An Electric Bill: Yankee Stadium

Each of the 500 floodlights at Yankee Stadium uses electrical energy at the rate of 1.0 kW. How much does it cost to run these lights during a 4-hour night game, if electricity costs 9.5¢/kWh (see Fig. 7-20)?

Solution

The total power consumption of the 500 lights is 500 kW. Since the power is constant, the total work done to run the lamps is given by Equation 7-19:

$$W = P\Delta t = (500\text{ kW})(4.0\text{ h}) = 2000\text{ kWh}.$$

The cost is then $(2000\text{ kWh})(9.5¢/\text{kWh}) = \$190$.

Note in this example that energy in kilowatt-hours is simply the product of power in kilowatts and time in hours.

EXERCISE New Hampshire's Seabrook nuclear power plant produces electrical energy at the rate of 1150 MW. (a) How much energy does it produce in a year? (b) At a wholesale price of 2¢/kWh, how much is this energy worth?

Answers: (a) 10^{10} kWh; (b) $200 million

Some problems similar to Example 7-13: 61, 64, 68

FIGURE 7-20 How much does it cost to run Yankee Stadium's lights for a night game? (Example 7-13)

APPLICATION	Energy and Society

We hear a great deal about today's energy-intensive industrial societies and about environmental consequences of our energy use. Just how much energy do we use, and what does it mean for a society to be energy intensive?

Example 7-12 showed that the average power output of the human body is about 100 W. Before our species harnessed fire and domesticated animals, that 100 W was all the power available to the average human being. At what rate, on the average, do *you* use energy? There's the 100 W associated with your own body. Then there's that 100-W light bulb you keep on several hours a day. Maybe your car burns an average of a gallon of gasoline a day; that gallon is equivalent to about 40 kWh (Appendix C lists this and many other fuel equivalents). On average, that's 40 kWh/24 h or about 1.7 kW. In the winter, your share of the heat may account for several kilowatts. The energy to cook your meals adds further. And what about the energy used to plow the fields that grew your food or to produce the fertilizers and pesticides used in agriculture? Or to manufacture all the goods you consume? In all, you use energy at a substantial rate. In the United States, at the end of the twentieth century, in fact, the

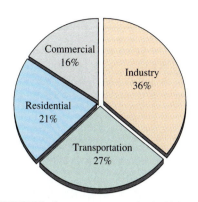

FIGURE 7-21 Per-capita energy consumption rate in the United States through the twentieth century. One "energy worker" is 100 W, about the average power output of the human body.

FIGURE 7-22 Current energy use in the United States.

current average energy consumption rate is just about 10 kW per person (see Fig. 7-21). Other industrial nations are within a factor of two of this value, most of them lower.

This quantity, 10 kW, is 10,000 W, or 100 times the average power output of the human body. If our energy were supplied by human labor, instead of gasoline engines and nuclear power plants, each of us would need about 100 laborers working around the clock. What do our 100 "energy workers" do? Figure 7-22 shows that 36 of them work in the industries that supply us with goods; 27 are in transportation, moving us and our goods around; 21 are domestic workers, heating our homes and running refrigerators, lights, televisions, and computers.

Finally, 16 are in the commercial sector, powering things like the vast banks of lights and air conditioners in shopping malls or the aisles of open freezer units in supermarkets.

Today, over 90% of our "energy workers" derive their power from the combustion of fossil fuels—coal, oil, or natural gas. Carbon dioxide released in that combustion is thought to be a major contributor to global warming. Both our rate of energy consumption and the sources of that energy are therefore coming under intense scrutiny. Much of what you learn in an introductory physics course is directly relevant to contemporary problems like energy use and global warming, and we'll focus on this again elsewhere in the book.

Tip

Don't Confuse Energy and Power Is that 10 kW per year, per day, or what? That question reflects a common confusion of energy and power. Power is the *rate* of energy use; it doesn't need any "per time" attached to it. It's just 10 kW—meaning energy is used at the average rate of 10,000 W, or 10,000 J/s, or, equivalently, 10 kWh per hour.

Power and Velocity

We can derive an expression relating power, applied force, and velocity by noting that the work ΔW done by a force $\mathbf{F}$ acting on an object that undergoes a small displacement $\Delta \mathbf{r}$ is given by Equation 7-5:

$$\Delta W = \mathbf{F} \cdot \Delta \mathbf{r}.$$

Dividing both sides by the time interval Δt in which the displacement $\Delta \mathbf{r}$ occurs, and taking the limit as $\Delta t \to 0$, we have

$$\lim_{\Delta t \to 0} \frac{\Delta W}{\Delta t} = \lim_{\Delta t \to 0} \mathbf{F} \cdot \frac{\Delta \mathbf{r}}{\Delta t} = \mathbf{F} \cdot \frac{d\mathbf{r}}{dt}.$$

But the limit of $\Delta W/\Delta t$ is just the instantaneous power, P, and $d\mathbf{r}/dt$ is the velocity, $\mathbf{v}$, so

$$P = \mathbf{F} \cdot \mathbf{v}. \tag{7-21}$$

EXAMPLE 7-14	*Bicycling*

As you ride your 14-kg bicycle on level ground, you do work against a 30-N force of air resistance (Fig. 7-23). If your mass is 65 kg, what is the power you must supply to maintain a steady 25 km/h (a) on level ground and (b) going up a 5° incline?

Solution

Air resistance opposes your motion; to overcome it, you must apply a force of equal magnitude in the direction of motion. The 25 km/h speed is equivalent to $(25 \times 10^3 \text{ m})/(3600 \text{ s}) = 6.9$ m/s, so the power you supply is

$$P = \mathbf{F} \cdot \mathbf{v} = Fv = (30 \text{ N})(6.9 \text{ m/s}) = 210 \text{ W},$$

or a little over one-fourth horsepower. (In writing $\mathbf{F} \cdot \mathbf{v} = Fv$, we used the fact that the force is in the same direction as the velocity, so the cosine in the dot product is 1.)

In climbing the hill, you must overcome not only air resistance but also the downslope component of the gravitational force. From Example 6-1, this downslope component is $mg \sin\theta$, here equal to $(14 \text{ kg} + 65 \text{ kg})(9.8 \text{ m/s}^2)(\sin 5°) = 67$ N. So the power you must supply is

$$P = Fv = (30 \text{ N} + 67 \text{ N})(6.9 \text{ m/s}) = 670 \text{ W},$$

or nearly one horsepower. Here again we wrote $P = Fv$ since the applied force is in the direction of the velocity.

Both our answers are considerably greater than the 100 W we've cited as the average human power output. That 100 W is

FIGURE 7-23 How much power does it take to overcome air resistance ($\mathbf{F}_a$) and the gravitational force ($\mathbf{F}_g$) as a bicycle climbs a hill?

only an average; many athletes can produce several hundred watts for sustained periods and several kilowatts in brief bursts.

EXERCISE A 1750-kg car delivers energy to its drive wheels at the rate of 35 kW. Neglecting air resistance, what is the greatest speed with which it can climb a 4.5° slope?

Answer: 94 km/h

Some problems similar to Example 7-14: 73, 83, 84, 92

CHAPTER SYNOPSIS

Summary

This chapter introduces the important concepts of work, energy, and power, whose meanings in physics are similar, but not identical, to their meanings in everyday language.

1. **Work** is the product of the component of force in the direction an object moves with the object's displacement.

$$W = F_x \Delta x.$$

The SI unit of work is the newton-meter, given the name **joule** (J).

2. The **scalar product** or **dot product** of two vectors provides a convenient shorthand for writing work in terms of the force and displacement vectors. The scalar product of any two vectors **A** and **B** is the product of their magnitudes with the cosine of the angle between them:

$$\mathbf{A} \cdot \mathbf{B} = AB \cos\theta.$$

In terms of the dot product, the work done by a force **F** acting on an object undergoing displacement $\Delta\mathbf{r}$ is

$$W = \mathbf{F} \cdot \Delta\mathbf{r}.$$

3. When force varies with distance, work must be calculated by summing the terms $\mathbf{F} \cdot \Delta\mathbf{r}$ in the limit of arbitrarily small $\Delta\mathbf{r}$, a process that defines the **definite integral**:

$$W = \int_{r_1}^{r_2} \mathbf{F} \cdot d\mathbf{r}.$$

For one-dimensional motion, this line integral reduces to

$$W = \int_{x_1}^{x_2} F \, dx.$$

4. Work done by a nonzero net force results in a change in an object's **kinetic energy**, a scalar quantity given by $K = \frac{1}{2}mv^2$. The **work-energy theorem** shows that the change in kinetic energy is exactly equal to the work done by the net force:

$$W_{\text{net}} = \Delta K = \frac{1}{2}mv_2^2 - \frac{1}{2}mv_1^2.$$

The units of energy are the same as those of work.

5. **Power** is the rate of doing work:

$$P = \frac{dW}{dt}.$$

The SI units of power is the **watt** (W), equal to 1 J/s. Power can also be written in terms of the force **F** acting on an object moving with velocity **v**:

$$P = \mathbf{F} \cdot \mathbf{v}.$$

Terms You Should Understand

(Pairs are closely related terms whose distinction is important; number in parentheses is chapter section where term first appears.)

work (7-1)
joule (7-1)
scalar or dot product (7-2)
definite integral (7-3)
line integral (7-4)
kinetic energy (7-5)
work-energy theorem (7-5)
power, energy (7-6)
watt (7-6)

Symbols You Should Recognize

W (7-1)
J (7-1)
$\mathbf{A} \cdot \mathbf{B}$ (7-2)
$\int_{x_1}^{x_2} F(x)\,dx$ (7-3)

$\int_{r_1}^{r_2} \mathbf{F} \cdot d\mathbf{r}$ (7-4)
K (7-5)
P (7-6)
W (7-6)

Problems You Should Be Able to Solve

calculating work done when a constant force acts on an object moving in one dimension (7-1)
evaluating scalar products for vectors specified either by magnitude and direction or in unit vector notation (7-2)
using the scalar product to evaluate work (7-2)
setting up and evaluating integrals for the work done by a force that varies with position in one dimension (7-3)
solving problems involving the work done in stretching and compressing springs (7-3)
setting up and evaluating line integrals for the work done by a force that varies with position in two dimensions (7-4)
calculating kinetic energy (7-5)
applying the work-energy theorem to relate kinetic energy changes to the total work done on an object (7-5)
converting among common energy units (7-5)
evaluating average and instantaneous power (7-6)
calculating work from power and time, using integration if the power varies with time (7-6)
calculating power from force and velocity (7-6)

Limitations to Keep in Mind

Simple multiplicative formulas for work given force and displacement apply only when the force is constant; otherwise, integration must be used to determine the work. The same holds for work determined from power and time, where integration must be used unless the power is constant.
Like much of Newtonian mechanics, the expression $K = \frac{1}{2}mv^2$ for kinetic energy holds only for speeds much less than the speed of light.

QUESTIONS

1. Give two examples of situations in which you might think you are doing work but in which, in the technical sense, you do no work.
2. If the scalar product of two nonzero vectors is zero, what can you conclude about their relative directions?
3. Must you do work to whirl a ball around on the end of a string? Explain.
4. If you pick up a suitcase and put it down, how much total work have *you* done on the suitcase? Does your answer change if you pick up the suitcase and drop it?
5. You lift a book from your desk to a bookshelf. It is initially at rest and ends up at rest, so its kinetic energy has not changed. Yet you have certainly done work on the book. Explain why this is not a violation of the work-energy theorem.
6. A given force F is applied to move a crate a fixed distance across the floor. Does the amount of work done by the force depend on the coefficient of friction? Does the total work done on the crate depend on the coefficient of friction?
7. Two cross-country skiers race up opposite sides of the mountain shown in Fig. 7-24. If the skier coming up the steeper side wins, compare the work and the average power associated with each skier. Assume that no work is done by friction (although static friction, which does no work, is what makes the climb possible).

FIGURE 7-24 Question 7.

8. You want to raise a piano a given height, using a ramp. With a fixed, nonzero coefficient of friction, will you have to do more work if the ramp is steeper or more gradual? Explain.

9. Does the gravitational force of the Sun do work on a planet in a circular orbit? On a comet in an elliptical orbit? Explain.

10. How does the dependence of a car's kinetic energy on speed affect its stopping distance, assuming a constant braking force?

11. Give an example showing that kinetic energy depends on frame of reference.

12. Can kinetic energy ever be negative? Explain.

13. A pendulum bob swings back and forth on the end of a string, describing a circular arc. Does the tension force in the string do any work?

14. In the preceding question, does the kinetic energy of the bob change as it swings back and forth? Why?

15. Does your car's kinetic energy change if you drive at constant speed for 1 hour?

16. A watt-second is a unit of what quantity? Relate it to a more standard SI unit.

17. A body collides with a spring and compresses it an amount Δx. How will Δx change if you double the impact velocity? Halve the mass of the body? Triple the spring constant?

18. Two particles of different mass have the same momentum. Compare their kinetic energies.

19. A truck is moving northward at 55 mph. Later, it is moving eastward at the same speed. Has its kinetic energy changed? Has its momentum changed? Has work been done on the truck? Has a force acted on the truck? Explain.

20. In a recent article, *The New York Times* described a new power plant by saying it "could yield 50 megawatts of electricity an hour . . . ." Criticize this phrase.

PROBLEMS

ActivPhysics can help with these problems:
Activity 5.1.

Section 7-1 Work

1. How much work do you do as you exert a 75-N force to push a shopping cart through a 12-m-long supermarket aisle?

2. If the coefficient of kinetic friction is 0.21, how much work do you do when you slide a 50-kg box at constant speed across a 4.8-m-wide room?

3. A crane lifts a 650-kg beam vertically upward 23 m, then swings it eastward 18 m. How much work does the crane do? Neglect friction, and assume the beam moves with constant speed.

4. You lift a 45-kg barbell from the ground to a height of 2.5 m. (a) How much work do you do on the barbell? (b) You hold the barbell aloft for 2.0 min. How much work do you do on the barbell during this time? (c) You lower the barbell to the ground. Now how much work do you do on it?

5. The world's highest waterfall, the Cherun-Meru in Venezuela, has a total drop of 980 m. How much work does gravity do on a cubic meter of water dropping down the Cherun-Meru?

6. A meteorite plunges to Earth, embedding itself 75 cm in the ground. If it does 140 MJ of work in the process, what average force does the meteorite exert on the ground?

7. You slide a box of books at constant speed up a 30° ramp, applying a force of 200 N directed up the slope. The coefficient of sliding friction is 0.18. (a) How much work have you done when the box has risen 1 m vertically? (b) What is the mass of the box?

8. Two people push a stalled car at its front doors, each applying a 280-N force at 25° to the forward direction, as shown in Fig. 7-25. How much work does each do in pushing the car 5.6 m?

FIGURE 7-25 Problem 8.

9. A locomotive does 7.9×10^{11} J of work in pulling a 3.4×10^{6}-kg train 180 km. What is the average force in the coupling between the locomotive and the rest of the train?

10. An elevator of mass m rises a distance h up a vertical shaft with upward acceleration equal to one-tenth g. How much work does the elevator cable do on the elevator?

Section 7-2 Work and the Scalar Product

11. Show that the scalar product obeys the distributive law: $\mathbf{A} \cdot (\mathbf{B} + \mathbf{C}) = \mathbf{A} \cdot \mathbf{B} + \mathbf{A} \cdot \mathbf{C}$.

12. (a) Find the scalar products $\hat{\imath} \cdot \hat{\imath}$, $\hat{\jmath} \cdot \hat{\jmath}$, and $\hat{k} \cdot \hat{k}$. (b) Find the scalar products $\hat{\imath} \cdot \hat{\jmath}$, $\hat{\jmath} \cdot \hat{k}$, $\hat{k} \cdot \hat{\imath}$. (c) Use the distributive law to multiply out the scalar product of two arbitrary vectors $\mathbf{A} = A_x\hat{\imath} + A_y\hat{\jmath} + A_z\hat{k}$ and $\mathbf{B} = B_x\hat{\imath} + B_y\hat{\jmath} + B_z\hat{k}$. Then use the results of parts (a) and (b) to verify Equation 7-4.

13. One vector has magnitude 15 units, and another 6.5 units. Find their scalar product if the angle between them is (a) 27° and (b) 78°.

14. Given the following vectors:

A: magnitude 10 at 30° counterclockwise from the *x* axis
B: magnitude 4.0 at 10° counterclockwise from the *y* axis
$\mathbf{C} = 5.6\hat{\imath} - 3.1\hat{\jmath}$
$\mathbf{D} = 1.9\hat{\imath} + 7.2\hat{\jmath}$,

compute the scalar products (a) $\mathbf{A} \cdot \mathbf{B}$; (b) $\mathbf{C} \cdot \mathbf{D}$; (c) $\mathbf{B} \cdot \mathbf{C}$.

15. (a) Find the scalar product of the vectors $a\hat{\imath} + b\hat{\jmath}$ and $b\hat{\imath} - a\hat{\jmath}$, and (b) determine the angle between them. (Here a and b are arbitrary constants.)

16. Rework Example 7-5 using Equation 7-3 instead of Equation 7-4.

17. Use Equations 7-3 and 7-4 to show that the angle between the vectors $\mathbf{A} = a_x\hat{\imath} + a_y\hat{\jmath}$ and $\mathbf{B} = b_x\hat{\imath} + b_y\hat{\jmath}$ is

$$\theta = \cos^{-1}\left\{\frac{a_xb_x + a_yb_y}{[(a_x^2 + a_y^2)(b_x^2 + b_y^2)]^{1/2}}\right\}.$$

18. Find the angles between all three pairs of the vectors $\mathbf{A} = 3\hat{\imath} + 2\hat{\jmath}$, $\mathbf{B} = -\hat{\imath} + 6\hat{\jmath}$, $\mathbf{C} = 7\hat{\imath} - 2\hat{\jmath}$.

19. Find the work done by a force $\mathbf{F} = 1.8\hat{\imath} + 2.2\hat{\jmath}$ N as it acts on an object moving from the origin to the point $\mathbf{r} = 56\hat{\imath} + 31\hat{\jmath}$ m.

20. A force $\mathbf{F} = 14\hat{\imath} + 11\hat{\jmath}$ N acts on an object. Find the work done by the force if the object moves from the origin to the point (a) $28\hat{\imath} + 22\hat{\jmath}$ m and (b) $22\hat{\imath} - 28\hat{\jmath}$ m.

21. A force $\mathbf{F} = 67\hat{\imath} + 23\hat{\jmath} + 55\hat{k}$ N is applied to a body as it moves in a straight line from $\mathbf{r}_1 = 16\hat{\imath} + 31\hat{\jmath}$ to $\mathbf{r}_2 = 21\hat{\imath} + 10\hat{\jmath} + 14\hat{k}$ m. How much work is done by the force?

22. A rope pulls a box a horizontal distance of 23 m, as shown in Fig. 7-26. If the rope tension is 120 N, and if the rope does 2500 J of work on the box, what angle does it make with the horizontal?

FIGURE 7-26 Problem 22.

Section 7-3 A Varying Force

23. Find the total work done by the force shown in Fig. 7-27 as the object on which it acts moves (a) from $x = 0$ to $x = 3$ km and (b) from $x = 3$ km to $x = 4$ km.

FIGURE 7-27 Problem 23.

24. Find the total work done by the force shown in Fig. 7-28, as the object on which it acts moves from $x = 0$ to $x = 5.0$ m.

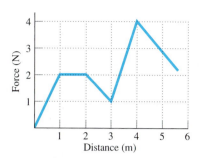

FIGURE 7-28 Problem 24.

25. A force F acts in the x direction, its magnitude given by $F = ax^2$, where x is in meters and a is exactly 5 N/m². (a) Find an exact value for the work done by this force as it acts on a particle moving from $x = 0$ to $x = 6$ m. Now find approximate values for the work by dividing the area under the force curve into rectangles of width (b) $\Delta x = 2$ m; (c) $\Delta x = 1$ m; (d) $\Delta x = \frac{1}{2}$ m with height equal to the magnitude of the force in the center of the interval. Calculate the per cent error in each case.

26. A spring has spring constant $k = 200$ N/m. How much work does it take to stretch the spring (a) 10 cm from equilibrium and (b) from 10 cm to 20 cm from equilibrium?

27. A certain amount of work is required to stretch spring A a certain distance. Twice as much work is required to stretch spring B half that distance. Compare the spring constants of the two springs.

28. On graph paper, draw an accurate force-distance curve for the force of Example 7-8, and obtain a solution to that example by determining graphically the area under the curve.

29. A force $\mathbf{F}$ acts in the x direction, its x component given by $F = F_0 \cos(x/x_0)$, where $F_0 = 51$ N and $x_0 = 13$ m. Calculate the work done by this force acting on an object as it moves from $x = 0$ to $x = 37$ m. *Hint:* Consult Appendix A for the integral of the cosine function and treat the argument of the cosine as a quantity in radians.

30. Work the preceding problem graphically, by making an accurate plot of the force versus distance curve on graph paper, and determining the area (in units of work) under the curve.

31. A force given by $F = a\sqrt{x}$ acts in the x direction, where $a = 9.5$ N/m$^{1/2}$. Calculate the work done by this force acting on an object as it moves (a) from $x = 0$ to $x = 3$ m; (b) from 3 m to 6 m; (c) from 6 m to 9 m.

32. A force given by $F = b/\sqrt{x}$ acts in the x direction, where b is a constant with the units N·m$^{1/2}$. Show that even though the force becomes arbitrarily large as x approaches 0, the work done in moving from x_1 to x_2 remains finite even as x_1 approaches zero. Find an expression for that work in the limit $x_1 \to 0$.

33. The force exerted by a rubber band is given approximately by

$$F = F_0\left[\frac{\ell_0 + x}{\ell_0} - \frac{\ell_0^2}{(\ell_0 + x)^2}\right],$$

where ℓ_0 is the unstretched length, x the stretch, and F_0 is a constant (although F_0 varies with temperature). Find the work needed to stretch the rubber band a distance x.

Section 7-4 Force and Work in Three Dimensions

34. A car drives 3.1 km southward, propelled by the 6.3-kN force of friction between its tires and the road. It then turns eastward and goes another 1.8 km; during this stretch the frictional force is 5.1 kN. Finally, the car turns toward the southeast and goes 2.6 km while the frictional force is 6.8 kN. Find the total work done on the car by the frictional force, assuming the force always acts in the direction of the car's motion.

35. A particle moves from point A to point B along the semicircular path of radius R, as shown in Fig. 7-29. It is subject to a force of constant magnitude F. Find the work done by the force (a) if the force always points upward in Fig. 7-29, (b) if the force always points to the right in Fig. 7-29, and (c) if the force always points in the direction of the particle's motion.

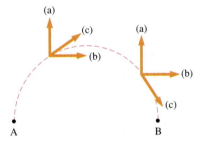

FIGURE 7-29 Problem 35. Arrows are force vectors, labeled to correspond to parts (a), (b), and (c) of the problem.

36. A cylindrical log of radius R lies half buried in the ground, as shown in Fig. 7-30. An ant of mass m climbs to the top of the log. Show that the work done by gravity on the ant is $-mgR$.

FIGURE 7-30 Problem 36.

37. A particle of mass m moves from the origin to the point $x = 3\,\text{m}$, $y = 6\,\text{m}$ along the curve $y = ax^2 - bx$, where

$a = 2\ \text{m}^{-1}$ and $b = 4$. It is subject to a force $\mathbf{F} = cxy\hat{\mathbf{i}} + d\hat{\mathbf{j}}$, where $c = 10\ \text{N/m}^2$ and $d = 15\ \text{N}$. Calculate the work done by the force.

38. Repeat the preceding problem for the case when the particle moves first along the x axis from the origin to the point (3,0), then parallel to the y axis until it reaches (3,6).

39. You put your little sister (mass m) on a swing whose chains have length ℓ, and pull slowly back until the swing makes an angle ϕ with the vertical. Show that the work you do is $mg\ell(1 - \cos\phi)$.

Section 7-5 Kinetic Energy

40. A 2.4×10^5-kg jet is cruising at 900 km/h. (a) What is its kinetic energy relative to the ground? A 65-kg passenger strolls down the aisle at 3.1 km/h. What is the passenger's kinetic energy in the reference frame of (b) the plane and (c) the ground?

41. Electrons in a color TV tube are accelerated to 25% of the speed of light. How much work does the TV tube do on each electron? (At this speed, relativity introduces small but measurable corrections; here you neglect these effects.) See inside front cover for the electron mass.

42. In a cyclotron used to produce radioactive isotopes for medical research, deuterium nuclei (mass 3.3×10^{-27} kg) are given kinetic energies of 8.8×10^{-13} J. What is their speed?

43. At what speed must a 950-kg subcompact car be moving to have the same kinetic energy as a 3.2×10^4-kg truck going 20 km/h?

44. A 60-kg skateboarder comes over the top of a hill at 5.0 m/s, and reaches 10 m/s at the bottom of the hill. Find the total work done on the skateboarder between the top and bottom of the hill.

45. Two unknown elementary particles pass through a detection chamber. If they have the same kinetic energy and their mass ratio is 4:1, what is the ratio of their speeds?

46. You do 8.5 J of work to stretch a spring of spring constant $k = 190\,\text{N/m}$, starting with the spring unstretched. How far does the spring stretch?

47. After a tornado, a 0.50-g drinking straw was found embedded 4.5 cm in a tree. Subsequent measurements showed that the tree would exert a stopping force of 70 N on the straw. What was the straw's speed when it hit the tree?

48. You drop a 150-g baseball from a sixth-story window 16 m above the ground. What are (a) its kinetic energy and (b) its speed when it hits the ground? Neglect air resistance.

49. A hospital patient's leg slipped off a stretcher and his heel hit the concrete floor. As a physicist, you are called to testify about this accident. You estimate that the foot and leg had an effective mass of 8 kg, that they dropped freely a distance of 70 cm, and that the stopping distance was 2 cm. What force can you claim the floor exerted on the foot? Give your answer in pounds for the jury's sake.

50. From what height would you have to drop a car for its impact to be equivalent to a collision at 20 mi/h?

51. Catapults run by high-pressure steam from the ship's nuclear reactor are used on the aircraft carrier Enterprise to launch jet aircraft to takeoff speed in only 76 m of deck space (see Fig. 7-31). A catapult exerts a 1.1×10^6 N force on a 3.3×10^4 kg aircraft. What are (a) the kinetic energy and (b) the speed of the aircraft as it leaves the catapult? (c) How long does the catapulting operation take? (d) What is the acceleration of the aircraft?

FIGURE 7-31 Problem 51.

Section 7-6 Power

52. A horse plows a 200-m-long furrow in 5.0 min, exerting a force of 750 N. What is its power output, measured in watts and in horsepower?

53. A typical car battery stores about 1 kWh of energy. What is its power output if it is drained completely in (a) 1 minute; (b) 1 hour; (c) 1 day?

54. A sprinter completes a 100-m dash in 10.6 s, doing 22.4 kJ of work. What is her average power output?

55. How much work can a 3.5-hp lawnmower engine do in 1 h?

56. Water drops over 49-m-high Niagara Falls at the rate of 6.0×10^6 kg/s. If all the energy of the falling water could be harnessed by a hydroelectric power plant, what would be the plant's power output?

57. A "mass driver" is designed to launch raw materials mined on the moon to a factory in lunar orbit. The driver can accelerate a 1000-kg package to 2.0 km/s (just under lunar escape speed) in 55 s. (a) What is its power output during a launch? (b) If the driver makes one launch every 30 min, what is its average power consumption?

58. A 75-kg long-jumper takes 3.1 s to reach a prejump speed of 10 m/s. What is his power output?

59. Estimate your power output as you do deep knee bends at the rate of one per second.

60. At what rate can a one-half horsepower well pump deliver water to a tank 60 m above the water level in the well? Give your answer in kg/s and gal/min.

61. In midday sunshine, solar energy strikes Earth at the rate of about 1 kW/m². How long would it take a perfectly efficient solar collector of 15 m² area to collect 40 kWh of energy? (This is roughly the energy content of a gallon of gasoline.)

62. It takes about 20 kJ to melt an ice cube. A typical microwave oven produces 625 W of microwave power. How long will it take to melt the ice cube in this oven?

63. The rate at which the United States imports oil, expressed in terms of the energy content of the imported oil, is nearly 700 GW. Using the "Energy Content of Fuels" table in Appendix C, convert this figure to gallons per day.

64. Which consumes more energy, a 1.2-kW hair dryer used for 10 min or a 7-W night-light left on for 24 h?

65. By measuring oxygen uptake, sports physiologists have found that the power output of long-distance runners is given approximately by $P = m(bv - c)$, where m and v are the runner's mass and speed, respectively, and where b and c are constants given by $b = 4.27$ J/kg·m and $c = 1.83$ W/kg. Determine the work done by a 54-kg runner who runs a 10-km race at a speed of 5.2 m/s.

66. A 65-kg runner running at $v_0 = 4.8$ m/s accelerates to 6.1 m/s over a 25-s interval. (a) By writing $v = v_0 + at$, where a is the runner's acceleration, use the formula in the previous problem to express the runner's power output as a function of time. (b) How much work does the runner do during the acceleration period?

67. A 1400-kg car ascends a mountain road at a steady 60 km/h. The force of air resistance on the car is 450 N. If the car's engine supplies energy to the drive wheels at the rate of 38 kW, what is the slope angle of the road?

68. A machine does work at a rate given by $P = ct^2$, where $c = 18$ W/s² and t is time. Find an expression for the work done by the machine between $t = 10$ s and $t = 20$ s.

Paired Problems

(Both problems in a pair involve the same principles and techniques. If you can get the first problem, you should be able to solve the second one.)

69. You apply a 470-N force to push a stalled car at a 17° angle to its direction of motion, doing 860 J of work in the process. How far do you push the car?

70. A tractor tows a jumbo jet from its airport gate, doing 8.7 MJ of work. The link from the plane to the tractor makes a 22° angle with the direction of the plane's motion, and the tension in the link is 4.1×10^5 N. How far does the tractor move the plane?

71. A force pointing in the x direction is given by $F = F_0(x/x_0)$, where F_0 and x_0 are constants and x is the position. Find an expression for the work done by this force as it acts on an object moving from $x = 0$ to $x = x_0$.

72. A force pointing in the x direction is given by $F = ax^{3/2}$, where $a = 0.75$ N/m$^{3/2}$. Find the work done by this force as it acts on an object moving from $x = 0$ to $x = 14$ m.

73. Two vectors have equal magnitude, and their scalar product is one-third of the square of their magnitude. Find the angle between them.

74. Vector **A** has magnitude A, vector **B** has magnitude $2A$, and $\mathbf{A} \cdot \mathbf{B} = A^2$. Find the angle between **A** and **B**.

75. A 460-kg piano is pushed at constant speed up a ramp, raising it a vertical distance of 1.9 m (see Fig. 7-32). If the coefficient of friction between ramp and piano is 0.62, find the work done by the agent pushing the piano if the ramp angle is (a) 15° and (b) 30°. Assume the force is applied parallel to the ramp.

FIGURE 7-32 Problem 75.

76. You have to do 2.2 kJ of work to push a 78-kg trunk 3.1 m along a slope inclined upward at 22°, pushing parallel to the slope. What is the coefficient of friction between trunk and slope?

77. (a) How much power is needed to push a 95-kg chest at 0.62 m/s along a horizontal floor where the coefficient of friction is 0.78? (b) How much work is done in pushing the chest 11 m?

78. You mix flour into a thick bread dough, exerting a 45-N force on the stirring spoon. If you move the spoon at 0.29 m/s, (a) what power do you supply? (b) How much work do you do if you stir for 1.0 min?

Supplementary Problems

79. The power output of a machine of mass m increases linearly with time, according to the formula $P = bt$, where b is a constant. (a) Find an expression for the work done between $t = 0$ and some arbitrary time t. (b) Suppose the machine is initially at rest and all the work it supplies goes into increasing its own speed. Use the work-energy theorem to show that the speed increases linearly with time, and find an expression for the acceleration.

80. You're trying to decide whether to buy an energy-efficient, 225-W refrigerator for $1150 or a standard, 425-W model for $850. The standard model will run 20% of the time, while better insulation means the energy-efficient model will run 11% of the time. If electricity costs 9.5¢/kWh, how long would you have to own the energy-efficient model to make up the difference in cost? Neglect interest you might earn on your money.

81. The per-capita energy consumption rate plotted in Fig. 7-21 can be approximated by the expression $P = P_0 + at + bt^2 + ct^3$, where $P_0 = 4.4$ kW, $a = -5.57 \times 10^{-2}$ kW/y, $b = 3.84 \times 10^{-3}$ kW/y^2, $c = -2.79 \times 10^{-5}$ kW/y^3, and t is the time in years since 1900 (i.e., 1960 is $t = 60$). Integrate this expression to find approximate values for the energy used per capita during the decades (a) from 1940 to 1950 and (b) from 1960 to 1970. It's easiest to give your answers in kilowatt-years.

82. A spring of spring constant k is attached to a mass m and the other end of the spring is pulled vertically in order to lift the mass. Find an expression for the amount of work that must be done on the spring *before* the mass begins to leave the ground.

83. Figure 7-33 shows the power a baseball bat delivers to the ball, as a function of time. Use graphical integration to determine the total work the bat does on the ball.

FIGURE 7-33 Power delivered by a baseball bat (Problem 83). (Adapted from Adair, "The Physics of Baseball," *Physics Today*, May 1995.)

84. A machine delivers power at a decreasing rate $P = P_0 t_0^2/(t + t_0)^2$, where P_0 and t_0 are constants. The machine starts at $t = 0$ and runs forever. Show that it nevertheless does only a finite amount of work, equal to $P_0 t_0$.

85. An unusual spring has the force-distance curve shown in Fig. 7-34 and described by $F = 100x^2$ for $0 \le x \le 1$ and $F = 100(4x - x^2 - 2)$ for $1 \le x \le 2$, where x is the displacement in meters from the spring's unstretched length and F is in newtons. Find the work done in stretching this spring (a) from $x = 0$ to $x = 1$ m and (b) from $x = 1$ m to $x = 2$ m.

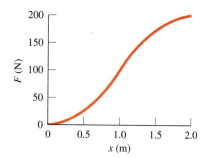

FIGURE 7-34 Problem 85.

86. A locomotive accelerates a freight train of total mass M from rest, applying constant power P. Determine the speed and position of the train as functions of time, assuming all the power goes to increasing the train's kinetic energy.

Conservation of Energy

8

The Yellowstone River plunges over Yellowstone Falls, converting gravitational potential energy into kinetic energy and then to sound and heat.

The rock climber of Fig. 8-1a does work as she ascends the vertical cliff. So does the mover of Fig. 8-1b, as he pushes a heavy chest across the floor. But there's a difference. If the rock climber lets go, down she goes; the work she put into the climb comes back as kinetic energy of her fall. If the mover lets go of the chest, though, he and the chest stay right where they are.

(a)   (b)

FIGURE 8-1 Both the rock climber (a) and the mover (b) do work, but only the climber can recover that work as kinetic energy.

The contrast between these two situations shows a distinction between two types of forces, called **conservative** and **nonconservative**, which we'll now examine in detail. From that distinction we'll develop one of the most important principles in all of physics: **conservation of energy**. In this chapter we consider conservation of **mechanical energy**, which includes kinetic energy that we introduced in Chapter 7 and **potential energy** that we'll become familiar with here. In later chapters, we'll expand the conservation of energy principle to include new forms of energy. Ultimately, in Chapter 38, we'll see how Einstein's relativity subsumes two great principles—conservation of energy and conservation of mass—into a single statement.

8-1 CONSERVATIVE AND NONCONSERVATIVE FORCES

Both the climber and the mover of Fig. 8-1 are working against external forces—gravity for the climber and friction for the mover. The difference between the two situations is this: if the climber lets go, the gravitational force "gives back" the work that she did; that work manifests itself as kinetic energy. But the frictional force does not "give back" the work that the mover did; that work cannot be recovered as kinetic energy.

We use the term **conservative force** to describe a force that, like gravity or a spring, "gives back" work that has been done against it. A force like friction is **nonconservative**. We can give a more precise mathematical sense of this distinction by considering the work involved in moving an object over a closed path—that is, a path that ends up at the same point where it started. Suppose our rock climber ascends a cliff of height h and then descends to her starting point. How much work has the gravitational force done on her? That force has magnitude mg, and points downward. Going up, the force is directed opposite to her motion, so the work done by gravity is $-mgh$. Coming down, the force is in the same direction as her motion, so the work done by gravity is $+mgh$. The total work that gravity does on the climber as she traverses the closed path from the bottom to the top of the cliff and back again is therefore zero.

Now suppose the mover of Fig. 8-1*b* pushes the chest a distance ℓ across a room, discovers it's the wrong room, and pushes it back to the door. Like the climber, the chest describes a closed path. How much work is done by the frictional force acting over this path? That force has magnitude μN, where the normal force in this case of horizontal motion is just *mg*. But the force of kinetic friction *always* acts to oppose the motion, so it *always* does negative work. With frictional force μmg opposing the motion, the work done in crossing the width ℓ of the room is $-\mu mg\ell$. Coming back, it is also $-\mu mg\ell$, so the total work done by the frictional force is $-2\mu mg\ell$.

The difference between our answers for the total work done by the gravitational and frictional forces acting over closed paths provides one precise definition of the distinction between conservative and nonconservative forces:

> **When the total work done by a force F acting as an object moves over any closed path is zero, then the force is conservative. Mathematically,**

$$\oint \mathbf{F} \cdot d\mathbf{r} = 0 . \quad \text{(conservative force)} \qquad (8\text{-}1)$$

The circle on the integral sign indicates that the integral is taken over a *closed* path. A force for which the integral is nonzero, like the frictional force, is nonconservative.

You can see why the mathematical definition given by Equation 8-1 is equivalent to our more physical statement that a conservative force "gives back" work that was done against it. When we do work against a conservative force, it simultaneously does negative work on us. But for the total work done by the conservative force to be zero, it must subsequently do positive work on us, "giving back" the work we did earlier.

Equation 8-1 suggests a related property of conservative forces. Suppose we move an object along the straight path between points *A* and *B* shown in Fig. 8-2, along which a conservative force acts; let the work done by the conservative force be W_{AB}. Since the work done by a conservative force over any closed path is zero, the work W_{BA} done in moving back from *B* to *A* must be $-W_{AB}$, whether we return along the straight path or the curved path or any other path. So, going from *A* to *B* involves work W_{AB}, regardless of the path taken. In other words:

> **The work done by a conservative force in moving between two points is independent of the path taken; mathematically, $\int_A^B \mathbf{F} \cdot d\mathbf{r}$ depends only on the endpoints *A* and *B*, not on the path between them.**

We saw this in Example 7-9, where we found that the work done by gravity does not depend on the details of the path taken (Fig. 8-3). In contrast, the work done by a nonconservative force does depend on the path. On a frictional surface, for example, the least work is done over a straight-line path; any other path involves more work (Fig. 8-4).

Important examples of conservative forces include gravity and the static electric force. The force of an ideal spring—fundamentally an electric force—is also conservative. Nonconservative forces include friction and the electric force in the presence of time-varying magnetic effects which we will encounter in Chapter 31.

FIGURE 8-2 Since the work done by a conservative force over a closed path is zero, the work done in moving from point *A* to point *B* is the same for the straight path, the curved path, or any other path.

FIGURE 8-3 Movers raise identical boxes a vertical distance *h*. The work done by gravity is the same for the box lifted vertically and for the box pushed up the ramp. (The horizontal location of the starting point doesn't matter here since gravity does no work on an object moved horizontally.)

FIGURE 8-4 Top view of boxes being pushed along a horizontal floor. The work done by friction is least for the straight-line path.

FIGURE 8-5 The archer's taut bow stores potential energy that can become kinetic energy of the arrow.

8-2 POTENTIAL ENERGY

Work done against a conservative force is somehow "stored," in the sense that we can get it back again in the form of kinetic energy. The climber of Fig. 8-1a is acutely aware of that "stored work"; it gives her the potential for a dangerous fall. So is the archer of Fig. 8-5; the work he did against the springiness of his bow has the potential to propel the arrow at high speed. "Potential" is an appropriate word here: we can consider the "stored work" as **potential energy** U, in the sense that it can be released as kinetic energy.

We define potential energy formally in terms of the work done by a conservative force. Specifically:

> **The change ΔU_{AB} in potential energy associated with a conservative force is the negative of the work done by that force as it acts over any path from point A to point B:**
>
> $$\Delta U_{AB} = -\int_A^B \mathbf{F} \cdot d\mathbf{r}. \qquad \text{(potential energy)} \qquad (8\text{-}2)$$

Why the minus sign? Because potential energy represents stored work. If a conservative force does *positive* work (as does gravity on a falling object), then potential energy must decrease—and that means ΔU must be *negative.* Conversely, if a conservative force does *negative* work—as does gravity on a weight being lifted—then energy is stored, and ΔU must be *positive.* The minus sign in Equation 8-2 handles both these cases. We will often drop the subscript AB and write simply ΔU for the potential energy change. Keeping the subscript is important, though, when we need to be clear about whether we're going from A to B or from B to A.

Our definition describes only *changes* in potential energy. Such changes are all that ever matter physically; the actual value of potential energy is physically meaningless. Often, though, it's convenient to establish a reference point at which the potential energy is defined to be zero. When we say "the potential energy U," we really mean the potential energy difference ΔU between that reference point and whatever other point we're considering. Our rock climber, for example, might find it convenient to take the zero of potential energy at the base of the cliff. But the choice is purely for convenience; only potential energy *differences* really matter.

Equation 8-2 is a completely general definition of potential energy, applicable in all circumstances. Often, though, we can consider a path where force and displacement are parallel (or antiparallel). Then Equation 8-2 simplifies to

$$\Delta U = -\int_{x_1}^{x_2} F(x)\, dx, \qquad (8\text{-}2a)$$

where x_1 and x_2 are the starting and ending points on the x axis, taken to coincide with the path. When the force is constant, this equation simplifies further to

$$\Delta U = -F(x_2 - x_1). \qquad (8\text{-}2b)$$

Understand Your Equations Equation 8-2b provides a very simple expression for potential energy changes, but it applies *only* when the force is constant. Equation 8-2b is a special case of Equation 8-2a that results when the force can be taken outside the integral sign—and that's allowed only when the force doesn't vary with position. Similarly, Equation 8-2a is a special case of Equation 8-2 that applies only when the force and path are parallel (or antiparallel).

Gravitational Potential Energy

We're frequently moving things up and down, causing changes in potential energy. Figure 8-6 shows two possible paths for a book that's lifted from the floor to a shelf of height h. Which path should we use to calculate the potential energy change? Since the gravitational force is conservative, it doesn't matter. It's easiest to use the path consisting of straight horizontal and vertical segments. There's no work or potential energy change associated with the horizontal motion since the gravitational force is perpendicular to the motion. For the vertical lift, the force of gravity is constant and Equation 8-2b gives immediately $\Delta U = mgh$, where the minus sign in Equation 8-2b cancels with the minus sign associated with the *downward* direction of gravity. This result is quite general; when a mass m undergoes a vertical displacement Δy near Earth's surface, its gravitational potential energy changes by

$$\Delta U = mg\,\Delta y . \qquad \text{(gravitational potential energy)} \qquad (8\text{-}3)$$

The quantity Δy can be positive or negative, depending on whether the object moves up or down; correspondingly, the potential energy can either increase or decrease.

FIGURE 8-6 The work done by gravity as the book moves from floor to shelf is the same for both paths shown, but is more easily calculated for the path composed of horizontal and vertical sections.

Know Your Limitations We emphasize that Equation 8-3 applies *near Earth's surface*—that is, for distances small compared with Earth's radius. That assumption allowed us to treat the gravitational force as constant over the path. For larger distances the gravitational force varies, and we must use the integral of Equation 8-2 to calculate the potential energy change. We'll explore this more general case in the next chapter.

We've found the *change* in the book's potential energy, but what about the potential energy itself? That depends on where we define the zero of potential energy. If we choose $U = 0$ at the floor, then $U = mgh$ on the shelf. But we could just as well take $U = 0$ at the shelf; then the book's potential energy on the floor would be $-mgh$. Negative potential energies arise frequently, and they're nothing to be concerned about because it's only *differences* in potential energy that really matter. Figure 8-7 shows a plot of potential energy versus height with $U = 0$ taken at the floor. The *linear* increase in potential energy with height reflects the *constant* gravitational force.

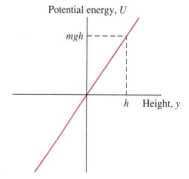

FIGURE 8-7 Since the gravitational force is constant, the potential energy increases linearly with height.

| **EXAMPLE 8-1** | *Gravitational Potential Energy* |

A 55-kg engineer leaves her office on the 33rd floor of a skyscraper and takes an elevator to the 59th floor. Later she descends to street level. If the engineer takes her office as the zero of potential energy and if the distance from one floor to the next is 3.5 m, what is the engineer's potential energy (a) in her office, (b) on the 59th floor, and (c) at street level?

Solution

In her office, the engineer's potential energy is zero since she defined it that way. The 59th floor is $59 - 33 = 26$ floors higher, so the potential energy there is

$$U_{59} = mg\,\Delta y = (55 \text{ kg})(9.8 \text{ m/s}^2)(26 \text{ floors})(3.5 \text{ m/floor})$$

$$= 49 \text{ kJ}.$$

Note that we can write U rather than ΔU since we're calculating the potential energy change from the place where $U = 0$. Similarly, street level is 32 floors *below* the engineer's office, so

$$U_{\text{street}} = mg\,\Delta y = (55 \text{ kg})(9.8 \text{ m/s}^2)(-32 \text{ floors})(3.5 \text{ m/floor})$$

$$= -60 \text{ kJ}.$$

EXERCISE You fly from Boston's Logan Airport, at sea level, to Denver (altitude 1.6 km). Taking your mass as 65 kg and the zero of potential energy at Boston, what is your gravitational potential energy (a) at the plane's 11-km cruising altitude and (b) in Denver?

Answers: (a) 7.0 MJ; (b) 1.0 MJ

Some problems similar to Example 8-1: 4, 5, 8, 10

| **APPLICATION** | *Pumped Storage* |

Electricity, which we'll study in detail in later chapters, is a wonderfully versatile form of energy. But it has a serious drawback: It's difficult to store electrical energy. Large electric power plants operate most efficiently on a continuous basis, yet electric power demand fluctuates. Energy storage can help by supplying extra energy at times of peak demand, ultimately reducing the need to build new power plants.

Gravitational potential energy provides a simple storage medium. In so-called pumped storage facilities, surplus power during times of low demand is used to pump water from a lower reservoir to a higher one, storing energy as gravitational potential energy of the water. When demand for electricity is high, water from the upper reservoir flows back down, turning electric generators to make electricity. (For reasons we'll see in Chapter 31, the same motors that run the pumps can also function as generators.)

Figure 8-8 shows an aerial view of the Northfield Mountain Pumped Storage Project in Massachusetts. The upper reservoir at this facility is 270 m above the pump/generators, and holds 1.6×10^{10} kg of water. According to Equation 8-3, the total energy stored is $U = mg\,\Delta y = (1.6 \times 10^{10} \text{ kg})(9.8 \text{ m/s}^2) \times (270 \text{ m}) = 4.2 \times 10^{13}$ J. The generators at Northfield Mountain have a total power output of 1080 MW. Since 1 MW $= 10^6$ J/s,

FIGURE 8-8 The Northfield Mountain Pumped Storage Project in Massachusetts stores surplus electrical energy as gravitational potential energy of water in this mountaintop reservoir, 270 m above the pump/generators.

it would take $(4.2 \times 10^{13} \text{ J})/(1080 \times 10^6 \text{ J/s}) = 3.9 \times 10^4$ s, or about 11 hours to drain the upper reservoir. In practice, the facility can generate electricity for almost this long before recharging the reservoir.

The Northfield facility is quite efficient: 86% of the energy used to pump the water is recovered as electricity.

Elastic Potential Energy

When you stretch or compress a spring or other elastic object, you do work against the spring force, and that work ends up as stored potential energy—called **elastic potential energy**. For an ideal spring, the force is $F = -kx$, where x is the distance the spring is stretched from equilibrium, and where the minus sign shows that the force opposes the stretching (or compression for $x < 0$). Since the force varies with position, we use Equation 8-2b to evaluate the potential energy:

$$\Delta U = -\int_{x_1}^{x_2} F(x)\, dx = -\int_{x_1}^{x_2} (-kx)\, dx = \tfrac{1}{2}kx_2^2 - \tfrac{1}{2}kx_1^2,$$

where x_1 and x_2 are the initial and final values of the stretch. If we take $U = 0$ when $x = 0$—that is, when the spring is neither stretched nor compressed—then we can use this result to write the potential energy at an arbitrary stretch (or compression) x as

$$U = \tfrac{1}{2}kx^2. \qquad \text{(elastic potential energy)} \qquad (8\text{-}4)$$

Comparison with Equation 7-10 shows that this is equal to the work done in stretching the spring. Of course: that work gets stored as potential energy of the spring. Figure 8-9 shows the potential energy as a function of the stretch or compression of a spring. The *parabolic* shape of the potential energy curve reflects the *linear* change of the spring force with stretch or compression.

FIGURE 8-9 The potential energy curve for a spring is a parabola.

EXAMPLE 8-2	*Energy Storage: Springs versus Gasoline*

How far would you have to stretch a spring of constant $k = 8500$ N/m in order to store the same amount of energy as is contained in 1.0 g of gasoline?

Solution

The "Energy Content of Fuels" table in Appendix C shows that 1 g of gasoline contains 44 kJ of energy. Solving Equation 8-4 for x then gives

$$x = \sqrt{\frac{2U}{k}} = \sqrt{\frac{(2)(44\times10^3 \text{ J})}{8500 \text{ N/m}}} = 3.2 \text{ m}.$$

Since $k = 8500$ N/m implies an extraordinarily stiff spring, this is an unrealistically large stretch. Furthermore, 1 gram isn't much gasoline. This example shows that springs, while useful energy storage devices, cannot compete with chemical fuels.

EXERCISE A hydrogen chloride (HCl) molecule can be modeled as a hydrogen and a chlorine atom connected by a spring of spring constant $k = 480$ N/m (Fig. 8-10). If the molecule is stretched from equilibrium until its potential energy is 5.0×10^{-22} J, by how much does the interatomic separation increase? (This model holds only for very small deviations from equilibrium; beyond that the "spring" ceases to obey Hooke's law.)

FIGURE 8-10 A hydrogen chloride molecule, modeled as two masses connected by a spring.

Answer: 1.4 pm = 1.4×10^{-12} m

Some problems similar to Example 8-2: 11–13

Other Forces

In Equations 8-3 and 8-4 we have the potential energy associated with two common forces—gravity and springs. In the gravitational case, calculation of the potential energy was easy because the gravitational force doesn't change with position. The spring force does change with position, but we've accounted for that by evaluating the integral in Equation 8-2a.

You will encounter other forces that vary with position. Unless you already have an expression for work or potential energy, you'll need to integrate—according to Equation 8-2 or Equation 8-2a—to evaluate the potential energy.

EXAMPLE 8-3	A Climbing Rope

Ropes used in rock climbing are "springy" so they cushion a climber's fall (Fig. 8-11). A particular rope has a force law given by $F = -kx + bx^2$, where $k = 223$ N/m, $b = 4.1$ N/m^2, and x is the amount of stretch. Find the potential energy stored in this rope when it's been stretched 2.62 m, taking $U = 0$ at $x = 0$.

Solution

For this one-dimensional case we use Equation 8-2a:

$$U = -\int_{x_1}^{x_2} F(x)\, dx = -\int_0^x (-kx + bx^2)\, dx$$

$$= \tfrac{1}{2}kx^2 - \tfrac{1}{3}bx^3 \Big|_0^x = \tfrac{1}{2}kx^2 - \tfrac{1}{3}bx^3$$

$$= (\tfrac{1}{2})(223 \text{ N/m})(2.62 \text{ m})^2 - (\tfrac{1}{3})(4.1 \text{ N/m}^2)(2.62 \text{ m})^3$$

$$= 741 \text{ J}.$$

This is about 3% less than the potential energy $U = \tfrac{1}{2}kx^2$ of an ideal spring with the same spring constant.

EXERCISE An elementary-school student stretches a rubber band between thumb and forefinger and takes aim at the teacher. The force law for this particular rubber band is $F = -1.0x + 0.12x^2$, where x is the stretch in centimeters and F is in newtons.

FIGURE 8-11 The right degree of "springiness" in the climbing rope is essential for safety.

How much energy is stored in the rubber band when the student has stretched it 4.3 cm?

Answer: 0.061 J

Some problems similar to Example 8-3: 14–17

8-3 CONSERVATION OF MECHANICAL ENERGY

The work-energy theorem, introduced in the preceding chapter, shows that the change ΔK in a body's kinetic energy is equal to the net work done on it:

$$\Delta K = W_{\text{net}}.$$

Consider separately the work W_c done by conservative forces and the work W_{nc} done by nonconservative forces, so

$$\Delta K = W_c + W_{nc}.$$

We have defined the change in potential energy, ΔU, as the negative of the work done by conservative forces. So we can write

$$\Delta K = -\Delta U + W_{nc},$$

or

$$\Delta K + \Delta U = W_{nc}. \tag{8-5}$$

5.4
Inventing Processes

We define the sum of the kinetic and potential energy as the **mechanical energy**. Then Equation 8-5 shows that the change in mechanical energy is equal to the work done by nonconservative forces.

In the absence of nonconservative forces, the mechanical energy is unchanged:

$$\Delta K + \Delta U = 0 \tag{8-6}$$

and, equivalently,

$$K + U = \text{constant} = K_0 + U_0, \qquad (8\text{-}7)$$

where K_0 and U_0 are the values of kinetic and potential energy of a body at some point and K and U their values when the body is at any other point. Equations 8-6 and 8-7 express the **law of conservation of mechanical energy**. They show that, in the absence of nonconservative forces, the mechanical energy $K + U$ remains always the same. The kinetic energy K may change, but that change is always compensated by an equal but opposite change in potential energy.

Conservation of mechanical energy is a powerful principle. Throughout physics, from the subatomic realm through practical problems in engineering and on to astrophysics, the principle of energy conservation is widely used in solving problems that would be intractable without it.

5.7
Inverse Bungee Jumper

Tip

Applying Conservation of Energy Applying the conservation of energy principle is as simple as writing $K + U = K_0 + U_0$. In classical physics, the kinetic energy is always given by $K = \frac{1}{2}mv^2$. But the form of the potential energy U depends on the particular conservative force; Equations 8-3 and 8-4 give expressions for the common forces of gravity and springs. You may be given other potential energy functions, or you may need to determine the form of the potential energy from a force law, as in Example 8-3. What about the constants K_0 and U_0? You can determine them from the conditions given in the problem; their sum is the mechanical energy that remains unchanged.

5.2
Ejector Pad

EXAMPLE 8-4	*Tranquilizing an Elephant*

A biologist uses a spring-loaded gun to shoot tranquilizer darts into an elephant. The gun's spring has spring constant $k = 940$ N/m and is compressed a distance $x_0 = 25$ cm before firing a 38-g dart. At what speed does the dart leave the gun?

Solution

Here we have a system in which energy is initially stored in the compressed spring; later, that energy gets transformed into the kinetic energy of the dart. Initially the dart is at rest, so $K_0 = 0$. The spring is compressed a distance x_0, so the initial potential energy is $U_0 = \frac{1}{2}kx_0^2$ from Equation 8-4. When the dart leaves the gun the spring is back in equilibrium, so the potential energy is $U = 0$, while the kinetic energy is that of the dart: $K = \frac{1}{2}mv^2$. So the statement that mechanical energy is conserved—Equation 8-7—becomes $U_0 = K$, or

$$\tfrac{1}{2}kx_0^2 = \tfrac{1}{2}mv^2 .$$

Solving for the dart speed v then gives

$$v = \sqrt{\frac{k}{m}}\, x = \left(\sqrt{\frac{940 \text{ N/m}}{0.038 \text{ kg}}} \right)(0.25 \text{ m}) = 39 \text{ m/s} .$$

Does this result make sense? Yes. In algebraic form, our answer $v = \sqrt{k/m}\, x$ shows that the stiffer the spring, the higher the speed; the greater the mass, the lower the speed, as we expect from Newton's second law. And the further we compress the spring, the greater the speed as well.

Notice how easy conservation of energy made this problem. Had we tried to calculate the speed using Newton's second law, we would have had a hard time because the force, and therefore the acceleration, is not constant.

EXERCISE In a railroad yard, a 35,000-kg boxcar moving at 7.5 m/s is brought to a stop by a spring-loaded bumper mounted at the end of the level track. If the spring has constant $k = 2.8$ MN/m, how far does it compress in stopping the boxcar?

Answer: 84 cm

Some problems similar to Example 8-4: 21, 22, 29

EXAMPLE 8-5 — Conservation of Energy: A Spring and Gravity

The spring in Fig. 8-12 has spring constant $k = 140$ N/m. A 50-g block is placed against the spring, which is then compressed 11 cm. When the block is released, how high up the slope does it rise? Both the horizontal surface and the slope are frictionless.

Solution

To solve this problem, we equate the total energy $K_0 + U_0$ in the initial position with the total energy $K_1 + U_1$ at the maximum height:

$$K_1 + U_1 = K_0 + U_0.$$

Initially, the block is at rest, so $K_0 = 0$. At maximum height on the slope, it is also at rest, so $K_1 = 0$. The initial potential energy is that of the compressed spring, or $\frac{1}{2}kx^2$. The final potential energy is the gravitational potential energy mgh. So our statement of energy conservation reads simply

FIGURE 8-12 Example 8-5.

$$\frac{1}{2}kx^2 = mgh.$$

Solving for the height h, we have

$$h = \frac{kx^2}{2mg} = \frac{(140 \text{ N/m})(0.11 \text{ m})^2}{(2)(0.050 \text{ kg})(9.8 \text{ m/s}^2)} = 1.7 \text{ m}.$$

Tip

Save Steps You might have been tempted in working this example to solve for the speed after the block left the spring and then equate $\frac{1}{2}mv^2$ to mgh to find the height. And you certainly could have done that. But you don't have to! Conservation of energy shortcuts all details of the motion and allows you to equate directly the total energy at two points of interest. Here the speed is zero at both these points, so you need not be concerned with kinetic energy.

EXERCISE You're designing a toy rocket to be launched by a spring. The launching apparatus has room for a spring that can be compressed 14 cm, and the rocket's mass is 65 g. If the rocket is to reach 35 m altitude, what should be the spring constant?

Answer: 2.3 kN/m

Some problems similar to Example 8-5: 23, 26, 30

EXAMPLE 8-6 — A Pendulum Fall

A climber attached to a rope of length ℓ is on a vertical rock face in a position where the rope makes an angle θ_0 with the vertical, as shown in Fig. 8-13. The climber loses grip and swings like a pendulum across the rock face. (a) How fast is the climber going at the lowest point? (b) Just as the rope becomes vertical, it catches on a protruding rock a distance a above the climber. As the climber keeps swinging, what is the maximum angle θ_1 that the rope will make with the vertical? Assume the rope remains taut, but neglect any stretching.

Solution

Here two forces are acting: the conservative force of gravity and the rope tension. But tension is perpendicular to the motion, so it does no work. The climber's total energy remains constant, and the potential energy is associated with the gravitational force alone:

$$K + U = K_0 + U_0.$$

To proceed, we need an expression for the potential energy as a function of angle. Figure 8-14 shows that an angle θ corresponds to a height $h = \ell - \ell \cos\theta$. Setting the zero of potential energy at the lowest point, we can then write $U_0 = mgh = mg\ell(1 - \cos\theta_0)$, where m is the climber's mass (we assume the rope has negligible mass). Since the climber falls from rest, $K_0 = 0$, so $K_0 + U_0 = mg\ell(1 - \cos\theta_0)$.

FIGURE 8-13 Example 8-6.

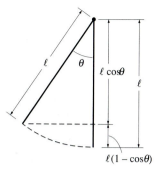

FIGURE 8-14 When the rope makes an angle θ with the vertical, it is a distance $h = \ell(1 - \cos\theta)$ above its lowest position.

(a) To find the speed at the bottom, we equate the energy at the bottom to the total energy $K_0 + U_0$. At the bottom, we have defined $U = 0$, so $K + U = \frac{1}{2}mv^2$ at the bottom. Then

$$\tfrac{1}{2}mv^2 = mg\ell(1 - \cos\theta_0),$$

so

$$v = \sqrt{2g\ell(1 - \cos\theta_0)}.$$

(b) To find the maximum angle as the climber swings to the right, we equate the energy in the rightmost position to the total energy $K_0 + U_0$. On the right, the geometry is the same as in Fig. 8-14 but with the length a replacing ℓ. So the potential energy in the rightmost position is $mga(1 - \cos\theta_1)$. Since the climber is instantaneously at rest in this position, $K = 0$, and conservation of energy becomes

$$mga(1 - \cos\theta_1) = mg\ell(1 - \cos\theta_0).$$

Solving for θ_1 gives

$$\theta_1 = \cos^{-1}\!\left(\frac{\ell}{a}\cos\theta_0 + \frac{a - \ell}{a}\right).$$

Does this result make sense? When $a = \ell$, so there's no protrusion to stop the rope, then $\theta_1 = \theta_0$, and the climber swings symmetrically about his lowest position. And no matter where the protruding rock, our conservation of energy statement shows that $a(1 - \cos\theta_1) = \ell(1 - \cos\theta_0)$; from Fig. 8-14, we see that this means the climber rises to the same height on either side. Of course he must! At his extreme positions, the climber has only gravitational potential energy. Since gravitational potential energy is mgh regardless of the details of the path taken to rise a distance h, the heights must be the same on both sides of the swing.

Will the rope really remain taut, as we've assumed? Not always! Problems 33 and 80 explore this question.

How long does it take the climber to complete the swing? That's a much harder question, one that energy conservation cannot answer. We'll solve Newton's second law for this situation in Chapter 15; only then can we determine the time dependence of the motion.

EXERCISE A wrecking ball is used to demolish a building. The 600-kg ball starts from rest, with its 37-m-long cable making a 22° angle with the vertical. It strikes the building when the cable is vertical. What is the speed of the ball on impact?

Answer: 7.3 m/s

Some problems similar to Example 8-6: 24, 33, 80

In the examples of this section we've neglected friction and other nonconservative forces such as air resistance. Under these circumstances the principle of mechanical energy conservation is exactly true. But in reality nonconservative forces are nearly always present, and in Section 8-6 we show how to deal with them. Often, though, the energy lost to nonconservative forces is small enough that it's a reasonable approximation to assume energy is strictly conserved.

8-4 POTENTIAL ENERGY CURVES

Figure 8-15 shows a frictionless roller-coaster track. How fast must a car be coasting at point A if it's to reach point D? Conservation of energy provides the

FIGURE 8-15 A roller-coaster track.

answer. To get to D, the car must clear peak C. Clearing C requires that its total energy exceed its potential energy at C; that is, $\frac{1}{2}mv_A^2 + mgh_A > mgh_C$, where we've taken the zero of potential energy at the bottom of the track. Solving for v_A gives $v_A > \sqrt{2g(h_C - h_A)}$. If v_A satisfies this inequality, the car will reach C with some kinetic energy remaining and will coast over the peak.

What if the car is moving a little more slowly at A? Then it will stop at some point to the left of C where its energy is entirely potential—that is, at a height h such that $\frac{1}{2}mv_A^2 + mgh_A = mgh$. Then it will head back, clearing peak B and again coming to a stop at the height h. So it will run back and forth between two **turning points** set by the value of its total energy. Lowering the speed still further would confine the car to the valley between points A and B.

Figure 8-15 is a drawing of the actual roller-coaster track. But because gravitational potential energy is directly proportional to height, it's also a plot of potential energy versus position: a **potential energy curve**. We can study the car's motion by plotting its total energy on the same graph as the potential energy curve. Since total energy is constant, the total energy plot is a straight line. Figure 8-16 shows the potential energy and total energy for several values of the total energy. In Fig. 8-16a, the total energy exceeds the potential energy at C; therefore the car will reach C with kinetic energy to spare and will make it all the way to D. In Fig. 8-16b, the total energy is less than the potential energy at C, and the motion is confined between two turning points where the total energy and potential energy curves intersect. In Fig. 8-16c the energy is still lower, and now the car is confined to the leftmost valley.

Even though the car in Figs. 8-16b and c cannot get to D, its total energy still exceeds the potential energy at D. But it's blocked from reaching D by the **potential barrier** of peak C. We say that it's **trapped** in a **potential well** between its turning points.

Potential energy curves are useful even with nongravitational forces where there is no direct correspondence with hills and valleys. The terminology used here—potential barriers, wells, and trapping—remains appropriate in such cases and indeed is widely used throughout physics.

FIGURE 8-16 Potential and total energy for a car on a roller coaster. (a) The total energy E_1 exceeds the potential energy at peak C, and the car can move over the entire track. (b) The total energy E_2 is lower than the potential energy at C, and the car's motion is confined between the turning points (purple dots) where the total and potential energy curves intersect. (c) The total energy E_3 is lower than the potential energy at B, further limiting the car's motion.

(a)

(b)

(c)

APPLICATION   *Keeping a Molecule Together*

Figure 8-17 shows the potential energy of a pair of hydrogen atoms as a function of their separation. This energy is associated with attractive and repulsive electrical forces involving the electrons and the nuclei of the two atoms. The potential energy curve

FIGURE 8-17 Potential energy curve for two hydrogen atoms. At total energy E_1 the atoms are trapped in the potential well, forming a hydrogen molecule (H_2). For energy E_2 and any other total energy above zero, the two atoms can move to arbitrarily large separations, so they don't constitute a molecule.

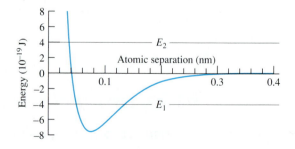

exhibits a potential well, showing that the atoms can form a **bound system** in which they are unable to separate fully. That bound system is a hydrogen molecule (H_2). The minimum energy, -7.6×10^{-19} J, corresponds to a separation of 0.074 nm; this is the equilibrium separation for the H_2 molecule. It's convenient to define the zero of potential energy when the atoms are infinitely far apart; Fig. 8-17 then shows that any total energy less than zero results in a bound system. At the energy marked E_1, for example, the atomic separation is limited to a narrow range defined by the interval where the $E = E_1$ line is above the potential energy curve.

What if the total energy is greater than zero? Then, as the line marked E_2 shows, the energy lies above the top of the potential well, and therefore, the atoms can be arbitrarily far apart. At positive energy the atoms are no longer bound together to form a molecule. So this potential energy curve allows a pair of hydrogen atoms two possibilities: Total energy less than zero means they're trapped in the potential well and form a molecule, while total energy above zero gives two separate, unbound atoms.

Readers of the extended version of this text will encounter many more details of molecular energy in Chapter 41.

EXAMPLE 8-7   *Molecular Energy*

Very near the bottom of the potential well in Fig. 8-17, the potential energy of the two hydrogen atoms is given approximately by $U = U_0 + a(x - x_e)^2$, with $U_0 = -7.6\times10^{-19}$ J, $a = 2.86\times10^{-16}$ J/nm^2 and $x_e = 0.0741$ nm. What range of atomic separations is allowed if the total energy is -7.17×10^{-19} J?

Solution

Figure 8-18 shows graphically what we want, namely, the points where the line $E = 0.40\times10^{-19}$ J intersects the curve $U = U_0 + a(x - x_e)^2$. We can find those points algebraically by writing $E = U_0 + a(x - x_e)^2$ and solving to get

$$x - x_e = \pm\sqrt{\frac{E - U_0}{a}}$$

$$= \pm\sqrt{\frac{-7.17\times10^{-19}\text{ J} - (-7.6\times10^{-19}\text{ J})}{2.86\times10^{-16}\text{ J/nm}^2}}$$

$$= \pm0.0123 \text{ nm}.$$

With $x_e = 0.0741$ nm, this gives

$$x = x_e \pm 0.0123 \text{ nm} = 0.086 \text{ nm or } 0.062 \text{ nm}.$$

In working this example we've assumed the atoms behave like classical particles. In fact, as we'll see in later chapters, quantum mechanics constrains the energies of the system to certain fixed values. Our choice of $E = 7.17\times10^{-19}$ J happens to be one of those values.

The fact that the potential energy curve is approximately parabolic (just like a spring's) near its minimum shows that the molecule can be modeled approximately as two atoms joined by

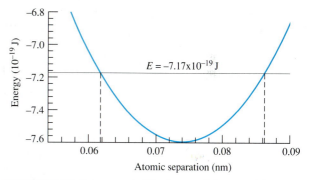

FIGURE 8-18 Enlargement of the bottom of the potential energy curve of Fig. 8-17 for two hydrogen atoms approximates a parabola. With total energy -7.17×10^{-19} J, the atoms are constrained to separations between 0.62 nm and 0.86 nm.

a spring, as we saw in Example 8-2 for the hydrogen chloride molecule (Fig. 8-10). But this approximation holds only for small displacements from the equilibrium separation; for larger displacements, the potential energy is given by the curve of Fig. 8-17, which looks quite different from the potential energy curve for a spring.

EXERCISE A particle is trapped in a potential well described by $U = a|x|$, where x is meters and $a = 3.8$ J/m. If the particle has total energy 5.0 J, find the turning points for its motion.

Answer: $x = \pm1.3$ m

Some problems similar to Example 8-7: 38–41

8-5 FORCE AND POTENTIAL ENERGY

The roller-coaster track shown in Fig. 8-15 is, as we argued in the preceding section, a graph of the gravitational potential energy of a roller-coaster car. But this graph also conveys information about the component of the gravitational

FIGURE 8-19 The gravitational force parallel to the track (designated $\mathbf{F}_\parallel$) is greatest where the track is steepest, and is zero at the peaks and valleys. In general, the slope of a potential energy curve is proportional to the force.

force acting to accelerate the car along the track: where the graph is steep—i.e., where the potential energy is changing most rapidly—the force is greatest (Fig. 8-19). At the peaks and valleys, there's no component of gravitational force parallel to the track. So it's the *slope* of the potential energy curve that tells about the force.

We can make the same argument for the potential energy curve of the hydrogen molecule in Fig. 8-17. It, too, conveys information about force—in this case the force acting between the two atoms. As the atoms get very close—to the left of the minimum energy point in Fig. 8-17—they experience a repulsive force. This is evident because the potential energy increases with decreasing distance, showing that you have to do work to move the atoms closer. How strong is that force? That depends on *how rapidly* the potential energy changes with position. If we change the separation by a small distance Δx—so small that the force F_x is essentially constant over this distance—then we can use Equation 8-2b to write $\Delta U = -F_x \Delta x$, or $F_x = -\Delta U / \Delta x$. In the limit $\Delta x \to 0$, this equation becomes exact, and $\Delta U / \Delta x$ becomes the derivative, and we have

$$F_x = -\frac{dU}{dx}. \tag{8-8}$$

This equation makes mathematical as well as physical sense; we've already written potential energy as the *integral* of force over distance, so it's no surprise that force is the *derivative* of potential energy.

We were careful to write F_x in Equation 8-8 because the rate at which the potential energy changes with position in the x direction tells only about the force component in that direction. The y and z components of force are, in analogy with Equation 8-8, the derivatives of the potential energy with respect to y and z. Taking derivatives with respect to all three coordinates thus determines the entire force vector.

In Fig. 8-17 we see that dU/dx is negative to the left of the energy minimum; Equation 8-8 then shows that the force is positive, or to the right—indicating a repulsion of the two atoms that tends to increase their separation. To the right of the minimum dU/dx is positive, and the force is to the left, showing that the atoms attract each other. What about the minimum itself? Here the slope dU/dx is zero, so there's no force on the atoms. That's the one place where they can remain at rest. We'll explore such **equilibrium points** further in Chapter 14.

Got It!

Why is there a minus sign in Equation 8-8? Explain by referring to Figures 8-17 and 8-19.

| EXAMPLE 8-8 | *Interatomic Forces* |

Find the force on the hydrogen atoms at the turning points given in Example 8-7.

Solution

Example 8-7 gives $U = a(x - x_e)^2$ for the potential energy near the bottom of the potential well. We then find the force from Equation 8-8:

$$F_x = -\frac{dU}{dx} = -\frac{d}{dx}[U_0 + a(x - x_e)^2] = -2a(x - x_e).$$

In Example 8-7 we found $x - x_e = \pm 0.0123 \times 10^{-9}$ m; then

$$F_x = (-2)(2.86 \times 10^{-16} \text{ J/nm}^2)(\pm 0.0123 \text{ nm}) = \mp 7.0 \text{ nN}.$$

The minus sign goes with the point to the right of the energy minimum, indicating a leftward (attractive) force, and vice versa.

EXERCISE The energy stored in a rubber band is given approximately by $U(x) = ax^2 - bx^3$, where $a = 90$ J/m^2, $b = 750$ J/m^3, and x is the stretch in meters. Find an expression for the force exerted by the rubber band as a function of stretch, and evaluate your result for a stretch of 2.5 cm.

Answers: $F = -2ax + 3bx^2$; $F(x = 2.5 \text{ cm}) = -3.1$ N (The minus sign indicates that the force opposes the stretch.)

Some problems similar to Example 8-8: 45, 47, 48

8-6 NONCONSERVATIVE FORCES

We developed the conservation of energy principle and the notion of potential energy on the assumption that only conservative forces were acting. But with nonconservative forces like friction, mechanical energy is not conserved and we must go back to Equation 8-5:

$$\Delta K + \Delta U = W_{nc}, \tag{8-5}$$

where K is the kinetic energy, U the potential energy associated with any conservative forces acting, and W_{nc} the work done by nonconservative forces. There is no potential energy associated with nonconservative forces since these forces do not "give back" work done against them.

If we have an expression for W_{nc} in Equation 8-5, we can use that equation as we did the conservation of energy principle to provide a shortcut to the solution of many practical problems.

5.3
Sliding on Snow and Grass

5.8
Spring-Launched Bowler

5.9
Skier Speed

5.11
Spring-Launched Ski Lift

| EXAMPLE 8-9 | *Lousy Skiing* |

A cross-country skier moving at 4.8 m/s on level ground encounters a nearly frictionless downward slope 6.1 m high. On the level ground below, the snow has been worn thin, and consequently, the coefficient of friction is 0.27. After coasting down the hill, how far will the skier glide across the level stretch?

Solution

The skier starts with mechanical energy $K + U = \frac{1}{2}mv_0^2 + mgh$, where v_0 is the speed at the top of the slope and h the height of the hill and where we've taken the zero of potential energy at the bottom of the slope. When the skier has stopped on the level stretch, both the kinetic and potential energy are zero; the total change in mechanical energy is therefore $\Delta K + \Delta U = -(\frac{1}{2}mv_0^2 + mgh)$. The work done by friction is the frictional

force times the displacement. On level ground, the frictional force has magnitude μmg; if we take the x direction as the direction of motion, the work is then $-\mu mg \Delta x$, where the minus sign arises because the force is opposite the direction of motion. Then Equation 8-5, $\Delta K + \Delta U = W_{nc}$, becomes

$$-(\tfrac{1}{2}mv_0^2 + mgh) = -\mu mg \Delta x,$$

so

$$\Delta x = \frac{\frac{1}{2}v_0^2}{\mu g} + \frac{h}{\mu} = \frac{(\frac{1}{2})(4.8 \text{ m/s})^2}{(0.27)(9.8 \text{ m/s}^2)} + \frac{6.1 \text{ m}}{0.27} = 27 \text{ m}.$$

Does this result make sense? Yes. As μ gets very small, Δx grows arbitrarily large, showing that the skier would coast forever in the absence of friction.

EXERCISE At the end of a factory production line, boxes are placed on a 30° ramp of height 2.7 m, as shown in Fig. 8-20. They slide down the ramp and drop into a waiting truck, whose bed lies 2.4 m below the end of the ramp. If a 10-kg box has kinetic energy 380 J when it lands in the truck, what is the coefficient of friction on the ramp?

Answer: 0.26

Some problems similar to Example 8-9: 50, 52, 59, 73, 74

FIGURE 8-20 What is the coefficient of friction on the ramp?

8-7 CONSERVATION OF ENERGY AND MASS-ENERGY

With conservative forces, mechanical energy is conserved—although it may change from kinetic to potential energy and vice versa. But what happens to the energy that nonconservative forces "take" and don't "give back"? It changes into other forms that we don't usually associate with mechanical energy—in particular, the random molecular motions called, loosely, heat. There are many other forms of energy, too. Fuels such as gasoline store energy in the chemical bonds of their molecules, energy ultimately associated with electric forces. The far stronger forces binding neutrons and protons in atomic nuclei store the awesome amounts of energy that are released in nuclear reactions. Electric and magnetic energy together make electromagnetic waves that, like the light from the Sun, carry energy over great distances.

Much of physics and engineering involves identifying or controlling the interchanges of energy among its different forms. In classical physics, one overriding principle governs those interchanges: the principle of **conservation of energy**. If we keep track of all forms, we find that energy is never lost in any interchange.

Alongside conservation of energy is the principle of conservation of mass. But a closer look shows that neither principle stands by itself. If we measure the mass of a system before it emits energy, and again afterward, in principle we will find the mass has decreased. Einstein's famous equation $E = mc^2$ describes this effect, saying that a quantity of mass m is equivalent to an amount of energy mc^2, where c is the speed of light.

Conversion of matter to energy is popularly associated with nuclear energy. That misconception does injustice to Einstein's universal statement of mass-energy equivalence. *Any* time a system loses energy E, its mass drops by E/c^2. This is as true in burning gasoline or in releasing the tension on a stretched spring as it is in fissioning uranium; it's just that nuclear reactions convert a far greater portion of their mass to energy, and so the effect is readily measurable only for nuclear reactions. Under extremely high-energy conditions the conversion of matter to energy and vice versa is even more obvious, as particles of matter form out of pure energy and annihilate to give again pure energy (Fig. 8-21). If we could extract all the energy mc^2 in a single raisin, it would be enough to supply the energy needs of a major city for a day!

FIGURE 8-21 The creation of matter out of energy. In this image from the Fermi National Accelerator Laboratory, a high-energy proton and antiproton have collided head-on. Each of the colored tracks represents a new particle created from the energy of the original proton-antiproton pair.

Einstein's mass-energy equivalence replaces the two separate conservation statements for mass and energy with a single statement: the **conservation of mass-energy**. Interchanges occur not only among different forms of energy but also among mass and energy, conserving only the total mass-energy. In this sense matter and energy are aspects of the same basic "stuff" that makes up our universe. We will see how mass-energy equivalence arises when we study relativity in Chapter 38.

CHAPTER SYNOPSIS

Summary

1. A **conservative force** "stores" work done against it. Mathematically, a conservative force is one that does zero work on an object moved around any closed path:

$$\oint \mathbf{F} \cdot d\mathbf{r} = 0 . \qquad \text{(conservative force)}$$

A corollary is that the work done by a conservative force as an object is moved between two points is independent of the path taken. Gravity is a familiar example of a conservative force.

2. With a **nonconservative force**, like friction, the work done by the force is not path-independent, and the total work done on an object describing a closed path need not be zero.

3. **Potential energy** describes the "stored work" associated with a conservative force. Mathematically, the potential energy difference as an object moves from point A to point B is defined as the negative of the work done on the object by the conservative force:

$$\Delta U_{AB} = -\int_{A}^{B} \mathbf{F} \cdot d\mathbf{r} . \qquad \text{(potential energy)}$$

Only potential energy differences have physical significance. We are free to assign zero potential energy to any point we choose; when we then speak of the potential energy U at some other point, we really mean the potential energy difference between that point and the point where $U = 0$.

The form of the potential energy function depends on the specific conservative force involved. Two commonly encountered cases include gravitational potential energy near Earth's surface:

$$U = mgh , \qquad \text{(gravitational potential energy)}$$

and the potential energy of an ideal spring or other elastic object:

$$U = \tfrac{1}{2}kx^2 . \qquad \text{(elastic potential energy)}$$

4. When only conservative forces act, the **mechanical energy**—the sum $K + U$ of the kinetic and potential energies—remains constant. This statement is the principle of **conservation of mechanical energy**. The conservation of energy principle allows us to solve easily problems that would be difficult to solve using Newton's second law.

5. Graphs of potential energy as a function of position—**potential energy curves**—reveal features of an object's motion. In particular, from such curves we can identify **turning points** where kinetic energy goes to zero; when there are two such points, the object is confined to a **potential well** by **potential barriers** on either side.

6. Potential energy is related to the integral of force over distance; inversely, force is the negative of the derivative of potential energy:

$$F_x = -\frac{dU}{dx} .$$

7. Energy takes many forms besides kinetic and potential. The **conservation of energy** principle states that energy is neither created nor destroyed as it undergoes changes among the various forms.

8. Einstein showed that energy and matter are interchangeable according to the equation $E = mc^2$. His theory of relativity therefore replaces the classical principles of conservation of energy and conservation of matter with the single **conservation of mass-energy** principle.

Terms You Should Understand

(Pairs are closely related terms whose distinction is important; number in parentheses is chapter section where term first appears.)

conservative force, nonconservative force (8-1)
potential energy (8-2)
mechanical energy (8-3)
potential energy curve (8-4)
turning point (8-4)
potential well (8-4)
potential barrier (8-4)
equilibrium point (8-5)
mass-energy (8-7)

Symbols You Should Recognize

ΔU, U (8-2)

E (8-7)

c (8-7)

Problems You Should Be Able to Solve

calculating gravitational potential energy near Earth's surface (8-2)

calculating the potential energy of a spring (8-2)

calculating potential energy given simple force laws (8-2)

applying conservation of mechanical energy in situations involving gravity, springs, or other simple forces alone or in combination (8-3)

evaluating motion given potential energy curves and total energy; determining turning points (8-4)

calculating force given potential energy as a function of position (8-5)

solving problems involving both nonconservative and conservative forces (8-6)

Limitations to Keep in Mind

Potential energy can be computed as the negative of the product of force and distance only when the force does not vary with position. Otherwise, integration must be used to evaluate the potential energy.

The simple expression $\Delta U = mg\,\Delta y$ for gravitational potential energy changes applies only near Earth's surface, where Δy is small compared with Earth's radius.

The expression $U = \frac{1}{2}kx^2$ applies to ideal springs whose force-distance curve is linear; real springs deviate from this law, especially when stretched or compressed substantially.

Mechanical energy is conserved only in the absence of non-conservative forces such as friction or air resistance. In reality these forces are almost always present, so mechanical energy generally decreases.

Conservation of energy is itself only approximately true; accurate treatment of highly energetic processes, especially, requires the principle of conservation of mass-energy.

QUESTIONS

1. Figure 8-22 shows force vectors at different points in space for two forces. Which is conservative and which nonconservative? Explain.

(a)   (b)

FIGURE 8-22 Question 1, Problem 3.

2. Is the conservation of energy principle related to Newton's laws, or is it an entirely separate physical principle? Discuss.

3. Why can't we define a potential energy associated with friction?

4. Why are you free to choose the zero of potential energy?

5. Can potential energy be negative? Can kinetic energy? Can total mechanical energy? Explain.

6. If the potential energy is zero at a point, must the force also be zero at that point? Give an example.

7. If the force is zero at a point, must the potential energy also be zero at that point? Give an example.

8. Explain how path independence of the work done by a conservative force follows from the fact that the work done over a closed path is zero.

9. If the difference in potential energy between two points is zero, does that necessarily mean that an object moving between those points experiences no force?

10. A tightrope walker follows an essentially horizontal rope between two mountain peaks of equal altitude. A climber descends from one peak and climbs the other. Compare the work done by the gravitational force on the tightrope walker and on the climber.

11. A bowling ball is tied to the end of a long rope and suspended from the ceiling. A student climbs a stool at one side of the room and holds the ball to her nose, then releases it from rest (Fig. 8-23a). Should she duck as it swings back (Fig. 8-23b)? Argue from conservation of energy.

FIGURE 8-23 Question 11.

12. An avalanche thunders down a mountainside. Discuss the various energy transfers that resulted in water from the ocean eventually ending up as snow in the avalanche.

13. Could you define a potential energy function for a velocity-dependent force?

14. A block of mass m is held against a spring of constant k while the spring is compressed a distance x. Discuss how the speed of the block when released scales with k, x, and m.

15. Figure 8-24 shows a potential energy curve along with total energies for three particles. If the particles are all initially at x_0 and moving to the right, describe qualitatively their subsequent motions.

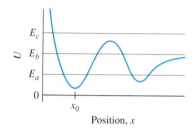

FIGURE 8-24 Question 15.

16. If conservation of energy is a law of nature, why do we have programs—like mileage requirements for cars or insulation standards for buildings—designed to encourage energy conservation?

17. Figure 8-25 shows the potential energy curve for a particle. At which of the labeled points (a) does the force have the greatest magnitude; (b) does the force point in the negative x direction; (c) is the force zero; (d) are the force and potential energy both zero?

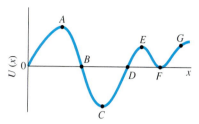

FIGURE 8-25 Question 17.

18. Why is it a misconception to apply $E = mc^2$ only to nuclear reactions?

19. High-energy physicists often give the mass of elementary particles in energy units. Explain.

20. You use a microwave oven to boil a cup of coffee. Assuming that your electricity comes from a hydroelectric power plant, trace the energy of your hot coffee as far back as you can.

21. In terms of potential energy, how do a new and a rundown battery differ?

PROBLEMS

ActivPhysics can help with these problems:
Activities in Section 5, Work and Energy

Section 8-1 Conservative and Nonconservative Forces

1. Determine the work done by the frictional force in moving a block of mass m from point 1 to point 2 over the two paths shown in Fig. 8-26. The coefficient of friction has the constant value μ over the surface. (The diagram lies in a horizontal plane.)

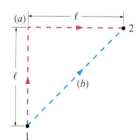

FIGURE 8-26 Problems 1, 2.

2. Now take Fig. 8-26 to lie in a vertical plane, and find the work done by the gravitational force as an object moves from point 1 to point 2 over each of the paths shown.

3. The force in Fig. 8-22a is given by $\mathbf{F} = F_0\hat{\jmath}$, where F_0 is a constant. The force in Fig. 8-22b is given by $\mathbf{F} = F_0(x/a)\hat{\jmath}$, where the origin is taken at the lower left corner of the box, a is the width of the square box, and the distance x increases horizontally to the right. Determine the work done by $\mathbf{F}$ on an object moved counterclockwise around each box, starting at the lower left corner.

Section 8-2 Potential Energy

4. Rework Example 8-1, now taking the zero of potential energy at street level.

5. Find the potential energy of a 70-kg hiker (a) atop New Hampshire's Mount Washington, 1900 m above sea level, and (b) in Death Valley, California, 86 m below sea level. Take the zero of potential energy at sea level.

6. An incline makes an angle θ with the horizontal. Find the gravitational potential energy associated with a mass m located a distance x measured along the incline. Take the zero of potential energy at the bottom of the incline.

7. Show using Equation 8-2b that the potential energy difference between the ground and a distance h above the ground is mgh regardless of whether you choose the y axis upward or downward.

8. The top of the volcano Haleakala on Maui, Hawaii, is 3050 m above sea level and 18 km inland from the sea. By how much does your gravitational potential energy change as you come down from the mountaintop observatory to swim in the ocean? Assume your mass is 75 kg.

9. A 1.50-kg brick measures 20.0 cm $\times$ 8.00 cm $\times$ 5.50 cm. Taking the zero of potential energy when the brick lies on its broadest face, what is the potential energy (a) when the brick is standing on end and (b) when it is balanced on its 8-cm edge, with its center directly above that edge? *Note:* You can treat the brick as though all its mass is concentrated at its center.

10. A 60-kg hiker ascending 1250-m-high Camel's Hump mountain in Vermont has potential energy -2.4×10^5 J; the zero of potential energy is taken at the mountaintop. What is her altitude?

11. How much energy can be stored in a spring with $k = 320$ N/m if the maximum allowed stretch is 18 cm?

12. A carbon monoxide molecule can be modeled as a carbon atom and an oxygen atom connected by a spring. If a displacement of the carbon by 1.6×10^{-12} m from its equilibrium position relative to the oxygen increases the molecule's potential energy by 0.015 eV, what is the spring constant?

13. How far would you have to stretch a spring of spring constant $k = 1.4$ kN/m until it stored 210 J of energy?

14. A more accurate expression for the force law of the rope in Example 8-3 is $F = -kx + bx^2 - cx^3$, where k and b have the values given in Example 8-3, and $c = 3.1$ N/m³. Find the energy stored in stretching the rope 2.62 m. By what percentage does your result differ from that of Example 8-3?

15. The force exerted by an unusual spring when it's compressed a distance x from equilibrium is given by $F = -kx - cx^3$, where $k = 220$ N/m and $c = 3.6$ kN/m³. Find the energy stored in this spring when it's been compressed 15 cm.

16. The force on a particle is given by $\mathbf{F} = A\hat{\mathbf{i}}/x^2$, where A is a positive constant. (a) Find the potential energy difference between two points x_1 and x_2, where $x_1 > x_2$. (b) Show that the potential energy difference remains finite even when $x_1 \to \infty$.

17. A particle moves along the x axis under the influence of a force $F = ax^2 + b$, where a and b are constants. Find its potential energy as a function of position, taking $U = 0$ at $x = 0$.

18. A 3.0-kg fish is hanging from a spring scale whose spring constant is 240 N/m. (a) What is the potential energy of the spring? (b) If the fish were moved slowly upward to the equilibrium position of the spring, by how much would its gravitational potential energy change? (c) In case (b), by how much would the spring's potential energy change? Explain any apparent discrepancies.

19. The force exerted by a rubber band is given approximately by

$$F = F_0\left[\frac{\ell + x}{\ell} - \frac{\ell^2}{(\ell + x)^2}\right],$$

where ℓ is the unstretched length and F_0 a constant. Find the potential energy of the rubber band as a function of the distance x it is stretched. Take the zero of potential energy in the unstretched position.

Section 8-3 Conservation of Mechanical Energy

20. A skier starts down a frictionless 32° slope. After a vertical drop of 25 m, the slope temporarily levels out, then drops at 20° an additional 38 m vertically before leveling out again. What is the skier's speed on the two level stretches?

21. A Navy jet of mass 10,000 kg lands on an aircraft carrier and snags a cable to slow it down. The cable is attached to a spring with spring constant 40,000 N/m. If the spring stretches 25 m to stop the plane, what was the landing speed of the plane?

22. A spring of constant k, compressed a distance x, is used to launch a mass m up a frictionless slope that makes an angle θ with the horizontal. Find an expression for the maximum distance along the slope that the mass moves after leaving the spring.

23. A 120-g arrow is shot vertically from a bow whose effective spring constant is 430 N/m. If the bow is drawn 71 cm before shooting the arrow, to what height does the arrow rise?

24. A child is on a swing whose 3.2-m-long chains make a maximum angle of 50° with the vertical. What is the child's maximum speed?

25. With $x - x_0 = h$ and $a = g$, Equation 2-11 gives the speed of an object thrown downward with initial speed v_0 after it has dropped a distance h: $v = \sqrt{v_0^2 + 2gh}$. Use conservation of energy to derive the same result.

26. In a switchyard, freight cars start from rest and roll down a 2.8-m incline and come to rest against a spring bumper at the end of the track (Fig. 8-27). If the spring constant is 4.3×10^6 N/m, how much is the spring compressed when hit by a 57,000-kg freight car?

FIGURE 8-27 Problem 26.

27. Two clever kids use a huge spring with $k = 890$ N/m to launch their toboggan at the top of a 9.5-m-high hill (Fig. 8-28). The mass of kids plus toboggan is 80 kg. If the kids manage to compress the spring 2.6 m, (a) what will be their speed at the bottom of the hill? (b) What fraction of their final kinetic energy was initially stored in the spring? Neglect friction.

FIGURE 8-28 Problem 27.

28. A 200-g block slides back and forth on a frictionless surface between two springs, as shown in Fig. 8-29. The left-hand spring has $k = 130$ N/m and its maximum compression is 16 cm. The right-hand spring has $k = 280$ N/m. Find (a) the maximum compression of the right-hand spring and (b) the speed of the block as it moves between the springs.

FIGURE 8-29 Problem 28.

29. An initial speed of 2.4 km/s (the "escape speed") is required for an object launched from the moon to get arbitrarily far from the moon. At a mining operation on the moon, 1000-kg packets of ore are to be launched to a smelting plant in orbit around the Earth. If they are launched with a large spring whose maximum compression is 15 m, what should be the spring constant of the spring?

30. A runaway truck lane heads uphill at $30°$ to the horizontal. If a 16,000-kg truck goes out of control and enters the lane going 110 km/h, how far along the ramp does it go? Neglect friction.

31. A low-damage bumper on a 1400-kg car is mounted on springs whose total effective spring constant is 7.0×10^5 N/m. The springs can undergo a maximum compression of 16 cm without damage to the bumper, springs, or car. What is the maximum speed at which the car can collide with a stationary object without sustaining damage?

32. A block slides on the frictionless loop-the-loop track shown in Fig. 8-30. What is the minimum height h at which it can start from rest and still make it around the loop?

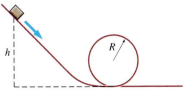

FIGURE 8-30 Problem 32.

33. Show that the rope in Example 8-6 can remain taut all the way to the top of its smaller loop only if $a \leq \frac{2}{5}\ell$. (Note that the maximum release angle is $90°$ for the rope to be taut on the way down.)

34. The maximum speed of the pendulum bob in a grandfather clock is 0.55 m/s. If the pendulum makes a maximum angle of $8.0°$ with the vertical, what is the length of the pendulum?

35. A 2.0-kg mass rests on a frictionless table and is connected over a frictionless pulley to a 4.0-kg mass, as shown in Fig. 8-31. Use conservation of energy to calculate the speed of the masses after they have moved 50 cm.

FIGURE 8-31 Problem 35.

36. The masses shown in Fig. 8-32 are connected by a massless string over a frictionless, massless pulley and are released from rest. Use energy conservation to find (a) the velocity of the 7.0-kg mass just before it hits the floor, (b) the maximum height reached by the 4.0-kg mass, and (c) the fraction of the system's initial mechanical energy lost when the 7.0-kg mass comes to rest on the floor.

FIGURE 8-32 Problem 32.

37. A mass m is dropped from a height h above the top of a spring of constant k that is mounted vertically on the floor (Fig. 8-33). Show that the maximum compression of the spring is given by $(mg/k)(1 + \sqrt{1 + 2kh/mg})$. What is the significance of the other root of the quadratic equation?

FIGURE 8-33 Problem 37.

Section 8-4 Potential Energy Curves

38. A particle slides along the frictionless track shown in Fig. 8-34, starting at rest from point A. Find (a) its speed at B, (b) its speed at C, and (c) the approximate location of its right-hand turning point.

FIGURE 8-34 Problem 38.

39. A particle slides back and forth on a frictionless track whose height as a function of horizontal position x is given by $y = ax^2$, where $a = 0.92 \ m^{-1}$. If the particle's maximum speed is 8.5 m/s, find the turning points of its motion.

40. A particle with total energy 3.5 J is trapped in a potential well described by $U = 7.0 - 8.0x + 1.7x^2$, where U is in joules and x in meters. Find its turning points.

41. The potential energy associated with a conservative force is shown in Fig. 8-35. Consider particles with total energies $E_1 = -1.5$ J, $E_2 = -0.5$ J, $E_3 = 0.5$ J, $E_4 = 1.5$ J, and $E_5 = 3.0$ J. Discuss the subsequent motion, including the approximate location of any turning points, if the particles are initially at point $x = 1$ m and moving in the $-x$ direction.

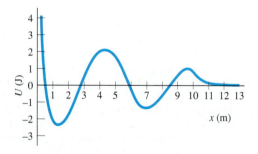

FIGURE 8-35 Problem 41.

42. Make an accurate potential energy curve, covering the region $-8 \ m < x < 8$ m, for potential energy $U = (ax^2 - b)e^{-x^2/c^2}$, where $a = 1.5 \ J/m^2$, $b = 5.0$ J, and $c = 3.0$ m. Discuss the subsequent motion of 1-kg particles starting from the origin and moving initially in the $+x$ direction with total energies of -3 J, 1 J, and 4 J. Include the location of any turning points. Determine also the speed of the highest energy particle when it is a great distance from the origin.

43. (a) Derive an expression for the potential energy of an object subject to a force $F_x = ax - bx^3$, where $a = 5$ N/m and $b = 2$ N/m³, taking $U = 0$ at $x = 0$. (b) Graph the potential energy curve for $x > 0$, and use it to find the turning points for an object whose total energy is -1 J.

Section 8-5 Force and Potential Energy

Note: In the following problems, motion is restricted to one dimension.

44. Figure 8-36 shows the potential energy curve for a certain particle. Find the force on the particle at each of the curve segments shown.

FIGURE 8-36 Problem 44.

45. A particle is trapped in a potential well described by $U(x) = 1.6x^2 - 4$, where U is in joules and x is in meters. Find the force on the particle when it's at (a) $x = 2.1$ m, (b) $x = 0$ m, and (c) $x = -1.4$ m.

46. In ionic solids such as NaCl (salt), the potential energy of a pair of ions takes the form $U = \dfrac{b}{r^n} - \dfrac{a}{r}$, where r is the separation of the ions. For NaCl, a and b have the SI values 4.04×10^{-28} and 5.52×10^{-98}, respectively, and $n = 8.22$. Find the equilibrium separation between ions in NaCl.

47. The potential energy associated with a certain conservative force is given by $U = bx^2$, where b is a constant. Show that the force always tends to accelerate a particle toward the origin if b is positive and away from the origin if b is negative.

48. A more accurate expression for the potential well in Fig. 8-18 than that provided in Example 8-7 is $U = 286(x - x_e)^2 - 6.22 \times 10^{12}(x - x_e)^3$ with U in joules and x in meters. Find the force on the hydrogen atoms when they are 0.10 nm apart.

49. The potential energy of a spring is given by $U = ax^2 - bx + c$, where $a = 5.20$ N/m, $b = 3.12$ N, and $c = 0.468$ J, and where x is the *overall* length of the spring (not the stretch). Find (a) the equilibrium length of the spring and (b) the spring constant.

Section 8-6 Nonconservative Forces

50. Repeat Problem 20 for the case when the coefficient of kinetic friction on both slopes is 0.11, while the level stretches remain frictionless.

51. A basketball dropped from a height of 2.40 m rebounds to a maximum height of 1.55 m. What fraction of the ball's initial energy is lost to nonconservative forces? Take the zero of potential energy at the floor.

52. A 1.5-kg block is launched up a 30° incline with an initial speed of 6.4 m/s. It comes to a halt after moving 3.4 m along the incline, as shown in Fig. 8-37. Find (a) the change in the block's kinetic energy; (b) the change in the block's potential energy; (c) the work done by friction; (d) the coefficient of kinetic friction.

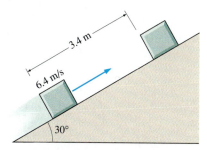

FIGURE 8-37 Problem 52.

53. A pumped-storage reservoir sits 140 m above its generating station and holds 8.5×10^9 kg of water. The power plant generates 330 MW of electric power while draining the reservoir over an 8.0-hour period. What fraction of the initial potential energy is lost to nonconservative forces (i.e., does not emerge as electricity)?

54. A spring of constant $k = 340$ N/m is used to launch a 1.5-kg block along a horizontal surface whose coefficient of sliding friction is 0.27. If the spring is compressed 18 cm, how far does the block slide?

55. A 2.5-kg block strikes a horizontal spring at a speed of 1.8 m/s, as shown in Fig. 8-38. The spring constant is 100 N/m. If the maximum compression of the spring is 21 cm, what is the coefficient of friction between the block and the surface on which it is sliding?

FIGURE 8-38 Problem 55.

56. A meteorite strikes Earth and embeds itself 1.7 m into the ground. Scientists dig up the meteorite and find that its mass is 400 g; they estimate that the ground exerted a retarding force of 10^6 N on the meteorite. Estimate the impact speed of the meteorite.

57. A surface is frictionless except for a region between $x = 1$ m and $x = 2$ m, where the coefficient of friction is given by $\mu = ax^2 + bx + c$, with $a = -2$ m^{-2}, $b = 6$ m^{-1}, and $c = -4$. A block is sliding in the $+x$ direction when it encounters this region. What is the minimum speed it must have to get all the way across the region?

58. A biologist uses a spring-loaded dart gun to shoot a 50-g tranquilizing dart into an elephant 21 m away. The gun's spring has spring constant $k = 690$ N/m and is pulled back 14 cm to launch the dart. The dart embeds itself 2.2 cm in the elephant. (a) What is the average stopping force exerted on the dart by the elephant's flesh? (b) How long does it take the dart to reach the elephant? Assume the dart's trajectory is nearly horizontal.

59. A skier starts from rest at the top of the left-hand peak in Fig. 8-39. What is the maximum coefficient of kinetic friction on the slopes that would allow the skier to coast to the second peak? (Your answer, of course, neglects air resistance.)

FIGURE 8-39 Problem 59.

60. A bug slides back and forth in a hemispherical bowl of 11 cm radius, starting from rest at the top, as shown in Fig. 8-40. The bowl is frictionless except for a 1.5-cm-wide sticky patch at the bottom, where the coefficient of friction is 0.61. How many times does the bug cross the sticky region?

FIGURE 8-40 Problem 60.

61. A 190-g block is launched by compressing a spring of constant $k = 200$ N/m a distance of 15 cm. The spring is mounted horizontally, and the surface directly under it is

frictionless. But beyond the equilibrium position of the spring end, the surface has coefficient of friction $\mu = 0.27$. This frictional surface extends 85 cm, followed by a frictionless curved rise, as shown in Fig. 8-41. After launch, where does the block finally come to rest? Measure from the left end of the frictional zone.

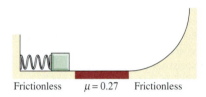

Frictionless $\mu = 0.27$ Frictionless

FIGURE 8-41   Problem 61.

Section 8-7 Conservation of Energy and Mass-Energy

62. Two deuterium nuclei fuse to form a helium nucleus. Each deuterium has mass 3.344×10^{-27} kg, and the helium has mass 6.645×10^{-27} kg. Find the energy released in this reaction.

63. A hypothetical power plant converts matter entirely into electrical energy. Each year, a worker at the plant buys a box of 1-g raisins, and each day drops one raisin into the plant's energy conversion unit. Estimate the average power output of the plant, and compare with a 500-MW coal-burning plant that consumes a 100-car trainload of coal every 3 days.

64. The Sun's total power output is 3.85×10^{26} W. What is the associated rate at which the Sun loses mass?

Paired Problems

(Both problems in a pair involve the same principles and techniques. If you can get the first problem, you should be able to solve the second one.)

65. A block slides down a frictionless incline that terminates in a ramp pointing up at a 45° angle, as shown in Fig. 8-42. Find an expression for the horizontal range x shown in the figure, as a function of the heights h_1 and h_2 shown.

FIGURE 8-42   Problem 65.

66. A block of mass m is launched horizontally from a compressed spring on a frictionless track that turns upward at a

45° angle, as shown in Fig. 8-43. Find an expression for the horizontal range x shown in the figure, as a function of the distance d by which the spring is initially compressed, the spring constant k, and the height h of the ramp.

FIGURE 8-43   Problem 66.

67. A ball of mass m is being whirled around on a string of length R in a vertical circle; the string does no work on the ball. (a) Show from force considerations that the speed at the top of the circle must be at least $\sqrt{Rg}$ if the string is to remain taut. (b) Show that, as long as the string remains taut, the speed at the bottom of the circle can be no more than $\sqrt{5}$ times the speed at the top.

68. An 840-kg roller-coaster car is launched from a giant spring of constant $k = 31$ kN/m into a frictionless loop-the-loop track of radius 6.2 m, as shown in Fig. 8-44. What is the minimum amount that the spring must be compressed if the car is to stay on the track?

FIGURE 8-44   Problem 68.

69. A pendulum consisting of a mass m on a string of length ℓ is pulled back so the string is horizontal, as shown in Fig. 8-45. The pendulum is then released. Find (a) the speed of the mass and (b) the magnitude of the string tension when the string makes a 45° angle with the horizontal.

FIGURE 8-45   Problem 69.

70. A particle of mass m slides down a frictionless quarter-circular track of radius R as shown in Fig. 8-46. If it starts from rest at the top of the track, find (a) its speed and (b) the magnitude of the normal force exerted by the track when the radius vector from the center of the track to the particle makes a 45° angle, as shown.

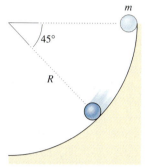

FIGURE 8-46 Problem 70.

71. A particle slides back and forth in a frictionless bowl whose height is given by $h(x) = 0.18x^2$, where x and h are both in meters. If the particle's maximum speed is 47 cm/s, find the x coordinates of its turning points.

72. A 1-kg particle slides on a frictionless track whose height is given by $y = ax^4 - bx^2$, where $a = 1$ m^{-3} and $b = 4$ m^{-1}. The particle's total energy is 20 J, where the zero of potential energy is at $y = 0$. Find the turning points of its motion.

73. A child sleds down a frictionless hill whose vertical drop is 7.2 m. At the bottom is a level but rough stretch where the coefficient of kinetic friction is 0.51. How far does she slide across the level stretch?

74. At the bottom of a frictionless ski slope is a 20-m wide stretch of rough snow where the coefficient of friction is 0.32. From what vertical height on the slope should a skier start at rest, in order to get through the rough patch and come out of it with a speed of 6.0 m/s?

Supplementary Problems

75. A uranium nucleus has a radius of 1.43×10^{-10} m. An alpha particle (mass 6.7×10^{-27} kg) leaves the surface of the nucleus with negligible speed, subject to a repulsive force whose magnitude is $F = A/x^2$, where $A = 4.1 \times 10^{-26}$ N·m^2 and where x is the distance from the alpha particle to the center of the nucleus. What is the speed of the alpha particle when it is (a) 4 nuclear radii from the nucleus; (b) 100 nuclear radii from the nucleus; (c) very far from the nucleus ($x \to \infty$)?

76. A mass m is attached to a spring of constant k that is hanging from the ceiling. (a) Taking the zero of potential energy with the spring in its normal unstretched position, derive an expression for the total potential energy (gravitational plus spring) as a function of distance y taken as positive down-ward. (b) Find the point where the potential energy is a minimum, and explain its significance. (c) Find a second point where the total potential energy is zero. Discuss its significance in terms of an experiment where you attach the mass to the unstretched spring and let go.

77. With the brick of Problem 9 standing on end, what is the minimum energy that can be given the brick to make it fall over?

78. A bug lands on top of the frictionless, spherical head of a bald man. It begins to slide down the head (Fig. 8-47). Show that the bug leaves the head when it has dropped a vertical distance one-third the radius of the head.

FIGURE 8-47 Problem 78.

79. Together, the springs in a 1200-kg car have an effective spring constant of 110,000 N/m and can compress a maximum distance of 40 cm. What is the maximum abrupt drop in road level (Fig. 8-48) that the car can tolerate without "bottoming out"—that is, without its springs reaching maximum compression? Assume the car is driving fast enough that it becomes temporarily airborne.

FIGURE 8-48 Problem 79.

80. Show that the rope in Example 8-6 will cease to be taut when the rope has caught on the rock and makes an angle

$$\theta = \cos^{-1}\left[\frac{2\ell}{3a}\left(\cos\theta_0 + \frac{a}{\ell} - 1\right)\right]$$

with the vertical. Show that your answer is consistent with that of Problem 33.

81. An electron with kinetic energy 0.85 fJ enters a region where its potential energy as a function of position is $U = ax^2 - bx$, where $a = 2.7$ fJ/cm^2 and $b = 4.2$ fJ/cm. (a) How far into the region does the electron penetrate? (b) At what position does the electron have its maximum speed? (c) What is this maximum speed?

82. A particle of mass m is subject to a force $\mathbf{F} = (a\sqrt{x})\hat{\imath}$, where a is a constant. The particle is initially at rest at the origin, and is given a slight nudge in the positive x direction. Find an expression for the particle's speed as a function of position x.

83. (a) Repeat the previous problem for the case of a force $\mathbf{F} = (ax - bx^3)\hat{\imath}$, where a and b are positive constants. (b) What is the significance of the negative square root that can occur for some values of x? (c) Find an expression for the particle's maximum speed.

84. A 17-m-long vine hangs vertically from a tree on one side of a 10-m-wide gorge, as shown in Fig. 8-49. Tarzan runs up, hoping to grab the vine, swing over the gorge, and drop vertically off the vine to land on the other side. At what minimum speed must he be running?

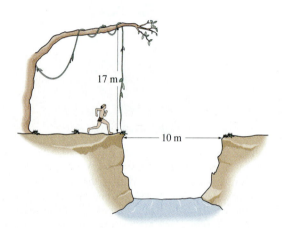

17 m

10 m

FIGURE 8-49 Problem 84.

85. A force points in the $-x$ direction with magnitude given by $F = ax^b$, where a and b are constants. Evaluate the potential energy as a function of position, taking $U = 0$ at some point $x_0 > 0$. Use your result to show that an object of mass m released at $x = \infty$ will reach x_0 with finite velocity provided $b < -1$. Find the velocity for this case.

86. A block slides on a horizontal surface with coefficient of sliding friction $\mu_k = 0.37$. It collides with a spring and stops at the point of maximum compression. If the block hit the spring at 1.79 m/s, and if the spring compressed 22 cm, and if these are the maximum speed and compression for which the block stops, show that the coefficient of static friction is twice the coefficient of sliding friction.

87. The climbing rope described in Example 8-3 is securely fastened at its lower end. At the upper end is a 65-kg climber. At a height 2.4 m directly below the climber, the rope passes through a carabiner (essentially a frictionless metal loop), as shown in Fig. 8-50. If the climber falls, through what maximum total distance—including the stretching of the rope—does he drop? *Hint:* Your statement of energy conservation should result in a cubic equation, which you can solve graphically, numerically, or analytically.

2.4 m

FIGURE 8-50 Before and after the fall (Problem 87).

Gravitation

The Russian Mir space station, viewed from an approaching American space shuttle. Precise application of Newton's laws of motion and gravity makes possible the space technology that is increasingly important in science, engineering, and communications.

Gravity is the most obvious of nature's fundamental forces. With your understanding of the laws of motion and mechanical energy, you're now in a position to explore some phenomena of gravitation. Historically, theories of gravity have led to clearer understandings of the nature and evolution of the universe beyond planet Earth. With the advent of the space age, we've used our knowledge of gravity to explore the solar system and to engineer a host of new space-based technologies. In all but the most exotic astrophysical applications, we still use the theory of gravity developed by Isaac Newton in the late 1600s.

FIGURE 9-1 Kepler's first law states that planetary orbits are ellipses with the Sun at one focus; the other focus is a point in empty space. The ellipse shown here is highly exaggerated; all planetary orbits except Pluto's are very nearly circular. (A circle is an ellipse in which both foci coincide at the center.) The straight line is the major axis of the ellipse; half its length is the semimajor axis that figures in Kepler's third law.

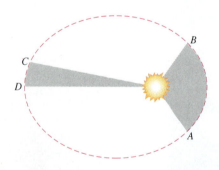

FIGURE 9-2 Kepler's equal-area law. If the planet takes the same time to go from *A* to *B* as from *C* to *D*, then the shaded regions have the same area. This means the planet must be moving faster when it's closer to the Sun.

FIGURE 9-3 In an Earth-centered universe, Venus would not show the complete range of phases from crescent to full, and its apparent size would remain constant because of its constant distance from Earth. Galileo's observations of Venus provided strong evidence for Copernicus's heliocentric theory.

9-1 TOWARD A LAW OF GRAVITY

Newton's theory of gravity was the culmination of two centuries of scientific revolution that began in 1543 with Polish astronomer Nicolaus Copernicus's radical suggestion that the planets orbit not Earth but the Sun. Before that time, views of the Greek philosopher-scientists Aristotle and Ptolemy dominated, holding that Earth was the center of the universe and the realm of imperfection. Terrestrial objects naturally moved toward Earth. Celestial objects, in contrast, were perfect and moved only in perfect circles. Even Copernicus maintained this sharp distinction between celestial and terrestrial realms, holding that planetary motions involved only perfect circles.

Fifty years after Copernicus's work was published, the Danish noble Tycho Brahe began a program of accurate planetary observations. After Tycho's death in 1601, his assistant Johannes Kepler worked to make sense of the observations. Success came when Kepler took a radical step: He gave up the requirement that planetary motion involved only perfect circles. Kepler summarized his new insights in three laws of planetary motion:

Kepler's first law: The planets orbit the Sun in ellipses, with the Sun at one focus (Fig. 9-1).

Kepler's second law: The line joining the Sun and a planet sweeps out equal areas in equal times (Fig. 9-2).

Kepler's third law: The square of a planet's orbital period is proportional to the cube of the semimajor axis of its orbit (Fig. 9-1).

Kepler's laws were based solely on observation and had no theoretical basis. So Kepler knew *how* the planets moved but not *why* they did so.

Shortly after Kepler published his first two laws, Galileo trained his first telescopes on the heavens. Among his discoveries were four moons orbiting Jupiter, sunspots that blemished the supposedly perfect sphere of the Sun, and the phases of Venus (Fig. 9-3). His observations called into question the notion that all celestial objects were perfect and also lent credence to the Copernican view of the Sun as the center of planetary motion. Galileo's advocacy of the Copernican theory led to his 1633 conviction and house arrest on charges of heresy. Only in 1992 did the Vatican admit formally to having been in error and offer praise for Galileo.

By Newton's time the intellectual climate was ripe for the culmination of the revolution that had begun with Copernicus. Legend has it that Newton was sitting under an apple tree when an apple struck him on the head, causing him to discover gravity. That story is probably a myth, but if it were true the other half would be that Newton was staring at the moon when the apple struck. Newton's stroke of genius was this:

> Newton realized that the motion of the apple and the motion of the moon were the *same;* that both were "falling" toward Earth under the influence of the same force.

Newton called this force **gravity**, after the Latin *gravitas,* meaning "heaviness." In one of the most sweeping syntheses in the history of human thought, Newton eliminated forever the distinction between terrestrial and celestial realms. Instead, he implied, the behavior of everything in the universe obeys the same set of physical laws.

9-2 UNIVERSAL GRAVITATION

Newton generalized his new understanding of gravity to suggest that any two particles in the universe exert attractive forces on each other, with magnitude given by

$$F = \frac{Gm_1 m_2}{r^2}. \quad \text{(universal gravitation)} \quad (9\text{-}1)$$

Here m_1 and m_2 are the particle masses, r the distance between them, and G the **constant of universal gravitation** whose value—determined after Newton's time—is $6.67 \times 10^{-11} \ \text{N} \cdot \text{m}^2/\text{kg}^2$. The constant G is truly a universal constant; observation and theory suggest that it has the same value throughout the universe.

The force of gravity acts *between* two particles. That is, m_1 exerts an attractive force on m_2, and m_2 exerts an equal but oppositely directed force on m_1. The two forces therefore obey Newton's third law.

Newton's law of universal gravitation applies strictly only to point particles that have no extent. But, as Newton showed using his newly developed calculus, it also holds for spherically symmetric objects of any size if the distance r is measured from their centers. It also applies approximately to arbitrarily shaped objects provided the distance between them is large compared with their sizes. For example, the gravitational force of Earth on a space shuttle is given accurately by Equation 9-1 because (1) Earth is essentially spherical and (2) the space shuttle, although irregular in shape, is much smaller than its distance from Earth's center.

EXAMPLE 9-1	*The Acceleration of Gravity*

Use the law of universal gravitation to find the force of Earth's gravity on a mass m, and apply Newton's second law to determine the corresponding acceleration. Evaluate your results at Earth's surface and at the 250-km altitude of a space shuttle. Finally, adapt your calculations to find the acceleration due to the moon's gravity at the lunar surface.

Solution

Since Earth is essentially spherical, Equation 9-1 gives the gravitational force on a mass m:

$$F = \frac{GM_E m}{r^2},$$

where M_E is Earth's mass. Newton's second law, $F = ma$, shows that the mass m has acceleration given by

$$a = \frac{F}{m} = \frac{GM_E}{r^2}. \quad (9\text{-}2)$$

The distance r is measured from the *center* of the object providing the gravitational force, so to find the acceleration at Earth's surface we use R_E, the radius of the Earth, for r. Taking R_E and M_E from inside the front cover (or from Appendix E), we have

$$a = \frac{GM_E}{R_E^2} = \frac{(6.67 \times 10^{-11} \ \text{N} \cdot \text{m}^2/\text{kg}^2)(5.97 \times 10^{24} \ \text{kg})}{(6.37 \times 10^6 \ \text{m})^2}$$

$$= 9.81 \ \text{m/s}^2.$$

This, of course, is just the value of g—the acceleration of gravity at Earth's surface. Note the difference between the two numbers G and g commonly associated with gravity: G is a universal constant, while g describes the gravitational acceleration at a particular place—namely, Earth's surface—and happens to have the value it does because of the size and mass of the Earth.

At the space shuttle altitude, we have $r = R_E + 250$ km, so

$$a = \frac{GM_E}{r^2} = \frac{(6.67 \times 10^{-11} \text{ N·m}^2/\text{kg}^2)(5.97 \times 10^{24} \text{ kg})}{(6.37 \times 10^6 \text{ m} + 250 \times 10^3 \text{ m})^2}$$

$$= 9.09 \text{ m/s}^2,$$

or about 93% of its surface value. This calculation supports our contention in Chapter 5 that weightlessness doesn't mean the absence of gravitational force; rather, weightlessness arises because—as Equation 9-2 shows—the gravitational acceleration of an object is independent of its mass, so all objects "fall" together with a common acceleration.

Finally, using values for the moon from Appendix E, we have

$$g_{\text{moon}} = \frac{GM_m}{R_m^2} = \frac{(6.67 \times 10^{-11} \text{ N·m}^2/\text{kg}^2)(7.35 \times 10^{22} \text{ kg})}{(1.74 \times 10^6 \text{ m})^2}$$

$$= 1.62 \text{ m/s}^2.$$

Although the moon's mass is only about 1% of Earth's, it's also a lot smaller, and the two effects combine to give a gravitational acceleration about one-sixth that of Earth.

Tip

Measure from the Center The law of universal gravitation applies to spherical objects when the distance r is measured *from the center*. If you're 100 m above Earth, the distance r in Equation 9-1 is $R_E + 100$ m, not just 100 m. "Distance between" in this context means between centers.

EXERCISE Calculate the gravitational acceleration at the surface of (a) Mars and (b) a neutron star with the Sun's mass crammed into a sphere 6.6 km in radius.

Answer: (a) $g_{\text{Mars}} = 3.75$ m/s^2; (b) $g_{ns} = 3.0 \times 10^{12}$ m/s^2

Some problems similar to Example 9-1: 1–4, 6

The variation of gravitational acceleration with distance from Earth's center provided Newton with one clue that the gravitational force should vary as the inverse square of the distance. Newton knew the moon's orbital period and distance from Earth; from these he could calculate its orbital speed and thus its acceleration v^2/r. Newton found—as you can in Problem 2—that the moon's acceleration is about 1/3600 the gravitational acceleration g at Earth's surface. The moon is about 60 times farther from Earth's center than is Earth's surface; since $60^2 = 3600$, the decrease in gravitational acceleration with distance from Earth's center is consistent with a gravitational force that varies as $1/r^2$.

Tip

Understanding "Inverse Square" Newton's universal gravitation (Equation 9-1) is the first of several "inverse square" force laws you'll encounter, and it's important to understand what this term means. In Equation 9-1 the distance r between the two masses appears *squared,* and it occurs in the *denominator;* hence the force depends on the *inverse square* of the distance. But practically, what does this mean? It means the force falls very rapidly with increasing distance. How rapidly? Double the distance, and the force drops to $1/2^2$, or 1/4 of its original value. Triple the distance, and it drops to $1/3^2$, or 1/9. Go 60 times as far away—as in going from Earth's surface to the moon's orbit—and it drops to $1/60^2$, or to 1/3600 of its value at Earth's surface. Although you can always grind through the arithmetic of Equation 9-1, you should get used to evaluating variations in force through these simple ratio calculations whenever possible.

Since acceleration is proportional to force, these considerations apply also to the variation of gravitational acceleration with distance from a gravitating body. Standing on the ground, you're one Earth radius from Earth's center; double that distance, and the acceleration of gravity for you will be $1/2^2 = 1/4$ its surface value, or about 2.5 m/s^2.

Figure 9-4 shows the inverse-square relation.

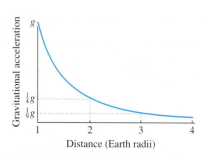

FIGURE 9-4 Variation in the gravitational acceleration with distance from Earth's center obeys the inverse-square law evident in Equation 9-1. At three Earth radii, for example, the gravitational acceleration is $1/3^2 = 1/9$ of its value g at Earth's surface.

EXAMPLE 9-2	*Gravity Is Weak!*

Estimate the gravitational force between a 55-kg woman and a 75-kg man when they're 1.6 m apart. Find also the gravitational force between two electrons 1.0 cm apart, and compare with the 2.3×10^{-24} N repulsive electric force between the electrons.

Solution

The people are hardly spherical, and their separation is not large compared with their sizes, so Equation 9-1 provides at best an order-of-magnitude estimate of the force:

$$F = \frac{Gm_1 m_2}{r^2} = \frac{(6.67 \times 10^{-11} \text{ N·m}^2/\text{kg}^2)(55 \text{ kg})(75 \text{ kg})}{(1.6 \text{ m})^2}$$

$$= 10^{-7} \text{ N}.$$

This is far smaller than forces typically experienced by people-size objects.

Electrons are essentially point particles, so Equation 9-1 applies exactly. Taking the electron mass from the table inside the front cover, we have

$$F = \frac{Gm_e^2}{r^2} = \frac{(6.67 \times 10^{-11} \text{ N·m}^2/\text{kg}^2)(9.11 \times 10^{-31} \text{ kg})^2}{(0.010 \text{ m})^2}$$

$$= 5.5 \times 10^{-67} \text{ N},$$

about 10^{-43} times smaller than the electric force. Gravitational forces are completely negligible in the subatomic realm.

EXERCISE Two boulders, one of mass 3×10^5 kg and the other 9×10^4 kg, are roughly spherical and sit 21 m apart on a mountain ridge. Calculate the gravitational force between them, and compare with the weight of a 1-g raisin.

Answer: 4×10^{-3} N, about half the weight of the raisin

Some problems similar to Example 9-2: 5, 7, 8, 10, 11

If gravity is so weak, why is it such an important force? Because, unlike the electric force, gravity is always attractive. No antigravity or negative mass has ever been found. So the gravitational force is always cumulative, and large concentrations of matter produce substantial gravitational forces. Electric forces, in contrast, can be attractive or repulsive because there are two kinds of electric charge. A large object such as Earth contains nearly equal amounts of positive and negative charge and, therefore, exerts no significant electric force. We'll explore this fundamental distinction between electric and gravitational forces further in Chapter 23.

The Cavendish Experiment: Weighing the Earth

Given the mass and radius of the Earth and the measured value of g, we could use Equation 9-1 to determine the universal constant G. Unfortunately, the only way to determine Earth's mass accurately is to measure its gravitational effect and then use Equation 9-1. But that requires knowing G.

To determine G we need to measure the gravitational force of a *known* mass. Given the weak gravitational force of normal-size objects, this is a challenging task. It was accomplished in 1798 through an ingenious experiment by the British physicist Henry Cavendish. Cavendish mounted two 5-cm-diameter lead spheres on the ends of a rod suspended from a thin fiber. He then brought two 30-cm lead spheres nearby (Fig. 9-5). Their gravitational attraction caused a slight movement of the small spheres, twisting the fiber. Knowing the properties of the fiber, Cavendish could determine the force. With the known masses and their separation, he then used Equation 9-1 to calculate G. His result determined the mass of the Earth; indeed, his published paper was entitled "On Weighing the Earth."

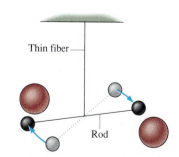

Thin fiber

Rod

FIGURE 9-5 The Cavendish experiment, used to determine G. Light shading indicates the original position of the small spheres.

Variations in the thickness and density of Earth's crust are associated with geological features and give rise to small variations in the surface value of the gravitational acceleration g. Geologists use sensitive instruments called gravimeters to measure these variations and infer the underlying rock structures. Gravimeters themselves are based on simple physical principles; the most common types employ fixed masses on sensitive springs. Ingeniously designed, these devices detect variations in g as small as 10^{-6} m/s^2.

Petroleum geologists find gravity measurements particularly useful since they readily reveal the presence of low-density salt domes that often occur with oil and gas deposits (Fig. 9-6). Gravity measurements also show that the extra mass of moun-

tains is partly compensated by low-density material in the regions below them. On a global scale, sensitive mapping of the height of the sea surface indicates the gravitational attraction of the underlying material and reveals a wealth of geological features (Fig. 9-7).

FIGURE 9-7 This map shows the gravitational acceleration at the ocean surface; lighter areas correspond to higher values of g and vice versa. The map was made using radar altimetry to determine the level of the ocean surface from the orbiting satellites; accuracy of the surface-height measurement is about 10 cm. Regions of high ocean surface correspond to higher gravity, as the underlying mass (a mountain ridge, for example) attracts water, causing it to pile up.

FIGURE 9-6 A "dome" of rock salt protrudes into the overlying rock layers. Since the salt has lower density, the value of g at the surface will be slightly lower than normal.

9-3 ORBITAL MOTION

Orbital motion occurs when gravity is the dominant force acting on a body. It's not just planets and spacecraft that are in orbit. An individual astronaut, floating outside a space shuttle, is in orbit about Earth. The Sun itself orbits the center of the galaxy, taking about 200 million years to complete one revolution. Neglecting air resistance, even a baseball is temporarily in orbit. Here we discuss quantitatively the special case of circular orbits, then describe qualitatively the general case.

Newton's genius was to recognize that the moon is held in its circular orbit by the same force that pulls an apple to the ground. From there, it was a short step for Newton to realize that human-made objects could be put into orbit. Nearly 300 years before the first artificial satellites, he imagined a projectile launched horizontally from a high mountain (Fig. 9-8). The projectile moves in a curve,

FIGURE 9-8 Newton's "thought experiment" convinced him that projectile and orbital motion are essentially the same.

FIGURE 9-9 An object in circular orbit is falling away from the straight-line path it would take in the absence of gravity. Light pink lines connect points on the orbit with positions where the object would be in the absence of gravity.

as gravity pulls it from the straight-line path it would follow if no force were acting. As its initial speed is increased, the projectile travels farther before striking Earth. Finally, there comes a speed for which the rate at which the projectile's path bends is exactly equal to the rate at which Earth's surface falls away beneath it. It is then in **circular orbit**, continuing forever unless a nongravitational force acts.

Why doesn't an orbiting object fall toward Earth? It does! Under the influence of gravity, it gets ever closer to Earth than it would be on a straight-line path (Fig. 9-9). It's behaving exactly as Newton's second law requires of an object under the influence of a force—by accelerating. For a *circular* orbit, that acceleration amounts to a change in the direction, but not the magnitude, of the orbiting object's velocity.

Remember that Newton's laws aren't so much about *motion* as they are about *changes* in motion. To ask why a satellite doesn't fall to Earth is to adopt the archaic Aristotelian view. The Newtonian question is this: Why doesn't the satellite move in a straight line? And the answer is simple: because a force is acting. That force—gravity—is exactly analogous to the tension force that keeps a ball on a string whirling on its circular path.

We can analyze circular orbits quantitatively because, as we learned in Section 4-4, a force of magnitude mv^2/r is required to keep an object of mass m and speed v in a circular path of radius r. In the case of an orbit that force is gravity, so we have

$$\frac{GMm}{r^2} = \frac{mv^2}{r},$$

where m is the mass of the orbiting object and M that of the object about which it's orbiting. We assume here that $M \gg m$, so the gravitating object can be considered essentially at rest—a reasonable approximation with Earth satellites or even for planets orbiting the much more massive Sun.

Solving for the orbital speed gives

$$v^2 = \frac{GM}{r}. \tag{9-3}$$

Often we're interested in the **orbital period**, or the time to complete one orbit. In one period T, the orbiting object moves the orbital circumference $2\pi r$, so its speed may be written $v = 2\pi r/T$. Then Equation 9-3 becomes

$$\left(\frac{2\pi r}{T}\right)^2 = \frac{GM}{r}$$

or

$$T^2 = \frac{4\pi^2 r^3}{GM}. \qquad \text{(orbital period, circular orbit)} \tag{9-4}$$

4.8
Satellites Orbit

In deriving Equation 9-4, we've proved Kepler's third law—that the square of the orbital period is proportional to the cube of the semimajor axis—for the special case of a circular orbit whose semimajor axis is just its radius.

Note that orbital speed and period are independent of the mass m of the orbiting object. This is another indication that all objects experience the same gravitational acceleration. Astronauts, for example, have the same orbital parameters as their space shuttle. That's why astronauts are weightless inside the shuttle and why they don't float away if they step outside (Fig. 9-10).

FIGURE 9-10 Astronaut Bruce McCandless floats freely outside a space shuttle. Because orbital parameters are independent of the orbiting mass, astronaut and shuttle remain in the same orbit, circling Earth at nearly 8 km/s.

EXAMPLE 9-3	*A Space Shuttle Orbit*

A space shuttle is in a circular orbit 250 km above Earth's surface. What are its orbital speed and period?

Solution
Remember that r appearing in Equations 9-3 and 9-4 is the distance from the center of the gravitating object. So here r is Earth's radius plus the 250-km altitude. Taking Earth's mass and radius from the table inside the front cover, Equation 9-3 gives

$$v = \sqrt{\frac{GM_E}{r}}$$

$$= \sqrt{\frac{(6.67\times10^{-11}\ \text{N·m}^2/\text{kg}^2)(5.97\times10^{24}\ \text{kg})}{(6.37\times10^6\ \text{m} + 250\times10^3\ \text{m})}}$$

$$= 7.8\ \text{km/s},$$

or about 17,400 mi/h. Astronauts have no choice; if they want a circular orbit 250 km up, they must have this speed.

We can get the orbital period from the speed and radius, or directly from Equation 9-4:

$$T = \sqrt{\frac{4\pi^2 r^3}{GM_E}}$$

$$= \sqrt{\frac{(4\pi^2)(6.37\times10^6\ \text{m} + 250\times10^3\ \text{m})^3}{(6.67\times10^{-11}\ \text{N·m}^2/\text{kg}^2)(5.97\times10^{24}\ \text{kg})}}$$

$$= 5.4\times10^3\ \text{s},$$

or 90 minutes. Again, there's no choice: As long as gravity is the only force acting, a circular orbit at this altitude will take this much time.

Since 250 km is small compared with Earth's radius, the orbital speed and 90-minute period found in this example are approximately correct for any near-Earth orbit. If it weren't for air resistance and mountains, a baseball could be put into orbit just above the ground—and its orbital period would be about 90 minutes. Of course, it would need to be thrown with about the same 7.8 km/s speed as the space shuttle.

EXERCISE The Mars Surveyor mapping spacecraft is in a circular orbit 400 km above Mars's surface. What is Surveyor's orbital period? Consult Appendix E for data.

Answer: 118 min

Example 9-3 shows that the orbital period in near-Earth orbit is about 90 minutes. The moon, on the other hand, takes 27 days to complete its nearly circular orbit. So there must be a distance where the orbital period is 24 hours—the same as Earth's rotation period. A satellite at this distance will remain fixed with respect to Earth's surface provided its orbit is parallel to the equator. Weather

FIGURE 9-11 Weather over Africa and the South Atlantic as photographed by the European Space Agency's METEOSAT satellite from geosynchronous orbit.

FIGURE 9-12 This TV satellite dish is trained on a communications satellite in geosynchronous orbit 36,000 km above the equator.

and communication satellites are often placed in this **geosynchronous orbit** (Fig. 9-11). Satellite TV, as well as some intercontinental telephone and data transmissions, use satellites in geosynchronous orbit (Fig. 9-12).

EXAMPLE 9-4	*Geosynchronous Orbit*

What altitude is required for geosynchronous orbit?

Solution

We want the period T to be 24 h or 8.64×10^4 s. Solving Equation 9-4 for r gives

$$r = \left(\frac{GM_E T^2}{4\pi^2} \right)^{1/3}$$

$$= \left(\frac{(6.67 \times 10^{-11} \ \text{N·m}^2/\text{kg}^2)(5.97 \times 10^{24} \ \text{kg})(8.64 \times 10^4 \ \text{s})^2}{4\pi^2} \right)^{1/3}$$

$$= 4.22 \times 10^7 \ \text{m} ,$$

or 42,200 km. This is the distance from Earth's center; the altitude above Earth's surface is then about 36,000 km or 22,000 miles.

A more careful calculation would use Earth's so-called sidereal rotation period, measured with respect to the distant stars rather than the Sun. Earth's sidereal period is 0.997 days. And, because Earth is not a perfect sphere, geosynchronous satellites drift from their intended positions. They fire small rocket thrusters every few weeks to correct for this effect.

EXERCISE Astronauts establish two separate bases on Mars, communicating via synchronous satellite. At what altitude should they place the satellite? (Consult Appendix E for Mars's mass, radius, and sidereal rotation period.)

Answer: 1.7×10^4 km

Some problems similar to Examples 9-3 and 9-4: 12–15, 17, 18, 21–23

APPLICATION	*Perpetual Sunshine*

Solar physicists have long wished for an observatory with an ininterrupted view of the Sun. In 1995 they got their wish, with the launch of the Solar and Heliospheric Observatory (SOHO), a joint venture by NASA and the European Space Agency. Other spacecraft have observed the Sun, most of them from Earth orbit. But Earth-orbiting spacecraft regularly pass behind the planet, which temporarily blocks the Sun. For studies requiring uninterrupted solar data, these blackouts are unacceptable.

SOHO's remarkable orbit solves the blackout problem, while keeping the spacecraft relatively close to Earth and in a position to observe the Sun from the same perspective as Earth.

SOHO is "parked" in an orbit that keeps it approximately 1.5 million km sunward of Earth at all times (this value is about 1% of the Earth-Sun distance). How is that possible? After all, Equation 9-4 shows the orbital period decreasing with decreasing orbital radius, and we know that both Venus and Mercury have shorter "years" than does Earth. But Equation 9-4 assumes an object in orbit around a single massive gravitating center. SOHO, although in solar orbit, is close enough to Earth that Earth's gravity is important. Along a line from Earth to Sun, the gravitational forces of Earth and Sun point in opposite directions. Close to Earth, the force of Earth's gravity is strongest. Far from Earth, the Sun's gravity dominates. Somewhere they just cancel, giving zero net force—but hold on, that's not where SOHO is. Further sunward, the net gravitational force is sunward and it gets stronger with increasing distance from Earth. Eventually, there's a point where the net gravitational force has just the right value to hold an object in circular orbit about the Sun with a period of exactly one year. At that point, and that point only, an object's orbit about the Sun will keep it in step with Earth's orbital motion. The object will remain always at the same point on the Earth-Sun line even as that line rotates with Earth's orbital period (Fig. 9-13).

The special point we've just described is where NASA engineers have "parked" SOHO. You can find that point's

FIGURE 9-14 Image of the Sun taken with the SOHO spacecraft's Extreme Ultraviolet Imaging Telescope. This particular instrument is sensitive to the light given off by ionized helium at temperatures of 60,000–80,000 K. A large tongue of solar material is erupting from the Sun at lower left.

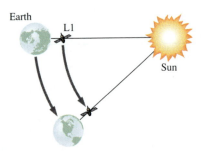

FIGURE 9-13 At the special point labeled L1, the net force of Earth's and Sun's gravity gives a spacecraft an orbital period of one year, so it stays in step with Earth's orbital motion. Figure is not to scale; L1 is actually sunward of Earth by only about 1% of the Earth-Sun distance.

precise location in Problem 66. From its special vantage point, SOHO has produced remarkable images and data with unprecedented resolution. Figure 9-14 shows a solar image from SOHO.

SOHO's position is one of several points, called Lagrangian points, where an object can orbit the Sun stably under the influence of both terrestrial and solar gravity. SOHO's Lagrangian point is called L1. In general, the motion of an object under the influence of two gravitating bodies presents a formidable mathematical problem, solvable exactly only in a few special cases—including that of the L1 point (Problem 66). Actually, SOHO is not fixed at L1 but rather describes an elongated orbit about that point.

Elliptical Orbits

Using his laws of motion and gravity, Newton was able to prove Kepler's assertion that the planets move in elliptical paths with the Sun at one focus. Circular orbits represent the special case where the two foci of the ellipse coincide, so the distance from the gravitating center remains constant. Most planetary orbits are nearly, but not quite, circular; Earth's distance from the Sun, for example, varies by about 3% throughout the year. But the orbits of comets and other smaller bodies are often highly elliptical (Fig. 9-15). Their orbital speeds also vary, as they gain speed "falling" toward the Sun, whip quickly around the Sun at the point of closest approach (the **perihelion**), and then "climb" ever more slowly to their most distant point (**aphelion**) before returning to the Sun's vicinity. Comet Halley, for example, visited the inner solar system in 1986 and will not do so again

FIGURE 9-15 Orbits of most known comets are highly elliptical. Those with longer periods, like Comet Halley (orbit marked with arrow), spend much of their time moving slowly through the outer reaches of the solar system. All comet orbits have the sun at one focus.

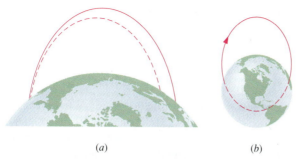

FIGURE 9-16 (*a*) For projectiles of limited range, the true elliptical trajectory (solid line) differs only slightly from the parabolic trajectory calculated on the assumption of a flat Earth. (*b*) Long-range trajectories, like those of intercontinental missiles, are clearly elliptical. Were Earth's mass concentrated at the center, such a projectile would continue forever in its elliptical orbit.

until 2061; most of its time will be spent moving slowly through the distant realms beyond the orbit of Uranus.

In Chapter 3 we showed that the trajectory of a projectile is a parabola. But our derivation neglected Earth's curvature and the associated variation in *g* with altitude. In fact, a projectile is just like any orbiting body. Neglecting air resistance, it too describes an elliptical orbit with Earth's center at one focus. Only for trajectories small compared with Earth's radius are the true elliptical path and the parabola of Chapter 3 essentially indistinguishable (Fig. 9-16).

Are missiles and baseballs really in orbit? Yes—but their orbits happen to intersect the Earth. At that point, nongravitational forces put an end to orbital motion. If Earth suddenly shrank to the size of a grapefruit, a baseball would continue happily in orbit, as Fig. 9-16*b* suggests. Newton's ingenious intuition was correct: Barring air resistance, there's truly no difference between the motion of everyday objects near Earth and the motion of celestial objects.

Open Orbits

With elliptical and circular orbits, the motion repeats indefinitely because the orbit is a closed path. But closed orbits aren't the only ones possible. Imagine again Newton's thought experiment, only now fire the projectile faster than necessary for a circular orbit (Fig. 9-17). It rises higher than before, describing an ellipse with its low point at the launch site. Faster, and the ellipse gets more elongated. But with great enough initial speed the projectile describes a trajectory that takes it ever farther from Earth (Fig. 9-18). We'll see in the next section how energy determines the type of orbit.

9-4 GRAVITATIONAL ENERGY

How much energy does it take to boost a satellite to geosynchronous altitude? Our simple answer *mgh* won't do here since *g* varies substantially over the distance involved. So, as we found in the preceding chapter, we have to integrate to determine the potential energy.

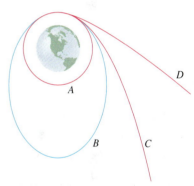

FIGURE 9-17 As projectile speed is increased above that needed for circular orbit (*A*), the trajectory becomes first an ellipse (*B*), then a parabola (*C*), and finally a hyperbola (*D*).

FIGURE 9-18 Hyperbolic orbit of a high-speed object passing a gravitating center like the Sun or Earth. Only near the gravitating center does the orbit deviate significantly from the straight-line asymptotes of the hyperbola.

FIGURE 9-19 The change in gravitational potential energy between points r_1 and r_2 is found by integrating the gravitational force; along the path of integration the force **F** and path element $d\mathbf{r}$ are oppositely directed.

Figure 9-19 shows two points at distances r_1 and r_2 from the center of a gravitating mass M, in this case, Earth. Equation 8-2 gives the change in potential energy associated with moving a mass m from r_1 to r_2:

$$\Delta U_{12} = -\int_{r_1}^{r_2} \mathbf{F} \cdot d\mathbf{r}.$$

Here the force points radially inward and has magnitude GMm/r^2, while the path element $d\mathbf{r}$ points radially outward. Then $\mathbf{F} \cdot d\mathbf{r} = -(GMm/r^2)dr$, where the minus sign comes from the factor $\cos 180°$ in the dot product of oppositely directed vectors. Then the potential energy difference is

$$\Delta U_{12} = \int_{r_1}^{r_2} \frac{GMm}{r^2} dr = GMm \int_{r_1}^{r_2} r^{-2} dr$$

$$= GMm \left.\frac{r^{-1}}{-1}\right|_{r_1}^{r_2} = GMm\left(\frac{1}{r_1} - \frac{1}{r_2}\right). \tag{9-5}$$

Does this make sense? Yes: For $r_1 < r_2$, ΔU_{12} is positive, showing that potential energy increases with height—consistent with our simpler result $\Delta U = mgh$ near Earth's surface. (In fact, as Problem 64 shows, $\Delta U = mgh$ is a special case of Equation 9-5 when $r_1 \simeq r_2 \simeq R_E$.) Although we derived Equation 9-5 for two points on a radial line, Fig. 9-20 shows that it holds for any two points at distances r_1 and r_2 from the gravitating center.

FIGURE 9-20 Since gravity is a conservative force, we can use any path to evaluate the potential energy change. For these two points not on a radial line, we choose a path consisting of an arc and a radial line. The potential energy doesn't change along the arc since it's perpendicular to the gravitational force. All the change occurs along the line and is given by Equation 9-5. So Equation 9-5 holds for any two points at radii r_1 and r_2.

EXAMPLE 9-5	Steps to the Moon

Materials to construct an 11,000-kg lunar observatory are boosted from Earth to geosynchronous orbit. There they are assembled, then launched to the moon, 384,000 km from Earth. Compare the work that must be done against Earth's gravity on the two legs of the trip.

Solution

As we saw in the preceding chapter, the work done against a conservative force is equal to the change in potential energy; here that change is given by Equation 9-5. For the first step we have $r_1 = R_E$ and, from Example 9-4, $r_2 = 42,200$ km. Since the quantity GM_Em that appears in Equation 9-5 will be used in both steps, we calculate it first: $GM_Em = 4.38 \times 10^{18}$ N·m². Then for the first step we have

$$W = \Delta U_{12} = GM_Em\left(\frac{1}{r_1} - \frac{1}{r_2}\right)$$

$$= (4.38 \times 10^{18}\ \text{N·m}^2)\left(\frac{1}{6.37 \times 10^6\ \text{m}} - \frac{1}{4.22 \times 10^7\ \text{m}}\right)$$

$$= 5.8 \times 10^{11}\ \text{J}.$$

From geosynchronous orbit to the moon a similar calculation gives

$$W = (4.38 \times 10^{18}\ \text{N·m}^2)\left(\frac{1}{4.22 \times 10^7\ \text{m}} - \frac{1}{3.84 \times 10^8\ \text{m}}\right)$$

$$= 9.2 \times 10^{10}\ \text{J}.$$

Even though the second step is much longer, the rapid drop-off in the gravitational force means that less work is required than for the shorter boost to geosynchronous altitude.

Our calculations here include only the work done against Earth's gravity; additional energy would be required to attain a circular geosynchronous orbit. On the other hand, the moon's gravitational attraction would lower the required energy somewhat.

EXERCISE How much energy must a 790-kg space probe have to get from Earth's vicinity to Jupiter's? Consider only the effect of the Sun's gravity, not the planets'. Consult Appendix E.

Answer: 5.6×10^{11} J

Some problems similar to Example 9-5: 28, 29

The Zero of Potential Energy

Equation 9-5 has an interesting feature—the potential energy difference remains finite even when the points are infinitely far apart, as you can see by setting either r_1 or r_2 to infinity. Although the gravitational force always acts, it weakens so rapidly with distance that its cumulative effect is finite even over infinite distances. This property makes it convenient to set the zero of potential energy at infinity. Setting $r_1 = \infty$ and dropping the subscript on r_2, we then have an expression for the potential energy at an arbitrary distance r from the gravitating center:

$$U(r) = -\frac{GMm}{r}. \quad \text{(gravitational potential energy)} \quad (9\text{-}6)$$

The potential energy is negative because we chose $U = 0$ at $r = \infty$; any other point is closer to the gravitating center and, therefore, has lower potential energy.

Knowing the gravitational potential energy allows us to apply the powerful conservation of energy principle. Figure 9-21 shows the potential energy curve obtained by plotting Equation 9-6. Superposing several values of total energy shows immediately that an object with $E < 0$ is in a bound orbit, with a maximum distance beyond which it cannot go. In general, the orbit for $E < 0$ is an ellipse. For $E > 0$, the object is not bound since it's energetically possible for it to move all the way to infinity. In this case the orbit is hyperbolic. The special case $E = 0$ corresponds to a parabolic orbit.

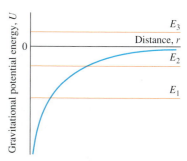

FIGURE 9-21 A gravitational potential energy curve, with the zero of potential energy taken at infinity. Total energies E_1 and E_2, both less than zero, correspond to bound (elliptical) orbits. Positive total energy E_3 corresponds to an unbound (hyperbolic) orbit.

EXAMPLE 9-6	*Blast-Off*

A rocket is launched vertically upward at 2.1 km/s. How high does it go?

Solution

This is a typical conservation of energy problem, like those of the preceding chapter. We write $K + U = K_0 + U_0$ to equate the total energies at two different points. At launch the rocket has both kinetic and potential energy, while at the peak of its trajectory its energy is all potential. As always, $K = \frac{1}{2}mv^2$, and here U is given by Equation 9-6. So we have

$$-\frac{GM_Em}{r} = \frac{1}{2}mv_0^2 - \frac{GM_Em}{R_E},$$

where m is the rocket's mass, r is the distance from Earth's center at the peak, and Earth's radius R_E is the distance at launch. Solving for r gives

$$r = \left(\frac{1}{R_E} - \frac{v_0^2}{2GM_E}\right)^{-1}$$

$$= \left(\frac{1}{6.37 \times 10^6 \text{ m}} - \frac{(2100 \text{ m/s})^2}{2(6.67 \times 10^{-11} \text{ N·m}^2/\text{kg}^2)(5.97 \times 10^{24} \text{ kg})}\right)^{-1}$$

$$= 6.603 \times 10^6 \text{ m}.$$

Again, this is the distance from Earth's center; subtracting Earth's radius then gives a peak altitude of 230 km.

Tip

All Conservation of Energy Problems Are the Same This problem is essentially the same as one from the preceding chapter where you throw a ball straight up and solve for its maximum height using $U = mgh$ for the potential energy. The only difference is the more complicated potential energy function $U = -GMm/r$ that arises because the variation in gravity becomes significant over the rocket's trajectory. Recognize what's common to all similar problems, and you'll begin to see physics for what it is—a powerful description based on a few simple principles, rather than a bewildering array of new and different things to learn.

| EXAMPLE 9-7 | *Bringing Satellite TV to Siberia* |

Viewed from extreme northern and southern latitudes, geosynchronous satellites are too low in the sky for reliable communications. Service to these regions can be provided by satellites in highly elliptical orbits that move very slowly high over the intended recipients, then drop down to make a rapid, much lower pass around the other side of the Earth. Television satellites serving northern Russia, for example, are in 12-hour orbits with altitudes ranging from 500 km to 40,000 km. If such a satellite passes its lowest point moving at 9.94 km/s, how fast will it be moving at the peak of its trajectory?

Solution

Here's another conservation of energy problem, the only difference from Example 9-6 being that we have both kinetic and potential energy at both points, and we're asked for speed rather than distance. Writing $K + U = K_0 + U_0$, we have

$$\tfrac{1}{2}mv^2 - \frac{GM_E m}{r} = \tfrac{1}{2}mv_0^2 - \frac{GM_E m}{r_0},$$

where m is the satellite's mass. Solving for the speed v gives

$$v = \sqrt{v_0^2 + 2GM_E\left(\frac{1}{r} - \frac{1}{r_0}\right)}.$$

The radii appearing here are measured *from Earth's center*, so we add Earth's radius (6.37×10^6 m) to the altitudes given. Then $r = 6.37 \times 10^6$ m $+ 40,000 \times 10^3$ m $= 46.37 \times 10^6$ m, and similarly, $r_0 = 6.87 \times 10^6$ m. Using these figures along with $M_E = 5.97 \times 10^{24}$ kg then gives $v = 233$ m/s. This low figure makes sense since the satellite has slowed in "climbing" so far against Earth's gravity.

EXERCISE At its perihelion in February 1986, Comet Halley was 8.79×10^7 km from the Sun and was moving at 54.6 km/s. What was its speed a month later at its encounter with the Giotto spacecraft, 1.16×10^8 km from the Sun?

Answer: 47.4 km/s

Some problems similar to Examples 9-6 and 9-7:
30–32, 34, 43, 49

Escape Speed

Throw a ball straight up, and eventually it comes down. Is this always true? Not if the ball has enough energy! Figure 9-21 shows that an object with total energy greater than zero can escape infinitely far from a gravitating body, never to return.

How fast should you throw the ball so it won't come back? If its total energy is exactly zero, it can just barely escape to infinity. Its speed is given by the conservation of energy principle, in this case with the total energy $K + U$ set to zero:

$$0 = K + U = \tfrac{1}{2}mv_{esc}^2 - \frac{GMm}{r},$$

where m is the mass of the ball or space probe or whatever, M the mass of the gravitating object, and r the distance from its center (i.e., $r = R_E$ for an object launched from Earth's surface). Solving for v_{esc} then gives

$$v_{esc} = \sqrt{\frac{2GM}{r}}. \qquad \text{(escape speed)} \qquad (9\text{-}7)$$

This is the **escape speed**—the speed that must be given an object at distance r from the gravitating center if it's to escape all the way to infinity. At Earth's surface, $v_{esc} = 11.2$ km/s. Earth-orbiting spacecraft have somewhat lower speeds. Moon-bound spacecraft have speeds just under v_{esc}, so if anything goes wrong (as with Apollo 13), they'll return to Earth. Planetary spacecraft have speeds greater than v_{esc}. Pioneer and Voyager missions to the outer solar system left Earth's vicinity at 14 km/s. They gained additional energy in their encounters with Jupiter (see "Application: Gravity's Slingshot" in Chapter 11) and now have escape speed relative to the Sun (Fig. 9-22).

FIGURE 9-22 Artist's conception of the Pioneer 10 spacecraft in interstellar space. With speeds in excess of solar escape speed, Pioneers 10 and 11 and two Voyager spacecraft are leaving the solar system to travel forever throughout the galaxy. In 1998 Voyager 1 passed Pioneer 10 to become the most distant human-made object. Both spacecraft were then more than 10 billion km from Earth, about twice as far as Pluto. The Pioneers and Voyagers were launched in the 1970s, and the Voyagers should continue to return data until about 2020.

Energy in Circular Orbits

In the special case of a circular orbit, kinetic and potential energies are related in a simple way. In Section 9-3 we found that the speed in a circular orbit is given by

$$v^2 = \frac{GM}{r},$$

where r is the distance from a gravitating center of mass M. So the kinetic energy of the orbiting object is

$$K = \tfrac{1}{2}mv^2 = \frac{GMm}{2r},$$

while the potential energy is given by Equation 9-6:

$$U = -\frac{GMm}{r}.$$

Comparison of these two expressions shows that $U = -2K$ for a circular orbit. The total energy is therefore

$$E = U + K = -2K + K = -K, \tag{9-8}$$

or, equivalently,

$$E = \tfrac{1}{2}U = -\frac{GMm}{2r}. \tag{9-9}$$

The total energy given by these equations is negative, showing that circular orbits are—obviously—bound orbits. We stress that these results apply only to *circular* orbits; in elliptical orbits there's a continual interchange between kinetic and potential energy as the orbiting object moves relative to the gravitating center.

Equation 9-8 shows that *higher* kinetic energy corresponds to *lower* total energy. This surprising result occurs because *higher* orbital speed corresponds to a *lower* orbit, with lower potential energy. The implications for space flight are counterintuitive. To get into a faster orbit a spacecraft must *lose* energy—as if a car, to speed up, had to apply its brakes. Astronauts attempting orbital rendezvous actually fire braking rockets in order to catch up with their target (Fig. 9-23).

(a)   (b)

FIGURE 9-23 Orbital maneuver. A space shuttle seeks to overtake a satellite further ahead in the same orbit; both spacecraft are moving from left to right. (a) Thrusting toward the target would take the shuttle into a higher-energy—and therefore higher but slower—orbit. (b) The correct maneuver is counterintuitive. The shuttle rotates and thrusts *away* from its target, decreasing its energy and changing its orbit to an ellipse. A second thrust circularizes the orbit, now lower and faster than the original circular orbit. After overtaking the target, the shuttle reverses these maneuvers.

| **EXAMPLE 9-8** | *Launching a Communications Satellite* |

A 740-kg communications satellite is carried in a space shuttle to a 250-km-high circular orbit. How much energy is required to launch it from there to geosynchronous orbit?

Solution

In the shuttle orbit the satellite already has some orbital energy; the energy needed to get it from there to geosynchronous orbit is the difference between the orbital energies at the two altitudes. Those energies are given by Equation 9-9; their difference is then

$$\Delta E = -\frac{GM_E m}{2r_2} - \left(-\frac{GM_E m}{2r_1}\right) = \frac{GM_E m}{2}\left(\frac{1}{r_1} - \frac{1}{r_2}\right)$$

where r_2 and r_1 are the radii of the geosynchronous and shuttle orbits, respectively. In Example 9-4 we found that the geosynchronous orbit radius is $r_2 = 42,000$ km; putting $r_1 = R_E + 250$ km $= 6.62\times10^6$ m, the expression above then

gives $\Delta E = 1.9\times10^{10}$ J. This is roughly the energy equivalent of 400 kg of chemical fuel.

Our answer in this problem includes everything—the energy needed to climb against Earth's gravity as well as the kinetic energy needed for the circular orbit. This is in contrast to Example 9-5, where we found only the work done against gravity.

EXERCISE A 73,000-kg space shuttle in a circular orbit at 250 km altitude is sent to repair the Hubble Space Telescope in its 610-km-altitude circular orbit. How much energy is required to get the shuttle into the new orbit?

Answer: 1.1×10^{11} J

Some problems similar to Example 9-8: 33, 36, 45

The orbital energy of a massive body like a planet is substantial. It's possible for spacecraft to tap that energy with negligible effect on the planet's motion. Pioneer and Voyager spacecraft were gravity-boosted by Jupiter to speeds sufficient to escape the Sun's gravity altogether. And recent probes to the outer planets—including Galileo to Jupiter and Cassini to Saturn—executed complicated trajectories that took them first to Venus for gravity-assisted energy gains (Fig. 9-24). Gravity assist is actually an example of a collision, and we give a more detailed account of how it works in Chapter 11.

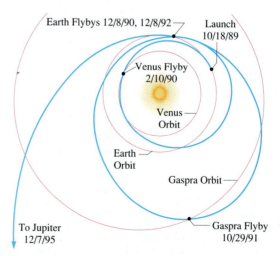

FIGURE 9-24 A close encounter with Venus and two encounters with Earth gave the Galileo probe enough energy to reach Jupiter.

9-5 THE GRAVITATIONAL FIELD

Our description of gravity so far suggests that a massive body like Earth somehow "reaches out" across empty space to pull on objects like falling apples, satellites, or the moon. This view—called **action-at-a-distance**—has bothered both physicists and philosophers for centuries. How can the moon, for example, "know" about the presence of the distant Earth?

An alternative view holds that Earth creates a **gravitational field** and that objects respond to the field in their immediate vicinity. The field is described by vectors that give the force per unit mass that would arise at each point if a mass were placed there. Near Earth's surface, for instance, the gravitational field vectors point vertically downward and have magnitude 9.8 N/kg. We could express this field vectorially by writing

$$\mathbf{g} = -g\,\hat{\mathbf{j}}. \qquad \text{(gravitational field near Earth's surface)} \qquad (9\text{-}10)$$

More generally, the field points toward a spherical gravitating center, and its strength drops inversely with the square of the distance:

$$\mathbf{g} = -\frac{GM}{r^2}\hat{\mathbf{r}}, \qquad \text{(gravitational field of a spherical mass } M) \qquad (9\text{-}11)$$

where $\hat{\mathbf{r}}$ is a unit vector that points radially outward. Figure 9-25 shows pictorial representations of Equations 9-10 and 9-11. You can show that the units of gravitational field (N/kg) are equivalent to those of acceleration (m/s²), so the field is really just a vectorial representation of g, the local acceleration of gravity.

What do we gain by this field description? As long as we deal with situations where nothing changes, the action-at-a-distance and field descriptions are equivalent. But what if, for example, Earth suddenly gains mass. How does the moon know to adjust its orbit? Under the field view its orbit doesn't change immediately; instead, it takes a small but nonzero time for the information about the more massive Earth to propagate out to the moon. The moon always responds to the gravitational field *in its immediate vicinity,* and it takes a short time for the field itself to change. That description is consistent with Einstein's notion that instantaneous transmission of information is impossible; the action-at-a-distance view is not consistent with Einstein.

More generally, the field view provides a powerful way of describing the interactions of physics. We'll see fields again when we study electricity and magnetism, and you'll gain a sense that fields aren't just mathematical or philosophical conveniences but are every bit as real as matter itself.

9-6 TIDAL FORCES

When the gravitational field is uniform, all parts of a freely falling body experience exactly the same gravitational acceleration. But over large enough scales gravity is always nonuniform, and the acceleration of gravity varies from place to place. The result is a force that tends to stretch or compress an object.

Ocean tides are an important manifestation of this force, in which the oceans are stretched by the nonuniform gravitational forces of the moon and Sun (Fig. 9-26). For that reason the forces associated with the variation in gravitational field from place to place are called **tidal forces.**

(a)

(b)

FIGURE 9-25 (*a*) Gravitational field vectors in a small region near Earth's surface have the same magnitude and direction. (*b*) On a larger scale the field vectors vary in both direction and magnitude.

Earth   Moon

FIGURE 9-26 Ocean tides result primarily from the nonuniform gravitational field of the moon. The gravitational force on the moonward side of the ocean is stronger than on the Earth itself, which in turn is stronger than the force on the distant ocean. The ocean therefore stretches into two "tidal bulges" that move as Earth rotates, giving rise to two high tides a day at most locations. (Not shown is the Sun, which produces a weaker tidal effect.)

FIGURE 9-27 Volcanic activity on Jupiter's moon Io probably originates from internal heating caused by tidal stresses. Insert in this Voyager spacecraft photo shows an enlargement of the eruption just visible on Io's limb.

FIGURE 9-28 Saturn's rings, in a Voyager spacecraft image. Planetary rings consist of myriad small chunks of orbiting material. They occur within the planet's Roche limit, where tidal forces overcome the gravitational forces that would hold a moon together.

Tidal forces arise not from gravity itself but from *differences* in gravity. As you can show in Problem 50, the tidal force therefore drops even more rapidly with distance than does gravity itself, being inversely proportional to the *cube* of the distance. That's why the moon is the dominant influence on ocean tides; even though the Sun's gravity is much stronger at Earth than is the moon's, the distance from the Sun is so great that the moon's *tidal* effect is greater.

Tidal forces exert stresses on any object in a nonuniform gravitational field, and the astronomical consequences are, therefore, numerous. The extensive volcanic activity of Jupiter's moon Io (Fig. 9-27) is thought to arise from heat generated by tidal stresses. Comets sometimes break apart under the influence of strong tidal forces as they pass near the Sun or even Jupiter. And stars in binary star systems are frequently distorted by tidal forces.

Close to a massive body like a planet, tidal forces can become strong enough to break up natural satellites held together by their own gravity. When the planet and its satellite have the same density, that occurs within about 2.5 planetary radii of the planet's center—a distance called the **Roche limit**. Within the Roche limits of Saturn and the other outer planets we find rings, rather than solid moons (Fig. 9-28)—showing that tidal forces prevent the formation of solid bodies held together by self-gravitation. We regularly place artificial satellites within Earth's Roche limit, but these aren't held together by gravity. Problem 52 explores the Roche limit.

9-7 GRAVITY AND THE GENERAL THEORY OF RELATIVITY

Newton's theory of gravity provided a brilliantly successful explanation of planetary motion and today guides space probes on billion-mile journeys throughout the solar system. But in very strong gravitational fields or in applications requiring high precision—like the satellite-based Global Positioning System—deviations from Newton's theory become evident. Those deviations are correctly described by the **general theory of relativity**, a radically different theory of gravity proposed by Einstein in 1916. Einstein's general theory is beyond the scope of this book; here we note only that Einstein describes gravity as a geometrical effect resulting from the curvature of space and time caused by the presence of matter. Objects moving under the influence of gravity follow the "straightest" possible paths in this curved space-time (Fig. 9-29).

FIGURE 9-29 (*a*) The "straightest" path between San Francisco and Tokyo is a great circle skirting the Aleutian Islands. (*b*) Similarly, the "straightest" path in the curved space-time near a massive object is not a truly straight line but a curve. Depression in the surface represents the effect of a massive object on space and time.

(*a*)   (*b*)

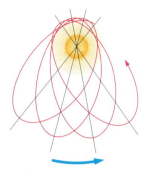

FIGURE 9-30 The axis (black lines) of Mercury's elliptical orbit precesses very slightly, an effect explained by general relativity but not by Newtonian gravitational theory. Both the shift and ellipticity are exaggerated; Mercury's orbit is nearly circular, and the shift amounts to only 43 seconds of arc (43/3600 degree) per century.

For decades the only orbital evidence for Einstein's theory was a very slight shift in the orbit of Mercury (Fig. 9-30). Differences between Einsteinian and Newtonian gravity become substantial only in regions where the escape speed approaches the speed of light, and that doesn't happen in our solar system. But astrophysicists have discovered extraordinarily dense collapsed stars whose properties must be explained using general relativity. At the general relativistic extreme are **black holes**—objects of such density that the escape speed exceeds that of light, making it impossible for anything to escape their gravitational grip. Black holes with several times the Sun's mass have been identified in some binary star systems, and massive black holes—a million or more solar masses—are believed to lurk at the centers of many galaxies, including our own (Fig. 9-31).

General relativity also predicts the existence of **gravitational waves**. Literally ripples in the fabric of space and time, these waves could be generated in violent stellar explosions and might be detected by the vibrations they induce in massive objects. Indirect detection of gravitational waves has already occurred; by analyzing changes in the motion of a pulsar in close orbit around another object, Joseph Taylor and Russell Hulse showed that the pulsar is losing energy at just the rate that would result from the emission of gravitational waves. Their work won Taylor and Hulse the 1993 Nobel Prize in Physics.

Although general relativity is mathematically complex, it's based in a simple observation that, prior to Einstein, seemed a coincidence. Equation 9-1, the law of universal gravitation, states that the attractive force between two particles depends on their masses. Equation 5-3, Newton's second law, states that the force needed to produce a given acceleration is proportional to an object's mass. Why should the same property—mass—that determines the attraction to other objects also determine an object's response to applied forces? For years physicists puzzled over this seeming coincidence; they even coined the distinct terms "gravitational mass" and "inertial mass" to describe the two properties which experiments—like Galileo's dropping objects from the Tower of Pisa—showed to have the same value. In formulating general relativity, Einstein assumed that the equivalence of gravitational and inertial mass is no coincidence but reflects instead an underlying equivalence between the effects of gravity and of acceleration. General relativity is a theory not only about gravity but also about motion in arbitrary—including accelerated—reference frames, and it is this **principle of equivalence** that provides a coherent basis for the theory.

FIGURE 9-31 Artist's conception of a black hole orbiting a large star. A disk of hot gas surrounds the hole.

CHAPTER SYNOPSIS

Summary

1. The concept of **universal gravitation** subsumes terrestrial and celestial motions under the same physical laws. In the 17th century this provided a major philosophical shift in human understanding of the universe.

2. Newton's **law of universal gravitation** states that any two particles exert a mutually attractive force of magnitude

$$F = \frac{Gm_1 m_2}{r^2},$$

where m_1 and m_2 are the particle masses and r the distance between them. Although the law applies strictly to point particles, Newton proved that it also holds exactly for the force between spherical masses. It is approximately true for arbitrarily shaped objects whose separation is large compared to their size. The **constant of universal gravitation** G has the approximate value $G = 6.67 \times 10^{-11}$ N·m^2/kg^2.

3. An **orbit** is the path of a body whose motion is dominated by gravity. For gravitational interaction involving only two bodies, the possible orbits have simple shapes:

   a. Bodies whose total energy is negative travel in closed, **elliptical orbits**.

   b. A special case of an ellipse is the **circular orbit**, for which gravity provides the centripetal force mv^2/r needed to maintain circular motion. For an object in orbit about a much greater mass M, the orbital period and radius are related by

$$T^2 = \frac{4\pi^2 r^3}{GM}. \qquad \text{(circular orbit)}$$

   An especially important orbit is the **geosynchronous orbit**, where a satellite's orbital period is equal to Earth's rotation period. The satellite then appears motionless above the equator. Geosynchronous orbit occurs about 36,000 km above Earth's surface.

   c. Objects whose total energy is greater than zero travel in open, **hyperbolic orbits** that take them infinitely far from the gravitating center. The intermediate case of zero energy corresponds to a parabolic orbit.

4. The gravitational potential energy of two masses M and m is given by

$$U = -\frac{GMm}{r}, \qquad \text{(gravitational potential energy)}$$

where r is the distance between their centers and where the zero of potential energy is taken at infinite separation.

   a. Because potential energy remains finite over infinite distances, it is possible to launch an object with enough energy that it will never return. The required **escape**

speed a distance r from a gravitating mass M is given by

$$v_{\text{esc}} = \sqrt{\frac{2GM}{r}}. \qquad \text{(escape speed)}$$

   b. For a circular orbit, the kinetic and potential energies are directly related:

$$U = -2K,$$

so the total energy is

$$E = \tfrac{1}{2}U = -\frac{GMm}{2r} = -K.$$

5. The **gravitational field** describes the gravitational force per unit mass at each point in space. The field concept replaces the outmoded action-at-a-distance view, holding instead that a massive body creates a gravitational field and that other objects respond to the field in their immediate vicinities.

6. **Tidal forces** result from differences in gravitational force over an extended body. They give rise to stresses on astronomical objects, including ocean tides on Earth. Within the **Roche limit**, tidal forces are strong enough to prevent self-gravitating satellites from forming.

7. The **general theory of relativity** is Einstein's description of gravity in terms of the geometry of space and time. It differs substantially from Newtonian theory in regions of very strong gravity—where the escape speed is comparable to the speed of light.

Terms You Should Understand

(Pairs are closely related terms whose distinction is important; number in parentheses is chapter section where term first appears.)

Copernicus, Brahe, Kepler, Galileo, Newton (9-1)
Kepler's laws (9-1)
law of universal gravitation (9-2)
G, g (9-2)
orbital motion (9-3)
orbital period (9-3)
geosynchronous orbit (9-3)
perihelion, aphelion (9-3)
circular, elliptical, parabolic, hyperbolic orbits (9-3)

gravitational potential energy (9-4)
escape speed (9-4)
action-at-a-distance (9-5)
gravitational field (9-5)
tidal forces (9-5)
Roche limit (9-5)
general theory of relativity (9-6)

Symbols You Should Recognize

G (9-2)   **g** (9-5) $\hat{\mathbf{r}}$ (9-5)

Problems You Should Be Able to Solve

calculating gravitational forces using the law of universal gravitation (9-2)

solving for speeds, periods, distances in circular orbits (9-3)

evaluating changes in gravitational potential energy (9-4)

solving conservation of energy problems involving gravitational energy (9-4)

evaluating escape speed for different bodies (9-4)

Limitations to Keep in Mind

Newton's law of universal gravitation applies exactly only to point particles or to spherical objects; it's a good approximation for other bodies at separations large compared with their sizes.

The quantity r that appears in the law of universal gravitation and in other equations derived from it is always the distance *from the center* of the gravitating body, not from its surface.

Our description of orbits as circular, elliptical, parabolic, or hyperbolic applies exactly only when the interaction involves just two gravitating bodies.

Newton's law of universal gravitation provides an accurate description of gravity only in regions where the escape speed is much less than the speed of light—a condition valid throughout the solar system and in most of the universe.

QUESTIONS

1. Why is Newton's assertion that planetary orbits are elliptical more satisfying than Kepler's?
2. What do Newton's apple and the moon have in common?
3. Explain the difference between G and g.
4. Earth's orbital motion is fastest in January and slowest in June. When is Earth closest to the Sun? Explain.
5. When you stand on Earth, the distance between you and Earth is zero. So why isn't the gravitational force infinite?
6. The force of gravity on an object is proportional to the object's mass, yet all objects fall with the same gravitational acceleration. Why?
7. A friend who knows nothing about physics asks what keeps an orbiting space shuttle from falling to Earth. Give an answer that will satisfy your friend.
8. Could you put a satellite in an orbit that kept it stationary over the south pole? Explain.
9. Why are satellites generally launched eastward from low latitudes? *Hint:* Think about Earth's rotation.
10. It takes more energy to launch a satellite into the polar orbit shown in Fig. 9-32 than into the equatorial orbit shown. Why?

FIGURE 9-32 Polar and equatorial orbits (Question 10).

11. Can you launch a projectile that will travel three-fourths of the way around the Earth, as suggested in Fig. 9-33? Why or why not?

FIGURE 9-33 Question 11.

12. Given the mass of the Earth, the distance to the moon, the period of the moon's orbit, and the value of G, could you calculate the moon's mass? How or why not?
13. How should a satellite be launched so its orbit takes it over every point on the (rotating) Earth?
14. Does the gravitational force of the Sun ever do work on a planet in a circular orbit? Explain.
15. Does the gravitational force of the Sun ever do work on a comet in an elliptical orbit? What is the net work done as the comet completes the entire orbit?
16. Why are the tides highest when Sun, moon, and Earth are in a line? At what phase(s) of the moon does this occur?
17. Why do we choose the zero of gravitational potential energy at infinity rather than, say, at Earth's surface?
18. Could you launch a projectile to the moon using a powerful slingshot mounted on Earth? Explain.
19. Could you launch a projectile into circular orbit using a powerful slingshot mounted on Earth? Explain.

20. Describe the maneuvers necessary for a spacecraft to catch up with another that is ahead of it in the same circular orbit.

21. If the Sun suddenly shrank to a white dwarf star with the same mass concentrated into the size of the Earth, what would happen to Earth's orbit?

22. Why is it significant whether the energy of a comet is more or less than zero?

23. Satellites in orbits lower than a few hundred kilometers experience frictional drag due to residual air at those altitudes. Assuming their orbits remain essentially circular, does this drag decrease or increase the satellites' speeds?

PROBLEMS

ActivPhysics can help with these problems:
Activity 4.8

Section 9-2 The Law of Universal Gravitation

1. Space explorers land on a planet with the same mass as Earth, but they find they weigh twice as much as they would on Earth. What is the radius of the planet?

2. Use data for the moon's orbit from Appendix E to compute the moon's acceleration in its circular orbit, and verify that the result is consistent with Newton's law of universal gravitation.

3. To what fraction of its current radius would Earth have to be shrunk (with no change in mass) for the gravitational acceleration at its surface to triple?

4. Calculate the gravitational acceleration at the surface of (a) Mercury and (b) Saturn's moon Titan.

5. Two identical lead spheres are 14 cm apart and attract each other with a force of 0.25 μN. What is their mass?

6. The gravitational acceleration at the surface of a planet is 22.5 m/s^2. Find the acceleration at a height above the surface equal to half the planet's radius.

7. What is the approximate value of the gravitational force between a 67-kg astronaut and a 73,000-kg space shuttle when they're 84 m apart?

8. Astronauts put their spaceship into orbit about a planet. They find that the acceleration of gravity at their orbital altitude is half that at the planet's surface. How far above the planet's surface are they orbiting? Answer in terms of the radius of the planet.

9. A sensitive gravimeter is carried to the top of Chicago's Sears Tower, where its reading for the acceleration of gravity is 0.00136 m/s^2 lower than at street level. Find the height of the building.

10. A roughly spherical volume of rock 1.3 km in radius is 30% denser than the surrounding rock, whose density is 2700 kg/m^3. The denser rock is centered 2.1 km below Earth's surface. By what percentage is the surface value of g directly above the denser rock increased due to its excess density? *Hint:* Treat the "extra" mass of the denser rock as a gravitating sphere, and calculate the gravitational acceleration it produces at Earth's surface.

11. If you're standing on the ground 15 m directly below the center of a spherical water tank containing 4×10^6 kg of water, by what fraction is your weight reduced due to the gravitational attraction of the water?

Section 9-3 Orbital Motion

12. At what altitude will a satellite complete a circular orbit of the Earth in 2.0 hours?

13. Find the speed of a satellite in geosynchronous orbit.

14. Mars's orbit has a diameter 1.52 times that of Earth's orbit. How long does it take Mars to orbit the Sun?

15. Calculate the orbital period for Jupiter's moon Io, which orbits 4.22×10^5 km from the center of the 1.9×10^{27} kg planet.

16. Given the orbital radius of 384,400 km and period of 27.3 days, calculate the acceleration of the moon in its circular orbit, and compare with the acceleration of gravity at Earth's surface. Show that the acceleration of the moon is smaller by the ratio of the square of Earth's radius to the square of the moon's orbital radius, thus confirming the inverse-square law for the gravitational force.

17. During the Apollo moon landings, one astronaut remained with the command module in lunar orbit, about 130 km above the surface. For half of each orbit, this astronaut was completely cut off from the rest of humanity, as the spacecraft rounded the far side of the moon (see Fig. 9-34). How long did this period last?

FIGURE 9-34 Problem 17.

18. A white dwarf is a collapsed star with roughly the mass of the Sun compressed into the size of the Earth. What would be (a) the orbital speed and (b) the orbital period for a spaceship in orbit just above the surface of such a white dwarf?

19. Given that our Sun orbits the galaxy with a period of 200 My at a distance of 2.6×10^{20} m from the galactic center, estimate the mass of the galaxy. Assume (incorrectly) that the galaxy is essentially spherical and that most of its mass lies interior to the Sun's orbit. To how many Sun-mass stars is your estimate equivalent?

20. Satellites *A* and *B* are in circular orbits, with *A* twice as far from Earth's center as *B*. How do their orbital periods compare?

21. Where should a satellite be placed to orbit the Sun in a circular orbit with a period of 100 days?

22. Determine the orbital period of the Hubble Space Telescope, which orbits Earth at an altitude of 610 km.

23. How far from the Sun's center would a satellite in circular orbit be heliosynchronous? *Hint:* Consult Appendix E, and remember that a synchronous orbit must parallel the equator. So which rotation period is appropriate?

24. Comets are thought to originate in a cloud of ice chunks in roughly circular orbits almost 1 light-year (the distance light travels in a year) from the Sun. Collisions among the ice chunks and gravitational effects of other stars occasionally send a chunk into an elliptical orbit to become an observed comet. What is the orbital period of the cometary ice chunks in their remote orbits?

25. The asteroid Pasachoff orbits the Sun with a period of 1417 days. What is the semimajor axis of its orbit? Determine using Kepler's third law in comparison with Earth's orbital radius and period.

26. We derived Equation 9-4 on the assumption that the massive gravitating center remains fixed. Now consider the case of two objects of equal mass *M* orbiting each other as shown in Fig. 9-35. Show that the orbital period is given by

$$T^2 = \frac{16\pi^2 r^3}{GM},$$

where *r* is the orbital radius (half the distance between the objects).

FIGURE 9-35 Problem 26.

27. Our galaxy belongs to a large group of galaxies known as the Virgo Cluster. The cluster contains about 1000 times the mass of our galaxy, which in turn contains about 10^{11} times the Sun's mass. We're roughly 50 million light-years from the center of the approximately spherical cluster. Could our galaxy have completed a full orbit of the cluster since the universe began, some 15 billion years ago?

Section 9-4 Gravitational Energy

28. Earth's distance from the Sun varies from 1.47×10^{11} m at perihelion to 1.52×10^{11} m at aphelion because its orbit is not quite circular. Find the change in potential energy as Earth goes from perihelion to aphelion.

29. How much energy does it take to launch a 230-kg instrument package on a vertical trajectory that peaks at an altitude of 1800 km?

30. One proposal for dealing with radioactive waste is to shoot it into the Sun. Suppose a waste canister were simply dropped, starting from rest in the vicinity of Earth's orbit. At what speed would it hit the Sun?

31. A rocket is launched vertically upward from Earth's surface at a speed of 3.1 km/s. What is its maximum altitude?

32. What vertical launch speed is necessary to get a rocket to 1100 km altitude?

33. Find the energy necessary to put 1 kg, initially at rest on Earth's surface, into geosynchronous orbit.

34. At its perihelion in February 1986, Comet Halley was 8.79×10^7 km from the Sun and was moving at 54.6 km/s. What will be its speed when it crosses Neptune's orbit, in 2006?

35. Neglecting air resistance, to what height would you have to fire a rocket for the constant acceleration equations of Chapter 2 to give a height that is in error by 1%? Would those methods over- or underestimate the height?

36. What is the total mechanical energy associated with Earth's orbital motion?

37. Drag due to small amounts of residual air causes satellites in low Earth orbit to lose energy and eventually spiral to Earth. What fraction of its orbital energy is lost as a satellite drops from 300 to 100 km, assuming its orbit remains essentially circular?

38. Show that an object released from rest very far from Earth ($r \gg R_E$) reaches Earth's surface at essentially escape speed.

39. By what factor must the speed of an object in circular orbit be increased to reach escape speed from its orbital altitude?

40. Astronomers discover a new comet. As it crosses Earth's orbit the comet is moving at 45 km/s. Is the comet in an open or closed orbit?

41. The escape speed from a planet of mass 2.9×10^{24} kg is 7.1 km/s. What is the planet's radius?

42. Determine the escape speed from (a) Jupiter's moon Callisto, with mass 1.07×10^{23} kg and radius 2.40 Mm, and (b) a neutron star, with the Sun's mass crammed into a sphere 6.0 km in radius.

43. Two meteoroids are 250,000 km from Earth and moving at 2.1 km/s. One is headed straight for Earth, while the other is on a path that will come within 8500 km of Earth's center (Fig. 9-36). (a) What is the speed of the first meteoroid when it strikes Earth? (b) What is the speed of the second meteoroid at its closest approach to Earth? (c) Will the second meteoroid ever return to Earth's vicinity?

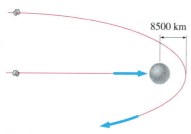

FIGURE 9-36 Partial trajectories of two meteoroids (Problem 43).

44. One component of the proposed "star wars" antimissile defense system calls for powerful laser beams aimed by mirrors in geosynchronous orbit. One simple countermeasure to this delicate technology is to put a truckload of rocks in the same orbit, going in the opposite direction. At what relative speed would the rocks hit the mirror?

45. Neglecting Earth's rotation, show that the energy needed to launch a satellite of mass m into circular orbit at altitude h is

$$\left(\frac{GM_E m}{R_E}\right)\left(\frac{R_E + 2h}{2(R_E + h)}\right).$$

46. Humanity currently consumes energy at the rate of about 10^{13} W. Suppose a method were developed to extract usable energy from the moon's orbital motion. If all our energy came from this source and if our energy use remained constant, by how much would (a) the moon's orbital radius and (b) its orbital period change in a century?

47. A projectile is launched vertically upward from a planet of mass M and radius R; its initial speed is twice the escape speed. Derive an expression for its speed as a function of the distance r from the center of the planet.

48. A spacecraft is in a circular Earth orbit at an altitude of 5500 km. By how much will its altitude decrease if it moves to a new circular orbit where (a) its orbital speed is 10% higher or (b) its orbital period is 10% shorter?

49. The Pioneer spacecraft left Earth's vicinity moving at about 38 km/s relative to the Sun (this figure combines the effect of rocket boost and Earth's orbital motion). How far out in the solar system could Pioneer get without additional rocket power or use of the "gravitational slingshot" effect?

Section 9-6 Tidal Forces

50. To get a feel for the behavior of tidal forces, consider an object consisting of two small masses m separated by a distance $2a$, a distance r from a body of mass M, as shown in Fig. 9-37. Use the law of universal gravitation to determine the gravitational force of the large mass on each of the small masses. Find an expression for the difference between the two forces, and put your expression over a common denominator. Show that, in the approximation where a^2 can be neglected compared with r^2, your expression for the force difference can be written

$$\Delta F = \frac{4GMma}{r^3}.$$

This is the tidal force, and your expression shows that it drops as the *cube* of the distance.

FIGURE 9-37 The tidal force on an object arises from the different gravitational forces experienced by different parts of the object (Problem 50).

51. Show that the force of the Sun's gravity on Earth is nearly 200 times that of the moon's gravity, but that the tidal force of the moon on Earth (see preceding problem) is about twice that of the Sun.

52. Suppose the composite object in Fig. 9-37 is held together by the gravitational attraction of the two small masses. Show that the tidal force of problem 50 is greater than the self-gravitational force of the object when $r^3 < 16Ma^3/m$. This defines the Roche limit for this simple example.

Paired Problems

(Both problems in a pair involve the same principles and techniques. If you get the first problem, you should be able to solve the second one.)

53. An astronaut hits a golf ball horizontally from the top of a lunar mountain so fast that it goes into circular orbit. What is its orbital period?

54. Find the period of a spacecraft in circular orbit 150 km above Mars's surface.

55. Two meteoroids are 160,000 km from Earth's center and heading straight toward Earth. One is moving at 10 km/s, the other at 20 km/s. At what speeds will they strike Earth?

56. Two rockets are launched from Earth's surface, one at 12 km/s and the other at 18 km/s. How fast is each moving when it crosses the moon's orbit?

57. A satellite is in an elliptical orbit at altitudes ranging from 230 to 890 km. At the high point it's moving at 7.23 km/s. How fast is it moving at the low point?

58. A missile's trajectory takes it to a maximum altitude of 1200 km. If its launch speed is 6.1 km/s, how fast is it moving at the peak of its trajectory?

59. To what radius would Earth have to be shrunk, with no loss of mass, for escape speed at its surface to be 30 km/s?

60. What is the mass of a planetary moon whose radius is 14 km and whose surface escape speed is 0.13 m/s?

61. A 720-kg spacecraft has total energy -5.3×10^{11} J and is in circular orbit about the Sun. Find (a) its orbital radius, (b) its kinetic energy, and (c) its speed.

62. A 2500-kg boulder is among the myriad particles making up Saturn's rings shown in Fig. 9-38. The boulder is in a circular orbit 95,000 km from the center of Saturn. Find (a) its total energy, (b) its orbital speed, and (c) its orbital period.

FIGURE 9-38 Saturn's rings shown in a composite image with several moons and a Voyager spacecraft (Problem 62).

Supplementary Problems

63. Mercury's orbital speed varies from 38.8 km/s at aphelion to 59.0 km/s at perihelion. If the planet is 6.99×10^{10} m from the Sun's center at aphelion, how far is it at perihelion?
64. Show that the form $\Delta U = mg\,\Delta r$ follows from Equation 9-5 when $r_1 \simeq r_2$. *Hint:* Write $r_2 = r_1 + \Delta r$, and apply the binomial approximation (see Appendix A).
65. A black hole is an object so dense that its escape speed exceeds the speed of light. Although a full description of black holes requires general relativity, the radius of a black hole can be calculated using Newtonian theory. (a) Show that the radius of a black hole of mass M is $2GM/c^2$, where c is the speed of light. What are the radii of black holes with (b) the mass of the Earth and (c) the mass of the Sun?
66. Find the point discussed in the Application: Perpetual Sunshine (pages 221–222)—that is, the point along the Earth-Sun line where an object will orbit the Sun with the same orbital period as does Earth. Express as a distance sunward of Earth, both in SI units and as a fraction of Earth's orbital radius. Use data from Appendix E. You may need to use numerical or graphical techniques.
67. Two satellites are in geosynchronous orbit, but in diametrically opposite positions (Fig. 9-39). Into how much lower a circular orbit should one spacecraft descend if it is to catch up with the other after 10 complete orbits? Neglect rocket firing times and time spent moving between the two circular orbits.

FIGURE 9-39 Problem 67.

10 Systems of Particles

A back flip on stilts. Most parts of the acrobat's body undergo complex motions (try following his head!). But one point follows a simple parabolic trajectory. Application of Newton's laws shows why, and helps us understand the behavior of many-particle systems.

So far we've treated objects as point particles, ignoring the fact that most objects are composed of smaller parts and have nonzero size. Here we deal explicitly with systems composed of many particles. These include **rigid bodies**—objects such as baseballs, cars, and planets whose constituent particles are stuck together in fixed orientations—as well as systems such as human bodies, exploding fireworks, or flowing rivers, whose constituent parts move relative to one another. Much contemporary research involves many-particle systems; for example, meteorologists are still struggling to understand and predict the motions of the air masses that determine our weather. In subsequent chapters we'll look at specific instances of many-particle systems, including the rotational motion of rigid bodies (Chapter 12) and the behavior of fluids (Chapter 18).

10-1 CENTER OF MASS

The motion of the acrobat in this chapter's opening photo is quite complex, with each part of his body moving on a different path. But the curve superimposed on the photograph shows that one point seems to follow the parabola that we expect of a point projectile (Section 4-3). This point is known as the **center of mass**; it represents a kind of "average position" of all the mass making up the acrobat and it behaves just as a particle of mass equal to that of the whole acrobat would.

How do we find the center of mass? The acrobat photo and Figure 10-1 both show that the center of mass obeys Newton's second law just as would a point particle. If we can find a point whose acceleration **A** obeys Newton's second law **F** = M**A**, where **F** is now the net force on an entire system and M the mass of that system, then we will have found the center of mass. (Note that we use capital letters for quantities associated with the center of mass.)

Consider a system consisting of many particles. To find the center of mass, we want an equation that looks like Newton's second law but involves the total mass of the system and the net force on the entire system. If we apply Newton's second law to the ith particle in the system, we have

$$\mathbf{F}_i = m_i\mathbf{a}_i = m_i\frac{d^2\mathbf{r}_i}{dt^2} = \frac{d^2m_i\mathbf{r}_i}{dt^2},$$

where $\mathbf{F}_i$ is the net force on the particle, m_i its mass, and where we've written the acceleration $\mathbf{a}_i$ as the second derivative of the position $\mathbf{r}_i$. The total force on the entire system is the sum of the forces acting on all N particles. We write this sum compactly using the summation symbol Σ:

$$\mathbf{F}_{\text{total}} = \sum_{i=1}^{N}\mathbf{F}_i = \sum_{i=1}^{N}\frac{d^2m_ir_i}{dt^2},$$

where the sum runs over all values of i from 1 to N—i.e., over all the particles comprising the system. But the sum of derivatives is the same as the derivative of the sum, so

$$\mathbf{F}_{\text{total}} = \frac{d^2\left(\sum m_i\mathbf{r}_i\right)}{dt^2}.$$

We can now put this equation in the form of Newton's second law. Multiplying and dividing the right-hand side by the total mass $M = \Sigma m_i$, and distributing this constant M through the differentiation, we have

$$\mathbf{F}_{\text{total}} = M\frac{d^2}{dt^2}\left(\frac{\sum m_i\mathbf{r}_i}{M}\right). \tag{10-1}$$

Equation 10-1 has the desired form **F** = M**A** = $M(d^2\mathbf{R}/dt^2)$ if we define

$$\mathbf{R} = \frac{\sum m_i\mathbf{r}_i}{M}. \quad \text{(center of mass)} \tag{10-2}$$

We've almost reached our goal of showing that the point **R** moves according to Newton's law **F** = $M\,d^2\mathbf{R}/dt^2$. Why aren't we there now? Because the force $\mathbf{F}_{\text{total}}$ in Equation 10-1 is the sum of *all* the forces acting on all the particles of the system, including the **internal forces** that act between the particles. We would like the force **F** in Newton's law to be the net **external force**—

FIGURE 10-1 A wrench slides along a frictionless surface, spinning as it goes. Most parts of the wrench undergo complex motions. But its center of mass moves in a straight line at constant speed, just like a particle subject to zero net force.

the net force applied from outside the system. We can write the force $\mathbf{F}_{total}$ in Equation 10-1—the total force on all the particles of the system—as

$$\mathbf{F}_{total} = \sum \mathbf{F}_{ext} + \sum \mathbf{F}_{int},$$

where $\sum \mathbf{F}_{ext}$ is the sum of all the external forces and $\sum \mathbf{F}_{int}$ the sum of the internal forces. According to Newton's third law of motion, each of the internal forces has an equal but oppositely directed force that itself acts on a particle of the system and is therefore included in the sum $\sum \mathbf{F}_{int}$. (Each external force is also part of a third-law pair, but forces paired with the external forces act *outside* the system and are therefore not included in the sum.) Added vectorially, the internal forces therefore cancel in pairs, so $\sum \mathbf{F}_{int} = \mathbf{0}$, and the force $\mathbf{F}_{total}$ in Equation 10-1 is just the net *external* force applied to the system. So the point $\mathbf{R}$ defined in Equation 10-2 does obey Newton's law, written in the form

$$\mathbf{F}_{net\ ext} = M \frac{d^2 \mathbf{R}}{dt^2}, \tag{10-3}$$

where $\mathbf{F}_{net\ ext}$ is the net external force applied to the system and M the total mass.

We have defined the center of mass $\mathbf{R}$ so we can apply Newton's second law to the entire system rather than to each individual particle. As far as its overall motion is concerned, a complex system acts as though all its mass were concentrated at the center of mass. The form of Equation 10-2 shows that the center of mass is indeed an average of the positions of the individual particles, each weighted according to its mass.

Finding the Center of Mass

Equation 10-2 expresses the center of mass in vector form; taking components gives three separate scalar equations for the *xyz* coordinates of the center of mass. If we consider only a one-dimensional situation, in which the constituent particles lie along a single line, then the center of mass must lie along that line. Similarly, for a two-dimensional object, the center of mass lies in the plane of the object. For the simple case of two-point masses, we can take the *x* axis along the line joining the masses and write Equation 10-2 in the form

$$X = \frac{m_1 x_1 + m_2 x_2}{m_1 + m_2}. \tag{10-4}$$

EXAMPLE 10-1	*Weightlifter*

You want to lift a barbell at its center of mass. (a) Suppose there are equal 60-kg masses at either end of the 1.5-m-long bar. (b) Suppose someone put unequal masses of 50 kg and 80 kg on the ends. Where is the center of mass in each case? Neglect the mass of the bar.

Solution

In (a) it's obvious that the center of mass must lie at the center of the barbell. If we choose the origin to lie at one of the masses, then $x_1 = 0$ m and $x_2 = 1.5$ m; applying Equation 10-4 then gives

$$X = \frac{m_1 x_1 + m_2 x_2}{m_1 + m_2} = \frac{(60\ \text{kg})(0\ \text{m}) + (60\ \text{kg})(1.5\ \text{m})}{60\ \text{kg} + 60\ \text{kg}}$$

$$= 0.75\ \text{m},$$

as expected. In case (b), with the origin at the 50-kg mass, we have

$$X = \frac{m_1 x_1 + m_2 x_2}{m_1 + m_2} = \frac{(50\ \text{kg})(0\ \text{m}) + (80\ \text{kg})(1.5\ \text{m})}{50\ \text{kg} + 80\ \text{kg}}$$

$$= 0.92\ \text{m}.$$

60 kg   60 kg
(a)

50 kg   80 kg
(b)

FIGURE 10-2 Center of mass of a barbell. (a) Two equal masses. (b) 50-kg and 80-kg masses.

Again, the result makes sense: the center of mass is closer to the more massive constituent of the system (Fig. 10-2).

EXERCISE Where is the center of mass of a canoe if a 76-kg paddler is 0.85 m from the stern and a 52-kg paddler is 3.9 m from the stern? Neglect the mass of the canoe itself.

Answer: 2.1 m from the stern

Some problems similar to Example 10-1: 1, 4, 6, 8

EXAMPLE 10-2   Center of Mass in a Plane: A Space Station

A space station consists of four identical modules of mass m arranged in a rectangle of width a and length b, as shown in Fig. 10-3. The modules are connected by tubes of negligible mass. Where is the center of mass of the station?

Solution

A convenient coordinate system has two sides of the station along the x and y axes, with one corner at the origin (Fig. 10-3). Then the x and y components of Equation 10-2 are

$$X = \frac{\sum m_i x_i}{M} = \frac{m(0 + b + b + 0)}{4m} = \frac{b}{2}$$

and

$$Y = \frac{\sum m_i y_i}{M} = \frac{m(0 + 0 + a + a)}{4m} = \frac{a}{2},$$

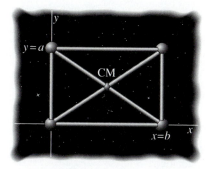

FIGURE 10-3 Example 10-2.

where in both cases we summed going counterclockwise around the space station, starting at the origin. Our result is hardly surprising: the center of mass lies at the center of the space station.

EXERCISE Three equal masses m lie at the vertices of a triangle with coordinates $(-a, 0)$, $(a, 0)$, and $(0, a)$. Find the center of mass.

Answer: $X = 0$, $Y = \dfrac{a}{3}$

Some problems similar to Example 10-2: 2, 3, 5, 8, 11

Continuous Distributions of Matter

We've expressed the center of mass in terms of sums over individual particles. Ultimately, matter *is* composed of individual particles. But it's often a convenient approximation to consider that matter is continuously distributed; after all, we don't want to deal with 10^{23} or so atoms to find the center of mass of a book or other macroscopic object. We can consider a chunk of continuous matter to be composed of individual pieces of mass Δm_i, with position vectors $\mathbf{r}_i$; we call these pieces **mass elements** (Fig. 10-4). The center of mass of the entire chunk is then given by Equation 10-2:

$$\mathbf{R} = \frac{\sum \Delta m_i \mathbf{r}_i}{M},$$

where $M = \sum \Delta m_i$ is the total mass. This expression is slightly vague, for we don't know exactly where within a mass element its position vector should terminate. But in the limit as the mass elements become arbitrarily small, like point particles, the expression becomes exact. As in Chapter 7, that limiting process defines an integral, giving

$$\mathbf{R} = \lim_{\Delta m_i \to 0} \frac{\sum \Delta m_i \mathbf{r}_i}{M} = \frac{1}{M} \int \mathbf{r}\, dm, \quad \left(\begin{array}{c}\text{center of mass,}\\ \text{continuous matter}\end{array}\right) \quad (10\text{-}5)$$

where the integration is over the entire volume of the object. Like the sum 10-2, the vector form 10-5 stands for three separate integrals for the three components of the center-of-mass position. Example 10-3 shows how to evaluate these integrals.

FIGURE 10-4 A chunk of continuous matter, showing one mass element Δm_i and its position vector $\mathbf{r}_i$ from an arbitrary origin.

EXAMPLE 10-3	An Aircraft Wing

The wing of a supersonic aircraft is an isosceles triangle of length ℓ, width w, and negligible thickness (Fig. 10-5). It has total mass M, distributed uniformly over the wing. Where is its center of mass?

Solution

Figure 10-5 shows the wing with a suitable coordinate system. Since the wing is flat and of negligible thickness, its center of mass must lie in the x-y plane. The wing is symmetric about the x axis, so the center of mass must lie on the x axis; that is, $Y = 0$. So we need to integrate only to find the x coordinate. Figure 10-5 shows an appropriate mass element, here a strip of width dx located a distance x along the axis. To find the mass dm of the strip, we first find its area. Figure 10-5 shows that the equations describing the sloping sides of the wing are $y = \pm wx/2\ell$, so our strip extends from $y = -wx/2\ell$ to $+wx/2\ell$; its length is therefore wx/ℓ. Since its width is dx, its

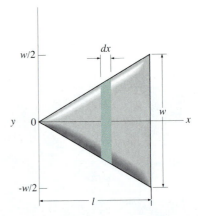

FIGURE 10-5 A supersonic aircraft wing. Green area is a mass element of width dx.

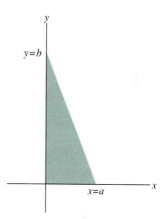

FIGURE 10-6 As the width dx of the strip becomes arbitrarily small, its area approaches that of a rectangle.

area is then $dA = (wx\,dx)/\ell$ (see Fig. 10-6). Since mass is distributed uniformly over the wing, the mass per unit area is just the total mass, M, divided by the total area, $A = \frac{1}{2}w\ell$. Multiplying the mass per unit area by the area dA gives the mass dm:

$$dm = \frac{M}{A}dA = \left(\frac{M}{\frac{1}{2}w\ell}\right)\left(\frac{wx\,dx}{\ell}\right),$$

$$= \frac{2Mx\,dx}{\ell^2}.$$

The x component of the center-of-mass position is given by the x component of Equation 10-5:

$$X = \frac{1}{M}\int x\,dm.$$

Using our expression for dm, and integrating over the entire triangle—that is, from $x = 0$ to $x = \ell$— we have

$$X = \frac{1}{M}\int_0^\ell \frac{2M}{\ell^2}x^2\,dx = \frac{2}{\ell^2}\frac{x^3}{3}\bigg|_0^\ell = \tfrac{2}{3}\ell.$$

Does this make sense? Yes. More of the wing's mass is concentrated near the wide end at $x = \ell$, so the center of mass should be located closer to the end.

EXERCISE Find the center of mass of the triangular slab shown in Fig. 10-7, assuming its mass is distributed uniformly.

FIGURE 10-7 Find the center of mass of the triangular slab.

Answer: $X = \dfrac{a}{3}$, $Y = \dfrac{b}{3}$

Some problems similar to Example 10-3: 10, 18, 57

With still more complex objects, it's convenient to find the centers of mass of major subpieces, then treat those subpieces as point particles to find the center of mass of the entire object. If the wing of Example 10-3 is placed on a cylindrical airplane fuselage, for example, we can find the center of mass of the entire plane by treating the wing and fuselage as point particles located at their respective centers of mass (Fig. 10-8). And an irregular object like that of

FIGURE 10-8 The center of mass of the airplane is found by treating the wing and fuselage as point particles located at their respective centers of mass. Given the center-of-mass location, is the wing or the fuselage more massive?

FIGURE 10-9 An irregular object, showing centers of mass of the constituent rectangles and of the object itself. Note that the center of mass lies outside the object.

FIGURE 10-10 The jumper clears the high jump bar, but his center of mass doesn't. This is possible because his entire body is not above the bar at the same time.

Fig. 10-9 is treated by locating the centers of mass of its three constituent rectangles (see Problem 7).

Figure 10-9 shows that the center of mass need not lie within the object. A high jumper (Fig. 10-10) takes advantage of this fact by arching his body into a shape qualitatively like that of Fig. 10-9. The jumper's center of mass never has to get as high as the bar, thus reducing the amount of work he must do against gravity. Similarly, a ballet dancer can appear to float through the air, her head and torso following a horizontal trajectory, by raising her legs and therefore the position of the center of mass relative to her torso. The center of mass, of course, follows a parabolic trajectory, but that's not what the audience notices (Fig. 10-11).

Got It!

A thick wire is bent into a semicircle, as shown in Fig. 10-12. Which of the points shown is most likely to be the center of mass?

FIGURE 10-12 Which point is the center of mass of the semicircular loop?

Motion of the Center of Mass

We defined the center of mass (Equation 10-2) so that its motion would obey Newton's law $\mathbf{F} = M\mathbf{A}$, where $\mathbf{F}$ is the net external force applied to a system and M the total mass. When, for example, gravity is the only external force acting on a system, the center of mass follows the trajectory appropriate to a

FIGURE 10-11 Performing a grand jeté, Jennifer Davis of the Pittsburgh Ballet Theatre keeps her head and torso moving nearly horizontally while her center of mass describes a parabolic trajectory.

point particle (as shown in Figs. 10-1 and 10-11). An example on a grander scale is the breakup of comet Biela into the Andromedid meteors as it passed the Sun in the mid-1800s. Today, the center of mass of the meteor swarm remains in the orbit of the original comet, despite the fact that there is no longer any matter there.

When the net external force on a system is zero, then the center of mass acceleration **A** is zero, and the center of mass moves with constant velocity. In the special case of a system at rest with zero net external force, the center of mass remains at rest despite any motions of the system's constituents.

EXAMPLE 10-4   *Leaping to Shore*

You're standing 1.8 m from the shoreward end of a 4.2-m-long boat; from the end to shore is another 1.1 m (Fig. 10-13). Your mass is 70 kg and the boat's mass is 150 kg. The center of mass of the boat lies at its center. You walk to the shoreward end of the boat, preparing to leap to shore. How far do you have to leap? Where is the boat at the instant you reach shore? Neglect any frictional effects.

FIGURE 10-13 Example 10-4.

Solution
The forces on you as you walk on the boat and then leap shoreward are contact forces from the boat; by Newton's third law, you exert oppositely directed forces that accelerate the boat away from shore. But all these forces are internal to the boat + you system, so the center of mass of the system stays fixed. Letting m_1 and x_1 be your mass and position, and m_2 and x_2 the mass and position of the boat (that is, of the boat's center of mass), and designating the initial and final values by the subscripts i and f, respectively, we equate the initial and final positions of the center of mass:

$$\frac{m_1x_{1i} + m_2x_{2i}}{m_1 + m_2} = \frac{m_1x_{1f} + m_2x_{2f}}{m_1 + m_2}.$$

The total mass $m_1 + m_2$ cancels, so

$$m_1x_{1i} + m_2x_{2i} = m_1x_{1f} + m_2x_{2f}. \qquad (10\text{-}6)$$

Since we're interested in the final position with respect to the shore, an appropriate choice of coordinate system has the origin at the shore. Then Fig. 10-12 shows that $x_{1i} = 1.1$ m + 1.8 m = 2.9 m and $x_{2i} = 1.1$ m + 2.1 m = 3.2 m. The points

x_{1f} and x_{2f} are still unknown. But they're related: when you reach the end of the boat, you're half a boat length closer to shore than the center of the boat. Therefore, $x_{2f} = x_{1f} + \frac{1}{2}L$, where L is the 4.2-m length of the boat. Using this result in Equation 10-6 gives

$$m_1x_{1i} + m_2x_{2i} = m_1x_{1f} + m_2(x_{1f} + \tfrac{1}{2}L).$$

Solving for x_{1f}, we then have

$$x_{1f} = \frac{m_1x_{1i} + m_2x_{2i} - \frac{1}{2}m_2L}{m_1 + m_2}$$

$$= (70 \text{ kg})(2.9 \text{ m}) + (150 \text{ kg})(3.2 \text{ m})$$
$$- \tfrac{1}{2}(150 \text{ kg})(4.2 \text{ m})70 \text{ kg} + 150 \text{ kg}$$
$$= 1.7 \text{ m}.$$

This is the distance you have to leap from the end of the boat to shore. When you reach shore, you are at the origin: $x_{1f} = 0$. Solving Equation 10-6 for the boat's position then gives

$$x_{2f} = \frac{m_1x_{1i} + m_2x_{2i}}{m_2} = \frac{(70 \text{ kg})(2.9 \text{ m}) + (150 \text{ kg})(3.2 \text{ m})}{150 \text{ kg}}$$
$$= 4.6 \text{ m}.$$

After the instant you reach shore, we can no longer argue that the center of mass remains fixed. Why not? Because an external force—the stopping force of the ground—has acted on part of the system, so the center of mass is no longer fixed. Indeed, the boat continues to drift away from shore. Question 10 explores this situation further.

EXERCISE A 940-kg horse trailer with essentially frictionless wheels is sitting in a level parking lot. The trailer is 5.1 m long, and its center of mass is at its center. Its passenger, a 480-kg horse, breaks free from its stall at one end of the trailer and walks to the other end. How far does the trailer move relative to the ground? Treat the horse as a point particle.

Answer: 1.7 m

Some problems similar to Example 10-4: 14–17

10-2 MOMENTUM

In Chapter 5 we defined the linear momentum $\mathbf{p}$ of a particle as $\mathbf{p} = m\mathbf{v}$, and first wrote Newton's law in the form $\mathbf{F} = d\mathbf{p}/dt$. We subsequently applied the law to single particles, using the form $\mathbf{F} = m\mathbf{a}$, but suggested that the momentum concept would play an important role in many-particle systems. We're now ready to explore that role.

The momentum of a system of particles is just the vector sum of the individual momenta:

$$\mathbf{P} = \sum \mathbf{p}_i = \sum m_i \mathbf{v}_i,$$

where m_i and $\mathbf{v}_i$ are the masses and velocities of the individual particles. But we really don't want to keep track of all the particles in the system. Is there a simpler way to express the total momentum? There is, and it comes from writing the individual particle velocities as time derivatives of position: $\mathbf{v} = d\mathbf{r}/dt$. Then we have

$$\mathbf{P} = \sum m_i \frac{d\mathbf{r}_i}{dt} = \frac{d}{dt} \sum m_i \mathbf{r}_i,$$

where the last step follows because the individual particle masses are constant and because the sum of derivatives is the derivative of the sum. In Section 10-1 we defined the center-of-mass position $\mathbf{R}$ as $\sum m_i \mathbf{r}_i / M$, where M is the total mass. So the total momentum can be written

$$\mathbf{P} = \frac{d}{dt} M\mathbf{R},$$

or, assuming the system mass M remains constant,

$$\mathbf{P} = M\frac{d\mathbf{R}}{dt} = M\mathbf{V}, \tag{10-7}$$

where $\mathbf{V} = d\mathbf{R}/dt$ is the center-of-mass velocity. So the momentum of a system is given by an expression similar to that of a single particle; it is the product of the system mass with the system velocity—that is, with the velocity of the center of mass. If this seems so obvious as not to need deriving, watch out! We'll see in Section 10-3 that the same is *not* true for the system's total energy.

If we differentiate Equation 10-7 with respect to time, we have

$$\frac{d\mathbf{P}}{dt} = M\frac{d\mathbf{V}}{dt} = M\mathbf{A},$$

where $\mathbf{A}$ is the center-of-mass acceleration. But we defined the center of mass so that its motion obeyed Newton's second law, $\mathbf{F} = M\mathbf{A}$, with $\mathbf{F}$ the net external force on the system. So we can write simply

$$\mathbf{F}_{\text{net ext}} = \frac{d\mathbf{P}}{dt}, \tag{10-8}$$

showing that the momentum of a system of particles changes only if there is a net external force on the system. Remember the hidden role of Newton's third law in all this: only because the forces *internal* to the system cancel in pairs can we ignore them and consider just the external force.

Conservation of Momentum

In the special case when the net external force is zero, Equation 10-8 gives

so
$$\frac{d\mathbf{P}}{dt} = \mathbf{0}, \quad \text{(zero net external force)}$$

$$\mathbf{P} = \text{constant}. \quad \text{(conservation of linear momentum)} \quad (10\text{-}9)$$

Equation 10-9 describes the **conservation of linear momentum**, one of the most fundamental laws of physics:

> *Conservation of linear momentum: When the net external force on a system is zero, the total momentum* **P** *of the system—the vector sum of the individual momenta m***v** *of its constituent particles—remains constant.*

Momentum conservation holds no matter how many particles are involved and no matter how they're moving. It applies to systems ranging in size from atomic nuclei to pool balls (Fig. 10-14), from colliding cars to galaxies. Although we derived Equation 10-9 from Newton's laws, momentum conservation is even more basic than those laws since it applies to subatomic and nuclear systems where the laws and even language of Newtonian physics are hopelessly inadequate. The following examples show the wide range and power of the momentum conservation principle.

FIGURE 10-14 Initially the momentum of a system of pool balls is that of the cue ball alone, shown coming from the left in this strobe photo. After that one ball has struck the others, the vector sum of all the balls' momenta remains what it was initially.

Got It!

A 500-g fireworks rocket is moving with velocity $\mathbf{v} = 60\mathbf{\hat{j}}$ m/s at the instant it explodes. If you were to add the momentum vectors of all its fragments just after the collision, what would be the result?

EXAMPLE 10-5	*Kayaking*

Jess (mass 53 kg) and Nick (mass 72 kg) are sitting in a kayak (mass 26 kg) at rest on frictionless water. She tosses him a 17-kg pack, giving it a speed of 3.1 m/s relative to the water. What is the speed of the kayak (a) while the pack is in the air and (b) after Nick catches it?

Solution

There's no net external force on the system consisting of kayak, paddlers, and pack, so the system's momentum is conserved. Everything is initially at rest, so that momentum is zero.

While the pack is in the air, it has horizontal momentum $m_p v_p$. The kayak and its passengers are all moving together; their horizontal momentum is $(m_j + m_n + m_k)v_k$, where m_j, m_n, and m_k are the masses of Jess, Nick, and the kayak, respectively, and v_k is the horizontal component of the kayak's velocity. Since the total momentum is conserved, it remains zero while the pack moves; thus

$$m_p v_p + (m_j + m_n + m_k)v_k = 0,$$

or

$$v_k = -\frac{m_p v_p}{m_j + m_n + m_k} = -\frac{(17 \text{ kg})(3.1 \text{ m/s})}{53 \text{ kg} + 72 \text{ kg} + 26 \text{ kg}}$$

$$= -0.35 \text{ m/s}.$$

The minus sign shows that the kayak moves in the opposite direction from the pack.

There's no need to calculate the speed after Nick catches the pack; kayak, passengers, and pack all have the same velocity then. For the total momentum to remain zero, that velocity must be zero.

EXERCISE A 28-kg dog leaps horizontally out of a 72-kg rowboat at a speed of 1.6 m/s relative to the water. If the rowboat is initially at rest, how fast is it moving after the dog leaps?

Answer: 0.62 m/s

Some problems similar to Example 10-5: 22, 31, 51, 52

EXAMPLE 10-6 | *A Speeding Puck*

A hockey coach enlists a physics student on the team to measure the speed of a hockey puck. The student loads a small styrofoam chest with sand, giving it a total mass of 6.4 kg. He places the chest, at rest on frictionless ice, in the path of the hockey puck, whose mass is 160 g. The puck embeds itself in the styrofoam, and the chest moves off at 1.2 m/s. What was the speed of the puck?

Solution

The only forces in this situation are between the puck and the chest, so if we choose our system to be puck plus chest, then the external force on the system is zero, and the system's momentum is conserved. Originally, all the momentum of the system is in the puck: $P = m_p v_p$, where we don't need vector notation because the motion is in one dimension. After the puck hits the chest, the two move off together at the same speed: $P = (m_p + m_c)v_c$. So the statement that momentum is conserved becomes

$$m_p v_p = (m_p + m_c)v_c .$$

Then

$$v_p = \frac{(m_p + m_c)v_c}{m_p} = \frac{(0.16 \text{ kg} + 6.4 \text{ kg})(1.2 \text{ m/s})}{0.16 \text{ kg}} = 49 \text{ m/s} .$$

Variations on this technique are routinely used to measure the speeds of rapidly moving objects such as bullets.

Tip

Spare the Details The power of conservation principles like conservation of linear momentum and conservation of energy lies in their ability to predict the outcomes of physical happenings without lots of intermediate detail. In this example, for instance, we didn't need to know anything about the interaction between hockey puck and styrofoam chest—for example, how the puck slowed down, or the acceleration of the chest. All we knew was that the system had a certain momentum before the interaction, and the conservation of momentum principle told us it had to have that same momentum after the interaction. That alone was enough to solve the problem. When confronted with a conservation-law problem, go straight from the initial to the final situation without trying to analyze the intermediate details.

EXERCISE A 42-kg child stands at rest on ice skates. She catches a 1.1-kg ball moving horizontally at 9.5 m/s. What is her speed after she's caught the ball?

Answer: 0.24 m/s

Some problems similar to Example 10-6: 23, 26, 30

EXAMPLE 10-7 | *Radioactive Decay*

A lithium-5 nucleus (^{5}Li) is moving at 1.6×10^6 m/s when it decays into a proton (^{1}H) and an alpha particle (^{4}He). [The superscripted numbers are the total number of nucleons (neutrons and protons) in a nucleus, and give the approximate nuclear mass in unified atomic mass units (u).] The alpha particle is detected moving at 1.4×10^6 m/s, at 33° to the original velocity of the ^{5}Li nucleus. What are the magnitude and direction of the proton's velocity?

Solution

Again, momentum is conserved. Before the decay, we have only the lithium nucleus. After the decay, there are two particles whose individual momenta contribute to the total. So the statement that momentum is conserved becomes

$$m_{\text{Li}}\mathbf{v}_{\text{Li}} = m_p \mathbf{v}_p + m_\alpha \mathbf{v}_\alpha ,$$

where we keep the full vector notation because the motion involves two dimensions. If we choose the x axis along the direction of $\mathbf{v}_{\text{Li}}$, then we can write separately the two components of the momentum conservation equation:

x component: $m_{\text{Li}} v_{\text{Li}} = m_p v_{px} + m_\alpha v_{\alpha x}$
y component: $0 = m_p v_{py} + m_\alpha v_{\alpha y} .$

FIGURE 10-15 Velocity diagram for the decay of ^{5}Li nucleus (Example 10-7).

The given information in this problem includes the speed v_{Li} of the lithium nucleus and the final speed v_α and direction ϕ of the alpha particle. From Fig. 10-15 we see that the components of the alpha particle velocity are $v_{\alpha x} = v_\alpha \cos \phi$ and $v_{\alpha y} = v_\alpha \sin \phi$. Solving our two equations for the unknown components of the proton velocity then gives

x component:

$$v_{px} = \frac{m_{\text{Li}} v_{\text{Li}} - m_\alpha v_{\alpha x}}{m_p} = \frac{m_{\text{Li}} v_{\text{Li}} - m_\alpha v_\alpha \cos \phi}{m_p}$$

$$= \frac{(5.0 \text{ u})(1.6 \text{ Mm/s}) - (4.0 \text{ u})(1.4 \text{ Mm/s})(\cos 33°)}{1.0 \text{ u}}$$

$$= 3.30 \text{ Mm/s}$$

y component: $v_{py} = -\frac{m_\alpha v_{\alpha y}}{m_p} = -\frac{m_\alpha v_\alpha \sin \phi}{m_p}$

$$= -\frac{(4.0 \text{ u})(1.4 \text{ Mm/s})(\sin 33°)}{1.0 \text{ u}}$$

$$= -3.05 \text{ Mm/s} .$$

Thus the proton's speed is

$$v_p = \sqrt{v_{px}^2 + v_{py}^2} = \sqrt{(3.30 \text{ Mm/s})^2 + (-3.05 \text{ Mm/s})^2}$$

$$= 4.5 \text{ Mm/s}$$

and its direction is given by

$$\theta = \tan^{-1}\left(\frac{v_{py}}{v_{px}}\right) = \tan^{-1}\left(\frac{-3.05 \text{ Mm/s}}{3.30 \text{ Mm/s}}\right) = -43°,$$

where the minus sign shows that the proton's velocity vector points below the x axis, as shown in Fig. 10-15.

We can see graphically that our results make sense by redrawing Fig. 10-15 as a momentum vector diagram—that is, by multiplying each velocity vector by the appropriate mass. The result, Fig. 10-16, shows that the y components of the alpha particle and proton momenta cancel, and that their x components sum to the momentum of the original nucleus.

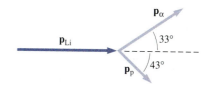

FIGURE 10-16 Momentum diagram for Example 10-7.

With no external forces acting, momentum had to be conserved in this decay. But kinetic energy is not conserved, as you will find if you evaluate the kinetic energies before and after decay (see Problem 41). Internal potential energy of the ^{5}Li nucleus is converted to kinetic energy in the decay process.

EXERCISE A skater embeds a firecracker in a large snowball and pushes it across a frozen pond at 7.6 m/s. The firecracker explodes, breaking the snowball into two equal-mass chunks. One chunk moves off at 9.3 m/s at $+19°$ to the original direction of motion. Find the speed and direction of the second chunk.

Answer: 7.1 m/s, $-25°$ to the original direction

Some problems similar to Example 10-7: 24, 36, 49, 50, 70

6.6
Saving an Astronaut

Defining the System: Internal and External Forces

How do we decide whether or not the forces acting on a system are external? That depends on our choice of what to include in the system. In Example 10-6, for instance, we chose to include both the hockey puck and the styrofoam chest in our system; the force exerted on the chest by the puck was then an internal force and we did not consider it explicitly. On the other hand, we could have chosen our system to include just the chest; then the force of the puck would be an external force, and the momentum of the system—the chest alone—would change. Of course, our definition of the system cannot affect what actually happens. Either description of the puck-chest interaction is equally valid; our choice was made so we could apply the conservation of momentum principle.

Got It!

Two skaters face each other and toss a basketball back and forth on frictionless ice. Does either skater's momentum change? Does the basketball's momentum change? Does the momentum of the system comprising the basketball and the two skaters change?

Sometimes we're interested in the force exerted on a particular object. Then it's convenient to redefine our system to include only that object, so the force of interest becomes an external force. The example below illustrates this situation.

EXAMPLE 10-8	*Fighting a Fire*

A firefighter directs a stream of water against the window of a burning building, hoping to break it so the water can get to the fire (Fig. 10-17). The hose delivers water at the rate of 45 kg/s; the water hits the window moving horizontally at 32 m/s. After hitting the window, the water drops vertically downward. What is the horizontal force on the window?

Solution

The horizontal motion of the water stops abruptly at the window; since the water is moving initially at 32 m/s, each kg of water loses 32 kg·m/s of momentum. But water strikes the window at the rate of 45 kg/s, so the rate of momentum loss is

$$\frac{dP}{dt} = (45 \text{ kg/s})(32 \text{ kg·m/s/kg}) = 1400 \text{ kg·m/s}^2 .$$

If we regard the water alone as our system, then this change in the system's momentum means an external force of 1400 N acts on the water. That force is provided by the window. By Newton's third law, the water must therefore exert an oppositely directed force of equal magnitude on the window. Because the window is attached to the building, and the building to Earth, the force does not give rise to any significant acceleration. Once the window breaks, though, the glass fragments will accelerate violently.

EXERCISE An airliner taxies directly away from the terminal building, its jet exhaust directed perpendicularly against the

FIGURE 10-17 What force does the water exert? (Example 10-8).

window of the terminal. The plane exhausts 94 kg of gas each second, and the gas strikes the window at 220 m/s and then moves parallel to the window surface. How much force must the window withstand?

Answer: 21 kN

Some problems similar to Example 10-8: 27, 32, 35, 53, 54

Rockets

Rockets provide our means of escaping Earth's gravity. And in the vacuum of space, where there's nothing for a wheel or propeller to push against, rockets are, at present, our only practical means of propulsion. Learning how rockets work will deepen your understanding of the principle of momentum conservation, and at the same time will give you an appreciation for this essential element of modern space technology.

Consider a rocket whose total mass $M + \Delta m$ includes fuel, moving at speed v relative to some reference frame (Fig. 10-18a). Its total momentum is therefore $P = (M + \Delta m)v$. Now the rocket fires for a short time Δt, expelling a small quantity Δm of fuel moving at speed v_{ex} relative to the rocket and therefore at $v - v_{ex}$ relative to our reference frame (Fig. 10-18b). The momentum of the expelled fuel is then $\Delta m(v - v_{ex})$. The rocket's mass drops to M, and its speed increases by a small amount Δv, so its momentum is now $M(v + \Delta v)$. But with no net external force the momentum of the (rocket + fuel) system is conserved, so the momenta of the rocket and the fuel must sum to the initial momentum,

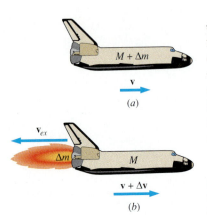

FIGURE 10-18 A rocket (a) before and (b) after it expels a small mass Δm of fuel. Rocket speed is relative to a nonaccelerating frame of reference; exhaust speed v_{ex} is relative to the rocket.

whose value is $P = (M + \Delta m)v$; thus

$$(M + \Delta m)v = M(v + \Delta v) + \Delta m(v - v_{ex}),$$

or, multiplying out and simplifying,

$$M \Delta v = v_{ex} \Delta m.$$

We can recast this equation in terms of the change in rocket mass M by noting that the expelled fuel Δm represents a *decrease* in the rocket mass; that is, the change ΔM in rocket mass is given by $\Delta M = -\Delta m$, where the minus sign signifies a mass decrease. If we also divide by the time Δt over which the fuel is expelled, our equation becomes

$$M \frac{\Delta v}{\Delta t} = -v_{ex} \frac{\Delta M}{\Delta t}. \qquad (10\text{-}10a)$$

Actually, the entire procedure leading to this equation is only approximate: The velocity of the rocket increases continuously as the fuel mass is expelled, and thus our assertion that the fuel velocity is $v - v_{ex}$ is itself only approximate. But in the limit of a vanishingly small fuel mass Δm expelled over a vanishingly small time Δt, the velocity change Δv becomes negligible, and the equation becomes exact. In that limit the ratios in Equation 10-10a become derivatives, and we have

$$M \frac{dv}{dt} = -v_{ex} \frac{dM}{dt}. \qquad (10\text{-}10b)$$

Rocket engineers call the quantity $-v_{ex}\,dM/dt$ the **thrust** of the rocket. Thrust has the dimensions of force (check the units!) and is indeed a measure of the force accelerating the rocket. Equation 10-10b shows that thrust can be increased by expelling the gases at a higher speed or by ejecting a greater mass of gas per unit time. The minus sign shows that an increase in speed—positive dv/dt—corresponds to a *decrease* in rocket mass—negative dM/dt. In practice the exhaust gas does not point straight backward, but fans out somewhat, thereby reducing the forward thrust (Fig. 10-19).

What force actually accelerates the rocket? The high-pressure gases inside the rocket push on all sides of the rocket chamber—except the back, where the exhaust port is. So the force associated with gas pushing on the *front* of the rocket chamber is not canceled by a corresponding force on the rear, and that net force is what gives the rocket its forward acceleration (Fig. 10-20).

Our analysis so far considered only a short rocket firing. We can find the effect of a longer firing by first multiplying both sides of Equation 10-10b by dt/M:

$$dv = -v_{ex} \frac{dM}{M}.$$

The overall change in velocity comes from summing—that is, integrating—all the small changes dv as the velocity goes from some initial value v_i to some final value v_f. During the same time the mass goes from M_i to M_f. So we have

$$\int_{v_i}^{v_f} dv = -v_{ex} \int_{M_i}^{M_f} \frac{dM}{M}.$$

FIGURE 10-19 The exhaust plume of a rocket fans out slightly, reducing thrust from the theoretical value given by Equation 10-10.

FIGURE 10-20 (*a*) In a closed container of pressurized gas, the gas exerts forces on all the container walls, and the net force is zero. (*b*) With a hole at the left end of the container, gas rushes out and some of the pressure force on the right end is not canceled. The resulting net force is what accelerates the container to the right.

The left-hand integral is just $v_f - v_i$, while the right-hand integral defines the natural logarithm. So

$$v_f - v_i = -v_{ex}[\ln(M_f) - \ln(M_i)] = v_{ex}[\ln(M_i) - \ln(M_f)].$$

But $\ln(a) - \ln(b) = \ln(a/b)$, so

$$v_f = v_i + v_{ex} \ln\left(\frac{M_i}{M_f}\right). \qquad (10\text{-}11)$$

Since $M_i > M_f$, this equation gives the expected result that speed increases as the rocket ejects fuel.

A rocket carries only a finite amount of fuel, so the mass ratio from fully loaded to fully empty fuel tanks sets the maximum achievable speed—the **terminal speed** of the rocket. For a given mass ratio, the terminal speed can be increased by increasing the velocity of the exhaust gases.

EXAMPLE 10-9	*Terminal Speed*

A spacecraft is being designed to probe the interstellar medium. The craft is to be boosted from Earth and sent on an outbound trajectory by conventional rockets. At the orbit of Pluto, it is to be moving away from the Sun at 35 km/s; at that point an advanced rocket engine will fire to accelerate the craft to its terminal speed of 150 km/s. If the mass of the spacecraft alone is 750 kg, and if the advanced rocket exhausts fuel at 47 km/s, how much fuel must be carried to Pluto's orbit?

Solution

We want the final mass M_f to be that of the spacecraft alone, while M_i is the mass of the spacecraft plus fuel. To solve Equation 10-11 for the fuel mass, we first write

$$\ln\left(\frac{M_i}{M_f}\right) = \frac{v_f - v_i}{v_{ex}} = \frac{150 \text{ km/s} - 35 \text{ km/s}}{47 \text{ km/s}} = 2.45,$$

so

$$\frac{M_i}{M_f} = e^{2.45} = 11.6,$$

where we used the fact that natural logarithm and exponential are inverse functions: $e^{\ln(x)} = x$. So the total mass before the rocket firing is $11.6M_f$, or 8700 kg. Subtracting the 750-kg spacecraft mass leaves 7950 kg of fuel. This example shows why the achievement of very high exhaust speeds is crucial to long-distance space travel; even in this case the useful payload is dwarfed by the fuel mass, and the situation would be far

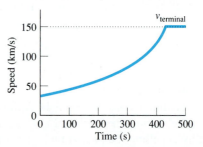

FIGURE 10-21 Speed versus time for the spacecraft of Example 10-9. The craft coasts at its terminal speed once all its fuel is exhaustd. Note that the acceleration increases as the craft loses mass. Calculation assumes an exhaust rate of 19 kg/s.

worse with present-day rockets whose exhaust speeds are typically several km/s.

As Fig. 10-21 shows, most of the acceleration takes place in the later stages of the firing, when the mass of the rocket system is greatly reduced.

EXERCISE Find the terminal speed of a 750-kg rocket that starts from rest carrying 2600 kg of fuel and that expels its exhaust gases at 1.8 km/s.

Answer: 2.7 km/s

Some problems similar to Example 10-9: 38–40, 69

10-3 KINETIC ENERGY IN MANY-PARTICLE SYSTEMS

We've seen in this chapter how the momentum of a many-particle system is determined entirely by the motion of its center of mass; the detailed behavior of the individual particles doesn't matter. For example, a firecracker sliding on ice has the same total momentum before and after it explodes.

The same, however, is *not* true of a system's kinetic energy. Energetically, our firecracker is very different after it explodes; internal potential energy has been converted to kinetic energy of the fragments. Nevertheless, the center-of-mass concept remains useful in categorizing the kinetic energy associated with a system of particles.

The total kinetic energy of a system is simply the sum of the kinetic energies of the constituent particles:

$$K = \sum \tfrac{1}{2} m_i v_i^2 .$$

But the velocity $\mathbf{v}_i$ of a particle can be written as the vector sum of the center-of-mass velocity $\mathbf{V}$ and a velocity $\tilde{\mathbf{v}}_i$ of that particle relative to the center of mass:

$$\mathbf{v}_i = \mathbf{V} + \tilde{\mathbf{v}}_i .$$

Then the total kinetic energy of the system is

$$
\begin{aligned}
K &= \sum \tfrac{1}{2} m_i (\mathbf{V} + \tilde{\mathbf{v}}_i) \cdot (\mathbf{V} + \tilde{\mathbf{v}}_i) \\
&= \sum \tfrac{1}{2} m_i V^2 + \sum m_i \mathbf{V} \cdot \tilde{\mathbf{v}}_i + \sum \tfrac{1}{2} m_i \tilde{v}_i^2 ,
\end{aligned}
\tag{10-12}
$$

where in the middle term the $\tfrac{1}{2}$ cancelled the 2 from the cross terms in multiplying out the dot product.

Let us examine the three sums making up the total kinetic energy. Since the center-of-mass speed V is common to all particles, it can be factored out of the first sum, so

$$\sum \tfrac{1}{2} m_i V^2 = \tfrac{1}{2} V^2 \sum m_i = \tfrac{1}{2} M V^2 ,$$

where M is the total mass. So what is this term? It's just the kinetic energy of a particle with mass M moving at speed V; we call this term K_{cm}, the **kinetic energy of the center of mass**.

The center-of-mass velocity can also be factored out of the second term in Equation 10-12, giving

$$\sum m_i \mathbf{V} \cdot \tilde{\mathbf{v}}_i = \mathbf{V} \cdot \sum m_i \tilde{\mathbf{v}}_i .$$

But what is $\sum m_i \tilde{\mathbf{v}}_i$? Because the $\tilde{\mathbf{v}}_i$'s are the particle velocities relative to the center of mass, that sum is just the total momentum measured in a frame of reference moving with the center of mass. But we found earlier that the total momentum is $\mathbf{P} = m\mathbf{V}$, with $\mathbf{V}$ the center-of-mass velocity. In a frame of reference where $\mathbf{V} = \mathbf{0}$—that is, a frame of reference moving with the center of mass—the total momentum must be zero. So the entire second term in Equation 10-12 is zero.

The third term in Equation 10-12, $\sum \tfrac{1}{2} m_i \tilde{v}_i^2$, is just the sum of the individual kinetic energies measured in a frame of reference moving with the center of mass. We call this term K_{int}, the **internal kinetic energy**.

With the middle term gone, Equation 10-12 shows that the kinetic energy of a system breaks down into two terms:

$$K = K_{cm} + K_{int}. \qquad (10\text{-}13)$$

6.7
Explosion Problems

The first term, the kinetic energy of the center of mass, depends only on the center-of-mass motion. In our firecracker example, K_{cm} doesn't change when the firecracker explodes. The second term, the internal kinetic energy, depends only on the motions of the individual particles relative to the center of mass. Explosion of the firecracker dramatically increases the internal kinetic energy.

EXAMPLE 10-10	*Separation*

A 325-kg booster rocket and a 732-kg satellite are coasting through space together at 5.22 km/s. Explosive bolts fire to separate the satellite from its booster, and after separation the satellite and booster are moving in their original direction at 6.69 km/s and 1.91 km/s, respectively. Find the center-of-mass and internal kinetic energies of the (booster + satellite) system before and after separation.

Solution

Before separation the two components are bolted together, so there is no internal kinetic energy. The center-of-mass kinetic energy is just the total kinetic energy:

$$K_{cm} = \tfrac{1}{2}MV^2 = (\tfrac{1}{2})(325 \text{ kg} + 732 \text{ kg})(5.22 \times 10^3 \text{ m/s})^2$$

$$= 14.4 \text{ GJ}.$$

After separation, momentum conservation assures us that the center-of-mass velocity V remains 5.22 km/s. Since the total mass is unchanged, so, too, is the center-of-mass kinetic energy. To find the internal kinetic energy we need the velocities $\tilde{v}$ relative to the center of mass; we get these by subtracting the center-of-mass velocity from the individual velocities:

$$\tilde{v}_s = 6.69 \text{ km/s} - 5.22 \text{ km/s} = 1.47 \text{ km/s}$$

$$\tilde{v}_b = 1.91 \text{ km/s} - 5.22 \text{ km/s} = -3.31 \text{ km/s},$$

where the minus sign indicates that the booster is moving backward relative to the center of mass. The internal kinetic energy is the sum of the energies associated with these internal motions:

$$K_{int} = \tfrac{1}{2}m_s\tilde{v}_s^2 + \tfrac{1}{2}m_b\tilde{v}_b^2$$

$$= (\tfrac{1}{2})(732 \text{ kg})(1.47 \times 10^3 \text{ m/s})^2$$

$$+ (\tfrac{1}{2})(325 \text{ kg})(-3.31 \times 10^3 \text{ m/s})^2 = 2.57 \text{ GJ}.$$

This extra energy comes from the conversion of chemical potential energy in the explosive bolt.

We can confirm that the center-of-mass energy remains constant by calculating the total energy after separation and subtracting the internal energy:

$$K_{total} - K_{internal} = \tfrac{1}{2}m_s v_s^2 + \tfrac{1}{2}m_b v_b^2 - K_{int}$$

$$= (\tfrac{1}{2})(732 \text{ kg})(6.69 \times 10^3 \text{ m/s})^2$$

$$+ (\tfrac{1}{2})(325 \text{ kg})(1.91 \times 10^3 \text{ m/s})^2 - 2.57 \text{ GJ}$$

$$= 14.4 \text{ GJ},$$

in agreement with our before-separation result for the center-of-mass kinetic energy.

Tip

Remember the SI Prefixes What's a GJ? If you encounter an unfamiliar SI prefix, refer to Table 1-1 (also inside the front cover). There you'll find that G stands for "giga," signifying multiplication by 10^9. So the center-of-mass energy is 14.4×10^9 J.

EXERCISE Find the center-of-mass and internal kinetic energies for the snowball in the exercise following Example 10-7. Take the mass of the snowball to be 14 kg. *Hint:* Here you'll need to do a vector subtraction to determine the velocities relative to the center of mass.

Answers: $K_{cm} = 404$ J; $K_{int} = 73$ J

Some problems similar to Example 10-10: 41, 42, 44

CHAPTER SYNOPSIS

Summary

1. A system of particles of total mass M has associated with it a point called the **center of mass** to which Newton's laws of motion apply as they do to a point particle:

$$\mathbf{F}_{\text{net ext}} = M\frac{d^2\mathbf{R}}{dt^2} = M\mathbf{A},$$

where $\mathbf{F}_{\text{net ext}}$ is the net external force on the system and $\mathbf{A}$ the acceleration of the center of mass. The position $\mathbf{R}$ of the center of mass is given by

$$\mathbf{R} = \frac{\sum m_i \mathbf{r}_i}{M}, \quad \text{(center of mass)}$$

where m_i and $\mathbf{r}_i$ represent the masses and positions of the individual particles in the system. For continuously distributed matter, the center-of-mass position is given by an integral:

$$\mathbf{R} = \frac{1}{M}\int \mathbf{r}\, dm,$$

where the integration is taken over the entire system. That the center-of-mass concept is useful is a consequence of Newton's third law, which requires that internal forces cancel in pairs, leaving the overall system motion determined only by external forces.

2. In the absence of a net external force, the center-of-mass velocity $\mathbf{V} = \sum m_i\mathbf{v}_i/M$ remains constant. In particular, if the center of mass is at rest, then it remains at rest regardless of the motions of the constituent particles.

3. The total momentum $\mathbf{P}$ of a system is the vector sum of the momenta $\mathbf{p}_i = m_i\mathbf{v}_i$ of the constituent particles: $\mathbf{P} = \sum m_i\mathbf{v}_i$. Application of Newton's third law, as embodied in the center-of-mass concept, shows that the system obeys Newton's second law in the form

$$\mathbf{F}_{\text{net ext}} = \frac{d\mathbf{P}}{dt},$$

where $\mathbf{F}$ is the net external force applied to the system.

4. When the net external force is zero, the momentum of a system remains constant. This statement is known as the **law of conservation of momentum**. It is a fundamental principle of physics, extending even into realms where Newtonian mechanics is not applicable.

5. The motion of a rocket is a manifestation of the momentum principle. The rate of change of a rocket's speed v is given by

$$M\frac{dv}{dt} = -v_{\text{ex}}\frac{dM}{dt},$$

where M is the rocket's mass, v_{ex} the speed of the exhaust gas relative to the rocket, and dM/dt the rate of change of the rocket's mass due to the ejection of gas.

6. The total kinetic energy of a system of particles includes the kinetic energy of the center of mass, given by

$$K_{cm} = \tfrac{1}{2}MV^2,$$

where M is the total mass and V the speed of the center of mass, and the **internal kinetic energy**, given by

$$K_{\text{int}} = \sum \tfrac{1}{2}m_i\tilde{v}_i^2,$$

where m_i is the mass of an individual particle and $\tilde{v}_i$ its speed relative to the center of mass. The total kinetic energy is the sum of these two:

$$K_{\text{total}} = K_{\text{cm}} + K_{\text{int}}.$$

Terms You Should Understand

(Pairs are closely related terms whose distinction is important; number in parentheses is chapter section where term first appears.)

rigid body (introduction)
center of mass (10-1)
internal force, external force (10-1)
mass element (10-1)
linear momentum (10-2)
conservation of linear momentum (10-2)
rocket (10-2)
thrust (10-2)
center-of-mass kinetic energy, internal kinetic energy (10-3)

Symbols You Should Recognize

$\mathbf{R}$, X, Y, Z (10-1)	$\mathbf{P}$ (10-2)
M (10-1)	$\mathbf{V}$, $\mathbf{v}_i$, $\tilde{\mathbf{v}}_i$ (10-3)
$\mathbf{F}_{\text{ext}}$, $\mathbf{F}_{\text{int}}$ (10-1)	K_{cm}, K_{int} (10-3)
$\int \mathbf{r}\, dm$ (10-1)	

Problems You Should Be Able to Solve

determining the center of mass of a system consisting of point particles on a line or in a plane (10-1)
determining the center of mass of a composite object from the centers of mass of its constituent parts (10-1)
determining the center of mass of a continuous distribution of matter using integration (10-1)
using center of mass to determine positions of the constituent objects of a system as the system is reconfigured (10-1)
applying conservation of momentum to determine the behavior of individual parts of a system (10-2)

using conservation of momentum to determine forces on objects being bombarded by a stream of particles (10-2)

analyzing rocket motion (10-2)

evaluating center-of-mass and internal energies of systems of particles (10-3)

Limitations to Keep in Mind

Conservation of momentum applies to a system only when the net external force on the system is zero.

QUESTIONS

1. Roughly where is your center of mass when you are standing?

2. Can you form your body into a shape such that your center of mass is not within your body? If not, why not? If so, describe.

3. Where is the center of mass of a solid wooden wheel? Of a bicycle wheel, with spokes?

4. Earth and moon are both in nearly circular orbits about a point 4700 km from the center of Earth. Explain in terms of the center-of-mass concept as applied to the Earth-moon system.

5. Hunters drive a herd of bison over the edge of a cliff. As they fall, what happens to the center of mass of the Earth + bison system? What happens to the centers of mass of the herd and Earth separately? Explain.

6. Explain why a high jumper's center of mass need not clear the bar.

7. Where would our derivation of the center-of-mass position **R** fail if the number of particles in the system were not constant?

8. The center of mass of a solid sphere is clearly at its center. If the sphere is cut in half, and the two halves are stacked as in Fig. 10-22, is the center of mass at the point where they touch? If not, roughly where is it? Explain.

FIGURE 10-22 Question 8.

9. How can a jet engine work when it takes air in the front as well as exhausting it out the back?

10. When you reach shore in Example 10-4, the center of mass of the (boat + you) system suddenly begins moving. What force accelerates it?

11. In Example 10-4, does the motion of the boat change when you reach shore?

12. Does the momentum of a basketball change as it rebounds off a backboard? What happens to the momentum of the backboard?

13. The momentum of a system of pool balls is the same before and after they are hit by the cue ball. Is it still the same after one of the balls strikes the edge of the table? Explain.

14. If all the cars in the world started driving eastward, what would happen to the length of the day?

15. A group of kids are pelting a wall with rocks. For a given rock speed and number of rocks thrown per unit time, will the force on the wall be greater (a) if the rocks stick to the wall or (b) if the rocks bounce off the wall, heading back in the direction from which they came? Explain.

16. Consider the system consisting of a shot putter and his shot; the mass of the shot is about 10% that of the shot putter. Describe the motion of the system's center of mass (a) if the shot putter is standing on a concrete pad with high coefficient of friction and (b) if he is standing on a frictionless surface.

17. An asteroid 100 km in diameter is discovered to be on a collision course with Earth. In a show of international cooperation and mutual disarmament, nations launch all their nuclear missiles at the asteroid and succeed in blowing it to smithereens. Will the center of mass of the asteroid still hit Earth?

18. Can you make a sailboat go by blowing air onto the sails with a fan mounted on the boat? With air from a compressed-air cylinder mounted on the boat?

19. When rocket pioneer Robert Goddard proposed using rocket propulsion for space travel, the January 13, 1920 issue of *The New York Times* criticized Goddard with the scathing words "Professor Goddard . . . does not know the relation of action to reaction, and of the need to have something better than a vacuum against which to react . . . he . . . seems to lack the knowledge ladled out daily in high schools." How can a rocket work if it doesn't have anything to "push against?" Who was right, the *Times* or Goddard? Explain.

20. An hourglass is inverted and placed on a scale. Compare scale readings (a) before sand begins to hit the bottom; (b) while sand is hitting the bottom; (c) when all the sand is on the bottom.

21. The momentum of the center of mass of a system is the sum of the momenta of the individual particles, but the same is not true for kinetic energy. Why not?

PROBLEMS

ActivPhysics can help with these problems:
Activities 6-6, 6-7

Section 10-1 Center of Mass

1. A 28-kg child sits at one end of a 3.5-m long seesaw. Where should her 65-kg father sit so the center of mass will be at the center of the seesaw?

2. Two particles of equal mass m are at the vertices of the base of an equilateral triangle. The center of mass of the triangle is midway between the base and the third vertex. What is mass at the third vertex?

3. Four trucks, with masses indicated in Fig. 10-23, are on a rectangular barge of mass 35 Mg whose center of mass is at its center. The trucks' individual centers of mass are located 25 m apart on the barge's long dimension and 10 m apart on the short dimension, as shown. Where is the center of mass of the entire system? Express in relation to the truck at lower left.

FIGURE 10-23 Top view of four trucks on a barge, with truck masses given. Dots mark individual trucks' centers of mass (Problems 3, 8).

4. Rework Example 10-1 with the origin at the center of the barbell, showing that the physical location of the center of mass is independent of the choice of coordinate system.

5. Three equal masses lie at the corners of an equilateral triangle of side ℓ. Where is the center of mass?

6. How far from the center of Earth is the center of mass of the Earth-moon system? *Hint:* Consult Appendix E.

7. Find the center of mass of the plane object shown in Fig. 10-9, assuming uniform density.

8. Where, on the barge of Fig. 10-23, would you park a 25-Mg cement truck to put the center of mass of the entire system right in the center of the barge?

9. Find the center of mass of a pentagon of side a with one triangle missing, as shown in Fig. 10-24. *Hint:* See Example 10-3, and treat the pentagon as a group of triangles.

FIGURE 10-24 Problem 9.

10. A solid cube of side a has a density that varies linearly from zero at the bottom to ρ_0 at the top, as suggested in Fig. 10-25; that is, $\rho = \rho_0 \dfrac{y}{a}$. Find expressions for (a) the cube's mass and (b) the y coordinate of its center of mass. *Hint:* Use a square mass element of thickness dy, as shown in the figure.

FIGURE 10-25 Cube for Problem 10. The dark band suggests a mass element in the form of a square slab with dimensions $a \times a \times dy$.

11. A water molecule (H_2O) consists of two hydrogen atoms, each of mass 1.0 u, and one oxygen atom of mass 16 u. The hydrogen atoms are 96 pm from the oxygen and are separated by an angle of 105° (Fig. 10-26). Where is the center of mass of the molecule?

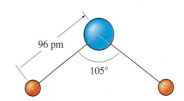

FIGURE 10-26 A water molecule (Problem 11).

12. A flat, T-shaped structure is made from two identical rectangles of length ℓ and width w (Fig. 10-27). Find its center of mass.

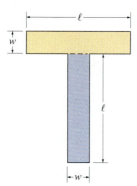

FIGURE 10-27 Problem 12.

13. Consider a system of three equal-mass particles moving in a plane; their positions are given by $a_i\hat{\mathbf{i}} + b_i\hat{\mathbf{j}}$, where a_i and b_i are functions of time with the units of position. Particle 1 has $a_1 = 3t^2 + 5$ and $b_1 = 0$; particle 2 has $a_2 = 7t + 2$ and $b_2 = 2$; particle 3 has $a_3 = 3t$ and $b_3 = 2t + 6$. Find the position, velocity, and acceleration of the center of mass as functions of time.

14. A 55-kg woman on a 450-kg boat hooks a 160-kg fish on the end of a nearly horizontal line 32 m long. If fish and boat are originally at rest on a frictionless sea, how far does the boat move as she reels in the fish?

15. Estimate how much Earth would move if its entire human population jumped simultaneously into the 1-mile-deep Grand Canyon.

16. You are with 19 other people on a boat at rest in frictionless water. Your total mass is 1500 kg, and the mass of the boat itself is 12,000 kg. The entire party walks the 6.5-m distance from bow to stern. How far does the boat move?

17. A hemispherical bowl is at rest on a frictionless kitchen counter. A mouse drops onto the rim of the bowl from a cabinet directly overhead. The mouse climbs down the inside of the bowl to eat the crumbs at the bottom. If the bowl moves along the counter a distance equal to one-tenth of its diameter, how does the mouse's mass compare with the bowl's mass?

18. Find the center of mass of the uniform, solid cone of height h and constant density ρ shown in Fig. 10-28. *Hint:* Integrate over disk-shaped mass elements of thickness dy, as shown in the figure.

Section 10-2 Momentum

19. A popcorn kernel in a hot pan bursts into two pieces, with masses of 91 mg and 64 mg. The more massive piece moves horizontally at 47 cm/s. Describe the motion of the second piece.

FIGURE 10-28 Cone for Problem 18 has base radius R and height h. Dark band shows a mass element for use in the integration. It is a disk with thickness dy and radius that depends on its position y.

20. A 60-kg ice skater, at rest on frictionless ice, tosses a 12-kg snowball with velocity given by $\mathbf{v} = 3.0\hat{\mathbf{i}} + 4.0\hat{\mathbf{j}}$ m/s, where the x and y axes are both in the horizontal plane. What is the subsequent velocity of the skater?

21. A firecracker, initially at rest, explodes into two fragments. The first, of mass 14 g, moves in the positive x direction at 48 m/s. The second moves at 32 m/s. Find its mass and the direction of its motion.

22. A rowboat with a mass of 94 kg carries a 61-kg rower and 34 kg of water that has accumulated in the bottom. It's drifting forward at 0.84 m/s when the rower scoops up 11 kg of water in a bucket of negligible mass and heaves it horizontally over the stern at a speed of 4.3 m/s relative to the boat. What is the subsequent speed of the boat?

23. A 680-g wood block is at rest on a frictionless table, when a 27-g bullet is fired into it. If the block with the embedded bullet moves off at 19 m/s, what was the original speed of the bullet?

24. A plutonium-239 nucleus at rest decays into a uranium-235 nucleus by emitting an alpha particle (^{4}He) with kinetic energy of 5.15 MeV. What is the speed of the uranium nucleus?

25. A runaway toboggan of mass 8.6 kg is moving horizontally at 23 km/h. As it passes under a tree, 15 kg of snow drop onto it. What is its subsequent speed?

26. A 950-kg airplane touches down on an icy runway, heading northward at 150 km/h. It collides with a 1200-kg plane taxiing eastward at 85 km/h. Find the speed and direction of the combined wreckage.

27. During a heavy storm, rain falls at the rate of 2.0 cm/hour; the speed of the individual raindrops is 25 m/s. (a) If the rain strikes a flat roof and then flows off the roof with negligible speed, what is the force exerted per square meter of roof area? (b) How much water would have to stand on the roof to exert the same force? The density of water is 1.0 g/cm^3.

28. A group of ice skaters with masses 50, 55, 60, 65, 70, and 75 kg are spaced evenly around a circle, as shown in Fig. 10-29. Simultaneously, they all skate toward the center at 4.0 m/s. At the center they hold each other in a

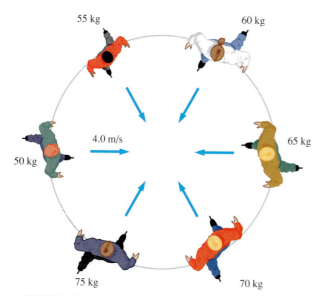

FIGURE 10-29 View from above of ice skaters heading toward the center of a circle (Problem 28).

tight bunch. Find the velocity of this bunch, in a coordinate system with the x axis to the right and the y axis upward in Fig. 10-29. Explain, in terms of the way the skaters are distributed, why your answer makes sense.

29. An 11,000-kg freight car rests against a spring bumper at the end of a railroad track. The spring has constant $k = 3.2 \times 10^5$ N/m. The car is hit by a second car of 9400 kg mass moving at 8.5 m/s, and the two cars couple together. (a) What is the maximum compression of the spring? (b) What is the speed of the two cars together when they rebound from the spring?

30. On an icy road, a 1200-kg car moving at 50 km/h strikes a 4400-kg truck moving in the same direction at 35 km/h. The combination is soon hit from behind by a 1500-kg car speeding at 65 km/h. If all three vehicles stick together, what is the speed of the wreckage?

31. A 1600-kg automobile is resting at one end of a 4500-kg railroad flatcar that is also at rest. The automobile then drives along the flatcar at 15 km/h relative to the flatcar. Unfortunately, the flatcar brakes are not set. How fast does it move?

32. A car of mass M is initially at rest on a frictionless surface. A jet of water carrying mass at the rate dm/dt and moving horizontally at speed v_0 strikes the rear window of the car, which makes a 45° angle with the horizontal; the water bounces off at the same relative speed with which it hit the window, as shown in Fig. 10-30. (a) Find an expression for the initial acceleration of the car. (b) What is the maximum speed reached by the car?

33. A 950-kg compact car is moving with velocity $\mathbf{v}_1 = 32\hat{\imath} + 17\hat{\jmath}$ m/s. It skids on a frictionless icy patch, and collides with a 450-kg hay wagon moving with velocity

FIGURE 10-30 Problem 32.

$\mathbf{v}_2 = 12\hat{\imath} + 14\hat{\jmath}$ m/s. If the two stay together, what is their velocity?

34. The 975-kg Giotto spacecraft, when it was close to Halley's Comet in 1986, passed through cometary dust of density 0.10 g/m³ at a speed of 200 m/s. Its frontal surface area was 10 m². Assuming that the dust stuck to the front of the spacecraft, at what rate was the spacecraft decelerated?

35. A biologist fires 20-g rubber bullets at a rhinoceros that is charging at 1.9 m/s. If the gun fires 5 bullets per second, with a speed of 1600 m/s, and if the biologist fires for 13 s to stop the rhino in its tracks, what is the mass of the rhino? Assume the bullets drop vertically after striking the rhino, and neglect forces exerted by the rhino's feet.

36. A ^{238}U nucleus is moving in the x direction at 5.0×10^5 m/s, when it decays into an alpha particle (^{4}He) and a ^{234}Th nucleus. If the alpha particle moves off at 22° above the x axis with a speed of 1.4×10^7 m/s, what is the recoil velocity of the thorium nucleus?

37. An Ariane rocket ejects 1.0×10^5 kg of fuel in the 90 s after launch. (a) How much thrust is developed if the fuel is ejected at 3.0 km/s with respect to the rocket? (b) What is the maximum total mass of the rocket if it is to get off the ground?

38. Eighty percent of a rocket's initial mass is fuel. If the fuel is exhausted at 2.5 km/s relative to the rocket, what is the terminal speed of the rocket?

39. If a rocket's exhaust speed is 200 m/s relative to the rocket, what fraction of its initial mass must be ejected to increase the rocket's speed by 50 m/s?

40. A space shuttle's main engines develop a thrust of 35×10^6 N as they eject gas at 2500 m/s relative to the shuttle. How much fuel must the shuttle carry to permit a 5-minute engine firing?

Section 10-3 Kinetic Energy in Many-Particle Systems

41. Determine the center-of-mass and internal kinetic energies before and after decay of the lithium nucleus of Example 10-7. Treat the individual nuclei as point particles.

42. A 150-g trick baseball is thrown at 60 km/h. It explodes in flight into two pieces, with a 38-g piece continuing straight ahead at 85 km/h. How much energy do the pieces gain in the explosion?

43. A 1200-kg car moving at 88 km/h collides with a 7600-kg truck moving in the same direction at 65 km/h. The two stick together, continuing in their original direction at 68 km/h. Determine the center-of-mass and internal energies of the (car + truck) system before and after the collision.

44. A sealed can of air contains 10^{21} air molecules moving randomly, on average, at 340 m/s. If the can is thrown at 10 m/s, compare the center-of-mass and internal energies of the air.

Paired Problems

(Both problems in a pair involve the same principles and techniques. If you can get the first problem, you should be able to solve the second one.)

45. A drinking glass is in the shape of a cylinder whose inside dimensions are 9.0 cm high and 8.0 cm in diameter as shown in Fig. 10-31. Its base has a mass of 140 g, while the mass of the curved, cylindrical sides is 85 g. (a) Where is its center of mass? (b) If the glass is three-quarters filled with juice (density 1.0 g/cm³), where is the center of mass of the glass-juice system? Assume the thickness of the glass is negligible.

FIGURE 10-31 Problems 45 and 68.

46. A cylindrical concrete silo is 4.0 m in diameter and 30 m high. It consists of a 6,000-kg concrete base and 38,000-kg cylindrical concrete walls. Locate the center of mass of the silo (a) when it's empty and (b) when it's two-thirds full of silage whose density is 800 kg/m³. Neglect the thickness of the silo walls and base.

47. Olympic-champion ice dancers Marina Klimova (mass 50 kg) and Sergei Ponomarenko (mass 70 kg) start from rest and push off each other on essentially frictionless ice. If Ponomarenko's speed is 2.8 m/s, how far apart are they after 3.0 s?

48. A 90-kg astronaut completes repairs on a 470-kg communications satellite, then pushes off from the satellite. When no longer in physical contact, the astronaut is moving at 62 cm/s relative to the satellite. What change in velocity has the astronaut given the satellite?

49. A 42-g firecracker is at rest at the origin when it explodes into three pieces. The first, with mass 12 g, moves along the x axis at 35 m/s. The second, with mass 21 g, moves along the y axis at 29 m/s. Find the velocity of the third piece.

50. A 60-kg astronaut floating in space simultaneously tosses away a 14-kg oxygen tank and a 5.8-kg camera. The tank moves in the x direction at 1.6 m/s, and the astronaut recoils at 0.85 m/s in a direction 200° counterclockwise from the x axis. Find the velocity of the camera.

51. A 4100-kg bull elephant is at one end of a 16,000-kg circus train car initially at rest on a frictionless track. The elephant charges the 17-m length of the car at a speed of 6.5 m/s, then stops when it hits the far wall. (a) How far does the car move during the elephant's charge? (b) How fast is the car moving during the charge? (c) What is the car's speed after the elephant has stopped? Assume the center of mass of the car is at its center, and treat the elephant as a particle.

52. A 65-m long ferry boat has a mass of 32,000 kg and is at rest with its shoreward end 55 m from shore. The center of mass of the boat is at its center. A stunt driver starts from the far end of the ferry and heads toward the shoreward end, accelerating from rest to 23 m/s relative to the boat at the instant he leaves the boat. The mass of car and driver is 1100 kg. (a) How much farther from shore is the end of the boat when the car reaches it? (b) How fast is the boat moving when the car departs?

53. Firefighters spray water horizontally at the rate of 41 kg/s from a nozzle mounted on a 12,000-kg fire truck. The water speed is 28 m/s relative to the truck. (a) Neglecting friction, what is the initial acceleration of the truck? (b) If the 12,000-kg truck mass includes 2400 kg of water, how fast will the truck be moving when the water is exhausted? *Hint:* Think about rockets.

54. A 36-kg child stands on frictionless ice, holding a box of negligible mass containing twenty 220-g snowballs. If the child tosses the snowballs one at a time, horizontally, at 14 m/s relative to herself, how fast will she be moving once the snowballs are gone? Use the approximation that the child ejects snow continuously—i.e., the rocket equation.

Supplementary Problems

55. A 55-kg sprinter is standing at the left end of a 240-kg cart moving to the left at 7.6 m/s. She runs to the right end and continues horizontally off the cart. What should be her speed relative to the cart in order to leave the cart with no horizontal velocity component relative to the ground?

56. The coefficient of static friction between the boots of a 78-kg firefighter and the ground is 0.63. The firefighter is holding a hose that spews water at 19 m/s. At what rate, in kilograms per second, can the hose supply water without the firefighter sliding backward?

57. Figure 10-32 shows a paraboloidal solid of constant density ρ. It extends a height h along the z axis, and is described by $z = ar^2$, where the units of a are m^{-1} and r is the radius in a plane perpendicular to the z axis. Find expressions for (a) the mass of the solid and (b) the z coordinate of its center of mass.

FIGURE 10-32 Problem 57.

58. Two canoes are gliding in parallel paths on water that offers essentially no resistance to their forward motion, one at 2.0 m/s and the other at 5.0 m/s. The mass of each canoe with its occupants and their gear is 210 kg. Just as the faster canoe comes alongside the slower one, occupants of the slower canoe toss gear into the faster one. (a) How much gear must they toss to bring the faster canoe's speed down to 4.5 m/s? (b) Could they make the speeds equal by tossing enough gear? (c) What happens to the slower canoe's speed? Assume the keels of the canoes prevent any sideways motion and that the gear is tossed perpendicular to the canoes' motion.

59. Cookie sheets move along a conveyor belt toward an oven, with mounds of unbaked dough dropping vertically onto the sheets at the rate of one 12-g mound every two seconds. What average force must the conveyor belt exert on a cookie sheet to keep it moving at a constant 50 cm/s?

60. The triangle of Fig. 10-33 has a density that varies in proportion to y^α, where α is a constant. Show that its center of mass is located at $y = (\alpha + 2)h/(\alpha + 3)$.

61. While standing on frictionless ice, you (mass 65.0 kg) toss a 4.50-kg rock with initial speed of 12.0 m/s. If the rock is 15.2 m from you when it lands, (a) at what angle did you toss it? (b) How fast are you moving?

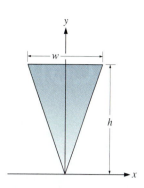

FIGURE 10-33 Problem 60.

62. A drunk driver in a 1600-kg car plows into a 1300-kg parked car with its brake set. Police measurements show that the two cars skid together a distance of 25 m before stopping. If the effective coefficient of friction is 0.77, how fast was the drunk going just before the collision?

63. A fireworks rocket is launched vertically upward at 40 m/s. At the peak of its trajectory, it explodes into two equal-mass fragments. One reaches the ground 2.87 s after the explosion. When does the second reach the ground?

64. A fire hose delivers 50 kg/s of water at 30 m/s. How many 75-kg firefighters are needed to hold the hose on muddy ground for which the coefficient of static friction is 0.35?

65. (a) Derive an expression for the thrust of a jet aircraft engine. Moving through the air with speed v, the engine takes in air at the rate dM_{in}/dt. It uses the air to burn fuel with a fuel/air ratio f (that is, f kg of fuel burned for each kg of air), and ejects the exhaust gases at speed v_{ex} with respect to the engine. (b) Use your result to find the thrust of a JT-8D engine on a Boeing 727 jetliner, for which $v_{ex} = 1034$ ft/s and $dM_{in}/dt = 323$ lb/s, and which consumes 3760 lb of fuel per hour while cruising at 605 mi/h.

66. Two blocks are sliding along a one-dimensional frictionless surface with speeds v_1 and v_2, when they collide. Use the conservation of momentum principle to show that the most kinetic energy is lost if they stick together.

67. An ideal spring of spring constant k rests on a frictionless surface. Blocks of mass m_1 and m_2 are pushed against the two ends of the spring until it is compressed a distance x from its equilibrium length. The blocks are then released. What are their speeds when they leave the spring?

68. (a) What depth of juice should be in the glass of Problem 45 to put the center of mass of the system at its lowest possible point? (b) Show that the center of mass is then at the surface of the juice.

11 Collisions

$\mathbf{v}_{in}$

$\mathbf{v}_{out}$

A collision is a brief interaction that involves large forces and abruptly changes the motion of one or both of the interacting bodies. Here a tennis ball and racket are about to collide; vectors represent incident and outgoing velocities.

On the highway, we try to avoid colliding with other cars. On the pool table, we tailor collisions to suit our purposes. In particle accelerators, we interpret collisions to reveal the innermost structure of matter. On a cosmic scale, we wonder if a collision between an asteroid and Earth led to the extinction of the dinosaurs (Fig. 11-1). Collisions are important features of our physical universe.

FIGURE 11-1 Celestial collisions are not uncommon in our solar system. This photo of Jupiter shows two bright spots (near bottom) that mark impacts of Comet Shoemaker-Levy 9 with the giant planet in 1994. The impact scars are approximately the size of Earth and were caused by comet fragments of roughly kilometer size, somewhat smaller than the object whose collision with Earth is believed responsible for the extinction of the dinosaurs.

A **collision** is a relatively violent interaction of objects that lasts for a short time. By "violent interaction" we mean that forces associated with the collision are much greater than any other forces that may be acting on the objects. By "short time" we mean short compared with time scales appropriate in describing the overall motion of the objects. A collision between two airplanes, for example, involves forces much greater than the gravitational and aerodynamic forces; the time interval over which the collision occurs is short compared with the overall flight times. Similarly, a collision between two galaxies may take millions of years, but that period is still short compared with the ages of the galaxies.

Our purpose in this chapter is to explore the principles that underlie the diversity of interactions that qualify as collisions, and to predict as much as possible about the outcome of a collision.

11-1 IMPULSE AND COLLISIONS

In a collision of two objects—like the foot and football in Fig. 11-2—the velocity of one or both objects is abruptly changed. We know, from Newton's laws of motion, that such a change means a force has been applied. The strong but short-duration force associated with a collision is called an **impulsive force**. Although the gravitational force also acts on the ball, during the collision the impulsive force is overwhelmingly dominant.

We can relate the impulsive force to the change in an object's momentum through Newton's second law:

$$\mathbf{F} = \frac{d\mathbf{p}}{dt}.$$

FIGURE 11-2 High-speed photo of a collision between a foot and a football. The strong impulsive force is evident in the deformation of the football. This force causes a rapid change in the ball's velocity. Vector $\mathbf{F}$ is the impulsive force on the ball; not shown is the paired force of the ball on the foot.

Multiplying this equation by dt and integrating from some time t_1 before the collision to a time t_2 after the collision, we have

$$\int_{t_1}^{t_2} \mathbf{F}\, dt = \int_{t_1}^{t_2} d\mathbf{p}.$$

The right-hand integral is just the change $\Delta\mathbf{p}$ that occurs during the collision. The integral on the left is known as the **impulse**, $\mathbf{I}$, associated with the collision. Our result then shows that the change in an object's momentum is equal to the

FIGURE 11-3 (*a*) Crash test of Volkswagen's New Beetle. (*b*) The impulsive force during such a crash is a complicated function of time. Average force is the height of the rectangle whose area is the same as that under the jagged curve.

(*a*)

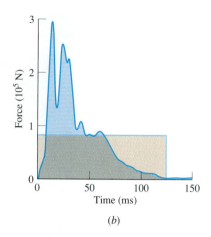

(*b*)

impulse:

$$I = \int_{t_1}^{t_2} F\, dt = \Delta p \,. \qquad (11\text{-}1)$$

The units of impulse are the same as those of momentum: kg·m/s, or, equivalently, N·s. Since the definite integral corresponds to the area under a curve, Equation 11-1 shows that the impulse is given geometrically by the area under the force-versus-time curve. It doesn't much matter whether the force curve includes any nonimpulsive forces that may be present, for our definition of a collision ensures that the change in momentum associated with nonimpulsive forces is small during the time of the collision.

Figure 11-3 shows the force as a function of time for an automobile crash test, the peaks and valleys of the curve occurring as parts of the car deform or break entirely. You might look at that graph, or at the dramatic distortion of the football in Fig. 11-2, and wonder how we're ever going to analyze such situations quantitatively. But that's just the point of treating collisions as short, intense events: we want to summarize the overall effect of a collision without treating the details of the interaction forces. That overall effect is summarized by the change in the momenta of the colliding objects. We can work backward from that change to determine the **average impulsive force** $\overline{\mathbf{F}}$—the force that, if applied constantly during the collision time Δt, would give the same change in momentum. That is,

$$\overline{\mathbf{F}} = \frac{\mathbf{I}}{\Delta t} = \frac{\Delta \mathbf{p}}{\Delta t} \,. \qquad (11\text{-}2)$$

Graphically, the average force is represented by the height of a rectangle whose area is the same as the actual impulse area $\int F\, dt$ (see Fig. 11-3).

Got It!

Which of the following qualify as collisions?
- A basketball rebounds off the backboard.
- Two magnets approach, their north poles facing. They repel and reverse direction without touching.
- A basketball flies through the air on a parabolic trajectory.

EXAMPLE 11-1	*Impulse*

A 150-g baseball is moving horizontally at 30 m/s just before reaching the bat. Bat and ball are then in contact for 2.0 ms. Find the impulse and the average impulsive force (a) if the hit is a line drive to center field at 45 m/s and (b) if the hit is a pop foul that starts straight up at 22 m/s.

Solution

In a coordinate system with x axis along the line from home plate to center field, the incoming momentum is

$$\mathbf{p}_1 = m\mathbf{v}_1 = (0.15 \text{ kg})(-30\hat{\imath} \text{ m/s}) = -4.5\hat{\imath} \text{ kg·m/s} .$$

For the line drive, the outgoing momentum is

$$\mathbf{p}_2 = m\mathbf{v}_2 = (0.15 \text{ kg})(45\hat{\imath} \text{ m/s}) = 6.8\hat{\imath} \text{ kg·m/s} ,$$

giving an impulse

$$\mathbf{I} = \Delta\mathbf{p} = (6.8\hat{\imath} \text{ kg·m/s}) - (-4.5\hat{\imath} \text{ kg·m/s}) = 11\hat{\imath} \text{ kg·m/s}$$

and an average force

$$\overline{\mathbf{F}} = \frac{\Delta\mathbf{p}}{\Delta t} = \frac{11\hat{\imath} \text{ kg·m/s}}{2.0\times10^{-3} \text{ s}} = 5.5\times10^3\hat{\imath} \text{ N} .$$

This is a large force, nearly 4000 times the gravitational force on the ball—thus justifying neglect of gravity during the collision.

For the pop foul, the outgoing momentum is in the y direction:

$$\mathbf{p}_2 = m\mathbf{v}_2 = (0.15 \text{ kg})(22\hat{\jmath} \text{ m/s}) = 3.3\hat{\jmath} \text{ kg·m/s} ,$$

so

$$\mathbf{I} = \Delta\mathbf{p} = (3.3\hat{\jmath} \text{ kg·m/s}) - (-4.5\hat{\imath} \text{ kg·m/s})$$
$$= 4.5\hat{\imath} + 3.3\hat{\jmath} \text{ kg·m/s}$$

and

$$\overline{\mathbf{F}} = \frac{\Delta\mathbf{p}}{\Delta t} = \frac{4.5\hat{\imath} + 3.3\hat{\jmath} \text{ kg·m/s}}{2.0\times10^{-3} \text{ s}}$$
$$= 2.3\times10^3\hat{\imath} + 1.7\times10^3\hat{\jmath} \text{ N} ,$$

or an average impulsive force of magnitude 2800 N. Large forces like this are typical of collisions, and explain why collisions often involve so much damage.

EXERCISE A 55-kg cyclist is riding a 10-kg bicycle at 7.5 m/s when she's struck by another cyclist. The collision lasts 0.11 s, after which the velocity of the first cyclist and her bicycle is $8.1\hat{\imath} + 3.2\hat{\jmath}$ m/s, where the x direction is that of the initial motion. Find the impulse and the magnitude of the average impulsive force on the cyclist, and compare the latter with her weight.

Answers: $\mathbf{I} = 39\hat{\imath} + 210\hat{\jmath}$ N·s; $F = 1900$ N, 3.5 times her weight

Some problems similar to Example 11-1: 2, 5, 6

11-2 COLLISIONS AND THE CONSERVATION LAWS

Often we know no more about the impulsive force of a collision than that it acts for a short time and produces abrupt changes in motion. Nevertheless, we can use the conservation laws developed in earlier chapters to relate the interacting objects' motions before and after collision. As always, conservation laws provide a "shortcut," giving us an overall picture lacking in some details. In the case of a collision involving an unknown impulsive force, those missing details are confined to the very short time of the collision.

Momentum

One thing we do know about impulsive forces between colliding objects is that they are *internal* to the system comprising those objects. But we found in the preceding chapter that only *external* forces can change a system's momentum. Therefore, the impulsive forces of a collision leave the total momentum of the colliding objects unchanged. And any *external* forces are, by the definition of a collision, negligible compared with the internal impulsive forces (as we found explicitly for the gravitational force on the baseball of Example 11-1). To a very good approximation, then, the total momentum of a colliding system is conserved during the collision.

FIGURE 11-4 (*a*) A rubber ball undergoes a nearly elastic collision with the ground, rebounding with outgoing speed v_{out} nearly equal to its incident speed v_{in}. (*b*) An automobile collision is invariably inelastic, with much of the kinetic energy lost to permanent deformation of the colliding vehicles.

(*a*)

(*b*)

Energy

What about kinetic energy? It may or may not be conserved during a collision. If kinetic energy is conserved, the collision is termed **elastic**. Like a completely frictionless surface, an **elastic collision** is an impossible idealization in the macroscopic world. In a macroscopic collision, some kinetic energy is inevitably transformed to other forms like sound, the random molecular motions that we call, loosely, "heat," or the energy associated with permanently deforming materials (Fig. 11-4). But some interactions in the atomic, nuclear, and elementary particle realms are elastic. And macroscopic objects such as billiard balls, trampolines, and hockey pucks undergo nearly elastic collisions. The important criterion is that in an elastic collision, the internal forces must be conservative. Then kinetic energy is stored temporarily as potential energy, all of which is again released as kinetic energy by the time the collision is over.

When mechanical energy is lost during a collision, the collision is **inelastic**. In a **totally inelastic collision**, the colliding objects stick together to form one composite object. Even then, mechanical energy is usually not all lost; complete loss of mechanical energy in most cases would violate conservation of momentum. But a totally inelastic collision involves the maximum loss of mechanical energy that is consistent with momentum conservation. In general, we can determine the motion after collision only for the case of elastic or totally inelastic collisions; in intermediate cases, like that shown in Fig. 11-5, we must know just how much energy is lost before we can solve for the post-collision motion. Problems 16, 66, 68, and 71 treat such intermediate cases.

FIGURE 11-5 An arrow passes through an apple. This is an example of a collision that's neither fully elastic nor fully inelastic.

11-3 INELASTIC COLLISIONS

6.2

Collisions and Elasticity

The motion after a totally inelastic collision is determined entirely by the conservation of momentum principle. We analyzed some totally inelastic collisions in the previous chapter; for instance, measuring the speed of the hockey puck in Example 10-6 involved a totally inelastic collision.

Consider two objects with masses m_1 and m_2 and initial velocities $\mathbf{v}_{1i}$ and $\mathbf{v}_{2i}$ that undergo a totally inelastic collision. That is, after collision they stick together to form a single composite body of mass $m_1 + m_2$ and final velocity $\mathbf{v}_f$. Conservation of momentum states that the initial and final momenta of this two-particle system must be the same:

$$m_1\mathbf{v}_1 + m_2\mathbf{v}_2 = (m_1 + m_2)\mathbf{v}_f. \quad \text{(totally inelastic collision)} \quad (11\text{-}3)$$

Given four of the five quantities m_1, $\mathbf{v}_{1i}$, m_2, $\mathbf{v}_{2i}$, and $\mathbf{v}_f$, we can solve for the fifth. Often, but not always, the unknown is the final velocity:

$$\mathbf{v}_f = \frac{m_1\mathbf{v}_{1i} + m_2\mathbf{v}_{2i}}{m_1 + m_2}. \qquad (11\text{-}4)$$

Calculating the total kinetic energy before and after the collision will convince you that this collision is indeed inelastic (see Problem 21).

EXAMPLE 11-2	*The Ballistic Pendulum*

The ballistic pendulum is a device used to measure the speeds of fast-moving objects such as bullets. It consists of a wooden block of mass M suspended from vertical strings (Fig. 11-6). When a bullet strikes the block, it undergoes an inelastic collision and embeds itself in the block. If the bullet has mass m, and if the block rises a maximum height h after the collision, show that the speed of the bullet is $[(m + M)/m]\sqrt{2gh}$.

Solution

To solve this problem, we deal separately first with the collision and then with the subsequent rise of the block. Understanding the difference in the way we handle these two steps will strengthen your confidence in applying the conservation laws.

1. The incoming bullet undergoes an inelastic collision with the block. Mechanical energy is not conserved. But because the collision takes such a short time, external forces—here gravity and the string tension—have little effect and the momentum of the bullet + block system is essentially conserved. So we can write:

$$mv = (m + M)V,$$

where v is the initial speed of the bullet and V the speed of the bullet/block combination after the collision. Solving for V gives $V = mv/(m + M)$.

2. As the block swings upward, the external forces of gravity and string tension act to alter the momentum of the bullet + block system. Momentum is not conserved. But gravity is a conservative force, and the string tension acts at right angles to the motion and therefore does no work. So mechanical energy is conserved in the upward swing of the block. Taking the zero of potential energy in the block's initial position, we can then equate the kinetic energy just after the collision to the potential energy when the block is at its maximum height:

$$\tfrac{1}{2}(m + M)V^2 = (m + M)gh.$$

Now we relate the two parts of the problem. Using our expression for V in the statement of energy conservation, we have

$$\frac{1}{2}\left(\frac{mv}{m + M}\right)^2 = gh,$$

FIGURE 11-6 A simplified ballistic pendulum (Example 11-2).

which we can solve for v to get

$$v = \left(\frac{m + M}{m}\right)\sqrt{2gh}.$$

Tip

Know When to Apply Conservation Laws This example emphasizes the different conditions under which the conservation laws for momentum and energy apply. In the first part of the example we had an inelastic collision in which energy was explicitly *not* conserved. But momentum *was* conserved because the collision took place so rapidly that any impulse from external forces acting on the bullet + block system was negligible. In the second part the presence of a nonzero net force due to gravity and string tension meant that momentum was not conserved. But one of those forces was conservative and the other did no work, so mechanical energy was conserved. We needed both conservation laws—applied at different stages in the event being analyzed—to work this example.

EXERCISE A 950-kg car is stopped on an icy road at the bottom of a hill, facing uphill. It's hit from behind by a 7600-kg truck moving at 50 km/h. If the collision is totally inelastic, to what vertical distance up the hill does the combined wreckage slide?

Answer: 7.8 m

Some problems similar to Example 11-2: 17, 19, 20, 63

EXAMPLE 11-3 | A Fusion Reaction

In a fusion reaction, two deuterium nuclei (^{2}H) combine to form a helium nucleus (^{4}He). One of the incident nuclei is initially moving in the $+x$ direction at 3.5 Mm/s, and the helium nucleus is subsequently detected moving at 2.3 Mm/s at an angle $\theta = 21°$ to the x axis (Fig. 11-7). Find the initial velocity of the second deuterium nucleus.

Solution

Momentum conservation, as stated in Equation 11-3, entirely determines the outcome of this totally inelastic collision. Solving that equation for the initial velocity $\mathbf{v}_2$ of the second deuterium nucleus, we have

$$\mathbf{v}_2 = \frac{(m_1 + m_2)\mathbf{v}_f - m_1\mathbf{v}_1}{m_2},$$

where $\mathbf{v}_f$ is the velocity of the resulting helium nucleus. Breaking this equation into components gives

x component:

$$v_{2x} = \frac{(m_1 + m_2)v_{fx} - m_1 v_{1x}}{m_2}$$

$$= \frac{(2.0 \text{ u} + 2.0 \text{ u})(2.3 \text{ Mm/s})\cos 21° - (2.0 \text{ u})(3.5 \text{ Mm/s})}{2.0 \text{ u}}$$

$$= 0.79 \text{ Mm/s}$$

y component:

$$v_{2y} = \frac{(m_1 + m_2)v_{fy}}{m_2} = \frac{(2.0 \text{ u} + 2.0 \text{ u})(2.3 \text{ Mm/s})\sin 21°}{2.0 \text{ u}}$$

$$= 1.65 \text{ Mm/s},$$

where we've used the fact that $\mathbf{v}_1$ is entirely in the x direction. The magnitude of $\mathbf{v}_2$ is then $v_2 = \sqrt{v_{2x}^2 + v_{2y}^2} = 1.8$ Mm/s, while $\mathbf{v}_2$ makes an angle $\phi = \tan^{-1}(v_{2y}/v_{2x}) = 64°$ with the x axis. Figure 11-7 shows the velocity vectors for all three nuclei.

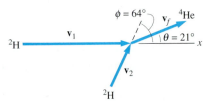

FIGURE 11-7 Velocity vectors for Example 11-3.

Does this problem remind you of the radioactive decay of Example 10-7? It should. Fusion and radioactive decay are essentially inverse processes. The same momentum conservation principle governs both, and the same mathematical techniques apply.

Tip

Know When to Avoid Unit Conversions Although we stress the importance of SI units, there are instances where unit conversions are unnecessary. The equations derived in this example have mass in both numerator and denominator, so mass units cancel, and therefore, it doesn't matter what units we use. The nuclear mass numbers (e.g., 2 in ^{2}H and 4 in ^{4}He) suffice, and there's no need to convert to kilograms.

EXERCISE A 9400-kg truck is moving eastward at 35 km/h on an icy road when it collides with a 2300-kg car. The two vehicles move off together at 14° north of east, at 41 km/h. Find the initial velocity of the car.

Answer: 78 km/h at 40° north of east

Some problems similar to Example 11-3: 22, 25, 28

11-4 ELASTIC COLLISIONS

We've seen that momentum is essentially conserved in any collision. In an elastic collision, kinetic energy is conserved as well. In the most general case of a two-body collision, we consider two objects of masses m_1 and m_2, moving initially with velocities $\mathbf{v}_{1i}$ and $\mathbf{v}_{2i}$, respectively. Their final velocities after collision are $\mathbf{v}_{1f}$ and $\mathbf{v}_{2f}$. Then the conservation statements for momentum and kinetic energy become

$$m_1\mathbf{v}_{1i} + m_2\mathbf{v}_{2i} = m_1\mathbf{v}_{1f} + m_2\mathbf{v}_{2f} \tag{11-5}$$

and

$$\tfrac{1}{2}m_1 v_{1i}^2 + \tfrac{1}{2}m_2 v_{2i}^2 = \tfrac{1}{2}m_1 v_{1f}^2 + \tfrac{1}{2}m_2 v_{2f}^2. \tag{11-6}$$

Given the initial velocities, we would like to predict the outcome of a collision. In the totally inelastic two-dimensional collision of the preceding section, we had two equations (Equations 11-3 and 11-4, the two components of the vector momentum conservation equation) and two unknowns (the magnitude and direction of the one final velocity, $\mathbf{v}_f$ in Equation 11-4). Mathematically, we had enough information to solve the system. Here, in the two-dimensional elastic case, we have the two components of the momentum conservation equation 11-5 and the single scalar equation for energy conservation 11-6. But we have four unknowns—the magnitudes and directions of both final velocities. With three equations and four unknowns, we don't have enough information to solve the general two-dimensional elastic collision. Later in this section we will see how other information can help us solve such problems. First, though, we look at the special case of a one-dimensional elastic collision.

Elastic Collisions in One Dimension

When two objects collide head-on, the internal forces act along the same line as the incident motion, and the objects' subsequent motion must therefore be along that same line (Fig. 11-8). Although such one-dimensional collisions are a very special case, they do occur and they provide much insight into the more general case.

In the one-dimensional case, the momentum conservation equation 11-5 has only one nontrivial component:

$$m_1 v_{1i} + m_2 v_{2i} = m_1 v_{1f} + m_2 v_{2f}. \tag{11-5a}$$

where the v's stand for velocity components, rather than magnitudes, and can therefore be positive or negative. If we collect together the terms in Equations 11-5a and 11-6 that are associated with each mass, we have

$$m_1(v_{1i} - v_{1f}) = m_2(v_{2f} - v_{2i}) \tag{11-5b}$$

and

$$m_1(v_{1i}^2 - v_{1f}^2) = m_2(v_{2f}^2 - v_{2i}^2). \tag{11-6a}$$

But $a^2 - b^2 = (a + b)(a - b)$, so Equation 11-6a can be written

$$m_1(v_{1i} - v_{1f})(v_{1i} + v_{1f}) = m_2(v_{2f} - v_{2i})(v_{2f} + v_{2i}). \tag{11-6b}$$

Dividing the left and right sides of Equation 11-6b by the corresponding sides of Equation 11-5b then gives

$$v_{1i} + v_{1f} = v_{2f} + v_{2i}. \tag{11-7}$$

Rearranging Equation 11-7 shows that

$$v_{1i} - v_{2i} = v_{2f} - v_{1f}. \tag{11-8}$$

What does this equation tell us? Both sides describe the relative velocity between the two particles; the equation therefore shows that the relative speed remains unchanged after the collision, although the direction reverses. If one object is approaching another at a relative speed of 5 m/s, then after collision it will be receding at 5 m/s.

Continuing our search for the final velocities, we solve Equation 11-8 for v_{2f}.

$$v_{2f} = v_{1i} - v_{2i} + v_{1f},$$

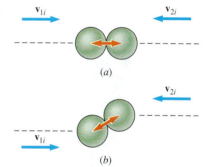

FIGURE 11-8 (a) When two objects collide head-on, internal forces act along the same line as the incident motion, and the subsequent motion is also along this line. The collision is one-dimensional. (b) If the collision is not head-on, internal forces act in new directions, and the motion is necessarily two-dimensional.

(a) Case 1

(b) Case 2

(c) Case 3

FIGURE 11-9 Three special cases of one-dimensional collisions. (a) In case 1, a ping-pong ball strikes a bowling ball and rebounds with essentially its initial speed; the bowling ball remains at rest. (b) In case 2 the colliding objects have equal masses. Here one pendulum bob strikes another of equal mass; the first stops, having transferred all its energy and momentum to the second. (c) In case 3 a more massive object (here a golf club) strikes a much less massive one (the ball). The club's motion continues unchanged while the ball takes off with essentially twice the club's speed.

and use this result in Equation 11-5a:

$$m_1 v_{1i} + m_2 v_{2i} = m_1 v_{1f} + m_2 (v_{1i} - v_{2i} + v_{1f}).$$

Solving for v_{1f} then gives

$$v_{1f} = \frac{m_1 - m_2}{m_1 + m_2} v_{1i} + \frac{2m_2}{m_1 + m_2} v_{2i}. \tag{11-9a}$$

Problem 46 asks you to show similarly that

$$v_{2f} = \frac{2m_1}{m_1 + m_2} v_{1i} + \frac{m_2 - m_1}{m_1 + m_2} v_{2i}. \tag{11-9b}$$

Equations 11-9a and 11-9b are our desired result, expressing the final velocities in terms of the initial velocities alone.

To see that these results make sense, we suppose that $v_{2i} = 0$. (This is really not a special case, since we can always work in a frame of reference in which m_2 is initially at rest.) We then consider the three special cases of one-dimensional elastic collisions illustrated in Fig. 11-9.

Case 1: $m_1 \ll m_2$ (Fig. 11-9a) For this case, picture a ping-pong ball colliding with a bowling ball (Fig. 11-9a), or any object colliding elastically with a perfectly rigid surface. Setting $v_{2i} = 0$ in Equations 11-9, and dropping m_1 as being negligible compared with m_2, Equations 11-9 become simply

$$v_{1f} = -v_{1i}$$

and

$$v_{2f} = 0.$$

That is, the lighter object rebounds with no change in speed, while the heavier object remains at rest. Does this make sense in light of the conservation laws that Equations 11-9 are supposed to reflect? Clearly energy is conserved: the kinetic energy of m_2 remains zero and the kinetic energy $\frac{1}{2}m_1 v_1^2$ is unchanged. But what about momentum? The momentum of the lighter object has changed, from $m_1 v_{1i}$ to $-m_1 v_{1i}$. But momentum *is* conserved; the momentum given up by the lighter object is absorbed by the heavier object. In the limit of an arbitrarily large m_2, the heavier object can absorb huge amounts of momentum mv without acquiring significant speed. If we "back off" from the extreme case that m_1 can be neglected altogether compared with m_2, we would find that the lighter object rebounds with slightly reduced speed and that the heavier object begins moving very slowly in the opposite direction (see Problem 67).

Case 2: $m_1 = m_2$ (Fig. 11-9b) Again setting $v_{2i} = 0$, Equations 11-9 now give

$$v_{1f} = 0$$

and

$$v_{2f} = v_{1i}.$$

So the first object stops abruptly, transferring all its energy and momentum to the second object. For purposes of energy transfer, two equal-mass particles are perfectly "matched." We'll encounter analogous instances of energy transfer "matching" when we discuss wave motion and again in connection with electric circuits.

*Activ*Physics

6.3
Momentum Conservation and Collisions

Case 3: $m_1 \gg m_2$ (Fig. 11-9c) Now, with v_{2i} again set to zero, Equations 11-9 give

$$v_{1f} = v_{1i}$$

and

$$v_{2f} = 2v_{1i},$$

where we've neglected m_2 compared with m_1. So here the more massive object barrels right on with no change in motion, while the lighter one heads off with twice the speed of the massive one. How are momentum and energy conserved in this case? In the extreme limit where we neglect the mass m_2 its energy and momentum are negligible. Essentially all the energy and momentum remain with the more massive object, and both these quantities are essentially unchanged in the collision.

Although we've found it convenient to consider these three special cases of elastic collisions, you might convince yourself that cases 1 and 3 are really the same. Both describe a collision between objects of very unequal mass—case 1 in the reference frame of the massive object and case 3 in the reference frame where the less massive object is initially at rest.

Got It!

An object strikes another, initially at rest. The collision reverses the incident object's direction of motion. Which object is more massive?

APPLICATION	*Nuclear Reactor Engineering*

Our analysis of three special cases shows that energy transfer occurs most efficiently in a collision between equal-mass objects. This fact has important implications for nuclear reactor engineering. The fission reactions that sustain a reactor are far more likely to occur if the neutrons striking uranium-235 nuclei are moving slowly. But the fission of U-235 releases fast neutrons. So the uranium fuel rods in a nuclear reactor are surrounded by a substance called a *moderator,* whose job is to slow down the fast neutrons. Our case 2 analysis shows that the most effective slowing down occurs in collisions of equal masses. Most reactors use water as the moderator; the protons comprising the nuclei of the hydrogen atoms have nearly the same mass as a neutron and are therefore especially good at slowing neutrons.

EXAMPLE 11-4	*Car-Truck Collisions*

A truck of mass $9M$ is moving at speed $v = 15$ km/h when it collides head-on with a parked car of mass M. Spring-mounted bumpers ensure that the collision is essentially elastic. Describe the subsequent motion of each vehicle. Repeat for the case of the car moving at speed $v = 15$ km/h and colliding with the stationary truck. What fraction of the incident vehicle's kinetic energy is transferred in each case?

Solution

For the first case, we can set $m_1 = 9M$, $v_{1i} = v = 15$ km/h, $m_2 = M$, and $v_{2i} = 0$. Then Equations 11-9 give

$$v_{1f} = \frac{9M - M}{9M + M}v, = \tfrac{4}{5}v = 12 \text{ km/h}$$

and

$$v_{2f} = \frac{(2)(9M)}{9M + M} v = \tfrac{9}{5} v = 27 \text{ km/h}.$$

So both vehicles move off in the same direction, with the truck's speed reduced by 20% and the car being propelled to 27 km/h. The initial energy of the truck is $\tfrac{9}{2} Mv^2$ or $4.5Mv^2$; the final energy of the car is $\tfrac{1}{2} M(\tfrac{9}{5}v)^2$ or $1.6Mv^2$. So 1.6/4.5, or 36% of the truck's energy is transferred in this case.

For the second collision, we set $m_1 = M$ and $m_2 = 9M$, giving

$$v_{1f} = \frac{M - 9M}{M + 9M} v = -\tfrac{4}{5} v = -12 \text{ km/h}$$

and

$$v_{2f} = \frac{2M}{M + 9M} v = \tfrac{1}{5} v = 3.0 \text{ km/h},$$

so the car rebounds with 80% of its initial speed and the truck picks up a relatively small speed. Now the initial energy of the

car is $\tfrac{1}{2} Mv^2$, while the final energy of the truck is $\tfrac{9}{2} M(\tfrac{1}{5}v)^2 = 0.18Mv^2$, so again 36% of the energy is transferred. Even though the mass ratio is quite large, neither collision approaches closely the case 1 or case 3 limit. Problem 40 explores the approach to those limits.

EXERCISE In a nuclear reactor, a neutron (mass 1 u) moving at 6.9×10^6 m/s collides elastically, head-on, with a carbon-12 nucleus (mass 12 u) initially at rest. Find the velocity of each particle after the collision, and the fraction of the neutron's kinetic energy transferred to the carbon nucleus.

Answers: $v_n = -5.8 \times 10^6$ m/s (minus indicates direction reversal); $v_c = 1.1 \times 10^6$ m/s; 28% of neutron energy transferred

Some problems similar to Example 11-4: 32, 34, 37, 40

EXAMPLE 11-5	"Weighing" an Elementary Particle

In a nuclear experiment, a particle of unknown mass moving at 460 km/s undergoes a head-on elastic collision with a carbon nucleus (^{12}C; mass 12 u) moving at 220 km/s in the same direction. After collision, the carbon continues in the same direction at 340 km/s as illustrated in Fig. 11-10a. Find the mass and final velocity of the unknown particle.

Solution

If we designate the carbon as particle 2, we then know all quantities in Equation 11-9b except the unknown mass m_1. Multiplying that equation through by $(m_1 + m_2)$, we have

$$(m_1 + m_2)v_{2f} = 2m_1 v_{1i} + (m_2 - m_1)v_{2i}.$$

Solving for m_1 then gives

$$m_1 = \frac{m_2(v_{2i} - v_{2f})}{v_{2f} - 2v_{1i} + v_{2i}}$$

$$= \frac{(12 \text{ u})(220 \text{ km/s} - 340 \text{ km/s})}{340 \text{ km/s} - (2)(460 \text{ km/s}) + 220 \text{ km/s}} = 4.0 \text{ u}.$$

The unknown particle is therefore probably an alpha particle (^{4}He, or helium nucleus). Knowing m_1, we use Equation 11-9a to find v_{1f}:

$$v_{1f} = \frac{4.0 \text{ u} - 12 \text{ u}}{16 \text{ u}} (460 \text{ km/s}) + \frac{(2)(12 \text{ u})}{16 \text{ u}} (220 \text{ km/s})$$

$$= 100 \text{ km/s}.$$

Are these results consistent with our earlier finding that a less massive particle should rebound off a more massive one? After all, both particles now seem to continue in the same direction. But there's no inconsistency; our earlier conclusion was based on one particle's being initially at rest, while here both have

FIGURE 11-10 The collision of Example 11-5 (a) in the original reference frame and (b) in a reference frame moving with the initial 220 km/s velocity of the carbon nucleus.

nonzero initial velocities. If we look at the situation in a reference frame where the carbon is initially at rest, we have $v_{1i} = 460$ km/s $- 220$ km/s $= 240$ km/s, while $v_{1f} = 100$ km/s $- 220$ km/s $= -120$ km/s. The less massive nucleus does rebound, as expected. Figure 11-10 summarizes the collision in both reference frames; the change of reference frames is explored further in Problem 41.

EXERCISE A 2.1×10^4 kg railroad freight car moving at 32 km/h is struck from behind by a second freight car moving at 43 km/h. The collision is elastic, and afterward the first car is moving at 38 km/h in its original direction. Find the mass and final velocity of the second car.

Answers: $m = 7.88 \times 10^3$ kg; $v = 27$ km/h (same direction)

Some problems similar to Example 11-5: 35, 36, 38

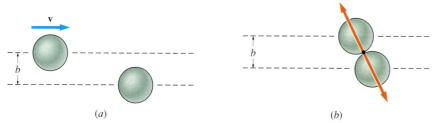

FIGURE 11-11 (*a*) The impact parameter is the perpendicular distance *b* between the centers of the colliding spheres. (*b*) The impact parameter determines where the spheres touch. Since the contact forces of the collision are perpendicular to the surfaces, the impact parameter carries information about the directions of the forces and therefore about the subsequent motion.

Elastic Collisions in Two Dimensions

To analyze an elastic collision in two dimensions, we must use the full vector statement of momentum conservation (Equation 11-5), along with the statement of energy conservation (Equation 11-6). But we found earlier that these equations alone don't provide enough information to solve the problem. In a collision between reasonably simple macroscopic objects, that information may be provided by the so-called **impact parameter**, a measure of how much the collision differs from being head-on (Fig. 11-11). More typically, though, and this is especially true with atomic and nuclear interactions, the necessary information must be supplied by measurements done after the collision. Knowing the direction of motion of one particle after collision, for example, provides enough information to analyze the collision if the masses and initial velocities are also known.

6.5
Car Collision: Two Dimensions

| **EXAMPLE 11-6** | *Croquet* |

A moving croquet ball strikes a stationary one of equal mass. The collision is elastic, and the incident ball goes off at 30° to its original direction (Fig. 11-12). In what direction does the other ball move?

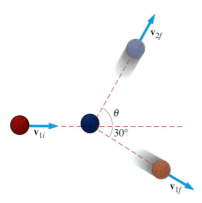

FIGURE 11-12 A collision between equal mass croquet balls (Example 11-6).

Solution

Momentum is always conserved in a collision, and since this collision is elastic, so is kinetic energy. So the physics of the problem is contained entirely in Equations 11-5 and 11-6, which state conservation of momentum and energy, respectively. The rest is algebra.

In a two-dimensional problem such as this one, the momentum equation 11-5 has two components, so we have a total of three equations. If we were asked to analyze the situation completely, we could solve these for three unknowns—the final speeds of both balls, and the direction of the struck ball. But here we're asked only for the direction of the struck ball. Although we could grind through all the algebra, a little cleverness will reduce the amount of math needed.

Since the two balls' masses are equal, the mass cancels from the conservation equations 11-5 and 11-6. Furthermore, the struck ball is initially at rest, so $\mathbf{v}_{2i} = 0$. Then the conservation equations become

$$\text{momentum:} \qquad \mathbf{v}_{1i} = \mathbf{v}_{1f} + \mathbf{v}_{2f}$$

and

$$\text{energy:} \qquad v_{1i}^2 = v_{1f}^2 + v_{2f}^2.$$

Now here's the clever part. The momentum equation is still a vector equation. Rather than write it as two component equations, however, let's take the dot product of each side of this vector equation with itself. Why do that? Two reasons: First, the dot product of vectors involves the angle between them—and an angle is what we're asked to find. Second, the energy equation contains the *squares* of the various speeds. Forming the dot product of the momentum equation with itself will also generate squares of the speeds, so we'll be able to combine the two equations.

The dot product is distributive and commutative, so here's what we get when we dot the momentum equation with itself:

$$\mathbf{v}_{1i} \cdot \mathbf{v}_{1i} = (\mathbf{v}_{1f} + \mathbf{v}_{2f}) \cdot (\mathbf{v}_{1f} + \mathbf{v}_{2f})$$

$$= \mathbf{v}_{1f} \cdot \mathbf{v}_{1f} + \mathbf{v}_{2f} \cdot \mathbf{v}_{2f} + 2\mathbf{v}_{1f} \cdot \mathbf{v}_{2f}.$$

Recall that the dot product of two vectors is the product of their magnitudes with the cosine of the angle between them: $\mathbf{A} \cdot \mathbf{B} = AB \cos\theta$. Since the angle between a vector and itself is zero, the dot product of a vector with itself is just the square of its magnitude: $\mathbf{A} \cdot \mathbf{A} = A^2 \cos(0) = A^2$. So our equation becomes

$$v_{1i}^2 = v_{1f}^2 + v_{2f}^2 + 2v_{1f}v_{2f}\cos(\theta + 30°),$$

where the argument of the cosine follows because, as Fig. 11-12 shows, the angle between $\mathbf{v}_{1f}$ and $\mathbf{v}_{2f}$ is $\theta + 30°$. We now subtract the energy equation from this new equation to get

$$2v_{1f}v_{2f}\cos(\theta + 30°) = 0.$$

But neither of the final speeds is zero, so this equation requires that $\cos(\theta + 30°) = 0$. Thus $\theta + 30° = 90°$, and our answer follows: $\theta = 60°$.

Note that the two post-collision velocities are at 90°. This result holds in any two-dimensional elastic collision between equal mass objects, in a frame where one object is initially at rest. Although this example did not ask about the post-collision speeds, those could be found from the components of the momentum equation once we found the unknown angle.

EXERCISE A proton moving at 1.45 Mm/s collides elastically with a stationary proton. The incident proton's velocity is deflected by 20° from its original direction. Find the final speeds of both protons.

Answer: 1.31 Mm/s, 0.613 Mm/s for incident and struck protons, respectively

Some problems similar to Example 11-6: 43, 44, 47, 48, 50, 55

The Center-of-Mass Frame

Two-dimensional collisions take a particularly simple form in a frame of reference moving with the center of mass of the colliding particles, since the total momentum in such a frame must be zero. That remains true after a collision, which involves only *internal* forces which, as we found in the preceding chapter, cannot affect the motion of the center of mass. Therefore, both the initial and final momenta form pairs of oppositely directed vectors of equal magnitude, as shown in Fig. 11-13a. In an elastic collision, energy conservation requires further that the incident and final momenta have the same values, so a single number—the angle θ in Fig. 11-13a—completely describes the collision.

It is often easier to analyze a collision by transforming to the center-of-mass frame, doing the analysis, and then transforming the resulting momentum and velocity vectors back to the original or "lab" frame. High-energy physicists routinely make such transformations as they seek to understand the fundamental forces between elementary particles. Those forces are described most simply in the center-of-mass frame of colliding particles, but in some experiments—those where lighter particles slam into massive nuclei or stationary targets—the physicists and their particle accelerators are not in the center-of-mass frame (Fig. 11-13b). (In contrast, many high-energy experiments involve collisions between oppositely directed beams of identical-mass particles. Here the center of mass of the opposing beams is at rest in the laboratory, so there's no need to make a transformation.)

(a)

(b)

FIGURE 11-13 (a) An elastic collision viewed in the center-of-mass frame. Since the system has zero momentum in this frame, the initial and final momentum vectors form pairs with equal magnitudes and opposite directions. (b) A collision between a high-energy proton (coming in from top) and a stationary proton results in a spray of particles. The particles' tracks are revealed by their interactions with atoms in a fluid background.

APPLICATION	*Gravity's Slingshot*

Interplanetary space travel provides an unusual example of elastic collisions. To get spacecraft such as the Galileo Jupiter probe or the Cassini Saturn mission to the outer planets, engineers direct them first inward to a close encounter with Venus and then on to another close pass by Earth. In both encounters the spacecraft picks up speed it needs for its outward journey. A similar effect occurred with the Pioneer and Voyager missions, where the spacecraft gained sufficient speed in close encounters with Jupiter to allow them to leave the solar system forever.

What do these space maneuvers have to do with collisions? A close encounter with a planet is a relatively short duration event in the years-long flight of an interplanetary spacecraft. And the $1/r^2$ falloff of the gravitational force ensures that the force a planet exerts on a spacecraft is significant only when close to the planet. So the planetary encounter meets our criteria for a collision: it's an event of limited duration during which a strong impulsive force acts. It doesn't matter that the impulsive force in this case is the attractive force of gravity; we've seen that details of the impulsive force don't matter when all we're interested in is the motion before and after the collision.

If we analyze the encounter in the reference frame of the spacecraft as it approaches the planet, it's a two-dimensional version of the case 3 collision we considered in Section 11-4. In this case a massive object collides with one of much lower mass, "kicking" the lighter object up to a higher speed. You can also understand the spacecraft's speed increase by considering the collision first in the planet's reference frame, then in the Sun's. In the planet's frame, energy conservation shows that the spacecraft approaches, speeds up as it falls toward the planet, swings around and recedes in a different direction with the same speed it had on approach (Fig. 11-14a). But in the Sun's reference frame, the planet is moving. If the spacecraft approaches the planet from behind, it leaves with additional

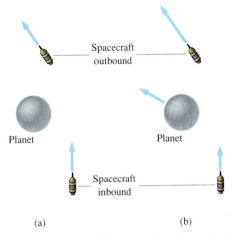

(a)   (b)

FIGURE 11-14 A gravity-assist spacecraft trajectory involves what is essentially an elastic collision with a planet. (a) In the planet's frame of reference, the spacecraft's inbound and outbound speeds are the same. (b) In the Sun's reference frame, the spacecraft gains energy from the planet's orbital motion.

kinetic energy gained from the planet's orbital motion (Fig. 11-14b). The planet actually slows very slightly, but the spacecraft's comparatively tiny mass makes this effect negligible.

Figure 11-15 shows the trajectory of the Cassini mission to Saturn, launched in 1997. This complicated flight path includes two Venus encounters, and one each with Earth and Jupiter, before arrival at Saturn in 2004. Energy gains at these planetary encounters reduce the overall flight time to 6.7 years; without them this trip would take many decades. Given existing rockets, some interplanetary missions would be impossible altogether without gravity assist.

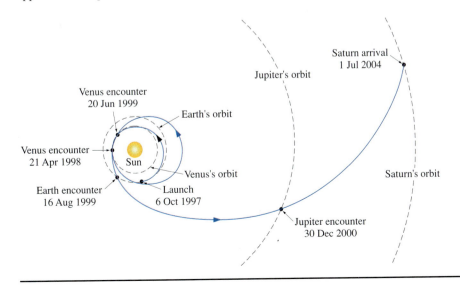

FIGURE 11-15 Trajectory of the Cassini mission to Saturn, showing two encounters with Venus and one each with Earth and Jupiter.

CHAPTER SYNOPSIS

Summary

1. A **collision** is a relatively violent interaction between two objects that takes place over a short period of time. An **impulsive force** acts between the colliding objects; this force is much stronger than any external force acting on either object.

2. The **impulse** imparted to an object is given by integrating the impulsive force over time; Newton's second law shows that the impulse is equal to the change in the object's momentum:

$$I = \int_{t_1}^{t_2} F \, dt = \Delta p \,.$$

The average value $\overline{F}$ of the impulsive force is given by the impulse divided by the time interval Δt over which the force acts:

$$\overline{F} = \frac{I}{\Delta t} = \frac{\Delta p}{\Delta t} \,.$$

3. Because impulsive forces acting during a collision are internal to the system of colliding objects, they cancel in pairs and therefore cannot change the momentum of the system. Any external forces are small compared with the impulsive forces, so to a good approximation **momentum is conserved during a collision**.

4. If kinetic energy is not conserved during a collision, the collision is **inelastic**. The maximum loss of kinetic energy occurs when the colliding objects stick together; then the collision is **totally inelastic**. In a totally inelastic collision, the final velocity $\mathbf{v}_f$ is determined entirely by the momentum conservation equation:

$$m_1 \mathbf{v}_{1i} + m_2 \mathbf{v}_{2i} = (m_1 + m_2) \mathbf{v}_f \,,$$

where m_1 and m_2 are the masses of the colliding objects.

5. In an **elastic collision**, kinetic energy is conserved. The relation between the initial and final velocities is governed by conservation of momentum and conservation of energy:

$$m_1 \mathbf{v}_{1i} + m_2 \mathbf{v}_{2i} = m_1 \mathbf{v}_{1f} + m_2 \mathbf{v}_{2f}$$
$$\tfrac{1}{2} m_1 v_{1i}^2 + \tfrac{1}{2} m_2 v_{2i}^2 = \tfrac{1}{2} m_1 v_{1f}^2 + \tfrac{1}{2} m_2 v_{2f}^2 \,.$$

In the general case, these equations are not sufficient to solve for the final velocities. Additional information, such as the direction of one of the final velocities or the details of the collision, must also be used. In the special case of a one-dimensional collision, the momentum and energy conservation equations combine to determine the final velocities:

$$v_{1f} = \frac{m_1 - m_2}{m_1 + m_2} v_{1i} + \frac{2m_2}{m_1 + m_2} v_{2i}$$

$$v_{2f} = \frac{2m_1}{m_1 + m_2} v_{1i} + \frac{m_2 - m_1}{m_1 + m_2} v_{2i} \,.$$

Terms You Should Understand

(Pairs are closely related terms whose distinction is important; number in parentheses is chapter section where term first appears.)

collision (introduction)
impulse (11-1)
impulsive force, average impulsive force (11-1)
elastic collision, inelastic collision (11-2)
totally inelastic collision (11-2)

Symbols You Should Recognize

I (11-1)

Problems You Should Be Able to Solve

calculating momentum changes given impulse (11-1)
calculating average impulsive force given momentum change and collision time (11-1)
solving for both components of the final velocity, or for any other pair of unknowns, in a totally inelastic collision (11-3)
solving for any two unknowns in a one-dimensional elastic collision (11-4)
solving for unknown quantities in a two-dimensional elastic collision, given sufficient information (11-4)

Limitations to Keep in Mind

Conservation of momentum holds during a collision only to the extent that the impulsive forces of the collision are far greater than any external forces acting on the system during the collision.
A perfectly elastic collision is an impossibility in the macroscopic realm.

QUESTIONS

1. Why do we require a short time interval and strong impulsive forces for an interaction to qualify as a collision? What is meant by "short" and "strong" in this context?
2. Two identical objects undergo collisions where the impulsive forces, as functions of time, are shown in Fig. 11-16. Which object's momentum undergoes the greater change?

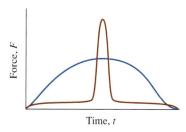

FIGURE 11-16 Question 2.

3. When a ball bounces off a wall, its momentum is reversed. How can this be, in view of the law of conservation of momentum?
4. A high jumper runs to the takeoff point with horizontal but no vertical momentum. When he jumps, where does his vertical momentum come from?
5. As you jump off a table, you bend your knees on landing. How does this lessen the shock to your body?
6. Figure 11-17 shows position-versus-time graphs for two objects that undergo a one-dimensional collision; which object is more massive? Explain.
7. Must the analysis of a collision between two objects ever require consideration of all three dimensions? Explain.
8. Why are cars designed so that their front ends crush during an accident?
9. Discuss the relative advantages and disadvantages of air bags and seat belts for automotive safety during collisions.
10. Give three everyday examples of inelastic collisions.
11. Is it possible to have an inelastic collision in which *all* the kinetic energy of the colliding objects is lost? If not, why not? If so, give an example.

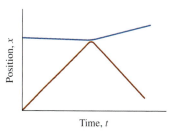

FIGURE 11-17 Position versus time graphs for two different objects, each represented by a different color (Question 6).

12. If you want to stop the neutrons in a reactor, why not use massive nuclei like lead?
13. Discuss the conservation principles used in the analysis of the ballistic pendulum. When is each valid?
14. A truck collides with an identical-looking truck initially at rest. The two move off together with more than half the original speed of the moving truck. What can you conclude about their relative loads?
15. Mark McGwire slides into home plate. His kinetic energy has been dissipated as heat, but where did his momentum go?
16. A pitched baseball moves no faster than the pitcher's hand. But a batted ball can move much faster than the bat. Why the difference?
17. Why is it relatively safe (though not recommended, of course!) to drop a lead weight on your foot if your foot is not in direct contact with the ground?
18. A downward-moving gas molecule collides with a downward-moving piston in an automobile engine. Comment on the speeds of each after the collision, and on any transfer of energy that might take place. How are such collisions important to the operation of the engine?
19. Two identical satellites are going in opposite directions in the same circular orbit, when they collide head-on. Describe their subsequent motion if the collision is (a) elastic or (b) inelastic.

PROBLEMS

ActivPhysics can help with these problems:
Activities 6.2–6.6.

Section 11-1 Impulse and Collisions

1. What is the impulse associated with a 650-N force acting for 80 ms?
2. A 7.5-kg object is moving in the positive x direction at 34 m/s when it undergoes a collision that lasts 0.22 s and

leaves it moving in the negative x direction at 51 m/s. Find (a) the impulse and (b) the average impulsive force associated with this collision.
3. A 62-kg parachutist hits the ground moving at 35 km/h and comes to a stop in 140 ms. Find the average impulsive force on the chutist, and compare with the chutist's weight.
4. (a) By how much does the momentum of a car change when it undergoes a collision during which an average impulsive

force of 1.2×10^5 N acts for 0.25 s? (b) If the car's mass is 1800 kg, for what initial speed would this collision bring the car to a stop?

5. A 240-g ball is moving with velocity $\mathbf{v}_i = 6.7\hat{\mathbf{i}}$ m/s when it undergoes a collision lasting 52 ms. After the collision its velocity is $\mathbf{v}_f = -4.3\hat{\mathbf{i}} + 3.1\hat{\mathbf{j}}$ m/s. Find (a) the impulse and (b) the average impulsive force associated with this collision.

6. A proton moving in the positive x direction at 4.3 Mm/s collides with a nucleus. The collision lasts 0.12 fs, and the average impulsive force is $42\hat{\mathbf{i}} + 17\hat{\mathbf{j}} \, \mu$N. (a) Find the velocity of the proton after the collision. (b) Through what angle has the proton's motion been deflected?

7. Safety standards call for a 1900-kg car colliding at 12 m/s with a concrete wall to experience an average impulsive force not greater than 50 kN. What is the minimum permissible time for the car to come to a stop during such a collision?

8. Explosive bolts separate a 950-kg communications satellite from its 640-kg booster rocket. If the impulse of the explosion is 350 N·s, at what relative speed do the satellite and booster separate?

9. A 727 jetliner in level flight with a total mass of 8.6×10^4 kg encounters a downdraft lasting 1.3 s. During this time, the plane acquires a downward velocity component of 85 m/s. Find (a) the impulse and (b) the average impulsive force on the plane.

10. A 2200-kg spacecraft on a gravity assist trajectory approaches a planet at 15.5 km/s. The spacecraft swings around the planet, and when again far from the planet, it is going opposite its original direction at 17.2 km/s. What is the magnitude of the impulse the spacecraft experiences during this encounter?

11. (a) Estimate the impulse imparted by the force shown in Fig. 11-18. (b) What is the average impulsive force?

FIGURE 11-18 Problem 11.

12. A 59-g tennis ball is thrown straight up, and at the peak of its trajectory is hit by a racket that exerts a horizontal force given by $F = at - bt^2$, where t is the time in milliseconds from the instant the racket first contacts the ball, and where $a = 1200$ N/ms and $b = 400$ N/ms^2. The ball separates from the racket after 3.0 ms. Find (a) the impulse, (b) the average impulsive force, and (c) the ball's speed just after it leaves the racket.

Section 11-2 Collisions and the Conservation Laws

13. At the peak of its trajectory, a 1.0-kg projectile moving horizontally at 15 m/s collides with a 2.0-kg projectile at the peak of a vertical trajectory. If the collision takes 0.10 s, how good is the assumption that momentum is conserved during the collision? To find out, compare the change in momentum of the colliding system with the system's total momentum.

14. An object like a ball used in a sporting event can be characterized by its **coefficient of restitution**, defined as the ratio of outgoing to incident speed when the ball collides with a rigid surface. The coefficient of restitution of a typical tennis ball is about 0.7. What fraction of the ball's kinetic energy is lost at each bounce?

15. An 1800-kg car moving at 25 m/s collides with an identical car moving in the same direction at 15 m/s. If an external frictional force of 6.1 kN acts on both cars, what is the minimum collision time that will ensure the system momentum changes by less than 0.1% during the collision?

16. A 340-g ball moving at 7.40 m/s collides with a 230-g ball initially at rest. After the collision the first ball is moving at 1.60 m/s and the second at 8.57 m/s, both in the initial direction of the first ball. (a) Calculate the momenta before and after the collision and show that, to three significant figures, momentum is conserved. (b) Is the collision elastic, totally inelastic, or somewhere in between? Justify your answer.

Section 11-3 Inelastic Collisions

17. In a railroad switchyard, a 56-ton freight car is sent at 7.0 mi/h toward a 31-ton car that is moving in the same direction at 2.6 mi/h. (a) What is the speed of the pair after they couple together? (b) What fraction of the initial kinetic energy was lost in the collision?

18. In a totally inelastic collision between two equal masses, one of which is initially at rest, show that half the initial kinetic energy is lost.

19. A sled and child with a total mass of 33 kg are moving horizontally at 10 m/s when a second child leaps on with negligible speed. If the sled's speed drops to 6.4 m/s, what is the mass of the second child?

20. In an ice-show stunt, a 70-kg skater dressed as a baseball player catches a 150-g baseball moving at 23 m/s. (a) If the skater was initially at rest, what is his final speed? (b) If the catch takes 36 ms, what is the average impulsive force exerted by the ball?

21. A mass m collides totally inelastically with a mass M initially at rest. Show that a fraction $M/(m + M)$ of the initial kinetic energy is lost in the collision.

22. A 1200-kg Toyota and a 2200-kg Buick collide at right angles in an intersection. They lock together and skid 22 m; the coefficient of friction is 0.91. Show that at least one car must have exceeded the 25 km/h speed limit in effect at the intersection.

23. Astronomers warn that there is a nonzero chance of Earth colliding inelastically with a substantial asteroid. Impact speed of the asteroid might be 10 km/s. Estimate the mass of an asteroid needed to alter Earth's orbital speed by 0.01%.

24. A 114-g Frisbee is caught in a tree. To dislodge it, you toss a 330-g lump of clay vertically upward. Clay and Frisbee stick together and rise to a maximum height of 4.1 m above the Frisbee's initial position. What was the speed of the clay as it hit the Frisbee?

25. A neutron (mass 1 u) strikes a deuteron (mass 2 u), and the two combine to form a tritium nucleus. If the neutron's initial velocity was $28\hat{\imath} + 17\hat{\jmath}$ Mm/s and if the tritium nucleus leaves the reaction with velocity $12\hat{\imath} + 20\hat{\jmath}$ Mm/s, what was the velocity of the deuteron?

26. Two identical trucks have mass 5500 kg when empty. One truck carries a 9500-kg load and is moving at 65 km/h. It collides inelastically with the second truck, which is initially at rest, and the pair moves off at 40 km/h. What is the load of the second truck?

27. Two identical pendulum bobs are suspended from strings of equal length, and one is released from a height h as shown in Fig. 11-19. When the first bob hits the second, the two stick together. Show that the maximum height to which the combination rises is $\frac{1}{4}h$.

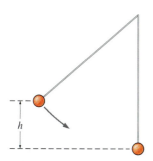

FIGURE 11-19 Problem 27.

28. A 5.4-kg hawk is diving at 18 m/s on a northward path at 65° to the horizontal when it grabs a 1.2-kg pigeon in its talons. If the pigeon was flying horizontally at 14 m/s in the same direction as the hawk's horizontal motion, what is the velocity of the pair just after the catch?

29. A 400-mg popcorn kernel is skittering across a nonstick frying pan at 8.2 cm/s when it pops and breaks into two equal-mass pieces. If one piece ends up at rest, how much energy was released in the popping?

30. A 1300-kg car moving at 10 km/h collides with a 1600-kg car moving in the same direction at 6.6 km/h. The first car is equipped with spring-loaded bumpers to prevent damage. If the spring constant is 28,000 N/m, find the maximum compression of the spring.

31. Two identical objects with the same initial speed collide and stick together. If the composite object moves with half the initial speed of either object, what was the angle between the initial velocities?

Section 11-4 Elastic Collisions

32. An alpha particle (^{4}He) strikes a stationary gold nucleus (^{197}Au) head-on. What fraction of the alpha particle's kinetic energy is transferred to the gold nucleus? Assume the collision is totally elastic.

33. While playing ball in the street, a child accidentally tosses a ball at 18 m/s toward the front of a car moving toward him at 14 m/s. What is the speed of the ball after it rebounds elastically from the car?

34. A block of mass m undergoes a one-dimensional elastic collision with a block of mass M initially at rest. If both blocks have the same speed after the collision, how are their masses related?

35. A proton moving at 6.9 Mm/s collides elastically and head-on with a second proton moving in the opposite direction at 11 Mm/s. Find their velocities after the collision.

36. A proton (mass 1 u) moving at 6.90 Mm/s collides elastically and head-on with a second particle moving in the opposite direction at 2.80 Mm/s. After the collision, the proton is moving opposite to its initial direction at 8.62 Mm/s. Find the mass and final velocity of the second particle.

37. Two objects, one initially at rest, undergo a one-dimensional elastic collision. If half the kinetic energy of the initially moving object is transferred to the other object, what is the ratio of their masses?

38. A 59.1-g tennis ball is moving at 14.5 m/s when it collides elastically and head-on with a basketball moving in the opposite direction at 9.63 m/s. If the tennis ball rebounds at twice its initial speed, find the mass and final velocity of the basketball.

39. Blocks B and C have masses $2m$ and m, respectively, and are at rest on a frictionless surface. Block A, also of mass m, is heading at speed v toward block B as shown in Fig. 11-20. If all subsequent collisions are elastic, determine the final velocity of each block.

FIGURE 11-20 Problem 39.

40. A block of mass m_1 undergoes a one-dimensional elastic collision with an initially stationary block of mass m_2. Find an expression for the fraction of the initial kinetic energy transferred to the second block, and plot your result for mass ratios m_1/m_2 from 0 to 20. Show also that, for a given mass ratio, the energy transfer is the same no matter which mass is initially at rest.

41. Rework Example 11-5 using a frame of reference in which the carbon nucleus is initially at rest.

42. Two buses approach each other, each going 60 km/h relative to the road. The driver of one bus tosses a tennis ball straight ahead at 20 km/h relative to his bus. The ball bounces elastically off the vertical windshield of the

second bus, and back to the driver who threw it. At what speed relative to the driver is it going when caught? Neglect gravity.

43. An object collides elastically with an equal-mass object initially at rest. If the collision is not head-on, show that the final velocity vectors are perpendicular.

44. On ice, a 3.2-kg rock moving at 1.0 m/s collides elastically with a 0.35-kg rock initially at rest. The smaller rock goes off at an angle of 45° to the larger rock's initial motion. What are the final speeds of the two rocks? What is the direction of the larger rock?

45. Two pendulums of equal length $\ell = 50$ cm are suspended from the same point. The pendulum bobs are steel spheres with masses of 140 and 390 g. The more massive bob is drawn back to make a 15° angle with the vertical (Fig. 11-21). When it is released the bobs collide elastically. What is the maximum angle made by the less massive pendulum?

15°

FIGURE 11-21 Problem 45.

46. Derive Equation 11-9b.

47. A particle of mass m is moving along the x axis when it collides elastically with a particle of mass $3m$. The more massive particle moves off at 1.2 m/s at 17° to the x axis, while the less massive particle moves off at 0.92 m/s at 48° to the x axis, as shown in Fig. 11-22. Find two sets of possible values for the initial speeds of both particles and the initial direction of the more massive particle.

m

$\mathbf{v}_{1f}$

$\mathbf{v}_{2f}$ $3m$

48°

17°

x

FIGURE 11-22 Problem 47.

48. A proton (mass 1 u) collides elastically with a stationary deuteron (mass 2 u). If the proton is deflected through 37°, what fraction of its kinetic energy does it transfer to the deuteron?

49. A tennis ball moving at 18 m/s strikes the 45° hatchback of a car moving away at 12 m/s, as shown in Fig. 11-23. Both speeds are given with respect to the ground. What is the velocity of the ball with respect to the ground after it rebounds elastically from the car? *Hint:* Work in the frame of reference of the car; then transform to the ground frame.

18 m/s   45°   12 m/s

FIGURE 11-23 Problem 49.

50. If the incident ball in Example 11-6 is moving initially at 1.1 m/s, what are the speeds of both balls after the collision?

51. Two identical billiard balls are initially at rest when they are struck symmetrically by a third identical ball moving with velocity $\mathbf{v}_0 = v_0\hat{\mathbf{i}}$, as shown in Fig. 11-24. Find the velocities of all three balls after they undergo an elastic collision.

v_0

FIGURE 11-24 Problem 51.

52. A particle of mass m, moving in the $+x$ direction at speed v_{1i}, undergoes an elastic collision with a particle of mass $2m$, moving in the $+y$ direction. After the collision, the first particle is moving in the $+y$ direction and the second particle in the $+x$ direction. Find the final speeds of both particles and the initial speed of the more massive particle, all in terms of v_{1i}.

Paired Problems

(Both problems in a pair involve the same principles and techniques. If you can get the first problem, you should be able to solve the second one.)

53. A 590-g basketball is moving at 9.2 m/s when it hits a backboard at 45°. It bounces off at a 45° angle, still moving at 9.2 m/s. If the ball is in contact with the backboard for 22 ms, find the average impulsive force on the ball.

54. A 330-g snowball moving at 13 m/s hits you square in the forehead, after which it crumbles and falls straight to the ground. If the collision lasts 54 ms, what average impulsive force does the snowball exert on your forehead?

55. A 2100-kg car is moving east at 75 km/h when it undergoes a totally inelastic collision with a 7900-kg truck moving northeast at 50 km/h. Find the final velocity of the combined wreckage.

56. A 32-u oxygen molecule (O_2) moving in the $+x$ direction at 580 m/s collides with an oxygen atom (mass 16 u) moving at 870 m/s at 27° to the x axis. The particles stick together to form an ozone molecule. Find the velocity of the ozone.

57. A truck slams into a parked car, and the resulting one-dimensional collision is elastic and transfers 41% of the truck's kinetic energy to the car. Compare the masses of the two vehicles.

58. A 4.0-u helium nucleus makes an elastic, head-on collision with another nucleus, initially at rest. If the helium's initial kinetic energy is 890 keV and if the collision transfers 240 keV to the second nucleus, what is the latter's mass?

59. A head-on, elastic collision between two particles with equal initial speed v leaves the more massive particle (mass m_1) at rest. Find (a) the ratio of the particle masses and (b) the final speed of the less massive particle.

60. A proton (mass 1.0 u) is moving at 9.7×10^5 m/s when it undergoes a head-on, elastic collision with an atomic nucleus moving in the same direction at one-fifth of the proton's speed. After the collision the two particles are moving in opposite directions, the proton at 3.6×10^5 m/s. What are (a) the mass and (b) the final speed of the nucleus?

61. A billiard ball moving at 1.8 m/s strikes an identical ball initially at rest as illustrated in Fig. 11-25. They undergo an elastic collision and the first ball moves off at 23° counterclockwise from its original direction. Find the final speeds of both balls and the direction of the second ball's motion.

FIGURE 11-25 Problem 61.

62. A proton (mass 1.0 u) collides elastically with a deuteron (mass 2.0 u) initially at rest. After collision the proton is moving at 6.2×10^5 m/s at 31° clockwise from its initial direction of motion. Find the initial speed of the proton, the final speed of the deuteron, and the direction of the deuteron's motion.

Supplementary Problems

63. A 114-g Frisbee is lodged on a tree branch 7.65 m above the ground. To free it, you lob a 240-g wad of mud vertically upward. The mud leaves your hand at a point 1.23 m above the ground, moving at 17.7 m/s. It sticks to the Frisbee. Find (a) the maximum height reached by the Frisbee-mud combination and (b) the speed with which the combination hits the ground.

64. You set a small ball of mass m atop a large ball of mass $M \gg m$ and drop the pair from a height h. Assuming the balls are perfectly elastic, show that the smaller ball rebounds to a height $9h$.

65. A 1400-kg car moving at 75 km/h runs into a 1200-kg car moving in the same direction at 50 km/h (Fig. 11-26). The two cars lock together and both drivers immediately slam on their brakes. If the cars come to rest in a distance of 18 m, what is the coefficient of friction?

FIGURE 11-26 Problem 65.

66. A car moving at speed v undergoes a one-dimensional collision with an identical car initially at rest. The collision is neither elastic nor fully inelastic; $\frac{5}{18}$ of the initial kinetic energy is lost. Find the velocities of the two cars after the collision.

67. Consider a one-dimensional elastic collision with $m_1 \ll m_2$ and m_2 initially at rest. In discussing this extreme case, we neglected m_1 altogether and showed that m_1 then rebounds with its initial speed. Now use the binomial theorem (see Appendix A) to show that a better approximation gives a rebound speed that is less than the incident speed by an amount $2m_1v_1/m_2$ for the case $m_1 \ll m_2$. In applying the binomial theorem, keep terms of order m_1/m_2, but neglect terms of order m_1^2/m_2^2.

68. A 1.0-kg block is sliding on a frictionless surface at 10 m/s when it undergoes a head-on collision with a 2.0-kg block initially at rest. The collision is neither elastic nor totally inelastic; 20 percent of the initial kinetic energy is lost. Find the velocities of the two blocks after the collision.

69. A 1.0-kg particle is moving in the $+x$ direction at 4.0 m/s when it collides elastically with a 4.0-kg particle moving in the $-x$ direction at 1.0 m/s. After colliding, the 1-kg particle moves off at 130° counterclockwise from the positive x axis. Find the final speeds of both particles and the direction of the more massive one.

70. A 200-g block is released from rest 25 cm high on a frictionless 30° incline. It slides down the incline, then along a frictionless surface until it collides elastically with an 800-g block at rest 1.4 m from the bottom of the incline (Fig. 11-27). How much later do the two blocks collide again?

FIGURE 11-27 Problem 70.

71. A 1200-kg car moving at 25 km/h undergoes a one-dimensional collision with an 1800-kg car initially at rest. The collision is neither elastic nor totally inelastic; the kinetic energy lost is 5800 J. Find the speeds of both cars after the collision.

72. A 14-kg projectile is launched at 380 m/s at a 55° angle to the horizontal. At the peak of its trajectory it collides with a second projectile moving horizontally, in the opposite direction, at 140 m/s. The two stick together and land 9.6 km horizontally downrange from the first projectile's launch point. Find the mass of the second projectile.

73. A block of mass M is moving at speed v_0 on a frictionless surface that ends in a rigid wall. Farther from the wall is a more massive block of mass αM, initially at rest (Fig. 11-28). The less massive block undergoes elastic collisions with the other block and with the wall, and the motion of both blocks is confined to one dimension. (a) Show that the two blocks will undergo only one collision if $\alpha \leq 3$. (b) Show that the two blocks will undergo two collisions if $\alpha = 4$, and determine their final speeds. (c) Find out how many collisions the two blocks will undergo if $\alpha = 10$, and determine their final speeds.

FIGURE 11-28 Problem 73.

Rotational Motion

Amusement park rides involve a variety of rotational motions.

You're sitting on a rotating planet. The wheels of your car rotate. Your favorite music comes from a rotating compact disc. A circular saw rotates at high speed to rip its way through a board. A dancer pirouettes, and a satellite spins about its axis. Even molecules rotate. Rotational motion is commonplace throughout the physical universe.

In principle, we could treat rotational motion by analyzing the motion of each particle making up a composite, rotating object. But that would be a hopeless task for any but the simplest objects. Instead, we'll develop a description of rotational motion that closely parallels our understanding of motion as described by Newton's laws.

This chapter parallels our study of one-dimensional motion in Chapters 2 and 5. In the next chapter we introduce a full vector description to treat multidimensional cases of rotational motion.

12-1 ANGULAR VELOCITY AND ACCELERATION

You slip a compact disc into its player, and it starts spinning. You could describe its motion by giving the speed and direction of each point on the disc. But it's much easier just to say that the disc is rotating at 200 revolutions per minute (rpm). As long as the disc is a **rigid body**—one whose parts remain in fixed positions relative to one another—then that single statement suffices to describe the motion of the entire disc.

Angular Velocity

The rate at which a body rotates is its **angular velocity**—a quantity that describes how rapidly the angular position of any point on the body changes. With our 200-rpm CD, our unit of angle was one full revolution (360°, or 2π radians), and our unit of time was the minute. But we could equally well express angular speed in revolutions per second (rev/s), degrees per second (°/s), or radians per second (rad/s or simply s^{-1} since radians are dimensionless). Because of the mathematically simple status of radian measure, we'll often use radians in calculations involving rotational motion.

Math Toolbox

Radian Measure We first introduced the radian in Chapter 1 as the SI measure of angle. Although you're more familiar with angular measure in degrees, the radian is widely used in physics and mathematics because it's the "natural" measure of angle and often simplifies mathematical expressions and calculations.

Figure 12-1 is a reminder of the definition of the radian we gave in Chapter 1. As the figure shows, the radian measure of an angle θ is the ratio of the length of the arc that subtends that angle to the radius of a circle centered at the angle's apex and of which that arc is a part. Here "subtends" means the arc extends between the two line segments that define the angle. Because the angle θ is a *ratio* of two lengths—the arc length s to the radius r—the radius itself doesn't matter. Double the radius r in Fig. 12-1, and you also double the circle's circumference and with it the arc length s. So the ratio $\theta = s/r$ remains the same.

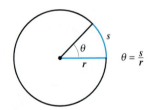

FIGURE 12-1 The angle θ in radians is the ratio of the arc length s to the radius r.

$$\theta = \frac{s}{r}$$

The definition in Fig. 12-1 also shows that a full circle comprises 2π radians. That's because when θ grows to encompass the full circle, then the arc length becomes the circumference $2\pi r$, so $\theta_{\text{full circle}} = 2\pi r/r = 2\pi$. Since a full circle is also 360°, that sets the conversion factor $360° = 2\pi$ rad, or 1 rad $= 360°/2\pi \approx 57.3°$.

We use the Greek symbol ω (omega) for angular velocity and define **average angular velocity** $\overline{\omega}$ as:

$$\overline{\omega} = \frac{\Delta\theta}{\Delta t}, \tag{12-1}$$

FIGURE 12-2 A rigid body—here, a forearm—rotates through the angle $\Delta\theta$ in time Δt. Its average angular speed is $\Delta\theta/\Delta t$.

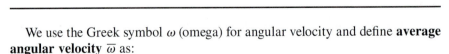

where $\Delta\theta$ is the **angular displacement**—i.e., the change in angular position—occurring in the time Δt (Fig. 12-2). When the angular velocity is constant, its value at any instant is the same as its average value. When angular velocity is changing, we define **instantaneous angular velocity** as the limit of the average angular velocity taken over arbitrarily short time intervals:

$$\omega = \lim_{\Delta t \to 0} \frac{\Delta \theta}{\Delta t} = \frac{d\theta}{dt}. \tag{12-2}$$

These definitions are analogous to our definitions of average and instantaneous linear velocity introduced in Chapter 2. The only difference is the use of angular displacement $\Delta \theta$, rather than linear displacement Δx.

Just as we use the term *speed* for the magnitude of velocity, so we define **angular speed** as the magnitude of the angular velocity.

What about direction? After all, we know that velocity is a vector quantity, with magnitude and direction. Is angular velocity also a vector? Yes—but, again, we emphasize that in this chapter we're treating rotational motion in analogy with Chapter 2's account of one-dimensional motion. There velocity was a quantity that could have one of two possible directions along a one-dimensional path; we distinguished those directions using positive and negative signs. Later, in Chapter 3, we introduced the full vector description of motion, and velocity became a full-fledged vector with magnitude and completely arbitrary direction.

We're doing the same thing here with rotational quantities. In this chapter, it's sufficient to know whether an object's rotation is clockwise or counterclockwise about a fixed axis—as suggested by the curved arrow in Fig. 12-2. The restriction to a fixed axis is analogous to Chapter 2's restriction of motion to a single one-dimensional path. In Chapter 13 we'll expand our treatment to include arbitrary and changeable directions for the rotation axis; then we'll give a full vector definition of angular velocity and the other quantities we introduce in this chapter. For now, be content with the terms *clockwise* (CW) and *counterclockwise* (CCW) for the direction of angular velocity and other rotational quantities. Be aware, though, that these quantities are really vectors and that we will expand our definitions in the next chapter.

Angular and Linear Speed

Individual points on a rotating object undergo circular motion. How fast is each point moving? Each point has an instantaneous linear velocity **v** with which it would continue if the forces holding the object together suddenly disappeared. We now relate the magnitude v —i.e., the linear speed—to the angular speed ω of a rotating object. The definition of angular measure in radians (see Math Toolbox and Fig. 12-1) gives

$$\theta = \frac{s}{r}. \tag{12-3}$$

Differentiating this expression with respect to time we have

$$\frac{d\theta}{dt} = \frac{1}{r}\frac{ds}{dt},$$

because the radius r is constant. But $d\theta/dt$ is the angular velocity, and ds/dt is the linear speed, v, so $\omega = v/r$, or

$$v = \omega r. \tag{12-4}$$

FIGURE 12-3 The linear speed of a point on a rotating object is proportional to the angular speed and the distance from the rotation axis. Here the point on the rim has a higher linear speed, as suggested by the greater magnitude of its velocity vector **v**.

Thus the linear speed of any point on a rotating object is proportional both to the angular speed of the object and to the distance from that point to the axis of rotation (Fig. 12-3).

Tip

Know When to Use Radian Measure Equation 12-4 was derived using the definition of angle *in radians* and therefore holds only for angular speed measured in radians per unit time. If you're given other angular measures—degrees or revolutions, for example—you should convert to radians before using Equation 12-4 (see Example 12-1 and Problem 3). Furthermore, Equation 12-4 is valid only for rotation about a fixed axis. In Section 12-5 we'll consider the more general case of an object—like a rolling wheel—whose rotation axis is itself in motion.

EXAMPLE 12-1	*Angular Speed*

A turbine in an electric power plant rotates at 3600 rpm. Find its angular speed in rad/s, and determine the linear speed of a point 72 cm from the rotation axis.

Solution
One revolution is 2π radians, and 1 minute is 60 s, so we have

$$\omega = 3600 \text{ rpm} = \frac{(3600 \text{ rev/min})(2\pi \text{ rad/rev})}{60 \text{ s/min}} = 377 \text{ rad/s}.$$

Then the speed of a point 72 cm from the axis is given by Equation 12-4:

$$v = \omega r = (377 \text{ rad/s})(0.72 \text{ m}) = 270 \text{ m/s},$$

where the units work out because radians are dimensionless.

EXERCISE An engineer is designing a helicopter blade to rotate at 260 rpm. (a) Find the rotation rate in rad/s, and (b) determine the maximum blade length (measured from the rotation axis) that will keep the blade speed everywhere subsonic (less than the speed of sound in air, about 340 m/s).

Answers: (a) 27.2 rad/s (b) 12.5 m

Some problems similar to Example 12-1: 2, 4, 7, 8

Angular Acceleration

7.8

ActivPhysics

Rotational Kinematics

If the angular velocity of a rotating object changes—as when a CD starts up after you turn on the power—then the object undergoes an **angular acceleration**, α, defined analogously to linear acceleration:

$$\alpha = \lim_{\Delta t \to 0} \frac{\Delta\omega}{\Delta t} = \frac{d\omega}{dt}. \tag{12-5}$$

Taking the limit in Equation 12-5 gives the instantaneous angular acceleration; if we don't take the limit, then we have an average value over the time interval Δt. The SI units for angular acceleration are rad/s², although we will sometimes use other units such as rpm/s or rev/s².

What about direction? As with angular velocity, in this chapter we distinguish only between clockwise and counterclockwise directions for the angular acceleration about a fixed axis. The angular acceleration has the same direction as the angular velocity if the angular speed is increasing, and the opposite direction if angular speed is decreasing. These situations are analogous, respectively, to a car accelerating or decelerating while moving in a straight line.

Earlier we related angular velocity to the linear velocity of a point on a rotating object (recall Equation 12-4). Now we do the same for angular acceleration. If a rotating object undergoes angular acceleration, individual points on the object either speed up or slow down. However, even if an object has no angular acceleration, individual points on it are still accelerating because they're in circular motion. We made this point when we dealt with nonuniform circular motion in Section 4-5, which you may want to review. There, we introduced the terms **tangential acceleration** a_t and **radial acceleration** a_r for the acceleration components tangential and perpendicular, respectively, to a circular path. Tangential acceleration is what's associated with a change in angular speed. If we differentiate Equation 12-4, we get a relation between angular acceleration α and the tangential acceleration a_t of a point a distance r from the axis of rotation:

$$a_t = \frac{dv}{dt} = r\frac{d\omega}{dt} = r\alpha. \tag{12-6}$$

There is also the radial acceleration a_r directed toward the rotation axis and given by

$$a_r = \frac{v^2}{r} = \omega^2 r, \tag{12-7}$$

where we've used Equation 12-4 to express v in terms of ω. Since Equations 12-6 and 12-7 were derived using Equation 12-4, they, too, require that the angular velocity ω be expressed in rad/s. Tangential and radial accelerations comprise two components of the full acceleration vector for a point on a rotating object. The magnitude of that acceleration ultimately determines the forces needed to keep the rotating object from flying apart (see Fig 12-4).

Because angular velocity and acceleration are defined in a way that is mathematically analogous to linear velocity and acceleration, all the relations among linear position, velocity, and acceleration automatically apply among angular position, angular velocity, and angular acceleration. For example, angular acceleration is the second time derivative of angular position; angular velocity is the integral of angular acceleration. And if angular acceleration is constant, then all our constant-acceleration formulas of Chapter 2 apply when we make the substitutions θ for x, ω for v, and α for a. Table 12-1 summarizes this direct analogy between linear and rotational quantities. With Table 12-1, problems involving rotational motion are analogous to the one-dimensional linear problems you solved in Chapter 2.

FIGURE 12-4 A circular saw blade. As it accelerates to full speed with angular acceleration α, the linear acceleration of a particular sawtooth has tangential component $a_t = r\alpha$ and radial component $\omega^2 r$. These components form the total acceleration **a**, whose magnitude determines, through Newton's second law, the force required to hold the sawtooth on the blade.

TABLE 12-1 *Angular and Linear Position, Velocity, and Acceleration*

LINEAR QUANTITY	ANGULAR QUANTITY
Position x	Angular position θ
Velocity $v = \dfrac{dx}{dt}$	Angular velocity $\omega = \dfrac{d\theta}{dt}$
Acceleration $a = \dfrac{dv}{dt} = \dfrac{d^2x}{dt^2}$	Angular acceleration $\alpha = \dfrac{d\omega}{dt} = \dfrac{d^2\theta}{dt^2}$

EQUATIONS FOR CONSTANT LINEAR ACCELERATION		EQUATIONS FOR CONSTANT ANGULAR ACCELERATION	
$\bar{v} = \frac{1}{2}(v_0 + v)$	(2-8)	$\bar{\omega} = \frac{1}{2}(\omega_0 + \omega)$	(12-8)
$v = v_0 + at$	(2-7)	$\omega = \omega_0 + \alpha t$	(12-9)
$x = x_0 + v_0 t + \frac{1}{2}at^2$	(2-10)	$\theta = \theta_0 + \omega_0 t + \frac{1}{2}\alpha t^2$	(12-10)
$v^2 = v_0^2 + 2a(x - x_0)$	(2-11)	$\omega^2 = \omega_0^2 + 2\alpha(\theta - \theta_0)$	(12-11)

EXAMPLE 12-2	*A Power Plant Shutdown*

During a power plant shutdown, the turbine of Example 12-1 coasts to a halt in 590 s. If the angular acceleration is constant, how many revolutions does the turbine make during this time?

Solution

With constant angular acceleration, the average angular speed during the 590-s stopping time is just the average of the initial 3600 rpm and the final 0 rpm (Equation 12-8). So the number of revolutions is

$$\theta = \overline{\omega}t = \tfrac{1}{2}(\omega_0 + \omega)t = \tfrac{1}{2}(3600 \text{ rpm} + 0 \text{ rpm})\left(\frac{590 \text{ s}}{60 \text{ s/min}}\right)$$

$$= 1.8\times10^4 \text{ rev}.$$

Alternatively, we could have solved for the angular acceleration using $\alpha = \Delta\omega/\Delta t$. Then Equation 12-10 would give the angular displacement $\theta - \theta_0$ during the stopping time. Or we could have used Equation 12-11, setting the final angular speed ω to zero and solving for $\theta - \theta_0$.

Tip

You Don't Always Need to Work in Radians Here, with speed given in rpm and the desired answer in revolutions, there was no need to convert angular measure to radians.

EXERCISE The blade in a food processor spins at 1700 rpm. After the machine is turned off, the blade comes to a stop in 3.7 s. How many revolutions does it make during this time, assuming constant angular deceleration?

Answer: 52

Some problems similar to Example 12-2: 6, 10, 11, 61, 62

EXAMPLE 12-3	*A Quick Stop*

A rotating wheel 80 cm in diameter is decelerating at 0.21 rad/s². What should be the initial angular speed if the wheel is to stop after exactly one revolution? What is the tangential linear deceleration of a point on the wheel's rim?

Solution

Can you see that this problem is exactly like one from Chapter 2 in which you're asked to find the initial vertical speed needed to throw a ball to a given height? We apply Equation 12-11, setting the final angular speed ω to zero and taking $\theta_0 = 0$ for convenience:

$$0 = \omega_0^2 + 2\alpha\theta.$$

Setting θ to 2π because we want exactly one revolution, and noting that α is negative because it's a deceleration, we solve for ω_0 to get

$$\omega_0 = \sqrt{-2\alpha\theta} = \sqrt{(-2)(-0.21 \text{ rad/s}^2)(2\pi)} = 1.6 \text{ rad/s}.$$

The tangential acceleration of a point on the rim is given by Equation 12-6:

$$a_t = r\alpha = (40 \text{ cm})(-0.21 \text{ rad/s}^2) = -8.4 \text{ cm/s}^2,$$

where the minus sign tells us that the tangential acceleration is directed oppositely to the linear velocity of the rim.

EXERCISE A circular saw blade is 25 cm in diameter and rotates at 3600 rpm. A magnetic brake brings the blade to a halt in just 10 revolutions. What are the magnitudes of (a) the angular deceleration and (b) the tangential deceleration of the blade teeth?

Answers: (a) 1.13 krad/s²; (b) 141 m/s²

Some problems similar to Example 12-3: 5, 9, 14

12-2 TORQUE

Newton's second law, $\mathbf{F} = m\mathbf{a}$, proved very powerful in our study of motion. Ultimately Newton's law governs all motion, but its application to every particle in a rotating object would be terribly cumbersome. Can we instead formulate an analogous law that deals with rotational quantities?

To develop such a law, we need rotational analogs of force, mass, and acceleration. Angular acceleration α is the analog of linear acceleration; in the next two sections we develop analogs for force and mass. In this chapter we consider only the one-dimensional form of Newton's law and its rotational analog; in the next chapter we'll develop the full vector description of rotational motion.

Figure 12-5 shows a child balancing her big sister on a seesaw. How can she do this? By sitting far from the seesaw's rotation axis, she's increased the effectiveness of the force she applies, and her smaller weight at a greater

FIGURE 12-5 The effectiveness of a force in effecting rotational motion depends on how far from the axis it's applied. That's why the small child can balance her big sister on the seesaw.

distance from the pivot is as effective as her sister's greater weight closer to the pivot. In general, the effectiveness of a force in bringing about changes in rotational motion—a quantity called **torque**—depends not only on the magnitude of the force, but also on how far from the rotation axis it's applied (Fig. 12-6). Effectiveness of the force also depends on the *direction* in which it's applied; pushing at right angles to the line from the rotation axis to the force application point is most effective (Fig. 12-7). In fact, as Fig. 12-7 suggests, only the component of force at right angles to that line has any rotational effect. Based on these considerations, we define torque—again, a measure of the effectiveness of a given force in producing a change in rotational motion—as the product of the distance r from the rotation axis with the component of force perpendicular to that axis. This quantity is given the symbol τ (Greek tau, pronounced to rhyme with "how"). Then we can write

$$\tau = rF \sin\theta, \tag{12-12}$$

where θ is the angle between the force vector and the vector $\mathbf{r}$ from the rotation axis to the force application point. Figure 12-8 shows two interpretations of Equation 12-12. In Fig. 12-8a, we think of the quantity $\tau = rF\sin\theta$ as the product of the distance r to the force application point with the force component $F\sin\theta$ in the direction perpendicular to $\mathbf{r}$. But we can also write $\tau = F(r\sin\theta)$; then we interpret τ as the product of the force with the component of $\mathbf{r}$ perpendicular to the force, namely $r\sin\theta$ (Fig. 12-8b). This quantity $r\sin\theta$—the perpendicular distance from the rotation axis to the force application point—is called the **lever arm**. Sometimes you'll be given the lever arm rather than the actual distance r and angle θ; that actually makes your calculations easier, since the lever arm already includes the factor $\sin\theta$.

(a)   (b)   (c)

FIGURE 12-6 Torque—a measure of a force's effectiveness in altering rotational motion—increases with the distance r from the rotation axis P to the force application point. The same force applied at the different points shown in (a), (b), and (c) produces the greatest torque in (c).

(a)   (b)   (c)

FIGURE 12-7 The torque is greatest with $\mathbf{F}$ and $\mathbf{r}$ at right angles, and diminishes to zero as they become colinear. You can see that pulling with the force shown in (c) produces no tendency for the object to rotate about the axis P. In general, only the component of force perpendicular to $\mathbf{r}$ contributes to the torque.

$F_\perp = F\sin\theta$

$r_\perp = r\sin\theta$

(a)   (b)

FIGURE 12-8 You can think of torque as either (a) the product of the distance r from the axis (P) to the force application point with the force component $F\sin\theta$ perpendicular to $\mathbf{r}$, or (b) as the product of F with the perpendicular distance $r\sin\theta$. The latter is the **lever arm**.

Torque, which you can think of as a "twisting force," is the rotational analog of Newton's second law. Equation 12-12 shows that torque is measured in N·m. Although this is the same unit as energy, torque is a different physical quantity, so we reserve the term *joule* (= 1 N·m) for energy.

| EXAMPLE 12-4 | *Changing a Tire* |

You're tightening your car's wheel nuts after changing a flat tire. The instructions specify a tightening torque of 95 N·m to ensure the nuts won't come loose. If your 45-cm-long wrench makes a 67° angle with the horizontal, as shown in Fig. 12-9, with what force must you pull horizontally to produce the required torque?

Solution

With the force applied horizontally, the angle θ in Equation 12-12 is $180° - 67° = 113°$ (see Fig. 12-9), so we can solve Equation 12-12 for the force F:

$$F = \frac{\tau}{r \sin \theta} = \frac{95 \text{ N·m}}{(0.45 \text{ m})(\sin 113°)} = 230 \text{ N}.$$

Tightening torques, as in this example, are often specified for nuts and bolts in critical applications. Mechanics use specially designed "torque wrenches" that provide direct indication of the applied torque.

FIGURE 12-9 Tightening the wheel nut.

FIGURE 12-10 A bicycle wheel. What torque arises from the weight of the valve stem?

EXERCISE You have your bicycle upside down for repairs. The front wheel is free to rotate and is perfectly balanced except for the 25-g valve stem. If the valve stem is 32 cm from the rotation axis and is located at 24° below the horizontal, as shown in Fig. 12-10, what is the resulting torque about the wheel's axis?

Answer: 0.072 N·m

Some problems similar to Example 12-4: 16, 18–20

Tip
Specify the Axis Torque depends not only on force but also on where the force is applied *relative to some rotation axis*. The same physical force gives rise to different torques about different axes. Any calculation involving torque implicitly or explicitly assumes a particular rotation axis. If the rotation axis isn't obvious, be sure to specify it before working problems involving torque.

Does torque have direction? In Fig. 12-9 the torque tends to rotate the nut clockwise, while in Fig. 12-10 the weight of the valve stem will cause a counter-clockwise rotation. For now we'll specify the direction of torque as being either clockwise or counterclockwise; these are analogous to the two directions $+x$ and $-x$ in one-dimensional motion. In the next chapter we'll expand our notion of torque to provide a vector description of its direction.

Got It!

The forces in Figs. 12-6*b* and 12-7*b* have the same magnitude. In which figure is the torque greater?

12-3 ROTATIONAL INERTIA AND THE ANALOG OF NEWTON'S LAW

Torque and angular acceleration are the rotational analogs of force and linear acceleration; to develop a rotational analog of Newton's law, we still need the rotational analog of mass.

The mass m in Newton's law is a measure of a body's inertia—of its resistance to changes in motion. We want a quantity that, analogously, describes resistance to changes in rotational motion. Figure 12-11 shows that it's easier to set an object rotating when its mass is concentrated near the rotation axis. So our rotational analog of inertia must depend not only on mass itself but also on the distribution of mass in relation to the rotation axis.

Suppose the composite object shown in Fig. 12-11 consists of an essentially massless rod of length R with a ball of mass m on the end. We allow the object to rotate about an axis through the free end of the rod and apply a force $\mathbf{F}$ to the ball, always at right angles to the rod (Fig. 12-12). The ball undergoes a tangential acceleration given by Newton's law: $F = ma_t$. (There's also a tension force in the rod, but because it acts along the rod, it doesn't contribute to the torque or angular acceleration.) We can use Equation 12-6 to express the tangential acceleration in terms of the angular acceleration α and the distance R from the rotation axis:

$$F = ma_t = m\alpha R. \qquad (12\text{-}13)$$

We can also express the force F in terms of its associated torque. Since the force is perpendicular to the rod, Equation 12-12 gives

$$\tau = RF.$$

Using F from Equation 12-13, we have

$$\tau = (mR^2)\alpha.$$

Here we have Newton's law, $F = ma$, written in terms of rotational quantities. The torque—analogous to force—is the product of the angular acceleration and the quantity mR^2, which must therefore be the rotational analog of mass. We call this quantity the **rotational inertia** or **moment of inertia** and give it the symbol I. Rotational inertia is measured in kg·m² and accounts for both an object's mass and the distribution of that mass. Like torque, the value of the rotational inertia depends on the location of the rotation axis. Given the rotational inertia I, our rotational analog of Newton's law becomes

$$\tau = I\alpha. \qquad (12\text{-}14)$$

Although we derived Equation 12-14 for a single, localized mass, we can apply it to extended objects if we interpret τ as the net torque on the object and I as the sum of the rotational inertias of the individual mass elements making up the object. A rigorous proof that Equation 12-14 applies to extended objects invokes Newton's third law to show that internal forces—and therefore torques—cancel in pairs, making the net torque indeed the sum of the external torques acting. That proof requires the additional condition—nearly always

FIGURE 12-11 A composite object consisting of a mass on the end of a rigid rod. Its resistance to changes in rotational motion depends on how the mass is distributed relative to the rotation axis. It's easier to set it rotating in the left-hand case, where the mass is concentrated near the axis.

FIGURE 12-12 A force applied perpendicular to the rod results in angular acceleration.

7.7

Rotational Inertia

FIGURE 12-13 Two mass elements exert equal but opposite forces on each other. If the forces act along the line joining the mass elements, then $r_1 \sin\theta_1 = r_2 \sin\theta_2$. Because the forces are equal but opposite, so are the torques $Fr \sin\theta$. Thus internal torques cancel in pairs, and the net torque on the object is the sum of the external torques only. (The angles shown are the supplements of the angles used in Equation 12-12, but that's ok since an angle and its supplement have the same sine.)

satisfied—that the internal forces act along the line joining two mass elements (Fig. 12-13).

We emphasize that the quantities in Equation 12-14—torque, rotational inertia, and angular acceleration—are defined relative to some rotation axis. Equation 12-14 is valid only if the same rotation axis is used for each quantity.

In the next two sections we show first how to calculate the rotational inertia of extended objects, and then how to apply Equation 12-14 to the dynamics of rotating objects.

Calculating the Rotational Inertia

When an object consists of a number of discrete mass points, its rotational inertia about an axis is just the sum of the rotational inertias of the individual mass points about that axis:

$$I = \sum m_i r_i^2 . \tag{12-15}$$

Here m_i is the mass of the ith mass point, and r_i its distance from the rotation axis.

EXAMPLE 12-5	*Rotational Inertia*

A dumbbell-shaped object consists of two equal masses $m = 0.64$ kg on the ends of a massless rod of length $\ell = 85$ cm. Calculate the rotational inertia of this object about an axis one-fourth of the way from one end of the rod and perpendicular to it. If the object is accelerated from rest by a torque of 1.2 N·m about the same axis, how many revolutions will it turn in 2.5 s?

Solution

The situation is shown in Fig. 12-14. Summing the individual rotational inertias, we have

$$I = \sum m_i r_i^2 = m(\tfrac{1}{4}\ell)^2 + m(\tfrac{3}{4}\ell)^2 = \tfrac{5}{8}m\ell^2$$

$$= \tfrac{5}{8}(0.64 \text{ kg})(0.85 \text{ m})^2 = 0.29 \text{ kg·m}^2 .$$

From Equation 12-14, the angular acceleration is

$$\alpha = \frac{\tau}{I} .$$

Using this result in Equation 12-10 then gives the angular displacement:

$$\theta = \tfrac{1}{2}\alpha t^2 = \frac{1}{2}\left(\frac{\tau}{I}\right)t^2 = \frac{1}{2}\left(\frac{1.2 \text{ N·m}}{0.29 \text{ kg·m}^2}\right)(2.5 \text{ s})^2$$

$$= 13 \text{ rad} = 2.1 \text{ rev} .$$

FIGURE 12-14 Example 12-5.

EXERCISE Three 1.2-kg masses are located at the vertices of an equilateral triangle 88 cm on a side, connected by rods of negligible mass. Find the rotational inertia of this object (a) about an axis through the center of the triangle and perpendicular to its plane and (b) about an axis that passes through one vertex and the midpoint of the opposite side.

Answers: (a) 0.93 kg·m²; (b) 0.46 kg·m²

Some problems similar to Example 12-5: 24, 27

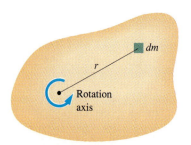

FIGURE 12-15 The rotational inertia of a solid object can be found by integrating the rotational inertias $r^2\, dm$ of all the infinitesimal mass elements making up the object.

When an object consists of a continuous distribution of matter, then we consider a large number of very small mass elements dm throughout the object, and sum the individual rotational inertias $r^2\, dm$ over the entire object (Fig. 12-15). In the limit of an arbitrarily large number of very small mass elements, the sum becomes an integral, and we have

$$I = \int r^2 dm, \qquad (12\text{-}16)$$

where the limits of integration are chosen to include the entire object.

The following three examples show integration can be used to find the rotational inertias of common shapes about particular axes.

EXAMPLE 12-6 | *Rotational Inertia of a Rod*

Find the rotational inertia of a uniform, narrow rod of mass M and length ℓ about an axis through its center and perpendicular to the rod.

Solution

Let the rod coincide with the x axis, with origin at the center of the rod, and consider mass elements of mass dm and length dx, as shown in Fig. 12-16. The distance x from the center of the rod to the mass element dm plays the role of r in Equation 12-16, so

$$I = \int_{x=-\ell/2}^{x=\ell/2} x^2 dm,$$

where we've chosen the limits to include the entire rod. To do the integration, we must somehow relate x and dm so we have a single variable under the integral sign. Here we have a rod of length ℓ and M, and we're told that the mass is distributed uniformly along the rod. So the mass per unit length is M/ℓ. Multiplying this quantity by an arbitrary length gives the mass contained within that length. Here we want the mass dm contained in the length dx; its value is thus

$$dm = \frac{M}{\ell} dx.$$

FIGURE 12-16 A uniform rod, showing a mass element of mass dm and length dx.

Using this result in our integral for I then gives

$$I = \int_{-\ell/2}^{\ell/2} \frac{M}{\ell} x^2 \, dx = \frac{M}{\ell} \int_{-\ell/2}^{\ell/2} x^2 \, dx \qquad (12\text{-}17)$$

$$= \frac{M}{\ell} \frac{x^3}{3} \Big|_{-\ell/2}^{\ell/2} = \tfrac{1}{12} M \ell^2 . \quad \text{(rod about bisector)}$$

Does this make sense? Yes. Much of the rod's mass is near the axis of rotation, and therefore contributes little to the rotational inertia. The result is a much lower rotational inertia than if all the mass were at the ends of the rod (as it was in Example 12-5).

Tip

Integrals It's baffling to confront an integral like $\int x^2 dm$ that seems to contain two variables. You can't do the integral unless the only variable under the integral sign is the same *something* that's in the $d(something)$ at the end of the integral. With integrals that arise in physics, there's always a clear link between two seemingly different variables. Often that link involves distributions of mass, electric charge, or other quantities in one, two, or three dimensions. In such cases it's often useful to define a density—for example, as mass per unit length, per unit area, or per unit volume, as appropriate—and use that to relate the variables. In Example 12-6 we had to relate x and dm—and we did so by invoking the mass per unit length (sometimes called the linear mass density, or line density), which we determined to be M/ℓ. Multiplying this mass per unit length by a length gives the mass in that length. For example, multiply M/ℓ by ℓ and you get the total mass M in the whole length ℓ of the rod; multiply by $\tfrac{1}{3}\ell$ and you get the mass $M/3$ in one-third of the rod. And, as we did in Example 12-6, multiply by an infinitesimal length dx to get the infinitesimal mass dm in that infinitesimal section of the rod. Then we had dm in terms of dx, leaving x the only variable in the integral, and we could proceed with the integration.

| **EXAMPLE 12-7** | *Rotational Inertia of a Ring* |

Find the rotational inertia of a thin ring of radius R and mass M about the ring's axis (Fig. 12-17).

Solution

We divide the ring into mass elements dm, one of which is shown in Fig. 12-17. All the mass elements in the ring are the same distance R from the rotation axis, so r in Equation 12-16 is the constant R, and the equation becomes

$$I = \int R^2 dm = R^2 \int dm,$$

where the integration is over the ring. But the sum of mass elements over the ring is just the total mass, M, so

$$I = MR^2. \quad \text{(thin ring)} \quad (12\text{-}18)$$

The rotational inertia of the ring is the same as if all the mass were concentrated in one place a distance R from the rotation axis; the angular distribution of the mass about the axis doesn't matter. Notice, too, that it doesn't matter whether the ring is narrow like a loop of wire or long like a section of hollow pipe, as long as it's thin enough that all of it is essentially equidistant from the rotation axis (Fig 12-18).

FIGURE 12-17 A thin ring, showing one mass element dm.

FIGURE 12-18 The rotational inertia is MR^2 for any thin ring, whether it's narrow like a wire loop (left) or long like a section of pipe (right).

| **EXAMPLE 12-8** | *Rotational Inertia of a Disk* |

A disk of radius R and mass M has uniform density. Find the rotational inertia of the disk about an axis through its center and perpendicular to the disk.

Solution

Not all parts of the disk are the same distance from the axis, so r is not constant in Equation 12-16. Since we already know the rotational inertia of a ring, we can divide the disk into mass elements that are themselves rings, as shown in Fig. 12-19. A given mass element is a ring of radius r, width dr, and mass dm. Its rotational inertia is $r^2 dm$, so the total rotational inertia of the disk is

$$I = \int_{r=0}^{r=R} r^2 dm,$$

where the limits include all the ring-shaped mass elements in the entire disk. Now we have the same problem we did in Example 12-6: to evaluate the integral we must relate the variables m and r. As the Tip after Example 12-6 suggests, the best way to do this is by defining an appropriate density. In Exam-

FIGURE 12-19 A disk may be divided into ring-shaped mass elements of mass dm, radius r, and width dr.

ple 12-6, that was the mass per unit length. Here, though, we're dealing with a disk whose mass is spread over an area. So we want the mass per unit area. Since the mass M is spread uniformly over the circular area πR^2, the mass per unit area is $M/\pi R^2$. To get the mass dm, we multiply by the area of the mass element dm. Since the ring is very thin, we can imagine "unwinding" it to get a thin rectangle of length $2\pi r$ and width

(a)   (b)

FIGURE 12-20 The mass element dm may be "unwound" into a thin rectangle of length $2\pi r$ and width dr.

FIGURE 12-21 The rotational inertia of a rod about an axis through one end is *not* twice that about an axis through the center. Why not?

dr (Fig. 12-20)—and therefore area $2\pi r\, dr$. Multiplying this infinitesimal ring area by the mass per unit area $M/\pi R^2$ gives the mass dm of the ring;

$$dm = (2\pi r\, dr)\left(\frac{M}{\pi R^2}\right) = \frac{2M}{R^2} r\, dr.$$

Using this result in our integral for I then gives

$$I = \int_{r=0}^{r=R} r^2\, dm = \int_0^R r^2 \frac{2M}{R^2} r\, dr = \frac{2M}{R^2} \int_0^R r^3\, dr$$

$$(12\text{-}19)$$

$$= \frac{2M}{R^2} \left.\frac{r^4}{4}\right|_0^R = \tfrac{1}{2} MR^2 . \quad \text{(disk)}$$

Does this make sense? In the disk, mass is distributed from the axis out to the edge. Mass nearer the axis contributes less to the rotational inertia, so we expect a lower rotational inertia for the disk than for a ring of the same mass and radius.

EXERCISE Find the rotational inertia of a thin rod of length ℓ and mass M when it's rotated about an axis through one end (Fig. 12-21). Why isn't your answer twice the answer for Example 12-6?

Answer: $I = \tfrac{1}{3} M\ell^2$

Some problems similar to Examples 12-6 through 12-8: 30, 36, 72, 73

Tip

Constants and Variables Note the different roles of R and r in Example 12-8. R represents a fixed quantity—the actual radius of the disk. Even though we haven't assigned it a specific numerical value, it's a constant quantity as far as the calculation is concerned—and therefore we can take it outside the integral sign. On the other hand, r is the *variable of integration.* It's the quantity that changes as we range from the disk's center to its edge, picking up the contributions all the infinitesimal ring-shaped mass elements make to the total rotational inertia. Because r is a variable over the region of integration, we can't take it outside the integral.

Where we have in the same problem a physical quantity like radius that appears as both a fixed value (e.g., the disk radius R) and a variable (e.g., r, the radial distance of an arbitrary point from the disk center), we'll frequently use capital letters for the constant and lowercase for the variable.

The rotational inertias of other shapes about various axes may be found by integration as in these examples. Table 12-2 lists results for some common shapes. Note that more than one rotational inertia is listed for some shapes, since the rotational inertia depends on the rotation axis.

TABLE 12-2 *Rotational Inertias*

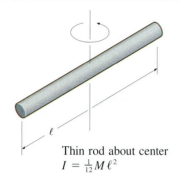

Thin rod about center
$I = \frac{1}{12}M\ell^2$

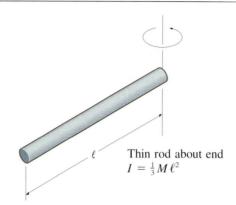

Thin rod about end
$I = \frac{1}{3}M\ell^2$

Thin ring or hollow cylinder
about its axis
$I = MR^2$

Disk or solid cylinder
about its axis
$I = \frac{1}{2}MR^2$

Solid cylinder about its perpendicular bisector
$I = \frac{1}{4}MR^2 + \frac{1}{12}M\ell^2$

Solid sphere about diameter
$I = \frac{2}{5}MR^2$

Hollow spherical shell about diameter
$I = \frac{2}{3}MR^2$

Solid sphere about tangent line
$I = \frac{7}{5}MR^2$

Flat plate about perpendicular axis
$I = \frac{1}{12}M(a^2 + b^2)$

Flat plate about central axis
$I = \frac{1}{12}Ma^2$

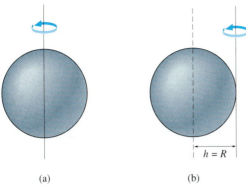

(a)   (b)

FIGURE 12-22 Meaning of the parallel-axis theorem, as applied to Example 12-9. (a) We know the rotational inertia of a solid sphere about an axis through its center, call that $I_{diameter}$. (b) We want the rotational inertia of the same object about a different axis, parallel to the first. Here the new axis is tangent to the sphere. The rotational inertia about the new axis is the known quantity $I_{diameter}$ plus the quantity Mh^2, where h is the distance between the parallel axes and M is the object's mass. Here $I_{diameter} = \frac{2}{5}MR^2$ and $h = R$, so the parallel-axis theorem gives $I_{tangent} = \frac{7}{5}MR^2$.

If we know the rotational inertia, I_{cm}, about an axis through the center of mass of a body, a useful relation called the **parallel-axis theorem** allows us to calculate the rotational inertia, I, through any parallel axis. The parallel-axis theorem states that

$$I = I_{cm} + Mh^2, \tag{12-20}$$

where h is the distance from the center of mass axis to the parallel axis and M the total mass of the object. Problem 37 explores the proof of this theorem, while Fig. 12-22 shows its meaning in the context of Example 12-9.

EXAMPLE 12-9	*The Parallel-Axis Theorem*

Use the parallel-axis theorem, along with Table 12-2's entry for the rotational inertia of a solid sphere about a diameter, to verify the table's entry for the sphere about a tangent line.

Solution

Table 12-2 gives $I_{diameter} = \frac{2}{5}MR^2$ for the sphere about a diameter. The tangent line is one radius R from the center, and parallel to a diameter (see Fig. 12-22), so we can apply the parallel-axis theorem:

$$I_{tangent} = I_{diameter} + MR^2 = \frac{2}{5}MR^2 + MR^2 = \frac{7}{5}MR^2.$$

Tip

Save Work Integrating to get the result of this example would have been exceedingly tedious. The parallel-axis theorem can save a lot of work! Similarly, you can often find the rotational inertia of a composite object by adding contributions from different parts if they have the shapes shown in Table 12-2.

EXERCISE Use the parallel-axis theorem and the result of Example 12-6 to verify the answer to the exercise following Example 12-8.

Some problems similar to Example 12-9: 31, 63, 64

Got It!

Explain why the rotational inertia of the solid sphere in Table 12-2 is less than that of the spherical shell with the same radius and the same mass.

Rotational Dynamics

7.10
Rotoride

Knowing a body's rotational inertia, we can use the rotational analog of Newton's second law (Equation 12-14) to determine its behavior, just as we used Newton's law itself to analyze linear motion. As with the force in Newton's law, the torque in Equation 12-14 is the *net* external torque—the sum of all external torques acting on the body.

EXAMPLE 12-10	*De-Spinning a Satellite*

A cylindrical satellite is 1.4 m in diameter, with its mass of 940 kg distributed approximately uniformly throughout its volume. The satellite is spinning at 10 rpm about its axis but must be stopped so that a space shuttle crew can make repairs. Two small gas jets, each with a thrust of 20 N, are mounted on opposite sides of the satellite and are aimed tangent to the satellite's surface (Fig. 12-23). How long must the jets be fired in order to stop the satellite's rotation?

Solution
The satellite's angular speed must change by $\Delta\omega = 10$ rpm. At constant angular acceleration α, this takes time

$$\Delta t = \frac{\Delta\omega}{\alpha} = \frac{\Delta\omega I}{\tau},$$

where we've used Equation 12-14 to write $\alpha = \tau/I$. From Table 12-2 the rotational inertia of the cylindrical satellite is $I = \frac{1}{2}MR^2$. The torque exerted by both jets, each a distance R from the rotation axis and directed perpendicular to the radius, is $\tau = 2RF$, with F the thrust of one jet. Then our expression for Δt becomes

$$\Delta t = \frac{(\Delta\omega)(\frac{1}{2}MR^2)}{2RF} = \frac{\Delta\omega MR}{4F}$$

$$= \frac{(10\text{ rpm})(2\pi\text{ rad/rev})}{60\text{ s/min}}\frac{(940\text{ kg})(0.70\text{ m})}{(4)(20\text{ N})} = 8.6\text{ s},$$

FIGURE 12-23 Satellite with gas jets (Example 12-10).

where we have converted the change in angular speed from rpm to rad/s.

EXERCISE Essentially all the mass of a 740-g bicycle wheel is concentrated in its rim, 34 cm from the rotation axis. You have the bicycle upside down, with the wheel spinning freely at 210 rpm, in order to adjust the brakes. What frictional force must the brakes apply to the wheel rim if they're to bring the wheel to a stop in 0.92 s?

Answer: 6.0 N

Some problems similar to Example 12-10: 39, 44

Often, rotational and linear motion are coupled in a single problem. Then we use the relations between linear and rotational motion to formulate equations containing all the unknowns of the problem. The following example illustrates this procedure:

EXAMPLE 12-11	*Rotational and Linear Dynamics*

A solid cylinder of mass M and radius R is mounted on a frictionless horizontal axle over a well, as shown in Fig. 12-24. A rope of negligible mass is wrapped around the cylinder, and a bucket of mass m is suspended from the rope. Find an expression for the acceleration of the bucket as it falls down the empty well shaft.

Solution
Were it not connected to the cylinder, the bucket would, of course, accelerate downward with linear acceleration g. But now the rope exerts an upward tension force T on the bucket, reducing the net downward force and at the same time exerting a torque on the cylinder. The downward force on the bucket is

FIGURE 12-24 Example 12-11.

FIGURE 12-25 Free-body diagram for the bucket. The net downward force is $mg - T$.

$F = mg - T$ (Fig. 12-25), so Newton's second law gives

$$ma = mg - T,$$

where a is the linear acceleration of the bucket. Looking at the cylinder end-on (Fig. 12-26), we see that the rope exerts a torque $\tau = RT$ on the cylinder, giving it an angular acceleration

$$\alpha = \frac{\tau}{I} = \frac{RT}{I},$$

where I is the rotational inertia.

As the rope unwinds, the tangential acceleration of the cylinder edge must be equal to the bucket's linear acceleration. Therefore $a = \alpha R$, or, using our expression for α,

FIGURE 12-26 End view of the cylinder, showing that the rope tension T exerts a torque RT about the cylinder axis.

$$a = \alpha R = \frac{R^2 T}{I}.$$

The tension T is the same throughout the massless rope. Solving the above equation for this tension and using the result in our statement of Newton's law gives

$$ma = mg - \frac{I}{R^2} a,$$

so

$$\left(m + \frac{I}{R^2}\right) a = mg.$$

Solving for the acceleration a, and noting that the rotational inertia of a solid cylinder about its axis is $I = \frac{1}{2}MR^2$, we have

$$a = \frac{mg}{m + \frac{1}{2}M}.$$

Is this result reasonable? If the cylinder mass M is small compared with the bucket mass m, the rotation of the cylinder is unimportant and the acceleration is simply g. But more generally, the gravitational force on the bucket provides not only the bucket's linear acceleration, but also the angular acceleration of the cylinder. As a result, the linear acceleration is decreased.

EXERCISE Two masses m_1 and m_2 are connected by a rope that passes without slipping over a massive pulley of radius R and rotational inertia I mounted on frictionless bearings, as shown in Fig. 12-27. If $m_1 > m_2$, find an expression for the downward acceleration of m_1, and show that your result makes sense as $I \to 0$. *Hint:* The rope tensions on m_1 and m_2 aren't the same since it's the difference in rope tensions that provides a net torque on the pulley.

Answer: $a = \dfrac{g(m_1 - m_2)}{m_1 + m_2 + (I/R^2)}$

Some problems similar to Example 12-11: 40–42, 45
ActivPhysics Activity 7.12 simulates this example.

7.12
Flywheel Elevator

FIGURE 12-27 As m_1 falls, it not only causes m_2 to accelerate upward but also imparts an angular acceleration to the pulley.

12-4 ROTATIONAL ENERGY

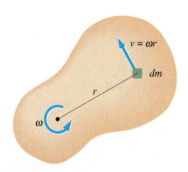

FIGURE 12-28 A mass element dm a distance r from the rotation axis has linear speed $v = \omega r$, giving it kinetic energy $dK = \frac{1}{2}(dm)(\omega r)^2$.

A rotating object clearly has kinetic energy. We define an object's **rotational kinetic energy** as the sum of the kinetic energies of all its mass elements, taken with respect to the rotation axis. (For a refresher on kinetic energy, see Section 7-5.) Figure 12-28 shows that an individual mass element dm a distance r from the rotation axis has kinetic energy given by

$$dK = \tfrac{1}{2}(dm)(v^2) = \tfrac{1}{2}(dm)(\omega r)^2 .$$

The rotational kinetic energy is given by summing—that is, integrating—over the entire object:

$$K_{\text{rot}} = \int dK = \int \tfrac{1}{2}(dm)(\omega r)^2 = \tfrac{1}{2}\omega^2 \int r^2 \, dm ,$$

where we've taken ω^2 outside the integral because it's a constant characterizing the rotation of the entire object. But the remaining integral is just the rotational inertia I, so we have

$$K_{\text{rot}} = \tfrac{1}{2}I\omega^2 . \tag{12-21}$$

This formula should come as no surprise: since I and ω are the rotational analogs of mass and speed, Equation 12-21 is the rotational equivalent of $K = \tfrac{1}{2}mv^2$.

APPLICATION	*Flywheel Energy Storage*

Energy storage is probably the biggest challenge to engineers designing electric and other low-emission vehicles. Traditional electric batteries are heavy, expensive, and simply don't store enough energy. A rotating disk or wheel has kinetic energy; mounted in a vehicle, such a **flywheel** can serve as an alternative energy storage device. Advances in ultrastrong materials and magnetic bearings have made high-speed, efficient flywheels a reality.

New generation car designs are focusing on gasoline-electric hybrids in which a small gasoline engine, running only when needed, produces mechanical energy that is then stored as rotational kinetic energy in a flywheel. The spinning flywheel powers an electric generator that drives electric motors that turn the car's wheels. A typical prototype flywheel stores some 10 MJ of energy in a 50-kg rotor spinning at 30,000 rpm or more. Such high speeds require very strong materials, since tension forces in the material must provide the force of magnitude $m\omega^2 r$ (recall Equation 12-7) needed to hold all parts of the rotor in circular motion. Advanced flywheel designs use carbon composite materials for this reason. To minimize frictional losses, high-speed flywheels use magnetic bearings that eliminate contact between spinning and stationary parts. The most advanced of these use high-temperature superconducting materials (more on these in the chapters on electromagnetism and modern physics); they achieve effective friction coefficients as low as 10^{-6} and lose only about 5 percent of their kinetic energy in an hour. Figure 12-29 shows a prototype flywheel design, while Problems 44, 46, and 52 explore the physics of flywheels.

FIGURE 12-29 This flywheel for a gas-electric hybrid car can store 16 MJ of rotational kinetic energy.

EXAMPLE 12-12	*Earth's Rotational Energy*

Estimate the rotational kinetic energy of Earth, assuming it to be a solid sphere of uniform density.

Solution

To use Equation 12-21 for rotational kinetic energy, we need the rotational inertia and angular velocity of Earth. From Table 12-2, we find that $I = \frac{2}{5}MR^2$ for a uniform solid sphere, so

$$K_{rot} = \frac{1}{2}I\omega^2 = \frac{1}{5}MR^2\omega^2.$$

Obtaining M and R from Appendix E, and converting Earth's angular speed of 1 rev/day to rad/s, we have

$$K_{rot} = \frac{(5.97\times10^{24}\text{ kg})(6.37\times10^6\text{ m})^2}{5}$$

$$\times\left(\frac{1.0\text{ rev/day})(2\pi\text{ rad/rev})}{(3600\text{ s/h})(24\text{ h/day})}\right)^2 = 2.56\times10^{29}\text{ J}.$$

Actually, more of Earth's mass is concentrated toward the center, reducing the rotational inertia and making this value an overestimate.

Tip

Know When to Use Radians We used Equation 12-5, $v = \omega r$, in deriving Equation 12-21. Since Equation 12-5 works only with radian measure, the same is true for Equation 12-21.

EXERCISE In the magnet laboratory at the Massachusetts Institute of Technology (MIT), huge flywheels are used to store energy that eventually powers strong electromagnets. Each flywheel is a solid disk 2.4 m in radius, with a mass of 7.7×10^4 kg. How much energy does each wheel store when it's rotating at 360 rpm?

Answer: 158 MJ

Some problems similar to Example 12-12: 47, 49, 52

Energy and Work in Rotational Motion

A force acting in one dimension does work on an object and changes the kinetic energy of its straight-line motion. Similarly, a torque does work on an object, changing its rotational kinetic energy. Suppose a torque τ acts to rotate a rigid body through a small angle $d\theta$, as suggested in Fig. 12-30. We can think of this torque as arising from the force **F** shown in the figure. If the force is applied a distance r from the rotation axis, then the force application point moves through a distance $ds = rd\theta$. Acting over this distance, the force does work $dW = Fds$. But $\tau = rF$, so $F = \tau/r$, and $dW = Fds$ becomes $dW = \tau d\theta$. If the torque is constant, the work done as the object rotates through any angle $\Delta\theta$ is then

$$W = \tau\Delta\theta. \quad \text{(constant torque)} \quad (12\text{-}22a)$$

If the torque varies with angular position then we need to integrate:

$$W = \int dW = \int \tau\, d\theta. \quad (12\text{-}22b)$$

FIGURE 12-30 The force **F** acts over a distance $ds = rd\theta$ while rotating the rigid body through a very small angle $d\theta$. The work done is Fds, and the torque is rF.

Equations 12-22a and 12-22b are equivalent, respectively, to $W = F\Delta x$ and $W = \int F dx$ that we developed in Sections 7-1 and 7-2 for straight-line motion. Problem 78 shows how Equation 12-22b leads to the rotational version of the work-energy theorem, which states that the work done by torques on a body rotating about a fixed axis is equal to the change in rotational kinetic energy:

$$W = \int_{\theta_0}^{\theta_f} \tau\, d\theta = \Delta K_{rot} = \frac{1}{2}I\omega_f^2 - \frac{1}{2}I\omega_0^2, \quad (12\text{-}23)$$

where the subscripts refer to the initial and final values. Equation 12-23 is the rotational analog of the work-energy theorem we derived in Chapter 7.

*Activ*Physics

7.14, 7.15
Energy Approach to Rotational Dynamics

EXAMPLE 12-13	*Spinning a Gyroscope*

A gyroscope consists of a ring of mass $M = 85$ g and radius $R = 2.6$ cm, connected by essentially massless spokes to an axle of negligible mass (Fig. 12-31). A massless string of length $\ell = 45$ cm is wrapped around the axle and pulled with a steady force $F = 3.7$ N. If the string unwinds without slipping, find the final speed of the gyroscope. If the torque due to the string is 7.4×10^{-3} N·m, how many revolutions does the gyroscope make while the string is being pulled?

Solution

We don't know the angular displacement $\Delta\theta$, so we can't immediately use $W = \tau\Delta\theta$ to determine the work. But we do know the work done by the agent pulling the string—with constant force, that's just $W = F\ell$. And since the string is massless, energy conservation ensures that all that work ends up as rotational kinetic energy. So we have

$$\tfrac{1}{2}I\omega^2 = F\ell \, .$$

Solving for ω and using $I = MR^2$ for the ring gives

$$\omega = \sqrt{\frac{2F\ell}{I}} = \sqrt{\frac{2F\ell}{MR^2}} = \sqrt{\frac{(2)(3.7 \text{ N})(0.45 \text{ m})}{(0.085 \text{ kg})(0.026 \text{ m})^2}}$$

$$= 240 \text{ rad/s} \, .$$

As with linear motion, conservation of energy provides a quick route to the final answer.

Since the work $F\ell$ done in pulling the string is equal to the work $\tau\Delta\theta$ done on the gyroscope, we must have

FIGURE 12-31 A gyroscope (Example 12-13).

$$\Delta\theta = \frac{F\ell}{\tau} = \frac{(3.7 \text{ N})(0.45 \text{ m})}{7.4 \times 10^{-3} \text{ N·m}} = 225 \text{ rad} = 36 \text{ rev} \, .$$

EXERCISE Mounted on its rim, an automobile tire has a radius of 38 cm and a rotational inertia of 2.7 kg·m^2. A tire testing machine spins up the tire by applying a force at the outer edge of the tire. If the force is at right angles to a radius, what should its magnitude be if the tire is to reach 690 rpm in 30 revolutions?

Answer: 98 N

Some problems similar to Example 12-13: 51, 65, 66

12-5 ROLLING MOTION

FIGURE 12-32 A rolling wheel has both translational and rotational motion.

A rolling object, like the wheel of Fig. 12-32, exhibits both rotational motion and translational motion—the latter meaning the motion of the whole object from place to place. How much kinetic energy is associated with each of these motions?

In Section 10-3, we found that the kinetic energy of a composite object comprises two terms: the kinetic energy of the center of mass and the so-called internal kinetic energy of the particles making up that object as they move with respect to the center of mass. We expressed this in Equation 10-13: $K = K_{cm} + K_{internal}$. In Fig. 12-32, the entire wheel moves with speed v; its center-of-mass kinetic energy is therefore $K_{cm} = \tfrac{1}{2}Mv^2$, where M is its total mass. In the center-of-mass frame, the wheel is simply rotating with angular speed ω about the center of mass. Its internal kinetic energy is therefore the kinetic energy of its rotation: $K_{internal} = \tfrac{1}{2}I_{cm}\omega^2$. Here we indicate explicitly that the rotational inertia is taken about the center of mass, since we want the energy of the wheel relative to the center of mass. We now sum K_{cm} and $K_{internal}$ to get the total kinetic energy:

$$K_{total} = \tfrac{1}{2}Mv^2 + \tfrac{1}{2}I_{cm}\omega^2 \, . \tag{12-24}$$

When a wheel is truly *rolling*—moving without slipping against the ground—its translational speed v and angular speed ω about its center of mass are related; we now explore that relation. Imagine a wheel that rolls for half a revolution. If it doesn't slip against the ground, it must cover a horizontal distance equal to half its circumference, as shown in Fig. 12-33. Let's say this happens in some time Δt. Then the wheel's angular speed is the angular displacement $\Delta\theta$, here half a revolution, or π radians, divided by the time Δt: $\omega = \pi/\Delta t$. Its translational speed is the actual distance the wheel travels divided by the same time interval. But we've just argued that it travels half a circumference, or πR, where R is the wheel's radius. So its translational speed is $v = \pi R/\Delta t$. Comparing our expressions for v and ω, we see immediately that

$$v = \omega R, \quad \text{(rolling motion)} \tag{12-25}$$

for a wheel rolling without slipping.

Equation 12-25 looks deceptively like Equation 12-4 at the beginning of the chapter. But it says more. In Equation 12-4, which reads $v = \omega r$, v is the linear speed of a point a distance r from the center of a rotating object. In Equation 12-25, v is the translational speed of the whole object and R its radius for an object that *rolls without slipping*. The two equations look similar because, as our argument leading to Equation 12-25 shows, an object that rolls without slipping moves with respect to the ground at the same rate that a point on its rim moves in the center-of-mass frame.

Our description of rolling motion leads to a point you may at first find absurd: in a rolling wheel, the point in contact with the ground is, instantaneously, at rest! Figure 12-34 shows how this comes about. Here we decompose a rolling wheel's motion into pure translation of the center of mass and pure rotation about the center of mass—just as we did in writing the separate kinetic energy terms in Equation 12-24. Figure 12-34 shows how these two motions sum to give rolling motion in which the wheel's axle moves with the center-of-mass velocity (no surprise here!), the top of the wheel moves twice as fast, and the bottom is instantaneously at rest.

FIGURE 12-33 A rolling wheel turns through half a revolution. If it doesn't slip, it moves horizontally a distance equal to half its circumference, or πR.

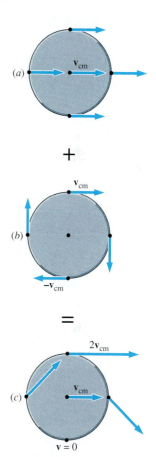

FIGURE 12-34 Motion of a rolling wheel can be decomposed into (a) pure translation of the entire wheel and (b) pure rotation about the center of mass. The actual motion (c) is the sum of these two, and shows that the center of mass moves with the wheel's speed v, while the top of the wheel moves twice as fast. Note especially that for the point in contact with the ground, the two velocity vectors in (a) and (b) sum to zero. The contact point is therefore instantaneously at rest.

Tip

Instantaneous Rest? How can that be, when the wheel is rolling? The key word is "instantaneous." The point that's *now* in contact with the ground and therefore isn't moving is only *instantaneously* at rest. It will be moving an instant later, leaving the ground as it participates in the wheel's rotation. Another point on the wheel will take its place on the ground. And so forth. This is really no more mysterious than saying that a ball thrown straight up is instantaneously at rest at the top of its trajectory. Just before that instant it was moving upward; just afterward it will be moving down—but for an instant it truly has zero velocity. It's the same for the point at the bottom of the wheel.

Why would an object roll without slipping? The answer is friction. Put a wheel on an icy slope and it would simply slide down, without rolling. But put it on a frictional slope and the force of static friction keeps it from sliding.

FIGURE 12-35 A wheel on a sloping surface. The force of static friction acts to keep the bottom of the wheel from slipping, so the wheel rolls rather than slides down the surface. Not shown are the gravitational force and the normal force on the wheel.

Instead, it rolls (Fig. 12-35). Because the contact point is at rest, the frictional force does no work and therefore mechanical energy is conserved. This fact lets us use the powerful conservation-of-energy principle, in conjunction with Equations 12-24 and 12-25, to analyze the motion of rolling objects. Example 12-14 shows how.

EXAMPLE 12-14	*Rolling Downhill*

A solid ball of M and radius R starts from rest and rolls without slipping down a hill; its center of mass drops a total distance h (Fig. 12-36). Find the ball's speed at the bottom of the hill.

Solution

Mechanical energy is conserved, so as usual we can equate the initial potential energy Mgh to the final kinetic energy. Now, however, the final kinetic energy consists of both rotational and translational energy, as given by Equation 12-24. So we have

$$Mgh = \tfrac{1}{2}I_{cm}\omega^2 + \tfrac{1}{2}Mv^2.$$

But $\omega = v/R$ for a rolling object, and Table 12-2 gives $I_{cm} = \tfrac{2}{5}MR^2$ for a solid sphere, so

$$Mgh = \tfrac{1}{5}MR^2\left(\frac{v}{R}\right)^2 + \tfrac{1}{2}Mv^2 = \tfrac{7}{10}Mv^2.$$

Solving for v then gives

$$v = \sqrt{\frac{10}{7}gh}.$$

This is less than the speed $v = \sqrt{2gh}$ for an object that slides without rolling down a frictionless incline. Why? Because some of the energy the rolling object gains goes into rotation, leaving less for translational motion.

FIGURE 12-36 How fast is the ball moving at the bottom of the hill (Example 12-14)?

EXERCISE You're about to change a flat tire, but when you get out the spare tire it rolls away down a hill. The 28-kg spare is 70 cm in diameter and has rotational inertia 1.7 kg·m². How fast is it rolling after it goes a vertical distance of 15 m?

Answer: 14 m/s

Some problems similar to Example 12-14: 53–55, 67, 68

ActivPhysics Activity 7.13 will help you understand this example.

7.13
Race between a Block and a Disk

Got It!

A solid ball and a hollow ball, both with the same mass and radius, roll down a ramp. Which reaches the bottom first?

CHAPTER SYNOPSIS

Summary

Rotational motion is described using quantities analogous to those of linear motion. These rotational quantities satisfy the same relations as their linear counterparts, making problems involving rotational motion similar to the linear motion problems of previous chapters. Table 12-3 summarizes the analogies between linear and rotational motion.

1. The rotational analog of displacement is **angular displacement**, defined as the angle through which an object has rotated. The SI unit of angular displacement is the radian. The first and second time derivatives of angular displacement are **angular velocity**, ω, and **angular acceleration**, α.

TABLE 12-3 *Linear and Angular Quantities*

LINEAR QUANTITY OR EQUATION	ANGULAR QUANTITY OR EQUATION	RELATION BETWEEN LINEAR AND ANGULAR QUANTITIES
Position x	Angular position θ	
Speed $v = dx/dt$	Angular speed $\omega = d\theta/dt$	$v_t = \omega r$
Acceleration a	Angular acceleration α	$a_t = \alpha r$
Mass m	Rotational inertia I	$I = \int r^2 dm$
Force F	Torque τ	$\tau = rF \sin\theta$

Newton's second law (constant mass or rotational inertia):

$F = ma$ $\qquad\qquad$ $\tau = I\alpha$

Kinetic energy:

$K_{\text{trans}} = \frac{1}{2}mv^2$ $\qquad\qquad$ $K_{\text{rot}} = \frac{1}{2}I\omega^2$

2. The rotational analog of mass is **rotational inertia**, a quantity that measures the resistance of a body to changes in rotational motion. Rotational inertia depends on the mass of a body and on the distribution of mass about the rotation axis, and is given by

$$I = \sum m_i r_i^2$$

for a body consisting of discrete masses, and by

$$I = \int r^2 \, dm$$

for a continuous distribution of matter.

3. **Torque** is the rotational analog of force; torque, rotational inertia, and angular acceleration are related by the rotational analog of Newton's second law:

$$\tau = I\alpha .$$

4. **Rotational kinetic energy** is calculated from rotational inertia and angular speed in the same way that translational kinetic energy is calculated from mass and linear speed.

$$K_{\text{rot}} = \frac{1}{2}I\omega^2 .$$

The total kinetic energy of a rigid, rotating object may be written as the sum of the translational kinetic energy of its center of mass and the rotational kinetic energy about its center of mass.

Terms You Should Understand

(Pairs are closely related terms whose distinction is important; number in parentheses is chapter section where term first appears.)

angular displacement (12-1)
angular velocity (average, instantaneous) (12-1)
angular acceleration (12-1)
torque (12-2)
rotational inertia (12-3)
parallel-axis theorem (12-3)
rotational kinetic energy (12-4)
rolling motion (12-5)

Symbols You Should Recognize

ω (12-1) $\qquad$ I (12-3)
α (12-1) $\qquad$ K_{rot} (12-4)
τ (12-2)

Problems You Should Be Able to Solve

calculating angular velocity and acceleration (12-1)
relating angular and linear velocities and accelerations (12-1)
solving rotational analogs of problems in one-dimensional motion with constant acceleration (12-1)
calculating torques (12-2)
calculating rotational inertias by summing over discrete masses (12-3)
calculating rotational inertias by integrating over solid objects (12-3)
solving for rotational motion given torque and rotational inertia (12-3)
solving problems that mix linear and rotational motion (12-3)
calculating rotational energies (12-4)
applying the work-energy theorem for rotational motion (12-4)
applying conservation of energy to the motion of rolling objects (12-5)

Limitations to Keep in Mind

Some problems, namely, all those derived using the relation $v = \omega r$ are valid only when angular quantities are given using radian measure.
The results given in this chapter apply only when the orientation of the rotation axis remains fixed.

QUESTIONS

1. Do all points on a rigid, rotating object have the same angular velocity? linear speed? radial acceleration?

2. Suppose you mount tires on your car that are slightly larger in diameter than factory-supplied tires. If you are in a 55 mi/h zone and your speedometer says 55 mi/h, are you speeding? Explain.

3. A wheel undergoes a constant angular acceleration. How do each of the following depend on time: (a) tangential acceleration of a point on the rim? (b) radial acceleration of a point on the rim? (c) angular velocity of the wheel?

4. Part of a train wheel extends below the point of contact with the rails, as shown in Fig. 12-37. It is often said that this part of the train moves backward. Explain.

FIGURE 12-37 Question 4.

5. A point on the rim of a rotating wheel has nonzero acceleration, since it is moving in a circular path. Does it necessarily follow that the wheel is undergoing angular acceleration?

6. Why doesn't it make sense to talk about a body's rotational inertia unless a rotation axis is specified?

7. Two different forces act on an object, but the net force is zero. Must the net torque be zero? If so, why? If not, give a counterexample.

8. Is it possible to apply a counterclockwise torque to an object that's rotating clockwise? If not, why not? If so, how will the object's motion change?

9. A solid sphere and a hollow sphere, of the same mass and radius, are rolling along level ground. If they have the same kinetic energy, which is moving faster?

10. A solid cylinder and a hollow cylinder, of the same mass and radius, are rolling along level ground at the same speed. Which has more kinetic energy?

11. As the wheel in Fig. 12-10 rotates, does the torque due to the weight of the valve stem remain constant? Explain.

12. What is meant by the statement that the point where a rotating wheel contacts the ground is instantaneously at rest? If it's true, how can the wheel be moving?

13. An electric circular saw takes a long time to stop rotating after the power is turned off. Without the saw blade mounted, the motor stops much more quickly when turned off. Why?

14. A solid sphere and a solid cube have the same mass, and the side of the cube is equal to the diameter of the sphere. Which has the greatest rotational inertia about an axis

through the center of mass? The rotational axis for the cube is perpendicular to two of the cube faces.

15. A badly unbalanced wheel has its center of mass located closer to its rim than to its geometrical center. The wheel is released from rest on a slope where it is free to roll without slipping. Describe its initial motion when released from each of the orientations shown in Fig. 12-38.

FIGURE 12-38 How will the wheel move? Red dot indicates its center of mass (Question 15).

16. The lower leg of a horse contains essentially no muscle. How does this help the horse to run fast? Explain in terms of rotational inertia.

17. You wish to store energy in a rotating flywheel. Given a fixed amount of a material, what shape should you make the flywheel so it will store the most energy at a given angular speed?

18. A ball starts from rest and rolls without slipping down a slope, then starts up a *frictionless* slope (Fig. 12-39). Compare its maximum height on the frictionless slope with its starting height on the first slope.

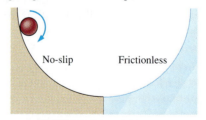

FIGURE 12-39 Question 18.

19. Two solid cylinders of the same mass but different radii are rolling with the same linear speed. How do their translational and rotational kinetic energies compare?

20. A raw egg and a hard-boiled egg, otherwise identical, are rolled down an incline. Which hits the bottom first? Explain.

21. What happens to the rotational inertia of a washing machine tub and its contents when the spin portion of the cycle starts?

PROBLEMS

ActivPhysics can help with these problems:
Activities 7.7, 7.8, 7.10, 7.12, 7.13, 7.14, 7.15

Section 12-1 Angular Velocity and Acceleration

1. Determine the angular speed, in rad/s, of (a) Earth about its axis; (b) the minute hand of a clock; (c) the hour hand of a clock; (d) an egg beater turning at 300 rpm.
2. What is the linear speed (a) of a point on Earth's equator? (b) At your latitude?
3. Express each of the following in radians per second: (a) 720 rpm; (b) 50°/h; (c) 1000 rev/s; (d) 1 rev/year (which is the angular speed of Earth in its orbit).
4. A 25-cm-diameter circular saw blade spins at 3500 rpm. How fast would you have to push a straight hand saw to have the teeth move through the wood at the same rate as the circular saw teeth?
5. A wheel turns through 2.0 revolutions while being accelerated from rest at 18 rpm/s. (a) What is the final angular speed? (b) How long does it take to turn the 2.0 revolutions?
6. You switch a food blender from its high to its low setting; the blade speed drops from 3600 rpm to 1800 rpm in 1.4 s. How many revolutions does it make during this time?
7. A compact disc (CD) player varies the rotation rate of the disc in order to keep the part of the disk from which information is being read moving at a constant linear speed of 1.30 m/s. Compare the rotation rates of a 12.0-cm-diameter CD when information is being read from (a) its outer edge and (b) a point 3.75 cm from the center. Give your answers in rad/s and rpm.
8. The maximum rotation rate of a compact disc is 500 rpm. What is the minimum distance from the center at which information is read from the disc? Refer to the preceding problem for necessary information.
9. The rotation rate of a compact disc varies from about 200 rpm to 500 rpm (see Problem 7). If the disc plays for 74 min, what is its average angular acceleration in (a) rpm/s and (b) rad/s²?
10. You rev your car's engine and watch the tachometer climb steadily from 1200 rpm to 5500 rpm in 2.7 s. (a) What is the angular acceleration of the engine? (b) What is the tangential acceleration of a point on the edge of the engine's 3.5-cm-diameter crankshaft? (c) How many revolutions does the engine make during this time?
11. During startup of a power plant, a turbine accelerates from rest at 0.52 rad/s². (a) How long does it take to reach its 3600-rpm operating speed? (b) How many revolutions does it make during this time?
12. A wheel is spinning at 47 rad/s when an acceleration of 0.72 rad/s² is applied. If the acceleration lasts for 140 revolutions, what is the final angular speed?
13. A piece of machinery is spinning at 680 rpm. When a brake is applied, its rotation rate drops to 440 rpm while it turns

through 180 revolutions. What is the magnitude of the angular deceleration?
14. A circular saw blade completes 1200 revolutions in 40 s while coasting to a stop after being turned off. Assuming constant deceleration, what are (a) the angular deceleration and (b) the initial angular speed?
15. The angular acceleration of a wheel in rad/s² is given by $24t^2 - 16t^3$, where t is the time in seconds. The wheel starts from rest at $t = 0$. (a) When is it again at rest? (b) How many revolutions has it turned between $t = 0$ and when it is again at rest?

Section 12-2 Torque

16. A frictional force of 320 N acts on the rim of a 1.0-m-diameter wheel to oppose its rotational motion. What is the torque about the wheel's central axis?
17. A torque of 110 N·m is required to start a revolving door rotating. If a child can push with a maximum force of 90 N, how far from the door's rotation axis must she apply this force?
18. A car tune-up manual calls for tightening the spark plugs to a torque of 35.0 N·m. To achieve this torque, with what force must you pull on the end of a 24.0-cm-long wrench if you pull (a) at right angles to the wrench shaft and (b) at 110° to the wrench shaft?
19. A 55-g mouse runs out to the end of the 17-cm-long minute hand of a grandfather clock when the clock reads 10 minutes past the hour. What torque does the mouse's weight exert about the rotation axis of the clock hand?
20. In a large steam engine, a horizontal rod is attached to a flywheel by means of a frictionless pivot 95 cm from the wheel's axis. If the rod pushes with 13 kN force, what is the torque about the wheel's axis in the configuration shown in Fig. 12-40?

FIGURE 12-40 Problems 20, 29.

21. A pulley 12 cm in diameter is free to rotate about a horizontal axle. A 220-g mass and a 470-g mass are tied to either end of a massless string, and the string is hung over the pulley. If the string does not slip, what torque must be applied to keep the pulley from rotating?

22. Two arm wrestlers are deadlocked in the position shown in Fig. 12-41. Each arm is 34 cm long and makes a 60° angle with the horizontal; the contact force at the hands is 180 N. What is the torque each exerts about the other's elbow? Neglect the weights of the wrestlers' arms.

FIGURE 12-41 Problem 22.

23. A 1.5-m-diameter wheel is mounted on an axle through its center. (a) Find the net torque about the axle due to the forces shown in Fig. 12-42. (b) Are there any forces that don't contribute to the torque?

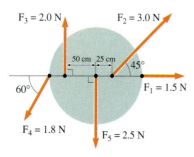

FIGURE 12-42 Problem 23.

Section 12-3 Rotational Inertia and the Analog of Newton's Law

24. Four equal masses m are located at the corners of a square of side ℓ, connected by essentially massless rods. Find the rotational inertia of this system about an axis (a) that coincides with one side and (b) that bisects two opposite sides.

25. The shaft connecting a turbine and electric generator in a power plant is a solid cylinder of mass 6.8×10^3 kg and diameter 85 cm. Find its rotational inertia.

26. The chamber of a rock-tumbling machine is a hollow cylinder with mass 65 g and radius 7.1 cm. The chamber is closed off by end caps in the form of uniform circular disks each of mass 22 g. (a) What is the rotational inertia of the chamber about its central axis? (b) What torque is necessary to give the chamber an angular acceleration of 3.4 rad/s²?

27. A square frame is made from four thin rods, each of length ℓ and mass m. Calculate its rotational inertia about the three axes shown in Fig. 12-43.

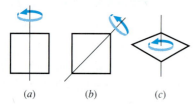

FIGURE 12-43 Problem 27.

28. The full diameter of a wheel is 92 cm, and its rotational inertia is 7.8 kg·m². (a) What is the minimum mass it could have? (b) How could it have more mass?

29. The wheel shown in Fig. 12-40 consists of a 120-kg outer rim 55 cm in radius, connected to the center by five 18-kg spokes. Treating the rim as a thin ring and the spokes as thin rods, determine the rotational inertia of the wheel.

30. Use integration to show that the rotational inertia of a thick ring of mass M and inner and outer radii R_1 and R_2 is given by $\frac{1}{2}M(R_1^2 + R_2^2)$. *Hint:* See Example 12-8.

31. A uniform rectangular flat plate has mass M and dimensions a by b. Use the parallel-axis theorem in conjunction with Table 12-2 to show that its rotational inertia about the side of length b is $\frac{1}{3}Ma^2$.

32. A rotating glass door is made from four rectangular panes, each 1.2 m wide by 2.4 m high, joined together along one long edge and at right angles to each other. The mass of each pane is 63 kg. Use the result of the previous problem to find the rotational inertia of the door about its central axis.

33. (a) Estimate the rotational inertia of Earth, assuming it to be a uniform solid sphere. (b) What torque would have to be applied to Earth to cause the length of the day to change by one second every century?

34. Each propeller on a King Air twin engine airplane consists of three blades, each of mass 10 kg and length 125 cm. The blades may be treated approximately as uniform, thin rods. (a) What is the rotational inertia of the propeller? (b) If the propeller is driven by an engine that develops a torque of 2700 N·m, how long will it take to change the propeller's angular speed from 1400 rpm to 1900 rpm? Neglect the rotational inertia of the engine and any aerodynamic forces on the propeller.

35. A neutron star is an extremely dense, rapidly spinning object that results from the collapse of a star at the end of its life. A neutron star of 1.8 times the Sun's mass has an approximately uniform density of 1×10^{18} kg/m³. (a) What is its rotational inertia? (b) The neutron star's spin rate slowly decreases as a result of torque associated with magnetic forces. If the spin-down rate is 5×10^{-5} rad/s², what is the magnetic torque?

36. Verify by direct integration the formula given in Table 12-2 for the rotational inertia of a flat plate about a central axis. *Hint:* Divide the plate into strips parallel to the axis.

37. Proof of the parallel-axis theorem: Fig. 12-44 shows an object of mass M with axes through the center of mass and through an arbitrary point A. Both axes are perpendicular to the page. Let $\mathbf{h}$ be a vector from the axis through the center of mass to the axis through point A, $\mathbf{r}_{cm}$ a vector from the axis through the CM to an arbitrary mass element dm, and $\mathbf{r}$ a vector from the axis through point A to the mass element dm, as shown. (a) Use the law of cosines (Appendix A; derived in Problem 3-65) to show that

$$r^2 = r_{cm}^2 + h^2 - 2\mathbf{h} \cdot \mathbf{r}_{cm}.$$

(b) Use this result in the expression $I = \int r^2 \, dm$ to calculate the rotational inertia of the object about the axis through A. Each of the three terms in your expression for r^2 leads to a separate integral. Identify one as the rotational inertia about the CM, another as the quantity Mh^2, and show that the third is zero because it involves the position of the center of mass relative to itself. Your result is then a statement of the parallel-axis theorem (Equation 12-20).

FIGURE 12-44 Problem 37.

38. A 108-g Frisbee is 24 cm in diameter and has about half its mass spread uniformly in a disk, and the other half concentrated in the rim. With a quarter-turn flick of the wrist, a student sets the Frisbee rotating at 550 rpm. (a) What is the rotational inertia of the Frisbee? (b) What is the magnitude of the torque, assumed constant, that the student applies?

39. A space station is constructed in the shape of a wheel 22 m in diameter, with essentially all of its 5.0×10^5-kg mass at the rim (Fig. 12-45). Once the station is completed, it is set rotating at a rate that requires an object at the rim to have radial acceleration g, thereby simulating Earth's surface gravity. This is accomplished using two small rockets, each with 100 N thrust, that are mounted on the rim of the station as shown. (a) How long will it take to reach the desired spin rate? (b) How many revolutions will the station make in this time?

FIGURE 12-45 Problem 39.

40. A motor is connected to a solid cylindrical drum with a diameter of 1.2 m and a mass of 51 kg. A massless rope is attached to the drum and tied at the other end to a 38-kg weight, so the rope will wind onto the drum as it turns. What torque must the motor apply if the weight is to be lifted with an acceleration of 1.1 m/s²?

41. The crane shown in Fig. 12-46 contains a hollow drum of mass 150 kg and radius 0.80 m that is driven by an engine to wind up a cable. The cable passes over a solid cylindrical 30-kg pulley 0.30 m in radius to lift a 2000-N weight. How much torque must the engine apply to the drum to lift the weight with an acceleration of 1.0 m/s²? Neglect the rotational inertia of the engine and the mass of the cable.

FIGURE 12-46 Problems 41, 66.

42. A 2.4-kg block rests on a 30° slope and is attached by a string of negligible mass to a solid drum of mass 0.85 kg and radius 5.0 cm, as shown in Fig. 12-47. When released, the block accelerates down the slope at 1.6 m/s². What is the coefficient of friction between block and slope?

FIGURE 12-47 Problem 42.

43. A bicycle is under repair and is upside-down with its 66-cm-diameter wheel spinning freely at 230 rpm. The mass of the wheel is 1.9 kg and is concentrated mostly at the rim. The cyclist holds a wrench against the tire for 3.1 s, with a normal force of 2.7 N. If the coefficient of friction between the wrench and the tire is 0.46, what is the final angular speed of the wheel?

44. At the MIT Magnet Laboratory, energy is stored in huge solid flywheels of mass 7.7×10^4 kg and radius 2.4 m. The flywheels ride on shafts 41 cm in diameter. If a frictional force of 34 kN acts tangentially on the shaft, how long will it take the flywheel to coast to a stop from its normal rotation rate of 360 rpm?

45. Two blocks of mass m_1 and m_2 are connected by a massless string that passes over a solid cylindrical pulley, as shown in Fig. 12-48. The surface under the block m_2 is frictionless, and the pulley rides on frictionless bearings. The string passes over the pulley without slipping. When released, the masses accelerate at $\frac{1}{3}g$. The tension in the lower half of the string is 2.7 N and that in the upper half, 1.9 N. What are the masses of the pulley and of the two blocks?

FIGURE 12-48 Problem 45.

Section 12-4 Rotational Energy

46. The flywheel of Problem 44 is used to generate a large amount of electric power for a short time. If the wheel's rotation rate is dropped from 390 to 300 rpm in 5.0 s, (a) what is the average power output and (b) what fraction of the rotational kinetic energy has been removed?

47. A 25-cm-diameter circular saw blade has a mass of 0.85 kg, distributed uniformly as in a disk. (a) What is its rotational kinetic energy at 3500 rpm? (b) What average power must be applied to bring the blade from rest to 3500 rpm in 3.2 s?

48. Humanity uses energy at the rate of about 10^{13} W. If we found a way to extract this energy from Earth's rotation, how long would it take before the length of the day increased by 1 minute?

49. A 150-g baseball is pitched at 33 m/s, spinning at 42 rad/s. What fraction of its kinetic energy is rotational? Treat the baseball as a uniform solid sphere of radius 3.7 cm.

50. A potter's wheel is a stone disk 90 cm in diameter with a mass of 120 kg. If the potter's foot pushes at the outer edge of the initially stationary wheel with a 75-N force for one-eighth of a revolution, what will be the final speed? Use the work-energy theorem.

51. A ship's anchor weighs 5000 N. Its cable passes over a roller of negligible mass and is wound around a hollow cylindrical drum of mass 380 kg and radius 1.1 m, as shown in Fig. 12-49. The drum is mounted on a frictionless axle. The anchor is released and drops 16 m to the water. Use energy considerations to determine the drum's rotation rate when the anchor hits the water. Neglect the mass of the cable.

FIGURE 12-49 Problem 51.

52. A flywheel for energy storage in a hybrid gasoline-electric car is a ring-shaped rotor of mass 48 kg, designed to rotate at 30,000 rpm; at that speed it stores 10 MJ of energy (equivalent to about a cup of gasoline). (a) What is the ring's diameter? (b) If the flywheel can supply power at the rate of 25 kW, how long will it take for its stored energy to be exhausted?

Section 12-5 Rolling Motion

53. A basketball rolls down a 30° incline. If it starts from rest, what is its speed after it's gone 8.4 m along the incline? (The basketball is hollow.)

54. Repeat the preceding problem for a solid baseball, assuming uniform density.

55. As long as its mass is distributed symmetrically about a central axis, a round object like a sphere or wheel may be characterized by a rotational inertia of the form $I = \alpha MR^2$, where α is a constant. Derive a formula for the final speed of such an object if it starts from rest and rolls without slipping down an incline of vertical height h.

56. A hollow ball is rolling along a horizontal surface at 3.7 m/s when it encounters an upward incline. If it rolls without slipping up the incline, what maximum height will it reach?

57. The rotational kinetic energy of a rolling automobile wheel is 40% of its translational kinetic energy. The wheel is then redesigned to have 10% lower rotational inertia and 20% less mass, while keeping its radius the same. By what percentage does its total kinetic energy at a given speed decrease?

58. Two solid cylinders of the same mass roll without slipping down an incline. If they start from the same height h, show that they reach the bottom with the same linear speed, even if their radii are not the same. What is the linear speed at the bottom?

59. A ball rolls without slipping down a slope of vertical height 34 cm, and reaches the bottom moving at 2.0 m/s. Is the ball hollow or solid?

60. A solid ball of mass M and radius R starts at rest at height h above the bottom of the path shown in Fig. 12-50. It rolls without slipping down the left side of the path. The right side of the path, starting at the bottom, is frictionless. To what height does the ball rise on the right?

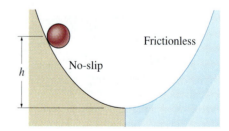

FIGURE 12-50 Problem 60.

Paired Problems

(Both problems in a pair involve the same principles and techniques. If you can get the first problem, you should be able to solve the second one.)

61. A merry-go-round starts from rest and accelerates with angular acceleration 0.010 rad/s^2 for 14 s. (a) How many revolutions does it make during this time? (b) What is its average angular speed during the spin-up time?

62. A wheel spinning initially at 440 rpm is slowed with a constant angular deceleration of 2.8 rad/s² applied for 6.1 s. (a) How many revolutions does it turn during this time? (b) What is its average angular speed during the slowdown?

63. A disk of radius R has an initial mass M. Then a hole of radius $\frac{1}{4}R$ is drilled, with its edge at the disk center (Fig. 12-51). Find the new rotational inertia about the central axis. *Hint:* Find the rotational inertia of the missing piece, and subtract from that of the whole disk. You'll need to determine what fraction the missing mass is of the total M, and you'll need to use the parallel-axis theorem.

FIGURE 12-51 Problems 63, 76.

64. To reduce its rotational inertia, an engineer proposes drilling three holes in a large wheel of radius R. The holes are to be centered midway between the center and edge of the wheel, as shown in Fig. 12-52. What should be their radii if drilling the holes is to reduce the rotational inertia by 15%?

FIGURE 12-52 Problem 64.

65. A 50-kg mass is tied to a massless rope wrapped around a solid cylindrical drum. The drum is mounted on a frictionless horizontal axle. When the mass is released, it falls with acceleration $a = 3.7$ m/s². Find (a) the tension in the rope and (b) the mass of the drum.

66. A crane like that shown in Fig. 12-46 has a hollow drum of mass 110 kg and radius 0.35 m. The pulley at the top of the crane has negligible mass. If a 520 N·m torque is applied to the drum, it undergoes an angular acceleration $\alpha = 1.2$ rad/s². Find the mass being lifted by the crane.

67. Your little sister is building a toy car. She attaches four spools to a 48-g milk carton. The spools are essentially solid cylinders, each with mass 25 g and radius 1.8 cm and are mounted on frictionless axles of negligible mass. Starting from rest, the contraption rolls without slipping down

a slope. (a) How fast is it going after it's dropped a vertical distance of 85 cm? (b) What per cent of its total kinetic energy is in the translational motion of the milk carton alone?

68. A 320-kg motorcycle includes two wheels, each of which is 52 cm in diameter and has rotational inertia 2.1 kg·m². The cycle and its 75-kg rider are coasting at 85 km/h on a flat road when they encounter a hill. If the cycle rolls up the hill with no applied power and no significant internal friction, what vertical height will it reach?

Supplementary Problems

69. A solid marble starts from rest and rolls without slipping on the loop-the-loop track shown in Fig. 12-53. Find the minimum starting height of the marble from which it will remain on the track through the loop. Assume the marble radius is small compared with R.

FIGURE 12-53 Problem 69.

70. A 100-g yo-yo consists of two disks joined by a narrower shaft. The rotational inertia of the yo-yo is 600 g·cm². A string 80 cm long is wound around the narrow shaft of the yo-yo. With the yo-yo initially 50 cm off the ground, the string is pulled vertically upward with a force of 0.98 N until the string comes entirely free of the yo-yo. The yo-yo then falls freely. What are its rotational and translational kinetic energies just before it hits the ground?

71. An object of rotational inertia I is initially at rest. A torque is then applied to the object, causing it to begin rotating. The torque is applied for only one-quarter of a revolution, during which time its magnitude is given by $\tau = A\cos\theta$, where A is a constant and θ is the angle through which the object has rotated. What is the final angular speed of the object?

72. A disk of radius R and thickness w has a mass density that increases from the center outward, being given by $\rho = \rho_0 r/R$, where r is the distance from the axis of the disk. (a) Calculate the total mass M of the disk. (b) Calculate the rotational inertia about the disk axis, in terms of M and R. Compare with the results for a solid disk of uniform density and for a ring.

73. A thin, uniform vane of mass M is in the shape of a right triangle, as shown in Fig. 12-54. Find the rotational inertia about a vertical axis through its apex, as shown in the figure. Express your answer in terms of the triangle's base width b and its mass M.

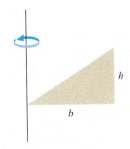

FIGURE 12-54 Problem 73.

74. A marble (solid) and a tennis ball (hollow) roll without slipping on the track shown in Fig. 12-55. Both start at a height of 1.8 m above the level stretch at the right. Find the horizontal range x of each ball.

FIGURE 12-55 Problem 74.

75. A uniform disk of radius R is free to rotate about a horizontal axis at its edge. If it's at its lowest position, as shown in

FIGURE 12-56 Problem 75.

Fig. 12-56, what is the minimum angular speed ω necessary to ensure that its motion describes a complete circle?

76. The wheel shown in Fig. 12-51 is rotating freely about a frictionless horizontal axle. Since the wheel is unbalanced, its angular speed varies as it rotates. If the maximum angular speed is ω_{max}, find an expression for the minimum speed. *Hint:* How does the potential energy change as the wheel rotates?

77. A thin solid rod of length ℓ and mass M is free to pivot about one end. If it makes an angle ϕ with the horizontal, find the torque due to gravity about the pivot point. You'll need to integrate the torques on the individual mass elements comprising the rod.

78. Proof of the work-energy theorem for rotational motion: Start with the expression $\tau = I\alpha$ and substitute $\alpha = d\omega/dt$. Then apply the chain rule for derivatives to write $d\omega/dt = (d\omega/d\theta)(d\theta/dt)$. Identify the term $d\theta/dt$, and substitute the quantity it's equal to. Then multiply the whole equation through by $d\theta$. You should then be able to integrate to get Equation 12-23.

Rotational Vectors and Angular Momentum

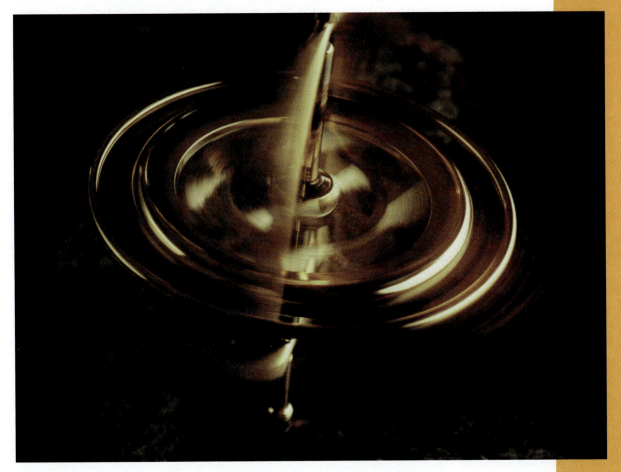

The spinning gyroscope seems to defy gravity, but actually it's just obeying Newton's laws.

Summer, fall, winter, spring—the cycle of the seasons continues indefinitely. Celebrated in music and poetry, that cycle is ultimately determined by the vector direction of Earth's angular velocity. The changing angular velocity of protons in living tissue produces MRI images that give physicians a noninvasive look inside the human body. A missile glides silently toward its target, its deadly accuracy assured by the unchanging angular velocity of a built-in gyroscope. Rising and rotating, moist, heated air forms itself into the ominous funnel of a tornado. A yo-yo drops to the end of its string, "sleeps," then rises suddenly on command. Computers on the Mir space station fail, and the media describe Mir as "spinning uncontrollably through space."

These diverse examples all involve rotational motion in which not only the magnitude but also the precise *direction* matters. They're best understood in terms of the rotational analog of Newton's law, which we will introduce in full vector form involving a rotational analog of momentum.

In Chapter 12 we restricted ourselves to rotational motion about a fixed axis, analogous to the one-dimensional linear motion of Chapter 2. With one-dimensional linear motion, force can change only an object's speed (or reverse its direction); arbitrary changes of direction are not possible under the restriction to one dimension. Analogously, in the rotational motion of Chapter 12, a torque could change only an object's angular velocity about a fixed axis, but we did not allow changes in the direction of that axis.

To explore the full and surprising richness of rotational motion requires that we allow for changes in the direction of an object's rotation axis. To do so we introduce a vector description of rotational motion that parallels the vector description of linear motion first used in Chapter 3. From that, we develop the rotational analog of Newton's law in full vector form and apply it to a broad spectrum of physical phenomena.

13-1 ANGULAR VELOCITY AND ACCELERATION VECTORS

So far we've ascribed direction to rotational motion using the terms "clockwise" and "counterclockwise." What more could we mean by "direction?" Figure 13-1 makes abundantly clear that rotation about a horizontal axis is not the same as rotation about a vertical axis. So we need to specify the direction of the rotation axis to describe fully the rotational motion. We therefore define **angular velocity ω** as a vector whose magnitude is the angular speed ω and whose direction is parallel to the rotation axis. Didn't we already define angular velocity in Chapter 12? Yes—and our new definition here is simply an extension that covers all possible orientations of the rotation axis. In Chapter 12 we considered the axis fixed, and could specify the direction of the angular velocity by indicating whether rotation was clockwise or counterclockwise. Now we're generalizing to the case where the direction of the rotation axis may change.

There's an ambiguity in this definition since there are two possible directions parallel to the axis. We resolve the ambiguity with the **right-hand rule**: If you curl the fingers of your right hand to follow the rotation, then your right thumb points in the direction of the angular velocity (Fig. 13-2). This refinement means

(a)

(b)

FIGURE 13-1 The direction of the rotation axis matters! (*a*) With its rotors spinning about vertical axes, this tilt-rotor aircraft rises vertically, like a helicopter. (*b*) With the rotors' axes horizontal, the aircraft cruises like a normal airplane.

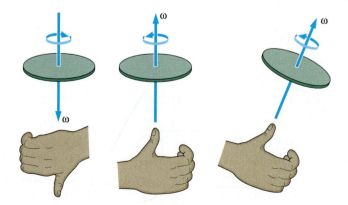

FIGURE 13-2 The direction of the angular velocity vector is given by the right-hand rule.

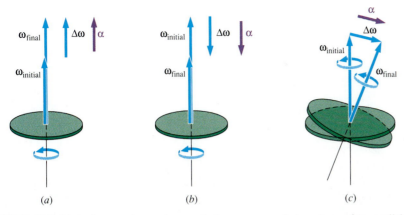

FIGURE 13-3 (a) An increase in angular speed alone corresponds to a change $\Delta\boldsymbol{\omega}$ parallel to the angular velocity $\boldsymbol{\omega}$ itself; therefore the angular acceleration vector $\boldsymbol{\alpha}$ is also parallel to $\boldsymbol{\omega}$. (b) With a decrease in ω, $\Delta\boldsymbol{\omega}$ and $\boldsymbol{\alpha}$ are antiparallel to $\boldsymbol{\omega}$. (c) When the angular velocity $\boldsymbol{\omega}$ changes only in direction, the small change $\Delta\boldsymbol{\omega}$ and, therefore, the angular acceleration $\boldsymbol{\alpha}$ are perpendicular to $\boldsymbol{\omega}$.

that $\boldsymbol{\omega}$ gives not only the angular speed and the direction of the rotation axis but distinguishes what we would have described previously as clockwise or counterclockwise rotation.

By analogy with the linear acceleration vector, we define angular acceleration as the rate of change of the angular velocity vector:

$$\boldsymbol{\alpha} = \lim_{\Delta t \to 0} \frac{\Delta\boldsymbol{\omega}}{\Delta t} = \frac{d\boldsymbol{\omega}}{dt}, \qquad (13\text{-}1)$$

where, as with Equation 12-2, we get the average angular acceleration if we don't take the limit.

Equation 13-1 says that angular acceleration points in the direction of the *change* in angular velocity. If that change is only in magnitude, then $\boldsymbol{\omega}$ simply grows or shrinks, and $\boldsymbol{\alpha}$ is parallel or antiparallel to the rotation axis (Fig. 13-3a, b). But a change in *direction* is also a change in angular velocity. When the angular velocity $\boldsymbol{\omega}$ changes only in direction, then the angular acceleration vector is perpendicular to $\boldsymbol{\omega}$ (Fig. 13-3c). More generally, both the magnitude and direction of $\boldsymbol{\omega}$ may change; then $\boldsymbol{\alpha}$ is neither parallel nor perpendicular to $\boldsymbol{\omega}$. These cases are exactly analogous to the situations we treated in Chapter 4, where acceleration parallel to velocity changes only the speed, while acceleration perpendicular to velocity changes only the direction of motion.

As with angular velocity, our new definition of angular acceleration is a generalization of Chapter 12's restricted definition that applied only for a fixed rotation axis. And just as the relaxation of Chapter 2's restriction to one-dimensional motion in Chapters 3 and 4 led to a rich new variety of motions where velocity and acceleration were not in the same direction, so here we will find a wide range of new possibilities when angular velocity and acceleration vectors have different directions

13-2 TORQUE AND THE VECTOR CROSS PRODUCT

Figure 13-4 shows a wheel, initially stationary, with a force applied at its rim. The torque associated with this force sets the wheel rotating in the direction shown; applying the right-hand rule we see that angular velocity vector $\boldsymbol{\omega}$ points

FIGURE 13-4 A force applied at the rim of the wheel will set it rotating with angular velocity $\boldsymbol{\omega}$ and angular acceleration $\boldsymbol{\alpha}$ both upward. For consistency with Newton's law, the associated torque vector should be in the same direction as the angular acceleration.

FIGURE 13-5 Three equivalent right-hand rules for the direction of torque and, more generally, for the cross product of two vectors. First, start with the vectors tail to tail. Note in each case that rotation of the first vector (**r**) onto the second (**F**) means rotating it through the smaller of two possible angles—that is, counterclockwise in this figure, rather than swinging **r** all the way round clockwise through an angle larger than 180°. The angle θ in the cross product is always this smaller angle.

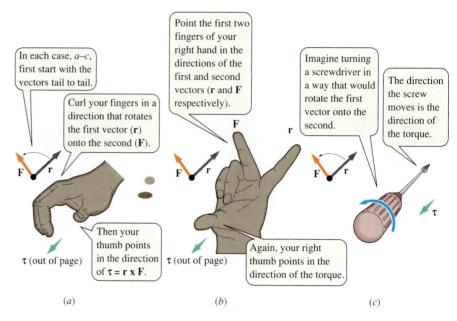

In each case, *a–c*, first start with the vectors tail to tail.

Curl your fingers in a direction that rotates the first vector (**r**) onto the second (**F**).

Then your thumb points in the direction of $\tau = \mathbf{r} \times \mathbf{F}$.

τ (out of page)

Point the first two fingers of your right hand in the directions of the first and second vectors (**r** and **F** respectively).

Again, your right thumb points in the direction of the torque.

τ (out of page)

Imagine turning a screwdriver in a way that would rotate the first vector onto the second.

The direction the screw moves is the direction of the torque.

τ

(a)   (b)   (c)

FIGURE 13-6 It's also appropriate to get the direction of the torque by curling your right fingers in the direction that the torque would rotate an initially stationary body; now your right thumb points along the torque vector. Here the torque about the wheel's axis arises from a downward force acting on the left edge.

τ (out of page)

upward. Since the angular speed is increasing, the angular acceleration $\boldsymbol{\alpha}$ also points upward. So that our rotational analog of Newton's law—angular acceleration proportional to torque—will hold for directions as well as magnitudes, we'd like the torque to have an upward direction, too.

We already know the magnitude of the torque: from Equation 12-12, it is $\tau = rF \sin\theta$, where r is the distance from the rotation axis to the force application point and θ is the angle between the corresponding vector **r** and the force vector **F**. The direction of the torque is defined as being perpendicular to both **r** and **F**. For the torque in Fig. 13-4, this gives one of two possible directions: upward or downward, parallel or antiparallel to the angular acceleration $\boldsymbol{\alpha}$. To specify that direction, we use a right-hand rule. The rule is described for the general case in Figs. 13-5 and 13-6. Practice the rule and then apply it to Fig. 13-4, noting from Fig. 13-5 that you first put the vectors together tail-to-tail. You should confirm that the torque in Fig. 13-5 is upward—in the *same* direction as the angular acceleration, just as the rotational analog of Newton's law would have it.

Tip

Choose a Right-Hand Rule The right-hand rules in Fig. 13-5 are fully equivalent. Choose the one you're most comfortable with and get familiar with it. You'll encounter the same rule in other areas of physics.

The Cross Product

The magnitude of the torque, $\tau = rF \sin\theta$, is determined by the magnitudes of the vectors **r** and **F** and the angle between them; we've now seen that the direction of the torque is also determined by the vectors **r** and **F** through the right-hand rule. So the torque vector is completely determined by the vectors **r** and **F**. This operation—forming from two vectors **A** and **B** a third vector **C** of magnitude $C = AB \sin \theta$ and direction given by the right-hand rule—occurs frequently in physics and is called the **cross product**:

> The cross product C of two vectors A and B is written
>
> $$C = A \times B,$$
>
> and is a vector with magnitude $AB \sin \theta$, where θ is the angle between A and B, and where the direction of C is given by the right-hand rule of Fig. 13-5.

See the accompanying Math Toolbox for more on the cross product.

Torque is an instance of the cross product, and we can write the torque vector simply as

$$\tau = r \times F. \tag{13-2}$$

Both direction and magnitude are described succinctly in this equation.

Math Toolbox

Multiplying Vectors The cross product $\mathbf{A} \times \mathbf{B}$ is the second way of multiplying vectors that you've encountered. The first was the vector dot product $\mathbf{A} \cdot \mathbf{B} = AB \cos \theta$ introduced in Chapter 7. Both depend on the product of the vector magnitudes and on the angle between them. But where the dot product depends on the *cosine* of the angle and is therefore maximum when the two vectors are parallel, the cross product depends on the *sine* and is therefore maximum for perpendicular vectors. In essence, the dot product samples how much directionality the two vectors have in common; it's the magnitude of vector **A** multiplied by the component of vector **B** in the direction of **A**. The cross product, in contrast, samples what the vectors don't have in common; its magnitude is that of vector **A** multiplied by the component of **B** in the direction perpendicular to **A** (see Fig. 13-7). That's why we suggested, in Fig. 12-7, using the lever arm—the perpendicular distance to the force application point—in calculating torques.

There's another crucial distinction between dot product and cross product: the dot product is a *scalar*—a single number, with no direction—while the cross product is a *vector*. That's why $AB \cos \theta$ completely specifies the dot product, while $AB \sin \theta$ gives only the magnitude of the cross product; it's also necessary to specify the direction via the right-hand rule.

The cross product obeys the usual distributive rule:

$$A \times (B + C) = A \times B + A \times C,$$

but it's *not* commutative; in fact, as you can see by rotating **F** onto **r** instead of **r** onto **F** in Fig. 13-5:

$$B \times A = -A \times B.$$

Problem 14 shows how to write a general cross product in unit vector notation, in analogy with Equation 7-4 for the dot product.

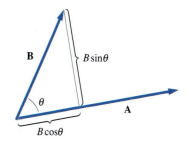

FIGURE 13-7 Two vectors **A** and **B** and the angle θ between them. The dot product $\mathbf{A} \cdot \mathbf{B}$ involves the component $B \cos \theta$ of **B** in the direction of **A**. The cross product involves the component $B \sin \theta$ of **B** in the direction perpendicular to **A**.

EXAMPLE 13-1	*Torque as a Cross Product*

A force $\mathbf{F} = \sqrt{3}\hat{\imath} + \hat{\jmath}$ N acts on a wheel whose rotation axis coincides with the z axis; the force is applied at the point $x = 3$ m, $y = 0$ m. Find the torque due to this force.

Solution

The torque is given by Equation 13-2: $\boldsymbol{\tau} = \mathbf{r} \times \mathbf{F}$. With the force applied at the point $(3, 0)$, we have $\mathbf{r} = 3\hat{\imath}$ m and the magnitude $r = 3$ m. (See Chapter 3, Section 3-3, if you need to review unit vector notation.) The magnitude of $\mathbf{F}$ is given by the pythagorean theorem:

$$F = \sqrt{F_x^2 + F_y^2} = \sqrt{3\ \text{N}^2 + 1\ \text{N}^2} = 2\ \text{N},$$

and the angle $\mathbf{F}$ makes with the x axis (and thus with $\mathbf{r}$) is

$$\theta = \tan^{-1}\left(\frac{1}{\sqrt{3}}\right) = 30°.$$

Then the magnitude of the cross product is

$$\tau = |\mathbf{r} \times \mathbf{F}| = rF\sin\theta = (3\ \text{m})(2\ \text{N})\sin 30° = 3\ \text{N·m}.$$

Rotating $\mathbf{r}$ into $\mathbf{F}$ shows that $\boldsymbol{\tau}$ is in the z direction (see Fig. 13-8); therefore, we can write

$$\boldsymbol{\tau} = \mathbf{r} \times \mathbf{F} = 3\hat{\mathbf{k}}\ \text{N·m}.$$

We could also obtain this result using unit vectors:

$$\boldsymbol{\tau} = \mathbf{r} \times \mathbf{F} = (3\hat{\imath}\ \text{m}) \times (\sqrt{3}\hat{\imath} + \hat{\jmath}\ \text{N})$$
$$= 3\sqrt{3}\hat{\imath} \times \hat{\imath} + 3\hat{\imath} \times \hat{\jmath}\ \text{N·m}.$$

But the unit vector $\hat{\imath}$ is parallel to itself, so the cross product $\hat{\imath} \times \hat{\imath}$ is zero. On the other hand, $\hat{\imath} \times \hat{\jmath} = \hat{\mathbf{k}}$, as Fig. 13-9 will convince you. So we again have $\boldsymbol{\tau} = 3\hat{\mathbf{k}}$ N·m.

FIGURE 13-8 With $\mathbf{r}$ along the x axis, and $\mathbf{F}$ in the x-y plane, the torque $\boldsymbol{\tau} = \mathbf{r} \times \mathbf{F}$ is in the z direction.

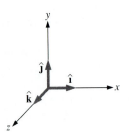

FIGURE 13-9 Rotate one unit vector onto another to see that the cross product is plus or minus the third unit vector. Use the plus sign when the vectors are in the order $\hat{\imath}\,\hat{\jmath}\,\hat{\mathbf{k}}\,\hat{\imath}$ . . . . The magnitude works out because each unit vector has magnitude 1 and the angle between any pair is 90°, so $\sin\theta = 1$. Cross products of unit vectors work out correctly only in a right-handed coordinate system; see the Tip box.

Tip

Stick with Right-Handed Coordinate Systems If you want to add a z axis to an x-y coordinate system, there are two possible directions for the positive z axis to point. You need to choose the one that makes $\hat{\imath} \times \hat{\jmath} = \hat{\mathbf{k}}$ according to the right-hand rule. The result is a right-handed coordinate system, consistent with all the right-hand rules used in physics.

If you're left-handed don't feel snubbed. Physics would have been equally consistent had we defined rotational vectors and cross products in terms of a left-hand rule and then used only left-handed coordinate systems.

EXERCISE A force $\mathbf{F} = 4.6\hat{\mathbf{k}}$ N is applied at the point $\mathbf{r} = 1.3\hat{\jmath} + 2.4\hat{\mathbf{k}}$ m. Find the torque exerted about the origin.

Answer: $6.0\hat{\imath}$ N·m

Some problems similar to Example 13-1: 7, 9, 11, 12

7.1
Calculating Torques

13-3 ANGULAR MOMENTUM

We first used Newton's law in the form $\mathbf{F} = m\mathbf{a}$, but later (in Chapter 10, Section 10-2) found the form $\mathbf{F} = d\mathbf{P}/dt$, with $\mathbf{P}$ the linear momentum of a system of particles, especially powerful. The same is true in rotational motion: To explore fully some surprising aspects of rotational dynamics, we need to define **angular momentum** and develop a relation between its rate of change and the applied torque. Once we've done that we'll be able to answer such diverse questions as why the gyroscope on page 313 doesn't fall over or how the behavior of protons' angular momentum vectors lead to the MRI images that help physicians to examine noninvasively your body's innards.

Like other rotational quantities, angular momentum is specified with respect to a given point or axis. We begin with the angular momentum **L** of a single particle:

> **If a particle with linear momentum p is at position r with respect to some point, then its angular momentum L about that point is**
>
> $$\mathbf{L} = \mathbf{r} \times \mathbf{p}. \tag{13-3}$$

EXAMPLE 13-2 | *Angular Momentum of a Particle*

A particle of mass m moves counterclockwise at speed v around a circle of radius r in the x-y plane. Find its angular momentum about the center of the circle, and express in terms of its angular velocity.

Solution

From Fig. 13-10 we see that the particle's linear momentum $m\mathbf{v}$ and the radius $\mathbf{r}$ are always at right angles, so the magnitude of the angular momentum **L** is just rmv. Applying the right-hand rule shows that **L** points in the z direction. So we have $\mathbf{L} = rmv\hat{\mathbf{k}}$. We can write this in terms of the angular velocity $\boldsymbol{\omega}$ by noting that $v = \omega r$ and by applying the right-hand rule to see that $\boldsymbol{\omega}$, too, points in the z direction; that is, $\boldsymbol{\omega} = \omega\hat{\mathbf{k}}$. Then we have

$$\mathbf{L} = rmv\hat{\mathbf{k}} = mr^2\omega\hat{\mathbf{k}} = mr^2\boldsymbol{\omega}.$$

EXERCISE Determine the angular momentum about Earth's center of a 540-kg communications satellite in geosynchronous orbit. *Hint:* Consult Example 9-4 and the answer to Problem 9-13.

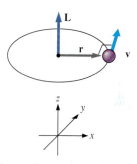

FIGURE 13-10 The angular momentum **L** of a particle moving at speed v around a circle of radius r has magnitude rmv and is perpendicular to the plane of the circle. Here **L** is calculated about the center of the circle.

Answer: 7.1×10^{13} kg·m²/s, northward

Some problems similar to Example 13-2: 19, 24, 26, 27

This angular momentum we've just defined in Equation 13-3 is the rotational analog of linear momentum $\mathbf{p} = m\mathbf{v}$. Since rotational inertia I is the analog of mass m, and angular velocity $\boldsymbol{\omega}$ is the analog of linear velocity $\mathbf{v}$, you might expect that we could write

$$\mathbf{L} = I\boldsymbol{\omega}. \tag{13-4}$$

Since the rotational inertia of a single particle is mr^2, the result of Example 13-2 can indeed be written $\mathbf{L} = I\boldsymbol{\omega}$. By defining the angular momentum of a system as the sum of the angular momenta of its constituent particles, Equation 13-4 can be shown to hold in the case of a symmetric object such as a wheel or sphere rotating about a symmetry axis that is itself stationary. But in the more general case, Equation 13-4 does not necessarily hold; surprisingly, **L** and $\boldsymbol{\omega}$ can actually have different directions. Even vector mathematics fails to describe such cases adequately, and the mathematical tools needed are best left for advanced courses in mechanics.

We'll deal mostly with situations for which Equation 13-4 does apply. In those cases it's usually easiest to calculate the angular momentum from Equation 13-4. But Equation 13-3—summed over all particles of a system—remains the fundamental definition of angular momentum.

Torque and Angular Momentum

We're now ready to develop the full vector analog of Newton's law in the form $\mathbf{F} = d\mathbf{P}/dt$. Recall that $\mathbf{F}$ here is the *net* external force on a system, and $\mathbf{P}$ is the system's momentum—the vector sum of the momenta of its constituent particles. Can we write, by analogy,

$$\boldsymbol{\tau} = \frac{d\mathbf{L}}{dt}?$$

To see that we can, we write the angular momentum of a system as the sum of the angular momenta of its constituent particles:

$$\mathbf{L} = \sum \mathbf{L}_i = \sum (\mathbf{r}_i \times \mathbf{p}_i),$$

where the subscript i refers to the ith particle of the system. Differentiating this equation with respect to time gives

$$\frac{d\mathbf{L}}{dt} = \sum \left(\mathbf{r}_i \times \frac{d\mathbf{p}_i}{dt} + \frac{d\mathbf{r}_i}{dt} \times \mathbf{p}_i \right),$$

where we've applied the product rule for differentiation, being careful to preserve the order of the cross product since it is not commutative. But $d\mathbf{r}_i/dt$ is the velocity of the ith particle, so the second term in the sum is the cross product of velocity $\mathbf{v}$ and momentum $\mathbf{p} = m\mathbf{v}$. Since these two vectors are parallel, their cross product is zero, and we're left with only the first term in the sum:

$$\frac{d\mathbf{L}}{dt} = \sum \left(\mathbf{r}_i \times \frac{d\mathbf{p}_i}{dt} \right) = \sum (\mathbf{r}_i \times \mathbf{F}_i),$$

where we've used Newton's law to write $d\mathbf{p}_i/dt = \mathbf{F}_i$. But $\mathbf{r}_i \times \mathbf{F}_i$ is the torque, $\boldsymbol{\tau}_i$, on the ith particle, so

$$\frac{d\mathbf{L}}{dt} = \sum \boldsymbol{\tau}_i.$$

As we discussed in Section 12-3, the internal torques cancel in pairs as long as the internal forces in a system of particles act along the lines between the particles. Under these conditions, the sum of all the torques on all the particles reduces to the net *external* torque on the system, and we have

$$\frac{d\mathbf{L}}{dt} = \boldsymbol{\tau}, \tag{13-5}$$

where $\boldsymbol{\tau}$ is the net external torque. Thus our analogy between linear and rotational motion holds for momentum as well as for the other quantities we've discussed.

7.16
Ball Hits Bat

7.17
Scattering

13-4 CONSERVATION OF ANGULAR MOMENTUM

When there is no external torque on a system, Equation 13-5 tells us that angular momentum is constant. This statement—that the angular momentum of an isolated system cannot change—is of fundamental importance in physics, and applies to systems ranging from subatomic particles to galaxies. In deriving Equation 13-5, we did not require that the system in question be a rigid object, so conservation of angular momentum applies even to systems that undergo changes in configuration and therefore in rotational inertia. The classic example is a figure skater, who starts spinning relatively slowly with arms extended, then pulls her arms in to spin much more rapidly (Fig. 13-11). Why? As the skater's arms move in, her mass is concentrated more toward the rotation axis, lowering her rotational inertia, I. But her angular momentum $I\omega$ is conserved, so her angular speed ω must increase. A much more dramatic example is illustrated in Example 13-3: the collapse of a star at the end of its lifetime. Again, the rotational inertia decreases, requiring an increase in the star's rotational speed.

FIGURE 13-11 As skater Kristi Yamaguchi pulls in her arms, her rotational inertia I decreases. To conserve her angular momentum $I\omega$, her angular speed ω must increase.

EXAMPLE 13-3	*Pulsars*

A star rotates about its axis once every 45 days. At the end of its life it undergoes a colossal outburst called a supernova explosion. Much of the star's mass is flung outward into the interstellar medium, where it will eventually condense into new stars and planets and perhaps find its way into living creatures (Fig. 13-12). But the inner core of the star, whose initial radius was 2×10^7 m, collapses into a neutron star, only 6 km in radius. Calculate the rotation rate of the neutron star, assuming that no torque acts on the stellar core during the collapse. Consider the core to be a uniform sphere both before and after collapse.

Solution

This situation is exactly like that of the figure skater: a decrease in rotational inertia requires an increase in angular speed. Conservation of angular momentum states that

$$I_1 \omega_1 = I_2 \omega_2 ,$$

where the subscripts 1 and 2 refer to conditions before and after the collapse, respectively. For a uniform sphere, $I = \frac{2}{5}MR^2$, so

$$\tfrac{2}{5}MR_1^2 \omega_1 = \tfrac{2}{5}MR_2^2 \omega_2 .$$

Solving for ω_2 and using the known values of ω_1, R_1, and R_2 gives

$$\omega_2 = \omega_1 \left(\frac{R_1}{R_2}\right)^2 = \left(\frac{1 \text{ rev}}{45 \text{ day}}\right)\left(\frac{2\times 10^7 \text{ m}}{6\times 10^3 \text{ m}}\right)^2$$

$$= 2.5\times 10^5 \text{ rev/day} = 2.9 \text{ rev/s} .$$

FIGURE 13-12 The Crab Nebula is the remains of a supernova explosion as it looks 1000 years after the explosion. At its center is a rapidly rotating neutron star.

This neutron star is a fantastic thing—an object with more mass than the entire Sun, rotating three times a second. Often intense radio waves, light, or x rays radiate in a narrow beam from the magnetic axis of the neutron star. As the star rotates, this beam sweeps through space like a searchlight, and we at Earth detect regular pulses of radiation that give the neutron star the name "pulsar."

Tip

You Don't Always Need Vectors Problems involving angular momentum where the direction of rotation doesn't change can be treated like other one-dimensional problems, without the need for vector notation. This example and the next one are both instances of one-dimensional angular momentum problems.

EXERCISE A 55-kg diver leaves the diving board in an essentially straight configuration, with an angular speed of 0.25 rev/s about her center of mass. She then goes into a tuck position with a radius of approximately 31 cm (Fig. 13-13). Approximating the diver with her outstretched arms first as a uniform thin rod 2.0 m long, then as a uniform sphere, estimate her rotation rate while in the tuck position.

FIGURE 13-13 How fast is the diver rotating when she goes into the tuck position?

Answer: 2.2 rev/s

Some problems similar to Example 13-3: 35, 36, 49, 50

EXAMPLE 13-4	*A Merry-Go-Round*

A merry-go-round of radius $R = 1.3$ m has a rotational inertia $I = 240$ kg·m² and is rotating freely at $\omega_1 = 11$ rpm. A boy of mass $m_1 = 28$ kg leaps onto the edge of the merry-go-round, heading directly toward the center (Fig. 13-14). What is the new angular speed of the merry-go-round? Later a girl, of mass $m_2 = 32$ kg, leaps onto the merry-go-round by running tangentially at speed $v = 3.7$ m/s. If the direction of her motion is the same as that of the merry-go-round (see Fig. 13-14), what is the new angular speed?

Solution

Moving directly toward the rotation axis, the boy carries no angular momentum relative to the axis, so the total angular momentum is $I\omega_1$. But sitting at the edge of the merry-go-round, he adds rotational inertia $m_1 R^2$ to the system. Then conservation of angular momentum may be written

$$I\omega_1 = (I + m_1 R^2)\omega_2 .$$

where ω_2 is the angular speed after the boy is on the merry-go-round. Solving for ω_2 gives

$$\omega_2 = \frac{I\omega_1}{I + m_1 R^2} = \frac{(240 \text{ kg·m}^2)(11 \text{ rpm})}{240 \text{ kg·m}^2 + (28 \text{ kg})(1.3 \text{ m})^2}$$

$$= 9.2 \text{ rpm} .$$

In this calculation, where we dealt with a ratio of angular speeds, we didn't need to convert from rpm to rad/s.

The girl, running tangentially to the merry-go-round, carries angular momentum $m_2 v R$, in the same direction as the merry-go-round's angular momentum, so the total angular momentum of the system is now $I\omega_1 + m_2 v R$. After she leaps on, the total rotational inertia includes that of the merry-go-round along with a contribution $m R^2$ from each child. Calling the final angular speed ω_3, conservation of angular momentum

FIGURE 13-14 Running straight toward its axis, the boy brings no angular momentum to the merry-go-round. But the girl, running tangentially at speed v, brings angular momentum $m v R$.

may then be written

$$I\omega_1 + m_2 v R = (I + m_1 R^2 + m_2 R^2)\omega_3 ,$$

so

$$\omega_3 = \frac{I\omega_1 + m_2 v R}{I + (m_1 + m_2)R^2} .$$

With m_2 in kilograms, v in meters per second, and R in meters, the angular momentum $m_2 v R$ of the second child has the units of kg·m²·rad/s, while all our other angular momenta have been expressed implicitly in kg·m²·rpm. To solve for ω_3 in rpm, we convert the girl's angular momentum into the latter unit, multiplying by the conversion factor $\omega = (1 \text{ rev}/2\pi \text{ rad})(60 \text{ s/min})$. The equation above then gives $\omega_3 = 12$ rpm.

Is mechanical energy conserved as the children leap onto the merry-go-round? No! In each case frictional forces act to bring children and merry-go-round to rest with respect to each other, so the situation is like an inelastic collision.

EXERCISE A circular bird feeder 19 cm in radius has rotational inertia 0.12 kg·m². The feeder is suspended by a thin wire
and is spinning slowly at 5.6 rpm. A 140-g bird lands on the rim
of the feeder, coming in tangent to the rim at 1.1 m/s in a
direction opposite the feeder's rotation. What is the rotation
rate after the bird lands?

Answer: 3.14 rpm

Some problems similar to Example 13-4: 30, 31, 49, 50

Got It!

The boy in Example 13-4 causes a change of 1.8 rpm in the merry-go-round's
rotational speed; the girl causes a 2.8 rpm change. Yet their masses are nearly
equal. Explain the main difference in their effects on the rotation rate.

In a popular demonstration of angular momentum conservation, a student
stands on a stationary turntable holding a wheel rotating about a vertical axis.
With the rotation direction shown in Fig. 13-15, the angular momentum vector
of the wheel, and thus of the wheel + student + turntable system, is upward.

The student stands on a
stationary turntable holding a
horizontal bicycle wheel that
rotates counterclockwise.

The student flips over the
moving wheel, and thereby
reverses its angular
momentum. The angular
momentum of the system,
however, is conserved, so
what happens to the student
and the turntable?

$\mathbf{L}_{ts}$

$\mathbf{L}_{w}$

$\mathbf{L}_{total} = \mathbf{L}_{w}$

$\mathbf{L}_{total}$

(a)   (b)

FIGURE 13-15 A popular
demonstration of angular momentum
conservation. Flipping the rotating
wheel upside down sets the originally
stationary student/turntable
combination rotating in order to
conserve the total angular momentum,
whose vector direction is upward. $\mathbf{L}_w$ is
the wheel's angular momentum. $\mathbf{L}_{ts}$ is
the angular momentum of the
turntable/student combination. In
(b), $\mathbf{L}_{ts}$ and $\mathbf{L}_w$ add vectorially to give
the total angular momentum, which is
the same in (a) and (b).

The student then turns the wheel upside down, reversing the direction of its angular momentum. Analysis of the complete process requires a full vector description, as the wheel's rotation axis gradually changes direction. But because the turntable is free to spin on essentially frictionless bearings, there's no torque in the vertical direction, so angular momentum of the system is conserved. But now the wheel has a downward angular momentum vector, so turntable and student must acquire an upward angular momentum of greater magnitude to maintain the original upward angular momentum vector. That means turntable and student start rotating in the same direction the wheel originally rotated.

Where does the rotation energy of student and turntable come from? It comes from work the student does in flipping the rotating wheel. That work is done against torques that develop within the student's body and between the student and the turntable—torques that in turn cause the angular acceleration associated with starting the student/turntable combination rotating (recall that in Equation 12-23 we gave the rotational version of the work-energy theorem). Since those torques are *internal* to the student/turntable/wheel system, they don't change the overall angular momentum of the entire system. Problem 40 explores this demonstration quantitatively.

13-5 ROTATIONAL DYNAMICS IN THREE DIMENSIONS

So far we've explored rotational dynamics only in cases where the direction of the rotation axis remains fixed. But when torque and angular momentum are in different directions, new and often startling behavior results. However strange this behavior may seem, you can understand it if you really accept the rotational analog of Newton's law—that the rate of change of the angular momentum *vector* is equal to the net torque *vector*.

Precession

A gyroscope seems to defy gravity, balanced on a single point with most of its mass unsupported (Fig. 13-16). Surprising though it is, this behavior follows directly from the rotational analog of Newton's law. The downward force of gravity produces a torque whose direction in Fig. 13-16 is into the page. Were the gyroscope not rotating, it would simply fall over, gaining angular momentum into the page about its bottom pivot (Fig. 13-17). The change in angular momentum—here simply an increase in magnitude—is indeed in the same direction as the torque, as the rotational analog of Newton's law requires.

When the gyroscope is rotating, the torque is still into the page, so that must still be the direction of the *change* in angular momentum as well. But now the gyroscope already has angular momentum that points along its rotation axis, so now the change in angular momentum is at right angles to the angular momentum itself. That means that only the direction, not the magnitude, of the angular

FIGURE 13-16 Why doesn't the spinning gyroscope fall over?

$\tau, \mathbf{L}, \Delta\mathbf{L}$
into page

FIGURE 13-17 If it weren't spinning, the torque due to the gravitational force *would* cause it to fall. It would gain angular momentum about its pivot, and both the torque and change in angular momentum would point into the page, obeying the rotational analog of Newton's law.

(b)

FIGURE 13-19 (a) A gyroscope spinning with its axis horizontal. (b) Top view, showing change in the angular momentum vector.

FIGURE 13-18 With **L** and **τ** at right angles, the gyroscope precesses, the end of its rotation axis describing a circle. The *change* in angular momentum is still in the direction of the torque.

momentum vector changes. As a result the gyroscope moves so its rotation axis sweeps out a circle—a phenomenon called **precession** (Fig. 13-18).

So why doesn't the gyroscope fall over? That's like asking why a satellite in circular orbit doesn't fall to Earth. There's a gravitational force pulling the satellite toward Earth, but it's just the right strength to keep the satellite in a circular path. Similarly, there's a torque on the gyroscope, but it's just sufficient to change the angular momentum at the rate that maintains precession.

We can analyze the gyroscope's behavior quantitatively through Fig. 13-19, which shows a gyroscope spinning with its axis in a horizontal plane. The downward force of gravity on the unbalanced gyroscope produces a torque into the page in Fig. 13-19a—that is, at right angles to the angular momentum vector. In a short time dt, the angular momentum vector changes by an amount $d\mathbf{L}$ given by Equation 13-5:

$$d\mathbf{L} = \boldsymbol{\tau}\, dt . \qquad (13\text{-}6)$$

This change is shown in Fig. 13-19b, and represents a rotation of the angular momentum vector through a small angle $d\phi$. For an arbitrarily small time interval dt, and correspondingly small angle $d\phi$, the magnitude dL of the change in angular momentum is essentially equal to the arc length through which the tip of the angular momentum vector swings. From the definition of angle (Equation 12-3), this arc length is just $L\, d\phi$, so

$$dL = L\, d\phi .$$

Combining this result with Equation 13-6 gives

$$\tau\, dt = L\, d\phi .$$

The angular speed of precession, called Ω, is the rate at which the angular momentum vector rotates, or $d\phi/dt$. Solving for this quantity gives

$$\Omega = \frac{d\phi}{dt} = \frac{\tau}{L} = \frac{mgd}{L}, \qquad (13\text{-}7)$$

where we wrote $\tau = mgd$ with d the distance from the pivot to the gyroscope's center of gravity. Although we derived Equation 13-7 for a gyroscope with its rotation axis horizontal, Problem 44 shows that the form $\Omega = mgd/L$ holds for any angle.

FIGURE 13-20 Magnetic resonance imaging uses electromagnetic signals from precessing protons to image the body's innards noninvasively. Both bone and soft tissues show in this MRI image.

Our assumption that the gyroscope's angular momentum is exactly horizontal isn't quite right. Because it's precessing, it also has a small vertical component of angular momentum. Equation 13-7 is therefore an approximation that holds when the precessional angular momentum is much smaller than that associated with rotation—an approximation that is usually valid.

Precession is not limited to the novel behavior of toy gyroscopes. Systems from elementary particles to planets exhibit precession; here we'll look at just a few examples:

The medical imaging technique known as MRI (*magnetic resonance imaging*) constructs images of the body's interior from signals produced by precessing protons that constitute the nuclei of hydrogen atoms. As we'll describe in Chapter 29 and again in Chapter 43 of the extended version of this text, protons precess because of the torque originating from a strong magnetic field. Protons in the hydrogen atoms of different chemical compounds "see" the magnetic field modified slightly by the effect of the surrounding electrons. As a result, each hydrogen-containing compound exhibits one or more different proton precession rates, depending on how many chemically different sites hydrogen atoms occupy in the compound. By combining electrical signals from many precessing protons, the MRI technique yields high-resolution images of internal body structures due to their variable density of protons (Fig. 13-20).

You may have used magnetic resonance in your chemistry or biochemistry courses, where the signal from precessing protons is used to chart the structure of chemical compounds. In this context the process is often called NMR—nuclear magnetic resonance. Our description of magnetic resonance here is from the viewpoint of classical physics; in Chapter 43 of the extended version we revisit magnetic resonance in more detail, from a quantum point of view.

On a much grander scale, Earth itself precesses. This happens because the planet bulges slightly at the equator (as you can see by applying Newton's law to a rotating, deformable object). The gravitational force of the Sun is weaker on the side of the bulge opposite the Sun and the resulting net force produces a torque on the tilted, spinning planet (Fig. 13-21; actually, the moon's effect is important too, but here we consider just the Sun for simplicity). In response, Earth's rotation axis precesses, taking about 26,000 years to describe a full circle. The axis now points to the star Polaris, which we therefore call the North Star, but Polaris won't always be the North Star!

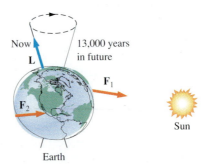

FIGURE 13-21 A highly exaggerated view of Earth's equatorial bulge. Since the Sun's gravitational force weakens with distance, the gravitational force on the far side of the bulge is weaker. The difference in forces results in a torque; if the planet were not rotating, you can see that the torque would tend to bring the rotation axis to a vertical orientation in the figure. Applying the right-hand rule shows that such a torque is into the page. But Earth is rotating, so, just as with a gyroscope, its angular momentum vector changes in the direction of the torque. The result is precession, here with period of some 26,000 years.

EXAMPLE 13-5	*Precession*

A gyroscope consists of a solid disk of radius $R = 10$ cm, mounted in the center of a shaft whose length $\ell = 32$ cm. One end of the shaft is mounted in a frictionless pivot, and the other end is free; the shaft has negligible mass. The disk mass $M = 840$ g. The disk is precessing horizontally at $\Omega = 1.2$ rad/s. Find the angular speed ω of rotation about the shaft.

Solution

We want the angular speed of the disk, but Equation 13-7 contains only the angular momentum, torque, and precession rate. But we can relate the angular speed and angular momentum through $L = I\omega$. (Although this relation is strictly correct only when the rotation axis is stationary, Equation 13-7's assumption that the precessional angular momentum is small allows us to use $L = I\omega$ here.) Solving Equation 13-7 for L then gives

$$L = I\omega = \frac{\tau}{\Omega}.$$

But $I = \frac{1}{2}MR^2$ for the solid disk, and $\tau = \frac{1}{2}\ell Mg$ because the disk (weight Mg) is mounted $\frac{1}{2}\ell$ from the pivot. Solving our equation for ω and using these expressions for I and τ, we then have

$$\omega = \frac{\tau}{I\Omega} = \frac{\frac{1}{2}\ell Mg}{\frac{1}{2}MR^2\Omega} = \frac{\ell g}{R^2\Omega} = \frac{(0.32 \text{ m})(9.8 \text{ m/s}^2)}{(0.10 \text{ m})^2(1.2 \text{ rad/s})}$$

$$= 260 \text{ rad/s} .$$

That $\omega \gg \Omega$ suggests that our assumption that the precessional angular momentum is small is a good one.

Tip

You Don't Always Need All the Information
Sometimes a problem contains superfluous information, in this case the disk mass M. It may not be obvious at first that the information is unnecessary, but if it cancels from your final equations then it indeed was. You can sometimes gain valuable physical insight by considering why the given information doesn't matter. In this case it's because an increased mass gives rise to a greater angular momentum, but also proportionately to a greater torque, so the relationship expressed in Equation 13-7 remains unchanged.

EXERCISE A solid sphere is mounted on a shaft of negligible mass and length 15 cm; the shaft end rests on a frictionless pivot, as shown in Fig. 13-22. The sphere is spinning at 280 rad/s and precessing in a horizontal circle at 1.9 rad/s. Find its radius.

FIGURE 13-22 How big is the sphere?

Answer: 11 cm

Some problems similar to Example 13-5: 42, 43, 45

Got It!

Which way would you have to push on the sphere in Fig. 13-22 to keep it from precessing?

Conservation of Angular Momentum in Three Dimensions

When no external torques act on a system, both the direction and magnitude of its angular momentum remain constant. A spinning gyroscope, suspended so as to be free of torques, keeps its rotation axis in the same direction even as it moves about the Earth. Gyroscopes are therefore used extensively in navigation systems. A gyrocompass is simply a gyroscope that always points in a preset direction. More elaborate so-called inertial guidance systems are built into modern aircraft, missiles, ships, and submarines. In these systems, a computer "remembers" every change in the rotation axis of a gyroscope relative to the vehicle. On-board accelerometers also sense the magnitude and direction of any acceleration. Together, this information is used to calculate the total vector displacement of the vehicle from its starting point, thus keeping track of the exact position.

APPLICATION	*Pointing a Satellite*

Some satellites use angular momentum conservation to orient themselves in space (Fig. 13-23). Such a satellite contains

three wheels whose axes are mutually perpendicular. Each wheel has a motor and brakes to control its rotation. When a wheel starts rotating, the satellite rotates in the opposite direction to conserve angular momentum. After the satellite has rotated through the desired angle, the wheel is stopped and the satellite also stops in its new orientation. Using three perpendicular wheels allows the satellite to point in any direction. Electricity generated by solar panels powers the motors and brakes, so there's no fuel to run out.

FIGURE 13-23 The Solar Maximum Mission satellite became the first to be repaired in space after an electrical failure crippled the reaction-wheel system that used angular momentum conservation to point the satellite at the Sun. Here a shuttle astronaut attempts to link with the slowly spinning satellite.

CHAPTER SYNOPSIS

Summary

1. Full description of rotational motion requires that rotational quantities be treated as vectors. **Angular velocity** is a vector whose magnitude is the angular speed ω and whose direction is that of the rotation axis, as established by the right-hand rule. The **angular acceleration** vector is the rate of change of the angular velocity.

2. The **torque** vector $\boldsymbol{\tau}$ has magnitude $rF\sin\theta$ as in Chapter 12, with its direction determined by applying the right-hand rule to the vectors $\mathbf{r}$ and $\mathbf{F}$ as shown in Fig. 13-5. The operation of forming from two vectors $\mathbf{r}$ and $\mathbf{F}$ a third vector with magnitude $rF\sin\theta$ and direction given by the right-hand rule is called the **cross product**. Torque is the cross product of $\mathbf{r}$ and $\mathbf{F}$, and is written

$$\boldsymbol{\tau} = \mathbf{r} \times \mathbf{F}.$$

3. The **angular momentum**, $\mathbf{L}$, of a particle about some point is the cross product of the radius vector from that point to the particle's location with the particle's linear momentum $\mathbf{p}$:

$$\mathbf{L} = \mathbf{r} \times \mathbf{p}.$$

The angular momentum of a system is the sum of the angular momenta of its constituent particles. For symmetrical systems with stationary rotation axes, the angular momentum can also be written $\mathbf{L} = I\boldsymbol{\omega}$.

4. The rate at which a system's angular momentum changes is equal to the net external torque applied to the system:

$$\frac{d\mathbf{L}}{dt} = \boldsymbol{\tau}.$$

This is Newton's law for rotational motion, in its full vector form.

5. In the absence of external torques, $d\mathbf{L}/dt = 0$ and a system's angular momentum remains constant in direction and magnitude.

6. **Precession**—circular motion of a spinning object's rotation axis—occurs when the applied torque has a component perpendicular to the rotation axis.

Terms You Should Understand

(Pairs are closely related terms whose distinction is important; number in parentheses is chapter section where term first appears.)

angular velocity, angular acceleration vectors (13-1)
right-hand rule (13-1, 13-2)
cross product (13-2)
torque vector (13-2)
angular momentum (13-3)
precession (13-5)

Symbols You Should Recognize

$\boldsymbol{\omega}$ (13-1)	$\mathbf{L}$ (13-3)
$\boldsymbol{\alpha}$ (13-1)	Ω (13-5)
$\mathbf{A} \times \mathbf{B}$ (13-2)	

Problems You Should Be Able to Solve

applying the right-hand rule to determine the direction of angular velocity and acceleration vectors (13-1)

evaluating cross products (13-2)

calculating torque vectors (13-2)

calculating angular momentum from linear velocity and position (13-3)

calculating angular momentum from rotational inertia and angular velocity (13-3)

solving problems involving the conservation of angular momentum in one dimension (13-4)

solving problems involving precession (13-5)

Limitations to Keep in Mind

The expression $\mathbf{L} = I\boldsymbol{\omega}$ applies exactly only when the rotation axis is stationary and is a symmetry axis.

The expression $\Omega = \tau/L$ applies only when the angular momentum associated with precession is much less than the rotational angular momentum.

QUESTIONS

1. Does Earth's angular velocity vector point north or south?
2. Must a torque necessarily change the angular speed of a rotating object?
3. Figure 13-24 shows four forces acting on a body. What are the directions of each of the associated torques about the point O? About the point P?

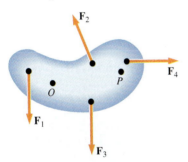

FIGURE 13-24 Question 3.

4. A satellite is small enough to be treated as a point particle. Can Earth's gravity exert a torque on the satellite about Earth's center?
5. From the result of the previous question, what can you conclude about the angular momentum associated with a satellite's orbital motion?
6. You tie a ball to the end of a string and whirl it in a vertical circle. Is its angular momentum constant? If not, why not?
7. Why isn't the cross product commutative?
8. Although it contains no parentheses, the expression $\mathbf{A} \times \mathbf{B} \cdot \mathbf{C}$ is unambiguous. Why?
9. Two vectors are parallel. What can you conclude about their cross product?
10. The dot product of two vectors is equal to the magnitude of their cross product. What can you conclude about the angle between them?
11. Why does a tether ball move faster as it winds up its pole?
12. A cloud of interstellar matter collapses to form a star. Under what conditions will the star *not* be rotating?

13. Why do helicopters have two rotors?
14. A bug, initially at rest on a stationary turntable, walks halfway around the circumference. Describe the motion of the turntable while the bug is walking and after it stops.
15. A group of polar bears are standing around the edge of a circular ice floe that's slowly rotating. If the bears all walk to the center, what will happen to the rotation rate?
16. Tornadoes in the northern hemisphere rotate counterclockwise as viewed from above. A far-fetched idea suggests that driving on the right side of the road may increase the frequency of tornadoes. Does this idea have *any* merit? Explain in terms of the angular momentum imparted to the air by passing cars.
17. How does angular momentum conservation help explain Earth's seasons?
18. Passengers on a cruise ship can party on in inclement weather, thanks to giant gyroscopes that help stabilize the ship in rough seas. How does such a gyroscope work? Which way(s) could you orient its rotation axis to minimize the ship's side-to-side rocking motion?
19. Does a particle moving at constant speed in a straight line have angular momentum about a point on the line? About a point not on the line? In either case, is its angular momentum constant?
20. Spacecraft are often set rotating. How does this help stabilize their orientations?
21. When you turn on a high-speed power tool such as a router, you feel the tool tending to twist in your hands. Why?
22. Does the center of mass of a car have angular momentum about the front axle? What does this have to do with the car's tendency to nose downward when braking hard? (*Note:* The front brakes do most of the stopping.)
23. A huge turbine in the engine room of a ship has its axis aligned with the ship and is spinning rapidly with angular momentum vector toward the ship's bow. If its lubrication fails and the turbine suddenly "seizes" and stops abruptly, what will happen to the ship?

24. A gyroscope is spinning with its rotation axis horizontal and is precessing about a vertical axis. If a weight is hung from the end of the gyroscope (Fig. 13-25), what will happen to the precession rate?

FIGURE 13-25 Question 24.

25. What happens if you push horizontally at right angles to the axis of the spinning gyroscope shown in Fig. 13-26?

FIGURE 13-26 Question 25.

PROBLEMS

ActivPhysics can help with these problems:
Activities 7.1, 7.16, 7.17.

Section 13-1 Angular Velocity and Acceleration Vectors

1. A car is headed north at 70 km/h. Give the magnitude and direction of the angular velocity of its 62-cm-diameter wheels.

2. If the car of Problem 1 makes a 90° left turn lasting 25 s, determine the average angular acceleration of the wheels.

3. A wheel is spinning at 45 rpm with its spin axis vertical. After 15 s, it's spinning at 60 rpm with its axis horizontal. Find (a) the magnitude of its average angular acceleration and (b) the angle the average angular acceleration vector makes with the horizontal.

4. A wheel is spinning about a horizontal axis, with angular speed 140 rad/s and with its angular velocity pointing east. Find the magnitude and direction of its angular velocity after an angular acceleration of 35 rad/s², pointing 68° west of north, is applied for 5.0 s.

5. A wheel is spinning with angular speed $\omega = 5.0$ rad/s, when a constant angular acceleration $\alpha = 0.85$ rad/s² is applied at right angles to the initial angular velocity. How long does it take for the angular speed to increase by 10 rad/s?

Section 13-2 Torque and the Vector Cross Product

6. A rod is free to pivot about one end, and a force **F** is applied at the other end, as shown in Fig. 13-27. What are the magnitude and direction of the torque about the pivot point?

7. A coordinate system lies with its x-y plane in the plane of this page, and its z axis coming out of the page. A force **F** is applied at the point $x = 1$, $y = 1$. What is the direction of the torque about the origin if **F** points (a) in the x direction, (b) in the y direction, and (c) in the z direction?

8. The disk in Fig. 13-28 has radius 35 cm. Give the magnitude and direction of the smallest force that you could apply at point P to produce a torque of magnitude 1.2 N·m (a) about an axis through the center of the disk and perpen-

FIGURE 13-27 Problem 6.

FIGURE 13-28 Problem 8.

dicular to the page and (b) about a vertical axis tangent to the left edge of the disk.

9. A 12-N force is applied at the point $x = 3$ m, $y = 1$ m. Find the torque about the origin if the force points in (a) the x direction, (b) the y direction, and (c) the z direction.

10. A sphere 1.0 m in radius is centered at the origin. At what x, y, and z coordinates on the surface of the sphere could you apply a 5.0-N force pointing in the y direction in order to produce, about the origin, (a) a 5.0 N·m torque pointing in the $-z$ direction, (b) a 3.4 N·m torque pointing in the $+z$ direction, and (c) a 3.4 N·m torque pointing in the $-x$ direction?

11. You slip a wrench over a bolt. Taking the origin at the bolt, the other end of the wrench is at $x = 18$ cm, $y = 5.5$ cm. You apply a force $\mathbf{F} = 88\hat{\mathbf{i}} - 23\hat{\mathbf{j}}$ to the end of the wrench. What is the torque on the bolt?

12. A force $\mathbf{F} = 1.3\hat{\mathbf{i}} + 2.7\hat{\mathbf{j}}$ N is applied at the point $x = 3.0$ m, $y = 0$ m. Find the torque about (a) the origin and (b) the point $x = -1.3$ m, $y = 2.4$ m.

13. Vector $\mathbf{A}$ points 30° counterclockwise from the x axis. Vector $\mathbf{B}$ is twice as long as $\mathbf{A}$. Their product $\mathbf{A} \times \mathbf{B}$ has length A^2, and points in the negative z direction. What is the direction of vector $\mathbf{B}$?

14. Show that the cross product of two arbitrary vectors $\mathbf{A} = A_x\hat{\mathbf{i}} + A_y\hat{\mathbf{j}} + A_z\hat{\mathbf{k}}$ and $\mathbf{B} = B_x\hat{\mathbf{i}} + B_y\hat{\mathbf{j}} + B_z\hat{\mathbf{k}}$ can be written $\mathbf{A} \times \mathbf{B} = (A_yB_z - A_zB_y)\hat{\mathbf{i}} + (A_zB_x - A_xB_z)\hat{\mathbf{j}} + (A_xB_y - A_yB_x)\hat{\mathbf{k}}$.

15. Show that $\mathbf{A} \cdot (\mathbf{A} \times \mathbf{B}) = 0$ for any vectors $\mathbf{A}$ and $\mathbf{B}$.

16. Find the cross product of the vectors $\mathbf{A} = \hat{\mathbf{i}} - 2\hat{\mathbf{j}} + 3\hat{\mathbf{k}}$ and $\mathbf{B} = 2\hat{\mathbf{i}} + 4\hat{\mathbf{j}} + 2\hat{\mathbf{k}}$.

17. Find a force vector that, when applied at the point $x = 2.0$ m, $y = 1.5$ m, will produce a torque $\boldsymbol{\tau} = 4.7\hat{\mathbf{k}}$ N·m about the origin. (There are many answers.)

Section 13-3 Angular Momentum

18. Express the units of angular momentum (a) using only the fundamental units kilogram, meter, and second; (b) in a form involving newtons; (c) in a form involving joules.

19. In the Olympic hammer throw, a contestant whirls a 7.3-kg steel ball on the end of a 1.2-m cable. If the contestant's arms reach an additional 90 cm from his axis of rotation and if the speed of the ball just prior to release is 27 m/s, what is the magnitude of its angular momentum?

20. An anemometer for measuring wind speed consists of four small metal cups, each of mass 120 g, mounted on the ends of essentially massless rods 32 cm long (Fig. 13-29). Find (a) the anemometer's rotational inertia about its central axis and (b) its angular momentum when it's spinning at 12 rev/s in the direction indicated. Treat the cups as point masses.

FIGURE 13-29 Problem 20.

21. A gymnast of rotational inertia 62 kg·m² is tumbling head over heels. If her angular momentum is 470 kg·m²/s, what is her angular speed?

22. A 640-g hoop 90 cm in diameter is rotating at 170 rpm about its central axis. What is its angular momentum?

23. A 7.4-cm-diameter baseball has a mass of 150 g and is spinning at 210 rad/s. What is the magnitude of its angular momentum? Treat the baseball as a solid sphere.

24. What is the magnitude of the angular momentum associated (a) with Earth's rotation about its own axis and

(b) with its revolution about the Sun? See Appendix E, and consider Earth to be a uniform sphere.

25. A weightlifter's barbell consists of two 25-kg masses on the ends of a 15-kg rod 1.6 m long. The weightlifter holds the rod at its center and spins it at 10 rpm about an axis perpendicular to the rod. What is the magnitude of the barbell's angular momentum?

26. A particle of mass m moves in a straight line at constant speed v. Show that its angular momentum about a point located a perpendicular distance b from its line of motion is mvb regardless of where the particle is on the line.

27. Two identical 1800-kg cars are traveling in opposite directions at 90 km/h. Each car's center of mass is 3.0 m from the center of the highway (Fig. 13-30). What are the magnitude and direction of the angular momentum of the system consisting of the two cars, about a point on the centerline of the highway?

FIGURE 13-30 Problem 27.

28. Figure 13-31 shows dimensions of a 880-g wooden baseball bat whose rotational inertia about its center of mass is 0.048 kg·m². If the bat is swung so its far end moves at 50 m/s, find (a) its angular momentum about the pivot point P and (b) the constant torque applied about P to achieve this angular momentum in 0.25 s. *Hint:* Remember the parallel axis theorem.

FIGURE 13-31 Problem 28.

29. Engineers redesign a car's wheels, with the goal of dropping each wheel's angular momentum by 30% for a given linear speed for the car. Other design considerations require that the wheel diameter go from 38 cm to 35 cm. If the old wheel had a rotational inertia of 0.32 kg·m², what must be the new wheel's rotational inertia if the engineers are to achieve their goal?

Section 13-4 Conservation of Angular Momentum

30. A potter's wheel, with rotational inertia 6.40 kg·m², is spinning freely at 19.0 rpm. The potter drops a 2.70-kg lump of clay onto the wheel, where it sticks a distance of 46.0 cm from the rotation axis. What is the subsequent angular speed of the wheel?

31. A 3.0-m-diameter merry-go-round with rotational inertia 120 kg·m² is spinning freely at 0.50 rev/s. Four 25-kg

children sit suddenly on the edge of the merry-go-round. (a) Find the new angular speed, and (b) determine the total energy lost to friction between the children and the merry-go-round.

32. Two ice skaters, both of mass 60 kg, approach on parallel paths 1.4 m apart. Both are moving at 3.2 m/s with their arms outstretched (Fig. 13-32). They join hands as they pass, still maintaining their 1.4-m separation, and begin rotating about one another. What is their angular speed?

1.4 m

FIGURE 13-32 Problem 32.

33. In Fig. 13-33 the lower disk, of mass 440 g and radius 3.5 cm, is rotating at 180 rpm on a frictionless shaft of negligible radius. The upper disk, of mass 270 g and radius 2.3 cm, is initially not rotating. It drops freely down the shaft onto the lower disk, and frictional forces act to bring the two disks to a common rotational speed. (a) What is that speed? (b) What fraction of the initial kinetic energy is lost to friction?

34. In the apparatus shown in Fig. 13-33, the lower disk is initially spinning about a frictionless shaft while the upper disk is stationary. The upper disk drops onto the lower one, and they come to a common angular speed. If one-third of the initial energy is lost in the process, how do the rotational inertias of the two disks compare?

35. A uniform, spherical cloud of interstellar gas has mass 2.0×10^{30} kg and radius 1.0×10^{13} m, and it is rotating with period 1.4×10^6 years. If the cloud collapses to form a star 7.0×10^8 m in radius, what will be the star's rotation period?

36. A skater's body has rotational inertia 4.2 kg·m² with his fists held to his chest and 5.7 kg·m² with arms outstretched. The skater is twirling at 3.0 rev/s while holding 2.5-kg weights in each outstretched hand; the weights are 76 cm from his rotation axis. If he pulls his hands in to his chest, how fast will he be twirling?

37. A turntable of radius 25 cm and rotational inertia 0.0154 kg·m² is spinning freely at 22.0 rpm about its central axis, with a 19.5-g mouse on its outer edge. The mouse walks from the edge to the center. Find (a) the new rotation speed and (b) the work done by the mouse.

38. A 17-kg dog is standing on the edge of a stationary, frictionless turntable of rotational inertia 95 kg·m² and radius 1.81 m. The dog walks once around the turntable. What fraction of a full circle does the dog's motion make with respect to the ground?

39. Two small beads of mass m are free to slide on a frictionless rod of mass M and length ℓ, as shown in Fig. 13-34. Initially the beads are held together at the rod center, and the rod is set spinning freely with initial angular speed ω_0 about a vertical axis coming out of the page in Fig. 13-35. The beads are released, and they slide to the ends of the rod and then off. Find the expressions for the angular speed of the rod (a) when the beads are halfway to the ends of the rod, (b) when they're at the ends, and (c) after the beads are gone. *Hint:* Two of the answers are the same. Why?

FIGURE 13-34 Problem 39.

40. A physics student is standing on an initially motionless, frictionless turntable with rotational inertia 0.31 kg·m². He's holding a wheel of rotational inertia 0.22 kg·m² spinning at 130 rpm about a vertical axis, as we showed in Fig. 13-15. When he turns the wheel upside down, student and turntable begin rotating at 70 rpm. (a) What is the student's mass, considering him to be a cylinder 30 cm in diameter? (b) How much work did he do in turning the wheel upside down? Neglect the distance between the axes of the turntable and wheel.

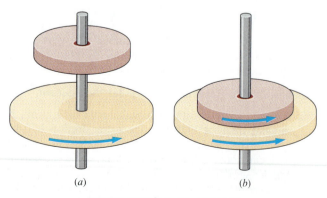

(a)   (b)

FIGURE 13-33 Problems 33, 34.

41. Eight 60-kg skaters join hands and skate down an ice rink at 4.6 m/s. Side by side, they form a line 12 m long. The skater at one end stops abruptly, and the line proceeds to rotate rigidly about that skater. Find (a) the angular speed, (b) the linear speed of the outermost skater, and (c) the force that must be exerted on the outermost skater.

Section 13-5 Rotational Dynamics in Three Dimensions

42. A gyroscope with rotational inertia 6.8×10^{-3} kg·m^2 is precessing in a horizontal plane at 0.42 rad/s under the influence of a 0.31 N·m torque caused by a force pointing vertically downward. How fast is the gyroscope spinning on its axis?

43. A gyroscope consists of a solid disk of radius 7.5 cm, mounted on one end of a shaft of negligible mass. The far end of the shaft is placed on a frictionless pivot and the disk set spinning at 950 rpm. The gyroscope then precesses at 2.1 rad/s. How long is the shaft?

44. Show that the final equality of Equation 13-7 holds for a gyroscope whose angular momentum vector is not necessarily in a horizontal plane.

45. A gyroscope consists of a disk and shaft mounted on frictionless bearings in a frame of diameter d, as shown in Fig. 13-35. Initially the gyroscope is spinning with angular speed ω and is perfectly balanced so it's not precessing. When a mass m is hung from the frame at one of the shaft bearings, the gyroscope precesses about a vertical axis with angular speed Ω. Find an expression for the rotational inertia of the gyroscope.

FIGURE 13-35 Problem 45.

46. Because it bulges slightly at the equator, Earth experiences a gravitational torque that causes its axis to precess with a period of about 26,000 years. Use this fact, and the result of Problem 24, to estimate the magnitude of the torque.

Paired Problems

(Both problems in a pair involve the same principles and techniques. If you can get the first problem, you should be able to solve the second one.)

47. The dot product of a pair of vectors is twice the magnitude of their cross product. What is the angle between the vectors?

48. A force $\mathbf{F}$ applied at the point $x = 2.0$ m, $y = 0$ produces a torque $\boldsymbol{\tau} = 4.6\hat{\mathbf{k}}$ N·m about the origin. If the x component of $\mathbf{F}$ is 3.1 N, what angle does it make with the x axis?

49. A student's rotational inertia about a vertical axis through his center is 4.5 kg·m^2 with his arms held to his chest and 5.6 kg·m^2 with his arms outstretched. In a physics demonstration, the student stands on a turntable rotating at 1.0 rev/s, clutching two 7.5-kg weights to his chest. The turntable's rotational inertia is 4.0 kg·m^2. If the student extends his arms fully so the weights are each 95 cm from his rotation axis, what will be his new angular speed?

50. Five ice skaters of equal mass join hands. With their elbows bent they form a tight circle 1.0 m in diameter, rotating once every 1.3 s about its center. If the skaters now extend their arms so the circle grows to 2.1 m in diameter, what is the new rotation period?

51. The turntable in Fig. 13-36 has rotational inertia 0.021 kg·m^2, and is rotating at 0.29 rad/s about a frictionless vertical axis. A wad of clay is tossed onto the turntable and sticks 15 cm from the rotation axis. The clay impacts with horizontal velocity component 1.3 m/s, at right angles to the turntable's radius, and in a direction that opposes the rotation, as suggested in Fig. 13-37. After the clay lands, the turntable has slowed to 0.085 rad/s. Find the mass of the clay.

FIGURE 13-36 Problem 51.

52. A uniform, solid, spherical asteroid with mass 1.2×10^{13} kg and radius 1.0 km is rotating with a period of 4.3 hours. A meteoroid moving in the asteroid's equatorial plane crashes into the equator at 8.4 km/s. It impacts at a 58° angle to the vertical and embeds itself at the surface. After the impact the asteroid's rotation period is 3.9 hours. Find the meteoroid's mass.

53. A dog of mass m is standing on the edge of a stationary, frictionless turntable of rotational inertia I and radius R. The dog walks once around the turntable. What fraction of a full circle does the dog's motion make with respect to the ground?

54. A dog of mass m is standing on the edge of a stationary, frictionless turntable of rotational inertia I and radius R. On the ground next to the dog is a tree. The dog walks around the turntable until it's again next to the tree. How many times around the turntable has the dog walked?

Supplementary Problems

55. An advanced civilization lives on a solid spherical planet of uniform density. Running out of room for their expanding population, the civilization's government calls an engineering firm specializing in planetary reconfiguration. Without adding any material or angular momentum, the engineers reshape the planet into a hollow shell whose thickness is one-fifth of its outer radius. Find the ratio of the new to the old (a) surface area and (b) length of day.

56. A massless spring of spring constant k is mounted on a turntable of rotational inertia I, as shown in Fig. 13-37. The turntable is on a frictionless vertical axle, though initially it's not rotating. The spring is compressed a distance Δx from its equilibrium, with a mass m placed against it. When the spring is released, the mass leaves the spring moving at right angles to a line through the center of the turntable, at a distance b from the center, and slides without friction across the table and off. Find expressions for (a) the linear speed of the mass and (b) the rotational speed of the turntable. *Hint:* What's conserved?

FIGURE 13-37 Problem 56.

57. If you're familiar with determinants, show that the cross product $\mathbf{A} \times \mathbf{B}$ can be written as a determinant:

$$\mathbf{A} \times \mathbf{B} = \begin{vmatrix} \hat{\imath} & \hat{\jmath} & \hat{k} \\ A_x & A_y & A_z \\ B_x & B_y & B_z \end{vmatrix}.$$

58. A 150-g baseball has angular momentum 7.7 kg·m²/s about a vertical axis through the batter. If it's moving at 43 m/s without spinning, by how much will it miss the batter's axis?

59. About 99.9% of the solar system's total mass lies in the Sun. Using data from Appendix E, estimate what fraction of the solar system's angular momentum about its center is associated with the Sun. Where is most of the rest of the angular momentum?

60. A 55-kg diver is spinning forward in a tuck position at 2.1 rev/s, as shown in Fig. 13-38a. In this position, the diver's rotational inertia is 3.9 kg·m². At the peak of her trajectory, the diver suddenly straightens out in a horizontal position as shown in Fig. 13-38b. In this new position,

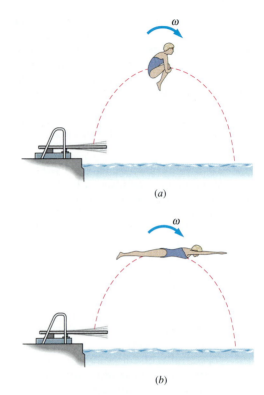

(a)

(b)

FIGURE 13-38 Problem 60.

the diver has an overall length of 2.2 m with center of mass midway along this length, and a rotational inertia of 21 kg·m² about the rotation axis. What is the minimum height of the diver above the water if she is to enter the water hands first? Neglect the diver's horizontal translational motion.

61. A rod of length ℓ and mass M is suspended from a pivot, as shown in Fig. 13-39. The rod is struck midway along its length by a wad of putty of mass m moving horizontally at speed v. The putty sticks to the rod. Find an expression for the minimum speed v that will result in the rod's making a complete circle rather than swinging like a pendulum.

FIGURE 13-39 Problem 61.

62. A 30-cm-diameter phonograph record is dropped onto a turntable being driven at $33\frac{1}{3}$ rpm. If the coefficient of friction between record and turntable is 0.19, how far will the turntable rotate between the time when the record first contacts it and when the record is rotating at the full $33\frac{1}{3}$ rpm? Assume that the record is a homogeneous disk. *Hint:* You'll need to do an integral to calculate the torque.

63. A solid disk of mass M and radius R is initially stationary on a frictionless horizontal axle. A blob of putty with mass m falls and strikes a small protrusion on the side of the disk, as shown in Fig. 13-40. The protrusion is initially level with the axle, and the protrusion sticks to it. The protrusion has negligible mass. Find (a) the angular speed of the disk immediately after the particle hits and (b) the lowest angular speed the disk subsequently obtains. (c) Find an expression for the minimum h such that the disk will rotate rather than oscillate back and forth after the particle hits.

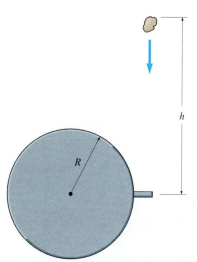

FIGURE 13-40 Problem 63.

64. A system has total angular momentum $\mathbf{L}$ about an axis O. Show that the system's angular momentum about a parallel axis O' is given by $\mathbf{L}' = \mathbf{L} - \mathbf{h} \times \mathbf{P}$, where $\mathbf{P}$ is the system's linear momentum and $\mathbf{h}$ is the displacement vector from O to O' (see Fig. 13-41).

FIGURE 13-41 An object of arbitrary shape comprises a system whose angular momentum about axis O is $\mathbf{L}$. What's its angular momentum about axis O'? Also shown is the displacement $\mathbf{h}$ from O to O', and vectors from each axis to the ith mass element of the system (Problem 64).

65. A solid ball of mass M and radius R is spinning with angular velocity ω_0 about a horizontal axis. It drops vertically onto a surface where the coefficient of kinetic friction with the ball is μ_k (Fig. 13-42). Find expressions for (a) the final angular velocity once it's achieved pure rolling motion and (b) the time it takes until it's in pure rolling motion.

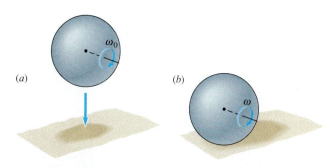

FIGURE 13-42 (a) A solid, spinning ball drops to the surface. (b) What's its angular speed once it's rolling without slipping? (Problem 65)

66. The contraption shown in Fig. 13-43 consists of two solid rubber wheels each of mass M and radius R mounted on an axle of negligible mass in a rigid square frame made of thin rods of mass m and length ℓ. The axle bearings are frictionless, and the wheels are mounted symmetrically about the center line of the frame, just far enough apart that they don't touch. The whole contraption is floating freely in space, and the frame is not rotating. The wheels are rotating with angular speed ω in the same direction, as shown. A mechanism built into the frame moves the axles very slightly so the wheels touch and frictional forces act between them. Describe quantitatively the motion of the system after the wheels have stopped.

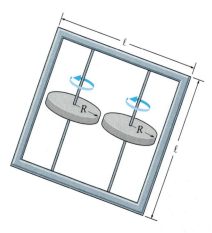

FIGURE 13-43 Problem 66.

14 Static Equilibrium

This rock is in static equilibrium, with zero net force and zero net torque.

What keeps the rock pictured above from tumbling down? Two things: First, the rock below supports it against the force of gravity, giving zero net force. Second, there's no tendency for the rock to tip in any direction—that is, the net torque on the rock is zero. Similarly, the steelworker and beam in Fig. 14-1 are supported by the tension force in the cable, which sums with gravity to give zero net force. But that's not enough—worker and beam are also balanced, so there's no net torque and thus no tendency for the beam to rotate. With zero net force *and* zero net torque, both the rock and the construction worker are in **static equilibrium**.

Understanding equilibrium is crucial for both engineers and scientists. Bridges, buildings, and other structures don't fall down because engineers design them to satisfy equilibrium conditions. Scientists grasp the structure of molecules—and, increasingly, design entirely new molecules—by applying equilibrium principles at the molecular level. In this chapter, we explore conditions that the laws of physics require for a system to be in equilibrium, and show how to apply those conditions in practical situations.

(a)

(b)

(c)

14-1 CONDITIONS FOR EQUILIBRIUM

A body is in **equilibrium** when the net external force and torque on the body are both zero. According to Newton's law, it may still be moving or rotating uniformly. In the special case where the body is also at rest and not rotating, then it is in **static equilibrium**. Formalizing our insights from Fig. 14-1, we write

> **A body is in static equilibrium when it is stationary and when the net external force and torque on the body are both zero.**

Systems in static equilibrium include not only the rock in this chapter's opening photo and the construction worker in Fig. 14-1, but also buildings and structures of all sorts, trees, molecules, your bones and muscles when you're sitting or standing at rest, and anything else that, by virtue of zero net force and zero net torque, remains stationary and is not rotating.

We can write the conditions for static equilibrium mathematically by setting the sums of all the external forces and torques both to zero:

$$\sum \mathbf{F}_i = 0 \tag{14-1}$$

and

$$\sum \boldsymbol{\tau}_i = \sum (\mathbf{r}_i \times \mathbf{F}_i) = 0. \tag{14-2}$$

Here the subscripts i label the different forces $\mathbf{F}$ acting on an object, the positions $\mathbf{r}$ of the force application points, and the associated torques $\boldsymbol{\tau}$.

In Chapters 12 and 13 we were careful to note that torque—and other rotational quantities, for that matter—depends on the choice of a rotation axis. Actually, the issue is not so much an axis but a single point—the point of origin of the vectors $\mathbf{r}$ that enter the expression $\boldsymbol{\tau} = \mathbf{r} \times \mathbf{F}$ for the torque. In this chapter, where we have objects in equilibrium so they aren't rotating, we'll talk of this "pivot point" rather than a rotation axis. So the torque $\boldsymbol{\tau} = \mathbf{r} \times \mathbf{F}$ depends on the choice of pivot point. Then there seems to be an ambiguity in Equation 14-2, since we haven't specified a pivot point.

For an object to be in equilibrium it can't rotate about *any* point, so Equation 14-2 must hold no matter what point we choose. Must we then check every possible point? Fortunately, no. If the first equilibrium condition holds—that is,

FIGURE 14-1 (*a*) With no net force or torque, steelworker and beam are in static equilibrium. A nonzero net force (*b*) or nonzero net torque (*c*) results in disaster.

7.2

A Tilted Beam; Torques and Equilibrium

if the net force on an object is zero—and if the net torque about *some* point is zero, then the net torque about *any other* point is also zero. Problem 8 leads you through the proof of this statement.

In solving equilibrium problems, we're thus free to choose any convenient point about which to evaluate the torques. An appropriate choice is often the application point of one of the forces acting; then $\mathbf{r} = \mathbf{0}$ for that force, and the associated torque $\mathbf{r} \times \mathbf{F}$ is zero. This leaves Equation 14-2 with one term fewer than it would otherwise have.

You might be bothered by having to choose a "pivot point" for an object that's supposed to be in equilibrium, so it's not pivoting or rotating. But don't worry: you can choose *any* point, show that Equations 14-1 and 14-2 are satisfied, and you're assured that the object won't be rotating. The point you choose needn't be on a physical axle, or at a hinge, or at an obvious point about which the object might rotate; it can be *any* point whatsoever. Example 14-1 shows explicitly that the choice of pivot point is arbitrary. However, the example also shows—as in Chapter 6 with the choice of a coordinate system for solving Newton's law problems—that a smart choice results in less algebra.

EXAMPLE 14-1 | *Choosing the Pivot Point*

A 5.0-m-long canoe is tied at bow and stern to a pair of posts so it rides parallel to the shore, as shown in Fig. 14-2. The tie ropes are perpendicular to the shore. A paddler boards the canoe 1.0 m from the stern, in the process exerting an outward force of 200 N at right angles to the shore. Find the tension in the bow rope if the canoe remains in static equilibrium in the horizontal plane.

Solution

All three horizontal forces are perpendicular to the shore, so the condition that there be no net force (Equation 14-1) has a single component:

$$T_b + T_s - 200 \text{ N} = 0,$$

where we take the shoreward direction as positive. Choosing the application point of one of the unknown tensions as our pivot will eliminate that unknown from the torque equation. If we choose the stern, the condition that there be no net torque (Equation 14-2) becomes

$$(5.0 \text{ m})(T_b) - (200 \text{ N})(1.0 \text{ m}) = 0,$$

where the first term is the torque due to the bow-rope tension and the second is due to the force of the paddler. Here we take a positive torque as one tending to produce counterclockwise rotation (torque vector out of the page in Fig. 14-2), so the paddler torque is negative. Solving for T_b gives

$$T_b = \frac{(200 \text{ N})(1.0 \text{ m})}{5.0 \text{ m}} = 40 \text{ N}.$$

FIGURE 14-2 Top view of the canoe in Example 14-1.

Another Pivot Point

Suppose we had chosen the center of the canoe as our pivot point. The force-balance equation would be unchanged, but the torque equation would now contain three terms:

$$(2.5 \text{ m})(T_b) + (1.5 \text{ m})(200 \text{ N}) - (2.5 \text{ m})(T_s) = 0.$$

The three terms are due to the bow rope, the paddler, and the stern rope, respectively, and the distances are measured from the canoe center. Note that now the bow-rope and paddler torques have the same sign, since both tend to produce counterclockwise rotation about the canoe center. We can solve the force equation for T_s to get

$$T_s = 200 \text{ N} - T_b.$$

Using this result in the torque equation gives

$$(2.5 \text{ m})(T_b) + (1.5 \text{ m})(200 \text{ N}) - (2.5 \text{ m})(200 \text{ N} - T_b) = 0,$$

so

$$T_b = \frac{(2.5 \text{ m})(200 \text{ N}) - (1.5 \text{ m})(200 \text{ N})}{5.0 \text{ m}} = 40 \text{ N},$$

as before. Although we get the same answer, the algebra is considerably more complicated with this choice of pivot point.

EXERCISE Inside a piece of machinery, a metal rod is secured in the horizontal plane by three horizontal springs, as shown in Fig. 14-3. Find the tension force $\mathbf{F}_3$ and point of attachment x for the right-hand spring that will maintain the rod in static equilibrium.

Answers: $F_3 = 14$ N; $x = 2.9$ cm

Some problems similar to Example 14-1: 2, 8, 13

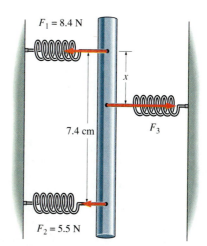

FIGURE 14-3 Where to attach $\mathbf{F}_3$? How big should it be? (The entire structure lies in the horizontal plane.)

Got It!

Figure 14-4 shows three pairs of forces acting on an object. Which pair, acting as the *only* forces on the object, results in static equilibrium? Explain why the other pairs don't.

FIGURE 14-4 Which pair of forces produces static equilibrium? Why don't the others? (Pairs are identified by color, rather than using the usual force-vector orange color.)

14-2 CENTER OF GRAVITY

One force often present is gravity, which acts on all parts of a body (Fig. 14-5). The vector sum of these gravitational forces is just $M\mathbf{g}$. But what about the torques due to the gravitational forces acting on different parts of the body? Summing these torques, we have

$$\boldsymbol{\tau} = \sum \mathbf{r}_i \times \mathbf{F}_i = \sum \mathbf{r}_i \times m_i \mathbf{g} = \left(\sum m_i \mathbf{r}_i \right) \times \mathbf{g},$$

FIGURE 14-5 The gravitational force acts everywhere on an extended body. In a uniform gravitational field, the force on equal-mass elements has the same magnitude and direction.

FIGURE 14-6 The gravitational force on the mass element m_i produces a torque about the point O.

where $\mathbf{F}_i$ is the gravitational force on the ith mass element, and $\mathbf{r}_i$ is the vector from some pivot point to that mass element (Fig. 14-6). We can rewrite this equation by multiplying the right-hand side by M/M, where M is the total mass of the body:

$$\boldsymbol{\tau} = \left(\frac{\sum m_i \mathbf{r}_i}{M} \right) \times M\mathbf{g} \,.$$

The term in parentheses is just the center of mass (see Section 10-1), while the right-hand term is the total weight of the body. Therefore, the net torque on the body due to gravity is just that of the gravitational force $M\mathbf{g}$ acting at the center of mass. In general, the point at which the gravitational force seems to act is called the **center of gravity**. We have just proven that the center of gravity coincides with the center of mass when the gravitational field is uniform—that is, when $\mathbf{g}$ is the same for all mass elements in the body. If a body is large enough that the variation in magnitude or direction of $\mathbf{g}$ is significant, then the two points may not coincide (this is obvious only for objects whose size is not insignificant compared with Earth's radius; see Problem 61), although this is not a situation we usually encounter.

We can easily locate the center of gravity by suspending an object from a string attached to its edge. The torque about the suspension point is due entirely to gravity and is zero only if the center of gravity lies directly beneath that point (Fig. 14-7). In equilibrium, a vertical line from the suspension point must therefore pass through the center of gravity. If we now change the suspension point, we can determine another line that passes through the center of gravity. These two lines intersect in a single point, which must be the center of gravity (Fig. 14-8).

FIGURE 14-8 The intersection of vertical lines from two suspension points marks the center of gravity.

$$\tau \neq 0$$
$$(a)$$

$$\tau = 0$$
$$(b)$$

FIGURE 14-7 A suspended object is in equilibrium only when its center of gravity lies directly below the suspension point. The nonzero torque in (a) tends to rotate the object to the equilibrium orientation in (b).

14-3 EXAMPLES OF STATIC EQUILIBRIUM

Example 14-1 is particularly simple because all the forces have a single common nonzero component (perpendicular to shore), and so do the torques (vertical), reducing the equilibrium conditions to two equations in two unknowns. Generally, forces act in different directions, so Equations 14-1 and 14-2 have additional components, and this results in additional equations. We'll restrict ourselves to the common situation in which all forces lie in a plane; then the force equation has two components while the torque equation has only one, so we end up with three equations in three unknowns.

Whatever the geometry, solving a static equilibrium problem is much like solving a Newton's law problem; after all, the equations for static equilibrium are Newton's law and its rotational analog, with the linear and angular acceleration set to zero. Here we adapt the strategy for Newton's law problems given in Chapter 6 to problems of static equilibrium:

7.3
Arm Levers

7.4
Two Painters on a Beam

7.5
The Back

Strategy

Static Equilibrium Problems

1. Identify the object in equilibrium.
2. Identify all the forces acting on the object, and draw a free-body diagram showing the force vectors. Since we're dealing with torques as well as forces, it's important where each force is applied. Instead of treating the object as a point particle with all forces acting at the same point, as we did in Chapter 6, it's essential here that the free-body diagram shows the forces drawn from their actual application points. If the direction of any force is unknown, draw a force vector you think looks appropriate and let the algebra take care of signs and angles.
3. Choose an appropriate coordinate system, and resolve all vectors into components.
4. Write Equation 14-1 (the condition that the forces sum to zero) as a set of equations, one for each component.
5. Choose a pivot point for calculating torques. The choice is yours, but a smart choice—usually at the application point of one of the forces—will simplify the algebra.
6. Calculate the torque associated with each force, and formulate Equation 14-2 (the condition that the torques sum to zero).
7. Solve your system of force and torque equations for the unknowns of the problem.

Here we've skipped the step of writing the relevant equations in vector form; it suffices to identify all the force vectors and write the components of the equilibrium equations in a chosen coordinate system. As always, it's a good idea to solve first for answers in symbolic form, and to ask if those answers make sense, before going on to obtain numerical answers. The examples that follow illustrate the use of this strategy in a range of practical situations.

EXAMPLE 14-2	*A Drop-Leaf Table*

A dining table extends with a leaf of length ℓ supported by a diagonal brace at angle $\theta = 40°$, as shown in Fig. 14-9a. If the maximum load is 120 N, centered on the center of the leaf, what is the force exerted by the hinge that connects the leaf to the table?

Solution
Here we'll follow the strategy above in numbered steps with detailed explanations; in subsequent examples, we'll be sure to take each step, but without numbering each explicitly.

1. The object of interest is the table leaf with the turkey on it; their combined weight can't exceed the maximum load of 120 N.
2. Forces on this object include the force $\mathbf{F}_1$ of the hinge, the load weight $\mathbf{W}$ of the table leaf and turkey together, and the compression force $\mathbf{F}_2$ of the diagonal brace. Figure 14-9b is a free-body diagram showing these forces at the points where they're applied. It's clear which way the diagonal brace and the weight act, but the hinge force $\mathbf{F}_1$ is less obvious. We've drawn it as shown because it clearly needs an upward component to keep the left edge of the table leaf from dropping, and, because the force of the diagonal brace has a rightward component, the hinge had better pull leftward if the table leaf is to be in equilibrium. But if we had drawn $\mathbf{F}_1$ "wrong," the algebra would still have given us correct answers.
3. With three forces in different directions, the best choice of coordinate system may not be obvious. But two of the force application points lie on a horizontal line, so it makes sense to make that line a coordinate axis. Thus we choose an xyz coordinate system as shown in Fig. 14-9. In this system the weight $\mathbf{W}$ has only a y component, which is clearly downward, so $W_y = -W$ and $W_x = 0$. You've taken enough vector components by now to see that $\mathbf{F}_2$ has components $F_{2x} = F_2 \cos\theta$ and $F_{2y} = F_2 \sin\theta$. Since we don't know the exact direction of the hinge force $\mathbf{F}_1$, we'll just call its components F_{1x} and F_{1y}, and treat them as unknowns. (Alternately, we could have specified an unknown angle and used the magnitude F_1 and that angle as unknowns.)
4. With the force components identified, we write the x and y components of Equation 14-1:

   x (horizontal): $\qquad F_{1x} + F_2 \cos\theta = 0$

   y (vertical): $\qquad F_{1y} - W + F_2 \sin\theta = 0$.

5. On to the torques. First we need a pivot point; as always, it's convenient to use one of the force application points. In this case the unknowns are the components of $\mathbf{F}_1$; if we choose $\mathbf{F}_1$'s application point, then $\mathbf{F}_1$ will not appear in the torque equation. That may simplify the algebra, since then the unknown components of $\mathbf{F}_1$ appear only once, each in a force equation. We've indicated this choice by putting the origin of our coordinate system at the hinge.
6. Now we calculate the torques. The torque due to $\mathbf{F}_1$ about our chosen pivot point is zero. The diagonal force $\mathbf{F}_2$ makes

(a)　　　　　　　　　(b)

FIGURE 14-9 (a) What is the force exerted by the drop-leaf table's hinge? (b) Free-body diagram for the table leaf.

an angle θ with a vector from the pivot to the application point of $\mathbf{F}_2$; the latter vector has magnitude ℓ. So the torque due to $\mathbf{F}_2$ has magnitude $F_2 \ell \sin\theta$. The right-hand rule shows that this torque would tend to rotate the leaf clockwise about the pivot; using Figs. 13-5 or 13-6 shows that the torque vector points out of the page, or in the $+z$ direction. Thus the z component of this torque is $\tau_{2z} = F_2 \ell \sin\theta$.

What about the torque due to the weight $\mathbf{W}$? Because of the turkey, we don't know the y coordinate of its application point. But recall Fig. 12-7, which shows that the magnitude of the torque is the product of the force with the lever arm— the perpendicular distance from the pivot point to the force application point. Here that distance is $\frac{1}{2}\ell$; thus the torque due to $\mathbf{W}$ has magnitude $\tau_W = \frac{1}{2}\ell W$. The right-hand rule shows that the direction of the torque vector is into the page, or in the $-z$ direction. Thus its z component is $\tau_{Wz} = \frac{1}{2}\ell W$. With both nonzero torques in the z direction, we have a single component of the torque equation (Equation 14-2). It reads

$$F_2 \ell \sin\theta - \tfrac{1}{2}\ell W = 0 \, .$$

7. Solving the torque equation for F_2 gives $F_2 = W/2\sin\theta$; using this result in the x-component force equation gives

$$F_{1x} = -F_2 \cos\theta = -\frac{W\cos\theta}{2\sin\theta} = -\tfrac{1}{2}W\cot\theta$$

$$= -(\tfrac{1}{2})(120 \text{ N})\cot 40° = -71.5 \text{ N} \, .$$

Does this make sense? With the positive x direction to the right, F_{1x} had better be negative to balance the rightward component from the diagonal brace. We also see that if $\theta \rightarrow 0$, F_{1x} becomes infinite—an impossibility. Of course: without a vertical component to the force at its right end, equilibrium as shown in Fig. 14-8 would be impossible; the leaf would swing downward.

Meanwhile, the y force equation gives

$$F_{1y} = W - F_2 \sin \theta = W - \tfrac{1}{2}W = \tfrac{1}{2}W = 60 \text{ N}.$$

This, too, makes sense. With the load weight in the center of the leaf, the vertical force components at the two ends should each equal half the load. Finally, we can find the magnitude of the hinge force $\mathbf{F}_1$:

$$F_1 = \sqrt{F_{1x}^2 + F_{1y}^2} = \sqrt{(-71.5 \text{ N})^2 + (60 \text{ N})^2} = 93 \text{ N}.$$

EXAMPLE 14-3 | A Drawbridge

The raised span of the drawbridge shown in Fig. 14-10a has its mass of 11,000 kg distributed uniformly over its 14-m length. Find the magnitude of the tension in the supporting cable and the magnitude and direction of the force exerted by the hinge.

Solution

Figure 14-10b is a free-body diagram showing the forces on the raised span, and an appropriate coordinate system. Resolving the forces into components and summing them to zero gives

x (horizontal): $F_h \cos \phi_1 - T \cos \phi_2 = 0$

y (vertical): $F_h \sin \phi_1 - mg - T \sin \phi_2 = 0.$

Choosing the pivot at the hinge eliminates the hinge force from the torque equation. Figure 14-10b shows that the angles θ_1 and θ_2 for calculating the torques are 120° and 165°, respectively. The two individual torques are both perpendicular to the plane of Fig. 14-10b, (i.e., in the z direction), so the torque equation has only a single component:

$$-\frac{L}{2} mg \sin \theta_1 + LT \sin \theta_2 = 0,$$

where L is the length of the span and where $L/2$ appears in the first term since the gravitational force acts at the center of mass, halfway along the span. The minus sign appears because the gravitational torque is into the page, i.e., in the $-z$ direction.

We're now ready to solve for the unknowns F_h, T, and ϕ_1. Our choice of pivot leaves the single unknown T in the torque equation, which we can solve to get

$$T = \frac{mg \sin \theta_1}{2 \sin \theta_2} = \frac{(11{,}000 \text{ kg})(9.8 \text{ m/s}^2)(\sin 120°)}{(2)(\sin 165°)}$$

$$= 1.80 \times 10^5 \text{ N}.$$

If we isolate the terms in the unknowns F_h and ϕ_1 on the left-hand sides of the two force equations and divide the resulting y equation by the x equation, we have

$$\frac{\sin \phi_1}{\cos \phi_1} \equiv \tan \phi_1 = \frac{mg + T \sin \phi_2}{T \cos \phi_2}$$

$$= \frac{(11{,}000 \text{ kg})(9.8 \text{ m/s}) + (1.80 \times 10^5 \text{ N})(\sin 15°)}{(1.80 \times 10^5 \text{ N})(\cos 15°)} = 0.887,$$

giving $\phi_1 = \tan^{-1}(0.887) = 41.6°$. Finally, we can solve the x component force equation for F_h:

$$F_h = \frac{T \cos \phi_2}{\cos \phi_1} = \frac{(1.80 \times 10^5 \text{ N})(\cos 15°)}{\cos 41.6°} = 2.3 \times 10^5 \text{ N}.$$

(a)

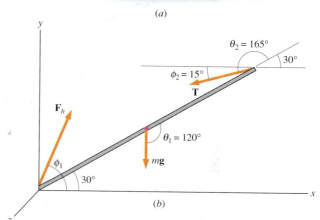

(b)

FIGURE 14-10 (a) How should the drawbridge cable and hinge be engineered to ensure adequate strength? (b) Side view of the bridge span, showing the force $\mathbf{F}_h$ exerted by the hinge, the gravitational force $m\mathbf{g}$ acting at the span's center of gravity, and the cable tension $\mathbf{T}$. Also shown are the unknown angle ϕ_1 and the angles θ_1 and θ_2 used in calculating the torques; these follow from the 30° inclination angle and the 15° cable angle.

Note that both the hinge force and the cable tension are considerably larger than the 1.1×10^5-N weight of the bridge span. Engineers are responsible for ensuring that the bridge components can handle these loads.

ActivPhysics Activity 7.5 is a physiological version of this example.

Some problems similar to Examples 14-2 and 14-3: 29, 41, 58

7.5
The Back

EXAMPLE 14-4	*Leaning a Board*

A board of mass m and length L is leaning against a wall, as shown in Fig. 14-11a. The wall is frictionless, and the coefficient of static friction between board and floor is μ. Find an expression for the minimum angle ϕ at which the board can be leaned without slipping.

Solution

Figure 14-11b shows the free-body diagram for the board, with an appropriate coordinate system. In addition to the board's weight $m\mathbf{g}$, there are normal forces $\mathbf{F}_1$ and $\mathbf{F}_2$ at the floor and wall, and a frictional force at the floor whose maximum possible magnitude μF_1 corresponds to the minimum board angle. Then the components of the force equation are

x (horizontal) $\mu F_1 - F_2 = 0$

y (vertical) $F_1 - mg = 0$.

A smart choice for the pivot point is the bottom of the board since then we eliminate two forces from the torque equation. The remaining torques are due to $\mathbf{F}_2$ and the gravitational force $m\mathbf{g}$, and they're both in the z direction (perpendicular to the page). Calculating and summing the z components of these torques gives

$$LF_2 \sin \phi - \frac{L}{2}mg \cos \phi = 0,$$

where Fig. 14-11b shows how the angles used to calculate the torques relate to the board angle ϕ. The actual angle for the first term is $180° - \phi$, but we wrote $\sin \phi$ since $\sin(180° - \phi) = \sin \phi$.

Having written the force and torque equations, we've completed the essential physics. The rest is algebra. The vertical force equation gives $F_1 = mg$; substituting this in the horizontal force equation then gives $F_2 = \mu mg$. Substituting this result in the torque equation then allows us to solve for the tangent of the unknown angle:

$$\frac{\sin \phi}{\cos \phi} \equiv \tan \phi = \frac{mg}{2F_2} = \frac{mg}{2\mu mg} = \frac{1}{2\mu},$$

giving $\phi = \tan^{-1}(1/2\mu)$.

This is a remarkably simple result—it doesn't depend on the mass or length of the board, nor on g. Does it make sense? As the coefficient of friction goes to zero, $\tan \phi$ grows without bound, and ϕ approaches 90°. With no friction, that says, we can lean the board against the wall only if it's vertical. Increasing the friction, on the other hand, allows us to lean the board at ever lower angles.

EXERCISE Climbers attempting to cross a stream place a 340-kg log against a vertical, frictionless ice cliff on the opposite side (Fig. 14-12). The log is inclined at 27°, and its center of gravity is one-third of the way along its 6.3-m length. If the coefficient of friction between the left end of the log and the ground is 0.92, what is the maximum mass for a climber and pack to cross without the log slipping?

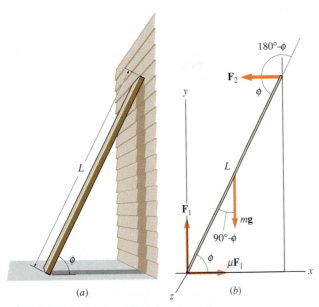

(a)

(b)

FIGURE 14-11 (a) At what angle will the board slip? (b) Forces on the board include its weight, the normal forces $\mathbf{F}_1$ and $\mathbf{F}_2$ at the floor and wall, and the frictional force of magnitude μF_1 at the floor. (Absence of friction at the wall means the contact force with the wall is entirely normal.) The angle used in calculating the gravitational torque is actually the supplement of $90 - \phi$, but the two have the same sine, namely $\sin(90° - \phi) = \cos \phi$.

FIGURE 14-12 How heavy a climber can cross the log? Dot marks the log's center of gravity.

Answer: 87 kg

Some problems similar to Example 14-4: 24, 28, 43, 44, 50

EXAMPLE 14-5	Equilibrium in the Human Body

Figure 14-13 depicts a human arm. The forearm measures 32 cm from elbow joint to center of palm and has a mass $m = 2.7$ kg, with center of mass located 14 cm from the elbow joint. The biceps muscle attaches to the radius (forearm bone) 3.6 cm from the elbow joint. With the humerus (upper arm bone) vertical and the forearm horizontal, the biceps muscle makes an 80° angle with the horizontal. If a pumpkin of mass $M = 4.5$ kg rests on the palm, what are the tension in the biceps and the force exerted on the elbow joint?

Solution

Figure 14-14 shows the forces acting on the forearm, including the weights $m\mathbf{g}$ and $M\mathbf{g}$ of the arm and pumpkin, the muscle tension $\mathbf{T}$, and the contact force $\mathbf{F}_c$. We can read the x and y components of force balance from the diagram:

$$x: \qquad F_{cx} - T\cos\theta = 0$$
$$y: \qquad T\sin\theta - F_{cy} - mg - Mg = 0.$$

Choosing the pivot at the elbow gives a torque equation in which the contact force doesn't appear:

$$x_1 T\sin\theta - x_2 mg - x_3 Mg = 0,$$

where the x's are the coordinates of the force application points. Solving for the biceps tension T gives

$$T = \frac{(x_2 m + x_3 M)g}{x_1\sin\theta}$$
$$= \frac{[(0.14\text{ m})(2.7\text{ kg}) + (0.32\text{ m})(4.5\text{ kg})](9.8\text{ N/kg})}{(0.036\text{ m})(\sin 80°)}$$
$$= 500\text{ N}.$$

The horizontal and vertical force equations then give the components of the elbow contact force:

$$F_{cx} = T\cos\theta = (500\text{ N})(\cos 80°) = 87\text{ N},$$

and

$$F_{cy} = T\sin\theta - (m + M)g$$
$$= (500\text{ N})(\sin 80°) - (2.7\text{ kg} + 4.5\text{ kg})(9.8\text{ N/kg})$$
$$= 420\text{ N},$$

making the total force on the elbow $F_c = \sqrt{(87\text{ N})^2 + (420\text{ N})^2} = 430$ N. This example shows how the human body often sustains forces far larger than the weights of objects it may be lifting.

EXERCISE A 95-kg horizontal tree branch has its center of gravity 2.2 m from the tree trunk. A rope helps support the branch, attached as shown in Fig. 14-15. A 4.5-kg swing hangs from a point 7.3 m out along the branch. How massive a child can sit stationary on the swing if the tension in the diagonal rope is not to exceed 1750 N? Neglect any supporting torque where the branch joins the trunk.

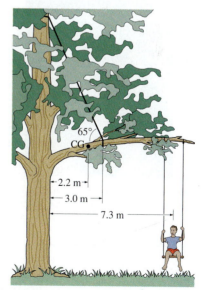

FIGURE 14-15 How heavy a child can sit on the swing?

Answer: 33.4 kg

FIGURE 14-13 Holding a pumpkin. The elbow and biceps provide the forces that support the forearm and pumpkin.

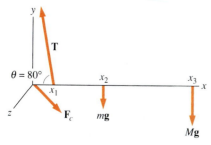

FIGURE 14-14 Forces on the forearm include its own weight $m\mathbf{g}$, the pumpkin weight $M\mathbf{g}$, the muscle tension $\mathbf{T}$, and the elbow contact force $\mathbf{F}_c$.

Some problems similar to Example 14-5: 19, 39, 40
ActivPhysics Activity 7.3 simulates this example, and also explores the triceps muscle.

APPLICATION	*Restoring the Statue of Liberty*

In 1986, workers completed major renovation of the Statue of Liberty, France's famous gift to the United States that was first dedicated in 1886. Although its designer, French sculptor Frédéric-Auguste Bartholdi, suggested that his creation should last as long as Egypt's pyramids, many factors conspired to make major renovation necessary after only one century. These include corrosion from air pollution and from a chemical reaction between the iron framework and the copper skin, as well as a deviation from engineering plans during construction that resulted in excess torques on the statue's structural members.

Sculptor Bartholdi was no engineer, and without the work of the French engineer Eiffel (of tower fame) the statue could not have maintained itself in static equilibrium. Eiffel designed an inner skeleton of iron to provide the forces necessary to counteract the weights and torques associated with components of the statue, as well as with the force exerted by wind

(Fig. 14-16). The statue was constructed in France in 300 separate pieces, then shipped to New York. During assembly, probably as a conscious aesthetic decision, Liberty's head and upraised arm were mounted 2 feet from their locations on Eiffel's plan, with the arm making a greater angle to the vertical than planned (Fig. 14-17). This made the arm exert a much greater torque about the shoulder than planned, resulting in greater forces on structural components. For historical integrity, renovators did not return to Eiffel's original design; instead, they reinforced the support structure to withstand better the excess forces and torques.

FIGURE 14-16 The Statue of Liberty's interior skeleton counteracts forces and torques acting on the statue. Computer-drawn images of Liberty's skeleton helped engineers and architects plan its renovation.

As built

Eiffel's plan

FIGURE 14-17 The statue's head and arm are offset from their planned positions, resulting in greater than anticipated forces and torques on structural members.

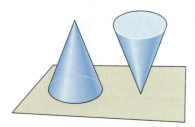

14-4 STABILITY OF EQUILIBRIA

What if a body is disturbed from static equilibrium? Then, in general, it experiences nonzero net forces or torques, and it accelerates or begins to rotate. Figure 14-18 shows two very different possibilities for the subsequent behavior

FIGURE 14-18 Stable (left) and unstable (right) equilibria.

of a body displaced slightly from equilibrium. Tip the cone on the left slightly, and a torque (due to the gravitational force) develops that brings it quickly back to equilibrium. Tip the cone on the right in Fig. 14-18, and over it goes. The torque arising from even a slight displacement swings the cone permanently away from its original equilibrium. The former situation is an example of **stable equilibrium**, the latter of **unstable equilibrium**. Nearly all the equilibria we encounter in nature are stable, since a body in unstable equilibrium will not remain so for any significant time. The slightest disturbance will set it in motion, and it will eventually stop in a very different equilibrium state.

The distinction between stable and unstable equilibria is often subtler than Fig. 14-18 would imply. Figure 14-19 shows a ball in four different equilibrium situations. Clearly situation (a) is stable, while (b) is unstable. Situation (c) is neither stable nor unstable; it is termed **neutrally stable**. But what about situation (d)? For very small disturbances, the ball will return to its original state, so the equilibrium is stable. But for larger disturbances—large enough to push the ball just over the highest points on the hill—it's unstable. Such an equilibrium is called **conditionally stable** or **metastable**. Many common equilibria are actually metastable, as Fig. 14-20 suggests.

We've defined a stable equilibrium as one in which a displaced system returns to its equilibrium state. Be aware, though, that that return may not take place immediately. In Fig. 14-19a, for example, displacing the ball will result in its rolling back and forth about equilibrium. Eventually friction will dissipate its energy, and it will come to rest at equilibrium. Back-and-forth motion is common to many systems—from nuclei and atoms to skyscrapers and bridges—that are displaced from stable equilibrium. Such motion is the topic of the next chapter.

Stability is closely associated with the potential energy of the system in equilibrium. Because gravitational potential energy is directly proportional to height, the shapes of the hills and valleys in Fig. 14-19 are in fact the potential energy curves for the balls shown in the figure. In all cases of equilibrium, the ball is at a minimum or maximum of the potential energy curve—at a place where the force (that is, the derivative of potential energy with respect to position) is zero. For the stable and metastable equilibria, the potential energy at equilibrium is a minimum, at least with respect to positions immediately adjacent to equilibrium. A deviation from equilibrium requires that work be done against a net force that tends to restore the ball to its equilibrium position. The unstable equilibrium, in contrast, occurs at a maximum in potential energy. Here, a deviation from equilibrium results in lower potential energy and in a net force that tends to accelerate the ball farther from equilibrium. For the neutrally stable equilibrium, there's no change whatever in potential energy as we move away from equilibrium; consequently the ball experiences no force.

As another example, consider the block shown in two orientations in Fig. 14-20. In either case, tipping the block requires raising the center of mass, thus raising the potential energy. So each orientation represents a local minimum in the potential energy. But tip the vertical block too far, and over it goes: the vertical equilibrium is only metastable, like the ball in Fig. 14-19d. In contrast, the horizontal block has the lowest possible potential energy, so it's stable like the ball of Fig. 14-19a. It's also possible to put the block into an unstable equilibrium, analogous to Fig. 14-19b, by balancing it on an edge with its center of mass directly above the edge.

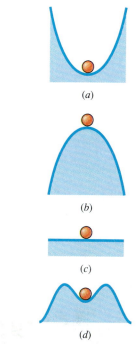

(a)

(b)

(c)

(d)

FIGURE 14-19 (a) Stable, (b) unstable, (c) neutrally stable, and (d) metastable equilibria.

FIGURE 14-20 Both equilibria are stable against very small disturbances, but a larger disturbance will knock the vertical block over. The vertical equilibrium is therefore metastable.

We can sum up our understanding of equilibrium and potential energy in two simple mathematical statements. First, the force must be zero; that requires a local maximum or minimum in the potential energy:

$$\frac{dU}{dx} = 0, \qquad \text{(equilibrium condition)} \qquad (14\text{-}3)$$

where U is the potential energy of a system and x is a variable describing the system's configuration. For the simple systems we've been considering, x measures the position or orientation of an object, but with more complicated systems it could be replaced by another quantity such as the system's volume or even its composition. For a stable equilibrium, we require a local minimum, so the potential energy curve is concave upward. (See the Math Toolbox to review the relevant calculus.) Mathematically,

$$\frac{d^2U}{dx^2} > 0. \qquad \text{(stable equilibrium)} \qquad (14\text{-}4)$$

This condition applies to metastable equilibria as well, for they are *locally* stable. In contrast, unstable equilibrium occurs where the potential energy has a local maximum, or

$$\frac{d^2U}{dx^2} < 0. \qquad \text{(unstable equilibrium)} \qquad (14\text{-}5)$$

The intermediate case $d^2U/dx^2 = 0$ corresponds to neutral stability.

Math Toolbox

Maxima, Minima, and Derivatives In calculus you've probably learned to find the maximum or minimum of a function by taking its derivative and setting it to zero (Problem 72 in Chapter 4 is an example). Why does this work? Because, as Figs. 14-19a, b, and d suggest, a hill or valley must be level right at its top or bottom. If you're on a mountain and the trail is still heading up, you can't be at the top! More generally, the slope of a curve—the derivative of the function describing that curve—must be zero at a maximum or minimum. We first introduced potential energy curves in Chapter 8, Section 8-4. In Section 8-5 we went on to show that force is the negative derivative of potential energy. For force to be zero, then, the slope of the potential energy curve must be zero—and that translates into our Equation 14-3.

What determines whether a point of zero slope is a maximum or minimum and whether the equilibrium is stable or unstable? That's also obvious from Fig. 14-19. If the slope is increasing as you move away from equilibrium in the positive x direction (Fig. 14-19a), then the equilibrium is stable. To say that the *slope* is increasing, rather than the function itself, is to say that the derivative of the function's derivative—what we call the second derivative, d^2U/dx^2—is positive. That's our condition 14-6. Similarly, a negative second derivative—as in Fig. 14-9b—describes unstable equilibrium (condition 14-7).

EXAMPLE 14-6	*Semiconductor Engineering*

Solid-state physicists developing a new semiconductor device theorize that the potential energy of an electron in a region of the device should be given by

$$U(x) = ax^2 - bx^4,$$

where x is the electron's position measured in nm, U is its energy in aJ (1 aJ $= 10^{-18}$ J), and constants a and b are given by $a = 8$ aJ/nm^2 and $b = 1$ aJ/nm^4. Locate the equilibrium positions for the electron, and describe their stability.

Solution

Equilibrium occurs where the potential energy has a minimum or maximum, so $dU/dx = 0$. Taking the derivative of the potential energy and setting it to zero gives

$$0 = \frac{dU}{dx} = 2ax - 4bx^3 = 2x(a - 2bx^2) = 2x(8 - 2x^2)$$

$$= 4x(4 - x^2) \text{ aJ/nm},$$

where for mathematical clarity we left off the units except in the final answer. This equation is satisfied if $x = 0$ or $x = \pm 2$. Therefore, the electron is in equilibrium at $x = -2$ nm, at $x = 0$ nm, or at $x = 2$ nm. To determine the stability of these equilibria, we evaluate the second derivative at each equilibrium position:

$$\frac{d^2U}{dx^2} = 2a - 12bx^2 = (16 - 12x^2) \text{ aJ/nm}^2,$$

so

$$\left(\frac{d^2U}{dx^2}\right)_{x=\pm2} = 16 - (12)(4) = -32 \text{ aJ/nm}^2$$

and

$$\left(\frac{d^2U}{dx^2}\right)_{x=0} = 16 - 0 = 16 \text{ aJ/nm}^2.$$

From conditions 14-6 and 14-7, we see that the equilibria at $x = \pm 2$ nm are unstable, while the equilibrium at $x = 0$ nm is locally stable. Figure 14-21 is a plot of the potential energy curve, which makes clear the location and stability of the equilibria.

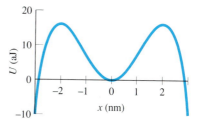

FIGURE 14-21 Potential energy curve for Example 14-6, showing that unstable equilibria occur at $x = \pm 2$ nm and stable equilibrium at $x = 0$.

EXERCISE A particle's potential energy as a function of position is given by $U = 2x^3 - 2x^2 - 7x + 10$, with x in meters and U in joules. Find the positions of any stable and unstable equilibria, and give the energy of each.

Answers: Stable at $x = 1.46$ m, $U = 1.74$ J; unstable at $x = -0.797$ m, $U = 13.3$ J

Some problems similar to Example 14-6: 34, 36, 37

Stability considerations apply to the overall arrangement of the particles that comprise matter. A mixture of hydrogen and oxygen, for example, is in metastable equilibrium at room temperature. Lighting a match puts some atoms over the maxima in their potential energy curves, at which point they rearrange into a state of lower potential energy—the state we call H_2O. Similarly, a uranium nucleus is at a local minimum of its potential energy curve, and a little excess energy can result in its splitting into two smaller nuclei whose total potential energy is much lower. That transition from a less stable to a more stable equilibrium describes the basic physics of nuclear fission.

Potential energy curves for complex structures like molecules or skyscrapers can't be described fully with one-dimensional graphs. If potential energy varies in different ways when the structure is altered in different directions, then in order to determine stability we need to consider all possible ways potential energy might vary. For example, a snowball sitting on a mountain pass—or any other system with a saddle-shaped potential energy curve—is stable against

FIGURE 14-22 A saddle-shaped potential energy curve. Point P is an equilibrium position that's stable in one direction and unstable in another.

displacements in one direction but not another (Fig. 14-22). Stability analysis of complex physical systems, ranging from nuclei and molecules to bridges and buildings and machinery, and on to stars and galaxies, is an important part of contemporary work in engineering and science.

CHAPTER SYNOPSIS

Summary

1. A body at rest is in **static equilibrium** when the net external force and torque on the body are both zero:

$$\sum \mathbf{F} = 0$$

and

$$\sum \boldsymbol{\tau} = 0.$$

If the first of these conditions is met, and the second holds for some point about which the torques are calculated, then it holds for all such points.

2. When the gravitational force acts on an extended body, the torque it produces is that of the body's weight acting at the **center of gravity**. When gravity is uniform over the entire body, then the center of gravity coincides with the center of mass.

3. Solving static equilibrium problems requires writing equations that set both the net force and net torque equal to zero. The result is a set of simultaneous equations that set conditions on the unknown quantities.

4. An equilibrium is **stable** if a small displacement from equilibrium results in forces and/or torques that tend to restore the equilibrium. An equilibrium is **unstable** if small displacements result in forces and/or torques that drive the system further from equilibrium. A **metastable** equilibrium is stable against very small displacements but unstable if larger displacements occur. Stable and metastable equilibria occur at local minima of a system's potential energy curve, while unstable equilibria occur at maxima. In one dimension, that is:

$$\frac{dU}{dx} = 0, \quad \text{(equilibrium condition)}$$

$$\frac{d^2U}{dx^2} > 0, \quad \text{(stable or metastable equilibrium)}$$

$$\frac{d^2U}{dx^2} < 0. \quad \text{(unstable equilibrium)}$$

The intermediate case $d^2U/dx^2 = 0$ is termed **neutral stability**.

Terms You Should Understand

(Pairs are closely related terms whose distinction is important; number in parentheses is chapter section where term first appears.)

static equilibrium (14-1)
center of gravity (14-2)
stable, unstable (14-4)
metastable (14-4)
neutrally stable (14-4)

Symbols You Should Recognize

$$\frac{dU}{dx}, \frac{d^2U}{dx^2} \quad (14\text{-}4)$$

Problems You Should Be Able to Solve

setting up and solving static equilibrium problems for any appropriate unknowns, including forces, torques, angles, and distances to force application points (14-2 and 14-3)
determining equilibrium points and their stability from potential energy curves (14-4)

Limitations to Keep in Mind

A body's center of gravity coincides with its center of mass only when gravity doesn't change significantly over the extent of the body.
The conditions for equilibrium give at most six equations, which may not be enough to solve for all unknowns in situations involving many forces.

QUESTIONS

1. Give an example of an object on which the net force is zero but which is not in static equilibrium.

2. Give an example of an object on which the net torque about the center of gravity is zero, but which is not in static equilibrium.

3. The net torque about a body's center of gravity is zero, but the body is undergoing linear acceleration. Is the net torque about a point other than the center of gravity necessarily zero? Explain.

4. The best way to lift a heavy weight is to squat with your back vertical, rather than to lean over. Why?

5. Pregnant women often assume a posture in which the shoulders are held well back of their normal position. Explain in terms of torque and center of gravity.

6. A large, irregularly shaped asteroid of uniform density is falling toward Earth in the orientation shown in Fig. 14-23. Which is closer to Earth, the asteroid's center of gravity or its center of mass? Explain.

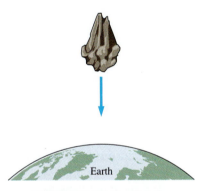

FIGURE 14-23 Question 6.

7. When you carry a bucket of water with one hand, you often find it easier if you extend your opposite arm. Why?

8. Is a ladder more likely to slip when you stand near the top or the bottom? Explain.

9. How does a heavy keel on a boat help keep the boat from tipping over?

10. In addition to the wings, most airplanes have a smaller set of horizontal surfaces near the tail. Why? What does this suggest about the center of gravity of the airplane?

11. Does choosing a pivot point in an equilibrium problem mean that something is necessarily going to rotate about that point?

12. If you take the pivot at the application point of a force in a static equilibrium problem, that force doesn't enter the torque equation. Does that make the force irrelevant to the problem? Explain.

13. You're hanging a heavy picture on a wall, using wire attached to the top corners of the picture. Is the wire more likely to break if you run it tightly between the corners or if you give it some slack? Explain.

14. A projectile is shot vertically upward. Is it in equilibrium at the top of its trajectory, when it's instantaneously at rest? Why or why not?

15. Suppose that the floor in Example 4-3 were frictionless but the wall were not. Would this change the minimum angle at which the board could lean? Explain.

16. In Fig. 14-24, why is the dancer's upper body leaning slightly to her left?

FIGURE 14-24 Why is the dancer leaning to her left? (Question 16)

17. A short dog and a tall person are standing on a slope. If the angle of the slope is increased, which will fall over first? Why?

18. A stiltwalker is standing motionless on one stilt. What can you say about the location of the stiltwalker's center of mass?

19. Why is a bottle less stable if stood on its top rather than on its bottom?

20. A metastable equilibrium represents a local minimum in the potential energy curve. What is meant here by the term *local*?

21. Given that hydrogen nuclei can fuse together with enormous energy release, is water really a fully stable configuration of matter?

PROBLEMS

ActivPhysics can help with these problems:
Activities 7.1–7.6.

Section 14-1 Conditions for Equilibrium

1. Five forces act on a rod, as shown in Fig. 14-25. Write the torque equations that must be satisfied for the rod to be in static equilibrium taking the torques (a) about the top of the rod and (b) about the center of the rod.

FIGURE 14-25 Problem 1.

2. A body is subject to three forces: $\mathbf{F}_1 = 2\hat{\imath} + 2\hat{\jmath}$ N, applied at the point $x = 2$ m, $y = 0$ m; $\mathbf{F}_2 = -2\hat{\imath} - 3\hat{\jmath}$ N, applied at $x = -1$ m, $y = 0$; and $\mathbf{F}_3 = 1\hat{\jmath}$ N, applied at $x = -7$ m, $y = 1$ m. (a) Show explicitly that the net force on the body is zero. (b) Show explicitly that the net torque about the origin is zero. (c) To confirm the assertion following Equation 14-4 that the net torque must be zero about any other point, evaluate the net torque about the point (3 m, 2 m), the point (−7 m, 1 m), and about any other point of your choosing.

3. Suppose the force $\mathbf{F}_3$ in the preceding problem is doubled so the forces no longer balance and the body is therefore accelerating. Show that (a) the torque about the point (−7 m, 1 m) is still zero, but that (b) the torque about the origin is no longer zero. What is the torque about the origin?

4. A rod of mass m and length ℓ is falling freely in a horizontal orientation, with no torque about its center of mass. Find the magnitude of the torque about either end. Why does your answer not violate the point made in Problem 8?

5. In Fig. 14-26 the forces shown all have the same magnitude F. For each of the cases shown, is it possible to place a third force so the three forces meet both conditions for static equilibrium? If so, specify the force and a suitable application point; if not, why not?

6. Are there any other application points for the force $\mathbf{F}_3$ in Problem 2 that will ensure that both static equilibrium conditions are met?

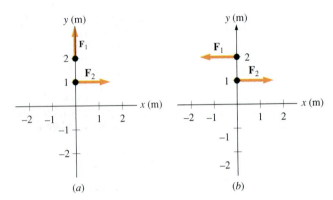

FIGURE 14-26 Problem 5.

7. Four forces act on a body, as shown in Fig. 14-27. Write the set of scalar equations that must hold for the body to be in equilibrium, evaluating the torques (a) about point O and (b) about point P.

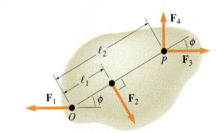

FIGURE 14-27 Problem 7.

8. In this problem you prove the statement in Section 14-1 that the choice of pivot point does not matter when applying the conditions for static equilibrium. Figure 14-28 shows an object on which the net force is assumed to be zero. Also, the net torque about the point O shown is zero. You're to show that the net torque about any other point P is also zero. To do so, write the net torque about P as $\boldsymbol{\tau}_P = \sum \mathbf{r}_{Pi} \times \mathbf{F}_i$, where the vectors $\mathbf{r}_P$ are from P to the force application points, and the index i labels the different

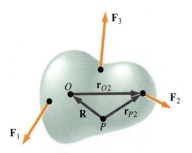

FIGURE 14-28 Problem 8.

forces. Note in Fig. 14-28 that $\mathbf{r}_{Pi} = \mathbf{r}_{Oi} + \mathbf{R}$, where $\mathbf{R}$ is a vector from P to O. Use this result in your expression for $\boldsymbol{\tau}_P$ and apply the distributive law to get two separate sums. Use the assumptions that $\mathbf{F}_{net} = 0$ and $\boldsymbol{\tau}_O = 0$ to argue that both terms are zero. This completes the proof.

Section 14-2 Center of Gravity

9. Figure 14-29a shows a thin, uniform square plate of mass m and side ℓ. The plate is in a vertical plane. Find the magnitude of the gravitational torque on the plate about each of the three points shown.

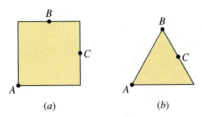

(a)   (b)

FIGURE 14-29 Problems 9, 10.

10. Figure 14-29b shows a thin, uniform plate of mass m in the shape of an equilateral triangle of side ℓ. The plate is in a vertical plane. Find the magnitude of the gravitational torque on the plate about each of the three points shown.

11. Three identical books of length L are stacked over the edge of a table as shown in Fig. 14-30. The top book overhangs the middle one by $\frac{1}{2}L$, so it just barely avoids falling. The middle book overhangs the bottom one by $\frac{1}{4}L$. How much of the bottom book can be allowed to overhang the edge of the table without the books falling?

FIGURE 14-30 How far can the bottom book overhang the edge? Problem 11.

12. A 60-kg uniform board 2.4 m long is supported by a pivot 80 cm from the left end, and by a scale at the right end (Fig. 14-31). How far from the left end should a 40-kg child sit if the scale is to read zero?

FIGURE 14-31 Problems 12, 13.

Section 14-3 Examples of Static Equilibrium

13. Where should the child in Fig. 14-31 sit if the scale is to read (a) 100 N and (b) 300 N?

14. A 4.2-m-long beam is supported by a cable at its center. A 65-kg steelworker stands at one end of the beam. Where should a 190-kg bucket of concrete be suspended if the beam is to be in static equilibrium?

15. Two pulleys are mounted on a horizontal axle, as shown in Fig. 14-32. The inner pulley has a diameter of 6.0 cm, the outer a diameter of 20 cm. Cords are wrapped around both pulleys so they don't slip. In the configuration shown, with what force must you pull on the outer rope in order to support the 40-kg mass?

FIGURE 14-32 Problem 15.

16. A 23-m-long log of irregular cross section is lying horizontally, supported by a wall at one end and a cable attached 4.0 m from the other end, as shown in Fig. 14-33. The log weighs 7.5×10^3 N, and the tension in the cable is 6.2×10^3 N. Where is the log's center of gravity?

FIGURE 14-33 Problem 16.

17. Figure 14-34 shows a traffic signal, with masses and positions of its various members indicated. The structure is mounted with two bolts, located symmetrically about the vertical member's centerline, as indicated. What tension force must the left-hand bolt be capable of withstanding?

FIGURE 14-34 Problem 17.

18. Figure 14-35 shows how a scale with a capacity of only 250 N can be used to weigh a heavier person. The board is 3.0 m long, has a mass of 3.4 kg, and is of uniform density. It is free to pivot about the end farthest from the scale. What is the weight of a person standing 1.2 m from the pivot end, if the scale reads 210 N? Assume that the beam remains nearly horizontal.

FIGURE 14-35 Problem 18.

19. Figure 14-36*a* shows an outstretched arm with a mass of 4.2 kg. The arm is 56 cm long, and its center of gravity is 21 cm from the shoulder. The hand at the end of the arm holds a 6.0-kg mass. (a) What is the torque about the shoulder due to the weights of the arm and the 6.0-kg mass? (b) If the arm is held in equilibrium by the deltoid

(*a*)

(*b*)

FIGURE 14-36 Problem 19.

muscle, whose force on the arm acts 5.0° below the horizontal at a point 18 cm from the shoulder joint (Fig. 14-36*b*), what is the force exerted by the muscle?

20. Figure 14-37 shows a portable infant seat that is supported by the edge of a table. The mass of the seat is 1.5 kg, and its center of mass is located 16 cm from the table edge. A 12-kg baby is sitting in the seat with her center of mass over the seat's center of mass. Find the forces F_A and F_B that the seat exerts on the table.

FIGURE 14-37 Problem 20.

21. A 15.0-kg door measures 2.00 m high by 75.0 cm wide. It hangs from hinges mounted 18.0 cm from top and bottom. Assuming that each hinge carries half the door's weight,

determine the horizontal and vertical forces that the door exerts on each hinge.

22. Figure 14-38 shows a popular system for mounting book-shelves. An aluminum bracket is mounted on a vertical aluminum support by small tabs inserted into vertical slots. If each bracket in a shelf system supports 32 kg of books, with the center of gravity 12 cm out from the vertical support, what is the horizontal component of the force exerted on the upper of the two bracket tabs? Assume contact between the bracket and support occurs only at the upper tab and at the bottom of the bracket, 4.5 cm below the upper tab.

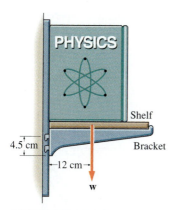

FIGURE 14-38 Problem 22.

23. Figure 14-39 shows a house designed to have high "cathedral" ceilings. Following a heavy snow, the total mass supported by each diagonal roof rafter is 170 kg, including building materials as well as snow. Under these conditions, what is the force in the horizontal tie beam near the roof peak? Is this force a compression or a tension? Neglect any horizontal component of force due to the vertical walls below the roof. Ignore the widths of the various structural components, treating contact forces as though

FIGURE 14-39 Problem 23.

they were concentrated at the roof peak and at the outside edge of the rafter/wall junction.

24. Repeat Example 14-4, now assuming that the coefficient of friction at the floor is μ_1 and that at the wall μ_2. Show that the minimum angle at which the board will not slip is now given by

$$\phi = \tan^{-1}\left(\frac{1 - \mu_1\mu_2}{2\mu_1}\right).$$

25. A uniform sphere of radius R is supported by a rope attached to a vertical wall, as shown in Fig. 14-40. The point where the rope is attached to the sphere is located so a continuation of the rope would intersect a horizontal line through the sphere's center a distance $R/2$ beyond the center, as shown. What is the smallest possible value for the coefficient of friction between wall and sphere?

FIGURE 14-40 Problems 25, 26.

26. Show that if the wall in the previous problem is frictionless, then a continuation of the rope line must pass through the center of the sphere.

27. A garden cart loaded with firewood is being pushed horizontally when it encounters a step 8.0 cm high, as shown in Fig. 14-41. The mass of the cart and its load is 55 kg, and the cart is balanced so that its center of mass is directly over the axle. The wheel diameter is 60 cm. What is the minimum horizontal force that will get the cart up the step?

FIGURE 14-41 Problem 27.

28. Figure 14-42 shows the foot and lower leg of a person standing on the ball of one foot. Three forces act on the foot to maintain this equilibrium: the tension force **T** in the Achilles tendon, contact force **F_c** at the ankle joint, and the normal force **N** of the ground that supports the person's weight. The person's mass is 70 kg, and the force application points are as indicated in Fig. 14-42. Find the magnitude of (a) the tension in the Achilles tendon and (b) the contact force at the ankle joint.

FIGURE 14-42 What are the forces on the foot? Note that the direction of **F_c** is not specified (Problem 28).

29. The leaning Tower of Pisa (Fig. 14-43) currently leans at a 4.7° angle to the vertical. Treating the tower as a solid cylinder, what is the maximum angle at which it can lean before falling over? Treat the tower as a uniform cylinder 7.0 m in diameter and 55 m high, and assume the ground supports the tower's weight but does not provide any torque.

FIGURE 14-43 How much farther can the Tower of Pisa lean?

30. A uniform 5.0-kg ladder is leaning against a frictionless vertical wall, with which it makes a 15° angle. The coefficient of friction between ladder and ground is 0.26. Can a 65-kg person climb to the top of the ladder without it slipping? If not, how high can the person climb? If so, how massive a person would make the ladder slip?

31. The boom in the crane of Fig. 14-44 is free to pivot about point P and is supported by the cable that joins halfway along its 18-m total length. The cable passes over a pulley and is anchored at the back of the crane. The boom has mass 1700 kg, distributed uniformly along its length, and the mass hanging from the end of the boom is 2200 kg. The boom makes a 50° angle with the horizontal. What is the tension in the cable that supports the boom?

FIGURE 14-44 Problem 31.

32. A uniform board of length ℓ and weight W is suspended between two vertical walls by ropes of length $\ell/2$ each. When a weight w is placed on the left end of the board, it assumes the configuration shown in Fig. 14-45. Find the weight w in terms of the board weight W.

FIGURE 14-45 Problem 32.

33. Figure 14-46 shows a 1250-kg car that has slipped over the edge of an embankment. A group of people are trying to hold the car in place by pulling on a horizontal rope, as shown. The car's bottom is pivoted on the edge of the embankment, and its center of mass lies further back, as shown. If the car makes a 34° angle with the horizontal, what force must the group apply to hold it in place?

FIGURE 14-46 Problem 33.

34. A uniform board of length ℓ is dangling over a *frictionless* edge, secured by a *horizontal* rope, as shown in Fig. 14-47. Show that the angle it makes with the horizontal must be
$\theta = \sin^{-1} \sqrt{\dfrac{2d}{\ell}}$, where d is the distance from the edge to the center of the board.

FIGURE 14-47 Problems 34, 35.

35. Figure 14-47 shows a uniform board dangling over a *frictionless* edge, secured by a *horizontal* rope. If the angle θ in Fig. 14-47 were 30°, what fraction would the distance d shown in the figure be of the board length ℓ?

Section 14-4 Stability of Equilibria

36. A portion of a roller coaster track is described by $h = 0.94x - 0.010x^2$, where h and x are the height and horizontal position in meters. (a) Find a point where the roller coaster car could be in static equilibrium on this track. (b) Is the equilibrium stable or unstable? (c) What is the height of the track at the equilibrium point?

37. A roly-poly toy clown is made from part of a sphere topped by a cone. The sphere is truncated at just the right point so that there is no discontinuity in angle as the surface changes from sphere to cone (Fig. 14-48a). If the clown always returns to an upright position, what is the maximum possible height for its center of mass? Would your answer change if the continuity-of-angle condition were not met, as in Fig. 14-48b?

(a)   (b)

FIGURE 14-48 Problem 37.

38. A uniform rectangular block is twice as long as it is wide. Letting θ be the angle that the long dimension makes with the horizontal, determine the angular positions of any static equilibria, and comment on their stability.

39. The potential energy as a function of position for a certain particle is given by
$$U(x) = U_0\left(\frac{x^3}{x_0^3} + a\frac{x^2}{x_0^2} + 4\frac{x}{x_0}\right),$$
where U_0, x_0, and a are constants. For what values of a will there be two static equilibria? Comment on the stability of these equilibria.

40. A cubical block rests on an inclined board with two sides parallel to the direction of the incline. The coefficient of static friction between block and board is 0.95. If the inclination angle of the board is increased, will the block first slide or first tip over?

Paired Problems

(Both problems in a pair involve the same principles and techniques. If you can get the first problem, you should be able to solve the second one.)

41. Figure 14-49 shows a 66-kg sign hung centered from a uniform rod of mass 8.2 kg and length 2.3 m. At one end the rod is attached to the wall by a pivot; at the other end it's supported by a cable that can withstand a maximum tension of 800 N. What is the minimum height h above the pivot for anchoring the cable to the wall?

42. A crane in a marble quarry is mounted on the rock walls of the quarry and is supporting a 2500-kg slab of marble

FIGURE 14-49 Problem 41 (the sign is centered beneath the rod).

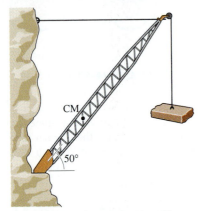

FIGURE 14-50 Problem 42.

as shown in Fig. 14-50. The center of mass of the 830-kg boom is located one-third of the way from the pivot end of its 15 m length, as shown. Find the tension in the horizontal cable that supports the boom.

43. A 4.2-kg plant hangs from the bracket shown in Fig. 14-51. The bracket has a mass of 0.85 kg, and its center of mass lies 9.0 cm from the wall. A single screw holds the bracket to the wall, as shown. Find the horizontal tension force in the screw. *Hint:* Imagine that the bracket is slightly loose and pivoting about its bottom end. Assume the wall is frictionless.

FIGURE 14-51 Problem 43.

44. A 160-kg highway sign of uniform density is 2.3 m wide and 1.4 m high. At one side it is secured to a pole with a single bolt, mounted a distance d from the top of the sign. The only other place where the sign contacts the pole is at its bottom corner. If the bolt can sustain a horizontal tension of 2100 N, what is the maximum permissible value for the distance d?

45. A 5.0-m-long ladder has mass 9.5 kg and is leaning against a frictionless wall, making a 66° angle with the horizontal. If the coefficient of friction between the ladder and ground is 0.42, what is the mass of the heaviest person who can safely ascend to the top of the ladder? (The center of mass of the ladder is at its center.)

46. To what vertical height on the ladder in the preceding problem could a 95-kg person reach before the ladder starts to slip?

47. A uniform, solid cube of mass m and side s is in stable equilibrium when sitting on a level tabletop. How much energy is required to bring it to an unstable equilibrium where it's resting on its corner?

48. An isosceles triangular block of mass m and height h is in stable equilibrium, resting on its base on a horizontal surface. How much energy does it take to bring it to unstable equilibrium, resting on its apex? *Hint:* Consult Example 10-3.

Supplementary Problems

49. A uniform pole of mass M is at rest on an incline of angle θ, secured by a horizontal rope as shown in Fig. 14-52. What is the minimum coefficient of friction that will keep the pole from slipping?

FIGURE 14-52 Problem 49.

50. For what angle does the situation of Problem 49 require the greatest coefficient of friction?

51. One end of a board of negligible mass is attached to a spring of spring constant k, while its other end rests on a frictionless surface, as shown in Fig. 14-53. If a mass m is placed on the middle of the board, by how much will the spring compress?

FIGURE 14-53 Problem 51.

52. A uniform ladder of mass m is leaning against a frictionless vertical wall with which it makes an angle θ. The coefficient of static friction at the floor is μ. Find an expression for the maximum mass for a person who is able to climb to the top of the ladder without its slipping. Use your result to show that *anyone* can climb to the top if $\mu \geq \tan\theta$, but that *no one* can if $\mu < \frac{1}{2}\tan\theta$.

53. Figure 14-54 shows a wheel on a slope with inclination angle $\theta = 20°$, where the coefficient of friction is adequate to prevent the wheel from slipping; however, it might still roll. The wheel is a uniform disk of mass 1.5 kg, and it is weighted at one point on the rim with an additional 0.95-kg mass m. Find the angle ϕ shown in the figure such that the wheel will be in static equilibrium.

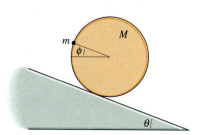

FIGURE 14-54 Problems 53, 54.

54. The wheel in Fig. 14-54 has mass M and is weighted with an additional mass m as shown. The slope angle is θ. Show that static equilibrium is possible only if $m > \dfrac{M\sin\theta}{1-\sin\theta}$.

55. A 2.0-m-long rod has a density described by $\lambda = a + bx$, where λ is the density in kilograms per meter of length, $a = 1.0$ kg/m, $b = 1.0$ kg/m², and x is the distance in meters from the left end of the rod. The rod rests horizontally with its ends each supported by a scale. What do the two scales read?

56. What horizontal force applied at its highest point is necessary to keep a wheel of mass M from rolling down a slope inclined at angle θ to the horizontal?

57. A rectangular block twice as high as it is wide is resting on a board. The coefficient of static friction between board and incline is 0.63. If the board is tilted as shown in Fig. 14-55, will the block first tip over or first begin sliding?

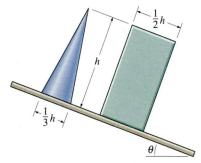

FIGURE 14-55 Problems 57 (block), 58 (block), 59 (cone).

58. What condition on the coefficient of friction in the preceding problem will cause the block to slide before it tips?

59. A uniform solid cone of height h and base diameter $\frac{1}{3}h$ is placed on the board of Fig. 14-55. The coefficient of static friction between the cone and incline is 0.63. As the slope of the board is increased, will the cone first tip over or begin sliding? *Hint:* Begin with an integration to find the center of mass.

60. In Fig. 14-56 a uniform boom of mass 350 kg is attached to a vertical wall by a pivot, and its far end is supported by a cable as shown. If the cable can withstand a maximum tension of 4.0 kN, what is the maximum value for the angle ϕ?

FIGURE 14-56 Problem 60.

61. An interstellar spacecraft from an advanced civilization is hovering above Earth, as shown in Fig. 14-57. The ship consists of two pods of mass m separated by a rigid shaft of negligible mass that is one Earth radius (R_E) long. Find (a) the magnitude and direction of the net gravitational force on the ship and (b) the net torque about the center of mass. (c) Show that the ship's center of gravity is displaced approximately $0.083R_E$ from its center of mass.

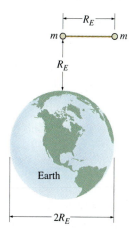

FIGURE 14-57 Problem 61.

PART 1 *Cumulative Problems*

These problems combine material from chapters throughout the entire part or, in addition, from chapters in earlier parts, or they present special challenges.

1. A 170-g apple sits atop a 2.8-m-high post. A 45-g arrow moving horizontally at 130 m/s passes horizontally through the apple and strikes the ground 36 m from the base of the post, as shown in Fig. 1. Where does the apple hit the ground? Neglect the effect of air resistance on either object as well as any friction between apple and post.

$v = 130$ m/s

2.8 m

FIGURE 1 Cumulative Problem 1.

2. A fire department's tanker truck has a total mass of 21×10^3 kg, including 15×10^3 kg of water. Its brakes fail at the top of a long 3° slope and it begins to roll downward, starting from rest. In an attempt to stop the truck, firefighters direct a stream of water parallel to the slope, as shown in Fig. 2, beginning as soon as the truck starts to roll. The water leaves the 6.0-cm-diameter hose nozzle at 50 m/s. Will the truck stop before it runs out of water? If so, when? If not, what is the minimum speed reached?

FIGURE 2 Cumulative Problem 2.

3. A block of mass m_1 is attached to the axle of a uniform solid cylinder of mass m_2 and radius R by massless strings. The two accelerate down a slope that makes an angle θ with the horizontal, as shown in Fig. 3. The cylinder rolls without slipping and the block slides with coefficient of kinetic friction μ between block and slope. The strings are attached to the cylinder's axle with frictionless loops so that the cylinder can roll freely without any torque from the string. Find an expression for the acceleration of the pair, assuming that the string remains taut.

FIGURE 3 Cumulative Problem 3.

4. A missile is launched from point A in Fig. 4, heading for target C. The launch angle is 45.0°, and the launch speed is 1.90 km/s. An antimissile defense system is located at point B, 310 km downrange from the launch site. It fires an interceptor rocket at a 65.0° launch angle, with the intention of hitting the attacking missile when the latter is 270 km downrange of its launch site. (a) What should be the interceptor's launch speed? (b) How long after the launch of the attacking missile should the interceptor be launched? (c) At what altitude does the interception take place?

270 km

310 km

A B C

FIGURE 4 Cumulative Problem 4.

5. A solid ball of radius R is set spinning with angular speed ω about a horizontal axis. The ball is then lowered vertically with negligible speed until it just touches a horizontal surface and is released (Fig. 5). If the coefficient of kinetic friction between the ball and the surface is μ, find (a) the linear speed of the ball once it achieves pure rolling motion and (b) the distance it travels before its motion is pure rolling.

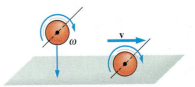

FIGURE 5 Cumulative Problem 5.

Part Two

Oscillations, Waves, and Fluids

High-speed photo taken just after a drop has struck calm water shows complex fluid behavior and circular waves propagating outward.

A giant wave crashes on the shore, dissipating energy that has traveled across thousands of kilometers of open ocean. Vibrations of an electric guitar string sound loudly through a rock concert arena. Inside your watch, a tiny quartz crystal vibrates 32,768 times each second to keep near perfect time. A radar-equipped police officer waits around the next turn in the highway ready to ticket your speeding car, while astrophysicists use the same principle to observe our expanding universe. A rafting party enters a narrow gorge, getting a wild ride as the river's speed rises dramatically. All these examples involve the collective motion of multi-particle systems. In the next four chapters, we explore first the simple, repetitive motion called oscillation, then show how oscillations of multi-particle systems lead to the phenomenon of wave motion. Finally, we show how the laws of motion govern the sometimes surprising and beautiful behavior of fluids like air and water.

15 Oscillatory Motion

A ball attached to a spring undergoes oscillatory motion. Photo was taken with a strobe light flashing to image the ball at different points in its oscillation cycle. At the same time the camera panned sideways, displacing successive images horizontally and thus producing a plot of the ball's vertical position as a function of time. The position is a sinusoidal function of time. Interval between strobe flashes is 90 ms.

When a system is disturbed from stable equilibrium, forces within the system tend to restore the equilibrium. But, like the ball in Fig. 15-1, the system may overshoot its equilibrium position. Again a restoring force develops and eventually the system turns back toward equilibrium. Again it may overshoot. The result is **oscillatory motion**—back and forth motion about equilibrium. In the absence of friction this oscillatory motion would continue forever; in reality the system eventually settles back into equilibrium.

A wide variety of physical systems exhibit oscillatory motion. A uranium nucleus oscillates before it fissions. Oscillatory motion of water molecules is what cooks the food in a microwave oven. The horrible squeaking noise of chalk on a blackboard results from oscillatory motion. The timekeeping mechanism of a watch—whether an old-fashioned spring and balance wheel or a modern quartz crystal—is a carefully engineered system in oscillatory motion. Even large-scale structures such as buildings and bridges undergo oscillatory motion, sometimes with disastrous results. And waves—from the sound waves that bring you music, a physics lecture, or a friend's voice; to ocean waves that can guide a surfboard or capsize a ship; and even to waves that propagate through the solid Earth to bring news of an earthquake to the farthest reaches of the planet—all these waves involve oscillatory motion in multiparticle systems.

Oscillatory motion is a universal phenomenon. That's because systems tend naturally toward a state of stable equilibrium, and, as Fig. 15-1 shows, oscillation results when a system is displaced from stable equilibrium. The restoring force on the ball in Fig. 15-1 is gravity, but it could be an electrical force between atoms in a molecule that's been stretched from its equilibrium, the force of a compressed spring in a car's suspension, the tension force in an oscillating violin string, the nuclear force in a distorted uranium nucleus, a pressure force driving oscillations of air in a sound wave, or the buoyant force of water on a bobbing boat.

It's not just the qualitative phenomenon of oscillation that's universal. Remarkably, the mathematical description of oscillatory motion is essentially the same for systems ranging from atoms and molecules through cars and bridges and on to stars and galaxies. We'll see in Section 15-5 how that common description results from a fundamental sameness of nearly all potential energy curves near equilibrium. First, though, we develop a general description of oscillatory motion and apply it in a range of practical situations.

15-1 PROPERTIES OF OSCILLATORY MOTION

Two quantities characterize oscillatory motion: **amplitude** is the maximum displacement from equilibrium, and **period** is the time it takes for the motion to repeat itself. Figure 15-2 shows both these quantities on plots of position versus time. Another way to express the time aspect of oscillatory motion is through **frequency**, or number of oscillation cycles per unit time. Frequency and period are complementary ways of conveying the same information, and mathematically they're just inverses:

$$f = \frac{1}{T},$$
(15-1)

where f is the frequency and T the period. The unit of frequency is the **hertz** (Hz), named after the German physicist, engineer, and mathematician Heinrich Hertz (1857–1894), who was the first to produce and detect radio waves. One hertz is equal to one oscillation cycle per second.

FIGURE 15-1 (*a*) A ball in stable equilibrium at the bottom of a valley. (*b*) Disturbed from equilibrium, the ball oscillates about its equilibrium position.

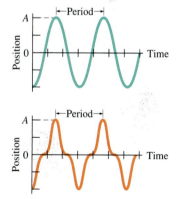

FIGURE 15-2 Position-versus-time graphs for two oscillatory motions. Both have the same amplitude (*A*) and frequency (and therefore period). Their differences reflect the different restoring forces acting on each system.

EXAMPLE 15-1	*An Oscillatory Distraction*

Tired of homework, a student holds one end of a flexible plastic ruler against a desk and idly strikes the other end, setting it into oscillation (Fig. 15-3). The student notes that 28 complete cycles occur in 10 s, and that the end of the ruler moves a total distance of 8.0 cm. What are the amplitude, period, and frequency of this oscillatory motion?

Solution
We've defined amplitude as the maximum displacement from equilibrium. Because the end of the ruler moves both sides of equilibrium, the amplitude of the motion is 4.0 cm. (The full 8.0-cm motion is called the **peak-to-peak** amplitude.) With 28 cycles in 10 s, the time per cycle, or period, is

$$T = \frac{10 \text{ s}}{28} = 0.36 \text{ s}.$$

The frequency in Hz is the inverse of the period:

$$f = \frac{1}{T} = \frac{1}{0.36 \text{ s}} = 2.8 \text{ Hz}.$$

FIGURE 15-3 Side view of a ruler undergoing oscillatory motion.

EXERCISE The top of a skyscraper sways back and forth, completing 9 oscillation cycles in one minute. Find the period and frequency of the motion.

Answers: $T = 6.7$ s; $f = 0.15$ Hz

Some problems similar to Example 15-1: 1–3

Amplitude and frequency don't provide all the details of oscillatory motion, since two quite different motions can have the same frequency and amplitude (Fig. 15-2). The differences reflect details of the restoring forces that tend to return systems to equilibrium.

Remarkably, though, restoring forces in many physical systems have the same mathematical form—a form we encountered before, when we introduced the force of an ideal spring in Chapter 5, Section 5-8. The rest of this chapter concentrates on this important case.

15-2 SIMPLE HARMONIC MOTION

In a wide variety of physical systems, the restoring force that develops when the system is displaced from equilibrium increases approximately in direct proportion to the displacement—meaning that if you displace the system twice as far from equilibrium, the force tending to restore equilibrium becomes twice as great. This approximation is especially good for small displacements. In the rest of this chapter, we therefore consider the case where the restoring force is directly proportional to displacement. We emphasize that this is an approximation for most real systems, but often a very good approximation, especially where displacements from equilibrium are small.

The type of motion that results from a restoring force proportional to displacement is called **simple harmonic motion**:

Simple harmonic motion is the motion that results when an object is subject to a restoring force proportional to its displacement from equilibrium.

Mathematically, we describe such a force by writing

$$F = -kx, \tag{15-2}$$

where F is the force, x the displacement, and k a constant giving the proportionality between them. The minus sign in Equation 15-2 indicates a *restoring* force: If the object is displaced in one direction, the force is in the *opposite* direction, so it tends to restore the equilibrium.

We've seen Equation 15-2 before: It's the force exerted by an ideal spring of spring constant k (see Chapter 5, Section 5-8). So a system consisting of a mass attached to a spring undergoes simple harmonic motion (Fig. 15-4). Many other systems—including atoms and molecules—can often be understood by modeling them as miniature mass-spring systems.

FIGURE 15-4 A mass attached to an ideal spring undergoes simple harmonic motion. The mass rides on a frictionless surface, and the spring exerts a force if it's either stretched or compressed from equilibrium.

We've defined simple harmonic motion, but we haven't described it. How does a body in simple harmonic motion actually move? We can find out by applying Newton's second law, $\mathbf{F} = m\mathbf{a}$, to the mass-spring system of Fig. 15-4. Here the force on the mass m is $-kx$, so Newton's law becomes

$$-kx = ma, \tag{15-3}$$

where we take the x axis along the direction of motion, with $x = 0$ at the equilibrium position. We want to know how the position x depends on time. Although time doesn't appear explicitly in Equation 15-3, it's implicit because the acceleration is the second time derivative of position. Thus Equation 15-3 may be written

$$m\frac{d^2x}{dt^2} = -kx. \tag{15-4}$$

The solution to this equation is the position x as a function of time. What sort of function might it be? Physical insight tells us to expect periodic motion, so we could try periodic functions—like sine and cosine. Suppose we pull the mass in Fig. 15-4 to the right and, at time $t = 0$, release it. Since it starts with a nonzero displacement, we might expect cosine to be the appropriate function (recall that $\cos(0) = 1$, while $\sin(0) = 0$). We still don't know the amplitude or frequency, so we'll try a form that has two unknown constants:

$$x(t) = A\cos\omega t. \tag{15-5}$$

Here we write $x(t)$ explicitly to remind you that position x is a function of time t.

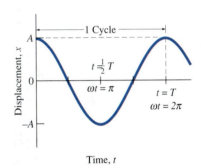

What's the physical significance of the constants in Equation 15-5? Because the cosine function itself varies between $+1$ and -1, the quantity A is just the amplitude—the greatest displacement from equilibrium (Fig. 15-5).

FIGURE 15-5 The function $A\cos\omega t$. This function varies between $\pm A$, and undergoes one full cycle as ωt increases by 2π.

What about the constant ω? The cosine function undergoes a full cycle as its argument increases by 2π radians, or $360°$, as shown in Fig. 15-5. In Equation 15-5, the argument of the cosine is ωt. Since the time for a full cycle is the period T, the argument ωt must go from 0 to 2π as the time t goes from 0 to T. So we have

$$\omega T = 2\pi,$$

or

$$T = \frac{2\pi}{\omega}. \tag{15-6}$$

The frequency of the motion is then

$$f = \frac{1}{T} = \frac{\omega}{2\pi}. \tag{15-7}$$

Equation 15-7 shows that ω is a measure of the frequency, although it differs from the frequency f by a factor of 2π. The quantity ω is called the **angular frequency**, and its units are radians per second or, since radians are dimensionless, simply inverse seconds (s^{-1}).

Tip

Why Radians? Here, as in Chapter 12's description of rotational motion, we use the angular quantity ω because it provides the simplest mathematical description of the motion. In fact, the relation between angular frequency and frequency in hertz is the same as Chapter 12's relation between angular speed in radians per second and in revolutions per second. Although there's no physical angle involved in our one-dimensional simple harmonic motion, the similarity between the descriptions of simple harmonic motion and of rotational motion is no coincidence. We'll explore that similarity further in Section 15-4.

Writing the displacement x in the form 15-5 doesn't guarantee that we have a solution; we must see if the assumed solution 15-5 satisfies Equation 15-4. If $x(t)$ is given by Equation 15-5, then its first derivative is

$$\frac{dx}{dt} = \frac{d}{dt}(A\cos\omega t) = -A\omega\sin\omega t,$$

where we've used the chain rule for differentiation (see Appendix A). Then the second time derivative is

$$\frac{d^2x}{dt^2} = \frac{d}{dt}\left(\frac{dx}{dt}\right) = \frac{d}{dt}(-A\omega\sin\omega t) = -A\omega^2\cos\omega t.$$

We can now try out the assumed solution for x (Equation 15-5), and its second time-derivative in Equation 15-4: Substituting $x(t)$ and d^2x/dt^2 in the appropriate places gives

$$m(-A\omega^2\cos\omega t) \stackrel{?}{=} -k(A\cos\omega t),$$

where the ? indicates that we're still trying to find out if this is indeed an equality. If it is, the equality must hold *for all values of time t.* Why? Because Newton's law holds at all times, and we derived our questionable equality from Newton's law. Fortunately, the time-dependent term $\cos\omega t$ appears on both sides of the equation, so we can cancel it. Also the amplitude A and the minus sign cancel from the equation, leaving only $m\omega^2 = k$, or

$$\omega = \sqrt{\frac{k}{m}}. \qquad \text{(Angular frequency, simple harmonic motion)} \qquad (15\text{-}8a)$$

Thus, Equation 15-5 *is* a solution of Equation 15-4, *provided* the angular frequency ω is given by Equation 15-8a.

Frequency and Period in Simple Harmonic Motion

We can recast Equation 15-8a in terms of the more familiar frequency f and period T using Equation 15-7, $f = \omega/2\pi$. This gives

$$f = \frac{\omega}{2\pi} = \frac{1}{2\pi}\sqrt{\frac{k}{m}}, \qquad (15\text{-}8b)$$

for the frequency in hertz, and

$$T = \frac{1}{f} = 2\pi\sqrt{\frac{m}{k}} \qquad (15\text{-}8c)$$

for the period.

FIGURE 15-6 A simple model for the hydrogen chloride (HCl) molecule pictures the hydrogen and chlorine atoms joined by a spring representing electric forces that tend to restore the atoms to their equilibrium separation if the molecule is stretched or compressed. The result is simple harmonic motion, as shown. Because the chlorine atom is much more massive than hydrogen, it can be treated as approximately fixed. The exercise following Example 15-2 deals quantitatively with this molecular system.

Do these relations make sense? If we increase the mass m, it becomes harder to accelerate and we expect slower oscillations. This is indeed reflected in Equations 15-8a and 15-8b, where m appears in the denominator. Increasing k, on the other hand, makes the spring stiffer and therefore results in greater force for a given displacement. That, in turn, increases the oscillation frequency—as shown by the presence of k in the numerators of Equations 15-8a and 15-8b. We've labeled the last three equations all as versions of 15-8a, to emphasize that the quantities ω, f, and T all convey essentially the same information about the motion—namely, how often or how rapidly it repeats.

Physical systems display a wide range of m and k values and a correspondingly large range of oscillation frequencies. A molecule, with its small mass and "springiness" provided by electric forces (Fig. 15-6), may oscillate at 10^{14} Hz or more. A massive skyscraper, in contrast, typically oscillates at about 0.1 Hz.

Amplitude in Simple Harmonic Motion

The amplitude A canceled from our equations, showing that our analysis works for *any* value of A. This means that the oscillation frequency does not depend on the oscillation amplitude. Independence of frequency and amplitude is a particularly simple feature of simple harmonic motion, and arises because the restoring force is *directly proportional* to displacement. When the restoring force does not have the simple form $F = -kx$, then frequency *does* depend on amplitude and the analysis of oscillatory motion becomes much more complicated (see Problem 72). In many systems the relation $F = -kx$ breaks down if the displacement x gets too big; for this reason, simple harmonic motion is often an approximation valid for relatively small oscillation amplitudes.

Phase

Equation 15-5 is not the only possible solution to Equation 15-4; you can readily show, for example, that $x = A \sin \omega t$ works just as well. We chose the cosine because we took time $t = 0$ at the point of maximum displacement. Had we set $t = 0$ as the mass passed through its equilibrium point, sine would have been the appropriate function. More generally we could take the zero of time at some arbitrary point in the oscillation cycle. Then, as Fig. 15-7 shows, we can represent the motion by the form

$$x(t) = A\cos(\omega t + \phi), \quad \text{(simple harmonic motion)} \qquad (15\text{-}9)$$

where the **phase constant** ϕ has the effect of shifting the cosine curve to the left or right but does not affect the frequency or amplitude.

9.1
Position Graphs and Equations

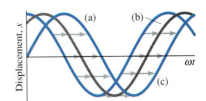

FIGURE 15-7 The phase constant ϕ determines the displacement x at time $t = 0$. (a) $\phi = 0$ corresponds to oscillation with maximum displacement at $t = 0$, while (b) $\phi = -\pi/4$ shifts the curve one-eighth cycle to the right. (c) $\phi = -\pi/2$ shifts the curve by one-fourth cycle and corresponds to motion that passes through equilibrium at $t = 0$—i.e., $x(t)$ becomes a sine curve.

Math Toolbox

Phase, Phase Constant, Phase Difference The trig functions sine and cosine go through a full cycle as their arguments go through 2π radians or 180°. It's therefore convenient to specify points in the cycle by giving the **phase**, which is another name for the argument of the function; at a phase of $\frac{\pi}{2}$ radians or 90°, for example, the sine function is at its peak and the cosine is zero. When we're dealing with sinusoidal functions of time, it's also important to know just where we are in the cycle at time $t = 0$. As Equation 15-9 shows, that quantity is the **phase constant**, ϕ, whose interpretation is shown in Fig. 15-7. We can compare two different sinusoidal functions by giving their **phase difference**. For example, the functions $\sin \omega t$ and $\sin(\omega t + \frac{\pi}{4})$ differ in phase by $\frac{\pi}{4}$ or 45°. Or, because $\sin \omega t = \cos(\omega t + \frac{\pi}{2})$, the sine and cosine functions differ in phase by $\frac{\pi}{2}$ or 90°. Phase differences are useful in describing related quantities that share a common periodic time dependence but that peak at different times. Such quantities include displacement, velocity, and acceleration in simple harmonic motion, as the next section shows.

9.2

Describing Vibrational Motion

Velocity and Acceleration in Simple Harmonic Motion

Equation 15-5 (or, more generally, Equation 15-9) gives the position of an object in simple harmonic motion as a function of time, so its first derivative must be the object's velocity. We took that derivative when we showed that Equation 15-5 really is a solution to Newton's law for a mass-spring system; here we do so again and identify the result as the time-dependent velocity $v(t)$:

$$v(t) = \frac{dx}{dt} = \frac{d}{dt}(A\cos \omega t) = -A\omega \sin \omega t. \tag{15-10}$$

Because the maximum value of the sine function is one, this expression shows that the maximum velocity has magnitude $A\omega$. This makes sense because a higher frequency oscillation requires that the object traverse the distance A (the amplitude of its motion) in a shorter time—so it must move faster. Equation 15-10 shows that the velocity $v(t)$ is a sine function when the displacement $x(t)$ is a cosine. Thus velocity is a maximum when displacement is zero, and vice versa; mathematically, we express this by saying that displacement and velocity differ in phase by $\frac{\pi}{2}$ radians or 90°. Does this make sense? Sure, because at the extremes of its motion, the oscillating object is instantaneously at rest as it reverses direction: maximum x, zero v. And when it passes through its equilibrium position $(x = 0)$, that's when the object is going fastest. Figure 15-8(a) and (b) show graphically the relation between displacement and velocity in simple harmonic motion.

Just as velocity is the derivative of position, so acceleration is the derivative of velocity, or the second derivative of position:

$$a(t) = \frac{dv}{dt} = \frac{d}{dt}(-A\omega \sin \omega t) = -A\omega^2 \cos \omega t. \tag{15-11}$$

Since the maximum value of cosine is one, the maximum acceleration has magnitude $A\omega^2$. Since acceleration is a cosine function if velocity is a sine, each reaches its maximum value when the other is zero (see Fig. 15-8b, c);

(a)

(b)

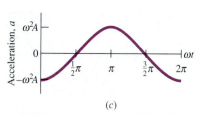

(c)

FIGURE 15-8 Displacement, velocity, and acceleration in simple harmonic motion. Note that the speed is greatest when the displacement is zero, and vice versa. Mathematically, displacement and velocity are $\frac{\pi}{2}$ out of phase, as are velocity and acceleration.

mathematically, they differ in phase by $\frac{\pi}{2}$ radians or 90°. But because acceleration and displacement are both cosine functions, they reach their extremes at the same time, but with opposite signs (they're π radians or 180° out of phase). This reflects the restoring force and Newton's law. Because $F = ma$, the acceleration is maximum when the force is maximum—and, because $F = -kx$, that occurs at the extremes of the displacement x from equilibrium. Displacement and acceleration have opposite signs because F is a *restoring* force: when x has its maximum positive value, F and a are negative as the object is being pulled back toward equilibrium; when x has its maximum negative value, F and a are positive as the object is once again being pulled back toward equilibrium. Figure 15-8 shows graphically the relation between displacement, velocity, and acceleration over one cycle of simple harmonic motion.

9.6, 9.7
Releasing a Vibrating Skier

9.9
Vibro-Ride

Got It!

Two identical mass-spring systems are displaced different amounts from equilibrium, then released at different times. Of the amplitudes, frequencies, periods, and phase constants of the resulting motions, which are the same for both systems and which are different?

EXAMPLE 15-2	*A Swaying Skyscraper*

The huge mass-spring system shown in Fig. 15-9 is on the top floor of New York's 300-m high Citicorp Tower. It is engineered to oscillate at the same frequency as the building itself, helping to reduce the overall oscillation amplitude of the building. The 3.73×10^5-kg concrete block completes one oscillation in 6.80 s, and the oscillation amplitude in a high wind is 110 cm. Determine the spring constant and the maximum speed and acceleration experienced by the concrete block.

Solution

Since we know the mass and period, we can solve Equation 15-8c for the spring constant k:

$$k = \frac{4\pi^2 m}{T^2} = \frac{(4\pi^2)(3.73 \times 10^5 \text{ kg})}{(6.80 \text{ s})^2} = 3.18 \times 10^5 \text{ N/m}.$$

Equations 15-10 and 15-11 show that the maximum speed and acceleration are $v_{max} = \omega A$ and $a_{max} = \omega^2 A$. In terms of the period, the angular frequency may be obtained from Equation 15-6:

$$\omega = \frac{2\pi}{T} = \frac{2\pi}{6.80 \text{ s}} = 0.924 \text{ s}^{-1},$$

FIGURE 15-9 (*a*) New York's 59-floor Citicorp Tower. (*b*) To reduce the building's tendency to oscillate, engineers designed this huge mass-spring system, mounted on the top floor. The 410-ton mass and springs have the same oscillation frequency as the building. The mass rides on a film of oil and oscillates 180° out of phase with the building, reducing the amplitude of the building's oscillation.

(*a*)   (*b*)

so

$$v_{max} = A\omega = (1.10 \text{ m})(0.924 \text{ s}^{-1}) = 1.02 \text{ m/s}$$

and

$$a_{max} = A\omega^2 = (1.10 \text{ m})(0.924 \text{ s}^{-1})^2 = 0.939 \text{ m/s}^2 .$$

The Citicorp tuned mass damper was the first such system installed on a large building. Today, similar systems are used on a variety of structures, from skyscrapers to airport control towers to ski-lift gondolas. Since they actively damp out structural vibrations, tuned mass dampers permit architects and engineers to design structures that do not need as much intrinsic stiffness; thus, they can be lighter and less expensive.

EXERCISE A hydrogen chloride molecule (HCl) can be modeled as a hydrogen atom attached by a spring to a chlorine atom; the chlorine atom is so massive that it remains essentially fixed as the hydrogen oscillates at a frequency of 8.66×10^{13} Hz. (a) Find the effective spring constant. (b) If the maximum speed of the hydrogen atom is 2.50×10^5 m/s, what is its maximum displacement from equilibrium?

Answers: (a) 494 N/m; (b) 0.459 nm

Some problems similar to Example 15-2: 6–9

15-3 APPLICATIONS OF SIMPLE HARMONIC MOTION

Simple harmonic motion occurs in any system where restoring force is directly proportional to the displacement from equilibrium. Analysis of such systems follows that of the mass-spring system we just considered, but often involves different physical quantities. Here we explore several systems that exhibit simple harmonic motion.

The Vertical Mass-Spring System

A mass hanging vertically from a spring is subject to gravity as well as the spring force (Fig. 15-10). In equilibrium the spring must be stretched enough for its force to balance gravity:

$$mg - kx_1 = 0,$$

where x_1 is the new equilibrium position and where we take the x axis vertically downward. Suppose we stretch the spring an additional amount Δx from its new equilibrium. Then the spring force is $F_{spring} = -k(x_1 + \Delta x)$ and the net force, including gravity, is

$$F = mg - k(x_1 + \Delta x) = mg - kx_1 - k\Delta x = -k\Delta x,$$

FIGURE 15-10 A vertical mass-spring system. (*a*) Equilibrium length of the spring without a mass attached. (*b*) Attaching a mass stretches the spring an amount x_1 to a new equilibrium length. The mass can then undergo simple harmonic motion about this new equilibrium.

where the last step follows because the equilibrium position x_1 satisfies the condition $mg - kx_1 = 0$. Thus the system is subject to a restoring force $-k\Delta x$ that is directly proportional to the displacement Δx from the new equilibrium. We can apply the analysis of Section 15-2, now with Δx playing the role of x, and the result is again simple harmonic motion with the same frequency $\omega = \sqrt{k/m}$. Thus gravity changes only the equilibrium position and doesn't affect the frequency at all.

9.4

Two Ways to Measure Young Tarzan's Mass

9.5

Ape Drops Tarzan

The Torsional Oscillator

In many cases a system displaced from equilibrium tends to undergo rotary oscillations, swinging back and forth through a range of angular positions. Such a system is called a **torsional oscillator**. Examples include pendulums of all sorts; any object suspended from a rope, cable, or other fiber and given an angular displacement that twists the supporting structure (Fig. 15-11); and the balance wheels that establish the timekeeping in old-fashioned mechanical watches (Fig. 15-12).

Because they involve angular displacements, torsional oscillators are best described in the language we introduced in Chapter 12 for rotational motion. Thus we'll speak of angular position θ rather than position x, rotational inertia I rather than mass m, and torque τ rather than force F. In particular, we'll be interested in the **restoring torque** that tends to drive such systems back toward equilibrium. When that torque is directly proportional to the angular displacement, we once again have simple harmonic motion—only now it's the angular position θ rather than position x that varies sinusoidally with time.

A simple example of a torsional oscillator is an object of rotational inertia I suspended from a fiber that develops a torque when twisted (Fig. 15-11). When the restoring torque is directly proportional to the angular displacement, we can write

$$\tau = -\kappa\theta, \tag{15-12}$$

where τ is the torque and θ the angular displacement. The constant κ is the **torsional constant**, and is the rotational analog of the spring constant.

The behavior of the torsional oscillator is described by the rotational analog of Newton's law (Equation 12-14):

$$\tau = I\alpha,$$

where α is the angular acceleration. Using Equation 15-12 for τ and writing α as the second time derivative of angular displacement, the analog of Newton's law becomes

$$I\frac{d^2\theta}{dt^2} = -\kappa\theta. \tag{15-13}$$

This equation is identical to Equation 15-4 for the linear oscillator, except that I replaces m, θ replaces x, and κ replaces k. In direct analogy with the solution of Equation 15-4, we can then write

$$\theta(t) = A\cos\omega t,$$

where A of Equation 15-4 is the amplitude (now in radians or degrees rather than units of length) and where ω is given by analogy with Equation 15-11:

$$\omega = \sqrt{\frac{\kappa}{I}}. \tag{15-14}$$

Expressions for the period and frequency in Hz follow directly from Equations 15-6 and 15-7. Note that ω in Equation 15-14 is the angular frequency of the oscillations (i.e., $2\pi f$, where f is the number of oscillation cycles per unit time), and *not* the angular velocity $d\theta/dt$; the latter could be obtained by differentiating the expression for angular position.

In addition to its timekeeping functions, the torsional oscillator provides an accurate way to measure rotational inertia, as the example below illustrates.

FIGURE 15-11 A torsional oscillator consisting of a disk suspended from a wire.

FIGURE 15-12 The balance wheel in a mechanical watch is a torsional oscillator whose period determines the timekeeping accuracy of the watch. A coil-shaped spring (not obvious in this photo) provides the restoring torque.

EXAMPLE 15-3	*Swinging*

A child mounts a swing consisting of a tire suspended from a rope of torsional constant 6.1 N·m/rad, and sets herself into torsional oscillations, rotating back and forth about the rope axis. (a) If 35 complete oscillation cycles occur in 2 minutes, what is the rotational inertia of child and swing about the rope? (b) If the maximum angular speed is 25°/s, what is the maximum angular displacement of the swing from equilibrium?

Solution

(a) Solving Equation 15-14 for I gives

$$I = \frac{\kappa}{\omega^2} = \frac{\kappa}{(2\pi f)^2} = \frac{6.1 \text{ N·m/rad}}{[(2\pi)(35 \text{ cycles/120 s})]^2} = 1.8 \text{ kg·m}^2 .$$

Torsional oscillators are often used to measure the rotational inertias of irregular objects, as in this example.

(b) The properties of a torsional oscillator are exactly analogous to those we developed for the linear oscillator in Section 15-2. There we found, arguing from Equation 15-10, that the maximum velocity is $A\omega$. So for the torsional oscillator the maximum *angular* velocity is $A\omega$, with the amplitude A now meaning the maximum *angular* displacement. (We could also get this result by differentiating the angular displacement $\theta(t) = A\cos\omega t$.) Here we're given that the maximum angular velocity is 25°/s, so we can solve to get

$$A = \frac{(d\theta/dt)_{max}}{\omega} = \frac{(d\theta/dt)_{max}}{2\pi f} = \frac{25°/s}{(2\pi)(35 \text{ cycles/120 s})} = 14°.$$

So the child swings 14° either side of equilibrium, twisting back and forth through a full angle twice this size.

EXERCISE The balance wheel in a watch has rotational inertia 1.24×10^{-7} kg·m². What should be the torsional constant of the hairspring if the period of the wheel's torsional oscillations is to be 1.00 s?

Answer: 4.9×10^{-6} N·m/rad

Some problems similar to Example 15-3: 19, 25, 59, 60

The Pendulum

A **simple pendulum** consists of a point mass suspended from a rope, string, or rod. Real systems approximate this idealization when the suspended object's size is negligible compared with the rope's length, while at the same time the rope's mass is negligible compared with the object's. Examples include a rock climber dangling from a long rope, or the pendulum in a grandfather clock.

Figure 15-13 shows a pendulum of mass m and length ℓ displaced slightly from equilibrium. The tension force **T** exerts no torque about the suspension

FIGURE 15-13 (*a*) Forces acting on a simple pendulum. The gravitational force produces a torque of magnitude $mg\ell\sin\theta$ about the suspension point. (*b*) The torque tends to rotate the displaced pendulum back toward its equilibrium, resulting in oscillatory motion. Here a multicolored strobe light was used to image a pendulum over one-half cycle of its motion. Distance between successive images shows that the speed is greatest as the pendulum swings through its equilibrium position.

(*a*)

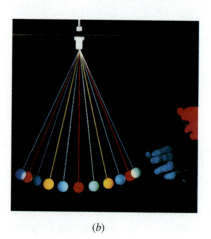

(*b*)

point because it lies on the line between the mass and suspension point. But the gravitational force $m\mathbf{g}$ does exert a torque, given by

$$\tau = -mg\ell \sin\theta,$$

where the minus sign indicates that the torque tends to rotate the pendulum back toward its equilibrium. The rotational analog of Newton's law, $\tau = I\alpha$, then becomes

$$I\frac{d^2\theta}{dt^2} = -mg\ell \sin\theta, \qquad (15\text{-}15)$$

where we've written the angular acceleration as the second derivative of the angular displacement.

Equation 15-15 looks somewhat like Equation 15-13 for the torsional oscillator—but not quite, since the torque involves $\sin\theta$ rather than θ itself. Thus the restoring torque is not *directly* proportional to the angular displacement, and the motion is therefore *not* simple harmonic. Problem 72 explores this more complex situation.

If, however, the amplitude of the motion is small, then it *approximates* simple harmonic motion. Figure 15-14 shows that for small angles—much less than 1 radian—$\sin\theta$ and θ are essentially equal. For a small-amplitude pendulum we can therefore replace $\sin\theta$ in Equation 15-15 with θ to get

$$I\frac{d^2\theta}{dt^2} = -mg\ell\theta.$$

This is essentially Equation 15-13, with $mg\ell$ playing the role of κ. So the small-amplitude pendulum undergoes simple harmonic motion, its angular frequency given by Equation 15-14 with $\kappa = mg\ell$:

$$\omega = \sqrt{\frac{mg\ell}{I}}. \qquad (15\text{-}16)$$

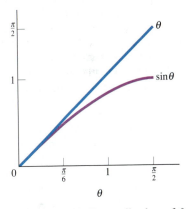

FIGURE 15-14 For small values of θ measured in radians, $\sin\theta$ and θ are nearly equal. Even at 30° ($\pi/6$, or 0.52 rad) the value of $\sin\theta$ (= 0.50) is within 4% of θ itself.

For a *simple* pendulum, the rotational inertia I is that of a point mass m a distance ℓ from the rotational axis, or $I = m\ell^2$ as we found in Chapter 12, Section 12-3. Then we have

$$\omega = \sqrt{\frac{mg\ell}{m\ell^2}} = \sqrt{\frac{g}{\ell}}, \quad \text{(simple pendulum)} \qquad (15\text{-}17)$$

or, from Equation 15-6,

$$T = \frac{2\pi}{\omega} = 2\pi\sqrt{\frac{\ell}{g}}. \quad \text{(simple pendulum)} \qquad (15\text{-}18)$$

9.10
Pendulum Frequency

9.11
Pendulum Timer

These equations show that the frequency and period of a simple pendulum are independent of its mass, depending only on length and gravitational acceleration.

EXAMPLE 15-4	*Rescuing Tarzan*

Tarzan stands on a branch, petrified with fear as a leopard approaches. Fortunately, Jane is on a branch of the same height in a nearby tree, holding a 25-m-long vine of negligible mass attached directly above the point midway between her and Tarzan (Fig. 15-15). Jane grasps the vine and steps off her branch with negligible initial velocity. (a) How soon does she reach Tarzan? (b) Find an expression for the maximum tension in the vine in terms of Jane's weight mg and the maximum angle the vine makes with the vertical.

Solution

(a) Jane and the vine constitute a pendulum that takes half a period to reach Tarzan. The period is given by Equation 15-18:

$$T = 2\pi\sqrt{\frac{\ell}{g}} = 2\pi\sqrt{\frac{25 \text{ m}}{9.8 \text{ m/s}^2}} = 10 \text{ s},$$

so Jane reaches Tarzan in 5.0 s. Since the period of a simple pendulum is independent of its mass, the return trip with Tarzan takes the same time.

(b) Here's a good example of a multistep problem that draws on material from different chapters. We're asked for the tension force, so this is basically a Newton's law problem. When will the tension be greatest? When Jane's moving fastest, so she has the greatest radial acceleration v^2/r—and, as always with simple harmonic motion, that happens as she swings through equilibrium, with the vine vertical. Figure 15-16 is a free-body diagram for Jane as she passes through equilibrium. The two forces acting are gravity and the vine tension; they sum to give the upward force that produces the acceleration v^2/r associated with the circular motion of Jane's swing. So, in a coordi-

FIGURE 15-16 Free-body diagram for Jane as she swings through equilibrium. The vine tension is greatest at this point.

nate system with the positive direction upward, Newton's second law becomes $T - mg = \dfrac{mv^2}{r}$.

In analogy with linear harmonic motion, the greatest angular velocity occurs as she swings through equilibrium; then, as we found in Example 15-3, $(d\theta/dt)_{\text{max}} = A\omega$. Multiplying by the radius—here the vine length ℓ—gives her maximum linear velocity: $v_{\text{max}} = A\omega\ell$. Using this result in our statement of Newton's law and solving for T then gives

$$T = \frac{mv^2}{r} + mg = \frac{mA^2\omega^2\ell^2}{\ell} + mg = mA^2g + mg$$

$$= mg(1 + A^2),$$

where we set r equal to the vine length ℓ and used Equation 15-17 for ω. The amplitude A is the vine angle shown in Fig. 15-15; from trigonometry, we have $\sin A = \dfrac{4.0 \text{ m}}{25 \text{ m}} = 0.16.$ The inverse sine is 0.1607 radians, showing that the approximation $\sin\theta \simeq \theta$ holds well in this example. So the fractional increase in tension over Jane's weight is given by A^2, which in this case is about 2.6%.

> **Tip**
>
> *Set Your Calculator for Radians* Most calculators assume that the arguments of trig functions are given in degrees. It's usually possible to set the calculator for radians instead. Make sure you do this before working with radian measure.

EXERCISE A 650-kg wrecking ball is suspended from a 20-m chain of negligible mass. The ball is hanging vertically, resting against the wall of a building. It is then withdrawn a distance much smaller than the chain length and released. How soon does it strike the building?

Answer: 2.2 s

Some problems similar to Example 15-4: 17, 18, 21, 63, 64

FIGURE 15-15 Tarzan in trouble (Example 15-4). Lengths are not to scale.

Got It!

What happens to the period of a pendulum if (a) its mass is doubled? (b) it's moved to a planet whose gravitational acceleration is one-fourth that of Earth? (c) its length is quadrupled?

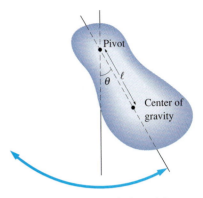

FIGURE 15-17 A physical pendulum.

The Physical Pendulum

A **physical pendulum** is an object of arbitrary shape that is free to swing (Fig. 15-17). It differs from a simple pendulum in that mass may be distributed over its entire length. Physical pendulums are everywhere: examples include the legs of humans and other animals (see Example 15-5), a skier on a chair lift, a boxer's punching bag, a frying pan hanging from a rack, and a crane lifting any object of significant extent. In our analysis of the simple pendulum, we used the fact that mass was concentrated at the bottom only in the final step, when we wrote $m\ell^2$ for the rotational inertia. Our analysis before that step therefore applies to the physical pendulum as well.

In particular, a physical pendulum displaced slightly from equilibrium undergoes simple harmonic motion with frequency given by Equation 15-16. But how are we to interpret the length ℓ that appears in that equation? Because gravity—which provides the restoring torque for *any* pendulum—acts on an object's center of gravity, ℓ must be the distance from the pivot to the center of gravity, as marked in Fig. 15-17.

EXAMPLE 15-5	*Walking*

When walking, the leg not in contact with the ground swings forward, acting essentially like a physical pendulum. Making the crude approximation that the leg acts like a uniform rod, find the period of this pendulum motion for leg length $L = 90$ cm.

Solution

With the uniform-rod assumption the center of gravity lies halfway along the leg, so ℓ in Equation 15-16 is $L/2$. Combining Equations 15-16 and 15-6 then gives the period:

$$T = \frac{2\pi}{\omega} = 2\pi\sqrt{\frac{I}{mgL/2}} = 2\pi\sqrt{\frac{mL^2}{3mgL/2}} = 2\pi\sqrt{\frac{2L}{3g}},$$

where we used Table 12-2's result $I = \frac{1}{3}mL^2$ for the rotational inertia. Using the 90-cm leg length gives $T = 1.55$ s, which is indeed about the time for one complete stride with both legs.

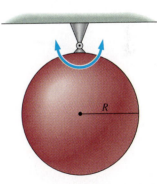

FIGURE 15-18 What's the period of this physical pendulum?

Answer: $2\pi\sqrt{\dfrac{7R}{5g}}$

EXERCISE A uniform solid ball of radius R hangs from a pivot attached to its surface (Fig. 15-18). What will be the period of small-amplitude oscillations about its equilibrium position?

Some problems similar to Example 15-5: 20, 28, 29, 57, 58

15-4 CIRCULAR MOTION AND SIMPLE HARMONIC MOTION: AN INTIMATE RELATION

An alien spacecraft hovers far above the Sun's polar region, looking down on the solar system so that alien astronomers can study the motion of planet Earth. And what do they see? As Fig. 15-19a shows, they see Earth executing essentially uniform circular motion about the Sun. Another alien spacecraft also watches Earth from the same great distance, but this time in the plane of the planets' circular orbits. What do its astronomers see? As Fig. 15-19b shows, they see Earth moving back and forth. Furthermore, the planet appears to slow as it approaches the endpoints of its motion, since then it's actually moving mostly toward or away from the observers. It appears to move faster as it passes in front of or behind the Sun. If the astronomers on this second spaceship plot Earth's apparent position as a function of time, they'll get the graph shown in Fig. 15-20.

Earth's position in Fig. 15-20 looks just like Fig. 15-5 for simple harmonic motion. That's no coincidence: simple harmonic motion and circular motion are intimately related, as we now show.

Figure 15-21 shows the position vector **r** for an object undergoing uniform circular motion. As the figure suggests, the components of this position vector are $x = r\cos\theta$ and $y = r\sin\theta$. In uniform circular motion, the angle θ increases steadily with time; if $\theta = 0$ when time $t = 0$, we can write $\theta = \omega t$, with ω the

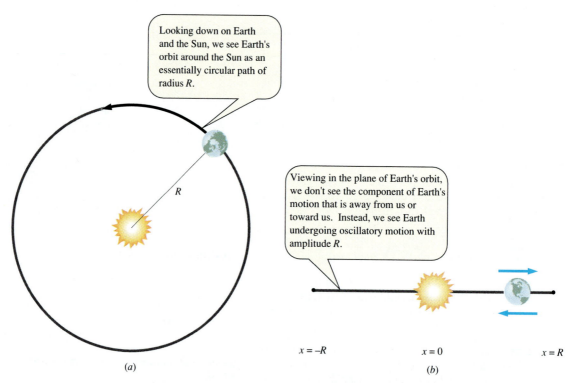

Looking down on Earth and the Sun, we see Earth's orbit around the Sun as an essentially circular path of radius R.

R

Viewing in the plane of Earth's orbit, we don't see the component of Earth's motion that is away from us or toward us. Instead, we see Earth undergoing oscillatory motion with amplitude R.

$x = -R$ $x = 0$ $x = R$

(a)   (b)

FIGURE 15-19 (a) From a vantage point perpendicular to the plane of Earth's orbit, the planet's essentially uniform circular motion is obvious. (b) From a vantage point in the plane of the orbit, Earth appears to move back and forth in oscillatory motion.

angular velocity of the circular motion. So the components of the object's position become

$$x(t) = r \cos \omega t$$

$$y(t) = r \sin \omega t .$$

But these are just the equations for two different simple harmonic motions, one in the x direction and the other in the y direction. Because one has a sine and the other a cosine, the two motions are out of phase by $\frac{\pi}{2}$ (see the Math Toolbox on page 368 to review phase differences).

We can think of circular motion as arising from two perpendicular simple harmonic motions, both with the same frequency and amplitude but $\frac{\pi}{2}$ out of phase. You could actually produce circular motion this way by starting a pendulum swinging in one direction; then, just as it's at its maximum displacement, give it a push in a perpendicular direction. If you give it just the right speed, the combination of two perpendicular swinging motions $\frac{\pi}{2}$ out of phase results in circular motion.

If we measure Earth's apparent displacement in Fig. 15-19b over time, we find simple harmonic motion.

FIGURE 15-20 Earth's apparent position versus time from the vantage point in Fig. 15-19b. What's the maximum time shown, in years?

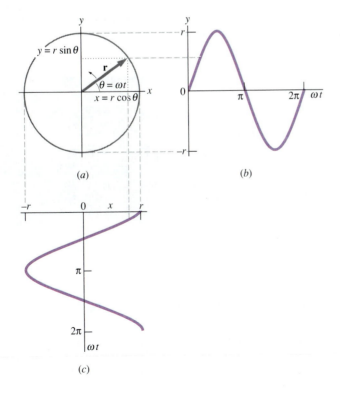

(a)

(b)

(c)

FIGURE 15-21 (a) The components of the position vector in uniform circular motion are $x = r \cos \theta$ and $y = r \sin \theta$, with $\theta = \omega t$. (b, c) The individual components show simple harmonic motion with the same amplitude as the circle's radius and the same angular frequency as the circular motion. Note that they're out of phase by $\frac{\pi}{2}$ or 90°, with one component at zero when the other is at its maximum.

(a)　　　　　(b)

(c)

Figure 15-21 should help you to understand why we use the term "angular frequency" for simple harmonic motion even though there's not necessarily any angle involved. If we think of simple harmonic motion as a component of uniform circular motion, then one cycle of the simple harmonic motion occurs in the time for one complete revolution in the corresponding circular motion. The argument ωt of the sine or cosine describing simple harmonic motion is the same as the physical angle $\theta = \omega t$ giving an object's angular position in circular motion. Similarly, the angular frequency ω is simply the angular velocity ω of the corresponding circular motion.

You can verify directly that two mutually perpendicular simple harmonic motions of the same amplitude and frequency sum vectorially to give circular motion (see Problem 36). But what if the amplitudes or frequencies aren't the same? Then interestingly complex motions occur, as suggested in Fig. 15-22.

FIGURE 15-22 When oscillation frequencies differ in different directions, the oscillating object traces out a complex path. Here we see paths for ratios of (a) 2:1 and (b) 2:3 for the vertical to horizontal frequency. (c) This pendulum deposits sand as it swings in two dimensions, producing complex patterns.

APPLICATION	*Of Engines and Sewing Machines*

The relation between circular and simple harmonic motion sees practical use in machinery that converts rotary motion to back-and-forth linear motion or vice versa. In a car's engine, for example, the up-and-down motion of the pistons, driven by pressure from the combustion of gasoline, is converted to the engine's rotational motion through the mechanism shown in Fig. 15-23a. The same thing happens in an old-fashioned steam locomotive (Fig. 15-23b), while a similar mechanism operating in reverse turns rotary motion from an electric motor into the up-and-down motion of a sewing machine's needle. It's hard to imagine a day going by that you don't use a device that incorporates this mechanism.

FIGURE 15-23 (a) Through the intermediary of the connecting rods, the up-down motion of pistons in a car engine is converted to rotary motion of the engine's crankshaft. Because the connecting rod angle changes, the piston's motion is not quite simple harmonic. (b) The connecting rod's role in driving the wheel is obvious in this steam locomotive.

Piston

Connecting rod

Crankshaft

(a)

(b)

15-5 ENERGY IN SIMPLE HARMONIC MOTION

If we displace a mass-spring system from equilibrium, we do work as we build up potential energy in the spring. When we release the mass it accelerates toward equilibrium, gaining kinetic energy at the expense of potential energy. The mass

FIGURE 15-24 Kinetic and potential energy in a simple harmonic oscillator. Figures show the extension or compression of the spring, the velocity of the mass, and the balance of kinetic and potential energy at different times spaced one-eighth of a cycle ($\pi/4$ or 45° in phase) apart. Vertical line at right marks the spring's equilibrium position. ActivPhysics Activity 9.3 includes an animation of this figure.

passes through its equilibrium position with maximum kinetic energy and no potential energy, then slows and builds potential energy as it compresses the spring. If there is no energy loss, this process continues indefinitely. In oscillatory motion, energy is continually transferred back and forth between its kinetic and potential forms (Fig. 15-24).

For a mass-spring system, the potential energy is given by Equation 8-4:

$$U = \tfrac{1}{2}kx^2 ,$$

where x is the displacement from equilibrium. Meanwhile, the kinetic energy is $K = \tfrac{1}{2}mv^2$. We can illustrate explicitly the interchange of kinetic and potential energy in simple harmonic motion by using x from Equation 15-5 and v from Equation 15-10 in the expressions for potential and kinetic energy. Then we have

$$U = \tfrac{1}{2}kx^2 = \tfrac{1}{2}k(A\cos\omega t)^2 = \tfrac{1}{2}kA^2\cos^2\omega t$$

and

$$K = \tfrac{1}{2}mv^2 = \tfrac{1}{2}m(-A\omega\sin\omega t)^2 = \tfrac{1}{2}m\omega^2 A^2\sin^2\omega t = \tfrac{1}{2}kA^2\sin^2\omega t ,$$

where we have used the fact that $\omega^2 = k/m$. Comparing our expressions for potential and kinetic energy, we see that both have the same maximum value—$\tfrac{1}{2}kA^2$—equal to the initial potential energy of the stretched spring. The crucial difference lies in their relative phase—the potential energy is a maximum when the kinetic energy is zero, and vice versa. What about the total energy? It is

$$E = U + K = \tfrac{1}{2}kA^2\cos^2\omega t + \tfrac{1}{2}kA^2\sin^2\omega t = \tfrac{1}{2}kA^2 ,$$

where we have used $\sin^2\omega t + \cos^2\omega t = 1$.

What is this result saying? It's a statement of conservation of mechanical energy—the principle we introduced in Chapter 8—applied to a simple harmonic oscillator. Although the kinetic and potential energies K and U both vary with time, their sum—the total energy E—does not (Fig. 15-25).

ActivPhysics

9.3
Vibrational Energy

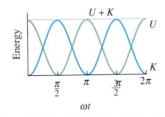

FIGURE 15-25 The potential energy U and kinetic energy K of a simple harmonic oscillator vary with time, but their sum remains constant.

EXAMPLE 15-6	*Energy in Simple Harmonic Motion*

A mass-spring system is undergoing simple harmonic motion with angular frequency ω and amplitude A. Find its speed at the point where the kinetic and potential energies are equal.

Solution

When the energies are equal, each must be half the total energy. Equation 15-10 shows that the maximum speed is $v_{max} = A\omega$. Since the maximum speed occurs when the energy is all kinetic, the total energy must be $E = \frac{1}{2}mv_{max}^2 = \frac{1}{2}mA^2\omega^2$. When the kinetic energy is half the total energy we then have

$$K = \tfrac{1}{2}mv^2 = \tfrac{1}{2}E = \tfrac{1}{2}(\tfrac{1}{2}mA^2\omega^2) = \tfrac{1}{4}mA^2\omega^2.$$

Solving for v gives the desired answer:

$$v = \frac{A\omega}{\sqrt{2}}.$$

EXERCISE Find the position x of the mass in Example 15-6 at the point when the kinetic and potential energies are equal.

Answer: $A/\sqrt{2}$

Some problems similar to Example 15-6: 41, 61, 62

FIGURE 15-26 Near their minima, potential energy curves often approximate parabolas. Simple harmonic motion can therefore occur about these minima, which are points of stable equilibrium.

Potential Energy Curves and Simple Harmonic Motion

We arrived at the expression $U = \frac{1}{2}kx^2$ for the potential energy of a spring by integrating the spring force, $-kx$, over distance. Since every simple harmonic oscillator has a restoring force or torque proportional to displacement, integration always results in a potential energy proportional to the *square* of the displacement—that is, in a parabolic potential energy curve. Conversely, any system with a parabolic potential energy curve exhibits simple harmonic motion. The simplest mathematical approximation to a smooth curve is a parabola, and for that reason potential energy curves for complex systems often approximate parabolas near their stable equilibrium points (Fig. 15-26). Small disturbances from these equilibria therefore result in simple harmonic motion.

15-6 DAMPED HARMONIC MOTION

In real oscillating systems, forces such as friction or air resistance normally dissipate the oscillation energy, preventing the oscillation from continuing forever. In a pendulum, for example, both air resistance and friction at the pivot contribute to energy dissipation; in a mass-spring system, energy dissipation occurs through friction between the mass and the surface it's sliding on, as well as through losses in the spring itself. This energy loss causes the oscillation amplitude to decrease, and the motion is then said to be **damped**.

If dissipation is sufficiently weak that only a small fraction of the system's energy is removed in each oscillation cycle, then we expect that the system should behave essentially as in the undamped case, except for a gradual decrease in the oscillation amplitude (Fig. 15-27).

In many systems the damping force is approximately proportional to the velocity, and in the opposite direction:

FIGURE 15-27 Weakly damped motion, showing sinusoidal oscillations confined within the "envelope" of a decaying exponential.

$$F_d = -bv = -b\frac{dx}{dt},$$

where b is a constant giving the strength of the damping. We can write Newton's law as before, now including the damping force along with the restoring force. For a mass-spring system, we have

$$m\frac{d^2x}{dt^2} = -kx - b\frac{dx}{dt},$$

or

$$m\frac{d^2x}{dt^2} + b\frac{dx}{dt} + kx = 0. \tag{15-19}$$

We will not solve this equation, but simply state that its solution can be written

$$x(t) = Ae^{-bt/2m}\cos(\omega t + \phi). \quad (15\text{-}20)$$

This solution describes sinusoidal motion whose amplitude decreases exponentially with time. How fast the amplitude drops depends on the damping constant b and mass m: when $t = 2m/b$, the amplitude has dropped to $1/e$ of its original value. When the damping is so weak that only a small fraction of the total energy is lost in each cycle, then the frequency ω in Equation 15-20 is essentially equal to the undamped frequency $\sqrt{k/m}$. But with stronger damping, the damping force slows the motion, and the frequency becomes lower. Also, the oscillation amplitude decreases more rapidly with time (Fig. 15-28, curve a). As long as oscillation occurs, the motion is said to be **underdamped**. For sufficiently strong damping, though, the effect of the damping force is as great as that of the spring force. Under this condition, called **critical damping**, the system returns to its equilibrium state without undergoing any oscillations (Fig. 15-28, curve b). If the damping is made still stronger, the system becomes **overdamped**. The damping force now dominates, so the system returns more slowly to equilibrium (Fig. 15-28, curve c).

Many physical systems, from atoms to the human leg, can be modeled as damped oscillators. Engineers often design systems with specific amounts of damping. Automobile shock absorbers, for example, are designed with the springs to give critical damping. This results in rapid return to equilibrium while absorbing energy imparted by road bumps (Fig. 15-29). Similarly, the strings of a piano are damped—although not critically—so notes die out relatively quickly.

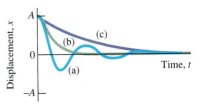

FIGURE 15-28 As the damping increases the amplitude falls more rapidly and the period increases slightly, as shown in curve a. With critical damping the oscillations cease altogether, as shown in curve b. Overdamping is shown in curve c.

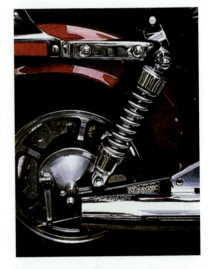

FIGURE 15-29 This motorcycle spring cushions the rider from road bumps. Cylinder inside the spring is a shock absorber that provides critical damping, thus preventing continuing oscillation.

EXAMPLE 15-7	*Bad Shocks*

A car and its suspension system act like a mass-spring system with $m = 1200$ kg and $k = 58$ kN/m. Its worn-out shock absorbers provide a damping constant $b = 230$ kg/s. The car hits a pothole that sets it oscillating. How many oscillations will it make before the oscillation amplitude drops to half its initial value?

Solution

The amplitude will be half its original value when the factor $e^{-bt/2m}$ in Equation 15-23 has the value one-half:

$$e^{-bt/2m} = \tfrac{1}{2}.$$

Taking the natural logarithm of both sides gives

$$\frac{-bt}{2m} = -\ln 2,$$

where we have used the facts that $\ln(x)$ and e^x are inverse functions and that $\ln(1/x) = -\ln(x)$. Then

$$t = \frac{2m}{b}\ln 2 = \frac{(2)(1200 \text{ kg})}{230 \text{ kg/s}}\ln 2 = 7.23 \text{ s}$$

is the time for the amplitude to drop to half its original value. For weak damping, the period is very close to the undamped period, which is

$$T = 2\pi\sqrt{\frac{m}{k}} = 2\pi\sqrt{\frac{1200 \text{ kg}}{58 \times 10^3 \text{ N/m}}} = 0.904 \text{ s}.$$

Then the number of cycles during the 7.23 s it takes the amplitude to drop in half is

$$\frac{7.23 \text{ s}}{0.904 \text{ s}} = 8.$$

That the number of oscillations is much greater than 1 tells us that the damping is weak, justifying our use of the undamped period.

EXERCISE Find the time it takes the system of Example 15-7 to drop to one-tenth of its initial amplitude.

Answer: 24 s

Some problems similar to Example 15-7: 47, 48

15-7 DRIVEN OSCILLATIONS AND RESONANCE

FIGURE 15-30 One way to drive a mass-spring system is to hold the end of the spring and move it up and down. The frequency of that motion is the driving frequency. You'll build up large-amplitude oscillations if the driving frequency is close to the natural frequency $\omega_0 = \sqrt{k/m}$.

Pushing a child on a swing, you can build up a large amplitude by giving a relatively small push once each oscillation cycle. If your pushing were not in step with the swing's natural oscillatory motion, then the same force would have little effect.

When an external force acts on an oscillatory system, we say that the system is **driven**. Consider a mass-spring system, which you might drive as suggested in Fig. 15-30. Suppose the driving force is given by $F_0 \cos \omega_d t$, where ω_d is called the **driving frequency**. Then Newton's law is

$$m\frac{d^2x}{dt^2} = -kx - b\frac{dx}{dt} + F_0 \cos \omega_d t, \qquad (15\text{-}21)$$

where the first term on the right-hand side is the restoring force, the second the damping force, and the third the driving force. Since the system is being driven at the frequency ω_d, we expect it to undergo oscillatory motion at this frequency. So we guess that the solution to Equation 15-21 might have the form

$$x = A \cos(\omega_d t + \phi). \qquad (15\text{-}22)$$

Substituting this expression and its derivatives into Equation 15-21 (see Problem 51) shows that the equation is satisfied if

$$A(\omega) = \frac{F_0}{m\sqrt{(\omega_d^2 - \omega_0^2)^2 + b^2\,\omega_d^2/m^2}}, \qquad (15\text{-}23)$$

where ω_0 is the undamped **natural frequency** $\sqrt{k/m}$, as distinguished from the driving frequency ω_d.

Equation 15-23 shows that the amplitude of the motion varies with driving frequency for a fixed driving force F_0. Figure 15-31 shows a **resonance curve**, which is just a plot of Equation 15-23 as a function of driving frequency, for

FIGURE 15-31 Resonance curves for several damping strengths. The quantity ω_0 is the undamped natural frequency $\sqrt{k/m}$.

several values of the damping constant. As long as the system is underdamped, the curve has a maximum at some nonzero frequency (see Problem 52), and for weak damping that maximum occurs at very nearly the natural frequency. The weaker the damping, the more sharply peaked is the resonance curve. Thus in weakly damped systems it is possible to build up large-amplitude oscillations with relatively small driving forces—a phenomenon known as **resonance**.

Most physical systems, from molecules to cars, and loudspeakers to buildings and bridges, exhibit one or more natural modes of oscillation. If these oscillations are weakly damped, then the buildup of large-amplitude oscillations through resonance can cause serious problems—sometimes even destroying the system (see Fig. 15-32). Engineers designing complex structures spend a lot of their time exploring all possible oscillation modes and taking steps to avoid resonance. In an earthquake-prone area, for example, a building's natural frequencies would be designed to avoid the frequency of typical earthquake motions. A loudspeaker should be engineered so its natural frequency isn't in the range of sound it's intended to reproduce. Damping systems such as the shock absorbers of Example 15-7 or the tuned mass damper of Example 15-2 help limit resonant oscillations in cases where natural frequencies aren't easily altered.

Resonance is also important in microscopic systems. The resonant behavior of electrons in a special tube called a magnetron produces the microwaves that cook food in a microwave oven; the same resonant process heats ionized gases in some experiments designed to harness fusion energy. Carbon dioxide in Earth's atmosphere absorbs infrared radiation because CO_2 molecules—acting like miniature mass-spring systems—resonate at some of the frequencies of infrared radiation. The result is the greenhouse effect, which many scientists believe threatens Earth with significant climatic change. At the nuclear level, the process called nuclear magnetic resonance (NMR) uses resonant behavior of protons to probe the structure of matter and to produce images used in medical diagnosis. In NMR, the resonance involves the natural precession frequency of the protons due to magnetic torques; we described the classical model of this process in Chapter 13.

(a)   (b)   (c)

FIGURE 15-32 (*a*, *b*) Collapse of the Tacoma Narrows Bridge—only four months after its opening in 1940—followed the growth of large-amplitude oscillations. That growth resulted from complex interactions between aerodynamic forces and the bridge itself. (*c*) The rebuilt bridge includes a much stiffer deck that damps out oscillations.

CHAPTER SYNOPSIS

Summary

1. **Oscillatory motion** is periodic motion back and forth about a system's equilibrium position. It occurs when a system subject to a restoring force is displaced from stable equilibrium.

2. **Simple harmonic motion** is the special case that occurs when the restoring force is proportional to displacement from equilibrium. Simple harmonic motion is described by

$$x(t) = A \cos(\omega t + \phi),$$

where A is the maximum displacement, or **amplitude**, ϕ the **phase constant**, and ω the **angular frequency** of oscillation. For a mass-spring system, $\omega = \sqrt{k/m}$. Analogous expressions hold for other systems, including torsional oscillators and pendulums. The frequency in hertz (or cycles per second) and the period are related to the angular frequency by the equations

$$f = \frac{\omega}{2\pi} \quad \text{and} \quad T = \frac{1}{f} = \frac{2\pi}{\omega}.$$

3. Simple harmonic motion and uniform circular motion are intimately related. Simple harmonic motion can be viewed as a component or projection of circular motion onto a line; conversely, two perpendicular simple harmonic motions that are out of phase by $\frac{\pi}{2}$ radians or 90° combine to produce uniform circular motion. The angular velocity ω of circular motion and the angular frequency ω of the corresponding simple harmonic motion are the same.

4. In oscillatory motion, energy is transferred back and forth between kinetic and potential forms; in the absence of loss mechanisms, the total energy remains constant. The special case of simple harmonic motion results when the potential energy is a quadratic function of displacement—a situation that is approximated for many systems near stable equilibrium.

5. Energy loss results in **damped harmonic motion**. In an **underdamped** system, the damping is relatively weak and the motion is described by

$$x(t) = A\, e^{-bt/2m} \cos(\omega t + \phi),$$

where b is a constant describing the strength of the damping. For very weak damping, ω is essentially the natural oscillation frequency of the system. As the damping increases, the frequency drops and eventually the system becomes **critically damped**, and then **overdamped**, in both cases returning to equilibrium without oscillating.

6. A driven oscillatory system responds with motion at the driving frequency. The amplitude peaks for driving frequencies near the system's natural frequency—the phenomenon of **resonance**. The amplitude of resonant oscillations is given by

$$A(\omega) = \frac{F_0}{m\sqrt{(\omega_d^2 - \omega_0^2)^2 + b^2\omega_d^2/m^2}},$$

where F_0 is the amplitude of the driving force, ω_d its frequency, m the mass, b the damping constant, and $\omega_0 = \sqrt{k/m}$ the undamped natural frequency of the system.

Terms You Should Understand

(Pairs are closely related terms whose distinction is important; number in parentheses is chapter section where term first appears.)

oscillatory motion (introduction)
amplitude (15-1)
period, frequency (15-1)
hertz (15-1)
simple harmonic motion (15-2)
phase (15-2)
torsional oscillator (15-3)
simple pendulum, physical pendulum (15-3)
damping (15-6)
underdamping, critical damping, overdamping (15-6)
driven oscillations (15-7)
driving frequency, natural frequency (15-7)
resonance (15-7)

Symbols You Should Recognize

ω, f, T (15-1)	κ (15-3)
ϕ (15-2)	ω_d, ω_0 (15-7)

Problems You Should Be Able to Solve

calculating frequency from period, and vice versa (15-1)
calculating frequency and period of mass-spring systems (15-2)
determining velocity and acceleration in simple harmonic motion (15-2)
solving problems involving torsional oscillators, simple pendulums, and physical pendulums (15-3)
finding kinetic and potential energies in simple harmonic motion (15-5)
analyzing damped harmonic motion (15-6)
determining amplitudes of resonant motion (15-7)

Limitations to Keep in Mind

Simple harmonic motion occurs only when the restoring force is strictly proportional to displacement from equilibrium. For many systems this is a reasonable approximation only for small amplitudes.

The expression $T = 2\pi\sqrt{g/\ell}$ for the period of a pendulum holds only for small angular displacements from vertical.

The total energy of most oscillating systems is only approximately constant, as energy loss mechanisms damp the motion.

Equation 15-20 for damped harmonic motion applies only to underdamped systems, and the frequency ω is only approximately the natural frequency of the system.

QUESTIONS

1. Is a vertically bouncing ball an example of oscillatory motion? Of simple harmonic motion? Explain.
2. The vibration frequencies of molecules are much higher than those of macroscopic mechanical systems. Why should this be?
3. What happens to the frequency of a simple harmonic oscillator when the spring constant is doubled? When the mass is doubled?
4. If the spring of a simple harmonic oscillator is cut in half, what happens to the frequency?
5. How does the frequency of a simple harmonic oscillator depend on its amplitude?
6. How would the frequency of a horizontal mass-spring system change if it were taken to the moon? Of a vertical mass-spring system? Of a simple pendulum?
7. In what ways is the motion of a damped pendulum not exactly periodic?
8. When is the acceleration of an undamped simple harmonic oscillator zero? When is the velocity zero?
9. Is the acceleration of a damped harmonic oscillator ever zero? Explain.
10. If the spring in a mass-spring system is not massless, how will this affect the frequency?
11. What will happen to the period of a mass-spring system if it is placed in a jetliner accelerating down the runway? What will happen to the period of a pendulum in the same situation?
12. Explain how simple harmonic motion might be used to determine the mass of objects in an orbiting spacecraft.
13. One pendulum consists of a solid rod of mass m and length ℓ, another of a compact ball of the same mass m on the end of a massless string of the same length ℓ. Which has the greater period? Why?
14. Why doesn't the period of a simple pendulum depend on its mass?
15. When the amplitude of a pendulum's motion becomes large enough that the approximation $\sin \theta \simeq \theta$ is no longer valid, the period lengthens with increasing amplitude. Why should this be?
16. The x and y components of motion of a body are both simple harmonic with the same frequency and amplitude. What shape is the path of the body if the component motions are (a) in phase; (b) $\pi/2$ out of phase; (c) $\pi/4$ out of phase?
17. Why is critical damping desirable in a car's suspension system?
18. Explain why the frequency of a damped system is lower than that of the equivalent undamped system.
19. The quantity $2m/b$ in Equation 15-20 has the units of time. How should this time compare with the period of the motion if damping is to be considered small?
20. Opera singers have been known to break glasses with their voices. How?
21. Depressing the rightmost pedal on a piano causes notes to sound much longer than usual. What quantity changes in Equation 15-20 when the pedal is pressed?
22. Real physical systems often have more than one resonant frequency. How can this come about?

PROBLEMS

ActivPhysics can help with these problems:
See ActivPhysics Section 9.

Sections 15-1 and 15-2 Oscillations and Simple Harmonic Motion

1. A doctor counts 77 heartbeats in one minute. What are the period and frequency of the heart's oscillations?
2. A violin string playing the note "A" oscillates at 440 Hz. What is the period of its oscillation?
3. The vibration frequency of a hydrogen chloride molecule is 8.66×10^{13} Hz. How long does it take the molecule to complete one oscillation?
4. Write expressions for simple harmonic motion (a) with amplitude 10 cm, frequency 5.0 Hz, and with maximum displacement at $t = 0$ and (b) with amplitude 2.5 cm, angular frequency 5.0 s^{-1}, and with maximum velocity at $t = 0$.
5. Determine the amplitude, angular frequency, and phase constant for each of the simple harmonic motions shown in Fig. 15-33.

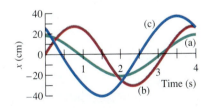

FIGURE 15-33 Problem 5.

6. A 200-g mass is attached to a spring of constant $k = 5.6$ N/m and set into oscillation with amplitude $A = 25$ cm. Determine (a) the frequency in hertz, (b) the period, (c) the maximum velocity, and (d) the maximum force in the spring.
7. An astronaut in an orbiting spacecraft is "weighed" by being strapped to a spring of constant $k = 400$ N/m, and set into simple harmonic motion. If the oscillation period is 2.5 s, what is the astronaut's mass?
8. A simple model for an automobile suspension consists of a mass attached to a spring. If the mass is 1900 kg and the

spring constant is 26 kN/m, with what frequency and period will the car undergo simple harmonic motion?

9. A simple model of a carbon dioxide (CO_2) molecule consists of three mass points (the atoms) connected by two springs (electrical forces), as suggested in Fig. 15-34. One way this system can oscillate is if the carbon atom stays fixed and the two oxygens move symmetrically on either side of it. If the frequency of this oscillation is 4.0×10^{13} Hz, what is the effective spring constant? The mass of an oxygen atom is 16 u.

FIGURE 15-34 Problem 9.

10. Sketch the following simple harmonic motions on the same graph: (a) $x = (15 \text{ cm})[\cos(2.5t + \pi/2)]$, (b) motion with amplitude 30 cm, period 5.0 s, phase constant 0; (c) motion with amplitude 15 cm, frequency 0.40 Hz, phase constant 0.

11. Two identical mass-spring systems consist of 430-g masses on springs of constant $k = 2.2$ N/m. Both are displaced from equilibrium and the first released at time $t = 0$. How much later should the second be released so the two oscillations differ in phase by $\pi/2$?

12. The quartz crystal in a digital quartz watch executes simple harmonic motion at 32,768 Hz. (This is 2^{15} Hz, chosen so 15 divisions by 2 give a signal at 1.00000 Hz.) If each face of the crystal undergoes a maximum displacement of 100 nm, find the maximum velocity and acceleration of the crystal faces.

13. A mass m slides along a frictionless horizontal surface at speed v_0. It strikes a spring of constant k attached to a rigid wall, as shown in Fig. 15-35. After a completely elastic encounter with the spring, the mass heads back in the direction it came from. In terms of k, m, and v_0, determine (a) how long the mass is in contact with the spring and (b) the maximum compression of the spring.

FIGURE 15-35 Problem 13.

14. A 50-g mass is attached to a spring and undergoes simple harmonic motion. Its maximum acceleration is 15 m/s² and its maximum speed is 3.5 m/s. Determine (a) the angular frequency, (b) the spring constant, and (c) the amplitude of the motion.

15. Show by substitution that $x(t) = A \sin \omega t$ is a solution to Equation 15-4.

16. Show by substitution that $x(t) = a \cos \omega t - b \sin \omega t$ is a solution to Equation 15-4, and that this form is equivalent to Equation 15-9 with $A = \sqrt{a^2 + b^2}$ and $\phi = \tan^{-1}(b/a)$.

Section 15-3 Applications of Simple Harmonic Motion

17. How long should you make a simple pendulum so its period is (a) 200 ms; (b) 5.0 s; (c) 2.0 min?

18. At the heart of a grandfather clock is a simple pendulum 1.45 m long; the clock ticks each time the pendulum reaches its maximum displacement in either direction. What is the time interval between ticks?

19. A 640-g hollow ball 21 cm in diameter is suspended by a wire and is undergoing torsional oscillations at a frequency of 0.78 Hz. What is the torsional constant of the wire?

20. A physics student, bored by a lecture on simple harmonic motion, idly picks up his pencil (mass 9.2 g, length 17 cm) by the tip with his frictionless fingers, and allows it to swing back and forth with small amplitude. If it completes 6279 full cycles during the lecture, how long does the lecture last? (*Hint:* See Example 15-5.)

21. A pendulum of length ℓ is mounted in a rocket. What is its period if the rocket is (a) at rest on its launch pad; (b) accelerating upward with acceleration $a = \frac{1}{2}g$; (c) accelerating downward with acceleration $a = \frac{1}{2}g$; (d) in free fall?

22. A 340-g mass is attached to a vertical spring and lowered slowly until it rests at a new equilibrium position, which is 30 cm below the spring's original equilibrium. The system is then set into simple harmonic motion. What is the period of the motion?

23. A mass is attached to a vertical spring, which then goes into oscillation. At the high point of the oscillation, the spring is in the original unstretched equilibrium position it had before the mass was attached; the low point is 5.8 cm below this. What is the period of oscillation?

24. Derive the period of a simple pendulum by considering the horizontal displacement x and the force acting on the bob, rather than the angular displacement and torque.

25. A solid disk of radius R is suspended from a spring of linear spring constant k and torsional constant κ, as shown in Fig. 15-36. In terms of k and κ, what value of R will give the same period for the vertical and torsional oscillations of this system?

FIGURE 15-36 Problem 25.

26. A thin steel beam 8.0 m long is suspended from a crane and is undergoing torsional oscillations. Two 75-kg steelworkers leap onto opposite ends of the beam, as shown in Fig. 15-37. If the frequency of torsional oscillations diminishes by 20%, what is the mass of the beam?

FIGURE 15-37 Problem 26.

27. Geologists use an instrument called a **gravimeter** to measure the local acceleration of gravity. A particular gravimeter uses the period of a 1-m-long pendulum to determine g. If g is to be measured to within 1 mgal (1 gal = 1 cm/s²) and if the period can be measured with arbitrary accuracy, how accurately must the length of the pendulum be known?

28. A pendulum consists of a 320-g solid ball 15.0 cm in diameter, suspended by an essentially massless string 80.0 cm long. Calculate the period of this pendulum, treating it first as a simple pendulum and then as a physical pendulum. How much error is introduced by the simple pendulum approximation? *Hint:* Remember the parallel-axis theorem.

29. A thin, uniform hoop of mass M and radius R is suspended from a thin horizontal rod and set oscillating with small amplitude, as shown in Fig. 15-38. Show that the period of the oscillations is $2\pi \sqrt{2R/g}$. *Hint:* You may find the parallel-axis theorem useful.

FIGURE 15-38 Problem 29.

30. A solid disk of mass M and radius R is mounted on a horizontal axle, as shown in Fig. 15-39. A spring of spring constant k is connected to the disk at a point $\frac{1}{2}R$ above the axle, and in equilibrium runs horizontally to a wall. If the

FIGURE 15-39 Problem 30.

disk is rotated slightly away from equilibrium, what is the angular frequency of the resulting oscillations? *Hint:* For small θ, $\sin\theta \simeq \theta$ and $\cos\theta \simeq 1$.

31. A point mass m is attached to the rim of an otherwise uniform solid disk of mass M and radius R (Fig. 15-40). The disk is rolled slightly away from its equilibrium position and released. It rolls back and forth without slipping. Show that the period of this motion is given by

$$T = 2\pi \sqrt{\frac{3MR}{2\,mg}}.$$

FIGURE 15-40 Problem 31.

32. Repeat the previous problem for the case when the disk does not contact the ground but is mounted on a frictionless horizontal axle through its center. Why is your answer different?

33. A cyclist turns her bicycle upside down to tinker with it. After she gets it upside down, she notices the front wheel executing a slow, small-amplitude back-and-forth rotational motion with a period of 12 s. Considering the wheel to be a thin ring of mass 600 g and radius 30 cm, whose only irregularity is the presence of the tire valve stem, determine the mass of the valve stem.

34. A mass m is mounted between two springs of constants k_1 and k_2, as shown in Fig. 15-41. Show that the angular frequency of oscillation is given by

$$\omega = \sqrt{\frac{k_1 + k_2}{m}}.$$

FIGURE 15-41 Problem 34.

35. Repeat the previous problem for the case when the springs are connected as in Fig. 15-42.

FIGURE 15-42 Problem 35.

Section 15-4 Circular Motion and Simple Harmonic Motion

36. An object undergoes simple harmonic motion in two mutually perpendicular directions, its position given by $\mathbf{r} = A \sin \omega t \, \hat{\mathbf{i}} + A \cos \omega t \, \hat{\mathbf{j}}$. (a) Show that the object remains a fixed distance from the origin—i.e., that its path is circular—and find that distance. (b) Find an expression for the object's velocity. (c) Show that the speed remains constant, and find its value. (d) What is the angular speed of the object in its circular path?

37. The equation for an ellipse is

$$\frac{x^2}{a^2} + \frac{y^2}{b^2} = 1.$$

Show that two-dimensional simple harmonic motion whose two components have different amplitudes and are $\pi/2$ out of phase gives rise to elliptical motion. How are a and b related to the amplitudes?

38. The x and y components of motion of a body are harmonic with frequency ratio $1.75 : 1$. How many oscillations must each component undergo before the body returns to its initial position?

Section 15-5 Energy in Simple Harmonic Motion

39. A 1400-kg car with poor shock absorbers is bouncing down the highway at 20 m/s, executing vertical harmonic motion at 0.67 Hz. If the amplitude of the oscillations is 18 cm, what is the total energy in the oscillations? What fraction of the car's kinetic energy is this? Neglect rotational energy of the wheels and the fact that not all the car's mass participates in the oscillation.

40. A 450-g mass on a spring is oscillating at 1.2 Hz. The total energy of the oscillation is 0.51 J. What is the amplitude of oscillation?

41. The motion of a particle is described by

$$x = (45 \text{ cm})[\sin(\pi t + \pi/6)],$$

with x in cm and t in seconds. At what time is the potential energy twice the kinetic energy? What is the position of the particle at this time?

42. A torsional oscillator of rotational inertia 1.6 kg·m^2 and torsional constant 3.4 N·m/rad has a total energy of 4.7 J. What are its maximum angular displacement and maximum angular speed?

43. Show that the potential energy of a simple pendulum is proportional to the square of the angular displacement in the small-amplitude limit.

44. The total energy of a mass-spring system is the sum of its kinetic and potential energy: $E = \frac{1}{2}mv^2 + \frac{1}{2}kx^2$. Assuming E remains constant, differentiate both sides of this expression with respect to time and show that Equation 15-4 results. *Hint:* Remember that $v = dx/dt$.

45. A solid cylinder of mass M and radius R is mounted on an axle through its center. The axle is attached to a horizontal spring of constant k, and the cylinder rolls back and forth without slipping (Fig. 15-43). Write the statement of energy conservation for this system, and differentiate it to obtain an equation analogous to Equation 15-4 (see previous problem). Comparing your result with Equation 15-4, determine the angular frequency of the motion.

FIGURE 15-43 Problem 45.

46. A mass m is free to slide on a frictionless track whose height y as a function of horizontal position x is given by $y = ax^2$, where a is a constant with the units of inverse length. The mass is given an initial displacement from the bottom of the track and then released. Find an expression for the period of the resulting motion.

Section 15-6 Damped Harmonic Motion

47. A 250-g mass is mounted on a spring of constant $k = 3.3$ N/m. The damping constant for this system is $b = 8.4 \times 10^{-3}$ kg/s. How many oscillations will the system undergo during the time the amplitude decays to $1/e$ of its original value?

48. The vibration of a piano string can be described by an equation analogous to Equation 15-20. If the quantity analogous to $b/2m$ in that equation has the value 2.8 s^{-1}, how long will it take the vibration amplitude to drop to half its original value?

Section 15-7 Driven Oscillations and Resonance

49. A mass-spring system has $b/m = \omega_0/5$, where b is the damping constant and ω_0 the natural frequency. How does its amplitude when driven at frequencies 10% above and below ω_0 compare with its amplitude at ω_0?

50. A car's front suspension has a natural frequency of 0.45 Hz. The car's front shock absorbers are worn out, so they no longer provide critical damping. The car is driving on a bumpy road with bumps 40 m apart. At a certain speed, the driver notices that the car begins to shake violently. What speed?

51. Show by direct substitution that Equation 15-22 satisfies Equation 15-21 with A given by Equation 15-23.

52. A harmonic oscillator is underdamped provided that the damping constant b is less than $\sqrt{2}m\omega_0$, where ω_0 is the natural frequency of undamped motion. Show that for an underdamped oscillator, Equation 15-23 has a maximum for a driving frequency less than ω_0.

Paired Problems

(Both problems in a pair involve the same principles and techniques. If you can get the first problem, you should be able to solve the second one.)

53. A particle undergoes simple harmonic motion with amplitude 25 cm and maximum speed 4.8 m/s. Find (a) the angular frequency, (b) the period, and (c) the maximum acceleration.

54. A particle undergoes simple harmonic motion with maximum speed 1.4 m/s and maximum acceleration 3.1 m/s². Find (a) the angular frequency, (b) the period, and (c) the amplitude of the motion.

55. A massless spring of spring constant $k = 74$ N/m is hanging from the ceiling. A 490-g mass is hooked onto the unstretched spring and allowed to drop. Find (a) the amplitude and (b) the period of the resulting motion.

56. A massless spring is hanging from the ceiling. A mass is hooked onto the end of the spring and allowed to drop. If the amplitude of the resulting motion is 20 cm, what is its frequency?

57. A meter stick is suspended from one end and set swinging. What is the period of the resulting oscillations, assuming they have small amplitude?

58. A meter stick is suspended from a frictionless rod inserted through a small hole at the 25 cm mark. What is the period of small-amplitude oscillations about the stick's equilibrium position?

59. Two balls each of unknown mass m are mounted on opposite ends of a 1.5-m-long rod of mass 850 g. The system is suspended from a wire attached to the center of the rod and set into torsional oscillations. If the torsional constant of the wire is 0.63 N·m/rad and the period of the oscillations is 5.6 s, what is the unknown mass m?

60. Figure 15-44 shows a bird feeder that consists of a 340-g solid circular disk 50 cm in diameter suspended by a wire attached at the center. Two 65-g birds land at opposite ends of a diameter, and the system goes into torsional

oscillation at 2.6 Hz. What is the torsional constant of the wire?

61. Two mass-spring systems with the same mass are undergoing oscillatory motion with the same amplitudes. System 1 has twice the frequency of system 2. How do (a) their energies and (b) their maximum accelerations compare?

62. Two mass-spring systems have the same mass and the same total energy. The amplitude of system 1 is twice that of system 2. How do (a) their frequencies and (b) their maximum accelerations compare?

Supplementary Problems

63. While waiting for your plane to take off, you suspend your keys from a thread and set the resulting pendulum oscillating. It completes exactly 90 cycles in 1 minute. You repeat the experiment as the plane accelerates down the runway, and now find the pendulum completes exactly 91 cycles in 1 minute. Find the plane's acceleration.

64. A 500-g mass is suspended from a thread 45 cm long that can sustain a maximum tension of 6.0 N before breaking. What is the maximum allowable amplitude for pendulum motion of this system?

65. A 500-g block on a frictionless surface is connected to a rather limp spring of constant $k = 8.7$ N/m. A second block rests on the first, and the whole system executes simple harmonic motion with a period of 1.8 s. When the amplitude of the motion is increased to 35 cm, the upper block just begins to slip. What is the coefficient of static friction between the blocks?

66. The potential energy of a 75-g particle is given by $U = ax^2 - bx^4$, where $a = 3.5$ J/m², $b = 1.2$ J/m⁴, and x is in meters. (a) Show that there is a metastable equilibrium at $x = 0$. (b) Find the frequency of small amplitude oscillations about this equilibrium. *Hint:* For small x, $x^4 \ll x^2$. (c) What is the maximum amplitude for oscillatory (but not necessarily simple harmonic) motion to occur?

67. Repeat Problem 46 for a small solid ball of mass M and radius R that rolls without slipping on the parabolic track.

68. A child twirls around on a swing, twisting the swing ropes, as shown in Fig. 15-45. As a result, the child and swing rise slightly, with the rise, h, in cm equal to the square of the number of full turns of the swing. When the child stops twisting up the swing, it goes into torsional oscillation. What is the period of this oscillation, assuming that all the potential energy of the system is gravitational? The combined mass of the child and swing is 20 kg, and the rotational inertia of the pair about the appropriate vertical axis is 0.12 kg·m².

FIGURE 15-44 Problem 60.

FIGURE 15-45 Problem 68.

69. A 1.2-kg block rests on a frictionless surface and is attached to a horizontal spring of constant $k = 23$ N/m (Fig. 15-46). The block is oscillating with amplitude 10 cm and with phase constant $\phi = -\pi/2$. A block of mass 0.80 kg is moving from the right at 1.7 m/s. It strikes the first block when the latter is at the rightmost point in its oscillation. The collision is completely inelastic, and the two blocks stick together. Determine the frequency, amplitude, and phase constant (relative to the *original* $t = 0$) of the resulting motion.

FIGURE 15-46 Problem 69.

70. The magnitude of the gravitational acceleration *inside* Earth is given approximately by $g(r) = g_0\frac{r}{R_E}$, where g_0 is the surface value, r is the distance from Earth's center, and R_E is Earth's radius; the acceleration is directed toward Earth's center. Suppose a narrow hole were drilled straight through the center of Earth and out the other side. Neglecting air resistance, show that an object dropped into this hole executes simple harmonic motion, and find an expression for the period. Evaluate and compare with the period of a satellite in a circular orbit not far above Earth's surface.

71. A small object of mass m slides without friction in a circular bowl of radius R. Derive an expression for small-amplitude oscillations about equilibrium, and compare with that of a simple pendulum.

72. A more exact expression than Equation 15-18 for the period of a simple pendulum is

$$T = T_0[1 + \tfrac{1}{4}\sin^2(\tfrac{1}{2}\theta_0) + \tfrac{9}{64}\sin^4(\tfrac{1}{2}\theta_0) + \cdots],$$

where $T_0 = 2\pi\sqrt{\ell/g}$ is the period in the limit of arbitrarily small amplitude, and θ_0 is the amplitude. The $\cdots$ indicates that additional terms (in fact, infinitely many more) are needed for an exact expression. For a pendulum with $T_0 = 1.00$ s, plot the period given above versus amplitude for amplitudes from 0 to 45°. By what percentage does the plotted period differ from T_0 for θ_0 of 30° and 45°?

73. A mass m is connected between two springs of length L, as shown in Fig. 15-47. At equilibrium, the tension force in each spring is F_0. Find the period of oscillations *perpendicular* to the springs, assuming sufficiently small amplitude that the magnitude of the spring tension is essentially unchanged.

FIGURE 15-47 Problem 73. This is a top view; the mass is moving on a frictionless horizontal surface.

74. A disk of radius R is suspended from a pivot somewhere between its center and edge (Fig. 15-48). For what pivot point will the period of this physical pendulum be a minimum?

FIGURE 15-48 Problem 74.

75. A uniform piece of wire is bent into a V-shape with angle θ between two legs of length ℓ. The wire is placed over a pivot, as shown in Fig. 15-49. Show that the angular frequency of small-amplitude oscillations about this equilibrium is given by

$$\omega = \sqrt{\frac{3g\cos(\theta/2)}{2\ell}}.$$

FIGURE 15-49 Problem 75.

76. Integrating the nonconstant acceleration of a harmonic oscillator over time from the time of maximum displacement to the time of zero displacement should give the velocity at zero displacement. Carry out this integration, using Equation 15-11 for the acceleration, and show that your answer is just the maximum velocity.

Wave Motion

Ocean waves carry energy thousands of kilometers before breaking on shore. These waves are produced by wind disturbing the ocean surface. Numerous smaller waves are superposed on the two large wave crests prominent in this photo.

It's a beautiful day at the beach, but the surf is a bit rough as ocean waves bring to shore energy imparted by a distant storm. Astronomers direct the Hubble Space Telescope to capture images of galaxies so distant that the light waves reaching Hubble have been traveling for 12 billion years. Your car breaks down and you use a cellular phone to summon help; your voice is carried on radio waves to the telephone network. A rock band energizes the air with its playing, and that energy is carried as sound waves to the audience's ears. An earthquake sends waves to the far corners of the planet, allowing geologists to pinpoint the quake and to study Earth's interior. Spectators in one section of a football stadium stand up, and soon a wave of standing fans sweeps around the stadium. Physicians probe the human body with ultrasound waves, whose reflections form images of inner structures (Fig. 16-1).

(a)

(b)

(c)

FIGURE 16-1 (a) Twin fetuses are evident in this image, produced by ultrasound waves reflecting in the human body. (b) This building in Kobe, Japan, was destroyed in the 1995 earthquake. Energy released in a quake propagates as a wave, shaking the ground as it passes. (c) Invisible electromagnetic waves carry cellular phone messages.

All of these examples involve **wave motion**. They have in common the motion—or **propagation**—of energy from one place to another. Matter, however, does not travel anywhere: those waves crashing on the beach don't carry water from the distant open ocean where the storm raged. Air does not travel from the rock band's loudspeakers to your ears. Spectators don't run around the football stadium. And though geologists across the planet know about the earthquake, no earth actually moves from the quake zone to distant seismographs. Our definition of a **wave** emphasizes this point:

▎ *A wave is a traveling disturbance that transports energy but not matter.*

16-1 KINDS OF WAVES

You're familiar with many kinds of waves. Sound waves carry energy and information through the air; sound also propagates in solids and liquids. Water waves are obvious on the surface of lakes and seas; earthquake waves propagate invisibly through Earth's solid and liquid interior. The vibrating strings of violins and pianos involve waves propagating back and forth along the strings. All these are examples of **mechanical waves**, so called because each involves disturbances of a mechanical medium such as air, water, solid Earth, or a stretched string.

Other common waves include the light waves by which you see, radio waves that carry radio and TV signals, microwaves that cook your food, X rays that image your body's innards, and ultraviolet waves that can burn your skin. All these are examples of **electromagnetic waves**. These waves have many properties in common with mechanical waves, including the same basic mathematical description. However, electromagnetic waves don't involve a mechanical medium. Less familiar are waves used in the quantum mechanical description of the physical world at the atomic scale. These so-called matter waves govern the behavior of particles such as electrons and protons.

We explore wave motion in this chapter and the next, concentrating primarily on mechanical waves. Many of the phenomena and mathematical techniques we develop here will apply also to electromagnetic waves, which we study in Chapters 34–38, and to matter waves, introduced in Chapter 39 and explored further in the extended version of this text.

Mechanical Waves

What does wave motion have to do with what we've studied in earlier chapters? For mechanical waves, the answer is quite a lot. Because such waves involve disturbance of a mechanical system, they're ultimately governed by the interplay between force and mass described by Newton's laws.

Both the physics and the mathematics of wave motion have much in common with oscillatory motion that we studied in the preceding chapter. The interactions among particles that make up bulk matter can often be modeled by considering the particles to be masses coupled by springs that represent the forces acting between them. A disturbance from equilibrium in one region of the material sets up an oscillation that is then coupled to other regions. The result

(a)

(b)

(c)

FIGURE 16-2 A long, narrow structure such as a stretched string or a rod can be modeled as a line of blocks connected by springs. (*a*) A disturbance from equilibrium sets the highlighted block at left oscillating, compressing and stretching the adjacent springs. (*b–c*) Because the blocks are coupled, the disturbance propagates to other regions of the medium, moving ever farther from its starting point as time advances. The propagating disturbance is a wave pulse.

is a propagating wave, carrying the disturbance throughout the material. Figure 16-2 illustrates this process.

The mass-spring model of Fig. 16-2 will help you understand wave motion by building on your knowledge of oscillatory motion. Those who go on to more advanced work in physics, engineering, or materials science will find many other examples—from semiconductor crystals to skyscrapers—where structures are effectively modeled as coupled mass-spring systems.

Tip

What Do You Mean, A Wave Doesn't Transport Matter? Our definition of a wave emphasizes the transport of energy but not matter. But in Fig. 16-2 it sure looks like the individual blocks move. They *do* move, temporarily, executing small oscillations about their equilibrium positions, as the wave goes by. But they aren't transported from place to place. That's the important distinction. A mechanical wave is a disturbance of a medium, and while the wave is passing the particles making up the medium do move. But they only oscillate; they don't undergo a bulk displacement from one place to another. In contrast, the wave energy—manifested in the oscillations of the individual blocks shown in Fig. 16-2—does move from place to place (see Fig. 16-3).

FIGURE 16-3 Waves on the open ocean disturb the boat, but it doesn't participate in their shoreward motion. Neither does the water itself, although water does move about locally as the wave passes (see Fig. 16-5).

16-2 WAVE PROPERTIES

Here we describe the physical properties that characterize different waves. You can visualize these properties and gain much more insight into wave motion through the wave animations provided in ActivPhysics Activity 10.1.

10.1
Properties of Mechanical Waves

(a)

(b)

FIGURE 16-4 Waves on a stretched spring, like a Slinky. (a) Compressing a section of the spring produces a longitudinal wave pulse. (b) Displacing the spring perpendicular to its length produces a transverse wave pulse.

Amplitude

A wave disturbs a medium from its equilibrium state. The maximum value of the disturbance is the wave **amplitude**; this is the same as the definition of amplitude we gave in Chapter 15 for oscillatory motion. Amplitude measures whatever physical property is affected by the wave—the height of a water wave from the undisturbed water surface, the excess pressure of a sound wave, the extra tension or compression forces in the springs of Figs. 16-2 and 16-4, or the maximum displacement of a violin string from equilibrium.

Longitudinal and Transverse Waves

Figure 16-4 shows a section of a stretched spring (a Slinky is a good example). Imagine compressing part of the spring and then releasing it. The compression moves along the spring, constituting a traveling wave pulse (Fig. 16-4a). As the pulse passes along the spring, coils of the spring move slightly back and forth to bunch up and then relax again to their equilibrium positions. A wave such as this one, in which the medium moves back and forth along the same line on which the wave is propagating, is called a **longitudinal wave**. Another example of a longitudinal wave is sound, in which air molecules oscillate back and forth in the direction of the sound's propagation. We'll study sound waves in the next chapter.

Figure 16-4b shows another way to set up a wave on the stretched spring. Disturbing the spring at right angles to its long dimension and then releasing it sends a pulse down the spring. As the pulse passes, a section of the spring moves back and forth at right angles to the spring's long dimension, taking on the pulse shape and then relaxing back to equilibrium. A wave such as this, where the medium moves back and forth at right angles to the wave motion, is called a **transverse wave**. Examples of transverse mechanical waves include some types of earthquake waves and waves on musical instrument strings. Electromagnetic waves in vacuum are also transverse, but since there's no medium involved it won't be fully clear until Chapter 34 just what that means.

Unlike solids, liquids and gases (collectively called fluids) do not develop restoring forces in response to so-called shearing motions that displace one layer of fluid sideways relative to another. As a result, liquids and gases cannot support fully transverse waves confined entirely within the bulk material of the fluid. In contrast, fluids can support longitudinal waves because they develop restoring forces in response to compression.

Things get more complicated at the interface between two fluids, for example, water and air, or even the warm and cool layers in lakes. At such interfaces waves can exist with both longitudinal and transverse components. The familiar waves on the surface of water provide an example (Fig. 16-5).

FIGURE 16-5 A water wave has both longitudinal and transverse components, as parcels of water describe nearly circular paths around their equilibrium positions.

Wave motion

Waveforms

Wave disturbances come in many shapes, called **waveforms** (Fig. 16-6). An isolated disturbance, traveling through an otherwise undisturbed medium, is a **pulse**. A pulse occurs when a medium is disturbed only briefly, as in Fig. 16-4. At the opposite extreme is a **continuous wave**, produced when a medium is disturbed in a regular, periodic way. A **wave train** results from the more realistic case when a periodic disturbance lasts for a finite time.

Wavelength and Period

A continuous wave repeats itself in both space and time. The **wavelength** λ is the *distance* over which the wave pattern repeats, as measured at a *fixed time* (Fig. 16-7). The wave **period** T is the *time* for one complete wave cycle to pass a *fixed position*. The **frequency** f, or number of wave cycles passing a given point per unit time, is the inverse of the period.

Wave Speed

A wave travels at a characteristic speed through its medium. Under typical conditions, the speed of sound in air is 340 m/s. Small ripples on the surface of a pond move at about 20 cm/s, while earthquake waves move through Earth's outer crust at about 6 km/s. The physical properties of the medium, in connection with Newton's laws, ultimately determine wave speed. In Section 16-4 we'll see how this works for one simple yet important case.

Wave speed, wavelength, and period are related. In one wave period, a fixed observer sees one complete wavelength go by (Fig. 16-8). Thus, the wave moves one wavelength in one period, so its speed is

$$v = \frac{\lambda}{T} = \lambda f, \tag{16-1}$$

where the second equality follows because the period and frequency are inverses.

16-3 MATHEMATICAL DESCRIPTION OF WAVE MOTION

Figure 16-9 shows a "snapshot" of a wave pulse at time $t = 0$. The pulse is moving to the right with speed v, and at $t = 0$ its peak coincides with $x = 0$. We can describe the pulse by giving the displacement y as a function of position x: $y = f(x)$, where the peak of the function f occurs where its argument is zero.

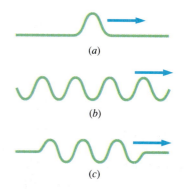

FIGURE 16-6 (*a*) A pulse, (*b*) a continuous wave, and (*c*) a wave train.

FIGURE 16-7 The wavelength λ is the distance over which the wave pattern repeats.

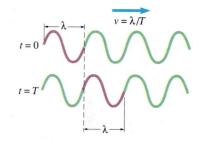

FIGURE 16-8 One full cycle—occupying a distance of one wavelength—passes a given point in one wave period. The wave speed is therefore $v = \lambda/T$.

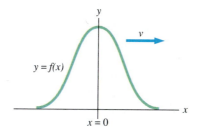

FIGURE 16-9 A "snapshot" of a wave pulse at time $t = 0$. The pulse is moving to the right with speed v.

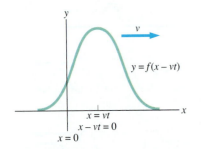

FIGURE 16-10 At a later time t the wave pulse has moved to the right a distance vt. It is described by the same function f, but now with argument $x - vt$.

Figure 16-10 shows the pulse some time t later. Moving at speed v, its peak is now located at $x = vt$. We can describe this displaced pulse by adjusting the function $y = f(x)$ so it peaks at $x = vt$ instead of at $x = 0$. The function f itself peaks where its argument is zero, so if we change the argument to $x - vt$ we will have just what we want: a function whose peak occurs when $x - vt = 0$, or $x = vt$. As time increases, so does vt and, therefore, the value of x that gives the location of the peak. Thus, the function $f(x - vt)$ correctly describes the moving pulse.

Although we considered a single pulse, the same argument applies to *any* function $f(x)$, including continuous waves. Quite generally, a wave moving in the positive x direction is described by some function of the form $f(x - vt)$, with v the wave speed. You can convince yourself that a wave moving in the negative x direction is described similarly by $f(x + vt)$.

A particularly important case is the **simple harmonic wave**, so called because the wave medium executes simple harmonic motion about equilibrium. We want a mathematical description of such a wave, starting first at a fixed time, say $t = 0$. Given such a description—which amounts to an expression for the wave displacement as a function of position x—we'll be able to generalize to all times by replacing x with $x - vt$, as we argued using Figs. 16-9 and 16-10.

A simple harmonic wave must be sinusoidal in shape, so a sine or cosine function will do. We'll choose cosine, an arbitrary choice that assumes the wave has its maximum displacement at $x = 0$. But what, exactly, should be the argument of that cosine function? Our wave has wavelength λ, so the interval from $x = 0$ to $x = \lambda$ should span one wavelength. The cosine function itself goes through a full cycle as its argument goes from 0 to 2π, so we want the argument of our cosine function to be zero at $x = 0$ and 2π when $x = \lambda$. Taking $2\pi x/\lambda$ for the argument of the cosine does this: substitute $x = 0$ and the result is zero; substitute $x = \lambda$ and the result is 2π. So our expression for the wave displacement at time $t = 0$ is

$$y(x, 0) = A\cos\left(\frac{2\pi x}{\lambda}\right),$$

where y is the displacement from equilibrium and A the amplitude (Fig. 16-11a). This expression holds at $t = 0$; to get an expression valid for all times, we replace x by $x \pm vt$:

$$y(x, t) = A\cos\left[\frac{2\pi(x \pm vt)}{\lambda}\right] = A\cos\left(\frac{2\pi x}{\lambda} \pm 2\pi ft\right), \qquad (16\text{-}2)$$

(a)

(b)

FIGURE 16-11 (a) "Snapshot," at time $t = 0$, of the simple harmonic wave described by Equation 16-2. The graph is the wave displacement as a function of position x. (b) The wave displacement at a fixed position, plotted as a function of *time*. The medium oscillates with angular frequency $\omega = 2\pi f = 2\pi/T$. Note the difference between (a) and (b); (a) shows the *spatial* variation at a *fixed time*, while (b) shows the *temporal* variation at a *fixed position*.

where the last step follows using $v/\lambda = f$ from Equation 16-1. Equation 16-2 shows that if we sit at a fixed position—say, $x = 0$—then the displacement varies in time as $y(0, t) = A\cos(2\pi ft)$, which we recognize as simple harmonic motion with **angular frequency** given by

$$\omega = 2\pi f = \frac{2\pi}{T}, \qquad (16\text{-}3)$$

as shown in Fig. 16-11b. Similarly, it is convenient to define the **wave number**, k:

$$k = \frac{2\pi}{\lambda}. \qquad (16\text{-}4)$$

The wave number is the spatial analog of frequency; the latter describes the number of radians of wave cycle per unit *time,* the former the number of radians per unit *distance.* The definition of k shows that its units are m^{-1}. Using ω and k, we can rewrite Equation 16-2:

$$y(x, t) = A\cos(kx \pm \omega t). \qquad (16\text{-}5)$$

The simple way in which k and ω enter this description of the wave is the reason these quantities are so often used. We can use Equation 16-1 with Equations 16-3 and 16-4 to write the wave speed in terms of ω and k:

$$v = \frac{\lambda}{T} = \frac{2\pi/k}{2\pi/\omega} = \frac{\omega}{k}. \qquad (16\text{-}6)$$

Sometimes, especially when we're dealing with multiple waves, we may add a phase constant in the argument of the cosine in Equation 16-5, as we described in the Math Toolbox "Phase, Phase Constant, Phase Difference" in Chapter 15.

EXAMPLE 16-1	*Surf's Up!*

A surfing physicist paddles out beyond the breaking surf to a deep-water region where the ocean waves are sinusoidal in shape, with crests 14 m apart. The surfer rises a vertical distance 3.6 m from wave trough to crest, a process that takes 1.5 s. Find the wave speed, and describe it with an equation of the same form as Equation 16-5. Take a wave crest to be at $x = 0$ at time $t = 0$, with the positive x direction toward the open ocean.

Solution

Figure 16-11*b* shows that the time from trough to crest is half a period, so $T = 3.0$ s. Then Equation 16-1 gives

$$v = \frac{\lambda}{T} = \frac{14 \text{ m}}{3.0 \text{ s}} = 4.67 \text{ m/s}.$$

To use the form of Equation 16-5 we need the amplitude A, wave number k, and angular frequency ω. Figure 16-11 shows that the amplitude is half the trough-to-crest displacement, or 1.8 m, while Equations 16-3 and 16-4 give ω and k:

$$\omega = \frac{2\pi}{T} = \frac{2\pi}{3.0 \text{ s}} = 2.09 \text{ s}^{-1}, \; k = \frac{2\pi}{\lambda} = \frac{2\pi}{14 \text{ m}} = 0.449 \text{ m}^{-1}.$$

With the wave propagating in the $-x$ direction—toward shore—we take the plus sign in Equation 16-5, so the wave description is

$$y(x, t) = 1.8\cos(0.449x + 2.09t) \text{ m}.$$

EXERCISE The temporal and spatial variation of the waves in a microwave oven are described by $\cos(50.3x - 15.1t)$, with t in nanoseconds and x in meters. Find (a) the wave frequency in hertz, (b) the wavelength, and (c) the wave speed.

Answers: (a) 2.4 GHz; (b) 12.5 cm; (c) 3.00×10^8 m/s

Some problems similar to Example 16-1: 10, 13, 14

16-4 WAVES ON A STRING

A Stretched String

What determines how fast waves propagate in a mechanical medium? The answer lies in Newton's laws and the physical properties of the medium. Calculating the speed and other characteristics of waves in different materials is a significant job for professional physicists and materials scientists. Only in the simplest cases can mathematical analysis at our level yield the wave speed. One

FIGURE 16-12 A pulse on a Slinky is an example of a transverse wave on an elongated structure. The pulse was produced by pulling the Slinky vertically at one point, then releasing.

such case is that of transverse waves on a stretched string, which we're now going to look at in detail. Our results are directly applicable to musical instrument strings, suspension bridge cables, and many other elongated structures (Fig. 16-12).

Our string has mass per unit length μ in kilograms per meter, and is stretched to a tension force F in newtons. In equilibrium, the string lies along the x axis. Suppose we distort a section of it slightly by displacing it in the y direction. We want to show that wave motion results when the string is released and to determine the wave speed.

To find the speed, we need to apply Newton's law to the motion of the string. Figure 16-13a shows the wave pulse moving to the right with some speed v. It's easiest to apply Newton's law in a frame of reference moving with the uniform velocity of the pulse; in that frame the entire string is moving to the *left* at speed v. As a section of the string encounters the pulse, which is stationary in this frame of reference, its motion deviates from a straight line as it rides up over the pulse (Fig. 16-13b).

Whatever the pulse shape, we can describe a small enough section at the top as a circular arc of some radius R, as shown in Fig. 16-13c. Then a small section of string right at the top of the pulse undergoes circular motion with speed v and radius R; if its mass is m, Newton's law requires that a force of magnitude mv^2/R act toward the center of curvature in order to keep the string section on its circular path. This force is provided by the difference in string tension between the two ends of the section; as Fig. 16-13c shows, the section's curvature means the tension vectors at the two ends point in different directions. The tension at each end contributes a component $F \sin\theta$ toward the center of curvature, where θ is shown in Fig. 16-13c. Then the net force on the segment has magnitude $2F \sin\theta$ and points toward the center of curvature.

Now we make an additional assumption: that the disturbance of the string is small, in the sense that the string remains almost horizontal even at the pulse. Then the angle θ is small, and we can apply the approximation $\sin\theta \simeq \theta$. Therefore the net force on the string section becomes approximately $2F\theta$. Furthermore, the small-disturbance approximation means that the tension doesn't vary significantly from its undisturbed value, so the F in this expression is essentially the same F we're using to characterize the tension throughout the string. Finally, our curved string section forms a circular arc whose length, from Fig. 16-13c, is $2\theta R$. Multiplying by the mass per unit length μ gives its mass:

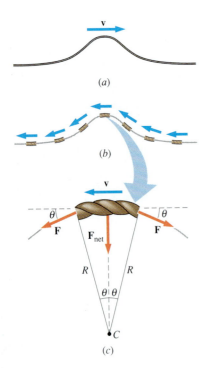

(a)

(b)

(c)

FIGURE 16-13 (a) A pulse moving to the right with speed v on a stretched string. (b) In the reference frame of the moving pulse, the string moves to the left. Individual segments of the string follow curved paths as they move through the pulse. (c) A blow-up of a small string segment at the top of the pulse. The net force on the segment is the vector sum of the tension forces **F** at the two ends; this force keeps the string segment in its path through the curved pulse. The angle θ is exaggerated; it is actually so small that $\sin\theta \simeq \theta$, making $F_{net} \simeq 2F\theta$. The quantity R is the curvature radius at the top of the pulse.

Remember that the analysis of (c) is done in a reference frame with the pulse at rest; in that frame, the string really does undergo circular motion at the top of the pulse. But in a reference frame in which the undisturbed string is at rest, the only motion is the back-and-forth motion of the string in the y direction (perpendicular to the string) as the pulse goes by.

$m = 2\theta R\mu$. Now we can apply Newton's law, equating the net force $2F\theta$ to the mass times acceleration:

$$2F\theta = \frac{mv^2}{R} = \frac{2\theta R\mu v^2}{R} = 2\theta\mu v^2.$$

Solving for the wave speed v then gives

$$v = \sqrt{\frac{F}{\mu}}. \qquad (16\text{-}7)$$

10.2
Speed of Waves on a String

Does this result make sense? The string tension provides the restoring force that drives the disturbed part of the string toward equilibrium. The greater the tension F, the greater the acceleration of the disturbed string, and thus the more rapidly the wave should propagate. The string's inertia, on the other hand, limits the acceleration with which the string responds to the force, and therefore a greater mass per unit length should slow the wave propagation. Equation 16-7, with F in the numerator and μ in the denominator, reflects both these trends.

We have made no assumption about wave shape other than to assume that the disturbance is small; therefore Equation 16-7 applies to small-amplitude pulses, continuous waves, and wave trains of any shape. In Section 16-6 we will derive Equation 16-7 using a more advanced analysis that gives a general equation shared by many systems that support propagating waves and will show explicitly that simple harmonic waves are among its solutions.

EXAMPLE 16-2	*Rock Climbing*

Two climbers are joined by a 43-m-long rope of total mass 5.0 kg. One climber strikes the rope with a fist, and 1.4 s later the second climber feels the effect. What is the rope tension?

Solution

Solving Equation 16-7 for the tension gives $F = \mu v^2$. Here $\mu = m/L$ and $v = L/t$, with L and m the rope length and mass and t the time interval. So we have

$$F = \mu v^2 = \left(\frac{m}{L}\right)\left(\frac{L}{t}\right)^2 = \frac{mL}{t^2} = \frac{(5.0\ \text{kg})(43\ \text{m})}{(1.4\ \text{s})^2} = 110\ \text{N}.$$

Is this number reasonable? A typical adult weighs between 500 and 1000 N, so the rope is supporting only a small fraction of the lower climber's weight—a reasonable situation.

EXERCISE A 4.5-g piano wire is under 680 N tension. If waves propagate along it at 320 m/s, what is its length?

Answer: 68 cm

Some problems similar to Example 16-2: 21, 24, 27, 29

16-5 WAVE POWER AND INTENSITY

A wave propagates because part of a medium communicates its motion to adjacent parts. In the process, energy passes through the medium. As always in mechanics, that energy is transferred by forces that do work.

In the case of a stretched string, it is the tension force that does work on the string, and this work results in energy transfer along the string in the direction of the wave propagation. As we showed in Section 7-7, power—the rate of

FIGURE 16-14 The force acting on the left end of the string is the tension force **F**. But since the string is moving downward, only the vertical component $F_y = F \sin \theta$ does any work. For small angles, $\sin \theta \simeq \theta \simeq \tan \theta$, and $\tan \theta$ is the slope—that is, the derivative dy/dx—of the string evaluated at the end of the segment.

FIGURE 16-15 The speed u of the disturbed string is not the same as the wave speed v! The pulse moves in the x direction, from left to right along the string, while a section of the string moves back and forth in the y direction, perpendicular to the wave propagation, as the pulse passes by. Both the directions and the magnitudes of the two velocities **u** and **v** are different.

doing work—is the dot product of the force with the velocity. Figure 16-14 shows the section of string we considered earlier, now in the reference frame of the string. In that frame the left end of the displaced segment is moving downward as the pulse passes to the right, and, as we found earlier, the vertical component of the tension force on the left end alone is very nearly $-F\theta$, with the minus sign indicating the downward direction. Then the rate at which work is done by this force is

$$P = F_y u = -F\theta u,$$

where u is the vertical speed of the string segment.

Tip

The Medium Is Not the Wave The speed u is the speed at which the disturbed medium moves and is *not* the same as the wave speed v. For this transverse wave, the string motion is in fact at right angles to the wave propagation. Figure 16-15 emphasizes this distinction.

This expression for power holds for any wave shape; we now specialize to the case of a simple harmonic wave, described by Equation 16-5. The velocity u at which the string moves vertically is simply the derivative of the string displacement $y(x, t) = A \cos(kx - \omega t)$ with respect to time:

$$u = \frac{\partial y}{\partial t} = \omega A \sin(kx - \omega t),$$

where we used the chain rule for differentiation, differentiating cosine to get $-$sine, then multiplying by the derivative, $-\omega$, of the cosine's argument $kx - \omega t$. As Fig. 16-14 shows, the tangent of the angle θ is the slope, $\partial y/\partial x$, at the left end of the segment. In the small angle approximation, $\theta \simeq \tan \theta$. Then we have

$$\theta \simeq \frac{\partial y}{\partial x} = -kA \sin(kx - \omega t).$$

The minus sign shows that θ is *positive*—as in Fig. 16-14—when $\sin(kx - \omega t)$ is *negative*. Thus, the force is downward when the velocity **u** is downward, indicating that the tension force does work on the string segment.

Math Toolbox

Partial Derivatives Equation 16-5 gives the displacement in a simple harmonic wave as a function of *both position and time*. Figure 16-14 is a "snapshot" of the string *at an instant in time*. Therefore, the derivative is to be taken *with time fixed*. This qualification is important because the string displacement is a function of both x and t and changes if *either* of these variables changes. With functions of more than one variable, we use the symbol ∂ instead of the usual d to indicate a rate of change with respect to one variable while other variables are held fixed. Such derivatives, like $\partial y/\partial t$ and $\partial y/\partial x$, are called **partial derivatives**.

The rules for partial derivatives are exactly the same as for ordinary derivatives; you just treat as constants all variables other than the one with respect to which you're taking the derivative. Thus, in computing the string's velocity $u = \partial y/\partial t$, we treat x as a constant.

Using our expressions for u and θ, we can then write the power transmitted along the wave as

$$P = -F\theta u = F\omega kA^2 \sin^2(kx - \omega t).$$

The term $\sin^2(kx - \omega t)$ shows that the power fluctuates throughout the wave cycle. We're usually more interested in the *average* power, which we get by noting that the average value of $\sin^2$ is $\frac{1}{2}$ (see Fig. 16-16). Then the average power is simply

$$\bar{P} = \tfrac{1}{2}F\omega kA^2.$$

We can give this expression more physical meaning if we use Equations 16-6 and 16-7 to write $k = \omega/v$ and $F = \mu v^2$, where v is the wave speed. Then we have

$$\bar{P} = \tfrac{1}{2}\mu\omega^2 A^2 v. \tag{16-8}$$

This equation makes sense since it shows that the power—the rate at which energy moves along the wave—is directly proportional to the wave speed v.

Although we derived Equation 16-8 for waves on a string, some aspects of the equation are common to all waves. In particular, wave power is always proportional to the wave speed and to the *square* of the wave amplitude.

FIGURE 16-16 The function $\sin^2 x$ swings symmetrically between 0 and 1, so its average value is $\frac{1}{2}$.

EXAMPLE 16-3	*Wave Power*

A garden hose with 440 g of mass per meter of length is lying on the ground. You pull on the hose, producing 12 N of tension, then shake it from side to side to make waves (Fig. 16-17). At what average rate must you do work if you displace the hose 25 cm either side of its equilibrium position, completing two full back-and-forth cycles every second? What will be the distance between wave crests?

Solution

The work you do is transmitted along the hose as the energy of the wave, so you do work at the rate given by Equation 16-8. To use this equation we need the wave speed v and angular frequency ω. The former is given by Equation 16-7:

$$v = \sqrt{\frac{F}{\mu}} = \sqrt{\frac{12\ \text{N}}{0.44\ \text{kg/m}}} = 5.22\ \text{m/s},$$

while the angular frequency is $\omega = 2\pi f = (2\pi)(2.0\ \text{Hz}) = 12.6\ \text{s}^{-1}$. Then the average power is

$$\bar{P} = \tfrac{1}{2}\mu\omega^2 A^2 v$$
$$= \tfrac{1}{2}(0.44\ \text{kg/m})(12.6\ \text{s}^{-1})^2(0.25\ \text{m})^2(5.22\ \text{m/s})$$
$$= 11\ \text{W}.$$

This answer neglects any work done against friction between hose and ground.

Finally, Equation 16-1 gives the wavelength—the distance between wave crests:

FIGURE 16-17 How much power does it take to send waves along the hose?

$$\lambda = \frac{v}{f} = \frac{5.22\ \text{m/s}}{2.0\ \text{Hz}} = 2.6\ \text{m}.$$

EXERCISE A suspension bridge cable has 3800 kg/m and is under 230 MN tension. What power is required to send a 15-Hz wave with amplitude 5.0 mm along this cable?

Answer: 100 kW

Some problems similar to Example 16-3: 33–35, 38

FIGURE 16-18 (a) A plane wave does not spread, so its intensity remains constant. (b) As a spherical wave spreads from a point source, its intensity decreases as the inverse square of the distance from the source.

Wave Intensity

The total power is useful in describing a wave confined to a narrow structure like a string for mechanical waves or a cable or optical fiber for electromagnetic waves. But when waves travel throughout a three-dimensional medium, like sound waves spreading out in air, it makes more sense to talk about the rate at which the wave carries energy across a unit area. This quantity defines the wave **intensity**:

> The intensity of a wave is the average rate at which the wave carries energy per unit area across a surface perpendicular to the wave propagation.

Since the rate of energy flow is power, the intensity is just the power per unit area carried by the wave; its units are W/m^2.

A **wavefront** is a surface over which the wave has constant phase. (Recall from Chapter 15 that *phase* means the argument of the function describing oscillatory motion; here we generalize to the argument of the function describing a wave. In the simple cases we've been dealing with, the wave phase is the quantity $x \pm vt$.) An example of a wavefront is a contiguous surface containing all points where the wave displacement is at its peak value. A **plane wave** is one whose wavefronts are planes. Since the wave energy doesn't spread out as the wave propagates, the intensity remains constant (Fig. 16-18a). But with waves from a localized source, the wave energy spreads over ever greater areas, and therefore the intensity decreases. **Spherical waves** originate from pointlike sources and their spherical wavefronts spread in all directions; since the area increases as the square of the distance from the source, the intensity decreases as the inverse square of the distance (Fig. 16-18b). If P is the total power emitted by the source, then the intensity at a distance r is given by

$$I = \frac{P}{A} = \frac{P}{4\pi r^2}, \quad \text{(spherical wave)} \tag{16-9}$$

since the area of a sphere is $4\pi r^2$. It isn't that wave energy is being lost; rather, the same energy is spread over ever greater areas as the waves propagate outward. Examples of spherical waves include light spreading out from a single light bulb, radio waves spreading from a small antenna, or sound from a localized source such as a single loudspeaker. In general, waves spreading out from a source are to a good approximation spherical at distances large compared to the source size.

Table 16-1 lists the intensities of various waves. For those entries whose sources are small compared with the distance listed, you can find the intensities at other distances using the inverse-square relation (see Problems 39–45).

TABLE 16-1 *Wave Intensities*

WAVE	INTENSITY, W/m^2
Sound, 4 m from loud rock band	1
Sound, jet aircraft at 50 m	10
Sound, whisper at 1 m	10^{-10}
Light, sunlight at Earth's orbit	1368
Light, sunlight at Jupiter's orbit	50
Light, 1 m from typical camera flash	4000
Light, at target of laser fusion experiment	10^{18}
TV signal, 5 km from 50 kW transmitter	1.6×10^{-4}
Microwaves, inside microwave oven	6000
Earthquake wave, 5 km from Richter 7.0 quake	4×10^4

EXAMPLE 16-4	*Reading Light*

The page of your book is 1.9 m from a 75-W light bulb, and the light is just barely adequate for reading. How far from a 40-W bulb would the page have to be to get the same light intensity? Treat the bulbs as sources of spherical light waves.

Solution

Equation 16-9 gives the intensity of a spherical wave in terms of the source power and distance. We want the same intensity from both bulbs; equating the intensities as given by Equation 16-9, we have

$$\frac{P_{75}}{4\pi r_{75}^2} = \frac{P_{40}}{4\pi r_{40}^2}$$

Solving for the unknown distance r_{40} then gives

$$r_{40} = r_{75}\sqrt{\frac{P_{40}}{P_{75}}} = (1.9 \text{ m})\sqrt{\frac{40 \text{ W}}{75 \text{ W}}} = 1.4 \text{ m}.$$

Although the 40-W bulb has only about half the power output, the decrease in distance is not as great because the intensity depends on the inverse *square* of the distance.

EXERCISE Use the entry in Table 16-1 for sunlight at Earth's orbit, along with Earth's distance from the Sun, to calculate the total power emitted by the Sun.

Answer: 3.9×10^{26} W

Some problems similar to Example 16-4: 39–41, 59

16-6 THE SUPERPOSITION PRINCIPLE AND WAVE INTERFERENCE

What happens if we launch two wave trains from opposite ends of a stretched string? Where they meet, experiment shows that the displacement of the string is just the sum of the displacements of the two wave trains (Fig. 16-19). It's also possible to prove this mathematically, under the small-amplitude approximation that led to Equation 16-7; we'll see this in the next section. The combining of two waves to form a composite wave is called **interference**. The interference is **constructive** if the waves reinforce each other (Fig. 16-19b) and **destructive** if they tend to cancel (Fig. 16-19c).

In most cases the displacement of a composite wave is the algebraic sum of the displacements of two or more interfering waves. This is generally true for waves whose amplitude is not too large, including most sound waves, and it's always true for light waves, at least in vacuum. Waves whose displacements simply add are said to obey the **superposition principle**.

Suppose we have two such waves, each described by Equation 16-5. Each could have a different frequency ω, wave number k, amplitude A, and propagation direction. Their relative phases might be different, so each might need a phase constant in Equation 16-5. If the two waves are given by

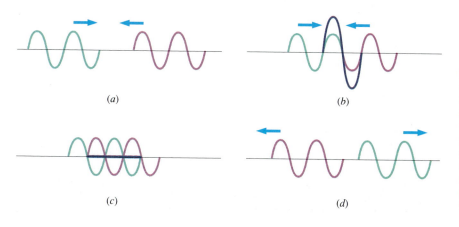

(a)   (b)

(c)   (d)

FIGURE 16-19 (a) Sinusoidal wave trains propagating in opposite directions. (b) As their crests overlap, they interfere constructively, producing the darker waveform; at this instant the two waves are said to be in phase. (c) A quarter cycle later, they are 180° or π radians out of phase and interfere destructively; the result is zero displacement (dark line). (d) The wave trains continue on their way, unaffected by their encounter.

$y_1(x, t) = A_1 \cos(k_1 x \pm \omega_1 t + \phi_1)$ and $y_2(x, t) = A_2 \cos(k_2 x \pm \omega_2 t + \phi_2)$, then their superposition is just

$$y(x, t) = A_1 \cos(k_1 x \pm \omega_1 t + \phi_1) + A_2 \cos(k_2 x \pm \omega_2 t + \phi_2). \quad (16\text{-}10)$$

That is, Equation 16-10 gives the displacement y at any position x and time t in the presence of the two waves whose displacements are $y_1(x, t)$ and $y_2(x, t)$.

Waves that do not obey the superposition principle include large-amplitude waves such as the sound waves from a thunderclap or explosion, the tidal bores that race up rivers in regions of high tides, and waves in complicated media. Mathematical analysis of these so-called nonlinear waves is quite difficult.

Wave interference and superposition occur throughout physics, from mechanical waves to light and sound, and even in the quantum-mechanical waves that govern behavior in the atomic and subatomic realms. Here and in the next chapter we present some interference phenomena, and we will consider the interference of light waves in much greater detail in Chapter 37.

Analysis of Complex Waves: Fourier Analysis

The superposition principle allows us to build complex wave shapes by superposing simpler ones—in particular, simple harmonic waves. Analysis of a complex wave in terms of its so-called harmonic components is termed **Fourier analysis**, after the French mathematician Jean Baptiste Joseph Fourier (1768–1830). Fourier showed that *any* periodic wave can be decomposed into a sum of simple harmonic terms. Figure 16-20 shows how a square wave—important, for example, as the waveform of the "clock" signal that determines the speed of your computer—can be represented as a superposition of individual sine waves. For this waveform the component sine waves have frequencies that are odd integer multiples of a fundamental frequency (e.g., the clock rate in your computer, for example: 350 MHz), and the higher frequencies decrease in amplitude as the inverse of the frequency. Mathematically, the time dependence of the square wave (e.g., its displacement at a fixed position, say $x = 0$) is given by

$$y(t) = A \sin(\omega t) + \tfrac{1}{3} A \sin(3\omega t) + \tfrac{1}{5} A \sin(5\omega t) + \ldots.$$

You can explore Fourier analysis for this and other examples with ActivPhysics Activity 10.10. Fourier analysis has many applications, ranging from music to structural engineering and communications because it helps us understand how a complex wave behaves if we know how its simple harmonic components behave. For example, the Fourier components of a complex sound waveform from a musical instrument determine the exact sound we hear (Fig. 16-21). Two different instruments playing the same note produce two different sets of Fourier components, so they sound different.

Dispersion

When wave speed is independent of wavelength, then the simple harmonic components making up a complex waveform travel at the same speed. As a

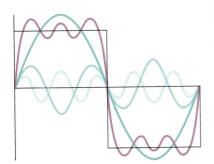

FIGURE 16-20 A square wave built up as a sum of simple harmonic waves, with frequencies in the ratio $1:3:5:\ldots$ and amplitudes in the ratio $1:\tfrac{1}{3}:\tfrac{1}{5}:\ldots$. Shown are the square wave (black), its first three harmonic components (green), and their sum (purple).

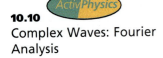

10.10
Complex Waves: Fourier Analysis

Time

(a)

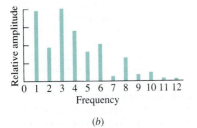

Frequency

(b)

FIGURE 16-21 An electric guitar plays the note E, producing a complex waveform of which two cycles are shown in (a) as a plot of sound wave pressure variation versus time. (b) Fourier analysis shows the relative strengths of individual sine waves whose sum forms the complex waveform. Numbers on the horizontal axis are multiples of the fundamental frequency, and the height of each bar measures the amplitude of that frequency component. To reproduce the waveform faithfully, an audio system must be capable of reproducing not only the fundamental frequency but also the higher frequencies of the harmonic components.

result, the waveform maintains its shape. But for some media, wave speed depends on wavelength. Then, individual harmonic waves travel at different speeds, and a complex waveform changes shape as it moves. This phenomenon is called **dispersion**, and is illustrated in Fig. 16-22. Waves on the surface of deep water, for example, have speed given by

$$v = \sqrt{\frac{\lambda g}{2\pi}}, \tag{16-11}$$

where λ is the wavelength and g the acceleration of gravity. Because v depends on λ, the waves are dispersive. Long-wavelength waves from a storm at sea have the highest speeds and therefore reach shore well in advance of both the storm and the shorter wavelength waves. Dispersion is also important in communications systems; for example, dispersion of the square wave pulses carrying digital data sets the maximum lengths for wires and optical fibers used in computer networks.

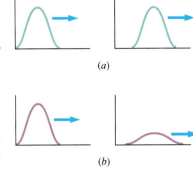

FIGURE 16-22 (*a*) A wave pulse in a nondispersive medium holds its shape as it propagates. (*b*) In a dispersive medium, the pulse changes shape as it propagates.

Beats

In Fig. 16-19 we saw the superposition of two waves of the same frequency and amplitude. When they were in phase, they interfered everywhere constructively; when they were 180° out of phase, the interference was everywhere destructive. But what if two waves with slightly different frequencies interfere? Then their interference is constructive at some points and destructive at others, resulting in a waveform whose amplitude itself varies (Fig. 16-23). We can analyze this phenomenon by writing the composite waveform as the sum of two equal-amplitude waves of slightly different frequencies, according to Equation 16-10. If we consider just the time variation at the fixed position $x = 0$, then this sum is

$$y(t) = A \cos \omega_1 t + A \cos \omega_2 t.$$

We can express this in a more enlightening form using the trigonometric identity $\cos \alpha + \cos \beta = 2 \cos\left(\frac{\alpha - \beta}{2}\right) \cos\left(\frac{\alpha + \beta}{2}\right)$ given in Appendix A. Then we have

$$y(t) = 2A \cos(\tfrac{1}{2}(\omega_1 - \omega_2)t) \cos(\tfrac{1}{2}(\omega_1 + \omega_2)t).$$

The second cosine factor in this equation represents a sinusoidal oscillation at the average of the two individual frequencies. The first term oscillates at a lower frequency—half the difference of the individual frequencies. If we think of the entire term $2A \cos(\tfrac{1}{2}(\omega_1 - \omega_2)t)$ as the "amplitude" of the higher frequency

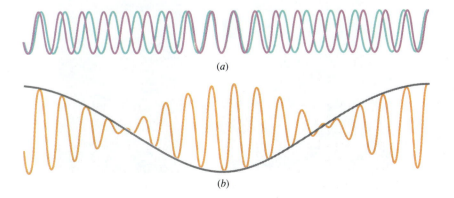

(*a*)

(*b*)

FIGURE 16-23 (*a*) Two waves with slightly different frequencies. Where the two are in phase, they interfere constructively. Where they are out of phase, the interference is destructive. The amplitude of the resulting waveform (*b*) varies with a frequency equal to the difference of the frequencies of the two interfering waves. The gray curve represents the term $2A \cos[\tfrac{1}{2}(\omega_1 - \omega_2)t]$ that describes this amplitude variation.

oscillation, then this amplitude itself varies with time, as Fig. 16-23 shows. Note that there are *two* amplitude peaks for each cycle of the slow oscillation, so the frequency with which the amplitude varies is simply $\omega_1 - \omega_2$.

For sound waves, interference of two nearly equal frequencies results in variations in sound intensity called **beats**; the closer the two frequencies, the longer the period between beats. In twin-engine aircraft, for example, pilots synchronize engine speeds by reducing the beat frequency toward zero. Beating of electromagnetic waves forms the basis for some very sensitive measurements; modern optical techniques, for example, allow us to detect beat frequencies in the millihertz range arising from the interference of light waves whose frequencies are around 10^{14} Hz.

ActivPhysics Activity 10.7 lets you experiment with beating waves of different frequencies; with ActivPhysics you can also hear actual beats from the interference of sound waves.

Interference in Two Dimensions

Waves propagating in two and three dimensions exhibit a rich variety of interference patterns. Figure 16-24 shows one of the simplest and most important examples—the interference of waves from two point sources oscillating at the same frequency. Points on a line passing perpendicular midway between the sources are equidistant from both sources, and therefore waves arrive at this line in phase. Thus, they interfere constructively, producing a high amplitude on this center line. Some distance away, though, is a set of points on which waves arrive exactly half a period out of phase. They therefore interfere destructively, giving rise to a **nodal line** on which the wave amplitude is very small. Since waves travel half a wavelength in half a period, the nodal line occurs where the distances to the two sources differ by half a wavelength. Additional nodal lines occur where those distances differ by $1\frac{1}{2}$ wavelengths, $2\frac{1}{2}$ wavelengths, and so forth.

Two-source interference also arises when plane waves pass through two small apertures which act as sources of circular or spherical wavefronts (Fig. 16-25a). Such two-slit interference experiments are of considerable importance in optics and in modern physics and are of historical interest because they were first used to demonstrate the wave nature of light (Fig. 16-25b). We will explore optical interference further in Chapter 37.

ActivPhysics
10.7
Beats and Beat Frequency

FIGURE 16-24 Interference of circular water waves from two point sources (at rear) shows clearly the pattern of nodal lines, or regions of low wave amplitude resulting from destructive interference.

FIGURE 16-25 (*a*) Interference pattern produced by passing plane waves through two apertures. Dark curves (purple) are nodal lines, with low wave amplitude; light curves (pink) mark constructive interference giving rise to high amplitude. The situation shown here is just like that of Fig. 16-24 except that now instead of two sources we use a barrier with two slits that turn plane waves into circular waves. (*b*) Interference pattern produced by shining laser light through two narrow slits. Photographic film was placed at the right end of an optical setup analogous to (*a*), thus capturing a pattern of alternating light and dark regions.

(*a*)

(*b*)

EXAMPLE 16-5	*Calm Water*

Ocean waves pass through two small openings in a breakwater. The openings are $d = 20$ m apart, as shown in Fig. 16-26. You're in a small boat on a perpendicular line midway between the two openings, 75 m from the breakwater. You row 33 m parallel to the breakwater and, for the first time, find yourself in relatively calm water. What is the wavelength of the waves?

Solution

Finding calm water means finding a point P where the waves interfere destructively. That means waves from openings A and B arrive at P out of phase by half a cycle—that is, waves from A arrive half a period later than those from B. The first time that happens is when AP is longer than BP by the distance the waves go in half a period—that is, by half a wavelength. Mathematically, $AP - BP = \frac{1}{2}\lambda$. In Fig. 16-26 we've lightly shaded two right triangles whose hypotenuses are the lengths AP and BP. Applying the Pythagorean theorem gives

$$AP = \sqrt{(75 \text{ m})^2 + (43 \text{ m})^2} = 86.5 \text{ m}$$
$$BP = \sqrt{(75 \text{ m})^2 + (23 \text{ m})^2} = 78.4 \text{ m}.$$

Then

$$\lambda = 2(AP - BP) = 2(86.5 \text{ m} - 78.4 \text{ m}) = 16 \text{ m}.$$

EXERCISE On another day waves of a different wavelength impinge on the breakwater in Fig. 16-26. Still 75 m from the breakwater, you now row 38 m from the center line and find yourself in the first region of *maximum* wave amplitude. What is the wavelength on this day?

FIGURE 16-26 Calm water at P implies that paths AP and BP differ by half a wavelength.

Answer: 9.0 m

Some problems similar to Example 16-5: 51, 52, 69, 70

16-7 THE WAVE EQUATION

Our only quantitative analysis of wave propagation in this chapter involved waves on a stretched string, and in that analysis we found only the speed of the waves. We did not explicitly show that wave functions of the form $f(x \pm vt)$ are compatible with Newton's law applied to the string. Here we derive the so-called linear **wave equation** that is satisfied not only by waves on a stretched string but by any other waves that satisfy the superposition principle. The wave equation gives a complete description of the wave motion. We will see the wave equation again in Chapter 34 when we consider electromagnetic waves.

Figure 16-27 again shows our stretched string and the forces at opposite ends of a small segment of the string with mass dm and extending from x to $x + dx$. Under the small-angle approximation, the net force is nearly vertical and Fig. 16-27 shows that its magnitude is

$$dF_y \simeq F\sin\theta_2 - F\sin\theta_1 \simeq F(\tan\theta_1 - \tan\theta_2),$$

where the last step follows because for small angles $\sin\theta \simeq \theta \simeq \tan\theta$. But the tangents are the slopes dy/dx at opposite ends of the string segment, so

$$dF_y = F(\tan\theta_1 - \tan\theta_2) = F\left(\frac{\partial y}{\partial x}\bigg|_{x+dx} - \frac{\partial y}{\partial x}\bigg|_{x}\right).$$

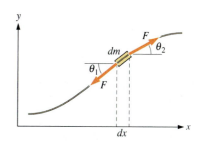

FIGURE 16-27 A portion of the stretched string, showing the forces on a short segment of mass dm. The forces at opposite ends point in slightly different directions, producing a net downward force. The vertical distortion is exaggerated for clarity; actually, the string remains very nearly horizontal.

(See the Math Toolbox on page 400 for the meaning of the symbol ∂.) The term in parentheses is the change in the first derivative over the interval dx; dividing through by dx would give the rate of change of the first derivative—that is, the second derivative $\partial^2 y/\partial x^2$. So we can write

$$dF_y = F\frac{\partial^2 y}{\partial x^2}dx$$

for the net force on the segment. Since the string has mass per unit length μ and is nearly horizontal, the segment's length is essentially dx and therefore its mass is $dm = \mu dx$. Knowing the force, we can then apply Newton's law $F_{net} = ma$ to get

$$F\frac{\partial^2 y}{\partial x^2}dx = \mu\, dx\frac{\partial^2 y}{\partial t^2},$$

where we have written the acceleration as the second time derivative of the displacement. Canceling dx, we can write

$$\frac{\partial^2 y}{\partial x^2} = \frac{\mu}{F}\frac{\partial^2 y}{\partial t^2}.$$

But Equation 16-7 shows that $\mu/F = 1/v^2$, with v the wave speed. So we have

$$\frac{\partial^2 y}{\partial x^2} = \frac{1}{v^2}\frac{\partial^2 y}{\partial t^2}. \tag{16-12}$$

This is the linear **wave equation**. Any time the analysis of a physical system leads to an equation of this form, then that system supports waves propagating with speed v—that is, with speed given by the inverse of the square root of whatever quantity multiplies $\partial^2 y/\partial t^2$. For our string wave that quantity was μ/F, but for another type of wave it would be some other combination of physical quantities (see Problem 53 for one example).

It's a simple matter to show that any harmonic wave of the form $y = A\cos(kx - \omega t)$ satisfies the wave equation. To do so, we twice differentiate this function with respect to x and t:

$$\frac{\partial^2}{\partial x^2}[A\cos(kx - \omega t)] = \frac{\partial}{\partial x}[-kA\sin(kx - \omega t)] = -k^2 A\cos(kx - \omega t)$$

$$\frac{\partial^2}{\partial t^2}[A\cos(kx - \omega t)] = \frac{\partial}{\partial t}[\omega A\sin(kx - \omega t)] = -\omega^2 A\cos(kx - \omega t).$$

Substituting these results in Equation 16-12 gives

$$-k^2 A\cos(kx - \omega t) = \frac{1}{v^2}[-\omega^2 A\cos(kx - \omega t)]$$

or, canceling the cosine term and the minus sign,

$$v^2 = \frac{\omega^2}{k^2}.$$

But we found earlier that $v = \omega/k$ for a harmonic wave, so this equation is an identity. Thus, we've shown by direct substitution that the harmonic wave $A\cos(kx - \omega t)$ satisfies the wave equation 16-12. In Problem 54 you can show that *any* function of the form $f(x \pm vt)$ also satisfies the wave equation. You can also show that the sum of two different solutions to the wave equation is also a solution, thus verifying that waves that satisfy this equation obey the superposition principle.

CHAPTER SYNOPSIS

Summary

1. A **wave** is a propagating disturbance that carries energy but not matter. A wave is **longitudinal** if the disturbance displaces the medium in the direction of propagation, and **transverse** if the displacement is perpendicular to the wave propagation. A wave may have any shape, from a single **pulse** to a **continuous wave**. The peak value of the wave disturbance is the wave **amplitude**.

2. A continuous wave is a periodic disturbance characterized by its **wavelength** λ—the distance between wave crests—and its **period** T—the time between crests measured at a fixed point. A wave travels one wavelength in one period, so its speed is

$$v = \frac{\lambda}{T} = f\lambda,$$

   where $f = 1/T$ is the wave **frequency**.

3. A wave propagating in the x direction is described by a function of the quantity $x \pm vt$. In the special case of a **simple harmonic wave**, that function is sinusoidal and may be written

$$y(x, t) = A\cos(kx \pm \omega t),$$

   where y is the displacement of the medium, A the amplitude, $k = 2\pi/\lambda$ the **wave number**, and $\omega = 2\pi f = 2\pi/T$ the **angular frequency**. The wave speed v is then $v = \lambda/T = \omega/k$.

4. Applying Newton's law for small-amplitude displacements of a stretched string shows that the waves propagate with speed $v = \sqrt{F/\mu}$, where F is the string tension and μ the mass per unit length.

5. Waves carry energy at a rate proportional to the wave speed and to the square of the wave amplitude. For waves propagating in three dimensions, the rate of energy flow is characterized by the **intensity**, or power per unit area through an area at right angles to the wave propagation. For **plane waves** the intensity remains constant as the wave propagates without spreading, but for the more realistic case of spherical waves from a localized source, the waves spread and their intensity drops as the inverse square of the distance from the source.

6. Many waves obey the **superposition principle**, meaning that their wave displacements simply add when the waves overlap or **interfere**. Wave interference is **constructive** if the overall amplitude is enhanced and **destructive** when it is diminished. In two dimensions, wave interference results in patterns including **nodal lines** where the combined wave amplitude is a minimum.

7. Complex waves may be analyzed as sums of simple harmonic waves of different wavelengths. When wave speed is independent of wavelength, a complex wave retains its shape. But if wave speed varies with wavelength, a complex waveform exhibits **dispersion**, changing shape as it propagates.

8. Many waves of sufficiently small amplitude satisfy the linear **wave equation**,

$$\frac{\partial^2 y}{\partial x^2} = \frac{1}{v^2}\frac{\partial^2 y}{\partial t^2},$$

   and those that do then obey the superposition principle.

Terms You Should Understand

(Pairs are closely related terms whose distinction is important; number in parentheses is chapter section where term first appears.)

wave, mechanical wave (16-1)
amplitude (16-2)
longitudinal wave, transverse wave (16-2)
pulse, continuous wave, wave train (16-2)
wavelength, period, frequency (16-2)
simple harmonic wave (16-3)
wave number, angular frequency (16-3)
partial derivative (16-4)
intensity (16-5)
plane wave, spherical wave (16-5)
superposition principle (16-6)
Fourier analysis (16-6)
dispersion (16-6)
interference, constructive and destructive (16-6)
beats (16-6)
nodal line (16-6)
wave equation (16-7)

Symbols You Should Recognize

k, ω (16-3)
$kx \pm \omega t$ (16-3)
μ (16-4)
∂ (16-4)

Problems You Should Be Able to Solve

solving for wavelength, period, or speed from the other two quantities (16-2)

solving for frequency, wavelength, or speed from the other two quantities (16-2)

converting among period, frequency, and angular frequency (16-3)

converting between wavelength and wave number (16-3)

solving for angular frequency, wave number, or speed from the other two quantities (16-3)

writing mathematical expressions for simple harmonic waves (16-3)

solving for speed, tension, or mass per unit length involved with waves on a stretched string, given two of those quantities (16-4)

calculating the wave power propagating on a stretched string (16-5)

calculating the intensity of spherical waves (16-5)

describing quantitatively simple interference situations, including beats and nodal lines in two dimensions (16-6)

Limitations to Keep in Mind

Many of the results developed in this chapter—including the wave speed on stretched strings and the superposition principle—apply only for small-amplitude waves.

QUESTIONS

1. What distinguishes a wave from an oscillation?
2. Red light has a longer wavelength than blue light. Compare their frequencies.
3. Consider a light wave and a sound wave with the same wavelength. Which has the higher frequency?
4. In what sense is "the wave" passing through the crowd at a football game really a wave?
5. A car stops suddenly. The subsequent stopping of cars behind it can be described as a "wave" that propagates back into the traffic. In what sense is this a wave? What are some factors that determine its speed?
6. Must a wave be either transverse or longitudinal? Explain.
7. Does a wave pulse have a period? A frequency? A speed? An amplitude? Explain.
8. Explain in words why the speed of a wave is given by λ/T.
9. As a wave propagates on a stretched string, the string moves back and forth sideways. Is the string speed related to the wave speed? Explain.
10. If you doubled the tension in a string, what would happen to the speed of waves on the string?
11. The wave number k is sometimes called the *spatial frequency*. Why is this name appropriate?
12. A heavy cable is hanging vertically, its bottom end free. How will the speed of transverse waves near the top and bottom of the cable compare? Why?
13. Why won't waves propagate on a string that's not under tension?
14. If you halve the amplitude of your side-to-side shaking of the garden hose in Example 16-3, what would happen to the power you need to supply?
15. As a wave propagates down an ideal, uniform string, does the rate at which it carries energy change?
16. The intensity of waves from a spherical source decreases as

the inverse square of the distance from the source. How does the wave amplitude depend on distance?

17. The intensity of light from a localized source decreases as the inverse square of the distance from the source. Does this mean that the light loses energy as it propagates?
18. The speed of small-amplitude waves on a stretched string is independent of wavelength. Do you expect that the speed of large-amplitude waves should increase or decrease with increasing wavelength? Give a physical reason for your answer.
19. An upward and a downward pulse, otherwise identical in shape, are propagating in opposite directions along a stretched string. At the instant they overlap completely, the displacement of the string is exactly zero everywhere. How does this situation differ from true equilibrium? *Hint:* Where is the wave energy?
20. A lightning flash in Earth's southern hemisphere produces radio waves that give a burst of static in nearby radios. But a radio receiver appropriately located in the northern hemisphere detects a long whistle whose pitch decreases with time. What does this say about the speed of these radio waves as a function of frequency? (Electrical properties of the upper atmosphere cause this phenomenon; in vacuum all radio and other electromagnetic waves travel at the same speed.)
21. Do the nodal lines in Fig. 16-24 move as the waves propagate?
22. Is the wave amplitude on a nodal line exactly zero? Why?
23. The maximum frequency the human ear can detect is about 20 kHz. If you walk into a room in which two sources are emitting sound waves at 100 kHz and 102 kHz, will you hear anything? Explain.

PROBLEMS

ActivPhysics can help with these problems:
Activities 10.1, 10.2, 10.7, 10.10.

Section 16-2 Wave Properties

1. Ocean waves with 18-m wavelength travel at 5.3 m/s. What is the time interval between wave crests passing under a boat moored at a fixed location?

2. Ripples in a shallow puddle are propagating at 34 cm/s. If the wave frequency is 5.2 Hz, what are (a) the period and (b) the wavelength?

3. An 88.7-MHz FM radio wave propagates at the speed of light. What is its wavelength?

4. One end of rope is tied to a wall. You shake the other end with a frequency of 2.2 Hz, producing waves whose wavelength is 1.6 m. What is their propagation speed?

5. A 145-MHz radio signal propagates along a cable. Measurement shows that the wave crests are spaced 1.25 m apart. What is the speed of the waves on the cable? Compare with the speed of light in vacuum.

6. Calculate the wavelengths of (a) a 1.0-MHz AM radio wave, (b) a channel 9 TV signal (190 MHz), (c) a police radar (10 GHz), (d) infrared radiation from a hot stove (4.0×10^{13} Hz), (e) green light (6.0×10^{14} Hz), and (f) 1.0×10^{18} Hz X rays. All are electromagnetic waves that propagate at 3.0×10^8 m/s.

7. Detecting objects by reflecting waves off them is effective only for objects larger than about one wavelength. (a) What is the smallest object that can be seen with visible light (maximum frequency 7.5×10^{14} Hz)? (b) What is the smallest object that can be detected with a medical ultrasound unit operating at 5 MHz? The speed of ultrasound waves in body tissue is about 1500 m/s.

8. A seismograph located 1200 km from an earthquake detects waves from the quake 5.0 min after the quake occurs. The seismograph oscillates in step with the waves, at a frequency of 3.1 Hz. Find the wavelength of the waves.

9. In Fig. 16-28 two boats are anchored offshore and are bobbing up and down on the waves at the rate of six complete cycles each minute. When one boat is up the other is down. If the waves propagate at 2.2 m/s, what is the minimum distance between the boats?

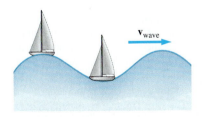

FIGURE 16-28 Problem 9.

Section 16-3 Mathematical Description of Wave Motion

10. Ultrasound used in a particular medical imager has frequency 4.8 MHz and wavelength 0.31 mm. Find (a) the angular frequency, (b) the wave number, and (c) the wave speed.

11. An ocean wave has period 4.1 s and wavelength 10.8 m. Find (a) its wave number and (b) its angular frequency.

12. Find (a) the amplitude, (b) the wavelength, (c) the period, and (d) the speed of a wave whose displacement is given by $y = 1.3 \cos(0.69x + 31t)$, where x and y are in cm and t is in seconds. (e) In which direction is the wave propagating?

13. A simple harmonic wave of wavelength 16 cm and amplitude 2.5 cm is propagating along a string in the negative x direction at 35 cm/s. Find (a) the angular frequency and (b) the wave number. (c) Write a mathematical expression describing the displacement y of this wave (in centimeters) as a function of position and time. Assume the displacement at $x = 0$ is a maximum when $t = 0$.

14. Figure 16-29 shows a simple harmonic wave at time $t = 0$ and later at $t = 2.6$ s. Write a mathematical description of this wave.

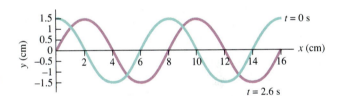

FIGURE 16-29 Problem 14.

15. What are (a) the amplitude, (b) the frequency in hertz, (c) the wavelength, and (d) the speed of a water wave whose displacement is $y = 0.25 \sin(0.52x - 2.3t)$, where x and y are in meters and t in seconds?

16. A sound wave with frequency 256 Hz (the musical note middle C) is propagating in air at 343 m/s. How far apart are two points on the wave that differ in phase by $\frac{\pi}{2}$ or 90°?

17. At time $t = 0$, the displacement in a transverse wave pulse is described by $y = \dfrac{2}{x^4 + 1}$, with both x and y in cm. Write an expression for the pulse as a function of position x and time t if it is propagating in the positive x direction at 3 cm/s.

18. Plot the answer to the previous problem as a function of position x for the two cases $t = 0$ and $t = 4$ s, and verify that your plots are consistent with the pulse speed of 3 cm/s.

19. Figure 16-30a shows a wave plotted as a function of position at time $t = 0$, while Fig. 16-30b shows the same wave plotted as a function of time at position $x = 0$. Find (a) the wavelength, (b) the period, (c) the wave speed, and (d) the direction of propagation.

(a)

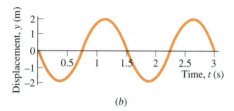

(b)

FIGURE 16-30 Problems 19, 20.

20. Write a mathematical description of the wave in the preceding problem.

Section 16-4 Waves on a String

21. The main cables supporting New York's George Washington Bridge have a mass per unit length of 4100 kg/m and are under tension of 250 MN. At what speed would a transverse wave propagate on these cables?

22. A transverse wave 1.2 cm in amplitude is propagating on a string; the wave frequency is 44 Hz. The string is under 21 N tension and has mass per unit length of 15 g/m. Determine (a) the wave speed and (b) the maximum speed of a point on the string.

23. A transverse wave with 3.0-cm amplitude and 75-cm wavelength is propagating on a stretched spring whose mass per unit length is 170 g/m. If the wave speed is 6.7 m/s, find (a) the spring tension and (b) the maximum speed of any point on the spring.

24. A rope is stretched between supports 12 m apart; its tension is 35 N. If one end of the rope is tweaked, the resulting disturbance reaches the other end 0.45 s later. What is the total mass of the rope?

25. A 3.1-kg mass hangs from a 2.7-m-long string whose total mass is 0.62 g. What is the speed of transverse waves on the string? *Hint:* You can ignore the string mass in calculating the tension but not in calculating the wave speed. Why?

26. Transverse waves propagate at 18 m/s on a string whose tension is 14 N. What will be the wave speed if the tension is increased to 40 N?

27. The density of copper is 8.29 g/cm^3. What is the tension in a 1.0-mm-diameter copper wire that propagates transverse waves at 120 m/s?

28. A 100-m-long wire has a mass of 130 g. A sample of the wire is tested and found to break at a tension of 150 N. What is the maximum propagation speed for transverse waves on this wire?

29. A 25-m-long piece of 1.0-mm-diameter wire is put under 85 N tension. If a transverse wave takes 0.21 s to travel the length of the wire, what is the density of the material comprising the wire?

30. A mass m_1 is attached to a wire of linear density 5.6 g/m, and the other end of the wire run over a pulley and tied to a wall as shown in Fig. 16-31. The speed of transverse waves on the horizontal section of wire is observed to be 20 m/s. If a second mass m_2 is added to the first, the wave speed increases to 45 m/s. Find the second mass. Assume the string does not stretch appreciably.

FIGURE 16-31 Problem 30.

31. A steel wire can tolerate a maximum tension per unit cross-sectional area of 2.7 GN/m^2 before it undergoes permanent distortion. What is the maximum possible speed for transverse waves in a steel wire if it is to remain undistorted? Steel has a density of 7.9 g/cm^3.

32. A uniform cable hangs vertically under its own weight. Show that the speed of waves on the cable is given by $v = \sqrt{yg}$, where y is the distance from the bottom of the cable.

Section 16-5 Wave Power and Intensity

33. A rope with 280 g of mass per meter is under 550 N tension. A wave with frequency 3.3 Hz and amplitude 6.1 cm is propagating on the rope. What is the average power carried by the wave?

34. A motor drives a mechanism that produces simple harmonic motion at one end of a stretched cable. The frequency of the motion is 30 Hz, and the motor can supply energy at an average rate of 350 W. If the cable has linear density 450 g/m and is under 1.7 kN tension, (a) what is the maximum wave amplitude that can be driven down the cable? (b) If the motor were replaced by a larger one capable of supplying 700 W, how would the maximum amplitude change?

35. A 600-g Slinky is stretched to a length of 10 m. You shake one end at the frequency of 1.8 Hz, applying a time-average power of 1.1 W. The resulting waves propagate along the Slinky at 2.3 m/s. What is the wave amplitude?

36. A simple harmonic wave of amplitude 5.0 cm, wavelength 70 cm, and frequency 14 Hz is propagating on a wire with linear density 40 g/m. Find the wave energy per unit length of the wire.

37. Figure 16-32 shows a wave train consisting of two cycles of a sine wave propagating along a string. Obtain an expression for the total energy in this wave train, in terms of the string tension F, the wave amplitude A, and the wavelength λ.

FIGURE 16-32 Problem 37.

38. A steel wire with linear density 5.0 g/m is under 450 N tension. What is the maximum power that can be carried by transverse waves on this wire if the wave amplitude is not to exceed 10% of the wavelength?

39. A loudspeaker emits energy at the rate of 50 W, spread in all directions. What is the intensity of sound 18 m from the speaker?

40. The light intensity 3.3 m from a light bulb is 0.73 W/m². What is the power output of the bulb, assuming it radiates equally in all directions?

41. Use data from Appendix E to determine the intensity of sunlight at (a) Mercury and (b) Pluto.

42. A 9-W laser produces a beam 2 mm in diameter. Compare its light intensity with that of sunlight at noon, about 1 kW/m².

43. Light emerges from a 5.0-mW laser in a beam 1.0 mm in diameter. The beam shines on a wall, producing a spot 3.6 cm in diameter. What are the beam intensities (a) at the laser and (b) at the wall?

44. A large boulder drops from a cliff into the ocean, producing circular waves. A small boat 18 m from the impact point measures the wave amplitude at 130 cm. At what distance will the amplitude be 50 cm?

45. Use Table 16-1 to determine how close to a rock band you should stand for it to sound as loud as a jet plane at 200 m. Treat the band and the plane as point sources. Is this assumption reasonable?

Section 16-6 The Superposition Principle and Wave Interference

46. Consider two functions $f(x \pm vt)$ and $g(x \pm vt)$ that both satisfy the wave equation (Equation 16-12). Show that their sum also satisfies the wave equation.

47. Two wave pulses are described by $y_1(x, t) = \dfrac{2}{(x - t)^2 + 1}$,

$y_2(x, t) = \dfrac{-2}{(x - 5 + t)^2 + 1}$, where x and y are in cm

and t in seconds. (a) What is the amplitude of each pulse? (b) At $t = 0$, where is the peak of each pulse, and in what direction is it moving? (c) At what time will the two pulses exactly cancel?

48. The triangular wave of Fig. 16-33 can be described by the following sum of simple harmonic terms:

$$y(x) = \frac{8}{\pi^2}\left(\frac{\sin x}{1^2} - \frac{\sin 3x}{3^2} + \frac{\sin 5x}{5^2} - \cdots\right).$$

Plot the sum of the first three terms in this series for x ranging from 0 to 2π, and compare with the first cycle shown in Fig. 16-33. (See also ActivPhysics Activity 10.7.)

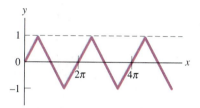

FIGURE 16-33 A triangular wave (Problem 48).

49. You're in an airplane whose two engines are running at 560 rpm and 570 rpm. How often do you hear the sound intensity increase as a result of wave interference?

50. Two waves have the same angular frequency ω, wave number k, and amplitude A, but they differ in phase: $y_1 = A\cos(kx - \omega t)$ and $y_2 = A\cos(kx - \omega t + \phi)$. Show that their superposition is also a simple harmonic wave, and determine its amplitude A_s as a function of the phase difference ϕ.

51. What is the wavelength of the ocean waves in Example 16-5 if the calm water you encounter at 33 m is the *second* calm region on your voyage from the center line?

52. The two loudspeakers shown in Fig. 16-34 emit identical 500-Hz sound waves. Point P is on the first nodal line of the interference pattern. Use the numbers shown to calculate the speed of the sound waves.

FIGURE 16-34 Problem 52.

Section 16-7 The Wave Equation

53. The following equation arises in analyzing the behavior of shallow water:

$$\frac{\partial^2 y}{\partial x^2} - \frac{1}{gh}\frac{\partial^2 y}{\partial t^2} = 0 ,$$

where h is the equilibrium depth and y the displacement from equilibrium. Give an expression for the speed of waves in shallow water. (Here *shallow* means the water depth is much less than the wavelength.)

54. Use the chain rule for differentiation to show explicitly that any function of the form $f(x \pm vt)$ satisfies the wave equation (Equation 16-12).

Paired Problems

(Both problems in a pair involve the same principles and techniques. If you can get the first problem, you should be able to solve the second one.)

55. A wave on a taut wire is described by the equation $y = 1.5\sin(0.10x - 560t)$, where x and y are in cm and t is in seconds. If the wire tension is 28 N, what are (a) the amplitude, (b) the wavelength, (c) the period, (d) the wave speed, and (e) the power carried by the wave?

56. A wave given by $y = 23\cos(0.025x - 350t)$, with x and y in mm and t in seconds, is propagating on a cable with mass per unit length 410 g/m. Find (a) the amplitude, (b) the wavelength, (c) the frequency in Hz, (d) the wave speed, and (e) the power carried by the wave.

57. A spring of mass m and spring constant k has an unstretched length ℓ_0. Find an expression for the speed of transverse waves on this spring when it has been stretched to a length ℓ.

58. When a 340-g spring is stretched to a total length of 40 cm, it supports transverse waves propagating at 4.5 m/s. When it's stretched to 60 cm, the waves propagate at 12 m/s. Find (a) the unstretched length of the spring and (b) its spring constant.

59. At a point 15 m from a source of spherical sound waves, you measure a sound intensity of 750 mW/m². How far do you need to walk, directly away from the source, until the intensity is 270 mW/m²?

60. Figure 16-35 shows two observers 20 m apart, on a line that connects them and a spherical light source. If the observer nearest the source measures a light intensity 50% greater than the other observer, how far is the nearest observer from the source?

61. Two motors in a factory produce sound waves with the same frequency as their rotation rates. If one motor is running at 3600 rpm and the other at 3602 rpm, how often will workers hear a peak in the sound intensity?

62. Two radio waves with frequencies of approximately 50 MHz interfere. The composite wave is detected and fed to a loudspeaker, which emits audible sound at 500 Hz. What is the percentage difference between the frequencies of the two radio waves?

Supplementary Problems

63. For a transverse wave on a stretched string, the requirement that the string be nearly horizontal is met if the amplitude is much less than the wavelength. (a) Show this by drawing an appropriate sketch. (b) Show that, under this approximation that $A \ll \lambda$, the maximum speed u of the string must be considerably less than the wave speed v. (c) If the amplitude is not to exceed 1% of the wavelength, how large can the string speed u be in relation to the wave speed v?

64. A 64-g spring has unstretched length 25 cm. With a 940-g mass attached, the spring undergoes simple harmonic motion with angular frequency 6.1 s^{-1}. What will be the speed of transverse waves on this spring when it's stretched to a total length of 40 cm?

65. An ideal spring is compressed until its total length is ℓ_1, and the speed of transverse waves on the spring is measured. When it's compressed further to a total length ℓ_2, waves propagate at the *same* speed. Show that the uncompressed spring length is just $\ell_1 + \ell_2$.

66. An ideal spring is stretched to a total length ℓ_1. When that length is doubled, the speed of transverse waves on the spring triples. Find an expression for the unstretched length of the spring.

67. A 1-megaton nuclear explosion produces a shock wave whose amplitude, measured as excess air pressure above normal atmospheric pressure, is 1.4×10^5 Pa (1 Pa = 1 N/m²) at a distance of 1.3 km from the explosion. An excess pressure of 3.5×10^4 Pa will destroy a typical wood-frame house. At what distance from the explosion will such houses be destroyed? Assume the wavefront is spherical.

68. Show that the time it takes a wave to propagate up the cable in Problem 32 is $t = 2\sqrt{\ell/g}$, where ℓ is the cable length.

69. In Example 16-5, how much farther would you have to row to reach a region of maximum wave amplitude?

70. Suppose the wavelength of the ocean waves in Example 16-5 were 8.4 m. How far would you have to row from the center line, staying 75 m from the breakwater, in order to find (a) the first and (b) the second region of relative calm?

FIGURE 16-35 Problem 60.

Sound and Other Wave Phenomena

A bat uses high-frequency sound waves to navigate and to find its prey.

Sound waves are longitudinal mechanical waves that propagate through gases, liquids, and solids. We think of sound waves primarily in connection with the sounds we hear, but **audible** sound comprises only a small part of the range of sound waves important both in the natural world and in technology. The human ear is sensitive to sounds in the range from approximately 20 Hz to 20 kHz; below this range is **infrasound** arising, for example, from the vibration of massive structures like buildings. Above the audible range lies **ultrasound**, used in medical diagnostics and treatment, location of underwater objects, analysis of materials, and even microscopy. Many animals can detect sounds above the range audible to humans; bats, in particular, use ultrasound for navigation.

The generation and propagation of sound waves involves a number of wave phenomena beyond those introduced in Chapter 16. Here we describe the properties of sound waves, then explore these additional wave phenomena.

17-1 SOUND WAVES IN GASES

All materials are, to some degree, compressible. That means a force applied to the material results in a change in volume. According to Newton's third law, the material in turn exerts a force. In gases it's simplest to characterize that force in terms of **pressure**, or force per unit area.

Applying a force to one part of a gas immediately compresses only that part. But the increased pressure is communicated to adjacent regions, and the result is a propagating longitudinal wave—a sound wave. Figure 17-1 shows a hollow

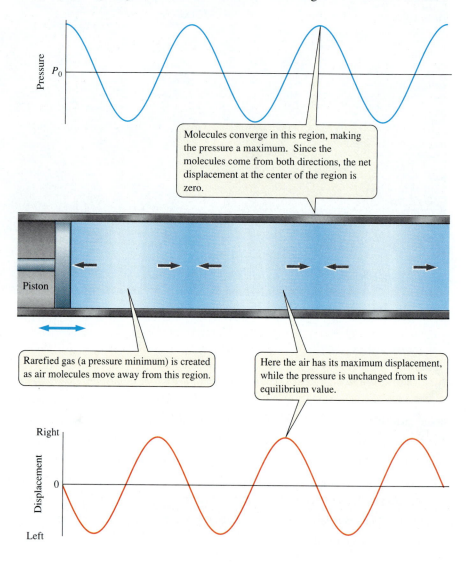

Molecules converge in this region, making the pressure a maximum. Since the molecules come from both directions, the net displacement at the center of the region is zero.

Rarefied gas (a pressure minimum) is created as air molecules move away from this region.

Here the air has its maximum displacement, while the pressure is unchanged from its equilibrium value.

FIGURE 17-1 A sound wave in a hollow pipe consists of alternating regions of compression and rarefaction propagating through the air. Arrows show the instantaneous displacements of the air from equilibrium as it undergoes oscillatory motion. Note that regions where the pressure is a maximum or minimum correspond to zero displacement. The displacement is highly exaggerated; normally, displacements of air in a sound wave are less than 1% of the wavelength. The pressure and displacement are $\pi/2$ or 90° out of phase. We assume that the pipe continues forever to the right; otherwise, the waves would spread out at the open end to make audible sound. However, they might also reflect back into the pipe and complicate the picture.

pipe closed at one end by a movable piston. Moving this piston back and forth alternately rarefies and compresses the air, with the pressure varying slightly about its equilibrium value. That equilibrium pressure itself arises from random motion of the air molecules, which we'll examine in detail in Chapter 20. Collisions among the rapidly moving molecules communicate changes in pressure to adjacent volumes of air, with the result that the compression and rarefaction induced by the piston propagate down the pipe as a sound wave.

The piston's movement communicates not only pressure changes but also motion to the air. As Fig. 17-1 shows, adjacent volumes of air have displacements in opposite directions; the region where those air volumes meet is either a pressure maximum or minimum, depending on whether air has moved into or out of the region. Since the displacement must be zero where oppositely displaced air masses meet, the displacement and pressure variation are therefore out of phase. So the sound wave consists of alternating regions of compression and rarefaction, and correspondingly of back-and-forth air motion, propagating down the pipe.

You might wonder whether you could hear the sound depicted in Fig. 17-1. We've assumed the pipe continues indefinitely, but if instead it's open at the right end, then the waves will spread through the surrounding air. If the piston is moving at a frequency in the audible range, then you'll hear the sound as a pure tone. An organ pipe is an obvious example of a system similar to our pipe; so are instruments such as trumpets and clarinets, with their flaring open ends designed to transfer the most sound energy to the surrounding air.

Tip

The Air Motion Is Not the Wave Motion Is Not the Molecular Motion As always, a wave transports energy but not matter. The back-and-forth motion of the air is a manifestation of the wave's passage, just as is the sideways motion of a string as a transverse wave passes. Although the air moves back and forth, it undergoes no overall change in position. And its speed is *not* the wave speed.

There's another important distinction to be made. The back-and-forth air motion refers to the *average* motion of a group of air molecules. Individually, those molecules are whizzing around with random motion at much higher speeds. In fact, for reasons we'll see in Chapter 20, the typical speed of that random motion is roughly the same as the wave speed. The back-and-forth motion of the air as the wave passes is just a small effect superposed on the individual random molecular motions.

The variations suggested in Fig. 17-1 are highly exaggerated. The pressure changes even in the loudest audible sound are about one ten-thousandth of the equilibrium air pressure, and the maximum displacement is a tiny fraction of a wavelength.

17-2 THE SPEED OF SOUND IN GASES

In the preceding chapter we found the speed of transverse waves on a stretched string to be given by $v = \sqrt{F/\mu}$. Here the string tension F is the force that tends to restore the string to equilibrium, while μ—the mass per unit length—measures the inertia associated with the string's mass. We might expect the speed of sound to depend on analogous factors—a restoring force and inertia. In a gas that restoring force is provided by the gas pressure P, while the density ρ—mass per unit volume—measures the inertia. So is the sound speed given by $v = \sqrt{P/\rho}$? Almost: dimensional analysis (see Problem 1) shows that this quantity does indeed have the units of velocity, but dimensional analysis cannot tell whether we have exactly the right constant factors. In fact, for reasons we'll see in Chapter 21, the exact expression is

$$v = \sqrt{\frac{\gamma P}{\rho}} \quad \text{(sound speed in a gas)}, \tag{17-1}$$

where γ is a constant that depends on the nature of the gas. For a gas consisting of simple particles—helium atoms, for example, or the electron-proton mixtures that characterize matter at very high temperatures—γ has the value $\frac{5}{3}$. For diatomic molecules like N_2 and O_2 that comprise air, γ takes the lower value $\frac{7}{5}$. And for more complicated molecules γ is lower still; in triatomic CO_2, for example, γ is close to $\frac{4}{3}$.

EXAMPLE 17-1	"Donald Duck" Talk

Under normal atmospheric conditions, air pressure is 1.01×10^5 N/m², and there are 2.51×10^{25} air molecules per cubic meter. Air is essentially 21% oxygen (O_2) and 79% nitrogen (N_2). (a) Find the speed of sound in air and in helium (He) with the same pressure and number of molecules per unit volume. (b) For each gas, find the frequency of a sound wave whose wavelength is 64 cm.

Solution
The masses of oxygen and nitrogen molecules are 32 u and 28 u respectively, so the density of air is

$$\rho = [(0.21)(32 \text{ u}) + (0.79)(28 \text{ u})]$$
$$\times (1.66 \times 10^{-27} \text{ kg/u})(2.51 \times 10^{25} \text{ m}^{-3}) = 1.20 \text{ kg/m}^3,$$

where we've weighted the masses of the individual molecules according to their abundances. Then we have

$$v = \sqrt{\frac{\gamma P}{\rho}} = \sqrt{\frac{(7/5)(1.01 \times 10^5 \text{ N/m}^2)}{1.20 \text{ kg/m}^3}} = 343 \text{ m/s}.$$

The atomic weight of helium is 4 u, giving $\rho = (4 \text{ u})(1.66 \times 10^{-27} \text{ kg/u})(2.51 \times 10^{25} \text{ m}^{-3}) = 0.167 \text{ kg/m}^3$. Then, using $\gamma = \frac{5}{3}$ for a monatomic gas, we have

$$v = \sqrt{\frac{\gamma P}{\rho}} = \sqrt{\frac{(5/3)(1.01 \times 10^5 \text{ N/m}^2)}{0.167 \text{ kg/m}^3}} = 1000 \text{ m/s}.$$

Both these speeds are, incidentally, close to the mean speeds of the random molecular motion in the two gases—not surprising, since it's ultimately collisions between gas molecules that transmit the wave energy.

Writing Equation 16-1 in terms of the frequency $f = 1/T$ then gives

$$f_{\text{air}} = \frac{v}{\lambda} = \frac{343 \text{ m/s}}{0.64 \text{ m}} = 536 \text{ Hz}$$

$$f_{\text{He}} = \frac{v}{\lambda} = \frac{1000 \text{ m/s}}{0.64 \text{ m}} = 1560 \text{ Hz}.$$

If you've ever heard someone speak after inhaling helium, you've experienced directly the effect of the different sound speeds calculated in this example. Wavelengths in human speech are set by the geometry of the vocal cords and throat, so a rise in sound speed increases the frequency—resulting in the high-pitched, "Donald Duck" speech of the helium inhaler.

EXERCISE Find the sound speed in hydrogen (H_2) under standard conditions. The number of particles per cubic meter in this case is the same as for air. Take $\gamma = \frac{7}{5}$ since hydrogen is diatomic.

Answer: 1.3 km/s

Some problems similar to Example 17-1: 6–8, 12, 14

17-3 SOUND INTENSITY

In Section 16-5 we calculated the power carried in a wave on a stretched string by finding the rate at which one section of string did work on the next section. That rate was $F_y u$, with F_y the y component of the string tension and u the speed *of the string*. Here we do the analogous calculation for sound waves.

Let s be the air's displacement from equilibrium, so $u = \partial s / \partial t$ is its speed. The air motion in a sound wave is driven by the force associated with the pressure *change* ΔP from the equilibrium value. Since pressure is force per unit area, the force exerted *by* one region of the air *on* an adjacent region of area A is ΔPA, and the power is therefore $\Delta PAu = \Delta PA(\partial s / \partial t)$. Dividing by A gives the power per unit area, or intensity:

$$I = \Delta P \frac{\partial s}{\partial t}.$$

In a simple harmonic wave both pressure and displacement vary sinusoidally in space and time with amplitudes ΔP_0 and s_0:

$$\Delta P = \Delta P_0 \cos(kx - \omega t) \qquad (17\text{-}2a)$$

$$s = -s_0 \sin(kx - \omega t), \qquad (17\text{-}2b)$$

where we've chosen cosine and sine, and the minus sign on s, for consistency with Fig. 17-1. Using these expressions in our equation for intensity gives

$$I = \Delta P \frac{\partial s}{\partial t} = \Delta P_0 \cos(kx - \omega t) \frac{\partial}{\partial t} [-s_0 \sin(kx - \omega t)]$$

$$= s_0 \omega \Delta P_0 \cos^2(kx - \omega t).$$

As in Chapter 16, we're more interested in the intensity averaged over one cycle; since the average of $\cos^2$ is $\frac{1}{2}$, we have

$$\bar{I} = \tfrac{1}{2} s_0 \omega \Delta P_0. \qquad (17\text{-}3a)$$

Finally, we can relate the pressure amplitude ΔP_0 and displacement amplitude s_0. Figure 17-2 shows a thin slab of air in a sound wave. On one side of the slab, whose thickness is dx, the pressure is P; on the other side, it is $P + dP$. The slab has area A, so the net force on it is $dF = [P - (P + dP)]A = -A\,dP$, where the minus sign indicates a leftward force in Fig. 17-2 when dP is positive. The volume of the slab is $A\,dx$, so its mass is $dm = A\rho\,dx$, with ρ the density. Solving Newton's law for acceleration gives $a = F/m$; here the force is dF and the mass is dm, so

$$a = \frac{dF}{dm} = \frac{-A\,dP}{A\rho\,dx} = -\frac{1}{\rho} \frac{\partial P}{\partial x}$$

is the acceleration of the slab. We've used the partial derivative because the pressure is a function of both position and time, and here we want its

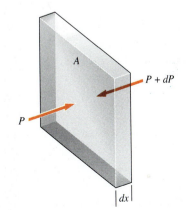

FIGURE 17-2 A thin slab of air in a sound wave has area A and thickness dx. The pressure on one side is P and on the other side $P + dP$, giving a net force of magnitude $A\,dP$ on the slab.

TABLE 17-1 *Sound Intensity*

SOURCE	INTENSITY, W/m^2	INTENSITY LEVEL, dB	
Space shuttle, at 50 m	10^5	170	
Eardrum ruptures	10^4	160	
Jet aircraft, at 50 m	10	130	
Rock band, at 4 m	1	120	← Threshold of pain
Subway	10^{-2}	100	
City traffic	10^{-4}	80	
Normal conversation, at 1 m	10^{-6}	60	
Mosquito	10^{-8}	40	
Whisper, at 1 m	10^{-10}	20	
Normal breathing	10^{-11}	10	
Threshold of hearing	10^{-12}	0	

variation with position only. Using Equations 17-2, we can write $a = \dfrac{\partial^2 s}{\partial t^2} = -s_0 \omega^2 \cos(kx - \omega t)$ and $\dfrac{\partial P}{\partial x} = -k\Delta P_0 \sin(kx - \omega t)$. So the acceleration amplitude is $s_0 \omega^2$ and the amplitude of $\partial P/\partial x$ is $k\Delta P_0$. Using our Newton's law equation to relate these amplitudes gives

$$s_0 \omega^2 = \frac{k\,\Delta P_0}{\rho}.$$

Solving this equation first for s_0 and then for ΔP_0 and using the results in Equation (17-3a) gives two alternative forms for the sound wave intensity:

$$\bar{I} = \tfrac{1}{2} s_0 \omega \Delta P_0 = \frac{\Delta P_0^2}{2\rho v} \tag{17-3b}$$

$$\bar{I} = \tfrac{1}{2} s_0 \omega \Delta P_0 = \tfrac{1}{2}\rho\omega^2 s_0^2 v, \tag{17-3c}$$

where we've used Equation 16-6 to write the wave speed $v = \omega/k$. Note that both these expressions depend on the *square* of the disturbed quantity, as advertised in Section 16-5. Table 17-1 lists intensities for some common sounds.

You might wonder whether "intensity" when applied to sound waves means the same thing as "loudness." Intensity does ultimately determine loudness, but the physiology of hearing is such that your perception of loudness is nowhere near directly proportional to sound intensity. In the next section we look specifically at the human ear and quantify the relation between intensity and loudness.

Sound and the Human Ear

The intensity of normal sound waves ranges widely from small to truly minuscule values, and the ear is a remarkable instrument both in its ability to respond to these weak waves and in the wide range of amplitudes it can handle. Figure 17-3 shows the minimum intensity and the threshold of pain for the human ear, as functions of frequency.

APPLICATION | Stereo Controls

Your stereo system probably has a "loudness" switch that you're supposed to turn on at low volumes. The shape of the curves in Fig. 17-3 is the reason for this switch. At high volumes (i.e., high intensities), the curves are not far from being flat, meaning that sounds of the same power but different frequencies are perceived at essentially the same volume. But at low volumes the curves turn upward at both ends of the frequency scale, showing that it takes greater intensity at high and low frequencies to give the same perceived volume. The "loudness" control switches in a circuit that boosts the high and low frequencies to compensate for this effect.

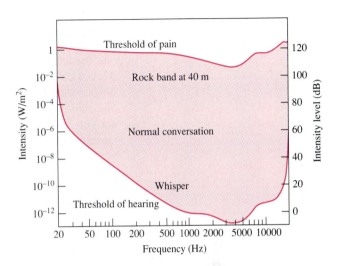

FIGURE 17-3 Minimum and maximum sound intensities for a typical human ear, as functions of frequency. The ear responds to sounds in the entire shaded region. Note the logarithmic scales. Intensities are shown in both watts per square meter and in decibels. Sounds above the threshold of pain are also heard, but prolonged exposure can damage the ears. Ranges for three common sounds are marked on the diagram.

EXAMPLE 17-2 | Response of the Human Ear

(a) Find the displacement and pressure amplitudes of the weakest sound to which the typical human ear can respond. (b) Over a wide frequency range, the threshold of pain is about 1 W/m². Find the displacement and pressure amplitudes for this sound.

Solution

(a) Figure 17-3 shows that the weakest sound for human perception is in the frequency range from 3 kHz to 4 kHz, where the minimum intensity is about 10^{-13} W/m². Equation 17-3b shows that the pressure amplitude is independent of frequency; solving for ΔP_0 then gives

$$\Delta P_0 = \sqrt{2\rho v \bar{I}} = \sqrt{(2)(1.2 \text{ kg/m}^3)(343 \text{ m/s})(10^{-13} \text{ W/m}^2)}$$
$$= 10^{-5} \text{ N/m}^2,$$

where we used the density and sound speed from Example 17-1. Since normal air pressure is 10^5 N/m², this amplitude represents a variation of only one part in ten billion! The corresponding displacement is also impressively small. Taking $f = 3.5$ kHz as typical of the frequency range for minimum intensity and solving Equation 17-3c for s_0 gives

$$s_0 = \sqrt{\frac{2\bar{I}}{\rho\omega^2 v}} = \sqrt{\frac{(2)(10^{-13} \text{ W/m}^2)}{(1.2 \text{ kg/m}^3)[2\pi(3500 \text{ Hz})]^2(343 \text{ m/s})}}$$
$$= 10^{-12} \text{ m},$$

where we used $\omega = 2\pi f$. This number is one hundredth of an atomic diameter! That your eardrum can detect and transmit to your brain information about such small amplitude motions is truly astounding. (b) With 1-kHz waves at the 1 W/m² threshold of pain, similar calculations give $\Delta P_0 = 29$ N/m² and $s_0 = 1 \times 10^{-5}$ m, or one hundredth of a millimeter.

EXERCISE In a whispered conversation, the sound intensity 1 m from the source is about 100 pW/m². Under these conditions, what are (a) the total power falling on a typical adult eardrum of area 60 mm² and (b) the displacement amplitude, assuming a frequency of 850 Hz?

Answers: (a) 6×10^{-15} W; (b) 0.13 nm

Some problems similar to Example 17-2: 15, 16, 18, 20

Decibels

The human ear responds to sound intensities and frequencies covering many orders of magnitude; that's why Fig. 17-3 is plotted with logarithmic scales. Because of this wide range, it makes sense to quantify sound levels with a unit proportional to the logarithm of the actual intensity. Such a unit is the **decibel** (dB), defined by

$$\beta = 10 \log\left(\frac{I}{I_0}\right), \tag{17-4}$$

where β is the sound **intensity level** in decibels and where $I_0 = 10^{-12}$ W/m^2 is a reference level chosen as the threshold of hearing at 1 kHz. The decibel is one-tenth of a bel, a less frequently used unit named for telephone inventor Alexander Graham Bell. Since the logarithm of 10 is 1, each factor-of-10 increase in sound intensity over the reference level of 10^{-12} W/m^2 represents an increase of 10 dB. Your actual perception of loudness is somewhat subjective, depending not only on the intensity level but also on frequency and duration; in general, for intensity levels above about 40 dB, the perceived loudness approximately doubles for every 10 dB increase in intensity level. One consequence of this relation is the enormous power increase needed to produce really loud sounds.

Sound levels over 120 dB are generally painful, while continuous exposure to levels in excess of 90 dB can lead to hearing loss. Table 17-1 includes common sound intensity levels in dB; we've also included a decibel scale on Fig. 17-3.

Got It!

Remember that the intensity of waves from a pointlike source falls off in proportion to the inverse square of the distance (see Equation 16-9). So a 10-fold increase in distance corresponds to a 100-fold drop in intensity. Does that mean the decibel level also drops by a factor of 100? If not, by how much does it drop?

EXAMPLE 17-3	*Turn Down the TV!*

Your little sister is watching TV, and the sound is blasting your ears at 75 dB. You yell to her to turn it down, and she drops the intensity level to 60 dB. By what factor has the power dropped?

Solution

The intensity level has dropped by 15 dB, corresponding to 1.5 orders of magnitude in actual intensity. So the intensity—and therefore the power emitted by the speakers—drops by a factor $10^{-1.5}$, or to about one thirtieth of its original value. We can get this result more formally by writing Equation 17-4 for each value and subtracting. Designating the initial and final values by the subscripts 1 and 2, we have:

$$\beta_2 - \beta_1 = 10 \log\left(\frac{I_2}{I_0}\right) - 10 \log\left(\frac{I_1}{I_0}\right) = 10 \log\left(\frac{I_2}{I_1}\right).$$

Solving for the logarithm gives $\log(I_2/I_1) = (\beta_2 - \beta_1)/10$; exponentiating in base 10 then gives

$$10^{\log(I_2/I_1)} = \frac{I_2}{I_1} = 10^{(\beta_2 - \beta_1)/10} = 10^{(60\,\text{dB} - 75\,\text{dB})/10}$$

$$= 10^{-1.5} = 0.032.$$

This substantial power reduction results in only a modest reduction in perceived loudness; since the loudness changes by roughly a factor of 2 for each 10 dB change in intensity level, the reduced volume will sound between one-fourth and one-half as loud as before.

Tip

Working with Decibels Decibels are designed for ease in calculating sound intensity levels. That's why we could do this example in a few sentences and get the same result as a paragraph of equations. Note also that decibels are dimensionless because the decibel measure always involves intensity ratios.

EXERCISE At the softest passage in a piece of music, your loudspeakers put out a sound level of 48 dB; the actual power delivered by the speakers at this time is 7.8 mW. If you perceive the loudest music to be eight times as loud as the softest, what will be the greatest power the speakers must deliver during this piece?

Answer: 7.8 W

Some problems similar to Example 17-3: 22, 24, 25, 28

17-4 SOUND WAVES IN LIQUIDS AND SOLIDS

Although less compressible than gases, liquids and solids also support longitudinal sound waves. In general, a material's compressibility is described by its **bulk modulus of elasticity**, or the ratio of the change in pressure to the fractional change in volume:

$$B = -\frac{\Delta P}{\Delta V/V}, \tag{17-5}$$

where the minus sign arises because a positive pressure increase corresponds to a decrease in volume. Because the denominator in this expression is dimensionless, B has the units of pressure. The bulk modulus is essentially a measure of a material's elasticity, with a large value of B describing a "stiff" material, one that is hard to compress. The stiffer the material, the stronger the restoring forces that develop in response to compression; at the same time, response to compressional forces depends on inertia as measured by the material density. Therefore, it's not surprising that the speed of sound in a material is given by

$$v = \sqrt{\frac{B}{\rho}}. \tag{17-6}$$

This is the analog of Equation 17-1 for solids and liquids. Table 17-2 lists sound speeds in some common materials. The stiffness of solids and liquids results in greater sound speeds than in gases, although greater density makes the increase less dramatic than it would otherwise be.

Wave propagation in solids is a complex subject. A simple model for a solid consists of individual atoms linked by springs representing the interatomic electrical forces (Fig. 17-4)—a three-dimensional version of the model system we used to introduce wave motion in Chapter 16 (see Fig. 16-2). Such a structure supports not only longitudinal but also transverse waves. Furthermore, unless the structure is perfectly symmetric, wave properties differ depending on propagation direction. The analysis of possible wave modes is the focus of much contemporary work by solid-state physicists.

TABLE 17-2 *Sound Speeds in Selected Materials**

MATERIAL	SOUND SPEED (m/s)
Gases	
Air (0°C)	331
Air (20°C)	343
Carbon dioxide	259
Hydrogen	1284
Liquids (at 25°)	
Benzene	1295
Mercury	1450
Water	1497
Solids	
Aluminum	6420
Copper	5010
Glass (Pyrex)	5640
Lead	1960
Neoprene	1600
Steel	5940

*At normal atmospheric pressure. Sound speed generally increases with temperature because, as we show in Chapter 20, sound speed is related to the random thermal speeds of molecules.

FIGURE 17-4 A simple model for a solid, showing atoms connected by springs. This structure supports both longitudinal and transverse waves.

17-5 WAVE REFLECTION AND REFRACTION

You shout in a mountain valley and hear echoes reverberating off the valley walls. You look in a mirror and see light from your face reflected off the silvered surface. A metal screen in your microwave oven's door turns back potentially harmful waves and keeps them where they'll heat your food. A doctor's ultrasound probes your body, bouncing back to reveal internal structures. A bat navigates flawlessly in response to echoes from a cave wall. All these are examples of wave **reflection**.

You can see that wave reflection *must* occur when a wave hits a medium in which it can't propagate; otherwise, where would the wave energy go? Figure 17-5 details the reflection process for waves on a stretched string, in the two cases where the string end is (*a*) clamped at a rigid wall and (*b*) free to move up and down. In the first case the wave amplitude must remain zero at the end, so

(*a*)   (*b*)

FIGURE 17-5 Reflection of a wave pulse at the end of a string. Conditions at the end determine the details of the reflection. In (*a*) the string is rigidly clamped, so the wave amplitude must be zero at the end and therefore the incident and reflected pulses interfere destructively. That means the reflected pulse must be inverted. In (*b*) the string is free to move up and down on a frictionless rod, and the wave displacement at the end is a maximum; therefore the pulse reflects without inverting.

FIGURE 17-6 Partial reflection at a junction between two different strings. Here the right-hand string is heavier, so the reflected pulse is inverted.

the incident and reflected pulses interfere destructively and the reflected wave is therefore inverted. In the second case the displacement is a maximum at the free end, and the reflected wave is not inverted.

Between the extremes of a rigid wall and a perfectly free end lies the case of one string connected to another with a different mass per unit length. In this case some wave energy is transmitted to the second string and some reflected back along the first (Fig. 17-6).

The phenomenon of partial reflection and transmission at a junction of strings has its analog in the behavior of all sorts of waves at interfaces between different media. For example, shallow water waves are partially reflected if the water depth changes abruptly. Light incident on even the clearest glass undergoes partial reflection because of the difference in light-transmitting capabilities of air and glass (Fig. 17-7). Partial reflection of ultrasound waves at interfaces of body tissues with different densities makes ultrasound a valuable medical diagnostic.

When waves strike an interface between two media at an oblique angle, and are capable of propagating in the second medium, then the phenomenon of **refraction** occurs. In refraction, the direction of wave propagation changes because of a difference in wave speed between the two media. Fig. 17-8 shows the refraction of water waves at an interface between two different water depths. It's often convenient to describe the direction of wave propagation, especially in cases of reflection and refraction where the direction changes, by drawing lines called **rays** that are perpendicular to the wavefronts. We've superposed some rays on Fig. 17-8; note in addition to the refracted ray, there's a weak reflected ray, as well. When the wave speed in a medium changes continuously with position, then the propagation direction also changes continuously and the rays become curves. We discuss the mathematics of refraction in Chapter 35.

FIGURE 17-7 Even though glass is transparent, partial reflection of light occurs at the interface between air and glass. Here the Dallas skyline is reflected in a glass-walled building.

FIGURE 17-8 Waves in shallow water refract—change direction—at the interface between two different water depths. Although most of the wave energy crosses the interface, some is reflected, as evidenced by the weak reflected waves. We've noted the directions of the incident, refracted, and reflected waves by drawing rays—that is, lines perpendicular to the wavefronts—where the waves cross the long edge of the shallow region.

Waves propagating and reflecting inside the Earth allow geologists to deduce the structure of the planet's interior, from its largest features to the locations of oil and gas deposits. The waves used include those generated naturally by earthquakes, as well as waves produced intentionally with explosives.

The interior of Earth supports two types of earthquake-generated waves. These are longitudinal waves, which geologists call P waves, and transverse waves called S waves (Fig. 17-9). (Additional wave types propagate near the surface, but not through the interior.) Recall that solids support both longitudinal and transverse waves, while only longitudinal waves can propagate in liquids. This fact provides our most direct evidence that Earth has a liquid core. Since the transverse S waves do not propagate in liquid, they leave a "shadow zone" as shown in Fig. 17-10. Measuring the extent of the shadow zone with a network of seismic stations lets geologists infer the size of the liquid core.

Longitudinal waves—or P-waves—do propagate through the liquid core. Detection of P-waves partially reflected from within the core led geologists to propose an inner core structure. Propagation times for waves passing through this inner core proved shorter than for those passing through the outer core alone, giving evidence that the inner core is solid, with a higher sound speed. Detailed analysis of P-waves from nuclear weapons tests led to geologists' best measurements of the core sizes; the solid inner core is about 1200 km in radius and is surrounded by the 2300-km-thick liquid outer core (Fig. 17-11).

Probing with seismic waves on a smaller scale helps in the search for oil and gas. Using small explosive charges or special machinery that vigorously "thumps" the ground, geologists generate seismic waves that reflect from rock layers a few hundred meters to a few kilometers down. They detect the reflected waves a short distance from their source. Increasingly, this technique is being used on even smaller scales by environmental scientists to map water supplies and the spread of pollutants in groundwater.

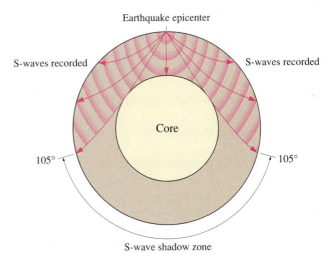

FIGURE 17-10 Transverse waves (S-waves) cannot propagate in liquids, so the presence of a shadow zone for earthquake-generated S-waves is evidence for Earth's liquid core. Bending of the rays occurs because of changes in wave speed with depth.

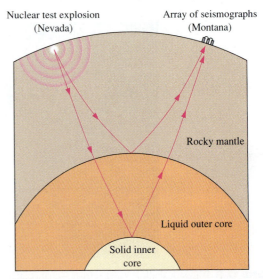

FIGURE 17-11 Longitudinal waves (P-waves) do propagate in the liquid core. The P-waves from nuclear explosions are partially reflected at the boundaries of the inner and outer cores; precise timing of these "echoes" gives the sizes of the cores.

FIGURE 17-9 The structure of compressional P waves and transverse S waves in Earth's interior. Only the P waves can propagate in both liquid and solid regions.

17-6 STANDING WAVES

Imagine a string clamped tightly at both ends. Waves can propagate back and forth on this string by reflecting at its ends. But because the ends are clamped, the wave displacement at the ends must always be zero. Only certain waves can satisfy this requirement; as Fig. 17-12 suggests, they're those for which an integer number of half wavelengths just fits on the length L of the string.

The wave structures shown in Fig. 17-12 are called **standing waves**, so named because they essentially stand still, confined to the length of the string, and they don't propagate anywhere. Instead, the string at each point executes simple harmonic motion perpendicular to the direction of the undisturbed string. We can understand and describe standing waves mathematically by considering that they arise from the superposition of two waves propagating in opposite directions and reflecting at the ends of the string. If we take the x axis to coincide with the string, then we can write the string displacements in two such waves as $y_1(x, t) = A\cos(kx - \omega t)$ for the wave propagating in the $+x$ direction (recall Equation 16-5), and $y_2(x, t) = -A\cos(kx + \omega t)$ for the wave propagating in the $-x$ direction. (The minus sign in y_2 accounts for the phase change that occurs on reflection.) Their superposition is then

$$y(x, t) = y_1 + y_2 = A[\cos(kx - \omega t) - \cos(kx + \omega t)].$$

Appendix A lists a trig identity for the difference of two cosines:

$$\cos\alpha - \cos\beta = -2\sin[\tfrac{1}{2}(\alpha + \beta)]\,\sin[\tfrac{1}{2}(\alpha - \beta)];$$

applying this identity with $\alpha = kx - \omega t$ and $\beta = kx + \omega t$ gives

$$y(x, t) = 2A\sin kx \sin \omega t. \tag{17-7}$$

Equation 17-7 is the mathematical description of a standing wave, and it affirms our qualitative description that each point on the string simply oscillates up and down. Pick any point—that is, any fixed value of x—and Equation 17-7 does indeed describe simple harmonic motion in the y direction, through the factor $\sin\omega t$. The amplitude of that motion depends on the point x you've chosen, and is given by the factor that multiplies $\sin\omega t$, namely $2A\sin kx$.

Because the string is clamped at both ends, the amplitude at the ends must be zero. Our amplitude factor $2A\sin kx$ does give $y = 0$ in Equation 17-7 at $x = 0$, but what about at $x = L$? Here we'll get zero only if $\sin kL = 0$—and that requires kL to be a multiple of π (recall that the sine function is zero when its argument is $0, \pi, 2\pi, \ldots$). So we must have $kL = m\pi$, where m is any integer. But the wave number, k, is related to the wavelength λ by $k = 2\pi/\lambda$. Our condition $kL = m\pi$ can then be written

$$L = \frac{m\lambda}{2}, \quad m = 1, 2, 3, \ldots \tag{17-8}$$

This is just the condition we already guessed at from Fig. 17-12, namely that the string length L be an integer number of half wavelengths.

Given a particular string length L, Equation 17-8 limits the allowed standing waves on the string to a discrete set whose wavelengths follow from the equation. Those allowed waves are called **modes**, and the integer m is the **mode number**. The $m = 1$ mode is the **fundamental**, and is the longest wavelength standing wave that can exist on the string. The higher modes are called **harmonics**. You can explore standing waves with ActivPhysics 10.4, 10.5, and 10.6.

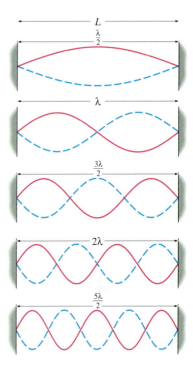

FIGURE 17-12 Standing waves on a string. Clamped rigidly at both ends, the string can accommodate only an integer number of half wavelengths. Shown are the fundamental and four harmonics. Solid line is the string at one instant, dashed line one-half cycle later. Nodes—points where the displacement is always zero—occur at the ends in all cases, and in between for the harmonics.

10.4, 10.5, 10.6

Standing Waves on a String

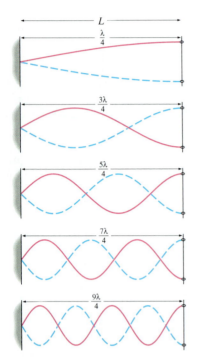

FIGURE 17-13 When one end of the string is fixed and the other free, the string can accommodate only an odd number of quarter wavelengths. (Here the string is clamped at the left end, but at the right end is attached to a ring that slides without friction along a vertical pole.)

Figure 17-12 shows that there are points where the string does not move at all. These include, obviously, the two clamped ends. For all but the fundamental, they also include one or more points in between. Points of zero displacement in a standing wave are called **nodes**. Points where the amplitude of the wave displacement is a maximum, in contrast, are **antinodes**.

When a string is clamped rigidly at one end but free at the other, its clamped end is a node but its free end is an antinode. Figure 17-13 shows that the string length must then be an odd multiple of a quarter wavelength—a result that you can also get from Equation 17-7 by requiring $\sin kL = 1$ to give maximum amplitude at $x = L$ (see Problem 41).

Standing Wave Resonance

We've discussed standing waves in terms of constraints on the wavelength λ rather than on the frequency f. But because waves on a string have a fixed speed v, and because $f\lambda = v$, Equation 17-8's discrete set of allowed wavelengths corresponds to a set of discrete frequencies, as well. The lowest allowed frequency, called the fundamental frequency, corresponds to the longest wavelength; the harmonics have higher frequencies. With ActivPhysics Activity 10.4 you can actually listen to the different harmonics of a vibrating string.

Because a stretched string can oscillate in any of its allowed frequencies, resonant behavior that we discussed in Chapter 15, Section 15-7, can occur close to any of those frequencies. Buildings and other structures, in analogy with our simple string, support a variety of standing wave modes. For example, a skyscraper is like the string of Fig. 17-13, its base clamped to Earth but its top free to swing. Engineers must be sure to identify all possible modes of structures they design, in order to avoid harmful resonances. The disastrous oscillations of the Tacoma Narrows Bridge shown in Fig. 15-32 are actually torsional standing waves.

ActivPhysics Activity 10.4 lets you try to get a string oscillating at *any* frequency you choose. You'll find that you can produce oscillations of significant amplitude only for frequencies very close to the allowed mode frequencies.

Other Standing Waves

Standing waves are common phenomena. Water waves in confined spaces exhibit standing waves, and entire lakes can develop very slow oscillations corresponding to low-mode-number standing waves. Standing electromagnetic waves occur inside closed metal cavities; in microwave ovens the nodes of the standing-wave pattern would result in "cold" spots were not either the food or the source of microwaves kept in motion. Standing waves are common in mechanical systems. And even atomic structure can be understood in terms of standing waves associated with electrons.

In a novel variant on musical wind instruments, engineers seeking to eliminate ozone-destroying chemicals now used in refrigerators have developed so-called thermoacoustic refrigerators, in which high-amplitude standing sound waves provide the compression and expansion necessary to extract heat (more on this in Chapter 22).

FIGURE 17-14 Complex standing wave patterns arise in two and three dimensions. Here, a computer model of standing-wave oscillations in the Sun provides insights into physical conditions deep in the solar interior. Red and blue areas represent oscillatory motion in opposite directions.

Standing-wave patterns in two- and three-dimensional systems can be quite complex, as Fig. 17-14 suggests.

Musical Instruments

Our analysis of standing waves on strings applies directly to stringed musical instruments such as violins, guitars, and pianos. Standing-wave vibrations in the instrument strings are communicated to the air as sound waves, usually through the intermediary of a sounding box or electronic amplifiers. For instruments in the violin family, the body of the instrument itself undergoes standing wave vibrations, excited by the vibration of the string, that establish each individual instrument's peculiar sound quality (Fig. 17-15a). Similarly, the stretched membranes of drums exhibit a variety of standing wave patterns representing the allowed modes on these two-dimensional surfaces (Fig. 17-15b).

Wind instruments, in contrast, generate standing sound waves in air columns, analogous to the pipe we considered in Fig. 17-1. These must be open at one end to allow sound to escape; in many instruments the column is effectively open at both ends. An open end has its pressure fixed at atmospheric pressure; it is therefore a pressure node and thus, from Fig. 17-1, a displacement antinode. As a result, an instrument open at one end supports odd integer multiples of a quarter wavelength (Fig. 17-16a), in analogy with Fig. 17-13. An instrument open at both ends, on the other hand, supports integer multiples of a half wavelength (Fig. 17-16b).

10.5 Tuning a Stringed Instrument

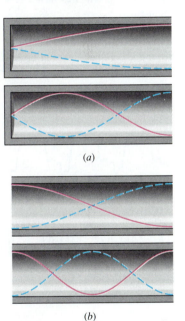

(a)

(b)

FIGURE 17-16 Graphs showing displacement of standing sound waves in wind instruments. Solid and dashed lines are one-half cycle apart. Shown are the fundamental and the lowest harmonic that the instrument can support. (a) An instrument with one end open must have a node at the closed end and an antinode at the open end, so it supports odd integer multiples of a quarter wavelength. (b) With both ends open antinodes occur at both ends, so the instrument supports integer multiples of a half wavelength.

(a)

(b)

FIGURE 17-15 (a) Standing waves on a violin, imaged using holographic interference of laser light waves. (b) Standing waves on a drum.

EXAMPLE 17-4	*The Double Bassoon*

The double bassoon (Fig. 17-17) is the lowest pitched instrument in a normal orchestra. The instrument is "folded" to achieve an effective air column 5.5 m long, and it acts like a pipe open at both ends. What is the frequency of the double bassoon's fundamental note?

Solution

Because the double bassoon acts like a pipe open at both ends, Fig. 17-16b shows that its fundamental mode has a wavelength twice that of the air column, or 11 m. Equation 16-1, $v = \lambda f$, then gives

$$f = \frac{v}{\lambda} = \frac{343 \text{ m/s}}{11 \text{ m}} = 31 \text{ Hz},$$

where we found the sound speed in Table 17-2. This frequency is the note B_0, and lies near the low-frequency limit of the human ear.

The actual length of the double bassoon's air column is 4.8 m, but the instrument's detailed shape alters the standing wave modes, giving a greater effective length. Like most wind

FIGURE 17-17 The double bassoon, whose air column is about 5 m long, is the lowest pitched instrument in a standard orchestra. The instrument is "folded" to achieve its long air column in a more compact space.

instruments, the bassoon has a number of holes that, when uncovered, alter the positions of the antinodes and therefore change the pitch.

EXERCISE The C clarinet has an effective length of 32.8 cm, and for its lowest notes it functions as a pipe closed at one end. What is the fundamental frequency of this instrument?

Answer: 261 Hz

Some problems similar to Example 17-4: 50, 52–55

A vibrating string or air column can support many modes, each corresponding to a different frequency and wavelength. In general, a mixture of modes exists simultaneously, a superposition of many simple harmonic waves. The method of Fourier analysis, introduced in Section 16-6, is useful in describing the distribution of individual modes. Different musical instruments favor different modes, which is what gives each its distinctive sound (Fig. 17-18).

FIGURE 17-18 Waveforms of a clarinet (above) and oboe (below) playing the same note. Although the fundamental frequencies are the same, the waveforms and the resulting sounds are quite different because of the different mixtures of standing wave modes in the two instruments.

EXAMPLE 17-5	*Measuring the Sound Speed*

Resonance in hollow pipes provides an accurate means of measuring the speed of sound. In a particular experiment, a pipe 1.300 m long is closed at one end with a diaphragm that can be made to oscillate at an arbitrary frequency, while the other end is open to the atmosphere. A microphone monitors the sound intensity at the open end. Experimentally, the lowest diaphragm frequency that causes the intensity to peak is found to be 66.29 Hz. (a) What is the sound speed in the pipe? (b) At what frequency will the next resonance occur?

Solution

Figure 17-16a shows that a pipe open at one end supports standing waves with the pipe length L an odd quarter multiple of a wavelength. Thus, for the 66.29-Hz fundamental, $L = \frac{1}{4}\lambda$, so $\lambda = 4L$, and the sound speed is

$$v = f\lambda = (66.29 \text{ Hz})(4)(1.300 \text{ m}) = 344.7 \text{ m/s}.$$

The next resonance occurs when $L = \frac{3}{4}\lambda$ or $\lambda = \frac{4}{3}L$; the corresponding frequency is

$$f = \frac{v}{\lambda} = \frac{344.7 \text{ m/s}}{(\frac{4}{3})(1.300)} = 198.9 \text{ Hz}.$$

EXERCISE In air at 20°C and 30% humidity, the speed of sound is 343.8 m/s. Under these conditions the fundamental resonant frequency in a hollow pipe is 1148 Hz. When the humidity increases to 80%, the resonant frequency rises to 1150 Hz. What is the sound speed at 80% humidity?

Answer: 344.4 m/s.

Some problems similar to Example 17-5: 43, 55

17-7 THE DOPPLER EFFECT

The speed v of a wave is its speed relative to the medium through which it propagates. A point source at rest in the medium radiates waves uniformly in all directions (Fig. 17-19). But when the source moves, wave crests bunch up in the direction toward which the source is moving, resulting in a decreased wavelength (Fig. 17-20). In the opposite direction, wave crests spread out and the wavelength increases. You can see this effect simulated with ActivPhysics Activity 10.8.

The wave speed is determined by the properties of the medium, so it doesn't change with source motion. Thus the relation $v = \lambda f$ still holds. This means that an observer in front of the moving source, where λ is smaller, experiences a higher wave frequency as more wave crests pass per unit time. Similarly, an observer behind the source experiences a lower frequency. This change in wavelength and frequency from a moving source is the **Doppler effect** or **Doppler shift**, after the Austrian physicist Christian Johann Doppler (1803–1853).

To analyze the Doppler effect, let λ be the wavelength measured when the source is stationary, and λ' the wavelength when the source is moving at speed u through a medium where the wave speed is v. At the source, the time between wave crests is the wave period T, and a wave crest moves one wavelength λ in this time. But during the same time T, the moving source covers a distance uT, after which it emits the next wave crest. So the distance between wave crests, as seen by an observer in front of the moving source, is

$$\lambda' = \lambda - uT.$$

Writing $T = \lambda/v$, this becomes

$$\lambda' = \lambda - u\frac{\lambda}{v} = \lambda\left(1 - \frac{u}{v}\right). \qquad \text{(source approaching)} \qquad (17\text{-}9a)$$

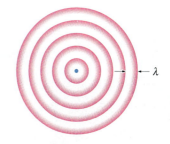

FIGURE 17-19 Circular waves from a source at rest with respect to the medium.

10.8, 10.9
Doppler Effect

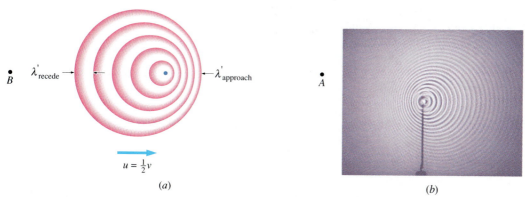

$$u = \tfrac{1}{2}v$$

(a)

(b)

FIGURE 17-20 (a) When the source moves through the medium, the wavelength is shortened in the direction of motion and increased in the opposite direction. Observers at A and B therefore detect higher and lower frequencies, respectively. In the case shown, the source speed u is half the wave speed v. (b) Doppler effect in water waves produced by a moving source tapping the water surface at regular intervals. Which way is the source moving?

FIGURE 17-21 Speed trap! Police radar works by measuring the Doppler shift of radio waves reflected off moving cars.

The situation is similar in the direction opposite the source motion, except that now the wavelength *increases* by the amount $\lambda u/v$, giving

$$\lambda' = \lambda\left(1 + \frac{u}{v}\right). \qquad \text{(source receding)} \qquad (17\text{-}9b)$$

We can recast these expressions in terms of frequency using the relations $\lambda = v/f$ and $\lambda' = v/f'$, where f' is the frequency of waves from the moving source as measured by an observer at rest in the medium. Substituting these relations in our expressions for λ' and solving for f' gives

$$f' = \frac{f}{1 \pm u/v}, \qquad \text{(Doppler shift, moving source)} \qquad (17\text{-}10)$$

for the Doppler-shifted frequency, where the $+$ and $-$ signs correspond to receding and approaching sources, respectively.

You've probably experienced the Doppler effect for sound when standing near a highway. A loud truck approaches with a high-pitched sound "aaaaaaaaaaa." As it passes, the pitch drops abruptly: "aaaaaaaaeioooooooooo," and stays low as the truck recedes. Practical uses of the Doppler effect are numerous. Measuring the Doppler shift in reflected ultrasound allows measurement of blood flow and fetal heartbeat. Police radar works by measuring the Doppler shift of high-frequency radio waves reflected from moving cars (Fig. 17-21). The Doppler shift of starlight reveals stellar motions, while Doppler-shifted light from distant galaxies is evidence that our entire universe is expanding.

EXAMPLE 17-6	*The Wrong Note*

A car speeds down the highway with its stereo blasting. An observer with perfect pitch is standing by the roadside and, as the car approaches, notices that a musical note that should be G ($f = 392$ Hz) sounds like A (440 Hz). How fast is the car moving?

EXERCISE What is the shift in frequency of a 1.2-kHz m ambulance siren when the ambulance is approaching at 130 km/h?

Solution
Solving Equation 17-10 for the source speed u, we have

$$u = v\left(1 - \frac{f}{f'}\right) = (343 \text{ m/s})\left(1 - \frac{392 \text{ Hz}}{440 \text{ Hz}}\right) = 37.4 \text{ m/s}$$

$$= 135 \text{ km/h}.$$

Answer: $\Delta f = 140$ Hz

Some problems similar to Example 17-6: 56, 57, 59

Moving Observers

A Doppler shift in frequency, but not wavelength, also occurs when a moving observer approaches a stationary source—meaning a source at rest with respect

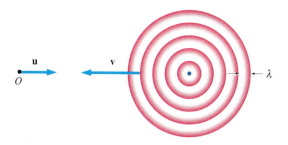

FIGURE 17-22 An observer O moving at speed u approaches a wave source stationary with respect to the wave medium. The wave speed relative to the medium is v, so it's $v + u$ relative to the moving observer. Wave crests pass the observer more frequently than if the observer were at rest, and therefore the moving observer measures a higher wave frequency.

to the wave medium. Figure 17-22 shows how this comes about. An observer moving with speed u toward a stationary source of waves with wave speed v is moving at speed $v + u$ relative to the wave crests (recall Chapter 3, Section 3-5 on relative motion). Since the distance between wave crests is the wavelength λ, the moving observer will measure a time T' between wave crests given by

$$T' = \frac{\lambda}{v + u}.$$

As far as the moving observer is concerned, this time T' is the wave period—the time for the wave cycle to repeat itself fully. Since frequency and period are inverses, the moving observer measures a wave frequency f' given by $f' = 1/T' = (v + u)/\lambda$. We can recast this expression in terms of the frequency f measured by an observer at rest by noting that, in the rest frame of the source, $f\lambda = v$ or $\lambda = v/f$. Using this result in our expression for the shifted frequency gives

$$f' = \frac{v + u}{\lambda} = f\frac{v + u}{v} = f(1 + u/v).$$

Had the observer been moving away from the source, the relative speed would have been $v - u$, and we would have $f' = f(1 - u/v)$. Thus, in general, the shifted frequency measured by a moving observer is

$$f' = f(1 \pm u/v), \quad \text{(Doppler shift, moving observer)} \qquad (17\text{-}11)$$

with the positive sign for an observer approaching the source, negative for an observer receding. For observer velocities u very small compared with the wave speed v, Equations 17-10 and 17-11 give essentially the same results, as you can show in Problem 61. Problem 76 shows how to combine Equations 17-10 and 17-11 to get a general expression for the Doppler shift when both source and observer are in motion. ActivPhysics Activities 10.8 and 10.9 simulate the Doppler effect for moving sources, moving observers, and situations where both source and observer move.

Waves from a stationary source that reflect from a moving object undergo a Doppler shift *twice*. First, because the frequency as received at the reflecting object is shifted, according to Equation 17-11, due to the object's motion relative to the source. Then a stationary observer sees the reflected waves as coming from a moving source, so there's another shift, this time given by Equation 17-10. Police radar and other Doppler-based speed measurements make use of this double Doppler shift that occurs on reflection (see Problems 77–80).

The Doppler Effect for Light

Although light and other electromagnetic waves do not require a material medium, they, too, are subject to the Doppler shift. Both Doppler formulas we've derived here apply to electromagnetic waves, but only in the limit where the relative speed between source and observer is much less than the 3×10^8 m/s speed of light.

The Doppler shift for electromagnetic waves is the same whether it's the source that moves or the observer. This reflects a profound fact at the root of Einstein's relativity, a fact that we hinted at in Chapter 3 and will explore in Chapter 38: that "stationary" and "moving" are meaningful only as relative terms. Electromagnetic waves, unlike mechanical waves, do not require a medium—and therefore terms such as "stationary source" and "moving observer" are meaningless. All that matters is the relative motion between source and observer.

17-8 SHOCK WAVES

Equation 17-9a suggests that wavelength goes to zero if a source approaches at exactly the wave speed. This happens because wave crests can't get away from the source, so they pile up just ahead of it to form a large-amplitude wave called a **shock wave** (Fig. 17-23a). When the source moves faster than the wave speed, waves pile up on a cone whose half angle is given by $\sin \theta = v/u$, as shown in Fig. 17-23b. The ratio u/v is called the **Mach number**, and the cone angle is the **Mach angle**. The speeds of supersonic aircraft are often stated in terms of Mach number; for example, the Concorde, the world's only supersonic passenger plane, flies at Mach 2.

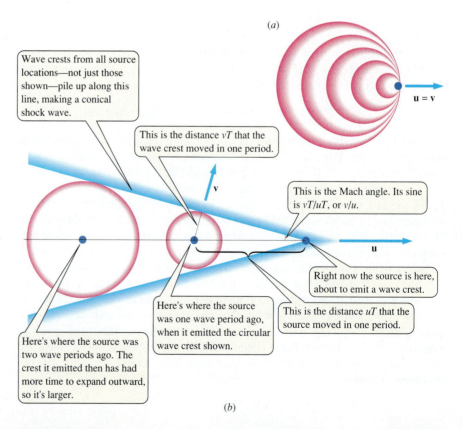

FIGURE 17-23 Formation of shock waves. (a) When the source (blue dot) moves at just the wave speed, wave crests emitted in the direction of the source motion remain right at the source. This pileup of wave crests at one place is the shock wave. (b) When the source moves faster than the wave speed, the source travels farther in a given time than do the expanding wave crests. The crests pile up along a cone whose half-angle is the Mach angle, $\sin^{-1}(v/u)$. Can you determine the Mach number from this diagram?

(a)

u = v

Wave crests from all source locations—not just those shown—pile up along this line, making a conical shock wave.

This is the distance vT that the wave crest moved in one period.

v

This is the Mach angle. Its sine is vT/uT, or v/u.

u

Right now the source is here, about to emit a wave crest.

Here's where the source was one wave period ago, when it emitted the circular wave crest shown.

This is the distance uT that the source moved in one period.

Here's where the source was two wave periods ago. The crest it emitted then has had more time to expand outward, so it's larger.

(b)

(a)

(b)

(c)

FIGURE 17-24 (a) Shock waves (red lines) trail from a model of a delta-winged orbiter in a wind tunnel. Shocks from real supersonic aircraft are the sonic booms that can damage buildings and marine life. (b) A bullet passes through a candle flame, trailing shock waves and disrupting the air flow above the flame. Photos (a) and (b) were both made with a technique that images regions of enhanced density, such as the air that "piles up" behind a shock wave. (c) A powerboat's wake is also a shock wave.

Shock waves occur in a wide variety of physical situations (Fig. 17-24). Sonic booms are shock waves from supersonic aircraft. The bow wave of a boat is a shock wave on the water surface. On a much larger scale, a huge shock wave forms in space as the solar wind—a high-speed flow of particles from the Sun—encounters Earth's magnetic field.

CHAPTER SYNOPSIS

Summary

1. **Sound waves** are longitudinal mechanical waves propagating in gases, liquids, or solids. The speed of sound in gases is given by

$$v = \sqrt{\frac{\gamma P}{\rho}},$$

with P the pressure, ρ the density, and γ a constant that depends on the nature of the gas molecules. More generally, the speed of sound is given by $v = \sqrt{B/\rho}$, where the **bulk modulus** B measures the elastic properties of the medium.

2. The intensity of sound, like that of any wave, depends on the square of the wave disturbance. In sound the medium undergoes both displacement and pressure changes, and the intensity can be written as

$$\bar{I} = \frac{\Delta P_0^2}{2\rho v} = \tfrac{1}{2}\rho\omega^2 s_0^2 v,$$

where ΔP_0 and s_0 are the pressure and displacement amplitudes, ω the angular frequency, and v the wave speed.

3. Audible sound covers many orders of magnitude in intensity, and the human ear responds logarithmically to sound intensity. A convenient measure of intensity is the **decibel** level, defined by

$$\beta = 10 \log\left(\frac{I}{I_0}\right),$$

where $I_0 = 10^{-12}$ W/m² is approximately the threshold of hearing at 1 kHz.

4. Wave **reflection** occurs whenever the medium changes abruptly. Complete reflection occurs if a wave cannot propagate in the new medium. More generally, a wave is partially reflected and partially transmitted at an interface between two media.

5. **Standing waves** arise when a vibrating medium is bounded. Each point in a standing wave undergoes simple harmonic motion. When the system is constrained so that there can be no displacement at either end, then its length must be an integer number of half wavelengths:

$$L = \frac{n\lambda}{2}.$$

If one end is fixed and the other free, then an odd integer number of quarter wavelengths must fit between the ends. The longest wavelength—and lowest frequency—standing wave is the **fundamental**; higher frequencies are the **harmonics**.

6. The **Doppler effect** is the change in frequency due to the motion of a wave source or observer. For mechanical waves, the Doppler-shifted frequency from a moving source is

$$f' = \frac{f}{1 \pm u/v},$$

where f is the frequency emitted when the source is at rest, v the wave speed, and u the source speed with respect to the medium. The positive sign applies to a source receding from the observer, the minus sign to an approaching source. For a stationary source and a moving observer, the Doppler shift is given by

$$f' = f(1 \pm u/v).$$

7. **Shock waves** are formed by sources moving through a medium at speeds greater than the wave speed. Shock waves are large-amplitude disturbances that form a cone of half angle $\theta = \sin^{-1}(v/u)$ with apex at the moving source.

Terms You Should Understand

(Pairs are closely related terms whose distinction is important; number in parentheses is chapter section where term first appears.)

audible sound, infrasound, ultrasound (introduction)
pressure (17-1)
decibel (17-3)
bulk modulus (17-4)
reflection, partial reflection (17-5)
refraction (17-5)
standing wave (17-6)
node, antinode (17-6)
mode (17-6)
Doppler effect (17-7)
shock wave (17-8)
Mach number, Mach angle (17-8)

Symbols You Should Recognize

γ (17-2) s (17-3)
P (17-2) β (17-3)
ρ (17-2) f', λ' (17-7)

Problems You Should be Able to Solve

calculating sound speed from pressure, density, and constant γ (17-2)
relating frequency and wavelength of waves in different gases (17-2)
solving for sound intensity, displacement amplitude, or pressure amplitude (17-3)
working with intensity level in decibels (17-3)
solving for reflected and transmitted amplitude with waves on strings (17-5)
finding frequency and wavelength of allowed standing wave modes (17-6)
determining Doppler-shifted frequency and wavelength (17-7)
evaluating shock-wave angles (17-8)

Limitations to Keep in Mind

Expressions for sound speed apply only for small-amplitude waves.

When applied to light and other electromagnetic waves, the Doppler shift formulas developed in this chapter are approximations good when the source speed is small compared with the speed of light.

QUESTIONS

1. Consider a light wave and a sound wave with the same wavelength. Which has the higher frequency?
2. If you double the pressure of a gas while keeping its density the same, what happens to the sound speed?
3. Water is about 1000 times more dense than air, yet the speed of sound in water is greater than in air. How is this possible?
4. Why can't astronauts on the moon communicate with sound?
5. In a sound wave, do the displacement and pressure peak at the same point or at different points? Why?
6. Does an increase of 1 dB in sound level correspond to a definite change in the intensity as measured in W/m^2? Explain.
7. If the decibel level drops by half, does the sound intensity in W/m^2 also drop by half? Explain.
8. What property of the human ear makes the decibel scale particularly useful?
9. A loudspeaker is blaring at only 10 dB below the threshold of pain. By what factor must its power be increased to reach that threshold?
10. Figure 17-3 is drawn for a typical human ear. How might the figure change as a person ages?
11. Is it meaningful to talk about sound with a negative decibel level? Explain.

12. Why do you see a reflection of yourself in a perfectly clear glass window?
13. Which string in Fig. 17-6 has the greater mass per unit length?
14. If you place a perfectly clear piece of glass in perfectly clear water, you can still see the glass. Why?
15. Standing waves don't propagate. In what sense, then, are they waves?
16. Do standing waves satisfy the wave equation? You can answer without doing any math; just think about the superposition principle.
17. Light from distant galaxies is red shifted relative to nearby galaxies. Assuming this red shift is due to the Doppler shift, what does it say about the distant galaxies' motion relative to Earth?
18. When a wave source moves relative to the medium, a stationary observer measures changes in both wavelength and frequency. But when the observer moves and the source is stationary, only the frequency changes. Why the difference?
19. Why does a boat easily produce a shock wave on the water surface, while it takes very high-speed aircraft to produce sonic booms?

PROBLEMS

ActivPhysics can help with these problems:
Activities 10.3, 10.4, 10.5, 10.6, 10.8, 10.9.

Sections 17-1 and 17-2 Sound Waves and the Speed of Sound in Gases

1. Show that the quantity $\sqrt{P/\rho}$ has the units of speed.
2. Dimensional analysis alone suggests that the sound speed in a gas should be given roughly by $\sqrt{P/\rho}$. By how much would an estimate based on this simple analysis be in error for a gas with $\gamma = \frac{7}{5}$?
3. Find the wavelength, period, angular frequency, and wave number of a 1.0-kHz sound wave in air under the conditions of Example 17-1.
4. (a) Determine an approximate value for the speed of sound in miles per second. (b) Suppose you see a lightning flash and, 10 s later, hear the thunder. How many miles away did the flash occur? Neglect the travel time for the light (why?)
5. Timers in sprint races start their watches when they see smoke from the starting gun, not when they hear the sound (Fig. 17-25). Why? How much error would be introduced by timing a 100-m race from the sound of the shot?

FIGURE 17-25 Problem 5.

6. The factor γ for nitrogen dioxide (NO_2) is 1.29. Find the sound speed in NO_2 at a pressure of 4.8×10^4 N/m^2 and density 0.35 kg/m^3.
7. At standard atmospheric pressure (1.0×10^5 N/m^2), what density of air would make the sound speed 1.0 km/s?
8. The Sun's outer atmosphere, or corona, has about 10^8 electrons and an equal number of protons per cubic centimeter. The pressure of this electron-proton gas is about 3×10^{-3} N/m^2, and it behaves like a monatomic gas with $\gamma = \frac{5}{3}$. To one significant figure, what is the sound speed in the corona?
9. A gas with density 1.0 kg/m^3 and pressure 8.0×10^4 N/m^2 has sound speed 365 m/s. Are the gas molecules monatomic or diatomic?
10. By what percentage would the sound speed in pure oxygen (O_2) differ from that in air with the same pressure and number of particles per unit volume? Consult Example 17-1.
11. Saturn's moon Titan has one of the solar system's thickest atmospheres. Near Titan's surface, atmospheric pressure is 50% greater than standard atmospheric pressure on Earth, while the density in molecules per unit volume is one-third that of Earth's atmosphere. If Titan's atmosphere is essentially all nitrogen (N_2), what is the sound speed?
12. Divers in an underwater habitat breathe a special mixture of oxygen and neon, with pressure 6.2×10^5 N/m^2 and density 4.5 kg/m^3. The effective γ value for the mixture is 1.61. Find the frequency in this mixture for a 50-cm-wavelength sound wave, and compare with its frequency in air under normal conditions.
13. You see an airplane straight overhead at an altitude of 5.2 km. Sound from the plane, however, seems to be coming from a point back along the plane's path at a 35° angle to the vertical (Fig. 17-26). What is the plane's speed, assuming an average 330 m/s sound speed?

FIGURE 17-26 Problem 13.

14. A mixture of oxygen and nitrogen with the pressure and molecules per cubic meter given in Example 17-1 has sound speed 339 m/s. What fraction of the molecules are oxygen?

Section 17-3 Sound Intensity

15. Sound intensity in normal conversation is about 1 μW/m^2. What is the displacement amplitude of air in a 2.5-kHz sound wave with this intensity?
16. The eardrum ruptures at a sound intensity of 10 kW/m^2. What is the amplitude of the sound-wave pressure variation at this intensity, in air under normal conditions? Compare with standard atmospheric pressure, about 10^5 N/m^2.
17. A speaker produces 440-Hz sound with total power 1.2 W, radiating equally in all directions. At a distance of 5.0 m, what are (a) the average intensity, (b) the decibel level, (c) the pressure amplitude, and (d) the displacement amplitude?

18. A "tweeter" loudspeaker emitting 5.0 kHz sound has an oscillation amplitude of 1 μm. What must be the oscillation amplitude of a "woofer" speaker producing the same sound intensity at 30 Hz?

19. What is the approximate frequency range over which sound with intensity 10^{-12} W/m^2 can be heard? Consult Fig. 17-3.

20. The radius of the hydrogen atom is 0.0529 nm. (a) What is the intensity of a 100-Hz sound wave whose displacement amplitude is this size? (b) Repeat for a 2.0 kHz wave. Is either sound audible? Consult Fig. 17-3.

21. What are the intensity and pressure amplitudes in sound waves with intensity levels of (a) 65 dB and (b) −5 dB?

22. A 1-dB increase in sound level is about the minimum change the human ear can perceive. By what factor is the sound intensity increased if the level changes by 1 dB?

23. (a) What is the decibel level of a sound wave whose pressure amplitude is $2.9{\times}10^{-4}$ N/m^2? (b) Consult Fig. 17-3 to determine the approximate lowest frequency at which this sound would be audible.

24. If the pressure amplitude of a sound wave doubles, what happens to (a) the intensity in W/m^2 and (b) the decibel level?

25. Show that a doubling of sound intensity corresponds to very nearly a 3 dB increase in the decibel level.

26. Sound intensity from a localized source decreases as the inverse square of the distance, according to Equation 16-9. If the distance from the source doubles, what happens to (a) the intensity and (b) the decibel level?

27. At a distance 2.0 m from a localized sound source you measure the intensity level as 75 dB. How far away must you be for the perceived loudness to drop in half (i.e., to an intensity level of 65 dB)?

28. An amplifier is supplying a loudspeaker with 50 mW of power, and the resulting sound level where you are sitting is 46 dB. How much power must the amplifier supply for you to perceive a fourfold increase in loudness?

29. Sound intensity from a certain extended source drops as $1/r^n$, where r is the distance from the source. If the intensity level drops by 3 dB every time the distance is doubled, what is n?

30. (a) Show that the decibel level may be written

$$\beta = 20 \log\left(\frac{\Delta P}{P_0}\right),$$

where ΔP is the sound-wave pressure amplitude and P_0 is a reference pressure. (b) Find the value of P_0.

Section 17-4 Sound Waves in Liquids and Solids

31. The bulk modulus for tungsten is $2.0{\times}10^{11}$ N/m^2, and its density is $1.94{\times}10^4$ kg/m^3. Find the sound speed in tungsten.

32. The density of aluminum is 2700 kg/m^3. Use the sound speed in Table 17-2 to find aluminum's bulk modulus.

33. The speed of sound in body tissues is essentially the same as in water. Find the wavelength of 2.0 MHz ultrasound used in medical diagnostics.

34. A 1-m-long lead bar and a 1-m-long steel bar are side by side. If they are simultaneously struck a blow on one end, how much sooner will the resulting pressure pulse arrive at the far end of the steel bar?

35. Mechanical vibration induces a sound wave in a mechanism consisting of a 12-cm-long steel rod attached to a 3.0-cm-long neoprene block. How long does it take the wave to propagate through this structure?

36. An acoustic microscope is a device that uses high-frequency ultrasound for imaging; such microscopes are especially useful in the semiconductor industry. The smallest structures that can be imaged by the acoustic microscope (or any other microscope that uses waves of any kind to probe its specimens) have sizes on the order of a wavelength. What is the smallest structure that can be imaged by an acoustic microscope using 4.5-GHz ultrasound in liquid helium, where the sound speed is 240 m/s?

37. The bulk modulus of the steel whose sound speed is given in Table 17-2 is $1.6{\times}10^{11}$ N/m^2. A 0.50-mm-diameter wire made from this steel can withstand a tension force of 50 N before it deforms permanently. Is it possible to put this wire under enough tension that the speed of transverse waves on the wire is the same as the sound speed in the wire? Answer by calculating the tension required.

Section 17-6 Standing Waves

38. A 2.0-m-long string is clamped at both ends. (a) What is the longest wavelength standing wave that can exist on this string? (b) If the wave speed is 56 m/s, what is the lowest standing-wave frequency?

39. When a stretched string is clamped at both ends, its fundamental standing-wave frequency is 140 Hz. (a) What is the next higher frequency? (b) If the same string, with the same tension, is now clamped at one end and free at the other, what is the fundamental frequency? (c) What is the next higher frequency in case (b)?

40. The A-string (440 Hz) on a piano is 38.9 cm long and is clamped tightly at both ends. If the string is under 667 N tension, what is its mass?

41. Show that only odd harmonics are allowed on a taut string with one end tight and the other free.

42. A string is clamped at both ends and tensioned until its fundamental vibration frequency is 85 Hz. If the string is then held rigidly at its midpoint, what is the lowest frequency at which it will vibrate?

43. Show that the standing-wave condition of Equation 17-8 is equivalent to the requirement that the time it takes a wave to make a round trip from one end of the medium to the other and back be an integer multiple of the wave period.

44. The wave speed on a taut wire is 320 m/s. If the wire is 80 cm long, and is vibrating at 800 Hz, how far apart are the nodes?

45. "Vibrato" in a violin is produced by sliding the finger back and forth along the vibrating string. The G-string on a particular violin measures 30 cm between the bridge and its far end and is clamped rigidly at both points. Its

fundamental frequency is 197 Hz. (a) How far from the end should the violinist place a finger so that the G-string plays the note A (440 Hz)? (b) If the violinist executes vibrato by moving the finger 0.50 cm to either side of the position in part (a), what range of frequencies results?

46. Estimate the fundamental frequency of the human vocal tract by assuming it to be a cylinder 15 cm long that is closed at one end.

47. A bathtub 1.7 m long contains 13 cm of water. By sloshing water back and forth with your hand, you can build up large-amplitude oscillations. Determine the lowest frequency possible for such a resonant oscillation, using the fact that the speed of waves in shallow water of depth h is $v = \sqrt{gh}$. *Hint:* At resonance in this case, the wave has a crest at one end and a trough at the other.

48. What length is necessary for an organ pipe (Fig. 17-27) to produce a 22-Hz tone (a) if the pipe is closed at one end and (b) if it's open at both ends?

FIGURE 17-27 What length pipe organ will produce a 22-Hz tone? (Problem 48)

49. What would be the fundamental frequency of the double bassoon of Example 17-4, if it were played in helium under conditions of Example 17-1?

50. An organ pipe is closed at one end and has a fundamental frequency of 50 Hz. What are the mode numbers and frequencies of the next two higher frequencies it can play?

51. An astronaut smuggles a double bassoon (Example 17-4) to Mars and plays the instrument's fundamental note. If it sounds at 23 Hz, what is the sound speed on Mars?

52. A guitar's G note that should be 392 Hz is playing a bit flat, at 381 Hz. By what percentage should the string tension be increased? Assume the string does not stretch significantly.

Section 17-7 The Doppler Effect

53. A car horn emits 380-Hz sound. If the car moves at 17 m/s with its horn blasting, what frequency will a person standing in front of the car hear?

54. The stationary siren on a firehouse is blaring at 85 Hz. What is the frequency perceived by a firefighter racing toward the station at 120 km/h?

55. A fire truck's siren at rest wails at 1400 Hz; standing by the roadside as the truck approaches, you hear it at 1600 Hz. How fast is the truck going?

56. Red light emitted by hydrogen atoms at rest in the laboratory has wavelength 656 nm. Light emitted in the same process on a distant galaxy is received at Earth with wavelength 708 nm. Describe the galaxy's motion relative to Earth.

57. The dominant frequency emitted by an airplane's engines is 1400 Hz. (a) What frequency will you measure if the plane approaches you at half the sound speed? (b) What frequency will you measure if the plane recedes at half the sound speed?

58. A wave source approaches you at constant speed, and you measure a wave frequency f_1. As the source passes and then recedes, you measure frequency f_2. Find expressions for (a) the source speed and (b) the frequency emitted if the source were stationary, both in terms of f_1, f_2, and the wave speed v.

59. You're standing by the roadside as a truck approaches, and you measure the dominant frequency in the truck noise at 1100 Hz. As the truck passes the frequency drops to 950 Hz. What is the truck's speed?

60. You're between two loudspeakers emitting 180-Hz tones. How fast would you have to walk or run to perceive a beat frequency of 1.5 Hz between the two?

61. Use the binomial approximation to show that Equations 17-10 and 17-11 give the same result in the limit $u \ll v$.

Section 17-8 Shock Waves

62. What will be the cone angle for a supersonic aircraft traveling at Mach 2.5 (2.5 times the sound speed)?

63. Figure 17-28 shows a projectile in supersonic flight, with shock waves clearly visible. By making appropriate

FIGURE 17-28 Problem 63.

measurements, determine the projectile's speed as compared with the sound speed.

64. A supersonic plane flies directly over you at 2.2 times the sound speed. You hear its sonic boom 19 s later. What is the plane's altitude, assuming a constant 340 m/s sound speed?

Paired Problems

(Both problems in a pair involve the same principles and techniques. If you can get the first problem, you should be able to solve the second one.)

65. A 1.0-W sound source emits uniformly in all directions. Find (a) the intensity and (b) the decibel level 12 m from the source.

66. At a distance 3.5 m from a localized sound source the intensity level is 84 dB. (a) What will it be 8.0 m from the source? (b) What is the total power emitted by the source?

67. A pipe 80 cm long is open at both ends. When the pipe is immersed in a gas mixture, the frequency of a certain harmonic is 280 Hz and the next higher harmonic is 350 Hz. Determine (a) the sound speed and (b) the mode numbers of the two harmonics.

68. A 1.5-m-long pipe has one end open. Among its possible standing-wave frequencies is 225 Hz; the next higher frequency is 375 Hz. Find (a) the fundamental frequency and (b) the sound speed.

69. Find the wave speed in a medium where a 28 m/s source speed causes a 3% increase in frequency measured by a stationary observer.

70. A wave source recedes from you at 8.2 m/s, and the wavelength you measure is 20% greater than what you would measure were the source at rest. What is the wave speed?

Supplementary Problems

71. The sound speed in air at 0°C is 331 m/s, and for temperatures within a few tens of degrees of 0°C it increases at the rate 0.590 m/s for every °C increase in temperature. How long would it take a sound wave to travel 150 m over a path where the temperature rises linearly from 5°C at one end to 15°C at the other end?

72. Rods of lead and steel are joined end-to-end; the total length is 6.0 m. If a sound wave takes 1.8 ms to traverse this structure, how long is the lead rod?

73. A rectangular trough is 2.5 m long and is much deeper than its length, so Equation 16-11 applies. Determine the wavelength and frequency of (a) the longest and (b) the next longest standing waves possible in this trough. Why isn't the higher frequency twice the lower?

74. Show by direct substitution (with appropriate differentiation) that Equation 17-7 satisfies the wave Equation 16-12.

75. A supersonic airplane flies directly over you at 6.5 km altitude. You hear its sonic boom 13 s later. What is the plane's Mach number?

76. A wave source moves at speed u_s through a medium where the wave speed is v. An observer moves with speed u_o. If the wave frequency as emitted by the source is f, show that the observer measures a frequency given by $f' = f(v \pm u_o)/(v \mp u_s)$, where the signs are interpreted as in Equations 17-10 and 17-11.

77. Consider an object moving at speed u through a medium, and reflecting sound waves from a stationary source back toward the source. The object receives the waves at the shifted frequency given by Equation 17-11, and when it re-emits them they are shifted once again, this time according to Equation 17-10. Find an expression for the overall frequency shift that results, and show that, for $u \ll v$, this shift is approximately $2fu/v$.

78. Obstetricians use ultrasound to monitor fetal heartbeat. If 5.0-MHz ultrasound reflects off the moving heart wall with a 100-Hz frequency shift, what is the speed of the heart wall? *Hint:* The heart *reflects* the waves, so consider the result of the preceding problem.

79. What is the frequency shift of a 70-GHz police radar signal when it reflects off a car moving at 120 km/h? (Radar waves travel at the speed of light.) *Hint:* See Problem 77.

80. In an extraordinarily sensitive experiment, physicists at Harvard University recently measured the growth rate of crystals by reflecting a laser beam off the crystal surface. The reflected and transmitted beams were combined, and the resulting beat frequency—arising from the very small Doppler shift—was measured. (a) For a laser frequency of 5×10^{14} Hz, what beat frequency results from a crystal growth rate of 0.2 nm/s? (b) What fraction is the frequency shift of the original laser frequency?

Fluid Motion

A tornado owes its destructive power to the swirling winds that develop as the fluid air responds to pressure and gravitational forces.

A tornado whirls across a darkened sky. A jetliner takes off, propelled by hot gases and supported by air pressure on its wings. A stream of gas leaves the surface of a giant star and forms a cosmic whirlpool before it plunges into a black hole. Your car brakes to a stop, the force of your foot on the brake pedal amplified by the effect of fluid in the brake cylinders. Your own body is sustained by air moving in and out of your lungs, and by the flow of blood throughout your tissues. All these examples involve fluid motion.

Fluid is matter that flows under the influence of external forces. The intermolecular forces are weaker in fluids than in solids, and as a result the molecules move around readily rather than being locked into the rigid structure that characterizes a solid. In a liquid, those forces are still significant enough to keep the molecules in close contact, while in a gas they are almost negligible and the molecules are usually widely spaced. In either case, mobility of the individual molecules means that fluids cannot resist so-called shear forces that tend to slide one layer of material past another. For example, you can't make a pile of water the way you can of, say, sand. This inability to resist shear forces means that a fluid spreads out to take the shape of its container.

18-1 DESCRIBING FLUIDS: DENSITY AND PRESSURE

If we could observe a fluid on the molecular scale, we would find large numbers of molecules in continuous motion, colliding frequently with each other and with the walls of their containers. This molecular behavior is governed by the laws of mechanics, and in principle we could study fluids by applying those laws to all the individual molecules. But even a drop of water contains about 10^{21} molecules; to calculate the motions of all those molecules would take the fastest computers many times the age of the universe!

Because the number of molecules is so large, we approximate a fluid by considering it to be continuous rather than composed of discrete particles. In this approximation, valid for fluid samples large compared with the distance between molecules, we describe the fluid by specifying macroscopic properties such as density and pressure.

Density

Density (symbol ρ, the Greek rho) measures the mass per unit volume; its SI units are kg/m³. The density of water under normal conditions is about 1000 kg/m³; that of air is about a factor of 1000 smaller. Because their molecules are essentially in contact, liquids are **incompressible**, meaning that their densities remain nearly constant. In contrast, gases, with relatively large distances between their molecules, are **compressible**; their densities change readily.

Pressure

Pressure measures the normal force per unit area exerted by a fluid (Fig. 18-1a). If the pressure is uniform over an area, then we have

$$P = \frac{F}{A};$$
(18-1a)

if pressure varies over an area, we consider the force dF on an infinitesimal area dA and write

$$P = \frac{dF}{dA}.$$
(18-1b)

The SI pressure unit is N/m², given the name **pascal** (Pa) after the French mathematician, scientist, and philosopher Blaise Pascal (1623–1662). Another commonly used pressure unit is the **atmosphere** (atm), defined as Earth's normal atmospheric pressure at sea level and equal to 1.013×10^5 Pa (14.7 pounds per square inch). Problems 6 and 7 introduce several other pressure units.

$d\mathbf{F}$ dA

(a)   *(b)*

Pressure is a scalar quantity; at a given point in a fluid, pressure is exerted equally in all directions (Fig. 18-1*b*), so it makes no sense to associate a direction with it. This property explains an aspect of pressure that you may find puzzling. Although the atmosphere bears down on your body with a pressure of 14.7 pounds on every square inch, you certainly don't feel that burden. Why not? Because the force associated with this pressure is everywhere perpendicular to your body, and your body fluids respond by compressing until they're at the same pressure. If you've had your ears "pop" in a fast elevator or airplane, or when diving underwater, you know the pain that can develop when pressure forces on your body are temporarily imbalanced.

18-2 FLUIDS AT REST: HYDROSTATIC EQUILIBRIUM

For a fluid to remain at rest, the net force everywhere in the fluid must be zero. When this condition is met, the fluid is in **hydrostatic equilibrium**. In the absence of any external forces, hydrostatic equilibrium requires that the pressure be constant throughout the fluid; otherwise pressure differences would result in forces acting on the fluid, and the fluid would move in response. As Fig. 18-2

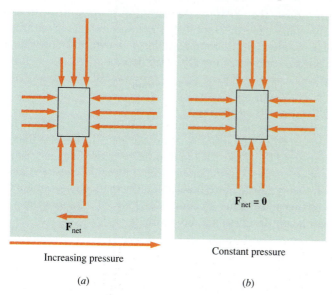

$\mathbf{F}_{net}$

Increasing pressure

(a)

$\mathbf{F}_{net} = 0$

Constant pressure

(b)

FIGURE 18-2 (*a*) If pressure varies with position, then there is a net pressure force on a volume of fluid. In the absence of external forces, the fluid then cannot be in hydrostatic equilibrium. (*b*) When the pressure is constant, the net pressure force is zero. In the absence of external forces, the fluid is then in hydrostatic equilibrium.

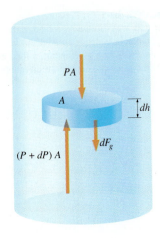

suggests, it is pressure *difference,* rather than pressure itself, that gives rise to net forces within fluids.

Hydrostatic Equilibrium with Gravity

For a fluid to be in hydrostatic equilibrium in the presence of gravity, there must be a pressure force to counteract the gravitational force. Since pressure forces arise only from pressure differences, the fluid pressure must therefore vary with depth.

Figure 18-3 shows the forces on a fluid element of area A, thickness dh, and mass dm. A gravitational force acts downward on this fluid element; for it to be in equilibrium there must therefore be an upward pressure force—and that requires a greater pressure on the lower side of the fluid element. Suppose the pressures at the top and bottom are P and $P + dP$, respectively. Since pressure is force per unit area, the net pressure force on the fluid element is therefore

$$dF_{\text{press}} = (P + dP)A - PA = A\, dP.$$

The gravitational force is $dF_{\text{grav}} = -g\, dm$, where the minus sign designates the downward direction. But the mass dm is the density times the volume, so

$$dF_{\text{grav}} = -g\, dm = -g\rho A\, dh.$$

Hydrostatic equilibrium requires that these forces sum to zero:

$$A\, dP - g\rho A\, dh = 0,$$

or

$$\frac{dP}{dh} = \rho g. \tag{18-2}$$

This equation shows that dP/dh—the variation in pressure with depth h—is positive, confirming our expectation that pressure increases with depth. For a liquid, which is essentially incompressible, ρ is constant and Equation 18-2 shows that pressure increases linearly with depth:

$$P = P_0 + \rho g h, \tag{18-3}$$

where P_0 is the pressure at the liquid surface.

Equation 18-2 applies to any fluid in a uniform gravitational field; Equation 18-3 follows from Equation 18-2 for the special case of a liquid. It's also possible to integrate Equation 18-2 to find the pressure in a gas, such as Earth's atmosphere, that's subject to the gravitational force. Because the gas density is not constant, this is a little more involved mathematically—but not beyond the reach of a first-year calculus student. Problem 70 explores the variation of pressure with height in Earth's atmosphere.

EXAMPLE 18-1 | *Ocean Depths*

(a) At what water depth is the pressure twice atmospheric pressure? (b) What is the water pressure at the bottom of the 11.3-km-deep Marianas trench in the North Pacific, the deepest point in the ocean? Atmospheric pressure P_0 is 1.0×10^5 Pa, and the density of water is $1000 \ kg/m^3$.

Solution

At twice atmospheric pressure, $P = 2P_0$ in Equation 18-2. Solving for the depth h then gives

$$h = \frac{P - P_0}{\rho g} = \frac{2.0 \times 10^5 \ \text{Pa} - 1.0 \times 10^5 \ \text{Pa}}{(1000 \ \text{kg/m}^3)(9.8 \ \text{m/s}^2)} = 10 \ \text{m} \ .$$

Since pressure increases linearly with depth, the pressure continues to increase by 1.0×10^5 Pa for every 10 m of depth. In the Marianas trench, 11.3×10^3 m deep, the pressure increase is then

$$P - P_0 = (11.3 \times 10^3 \ \text{m})(1.0 \times 10^5 \ \text{Pa}/10 \ \text{m}) = 1.1 \times 10^9 \ \text{Pa} \ .$$

This is over 1000 times atmospheric pressure, or more than 8 tons per square inch! Creatures living at these depths are in pressure equilibrium with their surroundings; to bring them to the surface for study, scientists must maintain their natural pressure or they will explode (Fig. 18-4). A similar plight awaits scuba divers who hold their breath while ascending; air in the lungs expands, bursting the alveoli.

EXERCISE A submarine is designed for depths to 1500 m. How much pressure must it withstand if its interior is maintained at normal atmospheric pressure?

FIGURE 18-4 Oceanographers bring deep ocean water to the surface in a container that maintains deep-sea creatures at their natural pressure.

Answer: 1.5×10^7 Pa

Some problems similar to Example 18-1: 17–19

EXAMPLE 18-2 | *A Swimming Pool*

A swimming pool is 15 m wide and, at the deep end, 3.0 m deep. Find the force of the water on the pool wall at the deep end.

Solution

The pressure in the pool varies from surface to bottom, so we can't simply multiply the pressure by the area to find the force. Instead, we consider the force on a small strip of height dh and pool width W, as shown in Fig. 18-5. This strip has area $dA = W dh$, so the force on it is $dF = P dA = PW dh$. Using Equation 18-3 for the pressure, and integrating to get the total force, we have

$$F = \int dF = \int_{h=0}^{h=H} (P_0 + \rho g h) W \, dh = W(P_0 h + \tfrac{1}{2}\rho g h^2)\big|_0^H$$

$$= P_0 WH + \tfrac{1}{2}\rho g WH^2 \ ,$$

FIGURE 18-5 Since pressure varies with depth, calculating the force on the pool wall involves integrating over the vertical position. A suitable area element is a strip of width W and height dh.

where H is the pool depth. Using $P_0 = 1.0 \times 10^5$ Pa for atmospheric pressure, $\rho = 1000$ kg/m^3 for water, and the pool dimensions gives $F = 5.2$ MN.

EXERCISE The spent fuel storage pool at a nuclear reactor measures 20 m long by 10 m wide by 6.5 m deep and is filled with water. What force must its longer sides be capable of withstanding?

Answer: 17 MN

Some problems similar to Example 18-2: 23, 24

FIGURE 18-6 A mercury barometer. Normal air pressure supports a mercury column 760 mm high.

Measuring Pressure

The variation in liquid pressure with depth is the basis of several common pressure-measuring instruments. Figure 18-6 shows a simple **barometer**. Atmospheric pressure acts on the open pool of liquid mercury, pushing the liquid into the evacuated tube. Since $P_0 = 0$ in the vacuum at the top of the tube, Equation 18-3 becomes simply $P = \rho g h$, showing that the height h of the mercury column is directly proportional to the atmospheric pressure P at the bottom of the column. In mercury, standard atmospheric pressure of 1.013×10^5 Pa supports a mercury column 760 mm or 29.92 inches high (see Problem 6). The actual value of atmospheric pressure usually varies slightly from one place to another, and is of interest to meteorologists because pressure variations drive the air motions we call wind and indirectly cause other weather phenomena. Weather forecasters often report atmospheric pressure in mm or inches of mercury.

Barometers use mercury because its high density makes for a relatively short instrument; Example 18-1 shows that a water-filled barometer would need to be 10 m long to measure atmospheric pressure. The same underlying fact—that atmospheric pressure can support a water column 10 m high—puts a limitation on water pumps that operate by suction. No matter how good a vacuum a suction pump can produce, atmospheric pressure can't push water up more than 10 m. Pumping from greater depths requires a submerged pump or one that somehow increases the pressure at the pumping depth.

Measurement of pressure differences is accomplished with a **manometer**, a U-shaped tube containing liquid and open at both ends (Fig. 18-7). A pressure difference between the ends of the tube results in a difference in height of the two liquid surfaces; Equation 18-3 shows that this height difference is directly proportional to the pressure difference.

Mercury barometers and manometers are the classic pressure measuring instruments, and understanding their simple operation helps elucidate the meaning of pressure. But pressure-measuring devices in use today are often electronic, using the pressure force on a solid material to alter electrical properties in a way that produces an electrical signal proportional to the pressure.

When one end of a manometer, or other pressure-difference instrument, senses atmospheric pressure, the pressure it reads is called **gauge pressure**, meaning the pressure in excess of atmospheric pressure. Inflation pressures for tires and sports equipment are given in gauge pressure; a tire inflated to 200 kPa (about 30 pounds/in^2) actually has an absolute pressure of about 300 kPa because the 100-kPa atmospheric pressure is not included in the specification. Tire gauges read gauge, not absolute, pressure.

FIGURE 18-7 A manometer used to measure pressure difference between a closed container and the ambient atmosphere. Height difference h is proportional to the pressure difference.

Pascal's Law

Equation 18-3 shows that an increase in surface pressure P_0 results in the same pressure increase throughout the fluid. More generally, a pressure increase anywhere in a fluid is felt throughout the fluid—a fact first recognized by Pascal and now known as **Pascal's law**. Pascal applied this principle in his invention of the hydraulic press; today hydraulic systems, based on Pascal's law, are used to control machinery ranging from automobile brake systems, to aircraft wings, to bulldozers, cranes, and robots (Fig. 18-8).

FIGURE 18-8 Arrows indicate the hydraulic cylinders that actuate this power shovel.

EXAMPLE 18-3	*A Hydraulic Lift*

In the hydraulic lift shown in Fig. 18-9, a 120-cm-diameter piston supports a car. If the total mass of the piston and car is 3200 kg, what should be the diameter of the smaller piston if an applied force of 450 N is to maintain the system in equilibrium? Neglect the mass of the smaller piston and any pressure variation with height.

Solution

The small piston exerts a pressure $P = F_1/A_1 = F/\pi r_1^2$, with r_1 its radius and F_1 the 450-N applied force. Pascal's law says that this pressure is transmitted equally throughout the system; at the large piston it produces a force $F_2 = PA_2$. This force supports the weight mg of piston and car; therefore we have

$$mg = PA_2 = P\pi r_2^2 = \frac{F_1}{\pi r_1^2}\pi r_2^2 = F_1\frac{r_2^2}{r_1^2}.$$

Solving for r_1 gives

$$r_1 = r_2\sqrt{\frac{F_1}{mg}} = (60 \text{ cm})\sqrt{\frac{450 \text{ N}}{(3200 \text{ kg})(9.8 \text{ N/kg})}} = 7.2 \text{ cm},$$

or a diameter of 14.4 cm. Note that the 450-N force is effectively multiplied by the ratio of the piston areas, ultimately supporting a weight of nearly 32,000 N.

FIGURE 18-9 A hydraulic lift (Example 18-3).

FIGURE 18-10 Simplified diagram of an automobile braking system, showing master cylinder and one of the slave cylinders. The slave cylinder pushes the brake pads against the rotating brake disk, stopping it and the attached wheel.

Are we getting something for nothing here? No. Work done in moving the small piston—the product of force with distance moved—is equal to the work done on the large piston. Since the force on the large piston is much greater, the distance moved is much smaller, and energy is conserved.

EXERCISE Figure 18-10 shows an automobile braking system. The brake pedal applies a force to a piston in the "master cylinder," and the resulting pressure increase is transmitted to "slave cylinders" that operate the brakes. The master cylinder has an interior diameter of 8.0 mm, and it operates two slave cylinders each with diameter 3.2 cm. (Two separate systems each operating two wheels are provided on modern cars for safety in the event of a hydraulic fluid leak.) If a 750-N force is applied to the master cylinder, what force does each of the two slave cylinders exert on its brake pads?

Answer: 12 kN

Some problems similar to Example 18-3: 28–30

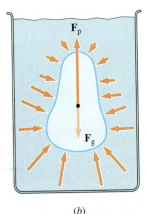

FIGURE 18-11 (*a*) In hydrostatic equilibrium, the upward pressure force $\mathbf{F}_p$ is equal to the weight $\mathbf{F}_g$ of any fluid volume. (*b*) If the fluid is replaced by a solid object, the pressure force remains the same but the gravitational force generally changes. The direction of the net force on the object depends on whether it is more or less dense than the fluid.

18-3 ARCHIMEDES' PRINCIPLE AND BUOYANCY

Drop a rock into water and it sinks. Drop a cork and it floats. Why the difference?

Figure 18-11*a* shows the upward pressure force on an arbitrary fluid volume balancing the downward gravitational force. Now imagine replacing the fluid volume by a solid object of identical shape (Fig. 18-11*b*). The remaining fluid hasn't changed, so it continues to exert an upward force on the object—a force whose magnitude equals the weight of the *original fluid volume*. This force is called the **buoyancy force**, and in giving its magnitude we've stated **Archimedes' principle**:

> *Archimedes' principle: The buoyant force on an object is equal to the weight of the fluid displaced by the object.*

If the submerged object weighs more than the displaced fluid, then the gravitational force exceeds the buoyancy force and it sinks. If the object weighs less than the displaced fluid, the buoyancy force is greater and it rises. Therefore, an object floats or sinks depending on whether its average density is greater or less than that of the fluid. In between is the case of **neutral buoyancy**, when an object's average density is the same as that of the fluid. Fish, submarines, and balloons are often in neutral buoyancy (Fig. 18-12).

(*a*)

(*b*)

FIGURE 18-12 (*a*) A hot-air balloon at constant altitude is in neutral buoyancy. (*b*) So is a fish, whose gas-filled swim bladder compresses or expands to maintain the same average density as water. In both cases the net buoyancy force is equal in magnitude to the gravitational force.

EXAMPLE 18-4	*Aerogels, Archimedes, and the King's Crown*

Physicists have developed new materials called *aerogels* that are at once amazingly light (Fig. 18-13*a*) and surprisingly strong (Fig. 18-13*b*). A particular piece of aerogel is made

(*a*)

(*b*)

FIGURE 18-13 (*a*) Aerogels, made from silicon dioxide, are so tenuous that the buoyant force of air significantly reduces the apparent weight. Here a ghostly blue slab of aerogel rests on freshly beaten egg whites. (*b*) Aerogels are surprisingly strong. Here an aerogel slab with mass under 1 g supports a 100-g mass.

from 1.00 g of silicon dioxide. Yet its apparent weight on a scale is 7.35 mN. How does the aerogel's density compare with that of air?

Solution

The aerogel's apparent weight is less than its actual weight $m_{gel}g = 9.8$ mN because of the upward buoyant force of the air. That force is equal to the weight of displaced air, or $F_b = m_{air}g$. The *volume* of displaced air is that of the aerogel, so $m_{air} = \rho_{air}V_{gel}$. But the aerogel's volume is $V_{gel} = m_{gel}/\rho_{gel}$. Putting this all together gives the buoyant force:

$$F_b = m_{air}g = \rho_{air}V_{gel}g = \rho_{air}\frac{m_{gel}}{\rho_{gel}}g = W_{gel}\frac{\rho_{air}}{\rho_{gel}},$$

where $W_{gel} = m_{gel}g$ is the gel's actual weight. Its apparent weight is then $W_{apparent} = W_{gel} - F_b$. Using our expression for F_b and solving for the density ratio ρ_{gel}/ρ_{air} then gives

$$\frac{\rho_{gel}}{\rho_{air}} = \frac{W_{gel}}{W_{gel} - W_{apparent}} = \frac{9.8 \text{ mN}}{9.8 \text{ mN} - 7.35 \text{ mN}} = 4.0.$$

The density of air is about 1.2 kg/m³, so the aerogel's density is only 4.8 kg/m³—compared with 1000 kg/m³ for water.

The buoyant force of air significantly reduces the aerogel's apparent weight because its density is only a few times that of air. Buoyancy actually lowers the apparent weights of all objects when weighed in air, but usually the effect is negligible because typical densities are on the order of 1000 times that of air.

Archimedes (c. 287–212 B.C.), one of the greatest scientists of ancient Greece, purportedly used his principle to determine

FIGURE 18-14 Archimedes purportedly verified that the king's crown was pure gold by finding its apparent weight when submerged in water.

the density of the king's crown, and thus verify that it was indeed made of gold. Archimedes achieved a nonnegligible buoyancy force by suspending the crown in water (see Fig. 18-14 and Problem 34).

EXERCISE Salvage experts recover a shipment of steel beams from a sunken ship. What will be the tension in a cable lifting a 750-kg beam through water with density 1.0 g/cm³? The density of the steel is 7.9 g/cm³ and the lifting is at constant speed.

Answer: 6.4 kN

Some problems similar to Example 18-4: 31–34

Floating Objects

Archimedes' principle still holds for a floating object. But now the buoyant force must balance the object's weight—and this can happen only if the fluid displaced by the submerged part of the object has a weight equal to that of the object. This condition determines how high in the water the object floats, as Fig. 18-15 and the following examples illustrate.

(a)   (b)

FIGURE 18-15 Supertankers, (a) empty and (b) fully loaded. In both cases the buoyant force supports the full weight of the ship and cargo. The buoyant force is equal to the weight of the displaced water, so the fully loaded ship must displace more water and therefore floats lower in the water.

Got It!

A glass of water, with an ice cube floating in it, is full to the brim. Will it overflow as the ice cube melts?

EXAMPLE 18-5	The Tip of the Iceberg

The average density of a typical arctic iceberg is 0.86 that of sea water. What fraction of an iceberg's volume is submerged?

Solution

The buoyant force supports the entire weight of the iceberg, so the weight of the displaced water is equal to the iceberg weight. If V_{sub} is the volume of ice that's submerged, then the weight of an equal volume of water—and therefore the magnitude of the buoyant force—is

$$F_b = W_{water} = m_{water}g = \rho_{water}V_{sub}g .$$

The weight of the iceberg is

$$W_{ice} = m_{ice}g = \rho_{ice}V_{ice}g ,$$

where V_{ice} is the volume of the entire iceberg. Equating the iceberg weight to the magnitude of the buoyant force, we have

$$\rho_{ice}V_{ice}g = \rho_{water}V_{sub}g ,$$

so

$$\frac{V_{sub}}{V_{ice}} = \frac{\rho_{ice}}{\rho_{water}} = 0.86 .$$

Roughly six-sevenths of an arctic iceberg is therefore submerged (Fig. 18-16).

FIGURE 18-16 Most of an iceberg's volume is submerged because its density is only slightly less than that of water.

EXAMPLE 18-6	An Overloaded Boat

A flat-bottomed rowboat has length $\ell = 3.2$ m, width $w = 1.1$ m, and is 28 cm deep. Empty, it has a mass of 130 kg. (a) How much of the boat is submerged when it is empty? (b) What is the total mass it could carry without taking on water?

Solution

In equilibrium, the total weight of the boat and its load must be supported by the buoyant force of the water. By Archimedes' principle, this force is equal to the weight of water displaced by the boat. Letting y be the depth to which the boat is submerged, we have

$$\ell wy\rho_{water}g = Mg .$$

Here ρ_{water} is the density of water, and ℓwy the submerged volume, so the term on the left is the weight of displaced water and is therefore equal to the magnitude of the buoyant force. The quantity M is the total mass of the boat plus its load, so the term on the right is the weight supported by the buoyant force. Solving for y, we have

$$y = \frac{M}{\ell w\rho_{water}} = \frac{(130\ \text{kg})}{(3.2\ \text{m})(1.1\ \text{m})(1000\ \text{kg/m}^3)} = 3.7\ \text{cm}$$

for the empty boat.

To find the absolute maximum load, we set y equal to the boat's 28-cm depth, and solve for M:

$$M = \ell wy\rho_{water} = (3.2\ \text{m})(1.1\ \text{m})(0.28\ \text{m})(1000\ \text{kg/m}^3)$$
$$= 986\ \text{kg} .$$

This is the total mass; subtracting the 130-kg boat mass gives 856 kg for the maximum load.

EXERCISE A rectangular bar of soap floats with 3.5 cm extending below the water surface and 1.5 cm above. What is its density?

Answer: 700 kg/m^3

Some problems similar to Examples 18-5 and 18-6: 35–37, 40

The Center of Buoyancy

A boat will float if its average density is less than that of water. But will it float upright? That depends. We found in Chapter 14 that the force of gravity acts as though it were all concentrated at a point called the center of gravity. Does the buoyancy force also act at the center of gravity? No: The buoyancy force on an object is precisely the force that would act on a volume of water identical in size and shape to the submerged part of the object. Since the buoyancy force and gravitational force would keep that water volume in equilibrium, the two forces must act at the same point—otherwise there could be torques that would set the water into rotation. So the buoyancy force acts at the center of gravity not of the object but of the water that would be there if the object weren't. Normally, therefore, the center of gravity and **center of buoyancy**, as it's called, are not the same point.

For a floating object to be in stable equilibrium, the forces of gravity and buoyancy must not only sum to zero, but they must also produce no net torque. Consider the boat shown in Fig. 18-17a, whose center of buoyancy lies above its center of gravity. If it tips a bit to the side, a torque develops that tends to restore it to equilibrium. But if the boat were so ill designed, or so overloaded, that its center of gravity was above its center of buoyancy, then any deviation from a perfectly upright position would produce a torque that would tip the boat over (Fig. 18-17b). So the first priority of a marine engineer is to ensure that any watercraft design puts the center of gravity below the center of buoyancy, and the first priority of any boat operator is to keep it that way!

Got It!

Explain, in terms of center of gravity and center of buoyancy, why you're not supposed to stand up in a canoe.

FIGURE 18-17 (a) When the center of buoyancy (CB) is above the center of gravity (CG), the torque that develops if the boat tips tends to restore it to its upright position. (b) If the center of gravity is above the center of buoyancy, a torque develops that tips the boat over.

18-4 FLUID DYNAMICS

We now turn our attention to moving fluids, which are described by the flow velocity at each point in the fluid and at each instant of time. Figure 18-18 shows some flow velocity vectors in a river. We can describe flow velocity either with individual vectors, as in Fig. 18-18a, or by drawing continuous lines called **streamlines** that are everywhere tangent to the local flow direction (Fig. 18-18b). Their spacing is a measure of flow speed, with closely spaced streamlines indicating high speed. Small particles, such as smoke or dyes, are

FIGURE 18-18 (a) Flow vectors in a river. Note the higher speed where the river narrows. (b) Streamlines are an alternative way of representing the flow. Note that lines are closer where the flow speed is higher.

FIGURE 18-20 (*a*) Smoke from a burning cigarette first rises in a steady flow, but soon the flow becomes unsteady. (*b*) Unsteady flows in Jupiter's atmosphere, photographed by a Voyager spacecraft.

FIGURE 18-19 In this aerodynamic test, smoke particles trace streamlines in the airflow over a car. Can you tell where the flow is fastest?

often introduced into moving fluids because they follow streamlines and therefore give a visual indication of the flow velocity pattern (Fig. 18-19).

We distinguish two types of fluid motion. In **steady flow**, the pattern of fluid motion remains the same at each point, even though individual fluid elements are in continual motion. When you look at a river in steady flow, for example, it always looks the same, even though you're not seeing the same water each time you look. At a given point in the river, the water velocity, density, and pressure are always the same. **Unsteady flow**, in contrast, involves fluid motion that changes with time even at a fixed point. The blood in your arteries is in unsteady flow; with each contraction of the heart ventricles, the pressure rises, and the flow velocity increases. Figure 18-20 shows other examples of steady and unsteady flow. We will restrict our quantitative description of fluid motion to steady flow.

Like all other motion in classical physics, fluid motion is governed by Newton's laws. Indeed, it is possible to write Newton's second law in a form that involves explicitly the fluid velocity as a function of position and time. But the resulting equation is difficult to solve in any but the simplest cases. Instead of applying Newton's law directly, we will approach fluid dynamics from the point of view of energy conservation. As in mechanics, energy conservation provides a shortcut to problem solving; the price of that shortcut is the lack of some details.

Conservation of Mass: The Continuity Equation

In mechanics we had no trouble keeping track of the individual objects. But a fluid is continuous and deformable, so it's not easy to follow an individual fluid element as it moves. Yet fluid is conserved; as it moves and deforms, new fluid is neither created nor destroyed. The **continuity equation** is a mathematical statement of this fact.

To develop the continuity equation, consider a steady fluid flow represented by streamlines, as shown in Fig. 18-21*a*. We have shaded a **flow tube**—a small tubelike region bounded on its sides by a set of streamlines and on its ends by areas at right angles to the streamlines. We choose the flow tube to have

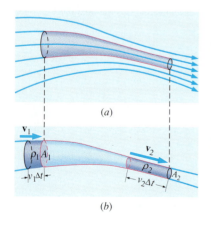

FIGURE 18-21 (*a*) A flow tube. In steady flow, the rate at which fluid enters the tube equals the rate at which it leaves the tube. (*b*) Fluid elements of equal mass entering and leaving the tube.

sufficiently small cross-sectional area that fluid velocity and other fluid properties do not vary significantly over any cross section; however, fluid properties
may vary along the flow tube. Although our flow tube has no physical
boundaries, it nevertheless acts like a pipe of the same shape because fluid flows
along, not across the streamlines. In steady flow, the rate at which fluid enters
the tube at its left end equals the rate at which it exits at the right; otherwise, the
amount of fluid in the pipe would change and the fluid properties would not be
independent of time.

Figure 18-21*b* shows a small fluid element just about to enter the flow tube,
a process that will take some time Δt. Suppose the fluid is moving at speed v_1;
since it takes time Δt to cross the tube end, its length is $v_1 \Delta t$. With cross-
sectional area A_1, length $v_1 \Delta t$, and density ρ_1, the mass of the entering fluid
element is

$$m = \rho_1 A_1 v_1 \Delta t .$$

Another fluid element is shown just about to leave the tube. Suppose it has the
same mass m as the entering fluid element. Then it must exit the tube in the *same*
time Δt, in order to keep the total mass in the tube constant. But its mass can be
written

$$m = \rho_2 A_2 v_2 \Delta t .$$

Equating our two expressions for m shows that

$$\rho_1 v_1 A_1 = \rho_2 v_2 A_2 . \tag{18-4a}$$

Since the endpoints of the tube are arbitrary, we conclude that the quantity $\rho v A$
must have the same value anywhere along the flow tube:

$$\rho v A = \text{constant along a flow tube} . \quad \text{(any fluid)} \tag{18-4b}$$

What is this quantity $\rho v A$ that is constant along a flow tube? Its SI units are
$(\text{kg/m}^3)(\text{m/s})(\text{m}^2)$, or simply kg/s. The quantity $\rho v A$ is therefore the **mass
flow rate** or mass of fluid per unit time passing through the flow tube. Equa-
tions 18-4a and 18-4b are equivalent expressions of the continuity equation,
both stating that the mass flow rate is constant along a flow tube in steady flow.

For a liquid, the density ρ is essentially constant, and the continuity equation 18-5 becomes simply

$$v A = \text{constant along a flow tube} . \quad \text{(liquid)} \tag{18-5}$$

Now the constant quantity is just $v A$, with units of $(\text{m/s})(\text{m}^2)$, or m^3/s. The
quantity $v A$ is the **volume flow rate**; in a fluid of constant density, constancy of
mass flow rate also implies constancy of volume flow rate because a given mass
of fluid does not change volume. In the form 18-5, the continuity equation
makes obvious physical sense. Where the liquid has a large cross-sectional area,
it can flow relatively slowly to transport a given volume of fluid per unit time.
But where the area is more constricted, the flow must be faster to carry the same
volume per unit time. With a gas, obeying Equation 18-4 but not necessarily
18-5, the situation is slightly more ambiguous, as density variations also play a
role in the continuity equation. For flow speeds below the speed of sound in a
gas, it turns out that lower area implies a higher flow speed just as for a liquid.
But when gas flow speed exceeds the sound speed, density changes become so
great that flow speed actually decreases with lower area.

EXAMPLE 18-7	*Ausable Chasm*

In the lower part of its valley, the Ausable River in upstate New York is about 40 m wide. Under typical early summer conditions, it is 2.2 m deep and flows at 4.5 m/s. Just before it reaches Lake Champlain, the river enters Ausable Chasm, a deep gorge cut through rock (Fig. 18-22). At its narrowest, the gorge is only 3.7 m wide at the river surface. If the flow rate in the gorge is 6.0 m/s, how deep is the river at this point? Assume that the river has a rectangular cross section, with uniform flow speed over a cross section.

Solution

Writing the cross-sectional area as the product of width w and depth d, Equation 18-5 becomes

$$v_1 w_1 d_1 = v_2 w_2 d_2 .$$

Solving for the gorge depth d_2 gives

$$d_2 = \frac{v_1 w_1 d_1}{v_2 w_2} = \frac{(4.5 \text{ m/s})(40 \text{ m})(2.2 \text{ m})}{(6.0 \text{ m/s})(3.7 \text{ m})} = 18 \text{ m} ,$$

or about 60 feet!

FIGURE 18-22 The Ausable River in upstate New York cuts through a narrow chasm. To accommodate the flow, water depth in the chasm is much greater than elsewhere.

EXERCISE A 2.5-cm-diameter pipe is full of water flowing at 1.8 m/s. If the pipe narrows to 2.0-cm diameter, what is the flow speed in the narrow section?

Answer: 2.8 m/s

Some problems similar to Example 18-7: 43–45

Conservation of Energy: Bernoulli's Equation

We now turn to conservation of fluid energy. Figure 18-23 shows the same fluid element of mass m as it enters and again as it leaves a flow tube. If it enters with

FIGURE 18-23 A flow tube showing the same fluid element entering and leaving. The work done by pressure and gravitational forces equals the change in kinetic energy of the fluid element.

speed v_1 and leaves with speed v_2, the change in its kinetic energy is

$$\Delta K = \tfrac{1}{2}m(v_2^2 - v_1^2).$$

The work-energy theorem (Equation 7-16) equates this change to the net work done on the fluid element. As the element enters the tube, it's subject to a pressure force P_1A_1 from the fluid to its left. This external force acts over the length Δx_1 of the fluid element as it enters, so it does work $W_1 = P_1A_1\Delta x_1$. Similarly, as it leaves the tube the fluid element experiences a force P_2A_2 from the fluid to its right. Because this force is opposite to the flow direction, it does negative work $W_2 = -P_2A_2\Delta x_2$. There are also pressure forces that adjacent volumes of fluid within the flow tube exert on each other, but by Newton's third law these internal forces cancel in pairs and therefore do no net work. Forces from adjacent flow tubes act at right angles to the flow, so they, too, do no net work. Finally, the fluid element rises a distance $y_2 - y_1$ as it traverses the tube; therefore gravity does negative work $W_3 = -mg(y_2 - y_1)$. (Here we assume the flow tube is narrow enough that height variations across either end of the tube are insignificant.) Summing the three contributions to the work and applying the work-energy theorem, we have

$$W_1 + W_2 + W_3 = \Delta K,$$

or

$$P_1A_1\Delta x_1 - P_2A_2\Delta x_2 - mg(y_2 - y_1) = \tfrac{1}{2}m(v_2^2 - v_1^2).$$

The quantities $A_1\Delta x_1$ and $A_2\Delta x_2$ are the volumes of the fluid element as it enters and leaves the flow, respectively. If we restrict ourselves to incompressible fluids, then those two volumes are equal. Dividing through by this common volume $V = A\Delta x$ and noting that $m/V = \rho$, our equation becomes

$$P_1 + \tfrac{1}{2}\rho v_1^2 + \rho g y_1 = P_2 + \tfrac{1}{2}\rho v_2^2 + \rho g y_2, \qquad (18\text{-}6a)$$

or

$$P + \tfrac{1}{2}\rho v^2 + \rho g y = \text{constant along a flow tube}. \qquad (18\text{-}6b)$$

This is called **Bernoulli's equation**, after the Swiss mathematician Daniel Bernoulli (1700–1782).

What do the terms in Bernoulli's equation mean? The quantity $\tfrac{1}{2}\rho v^2$ looks like the kinetic energy $\tfrac{1}{2}mv^2$, except it has mass per unit volume ρ instead of mass m. It's therefore the kinetic energy per unit volume, or kinetic energy density. Similarly, $\rho g y$ is the gravitational potential energy per unit volume. What about the pressure P? It, too, has the units of energy density, and represents the internal energy of the fluid. Bernoulli's equation therefore says that the total energy per unit volume of fluid is conserved as the fluid moves.

Bernoulli's equation in the form 18-6 applies to incompressible fluids. It neglects fluid friction, also called *viscosity,* that may dissipate fluid kinetic energy. It also neglects energy transfers associated with machinery such as turbines or pumps that may extract or add to the fluid's energy. Engineers often include those effects in deriving Bernoulli's equation.

18-5 APPLICATIONS OF FLUID DYNAMICS

The laws of mass and energy conservation we have just written for fluids can be used to analyze a wide variety of natural and technological phenomena involving fluid motion. As we give examples of their applications, remember that those laws are based in the same physical principles—particularly Newton's laws—that we used to describe mechanical systems.

EXAMPLE 18-8	*Draining a Tank*

A large, open tank is filled to a height h with liquid of density ρ. What is the speed of the liquid emerging from a small hole at the base of the tank (Fig. 18-24)?

Solution

We apply Bernoulli's equation to the emerging fluid, calculating the quantity $P + \frac{1}{2}\rho v^2 + \rho gy$ at the hole ($y = 0$) and at the tank top ($y = h$). At both these points the fluid is open to the atmosphere, so the pressure at both points is atmospheric pressure, P_a. If the tank area is large compared with the hole area, fluid at the tank top will be moving very slowly and we can make the approximation $v_{top} \simeq 0$. Then Bernoulli's equation

becomes

$$P_a + \tfrac{1}{2}\rho v_{hole}^2 = P_a + \rho gh.$$

Solving for the outflow speed at the hole gives

$$v_{hole} = \sqrt{2gh}.$$

This is the same result we would get by dropping an object through the distance h—and for the same reason: conservation of energy. Draining a gram of water from the hole is energetically equivalent to removing a gram of water from the top and dropping it through the distance h. Just as the speed of a falling object is independent of its mass, so is the speed of the liquid independent of its density.

As the liquid drains the height h decreases, and so does the flow rate. Problem 67 explores this situation further.

EXERCISE Suppose the top of the tank in Example 18-8 is sealed and pressurized to twice atmospheric pressure. What now is the outflow speed at the hole?

Answer: $\sqrt{2(P_a/\rho + gh)}$

FIGURE 18-24 Example 18-8. How fast does the liquid emerge from the tank?

Some problems similar to Example 18-8: 48, 49, 59, 67

Venturi Flows

A constriction in a pipe carrying incompressible fluid—a liquid or a gas moving at well below its sound speed—requires that flow speed increase in order to maintain constant mass flow. Such a constriction is called a **venturi**. Bernoulli's equation requires that the pressure be lower in the venturi. Example 18-9 shows how this effect is used to measure fluid flow.

| **EXAMPLE 18-9** | *A Venturi Flowmeter* |

Figure 18-25 shows a pipe of cross sectional area A_1 with a venturi constriction of area A_2. A pressure gauge senses pressure differences between the venturi and the unconstricted pipe. The pipe carries an incompressible fluid of density ρ. Find an expression for the flow speed in the unconstricted pipe as a function of the pressure difference ΔP.

Solution

The gravitational term in Bernoulli's equation is the same in the pipe and venturi, so the equation becomes simply

$$P_1 + \tfrac{1}{2}\rho v_1^2 = P_2 + \tfrac{1}{2}\rho v_2^2,$$

where the subscripts 1 and 2 refer to the unconstricted pipe and venturi, respectively. We can relate the two speeds using the continuity equation for an incompressible fluid, Equation 18-5:

$$v_1 A_1 = v_2 A_2.$$

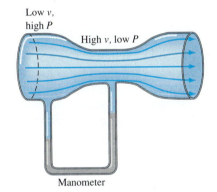

Low v, high P

High v, low P

Manometer

FIGURE 18-25 A venturi flowmeter, with a manometer used to measure the pressure difference between unconstricted pipe and venturi. Bernoulli's equation shows that the pressure difference depends on flow speed.

Solving for v_2 and using the result in Bernoulli's equation gives

$$P_1 - P_2 = \tfrac{1}{2}\rho v_2^2 - \tfrac{1}{2}\rho v_1^2 = \frac{1}{2}\rho\left(\frac{v_1 A_1}{A_2}\right)^2 - \tfrac{1}{2}\rho v_1^2$$
$$= \frac{1}{2}\rho v_1^2\left[\left(\frac{A_1}{A_2}\right)^2 - 1\right].$$

Solving for v_1 in terms of the pressure difference $\Delta P = P_1 - P_2$ then gives

$$v_1 = \sqrt{\frac{2\Delta P}{\rho[(A_1/A_2)^2 - 1]}}.$$

This is the flow speed; multiplying by the area A_1 would give the volume flow rate.

Tip

Combine Information Bernoulli's equation alone could not solve this example; instead we needed both Bernoulli's equation (conservation of energy) and the continuity equation (conservation of mass). You've frequently encountered problems like this where you need to invoke several distinct physical laws. As you attempt new problems, be sure to consider all the laws that might be applicable.

EXERCISE A 1.0-cm-diameter venturi flowmeter is inserted in a 2.0-cm-diameter pipe carrying water (density 1000 kg/m^3). What are (a) the flow speed in the pipe and (b) the volume flow rate if the pressure difference between venturi and unconstricted pipe is 17 kPa?

Answers: (a) 1.5 m/s; (b) 0.473 L/s

Some problems similar to Example 18-9: 46, 47, 51, 57, 58

The venturi phenomenon is put to good use in the carburetor, a device that mixes fuel with air to provide a combustible mixture to a gasoline engine. Liquid fuel is introduced at a venturi in the air stream heading to the engine. Lower pressure at the venturi causes fuel to be forced through a small nozzle, where it mixes thoroughly with the air (Fig. 18-26; see also Problem 65). Small gasoline engines and older cars use carburetors, but fuel injection systems have largely supplanted carburetors in modern cars.

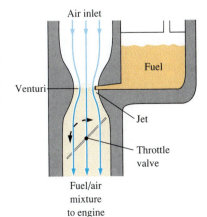

Air inlet

Fuel

Venturi

Jet

Throttle valve

Fuel/air mixture to engine

FIGURE 18-26 Simplified view of a carburetor. Pressure difference between the top of the fuel, at atmospheric pressure, and lower pressure in the venturi forces fuel into the air stream. Throttle plate controls the rate of air flow and therefore the engine speed; it's what's connected to the gas pedal in automobile engines using carburetors.

FIGURE 18-27 Do prairie dogs shape the entrances to their holes to provide ventilation by lowering air pressure above the hole?

The occurrence of lower pressure with higher flow speeds, and vice versa—often called the **Bernoulli effect**—has numerous manifestations. The dirt around a prairie dog's hole is mounded up in a way that forces wind to accelerate over the hole, resulting in lower pressure above the hole (Fig. 18-27). Biologists speculate that prairie dogs have evolved this design to provide natural ventilation. Sometimes the Bernoulli effect can be strikingly counterintuitive. Figure 18-28 shows a ping-pong ball suspended by a *downward* blowing airflow in an inverted funnel. Rapid divergence of the flow results in lower speed and therefore higher pressure below the ball.

Got It!

Cholesterol buildup reduces the diameter of a small section of a major artery. Will the blood pressure in this section be higher or lower than elsewhere? (Consider the flow as being steady, even though blood flow is decidedly not.)

FIGURE 18-28 A ping-pong ball supported by a downward-flowing air stream.

Flight and Lift

Airplanes, helicopters, and birds are supported in flight by aerodynamic forces resulting from their dynamic interaction with the air. Hydrofoil boats, water skis, and high-performance sailboards have analogous interactions with water. Projectiles such as baseballs and missiles, although not supported by the air, have their trajectories substantially modified by aerodynamic forces.

One of the simplest examples of aerodynamic **lift** is the helicopter. Its whirling blades are tilted so they force air downward as they move, just like a giant fan (Fig. 18-29). By Newton's third law, the air exerts an upward force on the blades, ultimately supporting the helicopter. An airplane wing works in the same way, except that it moves forward in a straight line instead of describing a circle. Wings are shaped to maximize the downward deflection of the air even with the wing horizontal, but in principle even a flat board would function as a

FIGURE 18-29 Helicopter blades are tilted to deflect air downward. By Newton's third law, the deflected air exerts an upward force on the blade, ultimately supporting the copter. Airflow is depicted in the frame of reference of the moving blade.

FIGURE 18-31 Vertical component (lift) of the aerodynamic force $\mathbf{F}_a$ supports the entire weight $\mathbf{F}_g$ (140 MN or 150 tons) of this A300 Airbus. Engine force $\mathbf{F}_e$ balances the horizontal component (drag) to keep the plane moving at constant speed.

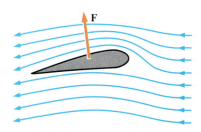

FIGURE 18-30 Flow past a wing. The wing deflects the initially horizontal flow downward; in reaction, the air exerts an upward lift force on the wing. Curved shape enhances lift, but is not essential. Note closer-spaced streamlines above the wing, indicating higher speed and therefore lower pressure.

wing if it were tilted to the oncoming air. Figure 18-30 shows the airflow around a wing. Note how the flow, initially horizontal, leaves the wing moving downward—a clear indication that the wing has exerted a downward force on the air. In a third-law pair with this downward force is the upward force that supports the airplane (Fig. 18-31).

A spinning ball provides another example of aerodynamic lift. Figure 18-32a shows the airflow around a baseball that's not spinning; the flow is symmetric on top and bottom of the ball. But if the pitcher sets the ball spinning in the direction shown in Fig. 18-32b, air dragged around the top is deflected downward. This does not happen symmetrically on the bottom because of differences in the flow pattern between the forward and backward directions. The result is a net downward air deflection and, therefore, an upward force on the ball. If the spin is reversed, the "lift" force will be downward; if the spin axis is turned vertical, the ball will veer left or right (Fig. 18-33).

Bernoulli's equation is frequently invoked to explain lift forces. It is true, as Figs. 18-30 and 18-31b suggest, that flow speeds are higher, and therefore—according to Bernoulli's equation—pressures are lower on top of a wing or a spinning ball. Forces associated with that pressure difference provide the lift, so Bernoulli's equation does help explain what's going on. But those pressure differences and the flow speeds associated with them are manifestations of a simpler underlying phenomenon—the force pairs of Newton's third law.

FIGURE 18-32 (a) Flow is symmetric around a non-spinning ball, so air passes the ball with no net deflection. Therefore there is no lift force on the ball. (b) When the ball spins it drags air with it, causing a downward air deflection and therefore giving rise to a lift force. Note also the higher flow speed and therefore lower pressure above the ball. Small curves represent turbulent eddies that form behind the ball.

FIGURE 18-33 Aerodynamic forces ($\mathbf{F}_a$) give the spinning curve ball its curved trajectory.

Bernoulli's equation states that fluid energy is conserved. If, however, we put moving machinery in a fluid flow, that machinery may add energy, as do pumps, or it may extract energy, as do windmills and other turbines (Fig. 18-34).

Where the wind is blowing with speed v, Bernoulli's equation shows that kinetic energy of fluid motion is present with density $\frac{1}{2}\rho v^2$. A wind turbine can extract fluid kinetic energy from the flow, converting it to the mechanical energy of moving machinery and ultimately to electricity.

What is the rate at which a turbine can extract energy from the wind? If the air approaching the turbine in Fig. 18-34 has speed v, then in time Δt a column of air with length $v\,\Delta t$ flows past the turbine. If the turbine sweeps out an area A, then the volume passing in time Δt is $vA\,\Delta t$. Since the kinetic energy density is $\frac{1}{2}\rho v^2$, the kinetic energy ΔK passing the turbine is

$$\Delta K = (\tfrac{1}{2}\rho v^2)(vA\,\Delta t) = \tfrac{1}{2}\rho v^3 A\,\Delta t.$$

Dividing through by $A\,\Delta t$ gives the energy per time per unit area—that is, the power per unit area available from the wind:

$$\text{Wind power per unit area} = \tfrac{1}{2}\rho v^3.$$

Unfortunately the wind turbine can't extract *all* the kinetic energy, for if it did the air would come to a complete stop behind the turbine and the pressure would build up, halting the flow. A thorough analysis shows that the maximum rate for wind energy extraction is $\frac{8}{27}\rho v^3$, amounting to about 59% of the total kinetic energy. For air (density 1.2 kg/m³) with a wind speed of 10 m/s, this gives 356 watts for every square meter swept out by the turbine. Under ideal conditions, the best practical wind turbines can achieve 80 percent of the theoretical maximum energy extraction.

Because wind power scales as the cube of the wind speed, regions where winds are strong and steady have considerable potential for producing wind energy. In the United States those regions are concentrated near the coasts and in the Great Plains; estimates suggest that large-scale wind development could supply 20% or more of the nation's electrical energy. Thanks to intensive wind development over the past two decades, California already gets 1% of its electricity from the wind, at costs competitive with conventional sources (Fig. 18-35).

Wind is rarely constant, so wind-generated energy must either be stored somehow or used to supplant other energy sources at those times when wind is available. The effect of

FIGURE 18-34 A set of rotating blades—a turbine—in a fluid flow. If external forces turn the turbine, then the turbine acts as a pump, doing work on the fluid and increasing fluid energy. If the fluid turns the turbine, then the turbine extracts energy from the fluid. Can you tell from the streamlines which this turbine is doing?

wind fluctuations can be minimized by connecting generators at diverse locations to a common electrical grid.

Wind generators have fewer adverse environmental effects than most other means of generating electricity. They may present aesthetic problems, especially on mountain ridges, and their mounting towers do take land area. On the other hand, activities such as farming and livestock grazing can continue even in dense "wind farms" like the one shown in Fig. 18-35.

FIGURE 18-35 "Wind farm" at Altamont Pass, California, has more than 6,000 wind turbines and produces an average power of more than 100 MW. California's total wind capacity of nearly 2 GW is the equivalent of two large nuclear or coal-fired power plants.

18-6 VISCOSITY AND TURBULENCE

Our discussion of the spinning baseball suggests that air is "dragged" by objects moving through it. This indeed happens, not only when a fluid is in motion relative to a solid object but even when it moves with different speeds on different streamlines. This phenomenon—called fluid friction or **viscosity**—ultimately arises from momentum transfers among individual molecules with components of motion perpendicular to the flow.

Viscosity is often negligible, especially when fluid is far from a solid boundary. But near such boundaries viscosity is always important because forces between fluid and boundary bring the fluid to a complete stop right at the boundary surface. It's this boundary effect that produces drag forces on objects moving through fluids—and it's the same viscous drag at the surfaces of airplane and ship propellers that exerts a force on the fluid. Without viscosity propellers would just spin uselessly and planes and ships would go nowhere.

Fluid flowing in narrow channels or pipes is always close to a solid boundary, so here viscosity is always important. The result is a nonuniform flow profile, as shown in Fig. 18-36. Viscosity is the dominant force in fluids confined to very small spaces, such as the lubricating oils separating metal surfaces in machinery. Similarly, viscosity plays a more important role in blood flow through capillaries than it does in major arteries and veins.

The importance of viscosity depends not only on the dimensions of the flow channel but also on the fluid itself. Water, for example, is relatively inviscid while molasses is extremely viscous. But again, it's a question of scale: viscosity plays only a small role in the flow of a river, but to a bacterium wiggling its flagella for propulsion, water is far more viscous than molasses dripping off a spoon.

Viscosity also plays an important role in stabilizing fluid flows that would otherwise become **turbulent**, or chaotically unsteady (Fig. 18-37). Turbulence ultimately results from the growth of waves that gain energy at the expense of the flow. When many wave modes are present at once the flow becomes completely chaotic, changing continuously in unpredictable ways. There is not yet a fully satisfactory theory of turbulence, so this area of fluid dynamics is the focus of much contemporary research. Researchers continue to find remarkable connections between the behavior of turbulent fluids and of seemingly unrelated phenomena such as the growth of crystals, the shapes of mountain ranges, and population fluctuations in ecological systems.

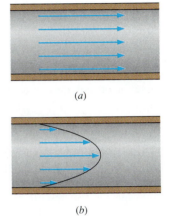

(a)

(b)

FIGURE 18-36 (a) Inviscid flow in a pipe would be uniform. (b) Viscosity reduces the flow velocity, especially near the walls, resulting in a nonuniform flow profile.

(a)   (b)

FIGURE 18-37 (a) An initially uniform flow of liquid (red area) soon becomes turbulent. (b) This turbulent flow shows a striking pattern of whirlpool-like eddies.

CHAPTER SYNOPSIS

Summary

1. **Fluid** is matter that readily deforms and flows under the influence of forces. Fluids are characterized by **density**, or mass per unit volume, and **pressure**, or force per unit area. Liquids are nearly **incompressible**, meaning liquid density hardly changes. Gases are **compressible**, capable of large density changes, but such changes generally occur only when flow speeds approach or exceed the sound speed.

2. In **hydrostatic equilibrium** there is no net force on any element of a fluid. In the absence of external forces, hydrostatic equilibrium implies uniform pressure throughout the fluid. In the presence of gravity, fluid pressure increases with depth so pressure forces balance the gravitational force; in a liquid, that increase is described by

$$P = P_0 + \rho g h,$$

where P_0 is the surface pressure and h the depth.

3. In hydrostatic equilibrium, a pressure increase at any point is transmitted throughout the fluid, a fact known as **Pascal's law**.

4. **Buoyancy** is the upward pressure force on an object wholly or partly immersed in a fluid. The buoyancy force is equal to the weight of fluid displaced by the object—a fact known as **Archimedes' principle**. If an object is less dense than the fluid, the buoyancy force exceeds the gravitational force, and the object rises.

5. A moving fluid is characterized by its flow velocity at each point in space and time. In **steady flow** the velocity is always the same at a given point; such flow is represented by **streamlines** that mark the paths of the fluid elements. In **unsteady flow** the flow velocity varies with time as well as position.

6. The laws of conservation of mass and conservation of energy provide a simplified description of a fluid in steady flow. Both laws are applied to a narrow **flow tube**—a volume bounded by nearby streamlines. Conservation of mass results in the **continuity equation**:

$$\rho v A = \text{constant along a flow tube},$$

where A is the tube area and $\rho v A$ the **mass flow rate**. In a liquid, or a gas with flow speed well below the sound speed, the density ρ is constant and therefore the **volume flow rate** $v A$ remains constant along a flow tube.

In steady, incompressible flow in the absence of viscosity or other forms of energy loss or addition, conservation of energy yields **Bernoulli's equation**:

$$P + \tfrac{1}{2}\rho v^2 + \rho g h = \text{constant along a flow tube}.$$

The continuity equation and Bernoulli's equation together help explain a great many fluid phenomena; other phenomena, such as airplane flight, are more simply explained through the paired forces of Newton's third law.

7. Fluid friction, or **viscosity**, is especially important near fluid boundaries, particularly in narrowly confined flows. Viscosity exerts a stabilizing influence on flows that would otherwise become **turbulent**, or chaotically unstable.

Terms You Should Understand

(Pairs are closely related terms whose distinction is important; number in parentheses is chapter section where term first appears.)

fluid (introduction)
density (18-1)
compressible, incompressible (18-1)
pressure (18-1)
pascal (18-1)
hydrostatic equilibrium (18-2)
barometer, manometer (18-2)
gauge pressure (18-2)
Pascal's law (18-2)
buoyancy force (18-3)
Archimedes' principle (18-3)
streamlines (18-4)
steady flow, unsteady flow (18-4)
flow tube (18-4)
continuity equation (18-4)
mass flow rate, volume flow rate (18-4)
Bernoulli's equation (18-4)
Bernoulli effect (18-5)
lift (18-5)
viscosity (18-6)
turbulence (18-6)

Symbols You Should Recognize

P (18-1)
ρ (18-1)
Pa (18-1)

Problems You Should Be Able to Solve

calculating pressure from force and vice versa (18-1)
calculating pressure as a function of depth in liquids (18-2)
analyzing simple hydraulic systems (18-2)
determining density given apparent weight of submerged objects (18-3)
determining floating position of buoyant objects (18-3)
using the continuity equation to determine flow speeds (18-4)
using the continuity equation and Bernoulli's equation together to solve fluid dynamics problems (18-5)

Limitations to Keep in Mind

Treating matter as a continuous fluid is an approximation valid only when the spacing between molecules is much smaller than any length of interest—including the wavelength of any significant wave motion.

Bernoulli's equation applies only to incompressible flows—that is, to liquids or to gases moving at much less than the sound speed.

QUESTIONS

1. Explain the difference between hydrostatic equilibrium, steady flow, and unsteady flow.
2. Why do your ears "pop" when you drive up a mountain?
3. The cabins of commercial jet aircraft are usually pressurized to the pressure of the atmosphere at about 2 km above sea level. Why don't you feel the lower pressure on your entire body?
4. Water pressure at the bottom of the ocean arises from the weight of the overlying water. Does this mean that the water exerts pressure only in the downward direction? Explain.
5. The three containers in Fig. 18-38 are filled to the same level and are open to the atmosphere. How do the pressures at the bottoms of the three containers compare?

FIGURE 18-38 Question 5.

6. Municipal water systems often include tanks or reservoirs mounted on hills or towers. Besides water storage, what function might these reservoirs have?
7. Why is it easier to float in the ocean than in fresh water?
8. Figure 18-39 shows a cork suspended from the bottom of a sealed container of water. The container is on a turntable rotating about a vertical axis, as shown. Explain the position of the cork.

FIGURE 18-39 Question 8.

9. An ice cube is floating in a cup of water. Will the water level rise, fall, or remain the same when the cube melts?

10. Meteorologists in the United States usually report barometer readings in "inches." What are they talking about?
11. A mountain stream, frothy with entrained air bubbles, presents a serious hazard to hikers who fall into it, for they may sink in the stream where they would float in calm water. Why?
12. Why are dams thicker at the bottom than at the top?
13. It's not possible to breathe through a snorkel from a depth greater than a meter or so (Fig. 18-40). Why not?

FIGURE 18-40 Why don't snorkels work at more than a meter or so of depth (Question 13)?

14. Most humans float naturally in fresh water. Yet the body of a drowning victim generally sinks, often rising several days later after bodily decomposition has set in. What might explain this sequence of floating, sinking, and floating again?
15. A helium-filled balloon stops rising long before it reaches the "top" of the atmosphere, while a cork released from the bottom of a lake rises all the way to the surface of the water. Explain the difference between these two behaviors.
16. A barge filled with steel beams overturns in a lake, spilling its cargo. Does the water level in the lake rise, fall, or remain the same?
17. Imagine a vertical cylinder filled with water and set rotating about its axis. If pieces of wood and stone are introduced into the cylinder, where will each end up?
18. When gas in steady, subsonic flow through a tube encounters a constriction, its flow speed increases. When it flows supersonically in the same situation, flow speed decreases in the constriction. What must be happening to the gas density at the constriction in the supersonic case?
19. Under what conditions can a gas be treated as incompressible?
20. As you drive along a highway and are passed by a large truck, your car may experience a force toward the truck. Explain the origin of this force in terms of the Bernoulli effect.

FIGURE 18-41 A ball supported by air from a hair dryer. Why is it in stable equilibrium? (Question 21)

21. A ball supported by an upward-flowing air column (Fig. 18-41) is essentially in stable equilibrium; if the ball is displaced slightly in any direction, it returns to its original position. Explain. *Hint:* How do you expect the flow speed to vary with horizontal position from the center of the air column?
22. A pump is submerged at the bottom of a 200-ft-deep well. Does it take more power to pump water to the surface when the well is full of water or nearly empty? Or doesn't it matter?
23. Why do airplanes take off into the wind?
24. Is the turbine in Fig. 18-34 adding or removing energy from the flow? How can you tell?
25. Is the flow speed behind a wind turbine greater or less than the flow speed in front? Is the pressure behind the turbine greater or less than in front? Is there a violation of Bernoulli's equation here? Explain.

PROBLEMS

Section 18-1 Describing Fluids: Density and Pressure

1. The density of molasses is 1600 kg/m^3. Find the mass of the molasses in a 0.75-liter jar.
2. Salad dressing is made from one part (by volume) of vinegar (density 1.0 g/cm^3) to three parts olive oil (density 0.92 g/cm^3). What is the average density of the dressing?
3. The density of atomic nuclei is about 10^{17} kg/m^3, while the density of water is 10^3 kg/m^3. Roughly what fraction of the volume of water is *not* empty space?
4. Compressed air with mass 8.8 kg is stored in a gas cylinder with a volume of 0.050 m^3. (a) What is the density of the compressed air? (b) How large a volume would the same gas occupy at typical atmospheric density of 1.2 kg/m^3?
5. A plant hangs from a 3.2-cm-diameter suction cup affixed to a smooth horizontal surface (Fig. 18-42). What is the maximum weight that can be suspended (a) at sea level and (b) in Denver, where atmospheric pressure is about 0.80 atm?

Suction cup

FIGURE 18-42 Problem 5.

6. The pressure unit **torr** is defined as the pressure that will support a column of mercury 1 mm high. Meteorologists often give barometric pressure in **inches of mercury**, defined analogously. Express each of these units in SI. The density of mercury is 1.36×10^4 kg/m^3.

7. Measurement of small pressure differences, for example, between the interior of a chimney and the ambient atmosphere, is often given in **inches of water**, where one inch of water is the pressure that will support a 1-in.-high water column. Express this unit in SI.
8. (a) What is the weight of a column of air with cross-sectional area 1 m^2 extending from Earth's surface to the top of the atmosphere? (b) What is the weight of the entire atmosphere?
9. The fuselage of a 747 jumbo jet is roughly a cylinder 60 m long and 6 m in diameter. If the interior of the plane is pressurized to 0.75 atm, what is the net pressure force tending to separate half the cylinder from the other half when the plane is flying at 10 km, where air pressure is about 0.25 atm? (The earliest commercial jets suffered structural failure from just such forces; modern planes are better engineered.)
10. A 4300-kg circus elephant balances on one foot (Fig. 18-43). If the foot is a circle 30 cm in diameter, what pressure does it exert on the ground?

FIGURE 18-43 Problem 10.

11. A paper clip is made from wire 1.5 mm in diameter. You unbend a paper clip and push the end against the wall. What force must you exert to give a pressure of 120 atm?

12. Continuously running exhaust hoods in a university chemistry building keep the inside air pressure slightly lower than outside. A student notices that a 150-N force is necessary to start opening a 1.2 m by 2.3 m door. The door is hinged on one of its 2.3-m vertical sides, and the handle is mounted on the other side. What is the pressure difference between inside and outside? Give in pascals and as a fraction of atmospheric pressure. *Hint:* Think about torque.

13. When a couple with a total mass of 120 kg lies on a water bed, the pressure in the bed increases by 4700 Pa. What surface area of the two bodies is in contact with the bed?

14. A fully loaded Volvo station wagon has a mass of 1950 kg. If each of its four tires is inflated to a gauge pressure of 230 kPa, what is the total tire area in contact with the road?

15. The emergency escape window of a DC-9 jetliner measures 50 cm by 90 cm. The interior pressure is 0.75 atm, and the plane is at an altitude where atmospheric pressure is 0.25 atm. Is there any danger that a passenger could open the window? Answer by calculating the force needed to pull the window straight inward.

Section 18-2 Fluids at Rest: Hydrostatic Equilibrium

16. Calculate the height of a mercury column that can be supported by air at 1.0 atm pressure. Mercury's density is 1.36×10^4 kg/m^3.

17. What is the density of a fluid whose pressure increases at the rate of 100 kPa for every 6.0 m of depth?

18. A research submarine can withstand external pressures of 50 MPa when its internal pressure is 100 kPa. How deep can it dive?

19. Scuba equipment provides the diver with air at the same pressure as the surrounding water. But at pressures greater than about 1 MPa, the nitrogen in air becomes dangerously narcotic. At what depth does nitrogen narcosis become a hazard?

20. Hot gases rising in a chimney produce a slightly lower air pressure in the chimney, which in turn ensures that these gases can't escape into the surrounding building. The pressure difference, called draft, is often measured with a manometer as shown in Fig. 18-44. If the difference in water levels in the manometer tube is 0.04 in. (typical of an oil furnace), by how much does the chimney pressure differ from atmospheric pressure?

21. A vertical tube open at the top contains 5.0 cm of oil (density 0.82 g/cm^3) floating on 5.0 cm of water. Find the *gauge* pressure at the bottom of the tube.

22. A vertical tube 1.0 cm in diameter and open at the top contains 5.0 g of oil (density 0.82 g/cm^3) floating on 5.0 g of water. Find the *gauge* pressure (a) at the oil-water interface and (b) at the bottom.

FIGURE 18-44 Water manometer used on a chimney (Problem 20).

23. A 1500-m-wide dam holds back a lake 95 m deep. What force does the water exert on the dam?

24. Show that the force on the wall in Example 18-2 can be found by multiplying the wall area by the average of the pressures at top and bottom of the wall. Why does this work?

25. A U-shaped tube open at both ends contains water and a quantity of oil occupying a 2.0-cm length of the tube, as shown in Fig. 18-45. If the oil's density is 0.82 times that of water, what is the height difference h?

FIGURE 18-45 Problem 25.

26. A child attempts to drink water through a 100-cm-long straw, but finds that the water rises only 75 cm. By how much has the child reduced the pressure in her mouth below atmospheric pressure?

27. Barometric pressure in the eye of a hurricane is 0.91 atm (27.2 inches of mercury). How does the level of the ocean surface under the eye compare with that under a distant fair-weather region where the pressure is 1.0 atm?

28. A hydraulic cylinder moving a robotic arm has a diameter of 5.0 cm and can exert a maximum force of 5.6 kN. (a) What pressure must the hydraulic lines be capable of withstanding? (b) The cylinder at the other end of the hydraulic system has a 1.0-cm diameter. What force must be applied to it to get the maximum force out of the cylinder driving the arm?

29. A garage lift has a 45-cm-diameter piston supporting the load. Compressed air with a maximum pressure of

500 kPa is applied to a small piston at the other end of the hydraulic system. What is the maximum mass the lift can support?

30. Figure 18-46 shows a hydraulic lift operated by pumping fluid into the hydraulic system. The large cylinder is 40 cm in diameter, while the small tube leaving the pump is 1.7 cm in diameter. A total load of 2800 kg is raised 2.3 m at a constant rate. (a) What volume of fluid passes through the pump? (b) What is the pressure at the pump outlet? (c) How much work does the pump do? (d) If the lifting takes 40 s, what is the pump power? Neglect pressure variations with height, and neglect also the weight of the fluid raised.

FIGURE 18-46 Problem 30 (diameters are not to scale).

Section 18-3 Archimedes' Principle and Buoyancy

31. On land, the most massive concrete block you can carry is 25 kg. How massive a block could you carry underwater, if the density of concrete is 2300 kg/m³?

32. A 5.4-g jewel has an apparent weight of 32 mN when submerged in water. Could the jewel be diamond (density 3.51 g/cm³)?

33. The density of styrofoam is 160 kg/m³. What per cent error is introduced by weighing a styrofoam block in air, which exerts an upward buoyancy force, rather than in vacuum? The density of air is 1.2 kg/m³.

34. Archimedes purportedly used his principle to verify that the king's crown was pure gold, by weighing the crown while it was submerged in water (see Fig. 18-14). Suppose the crown's actual weight was 25.0 N. What would be its apparent weight if it were made of (a) pure gold and (b) 75% gold and 25% silver, by volume? The densities of gold, silver, and water are 19.3 g/cm³, 10.5 g/cm³, and 1.00 g/cm³, respectively.

35. A partially full beer bottle with interior diameter 52 mm is floating upright in water, as shown in Fig. 18-47. A drinker takes a swig and replaces the bottle in the water, where it now floats 28 mm higher than before. How much beer did the drinker drink?

FIGURE 18-47 Problem 35.

36. A glass beaker measures 10 cm high by 4.0 cm in diameter. Empty, it floats in water with one-third of its height submerged. How many 15-g rocks can be placed in the beaker before it sinks?

37. A typical supertanker has mass 2.0×10^6 kg and carries twice that much oil. If 9.0 m of the ship is submerged when it's empty, what is the minimum water depth needed for it to navigate when full? Assume the sides of the ship are vertical.

38. A balloon contains gas of density ρ_g and is to lift a mass M, including the balloon but not the gas. Show that the minimum mass of gas required is

$$m = \frac{M\rho_g}{\rho_a - \rho_g},$$

where ρ_a is the atmospheric density.

39. (a) How much helium (density 0.18 kg/m³) is needed to lift a balloon carrying two people in a basket, if the total mass of people, basket, and balloon (but not gas) is 280 kg? (b) Repeat for a hot air balloon, whose air density is 10% less than that of the surrounding atmosphere.

40. A 55-kg swimmer climbs onto a styrofoam block whose density is 160 kg/m³. If the water level comes right to the top of the styrofoam, what is the block's volume?

Sections 18-4 and 18-5 Fluid Dynamics and Applications

41. A fluid is flowing steadily, roughly from left to right. At left it is flowing rapidly; it then slows down, and finally speeds up again. Its final speed at right is not as great as its initial speed at left. Sketch a streamline pattern that could represent this flow.

42. Show that pressure has the units of energy density.

43. A typical mass flow rate for the Mississippi River is 1.8×10^7 kg/s. Find (a) the volume flow rate and (b) the flow speed in a region where the river is 2.0 km wide and an average of 6.1 m deep.

44. A fire hose 10 cm in diameter delivers water at the rate of 15 kg/s. The hose terminates in a nozzle 2.5 cm in diameter. What are the flow speeds (a) in the hose and (b) in the nozzle?

45. A typical human aorta, or main artery from the heart, is 1.8 cm in diameter and carries blood at a speed of 35 cm/s. What will be the flow speed around a clot that reduces the flow area by 80%?

46. If the blood pressure in the unobstructed artery of the previous problem is 16 kPa gauge (about 120 mm of mercury, in the unit commonly reported by doctors), what will it be at the clot? The density of blood is 1060 kg/m^3. (Too low a pressure can actually collapse the artery, momentarily cutting off blood flow.)

47. In Fig. 18-48 a horizontal pipe of cross-sectional area A is joined to a lower pipe of cross-sectional area $\frac{1}{2}A$. The entire pipe is full of liquid with density ρ, and the left end is at atmospheric pressure P_a. A small open tube extends upward from the lower pipe. Find the height h_2 of liquid in the small tube (a) when the right end of the lower pipe is closed, so the liquid is in hydrostatic equilibrium, and (b) when the liquid flows with speed v in the upper pipe.

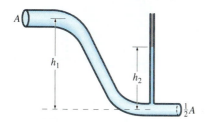

FIGURE 18-48 Problem 47.

48. A can of height h is full of water. At what height y should a small hole be cut so the water initially goes as far horizontally as it does vertically, as shown in Fig. 18-49?

FIGURE 18-49 Problem 48.

49. The water in a garden hose is at a gauge pressure of 140 kPa and is moving at negligible speed. The hose terminates in a sprinkler consisting of many small holes. What is the maximum height reached by the water emerging from the holes?

50. Water emerges from a faucet of diameter d_0 in steady, near vertical flow with speed v_0. Show that the diameter of the falling water column is given by $d = d_0[v_0^2/(v_0^2 + 2gh)]^{1/4}$, where h is the distance below the faucet (Fig. 18-50).

FIGURE 18-50 The diameter of the water column varies as the fourth root of the distance from the faucet (Problem 50).

51. The venturi flowmeter shown in Fig. 18-51 is used to measure the flow rate of water in a solar collector system. The flowmeter is inserted in a pipe with diameter 1.9 cm; at the venturi of the flowmeter the diameter is reduced to 0.64 cm. The manometer tube contains oil with density 0.82 times that of water. If the difference in oil levels on the two sides of the manometer tube is 1.4 cm, what is the volume flow rate?

FIGURE 18-51 Problem 51.

52. A drinking straw 20 cm long and 3.0 mm in diameter stands vertically in a cup of juice 8.0 cm in diameter. A section of straw 6.5 cm long extends above the juice. A child sucks on the straw, and the level of juice in the glass begins dropping at 0.20 cm/s. (a) By how much does the pressure in the child's mouth differ from atmospheric pressure? (b) What is the greatest height from which the child could drink, assuming this same mouth pressure?

Paired Problems

(Both problems in a pair involve the same principles and techniques. If you can get the first problem, you should be able to solve the second one.)

53. A steel drum has volume 0.23 m³ and mass 16 kg. Will it float in water when filled with (a) water or (b) gasoline (density 860 kg/m³)? Neglect the thickness of the steel.

54. A 260-g circular pan 20 cm in diameter has straight sides 6.0 cm high and is made from metal of negligible thickness. To what maximum depth can the pan be filled with water and still float on water?

55. A spherical rubber balloon with mass 0.85 g and diameter 30 cm is filled with helium (density 0.18 kg/m³). How many 1.0-g paper clips can you hang from the balloon before it loses its buoyancy?

56. A string of negligible diameter has mass per unit length 1.4 g/m. You tie a 3-m-long piece of the string to a spherical helium balloon 23 cm in diameter and find that the balloon floats with 1.8 m of string off the floor. Find the combined mass of the balloon and helium.

57. Water at a pressure of 230 kPa is flowing at 1.5 m/s through a pipe, when it encounters an obstruction where the pressure drops by 5%. What fraction of the pipe's area is obstructed?

58. A venturi flowmeter in an oil pipeline has a radius half that of the pipe. The flow speed in the unconstricted flow is 1.9 m/s. If the pressure difference between the unconstricted flow and the venturi is 16 kPa, what is the density of the oil?

59. Find an expression for the volume flow rate from the siphon shown in Fig. 18-52, assuming the siphon area A is much less than the tank area.

FIGURE 18-52 Problems 59, 60.

60. (a) Find the initial siphon flow speed in Fig. 18-52 if the tank is sealed, with its top at only one-fourth of atmospheric pressure. Answer in terms of atmospheric pressure P_a, liquid density ρ, height h, and g. (b) What is the maximum distance between the bend at the top of the siphon and the liquid level in the tank for which the siphon will work under these conditions, assuming the liquid is water? (Give a numerical value here.)

Supplementary Problems

61. A 1.0-m-diameter tank is filled with water to a depth of 2.0 m and is open to the atmosphere at the top. The water drains through a 1.0-cm-diameter pipe at the bottom; that pipe then joins a 1.5-cm-diameter pipe open to the atmosphere, as shown in Fig. 18-53. Find (a) the flow speed in the narrow section and (b) the water height in the *sealed* vertical tube shown.

FIGURE 18-53 Problem 61.

62. How massive an object can be supported by a 5.0-cm-diameter suction cup mounted on a vertical wall, if the coefficient of friction between cup and wall is 0.72? Assume normal atmospheric pressure.

63. Figure 18-54 shows a simplified diagram of a Pitot tube, used for measuring aircraft speeds. The tube is mounted on the underside of the aircraft wing with opening A at right angles to the flow and opening B pointing into the flow. The gauge prevents airflow through the tube. Use Bernoulli's equation to show that the air speed relative to the wing is given by $v = \sqrt{2\Delta P/\rho}$, where ΔP is the pressure difference between the tubes and ρ is the density of air. *Hint:* The flow must be stopped at B, but continues past A with its normal speed.

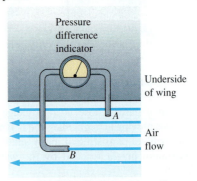

FIGURE 18-54 Problem 63.

64. A ship's hull has a V-shaped cross section, as shown in Fig. 18-55. The ship has vertical height h_0 from keel to deck and a total length ℓ perpendicular to the plane of Fig. 18-54. Empty, the hull extends underwater to a depth h_1, as shown. Find an expression for the maximum load the ship can carry, in terms of the water density ρ and the quantities h_0, h_1, ℓ, and θ shown in the figure.

FIGURE 18-55 Problems 64, 72.

65. With its throttle valve wide open, an automobile carburetor has a throat diameter of 2.4 cm. With each revolution, the engine draws 0.50 L of air through the carburetor. At an engine speed of 3000 rpm, what are (a) the volume flow rate, (b) the airflow speed, and (c) the difference between atmospheric pressure and air pressure in the carburetor throat? The density of air is 1.2 kg/m³.

66. A wind turbine has a blade diameter of 65 m. What is the theoretical maximum power output of this turbine in winds of (a) 10 m/s and (b) 15 m/s? (c) If the machine actually achieves 50% of its theoretical maximum output, how many such turbines would be needed to displace a 1-GW nuclear power plant, assuming an average wind speed of 12 m/s?

67. A can of height h and cross-sectional area A_0 is initially full of water. A small hole of area $A_1 \ll A_0$ is cut in the bottom of the can. Find an expression for the time it takes all the water to drain from the can. *Hint:* Call the water depth y, use the continuity equation to relate dy/dt to the outflow speed at the hole, then integrate.

68. A pencil is weighted so it floats vertically with length ℓ submerged. It's pushed vertically downward without being totally submerged, then released. Show that it undergoes simple harmonic motion with period $T = 2\pi\sqrt{\ell/g}$.

69. A circular pan of liquid (density ρ) is centered on a horizontal turntable rotating with angular speed ω. Its axis coincides with the rotation axis, as shown in Fig. 18-56. Atmospheric pressure is P_a. Find expressions for (a) the pressure at the bottom of the pan and (b) the height of the liquid surface as functions of the distance r from the axis, given that the height at the center is h_0.

FIGURE 18-56 Problem 69.

70. Density and pressure in Earth's atmosphere are proportional: $\rho = P/h_0g$, where h_0 is a constant with the approximate value 8200 m and g is the acceleration of gravity. (a) Integrate Equation 18-2 for this case to show that atmospheric pressure as a function of height h above the surface is given by $P = P_0e^{-h/h_0}$, where P_0 is the surface pressure. (b) At what height will the pressure have dropped to half its surface value?

71. (a) Use the result of the preceding problem to express Earth's atmospheric density as a function of height (this is simple). (b) Use the result of (a) to find the height below which half of Earth's atmospheric mass lies (this will require integration).

72. Find the center of buoyancy of the ship shown in Fig. 18-55.

PART 2 Cumulative Problems

1. A cylindrical log of total mass M and uniform diameter d has an uneven mass distribution that causes it to float in a vertical position, as shown in Fig. 1. (a) Find an expression for the length ℓ of the submerged portion of the log when it is floating in equilibrium, in terms of M, d, and the water density ρ. (b) If the log is displaced vertically from its equilibrium position and released, it will undergo simple harmonic motion. Find an expression for the period of this motion, neglecting viscosity and other frictional effects.

FIGURE 1 Cumulative Problem 1.

2. A cable of total mass m and length ℓ hangs vertically, with a mass M attached to its bottom end, as shown in Fig. 2. The mass is given a sudden sideways blow that starts a low-amplitude transverse pulse propagating up the cable. Show that the time it takes the pulse to reach the top of the cable is

$$t = 2\left(\sqrt{\frac{(m + M)\ell}{mg}} - \sqrt{\frac{M\ell}{mg}} \right).$$

FIGURE 2 Cumulative Problem 2.

3. Let P_0 and ρ_0 be the atmospheric pressure and density at Earth's surface. Assume that the ratio P/ρ is the same throughout the atmosphere (this implies that the temperature is uniform). Show that the pressure a vertical height z above the surface is given by $P(z) = P_0 e^{-\rho_0 gz/P_0}$, for z much less than Earth's radius (this amounts to neglecting Earth's curvature, and thus taking g to be constant).

4. A piece of rope of length ℓ and mass m has its two ends spliced together to form a continuous loop. The loop is set spinning at so high a rate that it forms a circle with essentially uniform tension. It is then placed in contact with the ground, where it rolls, without slipping, like a rigid hoop. The loop is rolling on level ground when it rolls over a stick that produces a small distortion (see Fig. 3). As a result, two pulses, initially coinciding, propagate along the loop in opposite directions. (a) Where will they again coincide? (b) Through what angle will the loop have rotated while the pulses are separated?

FIGURE 3 Cumulative Problem 4.

5. A U-shaped tube containing liquid is mounted on a table that tilts back and forth through a slight angle, as shown in Fig. 4. The diameter of the tube is much less than either the height of its arms or their separation. When the table is rocked very slowly or very rapidly, nothing particularly dramatic happens. But when the rocking takes place at a few times per second, the liquid level in the tube oscillates violently, with maximum amplitude at a rocking frequency of 1.7 Hz. Explain what is going on, and find the total length of the liquid including both vertical and horizontal portions.

FIGURE 4 Cumulative Problem 5.

Part Three

Thermodynamics

Coal burns, releasing its stored chemical energy as heat—here largely in the form of radiation from the hot, glowing chunks of coal. Burning coal supplies much of the world's electrical energy, as electric power plants convert a fraction of the heat released into useful work. Carbon dioxide from combustion of coal affects heat transfer in Earth's atmosphere, causing the global warming that scientists now believe is attributable to human activities. All these processes—heat transfer, conversion of thermal energy to useful work, and climate change—are governed by the laws of thermodynamics.

Without the Sun's heat, the Earth would be a lifeless, frozen rock. Without the heat from burning fuels, we humans would be confined to the tropics. Nearly all our transportation systems use engines driven by the heat released in combustion. Even our bodies could not function without mechanisms to regulate the flow of heat. The study of heat and temperature, and their connection with the all important concept of energy, comprises the branch of physics called thermodynamics. The next four chapters probe the fundamental physics and many practical applications of thermodynamics.

19 Temperature and Heat

Thermogram of a house, taken with an infrared scanning device, shows regions of greatest heat loss in red and yellow, lowest in blue and black. Understanding heat flow allows engineers to design systems that keep buildings comfortable and helps scientists predict the effect of human activities on Earth's climate.

The next four chapters deal with the physics of heat, temperature, and related phenomena. Our own bodies provide a qualitative sense of what it means for things to be "hot" or "cold." Here we'll quantify this sense and explore the behavior of matter under different thermal conditions. And we will learn something our sense of temperature could never tell us—namely, how thermal phenomena reflect the laws of mechanics operating on a microscopic scale.

19-1 MACROSCOPIC AND MICROSCOPIC DESCRIPTIONS

Some physical properties—for example, mass—apply equally to microscopic objects such as atoms and molecules and to macroscopic objects such as cars, gas cylinders, and planets. But others—for example, temperature and pressure—have no meaning on a microscopic scale. We speak of the temperature and pressure of air, but it makes no sense to ask about the temperature or pressure of an individual air molecule. The study of temperature, heat, and related macroscopic properties comprises the branch of physics called **thermodynamics**.

The thermodynamic behavior of matter is determined by the behavior of its constituent atoms and molecules in response to the laws of mechanics. **Statistical mechanics** is the branch of physics that relates the macroscopic description of matter to the underlying microscopic processes. Historically, thermodynamics was developed before the atomic theory of matter was well established. The subsequent explanation of thermodynamics in terms of statistical mechanics—the mechanics of atoms and molecules—was a triumph for classical physics. At the same time, the few thermodynamic phenomena that could not be explained successfully with classical physics helped point the way to the development of the quantum theory. In our study of thermal phenomena, we will interweave the macroscopic and microscopic descriptions to provide the fullest understanding of both viewpoints.

19-2 TEMPERATURE AND THERMODYNAMIC EQUILIBRIUM

Take a bottle of soda from the refrigerator and leave it on the kitchen counter. Eventually it reaches room temperature and then stays there. You don't need a scientific definition of temperature to recognize this; your sense of touch suffices to tell you that the soda's temperature eventually stops changing.

The key point here is that the soda and the room have reached a kind of equilibrium—not the static equilibrium of force balance that we explored in Chapter 14, but a **thermodynamic equilibrium**. We define this new type of equilibrium by saying that when two systems—in this case the soda bottle and the surrounding air—are placed together until no further change occurs in any macroscopic property, then the two have reached thermodynamic equilibrium with each other. When we use the term "equilibrium" in the next four chapters, we'll always mean thermodynamic equilibrium.

The concept of thermodynamic equilibrium does not require a prior notion of temperature. To determine whether two systems are in equilibrium, we can consider *any* macroscopic properties. Typical properties include length, volume, pressure, and electrical resistance, as well as temperature. If any macroscopic property changes when two systems are placed together, then the systems were not originally in thermodynamic equilibrium. Once changes cease, then the systems have reached equilibrium.

We've used the phrase "placed together" to describe arranging two systems so they can come to thermodynamic equilibrium. A more precise phrase would be "placed in *thermal contact*." Two systems are in **thermal contact** if heating one

FIGURE 19-1 (a) Systems A and C are each in thermal contact with B, but not with each other, and both A and C have reached thermodynamic equilibrium with B. (b) If A and C are put in thermal contact, their macroscopic properties don't change—showing that A and C were already in thermodynamic equilibrium.

FIGURE 19-2 The coil at the center of this thermostat is a bimetallic strip that bends with increasing temperature, actuating a switch that controls a furnace.

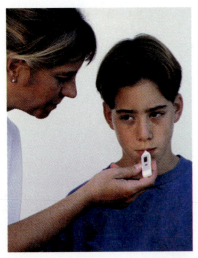

of them results in macroscopic changes in the other. For example, put two metal cups of water in contact, and place a heater in one of them; the water in both cups gets hotter. In that case the cups are in thermal contact. Do the same with styrofoam cups, or separate the metal cups with a layer of styrofoam, and heating one cup has little effect on the other. In that case the two systems are **thermally insulated**. Thermal contact need not imply direct physical contact and—as the styrofoam cups show—physical contact alone may not ensure thermal contact.

Using the concept of thermodynamic equilibrium, we can now define quantitatively what we mean by temperature. We first state what it means for two systems to have the same temperature:

> **Two systems have the same temperature if they are in thermodynamic equilibrium.**

Conversely, two systems that are not in thermodynamic equilibrium do not have the same temperature.

A simple experimental fact makes it possible to compare systems that aren't in thermal contact. Consider two systems A and C in thermal contact with a third system B, but not with each other (Fig. 19-1a). If we wait until A and C are both in thermodynamic equilibrium with B, then bring A and C into contact (Fig. 19-1b), we find that no further changes occur—indicating that A and C are already in equilibrium. This fact is so fundamental to the rest of thermodynamics that it is called the **zeroth law of thermodynamics**:

> *Zeroth law of thermodynamics: If two systems A and C each are in thermodynamic equilibrium with system B, then A and C are in thermodynamic equilibrium with each other.*

19-3 MEASURING TEMPERATURE

Rephrased in terms of temperature, the zeroth law says that if system A has the same temperature as system B, and system B has the same temperature as system C, then A and C have the same temperature. This property allows us to make quantitative measurements of temperature.

A **thermometer** is a system with some conveniently observed macroscopic property that changes with temperature. The length of the mercury column indicates temperature in a mercury thermometer. A strip made of two different metals bends when heated, turning the indicating needle on a dial-type thermometer or closing a switch that starts a furnace (Fig. 19-2). Electrical resistance has long been used in science and engineering to measure temperature and is rapidly replacing mercury in medical and other applications (Fig. 19-3).

To use a thermometer, we simply put it in contact with the system whose temperature we're trying to measure and let the two come to thermodynamic equilibrium. The value of whatever macroscopic property has changed then gives a quantitative indication of temperature. The zeroth law assures us that this process is consistent, in that two systems for which the thermometer gives the same reading must have the same temperature.

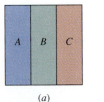

FIGURE 19-3 An electronic digital fever thermometer. For this thermometer, electrical resistance is the macroscopic property that changes with temperature.

The mercury in the left-hand tube is maintained constant at this level...

by moving the right-hand tube up or down.

System whose temperature is to be measured.

Vacuum

Gas

The height difference *h* between the two mercury levels is a measure of the gas pressure, and, therefore, of the temperature.

Mercury

Flexible tube

FIGURE 19-4 A constant-volume gas thermometer. The gas pressure increases with increasing temperature and decreases with decreasing temperature. The closed tube at right is raised or lowered to keep the mercury level in the left-hand tube constant, thus maintaining constant gas volume. The height difference *h* between the mercury levels is then a measure of gas pressure and, therefore, of temperature.

FIGURE 19-5 Kelvin temperature scale defined using a constant-volume gas thermometer.

Gas Thermometers and the Kelvin Scale

We need a standard against which to calibrate different types of thermometers. Gas thermometers—using either the pressure or the volume of a gas to indicate temperature—operate over an extremely wide temperature range and are therefore used to define the temperature scale.

Figure 19-4 shows a **constant-volume gas thermometer**, whose temperature indication is the pressure of gas held at constant volume. Temperature is taken to be a linear function of the gas pressure. Two points are needed to define a linear function. One point corresponds to zero gas pressure in the thermometer, and we define the temperature at that point to be zero (see Fig. 19-5). The second point is established by the **triple point** of water—the unique temperature at which solid, liquid, and gas phases of water can coexist in equilibrium (more on the triple point in Chapter 20). The SI temperature unit, the **kelvin** (symbol K; *not* "degrees kelvin" or °K), is defined by setting the triple point at exactly 273.16 K. The temperature of a constant-volume gas thermometer is then

$$T = 273.16 \frac{P}{P_3}, \tag{19-1}$$

where P is the thermometer pressure at an arbitrary temperature T and P_3 its pressure at the triple point (see Fig. 19-5).

Since a gas cannot have negative pressure, the zero of the kelvin scale represents an absolute lower limit on temperature, and is called **absolute zero**. We'll explore the meaning of absolute zero further in Chapter 22. Figure 19-6 shows some important physical situations on the kelvin scale.

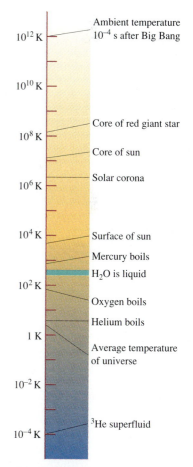

Ambient temperature 10^{-4} s after Big Bang

10^{12} K

10^{10} K

Core of red giant star

10^8 K

Core of sun

Solar corona

10^6 K

Surface of sun

10^4 K

Mercury boils

H_2O is liquid

10^2 K

Oxygen boils

Helium boils

1 K

Average temperature of universe

10^{-2} K

^{3}He superfluid

10^{-4} K

FIGURE 19-6 Some physical processes on the kelvin scale. Chart is logarithmic to display a wide temperature range. Because of the logarithmic scale, it's not possible to show absolute zero on the diagram.

What kind of gas should we use in our thermometer? It doesn't matter. That's the beauty of gas thermometry, and the reason it's used to set the temperature scale. What is important is the amount of gas: experimentally, we find that *all* gases behave exactly the same way as the quantity of gas in the thermometer becomes arbitrarily small (we'll see why in the next chapter). Thus Equation 19-1 is precisely valid only in the limit as the amount of gas shrinks to zero. But we don't really need to reach that limit; it suffices to take several measurements, using decreasing amounts of gas in each, and then extrapolate the ratio P/P_3 in Equation 19-1 to the value it would have as the amount of gas becomes arbitrarily small.

Other Temperature Scales

Other scales in common use include the Celsius (°C), Fahrenheit (°F), and Rankine (°R) scales (Fig. 19-7), although the latter two are largely limited to the United States. One Celsius degree represents the same temperature difference as one kelvin, but the zero of the Celsius scale occurs at 273.15 K, so

$$T_C = T - 273.15, \qquad (19\text{-}2)$$

where T_C is the Celsius temperature and T the temperature in kelvins. The Celsius scale was chosen so the melting point of ice at standard atmospheric pressure—the ice point—is at exactly 0°C, while the boiling point of water at standard atmospheric pressure—the steam point—is at 100°C. The triple point of water occurs at 0.01°C, which accounts for the 273.15 difference between the kelvin and Celsius scales as well as for the difference of 0.01 in the constants of Equations 19-1 and 19-2. Equation 19-2 shows that absolute zero occurs at −273.15°C.

The Fahrenheit scale, which is part of the British system of units, is defined with the ice point at 32°F and the steam point at 212°F (Fig. 19-7). As a result, the relation between the Fahrenheit and Celsius scales is

$$T_F = \tfrac{9}{5}T_C + 32. \qquad (19\text{-}3)$$

FIGURE 19-7 Relations among the four temperature scales.

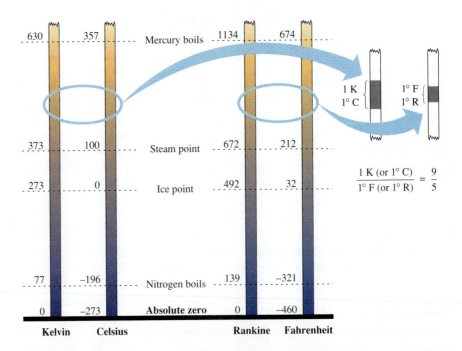

The Rankine scale is often used in engineering work in the United States. A Rankine degree is the same size as a Fahrenheit degree, but the zero of the Rankine scale coincides with the zero of the kelvin scale, so 0°R is absolute zero.

EXAMPLE 19-1	*Temperature Scales*

What is normal body temperature (98.6°F) on the Celsius and kelvin scales? If you have a fever of 101.6°F, by how much has your temperature risen on each of these scales?

Solution

Solving Equation 19-3 for T_C gives

$$T_C = \tfrac{5}{9}(T_F - 32) = \tfrac{5}{9}(98.6 - 32.0) = 37.0°C .$$

Then Equation 19-2 gives the kelvin temperature:

$$T = T_C + 273.2 = 310.2 \text{ K} .$$

A kelvin and a degree Celsius are the same size, and are both larger than a degree Fahrenheit by the factor $\tfrac{9}{5}$, so a rise of 3.0°F is equivalent to a rise of

$$\frac{3.0}{9/5} = 1.7°C = 1.7 \text{ K} .$$

EXERCISE A meteorologist on a Canadian radio station reports a high temperature of 24°C. What is the corresponding Fahrenheit temperature?

Answer: 75°F

Some problems similar to Example 19-1: 2–8

19-4 TEMPERATURE AND HEAT

A lighted match will burn your finger, yet it wouldn't provide much heat in a cold room. A large vat of water, although much cooler than the match, would do a better job heating the room. This example shows our intuitive sense of the difference between temperature and heat: Heat measures an *amount* of "something," while temperature measures the *strength* of that "something."

What is that "something"? Before the early 1800s, heat was considered a material fluid, called **caloric**, that flowed from hot bodies to colder ones. But observations made by the American-born scientist Benjamin Thompson in the late 1700s began to shed doubt on the caloric theory. Thompson was appointed director of the Bavarian arsenal, where he supervised the boring of cannon. Thompson recognized that essentially limitless amounts of heat could be produced in the boring process, and he concluded that heat could not be a conserved fluid. Instead, he suggested, heating was associated with mechanical work done by the boring tool.

In the half-century following Thompson's observations, the caloric theory gradually faded in popularity as a series of experiments confirmed the association between heating and mechanical energy. These experiments culminated in the work of the British physicist and brewer James Joule (1818–1889), who explored the relation between heat and mechanical, electrical, and chemical energy. In 1843, Joule quantified the relation between heat and energy, bringing thermal phenomena under the powerful conservation-of-energy law. In recognition of this major synthesis in physics, the SI unit of energy is named after Joule (Fig. 19-8). In Chapter 21 we will explore in detail the relation between heat and energy, and will show Joule's experiment in Fig. 21-2.

Our everyday experience of heat is nearly always associated with the movement of energy from one body to another. We rarely make statements about the actual amount of "heat" in an object—we're concerned instead that the temperature be appropriate. We want the furnace to transfer energy to our house in the winter and are satisfied when the house reaches a certain temperature, not when

FIGURE 19-8 In SI-based Australia, energy content of foods is given in joules rather than calories.

it contains a certain amount of "heat." The scientific definition of heat reflects this natural inclination to think of heat as energy in transit:

| Heat is energy being transferred from one object to another because of a temperature difference alone.

Strictly speaking, the word **heat** refers only to energy in transit. Once heat has been transferred to an object, we say that the **internal energy** of the object has increased, but not that it contains more heat. This distinction reflects the fact that processes other than heating—such as the transfer of mechanical or electrical energy—can also change an object's temperature. The next chapter explores this relation between heat and internal energy.

19-5 HEAT CAPACITY AND SPECIFIC HEAT

Experimentally, we find the heat ΔQ transferred to an object and the resulting change ΔT in the object's temperature are directly proportional. We write

$$\Delta Q = C\Delta T, \qquad (19\text{-}4)$$

where C is called the **heat capacity** of the object. Since heat is a measure of energy transfer, its unit is the joule, and therefore the units of heat capacity are J/K. The heat capacity C applies to a specific object and depends on its mass and on the substance from which it's made. We characterize different substances in terms of **specific heat** c, or heat capacity per unit mass. The heat capacity of an object is then the product of its mass and specific heat, so we can write

$$\Delta Q = mc\Delta T. \qquad (19\text{-}5)$$

The SI units of specific heat are J/kg·K. Figure 19-9 illustrates the difference between heat capacity and specific heat, while Table 19-1 lists specific heats of common materials.

Historically, thermodynamic phenomena were first studied before scientists knew the relation between heat and energy. Consequently other units were

Heat capacity
The heat capacity C of the iguana is the energy ΔQ per unit temperature change that must be transferred to the *whole iguana* to raise its temperature:

$$C = \frac{\Delta Q}{\Delta T} \quad \text{(SI units: J/K)}$$

Specific Heat
The specific heat c is the energy ΔQ per unit temperature change that must be transferred to the iguana *per unit mass* to raise its temperature:

$$c = \frac{\Delta Q}{m\Delta T} \text{ (SI units: J/kg·K)}$$

c is a property not of this particular iguana but of the material–mostly water–from which it's made.

FIGURE 19-9 The difference between heat capacity and specific heat, as exemplified by a Galapagos marine iguana. These cold-blooded organisms forage in cold shore waters, and to warm up they emerge periodically and bask on the hot black rocks of the shore.

TABLE 19-1 *Specific Heats of Some Common Materials**

	Specific Heat, *c*	
Substance	**SI Units: J/kg·K**	**cal/g·°C, kcal/kg·°C, or Btu/lb·°F**
Aluminum	900	0.215
Copper	386	0.0923
Iron	447	0.107
Glass	753	0.18
Mercury	140	0.033
Steel	502	0.12
Stone (granite)	840	0.20
Water:		
Liquid	4184	1.00
Ice, $-10°C$	2050	0.49
Wood	1400	0.33

*Temperature range 0°C to 100°C except as noted.

defined for heat. The **calorie** (cal) was defined as the heat needed to raise the temperature of one gram of water from 14.5°C to 15.5°; consequently, the specific heat of water in this temperature range is 1 cal/g·°C. Several different definitions of the calorie exist today, based on different methods for establishing the heat-energy equivalence. In this book we use the so-called thermochemical calorie, defined as exactly 4.184 J. The "calorie" used in describing the energy content of foods is actually a kilocalorie. In the English system, still widely used in engineering in the United States, the unit of heat is the **British thermal unit** (Btu). One Btu is the amount of heat needed to raise the temperature of one pound of water from 63°F to 64°F, and is equal to 1055 J.

EXAMPLE 19-2	*Waiting to Shower*

Your whole family has taken showers before you, dropping the temperature in the water heater to 18°C. If the heater holds 150 kg of water, how much energy will it take to bring it to 50°C? If the energy is supplied by a 5.0-kW electric heating element, how long will that take?

Solution

The heat required is given by Equation 19-5:

$$\Delta Q = mc\,\Delta T = (150 \text{ kg})(4184 \text{ J/kg·K})(50°C - 18°C)$$
$$= 2.0 \times 10^7 \text{ J},$$

where we found the specific heat of water in Table 19-1. The heating element supplies energy at the rate of 5.0 kW, or 5.0×10^3 J/s; at that rate the time needed to supply 2.0×10^7 J is

$$\Delta t = \frac{2.0 \times 10^7 \text{ J}}{5.0 \times 10^3 \text{ J/s}} = 4000 \text{ s}, \quad \text{or a little over an hour}.$$

Tip

Is That C or K? It doesn't matter when we're talking about temperature *differences*. That's why we could mix units, multiplying the specific heat in J/kg·K by the difference of Celsius temperatures.

EXERCISE (a) How much heat does it take to bring a 3.4-kg iron skillet from 20°C to 130°C? (b) If the heat is supplied by a stove burner at the rate of 2.0 kW, how long will it take to heat the pan?

Answers: (a) 166 kJ; (b) 84 s

Some problems similar to Example 19-2: 19, 23–25, 28

For many substances, the specific heat is nearly independent of temperature over wide temperature ranges. When the specific heat does vary significantly with temperature, we write Equation 19-5 in the limit of very small temperature change dT and heat dQ, and integrate to find the heat required for larger changes. Problem 73 explores this situation.

Strictly speaking, values of heat capacity and specific heat depend on whether an object's pressure or its volume changes as it's heated. For solids and liquids, which don't expand much, the distinction is not very important. But it makes a big difference whether a gas is confined to a fixed volume or allowed to expand when heated. Consequently, for gases we need to define two different specific heats, depending on which of volume or pressure is held constant. We'll deal with that issue in Chapter 21, where we explore the behavior of gases in the context of fundamental laws of thermodynamics.

The Equilibrium Temperature

When two objects at different temperatures are in thermal contact, heat flows from the hotter object to the cooler one until they reach thermodynamic equilibrium. If the two objects are thermally insulated from their surroundings, then all the energy leaving the hotter object ends up in the cooler one. Mathematically, this statement may be written

$$m_1 c_1 \, \Delta T_1 + m_2 c_2 \, \Delta T_2 = 0, \qquad (19\text{-}6)$$

where mc is the heat capacity of an object of mass m and specific heat c, and ΔT is the temperature change of that object. For the hotter object, ΔT is negative, so the two terms in Equation 19-6 have opposite signs. One term represents the outflow of heat from the hotter object, the other inflow into the cooler object.

Got It!

A hot rock with mass 250 g is dropped into an equal mass of cool water. Which temperature changes more, that of the rock or the water? Explain.

EXAMPLE 19-3	*Cooling Down*

An aluminum frying pan with mass 1.5 kg is heated on a stove to 180°C, then plunged into a sink containing 8.0 kg of water at room temperature (20°C). Assuming that none of the water boils, and that no heat is lost to the surroundings, what is the equilibrium temperature of the water and pan?

Solution

We write Equation 19-6 in the form

$$m_p c_p (T - T_p) + m_w c_w (T - T_w) = 0,$$

where the subscripts p and w refer to the pan and the water, and where the equilibrium temperature T is the same for both. Solving for T then gives

$$T = \frac{m_p c_p T_p + m_w c_w T_w}{m_p c_p + m_w c_w}.$$

Using the given values of m_p, T_p, m_w, and T_w, and taking c_p and c_w from Table 19-1, we find that $T = 26°C$.

EXERCISE You take a 1.0-L bottle of soda from a 4.0°C refrigerator and put it in an insulated cooler chest whose heat capacity is negligible. Also in the chest is a wooden cutting board of mass 2.1 kg and temperature 24°C. When you open the chest much later, what will be the temperature of the soda? Soda has essentially the same density (1.0 kg/L) and specific heat as water. Neglect the heat capacity of the soda bottle itself.

Answer: 12°C

Some problems similar to Example 19-3: 34–36, 59, 60

19-6 HEAT TRANSFER

How is heat transferred between two objects? Engineers need to know so they can design systems to control heat transfer, as in heating or cooling a building. Scientists need to know so they can anticipate temperature changes, as in the global warming that seems to be resulting from combustion of fossil fuels and other human activities.

Three heat-transfer mechanisms commonly occur. These are conduction, a process involving direct physical contact; convection, involving energy transfer by the bulk flow of a fluid; and radiation, or energy transfer by electromagnetic waves. In a given situation, one of the three may dominate, or we may have to take all three into account.

Conduction

Conduction is the transfer of heat through direct physical contact. Microscopically, conduction occurs because molecules in a hotter region transfer energy to those of an adjacent cooler region through collisions. The effect of these collisions in a given material is quantified by the material's **thermal conductivity**, k, whose SI units are W/m·K. Common materials exhibit a broad range of thermal conductivities, from about 400 W/m·K for copper—a good conductor of heat—to 0.029 W/m·K for styrofoam, a good thermal insulator.

Figure 19-10 shows a slab of material with thickness Δx and cross-sectional area A. Suppose one face of the material is held at temperature T and the other at $T + \Delta T$. Intuitively, we might expect the rate of heat flow through the slab to increase with increasing area A and to decrease with increasing thickness Δx. Of course, the heat-flow rate must also depend on the thermal conductivity of the material. We expect further that heat will flow from the hotter to the cooler face of the slab, with the heat-flow rate dependent also on the temperature difference between the two faces. Our intuition is borne out experimentally: for a slab of uniform thickness, the heat-flow rate H is given by

$$H = -kA\frac{\Delta T}{\Delta x}. \tag{19-7}$$

Since H is a rate of energy flow, its units are joules/second, or watts. The minus sign in Equation 19-7 shows that heat transfer is opposite to the direction of increasing temperature, that is, from hotter to cooler.

Table 19-2 lists thermal conductivities for some common materials. Both SI and British units are listed since the latter are commonly used in calculations involving heat loss in buildings. Note the wide range of thermal conductivities in Table 19-2. Metals are exceptionally good conductors because they contain free electrons that move quickly, transferring energy with them. Gases, on the other hand, are poor conductors because the wide spacing of their molecules makes for infrequent energy transfers. Good heat insulators, such as fiberglass and styrofoam, owe their insulating properties to a physical structure that traps small volumes of air or other gas.

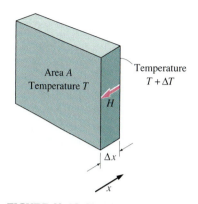

FIGURE 19-10 Heat flows from the hotter to the cooler face of the slab, at a rate H that depends on the slab area A, thickness Δx, temperature difference ΔT, and thermal conductivity k.

TABLE 19-2 *Thermal Conductivities**

Material	Thermal Conductivity, k	
	SI Units: W/m·K	**British Units: Btu·in./h·ft^2·°F**
Air	0.026	0.18
Aluminum	237	1644
Concrete (varies with mix)	1	7
Copper	401	2780
Fiberglass	0.042	0.29
Glass	0.7–0.9	5–6
Goose down	0.043	0.30
Helium	0.14	0.97
Iron	80.4	558
Steel	46	319
Styrofoam	0.029	0.20
Water	0.61	4.2
Wood (pine)	0.11	0.78

* Temperature range 0°C to 100°C.

EXAMPLE 19-4	*Warming a Lake*

A lake with a flat bottom and steep sides has surface area 1.5 km² and is 8.0 m deep. On a summer day, the surface water is at a temperature of 30°C, while the bottom water is at 4.0°C. What is the rate of heat conduction through the lake? Assume that the temperature declines uniformly from surface to bottom.

Solution

The lake resembles the slab of Fig. 19-10. Taking the thermal conductivity of water from Table 19-2, Equation 19-7 gives

$$H = -kA\frac{\Delta T}{\Delta x}$$

$$= -(0.61 \text{ W/m·K})(1.5\times10^6 \text{ m}^2)\frac{30°C - 4.0°C}{8.0 \text{ m}}$$

$$= -3.0\times10^6 \text{ W}.$$

The minus sign indicates that heat flows in the direction of decreasing temperature, or downward into the lake. Were the surface and bottom temperatures not maintained, heat flow would eventually bring the entire lake to a uniform temperature.

EXERCISE A concrete wall 20 cm thick measures 2.2 m high by 11 m wide. On the inside, the temperature is 20°C; outside, it's −10°C. What is the heat-flow rate through the wall?

Answer: 3.6 kW

Some problems similar to Example 19-4: 38, 39, 42, 46

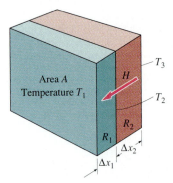

FIGURE 19-11 A composite slab. The heat-flow rate H is the same through both sections.

Equation 19-7 is strictly correct only when the temperature varies uniformly from one surface to the other. This is the case in practical problems where two surfaces at different temperatures have the same area. With other geometries—as in evaluating heat loss through the insulation surrounding a cylindrical pipe—we need to write $\Delta T/\Delta x$ as the derivative dT/dx and integrate to relate the heat loss and the temperature difference. Problems 74 and 75 explore this situation.

Often heat flows through several different materials. A building wall, for example, may contain wood, plaster, fiberglass insulation, and other materials. Figure 19-11 shows such a composite structure, with temperature T_1 on one side and T_3 on the other. The heat-flow rate H must be the same through both slabs since energy doesn't accumulate or disappear at the interface between the two. Then Equation 19-7 gives

$$H = -k_1 A\frac{T_2 - T_1}{\Delta x_1} = -k_2 A\frac{T_3 - T_2}{\Delta x_2}, \qquad (19\text{-}8)$$

where k_1 and k_2 are the thermal conductivities of the two materials, and T_2 is the temperature at the interface. We would like to express the heat-flow rate in terms of the surface temperatures T_1 and T_3 alone, without having to worry about the intermediate temperature T_2. To do so, it's convenient to define the **thermal resistance**, R, of each slab:

$$R = \frac{\Delta x}{kA}. \qquad (19\text{-}9)$$

The SI units of R are K/W. Unlike the thermal conductivity, k, which is a property of a *material*, R is a property of a *particular piece* of material, reflecting both its conductivity and its geometry. In terms of thermal resistance, Equation 19-8 becomes

$$H = -\frac{T_2 - T_1}{R_1} = -\frac{T_3 - T_2}{R_2},$$

so

$$R_1 H = T_1 - T_2$$

and

$$R_2 H = T_2 - T_3.$$

Adding these two equations gives

$$(R_1 + R_2)H = T_1 - T_2 + T_2 - T_3 = T_1 - T_3,$$

or

$$H = \frac{T_1 - T_3}{R_1 + R_2}. \qquad (19\text{-}10)$$

Equation 19-10 shows that the composite slab acts like a single slab whose thermal resistance is the sum of the resistances of the two slabs that compose it. We could easily extend this treatment to show that the thermal resistances of three or more slabs add when the slabs are arranged so the same heat flows through all of them.

In the United States, the insulating properties of building materials are usually described in terms of the **R-factor**, $\mathcal{R}$, which is the thermal resistance for a slab of unit area:

$$\mathcal{R} = RA = \frac{\Delta x}{k}. \qquad (19\text{-}11)$$

The units of $\mathcal{R}$, although rarely stated, are ft²·°F·h/Btu. This means that $\mathcal{R}$-19 fiberglass insulation, now in common use as a wall insulation in the northern part of the United States, has a heat loss of $\frac{1}{19}$ Btu per hour for each square foot of insulation for each degree Fahrenheit temperature difference across the insulation (see Fig. 19-12).

FIGURE 19-12 This $\mathcal{R}$-19 fiberglass insulation loses 1/19 Btu per hour per square foot for every °F temperature difference.

EXAMPLE 19-5	*Insulation, Heat Loss, and the Price of Oil*

Figure 19-13 shows a house whose walls consist of plaster ($\mathcal{R} = 0.17$), $\mathcal{R}$-11 fiberglass insulation, plywood ($\mathcal{R} = 0.65$), and cedar shingles ($\mathcal{R} = 0.55$). The roof is the same construction except it uses $\mathcal{R}$-30 fiberglass insulation. The average outdoor temperature in winter is 20°F, and the house is maintained at 70°F. The house's oil furnace produces 100,000 Btu for every gallon of oil, and oil costs 94¢ per gallon. How much does it cost to heat the house for a month?

Solution

The R-factors for the walls and roof are

$$\mathcal{R}_{\text{wall}} = \mathcal{R}_{\text{plaster}} + \mathcal{R}_{\text{fiberglass}} + \mathcal{R}_{\text{plywood}} + \mathcal{R}_{\text{shingles}}$$
$$= 0.17 + 11 + 0.65 + 0.55 = 12.4,$$

and

$$\mathcal{R}_{\text{roof}} = 0.17 + 30 + 0.65 + 0.55 = 31.4.$$

The total wall area is

$$A_{\text{wall}} = (28 \text{ ft} + 36 \text{ ft} + 28 \text{ ft} + 36 \text{ ft})(10 \text{ ft})$$
$$+ (28 \text{ ft})(8.08 \text{ ft}) = 1506 \text{ ft}^2,$$

where the second term in the sum is the area of the two triangular portions of the side walls, whose height is (14 ft)(tan30°), or 8.08 ft. These $\mathcal{R}$-12.4 walls lose 1/12.4 Btu/h·ft²·°F, and the temperature difference across them is 50°F, so the total heat-loss rate through the walls is

$$H_{\text{walls}} = \left(\tfrac{1}{12.4} \text{ Btu/h·ft}^2\text{·°F}\right)(1506 \text{ ft}^2)(50\text{°F}) = 6073 \text{ Btu/h}.$$

FIGURE 19-13 House for Example 19-5.

The area of the pitched roof is increased over that of a flat roof by the factor 1/cos30°, so the heat-loss rate through the roof is

$$H_{\text{roof}} = \left(\tfrac{1}{31.4} \text{ Btu/h·ft}^2\text{·°F}\right)\frac{(36 \text{ ft})(28 \text{ ft})}{\cos 30°}(50\text{°F})$$
$$= 1853 \text{ Btu/h}.$$

The total heat-loss rate is then

$$H = 6073 \text{ Btu/h} + 1853 \text{ Btu/h} = 7926 \text{ Btu/h}.$$

In a month, this results in a total heat loss of

$$Q = (7926 \text{ Btu/h})(30 \text{ days/month})(24 \text{ h/day})$$
$$= 5.71 \times 10^6 \text{ Btu}.$$

With 10^5 Btu per gallon of oil burned, this requires 57.1 gallons of oil, at a cost of (57.1 gal) ($0.94/gal) = $53.58.

This estimate is low; losses through windows and doors are substantial, and cold air infiltration results in additional heat loss. A more accurate analysis would also consider heat lost to the ground and solar energy gained through the windows. Problem 67 provides a more realistic look at heat loss in this house.

EXERCISE In the house of Example 19-5, how much money would be saved each month if the wall insulation were increased to the same $\mathcal{R} = 30$ as in the roof?

Answer: $24.80

Some problems similar to Example 19-5: 43, 45, 47, 48, 67

Convection

Convection is heat transfer by the bulk motion of a fluid. Convection occurs because a fluid becomes less dense when heated and therefore rises. Figure 19-14a shows two plates held at different temperatures, with fluid between them. Fluid heated by the lower plate rises and transfers heat to the upper plate. The cooled fluid then sinks, and the process repeats. The pattern of rising and sinking fluid often acquires a striking regularity, as shown in Fig. 19-14b.

Convection is important in many technological and natural environments. When you heat water on a stove, convection carries heat from the bottom of the pan to the top. Houses usually rely on convection from heat sources near floor level to circulate warm air throughout a room. Insulating materials such as fiberglass and goose down trap air and thereby inhibit convection that would otherwise cause excessive heat loss from our houses and our bodies. Convection associated with solar heating of Earth's surface drives the vast air movements that establish our overall climate. Violent convective movements, such as those in thunderstorms, are associated with localized temperature differences. On a much longer time scale, convection in Earth's mantle is involved in continental drift (Fig. 19-15). Convection plays a crucial role in many astrophysical processes, including the generation of magnetic fields in stars and planets.

As with conduction, the convective heat-loss rate often is approximately proportional to the temperature difference. But the calculation of convective heat loss is complicated because of the need to understand the details of the associated fluid motion. The study of convection processes is an important research area in many fields of contemporary science and engineering.

(a)

(b)

FIGURE 19-14 (a) Schematic diagram showing convection between two plates at different temperatures. (b) Top view of convection cells in a laboratory experiment.

Radiation

Turn an electric stove burner to "high," and it glows a brilliant red-orange. Set it on "low," and it does not appear hot, yet you can still tell it is by holding your hand near it. In both cases the burner is losing energy by emitting **radiation**. In later chapters, we will investigate the nature of radiation in terms of electromagnetic phenomena and atomic theory. Our stove-burner example suggests that radiation increases rapidly with temperature. Experiment confirms this: the rate of energy loss by radiation is given by the **Stefan-Boltzmann law**:

$$P = e\sigma AT^4, \tag{19-12}$$

where the energy loss rate P is in watts, A is the surface area of the emitting surface, T the temperature in kelvins, and σ a constant called the **Stefan-**

FIGURE 19-15 Slow convection in Earth's mantle brings up material at the mid-ocean ridges. Here continents A and B are drifting apart as the ocean widens.

Boltzmann constant, approximately 5.67×10^{-8} W/m^2·K^4. The quantity e is called the **emissivity** of the material. It is a dimensionless number ranging from 0 to 1 that measures the material's effectiveness in emitting radiation.

The rate of energy loss by radiation depends on the fourth power of the temperature. Therefore radiation is generally less important at low temperatures but dominates at high temperatures. A house loses only modest heat through radiation, while very hot things such as the Sun, light bulb filaments, or molten metal lose most of their energy by radiation (Fig. 19-16)—although any object above absolute zero radiates some energy. In vacuum, where conduction and convection cannot occur, all heat transfer occurs by radiation. That's why Thermos bottles and Dewar flasks—whose insulation is the vacuum between layers of glass—are coated with shiny material that reflects radiation.

FIGURE 19-16 Foundry worker pouring molten gold concentrate. Radiation is the dominant mode of heat loss from the hot liquid metal, as evidenced by its bright glow.

| **EXAMPLE 19-6** | *The Sun's Temperature* |

The Sun radiates energy at the rate $P = 3.9 \times 10^{26}$ W, and its radius is 7.0×10^8 m (Fig. 19-17). Assuming the Sun to be a blackbody (emissivity = 1), what is its surface temperature?

Solution

The radiated power is given by the Stefan-Boltzmann law, Equation 19-12. Solving this equation for T and using $4\pi R^2$ for the surface area of the Sun gives

$$T = \left(\frac{P}{4\pi R^2 \sigma} \right)^{1/4}$$

$$= \left[\frac{3.9 \times 10^{26} \text{ W}}{4\pi (7.0 \times 10^8 \text{ m})^2 (5.7 \times 10^{-8} \text{ W/m}^2 \cdot \text{K}^4)} \right]^{1/4}$$

$$= 5.8 \times 10^3 \text{ K},$$

in agreement with observational measurements.

EXERCISE What is the surface area of a 100-W light bulb filament at a temperature of 3100 K? Assume the filament has emissivity $e = 1$.

Answer: 1.9×10^{-5} m^2

FIGURE 19-17 What is the Sun's surface temperature?

Some problems similar to Example 19-6: 52–54, 63, 64

When an object is in thermodynamic equilibrium with its surroundings, it must emit and absorb radiation at the same rate; otherwise it would gain or lose energy and its temperature change from that of its surroundings. Then, since Equation 19-12 gives the rate of energy emission, it must also give the rate of absorption. Furthermore, for emission and absorption to be equal at a given temperature, the quantity e appearing in Equation 19-12 must be the same in both processes. A perfect emitter has $e = 1$ and must therefore also be a perfect absorber. Since it absorbs all radiation incident on it, such an object would appear black at room temperature and is therefore called a **blackbody**. (A blackbody would, however, glow brightly at high temperature.) A shiny object, in contrast, reflects radiation incident on it. So it has $e \simeq 0$, and is therefore also a poor emitter of radiation. That's why wood stoves and stovepipes are painted black; if they were shiny less heat would be radiated into the room to warm its occupants (and more would go up the chimney, by convection).

When an object is not in thermodynamic equilibrium, its temperature T differs from the surrounding temperature T_0. The object still emits energy at the rate $P_e = e\sigma AT^4$ set by its own temperature, but now it absorbs at the rate $P_a = e\sigma AT_0^4$ set by its surroundings. The net rate at which the object loses energy through radiation is the difference between these two quantities, or:

$$P_{\text{net}} = e\sigma A(T^4 - T_0^4) . \tag{19-13}$$

When $T = T_0$ we recover the result $P_{\text{net}} = 0$, as we argued must be the case for an object in equilibrium with its surroundings; when $T < T_0$ Equation 19-13 gives a negative energy loss rate, indicating that the object gains energy from its surroundings.

Examples of objects decidedly not in thermodynamic equilibrium with their surroundings include the Sun and the filament in Example 19-6. In that example, we were justified in neglecting the absorbed power because the surrounding temperature T_0 is in both cases so much less than the object's temperature that, when raised to the fourth power, it makes the absorbed power totally negligible.

Got It!

You set an electric stove burner on "high" but forget to put a pan on it; soon the burner glows red hot. What's the dominant mode of heat loss from the burner in this case? Now you put a pan of water on the burner and bring the water to a vigorous boil. What's the dominant mode of heat transfer (a) from burner to pan and (b) from the bottom of the pan to the top of the water surface?

19-7 THERMAL ENERGY BALANCE

When an object is in thermodynamic equilibrium with its surroundings, its temperature remains constant. But it could also maintain a constant temperature, different from its surroundings, by balancing energy gain and loss. A house in winter provides a good example of this **thermal energy balance**. Unheated, the house would come to equilibrium at the outdoor temperature. Heated, it loses energy because of the temperature difference between itself and its environment, but this loss is balanced by energy input from a furnace, solar collector, electricity, or other source (Fig. 19-18).

The principle of thermal energy balance is used throughout science and engineering to predict temperatures under different conditions. It's also used to determine the sizes of heat sources needed to achieve desired temperatures. When heat is supplied to an object, its temperature initially rises. But so does the heat-loss rate, which increases with the temperature difference between the object and its surroundings. Eventually the loss rate equals the rate of energy input. The object is then in thermal energy balance at a constant temperature. The following examples and application explore thermal energy balance.

FIGURE 19-18 A house in thermal energy balance. Energy from the furnace balances heat loss, maintaining the house at a constant temperature higher than that of its surroundings.

EXAMPLE 19-7	A Water Heater

A poorly insulated electric water heater loses heat at the rate of 40 W for each Celsius degree difference between the water and its surroundings. The tank is heated by a 2.5-kW electric heating element. If the heater is located in a 15°C basement, what will be its temperature if the heating element operates continuously?

Solution

The heating element supplies energy at the rate $H_{in} = 2.5$ kW, while the heater loses energy at the rate $H_{out} = (40 \text{ W/°C})(\Delta T)$, where ΔT is the temperature difference between the water and its surroundings. In thermal energy balance the heat input equals the heat loss, so we have

$$(40 \text{ W/°C})(\Delta T) = 2.5 \text{ kW},$$

or

$$\Delta T = \frac{2.5 \text{ kW}}{40 \text{ W/°C}} = 63°C.$$

With the basement at 15°C, the water temperature is then 78°C.

EXERCISE A home heating system supplies heat at the maximum rate of 40 kW. If the house loses 1.1 kW for each °C between inside and outside, what is the minimum outdoor temperature for which the heating system can maintain 20°C inside?

Answer: $-16°C$

Some problems similar to Example 19-7: 51, 54, 58, 65, 66

EXAMPLE 19-8	A Solar Greenhouse

Figure 19-19 shows a solar-heated greenhouse. The south-facing diagonal wall is made of double-pane glass ($\mathcal{R} = 1.8$), while the other walls are opaque and have R-factors of 30. Heat loss through the floor is negligible. The intensity of sunlight on the glass, averaged over a typical day, is 120 W/m². If the outdoor temperature is 15°F, what will be the temperature in the greenhouse?

Solution

We first calculate the heat-loss rate for the greenhouse. The total area of insulated wall is

$$A_w = (10 \text{ ft})(20 \text{ ft}) + 2[\tfrac{1}{2}(10 \text{ ft})^2] = 300 \text{ ft}^2,$$

so the heat-loss rate through these $\mathcal{R}$-30 walls is

$$H_w = \frac{A_w \Delta T}{\mathcal{R}_w} = \frac{300 \Delta T}{30} = 10\Delta T \text{ Btu/h·°F}.$$

Similarly, the glass area is

$$A_g = (20 \text{ ft})(10\sqrt{2} \text{ ft}) = 283 \text{ ft}^2,$$

so the heat-loss rate through the glass is

$$H_g = \frac{A_g \Delta T}{\mathcal{R}_g} = \frac{283 \Delta T}{1.8} = 157\Delta T \text{ Btu/h·°F}.$$

If the greenhouse is to be in thermal energy balance, the total heat-loss rate of $167\Delta T$ Btu/h·°F must be balanced by the energy gained from the Sun. The average solar input, which we denote S, is 120 W/m², or

$$S = (120 \text{ W/m}^2)[3.413(\text{Btu/h})/\text{W}](0.0929 \text{ m}^2/\text{ft}^2)$$
$$= 38.0 \text{ Btu/h·ft}^2,$$

where we obtained the conversion factors from Appendix C. Then the total solar gain on the 283-ft² glass is

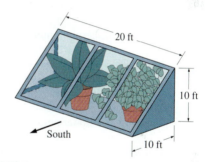

FIGURE 19-19 Solar greenhouse for Example 19-8.

$$(283 \text{ ft}^2)(38.0 \text{ Btu/h·ft}^2) = 1.075\times10^4 \text{ Btu/h}.$$

Equating the heat loss to the solar gain gives

$$167\Delta T \text{ Btu/h·°F} = 1.075\times10^4 \text{ Btu/h},$$

so

$$\Delta T = \frac{1.075\times10^4 \text{ Btu/h}}{167 \text{ Btu/h·°F}} = 64°F.$$

With the outdoors at 15°F, the greenhouse temperature is then 79°F.

EXERCISE A cubical doghouse measures 4.0 ft on a side, and its four walls and roof have $\mathcal{R} = 8.5$, including an insulated door. Heat loss to the ground is negligible. If the dog's metabolism produces energy at the average rate of 45 W, what will be the doghouse temperature when the outside temperature is $-5°F$?

Answer: 11°F

Some problems similar to Example 19-8: 55, 67

APPLICATION	*The Greenhouse Effect and Global Warming*

Among the most serious environmental challenges of the twenty-first century is global warming, brought on as human activity alters the composition of Earth's atmosphere (Fig. 19-20). Among the likely consequences are a rise in sea level and shifts in rainfall patterns that could jeopardize our ability to feed the burgeoning human population. With warming rates well in excess of naturally occurring climate change, many plant and animal species might perish from inability to adapt or migrate fast enough to escape inhospitable conditions. Less probable but potentially disastrous consequences include sudden, radical shifts in ocean circulation patterns that could leave Europe—now warmed by the Gulf Stream—with a climate like that of northern Labrador.

Scientific analysis of global warming is complex and not without controversy. By the mid-1990s, however, a substantial majority of climate scientists had concluded that signs of global warming were already evident, and that warming was likely to become much more obvious over the next few decades. In 1996, the authoritative Intergovernmental Panel on Climate Change (IPCC) published a carefully worded statement that "the balance of evidence suggests a discernible human influence on global climate."* IPCC scientists based their conclusion in part on direct evidence, including a rise in global temperature and the occurrence of record hottest years and even decades at the twentieth century's end. But equally compelling was indirect evidence from patterns of climatic change—for example, the occurrence of more intense precipitation—that corroborate computer model predictions for the effects of human-induced global warming. By now there is near-universal agreement in the scientific community that human activities will bring a still warmer climate in the coming decades. However, the details of how much warming, how fast, where, and with what consequences remain less certain.

But though the details are complex, the basic physics is straightforward. Earth itself is essentially in thermal energy balance. Sunlight heats the planet, which in turn radiates energy as infrared radiation. Earth's temperature is established by the balance between solar input and infrared radiation into space. Figure 19-21 shows that our planet presents an effective area πR_E^2 to the incident sunlight. The rate of solar energy input at the top of the atmosphere is then $\pi R_E^2 S$, where S is the power per unit area in sunlight. Above the atmosphere, $S = 1.37$ kW/m², but about 30% of the sunlight is reflected back into space, giving an effective solar intensity $S = 960$ W/m². Figure 19-21 also shows that Earth radiates from its entire surface area $4\pi R_E^2$. If Earth were a blackbody ($e = 1$), Equation 19-12 would give a total energy loss rate $P = \sigma 4\pi R_E^2 T^4$.

* *Climate Change 1995: The Science of Climate Change* (Contribution of Working Group I to the Second Assessment Report of the Intergovernmental Panel on Climate Change), J. T. Houghton et al., eds. (Cambridge University Press, 1996).

FIGURE 19-20 Global temperature changes according to a computer model simulating the period from 1880 to 2049, based on projected increases in carbon dioxide and atmospheric aerosols (particulate matter). Darkest red areas represent a 5°C temperature increase; darkest blue areas indicate a 2°C decrease. Simulation is for conditions during the northern hemisphere winter.

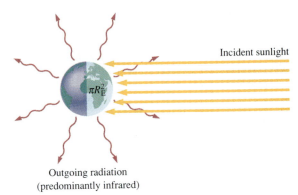

FIGURE 19-21 Earth's temperature is determined by the balance of incoming sunlight and outgoing infrared radiation. The planet presents an effective area πR_E^2 to sunlight, but radiates from its entire surface.

Equating energy gain and loss rates would give

$$\pi R_E^2 S = \sigma 4\pi R_E^2 T^4,$$

or

$$T = \left(\frac{S}{4\sigma}\right)^{1/4} = \left(\frac{960 \text{ W/m}^2}{(4)(5.67\times10^{-8}\text{ W/m}^2\text{·K})}\right)^{1/4}$$

$$= 255 \text{ K} = -18°C.$$

This number is certainly the right order of magnitude, but is considerably lower than the measured global average temperature of about 14°C.

What's missing in our simple calculation that would account for the 32°C discrepancy? The answer lies in the composition of Earth's atmosphere. A number of atmospheric gas molecules absorb infrared radiation, reradiating some to space but some back to Earth. As a result, Earth's surface temperature must be higher than it would be in the absence of those gases in order to achieve the same rate of infrared radiation escaping to outer space. This phenomenon is called the **greenhouse effect** because the infrared-absorbing gases play the same role as greenhouse glass: they let incident sunlight through but impede escaping infrared, helping to keep the greenhouse temperature higher than it otherwise would be.

The 32°C temperature increase we've just described is due to the **natural greenhouse effect**, caused primarily by atmospheric water vapor and carbon dioxide. It's good thing we have the natural greenhouse effect; otherwise Earth would be intolerably cold, as our calculation suggests. The planet Mars has insignificant quantities of greenhouse gases, and it's much colder relative to Earth than its greater distance from the Sun would imply. On the other hand the greenhouse effect can get out of control; Venus' surface temperature is hotter than an oven, thanks to an overabundance of greenhouse gases. Earth's temperature is in a delicate balance between too little and too much greenhouse effect.

Unfortunately that balance is changing. The single most significant human contribution to atmospheric greenhouse gases is carbon dioxide, which results primarily from burning fossil fuels and accounts for nearly two-thirds of the human-induced enhancement of the greenhouse effect. The CO_2 content of Earth's atmosphere has risen steadily throughout the industrial age (Fig. 19-22), and now produces roughly the same excess heating as would a 1.6-kW/m^2 increase in the intensity of sunlight.

CO_2 emissions continue to rise, driven by such factors as rapid industrialization in the developing world and decreases in average automobile fuel efficiency in the U.S. (recall Fig. 7-21). It's definitely too late to prevent global warming altogether. With a concerted effort, though, the average temperature increase might be held to about 2 C°—a rise that, although small, still implies significant climatic change. In 1997, a global conference on greenhouse warming produced the first international treaty with binding requirements on some nations to reduce their greenhouse gas emissions. The treaty reductions will help, but in themselves will not be enough to prevent continued increases in atmospheric CO_2 and with them a rise in global temperature.

Current projections, based on computer models that couple the physics and chemistry of the atmosphere and oceans with responses of the biosphere and assumptions about the development of human society, suggest a global average temperature increase of some 1–3.5°C over the next century, with 2°C a best estimate. These values may seem modest, but they represent a rate of change far in excess of what humankind has previously experienced (Fig. 19-23). Furthermore, the projected warming is not spread evenly over the planet, but tends to be greatest in the polar regions. Significant climatic change will almost certainly accompany even a global average temperature rise of 1–2°C.

There remain uncertainties in predicting both the extent of global warming and its effects. Physical, chemical, and biological mechanisms, many poorly understood, may help stabilize global warming, or they may exacerbate it. New technologies may help alleviate the problem or they may contribute to it. Global warming presents an enormous challenge to scientists and engineers—and to all the world's citizens.

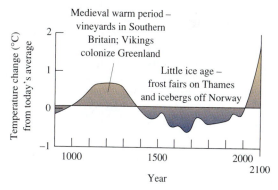

FIGURE 19-23 Global average temperature change over 1200 years, including the best estimate by the Intergovernmental Panel on Climate Change for the next century. The IPCC's 2°C projection is considerably larger than natural variations over the past thousand years; even the latter had obvious effects on climate. Furthermore, the projected increase due to global warming will occur far more rapidly than any recent natural changes, giving ecosystems little time to adapt. Although a 2°C rise may seem small, changes only a few times larger—but in the opposite direction—are associated with the difference between Earth's present climate and the last ice age.

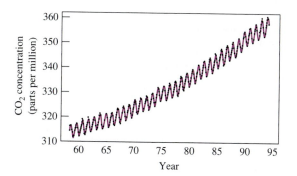

FIGURE 19-22 Atmospheric CO_2 concentration as measured at Mauna Loa, Hawaii, over the past four decades. Annual variations reflect seasonal changes in vegetation. The overall trend shows an increase that has been occurring since the beginning of the industrial age.

CHAPTER SYNOPSIS

Summary

1. Heat and related phenomena may be viewed from either the macroscopic viewpoint of **thermodynamics** or the microscopic viewpoint of **statistical mechanics**.
2. Two systems are in **thermodynamic equilibrium** if none of their macroscopic properties change when they are brought into thermal contact. Systems in thermodynamic equilibrium have the same **temperature**.
3. The **zeroth law of thermodynamics** states that two systems in thermodynamic equilibrium with a third system are in thermodynamic equilibrium with each other. This law allows the establishment of temperature scales.
4. A **thermometer** is a system with a convenient macroscopic property that serves to indicate temperature. **Gas thermometers** are used to establish the **kelvin** temperature scale of the SI system.
5. **Heat** is energy being transferred between objects as a result of a temperature difference.
6. **Specific heat** measures the ratio of heat to temperature change for a unit mass of a given material:

$$c = \frac{1}{m}\frac{\Delta Q}{\Delta T}.$$

Heat capacity is the ratio of heat to temperature change for a given object:

$$C = mc = \frac{\Delta Q}{\Delta T}.$$

7. Heat transfer occurs mainly by three distinct mechanisms:
   a. **Conduction** is direct transfer of heat through physical contact, and involves energy exchange through molecular collisions. The conduction rate H through a slab of material depends on the **thermal conductivity** k of the material, the slab thickness Δx and slab area A, and on the temperature difference across the slab:

   $$H = -kA\frac{\Delta T}{\Delta x}.$$

   Thermal resistance, $R = \Delta x/kA$ and **R-factor**, $\mathcal{R} = \Delta x/k$, also characterize heat conduction through materials.
   b. **Convection** is heat transfer through bulk motion of a fluid, as when heated air rises. Convection is difficult to describe quantitatively but is an important process in many natural and technological systems.
   c. **Radiation** is energy in the form of electromagnetic waves that can travel through empty space. The rate at which a hot surface of temperature T and area A loses energy by radiation is

   $$P = e\sigma AT^4,$$

   where e is a number between 0 and 1 that describes the effectiveness of the surface as a radiation emitter

and σ is the universal **Stefan-Boltzmann constant**, $\sigma = 5.67\times10^{-8}$ W/m²·K.
8. **Thermal energy balance** exists when an object gains and loses energy at the same rate, thereby maintaining a constant temperature. If either energy gain or loss changes, the temperature rises or falls until heat loss again balances gain.

Terms You Should Understand

(Pairs are closely related terms whose distinction is important; number in parentheses is chapter section where term first appears.)

thermodynamics, statistical mechanics (19-1)
thermodynamic equilibrium (19-2)
thermal contact, thermal insulation (19-2)
thermometer, gas thermometer (19-3)
kelvin (19-3)
calorie, British thermal unit (19-4)
specific heat, heat capacity (19-5)
conduction, convection, radiation (19-6)
thermal conductivity (19-6)
thermal resistance, R-factor (19-6)
Stefan-Boltzmann law (19-6)
emissivity (19-6)
blackbody (19-6)
thermal energy balance (19-7)
greenhouse effect (19-7)

Symbols You Should Recognize

T (19-3) k (19-6)
K, °C, °F (19-3) $R, \mathcal{R}$ (19-6)
cal, Btu (19-4) e (19-6)
c, C (19-5) σ (19-6)
H (19-6)

Problems You Should Be Able to Solve

converting among different temperature scales (19-3)
converting among different energy units (19-4)
calculating the equilibrium temperature of a mixture (19-5)
evaluating heat loss given thermal conductivity, resistance, or R-factor (19-6)
evaluating radiant heat loss (19-6)
determining temperature in thermal energy balance (19-7)

Limitations to Keep in Mind

When specific heat varies significantly over a temperature range, Equation 19-4 must be written in terms of the derivative dQ/dT and then integrated to find the heat.
Equation 19-7 applies exactly only when the thermal conductivity is independent of temperature and the geometry is that of a rectangular slab. Otherwise it must be written in terms of the derivative dT/dx and integrated to relate heat loss and temperature difference.

QUESTIONS

1. Two identical-looking physical systems are in the same macroscopic state. Must they be in the same microscopic state? Explain.
2. Two identical-looking physical systems are in the same microscopic state. Must they be in the same macroscopic state? Explain.
3. If system *A* is not in thermodynamic equilibrium with system *B*, and *B* is not in equilibrium with *C*, can you draw any conclusions about the temperatures of the three systems?
4. Given that there are three main mechanisms of heat transfer, how would you construct a good insulator?
5. Does a thermometer measure its own temperature, or the temperature of its surroundings? Explain.
6. To get an accurate body temperature measurement, you must hold a glass-and-mercury fever thermometer under your tongue for about 3 minutes. Some electronic fever thermometers require less than a minute. What might account for the difference?
7. Why is it better to define temperature scales in terms of a physical state, such as the triple point of water, rather than by having an official, standard thermometer stored at the International Bureau of Weights and Measures?
8. Compare the relative sizes of the kelvin, the degree Celsius, the degree Fahrenheit, and the degree Rankine.
9. Does a vacuum have temperature? Explain.
10. If you put a thermometer in direct sunlight, what do you measure? The air temperature? The temperature of the Sun? Some other temperature?
11. Why does the temperature in a stone building usually vary less than in a wooden building?
12. Why do large bodies of water exert a temperature-moderating effect on their surroundings?
13. A Thermos bottle consists of an evacuated, double-wall glass liner. The glass is coated with a thin layer of aluminum. How does a Thermos bottle work?
14. Stainless-steel cookware often has a layer of aluminum or copper embedded in the bottom. Why?
15. What method of energy transfer dominates in baking? In broiling?
16. After a calm, cold night the temperature a few feet above ground often drops just as the Sun comes up. Explain in terms of convection.
17. Solar collectors often have a copper absorber surface coated with a black paint, whose emissivity is nearly 1 for visible and infrared radiation. Better results can be achieved, though, with a "selective surface," whose emissivity is high for visible light but low for the infrared radiation associated with lower temperatures than the Sun's. Why is this?
18. Glass and fiberglass are made from the same material, yet have dramatically different thermal conductivities. Why?
19. A thin layer of glass does not offer much resistance to heat conduction. Yet double-glazed windows provide substantial energy savings. Why?
20. The insulating value of a double-glazed window actually decreases if the spacing is made too great. Why might this be?
21. To keep your hands warm while skiing, you should wear mittens instead of gloves. Why?
22. Since Earth is exposed to solar radiation, why doesn't Earth have the same temperature as the Sun?
23. On a clear night, a solar collector will often cool well below the ambient air temperature. Why? Why doesn't this happen on a cloudy night?
24. Is Earth in perfect energy balance? If not, why not?

PROBLEMS

Section 19-1 Macroscopic and Microscopic Descriptions

1. The macroscopic state of a carton capable of holding a half-dozen eggs is specified by giving the number of eggs in the carton. The microscopic state is specified by telling where each egg is in the carton. How many microscopic states correspond to the macroscopic state of a full carton?

Section 19-3 Measuring Temperature

2. A Canadian meteorologist predicts an overnight low of $-15°C$. How would a U.S. meteorologist express that same prediction?
3. Normal room temperature is $68°F$. What is this in Celsius?
4. The outdoor temperature rises by $10°C$. What is the rise in Fahrenheit?
5. At what temperature do the Fahrenheit and Celsius scales coincide?
6. Give equations for Rankine temperature in terms of (a) kelvins and (b) $°F$.
7. The normal boiling point of nitrogen is 77.3 K. Express this in Celsius and Fahrenheit.
8. A sick child's temperature reads 39.1 on a Celsius thermometer. What's the child's temperature on the Fahrenheit scale?
9. A constant-volume gas thermometer is filled with air whose pressure is 101 kPa at the normal melting point of ice. What would its pressure be at (a) the normal boiling point of water, (b) the normal boiling point of oxygen

(90.2 K), and (c) the normal boiling point of mercury (630 K)?

10. A constant-volume gas thermometer is at 55 kPa pressure at the triple point of water. By how much does its pressure change for each kelvin temperature change?

11. The temperature of a constant-pressure gas thermometer is directly proportional to the gas volume. If the volume is 1.00 L at the triple point of water, what is it at water's normal boiling point?

12. In the gas thermometer of Fig. 19-24, the height h is 60.0 mm at the triple point of water. When the thermometer is immersed in boiling sulfur dioxide the height drops to 57.8 mm. What is the boiling point of SO_2 in kelvins and in degrees Celsius?

FIGURE 19-24 Problem 12.

13. A constant-volume gas thermometer supports a 72.5-mm-high mercury column when it's immersed in liquid nitrogen at $-196°C$. What will be the column height when the thermometer is in molten lead at 350°C?

Sections 19-4 and 19-5 Temperature and Heat, Heat Capacity and Specific Heat

14. The average human diet contains about 2000 kcal per day. If all this food energy is released rather than being stored as fat, what is the approximate average power output of the human body?

15. If your mass is 60 kg, what is the minimum number of calories you would "burn off" climbing a 1700-m-high mountain? (The actual metabolic energy used would be much greater.)

16. Walking at 3 km/h requires an energy expenditure rate of about 200 W. How far would you have to walk to "burn off" a 300-kcal hamburger?

17. Typical fats contain about 9 kcal per gram. If the energy in body fat could be utilized with 100% efficiency, how much mass could a 78-kg person lose running a 26.2-mile marathon? The energy expenditure rate for that mass is 125 kcal/mile.

18. You expend 150 kcal while exercising for 5 minutes. If your mass is 60 kg and you're essentially water, by how much would your temperature increase if you had no heat loss?

19. A circular lake 1.0 km in diameter is 10 m deep (Fig. 19-25). Solar energy is incident on the lake at an average rate of 200 W/m². If the lake absorbs all this energy and does not exchange heat with its surroundings, how long will it take to warm from 10°C to 20°C?

FIGURE 19-25 Problem 19.

20. You bring a 350-g wrench into the house from your car. The house is 15°C warmer than the car, and it takes 2.52 kJ of energy to warm the wrench by this amount. Find (a) the heat capacity of the wrench and (b) the specific heat of the metal it's made from.

21. How much heat is required to raise an 800-g copper pan from 15°C to 90°C if (a) the pan is empty; (b) the pan contains 1.0 kg of water; (c) the pan contains 4.0 kg of mercury?

22. Initially, 100 g of water and 100 g of another substance listed in Table 19-1 are at 20°C. Heat is then transferred to each substance at the same rate for 1.0 min. At the end of that time the water is at 32°C and the other substance at 76°C. (a) What is the other substance? (b) What is the heating rate?

23. How much power does it take to raise the temperature of a 1.3-kg copper pipe by 15°C/s?

24. How long will it take a 625-W microwave oven to bring 250 mL of water from 10°C to the boiling point?

25. You insert your microwave oven's temperature probe in a roast and start it cooking. You notice that the temperature goes up 1°C every 20 s. If the roast has the same specific heat as water, and if the oven power is 500 W, what is the mass of the roast? Neglect heat loss.

26. Two neighbors return from Florida to find their houses at a frigid 15°F. Each house has a furnace with heat output of 100,000 Btu/h. One house is made of stone and weighs 75 tons. The other is made of wood and weighs 15 tons. How long does it take each house to reach 65°F? Neglect heat loss, and assume the entire house mass reaches the same 65°F temperature.

27. A stove burner supplies heat at the rate of 1.0 kW, a microwave oven at 625 W. You can heat water in the microwave in a paper cup of negligible heat capacity, but the stove requires a pan whose heat capacity is 1.4 kJ/K. (a) How much water do you need before it becomes quicker to heat on the stovetop? (b) What will be the rate at which the temperature of this much water rises?

28. When a nuclear power plant's reactor is shut down, radioactive decay continues to produce heat at about 10% of the reactor's normal power level of 3.0 GW. In a major accident, a pipe breaks and all the reactor cooling water is

lost. The reactor is immediately shut down, the break sealed, and 420 m³ of 20°C water injected into the reactor. If the water were not actively cooled, how long would it take to reach its normal boiling point?

29. A 1.2-kg iron tea kettle sits on a 2.0-kW stove burner. If it takes 5.4 min to bring the kettle and the water in it from 20°C to the boiling point, how much water is in the kettle?

30. An alpine rescue team finds a 73-kg hypothermia victim whose body temperature has dropped to 34°C. They wrap the victim in blankets, reducing his heat loss to near zero. Shivering violently, the victim's own metabolism releases energy at the rate of 190 W. (a) How long will it take to warm his body to the normal 37°C? Assume the body is essentially water. (b) How many 230-kcal chocolate bars would it take to supply the energy needed to heat the victim's body?

31. Two cars collide head-on at 90 km/h. If all their kinetic energy ended up as heat, what would be the temperature increase of the wrecks? The specific heat of the cars is essentially that of iron.

32. A 1500-kg car moving at 40 km/h is brought to a sudden stop. If all the car's energy is dissipated in heating its four 5.0-kg steel brake disks, by how much do the disk temperatures increase?

33. A leaf absorbs sunlight with intensity 600 W/m². The leaf has a mass per unit area of 100 g/m², and its specific heat is 3800 J/kg·K. In the absence of any heat loss, at what rate would the leaf's temperature rise?

34. A child complains that her cocoa is too hot. The cocoa is at 90°C. Her father pours 2 oz of milk at 3°C into the 6 oz of cocoa. Assuming milk and cocoa have the same specific heat as water, what is the new temperature of the cocoa?

35. A piece of copper at 300°C is dropped into 1.0 kg of water at 20°C. If the equilibrium temperature is 25°C, what is the mass of the copper?

36. Vegetables with mass 2.2 kg, specific heat 0.92 cal/g·°C, and temperature 4.0°C are added to 4.5 kg of soup stock (essentially water) at 80°C. What is the equilibrium temperature?

37. A thermometer of mass 83.0 g is used to measure the temperature of a 150-g water sample. The thermometer's specific heat is 0.190 cal/g·°C, and it reads 20.0°C before immersion in the water. The water temperature is initially 60.0°C. What does the thermometer read after it comes to equilibrium with the water?

Sections 19-6 and 19-7 Heat Transfer and Thermal Energy Balance

38. Find the heat-loss rate through a 1.0-m² slab of (a) wood and (b) styrofoam, each 2.0 cm thick, if one surface is at 20°C and the other at 0°C.

39. The top of a steel wood stove measures 90 cm × 40 cm, and is 0.45 cm thick. The fire maintains the inside surface of the stove top at 310°C, while the outside surface is at 295°C. Find the rate of heat conduction through the stove top.

40. How thick a concrete wall would be needed to give the same insulating value as 3½ inches of fiberglass?

41. Building heat loss in the United States is usually expressed in Btu/h. What is 1 Btu/h in SI?

42. An 8.0 m × 12 m house is built on a concrete slab 23 cm thick. What is the heat-loss rate through the floor if the interior is at 20°C while the ground is at 10°C?

43. What is the R-factor of a wall that loses 0.040 Btu each hour through each square foot for each °F temperature difference?

44. Compute the R-factors for 1-inch thicknesses of air, concrete, fiberglass, glass, styrofoam, and wood.

45. A biology lab's walk-in cooler measures 3.0 m × 2.0 m × 2.3 m and is insulated with 8.0-cm-thick styrofoam. If the surrounding building is at 20°C, at what average rate must the cooler's refrigeration unit remove heat in order to maintain 4.0°C in the cooler?

46. One end of an iron rod 40 cm long and 3.0 cm in diameter is in ice water, the other in boiling water. (See Fig. 19-26.) The rod is well insulated so there's no heat lost out the sides. What is the heat-flow rate along the rod?

Iron rod

Ice water   Boiling water

FIGURE 19-26 Problem 46.

47. (a) What is the R-factor for a wall consisting of ¼-in. pine paneling, ℛ-11 fiberglass insulation, ¾-in. pine sheathing, and 2.0-mm aluminum siding? (b) What is the heat-loss rate through a 20 ft × 8 ft section of wall when the temperature difference across the wall is 55°F?

48. You're considering installing a 5 ft × 8 ft picture window in a north-facing wall that now has ℛ-19 insulation. The window has ℛ = 2.1 ft²·°F·h/Btu. If you install the window, how much more oil, at 100,000 Btu per gallon, will you have to burn in a winter month when the outdoor temperature averages 15°F and the indoor temperature is 68°F?

49. Repeat the preceding problem for a south-facing window where the average sunlight intensity is 180 W/m².

50. A flat-roofed house measures 28 ft × 28 ft × 9 ft high and has ℛ = 30 for its roof and ℛ = 20 for its walls. The house next door has the same height, the same wall and roof construction, the same square shape, but twice the floor area. If the houses are kept at the same temperature, compare their heating bills. Neglect losses through the floors.

51. A house is insulated so its total heat loss is 370 W/°C. On a night when the outdoor temperature is 12°C the owner throws a party, and 40 people come. The average power output of the human body is 100 W. If there are no other

heat sources in the house, what will be the house temperature during the party?

52. A 1000-W electric clothes iron has surface area 300 cm² and emissivity $e = 0.97$. If the surface temperature of the iron is 500 K and its surroundings are at 300 K, (a) what is the *net* rate of energy transfer by radiation from the iron? (b) What must be the rate of energy transfer by conduction and convection?

53. An electric stove burner has surface area 325 cm² and emissivity $e = 1.0$. The burner is at 900 K and the electric power input to the burner is 1500 W. If room temperature is 300 K, what fraction of the burner's heat loss is by radiation?

54. An electric current passes through a metal strip 0.50 cm × 5.0 cm × 0.10 mm, heating it at the rate of 50 W. The strip has emissivity $e = 1.0$ and its surroundings are at 300 K. What will be the temperature of the strip if it's enclosed in (a) a vacuum bottle transparent to all radiation and (b) an insulating box with thermal resistance $R = 8.0$ K/W that blocks all radiation?

55. The average human body produces heat at the rate of 100 W and has total surface area of about 1.5 m². What is the coldest outdoor temperature in which a down sleeping bag with 4.0-cm loft (thickness) can be used without the body temperature dropping below 37°C? Consider only conductive heat loss.

56. The Intergovernmental Panel on Climate Change estimates that human-produced greenhouse gases currently have a climatic effect roughly equivalent to an increase in the intensity of sunlight of 2.5 W/m². What increase in global temperature should be attributable to these gases? (Your answer is only an estimate because your calculation ignores feedbacks and other important effects.)

57. Scientists worry that a nuclear war could inject enough dust into the upper atmosphere to reduce significantly the amount of solar energy reaching Earth's surface. If an 8% reduction in solar input occurred, what would happen to Earth's 287-K average temperature?

58. Sunlight intensity varies with the inverse square of the distance from the Sun; at Earth's orbit the intensity is 1.37 kW/m². Use data from Appendix E to calculate the average temperatures of Mars and Venus if those planets' atmospheres contained no greenhouse gases, and treating each as a blackbody ($e = 1$). Compare with the measured surface temperatures of about 220 K and 730 K, respectively. Does either planet have a significant greenhouse effect?

Paired Problems

(Both problems in a pair involve the same principles and techniques. If you can get the first problem, you should be able to solve the second one.)

59. A blacksmith heats a 1.1-kg iron horseshoe to 550°C, then plunges it into a bucket containing 15 kg of water at 20°C. What is the final temperature?

60. A 2.3-kg cast-iron frying pan is plunged into 7.5 kg of water at 22°C. If the equilibrium temperature is 30°C, what was the pan's initial temperature?

61. What is the power output of a microwave oven that can heat 430 g of water from 20°C to the boiling point in 5.0 minutes? Neglect the heat capacity of the container.

62. A nuclear power plant is being started up after refueling. If it takes 1.5 hours to bring the reactor's 5.4×10^6 kg of cooling water from 10°C to its 350°C operating temperature, what is the reactor's thermal power output? Neglect the heat capacity of the reactor vessel and plumbing.

63. A cylindrical log 15 cm in diameter and 65 cm long is glowing red hot in a fireplace. If it's emitting radiation at the rate of 34 kW, what is its temperature? The log's emissivity is essentially 1.

64. A star whose surface temperature is 50 kK radiates 4.0×10^{27} W. If the star behaves as a blackbody, what is its radius?

65. An enclosed rabbit hutch has a thermal resistance of 0.25 K/W. If you put a 50-W heat lamp in the hutch on a day when the outside temperature is −15°C, what will be the hutch temperature? Neglect the rabbit's metabolism.

66. The walls of a home refrigerator have a thermal resistance of 0.090 K/W. What is the average rate at which the refrigerator must transfer heat in order to maintain the interior at 4°C in a room where the temperature is 21°C?

Supplementary Problems

67. Rework Example 19-5, now assuming that the house has 10 single-glazed windows, each measuring 2.5 ft × 5.0 ft. Four of the windows are on the south, and admit solar energy at the average rate of 30 Btu/h·ft². *All* the windows lose heat; their R-factor is 0.90. (a) What is the total heating cost for the month? (b) How much is the solar gain worth?

68. What are the SI units of R-factor? Express the R-factor for 6-in fiberglass insulation ($\mathcal{R} = 19$ ft²·°F·h/Btu) in SI.

69. My house currently burns 160 gallons of oil in a typical winter month when the outdoor temperature averages 15°F and the indoor temperature averages 66°F. Roof insulation consists of $\mathcal{R} = 19$ fiberglass, and the roof area is 770 ft². If I double the thickness of the roof insulation, by what percentage will my heating bills drop? A gallon of oil yields about 100,000 Btu of heat.

70. A black woodstove with surface area 4.6 m² is made from cast iron 4.0 mm thick. The interior wall of the stove is at 650°C while the exterior is at 647°C. (a) What is the rate of heat conduction through the stove wall? (b) What is the rate of heat loss by radiation from the stove? (c) Use the results of (a) and (b) to find how much heat the stove loses by a combination of conduction and convection in the surrounding air.

71. A copper pan 1.5 mm thick and a cast iron pan 4.0 mm thick are sitting on electric stove burners; the bottom area of each pan is 300 cm². Each contains 2.0 kg of water

whose temperature is rising at the rate of 0.15 K/s. Find the temperature difference between the inside and outside bottom of each pan.

72. What should be the average temperature on Pluto, at its 5.9×10^{12}-m distance from the Sun? Treat Pluto as a blackbody.

73. At low temperatures the specific heat of a solid is approximately proportional to the cube of the temperature; for copper the specific heat is given by $c = 31(T/343 \text{ K})^3$ J/g·K. When heat capacity is not constant, Equations 19-4 and 19-5 must be written in terms of the derivative dQ/dT and integrated to get the total heat involved in a temperature change. Find the heat required to bring a 40-g sample of copper from 10 K to 25 K.

74. When area or heat conductivity are not constant, Equation 19-7 must be written in terms of the derivative dT/dx:

$$H = -kA\frac{dT}{dx} \qquad (19\text{-}14)$$

and must be integrated to get the relation between the temperature difference and heat loss. Consider a truncated cone with faces of radii R_1 and R_2 and length ℓ, as shown in Fig. 19-27. If the temperatures on the faces are T_1 and T_2, respectively, and if insulation prevents heat loss out the sides, show that the heat flow rate is given by $H = \pi k R_1 R_2 (T_1 - T_2)/\ell$. *Hint:* Divide the cone into thin slabs and write the area of each in terms of its distance x from the left face. Use this expression for the area in Equation 19-14, multiply through by dx/A, and integrate, noting that H must be the same throughout the cone.

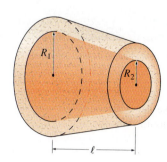

FIGURE 19-27 What is the heat flow rate through the cone? The insulation prevents heat loss out the sides (Problem 74).

75. A pipe of length ℓ and radius R_1 is surrounded by insulation of outer radius R_2 and thermal conductivity k. Use the methods of the preceding problem to show that the heat loss rate through the insulation is

$$H = \frac{2\pi k \ell (T_1 - T_2)}{\ln(R_2/R_1)}.$$

Hint: Consider the heat flow through a thin layer of thickness dr and temperature difference dT as shown in Fig. 19-28.

FIGURE 19-28 An insulated pipe. Blue cylinder is a layer of thickness dr for use in calculating the heat loss (Problem 75).

76. An object of heat capacity C J/K is surrounded by insulation with thermal resistance R K/W. The object is initially at temperature T_1 and its surroundings are at the constant temperature T_0. (a) If there is no source of heat in the object, show that its temperature T as a function of time t is described by the equation

$$C\frac{dT}{dt} = -\frac{1}{R}(T - T_0).$$

(b) Show by substitution that the solution to this equation is

$$T = T_0 + (T_1 - T_0)e^{-t/RC}.$$

Show that this solution gives reasonable results for $t = 0$ and as $t \to \infty$.

77. A house is at 20°C on a winter day when the outdoor temperature is -15°C. Suddenly the furnace fails. Use the result of the previous problem to determine how long it will take the house temperature to reach the freezing point. The heat capacity of the house is 6.5 MJ/K, and its thermal resistance is 6.67 mK/W.

20

The Thermal Behavior of Matter

Melting is one of the changes matter undergoes when its temperature increases. Here molten steel pours from a red-hot crucible.

Matter responds to heating in a variety of ways. It may get hotter or it may melt. It may experience changes in size or shape, or in pressure. In this chapter, we seek to understand the thermal behavior of matter. We start with a particularly simple state—the gaseous state—whose behavior can largely be explained by applying Newtonian mechanics at the molecular level. We then move to the more complicated cases of liquids and solids, whose behavior is still grounded in the molecular properties of matter, but whose description at the level of this text is necessarily more empirical.

20-1 GASES

Gas is matter in a rarefied state. Molecules of a gas are so far apart that they spend most of their time moving freely, and only rarely interact with one another. That makes gas behavior and its physical explanation particularly simple. In studying gas behavior, we will develop a clear understanding of the relation between macroscopic properties—such as temperature and pressure—and the underlying microscopic properties of gas molecules.

The Ideal Gas Law

The macroscopic state of a gas in thermodynamic equilibrium is determined completely by its temperature, pressure, and volume. Moreover, it turns out that all gases exhibit, to a very good approximation, the same relation among these three quantities.

A simple system for studying gas behavior consists of a gas-filled cylinder sealed by a movable piston (Fig. 20-1). As we explore this system here and in the next chapter, keep in mind that it's not just a pedagogical abstraction. Practical devices including engines, pumps, and air compressors contain piston-cylinder systems, while human lungs, balloons, the blood-borne gas bubbles that cause the "bends" in scuba divers, and many other natural systems involving confined gases are analogous to our piston-cylinder system. ActivPhysics Activity 8.4 provides a simulation of a gas in a piston-cylinder system.

FIGURE 20-1 A piston-cylinder system.

8.4
Ideal Gas Law

If we maintain the system of Fig. 20-1 at constant temperature (for example, by immersing it in a bath of water) and move the piston to vary the gas volume, we find that the pressure varies inversely with volume. If we increase the temperature while holding volume fixed, the pressure rises in direct proportion to the temperature. If we double the amount of gas while holding temperature and volume constant, we find that the pressure doubles. Putting all these experimental results together, we can write

$$PV = NkT, \tag{20-1}$$

with P, V, and T the pressure, volume, and temperature, respectively, and N the number of molecules in the gas. The constant k is **Boltzmann's constant**, after the Austrian physicist Ludwig Boltzmann (1844–1906), who was instrumental in developing the microscopic description of thermal phenomena. Its value is $k = 1.38 \times 10^{-23}$ J/K.

Equation 20-1 is the **ideal gas law**. Most real gases obey this law to a very good approximation. Later we'll see just why and how real gas behavior deviates, usually just slightly, from the ideal expressed in Equation 20-1.

Because the number of molecules, N, in a typical gas sample is astronomically large, we often express the ideal gas law in terms of the number of **moles** (mol) of gas molecules. The mole is an SI unit useful for measuring the amount of anything that comes in large numbers; one mole of anything consists of Avogadro's number of that thing, where Avogadro's number is approximately $N_A = 6.022 \times 10^{23}$. (Formally, Avogadro's number is defined as the number of carbon-12 atoms in 1 gram of carbon-12. It's named after the Italian chemist Amadeo Avogadro, 1776–1856.)

If we have n moles of a gas, then $N = nN_A$ is the number of molecules, so the ideal gas law becomes

$$PV = nN_A kT = nRT, \qquad (20\text{-}2)$$

where the constant $R = N_A k = 8.314$ J/K·mol is called the **universal gas constant**.

EXAMPLE 20-1	*STP*

What is the volume occupied by 1.00 mol of an ideal gas at standard temperature and pressure (STP), where $T = 0°C$ and $P = 101.3$ kPa?

Solution

Solving the ideal gas law for the volume V, and expressing temperature in kelvins, we have

$$V = \frac{nRT}{P} = \frac{(1.00 \text{ mol})(8.314 \text{ J/K·mol})(273 \text{ K})}{1.013 \times 10^5 \text{ Pa}}$$

$$= 22.4 \times 10^{-3} \text{ m}^3 = 22.4 \text{ L}.$$

EXERCISE If the gas of Example 20-1 is cooled to $-120°C$ and compressed into a 2.0-L container, what will be its pressure?

Answer: 636 kPa

Some problems similar to Example 20-1: 3, 6, 8, 11

The ideal gas law is remarkably simple. Neither the form of the law nor the constants k and R depend on the substance making up the gas or on the mass of the individual gas molecules. Yet most real gases follow the ideal gas law very closely over a wide range of pressures. This nearly ideal behavior is what gives gas thermometers their high precision over a wide temperature range.

Kinetic Theory of the Ideal Gas

Why do gases obey such a simple relation among temperature, pressure, and volume? Here we answer that question with a microscopic analysis of the ideal gas that is based ultimately in the laws of Newtonian mechanics.

To understand how matter in the gaseous state should behave, we make a number of simplifying assumptions:

1. The gas consists of a very large number of identical molecules, each with mass m but with negligible size and no internal structure. This assumption is approximately true for real gases when the distance between molecules is large compared with their size. The molecules' negligible size means that intermolecular collisions are so rare we can neglect them. (We'll see later that neglecting collisions is not essential, but it will simplify our analysis. ActivPhysics Activity 8.1 explores the role of molecular collisions.)

2. The molecules do not exert any action-at-a-distance forces on each other. This means there are no potential energy changes to be considered, so each molecule's kinetic energy remains unchanged. Thus the only form of molecular energy that's important is kinetic energy. This assumption is fundamental to the nature of an ideal gas.

3. The molecules are moving in random directions with a distribution of speeds that is independent of direction.

4. Collisions with the container walls are elastic, conserving the molecules' energy and momentum. This is where we'll tie our gas model to the laws of Newtonian mechanics.

8.1

Characteristics of a Gas

Consider N molecules of gas confined inside a rectangular container extending a length ℓ in the x direction (Fig. 20-2). Each time a gas molecule collides with a container wall, it exerts a force on the wall. There are so many molecules (assumption 1) that individual collisions aren't evident; instead the wall experiences an essentially constant average force. The gas pressure P is a measure of this force pushing on a unit area. We're going to find an expression for this pressure and show that it can be put in the same form as the ideal gas law.

To find the pressure, consider one molecule colliding with the right-hand wall in Fig. 20-2. Since the collision is elastic (assumption 4), the y component of the molecule's velocity remains unchanged, while the x component reverses sign (Fig. 20-3). Thus the molecule undergoes a momentum change of magnitude $2mv_{xi}$, where i labels this particular molecule. After colliding with the right-hand wall, nothing will change the molecule's x velocity (assumption 2) until it hits the left-hand wall and its x velocity again reverses. So it will be back at the right-hand wall in the time $\Delta t_i = 2\ell/v_{xi}$ that it takes to go back and forth along the container.

Now each time our molecule collides with the right-hand wall, it delivers momentum $2mv_{xi}$ to the wall. Newton's second law says that force is the rate of change of momentum; since we've just found the time interval between collisions, we can calculate the average force $\overline{F}_i$ due to the one molecule we're considering:

$$\overline{F}_i = \frac{\Delta p}{\Delta t} = \frac{2mv_{xi}}{(2\ell/v_{xi})} = \frac{mv_{xi}^2}{\ell}.$$

To get the total force on the wall, we sum over all N molecules with their different x velocities; dividing by the wall area A then gives the force per unit area, or pressure:

$$P = \frac{\overline{F}}{A} = \frac{\sum \overline{F}_i}{A} = \frac{\sum mv_{xi}^2/\ell}{A} = \frac{m \sum v_{xi}^2}{A\ell}.$$

The last step follows because both the box length ℓ and molecular mass m are the same for all molecules, so they factor out of the sum. We can simplify our expression for pressure by noting that the denominator $A\ell$ is just the volume, V, of the rectangular container. Let's also multiply by 1 in the form N/N, with N the number of molecules. Then we have

$$P = \frac{m \sum v_{xi}^2}{A\ell} = \frac{mN}{V} \frac{\sum v_{xi}^2}{N}.$$

In the final expression here, the term $\sum v_{xi}^2/N$ is just the average of the squares of all the x velocity components of all the molecules; we designate this quantity $\overline{v_x^2}$. So the pressure becomes

$$P = \frac{mN}{V} \overline{v_x^2}.$$

We still haven't used our assumption 3, that the molecules move in random directions with speed distribution independent of direction. If we grab a molecule at random, that means we're just as likely to find it moving in the x direction, the y direction, the z direction, or any direction in between—and its speed, on average, won't depend on its direction of motion. So the average quantities $\overline{v_x^2}$, $\overline{v_y^2}$, and $\overline{v_z^2}$ must be equal; otherwise one of the directions would be favored with molecules moving faster. Since the three directions x, y, and z are perpendicular, the average of the molecular speeds squared is given by

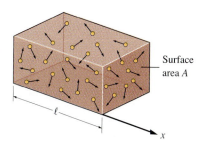

FIGURE 20-2 Gas molecules confined to a rectangular box.

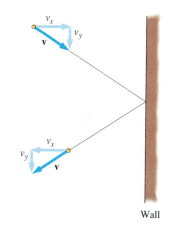

FIGURE 20-3 A molecule undergoes an elastic collision with the container wall, reversing its x component of velocity and transferring momentum $2mv_x$ to the wall.

$\overline{v^2} = \overline{v_x^2} + \overline{v_y^2} + \overline{v_z^2}$. Since we've just argued that all three terms on the right must be equal, we can then write $\overline{v^2} = 3\overline{v_x^2}$, or $\overline{v_x^2} = \frac{1}{3}\overline{v^2}$. Then our expression for pressure becomes

$$P = \frac{mN}{3V}\overline{v^2}.$$

Multiplying through by V, and by 1 in the form 2/2, we have

$$PV = \frac{2}{3}N(\frac{1}{2}m\overline{v^2}). \tag{20-3}$$

This looks a lot like the ideal gas law (Equation 20-1)! On the left is product PV, showing that pressure and volume are indeed inversely proportional if other quantities are held fixed. On the right is N, showing that pressure is indeed proportional to the amount of gas. But instead of kT we have $\frac{2}{3}(\frac{1}{2}m\overline{v^2})$. Take a good look at the quantity in parentheses: you'll see that it's just the average kinetic energy of a gas molecule.

Think about what we've done here. We applied the fundamental laws of mechanics to an ideal gas and came up with an equation (20-3) that looks like the experimentally verified ideal gas law, except that it's expressed in terms of a microscopic quantity—molecular kinetic energy—rather than the macroscopic quantity temperature. Since Equation 20-3 describes the behavior of an ideal gas, it *must be* the ideal gas law. Comparing our equation with the ideal gas law in the form 20-1, we see that for the equations to be equivalent, we must have

$$\frac{1}{2}m\overline{v^2} = \frac{3}{2}kT. \tag{20-4}$$

Our derivation leading to Equation 20-3 shows why, in terms of Newtonian mechanics, a gas obeying our four assumptions should obey the ideal gas law. In Equation 20-4 we get an added bonus—a microscopic understanding of the meaning of temperature:

> **Temperature measures the average kinetic energy associated with random translational motion of the molecules.**

EXAMPLE 20-2	*Molecular Energy*

What is the average kinetic energy of a molecule in air at room temperature? What would be the speed of a nitrogen molecule with this energy?

Solution

The average kinetic energy is given by Equation 20-4, where room temperature is about 20°C (293 K):

$$\frac{1}{2}m\overline{v^2} = \frac{3}{2}kT = \frac{3}{2}(1.38\times10^{-23}\text{ J/K})(293\text{ K})$$

$$= 6.07\times10^{-21}\text{ J}.$$

A nitrogen molecule consists of two nitrogen atoms (atomic mass 14 u; see Appendix D), so its mass is

$$m = 2(14\text{ u})(1.66\times10^{-27}\text{ kg/u}) = 4.65\times10^{-26}\text{ kg}.$$

The kinetic energy is $K = \frac{1}{2}m\overline{v^2}$, so

$$v = \sqrt{\frac{2K}{m}} = \sqrt{\frac{2(6.07\times10^{-21}\text{ J})}{4.65\times10^{-26}\text{ kg}}} = 511\text{ m/s}.$$

Not surprisingly, this is of the same order of magnitude as the sound speed (≈340 m/s) in air at room temperature. At the microscopic level, the speed of the individual molecules sets an approximate upper limit on the maximum rate at which information can be transmitted by disturbances—that is, sound waves—propagating through the gas.

EXERCISE Find the speed of a hydrogen molecule (H_2) with average kinetic energy at 300 K.

Answer: 1.9 km/s

Some problems similar to Example 20-2: 14–16

We'll call the speed calculated in Example 20-2 the **thermal speed**; in terms of temperature, Equation 20-4 shows that it's given by

$$v_{th} = \sqrt{\frac{3kT}{m}}. \tag{20-5}$$

v_{th} is also called the **root mean square** (rms) speed, because it comes from taking the square root of a quantity—the temperature T or average molecular kinetic energy K—that contains the average of the speeds squared.

The Distribution of Molecular Speeds

The quantity $\frac{3}{2}KT$ in Equation 20-4 gives the average kinetic energy of all the molecules in a gas, but it doesn't tell us about any one molecule. Similarly, the thermal speed of Equation 20-5 is a typical molecular speed, but again it doesn't tell us much about what to expect for the speed of any individual molecule.

Sometimes we want to know more than just these average quantities. For example, is the range of molecular speeds limited to a narrow band about the thermal speed? Or are there many molecules moving much faster? Such fast molecules would be important in determining, for example, the chemical reaction rates in a gas mixture, or the tendency of an atmosphere to escape the gravitational field of its planet.

In the 1860s, the Scottish physicist James Clerk Maxwell considered the sharing of energy that must result from collisions among the molecules of a gas. Although we've neglected such collisions, their presence changes none of our earlier conclusions as long as the collisions are elastic; in fact, collisions are responsible for bringing a gas into thermodynamic equilibrium. Maxwell showed that molecular collisions result in a speed distribution where the number of molecules in a small speed range Δv about some speed v is given by

8.2, 8.3
Maxwell-Boltzmann
Distribution

$$N(v)\,\Delta v = 4\pi N\left(\frac{m}{2\pi kT}\right)^{3/2} v^2 e^{-mv^2/2kT}\,\Delta v, \tag{20-6}$$

where N is the total number of molecules in the gas, m the molecular mass, k Boltzmann's constant, and T the temperature. The quantity $N(v)$ is the number of molecules per unit speed range; multiplying by a small speed range Δv gives $N(v)\Delta v$, the actual number of molecules in that range. Equation 20-6 is known as the **Maxwell-Boltzmann distribution**. Figure 20-4 shows plots of this distribution for the same gas sample at two different temperatures. Each curve exhibits a single peak; this is the most probable value for a molecule's speed. Because the curve is not symmetric about the peak, the most probable speed lies below the thermal speed (see Problem 72). Figure 20-4 shows what Equation 20-4 already told us: that an increase in temperature corresponds to an increase in mean thermal speed. But it also shows something averages alone could not reveal: that an increase in temperature results in a broader speed distribution, with relatively fewer molecules near the most probable speed. ActivPhysics Activity 8.2 lets you explore the Maxwell-Boltzmann distribution for a simulated gas; you can pick a speed range on a graph of the distribution and you'll see highlighted just which molecules in the gas have speeds in that range.

FIGURE 20-4 Maxwell-Boltzmann distribution of molecular speeds for 10^{20} nitrogen molecules (N_2) at temperatures of 80 K and 300 K. Also marked is the thermal speed $v_{th} = \sqrt{3kT/m}$; note that it isn't quite the same as the most probable speed, which is the speed value where the curve has its peak. Areas under both curves correspond to the total number of molecules and are therefore the same.

Our world would be very different if molecules in a gas all shared a single speed, or even if the distribution of molecular speeds were more symmetric than the Maxwell-Boltzmann distribution. Because the "tail" of the distribution extends to high speeds, there are always a significant number of high-energy molecules even in a relatively cool gas. It's easier for these high-energy molecules to break the bonds holding them in the liquid, so they're the ones that go first when the liquid evaporates. Without the high-energy tail of the Maxwell-Boltzmann distribution, Earth's atmosphere would be much drier and rain far less frequent. Loss of the highest-energy molecules during evaporation also leaves the average energy—and therefore the temperature—of the remaining molecules lower. That explains the process of evaporative cooling—a process our own bodies use to help regulate temperature.

The high-energy tail of the Maxwell-Boltzmann distribution also determines chemical reaction rates, and explains even such mundane phenomena as the spoiling of unrefrigerated food. Higher-energy molecules are more likely to collide vigorously enough to combine or break apart to form new chemical species. The exponential term in Equation 20-6 shows that increasing the temperature even slightly disproportionately increases the number of high-energy molecules (see Problem 22). For that reason, chemical reaction rates increase dramatically with increasing temperature. Biochemical reactions are no exception, and that's why even the roughly 20°C difference between refrigerator temperature and room temperature makes such a big difference in how long you can keep food before it spoils.

Real Gases

Though the ideal gas law is a good approximation to the behavior of real gases, the assumptions leading to its derivation are not entirely realistic. Real gases therefore exhibit deviations from ideal behavior.

Our derivation of the ideal gas law assumed gas molecules are noninteracting point particles. But real molecules take up space, and they do collide. Figure 20-5 shows that each molecule prevents others from approaching closer than one molecular radius, thereby reducing the total volume available to the molecules. When molecules are close, furthermore, electrical effects result in a weak attractive force called the **van der Waals force**. In Chapter 23 we'll see how the van der Waals force arises from fundamental principles of electricity (see Fig. 23-30). As molecules move apart they do work to overcome the van der Waals force, and as a result the molecular kinetic energy drops. Correcting for both the nonzero molecular size and the effect of the van der Waals force gives the **van der Waals equation**, which we state without further derivation:

$$\left(P + \frac{n^2a}{V^2}\right)(V - nb) = nRT, \tag{20-7}$$

where a and b are constants that depend on the particular gas. For low particle densities n/V, both correction terms in the van der Waals equation become negligible, showing that a rarefied gas closely follows the ideal gas law.

FIGURE 20-5 Two spherical gas molecules cannot get closer than a center-to-center separation of twice their radius. This effect reduces the total volume available to the molecules.

| **EXAMPLE 20-3** | *Van der Waals Effects* |

The constants a and b in the van der Waals equation for nitrogen have the values $a = 0.14$ Pa·m^6/mol^2, $b = 3.91 \times 10^{-5}$ m^3/mol. If 1.000 mol of nitrogen is confined to a volume of 2.000 L, and is at pressure of 10.00 atm, by how much does its temperature as predicted by the van der Waals equation differ from the ideal gas prediction?

Solution

Converting to SI units, we have $P = 1.013 \times 10^6$ Pa and $V = 2.000 \times 10^{-3}$ m^3. Then the ideal gas law predicts a temperature

$$T_{\text{ideal}} = \frac{PV}{nR} = \frac{(1.013 \times 10^6 \text{ Pa})(2.000 \times 10^{-3} \text{ m}^3)}{(1.000 \text{ mol})(8.314 \text{ J/K·mol})} = 244 \text{ K}.$$

The van der Waals equation predicts a temperature

$$T_{\text{van}} = \frac{(P + n^2 a/V^2)(V - nb)}{nR} = 247 \text{ K},$$

using the given values of a, b, n, P, and V. Under these conditions, nitrogen deviates from ideal gas behavior by only about 1%.

EXERCISE If the gas volume in Example 20-3 is halved while the pressure is held constant, by what percentage will the ideal and van der Waals temperature calculations differ?

Answer: 9.4%

Some problems similar to Example 20-3: 17–19

20-2 PHASE CHANGES

Step out of a steamy shower and you'll find the bathroom mirror all fogged up. Why? Because a gas of H_2O molecules has condensed on the cool mirror to make a film of liquid water. Climb a mountain on a winter day and you may be treated to the lovely spectacle of every rock, every branch, even every pine needle covered with a delicate coating of frost. Why? Because gaseous water from the air has solidified directly onto these surfaces. Spray a carbon-dioxide fire extinguisher and you'll see flakes of dry ice—solid CO_2 that formed directly from the rapidly cooling CO_2 gas expelled from the extinguisher.

What's happening here is a **phase change** that turns a gas into a liquid or even a solid. Intermolecular forces, negligible in the ideal gas approximation and weak in the van der Waals model, become dominant and bind the molecules into close proximity, sliding past each other in a liquid or locked into the rigid structure of a solid. You're familiar with other phase changes, too. You've observed ice melting and water freezing. You may have seen liquid nitrogen boiling at a mere 77 K ($-196°C$), or watched a welding torch melt its way through steel.

In this section we consider first such individual phase changes, then put phase changes in the broader context of the behavior of matter in response to general changes in temperature and pressure.

Heat and Phase Changes

Drop some ice cubes into a drink, stir, and wait a few minutes. What's the temperature of the drink? The answer is remarkably simple: it's 0°C, and it stays there as long as there's any ice left. The melting of a pure solid such as ice takes place at a fixed temperature (although, as we'll soon see, that temperature may depend on pressure). During the melting process, energy goes into breaking the molecular bonds that hold the material in its solid form. This increases the potential energy associated with separation of the molecules, but not their kinetic energy. We've just seen in Section 20-1 that temperature is related to molecular *kinetic* energy. Since molecular kinetic energy doesn't change during melting, neither does temperature.

FIGURE 20-6 Temperature versus time for what's initially a block of ice at −20°C, supplied with energy at a constant rate. The temperature doesn't change as the ice melts, nor when it boils; during these times the energy being absorbed goes into breaking molecular bonds. We've indicated a gap in the boiling time; otherwise this part of the graph would be inordinately long. Can you see from Table 20-1 why that would be? Can you tell from the graph whether ice or water has the greater specific heat?

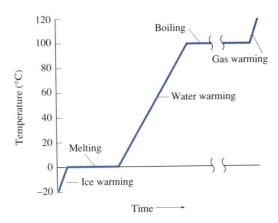

Figure 20-6 shows what happens if we take a block of ice from the freezer at, say, −20°C and supply energy at a constant rate, perhaps with a flame or by putting the ice in a microwave oven. At first the ice warms up, but soon it reaches its 0°C melting point. It continues to absorb energy, but with no temperature increase until it's all melted. Then its temperature once again increases. If we continue heating, the water eventually reaches its 100°C boiling point and then the temperature again remains constant as liquid water turns to gas. Finally, with continued heating, the gas temperature rises.

The amount of energy required to change the phase of a unit mass of material is called a **heat of transformation**; for the solid-to-liquid change it's the **heat of fusion**, L_f, and for the liquid-to-gas change it's the **heat of vaporization**, L_v. Less familiar is the **heat of sublimation** characterizing a change from solid directly to gas. Since the heat of transformation is the energy required per unit mass, the energy required to change the phase of a mass m is

$$Q = Lm. \qquad (20\text{-}8)$$

To reverse the phase change—for example, to freeze water—requires removing the energy given by Equation 20-8. Table 20-1 lists heats of transformation for some common materials at atmospheric pressure.

Got It!

You bring a pot of water to boil, then forget about it. Ten minutes later you come back to the kitchen to find the water still boiling. What's its temperature?

TABLE 20-1 *Heats of Transformation (At Atmospheric Pressure)*

SUBSTANCE	MELTING POINT, K	L_f, kJ/kg	BOILING POINT, K	L_v, kJ/kg
Alcohol, ethyl	159	109	351	879
Copper	1357	205	2840	4726
Lead	601	24.7	2013	858
Mercury	234	11.3	630	296
Oxygen	54.8	13.8	90.2	213
Sulfur	388	38.5	718	287
Water	273	334	373	2257
Uranium	1406	82.8	4091	1875

Heat transfers associated with phase changes are typically quite large. The heat of fusion of water, for example, is 334 kJ/kg or 80 cal/g—meaning that it takes as much energy to melt one gram of ice as it does to raise the resulting water from 0°C to 80°C.

| **EXAMPLE 20-4** | *Meltdown!* |

In a serious accident, a nuclear power plant's reactor vessel cracks, and all the cooling water drains out (Fig. 20-7). Although nuclear fission stops, radioactive decay continues to heat the reactor's 2.5×10^5-kg uranium core at the rate of 120 MW. Once the core reaches its melting point, how much energy will it take to melt the core? How long will the melting take?

Solution

Using the heat of fusion from Table 20-1 in Equation 20-8 gives

$$Q = mL_f = (2.5 \times 10^5 \text{ kg})(82.8 \text{ kJ/kg}) = 2.07 \times 10^{10} \text{ J}.$$

At a heating rate of 120 MW ($= 1.2 \times 10^8$ J/s), the melting will take

$$\frac{2.07 \times 10^{10} \text{ J}}{1.2 \times 10^8 \text{ J/s}} = 172 \text{ s},$$

or less than 3 minutes! Failsafe emergency cooling systems are essential in preventing nuclear meltdowns.

EXERCISE (a) Find the energy needed to melt a 500-g block of lead at its melting point. (b) If the energy is supplied with a 1.1-kW torch, how long will the melting take?

Answers: (a) 12.4 kJ; (b) 11 s

Some problems similar to Example 20-4: 30, 32, 34–37

FIGURE 20-7 Workers practice picking up radioactive debris in a full-scale model of the damaged Three Mile Island nuclear reactor. The TMI reactor experienced a partial meltdown, although its pressure vessel did not crack.

The heats of transformation measure only the energy associated with phase changes, during which temperature doesn't change. To calculate the heat needed to change first the temperature and then the phase, we need to consider both the specific heat and the heat of transformation:

| **EXAMPLE 20-5** | *Meltdown in the Kitchen?* |

You put 650 g of water at 20°C in a pan on a 1.5-kW stove burner and forget about it. How long will it take to boil the pan dry, assuming all the burner's energy goes into the water?

Solution

First we calculate the energy needed to raise the water to its boiling point. Using the appropriate specific heat from Table 19-1 in Equation 19-4 gives

$$Q_1 = mc\,\Delta T = (0.65 \text{ kg})(4.184 \text{ kJ/kg·K})(80 \text{ K}) = 218 \text{ kJ}.$$

Equation 20-8, with data from Table 20-1, then gives the energy needed to transform all the water to the gaseous state:

$$Q_2 = mL_v = (0.65 \text{ kg})(2257 \text{ kJ/kg}) = 1467 \text{ kJ}.$$

So total energy needed is 218 kJ + 1467 kJ = 1685 kJ; at a heating rate of 1.5 kW, this takes 1685 kJ/1.5 kJ/s = 1123 s, or about 19 minutes.

Tip

Break a Problem into Separate Parts To work this example required solving two separate problems, one about temperature change and one about boiling. You'll often need to break a complex problem into several simpler ones, as this example suggests.

EXERCISE You put 100 g of ice at 0°C in a 625-W microwave oven. How long will it take until you have water at 90°C?

Answer: 114 s

Some problems similar to Example 20-5: 37–42

EXAMPLE 20-6	*Enough Ice?*

200 g of ice at $-10°C$ is added to 1.0 kg of water at 15°C in an insulated container. Is there enough ice to cool the water to 0°C? If so, how much ice and water are present once equilibrium is reached?

Solution

First we determine whether there is enough ice. To bring the ice to its melting point and melt all of it requires

$$Q_1 = mc\,\Delta T + mL_f$$

$$= (0.20 \text{ kg})(2.05 \text{ kJ/kg·K})(10 \text{ K}) + (0.20 \text{ kg})(334 \text{ kJ/kg})$$

$$= 4.1 \text{ kJ} + 66.8 \text{ kJ} = 70.9 \text{ kJ},$$

where we used data from Tables 19-1 and 20-1, and where the temperature change in °C is equal to its value in kelvins. (Here we've algebraically combined the two subproblems mentioned in the tip in Example 20-5.)

Cooling the water to 0°C extracts an amount of heat given by

$$Q_2 = mc\,\Delta T = (1.0 \text{ kg})(4.184 \text{ kJ/kg·K})(15 \text{ K}) = 62.8 \text{ kJ}.$$

This is far more than the 4.1 kJ needed to bring the ice to 0°C, but not quite the 70.9 kJ needed to leave it all melted. So there's enough ice to cool the water to 0°C, with some left over. How much? Our calculation of Q_1 shows that 4.1 kJ go into raising the ice temperature. Of the 62.8 kJ extracted from the water, the remaining 58.7 kJ go to melting ice. From Equation 20-6, the amount of ice melted is then

$$m = \frac{Q}{L_f} = \frac{58.7 \text{ kJ}}{334 \text{ kJ/kg}} = 0.176 \text{ kg} = 176 \text{ g}.$$

Thus we're left with 24 g of ice in 1176 g of water, all at 0°C.

EXERCISE Determine the final mix and temperature in Example 20-6 if the initial amount of ice is 100 g.

Answer: all water at 5.9°C

Some problems similar to Example 20-6: 43–47, 49

Phase Diagrams

Mountaineers in the Himalayas can't get their coffee as hot as you can at a lower altitude. Why not? Because the boiling point of water drops with the decreasing pressure at higher altitudes. This makes good physical sense, since it's easier for molecules to escape the liquid when there's less pressure from the surrounding air. Remember that the temperature doesn't change while the water is boiling, so it won't do the mountaineers any good to turn up the flame or heat their coffee longer—eventually it will just boil away!

In general, the temperatures at which phase changes occur—the melting and boiling points—depend on pressure. We can explore these effects with a **phase diagram** that shows where the solid, liquid, and gas phases lie on a plot of pressure versus temperature. Each substance has a different phase diagram, although most are qualitatively similar. Figure 20-8 shows a phase diagram for a typical substance such as carbon dioxide. (Water, with whose phase changes you're most familiar, has a slightly unusual phase diagram that we discuss in the next section. However, most of our general discussion here applies to water as well.)

The phase diagram of Fig. 20-8 divides T-P space into three regions corresponding to the solid, liquid, and gas phases. The lines separating these regions mark the phase transitions. Our everyday experience suggests that heating brings a solid to its melting point, turns it to liquid, raises the liquid temperature to the boiling point, and then turns it to a gas—just as we showed for water in Fig. 20-6. But Fig. 20-8 shows that this sequence doesn't always occur. At low enough pressure (line AB in Fig. 20-8), heating brings the substance right across the solid-gas transition. For carbon dioxide, normal atmospheric pressure lies in this lower region of the curve; that's why dry ice (solid CO_2) turns directly into

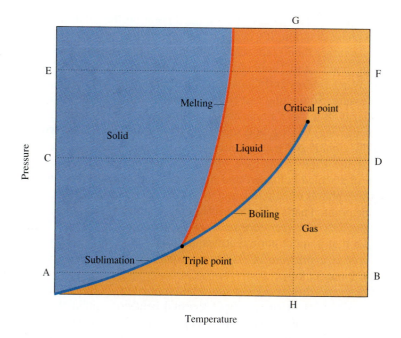

FIGURE 20-8 A phase diagram shows where solid, liquid, and gas phases lie in a plot of pressure versus temperature. Melting, boiling, and sublimation curves separate the different phases; on these curves, two phases can coexist in equilibrium. All three phases can coexist at the triple point.

FIGURE 20-9 Carbon dioxide subliming from solid to gas. The gray mist is actually a cloud of water droplets that condensed on contact with the cool CO_2 gas.

gas, a process called **sublimation** (Fig. 20-9). At higher pressures (line CD in Fig. 20-8), heating a substance gives the normal solid-liquid-gas sequence. (At room temperature, for example, a carbon-dioxide fire extinguisher is at a high enough pressure that the CO_2 is liquid.) But at still higher pressures (line EF), above the so-called **critical pressure** marked by the **critical point** in the phase diagram, heating turns the solid into a thick fluid whose properties gradually change from liquidlike to gaslike with continued heating; at these supercritical pressures, there's no sharp phase transition between liquid and gas.

We generally think of changing solid or liquid, or liquid to gas, by applying heat. But our phase diagram (Fig. 20-8) shows that we can also accomplish phase changes by varying the pressure. Lowering the pressure on a liquid at fixed temperature, for example (line GH in the phase diagram), will cause the liquid to boil and become a gas. You may have seen a demonstration in which water at room temperature is placed in an enclosed chamber and the air pumped out; when the pressure gets low enough, the water boils vigorously (Fig. 20-10).

Don't let Figure 20-8 fool you into thinking that phase transitions occur instantaneously as a substance jumps from, say, the solid to the liquid region of its phase diagram. If you started a substance at point C and supplied heat at a constant rate, keeping the pressure constant, the substance would move gradually across line CD in its phase diagram. Its temperature would increase at a rate determined by the power of the heat source and the specific heat of the solid; then it would pause on the solid-liquid transition for the time it took the entire sample to melt—a time determined by the heat of fusion. It would then move across the liquid region of the diagram, and then pause again on the liquid-gas transition until it had all turned to gas. This process is in fact just what we described for water in Fig. 20-6.

The dividing curves on Fig. 20-8 are regions where two phases can coexist in equilibrium. Ice floating in water at atmospheric pressure is one example; as long

FIGURE 20-10 Water boiling at room temperature in an evacuated flask.

as any ice remains, the system sits at a fixed point on the solid-liquid dividing line in the phase diagram. It's because melting, boiling, and sublimation occur along curves rather than at specific points in the phase diagram that terms such as "melting point" and "boiling point" are meaningless unless a pressure is specified. Water freezes at 0°C and boils at 100°C—but only at normal atmospheric pressure. So melting and boiling points do not make for good temperature standards. But there's one unique point in the phase diagram where the curves for melting, boiling, and sublimation all meet. That's the **triple point**, where solid, liquid, and gas can all coexist in equilibrium. Temperature and pressure at the triple point have unique, unambiguous values. If you put a substance in a sealed container and manipulate the temperature and pressure until all three phases remain indefinitely in the container, then you know you're at the triple point. That's why the triple point of water—at 273.16 K—is used to define the Kelvin temperature scale, as we discussed in Chapter 19. But you won't reach that point at normal atmospheric pressure; for the water the triple point occurs at a pressure of 0.006 atmospheres (that's the pressure at an altitude of about 35 km).

Phase diagrams display a lot of information in compact form. But even they can't do justice to the rich variety of thermal behavior exhibited by different substances. For example, a phase diagram doesn't show directly how volume changes with temperature and pressure. Furthermore, many substances have more complicated phase diagrams with different subphases, associated with changes in crystalline structure or molecular bonding. Full description of the thermal behavior of a given substance requires a three-dimensional diagram with axes representing temperature, pressure, and volume. We leave that for more advanced works on thermodynamics.

20-3 THERMAL EXPANSION

We've explored changes of temperature and phase that occur when matter is heated. But heating can also result in pressure or volume changes. For a gas held at constant pressure, for example, the ideal gas law shows that volume increases in direct proportion to the temperature rise.

The volume and pressure relations in the liquid and solid phases are not quite so simple. Liquids and solids are far less compressible than gases, so thermal expansion is less pronounced. On the microscopic level, the molecules in a liquid or solid are closely spaced; to move them requires that we do work against large (electrical) forces.

We can characterize the change in the volume of a substance with temperature in terms of its **coefficient of volume expansion**, β, defined as the fractional change in volume when the substance undergoes a small temperature change ΔT:

$$\beta = \frac{\Delta V/V}{\Delta T}. \tag{20-9}$$

This equation assumes that β is independent of temperature; if it varies significantly then we would need to define β in terms of the derivative dV/dT (see Problem 76). Our definition of β also assumes constant pressure; we could entirely inhibit thermal expansion with appropriate pressure increases.

Often we want to know how one linear dimension of a solid changes with temperature. This is especially true with long, rodlike structures where the absolute change is greatest along the long dimension (Fig. 20-11). We then

(a)

(b)

FIGURE 20-11 A power line sags as its length increases on a hot summer day.

TABLE 20-2 *Expansion Coefficients**

SOLIDS	$\alpha(K^{-1})$	LIQUIDS AND GASES	$\beta(K^{-1})$
Aluminum	24×10^{-6}	Air	3.7×10^{-3}
Brass	19×10^{-6}	Alcohol, ethyl	75×10^{-5}
Copper	17×10^{-6}	Gasoline	95×10^{-5}
Glass (Pyrex)	3.2×10^{-6}	Mercury	18×10^{-5}
Ice	51×10^{-6}	Water, 1°C	-4.8×10^{-5}
Invar†	0.9×10^{-6}	Water, 20°C	20×10^{-5}
Steel	12×10^{-6}	Water, 50°C	50×10^{-5}

*At approximately room temperature unless noted.

†Invar, consisting of 64% iron and 36% nickel, is an alloy designed to minimize thermal expansion.

speak of the **coefficient of linear expansion**, α, defined by

$$\alpha = \frac{\Delta L/L}{\Delta T}. \tag{20-10}$$

The volume expansion coefficient and linear expansion coefficient α are related in a simple way: $\beta = 3\alpha$, as you can show in Problem 79. This relation means that either of these coefficients fully characterizes the thermal expansion of a material. However, the linear expansion coefficient α is really only meaningful with solids, because liquids and gases deform readily and therefore do not generally expand proportionately in all directions. Table 20-2 lists expansion coefficients for some common substances.

EXAMPLE 20-7 | *Thermal Expansion*

A steel girder is 15 m long at $-20°C$. It is used in the construction of a building where temperature extremes of $-20°C$ to $40°C$ are expected. By how much does the girder length change between these extremes?

Solution

Table 20-2 gives the coefficient of linear expansion for steel: $\alpha = 12\times10^{-6}\ K^{-1}$. Equation 20-10 then gives

$\Delta L = \alpha L\,\Delta T = (12\times10^{-6}\ K^{-1})(15\ m)(60\ K) = 1.1\ cm$.

EXERCISE A telescope assembly includes an aluminum rod 1.3 m long at 10°C. What is the maximum allowable temperature if the rod length is not to increase by more than 0.50 mm?

Answer: 26°C

Some problems similar to Example 20-7: 51–54

What happens when a hollow object expands? In Fig. 20-12, you might expect that the hole would shrink as material expands into it. Actually, as Fig. 20-13 shows, *every* linear dimension expands in the same proportion, causing the interior space to expand, too.

FIGURE 20-12 How will the size of the hole change when the object expands?

FIGURE 20-13 A hollow solid made of rectangular slabs. As the slabs expand, so does the interior space.

EXAMPLE 20-8	Spilled Gasoline

A car's gasoline tank is made of steel and has internal dimensions 60 cm × 60 cm × 20 cm at 10°C. It is filled with gasoline at 10°C. If the temperature now increases to 30°C, by how much does the volume of the tank increase? How much gasoline spills out of the tank?

Solution

The initial volume of the tank is

$$V = (0.60 \text{ m})(0.60 \text{ m})(0.20 \text{ m}) = 0.072 \text{ m}^3 .$$

Equation 20-9 then gives the volume increases:

$$\Delta V = \beta V \Delta T ,$$

so

$$\Delta V_{tank} = (3)(12 \times 10^{-6} \text{ K}^{-1})(0.072 \text{ m}^3)(20 \text{ K})$$

$$= 5.18 \times 10^{-5} \text{ m}^3 ,$$

and

$$\Delta V_{gas} = (95 \times 10^{-5} \text{ K}^{-1})(0.072 \text{ m}^3)(20 \text{ K}) = 1.37 \times 10^{-3} \text{ m}^3 .$$

Since Table 20-2 gives the coefficient of linear expansion, α, for solids, we used $\beta = 3\alpha$ in calculating the volume change of the tank.

The expansion of the steel tank is negligible compared with that of the gasoline, so we lose $1.32 \times 10^{-3} \text{ m}^3$, or 1.32 L of gasoline. Don't fill your gas tank to the very top!

EXERCISE A farmer milks a cow into a 20-L steel milk pail; the milk comes from the cow at approximately 37°C. If the pail is initially full and also at 37°C, how much empty space will there be when it's been cooled to 3°C? The average thermal expansion coefficient for milk in this temperature range is $2.0 \times 10^{-4} \text{ K}^{-1}$.

Answer: 112 mL

Some problems similar to Example 20-8: 60, 62, 76

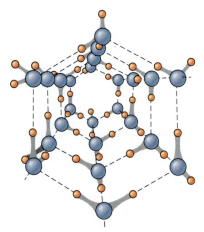

FIGURE 20-15 Water molecules in an ice crystal form an open structure, giving solid water a lower density than the liquid state.

Thermal Expansion of Water

The entry for water at 1°C in Table 20-2 is remarkable, for the negative expansion coefficient shows that water at this temperature actually *contracts* on heating (Fig. 20-14). This unusual behavior occurs because ice has a relatively open crystal structure (Fig. 20-15), and therefore is less dense than liquid water. That's why ice floats. Immediately above the melting point, the intermolecular forces (so-called hydrogen bonds) that hold H_2O molecules together in ice still exert an influence, giving cold liquid water a lower density than at slightly higher temperatures. At 4°C water reaches its maximum density, and above this temperature the effect of molecular kinetic energy in keeping molecules apart wins out over intermolecular forces. From there on water exhibits the more normal behavior of expansion with increasing temperature.

This unusual property of water near its melting point is reflected in its phase diagram, shown in Fig. 20-16. Notice that the solid-liquid boundary extends leftward from the triple point, in contrast to the more typical behavior we showed in Fig. 20-8. That means that ice at a fixed temperature will melt if the pressure is *increased*—an unusual property known as pressure melting (see Question 26 for more on this).

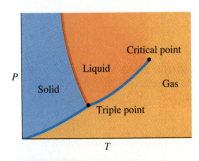

FIGURE 20-16 Phase diagram for water. Compare the solid-liquid boundary here with that of Fig. 20-8.

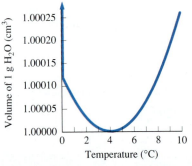

FIGURE 20-14 Volume of one gram of water near its melting point. Below 4°C, water actually expands when cooled. Graph rises vertically at 0°C, showing that solid ice would be way off scale at about 1.1 cm³. This is because ice's density is only about 90% of that of water.

The anomalous behavior of water has important consequences for life. If ice did not float, then ponds, lakes, and even oceans would freeze solid from the bottom up, making aquatic life impossible. What actually happens, instead, is that a thin layer of ice forms on the surface, insulating the water below and keeping it liquid; as a result, ice cover in temperate climates rarely exceeds a meter or so. Because water has the greatest density at 4°C, water at this temperature sinks to the bottom. At lake depths greater than a few meters, sunlight is inadequate to raise the temperature, which therefore remains year-round at 4°C.

Thermal Stresses

By enclosing a liquid or gas in a rigid container, or by tightly clamping the ends of a solid in place, we can inhibit thermal expansion. When heated, the material must then experience a pressure increase. If a container is unable to withstand this increase, it will burst (Fig. 20-17). If a solid is restrained along only one dimension, it will deform and perhaps crack (Fig. 20-18). Similarly, when a solid is clamped at both ends and cooled, tension forces develop that may cause it to break. Finally, if a solid is heated or cooled unevenly, part of the material expands or contracts at a different rate from the surrounding material. Again, the resulting forces may damage the material.

FIGURE 20-17 Industrial disaster! This boiler burst from overpressure caused by thermal expansion.

FIGURE 20-18 Thermal expansion distorted these railroad tracks, causing a derailment.

CHAPTER SYNOPSIS

Summary

1. An **ideal gas** is described by the **ideal gas law**, a relation among pressure, temperature, volume, and amount of gas.

$$PV = NkT.$$

Here N is the number of gas molecules and $k = 1.38 \times 10^{-23}$ J/K is **Boltzmann's constant**. The ideal gas law may also be written

$$PV = nRT,$$

where n is the number of moles and $R = 8.314$ J/K·mol is the **universal gas constant**.

2. **Kinetic theory** provides a description of the ideal gas in terms of the microscopic physics of large numbers of molecules. Kinetic theory relates temperature to the average translational kinetic energy of the gas molecules:

$$\tfrac{1}{2}m\overline{v^2} = \tfrac{3}{2}kT.$$

3. **Real gases** deviate from ideal behavior at high densities and low temperatures, where molecular size and intermolecular forces become significant. Real gases are described approximately by the **van der Waals equation**:

$$\left(P + \frac{n^2a}{V^2}\right)(V - nb) = nRT,$$

where a and b are constants describing a particular gas.

4. Most substances can exist in several **phases**, including solid, liquid, and gas. During a **phase change**, energy is transferred to or from a substance without any temperature change. The energy per unit mass associated with phase changes from solid to liquid and liquid to gas are, respectively, the **heat of fusion** and the **heat of vaporization**. The **heat of sublimation** characterizes the solid-gas transition.

5. A **phase diagram** shows solid, liquid, and gaseous phases as regions on a plot of pressure versus temperature. Important points in the diagram are the **triple point**, defining the

unique temperature and pressure where all three phases can coexist in equilibrium, and the **critical point**, where the boundary between liquid and gas phases ceases to be distinct.

6. Most substances expand when heated at constant pressure. The change in volume is given by

$$\Delta V = \beta V \Delta T,$$

where β is the **coefficient of volume expansion**. The change in length of a solid is given by a similar expression:

$$\Delta L = \alpha L \Delta T,$$

where $\alpha = \beta/3$ is the **coefficient of linear expansion**. Water provides an important exception to the general rule that substances expand when heated: In the range from 0°C to 4°C, water contracts on heating.

7. If a substance is held rigidly, so that thermal expansion or contraction cannot occur, then **thermal stresses** develop that may cause damage.

Terms You Should Understand

(Pairs are closely related terms whose distinction is important; number in parentheses is chapter section where term first appears.)

ideal gas (20-1)
ideal gas law (20-1)
Boltzmann's constant (20-1)
universal gas constant (20-1)
Maxwell-Boltzmann distribution (20-1)
van der Waals equation (20-1)
phase, phase change (20-2)
phase diagram (20-2)

heat of transformation; heats of fusion and vaporization (20-2)
critical point (20-2)
triple point (20-2)
coefficients of volume and linear expansion (20-3)

Symbols You Should Recognize

N (20-1)	$\overline{v^2}$ (20-1)
k (20-1)	L, L_f, L_v (20-2)
N_A (20-1)	α, β (20-3)
R (20-1)	

Problems You Should Be Able to Solve

evaluating ideal gas properties (20-1)
relating temperature and molecular kinetic energy (20-1)
evaluating gas properties in the van der Waals approximation (20-1)
determining energy involved in phase changes (20-2)
calculating thermal expansion (20-3)

Limitations to Keep in Mind

The ideal gas law is an approximation valid for rarefied gases where molecular size and intermolecular forces are not important. For most gases under normal conditions the law provides an excellent approximation.

Despite our everyday experience, the distinction between liquid and gas is not always clear-cut. Similarly, the temperature regimes in which the different phases can exist depend on pressure and may sometimes run counter to common experience.

Equations 20-7 and 20-8 are strictly valid only for temperature changes small enough that the expansion coefficients β and α remain essentially constant.

QUESTIONS

1. If the volume of an ideal gas is increased, must the pressure drop proportionately? Explain.
2. According to the ideal gas law, what should the volume of a gas be at absolute zero? Why is this result absurd?
3. Why are you supposed to check the pressure in a tire when the tire is cold?
4. The average *speed* of the molecules in a gas increases with increasing temperature. What about the average *velocity?*
5. Suppose you start running while holding a jar of air. Do you change the average speed of the air molecules? The average velocity? The temperature?
6. Do all molecules in a gas have the same speed? If so, how does this come about? If not, how can the notion of temperature be meaningful?
7. The speed of sound in a gas is closely related to the thermal speed of the molecules. Why?

8. Two different gases are at the same temperature, and both are at low enough densities that they behave like ideal gases. Do their molecules have the same thermal speeds? Explain.
9. The atmosphere of a small planet such as Earth contains very little of the lighter gases such as hydrogen and helium. The massive planet Jupiter has an atmosphere rich in light gases. Explain, using the concepts of thermal speed and escape speed (see Chapter 9, Section 9-4).
10. Is the van der Waals force attractive or repulsive? Justify your answer in terms of the sign of the term n^2a/V^2 appearing in the van der Waals equation, assuming that the parameter a is positive.
11. Some people think that ice and snow must be at 0°C. Is this always true? Under what circumstances must it be true? Could you paraphrase the same arguments for another substance? Try steel, for example.

12. What is the temperature of water just under the ice layer of a frozen lake? At the bottom of the lake?

13. Deep lakes usually "turn over" twice each year. During the overturn, water from the lake bottom gets mixed with surface water, while at other times deep water and surface water do not mix. Under what conditions should such an overturn occur?

14. What's the temperature at the bottom of Lake Michigan?

15. How is it possible to have liquid water at 0°C?

16. Some ice and water have been together in a glass for a long time. Is the water hotter than the ice?

17. Does it take more heat to melt a gram of ice at 0°C than to bring the resulting water to the boiling point? Once at the boiling point, does it take more heat to boil all the water than it did to bring it from the melting point to the boiling point?

18. Why does removing the plastic wrap from a package of frozen hamburger help it to thaw faster?

19. Why do we use the triple point of water for thermometer calibration? Why not just use the melting point or boiling point?

20. When the average temperature drops below freezing in winter, regions near large lakes remain warmer for some time. Why?

21. Must all substances exhibit solid, liquid, and gas phases? What might happen before a substance reaches the gas phase? Consider sugar, for example.

22. How is it possible to have boiling water at a temperature other than 100°C?

23. Why does the water in a car radiator boil explosively when you remove the radiator cap?

24. How does a pressure cooker work?

25. Why does a double boiler prevent food from burning?

26. Figure 20-19 shows a thin, flexible wire draped over an ice cube, with weights tied on either end of the wire. If the weights are heavy enough, the wire will gradually melt its

FIGURE 20-19 Questions 26–27.

way through the ice cube, nevertheless leaving the cube in one piece. Explain this phenomenon in terms of the phase diagram for water (Fig. 20-16).

27. Could you perform the experiment in Fig. 20-19 on a dry ice cube? Explain by comparing Figs. 20-8 and 20-16.

28. Earth's inner core is solid and is surrounded by a liquid outer core made of the same material but cooler. How is this possible?

29. Suppose mercury and glass had the same coefficient of volume expansion. Could you build a mercury thermometer?

30. Why are the coefficients of volume expansion generally greater for liquids than for solids?

31. A bimetallic strip consists of thin pieces of brass and steel bonded together (Fig. 20-20). Such strips are often used in thermostats. What will happen when the strip is heated? *Hint:* Consult Table 20-2.

Brass
Steel

FIGURE 20-20 Question 31.

32. Why are power lines more likely to break in winter?

PROBLEMS

ActivPhysics can help with these problems: Activities 8.1–8.4.

Section 20-1 Gases

1. At Mars's surface, the planet's atmosphere has a pressure only 0.0070 times that of Earth, and an average temperature of 218 K. What is the volume of 1 mole of the Martian atmosphere?

2. How many molecules are in an ideal gas sample at 350 K that occupies 8.5 L when the pressure is 180 kPa?

3. What is the pressure of an ideal gas if 3.5 moles occupy 2.0 L at a temperature of −150°C?

4. An ideal gas occupies a volume V at 100°C. If the gas pressure is held constant, by what factor does the volume change (a) if the Celsius temperature is doubled and (b) if the kelvin temperature is doubled?

5. If 2.0 mol of an ideal gas are at an initial temperature of 250 K and pressure of 1.5 atm, (a) what is the gas volume? (b) The pressure is now increased to 4.0 atm, and the gas volume drops to half its initial value. What is the new temperature?

6. The solar corona is an extended atmosphere of hot (2×10^6 K) gas surrounding the cooler visible surface of the Sun. The gas pressure in the solar corona is about 0.03 Pa. What is the coronal density in particles per cubic meter? Compare with Earth's atmosphere.

7. A pressure of 1.0×10^{-10} Pa is readily achievable with laboratory vacuum apparatus. If the residual air in this

"vacuum" is at 0°C, how many air molecules are in one liter?

8. A cubical metal box with thin walls measures 10 cm on each side. It is filled with 0.50 mol of an ideal gas at 180 K, and is surrounded by air at atmospheric pressure. What is the net pressure force on each side of the box?

9. A helium balloon occupies 8.0 L at 20°C and 1.0 atm pressure. The balloon rises to an altitude where air pressure is 0.65 atm and the temperature is −10°C. What is its volume when it reaches equilibrium at the new altitude? (Neglect tension forces in the material of the balloon.)

10. A compressed air cylinder stands 100 cm tall and has an internal diameter of 20.0 cm. At room temperature, the pressure is 180 atm. (a) How many moles of air are in the cylinder? (b) What volume would this air occupy at 1.0 atm and room temperature?

11. An aerosol can of whipped cream is pressurized at 440 kPa when it's refrigerated at 3°C. The can warns against temperatures in excess of 50°C. What is the maximum safe pressure for the can?

12. A student's dormitory room measures 3.0 m × 3.5 × 2.6 m. (a) How many air molecules does it contain? (b) What is the total translational kinetic energy of these molecules? (c) How does this energy compare with the kinetic energy of the student's 1200-kg car going 90 km/h?

13. A 3000-ml flask is initially open while in a room containing air at 1.00 atm and 20°C. The flask is then closed and immersed in a bath of boiling water. When the air in the flask has reached thermodynamic equilibrium, the flask is opened and air allowed to escape. The flask is then closed and cooled back to 20°C. (a) What is the maximum pressure reached in the flask? (b) How many moles escape when air is released from the flask? (c) What is the final pressure in the flask?

14. What is the thermal speed of hydrogen (H_2) molecules at 800 K?

15. In which gas are the molecules moving faster: hydrogen (H_2) at 75 K or sulfur dioxide (SO_2) at 350 K?

16. The principal gases in Earth's atmosphere are N_2, O_2, and Ar, with smaller amounts of CO_2 and H_2O. In air at 300 K, what are the thermal speeds of these gases?

17. The van der Waals constants for helium gas (He) are $a = 0.0341$ $L^2 \cdot atm/mol^2$ and $b = 0.0237$ L/mol. What is the temperature of 3.00 mol of helium at 90.0 atm pressure if the gas volume is 0.800 L? How does this result differ from the ideal gas prediction?

18. At what pressure does the van der Waals calculation of temperature for the gas of Example 20-3 differ by 10% from the ideal gas calculation?

19. Because the correction terms (n^2a/V^2 and $−nb$) in the van der Waals equation have opposite signs, there is a point at which the van der Waals and ideal gas equations predict the same temperature. For the gas of Example 20-3, at what pressure does that occur?

20. Plot the Maxwell-Boltzmann distribution of molecular speeds for samples of monatomic helium gas (He) containing 10^{18} atoms at temperatures of 50 K and 250 K.

21. In a sample of 10^{24} hydrogen (H_2) molecules, how many molecules have speeds between 900 and 901 m/s (a) at a temperature of 100 K and (b) at 450 K?

22. Room temperature (about 293 K) is only about 6.5% higher than a typical refrigerator temperature (about 275 K). To show how important the high-energy tail of the Boltzmann distribution is in determining food spoilage rates, find the percent increase in the number of oxygen molecules in air with speeds in the range 1350 m/s to 1351 m/s as the temperature goes from 275 K to 293 K. You should find it to be much greater than the corresponding 6.5% increase in temperature.

Section 20-2 Phase Changes

23. How much energy does it take to melt a 65-g ice cube?

24. It takes 200 J to melt an 8.0-g sample of one of the substances in Table 20-1. What is the substance?

25. If it takes 840 kJ to vaporize a sample of liquid oxygen, how large is the sample?

26. Carbon dioxide sublimes (changes from solid to gas) at 195 K. The heat of sublimation is 573 kJ/kg. How much heat must be extracted from 250 g of CO_2 gas at 195 K in order to solidify it?

27. Find the energy needed to convert 28 kg of liquid oxygen at its boiling point into gas.

28. A stove burner supplies heat to a pan at the rate of 1500 W. How long will it take to boil away 1.1 kg of water, from the time the water is at its boiling point?

29. If a 1-megaton nuclear bomb were exploded deep in the Greenland ice cap, how much ice would it melt? Assume the ice is initially at about its freezing point, and consult Appendix C for the appropriate energy conversion.

30. How much ice can a 625-W microwave oven melt in 1.0 min, if the ice is initially at 0°C?

31. What is the power of a microwave oven that takes 20 min to boil dry a 300-g cup of water initially at its boiling point?

32. At winter's end, Lake Superior's 82,000-km^2 surface is frozen to a depth of 1.3 m. The density of ice is 917 kg/m^3. (a) How much energy does it take to melt the ice? (b) If the ice disappears in 3 weeks, what is the average power supplied to melt it?

33. A refrigerator extracts energy from its contents at the rate of 95 W. How long will it take to freeze 750 g of water already at 0°C?

34. The size of industrial air conditioning and refrigeration equipment is often given in tons, meaning the number of tons of water at its melting point that the unit could freeze in one day. (This unit is a holdover from the days when ice was cut from lakes in winter.) What is the rate of heat extraction, in watts, of a 15-ton refrigeration unit?

35. At its "thaw" setting a microwave oven delivers 210 W. How long will it take to thaw a frozen 1.8-kg roast, assuming the roast is essentially water and is initially at 0°C?

36. An ice layer 50 cm thick covers a lake; soot from air pollution covers the ice and absorbs 75% of the incident sunlight, whose time-average intensity is 200 W/m². How long will it take to melt the ice, assuming an initial temperature of about 0°C? The density of ice is 917 kg/m³.

37. A 100-g block of ice, initially at −20°C, is placed in a 500-W microwave oven. (a) How long must the oven be on to produce water at 50°C? (b) Make a graph showing temperature versus time during this entire interval.

38. Repeat Example 20-6 if the initial mass of ice is 50 g.

39. How much energy does it take to melt 10 kg of ice initially at −10°C? Consult Table 19-1.

40. Water is brought to its boiling point and then allowed to boil away completely. If the energy needed to raise the water to the boiling point is one-tenth of that needed to boil it away, what was the initial temperature?

41. A 250-g piece of ice at 0°C is placed in a 500-W microwave oven and the oven run for 5.0 min. What is the temperature at the end of this time?

42. During a nuclear accident, 420 m³ of emergency cooling water at 20°C are injected into a reactor vessel where the reactor core is producing heat at the rate of 200 MW. If the water is allowed to boil at normal atmospheric pressure, how long will it take to boil the reactor dry?

43. What is the minimum amount of ice in Example 20-6 that will ensure a final temperature of 0°C?

44. What would have to be the initial ice temperature in Example 20-6 in order that the final mixture ends up with more than 200 g of ice?

45. A 500-g chunk of solid mercury at its 234 K melting point is added to 500 g of liquid mercury at room temperature (293 K). Determine the equilibrium mix and temperature.

46. Repeat the preceding problem if the initial amount of liquid is 1.0 kg.

47. A bowl contains 16 kg of punch (essentially water) at a warm 25°C. What is the minimum amount of ice at 0°C that will cool the punch to 0°C?

48. Water at 300 K is sprinkled onto 200 g of molten copper at its 1356-K melting point. The water boils away, leaving solid copper still at 1356 K. How much water does this take? Assume that the only heat loss from the copper is to the liquid water.

49. A 50-g ice cube at −10°C is placed in an equal mass of water. What must be the initial water temperature if the final mixture still contains equal amounts of ice and water?

50. A 40-kg block of aluminum is initially at 50°C. A jet of steam at 100°C hits the block and condenses, and the resulting water drops off before its temperature changes. How much steam must hit the block to raise its temperature to 100°C?

Section 20-3 Thermal Expansion

51. A Pyrex glass marble is 1.00000 cm in diameter at 20°C. What will be its diameter at 85°C?

52. At 0°C, the hole in a steel washer is 9.52 mm in diameter. To what temperature must it be heated in order to fit over a 9.55-mm-diameter bolt?

53. Suppose a single piece of welded steel railroad track stretched 5000 km across the continental United States. If the track were free to expand, by how much would its length change if the entire track went from a cold winter temperature of −25°C to a hot summer day at 40°C?

54. A glass marble 1.000 cm in diameter is to be dropped through a hole in a steel plate. At room temperature the hole diameter is 0.997 cm. By how much must the steel temperature be raised so that the marble will fit through the hole?

55. The tube in a mercury thermometer is 0.10 mm in diameter. What should be the volume of the thermometer bulb if a 1.0-mm rise is to correspond to a temperature change of 1.0°C? Neglect the expansion of the glass.

56. A 2000-mL graduated cylinder is filled with liquid at 350 K. When the liquid is cooled to 300 K, the cylinder is full only to the 1925-mL mark. Use Table 20-2 to identify the liquid.

57. A steel ball bearing is encased in a Pyrex glass cube 1.0 cm on a side. At 330 K, the ball bearing fits tightly in the cube. At what temperature will it have a clearance of 1.0 μm all around?

58. Gasoline comes from its underground tank at 10°C. On a summer day, how much gas can you put in your car's 60-L tank if the tank is not to overflow when the gas reaches the ambient temperature of 25°C?

59. A rod of length L_0 is clamped rigidly at both ends. Its temperature increases in the middle by an amount ΔT, and in the ensuing expansion it cracks to form two straight pieces, as shown in Fig. 20-21. Find an expression for the distance d shown in the figure, in terms of L_0, ΔT, and the coefficient of linear expansion, α.

FIGURE 20-21 Problem 59.

60. A 250-ml Pyrex glass beaker is filled to the brim with ethyl alcohol; both beaker and alcohol are at 20°C. How much alcohol spills over the top when the temperature is increased to 30°C?

Paired Problems

(Both problems in a pair involve the same principles and techniques. If you can get the first problem, you should be able to solve the second one.)

61. What is the density, in moles per m³, of air in a tire whose absolute pressure is 300 kPa at 34°C?

62. Venus's atmospheric pressure is 90 times that of Earth, and its average temperature is 730 K. What is the volume of 1 mole of Venus's atmosphere?

63. What power is needed to melt 20 kg of ice in 6.0 min?

64. How long will it take a 140-W heat source to vaporize 250 g of ethyl alcohol already at its boiling point?

65. You put 300 g of water into a 500-W microwave oven and accidentally set the time for 20 min instead of 2.0 min. If the water is initially at 20°C, how much is left at the end of 20 min?

66. If 4.5×10^5 kg of emergency cooling water at 10°C are dumped into a malfunctioning nuclear reactor whose core is producing energy at the rate of 200 MW, and if no circulation or cooling of the water is provided, how long will it be before half the water has boiled away?

67. Describe the composition and temperature of the equilibrium mixture after 1.0 kg of ice at −40°C is added to 1.0 kg of water at 5.0°C.

68. Repeat the preceding problem if the ice is initially at −80°C and if there are initially only 200 g of liquid water.

Supplementary Problems

69. How long will it take a 500-W microwave oven to vaporize completely a 500-g block of ice initially at 0°C?

70. The thermal resistance of a refrigerator's walls is 0.12 K/W. During a power failure you put a 15-kg block of ice at 0°C in the refrigerator, bringing the interior temperature to 0°C. If room temperature is 20°C, how long will the ice last?

71. A solar-heated house (Fig. 20-22) stores energy in 5.0 tons of Glauber salt ($Na_2SO_4 \cdot 10H_2O$), a substance that melts at 90°F. The heat of fusion of Glauber salt is 104 Btu/lb, and

the specific heats of the solid and liquid are, respectively, 0.46 Btu/lb·°F and 0.68 Btu/lb·°F. After a week of sunny weather, the storage medium is all liquid at 95°F. Then a cool, cloudy period sets in during which the house loses heat at an average rate of 20,000 Btu/h. (a) How long is it before the temperature of the storage medium drops below 60°F? (b) How much of this time is spent at 90°F?

72. By differentiating Equation 20-6, show that the most probable molecular speed in the Maxwell-Boltzmann distribution is lower than the thermal speed by a factor of $\sqrt{2/3}$.

73. Show that the coefficient of volume expansion of an ideal gas at constant pressure is just the reciprocal of its kelvin temperature.

74. A constant-volume gas thermometer is made from Pyrex glass. If the thermometer is calibrated at the triple point of water and then used to determine the boiling point of water, how much error will be introduced by ignoring the expansion of the glass?

75. Water's coefficient of volume expansion in the temperature range from 0°C to about 20°C is given approximately by $\beta = a + bT + cT^2$, where T is in Celsius and $a = -6.43 \times 10^{-5}$ °C^{-1}, $b = 1.70 \times 10^{-5}$ °C^{-2}, and $c = -2.02 \times 10^{-7}$ °C^{-3}. Show that water has its greatest density at approximately 4.0°C.

76. When the expansion coefficient varies with temperature, Equation 20-7 should be written $\beta = \dfrac{1}{V}\dfrac{dV}{dT}$. If a sample of water occupies 1.00000 L at 0°C, find its volume at 12°C. Use the information from the preceding problem, and integrate the equation above.

77. Ignoring air resistance, find the height from which you must drop an ice cube at 0°C so it melts completely on impact. Assume no heat exchange with the environment.

78. The timekeeping of an old clock is regulated by a brass pendulum 20.0 cm long. If the clock is accurate at 20°C but is in a room at 18°C, how long will it be before the clock is in error by 1 minute? Will it be too fast or too slow?

79. Prove the relation $\beta = 3\alpha$ (page 509) by considering a cube of side s and therefore volume $V = s^3$ that undergoes a small temperature change dT and corresponding length and volume changes ds and dV.

80. One of the dangers of global warming is a rise in sea level that could inundate some coastal areas. Most people assume such a rise would come from melting ice, but, in fact, the primary cause would be expansion of sea water. Estimate the rise due to expansion in the event of a 2°C rise in the average temperature of the entire ocean. Treat the ocean as a body of water of constant 3.8 km depth (the average depth of the oceans) at 20°C. Your answer is an overestimate; among other things, it doesn't include the effects of salinity changes, nor processes in the cold, deep ocean where, as Table 20-2 shows, water's expansion coefficient is very different than it is at 20°C.

FIGURE 20-22 A solar-heated house (Problem 71).

Heat, Work, and the First Law of Thermodynamics

21

A jet aircraft engine, shown here being repaired, converts energy released in burning fuel to mechanical motion. Jet engines, gasoline and diesel engines, and electric power plants all rely on thermodynamics to effect energy conversion.

How do we change the temperature of a substance? One approach involves heat transfer between substances at different temperatures. Another approach—which you've experienced if you ever pulled a rope too quickly through your hands, or touched a drill bit just after drilling a hole, or smelled your car's brakes burning as you went down a steep hill—involves mechanical energy. Here we explore this second approach to temperature change and, in the process, come to a deeper understanding of the relation between heat and mechanical energy.

21-1 THE FIRST LAW OF THERMODYNAMICS

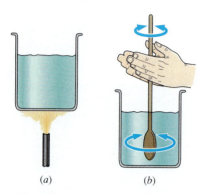

FIGURE 21-1 Either a flame or mechanical agitation will raise the water temperature.

8.6
Heat, Internal Energy, and First Law of Thermodynamics

Heat is energy being transferred from one object to another because of a temperature difference alone. As a result of heat transfer, a substance undergoes changes in its thermodynamic state—its temperature, pressure, and volume may change, and it may undergo a change of phase. But we can accomplish these same changes with mechanical energy. As Fig. 21-1 suggests, we can raise the temperature of water by heating with a flame or by stirring violently with a spoon. For the flame to heat the water, the flame temperature must exceed the water temperature. But the spoon can have the same temperature as the water, since it's the mechanical energy of the spoon's motion that raises the water temperature. We use the term **work** to describe energy transfer that does not require a temperature difference. This sense is consistent with our earlier use of the word *work* to describe mechanical energy transfer. Sometimes that energy ends up as stored potential energy, but often it results in a temperature change—as when we do work against frictional forces. That both heat and mechanical work can raise temperature is what made possible Joule's quantitative identification of heat as a form of energy (Fig. 21-2).

What happens to energy transferred to a system through either heat or mechanical work? It ends up changing the **internal energy** of the system—that is, the sum of the different kinds of energy associated with all the individual particles making up the system. For an ideal gas, internal energy is the total kinetic energy of the gas molecules. More complicated substances include potential energy as well; fuels such as gasoline or uranium, for example, have considerable internal potential energy. ActivPhysics Activity 8.6 explores the microscopic details of internal energy.

If we keep track of all energy entering and leaving a system—both heat and work—we find that the change in the system's internal energy depends only on the net amount of energy added to or removed from the system. In one sense this is hardly surprising; it's just an extension of the idea of energy conservation to include heat as well as mechanical work. But in another way it's remarkable: it doesn't matter at all *how* energy is transferred to or from the system—by heating, by mechanical work, or by some combination of the two. All that matters is the total energy transferred. This statement constitutes the **first law of thermodynamics**:

> *First law of thermodynamics: The change in the internal energy of a system depends only on the net heat transferred to the system and the net work done by the system, and is independent of the particular processes involved.*

Mathematically, the first law reads

$$\Delta U = Q - W, \qquad (21\text{-}1)$$

where ΔU is the change in a system's internal energy, Q the heat transferred *to* the system, and W the work done *by* the system. Thus a positive Q represents an energy gain for the system, while a positive W represents an energy loss; that's why the minus sign appears in Equation 21-1. This convention on the signs of Q and W is used because the first law was developed in connection with engines, which take heat from a source and give out mechanical work. Keeping track of energy transfers in an engine is easier if both the heat input and the work output are considered positive quantities; their difference is then the change in internal energy.

FIGURE 21-2 In Joule's apparatus, potential energy of the falling weights is converted to kinetic energy of the rotating paddle, which in turn becomes internal energy of the water.

The first law of thermodynamics says that the change in a system's internal energy doesn't depend on the details of the energy transfer—only on the total amount of energy transferred. We could transfer a given quantity of energy by heating, by mechanical work, or by some combination of the two, and the effect would be the same. For this reason internal energy is called a **thermodynamic state variable**, meaning a quantity whose value doesn't depend on how a system got into its particular state. Temperature and pressure are also thermodynamic state variables; heat and work are not.

We're frequently concerned with *rates* of energy flow. Differentiating the first law with respect to time gives a statement about these rates:

$$\frac{dU}{dt} = \frac{dQ}{dt} - \frac{dW}{dt}, \qquad (21\text{-}2)$$

where dU/dt is the rate of change of a system's internal energy, dQ/dt the rate of heat transfer to the system, and dW/dt the rate at which the system does work on its surroundings.

EXAMPLE 21-1 | *Nuclear Power, Thermal Pollution*

A nuclear power plant's reactor supplies energy at the rate of 3.0 GW ($1\ \text{GW} = 10^9\ \text{W}$), boiling water to produce steam that turns a turbine-generator (Fig. 21-3). The spent steam is then condensed through thermal contact with water taken from a river and sent back to the reactor. If the power plant produces electrical energy at the rate of 1.0 GW, at what rate is heat transferred to the river?

Solution

Here the system consists of the power plant and its reactor, so dU/dt in Equation 21-2 represents the rate of change of internal energy in the nuclear fuel. Since that internal energy is being converted to other forms, dU/dt is negative; its value is −3.0 GW. On the other hand, dW/dt is the rate at which the plant does work—i.e., the rate at which it supplies electrical

energy to the external world. Thus $dW/dt = +1.0\ \text{GW}$. Solving for the heat-transfer rate then gives

$$\frac{dQ}{dt} = \frac{dU}{dt} + \frac{dW}{dt} = -3.0\ \text{GW} + 1.0\ \text{GW} = -2.0\ \text{GW}.$$

Does this make sense? Since a positive Q represents heat transferred *to* the system, the minus sign in our answer shows that heat is transferred *from* the power plant to the river at the rate of 2.0 GW. The numbers in this example are typical for large nuclear and coal-burning power plants, and show that about two-thirds of the energy extracted from the fuel is wasted in heating the environment. We'll see in the next chapter just why this waste occurs.

Tip

Identify the System Thermodynamics problems often deal with energy flows into and out of a system. Before attacking a problem, be sure you're clear on just what constitutes the system. The first law holds no matter how you define the system, but the meanings of the various quantities change with that definition. In Example 21-1, for example, we could have excluded the nuclear fuel from the system. The net result— 2 GW dumped to the river—would have been the same, but now we would have had an additional heat input of 3 GW and no change in internal energy.

EXERCISE Gasoline burning in an automobile engine releases energy at the rate of 160 kW. Heat is exhausted through the car's radiator at the rate of 51 kW and out the exhaust at 50 kW. An additional 23 kW goes to frictional heating within the machinery of the car. What fraction of the fuel energy is available for propelling the car?

Answer: 22.5%

Some problems similar to Example 21-1: 4–6

FIGURE 21-3 A nuclear power plant, showing two reactor buildings and a large cooling tower. The plant takes in water from the river in the foreground. The water absorbs waste heat and then passes through the cooling tower before returning to the river. Example 21-1 shows that two-thirds of the energy produced in the reactor is discarded as waste heat.

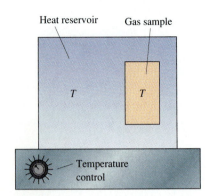

FIGURE 21-4 A quasi-static, or reversible, process. The gas sample is heated by immersion in a heat reservoir whose temperature is slowly increased. The entire gas sample is always at essentially the same temperature as the reservoir, so it is always in a well-defined thermodynamic state.

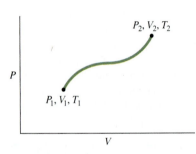

FIGURE 21-5 Because a system undergoing a quasi-static change is always in thermodynamic equilibrium, the change may be described by a succession of states—a continuous path—in its PV diagram.

21-2 THERMODYNAMIC PROCESSES

The first law relates two kinds of energy transfers—heat and work—that can change a system's thermodynamic state. Although the first law applies to *any* system, it is easiest to understand when applied to an ideal gas. The ideal gas law (Equation 20-2) relates the temperature, pressure, and volume of a given gas sample: $PV = nRT$. The thermodynamic state of the gas is completely determined by any two of the quantities P, V, or T. We'll find it convenient to work with pressure and volume, representing different states of a system as points on a coordinate system whose vertical and horizontal axes represent pressure and volume, respectively. This is called a **PV diagram**.

Reversible and Irreversible Processes

Imagine heating a gas sample by immersing it in a large reservoir of water whose temperature we can control (Fig. 21-4). If the gas and water temperatures are equal, the gas will stay in thermodynamic equilibrium. If we then raise the reservoir temperature very slowly, both water and gas temperatures will rise essentially in unison, and the gas will remain in equilibrium. Such a slow change is called a **quasi-static process**. Because a system undergoing a quasi-static process is always in thermodynamic equilibrium, its overall change from one state to another is then described by a continuous sequence of points—a curve—in its PV diagram (Fig. 21-5).

We could reverse this heating process by very slowly lowering the reservoir temperature; the gas would then cool while remaining essentially in thermodynamic equilibrium and would go back along the same path in its PV diagram. Because the system can be made to traverse the same path in the PV diagram going either way, a quasi-static process is also called a **reversible process**. A process like the sudden plunging of the gas sample into boiling water is, in contrast, **irreversible** (Fig. 21-6). During an irreversible process the system is not in equilibrium, and thermodynamic variables like temperature and pressure

FIGURE 21-6 Plunging a gas sample at 0°C into boiling water is an irreversible process. It takes some time for the gas to reach equilibrium at the higher temperature, during which time the gas itself has no well-defined thermodynamic state.

do not have well-defined values. It therefore makes no sense to think of a path in the *PV* diagram. A process may be irreversible even though it returns a system to its original state. The distinction lies not in the end states but in the *process* that takes the system between states.

There are many ways to change the thermodynamic state of a system. Here we consider several important special cases as they apply to an ideal gas system. These special cases illustrate the physical principles behind a myriad of technological devices and natural phenomena, from the operation of a gasoline engine to the propagation of a sound wave to the oscillations of a star.

Our system consists of an ideal gas confined to a cylinder sealed with a movable piston (Fig. 21-7). The piston and cylinder walls are perfectly insulating—they block all heat transfer—while the bottom is a perfect conductor of heat. We can change the thermodynamic state of the gas mechanically, by moving the piston, or thermally, by transferring heat through the bottom. We will consider only reversible processes, which we can describe by paths in the *PV* diagram for the gas.

FIGURE 21-7 A gas-cylinder system. The cylinder walls are perfectly insulating, but the bottom is a perfect conductor of heat.

Work and Volume Changes

Before examining specific processes, we develop a relation between volume change and work that holds for all processes. If *A* is the cross-sectional area of our piston and cylinder and *P* the gas pressure, then $F = PA$ is the force the gas exerts on the piston (Fig. 21-8*a*). If the piston moves a small distance Δx, then the work done by the gas is

$$\Delta W = F \Delta x = PA \Delta x = P \Delta V,$$

where $\Delta V = A \Delta x$ is the change in gas volume. The work ΔW is positive when the volume increases, indicating that the gas does work on the piston, and negative if ΔV is negative, indicating work done on the gas. Pressure may vary with volume, in which case our result is strictly valid only in the limit of very small volume changes. To find the work associated with a larger volume change, we take the limit $\Delta V \to 0$, and integrate over the volume change:

$$W = \int dW = \int_{V_1}^{V_2} P\, dV, \tag{21-3}$$

where V_1 and V_2 are the initial and final volumes. Figure 21-8*b* shows the geometrical interpretation of this equation: the work done by the gas is simply the area under the *PV* curve.

Now that we have a relation between pressure, volume, and work, we will explore several basic thermodynamic processes, in each of which we hold one of the thermodynamic variables constant. These processes approximate what goes on in a wide variety of real systems ranging from engines to sound waves to

ActivPhysics

8.5

Work Done by a Gas

(a)

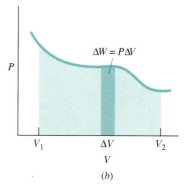

(b)

FIGURE 21-8 (*a*) The gas exerts a pressure force *PA* on the piston of area *A*, so the work done in moving the piston a small distance Δx is $PA \Delta x$, or $P\Delta V$. (*b*) On the *PV* diagram, this work corresponds to the area of the dark strip of width ΔV. The total work to take the system from volume V_1 to V_2 is the area under the *PV* curve between V_1 and V_2.

FIGURE 21-9 During an isothermal process, the piston moves slowly while the system is held in thermal contact with a heat reservoir at fixed temperature.

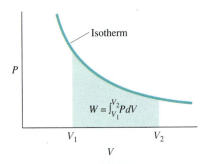

FIGURE 21-10 PV diagram for an isothermal process, showing a particular isotherm—a curve of constant temperature. Since $PV = nRT$ for an ideal gas, the pressure and volume are inversely related at constant temperature, so the isotherm is a hyperbola. The work done during an isothermal expansion from volume V_1 to V_2 is the area under the isotherm.

weather systems. We will restrict ourselves to quasi-static processes, so in each case the process in question is reversible and can be described by a path in the PV diagram.

Isothermal Processes

To perform a reversible **isothermal process**, we place the heat-conducting bottom of our gas cylinder in good thermal contact with a heat reservoir whose temperature is held constant (Fig. 21-9). We then move the piston to change the volume of the system, doing so slowly enough that the gas remains in equilibrium with the heat reservoir. The system then moves from its initial state to its final state along a curve of constant temperature—an **isotherm**—in the PV diagram (Fig. 21-10). The work done in the process is given by Equation 21-3 and is equal to the area under the isotherm.

For an ideal gas, we can relate pressure P and volume V through the ideal gas law:

$$P = \frac{nRT}{V}.$$

Then Equation 21-3 becomes

$$W = \int_{V_1}^{V_2} \frac{nRT}{V} \, dV.$$

For an isothermal process, the temperature T is constant, giving

$$W = nRT \int_{V_1}^{V_2} \frac{dV}{V} = nRT \ln V \Big|_{V_1}^{V_2} = nRT \ln\left(\frac{V_2}{V_1}\right).$$

The internal energy of an ideal gas consists only of the kinetic energy of its molecules which, in turn, depends only on the temperature. We showed this in the preceding chapter for a gas of structureless point particles and will extend it later in this chapter to gases consisting of more complicated molecules. Thus, there is no change in the internal energy of an ideal gas during an isothermal process. The first law of thermodynamics then gives

$$\Delta U = 0 = Q - W$$

so

$$Q = W = nRT \ln\left(\frac{V_2}{V_1}\right). \quad \text{(isothermal process)} \qquad (21\text{-}4)$$

Does this result $Q = W$ make sense? Recall that Q is the heat transferred to the gas, while W is the work done by the gas. Therefore, our result says that when an ideal gas does work W on the external world with no change in temperature, it must absorb an equal amount of heat from outside. Similarly, if work is done on the gas, then the gas must reject an equal amount of heat to the outside if its temperature is not to change. ActivPhysics Activity 8.10 lets you simulate the isothermal process described in our derivation of Equation 21-4.

8.10

Isothermal Process

EXAMPLE 21-2	A Diver Exhales

A scuba diver (Fig. 21-11) is swimming at a depth of 25 m, where the pressure is 3.5 atm (recall Example 18-1). The air she exhales forms bubbles 8.0 mm in radius. How much work is done by each bubble as it expands on rising to the surface? Assume that the bubbles remain at the uniform 300 K temperature of the surrounding water.

Solution

Since the bubbles remain at constant temperature, the process is isothermal and Equation 21-4 applies. Just before they break the surface, the bubbles are at essentially 1 atm pressure, so their pressure has decreased by a factor of 3.5. The ideal gas law, $PV = nRT$, shows that when temperature is constant, pressure and volume are inversely related. Therefore, the bubble volume has increased by a factor of 3.5. To apply Equation 21-4, we also need the quantity nRT for a bubble. We can get this from the ideal gas law using the given radius of the bubbles at 3.5 atm pressure:

$$nRT = PV = P(\tfrac{4}{3}\pi r^3),$$

so Equation 21-4 becomes

$$W = nRT \ln\left(\frac{V_2}{V_1}\right) = \tfrac{4}{3}\pi r^3 P \ln\left(\frac{V_2}{V_1}\right)$$

$$= \tfrac{4}{3}\pi (8.0 \times 10^{-3}\ \text{m})^3 (3.5\ \text{atm})(1.01 \times 10^5\ \text{Pa/atm}) \ln(3.5)$$

$$= 0.95\ \text{J}.$$

FIGURE 21-11 How much work do the diver's exhaled air bubbles do as they rise? (Example 21-2)

Where does this energy go? As a bubble expands, it pushes water outward and, ultimately, upward. It therefore raises the gravitational potential energy of the ocean. When the bubble breaks the surface, this excess potential energy becomes kinetic energy, appearing in the form of small waves on the water surface.

EXERCISE Consider 3.2 mol of an ideal gas in contact with a heat reservoir at 320 K. Find the work done by the gas if its volume doubles.

Answer: 5.9 kJ

Some problems similar to Example 21-2: 11, 13–16

Constant-Volume Processes and Specific Heat

A **constant-volume process** (also called an isometric, isochoric, or isovolumic process) occurs in a rigid, closed container whose volume cannot change. In our piston-cylinder arrangement, we could tightly clamp the piston for a constant-volume process. Because the piston doesn't move, the gas does no work, and the first law becomes simply

$$Q = \Delta U. \tag{21-5}$$

To express this result in terms of a temperature change ΔT, we introduce the **molar specific heat at constant volume**, C_V, defined by the equation

$$Q = nC_V\Delta T, \tag{21-6}$$

where n is the number of moles. This molar specific heat is like the specific heat defined in Chapter 19, except that with a gas it's more convenient to consider the heat per mole rather than per unit mass. Introducing the definition of C_V into Equation 21-5 gives

$$nC_V\Delta T = \Delta U. \tag{21-7}$$

Isochoric (Constant V) Process

Solving for C_V then gives

$$C_V = \frac{1}{n}\frac{\Delta U}{\Delta T}.$$ (21-8)

For an ideal gas, the internal energy is a function of temperature alone, so $\Delta U/\Delta T$ has the same value no matter what process the gas undergoes. Therefore Equation 21-7, relating the temperature change ΔT and internal energy change ΔU, applies not only to a constant-volume process, but also to *any* ideal gas process. Why, then, have we been so careful to label C_V the specific heat *at constant volume?* Although the relation $nC_V\Delta T = \Delta U$ holds for any process, it is only when no work is done that the first law allows us to write $Q = \Delta U$, and therefore only for a constant-volume process that Equation 21-6 holds.

Isobaric Processes and Specific Heat

Isobaric means constant pressure. Processes occurring in systems exposed to the nearly constant pressure of Earth's atmosphere, for example, are essentially isobaric. This includes most chemical and biochemical reactions. Even though these processes don't generally involve the gas phase, the fact of constant pressure nevertheless simplifies their thermodynamic analysis.

In a reversible isobaric process, a system moves along an isobar, or curve of constant pressure, in its PV diagram (Fig. 21-12). The work done as the volume changes from V_1 to V_2 is the area under the isobar, or

$$W = P(V_2 - V_1) = P\,\Delta V,$$ (21-9)

a result we could obtain formally by integrating Equation 21-3.

Solving the first law (Equation 21-1) for Q and using our expression for work gives

$$Q = \Delta U + W = \Delta U + P\,\Delta V.$$

For an ideal gas, we've just found that the change in internal energy is given by $\Delta U = nC_V\Delta T$ for *any* process. Therefore

$$Q = nC_V\Delta T + P\,\Delta V$$ (21-10)

for an ideal gas undergoing an isobaric process. We define the **molar specific heat at constant pressure**, C_P, as the heat required to raise one mole of gas through a unit temperature change at constant pressure, or

$$Q = nC_P\Delta T.$$

Equation 21-10 can then be written

$$nC_P\Delta T = nC_V\Delta T + P\,\Delta V. \quad \text{(isobaric process)}$$ (21-11)

This is a useful form for calculating temperature changes in an isobaric process, if we know both specific heats C_P and C_V. However, we really need only one of these specific heats, for a simple relation holds between the two. The ideal gas law, $PV = nRT$, allows us to write

$$P\,\Delta V = nR\,\Delta T$$

FIGURE 21-12 PV diagram for an isobaric process. The gas moves along the isobar from state 1 to state 2, doing work $P\Delta V$ in the process. Also shown are isotherms for the initial and final temperatures.

for an isobaric process. Using this expression in Equation 21-11 gives

$$nC_P\Delta T = nC_V\Delta T + nR\Delta T,$$

so
$$C_P = C_V + R.\qquad(21\text{-}12)$$

Does this result make sense? Specific heat measures the heat needed to cause a given temperature change. In a constant-volume process, no work is done and all the heat goes into raising the internal energy and thus the temperature of an ideal gas. In a constant-pressure process, work is done and some of the added heat ends up as mechanical energy, leaving less energy available for raising the temperature. Therefore, in a constant-pressure process, *more* heat is needed to achieve a given temperature change, so the specific heat at constant pressure is larger than at constant volume, as reflected in Equation 21-12.

Why didn't we distinguish specific heats at constant volume and constant pressure much earlier? Because we were concerned mostly with solids and liquids, whose coefficients of expansion are far lower than those of gases. As a result of its relatively small expansion, the work done by a solid or liquid is much less than that done by a gas. Since work is what gives rise to the difference between C_V and C_P, the distinction is less significant for solids and liquids. As a practical matter, measured specific heats are usually at constant pressure, because enormous forces would be needed to prevent volume changes in solids or liquids. The simulations in ActivPhysics Activity 8.7 will help you understand the difference between specific heats at constant volume and constant pressure.

8.7
Heat Capacity

8.9
Isobaric Process

Adiabatic Processes

In an **adiabatic process**, no heat transfer occurs between a system and its environment. The simplest way to achieve this is to surround the system with perfect thermal insulation. Even without insulation, processes that occur quickly are often approximately adiabatic because they're over before significant heat transfer has had time to occur. In a gasoline engine, for example, compression of the gasoline-air mixture and subsequent expansion of the combustion products are nearly adiabatic because they occur so rapidly that little heat flows through the cylinder walls during the process.

Since the heat Q is zero in an adiabatic process, the first law becomes simply

$$\Delta U = -W.\quad\text{(adiabatic process)}\qquad(21\text{-}13)$$

This says that if a system does work on its surroundings, then—in the absence of heat transfer—its internal energy must decrease by the same amount. Microscopically, this internal energy loss occurs in a gas-cylinder system when molecules collide with the moving piston, returning to the gas with less energy (Fig. 21-13).

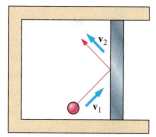

(a) Stationary piston

FIGURE 21-13 (a) Molecules bouncing off a stationary piston rebound with no loss of speed. Here the gas is doing no work, and its internal energy remains constant. (b) Molecules bouncing off an outward-moving piston give some energy to the piston and rebound with lower speed. The internal energy of the gas decreases as its molecules do work on the piston. If the piston were moving inward the molecules would gain energy, and the piston would be doing work on the gas.

(b) Moving piston

8.11

Adiabatic Process

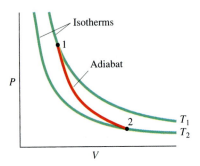

FIGURE 21-14 *PV* curve for an adiabatic process (red) shows that the pressure drops more than in an isothermal process going between the same two volumes. Two isotherms shown are for the initial and final temperatures of the adiabatic process. The adiabatic path is steeper because the gas loses internal energy as it does work.

As a gas expands adiabatically, its volume increases while its internal energy and temperature decrease. The ideal gas law, $PV = nRT$, then requires that the pressure decrease as well—and by more than it would in an isothermal process where T remains constant. In a *PV* diagram, the path of an adiabatic process—called an **adiabat**—therefore drops more steeply than the isotherms (Fig. 21-14).

The accompanying Math Toolbox details the mathematics involved in finding the shape of the adiabatic path; the result is

$$PV^{\gamma} = \text{constant} = P_0 V_0^{\gamma}, \quad \text{(adiabatic process)} \qquad (21\text{-}13a)$$

where $\gamma = C_P/C_V$ is the ratio of the specific heats and P_0 and V_0 are the values of P and V at some reference point, which could be any point in the process.

Because $C_P = C_V + R$, the ratio $\gamma = C_P/C_V$ is always greater than 1. Therefore an adiabatic process with a given volume change results in a greater pressure change than would a comparable isothermal process, as reflected in the steeper adiabatic path in Fig. 21-14. Physically, the adiabatic path is steeper because the gas loses internal energy as it does work, so its temperature drops.

Got It!

The ideal gas law says $PV = nRT$, but Equation 21-13a says $PV^{\gamma} = \text{constant}$. How can both equations be correct? Give an explanation that invokes the difference between adiabatic and isothermal processes.

We can find the temperature change in an adiabatic process by using the ideal gas law to eliminate pressure from Equation 21-13a. Writing that equation in the form $(PV)(V^{\gamma-1}) = (P_0 V_0)(V_0^{\gamma-1})$ and substituting for PV from the ideal gas law gives $nRTV^{\gamma-1} = nRT_0 V_0^{\gamma-1}$. Dividing both sides by nR gives

$$TV^{\gamma-1} = \text{constant} = T_0 V_0^{\gamma-1} \qquad (21\text{-}13b)$$

for the relation between temperature and volume in an adiabatic process. We could have written the adiabatic equation in yet a third way, eliminating V in favor of T and P (see Problem 28).

Math Toolbox

Deriving the Adiabatic Relation We derive the *PV* relation for an adiabatic process by integrating over a sequence of infinitesimal adiabatic changes. Equation 21-7, which holds for *any* process, shows that the internal energy change accompanying an infinitesimal temperature change is $dU = nC_V dT$. The work done in the process is $dW = P dV$ so, with $Q = 0$ for an adiabatic process, the first law becomes

$$nC_V dT = -P dV.$$

We now eliminate dT by differentiating the ideal gas law, allowing *both* P and V to change:

$$nR\, dT = d(PV) = P dV + V dP.$$

Solving for dT, substituting in our first-law statement, and multiplying through by R leads to

$$C_V V dP + (C_V + R) P dV = 0.$$

But $C_V + R = C_P$; substituting this and dividing through by $C_V PV$ gives

$$\frac{dP}{P} + \frac{C_P}{C_V}\frac{dV}{V} = 0 \,.$$

Defining $\gamma \equiv C_P/C_V$ and integrating gives

$$\ln P + \gamma \ln V = \ln(\text{constant}) \,,$$

where we've chosen to call the constant of integration $\ln(\text{constant})$. Since $\gamma \ln V = \ln V^\gamma$, it follows by exponentiation that

$$PV^\gamma = \text{constant} \,,$$

where the constant is the quantity $P_0 V_0^\gamma$ at a point where P and V have the known values P_0 and V_0.

EXAMPLE 21-3 | *Diesel Power*

Ignition of the fuel in a diesel engine (Fig. 21-15) occurs on contact with air heated by compression as the piston moves to the top of its stroke. (In this way a diesel differs from a gasoline engine, in which a spark ignites the fuel.) The compression occurs fast enough that very little heat flows out of the gas, so the process is essentially adiabatic. If a temperature of 500°C is required for ignition, what must be the compression ratio (ratio of maximum to minimum cylinder volume) of the diesel engine? Air has a specific heat ratio γ of 1.4, and before compression its temperature is 20°C.

Solution

Equation 21-13b gives the relation between temperature and volume in an adiabatic process. Writing T_0 and V_0 for the temperature and volume at the bottom of the piston stroke, and T_1 and V_1 for the top of the stroke, Equation 21-13b becomes

$$T_1 V_1^{\gamma-1} = T_0 V_0^{\gamma-1} \,.$$

Solving for the compression ratio V_0/V_1 gives

$$\frac{V_0}{V_1} = \left(\frac{T_1}{T_0}\right)^{1/(\gamma-1)} = \left(\frac{773\text{ K}}{293\text{ K}}\right)^{1/0.4} = 11 \,.$$

Practical diesel engines have considerably higher compression ratios to ensure reliable ignition. Conversely, compressional heating places an upper limit on the compression ratios of gasoline engines, where ignition by hot air would circumvent the carefully timed spark ignition system (see Problem 26).

(a)

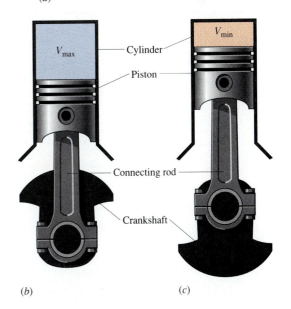

(b)   (c)

FIGURE 21-15 (a) Cutaway diagram of a diesel engine. (b) One cylinder of the engine, shown with the piston at the bottom of its stroke (maximum volume), and (c) with the piston at the top of its stroke (minimum volume). The compression ratio is the ratio V_{max}/V_{min}. In a diesel, this ratio is high enough that adiabatic compression alone brings the fuel-air mixture to ignition temperature. Expansion of the burning fuel-air mixture then pushes the piston down, and this is what powers the engine. Not shown are intake and exhaust valves, nor fuel injectors.

| EXAMPLE 21-4 | *Adiabatic and Isothermal Expansion* |

Two identical gas-cylinder systems each contain 0.060 mol of ideal gas at 300 K and 2.0 atm pressure. The specific heat ratio γ is 1.4. The gas samples are allowed to expand, one adiabatically and one isothermally, until both are at 1.0 atm pressure. What are the final temperatures and volumes of each?

Solution

The initial volume V_0 of both samples may be obtained from the ideal gas law, $PV = nRT$. Solving for V gives

$$V_0 = \frac{nRT_0}{P_0} = \frac{(0.060 \text{ mol})(8.314 \text{ J/K·mol})(300 \text{ K})}{(2.0 \text{ atm})(1.013 \times 10^5 \text{ Pa/atm})}$$

$$= 7.39 \times 10^{-4} \text{ m}^3 = 0.739 \text{ L}.$$

For the isothermal sample, T remains constant at 300 K. With constant temperature, $PV = $ constant, so as the pressure drops in half, the volume doubles, becoming 1.48 L.

For the adiabatic expansion, solving Equation 21-13a for the volume gives

$$V = \left(\frac{P_0}{P}\right)^{1/\gamma} V_0 = \left(\frac{2.0 \text{ atm}}{1.0 \text{ atm}}\right)^{1/1.4} (0.739 \text{ L}) = 1.21 \text{ L}.$$

The temperature follows from Equation 21-13b:

$$TV^{\gamma-1} = \text{constant} = T_0 V_0^{\gamma-1},$$

or

$$T = T_0 \left(\frac{V_0}{V}\right)^{\gamma-1} = (300 \text{ K})\left(\frac{0.739 \text{ L}}{1.21 \text{ L}}\right)^{0.4} = 246 \text{ K}.$$

Since we knew both P and V, we could equally well have determined the temperature from the ideal gas law.

In this example, both gas samples do work against the outside world as they expand. In the isothermal process, energy leaving the system as work is replaced by energy entering as

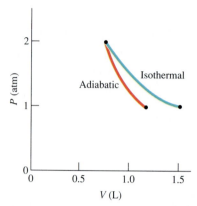

FIGURE 21-16 *PV* diagram showing isothermal and adiabatic processes of Example 21-4.

heat, so the temperature and internal energy remain constant. But heat cannot flow during the adiabatic process, so the work done is at the expense of the internal energy of the gas. As a result, the gas temperature drops, and the volume does not increase as much. Figure 21-16 shows both processes on a *PV* diagram.

EXERCISE A bicycle pump compresses 0.30 L of air, initially at 14°C and 1 atm pressure, to 4 times atmospheric pressure. The process occurs rapidly enough that it is essentially adiabatic. What are the volume and temperature of the compressed air? For air, $\gamma = 1.4$.

Answers: $V = 0.11$ L, $T = 153$°C

Some problems similar to Examples 21-3 and 21-4: 19, 22–26

How much work is done during an adiabatic process? Since there's no heat transfer, $W = -\Delta U$. But we've found that $\Delta U = nC_V\Delta T$ for *any* process. Therefore in an adiabatic process

$$W = -nC_V\Delta T = nC_V(T_1 - T_2),$$

where T_1 and T_2 are the initial and final temperatures. We can express this result in terms of pressure and volume changes by solving the ideal gas law, $PV = nRT$, for temperature and using the result in the equation above:

$$W = nC_V \frac{P_1 V_1 - P_2 V_2}{nR}.$$

But $R = C_P - C_V$, so

$$\frac{C_V}{R} = \frac{C_V}{C_P - C_V} = \frac{1}{(C_P/C_V) - 1} = \frac{1}{\gamma - 1}.$$

Then our expression for the adiabatic work becomes

$$W = \frac{P_1 V_1 - P_2 V_2}{\gamma - 1}. \tag{21-14}$$

We could also have obtained this result by direct integration of Equation 21-3 for an adiabatic process (see Problem 61).

APPLICATION	*Smog Alert!*

The smog shown in Fig. 21-17*a* is an unfortunate manifestation of our high-energy industrial society. The presence of that smog is closely related to the adiabatic processes we've just considered.

Normally, atmospheric temperature decreases with altitude at a so-called **lapse rate** of about 6.5°C per kilometer. The main reason for the decrease is that sunlight first heats Earth's surface, which then transfers heat to the atmosphere. Now consider a parcel of air that for some reason starts moving upward. That initial rise could occur because the air is over a darker region, like pavement, that absorbs more solar energy. The heated air parcel, being less dense than the surrounding air, then rises under the influence of the buoyancy force we discussed in Chapter 18. Or the rise could occur as horizontally moving air is forced upward to clear an obstruction. Or it could be that hot air and other gases are belched out of a smokestack or automobile exhaust pipe. Whatever the reason, the air parcel starts upward. We want to know what happens next.

(a)

(b)

FIGURE 21-17 (a) Smog over Los Angeles. The smog is trapped because adiabatic expansion cools rising smog to the same temperature as the surrounding air. (b) In the violently unstable thunderstorm, adiabatic cooling is not sufficient to bring rising or falling parcels of air to thermal equilibrium.

As the air parcel rises, the pressure of the surrounding air drops, and the parcel therefore expands to maintain pressure equilibrium. Now, air is a good thermal insulator, so a parcel of reasonable size exchanges little heat with its surroundings. Its expansion is therefore adiabatic, and thus, its temperature drops as it expands. The decrease in pressure with altitude is such that dry air cools adiabatically at the rate of about 10°C per kilometer as it rises. If the surrounding air has the typical lapse rate of 6.5°C/km, then the rising parcel cools faster. Even if it started out hotter than its surroundings, it will soon reach an altitude where it is at the same temperature (Fig. 21-18*a*). Then it will no longer be buoyant, and its upward motion will

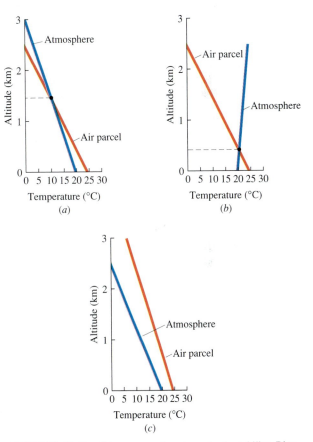

FIGURE 21-18 Conditions governing atmospheric stability. Blue lines show temperature versus altitude in the stationary atmosphere. Red lines are the rates at which rising air parcels cool adiabatically with increasing altitude. (a) Under normal stable conditions, adiabatic cooling occurs more rapidly and a parcel heated at ground level soon reaches equilibrium with the surrounding air, here at about 1.4 km. (b) A temperature inversion. Blue line shows air temperature increasing with altitude. Here equilibrium of a heated parcel occurs at low altitude, trapping pollutants near the ground. (c) When the lapse rate exceeds the adiabatic cooling rate, the air is unstable. A rising parcel continues to rise, without reaching equilibrium.

soon cease. Air under these conditions is therefore stable, in that a rising parcel soon reaches an equilibrium altitude. You can convince yourself that a falling parcel—falling because it's cooler than its surroundings—will also reach equilibrium.

Under stable conditions, smog-forming pollutants cannot escape to the upper atmosphere. Instead, they're trapped at an altitude where adiabatic cooling brings them to the same temperature as the surrounding air. The greater the difference between the actual lapse rate and the approximately 10°C/km adiabatic cooling rate, the stronger the "trapping" of the air and its pollutants. The most serious problems arise during a **temperature inversion**, in which the air temperature actually increases with height (Fig. 21-18b). A rising parcel still cools adiabatically, and now its temperature drops so quickly relative to its surroundings that the parcel is strongly trapped at low altitudes.

Sometimes the atmospheric lapse rate exceeds the rate of adiabatic cooling. This can occur on crisp, clear days when the ground is strongly heated, or it can occur with moist air for which the adiabatic cooling rate is only about 6°C/km. In this case a rising parcel cools more slowly than its surroundings, so its buoyancy increases and it accelerates upward (Fig. 21-18c). A falling parcel, similarly, accelerates downward. Under these conditions the air is unstable. The puffy cumulus clouds that form on an otherwise clear summer day are associated with plumes of warm air that rise through the unstable air until they're cool enough that moisture condenses to form clouds. A more dramatic example is the thunderstorm of Fig. 21-17b, in which unstable air undergoes violent up- and downdrafts driven by the heat of vaporization released as water vapor condenses. Problem 41 explores these issues of atmospheric stability.

Cyclic Processes

8.12, 8.13
Cyclic Process

Many natural and technological systems undergo **cyclic processes**, in which the system returns periodically to the same thermodynamic state. Engineering examples include engines, refrigerators, and air compressors, whose mechanical construction ensures cyclic behavior. Many natural oscillations, like those of a sound wave or a pulsating star, are essentially cyclic.

Cyclic processes often involve the four simple processes we've just outlined, which are summarized in Table 21-1. We've seen that the work done in any reversible process is just the area under the PV curve describing that process. A cyclic process returns to the same point in the PV diagram, so it generally involves both expansion and compression of the gas (Fig. 21-19). During expansion the gas does work on its surroundings; during compression work gets done on the gas. The net work is the difference between the two. Figure 21-19b shows that this work is the area—measured as pressure times volume—enclosed by the cyclic path in the PV diagram.

TABLE 21-1 *Ideal Gas Processes*

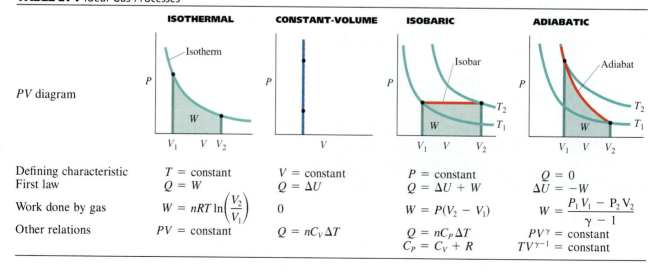

	ISOTHERMAL	CONSTANT-VOLUME	ISOBARIC	ADIABATIC
PV diagram				
Defining characteristic	$T = \text{constant}$	$V = \text{constant}$	$P = \text{constant}$	$Q = 0$
First law	$Q = W$	$Q = \Delta U$	$Q = \Delta U + W$	$\Delta U = -W$
Work done by gas	$W = nRT \ln\left(\dfrac{V_2}{V_1}\right)$	0	$W = P(V_2 - V_1)$	$W = \dfrac{P_1 V_1 - P_2 V_2}{\gamma - 1}$
Other relations	$PV = \text{constant}$	$Q = nC_V \Delta T$	$Q = nC_P \Delta T$ $C_P = C_V + R$	$PV^\gamma = \text{constant}$ $TV^{\gamma-1} = \text{constant}$

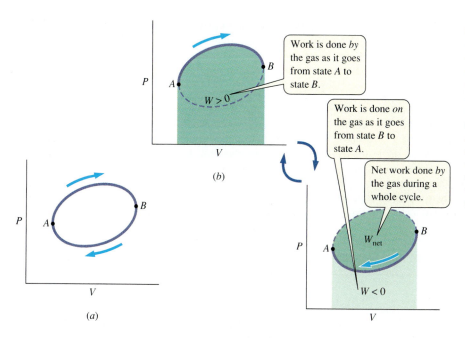

FIGURE 21-19 (*a*) A cyclic path for an ideal gas, traversed clockwise in the *PV* diagram. (*b*) The work done during a cycle. Work is done *by* the gas as it goes from state *A* to state *B*, and work is done *on* the gas as it returns from state *B* to state *A*. Since the area under each curve represents the associated work, the area inside the cycle represents the net work done by the gas. If the cycle were traversed counterclockwise rather than clockwise, the area inside the cycle would instead be the net work done *on* the gas.

EXAMPLE 21-5	*A Cyclic Process*

An ideal gas with $\gamma = 1.4$ occupies 4.0 L at 300 K and 100 kPa pressure. It is compressed adiabatically to one-fourth of its original volume, then cooled at constant volume to 300 K, and finally allowed to expand isothermally to its original volume. How much work is done on the gas?

Solution

Figure 21-20 shows the cyclic path *ABCA* in the *PV* diagram. To calculate the work done on the gas, we consider the work involved in moving along each of the sections *AB*, *BC*, and *CA*. The adiabatic work W_{AB} is given by Equation 21-14:

$$W_{AB} = \frac{P_A V_A - P_B V_B}{\gamma - 1}.$$

We know P_A, V_A, and V_B. To get P_B, we solve the adiabatic relation $P_B V_B^\gamma = P_A V_A^\gamma$ to obtain

$$P_B = P_A\left(\frac{V_A}{V_B}\right)^\gamma.$$

Then the adiabatic work is

$$W_{AB} = \frac{P_A[V_A - (V_A/V_B)^\gamma V_B]}{\gamma - 1}$$

$$= \frac{(1.0\times10^5 \text{ Pa})[4.0\times10^{-3} \text{ m}^3 - (4^{1/4})(1.0\times10^{-3} \text{ m}^3)]}{0.4}$$

$$= -741 \text{ J}.$$

The minus sign indicates that work is done *on* the gas during this adiabatic compression.

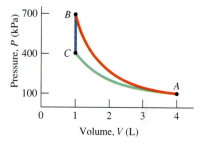

FIGURE 21-20 The cyclic process *ABCA* of Example 21-5 includes adiabatic (*AB*), constant volume (*BC*), and isothermal (*CA*) sections.

No work is done during the constant-volume process *BC*, while the isothermal work W_{CA} is given by Equation 21-4:

$$W_{CA} = nRT \ln\left(\frac{V_A}{V_C}\right).$$

The quantity nRT is given by the ideal gas law, $nRT = PV$, where we can evaluate P and V at any point along the isotherm because it's a curve of constant temperature. We know these values at point *A*, so the isothermal work becomes

$$W_{CA} = P_A V_A \ln\left(\frac{V_A}{V_C}\right)$$

$$= (1.0\times10^5 \text{ Pa})(4.0\times10^{-3} \text{ m}^3)\ln\left(\frac{4.0 \text{ L}}{1.0 \text{ L}}\right) = 555 \text{ J}.$$

The net work is then

$$W_{ABC} = W_{AB} + W_{BC} + W_{CA}$$
$$= -741 \text{ J} + 0 \text{ J} + 555 \text{ J} = -187 \text{ J}.$$

The minus sign indicates that net work is done on the gas.

We could achieve the cyclic process described here with our simple gas-cylinder system by first insulating the bottom of the cylinder and moving the piston to compress the gas to one-fourth its original volume. We would then clamp the piston in place to maintain constant volume and cool the gas to 300 K by placing the cylinder in contact with a heat reservoir whose temperature was slowly decreased. Finally, we would maintain contact with the 300 K heat reservoir while allowing the gas to expand to its original volume.

Since the system returns to its original state, its internal energy undergoes no net change. That means any work done on

it must be rejected to its surroundings as heat. Since no heat flows during the adiabatic process AB, and since the gas *absorbs* heat during its isothermal expansion CA, the heat rejection takes place entirely during the constant-volume cooling period BC.

EXERCISE The gas of this example starts at state A in Fig. 21-20 and is compressed adiabatically until its temperature is 400 K. It's then cooled while maintaining constant volume until it reaches 300 K, then allowed to expand isothermally back to state A. Find (a) the net work done on the gas and (b) the minimum volume reached.

Answers: (a) 45.7 J; (b) 1.95 L

Some problems similar to Example 21-5: 20, 21, 27, 31–33, 55, 56, 63

21-3 SPECIFIC HEATS OF AN IDEAL GAS

We've found that the thermodynamic behavior of an ideal gas depends on the specific heats C_V and C_P. What are the values of those quantities?

Our ideal gas model of Chapter 20 assumed the gas molecules were structureless point particles. The only energy of such particles is their translational kinetic energy, and the internal energy U of the gas is the sum of all the molecular translational energies. But the average kinetic energy is directly proportional to the temperature:

$$\tfrac{1}{2}m\overline{v^2} = \tfrac{3}{2}kT.$$

If we have n moles of gas, the internal energy is then

$$U = nN_A\left(\tfrac{1}{2}m\overline{v^2}\right) = \tfrac{3}{2}nN_A kT,$$

where N_A is Avogadro's number. But $N_A k = R$, the gas constant, so

$$U = \tfrac{3}{2}nRT.$$

Using this result in Equation 21-8 for the molar specific heat gives

$$C_V = \frac{1}{n}\frac{\Delta U}{\Delta T} = \tfrac{3}{2}R. \tag{21-15}$$

For this simple gas of structureless particles, the adiabatic exponent γ is then

$$\gamma = \frac{C_P}{C_V} = \frac{C_V + R}{C_V} = \frac{\tfrac{5}{2}R}{\tfrac{3}{2}R} = \frac{5}{3} = 1.67. \tag{21-16}$$

Some gases, notably the inert gases helium (He), neon (Ne), argon (Ar), and others in the last column of the periodic table, have adiabatic exponents and specific heats given by these equations. But others do not. At room temperature, for example, hydrogen (H_2), oxygen (O_2), and nitrogen (N_2) obey adiabatic laws with γ very nearly $\frac{7}{5}$ ($ = 1.4$). Solving Equation 21-16 for C_V shows that for these gases

$$C_V = \frac{R}{\gamma - 1} = \frac{R}{\frac{7}{5} - 1} = \frac{5}{2}R.$$

On the other hand, sulfur dioxide (SO_2) and nitrogen dioxide (NO_2) have specific heat ratios close to 1.3 and therefore volume specific heats of about $3.4R$.

What's going on here? A clue lies in the structure of individual gas molecules, reflected in their chemical formulas. The inert gas molecules are **monatomic**, consisting of single atoms. To the extent that these atoms behave like our model's structureless mass points, the only kind of energy they can have is kinetic energy associated with their translational motion. We can think of that kinetic energy as being a sum of *three* terms, each associated with motion in one of the three mutually perpendicular directions. We call each separate term in the expression for the energy of a system a **degree of freedom**, meaning a way that system can take on energy. So a monatomic molecule has three degrees of freedom.

In contrast, hydrogen, oxygen, and nitrogen molecules are **diatomic**, as shown in Fig. 21-21a. Although a gas of such molecules should still obey the ideal gas law $PV = nRT$, the molecules differ in one important respect from mass points: In addition to translational kinetic energy, they can have rotational energy as well. If we continue to model individual atoms as structureless mass points, then a diatomic molecule should be able to rotate about either of two axes, both mutually perpendicular and also perpendicular to the line joining the atoms, as suggested in Fig. 21-21b. Rotation about the axis joining the atoms is meaningless if the atoms are true mass points. Then the kinetic energy of a diatomic molecule consists of *five* terms, three for the three directions of translational motion and two for rotational motions about the two mutually perpendicular axes. So a diatomic molecule has five degrees of freedom. We'll now see how this difference between *three* degrees of freedom for monatomic molecules versus *five* for diatomic molecules accounts for the difference between their specific heats.

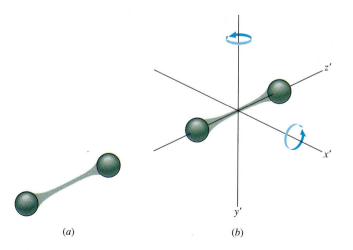

(a)   (b)

FIGURE 21-21 (a) "Dumbbell" model of a diatomic molecule, (b) showing that the diatomic molecule can rotate about two of three mutually perpendicular axes.

The Equipartition Theorem

We showed in Chapter 20 that the average translational kinetic energy associated with a gas molecule's motion in one direction is $\frac{1}{2}kT$. We then argued that all three directions of motion are equally probable, making the molecular kinetic energy, on average, $\frac{3}{2}kT$. The argument from one direction to three is statistical, based on the assumption that random collisions will "share" energy equally among the possible motions. When a molecule can rotate as well as translate, energy should be shared also among possible rotational motions.

Not only is energy shared, but it's shared equally. The nineteenth century Scottish physicist James Clerk Maxwell first proved this fact, which is now known as the **equipartition theorem**:

> *Equipartition theorem: When a system is in thermodynamic equilibrium, the average energy per molecule is $\frac{1}{2}kT$ for each degree of freedom.*

We can use the equipartition theorem to calculate the specific heat of a diatomic molecule. Each molecule has five degrees of freedom, three translational and two rotational. The average energy of a molecule is then $5(\frac{1}{2}kT) = \frac{5}{2}kT$, so the total internal energy in n moles of a diatomic gas is

$$U = nN_A(\tfrac{5}{2}kT) = \tfrac{5}{2}nRT.$$

Equation 21-8 then gives the specific heat at constant volume:

$$C_V = \frac{1}{n}\frac{\Delta U}{\Delta T} = \tfrac{5}{2}R. \qquad \text{(diatomic molecule)}$$

Our result $C_P = C_V + R$ still holds, since it was derived from the first law of thermodynamics without regard to molecular structure, so

$$C_P = \tfrac{7}{2}R$$

and

$$\gamma = \frac{C_P}{C_V} = \frac{7}{5} = 1.4.$$

These results describe the observed behavior of diatomic gases like hydrogen, oxygen, and nitrogen at room temperature.

EXAMPLE 21-6	*Mixing Gases*

A gas mixture consists of 2.0 mol of oxygen (O_2) and 1.0 mol of argon (Ar). What is the volume specific heat of the mixture?

Solution

Being diatomic, each oxygen molecule has five degrees of freedom. Then the equipartition theorem gives the total internal energy of all the oxygen molecules:

$$U_{O_2} = nN_A(\tfrac{5}{2}kT) = (2.0 \text{ mol})(\tfrac{5}{2}RT) = 5.0RT,$$

where we used $N_A k = R$. Similarly, the internal energy associated with all the monatomic argon molecules is

$$U_{Ar} = nN_A(\tfrac{3}{2}kT) = (1.0 \text{ mol})(\tfrac{3}{2}RT) = 1.5RT.$$

Then the total internal energy of the gas is

$$U = U_{O_2} + U_{Ar} = 6.5RT,$$

so

$$C_V = \frac{1}{n}\frac{\Delta U}{\Delta T} = \frac{6.5R}{3.0 \text{ mol}} = 2.2R.$$

EXERCISE Find the specific heat at constant volume and the adiabatic index γ for a mixture of equal numbers of nitrogen (N_2) and helium (He) molecules.

Answers: $C_V = 2R$, $\gamma = 1.5$

Some problems similar to Example 21-6: 42–45

A polyatomic molecule like NO_2 (Fig. 21-22) can rotate about any of three perpendicular axes and therefore has three rotational degrees of freedom. With a total of six degrees of freedom, the internal energy of n moles is then

$$U = (nN_A)(6)(\tfrac{1}{2}kT) = 3nRT,$$

so

$$C_V = \frac{1}{n}\frac{dU}{dT} = 3R,$$

$$C_P = C_V + R = 4R,$$

and

$$\gamma = \frac{C_P}{C_V} = \frac{4}{3} = 1.33.$$

These values are reasonably close to the experimental values $\gamma = 1.29$ and $C_V = 3.47R$, although the agreement is noticeably poorer than for monatomic and diatomic gases.

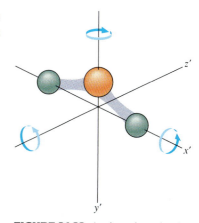

FIGURE 21-22 A triatomic molecule like NO_2 has significant rotational inertia about each of the three axes, and therefore has three rotational degrees of freedom.

Quantum Effects

Accounting for the effect of molecular structure on gas behavior seems a remarkable triumph for Newtonian physics. But hidden in our treatment of the specific heats of gases is an assumption that Newtonian physics alone can't justify, namely the treatment of atoms as structureless mass points. After all, real atoms have size and should be able to rotate. So why doesn't even a monatomic molecule have six degrees of freedom, three for rotation as well as three for translation? And if real atoms have size, a dumbbell-shaped diatomic molecule should be able to rotate about an axis through its atoms, giving it, too, three rotational degrees of freedom. Thus the fact that atoms have nonzero size suggests that both monatomic and diatomic molecules should have the same specific heat—whose value should be different from what's observed in either case. This difficulty greatly perplexed physicists at the end of the 19th century. What's wrong?

In trying to model individual atoms and molecules, we're pushing the limits of classical physics, approaching a realm where a quantum-mechanical description is necessary. In quantum mechanics, the energy associated with a periodic motion such as molecular rotation comes only in discrete multiples of some minimum amount. The minimum energy needed for rotation of monatomic molecules, or of diatomic molecules about the axis through the two atoms, is so large that at normal temperatures there isn't enough thermal energy to get these rotations going. So the atoms really do behave like structureless mass points—not because they are, but because they can't rotate. Our analysis of the specific heats of gases based on molecular structure is therefore correct—but only because of a hidden conclusion from quantum mechanics that lets us treat the individual atoms as nonrotating mass points.*

The fact of **quantization**—the restriction of energies to certain discrete values—is also evident in the behavior of specific heats as a function of temper-

---

*For more on this issue, see "Specific heats and the equipartition law," by Clayton A. Gearhart, *American Journal of Physics,* vol. 64, August 1996, p. 995.

FIGURE 21-23 Volume specific heat of H_2 gas as a function of temperature. Below 20 K hydrogen is liquid and above 3200 K it dissociates into individual atoms.

FIGURE 21-24 At high temperatures a diatomic molecule has enough energy to undergo vibrational motion.

ature, shown for hydrogen (H_2) in Fig. 21-23. In the region from about 250 K to 750 K, the specific heat has very nearly the value $\frac{5}{2}R$ that our dumbbell model predicts. But below about 100 K, hydrogen's specific heat is close to the $\frac{3}{2}R$ we expect for a monatomic molecule. There's a good reason for this: at these low temperatures, the thermal energy is well below the minimum needed for molecular rotation. So the molecules, although diatomic, can't rotate and therefore have only their three translational degrees of freedom. Thus at low temperatures, hydrogen's specific heat is that of a monatomic gas.

As the temperature rises, rotation becomes possible and the specific heat rises to the value $\frac{5}{2}R$ characteristic of diatomic molecules. At still higher temperatures, above about 3000 K, it rises to approximately $\frac{7}{2}R$. Here a new motion has become energetically possible, namely the vibration of molecules like miniature mass-spring systems (Fig. 21-24). Each molecule gains two more degrees of freedom, one for the kinetic energy and one for the potential energy associated with this vibrational motion, and so the specific heat goes up.

Are you bothered by the strange restrictions quantum mechanics imposes on the rotation and vibration of molecules? You should be! Nothing in the physics you've studied until now, and nothing in your everyday experience, suggests that a rotating object can't have any amount of energy you care to give it. But quantum mechanics deals with a realm of objects much smaller than those of our daily experience. The quantization of energy levels is only one of many unusual things that occur in the quantum realm. We will explore more quantum phenomena in Chapter 39.

CHAPTER SYNOPSIS

Summary

1. The **first law of thermodynamics** states that the change in a system's internal energy depends only on the net energy transfer to or from the system by any combination of heat or work. Thus the first law extends energy conservation to processes involving heat transfer. Mathematically, the change ΔU in a system's internal energy is the difference between the heat Q transferred *to* the system and the work W done *by* the system:

$$\Delta U = Q - W.$$

2. A **thermodynamic process** takes a system from one thermodynamic state to another. A **quasi-static process** occurs slowly enough that the system moves through a sequence of equilibrium states, so the process can be described by a path in the PV diagram. The work done by a system undergoing a quasi-static process that takes its volume from V_1 to V_2 is

$$W = \int_{V_1}^{V_2} P\,dV.$$

3. Four basic processes are **isothermal** (constant temperature), **constant volume**, **isobaric** (constant pressure), and **adiabatic** (no heat transfer). For an ideal gas, the work done and the relations among various thermodynamic variables are summarized in Table 21-1 in the text. A **cyclic process** takes a system around a closed path in its PV diagram, returning to its original state.

4. An ideal gas is characterized by its **molar specific heat at constant volume**, C_V, and its **molar specific heat at constant pressure**, C_P. The heat Q required to raise the temperature of n moles an amount ΔT is given by $Q = nC\Delta T$, where C is the specific heat appropriate to the condition—constant volume or pressure—under which the temperature change occurs. The specific heats are related by $C_P = C_V + R$, where R is the gas constant.

5. The **equipartition theorem** states that the average molecular energy per **degree of freedom** in thermodynamic equilibrium is $\frac{1}{2}kT$. Monatomic molecules have three degrees of freedom, associated with the three directions of translational motion; this leads to a volume specific heat $C_V = \frac{3}{2}R$. Diatomic molecules also undergo rotation, adding two more degrees of freedom and giving a volume specific heat of $\frac{5}{2}R$.

Terms You Should Understand

(Pairs are closely related terms whose distinction is important; number in parentheses is chapter section where term first appears.)

work (21-1)
internal energy (21-1)
first law of thermodynamics (21-1)
thermodynamic state, state variable (21-1)
quasi-static process (21-2)
reversible process, irreversible process (21-2)
isothermal process (21-2)
constant-volume process (21-2)
isobaric process (21-2)
molar specific heat at constant volume,
 . . . at constant pressure (21-2)
adiabatic process (21-2)
cyclic process (21-2)
degrees of freedom (21-3)
equipartition theorem (21-3)

Symbols You Should Recognize

ΔU (21-1) C_V, C_P (21-2) γ (21-2)

Problems You Should Be Able to Solve

calculating internal energy change, heat transfer, or work from the other two (21-1)
relating volume, pressure, and temperature changes for the basic ideal gas processes (21-2)
determining work done in basic ideal gas processes (21-2)
determining work involved in cyclic processes (21-2)
evaluating specific heats based on molecular structure (21-3)

Limitations to Keep in Mind

The ideal gas, with its internal energy a function of temperature alone, is an approximation. In real gases the weak forces among molecules make the internal energy depend slightly on volume as well.
Most relations developed in this chapter are valid only in the quasi-static limit; real processes may approach but not actually achieve this limit.

QUESTIONS

1. In Chapter 8 we wrote the conservation of energy principle in the form $K + U =$ constant. In what way is the first law of thermodynamics a broader statement than that?
2. The temperature of the water in a jar is raised by violently shaking the jar. Which of the terms Q and W in the first law of thermodynamics is involved in this case?
3. In Example 21-1, we considered the electric power leaving a power plant as part of the work done by the power plant. Why did we include the electric power with the work rather than with the heat?
4. What is the difference between heat and internal energy?
5. Some water is tightly sealed in a perfectly insulated container. Is it possible to change the water temperature? Explain.
6. Is the internal energy of a van der Waals gas a function of temperature alone? Why or why not?
7. Are the initial and final equilibrium states of an irreversible process describable by points in a PV diagram? Explain.
8. Why can an irreversible process not be described by a path in a PV diagram?
9. Does the first law of thermodynamics apply to an irreversible process?
10. Is it possible to have a process that is isothermal but irreversible? Explain.
11. A quasi-static process begins and ends at the same temperature. Is the process necessarily isothermal?

12. Figure 21-25 shows two processes, A and B, which connect the same initial and final states, 1 and 2. For which process is more heat added to the system?

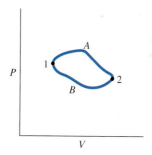

FIGURE 21-25 Question 12.

13. Two identical gas-cylinder systems are taken from the same initial state to the same final state, but by different processes. Is the work done in each case necessarily the same? The heat added? The change in internal energy?
14. When you let air out of a tire, the air seems cool. Why? What kind of process is occurring?
15. Blow on the back of your hand with your mouth wide open. Your breath will feel hot. Now tighten your lips into a small opening, and blow again. Now your breath feels cool. Why?
16. How is it possible to have $PV^{\gamma} =$ constant in an adiabatic process and yet have $PV = nRT$?

17. Water is boiled in an open pan. Of which of the four specific processes we considered is this an example?

18. Is it possible to involve an ideal gas in a process that is simultaneously isothermal and isobaric? Is there any real substance that could undergo such a process? Give an example.

19. Three identical gas-cylinder systems expand from the same initial state to final states that have the same volume. One system expands isothermally, one adiabatically, and one isobarically. Which does the most work? Which does the least work?

20. If the relation $\Delta U = nC_V\Delta T$ holds for any ideal gas process, why do we call C_V the molar specific heat at constant volume?

21. Why is the specific heat at constant pressure greater than at constant volume?

22. Imagine a gas of very complicated molecules, each with several hundred degrees of freedom. What, approximately, is the specific heat ratio γ of this gas? Is it easy or hard to change the gas temperature?

23. In what sense can a gas of diatomic molecules be considered an ideal gas, given that its molecules are not point particles?

PROBLEMS

ActivPhysics can help with these problems:
Activities 8.5–8.13.

Section 21-1 The First Law of Thermodynamics

1. In a perfectly insulated container, 1.0 kg of water is stirred vigorously until its temperature rises by 7.0°C. How much work was done on the water?

2. In a closed but uninsulated container, 500 g of water is shaken violently until its temperature rises by 3.0°C. The mechanical work required in the process is 9.0 kJ. (a) How much heat is transferred during the shaking? (b) How much mechanical energy would have been required had the container been perfectly insulated?

3. A 40-W heat source is applied to a gas sample for 25 s, during which time the gas expands and does 750 J of work on its surroundings. By how much does the internal energy of the gas change?

4. What is the rate of heat flow into a system whose internal energy is increasing at the rate of 45 W, given that the system is doing work at the rate of 165 W?

5. The most efficient large-scale electric power generating systems use high-temperature gas turbines and a so-called combined cycle system that maximizes the conversion of thermal energy into useful work. One such plant produces electrical energy at the rate of 360 MW, while extracting energy from its natural gas fuel at the rate of 670 MW. (a) At what rate does it reject waste heat to the environment? (b) Find its efficiency, defined as the percent of the total energy extracted from the fuel that ends up as electrical energy.

6. In a certain automobile engine, 17% of the total energy released in burning gasoline ends up as mechanical work. What is the engine's mechanical power output if its heat output is 68 kW?

7. Water flows over Niagara Falls (height 50 m) at the rate of about 10^6 kg/s. Suppose that all the water passes through a turbine connected to an electric generator producing 400 MW of electric power. If the water has negligible kinetic energy after leaving the turbine, by how much

has its temperature increased between the top of the falls and the outlet of the turbine?

Section 21-2 Thermodynamic Processes

8. An ideal gas expands from the state (P_1, V_1) to the state (P_2, V_2), where $P_2 = 2P_1$ and $V_2 = 2V_1$. The expansion proceeds along the straight diagonal path AB shown in Fig. 21-26. Find an expression for the work done by the gas during this process.

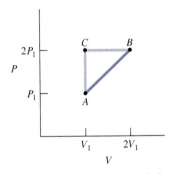

FIGURE 21-26 Poblems 8, 9.

9. Repeat the preceding problem for a process that follows the path ACB in Fig. 21-26.

10. Oceanographers lower an underwater habitat to the ocean floor. A hatch at the bottom of the habitat is open, so water can enter to compress the air and thus keep the air pressure inside equal to the pressure of the surrounding water. The habitat is lowered slowly enough that the inside air remains at the same temperature as the water. But the water temperature decreases with depth, in such a way that the air pressure and volume are related by $P = P_0\sqrt{V_0/V}$, where P_0 and V_0 are the surface values. The habitat's volume is 17 m^3 and it's initially full of air at normal atmospheric pressure. It's then lowered to a depth where the pressure is 1.4 atmospheres. Find (a) the air volume at this depth and (b) the work done on the air as the habitat is lowered. *Hint:* You'll need to do an integral.

11. A balloon contains 0.30 mol of helium. It rises, while maintaining a constant 300 K temperature, to an altitude where its volume has expanded 5 times. How much work is done by the gas in the balloon during this isothermal expansion? Neglect tension forces in the balloon.

12. The balloon of the preceding problem starts at a pressure of 100 kPa and rises to an altitude where the pressure is 75 kPa, maintaining a constant 300 K temperature. (a) By what factor does its volume increase? (b) How much work does the gas in the balloon do?

13. How much work does it take to compress 2.5 mol of an ideal gas to half its original volume while maintaining a constant 300 K temperature?

14. An ideal gas expands to 10 times its original volume, maintaining a constant 440 K temperature. If the gas does 3.3 kJ of work on its surroundings, (a) how much heat does it absorb, and (b) how many moles of gas are there?

15. A 0.25 mol sample of an ideal gas initially occupies 3.5 L. If it takes 61 J of work to compress the gas isothermally to 3.0 L, what is the temperature?

16. As the heart beats, blood pressure in an artery varies from a high of 125 mm of mercury to a low of 80 mm of mercury. These values are gauge pressures—i.e., excesses over atmospheric pressure. An air bubble trapped in the artery has diameter 1.52 mm when the blood pressure is at its minimum. (a) What will be its diameter at maximum pressure? (b) How much work does the blood (and ultimately the heart) do in compressing this bubble, assuming the air remains at the same 37.0°C temperature as the blood?

17. It takes 600 J to compress a gas isothermally to half its original volume. How much work would it take to compress it by a factor of 10 starting from its original volume?

18. A gas undergoes an adiabatic compression during which its volume drops to half its original value. If the gas pressure increases by a factor of 2.55, what is its specific heat ratio γ?

19. A gas with $\gamma = 1.4$ is at 100 kPa pressure and occupies 5.00 L. (a) How much work does it take to compress the gas adiabatically to 2.50 L? (b) What is its final pressure?

20. A gas sample undergoes the cyclic process $ABCA$ shown in Fig. 21-27, where AB lies on an isotherm. The pressure at point A is 60 kPa. Find (a) the pressure at B and (b) the net work done on the gas.

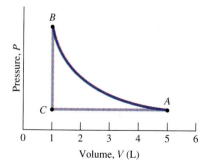

FIGURE 21-27 Problems 20, 21.

21. Repeat the preceding problem taking AB to be on an adiabat and using a specific heat ratio of $\gamma = 1.4$.

22. Warm winds called Chinooks (a Native American term meaning "snow eaters") sometimes sweep across the plains just east of the Rocky Mountains. These winds carry air from high in the mountains down to the plains rapidly enough that the air has no time to exchange significant heat with its surroundings (Fig. 21-28). On the day of a Chinook wind, pressure and temperature high in the Colorado Rockies are 62.0 kPa and −11.0°C, respectively. (a) What will be the air temperature when the Chinook has carried it to the plain where pressure is 86.5 kPa? (b) How much work is done on what was initially a cubic meter of air as it descends to the plain?

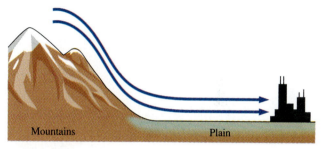

FIGURE 21-28 Chinook winds carry air from the low pressure and low temperature of the high Rocky Mountains to the higher pressure at the plains. How much does the air temperature increase? (Problem 22)

23. A gasoline engine has a compression ratio of 8.5. If the fuel-air mixture enters the engine at 30°C, what will be its temperature at maximum compression? Assume the compression is adiabatic and that the mixture has $\gamma = 1.4$.

24. By how much must the volume of a gas with $\gamma = 1.4$ be changed in an adiabatic process if the pressure is to double?

25. By how much must the volume of a gas with $\gamma = 1.4$ be changed in an adiabatic process if the kelvin temperature is to double?

26. Volvo's B5340 engine, used in the V70 series cars, has a compression ratio of 10.2 (see Example 21-3 for the meaning of this term). If air at 320 K and atmospheric pressure fills an engine cylinder at its maximum volume, (a) what will be the air temperature at the point of maximum compression? (b) What will be the pressure at this point? Assume the compression is adiabatic, with $\gamma = 1.4$.

27. A gas expands isothermally from state A to state B, in the process absorbing 35 J of heat. It is then compressed isobarically to state C, where its volume equals that of state A. During the compression, 22 J of work are done on the gas. The gas is then heated at constant volume until it returns to state A. (a) Draw a PV diagram for this process. (b) How much work is done on or by the gas during the complete cycle? (c) How much heat is transferred to or from the gas as it goes from B to C to A?

28. Derive an equation relating pressure and temperature in an adiabatic process.

29. A 2.0 mol sample of ideal gas with molar specific heat $C_V = \frac{5}{2}R$ is initially at 300 K and 100 kPa pressure. Determine the final temperature and the work done by the gas when 1.5 kJ of heat is added to the gas (a) isothermally, (b) at constant volume, and (c) isobarically.

30. Prove that the slope of an adiabat at a given point in a PV diagram is γ times the slope of the isotherm passing through the same point.

31. An ideal gas with $\gamma = 1.67$ starts at point A in Fig. 21-29, where its volume and pressure are 1.00 m^3 and 250 kPa, respectively. It then undergoes an adiabatic expansion that triples its volume, ending at point B. It's then heated at constant volume to point C, then compressed isothermally back to A. Find (a) the pressure at B, (b) the pressure at C, and (c) the net work done on the gas.

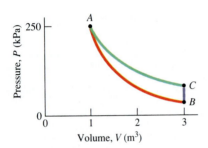

FIGURE 21-29 Problem 31.

32. The gas of Example 21-5 starts at state A in Fig. 21-20 and is compressed adiabatically until its volume is 2.0 L. It's then cooled while maintaining constant pressure until it reaches 300 K, then allowed to expand isothermally back to state A. Find (a) the net work done on the gas and (b) the minimum volume reached.

33. The gas of Example 21-5 starts at state A in Fig. 21-20 and is heated at constant volume until its pressure has doubled. It's then compressed adiabatically until its volume is one-fourth its original value, then cooled at constant volume to 300 K, and finally allowed to expand isothermally to its original state. Find the net work done on the gas.

34. A 25 L sample of an ideal gas with $\gamma = 1.67$ is at 250 K and 50 kPa. The gas is compressed isothermally to one-third of its original volume, then heated at constant volume until its state lies on the adiabatic curve that passes through its original state, and then allowed to expand adiabatically to that original state. Find the net work involved. Is work done on or by the gas?

35. A 25 L sample of an ideal gas with $\gamma = 1.67$ is at 250 K and 50 kPa. The gas is compressed adiabatically until its pressure triples, then cooled at constant volume back to 250 K, and finally allowed to expand iothermally to its original state. (a) How much work is done on the gas? (b) What is the minimum volume reached? (c) Sketch this cyclic process in a PV diagram.

36. A 25 L sample of ideal gas is at 250 K and 50 kPa. The gas is heated at constant volume until its pressure triples, then cooled at constant pressure until its temperature is back to 250 K, and finally allowed to expand isothermally to its original state. (a) How much work is done on the gas? (b) What is the minimum volume reached? (c) Sketch this cyclic process in a PV diagram.

37. A bicycle pump consists of a cylinder 30 cm long when the pump handle is all the way out. The pump contains air ($\gamma = 1.4$) at 20°C. If the pump outlet is blocked and the handle pushed until the internal length of the pump cylinder is 17 cm, by how much does the air temperature rise? Assume that no heat is lost.

38. A tightly sealed flask contains 5.0 L of air at 0°C and 100 kPa pressure. How much heat is required to raise the air temperature to 20°C? The molar specific heat of air at constant volume is 2.5R.

39. A balloon contains 5.0 L of air at 0°C and 100 kPa pressure. How much heat is required to raise the air temperature to 20°C, assuming the gas stays in pressure equilibrium with its surroundings? Neglect tension forces in the balloon. The molar specific heat of air at constant volume is 2.5R.

40. A piston-cylinder system has initial volume 1.0 L and contains ideal gas at 300 K and 1.0 atm, with $C_V = 2.5R$. The piston is held fixed and the cylinder placed in contact with a heat reservoir at 600 K. Once equilibrium is reached, the gas is allowed to expand isothermally. When the pressure reaches 1.0 atm, the gas is cooled at constant pressure to 300 K. This cyclic process is repeated once a second. (a) Draw a PV diagram for the process. (b) What is the rate at which the gas does work?

41. Problem 70 in Chapter 18 shows that pressure as a function of height in Earth's atmosphere is given approximately by $P = P_0 e^{-h/h_0}$, where P_0 is the surface pressure and $h_0 = 8.2$ km. A parcel of air, initially at the surface and at a temperature of 10°C, rises as described in Application: Smog Alert on page 529. (a) What will be its temperature when it reaches 2.0 km altitude? (b) If the temperature of the surrounding air decreases at the normal lapse rate of 6.5°C/km, is the atmosphere stable or unstable under the conditions of this problem?

Section 21-3 Specific Heats of an Ideal Gas

42. A gas mixture contains 2.5 mol O_2 and 3.0 mol Ar. What are the molar specific heats at constant volume and pressure for this mixture?

43. A mixture of monatomic and diatomic gases has specific heat ratio $\gamma = 1.52$. What fraction of the molecules are monatomic?

44. What should be the approximate specific heat ratio of a gas consisting of 50% NO_2 ($\gamma = 1.29$), 30% O_2 ($\gamma = 1.4$), and 20% Ar ($\gamma = 1.67$)?

45. A gas mixture contains monatomic argon and diatomic oxygen. An adiabatic expansion that doubles its volume results in the pressure dropping to one-third of its original value. What fraction of the molecules are argon?

46. You have 2.0 mol of an ideal diatomic gas whose molecules can rotate but not vibrate. Suppose you arrange to give the gas 8.0 kJ of energy in such a way that it all goes initially into translational motion of the molecules. When equilibrium is reached, what will be the gas temperature?

47. How much of a triatomic gas with $C_V = 3R$ would you have to add to 10 mol of monatomic gas to get a mixture whose thermodynamic behavior was like that of a diatomic gas?

48. By how much does the temperature of (a) an ideal monatomic gas and (b) an ideal diatomic gas (with molecular rotation but no vibration) change in an adiabatic process in which 2.5 kJ of work are done on each mole of gas?

Paired Problems

(Both problems in a pair involve the same principles and techniques. If you can get the first problem, you should be able to solve the second one.)

49. A 5.0 mol sample of ideal gas with $C_V = \frac{5}{2}R$ undergoes an expansion during which the gas does 5.1 kJ of work. If it absorbs 2.7 kJ of heat during the process, by how much does its temperature change? *Hint:* Remember that Equation 21-7 holds for *any* ideal gas process.

50. External forces compress 21 mol of ideal monatomic gas; during the process the gas transfers 15 kJ of heat to its surroundings, yet its temperature rises by 160 K. How much work was done on the gas?

51. A gas with $\gamma = \frac{5}{3}$ is at 450 K at the start of an expansion that triples its volume. The expansion is isothermal until the volume has doubled, then adiabatic the rest of the way. What is the final gas temperature?

52. A gas with $\gamma = \frac{7}{5}$ is at 273 K when it's compressed isothermally to one-third of its original volume, then further compressed adiabatically to one-fifth of its original volume. What is its final temperature?

53. An ideal gas with $\gamma = 1.4$ is initially at 273 K and 100 kPa. The gas expands adiabatically until its temperature drops to 190 K. What is its final pressure?

54. An ideal gas with $\gamma = 1.3$ is initially at 273 K and 100 kPa. The gas is compressed adiabatically to 240 kPa pressure. What is its final temperature?

55. The curved path in Fig. 21-30 lies on the 350-K isotherm for an ideal gas with $\gamma = 1.4$. (a) Calculate the net work done on the gas as it goes around the cyclic path *ABCA*. (b) How much heat flows into or out of the gas on the segment *AB*?

56. Repeat part (a) of the preceding problem for the path *ACDA* in Fig. 21-30. (b) How much heat flows into or out of the gas on the segment *CD*?

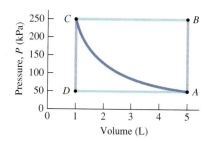

FIGURE 21-30 Problems 55, 56.

Supplementary Problems

57. An 8.5-kg rock at 0°C is dropped into a well-insulated vat containing a mixture of ice and water at 0°C. When equilibrium is reached there are 6.3 g less ice. From what height was the rock dropped?

58. A piston-cylinder arrangement containing 0.30 mol of nitrogen at high pressure is in thermal equilibrium with an ice-water bath containing 200 g of ice. The pressure of the ambient air is 1.0 atm. The gas is allowed to expand isothermally until it is in pressure balance with its surroundings. After the process is complete, the bath contains 210 g of ice. What was the original gas pressure?

59. Repeat Problem 8 for the case when the gas expands along a path given by $P = P_1 \left[1 + \left(\dfrac{V - V_1}{V_1} \right)^2 \right]$. Sketch the path in the *PV* diagram, and determine the work done.

60. A piston-cylinder arrangement contains 1.0 g of water at 50°C. The piston, which has negligible mass, is free to move and is exposed to atmospheric pressure (1.0 atm). The system is heated to 200°C. Assuming that liquid water is incompressible and that steam is an ideal gas with volume specific heat 4.3R, determine (a) the work done by the system and (b) the heat added to it.

61. Show that the application of Equation 21-3 to an adiabatic process results in Equation 21-14.

62. Find an expression for the molar specific heat at constant volume of an ideal gas in terms of its adiabatic exponent γ.

63. An ideal gas is taken clockwise around the circular path shown in Fig. 21-31. (a) How much work does the gas do? (b) If there are 1.3 moles of gas, what is the maximum temperature reached?

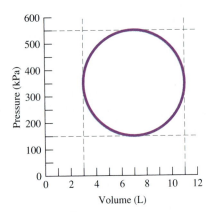

FIGURE 21-31 Problem 63.

64. A piston-cylinder system contains 0.50 mol of hydrogen (H_2) at 400 K and 300 kPa. An identical system contains 0.50 mol of helium (He) under identical conditions. Each gas undergoes an expansion that quadruples the system volume. Calculate the work done by each, if the expansion is (a) isothermal and (b) adiabatic.

65. Show that the work done by a van der Waals gas undergoing isothermal expansion from volume V_1 to V_2 is

$$W = nRT \ln\left(\frac{V_2 - nb}{V_1 - nb}\right) + an^2\left(\frac{1}{V_2} - \frac{1}{V_1}\right),$$

where a and b are the constants in Equation 20-5.

66. The compression and rarefaction in a sound wave occur fast enough that very little heat flow occurs, making the process essentially adiabatic. Show in this case that the bulk modulus (Equation 17-5) becomes $B = \gamma P$, and then show that Equation 17-6 leads to Equation 17-1 for the sound speed. *Hint:* Write Equation 17-5 in derivative form:

$$B = -V\frac{dP}{dV}.$$

67. A horizontal piston-cylinder system containing n mol of ideal gas is surrounded by air at temperature T_0 and pressure P_0. If the piston is displaced slightly from equilibrium, show that it executes simple harmonic motion with angular frequency $\omega = AP_0/\sqrt{MnRT_0}$, where A and M are the piston area and mass, respectively. Assume the gas temperature remains constant.

68. Repeat the preceding problem, now assuming that no heat flows into or out of the gas.

69. A cylinder of cross-sectional area A is closed by a massless piston. The cylinder contains n mol of ideal gas with specific heat ratio γ, and is initially in equilibrium with the surrounding air at temperature T_0 and pressure P_0. The piston is initially at height h_1 above the bottom of the cylinder. Sand is gradually sprinkled onto the piston until it has moved downward to a final height h_2. Find the total mass of the sand if the process is (a) isothermal and (b) adiabatic.

The Second Law of Thermodynamics

22

A power plant's cooling towers transfer waste heat to the environment. In a typical power plant, two-thirds of the energy released from the fuel ends up as waste heat—a consequence of the second law of thermodynamics.

T he first law of thermodynamics relates heat and other forms of energy. Much of our world works because of this relation. Cars run on energy extracted from the heat of burning gasoline. Most of the electrical energy that powers lights and motors and computers originates in heat released in burning fuels or fissioning uranium. Our own bodies run on energy that was once released as heat deep in the Sun's core. But the first law doesn't tell the whole story. Heat and mechanical energy are not exactly the same thing, and the difference between them makes the conversion of heat to work a more subtle task than the first law alone would imply.

Time ➡
(a)

(b)

FIGURE 22-1 A movie of a bouncing ball makes sense whether it's shown forward or backward.

Time ➡
(a)

(b)

FIGURE 22-2 Movie of a block warming as friction dissipates its kinetic energy. The reverse sequence would never happen, even though it does not violate energy conservation.

22-1 REVERSIBILITY AND IRREVERSIBILITY

Figure 22-1 shows a movie of a bouncing ball. We can run it forward or backward and still have a plausible sequence of physical events. Figure 22-2 shows a movie of another simple physical process. A block slides along a table, eventually coming to a stop. Friction warms the block, so we see its temperature rise. Play this one in reverse, and it makes no sense. We never see a block at rest suddenly start to move, cooling in the process. Yet energy could be conserved if it did, so the first law of thermodynamics would be satisfied.

Beat an egg, and the yolk and white quickly blend. You would be surprised if, on reversing the beater, the scrambled yolk and white separated—yet nothing in the laws of mechanics would prevent it. Or put cups of cold and hot water in thermal contact. The hot water gets colder, and the cold water gets hotter. The reverse never occurs—even though energy would be conserved if it did.

Most events are **irreversible**, in the sense of the block, the egg, and the water. What is the origin of this irreversibility? In each case we start with matter in an organized state. In the sliding block all molecules share a common motion. The egg is organized so all the yolk molecules are in one place. The hot water has a greater number of energetic molecules. Of all the possible states into which matter might arrange itself, these *organized* states are relatively rare. There are many more *chaotic* states—for instance, all the possible arrangements of molecules in a scrambled egg—that have less organization. When a system evolves, chances are it will end up in a less organized state, simply because there are far more such states available to it. It's then very unlikely to assume spontaneously a more organized state.

A key word here is *spontaneous.* We could restore a system to a more organized state—for example, by putting one cup of lukewarm water on the stove and the other in the refrigerator—but then we have to carry out a rather deliberate and energy-consuming process.

Thermodynamic processes can also be irreversible, as we discussed in the preceding chapter. Plunging a cool gas sample into boiling water, for example, creates a temporarily more organized state in which the gas is separated into a hotter region—i.e., a region of higher mean molecular energy—right near the container walls and a cooler region in the interior (recall Fig. 21-6). But this is not a state of thermodynamic equilibrium, and molecular collisions soon equalize the mean molecular energy throughout the gas, restoring thermodynamic equilibrium. At the same time, the organization represented by separate hotter and cooler regions disappears. A spontaneous return to the organized state is highly improbable, and in this sense the process is irreversible.

Irreversibility is a probabilistic notion. Events that *could* occur without violating the principles of Newtonian physics nevertheless *don't* occur because they're too improbable. A practical consequence is that it's difficult to harness the considerable energy tied up as internal energy associated with random molecular motions because those motions won't spontaneously become organized. That makes much of the world's energy unavailable for doing useful work.

22-2 THE SECOND LAW OF THERMODYNAMICS

Heat Engines

It is impossible to convert *all* the internal energy of a system to useful work. But devices called **heat engines** can extract *some* of that internal energy. Examples of

FIGURE 22-3 (*a*) Energy flow diagram for a perfect heat engine, which extracts heat Q from a reservoir and delivers an equal amount of work. (*b*) A real engine delivers as work only a fraction of the heat Q_h extracted from the high-temperature reservoir; the remainder is rejected to the low-temperature reservoir.

heat engines include gasoline and diesel engines, fossil-fueled and nuclear power plants, and jet aircraft engines.

Conceptually, we characterize a heat engine with a diagram showing heat flowing into the engine and work emerging. Figure 22-3*a* is such an energy-flow diagram for a "perfect" heat engine—one that extracts heat from a heat reservoir and converts it all to work. Such an engine would do exactly what we argued against in the preceding section—it would convert the random energy of thermal motion entirely into the ordered motion associated with mechanical work. In fact a perfect heat engine is impossible, for the same reason that we can't unscramble an egg or cause a block to accelerate spontaneously at the expense of its internal energy. This fact comprises one statement of the **second law of thermodynamics**:

> *Second law of thermodynamics (Kelvin-Planck statement): It is impossible to construct a heat engine operating in a cycle that extracts heat from a reservoir and delivers an equal amount of work.*

This version of the second law was formulated by Lord Kelvin and Max Planck. The phrase "in a cycle" means that a practical engine must go through a repeated sequence of steps, as in the back-and-forth motions of the pistons in a gasoline engine.

A simple heat engine consists of a gas-cylinder system and a heat reservoir, the latter kept hot, perhaps, by burning a fuel. With the gas initially at high pressure, we place the cylinder in contact with the heat reservoir. The gas expands and does work W on the piston. In this isothermal process, the gas extracts heat $Q = W$ from the reservoir. Eventually the gas reaches pressure equilibrium and stops expanding. The piston must then be returned to its original position if it's to do more work.

If we just push the piston back, we'll have to do as much work as was extracted during the expansion, and our engine will produce no net work. Instead we can cool the gas to reduce its volume, through thermal contact with a cool reservoir. But then some energy leaves the system as heat rather than work, as shown conceptually in Fig. 22-3*b*. Our engine extracts heat from a source and delivers mechanical work, but over a full cycle the amount of work is always less than the heat extracted. The remaining energy is rejected to the lower temperature reservoir, usually the environment. In practical terms, much of the energy

(a)

(b)

FIGURE 22-4 Real heat engines necessarily reject heat to the environment. (a) Water circulates through a car engine, absorbing waste heat, then on through the car's radiator. The radiator, a system of thin tubes exposed to the flow of air through the car's front grille, transfers waste heat to the air. Here a motorist adds antifreeze to the cooling water. (b) Power plants usually transfer waste heat to a nearby body of water. This infrared photo shows hot water (red) discharged from a power plant at the right end of the photo; black areas represent land, while yellow and gray regions are cooler parts of the river. Downstream is to the left.

released from fuels in car engines and power plants ends up as waste heat (Fig. 22-4).

The second law of thermodynamics states that we can't build a perfect heat engine. But how close can we come? Since we pay for the fuel that heats the high-temperature reservoir, it's clearly advantageous to minimize the rejected heat. We define the **efficiency** of an engine as the ratio of work W output by the engine in one cycle to the heat Q_h absorbed from the high-temperature reservoir,

$$e = \frac{W}{Q_h}.$$

Since the process is cyclic, there's no net change in internal energy over one cycle. Then the first law of thermodynamics, $\Delta U = Q - W$, ensures that the work done is the difference between the heat Q_h extracted from the high-temperature reservoir and the heat Q_c rejected to the cool reservoir. So the efficiency is

$$e = \frac{Q_h - Q_c}{Q_h} = 1 - \frac{Q_c}{Q_h}. \tag{22-1}$$

Figure 22-5 shows a simple heat engine whose efficiency we can readily calculate. The engine consists of a cylinder containing an ideal gas, sealed by a movable piston. The piston is connected to a rod that drives a wheel; as the piston goes back and forth, the wheel turns continually. The engine gets its energy from a heat reservoir maintained at a high temperature T_h, and it rejects heat to a cooler reservoir at temperature T_c.

Figure 22-6 shows how the engine works. It starts with the piston in its leftmost position, so the gas volume is at its minimum. This state is point A in the PV diagram of Fig. 22-6. At this point, we bring the high-temperature reservoir into thermal contact with the cylinder. The gas absorbs an amount of heat Q_h from the

FIGURE 22-5 A simple heat engine. The gas absorbs heat from the hot reservoir, does work on the piston and wheel, and rejects heat to the cool reservoir. The two heat reservoirs can be moved to bring either one into thermal contact with the cylinder.

FIGURE 22-6 *PV* diagram for the engine of Fig. 22-5. *AB* and *DC* are isotherms at the temperatures of the hot and cool reservoirs, respectively; *AD* and *BC* are adiabatic curves.

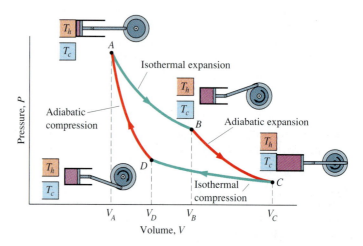

hot reservoir and expands isothermally along path AB in the PV diagram. Since the temperature remains constant during this process, so does the internal energy. The first law then shows that the engine does work $W = Q$ on the piston and wheel. At state B, we remove the hot reservoir. The expansion is now adiabatic, and follows path BC in the PV diagram. We design the engine so that, when the piston reaches its rightmost position, the gas temperature has cooled to T_c. This state is point C in the PV diagram, and is the state of maximum gas volume. We then bring the cool reservoir into thermal contact with the cylinder. The wheel's inertia keeps it turning, and the wheel does work on the gas, compressing it isothermally from state C to state D. This work ends up as heat rejected to the cool reservoir. Finally, at state D, we remove the cool reservoir from contact with the cylinder and allow the compression to continue adiabatically until the gas temperature has risen to T_h and the piston is once again in its leftmost position, with the gas compressed to its minimum volume. ActivPhysics Activity 8.14 provides a simulation of the entire cycle that shows this process more clearly than can a drawn picture.

8.14
ActivPhysics
Carnot Cycle

The engine we have just described undergoes a cyclic process consisting of four reversible steps, two isothermal and two adiabatic. This cycle is called a **Carnot cycle**, and the engine a **Carnot engine**, after the French engineer Sadi Carnot (1796–1832), who explored the properties of such an engine even before the first law of thermodynamics was formulated. The particular configuration of the engine is not important, nor is the choice of an ideal gas as the engine's **working fluid**. What distinguishes the Carnot cycle from others is the sequence of thermodynamic processes and the fact that these processes are reversible. The Carnot engine is an example of a **reversible engine**—one in which thermodynamic equilibrium is maintained so that all steps could, in principle, be reversed.

What is the efficiency of a Carnot engine? To find out, we need the heats Q_h and Q_c absorbed and rejected during the isothermal parts of the cycle shown in Fig. 22-6. We developed Equation 21-4 to deal with such isothermal processes. Applying that equation gives the heat Q_h absorbed during the isothermal expansion AB:

$$Q_h = nRT_h \ln\left(\frac{V_B}{V_A}\right),$$

and the heat Q_c rejected during the isothermal compression CD:

$$Q_c = -nRT_c \ln\left(\frac{V_D}{V_C}\right) = nRT_c \ln\left(\frac{V_C}{V_D}\right).$$

We put the minus sign here because our statement of the first law describes Q as the heat *absorbed*, while Equation 22-1 for the engine efficiency requires that Q_c be the heat *rejected*. To calculate engine efficiency according to Equation 22-1, we need the ratio Q_c/Q_h:

$$\frac{Q_c}{Q_h} = \frac{T_c \ln(V_C/V_D)}{T_h \ln(V_B/V_A)}. \tag{22-2}$$

This expression can be simplified by applying Equation 21-13b to the adiabatic processes BC and DA in the Carnot cycle:

$$T_h V_B^{\gamma-1} = T_c V_C^{\gamma-1} \quad \text{and} \quad T_h V_A^{\gamma-1} = T_c V_D^{\gamma-1}.$$

Dividing these two equations gives

$$\left(\frac{V_B}{V_A}\right)^{\gamma-1} = \left(\frac{V_C}{V_D}\right)^{\gamma-1} \quad \text{or} \quad \frac{V_B}{V_A} = \frac{V_C}{V_D},$$

so Equation 22-2 becomes simply

$$\frac{Q_c}{Q_h} = \frac{T_c}{T_h}.$$

Using this result in Equation 22-1 then gives the efficiency of the Carnot engine:

$$e_{\text{Carnot}} = 1 - \frac{T_c}{T_h}, \tag{22-3}$$

where the temperatures are measured on an absolute scale (Kelvin or Rankine). Equation 22-3 tells us that the efficiency of a Carnot engine depends only on the highest and lowest temperatures of the working fluid. For a practical engine, the low temperature is usually the ambient temperature of the environment. Then to maximize the efficiency, we must make the high temperature as high as possible. Real engines represent a compromise between efficiency and the ability of materials to withstand high temperatures and pressures.

EXAMPLE 22-1   A Carnot Engine

A Carnot engine extracts 240 J of heat from a high-temperature reservoir during each cycle. It rejects 100 J of heat to a reservoir at 15°C. How much work does the engine do in one cycle? What is its efficiency? What is the temperature of the hot reservoir?

Solution
The first law of thermodynamics requires that energy not rejected as heat be delivered as work, so the engine does

$$W = 240 \text{ J} - 100 \text{ J} = 140 \text{ J}$$

of work. The efficiency is defined by Equation 22-1 as the ratio of work to heat extracted from the hot reservoir:

$$e = \frac{W}{Q_h} = \frac{140 \text{ J}}{240 \text{ J}} = 0.583 = 58.3\%.$$

Knowing the efficiency, we can solve Equation 22-3 for the high temperature to get

$$T_h = \frac{T_c}{1 - e} = \frac{288 \text{ K}}{1 - 0.583} = 691 \text{ K} = 418°C.$$

Note that in using Equation 22-3 we must work with absolute temperatures.

EXERCISE A Carnot engine operates between heat reservoirs at 520 K and 280 K. (a) What is its efficiency? (b) If it produces useful work at the rate of 400 W, at what rate does it reject waste heat?

Answers: (a) 46%; (b) 467 W

Some problems similar to Example 22-1: 5–8

Engines, Refrigerators, and the Second Law

Why are we putting so much emphasis on one particular device, namely the Carnot engine? Because our understanding of the Carnot engine will lead to insights into the broader question of how much useful work we can hope to extract from the internal thermal energy of *any* system. That, in turn, will help us to understand practical limitations on humankind's attempts to harness even more energy, and will ultimately bring us to a deeper and more universal understanding of the second law of thermodynamics.

So why is the Carnot engine so special? Couldn't we build a different kind of engine with greater efficiency? The answer is no. The special role of the Carnot cycle is embodied in **Carnot's theorem**:

> **Carnot's theorem: All reversible Carnot engines operating between temperatures T_h and T_c have the same efficiency (given by Equation 22-3), and no other engine operating between the same two temperatures can have a greater efficiency.**

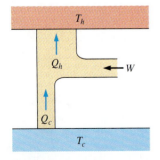

FIGURE 22-7 Energy flow diagram for a real refrigerator. The device takes in mechanical work and transfers heat from the cool to the hot reservoir.

To prove Carnot's theorem, we introduce the **refrigerator**. A refrigerator is the opposite of an engine: It extracts heat from a cool reservoir and rejects it to a hotter one, taking in work in the process (Fig. 22-7). A refrigerator forces heat

FIGURE 22-8 A perfect refrigerator would require no work to transfer heat from a cool object to a hotter one. The second law of thermodynamics rules out such a device.

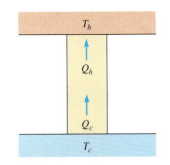

to flow the way it doesn't spontaneously go—from cold to hot—but to do so it requires work. A household refrigerator cools its contents and warms the house (you can feel the heat coming out the back), but in the process it uses electricity. That heat doesn't flow spontaneously from cold to hot constitutes another statement of the second law of thermodynamics, this one due to the German physicist Rudolph Clausius (1822–1888):

> **Second law of thermodynamics (Clausius statement): It is impossible to construct a refrigerator operating in a cycle whose sole effect is to transfer heat from a cooler object to a hotter one.**

The Clausius statement rules out a "perfect" refrigerator, like that shown in Fig. 22-8.

Suppose the Clausius statement were false. Then we could build the device of Fig. 22-9a, consisting of a reversible Carnot engine and a perfect refrigerator. In each cycle the engine would extract, say, 100 J from the hot reservoir, put out 60 J of useful work, and reject 40 J to the cool reservoir. The perfect refrigerator could transfer the 40 J back to the hot reservoir. The net effect would then be to extract 60 J from the hot reservoir and convert it entirely to work (Fig. 22-9b)—and we would have a perfect heat engine, in violation of the Kelvin-Planck statement of the second law. A similar argument shows that if a perfect heat engine is possible, so is a perfect refrigerator (see Problem 27). So the Clausius and Kelvin-Planck statements of the second law of thermodynamics are equivalent, in that if one is false then so is the other.

Because the Carnot engine is reversible, we could run it backward and reverse its path in the *PV* diagram of Fig. 22-6. Each process would run in reverse, and the engine would extract heat from the cool reservoir, take in work, and reject heat to the hot reservoir. It would be a refrigerator. Although real refrigerators are not designed exactly like engines, the two are, in principle, interchangeable.

We're now ready to prove Carnot's assertion that Equation 22-3 gives the maximum engine efficiency. Consider again the Carnot engine shown in Fig. 22-9a. It extracts 100 J of heat and delivers 60 J of work, so it's 60% efficient. Suppose we had another engine operating between the same two reservoirs, but with 70% efficiency. Since the Carnot engine is reversible, we can run it as a refrigerator. If we then put the two together, we get the device of Fig. 22-10a. Its

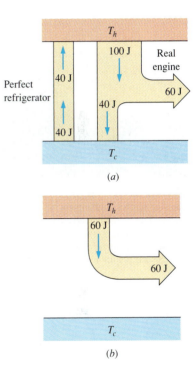

FIGURE 22-9 (a) A real heat engine combined with a perfect refrigerator. (b) The combination is equivalent to a perfect heat engine.

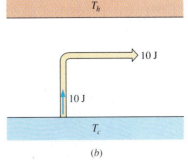

FIGURE 22-10 (a) A 60% efficient reversible engine run as a refrigerator, along with a hypothetical engine with 70% efficiency. (b) The combination is equivalent to a perfect heat engine delivering 10 J per cycle.

net effect is to extract 10 J of heat from the cool reservoir and deliver 10 J of work—so it's a perfect heat engine, in violation of the second law (Fig. 22-10*b*). We could make the same argument for any combination of a reversible Carnot engine and another, more efficient engine. It's therefore impossible to make an engine that's more efficient than a reversible Carnot engine, and thus, Equation 22-3 gives the maximum possible efficiency for *any* heat engine operating between the same two fixed temperatures.

Irreversible engines, because they involve processes that dissipate organized motion, are necessarily *less* efficient. So are many reversible engines, if their heat exchange does not take place solely at the highest and lowest temperatures available (see Problem 54). The ordinary gasoline engine is a case in point; even if it could be made perfectly reversible, its efficiency would be less than that of a comparable Carnot engine (see Problem 61).

22-3 APPLICATIONS OF THE SECOND LAW OF THERMODYNAMICS

The world abounds with thermal energy, but the second law of thermodynamics imposes a fundamental limitation on our ability to turn that energy to our own uses. Any device we construct that involves the interchange of heat and work is a heat engine or refrigerator, and is therefore subject to the second law.

Limitations on Heat Engines

FIGURE 22-11 A nuclear power plant, showing reactor containment vessel at left, and large cooling towers at right. The cooling towers transfer some waste heat to the air, reducing but not eliminating thermal pollution of adjoining waters.

Most of the electricity used in the United States is produced in large power plants that are basically heat engines powered by fossil fuels such as coal, oil, or natural gas, or by nuclear fission of uranium (Fig. 22-11). Figure 22-12 shows a schematic diagram of such a power plant. The working fluid is water, heated in a boiler and converted to steam at high pressure. The steam expands adiabatically against the blades of a turbine—a fanlike device that spins when struck by the steam. The turbine turns a generator that converts mechanical work into electrical energy (more on this in Chapter 31).

Steam leaving the turbine is still in the gaseous state, and is hotter than the water supplied to the boiler. Here's where the second law enters! Had the water

FIGURE 22-12 Schematic diagram of a typical electric power plant. Temperature of the working fluid (steam/water) is indicated at three points. $T_2 < T_1$ because the turbine has converted some of the steam's internal energy into mechanical work. $T_3 < T_2$ because the condenser has extracted additional internal energy and rejected it as waste heat. More significant is the energy extraction associated with the phase change from gas to liquid in the condenser; this energy, too, is sent to the environment as waste heat.

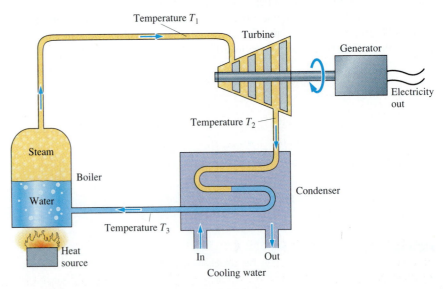

returned to its original state, we would have extracted as work all the energy acquired in the boiler, in violation of the second law. To use the steam again, we run it through a **condenser**—a device where pipes carrying the steam are in contact with large volumes of cool water, typically from a river, lake, or ocean. The condensed steam, now cool water, is fed back into the boiler to repeat the cycle.

The maximum steam temperature in a power plant is limited by the materials used in its construction. For a fossil-fueled plant, current technology permits high temperatures around 650 K. Potential damage to nuclear fuel rods limits the temperature in a nuclear plant to around 570 K. Cooling-water temperature averages about 40°C (310 K), so the maximum possible efficiencies for these power plants, given by Equation 22-3, are

$$e_{fossil} = 1 - \frac{310 \text{ K}}{650 \text{ K}} = 0.52 = 52\%$$

and

$$e_{nuclear} = 1 - \frac{310 \text{ K}}{570 \text{ K}} = 0.46 = 46\% .$$

Temperature differences between the exhausted steam and the cooling water, mechanical friction, and the need to divert energy for driving pumps and pollution control devices all reduce efficiency further, to about 40% for fossil-fueled plants and 34% for nuclear plants. This means that, when we make electricity, roughly two-thirds of the fuel energy released ends up as waste heat.

A typical large power plant produces 1000 MW of electricity, so another 2000 MW of waste heat is dumped into the cooling water. This rate of energy addition can cause a large temperature rise in even a major river, and can lead to serious ecological problems. The need for power plant cooling water—imposed on us by the second law of thermodynamics—is so great that a substantial fraction of all rainwater falling on the United States eventually finds its way through the condensers of power plants (see Problem 13).

To reduce this "thermal pollution," power plants employ cooling towers—expensive devices which release waste heat to the air rather than to water. Environmental effects of the heat released to the air are less serious than with heated water, although the increase in humidity can bring about unfortunate changes in local weather (Fig. 22-13).

FIGURE 22-13 Fog forms above the cooling towers of a large coal-fired electric power plant.

EXAMPLE 22-2	*Vermont Yankee*

The Vermont Yankee nuclear power plant at Vernon, Vermont, produces 540 MW of electric power, while energy from nuclear fission is released as heat at the rate of 1590 MW. Steam produced in the reactor enters the turbine at a temperature of 556 K and is discharged to the condenser at 313 K. Water from the Connecticut River is pumped through the condenser at the rate of 2.27×10^4 kg/s.

What is the maximum efficiency of the power plant, as limited by the second law of thermodynamics? What is the actual efficiency? How much does the temperature of the cooling water rise? How many houses like that of Example 19-5 could be heated with the waste heat from Vermont Yankee?

Solution

The second-law efficiency is given by Equation 22-3:

$$e = 1 - \frac{T_c}{T_h} = 1 - \frac{313 \text{ K}}{556 \text{ K}} = 0.437 = 43.7\% .$$

The actual efficiency is the ratio of electric power output to the rate of heat extraction from the nuclear fuel:

$$e = \frac{dW/dt}{dQ_h/dt} = \frac{540 \text{ MW}}{1590 \text{ MW}} = 0.340 = 34.0\% .$$

Waste heat is discharged to the river at a rate given by the difference between the thermal power output and the electric power output:

$$\frac{dQ_c}{dt} = \frac{dQ_h}{dt} - \frac{dW}{dt} = 1590 \text{ MW} - 540 \text{ MW} = 1050 \text{ MW} .$$

We can relate the waste power output to the temperature rise using Equation 19-5:

$$\Delta T = \frac{\Delta Q_c}{mc} = \frac{dQ_c/dt}{c\ dm/dt}$$

$$= \frac{1050 \times 10^6\ \text{W}}{(4184\ \text{J/kg·°C})(2.27 \times 10^4\ \text{kg/s})} = 11.1°\text{C},$$

where we used the given values of heat and mass per unit time for the ratio $\Delta Q/m$. The house of Example 19-5 uses 7926 Btu/h, or 2.3×10^{-3} MW. Then the waste heat from Vermont Yankee could heat $(1050\ \text{MW})/(2.4 \times 10^{-3}\ \text{MW/house}) = 457{,}000$ houses. This number is unrealistic because most houses aren't as energy efficient as the one in Example 19-5; nevertheless, it shows that waste heat from power plants is a potentially valuable source for heating buildings.

EXERCISE A 40% efficient coal-fired power plant produces 1100 MW of electric power. (a) If spent steam leaves the turbine at 350 K, what is the lowest possible value for the steam temperature as it leaves the boiler? (b) If the plant is cooled with essentially the entire 4.4×10^4-kg/s flow of a river, by how much does the river temperature rise?

Answers: (a) 583 K; (b) 9.0°C

Some problems similar to Example 22-2: 10–12, 47, 48, 60

FIGURE 22-14 Artist's conception of an OTEC power plant.

Gasoline and diesel engines provide another pervasive example of heat engines. A typical automobile engine has a theoretical maximum efficiency of just over 50%, but irreversible thermodynamic processes make the actual efficiency much lower. Mechanical friction dissipates additional energy, and the end result is that less than 20% of the fuel energy is available at the driving wheels. Problems 61 and 62 explore the thermodynamics of the gasoline engine.

We wouldn't be so concerned with efficiency if we didn't have to pay for fuel. Even a very small temperature difference can drive a heat engine, although with low efficiency. Surface temperatures in the tropical oceans are around 25°C (298 K), while hundreds of meters down the water temperature is only about 5°C (278 K). A heat engine operating between these temperatures would have an efficiency of only 1 − 278 K/298 K = 0.07 or 7%. Nevertheless, there are large amounts of warm ocean water, and its energy—solar in origin—is free. Substantial engineering problems remain before such **ocean thermal energy conversion** (OTEC) becomes practical, but pilot plants are already being tested (Fig. 22-14).

Another solar-powered heat engine uses mirrors to concentrate sunlight, heating a fluid and driving a turbine. Several hundred megawatts of such **solar-thermal power plants** have been built in California, and are generating power at rates just a few cents above those of conventional power plants (Fig. 22-15).

FIGURE 22-15 This solar-thermal power plant in California's Mojave Desert generates 90 MW of electricity. Sun-tracking parabolic reflectors concentrate sunlight on pipes carrying synthetic oil, which then transfers the energy to boil water that drives a steam turbine.

Refrigerators and Heat Pumps

Reversing a heat engine gives a refrigerator, which takes in mechanical work and transfers heat from cooler to hotter (Fig. 22-16). The heat coming out the back of your home refrigerator comprises both the energy removed from the refrigerator's contents as well as the energy that was supplied as electricity to run the refrigerator. A well-designed refrigerator should minimize the amount of work (or its equivalent, electrical energy) needed to extract a given amount of heat. But again, the second law of thermodynamics imposes limitations on even the best refrigerator.

The **coefficient of performance** (COP) is the ratio of heat extracted at the lower temperature to work input by a refrigerator:

$$\text{COP} = \frac{Q_c}{W} = \frac{Q_c}{Q_h - Q_c}. \tag{22-4}$$

For a reversible Carnot engine, we found in deriving Equation 22-3 that the heat ratio Q_c/Q_h is equal to the temperature ratio T_c/T_h. The best refrigerator we can build operates in a reversible Carnot cycle, so for this refrigerator the heat and temperature ratios are also equal. Then the COP becomes

$$COP = \frac{T_c}{T_h - T_c}.$$ (22-5)

As the high and low temperatures become arbitrarily close, Equation 22-5 shows that the COP becomes large—meaning that the refrigerator requires relatively little work to do its job. But if we wish to effect heat transfer between two widely separated temperatures, then the COP drops and the work becomes considerable. In the limit of very large T_h, the COP approaches zero, indicating that we're simply converting mechanical work into a nearly equal amount of heat, and transferring very little additional heat from the cool reservoir. In operating a real refrigerator, we would like to minimize the work needed. But Equation 22-5—like Equation 22-3 for a heat engine—imposes a fundamental limitation on that minimum amount of work.

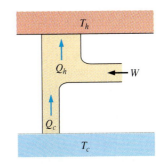

FIGURE 22-16 Energy flow diagram for a refrigerator.

EXAMPLE 22-3 | A Home Freezer

A typical home freezer operates between a low of 0°F (-18°C) and a high of 86°F (30°C). What is the maximum possible COP of this freezer? With this COP, how much electrical energy would be required to freeze 500 g of water, initially at 0°C?

Solution

Equation 22-5 gives the COP:

$$COP = \frac{T_c}{T_h - T_c} = \frac{255 \text{ K}}{303 \text{ K} - 255 \text{ K}} = 5.3.$$

To produce 500 g of ice takes

$$Q_c = mL_f = (0.50 \text{ kg})(334 \text{ kJ/kg}) = 170 \text{ kJ},$$

where we obtained the heat of fusion from Table 20-1. This Q_c is the heat that must be removed from the low-temperature end

of the freezer. The COP is the ratio of the heat removed to the work done, so

$$W = \frac{Q_c}{COP} = \frac{170 \text{ kJ}}{5.3} = 32 \text{ kJ}.$$

In a real freezer, the COP would be lower, and the work correspondingly higher, because of irreversible processes in the refrigeration cycle.

EXERCISE (a) What is the COP of a refrigerator that maintains its interior at 4°C while exhausting heat at 40°C? (b) At what average rate does the refrigerator consume electricity if it extracts heat from its contents at the rate of 300 W?

Answers: (a) 7.7; (b) 39 W

Some problems similar to Example 22-3: 16–20

Refrigerators are not confined to kitchens. An air conditioner is a refrigerator designed to cool an entire room or building. A heat pump is a refrigerator that cools a building in the summer and heats it in the winter (Fig. 22-17). Heat pumps are widely used in the southern United States, where in winter they pump energy from the cool outside air to the warm house. A heat pump requires electricity, but it supplies more energy as heat than it uses in electricity. The excess energy comes from the outdoor environment. Heat pumps operating from the constant 10°C temperature found two meters below the ground have been used for years in Scandinavian countries and are becoming more popular in the northern United States and Canada.

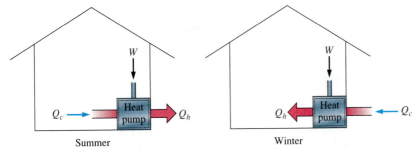

Summer   Winter

FIGURE 22-17 A heat pump. In summer the device acts as a refrigerator that cools the house interior by transferring heat to the outdoor environment. In winter its operation reverses, so it pumps heat from outdoors into the house. The work, W, is typically in the form of electricity.

EXAMPLE 22-4	A Heat Pump

A Carnot heat pump extracts energy from the ground at 10°C and transfers it to water at 70°C. The water is circulated to heat a building. (a) What is the COP of the heat pump? (b) What is its electrical power consumption if it supplies heat at the rate of 20 kW? (c) Compare the operating cost of the heat pump with that of an oil furnace if oil costs 93¢ per gallon and electricity costs 10¢ per kWh. (A gallon of oil releases about 30 kWh of heat when burned.)

Solution

Equation 22-5 gives the COP:

$$\text{COP} = \frac{T_c}{T_h - T_c} = \frac{283 \text{ K}}{343 \text{ K} - 283 \text{ K}} = 4.7 \,.$$

Equation 22-4 shows what this means: for every kWh of electricity used, the pump transfers an additional 4.7 kWh of heat from the ground, providing a total of 5.7 kWh. The pump supplies heat at the rate of 20 kW, so the electrical power needed is

$$P_{\text{electric}} = \frac{20 \text{ kW}}{5.7} = 3.5 \text{ kW} \,.$$

At 10¢/kWh, it costs 35¢ per hour to run the pump. Since oil supplies 30 kWh/gallon, we would need to burn two-thirds of a gallon per hour to get 20 kW, at a cost of $(\frac{2}{3}$ gal/h$)(93$¢/gal$)$ = 62¢ per hour.

Real heat pumps run at closer to half their theoretical maximum COP, and initial installation costs are much more expensive than for oil heat, so economics do not necessarily favor heat pumps.

If we're concerned about energy and not just cost, we should also consider the source of electricity. If this is a thermal power plant operating at an efficiency of, say, 33%, then the power plant uses three units of fuel energy for each unit it supplies to the heat pump. The overall efficiency of heat pump and power plant could actually be less than that of the oil furnace (see Problem 24).

EXERCISE A house requires 12 kW of heating power. If electricity costs 8.5¢/kWh, what is the minimum COP required if a heat pump is to operate for less than $5 per day?

Answer: 3.9

Some problems similar to Example 22-4: 22, 23, 63

22-4 THE THERMODYNAMIC TEMPERATURE SCALE

None of the practical thermometers we introduced in Chapter 19 works at all temperatures; even helium gas thermometers become useless below about 1 K.

The operation of a reversible Carnot engine between two fixed temperatures provides another way of measuring temperature that works at *any* temperature. Measuring the heats Q_c and Q_h, or one of these and the work output, allows us to calculate the temperature ratio. If one temperature is known, we can then determine the other. Although this may seem a rather obscure way to measure temperature, it is actually used in certain experiments at very low temperature. And it provides an absolute way of defining temperature that can, in principle, be used at any temperature. The temperature scale so defined is called the **thermodynamic temperature scale**.

The zero of the thermodynamic scale—**absolute zero**—is absolute in that it represents a state of maximum order. This is reflected in the fact that a heat engine rejecting heat at absolute zero would operate at 100% efficiency, as suggested by Equation 22-3 with $T_c = 0$. Unfortunately, there are no heat reservoirs at absolute zero, and it can be shown that it is impossible to cool anything to this temperature in a finite number of steps. The statement that it is impossible to reach absolute zero in a finite number of steps is called the **third law of thermodynamics**.

22-5 ENTROPY AND THE QUALITY OF ENERGY

If offered a joule of energy, would you rather have it delivered in the form of mechanical work, heat from an object at 1000 K, or heat from an object at 300 K? Your answer might depend on what you want to do. To lift or accelerate a mass, you would be smart to take your energy as work. But if you want to keep warm, then heat from the 300 K object would be perfectly acceptable.

If, on the other hand, you're not sure what you want to do with the energy, then which should you take? The second law of thermodynamics makes the answer clear: you should take the work. Why? Because you could use it directly as mechanical energy, or you could, through friction or other irreversible processes, use it to raise the temperature of something.

If you chose 300-K heat for your joule of energy, then you could supply a full joule only to objects cooler than 300 K. You couldn't do mechanical work unless you ran a heat engine. With its maximum temperature only a little above ambient, your engine would be very inefficient, and you could only extract a small fraction of a joule of mechanical energy. Nor could you heat anything hotter than 300 K, unless you ran a refrigerator—and that would take additional work. You would be better off with 1000-K heat since you could transfer it to anything cooler than 1000 K, or could run a heat engine to produce up to 0.70 joule of mechanical energy.

Taking your energy in the form of work gives you the most options. Anything you can do with a joule of energy, you can do with the work. Heat is less versatile, with 300-K heat the least useful of the three. We're not talking here about the quantity of energy—we have exactly one joule in each case—but about **energy quality**, indicated by its ability to do a variety of useful tasks. Schematically, we can describe energy quality on a diagram like Fig. 22-18. We can readily convert an entire amount of energy from higher to lower quality, but the second law of thermodynamics prevents us from going in the opposite direction with 100% efficiency.

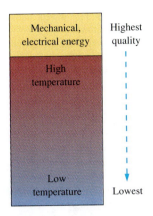

FIGURE 22-18 Energy quality measures the versatility of different energy forms. Electrical energy ranks with mechanical energy because it flows without the need for a temperature difference, thus qualifying as work.

APPLICATION	*Energy Quality, End Use, and Cogeneration*

Energy quality has important implications for our efficient use of energy, suggesting that we try to match the quality of available energy sources to our energy needs. Figure 22-19 shows a breakdown of United States energy use by quality; it makes clear that much of our energy demand is for relatively low-quality heat. Although we can do anything we want with a high-quality energy source like flowing water or electricity, it makes sense to put our high-quality energy to high-quality uses, and use lower-quality sources to meet other needs. For example, we often heat water with electricity—a great convenience to the homeowner, but a thermodynamic folly, for in so doing we convert the highest-quality form of energy into low-grade heat. If our electricity comes from a thermal power plant, we already threw away two-thirds of the energy from fuel as waste heat. It makes little sense to run an elaborate and inefficient heat engine only to have its high-quality output of electricity used for low-temperature heating. On the other hand, if we heat our water by burning a fuel directly at the water heater, then we can, in principle, transfer all the fuel's energy to the water. Another approach to matching energy quality with energy needs is to combine the production of steam for heating with the generation of electricity. Used in Europe for years, such **cogeneration** is gaining popularity in the United States.

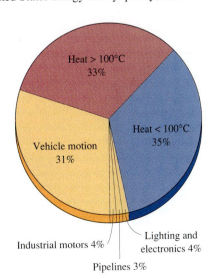

FIGURE 22-19 Energy use in the United States, organized by energy quality.

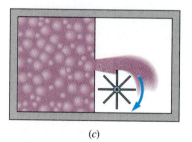

FIGURE 22-20 Two objects, initially at different temperatures, come to equilibrium at an intermediate temperature T_f. No energy is lost, but the system does lose its ability to do work.

FIGURE 22-21 (a, b) Adiabatic free expansion. Gas initially confined to one side of an insulated container expands to fill the entire container. The gas energy remains constant but its quality deteriorates. (c) A means of extracting useful work from the gas in the initial state of Fig. 22-21.

Entropy

How can we quantify the notion of energy quality? Imagine bringing two identical objects, initially at different temperatures, into thermal contact (Fig. 22-20). Heat flows from the hotter to the cooler object until they reach the same temperature. If they're thermally insulated from their environment there's no energy lost in the process. But something has changed: The system has lost the ability to do useful work. In the initial state we could have run a heat engine using the two objects as its hot and cool reservoirs. In the final state there's no temperature difference and therefore no way to run a heat engine. The quantity of energy has stayed the same, but its quality has decreased. Can we find some system property that reflects this change?

Figure 22-21 shows another system whose energy quality deteriorates without any loss of total energy. We start with a gas confined to one side of an insulated container; the other side is evacuated. Remove the partition, and the gas expands freely to fill the container. Since the container is insulated, the process is adiabatic, and no heat flows out. Since the gas expands into a vacuum, it does no work either. Therefore, its energy stays constant. But again we've lost the ability to do work. Starting with the initial state, we could have made the gas run a turbine between the high pressure region and the vacuum, extracting useful work (Fig. 22-21c). In the final state there's no pressure difference and therefore no way to run the turbine. Again, can we find a quantity that describes this decrease in energy quality?

To find the quantity we're after, consider an ideal gas undergoing a Carnot cycle—that is, a cycle of two isothermal and two adiabatic processes (recall Fig. 22-6). In deriving Equation 22-3 for the efficiency of this cycle we found that

$$\frac{Q_c}{Q_h} = \frac{T_c}{T_h},$$
(22-6)

where Q_c was the heat *rejected* from the system to the low-temperature reservoir at T_c and Q_h the heat *added* from the reservoir at T_h.

We now change the definition of Q_c so it also means heat *added* to the system. This redefinition just changes the sign of Q_c, so now Equation 22-6 can be written

$$\frac{Q_c}{T_c} + \frac{Q_h}{T_h} = 0.$$

We can generalize this result to any reversible cycle by approximating the cycle as a sequence of adiabatic and isothermal steps (Fig. 22-22). Figure 22-22's caption shows how summing over the individual hot and cold isothermal segments then gives

$$\sum \frac{Q}{T} = 0.$$

We can approximate the closed cycle ever closer by more and more adiabatic and isothermal segments. In the limit the approximation becomes exact and the sum becomes an integral:

$$\oint \frac{dQ}{T} = 0,$$
(22-7)

where the circle on the integral sign indicates that we integrate over all the heat transfers along a *closed* path.

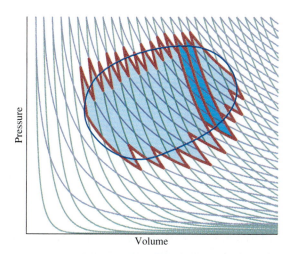

Equation 22-7 tells us that there is some quantity S, a small amount of which is given by $dS = dQ/T$, that does not change when we take a system around a cyclic path. This quantity S is called **entropy**. If we take a system around a path that isn't closed, then its entropy will, in general, change. That change is given by integrating $dS = dQ/T$ over the path in question:

$$\Delta S = \int_1^2 \frac{dQ}{T}, \qquad (22\text{-}8)$$

where ΔS is the change in entropy between the two thermodynamic states 1 and 2. Note that entropy has the units J/K.

What good is this concept of entropy? Equation 22-8 shows that there's no entropy change when we take a system from some initial state and eventually return it to that state. Now suppose we take a system part way around a closed path, from state 1 to state 2 shown in Fig. 22-23. The entropy change from state 2 back to state 1 must be exactly opposite the change from 1 to 2, so that the change going around the closed path is zero. But this must be true no matter how we get from state 2 to state 1, as suggested by the two possible paths in Fig. 22-23. That is, the entropy change given by Equation 22-8 is independent of path; it is a property only of the initial and final states themselves. Like pressure, temperature, and volume, entropy is a thermodynamic state variable—a quantity that characterizes a given state independently of how a system got into that state.

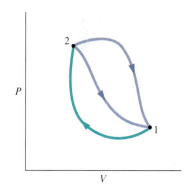

FIGURE 22-23 Entropy change is zero when the system returns to its original state. Therefore the entropy change from state 2 to state 1 is the same on both return paths shown. In fact, entropy change is always independent of path.

EXAMPLE 22-5	*Entropy*

An object of mass m and specific heat c is heated from temperature T_1 to temperature T_2. What is the change in its entropy?

Solution

Equation 22-8 gives the entropy change. To evaluate the integral in this equation we must relate dQ and T. Here we can do so because we know the specific heat: a small temperature change dT requires a heat dQ given by

$$dQ = mc\,dT.$$

Then Equation 22-8 becomes

$$\Delta S = \int_1^2 \frac{dQ}{T} = \int_{T_1}^{T_2} mc\,\frac{dT}{T} = mc\ln\left(\frac{T_2}{T_1}\right). \qquad (22\text{-}9)$$

EXERCISE What is the specific heat of a substance if 1.0 kg of it undergoes an entropy increase of 260 J/K when its temperature doubles?

Answer: 375 J/kg·K

Some problems similar to Example 22-5: 32, 33, 37, 38

Equation 22-8 is meaningful only for reversible processes since an irreversible process takes a system temporarily into thermodynamic disequilibrium, in which temperature is not well defined. But because entropy doesn't depend on how a system got into its thermodynamic state, we can calculate the entropy change during an *irreversible* process by finding a *reversible* process that takes the system between the same two states, then using Equation 22-8 to calculate the entropy change for the reversible process.

At the beginning of this section we considered two irreversible processes in which energy quality deteriorated even though total energy remained constant. We can come to understand the meaning of entropy by calculating entropy changes for these two processes.

Irreversible Heat Transfer

FIGURE 22-24 The two objects of Fig. 22-20, with a temperature scale showing the intermediate temperatures T_1 and T_2 used in evaluating the entropy change.

Figure 22-24 repeats Fig. 22-20, showing two objects, initially at temperatures T_h and T_c, placed in thermal contact until they reach a common temperature T_f. The total energy of the system remains unchanged, but energy quality deteriorates. We can calculate the entropy change by considering reversible processes that take the two objects to the final temperature T_f. We could, for example, place each in contact with a heat reservoir at its initial temperature and then gradually change the temperature until it reaches T_f. The entropy change for the cool object would then be

$$\Delta S_c = \int_{T_c}^{T_f} \frac{dQ}{T}.$$

Although we might evaluate this integral (see Problem 42), note instead that there must be some intermediate temperature T_1 *that lies between* T_c and T_f, for which

$$\Delta S_c = \frac{Q_c}{T_1},$$

where Q_c is the heat absorbed by the cool object. We've marked T_1 on Fig. 22-24. Similarly, the entropy change for the hot object is

$$\Delta S_h = \int_{T_h}^{T_f} \frac{dQ}{T} = \frac{Q_h}{T_2},$$

where T_2 *lies between* T_h and T_f.

The entropy change of the system is then

$$\Delta S = \Delta S_c + \Delta S_h = \frac{Q_c}{T_1} + \frac{Q_h}{T_2}.$$

But the two objects are insulated, so any heat gained by the cool object in the actual irreversible process is equal to the heat lost by the hot object. Thus $Q_h = -Q_c$, and the entropy change becomes

$$\Delta S = \frac{Q_c}{T_1} - \frac{Q_c}{T_2} = Q_c \left(\frac{1}{T_1} - \frac{1}{T_2} \right).$$

Now T_1 lies *below* the equilibrium temperature T_f and T_2 lies *above* T_f. That makes ΔS a *positive* quantity—meaning that entropy has *increased* during the irreversible heat transfer.

Adiabatic Free Expansion

Figure 22-21 showed a gas undergoing an irreversible adiabatic free expansion. Neither the temperature nor the internal energy changes during the process, but energy quality deteriorates. We can calculate the entropy change by considering a reversible process that takes the gas between the same initial and final states. Since the final and initial temperatures are equal, one such process is an isothermal expansion. Equation 21-4 gives the heat added during such an expansion:

$$Q = nRT \ln\left(\frac{V_2}{V_1}\right).$$

Since the temperature is constant, the entropy change of Equation 22-9 becomes

$$\Delta S = \int \frac{dQ}{T} = \frac{1}{T}\int dQ = \frac{Q}{T} = nR \ln\left(\frac{V_2}{V_1}\right). \tag{22-10}$$

Since the final volume V_2 is larger than V_1, the entropy has *increased*.

In calculating this entropy change, we used the heat Q that would be required during a reversible isothermal process. Of course, no heat is transferred during the actual adiabatic free expansion. Nevertheless the entropy change is the same as for the reversible isothermal process that takes the system between the same initial and final states—and that process does involve heat transfer.

Entropy and the Availability of Work

Entropy increases during both the irreversible processes we just considered. Earlier, we argued that those processes result in a deterioration of energy quality, in that both systems lose the ability to do work. Suppose we had let the gas in Fig. 22-21 undergo a reversible isothermal expansion instead of the adiabatic free expansion. Then it would have done work given by Equation 21-4:

$$W = nRT \ln\left(\frac{V_2}{V_1}\right).$$

After the irreversible free expansion, the gas can no longer do this work, even though its energy is unchanged. Comparing with the entropy change of Equation 22-10, we see that the energy that becomes unavailable to do work is

$$E_{\text{unavailable}} = T\Delta S. \tag{22-11}$$

Equation 22-11 is an example of a more general relation between entropy and the quality of energy:

> **Entropy and the Quality of Energy:** During an irreversible process in which the entropy of a system increases by ΔS, energy $E = T_{\text{min}}\Delta S$ becomes unavailable to do work, where T_{min} is coolest temperature available to the system.

This statement shows that entropy provides our desired measure of energy quality. Given two systems with identical energy content, the one with the lower entropy contains the higher-quality energy. An entropy increase always corresponds to a degradation in energy quality, in that some energy becomes unavailable to do work.

EXAMPLE 22-6	*Entropy and Energy Quality*

A cylinder contains 5.0 mol of compressed gas at 300 K, confined to 2.0 L. If the cylinder is discharged into a 150-L vacuum chamber and its temperature remains at 300 K, how much energy becomes unavailable to do work?

Solution

This is essentially an adiabatic free expansion, so Equations 22-10 and 22-11 give

$$E_{unavailable} = T\Delta S = nRT \ln\left(\frac{V_2}{V_1}\right)$$

$$= (5.0 \text{ mol})(8.314 \text{ J/K} \cdot \text{mol})(300 \text{ K}) \ln\left(\frac{152 \text{ L}}{2.0 \text{ L}}\right)$$

$$= 54 \text{ kJ}.$$

EXERCISE Astronauts pressurize an evacuated space station by discharging 670 mol of air from a 200-L cylinder into the station's 15-m^3 volume. The gas temperature remains at 290 K. How much work becomes unavailable as a result of this process?

Answer: 7.0 MJ

Some problems similar to Example 22-6: 44, 45

Entropy and the Second Law of Thermodynamics

We started this chapter by arguing that natural processes are generally irreversible, going from ordered states to disordered states. It's this loss of order—as when a hot and a cold object eventually reach the same temperature—that makes energy unavailable to do work. Entropy is a measure of this disorder. Given the tendency of systems to evolve toward disordered states, we can make a statement about entropy that is, in fact, a general statement of the second law of thermodynamics:

> *Second law of thermodynamics: The entropy of a closed system can never decrease.*

At best, the entropy of a closed system remains constant—and this happens only in an ideal, reversible process. If anything irreversible occurs—a slight amount of friction or a deviation from exact thermodynamic equilibrium—then entropy increases. There's no going back. As entropy increases, some energy becomes unavailable to do work, and nothing within the closed system can restore that energy to its original quality. This statement of the second law in terms of entropy is equivalent to our previous statements about the impossibility of perfect heat engines and refrigerators, for the operation of either device would require a decrease in entropy.

What about a system that isn't closed? Can't we decrease its entropy? Yes— but only by supplying high-quality energy from outside. Running a refrigerator decreases the entropy of its contents (Fig. 22-25). But we must do work on the refrigerator to effect this entropy decrease—to make heat flow in the direction it doesn't normally go. If we enlarge our closed system to include the power plant or whatever else supplies the refrigerator with work, we would find that the entropy of this new closed system does not decrease. The entropy decrease at the refrigerator is offset by entropy increases elsewhere in the system (Fig. 22-26). If irreversible processes occur anywhere in the system, then there is a net entropy increase.

Any system whose entropy seems to decrease—that gets more rather than less organized—cannot be a closed system. If we enlarge the system boundaries to encompass anything that might exchange energy with the original system, then the entropy of the larger system will not decrease. Ultimately, we can enlarge the system to include the entire universe. Then we have the ultimate statement of the second law:

FIGURE 22-25 A refrigerator decreases the entropy of its contents, but only when work is done on the system from outside.

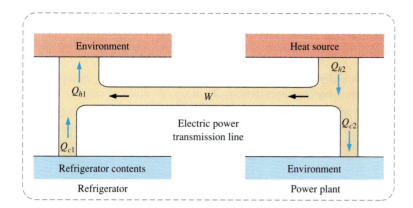

FIGURE 22-26 When the source of work for the refrigerator is included in the system, then the entropy of the entire system can at best remain constant.

Second law of thermodynamics: The entropy of the universe can never decrease.

As examples of this broad statement, consider the growth of a living thing from the random mix of molecules in its environment, or the construction of a skyscraper from materials that were originally dispersed about Earth, or the appearance of ordered symbols on a printed page from a bottle of ink. All these are processes in which matter goes from near chaos to a highly organized state—akin to separating yolk and white from a scrambled egg. They are certainly processes in which entropy decreases. But Earth is not a closed system. It gets high-quality energy from the Sun, energy that is ultimately responsible for life and all its actions. If we consider the Earth-Sun system, then the entropy decrease associated with life and civilization is more than balanced by the entropy increase associated with nuclear fusion inside the Sun. We living things represent a remarkable phenomenon—the organization of matter in a universe governed by a tendency toward disorder. But we do not escape the second law of thermodynamics. Our highly organized selves and society, and the entropy decreases they represent, come into being only at the expense of greater entropy increases elsewhere in the universe.

CHAPTER SYNOPSIS

Summary

1. **Irreversible processes** decrease a system's organization or order. Because there are many more ways to arrange matter in disorganized states, the probability that a disorganized state will become spontaneously organized is impossibly small. The many equivalent statements of the **second law of thermodynamics** embody this fact.

2. A **heat engine** extracts heat from a hot reservoir and converts some of it to useful work. Applied to heat engines, the second law says that it is impossible to build a perfect heat engine that converts all the heat to work. In particular, no engine operating between temperatures T_h and T_c can be more efficient than a reversible **Carnot engine**; thus

$$e = \frac{W}{Q_h} \le e_{\text{Carnot}} = 1 - \frac{T_c}{T_h} .$$

This second-law limitation on efficiency means that real

engines like automobile engines and power plants reject a great deal of waste heat to their environments.

3. A **refrigerator** extracts heat Q_c from a cool reservoir and transfers it to a hotter one. The second law of thermodynamics implies that a perfect refrigerator is impossible; real refrigerators must take in work W. The **coefficient of performance** measures the efficiency of a refrigerator:

$$\text{COP} = \frac{Q_c}{W} \le \text{COP}_{\text{Carnot}} = \frac{T_c}{T_h - T_c} ,$$

where the inequality shows that no refrigerator can have a higher COP than a reversible refrigerator operating on a Carnot cycle.

4. The second-law limit on the efficiency of a heat engine defines the **thermodynamic temperature scale**. **Absolute zero** corresponds to a state of maximum order, but the **third**

law of thermodynamics states that it is impossible to reach absolute zero in a finite number of thermodynamic steps.

5. **Energy quality** describes the ability of a given quantity of energy to do work. The highest-quality energy is mechanical or electrical, followed by the energy associated with large temperature differences, followed by ever smaller temperature differences. Higher-quality energy can be converted to lower quality with 100% efficiency, but the second law prohibits the reverse process from occurring with 100% efficiency.

6. **Entropy** measures the relative disorder of a system, so increasing entropy corresponds to decreasing energy quality. Entropy is a thermodynamic state variable; its value depends only on the state of a system and not on how the system got into that state. The entropy difference between two states can be found by evaluating the expression

$$\Delta S = \int_1^2 \frac{dQ}{T}$$

for any reversible process connecting those states.

7. In terms of entropy, the second law of thermodynamics asserts that the entropy of the universe can never decrease. In this form, the second law is a universal statement about the tendency of systems to evolve toward states of greater disorder.

Terms You Should Understand

(Pairs are closely related terms whose distinction is important; number in parentheses is chapter section where term first appears.)

irreversible process (22-1)
second law of thermodynamics (22-2, 22-5)

heat engine, refrigerator (22-2)
efficiency (22-2), coefficient of performance (22-3)
thermodynamic temperature scale (22-4)
absolute zero (22-4)
third law of thermodynamics (22-4)
energy quality (22-5)
entropy (22-5)

Symbols You Should Recognize

T_c, T_h (22-2)	COP (22-3)
Q_c, Q_h (22-2)	ΔS (22-5)
e (22-2)	

Problems You Should Be Able to Solve

calculating efficiencies and waste heat of engines (22-2, 22-3)
calculating COP and related quantities for refrigerators and heat pumps (22-3)
calculating entropy changes for simple thermodynamic processes (22-5)
calculating loss of available work associated with entropy increase (22-5)

Limitations to Keep in Mind

The second law of thermodynamics, unlike physical laws you have encountered previously, is fundamentally *statistical*. It rules out events not because they violate basic laws of mechanics but because they're simply too improbable.

A completely reversible process is an idealization that cannot be realized in the macroscopic world where friction and other energy-dissipation mechanisms are present.

QUESTIONS

1. Which of the following processes is irreversible?
   a. Stirring sugar into coffee
   b. Building a house
   c. Demolishing a house with a wrecking crane
   d. Demolishing a house by taking it apart piece-by-piece
   e. Warming a bottle of milk by transferring it directly from a refrigerator to stove top
   f. Writing a sentence
   g. Harnessing the energy of falling water in order to drive machinery

2. Could you cool the kitchen by leaving the refrigerator door open? Explain.

3. Could you heat the kitchen by leaving the oven open? Explain.

4. Why don't we simply refrigerate the cooling water of a power plant before it goes to the plant, thereby increasing the plant's efficiency?

5. Should a car get better mileage in the summer or the winter? Explain.

6. Is there a limit to the maximum temperature that can be achieved by focusing sunlight with a lens? If so, what is it?

7. Name some irreversible processes that occur in a real engine.

8. A power company claims that electric heat is one hundred per cent efficient. Discuss this claim.

9. A hydroelectric power plant, using the energy of falling water, can operate with an efficiency arbitrarily close to one hundred per cent. Why?

10. To maximize the COP of a refrigerator, should you strive for a large or a small temperature difference? Explain.

11. The manufacturer of a heat pump claims that the device will heat your home using only energy already available in the ground. Is this true?

12. Why are heat pumps more widely used in warmer climates?

13. Proponents of ocean thermal energy conversion don't seem bothered by efficiencies so low as to be intolerable in fossil-fueled or nuclear power plants. Why the difference?

14. What might be done with the waste heat from power plants?

15. Does sunlight represent high- or low-quality energy? Explain; see also Question 6.

16. If new materials were developed that could withstand higher temperatures than those now encountered in power plants, how would that help us save energy?

17. The heat Q added during adiabatic free expansion is zero. Why can't we then argue from Equation 22-8 that the entropy change is zero?

18. Energy is conserved, so why can't we recycle it as we do materials?

19. A power plant provides electricity to run a heat pump. Can the heat output of the pump be greater than the heat extracted from the power plant's fuel?

20. Why does the evolution of human civilization not violate the second law of thermodynamics?

PROBLEMS

ActivPhysics can help with these problems:
Activity 8.14.

Section 22-1 Reversibility and Irreversibility

1. The egg carton shown in Fig. 22-27 has places for one dozen eggs. (a) How many distinct ways are there to arrange six eggs in the carton? (b) Of these, what fraction correspond to all six eggs being in the left half of the carton? Treat the eggs as distinguishable, so an interchange of two eggs gives rise to a new state.

FIGURE 22-27 An egg carton (Problem 1).

2. A gas consists of four distinguishable molecules, all moving with the same speed v either to the left or to the right. A microscopic state is specified by telling which molecules are moving in which direction. (a) How many possible microscopic states are there? (b) How many of these correspond to all four molecules moving in the same direction? (c) What is the probability of finding the gas with all its molecules moving in one direction? Repeat parts (a–c) for a gas of (d) 10 molecules and (e) a more typical value, 10^{23} molecules.

3. Estimate the energy that could be extracted by cooling the world's oceans by 1°C. How does your estimate compare with humanity's yearly energy consumption of about 2.5×10^{20} J?

4. Two grains of salt and two grains of pepper are mixed. (a) If the mixture is shaken randomly and then divided into two equal parts, what is the approximate probability that all the salt will be in one part and all the pepper in another? Repeat for the case when (b) 10 grains and (c) 1000 grains of each are mixed.

Sections 22-2 and 22-3 The Second Law and Its Applications

5. What are the efficiencies of reversible heat engines operating between (a) the normal freezing and boiling points of water, (b) the 25°C temperature at the surface of a tropical ocean and deep water at 4°C, and (c) a 1000°C candle flame and room temperature?

6. A cosmic heat engine might operate between the Sun's 5600-K surface and the 2.7-K temperature of intergalactic space. What would be its efficiency?

7. A reversible Carnot engine operating between helium's melting point and its 4.25-K boiling point has an efficiency of 77.7%. What is the melting point?

8. A Carnot engine extracts 890 J from a 550-K reservoir during each cycle and rejects 470 J to a cooler reservoir. (a) How much work does it do each cycle? (b) What is its efficiency? (c) What is the temperature of the cool reservoir? (d) If the engine undergoes 22 cycles per second, what is its mechanical power output?

9. The maximum temperature in a nuclear power plant is 570 K. The plant rejects heat to a river where the temperature is 0°C in the winter and 25°C in the summer. What are the maximum possible efficiencies for the plant in these seasons? Why might the plant not achieve these efficiencies?

10. The minimum flow in the Connecticut River is 3.40×10^4 kg/s. By how much will the Vermont Yankee nuclear power plant described in Example 22-2 heat the entire river?

11. A power plant's electrical output is 750 MW. Cooling water at 15°C flows through the plant at 2.8×10^4 kg/s, and its temperature rises by 8.5°C. Assuming the plant's only energy loss is to the cooling water and that the cooling water is effectively the low-temperature reservoir, find (a) the rate of energy extraction from the fuel, (b) the plant's efficiency, and (c) its highest temperature.

12. A power plant extracts energy from steam at 250°C and delivers 800 MW of electric power. It discharges waste heat to a river at 30°C. The overall efficiency of the plant is 28%. (a) How does this efficiency compare with the maximum possible at these temperatures? (b) What is the rate of waste heat discharge to the river? (c) How many houses, each requiring 18 kW of heating power, could be heated with the waste heat from this plant?

13. The electric power output of all the thermal electric power plants in the United States is about 2×10^{11} W, and these plants operate at an average efficiency around 33%. What is the rate at which all these plants use cooling water, assuming an average 5°C rise in cooling-water temperature? Compare

with the 1.8×10^7 kg/s average flow at the mouth of the Mississippi River.

14. Consider a Carnot engine operating between temperatures T_h and T_c, where T_c is still above the ambient temperature T_0 (Fig. 22-28). It should be possible to operate a second engine between T_c and T_0. Show that the maximum overall efficiency of such a two-stage engine is the same as that of a single engine operating between T_h and T_0.

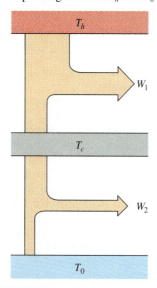

FIGURE 22-28 A two-stage engine (Problem 14).

15. A Carnot engine absorbs 900 J of heat each cycle and provides 350 J of work. (a) What is its efficiency? (b) How much heat is rejected each cycle? (c) If the engine rejects heat at 10°C, what is its maximum temperature?

16. What is the COP of a reversible refrigerator operating between 0°C and 30°C?

17. How much work does a refrigerator with a COP of 4.2 require to freeze 670 g of water already at its freezing point?

18. An industrial freezer operates between 0°C and 32°C, consuming electrical energy at the rate of 12 kW. Assuming the freezer is perfectly reversible, (a) what is its COP? (b) How much water at 0°C can it freeze in 1 hour?

19. A 4.0 L sample of water at 9.0°C is put into a refrigerator. The refrigerator's 130-W motor then runs for 4.0 min to cool the water to the refrigerator's low temperature of 1.0°C. (a) What is the COP of the refrigerator? (b) How does this compare with the maximum possible COP if the refrigerator exhausts heat at 25°C?

20. A refrigerator maintains an interior temperature of 4°C while the temperature near its heat exhaust is 30°C. The refrigerator's insulation is imperfect, and heat leaks into the refrigerator at the rate of 340 W. Assuming the refrigerator is reversible, at what rate must it consume electrical energy to maintain a constant 4°C interior?

21. A heat pump consumes electrical energy at the rate P_e. Show that it delivers heat at the rate $(COP + 1)P_e$.

22. A store is heated by an oil furnace that supplies 30 kWh of heat from each gallon. The store's owners are considering switching to a heat pump system. Oil costs 87¢/gallon, and electricity costs 7.8¢/kWh. What is the minimum heat pump COP that will result in a savings in heating costs?

23. A heat pump transfers heat between the interior of a house and the outside air. In the summer the outside air averages 26°C, and the pump operates by chilling water to 5°C for circulation throughout the house. In winter the outside air averages 2°C, and the pump operates by heating water to 80°C for circulation throughout the house. (a) Find the coefficients of performance in summer and winter. How much work does the pump require (b) for each joule of heat removed from the house in summer and (c) for each joule supplied to the house in winter?

24. A house is heated by a heat pump with COP = 2.3. The heat pump is run by electricity generated in a power plant whose efficiency is 28%. (a) What is the overall efficiency of this process, defined as the ratio of heat delivered to the house to heat released from fuel at the power plant? (b) Could the efficiency so defined ever exceed 100%?

25. A 0.20-mol sample of an ideal gas goes through the Carnot cycle of Fig. 22-29. Calculate (a) the heat Q_h absorbed, (b) the heat Q_c rejected, and (c) the work done. (d) Use these quantities to determine the efficiency. (e) Find the maximum and minimum temperatures, and show explicitly that the efficiency as defined in Equation 22-1 is equal to the Carnot efficiency of Equation 22-3.

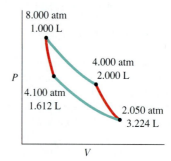

FIGURE 22-29 Problem 25 (diagram is not to scale).

26. Show that it is impossible for two adiabats to intersect. *Hint:* Suppose two adiabats do intersect. Connect them by a suitable isotherm to form a three-step cycle. Show that a heat engine operating in this cycle would have 100% efficiency, in violation of the second law.

27. Use appropriate energy flow diagrams to show that the existence of a perfect heat engine would permit the construction of a perfect refrigerator, thus violating the Clausius statement of the second law.

Section 22-4 The Thermodynamic Temperature Scale

28. A small sample of material is taken through a Carnot cycle between a reservoir of boiling helium at 1.76 K and an unknown lower temperature. During the process, 7.5 mJ of heat are absorbed from the helium, and 0.44 mJ rejected at the lower temperature. What is the unknown low temperature?

29. A Carnot engine operating between a vat of boiling sulfur and a bath of water at its triple point has an efficiency of 61.95%. What is the boiling point of sulfur?

30. A heat engine operating between a hotter reservoir of boiling hydrogen and a cooler one of boiling helium has 79.1% efficiency. What is the ratio of hydrogen to helium boiling temperatures?

Section 22-5 Entropy and the Quality of Energy

31. Calculate the entropy change associated with melting 1.0 kg of ice at 0°C.

32. You heat 250 g of water from 10°C to 95°C. By how much does the entropy of the water increase?

33. A 2.0-kg sample of water is heated to 35°C. If the entropy change is 740 J/K, what was the initial temperature?

34. Melting a block of lead already at its melting point results in an entropy increase of 900 J/K. What is the mass of the lead? *Hint:* Consult Table 20-1.

35. A shallow pond contains 94,000 kg of water. In winter it's entirely frozen. By how much does the entropy of the pond increase when the ice, already at 0°C, melts and then heats to its summer temperature of 15°C?

36. Figure 22-30 shows a 500-g copper block at 80°C dropped into 1.0 kg of water at 10°C. (a) What is the final temperature? (b) What is the entropy change of the system?

FIGURE 22-30 Problem 36.

37. The temperature of n moles of ideal gas is changed from T_1 to T_2 while the gas volume is held constant. Show that the corresponding entropy change is $\Delta S = nC_V \ln(T_2/T_1)$.

38. The temperature of n moles of ideal gas is changed from T_1 to T_2 while gas pressure is held constant. Show that the corresponding entropy change is $\Delta S = nC_P \ln(T_2/T_1)$.

39. A 5.0-mol sample of an ideal diatomic gas $(C_V = \frac{5}{2}R)$ is initially at 1.0 atm pressure and 300 K. What is the entropy change if the gas is heated to 500 K (a) at constant volume, (b) at constant pressure, and (c) adiabatically?

40. The interior of a house is maintained at 20°C while the outdoor temperature is $-10°C$. The house loses heat at the rate of 30 kW. At what rate does the entropy of the universe increase because of this irreversible heat flow?

41. A 250-g sample of water at 80°C is mixed with 250 g of water at 10°C. Find the entropy changes for (a) the hot water, (b) the cool water, and (c) the system.

42. Two identical objects of mass m and specific heat c at initial temperatures T_h and T_c are placed together in an insulated box and allowed to come to equilibrium. Show that the system's entropy increase is $\Delta S = mc \ln \dfrac{(T_h + T_c)^2}{4T_h T_c}$.

43. A 5.0-mol sample of ideal monatomic gas undergoes the cycle shown in Fig. 22-31, in which the process BC is isothermal. Calculate the entropy change associated with each of the three steps, and show explicitly that there is zero net entropy change over the full cycle.

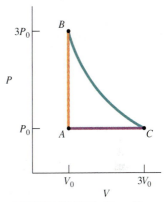

FIGURE 22-31 Problem 43.

44. In an adiabatic free expansion, 8.7 mol of ideal gas at 450 K expand 10-fold in volume. How much energy becomes unavailable to do work?

45. Ideal gas occupying 1.0 cm³ is placed in a 1.0-m³ vacuum chamber, where it expands adiabatically. If 6.5 J of energy become unavailable to do work, what was the initial gas pressure?

46. Make an argument based on Fig. 22-20 to show that a perfect refrigerator would decrease the entropy of the universe, in violation of the second law.

Paired Problems

(Both problems in a pair involve the same principles and techniques. If you can get the first problem, you should be able to solve the second one.)

47. Cooling water circulates through a reversible Carnot engine at 3.2 kg/s. The water enters at 23°C and leaves at 28°C; the average temperature is essentially that of the engine's cool reservoir. If the engine's mechanical power output is 150 kW, what are (a) its efficiency and (b) its highest temperature?

48. A reversible Carnot engine operates between 300 K and 640 K, running at 45 cycles per second. In each cycle the engine extracts 2.7 kJ from the high-temperature reservoir. Find (a) the efficiency and (b) the mechanical power output. (c) The low-temperature reservoir is provided by a flow of 300-K cooling water. If the water temperature increases 2.5°C, what is the flow rate?

49. Which would provide the greatest increase in efficiency of a Carnot engine, a 10 K increase in the maximum temperature or a 10 K decrease in the minimum temperature?

50. Which would provide the greatest increase in the COP of a reversible refrigerator, a decrease of 10 K in the maximum temperature or an increase of 10 K in the minimum temperature?

51. It costs $180 to heat a house with electricity in a typical winter month. (Electric heat simply converts all the incoming electrical energy to heat.) What would be the monthly heating bill following conversion to an electrically powered heat pump system with COP = 2.1?

52. It costs $140 each summer to operate a home air conditioner with a COP of 1.7. What will be the yearly savings in upgrading to a more efficient model with a COP of 2.4, assuming the same amount of heat is to be extracted from the house?

53. A reversible engine contains 0.20 mol of ideal monatomic gas, initially at 600 K and confined to 2.0 L. The gas undergoes the following cycle:

   - Isothermal expansion to 4.0 L.
   - Isovolumic cooling to 300 K.
   - Isothermal compression to 2.0 L.
   - Isovolumic heating to 600 K.

   (a) Calculate the net heat added during the cycle and the net work done. (b) Determine the engine's efficiency, defined as the ratio of the work done to only the heat *absorbed* during the cycle.

54. (a) Determine the efficiency for the cycle shown in Fig. 22-32, using the definition given in the preceding problem. (b) Compare with the efficiency of a Carnot engine operating between the same temperature extremes. Why are the two efficiencies different?

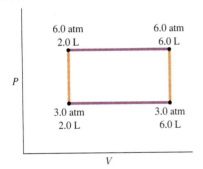

FIGURE 22-32 Problem 54.

55. You dump three 10-kg buckets of 10°C water into an empty tub, then add one 10-kg bucket of 70°C water. By how much does the entropy of the water increase?

56. Find the entropy change when a 2.4-kg aluminum pan at 155°C is plunged into 3.5 kg of water at 15°C.

Supplementary Problems

57. You're lying in a bathtub of water at 42°C. Suppose, in violation of the second law of thermodynamics, that the water spontaneously cooled to room temperature (20°C) and that the energy so released was transformed into your gravitational potential energy. Estimate the height to which you would rise above the bathtub.

58. An engine with mechanical power output 8.5 kW extracts heat from a source at 420 K and rejects it to a 1000-kg block of ice at its melting point. (a) What is its efficiency? (b) How long can it maintain this efficiency if the ice is not replenished?

59. A solar-thermal power plant is to be built in a desert location where the only source of cooling water is a small creek with average flow of 100 kg/s and an average temperature of 30°C. The plant is to cool itself by boiling away the entire creek. If the maximum temperature achieved in the plant is 500 K, what is the maximum electric power output it can sustain without running out of cooling water?

60. The McNeil generating station in Burlington, Vermont, is one of the world's largest wood-fired power plants. Here are some facts about the McNeil plant:

   - The electric power output is 59 MW.
   - Fuel consumption is 1.2×10^6 kg of wood per day. The wood's energy content is 1.4×10^7 J/kg, and 85% of this energy is released in burning.
   - Steam enters the plant's turbine at 1000°F and leaves at 200°F.
   - Cooling water circulates through the condenser at 1.8×10^5 kg/min, and its temperature increases by 18°F.

   Calculate the plant's efficiency in three ways: (a) Using only the third fact above to get the maximum possible efficiency; (b) using only the first and second facts; and (c) using only the first and fourth facts. What might account for the discrepancy between the second and third parts?

61. Gasoline engines operate approximately on the **Otto cycle**, consisting of two adiabatic and two constant-volume segments. The Otto cycle for a particular engine is shown in Fig. 22-33. (a) If the gas in the engine has specific heat ratio γ, find the engine's efficiency, assuming all processes are reversible. (b) Find the maximum temperature, in terms of the minimum temperature T_{min}. (c) How does the efficiency compare with that of a Carnot engine operating between the same two temperature extremes? *Note:* Fig. 22-33 neglects the intake of fuel-air and the exhaust of combustion products, which together involve essentially no net work.

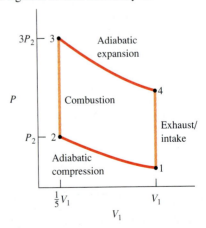

FIGURE 22-33 Otto cycle (Problems 61, 62).

62. The compression ratio r of an engine is the ratio of maximum to minimum gas volume. For the engine of the preceding problem, Fig. 22-33 shows that the compression ratio is 5. (a) Find an expression for the engine efficiency as a function of compression ratio. Assume that pressure continues to triple during the combustion phase, as shown in Fig. 22-33. (b) Make a graph of efficiency versus r, and on the same plot show also the efficiency of a Carnot engine operating between the same temperature extremes.

63. A heat pump designed for southern climates extracts heat from outside air and delivers air at 40°C to the inside of a house. (a) If the average outside temperature is 5°C, what is the average COP of the heat pump? (b) Suppose the pump is used in a northern climate where the average winter temperature is −10°C. Now what is the COP? (c) Two *identical* houses, one in the north and one in the south, are heated by this pump. Both houses maintain indoor temperatures of 19°C. What is the ratio of electric power consumption in the two houses? *Hint:* Think about heat loss as well as COP!

64. The specific heat of copper in the range from a few K to about 50 K is given by $c = aT^3$, where $a = 7.68 \times 10^{-4}$ J/kg·K^4. Find the entropy change in a 200-g piece of copper as it's heated from 10 K to 25 K.

65. A Carnot engine extracts heat from a block of mass m and specific heat c that is initially at temperature T_{h0} but which has no heat source to maintain that temperature. The engine rejects heat to a reservoir at a constant temperature T_c. The engine is operated so its mechanical power output is proportional to the temperature difference $T_h - T_c$:

$$P = P_0 \frac{T_h - T_c}{T_{h0} - T_c},$$

where T_h is the instantaneous temperature of the hot block and P_0 is the initial power output. (a) Find an expression for T_h as a function of time, and (b) determine how long it takes for the engine's power output to reach zero.

66. You have 50 kg of steam at 100°C, but no heat source to maintain it in that condition. You also have a heat reservoir at 0°C. Suppose you operate a reversible heat engine with

this system, so the steam gradually condenses and cools until it reaches 0°C. (a) Calculate the total entropy change of the steam and subsequent water. (b) Calculate the total entropy change of the reservoir. (c) Find the total amount of work that the engine can do. *Hint:* Consider the entropy change of the entire system. This change occurs as the result of a reversible process that supplies useful work. But if it had occurred irreversibly, how much energy would have become unavailable to do work?

67. An ideal diatomic gas undergoes the cyclic process described in Fig. 22-34. Fill in the blank spaces in the table below:

	P	V	T	$U - U_A$	$S - S_A$
A	P_0	V_0	T_0	0	0
B	$3.4P_0$	V_0			
C					
D	P_0	$3.0V_0$			

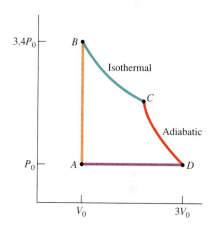

FIGURE 22-34 Cyclic process for Problem 67. Process *BC* is isothermal while *CD* is adiabatic. Diagram is not accurately scaled, and the location of point *C* is not quantitatively correct.

PART 3 *Cumulative Problems*

1. Figure 1 shows the thermodynamic cycle of a diesel engine. Note that this cycle differs from that of a gasoline engine (see Fig. 22-33) in that combustion takes place isobarically. As with the gasoline engine, the compression ratio r is the ratio of maximum to minimum volume; $r = V_1/V_2$. In addition, the so-called *cutoff ratio* is defined by $r_c = V_3/V_2$. Find an expression for the engine's efficiency, in terms of the ratios r and r_c and the specific heat ratio γ. Although your expression suggests that the diesel engine might be less efficient than the gasoline engine (see Problem 61 of Chapter 22), the diesel's higher compression ratio more than compensates, giving it a higher efficiency.

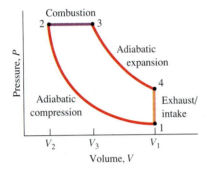

FIGURE 1 Cumulative Problem 1.

2. Deep in intergalactic space, an astronaut releases a thin-walled spherical container of radius R and negligible mass, containing a mass M of liquid water at temperature T_0 (Fig. 2). The container's surface is painted black to give it emissivity $e = 1$. The amount of radiation incident on the sphere from outside is negligible (since the temperature of intergalactic space is only 2.7 K). (a) Find an expression for the temperature of the liquid water as a function of time, assuming its heat conductivity is high enough that the water remains at essentially uniform temperature. (b) Taking $M = 100$ kg, $R = 29$ cm, and $T_0 = 300$ K, find the time from when the sphere is deployed until the water is completely frozen.

FIGURE 2 Cumulative Problem 2.

3. Equation 21-4 gives the work done by an ideal gas undergoing an isothermal expansion from volume V_1 to volume V_2. Find the analogous expression for a van der Waals gas described by Equation 20-7. Is the work done equal to the heat transferred to the gas in this case? Why or why not?

4. A solid sphere of mass m and radius R is made from a material with specific heat c, and is initially at a uniform temperature T_1. The sphere is surrounded by insulation of thermal conductivity k and thickness a (see Fig. 3). The temperature outside the insulation is fixed at T_0. (a) Assuming conduction is the only significant heat-loss mechanism, find an expression for the magnitude of the sphere's heat-loss rate as a function of its temperature T. (b) Assuming the temperature throughout the sphere remains uniform, find an expression for the temperature T as a function of time.

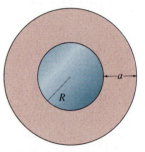

FIGURE 3 Cumulative Problem 4.

5. The ideal Carnot engine shown in Fig. 4 operates between a heat reservoir and a block of ice with mass M. An external energy source maintains the reservoir at a constant temperature T_h. At time $t = 0$ the ice is at its melting point T_0, but it is insulated from everything except the engine, so it is free to change state and temperature. The engine is operated in such a way that it extracts heat from the reservoir at a constant rate P_h. (a) Find an expression for the time t_1 at which the ice is all melted, in terms of the quantities given and any other appropriate thermodynamic parameters. (b) Find an expression for the mechanical power output of the engine as a function of time for times $t > t_1$. (c) Your expression in (b) holds only up to some maximum time t_2. Why? Find an expression for t_2.

FIGURE 4 Cumulative Problem 5.

Part Four

Electromagnetism

A portion of an integrated circuit, or "chip," magnified 100 times. Integrated circuits are at the heart of computers and many other electronic devices. A single integrated circuit can contain millions of transistors and other electronic components. These miniaturized circuits are but one of a myriad of electromagnetic technologies that we use every day.

Electromagnetism is a fundamental force, and governs the behavior of matter from the atomic scale into the macroscopic world. Electromagnetic technology, from computer microchips to large electric motors and generators, is essential to our technological society. Even our bodies—with their electrochemical nerve impulses, electrically polarized muscle cells, and carefully paced electrical signals controlling heartbeat—rely heavily on electromagnetism.

Four fundamental laws describe electricity and magnetism. Two deal separately with the two phenomena, while the other two reveal profound connections that show electricity and magnetism to be aspects of a single phenomenon—electromagnetism. The twelve chapters in this part will give you a thorough grounding in electromagnetism. You'll come to understand the fundamental laws that govern all electromagnetic phenomena, learn how electromagnetism determines the structure and behavior of nearly all matter, and explore the electromagnetic technologies that play so important a role in your life.

23 Electric Charge, Force, and Field

Lightning strikes at Kitt Peak National Observatory in Arizona relieve the buildup of electric charge in the atmosphere.

What force keeps the molecules in your body together? What force keeps a skyscraper standing or prevents a mountain from spreading into a flat blob? What force holds your car on the road as you round a turn? What force accelerates the electrons that paint the picture on your TV screen? What force underlies the awesome beauty of a thunderstorm?

Remarkably, these and all other forces except gravity that we encounter in our everyday lives—and in nearly all scientific work—are manifestations of a single force: the **electromagnetic force**. The friction, tension, and normal forces of mechanics are ultimately electromagnetic. So are interactions as diverse as the focusing of light in the lens of your eye, the extraction of information from a computer disk, or the formation of a water molecule from separate atoms. Electromagnetism is so important in science and engineering that we devote the next twelve chapters to it.

23-1 ELECTROMAGNETISM

Electromagnetism is among the fundamental forces of nature that we introduced in Chapter 5 (see Fig. 5-9) and is the dominant force in a vast range of natural and technological phenomena. Other than gravity, electromagnetism is the only force most of us will ever deal with.

Three distinct themes motivate our study of electromagnetism:

1. The electromagnetic force is solely responsible for the structure of matter from atoms to objects of roughly human size (Fig. 23-1). Much of physics, all of chemistry, and most of biology deal in this realm. Only at much smaller scales do the color and weak forces become important; only at larger scales is gravity significant.

   The wonderful diversity of chemical compounds is testimony to the rich possibilities contained in the electromagnetic interaction. Even life itself, and the DNA replicating mechanism at its heart, are manifestations of electromagnetism (Fig. 23-1). For students of physical and biological sciences, understanding electromagnetism means understanding the most fundamental basis of these disciplines.

2. We live in a technological world increasingly dominated by devices that operate on electromagnetic principles. Electric lights, motors, batteries, and generators have been essential for over 100 years. More recently, electronic technology has led to the proliferation of devices for storing and processing information, for sensing and measuring, and for sophisticated control of industrial, scientific, medical, automotive, and household systems (Fig. 23-2).

3. Studying electromagnetism leads to an understanding of the nature of light and from there to the theory of relativity. Relativity profoundly alters our ideas of space and time—the very basis of physical reality.

We've been speaking of electromagnetism, yet you're probably more familiar with electricity and magnetism separately. Although we begin with separate studies of these seemingly distinct phenomena, the relation between the two will become increasingly central. Eventually you will understand electricity and magnetism as two aspects of a single phenomenon that is basic to the workings of the universe.

FIGURE 23-1 Electric forces govern the transmission of nerve impulses, shape the DNA molecule, and hold atoms together.

FIGURE 23-2 Inside a computer, components as mundane as the cooling fan motor and as sophisticated as a memory chip work on electromagnetic principles. Blowup shows the computer's microprocessor, which includes millions of electronic components on a single silicon chip.

23-2 ELECTRIC CHARGE

Electric charge is a fundamental property of nature. Of the three building blocks of ordinary matter—the electron, the proton, and the neutron—two carry electric charge. What is electric charge? At the most fundamental level, we don't know. We don't know what mass "really" is either, but we're familiar with it because we've spent our lives pushing objects around. By studying electrical interactions we gain a similar familiarity with charge that is as close as we can get to understanding what it "really" is.

Two Kinds of Charge

Electric charge comes in two varieties, which Benjamin Franklin designated **positive** and **negative**. These are convenient labels, but they have no physical significance. There's nothing "missing" about negative charge. Positive and negative charge are complementary properties, not the presence and absence of something. The utility in the names is mathematical, since it's the algebraic sum of charges—described with positive and negative numbers—that has physical significance.

Quantities of Charge

All electrons carry the same charge, and all protons carry the same charge. The proton's charge has *exactly* the same magnitude as the electron's, but with opposite sign. Given that electrons and protons differ substantially in other properties—like mass—this electrical relation is remarkable. Problem 1 shows how dramatically different our world would be if there were even a slight difference between the magnitudes of the electron and proton charges.

The magnitude of the electron or proton charge is the **elementary charge**, *e*. Electric charge is **quantized**—that is, it comes only in discrete amounts. In a famous experiment in 1909, the American physicist R. A. Millikan used electric forces to suspend small oil drops. From the electric force he computed the charge on each drop and found it was always a multiple of a basic value we now know as the elementary charge (Fig. 23-3).

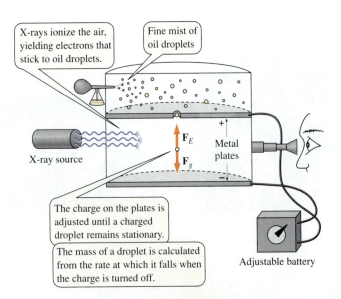

X-rays ionize the air, yielding electrons that stick to oil droplets.

Fine mist of oil droplets

$\mathbf{F}_E$

$\mathbf{F}_g$

Metal plates

X-ray source

The charge on the plates is adjusted until a charged droplet remains stationary.

The mass of a droplet is calculated from the rate at which it falls when the charge is turned off.

Adjustable battery

FIGURE 23-3 Millikan's oil-drop experiment. By balancing the electric force $\mathbf{F}_E$ and gravitational force $\mathbf{F}_g$ on oil drops, Millikan showed that charge is quantized.

Modern elementary particle theories suggest that the most basic unit of charge is actually $\frac{1}{3}e$. Such "fractional charges" reside on quarks, the basic building blocks of protons, neutrons, and many other particles. Quarks always join to produce particles with integer multiples of the full elementary charge, and it seems impossible to isolate individual quarks.

The SI unit of charge is the **coulomb** (C), named for the French physicist Charles Augustin de Coulomb (1736–1806). Although the coulomb's formal definition is in terms of electric current, it's convenient to describe one coulomb as being about 6.25×10^{18} elementary charges, making the elementary charge approximately 1.60×10^{-19} C.

Charge Conservation

Electric charge is a conserved quantity, meaning that the algebraic sum of the electric charges—i.e., the **net charge**—in a closed region remains constant. Charged particles may be created or annihilated, but always in pairs of equal and opposite charge (Fig. 23-4). The net charge always remains the same.

FIGURE 23-4 The creation of an electron and its antiparticle, a positron. The two particles' paths are the oppositely directed spirals that originate in a common point where the pair was created. The net charge remains zero before and after the particle creation. (The curved paths result from a magnetic force.)

23-3 COULOMB'S LAW

You can transfer charge to a balloon by rubbing it on your clothing; you'll then find that the balloon sticks to you. Charge another balloon and the two balloons will repel each other (Fig. 23-5). You're seeing a manifestation of the fundamental fact that unlike charges attract and like charges repel. Socks clinging to other clothes when they come out of a dryer, dust attracted to the front of a TV screen or computer monitor, and the shocks you get when you cross a carpet and touch a doorknob are other common examples where you're directly aware of this electrical interaction.

But electricity would be rather unimportant if the only significant electrical interactions were these obvious ones. In fact, all interactions of everyday matter—from the motion of a car to the movement of a muscle to the growth of a tree—are dominated by the electric force. It's just that matter on the large scale is nearly perfectly neutral, so electrical effects in bulk matter are not obvious. At the molecular or even cellular level the appearance of individual charged particles makes the electrical nature of matter immediately obvious (Fig. 23-6).

The attraction and repulsion of electric charges implies that a force acts between them. Scientists Joseph Priestley and Charles Augustin de Coulomb investigated this force in the late 1700s. They found that the force between two charges acts along the line joining them, with a magnitude proportional to the product of the charges and inversely proportional to the square of the distance

FIGURE 23-5 Two balloons carrying similar electric charge repel each other.

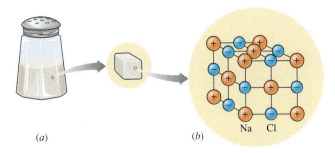

(a)   (b)

FIGURE 23-6 (a) The salt shaker and even a single salt grain are electrically neutral, so the role of electric forces in these structures is not obvious. (b) At the atomic scale, electric forces bind individual sodium and chloride ions together and are, in fact, responsible for the cubical shape of the salt crystal.

FIGURE 23-7 Quantities in Coulomb's law used in calculating the electric force of charge q_1 on q_2. The unit vector $\hat{\mathbf{r}}$ always points in the direction from q_1 toward q_2, regardless of the signs of the charges. The force $\mathbf{F}_{12}$ points in the same direction as $\hat{\mathbf{r}}$ if the two charges have the same sign, and otherwise in the opposite direction.

11.1
Electric Force: Coulomb's Law

between them. These results are summarized in **Coulomb's law**:

$$\mathbf{F}_{12} = \frac{kq_1q_2}{r^2}\hat{\mathbf{r}} \qquad \text{Coulomb's law .} \qquad (23\text{-}1)$$

Here $\mathbf{F}_{12}$ is the force exerted *by* the charge q_1 *on* the charge q_2 and r is the distance between the two. The quantity k is a proportionality constant whose value in SI units is approximately 9.0×10^9 N·m²/C². The force $\mathbf{F}_{12}$ is a vector, and $\hat{\mathbf{r}}$ is a unit vector giving its direction. Figure 23-7 shows that $\hat{\mathbf{r}}$ lies on the line passing through the two charges and points in the direction *from q_1 toward q_2*.

Coulomb's law is a vector equation that covers all possible combinations of charges and the associated attractive and repulsive forces. If q_1 and q_2 have the same sign—either positive or negative—then the product q_1q_2 is positive, and the force points in the same direction as $\hat{\mathbf{r}}$. The force on q_2 is thus away from q_1, or repulsive, as it should be. But if q_1 and q_2 have opposite signs, then q_1q_2 is negative and the direction of the force is opposite that of $\hat{\mathbf{r}}$—that is, attractive.

What about the force $\mathbf{F}_{21}$ that q_2 exerts on q_1? Equation 23-1 shows it has the same magnitude as $\mathbf{F}_{12}$, but a drawing like Fig. 23-7 gives the opposite direction. Thus the electric force obeys Newton's third law. ActivPhysics Activity 11.1 lets you explore the forces between pairs of electric charges.

EXAMPLE 23-1	*Two Charges*

A 1.0-μC charge is located at $x = 1.0$ cm, and a -1.5-μC charge at $x = 3.0$ cm. (a) What force does the positive charge exert on the negative one? (b) How would the force change if the distance between the charges were tripled?

Solution

(a) A vector from the positive charge toward the negative charge points in the $+x$ direction, so $\hat{\mathbf{r}}$ is simply the unit vector $\hat{\mathbf{i}}$. Then Equation 23-1 becomes

$$\mathbf{F} = \frac{kq_1q_2}{r^2}\hat{\mathbf{r}}$$

$$= \frac{(9.0 \times 10^9 \text{ N·m}^2/\text{C}^2)(1.0 \times 10^{-6} \text{ C})(-1.5 \times 10^{-6} \text{ C})}{(0.020 \text{ m})^2}\hat{\mathbf{i}}$$

$$= -34\hat{\mathbf{i}} \text{ N} .$$

The minus sign shows that the force is in the negative x direction—toward the positive charge, or attractive.

(b) If the distance were tripled the force would drop by a factor of $1/3^2$, to $-3.8\hat{\mathbf{i}}$ N.

Tip

Let the Algebra Take Care of the Signs Equation 23-1 accounts for all aspects of the force calculation. If you correctly take $\hat{\mathbf{r}}$ to be a unit vector pointing *away* from the charge giving rise to the force—whatever its sign—and *toward* the charge being acted on—whatever its sign—then calculation of $\frac{kq_1q_2}{r^2}\hat{\mathbf{r}}$ gives correctly the magnitude and direction of the force. You should, of course, check that your mathematical answer makes sense.

EXERCISE A 10-μC charge is at the origin. Find the force it exerts on a 5-μC charge at the point $x = 4$ m, $y = 3$ m. *Note:* You may need help with this one; see the Math Toolbox following this example.

Answer: $1.44\hat{\mathbf{i}} + 1.08\hat{\mathbf{j}}$ mN

Some problems similar to Example 23-1: 7, 12, 13

Math Toolbox

Finding the Unit Vector In Example 23-1, both charges lay on the x axis and it was obvious that a unit vector from the 1 μC charge toward the -1.5 μC charge is the vector $\hat{\mathbf{i}}$, so in that case $\hat{\mathbf{r}} = \hat{\mathbf{i}}$. But what's $\hat{\mathbf{r}}$ in the exercise with Example 23-1?

Coulomb's law says that $\hat{\mathbf{r}}$ is in the direction from q_1 toward q_2. But that's the same direction as the displacement vector $\mathbf{r}_{12}$ from q_1 to q_2. So $\mathbf{r}_{12}$ has the right direction; it just isn't a *unit* vector. But dividing by its magnitude makes a unit vector, as you can prove in Problem 12. Figure 23-8 shows that $\mathbf{r}_{12} = 4\hat{\mathbf{i}} + 3\hat{\mathbf{j}}$ m, so its magnitude is r = $\sqrt{(4 \text{ m})^2 + (3 \text{ m})^2}$ = 5 m. Then the unit vector from q_1 toward q_2 is

$$\hat{\mathbf{r}} = \frac{4\hat{\mathbf{i}} + 3\hat{\mathbf{j}} \text{ m}}{5 \text{ m}} = 0.80\hat{\mathbf{i}} + 0.60\hat{\mathbf{j}}.$$

Then we're ready to calculate the force, using Coulomb's law (Equation 23-1):

$$\mathbf{F}_{12} = \frac{kq_1q_2}{r^2}\hat{\mathbf{r}} = \frac{(9.0 \times 10^9 \text{ N·m}^2/\text{C}^2)(10 \ \mu\text{C})(5.0 \ \mu\text{C})}{(5.0 \text{ m})^2}(0.80\hat{\mathbf{i}} + 0.60\hat{\mathbf{j}})$$

$$= 1.44\hat{\mathbf{i}} + 1.08\hat{\mathbf{j}} \text{ mN}.$$

And that's it: a full vector expression for the force. More generally, given the vector $\mathbf{r}_{12}$ from q_1 to q_2, we can write the unit vector as

$$\hat{\mathbf{r}} = \frac{\mathbf{r}_{12}}{r}, \tag{23-2a}$$

where r is the magnitude of $\mathbf{r}_{12}$—i.e., the distance between the charges.

Equivalently, you can find the unit vector using trigonometry. Let θ be the angle that the vector $\mathbf{r}_{12}$ from q_1 to q_2 makes with the positive x axis, as marked in Fig. 23-8. Then the unit vector is

$$\hat{\mathbf{r}} = \cos\theta \, \hat{\mathbf{i}} + \sin\theta \, \hat{\mathbf{j}}. \tag{23-2b}$$

You can see this is a unit vector because it has magnitude $\sin^2\theta + \cos^2\theta = 1$, and the geometry of Fig. 23-8 shows clearly that $\hat{\mathbf{r}}$ as defined in Equation 23-2b is in the direction of $\mathbf{r}_{12}$. Finally, with the hypotenuse $r_{12} = 5$ in Fig. 23-8, the figure shows that $\cos\theta = 4/5$ and $\sin\theta = 3/5$. Thus $\hat{\mathbf{r}} = 0.80\hat{\mathbf{i}} + 0.60\hat{\mathbf{j}}$, as before. The methods of Equations 23-2a and 23-2b are completely equivalent. Equation 23-2a may seem less familiar, but it gives the unit vector directly without the intermediary of trigonometry.

Still another approach is to use Equation 23-1 to find just the magnitude of the force, then figure out whether the force is attractive or repulsive, and then find its components in a chosen coordinate system. This method is completely equivalent to our more elegant and straightforward approach using unit vectors.

Coulomb's law for the electric force is similar to Newton's law for the gravitational force. Both forces show the same inverse-square decrease with distance, and both are proportional to the product of the interacting charges or masses. But there is an important difference: There's only one kind of mass (even antimatter has "positive mass"), and the gravitational force it produces is always attractive. That means large concentrations of mass give rise to large gravitational forces. But charge comes in two varieties that attract each other, so large concentrations of charge tend to be electrically neutral and therefore give rise to weak electric forces. The electric force between individual particles is vastly stronger than the gravitational force between the same particles (see Problem 6), and it's only because of the nearly complete cancellation of positive and negative charge in bulk matter that gravity becomes important on the macroscopic scale.

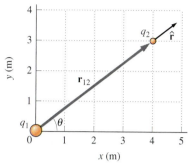

FIGURE 23-8 The two charges in the exercise with Example 23-1. You could get from q_1 to q_2 by going 4 m in the x direction and then 3 m in the y direction, so the displacement vector $\mathbf{r}_{12}$ is $\mathbf{r}_{12} = 4\hat{\mathbf{i}} + 3\hat{\mathbf{j}}$ m. The unit vector $\hat{\mathbf{r}}$ in Coulomb's law has the same direction as $\mathbf{r}_{12}$ but magnitude 1, so it's given by $\mathbf{r}_{12}$ divided by $\mathbf{r}_{12}$'s magnitude r, here $\sqrt{(4 \text{ m})^2 + (3 \text{ m})^2}$ = 5 m. More generally, the unit vector in the direction from q_1 toward q_2 is $\hat{\mathbf{r}} = \mathbf{r}_{12}/r$. Equivalently, the unit vector is $\hat{\mathbf{r}} = \cos\theta \, \hat{\mathbf{i}} + \sin\theta \, \hat{\mathbf{j}}$, with θ the angle between $\mathbf{r}_{12}$ and the positive x axis.

Got It!

Charge q_1 is located at $x = 1$ m, $y = 0$. What should you use for the unit vector $\hat{r}$ in Coulomb's law if you're calculating the force q_1 exerts on a charge q_2 located at (a) the origin and (b) the point $x = 0$, $y = 1$ m? Explain why you can answer this question without being told the signs of either charge.

Point Charges and the Superposition Principle

Coulomb's law is strictly true only for **point charges**—charged objects of negligible size. Electrons and protons can usually be treated as point charges; so, approximately, can any two charged objects if their separation is large compared to their size. But often we're interested in the electrical effects of **charge distributions**—arrangements of charge spread over space. The DNA molecule shown in Fig. 23-1 is a very complicated charge distribution. Other charge distributions include water molecules, the innards of a TV tube, a memory cell in a computer memory chip, your heart, and a thundercloud. We need to know how to combine the effects of two or more charges to find the electrical effects of such charge distributions.

Figure 23-9 shows two charges q_1 and q_2 which constitute a simple charge distribution. We want to know the net force on a third charge q_3 from the combination of q_1 and q_2. To find that net force, you might calculate the forces $\mathbf{F}_{12}$ and $\mathbf{F}_{13}$ from Equation 23-1, and then vectorially add them. And you'd be right: the force that q_1 exerts on q_3 is unaffected by the presence of q_2, and vice versa, so you can apply Coulomb's law separately to the pairs q_1q_3 and q_2q_3 and then combine the results. That may seem obvious, but nature needn't have been so simple.

The fact that electric forces add vectorially is called the **superposition principle**. Our confidence in this principle is ultimately based on experiments that show electric and indeed electromagnetic phenomena behave according to the principle. With superposition we can solve relatively complicated problems by breaking them into simpler parts. If the superposition principle did not hold, the mathematical description of electromagnetism would be far more complicated than it is. ActivPhysics Activities 11.2 and 11.3 let you explore the superposition principle.

Although the force that one point charge exerts on another decreases with the inverse square of the distance between them, it's important to recognize that the same is usually not true of the force arising from a charge distribution. The superposition of forces from different charges in a distribution may result in a very different distance dependence of the force due to a charge distribution (see Fig. 23-10). Example 23-2 on the next page provides a case in point.

FIGURE 23-9 The superposition principle allows us to add vectorially the forces from two or more charges.

11.2, 11.3

Electric Force: Superposition Principle

FIGURE 23-10 (*a*) For a charge distribution distant enough to resemble a point charge, the inverse-square law holds approximately. (*b*) Close to charge distribution, the inverse-square law usually does not hold. That's because individual charges in the distribution are located at different distances and directions from the charge experiencing the force.

| EXAMPLE 23-2 | *Raindrops* |

The charging of individual raindrops is ultimately responsible for the electrical activity of a thunderstorm. Suppose two drops with equal charge q are located on the x axis at $\pm a$, as shown in Fig. 23-11. Find the electric force on a third drop with charge Q located at an arbitrary point on the y axis.

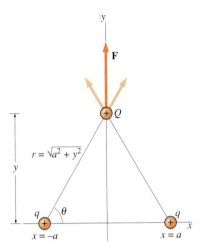

FIGURE 23-11 The force on Q is the vector sum of the forces from the individual charges.

Solution

Charge Q is the same distance $r = \sqrt{a^2 + y^2}$ from the two other drops, so the force from each has the same magnitude. Then it's obvious from Fig. 23-11 that the x components of the two forces cancel, while the y components are the same. Fig. 23-11 and Equation 23-2b show that the y components of the unit vectors from the two charges q toward Q are both given by $\hat{r}_y = \sin\theta = y/\sqrt{a^2 + y^2}$. Then the y component of each force is given by $F_y = (kqQ/r^2)\hat{r}_y$, and the net force on Q becomes

$$\mathbf{F} = F_y\hat{\mathbf{j}} = \left(\frac{2kqQ}{a^2 + y^2}\right)\left(\frac{y}{\sqrt{a^2 + y^2}}\right)\hat{\mathbf{j}} = \frac{2kqQ}{(a^2 + y^2)^{3/2}}\hat{\mathbf{j}},$$

where the factor of two comes from adding the y components of the forces from both charges q.

Does our result make sense? Evaluating $\mathbf{F}$ at $y = 0$ gives zero force. Here, midway between the two charges, Q experi-

ences equal but opposite forces from the two q's, so the net force must be zero. At very large distances such that $y \gg a$, on the other hand, we can neglect a^2 compared with y^2, and the force becomes

$$\mathbf{F} = \frac{k(2q)Q}{y^2}\hat{\mathbf{j}}. \qquad (y \gg a)$$

This is just the force we would expect from a single charge of magnitude $2q$ located a distance y from Q—showing that this system of two charges acts like a single charge $2q$ at distances large compared with the charge separation. But this is true only at distances large compared with the charge separation. In closer, where the detailed arrangement of the individual charges is important, the behavior of the field is more complicated. In fact, our result shows the field initially increasing as y increases, and only later beginning to decrease with increasing y.

In drawing Fig. 23-11 we tacitly assumed that q and Q have the same signs. But our analysis holds even if they don't; in that case the product qQ is negative, and $\mathbf{F}$ therefore points in the opposite direction from $\hat{\mathbf{j}}$.

EXERCISE Find the net force on the charge located at the origin in Fig. 23-12.

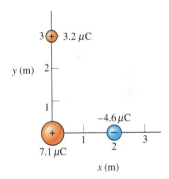

FIGURE 23-12 What is the force on the charge at the origin?

Answer: $73\hat{\mathbf{i}} - 23\hat{\mathbf{j}}$ mN

Some problems similar to Example 23-2: 19–22, 34

| EXAMPLE 23-3 | *Balancing Forces* |

A positive charge $+2q$ lies on the x axis at $x = -a$, and a charge $-q$ lies at $x = +a$, as shown in Fig. 23-13. Find a point where the electric force on a third charge Q would be zero.

Solution

The point must lie on the x axis since off axis the individual force vectors cannot point in opposite directions. But where on

FIGURE 23-13 Where will a third charge experience no net force (Example 23-3)?

the axis? In between the two charges the repulsion of one and attraction of the other would add to give a nonzero net force. To the left of $+2q$, a third charge Q would always be closer to $+2q$ than to $-q$. The force from $+2q$ would always be greater, partly because Q would be closer to it and partly because of its greater charge. So the only place the forces from the two charges might cancel is to the right of $-q$.

So suppose the third charge Q lies at some point x to the right of $-q$, so $x > a$. Then a unit vector from either $+2q$ or $-q$ toward Q points in the $+x$ direction, so is the vector $\hat{\mathbf{i}}$. Summing the two forces as given by Equation 23-1 and setting the result to zero then gives

$$\mathbf{F} = \mathbf{F}_{2q} + \mathbf{F}_{-q} = \frac{k(2q)Q}{(x+a)^2}\hat{\mathbf{i}} + \frac{k(-q)Q}{(x-a)^2}\hat{\mathbf{i}} = \mathbf{0},$$

where the denominators are the distances from any point $x > a$ to the charges located at $x = -a$ and $x = +a$, respectively. Note that Q cancels from the equation, showing that the point we're finding will be a point of zero force for *any* charge, no matter what its sign or magnitude. The quantities k and q also cancel, so the x component of our equation for the net force becomes

$$\frac{2}{(x+a)^2} = \frac{1}{(x-a)^2}.$$

Inverting and taking square roots gives

$$\frac{x+a}{\sqrt{2}} = \pm(x-a).$$

We solve separately for the two possible signs. For the $+$ sign, we have

$$x = a\frac{\sqrt{2}+1}{\sqrt{2}-1} = a\frac{(\sqrt{2}+1)^2}{(\sqrt{2}-1)(\sqrt{2}+1)}$$
$$= (3 + 2\sqrt{2})a = 5.83a.$$

Since this value of x is greater than a, this point does indeed lie to the right of $-q$. So it's the point where the two forces balance. Move a little to the left, and the negative charge dominates, exerting a leftward force on a positive Q. Move a little to the right, and the net positive charge of the whole distribution dominates, exerting a rightward force on a positive Q. In between is the point of zero force.

You can verify that the solution for the minus sign lies to the left of $-q$ and is therefore inconsistent with our choice of direction for the unit vector from $-q$. This second solution is therefore not a meaningful answer.

Tip

Let the Algebra Take Care of Signs Once again, Equation 23-1 tells it all—including the direction of the force once you choose the unit vector correctly. You may be tempted in a problem like Example 23-3 simply to set the magnitudes of the two forces equal and solve for x. That may work if you're careful, but it's safer to remember that you're really solving for a point where *the vector sum of two forces is zero*. You can't go wrong if you write those forces carefully with the correct vector directions and then sum them.

EXERCISE Repeat Example 23-3 with the charge $-q$ changed to $+q$.

Answer: $(3 - 2\sqrt{2})a = 0.17a$

Some problems similar to Example 23-3: 16–18, 32, 34

23-4 THE ELECTRIC FIELD

In Chapter 9 we defined the gravitational field at a point as the gravitational force per unit mass that an object at that point would experience. Even without Chapter 9, you're still familiar with this concept. You know that the force on an object of mass m near Earth's surface has magnitude mg and points downward. So we can think of g as a measure of the *force per unit mass* that any object would experience due to Earth's gravity. Full specification of that force includes its direction, which in this case is downward. So we can picture the gravitational field as a set of vectors giving the magnitude and direction of the gravitational force per unit mass at each point (Fig. 23-14a). In so doing, we've generalized to describe the force Earth would exert on *any* mass, rather than just its force on some particular mass.

It's convenient to do the same thing with the electric force. Rather than finding the force that a charge distribution exerts on some particular charge, we define the **electric field** as the force per unit charge:

> **The electric field at any point is the force per unit charge that would be experienced by a charge at that point. Mathematically,**

$$\mathbf{E} = \frac{\mathbf{F}}{q}.$$

(23-3a)

We emphasize that the electric field is a continuous entity, existing at every point in space. When we represent the field by vectors, we can't draw one everywhere, but that doesn't mean there isn't field at all points. Furthermore, we draw vectors as extended arrows, but each vector represents the field at only one point, namely the tail end of the vector. Figure 23-14b illustrates this for the electric field of a point charge.

The field concept implies a shift in our thinking about forces. Instead of the "action-at-a-distance" idea that Earth reaches out across empty space to pull on the moon, the gravitational field concept says that Earth creates a gravitational field and that the moon responds to the field at its location. The same is true for the electric field. Instead of thinking of one charge attracting or repelling another, we view a charge as creating an electric field throughout the space surrounding it. A second charge then responds to the field at its immediate location. Although the field only reveals itself through its effect on a charge, we nevertheless consider that the field exists at all points, whether or not there are charges present to feel a force. Right now you probably find the field concept to be a bit abstract, but as you advance in your study of electromagnetism you'll come to appreciate that fields are an essential feature of our universe, every bit as real as matter itself.

We can use Equation 23-3a as a prescription for measuring electric fields. Place a point charge at some point, measure the electric force it experiences, and divide by the charge to get the field. In practice, we need to be careful because the field generally arises from some distribution of charges, which we call the **source charges**. If the charge we're using to probe the field—the **test charge**—is large, the field it creates may disturb the source charges, altering their configuration and thus the field they create. For that reason, it's important to use a very small test charge.

If we know the electric field $\mathbf{E}$ at a point, we can rearrange Equation 23-3a to find the force on any point charge q placed at that point:

$$\mathbf{F} = q\mathbf{E}.$$

(23-3b)

If the charge q is positive, then this force is in the same direction as the field, but if q is negative then the force it experiences is opposite to the field direction.

Equations 23-3 show that the units of electric field are newtons per coulomb. Fields of hundreds to thousands of N/C are commonplace, while fields of 3×10^6 N/C will tear electrons from air molecules. Electric fields within atoms can exceed 10^{12} N/C.

FIGURE 23-14 (a) Representing the gravitational field near Earth's surface as a set of vectors. Each has magnitude $g = 9.8$ N/C and points downward. Each field vector gives the force per unit mass at a single point, namely the tail of the vector. Blowup shows that the field exists everywhere; we just can't draw vectors everywhere. (b) The electric field of a positive point charge points radially outward and its magnitude decreases with distance from the point charge (here the arrow lengths don't accurately reflect the exact inverse-square falloff). Each field vector gives the force per unit charge at a single point, namely the tail of the vector. As the blowup suggests, the field is continuous, with a field vector for each point in space. Figure is a 2-dimensional cross section of the field; in three dimensions, field vectors extend radially outward in all directions.

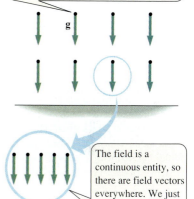

Right at this point the gravitational field is described by the vector **g**. That means a mass m placed here would experience a gravitational force $m\mathbf{g}$.

The field is a continuous entity, so there are field vectors everywhere. We just can't draw them all.

(a)

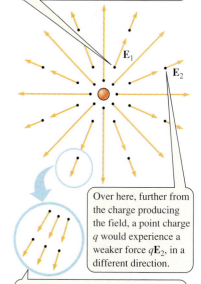

Right at this point the electric field is described by the vector $\mathbf{E}_1$. That means a point charge q placed here would experience an electric force $q\mathbf{E}_1$.

Over here, further from the charge producing the field, a point charge q would experience a weaker force $q\mathbf{E}_2$, in a different direction.

The field is a continuous entity, so there are field vectors everywhere. We just can't draw them all.

(b)

EXAMPLE 23-4	*A Thunderstorm: Force and Field*

A charged raindrop carrying 10 μC experiences an electric force of 0.30 N in the $+x$ direction. What is the electric field at its location? What would be the force on a -5.0-μC drop at the same location?

Solution

Equation 23-2a defines the electric field; here the force is $0.30\hat{\imath}$ N, so

$$\mathbf{E} = \frac{\mathbf{F}}{q} = \frac{0.30\hat{\imath}\ \text{N}}{10\times10^{-6}\ \text{C}} = 30\hat{\imath}\ \text{kN/C}.$$

Acting on a -5.0-μC charge, this field would result in a force

$$\mathbf{F} = q\mathbf{E} = (-5.0\ \mu\text{C})(30\hat{\imath}\ \text{kN/C}) = -0.15\hat{\imath}\ \text{N}.$$

Tip

The Field Is Independent of the Test Charge You might wonder if the field should point in the $-x$ direction when we talk about putting a negative charge in the field. It doesn't—because the whole point of the field concept is to provide a description that's independent of the particular charge experiencing that force.

The electric field in this example points in the $+x$ direction *no matter what charge* we may choose to put in the field. For a positive charge the force $q\mathbf{E}$ points in the *same* direction as the field; for a negative charge $q < 0$, and the force is *opposite* the field direction. As always, the algebra takes care of the signs—although you should check that your algebraic answers make physical sense.

EXERCISE An electric field $\mathbf{E} = -450\hat{\imath}$ kN/C is used to accelerate electrons in a portion of a TV picture tube, where the x axis points from the back to the front of the tube. Find the force in this field experienced by (a) an electron and (b) an ion carrying $+2$ elementary charges. (c) Which particle will be accelerated toward the front of the tube?

Answers: (a) $7.2\times10^{-14}\hat{\imath}$ N; (b) $-1.4\times10^{-13}\hat{\imath}$ N; (c) the electron

Some problems similar to Example 23-4: 26–28

The Field of a Point Charge

Once we know the field of a charge distribution we can calculate its effect on other charges. The simplest charge distribution is a single point charge. Coulomb's law gives the force on a test charge q_1 located a distance r from a point charge q:

$$\mathbf{F} = \frac{kqq_1}{r^2}\hat{\mathbf{r}},$$

where $\hat{\mathbf{r}}$ is a unit vector pointing *away* from q. The electric field arising from q is the force per unit charge, or

$$\mathbf{E} = \frac{\mathbf{F}}{q_1} = \frac{kq}{r^2}\hat{\mathbf{r}}. \qquad \text{(field of a point charge)} \qquad (23\text{-}4)$$

Since it is so closely related to Coulomb's law for the electric force, we also refer to Equation 23-4 as Coulomb's law. Note that the equation contains no reference to the test charge q_1, since the field of q exists independently of any other charge. Since $\hat{\mathbf{r}}$ always points *away* from q, the direction of $\mathbf{E}$ is radially outward if q is positive and radially inward if q is negative. Figure 23-15 shows some field

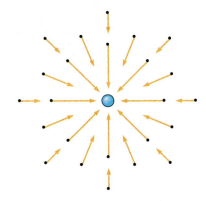

FIGURE 23-15 Field vectors for a negative point charge point radially inward, and their magnitude falls off with increasing distance from the point charge. As in Fig. 23-14b, each vector gives the force per unit charge that a test charge would experience when placed at the vector's tail. In three dimensions the vectors would fill all space in a spherically symmetric fashion.

vectors for a negative point charge, analogous to those of the positive point charge in Fig. 23-14*b*. ActivPhysics Activity 11.4 explores the point charge electric field.

11.4

Electric Field: Point Charge

23-5 ELECTRIC FIELDS OF CHARGE DISTRIBUTIONS

The electric field is the electric force per unit charge. Since the electric force obeys the superposition principle, so does the electric field. That means the field of a charge distribution is the vector sum of the fields of the individual point charges comprising the distribution:

$$\mathbf{E} = \mathbf{E}_1 + \mathbf{E}_2 + \mathbf{E}_3 + \cdots = \sum_i \mathbf{E}_i = \sum_i \frac{kq_i}{r_i^2}\hat{\mathbf{r}}_i, \qquad (23\text{-}5)$$

where the $\mathbf{E}_i$'s are the fields of the point charges q_i located at distances r_i from the point where we're evaluating the field, and where the $\hat{\mathbf{r}}_i$'s are unit vectors pointing *from* each point charge *toward* where we're evaluating the field. In principle, Equation 23-5 gives the electric field of *any* charge distribution. In practice, the process of summing the individual field vectors is often complicated unless the charge distribution contains relatively few charges arranged in a symmetric way.

EXAMPLE 23-5	*Two Protons*

Two protons are 3.6 nm apart. (a) Find the electric field at the point P shown in Fig. 23-16. (b) Find the force on an electron at point P.

Solution

If we take the x axis along the line joining the protons, then $\hat{\mathbf{r}}_1$ is just $\hat{\mathbf{i}}$ and $\hat{\mathbf{r}}_2$ is $-\hat{\mathbf{i}}$, where the subscripts 1 and 2 refer to the left and right protons, respectively. Then Equation 23-5 gives

$$\mathbf{E} = \mathbf{E}_1 + \mathbf{E}_2 = \frac{ke}{r_1^2}\hat{\mathbf{i}} + \frac{ke}{r_2^2}(-\hat{\mathbf{i}}) = ke\left(\frac{1}{r_1^2} - \frac{1}{r_2^2}\right)\hat{\mathbf{i}}$$

$$= (9.0\times10^9 \text{ N·m}^2/\text{C}^2)(1.6\times10^{-19} \text{ C})$$

$$\times \left[\frac{1}{(1.2\times10^{-9} \text{ m})^2} - \frac{1}{(2.4\times10^{-9} \text{ m})^2}\right]\hat{\mathbf{i}}$$

$$= 750\hat{\mathbf{i}} \text{ MN/C}.$$

FIGURE 23-16 What is the electric field at P (Example 23-5)?

An electron in this field will experience a force

$$\mathbf{F} = q\mathbf{E} = (-1.6\times10^{-19} \text{ C})(750\times10^6 \ \hat{\mathbf{i}} \text{ N/C})$$

$$= -1.2\times10^{-10}\hat{\mathbf{i}} \text{ N}.$$

EXERCISE Find the magnitude of the electric field (a) 4.8 nm and (b) 200 nm to the right of the right-hand proton in Fig. 23-16. (c) Show that your answer to (b) is nearly equal to the field of a single charge $2e$ located midway between the two protons.

Answers: (a) 82.9 MN/C; (b) 70.7 kN/C

Some problems similar to Example 23-5: 31–34

The Electric Dipole

One of the most important charge distributions is the **electric dipole**, consisting of two point charges of equal magnitude but opposite sign held a fixed distance apart. Many molecules are essentially electric dipoles, so an understanding of

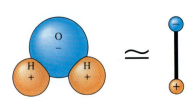

FIGURE 23-17 (left) A water molecule. Electrons spend more time in the vicinity of the single oxygen atom, giving rise to separate regions of negative and positive charge. The molecule therefore approximates the dipole shown at right, and results in an electric field like that of Example 23-6.

the dipole helps explain molecular behavior (Fig. 23-17). During contraction the heart muscle becomes essentially a dipole, and physicians performing electrocardiography are measuring, among other things, the strength and orientation of that dipole. The dipole configuration is also used in a number of technological devices such as radio and TV antennas.

EXAMPLE 23-6	*Modeling a Molecule*

A molecule consists of separated regions of positive and negative charge, modeled approximately as a positive charge q at $x = a$ and a negative charge $-q$ at $x = -a$, as shown in Fig. 23-18. Find a general expression for the electric field at any point on the y axis, and an approximate expression valid at large distances ($y \gg a$).

Solution

Figure 23-18 shows the individual field vectors $\mathbf{E}_-$ and $\mathbf{E}_+$, along with their sum. The y components cancel to give a net field parallel to the x axis, so we can get the net field by summing the two x components. Figure 23-18 and Equation 23-2b show that the x component of the unit vector from the negative charge toward the field point is $\cos\theta$, where $\cos\theta = a/r$; the x component of the unit vector from the positive charge is then $-a/r$. So the net field on the y axis becomes

$$\mathbf{E} = \frac{k(-q)}{r^2}\left(\frac{a}{r}\right)\hat{\imath} + \frac{kq}{r^2}\left(-\frac{a}{r}\right)\hat{\imath} = -\frac{2kqa}{(y^2+a^2)^{3/2}}\hat{\imath},$$

where the two terms in the sum correspond to the negative and positive charges, and where in the last step we used $r = \sqrt{y^2 + a^2}$. Although the x components of the unit vectors from the two charges have opposite signs, so do the charges— and thus the x components of the fields themselves are actually the same, as is obvious in Fig. 23-18.

Does this result make sense? Midway between the charges the fields from each charge point in the same direction and have the same magnitude, so we expect a resultant field twice that of either charge alone. Setting $y = 0$ at the midpoint gives

$$\mathbf{E}(y=0) = -\frac{2kqa}{(a^2)^{3/2}}\hat{\imath} = -\frac{k(2q)}{a^2}\hat{\imath},$$

which is indeed twice the field of either charge at the distance a.

We're frequently interested in the field far from a dipole, which is why this example asks for an approximate expression for $y \gg a$. (One needn't go very far from a molecule for its size to be insignificant.) Under this approximation we can neglect a^2 compared with y^2 in our expression for the field, giving

$$\mathbf{E} = -\frac{2kqa}{y^3}\hat{\imath}, \qquad y \gg a.$$

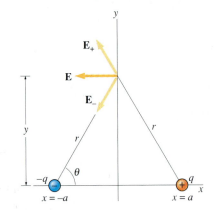

FIGURE 23-18 An electric dipole. The electric field on the dipole's perpendicular bisector (here the y axis) is parallel to the dipole axis.

We'll see later how forces associated with such molecular electric fields contribute to the van der Waals interaction that we considered in Chapter 20.

Tip

Approximations Making approximations requires some care. Here we're basically asking for the field when y is so large that a is negligible *compared with* y. So we neglect a^2 compared with y^2 when the two are summed, but we *don't* neglect a when it appears in the numerator, where it's not summed with y.

EXERCISE Find (a) a general expression for the dipole field at points on the x axis to the right of $x = a$ in Fig. 23-18, and (b) an approximate expression valid for $x \gg a$.

Answers: (a) $\mathbf{E} = \dfrac{4kqax}{(x^2 - a^2)^2}\hat{\imath}$; (b) $\mathbf{E} = \dfrac{4kqa}{x^3}\hat{\imath}$

Some problems similar to Example 23-6: 31, 37, 38, 41

The dipole fields in Example 23-6 and its exercise both decrease, at large distances, as the inverse *cube* of distance. Physically, this is because the dipole has zero *net* charge. Its field arises entirely from the slight separation of two opposite charges. Because of this separation the dipole field isn't exactly zero, but it is weaker and more localized than the field of a point charge. Many complicated charge distributions exhibit the essential characteristic of a dipole—namely, they're neutral but consist of separated regions of positive and negative charge—and at large distances such distributions all have essentially the same field configuration (see Problems 46 and 82). ActivPhysics Activity 11.5 explores the dipole field. By placing the two charges in simulation 1 close together you can verify approximately the inverse-cube dependence of the dipole field.

11.5
Electric Field:
Due to a Dipole

At large distances the results of Example 23-6 and its exercise show that the dipole's physical characteristics q and a enter the equations for the electric field only through the product qa. We could double q (that is, double both the positive and the negative charge) and halve a, and the dipole's electric field would remain unchanged. In general, a dipole's electrical properties are characterized completely by its **electric dipole moment**, p, defined as the product of the charge q and the separation d between the two charges making up the dipole:

$$p = qd. \quad \text{(dipole moment)} \qquad (23\text{-}6)$$

In Example 23-6 the charge separation was $d = 2a$, so there the dipole moment was $p = 2aq$. In terms of the dipole moment, the fields we derived in Example 23-6 can then be written

$$\mathbf{E} = -\frac{kp}{y^3}\hat{\mathbf{i}} \quad \left(\begin{array}{l}\text{dipole field for } y \gg a, \\ \text{on perpendicular bisector}\end{array}\right) \qquad (23\text{-}7a)$$

and

$$\mathbf{E} = \frac{2kp}{x^3}\hat{\mathbf{i}} \quad \left(\begin{array}{l}\text{dipole field} \\ \text{for } x \gg a, \text{ on axis}\end{array}\right). \qquad (23\text{-}7b)$$

Because the dipole isn't spherically symmetric, its field depends not only on distance but also on orientation; for instance, Equations 23-7a and b show that the field along the dipole axis at a given distance is twice as strong as along the bisector. So it's important to know the orientation of a dipole in space, and therefore we generalize our definition of the dipole moment to make it a vector, of magnitude $p = qd$, and in the direction from the negative toward the positive charge (Fig. 23-19).

FIGURE 23-19 The dipole moment vector has magnitude $p = qd$ given by the product of the charge and separation, and it points from the negative toward the positive charge.

Got It!

Far from a charge distribution, you measure an electric field strength of 800 N/C. What will be the field strength if you double your distance from the charge distribution, if the distribution consists of (a) a point charge or (b) a dipole?

Continuous Charge Distributions

Although any charge distribution ultimately consists of pointlike electrons and protons, it would be impossible in practice to sum all the field vectors from the 10^{23} or so particles in a typical piece of matter. Instead, it's convenient to make the approximation that charge is spread continuously over the distribution. If the charge distribution extends throughout a volume, we describe it in terms of the **volume charge density**, ρ, with units of C/m³. For charge distributions spread over surfaces or lines the corresponding quantities are the **surface charge density**, σ, and **line charge density**, λ. Their units are C/m² and C/m, respectively.

To calculate the field of a continuous charge distribution, we break the charged region into very many small charge elements dq, each small enough that it is essentially a point charge. Each dq then produces an electric field $d\mathbf{E}$ given by Equation 23-3:

$$d\mathbf{E} = \frac{k\,dq}{r^2}\hat{\mathbf{r}}. \tag{23-8a}$$

We then form the vector sum of all the $d\mathbf{E}$'s. In the limit of infinitely many infinitesimally small dq's and their corresponding $d\mathbf{E}$'s, that sum becomes an integral and we have

$$\mathbf{E} = \int d\mathbf{E} = \int \frac{k\,dq}{r^2}\hat{\mathbf{r}}. \tag{23-8b}$$

The limits of this integral are chosen to include the entire charge distribution. Figure 23-20 shows the meaning of Equation 23-8b; note in particular that both the distance r and the direction specified by $\hat{\mathbf{r}}$ generally vary with position.

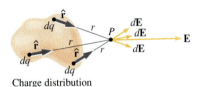

Charge distribution

FIGURE 23-20 The electric field at point P, given by Equation 23-8b, is the sum of the vectors $d\mathbf{E}$ arising from the individual charge elements dq in the entire distribution, each calculated using the appropriate distance r and unit vector $\hat{\mathbf{r}}$.

EXAMPLE 23-7	A Charged Rod

Wires, antennas, and similar elongated structures can often be treated as thin rods carrying electric charge. Suppose such a rod of length ℓ carries a positive charge Q distributed uniformly over its length. Find the electric field at point P in Fig. 23-21, a distance a from the end of the rod.

FIGURE 23-21 The field at P is the sum—or integral—of the fields arising from all the infinitesimal charge elements dq along the rod.

Solution

Let the y axis lie along the rod, with origin at P. Consider a small length dy of the rod, containing charge dq, and located a distance y from P. A unit vector from dq toward P is $-\hat{\mathbf{j}}$, so the field at P due to dq is

$$d\mathbf{E} = -\frac{k\,dq}{y^2}\hat{\mathbf{j}}.$$

The net field at P is the sum—that is, the integral—of all the fields $d\mathbf{E}$ arising from all the dq's along the rod:

$$\mathbf{E} = \int d\mathbf{E} = -\hat{\mathbf{j}} \int_{y=a}^{y=a+\ell} \frac{k\,dq}{y^2},$$

where we've chosen the limits to cover the entire rod. To evaluate the integral we must relate dq and y. How? The rod carries total charge Q, distributed uniformly over its length ℓ. The line charge density is therefore $\lambda = Q/\ell$. This is the charge per unit length; a length dy therefore carries charge $dq = \lambda\,dy$, or $dq = Q\,dy/\ell$. Then our integral becomes

$$\mathbf{E} = -\hat{\mathbf{j}} \int_a^{a+\ell} \frac{k(Q\,dy/\ell)}{y^2} = -\frac{kQ}{\ell}\hat{\mathbf{j}} \int_a^{a+\ell} \frac{dy}{y^2}$$

$$= -\frac{kQ}{\ell}\hat{\mathbf{j}}\left[-\frac{1}{y}\right]_a^{a+\ell} = -\frac{kQ}{\ell}\hat{\mathbf{j}}\left(\frac{1}{a} - \frac{1}{a+\ell}\right) = -\frac{kQ}{a(a+\ell)}\hat{\mathbf{j}},$$

where we took k, Q, ℓ, and $\hat{\mathbf{j}}$ outside the integral because they are constants.

Does this result make sense? First consider the direction: The negative sign shows that the field is downward for positive Q and upward for negative Q, as we should expect. Now suppose P is very far from the rod, so $a \gg \ell$. Then our result becomes approximately

$$\mathbf{E} = -\frac{kQ}{a^2}\hat{\mathbf{j}}, \qquad (a \gg \ell),$$

which is just what we expect for the field of a point charge Q. In this case we're so far from the rod that its length becomes negligible, and indeed it acts like a point charge. But as we move closer, the field becomes a more complicated superposition of the fields of all the dq's at different locations along the rod, and the field no longer exhibits the inverse-square dependence of the point-charge field.

Knowing the field of the charged rod, we can use superposition to find the fields of charge distributions involving more than one rod or a combination of rods and point charges (see Problems 44 and 46).

Tip

Find a Single Integration Variable Evaluating the integral in Equation 23-8b requires that we relate the charge element dq and the position variable r so we'll have the integral expressed in terms of a single vari-

able. The charge density provides the link needed, since it allows us to write dq as the charge density multiplied by an appropriate element of volume, area, or length:

$$dq = \rho\,dV, \quad dq = \sigma\,dA, \quad \text{or} \quad dq = \lambda\,dx.$$

Which of these we use depends on whether charge is distributed over a volume, area, or length; for the thin rod of Example 23-7, the appropriate charge density was the line charge density λ and the position variable was y, so we had $dq = \lambda\,dy$. Sometimes you'll be given the charge density explicitly, and other times you can compute it from the charge and dimensions of the charge distribution.

EXERCISE A thin rod of length ℓ lies along the y axis with its bottom end at the origin. It carries a line charge density λ that varies with position, being given by $\lambda = Q_0\dfrac{y^3}{\ell^4}$, where Q_0 is a constant and y is the distance from the origin. Find the magnitude of the electric field at $y = 0$.

Answer: $\dfrac{kQ_0}{2\ell^2}$

Some problems similar to Example 23-7: 43–46, 71, 72, 82

Got It!

The point P in Fig. 23-21 is a distance a from the charged rod carrying total charge Q. So why can't you just write kQ/a^2 for the magnitude of the field at P?

EXAMPLE 23-8	*A Charged Ring*

A thin ring of radius a is centered on the origin and carries a total charge Q distributed uniformly around the ring, as shown in Fig. 23-22. Find the electric field at a point P located a distance x along the axis of the ring, and show that the result makes sense when $x \gg a$.

Solution

In Example 23-7 the magnitude but not direction of the individual field vectors $d\mathbf{E}$ from all the charge elements dq varied. Here we have the opposite situation: a point on the ring axis is equidistant from all points on the ring, so the field magnitudes $d\mathbf{E}$ are the same but their directions vary. Figure 23-22 shows, however, that components perpendicular to the x axis cancel for any pair of charge elements on opposite sides of the ring,

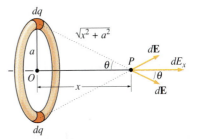

FIGURE 23-22 The electric field of a charged ring points along the ring axis since field components perpendicular to the axis cancel in pairs.

leaving a net field in the x direction. Each charge element contributes an amount dE_x to the field:

$$dE_x = \frac{k\,dq}{r^2}\cos\theta = \frac{k\,dq}{x^2 + a^2}\frac{x}{\sqrt{x^2 + a^2}} = \frac{kx\,dq}{(x^2 + a^2)^{3/2}},$$

where the geometry of Fig. 23-22 gives $r = \sqrt{x^2 + a^2}$ and $\cos\theta = x/\sqrt{x^2 + a^2}$; here $\cos\theta$ is the x component of the unit vector in Equation 23-8a. We now need to integrate this expression over the entire ring. In this integration k, a, and x are all constants—they don't change as we move around the ring. So we have

$$E = E_x = \int_{\text{ring}} dE_x = \int_{\text{ring}} \frac{kx\,dq}{(x^2 + a^2)^{3/2}}$$
$$= \frac{kx}{(x^2 + a^2)^{3/2}}\int_{\text{ring}} dq = \frac{kx\,Q}{(x^2 + a^2)^{3/2}},$$

where the last step follows because $\int_{\text{ring}} dq$ simply means the total charge on the ring. For positive Q this field points away from the ring.

Does this result make sense? At large distances from the ring we can neglect its size a compared with the distance x, and our result reduces to $E = \dfrac{kQ}{x^2}$—just what we would expect for

a point charge Q. As always, a finite-size charge distribution looks essentially like a point charge at distances large compared with its size.

Tip

How Can x Be a Constant? In this exercise x is constant because it's the distance from the center of the ring to the point where we're evaluating the field—that is, it's the distance from the origin to the *field point*, *P*. In the integration to find the field we're supposed to consider all *source points*—all points where charge is located that contributes to the field at *P*. Moving around the ring doesn't affect the value of x, so x is a constant for this integration. However, x is arbitrary, so our result holds for *any* value of x.

EXERCISE Find the point on the x axis where the electric field of the ring in Example 23-8 has its greatest magnitude.

Answer: $x = a/\sqrt{2}$

Some problems similar to Example 23-8: 47–50, 76, 83

EXAMPLE 23-9	*A Power Line's Field*

A long, straight electric power line coincides with the x axis and carries a line charge density λ C/m. What is the electric field at a point P on the y axis? Use the approximation that the line is infinitely long.

Solution

Here *both* the direction and magnitude of the field element $d\mathbf{E}$ arising from a charge element on the line vary with the position x of the charge element. But Fig. 23-23 shows that charge

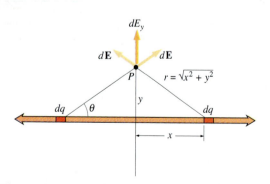

FIGURE 23-23 The field of a charged line is the vector sum of the fields $d\mathbf{E}$ from all the individual charge elements dq along the line. The x components from each pair of charge elements cancel, giving a net field that points directly away from the line.

elements on opposite sides of the y axis give rise to electric fields whose x components cancel. Thus the net field points in the y direction—that is, away from the line if λ is positive. So each charge element contributes an amount dE_y to the net field:

$$dE_y = \frac{k\,dq}{r^2}\sin\theta = \frac{k\lambda\,dx}{x^2 + y^2}\frac{y}{\sqrt{x^2 + y^2}} = \frac{k\lambda y\,dx}{(x^2 + y^2)^{3/2}},$$

where we've written $dq = \lambda\,dx$ and used the geometry of Fig. 23-23 to write $r = \sqrt{x^2 + y^2}$ and $\sin\theta = y/r$. Here, as usual, $\sin\theta$ is the y component of the unit vector $\hat{\mathbf{r}}$. To find the net field, we integrate over the entire line, from $x = -\infty$ to $x = +\infty$. The quantities k, λ, and y don't change as we move along the line, so we have

$$E = E_y = \int_{x=-\infty}^{x=\infty} \frac{k\lambda y\,dx}{(x^2 + y^2)^{3/2}} = k\lambda y \int_{-\infty}^{\infty} \frac{dx}{(x^2 + y^2)^{3/2}}$$
$$= k\lambda y \left[\frac{x}{y^2\sqrt{x^2 + y^2}}\right]_{-\infty}^{\infty} = k\lambda y\left[\frac{1}{y^2} - \left(-\frac{1}{y^2}\right)\right] = \frac{2k\lambda}{y}.$$

$$(23\text{-}9)$$

Here we evaluated the integral using the integral table in Appendix A and applied the limits $\pm\infty$ by noting that as $x \to \pm\infty$ the term y^2 becomes negligible compared with x^2, giving $x/\sqrt{x^2 + y^2} \to x/\sqrt{x^2} = \pm 1$. The integral could also be evaluated by rewriting it in terms of the angle θ (see Problem 87).

Since the line is infinite in both directions and has cylindrical symmetry, Equation 23-9 holds for *any* point a distance y from the line. Our result thus shows that the electric field of a long line of positive charge points radially away from the line, with magnitude that drops inversely with distance from the line (Fig. 23-24).

FIGURE 23-24 Field vectors for an infinite line of positive charge point radially outward from the line, with magnitude decreasing inversely with distance.

What about the field at large distances? Shouldn't it resemble that of a point charge, falling with the inverse square of the distance? No: The charged line is infinitely long, so no matter how far away we go it never resembles a point. Its slower dropoff reflects that fact.

Of course our infinite line is an impossibility. But many real charge distributions, including the power line of this example, have long, thin shapes that approximate an infinite line. Equation 23-9 is therefore a good approximation to the field of a *finite* line as long as we're much closer to it than its length, and not too near either end. Very far from a *finite* line, on the other hand, the field does approach that of a point charge.

EXERCISE A thin rod 2.0 m long carries 50 μC distributed uniformly over its length. Find the electric field strength (a) 1.0 cm from the rod axis, not near either end and (b) 500 m from the rod. Make suitable approximations in both cases.

Answers: (a) 45 MN/C; (b) 1.8 N/C

Some problems similar to Example 23-9: 50–54

23-6 MATTER IN ELECTRIC FIELDS

We're ultimately interested in electric fields since they give rise to forces on charged particles. Because matter consists of such particles, much of the behavior of matter is fundamentally determined by electric fields.

Point Charges in Electric Fields

The motion of a single charge in an electric field is governed by the definition of the electric field (Equation 23-3b):

$$\mathbf{F} = q\mathbf{E}$$

and Newton's law:

$$\mathbf{F} = m\mathbf{a}.$$

Combining these equations gives the acceleration of a particle with charge q and mass m in an electric field $\mathbf{E}$:

$$\mathbf{a} = \frac{q}{m}\mathbf{E}. \tag{23-10}$$

This equation shows that it's the charge-to-mass ratio, q/m, that determines a particle's response to an electric field. Electrons, nearly 2000 times less massive than protons but carrying the same charge, are readily accelerated by electric fields. Many practical devices, from x-ray machines to TV tubes, make use of electrons accelerated in electric fields.

When the electric field is uniform, problems involving the motion of charged particles reduce to the constant-acceleration problems we considered in Chapter 2. We'll see in the next chapter that uniform fields are easily produced by flat, uniformly charged plates. ActivPhysics Activities 11.7 and 11.8 simulate charged-particle motion in uniform electric fields.

ActivPhysics

11.7, 11.8

Motion in an Electric Field

EXAMPLE 23-10   Inside a Heart Monitor

A heart monitor used in a hospital's intensive care unit includes a cathode-ray tube that gives continuous visual display of a patient's heartbeat (Fig. 23-25). An electron beam "paints" the display on a phosphor screen at the front of the tube, being "steered" to different parts of the screen by electric forces. Figure 23-26 shows a side view of the "steering" region of the tube. The region is 2.0 cm long and contains a uniform electric field of 1.0 kN/C. (The field is produced by charging two flat metal plates with opposite charges, as we'll see in the next chapter.) Electrons enter this region moving horizontally at 4.0 Mm/s, as shown. In what direction are the electrons moving as they leave the field region?

FIGURE 23-25 This heart monitor uses an electron beam deflected by electric fields to display patients' heartbeats.

FIGURE 23-26 A uniform electric field deflects an electron from its straight-line path (Example 23-10).

Solution

As usual in two-dimensional motion, the vertical force due to the electric field does not affect the horizontal component of an electron's velocity. Therefore each electron spends a time $t = \Delta x/v_x$ in the field region. During this time it experiences a vertical acceleration qE/m, and therefore gains a vertical velocity component given by

$$v_y = a_y t = \frac{qE_y}{m} \frac{\Delta x}{v_x}$$

$$= \frac{(-1.6 \times 10^{-19} \text{ C})(-1.0 \times 10^3 \text{ N/C})}{9.11 \times 10^{-31} \text{ kg}} \left(\frac{2.0 \times 10^{-2} \text{ m}}{4.0 \times 10^6 \text{ m/s}} \right)$$

$$= 8.78 \times 10^5 \text{ m/s}.$$

Note that the field points downward, as reflected by the minus sign, and combined with the electron's negative charge thus results in an upward velocity. The electron thus leaves the field region moving at an angle of

$$\theta = \tan^{-1}\left(\frac{v_y}{v_x}\right) = \tan^{-1}\left(\frac{8.78 \times 10^5 \text{ m/s}}{4.0 \times 10^6 \text{ m/s}}\right) = 12.4°$$

to the horizontal.

As it traverses the field region the electron describes the parabolic trajectory of an object undergoing constant acceleration in two dimensions; once outside the field it continues in a straight line with its new velocity, as indicated in Fig. 23-26. Field configurations like this one are used to "steer" electron beams not only in heart monitors but also in oscilloscopes and other electronic instrumentation.

EXERCISE What electric field strength would be needed to cause the electron of Example 23-10 to leave the field region at a point 4.6 mm above where it entered?

Answer: 2.1 kN/C

Some problems similar to Example 23-10: 57–61, 75, 76

An application of charge motion in uniform electric fields that's important to biochemists is the process of electrophoresis. Here, charged molecules move through a gel substrate under the influence of a uniform electric field. The drag force of the gel (ultimately electric in origin) counters the $q\mathbf{E}$ force of the electric field, resulting in each molecule having a constant velocity that is greater for molecules of lower mass. The field is applied for a given time, and molecules migrate different distances through the gel. The resulting pattern provides an indication of the different molecular species present (Fig. 23-27). A variation on this technique is the most widely used method of determining the molecular weights of proteins. Electrophoresis is also used to separate particles of all sizes

FIGURE 23-27 Gel electrophoresis of DNA produced these characteristic patterns. Each band marks the final position of a different DNA strand.

in studies of such diverse mixtures as blood and geological sediments. It's sometimes coupled with laser Doppler shift measurements (see Chapter 17) to provide the speeds of the migrating charged particles and give high-precision results in very short times.

When the field is not uniform it's generally difficult to calculate particle trajectories. An important exception is the case of a particle moving at right angles to a field that points radially. In that case—the subject of the following example—the electric force changes the particle's direction but not its speed, so the motion is uniform circular.

EXAMPLE 23-11	*An Electrostatic Analyzer*

Two curved metal plates are used to establish an electric field given by

$$E = E_0 \frac{b}{r},$$

where $E_0 = 24$ kN/C and $b = 5.0$ cm. The field points toward the center of curvature, as shown in Fig. 23-28, and r is the distance from that center. A beam of protons with a mix of speeds is incident on the device. Find the speed v for which an incident proton will leave the analyzer moving horizontally in Fig. 23-28.

Solution

To exit with its velocity horizontal, a proton must describe a circular arc while inside the analyzer. The field provides the v^2/r acceleration required for that circular motion:

$$a = \frac{v^2}{r} = \frac{eE}{m} = \frac{e}{m} E_0 \frac{b}{r}.$$

Solving for v gives

$$v = \sqrt{\frac{eE_0 b}{m}} = \sqrt{\frac{(1.6\times10^{-19}\text{ C})(2.4\times10^4\text{ N/C})(0.050\text{ m})}{1.67\times10^{-27}\text{ kg}}}$$

$$= 3.4\times10^5 \text{ m/s}.$$

Note that it doesn't matter where the protons enter the analyzer since the $1/r$ decrease in field strength matches the $1/r$ depen-

FIGURE 23-28 An electrostatic analyzer, showing the trajectories of protons in the radial electric field. Only those entering with the right speed will emerge at the top moving horizontally. Collimators block protons not moving at right angles to the field.

dence of the acceleration. Devices of this sort have been used on spacecraft to analyze charged particles in interplanetary space.

EXERCISE A proton is in circular motion centered on a long charged wire carrying uniform negative line charge density $-\lambda$. Find its speed. *Hint:* Consult Example 23-9 for the field of the charged wire.

Answer: $v = \sqrt{2k\lambda e/m}$, with m the proton mass

Some problems similar to Example 23-11: 60–64

Dipoles in Electric Fields

Earlier in this chapter we calculated the field of an electric dipole, which consists of two opposite charges of equal magnitude. Here we study a dipole's response to electric fields. Since the dipole configuration provides a simple model for many molecules, our results help explain molecular behavior.

Figure 23-29 shows a dipole with charges $\pm q$ separated by a distance d, located in a uniform electric field. The dipole moment vector **p** has magnitude qd and points from the negative to the positive charge (recall Fig. 23-19). Since the field is uniform, it's the same at both ends of the dipole. Since the dipole charges are equal in magnitude but opposite in sign, they experience equal but opposite forces $\pm q\mathbf{E}$—and therefore there's no net force on the dipole.

FIGURE 23-29 A dipole in a uniform electric field experiences no net force, but it does experience a torque.

However, Fig. 23-29 shows that the dipole does experience a torque that tends to align it with the field. In Chapter 13 we described torque as the cross product of the position vector with the force: $\boldsymbol{\tau} = \mathbf{r} \times \mathbf{F}$, where the magnitude of the torque vector is $rF \sin\theta$ and its direction is given by the right-hand rule. Figure 23-29 thus shows that the torque about the center of the dipole due to the force on the positive charge has magnitude

$$\tau_+ = rF \sin\theta = \tfrac{1}{2}d\, qE \sin\theta.$$

The torque associated with the negative charge has the same magnitude and both torques are in the same direction since both tend to rotate the dipole in Fig. 23-29 clockwise. Thus the net torque has magnitude $\tau = qdE \sin\theta$; applying the right-hand rule shows that this torque is into the page. But qd is the magnitude of the dipole moment $\mathbf{p}$, and Fig. 23-29 shows that θ is the angle between the dipole moment vector and the electric field $\mathbf{E}$; therefore we can write the torque vectorially as

$$\boldsymbol{\tau} = \mathbf{p} \times \mathbf{E}. \qquad \text{(torque on a dipole)} \qquad (23\text{-}11)$$

Because of this torque, it takes work to rotate a dipole in an electric field. If we start with the dipole oriented at right angles to the field ($\theta = \pi/2$), then Equation 12-22b gives the work required to rotate it to a new angle θ:

$$W = \int_{\pi/2}^{\theta} \tau\, d\theta = \int_{\pi/2}^{\theta} pE \sin\theta\, d\theta = pE\, [-\cos\theta]_{\pi/2}^{\theta} = -pE \cos\theta,$$

where the last step follows because $\cos(\pi/2) = 0$. This work ends up as stored potential energy U. Since the product of two vector magnitudes with the cosine of the angle between the vectors defines the dot product, we can write the potential energy in compact form as

$$U = -\mathbf{p} \cdot \mathbf{E}, \qquad (23\text{-}12)$$

where the zero of potential energy corresponds to the dipole at right angles to the field.

APPLICATION   *Microwave Cooking and Liquid Crystals*

The torque on dipoles in electric fields forms the basis of two widespread contemporary technologies: the microwave oven and the liquid crystal display (LCD).

A microwave oven works by generating an electric field whose direction changes several billion times per second. Water molecules, whose dipole moment is much greater than that of most other molecules, respond by attempting to align with the field. But the field is constantly changing, so the molecules swing rapidly back and forth. As they jostle against each other, the energy they gain from the field is dissipated as heat that cooks the food (see Fig. 23-30).

FIGURE 23-30 Water heats in a microwave oven because individual water molecules act as electric dipoles, experiencing torques in the oven's rapidly reversing electric field.

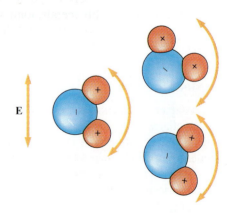

Calculators, laptop computers, gas pumps, watches, and many other devices display numerical and alphabetic information with liquid crystals. This unique state of matter combines the fluidity of a liquid with the order of a solid. The liquid crystal consists of long molecules whose chemical structure gives rise to a dipole-like charge separation. In response to each others' electric fields, the molecules tend to align with each other (see Fig. 23-31). But an external electric field can rotate the liquid crystal dipoles, altering the optical properties of the material. Using optical components we'll study in Chapter 34, different sections of a liquid crystal display can then be made to appear visible or invisible (Fig. 23-32). Liquid crystal displays have the advantage that they consume very little power. On the other hand they generate no light of their own, and therefore an external light source is needed to illuminate the display when it's dark.

Normal
liquid

Liquid
crystal

FIGURE 23-31 Liquid crystals consist of dipole-like molecules that all align in the same direction, in contrast to the random orientation of molecules in an ordinary liquid. Applying an electric field can change the orientation of the liquid-crystal molecules.

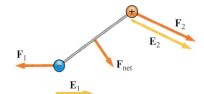

FIGURE 23-32 Changing the orientation of the liquid-crystal molecules alters the optical properties of the liquid crystal, making individual segments of this liquid-crystal display either visible or invisible. (More on liquid-crystal displays in Chapter 34.)

When the electric field is not uniform, the charges at opposite ends of the dipole experience forces that differ in magnitude and/or are not exactly opposite in direction. Then the dipole experiences a net force as well as a torque (Fig. 23-33). An important instance of this effect is the force on a dipole in the field of another dipole (Fig. 23-34). Because the dipole field falls off rapidly with distance and because the dipole responding to the field has closely spaced charges of equal magnitude but opposite sign, the dipole-dipole force is quite weak and falls extremely rapidly with distance. This weak force, which Fig. 23-34 shows to be attractive, is partly responsible for the van der Waals interaction between gas molecules that we considered in Chapter 20. Problems 68 and 85 deal with forces on dipoles in nonuniform fields.

FIGURE 23-33 When the electric field differs in magnitude or direction at the two ends of the dipole, then the dipole experiences a nonzero net force as well as a torque.

Conductors, Insulators, and Dielectrics

Bulk matter contains vast numbers of point charges, namely electrons and protons. In some matter—notably metals, ionic solutions, and ionized gases—individual charges are free to move throughout the material. In such materials—called **conductors**—the application of an electric field results in the ordered motion of electric charge that we call **electric current**. We'll consider the behavior of conductors and related materials called semiconductors in subsequent chapters.

Materials in which charge is not free to move are called **insulators**, since they do not support electric current. Insulators, however, still contain charges—it's just that their charges are bound into neutral molecules. Some molecules, such as water, have intrinsic dipole moments and therefore rotate in response to an applied electric field. Even if they don't have dipole moments, molecules may respond to an electric field by stretching and acquiring **induced dipole**

FIGURE 23-34 Dipole B is aligned with the electric field of dipole A. Since the field of A is stronger at the negative end of B, F_- is greater in magnitude than F_+, so dipole B experiences a net force toward dipole A. This is the origin of the van der Waals force between gas molecules.

FIGURE 23-35 (*a*) A molecule with no dipole moment has negative charge concentric with positive charge. (*b*) In an applied electric field, the molecule stretches and acquires a dipole moment.

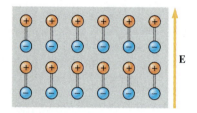

FIGURE 23-36 The alignment of molecular dipoles in a dielectric results in a reduction of the electric field within the dielectric.

moments (Fig. 23-35). In either case, the application of an electric field results in the alignment of molecular dipoles with the field (Fig. 23-36). The fields of the dipoles, pointing from their positive to their negative charges, then reduce the applied electric field within the material. We'll explore the consequences of this effect further in Chapter 26. Materials in which molecules have either intrinsic dipole moments or acquire induced moments are called **dielectrics**.

If the electric field applied to a dielectric becomes too great, individual charges are ripped free, and the material then acts like a conductor. Such **dielectric breakdown** can cause severe damage in electrical equipment (Fig. 23-37). On a larger scale, lightning results from dielectric breakdown in air.

FIGURE 23-37 (*a*) Dielectric breakdown in air results in sparks jumping between two highly charged wires. (*b*) Dielectric breakdown in a solid produced this treelike pattern.

CHAPTER SYNOPSIS

Summary

1. **Electromagnetism** is among the fundamental forces of nature. Electromagnetism comprises electricity and magnetism, seemingly distinct phenomena that are actually intimately related.

2. **Electric charge** is a fundamental property of matter. Charge comes in two types, arbitrarily called positive and negative. Charge is **quantized**, with one elementary charge—the magnitude of the electron or proton charge—equal to 1.60×10^{-19} C, where the coulomb (C) is the SI unit of charge. Charge is also **conserved**, in that the algebraic sum of the charges in a closed system never changes.

3. Charges interact via the **electric force**. This force is proportional to the product of the charges and inversely proportional to the square of the distance between them. **Coulomb's law** provides a mathematical description of the electric force between point charges:

$$\mathbf{F}_{12} = \frac{kq_1q_2}{r^2}\hat{\mathbf{r}}.$$

4. The **superposition principle** states that the electric force on a charge arising from two or more other charges is the vector sum of the force arising from each according to Coulomb's law. The superposition principle greatly simplifies the calculation of electrical effects of various **charge distributions**.

5. The electric field at a point is a vector giving the electric force per unit charge that would be experienced by a charge at that point:

$$E = \frac{F}{q}.$$

The electric field of a point charge q is therefore

$$E = \frac{kq}{r^2}\hat{r}.$$

6. The superposition principle shows that the electric field of a charge distribution is the sum of the fields of its individual point charges:

$$E = \sum_i E_i = \sum_i \frac{kq_i}{r_i^2}\hat{r}_i.$$

A particularly important charge distribution is the **electric dipole**, consisting of two point charges with equal magnitude but opposite sign, separated by a fixed distance. At large distances from a dipole the field decreases as the inverse cube of the distance.

7. With continuous distributions of charge, the sum over all point charges becomes an integral, giving

$$E = \int dE = \int \frac{k\,dq}{r^2}\hat{r}.$$

For any finite charge distribution with nonzero net charge, the field approaches that of a point charge at large distances.

8. A point charge in an electric field experiences a force $F = qE$; if this is the only force acting, the charge undergoes an acceleration $a = (q/m)E$ in accordance with Newton's law.

9. Because it consists of two equal but opposite point charges, an electric dipole experiences no net force in a uniform electric field. It does, however, experience a torque given by $\tau = p \times E$, where p is the dipole moment vector. A dipole in an electric field has potential energy given by $U = -p \cdot E$, where the zero of potential energy corresponds to the dipole oriented perpendicular to the field. In a nonuniform field, a dipole experiences both a torque and a net force.

Terms You Should Understand

(Pairs are closely related terms whose distinction is important; number in parentheses is chapter section where term first appears.)

electromagnetism (23-1)
electric charge (23-2)
coulomb (23-2)
Coulomb's law (23-3)
superposition principle (23-3)
point charge, charge distribution (23-3)
electric field (23-4)
electric dipole (23-5)
dipole moment (23-5)
volume, surface, and line charge density (23-5)
conductor, insulator, dielectric (23-6)
dielectric breakdown (23-6)

Symbols You Should Recognize

C (23-2)
e (23-2)
k (23-3)
q (23-3)
$\hat{r}$ (23-3)
E (23-4)
p (23-5)
ρ, σ, λ (23-5)

Problems You Should Be Able to Solve

calculating electric forces arising from one or more charges acting on another (23-3)
calculating electric fields of distributions of discrete charges (23-5)
calculating electric fields of continuous charge distributions (23-5)
approximating electric fields at large distances from charge distributions (23-5)
evaluating forces on charges in electric fields (23-4, 23-6)
describing the motion of charged particles in uniform and radial electric fields (23-6)
evaluating torques on dipoles in electric fields (23-6)

Limitations to Keep in Mind

Coulomb's law applies strictly only to one point charge acting on another. The forces and electric fields arising from more than one point charge or from a continuous distribution must be calculated using the superposition principle.
At large distances, the field of a charge distribution approaches that of a point charge only if the distribution is both finite in size and has nonzero net charge.
The dipole field decreases with the inverse cube of the distance only for distances large compared with the dipole's charge separation.

QUESTIONS

1. Discuss this statement: It is precisely because the electric force is so strong that the electrical nature of most everyday interactions is not obvious.
2. The gravitational force between an electron and proton is about 10^{-40} times weaker than the electrical force between the two. Since matter consists largely of electrons and protons, why is the gravitational force ever important?
3. You are given two electric charges. Could you determine whether they had the same or opposite signs? Could you determine the signs of each?
4. In Example 23-3 we found a point where the electric force on a third charge would be zero. Would a charge placed at that point be in stable equilibrium? Why or why not?
5. The gravitational force between an electron and a proton is about 10^{-40} times the electrical force between them. Does this ratio depend on how far apart they are? Explain.
6. In which of the following phenomena does electromagnetism play a dominant role?
   a. Gasoline burns in a car engine.
   b. The moon orbits Earth.
   c. A nerve impulse travels from your brain to a muscle.
   d. Protons and neutrons join to form an atomic nucleus.
   e. A chemist synthesizes a new polymer.
   f. You sit in a chair and the chair doesn't collapse.
7. A free neutron is unstable, and soon decays into other particles. One of the decay products is a proton. Must there be others? If so, what electrical properties must they have?
8. Where in Fig. 23-9 could you put a third charge so it would experience no net force? Would it be in stable or unstable equilibrium?
9. Why should the test charge used to measure an electric field be small?
10. Equation 23-4 gives the electric field of a point charge. Does the direction of $\hat{r}$ depend on whether the charge is positive or negative? Does the direction of $\mathbf{E}$ depend on the sign of the charge?
11. Is the electric force on a charged particle always in the direction of the field? Explain.
12. Why does a dipole produce an electric field at all? After all, the dipole has no net charge.
13. The ring in Example 23-8 carries total charge Q, and the point P is the same distance $r = \sqrt{x^2 + a^2}$ from all parts of the ring. So why isn't the electric field of the ring just kQ/r^2?
14. The field of a dipole decreases with the inverse cube of the distance. Why doesn't this violate our assertion that the field of a finite size charge distribution with nonzero net charge approaches that of a point charge at large distances?
15. A spherical balloon is initially uncharged. If you spread positive charge uniformly over the balloon's surface, would it expand or contract? What would happen if you spread negative charge instead?
16. Suppose someone argued that the force we call gravity is really an electric force, arising from a net electric charge on Earth. How could you disprove this?
17. Two cubical blocks of wood are each 10 cm on a side and carry electric charge spread over their surfaces. If they're 5 cm apart, would you be justified in writing kq_1q_2/r^2 for the force between them? How about if they're 5 m apart? Explain the difference.
18. A deuteron (heavy hydrogen nucleus) has twice the mass but the same charge as a normal hydrogen nucleus (a proton). Both are released from rest in the same uniform electric field. Compare the distances each goes in the same time.
19. Under what circumstances is the path of a charged particle a parabola? A circle?
20. Explain why a nonuniform field is required for a net force on a dipole.
21. Why should there be a force between two dipoles? After all, each has zero net charge.
22. Dipoles A and B are both located in the field of a point charge Q, as shown in Fig. 23-38. Does either experience a net torque? A net force? If each dipole is released from rest, describe qualitatively its subsequent motion.

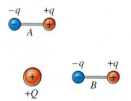

FIGURE 23-38 Question 22.

PROBLEMS

ActivPhysics can help with these problems:
Activities 11.1–11.8

Section 23-2 Electric Charge

1. Suppose the electron and proton charges differed by one part in one billion. Estimate the net charge you would carry.
2. A typical lightning flash delivers about 25 C of negativ charge from cloud to ground. How many electrons are involved?
3. Protons and neutrons are made from combinations of the two most common quarks, the u quark and the d quark. The u quark's charge is $+\frac{2}{3}e$ while the d quark carries

$-\frac{1}{3}e$. How could three of these quarks combine to make (a) a proton and (b) a neutron?

4. A 2-g ping-pong ball rubbed against a wool jacket acquires a net positive charge of 1 μC. Estimate the fraction of the ball's electrons that have been removed.

Section 23-3 Coulomb's Law

5. If the charge imbalance of Problem 1 existed, what would be the approximate force between you and another person 10 m away? Treat the people as point charges, and compare the answer with your weight.

6. Find the ratio of the electrical force between a proton and an electron to the gravitational force between the two. Why doesn't it matter that you aren't told the distance between them?

7. The electron and proton in a hydrogen atom are 52.9 pm apart. What is the magnitude of the electric force between them?

8. How far apart should an electron and proton be so the force of Earth's gravity on the electron is equal to the electric force arising from the proton? Your answer shows why gravity is unimportant on the molecular scale!

9. Two charges, one twice as large as the other, are located 15 cm apart and experience a repulsive force of 95 N. What is the magnitude of the larger charge?

10. Earth carries a net charge of -4.3×10^5 C. The force due to this charge is the same as if it were concentrated at Earth's center. How much charge would you have to place on a 1.0-g mass in order for the electrical and gravitational forces on it to balance?

11. A proton is on the x axis at $x = 1.6$ nm. An electron is on the y axis at $y = 0.85$ nm. Find the net force the two exert on a helium nucleus (charge $+2e$) at the origin.

12. Let $\mathbf{V} = V_x\hat{\mathbf{i}} + V_y\hat{\mathbf{j}}$ be an arbitrary vector, with V its magnitude. Show that the vector $\mathbf{V}/V$ is a unit vector—i.e., that its magnitude is 1.

13. A charge q is at the point $x = 1$ m, $y = 0$. Write expressions for the unit vectors you would use in Coulomb's law if you were finding the force that q exerts on other charges located at (a) $x = 1$ m, $y = 1$ m; (b) the origin; (c) $x = 2$ m, $y = 3$ m. Note that you don't know the sign of q. Why doesn't this matter?

14. A proton is at the origin and an electron is at the point $x = 0.41$ nm, $y = 0.36$ nm. Find the electric force on the proton.

15. A 9.5-μC charge is at $x = 16$ cm, $y = 5.0$ cm, and a -3.2-μC charge is at $x = 4.4$ cm, $y = 11$ cm. Find the force on the negative charge.

16. A charge 3q is at the origin, and a charge $-2q$ is on the positive x axis at $x = a$. Where would you place a third charge so it would experience no net electric force?

17. A 60-μC charge is at the origin, and a second charge is on the positive x axis at $x = 75$ cm. If a third charge placed at $x = 50$ cm experiences no net force, what is the second charge?

18. You have two charges $+4q$ and one charge $-q$. (a) How would you place them along a line so there's no net force on any of the three? (b) Is this equilibrium stable or unstable?

19. In Fig. 23-39 take $q_1 = 68$ μC, $q_2 = -34$ μC, and $q_3 = 15$ μC. Find the electric force on q_3.

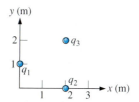

FIGURE 23-39 Problems 19, 20.

20. In Fig. 23-39 take $q_1 = 25$ μC and $q_2 = 20$ μC. If the force on q_1 points in the $-x$ direction, (a) what is q_3 and (b) what is the magnitude of the force on q_1?

21. Four identical charges q form a square of side a. Find the magnitude of the electric force on any of the charges.

22. Three identical charges $+q$ and a fourth charge $-q$ form a square of side a. (a) Find the magnitude of the electric force on a charge Q placed at the center of the square. (b) Describe the direction of this force.

23. Three charges lie in the x-y plane: $q_1 = 55$ μC at $x = 0$, $y = 2.0$ m; q_2 at $x = 3.0$ m, $y = 0$; and q_3 at $x = 4.0$ m, $y = 3.0$ m. If the force on q_3 is $8.0\hat{\mathbf{i}} + 15\hat{\mathbf{j}}$ N, find q_2 and q_3.

24. Two identical small metal spheres initially carry charges q_1 and q_2, respectively. When they're 1.0 m apart they experience a 2.5-N attractive force. Then they're brought together so charge moves from one to the other until they have the same net charge. They're again placed 1.0 m apart, and now they repel with a 2.5-N force. What were the original values of q_1 and q_2?

Section 23-4 The Electric Field

25. An electron placed in an electric field experiences a 6.1×10^{-10} N electric force. What is the field strength?

26. What is the magnitude of the force on a 2.0-μC charge in a 100 N/C electric field?

27. A 68-nC charge experiences a 150-mN force in a certain electric field. Find (a) the field strength and (b) the force that a 35-μC charge would experience in the same field.

28. A -1.0-μC charge experiences a $10\hat{\mathbf{i}}$-N electric force in a certain electric field. What force would a proton experience in the same field?

29. The electron in a hydrogen atom is 0.0529 nm from the proton. What is the proton's electric field strength at this distance?

30. A 65-μC point charge is at the origin. Find the electric field at the points (a) $x = 50$ cm, $y = 0$; (b) $x = 50$ cm, $y = 50$ cm; (c) $x = -25$ cm, $y = 75$ cm.

Section 23-5 Electric Fields of Charge Distributions

31. In Fig. 23-40, point P is midway between the two charges. Find the electric field in the plane of the page (a) 5.0 cm directly above P, (b) 5.0 cm directly to the right of P, and (c) at P.

$$+ 2.0\,\mu C$$

5.0 cm   •P

$$- 2.0\,\mu C$$

FIGURE 23-40 Problem 31.

32. A 1.0-μC charge and a 2.0-μC charge are 10 cm apart, as shown in Fig. 23-41. Find a point where the electric field is zero.

————10 cm————
$1.0\,\mu C$ $2.0\,\mu C$

FIGURE 23-41 Problem 32.

33. A proton is at the origin and an ion is at $x = 5.0$ nm. If the electric field is zero at $x = -5$ nm, what is the charge on the ion?

34. For the situation of Example 23-3, (a) write an expression for the electric field as a function of x for points to the right of the charge $-q$ shown in Fig. 23-13. (b) Taking $q = 1.0\ \mu C$ and $a = 1.0$ m, plot the field as a function of position for $x = 5$ m to $x = 25$ m.

35. (a) Find an expression for the electric field on the y axis due to the two charges q in Fig. 23-11. (b) At what point is the field on the y axis a maximum?

36. Write an expression for the dipole moment vector of the dipole shown in Fig. 23-18.

37. A dipole lies on the y axis, and consists of an electron at $y = 0.60$ nm and a proton at $y = -0.60$ nm. Find the electric field (a) midway between the two charges, (b) at the point $x = 2.0$ nm, $y = 0$, and (c) at the point $x = -20$ nm, $y = 0$.

38. What is the electric field strength 10 cm from a point dipole with dipole moment 3.8 μC·m (a) on the dipole's perpendicular bisector and (b) on its axis?

39. The dipole moment of the water molecule is 6.2×10^{-30} C·m. What would be the separation distance if the molecule consisted of charges $\pm e$? (The effective charge is actually less because electrons are shared by the oxygen and hydrogen atoms.)

40. You're 1.5 m from a charge distribution whose size is much less than 1 m. You measure an electric field strength of 282 N/C. You move to a distance of 2.0 m and the field strength becomes 119 N/C. What is the net charge of the distribution? *Hint:* Don't try to calculate the charge. Determine instead how the field decreases with distance, and from that infer the charge.

41. Three charges form an equilateral triangle of side a. At one vertex is a charge $+2q$; at the other two vertices are charges $-q$. The triangle is oriented with the charge $2q$ on the positive x axis and both charges $-q$ on the y axis. (a) Find an expression for the electric field on the x axis, in the approximation $x \gg a$. (b) Compare with Equation 23-7b to show that your result in (a) is a dipole field, and give an expression for the magnitude of the triangle's dipole moment.

42. Three identical charges q form an equilateral triangle of side a, with two charges on the x axis and one on the positive y axis. (a) Find an expression for the electric field at points on the y axis above the uppermost charge. (b) Show that your result reduces to the field of a point charge $3q$ for $y \gg a$.

43. A 30-cm-long rod carries a charge of 80 μC spread uniformly over its length. Find the electric field strength on the rod axis, 45 cm from the end of the rod.

44. A thin rod of length ℓ carries charge Q distributed evenly over its length. A point charge with the same charge Q lies a distance b from the end of the rod, as shown in Fig. 23-42. Find a point where the electric field is zero.

FIGURE 23-42 Problem 44.

45. A thin rod of length ℓ has its left end at the origin and its right end at $x = \ell$. It carries a line charge density given by $\lambda = \lambda_0 \dfrac{x^2}{\ell^2} \sin(\pi x/\ell)$, where λ_0 is a constant. Find the electric field strength at the origin.

46. Two identical rods of length ℓ lie on the x axis and carry uniform charges $\pm Q$, as shown in Fig. 23-43. (a) Find an expression for the electric field strength as a function of position x for points to the right of the right-hand rod. (b) Show that your result has the $1/x^3$ dependence of a dipole field for $x \gg \ell$. (c) What is the dipole moment of this configuration? *Hint:* See Equation 23-7b.

$$-Q \qquad +Q$$
$$x = -\ell \qquad x = 0 \qquad x = \ell$$

FIGURE 23-43 Problem 46.

47. A uniformly charged ring is 1.0 cm in radius. The electric field on the axis 2.0 cm from the center of the ring has magnitude 2.2 MN/C and points toward the ring center. Find the charge on the ring.

48. Figure 23-44 shows a thin, uniformly charged disk of radius R. Imagine the disk divided into rings of varying radii r, as suggested in the figure. (a) Show that the area of such a ring is very nearly $2\pi r\, dr$. (b) If the surface charge density on the disk is σ C/m², use the result of (a) to write an expression for the charge dq on an infinitesimal ring. (c) Use the result of (b) along with the result of Example 23-8 to write the infinitesimal electric field dE of this ring at a point on the disk axis, taken to be the positive x axis. (d) Integrate over all such rings (that is, from $r = 0$ to $r = R$), to show that the net electric field on the disk axis is

$$E = 2\pi k \sigma\left(1 - \frac{x}{\sqrt{x^2 + R^2}}\right).$$

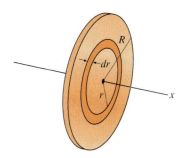

FIGURE 23-44 Problem 48.

49. Use the result of the preceding problem to show that the field of an *infinite,* uniformly charged flat sheet is $2\pi k\sigma$, where σ is the surface charge density. Note that this result is independent of distance from the sheet.

50. A semicircular loop of radius a carries positive charge Q distributed uniformly over its length. Find the electric field at the center of the loop (point P in Fig. 23-45). *Hint:* Divide the loop into charge elements dq as shown in Fig. 23-45, and write dq in terms of the angle $d\theta$. Then integrate over θ to get the net field at P.

FIGURE 23-45 Problem 50.

51. The electric field 22 cm from a long wire carrying a uniform line charge density is 1.9 kN/C. What will be the field strength 38 cm from the wire?

52. What is the line charge density on a long wire if the electric field 45 cm from the wire has magnitude 260 kN/C and points toward the wire?

53. A straight wire 10 m long carries 25 μC distributed uniformly over its length. (a) What is the line charge density

on the wire? Find the electric field strength (b) 15 cm from the wire axis, not near either end and (c) 350 m from the wire. Make suitable approximations in both cases.

54. Figure 23-46 shows a thin rod of length ℓ carrying charge Q distributed uniformly over its length. (a) What is the line charge density on the rod? (b) What must be the electric field direction on the rod's perpendicular bisector (taken to be the y axis)? (c) Modify the calculation of Example 23-9 to find an expression for the electric field at a point P a distance y along the perpendicular bisector. (d) Show that your result for (c) reduces to the field of a point charge Q for $y \gg \ell$.

FIGURE 23-46 Problem 54.

Section 23-6 Matter in Electric Fields

55. In his famous 1909 experiment that demonstrated quantization of electric charge, R. A. Millikan suspended small oil drops in an electric field. With a field strength of 20 MN/C, what mass drop can be suspended when the drop carries a net charge of 10 elementary charges?

56. How strong an electric field is needed to accelerate electrons in a TV tube from rest to one-tenth the speed of light in a distance of 5.0 cm?

57. A proton moving to the right at 3.8×10^5 m/s enters a region where a 56 kN/C electric field points to the left. (a) How far will the proton get before its speed reaches zero? (b) Describe its subsequent motion.

58. An oscilloscope display requires that a beam of electrons moving at 8.2 Mm/s be deflected through an angle of 22° by a uniform electric field that occupies a region 5.0 cm long. What should be the field strength?

59. An ink-jet printer works by "steering" charged ink drops to the right place on the page by passing moving drops through a uniform electric field that deflects them by the appropriate amount. Figure 23-47 shows an ink drop approaching the field region, which has length ℓ and width d between the charged plates that establish the field. Find an expression for the minimum speed a drop with mass m and

FIGURE 23-47 Problem 59.

charge q must have if it is to get through the region without hitting either plate.

60. An electrostatic analyzer like that of Example 23-11 has $b = 7.5$ cm. What should be the value of E_0 if the device is to select protons moving at 84 km/s?

61. An electron is moving in a circular path around a long, uniformly charged wire carrying 2.5 nC/m. What is the electron's speed?

62. Figure 23-48 shows a device its inventor claims will separate isotopes of a particular element. (Isotopes of the same element have nuclei with the same charge but different masses). Atoms of the element are first stripped completely of their electrons, then accelerated from rest through an electric field chosen to give the desired isotope exactly the right speed to pass through the electrostatic analyzer (see Example 23-11). Prove that the device won't work—that is, that it won't separate different isotopes.

FIGURE 23-48 An isotope separator that won't work (Problem 62).

63. What is the line charge density on a long wire if a 6.8-μg particle carrying 2.1 nC describes a circular orbit about the wire with speed 280 m/s?

64. The electron in a hydrogen atom has kinetic energy 2.18×10^{-18} J. Assuming the electron is in a circular orbit around the central proton, estimate the size of the atom. (Although this problem gives a reasonable answer, the simple model of an electron orbiting a proton is not consonant with the quantum mechanical description of the atom.)

65. A dipole with dipole moment 1.5 nC·m is oriented at 30° to a 4.0-MN/C electric field. (a) What is the magnitude of the torque on the dipole? (b) How much work is required to rotate the dipole until it's antiparallel to the field?

66. A molecule has its dipole moment aligned with a 1.2-kN/C electric field. If it takes 3.1×10^{-27} J to reverse the molecule's orientation, what is its dipole moment?

67. Two identical dipoles, each of charge q and separation a, are a distance x apart as shown in Fig. 23-49. By considering forces between pairs of charges in the different dipoles, calculate the net force between the dipoles. (a) Show that, in the limit $a \ll x$, the force has magnitude $6kp^2/x^4$, where $p = qa$ is the dipole moment. (b) Is the force attractive or repulsive?

FIGURE 23-49 Problem 67.

68. A dipole with charges $\pm q$ and separation $2a$ is located a distance x from a point charge $+Q$, with its dipole moment vector perpendicular to the x axis, as shown in Fig. 23-50. Find expressions for the magnitude of (a) the net torque and (b) the net force on the dipole, both in the limit $x \gg a$. (c) What is the direction of the net force?

FIGURE 23-50 Problem 68.

Paired Problems

(Both problems in a pair involve the same principles and techniques. If you can get the first problem, you should be able to solve the second one.)

69. An electron is at the origin and an ion with charge $+5e$ is at $x = 10$ nm. Find a point where the electric field is zero.

70. A proton is at the origin and an ion is at $x = 5.0$ nm. If the electric field is zero at $x = -6.83$ nm, what is the charge on the ion?

71. A thin rod of length ℓ has its left end at $x = -\ell$ and its right end at the origin. It carries a line charge density given by $\lambda = \lambda_0 \frac{x^2}{\ell^2}$, where λ_0 is a constant. Find the electric field at the origin.

72. Repeat the preceding problem for the case when $\lambda = \lambda_0 \frac{x^4}{\ell^4}$.

73. A thin, flexible rod carrying charge Q spread uniformly over its length is bent into a quarter circle of radius a, as shown in Fig. 23-51a. Find the electric field strength at the point P, which is the center of the circle. *Hint:* Consult Problem 50.

74. A thin, flexible rod carrying charge Q spread uniformly over its length is bent into a circular arc of radius a, as shown in Fig. 23-51b. Find the electric field strength at the point P, which is the center of the circular arc.

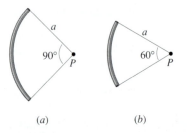

(a)   (b)

FIGURE 23-51 Problems 73, 74.

75. Ink-jet printers work by deflecting moving ink droplets with an electric field so they hit the right place on the paper. Droplets in a particular printer have mass 1.1×10^{-10} kg, charge 2.1 pC, speed 12 m/s, and pass through a uniform 97-kN/C electric field in order to be deflected through a 10° angle. What is the length of the field region?

76. If the drop speed in the printer of Problem 75 is doubled, what should be done to the electric field to have the drops hit the same point on the paper?

Supplementary Problems

77. A spring of spring constant 100 N/m is stretched 10 cm beyond its 90-cm equilibrium length. If you want to keep it stretched by attaching equal electric charges to the opposite ends, what magnitude of charge should you use?

78. Two small spheres with the same mass m and charge q are suspended from massless strings of length ℓ, as shown in Fig. 23-52. Each string makes an angle θ with the vertical. Show that the charge on each sphere is $q = \pm 2\ell \sin \theta \sqrt{mg \tan \theta / k}$.

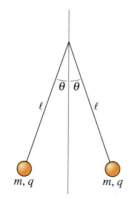

FIGURE 23-52 Problem 78.

79. A charge $-q$ and a charge $\frac{4}{9}q$ are located a distance a apart, as shown in Fig. 23-53. Where would you place a third charge so that all three are in static equilibrium? What should be the sign and magnitude of the third charge?

FIGURE 23-53 Problem 79.

80. Two 34-μC charges are attached to the opposite ends of a spring of spring constant 150 N/m and equilibrium length 50 cm. By how much does the spring stretch?

81. A 3.8-g particle with a 4.0-μC charge experiences a downward force of 0.24 N in a uniform electric field. Find the electric field, assuming that the gravitational force is *not* negligible.

82. A rod of length 2ℓ lies on the x axis, centered on the origin. It carries a line charge density given by $\lambda = \lambda_0 \dfrac{x}{\ell}$, where λ_0 is a constant. (a) What is the net charge on the rod? (b) Find an expression for electric field strength at all points $x > \ell$. (c) Show that your result has the $1/x^3$ dependence of a dipole field when $x \gg \ell$. *Hint:* For $\ell \ll x$, $\ln\left(\dfrac{x - \ell}{x + \ell}\right)$ becomes approximately $-\dfrac{2\ell}{x} - \dfrac{2\ell^3}{3x^3}$. (d) By comparing with Equation 23-7b, determine the dipole moment of the rod.

83. The electric field on the axis of a uniformly charged ring has magnitude 380 kN/C at a point 5.0 cm from the ring center. The magnitude 15 cm from the center is 160 kN/C; in both cases the field points away from the ring. Find the radius and charge of the ring.

84. Use the binomial theorem to show that, for $x \gg R$, the result of Problem 48 reduces to the field of a point charge whose total charge is the charge density σ times the disk area.

85. A molecule with dipole moment p is located a distance r from a proton, oriented with its dipole moment vector $\mathbf{p}$ as shown in Fig. 23-54. (a) Use Equation 23-7b to find the force the molecule exerts on the proton. (b) Now find the net force on the molecule in the proton's nonuniform electric field by considering that the molecule consists of two opposite charges $\pm q$, separated by a distance d such that $qd = p$. Take the limit as d becomes very small compared with r, and show that the resulting force has the same magnitude as that of part (a), as required by Newton's third law.

FIGURE 23-54 Problem 85.

86. An *electric quadrupole* consists of two oppositely directed dipoles in close proximity. (a) Calculate the field of the quadrupole shown in Fig. 23-55 for points to the right of $x = a$, and (b) show that for $x \gg a$ the quadrupole field falls off as $1/x^4$.

FIGURE 23-55 Problem 86.

87. Derive Equation 23-9 in Example 23-9 by making θ the integration variable, then evaluating the resulting integral.

24 Gauss's Law

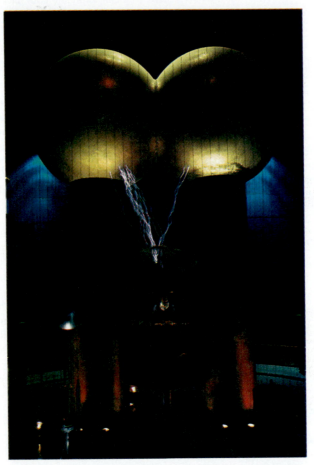

Huge sparks jump to the operator's cage in the Hall of Electricity at the Boston Museum of Science. But the operator is unharmed, for reasons that will become evident in this chapter.

We've seen how it's possible, in principle, to calculate the electric field of any charge distribution by summing the contributions of the many individual charges comprising the distribution. But in practice that process involves a vector integration that becomes difficult for all but the simplest charge distributions. How can we hope to calculate the field of a solid ball of charge, for example, when the individual charge elements are varying distances from the field point and their field vectors point in different directions (Fig. 24-1)?

In this chapter we introduce an elegant way of describing electric fields that makes almost trivial the calculation of fields from certain charge distributions. In the process we will formulate one of the four fundamental laws of electromagnetism—a statement that is equivalent to Coulomb's law but that gives deeper insights into the behavior of the electric field.

24-1 ELECTRIC FIELD LINES

The electric field is a set of vectors defined at all points in space, and we've therefore been representing fields by drawing a number of field vectors. A simpler way to visualize electric fields is with **electric field lines**, continuous lines whose direction is everywhere that of the electric field. To draw a field line, start at some point, and determine the field direction there. Move a small distance in the direction of the field, and evaluate the field direction at the new point. Extending this process in both directions from the starting point traces out an electric field line. The resulting line is a path whose direction at any point is that of the electric field at that point. Drawing many such lines gives a visualization of the overall field structure.

Tracing the field lines of a point charge is particularly simple. Starting at any point near a positive point charge, we find field vectors pointing radially outward from the charge. Move a little way outward, and the field still points in the same direction. So the field lines are straight lines, starting at the point charge and extending radially outward indefinitely (Fig. 24-2).

Field lines show the direction of the field, but what about its magnitude? In Fig. 24-2 the field lines spread apart as they extend farther from the point charge. Coulomb's law tells us that the field weakens farther from the charge. So in Fig. 24-2 the field is stronger where the lines are closer and weaker where they're farther apart. This is generally true, and allows us to infer relative field strength as well as field direction from field line pictures. ActivPhysics Activity 11.4 draws field lines for a point charge.

To trace the field lines of charge distributions, we follow the net field—the vector sum of the field contributions from all the charges in the distribution. Usually the direction of the field varies as we move along a field line, so the line itself is curved. Nevertheless, closeness of the field lines remains a measure of the

FIGURE 24-1 It would be difficult to find the field of a charged ball by summing vectorially the contributions of all the individual charge elements, three of which are shown here.

11.4

Electric Field: Point Charge

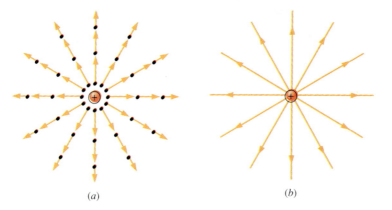

(a)   *(b)*

FIGURE 24-2 Vectors and field lines provide two ways to visualize the electric field. (*a*) The vector picture, introduced in the preceding chapter, uses individual field vectors drawn at selected points. Each vector gives the magnitude and direction of the field at that point, with the length of the arrow representing the magnitude. (*b*) Field lines are continuous lines that have the same direction as the field. For the point charge shown here, the field lines start at the charge and extend to infinity. The field magnitude is larger where the lines are closer together.

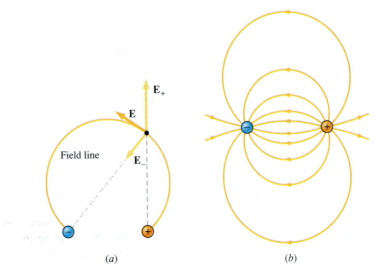

(a) (b)

FIGURE 24-3 (a) Tracing a field line for an electric dipole. At each point the direction of the field line is that of the *net* electric field $\mathbf{E} = \mathbf{E}_+ + \mathbf{E}_-$. (b) Tracing several field lines gives an overall sense of the dipole field. Near each charge the field has the radial structure of a point-charge field, but farther away the influence of both charges becomes important and the field lines curve. Field is stronger where field lines are closer—namely, near the charges and in the region between them.

field strength. Figure 24-3 shows some field lines for a dipole; you can see immediately from Fig. 24-3b that the field is strongest near the individual charges and in the region directly between them.

You might argue that "closeness of field lines" is vague because the electric field exists everywhere and therefore we can always draw as many field lines as we want. To make the field-line picture more precise, we associate a fixed number of field lines with a charge of given magnitude. In Fig. 24-4, for example, eight field

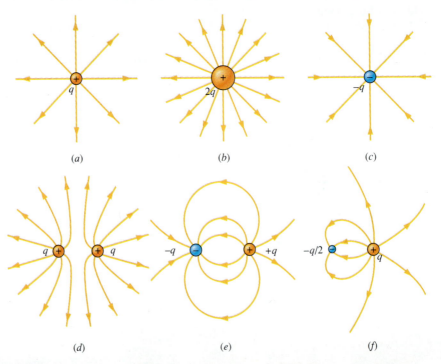

FIGURE 24-4 Field lines for (a) a positive charge q, (b) 2q, (c) −q, (d) two identical charges q, (e) a dipole, consisting of two equal but opposite charges ±q, and (f) opposite and unequal charges q and −q/2. In each drawing eight lines are used to represent a charge of magnitude q. Note in (d) and (f) that the field at large distances begins to resemble that of a single point charge.

lines correspond to a charge of magnitude q. Then eight lines *begin* on the *positive* charge $+q$ (Fig. 24-4a), and 16 on $+2q$ (Fig. 24-4b). Eight lines *end* on the *negative* charge $-q$ in Fig. 24-4c. Figures 24-4d–f show the fields of some two-charge distributions, drawn with the same eight-line convention. Note that field lines always *begin* on *positive* charges and *end* on *negative* charges. Activ-Physics Activity 11.6 draws field lines for other two-charge distributions of your choice.

11.6

Electric Field

24-2 ELECTRIC FLUX

Counting Field Lines

Figure 24-5 shows the charge distributions of Fig. 24-4, each surrounded by several surfaces. (The figure shows only the two-dimensional cross section of each surface.) Each surface is closed, meaning it's impossible to get from inside to outside without crossing the surface. We now ask a simple question: How many field lines emerge from inside each surface?

In Fig. 24-5a the answer for surfaces 1 and 2 is obvious: eight. With surface 3 one field line crosses three times, twice going out and once going in. If we count a field line going inward as negative, then the algebraic sum of field lines is again eight. In fact, any *closed* surface you can draw around $+q$ will have eight field lines emerging from within. That's because eight lines begin on the charge and extend indefinitely outward, so they cross *any* closed surface surrounding the charge.

What about surface 4? Two lines cross going inward and two going outward, so the net number of field lines emerging from this surface is zero. What's different about surface 4 is that it doesn't enclose the charge. By drawing other surfaces you can convince yourself that any surface not enclosing the charge will have as many lines going in as out, and will therefore have zero net field lines emerging.

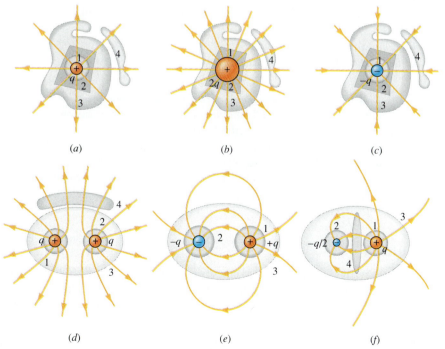

FIGURE 24-5 In all cases, the number of field lines emerging from a closed surface is proportional to the charge enclosed.

Figure 24-5*b* is identical except that now those surfaces enclosing the charge have 16 field lines emerging, reflecting the greater magnitude of the charge. Surfaces that don't enclose the charge still have zero net field lines emerging. Figure 24-5*c* is also like Fig. 24-5*a*, except that now the charge is negative so all field lines point inward. According to our sign convention, −8 field lines emerge from any surface enclosing the charge −*q*.

In Fig. 24-5*d*, surfaces 1 and 2 each enclose one of the charges *q*, and each has eight field lines emerging. Surface 3 encloses *both* charges, for a total enclosed charge +2*q*, and has 16 field lines emerging. Finally, surface 4 encloses no charge and has zero net field lines emerging.

On to Fig. 24-5*e*, the dipole. Surface 1 encloses charge *q* and has eight field lines emerging. Surface 2 encloses −*q* and has −8 field lines emerging. Surface 3 encloses both +*q* and −*q*, giving zero net charge enclosed. And as many field lines enter surface 3 as leave it, giving zero net field lines emerging.

Finally, in Fig. 24-5*f* eight field lines emerge from surface 1—and that surface encloses +*q*. Surface 2 encloses −*q*/2, and has −4 field lines emerging. Surface 3 encloses both charges, for a net enclosed charge +*q*/2—and four field lines emerge from this surface. Surface 4 encloses no charge and has zero net field lines emerging.

Counting the field lines in Fig. 24-5 leads to a simple statement about how electric fields must behave:

> **The number of electric field lines emerging from any closed surface is proportional to the charge enclosed.**

This statement is very general: It doesn't matter what shape the surface is or whether the enclosed charge is a single point charge or a lot of charges adding to the same net charge. Nor does it matter how the charges are arranged, as long as they're *enclosed* by the surface in question. And the presence of charges *outside* the surface doesn't alter the conclusion about the number of field lines emerging— although it may alter the shape of the individual lines. You can explore this statement as applied to the fields of two-charge distributions using ActivPhysics Activity 11.6.

We'll now rephrase our statement in a more mathematically rigorous way, obtaining one of the four fundamental laws of electromagnetism.

Tip

Remember Fig. 24-5 As we define new terms and write equations involving integrals, remember that the mathematics just reflects in a concise way what's clear from Fig. 24-5—that the number of field lines emerging from a closed surface depends only on the net charge enclosed. Go back to that figure any time you begin to lose the physical significance of the mathematics.

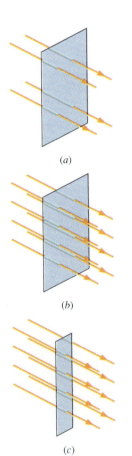

FIGURE 24-6 (*a*) Four field lines cross the surface shown. (*b*) Here the field strength has doubled, and eight lines cross the surface. (*c*) With the same field strength as in (*b*), but with half the area, only four lines cross the surface. In general, the number of field lines crossing a surface is proportional to the surface area and to the field strength.

Electric Flux

We can make the "number of field lines" more rigorous with Fig. 24-6, which shows several flat surfaces in uniform electric fields. Study the figure and its caption, and you'll see that the number of field lines crossing each surface is

FIGURE 24-7 The number of field lines crossing a surface also depends on the surface orientation relative to the field **E**. The orientation is specified by a vector **A** normal to the surface. In (a) the surface is perpendicular to the field, so **A** and **E** are parallel; then $\theta = 0$, $\cos\theta = 1$, and the number of field lines crossing the surface is a maximum. In (b) the surface is parallel to the field, so **A** and **E** are perpendicular; here $\theta = 90°$, $\cos\theta = 0$, and no lines cross the surface. (c) In general, the number of field lines varies as $\cos\theta$, where θ is the angle between **E** and **A**.

(a)

(b)

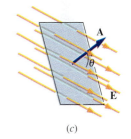

(c)

proportional to the surface area A and the field strength E. Figure 24-7 shows that it also depends on the orientation of the surface, specified by a vector normal to the surface. As Fig. 24-7 suggests, the number of field lines crossing the surface is proportional to the cosine of the angle between that normal vector **A** and the field **E**. Putting this all together, we have

$$\text{Number of field lines} \propto E\,A\cos\theta.$$

The quantity on the right-hand side of this equation has a definite value that captures the spirit of the more vague expression "number of field lines crossing a surface." We call this quantity the **electric flux**, ϕ, through the surface. If we make the magnitude of the surface normal vector **A** equal to the surface area A, then we can define the flux compactly using the vector dot product:

$$\phi = \mathbf{E} \cdot \mathbf{A}, \qquad (24\text{-}1)$$

where the dot product, defined in Chapter 7, is the product of the two vector magnitudes with the cosine of the angle between them. Since the units of **E** are N/C, flux is measured in N·m²/C.

For the open surfaces of Fig. 24-6 and 24-7 there's an ambiguity in the sign of ϕ, since we could have taken **A** in either of the two directions along the perpendicular to the surface. But for *closed* surfaces, we unambiguously define the direction of **A** as that of the outward-pointing normal to the surface.

Tip

The Flux Is Not the Field The flux ϕ and field **E** are related but distinct quantities. The field is a vector defined at each point in space. Flux is a global property of the field, depending not on a single point but on how the field behaves over an extended surface. Unlike field, flux is a scalar quantity; it's simply a quantification of the "amount of field" or "number of field lines" crossing a surface.

What if a surface is curved and/or the field varies with position? Then we divide the surface into many small patches, each small enough that it's essentially flat and that the field is essentially uniform over each (Fig. 24-8). If a patch has area dA, then Equation 24-1 gives the flux through it:

$$d\phi = \mathbf{E} \cdot d\mathbf{A},$$

where the vector $d\mathbf{A}$ is normal to the patch. The total flux through the surface is then the sum over all the patches. If we make the patches arbitrarily small that sum becomes an integral, and the flux is

$$\phi = \int_{\text{surface}} \mathbf{E} \cdot d\mathbf{A}. \qquad (24\text{-}2)$$

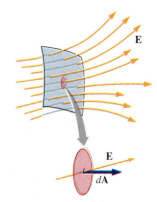

FIGURE 24-8 Even though the surface is curved and the field varies, a small enough patch of surface is essentially flat and the field is uniform over it, so the flux through the patch is $d\phi = \mathbf{E} \cdot d\mathbf{A}$.

FIGURE 24-9 What's the flux through each of the cube faces shown?

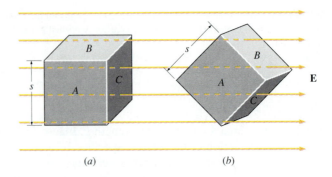

(a)   (b)

The limits of the integral range over the entire surface, picking up contributions from all the patches $d\mathbf{A}$. Although the integral can be difficult to evaluate, we'll find it most useful in cases where its evaluation is almost trivial. Again, remember what Equation 24-2 means: The flux ϕ simply serves as a more precise measure of the "number of field lines" crossing a surface.

Got It!

Figure 24-9 shows a cube of side s in a uniform electric field $\mathbf{E}$. What is the flux through each of the three cube faces A, B, C with the cube oriented as in (a)? Repeat for the orientation in (b), where the cube has been rotated through 45°.

24-3 GAUSS'S LAW

We showed in the preceding section that the number of field lines emerging from a closed surface is proportional to the charge enclosed. Now that we've developed electric flux to express more rigorously the notion "number of field lines," we can state the following:

> The electric flux through any closed surface is proportional to the charge enclosed by that surface.

Writing the same thing mathematically gives

$$\phi = \oint \mathbf{E} \cdot d\mathbf{A} \propto q_{\text{enclosed}},$$

where the circle on the integral sign indicates that the integral is over a *closed* surface.

To evaluate the proportionality between flux and enclosed charge, consider a positive point charge q and a spherical surface of radius r centered on the charge (Fig. 24-10a). The flux through this surface is given by Equation 24-2:

$$\phi = \oint \mathbf{E} \cdot d\mathbf{A} = \oint E \, dA \cos \theta.$$

But Fig. 24-10b shows that the surface normal $d\mathbf{A}$ and the electric field $\mathbf{E}$ are parallel at any point on the sphere, so $\cos \theta = 1$. Since the electric field varies as

(a)

(b)

FIGURE 24-10 (a) The electric field of a point charge has the same magnitude everywhere on a spherical surface centered on the charge. (b) At each point on the surface the field and the surface normal $d\mathbf{A}$ are parallel.

$1/r^2$ its magnitude is the same everywhere at the fixed radius r of our sphere. Thus, we can take E outside the integral, giving

$$\phi = \oint_{\text{sphere}} E\, dA = E \oint_{\text{sphere}} dA = E(4\pi r^2),$$

where the last step follows because $\oint dA$ just means the surface area of the sphere. Now, the electric field of a point charge is given by Equation 23-4: $E = kq/r^2$. So we have

$$\phi = E(4\pi r^2) = \left(\frac{kq}{r^2}\right)(4\pi r^2) = 4\pi kq.$$

Since the point charge q is the only charge inside our spherical surface, we see that the proportionality constant between flux and enclosed charge is just $4\pi k$.

Before proceeding, we introduce the so-called permittivity constant, ε_0, defined by the relation

$$\varepsilon_0 = \frac{1}{4\pi k}, \tag{24-3}$$

where k is the Coulomb constant. The value of ε_0 is 8.85×10^{-12} C^2/N·m^2.

Tip

Why Two Constants? There's no physics in Equation 24-3; it's just a definition of a new symbol. The SI unit system requires a proportionality constant in Coulomb's law or, equivalently, in the relation between flux and enclosed charge. The value of that constant conveys information about the strength of the electric force. That same information is contained in the constants k and ε_0; both are different ways of expressing the same thing. That there are two constants in use is purely a historical artifact, and we switch now from k to ε_0 only because doing so makes subsequent formulas simpler. It would have been better to define the units of electric charge so that Coulomb's law didn't need a proportionality constant. There are unit systems where that's done—but they aren't the internationally adopted SI system.

In terms of the new constant ε_0, the proportionality $4\pi k$ between flux and enclosed charge becomes $1/\varepsilon_0$. So our statement that the flux through any closed surface is proportional to the net charge enclosed becomes

$$\oint \mathbf{E} \cdot d\mathbf{A} = \frac{q_{\text{enclosed}}}{\varepsilon_0}. \quad \text{(Gauss's law)} \tag{24-4}$$

Here the integral is taken over *any closed surface,* and q_{enclosed} is the charge enclosed *by that surface.*

Equation 24-4 is **Gauss's law**, after the German mathematician Karl Friedrich Gauss (1777–1855). Gauss's law is one of four fundamental relations that govern the behavior of electromagnetic fields throughout the universe. Whether you journey into a star in some remote galaxy, down among the strands of a DNA molecule, or into the microprocessor chip at the heart of your computer, you will

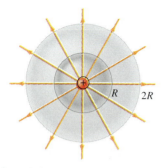

FIGURE 24-11 The outer sphere has twice the radius of the inner sphere, and thus four times the surface area. Since the same number of field lines crosses both spheres, the density of field lines at the outer sphere has one-fourth its value at the inner sphere. Thus the field-line density accurately reflects the inverse-square falloff of the electric field. If the inverse-square law did not hold, we would have to begin new field lines (or stop them) at different distances from the point charge, and the number of field lines crossing a surface would not depend only on the enclosed charge.

find that the flux of the electric field through any closed surface depends only on the enclosed charge. In over a century of experiments, no electric field has ever been observed to violate Gauss's law.

We stress that Gauss's law, although clothed in the mathematical finery of a surface integral, is just a more rigorous way of saying what's clear in Fig. 24-5: that the number of field lines emerging from a closed surface is proportional to the enclosed charge.

Gauss and Coulomb

Gauss's law and Coulomb's law look completely different, but they're actually equivalent. Figure 24-11 shows that the heart of this equivalence is the inverse-square law. The figure shows two spherical surfaces surrounding a point charge q. Gauss's law tells us that the flux through each surface is the same, and is equal to q/ε_0. But why? Because, as our arguments leading to Gauss's law show, the flux through a spherical surface of radius r centered on a point charge is the product of the surface area $4\pi r^2$ with the electric field strength E at the surface. But Coulomb's law says that the electric field drops off as $1/r^2$. As r increases, the surface area grows as r^2, but the $1/r^2$ decrease in field strength just compensates, giving a constant value for the flux that depends only on the enclosed charge. If the inverse-square law (e.g., Coulomb's law) didn't hold, then the flux would not be constant and Gauss's law wouldn't hold either.

It's also the inverse-square law that makes electric field line pictures useful for visualizing fields. Field lines begin or end only on charges; otherwise they go off to infinity. As the field lines of a point charge spread in three dimensions, the number crossing any spherical surface (or any closed surface, for that matter) remains the same. But larger spheres have larger surface areas, in proportion to r^2—and that means the density of field lines drops as $1/r^2$, accurately reflecting the strength of the field. If the inverse-square law didn't hold, we would have to start additional field lines beyond the point charge (or stop them) to represent the field strength quantitatively, and thus the number of field lines crossing a closed surface would not remain the same. Once again, the inverse-square law (Coulomb) and the relation between flux and enclosed charge (Gauss) are intimately connected. Incidentally, field-line pictures printed in a book or drawn on a blackboard generally cannot be quantitatively correct because they don't show the spreading of field lines in all three dimensions.

We've been talking here only about isolated point charges, but we emphasize that Gauss's law applies to *all* electric fields, no matter how complicated the charge distributions producing them. That's because of the superposition principle. We already know that superposition allows us to add vectorially the electric fields described individually by Coulomb's law for the point-charge field. Since Gauss's and Coulomb's law are equivalent, our argument leading to Gauss's law still applies when the field **E** is a superposition of point-charge fields.

Got It!

A spherical surface surrounds an isolated point charge. If a second point charge is brought to a point just outside the surface, will the flux through the surface change? Will the electric field at points on the surface change?

24-4 USING GAUSS'S LAW

Gauss's law is true for *any* surface enclosing *any* charge distribution; it's a universal statement of how electric fields everywhere must behave. In a few specialized cases Gauss's law can be used to calculate the electric field. In those cases, which we treat in this section, Gauss provides a powerful alternative to Coulomb's law, an alternative that makes electric-field calculations much easier. But despite this section's emphasis on using Gauss's law to calculate the field, remember that the law holds *universally,* even in cases where it's not useful for field calculations.

We can use Gauss to calculate the field when it's possible to evaluate the flux integral without actually knowing **E**. That happens only when the charge distribution has sufficient symmetry. We now illustrate the use of Gauss's law for three important symmetries.

Spherical Symmetry

A charge distribution is spherically symmetric if the charge density depends only on the distance from a central point. A point charge, a uniformly charged solid sphere, and a spherical surface carrying uniform surface charge density are all spherically symmetric charge distributions. Spherical symmetry implies that the magnitude of the electric field depends only on the distance r from the center of symmetry, and that the field direction is radial (Fig. 24-12).

Gauss's law relates the electric flux through a closed surface to the enclosed charge. The law holds for *any* surface whatsoever, provided it's a *closed* surface. The surface over which we're evaluating the flux is called a **gaussian surface**; it's not a real, physical surface but just an imaginary, mathematical surface that we envision for the purpose of applying Gauss's law. Although Gauss holds for *any* surface, it's useful for calculating electric fields only for surfaces that share the symmetry of the charge distribution.

In the case of spherical symmetry, the appropriate surface is a sphere of arbitrary radius r centered on the point of symmetry. Two such surfaces are shown in Fig. 24-13. With spherical symmetry, the magnitude E of the electric field must be the same everywhere on such a gaussian sphere. Furthermore, **E** is everywhere in the same direction as the perpendicular to the surface, so $\cos \theta = 1$. Thus, although the direction of **E** and of the surface vary, the product $E \cos \theta$ remains constant and is simply the field magnitude E. Then the flux through a gaussian sphere becomes

$$\phi = \oint \mathbf{E} \cdot d\mathbf{A} = \oint E \cos \theta \, dA = E \oint dA = 4\pi r^2 E, \qquad (24\text{-}5)$$

where the last step follows because $\oint dA$ is just the surface area of the sphere, $4\pi r^2$. This expression for the flux does not depend on the details of the charge distribution, so long as it is spherically symmetric.

Gauss's law says that the flux through the sphere is given by $q_{\text{enclosed}}/\varepsilon_0$, where q_{enclosed} is the net charge enclosed *by the sphere*. Suppose our spherically symmetric charge distribution carries total charge Q and has radius R. That is, whatever the particular distribution of charge for $r \leq R$, there is no charge at $r > R$. For any gaussian sphere with $r > R$, like the surface 1 in Fig. 24-13,

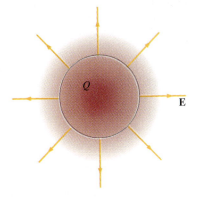

FIGURE 24-12 For a spherically symmetric charge distribution, the field vectors at a given radius all have the same magnitude and point in the radial direction—outward for a positive charge, as shown, or inward for a negative charge.

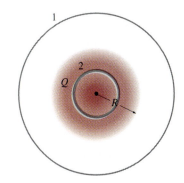

FIGURE 24-13 Two gaussian surfaces surrounding a spherical charge distribution. Surface 1 lies outside the distribution, and encloses all the charge Q. Surface 2 lies inside the distribution, and encloses only part of the charge.

FIGURE 24-14 Hairs on a highly charged person's head trace out the electric field. The essentially spherical head produces a field like that of a point charge.

the enclosed charge is the total charge Q. Equating the flux in Equation 24-5 to Q/ε_0 gives

$$4\pi r^2 E = \frac{Q}{\varepsilon_0},$$

or

$$E = \frac{1}{4\pi\varepsilon_0}\frac{Q}{r^2} = \frac{kQ}{r^2}, \quad (r > R) \tag{24-6}$$

where the last step follows because $1/4\pi\varepsilon_0$ is just the Coulomb constant, k. But this is just the field of a point charge! Equation 24-6 says that *outside* any spherically symmetric distribution of charge, the field is identical to that of a point charge located at the center of symmetry (Fig. 24-14). This is *not* an approximation—it is exactly true right up to the surface $r = R$! Imagine how hard it would have been to calculate this field using the superposition principle! Yet somehow all the charge elements throughout the spherically symmetric distribution produce $d\mathbf{E}$'s that add vectorially to give the same field as a single point charge. Like Gauss's law itself, this result is a manifestation of the inverse-square force law.

The field *inside* the charge distribution depends on how charge is distributed. This is because a gaussian sphere with $r < R$, such as surface 2 of Fig. 24-13, does not enclose the entire charge Q. How much it encloses depends on the charge distribution. In the examples below, we consider two important special cases.

EXAMPLE 24-1	*A Uniformly Charged Sphere*

A total charge Q is spread uniformly throughout a sphere of radius R. What is the electric field at all points in space?

Solution

This charge distribution is spherically symmetric, so the field for $r > R$ is like that of a point charge, given by Equation 24-6.

Inside the charged sphere, our gaussian surface is a sphere like surface 2 in Fig. 24-13. Equation 24-5 for the flux still holds, but now the charge enclosed is some fraction of Q. What fraction? The volume of the sphere is $\frac{4}{3}\pi R^3$, and it contains a total charge Q. Since charge is spread uniformly throughout the sphere, the volume charge density is given by

$$\rho = \frac{Q}{V} = \frac{Q}{\frac{4}{3}\pi R^3}.$$

Then the charge enclosed by our gaussian sphere of radius r is just the volume of that sphere multiplied by the volume charge density:

$$q_{enclosed} = V\rho = \frac{4}{3}\pi r^3\frac{Q}{\frac{4}{3}\pi R^3} = Q\frac{r^3}{R^3}.$$

Equating the flux from Equation 24-5 to $q_{enclosed}/\varepsilon_0$, we have

$$4\pi r^2 E = \frac{Qr^3}{\varepsilon_0 R^3},$$

or

$$E = \frac{1}{4\pi\varepsilon_0}\frac{Qr}{R^3} = \frac{\rho r}{3\varepsilon_0}, \quad (r < R) \tag{24-7}$$

where we've written the field in terms of both the total charge Q and the charge density $\rho = Q/\frac{4}{3}\pi R^3$. Equation 24-7 shows that the field *inside* the charge distribution increases linearly with distance from the center. This result is entirely consistent with the inverse-square law for point charges. Although the field of each charge element decreases as $1/r^2$, in this case the amount of charge enclosed increases more rapidly—as r^3—resulting in a field that increases linearly with r. Figure 24-15 shows the combined results for the fields both inside and outside the sphere. The field direction is, of course, radial, pointing outward if Q is positive and inward if Q is negative.

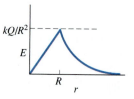

FIGURE 24-15 Field strength versus radial distance for a uniformly charged sphere of radius R. For $r > R$ the field has the inverse-square dependence of a point-charge field.

EXAMPLE 24-2	*A Thin Spherical Shell*

The thin spherical shell of radius R shown in Fig. 24-16 carries a total charge Q distributed uniformly over its surface. What is the electric field inside and outside the shell?

Solution

Since this distribution is spherically symmetric, we already know that the field outside is just the point-charge field of Equation 24-6.

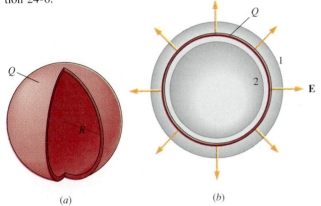

(a)   (b)

FIGURE 24-16 (*a*) A thin spherical shell carries charge Q distributed uniformly over its surface of radius R. (*b*) Cross-sectional view, showing two spherical gaussian surfaces. Surface 1 encloses the entire charge Q, while surface 2 encloses zero charge.

For any gaussian sphere inside the shell, the enclosed charge is zero. Equating the flux from Equation 24-5 to this zero enclosed charge gives

$$4\pi r^2 E = 0$$

so the field is zero everywhere inside the shell! How can this be? Again, it's a manifestation of the inverse-square law. At any point inside the shell, the larger fields of nearby portions of the shell are exactly canceled by the weaker fields of more distant, but more extensive, parts of the shell (Fig. 24-17).

FIGURE 24-17 At any point P inside a charged shell, the field arising from the relatively few but nearby charges in region A is exactly canceled by the field arising from the more numerous but more distant charges in region B.

Got It!

A spherical shell carries a charge Q, uniformly distributed over the shell. If the charge on the shell is doubled, what happens to the electric field (a) inside and (b) outside the shell?

EXAMPLE 24-3	*A Point Charge Inside a Shell*

A point charge $+q$ is at the center of a spherical shell of radius R carrying total charge $-2q$, distributed uniformly over its surface. (a) Draw the electric field lines for this configuration, using eight lines to represent a charge of magnitude q. Find expressions for the field strength for (b) $r < R$ and (c) $r > R$.

Solution

(a) The situation has spherical symmetry and so must the field. Gauss's law tells us that eight field lines must emerge from any surface surrounding $+q$ alone, and that eight field lines must go into any surface surrounding the entire distribution with its net charge $-q$. Fig. 24-18 shows the only way to draw the field that's compatible with Gauss's law. Notice a total of 16 lines end on the charged shell, consistent with its charge of $-2q$.

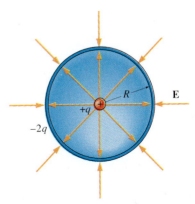

FIGURE 24-18 Field lines for a charge q surrounded by shell carrying $-2q$ (Example 24-3).

(b) For $r < R$ we're inside the shell, so the enclosed charge is just q. Solving Equation 24-4 for E then gives

$$E = \frac{kq}{r^2}.$$

What about the shell? Didn't we forget to take it into account? No! The shell and its charge are *irrelevant* as long as they preserve the spherical symmetry. Example 24-2 showed that the field inside a charged shell *due to the shell itself* is zero. Here we're inside the shell, so the only field we see is that of the point charge.

(c) Outside the shell, a spherical gaussian surface encloses net charge $-q$, so the field we see is that of a point charge $-q$; it has magnitude $E = q/4\pi\varepsilon_0 r^2$, and points radially inward.

What about the field at $r = R$? That's ambiguous; just inside the shell the field points outward, while just outside it points inward. In fact, the field undergoes a discontinuous jump across the infinitesimally thin surface charge layer on the shell.

Tip

Trust Gauss Gauss's law says that the flux—or number of field lines—emerging from any closed surface depends *only* on the *enclosed* charge—not on any other charge that may happen to be outside the surface. (Consult Fig. 24-5 to convince yourself of this.) *When there is enough symmetry* that often means that external charges are totally irrelevant in a field calculation, as is the shell in Example 24-3 for points with $r < R$. But *symmetry matters*: Without enough symmetry, zero net charge inside a gaussian surface is *not* sufficient to ensure that the field on the surface is zero (Fig. 24-19).

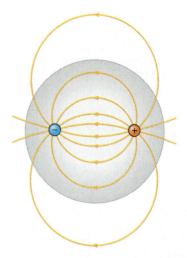

FIGURE 24-19 The net charge enclosed by the gaussian sphere (gray) is zero, but the field on the sphere is not zero. Here the charge distribution—a dipole—is not spherically symmetric, so Equation 24-5 is not a valid expression for the flux.

EXERCISE A solid sphere 10 cm in radius carries a uniform 40-μC charge distributed throughout its volume. It is surrounded by a concentric shell 20 cm in radius, also uniformly charged with 40 μC. Find the electric field (a) 5.0 cm, (b) 15 cm, and (c) 30 cm from the center.

Answers: (a) 18 MN/C; (b) 16 MN/C; (c) 8.0 MN/C

Some problems similar to Examples 24-1 through 24-3: 17–26, 66

Strategy

Using Gauss's Law This section illustrated the steps needed to calculate the electric field using Gauss's law:

1. Study the symmetry to see if you can construct a gaussian surface on which the field magnitude and its direction relative to the surface are constant. (With spherical symmetry that surface was spherical.) If you can't find such a surface then Gauss's law, while still true, won't help in calculating the field.
2. Evaluate the flux. This should be easy because your choice of gaussian surface makes $E\cos\theta$ constant over the surface. This term then comes outside the integral, leaving the integral equal to the surface area.
3. Evaluate the *enclosed* charge. This is not the same as the total charge if the gaussian surface lies *within* the charge distribution.
4. Equate the flux to $q_{enclosed}/\varepsilon_0$, and solve for E. The direction of **E** should be evident from the symmetry.

Once steps 1 and 2 are done for a particular symmetry, you'll have an equation like Equation 24-5 for the flux, and you can jump right to step 3 to calculate the field in a specific case—just as we did in Examples 24-1 and 24-2.

FIGURE 24-20 A positive charge distribution with line symmetry (red) extends infinitely in both directions, and its charge density depends only on the perpendicular distance from the symmetry axis. A cylindrical gaussian surface (gray) of length ℓ and radius r surrounds the charge distribution. Symmetry requires that the electric field on the surface point radially outward, and that the field magnitude E be constant over the surface. With a negative charge the field would point radially inward.

Line Symmetry

A charge distribution has line symmetry when its charge density depends only on the perpendicular distance r from a line, called the symmetry axis (Fig. 24-20). Symmetry then requires that the field point radially and that the field magnitude depend only on distance from the axis. An appropriate gaussian surface is the cylinder of length ℓ and radius r shown in Fig. 24-20. Being radial, field lines don't cross the circular ends of the cylinder, so there's no flux through these ends. The field is everywhere perpendicular to the curved part of the surface, so $\cos\theta = 1$ in the expression for flux through this part. Since the field magnitude is constant at the fixed radius r of the curved surface, the flux becomes

$$\phi = \int \mathbf{E} \cdot d\mathbf{A} = \int E\, dA \cos\theta = E\int dA = 2\pi r\ell E, \qquad (24\text{-}8)$$

where the last step follows because the cylinder "unrolls" into a rectangular sheet of length ℓ and width $2\pi r$ (Fig. 24-21). Since there is no flux through the cylinder ends, Equation 24-8 gives the total flux through our entire gaussian surface. Solving for the electric field in any situation with line symmetry then amounts to equating the flux given in Equation 24-8 to the enclosed charge divided by ε_0, then solving for E—exactly as we did for spherical symmetry using the analogous flux equation, Equation 24-5. There is one quantity in Equation 24-8 that has no analog in Equation 24-5, namely the length ℓ of the gaussian cylinder. As the following examples show, however, that length also appears in the calculation of the enclosed charge, so it always cancels from the final result.

FIGURE 24-21 (*a*) A cylindrical gaussian surface. (*b*) Unrolling the cylinder gives a flat sheet of area $2\pi r\ell$.

| **EXAMPLE 24-4** | *An Infinite Line of Charge* |

Use Gauss's law to calculate the electric field of an infinite line carrying line charge density λ.

Solution

This is the same problem we solved in Example 23-9 through a tedious Coulomb's law calculation. With line charge density λ, the charge enclosed by a gaussian cylinder of length ℓ is $q_{\text{enclosed}} = \lambda\ell$. Setting the flux given in Equation 24-8 to $q_{\text{enclosed}}/\varepsilon_0$ and solving for E then gives

$$E = \frac{\lambda\ell}{2\pi\varepsilon_0 r\ell} = \frac{\lambda}{2\pi\varepsilon_0 r}.$$

Since $1/2\pi\varepsilon_0 = 2k$, this is the same result we found in Example 23-9. The Gauss's law calculation is far simpler; symmetry and an intelligent choice of gaussian surface helped us bypass the entire integration of Example 23-9.

Although this problem dealt with an infinitesimally thin charged line, you can see that the same result must hold *outside* any charge distribution with line symmetry. And, as we argued in Example 23-9, the result is a good approximation for long, thin structures of finite length provided we're not too far away nor too close to the ends.

| **EXAMPLE 24-5** | *A Hollow Pipe* |

A thin-walled pipe 3.0 m long and 2.0 cm in radius carries a net charge $q = 5.7$ μC, distributed uniformly over its surface. Find the electric field (a) 8.0 mm and (b) 8.0 cm from the pipe axis, not near either end.

Solution

Since the pipe is much longer than its diameter, we can approximate its field as that of an infinitely long charge distribution with line symmetry.

(a) A point 8.0 mm from the axis lies inside the pipe. An 8.0-mm-radius gaussian cylinder therefore encloses zero net charge; equating the flux from Equation 24-8 to zero then shows that the field at this radius—and indeed anywhere deep within the hollow pipe—is zero.

(b) For a point outside the pipe, a gaussian cylinder of length ℓ encloses charge $\lambda\ell$, where the line charge density λ is 5.7 μC/3.0 m = 1.9 μC/m. Setting the flux from Equation 24-8 to this $q_{enclosed}$ and solving for E then gives

$$E = \frac{q_{enclosed}}{2\pi\varepsilon_0 r\ell} = \frac{\lambda}{2\pi\varepsilon_0 r}$$

$$= \frac{1.9\times10^{-6}\text{ C/m}}{(2\pi)(8.85\times10^{-12}\text{ C}^2/\text{N·m}^2)(8.0\times10^{-2}\text{ m})}$$

$$= 4.3\times10^5\text{ N/C}.$$

In this region the field points radially outward and falls inversely with distance from the axis.

> **Tip**
>
> *That's Distance from the Symmetry Axis* The distance r that arises in applying Gauss's law to situations with spherical or line symmetry is always the distance *from the point or line of symmetry*—as you can see from the derivations of Equations 24-4 and 24-8. Equations for the field are therefore most simply expressed in terms of that distance—*not* in terms of distance from the edge of the charge distribution.

EXERCISE Suppose the pipe in Example 24-5 were surrounded concentrically by a second pipe of the same length and 5.0 cm in diameter. What should be (a) the total charge and (b) the surface charge density (assumed uniform) on this outer pipe in order that there be no electric field outside the entire structure?

Answers: (a) -5.7 μC; (b) -12 μC/m^2

Some problems similar to Examples 24-4 and 24-5: 28, 29, 31, 32

Plane Symmetry

A charge distribution has plane symmetry when its charge density depends only on the distance from a plane. The only electric-field direction consistent with this symmetry is perpendicular to the symmetry plane (Fig. 24-22). We can evaluate the flux integral in Gauss's law using a gaussian surface with sides perpendicular to the symmetry plane, ends of area A parallel to the plane, and which straddles the symmetry plane to extend equal distances on either side of it (Fig. 24-22). Since no field lines cross the sides, the flux through them is zero. Symmetry of the situation implies that the field magnitude E cannot depend on position parallel to the symmetry plane. Therefore E is uniform over each end of the gaussian cylinder so, with the field perpendicular to the ends, the flux through each end is just EA, where A is the end area. Since the ends are the same distance from the symmetry plane, they must have the same field strength E. The total flux through the gaussian surface is therefore

$$\phi = 2EA. \qquad (24\text{-}9)$$

This equation holds for any charge distribution with plane symmetry; to find the field we evaluate the charge enclosed by the gaussian surface, then apply Gauss's law.

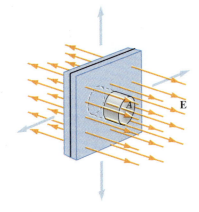

FIGURE 24-22 A charge distribution with plane symmetry. The charge density depends only on the distance from the plane of symmetry (black), and extends infinitely in both directions parallel to that plane. Also shown are the electric field and a gaussian surface with its sides perpendicular and ends parallel to the plane. Dashed lines show that the gaussian surface extends equal distances on both sides of the symmetry plane.

EXAMPLE 24-6	*A Sheet of Charge*

An infinite sheet of charge carries a uniform surface charge density σ. What is the electric field arising from this sheet?

Solution

Since the surface charge density is uniform, this charge distribution has plane symmetry. Figure 24-23 shows the sheet and an appropriate gaussian surface. The sheet area enclosed by the gaussian surface is clearly equal to the end area A. The surface charge density—charge per unit area—is σ, so the enclosed charge is $q_{enclosed} = \sigma A$. Setting $q_{enclosed}/\varepsilon_0$ to the flux $\phi = 2EA$ given by Equation 24-9 and solving for E then gives

$$E = \frac{\sigma}{2\varepsilon_0}. \qquad (24\text{-}10)$$

This simple result says that the field strength does not depend on distance from the sheet. How can this be? By symmetry, the field must point perpendicular to the sheet. There is no charge anywhere but on the sheet, so that's the only place where field lines can begin or end. Therefore the density of field lines—the measure of field strength—is the same everywhere. Figure 24-24 shows how this result is fully consistent with Coulomb's law.

Although this example treated only an infinitesimally thin sheet of charge, we would find a uniform electric field *outside* any charge distribution with plane symmetry. The field *inside* such a distribution would depend on how the charge density varies in the direction perpendicular to the symmetry plane (see Problem 36).

Perfect plane symmetry requires a charge distribution that is infinite in extent. But close to any large, flat, uniformly charged surface and not near an edge, the assumption of plane symmetry becomes a good approximation, and Equation 24-10 becomes reasonably accurate. We make the same approximation when we treat the acceleration of Earth's gravity as a constant; we're neglecting Earth's curvature and therefore its finite size, and approximating its gravitational field as the uniform field of an infinite sheet of mass.

EXERCISE An electron close to a large, flat sheet of charge is repelled from the sheet with a 1.8×10^{-12} N force. Find the surface charge density on the sheet.

FIGURE 24-23 The area of the charged sheet enclosed by the gaussian surface is the same as the area A of its ends; the enclosed charge is therefore σA.

FIGURE 24-24 As we rise above an infinite sheet, the amount of charge within a given angular region increases just enough to compensate for the inverse-square decrease in field strengths of the individual charges. The result is a field that does not depend on distance from the sheet.

Answer: $-200\ \mu$C/m^2

Some problems similar to Example 24-6: 34–37

24-5 FIELDS OF ARBITRARY CHARGE DISTRIBUTIONS

The examples of Section 24-4 show how easy Gauss's law can sometimes make problems that would be difficult to solve using Coulomb's law. In each case the symmetry allowed us to construct a gaussian surface on which $E\cos\theta$ was constant. Only then could we take E outside the integral and solve for it. But many situations do not possess the symmetry needed to apply Gauss's law in calculating the field. Try, for example, to calculate the field of a dipole using Gauss's law. The attempt fails because it is impossible to draw an appropriate surface.

FIGURE 24-25 The fields of a dipole, a point charge, a charged line, and a charged plane.

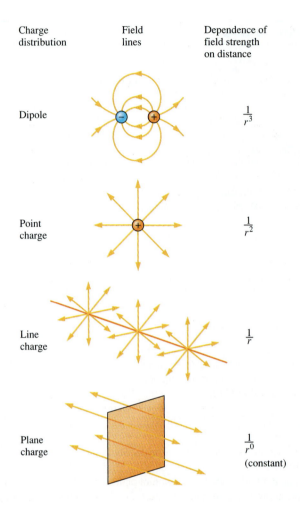

Charge distribution	Field lines	Dependence of field strength on distance
Dipole		$\frac{1}{r^3}$
Point charge		$\frac{1}{r^2}$
Line charge		$\frac{1}{r}$
Plane charge		$\frac{1}{r^0}$ (constant)

We can understand the fields associated with more complicated charge distributions by considering the fields of simpler distributions that we have already calculated using either Coulomb's law or Gauss's law. Figure 24-25 summarizes the fields of a dipole, a point charge, a uniformly charged line, and a uniformly charged plane. For the last three, note the simple relation between the number of dimensions in the charge distribution and the way the field strength depends on distance. The plane has two dimensions and its field strength is independent of distance. The line has one dimension and its field falls as $1/r$. The point has no dimensions and its field falls as $1/r^2$. In a sense, the dipole continues this progression, for it consists of two opposite point charges whose effects very nearly cancel. No wonder its field falls even faster, as $1/r^3$. In fact, one can construct a hierarchy of charge distributions whose fields fall off ever faster as dipoles nearly cancel dipoles, and so on. Such distributions are useful in the mathematical analysis of complicated charge distributions such as complex molecules or radio antennas.

Frequently we have a charge distribution that lacks the symmetry required to make Gauss's law useful and for which a Coulomb's law calculation would be impossibly difficult. Good thinking coupled with knowledge of simpler charge distributions can go a long way toward providing a reasonable approximation to the field. Consider, for example, the uniformly charged disk shown in Fig. 24-26. For points much closer to the disk surface than to the edge, the disk looks almost

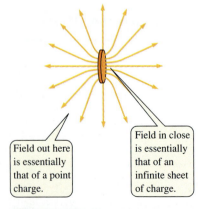

Field out here is essentially that of a point charge.

Field in close is essentially that of an infinite sheet of charge.

FIGURE 24-26 The field of a uniformly charged disk.

like an infinite flat plane of charge. For these points the field is approximately that of an infinite plane—a field that points directly away from the plane and does not fall off with distance. Far from the disk, meanwhile, its exact size and shape are unimportant. Its field closely resembles that of a single charged point: far from the disk the field points radially outward in all directions and falls off as the inverse square of the distance from the disk. The field at intermediate distances is harder to determine. But somehow the infinite-plane field lines close to the disk must connect smoothly to the point-charge field lines far away. If we sketch these in, as in Fig. 24-26, we have a rough picture of the field everywhere. Don't underestimate the value of a simple approximation like this one! It can often tell all we need to know about a situation and may provide a much clearer understanding than would a detailed calculation.

Got It!

A uniformly charged sheet measures 1 m on each side, and you're told the total charge Q. What expressions would you use to get approximate values for the field magnitude (a) 1 cm from the sheet (but not near an edge) and (b) 1 km from the sheet?

24-6 GAUSS'S LAW AND CONDUCTORS

Electrostatic Equilibrium

In the preceding chapter we defined electrical conductors as materials containing free charges—like the free electrons in metals. Figure 24-27 shows what happens when an electric field is applied to a piece of conducting material. Free charges respond to the electric force $q\mathbf{E}$ by moving—in the direction of the field if they are positive, opposite the field if negative. The resulting charge separation gives rise to an electric field within the material that is opposite to the applied field. As more charge moves this internal field becomes stronger until its magnitude eventually equals that of the applied field. At that point free charges within the conductor experience zero net force, and the conductor is in **electrostatic equilibrium**. Although individual charges continue to move about in random thermal motion, there is no longer any net motion of charge. Once equilibrium is reached the internal and applied fields are equal but opposite, and therefore,

| The electric field is zero inside a conductor in electrostatic equilibrium.

It could not be otherwise: Since a conductor contains free charges, the presence of any internal electric field would result in bulk charge motion, and we would not have equilibrium. This result does not depend on the size or shape of the conductor, the magnitude or direction of the applied field, or even the nature of the material as long as it's a conductor. This ability of a conductor to cancel applied fields is the basis of shielding—the use of conductive enclosures to keep out unwanted electric fields.

This discussion of equilibrium is a macroscopic one; it considers only overall average fields within the material. At the atomic and molecular level there are still strong electric fields near individual electrons and protons. But the *average* field, taken over distances many times the separation between individual charges, is zero in electrostatic equilibrium.

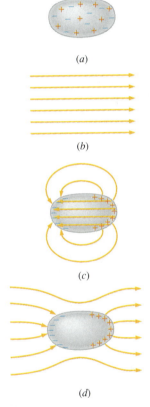

FIGURE 24-27 (a) A piece of conducting material contains positive and negative charge. (b) A uniform electric field, arising from charges outside the region shown. (c) Charges in the conductor separate in response to the field, resulting in an internal field that cancels the applied field. (d) The net field is the vector sum of the applied field and the field resulting from the redistribution of charge within the conductor. Note that field lines, as always, begin and end on charges.

FIGURE 24-28 Excess charge accumulates at the surface of a charged conductor. In this elongated conductor, mutual repulsion of the excess electrons results in the greatest charge accumulation at the opposite ends.

Gaussian surface

Material surface

FIGURE 24-29 Since the electric field inside the conductor is zero, a gaussian surface within the conductor encloses zero net charge. Any excess charge therefore resides on the conductor surface.

Charged Conductors

Although they contain free charges, conductors are normally electrically neutral since they include equal numbers of electrons and protons. But suppose we give a conductor a nonzero net charge, for example, by injecting excess electrons into its interior. There will be a mutual repulsion among the electrons and, because these are *excess* electrons, there is no compensating attraction from protons. We might expect, therefore, that the electrons will move as far apart as possible—namely to the surface of the conductor (Fig. 24-28). (Electrons might even leave the material—but that only occurs with very high charge densities.)

We now use Gauss's law to prove rigorously that excess charge *must* be at the surface of a conductor in electrostatic equilibrium. Figure 24-29 shows a piece of conducting material with a gaussian surface drawn just below the material surface. In equilibrium there is no electric field within the conductor, and thus the field is zero everywhere on the gaussian surface. The flux, $\oint \mathbf{E} \cdot d\mathbf{A}$, through the gaussian surface is therefore also zero. But Gauss's law says that the flux through a closed surface is proportional to the net charge enclosed, and therefore the net charge within our gaussian surface must be zero. This is true no matter where the gaussian surface is as long as it is *inside* the conductor. We can move the gaussian surface arbitrarily close to the conductor surface and it still encloses no net charge. If there is a net charge on the conductor it lies outside the gaussian surface, and therefore we conclude that

If a conductor in electrostatic equilibrium carries a net charge, all excess charge resides on the conductor surface.

EXAMPLE 24-7   *A Hollow Conductor*

An irregularly shaped conductor has a hollow cavity, as shown in Fig. 24-30. The conductor carries a net charge of 1.0 μC. A 2.0-μC point charge is inside the cavity, not touching the conductor. Find the net charge on the cavity wall and on the outer surface of the conductor, assuming electrostatic equilibrium.

+2.0 μC

Gaussian surface

FIGURE 24-30 A conductor with a hollow cavity containing a charge. The gaussian surface shown encloses no net charge, so the charge on the inner wall must be equal but opposite that of the charge within the cavity.

Solution

The electric field is zero everywhere within the conductor, and therefore is zero at all points on the gaussian surface shown in Fig. 24-30. The flux through this surface is thus zero, and Gauss's law tells us that the surface therefore encloses zero net charge. But there is a 2.0-μC charge within the cavity. In order for the gaussian surface to enclose zero net charge, the cavity wall must therefore carry -2.0 μC.

Since the conductor's net charge is 1.0 μC and there is -2.0 μC on its inner wall, the outer surface of the conductor surface must carry 3.0 μC.

EXERCISE A point charge $+q$ is placed inside a hollow conducting shell carrying a net charge $-3q$. What is the total charge on the outside surface of the shell?

Answer: $-2q$

Some problems similar to Example 24-7: 46–49

Got It!

A piece of conductor carries a net charge $+Q$. There's a hollow cavity within the conductor, and in it is a point charge $-Q$. In equilibrium, is there any charge on the outer surface of the conductor?

Experimental Tests of Gauss's Law

The fact that excess charge resides only on a conductor surface provides a very sensitive test of Gauss's law, and thus of the inverse-square law for the electric field. Figure 24-31 shows a charged conducting ball being placed inside a hollow, initially neutral conductor. When the two conductors touch, all the excess charge flows to the outer surface of the hollow conductor, leaving no net charge on the ball. In practice the experiment is often done in reverse, with an uncharged conducting ball placed within a hollow conductor. The outer conductor is then charged, and sensitive instruments used detect any charge moving to the ball. Absence of such charge motion confirms the inverse-square law. Recent experiments of this type show that the exponent 2 appearing in the inverse-square law is indeed 2 to within 3×10^{-16}. Such tests are far more sensitive than direct measurements of how the electric force varies with distance.

FIGURE 24-31 Experimental test of Gauss's law. When the small charged conductor contacts the interior of the hollow conductor, all its charge moves to the outside of the hollow conductor.

The Field at a Conductor Surface

There can be no electric field *within* a conductor in electrostatic equilibrium, but there *may* be a field right *at* the conductor surface. Such a field, though, cannot have a component parallel to the surface; if it did, charge would move along the surface and we would not have equilibrium. So the field at a conductor surface must be perpendicular to the surface (Fig. 24-32a).

We can compute the field strength by considering a small gaussian surface that straddles the conductor surface, as shown in Fig. 24-32b. We make the gaussian surface so small that curvature of the conductor becomes negligible, and we orient the gaussian surface with its sides perpendicular and its top parallel to the conductor surface. Since the field is perpendicular to the conductor, there is then no flux through the sides of the gaussian surface. Since the field is zero inside the conductor, there is also no flux through the inner end of the gaussian surface. The only

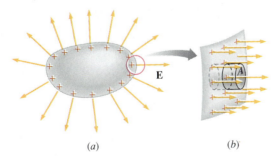

(a) (b)

FIGURE 24-32 (a) The electric field at the surface of a charged conductor is perpendicular to the conductor surface. (b) A small gaussian surface straddles the conductor surface.

FIGURE 24-33 During thunderstorms, a large charge density builds up at the pointed tip of the Empire State Building. The associated electric field can be strong enough to cause dielectric breakdown in the surrounding air, initiating frequent lightning strikes.

flux is through the outer end, whose area is A. Since the field is essentially uniform and perpendicular to this end, the flux is just EA. The only charge enclosed is right at the conductor surface, where it occupies the same area A. If the surface charge density is σ, then the enclosed charge is σA. Gauss's law equates the flux to $q_{\text{enclosed}}/\varepsilon_0$, so we have

$$EA = \frac{\sigma A}{\varepsilon_0}$$

or

$$E = \frac{\sigma}{\varepsilon_0}. \qquad \text{(field at conductor surface)} \qquad (24\text{-}11)$$

This result applies to any conductor in electrostatic equilibrium and shows that large electric fields develop where the charge density is high. Engineers designing electrical devices must avoid high charge densities whose associated fields could lead to sparks, arcing, and breakdown of electrical insulation (Fig. 24-33).

EXAMPLE 24-8	*Earth's Field*

Earth, which is an electrical conductor, carries a net charge of -4.3×10^5 C distributed approximately uniformly over its surface. Find the surface charge density, and use Equation 24-11 to calculate the electric field at Earth's surface.

Solution

Let Q be Earth's charge and R_E its radius (which is given inside the front cover and in Appendix E). Then the surface charge density is

$$\sigma = \frac{Q}{A} = \frac{Q}{4\pi R_E^2} = \frac{-4.3 \times 10^5 \text{ C}}{(4\pi)(6.37 \times 10^6 \text{ m})^2}$$

$$= -8.43 \times 10^{-10} \text{ C/m}^2.$$

Equation 24-11 then gives the electric field at Earth's surface:

$$E = \frac{\sigma}{\varepsilon_0} = \frac{-8.43 \times 10^{-10} \text{ C/m}^2}{8.85 \times 10^{-12} \text{ C}^2/\text{N·m}^2} = -95 \text{ N/C},$$

where the minus sign indicates that the field direction is downward. This modest field is present near Earth's surface in fair weather; in thunderstorms the local field exceeds this value by many orders of magnitude.

Does our result make sense? We could also treat Earth as a spherical charge distribution, whence its surface field strength would be $E = Q/4\pi \varepsilon_0 R_E^2$. Using the symbolic form of our result for σ in Equation 24-11 gives precisely this expression, showing that these two approaches to the field are indeed consistent.

EXERCISE Dielectric breakdown of air occurs with fields of about 3×10^6 N/C, and results in sparks jumping through the air. What is the maximum surface charge density permissible on a conductor if dielectric breakdown of the surrounding air is to be avoided?

Answer: 27 μC/m^2

Some problems similar to Example 24-8: 43, 44, 51

Equation 24-11 gives a field that depends only on the local charge density. Does that mean the field at any point on a conductor surface arises only from the charge right at that point? No! As always, the field at any point is the vector sum of contributions from all charge elements making up the charge distribution. Remarkably, Gauss's law requires that charges on a conductor arrange themselves in such a way that the field at any point on the conductor surface depends only on

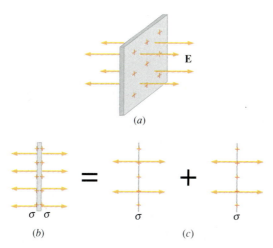

(a)

(b)   (c)

FIGURE 24-34 (a) An isolated, charged conducting plate. Its field points outward from both faces. (b) Edge-on view of the plate. If the plate is isolated, symmetry requires that there be equal charge densities on both faces. (c) The field anywhere is the sum of the fields of the two faces, each treated as a single charged sheet. Within the plate the fields cancel, while outside they sum to give a net field σ/ε_0.

the surface charge density right at that point—even though that field arises from *all* the charges on the surface (as well as from charges elsewhere if there are such)!

Consider a thin, flat, isolated, conducting sheet that has charge density σ on one of its two faces (Fig. 24-34a). Equation 24-11 shows immediately that the field at the surface of this plate is σ/ε_0. But if the plate is large and flat we can approximate it as an infinite sheet of charge—for which we found earlier (Equation 24-10 in Example 24-6) that the field should be $\sigma/2\varepsilon_0$. Is there a contradiction here? No! If the plate is isolated from other conductors or charges, then symmetry requires that charge spread itself evenly over *both* faces. If one face has charge density σ, so must the other—so we really have *two* charge sheets, each with density σ (Fig. 24-34b). Each gives rise to a field of magnitude $\sigma/2\varepsilon_0$, and *outside* the conductor those fields superpose to give the net field σ/ε_0 (Fig. 24-34c). *Inside* the conductor they also superpose, but here their directions are opposite and the result is that there is no field inside the conductor. Application of Equation 24-11 skips all these details. But because Equation 24-11 was derived on the assumption that the field inside the conductor is zero, it "knows" about charges everywhere on the conductor—and in this case that means on the second face of the conductor.

Equation 24-11 also applies to the pair of oppositely charged conducting plates shown in Fig. 24-35; the result, for the field between the plates, is σ/ε_0, where σ is the surface charge density on either plate. Why not $2\sigma/\varepsilon_0$? Again, Equation 24-11 always gives the field at a conductor surface—and it takes into account other charges that may be present. In this case neither plate is isolated, so the symmetry is broken, and charge builds up only on the inner faces of the two plates. Now each plate is a single charge layer, giving rise to a field $\sigma/2\varepsilon_0$, and between the plates the fields sum to Equation 24-11's result, σ/ε_0. Beyond the plates the fields sum to zero—a result that also follows from Equation 24-11 because now there is zero surface charge on the outer faces.

FIGURE 24-35 Edge view of two parallel conducting plates carrying opposite charges. Electrical attraction brings the excess charges to the inner faces. Each face constitutes a charge layer whose surface charge density has magnitude σ; between the plates their fields add to give field strength σ/ε_0.

CHAPTER SYNOPSIS

Summary

1. **Electric field lines** provide a visual representation of the electric field. The direction of a field line is that of the electric field, and the closeness of field lines is a measure of field strength. Electric field lines begin and end only on charges.

2. **Electric flux** quantifies the notion "number of field lines crossing a surface." Flux is the integral of the electric field over the surface:

$$\phi = \int \mathbf{E} \cdot d\mathbf{A},$$

where $d\mathbf{A}$ is an infinitesimal vector perpendicular to the surface at each point.

3. **Gauss's law** is a fundamental relation governing the behavior of electric fields throughout the universe. Gauss's law states that the electric flux emerging from any closed surface is proportional to the charge enclosed:

$$\oint \mathbf{E} \cdot d\mathbf{A} = \frac{q_{enclosed}}{\varepsilon_0},$$

where $\varepsilon_0 = 1/4\pi k$.

4. Gauss's law is true for any surface and any distribution of charge, but it proves useful in calculating the electric field only in cases with sufficient symmetry—in particular, spherical symmetry, line symmetry, and plane symmetry. Table 24-1 lists some fields calculated with Gauss's law. The fields of more realistic charge distributions are often approximated by the fields associated with these symmetries.

5. There is no electric field inside a conductor in **electrostatic equilibrium**. Gauss's law shows that any excess charge on the conductor resides on the conductor surface, and that the field at the conductor surface is perpendicular to the surface and has magnitude σ/ε_0, with σ the surface charge density.

TABLE 24-1 *Some Results from Gauss's Law*

CHARGE DISTRIBUTION	FIELD	WHERE VALID	DERIVED IN . . .
Any spherically symmetric	$E = \dfrac{kQ}{r^2} = \dfrac{Q}{4\pi\varepsilon_0 r^2}$	Outside the charge distribution	Section 24-4
Solid, uniformly charged sphere of radius R	$E = \dfrac{kQr}{r^3}$ $= \dfrac{Qr}{4\pi\varepsilon_0 r^3} = \dfrac{\rho r}{3\varepsilon_0}$	Inside ($r < R$)	Example 24-1
Uniform spherical shell of charge	$E = 0$	Inside	Example 24-2
Any cylindrically symmetric distribution with line charge density λ	$E = \dfrac{2k\lambda}{r} = \dfrac{\lambda}{2\pi e_0 r}$	Outside the charge distribution	Section 24-4
Solid, charged cylinder of radius R, uniform volume charge density ρ	$E = \dfrac{\rho r}{2\varepsilon_0 r}$	Inside ($r < R$)	Problem 24-31
Hollow, uniformly charged pipe	$E = 0$	Inside	Example 24-5
Infinite flat sheet, uniform surface charge density σ	$E = \dfrac{\sigma}{2\varepsilon_0}$	Outside	Example 24-6
Conductor in electrostatic equilibrium	$E = 0$	Inside	Section 24-6
Conductor in electrostatic equilibrium	$E = \dfrac{\sigma}{\varepsilon_0}$	At conductor surface	Section 24-6

Terms You Should Understand

(Pairs are closely related terms whose distinction is important; number in parentheses is chapter section where term first appears.)

electric field lines (24-1)
electric flux (24-2)
Gauss's law (24-3)
electrostatic equilibrium (24-6)

Symbols You Should Recognize

ϕ (24-2)

$\oint \mathbf{E} \cdot d\mathbf{A}$ (24-2)

$\mathbf{A}, d\mathbf{A}$ (24-2)

$\int$ (24-2)

$\oint$ (24-2)

k, ε_0 (24-3)

σ (24-6)

Problems You Should Be Able to Solve

drawing and interpreting field line patterns for simple charge distributions (24-1)
calculating electric flux (24-2)
using Gauss's law to calculate electric fields with spherical, line, or plane symmetry (24-4)
describing charge distributions in electrostatic equilibrium (24-6)
calculating electric fields at conductor surfaces (24-6)

Limitations to Keep in Mind

Gauss's law is universally true, but it can be used to calculate electric fields only with sufficient symmetry.

QUESTIONS

1. Can electric field lines ever cross? Why or why not?
2. If identical charged particles are placed at points *A* and *B* in Fig. 24-36, which will experience the greater force?

FIGURE 24-36 Question 2.

3. The electric flux through a closed surface is zero. Must the electric field be zero on that surface? If not, give an example.
4. If the flux of the gravitational field through a closed surface is zero, what can you conclude about the region interior to the surface?
5. Under what conditions can the electric flux through a surface be written as *EA*, where *A* is the surface area?
6. Eight field lines emerge from a closed surface surrounding an isolated point charge. Would this fact change if a second identical charge were brought to a point just *outside* the surface? If not, would anything change? Explain.
7. In what sense is Gauss's law equivalent to the inverse-square law?
8. If a charged particle were released from rest on a curved field line, would its subsequent motion follow the field line? Explain.
9. Gauss' law describes the flux of the electric field through a surface that may enclose charge. Must the field in Gauss's law arise only from charges within the closed surface?

10. In a certain region the electric field points to the right and its magnitude increases as you move to the right, as shown in Fig. 24-37. Does the region contain net positive charge, net negative charge, or zero net charge?

FIGURE 24-37 Question 10. (Left ends mark the beginnings of the field lines, which extend indefinitely to the right.)

11. A point charge is located a fixed distance from a uniformly charged sphere, outside the sphere. If the sphere shrinks in size without losing any charge, what happens to the force on the point charge?
12. In applying Equation 24-6 for the field outside a spherically symmetric charge distribution, is *r* the distance from the center or from the edge of the distribution?
13. The field of an infinite line of charge falls as $1/r$. How is this not a violation of the inverse-square law?
14. Why can't you use Gauss's law to determine the field of a uniformly charged cube? Why wouldn't it work to draw a cubical gaussian surface?
15. You're sitting inside an uncharged hollow spherical shell. Suddenly someone dumps a billion coulombs of charge on the shell, distributed uniformly. What happens to the electric field at your location?
16. Why is it that the field inside a uniformly charged sphere actually increases with distance from the center? How is this consistent with Coulomb's law?

17. There is a nonzero flux through each of the surfaces in Fig. 24-6, yet there is no charge in the region shown. Why is this not a violation of Gauss's law?

18. Does Gauss's law apply to a spherical surface not centered on a point charge, as shown in Fig. 24-38? Would this be a useful surface to use in calculating the electric field?

FIGURE 24-38 Question 18.

19. An insulating sphere carries charge spread uniformly throughout its volume. A conducting sphere has the same radius and net charge, but of course the charge is spread over its surface only. How do the electric fields outside these two charge distributions compare?

20. Why must the electric field be zero inside a conductor in electrostatic equilibrium?

21. Why must the electric field at the surface of a conductor in electrostatic equilibrium be perpendicular to the surface?

22. Where in Fig. 24-28 would you find the strongest electric field?

23. The electric field of a flat sheet of charge is $\sigma/2\varepsilon_0$. Yet the field of a flat conducting sheet—even a thin one, like a piece of aluminum foil—is σ/ε_0. Explain this apparent discrepancy.

24. A metal contains free electrons not bound to individual atoms. Does Gauss's law require that all these free electrons be on the metal surface?

PROBLEMS

ActivPhysics can help with these problems:
Activities 11.4–11.6

Section 24-1 Electric Field Lines

1. What is the net charge shown in Fig. 24-39? The magnitude of the middle charge is 3 μC.

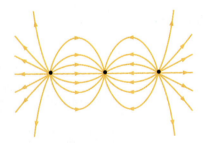

FIGURE 24-39 Problem 1.

2. A charge $+2q$ and a charge $-q$ are near each other. Sketch some field lines for this charge distribution, using the convention of eight lines for a charge of magnitude q.

3. Two charges $+q$ and a charge $-q$ are at the vertices of an equilateral triangle. Sketch some field lines for this charge distribution.

4. The net charge shown in Fig. 24-40 is $+Q$. Identify each of the charges A, B, C shown.

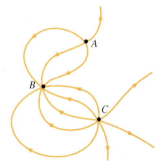

FIGURE 24-40 Problem 4.

Section 24-2 Electric Flux

5. A flat surface with area 2.0 m² is in a uniform electric field of 850 N/C. What is the electric flux through the surface when it is (a) at right angles to the field, (b) at 45° to the field, and (c) parallel to the field?

6. What is the electric field strength in a region where the flux through a 1.0 cm × 1.0 cm flat surface is 65 N·m²/C, if the field is uniform and the surface is at right angles to the field?

7. A flat surface with area 0.14 m² lies in the x-y plane, in a uniform electric field given by $\mathbf{E} = 5.1\hat{\imath} + 2.1\hat{\jmath} + 3.5\hat{k}$ kN/C. Find the flux through this surface.

8. The electric field on the surface of a 10-cm-diameter sphere is perpendicular to the sphere and has magnitude 47 kN/C. What is the electric flux through the sphere?

9. What is the flux through the hemispherical open surface of radius R shown in Fig. 24-41? The uniform field has magnitude E. *Hint:* Don't do a messy integral! Imagine closing the surface with a flat, circular piece across the open end. What would be the flux through the entire closed surface? And what's the flux through the flat end? So what's the answer?

FIGURE 24-41 Problem 9.

10. The electric field shown in Fig. 24-42 is given by $\mathbf{E} = E_0 \dfrac{y}{a}\hat{\mathbf{k}}$, where E_0 and a are constants. Find the flux through the square of side a shown.

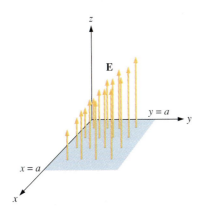

FIGURE 24-42 Problem 10.

Section 24-3 Gauss's Law

11. What is the electric flux through each closed surface shown in Fig. 24-43?

FIGURE 24-43 Problem 11.

12. A 6.8-μC charge and a $-4.7\ \mu$C charge are inside an uncharged sphere. What is the electric flux through the sphere?

13. A 2.6-μC charge is at the center of a cube 7.5 cm on each side. What is the electric flux through one face of the cube? *Hint:* Think about symmetry, and don't do an integral.

14. If the charge in the preceding problem is still inside the cube but not at the center, (a) what is the flux through the *entire* cube? (b) Could you still calculate the flux through one face without doing an integral?

15. A dipole consists of two charges $\pm 6.1\ \mu$C located 1.2 cm apart. What is the electric flux through each surface shown in Fig. 24-44?

FIGURE 24-44 Problem 15.

16. The electric field in a certain region is given by $\mathbf{E} = 40x\hat{\mathbf{i}}$ N/C, with x in meters. What is the volume charge density in the region? *Hint:* Apply Gauss's law to a cube 1 meter on a side.

Section 24-4 Using Gauss's Law

17. The electric field at the surface of a uniformly charged sphere of radius 5.0 cm is 90 kN/C. What would be the field strength 10 cm from the surface?

18. A solid sphere 25 cm in radius carries 14 μC, distributed uniformly throughout its volume. Find the electric field strength (a) 15 cm, (b) 25 cm, and (c) 50 cm from the sphere's center.

19. A crude model for the hydrogen atom treats it as a point charge $+e$ (the proton) surrounded by a uniform cloud of negative charge with total charge $-e$ and radius 0.0529 nm. What would be the electric field strength inside such an atom, halfway from the proton to the edge of the charge cloud?

20. Positive charge is spread uniformly over the surface of a spherical balloon 70 cm in radius, resulting in an electric field of 26 kN/C at the balloon's surface. Find the field strength (a) 50 cm from the balloon's center and (b) 190 cm from the center. (c) What is the net charge on the balloon?

21. A 10-nC point charge is located at the center of a thin spherical shell of radius 8.0 cm carrying -20 nC distributed uniformly over its surface. What are the magnitude and direction of the electric field (a) 2.0 cm, (b) 6.0 cm, and (c) 15 cm from the point charge?

22. A solid sphere 2.0 cm in radius carries a uniform volume charge density. The electric field 1.0 cm from the sphere's center has magnitude 39 kN/C. (a) At what other distance does the field have this magnitude? (b) What is the net charge on the sphere?

23. A point charge $-2Q$ is at the center of a spherical shell of radius R carrying charge Q spread uniformly over its surface. What is the electric field at (a) $r = \frac{1}{2}R$ and (b) $r = 2R$? (c) How would your answers change if the charge on the shell were doubled?

24. A spherical shell of radius 15 cm carries 4.8 μC, distributed uniformly over its surface. At the center of the shell is a point charge. (a) If the electric field at the surface of the sphere is 750 kN/C and points outward, what is the charge of the point charge? (b) What is the field just inside the shell?

25. A spherical shell 30 cm in diameter carries a total charge 85 μC distributed uniformly over its surface. A 1.0-μC point charge is located at the center of the shell. What is the electric field strength (a) 5.0 cm from the center and (b) 45 cm from the center? (c) How would your answers change if the charge on the shell were doubled?

26. The thick, spherical shell of inner radius a and outer radius b shown in Fig. 24-45 carries a uniform volume charge density ρ. Find an expression for the electric field strength in the region $a < r < b$, and show that your result is consistent with Equation 24-7 when $a = 0$.

FIGURE 24-45 Problems 26, 32.

27. How should the charge density within a solid sphere vary with distance from the center in order that the magnitude of the electric field in the sphere be constant?

28. A long, thin wire carrying 5.6 nC/m runs down the center of a long, thin-walled, hollow pipe with radius 1.0 cm carrying −4.2 nC/m spread uniformly over its surface. Find the electric field (a) 0.50 cm from the wire and (b) 1.5 cm from the wire.

29. A long solid rod 4.5 cm in radius carries a uniform volume charge density. If the electric field strength at the surface of the rod (not near either end) is 16 kN/C, what is the volume charge density?

30. The electric field strength outside a charge distribution and 18 cm from its center has magnitude 55 kN/C. At 23 cm the field strength is 43 kN/C. Does the distribution have spherical or line symmetry?

31. An infinitely long rod of radius R carries a uniform volume charge density ρ. Show that the electric field strengths outside and inside the rod are given, respectively, by $E = \rho R^2/2\varepsilon_0 r$ and $E = \rho r/2\varepsilon_0$, where r is the distance from the rod axis.

32. Repeat Problem 26, assuming that Fig. 24-45 represents the cross section of a long, thick-walled pipe. Now the case $a = 0$ should be consistent with the result of Problem 31 for the interior of the rod.

33. A long, thin wire carries a uniform line charge density $\lambda = -6.8$ μC/m. It is surrounded by a thick concentric cylindrical shell of inner radius 2.5 cm and outer radius 3.5 cm. What uniform volume charge density in the shell will result in zero electric field outside the shell?

34. A square nonconducting plate measures 4.5 m on a side and carries charge spread uniformly over its surface. The electric field 10 cm from the plate and not near an edge has magnitude 430 N/C and points toward the plate. Find (a) the surface charge density on the plate and (b) the total charge on the plate. (c) What is the electric field strength 20 cm from the plate?

35. If you "painted" positive charge on the floor, what surface charge density would be necessary in order to suspend a 15-μC, 5.0-g particle above the floor?

36. A slab of charge extends infinitely in two dimensions and has thickness d in the third dimension, as shown in Fig. 24-46. The slab carries a uniform volume charge density ρ. Find expressions for the electric field strength (a) inside and (b) outside the slab, as functions of the distance x from the center plane.

FIGURE 24-46 Section of an infinite slab of charge (Problem 36).

37. Figure 24-47 shows sections of three infinite flat sheets of charge, each carrying surface charge density with the same magnitude σ. Find the magnitude and direction of the electric field in each of the four regions shown.

FIGURE 24-47 Problem 37.

Section 24-5 Fields of Arbitrary Charge Distributions

38. A rod 50 cm long and 1.0 cm in radius carries a 2.0-μC charge distributed uniformly over its length. What is the approximate magnitude of the electric field (a) 4.0 mm from the rod surface, not near either end, and (b) 23 m from the rod?

39. A nonconducting square plate 75 cm on a side carries a uniform surface charge density. The electric field strength 1 cm from the plate, not near an edge, is 45 kN/C. What is the approximate field strength 15 m from the plate?

40. Two circular plates 10 cm in diameter and 2.0 mm apart carry equal but opposite charges ± 0.50 μC distributed uniformly over their facing surfaces. What is the electric field strength (a) between the plates but not near either edge? (b) 2.5 m from the plates on a plane passing midway between them? *Hint* for (b): See Example 23-6.

41. The electric field strength on the axis of a uniformly charged disk is given by $E = 2\pi k\sigma(1 - x/\sqrt{x^2 + a^2})$, with σ the surface charge density, a the disk radius, and x the distance from the disk center. If $a = 20$ cm, (a) for what range of x values does treating the disk as an infinite sheet give an approximation to the field that is good to within 10%? (b) For what range of x values is the point-charge approximation good to 10%?

42. A nonconducting square 2.0 cm on a side carries a 45-nC charge spread uniformly over its surface. The x axis runs through the plate center, perpendicular to the plate, with $x = 0$ at the plate center. A -45-nC point charge is at $x = 5.0$ cm. Find approximate values for the electric field strength on the x axis at (a) $x = 1.0$ mm; (b) $x = 4.8$ cm; (c) $x = 2.5$ m. *Hint* for (c): Consult Example 23-6.

Section 24-6 Gauss's Law and Conductors

43. What is the electric field strength just outside the surface of a conducting sphere carrying surface charge density 1.4 $\mu C/m^2$?

44. Calculate the acceleration of a proton at the surface of a conductor carrying surface charge density 0.60 C/m^2.

45. A net charge of 5.0 μC is applied on one side of a solid metal sphere 2.0 cm in diameter. After electrostatic equilibrium is reached, what are (a) the volume charge density inside the sphere and (b) the surface charge density on the sphere? Assume there are no other charges or conductors nearby. (c) Which of your answers depends on this assumption, and why?

46. A point charge $+q$ lies at the center of a spherical conducting shell carrying a net charge $\frac{3}{2}q$. Sketch the field lines both inside and outside the shell, using 8 field lines to represent a charge of magnitude q.

47. A 250-nC point charge is placed at the center of an uncharged spherical conducting shell 20 cm in radius. (a) What is the surface charge density on the outer surface of the shell? (b) What is the electric field strength at the shell's outer surface?

48. A point charge is placed at the center of an uncharged spherical conducting shell of inner radius 2.5 cm and outer radius 4.0 cm (Fig. 24-48). As a result, the outer surface of the shell acquires a surface charge density $\sigma = 71$ nC/cm^2. Find (a) the value of the point charge and (b) the surface charge density on the inner wall of the shell.

FIGURE 24-48 Problem 48.

49. An irregular conductor containing an irregular, empty cavity carries a net charge Q. (a) Show that the electric field inside the cavity must be zero. (b) If you put a point charge inside the cavity, what value must it have in order to make the surface charge density on the outer surface of the conductor everywhere zero?

50. A neutral dime is placed in a uniform electric field of 6.2×10^5 N/C, with its faces perpendicular to the field. (a) What is the approximate charge density on the faces of the dime? (b) What is the total charge on each face? (Measure a dime!)

51. A total charge of 18 μC is applied to a thin, square metal plate 75 cm on a side. Find the electric field strength near the plate's surface.

52. Two closely spaced parallel metal plates carry surface charge densities ± 95 nC/m^2 on their facing surfaces, with no charge on their outer surfaces. Find the electric field

strength (a) between the plates and (b) outside the plates. Treat the plates as infinite in extent.

53. A conducting sphere 2.0 cm in radius is concentric with a spherical conducting shell with inner radius 8.0 cm and outer radius 10 cm. The small sphere carries 50 nC charge and the shell has no net charge. Find the electric field strength (a) 1.0 cm, (b) 5.0 cm, (c) 9.0 cm, and (d) 15 cm from the center.

54. A coaxial cable consists of an inner wire and a concentric cylindrical outer conductor (Fig. 24-49). If the conductors carry equal but opposite charges, show that there is no net charge on the *outside* of the outer conductor.

FIGURE 24-49 Problem 54.

Paired Problems

(Both problems in a pair involve the same principles and techniques. If you can get the first problem, you should be able to solve the second one.)

55. A point charge $-q$ is at the center of a spherical shell carrying charge $+2q$. That shell, in turn, is concentric with a larger shell carrying charge $-\frac{3}{2}q$. Draw a cross section of this structure, and sketch the electric field lines using the convention that 8 lines correspond to a charge of magnitude q.

56. A point charge $-q$ is at the center of a spherical shell carrying charge $-\frac{3}{2}q$. That shell, in turn, is concentric with a larger shell carrying charge $+2q$. Draw a cross section of this structure, and sketch the electric field lines using the convention that 8 lines correspond to a charge of magnitude q.

57. A point charge q is at the center of a spherical shell of radius R carrying charge $2q$ spread uniformly over its surface. Write expressions for the electric field strength at (a) $\frac{1}{2}R$ and (b) $2R$.

58. A point charge q is at the center of a spherical shell of radius R carrying charge $5q$. At what other distance does the electric field have the same value it does at a point halfway from the center to the shell?

59. A long, thin hollow pipe 4.0 cm in diameter carries charge at a density of $-2.6\,\mu C/m$, uniformly distributed over the pipe. It is concentric with 10-cm diameter pipe carrying $+2.6\,\mu C/m$, also uniformly distributed. Find the magnitude of the electric field at (a) 0.50 cm, (b) 3.5 cm, and (c) 12 cm from the axis of the pipes.

60. Two concentric hollow pipes are 5.0 cm and 12 cm in diameter, respectively. Both carry uniformly distributed electric charges. The electric field 4.0 cm from their common axis is 630 kN/C, radially outward. The field 10 cm from their common axis is 126 kN/C, radially outward. (a) Find the linear charge densities on the two pipes. (b) How would the electric field strengths at 4.0 cm and 10 cm change if the charge density on the outer pipe were doubled?

61. An early (and incorrect) model for the atom pictured its positive charge as spread uniformly throughout the spherical atomic volume. For a hydrogen atom of radius 0.0529 nm, what would be the electric field due to such a distribution of positive charge (a) 0.020 nm from the center and (b) 0.20 nm from the center?

62. A solid sphere of radius R carries a charge spread uniformly throughout its volume. At what point outside the sphere is the electric field strength equal to that at a point halfway from the center to the edge? Express your answer as a distance from the center.

63. A sphere of radius $2a$ has a hole of radius a, as shown in Fig. 24-50. The solid portion carries a uniform volume charge density ρ. Find an expression for the electric field strength within the solid portion, as a function of the distance r from the center.

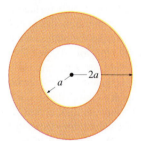

FIGURE 24-50 Problems 63, 64.

64. Repeat the previous problem, now considering that the figure represents the cross section of a thick cylindrical pipe.

Supplementary Problems

65. Repeat Problem 10 for the case $\mathbf{E} = E_0\left(\dfrac{y}{a}\right)^2\hat{\mathbf{k}}$.

66. The volume charge density inside a solid sphere of radius a is given by $\rho = \rho_0 r/a$, where ρ_0 is a constant. Find (a) the total charge and (b) the electric field strength within the sphere, as a function of distance r from the center.

67. A proton is released from rest 1.0 cm from a large sheet carrying a surface charge density of $-24\,nC/m^2$. How much later does it strike the sheet?

68. Fig. 24-51 shows a rectangular box with sides $2a$ and length ℓ surrounding a line of charge with uniform line charge density λ. The line passes directly through the center of the box faces. Using an expression for the field of a line charge, integrate over strips of width dx as shown to find the electric flux through one face of the box. Multiply by 4 to get the total flux through the box, and show that your result is consistent with Gauss's law.

FIGURE 24-51 Problem 68.

69. Repeat Problem 36 for the case when the charge density in the slab is given by $\rho = \rho_0 |x/d|$, where ρ_0 is a constant.
70. The charge density within a uniformly charged sphere of radius R is given by $\rho = \rho_0 - ar^2$, where ρ_0 and a are constants, and r is the distance from the center. Find an expression for a such that the electric field outside the sphere is zero.
71. A small object of mass m and charge q is attached by a thread of length ℓ to a large, flat, nonconducting plate carrying a uniform surface charge density σ with the same sign as q (Fig. 24-52). If the object is displaced slightly sideways from its equilibrium, show that it undergoes simple harmonic motion with period $T = 2\pi\sqrt{2\epsilon_0 m\ell/q\sigma}$. Assume the gravitational force is negligible.

FIGURE 24-52 Problem 71.

72. An infinitely long nonconducting rod of radius R carries a volume charge density given by $\rho = \rho_0(r/R)$, where ρ_0 is a constant. Find the electric field strength (a) inside and (b) outside the rod, as functions of the distance r from the rod axis.

73. A thick spherical shell of inner radius a and outer radius b carries a charge density given by $\rho = \dfrac{ce^{-r/a}}{r^2}$, where a and c are constants. Find expressions for the electric field strength for (a) $r < a$, (b) $a < r < b$, and (c) $r > b$.
74. A solid sphere of radius R carries a nonuniform volume charge density given by $\rho = \pi^2\rho_0 \sin(\pi r/R)$, where r is the distance from the center and ρ_0 is a positive constant. Find the magnitude and direction of the electric field at the sphere's surface.
75. A solid sphere of radius R carries a uniform volume charge density ρ. A hole of radius $R/2$ occupies a region from the center to the edge of the sphere, as shown in Fig. 24-53. Show that the electric field everywhere in the hole points horizontally and has magnitude $\rho R/6\epsilon_0$. *Hint:* Treat the hole as a superposition of two charged spheres of opposite charge.

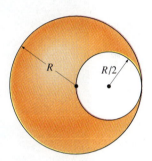

FIGURE 24-53 Problem 75.

76. You're 5.0 m from a charge distribution and you measure an electric field strength of 850 N/C. At 2.5 m the field strength has increased to about 3.4 kN/C. When you're 5.0 mm from the center of the distribution the field strength is 42.5 MN/C, and it increases to 85 MN/C at 2.5 mm. Describe the distribution as fully as you can, including its shape, any dimensions you can find, its total charge, and any appropriate charge density.
77. Two flat, parallel, closely spaced metal plates of area 0.080 m^2 carry total charges of -2.1 μC and $+3.8$ μC. Find the surface charge densities on the inner and outer faces of each plate.
78. Since the gravitational force of a point mass goes as $1/r^2$, the gravitational field **g** also obeys a form of Gauss's law. (a) Formulate this law, and (b) use it to find an expression for the gravitational field strength *within* Earth, as a function of distance r from the center. Treat Earth as a sphere of uniform density.

25 Electric Potential

Lines of constant electric potential on the surface of the human body reflect the electric dipole structure of the heart.

You have to do work to lift your book against Earth's gravitational field. The work you do gets stored as potential energy, which is released if you lower the book. In Chapter 8 we introduced the term **conservative** to describe a force or field that, like gravity, "gives back" all the stored energy. With conservative forces we could associate a potential energy, and then use the powerful conservation of energy principle to solve practical problems.

The electric field of a static charge distribution is also conservative—an experimental fact that's also suggested theoretically by the similarity between Coulomb's law and Newton's law of universal gravitation. Because the electric field is conservative, it is meaningful to talk about potential energy in electrostatic systems. If you do work moving a charge against the electric force, for example, that work ends up stored as electric potential energy.

In this chapter we deal with electric potential, a useful and easily measured quantity that derives from the concept of potential energy. We'll see how the use of electric potential can provide a simpler approach to calculating electric fields, and how electric potential relates to the properties of everyday devices like batteries.

25-1 POTENTIAL ENERGY, WORK, AND THE ELECTRIC FIELD

In Chapter 8 we defined potential energy difference ΔU_{AB} as the negative of the work W_{AB} done by a conservative force $\mathbf{F}$ on an object moved from point A to point B:

$$\Delta U_{AB} = U_B - U_A = -W_{AB} = -\int_A^B \mathbf{F} \cdot d\boldsymbol{\ell}, \qquad (25\text{-}1)$$

where $d\boldsymbol{\ell}$ is a small element of the path from A to B. We also showed that this potential energy difference is independent of the path taken between points A and B (Fig. 25-1).

We'll now look at potential energy changes associated with moving charged objects in an electric field. First, consider a positive charge q being moved between two points A and B a distance ℓ apart in a uniform electric field $\mathbf{E}$, as shown in Fig. 25-2. A conservative electric force $q\mathbf{E}$ acts on the charge, and since the field is uniform that force doesn't vary as we move from A to B. Therefore, we can dispense with the integral and write

$$\Delta U_{AB} = -W_{AB} = -\mathbf{F} \cdot \boldsymbol{\ell} = -q\mathbf{E} \cdot \boldsymbol{\ell} = -qE\ell \cos(180°) = qE\ell,$$

where $\boldsymbol{\ell}$ is a vector from A to B and where the factor $\cos 180° = -1$ appears because the vectors $\mathbf{E}$ and $\boldsymbol{\ell}$ are in opposite directions. Does this result make sense? Pushing a positive charge against the electric field is like pushing a car up a hill: We do positive work, gravity does negative work, and the gravitational potential energy increases. Here we must do positive work to move the charge from A to B, the electric field does negative work, and the electric potential energy change—the *negative* of the work done by the conservative electric force—is positive. Let go of the charge and the field will accelerate it back toward B, changing potential to kinetic energy, just as gravity would accelerate the car back down the hill.

FIGURE 25-1 The gravitational field is conservative, and therefore the net work required to move between two points is independent of the path taken.

FIGURE 25-2 The work required to move a charge q from A to B in a *uniform* electric field is $qE\ell$.

25-2 POTENTIAL DIFFERENCE

We've just found the potential energy change in moving a charge q from point A to point B in Fig. 25-2. If we had moved a charge $2q$ the potential energy change would have been twice as great, and it would have required twice as much work; $\frac{1}{4}q$ would have one-fourth the potential energy change and would require one-fourth the work. Since the potential energy change is directly proportional to the charge it's convenient to consider the *potential energy change per unit charge* involved in moving between two points. We call this quantity the **electric potential difference**, ΔV. Mathematically, we express the potential difference by writing $\mathbf{F} = q\mathbf{E}$ in Equation 25-1 and dividing by q:

$$\Delta V_{AB} = \frac{\Delta U_{AB}}{q} = -\frac{1}{q}\int_A^B q\mathbf{E} \cdot d\boldsymbol{\ell} = -\int_A^B \mathbf{E} \cdot d\boldsymbol{\ell}.$$

Then our definition of potential difference becomes:

> *The electric potential difference from point A to point B is the potential energy change per unit charge in moving from A to B:*

$$\Delta V_{AB} = -\int_A^B \mathbf{E} \cdot d\boldsymbol{\ell}. \qquad \text{(electric potential difference)} \quad (25\text{-}2a)$$

Here we use the Δ and the subscripts AB to show explicitly that we're talking about a *change* or *difference* from one point to another. We'll sometimes use just the symbol V for potential difference, in cases where the starting point A is understood. Note that potential difference, although computed from the dot product of vectors, is itself a scalar quantity.

The change from potential energy to electric potential is analogous to the change we made in Chapter 23 when we introduced the electric field as the electric force *per unit charge;* similarly, electric potential difference is the change in potential energy *per unit charge.* Again, the reason is the same: we want to express the electrical properties of a system in terms that don't involve the specific charges we may put in the vicinity of that system. Table 25-1 summarizes the relations among force and field, potential energy and electric potential.

In the special case of a uniform field, Equation 25-2a reduces to

$$\Delta V_{AB} = -\mathbf{E} \cdot \boldsymbol{\ell}, \quad \text{(uniform field)} \qquad (25\text{-}2b)$$

where $\boldsymbol{\ell}$ is a vector from A to B. Figure 25-2 shows the special case when the field $\mathbf{E}$ and path $\boldsymbol{\ell}$ are in opposite directions; here, Equation 25-2b gives $\Delta V_{AB} = E\ell$.

Equations 25-2 show that potential difference can be positive or negative, depending on whether the path goes against or with the field. Moving a positive charge through a positive potential difference is like going uphill: We must do work on the charge, and its potential energy increases. Moving a positive charge through a negative potential difference is like going downhill: We do negative work or, equivalently, the field does work on the charge, and its potential energy decreases. In both cases the opposite is true for a negative charge; even though the potential difference remains the same, the work and potential energy reverse because of the negative sign on the charge.

We emphasize that potential difference is a property *of two points;* it doesn't depend on the path taken between those points. In Fig. 25-2, considering a straight path from A to B made the calculation of potential difference easy, but we would have found the same result—albeit with much more work—using any path (Fig. 25-3).

TABLE 25-1 *Force and Field, Potential Energy and Potential*

GENERAL QUANTITY	ELECTRICAL QUANTITY
Force **F** (Unit: N)	Electric field $\mathbf{E} = \dfrac{\mathbf{F}}{q}$ (Unit: N/C or V/m)
Potential energy difference ΔU $\Delta U = -\int_A^B \mathbf{F} \cdot d\boldsymbol{\ell}$ (Unit: J)	Electric potential difference $\Delta V = \dfrac{\Delta U}{q}$ $\Delta V = -\int_A^B \mathbf{E} \cdot d\boldsymbol{\ell}$ (Unit: J/C or V)

FIGURE 25-3 The potential difference ΔV_{AB} depends only on the points A and B, not on the path taken. Application of Equation 25-2a to any of the three paths shown would give the same result, namely $\Delta V_{AB} = E\ell$.

Got It!

What would happen to the potential difference V_{AB} in Fig. 25-2 if (a) the electric field strength were doubled; (b) the length ℓ were doubled; (c) the points were moved so the path lay at right angles to the field; (d) the positions of A and B were interchanged?

The Volt and the Electron Volt

The definition of potential difference shows that its units are joules/coulomb. Potential difference is important enough that 1 J/C has a special name—the **volt** (V). To say that a car has a 12-V battery, for example, means that the battery does 12 J of work on every coulomb that moves between its two terminals. Table 25-2 lists some common potential differences.

We often use the term **voltage** to speak of potential difference, especially in describing electric circuits. Strictly speaking the two terms are not synonymous, since voltage is used even in nonconservative situations that arise when fields change with time. But in common usage this subtle distinction is usually not bothersome.

Tip

Potential Difference Depends on Two Points Specifically, it is the energy per unit charge involved in moving *between those points*. Always think of potential difference in terms of two points. This is ultimately a very practical matter; if you forget it you won't be able to hook up a voltmeter properly, or connect jumper cables safely to your car battery! Figure 25-4 provides a dramatic illustration of this point.

Sometimes we speak of "the potential (or the voltage) at point *P*." This is *always* a shorthand way of talking, and we *must* have in mind some other point. What we mean is the potential difference going from that other point to point *P*.

In molecular, atomic, and nuclear systems it's often convenient to measure energy in **electron volts** (eV), defined as follows:

One electron volt is the energy gained by a particle carrying one elementary charge when it moves through a potential difference of one volt.

Since one elementary charge is 1.6×10^{-19} C, 1 eV is 1.6×10^{-19} J. Energy in eV is particularly easy to calculate when charge is given in elementary charges. However, the eV is *not* an SI unit and should be converted to joules before calculating other quantities.

Got It!

A proton (charge e) and an alpha particle (charge $2e$) each move through the same potential difference. Compare the work done on each.

TABLE 25-2 *Typical Potential Differences*

Between human arm and leg due to heart's electrical activity	1 mV
Across biological cell membrane	80 mV
Between terminals of flashlight battery	1.5 V
Car battery	12 V
Across loudspeaker operating at 50 watts	20 V
Electrical outlet, United States	120 V
Electrical outlet, Europe	230 V
Between accelerating electrodes in TV picture tube	30 kV
Between long-distance electric transmission line and ground	365 kV
Between base of thunderstorm cloud and ground	100 MV

FIGURE 25-4 Potential difference depends on *two* points. This parasailer landed on a 138,000-V power line, but he's not being electrocuted because his body is not contacting *two* points with a potential difference between them.

EXAMPLE 25-1 | A TV Picture Tube: Potential Difference, Work, and Energy

At the back end of a TV picture tube, a uniform electric field of 600 kN/C extends over a distance of 5.0 cm and points toward the back of the tube (Fig. 25-5). (a) Find the potential difference between the back and the front end of this field region. (b) How much work would it take to move an ion with charge $+2e$ from the back to the front of the field region? (c) What would happen to an electron released at the back of the field region?

Solution

(a) With a uniform field the potential difference is given by Equation 25-2b:

$$V_{AB} = -\mathbf{E} \cdot \boldsymbol{\ell} = E\ell = (600 \times 10^3 \text{ N/C})(0.050 \text{ m})$$
$$= 30 \text{ kV},$$

where the second equality follows because a path from the back toward the front is opposite the field direction, as shown in Fig. 25-2, so $\cos\theta = -1$.

(b) Potential difference is the potential energy change per unit charge, or, equivalently, the work per unit charge needed to move charge between two points. Thus, the work to move the ion of charge $q = 2e$ against the 30-kV potential difference is

$$W_{\text{ion}} = q\Delta V = (2)(1.6 \times 10^{-19} \text{ C})(30 \text{ kV}) = 9.6 \times 10^{-15} \text{ J},$$

where the units work out because $1 \text{ V} = 1 \text{ J/C}$. Since the ion carries two elementary charges, we could also express this energy as $(2e)(30 \text{ kV}) = 60 \text{ keV}$.

FIGURE 25-5 A potential difference on the order of 30 kV is used to accelerate the electrons that "paint" the picture on the screen of a TV tube, shown here in a cutaway view.

(c) With its negative charge, the electron would *gain* energy given by $e\Delta V$, or 4.8×10^{-15} J (more simply calculated as 30 keV). But energy is conserved, so this gain—an increase in the electron's kinetic energy $\frac{1}{2}mv^2$—comes at the expense of a decrease in potential energy.

EXERCISE A 1.2-μC charge is accelerated through a 3400-V potential difference. How much energy does it gain?

Answer: 4.1 mJ

EXAMPLE 25-2 | Potential of a Charged Sheet

An isolated, infinite charged sheet carries a uniform surface charge density σ. (a) Find an expression for the potential difference from the sheet to a point a perpendicular distance x from the sheet. (b) What is the potential difference between two points the same distance from the sheet?

Solution

Equation 24-10 gives $E = \dfrac{\sigma}{2\varepsilon_0}$ for the field of a single, isolated sheet of charge. Since the field is uniform we can apply Equation 25-2b. Moving away from the sheet in either direction is going *with* the field (assuming positive σ), so the dot product in Equation 25-2b is positive and therefore the potential difference is negative. Taking $\ell = x$ in Equation 25-2b then gives

$$\Delta V_{0x} = -Ex = -\frac{\sigma x}{2\varepsilon_0},$$

where the subscript $0x$ means we're taking the potential difference from the sheet ($x = 0$) to the point x. Our result makes two important points. First, the minus sign reaffirms that moving in the direction of the electric field entails a decrease in electric potential. Second, the fact that ΔV is directly proportional to x shows that the potential in a *uniform* field varies *linearly* with distance along the field direction. (Here we're beginning to use the term "potential" as a shorthand for, in this case, "the potential difference between the sheet and another point." When we speak of "the potential," we always mean potential difference between two points, one of which is a common reference point—in this case the position of the charged sheet.)

If, on the other hand, we consider moving charge between two points equidistant from the sheet, then the charge moves perpendicular to the field and there is no change in its potential energy; thus, the potential difference between such points is zero.

EXERCISE Two nonconducting charged sheets carry equal but opposite surface charge densities ± 53 nC/m². The negative sheet is located at $x = 0$, the positive sheet at $x = 10$ cm. Find expressions for the potential difference from the negative sheet to the points (a) $x = 2.0$ cm, (b) $x = 5.0$ cm, (c) $x = 25$ cm, and (d) $x = -10$ cm. *Hint:* Think about the different fields *between* and *beyond* the plates.

Answers: (a) 120 V; (b) 300 V; (c) 600 V; (d) 0 V

Some problems similar to Examples 25-1 and 25-2: 5, 7–9, 18

Got It!

Does a proton tend to move in the direction of positive or negative potential difference, as measured from its starting point? How about an electron?

Curved Paths and Nonuniform Fields

Equations 25-2 contain a dot product that accounts for the orientation of the path relative to the field. Figure 25-6, for example, shows several straight paths of the same length ℓ in a uniform electric field. Path AB is the same path we considered in Fig. 25-2; the potential difference between its ends is just $\Delta V_{AB} = E\ell$ because the angle between $\mathbf{E}$ and $\boldsymbol{\ell}$ is 180°. Path AC is at 135° to the field direction, giving a potential difference $\Delta V_{AC} = -E\ell \cos 135° = E\ell/\sqrt{2}$. Finally, path AD is perpendicular to the field, giving $\Delta V_{AD} = 0$. Quite generally, as Fig. 25-6 suggests, the potential difference depends only on the component of the path *along* the field direction. This is analogous to the situation with gravity, where the work *mgh* needed to lift a mass depends only on the *vertical* distance h and not on any horizontal component of the motion.

If the field is not uniform or the path is not straight, then we must use Equation 25-2a to calculate the potential because the magnitude of $\mathbf{E}$ and/or the angle between $\mathbf{E}$ and the path is changing. Figure 25-7 shows that in such cases we can view the integral in Equation 25-2b as the sum of infinitely many infinitesimal potential differences dV. Each is taken over a path segment $d\boldsymbol{\ell}$ so short that it's essentially straight and the field is essentially uniform over the segment. The limits of the integral are the endpoints of the path, and thus include all the infinitesimal potential differences dVs along the path. Because the electric field is conservative, we can evaluate the integral over any path between the given endpoints. Several examples in the next section illustrate the use of Equation 25-2a.

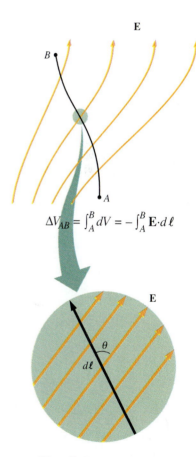

$$\Delta V_{AB} = \int_A^B dV = -\int_A^B \mathbf{E} \cdot d\boldsymbol{\ell}$$

$$dV = -\mathbf{E} \cdot d\boldsymbol{\ell} = -E\,d\ell \cos\theta$$

FIGURE 25-7 The line integral in Equation 25-2a is the sum of infinitely many infinitesimally small potential differences dV. Each dV is taken over a segment $d\boldsymbol{\ell}$ of the overall path short enough that it's essentially straight and that the electric field is essentially uniform over the segment. Then each dV is given by Equation 25-2b for a straight path in a uniform field: $dV = -\mathbf{E} \cdot d\boldsymbol{\ell}$. Summing—that is, integrating—over the whole path gives Equation 25-2a: $\Delta V_{AB} = -\int_A^B \mathbf{E} \cdot d\boldsymbol{\ell}$.

FIGURE 25-6 The potential difference depends only on the component of the path *along* the field. Mathematically, $\Delta V = -\mathbf{E} \cdot \boldsymbol{\ell} = -E\ell \cos\theta$, where the quantity $-\ell \cos\theta$ can be interpreted as the path component along the field.

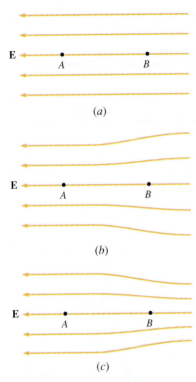

FIGURE 25-8 Which of the potential differences ΔV_{AB} is the lowest? The highest?

Figure 25-8 shows three straight paths AB of the same length, each in a different electric field. The field strength at A is the same in each. Rank the potential differences ΔV_{AB} from lowest to highest.

25-3 CALCULATING POTENTIAL DIFFERENCE

Here we use Equation 25-2a to calculate potential differences for a variety of charge distributions. Most important of these is the point charge. Understanding potential differences in the field of a point charge will deepen your understanding of the concept of electric potential, and provides an easy way to compute potential differences in the fields of more complicated charge distributions.

The Potential of a Point Charge

The electric field of a point charge q is given by Equation 23-3:

$$\mathbf{E} = \frac{kq}{r^2}\hat{\mathbf{r}},$$

where $\hat{\mathbf{r}}$ is a unit vector from the charge toward the point where the field is being evaluated. Consider two points A and B at distances r_A and r_B from a positive point charge, as shown in Fig. 25-9. What is the potential difference between these points? The distance between them is $r_B - r_A$, but we can't just multiply this distance by the electric field because the field varies with position. Instead we integrate, using Equation 25-2a:

$$\Delta V_{AB} = -\int_{r_A}^{r_B} \mathbf{E} \cdot d\ell = -\int_{r_A}^{r_B} \frac{kq}{r^2}\hat{\mathbf{r}} \cdot d\ell.$$

As we move from r_A toward r_B, the path element vectors $d\ell$ correspond to small increments dr in the radial direction, so we write $d\ell = \hat{\mathbf{r}}dr$. Then the potential becomes

$$\Delta V_{AB} = -\int_{r_A}^{r_B} \frac{kq}{r^2}\hat{\mathbf{r}} \cdot \hat{\mathbf{r}}dr = -kq\int_{r_A}^{r_B} r^{-2} dr,$$

since the dot product of the unit vector $\hat{\mathbf{r}}$ with itself is simply 1. Evaluating the integral gives

$$\Delta V_{AB} = -kq\left[-\frac{1}{r}\right]_{r_A}^{r_B} = kq\left(\frac{1}{r_B} - \frac{1}{r_A}\right). \tag{25-3}$$

FIGURE 25-9 The potential difference between points A and B is found by integrating between r_A and r_B.

Does this result make sense? For $r_B > r_A$ the potential difference is negative, showing that a positive test charge at r_A would "fall down" the potential "hill" toward r_B. Going the other way would require that positive work be done on a positive charge, as it's pushed "up" the potential "hill" against the repulsive force of the charge q. Although we considered q to be positive, our result holds as well for $q < 0$, in which case the sign of the potential difference changes.

Although we derived Equation 25-3 for two points on the same radial line, Fig. 25-10 shows that the result holds for *any* two points in the field of a charge q. It doesn't matter which point is at the greater distance either; if $r_B < r_A$ Equation 25-3 still gives the correct potential difference, which then becomes positive to indicate that work must be done moving a positive test charge *toward* a positive *q*.

The Zero of Potential

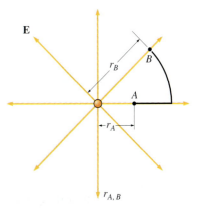

So far we've only talked about potential differences, symbolized by the expression ΔV_{AB}. That's because only differences in potential energy—and thus in electric potential, which is potential energy per unit charge—have physical significance. But as we did with potential energy, it's often convenient to define the **electric potential** at some point as zero and then to measure potential differences relative to that point. We then speak of "the potential at point *P*," designated $V(P)$ or V_P, and meaning the potential difference V_{OP} *from* our reference point *to* point *P*. Once we've defined a zero of potential, we can then write potential differences as differences in potential between two points; thus, our terminology ΔV_{AB} can equally well be written $V(B) - V(A)$ or $V_B - V_A$. The choice for the zero of potential is arbitrary and is usually made on the basis of mathematical or physical convenience. In electric power systems, Earth, called "ground," is usually taken as the zero. In automobile electric systems, the car's metal structure makes a convenient zero; this is usually connected electrically to the negative battery terminal. (As we'll soon see, every point on a conductor is at the same potential, so it's appropriate to consider an entire conductor like Earth or a car's metal structure as the "point" of zero potential.)

In dealing with isolated point charges, Equation 25-3 shows that it is convenient to choose the zero of potential at infinity. If we let r_A become arbitrarily large, and drop the subscript on r_B because it can be at any radial distance r, Equation 25-3 becomes

$$V_{\infty r} = V(r) = \frac{kq}{r}. \quad \text{(point-charge potential)} \quad (25\text{-}4)$$

When we call this expression $V(r)$ "the potential of a point charge," we really mean that $V(r)$ is the potential difference going from a point very far from a charge *q* to a point a distance *r* from the charge—an interpretation that is consistent with our definition of potential difference as depending on *two* points. Because the field outside any spherically symmetric charge distribution is that of a point charge, Equation 25-4 also gives the potential outside a spherically symmetric charge distribution.

Does it bother you that potential difference can be finite over an infinite distance? The reason lies in the inverse-square dependence of the field, which drops so rapidly that the work done in moving a charge from infinity to the vicinity of a point charge remains finite. We found an analogous result in Chapter 9, where it took only a finite amount of energy—and therefore a finite "escape speed"—to escape completely from a planet's gravitational attraction. As long as a charge distribution is finite in size—so its field at large distances falls at least as fast as $1/r^2$, then it makes sense to take the zero of potential at infinity.

FIGURE 25-10 Here points *A* and *B* do not lie on the same radial line. But potential difference is independent of path, and one path between *A* and *B* consists of a radial segment and a circular arc. Since **E** is perpendicular to the arc, it takes no work to move a charge along the arc. The potential difference ΔV_{AB} results only from the radial segment, and is therefore given by Equation 25-3. Any other path from *A* to *B* would also give the same result.

Got It!

You measure a potential difference of 50 V between two points a distance 10 cm apart in the field of a point charge. If you move closer to the charge and measure the potential difference over another 10 cm interval, will it be more, less, or the same?

EXAMPLE 25-3	*A Huge Van de Graaff Generator*

The Hall of Electricity at the Boston Museum of Science contains the world's largest air-insulated Van de Graaff generator, a device that builds up charge on a metal sphere (Fig. 25-11; you may have seen a smaller version used for demonstrations in your physics course). The Boston museum's generator has a sphere of radius $R = 2.3$ m that develops a charge of 640 μC, spread essentially uniformly over its surface. (a) What is the potential at the sphere's surface, with the zero of potential taken at infinity? (b) How much work would it take to bring a proton from infinity to the sphere's surface? (c) What is the potential difference from the sphere's surface to a point located $2R$ from its center?

Solution

(a) The field outside the sphere is that of a point charge Q located at the sphere's center, so the potential difference between infinity and any point *outside* the sphere is given by Equation 25-4. Therefore the potential at the sphere's surface is

$$V(R) = \frac{kQ}{R} = 2.5 \text{ MV} ,$$

with the numbers given for the museum's device.

(b) This quantity, 2.5 MV, is the work per unit charge needed to move from infinity to the sphere's surface, so the work required for a specific charge q is qV. Since a proton carries one elementary charge e, the work needed to bring the proton to the sphere is 2.5 MeV or 4.0×10^{-13} J.

(c) To get the potential difference from the surface ($r = R$) to $2R$, we could use Equation 25-3 with $r_B = 2R$ and $r_A = R$. But it's perhaps easiest to keep in mind just Equation 25-4 and then find the potential difference by subtracting the potentials at the two points:

$$\Delta V_{R\,2R} = V(2R) - V(R) = \frac{kQ}{2R} - \frac{kQ}{R} = -\frac{kQ}{2R},$$

or -1.25 MV in this example. Does this make sense? Yes: the negative result shows that electric potential decreases as we move in the direction of the electric field—that is, away from the positively charged sphere. Our result also shows that fully half the potential difference between the sphere and infinity

FIGURE 25-11 This Van de Graaff generator at the Boston Museum of Science puts some 640 μC on a 2.3-m-radius sphere, developing a potential difference of several million volts between the sphere and its surroundings. Here, sparks jump to a nearby conductor as the local electric field exceeds the breakdown field in air.

occurs within one radius of the sphere's surface—a consequence of the rapid $1/r^2$ decrease in the field.

You can convince yourself that with a 640-μC charge, the electric field at the sphere's surface is close to the 3 N/C breakdown field in air. Bringing another conductor nearby increases the local field, drawing the sparks shown in Fig. 25-11.

EXERCISE The potential at the surface of a 10-cm-radius sphere is 4.8 kV. (a) What is the charge on the sphere, assuming it's distributed in a spherically symmetric fashion? (b) What is the electric field at its surface? Assume here—and anytime it's not specified—that potential differences are taken from infinity.

Answers: (a) 53 nC; (b) 48 kN/C

Some problems similar to Example 25-3: 19–23, 25, 26, 52, 63, 69

Potentials of Arbitrary Charge Distributions

If we already know the field of a charge distribution, we can calculate potential differences by applying Equation 25-2a, as we did for the point-charge field. Example 25-4 illustrates this approach.

EXAMPLE 25-4	*A Power Line*

A long, straight power line is made from wire with radius $r_A = 1.0$ cm and carries a line charge density $\lambda = 2.6\ \mu C/m$ (Fig. 25-12). Assuming no other charges are present, what is the potential difference between the surface of the wire and the ground, a distance $r_B = 22$ m below?

Solution

We treat the wire as an infinitely long, charged rod. In the preceding chapter we used Gauss's law to show that the electric field outside any cylindrically symmetric charge distribution is the same as that of a line charge, namely

$$E = \frac{\lambda}{2\pi\varepsilon_0 r}\hat{r}.$$

We want to evaluate the potential difference in this field from the wire surface at r_A to the ground at r_B, as suggested in Fig. 25-12b. For a straight path between these points, we can again write $d\ell = \hat{r}\,dr$ just as we did in evaluating the point-charge potential. Then Equation 25-2a becomes

$$\Delta V_{AB} = -\int_{r_A}^{r_B} \mathbf{E}\cdot d\ell = -\int_{r_A}^{r_B} \frac{\lambda}{2\pi\varepsilon_0 r}\hat{r}\cdot\hat{r}\,dr$$

$$= -\frac{\lambda}{2\pi\varepsilon_0}\int_{r_A}^{r_B}\frac{dr}{r} = -\frac{\lambda}{2\pi\varepsilon_0}\ln r\,\Big|_{r_A}^{r_B} \qquad (25\text{-}5)$$

$$= \frac{\lambda}{2\pi\varepsilon_0}\ln\!\left(\frac{r_A}{r_B}\right),$$

where the last step follows because $\ln x - \ln y = \ln(x/y)$. For the numbers of this example, this result gives $\Delta V = -360$ kV, a value typical of long-distance electric power transmission lines. Why negative? Because the charge on the wire is positive, so moving away from the wire means moving in the direction of the field—which is always the direction of lower potential.

Note that we cannot let r_B go to infinity in the case of a truly infinite wire, for that would give an infinite potential difference. Physically, this reflects the fact that the charge distribution is itself of infinite extent. Mathematically, it reflects the slow $1/r$ decrease in field strength.

The calculation in this example is not entirely accurate, because the nearby presence of other wires and of charges drawn to the surface of the ground alters the field somewhat.

(a)

(b)

FIGURE 25-12 (a) A long, straight power line can be approximated as an infinite charged rod whose field is that of a line charge. (b) We want the potential difference from the wire surface, a distance r_A from the wire's axis, to the ground a distance r_B below. The wire carries uniform line charge density λ, and extends indefinitely to left and right. Diagram is not to scale, and we're ignoring the presence of other nearby wires.

Nevertheless, the example correctly illustrates the logarithmic dependence of potential on position in the $1/r$ field of a line charge.

EXERCISE An infinitely long rod of radius R carries a uniform volume charge density ρ; Problem 24-31 shows that the electric field *inside* this rod points radially outward and has magnitude $E = \rho r/2\varepsilon_0$. Use Equation 25-2a to find the potential difference from the rod's surface to its axis.

Answer: $\rho R^2/4\varepsilon_0$

Some problems similar to Example 25-4: 28, 29, 64, 73

Finding Potential Differences Using Superposition

When we don't know the field of a charge distribution, or the field is too complicated to integrate easily, we can find the potential using superposition. This often provides an easier approach to calculating the field as well.

Consider a charge q being brought from infinity to a point P in the vicinity of some other charges. We want to know the potential at P—by which we mean the work per unit charge required to move from infinity to P. The superposition principle states that the electric field of a charge distribution is the sum of the fields of the individual charges comprising the distribution. Therefore the work per unit charge—that is, the potential difference—between infinity and P is just the sum of the potential differences associated with the individual point charges. Mathematically, we find $V(P)$ by summing Equation 25-4 over the individual point charges q_i:

$$V(P) = \sum_i \frac{kq_i}{r_i}, \tag{25-6}$$

where the r_i's are the distances from each of the charges to the point P. Equation 25-6 has one enormous advantage over its counterpart for the electric field, Equation 23-4. Electric potential is a *scalar,* so the sum in Equation 25-6 is a scalar sum, and there's no need to consider angles, vector components, or unit vectors.

EXAMPLE 25-5	*The Dipole Potential*

The dipole of Fig. 25-13 consists of two point charges $\pm q$ separated by a distance $2a$. Find the potential at an arbitrary point P, taking the zero of potential at infinity.

Solution

Note first that this is a more ambitious example than the dipole field calculations in Chapter 23, which for mathematical simplicity were restricted to the dipole axis and perpendicular bisector. Here, since potential is a scalar, we can easily calculate the dipole potential *anywhere*. To do so, we sum the potentials of the individual point charges, as Equation 25-6 suggests:

$$V(P) = \sum_i \frac{kq_i}{r_i} = \frac{kq}{r_1} + \frac{k(-q)}{r_2} = kq\left(\frac{1}{r_1} - \frac{1}{r_2}\right)$$

$$= \frac{kq(r_2 - r_1)}{r_1 r_2},$$

where r_1 and r_2 are the distances from P to the positive and negative charges, respectively.

We're often interested in the electrical effects of a dipole at distances great compared with the separation of its two charges. For example, we saw in Chapter 23 how many molecules can be modeled as dipoles, and how effects such as the van der Waals force involve interactions among distant molecules. If r is the distance from the dipole's center to P, then in the limit $r \gg a$ the quantity $r_1 r_2$ becomes approximately r^2, and, as Fig. 25-13 shows, $r_2 - r_1 \simeq 2a\cos\theta$. Then the dipole potential for $r \gg a$ becomes

$$V(r, \theta) = \frac{k(2aq)\cos\theta}{r^2} = \frac{kp\cos\theta}{r^2}, \tag{25-7}$$

with $p = 2aq$ the dipole moment.

Note that the dipole potential drops more rapidly with distance than the point-charge potential, just as the dipole field drops more rapidly with distance than the point-charge field. Note also that Equation 25-7 gives $V = 0$ along the perpendic-

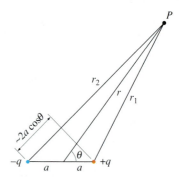

FIGURE 25-13 A dipole and a point P where its potential is to be evaluated. When P is far from the dipole, then r_2 is longer than r_1 by approximately $2a\cos\theta$. (The angle whose vertex is $-q$ is very nearly θ.)

ular bisector of the dipole ($\theta = 90°$). That makes sense because a charge approaching the dipole along its bisector moves at right angles to the dipole field, so no work need be done. Since potential difference is path independent, that means it takes no net work to move on *any* path from infinity to a point on the dipole's bisector (see Question 20).

Figure 25-14 shows a three-dimensional plot of the dipole potential (Equation 25-7) in the plane of Fig. 25-13. The positive charge corresponds to a "hill" of high potential and the negative charge to a deep "hole." Points on the right side of the diagram are closer to the positive charge and are therefore elevated relative to the zero of potential; this is reflected in the positive value of $\cos\theta$ for $\theta < 90°$ in Equation 25-7. Points on the left side are closer to the negative charge and are all depressed relative to zero potential; here $\cos\theta$ in Equation 25-7 is negative. The perpendicular bisector, with $\cos\theta = 0$ and therefore $V = 0$, is a level, straight line, neither elevated nor depressed.

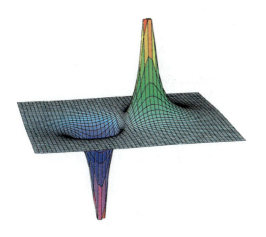

FIGURE 25-14 Three-dimensional plot of potential as a function of position in the plane of Fig. 25-13. Edges of the diagram are at nearly the zero of potential; perpendicular bisector is at exactly $V = 0$.

EXERCISE The dipole moment of a water molecule is 6.2×10^{-30} C·m. (a) Find the potential difference $V_B - V_A$ between two points on the axis of the molecular dipole, where points A and B are 8.2 nm and 5.1 nm, respectively, from the center. Both points are closer to the positive end. (b) How much work would it take to move a proton from A to B?

Answers: (a) 1.32 mV; (b) 1.32 meV $= 2.1 \times 10^{-22}$ J

Some problems similar to Example 25-5: 31–34, 74

Continuous Charge Distributions

We can calculate the potential of a continuous charge distribution by considering it to be made up of infinitely many infinitesimal charge elements dq. Each acts like a point charge and therefore contributes to the potential at some point P an amount dV given by

$$dV = \frac{k\,dq}{r},$$

where the zero of potential is at infinity. The potential at P is the sum—in this case an integral—of the contributions dV from all the charge elements:

$$V = \int dV = \int \frac{k\,dq}{r}, \qquad (25\text{-}8)$$

where the integration is over the entire charge distribution.

The examples that follow illustrate the use of Equation 25-8 for some charge distributions whose simple shapes make the integration reasonably straightforward. Simple cases such as these can often serve as approximations to more complicated charge distributions.

EXAMPLE 25-6	*A Charged Ring*

A total charge Q is distributed uniformly around a thin ring of radius a, as shown in Fig. 25-15. What is the potential on the axis of this charged ring?

Solution

Let x be the distance from the center of the ring to some arbitrary point P on the axis. The distance from each point on the ring to P is the same, and is given by $r = \sqrt{x^2 + a^2}$. The potential on the axis is the sum of the potentials dV of all the charge elements dq around the ring, as described by

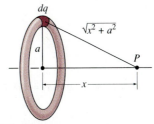

FIGURE 25-15 A charged ring (Example 25-6).

Equation 25-8:

$$V(x) = k \int_{ring} \frac{dq}{r} = \frac{k}{\sqrt{x^2 + a^2}} \int_{ring} dq \,,$$

where we've taken $r = \sqrt{x^2 + a^2}$ outside the integral because it's the same for all charge elements. The remaining integral is just the total charge Q, so we have

$$V(x) = \frac{kQ}{\sqrt{x^2 + a^2}} \,. \qquad (25\text{-}9)$$

Does this result make sense? At great distances from the ring ($x \gg a$), a^2 in the denominator becomes negligible, and our result becomes

$$V(x) = \frac{kQ}{x} \,,$$

which is just the potential of a point charge Q—as we would expect when we're so far from the ring that its size is no longer significant. At the center of the ring, on the other hand, Equation 25-9 gives

$$V(o) = \frac{kQ}{a} \,.$$

Here we're a distance a from all parts of the ring, and, since potential is a *scalar* the directions to those parts don't matter. The result is therefore the same as being a distance a from a point charge Q.

EXAMPLE 25-7	*A Charged Disk*

A charged disk of radius a carries a total charge Q distributed uniformly over its surface. What is the potential at a point P on the disk axis, a distance x from the disk?

Solution

To use Equation 25-8, we must divide the disk into charge elements dq. In the preceding example we found the potential of a charged ring, so we can take the charge elements of our disk to be thin rings (see Fig. 25-16), and integrate over all the rings that make up the disk. If a ring-shaped charge element has charge dq and radius r, then Equation 25-9 gives its potential dV a distance x from the disk center:

$$dV = \frac{k \, dq}{\sqrt{x^2 + r^2}} \,.$$

Then the potential of the entire disk is

$$V(x) = \int_{ring} dV = \int_{r=0}^{r=a} \frac{k \, dq}{\sqrt{x^2 + r^2}} \,.$$

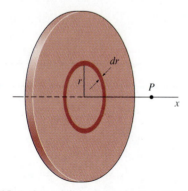

FIGURE 25-16 A charged disk, showing a ring-shaped charge element dq of radius r and width dr.

FIGURE 25-17 Unwinding the thin ring gives a strip of width dr and length $2\pi r$.

To evaluate this integral, we must relate r and dq. "Unwinding" the ring gives a strip of area $2\pi r \, dr$ (Fig. 25-17). The surface charge density σ is the total charge divided by the disk area: $\sigma = Q/\pi a^2$. Then the charge dq on our infinitesimal ring of area $2\pi r \, dr$ is

$$dq = \sigma \, 2\pi r \, dr = \frac{Q}{\pi a^2} 2\pi r \, dr = \frac{2Q}{a^2} r \, dr \,.$$

Using this result in the integral for the potential gives

$$V(x) = \int_0^a \frac{2kQ}{a^2} \frac{r \, dr}{\sqrt{x^2 + r^2}} = \frac{kQ}{a^2} \int_0^a \frac{2r \, dr}{\sqrt{x^2 + r^2}} \,.$$

Note that $2r \, dr = d(r^2) = d(x^2 + r^2)$ since x is a constant with respect to the integration. The integral therefore has the form $u^{-1/2} \, du$, where $u = x^2 + r^2$, and the result is $2u^{1/2}$ or

$$V(x) = \frac{2kQ}{a^2} \sqrt{x^2 + r^2} \, \Big|_{r=0}^{r=a} = \frac{2kQ}{a^2} \left(\sqrt{x^2 + a^2} - |x| \right) .$$

Figure 25-18 shows that this complicated-looking result makes sense: Close to the sheet, the potential resembles that of an infinite sheet, while far from the disk it approaches the potential of a point charge. Example 25-9 and Problem 70 explore these limiting cases further.

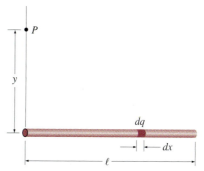

FIGURE 25-18 Charged-disk potential of Equation 25-10 approaches the potential of an infinite sheet for points close to the disk, and that of a point charge far from the disk.

FIGURE 25-19 What is the potential at P? Figure shows a charge element dq, of length dx, to use in the integration for the potential.

EXERCISE Point P in Fig. 25-19 lies a perpendicular distance y from the end of a uniformly charged rod of length ℓ and total charge Q. Find an expression for the potential at P, taking the zero of potential at infinity.

Answer: $V(y) = \dfrac{kQ}{\ell} \ln \left(\dfrac{\ell + \sqrt{\ell^2 + y^2}}{y} \right)$

Some problems similar to Examples 25-6 and 25-7: 36–39, 71, 78

25-4 POTENTIAL DIFFERENCE AND THE ELECTRIC FIELD

Equipotentials

It takes no work to move a charge at right angles to an electric field. Therefore there can be no potential difference between two points on a surface that is everywhere perpendicular to the electric field. Such surfaces are called **equipotential surfaces**, or simply **equipotentials**. Figure 25-20 shows some equipotential surfaces for both uniform and nonuniform electric fields.

Equipotentials are like contour lines that show land elevation on a map (Fig. 25-21). A contour line is a line of constant elevation, and therefore, it takes

(a)

(b)

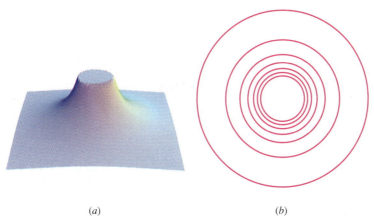

(a)   (b)

FIGURE 25-21 (a) A flat-topped hill and (b) its representation as a contour map. Closely spaced contours indicate steep slopes. Figures can also represent the potential of a uniformly charged spherical shell whose potential is constant inside, where **E** = 0, and falls as $1/r$ outside. In this case (a) is a 3-dimensional plot of the potential in a plane through the center of the sphere, and (b) shows the intersection of the three-dimensional equipotential surfaces (as shown in Fig. 25-20b) with this plane. Closely spaced contours indicate strong electric field.

FIGURE 25-20 (a) Equipotential surfaces in a uniform electric field are planes perpendicular to the field. (b) In a nonuniform field (here that of a point charge) the equipotential surfaces are curved (here they're spherical), but are still perpendicular to the field.

FIGURE 25-22 Equipotentials and field lines for a dipole, in a plane containing the dipole. The two sets of curves are everywhere perpendicular. Equipotentials on the left side represent negative values of potential; those on the right positive values. The perpendicular bisector is the special equipotential on which $V = 0$. In three dimensions it would be a plane and the other equipotentials would be closed surfaces. You should convince yourself that this figure is essentially a contour map of Fig. 25-14.

no work to move along a contour line. Contour lines are usually spaced at even increments of elevation. Where lines are closely spaced, the elevation changes rapidly. Similarly, closely spaced equipotentials indicate large potential differences between nearby points. That, in turn, means it takes a lot of work to move charge between those points—and therefore there must be a large electric field present. Figure 25-21 might just as well represent electric potential, in which case regions with closely spaced equipotentials—steep slopes on the "potential hill"—indicate large electric fields. Similarly, the equipotentials for a dipole (Fig. 25-22) describe the steep "hill" of the positive charge and a correspondingly deep "hole" of the negative charge that we showed in Fig. 25-14. ActivPhysics Activity 11.9 draws equipotentials for common charge distributions.

11.9
Electric Potential

Got It!

Figure 25-23 shows cross sections through two sets of equipotential surfaces. In both figures the potential difference between adjacent equipotentials is the same. Which could represent the potential of a point charge? Explain.

(a)

(b)

FIGURE 25-23 Which equipotential diagram is for a point charge?

Calculating the Field from the Potential

Given electric field lines, we can construct equipotentials. Conversely, given equipotentials we can reconstruct the field by sketching field lines at right angles to the equipotentials. Specifying the potential at each point thus conveys all the information needed to determine the field.

We can quantify the relation between potential and field by writing the potential difference dV between two points separated by an infinitesimal displacement $d\ell$:

$$dV = -\mathbf{E} \cdot d\ell = -E_\ell \, d\ell \,,$$

where E_ℓ designates the field component in the direction of $d\ell$. Rearranging this equation gives

$$E_\ell = -\frac{dV}{d\ell}. \qquad (25\text{-}10)$$

This equation confirms our statement that the electric field is strong where potential changes rapidly with distance. The minus sign in Equation 25-10 is the same one that appears in Equation 25-2; here it tells us that if we move in the direction of *increasing* potential, then we must be moving *against* the electric field. If we want to find the field components in a chosen coordinate system, we simply choose $d\ell$ along one of the coordinate axes and apply Equation 25-10; the x component of the field, for example, is given by $E_x = -dV/dx$. (If V is a function of all three coordinates we should, strictly speaking, write E_x in terms of the *partial* derivative, $\partial V/\partial x$, that we introduced in Chapter 16.) ActivPhysics Activity 11.10 explores graphically the relation between potential and electric field.

11.10
Electric Potential, Field, and Force

Equation 25-10 also shows that the units of electric field—introduced in Chapter 23 as N/C—can be written, equivalently, as V/m. You can see from an equipotential diagram why this unit makes sense: where the equipotentials are close, and the field therefore strong, you traverse a greater potential difference in a given distance—i.e., more "volts per meter." In fact, the electric field is sometimes called the "potential gradient," meaning the rate of change of potential with respect to position.

EXAMPLE 25-8 | *The Field of a Point Charge*

Use the point-charge potential of Equation 25-4 to derive the electric field of a point charge.

Solution

The point-charge potential, $V(r) = kq/r$, depends only on r. Therefore the electric field points in the radial direction, and has the form $\mathbf{E} = E_r\hat{\mathbf{r}}$. Choosing $d\ell = dr$ in Equation 25-10

gives the field component:

$$E_r = -\frac{dV}{dr} = -\frac{d}{dr}\left(\frac{kq}{r}\right) = -kq\frac{d(r^{-1})}{dr} = kqr^{-2} = \frac{kq}{r^2}.$$

Thus $\mathbf{E} = \dfrac{kq}{r^2}\hat{\mathbf{r}}$, as expected.

EXAMPLE 25-9 | *The Field of a Charged Disk*

Use the result of Example 25-7 to find the electric field on the axis of a charged disk.

Solution

Symmetry shows that the field must point along the disk axis, which is the x axis in Fig. 25-16. So the field has only an x component, given by applying Equation 25-10 to the disk potential:

$$E_x = -\frac{dV}{dx} = -\frac{d}{dx}\left(\frac{2kQ}{a^2}(\sqrt{x^2 + a^2} - |x|)\right)$$

$$= \frac{2kQ}{a^2}\left(1 - \frac{|x|}{\sqrt{x^2 + a^2}}\right).$$

To see that this makes sense, consider the case $x \ll a$, for which the field becomes approximately $2kQ/a^2$. Writing Q as the surface density σ times the area πa^2 gives $E_x = 2\pi k\sigma = \sigma/2\varepsilon_0$, which is the field of an infinite charged sheet. Of course—very close to the disk it looks effectively infinite, and its field should be well approximated by that of an infinite sheet. Problem 70 shows that the field far from the disk approaches that of a point charge Q.

EXERCISE Use Equations 25-7 and 25-10 to calculate the electric field on the axis of a point dipole, and show that your result is equivalent to Equation 23-5b.

Some problems similar to Examples 25-8 and 25-9: 47–49, 78

Examples 25-8 and 25-9 show that it is often much easier to calculate the electric field by first finding the potential and then differentiating, rather than doing a vector integration to get the field of a complicated charge distribution.

It's important to recognize that the *values* of the field and potential are not directly related; rather, as Equation 25-10 indicates, the field measures the *rate of change* of the potential. Field and potential are like acceleration and velocity; the *values* of the two are quite independent, with the former depending on the *rate of change* of the latter. Figure 25-24 and Example 25-10 illustrate the relation between potential and field.

Got It!

Is it possible to have a point where the electric field is zero but the potential is not? What about a point where the potential is zero but the field is not?

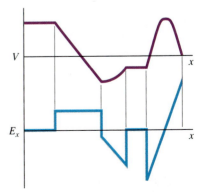

FIGURE 25-24 The x component of the electric field is the negative rate of change of the potential with respect to x.

| EXAMPLE 25-10 | *Potential and Field* |

A positive charge $+2q$ lies at $x = -a$, and a charge $-q$ lies at $x = +a$ as shown in Fig. 25-25. (a) Derive an expression for the potential on the x axis, and find a point on the axis in the region $x > a$ where the potential (with respect to infinity) is zero. (b) Use your expression for potential to find the electric field for $x > a$. Is the electric field zero where the potential is zero? If not, where is the field zero?

Solution

(a) The distance from any point x to the positive charge at $-a$ is $r_+ = |x - (-a)| = |x + a|$; similarly, the distance to the negative charge is $r_- = |x - a|$. Thus, the potential on the axis is

$$V(x) = \frac{k(2q)}{r_+} + \frac{k(-q)}{r_-} = kq\left(\frac{2}{|x+a|} - \frac{1}{|x-a|}\right).$$

We can find where $V = 0$ by setting the quantity in parentheses to zero. For $x > a$ both denominators are positive and we can remove the absolute value signs. For $V = 0$ we then have

$$\frac{2}{x+a} = \frac{1}{x-a}.$$

Solving for x gives $x = 3a$.

(b) The field clearly has only an x component, and Equation 25-10 then gives

$$E_x = -\frac{dV}{dx} = -kq\frac{d}{dx}\left(\frac{2}{x+a} - \frac{1}{x-a}\right)$$
$$= \frac{2kQ}{(x+a)^2} - \frac{kQ}{(x-a)^2}.$$

This result is hardly surprising: It's just the sum of two point-charge fields. We actually solved for the zero-field point in this configuration in Example 23-3; there we found that the electric force would be zero at $x = 5.83a$, which is *not* the same place where the potential is zero.

Figure 25-26 shows the potential of this charge distribution in the region $x > a$, showing clearly the point $x = 3a$ where

FIGURE 25-25 Two opposite but unequal charges.

FIGURE 25-26 Potential on the x axis for a charge distribution consisting of $+2q$ at $x = -a$ and $-q$ at $x = +a$. Shown here is the region $x > a$, including the point $x = 3a$ where the potential is zero and the point $x = 5.83a$ where the electric field—proportional to the *slope* of the potential curve—is zero. This graph shows potential along the x axis only in the region to the right of the negative charge. Leftmost part of curve shows the potential "hole" associated with the negative charge.

$V = 0$. Getting a charge to this point from infinity would take no *net* work, although it would require going up and then down a potential "hill." Also clear in Fig. 25-26 is the point $x = 5.83a$ where the electric field is zero. Note that this is the point where the *slope* of the potential curve is zero, *not* where the potential itself is zero.

There are actually two points on the x axis where $V = 0$; the second lies between the charges. Both lie on an equipotential surface of zero potential that surrounds the negative charge.

Tip

Field and Potential Are Not Proportional In particular, where one is zero, the other need not be zero. You can see that in Fig. 25-26, where it clearly takes work to get from infinity to the point where $E = 0$. Just because a mountaintop is flat doesn't mean it didn't take work to climb it! Potential depends not on the field at a point but on the field over an entire path from infinity to that point. Similarly, the potential can be zero at points where the field is not, as evidenced by the steep slope of the potential curve in Fig. 25-26 at the point where it crosses zero.

EXERCISE Find the second point on the x axis in Example 25-10 where the potential is zero.

Answer: $x = a/3$

Some problems similar to Example 25-10: 50, 77

25-5 POTENTIALS OF CHARGED CONDUCTORS

There is no electric field inside a conductor in electrostatic equilibrium, as we found in Chapter 24, so it takes no work to move a test charge around inside the conductor. We also found that the field at the conductor surface is perpendicular to the surface, so it takes no work to move a test charge along the surface, either. Therefore the potential difference between two points in or on a conductor must be zero, and thus,

A conductor in electrostatic equilibrium is an equipotential.

Consider an isolated, spherical conductor of radius R carrying charge Q. Since the conductor is isolated, charge is distributed uniformly over its surface, so the field and potential outside the sphere are that of a point charge. Then the potential at its surface is

$$V(R) = \frac{kQ}{R},\qquad (25\text{-}11)$$

as we found in Example 25-3. The sphere itself is an equipotential, so the potential *difference* between two points *on the sphere* is zero. But that doesn't mean the potential difference between *infinity* and the sphere is zero; since the sphere is charged, it takes work to move charge to its surface from infinity, and that's what Equation 25-11 says.

Now consider two widely separated spheres of different sizes. If we connect them by a thin conducting wire, as shown in Fig. 25-27, then the system constitutes a single conductor, and charge will move through the wire until both spheres are at the same potential. But since the spheres are widely separated, each still has an essentially spherical charge distribution, so Equation 25-11 applies to each. Since the spheres have the same potential, Equation 25-11 implies that

$$\frac{kQ_1}{R_1} = \frac{kQ_2}{R_2},$$

where the subscripts label the two spheres. We can write each charge as the surface area of the sphere multiplied by the surface charge density: $Q = 4\pi R^2 \sigma$. Substituting for the Q's in the above equation and solving for the ratio of surface charge densities then gives

$$\frac{\sigma_1}{\sigma_2} = \frac{R_2}{R_1}.$$

Thus the *smaller* sphere has the *larger* surface charge density. Since the electric field at a conductor surface has magnitude $E = \sigma/\varepsilon_0$, the field must be stronger at the smaller sphere.

This discussion of spherical conductors provides a qualitative description of nonspherical conductors as well. All parts of an irregularly shaped conductor must be at the same potential. Where the conductor surface curves sharply, it is like a small sphere and therefore has a higher surface charge density and a stronger electric field. In general, the field is strongest where the surface curves most sharply.

Because a conductor surface is an equipotential and the electric field is perpendicular to the conductor surface, equipotentials just above the surface must have approximately the same shape as the surface. Because the electric field is stronger where the conductor surface curves sharply, there must be more

FIGURE 25-27 Two conducting spheres held at the same potential by a conducting wire. The surface charge density is greater on the smaller sphere, in inverse proportion to its radius.

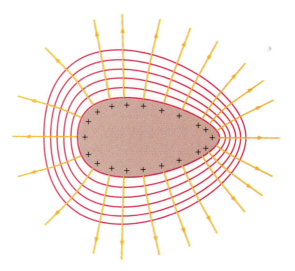

FIGURE 25-28 A charged conductor of irregular shape. Equipotentials near the conductor have approximately its shape, and the field is strongest—and therefore the equipotentials closest—where the conductor curves most sharply.

field lines emerging from such regions. Far from a charged conductor, on the other hand, its field must resemble that of a point charge, with radial field lines and circular equipotentials. With these limiting cases in mind, we can sketch the approximate form for the field of an arbitrarily shaped conductor (Fig. 25-28).

We stress that our conclusion about surface charge density and curvature applies only to *isolated* conductors—those far from any other charges. The field of a nearby charge will modify the charge distribution of a conductor, altering the surface charge distribution (Fig. 25-29).

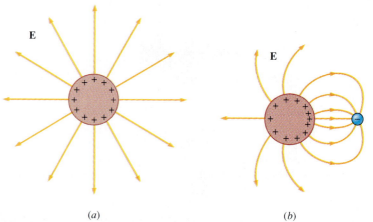

(a)   (b)

FIGURE 25-29 (a) An isolated conducting sphere carries a uniform surface charge density and has a spherically symmetric electric field. (b) The presence of a nearby charge distorts the surface charge distribution and therefore the electric field.

The large electric fields that develop where a charged conductor is sharply curved can cause serious problems in electrical equipment; in other applications those fields are put to good use. Fields above 3 MN/C are strong enough to strip electrons from air molecules, making the air a conductor. Breakdown of air is often evidenced by a blue glow around sharply-pointed conductors (Fig. 25-30). Called **corona discharge**, this glow results from the recombination of electrons with atoms. Corona discharge causes loss of power from high-voltage transmission lines, and engineers try to avoid it by eliminating sharp edges on wires and other conducting structures.

Corona discharge is put to good use in the **electrostatic precipitator**, a pollution-control device used especially on coal-burning power plants (Fig. 25-31). A typical precipitator consists of parallel metal plates with thin wires running between them. Application of a high voltage between plates and wires sets up large electric fields near the wires. Exhaust gases flow between the plates and the field ionizes some gas molecules. These charged molecules, in turn, attach themselves to pollutant particles. The charged particles are driven to the collecting plates by the electric field. Every few minutes a mechanical vibrator taps the plates and the particles fall into a hopper, where they can be trucked away to use for fill or in making products such as cinder blocks. A typical power plant produces some 30 pounds of particulates every second, and electrostatic precipitators remove up to 99 percent of this. Since the implementation of the Clean Air Act in the early 1960s, widespread use of electrostatic precipitators has significantly reduced particulate air pollution in the United States. However, precipitators do not remove gases like SO_2 that causes acid rain or CO_2 that contributes to global warming, and they also consume several percent of a power plant's electrical output.

(a)

(b)

FIGURE 25-31 (*a*) Electrostatic precipitators at a 1300-MW coal-burning power plant. (*b*) In the electrostatic precipitator, high voltage applied between the metal chamber and the thin central wire results in a strong, nonuniform electric field near the wire. This field ionizes air molecules, which attach to soot particles with the result that the particles are accelerated to the chamber walls. Mechanical vibration then dislodges the particles into the hopper for eventual collection. Parallel metal plates are often used instead of the cylindrical chamber shown here.

FIGURE 25-30 Corona discharge on a power-line insulator occurs because of strong electric fields that develop where a highly charged conducting wire is attached to the top of the insulator.

Xerography (literally, "dry writing") used in copiers and laser printers is another widespread application of corona discharge. The process starts with the uniform charging of a special photoconductive plate by corona discharge from a thin wire maintained at about 5 kV relative to the plate (Fig. 25-32a). Light, imaged in a copier from the document being copied or from a computer-controlled scanning laser

FIGURE 25-32 A step-by-step look at the xerography process, widely used in copiers and laser printers.

Corona discharge from a moving, thin wire lays positive charge over the light-sensitive surface (photoconductive plate).

The photoconductive surface is a good insulator in the dark and becomes a good conductor when exposed to light.

Corona wire

Metal

The potential difference between the wire and the metal below the photoconductive surface is approximately 5000 V.

(a)

Light is projected onto the original to be copied.

Light falls on the plate, except in the areas where the original is dark.

Lens

Photoconductive plate

Original   Light

Where light falls, the photoconductive plate is neutralized.

A positive charge pattern remains, corresponding to the dark areas of the image.

(b)

Negatively charged toner particles are carried toward the plate on a larger carrier particle, which they cling to due to electrostatic attraction.

As they near the plate, the toner particles are attracted to areas of the plate that are positively charged.

(c)

The negatively charged toner is attracted to the positively charged paper.

Heat is used to fuse the toner to the paper.

(d)

beam in a printer, then strikes the plate. The photoconductive material has the property that it is a good insulator in the dark, but the energy contained in light incident on it can dislodge electrons, creating free charge and making illuminated areas of the material a conductor. These free charges flow to neutralize the surface charge on illuminated areas of the plate, but dark areas retain their charge. At this point, then, the photoconductive plate contains an electrostatic version of the image being reproduced (Fig. 25-32b).

Next, a fine dusting of charged particles called toner is spread over the plate, often delivered on larger so-called carrier particles (Fig. 25-32c). The toner sticks to the charged parts of the photoconductive plate, and is then transferred to a sheet of charged paper (Fig. 25-32d). Finally, heating fuses the toner particles into the paper, making a permanent image.

In practical copiers the photoconductive surface may take the form of a flat plate charged by a moving corona wire, as we've shown in Fig. 25-32, or a moving belt or rotating drum with a fixed wire. The charge spread on the plate may be positive or negative, depending on the particular photoconductive material; inorganic silicon or selenium-based materials are positively charged, as shown in Fig. 25-32, while organic photoconductors, incorporating zinc oxide or cadmium sulfide, are charged negatively. Some copiers, especially smaller ones designed for intermittent use, eliminate the reusable carrier particles that transfer toner to the plate, and instead incorporate magnetic materials within the toner and employ magnets to effect the transfer. Either way, the basic copy process is electrostatic, with toner particles clinging to the unexposed parts of the plate because of the electric force.

CHAPTER SYNOPSIS

Summary

1. The **electric potential difference** between two points is the change in potential energy per unit charge for a charge moved between those points. Its unit is the joule/coulomb, or **volt** (V). Potential difference is a property of two points; because the electric field is conservative, the potential difference between two points is independent of the path taken between them. The potential difference ΔV_{AB} between points A and B is given by

$$\Delta V_{AB} = -\int_A^B \mathbf{E} \cdot d\boldsymbol{\ell} \, .$$

When the field is uniform, this expression reduces to

$$\Delta V_{AB} = -\mathbf{E} \cdot \boldsymbol{\ell} \, .$$

2. Defining the potential to be zero at some point allows us to speak of "the potential at a point," meaning the potential difference from the reference point to the point in question. For isolated point charges, a convenient zero is infinitely far from the charge; then the potential at an arbitrary point a distance r from the point charge q is

$$V(r) = \frac{kq}{r} \, . \qquad \text{(point-charge potential)}$$

The potentials of charge distributions may be found by taking the line integral of the field, if the latter is known, or by summing the potentials of the point charges making up the distribution:

$$V = \sum_i \frac{kq_i}{r_i}, \left(\begin{matrix}\text{discrete} \\ \text{charges}\end{matrix}\right) \quad \text{or}$$

$$V = \int \frac{k\,dq}{r} . \left(\begin{matrix}\text{continuous charge} \\ \text{distribution}\end{matrix}\right)$$

3. **Equipotentials** are surfaces over which the potential has a constant value. Equipotentials are everywhere perpendicular to the electric field. The field is strong where equipotentials are closely spaced and vice versa. Mathematically, the field component in a given direction is related to the rate of change of potential with position in that direction:

$$E_\ell = -\frac{dV}{d\ell} \, .$$

4. A conductor in electrostatic equilibrium is an equipotential. The surface charge density and therefore the electric field at the conductor surface are usually greatest where the conductor curves most sharply. Very strong electric fields occur at sharp bends; if strong enough, these fields can result in **corona discharge**, in which the surrounding air becomes a conductor and charge leaks off the charged conductor.

Terms You Should Understand

(Pairs are closely related terms whose distinction is important; number in parentheses is chapter section where term first appears.)

conservative field (introduction)
potential difference (25-2)
volt, electron volt (25-2)
line integral (25-2)
equipotential (25-4)
corona discharge (25-5)

Symbols You Should Recognize

ΔV_{AB} (25-2) $V(P)$ (25-3)
V, eV (25-2) $d\ell$ (25-2)

Problems You Should Be Able to Solve

calculating the work needed to move a given charge through a given potential difference (25-2)
calculating potential differences in uniform electric fields (25-2)
calculating potential differences using the line integral of a known electric field (25-3)
evaluating potentials by summing or integrating over point charges (25-3)
finding electric field components given potential as a function of position (25-4)
sketching equipotentials of simple charge distributions (25-4)
sketching equipotentials and fields around conductors (25-5)

Limitations to Keep in Mind

Electric potential difference depends on *two points*.
Phrases like "the potential at point P" or "the potential of a point charge" are always shorthand ways of talking about the potential difference between two points. When the second point is not specified, it is often taken to be at infinity.

QUESTIONS

1. Why can a bird perch on a high-voltage power line without getting electrocuted?
2. One proton is accelerated from rest by a uniform electric field, the other by a nonuniform electric field. If they move through the same potential difference, how do their final speeds compare?
3. Would a free electron move toward higher or lower potential?
4. The potential difference from A to B in Fig. 25-33 is zero since the two points are equidistant from the charge Q. How can this be, when a charge moving along the path shown clearly experiences an electric force not perpendicular to the path?

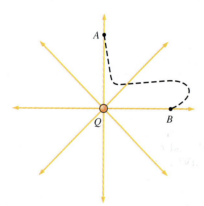

FIGURE 25-33 Question 4.

5. A proton and a positron (a particle with the electron's mass carrying charge +e) are accelerated through the same potential difference. How do their final energies compare? Their final speeds?
6. The electric field at the center of a uniformly charged ring is obviously zero, yet Example 25-6 shows that the potential at the center is not zero. How is this possible?
7. Must the potential be zero at any point where the electric field is zero? Explain.
8. Must the electric field be zero at any point where the potential is zero? Explain.
9. The potential is constant throughout an entire volume. What must be true of the electric field within that volume?
10. In considering the potential of an infinite flat sheet, why is it not useful to take the zero of potential at infinity?
11. The potential of a point charge is given by kq/r. Is r the distance between the two points for which this is the potential difference? Explain.
12. "Cherry picker" trucks for working in trees or power lines often carry the warning sign shown in Fig. 25-34. Explain

FIGURE 25-34 Question 12.

how this hazard arises and why it might be more of a danger to someone on the ground than to a worker on the truck.
13. The electric field midway between two equal positive charges is, clearly, zero. Is the potential at this point also zero? (Take the zero of potential at infinity.) Are there any other points (other than infinity) where the potential of this system is zero?
14. Is it possible for equipotential surfaces to intersect? Explain.
15. Is the potential at the center of a hollow, uniformly charged spherical shell higher, lower, or the same as at the surface?
16. A solid sphere contains positive charge uniformly distributed throughout its volume. Is the potential at its center higher, lower, or the same as at the surface?
17. Why do the spheres in Fig. 25-27 need to be far apart for the conclusion that surface charge density is inversely proportional to radius to hold accurately?
18. Figure 25-35 shows a cross section of some equipotential surfaces. Where does the electric field have the greatest magnitude, and in this region what is its approximate direction?

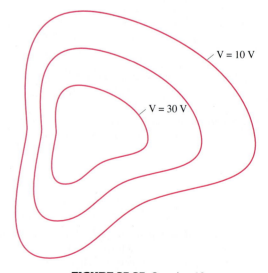

FIGURE 25-35 Question 18.

19. Two equal but opposite charges form a dipole. Describe the equipotential surface on which $V = 0$.

20. Figure 25-36 shows three paths leading from infinity to a point P on the perpendicular bisector of a dipole. For each path, how much work is needed to bring a charge q from infinity to P?

21. The electric potential in a region increases linearly with distance. What can you conclude about the electric field in this region?

22. In Fig. 25-29b the charge density on the conducting sphere is not uniform, yet the field inside must still be zero since the system is in electrostatic equilibrium. How is this possible?

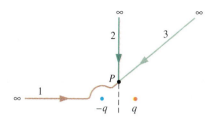

FIGURE 25-36 Question 20.

23. Why is lightning likely to strike an isolated tree?

24. What is the difference between a volt and an electron volt?

PROBLEMS

ActivPhysics can help with these problems:
Activities 11.9, 11.10.

Section 25-2 Potential Difference

1. How much work does it take to move a 50-μC charge against a 12-V potential difference?

2. The potential difference between the two sides of an ordinary electrical outlet is 120 V. How much energy does an electron gain when it moves from one side to the other?

3. It takes 45 J to move a 15-mC charge from point A to point B. What is the potential difference ΔV_{AB}?

4. Show that 1 V/m is the same as 1 N/C.

5. Find the magnitude of the potential difference between two points located 1.4 m apart in a uniform 650 N/C electric field, if a line between the points is parallel to the field.

6. A charge of 3.1 C moves from the positive to the negative terminal of a 9.0-V battery. How much energy does the battery impart to the charge?

7. Two points A and B lie 15 cm apart in a uniform electric field, with the path AB parallel to the field. If the potential difference ΔV_{AB} is 840 V, what is the field strength?

8. Figure 25-37 shows a uniform electric field of magnitude E. Find expressions for (a) the potential difference ΔV_{AB} and (b) ΔV_{BC}. (c) Use your result to determine ΔV_{AC}.

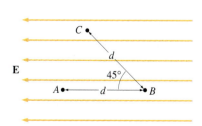

FIGURE 25-37 Problem 8.

9. A proton, an alpha particle (a bare helium nucleus), and a singly ionized helium atom are accelerated through a potential difference of 100 V. Find the energy each gains.

10. The electric field within the membrane separating the inside and outside of a biological cell is approximately 8.0 MV/m, and is essentially uniform. If the membrane is 10 nm thick, what is the potential difference across the membrane?

11. What is the potential difference between the terminals of a battery that can impart 7.2×10^{-19} J to each electron that moves between the terminals?

12. Electrons in a TV tube are accelerated from rest through a 25-kV potential difference. With what speed do they hit the TV screen?

13. A 12-V car battery stores 2.8 MJ of energy. How much charge can move between the battery terminals before it is totally discharged? Assume the potential difference remains at 12 V, an assumption that is not realistic.

14. What is the charge on an ion that gains 1.6×10^{-15} J when it moves through a potential difference of 2500 V?

15. Two large, flat metal plates are a distance d apart, where d is small compared with the plate size. If the plates carry surface charge densities $\pm \sigma$, show that the magnitude of the potential difference between them is $V = \sigma d / \varepsilon_0$.

16. An electron passes point A moving at 6.5 Mm/s. At point B the electron has come to a complete stop. Find the potential difference ΔV_{AB}.

17. A 5.0-g object carries a net charge of 3.8 μC. It acquires a speed v when accelerated from rest through a potential difference V. A 2.0-g object acquires twice the speed under the same circumstances. What is its charge?

Section 25-3 Calculating Potential Difference

Note: In these problems, the zero of potential is taken at infinity unless noted otherwise.

18. An electric field is given by $\mathbf{E} = E_0\hat{\mathbf{j}}$, where E_0 is a constant. Find the potential as a function of position, taking $V = 0$ at $y = 0$.

19. The classical picture of the hydrogen atom has a single electron in orbit a distance 0.0529 nm from the proton. Calculate the electric potential associated with the proton's electric field at this distance.

20. Earth carries an electric charge of -4.3×10^5 C, distributed essentially uniformly over its surface. What is the potential difference between Earth's surface and the base of the ionosphere, about 80 km above the surface?

21. Points A and B lie 20 cm apart on a line extending radially from a point charge Q, and the potentials at these points are $V_A = 280$ V, $V_B = 130$ V. Find Q and the distance r between A and the charge.

22. What is the maximum potential allowable on a 5.0-cm-diameter metal sphere if the electric field at the sphere's surface is not to exceed the 3 MV/m breakdown field in air?

23. A 3.5-cm-diameter isolated metal sphere carries a net charge of 0.86 μC. (a) What is the potential at the sphere's surface? (b) If a proton were released from rest at the sphere's surface, what would be its speed far from the sphere?

24. A sphere of radius R carries a negative charge of magnitude Q, distributed in a spherically symmetric way. Find the "escape speed" for a proton at the sphere's surface—that is, the speed that would enable the proton to escape to arbitrarily large distances.

25. A thin spherical shell of charge has radius R and total charge Q distributed uniformly over its surface. What is the potential at its center?

26. A solid sphere of radius R carries a net charge Q distributed uniformly throughout its volume. Find the potential difference from the sphere's surface to its center. *Hint:* Consult Example 24-1.

27. Find the potential as a function of position in an electric field given by $\mathbf{E} = ax\hat{\mathbf{i}}$, where a is a constant and where $V = 0$ at $x = 0$.

28. A coaxial cable consists of a 2.0-mm-diameter inner conductor and an outer conductor of diameter 1.6 cm and negligible thickness (Fig. 25-38). If the conductors carry line charge densities ± 0.56 nC/m, what is the magnitude of the potential difference between them?

29. The potential difference between the surface of a 3.0-cm-diameter power line and a point 1.0 m distant is 3.9 kV. What is the line charge density on the power line?

FIGURE 25-38 Problem 28.

30. Three equal charges q form an equilateral triangle of side a. Find the potential at the center of the triangle.

31. A charge $+Q$ lies at the origin, and $-3Q$ at $x = a$. Find two points on the x axis where $V = 0$.

32. Two identical charges q lie on the x axis at $\pm a$. (a) Find an expression for the potential at all points in the x-y plane. (b) Show that your result reduces to the potential of a point charge for distances large compared with a.

33. Find the potential 10 cm from a dipole of moment $p = 2.9$ nC·m (a) on the dipole axis, (b) at 45° to the axis, and (c) on the perpendicular bisector. The dipole separation is much less than 10 cm.

34. Two points A and B lie 55 cm from a dipole of moment $p = 6.4$ nC·m, whose charge separation is much less than 55 cm. A line from the dipole to A makes a 20° angle with the dipole axis, and a line to B makes a 50° angle. Find the potential difference $V_B - V_A$.

35. A hollow, spherical conducting shell of inner radius b and outer radius c surrounds is concentric with a solid conducting sphere of radius a, as shown in Fig. 25-39. The sphere carries a net charge $-Q$ and the shell carries a net charge

FIGURE 25-39 Problem 35.

+3Q. Both conductors are in electrostatic equilibrium. Find an expression for the potential difference from infinity to the surface of the sphere.

36. A thin plastic rod 20 cm long carries 3.2 nC distributed uniformly over its length. (a) If the rod is bent into a ring, find the potential at its center. (b) If the rod is bent into a semicircle, find the potential at the center (i.e., at the center of the circle of which the semicircle is part).

37. A thin ring of radius R carries a charge $3Q$ distributed uniformly over three-fourths of its circumference, and $-Q$ over the rest. What is the potential at the center of the ring?

38. The potential at the center of a uniformly charged ring is 45 kV, and 15 cm along the ring axis the potential is 33 kV. Find the ring's radius and its total charge.

39. The annulus shown in Fig. 25-40 carries a uniform surface charge density σ. Find an expression for the potential at an arbitrary point P on its axis.

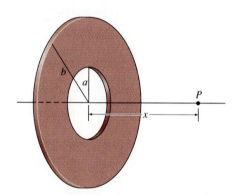

FIGURE 25-40 Problem 39.

40. A thin rod of length ℓ carries a charge Q distributed uniformly over its length. (a) Show that the potential in the plane that perpendicularly bisects the rod is given by

$$V(r) = \frac{2kQ}{\ell} \ln\left[\frac{\ell}{2r} + \sqrt{1 + \frac{\ell^2}{4r^2}}\right],$$

where r is the distance from the rod center. (b) Show that this expression reduces to an expected result when $r \gg \ell$. *Hint:* See Appendix A for a series expansion of the logarithm.

41. (a) Find the potential as a function of position in the electric field $\mathbf{E} = E_0(\hat{\mathbf{i}} + \hat{\mathbf{j}})$, where $E_0 = 150$ V/m. Take the zero of potential at the origin. (b) Find the potential difference from the point $x = 2.0$ m, $y = 1.0$ m to the point $x = 3.5$ m, $y = -1.5$ m.

Section 25-4 Potential Difference and the Electric Field

42. In a uniform electric field, equipotential planes that differ by 1.0 V are 2.5 cm apart. What is the field strength?

43. Figure 25-41 shows a plot of potential versus position along the x axis. Make a plot of the x component of the electric field for this situation.

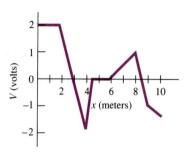

FIGURE 25-41 Problem 43.

44. Figure 25-42 shows some equipotentials in the x-y plane. (a) In what region is the electric field strongest? What are (b) the direction and (c) the magnitude of the field in this region?

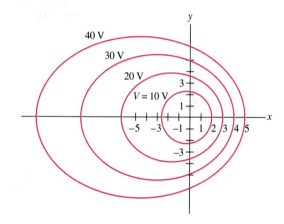

FIGURE 25-42 Problem 44.

45. The potential in a certain region is given by $V = axy$, where a is a constant. (a) Determine the electric field in the region. (b) Sketch some equipotentials and field lines.

46. Sketch some equipotentials and field lines for a distribution consisting of two equal point charges.

47. The electric potential in a region of space is given by $V = 2xy - 3zx + 5y^2$, with V in volts and the coordinates in meters. If point P is at $x = 1$ m, $y = 1$ m, $z = 1$ m, find

(a) the potential at P and (b) the x, y, and z components of the electric field at P.

48. Use Equation 25-7 to calculate the electric field on the perpendicular bisector of a point dipole, and show that your result is equivalent to Equation 23-7a.

49. Use the result of Example 25-6 to determine the on-axis field of a charged ring, and verify that your answer agrees with the result of Example 23-8.

50. A charge $+4q$ is located at the origin and a charge $-q$ is on the x axis at $x = a$. (a) Write an expression for the potential on the x axis for $x > a$. (b) Find a point in this region where $V = 0$. (c) Use the result of (a) to find the electric field on the x axis for $x > a$ and (d) find a point where $\mathbf{E} = \mathbf{0}$.

51. The electric potential in a region is given by $V = -V_0(r/R)$, where V_0 and R are constants, r is the radial distance from the origin, and where the zero of potential is taken at $r = 0$. Find the magnitude and direction of the electric field in this region.

Section 25-5 Potentials of Charged Conductors

52. (a) What is the maximum potential (measured from infinity) for the sphere of Example 25-3 before dielectric breakdown of air occurs at the sphere's surface? (Breakdown of air occurs at a field strength of 3 MV/m.) (b) What is the charge on the sphere when it's at this potential?

53. The spark plug in an automobile engine has a center electrode made from wire 2.0 mm in diameter. The electrode is worn to a hemispherical shape, so it behaves approximately like a charged sphere. What is the minimum potential on this electrode that will ensure the plug sparks in air? Neglect the presence of the second electrode.

54. A large metal sphere has three times the diameter of a smaller sphere and carries three times as much charge. Both spheres are isolated, so their surface charge densities are uniform. Compare (a) the potentials and (b) the electric field strengths at their surfaces.

55. Two metal spheres each 1.0 cm in radius are far apart. One sphere carries 38 nC of charge, the other -10 nC. (a) What is the potential on each? (b) If the spheres are connected by a thin wire, what will be the potential on each once equilibrium is reached? (c) How much charge must move between the spheres in order to achieve equilibrium?

56. Sketch some equipotentials and field lines for the isolated, charged conductor shown in Fig. 25-43.

57. Two conducting spheres are each 5.0 cm in diameter and each carries 0.12 μC. They are 8.0 m apart. Determine (a) the potential on each sphere; (b) the field strength at the surface of each sphere; (c) the potential midway between the spheres; (d) the potential difference between the spheres.

FIGURE 25-43 Problem 56.

58. Two small metal spheres are located 2.0 m apart. One has radius 0.50 cm and carries 0.20 μC. The other has radius 1.0 cm and carries 0.080 μC. (a) What is the potential difference between the spheres? (b) If they were connected by a thin wire, how much charge would move along it, and in which direciton?

Paired Problems

(Both problems in a pair involve the same principles and techniques. If you can get the first problem, you should be able to solve the second one.)

59. Three 50-pC charges sit at the vertices of an equilateral triangle 1.5 mm on a side. How much work would it take to bring a proton from very far away to the midpoint of one of the triangle's sides?

60. Repeat the preceding problem for the case when one of the charges is -50 pC and the proton is brought to the midpoint of the side between the two positive charges.

61. A pair of equal charges q lies on the x axis at $x = \pm a$. (a) Find expressions for the potential at points on the x axis for which $x > a$ and (b) show that your result reduces to a point-charge potential for $x \gg a$.

62. (a) For the charge distribution of the preceding problem, find an expression for the potential at *all* points on the y axis. (b) Show that your result reduces to a point-charge potential for $y \gg a$.

63. A 2.0-cm-radius metal sphere carries 75 nC and is surrounded by a concentric spherical conducting shell of radius 10 cm carrying -75 nC. (a) Find the potential difference between the shell and the sphere. (b) How would your answer change if the shell charge were changed to $+150$ nC?

64. A coaxial cable consists of a 2.0-mm-radius central wire carrying 75 nC/m, and a concentric outer conductor of radius 10 mm carrying -75 nC/m. (a) Find the potential

difference between the outer and inner conductor. (b) How would your answer change if the outer conductor were charged to $+150$ nC/m?

65. On the x axis, the electric field of a certain charge distribution is given by $\mathbf{E} = a/x^4\hat{\imath}$, where $a = 55$ V·m³. Find the potential difference from the point $x = 1.3$ m to the point $x = 2.8$ m.

66. A sphere of radius R carries a nonuniform but spherically symmetric volume charge density that results in an electric field in the sphere given by $\mathbf{E} = E_0(r/R)^2\hat{\mathbf{r}}$, where E_0 is a constant. Find the potential difference from the sphere's surface to its center.

67. The potential as a function of position in a certain region is given by $V(x) = 3x - 2x^2 - x^3$, with x in meters and V in volts. Find (a) all points on the x axis where $V = 0$, (b) an expression for the electric field, and (c) all points on the x axis where $\mathbf{E} = \mathbf{0}$.

68. The potential in a certain region is given by $V(x, y) = -[2x^2 + (y - 1)^2 - 1]$. Find (a) a point where $V = 0$, (b) an expression for the electric field, and (c) a point in the x-y plane where $\mathbf{E} = \mathbf{0}$.

Supplementary Problems

69. A conducting sphere 5.0 cm in radius carries 60 nC. It is surrounded by a concentric spherical conducting shell of radius 15 cm carrying -60 nC. (a) Find the potential at the sphere's surface, taking the zero of potential at infinity. (b) Repeat for the case when the shell also carries $+60$ nC.

70. Show that the result of Example 25-9 approaches the field of a point charge for $x \gg a$. *Hint:* You will need to apply the binomial theorem to the quantity $1/\sqrt{x^2 + a^2}$.

71. The potential on the axis of a uniformly charged disk at 5.0 cm from the disk center is 150 V; the potential 10 cm from the disk center is 110 V. Find the disk radius and its total charge.

72. A uranium nucleus (mass 238 u, charge $92e$) decays, emitting an alpha particle (mass 4 u, charge $2e$) and leaving a thorium nucleus (mass 234 u, charge $90e$). At the instant

the alpha particle leaves the nucleus, the centers of the two are 7.4 fm apart and are essentially at rest. Find their speeds when they are a great distance apart. Treat each particle as a spherical charge distribution.

73. A power line consists of two parallel wires 3.0 cm in diameter spaced 2.0 m apart. If the potential difference between the wires is 4.0 kV, what is the charge per unit length on each wire? The wires carry equal but opposite charges. *Hint:* The wires are far enough apart that they don't greatly affect each other's fields.

74. For the dipole of Example 25-5, show that the electric field at an arbitrary point far from the dipole can be written

$$\mathbf{E} = \frac{kp}{r^3}[(3\cos^2\theta - 1)\hat{\imath} + 3\sin\theta\cos\theta\hat{\jmath}]\,.$$

75. A thin rod of length ℓ lies on the x axis with its center at the origin. It carries a line charge density given by $\lambda = \lambda_0(x/\ell)^2$, where λ_0 is a constant. (a) Find an expression for the potential on the x axis for $x > \ell/2$. (b) Integrate the charge density to find the total charge on the rod. (c) Show that your answer for (a) reduces to the potential of a point charge whose charge is the answer to (b), for $x \gg \ell$.

76. Repeat the preceding problem for the case $\lambda = \lambda_0(x/\ell)$. Why is your answer for $x \gg \ell$ different? *Hint:* What does this charge distribution resemble at large distances?

77. For the situation of Example 25-10, find an equation for the equipotential with $V = 0$ in the x-y plane. Plot the equipotential, and show that it passes through the points described in Example 25-10 and its exercise.

78. A disk of radius a carries a nonuniform surface charge density given by $\sigma = \sigma_0(r/a)$, where σ_0 is a constant. (a) Find the potential at an arbitrary point on the disk axis, a distance x from the disk center. (b) Use the result of (a) to find the electric field on the disk axis, and (c) show that the field reduces to an expected form for $x \gg a$.

79. An open-ended cylinder of radius a and length $2a$ carries charge q spread uniformly over its surface. Find the potential on the cylinder axis at its center. *Hint:* Treat the cylinder as a stack of charged rings, and integrate.

26 Electrostatic Energy and Capacitors

A test firing of the Particle Beam Fusion Accelerator at Sandia National Laboratories involves the sudden release of energy stored in electric fields.

S uppose you hold two positive charges in your outstretched arms (Fig. 26-1). Bringing them closer takes work, as you move each charge against the other's electric field. That work is stored as potential energy associated with the new distribution of charge you create by moving the charges closer together. Because the static electric field is conservative, you could recover the stored energy by releasing the charges and letting them accelerate.

The example of Fig. 26-1 is trivial, but its implications are not. Energy storage in configurations of electric charge is a vital aspect of the natural and technological worlds. The energy produced in chemical reactions—including the metabolizing of food and the burning of coal, oil, and other fuels—is electrical energy released in the rearrangement of molecular charge distributions. Energy storage in systems of charged conductors is essential to the workings of electronic equipment and is important in devices that require large amounts of energy delivered in a short time. In this chapter we explore the energy of charge distributions and their electric fields, and we introduce a practical device—the capacitor—whose function is electrical energy storage.

(a)

(b)

FIGURE 26-1 (a) Widely separated charges exert little force on each other. (b) Moving them together takes work, which is stored as potential energy. Note how the bending of the field lines suggests the repulsive force.

26-1 ENERGY OF A CHARGE DISTRIBUTION

In the preceding chapter we defined the electric potential difference between two points as the change in potential energy per unit charge associated with moving charge between those points. To move charge between the two points takes work equal to the change in potential energy—equal, that is, to the electric potential difference multiplied by the charge being moved. In the simple case of two point charges, suppose charge q_1 is initially an infinite distance from a fixed charge q_2. You can assemble a new charge distribution by moving q_1 to a distance r from q_2. Equation 25-4 gives the electric potential difference from infinity to any point a distance r from q_2:

$$V_{\infty r} = \frac{kq_2}{r}.$$

Multiplying by q_1 gives the work you must do to bring q_1 in from infinity—that is, to assemble the new charge distribution. Since that work, W, gets stored as potential energy, U, we can write

$$W = U = \frac{kq_1q_2}{r}, \tag{26-1}$$

where we've taken the zero of potential energy when the charges are infinitely far apart.

Equation 26-1 gives the **electrostatic potential energy** of two point charges. The equation shows that the potential energy is positive if the charges have the same sign and negative if they have opposite signs. In the latter case, it would take positive work to separate the charges. We would have obtained the same potential energy had we moved q_2 in the field of q_1, showing that the potential energy of a charge distribution is independent of how it is assembled.

These considerations hold for any charge distribution. In general, it takes work to assemble a charge distribution and that work is stored as potential energy. The potential energy can be positive, zero, or negative. Because the electric force obeys the superposition principle, the potential energy is independent of how the charge distribution is assembled: the total energy is simply the sum of the potential energies of every charge pair making up the distribution.

11.11

Electrical Potential Energy and Potential

| EXAMPLE 26-1 | *The Energy of a Charge Distribution* |

Three point charges each carrying $+q$ and a fourth carrying $-q/2$ are initially infinitely far apart. They are brought together to form the square charge distribution shown in Fig. 26-2. What is the electrostatic potential energy of this charge distribution?

Solution

We can assemble the charge distribution in any order. Assume that the positive charge at the upper left is brought in first. This takes no work because no other charge is present. Next the positive charge q at the upper right is brought to a distance a from the first positive charge. Equation 26-1 tells us that the work required is

$$W_2 = k\frac{q^2}{a}.$$

Now the third positive charge is brought to its place at the lower left. This point is a distance a from the first charge q and $\sqrt{2}a$ from the second, so the work required is

$$W_3 = k\left(\frac{q^2}{a} + \frac{q^2}{\sqrt{2}a}\right).$$

Finally, the negative charge $-q/2$ is brought to a point a distance a from the second and third charges and $\sqrt{2}a$ from the first charge. The work required is again the sum of the potential differences multiplied by the charge $-q/2$:

$$W_4 = k\left(-\frac{q^2}{2a} - \frac{q^2}{2a} - \frac{q^2}{2\sqrt{2}a}\right).$$

This work is negative, indicating that it would take positive work to remove the negative charge. Adding the work required

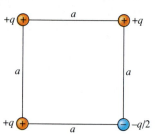

FIGURE 26-2 How much energy is stored in this square charge distribution? (Example 26-1).

to bring in the second, third, and fourth charges gives the electrostatic potential energy of the charge distribution:

$$W = W_2 + W_3 + W_4$$
$$= k\left(\frac{q^2}{a} + \frac{q^2}{a} + \frac{q^2}{\sqrt{2}a} - \frac{q^2}{2a} - \frac{q^2}{2a} - \frac{q^2}{2\sqrt{2}a}\right)$$
$$= \frac{kq^2(2\sqrt{2} + 1)}{2\sqrt{2}}.$$

That this is a positive quantity indicates that the work needed to assemble the three positive charges is greater than the energy gained bringing in the negative charge.

EXERCISE Repeat Example 26-1 for the case when the charge in the upper left corner is changed to $-q$.

Answer: $-3kq^2[1 - 1/(2\sqrt{2})]/a$

Some problems similar to Example 26-1: 1–4, 7, 79

26-2 TWO ISOLATED CONDUCTORS

(a)

(b)

A charge distribution useful for storing electrostatic energy consists of two isolated conductors carrying equal but opposite charges. Figure 26-3 shows two such conductors, each initially uncharged. Imagine moving a small quantity of charge from one conductor to the other, resulting in a net positive charge on one and a net negative charge on the other. This results in an electric field and therefore in a potential difference between the conductors. If we transfer more charge between the conductors, we do work traversing this potential difference. The more charge we move, the harder it gets to transfer additional charge. The work it takes to transfer the charge is stored as potential energy of the charge distribution.

It is generally difficult to calculate the stored potential energy for a pair of irregularly shaped conductors such as those of Fig. 26-3. An important practical case for which the potential energy may be calculated more easily is a pair of identical, flat, parallel conducting plates whose separation is small compared

FIGURE 26-3 A pair of isolated conductors. (a) Initially they are uncharged, and there is no potential difference between them. (b) When they carry opposite charges, there is an electric field and consequently a potential difference between them.

with their width (Fig. 26-4a). We start with the plates uncharged, and then transfer charge Q from one plate to the other. (In practice, we would accomplish this by connecting the plates to the terminals of a battery.) Charging the plates results in an electric field between them. For closely spaced plates, this field is essentially uniform except very near the edges (Fig. 26-4b), and we may neglect this nonuniform "fringing field."

What is the electric field strength between the plates? In Chapter 24 we used Gauss's law to show that the field near the surface of a conductor carrying surface charge density σ is given by

$$E = \frac{\sigma}{\varepsilon_0}.$$

As we discussed in Section 24-6, charge gathers entirely on the facing surfaces of the two plates, resulting in a charge density of magnitude $\sigma = q/A$, where A is the plate area. So the electric field between the plates is

$$E = \frac{\sigma}{\varepsilon_0} = \frac{q}{\varepsilon_0 A},$$

where q is the magnitude of the charge on either plate. Shouldn't this result be doubled because there are two plates? No! Review the discussion accompanying Figs. 24-34 and 24-35 to convince yourself of this point.

The presence of the electric field means there is a potential difference between the plates. Since the field is uniform, this potential difference is the product of the field strength and the distance d between the plates:

$$V = Ed = \frac{qd}{\varepsilon_0 A},$$

where we're now using V rather than ΔV_{AB} for the potential difference.

Now imagine moving an additional very small positive charge dq from the negative to the positive plate. How much work does this take? That depends on the potential difference between the plates, which, as our expression for V shows, depends on how much charge has already been transferred. Because potential difference is work per unit charge, the work dW required to move the charge dq between the plates is

$$dW = V\,dq = \frac{qd}{\varepsilon_0 A}\,dq.$$

Suppose we start with zero net charge on either plate and gradually transfer a total charge Q from one plate to the other. Each dq that we move requires work dW as given above, so the total work is the sum of all the dW's associated with all the small quantities of charge dq that make up Q. In the limit of infinitely many infinitesimal charges dq, this sum becomes an integral, and we have

$$W = \int_0^Q dW = \int_0^Q \frac{qd}{\varepsilon_0 A}\,dq = \frac{d}{\varepsilon_0 A}\int_0^Q q\,dq.$$

That the variable q remains under the integral sign reflects the physical fact that the continually increasing charge on the plates results in an increasing potential difference and therefore makes it harder to move each additional charge dq. Continuing the integration gives

$$W = \frac{d}{\varepsilon_0 A}\frac{q^2}{2}\bigg|_0^Q = \frac{d}{2\varepsilon_0 A}Q^2.$$

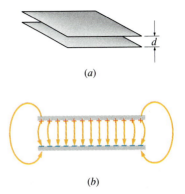

FIGURE 26-4 (a) A pair of closely spaced conducting plates. (b) Edge-on view of the plates when oppositely charged. For closely spaced plates the electric field is essentially uniform, except very near the edges, and the field outside the region between the plates is very small. Neglecting these small "fringing fields" is a good approximation.

Thus the work required to charge the plates increases as the square of the charge Q. The work done in charging the plates ends up as stored potential energy of the final charge distribution, so the stored energy is

$$U = W = \frac{d}{2\varepsilon_0 A} Q^2 . \qquad (26\text{-}2)$$

Note that the stored energy in Equation 26-2 depends on the *square* of the charge. Thus a pair of parallel plates on which we can build up lots of charge represents an excellent device for storing electrostatic energy. We'll see later in this chapter how widespread the technological applications of such devices are.

26-3 ENERGY AND THE ELECTRIC FIELD

We've seen that the work required to assemble a distribution of electric charge ends up as electrostatic potential energy. Just where is the energy stored? In Example 26-1, we considered the assembly of four point charges to form a square. Surely the point charges themselves did not change; we only moved them closer together. Similarly, when we charged our pair of metal plates we didn't alter the individual charges; we only moved them from one plate to another. So what has changed in both these cases? The electric field has changed. In the first case we started with four isolated point charges and an electric field that looked like four isolated point-charge fields. We ended with a new charge distribution whose field did not look at all like a point-charge field.

In the case of the parallel plates, we started with uncharged plates and no electric field. As soon as we began transferring charge from one plate to the other, an electric field appeared between the plates, and this field grew in strength as more charge was transferred.

So where is the energy stored? It is stored in the electric field. As we create or alter a charge distribution, we do work and an altered electric field configuration develops. The work done in moving the charges becomes energy stored in the electric field. If that work is positive, the new field configuration contains more energy; if the work is negative, the field has released energy and the new field contains less energy.

Every electric field represents stored energy. Because electric forces are primarily responsible for the behavior of everyday matter, many seemingly different forms of energy storage really involve electric field energy. When you burn gasoline or metabolize food, for example, you are rearranging the charge distributions we call molecules into new configurations whose electric fields contain less energy (Fig. 26-5).

If electric fields store energy, then the amount of stored energy should depend on the field strength. Since the field strength may vary with position, we describe the stored energy in terms of **energy density**, or energy stored per unit volume. We can readily determine the energy density for our parallel plates. There we found that the field strength is given by $E = Q/\varepsilon_0 A$; solving for Q and using the result in Equation 26-2 for the stored energy gives

$$U = \frac{d}{2\varepsilon_0 A} Q^2 = \frac{d}{2\varepsilon_0 A} (\varepsilon_0 A E)^2 = \tfrac{1}{2}\varepsilon_0 E^2 A d .$$

Our assumption that the plates are very close together allowed us to conclude that the field is very nearly uniform between the plates and essentially zero

FIGURE 26-5 Combustion involves the rearrangement of atoms into new molecular structures. Energy released as light and heat comes ultimately from the electric fields associated with the charge distribution in the molecules.

outside the plates. Therefore, the energy U is stored in the region between the plates, and is distributed uniformly because the field is uniform. The volume between the plates is just the plate area times the separation, or Ad, and therefore the energy density u_E is given by $u_E = U/Ad$, or

$$u_E = \tfrac{1}{2}\varepsilon_0 E^2. \quad \text{(electric energy density)} \quad (26\text{-}3)$$

Although we derived this expression for the uniform field between two parallel plates, it is in fact a universal expression that holds for *any* electric field. At any point where an electric field exists, there is stored energy whose density, in J/m³, is given by Equation 26-3.

The deepest significance of Equation 26-3 lies in its statement that every electric field represents stored energy. As we observe a variety of physical phenomena, from everyday happenings on Earth to events in distant galaxies, we can understand that the driving energy for many of these phenomena comes from the release of energy stored in electric fields.

EXAMPLE 26-2	*Electrical Energy of a Thunderstorm*

Electric fields inside a thunderstorm (Fig. 26-6) have typical values of 10^5 V/m and get even higher just before electrical energy is unleashed as lightning (recall that 3×10^6 V/m is the field at which air ionizes and becomes a conductor—which is what happens in a lightning strike). The origin of these fields and hence of the energy stored in them is believed to be associated with charge transfer to rising and falling water droplets or ice crystals in the intense updrafts and downdrafts of the thunderstorm. Consider a typical thundercloud that rises to an altitude of 10 km and has a diameter of 20 km. Assuming an average field strength of 10^5 V/m, estimate the total electrostatic energy stored in the cloud. How many gallons of gasoline would you have to burn to release the same amount of energy?

Solution
The energy density is given by Equation 26-3:

$$u_E = \tfrac{1}{2}\varepsilon_0 E^2 = \tfrac{1}{2}(8.85\times10^{-12}\ \text{C}^2/\text{N}\cdot\text{m}^2)(10^5\ \text{V/m})^2$$
$$= 4.4\times10^{-2}\ \text{J/m}^3 .$$

(You should verify that the units work out!) We are assuming that this energy density is the same throughout the storm, so we find the total energy by multiplying the energy density by the volume. The storm is roughly cylindrical in shape, so its volume is

$$V = \pi r^2 h = \pi(10\ \text{km})^2(10\ \text{km}) = 3100\ \text{km}^3$$
$$= 3.1\times10^{12}\ \text{m}^3 .$$

Then the total stored energy is

$$U = u_E V = (4.4\times10^{-2}\ \text{J/m}^3)(3.1\times10^{12}\ \text{m}^3) = 1.4\times10^{11}\ \text{J} .$$

A gallon of gasoline contains about 10^8 J (see Appendix C), so the electrical energy stored in a thunderstorm at any given instant is equivalent to about 1000 gallons or 4000 L of gasoline. This comparison is not quite fair to the thunderstorm,

FIGURE 26-6 Lightning is the sudden release of energy stored in atmospheric electric fields. The most common form of cloud-to-ground lightning, shown here, involves a negative charge layer at the cloud base, and a corresponding positive charge induced in the ground below. Other charge layers exist within the cloud, so electrostatic energy is stored both below and within the cloud.

though, because its electrical energy is continually dissipated in lightning strikes and at the same time renewed by the violent motion of the air. Problem 77 explores thunderstorm energetics in more detail.

EXERCISE In fair weather, Earth's atmospheric electric field is about 100 V/m. Find the energy stored in each km³ of the fair-weather atmosphere.

Answer: 44 J

Some problems similar to Example 26-2: 16–18

When the electric field is uniform, as in our thunderstorm example, we can find the stored energy simply by multiplying the energy density by the volume. But when the field changes with position we must resort to calculus. Consider a small volume element dV, so small that the electric field is essentially uniform over this volume. The stored energy dU in the volume element is just the energy density times the volume, or

$$dU = u_E\, dV = \tfrac{1}{2}\varepsilon_0 E^2\, dV.$$

The total energy U is then the sum of all the dUs. In the limit of infinitesimally small volumes dV and energies dU, this sum becomes an integral:

$$U = \tfrac{1}{2}\varepsilon_0 \int E^2\, dV, \tag{26-4}$$

where the limits on the integral are chosen to cover the entire region in which the electric field of interest exists.

We derived Equation 26-4 for the electric field energy using our previously determined expression for the work needed to assemble a simple charge distribution. We can also reverse that process, using the electric field of a charge distribution to calculate the energy density and from it the stored energy and therefore the work needed to assemble the distribution. Example 26-3 illustrates this procedure for a case when the energy density varies with position.

EXAMPLE 26-3	*A Shrinking Sphere*

A sphere of radius R_1 carries a total charge Q distributed evenly over its surface (Fig. 26-7a). How much work does it take to shrink the sphere to a smaller radius R_2? Practical applications in which this question might prove important include the behavior of cell membranes, charged bubbles, and raindrops in thunderclouds.

Solution

Shrinking the sphere moves all the charges on its surface closer together, and therefore requires positive work. That work is equal to the change in stored electric field energy given by Equation 26-4. With all charge distributed evenly over the sphere's surface, Gauss's law tells us that there is no electric field within the sphere. Because of the spherical symmetry, Gauss's law also tells us that the field outside the sphere is identical to that of a point charge Q at the sphere's center. This means that the field at and beyond the original radius R_1 does not change as we shrink the sphere. What does change is the field between R_1 and R_2 (Fig. 26-7b). Originally this field was zero. After the sphere has shrunk, this region, too, is filled with a point-charge field. This newly created field is the site of the additional energy stored in shrinking the sphere.

Because the point-charge field between R_1 and R_2 changes with position, we must use the integral form 26-4 to calculate the stored energy. The electric field outside the sphere is that of a point charge:

$$E = \frac{kQ}{r^2},$$

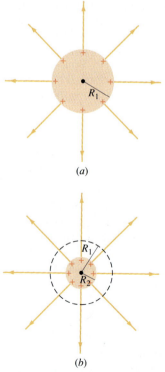

FIGURE 26-7 (a) A charged sphere and its electric field. (b) Shrinking the sphere creates new field in the region $R_2 < r < R_1$.

so, from Equation 26-3, the energy density as a function of r is

$$u_E(r) = \tfrac{1}{2}\varepsilon_0 E^2 = \tfrac{1}{2}\varepsilon_0\left(\frac{kQ}{r^2}\right)^2 = \frac{kQ^2}{8\pi r^4},$$

where we used $k = 1/4\pi\varepsilon_0$.

To determine the total stored energy we integrate this energy density over the volume between R_2 and R_1. Because of the spherical symmetry we consider volume elements made of thin spherical shells of thickness dr. Figure 26-8 shows that the volume of the shell is $dV = 4\pi r^2\,dr$, so Equation 26-4 becomes

$$U = \int_{R_2}^{R_1} u_E\,dV = \int_{R_2}^{R_1} \frac{kQ^2}{8\pi r^4}\,4\pi r^2\,dr$$

$$= \frac{kQ^2}{2}\int_{R_2}^{R_1} r^{-2}\,dr = \frac{kQ^2}{2}\left.\left(-\frac{1}{r}\right)\right|_{R_2}^{R_1}$$

$$= \frac{kQ^2}{2}\left(\frac{1}{R_2} - \frac{1}{R_1}\right).$$

This is the total energy stored in the new electric field between R_2 and R_1, and is therefore also the work done in shrinking the sphere from R_1 to R_2. If we let R_1 go to infinity, our result becomes the work required to assemble a sphere of radius R_2 carrying surface charge Q, or equivalently, the energy stored in the field of the sphere. Because the stored energy becomes infinite as R_2 approaches zero, our result suggests that the notion of a point charge is an impossible idealization. Problem 90 explores some implications of this result in the theory of elementary particles.

FIGURE 26-8 A thin spherical shell of thickness dr and radius r. Because the shell is very thin, its inner and outer surfaces have essentially the same area, namely $4\pi r^2$. Its volume is therefore $dV = 4\pi r^2\,dr$.

FIGURE 26-9 How much energy is stored in a length ℓ of the cable? (The cable is much longer than the outer conductor radius b.)

EXERCISE A long coaxial cable consists of an inner cylindrical conductor of radius a and an outer cylindrical conducting shell of radius b (Fig. 26-9). The conductors carry equal but opposite line charge densities $\pm\lambda$. Find the electric energy stored in a length ℓ of this cable.

Answer: $k\lambda^2\ell\,\ln(b/a)$

Some problems similar to Example 26-3: 21–23, 26, 27

26-4 CAPACITORS

In electrical and electronic equipment, electrical energy is often stored using a pair of charged conductors. Such a device is called a **capacitor**. Capacitors are typically used for short-term energy storage in situations where it is necessary to release electrical energy quickly. Most practical electronic devices, including radio, TV, computers, and audio equipment, would be virtually impossible to construct without capacitors. When you tune a radio, you're adjusting a capacitor. Your computer's memory stores information in millions of microscopic capacitors. Failure of a capacitor in your car's ignition system could leave you stranded on the highway. And many high-energy experiments in physics and engineering use so much power that, were it not for capacitors, they could not be done without disrupting the supply of electric power to the entire world!

In an uncharged capacitor both conductors are neutral. A capacitor is charged by transferring charge (usually electrons) from one conductor to the other. The work required is supplied by a source of electrical energy—for example, a battery—connected by wires to the capacitor's two conductors. An electric field develops as a result of the separation of positive and negative charge on the two conductors, and the stored energy resides in this field.

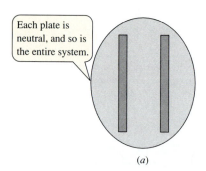

Each plate is neutral, and so is the entire system.

(a)

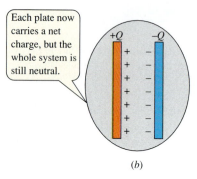

Each plate now carries a net charge, but the whole system is still neutral.

$+Q$ $-Q$

(b)

FIGURE 26-10 *(a)* In an uncharged capacitor both plates are neutral. *(b)* In a charged capacitor, the two plates carry opposite charges of equal magnitude. The entire system of two plates remains neutral.

FIGURE 26-11 Typical capacitors. The large blue unit is an 18-mF electrolytic capacitor. At top right is an air-insulated variable capacitor in which a set of metal plates rotates with respect to fixed plates in order to change the capacitance. The remaining smaller capacitors range from 43 pF to 10 μF.

Since there's an electric field in a charged capacitor, there's also a potential difference between its two conductors. The more charge, the greater the electric field, and, proportionately, the greater the potential difference. Thus a capacitor's charge and the potential difference between its conductors are proportional. In practice, we impose a potential difference between the two conductors, and a proportionate charge buildup occurs (that's because common electrical energy sources—such as batteries—produce a fixed potential difference rather than a fixed amount of charge). The ratio of charge to potential difference is characteristic of a given capacitor and is called its **capacitance**:

$$C = \frac{Q}{V}. \tag{26-5}$$

Here Q is the magnitude of the charge on either conductor and V the potential difference (or voltage) between the conductors. Clearly the units of capacitance are coulombs/volt. One coulomb/volt is given the name **farad** (F), in honor of the nineteenth century scientist Michael Faraday. One farad is so large a capacitance that the smaller units microfarad (10^{-6} F; abbreviated μF) and picofarad (10^{-12} F; abbreviated pF and often pronounced "puff") are widely used.

Capacitance depends on the physical construction of a capacitor—the shapes of its two conductors, their separation, and the choice of insulating material between them. Although Q and V enter the defining relation 26-5, capacitance is a constant. If V is increased, Q increases proportionately, maintaining the constant ratio C that characterizes the capacitor.

Tip

Charged but Neutral When we speak of a "charged capacitor," we mean a capacitor with one conductor positive and the other negative; the net charge on the entire capacitor—i.e., on *both* plates—remains zero. Similarly, when we say "the charge on a capacitor is Q," we mean that one conductor carries $+Q$ and the other $-Q$. Overall, the capacitor remains neutral even when it's "charged" (Fig. 26-10).

Any arrangement of two insulated conductors constitutes a capacitor. Practical capacitors are manufactured in a variety of configurations (Fig. 26-11). Often they are made from two long strips of aluminum foil separated by thin layers of plastic or paper. This foil "sandwich" is then rolled into a compact cylinder, wires attached, and the whole assembly covered with a protective coating. Another common arrangement is the variable capacitor, whose configuration can be altered to change its capacitance. This change can be accomplished mechanically or, as in many modern electronic devices, electrically. Very large capacitances are achieved with so-called electrolytic capacitors, in which a thin insulating layer develops chemically under the influence of the applied voltage. We'll consider the role of insulating materials further in Section 26-7.

Got It!

One capacitor has ± 50 μC on its plates when the voltage between the plates is 6 V. A second capacitor has ± 100 μC on its plates when the voltage between them is 12 V. Compare the two capacitances.

Calculating Capacitance

Capacitance is defined through Equation 26-5 as the ratio of charge to potential difference. To calculate the capacitance of a particular configuration, we assume there is a charge Q on the capacitor and calculate the corresponding potential difference. When the capacitor design includes sufficient symmetry, this calculation is straightforward.

By far the most important capacitor design is the parallel-plate configuration. In Section 26-2 we examined such a capacitor in some detail, although at that time we did not call the configuration a capacitor. There we found that the potential difference between plates of area A separated by a distance d is

$$V = \frac{Qd}{\varepsilon_0 A}.$$

Solving for the ratio $C = Q/V$ gives

$$C = \frac{\varepsilon_0 A}{d}. \qquad \text{(parallel-plate capacitor)} \qquad (26\text{-}6)$$

Equation 26-6 gives the capacitance of a parallel-plate capacitor in terms of the universal constant ε_0 and factors that describe the physical configuration of the capacitor. (Strictly speaking, this expression holds only for capacitors insulated by vacuum. In Section 26-7 we will modify Equation 26-6 to account for other insulating materials.) Note that neither charge nor potential difference enters the final expression for capacitance, showing that the capacitance is indeed a constant, independent of Q and V. Equation 26-6 suggests that the way to make a capacitor with large capacitance is to use two plates of large area but small separation. Incidentally, Equation 26-6 shows that the units of ε_0 may be expressed as farads/meter (F/m); see Problem 32.

APPLICATION	*Microphones, Keyboards, Elevators, Barometers . . .*

Capacitance depends on the geometrical arrangement of two conductors, and capacitance is an electrical quantity that's relatively easy to measure (you'll see why after you're studied Chapter 33). Those facts make capacitors ideal **transducers**—devices that convert physical quantities into electrical signals for measurement and control purposes.

The mechanical displacement of an object can be measured precisely by linking one plate of a capacitor to the object; capacitance changes as the object moves, and the change in capacitance provides a measure of displacement. This principle is used not only in direct displacement measurement, but also in capacitive microphones, where a metal diaphragm forming one capacitor plate vibrates in response to sound waves, changing the capacitance. Similarly, capacitive pressure transducers use the deflection of a capacitor-plate diaphragm to measure changes in air pressure. And, in an application you may use literally thousands of times a day, pressing a key on a computer keyboard varies the spacing of capacitor plates, changing the capacitance and signaling the computer that the key has been pressed (Fig. 26-12).

Contact or even nearby presence of a conducting object can change the charge distribution on capacitor plates, effectively

FIGURE 26-12 The keys of a computer keyboard move capacitor plates, altering the capacitance and signaling which key has been pressed.

altering the capacitance. "Touch sensitive" buttons in elevators and other applications work on this principle; as your finger approaches the button, charge movement in your body alters the charge on a capacitor behind the button, signaling your floor choice to the elevator. Lamps that turn on or off at the touch of a finger work on the same principle.

| EXAMPLE 26-4 | A Parallel-Plate Capacitor |

A capacitor consists of two circular metal plates of radius 10 cm separated by an air gap of 5.0 mm (Fig. 26-13). What is its capacitance? When a 12-volt battery is connected to the capacitor, how much charge appears on the plates?

Solution

Since the plate spacing is much smaller than the plate size, Equation 26-6 holds and the capacitance is

$$C = \frac{\varepsilon_0 A}{d} = \frac{\varepsilon_0 \pi r^2}{d} = \frac{(8.85 \times 10^{-12} \text{ F/m})(\pi)(0.10 \text{ m})^2}{5.0 \times 10^{-3} \text{ m}}$$

$$= 5.6 \times 10^{-11} \text{ F} = 56 \text{ pF}.$$

Equation 26-5 defines capacitance as the ratio of charge to potential difference. We can rewrite this defining relation to solve for the charge:

$$Q = CV = (56 \text{ pF})(12 \text{ V}) = 670 \text{ pC}.$$

What this really means, of course, is that the positive plate carries 670 pC and the negative plate −670 pC. Overall, the capacitor remains neutral. Note that by working with the capacitance in pF, the charge automatically comes out in pC.

EXERCISE A parallel-plate capacitor is to be made from two square pieces of aluminum foil each 8.0 cm on a side. (a) What

FIGURE 26-13 A parallel-plate capacitor connected to a battery. Drawing is not to scale (Example 26-4).

should be the spacing between them if the capacitance is to be 47 pF? (b) What applied voltage will put ±95 nC on the plates?

Answers: (a) 1.2 mm; (b) 2.0 kV

Some problems similar to Example 26-5: 35, 36, 67

| EXAMPLE 26-5 | A Cylindrical Capacitor |

A capacitor consists of two long concentric metal cylinders of length L, as shown in Fig. 26-14. The inner and outer cylinders have radii a and b, respectively. What is the capacitance?

Solution

Equation 26-6 does not apply to this configuration because the field between the cylinders is not uniform. To find the capacitance, we need a relation between charge and potential difference for the cylindrical configuration. In Example 25-4, we found that the potential difference between two points outside a charge distribution with line symmetry can be written

$$V(a) - V(b) = \frac{\lambda}{2\pi \varepsilon_0} \ln\left(\frac{b}{a}\right),$$

where λ is the line charge density. Because our capacitor is long compared with its diameter, this expression is a good approximation to the potential difference due to the field of the inner conductor. What about the outer conductor? Recall (Example 24-5) that the electric field inside an empty, hollow pipe is zero; therefore, the outer conductor contributes nothing to the electric field or the potential difference between the conductors. If the magnitude of the charge on either conductor is Q, then the line charge density is $\lambda = Q/L$, and our expression for

FIGURE 26-14 A cylindrical capacitor (Example 26-5).

potential difference becomes

$$V = V(a) - V(b) = \frac{Q}{2\pi \varepsilon_0 L} \ln\left(\frac{b}{a}\right).$$

Capacitance is the ratio of charge to potential difference, so we have

$$C = \frac{Q}{V} = \frac{Q}{(q/2\pi \varepsilon_0 L)\ln(b/a)} = \frac{2\pi \varepsilon_0 L}{\ln(b/a)}. \quad (26\text{-}7)$$

Does this result make sense? We already found that the capacitance of a parallel-plate capacitor increases with increasing plate area or with decreasing plate separation. With the cylindrical capacitor we can increase the area of both conductors by increasing the length L of the capacitor, and indeed Equation 26-7 shows the capacitance increasing proportionately. We can decrease the spacing of the conductors by making the radii a and b more nearly equal. This makes b/a closer to one, and $\ln(b/a)$ closer to zero, again increasing the capacitance. Although the geometries of the cylindrical and parallel-plate capacitors are quite different, the same physical considerations apply to both: a large capacitance is achieved with large

conductor areas and small separation. When the separation is very small, the curvature of the cylindrical capacitor cannot matter, and Equation 26-7 should reduce to Equation 26-6 for the parallel-plate capacitor (see Problem 84).

EXERCISE A conducting sphere of radius R is enclosed in a concentric spherical conducting shell of radius $\frac{3}{2}R$. What is the capacitance of this configuration?

Answer: $3R/k$

Some problems similar to Example 26-5: 35, 36, 67

Working Voltage

The most important consideration in using a capacitor is whether its capacitance is right for the particular application. But it's also important not to exceed a capacitor's **working voltage**, a safety rating set somewhat below the potential difference that would cause dielectric breakdown of the material between the capacitor plates.

Large capacitances are most easily achieved using small plate separations, as Equation 26-6 suggests. But a small plate separation implies a large electric field for a given voltage. Thus in practical capacitors there is a trade-off between capacitance and working voltage. High working voltage and high capacitance together require large plate separation to keep the electric field small and avoid dielectric breakdown, while at the same time requiring large plate area to keep the capacitance up. Thus large, high-voltage capacitors are physically bulky and expensive to build. Often economics as well as physics dictates the final design of a circuit involving capacitors.

26-5 ENERGY STORAGE IN CAPACITORS

In Section 26-3 we found that any electric field represents stored energy. The example that guided us to that conclusion was a parallel-plate capacitor. For that configuration, the stored energy U is given by Equation 26-2:

$$U = \frac{d}{2\varepsilon_0 A} Q^2 .$$

Since $\varepsilon_0 A/d$ is the capacitance of the parallel-plate capacitor, this stored energy may be written

$$U = \frac{Q^2}{2C}. \quad \text{(energy in a capacitor)} \quad \text{(26-8a)}$$

It is usually easier to measure voltage than charge. To express the stored energy in terms of voltage, we can solve the equation defining capacitance, $C = Q/V$, for Q and use the result in Equation 26-8a:

$$U = \frac{Q^2}{2C} = \frac{(CV)^2}{2C} = \tfrac{1}{2}CV^2 . \quad \text{(energy in capacitor)} \quad \text{(26-8b)}$$

Although Equations 26-8a and b were derived for a parallel-plate capacitor, they hold for any capacitor regardless of its configuration (see Problem 49).

FIGURE 26-15 The large black cylinders are 4700-μF electrolytic capacitors used in the power supply of a stereo amplifier. They store and release electrical energy to smooth out the voltage variations of the power line, and can retain significant charge after the stereo has been turned off.

That the stored energy depends on the *square* of the potential difference implies that more energy can be stored in a small capacitor at high voltage than in a larger one at low voltage. Practically, the difficulties of handling high voltages mitigate this conclusion somewhat, but the fact remains that the stored energy in a capacitor increases rapidly with increasing voltage.

Capacitors can store energy for significant times. In VCRs, for example, capacitors maintain program memory in the event of a power failure lasting up to an hour or so. Large capacitors used to produce steady direct current in TVs, stereos, and other electronic devices may retain their charge after the device is turned off (Fig. 26-15); before beginning work, repair technicians routinely discharge these capacitors by connecting a screwdriver across their terminals (Fig. 26-16). However, capacitors cannot store arbitrarily large amounts of energy indefinitely. One reason is that all capacitors "leak" charge through their imperfect insulation, gradually losing their energy; another is that dielectric breakdown sets a limit on the magnitude of the electric field in a capacitor. In Problem 18, for example, you can show that the maximum energy density for an electric field in air is far less than the energy density stored in gasoline. Thus you'll not see electric cars powered by the energy stored in capacitors. Capacitors do excel as energy storage devices in situations that call for rapid delivery of stored energy. We'll look at several such applications after Example 26-6.

FIGURE 26-16 This screwdriver has been used repeatedly to discharge a large capacitor. Steel vaporized in each of the pitted areas.

EXAMPLE 26-6	*Which Capacitor?*

Solution

A 100-μF capacitor has a working voltage of 20 V, while a 1.0-μF capacitor has a 300-V working voltage. Which can store the most energy? The most charge?

Solution

Applying Equation 26-8b with V set to the working voltage gives

$$U_{100\,\mu F} = \tfrac{1}{2}CV^2 = \tfrac{1}{2}(100 \ \mu F)(20 \ V)^2 = 20\times10^3 \ \mu J = 20 \ mJ$$

and

$$U_{1.0\,\mu F} = \tfrac{1}{2}CV^2 = \tfrac{1}{2}(1.0 \ \mu F)(300 \ V)^2$$
$$= 45\times10^3 \ \mu J = 45 \ mJ .$$

Because of its higher working voltage, the smaller capacitor can store more energy. On the other hand, the larger capacitor stores more charge, as shown by solving the defining relation $C = Q/V$:

$$Q_{100\,\mu F} = CV = (100 \ \mu F)(20 \ V) = 2000 \ \mu C = 2.0 \ mC$$

and

$$Q_{1.0\,\mu F} = CV = (1.0 \ \mu F)(300 \ V) = 300 \ \mu C = 0.30 \ mC .$$

Again, these numbers refer to the magnitude of the charge on each plate; overall, each capacitor remains neutral.

EXERCISE The "memory" capacitor in a VCR stores 25 J of energy with a potential difference of 3.5 V. (a) What is its capacitance? (b) What is the magnitude of the charge on each plate?

Answers: (a) 4.1 F; (b) 14 C

Some problems similar to Example 26-6: 38–41, 43, 44

Got It!

You need to replace a capacitor with one that can store more energy. Which will allow a greater increase in stored energy, a replacement capacitor with twice the capacitance and the same working voltage, or one with the same capacitance but twice the working voltage?

APPLICATION	*Camera Flashes, Toilet Flushes, Defibrillators, and Fusion*

You've probably used a camera equipped with a flash. After you snap a picture, you have to wait about 10 seconds before the flash is ready again. Why? Because the power required by the flash is far greater than a small battery could supply. So the battery is used to charge a capacitor at a slow rate. Once the capacitor is charged its stored energy can be dumped suddenly into the flash tube, producing a short burst of intense light. You can't use the flash again until the capacitor is recharged. The capacitor acts as a reservoir, accumulating energy slowly and then releasing it quickly. The average power—averaged over the relatively long capacitor-charging time—is modest and well within the battery's capability. The instantaneous power, during the millisecond or so of the flash, is much larger—and that's why the capacitor is needed. Problem 45 explores the camera flash.

The camera flash and its capacitor are analogous to a situation you encounter every day with household plumbing. Flushing a toilet requires a large amount of water in a short time—far more than typical household plumbing could supply in that time. So the water is accumulated gradually in the toilet tank, then suddenly dumped when needed for flushing. In this analogy the household plumbing corresponds to the small battery of the camera flash. The toilet tank, which gradually accumulates water, corresponds to the capacitor, which gradually accumulates electrical energy. Of course you need to wait between flushes for the toilet tank to fill, just as you need to wait between flash pictures for the capacitor to charge.

Professional photographers needing to take flash pictures in rapid succession often carry around a large, heavy battery pack capable of supplying the flash power directly. Similarly, institutional buildings with large, high-pressure water pipes often have toilets without tanks that can be flushed in rapid succession.

The example of the camera flash, scaled up in size, shows how large amounts of power may be obtained for brief intervals. An analogous medical application is the defibrillator, used to restore rhythmic beating of a heart undergoing the random, ineffectual muscle contractions called fibrillation. Successful defibrillation requires the delivery of several hundred joules of electrical energy in a few milliseconds (Fig. 26-17)—an impossibility for a battery-powered instrument that needs portability for use in medical emergencies. So, just as in the camera, capacitors are used to store the energy and make it available for instant use. Problem 44 explores the energetics of defibrillation.

At a grander scale, experiments involving high-powered lasers for nuclear fusion research require more power than all

FIGURE 26-17 A defibrillator delivers several hundred joules of electrical energy to restore the heart's normal beating. That energy is stored in capacitors which discharge in a few milliseconds.

FIGURE 26-18 This huge capacitor bank stores 60 MJ of energy to drive the Nova laser fusion experiment at Lawrence Livermore National Laboratory. The capacitors can discharge a significant fraction of their energy in 1 ns.

the world's electric generating stations produce (Fig. 26-18). The required energy is accumulated in huge banks of capacitors, which are suddenly discharged to provide energy to the laser. Think here about the difference between energy and power! The pulsed laser is only on for about 10^{-9} seconds, so although it consumes energy at an enormous rate while on, it does not use all that much total energy (see Problem 46). The laser is not fired very often, so there's plenty of time to charge the capacitors. The *average* power consumption of the experiment is modest.

26-6 CONNECTING CAPACITORS

Often a single capacitor with a desired combination of capacitance and working voltage is not available. But we can obtain the combination by connecting two or more capacitors together; that's how the large capacitance needed for laser fusion

(a)   (b)

FIGURE 26-19 Connecting capacitors together. (a) Parallel; (b) series. $\perp$ is the standard circuit symbol for a capacitor.

is achieved, for example. There are only two ways to connect two capacitors (and indeed any electrical components with only two wires coming from them). Called **parallel** and **series**, these two possible connections are shown in Fig. 26-19. We would like to know the equivalent capacitance of each combination.

Capacitors in Parallel

Consider first the parallel combination of Fig. 26-19a. If we impose a potential difference V across the two wires coming from the combination, what will be the potential difference across each capacitor? The key to answering this question is the recognition that the wires connecting the capacitors are conductors and that in electrostatic equilibrium there can be no potential difference between any points connected to the same wire.* Thus all points connected directly together—including the top plates of each capacitor—are at the same potential. Similarly, the bottom plates and the wires connecting them are all at the same potential. Therefore, the potential differences across the two capacitors are equal. This is a very important point in the practical understanding of electric circuits, and applies to any two circuit components that are connected in parallel:

▌ The potential differences across two electrical components in parallel are equal.

Recognizing this simple fact is essential in developing your understanding of electric circuits!

The equivalent capacitance is the ratio of the total charge on both capacitors to the voltage across the parallel combination. Solving the defining relation $C = Q/V$ for charge, we can write the charges on the two capacitors as

$$Q_1 = C_1 V \quad \text{and} \quad Q_2 = C_2 V.$$

The potential difference V is the *same* in both cases because the capacitors are connected in *parallel*. Thus the total charge is

$$Q = Q_1 + Q_2 = C_1 V + C_2 V = (C_1 + C_2)V.$$

Taking the ratio of total charge Q to the voltage V across the parallel combination gives the equivalent capacitance:

$$C = C_1 + C_2. \quad \text{(parallel capacitors)} \quad (26\text{-}9a)$$

Equation 26-9a is frequently stated as "capacitors in parallel add." You can understand this result physically by considering two parallel-plate capacitors with equal spacing. Connecting them in parallel amounts to adding their plate areas, giving a larger capacitance. Although we derived Equation 26-9a for two parallel capacitors, the result that parallel capacitances add is easily extended to three or more capacitors (see Problem 56):

$$C = C_1 + C_2 + C_3 + \cdots \quad \text{(parallel capacitors)} \quad (26\text{-}9b)$$

What about the working voltage of the parallel combination? Both capacitors experience the full potential difference V, so the working voltage of the combination is that of whichever capacitor has the lower working voltage.

Capacitors in Series

Suppose we charge the series capacitor system of Fig. 26-19b, putting $+Q$ on the upper plate of C_1 and $-Q$ on the lower plate of C_2. The positive charge on the

*Even when we relax the equilibrium assumption, this conclusion will still hold in the approximation that the wires are perfect conductors.

uppermost plate attracts $-Q$ to the lower plate of C_1 and the negative charge $-Q$ on the lowermost plate attracts $+Q$ to the upper plate of C_2 (Fig. 26-20). Note that this leaves the middle two plates together with zero net charge, which must be the case since these two plates are not connected to any external source of charge. With charge of magnitude Q on every plate, we can conclude that

▌Capacitors in series carry the same charge.

To find the equivalent capacitance, we first solve the relation $C = Q/V$ for the voltages across the two capacitors:

$$V_1 = \frac{Q}{C_1} \quad \text{and} \quad V_2 = \frac{Q}{C_2}.$$

FIGURE 26-20 Capacitors in series carry the same charge.

Here there's no need to label the Q's since series capacitors carry the same charge. But now the voltages need not be the same. Since the electric fields in the two capacitors point the same way (Fig. 26-20), the voltage across the series combination is just

$$V = V_1 + V_2.$$

Inserting our expressions for the individual potential difference gives

$$V = \frac{Q}{C_1} + \frac{Q}{C_2} = Q\left(\frac{1}{C_1} + \frac{1}{C_2}\right).$$

Dividing by Q gives V/Q, which the relation $C = Q/V$ shows is the reciprocal of the equivalent capacitance:

$$\frac{1}{C} = \frac{1}{C_1} + \frac{1}{C_2}. \qquad \text{(series capacitors)} \qquad \text{(26-10a)}$$

This result is frequently described by saying that "capacitors in series add reciprocally." The result is easily extended to three or more capacitors (see Problem 56):

$$\frac{1}{C} = \frac{1}{C_1} + \frac{1}{C_2} + \frac{1}{C_3} + \cdots. \qquad \text{(series capacitors)} \qquad \text{(26-10b)}$$

Equations 26-10 show that the combined capacitance of two series capacitors is less than the capacitance of either. You can make physical sense of this by considering parallel-plate capacitors with equal plate areas. Putting them in series effectively adds the plate separations of the two capacitors, yielding a smaller overall capacitance.

What about the voltage rating of a series combination? The full applied voltage V is the sum of the voltages across each capacitor, so each can be rated for less than the full applied voltage. The fraction of the applied voltage that appears across each capacitor depends on the relative capacitances.

Got It!

You have two identical capacitors, each with capacitance C. How would you connect the two to get equivalent capacitances of (a) $2C$ and (b) $\frac{1}{2}C$? (c) Which equivalent capacitor has the higher working voltage?

| EXAMPLE 26-7 | *Connecting Capacitors* |

(a) Find the equivalent capacitance of the combination shown in Fig. 26-21a. (b) If the maximum voltage applied between points A and B is 100 V, what should be the working voltage of C_2?

Solution

This is a problem about an electric circuit—an assemblage of interconnected electrical components, in this case four capacitors. The way to handle many such circuit problems is to reduce the circuit to a simpler one by recognizing combinations of series and parallel components, as shown in Fig. 26-21. Here C_3 and C_4 are in parallel, so they add to give an equivalent capacitance of 4.0 μF; the circuit then looks like Fig. 26-21b. This parallel combination C_{34} is in series with C_2; solving

Equation 26-10a then gives

$$C_{234} = \frac{C_2 C_{34}}{C_2 + C_{34}} = \frac{(12\ \mu\text{F})(4.0\ \mu\text{F})}{12\ \mu\text{F} + 4.0\ \mu\text{F}} = 3.0\ \mu\text{F}.$$

Now the circuit looks like Fig. 26-21c, with C_1 and C_{234} in parallel. The equivalent capacitance of the entire circuit is their sum, or 7.0 μF (Fig. 26-21d).

To find the working voltage needed for C_2, we need to know the voltage across C_2 with 100 V across the entire combination. Since C_1 and the combination C_{234} are in parallel and connected to points A and B, both these capacitors experience the full 100 V. We can then use the defining relation $C = Q/V$ to find the charge on C_{234}:

$$Q_{234} = C_{234} V = (3.0\ \mu\text{F})(100\ \text{V}) = 300\ \mu\text{C}.$$

But C_{234} is the series combination of C_2 and C_{34} (Fig. 26-21b, c), and the charge on series capacitors is the same. So $Q_2 = 300\ \mu$C as well. We again use the defining relation $C = Q/V$, now to find the voltage across C_2:

$$V_2 = \frac{Q_2}{C_2} = \frac{300\ \mu\text{C}}{12\ \mu\text{F}} = 25\ \text{V}.$$

This is the required working voltage for C_2.

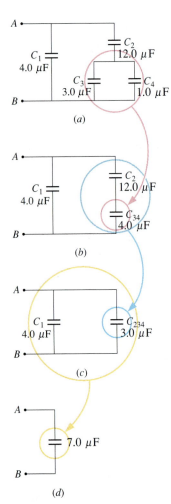

(a)

(b)

(c)

(d)

FIGURE 26-21 What is the equivalent capacitance (Example 26-7)? Analyzing the circuit involves reducing parallel and series combinations using Equations 26-9 and 26-10.

Tip

Analyzing Circuits This example illustrates a very general approach to circuit analysis. You reduce the circuit to its simplest form by recognizing series and parallel combinations, then gradually build back up to find the quantity of interest. The reduction is essential, even when you're only interested in what's happening with one component. Here, for instance, we wanted to know the voltage on C_2 with 100 V across the whole combination. But to find that we had to analyze the entire circuit, and only then could we focus on C_2.

Tip

Recognize Series and Parallel Parallel components have their two ends, respectively, connected *directly* together, as in Fig. 26-19a. Series components are connected in such a way that if you imagine moving through one component, then the *only* place you can go is into the next component (Fig. 26-19b). Many connections are neither; C_2 and C_3 in Fig. 26-21a, for example, are *not* in series because after you go through C_2 the circuit splits and you could go through either C_3 or C_4. And C_1 and C_2 are *not* in parallel; even though their top plates are connected directly together, their bottom plates are not. The series and parallel formulas we've derived apply *only* to true series and parallel combinations.

EXERCISE (a) With $V_{AB} = 100$ V in Fig. 26-21, what should be C_3's working voltage? (b) What will be the charges on C_1, C_3, and C_4?

Answers: (a) 75 V; (b) $Q_1 = 400$ μC, $Q_3 = 225$ μC, $Q_4 = 75$ μC

Some problems similar to Example 26-7: 52, 54, 57, 58

26-7 CAPACITORS AND DIELECTRICS

The insulating material between the plates of a capacitor serves several purposes. It maintains physical separation of the plates and minimizes charge leakage. Its molecular properties also influence the capacitance. In Chapter 23 we found that electric dipoles tend to align with an applied electric field, and we defined **dielectrics** as materials whose molecules behave as dipoles. The molecular dipole moments may be intrinsic to the molecules, or may be induced by an applied electric field, as we showed in Fig. 23-35. Essentially all insulators are dielectrics.

Suppose we have a parallel-plate capacitor charged to some voltage V_0, with air or vacuum between its plates. What happens if we insert a slab of dielectric material that fills the space between the plates? If the molecules of the dielectric have permanent dipole moments, they'll tend to align with the field, although thermal agitation prevents perfect alignment. If the molecular dipoles are induced by the electric field of the capacitor plates (recall Fig. 23-35), then the induced dipoles form in alignment with the field. Either way, as Fig. 26-22 shows for the case of induced dipoles, the fields of the dipoles themselves *oppose* the capacitor field. The result is a reduction in the net electric field between the plates. How much reduction depends on details of molecular structure and molecular interactions; empirically, though, we find that a given material may be characterized by its **dielectric constant**, κ, which describes the reduction in field. If E_0 is the original field, then the field after insertion of the dielectric will be decreased by a factor $1/\kappa$: $E = E_0/\kappa$.

If the capacitor is not connected to anything, then there's no way for the charge on its plates to change. But the field between the plates has been reduced, and therefore the potential difference $V = Ed$ has decreased by the same factor $1/\kappa$; $V = V_0/\kappa$. But capacitance is the ratio of charge to voltage, so with the dielectric in place we have

FIGURE 26-22 A capacitor with a dielectric between its plates. Molecular dipoles align with the capacitor's electric field, and their own fields point opposite to the original field. The result is a reduction in field strength.

$$C = \frac{Q}{V} = \frac{Q}{(V_0/\kappa)} = \frac{\kappa Q}{V_0} = \kappa C_0, \qquad (26\text{-}11)$$

where $C_0 = Q/V_0$ is the original capacitance. Thus insertion of the dielectric increases the capacitance by a factor κ.

Capacitors are among the most difficult electronic components to miniaturize, so the ongoing revolution in microelectronics has spurred a search for suitable dielectrics with large dielectric constants, good insulating properties, and high breakdown fields. Exotic materials such as tantalum oxide and strontium titanate have become widely used in recent years because of their high dielectric constants. In a few unusual applications water, with its dielectric constant of 78, is used as a dielectric. In high-energy experiments where it is necessary to store a large amount of energy for a short time, water's large dielectric

TABLE 26-1 *Properties of Some Common Dielectrics*

DIELECTRIC MATERIAL	DIELECTRIC CONSTANT	BREAKDOWN FIELD (kV/mm)
Air	1.0006	3
Aluminum oxide	8.4	670
Glass (Pyrex)	5.6	14
Paper	3.5	14
Plexiglass	3.4	40
Polyethylene	2.3	50
Polystyrene	2.6	25
Quartz	3.8	8
Tantalum oxide	26	500
Teflon	2.1	60
Water	78	—

constant outweighs the disadvantage of poor insulating quality. Table 26-1 lists dielectric constants and breakdown fields of selected materials.

In addition to helping build better capacitors, the relation between capacitance and dielectric constant serves as a useful probe of the structure of matter. Introducing a dielectric material between capacitor plates lowers the potential difference and therefore allows us to calculate the dielectric constant. This, in turn, gives information about the density and structure of the individual molecular dipoles. Conversely, we can use the measured dielectric constant to help identify an unknown material.

EXAMPLE 26-8   *Capacitors and Dielectrics*

An air-insulated capacitor is charged by connecting it to a 12-V battery. The battery is then disconnected. When the space between capacitor plates is filled with an unknown plastic, the voltage between the plates drops to 4.6 V. What is the unknown material? If the plate spacing is 0.10 mm, how much voltage can the capacitor withstand with this material between its plates?

Solution
The voltage has dropped by a factor $1/\kappa = 4.6/12 = 1/2.6$. From Table 26-1, we see that a plastic with $\kappa = 2.6$ is polystyrene. With a dielectric breakdown field of 25 kV/mm, the 0.1-mm-thick piece of polystyrene can withstand 2.5 kV.

The rated working voltage would actually be lower, to allow a margin of safety.

EXERCISE An air-insulated capacitor with $C = 25\ \mu\text{F}$ is connected to a 10-V battery and the battery is left connected as a quartz slab is inserted to fill the space between the plates. Find the charge on the capacitor (a) before and (b) after the slab is inserted. *Hint:* The battery maintains a fixed 10 V across the plates, but now charge can move from the battery to the plates.

Answers: (a) 250 μC; (b) 950 μC

Some problems similar to Example 26-8: 64–66

What happens to the energy stored in a capacitor when a dielectric is inserted between its plates? The dielectric increases the capacitance by a factor κ, but it also decreases the potential difference by the same factor. If the energy is initially $U_0 = \frac{1}{2} C_0 V_0^2$, then after the dielectric is inserted it becomes

$$U = \tfrac{1}{2}(\kappa C_0)\left(\frac{V_0}{\kappa}\right)^2 = \frac{1}{2\kappa} C_0 V_0^2 = \frac{U_0}{\kappa}. \tag{26-12}$$

Since $\kappa > 1$, the energy has decreased. Where has it gone? As the dielectric moves into the capacitor, the electric field causes charge separation and rotation of the molecular dipoles. The dipoles thus gain energy from the field. In a solid the molecules interact strongly, and the energy is quickly dissipated as heat.

FIGURE 26-23 The nonuniform fringing field outside the capacitor is stronger nearer the plates and therefore results in a net force on the molecular dipoles in the dielectric slab. As a result, the dielectric is pulled into the capacitor.

That the energy of a capacitor is lower with a dielectric inserted suggests that some attractive force must pull the dielectric slab into the capacitor. Figure 26-23 shows that this force originates in something we have heretofore intentionally ignored—the nonuniform fringing field beyond the plates of the capacitor. This nonuniform field acts on the dipoles in the dielectric to produce a net force toward the interior of the capacitor (see Problem 81).

CHAPTER SYNOPSIS

Summary

1. The work required to assemble a charge distribution is stored as the **electrostatic potential energy** of the distribution. Electrostatic potential energy resides in the electric field. Whenever an electric field is altered, energy is added to or removed from the field.

   a. The **electric field energy density** is given by

   $$u_E = \tfrac{1}{2}\varepsilon_0 E^2,$$

   where the SI units of u_E are J/m³.

   b. The electrostatic potential energy of a charge distribution may be determined either by computing the work required to assemble the individual charges of the distribution or, knowing the electric field of the distribution, by integrating the energy density over the volume containing the field:

   $$U = \int u_E \, dV = \tfrac{1}{2}\varepsilon_0 \int E^2 \, dV.$$

2. A **capacitor** is an arrangement of two conductors separated by an insulator. Transferring charge from one conductor to the other results in an electric field in the region between the conductors, and energy is stored in the field.

   a. The **capacitance** of a capacitor is the ratio of the charge to the potential difference between its conductors:

   $$C = \frac{Q}{V}.$$

   The capacitance of a parallel-plate capacitor is given by

   $$C = \frac{\varepsilon_0 A}{d},$$

   where A is the plate area and d the spacing. The capacitance of other configurations may be determined by assuming a charge, computing the associated potential difference, and taking the ratio $C = Q/V$.

   b. The energy stored in a capacitor depends on the capacitance and on the square of the potential difference:

   $$U = \tfrac{1}{2}CV^2.$$

   c. Capacitors may be connected in **series** or **parallel**. The capacitances of parallel capacitors add:

   $$C = C_1 + C_2 + C_3 + \cdots. \quad \text{(parallel capacitors)}$$

   The capacitances of series capacitors add reciprocally:

   $$\frac{1}{C} = \frac{1}{C_1} + \frac{1}{C_2} + \frac{1}{C_3} + \cdots. \quad \text{(series capacitors)}$$

   d. The **working voltage** of a capacitor is the maximum potential difference that should be applied across the capacitor without risk of dielectric breakdown in the insulating material.

   e. The **dielectric constant**, κ, of the insulating material used in a capacitor affects the capacitance, increasing it by this factor κ.

Terms You Should Understand

(Pairs are closely related terms whose distinction is important; number in parentheses is chapter section where term first appears.)

electrostatic potential energy (26-1)
energy density (26-3)
capacitor (26-4)
capacitance (26-4)
working voltage (26-6)
series, parallel (26-6)
dielectric constant (26-7)

Symbols You Should Recognize

U, u (26-2, 26-3)
C (26-4)
κ (26-7)

Problems You Should Be Able to Solve

calculating the work needed to assemble a distribution of discrete charges (26-1)
calculating electrostatic energy by integrating electric field energy density (26-3)

determining capacitance of simple capacitor configurations (26-4)

evaluating energy stored in capacitors (26-5)

analyzing parallel and series capacitor combinations (26-6)

determining the effect of dielectric materials in capacitors (26-7)

Limitations to Keep in Mind

Equation 26-6 for a parallel-plate capacitor is an approximation that neglects fringing fields at the plate edges; the approximation is good for capacitor plates much larger than their spacing.

QUESTIONS

1. Two positive point charges are initially infinitely far apart. Is it possible, using only a finite amount of work, to move them until they are located a small distance d apart?

2. How does the energy density a certain distance from a negative point charge compare with the energy density the same distance from a positive point charge of equal magnitude?

3. A dipole consists of two equal but opposite charges. Is the total energy stored in the field of the dipole zero? Why or why not?

4. Charge is spread over the surface of a balloon. The balloon is then allowed to expand. What happens to the energy of the electric field? If it is reduced, where does it go? If it is increased, where does the extra energy come from?

5. Why doesn't the superposition principle hold for electric field energy densities? That is, if you double the field strength at some point, why don't you simply double the energy density as well?

6. A student argues that the total energy associated with the electric field of a charged sphere must be infinite because its field extends throughout an infinite volume. Criticize this argument.

7. A capacitor is said to carry a charge Q. What is the net charge on the entire capacitor?

8. Does the capacitance of a capacitor describe the maximum amount of charge it can hold, in the same way that the capacity of a bucket describes the maximum amount of water it can hold? Explain and compare the meanings of capacitance and capacity.

9. A cylinder for storing compressed gas has a fixed volume, yet knowing this volume does not tell how much gas the cylinder can hold. Why not? How is the cylinder like a capacitor? Form analogies between quantities used in describing a capacitor and the amount of gas in the cylinder, the cylinder pressure, and the maximum pressure the cylinder can withstand.

10. A capacitor of capacitance C is charged to a potential difference V and carries charge Q. Why isn't the stored energy given simply by CV^2? After all, the work required to move a charge Q against a potential difference V is QV, and $C = Q/V$, so $Q = CV$.

11. Is a force needed to hold the plates of a charged capacitor in place? Explain.

12. Why do we say that capacitance depends only on the physical configuration of conductors making up a capacitor, not on the charge or potential difference, and yet we define capacitance as $C = Q/V$?

13. Why can't useful capacitors of arbitrarily large capacitance be made by simply reducing the spacing between parallel plates?

14. A solid conducting slab is inserted between the plates of a capacitor, as shown in Fig. 26-24. Does the capacitance increase, decrease, or remain the same?

FIGURE 26-24 Question 14.

15. Why is a capacitor needed for energy storage in a camera flash? After all, the battery is the ultimate source of the flash energy, so it should be capable of supplying the needed energy.

16. Two capacitors are connected in series. Is the equivalent capacitance more or less than that of either one?

17. Two capacitors are connected in series; they have capacitances C_1 and C_2, with $C_1 > C_2$. A potential difference V is imposed across the combination. Is the voltage across the two capacitors the same? If not, which has the greater voltage? Is the charge on each the same? If not, which has the greater charge?

18. Explain why the potential differences across parallel capacitors must be the same.

19. Two capacitors are storing equal amounts of energy, yet one has twice the capacitance of the other. How do their voltages compare?

20. Explain why inserting a dielectric between capacitor plates increases the capacitance.

21. An air-insulated parallel-plate capacitor is connected to a battery that imposes a potential difference V across the capacitor. If a dielectric slab is inserted between the capacitor plates, what happens to (a) the potential difference; (b) the capacitor charge; and (c) the capacitance?

22. A capacitor is charged and left connected to the charging battery. If you insert a dielectric slab between the capacitor plates, do you do work on the slab, or does it do work on you? Explain.

PROBLEMS

Section 26-1 Energy of a Charge Distribution

1. Three point charges, each of $+q$, are moved from infinity to the vertices of an equilateral triangle of side ℓ. How much work is required?

2. Repeat the preceding problem for the case of two charges $+q$ and one $-q$.

3. Four 50-μC charges are brought from far apart onto a line where they are spaced at 2.0-cm intervals. How much work does it take to assemble this charge distribution?

4. Repeat Example 26-1 for the case when the negative charge is $-q$ rather than $-q/2$.

5. Suppose two of the charges in Problem 1 are held in place, while the third is allowed to move freely. If this third charge has mass m, what will be its speed when it's far from the other two charges?

6. To a very crude approximation, a water molecule consists of a negatively charged oxygen atom and two "bare" protons, as shown in Fig. 26-25. Calculate the electrostatic energy of this configuration, which is therefore the magnitude of the energy released in forming this molecule from widely separated atoms. Your answer is an overestimate because electrons are actually "shared" among the three atoms, spending more time near the oxygen.

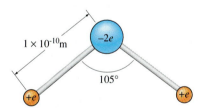

FIGURE 26-25 Problem 6.

7. Four identical charges q, initially widely separated, are brought to the vertices of a tetrahedron of side a (Fig. 26-26). Find the electrostatic energy of this configuration.

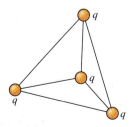

FIGURE 26-26 Problem 7 (All sides have equal length a).

8. A charge Q_0 is at the origin. A second charge, $Q_x = 2Q_0$, is brought to the point $x = a$, $y = 0$. Then a third charge Q_y is brought to the point $x = 0$, $y = a$. If it takes twice as much work to bring in Q_y as it did Q_x, what is Q_y in terms of Q_0?

Section 26-2 Two Isolated Conductors

9. Two square conducting plates 25 cm on a side and 5.0 mm apart carry charges $\pm 1.1 \ \mu$C. Find (a) the electric field between the plates, (b) the potential difference between the plates, and (c) the stored energy.

10. Two square conducting plates measure 5.0 cm on a side. The plates are parallel, spaced 1.2 mm apart, and initially uncharged. (a) How much work is required to transfer 7.2 μC from one plate to the other? (b) How much work is required to transfer a second 7.2 μC?

11. (a) How much charge must be transferred between the initially uncharged plates of the preceding problem in order to store 15 mJ of energy? (b) What will be the potential difference between the plates?

12. Two parallel, circular metal plates of 15 cm radius are initially uncharged. It takes 6.3 J to transfer 45 μC from one plate to the other. How far apart are the plates?

13. A conducting sphere of radius a is surrounded by a concentric spherical shell of radius b. Both are initially uncharged. How much work does it take to transfer charge from one to the other until they carry charges $\pm Q$?

14. Show that the energy given by Equation 26-2 can be written as the product of the charge transferred with the *average* value of the potential during the transfer.

15. Two conducting spheres of radius a are separated by a distance $\ell \gg a$; since the distance is large, neither sphere affects the other's electric field significantly, and the fields remain spherically symmetric. (a) If the spheres carry equal but opposite charges $\pm q$, show that the potential difference between them is $2kq/a$. (b) Write an expression for the work dW involved in moving an infinitesimal charge dq from the negative to the positive sphere. (c) Integrate your expression to find the work involved in transferring a charge Q from one sphere to the other, assuming both are initially uncharged.

Section 26-3 Energy and the Electric Field

16. The energy density in a uniform electric field is 3.0 J/m^3. What is the field strength?

17. A car battery stores about 4 MJ of energy. If all this energy were used to create a uniform electric field of 30 kV/m, what volume would it occupy?

18. Air undergoes dielectric breakdown at a field strength of 3 MV/m. Could you store energy in a uniform electric field in air with the same energy density as that of liquid gasoline? (See Appendix C.)

19. Find the electric field energy density at the surface of a proton, taken to be a uniformly charged sphere 1 fm in radius.

20. A pair of closely spaced square conducting plates measure 10 cm on a side. The electric field energy density between the plates is 4.5 kJ/m^3. What is the charge on the plates?

21. The electric field strength as a function of position x in a certain region is given by $E = E_0(x/x_0)$, where $E_0 = 24$ kV/m and $x_0 = 6.0$ m. Find the total energy stored in a cube 1.0 m on a side, located between $x = 0$ and $x = 1.0$ m. (The field strength is independent of y and z.)

22. A sphere of radius R contains charge Q spread uniformly throughout its volume. Find an expression for the electrostatic energy contained within the sphere itself. *Hint:* Consult Example 24-1.

23. A sphere of radius R carries a total charge Q distributed over its surface. Show that the total energy stored in its electric field is $U = kQ^2/2R$.

24. A uranium-235 nucleus contains 92 protons and 143 neutrons, and has a diameter of 6.6 fm. Assuming that the proton charge is distributed uniformly throughout the nucleus, calculate the total electrostatic energy of this configuration. *Hint:* See the preceding two problems.

25. Two 4.0-mm-diameter water drops each carry 15 nC. They are initially separated by a great distance. Find the change in the electrostatic potential energy if they are brought together to form a single spherical drop. Assume all charge resides on the drops' surfaces.

26. A 2.1-mm-diameter wire carries a uniform line charge density $\lambda = 28$ μC/m. How much energy is contained in a space 1.0 m long within one wire diameter of the wire surface?

27. A long, solid rod of radius a carries uniform volume charge density ρ. Find an expression for the electrostatic energy per unit length contained *within* the rod. *Hint:* See Problem 24-31.

Sections 26-4 Capacitors

28. A capacitor's plates hold 1.3 μC when charged to 60 V. What is its capacitance?

29. The "memory" capacitor in a VCR has a capacitance of 4.0 F and is charged to 3.5 V. What is the charge on its plates?

30. What voltage is needed to put 1.6 mC on a 100-μF capacitor?

31. Figure 26-27 shows data from an experiment in which known amounts of charge are placed on a capacitor and the resulting voltage measured. Fit a line to the data, and use it to determine the capacitance.

FIGURE 26-27 Problem 31 (data plot).

32. Show that the units of ε_0 may be written as F/m.

33. Find the capacitance of a parallel-plate capacitor consisting of circular plates 20 cm in radius separated by 1.5 mm.

34. A parallel-plate capacitor with 1.1-mm plate spacing has ± 2.3 μC on its plates when charged to 150 V. What is the plate area?

35. Find the capacitance of a 1.0-m-long piece of coaxial cable whose inner conductor radius is 0.80 mm and whose outer conductor radius is 2.2 mm, with air in between.

36. A capacitor consists of a conducting sphere of radius a surrounded by a concentric conducting shell of radius b.
Show that its capacitance is $C = \dfrac{ab}{k(b - a)}$.

37. Figure 26-28 shows a capacitor consisting of two electrically connected plates with a third plate between them, spaced so its surfaces are a distance d from the other plates. The plates have area A. Neglecting edge effects, show that the capacitance is $2\varepsilon_0 A/d$.

FIGURE 26-28 Problem 37.

Section 26-5 Energy Storage in Capacitors

38. The power supply of a stereo receiver contains a 2500-μF capacitor charged to 35 V. How much energy does it store?

39. Find the capacitance of a capacitor that stores 350 μJ when the potential difference across its plates is 100 V.

40. A certain capacitor stores 40 mJ of energy when charged to 100 V. (a) How much would it store when charged to 25 V? (b) What is its capacitance?

41. Which can store more energy, a 1-μF capacitor rated at 250 V or a 470 pF capacitor rated at 3 kV?

42. A circuit application calls for a 10-μF capacitor that can store 12 mJ. What should be its voltage rating? The capacitors are available with voltage ratings that are multiples of 25 V.

43. A 0.01-μF, 300-V capacitor costs 25¢, a 0.1-μF, 100-V capacitor costs 35¢, and a 30-μF, 5-V capacitor costs 88¢. (a) Which can store the most charge? (b) Which can store the most energy? (c) Which is the most cost-effective energy storage device, as measured by energy stored per unit cost?

44. A medical defibrillator stores 950 J of energy in a 100-μF capacitor. (a) What is the voltage across the capacitor? (b) If the capacitor discharges 300 J of its stored energy in 2.5 ms, what is the power delivered during this time?

45. A camera flashtube requires 5.0 J of energy per flash. The flash duration is 1.0 ms. (a) What is the power used by the flashtube *while it is actually flashing*? (b) If the flashtube operates at 200 V, what size capacitor is needed to supply the flash energy? (c) If the flashtube is fired once every 10 s, what is its *average* power consumption?

46. The NOVA laser fusion experiment at Lawrence Livermore Laboratory in California can deliver 10^{14} W (roughly 100 times the output of all the world's power plants) of light energy when its lasers are on. But the laser pulse lasts only 10^{-9} s. (a) How much energy is delivered in one pulse? (b) The capacitor bank supplying this energy has a total capacitance of 0.26 F. Only about 0.17% (i.e., 0.0017) of the capacitor energy actually appears as light. To what voltage must the capacitor bank be charged?

47. A solid conducting slab is inserted between the plates of a charged capacitor, as shown in Fig. 26-29. The slab thickness is 60% of the plate spacing, and its area is the same as the plates'. (a) What happens to the capacitance? (b) What happens to the stored energy, assuming the capacitor is not connected to anything?

FIGURE 26-29 Problem 47.

48. Consider the two widely separated spheres of Problem 15 as a capacitor. Use energy considerations (i.e., the equation $U = \frac{1}{2}CV^2$ applies to *any* capacitor) and the answers to Problem 15 to find the capacitance.

49. The cylindrical capacitor of Example 26-5 is charged to a voltage V. Obtain an expression for the energy density as a function of radial position in the capacitor, and integrate to show explicitly that the stored energy is $\frac{1}{2}CV^2$.

Section 26-6 Connecting Capacitors

50. You have a 1.0-μF and a 2.0 μF capacitor. What values of capacitance could you get by connecting them in series or parallel?

51. Two capacitors are connected in series and the combination charged to 100 V. If the voltage across each capacitor is 50 V, how do their capacitances compare?

52. (a) What is the equivalent capacitance of the combination shown in Fig. 26-30? (b) If a 100-V battery is connected across the combination, what is the charge on each capacitor? (c) What is the voltage across each?

FIGURE 26-30 Problems 52.

53. You're given three capacitors: 1.0 μF, 2.0 μF, and 3.0 μF. Find (a) the maximum, (b) the minimum, and (c) two intermediate values of capacitance you could achieve with various combinations of all three capacitors.

54. What is the equivalent capacitance of the four identical capacitors in Fig. 26-31, measured between A and B?

FIGURE 26-31 Problem 54.

55. You have an unlimited supply of 2.0-μF, 50-V capacitors. Describe combinations that would be equivalent to (a) a 2.0-μF, 100-V capacitor and (b) a 0.50-μF, 200-V capacitor.

56. Repeat the derivations for parallel and series capacitors, now using combinations of three capacitors.

57. What is the equivalent capacitance in Fig. 26-32?

FIGURE 26-32 Problems 57, 58.

58. In Fig. 26-32, find the energy stored in the 1-μF capacitor when a 50-V battery is connected between points A and B.

59. Two capacitors C_1 and C_2 are in series, with a voltage V across the combination. Show that the voltages across the individual capacitors are

$$V_1 = \frac{C_2\,V}{C_1 + C_2} \quad \text{and} \quad V_2 = \frac{C_1\,V}{C_1 + C_2}.$$

60. A 0.10-μF capacitor rated at 50 V is in series with a 0.20-μF capacitor rated at 200 V. What is the maximum voltage that should be applied across the series combination? *Hint:* See the preceding problem.

61. A variable "trimmer" capacitor used to make fine adjustments has a capacitance range from 10 to 30 pF. The trimmer is in parallel with a capacitor of about 0.001 μF. Over what percentage range can the capacitance of the combination be varied?

62. Capacitors are often marked with a nominal value for the capacitance and a tolerance range within which the actual capacitance lies. For example, a 1-μF, $\pm$20% capacitor has capacitance between 0.8 μF and 1.2 μF. If you connect a 0.01-μF $\pm$ 20% capacitor in series with a 0.02 μF $\pm$ 30% capacitor, in what range will the resulting capacitance lie? Express as a capacitance and its associated tolerance.

63. A 5.0-μF capacitor is charged to 50 V, and a 2.0-μF capacitor is charged to 100 V. The two are disconnected from their charging batteries and connected in parallel, positive to positive. (a) What is the common voltage across each after they are connected? *Hint:* Charge is conserved. (b) Compare the total electrostatic energy before and after the capacitors are connected. Speculate on the discrepancy.

Section 26-7 Capacitors and Dielectrics

64. A parallel-plate capacitor has plates with 50 cm² area separated by a 25-μm layer of polyethylene. Find (a) its capacitance and (b) its working voltage.

65. A 470-pF capacitor consists of two circular plates 15 cm in radius, separated by a sheet of polystyrene. (a) What is the thickness of the sheet? (b) What is the working voltage?

66. An electrolytic capacitor is essentially a parallel-plate configuration in which aluminum plates are separated by a thin layer of aluminum oxide created by chemical action when a voltage is applied. If the effective plate area of a 2000-μF capacitor is 2.5 m², what are (a) the oxide layer thickness and (b) the working voltage?

67. Repeat Problem 35 for the more realistic case of a cable insulated with polyethylene.

68. An air-insulated parallel-plate capacitor has plate area 76 cm² and spacing 1.2 mm. It is charged to 900 V and then disconnected from the charging battery. A plexiglass sheet is then inserted to fill the space between the plates. What are (a) the capacitance, (b) the potential difference between the plates, and (c) the stored energy both before and after the plexiglass is inserted?

69. The capacitor of the preceding problem is connected to its 900-V charging battery and left connected as the plexiglass sheet is inserted, so the potential difference remains at 900 V. What are (a) the charge on the plates and (b) the stored energy both before and after the plexiglass is inserted?

70. The first accurate estimate of the thickness of biological cell membranes used a capacitive technique, in which the capacitance per unit area of cell membrane was determined through a macroscopic measurement of the electrical properties of a suspension of cells; the result was a value of about 1 μF/cm² for a wide range of cells. Assuming a dielectric constant of about 3 for the membrane material, find the membrane thickness. (Your answer is the thickness of the bipolar lipid layer alone, and is lower by a factor of about 3 than values based on x-ray techniques; the full membrane may be thicker still.)

Paired Problems

(Both problems in a pair involve the same principles and techniques. If you can get the first problem, you should be able to solve the second one.)

71. A pair of parallel conducting plates of area 0.025 m² carrying equal but opposite charges stores 1.6 J in its electric field. When the magnitude of the charge on both plates is increased by 5.0 μC, the stored energy increases to 2.4 J. Find the plate separation.

72. A capacitor stores 50 mJ of energy at voltage V_0. When the voltage is increased by 150 V, the stored energy increases to 75 mJ. Find the capacitance.

73. A 20-μF air-insulated parallel-plate capacitor is charged to 300 V. The capacitor is then disconnected from the charging battery, and its plate separation is doubled. Find the stored energy (a) before and (b) after the plate separation increases. Where does the extra energy come from?

74. Repeat the preceding problem, except that now the capacitor remains connected to the 300-V battery while the plates are separated.

75. In the capacitor network of Fig. 26-33, take $C = 6.0\ \mu$F. Find (a) the equivalent capacitance between A and B and (b) the charge on C when 30 V is applied between A and B.

FIGURE 26-33 Problems 75, 76.

76. Take C in Fig. 26-33 as an unknown capacitance. If 100 V is applied between A and B, the network stores 5.8 mJ of energy. Find C.

Supplementary Problems

77. A typical lightning flash transfers 30 C across a potential difference of 30 MV. Assuming such flashes occur every 5 s in the thunderstorm of Example 26-2, roughly how long could the storm continue if its electrical energy were not replenished?

78. A capacitor is constructed from a "sandwich" consisting of two long strips of aluminum foil each 2.0 cm wide and 1.6 m long, separated by two strips of 5.0-μm-thick polyethylene (Fig. 26-34). The capacitor is rolled up to make a compact cylinder. Find its capacitance. *Hint:* Because the strips are thin and closely spaced, you can treat this as a parallel-plate capacitor. But note that each foil layer in the rolled-up capacitor "sees" an oppositely charged layer on *both* sides.

FIGURE 26-34 Problem 78.

79. Six charges $\pm q$, initially widely separated, are positioned to form a hexagon of side a, as shown in Fig. 26-35. What is the electrostatic energy of this configuration?

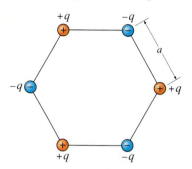

FIGURE 26-35 Problem 79.

80. Show that the result of Problem 36 reduces to that of a parallel-plate capacitor when the separation $b - a$ is much less than the radius a.

81. An air-insulated parallel-plate capacitor of capacitance C_0 is charged to voltage V_0 and then disconnected from the charging battery. A slab of material with dielectric constant κ, whose thickness is essentially equal to the capacitor spacing, is then inserted halfway into the capacitor (Fig. 26-36). Determine (a) the new capacitance, (b) the stored energy, and (c) the force on the slab in terms of C_0, V_0, κ, and the capacitor plate length L.

FIGURE 26-36 Problem 81.

82. Repeat parts (b) and (c) of the preceding problem, now assuming the battery remains connected while the slab is inserted.

83. We live inside a giant capacitor! Its plates are Earth's surface and the ionosphere, a conducting layer of the atmosphere beginning at about 60 km altitude. (a) What is its capacitance? *Hint:* You can treat it as either a spherical or a parallel-plate capacitor. Why? (b) The potential difference between Earth and ionosphere is about 6 MV. Find the total energy stored in this planetary capacitor.

84. Show that the result of Example 26-5 reduces to that of a parallel-plate capacitor when the separation $b - a$ is much less than the radius a. *Hint:* See Appendix A for an approximation to the logarithm.

85. Equation 26-2 gives the potential energy of a pair of oppositely charged plates. (a) Differentiate this expression with respect to the plate spacing to find the magnitude of the attractive force between the plates. (b) Compare with the

answer you would get by multiplying one plate's charge by the electric field between the plates. Why do your answers differ? Which is right?

86. A solid sphere contains a uniform volume charge density. What fraction of the total electrostatic energy of this configuration is contained *within* the sphere?

87. A small dipole lies on the x axis, centered at the origin. Find an expression for the total electrostatic energy contained in a thin cylindrical volume of diameter d and length ℓ, with its left end a distance ℓ from the dipole center, as shown in Fig. 26-37. Assume that ℓ is much greater than the dipole spacing. *Hint:* Since the cylinder is very thin, you can use the on-axis dipole field (Equation 23-5b) for the field throughout the cylinder.

FIGURE 26-37 Problem 87.

88. A coaxial cable 15 m long consists of an inner conductor 1.0 mm in radius and an outer conductor 3.0 mm in radius, separated by polyethylene insulation. What is the electrostatic energy contained within this cable when a potential difference of 300 V is applied between its two conductors?

89. A TV antenna cable consists of two 0.50-mm-diameter wires spaced 12 mm apart. Estimate the capacitance per unit length of this cable, neglecting dielectric effects of the insulation.

90. A classical view of the electron pictures it as a purely electrical entity, whose rest mass energy mc^2 (see Section 8-7) is the energy stored in its electric field. If the electron were a sphere with charge distributed uniformly over its surface, what radius would it have to satisfy this condition? (Your answer for the electron's "size" is not consistent with modern quantum mechanics nor with experiments that suggest the electron is a true point particle.)

91. Use the fact that the static electric field is conservative to argue that there *must* be fringing field at the edges of a parallel plate capacitor. *Hint:* Remember that the plates are equipotentials, and consider the potential differences V_{AB} and V_{CD} in Fig. 26-38. What does your argument say about the strength of the fringing field relative to the field between the plates?

FIGURE 26-38 Problem 91.

27 Electric Current

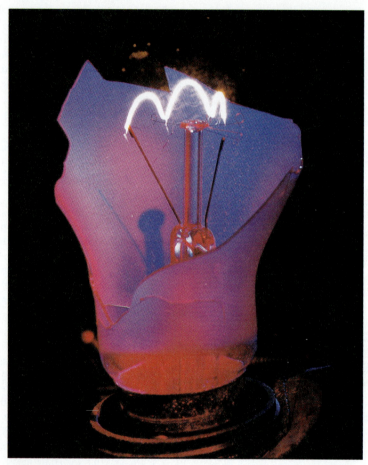

Electrical energy is converted to heat and light as a current of electrons flows through a lightbulb's filament.

So far our discussion of electrical phenomena has been based on the assumption of electrostatic equilibrium. We now relax that assumption, and instead of considering charges at rest, we'll consider situations in which charges are moving. Such motion usually occurs only in materials containing free charges, so our discussion will emphasize electrical conductors.

27-1 ELECTRIC CURRENT

Moving electric charge constitutes **electric current**. Electric currents are essential to many technological and natural processes. Currents flowing in light bulbs, toasters, and electric stoves produce heat and light. Currents in electric motors run our computers' disk drives, our refrigerators and washing machines, subway and railroad locomotives, and, increasingly, even advanced-technology electric cars. Your computer can plot a graph for your physics lab or search for a word in your English paper; fundamentally, these processes involve electric currents within the microchips at the heart of computers and other modern electronic devices. Currents in your body help your brain process information, regulate your heartbeat, and tell your muscles to move. Electric eels sense and kill their prey with electric currents they send through the surrounding water. A lightning strike is a strong but brief flow of current through the atmosphere. Currents in Earth's liquid outer core produce the planetary magnetic field that protects us from cosmic radiation, and currents in the ionized gases making up the stars greatly influence stellar behavior.

The measure of current is the net rate at which charge crosses a given area. Accordingly, its units are coulombs per second (C/s). This unit is given the special name **ampere** (A) after the French physicist André Marie Ampère:

$$1 \text{ A} = 1 \text{ C/s}.$$

In electronics, biomedical applications, and many other practical situations currents are small enough that the milliampere (mA) and microampere (μA) are frequently used. When the current I is steady we write

$$I = \frac{\Delta q}{\Delta t}, \qquad \text{(steady current)} \qquad (27\text{-}1a)$$

where Δq is the net charge crossing the given area in time Δt. If the current is not steady, we consider the ratio of charge to time for arbitrarily small time intervals, giving an instantaneous current that may vary with time:

$$I = \frac{dq}{dt}. \qquad \text{(instantaneous current)} \qquad (27\text{-}1b)$$

The direction of current is the direction in which *positive* charge flows. If the moving charge is negative, as with electrons in a metal, then the current is opposite the charge motion. You can blame Benjamin Franklin for this confusing situation! It was Franklin who assigned the names "positive" and "negative" to the two kinds of electric charge. Had Franklin known that free charges in metals are electrons, he might well have reversed his terminology.

An electric current may consist of only one sign of charge in motion, or it may involve both positive and negative charge. In that case the current is determined by the *net* charge motion—that is, by the algebraic sum of the currents associated with both kinds of charge (Fig. 27-1). That's why the bulk motion of a neutral object—even though it contains many coulombs of positive and of negative charge—does not constitute a current (Fig. 27-1b).

(a)

(b)

FIGURE 27-1 (a) Protons moving to the right constitute a current to the right. Since electrons are negative, *leftward* moving electrons also constitute a current to the *right*. The result in this case is a net current to the right. (b) In this bulk motion of neutral matter, the protons constitute a current to the right. But the negative electrons, also moving to the right, constitute a current to the *left*. So the net current is zero. Bulk motion of a *charged* object would, however, constitute a current.

Got It!

In which of the following situations is there a nonzero net current, and in which direction is that current flowing? (a) A beam of electrons moves from left to right; (b) a beam of protons moves upward; (c) in a solution, positive ions move to the left and negative ions to the right; (d) blood, carrying positive and negative ions at the same velocity, flows upward through a vein in your leg; (e) a metal car with no net charge moves westward on a highway.

A Microscopic Look at Current

Current—the rate at which charge crosses a given area—depends on the speed of the charge carriers, their density, and the charge carried by each. Consider a conductor containing n charges per unit volume, each carrying charge q and moving with speed v_d, as shown in Fig. 27-2. The quantity n is called the **number density**, and v_d is the **drift speed**. In some cases—a beam of electrons, for example—v_d is the actual particle speed. More commonly, v_d represents the time-average speed of the charge carriers, averaging out the effects of much faster but random thermal motion and collisions. If A is the conductor's cross-sectional area, then a length ℓ has volume $A\ell$ and therefore contains $nA\ell$ charges. Since each carries charge q, the total charge is $\Delta Q = nA\ell q$. With drift speed v_d, the length ℓ of charge moves past a given point in time $\Delta t = \ell/v_d$, so the current is

$v_d \longrightarrow$

n Charges/unit volume

A

ℓ

FIGURE 27-2 A conductor of cross-sectional area A containing n charge carriers per unit volume. Each moves with speed v_d and carries charge q. The total charge in a region of length ℓ is $nA\ell q$, and the current is therefore $nAqv_d$. Although we show positive charge moving, in the most common conductors—metals—charges carrying the current are actually negative electrons.

$$I = \frac{\Delta Q}{\Delta t} = \frac{nA\ell q}{\ell/v_d} = nAqv_d. \qquad (27\text{-}2)$$

| **EXAMPLE 27-1** | *Current in a Wire* |

A copper wire with a cross-sectional area of 1.0 mm² carries a current of 5.0 A. The charge carriers in copper are electrons, and each copper atom contributes, on average, 1.3 free electrons. What is the drift speed of the electrons?

Solution
The density of copper (see inside back cover) is 8920 kg/m³, and the periodic table (also inside back cover) lists copper's atomic weight as 63.55—meaning that the mass per atom is 63.55 u. So the number density of copper atoms is

$$n = \frac{8920 \text{ kg/m}^3}{(63.55 \text{ u/atom})(1.66 \times 10^{-27} \text{ kg/u})}$$

$$= 8.46 \times 10^{28} \text{ atoms/m}^3 .$$

Since each atom contributes 1.3 free electrons, the electron density is $(1.3)(8.46 \times 10^{28} \text{ m}^{-3}) = 1.10 \times 10^{29} \text{ m}^{-3}$. Solving Equation 27-2 for v_d then gives

$$v_d = \frac{I}{nAq} = \frac{5.0 \text{ A}}{(1.10 \times 10^{29} \text{ m}^{-3})(1.0 \times 10^{-6} \text{ m}^2)(1.6 \times 10^{-19} \text{C})}$$

$$= 0.284 \text{ mm/s} .$$

This remarkably small value is typical of drift speeds in metallic conductors.

EXERCISE A thin layer of gold, 0.10 mm wide and 3.2 μm thick, is used for connections to an integrated circuit. Find (a) the free electron density in gold and (b) the drift speed of electrons in the gold layer when it carries a current of 140 μA. The density of gold is 1.93×10^4 kg/m³, and each gold atom contributes, on average, 1.5 free electrons.

Answers: (a) 8.85×10^{28} m^{-3}; (b) 31 μm/s

Some problems similar to Example 27-1: 8, 55, 56

How can the drift speed be so small? When you turn on a light switch, the light comes on immediately, not several thousand seconds later as the result of Example 27-1 might imply. Here it's important to distinguish between the speed of the electrons and that of the electrical signal in the wire. As soon as electrons at one end of the wire begin moving, their electric fields affect adjacent electrons, which also begin moving. This effect propagates down the wire at what is in fact nearly the speed of light, so the current begins everywhere almost simultaneously. The same thing happens when you turn on a garden hose full of water: Water comes out the far end even though water at the faucet has not had time to travel down the hose.

Current Density

In many cases electric currents are not neatly confined in a wire. Examples include currents in Earth, in the atmosphere, in chemical solutions, and in the ionized gases that make up the stars and indeed much of the matter in the universe (Fig. 27-3). In these situations the current is spread over a rather ill-defined area, and its magnitude and direction may vary from point to point. It's useful to characterize such diffuse currents in terms of **current density**, J, defined as the current per unit area at a given point. Dividing Equation 27-2 by the area gives

$$J = \frac{I}{A} = nqv_d. \qquad (27\text{-}3a)$$

The flow of charge can vary in both magnitude and direction, so current density is more generally written as a vector quantity:

$$\mathbf{J} = nq\mathbf{v}_d, \qquad (27\text{-}3b)$$

where $\mathbf{v}_d$ is the drift velocity.

If current density is uniform, as in a wire, then the total current is simply the product of the current density with the wire's cross-sectional area. When the current density varies with position, then integration is necessary to calculate the total current. Problem 65 explores this case.

FIGURE 27-3 Strong electric currents flow in the bright yellow loops of ionized gas that arch above the Sun's surface in this image made with an orbiting x-ray telescope on the Japanese satellite Yohkoh.

EXAMPLE 27-2	*Through the Cell Membrane*

An ion channel is a narrow pore, formed from a special protein molecule, that allows specific ions to pass through a biological cell membrane (Fig. 27-4). A particular channel carries a current of 1.8 pA, with the charges being singly ionized potassium (K^+). The channel has a circular cross section 0.30 nm in diameter. (a) If the channel is open for 1.0 ms, how many ions pass through it? (b) What is the magnitude of the current density in the channel?

Ion channels

~0.3 nm

Lipid molecules

FIGURE 27-4 Diagram of a cell membrane, showing two ion channels. An ion current is passing through the frontmost channel, shown in cutaway. The current is driven in part by the electric field associated with the charge distribution on the lipid molecules that make up the membrane.

Solution

(a) A current of 1.8 pA means 1.8 pC/s, so the total charge passing through the channel in 1.0 ms is $(1.8 \text{ pC/s})(1.0 \text{ ms}) = 1.8$ fC, where we use the SI prefixes p $= 10^{-12}$, m $= 10^{-3}$, and f $= 10^{-15}$. Each ion carries one elementary charge, so the number of ions in 1 ms is

$$N = \frac{1.8 \times 10^{-15} \text{ C}}{1.6 \times 10^{-19} \text{ C/ion}} = 1.1 \times 10^4 \text{ ions} .$$

(b) Current density is current per unit area, so

$$J = \frac{I}{A} = \frac{I}{\pi r^2} = \frac{1.8 \times 10^{-12} \text{ A}}{(\pi)(0.15 \times 10^{-9} \text{ m})^2} = 2.5 \times 10^7 \text{ A/m}^2 .$$

This value is about four times the maximum safe current density in copper wire used in household wiring! (See the exercise with this example.) Of course, the ion channel is so narrow that the total current is minuscule.

Tip

Don't Just Plug In! Do you search for an equation as soon as you start a problem? Think first! If you really know what the concepts mean, you may not always need equations. Here we solved the problem entirely by knowing the meanings of the terms *current* and *current density*.

EXERCISE The maximum safe current density in copper wire used in household wiring is about 6 MA/m². (Beyond this level the wire overheats.) What is the minimum safe wire diameter in a circuit that can carry up to 15 A?

Answer: 1.8 mm

Some problems similar to Example 27-2: 2, 5–7, 10, 11

27-2 CONDUCTION MECHANISMS

What causes electric current? Electric charges experience forces in electric fields, so applying a field to a conductor should result in a current. (The simplest way to produce such a field is to connect a battery—a device that provides a fixed potential difference between two points—across the conductor.) You might think that it would suffice to apply the field briefly to get the charges moving; Newton's law suggests they would then keep moving. In most conductors, however, charges do not move unimpeded. They bump into things—usually ions—and quickly lose any energy they've gained from the field. To sustain a current in most materials, it is therefore necessary to maintain an electric field within the material. Having such a field does not violate our conclusion that there can be no electric field in a conductor in electrostatic equilibrium since we're explicitly considering moving charges and are therefore no longer talking about equilibrium.

Although it is generally true that electric fields result in currents, the detailed relation between current and field depends on the type of conductor. In addition to metals, important conductors include ionic solutions, plasmas (ionized gases), semiconductors, and superconductors, all of which we will consider briefly in this section.

In most materials the current density and the electric field are in the same direction, and we can therefore characterize the relation between the two using the equation

$$\mathbf{J} = \sigma \mathbf{E},$$ (27-4a)

where σ is called the **conductivity** of the material. Equation 27-4a shows that conductivity is the ratio of the magnitude of the current density to the magnitude of the electric field.

Ohm's Law: A Microscopic View

For many common conductors, including metals, the conductivity σ is independent of the electric field. Such materials are called **ohmic**, and for these materials Equation 27-4a is one way of stating what is known as **Ohm's law**, namely that the current density at any point in a conductor is proportional to the electric field at that point. In **nonohmic** materials, in contrast, conductivity does depend on field, and therefore $\mathbf{J}$ and $\mathbf{E}$ are not directly proportional.

You may already be familiar with the *macroscopic* version of Ohm's law, which makes the equivalent statement that the total current through a piece of material is proportional to the potential difference, or voltage, across it. In Equation 27-4a we have the *microscopic* version of Ohm's law, which describes what happens at a single point in a material in terms of the electric field and current density at that point. The macroscopic version, in contrast, links the current (a quantity related to current density) and voltage (related, as we saw in Chapter 25, to the electric field) associated with an entire piece of material. We'll derive the macroscopic version in section 27-3, and will find it very useful for analyzing electric circuits. But the microscopic version remains important for many applications in biophysics, geophysics, astrophysics, semiconductor engineering, and other areas where electric fields in conducting materials may vary with position, and where we therefore need to know what's going on at each point.

The conductivity σ tells how large a current density will result from a given electric field; it's thus a measure of how easy it is for an electric field to cause free charges in a material to move. A perfect conductor would have $\sigma = \infty$; a perfect insulator, $\sigma = 0$. A lot of subtle physics goes into determining the conductivity, as we'll soon see for metallic conductors. An equivalent quantity for describing the relation between current density and electric field in a material is the material's **resistivity**, ρ, defined as the reciprocal of the conductivity:

$$\rho = \frac{1}{\sigma},$$

so Equation 27-4a can also be written

$$\mathbf{J} = \frac{\mathbf{E}}{\rho}.$$ (27-4b)

Where conductivity tells how *easy* it is for a field to cause current in a material, its reciprocal, resistivity, tells how *hard* it is. Thus the larger the resistivity, the greater the electric field needed to produce a given current density. You may be familiar with electrical *resistance,* which we'll soon see is an electrical property of specific objects that relates to the underlying *resistivity* of the materials they're made from.

TABLE 27-1 *Resistivities*

MATERIAL	RESISTIVITY ($\Omega \cdot m$)
Metallic conductors (at 20°C)	
Aluminum	2.65×10^{-8}
Copper	1.68×10^{-8}
Gold	2.24×10^{-8}
Iron	9.71×10^{-8}
Mercury	9.84×10^{-7}
Silver	1.59×10^{-8}
Ionic solutions (in water at 18°C)	
1-molar copper sulfate ($CuSO_4$)	3.9×10^{-4}
1-molar hydrochloric acid (HCl)	1.7×10^{-2}
1-molar sodium chloride (NaCl)	1.4×10^{-4}
Water, pure (H_2O)	2.6×10^5
Blood, human	0.70
Sea water (typical value)	0.22
Semiconductors (pure, at 20°C)	
Germanium	0.45
Silicon	640
Insulators	
Ceramics	$10^{11} – 10^{14}$
Glass	$10^{10} – 10^{14}$
Polystyrene	$10^{15} – 10^{17}$
Rubber	$10^{13} – 10^{16}$
Wood (dry)	$10^8 – 10^{14}$

Equation 27-4b shows that the units of resistivity are V·m/A. One V/A is given the name **ohm** (symbol Ω), after the German physicist Georg Ohm (1789–1854), whose experiments clarified the relation between voltage and current. Thus the SI units of resistivity can be written $\Omega \cdot m$. Reciprocally, the units of conductivity are $(\Omega \cdot m)^{-1}$.

Conductivity and resistivity vary dramatically among different materials; indeed, their measurable range is one of the broadest of any physical quantity, spanning some 24 orders of magnitude. Table 27-1 lists some typical resistivities. In addition to telling us how well materials conduct electricity, measurement of resistivity or conductivity can also provide information on structure or composition. Some devices for routine blood analysis, for example, make use of conductivity measurements, while measurement of blood conductivity in laboratory animals has been used experimentally to assess changes in metabolic activity.

EXAMPLE 27-3 | *Household Wiring: The Electric Field*

A 1.8-mm-diameter copper wire carries 15 A to a household appliance. What is the electric field in the wire?

Solution
The current density is $J = I/A$; using this result in Equation 27-4b and solving for E gives

$$E = \frac{I\rho}{A} = \frac{(15 \text{ A})(1.68 \times 10^{-8} \ \Omega \cdot m)}{(\pi)(0.90 \times 10^{-3} \text{ m})^2} = 99 \text{ mV/m},$$

where we found the resistivity of copper in Table 27-1. This result is much smaller than the fields we've been discussing in electrostatic situations. Because copper is such a good conductor, only a very small field is needed to drive even a substantial current. In analyzing electric circuits we will often make the approximation that the fields and therefore potential differences in copper wires are essentially zero.

EXERCISE A uniform electric field of 0.76 V/m drives a 10-A current in an iron wire. Find the wire diameter.

Answer: 1.3 mm

Some problems similar to Example 27-3: 17–19

Conduction in Metals

Metals are good conductors because they contain large numbers of free electrons, which respond readily to electric fields. Each atom in the metal contributes, on average, about one electron to this "sea" of free electrons. The resulting positive ions combine in a regular structure, called the crystal lattice (Fig. 27-5). In the absence of an electric field, electrons move randomly through the lattice at high speeds of typically 10^6 m/s. They collide frequently with the ions, bouncing off in random directions. There's no net flow of electrons in any one direction, so there's no electric current. And because the whole system is in thermal equilibrium, there's no net energy transfer from electrons to ions or vice versa.

We'll use this simple description of a metal to develop an understanding of what happens when we apply an electric field to a metal—i.e., the conduction process. Although this will help you see why metals obey Ohm's law, be aware that our explanation is incomplete; a full description of metallic conduction necessarily involves quantum mechanics.

Applying an electric field to a metal gives the negative electrons an acceleration in the direction opposite the field. But the electrons are already whizzing around at high speed, colliding frequently with the ions. So an electron doesn't gain much energy or speed from the electric field before it collides with an ion. When it does, it gives up whatever energy it gained from the field, and rebounds with a random velocity. But the field is still there, and the electron again accelerates (Fig. 27-6). The result is that the electrons acquire an additional, very small average velocity in the direction opposite the field. This is the drift velocity $\mathbf{v}_d$ that we introduced earlier. Unlike their random thermal velocities, all electrons share a common drift velocity, and thus their motion constitutes a net current that is proportional to $\mathbf{v}_d$.

The electrons' behavior in metallic conduction is somewhat like driving through stop-and-go city traffic; you spend a lot of time accelerating, but soon you have to stop again. As a result, you acquire a rather slow average speed through the city. But this analogy is imperfect: your car accelerates from rest at each red light, while the electrons' acceleration introduces only a minuscule velocity change compared with their already high thermal velocity.

What happens to the energy the electrons gain from the field? They give it up in collisions with the ions, ultimately increasing the internal energy of the material. We saw in Chapter 21 that temperature is a measure of internal energy, so the metal's temperature increases when a current flows through it. That's the ultimate cause of heating in electric stoves, hair dryers, water heaters, toasters, and myriad other everyday devices.

So now we have the electrons drifting slowly in a direction opposite the electric field, with velocity $\mathbf{v}_d$. That drift velocity depends on two things: the acceleration of the electrons and the rate at which they undergo collisions. The electric force $-e\mathbf{E}$ gives an acceleration $\mathbf{a} = \mathbf{F}/m = -e\mathbf{E}/m$, with m the electron mass and $-e$ its charge. If we pick a random electron and ask when it last underwent a collision, the answer will be some mean time τ called the **collision time**. During that time the electron has been accelerating with acceleration $\mathbf{a} = -e\mathbf{E}/m$, and therefore its average velocity due to the presence of the electric field—i.e., the drift velocity $\mathbf{v}_d$—will be

$$\mathbf{v}_d = -\frac{e\mathbf{E}}{m}\tau.$$

FIGURE 27-5 Atoms of a metal form a regular structure, or crystal lattice. This image, made with a scanning tunneling microscope that uses the quantum mechanical behavior of electrons to image individual atoms, shows the arrangement of atoms at the surface of a metallic nickel crystal.

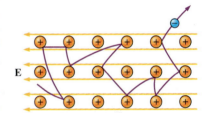

FIGURE 27-6 The path of an electron moving through a metal. The motion is almost completely random, but in the presence of an electric field there is a very slight drift antiparallel to the field.

Of course the electron also has its random thermal motion, but over many collisions this averages to zero while the velocity resulting from the electric field does not. Using our expression for the drift velocity in Equation 27-3b gives

$$\mathbf{J} = nq\mathbf{v}_d = n(-e)\mathbf{v}_d = \frac{ne^2\mathbf{E}}{m}\tau.$$

Comparing this expression with Equation 27-4a shows that the conductivity is

$$\sigma = \frac{ne^2}{m}\tau. \tag{27-5}$$

The collision time τ depends on several factors. Obviously, the spacing of ions in the crystal lattice influences how often collisions occur. Less obvious is the fact that the presence of impurities—i.e., atoms of other materials—has a dramatic influence on electron-ion collisions and thus on conductivity. And, also obviously, τ depends on how fast the electrons are moving; the faster they go, the more frequent their collisions, and the lower τ should be. The electrons have two kinds of motion: their random thermal motion and the drift velocity $\mathbf{v}_d$ acquired from the electric field. In Example 27-1 we found that a typical drift speed is on the order 1 mm/s, while thermal speeds are around 10^6 m/s. The drift speed is therefore completely negligible in determining the collision time. That means the collision time and hence the conductivity are essentially independent of the applied electric field—and that makes Equation 27-4a a linear relation for metallic conductors. In other words, metals obey Ohm's law. We stress that this conclusion is only approximate, and that Ohm's law, unlike Gauss's law, is *not* an exact, universal statement that holds everywhere and for all materials.

Although the conductivity of a metal is independent of the applied electric field, it does depend on other factors, especially temperature. From Chapter 20 we know that classical physics gives a thermal speed proportional to the square root of the temperature, so we might expect conductivity to be proportional to $1/\sqrt{T}$ and thus resistivity to $\sqrt{T}$. Experiment, however, shows that resistivity is very nearly proportional to temperature rather than to its square root. We show this relation for copper in Fig. 27-7, and explore it further in Problem 25. Here we've reached the limits of classical physics, which cannot describe fully the behavior of the free electrons in a metal. Readers of the extended version of this text will explore quantum mechanics and how it deals with electrical conduction.

FIGURE 27-7 Resistivity of copper—the inverse of conductivity—shows a nearly linear dependence on temperature, in contrast to the classical prediction of a $\sqrt{T}$ dependence.

EXAMPLE 27-4	*Conductivity and Collision Time*

Copper at room temperature contains 1.1×10^{29} free electrons per cubic meter. What is the collision time for these electrons?

Solution

Writing $\sigma = 1/\rho$ and solving Equation 27-5 for the collision time gives

$$\tau = \frac{m}{ne^2\rho}$$

$$= \frac{9.11\times10^{-31}\ \text{kg}}{(1.1\times10^{29}\ \text{m}^{-3})(1.6\times10^{-19}\ \text{C})^2(1.68\times10^{-8}\ \Omega\cdot\text{m})}$$

$$= 1.9\times10^{-14}\ \text{s},$$

where we found the resistivity of copper in Table 27-1. Problem 66 uses this result to estimate the mean thermal speed of the electrons.

EXERCISE Sodium contains 2.5×10^{28} free electrons per cubic meter, and the collision time is 3.4×10^{-14} s. What is the resistivity of sodium?

Answer: $4.2\times10^{-8}\ \Omega\cdot\text{m}$

Some problems similar to Example 27-4: 21, 66

APPLICATION	*Noise in Electronic Equipment*

Although the time-average current associated with random thermal motion of charge carriers is zero, at any given instant random fluctuations may result in more charge carriers moving in one direction than in another. The result is a very small current, whose sign and magnitude fluctuate randomly. Called thermal noise, this current may disturb or even overwhelm currents of interest in sensitive electronic instruments. Thermal motion decreases at low temperatures, and sensitive circuits such as the amplifiers in radio telescopes are often cooled to liquid helium temperatures, around 4 K (Fig. 27-8). That way, the very weak signals reaching Earth from cosmic sources are not overwhelmed by thermal noise. Ultimately thermal noise limits our ability to detect and study very weak electrical signals.

FIGURE 27-8 This 12-m radio telescope at Kitt Peak National Observatory uses amplifiers cooled to 4 K with liquid helium in order to reduce electrical noise.

Ionic Solutions

An ionic solution contains positive and negative ions that respond to an electric field by moving in opposite directions, resulting in a net current. Conductivity of the solution is limited by collisions between the ions and neutral atoms. In addition to heating the solution, some of the energy of these collisions may go into chemical reactions that store energy—as in charging a rechargable battery.

Conduction in ionic solutions is essential to life, as the flow of sodium, potassium, and other ions through cell membranes occurs through the process of ionic conduction. Electric eels set up currents in the surrounding water, using ionic conduction to sense and kill their prey (Fig. 27-9). Technological processes that use ionic conduction include electroplating of thin layers of one material onto another, and electrolysis of water to produce hydrogen and oxygen gas. Ionic conduction also plays an important role in the corrosion of metals, for example those exposed to salt solutions. And the presence of an ionic solution—sweat—increases our vulnerability to electric shock. Table 27-1 includes the resistivities of some ionic solutions. Note that these solutions are poorer conductors than metals.

FIGURE 27-9 The electric eel sets up currents in the surrounding water, and can sense the presence of nearby objects by subtle variations in conductivity. It uses larger currents to kill its prey.

Plasmas

Plasma is ionized gas that conducts because it contains free electrons and positive ions. It takes substantial energy to ionize atoms, so plasmas usually occur only in high-temperature environments. The few examples of plasmas on Earth occur in fluorescent lamps, neon signs, devices for fusion research, the ionosphere, flames, and lightning flashes (Fig. 27-10). Yet most of the matter in the universe is probably in the plasma state; the stars, in particular, are almost entirely plasma.

The electrical properties of plasma make it so different from ordinary gas that plasma is often called "the fourth state of matter." Some plasmas, especially in astrophysical situations, are so diffuse that collisions between particles are rare. These "collisionless" plasmas are sometimes far better conductors than metals, and they can sustain large electric currents with very modest electric fields.

FIGURE 27-10 Plasma, or ionized gas, is an excellent electrical conductor. Photo shows glowing plasma in the Tokamak Fusion Test Reactor at the Princeton Plasma Physics Laboratory.

Semiconductors

Even in the best insulators, random thermal motions occasionally dislodge electrons, giving these materials very modest conductivity. This effect is usually insignificant at normal temperatures. But a few materials—notably the element silicon—have more electrons dislodged by thermal motion even at room temperature, and therefore exhibit significant conductivity. Because their conductivity lies between that of insulators and that of good conductors, such materials are called **semiconductors**. The electrical properties of semiconductors make possible the microelectronic technology that plays a pervasive role in modern civilization. Here we give a qualitative description of semiconductors based on classical physics; the extended version of this text revisits semiconductors from a quantum perspective in Chapter 42.

Conduction in semiconductors involves not only electrons dislodged from their places in the material structure, but also the "holes" left behind by those electrons. Nudged by the electric field, an adjacent electron can "fall" into the hole, with the effective result that the hole has moved in the direction of the field (Fig. 27-11). Thus holes act as positive charge carriers, and a pure semiconductor such as silicon contains equal numbers of negative charge carriers (free electrons) and positive charge carriers (holes).

A pure semiconductor has rather low conductivity and is useful only in a few applications. The key to semiconductor technology lies in the control of conductivity by adding very small amounts of impurities—a process called **doping**. Adding an element with five electrons in its outermost shell—as opposed to silicon's four—results in large numbers of free electrons and a much more conductive material whose charge carriers are predominantly negative (Fig. 27-12). Since its charge carriers are negative, such a material is called an **N-type** semiconductor. In contrast, doping with an element containing only three outermost electrons results in a **P-type** semiconductor, whose charge carriers are predominantly positive holes.

The key element in nearly all semiconductor devices is the **PN junction**, where *P*- and *N*-type semiconductors meet. When such a junction forms, free

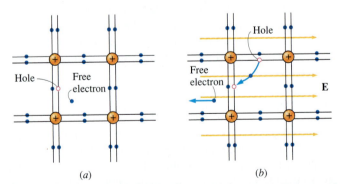

(a) *(b)*

FIGURE 27-11 *(a)* Structure of a silicon crystal, showing each atom bound to each of its neighbors by two shared electrons. Thermal motion has dislodged one of the electrons from the crystal structure, leaving behind a hole. *(b)* In the presence of an electric field, the free electron drifts opposite the field direction. In addition, a nearby bound electron falls into the hole, effectively moving the hole in the direction of the field. Holes thus act as positive charge carriers.

FIGURE 27-12 (*a*) An arsenic atom, showing its five valence electrons. (*b*) Incorporated into a silicon crystal, the arsenic atom does its best to fit into the crystal structure. One of its electrons cannot participate in the bonding, but moves throughout the crystal lattice as a free conduction electron. Because its free charge carriers are predominantly electrons, the arsenic-doped silicon is an *N*-type semiconductor. Doping with aluminum, which has three valence electrons, would result similarly in excess holes, making a *P*-type material. In either case the material remains neutral; *P* and *N* refer to the sign of the free charges, not to a net charge on the material.

(*a*)

(*b*)

electrons, abundant in the *N*-type material but rare in the *P*, diffuse across the junction and combine with ions on the *P* side of the junction (Fig. 27-13*a*). Similarly, holes diffuse the other way and combine with electrons. (This diffusion process is similar to what happens when you open a bottle of perfume or drop food coloring into water; molecules of the substance spread from regions of high concentration to regions of low concentration.) Eventually diffusion stops because buildup of charge on opposite sides of the junction results in an electric field opposing further diffusion. But by now the junction region is depleted of free charges, and is therefore a poor conductor.

A single *PN* junction does conduct, but only in one direction. Applying a potential difference with positive at the *N*-type material only reinforces the charge depletion at the junction, further reducing its conductivity (Fig. 27-13*b*) and preventing significant current from flowing. This situation is called **reverse bias**. In contrast, making the *P*-type material positive reduces the internal electric field, shrinking the depleted region and greatly increasing its conductivity (Fig. 27-13*c*). A substantial current thus flows in this case of **forward bias**. We'll see in Chapter 33 how this "one-way" property of the *PN* junction is used to convert alternating current from household power sources into the direct current needed to power electronic devices.

The wide range of semiconductor devices in use today results largely from carefully engineered combinations of *PN* junctions. The following application presents one of the most important such devices.

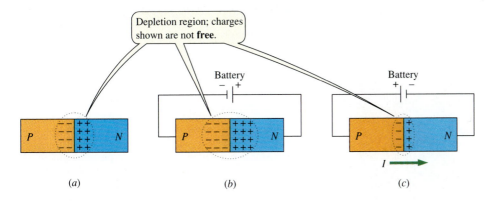

Depletion region; charges shown are not **free**.

Battery

(*a*)   (*b*)   (*c*)

FIGURE 27-13 (*a*) When a *PN* junction is first established, electrons diffuse from the *N*-type material into the *P*, where they combine with holes. The result is a net negative charge to the left of the junction, but few free charges. Similarly, holes diffuse the other way, resulting in net positive charge and few free charges to the right of the junction. (*b*) Applying a potential difference from *N* to *P* reinforces the depletion, and very little current flows. (*c*) Applying a potential difference from *P* to *N* narrows the depletion region and results in substantial current flow.

Few inventions have revolutionized human society as much as the transistor. Transistors are the basis of all modern electronic devices, from stereo amplifiers to automobile ignition systems to VCRs, laboratory instruments, and computers.

Figure 27-14 shows a widely used type of transistor, called the field effect transistor (FET). This particular FET consists of a slab of P-type material with two embedded N-type regions. Wires connect these N-type regions to external circuitry, but normally no current can flow through the transistor in either direction because one of the two PN junctions will be reverse biased. Coated on top of the P region is a layer of silicon dioxide (SiO_2), an excellent insulator, and over that is a metal layer called the *gate*. Suppose the gate is charged positively, by connecting it to a battery. This charge will repel positive holes in the P-type channel below the gate, and attract electrons. As a result, the channel becomes temporarily N-type, and the PN junctions disappear. The transistor therefore conducts electric current (Fig. 27-14b).

Varying the gate charge continuously varies the conductivity and therefore the current; the transistor then functions as an *amplifier,* in which a weak signal applied to the gate controls a stronger signal in the form of the current through the transistor.

Audio and video systems all contain amplifying transistors; ultimately, for example, the weak signal from a microphone or guitar pickup is amplified enough to drive a loudspeaker. In digital circuits like computers, in contrast, the transistor functions as a switch, with its drain–source channel either fully "on" (conducting) or "off" (nonconducting).

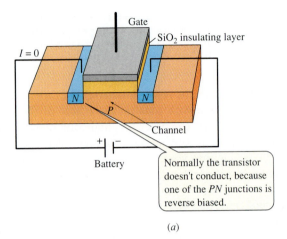

Normally the transistor doesn't conduct, because one of the PN junctions is reverse biased.

(a)

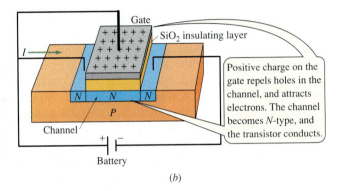

Positive charge on the gate repels holes in the channel, and attracts electrons. The channel becomes N-type, and the transistor conducts.

(b)

FIGURE 27-14 A field-effect transistor, or FET. (*a*) Normally current flow between the N-type regions is impossible, because one of the two PN junctions is necessarily reverse biased. (*b*) Positive charge on the gate makes the channel temporarily N-type, allowing current to flow.

FIGURE 27-15 The PowerPC chip is a complex integrated circuit at the heart of Apple's Macintosh computers.

A transistor is fabricated from a single piece of silicon. By exposing various parts of the surface to dopant chemicals, oxygen, and metal atoms, the various N and P regions as well as the SiO_2 insulator and metallic gate are formed. The same process is used to produce entire circuits containing millions of transistors (Fig. 27-15). These **integrated circuits**—also called **chips**—make possible the complexity, miniaturization, and sophistication of modern electronic devices.

Superconductors

In 1911 the Dutch physicist H. Kamerlingh Onnes, studying the electrical properties of mercury at very low temperatures, found a sudden drop in resistivity at a temperature of 4.2 K. The resistivity below this temperature proved immeasurably low. Subsequent research has identified thousands of substances that become **superconductors** at sufficiently low temperatures. Currents in superconductors persist for years without any measurable decrease, suggesting that the resistivity of a superconductor is truly zero (Fig. 27-16).

FIGURE 27-16 Resistivity versus temperature for a thin film of yttrium-barium-copper-oxide. Below the 93-K transition temperature the resistivity is truly zero.

For decades the known superconductors were largely metals and metal alloys that required cooling in liquid helium to achieve their superconductivity. Then, in 1986, physicists J. Georg Bednorz and K. Alex Müller of IBM's Zurich research laboratory made the stunning discovery that a class of ceramic materials becomes superconducting at temperatures around 100 K—high enough that these materials superconduct when cooled with liquid nitrogen. A flurry of research followed, soon pushing the highest superconducting temperature to well over 100 K. Bednorz and Müller received the 1987 Nobel Prize in physics, only a year after their discovery. The search for higher temperature superconductors continues, with the highest reported temperatures now over 160 K. Sporadic reports of superconductivity at or close to room temperature have appeared in the literature, but so far none have met the test of repeatability. Development of a room-temperature superconductor would revolutionize electromagnetic technology.

Superconductivity offers loss-free flow of electric current. Electromagnets made from metal and metal alloy superconductors cooled with liquid helium have been used for years in such applications as nuclear magnetic resonance spectrometers (your chemistry lab may have one) and, more recently, in magnetic resonance imagers used in medicine. Electric current in these devices, once started, continues forever with no power source—as long as the liquid helium is regularly replenished (Fig. 27-17).

The liquid nitrogen coolant adequate for high-temperature superconductors is far less expensive than liquid helium, so scientists and engineers are developing a wide array of commercial applications of these materials. Devices based on thin films of high-T superconductors measure weak magnetic fields in biomedical and geophysical applications, sense radiant energy, and produce and process microwaves. Finally, high-T superconducting wires are now commercially available in kilometer lengths.

FIGURE 27-17 This superconducting electromagnet at Lawrence Berkeley Laboratory is among the strongest of its kind. It uses 14 miles of niobium-tin superconducting wire, and is cooled with liquid helium.

Although superconductivity was discovered in 1911, a satisfactory explanation of the phenomenon was not given until 1957. In that year John Bardeen, Leon Cooper, and J. Robert Schrieffer showed how superconductivity in the traditional low-temperature materials arises from a quantum-mechanical interaction among the conduction electrons. In a way that has no analog in classical physics, all the electrons move coherently through the crystal lattice, with no energy loss. Their theory earned Bardeen, Cooper, and Schrieffer the 1972 Nobel Prize in physics. A comprehensive theory of the newer, high-temperature superconducting materials has yet to be fully developed. Readers of the extended version of this text will revisit superconductivity in Chapter 42.

27-3 RESISTANCE AND OHM'S LAW

How much current does it take to run this hair dryer? Do I risk a fatal shock if I touch this wire? How long an extension cord can I use with this electric saw? Why are these jumper cables so thick? How long will it take to recharge my dead battery? Is the wiring in my house safe, or could it overheat and cause a fire? All these questions are ultimately about the total electric current flowing in wires, bodies, batteries, and other objects. The answer in each case depends on two things: the voltage (i.e., potential difference), V, applied across the object, and the **resistance**, R, that the object offers to the flow of electric current.

The macroscopic version of Ohm's law—with which you may already be familiar—relates voltage, current, and resistance. Ohm's law states that the current through an object is proportional to the voltage across it and inversely proportional to the object's resistance:

$$I = \frac{V}{R}. \quad \text{(Ohm's law)} \tag{27-6}$$

Ohm's law in this form makes good sense, for it shows that a given voltage can push more current through a lower resistance. It's worth noting two extreme cases: An **open circuit** is a nonconducting gap with infinite resistance. No matter what the voltage across an open circuit, Equation 27-6 shows that no current can flow. A common example of an open circuit is a switch in its "off" position. A **short circuit**, in contrast, has zero resistance. In a short circuit, current of any magnitude is possible without any voltage or electric field. A closed switch approximates a short circuit. An unintentional short circuit is often dangerous; short circuits in household wiring, for example, are a leading cause of fires because they allow large currents to flow, resulting in excessive heating. All real situations, with the exception of superconductors, lie between the extremes of short and open circuits.

We can understand how the macroscopic version of Ohm's law, Equation 27-6, follows from the microscopic version by considering the cylindrical conductor shown in Fig. 27-18. Suppose there is a uniform electric field **E** within the conductor. Then there must be a uniform current density given by Equation 27-4b:

$$\mathbf{J} = \frac{\mathbf{E}}{\rho},$$

where ρ is the resistivity of the material. Then the total current is

$$I = JA = \frac{EA}{\rho},$$

where A is the conductor's cross-sectional area. If the conductor has length ℓ then the potential difference between its ends is

$$V = E\ell,$$

FIGURE 27-18 A cylindrical conductor made from a material with resistivity ρ. The uniform electric field **E** drives a uniform current density **J**, giving a total current $I = JA$ through the conductor's cross-sectional area A. The electric field is associated with a potential difference V across the length ℓ of the conductor.

since the electric field is uniform. Solving to get $E = V/\ell$ and using the result in our expression for I gives

$$I = \frac{VA}{\ell\rho} = \frac{V}{(\rho\ell/A)}.$$

Comparison with the macroscopic Ohm's law, Equation 27-6, lets us identify the resistance with the term $\rho\ell/A$. Thus resistance depends on the resistivity ρ and the geometry—length and area—of the particular piece of material:

$$R = \frac{\rho\ell}{A}. \qquad (27\text{-}7)$$

We derived this expression for a conductor of uniform cross section; although Ohm's law still holds for a nonuniform conductor, integration is required to calculate the resistance (see Problems 71 and 72). Incidentally, Equations 27-6 and 27-7 both show that the units of resistance are ohms (Ω).

We emphasize again that neither the microscopic nor the macroscopic version of Ohm's law is fundamental, but rather that each is an empirical law that provides a good description of electrical conductivity in some materials. Table 27-2 summarizes the relation between microscopic and macroscopic quantities in Ohm's law.

TABLE 27-2 *Microscopic and Macroscopic Quantities and Ohm's Law*

MICROSCOPIC QUANTITY	MACROSCOPIC QUANTITY	RELATION
Electric field, $\mathbf{E}$	Voltage, V	$\mathbf{E}$ is defined at each point in a material; V is the integral of $\mathbf{E}$ over a path containing many points. In a uniform field, $V = E\ell$.
Current density, $\mathbf{J}$	Current, I	$\mathbf{J}$ is defined at each point in a material; I is the integral of $\mathbf{J}$ over an area containing many points. With uniform current density, $I = JA$.
Resistivity, ρ	Resistance, R	ρ is a property of a given material; R is a property of a particular piece of the material. In a piece of uniform cross section, $R = \dfrac{\rho\ell}{A}$.
Ohm's law $\mathbf{J} = \dfrac{\mathbf{E}}{\rho}$	Ohm's law $I = \dfrac{V}{R}$	Microscopic version relates current density to electric field at a point in a material of specified resistivity; macroscopic version relates current through to voltage across a given piece of material with specified resistance.

| EXAMPLE 27-5 | *Resistance and Ohm's Law* |

A copper wire 0.50 cm in diameter and 70 cm long is used to connect a car battery to the starter motor. What is the wire's resistance? If the starter motor draws a current of 170 A, what is the potential difference across the wire?

Solution

Table 27-1 gives 1.68×10^{-8} Ω·m for the resistivity of copper. Then Equation 27-6 gives

$$R = \frac{\rho\ell}{A} = \frac{(1.68 \times 10^{-8} \text{ Ω·m})(0.70 \text{ m})}{(\pi)(0.25 \times 10^{-2} \text{ m})^2} = 6.0 \times 10^{-4} \text{ Ω} .$$

This low resistance is necessary because the starter motor draws such a large current. We now apply Ohm's law to find the voltage across the wire:

$$V = IR = (170 \text{ A})(6.0 \times 10^{-4} \text{ Ω}) = 0.10 \text{ V} .$$

This is small compared with the 12 volts available from the car battery, showing that the wire is well chosen for this application (Fig. 27-19). A larger voltage difference—which would occur with a thinner wire—would mean a significant reduction in current to the motor.

FIGURE 27-19 Thick jumper cables are necessary to carry the large current used by a car's starter motor.

EXERCISE What should be the diameter of an aluminum wire that carries 15 A when the voltage across 1.0 m of the wire is 0.25 V?

Answer: 1.4 mm

Some problems similar to Example 27-5: 30, 35, 36, 38

FIGURE 27-20 Typical resistors. The large unit at the upper left is a wire-wound resistor that can dissipate 30 watts. At upper right is a variable resistor, in which a rotating contact can be positioned at different points on a coil of resistance wire. Colored stripes on the smaller resistors code their resistance values. The smallest resistor shown is a carbon-film resistor that can dissipate at most $\frac{1}{4}$ watt.

A **resistor** is a piece of conductor made to have a specific resistance. Heating elements used in electric stoves, hair dryers, irons, space heaters, and the like are all essentially resistors; so are the filaments of ordinary incandescent light bulbs. In all these cases the resistance—ultimately resulting from collisions between conduction electrons and lattice ions—provides a means of turning electrical energy into heat. Resistors are also used to set appropriate values of current and voltage in electronic circuits; for this purpose, they are made in a wide range of resistances. Resistors are rated not only by their resistance but also by the maximum power they can dissipate without overheating. Figure 27-20 shows some typical resistors.

Got It!

Figure 27-21 shows three pieces of wire. (1) and (2) are made from the same material, while (3) is made from a material with twice the resistivity. (a) Which has the greatest resistance? (b) If the same voltage is applied across each, which will pass the greatest current?

(1)   (2)   (3)

FIGURE 27-21 Which wire has the greatest resistance?

27-4 ELECTRIC POWER

Suppose a potential difference V is imposed across a resistor, driving a current I through it. The quantity V is the energy gained per unit charge as charge "falls" through the potential difference. In a resistor, that energy is dissipated through collisions, heating the material. So V is also the energy per unit charge going into heating. Meanwhile, the current I is the rate at which charge flows through the resistor. Then the energy per unit time—that is, the power dissipated in heating the resistor—is the product of the energy per unit charge times the rate at which charge moves through the conductor:

$$P = IV. \quad \text{(electric power)} \tag{27-8}$$

Although we developed Equation 27-8 for power dissipated as heat in a resistance, it holds any time electrical energy is being converted to some other form. If, for example, we measure 5 V across an electric motor and 2 A through the motor, we can conclude that the motor is converting electrical to mechanical energy at the rate of 10 W (actually somewhat less because some of the power goes into heating).

Solving Ohm's law for V and putting the result in Equation 27-8 gives

$$P = I^2 R; \tag{27-9a}$$

solving instead for I gives

$$P = \frac{V^2}{R}. \tag{27-9b}$$

These are useful forms when we know the resistance and either the voltage or current. Although they may seem contradictory, the forms are equivalent and both are equivalent to the more general Equation 27-8 for the case when current and voltage are related by Ohm's law.

Tip

Think about What's Constant Equation 27-9a seems to imply that power increases with increasing resistance, while Equation 27-9b seems to suggest the opposite. Both implications are correct—*if I* in Equation 27-9a and V in Equation 27-9b are constants. But there's no contradiction because I and V can't both be constant while the resistance R—the ratio of V to I—changes. In most cases we work with sources of constant voltage—for example, the power company promises to maintain 120 V between the two contacts in a household electrical outlet—and in this case the power dissipated is inversely proportional to the resistance we connect across that voltage, as shown by Equation 27-9b. See Question 20 for more on this point.

EXAMPLE 27-6	A Light Bulb

The voltage in typical household wiring is 120 V. How much current does a 100-W light bulb draw? What is the bulb's resistance under these conditions?

Solution

Solving Equation 27-8 for I gives

$$I = \frac{P}{V} = \frac{100 \text{ W}}{120 \text{ V}} = 0.833 \text{ A} .$$

Since we know the current, we can determine the resistance directly from Ohm's law:

$$R = \frac{V}{I} = \frac{120 \text{ V}}{0.833 \text{ A}} = 144 \ \Omega .$$

We could have bypassed the calculation of current and obtained R directly from Equation 27-9b:

$$R = \frac{V^2}{P} = \frac{(120 \text{ V})^2}{100 \text{ W}} = 144 \ \Omega .$$

Finally, had we known the current but not the voltage, we could have used Equation 27-9a:

$$R = \frac{P}{I^2} = \frac{100 \text{ W}}{(0.833 \text{ A})^2} = 144 \ \Omega .$$

The three approaches are equivalent. Use of Equation 27-9a or b merely amounts to solving symbolically for V or I before using Equation 27-8.

Because a light bulb filament undergoes a huge temperature change when turned on, its resistance is not independent of voltage and current. Our value 144 Ω holds when the light is on. When off, it is cool, and its resistance is much lower.

EXERCISE A power line has 0.20 Ω resistance per kilometer of length. If it carries 300 A of current, find (a) the voltage across 1.0 km of the wire and (b) the power dissipated in each km of wire.

Answers: (a) 60 V; (b) 18 kW

Some problems similar to Example 27-6: 44–46

The exercise with Example 27-6 suggests that high currents result in significant power loss even in wires of low resistance—as the quadratic dependence of power on current in Equation 27-9b confirms. That result has important implications for electric power transmission, showing that power companies are better off transmitting a given power $P = IV$ at high voltage and low current rather than vice versa. We'll examine this situation in more detail in Chapter 33, once we've seen how to effect transformations among different voltage levels (see the Application: Electric Power Distribution, on page 873).

The Kilowatt-Hour

The SI unit of power is the watt (W), defined as 1 J/s and thus reflecting the definition of power as energy per time. We could equally well have defined the watt first, then defined the Joule as 1 W·s. The **kilowatt-hour** (kWh), a unit commonly used for electrical energy, is in fact defined in an analogous way. Just as 1 joule is the energy used by a device consuming 1 watt for 1 second, so a kilowatt-hour is the energy used by a device consuming 1 kW for 1 hour. Your household electric bill shows your electrical energy consumption in kWh; your cost for 1 kWh of electrical energy is typically in the range from 5¢ to 15¢. Since there are 3600 s in an hour, 1 kWh is equal to (1000 W)(3600 s) = 3.6 MJ. Burning a 100-W light bulb for 1 hour, for example, uses 100 watt-hours or 0.1 kWh. Although it is usually used only with electrical energy, the kWh is a perfectly good non-SI unit for describing any kind of energy; for example, it's useful to remember that the energy content of a gallon of oil or gasoline is about 40 kWh. If all that energy could be converted to electrical energy, it could power a 100-W light bulb for 400 hours.

CHAPTER SYNOPSIS

Summary

1. **Electric current** is a net flow of electric charge, specified as the charge per unit time crossing a given area:

$$I = \frac{dq}{dt}.$$

If a material contains n free charges q per unit volume, moving with average speed v_d (called the **drift speed**), then the current through an area A perpendicular to the flow is

$$I = nqAv_d.$$

Current density is a vector specifying the current per unit area:

$$\mathbf{J} = nq\mathbf{v}_d.$$

2. **Conductivity**, σ, is a property of a given material describing the ratio of current density to electric field in the material:

$$\mathbf{J} = \sigma\mathbf{E}.$$

For **ohmic** materials conductivity is independent of electric field and this relation constitutes the microscopic version of **Ohm's law**.

Resistivity, ρ, is the inverse of conductivity.

3. Conduction mechanisms vary with material, and include:
   a. **Metals**, in which the charge carriers are free electrons. Metals are ohmic materials in which resistivity arises from collisions of free electrons with ions.
   b. **Ionic solutions** are conductors because of the presence of negative and positive ions that can move through the solution.
   c. **Plasmas** are ionized gases, often with extremely high conductivity. Plasmas are rare on Earth but comprise much of the matter in the universe.
   d. **Semiconductors** conduct only poorly in their pure state, but their electrical properties can be radically altered by doping with impurities. Charge carriers in semiconductors can be electrons, positive "holes," or both. Semiconductors are the basis of modern electronic technology.
   e. **Superconductors** exhibit zero resistivity at sufficiently low temperatures, and consequently require no electric field or potential difference to drive a current.

4. The macroscopic version of **Ohm's law** relates current I, voltage V, and **resistance** R:

$$I = \frac{V}{R}.$$

Resistance depends on resistivity and physical dimensions. For an object of resistivity ρ, length ℓ, and uniform cross-sectional area A, the resistance is $R = \rho\ell/A$.

5. The rate at which electrical energy is converted to other forms—i.e., the power, P—is the product of the current I through a device and the potential difference V across it:

$$P = IV.$$

In a resistance the electrical energy is converted to heat, and the power can be written in the two equivalent forms

$$P = I^2R \quad \text{and} \quad P = \frac{V^2}{R}.$$

Terms You Should Understand

(Pairs are closely related terms whose distinction is important; number in parentheses is chapter section where term first appears.)

electric current, current density (27-1)
ampere (27-1)
drift speed, drift velocity (27-1)
conductivity, resistivity (27-2)
ohm (27-2)
ohmic, nonohmic materials (27-2)
Ohm's law (27-2, 27-3)
plasma (27-2)
semiconductor (27-2)
superconductor (27-2)
resistance (27-3)
open circuit, short circuit (27-3)

Symbols You Should Recognize

I (27-1)	σ, ρ (27-2)
v_d (27-1)	Ω (27-2)
$\mathbf{J}$ (27-1)	R (27-3)

Problems You Should Be Able to Solve

calculating current from drift speed and material properties (27-1)
relating current and current density (27-1)
relating electric field, current density, and conductivity or resistivity (27-2)
calculating resistance from resistivity and dimensions (27-3)
using Ohm's law to relate current, voltage, and resistance (27-3)
calculating electric power (27-4)

Limitations to Keep in Mind

Ohm's law is not a universal statement but an approximate empirical relation that holds with high accuracy for some materials, such as metals.

QUESTIONS

1. If you physically move an electrical conductor, does this constitute a current?
2. In previous chapters we've stressed the absence of electric fields inside conductors in equilibrium. Why now do we allow such fields?
3. A wire carries a steady current. If the wire diameter decreases in the direction of the current, what happens to the current density?
4. When you talk on the telephone, your voice is heard almost immediately at the other end. Yet the drift speed of electrons in the telephone wire is on the order of millimeters per second. Explain the apparent discrepancy.
5. What is the difference between current and current density?
6. A constant electric field generally produces a constant drift velocity. How is this consistent with Newton's assertion that force results in acceleration, not velocity?
7. When caught in the open in a lightning storm, it is better to crouch low with the feet close together rather than lie flat on the ground. Why?
8. Why does the conductivity of a metal depend on the *square* of the electron charge?
9. What are *P*- and *N*-type semiconductors? Does either carry a net electric charge?
10. Good conductors of electricity are often good conductors of heat. Why might this be?
11. Why can current persist forever in a superconductor with no applied voltage?
12. A plasma contains equal densities of free electrons and protons. Do you expect each to contribute equally to the net current? Explain.
13. Does an electric stove burner draw more current when it is first turned on or when it's fully hot?
14. A person and a cow are standing in a field when lightning strikes the ground nearby. Why is the cow more likely to be electrocuted?
15. You put a 1.5-V battery across a piece of material and a 100-mA current flows through the material. With a 9-V battery the current increases to 400 mA. Is the material ohmic or not?
16. The resistance of a metal increases with increasing temperature, while the resistance of a semiconductor decreases. Why the difference?
17. How does the fact that the drift speed of electrons in a metal is much less than their thermal speed imply that metals are ohmic conductors?
18. A 50-W and a 100-W light bulb are both designed to operate at 120 V. Which has the lower resistance?
19. A power line with a small but nonzero resistance is used to carry 450 MW of electric power from a nuclear power plant to a city. Is it most efficient to transmit this power at high voltage and low current or vice versa? Explain.
20. Equation 27-9a suggests that no power can be dissipated in a superconductor, since $R = 0$. But Equation 27-9b suggests the power should be infinite. Which is right, and why?
21. A motor made with superconducting wire and frictionless bearings is turning at constant speed and doing no mechanical work. Make an argument showing that the motor cannot be drawing current, even if it's connected to a battery. What would happen if the motor started to do mechanical work, like lifting a weight?
22. The resistivity of a pure semiconductor decreases with increasing temperature. Speculate on what might happen if a fixed voltage were applied across a piece of such material.

PROBLEMS

Section 27-1 Electric Current

1. A wire carries 1.5 A. How many electrons pass through the wire in each second?
2. In an ionic solution, 4.1×10^{15} ions, each carrying charge $+2e$, pass to the right each second; 3.6×10^{15} ions, each carrying $-e$, pass to the left in the same time. What is the net current?
3. A 12-V car battery is rated at 80 ampere-hours, meaning it can supply 80 A of current for 1 hour before it becomes discharged. If you accidentally leave the headlights on until the battery discharges, how much charge moves through the lights?
4. The electron beam that "paints" the image on a computer screen contains 5.0×10^6 electrons per cm of its length. If the electrons move toward the screen at 6.0×10^7 m/s, how much current does the beam carry? What is the direction of this current?
5. Microbiologists measure total current due to potassium ions (K^+) moving through a cell membrane of a rock crab neuron cell to be 30 nA. How many ions pass through the membrane each second?
6. An ion channel in a cell membrane carries 2.4 pA when it's open, but it's only open 20% of the time. (a) What is the average current in the channel? (b) If the channel opens for 1.0 ms, how many singly ionized ions pass through it in this time?
7. The National Electrical Code specifies a maximum current of 10 A in 16-gauge (0.129 cm diameter) copper wire. What is the corresponding current density?
8. Each atom in aluminum contributes about 3.5 conduction electrons. What is the drift speed in a 0.21-cm-diameter aluminum wire carrying 20 A?
9. What is the drift speed in a silver wire carrying a current density of 150 A/mm²? Each silver atom contributes 1.3 free electrons.

10. The filament of the light bulb in Example 27-6 has a diameter of 0.050 mm. What is the current density in the filament? Compare with the current density in a 12-gauge wire (diameter 0.21 cm) supplying current to the light bulb.

11. A gold film in an integrated circuit measures 2.5 μm thick by 0.18 mm wide. It carries a current density of 6.8×10^5 A/m². What is the total current?

12. A piece of copper wire joins a piece of aluminum wire whose diameter is twice that of the copper. The same current flows in both wires. The density of conduction electrons in copper is 1.1×10^{29} m⁻³; in aluminum it is 2.1×10^{29} m⁻³. Compare (a) the drift speeds and (b) the current densities in each.

13. A plasma used in fusion research contains 5.0×10^{18} electrons and an equal number of protons per cubic meter. Under the influence of an electric field the electrons drift in one direction at 40 m/s, while the protons drift in the opposite direction at 6.5 m/s. (a) What is the current density? (b) What fraction of the current is carried by the electrons?

14. In Fig. 27-22, a 100-mA current flows through a copper wire 0.10 mm in diameter, a 1.0-cm-diameter glass tube containing a salt solution, and a vacuum tube where the current is carried by an electron beam 1.0 mm in diameter. The density of conduction electrons in copper is 1.1×10^{29} m⁻³. The current in the solution is carried equally by positive and negative ions with charges $\pm 2e$; the density of each ion species is 6.1×10^{23} m⁻³. The electron density in the beam is 2.2×10^{16} m⁻³. Find the drift speed in each region.

FIGURE 27-22 Problem 14.

15. In a study of proteins mediating cell membrane transport, microbiologists measure current versus time through the cell membranes of oocytes (nearly mature egg cells) taken from the African clawed frog, *Xenopus*. The measured current versus time is given approximately by $I = 60t + 200t^2 + 4.0t^3$, with t in seconds and I in nA. Find the total charge that flows through the cell membrane in the interval from $t = 0$ to $t = 5.0$ s.

Section 27-2 Conduction Mechanisms

16. The electric field in an aluminum wire is 0.085 V/m. What is the current density in the wire?

17. What electric field is necessary to drive a 7.5-A current through a silver wire 0.95 mm in diameter?

18. A cylindrical tube of sea water carries a total electric current of 350 mA. If the electric field in the water is 21 V/m, what is the diameter of the tube?

19. A 1.0-cm-diameter rod carries a 50-A current when the electric field in the rod is 1.4 V/m. What is the resistivity of the rod material?

20. There is a potential difference of 2.5 V between opposite ends of a 6.0-m-long iron wire. (a) Assuming a uniform electric field in the wire, what is the current density? (b) If the wire diameter is 1.0 mm, what is the total current?

21. Use Table 27-1 to determine the conductivity of (a) copper and (b) sea water.

22. The maximum safe current in 12-gauge (0.21-cm-diameter) copper wire is 20 A. What are (a) the current density and (b) the electric field under these conditions?

23. The free-electron density in aluminum is 2.1×10^{29} m⁻³. What is the collision time in aluminum?

24. A pure silicon crystal contains 4.9×10^{28} atoms/m³. At room temperature, the density of electron-hole pairs is 1×10^{16} m⁻³. In what concentration (aluminum atoms per silicon atom) must aluminum be added to give a conductivity 1000 times that of pure silicon? Assume that each aluminum atom contributes one extra hole, and that the conductivity is proportional to the density of charge carriers.

25. The resistivity of copper as a function of temperature is given approximately by $\rho = \rho_0[1 + \alpha(T - T_0)]$, where ρ_0 is the value listed in Table 27-1 for 20°C, $T_0 = 20°C$, and $\alpha = 4.3 \times 10^{-3}°C^{-1}$. Find the temperature at which copper's resistivity is twice its room-temperature value.

26. Manganin is an alloy whose resistivity hardly changes with temperature; its resistivity is given by the same equation as in the previous problem, but with $\rho_0 = 48.8 \times 10^{-8}$ Ω·m and $\alpha = 2.0 \times 10^{-6}°C^{-1}$. At what temperature does manganin have a resistivity 10 times that of copper?

Section 27-3 Resistance and Ohm's Law

27. What is the resistance of a heating coil that draws 4.8 A when the voltage across it is 120 V?

28. What voltage does it take to drive 300 mA through a 1.2-kΩ resistance?

29. What is the current in a 47-kΩ resistor with 110 V across it?

30. The "third rail" that carries the electric power to a subway train is a rectangular iron bar whose cross section measures 10 cm × 15 cm, as shown in Fig. 27-23. What is the resistance of a 5.0-km piece of this rail?

FIGURE 27-23 A "third rail" (Problem 30).

31. What current flows when a 45-V potential difference is imposed across a 1.8-kΩ resistor?

32. A silver and an iron wire of the same length and diameter carry the same current. How do the voltages across the two compare?

33. The presence of a few ions makes air a conductor, albeit a poor one. If the total resistance between the ionosphere and Earth is 200 Ω, how much current flows as a result of a 300-kV potential difference between Earth and ionosphere?

34. A uniform wire of resistance R is stretched until its length doubles. Assuming its density and resistivity remain constant, what is its new resistance?

35. A cylindrical iron rod measures 88 cm long and 0.25 cm in diameter. (a) Find its resistance. If a 1.5-V potential difference is applied between the ends of the rod, find (b) the current, (c) the current density, and (d) the electric field in the rod.

36. You have a cylindrical piece of material 2.4 cm long and 2.0 mm in diameter. When you attach a 9-V battery to the ends of the piece, a current of 2.6 mA results. Which material from Table 27-1 do you have?

37. How must the diameters of copper and aluminum wire be related if they are to have the same resistance per unit length?

38. Extension cords are often made from 18-gauge copper wire (diameter 1.0 mm). (a) What is the resistance per unit length of this wire? (b) An electric saw that draws 7.0 A is operated at the end of an 8.0-m-long extension cord. What is the potential difference between the wall outlet and the saw?

39. Engineers call for a power line with a resistance per unit length of 50 mΩ/km. What wire diameter is required if the line is made of (a) copper or (b) aluminum? (c) If the costs of copper and aluminum wire are $1.53/kg and $1.34/kg, which material is more economical? The densities of copper and aluminum are 8.9 g/cm³ and 2.7 g/cm³, respectively.

40. A solid, rectangular iron bar measures 0.50 cm by 1.0 cm by 20 cm. Find the resistance between each of the three pairs of opposing faces, assuming that the faces in question are equipotentials.

41. Corrosion at battery terminals results in increased resistance, and is a frequent cause of hard starting in cars. In an effort to diagnose hard starting, a mechanic measures the voltage between the battery terminal and the wire carrying current to the starter motor. While the motor is cranking, this voltage is 4.2 V. If the motor draws 125 A, what is the resistance at the battery terminal?

42. A clear plastic trough 2.5 cm wide, 5.0 cm high, and 15 cm long has the insides of its two long sides coated with metal, as shown in Fig. 27-24. If a 60-V potential difference is applied between these sides, how much current flows when the trough contains (a) pure water and (b) sea water?

FIGURE 27-24 Problem 42.

Section 27-4 Electric Power

43. A car's starter motor draws 125 A with 11 V across its terminals. What is its power consumption?

44. A 4.5-W flashlight bulb draws 750 mA. (a) At what voltage does it operate? (b) What is its resistance?

45. A watch uses energy at the rate of 240 μW. How much current does it draw from its 1.5-V battery?

46. An electric stove burner with 35 Ω resistance consumes 1.5 kW of power. At what voltage does it operate?

47. What is the resistance of a standard 120-V, 60-W light bulb?

48. Use the numbers from Problem 33 to find the electric power dissipation in Earth's atmosphere. If we could harness this power, would it make a dent in humanity's 10^{12}-W electric power consumption?

49. If the electrons of Problem 4 are accelerated through a potential difference of 10 kV, how much power must be supplied to produce the electron beam?

50. The "instant on" feature of all the television sets in the United States requires the continuous power output of a typical large power plant—about 1000 MW. If there are 10^8 TVs in the United States, how much current does the "instant on" circuit of each draw from the 120-V power line?

51. How much total energy could the 12-V battery of Problem 3 supply?

52. During a "brownout," the power line voltage drops from 120 V to 105 V. By how much does the thermal power output of a 1500-W stove burner drop, assuming its resistance remains constant?

53. Two cylindrical resistors are made from the same material and have the same length. When connected across the same battery, one dissipates twice as much power as the other. How do their diameters compare?

54. Your author's house uses approximately 110 kWh of electrical energy each week. If that energy is supplied at 240 V, what average resistance does the house present to the power line?

55. A 2000-horsepower electric railroad locomotive gets its power from an overhead wire with 0.20 Ω/km. The potential difference between wire and track is 10 kV. Current returns through the track, whose resistance is negligible. (a) How much current does the locomotive draw? (b) How far from the power plant can the train go before 1% of the energy is lost in the wire?

56. A 100% efficient electric motor is lifting a 15-N weight at 25 cm/s. If the motor is connected to a 6.0-V battery, how much current does it draw?

Paired Problems

(Both problems in a pair involve the same principles and techniques. If you can get the first problem, you should be able to solve the second one.)

57. Electrons in a fine silver wire 20 μm in diameter drift at 0.14 mm/s. What is the current in the wire? Each silver atom contributes 1.3 free electrons.

58. A potassium slab carries a current density of 470 kA/m², and the drift speed of the electrons is 0.20 mm/s. If the density of potassium is 860 kg/m³, what is the average number of free electrons contributed by each atom?

59. What is the resistance of a column of mercury 0.75 m long and 1.0 mm in diameter?

60. An integrated circuit design calls for a 470-Ω resistor. The resistor is to be 10 μm long, 1.4 μm wide, and 0.85 μm thick, with connections made at the ends 10 μm apart. Its resistivity is to be set by the appropriate amount of doping. What should that resistivity be?

61. A power plant produces 1000 MW to supply a city 40 km away. Current flows from the power plant on a single wire of resistance 0.050 Ω/km, through the city, and returns via the ground, assumed to have negligible resistance. At the power plant the voltage between the wire and ground is 115 kV. (a) What is the current in the wire? (b) What fraction of the power is lost in transmission?

62. What should be the power line voltage in the preceding problem if the transmission loss is not to exceed 2%?

63. A 240-V electric motor is 90% efficient, meaning that 90% of the energy supplied to it ends up as mechanical work. If the motor lifts a 200-N weight at 3.1 m/s, how much current does it draw?

64. An 8.5-kN elevator is powered by a 480-V electric motor that draws 24 A. If the motor is 85% efficient, how long does it take to lift the elevator 18 m?

Supplementary Problems

65. A metal bar has a rectangular cross section 5.0 cm by 10 cm, as shown in Fig. 27-25. The bar has a nonuniform conductivity, ranging from zero at the bottom to a maximum at the top. As a result, the current density increases linearly from zero at the bottom to 0.10 A/cm² at the top. What is the total current in the bar?

FIGURE 27-25 Problem 65.

66. Metallic copper (atomic weight 64, density 8.9 g/cm²) forms a crystal structure with copper atoms located at the corners of cubes. (a) Use the density and atomic weight to determine the distance between copper atoms. (b) Use your result, and the collision time from Example 27-4, to estimate the mean thermal speed of the electrons in copper. Consider τ to be the mean time between collisions.

67. General Motors' EV1 electric car has a mass of 1500 kg and is powered by 26 12-V batteries connected in series, for a total of 312 V. About 85% of the electrical energy from the batteries ends up as mechanical energy at the drive wheels. How much current do the batteries supply when the car is climbing a 10° slope at 45 km/h? Neglect frictional losses and air resistance.

FIGURE 27-26 General Motors' EV1 electric car is powered by 26 12-V batteries driving a 102 kW (137 horsepower) electric motor. It can accelerate from 0 to 60 mi/h in 9 s, and can travel up to 90 miles before recharging (Problem 67).

68. An immersion-type heating coil is connected to a 120-V outlet and immersed in a 250-ml cup of water initially at 10°C. The water comes to a boil in 85 s. What are (a) the power and (b) the resistance of the heater? Assume no heat loss, and neglect the mass of the heater.

69. A 100-Ω resistor of negligible mass is mounted inside a calorimeter. When a 12-V battery is connected for 5.0 min, the temperature inside the calorimeter rises by 26°C. What is the heat capacity of the calorimeter contents?

70. A parallel-plate capacitor has plates of 10 cm² area separated by a 1.0-mm layer of glass insulation with resistivity

$\rho = 1.2 \times 10^{13}$ Ω·m and dielectric constant $\kappa = 5.6$. The capacitor is charged to 100 V and the charging battery disconnected. (a) What is the initial rate of discharge (i.e., the current through the insulation)? (b) At this rate, how long would it take the capacitor to discharge fully? (The rate does not remain constant; more on this in the next chapter.)

71. Figure 27-27 shows a resistor made from a truncated cone of material with uniform resistivity ρ. Consider the cone to be made of thin slices of thickness dx, like the one shown; Equation 27-6 shows that the resistance of each slab is $dR = \rho\,dx/A$. By integrating over all such slices, show that the resistance between the two flat faces is $R = \rho\ell/\pi ab$. (This method assumes the equipotentials are planes, which is only approximately true.)

72. A circular pan of radius b has a plastic bottom and metallic side wall of height h. It is filled with a solution of resistivity ρ. A metal disk of radius a and height h is placed at the center of the pan, as shown in Fig. 27-28. The side and disk are essentially perfect conductors. Show that the resistance measured from side to disk is $\rho \ln(b/a)/2\pi h$.

FIGURE 27-28 Problem 72.

73. At some point in a material of resistivity ρ the current density is J. Show that the power per unit volume dissipated at that point is $J^2\rho$.

74. A thermally insulated container of sea water carries a uniform current density of 75 mA/cm². How long does it take to raise its temperature from 15°C to 20°C? Use the result of the preceding problem, and assume that both the specific heat (assumed the same as pure water) and the resistivity are constant over this range.

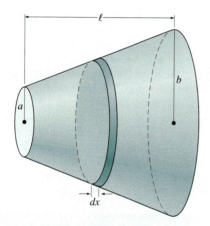

FIGURE 27-27 Problem 71.

Electric Circuits

This circuit board is a complex interconnection of electronic components, including resistors, capacitors, transistors, light-emitting diodes, and integrated circuits.

28-1 CIRCUITS AND SYMBOLS

An **electric circuit** is a collection of electrical devices, called **circuit elements**, connected by conductors. Most circuits include a source of electrical energy. You're most familiar with human-made electrical circuits, which range from simple flashlights to computers, but important circuits also exist in nature. Examples include nervous systems in living organisms and Earth's global atmospheric circuit, in which thunderstorms are the batteries and the atmosphere a resistor. Your study of electric circuits should prove immensely practical, for it will help you to understand and to use effectively and safely the growing myriad of electrical and electronic devices you encounter. Basic circuit knowledge can even help you design new devices and troubleshoot old ones.

Circuit symbols

Resistor Capacitor Source Voltmeter Switch
of emf

Ammeter Variable Variable Ground Fuse
resistor capacitor

FIGURE 28-1 Common circuit symbols.

FIGURE 28-2 Chemical reactions in this alkaline battery separate electric charges, resulting in a positive charge at the + end (left) and negative charge at the − end (right).

FIGURE 28-3 A gravitational analog of a source of emf. The person lifting the balls does work against the gravitational field **g** to maintain a steady flow of balls. This represents the energy conversion process in the emf, which does work lifting charge against the electric field. The balls roll down the ramp driven by the gravitational field. They bump into the pegs and dissipate their energy. The ramp and pegs are analogous to an external resistance connected across the emf.

It's often helpful to represent circuits symbolically. We do so using standard symbols for circuit elements, with lines to represent the wires connecting them. We usually assume that the wires are perfect conductors, so all points connected by wires alone are at the same potential; such points are electrically equivalent. Realizing this will greatly facilitate your interpretation of circuit diagrams! Figure 28-1 shows some common circuit symbols. With ActivPhysics you can "build" and simulate circuits using such symbols.

28-2 ELECTROMOTIVE FORCE

In the preceding chapter, we found that an electric field is necessary to drive a current in any conductor with nonzero resistance. But if we simply apply an electric field, say by putting excess charge on one end of the conductor, the charge will quickly redistribute itself until electrostatic equilibrium is reached and the electric field disappears. Somehow we must maintain the electric field, and with it the current, despite the tendency toward equilibrium. To keep current flowing through a conductor with nonzero resistance, we need to maintain a potential difference between the ends of the conductor. Otherwise the conductor would quickly come to electrostatic equilibrium, with no electric field to drive the current.

A device that can maintain a fixed potential difference and thus an electric field, despite the flow of current, is called a source of **electromotive force**, or **emf**. (This name, which has historical origins, is not accurate; emf is not a force but a potential difference.) Most sources of emf have two electrical contacts, or **terminals**, for connection to other circuit elements. A source of emf converts some other form of energy into electrical energy by separating charge to maintain the fixed potential difference between its two terminals. The circuit symbol for a source of emf is shown in Fig. 28-1. The most familiar example is a battery, in which chemical energy drives opposite charges to the two terminals (Fig. 28-2). Others include electric generators, which convert mechanical energy to electrical energy; photovoltaic cells, which convert sunlight; fuel cells, which "burn" hydrogen to produce electrical energy and water; and biological cell membranes, which separate charge to control the movement of ions into the cell.

When a source of emf is connected to an external circuit, current flows through the circuit from the emf's positive to the negative terminal. Energy conversion processes within the emf then "lift" charge against the internal electric field, boosting the charge's energy and thus maintaining a fixed voltage across the emf's terminals. The charge then "falls" through the external circuit, dissipating its energy in the circuit resistance. The process repeats as the charge returns to the negative terminal of the emf, and the result is a steady current and a constant voltage across the emf. Figure 28-3 shows a gravitational analogy for an emf with a resistance connected across it.

Electromotive force is quantified by the work per unit charge done as the emf "lifts" charge against the electric field. The units of emf are therefore volts. An **ideal source of emf**—one with no internal energy losses—maintains the same voltage across its terminals under all conditions. Real sources always have internal energy losses, so the terminal voltage may not equal the rated emf. We discuss this situation in the next section.

28-3 SIMPLE CIRCUITS: SERIES AND PARALLEL RESISTORS

In the circuit of Fig. 28-4 an ideal battery of emf $\mathcal{E}$ drives a current through the resistor R. How much current? The voltage across the battery is its emf $\mathcal{E}$. The battery is connected to the resistor by wires, assumed to have zero resistance. Because they have zero resistance, there is no potential difference across either wire. Therefore the voltage across the resistor is the same as the voltage across the battery, and we can immediately apply Ohm's law to find the current:

$$I = \frac{\mathcal{E}}{R}.$$

Energetically, this circuit is analogous to Fig. 28-3. Charge gains energy in the amount $\mathcal{E}$ joules per coulomb as it's "lifted" against the electric field inside the battery, then dissipates that energy in heating the resistor.

(a)

(b)

FIGURE 28-4 A circuit containing a battery and a resistor. (a) Physical circuit. (b) Schematic diagram, using the symbols of Fig. 28-1. Colored stripes on small resistors, like that shown here, code for the value of the resistance.

Tip

Don't Get Hung Up about Wires We assume the wires connecting circuit elements to be essentially perfect conductors—so it takes no potential difference between the ends of a wire to drive current through it. Thus all points on a wire are at the same potential, and are electrically equivalent. That means there are many ways to diagram the same circuit; as long as two components are shown as connected by a wire, that's all that matters. Of course real wires have some resistance, but if it's negligible compared with other resistances in the circuit, then we can approximate the wires as being ideal.

Series Resistors

Figure 28-5 shows a circuit containing two resistors in series. What's the current through these resistors? What's the voltage across each? Note that neither resistor is connected directly across the battery, so we can't argue that the voltage across either is the battery voltage. But we *can* argue that the current through the two resistors is the same. Why? Because the resistors are connected in series, so the only place for current to go after it flows through R_1 is through R_2. In a steady state, with no buildup of charge in the circuit, the current through both resistors—and, for that matter, through the battery as well—must be the same. This situation holds whenever circuit elements are in series:

12.1

DC Series Circuits

▌ **The current through each circuit element connected in series is the same.**

(a)

(b)

FIGURE 28-5 A battery and two resistors in series. (a) Physical circuit. (b) Schematic diagram.

If I is the current in the circuit of Fig. 28-5, then there must be a voltage $V_1 = IR_1$ across R_1 to drive the current through this resistor. Similarly, the voltage across R_2 is $V_2 = IR_2$. Thus, the voltage across the two resistors together is $V_1 + V_2 = IR_1 + IR_2$. But the battery is connected directly across this series combination, so we have

$$IR_1 + IR_2 = \mathcal{E},$$

or

$$I = \frac{\mathcal{E}}{R_1 + R_2}.$$

Comparison with Ohm's law in the form $I = V/R$ shows that the two resistors in series behave like an equivalent resistance equal to the sum of their resistances. In an obvious generalization to more resistors in series, we have

$$R_{\text{series}} = R_1 + R_2 + R_3 + \cdots \tag{28-1}$$

In other words, resistors in series add.

Given the current, we can use Ohm's law in the form $V = IR$ to solve for the voltage across each resistor:

$$V_1 = \frac{R_1}{R_1 + R_2}\mathcal{E} \tag{28-2a}$$

and

$$V_2 = \frac{R_2}{R_1 + R_2}\mathcal{E}. \tag{28-2b}$$

These expressions show that the battery voltage divides between the two resistors in proportion to their resistance. For this reason a series combination of resistors is called a **voltage divider**. Figure 28-6 depicts the voltages throughout the circuit of Fig. 28-5, and shows explicitly that the resistors divide the battery voltage.

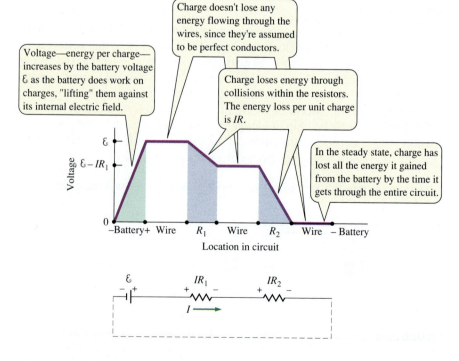

FIGURE 28-6 Voltages in the circuit of Fig. 28-5, with $V = 0$ at the negative battery terminal. Note that there is no potential difference across the wires, since they have negligible resistance, and that potential increases across the battery and decreases across the resistors. Can you tell from the graph which resistance is greater? (Here we've "unrolled" the circuit so we can clearly show the voltage as a function of position around the circuit. But remember that the circuit is a closed loop, so the left and right ends of the graph represent the same physical point, namely the negative battery terminal.)

Tip

How Does the Battery Know? How does the battery in Fig. 28-5 "know" how much current to supply? How does it even "know" there are two resistors, and what their values are? For the brief instant when the circuit is first connected, the battery doesn't "know," and some rather complicated action occurs as charge moves from the battery, encounters resistance, and accumulates to establish the potential differences across the resistors. During that brief time the current is not the same everywhere. But very soon the circuit reaches a steady state, with the same current throughout. Later in this chapter, when we consider circuits with capacitors, we'll look in more detail at the approach to the steady state; for now, our analyses assume that circuits have already reached that state.

EXAMPLE 28-1	*Designing a Voltage Divider*

A light bulb with a resistance (when on) of 5.0 Ω is designed to operate at a current of 600 mA. To operate this lamp from a 12-V battery, what resistance should you place in series with it?

Solution

Let R_2 be the lamp and R_1 the unknown series resistor. Since resistors in series add, the current through both resistors is $I = \mathcal{E}/(R_1 + R_2)$, which is supposed to be 600 mA or 0.60 A. Solving for R_1 gives

$$R_1 = \frac{\mathcal{E} - IR_2}{I} = \frac{12\ \text{V} - (0.60\ \text{A})(5.0\ \Omega)}{0.60\ \text{A}} = 15\ \Omega.$$

You can also get this result by noting that the light bulb's proper operating voltage is $V = IR_2 = (0.60\ \text{A})(5.0\ \Omega) = 3.0$ V. This is one-fourth of the battery voltage, so the light bulb's 5-Ω resistance should be one-fourth of the total. That makes the total 20 Ω, leaving 15 Ω for R_1.

EXERCISE Suppose that in Fig. 28-5 $R_1 = 470\ \Omega$. If the voltage across R_2 is 59% of the battery voltage, find R_2.

Answer: 676 Ω

Some problems similar to Example 28-1: 23–25

Got It!

What is the voltage across the resistor R at the top of each circuit shown in Fig. 28-7? In (*a*) the second resistor has the same resistance R, and in (*b*) the gap is an open circuit (infinite resistance). Think about it first, then verify your answers using Equations 28-2.

(*a*)   (*b*)   (*c*)

FIGURE 28-7 What's the voltage across the upper resistor in each circuit?

FIGURE 28-8 A 1.5-V calculator battery and a 1.5-V D-cell flashlight battery have the same voltage, but the internal resistance of the calculator battery is higher.

Real Batteries

What's the difference between the two 1.5-V batteries shown in Fig. 28-8? If both were ideal there would be no difference because both would maintain 1.5 V across their terminals no matter how much current was flowing. But these are real batteries. The rate at which internal chemical reactions take place limits the amount of current each can supply. Not surprisingly, the larger battery can supply more current.

We can model a real battery by considering it to be an ideal emf in series with an **internal resistance**, as shown in Fig. 28-9. Of course this is not how batteries are made since no manufacturer can make an ideal emf! The internal resistance is intrinsic to the battery, and there is no way to circumvent it. Some of the internal resistance is actual resistance of the battery materials, but most represents the limited rate of the chemical reactions that power the battery. The more powerful battery is the one with lower internal resistance; it approaches more closely the ideal of zero internal resistance and can therefore supply more current.

We can understand the effect of internal resistance by considering the circuit of Fig. 28-10. This is just the series circuit of Fig. 28-5, with R_1 the internal resistance R_{int} and R_2 the external resistance R_L. R_L is called the *load resistor* because it is the component to which we wish to deliver electric power; it is the electrical load on the battery. From Equation 28-2b we see that if R_{int} is small compared with R_L, then the voltage across the load resistance will be very close to the battery's internal emf. In this case the battery's behavior is nearly ideal, since it has essentially $\mathcal{E}$ volts across its terminals. But if we lower R_L so it becomes comparable with R_{int}, then the voltage across R_L decreases and the battery no longer seems ideal. As we lower R_L we draw more current from the battery. It takes a higher voltage to drive this current through the fixed resistance R_{int}, so more voltage drops across R_{int}, leaving less across R_L. Even if we short-circuit the battery terminals (which is not good for the battery!) we will not get infinite current—in fact, we will simply have

$$I = \frac{\mathcal{E}}{R_{int}}. \quad \text{(battery short-circuited)}$$

We conclude that a battery or other source of emf behaves more or less ideally depending on the size of its load resistance relative to its internal resistance. A calculator, for example, has a very high resistance and draws little current. It is quite happy with a small battery whose internal resistance, while high, is still small compared with the calculator's resistance. A car starter motor, on the other hand, draws a large current and thus requires a much larger battery with very low internal resistance.

FIGURE 28-9 A real battery modeled as an ideal emf in series with an internal resistance.

FIGURE 28-10 A real battery connected to an external load. Some voltage drops across the internal resistance, making the voltage across the battery terminals less than the battery's rated voltage.

EXAMPLE 28-2	*Starting a Car*

Your car's starter motor draws 125 A. The car has a 12-V battery, but while the starter motor is running the voltage across the battery terminals measures only 9.5 V. What is the internal resistance of the battery?

Solution

This circuit is just that of Fig. 28-10, with the starter being the load. With 9.5 V across the starter, there must be 2.5 V left across the internal resistance to make a total of 12 V. The current is the same throughout this series circuit, so 125 A is the current through R_{int}. Knowing current and voltage, we apply Ohm's law:

$$R = \frac{V}{I} = \frac{2.5 \text{ V}}{125 \text{ A}} = 0.020 \ \Omega.$$

A battery voltage between 9 and 11 volts is typical of a car being started. A battery voltage much below 9 volts usually indicates a weak battery, a defective starter motor, or very cold weather!

EXERCISE A 9-V battery has an internal resistance of 13 Ω. What is the maximum current that can be drawn from the battery if its terminal voltage is to remain above 8.0 V?

Answer: 77 mA

Some problems similar to Example 28-2: 12, 13, 15, 17

Parallel Resistors

Figure 28-11 shows two resistors in parallel, connected across an ideal battery. What is the equivalent resistance of this parallel combination? Since the two resistors are connected at top and bottom by ideal wires, the voltage across each must be the same. We made this point in Chapter 26 when we discussed parallel capacitors, and it's worth repeating here:

▌ The voltage across circuit elements in parallel is the same.

The parallel resistors are connected directly across the battery, so their common voltage is the battery emf $\mathcal{E}$. Applying Ohm's law then gives the current through each resistor:

$$I_1 = \frac{\mathcal{E}}{R_1}$$

and

$$I_2 = \frac{\mathcal{E}}{R_2}.$$

At the point marked A in Fig. 28-11, a current I brings in charge from the battery, while the currents I_1 and I_2 carry charge away. If charge is not to accumulate (see Problem 69), the incoming and outgoing currents must be equal; that is,

$$I = I_1 + I_2.$$

Using our expressions for the two resistor currents gives

$$I = \frac{\mathcal{E}}{R_1} + \frac{\mathcal{E}}{R_2} = \mathcal{E}\left(\frac{1}{R_1} + \frac{1}{R_2}\right).$$

Comparison with Ohm's law in the form $I = V/R$ shows that the equivalent resistance of the parallel combination is given by

$$\frac{1}{R_{parallel}} = \frac{1}{R_1} + \frac{1}{R_2}. \qquad (28\text{-}3a)$$

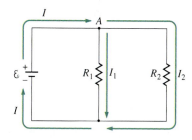

FIGURE 28-11 Parallel resistors connected across a battery. The resistor currents I_1 and I_2 sum to the battery current I.

12.2
DC Parallel Circuits

This result is readily generalized to more than two parallel resistors:

$$\frac{1}{R_{\text{parallel}}} = \frac{1}{R_1} + \frac{1}{R_2} + \frac{1}{R_3} + \cdots . \qquad (28\text{-}3b)$$

In other words, resistors in parallel add reciprocally. Equation 28-3b shows that the resistance of a parallel combination is always lower than that of the lowest resistance in the combination.

An analogy with highway traffic shows why this makes sense: adding a lane to a crowded highway eases congestion (i.e., lowers the overall resistance), allowing a greater traffic flow (e.g., a greater current). Putting one resistor in parallel with another is like adding an extra traffic lane.

When there are only two parallel resistors, we can rewrite Equation 28-3a using a common denominator to obtain

$$R_{\text{parallel}} = \frac{R_1 R_2}{R_1 + R_2} . \qquad (28\text{-}3c)$$

Note that *parallel* resistors combine in the same way as *series* capacitors, and vice versa.

Got It!

What's the equivalent resistance if you connect two identical resistors R (a) in series and (b) in parallel?

EXAMPLE 28-3 | *Parallel and Series Resistors*

You have available three 2.0-Ω resistors. What different resistances can you make by combining all three resistors?

Solution
Figure 28-12 shows the four possible combinations. Resistors in series add, so combination (*a*) has 6.0 Ω. Resistors in parallel reciprocally add, so combination (*b*) has

$$\frac{1}{R} = \frac{1}{2.0\ \Omega} + \frac{1}{2.0\ \Omega} + \frac{1}{2.0\ \Omega} = 1.5\ \Omega^{-1},$$

for a resistance of 0.67 Ω. Combination (*c*) has two resistors in series, giving 4.0 Ω. This 4.0-Ω combination is in parallel with 2.0 Ω, so Equation 28-3c gives

$$R = \frac{(2.0\ \Omega)(4.0\ \Omega)}{2.0\ \Omega + 4.0\ \Omega} = 1.3\ \Omega .$$

Finally, combination (*d*) has two resistors in parallel, giving 1.0 Ω. This combination is in series with 2.0 Ω, for a total of 3.0 Ω. Thus you can make combinations ranging from 0.67 Ω to 6.0 Ω with these three equal resistors.

EXERCISE A 270-Ω and a 470-Ω resistor are connected in parallel, and the combination is connected in series with a 150-Ω resistor. Find the equivalent resistance of this combination.

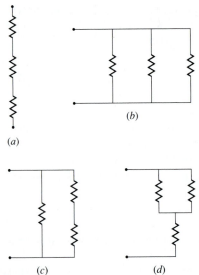

FIGURE 28-12 The four possible combinations of three equal resistors (Example 28-3).

Answer: 321 Ω

Some problems similar to Example 28-3: 16, 18, 19, 59, 60

Analyzing Circuits

Many circuits contain series and parallel combinations of basic circuit elements. We can simplify these circuits by treating each series or parallel combination as a single element, continuing the process until we can determine the voltages and currents throughout the entire circuit. Example 28-4 illustrates this procedure, which is similar to the way we dealt with capacitor combinations in Chapter 26.

12.3 ActivPhysics
DC Circuit Puzzles

EXAMPLE 28-4 | *Analyzing a Circuit*

In the circuit of Fig. 28-13, what is the current through the 2-Ω resistor?

FIGURE 28-13 Circuit for Example 28-4.

Solution

We approach this problem by simplifying the circuit until we can solve for something—in this case the total current. Then we reverse the process, analyzing the circuit details until we can solve for the quantity we want. Figure 28-14 shows the steps in simplifying the circuit. We get from the original circuit, Fig. 28-14a, to Fig. 28-14b by calculating the resistance of the parallel combination of 2 Ω and 4 Ω:

$$R_{\parallel} = \frac{(2.0\ \Omega)(4.0\ \Omega)}{2.0\ \Omega + 4.0\ \Omega} = 1.33\ \Omega.$$

Figure 28-14b shows three resistors in series, which add to get the single-resistor circuit of Fig. 28-14c. From here we can calculate the total current:

$$I = \frac{\mathcal{E}}{R} = \frac{12\ \text{V}}{5.33\ \Omega} = 2.25\ \text{A}.$$

Where does this current flow? It flows from the battery through the 1-Ω resistor, then on through the parallel combination of the 2-Ω and 4-Ω resistors, then through the 3-Ω resistor and back to the battery. It does *not* all flow through the 2-Ω resistor because there are two paths the current can take when it gets to the parallel combination. However, it does all flow through the parallel combination. We already found that this combination has a resistance of 1.33 Ω, and now we know that 2.25 A flows through the combination. So the voltage across the combination is

$$V = IR = (2.25\ \text{A})(1.33\ \Omega) = 2.99\ \text{V}.$$

This same voltage appears across each of the two resistors making up the parallel combination so the current through the 2-Ω resistor is

$$I = \frac{V}{R} = \frac{2.99\ \text{V}}{2.0\ \Omega} = 1.5\ \text{A}.$$

In solving for this current we effectively reversed our original simplification of the circuit, first considering Fig. 28-14b to get the voltage across the parallel combination, and then going to the full circuit to get the answer. At each stage we applied Ohm's law to solve for either a voltage or a current as needed.

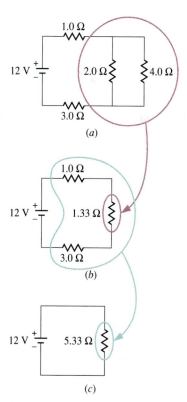

FIGURE 28-14 Simplifying the circuit by forming parallel and series combinations.

Don't Abuse Ohm's Law Ohm's law relates the voltage *across a resistor* to the current *through that resistor*. It does *not* relate arbitrary voltages and currents anywhere in a circuit. Just because there is a 12-V battery in Fig. 28-13, for example, does *not* mean that 12 V appears across the 2-Ω resistor. Be careful, too, with series and parallel combinations. As it stands, the only individual resistors in Fig. 28-13 in either series or parallel are the parallel pair of 2 Ω and 4 Ω. The 1-Ω and 2-Ω resistors are *not* in series because current flowing through the 1-Ω resistor need not all go through the 2-Ω resistor; some can go through the 4-Ω resistor instead. Equations 28-1 and 28-3 apply *only* to combinations that are strictly series or parallel, respectively.

FIGURE 28-15 What is the voltage across the 180-Ω resistor?

EXERCISE In Fig. 28-15, find (a) the current supplied by the battery and (b) the voltage across the 180-Ω resistor.

Answers: (a) 30 mA; (b) 2.9 V

Some problems similar to Example 28-4: 26–28

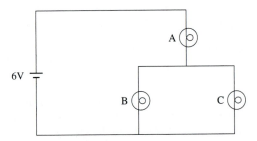

FIGURE 28-16 Which bulb will be brightest? What happens if you disconnect bulb C?

Got It!

Figure 28-16 shows a circuit with a 6-V battery and identical 6-V light bulbs— that is, bulbs that light at full brightness when there's a 6-V potential difference between their terminals. You can treat all three bulbs as being resistors. Which, if any, of the bulbs will be brightest? What will happen to the other two bulbs if you disconnect bulb C?

28-4 KIRCHHOFF'S LAWS AND MULTILOOP CIRCUITS

Some circuits cannot be simplified using series and parallel combinations. This often happens when there is more than one source of emf or when circuit elements are connected in complicated ways. In Fig. 28-17, for example, are

FIGURE 28-17 This circuit cannot be analyzed using series and parallel combinations.

resistors R_1 and R_2 in parallel? No, because R_3 separates their lower ends. Are R_1 and R_3 in series? No, because current flowing out the bottom of R_1 can go through either R_3 or R_4. Solving circuits that aren't reducible to series and parallel combinations usually requires more general techniques than we've used so far.

Kirchhoff's Laws

In Fig. 28-6 we looked at changes in electric potential around the loop comprising a simple series circuit. The result was an increase in potential at the battery, followed by decreases at both resistors that summed to the gain in the battery. If we count the increase as a positive change and the decreases as negative changes, we can state the following:

| **The sum of the voltage changes across all the circuit elements around any closed loop is zero.**

This statement is known as **Kirchhoff's loop law**, and it applies not just to Fig. 28-6 but to *any* closed loop in a circuit. The loop law is ultimately about energy conservation; it says that charge moving around a loop gains as much energy from batteries or other sources as it loses in resistors or other energy-conversion devices.

In analyzing parallel resistors with Fig. 28-11 we noted that the current flowing into point A must equal the total current flowing out through the two parallel resistors. This is really a statement about conservation of charge. It applies to any point in a circuit carrying steady currents since under steady-state conditions charge cannot build up or be depleted. The statement is most useful at a point where three or more wires join; such a point, like A in Fig. 28-11, is called a **node**. If we count currents flowing into a node as positive, and currents flowing out as negative, then the statement of charge conservation becomes the following:

| **The sum of the currents at any node is zero.**

This is **Kirchhoff's node law**.

Analyzing Multiloop Circuits

Even the most complex circuits can be analyzed using Kirchhoff's laws. Applying the laws amounts to writing equations expressing the loop law and node law for the distinct loops and nodes in the circuit. The number of equations needed is generally one less than the number of loops plus one less than the number of nodes; this is because the quantities in one loop and one node can be expressed entirely in terms of other loops and nodes, making one loop and one node equation each redundant. Here we give just two examples; electrical engineers take entire courses in circuit analysis using these laws.

12.5
Using Kirchhoff's Laws

<table>
<tr><td>**EXAMPLE 28-5**</td><td>*Rate the Resistor*</td></tr>
</table>

What power dissipation must resistor R_3 of Fig. 28-18a be able to tolerate?

Solution

This is a multiloop circuit in which none of the resistors are in either series or parallel with the others, so we need to use Kirchhoff's laws. In Figure 28-18b we identify three loops and two nodes. It's not always obvious in a multiloop circuit which way the currents flow, so in Fig. 28-18b we've arbitrarily assigned directions to the three currents. If an answer comes out negative, that just means the current is flowing in the opposite direction.

Here we need to know I_3 to find the power dissipation in R_3. Rather than solving symbolically, it will be simpler if we write the equations directly with their numerical values. Let's go counterclockwise around loop 1; starting at node A, the loop law becomes

$$6 - 2I_1 - I_3 = 0, \quad \text{(loop 1)}$$

where we've temporarily dropped the units. Starting from A and going clockwise around loop 2 (remember, the direction is arbitrary), we have

$$9 + 4I_2 - I_3 = 0. \quad \text{(loop 2)}$$

Why did we make the second term positive? Because this quantity is the voltage drop $I_2 R_2$ across the 4-Ω resistor R_2, and we're going through the resistor *against* the direction we've assigned for the current. This implies a voltage *increase* going in this direction. Finally, the node equation at node A reads

$$-I_1 + I_2 + I_3 = 0, \quad \text{(node A)}$$

where the first term is negative because I_1 is indicated as flowing *away* from the node. The equations for node B and loop 3 are redundant, so we're ready to solve the system. The node equation gives $I_1 = I_2 + I_3$; substituting in the loop 1 equation, we have $6 - 2I_2 - 3I_3 = 0$, or

$$I_2 = \tfrac{1}{2}(6 - 3I_3).$$

Finally, we can use this result in the loop 2 equation to get $9 + 2(6 - 3I_3) - I_3 = 0$ or

$$21 - 7I_3 = 0,$$

giving $I_3 = 3$ A. That this answer is positive indicates that I_3 is indeed upward in Fig. 28-18. The power dissipated in R_3 is therefore

$$P_3 = I_3^2 R_3 = (3 \text{ A})^2(1 \text{ }\Omega) = 9 \text{ W},$$

using Equation 27-9a. A 10-W resistor, the next larger size commercially available, would be just adequate.

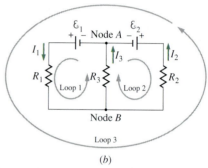

FIGURE 28-18 (a) A circuit that cannot be analyzed using series and parallel combinations. (b) There are 3 loops, 2 nodes, and 3 unknown currents whose direction assignments are, arbitrary (Example 28-5).

Tip

Getting Those Signs Right It really doesn't matter what direction you assign to the currents in a multiloop circuit, so don't spend a lot of time fretting about it; the algebra really will take care of signs. Here we found $I_3 = +3$ A, indicating that our upward direction in Fig. 28-18b was correct. But we found that I_2 was given by $I_2 = \tfrac{1}{2}(6 - 3I_3)$, so, with $I_3 = 3$ A, $I_2 = -1.5$ A. The minus sign says that I_2 is actually flowing downward through R_2, opposite the direction we assigned. Had we assigned a downward direction originally, we would have had a positive answer—but the physical situation would be identical.

The exercise with this example shows that I_2 goes to zero when $\mathscr{E}_2$ drops to 2 V. If $\mathscr{E}_2$ drops lower still, I_2 really will be upward—and then the algebra will give a positive answer.

It also doesn't matter what direction you choose to go around the circuit loops; changing direction will change the sign of *all* terms in the loop equation— leaving the mathematical content of the equation unchanged.

EXERCISE To what value should $\mathscr{E}_2$ in Fig. 28-18 be changed so that the current I_2 becomes zero?

Answer: 2.0 V

EXAMPLE 28-6	*The Cell Membrane: A Microbiological Circuit*

Figure 28-19 shows a simplified version of the so-called Hodgkin-Huxley model, which microbiologists use to describe the flow of ions through cell membranes (Hodgkin and Huxley won the 1963 Nobel Prize for physiology or medicine for development of this model). The batteries labeled $\mathcal{E}_K$, $\mathcal{E}_{Na}$, and $\mathcal{E}_L$ represent, respectively, the electrochemical effects of potassium, sodium, and other ions. (Sodium and potassium dominate, and currents associated with other ions constitute a small "leakage current"; hence the subscript L.) The resistances describe just that—the resistance the cell membrane offers to each ion species passing through it (although the resistances vary with electrical activity of the cell). Find an expression for the voltage across the cell membrane, V_M in Fig. 28-19, in terms of the other quantities shown.

Solution

V_M is clearly the sum of any one battery voltage minus the drop across the corresponding resistor, so we need the current in any one of the resistors. Here we'll go for I_K. We've identified two loops and one node, and marked them on Fig. 28-19, and have assigned directions to all three currents (obviously, they can't all be flowing upward, but once again we'll let the algebra handle that).

All the physics is in writing the loop and node equations. We'll start with the two loop equations, first going clockwise (an arbitrary choice) around loop 1, from the bottom; taking the sum of the voltage differences and setting it to zero gives

$$\mathcal{E}_K - I_K R_K + I_{Na} R_{Na} - \mathcal{E}_{Na} = 0 \, .$$

Here the voltage drop $I_{Na} R_{Na}$ across R_{Na} enters with a positive sign, since we're going *against* the direction we've assigned for the current through this resistor. Similarly, $\mathcal{E}_{Na}$ enters with a negative sign since we're going from the positive to the negative terminal of this battery—that is, in the direction of lower energy per unit charge. Similarly, going clockwise around loop 2 gives

$$\mathcal{E}_{Na} - I_{Na} R_{Na} + I_L R_L - \mathcal{E}_L = 0 \, .$$

Finally, we have an equation for node A. All our currents are assigned as flowing into the node, so

$$I_K + I_{Na} + I_L = 0 \, ,$$

which affirms what should be obvious already: that all three currents can't really flow upward, since all three can't have positive signs and satisfy this equation.

We now have three equations in the three unknown currents, and the rest is algebra. You can either solve and substitute for I_L, then I_{Na}, until you finally have one equation in the single unknown I_K, or you can use the methods of linear algebra if

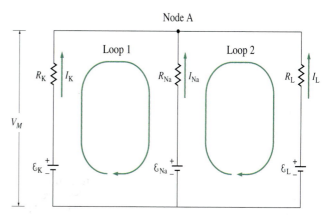

FIGURE 28-19 Simplified version of the Hodgkin-Huxley model for a biological cell membrane.

you've studied them. Either way, we'll skip the algebra and just give the result:

$$I_K = \frac{(\mathcal{E}_K - \mathcal{E}_{Na}) R_L + (\mathcal{E}_K - \mathcal{E}_L) R_{Na}}{R_K R_L + R_K R_{Na} + R_L R_{Na}} \, .$$

The membrane voltage itself is then $V_M = \mathcal{E}_K - R_K I_K$. In typical situations this quantity has a value measured in tens of millivolts.

EXERCISE In Fig. 28-20, find an expression for the current through R_3 in terms of the quantities listed.

FIGURE 28-20 What's the current through R_3?

Answer: $I_K = \dfrac{(\mathcal{E}_1 - \mathcal{E}_3) R_2 - (\mathcal{E}_2 + \mathcal{E}_3) R_1}{R_1 R_2 + R_1 R_3 + R_2 R_3}$, with a positive value indicating current from left to right in Fig. 28-20.

Some problems similar to Examples 28-5 and 28-6: 32–38

Strategy

Multiloop Circuits Examples 28-5 and 28-6 illustrate the strategy for solving multiloop circuits, for which simple series-parallel reductions don't work. Here we outline the steps in that strategy.

1. Identify circuit nodes and loops.
2. Assign directions to each current. The directions you assign are completely arbitrary, but once you assign them, use those directions consistently throughout.
3. Go around all but one of the loops you've identified, either clockwise or counterclockwise; the direction doesn't matter (you don't need to do all the loops because one is always redundant). As you go, sum the voltage changes across each circuit element you encounter, following these rules (all of which give the energy change per unit charge in traversing the circuit elements):
   a. For batteries traversed from the negative to the positive terminal, the voltage change is $+\mathcal{E}$, where $\mathcal{E}$ is the battery voltage.
   b. For batteries traversed from positive to negative, the voltage change is $-\mathcal{E}$.
   c. For resistors traversed in the direction you've assigned to the current I through the resistor, the voltage change is $-IR$.
   d. For resistors traversed opposite the direction you've assigned to the current I through the resistor, the voltage change is $+IR$.
   e. For other circuit elements (which we haven't yet encountered) use the characteristics of that element to determine the change in voltage across the element.
   For each loop, set the resulting sum to zero, reflecting the fact that charges going around a circuit gain as much energy as they lose. You then have one equation for each circuit loop but one.
4. For all but one node, sum the currents into the node and set the result to zero, reflecting the fact that there's no charge buildup in the steady state. Use the convention that a current whose assigned direction has it flowing *into* the node is positive, while a current flowing *out* of the node is negative. You now have one equation for each node but one; again, the last node is always redundant.
5. You now have as many equations as there are unknown currents. Solve these as a system of simultaneous equations. Use the algebraic signs of your answers to find the actual current directions. If an answer is positive, your assigned direction is correct; if not, the actual current direction is opposite what you've assigned.

28-5 ELECTRICAL MEASURING INSTRUMENTS

12.4

Using Ammeters and Voltmeters

Voltmeters

A **voltmeter** is a device that indicates the potential difference across its two terminals. The indication is usually by a digital readout, although older meters

FIGURE 28-21 (a) Most voltmeters today have digital displays, although (b) analog—or moving-needle—meters are still found in older instruments. (c) An oscilloscope is essentially a pair of voltmeters in which two different voltages are indicated by the horizontal and vertical deflection of an electron beam. When the horizontal voltage varies linearly with time, the result is a plot of the vertical voltage versus time.

(a)

use a moving needle, and oscilloscopes use the deflection of an electron beam (Fig. 28-21). Potential difference—voltage—is a property of two points, and therefore to measure the voltage between two points we connect the two terminals of the voltmeter to those points. So to measure the voltage across resistor R_2 in Fig. 28-22a, we connect the voltmeter *across* R_2, as shown. We do *not* break the circuit and insert the meter, as in Fig. 28-22b, for then we would not be measuring the voltage *across* the resistor; in fact, we would radically alter the circuit.

(b)

How good is our voltage measurement? That depends on two things: first, obviously, is the accuracy of the meter in reading the voltage across it. The second is more subtle: unless the voltmeter in Fig. 28-22 has infinite resistance, its presence will alter the circuit and change the voltage across R_2 from what it was without the meter. Even if the meter is perfectly accurate, it still will not read exactly what we want, namely the voltage that was across R_2 before we connected the meter.

An ideal voltmeter, therefore, should have infinite resistance so it doesn't draw any current and therefore doesn't alter the circuit it's measuring. Practically speaking, a voltmeter's resistance should be large compared with resistances in the circuit where the meter is being used. As a rough rule of thumb, you'll get accuracy within 1% if you use a meter whose resistance is 100 times the circuit resistance.

(c)

Older moving-needle meters (Fig. 28-21b) fall short of the ideal because they rely on current drawn from the circuit to produce a magnetic force that deflects the needle (more on magnetic force in the next chapter). Modern digital meters (Fig. 28-21a) contain amplifiers that greatly reduce current drawn from the circuit; typical meter resistances are around 10 MΩ and can easily be made much higher. Today's digital meters include amplifier, digital converter, and digital display in a single integrated-circuit package, making them the most economical, reliable, and accurate variety.

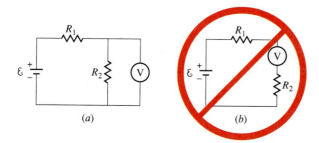

(a)   (b)

FIGURE 28-22 (a) Correct and (b) incorrect ways to measure the voltage across R_2.

EXAMPLE 28-7	*Voltmeters*

You wish to measure the voltage across the 40-Ω resistor of Fig. 28-23. What reading would an ideal voltmeter give? A voltmeter with a resistance of 1000 Ω?

Solution

An ideal voltmeter has infinite resistance and therefore would not alter the circuit, which is a simple voltage divider. Applying Equation 28-2b to this divider circuit gives the voltage across the 40-Ω resistor:

$$V_{40} = \frac{(40\ \Omega)(12\ \text{V})}{80\ \Omega\ +\ 40\ \Omega} = 4.0\ \text{V} .$$

Because the meter is connected in parallel with the resistor, this is also the voltage read by the meter.

With the nonideal voltmeter in place, the circuit becomes that of Fig. 28-24. The meter and 40-Ω resistor form a parallel combination whose resistance is given by Equation 28-3c:

$$R_{\parallel} = \frac{(40\ \Omega)(1000\ \Omega)}{40\ \Omega\ +\ 1000\ \Omega} = 38.5\ \Omega .$$

The circuit now looks like a voltage divider with $R_{\parallel}$ the lower resistor. Applying Equation 28-2b to this circuit gives

FIGURE 28-23 What is the voltage across the 40-Ω resistor?

FIGURE 28-24 A nonideal voltmeter alters the circuit, lowering the overall resistance.

$$V_{\parallel} = \frac{(38.5\ \Omega)(12\ \text{V})}{80\ \Omega\ +\ 38.5\ \Omega} = 3.9\ \text{V} .$$

This $V_{\parallel}$ is the voltage across the parallel combination consisting of the meter and 40-Ω resistor. Since the voltage across parallel circuit elements is the same, $V_{\parallel}$ is both the meter reading and the voltage across the 40-Ω resistor. And this value is 0.10 V—about 2.5%—lower than the value indicated by an ideal voltmeter.

EXERCISE A 100-kΩ resistor and a 150-kΩ resistor are in series, with a 250-V potential difference across the combination. A digital meter with a 3-significant-digit display and 1.0-MΩ resistance is used to measure the voltage across the 150-kΩ resistor. (a) What does it read? (b) By what percentage does this reading differ from that of an ideal voltmeter?

Answers: (a) 142 V; (b) 5.3%

Some problems similar to Example 28-7: 39, 40, 41, 61

Ammeters

An **ammeter** measures the current flowing *through* itself. To measure the current through a circuit element it is necessary to break the circuit and insert the ammeter in series with that element (Fig. 28-25); only then will all the current through the element also go through the meter. Connecting the meter across the resistor in Fig. 28-25 would be wrong, for then the current through the resistor would not be going through the meter.

FIGURE 28-25 An ammeter goes in series with the circuit element whose current it is to measure. It doesn't matter whether the meter goes (*a*) before or (*b*) after the circuit element, in this case the resistor *R*. (*c*) Connecting it across the resistor is incorrect, since then the resistor current does not flow through the meter. In fact, this connection would probably destroy the meter!

(*a*)

(*b*)

(*c*)

What electrical properties should the ammeter have so it doesn't alter the circuit in which it is connected? If the meter had any resistance, then the total resistance of the circuit would increase with the meter connected in series. This in turn would decrease the current, resulting in an incorrect reading. We conclude that an ideal ammeter should have zero resistance. In practice, ammeter resistance should be much lower than typical resistances in the circuit being measured.

Tip

Watch Your Language When Connecting Meters A voltmeter measures potential difference *between* two points; hence, we connect it *across*—i.e., in parallel with—the circuit element whose voltage we wish to measure. An ammeter measures the current *through* itself; hence, we connect it in *series* with the circuit element whose current we wish to measure. If you get used to voltages appearing *across* things and currents flowing *through* them, you'll have no trouble connecting meters. But if you insist on talking about "the voltage through" something, then you'll be unable to hook up meters accurately or safely. The ways to connect meters, and the words *across* for voltage and *through* for current, go right back to the definitions of potential difference as a property of two points and of current as a flow.

FIGURE 28-26 A simple ohmmeter consists of a known emf and an ammeter. When an unknown resistance is connected across the pair, its resistance may be determined from Ohm's law in the form $R = \mathcal{E}/I$.

Ohmmeters and Multimeters

Often we would like to measure the resistance of a particular circuit element. We can do this by connecting a source of known voltage in series with an ammeter and the unknown resistance, as in Fig. 28-26. Knowing the voltage and measuring the current then allows us to calculate the unknown resistance. A meter used for this purpose can be calibrated directly in ohms even though it is really measuring current; it is then called an **ohmmeter**.

The functions of voltmeter, ammeter, and ohmmeter are often combined in a single instrument called a **multimeter**. Multimeters include switches for selecting the quantity and range to be measured, and may be either analog or digital. Figure 28-27 shows a modern digital multimeter, or DMM.

Potentiometric Measurement

An elegant way to measure voltage is to compare the unknown voltage with an accurate standard, in much the same way that a pan balance weighs an unknown mass by balancing it against standard masses. Figure 28-28 shows how this scheme works. An accurately known emf $\mathcal{E}_0$ is connected across a resistor along which a sliding contact moves, forming a variable voltage divider in which the position of the sliding contact determines the voltage. The output of this voltage divider—called a **potentiometer**—is connected to the unknown voltage through a meter. The potentiometer is adjusted until the meter reads zero, at which point the potentiometer voltage—which can be read off its calibrated dial—must equal the unknown voltage. The great virtue of this method is that when the system is at null—the condition where source and unknown voltages are equal—then there is no current being drawn from the unknown regardless of the meter resistance, and therefore the method has, in principle, no effect on the circuit being measured.

FIGURE 28-27 This digital multimeter measures voltage, current, and resistance.

FIGURE 28-28 Potentiometric voltage measurement compares the unknown voltage with an accurately known voltage.

In the past, potentiometric measurements were made with circuits like that of Fig. 28-28, with special batteries of precisely known emf and accurately calibrated potentiometers. Manual adjustment was used to achieve the null condition. Today, nulling is accomplished electronically or electromechanically through a process known as negative feedback. Circuits using the potentiometric technique are the basis of many powerful measurement and control devices.

28-6 CIRCUITS WITH CAPACITORS

So far we've considered only circuits in which current and voltage are steady in all components. When you turn on a flashlight, for example, current starts to flow almost immediately through the bulb, batteries, and connecting metal parts. The current continues to flow steadily until you turn off the switch.

With a capacitor in a circuit, this picture changes. Circuit quantities change more gradually because of the capacitor. Why is this? Recall that a capacitor is a pair of insulated conductors that stores electrical energy when opposite charges are put on the conductors. A capacitor is characterized by its capacitance

$$C = \frac{Q}{V},$$

where Q is the magnitude of the charge on either conductor and V the voltage between the conductors. (See Section 26-4 for a review of capacitors.) Because charge and voltage are proportional in a capacitor, a change in a capacitor's voltage requires a change in its charge. In a circuit, a capacitor's charge changes only when current flows through the wires connecting the capacitor plates to the rest of the circuit. The magnitude of the current is the rate at which charge enters or leaves the capacitor. Since the current in any real circuit is finite, the charge on the capacitor cannot change instantaneously. But a capacitor's voltage is proportional to its charge, so:

❚ **The voltage across a capacitor cannot change instantaneously.**

This simple statement is the key to understanding circuits containing capacitors, so make sure you're clear on what it means. It says that you'll never see the voltage on a capacitor jump abruptly from one value to a different one; mathematically, capacitor voltage V_C must be a continuous function of time, with its derivative always finite. Just how rapidly the voltage can change depends on capacitance and other circuit quantities, as we'll soon see.

We now consider a simple circuit containing a resistor and a capacitor, and therefore called an **RC circuit**. *RC* circuits are ubiquitous, appearing everywhere from microbiological structures to stereo amplifiers to giant energy storage systems. We examine separately the two cases in which the capacitor is (1) charging and (2) discharging.

The *RC* Circuit: Charging

Consider the circuit of Fig. 28-29. The capacitor is initially uncharged, so the voltage across it is zero. What happens when we close the switch?

FIGURE 28-29 An *RC* circuit. The switch is closed at time $t = 0$.

The switch connects the left end of the resistor to the battery's positive terminal, so the left end of the resistor goes to $\mathscr{E}$ volts (here we take the zero of potential at the battery's negative terminal). The right end of the resistor is at the same voltage as the upper capacitor plate. But the voltage across the capacitor cannot change instantaneously, and therefore remains zero just after the switch is closed. With the capacitor plates both at zero volts, the full battery voltage $\mathscr{E}$ appears across the resistor. With $\mathscr{E}$ volts across the resistor, there must be a current $I = \mathscr{E}/R$ through the resistor. This current cannot flow "through" the capacitor but serves instead to pile positive charge on the upper plate, negative charge on the lower. The same current I flows everywhere except in the insulated gap between the capacitor plates.

Now that current is flowing, charge accumulates on the capacitor, and the capacitor voltage increases in proportion to this charge. As the capacitor voltage rises, the resistor voltage falls because the voltage across the series combination of resistor and capacitor is the battery voltage $\mathscr{E}$. But the current through the resistor is proportional to the resistor voltage, so the resistor current falls as well. This in turn decreases the *rate* at which charge accumulates on the capacitor plates, lowering the rate at which the capacitor voltage increases. The voltage across the capacitor continues to increase, and the current through the resistor to decrease, but at an ever slower rate.

What happens if we wait a long time? As the capacitor voltage approaches the battery voltage, the voltage across the resistor, hence the current through the resistor, and therefore the rate of charge buildup on the capacitor, all become very small. The whole system tends more and more slowly toward a final state in which the capacitor is charged to the full battery voltage and the current in the circuit is zero. Figure 28-30 summarizes the interplay among current, charge, and voltage.

We can analyze this circuit quantitatively using the loop law. Going clockwise around the loop, we first encounter a voltage increase $\mathscr{E}$ across the battery, then a drop IR across the resistor, then a drop V_C from the upper to lower capacitor

12.6
Capacitance

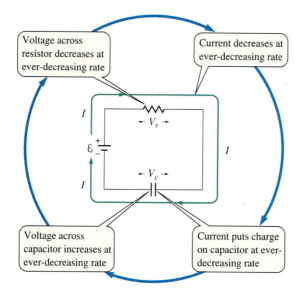

FIGURE 28-30 Interrelationships among circuit quantities in a charging *RC* circuit.

FIGURE 28-31 Voltage changes in a charging RC circuit. Since they sum to zero, the loop equation for this circuit is $\mathcal{E} - (IR) - (Q/C) = 0$.

plate (Fig. 28-31). But the definition of capacitance gives $V_C = Q/C$, so the loop equation becomes

$$\mathcal{E} - IR - \frac{Q}{C} = 0.$$

This equation contains the two unknown quantities I and Q. Can we relate them? Yes, because the current is the rate at which charge is accumulating on the capacitor. That is:

$$I = \frac{dQ}{dt}.$$

To use this relation, we take the time derivative of the loop equation:

$$-R\frac{dI}{dt} - \frac{1}{C}\frac{dQ}{dt} = 0.$$

The battery voltage $\mathcal{E}$ does not appear in this differentiated equation because it is constant and thus its derivative is zero. Using $I = dQ/dt$ and rearranging the equation slightly gives

$$\frac{dI}{dt} = -\frac{I}{RC}. \tag{28-4}$$

This equation shows that the rate of change of current is proportional to the current itself, expressing mathematically what Fig. 28-30 shows schematically. Equations like this arise whenever the rate of change of a quantity is proportional to the quantity itself. Population growth, the increase of money in a bank account, and the decay of a radioactive element are all described by similar equations.

Like the equation for simple harmonic motion in Chapter 15, Equation 28-4 is a *differential* equation, so called because the unknown quantity I occurs in a derivative. The solution to a differential equation is not a single number but rather a function expressing the relation between the unknown quantity—in this case current—and the independent variable—in this case time. We can solve this particular differential equation by multiplying both sides by dt/I, in order to collect all terms involving I on one side of the equation. This gives

$$\frac{dI}{I} = -\frac{dt}{RC}.$$

We then integrate both sides, noting that RC is constant:

$$\int_{I_0}^{I} \frac{dI}{I} = -\frac{1}{RC}\int_{0}^{t} dt,$$

where $I_0 = \mathcal{E}/R$ is the initial current at the time $t = 0$ just after the switch is closed and where the integration runs from $t = 0$ to some arbitrary time t. The integral on the left is just the natural logarithm, and that on the right is just t. Then we have

$$\ln(I/I_0) = -\frac{t}{RC},$$

where we used $\ln I - \ln I_0 = \ln(I/I_0)$. To get an equation for I we exponentiate both sides, recalling that $e^{\ln x} = x$. This gives

$$\frac{I}{I_0} = e^{-t/RC},$$

or, since $I_0 = \mathcal{E}/R$,

$$I = \frac{\mathcal{E}}{R} e^{-t/RC}. \qquad (28\text{-}5)$$

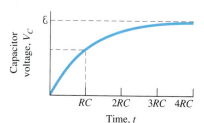

Thus the current in the circuit decreases exponentially with time, in agreement with our qualitative analysis.

What about the capacitor voltage? The capacitor and resistor voltages must add to the battery voltage $\mathcal{E}$, and the resistor voltage is just $V_R = IR$, or

$$V_R = \mathcal{E}e^{-t/RC}.$$

Thus the capacitor voltage is $V_C = \mathcal{E} - V_R$, or

$$V_C = \mathcal{E}(1 - e^{-t/RC}). \qquad (RC \text{ circuit, charging}) \qquad (28\text{-}6)$$

Equation 28-6 shows the capacitor voltage starting at zero, and rising rapidly at first but with its rate of rise ever slowing, as it gradually approaches the battery voltage $\mathcal{E}$—just as we reasoned in our qualitative analysis. Figure 28-32 shows plots of capacitor voltage, charge, and current using the equations we've just derived.

When is the capacitor fully charged? Never, according to our equations! But the rate at which it approaches full charge is determined by the quantity RC that appears in Equations 28-5 and 28-6. (Problem 45 will convince you that this quantity has the units of time.) Called the **time constant**, RC is a characteristic time for changes to occur in a circuit containing a capacitor. Equation 28-6 shows that in one time constant, the voltage rises to $\mathcal{E}(1 - 1/e)$, or to about two-thirds of the battery voltage. A practical rule of thumb says that in five time constants ($t = 5RC$) a capacitor is 99% charged (see Problem 47). The RC time constant clarifies our statement that the voltage across a capacitor cannot change instantaneously. We can now say that in times small compared with the time constant, the voltage across a capacitor cannot change appreciably. On the other hand, if we wait a long time—many time constants—we will find essentially no current flowing to the capacitor. We've shown quantitatively the role of the time constant RC by marking the time in units of RC on Fig. 28-32.

Resistors and capacitors are available in a wide range of values, so practical values for RC span many orders of magnitude. RC circuits with time constants from microseconds to hours are widely used in electronic devices to control the rates at which electrical quantities vary. For example, circuits with RC many times the sixtieth-of-a-second period of standard AC power are used to produce steady, direct current power for audio and video equipment. Bass and treble controls, or equalizers in more sophisticated audio systems, are simply variable resistances in RC circuits; changing the resistance changes the time constant and therefore the way the circuit handles rapidly changing audio signals. Sometimes, though, the time constant can be a nuisance. Capacitance in audio systems can limit high-frequency response, decreasing the quality of music reproduction. As computers reach speeds in the GHz range—meaning basic operations occur a billion times a second—even tiny, unintentional RC time constants associated with the resistance of wires and the capacitance of nearby conductors must be eliminated.

FIGURE 28-32 Time dependence of capacitor voltage, capacitor charge, and current in a charging RC circuit. In one time constant RC the capacitor voltage and charge rise to about 2/3 (actually $1 - 1/e$) of their final value, while the current drops to about 1/3 (actually $1/e$) of its initial value.

FIGURE 28-33 A discharging RC circuit.

The RC Circuit: Discharging

Suppose we connect a charged capacitor across a resistor, as shown in Fig. 28-33. If the capacitor voltage is initially V_0, then when the circuit is connected this voltage will drive a current $I_0 = V_0/R$ through the resistor. This current transfers charge from the positive to the negative capacitor plate, lowering the charge on the capacitor. Since capacitor charge and voltage are proportional, the capacitor voltage drops, too. So, therefore, does the current, and therefore the rate at which the capacitor discharges. We therefore expect both the voltage and current in this circuit to decay toward zero. In terms of energy, that happens because the energy stored in the capacitor's electric field is gradually dissipated as heat in the resistor.

The loop equation for Fig. 28-33 is particularly simple; going clockwise, we have

$$\frac{Q}{C} - IR = 0 \,,$$

where the two terms are the voltage changes across the capacitor and resistor, respectively. Since we've indicated positive current in Fig. 28-33 in the direction that would *reduce* the capacitor charge Q, the rate of change dQ/dt and the current must have opposite signs: $I = -dQ/dt$. Differentiating our loop equation and substituting this expression for I gives

$$\frac{dI}{dt} = -\frac{I}{RC} \,.$$

This is Equation 28-4; the solution is therefore Equation 28-5, but with $I_0 = V_0/R$ instead of $\mathscr{E}/R$:

$$I = \frac{V_0}{R} e^{-t/RC} \,. \tag{28-7}$$

12.7

Circuit Time Constant

In this circuit the capacitor and resistor voltage are the same since the two are in parallel. Since the resistor voltage and current are proportional, the voltage across the capacitor and resistor is

$$V = V_0 e^{-t/RC} \,. \qquad \text{(RC circuit, discharging)} \tag{28-8}$$

Equations 28-7 and 28-8 show that the capacitor discharges with the same characteristic time constant RC that governs its charging.

EXAMPLE 28-8	*A Camera Flash*

In Chapter 26 we considered an electronic camera flash using a capacitor to store energy. A particular camera flashtube obtains its energy from a 150-μF capacitor and requires 170 V to fire. If the capacitor is charged by a 200-V source through a 30-kΩ resistor, how long must the photographer wait between flashes? What is the peak power drawn from the power source? Assume the capacitor is fully discharged during a flash.

Solution

The time between flashes is the time it takes the capacitor voltage to reach 170 V. To find this time, we solve Equa-

tion 28-6 for the exponential term that contains the time:

$$e^{-t/RC} = 1 - \frac{V_C}{\mathscr{E}} \,.$$

We then take the natural logarithm of both sides, recalling that $\ln e^x = x$, so

$$-\frac{t}{RC} = \ln\left(1 - \frac{V_C}{\mathscr{E}}\right) \,.$$

Solving for t and setting $V_C = 170$ V, $\mathscr{E} = 200$ V, $R = 30$ kΩ, and $C = 150$ μF gives

$$t = -RC \ln\left(1 - \frac{V_C}{\mathcal{E}}\right)$$

$$= -(30 \times 10^3 \ \Omega)(150 \times 10^{-6} \ \text{F}) \ln\left(1 - \frac{170 \ \text{V}}{200 \ \text{V}}\right) = 8.5 \ \text{s}.$$

Problem 74 explores the question of power in this circuit, and shows that energy from the source cannot all end up in the capacitor.

EXERCISE If the flash lamp in Example 28-8 has an effective resistance of 10 Ω, how long does it take the capacitor voltage to drop to 100 V as it discharges through the lamp?

Answer: 0.80 ms

Some problems similar to Example 28-8: 47–49, 51

RC Circuits: Long- and Short-Term Behavior

It's not always necessary to solve exponential equations in analyzing RC circuits. If we're concerned only with times short compared with the time constant, it suffices to remember that the voltage across a capacitor cannot change instantaneously. And after many time constants have passed a capacitor has essentially reached its final voltage, and there will be no current flowing to it. These two conditions are sufficient to analyze circuits on short and long time scales.

EXAMPLE 28-9	*Long- and Short-Time Behavior of an RC Circuit*

In Fig. 28-34*a* the capacitor is initially uncharged. What is the current through R_1 the instant after the switch is closed? A long time after the switch has been closed?

Solution
The capacitor voltage cannot change instantaneously, so just after the switch is closed there can be no voltage across the capacitor and therefore none across R_2. Then the full battery voltage is across R_1, so the current in R_1 is $\mathcal{E}/R_1$. After a very long time the capacitor will be fully charged (to what voltage? —see the exercise below), and no current will flow into it. The capacitor then acts like an open circuit, and we simply have two resistors in series. The current in each is $\mathcal{E}/(R_1 + R_2)$.

How simple this example is! The uncharged capacitor has no voltage across it, so it acts instantaneously like a short circuit. The fully charged capacitor has no current into it, so it acts like an open circuit. To solve the problem we could simply re-draw the circuit, once with the capacitor replaced by a wire (Fig. 28-34*b*), the second time with the capacitor simply erased from the circuit diagram (Fig. 28-34*c*). Only if we wanted to know what was happening at intermediate times would we have to resort to the solution of an equation describing the circuit.

EXERCISE When the capacitor in Example 28-9 is fully charged, what will be the voltage across it?

Answer: $\mathcal{E}R_2/(R_1 + R_2)$

Some problems similar to Example 28-9: 55–57

(a)

(b)

(c)

FIGURE 28-34 (*a*) A circuit with two resistors and a capacitor. (*b*) Just after the switch is closed the voltage across the capacitor is still zero, so the capacitor acts like a short circuit. (*c*) Long after the switch is closed the capacitor is fully charged. No more current flows into it, so it acts like an open circuit.

FIGURE 28-35 What's the current in the 2-kΩ resistor when a charged capacitor is connected between points A and B?

Got It!

A capacitor is charged to 12 V and then connected between points A and B in Fig. 28-35, with its positive plate to A. What is the current through the 2-kΩ resistor (a) immediately after the capacitor is connected and (b) a long time (i.e., many time constants) after it's connected?

28-7 ELECTRICAL SAFETY

Whether you find yourself in a laboratory hooking up electronic equipment, or in a hospital connecting instrumentation to a patient, or on a job designing electrical devices, or simply at home plugging in appliances and tools, you should be concerned with electrical safety.

Everyone knows enough to be wary of "high voltage." People with a little more electrical sophistication are fond of saying "it isn't the voltage but the current that kills you." In fact, both points of view are partially correct. Current through the body is dangerous, but as with any resistor it takes voltage to drive that current.

Table 28-1 shows typical effects of electric currents introduced into the body through skin contact. A primary danger is disturbance of the biologically generated electrical signals that pace heartbeat; this is reflected in the lethal zone of 100 to 200 mA at which currents the heart is thrown into fibrillation—uncontrolled spasms of the cardiac muscle. With electrical signals applied internally to local regions of the body, much smaller currents can be lethal. Doctors performing cardiac catheterization, for example, must worry about currents at the microampere level.

Above 200 mA, complete cardiac arrest may occur, breathing may stop, and there may be severe burns both internally and at the points of skin contact. Sometimes such high currents are useful: when a heart is fibrillating, doctors or emergency technicians briefly apply a high enough current to stop the heart (Fig. 28-36). The heart often restarts, beating normally. The figures of Table 28-1 are rough averages, and vary widely from person to person as well as with duration of the shock and whether alternating or direct current is involved. In particular, very young children and people with heart conditions are at higher risk.

Under dry conditions, the typical human being has a resistance from one point to another on unbroken skin of about 10^5 Ω. What voltages are dangerous to such a person? At 10^5 Ω it takes

$$V = IR = (0.1\ \text{A})(10^5\ \Omega) = 10,000\ \text{V}$$

to drive the fatal 100 mA. But a person who is wet or sweaty has a much lower resistance and may be electrocuted by 120-V household electricity. People have been electrocuted at voltages as low as 30 V, although such cases are rare.

It takes current to harm a person, but it takes voltage to drive that current. To be dangerous, an electric circuit must have high voltage *and* be capable of

FIGURE 28-36 Defibrillation of a heart attack victim uses a current pulse of some 20 A, delivered over a few milliseconds. This high current shocks the heart out of ineffectual, chaotic muscle spasms called fibrillation. It may then restart with its normal rhythm.

TABLE 28-1 *Effects of Externally Applied Current on the Human Organism*

CURRENT RANGE	EFFECT
0.5–2 mA	Threshold of sensation
10–15 mA	Involuntary muscle contractions; can't let go
15–100 mA	Severe shock; muscle control lost; breathing difficult
100–200 mA	Fibrillation of heart; death within minutes
>200 mA	Cardiac arrest; breathing stops; severe burns

(a)   (b)

FIGURE 28-37 (a) A short circuit in an ungrounded tool could result in a lethal shock. (b) With a grounded tool, the short circuit causes a blown fuse or circuit breaker, thereby protecting the operator.

driving sufficient current. For example, a car battery can deliver 300 A, but it cannot electrocute you because its 12 volts will not drive much current through you (although you could get a bad burn, or be struck by vaporizing metal, if you accidentally short-circuit such a powerful battery). On the other hand the 20,000 V that runs your car's spark plugs will not electrocute you either, since the internal resistance of this high-voltage circuit is so high that it cannot deliver more than a few mA.

Because potential difference is a property of two points, receiving an electric shock requires that two parts of the body be in contact with conductors at different potentials. In typical 120-V wiring used throughout North America, one of the two wires is connected physically to the ground. This ground connection is to prevent the wiring from reaching arbitrarily high potentials with respect to the ground, as might otherwise happen in a thunderstorm or if a short circuit occurred in a power line. At the same time it means that an individual contacting the "hot" side of the circuit and any grounded conductor such as the ground, a water pipe, or a bathtub will receive a shock.

A potentially dangerous situation occurs when power tools, instruments, or appliances are used by an operator who is likely to be in contact with a grounded conductor. Examples include working outdoors with an electric drill, in a kitchen with an electric mixer, or in a laboratory with an oscilloscope. Suppose you're using a power tool that is plugged in through a regular two-wire cord. Normally exposed metal parts of the tool are not connected to either wire. Now suppose something goes wrong in the tool and a wire short-circuits to the metal case. If it happens to be the wire that's plugged into the grounded side of the power line there's no problem, but if it's the other wire the metal is suddenly 120 V above ground. If you're standing on the ground, or in a damp basement, or are leaning on the kitchen sink, you will receive a potentially lethal shock (Fig. 28-37a).

To avoid this danger many electrical devices have three-wire cords (Fig. 28-38). The third wire runs from exposed metal parts to a grounded wire in the outlet, and normally carries no current. If a short circuit occurs the third wire provides a very low resistance path to ground (Fig. 28-37b). A large current will flow and will blow the circuit breaker or fuse, shutting off the current. Held at ground potential by the ground wire, the operator of the device will be safe.

Because many older homes are not wired with grounded outlets, some manufacturers produce two-wire tools and other devices that are "double-insulated"

FIGURE 28-38 Plugs. (Left) grounded; (right) polarized.

FIGURE 28-39 A ground-fault interrupter protects against shock by shutting off the power when it senses small currents leaking to ground. It must then be reset manually by pushing the reset button.

to provide an extra margin of safety. Newer appliances are equipped with "polarized plugs," which can only be plugged in one way (Fig. 28-38), ensuring that exposed metal parts are most likely to end up at ground potential. Finally, electronic devices called ground-fault interrupters (Fig. 28-39) are used in kitchen, bathroom, basement, and other hazardous circuits in new homes. These devices sense a slight imbalance—5 mA or less—in current flowing in the two wires of a circuit, and shut off the circuit in less than a millisecond on the assumption that the excess current is leaking to ground—perhaps through a person. (Do ground-fault interrupters know about the node law?)

CHAPTER SYNOPSIS

Summary

1. A source of **electromotive force (emf)** is a device—like a battery—that converts some form of energy into the electrical energy associated with the buildup of positive and negative charge at its two terminals. An ideal emf maintains a constant potential difference between its terminals, but energy losses in a real emf result in terminal voltage that decreases as more current is drawn from the device.

2. Electric circuits may often be analyzed using series and parallel resistor combinations. Resistors in series add:

$$R_{series} = R_1 + R_2 + R_3 + \cdots,$$

while resistors in parallel add reciprocally:

$$\frac{1}{R_{parallel}} = \frac{1}{R_1} + \frac{1}{R_2} + \frac{1}{R_3} + \cdots.$$

3. More complicated circuits may be analyzed using **Kirchhoff's laws**. The **loop law** follows from conservation of energy and states that the sum of the voltage differences around any circuit loop is zero. The **node law** follows from conservation of charge and states that the sum of the currents at any circuit node is zero.

4. Measuring instruments should not alter the circuit they're measuring. An ideal **voltmeter** has infinite resistance, and should be connected in parallel with the component whose voltage is being measured. An ideal **ammeter** has zero resistance, and should be connected in series with the component whose current is being measured.

5. The voltage across a capacitor cannot change instantaneously. Quantities in a resistor-capacitor (*RC*) circuit change on a characteristic time scale given by the product *RC*. When an emf $\mathscr{E}$ charges a capacitor C through a resistor R, the capacitor voltage and circuit current vary with time according to

$$V_C = \mathscr{E}(1 - e^{-t/RC})$$

$$I = \frac{\mathscr{E}}{R}e^{-t/RC}.$$

For a discharging capacitor, both voltage and current decrease exponentially with the same time constant *RC*.

6. **Electrical safety** is a matter of avoiding currents high enough to cause biological damage. The danger of electric shock depends on the current at which such damage occurs, the resistance of the organism, and the voltage available to drive the current.

Terms You Should Understand

(Pairs are closely related terms whose distinction is important; number in parentheses is chapter section where term first appears.)

circuit, circuit element (28-1)
electromotive force (emf) (28-2)
ideal, real emfs (28-2, 28-3)
voltage divider (28-3)
internal resistance (28-3)
Kirchhoff's loop and node laws (28-4)
voltmeter, ammeter, ohmmeter (28-5)
RC circuit (28-6)
time constant (28-6)

Symbols You Should Recognize

electric circuit symbols (Fig. 28-1)
$\mathscr{E}$ (28-1)

Problems You Should Be Able to Solve

analyzing simple circuits with series and parallel resistors (28-3)
analyzing circuits with the loop and node laws (28-4)
determining the effects of nonideal measuring instruments (28-5)
analyzing charging and discharging *RC* circuits (28-6)
quickly determining short- and long-term behavior of *RC* circuits (28-6)
assessing electrical hazards (28-7)

Limitations to Keep in Mind

Real circuit elements deviate from their idealizations. Thus the voltage across a real battery may not be exactly its rated voltage, and voltage drops occur in real wires. Attention to circuit design will minimize these nonideal effects.

Electrical measuring instruments may affect the circuits they are measuring.

Currents may be far more dangerous than Table 28-1 implies if they are introduced beneath the skin.

QUESTIONS

1. In each of the circuits of Fig. 28-40, which, if any, of the resistors are in series? In parallel?

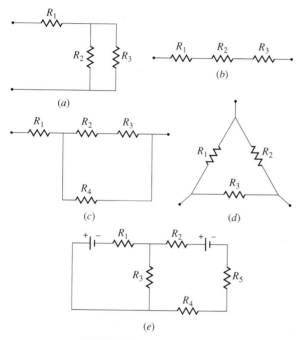

FIGURE 28-40 Question 1.

2. Are the electrical outlets in a home connected in series or parallel? How do you know?
3. In which of the circuits of Fig. 28-41 does the battery supply the same current? All the resistors have the same resistance.

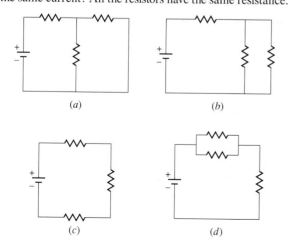

FIGURE 28-41 Question 3.

4. Can the voltage across a battery's terminals differ from the rated voltage of the battery? Explain.
5. Can the voltage across a battery's terminals be higher than the rated voltage of the battery? Explain.
6. In some cities, streetlights are wired in such a way that when one light burns out, they all go out. Are the lights in series or parallel?
7. If you know the battery voltage in Fig. 28-42, can you determine the voltage between points B and C without knowing the resistance R?

FIGURE 28-42 Questions 7, 16.

8. When the switch in Fig 28-43 is open, what is the voltage across the resistor? Across the switch?

FIGURE 28-43 Question 8.

9. Two identical resistors in series dissipate equal power. How can this be, when electric charge loses energy in flowing through the first resistor?
10. What is the current through resistor R_2 in Fig. 28-44? Assume all the wires are ideal.

FIGURE 28-44 Question 10.

11. The resistors in Fig. 28-45 all have the same resistance. If an ideal voltmeter is connected between points A and B, what will it read?

FIGURE 28-45 Question 11.

12. When a large electrical load such as a washing machine, oven, or oil burner comes on, lights throughout a house often dim. Why is this? *Hint:* Think about real wires.

13. If the node law were not obeyed at some node in an electric circuit, what would happen to the voltage at that node?

14. How would you connect a pair of equal resistors across an ideal battery in order to get the most power dissipation in the resistors?

15. You have a battery whose voltage and internal resistance are unknown. Using an ideal voltmeter and an ideal ammeter, how would you determine both these battery characteristics?

16. An ideal voltmeter is used to measure the voltages between points A and C and between B and C in the circuit of Fig. 28-42. How do the measurements compare?

17. You wish to measure the resistance R_2 in Fig. 28-46 with an ohmmeter. Can you do so while R_2 is in the circuit? Why or why not?

FIGURE 28-46 Question 17.

18. A student who is confused about voltage and current hooks a nearly ideal ammeter across a car battery. What happens?

19. A student who is confused about voltage and current tries to measure the voltage across a lighted light bulb by inserting a voltmeter in series with the bulb. What happens to the bulb? Explain.

20. Four identical light bulbs are connected to a battery as shown in Fig. 28-47. How does the brightness of each compare? Explain.

FIGURE 28-47 Questions 20, 21.

21. Suppose bulb A in Fig. 28-47 is unscrewed from its socket. How will the brightness of the three remaining bulbs change? How does the brightness of the three compare?

22. What does it mean for a capacitor to be "fully charged"?

23. Is the current into a charging capacitor in an RC circuit greatest when the capacitor voltage is greatest or when it is smallest?

24. If it takes forever to charge a capacitor fully, why is the RC time constant of any significance in describing the charging?

25. The two resistors in Fig. 28-48 have equal resistance. If the circuit has been connected for a long time, what is the voltage across the capacitor?

FIGURE 28-48 Question 25.

26. In one time constant, a charging capacitor reaches approximately $\frac{2}{3}$ of full charge. In one time constant, the voltage across a discharging capacitor falls to approximately $\frac{1}{3}$ of its original value. What is the origin of the approximate numerical factors $\frac{2}{3}$ and $\frac{1}{3}$ in these statements?

27. What's wrong with this news report: "A power-line worker was seriously injured when 4000 volts passed through his body"?

PROBLEMS

ActivPhysics can help with these problems:
Section 12, "DC Circuits."

Section 28-1 Circuits and Symbols

1. Sketch a circuit diagram for a circuit that includes a resistor R_1 connected to the positive terminal of a battery, a pair of parallel resistors R_2 and R_3 connected to the lower-voltage end of R_1, then returned to the battery's negative terminal, and a capacitor across R_2.

2. A circuit consists of two batteries, a resistor, and a capacitor, all in series. Sketch this circuit. Does the description allow any flexibility in how you draw the circuit?

3. Resistors R_1 and R_2 are connected in series, and this series combination is in parallel with R_3. This parallel combination is connected across a battery whose internal resistance is R_{int}. Draw a diagram representing this circuit.

Section 28-2 Electromotive Force

4. What is the emf of a battery that delivers 27 J of energy as it moves 3.0 C between its terminals?

5. A 1.5-V battery stores 4.5 kJ of energy. How long can it light a flashlight bulb that draws 0.60 A?

6. If you accidentally leave your car headlights (current drain 5 A) on for an hour, how much of the 12-V battery's chemical energy is used up?

7. A battery stores 50 W·h of chemical energy. If it uses up this energy moving 3.0×10^4 C through a circuit, what is its voltage?

Section 28-3 Simple Circuits: Series and Parallel Resistors

8. A 47-kΩ resistor and a 39-kΩ resistor are in parallel, and the pair is in series with a 22-kΩ resistor. What is the resistance of the combination?

9. What resistance should be placed in parallel with a 56-kΩ resistor to make an equivalent resistance of 45 kΩ?

10. In Fig. 28-49 all resistors have the same value, R. What will be the resistance measured (a) between A and B or (b) between A and C?

FIGURE 28-49 Problems 10, 11.

11. In Fig. 28-49, take all resistors to be 1.0 Ω. If a 6.0-V battery is connected between points A and B, what will be the current in the vertical resistor?

12. A defective starter motor in a car draws 300 A from the car's 12-V battery, dropping the battery terminal voltage to only 6 V. A good starter motor should draw only 100 A. What will the battery terminal voltage be with a good starter?

13. What is the internal resistance of the battery in the preceding problem?

14. Three 1.5-V batteries, with internal resistances of 0.01 Ω, 0.1 Ω, and 1 Ω, each have 1-Ω resistors connected across their terminals. To three significant figures, what is the voltage across each resistor?

15. When a 9-V battery is temporarily short-circuited, a 200-mA current flows. What is the internal resistance of the battery?

16. What possible resistance combinations can you form using three resistors whose values are 1.0 Ω, 2.0 Ω, and 3.0 Ω? (Use all three resistors.)

17. A partially discharged car battery can be modeled as a 9-V emf in series with an internal resistance of 0.08 Ω. Jumper cables are used to connect this battery to a fully charged battery, modeled as a 12-V emf in series with a 0.02-Ω internal resistance. How much current flows through the discharged battery?

18. You have a number of 50-Ω resistors, each capable of dissipating 0.50 W without overheating. How many resistors would you need, and how would you connect them, so as to make a 50-Ω combination that could be connected safely across a 12-V battery?

19. What is the equivalent resistance between A and B in each of the circuits shown in Fig. 28-50? *Hint*: In (c), think about symmetry and the current that would flow through R_2.

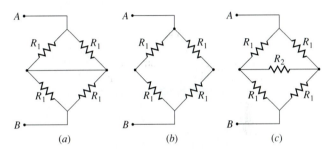

FIGURE 28-50 Problem 19.

20. A 6.0-V battery has an internal resistance of 2.5 Ω. If the battery is short circuited, what is the rate of energy dissipation in its internal resistance?

21. How many 100-W, 120-V light bulbs can be connected in parallel before they blow a 20-A circuit breaker?

22. What is the current through the 3-Ω resistor in the circuit of Fig. 28-51? *Hint*: This is trivial. Can you see why?

FIGURE 28-51 Problem 22.

23. Take $\mathscr{E} = 12$ V and $R_1 = 270$ Ω in the voltage divider of Fig. 28-5. (a) What should be the value of R_2 in order that 4.5 V appear across R_2? (b) What will be the power dissipation in R_2?

24. A voltage divider consists of two 1.0-kΩ resistors connected in series across a 160-V emf. If a 10-kΩ resistor is connected across one of the 1.0-kΩ resistors, what will be the voltage across it?

25. In the circuit of Fig. 28-52, R_1 is a variable resistor, and the other two resistors have equal resistances R. (a) Find an expression for the voltage across R_1, and (b) sketch a graph of this quantity as a function of R_1 as R_1 varies from 0 to 10R. (c) What is the limiting value as $R_1 \to \infty$?

FIGURE 28-52 Problem 25.

26. In the circuit of Fig. 28-53 find (a) the current supplied by the battery and (b) the current through the 6-Ω resistor.

FIGURE 28-53 Problems 26, 27.

27. In the circuit of Fig. 28-53, how much power is being dissipated in the 4-Ω resistor?

28. A 50-Ω resistor is connected across a battery, and a 26-mA current flows. When the 50-Ω resistor is replaced with a 22-Ω resistor, a 43-mA current flows. What are the battery's voltage and internal resistance?

Section 28-4 Kirchhoff's Laws and Multiloop Circuits

29. In the circuit of Fig. 28-54 it makes no difference whether the switch is open or closed. What is $\mathscr{E}_3$ in terms of the other quantities shown?

FIGURE 28-54 Problem 29.

30. What is the current through the ammeter in Fig. 28-55?

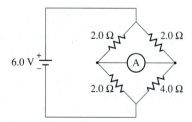

FIGURE 28-55 Problem 30.

31. In Fig. 28-56, what is the equivalent resistance measured between points A and B?

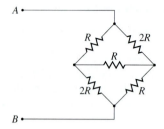

FIGURE 28-56 Problem 31.

32. Find all three currents in the circuit of Fig. 28-18, but now with $\mathscr{E}_2 = 1.0$ V.

33. Find all three currents in the circuit of Fig. 28-18 with the values given, but with battery $\mathscr{E}_2$ reversed.

34. In Fig. 28-57, take $\mathscr{E}_1 = 6.0$ V, $\mathscr{E}_2 = 1.5$ V, $\mathscr{E}_3 = 4.5$ V, $R_1 = 270\ \Omega$, $R_2 = 150\ \Omega$, $R_3 = 560\ \Omega$, and $R_4 = 820\ \Omega$. Find the current in R_3, and give its direction.

FIGURE 28-57 Problems 34, 35, 36.

35. With all the values except $\mathscr{E}_2$ in Fig. 28-57 as given in the preceding problem, find the condition on $\mathscr{E}_2$ that will make the current in R_3 flow upward.

36. Suppose that all resistors in Fig. 28-57 have the same value R and that $\mathscr{E}_1 = \mathscr{E}_3 = \mathscr{E}$ and $\mathscr{E}_2 = 2\mathscr{E}$. Find expressions for the currents in the four resistors, and give their directions.

37. Figure 28-58 shows a portion of a circuit used to model the electrical behavior of long, cylindrical biological cells such as muscle cells or the axons of neurons. Find the current through the emf $\mathscr{E}_3$, given that all resistors have the same value $R = 1.5$ MΩ and that $\mathscr{E}_1 = 75$ mV, $\mathscr{E}_2 = 45$ mV, and $\mathscr{E}_3 = 20$ mV. Be sure to specify the direction of the current.

FIGURE 28-58 Problems 37, 38.

38. An electrochemical impulse traveling along the cell modeled in Fig. 28-58 changes the value of emf $\mathscr{E}_3$ so that now it supplies an upward current of 40 nA. Assuming the rest of the circuit remains as described in the preceding problem, what is the new value of $\mathscr{E}_3$?

Section 28-5 Electrical Measuring Instruments

39. A voltmeter with 200-kΩ resistance is used to measure the voltage across the 10-kΩ resistor in Fig. 28-59. By what percentage is the measurement in error because of the finite meter resistance?

FIGURE 28-59 Problems 39, 40.

40. An ammeter with 100-Ω resistance is inserted in the circuit of Fig. 28-59. By what percentage is the measurement in error because of the nonzero meter resistance?

41. A neophyte mechanic foolishly connects an ammeter with 0.1-Ω resistance directly across a 12-V car battery whose internal resistance is 0.01 Ω. What is the power dissipation in the meter? No wonder it gets destroyed!

42. The voltage across the 30-kΩ resistor in Fig. 28-60 is measured with (a) a 50-kΩ voltmeter, (b) a 250-kΩ voltmeter, and (c) a digital meter with 10-MΩ resistance. To two significant figures, what does each read?

FIGURE 28-60 Problem 42.

43. In Fig. 28-61 what are the meter readings when (a) an ideal voltmeter or (b) an ideal ammeter is connected between points A and B?

FIGURE 28-61 Problem 43.

44. A resistor draws 1.00 A from an ideal 12.0-V battery. (a) If an ammeter with 0.10-Ω resistance is inserted in the circuit, what will it read? (b) If this current is used to calculate the resistance, how will the calculated value compare with the actual value?

Section 28-6 Circuits with Capacitors

45. Show that the quantity RC has the units of time (seconds).

46. If capacitance is given in μF, what will be the units of the RC time constant when resistance is given in (a) Ω, (b) kΩ, (c) MΩ? Your answers eliminate the need for tedious power-of-10 conversions.

47. Show that a capacitor is charged to approximately 99% of the applied voltage in five time constants.

48. An uncharged 10-μF capacitor and a 470-kΩ resistor are connected in series, and 250 V applied across the combination. How long does it take the capacitor voltage to reach 200 V?

49. Figure 28-62 shows the voltage across a capacitor that is charging through a 4700-Ω resistor in the circuit of Fig. 28-29. Use the graph to determine (a) the battery voltage, (b) the time constant, and (c) the capacitance.

FIGURE 28-62 Problem 49.

50. The voltage across a charging capacitor in an RC circuit rises to $1 - 1/e$ of the battery voltage in 5.0 ms. (a) How long will it take to reach $1 - 1/e^3$ of the battery voltage? (b) If the capacitor is charging through a 22-kΩ resistor, what is its capacitance?

51. A 1.0-μF capacitor is charged to 10.0 V. It is then connected across a 500-kΩ resistor. How long does it take (a) for the capacitor voltage to reach 5.0 V and (b) for the energy stored in the capacitor to decrease to half its initial value?

52. A capacitor used to provide steady voltages in the power supply of a stereo amplifier charges rapidly to 35 V every 1/60 of a second. It must then hold that voltage to within 1.0 V for the next 1/60 s while it discharges through the amplifier circuit. If the circuit draws 1.2 A from the 35-V supply (a) what is its effective resistance and (b) what value of capacitance is needed?

53. A capacitor is charged until it holds 5.0 J of energy. It is then connected across a 10-kΩ resistor. In 8.6 ms, the resistor dissipates 2.0 J. What is the capacitance?

54. A 2.0-μF capacitor is charged to 150 V. It is then connected to an uncharged 1.0-μF capacitor through a 2.2-kΩ resistor, by closing switch S in Fig. 28-63. Find the total energy dissipated in the resistor as the circuit comes to equilibrium. *Hint:* Think about charge conservation.

55. For the circuit of Example 28-9, take $\mathscr{E} = 100$ V, $R_1 = 4.0$ kΩ, and $R_2 = 6.0$ kΩ, and assume the capacitor is

FIGURE 28-63 Problem 54.

initially uncharged. What are the currents in both resistors and the voltage across the capacitor (a) just after the switch is closed and (b) a long time after the switch is closed? Long after the switch is closed it is again opened. What are I_1, I_2, and V_C (c) just after this switch opening and (d) a long time later?

56. In the circuit of Fig. 28-64 the switch is initially open and both capacitors initially uncharged. All resistors have the same value R. Find expressions for the current in R_2 (a) just after the switch is closed and (b) a long time after the switch is closed. (c) Describe qualitatively how you expect the current in R_3 to behave after the switch is closed.

FIGURE 28-64 Problem 56.

57. In the circuit of Fig. 28-65 the switch is initially open and the capacitor is uncharged. Find expressions for the current I supplied by the battery (a) just after the switch is closed and (b) a long time after the switch is closed.

FIGURE 28-65 Problem 57.

58. Obtain an expression for the rate (dV/dt) at which the voltage across a charging capacitor increases. Evaluate your result at time $t = 0$, and show that if the capacitor continued charging steadily at this rate it would be fully charged in exactly one time constant.

Paired Problems

(Both problems in a pair involve the same principles and techniques. If you can get the first problem, you should be able to solve the second one.)

59. A 3.3-kΩ resistor and a 4.7-kΩ resistor are connected in parallel, and the pair is in series with a 1.5-kΩ resistor. What is the resistance of the combination?

60. Find the value of R in Fig. 28-66 that will make the resistance between points A and B equal to R.

FIGURE 28-66 Problem 60.

61. A battery's voltage is measured with a voltmeter whose resistance is 1000 Ω; the result is 4.36 V. When the measurement is repeated with a 1500-Ω meter the result is 4.41 V. What are (a) the battery voltage and (b) its internal resistance?

62. An ammeter with a resistance of 1.4 Ω is connected momentarily across a battery (not the way to treat an ammeter!) and it reads 9.78 A. When the measurement is repeated with a meter whose resistance is 2.1 Ω the reading is 7.46 A. What are (a) the battery voltage and (b) its internal resistance?

63. In Fig. 28-67, take $\mathcal{E}_1 = 12$ V, $\mathcal{E}_2 = 6.0$ V, $\mathcal{E}_3 = 3.0$ V, $R_1 = 1.0$ Ω, $R_2 = 2.0$ Ω, and $R_3 = 4.0$ Ω. Find the current in R_2 and give its direction.

FIGURE 28-67 Problems 63, 64.

64. (a) With all values except $\mathcal{E}_2$ as given in the preceding problem, find $\mathcal{E}_2$ such that there is no current in this battery. (b) What are the currents in R_1 and R_2 under these conditions?

65. In Fig. 28-68 what are the meter readings when (a) an ideal voltmeter or (b) an ideal ammeter is connected between points A and B?

FIGURE 28-68 Problems 65, 66.

66. In Fig. 28-68 what are the meter readings when (a) a voltmeter with 50-kΩ resistance or (b) an ammeter with 150-Ω resistance is connected between points A and B?

67. An initially uncharged capacitor in an RC circuit reaches 75% of its full charge in 22.0 ms. What is the time constant?

68. Find the resistance needed in an RC circuit to bring a 20-μF capacitor from zero charge to 45% of its full charge in 140 ms.

Supplementary Problems

69. Suppose the currents into and out of a circuit node differed by 1 μA. If the node consists of a small metal sphere with diameter 1 mm, how long would it take for the electric field around the node to reach the breakdown field in air (3 MV/m)?

70. A problem on dairy farms is "stray voltage," caused by corroded wiring, poor wiring practices, or ground currents associated with nearby power lines. These conditions can result in several volts of potential difference between metal objects such as watering bowls, feed troughs, or milking equipment, and the ground. Cows feel slight shocks that make them nervous, resulting in reduced milk output. As a result, farmers can face serious financial losses. Figure 28-69 shows a circuit model for a stray voltage situation; the 1.5-kΩ resistor represents the resistance of corroded connections and poor wiring; you can assume the ground has negligible resistance. (a) The resistance from a cow's mouth to hoof is approximately 350Ω. How much current will flow through the cow in the situation shown? (It takes only about 1 mA to affect milk production.) In an effort to diagnose the problem, the farmer moves the cow aside and connects a multimeter between the watering bowl and ground. What will it read if it's set to measure (b) voltage and (c) current?

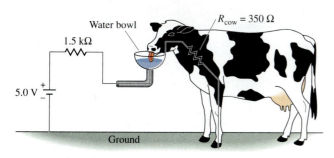

FIGURE 28-69 Stray voltage can bankrupt a dairy farm. (Problem 70)

71. In Fig. 28-70, what is the current in the 4-Ω resistor when each of the following circuit elements is connected between points A and B: (a) an ideal ammeter; (b) an ideal voltmeter; (c) another 4.0-Ω resistor; (d) an uncharged capacitor, right after it's connected; (e) long after the capacitor of part (d) is connected; (f) an ideal 12-V battery, with its positive terminal at A; (g) a capacitor initially charged to 12 V, right after

FIGURE 28-70 Problem 71.

it's connected with its positive plate at A; (h) long after the capacitor in part (g) is connected?

72. A resistance R is connected across a battery with internal resistance R_{int}. Show that the maximum power dissipation in R occurs when $R = R_{int}$. *Note:* This is not the way to treat a battery! But it is the basis for matching loads in amplifiers and other devices; for example, a stereo amplifier designed to drive 8-Ω speakers has internal resistance close to 8 Ω.

73. A parallel-plate capacitor is insulated with a material of dielectric constant κ and resistivity ρ. Since the resistivity is finite, the capacitor "leaks" charge and can be modeled as an ideal capacitor in parallel with a resistor. (a) Show that the time constant of the capacitor is independent of its dimensions (provided the spacing is small enough that the usual parallel-plate approximation applies) and is given by $\varepsilon_0\kappa\rho$. (b) If the insulating material is polystyrene ($\kappa = 2.6$, $\rho = 10^{16}$ Ω·m), how long will it take for the stored energy in the capacitor to decrease by a factor of 2?

74. Of the total energy drawn from a battery in charging an RC circuit, show that only half ends up as stored energy in the capacitor. *Hint:* What happens to the rest of it? You will need to integrate.

75. Write the loop and node laws for the circuit of Fig. 28-71, and show that the time constant for this circuit is $R_1 R_2 C/(R_1 + R_2)$.

FIGURE 28-71 Problem 75.

76. The circuit in Fig. 28-72 extends forever to the right, and all the resistors have the same value R. Show that the equivalent resistance measured across the two terminals at left is $\frac{1}{2}R(1 + \sqrt{5})$. *Hint:* You don't need to sum an infinite series.

FIGURE 28-72 Problem 76.

29 The Magnetic Field

Magnetic fields shape delicate loops and other structures in the Sun's atmosphere, imaged here in X rays by the Japanese satellite Yohkoh.

People are fascinated with magnets. Magnetism—the seemingly mysterious force you feel when you try to push two magnets together in a way they don't want to go—is always intriguing. Some uses of magnets, like holding notes on refrigerators, are mundane. But others—holding gas at a temperature of one hundred million K in a nuclear fusion reactor, or converting electrical into mechanical energy in the motors of a railroad locomotive—are more impressive. And magnetism, like electricity, is at the heart of many natural phenomena and technological devices. Video and audio cassette recorders, electric motors, TV picture tubes, computer disks, and electric power plants would be impossible without magnetism.

Earth's magnetism helps us find our way around, provides historical evidence for the evolution of our planet, and protects us from harmful radiation. Birds, sea turtles, and some bacteria use Earth's magnetism for navigation. Without magnetism we would not even see, for light itself originates in an interaction between magnetism and electricity. As with electricity, we often do not recognize the magnetic character of everyday phenomena.

In this chapter we introduce magnetism, and will find immediately that it's intimately connected with electricity. In subsequent chapters we explore further the deep relation between electricity and magnetism, and will eventually come to see electricity and magnetism as two inseparable aspects of the same underlying phenomenon.

29-1 WHAT IS MAGNETISM?

You know about magnetism because you've played with magnets or used them in everyday tasks such as sticking notes to your refrigerator. You know that magnets exert forces on each other and on certain materials, such as iron and steel. It's convenient to describe that interaction in terms of a **magnetic field** (symbol **B**). We say that one magnet produces a magnetic field, and that a second magnet responds to the field in its immediate vicinity. That way we avoid the awkward "action at a distance" picture, in which one magnet somehow reaches out across empty space to pull on another. We can picture a magnetic field using field lines, just as we did for electric fields, and can trace out magnetic field lines using small iron filings that align themselves with the field (Fig. 29-1).

FIGURE 29-1 Iron filings align with the magnetic field, tracing out the field from a pair of bar magnets. The field is strongest near the magnetic poles. We'll see in the next chapter why iron is a special magnetic material.

You may think we're now going to give rules for finding the magnetic field produced by a given magnet, and for the force a magnet experiences in a magnetic field. But we're not. That's because the magnetism you're familiar with—involving magnets and their interaction with specific materials such as iron—is not particularly fundamental. Rather, the magnetism that's familiar to you is a specialized and limited manifestation of a more fundamental and universal phenomenon. Here we'll go straight to the basics of magnetism, and later (in the next chapter) will come back to understand how the magnets you're familiar with fit into the larger picture.

In Chapters 23–28 we studied electrical phenomena, all of which ultimately involve electric charge. We saw how a charge produces an electric field, and how other charges respond to that field. We're now dealing with the magnetic field, so you might expect that we're about to introduce magnetic charge and tell how it gives rise to the magnetic field. But again, no. The fact is that no one has ever found a magnetic charge, an entity that would produce a radially outward magnetic field like the electric field of a point charge. Some theories of elementary particles and the origin of the universe suggest that such magnetic charges—called **magnetic monopoles**—should exist. But they've never been observed, and even if they exist, they play no role in the magnetic phenomena with which we're familiar. We'll have more to say about magnetic monopoles in the next chapter.

So if it's not about magnets or magnetic charge, what *is* magnetism about? Simple: it's about *electric* charge—the same electric charge we've been dealing with since Chapter 23. But whereas the phenomena of electricity involve electric charge, period,

▮ **the phenomena of magnetism involve *moving* electric charge.**

In particular, *moving* electric charge is the source of magnetic fields, and *moving* electric charges experience forces from magnetic fields. In this chapter we'll assume we have a magnetic field and will explore the magnetic force on moving electric charges that results from that field. In the next chapter we'll see just how moving electric charges give rise to magnetic fields. That will lead us to understand technological applications such as electromagnets, the magnetic fields of Earth and other astrophysical bodies, and how the familiar magnetism of materials such as iron arises ultimately from the motions of the electrons in those materials.

29-2 THE MAGNETIC FORCE ON A MOVING CHARGE

In Chapter 23 we defined the electric field **E** through the relation $\mathbf{F}_E = q\mathbf{E}$, where $\mathbf{F}_E$ is the electric force on a charge q. We're now going to develop the analogous relation between a *moving* charge q and the force $\mathbf{F}_B$ it experiences in a magnetic field **B**.

Consider a region with no electric field, but in which a magnetic field is present. You could verify the presence of the magnetic field and determine its direction with a compass, which itself is just a small magnet that's free to pivot into alignment with the magnetic field. More fundamentally, you can take our description of the force experienced by a moving charge as defining what it means for there to be a magnetic field present.

Now let's put a point charge q in the magnetic field. If the charge is stationary, we find that it experiences no magnetic force. But suppose the charge is moving. We won't worry about how it got moving—except that, as we'll soon see, magnetic force can't be responsible. Experiment shows that the moving charge experiences a magnetic force such that

1. The magnetic force is always at right angles both to the velocity **v** of the charge and to the magnetic field **B** (Fig. 29-2).
2. The strength of the magnetic force is proportional to the product of the charge q, its speed v, and the magnetic field strength B.
3. The force is greatest if the charged particle is moving at right angles to the magnetic field **B** and is zero if the charge velocity **v** is parallel or antiparallel to the field. In general, the magnetic force is proportional to the sine of the angle between the vectors **v** and **B** (see Fig. 29-2).

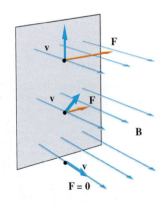

FIGURE 29-2 The magnetic force on a charged particle is perpendicular to the particle's velocity **v** and to the magnetic field **B**. The magnitude of the force depends on the angle between **v** and **B**, and is greatest when **v** and **B** are perpendicular (top). When **v** and **B** are parallel there is no magnetic force (bottom).

Putting these facts together allows us to write the magnetic force compactly in terms of the vector cross product introduced in Chapter 13:

$$\mathbf{F}_B = q\mathbf{v} \times \mathbf{B}, \quad \text{(magnetic force)} \qquad (29\text{-}1a)$$

where $\mathbf{F}_B$ is the magnetic force on a particle of charge q moving with velocity **v** at a point where the magnetic field is **B**. Recall from Chapter 13 that the cross product $\mathbf{v} \times \mathbf{B}$ is a vector of magnitude $vB\sin\theta$, where θ is the angle between

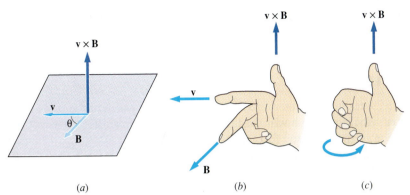

FIGURE 29-3 Ways to apply the right-hand rule. (a) Two vectors **v** and **B** and their cross product. The two vectors define a plane, and the cross product is always perpendicular to that plane. (b)–(c) All the right-hand rule does is distinguish between the two possible directions perpendicular to the plane. In (b), the fingers of the right hand point in the directions of the vectors **v** and **B**, and the cross product **v** × **B** in the direction of the thumb; in (c) the curved arrow describes a rotation that would take the vector **v** onto the vector **B**.

v and **B**. Thus the magnetic force has magnitude

$$F = qvB\sin\theta. \tag{29-1b}$$

The direction of **v** × **B** is perpendicular to both **v** and **B**, with the choice of the two possible perpendicular directions being made by the right-hand rule (Fig. 29-3). Because the charge q also enters Equation 29-1, the direction of the magnetic force is that of **v** × **B** for a positive charge but opposite **v** × **B** for a negative charge (Fig. 29-4).

We can regard Equation 29-1 as the definition of the magnetic field. If we put a particle of charge q moving with velocity **v** in a region free of other influences (i.e., electric and gravitational fields), then the presence of a force **F** on the particle shows that there is a magnetic field **B** implied by Equation 29-1a. Equations 29-1 show that the SI units of magnetic field are N·s/C·m, a unit given the name **tesla** (T) after the Serbian-American inventor Nikola Tesla (1865–1943). One tesla is a strong magnetic field, and a smaller unit called the gauss (G), equal to 10^{-4} T, is often used. Earth's magnetic field, for example, is a little under 1 G, while the field at the poles of a toy magnet may be 100 G. Strong laboratory magnets (Fig. 29-5) produce fields ranging from several T to

FIGURE 29-5 This superconducting electromagnet is used to steer high-energy beams of heavy atomic nuclei at the Laboratory of High Energies in Dubna, Russia. The Dubna laboratory is one of the world's leading facilities for the production and study of heavy nuclei.

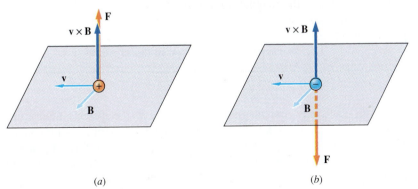

FIGURE 29-4 (a) When the charge is positive, the magnetic force is in the same direction as the cross product **v** × **B**. (b) When the charge is negative, the force q**v** × **B** is opposite **v** × **B**.

nearly 40 T, while magnetars—incredibly dense, rapidly rotating collapsed stars first identified in 1998—have fields up to 10^{11} T.

Got It!

Figure 29-6 shows a proton in a magnetic field. For which of the three possible proton velocities shown will the magnetic force be greatest? What will be the direction of the magnetic force in each case?

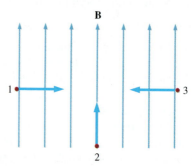

FIGURE 29-6 For which velocity is the magnetic force greatest? (The speed is the same in all three cases.)

| **EXAMPLE 29-1** | *Steering Protons* |

A magnetic field of 0.10 T is used to steer charged-particle beams in a nuclear physics experiment. The field points vertically upward. Three protons enter the field region, two moving horizontally and one vertically as shown in Fig. 29-7. All three are moving at 2.0×10^6 m/s. What is the magnetic force on each?

Solution

Proton 2 is moving parallel to the field. For it, $\mathbf{v} \times \mathbf{B} = \mathbf{0}$ and it experiences no magnetic force. Protons 1 and 3 are moving at right angles to the field, so $\sin\theta = 1$ and Equation 29-1b gives

$$F = qvB = (1.6\times10^{-19}\ \text{C})(2.0\times10^6\ \text{m/s})(0.10\ \text{T})$$

$$= 3.2\times10^{-14}\ \text{N}.$$

Since the protons carry positive charge, the direction of the force is that of the product $\mathbf{v} \times \mathbf{B}$. For proton 1, moving to the right, $\mathbf{v} \times \mathbf{B}$ is out of the page. For proton 3, moving to the left, the force is into the page. This example shows that the magnetic field alone does not determine the magnetic force. Identical particles in the same field experience different forces if their velocities are different. Had the particles been electrons the forces would have been in the opposite directions. (Why?)

FIGURE 29-7 What is the magnetic force on each proton? (Example 29-1)

EXERCISE A 1.3-T magnetic field points in the x direction. A particle carrying 1.0 μC is moving at 20 m/s in the x-y plane and experiences a magnetic force of 1.4×10^{-5} N. What angle does the particle's velocity make with the x axis?

Answer: 33°

Some problems similar to Example 29-1: 1–11

Although electricity and magnetism are related, the electric field and the magnetic field are distinct. In particular, both may be present simultaneously. In that case, a charged particle experiences both the magnetic force $\mathbf{F}_B$ of Equation 29-1 and also the electric force $q\mathbf{E}$, for a net **electromagnetic force** given by

$$\mathbf{F} = q\mathbf{E} + q\mathbf{v} \times \mathbf{B}. \qquad \text{(electromagnetic force)} \qquad (29\text{-}2)$$

EXAMPLE 29-2	*A Velocity Selector*

A wide range of applications, from manufacturing computer chips to cancer treatment, require charged-particle beams with precise velocities. In other cases—like analyzing charged-particle populations in interplanetary space—scientists need to classify particles by their speeds. Both tasks can be accomplished by a **velocity selector**, a device that uses electric and magnetic fields together to pass only particles with a specific velocity.

Figure 29-8 shows the perpendicular electric and magnetic fields used in a velocity selector; the fields have magnitudes E and B, respectively. A charged particle enters the field region, moving perpendicular to both fields, as shown. What speed must it have if it's to pass through the region undeflected?

Solution

The net force on a particle must be zero if it is to be undeflected. Consider a positively charged particle heading into the page in Fig. 29-8. The electric field points to the right, so the electric force $q\mathbf{E}$ is to the right. Applying the right-hand rule with the velocity vector $\mathbf{v}$ into the page and the magnetic field $\mathbf{B}$ downward gives a magnetic force to the left; since v and B are at right angles, the magnitude of the magnetic force is qvB. So the electric and magnetic forces are in opposite directions; for them to cancel their magnitudes must be equal:

$$qE = qvB,$$

or
$$v = \frac{E}{B}.$$

Particles with any other velocity will be deflected by a nonzero net force, so only those particles emerging undeflected have the precise speed $v = E/B$. Note that this selected speed is independent of the charge—and even of its sign, since the directions of both forces would reverse for a negative charge.

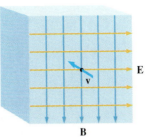

FIGURE 29-8 Crossed electric and magnetic fields give rise to oppositely directed forces on charged particles moving perpendicular to the fields. The magnetic force depends on the particle speed, but the electric force does not; therefore, only those particles with just the right speed can traverse the field region undeflected.

The velocity selector makes use of an important difference between the electric and magnetic forces: the electric force does not depend on a charged particle's velocity, while the magnetic force does. That's what makes possible the velocity selector's cancellation of the two forces at only one specific velocity. You can explore the velocity selector further with ActivPhysics Activity 13.8.

EXERCISE You have a magnet that produces a 0.25-T field. What strength electric field should you apply to make a velocity selector that passes 2.8×10^5 m/s particles undeflected?

Answer: 70 kV/m

Some problems similar to Example 29-2: 12–14

13.8
Velocity Selector

29-3 THE MOTION OF CHARGED PARTICLES IN MAGNETIC FIELDS

Like any force, the magnetic force deflects a particle from the straight-line path that Newton's first law says it would otherwise follow (Fig. 29-9). Use of magnetic forces to "steer" charged particles is the basis of many practical devices, from TV tubes to giant particle accelerators. Magnetic forces shape the trajectories of charged particles in a range of natural situations, especially in astrophysics.

FIGURE 29-9 (*a*) In the absence of a magnetic field, an electron beam moves in a straight line. (*b*) A magnetic field causes the beam to deflect. If the electrons are moving upward in the photo, which way is the field pointing?

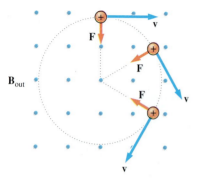

FIGURE 29-10 A positively charged particle moving at right angles to a uniform magnetic field describes a circular path. Note the convention that dots represent magnetic field lines emerging from the page; we designate this field by $\mathbf{B}_{out}$. Crosses, in contrast, would represent field lines going into the page. You can think of the dots as the tips of arrows and crosses as the feathers at the tails.

Unlike most other forces, the magnetic force is necessarily at right angles to the particle velocity. That means force and particle displacement are perpendicular. Since work is the dot product of force with displacement (Equation 7-5; $W = \mathbf{F} \cdot \Delta \mathbf{r}$), and the dot product of perpendicular vectors is zero, we can conclude that

❚ The magnetic force does no work on a charged particle.

Both the kinetic energy and thus the speed of a charged particle subject only to a magnetic force are therefore constant. The magnetic force changes only the direction of the particle's velocity, not its magnitude. What sort of motion results from the magnetic force? Suppose a particle with positive charge q is moving at right angles to a uniform magnetic field $\mathbf{B}$, as shown in Fig. 29-10. At the instant the particle's velocity is to the right, the outward-pointing magnetic field gives a force $q\mathbf{v} \times \mathbf{B}$ that is downward. Since this force is at right angles to the velocity, it changes the direction but not the magnitude of the velocity. The magnetic force on the particle with its new velocity is still perpendicular to the velocity, and since the magnitude of the velocity is unchanged, so is the magnitude of the force. What we've just described—a force of constant magnitude always at right angles to a particle's velocity—is the prescription for uniform circular motion. Thus, a charged particle moving in a plane perpendicular to a uniform magnetic field describes a circular path. The magnetic force acts exactly like the tension in a string when you tie a mass to the string and whirl it around in a circle. The tension is perpendicular to the motion and changes its direction but not its speed.

How big is the circle, and how long does it take to get around? We can answer these questions like we do any questions about the effects of forces—namely, by using Newton's second law. In its circular path, the charged particle undergoes an acceleration v^2/r, directed toward the center of the circle. What causes this acceleration? The magnetic force! With the field and velocity at right angles, the magnitude of the magnetic force is just

$$F = qvB,$$

and the force points toward the center of the circle. Writing Newton's law $\mathbf{F} = m\mathbf{a}$ then gives

$$qvB = m\frac{v^2}{r},$$

so

$$r = \frac{mv}{qB}. \tag{29-3}$$

This result makes sense: the larger the particle's momentum mv, the harder it is for the magnetic force to bend it out of a straight line, so the larger the radius of the orbit. On the other hand, if we make the field or charge larger, then the magnetic force increases, giving a tighter orbit.

This variation of orbital radius is used in the mass spectrometer, a device that sorts ionized atoms and molecules according to their charge-to-mass ratio. Problem 27 and ActivPhysics Activity 13.7 show how the mass spectrometer works. Another practical application is the television picture tube, described in the example below.

13.7
Mass Spectrometer

Got It!

A uniform magnetic field points out of this page. Will an electron circle clockwise or counterclockwise as viewed from above the page?

EXAMPLE 29-3	*A TV Picture Tube*

In a TV picture tube, deflection of the electron beam that "paints" the TV picture is accomplished using magnetic fields. The geometry of a certain tube requires that the electron beam be bent in a circular arc with a minimum radius of 4.5 cm (Fig. 29-11). If the electrons are accelerated from rest through a 25-kV potential difference before they enter the magnetic field region, what is the magnetic field strength required? In what direction should the field point to accomplish the deflection shown in Fig. 29-11? Assume that the field is uniform over the deflecting region and zero elsewhere.

FIGURE 29-11 A TV picture tube requiring a 4.5-cm bending radius (marked with a diagonal line) for maximum deflection of the electron beam. Which way should the magnetic field point to deflect an electron in the direction indicated?

Solution

Solving Equation 29-3 for the magnetic field strength B gives

$$B = \frac{mv}{er},$$

with e the elementary charge. "Falling" through a potential difference $V = 25$ kV, the electron of charge e acquires a kinetic energy $\frac{1}{2}mv^2 = Ve$, so its speed is

$$v = \sqrt{\frac{2Ve}{m}}.$$

Our expression for the field then becomes

$$B = \frac{m}{er}\sqrt{\frac{2Ve}{m}} = \frac{1}{r}\sqrt{\frac{2mV}{e}}$$

$$= \frac{1}{0.045 \text{ m}}\left(\frac{(2)(9.1\times10^{-31} \text{ kg})(25\times10^3 \text{ V})}{1.6\times10^{-19} \text{ C}}\right)^{1/2}$$

$$= 0.012 \text{ T}.$$

To achieve an initially downward deflection, the force $q\mathbf{v} \times \mathbf{B}$ must be initially downward. But the electron charge is negative, so $\mathbf{v} \times \mathbf{B}$ must be upward. Application of the right-hand rule to the rightward-moving electrons shows that the magnetic field $\mathbf{B}$ must be into the page in Fig. 29-11.

How does deflection of the electron beam result in a TV picture? In conventional TV, the magnetic field is varied so that three electron beams—one for each of the colors red, green, and blue—sweeps across the front of the screen in horizontal lines, starting at the top of the screen and working downward. A scan of the entire screen occurs thirty times each second. The electron current in each beam varies to match the brightness of its color at each point in the picture to be displayed, controlled by varying electric fields in the TV tube that themselves follow the signal coming into the TV from an antenna, cable, or VCR. The screen itself is coated with materials that glow in red, green, or blue when struck by the electrons, so the result is a reconstruction of the image that entered the TV as an electrical signal.

EXERCISE A beam of protons moving at 2.5×10^5 m/s is deflected through a 90° turn by a 10-mT magnetic field oriented perpendicular to the beam's velocity. What is the radius of the turn?

Answer: 26 cm

Some problems similar to Example 29-3: 15, 18, 21

The Cyclotron Frequency

How long does it take a charged particle to complete its circular orbit in a uniform magnetic field? The circumference of the orbit is $2\pi r$, so the period T of the circular motion is

$$T = \frac{2\pi r}{v}.$$

Using Equation 29-3 for the radius r gives

$$T = \frac{2\pi r}{v} = \frac{2\pi}{v}\frac{mv}{qB} = \frac{2\pi m}{qB}. \qquad (29\text{-}4)$$

13.4

Magnetic Force on a Particle

FIGURE 29-12 The Crab Nebula, remnant of a supernova explosion observed nearly 1000 years ago. Intense radio emission occurs as electrons undergo circular motion in the Crab's magnetic field. The frequency of the emission is related to the cyclotron frequency of the electrons' motion, and its measurement therefore allows determination of the magnetic field.

This remarkable result shows that the period of the circular motion is independent of the particle's speed and the size of its orbit. You can see why from Equation 29-3: the larger the speed v the larger the radius r, and therefore the circumference, in direct proportion to the speed. So a faster particle describes a larger circle, and ends up taking the same time to go around. Physically, that's because the magnetic force depends on the particle's speed.

Equivalently, we can describe the particle's circular motion in terms of its frequency, in revolutions per second, which is just the inverse of the period:

$$f = \frac{qB}{2\pi m}. \tag{29-5}$$

This quantity is called the **cyclotron frequency**, since it's the frequency at which charged particles circulate in a cyclotron particle accelerator. Because the cyclotron frequency depends only on the magnetic field and the particle's charge-to-mass ratio, observing cyclotron motion provides astrophysicists a direct measure of magnetic fields in distant astrophysical objects (Fig. 29-12). Conversely, a fixed magnetic field guarantees a specific cyclotron frequency, regardless of the particles' speeds. Microwave ovens exploit this fact, their microwaves generated by electrons circling 2.4 billion times each second in a special tube called a magnetron (see Problem 21).

APPLICATION	The Cyclotron

Physicists studying the basic structure of matter need tools that can probe the atomic nucleus and its constituent particles. The only probes sufficiently small are subatomic particles themselves, accelerated to high enough energies that they can disrupt the strong nuclear force. How is this acceleration accomplished? One way is to accelerate particles of charge q through a large potential difference V, giving each particle energy qV. But there are practical problems in the generation and handling of potential differences much over a million volts. To achieve higher energies, devices are used that circumvent the need for a single large potential difference. One of the earliest and most successful such devices is the **cyclotron** (Fig. 29-13). The device consists of an evacuated chamber between the poles of a magnet. At the center of the chamber is a source of the particles to be accelerated, usually protons or light ions. The ions undergo circular motion in the magnetic field.

Also within the evacuated chamber are two hollow conducting structures each shaped like the letter D (Fig. 29-12). A modest potential difference is applied across these two "dees," and this potential difference is made to alternate in polarity with the same frequency as the circular motion of the ions. Recall that this frequency depends only on the magnetic field strength and the charge-to-mass ratio of the ions, but not on their energy. As the ions circle around in the cyclotron, they are accelerated across the gap between the dees by the strong electric field associated with the potential difference. Because each

dee is a hollow, nearly closed conducting structure, there is no electric field within the dees.

Once inside a dee, the ions simply follow a circle in the magnetic field. Halfway round they again cross the gap between dees. If the electric field were steady, the ions would be *decelerated* at this crossing. But the electric field changes direction in step with the ions' circular motion, so each time the ions cross the dee gap they are accelerated and gain more energy. They move faster and in ever larger circles, but always

FIGURE 29-13 A cyclotron, showing one magnet pole, dees, and a typical ion trajectory (in red). Not shown are the vacuum chamber surrounding the dees, upper pole, and frame supporting pole pieces and electromagnet windings.

with the same orbital period. Eventually the ion orbits become nearly the size of the machine. At this point an electrostatic field provided by a high-voltage electrode deflects the ions out of the magnetic field and toward a target, where their interactions with target nuclei cause nuclear reactions.

In addition to providing experimental data on nuclear structure, cyclotrons are valuable in producing short-lived radioactive isotopes for a variety of purposes, particularly medical research and diagnosis. A number of large hospitals have their own cyclotrons (Fig. 29-14); in particular, the diagnostic procedure known as positron emission tomography (PET) requires cyclotron-produced radioisotopes.

At very high energies, the theory of relativity (Chapter 38) comes into play and alters our conclusion that the cyclotron frequency is independent of particle energy. As a result, the cyclotron cannot be used to achieve these relativistic energies. An alternate accelerator design is the **synchrotron**, in which both the magnetic field and frequency of an alternating electric field are varied to account for increasing particle energy, while the orbital radius is held constant (Fig. 29-15).

FIGURE 29-14 This cyclotron at Massachusetts General Hospital was used to produce radioisotopes for research leading to the development of the medical diagnostic procedure known as positron emission tomography (PET).

FIGURE 29-15 Aerial view of Fermilab, the Fermi National Accelerator Laboratory at Batavia, Illinois. Large circle is the 2-km diameter Tevatron, a synchrotron that accelerates protons to energies approaching 1 TeV (10^{12} eV).

EXAMPLE 29-4   *Designing a Cyclotron*

A cyclotron is to accelerate protons to a kinetic energy of 5.0 MeV. If the magnetic field in the cyclotron is 2.0 T, what must be the radius of the cyclotron and the frequency at which the dee voltage is alternated?

Solution
The cyclotron frequency is given by Equation 29-5:

$$f = \frac{qB}{2\pi m} = \frac{(1.6\times10^{-19}\ \text{C})(2.0\ \text{T})}{(2\pi)(1.67\times10^{-27}\ \text{kg})} = 3.0\times10^7\ \text{Hz}.$$

This is the frequency required to accelerate protons at each crossing of the dee gap; incidentally, it is about the frequency of a citizens band (CB) radio transmitter.

An energy of 5.0 MeV is equal to

$$(5.0\times10^6\ \text{eV})(1.6\times10^{-19}\ \text{J/eV}) = 8.0\times10^{-13}\ \text{J},$$

so the proton kinetic energy is

$$K = \tfrac{1}{2}mv^2 = 8.0\times10^{-13}\ \text{J}.$$

Solving for the speed v gives

$$v = \sqrt{\frac{2K}{m}} = \sqrt{\frac{(2)(8.0\times10^{-13}\ \text{J})}{1.67\times10^{-27}\ \text{kg}}} = 3.1\times10^7\ \text{m/s}.$$

Equation 29-3 then gives the radius needed to accommodate 5-MeV protons:

$$r = \frac{mv}{qB} = \frac{(1.67\times10^{-27}\ \text{kg})(3.1\times10^7\ \text{m/s})}{(1.6\times10^{-19}\ \text{C})(2.0\ \text{T})} = 0.16\ \text{m}.$$

To ensure a uniform magnetic field over the particle trajectories, the radii of the magnet pole pieces would have to be somewhat larger than this value.

EXERCISE A microwave oven uses 2.4-GHz microwaves, generated by electrons circling at this frequency in the magnetic field of a magnetron tube. (a) What is the magnetic field strength? (b) If the energy associated with an electron's circular motion is 890 eV, what is the radius of its circular path?

Answers: (a) 86 mT; (b) 1.2 mm

Some problems similar to Example 29-4: 17, 25, 26

FIGURE 29-16 A particle in a uniform magnetic field describes a spiral path, its motion along the field direction unaffected by the magnetic force.

(a)

(b)

FIGURE 29-17 (a) Charged particles undergoing spiral motion about the magnetic field direction are "frozen" to the field like (b) beads sliding along a wire.

FIGURE 29-18 Magnetic fields govern the behavior of matter throughout much of the universe. Here, concentrations of ionized gas trace out magnetic field loops in the Sun's atmosphere.

Particle Trajectories in Three Dimensions

What if a particle's motion is not confined to a plane perpendicular to the magnetic field? Then we can resolve its velocity into two vectors, one perpendicular and the other parallel to the magnetic field. Since the magnetic force is always perpendicular to the field, there is no component of force along the field direction—and therefore the velocity component in this direction is unaffected by the magnetic force. The force acts only on the velocity component perpendicular to the field, and here our previous analysis applies: in the plane perpendicular to the field, the particle's motion is circular with frequency given by Equation 29-5. In the absence of other forces the particle moves uniformly along the field direction while executing circular motion perpendicular to the field. The resulting trajectory is a spiral, as shown in Fig. 29-16.

The absence of magnetic force along the field direction means that particles move readily along the field. But if you try to push them at right angles to the field, they simply move in larger circles about the field direction. As a result, charged particles are often described as being "frozen" to the magnetic field (Fig. 29-17). Nonuniform fields and collisions between particles make this "freezing" of particles and field less than perfect, but in many cases the particle density is low enough that the "frozen" assumption is an excellent approximation. Unlike our relatively cool planet Earth, much of the universe consists of free electrons and protons, not bound into neutral atoms. As a result, magnetic fields are a dominant influence on matter throughout much of the universe (Fig. 29-18).

An important terrestrial application of this "trapping" of particles on magnetic field lines occurs in nuclear fusion reactors. These experimental devices—whose successful development would make 1 gallon of sea water the energy equivalent of more than 300 gallons of gasoline—have to contain ionized gas (plasma) at temperatures around 100 million kelvins. They do so with "magnetic bottles," most commonly toroidal (doughnut-shaped) chambers whose circular magnetic fields never intersect the chamber walls and therefore keep the hot plasma from touching the walls (Fig. 29-19).

(a)

(b)

FIGURE 29-19 (a) Charged particles spiral about the circular field lines in a simplified fusion reactor. With its toroidal shape, the machine has no "ends" from which magnetic field lines emerge. The field therefore keeps charged particles away from the chamber walls. (b) The Tokamak Fusion Test Reactor at Princeton University. This view, taken during construction, shows clearly the machine's toroidal shape.

Earth possesses a magnetic field whose origin we'll consider in the next chapter. This field shields Earth's surface from the direct impact of high-energy particles from the Sun and elsewhere in the cosmos. Particles reaching Earth's vicinity are trapped into spiral motion about the magnetic field, so they can't penetrate directly to the surface. This trapping generally occurs on the field lines that intersect Earth in the polar regions (Fig. 29-20*a*). High-energy particles moving along these field lines slam into the upper atmosphere near the poles, exciting oxygen and nitrogen atoms and thereby producing the spectacular displays we call the aurora (Fig. 29-20*b, c*). Bursts of solar particles also buffet Earth's magnetic field, causing "magnetic storms" that can severely disrupt communications and electric power transmission.

Fig. 29-21 shows a particle spiraling into a region of stronger magnetic field, like the polar regions in Fig. 29-20*a*. Note that there is a component of magnetic force opposite to the general direction of motion. This force eventually reverses the particle's forward motion, with the result that the stronger field region acts like a **magnetic mirror**, reflecting particles that attempt to penetrate. This means that particles trapped in Earth's magnetic field bounce back and forth between northern and southern hemispheres, reflected by the magnetic mirrors of higher field strength near the poles. Auroral displays in opposite hemispheres are often strikingly similar since they are caused by the same particle populations mirroring back and forth. Particles that penetrate the upper atmosphere and cause auroral displays combine with atmospheric atoms and are lost to the mirroring particle population, but they're continually replaced with new particles arriving from the Sun.

(*a*)

(*b*)

(*c*)

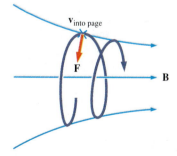

FIGURE 29-21 The magnetic mirror effect. A charged particle is spiraling into a region of stronger magnetic field. At the point shown its velocity is into the page, and the magnetic force—proportional to **v** × **B**—has a component to the left. This force eventually reverses the rightward motion of the particle.

FIGURE 29-20 The aurora arises from the interaction of high-energy particles trapped in Earth's magnetic field. (*a*) Particles trapped in the magnetic field spiral between the northern and southern polar regions. Diagram is highly simplified; Earth's field is actually more complicated because of interactions with the solar wind, a stream of ionized gas flowing outward from the Sun.
(*b*) A colorful aurora viewed from Canada's Prince Edward Island.
(*c*) The aurora appears as a circle surrounding Earth's north magnetic pole in this satellite image.

29-4 THE MAGNETIC FORCE ON A CURRENT

So far we've considered the magnetic force on individual charged particles. An electric current is simply a group of charged particles sharing a common motion, so we should expect a current to interact with a magnetic field.

The Force on a Straight Wire

Imagine a long straight wire carrying a current I through a uniform magnetic field $\mathbf{B}$, as shown in Fig. 29-22. If each charge carrier has a drift velocity $\mathbf{v}_d$ along the wire, and if each carries charge q, then the magnetic force on each charge carrier is given by Equation 29-1:

$$\mathbf{F}_q = q\mathbf{v}_d \times \mathbf{B}.$$

(Of course the charge carriers also have random thermal velocities. But these average to zero and therefore make no net contribution to the magnetic force.) If the wire has cross-sectional area A and contains n charge carriers per unit volume, then the net force on all the charge carriers in a length ℓ of the wire is

$$\mathbf{F} = nA\ell q\mathbf{v}_d \times \mathbf{B}.$$

The product $nAqv_d$ is just the current I, as we found in deriving Equation 27-2. If we define a vector $\boldsymbol{\ell}$ whose magnitude is the length ℓ of the wire and whose direction is along the current, then we can write

$$\mathbf{F} = I\boldsymbol{\ell} \times \mathbf{B}. \qquad \text{(magnetic force on a current)} \qquad (29\text{-}6)$$

The direction of this force is at right angles to both the current and the magnetic field, or out of the page in Fig. 29-22. For a given direction of the current, the direction of the force does not depend on the sign of the charge carriers. If the current is to the right, then positive charges move to the right and the force on each is out of the page. If the charges are negative, they move to the left and the force is still out of the page because both the sign of the velocity and the sign of the charge are reversed, given the same sign for the force $q\mathbf{v} \times \mathbf{B}$.

Strictly speaking, Equation 29-6 gives the net magnetic force only on the charge carriers in the wire. But the motion of the charge carriers—typically electrons—under the influence of the magnetic force causes charge separation in the wire, and the resulting electric field exerts a force on the fixed charges—typically ions—in the wire (Fig. 29-23). Thus the entire wire experiences the force. Although its origin is not entirely magnetic, we loosely call the force given by Equation 29-6 the magnetic force on the wire.

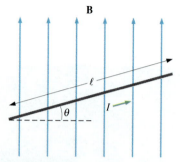

FIGURE 29-22 A straight wire carrying current I through a uniform magnetic field. The charge carriers in the wire experience a magnetic force, in this case out of the page.

FIGURE 29-23 Electrons moving to the left in a wire are deflected upward by the magnetic force, resulting in charge separation and therefore in an upward electric force on the fixed ions. As a result the entire wire is ultimately influenced by the magnetic force on the moving electrons.

The magnetic force on a current-carrying wire is the basis for many practical devices, including loudspeakers and the electric motors that start cars and run refrigerators, CD players, computer disk drives, subway trains, pumps, food processors, power tools, and myriad other useful instruments of modern society. At the end of this chapter we'll see just how electric motors work.

Got It!

Figure 29-24 shows a flexible, current-carrying wire passing through a region where a magnetic field points out of the page. The wire is deflected to the right, as shown in Fig. 29-24. Is the current flowing upward or downward in the wire?

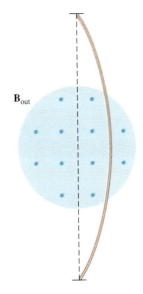

FIGURE 29-24 A flexible wire passes through a region containing a magnetic field pointing out of the page. Which direction is the current in the wire when it's deflected as shown?

EXAMPLE 29-5	*Magnetic Force on a Power Line*

A power line runs along Earth's equator, where Earth's magnetic field points horizontally from south to north and has a strength of about 0.5 G. The current in the power line is 500 A, flowing from west to east. What are the magnitude and direction of the magnetic force on 1 km of the power line?

Solution

Let eastward be the x direction, northward the y direction, and upward the z direction. After we convert gauss to tesla, Equation 29-6 gives

$$\mathbf{F} = I\boldsymbol{\ell} \times \mathbf{B} = (500 \text{ A})(1000\hat{\mathbf{i}} \text{ m}) \times (0.5 \times 10^{-4}\,\hat{\mathbf{j}} \text{ T})$$
$$= 25\hat{\mathbf{k}} \text{ N}.$$

This 25-N upward force is negligible compared with the weight—on the order of 2×10^4 N—of 1 km of power line.

EXERCISE A 2.0-m-long wire has a mass of 37 g. The wire extends horizontally, at 40° to a horizontal magnetic field of 0.075 T. What current in the wire will result in the magnetic force suspending it against gravity?

Answer: 3.8 A

Some problems similar to Example 29-5: 33, 35, 37

APPLICATION	*Magnetic Levitation and Propulsion*

Engineers throughout the world are at work on transportation systems whose operation results directly from the magnetic force on a straight current-carrying conductor. In so-called maglev vehicles, magnetic forces levitate the vehicle just a few centimeters above a conducting guideway and also provide the horizontal force that propels the vehicle (Fig. 29-25). Such vehicles should be capable of 500-km/h speeds, well above the 300 km/h maximum for high-speed rail systems. Maglev vehicles should prove especially effective for travel between cities in densely populated regions.

A related application is so-called magnetohydrodynamic (MHD) propulsion, a kind of jet propulsion in which a

FIGURE 29-25 A magnetically levitated vehicle under development in Japan.

(a)

Source: Mitsubishi Heavy Industries

(b)

conducting fluid is accelerated by the magnetic force. Engineers are currently experimenting with MHD propulsion for ships. Because sea water is a reasonably good electrical conductor, passage of a current through sea water in a magnetic field results in a magnetic force on the water. Figure 29-26 shows the experimental Japanese ship Yamato-1 and its MHD propulsion system.

FIGURE 29-26 (*a*) The Japanese ship Yamato-1 uses MHD propulsion. (*b*) Schematic diagram of the MHD propulsion unit. Superconducting electromagnet produces a magnetic field; current flowing in the sea water between the two electrodes then experiences a magnetic force that ejects a jet of water at right.

APPLICATION	*The Hall Effect*

The force on a current-carrying conductor is independent of the sign of the charge carriers. But there's a subtle difference. Fig. 29-27 shows two conductors, each with the same current I to the right and magnetic field $\mathbf{B}$ pointing into the page. In Fig. 29-27*a* the current is carried by electrons moving to the *left*. The product $\mathbf{v} \times \mathbf{B}$ is downward, but since electrons are negative the force $q\mathbf{v} \times \mathbf{B}$ is upward. As a result, the upper edge of the conductor is negative with respect to the lower edge. In Fig. 29-27*b* the current is carried by protons moving to the *right*. Again the force $q\mathbf{v} \times \mathbf{B}$ is upward, so now the upper edge of the conductor is positive.

This phenomenon of charge separation is the **Hall effect**. The separated charge gives rise to an electric field and therefore to a measurable potential difference—the **Hall potential**—between opposite edges of the conductor. The sign of the Hall potential depends on the sign of the charge carriers. Charge separation will stop once the electric force on the charge carriers cancels the magnetic force. The electric force has magnitude qE and, with $\mathbf{B}$ perpendicular to the current, the magnetic force has magnitude $qv_d B$, with v_d the charge-carrier drift speed. Equating these magnitudes gives $E = v_d B$. In a rectangular conductor this field will be essentially uniform, so the Hall potential becomes

$$V_H = Eh = v_d Bh,$$

where h is the conductor height shown in Fig. 29-27. But Equation 27-2 gives $I = nAqv_d$, with n the number density of charge carriers, A the conductor's cross-sectional area, and q

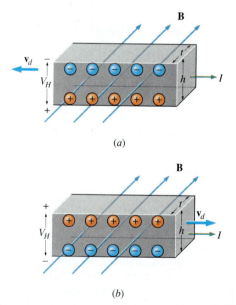

(a)

(b)

FIGURE 29-27 The Hall potential V_H arises from the deflection of charge carriers by the magnetic force when a current-carrying conductor is in a magnetic field. Although the magnetic force on the conductor is independent of the sign of the charge carriers, the sign of the Hall potential does depend on the sign of the charge carriers. In both (*a*) and (*b*) the current is to the right, carried in (*a*) by negative charge carriers moving to the left and in (*b*) by positive charge carriers moving to the right.

the charge on each carrier. Solving for v_d and using the result in our expression for V_H gives

$$V_H = \frac{IBh}{nAq},$$

or, since $A = ht$ with t the conductor thickness shown in Fig. 29-27,

$$V_H = \frac{IB}{nqt}. \qquad (29\text{-}7)$$

The quantity $1/nq$ is the **Hall coefficient**. Measurement of V_H in a sample of known thickness carrying known current in a known magnetic field yields the value of this coefficient and, thus, gives information on the nature and density of the charge carriers. Alternatively, measurement of V_H in a material with known Hall coefficient carrying a known current provides a direct measure of the magnetic field strength (see Problem 45).

Nonuniform Fields and Curved Conductors

Equation 29-6 gives the force, $\mathbf{F} = I\boldsymbol{\ell} \times \mathbf{B}$, on a straight conductor of length ℓ carrying current I in a uniform magnetic field $\mathbf{B}$. We can still use this equation if the conductor bends or the field varies with position, if we apply it only to a very small segment of this conductor—so small that the segment is essentially straight and the field essentially uniform over the segment. Designating this segment by $d\boldsymbol{\ell}$, Equation 29-6 becomes

$$d\mathbf{F} = I\,d\boldsymbol{\ell} \times \mathbf{B}$$

for the small force on the segment (Fig. 29-28). To find the total force on the conductor, we sum the forces on all such segments. In the limit of very small segments, this sum becomes an integral, and we have

$$\mathbf{F} = \int d\mathbf{F} = \int I\,d\boldsymbol{\ell} \times \mathbf{B}. \qquad (29\text{-}8)$$

The integration is taken over the entire section of conductor on which we are calculating the force.

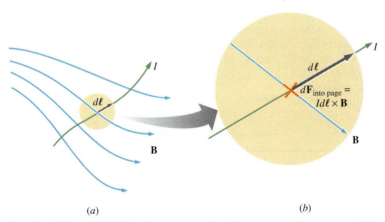

(a)   (b)

FIGURE 29-28 (a) A curved conductor in a nonuniform magnetic field. (b) A small segment $d\boldsymbol{\ell}$ can be treated as a straight wire in a uniform field; the magnetic force on the segment is $d\mathbf{F} = I\,d\boldsymbol{\ell} \times \mathbf{B}$.

EXAMPLE 29-6	*The Force on a Curved Conductor*

A semicircular wire connects two points C and D a horizontal distance $2R$ apart (Fig. 29-29a). The wire carries a current I from C to D and is in a uniform magnetic field $\mathbf{B}$ pointing upward. Show that the magnetic force on this semicircular wire is the same as the force that a straight wire from C to D would experience if it carried the same current I.

Solution

Since the orientation of the wire relative to the field varies, we use the integral in Equation 29-8 to calculate the force. Figure 29-29a shows an infinitesimal segment $d\ell$ of the wire, and the angle θ that specifies its position on the semicircular arc. This infinitesimal segment subtends an infinitesimal angle $d\theta$, as shown. A blown-up view of the segment (Fig. 29-29b) shows that the angle between the segment $d\ell$ and the magnetic field $\mathbf{B}$ is also θ. Then the magnitude of the force on the segment is

$$dF = I\,d\ell\,B\sin\theta.$$

Application of the right-hand rule shows that the direction of the force element is out of the page for all values of θ on the semicircle—that is, for $0 \le \theta \le \pi$. Therefore, the integral in Equation 29-8 describes a sum of vectors all of which point in the same direction, so the magnitude of the net force is

$$F = \int dF = \int_0^\pi IB\sin\theta\,d\ell.$$

But $d\ell$ subtends the angle $d\theta$, so $d\ell = R\,d\theta$ (Fig. 29-30). Then, taking the constants I, B, and R outside the integral, we have

$$F = IBR\int_0^\pi \sin\theta\,d\theta = IBR\,(-\cos\theta)\Big|_0^\pi$$
$$= IBR[-(-1-1)] = IB(2R).$$

This is just the force we would get from Equation 29-6 for a straight wire of length $2R$ carrying current I perpendicular to a magnetic field $\mathbf{B}$. You can see why this is: Equation 29-6 shows that the magnetic force depends on the quantity $d\ell \sin\theta$, which is the component of the segment $d\ell$ perpendicular to the field. That component is what you get if you take the straight path from C to D instead of the semicircle. Indeed, the force on any piece of wire carrying the same current from C to D would be the same as long as it stayed in the region of uniform field. A corollary is that the net force on any *closed* loop of current in a uniform magnetic field must be zero (see Problem 43).

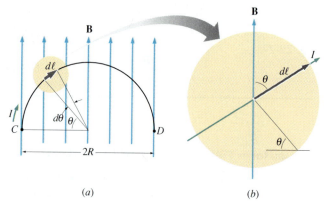

(a)   (b)

FIGURE 29-29 (a) A semicircular wire carries current I between points C and D. (b) Blowup of an infinitesimal segment $d\ell$ of the wire, showing that the segment makes an angle θ with the magnetic field.

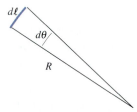

FIGURE 29-30 An angle in radians is defined as the ratio of subtended arc to radius. Here the angle $d\theta$ is so small that the difference between a circular arc and the straight segment $d\ell$ is insignificant. Therefore $d\ell = R\,d\theta$.

EXERCISE A 15-cm-long wire carrying 4.8 A is bent into a quarter circle and oriented like the left half of the semicircular wire in Fig. 29-29a (i.e., from point C to the top of the semicircle). If the magnetic field shown in Fig. 29-29a has magnitude 0.65 T, what is the magnetic force on the wire?

Answer: 0.30 N

Some problems similar to Example 29-6: 40–43

A common application using the force on a current-carrying wire is the loudspeaker, shown in Fig. 29-31. Here an unusually shaped magnet produces a nonuniform magnetic field that results in a net force on a current-carrying coil. The current in the coil alternates direction in accordance with the audio signal

(a)

(b)

FIGURE 29-31 A loudspeaker uses the magnetic force on a current-carrying coil to convert electrical energy into sound. (*a*) Cutaway view; (*b*) top view of the magnet, showing the nonuniform field and placement of the coil. With the current direction indicated, the net force is into the page. There's a net force on the loop only because the field is nonuniform.

from an amplifier, and this results in an alternating force that moves the coil back and forth. The coil, in turn, is connected to a flexible cone that moves to produce sound waves.

29-5 A CURRENT LOOP IN A MAGNETIC FIELD

Closed loops of current are important in a wide variety of natural and technological systems. Loops of current-carrying wire are at the heart of every electric motor, while miniature current loops associated with charged quarks circulating within the proton are responsible for nuclear magnetic resonance (NMR), widely used to determine the structure of chemical compounds and as the basis of the medical technique called magnetic resonance imaging (MRI). We now show that the magnetic forces on different parts of a current loop result in a torque on the loop; it's that torque that drives electric motors and the motion of protons in NMR.

Consider a rectangular current loop in a uniform magnetic field, with the normal to the loop making an angle θ with the magnetic field, as shown in Fig. 29-32a. Since current flows in opposite directions on opposite sides and since the field is uniform, the magnetic forces on opposite sides cancel and there is no net magnetic force on the loop. The right-hand rule shows that the forces on the top and bottom of the loop point directly upward and downward, respectively, and therefore result in no net torque.

The forces on the vertical sections of the loop, however, do produce a torque. Figure 29-32b shows a top view of the loop, with the forces resulting from the

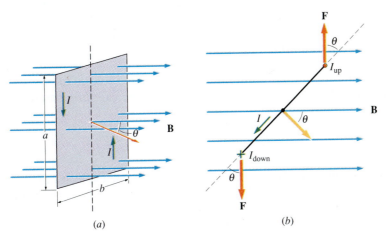

(a)

(b)

FIGURE 29-32 (*a*) A rectangular current loop in a uniform magnetic field. Shading indicates the plane of the loop. The angle between the loop normal and the magnetic field is θ. (*b*) Top view of the current loop, showing that magnetic forces on the vertical sides result in a net torque. The angles used in the torque calculation are the same as the angle θ between the loop normal and the magnetic field.

upward- and downward-flowing currents in the vertical sides. From the figure, it's clear that these forces give rise to a net torque twisting the loop counterclockwise. Each vertical side is a straight wire of length a carrying current I at right angles to the horizontally directed magnetic field $\mathbf{B}$, so the magnitude of the force on each side is simply

$$F_{\text{side}} = IaB .$$

The distance from the loop's central axis to the sides where this force acts is half the loop width, or $b/2$. The geometry of Fig. 29-32b shows that the angle used in calculating the torque is the same as the angle θ between the loop normal and the magnetic field. Therefore, the torque due to the force on each side is

$$\tau_{\text{side}} = F\frac{b}{2}\sin\theta = Ia\frac{b}{2}B\sin\theta .$$

Accounting for the contributions from both sides gives the magnitude of the net torque on the loop:

$$\tau = IabB\sin\theta .$$

We can express the torque in vector notation if we define a vector $\mathbf{A}$ whose magnitude is the area ab of the loop and which is perpendicular to the loop. We choose the direction of $\mathbf{A}$ by the right-hand rule: wrap your fingers around the loop in the direction of the current and your thumb points in the direction of $\mathbf{A}$. This is the same direction as the loop normal shown in Fig. 29-32. Then we can write

$$\tau = I\mathbf{A} \times \mathbf{B} . \qquad (29\text{-}9)$$

Although we derived this equation for a rectangular loop, it holds in fact for any current loop. The torque on a current loop depends on the current, the loop area, the magnetic field, and the orientation between loop and field.

Equation 29-9 should remind you of Equation 23-12 for the torque on an electric dipole in an electric field. There we had

$$\tau = \mathbf{p} \times \mathbf{E} ,$$

where $\mathbf{p}$ is the electric dipole moment and $\mathbf{E}$ the electric field. Comparison with Equation 29-9 suggests that a current loop in a magnetic field behaves analogously to an electric dipole in an electric field. As far as its response to magnetic fields is concerned, therefore,

▌ **A current loop constitutes a magnetic dipole.**

The quantity $I\mathbf{A}$ in Equation 29-9 plays the same role as the electric dipole moment in the equation $\tau = \mathbf{p} \times \mathbf{E}$. We therefore call this quantity the **magnetic dipole moment, $\boldsymbol{\mu}$**:

$$\boldsymbol{\mu} = I\mathbf{A} . \qquad \text{(single-turn loop)}$$

The direction of the vector $\boldsymbol{\mu}$ is the same as the direction we defined for $\mathbf{A}$: curl your right fingers in the direction of the loop current, and your thumb points in the direction of $\boldsymbol{\mu}$ (Fig. 29-33). (With ActivPhysics Activity 13.6 you can

FIGURE 29-33 Using the right-hand rule to find the direction of a current loop's magnetic moment.

graphically resize a current loop to see the effect on magnetic moment and torque.) More generally, a loop may consist of N turns of conducting wire; then each contributes $I\mathbf{A}$ to give the total magnetic moment:

13.6

Torque on a Current Loop

$$\boldsymbol{\mu} = NI\mathbf{A}. \qquad \text{(magnetic dipole moment)} \qquad (29\text{-}10)$$

Clearly the units of magnetic moment are A·m². Using the magnetic moment vector, Equation 29-9 then becomes

$$\boldsymbol{\tau} = \boldsymbol{\mu} \times \mathbf{B}, \qquad \text{(torque on a current loop)} \qquad (29\text{-}11)$$

in analogy with the electric case. The magnetic moment vector of a current loop is perpendicular to the plane of the loop, and the torque given in Equation 29-11 tends to align the magnetic moment with the field (Fig. 29-34). It takes work to twist the loop's magnetic moment vector out of alignment with the field. In exact analogy with the electric-dipole case summarized in Equation 23-10, we express the associated potential energy as

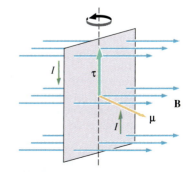

FIGURE 29-34 The torque on a current loop tends to align the loop's magnetic moment vector with the magnetic field.

$$U_{\text{magnetic}} = -\boldsymbol{\mu} \cdot \mathbf{B}. \qquad (29\text{-}12)$$

EXAMPLE 29-7	*Pointing a Satellite*

Solution

Some satellites use the magnetic torque on current loops to point themselves in space. Earth itself provides the magnetic field, while electricity from solar panels powers coils that constitute the current loops; unlike rocket-based pointing systems, there's no fuel to run out. Three mutually perpendicular coils allow the satellite to point itself in any direction. One satellite uses 30-cm-diameter circular coils, each with 1000 turns. (a) If the satellite orbits at an altitude where Earth's magnetic field is 0.24 G, and if specifications call for a maximum torque of 1.3 mN·m from each coil, what should be the coil current? (b) How much work is done on the coil to rotate it from its maximum-torque orientation to an angle of 120° to the field?

Solution

(a) The maximum torque occurs when the coil's magnetic moment is perpendicular to the field; Equation 29-11 shows that this maximum torque has magnitude $\tau_{\text{max}} = \mu B$. The magnetic moment of the coil is the product of the number of turns, the current, and the coil area πR^2, as given by Equation 29-10. Thus the maximum torque is

$$\tau_{\text{max}} = NI\pi R^2 B.$$

Solving for the current gives

$$I = \frac{\tau_{\text{max}}}{N\pi R^2 B} = \frac{1.3\times10^{-3}\ \text{N·m}}{(1000)(\pi)(0.15\ \text{m})^2(0.24\times10^{-4}\ \text{T})}$$

$$= 0.766\ \text{A}.$$

(b) The loop's potential energy is given by Equation 29-12: $U = -\boldsymbol{\mu} \cdot \mathbf{B} = -\mu B\cos\theta$. Maximum torque occurs when $\theta = 90°$, so the work in rotating the coil—equal to the difference in its potential energies in the two orientations—is

$$W = U_{120°} - U_{90°} = -\mu B\cos 120° - (-\mu B\cos 90°)$$

$$= (-1.3\times10^{-3}\ \text{N·m})(\cos 120°)$$

$$= 0.65\ \text{mJ},$$

where we recognized the quantity μB as the maximum torque defined earlier.

EXERCISE An electric motor consists of a 550-turn loop with area 100 cm² in a 0.23-T magnetic field. What loop current is necessary if the motor is to develop a maximum torque of 3.7 N·m?

Answer: 2.9 A

Some problems similar to Example 29-7: 47, 48, 50–52

APPLICATION	*Electric Motors*

Electric motors are so much a part of our lives that we hardly think of them. But CD players, car starters, refrigerators, vacuum cleaners, power saws, subway trains, computer disk drives, food processors, washing machines, fans, hair dryers, water pumps, oil burners, and most industrial machinery would be difficult or impossible to build without electric motors (Fig. 29-35).

At the heart of every electric motor is a current loop in a magnetic field. But instead of a steady current, the loop carries a current that reverses periodically. In direct-current (DC) motors, this reversal is achieved through the electrical contacts

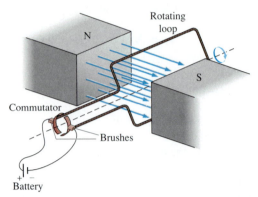

FIGURE 29-36 A simple electric motor. Current flows from the battery through the stationary brushes to the rotating commutator and loop. The direction of the loop current reverses as the two halves of the commutator rotate to contact different brushes.

FIGURE 29-35 (*a*) A small electric motor, partially disassembled. At left is the rotating coil (1), surrounded by permanent magnets (2). The commutator (3) is on the forward shaft. At right are the brushes (4), which fit around the commutator to supply current to the rotating coils. (*b*) This electric motor powers General Motors' EV1 electric car.

that provide current to the loop. Figure 29-36 shows a simple motor consisting of a loop in the field of a permanent magnet. Current from an external battery reaches the loop through a set of stationary "brushes," which make contact with a pair of semicircular conductors called the "commutator." The commutator is attached rigidly to the loop, which rotates to align its dipole moment with the field. Just as it reaches alignment, however, the brushes cross the gaps in the commutator. This reverses the connections to the battery, reversing the loop current. This in turn reverses the magnetic moment of the loop, so it's no longer aligned with the field. The loop then rotates another 180° to align its new magnetic moment vector with the field. Just as it reaches alignment, the current again reverses. This process repeats, resulting in continuous rotation of the loop. A rigid shaft through loop and commutator delivers mechanical work to the device powered by the motor. The source of this work is the battery or whatever supplies electrical energy to the motor. The motor itself is a device that converts electrical to mechanical energy; the magnetic field is an intermediary in this conversion.

CHAPTER SYNOPSIS

Summary

1. **Magnetism** is a fundamental interaction described in terms of **magnetic fields**. Magnetic fields interact with **moving electric charges**. A moving charged particle experiences a force that depends on its charge, its velocity, and the magnetic field. The force is at right angles to both velocity and field, and is given by

$$\mathbf{F} = q\mathbf{v} \times \mathbf{B}.$$

Because it's at right angles to the particle's velocity, the magnetic force does no work on a charged particle. In a uniform magnetic field, a particle's trajectory is a circle or spiral, with orbital period independent of the particle's speed.

2. An electric current is made up of moving electric charges, so there is a net magnetic force on an electric current. For a straight wire of length ℓ carrying current I in a magnetic

field **B**, the force is

$$\mathbf{F} = I\boldsymbol{\ell} \times \mathbf{B}.$$

3. A particularly important case of a current in a magnetic field is a closed current loop. Such a loop behaves like a **magnetic dipole** with magnetic dipole moment

$$\boldsymbol{\mu} = NI\mathbf{A},$$

where N is the number of turns in the loop, I the loop current, and **A** a vector perpendicular to the plane of the loop and whose magnitude is the loop area. A current loop in a magnetic field experiences a torque given by $\boldsymbol{\tau} = \boldsymbol{\mu} \times \mathbf{B}$, and the associated potential energy is $U_B = -\boldsymbol{\mu} \cdot \mathbf{B}$.

Terms You Should Understand

(Pairs are closely related terms whose distinction is important; number in parentheses is chapter section where term first appears.)

magnetic field (29-1, 29-2)
magnetic force, electromagnetic force (29-2)
tesla, gauss (29-2)
cyclotron frequency (29-3)
cyclotron, synchrotron (29-3)
magnetic mirror (29-3)
Hall effect, Hall potential (29-4)
current loop (29-5)

magnetic dipole moment (29-5)
electric motor (29-5)

Symbols You Should Recognize

B (29-1, 29-2)
T (29-2)
$\boldsymbol{\mu}$ (29-5)

Problems You Should Be Able to Solve

calculating magnetic force vectors given charge, velocity, and magnetic field (29-2)
analyzing charged-particle trajectories in uniform magnetic fields (29-3)
finding magnetic forces on straight conductors in uniform fields (29-4)
using integration to determine magnetic forces with curved conductors and/or nonuniform fields (29-4)
determining magnetic dipole moments of current loops (29-5)
evaluating torque and potential energy for current loops in magnetic fields (29-5)

Limitations to Keep in Mind

Magnetic forces arise only when charges are *moving*.
The cyclotron frequency is independent of particle energy only for speeds much less than the speed of light.

QUESTIONS

1. A charged particle moves through a region containing only a magnetic field. Under what condition will the particle experience no force?
2. An electron moving with velocity **v** through a magnetic field **B** experiences a magnetic force **F**. Which of the vectors **F**, **v**, and **B** must be at right angles?
3. In Fig. 29-37 a high-energy gamma ray has decayed into an electron and its positively charged antiparticle, a positron. A magnetic field points out of the plane of the photograph, and the electron and positron spiral in this field. Which path belongs to which particle?
4. A magnetic field points out of this page. Will a positively charged particle moving in the plane of the page circle clockwise or counterclockwise as viewed from above?
5. An electron moves through a region in a straight line at constant speed. Can you conclude that there is no magnetic field in the region? Could you so conclude if you knew that there were no electric or gravitational forces on the electron? Explain.
6. High-resolution color TV monitors sometimes have a built-in circuit that compensates for changes in the orientation of Earth's magnetic field relative to the TV picture tube as the monitor is moved from one place to another. Why is this necessary?
7. What is meant by the statement that charged particles can be "trapped" by magnetic fields?
8. An electron beam comes straight to the center of a TV screen, where it makes a spot of light. If you hold the north pole of a bar magnet on the left side of the picture tube, which way will the spot move? (Magnetic field lines emerge from the north pole of a magnet.)

FIGURE 29-37 Creation of an electron-positron pair in the decay of a gamma ray incident from the top of the figure. Both particles come into existence moving essentially downward in the photo, at the point where the two trajectories diverge. (Question 3)

9. Do particles in a cyclotron gain energy from the electric field, the magnetic field, or both? Explain.

10. A cyclotron is designed to accelerate either hydrogen or deuterium nuclei. If the magnetic field is unchanged, how must the frequency of the alternating dee voltage be changed in order to switch from hydrogen to deuterium?

11. An electron and a proton moving at the same speed enter a region containing a uniform magnetic field. Which is deflected more from its original path?

12. An electron and a proton with the same kinetic energy enter a region containing a uniform magnetic field. Which is deflected more from its original path?

13. For what orientation of electric and magnetic fields could the net force on a particle be zero?

14. Will the velocity selector of Example 29-2 work for particles coming out of the page in Fig. 29-8? Why or why not?

15. What does magnetism have to do with the fact that auroras are seen near Earth's poles?

16. In a certain region uniform electric and magnetic fields are at right angles to one another. A positively charged particle is released from rest in this region. Describe qualitatively its subsequent motion.

17. How do the period and radius of an electron's orbit in a magnetic field depend on its velocity?

18. Current in a certain ionic solution is carried equally by positive and negative ions. Would you expect the Hall effect to occur in this solution?

19. Two identical particles carrying equal charge are moving in opposite directions along a magnetic field, when they collide elastically head-on. Describe their subsequent motion.

20. Repeat the above question for the case when the two particles are moving instantaneously perpendicular to the field when they collide.

21. Under what conditions will a current loop in a magnetic field experience zero torque?

22. What would happen to a motor with no commutator?

PROBLEMS

ActivPhysics can help with these problems:
Activities 13.4, 13.6, 13.7, 13.8

Section 29-2 The Magnetic Force on a Moving Charge

1. (a) What is the minimum magnetic field needed to exert a 5.4×10^{-15}-N force on an electron moving at 2.1×10^7 m/s? (b) What magnetic field strength would be required if the field were at 45° to the electron's velocity?

2. An electron moving at right angles to a 0.10-T magnetic field experiences an acceleration of 6.0×10^{15} m/s². (a) What is the electron's speed? (b) By how much does its *speed* change in 1 ns ($= 10^{-9}$ s)?

3. What is the magnitude of the magnetic force on a proton moving at 2.5×10^5 m/s (a) at right angles; (b) at 30°; (c) parallel to a magnetic field of 0.50 T?

4. A magnetic field of 0.10 T points in the x direction. A charged particle carrying 1.0 μC enters the field region moving at 20 m/s. What are the magnitude and direction of the force on the particle when it first enters the field region if it does so moving (a) along the x axis; (b) along the y axis; (c) along the z axis; (d) at 45° to both x and y axes?

5. A particle carrying a 50-μC charge moves with velocity $\mathbf{v} = 5.0\hat{\mathbf{i}} + 3.2\hat{\mathbf{k}}$ m/s through a uniform magnetic field $\mathbf{B} = 9.4\hat{\mathbf{i}} + 6.7\hat{\mathbf{j}}$ T. (a) What is the force on the particle? (b) Form the dot products $\mathbf{F} \cdot \mathbf{v}$ and $\mathbf{F} \cdot \mathbf{B}$ to show explicitly that the force is perpendicular to both $\mathbf{v}$ and $\mathbf{B}$.

6. Moving in the x direction, a particle carrying 1.0 μC experiences no force. Moving with speed v at 30° to the x axis, the particle experiences a magnetic force of 2.0 N. What magnetic force would it experience if it moved along the y axis with speed v?

7. A proton moving with velocity $\mathbf{v}_1 = 3.6\times10^4 \hat{\mathbf{j}}$ m/s experiences a magnetic force of $7.4\times10^{-16} \hat{\mathbf{i}}$ N. A second proton moving on the x axis experiences a magnetic force of $2.8\times10^{-16} \hat{\mathbf{j}}$ N. Find the magnitude and direction of the magnetic field, and the velocity of the second proton.

8. The magnitude of Earth's magnetic field is a little less than 1 G near Earth's surface. What is the maximum possible magnetic force on an electron with kinetic energy of 1 keV? Compare with the gravitational force on the same electron.

9. An alpha particle (2 protons, 2 neutrons) is moving with velocity $\mathbf{v} = 150\hat{\mathbf{i}} + 320\hat{\mathbf{j}} - 190\hat{\mathbf{k}}$ km/s in a magnetic field $\mathbf{B} = 0.66\hat{\mathbf{i}} - 0.41\hat{\mathbf{j}}$ T. Find the magnetic force on the particle.

10. How much charge would you need to put on a 2.7-g ping-pong ball so the magnetic force when it's moving at 6.0 m/s at right angles to Earth's 44-μT magnetic field is equal to its weight? Is this realistic?

11. A 1.4-μC charge moving at 185 m/s experiences a magnetic force $\mathbf{F}_B = 2.5\hat{\mathbf{i}} + 7.0\hat{\mathbf{j}}$ μN in a magnetic field $\mathbf{B} = 42\hat{\mathbf{i}} - 15\hat{\mathbf{j}}$ mT. What is the angle between the particle's velocity and the magnetic field?

12. A velocity selector uses a 60-mT magnetic field and a 24 kN/C electric field. At what speed will charged particles pass through the selector undeflected?

13. A region contains an electric field $\mathbf{E} = 7.4\hat{\mathbf{i}} + 2.8\hat{\mathbf{j}}$ kN/C and a magnetic field $\mathbf{B} = 15\hat{\mathbf{j}} + 36\hat{\mathbf{k}}$ mT. Find the electromagnetic force on (a) a stationary proton, (b) an electron moving with velocity $\mathbf{v} = 6.1\hat{\mathbf{i}}$ Mm/s.

14. A charged particle is moving at right angles to both a 1.1 kN/C electric field and a 0.75-T magnetic field. If the magnitude of the electric force on the particle is twice that of the magnetic force, what is the particle's speed?

Section 29-3 The Motion of Charged Particles in Magnetic Fields

15. What is the radius of the circular path described by a proton moving at 15 km/s in a plane perpendicular to a 400-G magnetic field?

16. How long does it take an electron to complete a circular orbit at right angles to a 1.0-G magnetic field?

17. Radio astronomers detect electromagnetic radiation at a frequency of 42 MHz from an interstellar gas cloud. If this radiation is caused by electrons spiraling in a magnetic field, what is the field strength in the gas cloud?

18. A beam of electrons moving in the x direction at 8.7×10^6 m/s enters a region where a uniform magnetic field of 180 G points in the y direction. How far into the field region does the beam penetrate?

19. Electrons and protons with the same kinetic energy are moving at right angles to a uniform magnetic field. How do their orbital radii compare?

20. The Van Allen belts are regions in space where high-energy charged particles are trapped in Earth's magnetic field. If the field strength at the Van Allen belts is 0.10 G, what are the period and radius of the spiral path described (a) by a proton with a 1.0-MeV kinetic energy? (b) by a 10-MeV proton?

21. Microwaves in a microwave oven are produced by electrons circling in a magnetic field at a frequency of 2.4 GHz. (a) What is the magnetic field strength? (b) The electrons' motion takes place inside a special tube called a magnetron. If the magnetron can accommodate electron orbits with a maximum diameter of 2.5 mm, what is the maximum electron energy?

22. Show that the orbital radius of a charged particle moving at right angles to a magnetic field B can be written

$$r = \frac{\sqrt{2Km}}{qB},$$

where K is the kinetic energy in joules, m the particle mass, and q its charge.

23. Two protons, moving in a plane perpendicular to a uniform magnetic field of 500 G, undergo an elastic head-on collision. How much time elapses before they collide again? *Hint:* Draw a picture.

24. Repeat the preceding problem for the case of a proton and an antiproton colliding head-on (a) if they have the same speed and (b) if they have different speeds. (An antiproton has the same mass as a proton, but carries the opposite charge.)

25. A cyclotron is designed to accelerate deuterium nuclei. (Deuterium has one proton and one neutron in its nucleus.)

(a) If the cyclotron uses a 2.0-T magnetic field, at what frequency should the dee voltage be alternated? (b) If the vacuum chamber has a diameter of 0.90 m, what is the maximum kinetic energy of the deuterons? (c) If the magnitude of the potential difference between the dees is 1500 V, how many orbits do the deuterons complete before achieving the energy of part (b)?

26. Without changing the magnetic field, how could the cyclotron of the preceding problem be modified to accelerate (a) protons and (b) alpha particles (two protons and two neutrons)? What would be the maximum energy achievable with (c) protons and (d) alpha particles?

27. Figure 29-38 shows a simple mass spectrometer, designed to analyze and separate atomic and molecular ions with different charge-to-mass ratios. In the design shown, ions are accelerated through a potential difference V, after which they enter a region containing a uniform magnetic field. They describe semicircular paths in the magnetic field, and land on a detector a lateral distance x from where they entered the field region, as shown. Show that x is given by

$$x = \frac{2}{B}\sqrt{\frac{2V}{(q/m)}},$$

where B is the magnetic field strength, V the accelerating potential, and q/m the charge-to-mass ratio of the ion. By counting the number of ions accumulated at different positions x, one can determine the relative abundances of different atomic or molecular species in a sample.

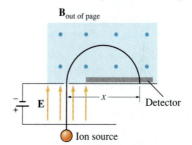

FIGURE 29-38 A mass spectrometer (Problem 27).

28. A mass spectrometer like that of the preceding problem has $V = 2000$ V and $B = 1000$ G. It is used to analyze a gas sample suspected of containing Ne, O_2, CO, SO_2, and NO_2. Ions are detected at distances of 58 cm, 68 cm, and 87 cm from the entrance to the field region. Which gases are actually present? Assume that all molecules are singly ionized.

29. A mass spectrometer is used to separate the fissionable uranium isotope U-235 from the much more abundant isotope U-238. To within what percentage must the magnetic field be held constant if there is to be no overlap of these two isotopes? Both isotopes appear as constituents of uranium hexafluoride gas (UF_6), and the gas molecules are all singly ionized.

30. An electron is moving in a uniform magnetic field of 0.25 T; its velocity components parallel and perpendicular to the field are both equal to 3.1×10^6 m/s. (a) What is the radius of the electron's spiral path? (b) How far does it move along the field direction in the time it takes to complete a full orbit about the field direction?

31. An electron moving at 3.8×10^6 m/s enters a region containing a uniform magnetic field $\mathbf{B} = 18\hat{\mathbf{k}}$ mT. The electron is moving at $70°$ to the field direction, as shown in Fig. 29-39. Find the radius r and pitch p of its spiral path, as indicated in the figure.

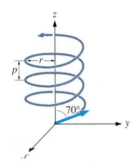

FIGURE 29-39 Problems 31, 32.

32. A proton in interstellar space describes a spiral path about a 15-mG magnetic field, with velocity component 40 km/s perpendicular to the field. If the pitch of the helix (see Fig. 29-39) is 8.7 km, what is the proton's velocity component parallel to the field?

Section 29-4 The Magnetic Force on a Current

33. What is the magnitude of the force on a 50-cm-long wire carrying 15 A at right angles to a 500-G magnetic field?

34. A wire coincides with the x axis, carrying 2.4 A in the $+x$ direction. The wire passes through a region containing a uniform magnetic field $\mathbf{B} = 0.17\hat{\mathbf{i}} + 0.32\hat{\mathbf{j}} - 0.21\hat{\mathbf{k}}$ T. Find a vector expression for the force per unit length on the wire in the magnetic field region.

35. A wire carrying 15 A makes a $25°$ angle with a uniform magnetic field. The magnetic force per unit length of wire is 0.31 N/m. (a) What is the magnetic field strength? (b) What is the maximum force per unit length that could be achieved by reorienting the wire in this field?

36. A wire of negligible resistance is bent into a rectangle as shown in Fig. 29-40, and a battery and resistor are connected as shown. The right-hand side of the circuit extends

FIGURE 29-40 Problem 36.

into a region containing a uniform magnetic field of 38 mT pointing into the page. Find the magnitude and direction of the net force on the circuit.

37. In a high-magnetic-field experiment, a conducting bar carrying 7.5 kA passes through a 30-cm-long region containing a 22-T magnetic field. If the bar makes a $60°$ angle with the field direction, what force is necessary to hold it in place?

38. A 20-cm-long conducting rod with mass 18 g is suspended by wires of negligible mass, as shown in Fig. 29-41. The rod is in a region containing a uniform magnetic field of 0.15 T pointing horizontally into the page, as shown. An external circuit supplies current between the support points A and B. (a) What is the minimum current necessary to move the bar to the upper position shown? (b) Which direction should the current flow?

FIGURE 29-41 Problem 38.

39. A piece of wire with mass per unit length 75 g/m runs horizontally at right angles to a horizontal magnetic field. A 6.2-A current in the wire results in its being suspended against gravity. What is the magnetic field strength?

40. A nonuniform magnetic field points out of the page, as shown in Fig. 29-42. The field strength increases at the rate of 2.0 mT/cm as you move to the right. A square wire loop 15 cm on a side lies in a plane perpendicular to the field, and a 2.5-A current circles the loop in the counterclockwise direction. What are the magnitude and direction of the net magnetic force on the loop?

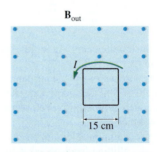

FIGURE 29-42 Problem 40.

41. A wire carrying 1.5 A passes through a region containing a 48-mT magnetic field. The wire is perpendicular to the field and makes a quarter-circle turn of radius 21 cm as it passes through the field region, as shown in Fig. 29-43. Find the magnitude and direction of the magnetic force on this section of wire

FIGURE 29-43 Problem 41.

42. A wire coincides with the x axis, and carries a current $I = 2.0$ A in the $+x$ direction. A nonuniform magnetic field points in the y direction, given by $\mathbf{B} = B_0(x/x_0)^2 \hat{\mathbf{j}}$, where $B_0 = 0.22$ T, $x_0 = 1.0$ m, and x is the x coordinate. Find the force on the section of wire between $x = 1.0$ m and $x = 3.5$ m.

43. Apply Equation 29-8 to a closed current loop of arbitrary shape in a *uniform* magnetic field, and show that the net force on the loop is zero. *Hint:* Both I and B are constant as you go around the loop, so you can take them out of the integral. What is the remaining vector integral?

44. A rectangular copper strip measures 1.0 mm in the direction of a uniform 2.4-T magnetic field. When the strip carries a 6.8-A current at right angles to the field, the Hall voltage across the strip is 1.2 μV. Find the number density of free electrons in the copper.

45. The probe in a Hall-effect magnetometer uses a semiconductor doped to a charge-carrier density of 7.5×10^{20} m^{-3}. The probe measures 0.35 mm thick in the direction of the magnetic field being measured, and carries a 2.5-mA current perpendicular to the field. If its Hall potential is 4.5 mV, what is the magnetic field strength?

Section 29-5 A Current Loop in a Magnetic Field

46. Earth has a magnetic dipole moment associated with currents flowing in the planet's liquid outer core. Suppose that current flowed in a single loop at the outer edge of the liquid core (radius 3000 km). What current would be needed to give the observed dipole moment of 8.0×10^{22} A·m^2? (The actual current structure is more complex than a single loop.)

47. A single-turn square wire loop 5.0 cm on a side carries a 450-mA current. (a) What is the magnetic moment of the loop? (b) If the loop is in a uniform 1.4-T magnetic field with its dipole moment vector at 40° to the field direction, what is the magnitude of the torque it experiences?

48. An electric motor contains a 250-turn circular coil 6.2 cm in diameter. If it is to develop a maximum torque of 1.2 N·m at a current of 3.3 A, what should be the magnetic field strength?

49. A bar magnet experiences a 12-mN·m torque when it is oriented at 55° to a 100-mT magnetic field. What is the magnitude of its magnetic dipole moment?

50. A single-turn wire loop 10 cm in diameter carries a 12-A current. It experiences a torque of 0.015 N·m when the

normal to the loop plane makes a 25° angle with a uniform magnetic field. What is the magnetic field strength?

51. A simple electric motor like that of Fig. 29-36 consists of a 100-turn coil 3.0 cm in diameter, mounted between the poles of a magnet that produces a 0.12-T field. When a 5.0-A current flows in the coil, what are (a) its magnetic dipole moment and (b) the maximum torque developed by the motor?

52. A satellite with rotational inertia 20 kg·m^2 is in orbit at a height where Earth's magnetic field strength is 0.18 G. It has a magnetic torquing system, as described in Example 29-7, that uses a 1000-turn coil 30 cm in diameter. What should be the current in the coil if the magnetic torque is to give the satellite a maximum angular acceleration of 0.0015 s^{-2}?

53. Nuclear magnetic resonance (NMR) is a technique for analyzing chemical structures and is also the basis of magnetic resonance imaging used for medical diagnosis. The NMR technique relies on sensitive measurements of the energy needed to flip atomic nuclei upside-down in a given magnetic field. In an NMR apparatus with a 7.0-T magnetic field, how much energy is needed to flip a proton ($\mu = 1.41 \times 10^{-26}$ A·m^2) from parallel to antiparallel to the field?

54. A wire of length ℓ carries a current I. (a) Find an expression for the magnetic dipole moment that results when the wire is wound into an N-turn circular coil. (b) For what integer value of N is this moment a maximum?

Paired Problems

(Both problems in a pair involve the same principles and techniques. If you can get the first problem, you should be able to solve the second one.)

55. Find the magnetic force on an electron moving with velocity $\mathbf{v} = 8.6 \times 10^5 \hat{\mathbf{i}} - 4.1 \times 10^5 \hat{\mathbf{j}}$ m/s in a magnetic field $\mathbf{B} = 0.18 \hat{\mathbf{j}} + 0.64 \hat{\mathbf{k}}$ T.

56. A proton moving with velocity $\mathbf{v} = 2.0 \times 10^5 \hat{\mathbf{i}} + 4.0 \times 10^5 \hat{\mathbf{j}}$ m/s experiences a magnetic force $\mathbf{F} = 10 \hat{\mathbf{i}} - 5.0 \hat{\mathbf{j}} + 21 \hat{\mathbf{k}}$ fN. What is the z component of the magnetic field?

57. Proponents of space-based particle-beam weapons have to confront the effect of Earth's magnetic field on their beams. If a beam of protons with kinetic energy 100 MeV is aimed in a straight line perpendicular to Earth's magnetic field in a region where the field strength is 48 μT, what will be the radius of the protons' circular path?

58. Electrons are accelerated through a 30-kV potential difference at the rear of a TV tube. The electron beam is initially headed straight toward the center of the tube. The TV is oriented so the beam is perpendicular to Earth's magnetic field, in a location where the field strength is 62 μT. What will be the radius of the electron beam's curved path?

59. A 170-mT magnetic field points into the page, confined to a square region as shown in Fig. 29-44. A square conducting loop 32 cm on a side carrying a 5.0-A current in the

FIGURE 29-44 Problems 59, 60.

clockwise sense extends partly into the field region, as shown. Find the magnetic force on the loop.

60. Find the force on the circular current loop shown at the right of Fig. 29-44. The loop carries 5.0 A clockwise, has radius 16 cm, and extends 10 cm into the field region.

61. An old-fashioned analog meter uses a wire coil in a magnetic field to deflect the meter needle. If the coil is 2.0 cm in diameter and consists of 500 turns of wire, what should be the magnetic field strength if the maximum torque is to be 1.6 μN·m when the current in the coil is 1.0 mA?

62. A circular wire coil 15 cm in diameter carries a 460-mA current and experiences a 0.020-N·m torque when the normal to the coil makes a 27° angle with a 42-mT magnetic field. How many turns are in the coil?

Supplementary Problems

63. Electrons in a TV picture tube are accelerated through a 30-kV potential difference and head straight for the center of the tube, 40 cm away. If the electrons are moving at right angles to Earth's 0.50-G magnetic field, by how much do they miss the screen's exact center?

64. The coil in the loudspeaker of Fig. 29-31 consists of 100 turns of wire, 3.5 cm in diameter. The magnetic field strength at the coil is 0.64 T. Find the magnitude of the force on the speaker coil when the current in the coil is 2.1 A.

65. A conducting bar with mass 15.0 g and length 22.0 cm is suspended from a spring in a region where a 0.350-T magnetic field points into the page, as shown in Fig. 29-45. With no current in the bar, the spring length is 26.0 cm. The bar is supplied with current from outside the field

region, using wires of negligible mass. When a 2.00-A current flows from left to right in the bar, it rises 1.2 cm from its equilibrium position. Find (a) the spring constant and (b) the unstretched length of the spring.

66. In 2.0 μs, an electron moves 15 cm in the direction of a 0.10-T magnetic field. If the electron's velocity components perpendicular and parallel to the field are equal, (a) what is the length of its actual spiral trajectory and (b) how many orbits about the field direction does it complete?

67. A solid disk of mass M and thickness d sits on an incline, as shown in Fig. 29-46. A loop of wire is wrapped around the disk, running along a diameter and oriented so the loop is parallel to the incline. A uniform magnetic field **B** points vertically upward. Find an expression for the current I in the loop that will keep it from rolling down the incline.

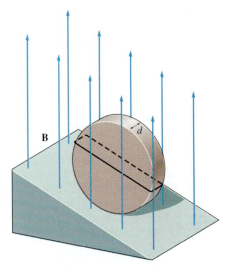

FIGURE 29-46 Problem 67.

68. A disk of radius R carries a uniform surface charge density σ and is rotating with angular frequency ω. Show that its magnetic dipole moment is $\frac{1}{4}\pi\sigma\omega R^4$. *Hint:* Divide the disk into concentric rings. Treat each as a loop carrying an infinitesimal current, and integrate over all the loops.

69. A 10-turn wire loop measuring 8.0 cm by 16 cm carrying 2.0 A lies in a horizontal plane but is free to rotate about the axis shown in Fig. 29-47. A 50-g mass hangs from one

FIGURE 29-45 Problem 65.

FIGURE 29-47 Problem 69.

side of the loop, and a uniform magnetic field points horizontally, as shown. What magnetic field strength is required to hold the loop in its horizontal position?

70. A closed current loop is made from two semicircular wire arcs of radius R, joined at right angles as shown in Fig. 29-48. The loop carries a current I and is oriented with the plane of one semicircle perpendicular to a uniform magnetic field **B**, as shown. Find (a) the magnetic moment of this nonplanar loop and (b) the torque on the loop. *Hint:* You can think of the loop as a superposition of two semicircular loops, each closed along the dashed line shown (why?).

FIGURE 29-49 Problem 71.

FIGURE 29-48 Problem 70.

71. A circular wire loop of mass m and radius R carries a current I. The loop is hanging horizontally below a cylindrical bar magnet, suspended by the magnetic force, as shown in Fig. 29-49. If the field lines crossing the loop make an angle θ with the vertical, show that the strength of the magnet's field at the loop's position is $B = mg/2\pi RI\sin\theta$.

72. A square wire loop of mass m carries a current I. It is initially in equilibrium, with its magnetic moment vector aligned with a uniform magnetic field **B**. The loop is rotated slightly out of equilibrium about an axis through the centers of two opposite sides and then released. Show that it executes simple harmonic motion with period given by $T = 2\pi\sqrt{m/6IB}$.

73. Early models pictured the electron in a hydrogen atom as being in a circular orbit of radius 5.29×10^{-11} m about the stationary proton, held in orbit by the electric force. Find the magnetic dipole moment of such an atom. This quantity is called the *Bohr magneton* and is typical of atomic-sized magnetic moments. *Hint:* The full electron charge passes any given point in the orbit once per orbital period. Use this fact to calculate the average current.

30 Sources of the Magnetic Field

Moving electric charge produces magnetic fields. Here a large electromagnet lifts scrap metal in a recycling operation. When the current through the electromagnet is switched off, it will drop the metal.

The preceding chapter introduced the magnetic field and its effect on matter. Here we consider the opposite question: How does matter produce magnetic fields in the first place? We've seen that magnetic fields exert forces on moving electric charges—a fact that implies a deep relation between electricity and magnetism. That relation in fact goes two ways: Not only do magnetic fields affect moving electric charges, but moving charges themselves produce magnetic fields.

30-1 THE BIOT-SAVART LAW

The first inkling of a relation between electricity and magnetism came in 1820 when the Danish scientist Hans Christian Oersted discovered that a compass needle is deflected by an electric current (Fig. 30-1). A mere month after Oersted's discovery became known in Paris, the French scientists Jean Baptiste Biot and Félix Savart had experimentally determined the form of the magnetic field arising from a steady current. Biot and Savart's result gives the contribution $d\mathbf{B}$ to the magnetic field at some point P due to a small element of current, just as Coulomb's law in the form of Equation 23-9a gives the contribution $d\mathbf{E}$ to the electric field from a small charge element dq:

$$d\mathbf{E} = \frac{k\,dq}{r^2}\hat{\mathbf{r}}$$

(see Fig. 30-2a). In this expression the field $d\mathbf{E}$ depends directly on the charge element dq, inversely on the square of the distance r, and on a universal constant, k (or, equivalently, $1/4\pi\varepsilon_0$). The direction of $d\mathbf{E}$ is determined by the unit vector $\hat{\mathbf{r}}$ from the charge element toward the field point P.

Biot and Savart found similar results for the magnetic field, as described in Fig. 30-2b. Here a steady current I is flowing, and we consider the contribution $d\mathbf{B}$ that a small length $d\ell$ of this current makes to the magnetic field at point P. The product $I\,d\ell$ plays the same role as does dq in Coulomb's law. Both dq and $I\,d\ell$ describe sources of the fields, charge for the electric field, and moving charge for the magnetic field. The quantity $I\,d\ell$ has the units of charge multiplied by velocity—showing that *moving* charge is at the heart of magnetism. Furthermore, the magnetic field due to the current element $I\,d\ell$ falls off inversely as the square of the distance, just like the electric field of a charge element dq.

FIGURE 30-1 Oersted's experiment linking electricity and magnetism is commemorated on the Oersted medal, awarded by the American Association of Physics Teachers to honor "notable contributions to the teaching of physics."

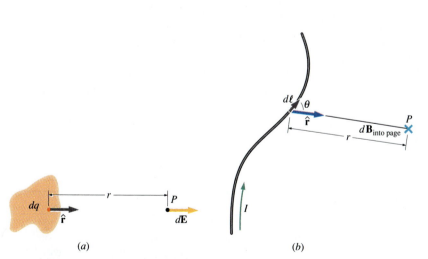

FIGURE 30-2 (a) Coulomb's law gives the electric field $d\mathbf{E}$ at point P due to an infinitesimal charge element dq. (b) The Biot-Savart law gives the magnetic field $d\mathbf{B}$ at point P arising from the current I flowing along the infinitesimal vector $d\ell$. The unit vector $\hat{\mathbf{r}}$ points from the current element $I\,d\ell$ toward the field point P.

But there are also important differences. The source of the electric field—charge—is a scalar quantity, whereas the source of the magnetic field is *moving* charge, and movement has direction. We can account for the direction of the current in Fig. 30-2b by defining a vector $d\boldsymbol{\ell}$ whose magnitude is the length $d\ell$ and which points in the direction of the current. Biot and Savart found that the magnetic field $d\mathbf{B}$ depends on sine of the angle θ between this vector $d\boldsymbol{\ell}$ and the unit vector $\hat{\mathbf{r}}$ from the current element $I\,d\ell$ toward the field point P, and that the direction of $d\mathbf{B}$ is perpendicular to both vectors. Mathematically, the $\sin\theta$ dependence and perpendicular direction together are described by a cross product. Thus our results for the magnetic field $d\mathbf{B}$ can be summarized in a compact vector equation, called the **Biot-Savart law**:

$$d\mathbf{B} = \frac{\mu_0}{4\pi}\frac{I\,d\boldsymbol{\ell}\times\hat{\mathbf{r}}}{r^2}, \quad \text{(Biot-Savart law)} \tag{30-1}$$

where μ_0 is a constant called the permeability constant, which has the exact value $4\pi\times10^{-7}\text{ N/A}^2$.

Besides the more complicated directionality evidenced by the cross product in the Biot-Savart law, there's another distinction between the Biot-Savart law and Coulomb's law. Both describe the fields of localized structures—current elements and point charges—that are sources of the fields. It makes sense to talk about the electric field of an isolated point charge. But can we have an isolated current element? Not in a steady-state situation, where the current flowing into a current element must be the same as the current flowing out. Thus any Biot-Savart calculation necessarily involves the fields produced by many small current elements from an entire circuit. Experimentally, we find that the magnetic field obeys the superposition principle, so the net field at any point is the vector sum—or integral—of the fields of individual current elements:

$$\mathbf{B} = \int d\mathbf{B} = \int \frac{\mu_0}{4\pi}\frac{I\,d\boldsymbol{\ell}\times\hat{\mathbf{r}}}{r^2}, \tag{30-2}$$

where the integration is taken over the entire circuit in which the current I flows. The field given by Equation 30-2 depends on the details of the current configuration, but the directionality associated with the cross product means that, quite generally, magnetic field lines encircle the current that is their source (Fig. 30-3).

FIGURE 30-3 Magnetic field lines generally encircle a current. The field direction is given by the right-hand rule: Point your right thumb in the direction of the current, and your fingers curl in the direction of the field.

EXAMPLE 30-1	*The Field of a Current Loop*

Find the magnetic field at an arbitrary point P on the axis of a circular loop of radius a carrying current I.

Solution

Let the loop axis be the x axis, with the origin at the loop center. Figure 30-4a shows the field contribution $d\mathbf{B}$ at P arising from a current element $I\,d\boldsymbol{\ell}$ at the top of the loop, with its direction given by the cross product $d\boldsymbol{\ell}\times\hat{\mathbf{r}}$. The symmetry of the situa-tion shows that all points on the loop produce similar field elements $d\mathbf{B}$, each making the same angle θ with the axis, giving a net field that points along the axis (Fig. 30-4b). To find that net field we therefore need sum only the x components of the field contributions from around the loop.

Figure 30-4a also shows that the vectors $d\boldsymbol{\ell}$ and $\hat{\mathbf{r}}$ are per-pendicular; therefore, the product $d\boldsymbol{\ell}\times\hat{\mathbf{r}}$ has magnitude $|d\boldsymbol{\ell}||\hat{\mathbf{r}}|\sin90° = d\ell$ since $\hat{\mathbf{r}}$ is a unit vector. Then the

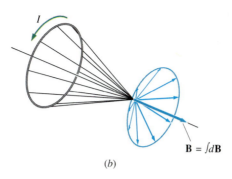

FIGURE 30-4 A current loop whose axis is the x axis. (a) The magnetic field $d\mathbf{B}$ arising from a current element of length $d\boldsymbol{\ell}$ on the loop is perpendicular to the vectors $d\boldsymbol{\ell}$ and $\hat{\mathbf{r}}$, and thus makes the angle θ with the loop axis. (b) Current elements all around the loop produce similar field elements $d\mathbf{B}$, with the result that the net field $\mathbf{B}$ points along the axis.

$\mathbf{B} = \int d\mathbf{B}$

(a)   (b)

magnitude of the field contribution $d\mathbf{B}$, as given by the Biot-Savart law, is

$$dB = \frac{\mu_0 I}{4\pi} \frac{|d\boldsymbol{\ell} \times \hat{\mathbf{r}}|}{r^2} = \frac{\mu_0 I}{4\pi} \frac{d\ell}{x^2 + a^2}.$$

To find the net field, we need to sum the x components $dB_x = dB\cos\theta$, which are the same for all current elements around the loop. Figure 30-4a shows that $\cos\theta = a/r = a/\sqrt{x^2 + a^2}$, so the net field becomes

$$B = \int_{\text{loop}} dB\cos\theta$$

$$= \int_{\text{loop}} \left(\frac{\mu_0 I}{4\pi} \frac{d\ell}{x^2 + a^2}\right)\left(\frac{a}{\sqrt{x^2 + a^2}}\right)$$

$$= \frac{\mu_0 Ia}{4\pi(x^2 + a^2)^{3/2}} \int_{\text{loop}} d\ell,$$

where the integral reduces to such a simple form because the distance x is the same for all points on the loop. The remaining integral just means the sum of all the infinitesimal segments $d\ell$

around the loop—or the loop circumference $2\pi a$. Thus, the magnitude of the magnetic field on the loop axis becomes

$$B = \frac{\mu_0 Ia^2}{2(x^2 + a^2)^{3/2}}. \qquad (30\text{-}3)$$

ActivPhysics Activity 13.2 shows you the entire field of this current loop.

EXERCISE Earth's magnetic field at temperate latitudes is about 50 μT. You're experimenting with the effect of magnetic fields on living cells and need a control point where the magnetic field is zero. To get such a point, you orient a 12-cm-diameter wire loop so the field at its center just cancels Earth's field. What loop current is required?

Answer: 4.8 A

Some problems similar to Example 30-1: 1–3, 5, 15, 17

13.2   Magnetic Field of a Loop

We found in the preceding chapter that a current loop behaves like a magnetic dipole when it's in an external magnetic field. Does the loop also produce a dipole-like field? At points far from the loop ($x \gg a$), we can neglect a^2 compared with x^2 in the denominator of Equation 30-3, which then becomes

$$B = \frac{\mu_0 Ia^2}{2x^3} = \frac{\mu_0}{2\pi} \frac{\mu}{x^3}, \qquad (x \gg a) \qquad (30\text{-}4)$$

where the second equality follows by introducing the loop's magnetic dipole moment $\mu = I\pi a^2$ as defined in Equation 29-10. Equation 30-4 shows the inverse-cube behavior we found earlier for the field of an *electric* dipole. Although we derived it for a circular loop, Equation 30-4 in fact holds at large distances from a current loop of *any* shape, suggesting that the field is essentially that of a magnetic dipole. A much more difficult calculation would confirm that the distant field off the axis also shows an inverse-cube dependence and exhibits the angular dependence typical of a dipole. We conclude that, in both its response to magnetic fields and its production of magnetic fields:

A current loop constitutes a magnetic dipole.

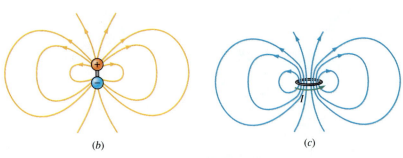

(a)

(b)

(c)

FIGURE 30-5 (a) The magnetic field of a current loop, as traced by iron filings. Note that field lines encircle the current-carrying wire. (b) The electric field of an electric dipole and (c) the magnetic field of a current loop. Far from their sources, the field patterns are identical, and exhibit the $1/r^3$ dependence of the dipole field.

Figure 30-5a shows the field of a current loop as traced by iron filings, while Figs. 30-5b, c compare the fields of an electric dipole and a magnetic dipole. It's the similarity of the overall field patterns—becoming mathematically identical at large distances, including the $1/r^3$ dependence—that leads us to identify the current loop as a magnetic dipole. Physically, a current-loop dipole doesn't look anything like its electric analog, a pair of opposite electric charges. But its behavior, both in response to magnetic fields and in producing magnetic fields, is completely analogous to that of an electric dipole with respect to electric fields. We'll see later that the familiar bar magnet is nothing but a collection of current-loop magnetic dipoles; what we call the north pole isn't a pole at all but just the end where magnetic field lines emerge from the current loops. The current loop in Fig. 30-5c acts essentially like a very short bar magnet, with its north end upward and south end downward. In fact, the electromagnet shown in the opening photo for this chapter is nothing but a current loop (actually many turns of wire), which produces a strong magnetic field when the current is on. We'll take a deeper look at electric and magnetic dipoles, and magnets, at the end of this chapter.

APPLICATION	*Magnetic Fields of Earth and Sun*

Earth, Sun, and many other astronomical objects possess magnetic fields. Reasonably close to Earth, the field approximates that of a magnetic dipole of dipole moment $\mu = 8.0 \times 10^{22}$ A·m² (Fig. 30-6). The direction of the dipole moment vector differs by about 11° from that of Earth's rotation axis, and this accounts for the difference between magnetic and true north. Locally, the field often deviates significantly from a pure dipole form, and these deviations provide geologists with

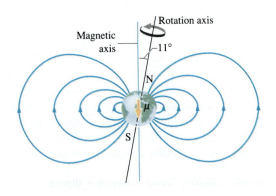

FIGURE 30-6 Earth's magnetic field approximates that of a magnetic dipole located near the center of the Earth and inclined at 11° to the rotation axis. Note from the field direction that Earth's "north" pole is really a magnetic south pole.

FIGURE 30-7 Magma emerges at the midocean ridges, pushing older portions of the ocean floor farther apart. As the magma solidifies, it becomes magnetized in the direction of Earth's magnetic field. (This occurs as atomic-scale current loops in magnetic materials such as iron align with the field and then retain permanently their magnetization, as we'll see later in the chapter.) Analysis of the ocean floor reveals bands of alternating magnetic polarity, showing that Earth's magnetic field reverses on a time scale of 10^5 to 10^6 years. Dark bands represent regions with Earth's present magnetic polarity.

clues to the detailed structure of the planet. The field is not constant; locally, its direction varies significantly over times as short as a few years, and the overall field reverses about every half million years or so (Fig. 30-7). At substantial distances from Earth the field is distorted from its dipole form by the solar wind, a flow of high-speed particles from the Sun (see Fig. 30-57, with Problem 30).

What causes Earth's magnetic field? We know that electric currents produce magnetic fields. Deep inside Earth are a solid inner core and a liquid outer core, both rich in iron. Through an interaction not yet fully understood, the planet's rotation combined with convective motions due to internal heating produces electric currents in the liquid core. For reasons even less well understood, those currents and the resulting magnetic field undergo reversals on a time scale of approximately a million years. Problems 5 and 6 deal with Earth's magnetic field and its origin.

Earth's magnetic field is crucial to our well-being. As we saw in the preceding chapter, high-energy particles from the Sun and elsewhere are trapped in the magnetic field and have difficulty reaching Earth's surface. Thus the field protects us from harmful particulate radiation. During the field reversals, which last about 10,000 years, the magnetic field is significantly reduced and surface exposure to high-energy particulate radiation is accordingly increased. Some scientists speculate that evolutionary changes due to radiation-induced mutations may accelerate at these times.

The Sun's magnetic field probably arises in the same way as does Earth's, although the gaseous nature of the star and the intense energy flow resulting from nuclear fusion in the Sun's core make its magnetic field much more dynamic. The Sun's field reverses every 11 years, giving rise to the solar activity cycle whose best-known indicator is the count of sunspots—regions of intense magnetic field at the solar surface (Fig. 30-8).

The complex behavior of astrophysical magnetic fields is governed entirely by Newton's laws and the laws of electromagnetism. That we do not yet fully understand these magnetic fields is testimony to the rich variety of phenomena subsumed under those laws.

(a)

(b)

FIGURE 30-8 (a) Sunspots are regions of intense magnetic field at the Sun's surface. (b) The solar magnetic activity cycle is clearly evident in this plot of the number of sunspots.

Any steady current ultimately flows in a complete, closed circuit, and therefore at great distances its magnetic field is dipolar. But closer in the field configuration depends on the details of the current. An important case is the field near a straight stretch of current. We can approximate this field as that of an infinite line of current, which we calculate in Example 30-2.

EXAMPLE 30-2	*The Field of a Straight Wire*

What is the magnetic field produced by an infinitely long straight wire carrying a steady current I?

Solution

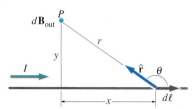

FIGURE 30-9 Geometry for calculating the field at P due to an infinite straight wire carrying a steady current I along the x axis. All current elements along the wire contribute fields at P that point out of the page.

Let the wire coincide with the x axis, and consider an arbitrary point P on the y axis. Figure 30-9 shows a current element $I\,d\boldsymbol{\ell}$ on the wire. At point P the field $d\mathbf{B}$ of this element is perpendicular to both the wire and the vector $\hat{\mathbf{r}}$—that is, $d\mathbf{B}$ points out of the page. Clearly this is true for all current elements along the wire, so we can find the net field by integrating the field contributions dB without needing a vector integration. Using the Biot-Savart law, we have

$$dB = \frac{\mu_0 I}{4\pi}\frac{|d\boldsymbol{\ell}\times\hat{\mathbf{r}}|}{r^2} = \frac{\mu_0 I}{4\pi}\frac{d\ell\sin\theta}{r^2},$$

where we used the fact that $\hat{\mathbf{r}}$ is a unit vector making an angle θ with $d\boldsymbol{\ell}$. Figure 30-9 shows that $r^2 = x^2 + y^2$ and $\sin\theta = y/r = y/\sqrt{x^2 + y^2}$. And, since the segment $d\boldsymbol{\ell}$ lies along the x axis, $d\ell = dx$. Making these substitutions and integrating over the entire wire (from $x = -\infty$ to $x = +\infty$) gives the net field at point P:

$$B = \int dB = \int_{-\infty}^{\infty} \frac{\mu_0 I}{4\pi}\frac{y\,dx}{(x^2 + y^2)^{3/2}}$$

$$= \frac{\mu_0 Iy}{4\pi}\frac{x}{y^2\sqrt{x^2 + y^2}}\bigg|_{-\infty}^{\infty},$$

where we found the integral in the table of integrals in Appendix A. (See Problem 71 for another approach.) At the limits $x = \pm\infty$ the expression $x/\sqrt{x^2 + y^2}$ takes on the values ± 1, so we have

$$B = \frac{\mu_0 I}{4\pi y}[1 - (-1)] = \frac{\mu_0 I}{2\pi y}. \qquad (30\text{-}5)$$

Since the wire has cylindrical symmetry this result must hold anywhere, and the result is circular field lines encircling the wire, as shown in Fig. 30-10 and explored further in ActivPhysics Activity 13.1.

The field given by Equation 30-5 falls as the inverse of the distance from the wire. This should not be surprising: we found

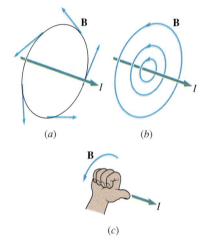

FIGURE 30-10 (a) Some magnetic field vectors associated with a straight wire carrying a steady current. (b) The corresponding magnetic field lines are circles, concentric with the wire. (c) The right-hand rule gives their direction.

the same dependence on distance for the *electric* field of an infinitely long charged line. The field patterns differ, though, in that the electric field points radially from the charged line while the magnetic field encircles the current-carrying wire. Although Equation 30-5 applies strictly only to an infinitely long wire, it is a good approximation for a finite wire at distances small compared with the wire length (Fig. 30-11).

EXERCISE A power line carries 450 A. How close would you have to be to the line for its magnetic field to equal Earth's $50\text{-}\mu\text{T}$ field?

Answer: 1.8 m

Some problems similar to Example 30-2: 4, 11, 57, 58

FIGURE 30-11 Iron filings trace out the circular magnetic field surrounding a current-carrying wire.

13.1
Magnetic Field of a Wire

Got It!

Figure 30-12 shows two wire loops bent into shapes consisting of straight and semicircular sections. Both loops carry the same steady current in the direction shown. (a) What will be the directions of the magnetic fields at the points P and Q? (b) At which point will the field be stronger?

FIGURE 30-12 Think about the magnetic fields at points P and Q.

30-2 THE MAGNETIC FORCE BETWEEN TWO CONDUCTORS

In the preceding chapter we found the force on a straight wire of length ℓ carrying a current I through a magnetic field **B**:

$$\mathbf{F} = I\boldsymbol{\ell} \times \mathbf{B},$$

where the vector $\boldsymbol{\ell}$ is in the direction of the current flow. Through Equation 30-5 we now know the magnetic field produced by a long wire. If two long, parallel wires carry current in the same direction, as shown in Fig. 30-13, then each will experience a force arising from the other's field. We now determine that force.

If d is the distance between the wires, then at wire 2 the field magnitude B_1 due to the current I_1 is, from Equation 30-5,

$$B_1 = \frac{\mu_0 I_1}{2\pi d}.$$

The field is perpendicular to wire 2, so the magnitude of the force on a length ℓ of wire 2 is

$$F_2 = I_2 \ell B_1 = \frac{\mu_0 I_1 I_2 \ell}{2\pi d}. \tag{30-6}$$

Calculating the force on a length ℓ of wire 1 would amount to interchanging the subscripts 1 and 2, giving a force of the same magnitude.

What is the direction of the force? Evaluating the cross product of $\boldsymbol{\ell}$ and **B** in Fig. 30-13 shows that the force on wire 2 is toward wire 1, and vice versa. By using the right-hand rule, you can convince yourself that reversing one of the currents would reverse the directions of both forces. So we conclude that currents in the same direction experience an attractive magnetic force, while currents in the opposite direction experience a magnetic repulsion.

The force between nearby conductors must be considered in the construction of electrical devices carrying large currents. In electromagnets—coils of wire designed to produce large magnetic fields that can be turned on or off with the current in the coils—nearby conductors must have enough physical support that magnetic forces do not destroy the device (Fig. 30-14).

The hum you often hear around electrical equipment comes from the mechanical vibration of tightly wound conductors in transformers and other electrical components. This vibration results from the changing magnetic force associated with the 60-Hz alternating current.

The magnetic force between conductors is the basis for the definition of the ampere and, consequently, the coulomb. One ampere is defined as the current flowing in two long, parallel conductors 1 m apart when they carry equal currents and experience a magnetic force of 2×10^{-7} N on each meter of their length. It then follows that 1 coulomb is the amount of charge passing in 1 s through a wire carrying 1 A.

FIGURE 30-13 The magnetic force between two parallel wires carrying current in the same direction is attractive.

13.5

Magnetic Force on a Wire

FIGURE 30-14 This superconducting electromagnet was torn apart by the magnetic forces from a current of 50 kA flowing in its coils. The magnetic field reached 55 T—over one million times Earth's field. Coils were made from copper/niobium composite with the strength of steel and were reinforced with Kevlar and a steel casing. The coils originally encircled the channel where a pencil has been placed to show the scale.

FIGURE 30-15 Will the spiral tighten or loosen when current flows as shown?

Got It!

A piece of wire is wound into a flat spiral as shown in Fig. 30-15. If a current is passed through the coil (supplied by flexible wires that aren't shown), will the coil tighten up or become looser? Will your answer change if the current direction reverses?

30-3 AMPÈRE'S LAW

In Chapter 23 we did several relatively cumbersome electric field calculations using Coulomb's law. For example, we found the field of an infinite line charge by integrating over all the charge elements along the line. Then in Chapter 24 we introduced Gauss's law and showed how it made electric field calculations much easier in situations with sufficient symmetry.

Can we make a statement that would enable us to calculate magnetic fields with comparable ease? Figure 30-16 shows two of the circular magnetic field lines surrounding a long wire carrying current I out of the page. Imagine moving around the inner circle. As you move a short way, form the product of the distance $d\ell$ that you travel with the component of the magnetic field in the direction you're going. Here the field is entirely in the direction of your path, so that product is simply $B \, d\ell$, where B is the field magnitude; more generally, it would be the dot product $\mathbf{B} \cdot d\ell$ to account for an arbitrary angle between the field and your path. Now consider adding up all these products as you go around a complete circle. Formally, the result is the line integral $\oint \mathbf{B} \cdot d\ell$, or, in this case where the directions of the path and field coincide, just $\oint B \, d\ell$. Here the circle indicates that the integration is done around a *closed* path. The magnitude of $\mathbf{B}$

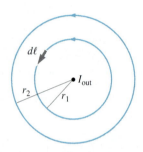

FIGURE 30-16 Two magnetic field lines surrounding a wire carrying current out of the page. The vector $d\ell$ denotes an infinitesimal portion of a circular path that coincides with the inner field line.

is given by Equation 30-5: $B = \dfrac{\mu_0 I}{2\pi r_1}$, where we've replaced y by the radius r_1. Evaluating $\oint \mathbf{B} \cdot d\ell$ then gives

$$\oint \mathbf{B} \cdot d\ell = \frac{\mu_0 I}{2\pi r_1} \oint d\ell = \frac{\mu_0 I}{2\pi r_1} (2\pi r_1) = \mu_0 I,$$

where we took $B = \mu_0 I / 2\pi r_1$ outside the integral because r_1 is the constant radius of the circular field line. What remains of the integral, $\oint d\ell$, is just the circumference, $2\pi r_1$. Our final answer, $\mu_0 I$, is thus independent of the radius r_1. We would get the same answer going around the outer circle, or indeed any circular path. On a larger path the distance is greater, but the field—dropping as $1/r$—is correspondingly weaker, making the value of $\oint \mathbf{B} \cdot d\ell$ the same. Thus the line integral $\oint \mathbf{B} \cdot d\ell$ does not depend on the radius of the circular path, but only on the current I encircled by that path.

We'll get the same result even if the path doesn't correspond to a field line. Figure 30-17 shows why for a path consisting of two circular arcs and radial lines joining them. The radial segments DA and BC contribute nothing to the quanity $\oint \mathbf{B} \cdot d\ell$ because the field is perpendicular to the path, and the large arc CD gives the same contribution as would the smaller arc BA because the field is weaker by just the right amount to compensate for arc CD's greater length. So going around the path shown in Fig. 30-17 gives the same value for the line integral—namely, $\mu_0 I$—as would going around a purely circular path. We can generalize this result to an arbitrary path by approximating the path as a series

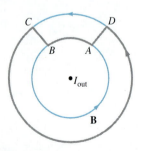

FIGURE 30-17 A closed loop that does not coincide with a single field line. The line integral of the magnetic field around this loop has the same value— $\mu_0 I$—that it has around a circular loop coinciding with a field line.

FIGURE 30-18 Approximating an irregular loop as a series of arcs and radial segments shows that the line integral of the magnetic field is $\mu_0 I$ for *any* closed loop.

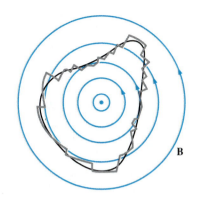

of circular arcs and radial segments (Fig. 30-18). Thus the quantity $\oint \mathbf{B} \cdot d\boldsymbol{\ell}$ has the same value, $\mu_0 I$, around *any* path surrounding a line current I. And because the superposition principle holds for magnetic fields, the result must be true for *any* distribution of current, not just the single line current we considered here. This result is in fact a universal statement about the relation between current and magnetic field:

> The value of the line integral $\oint \mathbf{B} \cdot d\boldsymbol{\ell}$ around any closed loop is proportional to the current encircled by that loop. Mathematically,
>
> $$\oint \mathbf{B} \cdot d\boldsymbol{\ell} = \mu_0 I_{\text{encircled}} . \quad \text{(Ampère's law, steady currents)} \qquad (30\text{-}7)$$

This statement is a form of **Ampère's law**, one of the four fundamental laws of electromagnetism. Ampère's law says that whatever arrangement of currents we might have, and however complicated the resulting magnetic field, that field is such that the line integral $\oint \mathbf{B} \cdot d\boldsymbol{\ell}$ around any closed loop will have the value $\mu_0 I$, where I is the net current *encircled* by that loop. Compare this with Gauss's law, which says that whatever arrangement of electric charges we might have, the resulting electric field is such that the surface integral $\oint \mathbf{E} \cdot d\mathbf{A}$ has the value q/ε_0, where q is the *enclosed* charge.

There's one important restriction on Ampère's law as expressed in Equation 30-7: it's exactly correct only for *steady* currents—that is, currents that don't change with time. We'll show in Chapter 34 how to relax that restriction—with profound implications. Until then, we restrict ourselves to steady currents for which Equation 30-7 holds, or to currents that change only slowly, for which it's a good approximation.

With the restriction to steady currents, our statement of Ampère's law is true for *any* closed loop whatsoever, no matter what its shape or orientation: for any loop, the line integral of the magnetic field around the loop is proportional to the encircled current. It doesn't matter whether the current is in a single wire or in a number of wires or distributed throughout space; in any case, we simply add the currents to obtain the net current encircled by the loop. If there are currents flowing in opposite directions we add them with appropriate algebraic signs. A current counts as positive if, when you curl the fingers of your right hand in the direction of the loop, your right thumb points in the general direction of the current.

Although Ampère's law describes the relation between the magnetic field on a loop and the current *encircled* by that loop, we emphasize that the field $\mathbf{B}$ in Ampère's law is the *net field* from all currents, whether inside the loop or not. We found the same thing with Gauss's law, which relates the electric field $\mathbf{E}$ on a closed surface to the enclosed charge; $\mathbf{E}$ itself, however, is the *net field* arising from all sources, whether enclosed or not.

Ampère's law, like Gauss's, is a truly universal statement describing the relation between magnetic field and electric current. It holds in the electromagnetic devices we build, in atomic and molecular systems, in the interaction of fluid motion and electric charge that gives rise to Earth's magnetic field, and in distant astrophysical objects (Fig. 30-19). Although it is difficult to show mathematically, the Biot-Savart law follows logically from Ampère's law in the same sense that Coulomb's law follows from Gauss's.

(a)

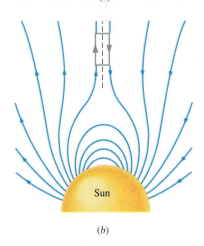

(b)

FIGURE 30-19 (*a*) A coronal streamer in the Sun's outer atmosphere contains oppositely directed magnetic fields in close proximity. (*b*) A model calculation of the coronal magnetic field. Since $\oint \mathbf{B} \cdot d\boldsymbol{\ell}$ is clearly nonzero around the loop shown, there must be current in the region encircled by the loop.

EXAMPLE 30-3	*Solar Currents*

The long dimension of the rectangular loop in Fig. 30-19*b* is 4×10^8 m, and the magnetic field strength in the vicinity of the loop is essentially constant at 2 mT. Find the total current encircled by the rectangle. In what direction is this current flowing?

Solution

We can't insert an ammeter into the Sun's atmosphere, but we can determine the current using Ampère's law. The short ends of the rectangle in Fig. 30-19*b* are perpendicular to the field, so here $\mathbf{B} \cdot d\boldsymbol{\ell} = 0$ and there is no contribution to the line integral around the loop. Moving around the loop in the direction shown means going *with* the field along both long dimensions (note that this is because the field direction reverses across the dashed line). Since the field is uniform, the contribution to the line integral from each side is just $B\ell$. Thus $\oint \mathbf{B} \cdot d\boldsymbol{\ell} = 2B\ell$. Ampère's law tells us that the line integral of the magnetic field around a closed loop has the value $\mu_0 I$, so

$$2B\ell = \mu_0 I,$$

or

$$I = \frac{2B\ell}{\mu_0} = \frac{(2)(2\times10^{-3}\ \text{T})(4\times10^8\ \text{m})}{4\pi\times10^{-7}\ \text{N/A}^2} = 1\times10^{12}\ \text{A}.$$

This is a colossal current by terrestrial standards, but is typical of large-scale currents on the Sun.

Since the line integral is positive, we curl our right fingers around the loop in the direction shown by the arrows and our thumb must point in the direction of the current—that is, into the page in Fig. 30-19. In three dimensions this current flows around the Sun in approximately the equatorial plane.

Tip

Amperian Loops The loop used with Ampère's law is truly arbitrary. It need not coincide with a field line, as Fig. 30-18 showed. Example 30-3 showed this, too; here, the rectangular loop coincided with the straight field lines over its long sides but not along its shorter ends. The loop used with Ampère's law is called an **amperian loop**. Don't confuse amperian loops with field lines!

EXERCISE Figure 30-20 shows a cross-sectional view of three wires carrying current perpendicular to the plane of the page. Wire *A* carries 20 A out of the page. $\oint \mathbf{B} \cdot d\boldsymbol{\ell}$ around loop 1 in the direction shown has the value 1.26×10^{-5} T·m, and the line integral around loop 2 has the value -6.28×10^{-6} T·m. Find the currents in wires *B* and *C*, and the directions of those currents.

Answers: *B*: 10 A into page; *C*: 5 A out of page

Some problems similar to Example 30-3: 28–30

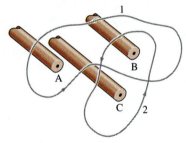

FIGURE 30-20 What are the currents in wires *B* and *C*?

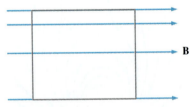

FIGURE 30-21 Which way is the current in this region? Gray rectangle is an amperian loop.

Got It!

Figure 30-21 shows a magnetic field that points to the right but increases in strength as you move up the page. A rectangular amperian loop is also shown. Use Ampère's law to argue that there must be current flowing in this region, and find its direction.

30-4 USING AMPÈRE'S LAW

For charge distributions with sufficient symmetry we used Gauss's law to solve for the electric field in a simple and elegant way. Similarly, for current distributions with sufficient symmetry we can use Ampère's law to solve for the magnetic field. Doing so requires finding suitable amperian loops over which we can evaluate the line integral of the magnetic field.

The Field of a Straight Wire

Here we use Ampère's law to determine the field of an infinite straight wire. This is the same calculation we did in Example 30-2 using the Biot-Savart law.

Figure 30-22 shows the wire, which carries current I. We know that magnetic field lines generally encircle the currents that are their sources. Here cylindrical symmetry requires that those field lines be circles centered on the wire and that the magnetic field strength cannot depend on angular position around the wire. Thus B must be constant on a field line. Applying the right-hand rule—thumb along the current, curling the fingers of the right hand—shows that the magnetic field circles counterclockwise around the wire. And since the wire is infinitely long, Fig. 30-22 represents the field anywhere along the wire.

Given the symmetry, an appropriate amperian loop for evaluating the line integral is itself a circle, also shown in Fig. 30-22. The magnetic field everywhere on this amperian loop is in the same direction as the loop, so the dot product $\mathbf{B} \cdot d\boldsymbol{\ell}$ becomes simply $B\,d\ell$. Then the line integral around the loop is

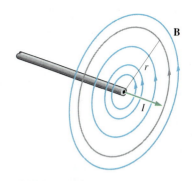

FIGURE 30-22 Circular field lines surrounding an infinitely long wire. Gray circle is an amperian loop for evaluating the line integral of the magnetic field. Although we've drawn only four field lines, the field exists everywhere, including on the amperian loop.

$$\oint_{\text{loop}} \mathbf{B} \cdot d\boldsymbol{\ell} = \oint_{\text{loop}} B\,d\ell = B \oint_{\text{loop}} d\ell = 2\pi r B.$$

Here we can take the field magnitude B outside the integral because it's constant on the circular amperian loop; the remaining integral is then the loop circumference $2\pi r$. Ampère's law equates this line integral to μ_0 times the encircled current, so

$$2\pi r B = \mu_0 I,$$

or

$$B = \frac{\mu_0 I}{2\pi r}. \tag{30-8}$$

This result is the same as Equation 30-5, but here we derived it in a much simpler way.

> **Tip**
>
> *Symmetry Is Crucial* Our use of Ampère's law to derive the field of a long wire depends crucially on symmetry. We cannot arbitrarily pull B outside the integral unless we know—as we do here from symmetry—that it is constant in magnitude and in direction relative to our amperian loop.

Our calculation made no assumptions about the diameter of the wire. Therefore Equation 30-8 holds for any long cylindrical wire, thick or thin, as long as we restrict ourselves to points *outside* the wire so that our amperian loop encircles the *entire* current. In fact, you can easily convince yourself that Equation 30-8 must hold *outside* any current distribution with cylindrical symmetry. To calculate the field *inside* a current distribution, however, we must be careful to use only the actual current encircled by our amperian loop. Example 30-4 illustrates this point.

EXAMPLE 30-4	*Inside a Wire*

A long, straight wire of radius R carries a current I uniformly distributed over its cross-sectional area. What is the magnetic field as a function of position within the wire?

Solution

All the symmetry arguments we used to find the field outside a wire still apply here, so the line integral around a circular amperian loop of radius r is still $2\pi rB$. What's different is that an amperian loop within the wire no longer encircles the entire current (Fig. 30-23). How much current is encircled? The current is distributed uniformly, giving a current density (current per unit area) $J = I/A = I/\pi R^2$. The encircled current is then the current density times the loop area, or

$$I_{\text{encircled}} = \left(\frac{I}{\pi R^2}\right)(\pi r^2) = I\frac{r^2}{R^2}.$$

Equating the line integral $2\pi rB$ to μ_0 times this encircled current gives

$$2\pi rB = \mu_0 I\frac{r^2}{R^2},$$

or
$$B = \frac{\mu_0 Ir}{2\pi R^2}. \tag{30-9}$$

FIGURE 30-23 Cross section of a long cylindrical wire carrying current out of the page. Symmetry requires that the magnetic field be circular inside as well as outside the wire. Current is distributed uniformly over the wire; in applying Ampère's law to the amperian loop shown in gray we need the fraction of the total current encircled by the loop.

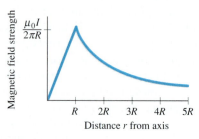

FIGURE 30-24 The magnetic field inside a wire is zero at the wire's axis and increases linearly with radial distance, while beyond the wire radius R it drops as $1/r$.

Does this result make sense? The field increases linearly with distance from the axis—just as we found for the *electric* field *inside* a uniformly charged cylinder. Here the increase occurs because we encircle more and more current—with $I_{\text{encircled}}$ growing as r^2—as long as we're inside the wire. Once we reach the surface, of course, the encircled current remains constant and the field begins to decrease inversely with distance, as described in Equation 30-8. Figure 30-24 plots the field strengths both inside and outside the wire.

This example is not merely academic; in superconducting wires, for example, strong magnetic fields can destroy superconductivity, so it's important to know the field throughout the wire.

EXERCISE A power line 4.0 cm in diameter carries 1.5 kA. Find the magnetic field (a) 1.0 cm from the axis of the wire and (b) 10 cm from the axis.

Answers: (a) 7.5 mT; (b) 3.0 mT

Some problems similar to Example 30-4: 32, 33, 37, 65

Got It!

A coaxial cable consists of an inner wire carrying current I in one direction, and an outer cylindrical conductor carrying the same current in the opposite direction; the current is distributed symmetrically in the outer conductor. (See Fig. 30-60 if the configuration isn't clear). If the current in the outer conductor only is doubled, will the magnetic field change (a) in between the two conductors or (b) outside the outer conductor?

EXAMPLE 30-5	*A Current Sheet*

An infinite flat sheet carries a current out of the page, as shown in Fig. 30-25. The current is distributed uniformly along the sheet, with the current per unit width along the sheet given by J_s. Find the magnetic field of this sheet.

Solution

What might the field of this sheet look like? Figure 30-26 suggests that we can consider the sheet to be made of many parallel wires. The vector sum of the fields of these wires gives a net field to the left above and to the right below the sheet. We can also argue from symmetry that the fields must point horizontally and with magnitude that is independent of position parallel to the sheet; since the sheet extends infinitely to the right and left, there's nothing to favor an upward or downward deflection of the field lines or any variation in field magnitude

FIGURE 30-25 A current sheet (gray) extends infinitely to the left and right, as well as in and out of the page. Field lines and a rectangular amperian loop are also shown.

parallel to the sheet. We've drawn these horizontal field lines, and an appropriate amperian loop, in Fig. 30-25.

We already evaluated $\oint \mathbf{B} \cdot d\boldsymbol{\ell}$ for a similar geometry in Example 30-3; the result is simply $2B\ell$, with ℓ the width of the amperian rectangle. The current per unit width of the sheet is J_s, so our rectangular loop of width ℓ encircles a current $I = J_s\ell$. Equating μ_0 times this encircled current to the line integral $\oint \mathbf{B} \cdot d\boldsymbol{\ell} = 2B\ell$ gives

$$2B\ell = \mu_0 J_s \ell,$$

or

$$B = \tfrac{1}{2}\mu_0 J_s. \qquad (30\text{-}10)$$

Thus the magnetic field of an infinite current sheet is independent of distance from the sheet. We found the same result for the electric field of an infinite charged plane. Although the infinite sheet is an idealization, Equation 30-10 is a good approximation to the field near long, wide, flat conductors. Thin current sheets also form in conducting plasmas like those in fusion reactors and in the Sun's atmosphere, where they can lead to sudden dissipation of energy.

EXERCISE Current in a printed circuit board is carried in a long copper strip 2.1 mm wide and much thinner than its width. If the current in the strip is 35 mA, spread uniformly over its cross section, find the magnetic field strength near the strip's surface.

Answer: 10 μT

Some problems similar to Example 30-5: 38, 39, 42

FIGURE 30-26 A current sheet approximated by closely spaced parallel wires. The magnetic field of the sheet is the vector superposition of the fields of the individual wires. In the limit of infinitesimally spaced wires, the field lines become straight and strictly horizontal.

Fields of Simple Current Distributions

We've just used Ampère's law to calculate the magnetic fields of two simple, symmetric current distributions. Although those magnetic fields may look quite different from the electric fields of correspondingly symmetric charge distributions, they exhibit the same dependences on distance. Table 30-1 summarizes the electric and magnetic fields of several simple charge and current distributions. Real distributions are usually more complicated, but often they can be approximated by these simple cases. Far from any current loop, for example, the magnetic field is that of a dipole. Very near *any* wire, its magnetic field is essentially that

TABLE 30-1 *Fields of Some Simple Charge and Current Distributions*

DISTRIBUTION	FIELD DEPENDENCE ON DISTANCE*	ELECTRIC OR MAGNETIC FIELD
Electric dipole	$\dfrac{1}{r^3}$	
Magnetic dipole	$\dfrac{1}{r^3}$	
Spherically symmetric charge distribution	$\dfrac{1}{r^2}$	
Spherically symmetric current distribution	Impossible for steady current	
Charge distribution with line symmetry	$\dfrac{1}{r}$	
Current distribution with line symmetry	$\dfrac{1}{r}$	
Infinite flat sheet of change	Uniform field; no variation	
Current sheet	Uniform field; no variation	

* For field *outside* distribution.

of a long straight wire. For situations that lack symmetry and in which approximations are not adequately accurate, we can always calculate the magnetic field of a steady current distribution from the Biot-Savart law, just as we can always calculate the electric field of an arbitrary charge distribution from Coulomb's law.

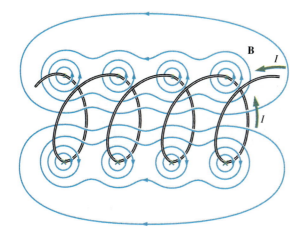

FIGURE 30-27 The magnetic field arising from the current in a loosely wound coil of wire is strongest within the coil and weaker outside. Field is shown only in the plane of the page; dots show current emerging from the page and crosses mark current going into the page.

30-5 SOLENOIDS AND TOROIDS

We found in Chapter 26 that we can produce a uniform electric field between the two closely spaced, charged conducting plates of a capacitor. Is there an analogous device that will produce a uniform magnetic field?

Figure 30-27 shows a coil of wire carrying current I. Close to the wire are magnetic field lines encircling the wire. We show these field lines in Fig. 30-27 at the top and bottom of the coil, where they cross the plane of the page. The net field anywhere is, of course, just the vector sum of the field contributions from all parts of the coil. You can see that inside the coil, the fields from current elements at the top and bottom all have a component to the right and so tend to reinforce. Outside the coil, though, field components from top and bottom are in opposite directions and thus reduce the net field, which points to the left as shown in the figure.*

Imagine making the coil longer and winding it more tightly. Such a long, tightly wound coil is a **solenoid**. Figure 30-28 shows what happens as the solenoid gets longer: the interior field stays essentially the same, but exterior field lines spread into more distant regions before closing back on themselves. Therefore, the field strength outside the solenoid—as evidenced by the density of field lines— decreases. In the limit of an infinitely long solenoid, the interior field becomes perfectly straight and the exterior field goes to zero. A real solenoid approaches this ideal limit when its length is much greater than its diameter. Figure 30-29 shows the field of a solenoid as traced by iron filings. Incidentally, the solenoid fields of Figs. 30-28 and 30-29 might remind you of the field of a bar magnet. They should: we'll soon see that a bar magnet and a solenoid, although superficially very different things, are magnetically very similar.

---

* Because the coil carries a net current from right to left, there is also a weak field component outside that encircles the coil. This component plays no role in the discussion that follows, and we ignore it.

FIGURE 30-28 As a solenoid gets longer, the interior field stays nearly constant but the exterior field weakens as the field lines spread ever farther apart.

13.3
Magnetic Field of a Solenoid

FIGURE 30-29 Iron filings trace the magnetic field of a solenoid. Note that the field is strong inside the solenoid, causing the filings to align strongly, and relatively weak outside, except near the ends. (With ActivPhysics Activity 13.3 you can simulate the pattern of iron filings around a solenoid.)

FIGURE 30-30 Cross section of a long solenoid, showing a rectangular amperian loop straddling the region where the solenoid coils emerge from the plane of the page.

In the long-solenoid limit, we can use Ampère's law to find the field in the solenoid. Figure 30-30 shows a cross section through a long solenoid, with a rectangular amperian loop. Since the exterior field is zero, there's no contribution to the line integral $\oint \mathbf{B} \cdot d\boldsymbol{\ell}$ from the top of the amperian loop. The loop's vertical sides are at right angles to the field, so they, too, contribute nothing to the line integral. The only contribution is from the bottom of the loop. Going counterclockwise around the loop, we move with the field on this segment. Since the field cannot vary with position along the infinite solenoid, the contribution to the line integral is just $B\ell$; since the other three sides contribute nothing, this is the value of $\oint \mathbf{B} \cdot d\boldsymbol{\ell}$.

To apply Ampère's law we need the encircled current. If there are n turns per unit length of solenoid, the amperian loop encircles $n\ell$ turns. The same current I flows in each turn, so the encircled current is $n\ell I$. Applying Ampère's law then gives

$$B\ell = \mu_0 n \ell I,$$

or $$B = \mu_0 n I. \quad \text{(solenoid)} \quad (30\text{-}11)$$

Since the vertical dimension of the amperian rectangle never entered our calculation, this field magnitude is the same anywhere inside the solenoid. The magnetic field in the solenoid is therefore uniform. Although it looks very different, the long solenoid with its uniform magnetic field is the magnetic analog of a closely spaced parallel-plate capacitor, which produces a uniform electric field.

Although Figs. 30-27 and 30-28 depict circular coils, the derivation of Equation 30-11 is based only on Fig. 30-30, which could represent a solenoid whose coils are circular, square, or any other shape.

APPLICATION	*Everyday Solenoids, Medical Solenoids*

Solenoids of all sizes are used in a wide variety of experimental and practical devices. Because a solenoid is hollow, magnetic materials such as iron will be pulled into the solenoid by the nonuniform magnetic field near its ends, and solenoids are therefore used to produce straight-line motion in mechanical devices. For example, turning the key to start your car sends current through a solenoid in the car's starter motor. A magnetic field develops in the solenoid, pulling in a steel plunger. Movement of the plunger joins a set of electrical contacts allowing current to flow to the starter motor. At the same time, the rod moves a small gear to the end of the motor shaft, engaging a gear on the engine's flywheel so that the starter motor can turn the engine (Fig. 30-31).

FIGURE 30-31 Cross section of a car starter motor, showing the workings of the solenoid. Turning the key to start the car sends current through the solenoid coils, creating a magnetic field that pulls the steel plunger into the solenoid. The lever attached to the plunger then pushes the gear outward on the shaft, engaging a larger gear on the gasoline engine. The electric starter motor turns to start the engine. Armature of the motor is the coil that forms the heart of the motor (recall Figs. 29-35 and 29-36).

Running a dishwasher or washing machine also involves solenoids. The valves that control the flow of water in these machines are solenoid valves, opened and closed as a steel rod moves in or out of a solenoid.

Finally, huge solenoids with human-size interiors are used to produce the strong, uniform magnetic fields needed for magnetic resonance imaging (MRI). This high-tech medical technique images the body's interior without the need for X rays or other radiation (Fig. 30-32). The MRI solenoids use superconducting wire cooled with liquid helium to achieve high currents and correspondingly high magnetic fields.

FIGURE 30-32 Patient being inserted into a superconducting solenoid used for magnetic resonance imaging (MRI), a powerful and relatively new medical diagnostic technique.

| **EXAMPLE 30-6** | *An MRI Solenoid* |

A solenoid used in magnetic resonance imaging is 2.4 m long and 95 cm in diameter. It is wound from a niobium-titanium superconducting wire 2.0 mm in diameter, with adjacent turns separated by an insulating layer of negligible thickness. What current is necessary to produce a 1.5-T magnetic field inside the solenoid?

Solution

The magnetic field is given by Equation 30-12, $B = \mu_0 nI$, so if we know n—the number of turns per unit length—we can solve for I. Since the wire has diameter $d = 2.0$ mm, 5 turns will occupy 1 cm and therefore $n = 500$ turns/meter. Solving

Equation 30-11 for I then gives

$$I = \frac{B}{\mu_0 n} = \frac{(1.5 \text{ T})}{(4\pi \times 10^{-7})(500 \text{ m}^{-1})} = 2.4 \text{ kA}.$$

This is a large current, but readily handled by the niobium-titanium superconductor.

EXERCISE Copper wire 0.40 mm in diameter is tightly wound into a long solenoid, and a 3.6-A current passed through it. What is the magnetic field in the solenoid?

Answer: 11 mT

Some problems similar to Example 30-6: 43–45, 48

Toroids

A **toroid** is a solenoid bent into a doughnut shape (Fig. 30-33). Toroidal geometry is widely used in fusion reactors, as discussed in the preceding chapter, and toroidal coils help produce the magnetic field that confines the fusion plasma.

Symmetry requires that the toroid's field lines be circular, with constant magnitude on any line. We can readily calculate the line integral of this magnetic field around a circular amperian loop, like that shown in Fig. 30-34. This loop coincides with a field line, and symmetry ensures that the magnetic field has the same magnitude over the loop. Therefore the line integral becomes

$$\underset{\text{loop}}{\oint} \mathbf{B} \cdot d\boldsymbol{\ell} = \underset{\text{loop}}{\oint} B \, d\ell = B \underset{\text{loop}}{\oint} d\ell = 2\pi r B.$$

FIGURE 30-33 A toroidal coil.

To apply Ampère's law we equate this quantity to μ_0 times the encircled current. If the toroid consists of N turns and carries a current I, then an amperian loop inside the toroid encircles a total current NI. Then Ampère's law becomes

$$2\pi r B = \mu_0 NI,$$

or

$$B = \frac{\mu_0 NI}{2\pi r}. \qquad \text{(toroid)} \qquad (30\text{-}12)$$

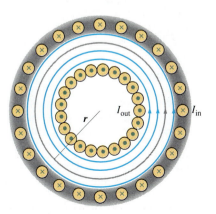

FIGURE 30-34 Cross section of a toroid showing current emerging at inner edge of coils and descending into plane of page at outer edge. Also shown are circular field lines and an amperian loop of radius r (gray) for use in calculating the field. You can confirm the field direction using the right-hand rule.

This result holds when the amperian loop is within the toroid itself. But if it's inside the inner edge (inside the "doughnut's hole"), there's no encircled current and, therefore, no magnetic field. And beyond the outer edge, the amperian loop encircles equal but opposite currents, giving zero net current and again no magnetic field. As with a solenoid, the individual turns of a toroid need not be circular.

The toroidal field of Equation 30-12 is not uniform but exhibits a $1/r$ decrease. This nonuniformity causes problems with plasma confinement in fusion reactors, where it causes a drift of particles perpendicular to the field and therefore toward the walls of the machine.

30-6 MAGNETIC MATTER

We began our study of magnetism in Chapter 29 with a discussion of magnets. But we quickly moved on to concentrate on the behavior of electric charges in magnetic fields. In this chapter we've further developed the relation between magnetism and electric charge, as we've seen that moving electric charge is the source of magnetic fields. What does electric charge have to do with the familiar magnets we used to introduce magnetism?

In fact the two are one and the same phenomenon. When an electron orbits an atomic nucleus, its circular motion and charge make a miniature current loop, and it therefore constitutes a magnetic dipole (Fig. 30-35); if you worked Problem 73 in the preceding chapter then you've calculated the dipole moment for a simple atomic model. In addition the electron possesses an intrinsic magnetic dipole moment associated with an intrinsic angular momentum called "spin." Interactions among these magnetic dipole moments determine the magnetic properties of individual atoms and of bulk matter. Although an accurate description of magnetism in matter necessarily involves quantum mechanics, we can nevertheless use our knowledge of magnetic dipoles to gain a qualitative understanding of magnetic matter.

FIGURE 30-35 In the classical model of the atom, the circling electron constitutes a miniature current loop. The atom is therefore a magnetic dipole. Here the current—carried by the *negative* electron and therefore opposite the electron's motion—is counterclockwise when viewed from above, so the magnetic moment points upward.

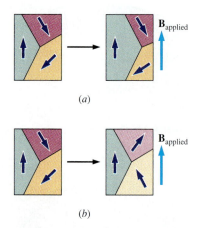

FIGURE 30-36 Domain changes in a ferromagnetic material occur through (*a*) domain growth and (*b*) domain re-alignment. These changes occur when a magnetic field is applied, and result in the material acquiring a net magnetic moment.

Ferromagnetism

Experiment reveals three types of magnetic behavior in bulk matter. **Ferromagnetism**, the most familiar, is actually limited to a few substances, notably the elements iron, nickel, and cobalt, and some compounds. In a ferromagnetic material, a quantum-mechanical interaction among nearby atomic magnetic moments results in regions—called **magnetic domains**—in which all the atomic magnetic moments point in the same direction. A typical domain contains 10^{17} to 10^{21} atoms and occupies a volume on the order of 10^{-12} to 10^{-8} m^3. The magnetic moment of a single domain can be large since it's the sum of many atomic magnetic moment vectors all pointing in the same direction. A typical piece of ferromagnetic material, however, contains many domains with their moments in random directions and, therefore, exhibits no net magnetic moment. But when an external magnetic field is applied, a net magnetic moment develops. This occurs because domains that already happen to be aligned with the field can grow by realignment of individual atomic moments in adjacent domains (Fig. 30-36*a*). In addition, the magnetic moments of entire domains can rotate (Fig. 30-36*b*).

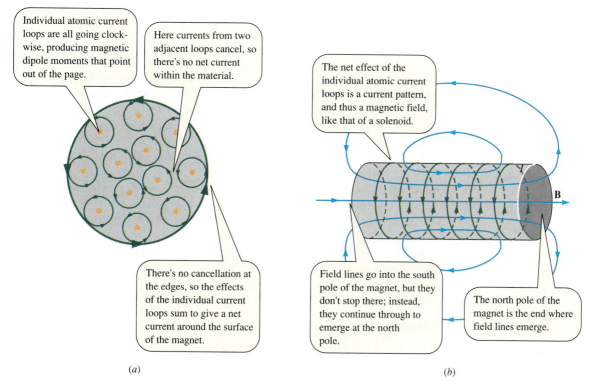

FIGURE 30-37 (a) Cross section of a bar magnet, showing individual atomic current loops all aligned the same way (dots represent the magnetic moment vectors). *Within* the material, adjacent atomic currents cancel. But they don't cancel at the edges, leaving a net current encircling the magnet. (b) Side view shows that this magnetization current is similar to the current in the coils of a solenoid. The bar magnet's field is therefore similar to that of a solenoid.

Since any dipole experiences a force in a nonuniform field, a piece of ferromagnetic material in such a field experiences a net force; this is why iron and other ferromagnetic materials are attracted to magnets even though they themselves are not magnets.

Some ferromagnetic materials retain significant magnetization even after the applied field has been removed. These so-called *hard* ferromagnetic materials make permanent magnets. A common bar magnet is a piece of hard ferromagnetic material that's been magnetized with its internal magnetic dipoles aligned along its long dimension. We suggested earlier that a bar magnet is magnetically similar to a solenoid, and Fig. 30-37 shows why: the internal atomic current loops give a net current flowing around the magnet, just like the current in a solenoid. This so-called magnetization current, however, arises not from the steady flow of charge in the material, but as the sum of the individual atomic current loops.

Permanent magnetization persists unless a strong magnetic field is applied that changes its direction or strength. Computer disks, credit cards, and audio- and videotapes (Fig. 30-38) make use of hard ferromagnetic materials that

FIGURE 30-38 Videotapes, credit cards, and computer disks all store information using hard ferromagnetic materials.

retain information as patterns of permanent magnetization; these magnetic media can be "rewritten" by applying a magnetic field strong enough to alter the magnetization and thus the stored information. We'll take a closer look at magnetic recording in the next chapter.

Permanent magnetization in so-called "soft" ferromagnetic materials, in contrast, is negligible. Such materials are used in applications that require magnetization to be turned on and off rapidly; these include the "heads" that read and write information on computer disks and audio- and videotapes, as well as electromagnets such as the one shown at the beginning of this chapter.

Random thermal motions tend to disrupt the alignment of individual magnetic moments. Thus ferromagnetic effects weaken with increasing temperature. Above the so-called **Curie temperature**, ferromagnetism ceases altogether. Curie temperatures for the common ferromagnetic elements nickel, iron, and cobalt are 631, 1043, and 1395 K, respectively. The rarer ferromagnetic elements dysprosium and gadolinium have much lower Curie temperatures of 85 and 289 K, respectively. The disappearance of ferromagnetism at the Curie temperature is an example of a phase transition, analogous to the solid/liquid/gas transitions we studied in Chapter 20.

Paramagnetism

Many substances that are not ferromagnetic nevertheless consist of atoms or molecules with permanent magnetic dipole moments. What distinguishes these **paramagnetic** materials from ferromagnetic substances is the absence of a strong interaction that tends to align nearby moments. As a result, individual atomic moments are not organized into domains, but point in random directions. An applied magnetic field still brings the atomic magnetic moments into some degree of alignment, but at all but the coldest temperatures this alignment is far less complete than in a ferromagnetic material. Therefore paramagnetic materials are attracted only weakly to magnets (Fig. 30-39), and paramagnetism decreases with increasing temperature. Unlike ferromagnetism, paramagnetism is not a strong enough effect to have many technological applications, but it does provide an important way of probing the structure of materials and can also be exploited to help achieve very low temperatures.

FIGURE 30-39 Liquid oxygen (O_2) is one of the more strongly paramagnetic materials. Here liquid oxygen is suspended between the poles of a magnet.

Diamagnetism

Even materials with no intrinsic magnetic moments can have magnetic moments induced when a magnet approaches or when an applied magnetic field otherwise changes. Such materials are termed **diamagnetic**. In contrast to paramagnetic and ferromagnetic materials, diamagnetic materials are repelled by magnets. We will explore the origins of diamagnetism in the next chapter.

Magnetic Susceptibility

We can characterize the effect of atomic magnetic dipoles on bulk matter just as we did in Chapter 23 for electric dipoles in dielectrics. There we found that atomic electric dipoles align with an electric field to reduce the field within the material, and we introduced the dielectric constant κ as the factor quantifying that reduction.

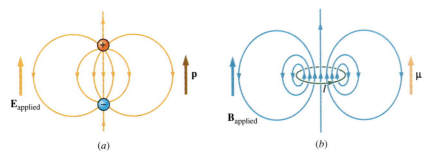

FIGURE 30-40 Although the electric fields far from electric and magnetic dipoles have the same form, the fields *within* the atomic structure giving rise to the different dipole moments have opposite directions. This is because electric dipoles consist of separated point charges, while magnetic dipoles are current loops. When external electric and magnetic fields are applied, respectively, to these two structures, the result is a reduction in the net electric field but an increase in the net magnetic field.

In a magnetic material, alignment of atomic magnetic dipoles has the opposite effect: the field in the material is increased. Figure 30-40 shows why. An electric dipole consists of two separated point charges. The strongest field associated with this dipole is the internal field pointing straight from the positive to the negative charge. When the dipole aligns with an applied electric field, this internal field is *opposite* the applied field and, therefore, *reduces* the net electric field (Fig. 30-40a). But, as we've seen, magnetic field lines always *encircle* a current. As Fig. 30-40b shows, the field inside the current loop therefore points in the *same* direction as the applied field and, therefore, *increases* the net magnetic field.

Because of the very strong alignment of atomic dipoles that occurs in ferromagnetic materials, these materials greatly increase an applied magnetic field. For that reason the coils of electromagnets, including the heads of computer disk drives and VCRs, are usually wound on a ferromagnetic core to give a much stronger field than would be provided by the coil current alone.

In analogy with the dielectric constant, we introduce the quantity κ_M, called the **relative permeability**, as the factor by which the magnetic field within a material increases as a result of the alignment of atomic magnetic dipoles. For paramagnetic materials, κ_M is slightly greater than 1; for ferromagnetic materials it is much greater than 1. In diamagnetic materials the dipoles align antiparallel to the field; this makes $\kappa_M < 1$ for these materials. Because the relative permeabilities of paramagnetic and diamagnetic materials are very close to 1, it's more convenient to work with the **magnetic susceptibility** χ_M, defined by

$$\chi_M = \kappa_M - 1.$$

The internal field in the material is then given by

$$B_{int} = \kappa_M B_{applied} = (\chi_M + 1)B_{applied}. \tag{30-13}$$

Equation 30-13 is most useful for paramagnetic and diamagnetic materials. In a ferromagnetic material, the internal and external fields are not proportional, and the internal field depends on the past history of the material's exposure to magnetic fields. This phenomenon, called **hysteresis**, is what makes possible

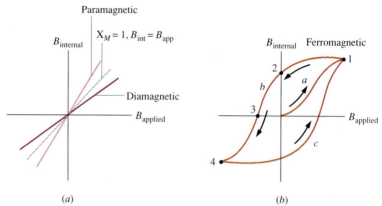

FIGURE 30-41 Internal versus applied magnetic field for different types of magnetic materials. (*a*) In diamagnetic and paramagnetic materials the relationship is linear; paramagnetic materials strengthen the applied field slightly, while diamagnetic materials weaken it slightly. (*b*) In ferromagnetic materials, the relationship depends on the strength of the applied field and on the past history of the material. As the applied field is increased, an initially unmagnetized ferromagnetic material responds by developing an increasing internal field (curve *a*). Eventually the field saturates (point 1) at its maximum possible value. Decreasing the applied field to zero leaves the material with a permanent magnetization (point 2); only a strong field in the opposite direction can eliminate (point 3) and eventually reverse the magnetization (point 4). Curve is for a "hard" ferromagnetic material that retains strong permanent magnetization; curve for a "soft" material would be much narrower, with a much smaller internal field at point 2. Axes are not to scale; field strengths on the vertical axis are much larger, reflecting the high magnetic susceptibility of a ferromagnetic material. Arrows indicate that the applied field is increased (curve *a*), decreased (curve *b*), and increased again (curve *c*).

permanent magnets. Figure 30-41 shows a ferromagnetic material's response to an externally applied magnetic field. If the material is initially unmagnetized, its internal field first increases with increasing applied field (curve *a* in Fig. 30-41). Eventually, though, increasing the applied field leads to little or no increase in the internal field; the material is then **saturated**, and no higher internal field is possible. Saturation occurs when essentially all the magnetic domains in the material are aligned, so there's no way to increase the internal field further. If the applied field is then reduced, the internal field also falls, but not as quickly. Even at zero applied field, there can remain a strong internal field due to the permanent magnetization we discussed earlier (point 2 in Fig. 30-41). Finally, a sufficiently strong field in the opposite direction results in saturation with the opposite magnetization direction.

Table 30-2 lists some magnetic susceptibilities for all three types of magnetic materials. That the ferromagnetic materials listed have susceptibilities many orders of magnitude higher than others shows why we normally think of magnetism only in the context of these special materials. The highest susceptibilities are achieved with special alloys such as permalloy and supermalloy; these are used in making high-field permanent magnets for a variety of applications. The material called "mu metal" is used for magnetic shielding—for example, to prevent distortion by external fields in TV picture tubes and computer monitors, or to shield the magnets used in loudspeakers (recall Fig. 29-31) so they can be placed near videotapes or TV sets without causing damage or distortion. Of the paramagnetic materials listed, liquid oxygen has by far the highest susceptibility, showing again the effect of temperature on paramagnetism. Finally, note the entry for superconductors, which are perfectly diamagnetic. Their susceptibility of -1 implies that $\kappa_M = 0$, showing that they completely exclude magnetic fields. We will explore the reasons for this in the next chapter.

TABLE 30-2 *Magnetic Susceptibilities**

MATERIAL	MAGNETIC SUSCEPTIBILITY, χ_M
Diamagnetic materials	
Copper	-9.6×10^{-6}
Lead	-1.6×10^{-5}
Mercury	-2.8×10^{-5}
Nitrogen (gas, 293 K)	-6.7×10^{-9}
Sodium chloride	-1.4×10^{-5}
Any superconductor	-1
Water	-9.1×10^{-6}
Paramagnetic materials	
Aluminum	2.1×10^{-5}
Chromium	3.1×10^{-4}
Oxygen (gas, 293 K)	1.9×10^{-6}
Oxygen (liquid, 90 K)	3.5×10^{-3}
Sodium	8.5×10^{-6}
Ferromagnetic materials (field and history dependent; maximum value listed)	
Iron (annealed)	5.5×10^{3}
Permalloy (55% Fe, 45% Ni)	2.5×10^{4}
Supermalloy (15.7% Fe, 79% Ni, 5.0% Mo; 0.30% Mn)	8.0×10^{5}
μ-metal (77% Ni, 16% Fe, 5% Cu, 2% Cr)	1.0×10^{5}

*At 300 K unless noted.

30-7 MAGNETIC MONOPOLES AND GAUSS'S LAW

Electric and magnetic fields, at least as we've studied them so far, have very different configurations. Electric fields begin and end on their sources—namely electric charges. Magnetic fields, in contrast, encircle their sources—namely *moving* electric charges. Magnetic fields generally form closed loops, while the electric fields we've encountered so far do not (Fig. 30-42).

Are there particles analogous to electric charges, from which magnetic field lines might originate? There might be. Symmetry arguments based on the existence of electric charge and the many similarities between electricity and magnetism have long suggested to physicists that such **magnetic monopoles**— isolated magnetic north or south poles—might exist. Furthermore, theories of elementary particles suggest that magnetic monopoles should have been created in the Big Bang event that began our universe. However, recent versions of the

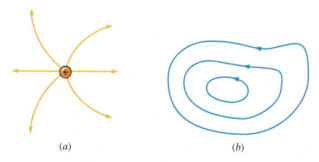

(a)   *(b)*

FIGURE 30-42 At this point in our study of electromagnetism, electric and magnetic field configurations are clearly distinguished. Electric fields *(a)* begin and end on electric charges, while magnetic fields *(b)* generally form closed loops.

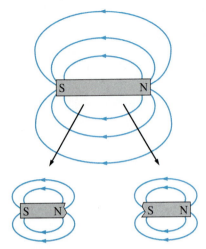

FIGURE 30-43 You can't separate the north and south poles of a bar magnet by cutting it in half; that only produces smaller bar magnets, each with a north and a south pole and thus each a magnetic dipole. That's because the field of a bar magnet arises from atomic current loops (recall Fig. 30-37), not from separate magnetic north and south poles, or monopoles.

Big Bang theory suggest that monopoles should be spread so thinly as to make the chance of detecting one completely negligible.

If they existed, magnetic monopoles would be to the magnetic field what electric charges are to the electric field. Isolated monopoles would give rise to radial magnetic fields like the electric fields of point charges. Monopoles would experience forces in magnetic fields, forces given simply by the product of the monopole's "magnetic charge" and the magnetic field. And *moving* magnetic monopoles would produce electric fields—just as moving electric charges produce magnetic fields.

No one has yet found a magnetic monopole, however, although serious experimental searches continue. Every magnetic field we've ever seen has its origin in moving electric charge, not in separate magnetic north and south poles. That's why you can't make an isolated magnetic north pole by chopping a bar magnet in half (Fig. 30-43). The observed absence of magnetic monopoles means that the most fundamental magnetic field configuration is that of the dipole—in contrast to the simpler electric case, where the spherically symmetric point-charge field is possible. That's why Table 30-1 contains no magnetic entry under spherical geometry.

In the absence of magnetic monopoles, there is no place where magnetic field lines begin or end. That means there is no closed surface through which a nonzero net number of magnetic field lines emerges. In complete analogy with our discussion of Gauss's law in Chapter 24, we can say that the **magnetic flux**—mathematically, the surface integral $\oint \mathbf{B} \cdot d\mathbf{A}$—is zero for every closed surface. This statement is **Gauss's Law for magnetism**:

$$\oint \mathbf{B} \cdot d\mathbf{A} = 0. \tag{30-14}$$

Equation 30-14 is another of the four fundamental laws of electromagnetism. We've now seen three of them: Gauss's law for electricity, Ampère's law (still incomplete because of its restriction to *steady* currents), and Gauss's law for magnetism. In the next chapter we'll encounter the fourth of these fundamental laws.

Although Gauss's law for magnetism has zero on its right-hand side, the law is far from being devoid of content. It says what we've already found to be the case: that magnetic fields must configure themselves so they have no beginnings or endings.

CHAPTER SYNOPSIS

Summary

1. Magnetic fields arise from **moving electric charges**. The field at some point P arising from a steady electric current is described by the **Biot-Savart law**:

$$d\mathbf{B} = \frac{\mu_0}{4\pi} \frac{I \, d\boldsymbol{\ell} \times \hat{\mathbf{r}}}{r^2},$$

where $d\mathbf{B}$ is the contribution to the field from a current element flowing along the infinitesimal vector $d\boldsymbol{\ell}$ a distance r from the point P, and $\hat{\mathbf{r}}$ is a unit vector from the current element toward P. The field at P of an entire current distribution is found by integrating all its contributions $d\mathbf{B}$.

Important special cases include a current loop, which at large distances produces a dipole field, and an infinite straight current, whose field encircles the current and decreases as $1/r$.

2. The field arising from a current exerts a magnetic force on nearby currents; as a result, parallel currents in the same direction attract and those in opposite directions repel.

3. **Ampère's law** relates the line integral of the magnetic field around an arbitrary closed loop to the current encircled by that loop:

$$\oint_{\text{loop}} \mathbf{B} \cdot d\boldsymbol{\ell} = \mu_0 I_{\text{encircled}}.$$

This form holds for all steady currents. It may be used to calculate magnetic fields in cases with sufficient symmetry, including line symmetry (straight wires), plane symmetry (current sheets), solenoids, and toroids.

4. Individual elementary particles and orbiting atomic electrons constitute miniature current loops, which are responsible for magnetic effects in bulk matter. The **relative permeability**, κ_M, gives the ratio of the internal magnetic field in a material to the applied field; this relation is also described by the **magnetic susceptibility**, $\chi_M = \kappa_M - 1$.

   a. In **ferromagnetic** materials, atomic magnetic moments group into domains with net magnetic moments. These align with an applied field, greatly increasing the field within the material. Ferromagnetic materials retain magnetization even after the applied field is removed; this phenomenon of **hysteresis** accounts for permanent magnets. $\kappa_M \gg 1$ for ferromagnetic materials, although the internal field depends on both the applied field and the material's history.

   b. In **paramagnetic** materials, individual atomic magnetic moments become partially aligned with an applied field, but there is no cooperative interaction among the individual moments. $\kappa_M > 1$ for paramagnetic materials.

   c. Diamagnetic materials have no intrinsic magnetic moments. They have $\kappa_M < 1$ and are weakly repelled from magnets.

5. No **magnetic monopoles**, or magnetic analogs of electric charge, have ever been found. Magnetic fields—originating from moving electric charge—therefore form closed loops without beginnings or ends. In the absence of magnetic monopoles, **Gauss's law for magnetism** says that the flux of the magnetic field through any closed surface is zero:

$$\oint \mathbf{B} \cdot d\mathbf{A} = 0.$$

Terms You Should Understand

(Pairs are closely related terms whose distinction is important; number in parentheses is chapter section where term first appears.)

Biot-Savart law (30-1)
Ampère's law (30-3)
solenoid, toroid (30-5)
ferromagnetism, paramagnetism, diamagnetism (30-6)
permeability, susceptibility (30-6)
magnetic monopole (30-7)
Gauss's law for magnetism (30-7)

Symbols You Should Recognize

μ_0 (30-1)

$\oint \mathbf{B} \cdot d\boldsymbol{\ell}$ (30-3)

κ_M, χ_M (30-6)

Problems You Should Be Able to Solve

calculating magnetic fields of simple current distributions by integration using the Biot-Savart law (30-1)
evaluating forces between adjacent conductors (30-2)
evaluating magnetic fields using Ampère's law in situations with sufficient symmetry (30-4)
applying results derived in the text for the fields of straight wires, current loops, solenoids, and toroids (30-1–30-5)
relating internal and applied magnetic fields given magnetic susceptibility (30-6)

Limitations to Keep in Mind

The Biot-Savart law, and Ampère's law as expressed in this chapter, are exactly valid only for *steady* currents—those that never change with time.

QUESTIONS

1. In what two senses does a current loop behave like a magnetic dipole?

2. The electric field far from a pair of equal but opposite charges has the same configuration as the magnetic field far from a current loop. Yet inside the structure giving rise to the fields, the two point in opposite directions. Why?

3. The Biot-Savart law shows that the magnetic field of a current element decreases as $1/r^2$. Could you put together a complete circuit whose field exhibits this $1/r^2$ decrease? Why or why not?

4. Do currents in the same direction attract or repel? Explain.

5. If a current is passed through an unstretched spring, will the spring contract or expand? Explain.

6. Why is it advantageous to define the ampere in terms of magnetic force rather than a standard ammeter?

7. An intense beam of electrons or other charged particles tends to "pinch" or compress to a smaller diameter. Explain the origin of this "pinch effect" in terms of magnetic forces.

8. The field of a long, straight wire consists of circular field lines. Does Ampère's law hold for a square loop surrounding the wire? For a circular loop not concentric with the wire? See Fig. 30-44.

9. If the line integral around a closed loop is zero, does that mean the magnetic field on the loop is zero?

10. Must the integration path in Ampère's law coincide with a field line?

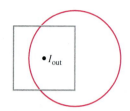

FIGURE 30-44 Question 8.

11. What must be going on inside Earth in order that it have a magnetic field?

12. Figure 30-45 shows some magnetic field lines associated with two parallel wires carrying equal currents perpendicular to the page. Are the currents in the same or opposite directions? How can you tell?

FIGURE 30-45 Question 12.

13. A solid cylinder and a hollow pipe of the same outer diameter carry the same current along their long dimensions, with the current distributed symmetrically about their axes. How do the magnetic fields at their surfaces compare?

14. Why is a piece of iron attracted into a solenoid?

15. Would there be a net magnetic force on a piece of iron deep inside a long solenoid? Explain.

16. In what sense is a long solenoid the magnetic analog of a parallel-plate capacitor?

17. What would happen to the magnetic field inside a solenoid if you (a) doubled the solenoid length without changing the number of turns per unit length or (b) doubled the length without changing the total number of turns?

18. Identify *three* regions in the magnetic field of Fig. 30-46 where there *must* be a current. Which way is the current flowing in each region?

FIGURE 30-46 Question 18.

19. An unmagnetized piece of iron has no net magnetic dipole moment. Yet it is attracted to either pole of a bar magnet. Why?

20. How would you determine experimentally whether a substance was paramagnetic or diamagnetic?

21. Would permanent magnets be possible if the relative permeability of ferromagnetic materials were strictly constant? Explain.

22. Why do paramagnetic and ferromagnetic effects weaken with increasing temperature?

23. If magnetic monopoles existed, then a net motion of monopoles would constitute a "magnetic current." What sort of field should arise from such a "current?"

24. In the absence of magnetic monopoles, why do we even bother to write Gauss's law for magnetism? Does the law have any physical significance?

PROBLEMS

ActivPhysics can help with these problems:
Activities 13.1–13.3, 13.5

Section 30-1 The Biot-Savart Law

1. A wire carries 15 A. You form the wire into a single-turn circular loop with magnetic field 80 μT at the loop center. What is the loop radius?

2. A single-turn wire loop is 2.0 cm in diameter and carries a 650-mA current. Find the magnetic field strength (a) at the loop center and (b) on the loop axis, 20 cm from the center.

3. A 2.2-m-long wire carrying 3.5 A is wound into a tight, loop-shaped coil 5.0 cm in diameter. What is the magnetic field at its center?

4. What is the current in a long wire if the magnetic field strength 1.2 cm from the wire's axis is 67 μT?

5. Suppose Earth's magnetic field arose from a single loop of current at the outer edge of the planet's liquid core (core radius 3000 km), concentric with Earth's center. What current would be necessary to give the observed field strength of 62 μT at the north pole? (The currents responsible for Earth's field are more complicated than this problem suggests.)

6. Earth's magnetic dipole moment is 8.0×10^{22} A·m^2. What is the magnetic field strength on Earth's surface at either pole?

7. A single-turn current loop carrying 25 A produces a magnetic field of 3.5 nT at a point on its axis 50 cm from the loop

center. What is the loop area, assuming the loop diameter is much less than 50 cm?

8. Two identical current loops are 10 cm in diameter and carry 20-A currents. They are placed 1.0 cm apart, as shown in Fig. 30-47. Find the magnetic field strength at the center of either loop when their currents are in (a) the same and (b) opposite directions.

10 cm

1.0 cm

FIGURE 30-47 Problem 8.

9. You have a spool of thin wire that can handle a maximum current of 0.50 A. If you wind the wire into a looplike coil 20 cm in diameter, how many turns should the coil have if the magnetic field at its center is to be 2.3 mT at this maximum current?

10. A single piece of wire is bent so that it includes a circular loop of radius a, as shown in Fig. 30-48. A current I flows in the direction shown. Find an expression for the magnetic field at the center of the loop.

FIGURE 30-48 Problem 10.

11. Two long, parallel wires are 6.0 cm apart. One carries 5.0 A and the other 10 A, with both currents in the same direction. Where on a line perpendicular to both wires is the magnetic field zero?

12. Four long, parallel wires are located at the corners of a square 15 cm on a side. Each carries a current of 2.5 A, with the top two currents into the page in Fig. 30-49 and the bottom two out of the page. Find the magnetic field at the center of the square.

13. A power line carries a 500-A current toward magnetic north and is suspended 10 m above the ground. The horizontal component of Earth's magnetic field at the power line's latitude is 0.24 G. If a magnetic compass is placed on the ground directly below the power line, in what direction will it point?

I_{in}

15 cm

I_{out}

15 cm

FIGURE 30-49 Problems 12, 23.

14. An electron is moving at 3.1×10^6 m/s parallel to a 1.0-mm-diameter wire carrying 20 A. If the electron is 2.0 mm from the center of the wire, with its velocity in the same direction as the current, what are the magnitude and direction of the force it experiences?

15. Part of a long wire is bent into a semicircle of radius a, as shown in Fig. 30-50. A current I flows in the direction shown. Use the Biot-Savart law to find the magnetic field at the center of the semicircle (point P).

I

a

P

FIGURE 30-50 Problem 15.

16. Use the result given in Problem 57 to find the magnetic field strength at the center of a square loop of side a carrying current I.

17. Figure 30-51 shows a conducting loop formed from concentric semicircles of radii a and b. If the loop carries a current I as shown, find the magnetic field at point P, the common center.

I

P

a b

FIGURE 30-51 Problem 17.

Section 30-2 The Magnetic Force between Two Conductors

18. In standard household wiring, parallel wires about 1 cm apart carry currents around 15 A. What is the magnitude of the force per unit length between such wires?

19. It would take a rather large apparatus to implement the definition of the ampere given at the end of Section 30-2. Suppose you wanted to use a smaller apparatus, with wires 50 cm long separated by 2.0 cm. What force would correspond to a current of 1 A?

20. Two parallel copper rods supply power to a high-energy experiment, carrying the same current in opposite directions. The rods are held 8.0 cm apart by insulating blocks mounted every 1.5 m. If each block can tolerate a maximum tension force of 200 N, what is the maximum allowable current?

21. The structure shown in Fig. 30-52 is made from conducting rods. The upper horizontal rod is free to slide vertically on the uprights, while maintaining electrical contact with them. The upper rod has mass 22 g and length 95 cm. A battery connected across the insulating gap at the bottom of the left-hand upright drives a 66-A current through the structure. At what height h will the upper wire be in equilibrium?

FIGURE 30-52 Problem 21.

22. Three parallel wires 4.6 m long each carry 20 A in the same direction. They are spaced at the vertices of an equilateral triangle 3.5 cm on a side. Find the magnitude of the force on each wire.

23. The wires in Fig. 30-49 carry 2.5-A currents in the directions indicated. Find the net force per unit length on the wire at lower left.

24. A long, straight wire carries 20 A. A 5.0-cm by 10-cm rectangular wire loop carrying 500 mA is located 2.0 cm from the wire, as shown in Fig. 30-53. Find the net magnetic force on the loop.

25. A solenoid 10 cm in diameter is made with 2.1-mm-diameter copper wire wound so tightly that adjacent turns touch, separated only by enamel insulation of negligible thickness. The solenoid carries a 28-A current. In the long, straight wire approximation, what is the net force between two adjacent turns of the solenoid?

FIGURE 30-53 Problem 24.

26. A long, flat conducting ribbon of width w is parallel to a long straight wire, with its near edge a distance a from the wire (Fig. 30-54). Wire and ribbon carry the same current I; this current is distributed uniformly over the ribbon. Use integration to show that the force per unit length between the two has magnitude $\dfrac{\mu_0 I^2}{2\pi w}\ln\left(\dfrac{a+w}{a}\right)$.

FIGURE 30-54 Problem 26.

Section 30-3 Ampère's Law

27. The line integral of the magnetic field on a closed path surrounding a wire has the value 8.8 μT·m. What is the current in the wire?

28. In Fig. 30-55, $I_1 = 2$ A flowing out of the page; $I_2 = 1$ A, also out of the page, and $I_3 = 2$ A, into the page. What is the line integral of the magnetic field taken counterclockwise around each loop shown?

29. The magnetic field shown in Fig. 30-56 has uniform magnitude 75 μT, but its direction reverses abruptly. How much current is encircled by the rectangular loop shown?

30. The solar wind drags Earth's magnetic field out into a long "magnetotail," where the field reverses direction abruptly

FIGURE 30-55 Problem 28.

FIGURE 30-56 Problem 29.

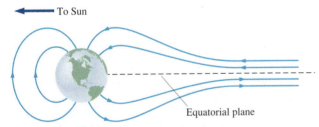

To Sun

Equatorial plane

FIGURE 30-57 A simplified view of Earth's magnetic field, showing the long "magnetotail" on the nighttime side, caused by the solar wind dragging Earth's field lines with it. What's the current in the region to the right, where the field lines are essentially straight? (Problem 30)

across the equatorial plane (Fig. 30-57). (a) If the field strength in a section of the magnetotail is 20 nT, what is the current per unit length flowing in the magnetotail? (b) What is the direction of this current in Fig. 30-57?

31. Figure 30-58 shows a magnetic field pointing in the x direction. Its strength, however, varies with position in the y direction. At the top and bottom of the rectangular loop shown the field strengths are 3.4 μT and 1.2 μT, respectively. How much current flows through the area encircled by the loop?

FIGURE 30-58 Problems 31, 66.

Section 30-4 Using Ampère's Law

32. (a) What is the magnetic field strength 0.10 mm from the axis of a 1.0-mm-diameter wire carrying 5.0 A distributed uniformly over its cross section? (b) What is the field strength at the surface of the wire?

33. A solid wire 2.1 mm in diameter carries a 10-A current with uniform current density. What is the magnetic field strength (a) at the axis of the wire, (b) 0.20 mm from the axis, (c) at the surface of the wire, and (d) 4.0 mm from the wire axis?

34. Show that Equations 30-8 and 30-9 give the same results when evaluated at the surface of the wire.

35. A long conducting rod of radius R carries a nonuniform current density given by $J = J_0 r/R$, where J_0 is a constant and r is the radial distance from the rod's axis. Find expressions for the magnetic field strength (a) inside and (b) outside the rod.

36. A long, hollow conducting pipe of radius R carries a uniform current I along the pipe, as shown in Fig. 30-59. Use Ampère's law to find the magnetic field strength (a) inside and (b) outside the pipe.

FIGURE 30-59 Problem 36.

37. Typically, cylindrical wires made from yttrium-barium-copper-oxide superconductor can carry a maximum current density of 6.0 MA/m² at a temperature of 77 K, as long as magnetic field at the conductor surface does not exceed 10 mT. Suppose such a wire is to carry the maximum current density. (a) At what wire diameter would the surface magnetic field equal the 10-mT limit? (b) Is this a maximum or minimum value for the diameter if the field is not to exceed the limit? (c) What current would a wire with this diameter carry?

38. A copper ribbon 1.0 cm wide and 0.15 mm thick is rated for a maximum safe current density of 8.8×10^6 A/m².

What is the maximum magnetic field strength achievable at the surface of this ribbon?

39. Two large, flat conducting plates lie parallel to the x-y plane. They carry equal currents, one in the $+x$ and the other in the $-x$ direction. In each plate the current per meter of width in the y direction is J_s. Find the magnetic field strength (a) between and (b) outside the plates.

40. The coaxial cable shown in Fig. 30-60 consists of a solid inner conductor of radius a and a hollow outer conductor of inner radius b and thickness c. The two carry equal but opposite currents I, uniformly distributed. Find expressions for the magnetic field strength as a function of radial position r (a) within the inner conductor, (b) between the inner and outer conductors, and (c) beyond the outer conductor.

FIGURE 30-60 Problems 40, 61.

41. A hollow conducting pipe of inner radius a and outer radius b carries a current I parallel to its axis and distributed uniformly through the pipe material (Fig. 30-61). Find expressions for the magnetic field for (a) $r < a$, (b) $a < r < b$, and (c) $r > b$, where r is the radial distance from the pipe axis.

FIGURE 30-61 Problem 41.

42. A conducting slab extends infinitely in the x and y directions and has thickness h in the z direction. It carries a uniform current density $\mathbf{J} = J\hat{\imath}$. Find the magnetic field strength (a) inside and (b) outside the slab, as functions of the distance z from the center plane of the slab.

Section 30-5 Solenoids and Toroids

43. A superconducting solenoid has 3300 turns per meter and can carry a maximum current of 4.1 kA. What is the magnetic field strength in the solenoid?

44. A solenoid used in a plasma physics experiment is 10 cm in diameter, 1.0 m long, and carries a 35-A current to produce a 100-mT magnetic field. (a) How many turns are in the solenoid? (b) If the solenoid resistance is 2.7 Ω, how much power does it dissipate?

45. You have 10 m of 0.50-mm-diameter copper wire and a battery capable of passing 15 A through the wire. What magnetic field strengths could you obtain (a) inside a 2.0-cm-diameter solenoid wound with the wire as closely spaced as possible and (b) at the center of a single circular loop made from the wire?

46. A toroidal coil of inner radius 15 cm and outer radius 17 cm is wound from 1200 turns of wire. What are (a) the minimum and (b) the maximum magnetic field strengths within the toroid when it carries a 10-A current?

47. A toroidal fusion reactor requires a magnetic field that varies by no more than 10% from its central value of 1.5 T. If the minor radius of the toroidal coil producing this field is 30 cm, what is the minimum value for the major radius of the device?

48. A long solenoid with n turns per unit length carries a current I. The current returns to its driving battery along a wire of radius R that passes through the solenoid, along its axis. Find expressions for (a) the magnetic field strength at the surface of the wire and (b) the angle the field at the wire surface makes with the solenoid axis.

49. We noted that there is a nonzero magnetic field component outside a solenoid, encircling the device, associated with the component of current flow parallel to the solenoid axis. For a long solenoid of radius R, find an expression for the ratio of this external encircling field just outside the solenoid to the field inside, and show explicitly that this ratio tends to zero as the number of turns per unit length becomes large.

50. Derive Equation 30-11 for the field of a solenoid by considering the solenoid to be made of a large number of adjacent current loops. Use Equation 30-3 for the field of a current loop, and integrate over all loops.

Section 30-6 Magnetic Matter

51. When a sample of a certain substance is placed in a 250.0-mT magnetic field, the field inside the sample is 249.6 mT. Find the magnetic susceptibility of the substance. Is it ferromagnetic, paramagnetic, or diamagnetic?

52. A container of liquid oxygen at 90 K is placed in a 500.0-G magnetic field. What is the field strength within the liquid oxygen?

53. A ferromagnetic material is placed in a 2.5-G magnetic field and the field within the material is determined to be 1.8 T. What is the magnetic susceptibility of this material?

54. Figure 30-62 shows the hysteresis curve for the ferromagnetic alloy Alnico V, commonly used in permanent magnets. Use the graph to find approximate values for the maximum field strength obtainable inside this material, (a) in the absence and (b) in the presence of an externally applied field.

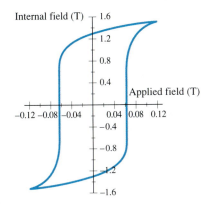

FIGURE 30-62 Problem 54.

Paired Problems

(Both problems in a pair involve the same principles and techniques. If you can get the first problem, you should be able to solve the second one.)

55. Two concentric, coplanar circular current loops have radii a and $2a$. If the magnetic field is zero at their common center, how does the current in the outer loop compare with that in the inner loop?

56. A thin conducting washer of inner radius a and outer radius $2a$ carries a current I distributed uniformly with radial position, as suggested in Fig. 30-63. Find an expression for the magnetic field strength at its center.

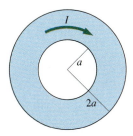

FIGURE 30-63 Problem 56.

57. Figure 30-64 shows a wire of length ℓ carrying current fed by other wires that are not shown. Point A lies on the perpendicular bisector, a distance y from the wire. Adapt the calculation of Example 30-2 to show that the magnetic field at A due to the straight wire alone has magnitude $\dfrac{\mu_0 I \ell}{2\pi y \sqrt{\ell^2 + 4y^2}}$. What is the field direction?

FIGURE 30-64 Problems 57, 58.

58. Point B in Fig. 30-64 lies a distance y perpendicular to the end of the wire. Show that the magnetic field at B has magnitude $\dfrac{\mu_0 I \ell}{4\pi y \sqrt{\ell^2 + y^2}}$. What is the field direction?

59. The largest lightning strikes have peak currents around 250 kA, flowing in essentially cylindrical channels of ionized air. How far from such a flash would the resulting magnetic field be equal to Earth's magnetic field strength, about 50 μT?

60. A particle-beam weapon being tested for ballistic missile defense delivers a 2.5-cm-diameter electron beam carrying a current of 10 kA at an altitude where Earth's magnetic field is 30 μT. How close to the beam would an adversary's surveillance apparatus need to be in order to detect the beam by observing a 1% change in the local magnetic field strength? Assume the beam's magnetic field is parallel to Earth's at the point of detection.

61. A coaxial cable like that shown in Fig. 30-60 consists of a 1.0-mm-diameter inner conductor and an outer conductor of inner diameter 1.0 cm and 0.20 mm thickness. A 100-mA current flows down the center conductor and back along the outer conductor. Find the magnetic field strength (a) 0.10 mm, (b) 5.0 mm, and (c) 2.0 cm from the cable axis.

62. Repeat the preceding problem if the current in the outer conductor only is increased to 200 mA.

Supplementary Problems

63. A circular wire loop of radius 15 cm and negligible thickness carries a 2.0-A current. Use suitable approximations to find the magnetic field of this loop (a) in the loop plane, 1.0 mm outside the loop, and (b) on the loop axis, 3.0 m from the loop center.

64. A long, flat conducting bar of width w carries a total current I distributed uniformly, as shown in Fig. 30-65. Use suitable approximations to write expressions for the

magnetic field strength (a) near the conductor surface ($r \ll w$) and (b) very far from the conductor ($r \gg w$).

FIGURE 30-65 Problem 64.

65. A long, hollow conducting pipe of radius R and length ℓ carries a uniform current I flowing around the pipe, as shown in Fig. 30-66. Find expressions for the magnetic field (a) inside and (b) outside the pipe. *Hint:* What configuration does this pipe resemble?

FIGURE 30-66 Problem 65.

66. The magnetic field in Fig. 30-58 is given by $\mathbf{B} = by\hat{\imath}$, where $b = 55$ μT/m and y is the vertical coordinate in Fig. 30-58, measured in meters. Find the current density in the region.
67. A wide, flat conducting spring of spring constant $k = 20$ N/m and negligible mass consists of two 6.0-cm-diameter turns, as shown in Fig. 30-67. In its unstretched configuration the coils are nearly touching. A 10-g mass is

hung from the spring, and at the same time a current I is passed through it. The spring stretches 2.0 mm. Find I, assuming the coils remain close enough to be treated as parallel wires.

FIGURE 30-67 Problem 67.

68. A solid conducting wire of radius R runs parallel to the z axis and carries a current density given by $\mathbf{J} = J_0(1 - r/R)\hat{\mathbf{k}}$, where J_0 is a constant and r the radial distance from the wire axis. Find expressions for (a) the total current in the wire, (b) the magnetic field strength for $r > R$, and (c) the magnetic field strength for $r < R$.
69. A disk of radius a carries a uniform surface charge density σ, and is rotating with angular speed ω about the central axis perpendicular to the disk. Show that the magnetic field at the disk's center is $\frac{1}{2}\mu_0\sigma\omega a$.
70. Calculate the magnetic field of an infinite current sheet by considering the sheet to be made up of infinitesimal line currents, as suggested in Fig. 30-26, and integrating the fields of these line currents.
71. Work Example 30-2 by expressing all variables in terms of the angle θ and integrating over the appropriate range in θ.

Electromagnetic Induction 31

These wind-driven electric generators use electromagnetic induction to convert the mechanical energy of wind into electrical energy. Underground cables combine the electric power produced by all the generators and the power is then fed into the utility company's power grid. Most of the world's electrical energy is produced by generators driven by steam from burning fossil fuels or from nuclear fission—and all such generators use electromagnetic induction. So do videotapes, computer disks, credit cards, and other magnetic information storage systems.

All the electric and magnetic fields we encountered in the previous chapters had their ultimate origins in electric charge, either stationary or moving. We stressed a relation between electricity and magnetism, whereby electric charge gives rise to and interacts with both the electric field and the magnetic field. The remainder of our study of electromagnetism is devoted to a much more intimate relation between electricity and magnetism, a relation in which the fields themselves interact directly. This interaction forms the basis of new electromagnetic technologies, leads toward an understanding of the nature of light, and points the way to the theory of relativity.

31-1 INDUCED CURRENTS

In 1831, the English scientist Michael Faraday and the American Joseph Henry independently carried out experiments in which electric currents arose in circuits subjected to changing magnetic fields. We now describe four simple experiments that illustrate this phenomenon:

Experiment 1 (Fig. 31-1): A bar magnet is moved in the presence of a circuit consisting of a coil of wire connected to an ammeter. There's no battery or other obvious source of emf in the circuit. As long as the magnet is stationary, there's no current. But when the magnet moves, the ammeter registers a current—which we call an **induced current**, because it's been somehow induced by the movement of the magnet. If we move the magnet faster, the induced current increases. If we reverse the direction of the magnet's motion, the current reverses.

Experiment 2 (Fig. 31-2): A coil is moved in the presence of a stationary magnet. An induced current results that behaves exactly like the current in Experiment 1. So we get the same results whether we move the magnet or the circuit; all that matters is the relative motion between magnet and circuit.

Experiment 3 (Fig. 31-3): Replace the bar magnet with an electromagnet made from a coil of wire carrying a steady current driven by a battery. The new coil creates a magnetic field like that of the bar magnet, and, not surprisingly given the results of Experiments 1 and 2, we get an induced current that depends on the relative motion of the two coils.

Experiment 4 (Fig. 31-4): Hold both coils stationary; then there's no induced current, just as there was none in Experiments 1 and 2 when the magnet and coil were not in relative motion. But now open the switch connecting the battery to the left-hand coil. The current drops quickly to zero, and during the brief interval while it's doing so, the ammeter registers a current in the right-hand coil. Then the induced current ceases as the current in the left-hand coil remains at zero. Now close the switch again: as the current briefly builds up in the left-hand coil, the ammeter registers an induced current in the right-hand coil—and its direction is opposite what it was when the switch was opened. Once the current reaches a steady value, the induced current again ceases.

The common feature in these experiments is a *changing magnetic field*. It does not matter whether the field changes because a magnet is moved, or because a circuit is moved near a magnet, or because the current giving rise to the

FIGURE 31-1 When a magnet is moved near a closed circuit, current flows in the circuit.

FIGURE 31-2 We get the same results if we move the coil instead of the magnet.

FIGURE 31-3 An induced current also arises when the magnet is replaced by a current-carrying circuit.

FIGURE 31-4 A current is also induced—even in the absence of any motion—when the current in an adjacent circuit changes.

field changes. In each case, an induced current appears in a circuit subjected to a changing magnetic field. We are observing here a new phenomenon— **electromagnetic induction**—whereby electrical effects arise from *changing* magnetic fields.

31-2 FARADAY'S LAW

We know from Chapter 27 that a source of electromotive force—such as a battery that supplies energy to electric charges—is needed to establish a current in a circuit. When an induced current flows in a circuit, even though there's no battery present, there must still be an emf. This so-called **induced emf** is usually not localized at one point in the circuit, as in a battery, but may be spread throughout the conductors making up the circuit.

Experimentally, we find that the induced emf in a circuit depends on the rate of change of **magnetic flux** through the circuit. Before quantifying this relationship, we show how to calculate magnetic flux.

Magnetic Flux

We introduced magnetic flux at the end of the preceding chapter, and showed that the magnetic flux through any *closed* surface is zero. Here we're interested in the flux through *open* surfaces, which need not be zero (Fig. 31-5). Like the electric flux defined in Chapter 24, magnetic flux is the integral of the magnetic field over a surface:

$$\phi_B = \int \mathbf{B} \cdot d\mathbf{A}. \tag{31-1}$$

As with electric flux, magnetic flux is proportional to the number of field lines passing through the surface. With electromagnetic induction, we're interested in the flux through a surface bounded by the circuit in question. For a circular loop such as the one in Fig. 31-5, that surface can be the circular disk whose circumference is the loop. More generally, the surface can be *any* surface bounded by the loop.

For a flat surface perpendicular to a uniform magnetic field, as in the example below, Equation 31-1 reduces to the simple expression $\phi_B = BA$. Note that the units of magnetic flux are $T \cdot m^2$.

FIGURE 31-5 A circular wire loop in the magnetic field of a bar magnet. The flux ϕ_B is proportional to the number of field lines crossing the circular surface bounded by the loop. If the magnet moves closer to the loop, the number of field lines—and hence the flux— increases.

EXAMPLE 31-1	*The Magnetic Flux through a Solenoid*

A solenoid of circular cross section has radius R, consists of n turns per unit length, and carries a current I. What is the magnetic flux through each turn of the solenoid?

Solution

The field of a solenoid is uniform and parallel to the solenoid axis, as we found in deriving Equation 30-11:

$$B = \mu_0 nI.$$

A flat surface bounded by one turn of the solenoid lies at right angles to this uniform field, so the flux is simply the product of the magnetic field and the area:

$$\phi_B = \int \mathbf{B} \cdot d\mathbf{A} = BA = \mu_0 nI\pi R^2.$$

We're being a little loose here in thinking of a single turn of the solenoid as a closed loop, but if the solenoid is tightly wound this is an excellent approximation. We will be concerned frequently with the flux through a multiturn coil, and in calculating this flux it's convenient to view each turn as an individual loop. The flux through an N-turn coil in a uniform magnetic field is just N times the flux through each turn.

EXERCISE A rectangular wire loop measuring 10 cm by 15 cm is oriented so the normal to the loop makes a 30° angle with a uniform 50-mT magnetic field. Find the magnetic flux through the loop.

Answer: 6.5×10^{-4} T·m^2

Some problems similar to Example 31-1: 3, 4

| EXAMPLE 31-2 | *Magnetic Flux in a Nonuniform Field* |

A long, straight wire carries a current I. A rectangular wire loop of dimensions ℓ by w lies with its closest edge a distance a from the wire, as shown in Fig. 31-6. What is the magnetic flux through the loop?

Solution

The magnetic field of the wire is given by Equation 30-8:

$$B = \frac{\mu_0 I}{2\pi r},$$

where r is the distance from the wire. At the site of the loop, this field points straight into the page, perpendicular to the plane of the loop. However, the field varies with distance from the straight wire, so we can't simply multiply the field by the loop area to get the flux. Instead, we divide the loop into thin strips of width dr and area $dA = \ell\, dr$, as shown in Fig. 31-6. With the field at right angles to each strip, $\mathbf{B} \cdot d\mathbf{A} = B\, dA$, and the flux through any strip is

$$d\phi_B = B\, dA = B\ell\, dr = \frac{\mu_0 I}{2\pi r}\, \ell\, dr.$$

Then the total flux through the loop is the integral over all such strips contained within the loop, that is, over all strips between $r = a$ and $r = a + w$:

$$\phi_B = \int_a^{a+w} \frac{\mu_0 I}{2\pi r}\, \ell\, dr = \frac{\mu_0 I \ell}{2\pi} \int_a^{a+w} \frac{dr}{r} = \frac{\mu_0 I \ell}{2\pi} \ln r \bigg|_a^{a+w}$$

$$= \frac{\mu_0 I \ell}{2\pi} \ln\!\left(\frac{a + w}{a}\right).$$

FIGURE 31-6 A rectangular loop in the magnetic field of a long wire. The field to the right of the wire points into the plane of the page, and its magnitude drops inversely with distance from the wire. Area elements for the flux calculation are strips of length ℓ and infinitesimal width dr.

EXERCISE A square wire loop 45 cm on a side lies in the plane of this page, taken to be the x-y plane. The left edge of the loop coincides with the y axis. A magnetic field points into the page; its magnitude varies with position, being given by $B = ax$, where $a = 2.0$ T/m and x is position in meters. Find the flux through this loop.

Answer: 91 mT·m²

Some problems similar to Example 31-2: 43, 44

Flux and Induced EMF

Having quantified the notion of magnetic flux, we are now ready to state rigorously the experimental fact that changing magnetic flux induces an emf in a circuit. Our statement is a special case of **Faraday's law of induction**, which constitutes another of the four basic laws of electromagnetism:

> The induced emf in a circuit is proportional to the rate of change of magnetic flux through any surface bounded by that circuit.

This statement is a special case of Faraday's law that describes electromagnetic induction specifically in circuits; later we'll present a more general form that applies even when no circuit is present. The induced emf tends to oppose the change in flux—a crucial point to which we'll devote all of Section 31-3—and so in SI units the proportionality between emf and rate of change of flux is just -1. Thus Faraday's law is

$$\mathcal{E} = -\frac{d\phi_B}{dt}, \tag{31-2}$$

where $\mathcal{E}$ is the emf induced in a circuit and ϕ_B the magnetic flux through any surface bounded by that circuit. Problem 1 will help convince you that the units of the rate of change of magnetic flux are indeed volts, the same as the units of emf.

Faraday's law relates the induced emf to the *change* in flux. It isn't magnetic flux or magnetic field that causes an induced emf—it's the *change* in flux. The relation between emf and flux is like the relation between acceleration and velocity, where the acceleration depends not on the actual value of the velocity, but on its *rate of change*. In Fig. 31-1 we changed the flux by moving a magnet near a coil, increasing the flux as more field lines went through the area bounded by the coil. In Fig. 31-4 we changed the current in an adjacent coil, changing the magnetic field and thus the flux. More generally, since the flux $\mathbf{B} \cdot \mathbf{A} = BA\cos\theta$, we can change flux by changing the field strength B, the area A, or the orientation of the surface to the field (i.e., the angle θ between the field and the normal to the surface). The following examples explore these different ways of changing magnetic flux.

13.9

Electromagnetic Induction

| **EXAMPLE 31-3** | *Changing Magnetic Field* |

A wire loop of radius 10 cm has a resistance of 2.0 Ω. The loop is at right angles to a uniform magnetic field $\mathbf{B}$, as shown in Fig. 31-7. The field strength is increasing at 0.10 tesla/second. What is the magnitude of the induced current in the loop?

Solution

To find the induced current, we need to know the induced emf. Faraday's law tells us that the induced emf is related to the rate of change of magnetic flux through the circuit. Here the field is uniform and at right angles to the loop, so the flux is just the product of the field with the loop area:

$$\phi_B = \int \mathbf{B} \cdot d\mathbf{A} = \pi r^2 B.$$

Why could we take B outside the integral when the field is changing? Because it's changing with *time,* and the integral is over *space*. At any given instant the field is *uniform* in space, and that's all we need to reduce the flux integral to a simple product.

We don't know B, but this doesn't matter because we are really interested in the *rate of change* of the flux, not in the flux itself. With the loop area constant, the rate of change of flux is

$$\frac{d\phi_B}{dt} = \pi r^2 \frac{dB}{dt} = (\pi)(0.10\text{ m})^2(0.10\text{ T/s}) = 3.14\times10^{-3}\text{ V}.$$

By Faraday's law, this is the magnitude of the induced emf. We then calculate the current using Ohm's law, as we would for any emf:

$$I = \frac{\mathcal{E}}{R} = \frac{3.14\times10^{-3}\text{ V}}{2.0\ \Omega} = 1.6\times10^{-3}\text{ A} = 1.6\text{ mA}.$$

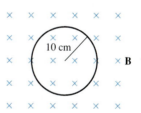

FIGURE 31-7 A circular conducting loop at right angles to a uniform magnetic field.

Tip

It's the Change That Counts Faraday's law relates induced emf to the *rate of change* of magnetic flux. The actual value of the flux—or of the magnetic field if that is what's changing—doesn't matter. You may be troubled by induction problems where the value of the field is not given. You don't need it; what you do need or may be asked to find is the *rate of change* of the field.

EXERCISE A square conducting loop 25 cm on a side lies at right angles to a uniform magnetic field. The loop's resistance is 8.0 Ω, and it carries a current of 14 mA. At what rate is the magnetic field changing?

Answer: 1.8 T/s

Some problems similar to Example 31-3: 4–8

EXAMPLE 31-4	*Changing Area*

A circuit consists of two parallel conducting rails a distance ℓ apart connected at one end by a resistance R. A conducting bar completes the circuit, joining the two rails electrically but being free to slide along them. The whole circuit is in a constant, uniform magnetic field $\mathbf{B}$ at right angles to the plane of the circuit, as shown in Fig. 31-8. The bar is pulled to the right with constant speed v, increasing the area of the circuit as it moves. What is the current in the circuit? Assume the bar and rails are ideal conductors, so the total circuit resistance is R.

Solution

Here the current is driven by an induced emf arising from the change in magnetic flux that occurs as the circuit area increases. We determine the emf using Faraday's law, $\mathcal{E} = -d\phi_B/dt$. The circuit area is the rail spacing ℓ times the distance x from resistor to bar. With a uniform field perpendicular to the circuit, the flux integral $\int \mathbf{B} \cdot d\mathbf{A}$ reduces to the product of field strength with the area:

$$\phi_B = \int \mathbf{B} \cdot d\mathbf{A} = BA = B\ell x.$$

Never mind that we don't know x—we do know its rate of change and that's all we need. With the field and the rail spacing constant, the rate of change of flux is

$$\frac{d\phi_B}{dt} = B\ell\frac{dx}{dt} = B\ell v,$$

since dx/dt is just the bar velocity v. Faraday's law tells us that the magnitude of the induced emf is equal to the rate of change of flux, so

$$|\mathcal{E}| = B\ell v.$$

This emf drives a current I around the circuit:

$$|I| = \frac{|\mathcal{E}|}{R} = \frac{B\ell v}{R}.$$

ActivPhysics Activity 13.10 provides a simulation of this example.

FIGURE 31-8 Pulling the bar to the right increases the circuit area, thereby increasing the magnetic flux and inducing an emf that drives a current.

EXERCISE A square wire loop 25 cm on a side is moving into a region containing a uniform 1.2-T magnetic field oriented at right angles to the loop, as shown in Fig. 31-9. The loop wire is essentially resistanceless, but inserted in the loop is a 3-V flashlight bulb. How fast must the loop move to keep the bulb lit at its normal brightness?

Answer: 10 m/s

Some problems similar to Example 31-4: 9, 10, 16, 27, 35

FIGURE 31-9 How fast must the loop move to light the 3-V bulb?

13.10
Motional EMF

EXAMPLE 31-5	*Changing Orientation: An Electric Generator*

A circular wire loop of radius a and resistance R is initially perpendicular to a constant, uniform magnetic field B. The loop rotates with angular velocity ω about an axis through a diameter, as shown in Fig. 31-10. What is the current in the loop?

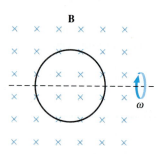

FIGURE 31-10 A wire loop rotating in a uniform magnetic field. The flux changes because of the changing orientation of the loop relative to the field, thereby inducing an emf that drives a current around the loop.

Solution

Again, we must find the rate of change of magnetic flux, from which we can get the induced emf and then the current. Here the field is uniform over the area, but the orientation of the field relative to the area is changing. The definition of magnetic flux contains a dot product to account for this orientation. Evaluating the flux, we have

$$\phi_B = \int \mathbf{B} \cdot d\mathbf{A} = \int B\,dA\cos\theta = B\cos\theta \int dA$$
$$= \pi a^2 B\cos\theta,$$

where θ is the angle between the field and a perpendicular to the loop area. Here we could take the field magnitude B outside the integral because the field is uniform over the loop. And even though the orientation between loop and field changes with *time*, it does not change with *position* at a given instant, so we could also take $\cos\theta$ outside the integral.

The changing orientation is described by giving θ as a function of time. Since the loop rotates with constant angular velocity ω, we can write simply $\theta = \omega t$, where we take the zero of time when $\theta = 0$. Then the flux is

$$\phi_B = \pi a^2 B\cos\omega t,$$

so

$$\frac{d\phi_B}{dt} = \pi a^2 B\,\frac{d}{dt}(\cos\omega t) = -\pi a^2 B\omega\sin\omega t.$$

By Faraday's law, the emf is then

$$\mathcal{E} = -\frac{d\phi_B}{dt} = \pi a^2 B\omega\sin\omega t,$$

giving a current

$$I = \frac{\mathcal{E}}{R} = \frac{\pi a^2 B\omega}{R}\sin\omega t.$$

(Check the units!)

Unlike the current in the previous two examples, this one changes with time. Its sinusoidal time dependence is in fact just like that of standard alternating current used for electric power—and with good reason: our rotating loop constitutes a simple alternating-current generator. Sinusoidally varying emf's and currents occur whenever conducting loops rotate in uniform magnetic fields.

Tip

Peak Values You'll often be asked for the peak value of voltage or current when either quantity is changing with time (more on this in Chapter 33). You've derived a formula like $\mathcal{E} = \pi a^2 B\omega\sin\omega t$ in Example 31-5, but you don't have a value for the time t. It doesn't matter! The peak value occurs when $\sin\omega t = 1$, so just replace $\sin\omega t$ by 1. In Example 31-5, for example, the peak emf is just $\mathcal{E}_p = \pi a^2 B\omega$.

EXERCISE Take the radius $a = 11$ cm in Example 31-5 and the magnetic field strength $B = 0.63$ T. With what angular speed ω must the loop rotate in order to produce a peak emf of 6.0 V?

Answer: $250\ \text{s}^{-1}$

Some problems similar to Example 31-5: 12, 24, 58, 63

You might wonder about the direction of the induced emf and current in these examples since we were concerned only with magnitudes. Formally, that direction follows mathematically from the minus sign in Faraday's law. But in the next section we'll provide a physical justification for the minus sign that makes it much clearer how to determine the direction of induced emf's and currents.

31-3 INDUCTION AND THE CONSERVATION OF ENERGY

Move a bar magnet toward a wire loop, as shown in Fig. 31-11. Without the loop present, it would take no work to move the magnet horizontally at constant

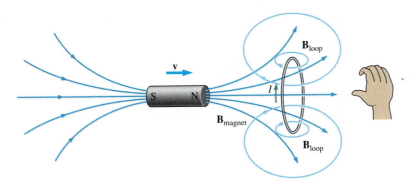

FIGURE 31-11 As the bar magnet moves toward the conducting loop, the changing magnetic flux through the loop induces an emf that drives a current around the loop. Conservation of energy requires that the magnetic field produced by this current *oppose* the motion of the magnet, so the agent moving the magnet does work that ends up heating the loop.

velocity. But with the loop present, moving the magnet induces a current in the loop. Electrical energy is dissipated in the loop's resistance, heating the loop. Where does the energy come from?

There's only one source for the energy—the agent moving the magnet. As you move the magnet, you must be doing positive work. Otherwise you would be getting energy—ultimately heating the loop—for nothing. So you must have to push the magnet against some force. What force? A magnetic force, caused by the interaction of the magnet with the magnetic field produced by the induced current. Think about this! The induced current, like any current, produces a magnetic field. The magnet experiences a force in this field, and you must do work to move the magnet through that field. With the magnetic field as intermediary, the work you do ultimately ends up heating the loop.

As you push the magnet toward the loop, the force the loop's field exerts on the magnet must be repulsive in order that you do positive work on the magnet. In Fig. 31-11 the bar magnet's north pole is toward the loop. To provide a repulsive force the loop must therefore present a north pole to the approaching magnet; that is, field lines must emerge from the loop's interior pointing to the left. What current direction will provide such a field? Application of the right-hand rule gives the answer: Wrap the fingers of your right hand around the loop in the direction of the current, and your right thumb points in the direction of the field in the loop's interior. Thus the current direction is as shown in Fig. 31-11.

This analysis leading to the direction of the induced current was based on conservation of energy, a fundamental principle that we believe applies universally. For electromagnetic induction, we've just seen that conservation of energy requires the following:

> **The direction of the induced emf and current is such that the magnetic field created by the induced current opposes the change in magnetic flux.**

This statement, called **Lenz's law**, is represented mathematically in the minus sign on the right-hand side of Faraday's law (Equation 31-2).

What happens, for example, if you pull the bar magnet away from the loop in Fig. 31-11? Now the loop must present a south pole to the receding magnet, creating an attractive force opposing the magnet's withdrawal (Fig. 31-12). The loop current must be opposite its direction in Fig. 31-11, as again you do work to overcome the magnetic force.

FIGURE 31-12 When the bar magnet is pulled away from the loop, the direction of the induced current is such that the magnetic force opposes the magnet's withdrawal.

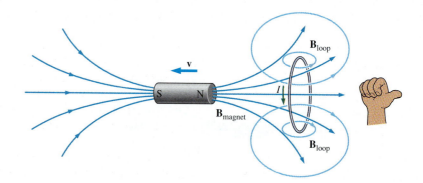

Got It!

You push a bar magnet toward a loop, with the north pole toward the loop as in Fig. 31-11. If you keep pushing the magnet straight through the loop, what will be the direction of the current as you pull it out the other side? Will you need to do work, or will work be done on you?

Motional EMF and Lenz's Law

When a conductor moves through a magnetic field, we can understand the origin of the induced emf in terms of the magnetic force on charge carriers in the wire; this emf is called **motional emf**. In the case of motional emf we can show explicitly that Lenz's law requires energy conservation.

Consider a square conducting loop of side ℓ and resistance R being pulled with constant speed v out of a uniform magnetic field **B**, as shown in Fig. 31-13. Since the magnetic flux through the loop is changing, there's an induced emf, and that emf drives a current. Energy is dissipated as heat because of the loop's resistance, and so, as we've just argued, the agent pulling the loop must do work. We'll now demonstrate quantitatively that energy is conserved, by showing that rate of heating in the loop is exactly equal to the rate at which the agent pulling the loop does work.

In Chapter 29 we found that the magnetic force on a charge is given by $\mathbf{F} = q\mathbf{v} \times \mathbf{B}$. Pulling the loop to the right moves its free electrons through the magnetic field; the magnetic force $q\mathbf{v} \times \mathbf{B}$ on these electrons is downward in Fig. 31-13 (opposite $\mathbf{v} \times \mathbf{B}$ since electrons are negative). The resulting downward motion of the negative electrons in the left-hand side of the loop constitutes an upward current. This current continues clockwise around the loop, driven by an electric field associated with the separation of charge in the loop's left side.

Now we have a current I in the loop. We found in Chapter 29 that the magnetic force on a current-carrying conductor of length ℓ is $\mathbf{F} = I\boldsymbol{\ell} \times \mathbf{B}$. Applying this expression to the conducting loop in Fig. 31-13 shows that there is no magnetic force on the right-hand side (since $\mathbf{B} = \mathbf{0}$ there) and that the forces on top and bottom cancel (Fig. 31-14). So the total magnetic force on the loop is that on the left side alone; since the current is upward while the magnetic field is into the page, the magnitude of this force is $I\ell B$, and the right-hand rule shows that it points to the left. This leftward magnetic force has just the direction needed to cancel the rightward applied force, giving the zero net force that Newton's law requires for the loop to move with constant velocity.

We could equally well determine the current direction from magnetic flux considerations. As the loop leaves the field region, the flux through it decreases. The direction of the induced current is such as to oppose this decrease in flux. Therefore the magnetic field of the induced current points into the page, as the induced current tries to maintain the flux. By the right-hand rule, a field within the loop and into the page requires that the induced current flow clockwise.

To calculate the current, we must find the induced emf, which in turn is related to the rate of change of magnetic flux through the loop. With the field and

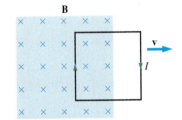

FIGURE 31-13 A conducting loop being withdrawn from a magnetic field. The magnetic force $q\mathbf{v} \times \mathbf{B}$ on charge carriers in the left side of the loop drives a current clockwise around the loop. The current direction also follows from Lenz's law: The magnetic field produced by the loop current acts to oppose the *decrease* in flux through the loop, and therefore points in the *same* direction as the original field. This requires a clockwise loop current.

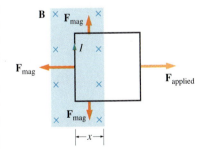

FIGURE 31-14 Forces on the loop. The total magnetic force is that on the left side alone, and the agent pulling the loop must exert an equal but opposite force to maintain constant velocity.

loop perpendicular, and with the field uniform in the region where it is nonzero, the magnetic flux is the product of the magnetic field strength and the loop area that lies within the field:

$$\phi_B = B\ell x,$$

where x is the distance between the left edge of the loop and the right edge of the magnetic field region. The magnetic field remains constant, but as the loop moves the distance x decreases at the rate $dx/dt = -v$ (the minus sign indicates a decrease). Then the rate of change of flux is

$$\frac{d\phi_B}{dt} = \frac{d(B\ell x)}{dt} = B\ell\frac{dx}{dt} = -B\ell v,$$

so Faraday's law gives

$$\mathscr{E} = -\frac{d\phi_B}{dt} = B\ell v.$$

This induced emf drives a current I around the loop, where

$$I = \frac{\mathscr{E}}{R} = \frac{B\ell v}{R}.$$

The rate of energy dissipation in the loop is the product of the emf and the current (Equation 27-8):

$$P = I\mathscr{E} = \frac{B\ell v}{R}B\ell v = \frac{B^2\ell^2 v^2}{R}. \qquad \left(\begin{array}{c}\text{power dissipated} \\ \text{in loop}\end{array}\right)$$

We've found that the magnetic force on the loop has magnitude $I\ell B$; since the loop is moving with constant velocity, this is also the magnitude of the applied force. Equation 7-21 shows that the rate at which work is done by a force $\mathbf{F}$ acting on an object moving with velocity $\mathbf{v}$ is $P = \mathbf{F} \cdot \mathbf{v}$; here, with the applied force and velocity in the same direction, we have

$$P = Fv = I\ell Bv = \frac{B\ell v}{R}\ell Bv = \frac{B^2\ell^2 v^2}{R}, \qquad \left(\begin{array}{c}\text{power supplied} \\ \text{to pull loop}\end{array}\right)$$

in agreement with our expression for the electric power dissipated in the loop. Thus, all the work done by the agent pulling the loop ends up heating the resistor, showing explicitly that energy is indeed conserved.

Got It!

What will be the direction of the current when the loop in Fig. 31-13 first enters the field, coming in from the left side?

Electromagnetic induction is the principle behind many important technologies, from information storage on computer disks and credit cards to electric power generation. Induction also gives us the flexibility to transform voltage levels in electric power systems, and to provide wireless charging systems for devices ranging from electric cars to toothbrushes. The applications that follow explore some uses of induction.

APPLICATION	*Electric Generators*

Probably the most important technological application of induction is the electric generator. The world currently uses electrical energy at the phenomenal rate of about 10^{13} watts—roughly equal to the power output of 100 billion human bodies—and virtually all this power comes from generators. A generator is just a system of conductors in a magnetic field (Fig. 31-15). Mechanical energy is supplied to rotate the conductors, resulting in a changing magnetic flux. An emf is induced and current flows through the generator and on to whatever electrical loads are connected to it. Because the changing flux results from a change in the orientation of the loop relative to the field—i.e., a change in θ in the expression $\phi_B = BA\cos\theta$—a generator such as that of Fig. 31-15 produces an alternating emf that varies sinusoidally with time (Fig. 31-16), as we saw in Example 31-5.

Any source of mechanical energy can power the generator, but the most common is steam from burning fossil fuels or from nuclear fission (Fig. 31-17). Electrical energy may be generated from the kinetic energy of water or wind—as shown in this chapter's opening photo. A small electric generator, driven by the car's gasoline engine, is used to recharge a car's battery.

Lenz's law, the conservation of energy in electromagnetic induction, is very much applicable to electric generators. Were it not for Lenz's law, which requires that induced currents *oppose* the changes giving rise to them, generators would turn on their own and happily supply electricity without the need for coal, oil, or uranium! The voluminous quantities of fuel (Fig. 31-18) consumed by power plants are dramatic testimony to the minus sign appearing on the right-hand side of Equation 31-2!

An instructive introduction to Lenz's law comes about if you have access to a hand-cranked electric generator. Without any electrical load across the generator, it is easy to turn. But as you switch on increasingly heavy loads the generator gets

FIGURE 31-15 Simplified diagram of an electric generator. As the loop rotates in the magnetic field, the changing flux induces an emf that drives a current through the rotating contacts and stationary brushes and on through the electrical load.

FIGURE 31-17 This large power-plant generator produces over 1000 MW of electric power. It's basically a large version of the generator shown in Fig. 31-15.

FIGURE 31-16 A generator such as that shown in Fig. 31-15 produces an alternating emf whose period is the rotation period of the conducting loop.

FIGURE 31-18 A 110-car trainload of coal arriving at a power plant in Texas. Some fourteen such trains arrive at the plant each week—a testimony to the minus sign in Equation 31-2!

(a)

(b)

FIGURE 31-19 (a) With no electrical load, a hand-cranked generator is easy to turn. (b) With 200 watts of light bulbs connected, turning the generator becomes much more difficult. The generator emf is the same in both cases, because the generator is being turned at the same rate. But only in (b) is current flowing, giving nonzero power $P = IV$ that must be supplied by turning the generator.

harder to turn (Fig. 31-19). Most people find they can just sustain a 100-W light bulb with a hand generator. Think about this next time you leave a light on! You also experience Lenz's law when you turn on the headlights of a car that's idling slowly. You can hear the engine speed drop, and the car may even stall, as the car's generator gets harder for the engine to turn.

Got It!

If you lower the resistance across an electric generator, while turning the generator at a constant speed, will the generator get easier or harder to turn?

EXAMPLE 31-6	*Designing a Generator*

An electric generator consists of a 10-turn square wire loop 50 cm on a side. The loop is turned at 60 revolutions per second, to produce standard 60-Hz alternating current like that used throughout the United States and Canada. How strong must the magnetic field be for the peak output voltage of the generator to be 170 V? (This is actually the peak voltage of standard 120-V household wiring; 120 V is an appropriate average value.)

Solution

We need to evaluate the induced emf as a function of magnetic field strength. With a uniform magnetic field, the flux through one turn of the loop is $\int \mathbf{B} \cdot d\mathbf{A} = BA\cos\theta$, where θ is the angle between the field and the normal to the loop. But the loop rotates with angular frequency $\omega = 2\pi f$, so $\theta = 2\pi ft$. The loop area A is s^2, with s the length of the loop side, so the flux through N turns of the loop is

$$\phi_B = NBs^2\cos(2\pi ft).$$

To find the induced emf, we take the time rate of change of this flux:

$$\mathscr{E} = -\frac{d\phi_B}{dt} = -NBs^2\left[-2\pi f\sin(2\pi ft)\right]$$

$$= 2\pi NfBs^2\sin(2\pi ft).$$

The peak emf is the quantity multiplying the sine; we want this to be 170 V. Solving for the unknown magnetic field B then gives

$$B = \frac{\mathscr{E}_{peak}}{2\pi Nfs^2} = \frac{170\ \text{V}}{(2\pi)(10)(60\ \text{Hz})(0.50\ \text{m})^2} = 0.18\ \text{T}.$$

This is a typical field strength near the poles of a strong permanent magnet.

EXERCISE A generator includes a circular coil 30 cm in diameter, spinning at 3600 rpm in a uniform 0.50-T magnetic field. How many turns should it have if the peak output voltage is to be 2400 V?

Answer: 180

Some problems similar to Example 31-6: 24, 26, 49, 50

Magnetic materials are widely used as information storage media. Examples include audio- and videocassette tapes, computer disks, and the magnetic strips on credit cards. Retrieving the stored information involves electromagnetic induction.

In a typical magnetic recording system the magnetic medium—usually a plastic tape or a circular disk coated with ferromagnetic oxides—moves past a small coil called the **head**. While recording, current passing through the coil creates a magnetic field that impresses a magnetization pattern on the tape or disk (Fig. 31-20). With analog systems, like most audio- and videotapes, the current varies continuously and produces a smoothly varying magnetization pattern. With digital systems, including computer data storage and the newer digital audio and video formats, coil currents of the same magnitude but opposite polarity produce regions of oppositely directed magnetization; these represent the 1's and 0's in which digital information is coded.

To retrieve the stored information, the magnetic medium is again moved past a coil, which may be the same one used for recording. The changing magnetization on the medium results in a varying magnetic flux through the coil, which induces an emf that's amplified and processed to produce images, sound, or digital data.

The rate at which information can be stored and extracted depends on how densely the regions of varying magnetization can be packed without interfering and on how fast the medium moves in relation to the heads. Audiocassette tapes move past the heads at a mere 4.8 cm/s, a speed that limits these tapes' ability to record high-frequency sound faithfully. The much higher information content of video images requires higher tape-to-head speeds; in standard videocassette recorders a speed of 39.52 m/s is achieved by moving the tape past rapidly spinning heads. High-speed computer disks boast even greater speeds, allowing rapid data storage and retrieval (Fig. 31-21).

FIGURE 31-20 Recording on magnetic tape. The iron body of the head confines the magnetic field of the coil except at the gap, where a fringing field emerges to impose a magnetization pattern on the moving tape. When the tape is played back, its changing magnetization pattern imposes a changing magnetic flux at the head, inducing an emf in the head coil.

FIGURE 31-21 Mechanism of a computer disk drive includes a head (arrow) that literally flies as close as 0.25 μm above a spinning aluminum disk coated with ferromagnetic material.

Our discussion of induced currents has centered on conducting loops. But induced currents also appear in solid conductors through which magnetic flux is changing. The resistance of a solid piece of conductor is low, so the induced currents are large, resulting in substantial energy dissipation. The presence of these **eddy currents** can make it difficult to move a conduc-

tor rapidly through a magnetic field. For example, if you try to push a piece of metal—it need not be a ferrous metal like iron—between the poles of a magnet, you'll find yourself working against a magnetic force.

A common demonstration of eddy currents consists of a pendulum with a metal bob that swings between the poles of a

(a)   (b)

FIGURE 31-22 (a) An eddy-current pendulum consists of a conductor swinging between magnet poles. As it enters the field region, the conductor experiences a changing magnetic flux that induces a current. You should convince yourself that the current is in the direction shown as the bob begins to enter the field region. (b) The current dissipates energy in the resistance of the conductor, at the expense of its kinetic energy. Strobe photo shows rapid deceleration as the bob passes between the magnet poles.

magnet (Fig. 31-22). As it swings toward the magnet, the pendulum experiences an increasing magnetic flux that induces eddy currents. The energy dissipated by these currents comes ultimately from the kinetic energy of the pendulum, which therefore slows abruptly between the magnet poles.

Eddy currents provide an alternative to friction brakes for stopping moving machinery. Rapidly rotating saw blades, for example, can be stopped abruptly by an electromagnet activated next to the blade. Similarly, eddy-current brakes are

sometimes used on trains and in other applications involving rotating conductors.

In some instances eddy currents are a nuisance, acting just like friction in reducing the efficiency of machinery. To solve this problem, slots are often cut into moving conductors to make the current paths longer, thus increasing the electrical resistance and reducing the eddy currents. For example, if the solid pendulum bob in Fig. 31-22 is replaced by a slotted piece, it then swings more freely through the magnet.

Lenz's Law and Changing Magnetic Fields

Lenz's law—conservation of energy applied to electromagnetic induction—determines the direction of the induced current even when no motion is involved. Figure 31-23 shows a conducting loop in a magnetic field that points into the page. Suppose the field strength—and, therefore, the magnetic flux through the loop—is *decreasing*. Then the direction of the induced current must be such that the magnetic field it creates *opposes* this decrease. Therefore, the loop's field must reinforce the existing field, which means that the loop's field points into the page. Applying the right-hand rule then shows that the loop current is clockwise in Fig. 31-23.

What if the magnetic field in Fig. 31-23 had been increasing in strength? Then the loop current would have been in the opposite direction, to create a magnetic field opposite the existing field in order to oppose its increase.

FIGURE 31-23 A uniform magnetic field is decreasing in strength, causing a decrease in magnetic flux through the conducting loop. The induced current in the loop must *oppose* this *decrease,* and therefore loop current goes clockwise in order to produce a magnetic field within the loop that reinforces the original field.

Tip

Induction Opposes Change   Faraday's law relates the induced emf to the *rate of change* of magnetic flux. Lenz's law says that the induced emf and current are in such a direction as to oppose that *change* in flux—not the flux or the field itself. Figure 31-23 is a case in point; here the induced current is in a direction that actually reinforces the original field and flux—precisely because they are both *decreasing*. The same thing happened in Fig. 31-13, where movement of the loop decreased the flux, giving an induced current that reinforced the existing field.

| **EXAMPLE 31-7** | *Lenz's Law* |

Two coils are arranged as shown in Fig. 31-24. If the resistance of the variable resistor is being increased, what is the direction of the induced current in the fixed resistor *R*?

Solution

Applying the right-hand rule, we find that the magnetic field of coil *A* emerges from the right side of the coil, pointing toward coil *B*. As the resistance increases, the current in coil *A* decreases, and with it the strength of coil *A*'s magnetic field. This results in a decrease in the magnetic flux through coil *B*. The induced current in coil *B* acts to oppose this decrease in flux, so the magnetic field resulting from the induced current reinforces the field from coil *A*. Thus the field of coil *B* emerges from the right end of the coil and enters on the left end. By the right-hand rule, this requires a current from right to left in the fixed resistor.

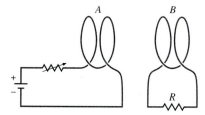

FIGURE 31-24   As the variable resistance is increased, the current in coil *A* decreases. This decreases the magnetic flux through coil *B*, resulting in an induced current whose direction is such that the magnetic field it creates in the interior of coil *B* reinforces the field from coil *A*, thereby opposing the decrease in flux through *B*.

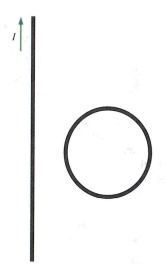

FIGURE 31-25   Which way is the current in the circular loop?

EXERCISE   A circular conducting loop lies next to a long, straight wire carrying current in the direction indicated in Fig. 31-25. In which direction is the induced current in the loop when the current in the wire is (a) increasing and (b) decreasing?

Answers: (a) counterclockwise; (b) clockwise

Some problems similar to Example 31-7: 4, 10, 19, 27, 32

Got It!

A wire loop lies in the plane of this page, and a uniform magnetic field points directly out of the page. What is the direction of the current in the loop if the magnetic field strength is (a) increasing or (b) decreasing?

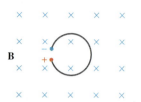

FIGURE 31-26 An open loop. In a changing magnetic field, there is an induced emf that results in charge buildup at the gap. The polarity shown results when the magnetic field strength is decreasing.

Induction in Open Circuits

An induced emf also arises in an open circuit subject to a changing magnetic field, but here the emf cannot drive a steady current. Figure 31-26 shows the loop and magnetic field of Fig. 31-23, but now with a small gap in the loop. Although the loop is not quite closed, there is still an induced emf. In response to this emf, charge piles up on either side of the gap, creating a voltage across it. Once the gap voltage equals the induced emf, the electric field associated with the separated charge opposes the emf's tendency to move charge, and a steady state is reached. In the open-circuit case, the entire emf implied by Equation 31-2 is available at the gap. The polarity can be determined by considering what would happen if current did flow. Since current flowed clockwise in the closed loop of Fig. 31-23, positive charge will accumulate at the bottom of the gap, as shown in Fig. 31-26.

Another example of an induced emf in an open circuit is the motional emf arising as a single conductor moves through a magnetic field. Example 31-8 treats this case quantitatively.

EXAMPLE 31-8	*The Tethered Satellite*

In 1996 astronauts on the space shuttle Columbia performed a novel experiment to explore a new method of generating electric power in space. Once in orbit, Columbia deployed a 520-kg satellite attached to the shuttle through a 20-km long conducting tether (Fig. 31-27). With the tethered satellite flying vertically above Columbia, the two moved at approximately right angles to Earth's magnetic field, whose strength was about 30 μT at the orbital position. Find the motional emf that developed between the tethered satellite and the shuttle with the tether extended its full 20-km length. (Unfortunately the tether broke just short of its full length, but five hours of data collected during deployment clearly demonstrated the power-generating potential of the tethered satellite.)

Solution

Figure 31-28 shows the pair flying at right angles to the magnetic field. We can imagine forming a closed circuit by letting the satellite and shuttle slide along a system of conducting rails, just like that of Example 31-4. The system is then identical to that example, and we have

$$\mathcal{E} = B\ell v = (30\times10^{-6}\text{ T})(20\times10^{3}\text{ m})(7.8\times10^{3}\text{ m/s})$$
$$= 4.7\text{ kV},$$

where we used the orbital speed calculated in Example 9-3.

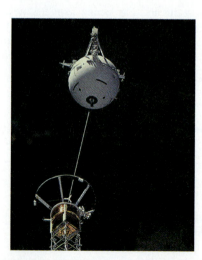

FIGURE 31-27 Tethered satellite being deployed from the space shuttle.

FIGURE 31-28 The tethered satellite generates electric power from the motional emf developed between the spacecraft and a satellite connected by a conducting tether. The system is analogous to the bar and rails shown in Fig. 31-8.

Since the magnetic flux through the rail arrangement would be increasing, the current would flow counterclockwise so that the magnetic field of the induced current would oppose this increase. That means positive charge will accumulate on the satellite and negative charge on the shuttle—a result that can also be obtained by considering the magnetic force on free charges in the tether.

At the shuttle's orbital altitude there are enough free electrons from ionization of the upper atmosphere for the tenuous gas surrounding the shuttle to carry a current, completing a circuit and allowing exploitation of the induced emf for electric power generation.

EXERCISE An airplane with a wingspan of 44 m is in level flight at 300 m/s over the north pole, where Earth's magnetic field has magnitude 0.62 G and points vertically downward. Find the induced emf between the wing tips.

Answer: 0.82 V

Some problems similar to Example 31-8: 10, 13, 56

31-4 INDUCED ELECTRIC FIELDS

What do we really mean by an induced emf? In a circuit containing a battery, the notion of emf is clear—the emf arises in a specific device where chemical energy is converted to electrical energy associated with charge separation. This charge separation sets up an electric field that drives current in an external circuit, as we discussed in Chapter 28. In the case of motional induced emf we also have a clear picture: the emf arises from the separation of charge associated with magnetic forces on the free charges in a moving conductor; again, the electric field associated with this charge separation may drive a current.

Now consider the current induced in a conducting loop by a magnetic field that changes with time. No motion is involved, yet there must be a force on the free charges in the conductor. The one force we know that acts on stationary charges is the electric force. Electric forces arise from electric fields, so there must be an electric field in a conducting loop in a changing magnetic field. This field is called an **induced electric field**. It has the same effect on charges— exerting a force $q\mathbf{E}$—as do the electric fields we considered earlier. The field itself, however, originates not in electric charges but in changing magnetic fields.

An induced electric field results whenever a magnetic field changes with time—whether or not an electric circuit is present. When a circuit is present, then the induced field may drive a current. But the induced field, not the current, is fundamental. A single, stationary electron placed in a changing magnetic field will experience an *electric* force—clear evidence for the existence of an electric field.

Until now we've been thinking of Faraday's law as a relation between the emf induced in a circuit and the rate of change of magnetic flux through that circuit. But we've just seen that induced electric fields are the fundamental manifestation of changing magnetic flux, and that these fields arise whether or not circuits are present. So we need to reformulate Faraday's law to describe induced electric fields without reference to circuits. The induced emf $\mathscr{E}$ that we've been writing on the left-hand side of Faraday's law means simply the work per unit charge gained by a test charge moved around a circuit. Since work is the line integral of force over distance, and electric field is the force per unit charge, we can write the emf as the line integral of the electric field. Then Faraday's law becomes

$$\oint \mathbf{E} \cdot d\boldsymbol{\ell} = -\frac{d\phi_B}{dt} \quad \text{(Faraday's law)} \qquad (31\text{-}3)$$

(a)

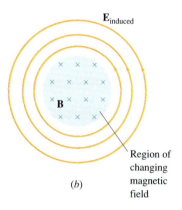

$E_{induced}$

B

Region of changing magnetic field

(b)

FIGURE 31-29 (a) Electric field lines arising from electric charges begin and end on the charges, or extend to infinity. (b) In contrast, the lines of induced electric fields have no beginning or ending points, but generally form closed loops encircling regions of changing magnetic field.

Here the line integral on the left-hand side is taken over *any* closed loop, which need not coincide with a circuit. The flux on the right-hand side is the surface integral of the magnetic field over *any* open surface bounded by the loop on the left-hand side.

Faraday's law in the form 31-3 makes no reference to wires or other circuits. It simply describes induced electric fields, which occur whenever there are changing magnetic fields. If electric circuits are present, then induced currents occur as well—but it is the induced electric fields that are fundamental. We can state Faraday's law loosely but powerfully by saying the following:

▌ **A changing magnetic field creates an electric field.**

This direct interaction between the fields is the basis for numerous practical devices and, as we'll see in Chapter 34, is essential to the existence of light.

Note the similarity between Faraday's law and Ampère's law (Equation 30-7). Faraday's law gives the line integral of the electric field around a closed loop in terms of the rate of change of magnetic flux through the loop. Ampère's law gives the line integral of the magnetic field around a closed loop in terms of the current through the loop. Both give fields that *encircle* their sources—current for the source of magnetic field and changing magnetic field for the induced electric field. That means the configuration of an induced electric field is very different from that of an electric field originating in electric charge. Induced fields have no beginning or end; their field lines generally form closed loops encircling regions of changing magnetic field (see Fig. 31-29).

When a changing magnetic field has sufficient symmetry, we can evaluate the induced electric field in the same way we did the magnetic field of a symmetric current distribution. Example 31-9 illustrates this procedure.

EXAMPLE 31-9	*An Induced Electric Field*

A long solenoid has circular cross section of radius R. The current in the solenoid is increasing and, as a result, the uniform magnetic field within the solenoid increases with time; the field magnitude is given by $B = bt$, with b a constant and t the time. Find the induced electric field outside the solenoid, a distance r from the solenoid axis.

Solution

The induced electric field has no beginning or end, so the field lines must encircle the solenoid. The only field consistent with the symmetry consists of circular field lines centered on the solenoid axis, as suggested in Fig. 31-30. Since the solenoid field points into the page and is increasing in strength, the direction of the induced electric field must be such that any current it might drive would produce a magnetic field *opposing* the increase in the solenoid field. Applying the right-hand rule then shows that the induced electric field runs counterclockwise.

Faraday's law relates the line integral of the electric field to the rate of change of the encircled magnetic flux. Here a suit-

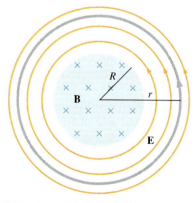

FIGURE 31-30 Cross section of a solenoid of radius R whose magnetic field is increasing with time. Field lines of the induced electric field are circles concentric with the solenoid axis. Also shown is a circular loop (gray) of radius r for evaluating the line integral in Faraday's law.

able integration loop is itself a circle centered on the solenoid axis. Symmetry shows that the field magnitude is constant over this loop, and if we circle the loop in the direction of the field then $\cos\theta$ in the dot product $\mathbf{E}\cdot d\boldsymbol{\ell}$ is 1. Thus

$$\oint \mathbf{E}\cdot d\boldsymbol{\ell} = \oint E\,d\ell = E\oint d\ell = 2\pi rE,$$

since $\oint d\ell$ is just the loop circumference. Faraday's law relates this quantity to the rate of change of the encircled magnetic flux. Here the flux is due to the uniform magnetic field inside the solenoid, perpendicular to our loop and confined to a circular area of radius R. (We use the long-solenoid approximation, neglecting the small magnetic field that must exist outside a solenoid of finite length.) So the encircled flux is just $\phi_B = \pi R^2 B = \pi R^2 bt$, and its rate of change is

$$\frac{d\phi_B}{dt} = \frac{d}{dt}(\pi R^2 bt) = \pi R^2 b.$$

Then Faraday's law gives

$$2\pi rE = -\pi R^2 b,$$

or

$$E = -\frac{R^2 b}{2r}.$$

We've already accounted for the minus sign in arguing that the field circles counterclockwise. The $1/r$ dependence of the field strength on distance should come as no surprise; points with $r > R$ are outside a cylindrically symmetric distribution, in this case a distribution of changing magnetic flux. We found the same $1/r$ dependence for the electric and magnetic fields outside, respectively, a cylindrically symmetric charge distribution and a cylindrically symmetric current distribution.

EXERCISE Show that the electric field at points *inside* the solenoid has magnitude $br/2$.

Some problems similar to Example 31-9: 36–38, 41, 42

In Chapter 30 we derived the magnetic field of a solenoid using Ampère's law—which, as we've formulated it so far, applies only to steady currents. But a solenoid whose field is changing—as in Example 31-9—must have a changing current, so how can we talk about it? In fact, Ampère's law gives a good approximation to the field produced by changing current, provided that change is sufficiently slow. In the examples and problems of this chapter we assume that to be the case. In Chapter 34 we'll see just what "sufficiently slow" means, and will explore what happens if we relax the assumption of slowly changing currents.

Conservative and Nonconservative Electric Fields

We've seen that static electric fields—those beginning and ending on stationary charge distributions—are conservative, meaning that the work required to move a charge between two points is independent of the path taken. A consequence is that it takes no work to move around a closed path in an electrostatic field; mathematically, we express this by writing

$$\oint \mathbf{E}\cdot d\boldsymbol{\ell} = 0. \qquad \text{(electrostatic field)}$$

In contrast, induced electric fields generally form closed loops, and Faraday's law shows that the line integral of the electric field around a closed path in such a field is decidedly not zero. That means the induced electric field does work on a charge moved around a *closed* path and that the work done in moving between two points cannot be independent of the path taken (Fig. 31-31). The induced electric field is therefore not conservative.

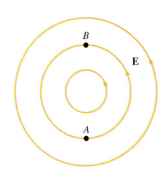

FIGURE 31-31 Two points in an induced electric field. If a positively charged particle moves counterclockwise along the field line from A to B the field does work on it. But if it moves from A to B in the clockwise direction the field does negative work; that is, an external force must do work on the charge. The work done is not path independent, and the induced electric field is not conservative.

FIGURE 31-32 This induction cooktop has no burners. Instead, coils beneath the cooktop produce time-varying magnetic fields that induce currents in the conducting cookware. Resistance in the cookware then results in heating. The cooktop itself remains cool because it's not a conductor.

The work done on charges moving around closed paths in nonconservative electric fields can be useful. A simple example is the induction cooktop (Fig. 31-32), where food cooks in a special conducting pan heated by currents in the pan itself. Those currents are driven by an induced electric field originating from a changing magnetic field in coils just below the cooktop's surface. Much more generally, any electrical device that derives its power from a generator—and that includes almost every electrical thing you use—is part of a circuit in which a nonconservative electric field drives the current.

APPLICATION	The Tokamak

In Chapter 29 we described fusion reactors, devices that may someday yield copious amounts of energy through nuclear fusion of hydrogen nuclei, using fuel derived from seawater. We saw how magnetic fields confine very hot plasma in fusion reactors and showed why most reactors have a toroidal shape. The most promising of the toroidal reactor designs is the **tokamak**, in which the confining magnetic field arises in part from current within the plasma itself. Discharging a large capacitor bank through a coil produces a rapidly changing magnetic field in the "hole" of the toroidal "doughnut," resulting in an induced electric field within the torus. This field drives the plasma current that produces a magnetic field component around the minor radius of the device. Other coils around the torus provide a magnetic field component around the long dimension of the torus, giving a net magnetic field that spirals around the plasma (Fig. 31-33).

As in any conductor, particle collisions dissipate energy gained from the electric field, in this case heating the plasma. Unfortunately the resistance of a plasma drops at high temperature, making it difficult to achieve the temperature needed for fusion with resistive heating alone. Nevertheless, the induced electric field helps bring the plasma close to the fusion temperature, as well as driving currents that produce the confining magnetic field.

Since the tokamak uses an induced electric field, its operation requires a changing magnetic field. Therefore, the tokamak

FIGURE 31-33 A tokamak fusion reactor. Current in the plasma is driven by an electric field induced by the magnetic field change associated with a rapid change in current through the central coil. Additional coils wound around the toroid give a steady magnetic field in the same direction as the plasma current. Combining with the field from the plasma current gives a net field that spirals around the plasma.

cannot run continuously but operates instead in a pulsed mode as current builds up rapidly and then decays in preparation for another pulse. Today's experimental tokamaks can achieve pulse durations of 10 s or more, during which they produce significant fusion energy.

The nonconservative nature of the induced electric field is strikingly demonstrated if you attempt to measure potential differences in nonconservative fields. In Chapter 25, we defined potential difference as the work required to move a unit charge between two points, and stressed that this work is independent of path for a conservative field. But when the field is nonconservative, the work is not independent of path, and the concept of potential becomes ambiguous.

Figure 31-34 shows an end view of a long solenoid surrounded by three identical resistors bent into circular arcs. If the solenoid current is increasing, an induced electric field appears in the resistors, and drives a current I in the counterclockwise direction.

Because they have the same resistance and carry the same current, the potential difference across each resistor should be the same. We could try to measure the potential difference across one resistor, for example, by connecting a voltmeter as with the right-hand meter in Fig. 31-34. With current I flowing through the resis-tance R, this meter reads IR. Since the current flows counterclockwise, we must connect the positive voltmeter terminal to point B.

But now try to measure the potential difference across the other two resistors together, as with the left-hand meter in Fig. 31-34. With the current I flowing through the total resis-tance $2R$, the meter now reads $2IR$. We have two voltmeters with their terminals connected to the same points, and yet they indicate different voltages. Not only are the magnitudes of the voltages different, but even their polarities differ. How can this be? It's because of the nonconservative nature of the induced

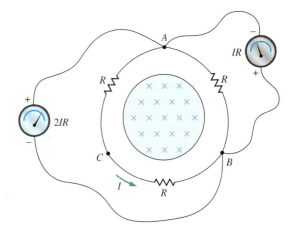

FIGURE 31-34 End view of a long solenoid surrounded by three resistors in series. A changing magnetic field in the solenoid induces an emf in the resistors, and the same current I flows through each. A voltmeter connected between points A and B indicates the voltage IR across one resistor. A second voltmeter connected to the *same points* indicates voltage $2IR$ with the opposite sign.

electric field. The two voltmeters are positioned differently with respect to the changing magnetic flux, so they sample different regions of the induced electric field. Even though the meters are connected to the same points, they measure the line integral of the induced electric field over *different* paths, and so they don't read the same voltage.

31-5 DIAMAGNETISM

In Section 30-6 we discussed paramagnetic and ferromagnetic materials, in which atomic magnetic dipoles align with an applied magnetic field, causing an attractive interaction between the material and a magnet. We also mentioned diamagnetic materials, in which induced magnetic dipoles align antiparallel to the applied field, causing a repulsive force. We are now ready to understand diamagnetism as a manifestation of Faraday's law at the microscopic level.

In a purely diamagnetic material, current loops associated with pairs of atomic electrons exactly cancel, leaving atoms with no intrinsic magnetic moments. Figure 31-35a shows a simplified model to describe such an atom.

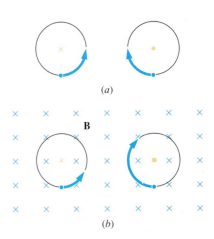

FIGURE 31-35 Simplified, classical model for a diamagnetic atom. (*a*) In the absence of an applied field, magnetic moments (cross and dot) associated with a pair of electrons exactly cancel. (*b*) The changing flux associated with an increasing magnetic field induces an electric field that speeds up one electron and slows down the other, giving rise to a net magnetic moment. (In applying the right-hand rule, remember that the electrons are negative.)

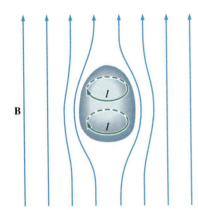

FIGURE 31-36 Induced currents in a superconductor completely cancel an applied magnetic field. Net result is that a magnetic field cannot penetrate the superconductor.

FIGURE 31-37 A small magnet is levitated above a wafer of high-temperature superconductor in a bath of liquid nitrogen at 77 K.

The picture should not be taken too literally, for it uses classical physics to describe a phenomenon properly within the domain of quantum mechanics. Nevertheless, it shows qualitatively how diamagnetism is an electromagnetic induction effect.

The electron orbiting clockwise in Fig. 31-35a has a magnetic moment pointing out of the page (apply the right-hand rule and remember that the electron carries a negative charge). In the absence of an applied magnetic field, this moment is exactly cancelled by the equal but oppositely directed moment of the other electron. But now suppose a magnetic field is applied, for example by moving the north pole of a magnet down toward the plane of Fig. 31-35. This produces a changing magnetic field in the plane of the figure, resulting in an induced electric field that alters the speeds of the orbiting electrons. The direction of this effect must be such as to oppose the increase in field. Thus the electron whose magnetic moment points out of the page has its moment increase, while the moment pointing into the page decreases. Figure 31-35b shows how these changes result from the alteration of electron speeds by the induced electric field.

Once the field is applied and the orbital speeds of the two electrons are no longer identical, the atom now has a net magnetic moment that points out of the page in Fig. 31-35, opposing the incoming magnet and resulting in a repulsive force. This repulsion is the distinguishing characteristic of diamagnetism. We listed a number of diamagnetic materials in Table 30-2.

A material that is entirely superconducting is perfectly diamagnetic, with magnetic susceptibility -1. This means that the magnetic field resulting from induced currents within the material completely cancels any applied field. Since these induced currents persist in the zero-resistance superconductor, the material completely excludes magnetic fields from its interior, a phenomenon known as the Meissner effect (Fig. 31-36). The repulsive force associated with the magnetic moments of a permanent magnet and a nearby superconductor results in the widely publicized phenomenon of magnetic levitation (Fig. 31-37). Readers of the extended version of this text will explore superconductivity further in Chapter 42.

CHAPTER SYNOPSIS

Summary

1. **Electromagnetic induction** is a fundamental phenomenon linking magnetism and electricity. Induction is described by **Faraday's law**, which states that a **changing magnetic field** produces an **induced electric field**. Unlike the conservative electrostatic field of an electric charge, this induced field is **nonconservative**, meaning it can do work on charges as they move around a closed loop. Faraday's law relates the line integral of this nonconservative electric field around an arbitrary loop to the rate of change of magnetic flux through a surface bounded by that same loop:

$$\oint \mathbf{E} \cdot d\boldsymbol{\ell} = -\frac{d\phi_B}{dt}.$$

2. In order for energy to be conserved, the induced electric field is in such a direction as to oppose the change in flux that gives rise to it. This energy-conserving aspect of Faraday's law is called **Lenz's law** and is reflected mathematically in the minus sign on the right-hand side of Faraday's law.

3. When a conductor is present, the nonconservative electric field manifests itself as an **induced emf**:

$$\mathcal{E} = -\frac{d\phi_B}{dt}.$$

This emf drives an **induced current** in any circuit with finite resistance. It does not matter whether the magnetic flux is changed by moving a conductor in a magnetic field, or by moving a magnetic field near a conductor, or by altering the shape or orientation of the conductor. The generation of electric power by moving conducting loops in magnetic fields is an important technological example of induced currents.

4. **Diamagnetism** is a manifestation of electromagnetic induction on the atomic scale. Application of a magnetic field to a diamagnetic material results in induced atomic magnetic moments that cause the material to be repelled from a magnet.

Terms You Should Understand

(Pairs are closely related terms whose distinction is important; number in parentheses is chapter section where term first appears.)

electromagnetic induction (31-1)
induced current, induced emf (31-1, 31-2)
magnetic flux (31-2)
Faraday's law, Lenz's law (31-2, 31-3)
motional emf (31-3)

generator (31-3)
eddy currents (31-3)
induced electric field (31-4)

Symbols You Should Recognize

ϕ_B (31-2)
$\oint \mathbf{E} \cdot d\boldsymbol{\ell}$ (31-4)

Problems You Should Be Able to Solve

calculating magnetic flux (31-2)
calculating induced emf's (31-2)
finding directions of induced emf's and currents (31-3)
calculating induced electric fields (31-4)

Limitations to Keep in Mind

Electromagnetic induction requires a *change* in magnetic flux. Values of magnetic field or flux alone don't matter; only the rate of change of those quantities is important.

QUESTIONS

1. A copper penny falls on a vertical path that takes it between the poles of a magnet. Does it hit the ground faster or slower than if no magnet were present?

2. A bar magnet is moved toward a conducting ring, as shown in Fig. 31-38. What is the direction of the induced current in the ring?

FIGURE 31-38 Question 2.

3. Figure 31-39 shows two concentric conducting loops, the outer connected to a battery and a switch. The switch is initially open. It is then closed, left closed for a while, then

FIGURE 31-39 Question 3.

opened again. Describe the currents in the inner loop during the entire procedure.

4. An electric generator is being turned at constant speed. A load resistor R is connected across the generator terminals. If the electrical resistance of the load is lowered, does the generator get easier or harder to turn?

5. Service manuals for cars often tell you to set the idle speed of the engine with the headlights on. Why? What does this have to do with electromagnetic induction?

6. Figure 31-40 shows two square wire loops, the first containing a battery and variable resistor. The resistor is initially at the midpoint of its resistance range. Should its resistance be lowered or raised in order to induce a clockwise current in the right-hand loop?

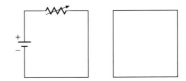

FIGURE 31-40 Question 6.

7. Consider the simple motor shown in Fig. 29-36. What happens if you connect a resistor across the motor terminals, and turn the motor by hand? What is the difference between a motor and a generator?

8. Figure 31-41 shows an open wire loop in a magnetic field. The field is changing, and charge has piled up at the loop gap with the polarity indicated. Is the magnetic field strength increasing or decreasing?

FIGURE 31-41 Question 8.

9. A constant, uniform magnetic field points into the page. A flexible, circular conducting ring lies in the plane of the page. If the ring is stretched, maintaining its circular shape, what is the direction of the induced current?

10. When a magnet is moved near a superconductor, the magnetic field lines never enter the superconductor. Why not?

11. Is it possible to produce an induced current that never changes? How or why not? Could you produce an induced current that was steady for some finite time? How or why not?

12. When you push a bar magnet into a conducting loop, you do work. What happens when you pull it out the other side?

13. You are turning a generator in such a way that the current it delivers remains constant. As you lower the load resistance across the generator, does the generator get easier or harder to turn?

14. Devise a way of measuring a magnetic field using Faraday's law.

15. In Fig. 31-42, a copper ring was originally resting on the wooden structure, surrounding the coil. When a rapidly

FIGURE 31-42 Question 15.

changing current was applied to the coil, the ring was ejected into the air. Explain this phenomenon.

16. Fluctuations in Earth's magnetic field due to changing solar activity can wreak havoc with communications, even those using underground cables. How is this possible?

17. Why is it not possible to run a tokamak on a continuous basis?

18. Conventional brakes on a car need large surface areas to dissipate the heat of friction when the brakes are applied. Would eddy-current brakes have the same problem?

19. Which way would the eddy currents flow in Fig. 31-22a as the bob continues its swing and begins to emerge from the field?

20. In Chapter 29, we pointed out that a static magnetic field cannot change the energy of a charged particle. Is this true of a changing magnetic field? Discuss.

21. A long solenoid of circular cross section is oriented so that its magnetic field points out of the page, as shown in Fig. 31-43. The solenoid current is increasing. (a) What is the direction of the induced electric field at points A and B in the figure? (b) What is the magnitude of the induced electric field in the center of the solenoid? (Don't calculate! Argue from symmetry.)

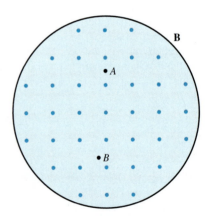

FIGURE 31-43 Question 21.

22. Is the concept of electric potential (Chapter 25) useful in a nonconservative electric field? Give an example to substantiate your answer.

23. Can an induced electric field exist in the absence of a conductor?

24. Could you tell whether a given electric field arises from electric charge or from a changing magnetic field? How or why not?

25. Does a diamagnetic material experience a force in a uniform magnetic field?

PROBLEMS

ActivPhysics can help with these problems:
Activities 13.9, 13.10

Sections 31-2 and 31-3 Faraday's Law and Induction and the Conservation of Energy

1. Show that the volt is the correct SI unit for the rate of change of magnetic flux, making Faraday's law dimensionally correct.
2. A bar magnet is moved steadily through a conducting ring, as shown in Fig. 31-44. Sketch qualitatively the current and power dissipation in the ring as functions of time. Take as positive a current flowing out of the plane of the page at the top of the ring, and indicate the position of the magnet on your time axis.

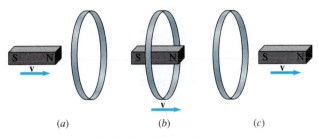

(a)   (b)   (c)

FIGURE 31-44 Problem 2.

3. Find the magnetic flux through a circular loop 5.0 cm in diameter oriented with the loop normal at $30°$ to a uniform 80-mT magnetic field.
4. A circular wire loop 40 cm in diameter has 100-Ω resistance and lies in a horizontal plane. A uniform magnetic field points vertically downward, and in 25 ms it increases linearly from 5.0 mT to 55 mT. Find the magnetic flux through the loop at (a) the beginning and (b) the end of the 25 ms period. (c) What is the loop current during this time? (d) Which way does this current flow?
5. A conducting loop of area 240 cm^2 and resistance 12 Ω lies at right angles to a spatially uniform magnetic field. The loop carries an induced current of 320 mA. At what rate is the magnetic field changing?
6. A conducting loop of area A and resistance R lies at right angles to a spatially uniform magnetic field. At time $t = 0$ the magnetic field and loop current are both zero. Subsequently, the current increases according to $I = bt^2$, where b is a constant with the units A/s^2. Find an expression for the magnetic field strength as a function of time.
7. A conducting loop with area 0.15 m^2 and resistance 6.0 Ω lies in the x-y plane. A spatially uniform magnetic field points in the z direction. The field varies with time according to $B_z = at^2 - b$, where $a = 2.0$ T/s^2 and $b = 8.0$ T.

Find the loop current (a) when $t = 3.0$ s and (b) when $B_z = 0$.

8. The magnetic field inside a 20-cm-diameter solenoid is increasing at the rate of 2.4 T/s. How many turns should a coil wrapped around the outside of the solenoid have in order that the emf induced in the coil be 15 V?
9. A square wire loop of side ℓ and resistance R is pulled with constant speed v from a region of no magnetic field until it is fully inside a region of constant, uniform magnetic field **B** perpendicular to the loop plane. The boundary of the field region is parallel to one side of the loop. Find an expression for the total work done by the agent pulling the loop.
10. A 1.8-m high runner sprints eastward at 9.5 m/s along the equator, where Earth's magnetic field points horizontally with a strength of 31 μT. (a) What is the magnitude of the emf induced between the runner's head and feet? (b) Which end is positive?
11. In Fig. 31-26 the loop radius is 15 cm, and the magnetic field is decreasing at the rate of 550 T/s. If the gap width is small compared with the loop circumference, what is the voltage across the gap?
12. A 5-turn coil 1.0 cm in diameter is rotated at 10 rev/s about an axis perpendicular to a uniform magnetic field. A voltmeter connected to the coil through rotating contacts reads a peak value of 360 μV. What is the magnetic field strength?
13. The wingspan of a 747 jetliner is 60 m. If the plane is flying at 960 km/h in a region where the vertical component of Earth's magnetic field is 0.20 G, what emf develops between the plane's wingtips?
14. A square wire loop 3.0 m on a side is perpendicular to a uniform magnetic field of 2.0 T. A 6-V light bulb is in series with the loop, as shown in Fig. 31-45. The magnetic field is reduced steadily to zero over a time Δt. (a) Find Δt such that the light will shine at full brightness during this time. (b) Which way will the loop current flow?

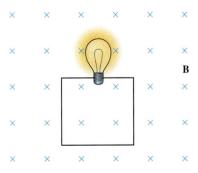

FIGURE 31-45 Problem 14.

15. In Example 31-2 take $a = 1.0$ cm, $w = 3.5$ cm, and $\ell = 6.0$ cm. Suppose the rectangular loop is a conductor with resistance 50 mΩ and that the current I in the long wire is increasing at the rate of 25 A/s. Find the induced current in the loop. In what direction does it flow?

16. A windmill with conducting blades of length ℓ is rotating with angular speed ω about a horizontal axis; the horizontal component of Earth's magnetic field at its location is B_x. Find an expression for the emf developed between the blade tips and the central axis.

17. A square conducting loop of side $s = 0.50$ m and resistance $R = 5.0\ \Omega$ moves to the right with speed $v = 0.25$ m/s. At time $t = 0$ its rightmost edge enters a uniform magnetic field $B = 1.0$ T pointing into the page, as shown in Fig. 31-46. The magnetic field covers a region of width $w = 0.75$ m. Plot (a) the current and (b) the power dissipation in the loop as functions of time, taking a clockwise current as positive and covering the time until the entire loop has exited the field region.

FIGURE 31-47 Problems 19–21.

FIGURE 31-48 Problem 20.

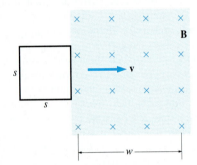

FIGURE 31-46 Problem 17.

18. A 2.0-m-long solenoid is 15 cm in diameter and consists of 2000 turns of wire. The current in the solenoid is increasing at the rate of 1.0 kA/s. (a) Find the current in a wire loop with diameter 10 cm and resistance 5.0 Ω, lying inside the solenoid in a plane perpendicular to the loop axis. (b) Repeat for a similarly oriented loop with diameter 25 cm, lying entirely outside the solenoid.

19. A solenoid 2.0 m long and 30 cm in diameter consists of 5000 turns of wire. A 5-turn coil with negligible resistance is wrapped around the solenoid and connected to a 180-Ω resistor, as shown in Fig. 31-47. The direction of the current in the solenoid is such that the solenoid's magnetic field points to the right. At time $t = 0$ the solenoid current begins to decay exponentially, being given by $I = I_0 e^{-t/\tau}$, where $I_0 = 85$ A, $\tau = 2.5$ s, and t is the time in seconds. (a) What is the direction of the current in the resistor as the solenoid current decays? What is the value of the resistor current at (b) $t = 1.0$ s and (c) $t = 5.0$ s?

20. Make a qualitative plot of the resistor current in the preceding problem as a function of time if the solenoid current

has the form shown in Fig. 31-48. Take a left-to-right resistor current as positive.

21. (a) Find an expression for the resistor current in Problem 19 if the solenoid current is given by $I = I_0 \sin \omega t$, where $I_0 = 85$ A and $\omega = 210$ s^{-1}. (b) What is the peak current in the resistor? (c) What is the resistor current when the solenoid current is a maximum?

22. A magnetic field is described by $\mathbf{B} = B_0 \sin \omega t\ \hat{\mathbf{k}}$, where $B_0 = 2.0$ T and $\omega = 10$ s^{-1}. A conducting loop with area 150 cm^2 and resistance 5.0 Ω lies in the x-y plane. Find the induced current in the loop (a) at $t = 0$ and (b) at $t = 0.10$ s.

23. In the preceding problem, what is the first time after $t = 0$ when the loop current will be zero?

24. A car alternator consists of a 250-turn coil 10 cm in diameter in a magnetic field of 0.10 T. If the alternator is turning at 1000 revolutions per minute, what is its peak output voltage?

25. A credit-card reader extracts information from the card's magnetic stripe as it is pulled past the reader's head. At some instant the card motion results in a magnetic field at the head that is changing at the rate of 450 μT/ms. If this field passes perpendicularly through a 5000-turn head coil 2.0 mm in diameter, what will be the induced emf?

26. A generator consists of a rectangular coil 75 cm by 1.3 m, spinning in a 0.14-T magnetic field. If it is to produce a 60-Hz alternating emf (i.e., $\mathscr{E} = \mathscr{E}_0 \sin 2\pi ft$, where $f = 60$ Hz) with peak value 6.7 kV, how many turns must it have?

27. Figure 31-49 shows a pair of parallel conducting rails a distance ℓ apart in a uniform magnetic field **B**. A resistance R is connected across the rails, and a conducting bar of negligible resistance is being pulled along the rails with velocity **v** to the right. (a) What is the direction of the current in the resistor? (b) At what rate must work be done by the agent pulling the bar?

FIGURE 31-49 Problems 27–29, 33, 60.

28. The resistor in the preceding problem is replaced by an ideal voltmeter. (a) To which rail should the positive meter terminal be connected if the meter is to indicate a positive voltage? (b) At what rate must work be done by the agent pulling the bar?

29. A battery of emf $\mathscr{E}$ is inserted in series with the resistor in Fig. 31-49, with its positive terminal toward the top rail. The bar is initially at rest, and now no agent pulls it. (a) Describe the bar's subsequent motion. (b) The bar eventually reaches a constant speed. Why? (c) What is that constant speed? Express in terms of the magnetic field, the battery emf, and the rail spacing ℓ. Does the resistance R affect the final speed? If not, what role does it play?

30. A toroidal coil of square cross section has inner radius a and outer radius b. It consists of N turns of wire and carries a time-varying current $I = I_0 \sin \omega t$. A single-turn wire loop encircles the toroid, passing through its center hole as shown in Fig. 31-50. Find an expression for the peak emf induced in the loop.

FIGURE 31-50 Problem 30.

31. A pair of parallel conducting rails 10 cm apart lie at right angles to a uniform magnetic field **B** of magnitude 2.0 T, as

shown in Fig. 31-51. A 5.0-Ω and a 10-Ω resistor lie across the rails and are free to slide along them. (a) The 5-Ω resistor is held fixed, and the 10-Ω resistor is pulled to the right at 50 cm/s. What are the direction and magnitude of the induced current? (b) Now the 10-Ω resistor is held fixed, and the 5-Ω resistor is pulled to the left at 50 cm/s. What are the direction and magnitude of the induced current? (c) What is the power dissipation in the 10-Ω resistor in both cases?

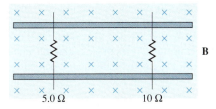

FIGURE 31-51 Problems 31, 32, and 64.

32. In Fig. 31-51 the 10-Ω resistor is being moved to the right at a constant 50 cm/s. The 5-Ω resistor, initially at rest, is placed across the conducting rails. Describe qualitatively its subsequent motion, and determine its final speed.

33. In Fig. 31-49, take $\ell = 10$ cm, $B = 0.50$ T, $R = 4.0\ \Omega$, and $v = 2.0$ m/s. Find (a) the current in the resistor, (b) the magnetic force on the bar, (c) the power dissipation in the resistor, and (d) the mechanical work done by the agent pulling the bar. Compare your answers to (c) and (d).

34. A rectangular conducting loop of resistance R, mass m, and width w falls into a uniform magnetic field **B**, as shown in Fig. 31-52. If the loop is long enough and the field region has a great enough vertical extent, the loop will reach a terminal speed. (a) Why? (b) Find an expression for the terminal speed. (c) What will be the direction of the loop current as the loop enters the field?

FIGURE 31-52 Problem 34.

35. A circular loop 40 cm in diameter is made from a flexible conductor and lies at right angles to a uniform 12-T magnetic field. At time $t = 0$ the loop starts to expand, its radius increasing at the rate of 5.0 mm/s. Find the induced emf in the loop (a) at $t = 1.0$ s and (b) at $t = 10$ s.

Section 31-4 Induced Electric Fields

36. The induced electric field 12 cm from the axis of a solenoid with 10 cm radius is 45 V/m. Find the rate of change of the solenoid's magnetic field.

37. Find the electric force on a 50-μC charge inside the solenoid of Problem 18, if the charge is 5.0 cm from the solenoid axis.

38. Figure 31-53 shows a top view of a tokamak. The magnetic field in the center is confined to a circular area of radius 50 cm, and during a pulse it increases at the rate of 5.1 T/ms. (a) What is the magnitude of the induced electric field in the tokamak, 1.2 m from the center of the field region in Fig. 31-53? (b) What is the field direction? (c) If a proton circles the tokamak once at this radius, going with the electric field, how much energy does it gain?

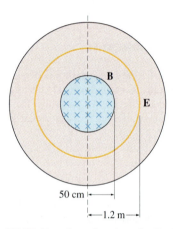

FIGURE 31-53 Top view of a tokamak. (Problem 38)

39. A uniform magnetic field points into the page in Fig. 31-54. In the same region an electric field points straight up, but increases with position at the rate of 10 V/m^2 as you move to the right. Apply Faraday's law to a rectangular loop to show that the magnetic field must be changing with time, and calculate the rate of change.

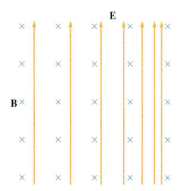

FIGURE 31-54 The magnetic field must be changing. Why? (Problem 39)

40. Use Faraday's law to show that the electric field produced by charges on the plates of a parallel-plate capacitor cannot end abruptly at the edges of the plates. *Hint:* Apply Faraday's law to the loop shown in Fig. 31-55.

FIGURE 31-55 Problem 40.

41. Figure 31-56 shows a magnetic field pointing into the page; the field is confined to a layer of thickness h in the vertical direction but extends infinitely to the left and right. The field strength is increasing with time: $B = bt$, where b is a constant. Find an expression for the electric field at all points outside the field region. *Hint:* Consult Example 30-5.

FIGURE 31-56 Problem 41.

42. The magnetic field inside a solenoid of circular cross section is given by $\mathbf{B} = bt\,\hat{\mathbf{k}}$, where $b = 2.1$ T/ms. At time $t = 0.40\ \mu$s a proton is inside the solenoid at the point $x = 5.0$ cm, $y = 0$, $z = 0$ and is moving with velocity $\mathbf{v} = 4.8 \times 10^6\,\hat{\mathbf{j}}$ m/s. Find the net electromagnetic force on the proton.

Paired Problems

(Both problems in a pair involve the same principles and techniques. If you can get the first problem, you should be able to solve the second one.)

43. A magnetic field is given by $\mathbf{B} = B_0(x/x_0)^2\,\hat{\mathbf{k}}$, where B_0 and x_0 are constants. Find an expression for the magnetic flux through a square of side $2x_0$ that lies in the x-y plane with one corner at the origin and two sides coinciding with the positive x and y axes.

44. A circular region of radius R lies in the x-y plane and contains a magnetic field given by $\mathbf{B} = B_0\dfrac{r}{R}\hat{\mathbf{k}}$, where r is the radial distance from the central axis of the field region. Find an expression for the magnetic flux through this region.

45. A uniform magnetic field is given by $\mathbf{B} = bt\,\hat{\mathbf{k}}$, where $b = 0.35$ T/s. Find the current in a conducting loop with area 240 cm^2 and resistance 0.20 Ω that lies in the x-y plane. In what direction is the current, as viewed from the positive z axis?

46. A uniform magnetic field is given by $\mathbf{B} = bt^3\,\hat{\mathbf{k}}$. A square conducting loop 15 cm on a side has 0.32-Ω resistance and lies in the x-y plane. At time $t = 2.5$ s, the current in the loop is 4.1 A. Find b.

47. A pair of vertical conducting rods are a distance ℓ apart and are connected at the bottom by a resistance R. A conducting bar of mass m runs horizontally between the rods and can slide freely down them while maintaining electrical contact. The whole apparatus is in a uniform magnetic field **B** pointing horizontally and perpendicular to the bar. When the bar is released from rest it soon reaches a constant speed. Find this speed.

48. A conducting bar of mass m slides down the conducting wedges shown in Fig. 31-57. The wedges are separated by a distance ℓ, connected at the top by a resistance R, and make an angle θ with the vertical. A uniform magnetic field **B** points horizontally, as shown. When released from rest the bar soon reaches a constant speed. Find an expression for this speed.

FIGURE 31-57 Problem 48.

49. Figure 31-58 shows an unusual design for a generator, consisting of a conducting bar that rotates about a central axis while making contact with a conducting ring of radius R. A uniform magnetic field is perpendicular to the ring. Wires from the axis and ring carry power to a load. Find an expression for the emf induced in this generator when the bar rotates with angular speed ω.

FIGURE 31-58 Problem 49.

50. A copper disk 90 cm in diameter is spinning at 3600 rpm about a conducting axle through its center, as shown in Fig. 31-59. A uniform 1.5-T magnetic field is perpendicular to the disk, as shown. A stationary conducting brush maintains contact with the disk's rim, and a voltmeter is

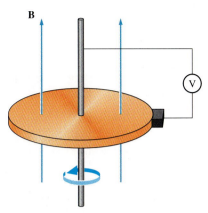

FIGURE 31-59 Problem 50.

connected between the brush and the axle. (a) What does the voltmeter read? (b) Which voltmeter lead is positive?

51. An electron is inside a solenoid, 28 cm from the solenoid axis. It experiences an electric force of magnitude 1.3 fN. At what rate is the solenoid's magnetic field changing?

52. It takes 0.43 J to push a 84-μC charge around a closed path surrounding a 1.5-m-diameter solenoid. At what rate is the solenoid's magnetic field changing?

Supplementary Problems

53. At times prior to $t = 0$, there is no current in either the solenoid or the small coil of Problem 19. Subsequently, the current in the small coil is observed to increase at 10 μA/s. What is the solenoid current as a function of time?

54. A conducting loop of area A and resistance R lies perpendicular to a uniform magnetic field B. The loop is then rotated at a uniform rate until it is upside down; this takes time Δt. Find an expression for the work done in flipping the loop.

55. So-called magnetohydrodynamic generators have been proposed as a means of extracting electrical energy from charged particles released in fusion reactions; they've also been suggested as a way to generate electricity from flowing water. An MHD generator consists of two metal plates on either side of a channel carrying conducting fluid in a magnetic field, as shown in Fig. 31-60. The magnetic force on free charges in the fluid drives positive charge to one plate, negative to the other. If there's no electrical load connected across the plates, the electric field that develops eventually halts any further charge motion. (a) Show in this case that the voltage between the plates is $V = vBd$, where v is the fluid velocity and d the plate spacing. (b) Now suppose a resistance R is connected between the plates. Show that the current through R is $I = \dfrac{vABd}{\rho d + AR}$, where A is the plate area and ρ is the resistivity of the fluid.

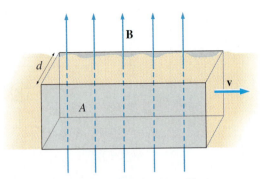

FIGURE 31-60 Problem 55.

56. The tethered satellite system of Example 31-8 is flown in a low circular orbit about a planet of mass M and radius R. If the tether has length ℓ and generates an emf $\mathcal{E}$, find an expression for the planet's magnetic field strength.

57. Clever farmers whose lands are crossed by large power lines have been known to steal power by stringing wire near the power line and making use of the induced current—a practice that has been ruled legally to be theft. The scene of a particular crime is shown in Fig. 31-61. The power line carries 60-Hz alternating current with a peak current of 10 kA (that is, the current is given by $I = I_0 \sin \omega t$, where $I_0 = 10$ kA and $\omega = 2\pi f$, with $f = 60$ Hz). (a) If the farmer wants a peak voltage of 170 V, what should be the length ℓ of the loop shown in Fig. 31-61? (170 V is the peak of standard 120-V AC power.) (b) If all the equipment the farmer connects to the loop has an equivalent resistance of 5.0 Ω, what is the farmer's average power consumption? *Note:* The *average* power consumption is half the product of the peak voltage and peak current. (c) If the power company charges 10¢ per kWh, what is the monetary value of the energy stolen each day? (d) Without examining the farmer's lands, how, in principle, could the power company know that a crime is being committed?

FIGURE 31-61 Problem 57.

58. A circular wire loop of resistance R and radius a lies with its plane perpendicular to a uniform magnetic field. The field strength changes from an initial value B_1 to a final value B_2. Show, by integrating the loop current over time, that the total charge that moves around the ring is

$$q = \frac{\pi a^2}{R}(B_2 - B_1).$$

Note that this result is independent of how the field changes with time.

59. A conducting disk with radius a, thickness h, and resistivity ρ is inside a solenoid of circular cross section. The disk axis coincides with the solenoid axis. The magnetic field in the solenoid is given by $B = bt$, with b a constant. Find expressions for (a) the current density in the disk as a function of the distance r from the disk center and (b) the rate of power dissipation in the entire disk. *Hint:* Consider the disk to be made up of infinitesimal conducting loops.

60. The bar in Problem 27 has mass m and is initially at rest. A constant force F is applied to the bar, pulling it to the right. (a) Formulate Newton's second law for the bar as an equation involving both v and $a = dv/dt$. (b) Use your equation to show that the bar's acceleration becomes zero when its speed reaches the value $FR/B^2\ell^2$. (c) Show by direct substitution that your equation is satisfied if v as a function of time is given by $v(t) = \dfrac{FR}{B^2\ell^2}(1 - e^{-B^2\ell^2 t/mR})$.

61. Find an expression for the speed of the left-hand resistor in Problem 32 as a function of time, in terms of its mass m, the field strength B, the speed v of the right-hand bar, the time t, and the resistances R_{left} and R_{right}.

62. A pendulum consists of a mass m suspended from two identical copper wires of negligible mass. At equilibrium the mass is a vertical distance ℓ below its supports, and the wires make 45° angles with the vertical, as shown in Fig. 31-62. A uniform magnetic field **B** points into the page. The pendulum is displaced from the plane of the page by a small angle θ_0, and at time $t = 0$ it is released. Find an expression for the voltmeter reading as a function of time.

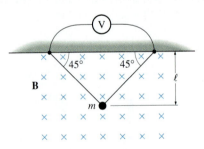

FIGURE 31-62 Problem 62.

63. A *flip coil* consists of a small coil used to measure magnetic fields. The flip coil is placed in a magnetic field with its plane perpendicular to the field, and then rotated abruptly through 180° about an axis in the plane of the coil. The coil is connected to instrumentation to measure the total charge Q that flows during this process. If the coil has N turns of area A and if its rotation axis is perpendicular to the magnetic field, show that the field strength is given by $B = QR/2NA$, where R is the coil resistance.

Inductance and Magnetic Energy

This transformer at an electrical substation uses mutual inductance to change the voltage at which power is transmitted.

Faraday's law implies that a changing magnetic flux through a circuit produces an induced emf in the circuit. In this chapter we consider the special case when that changing flux is itself caused by a changing current in an electric circuit. We then speak of the **inductance** of the circuit.

32-1 MUTUAL INDUCTANCE

FIGURE 32-1 The mutual inductance between two coils is the ratio of magnetic flux through one coil to the current in the other coil. A changing current in one coil induces an emf in the other.

Consider two coils arranged so that some of the magnetic flux associated with current in one coil also passes through the second coil, as in Fig. 32-1. If we change the current I_1 in the first coil, an induced emf $\mathcal{E}_2$ appears in the second. As we discussed in the preceding chapter, $\mathcal{E}_2$ depends on the rate of change of magnetic flux through the second coil. The magnetic flux depends, in turn, on the current in the first coil and on the geometrical arrangement of the two coils which determines how much flux from the first coil actually links the second. We characterize this geometrical arrangement by the ratio of the total magnetic flux through the second coil to the current in the first coil. This ratio defines the **mutual inductance**, M, of the two coils:

$$M = \frac{\phi_2}{I_1}. \tag{32-1}$$

Solving Equation 32-1 for ϕ_2 and differentiating, we obtain

$$\frac{d\phi_2}{dt} = M\frac{dI_1}{dt}.$$

Faraday's law says that $d\phi_2/dt$ is $-\mathcal{E}_2$, the induced emf in coil 2. So we have

$$\mathcal{E}_2 = -M\frac{dI_1}{dt}, \tag{32-2}$$

where the minus sign describes the polarity of the induced emf.

In the context of Fig. 32-1, our discussion of mutual inductance assumed that a changing current in the left-hand coil caused an induced emf in the right-hand coil. But we could have equally well considered the effect a changing current in the right-hand coil would have on the left-hand coil. Although it's not at all obvious, the mutual inductance M is the same either way; it's a constant that characterizes the physical arrangement of two coils regardless of which is the source of the changing magnetic flux.

From Equation 32-2, we see that the unit of mutual inductance is the volt-second/ampere. This unit is given the name henry (H) in honor of the American scientist Joseph Henry (1797–1878), who was also the first secretary of the Smithsonian Institution. Mutual inductances found in common electronic circuits usually range from microhenrys (μH) on up to several henrys.

EXAMPLE 32-1	*Mutual Inductance*

A 2-turn coil is wrapped around a long solenoid with cross-sectional area $A = 26$ cm^2, wound with $n = 3500$ turns per meter of length (Fig. 32-2). Find the mutual inductance of this arrangement.

Solution
Since the solenoid field is uniform and confined to the solenoid interior, the flux through each turn of the small coil is just BA. Accounting for the two turns and using Equation 30-11 for the solenoid's magnetic field, the total magnetic flux through the small coil becomes

$$\phi_2 = 2BA = 2\mu_0 nIA,$$

FIGURE 32-2 What is the mutual inductance of the two coils? (Example 32-1)

where I is the solenoid current. Equation 32-1 shows that mutual inductance is the ratio of the flux in one coil to the current in the other, or

$$M = \frac{\phi_2}{I} = \frac{2\mu_0 nIA}{I} = 2\mu_0 nA$$

$$= (2)(4\pi \times 10^{-7} \text{ N/A}^2)(3500)(26 \times 10^{-4} \text{ m}^2)$$

$$= 23 \ \mu\text{H}.$$

EXERCISE Suppose the solenoid of Example 32-1 has circular cross section, and that the smaller coil is *inside* the solenoid, with its diameter half that of the solenoid. Find the mutual inductance.

Answer: 5.7 μH

Some problems similar to Example 32-1: 6, 7, 10

Mutual inductance is the basis of **transformers** and similar devices that use the mutual inductance of two adjacent coils to transfer electric power from one circuit to another without direct electrical contact. Transformers also shift voltage levels, allowing great flexibility in the handling and use of electric power. But because they're based fundamentally on Faraday's law, these devices work only with alternating current or in situations where current is interrupted to make it change with time. We'll discuss transformers more in Chapter 33; for now, Example 32-2 and its exercise illustrate two transformer-like devices using mutual induction.

EXAMPLE 32-2	*Spark Plugs and Toothbrushes*

Electric sparks ignite the gasoline that powers your car's engine. High voltage to fire the spark plugs is provided by the ignition coil, an arrangement of two different coils with mutual inductance. Current from the car's 12-V battery flows through the coil with fewer turns, and is interrupted periodically by a switch in the car's distributor. The sudden change in current induces a large emf in the coil with more turns, and this emf drives the spark.

A typical ignition coil draws 3.0 A and supplies 20 kV to the spark plugs. If the current decays in 0.10 ms when the switch opens, what is the mutual inductance of the ignition coil?

Solution

The rate of change of current is

$$\frac{dI}{dt} = \frac{3.0 \text{ A}}{0.10 \times 10^{-3} \text{ s}} = 3.0 \times 10^4 \text{ A/s}.$$

Solving Equation 32-2 for M then gives

$$M = \frac{|\mathscr{E}|}{|dI/dt|} = \frac{20 \times 10^3 \text{ V}}{3.0 \times 10^4 \text{ A}} = 0.67 \text{ H}.$$

EXERCISE An electric toothbrush has no electrical connection to the power line (Fig. 32-3). But when the toothbrush is in its stand, a coil inside the toothbrush itself rests inside another coil in the stand, and alternating current from the power line flows in the stand coil. The mutual inductance of the two coils results in an induced current in the toothbrush

FIGURE 32-3 The batteries in this electric toothbrush are charged with energy transferred via mutual induction of coils located in the base unit, which is connected to the AC power line, and in the bottom of the brush unit. There is no direct electrical connection to the brush unit.

coil, and this current charges the batteries that power the toothbrush. Suppose the mutual inductance of this arrangement is 100 mH. At an instant when the current in the stand coil is changing at the rate of 40 A/s, what is the emf in the toothbrush coil?

Answer: 4.0 V

Some problems similar to Example 32-2: 1–4

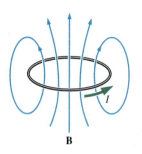

FIGURE 32-4 Magnetic flux from a circular current loop passes through the loop itself.

32-2 SELF-INDUCTANCE

So far we've considered emf and current induced in a circuit by changes—like moving a magnet or varying the current in another circuit—that were external to the circuit in question. But the changing magnetic field associated with the changing current in a circuit also affects that same circuit.

Consider a circular loop carrying current I, as shown in Fig. 32-4. Magnetic field lines arising from this current loop pass through the loop, making a magnetic flux through the loop. If the current is steady, this flux is constant, and there is no induced electric field. But if we change the loop current, then the flux changes, and an induced electric field arises. In order to conserve energy this field opposes the change that causes it—in this case the change in loop current. If the current is counterclockwise and we increase its strength, an induced electric field will appear in the clockwise direction to oppose the current increase. If we decrease the current, the induced electric field will have the opposite sense, now trying to maintain the current. The induced electric field therefore makes it difficult to change the current in the circuit.

This property of a circuit whereby its own magnetic field opposes changes in current is termed **self-inductance**. All circuits possess self-inductance, but this inductance is important only when the circuit encircles a great many of its own magnetic field lines or when current changes very rapidly. A simple piece of wire exhibits very little opposition to current changes in the 60-Hz alternating current used in electric power systems. But in a TV or computer, where currents change on time scales of billionths of a second, self-inductance of the wires themselves must be taken into account.

An **inductor** is a device designed specifically to exhibit self-inductance. Inductors have many uses in electric circuits, including establishing the frequencies of radio transmitters or the channel settings of TV sets, and helping "steer" high and low frequency signals to the tweeters and woofers of loudspeaker systems. We'll explore some of these uses in the next chapter. A typical inductor consists of a coil of wire, constructed so that a great deal of its own magnetic flux is encircled. Some inductors are wound on iron cores to promote flux concentration (Fig. 32-5). Ideally, the only electrical property of an inductor is its inductance. But real inductors are made from wire, so they have resistance as well.

As long as the current in an inductor is steady, the magnetic flux is constant, so there's no induced emf and the inductor acts just like a piece of wire. But when the current changes, the changing magnetic flux induces an emf that opposes the change in current. The more rapidly the current changes, the greater the rate of change of flux and so the greater the emf. The induced emf depends also on how much of its own magnetic flux the inductor encircles; consequently, we define self-inductance, L, as the ratio of magnetic flux through the inductor to current in the inductor:

$$L = \frac{\phi_B}{I}. \tag{32-3}$$

FIGURE 32-5 Typical inductors. At left is a 20-H unit, wound on an iron core for increased inductance. The others have inductances in the mH range.

The unit of self-inductance, like that of mutual inductance, is the henry. Inductance is a constant determined by the physical design of an inductor. In principle, we can calculate the inductance of any inductor, but in practice this is difficult unless the geometry is particularly simple. Inductors for use in electronic circuits are available commercially in a wide range of inductance values.

| **EXAMPLE 32-3** | *Inductance of a Solenoid* |

A long solenoid of cross-sectional area A and length ℓ has n turns per unit length. What is its self-inductance?

Solution

Equation 32-3 shows that self-inductance is the ratio of magnetic flux to current. In Chapter 30 we used Ampère's law to find the magnetic field of a long solenoid: $B = \mu_0 nI$. Since the field is uniform and perpendicular to the solenoid coils, the flux through each turn is just BA. With n turns per unit length, our solenoid has $N = n\ell$ turns. The total flux through the solenoid is then

$$\phi_B = NBA = (n\ell)(\mu_0 nI)(A) = \mu_0 n^2 A\ell I.$$

Then Equation 32-3 gives

$$L = \frac{\phi_B}{I} = \mu_0 n^2 A\ell. \tag{32-4}$$

Does this result make sense? As the area increases, so does the flux and therefore the inductance. As the length increases so does the number of turns, and therefore the flux and the inductance increase. Equation 32-4 reflects these trends. Can you see why the inductance should be proportional to the *square* of the number of turns per unit length?

EXERCISE What is the self-inductance of the MRI solenoid in Example 30-6 (page 787)?

Answer: 0.53 H

Some problems similar to Example 32-3: 11, 15, 20

The induced emf in an inductor is determined by Faraday's law, which relates the emf to the rate of change of magnetic flux:

$$\mathcal{E} = -\frac{d\phi_B}{dt}.$$

Differentiating Equation 32-3, the definition of inductance, gives

$$\frac{d\phi_B}{dt} = L\frac{dI}{dt}.$$

Then Faraday's law becomes

$$\mathcal{E} = -L\frac{dI}{dt}. \tag{32-5}$$

This equation gives the emf $\mathcal{E}$ induced in an inductor L when the current in the inductor is changing at the rate dI/dt. The minus sign again tells us that the emf *opposes* the change in current. For this reason the inductor emf is often called a **back emf**; it works *against* changes brought about by an externally applied emf. Figure 32-6 shows how to interpret the signs in Equation 32-5.

When the current in an inductor is steady, then $dI/dt = 0$ and there is no emf in the inductor. In this case, the inductor acts just like a piece of wire. But when the current changes the inductor responds by producing a back emf that opposes the change in current. Now the inductor acts very much like a battery, with the magnitude of its emf dependent on how fast the current changes. If we try to start or stop current suddenly, dI/dt is very large and a very large back emf appears. This is not just mathematics! Rapid switching of inductive devices such as solenoids, solenoid valves, or motors can result in destruction of delicate electronic devices by induced currents. And people have been killed opening switches in circuits containing large inductors. In the next section we'll take a closer look at the effect the rapid opening and closing of switches has in circuits containing inductors.

FIGURE 32-6 The inductor emf of Equation 32-5 is positive if, when going in the direction of the inductor current, you encounter the negative end of the inductor first. Because of the minus sign in Equation 32-5, this happens when the current is *decreasing* ($dI/dt < 0$).

FIGURE 32-7 Is the current increasing, decreasing, or steady?

Current flows from left to right through the inductor shown in Fig. 32-7. A voltmeter connected across the inductor gives a constant reading, and shows that the left end of the inductor is positive. Is the current in the inductor increasing, decreasing, or steady?

EXAMPLE 32-4	A Dangerous Inductor

A current of 5.0 A is flowing in a 2.0-H inductor. The current is reduced steadily to zero in 1.0 ms. What is the magnitude of the emf in the inductor while the current is being turned off?

Solution

Because the current changes steadily, its time rate of change has magnitude

$$\frac{dI}{dt} = \frac{5.0 \text{ A}}{1.0 \text{ ms}} = 5000 \text{ A/s},$$

so

$$|\mathcal{E}| = L\frac{dI}{dt} = (2.0 \text{ H})(5000 \text{ A/s}) = 10{,}000 \text{ V},$$

enough to produce a lethal shock. Note that this voltage is quite unrelated to the voltage of the battery or whatever else was supplying the inductor current. We could have a 6-volt battery and still be electrocuted trying to open the circuit rapidly when a large inductance is present.

EXERCISE A neon lamp that glows only when the voltage across it exceeds 90 V is connected across a 1.2-H inductor carrying 750 mA. When the current is interrupted the lamp flashes. Find the maximum time over which the current could have dropped to zero, assuming a steady decrease.

Answer: 10 ms

Some problems similar to Example 32-4: 12–14

32-3 INDUCTORS IN CIRCUITS

Here we examine circuits containing batteries, resistors, and inductors, analogous to the *RC* circuits of Chapter 28. In the qualitative analysis of *RC* circuits we found a useful guiding principle: The voltage across a capacitor cannot change instantaneously. We can make an analogous statement for inductors. Because the inductor emf is proportional to the rate of change of current in the inductor and because an infinite emf is physically impossible, we conclude that

> The current through an inductor cannot change instantaneously.

Thus, the effect an inductor has on current is analogous to the effect a capacitor has on voltage. Much of our understanding of capacitors can be applied to inductors if we interchange the words *voltage* and *current*.

Building Up the Current

Figure 32-8a shows a circuit containing a battery, switch, resistor, and inductor (symbol ⌇⌇⌇). What happens when we close the switch? Initially the inductor current is zero; since it can't change instantaneously, it must remain zero immediately after the switch is closed. But this is a series circuit, so the inductor

FIGURE 32-8 (*a*) An *RL* circuit. With the switch open no current flows. (*b*) Immediately after the switch is closed there is still no current. The inductor produces a back emf equal but opposite the battery emf, and therefore the rate of change of current is not zero. (*c*) After a long time, the rate of change of current and therefore the inductor emf approach zero. The inductor then acts like a piece of wire.

and resistor currents are equal. With zero current immediately after the switch is closed, there must be no voltage across the resistor. Therefore the inductor must produce a back emf equal to that of the battery, with the polarity shown in Fig. 32-8*b*. Even though there is, at this instant, no current in the inductor, the presence of an emf indicates that the *rate of change* of the current is not zero. Going around the circuit in the direction that the battery would drive a current, the inductor polarity indicated in Fig. 32-8*b* shows that the inductor emf is *negative*—and Equation 32-5 therefore shows that dI/dt is *positive*—i.e., the current is *increasing*.

As the current rises, so does the voltage across the resistor (since $V_R = IR$). Since the battery emf is constant, that means the inductor emf goes *down*—and that means the rate of change of current goes down. Thus, the current in the circuit builds up, but at an ever-decreasing rate. Concurrently, the inductor emf goes down. Eventually the current reaches a steady value, at which point dI/dt and, therefore, the inductor emf are zero. In this ultimate steady state the inductor acts like a piece of wire, and the circuit looks like Fig. 32-8*c*. The steady-state current is just $\mathcal{E}_0/R$, where $\mathcal{E}_0$ is the battery emf. Figure 32-9 summarizes this qualitative analysis of the *RL* circuit, while Fig. 32-10 shows the behavior of the current and inductor emf over time.

14.1
The *RL* Circuit

As current increases, so does resistor voltage *IR*, at an ever decreasing rate.

Current *I* increases at an ever decreasing rate.

Battery emf stays constant. Resistor and inductor voltages sum to the battery voltage.

Change in current results in an emf in the inductor. Emf decreases with decreasing rate of current change.

FIGURE 32-9 Interrelationships among circuit quantities as current builds up in an *RL* circuit. Compare with Fig. 28-30, which is a related diagram for a charging capacitor.

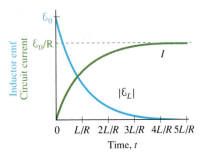

FIGURE 32-10 Inductor current and magnitude of the inductor emf as functions of time. Vertical axis represents either current or voltage.

To analyze the *RL* circuit quantitatively, we apply the loop law. Going clockwise from the negative terminal of the battery, we first encounter a voltage increase $\mathcal{E}_0$ due to the battery. Then the voltage decreases by IR in the resistor. Finally, there is a voltage change $\mathcal{E}_L$ in the inductor. This change is actually a decrease, because the inductor emf opposes the increase in current. However, we'll simply call the inductor emf $\mathcal{E}_L$ and let Equation 32-5 take care of the signs. Then the loop law becomes

$$\mathcal{E}_0 - IR + \mathcal{E}_L = 0. \tag{32-6a}$$

If we differentiate this equation with respect to time, the battery emf $\mathcal{E}_0$ drops out because it's constant, giving

$$\frac{d\mathcal{E}_L}{dt} = R\frac{dI}{dt}.$$

Equation 32-5 shows that $dI/dt = -\mathcal{E}_L/L$, so our differentiated loop equation becomes

$$\frac{d\mathcal{E}_L}{dt} = -R\frac{\mathcal{E}_L}{L}. \tag{32-6b}$$

This differential equation describes a quantity—$\mathcal{E}_L$—whose rate of change is proportional to itself. We discussed such equations in Chapter 28 when we considered the *RC* circuit. Equation 32-6b is similar to Equation 28-4, but with current *I* replaced by the inductor emf $\mathcal{E}_L$, capacitance *C* by *L*, and *R* by $1/R$. The solution to Equation 32-6b is that of Equation 28-4, provided we make the appropriate substitutions for *I*, *C*, and *R*:

$$\mathcal{E}_L = -\mathcal{E}_0 e^{-Rt/L}. \tag{32-7}$$

This equation shows that the inductor emf decays exponentially to zero, starting from an initial value of $-\mathcal{E}_0$ (negative because the inductor emf *opposes* the battery emf). We can now solve for the current using Equation 32-6a:

$$I = \frac{\mathcal{E}_0 + \mathcal{E}_L}{R} = \frac{\mathcal{E}_0 + (-\mathcal{E}_0 e^{-Rt/L})}{R} = \frac{\mathcal{E}_0}{R}(1 - e^{-Rt/L}). \tag{32-8}$$

With a capacitor, we characterized the exponentially changing quantities in terms of the capacitive time constant *RC*. With an inductor, we have an **inductive time constant** *L/R*. Significant changes in current cannot occur on time scales much shorter than *L/R*. On the other hand, an *RL* circuit will approach a steady state, with zero $\mathcal{E}_L$, only after many inductive time constants.

We include inductors in circuits when we want to limit the rate at which current can change, and we select *L* in conjunction with the circuit resistance *R* to give the desired time constant. But self-inductance occurs in *any* circuit, whether or not there's an explicit inductor present, and in high-speed circuits such as computers and TVs it's important to keep the time constant *L/R* small to allow rapid current changes.

Why is the inductive time constant a quotient of *L* and *R* rather than a product, as in the capacitor case? In Problem 23 you can convince yourself that *L/R* has the units of seconds. But you can also understand this physically. The instant the switch is closed in Fig. 32-8, the inductor emf must equal the battery emf to keep the current instantaneously at zero. The *larger* the inductance *L*, the smaller the rate of current change, *dI/dt*, needed to produce that emf—and so the longer it will take to build up the current. And the *smaller* the resistance, the larger the final current and therefore, again, the longer it will take to build up that current.

EXAMPLE 32-5	*Firing Up an Electromagnet*

A large electromagnet used for lifting scrap metal has a self-inductance of 56 H. It is connected through a switch to a constant 440-V power source; the total resistance of the circuit is 2.8 Ω. When the switch is closed, how long does it take to bring the magnet current to 75% of its final value?

Solution

Letting $t \to \infty$ in Equation 32-8 shows that the final current is $I_{\text{final}} = \mathcal{E}_0/R$, as we argued in our qualitative analysis. Setting the current I in Equation 32-8 to $0.75\mathcal{E}_0/R$ gives

$$0.75 = 1 - e^{-Rt/L},$$

or

$$e^{-Rt/L} = 0.25.$$

Taking the natural logarithm of both sides (recall that $\ln e^x = x$) gives

$$-Rt/L = \ln(0.25),$$

or

$$t = -\frac{L}{R}\ln(0.25) = -\frac{56\ \text{H}}{2.8\ \Omega}\ln(0.25) = 28\ \text{s}.$$

(The minus sign canceled since the logarithm of a number less than 1 is negative.) Our answer is approximately one time constant ($L/R = 20$ s). This should not be surprising since we found with RC circuits that quantities following equations such as Equation 28-6 (and, therefore, its analog, Equation 32-8) reach $1 - 1/e$, or about two-thirds, of their final value in one time constant.

EXERCISE A 1.0-kΩ resistor is in series with an inductor, and a 12-V battery is connected across the pair. The current rises to 8.5 mA in 21 μs. Find the inductance.

Answer: 17 mH

Some problems similar to Example 32-5: 27–29, 32

The Current Decays

Figure 32-11a shows an *RL* circuit with a two-way switch. Throwing the switch to position *A* allows current to build up in the inductor as we've already described. Then, at time $t = 0$, we throw it to position *B*. This disconnects the battery, leaving a circuit electrically equivalent to Fig. 32-11b. Just prior to $t = 0$ there was some current I_0 flowing downward in the inductor. Since the inductor current cannot change instantaneously, that current must continue just after the switch is closed, as shown in Fig. 32-11b. To drive this current, the inductor must develop an emf in the direction shown. Now the inductor emf is positive, so Equation 32-5 shows that the current is *decreasing,* as we might well expect since the battery has been disconnected. As the current decreases, so does the voltage across the resistor. So, therefore, does the inductor emf and, therefore, the rate of change of current. We thus expect both the current and the inductor emf to decrease, but at an ever decreasing rate.

Note that the inductor emf here is like any other induced emf: it *opposes* the change giving rise to it. In this case that change is the decrease in current caused by disconnecting the battery. The inductor responds with an emf in such a direction as to keep that current flowing.

(a)   *(b)*

FIGURE 32-11 (*a*) Throwing the switch to position *A* allows current to build up in the inductor. (*b*) Throwing it to position *B* gives a circuit containing only the inductor and resistor. The current then decays exponentially.

Applying the loop law to Fig. 32-11*b* gives

$$\mathcal{E}_L - IR = 0.$$

Using $\mathcal{E}_L = -L\,dI/dt$ from Equation 32-5, the loop equation becomes

$$\frac{dI}{dt} = -\frac{R}{L}I.$$

This is just like Equation 32-6b, but with I replacing $\mathcal{E}_L$. The solution follows by analogy with Equation 32-7:

$$I = I_0 e^{-Rt/L}, \tag{32-9}$$

where I_0 is the inductor current when the switch is thrown from A to B. Equation 32-9 shows that the current decays with the same exponential time constant L/R that described its buildup (Fig. 32-12). The resistor voltage IR and therefore the inductor emf also decay in the same way.

It is not always necessary to use Equations 32-8 and 32-9 in describing RL circuits. For times very short compared with the time constant L/R, it suffices to use the fact that inductor currents cannot change instantaneously. And after many time constants, inductors in a circuit containing only steady sources will act like wires. Example 32-6 explores this situation.

FIGURE 32-12 Exponential decay of the current in the circuit of Fig. 32-11*b*.

EXAMPLE 32-6	*Short Times, Long Times*

In the circuit of Fig. 32-13*a*, the switch is initially open. What is the current in resistor R_2 immediately after the switch is closed? A long time after the switch is closed? Long after the switch is closed, it is again opened. What is the current in R_2 just after it is opened? A long time after?

Solution

Just before we close the switch, the current in the inductor is zero. The current cannot change instantaneously, so it remains zero just after the switch is closed. At this instant the inductor might as well be an open circuit, giving the circuit shown in Fig. 32-13*b*. Then all the current from R_1 flows through R_2, so

$$I = \frac{\mathcal{E}_0}{R_1 + R_2}.$$

If we wait long enough, the circuit will reach a steady state in which $dI/dt = 0$. So then there is no inductor emf, and the inductor acts like a wire. We can redraw the circuit as Fig. 32-13*c*, in which all the current from R_1 goes through L, and none through R_2. The resulting current in R_1 and L is just $\mathcal{E}_0/R_1$.

Now the switch is opened again. Current in R_1 stops abruptly since there is no way charge can get through the open switch. But the current through the inductor, which was $\mathcal{E}_0/R_1$ just before the switch was opened, remains $\mathcal{E}_0/R_1$ the instant after the switch is opened. There is only one place this current can

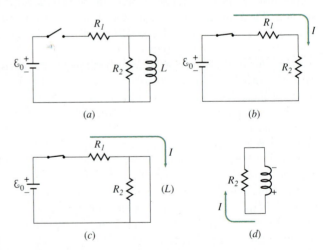

FIGURE 32-13 (*a*) Circuit for Example 32-6. (*b*) Just after the switch is closed the inductor acts like an open circuit. (*c*) A long time later the inductor emf is zero, so it acts like a wire. (*d*) When the switch opens again, current continues to flow in the inductor and on through R_2.

go—through R_2, from bottom to top (Fig. 32-13*d*). So just after the switch is opened, the current in R_2 is $\mathcal{E}_0/R_1$. Notice that the value of R_2 has no effect on this current, which is determined entirely by the battery emf and the resistance R_1.

What about the voltage across R_2? This is given by Ohm's law:

$$V_2 = I_2 R_2 = \frac{\mathscr{E}_0 R_2}{R_1}.$$

The larger R_2, the larger the voltage that appears when the switch is opened. If there's no resistor connected across the inductor (i.e., $R_2 = \infty$), then the voltage will be arbitrarily large as the inductor seeks at all cost to keep the current flowing. This dangerous situation can result in arcing and vaporization of circuit conductors, and even in electric shock. In circuits with large inductance, resistors are often placed in parallel with inductors to alleviate these dangers.

Finally, the current in Fig. 32-13d decays exponentially to zero. Plots of the currents in R_2 and L as functions of time are shown in Fig. 32-14.

EXERCISE In Fig. 32-13 take $\mathscr{E}_0 = 12$ V, $R_1 = 56$ Ω, $L = 48$ mH, and suppose the switch has been closed for a long time. What is the maximum value of R_2 for which the inductor emf will not exceed 100 V when the switch is opened?

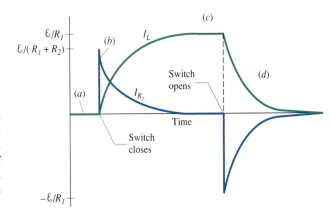

FIGURE 32-14 Currents in R_2 and L for Example 32-6. Note that the time constants before and after the switch opens are different; this reflects the fact that R_1 is out of the circuit after the switch opens. (a)–(d) indicate portions of the graph that correspond to the diagrams in Fig. 32-13.

Answer: 467 Ω

Some problems similar to Example 32-6: 36, 37, 61, 62

Got It!

In a circuit such as that of Fig. 32-13a, can the inductor emf ever exceed the battery emf? If so, can that happen (a) when the switch is closed or (b) when it's opened?

32-4 MAGNETIC ENERGY

In the situations we considered in Figs. 32-11b and 32-13d, current flows in circuits containing only a resistor and an inductor. Energy is dissipated, heating the resistor. Where does this energy come from?

Because there is a current in the inductor, there is also a magnetic field. The change in that magnetic field is what produces the emf that drives current around the circuit. As the current decreases, so does the inductor's magnetic field. Eventually the circuit reaches a state where there is no current, no magnetic field—and a hot resistor. So where did the resistor's thermal energy come from? It came from the magnetic field.

Like the electric field, the magnetic field contains stored energy. Our decaying RL circuit is analogous to a discharging RC circuit, in which the electric field between the capacitor plates disappears as thermal energy appears in the resistor. As in the electric case, magnetic energy is not limited to circuits. Any magnetic field contains energy. Release of magnetic energy drives a number of practical devices and also powers violent events throughout the universe (Fig. 32-15).

We can reinterpret the RL circuit of Fig. 32-11 in terms of energy. With the switch in position A, the battery supplies energy to the resistor and inductor. In the resistor the energy is dissipated as heat, but in the inductor it gets stored as magnetic field energy. When the switch is thrown to position B the battery—the

FIGURE 32-15 This eruption of a huge prominence from the Sun's surface involves the release of energy stored in magnetic fields. The intense magnetic fields responsible for such eruptive solar events are often associated with sunspots.

FIGURE 32-16 Energy transfers in the circuit of Fig. 32-11.

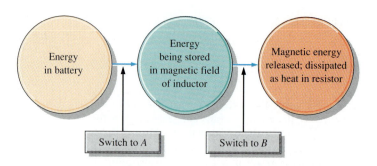

ultimate energy source for the circuit—is disconnected. Energy dissipated in the resistor now comes from the decaying magnetic field of the inductor. That energy came originally from the battery but was stored temporarily in the magnetic field. Figure 32-16 outlines these energy transfers.

Magnetic Energy in an Inductor

How much energy is stored in an inductor's magnetic field? We can answer this by considering first the *rate* of energy storage. If we multiply Equation 32-6a— the loop law for an *RL* circuit—by the current *I*, the result is

$$I\mathcal{E}_0 - I^2R + I\mathcal{E}_L = 0,$$

or, using Equation 32-5 for $\mathcal{E}_L$,

$$I\mathcal{E}_0 - I^2R - LI\frac{dI}{dt} = 0.$$

What do the terms in this equation mean? The first is the product of the battery's current and emf—a product we know gives electrical power. That this term is positive means the battery supplies energy *to* the circuit at the rate $I\mathcal{E}_0$. The second term, I^2R, is the rate of energy dissipation in the resistor (recall Equation 27-9). The negative sign means that this energy is taken *from* the circuit. The third term is also negative (since the current is increasing, dI/dt is positive) and represents the rate at which the inductor takes energy from the circuit. But the inductor does not dissipate this energy; instead, it stores the energy in its growing magnetic field. The rate at which the inductor stores energy is thus

$$P = LI\frac{dI}{dt}.$$

Suppose we increase the current in an inductor by some small amount dI over a small time interval dt. Since the power is the rate of energy storage, the energy dU stored during this time is thus

$$dU = P\,dt = LI\,dI$$

We find the total energy stored in bringing the inductor current from zero to some final value *I* by summing—that is, integrating—all the dU's:

$$U = \int dU = \int P\,dt = \int_0^I LI\,dI = \tfrac{1}{2}LI^2\big|_0^I$$

Evaluating at the two limits then gives the stored energy:

$$U = \tfrac{1}{2}LI^2. \tag{32-10}$$

This much energy is therefore released when the magnetic field decays.

EXAMPLE 32-7	*Quenching a Superconducting Magnet*

Loss of coolant is a danger in superconducting electromagnets. The current is suddenly left without its zero-resistance path, and energy stored in the magnetic field is rapidly released. To prevent explosive energy release, copper or silver is incorporated into the conducting system to lengthen the time constant L/R in the event of such a "quench" (Fig. 32-17). A superconducting MRI solenoid carries a 2.4-kA current and has 0.53-H inductance. In its nonsuperconducting state, the total resistance is 31 mΩ. (a) How much energy is stored in the solenoid's magnetic field? (b) If the coils suddenly lose their superconductivity, what is the initial rate of energy release?

Solution

(a) Equation 32-10 gives the magnetic energy:

$$U = \tfrac{1}{2}LI^2 = (\tfrac{1}{2})(0.53 \text{ H})(2.4\times10^3 \text{ A})^2 = 1.53 \text{ MJ}.$$

(b) When superconducting ceases, the current decays according to Equation 32-9. At the instant the decay starts the current still has its original value. Since the magnetic energy released is dissipated in the resistor, the rate of energy release is just I^2R, or

$$P = I^2R = (2.4\times10^3 \text{ A})^2(0.031 \text{ }\Omega) = 180 \text{ kW}.$$

This is a substantial power; equivalent to 1,800 100-W light bulbs burning in the space of this roughly human-size device.

FIGURE 32-17 Superconducting cables in various stages of manufacture. The hollow tubes are made of silver, and are packed with superconducting material. In the event of a coolant loss, the silver—the best metallic conductor—will carry the current and thus prevent explosive release of magnetic energy.

The following exercise explores the duration of this power surge.

EXERCISE How long is it before 90% of the magnetic energy in Example 32-7 has been dissipated?

Answer: 20 s

Some problems similar to Example 32-7: 42, 44, 47

Magnetic Energy Density

A long solenoid is a particularly simple inductor in which the magnetic field is essentially uniform. We can readily evaluate the energy density using this magnetic field, just as we found the electric field energy density using a parallel-plate capacitor.

In Example 32-3 we found that the inductance of a long solenoid of length ℓ and cross-sectional area A is $L = \mu_0 n^2 A\ell$, with n the number of turns per unit length. Equation 32-10 then gives the magnetic energy stored in the solenoid when it carries current I:

$$U = \tfrac{1}{2}LI^2 = \tfrac{1}{2}\mu_0 n^2 A\ell I^2 = \frac{1}{2\mu_0}(\mu_0 nI)^2 A\ell = \frac{B^2}{2\mu_0}A\ell,$$

where we recognized the quantity $\mu_0 nI$ as B, the magnetic field in the solenoid (Equation 30-11). The quantity $A\ell$ is the volume containing this field, so the energy per unit volume—the **magnetic energy density**—is

$$u_B = \frac{B^2}{2\mu_0}. \quad \text{(magnetic energy density)} \quad (32\text{-}11)$$

Although we derived this expression for the field of a solenoid, it is, in fact, a universal expression for the local magnetic energy density. Wherever there is a magnetic field, there is stored energy.

Compare Equation 32-11 with Equation 26-3 for the energy density in an electric field:

$$u_E = \tfrac{1}{2}\varepsilon_0 E^2.$$

The expressions for electric and magnetic energy densities are similar. Each is proportional to the *square* of the field strength, and each contains the appropriate constant. That the constant appears in the numerator in one case and the denominator in the other has no deep significance; it is merely a consequence of the way SI units are defined.

EXAMPLE 32-8   *Energy in Earth's Magnetic Field*

The magnetic field strength near Earth's surface is about 50 μT. (a) How much energy is contained in 1 cubic kilometer of this field? (b) How does this compare with the electrical energy in the same volume, given a fair-weather electric field of 100 V/m?

Solution

(a) The magnetic field is essentially constant over this volume, so the total energy is the product of the energy density with the volume V:

$$U = u_B V = \frac{B^2}{2\mu_0}V = \frac{(50\times10^{-6}\ \text{T})^2}{(2)(4\pi\times10^{-7}\ \text{N/A}^2)}(1\times10^3\ \text{m})^3$$

$$= 1\ \text{MJ}.$$

This is not a particularly large energy; a mere gallon of gasoline, for example, stores about 100 times as much.

(b) Since we're considering equal volumes, it suffices to compare energy densities. Then

$$\frac{u_B}{u_E} = \frac{B^2/2\mu_0}{\tfrac{1}{2}\varepsilon_0 E^2} = \frac{B^2}{\mu_0\varepsilon_0 E^2}$$

$$= \frac{(50\times10^{-6}\ \text{T})^2}{(4\pi\times10^{-7}\ \text{N/A}^2)(8.85\times10^{-12}\ \text{F/m})(100\ \text{V/m})^2}$$

$$= 2\times10^4$$

Thus the electrical energy is even smaller, by a factor of 20,000. The energy stored in both of Earth's electromagnetic fields is very small compared, for example, with the gravitational energy or thermal energy of an equivalent volume of air. In other systems, though, including the atmospheres of stars or lab experiments in plasma physics, magnetic energy may dominate.

EXERCISE A typical sunspot is about 50,000 km in diameter, and extends into the Sun as a cylinder about 30,000 km long. Its magnetic field is about 0.2 T. What is the magnetic energy in such a spot?

Answer: 9×10^{26} J

Some problems similar to Example 32-8: 51, 52

CHAPTER SYNOPSIS

Summary

1. The **mutual inductance** of a pair of coils is defined as the ratio of the total flux in the second coil to the current in the first:

$$M = \frac{\phi_2}{I_1}.$$

By Faraday's law, the emf in the second coil is proportional to the rate of change of current in the first:

$$\mathcal{E}_2 = -M\frac{dI_1}{dt}.$$

The same mutual inductance M describes the emf developed in the first coil as a result of changing current in the second coil.

2. A changing current in a coil or circuit results in a changing magnetic flux that gives rise to an induced electric field opposing the original change in current. A device constructed to exploit this property of **self-inductance** is called an **inductor**. The self-inductance L of an inductor is the ratio of magnetic flux to current:

$$L = \frac{\phi}{I}.$$

Faraday's law relates the emf in an inductor to the rate of change of current:

$$\mathcal{E} = -L\frac{dI}{dt}.$$

The direction of the emf is such as to oppose changes in the inductor current. Self-inductance prevents the inductor current from changing instantaneously.

3. In a circuit containing a resistor R and inductor L, changes occur exponentially with an **inductive time constant** L/R. The rising current in a series RL circuit is given by

$$I = \frac{\mathcal{E}_0}{R}(1 - e^{-Rt/L}),$$

where $\mathcal{E}_0$ is the battery emf and t the time. If the current is subsequently allowed to decay, it goes exponentially to zero:

$$I = I_0 e^{-Rt/L},$$

where t is measured from the start of the decay.

4. Electrical energy supplied to an inductor ends up stored in the inductor's magnetic field. When an inductance L carries current I, the stored magnetic energy is

$$U = \tfrac{1}{2}LI^2.$$

5. All magnetic fields, not only those of inductors, contain stored energy, with the **magnetic energy density** given by

$$u_B = \frac{B^2}{2\mu_0}.$$

Terms You Should Understand

(Pairs are closely related terms whose distinction is important; number in parentheses is chapter section where term first appears.)

mutual inductance, self-inductance (32-1, 32-2)
inductor (32-2)
back emf (32-2)
inductive time constant (32-3)
magnetic energy, magnetic energy density (32-4)

Symbols You Should Recognize

M, L (32-1, 32-2)
u_B (32-4)

Problems You Should Be Able to Solve

calculating mutual inductance for simple coil configurations (32-1)
finding induced emf in a second coil given mutual inductance and rate of change of current in the first coil (32-1)
calculating self-inductance for simple configurations (32-2)
calculating back emf given self-inductance and rate of change of current (32-2)
analyzing time-dependent behavior of RL circuits (32-3)
calculating magnetic energy (32-4)

Limitations to Keep in Mind

Real inductors, other than those made from superconductors, have resistance as well as inductance.

QUESTIONS

1. Figure 32-18 shows two pairs of identical coils in different geometrical arrangements. For which arrangement is the mutual inductance greatest? Why?

(a)   *(b)*

FIGURE 32-18 Question 1.

2. A car battery has an emf of 12 V, yet energy from the battery provides the 20,000-V spark that ignites the gasoline. How is this possible?

3. When two coils are connected in series but are physically far apart, they behave as a single inductor whose inductance is the sum of the individual inductances. Why might this not be true if they are close together?

4. You have a fixed length of wire to wind into an inductor. Will you get more inductance if you wind a short coil with large diameter, or a long coil with small diameter?

5. You have a fixed length of wire of resistance R. You want to wind the wire into a small space and use it as a resistor. How would you wind it so as to minimize its self-inductance?

6. In wiring circuits that operate at high frequencies, like TV sets or computers, it is important to avoid extraneous loops in wires. Why?

7. In a popular demonstration of induced emf, a light bulb is connected across a large inductor in an LR circuit, as shown in Fig. 32-19. When the switch is opened, the bulb flashes brightly and burns out. Why?

FIGURE 32-19 Question 7.

8. In the RL circuit of Fig. 32-8a, can the inductor emf exceed the battery emf (a) when the switch is first closed?

(b) When the switch is opened after being closed for a long time?

9. Does it take more or less than one time constant for current in an *RL* circuit to build up to half its steady-state value?

10. If you increase the resistance in an *RL* circuit, what effect does this have on the inductive time constant?

11. Speculate on what would happen if you connected an ideal battery directly across an ideal inductor, with no resistance anywhere in the circuit.

12. How could you modify the simple *RL* circuit of Fig. 32-8a to prevent dangerous voltages from developing when the switch is opened?

13. List some similarities and differences between inductors and capacitors.

14. A 1-H inductor carries 10 A, and a 10-H inductor carries 1 A. Which inductor contains more stored energy?

15. Does the energy density in a magnetic field depend on the direction of the field?

16. The field of a magnetic dipole extends to infinity. Is there an infinite amount of energy stored in the dipole field? Why or why not?

17. It takes work to push two bar magnets together with like poles facing each other. Where does this energy go?

PROBLEMS

ActivPhysics can help with these problems:
Activity 14.1

Section 32-1 Mutual Inductance

1. Two coils have a mutual inductance of 2.0 H. If current in the first coil is changing at the rate of 60 A/s, what is the emf in the second coil?

2. A 500-V emf appears in a coil when the current in an adjacent coil changes at the rate of 3.5 A/ms. What is the mutual inductance of the coils?

3. The current in one coil is given by $I = I_p \sin 2\pi ft$, where $I_p = 75$ mA, $f = 60$ Hz, and $t =$ time. Find the peak emf in a second coil if the mutual inductance between the coils is 440 mH.

4. Two coils have a mutual inductance of 580 mH. One coil is supplied with a current given by $I = 3t^2 - 2t + 4$, where I is in amperes and t in seconds. What is the induced emf in the other coil at time $t = 2.5$ s?

5. An alternating current given by $I_p \sin 2\pi ft$ is supplied to one of two coils whose mutual inductance is M. (a) Find an expression for the emf in the second coil. (b) When $I_p = 1.0$ A and $f = 60$ Hz, the peak emf in the second coil is measured at 50 V. What is the mutual inductance?

6. Find the mutual inductance of the two-coil system described in Problem 19 of Chapter 31.

7. Two long solenoids of length ℓ both have n turns per unit length. They have circular cross sections with radii R and $2R$, respectively. The smaller solenoid is mounted inside the larger one, with their axes coinciding. Find the mutual inductance of this arrangement, neglecting any nonuniformity in the magnetic field near the ends.

8. Coils A and B have mutual inductance 25 mH. At time $t = 0$ the current in coil A is zero. Subsequently a time-varying current is supplied to A, and the induced emf in coil B is given by $\mathcal{E} = 50 + 0.2t$, with $\mathcal{E}$ in V and t in ms. Find an expression for the time-varying current in coil A.

9. A rectangular loop of length ℓ and width w is located a distance a from a long, straight wire, as shown in Fig. 32-20. What is the mutual inductance of this arrangement?

FIGURE 32-20 Problem 9.

10. Two wire loops of radii a and b lie in the same plane and have a common center. Find the mutual inductance of this arrangement, assuming $b \gg a$. *Hint:* With $b \gg a$ the magnetic field will be essentially uniform over the smaller loop. See Example 30-1.

Section 32-2 Self-Inductance

11. What is the self-inductance of a solenoid 50 cm long and 4.0 cm in diameter that contains 1,000 turns of wire?

12. The current in an inductor is changing at the rate of 100 A/s, and the inductor emf is 40 V. What is its self-inductance?

13. A 2.0-A current is flowing in a 20-H inductor. A switch is opened, interrupting the current in 1.0 ms. What emf is induced in the inductor?

14. A 60-mA current is flowing in a 100-mH inductor. Over a period of 1.0 ms the current is reversed, going steadily to 60 mA in the opposite direction. What is the inductor emf during this time?

15. A cardboard tube measures 15 cm long by 2.2 cm in diameter. How many turns of wire must be wound on the full length of the tube to make a 5.8-mH inductor?

16. The current in a 2.0-H inductor is given by $I = 3t^2 + 15t + 8$, where t is in seconds and I in amperes. Find an expression for the magnitude of the inductor emf.

17. The emf in a 50-mH inductor has magnitude $|\mathcal{E}| = 0.020t$, with t in seconds and $\mathcal{E}$ in volts. At $t = 0$ the inductor current is 300 mA. (a) If the current is increasing, what will be its value at $t = 3.0$ s? (b) Repeat for the case when the current is decreasing.

18. The current in a 40-mH inductor is given by $I = I_0 e^{-bt}$, where $I_0 = 10$ A and $b = 20$ s^{-1}. What is the magnitude of the inductor emf at (a) $t = 0$, (b) $t = 25$ ms, and (c) $t = 50$ ms?

19. A 2,000-turn solenoid is 65 cm long and has cross-sectional area 30 cm^2. What rate of change of current will produce a 600-V emf in this solenoid?

20. You have a plastic rod 20 cm long and 1.5 cm in diameter. What inductance will you get if you wind the entire rod with a single layer of (a) 22-gauge (0.64-mm-diameter) and (b) 34-gauge (0.16-mm-diameter) wire? Assume adjacent turns are touching, separated only by a negligible thickness of enamel insulation.

21. The emf in a 50-mH inductor is given by $\mathcal{E} = \mathcal{E}_p \sin \omega t$, where $\mathcal{E}_p = 75$ V and $\omega = 140$ s^{-1}. What is the peak current in the inductor? (Assume the current swings symmetrically about zero.)

22. A coaxial cable consists of an inner conductor of radius a and outer conductor of radius b, as shown in Fig. 32-21. Current flows along one conductor and back along the other. Show that the inductance per unit length of the cable is
$\frac{\mu_0}{2\pi} \ln(b/a)$.

FIGURE 32-21 Problems 22, 68.

Section 32-3 Inductors in Circuits

23. Show that the inductive time constant has the units of seconds.

24. What inductance should you put in series with a 100-Ω resistor to give a time constant of 2.2 ms?

25. The current in a series RL circuit rises to 20% of its final value in 3.1 μs. If $L = 1.8$ mH, what is the resistance R?

26. The current in a series RL circuit rises to half its final value in 7.6 s. What is the time constant?

27. A 10-H inductor is wound of wire with resistance 2.0 Ω. If the inductor is connected across an ideal 12-V battery, how long will it take the current to reach 95% of its final value?

28. In a series RL circuit like Fig. 32-8a, $\mathcal{E}_0 = 45$ V, $R = 3.3$ Ω, and $L = 2.1$ H. If the current is 9.5 A, how long has the switch been closed?

29. In Fig. 32-8a, take $R = 2.5$ kΩ and $\mathcal{E}_0 = 50$ V. When the switch is closed, the current through the inductor rises to 10 mA in 30 μs. (a) What is the inductance? (b) What will be the current in the circuit after many time constants?

30. A series RL circuit like Fig. 32-8a has $\mathcal{E}_0 = 60$ V, $R = 22$ Ω, and $L = 1.5$ H. Find the rate of change of the current (a) immediately after the switch is closed and (b) 0.10 s later.

31. In Fig. 32-8a, take $R = 100$ Ω, $L = 2.0$ H, and $\mathcal{E}_0 = 12$ V. At 20 ms after the switch is closed, what are (a) the circuit current, (b) the inductor emf, (c) the resistor voltage, (d) the rate of change of the circuit current, and (e) the power dissipation in the resistor?

32. Show that a series RL circuit reaches 99% of its final current in approximately 5 time constants.

33. Resistor R_2 in Fig. 32-22 is to limit the emf that develops when the switch is opened. What should be its value in order that the inductor emf not exceed 100 V?

FIGURE 32-22 Problem 33.

34. In Fig. 32-11a take $\mathcal{E}_0 = 12$ V, $R = 2.7$ Ω, and $L = 20$ H. Initially the switch is in position B and there is no current anywhere. At $t = 0$ the switch is thrown to position A, and at $t = 10$ s it is thrown back to position B. Find the inductor current at (a) $t = 5.0$ s and (b) $t = 15$ s.

35. A 5.0-A current is flowing through a nonideal inductor with $L = 500$ mH. If the inductor is suddenly short circuited, the inductor current drops to 2.5 A in 6.9 ms. What is the resistance of the inductor?

36. In Fig. 32-23, take $\mathcal{E}_0 = 12$ V, $R_1 = 4.0$ Ω, $R_2 = 8.0$ Ω, $R_3 = 2.0$ Ω, and $L = 2.0$ H. What is the current I_2 (a) immediately after the switch is first closed and (b) a long time after the switch is closed? (c) After a long time the switch is again opened. Now what is I_2?

FIGURE 32-23 Problem 36.

37. In Fig. 32-24, take $\mathcal{E}_0 = 20$ V, $R_1 = 10$ Ω, $R_2 = 5.0$ Ω, and assume the switch has been open for a long time. (a) What is the inductor current immediately after the switch is closed? (b) What is the inductor current a long time after the switch is closed? (c) If after a long time the switch is again opened, what will be the voltage across R_1 immediately afterward?

FIGURE 32-24 Problem 37.

Section 32-4 Magnetic Energy

38. How much energy is stored in a 5.0-H inductor carrying 35 A?

39. What is the current in a 10-mH inductor when the stored energy is 50 μJ?

40. A 220-mH inductor carries 350 mA. How much energy must be supplied to the inductor in raising the current to 800 mA?

41. A 12-V battery, 5.0-Ω resistor, and 18-H inductor are connected in series and allowed to reach a steady state. (a) What is the energy stored in the inductor? (b) Once in the steady state, over what time interval is the energy dissipated in the resistor equal to that stored in the inductor?

42. A battery, switch, resistor, and inductor are connected in series. When the switch is closed the current rises to half its steady-state value in 1.0 ms. How long does it take for the magnetic energy in the inductor to rise to half its steady-state value?

43. The current in a 2.0-H inductor is decreased linearly from 5.0 A to zero over 10 ms. (a) What is the average rate at which energy is being extracted from the inductor during this time? (b) Is the instantaneous rate constant?

44. When a nonideal 1.0-H inductor is short-circuited, its magnetic energy drops to one-fourth of its original value in 3.6 s. What is its resistance?

45. The current in a 2.0-H inductor is increasing. At some instant, the current is 3.0 A and the inductor emf is 5.0 V. At what rate is the inductor's magnetic energy increasing at this instant?

46. A 500-turn solenoid is 23 cm long, 1.5 cm in diameter, and carries 65 mA. How much magnetic energy does it contain?

47. A superconducting solenoid with inductance $L = 3.5$ H carries 1.8 kA. Copper is embedded in the coils to carry the current in the event of a quench (see Example 32-7). (a) What is the magnetic energy in the solenoid? (b) What is the maximum resistance of the copper that will limit the power dissipation to 100 kW immediately after a loss of superconductivity? (c) With this resistance, how long will it take the power to drop to 50 kW?

48. Show that the quantity $B^2/2\mu_0$ has the units of energy density (J/m^3).

49. The Alcator fusion experiment at MIT has a 50-T magnetic field. What is the magnetic energy density in Alcator?

50. What is the magnetic field strength in a region where the magnetic energy density is 7.8 J/cm^3?

51. The magnetic field of a neutron star is about 10^8 T. How does the energy density in this field compare with the energy density stored in (a) gasoline and (b) pure uranium-235 (mass density 19×10^3 kg/m^3)? Consult Appendix C.

52. A loop of magnetic field arches above the Sun's surface, forming a tube approximately 10^5 km long and 10^4 km in diameter. If the magnetic field strength in the tube is 50 G, what is its magnetic energy content?

53. A single-turn loop of radius R carries current I. How does the magnetic energy density at the loop center compare with that of a long solenoid of the same radius, carrying the same current, and consisting of n turns per unit length?

54. A magnetic field is given by $\mathbf{B} = B_0(x/a)^2\hat{\mathbf{j}}$, where B_0 and a are constants. Find an expression for the magnetic energy in a cube of side a with one corner at the origin and sides extending along the coordinate axes.

55. A toroidal coil has inner radius R and a square cross section of side ℓ (Fig. 32-25). It is wound with N turns of wire, and carries a current I. Show that the magnetic energy in the toroid is given by

$$U = \frac{\mu_0 N^2 I^2 \ell}{4\pi} \ln\left(\frac{R + \ell}{R}\right).$$

FIGURE 32-25 Cross section of a toroidal coil. Also shown is a part of a volume element, in the shape of a ring of thickness dr.

56. A toroid of inner radius 1.5 m and square cross section is wound with 2,500 turns. What must be the length ℓ of its cross-sectional square if the toroid contains 80 J of magnetic energy at a current of 63 A?

Paired Problems

(Both problems in a pair involve the same principles and techniques. If you can get the first problem, you should be able to solve the second one.)

57. Two coils have mutual inductance M. The current supplied to coil A is given by $I = bt^2$. Find an expression for the magnitude of the induced emf in coil B.

58. Two coils have mutual inductance M, and a time-varying current is supplied to coil A; at time $t = 0$ that current is zero. The magnitude of the induced emf in coil B is given by $\mathcal{E} = b\sqrt{t}$. Find an expression for the current in coil A.

59. In the circuit of Fig. 32-8a, take $\mathcal{E}_0 = 5.0$ V and $R = 1.8\ \Omega$. At 2.5 s after the switch is closed, the circuit current is 250 mA. Find the inductance.

60. In the circuit of Fig. 32-8a, take $\mathcal{E}_0 = 5.0$ V and $R = 1.8\ \Omega$. At 2.5 s after the switch is closed, the inductor emf is 2.1 V. Find the inductance.

61. In Fig. 32-13a, take $\mathcal{E}_0 = 25$ V, $R_1 = 1.5\ \Omega$, and $R_2 = 4.2\ \Omega$. What is the voltage across R_2 (a) immediately after the switch is first closed and (b) a long time after the switch is closed? (c) Long after the switch is closed it is again opened. Now what is the voltage across R_2?

62. In Fig. 32-13, take $R_2 = 5R_1$. If the maximum possible value for the inductor emf in this circuit is 300 V, what is the battery emf $\mathcal{E}_0$?

63. A wire of radius R carries a current I distributed uniformly over its cross section. Find an expression for the magnetic energy per unit length in the region from R to $100R$.

64. A wire of radius R carries a current I distributed uniformly over its cross section. Find an expression for the total magnetic energy per unit length *within* the wire.

Supplementary Problems

65. (a) Use the result of Problem 55 to determine the inductance of a toroid. (b) Show that your result reduces to the inductance of a long solenoid when $R \gg \ell$.

66. Two long, flat parallel bars of width w and spacing d carry equal but opposite currents I, as shown in Fig. 32-26. (a) Use Ampère's law to find the magnetic field between the bars. Take $d \ll w$ so you can neglect fringing fields. (b) Use your result to find the magnetic energy per unit length stored between the bars. (c) Compare your result in (b) with the expression $U = \frac{1}{2}LI^2$ to find an expression for the inductance per unit length of the bars.

FIGURE 32-26 Problem 66.

67. (a) Use Equation 32-9 to write an expression for the power dissipation in the resistor as a function of time, and (b) integrate from $t = 0$ to $t = \infty$ to show that the total energy dissipated is equal to the energy initially stored in the inductor, namely, $\frac{1}{2}LI_0^2$.

68. (a) Find the magnetic energy density as a function of radial distance for the coaxial cable of Problem 22. (b) Integrate over the volume between the cable conductors to show that the total energy per unit length of the cable is

$$U = \frac{\mu_0}{4\pi}I^2\ln(b/a)\ .$$

Hint: Your volume element should be a cylindrical shell of radius r, thickness dr, and length ℓ. What is its volume dV? (c) Use the expression $U = \frac{1}{2}LI^2$ to find the inductance per unit length, and show that your result agrees with that of Problem 22.

69. An electric field and a magnetic field have the same energy density. Obtain an expression for the ratio E/B, and evaluate this ratio numerically. What are its units? Is your answer close to any of the fundamental constants listed inside the front cover?

70. Two long, straight, parallel wires are a distance d apart. The wires have radius a, where $a \ll d$. Current flows down one wire and back along the other. Find the inductance per unit length of the parallel wires. Assume the wire radius is so small that you can neglect the magnetic flux within the wires themselves.

71. The switch in the circuit of Fig. 32-27 is closed at time $t = 0$, at which instant the inductor current is zero. Write the loop and node laws for this circuit, and show that they are satisfied if the inductor current is given by $I = (\mathcal{E}_0/R_1)(1 - e^{-R_\parallel t/L})$, where $R_\parallel$ is the resistance of R_1 and R_2 were they connected in parallel.

FIGURE 32-27 Problem 71.

72. Earth's magnetic field ends abruptly on the sunward side at approximately the point where the magnetic energy density has dropped to the same value as the kinetic energy density in the solar wind. Near Earth, the solar wind contains about 5 protons and 5 electrons per cubic centimeter, and flows at 400 km/s. Treating Earth's field as that of a dipole with dipole moment 8×10^{22} J/T, estimate the distance to the point above the equator where the field ends.

33 Alternating-Current Circuits

Nearly all electric power systems use alternating current (AC) at a frequency of 50–60 Hz. Higher frequency AC is essential to radio, television, and computers.

Chapter 28 considered direct-current (DC) circuits, in which the source of electrical energy is a battery or other device whose emf does not change with time. When we turn on a circuit containing only resistors and a DC emf, current starts to flow immediately and remains steady until the circuit is turned off. Even when we add capacitance, as in Section 28-6, or inductance, as in Section 32-3, all currents and voltages eventually reach steady values.

We now turn our attention to alternating-current (AC) circuits, in which sources of electrical energy vary with time. Alternating current is used almost universally for electric power, for reasons we'll discuss in Section 33-6, so you make use of AC circuits every time you switch on a light, a toaster, a stereo, or another device plugged into your household wiring. More rapidly varying alternating currents include the audio and video signals inside stereos and TVs, and the "clock" signal that sets the basic speed of your computer.

In this chapter we'll show first how to characterize AC current and voltage, and then will look at the behavior of resistors, capacitors, and inductors in AC circuits.

33-1 ALTERNATING CURRENT

We saw in Chapter 31 how the rotation of conducting loops in electric power generators naturally leads to voltage and current that vary sinusoidally with time. In audio and video equipment, computers, and other electronic devices, AC signals may exhibit more complicated time variation. But, as we described in Section 16-6, these more complicated variations can be analyzed as superpositions of sinusoidal functions. For that reason we can limit our description of AC circuits to those where current and voltage vary sinusoidally with time.

A sinusoidal AC voltage or current is characterized by its amplitude, frequency, and phase constant—the same quantities we developed in Chapter 15 to describe simple harmonic motion. Amplitude is specified by giving the peak value (V_p, I_p) or the **root-mean-square** value (V_{rms}, I_{rms}). The rms value is an average obtained by squaring the signal, taking the time average, and then taking the square root. This procedure is used because the direct average of an AC signal is zero since it spends as much time below zero as above. Use of rms values also facilitates the calculation of power in AC circuits. For a sine wave, rms and peak values are related by

$$V_{rms} = \frac{V_p}{\sqrt{2}} \quad \text{and} \quad I_{rms} = \frac{I_p}{\sqrt{2}}, \tag{33-1}$$

as you can show in Problem 7. When we speak of 120-V household wiring, for example, we are giving the rms voltage. Figure 33-1 shows graphically the relation between rms and peak values.

In practical and engineering situations we usually describe frequency f in cycles per second, or hertz (Hz). In mathematical analysis of alternating current, it's usually more convenient to use the angular frequency ω, measured in radians per second or, equivalently, inverse seconds (s^{-1}). The relation between the two,

$$\omega = 2\pi f, \tag{33-2}$$

is the same as for rotational and simple harmonic motion, and for the same reason: a full cycle contains 2π radians.

Sometimes we are interested in the phase constant ϕ of an AC signal, which describes when the sine curve crosses zero (see Fig. 33-1). A full mathematical description of an AC voltage or current then includes its amplitude (V_p, I_p), frequency (ω), and phase constant (ϕ):

$$V = V_p \sin(\omega t + \phi_V) \quad \text{and} \quad I = I_p \sin(\omega t + \phi_I). \tag{33-3}$$

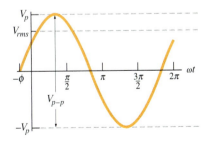

FIGURE 33-1 A sinusoidally varying AC voltage, showing peak, rms, and peak-to-peak amplitudes; the latter is just the difference between the extreme values, here equal to $2V_p$. The waveform completes a full cycle as ωt increases by 2π. The phase constant ϕ is $\pi/6$ or 30°; note that a positive phase constant shifts the curve to the left.

Here we've labeled the phase constants with subscripts V and I to indicate that voltage and current—even in the same circuit element—need not have the same phase constant. We will often take one phase constant to be zero; then the other describes the *phase difference* between the voltage and current. Phase difference, rather than the actual value of the phase constant, is the important quantity in AC circuits.

EXAMPLE 33-1	*Household Voltage*

Standard household wiring in North America supplies 120 V rms at 60 Hz. Express this voltage mathematically in the form of Equation 33-3, assuming that the voltage is rising through zero at time $t = 0$.

Solution

The rms and peak voltages are related by Equation 33-1, so

$$V_p = \sqrt{2}V_{\text{rms}} = (\sqrt{2})(120\text{ V}) = 170\text{ V}.$$

The angular frequency is 2π times the frequency in Hz, so

$$\omega = 2\pi f = (2\pi)(60\text{ Hz}) = 377\text{ s}^{-1}.$$

When $t = 0$ we want Equation 33-3 to give $V = 0$; that requires $\phi = 0$ or $\phi = \pi$. But only with $\phi = 0$ will the curve be *rising* at $t = 0$, so Equation 33-3 becomes

$$V = 170\sin(377t),$$

with V in volts and t in seconds. We will frequently take the phase constant to be zero as in this example; only when we're

comparing signals with different phase does the value of ϕ become significant.

Although household outlets in North America provide 120 V rms (or 170 V peak, as we just calculated), wires entering the house actually carry a 240-V potential difference. The full 240 V is available for major appliances such as electric dryers, stoves, and water heaters; it's split into separate 120-V circuits that supply groups of outlets and lights. In Europe, in contrast, the standard outlet voltage is about 230 V, and the frequency is 50 Hz.

EXERCISE A 1.0-kHz sinusoidal current with rms amplitude 1.5 A drives a loudspeaker in a test of a stereo system. Express this current in the form of Equation 33-3, assuming zero phase constant.

Answer: $I = 2.12\sin(6.28\times10^3 t)$, with I in A and t in s.

Some problems similar to Example 33-1: 1, 4, 5

33-2 CIRCUIT ELEMENTS IN AC CIRCUITS

Here we examine separately the AC behavior of resistors, capacitors, and inductors so we can subsequently understand what happens when we combine these elements in AC circuits.

Resistors

An ideal resistor is a device whose current and voltage are always proportional:

$$I = \frac{V}{R}.$$

$V_p \sin\omega t$ ⬡ ⚡R

FIGURE 33-2 A resistor connected across an AC generator (symbol ⊝).

Figure 33-2 shows a resistor R connected across an AC generator, making the voltage across the resistor equal to the generator voltage. The generator voltage is described by Equation 33-3, where we take the phase constant $\phi_V = 0$. Then the current is

$$I = \frac{V}{R} = \frac{V_p \sin\omega t}{R} = \frac{V_p}{R}\sin\omega t.$$

The current has the same frequency as the voltage, and, since its phase constant is also zero, the voltage and current are *in phase*—that is, they peak at the same time. The peak current is simply the peak voltage divided by the resistance: $I_p = V_p/R$. Because both voltage and current are sinusoidal, their rms values are in the same ratio as their peak values; thus $I_{\text{rms}} = V_{\text{rms}}/R$.

Capacitors

Figure 33-3 shows a capacitor connected across an AC generator. In Chapter 26, we defined a capacitor as a device in which voltage and charge are directly proportional:

$$q = CV.$$

Differentiating this relation gives

$$\frac{dq}{dt} = C\frac{dV}{dt}.$$

FIGURE 33-3 A capacitor across an AC generator.

But dq/dt is the current flowing to the capacitor plates (which we'll call the "capacitor current" even though charge doesn't actually flow through the space between the capacitor plates). So we have

$$I = C\frac{dV}{dt}.$$

The generator voltage $V_p \sin \omega t$ appears directly across the capacitor, so the capacitor voltage V is the generator voltage, and therefore

$$I = C\frac{d}{dt}(V_p \sin \omega t)$$

$$= \omega CV_p \cos \omega t = \omega CV_p \sin(\omega t + \pi/2). \qquad (33\text{-}4)$$

This equation shows clearly the phase and amplitude relations between current and voltage in a capacitor. Because the cosine curve is just a sine curve shifted left by $\pi/2$ or 90°, Equation 33-4 tells us that:

The current in a capacitor leads the voltage by 90°.

Figure 33-4 shows graphically this relation between current and voltage in a capacitor.

The term ωCV_p multiplying the cosine in Equation 33-4 is the amplitude of the current, so we can write

$$I_p = \omega CV_p,$$

or, in a form resembling Ohm's law,

$$I_p = \frac{V_p}{1/(\omega C)} = \frac{V_p}{X_C}, \qquad (33\text{-}5)$$

where we have defined $X_C = 1/\omega C$.

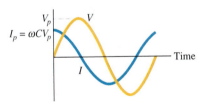

FIGURE 33-4 Current in a capacitor leads the voltage by $\pi/2$ or 90°, meaning that the current peaks *before* the voltage by one-fourth of a full cycle.

Equation 33-5 shows that the capacitor acts somewhat like a resistor of resistance $X_C = 1/\omega C$. But not quite! This "resistance" does give the relation between the peak voltage and peak current, but it doesn't tell the whole story. The capacitor also introduces a phase difference between voltage and current. This phase difference reflects a fundamental physical difference between resistors and capacitors. A resistor dissipates electrical energy as heat. A capacitor stores and releases electrical energy. Over a complete cycle, the agent turning the generator in Fig. 33-3 does no net work, while the agent turning the generator with the resistive load of Fig. 33-2 continually does work that gets dissipated as heat in the resistor. Because the quantity X_C in Equation 33-5 does not act quite like a resistance, we give it the special name **capacitive reactance**. Like resistance, reactance is measured in ohms (Ω).

Does it make sense that X_C depends on frequency? Yes—as frequency goes to zero, X_C goes to infinity. At zero frequency nothing is changing; there is no need to move charge on or off the plates, so no current flows, and the capacitor might as well be an open circuit. As frequency increases, larger currents flow to move charge on and off the capacitor plates in ever shorter times, so the capacitor looks increasingly like a short circuit. We often summarize this behavior qualitatively by saying that a capacitor at low frequencies acts like an open circuit, while at high frequencies it acts like a short circuit.

Why does the capacitor current *lead* the voltage? Because the capacitor voltage is proportional to its charge, and it takes current to move charge onto the capacitor plates. Therefore current must flow *before* the voltage can change significantly. We found the same thing with the *RC* circuit of Chapter 28; there current flowed as soon as the switch was closed, but it took time to build up the capacitor voltage.

Inductors

Figure 33-5 shows an inductor connected across an AC generator. The loop law for this circuit is

$$V_p \sin \omega t + \mathcal{E}_L = 0.$$

From the preceding chapter, we know that the inductor emf is given by $\mathcal{E}_L = -L\dfrac{dI}{dt}$, so the loop law becomes

$$V_p \sin \omega t = L\frac{dI}{dt}.$$

To obtain a relation involving the current I rather than its derivative, we integrate this equation:

$$\int V_p \sin \omega t \, dt = \int L\frac{dI}{dt} dt = \int L \, dI,$$

or

$$-\frac{V_p}{\omega} \cos \omega t = LI.$$

Here we have set the integration constants to zero because nonzero values would represent a DC emf and current that are absent in this circuit. Solving for I then gives

$$I = -\frac{V_p}{\omega L} \cos \omega t = \frac{V_p}{\omega L} \sin(\omega t - \pi/2), \tag{33-6}$$

where the last step follows because $\sin(\alpha - \pi/2) = -\cos \alpha$ for any α.

Equation 33-6 shows that the current in the inductor lags the applied voltage by $\pi/2$ or 90° (i.e., Equation 33-6 is Equation 33-3 with $\phi = -\pi/2$). Equivalently:

┃ The voltage across an inductor leads the inductor current by 90°.

Figure 33-6 plots this phase relation.

Equation 33-6 also shows that the peak current is

$$I_p = \frac{V_p}{\omega L} = \frac{V_p}{X_L}. \tag{33-7}$$

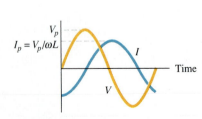

FIGURE 33-5 An inductor across an AC generator.

FIGURE 33-6 Voltage across an inductor leads the current by $\pi/2$ or 90°.

TABLE 33-1 *Phase and Amplitude Relations in Circuit Elements*

CIRCUIT ELEMENT	PEAK CURRENT/VOLTAGE	PHASE RELATION
Resistor	$I_p = \dfrac{V_p}{R}$	V, I in phase
Capacitor	$I_p = \dfrac{V_p}{X_C} = \dfrac{V_p}{1/\omega C}$	I leads V by $90°$
Inductor	$I_p = \dfrac{V_p}{X_L} = \dfrac{V_p}{\omega L}$	V leads I by $90°$

Again, this equation resembles Ohm's law, with a "resistance" $X_L = \omega L$. But as with the capacitor, no power is dissipated in the inductor. Instead, energy is alternately stored and released as the inductor's magnetic field builds up, then decays. To distinguish it from dissipative resistance, we call X_L the **inductive reactance**. Inductive reactance, too, is measured in ohms.

Does it make sense that the inductive reactance increases with increasing ω and increasing L? An inductor is a device that, through its induced back emf, opposes changes in current. The greater the inductance, the greater the opposition to changing current. And the more rapidly the current is changing, the more vigorously the inductor opposes the change, so the inductive reactance increases at high frequencies. In the extreme case of very high frequencies, an inductor looks like an open circuit. But at very low frequencies it looks more and more like a short circuit, until with direct current (zero frequency), an inductor exhibits zero reactance because there is no change in current.

Why does the inductor voltage *lead* the current? Because a changing current in an inductor induces an emf. *Before* the current can build up significantly there must first, therefore, be voltage across the inductor.

Table 33-1 summarizes the phase and amplitude relations in resistors, capacitors, and inductors.

Got It!

A capacitor and an inductor are connected across separate but identical electric generators, and the same current flows in each. If the frequency of the generators is doubled, which component will now carry the most current?

EXAMPLE 33-2	*Inductors and Capacitors*

A capacitor is connected across the 60-Hz, 120-V rms power line, and an rms current of 200 mA flows. What is the capacitance? What inductance would have to be connected across the power line for the same current to flow? Would there be anything different about the circuit containing the inductor?

Solution

The peak current and voltage are related through Equation 33-5: so

$$I_p = \frac{V_p}{1/\omega C},$$

$$C = \frac{I_p}{\omega V_p}.$$

We are given the rms voltage and current, but since only the ratio of these quantities appears in our equation, it doesn't matter whether we use rms or peak values. With $f = 60$ Hz, $\omega = 2\pi f$ or $377\ \mathrm{s}^{-1}$, so

$$C = \frac{I}{\omega V} = \frac{0.20\ \mathrm{A}}{(377\ \mathrm{s}^{-1})(120\ \mathrm{V})} = 4.4\ \mu\mathrm{F}.$$

An inductor that passes the same current must have the same reactance, so

$$\omega L = \frac{1}{\omega C},$$

or

$$L = \frac{1}{\omega^2 C} = \frac{1}{(377\ \mathrm{s}^{-1})^2(4.4\times10^{-6}\ \mathrm{F})} = 1.6\ \mathrm{H}.$$

Although the currents are the same, the two situations differ in that current leads voltage by 90° in the capacitor and lags by 90° in the inductor.

EXERCISE Inductors (called "ballast") are often used to limit the current in fluorescent lamps. In a particular lamp operating at 60 Hz, 80 V (rms) appears across a 0.53-H ballast inductor.

(a) What is the rms inductor current? (b) What capacitance could be used in place of the inductor to provide the same current?

Answers: (a) 400 mA; (b) 13 μF

Some problems similar to Example 33-2: 13, 14, 17, 20

Phasor Diagrams

Phase and amplitude relations in AC circuits may be summarized graphically in **phasor diagrams**. A phasor is an arrow whose fixed length represents the amplitude of an AC voltage or current. The phasor rotates counterclockwise about the origin with the angular frequency ω of the AC quantity. The component of the phasor on the vertical axis then represents the sinusoidally varying AC signal. Figure 33-7a shows phasors for the current and voltage in a resistor.

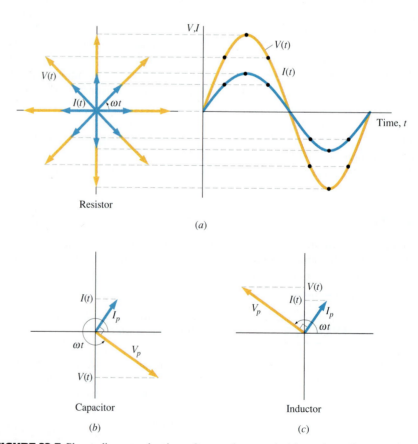

FIGURE 33-7 Phasor diagrams showing voltage and current in (*a*) a resistor, (*b*) a capacitor, and (*c*) an inductor. Lengths of phasors correspond to amplitudes V_p and I_p, while projection on the vertical axis gives the instantaneous value. Angle between voltage and current phasors gives their relative phase. In (*a*), the phasors are shown at several times; projection of the vertical components onto a plot of current and voltage versus time then shows that these quantities vary sinusoidally with time.

The lengths of the phasors are related by Ohm's law, $V_p = I_p R$. The current and voltage phasors always point in the same direction, showing that current and voltage in the resistor are in phase. For this case we show the phasors at several times in the cycle, to illustrate how, through their rotation, the phasors contain information about the time variation of the quantities they represent. Normally, however, it suffices to show phasors at one arbitrary time. We've done this in Figs. 33-7b and c for a capacitor and an inductor. The phasors are at right angles in each case, indicating the phase relations between current and voltage. Their lengths are related by the appropriate reactance, so $V_p = I_p X$. As phasors rotate, a diagram such as Fig. 33-7a would show them tracing out current and voltage graphs like those of Figs. 33-4 and 33-6. You should convince yourself that all the relationships of Table 33-1 are correctly described by the phasor diagrams of Fig. 33-7. Although phasor diagrams do not add much to our understanding of AC circuits containing only one circuit element, they will greatly simplify the analysis of more complicated circuits.

Capacitors and Inductors: A Comparison

Here and in previous chapters, we have considered separately the behavior of capacitors and inductors. Many of the properties of these devices are analogous. A capacitor opposes instantaneous changes in voltage, while an inductor opposes instantaneous changes in current. In an RC circuit with a DC emf, voltage builds up exponentially across the capacitor, with time constant RC. In the analogous RL circuit, current builds up exponentially in the inductor, with time constant L/R. A capacitor stores electrical energy given by $\frac{1}{2}CV^2$. An inductor stores magnetic energy given by $\frac{1}{2}LI^2$. A capacitor acts like an open circuit at low frequencies, an inductor like a short circuit at low frequencies. Each exhibits the opposite behavior at high frequencies.

Capacitors and inductors are complementary devices, reflecting a deeper complementarity between electric and magnetic fields. Any verbal description of a capacitor applies to an inductor if we replace the words "capacitor" with "inductor," "electric" with "magnetic," and "voltage" with "current." Table 33-2 summarizes the complementary aspects of capacitors and inductors.

TABLE 33-2 *Capacitors and Inductors*

	CAPACITOR	**INDUCTOR**
Defining relation	$C = \dfrac{q}{V}$	$L = \dfrac{\phi_B}{I}$
Defining relation, differential form	$I = C\dfrac{dV}{dt}$	$\mathcal{E} = -L\dfrac{dI}{dt}$
Opposes changes in	Voltage	Current
Energy storage	In electric field $U = \frac{1}{2}CV^2$	In magnetic field $U = \frac{1}{2}LI^2$
Behavior in low-frequency limit	Open circuit	Short circuit
Behavior in high-frequency limit	Short circuit	Open circuit
Reactance	$X_C = 1/\omega C$	$X_L = \omega L$
Phase	Current leads by 90°	Voltage leads by 90°

APPLICATION	*Loudspeaker Systems*

Loudspeakers in high-quality audio systems invariably contain two or more individual *drivers*—devices for converting electrical energy to sound—within the same enclosure (Fig. 33-8*a*). The most common form of driver includes a wire coil attached to a diaphragm and suspended in the field of a permanent magnet (Fig. 33-8*b*). Varying current in the coil then leads to a varying force that drives the diaphragm back and forth to produce sound.

Faithful reproduction of low-frequency sound requires a large driver, called a *woofer*. The woofer is large both because much of the sound power in music lies in the low-frequency range (think of a drum versus a flute!) and because the human ear is much less sensitive to low frequencies (recall Fig. 17-3). But the woofer's large size gives it a large mechanical inertia, so it can't undergo the rapid movements needed to reproduce high-frequency sound. Consequently, a much smaller driver, the *tweeter,* is used for high frequencies.

Power from an amplifier doesn't "know" about the mechanical properties of the drivers, so connecting both drivers directly to the same amplifier would result in low-frequency power being dissipated ineffectually in the tweeter and high-

frequency power in the woofer. To prevent this inefficiency, a speaker system contains a *crossover network* to "steer" power to the appropriate drivers. Figure 33-8*c* shows a simple crossover network that exploits the frequency-dependent behavior of capacitors and inductors. At low frequencies the inductor reactance ωL is low, and current flows readily through the inductor to the woofer coil. But at high frequencies the inductor reactance is high, and little high-frequency power reaches the woofer. The capacitor's behavior is the opposite: It blocks low-frequency power from reaching the tweeter, while passing high-frequency power. Many speaker systems also employ a *midrange* driver, with a capacitor and inductor in series to block power at both high- and low-frequency extremes. Example 33-4, later in this chapter, explores quantitatively the behavior of the midrange circuitry.

The circuits of Fig. 33-8*c* are examples of *filters,* widely used in electronic systems to pass preferentially a range of frequencies. For instance, bass and treble controls on audio systems adjust filter properties to boost low or high frequencies as desired. Problem 74 explores a simple filter.

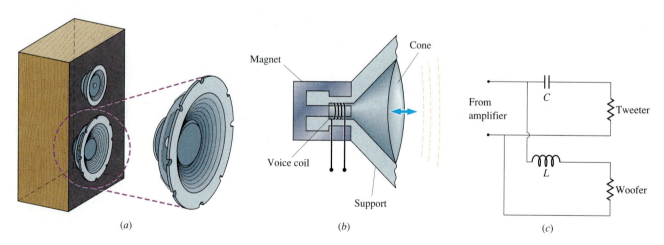

FIGURE 33-8 (*a*) A loudspeaker system, showing the woofer and tweeter drivers for low- and high-frequency sound production. (*b*) Cutaway view of a moving-coil driver. (*c*) The crossover network "steers" power at the appropriate frequencies to the woofer and tweeter. Resistances represent the coils in the two drivers.

33-3 *LC* CIRCUITS

In this section we consider circuits containing both inductors and capacitors. The properties of these circuits reflect directly the complementary nature of the two devices.

LC Oscillations

Figure 33-9 shows a circuit with a capacitor C and inductor L. Suppose the capacitor is initially charged to some voltage V_p and corresponding charge q_p, and is then connected to the inductor. What happens?

Initially, the capacitor is fully charged, while the inductor current is zero. There is electrical energy stored in the capacitor, but none in the inductor. This initial state is shown in Fig. 33-10a. Then the capacitor begins to discharge through the inductor. It cannot do so all at once, because the inductor opposes changes in current. So current in the inductor rises gradually, and with it the magnetic energy stored in the inductor. At the same time the capacitor voltage, charge, and stored electrical energy decrease. Some time later, the initial energy is divided equally between the capacitor and inductor, as in Fig. 33-10b. But the capacitor keeps discharging, eventually reaching zero charge, as in Fig. 33-10c. Now there is no voltage across the capacitor and no stored electrical energy. All the energy that was initially in the electric field of the capacitor is in the magnetic field of the inductor.

Does everything stop at this point? No, because current is flowing in the inductor. Current in an inductor cannot change abruptly, so the current keeps flowing and piles positive charge on the bottom plate of the capacitor (Fig. 33-10d). Stored electrical energy increases as the capacitor charges,

FIGURE 33-9 An *LC* circuit.

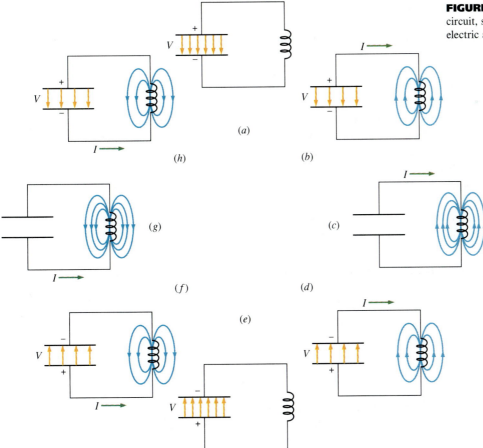

FIGURE 33-10 Oscillation in an *LC* circuit, showing energy transfer between electric and magnetic fields.

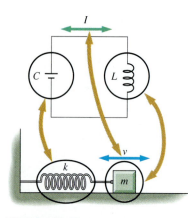

FIGURE 33-11 An LC circuit is the electrical analog of a mass-spring system. The capacitor corresponds to the spring, the inductor to the mass, and current to velocity.

TABLE 33-3 *LC Circuits and Mass-Spring Systems*

LC CIRCUIT	MASS-SPRING
Charge q	Displacement x
Current $I = dq/dt$	Velocity $v = dx/dt$
Inductance L	Mass m
Capacitance C	$1/k$ (k = spring constant)
Magnetic energy $U_B = \frac{1}{2}LI^2$	Kinetic energy $U_K = \frac{1}{2}mv^2$
Electric energy $U_E = \frac{1}{2}(1/C)q^2$	Potential energy $U = \frac{1}{2}kx^2$
Frequency $\omega = 1/\sqrt{LC}$	Frequency $\omega = \sqrt{k/m}$
Resistance	Friction

and the inductor current and stored magnetic energy decrease. Eventually (Fig. 33-10e), the capacitor is fully charged in the opposite direction from its initial state. Again all the energy is in the capacitor. Again the capacitor begins to discharge, and the process repeats, now with a counterclockwise current (Fig. 33-10f). All the energy is transferred to the inductor (Fig. 33-10g), and then back to the capacitor, which again attains its initial state (Fig. 33-10a). Provided there is no energy loss, the oscillation repeats indefinitely.

This LC oscillation should remind you of the mass-spring system we studied in Chapter 15. There, energy was transferred back and forth between kinetic energy of the mass and potential energy of the spring. Here, energy is transferred back and forth between magnetic energy of the inductor and electrical energy of the capacitor. The mass-spring system oscillates with frequency determined by the mass m and spring constant k. Similarly, the LC circuit oscillates with frequency determined by the inductance L and capacitance C. Figure 33-11 shows the corresponding elements of each system and Table 33-3 shows some analogies between mass-spring systems and LC circuits. We will develop these analogies more rigorously in the next section.

Analogies with LC circuits are so useful that engineers sometimes simulate complicated systems, such as bridges, automobile suspensions, or world energy usage, with networks of LC circuits. Such a network is called an analog computer because its behavior is analogous to that of the system under study.

Analyzing the *LC* Circuit

We described the LC circuit qualitatively in terms of transfer between electric and magnetic energy. This description suggests a way to analyze the circuit quantitatively. The total energy in the circuit is the sum of the magnetic and electric energy:

$$U = U_B + U_E = \frac{1}{2}LI^2 + \frac{1}{2}\frac{q^2}{C}.$$

The time derivative of this equation is

$$\frac{dU}{dt} = \frac{d}{dt}\left(\frac{1}{2}LI^2 + \frac{1}{2}\frac{q^2}{C}\right).$$

But since the total energy in our ideal circuit does not change, $dU/dt = 0$. Carrying out the differentiations in our expression for dU/dt, we then have

$$LI\frac{dI}{dt} + \frac{q}{C}\frac{dq}{dt} = 0. \tag{33-8}$$

Substituting $I = dq/dt$ and $dI/dt = d^2q/dt^2$ gives

$$L\frac{d^2q}{dt^2} + \frac{1}{C}q = 0. \tag{33-9}$$

Equation 33-9 is a differential equation describing the capacitor charge as a function of time. We encountered a similar equation in Chapter 15 when we studied the mass-spring system:

$$m\frac{d^2x}{dt^2} + kx = 0. \tag{15-4}$$

We found that Equation 15-4 could be satisfied by a sinusoidal function of time, with frequency given by

$$\omega = \sqrt{k/m}. \tag{15-11}$$

Equation 33-9 is identical to Equation 15-4 except that q replaces x, L replaces m, and $1/C$ replaces k. Therefore the solution of Equation 33-9 is a sinusoidal oscillation,

$$q(t) = q_p \cos \omega t, \tag{33-10}$$

whose frequency is given by Equation 15-8a with L replacing m and $1/C$ replacing k:

where
$$\omega = \frac{1}{\sqrt{LC}}. \tag{33-11}$$

Here we chose cosine rather than sine since our qualitative description (Fig. 33-10) started with the capacitor charge at its peak value. Differentiating the charge (Equation 33-10) gives the current:

$$I(t) = \frac{dq}{dt} = \frac{d}{dt}(q_p \cos \omega t) = -\omega q_p \sin \omega t. \tag{33-12}$$

All other circuit quantities follow from Equations 33-10 and 33-12. The capacitor voltage, obtained from the relation $q = CV$, is

$$V_C(t) = \frac{q}{C} = \frac{q_p}{C}\cos \omega t.$$

The electrical energy in the capacitor is, therefore,

$$U_E = \tfrac{1}{2}CV^2 = (\tfrac{1}{2}C)\left(\frac{q_p}{C}\cos \omega t\right)^2 = \frac{q_p^2}{2C}\cos^2 \omega t,$$

while the magnetic energy in the inductor is

$$U_B = \tfrac{1}{2}LI^2 = \tfrac{1}{2}L(-\omega q_p \sin \omega t)^2 = \tfrac{1}{2}L\omega^2 q_p^2 \sin^2 \omega t.$$

We can verify that our solution conserves energy by adding the electric and magnetic energies:

$$U_{\text{total}} = U_E + U_B = \frac{q_p^2}{2C}\cos^2 \omega t + \tfrac{1}{2}L\omega^2 q_p^2 \sin^2 \omega t.$$

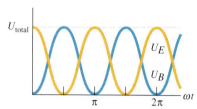

FIGURE 33-12 Electric and magnetic energies in an LC circuit. Their sum is constant.

14.2
The RLC Oscillator

But Equation 33-11 shows that $\omega^2 = 1/LC$, so we have

$$U_{total} = \frac{q_p^2}{2C}\cos^2\omega t + \tfrac{1}{2}\frac{L}{LC}q_p^2\sin^2\omega t$$

$$= \frac{q_p^2}{2C}(\cos^2\omega t + \sin^2\omega t) = \frac{q_p^2}{2C},$$

since $\cos^2\omega t + \sin^2\omega t = 1$. Thus the total energy is independent of time and is equal to the initial energy stored in the capacitor. Figure 33-12 is a plot of the electric and magnetic energies as functions of time, showing that the two always sum to a constant.

You can simulate the LC circuit we've just analyzed with ActivPhysics Activity 14.2 if you set $R = 0$ in that simulation.

Got It!

You have an LC circuit that oscillates at a typical AM radio frequency, namely 1 MHz. If you want to change the capacitor so that the circuit will now oscillate at a typical FM radio frequency of 100 MHz, should you make the capacitance larger or smaller? By what factor?

EXAMPLE 33-3	*A Piano Tuner*

You wish to make an LC circuit oscillate at 440 Hz (the note A above middle C); connected to an amplifier and loudspeaker it will produce a pure tone to be used in tuning pianos. You have available a 2.0-H inductor. What value of capacitance should you use? If you initially charge the capacitor to 5.0 V, what will be the peak charge on the capacitor and the peak current in the circuit?

Solution

The oscillation frequency is given by Equation 33-11. Solving for C gives

$$C = \frac{1}{\omega^2 L} = \frac{1}{(2\pi f)^2 L} = \frac{1}{[(2\pi)(440\text{ Hz})]^2(2.0\text{ H})} = 65.4\text{ nF}.$$

The capacitor charge and voltage are related through $C = q/V$, so

$$q_p = CV_p = (65.4\text{ nF})(5.0\text{ V}) = 327\text{ nC}.$$

Equation 33-12 then shows that the peak current is

$$I_p = \omega q_p = 2\pi f q_p = (2\pi)(440\text{ Hz})(327\text{ nC}) = 0.90\text{ mA}.$$

Problem 38 shows how the current also follows from energy considerations.

EXERCISE An FM radio transmitter requires an LC circuit that oscillates at the 89.5-MHz transmitter frequency. What should be the inductance if the circuit capacitance is 47 pF?

Answer: 67 nH

Some problems similar to Example 33-3: 27, 28, 31, 32

Resistance in LC Circuits—Damping

Real inductors, capacitors, and wires have resistance. Both this intrinsic resistance and any external resistance are represented by the resistor R in Fig. 33-13. What happens in such a resistive LC circuit?

Provided the resistance is small—small enough that only a small fraction of the energy is lost in one cycle—then our analysis of the preceding section applies. The circuit oscillates at a frequency given very nearly by Equation 33-11. But as current flows back and forth through the resistor, energy is dissipated as heat. On each successive cycle, the total energy decreases. Consequently, the amplitude of the oscillations decreases with time.

FIGURE 33-13 An RLC circuit.

We can analyze this *RLC* circuit by starting with Equation 33-8, except that now energy is being lost at the rate I^2R (the power dissipation in a resistor; recall Equation 27-9a). So instead of zero, the right side of Equation 33-8 becomes $-I^2R$, with the minus sign indicating energy loss from the circuit:

$$LI\frac{dI}{dt} + \frac{q}{C}\frac{dq}{dt} = -I^2R.$$

Writing $I = dq/dt$ as we did in the preceding section leads to

$$L\frac{d^2q}{dt^2} + R\frac{dq}{dt} + \frac{q}{C} = 0.$$

This equation is mathematically identical to Equation 15-19 for damped simple harmonic motion, showing that our analogies of Table 33-3 continue to hold when resistance is present. Using Equation 15-20, which is the solution to Equation 15-19, and the appropriate analogies from Table 33-3, we can construct the solution for our decaying *RLC* circuit:

$$q(t) = q_p e^{-Rt/2L}\cos\omega t. \qquad (33\text{-}13)$$

Other quantities show similar behavior, with oscillation amplitude decaying exponentially with time constant $2L/R$. Figure 33-14 shows an oscilloscope trace of the capacitor voltage in a circuit undergoing damped oscillations.

As the electrical resistance increases, the oscillations decay more rapidly and the frequency of oscillation decreases. Finally, when the exponential time constant $2L/R$ equals the inverse of the natural frequency given by Equation 33-11, much of the energy is lost in the time of one undamped oscillation period. This situation is termed **critical damping**, and at this value of *R* circuit quantities decay exponentially to zero, in analogy with a critically damped mechanical system (Section 15-6). For greater values of *R*, the circuit is **overdamped** and also exhibits no oscillation. In circuits that are designed to oscillate, such as radio transmitters or TV tuners, engineers obviously want to minimize damping. But in other situations, circuit oscillations would be a nuisance, and then it's important to introduce enough resistance to suppress oscillation. You can simulate the *RLC* circuit with ActivPhysics Activity 14.2.

FIGURE 33-14 An oscilloscope displays the capacitor voltage in an *RLC* circuit. Note the exponential decline in amplitude of the oscillations.

33-4 DRIVEN *RLC* CIRCUITS AND RESONANCE

Figure 33-15 shows an *RLC* circuit connected across an AC generator. The *RLC* circuit itself is analogous to a mass-spring system, so adding the generator is like adding the external driving force on the mechanical oscillator that we considered in Section 15-7. We'll call the generator frequency ω_d, the driving frequency, just as we did in Chapter 15. Pursuing the mechanical analogy, we expect the driven *RLC* circuit to exhibit resonant behavior as we discussed in Section 15-7. Such electrical resonance is crucial to the operation of radio, television, and other frequency-specific devices.

FIGURE 33-15 A series *RLC* circuit driven by an AC generator.

Resonance in the *RLC* Circuit

Suppose we vary the generator frequency ω_d in Fig. 33-15 while keeping the generator's peak voltage constant. How much current flows in the *RLC* circuit? At low frequencies the capacitor acts almost like an open circuit (its reactance $X_C = 1/\omega C$ is large), so little current flows. At high frequencies the inductor acts almost like an open circuit (its reactance $X_L = \omega L$ is large), so little current

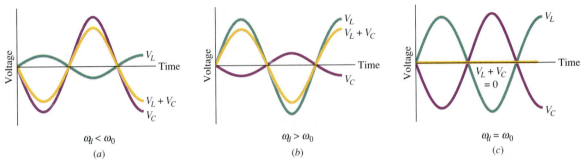

FIGURE 33-16 In a series RLC circuit, capacitor and inductor voltages are 180° out of phase at all frequencies. (*a*) At low frequencies, the voltage is greatest across the capacitor. (*b*) At high frequencies, the voltage is greatest across the inductor. (*c*) At resonance, capacitor and inductor voltages have equal amplitude, and therefore they cancel completely.

flows. At some intermediate frequency the current must be a maximum. We now show that this **resonant frequency** is in fact the undamped natural frequency $\omega_0 = 1/\sqrt{LC}$.

Figure 33-15 is a series circuit, so the *same* current flows through all the components. We know that the voltage in a capacitor lags the current by 90°, while the voltage in an inductor leads by 90°. Since the same current flows through the inductor and capacitor, the inductor and capacitor voltages are therefore 180° out of phase. This phase relation holds at *any* frequency. At low frequencies, however, the capacitor's reactance is greatest and the capacitor voltage is therefore greater than the inductor voltage (Fig. 33-16a). At high frequencies the opposite is true, with the inductor voltage being greatest (Fig. 33-16b). Since the two voltages are 180° out of phase, they tend to cancel, but at high or low frequencies Figs. 33-16a and b show that their different amplitudes mean this cancellation is not complete.

Is there some frequency, ω_0, at which the capacitor and inductor voltages exactly cancel? The peak current and voltage in these two components are related by Equations 33-5 and 33-7, respectively. Since the current is the same, comparison of these equations shows that the voltages will be the same when the capacitive reactance $1/\omega C$ is equal to the inductive reactance ωL, which gives

$$\omega_0^2 = \frac{1}{LC}. \quad \text{(resonant frequency)}$$

This is precisely Equation 33-11's condition for the undamped natural frequency.

At resonance, then, the capacitor and inductor voltages completely cancel. The voltage across the pair together is zero, and—at the resonant frequency only—the pair behave just like a wire. The circuit current at resonance is determined entirely by the resistance. At any other frequency the effects of capacitance and inductance do not cancel completely, and the current is lower.

14.3
The Driven Oscillator

Got It!

You measure the capacitor and inductor voltages in a driven RLC circuit, and find 10 V for the rms capacitor voltage and 15 V for the rms inductor voltage. Is the driving frequency above or below resonance?

Frequency Response of the *RLC* Circuit

Here we derive a general expression for the current as a function of frequency in the series *RLC* circuit, using the phasor diagrams introduced in Section 33-2. Since the same current flows through all components of the series circuit, we represent this current by a single phasor of length I_p in Fig. 33-17. Also shown are phasors for the resistor, capacitor, and inductor voltages. The resistor voltage phasor is in the same direction as the current because these two are in phase, but the capacitor and inductor voltages are at 90° relative to the current.

In analyzing circuits, we've often used the fact that the sum of the voltage differences around a circuit is zero. This statement is true *at each instant,* meaning that it applies to *instantaneous* values of the voltages. Because they have different phases, the voltages in the circuit of Fig. 33-15 peak at different times—so we can't simply sum the peak voltages around the circuit and set the result to zero. Instead, we have to sum the instantaneous voltages. We can do that by adding the voltage phasors *vectorially*—a process that accounts for both magnitude and phase. Figure 33-17*b* shows that this vector addition gives the following relation between the peak generator voltage, V_p, and the voltages across the individual components:

$$V_p^2 = V_{Rp}^2 + (V_{Lp} - V_{Cp})^2 .$$

Expressing this in terms of the current and the resistances and reactances gives

$$V_p^2 = I_p^2 R^2 + (I_p X_L - I_p X_C)^2 ,$$

or

$$I_p = \frac{V_p}{\sqrt{R^2 + (X_L - X_C)^2}} = \frac{V_p}{Z} , \qquad (33\text{-}14)$$

where we have defined

$$Z = \sqrt{R^2 + (X_L - X_C)^2} .$$

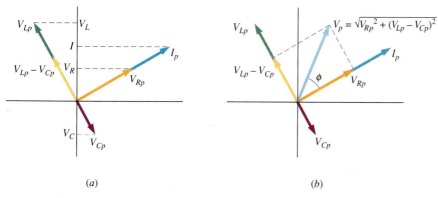

(*a*)　　　　　　　　　　　　(*b*)

FIGURE 33-17 Phasor diagrams for the driven *RLC* circuit. As usual, the length of each phasor indicates the peak value of voltage or current, while the projection on the vertical axis is the instantaneous value. As the phasors rotate with angular frequency ω_d, the instantaneous values vary sinusoidally with time. (*a*) The current in the three circuit elements is the same, and is in phase with the resistor voltage. The voltages differ, and are out of phase with each other. (*b*) Voltage phasors for the inductor, capacitor, and resistor sum vectorially to give the generator voltage V. In this case the inductor voltage exceeds the capacitor voltage, so the driving voltage V leads the current. The phase difference ϕ between V and I is given by Equation 33-16.

Equation 33-14 has the form of Ohm's law, with Z playing the role of resistance. We call Z the **impedance** of the circuit. Impedance is a generalization of resistance to include the frequency-dependent effects of capacitance and inductance. Putting in our expressions for the reactances gives

$$Z = \sqrt{R^2 + \left(\omega L - \frac{1}{\omega C}\right)^2}. \qquad (33\text{-}15)$$

In agreement with our earlier analysis, this equation shows that the circuit impedance becomes very large at high and low frequencies, and has its lowest value, R, at resonance.

Figure 33-18 is a plot of Equation 33-14, showing peak current versus frequency for several values of resistance. As we lower the resistance, the peak current at resonance rises. Although the current at other frequencies rises, too, it does so to a much lower extent than at resonance. This is because the impedance at resonance depends only on the resistance, but includes reactive effects at other frequencies. As a result, the resonance curve becomes more sharply peaked as the resistance drops. For a circuit with very low resistance, the current at resonance is dramatically different from that at even a slightly different frequency. Such a circuit, called a **high-Q** (for high-quality) circuit, does a good job of distinguishing its resonant frequency from nearby frequencies. A rigorous definition of Q can be given in terms of the width of the resonance curve (see Problem 81). High-Q circuits are important in radio and TV transmitters, where they help establish the precise broadcast frequency. At the receiving end, when you tune a simple radio, you're adjusting the variable capacitor in a high-Q LC circuit that selects the desired station from among the hodgepodge of radio signals reaching the antenna (Fig. 33-19).

Equation 33-14 relates the peak current in the RLC circuit and the voltage across it, but that equation doesn't tell the whole story. In general, current and voltage are not in phase. Figure 33-17b shows that the phase difference ϕ between the driving voltage and the circuit current is

$$\tan \phi = \frac{V_{Lp} - V_{Cp}}{V_{Rp}}.$$

Because the voltages are proportional to the reactances and resistance, this expression may be written

$$\tan \phi = \frac{X_L - X_C}{R} = \frac{\omega L - 1/\omega C}{R}. \qquad (33\text{-}16)$$

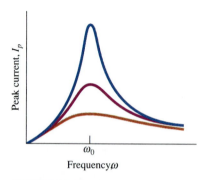

FIGURE 33-18 Resonance curves for an RLC circuit with three different resistance values. Upper curve is for half the resistance, and lower curve for twice the resistance, of the middle curve.

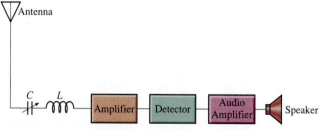

FIGURE 33-19 Diagram of a simple radio, using an LC circuit with a variable capacitor to select the desired station frequency. The signal is subsequently amplified, the audio information is extracted in the detector, and the amplified audio signal drives the loudspeaker. More sophisticated receivers often use digital circuitry in place of the LC frequency selector.

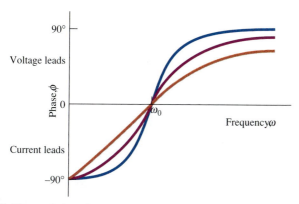

FIGURE 33-20 Phase relations for the *RLC* circuits whose resonance curves are shown in Fig. 33-18.

Does this equation make sense? At resonance, $X_L = X_C$ and the phase difference is zero. Here the effects of capacitance and inductance cancel, and the circuit behaves like a pure resistance. At frequencies below resonance, capacitive reactance is greatest and the phase difference is negative, indicating that current leads voltage—as we expect in a circuit dominated by capacitance. Above resonance $X_L > X_C$ and the phase difference is positive, indicating that voltage leads current—as we expect in a circuit dominated by inductance. At high- and low-frequency extremes, $\tan \phi$ becomes arbitrarily large and the phase differences approach 90°, as shown in Fig. 33-20.

We've defined the phase difference ϕ in Equation 33-16 as negative when the current leads. This means that if we describe voltage and current with Equation 33-3, then the arbitrary choice $\phi_V = 0$ requires $\phi_I = -\phi$. Conversely, if we choose $\phi_I = 0$, then $\phi_V = +\phi$.

Tip

Phase Matters You can't analyze an AC circuit by treating resistors, capacitors, and inductors all as "resistors" with resistances R, X_C, and X_L. Why not? Because associated with each component is a different phase relation between current and voltage. Only a phasor diagram—or mathematical analysis that includes phase relations—correctly characterizes the circuit. The phase relations in a series *RLC* circuit show up in the minus sign joining the capacitive and inductive reactance, and in the Pythagorean-like addition of the resistance and reactances in Equations 33-14 and 33-15.

EXAMPLE 33-4	*Designing a Loudspeaker System*

Current flows to the midrange speaker in a loudspeaker system through a 2.2-mH inductor and a capacitor, in series. (See *Application: Loudspeaker Systems,* earlier in this chapter.) (a) What should be the capacitance in order that a given applied voltage produces the maximum current at a frequency of 1.0 kHz? (b) What should be the speaker's resistance in order that the same voltage produces a current with half the maximum value at 600 Hz? (c) If the peak output voltage of the amplifier is 20 V, what should be the capacitor's peak voltage rating?

Solution

(a) Inductor, capacitor, and resistor comprise a series *RLC* circuit, with resonant frequency $f_0 = \omega_0/2\pi = 1/2\pi\sqrt{LC}$. Solving for C gives

$$C = \frac{1}{4\pi^2 f_0^2 L} = \frac{1}{(4\pi^2)(1.0\times10^3 \text{ Hz})^2(2.2\times10^{-3} \text{ H})} = 11.5 \,\mu\text{F} .$$

(b) Equation 33-14 gives the current in an *RLC* circuit. The denominator in this equation—the impedance $Z = \sqrt{R^2 + (X_L - X_C)^2}$—has the value R at resonance, when

$X_L = X_C$. Thus the current will have half its maximum value where the $Z = 2R$. Using $X_L = \omega L$ and $X_C = 1/\omega C$, we want R such that

$$Z = \sqrt{R^2 + \left(\omega L - \frac{1}{\omega C}\right)^2} = 2R$$

when $f = \omega/2\pi = 600$ Hz, or $\omega = 3.77 \times 10^3$ s^{-1}. Squaring and solving for R gives

$$R = \frac{1}{\sqrt{3}} \left|\omega L - \frac{1}{\omega C}\right| = 8.53 \ \Omega,$$

where we used the 11.5-μF answer to part (a) for the capacitance C. This resistance value is typical for a loudspeaker. The exercise below shows that the current also has half its maximum value at 1.7 kHz, so the midrange speaker gets at least half its maximum current in the range from about 600 to 1700 Hz.

(c) The maximum current flows at the resonant frequency, so the Ohm's-law-like Equation 33-5 shows that the maximum capacitor voltage also occurs at this frequency and is given by

$$V_{Cp} = I_p X_C = \left(\frac{V_p}{R}\right)\left(\frac{1}{\omega C}\right)$$

$$= \left(\frac{20 \ V}{8.53 \ \Omega}\right)\left(\frac{1}{(2\pi)(1000 \ \text{Hz})(11.5 \times 10^{-6} \ \text{F})}\right)$$

$$= 32 \ V \ .$$

How can this value be *greater* than the peak applied voltage? Remember that there's another source of emf in the circuit—the inductor, whose emf depends on the rate of change of current and may therefore exceed the applied voltage. In this relatively low-Q circuit the peak capacitor voltage is not too much greater than the peak applied voltage, but in high-Q circuits like those used in radio transmitters, capacitors may have to withstand voltages hundreds of times those applied to the circuit.

EXERCISE Find a second frequency where the speaker current in Example 33-4 has half its maximum value. *Hint:* Square Equation 33-15, isolate the frequency-dependent terms, take a square root, and solve a quadratic equation. Or use graphical techniques.

Answer: 1.7 kHz

Some problems similar to Example 33-4: 43, 44, 46, 69, 70, 76

33-5 POWER IN AC CIRCUITS

In Section 33-2, we noted that average power dissipation is zero in a circuit containing only a capacitor or an inductor. We can understand this physically because the reactive element alternately stores and releases energy rather than dissipating it as heat. Mathematically, we can see this from Fig. 33-21a, which

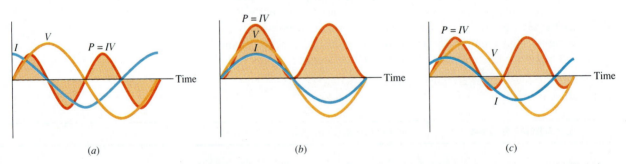

FIGURE 33-21 Current I, voltage V, and power consumption IV. (a) Current and voltage in a capacitor are out of phase by 90°. The power is alternately positive (absorbing energy from the source) and negative (returning energy to the source), and the net energy consumption (shaded area) over one cycle is zero. (b) Current and voltage are in phase in a resistor and therefore the power is always positive, meaning that the resistor is a net energy consumer. (c) Average power consumption decreases as current and voltage go out of phase.

shows the current, voltage, and instantaneous power in a capacitor. The power is the product of the current and voltage. Because these two are out of phase, the power is positive half the time, and negative half the time. When the power is positive, the capacitor absorbs energy from the source that drives the current. When the power is negative, the capacitor returns energy to the driving source. The net energy transferred to the capacitor over one cycle is $\int P\,dt$, or the area under the power-versus-time curve, and is zero in this case. Figure 33-21b, in contrast, shows current, voltage, and instantaneous power in a resistor. Since current and voltage are always in phase, the power is always positive, and the resistor always takes energy from the source. Comparison of Figs. 33-21a and b suggests that the phase difference between current and voltage is important in determining the average power consumption of an AC circuit. We can see this more clearly if we imagine slipping the current and voltage just slightly out of phase, as in Fig. 33-21c. Then there are narrow regions where the power is negative, so the average power over one cycle is slightly less than in the resistor case. As the phase difference increases, so does the time that the power is negative, until at 90° phase difference, the time-average power is zero.

We can develop a general expression for power in AC circuits by considering the time-average product of voltage and current with arbitrary phase difference ϕ:

$$\langle P \rangle = \langle [I_p \sin(\omega t + \phi)][V_p \sin \omega t] \rangle,$$

where $\langle \rangle$ indicates a time average over one cycle. Expanding the current term using a trig identity (see Appendix A) gives

$$\langle P \rangle = I_p V_p \langle (\sin^2 \omega t)(\cos \phi) + (\sin \omega t)(\cos \omega t)(\sin \phi) \rangle.$$

The average of $(\sin \omega t)(\cos \omega t)$ is zero, as we've just shown for two signals 90° out of phase. The quantity $\sin^2 \omega t$ swings from 0 to 1, and is symmetric about $\frac{1}{2}$, so its average value is $\frac{1}{2}$ recall (recall Fig. 16-16). Then we have

$$\langle P \rangle = \tfrac{1}{2} I_p V_p \cos \phi.$$

Writing the peak values as $\sqrt{2}$ times the rms values gives

$$\langle P \rangle = \tfrac{1}{2}\sqrt{2} I_{\text{rms}} \sqrt{2} V_{\text{rms}} \cos \phi = I_{\text{rms}} V_{\text{rms}} \cos \phi. \tag{33-17}$$

This equation confirms our earlier graphical arguments. When the voltage and current are in phase, the average power is just the product $I_{\text{rms}} V_{\text{rms}}$. (This, in fact, is a principal reason for using rms values: with them, the expression for average power is the same as in the DC case.) But with current and voltage out of phase, the average power is smaller; at 90° phase difference it is zero.

The factor $\cos \phi$ is called the **power factor**. A purely resistive circuit has a power factor of 1, while a circuit with only inductance and capacitance has a power factor of zero. In circuits containing resistance along with capacitance and/or inductance, the power factor generally depends on frequency; in the series *RLC* circuit, for example, it is 1 at resonance but lower at other frequencies.

Equation 33-17 shows that delivering a given average power at a fixed voltage requires greater current when the power factor is less than 1. Because energy is dissipated at the rate I^2R in the resistance of transmission lines, motor coils, and the like, electrical loads with low power factors result in wasted energy. For that reason, electric power engineers often add capacitance to inductive devices such as motors, bringing the power factor closer to 1 and thus lowering the current and therefore the resistive energy losses.

33-6 TRANSFORMERS AND POWER SUPPLIES

A **transformer** is a pair of wire coils in close proximity. We analyzed such a coil pair in Section 32-1, and showed how a change in current in one coil—which we'll call the **primary**—results in a changing magnetic flux and therefore, by Faraday's law, an emf in the other coil, or **secondary**. This emf can drive a current in circuitry connected to the secondary coil. Thus, the transformer transfers electrical energy from the primary circuit to the secondary circuit, even though there is no direct electrical connection between the two.

Practical transformers are often wound on iron cores that concentrate flux, ensuring that essentially all the magnetic flux produced by the primary coil goes through the secondary. Figure 33-22 shows a simplified diagram of a transformer, along with its circuit symbol.

The transformer in Fig. 33-22a has two turns in its primary and four in its secondary. Since the same changing flux passes through each turn of each coil, the total emf induced in the secondary must be twice that of the primary. This transformer is therefore a **step-up transformer**; it steps up the voltage by a factor of 2. Interchanging primary and secondary would give a **step-down** transformer, with the secondary voltage half that of the primary. In general, the ratio of the peak (or rms) primary voltage V_1 to the peak (or rms) secondary voltage V_2 is the same as the ratio of the numbers of turns in the two coils:

Primary   Secondary

(a)   *(b)*

FIGURE 33-22 *(a)* A transformer, consisting of two coils wound on an iron core. *(b)* Transformer circuit symbol.

$$V_2 = \frac{N_2}{N_1} V_1 . \qquad (33\text{-}18)$$

Aren't we getting something for nothing with a step-up transformer? No—a step-up transformer increases voltage but not power. In an ideal transformer, all the power supplied to the primary is transferred to the secondary; therefore,

$$I_1 V_1 = I_2 V_2 . \qquad (33\text{-}19)$$

If the voltage goes up, the current goes down, and vice versa. Real transformers have losses associated with resistance in their windings and heating of their iron cores, but good engineering holds these losses to a few per cent of the total power.

Transformers are widely used to provide voltages different from those of available sources. Most electronic circuits, for example, require a few tens of volts or less; step-down transformers bring the 120-V AC power line down to this level. Television tubes and computer monitors require tens of kV, calling for step-up transformers.

Transformers work only with alternating current, since they make use of electromagnetic induction and therefore require *changing* current for their operation. With the sinusoidally varying currents in AC power systems, the rate of change of current is also a sinusoidal function (the derivative of sine is cosine), so both the primary and secondary currents are sinusoidally varying AC. One of the main reasons for the near-universal use of AC power is the ease with which it can be transformed from one voltage level to another. To use transformers with DC—from a battery, for example—requires that the current be interrupted periodically. The car ignition coil of Example 32-2 is, in fact, a step-up transformer that works only because the car's distributor regularly interrupts the current to the coil's primary.

| **APPLICATION** | *Electric Power Distribution* |

The power loss in a resistance R carrying current I is given by I^2R. That means it's most efficient to transmit electric power at high voltage and low current. Lower voltages, on the other hand, are safer and easier to handle. How can we satisfy both these considerations in practical power systems? With transformers!

Power-plant generators operate at about 20 kV. Transformers at the power plant then step this up to several hundred kilovolts for long-distance transmission. At a city or town the voltage is dropped to several kilovolts for distribution within the municipality. Transformers reduce the voltage further for use in individual homes and businesses. The typical household voltage levels of 120 V and 240 V represent a compromise between the desire to minimize shock hazards—best met with low voltages—and the need to keep currents low. Low current allows the use of thinner wiring and also minimizes the danger of fire—but requires higher voltage to deliver a given power. Individual electrical devices within a building use transformers to meet their particular voltage requirements. Increasingly, small electrical devices such as modems, answering machines, portable stereos, and the like use external transformers that plug right into the wall; the power cord to the device then carries only low-voltage power. Figure 33-23 outlines the voltage transformations in power transmission.

FIGURE 33-23 Transformers are used throughout the power distribution network.

FIGURE 33-24 Circuit symbol for a diode, with preferred direction of current indicated.

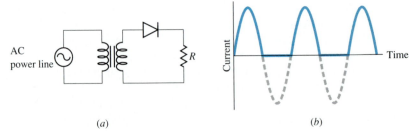

(a)   (b)

FIGURE 33-25 (a) A simple DC power supply consists of a transformer and diode, which supply current to the load resistance. (b) The diode passes current in only one direction, cutting off the negative half of each cycle (dashed gray) and giving the load current shown in blue.

DC Power Supplies

Devices such as light bulbs and electric heaters work equally well on AC or DC. But others, especially electronic circuits, require DC power. How do we get DC from the AC power line?

In Chapter 27's discussion of semiconductors, we showed how a junction between P-type and N-type semiconductors passes current in one direction but not the other. A **diode** is a PN junction designed specifically to be such a "one-way valve" for electric current. An ideal diode acts like a short circuit to current flowing in the preferred direction and like an open circuit in the opposite direction (Fig. 33-24).

Figure 33-25a shows a diode and resistor connected to the secondary of a transformer. The resistor represents the load—that is, whatever circuit we wish to supply with DC power. The transformer brings the 120-V AC power line to a level appropriate to the load. The diode passes current in only one direction, resulting in the load current shown in Fig. 33-25b.

Although the load current in Fig. 33-25 flows in one direction, it still varies drastically with time. If the load were a stereo amplifier, for example, its speakers would emit a loud hum. So we smooth, or **filter**, the output of the diode. The simplest filter is a capacitor, as shown in Fig. 33-26a. As the voltage on the left side of the diode rises, the capacitor voltage rises rapidly because of the short time constant associated with the low resistance of the diode in its preferred direction. But then the AC voltage begins to fall, and the diode "turns off." The capacitor cannot discharge from right to left through the diode but only through

(a)   (b)

FIGURE 33-26 (a) Adding a capacitor reduces variations in the load voltage and therefore in the load current. This circuit is a complete DC power supply. (b) Load voltage as a function of time.

the load resistance. If the time constant RC is long enough, the capacitor voltage will drop only slightly before the AC voltage again rises and sends a new surge of current through the diode to bring the capacitor to its maximum charge (Fig. 33-26b). By making the capacitance large enough—so large that the time constant is much longer than the period of the AC power—we can make load current and voltage arbitrarily smooth. Large capacitors are expensive, so in practice additional filters—often using transistors or integrated circuits—are added to the simple capacitive filter in critical applications. High-quality power supplies for audio equipment or electronic instrumentation achieve so-called ripple factors—the ratio of the fluctuation amplitude to the DC level—of 10^{-5} or better. More complicated diode circuits can also be used to produce signals requiring less filtering (see Problem 80).

CHAPTER SYNOPSIS

Summary

1. **Alternating current** varies with time. A sinusoidal AC signal is characterized by its peak amplitude, frequency, and phase constant; for example:

$$I = I_p \sin(\omega t + \phi).$$

The root-mean-square (rms) amplitude of a sinusoidal AC signal is the peak value divided by $\sqrt{2}$; here $I_{rms} = I_p/\sqrt{2}$.

2. In a resistor, the ratio of voltage to current is always constant, so

$$I_p = \frac{V_p}{R},$$

and the current and voltage are in phase.

3. In a capacitor the ratio of peak voltage and current is determined by the **capacitive reactance**:

$$I_p = \frac{V_p}{X_C}, \quad \text{where} \quad X_C = \frac{1}{\omega C}.$$

The current in the capacitor **leads** the voltage by $90°$.

4. In an inductor the ratio of peak voltage and current is determined by the **inductive reactance**:

$$I_p = \frac{V_p}{X_L}, \quad \text{where} \quad X_L = \omega L.$$

The current in the inductor **lags** the voltage by $90°$.

5. **Phasors** are vector-like arrows showing the amplitude and phase of AC signals, and are useful in analyzing AC circuits.

6. In an undriven LC circuit, energy oscillates between electric and magnetic forms at the **resonant frequency** $\omega_0 = 1/\sqrt{LC}$. The amplitude of the oscillation decays exponentially as energy is dissipated in the circuit resistance.

7. In a series RLC circuit, the effects of inductance and capacitance exactly cancel at the resonant frequency. At this frequency the circuit exhibits the minimum **impedance**,

and therefore passes the maximum current. At resonance the current and voltage are in phase. At lower frequencies the capacitor dominates and current leads voltage, while at higher frequencies the inductor dominates and voltage leads current. The impedance of a series RLC circuit is

$$Z = \sqrt{R^2 + (X_L - X_C)^2},$$

while the phase difference between current and voltage is given by

$$\tan \phi = \frac{X_L - X_C}{R}.$$

8. The power dissipated in an AC circuit depends on the relative effects of resistance and reactance. In a purely reactive circuit, current and voltage are $90°$ out of phase, and no power is dissipated. In a purely resistive circuit, the average power dissipation is $I_{rms} V_{rms}$. When both resistance and reactance are present, the power dissipation depends on the **power factor**, $\cos \phi$, where ϕ is the phase difference between current and voltage. In general, the time-average power consumed in an AC circuit is

$$\langle P \rangle = I_{rms} V_{rms} \cos \phi.$$

9. A **transformer** uses electromagnetic induction to transfer electric power between two circuits. The ratio of the peak or rms voltages in the transformer's two windings is the same as the ratio of the numbers of turns in the windings:

$$V_2 = \frac{N_2}{N_1} V_1,$$

while the power VI is the same in each winding of an ideal transformer.

10. DC **power supplies** use **diodes** to change alternating to direct power. Capacitors then smooth out the remaining time variation to produce the steady voltages and currents needed to power electronic equipment.

Terms You Should Understand

(Pairs are closely related terms whose distinction is important; number in parentheses is chapter section where term first appears.)

AC, DC (introduction)
peak, rms amplitudes (33-1)
frequency, angular frequency (33-1)
capacitive reactance, inductive reactance (33-2)
phasor (33-2)
resonant frequency (33-4)
impedance (33-4)
power factor (33-5)
transformer (33-6)
diode (33-6)

Symbols You Should Recognize

I_p, V_p; I_{rms}, V_{rms} (33-1) f, ω (33-1)
ϕ (33-1) X_C, X_L (33-2)
Z (33-4)

Problems You Should Be Able to Solve

calculating current and voltage in AC circuits involving individual resistors, capacitors, and inductors (33-2)
analyzing oscillating *LC* circuits (33-3)
analyzing driven *RLC* circuits (33-4)
calculating power in AC circuits (33-5)
designing simple power supplies using transformers, diodes, and capacitive filters (33-6)

Limitations to Keep in Mind

This chapter considers only sinusoidally varying AC signals. More complex time variations must first be analyzed as sums of sinusoidal terms, using techniques mentioned in Chapter 16.
Care must be taken in adding AC signals with different phases. Phasor diagrams provide a convenient way of doing this.

QUESTIONS

1. Two AC signals have the same amplitude but different frequencies. Are their rms amplitudes the same?
2. Does it make sense to talk about the phase difference between two AC signals of different frequencies? Sketch a diagram to confirm your answer.
3. What is meant by the statement "a capacitor is a DC open circuit"?
4. How can current keep flowing in an AC circuit containing a capacitor? After all, a capacitor contains a gap between two conductors, and no charge can cross this gap.
5. Why does it make sense that inductive reactance increases with frequency?
6. The same AC voltage appears across a capacitor and a resistor, and the same rms current flows in each. Is the power dissipation the same in each?
7. When a particular inductor and capacitor are connected across the same AC voltage, the current in the inductor is larger than in the capacitor. Will this be true at all frequencies?
8. An inductor and capacitor are connected in series across an AC generator, and the rms voltage across the inductor is found to be larger than that across the capacitor. Is the generator frequency above or below resonance?
9. When the capacitor voltage in an undriven *LC* circuit reaches zero, why don't the oscillations stop?
10. Why is the quantity ωL not called the resistance of an inductor?
11. Why is Equation 33-5 not a full description of the relation between voltage and current in a capacitor?
12. If you double both the capacitance and inductance in an *LC* circuit, what effect does this have on the resonant frequency?

13. In a series *RLC* circuit, the applied voltage lags the current. Is the frequency above or below resonance?
14. In a series *RLC* circuit, the applied voltage leads the current. Is the peak voltage greater across the capacitor or the inductor?
15. What does it mean to say that the capacitor in an *RLC* circuit dominates at low frequencies?
16. The voltage across two circuit elements in series is zero. Is it possible that the voltages across the individual elements are nevertheless not zero? Give an example.
17. If you measure the rms voltages across the resistor, capacitor, and inductor in a series *RLC* circuit, will they add to the rms value of the generator voltage? Reconcile your answer with the loop law. (See also Problem 47.)
18. In a fluorescent light fixture an inductor, called the ballast, is used to limit current to the lamp. Why is an inductor preferable to a resistor?
19. What is the power factor in a circuit containing only a resistor? Does this power factor change with frequency?
20. To save electrical energy, should you strive for a large or small power factor?
21. When an AC motor runs with no significant mechanical load, its power factor is very nearly zero. What must happen when the motor begins doing mechanical work?
22. A step-up transformer increases voltage, or energy per unit charge. How is this possible without violating conservation of energy?
23. A battery charger runs off the 120-V AC power line. It supplies up to 30 A to recharge a 12-V car battery, yet it can be plugged into a 15-A circuit without blowing the circuit breaker. How is this possible?

PROBLEMS

ActivPhysics can help with these problems:
Activities 14.2, 14.3

Section 33-1 Alternating Current

1. Much of Europe uses AC power at 230 V rms and 50 Hz. Express this AC voltage in the form of Equation 33-3, taking $\phi = 0$.
2. An rms voltmeter connected across the filament of a TV picture tube reads 6.3 V. What is the peak voltage across the filament?
3. An oscilloscope displays a sinusoidal signal whose peak-to-peak voltage (see Fig. 33-1) is 28 V. What is the rms voltage?
4. An industrial electric motor runs at 208 V rms and 400 Hz. What are (a) the peak voltage and (b) the angular frequency?
5. An AC current is given by $I = 495 \sin(9.43t)$, with I in milliamperes and t in milliseconds. Find (a) the rms current and (b) the frequency in Hz.
6. What are the phase constants for each of the signals shown in Fig. 33-27?

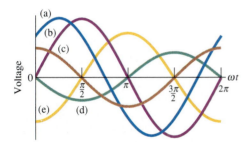

FIGURE 33-27 Problem 6.

7. The rms amplitude is defined as the square root of the average of the square of the signal. For a periodic function the time average is the integral over one period, divided by the period. For a sinusoidal voltage given by $V = V_p \sin \omega t$, show explicitly that $V_{rms} = V_p/\sqrt{2}$.
8. How are the rms and peak voltages related for the square wave shown in Fig. 33-28? See Problem 7.

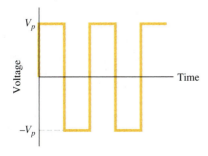

FIGURE 33-28 A square wave (Problem 8).

9. How are the rms and peak voltages related for the triangle wave in Fig. 33-29? See Problem 7.

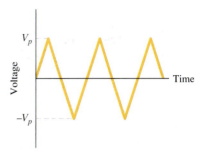

FIGURE 33-29 A triangle wave (Problem 9).

10. A 10-V rms AC signal with frequency 1.0 kHz is 90° ahead of another signal of the same frequency but with peak voltage 7.1 V. On the same graph, plot voltage versus time for both these signals. Choose scales appropriate to display one full cycle.
11. The most general expression for a sinusoidal AC current may be written either $I = I_1 \sin \omega t + I_2 \cos \omega t$ or $I = I_p \sin(\omega t + \phi)$. Find relations between I_1, I_2, I_p, and ϕ that make these expressions equivalent. (See Appendix A for trig identities.)

Section 33-2 Circuit Elements in AC Circuits

12. Show that the unit of both capacitive and inductive reactance is the ohm.
13. What is the rms current in a 1.0-μF capacitor connected across the 120-V rms, 60-Hz AC line?
14. A 470-Ω resistor, 10-μF capacitor, and 750-mH inductor are each connected across 6.3-V rms, 60-Hz AC power sources. Find the rms current in each.
15. Find the reactance of a 3.3-μF capacitor at (a) 60 Hz, (b) 1.0 kHz, and (c) 20 kHz.
16. A 15-μF capacitor carries an rms current of 1.4 A. What is the minimum safe voltage rating for the capacitor if the frequency is (a) 60 Hz or (b) 1.0 kHz?
17. A capacitor and a 1.8-kΩ resistor pass the same current when each is separately connected across a 60-Hz power line. What is the capacitance?
18. (a) A 2.2-H inductor is connected across the 120-V rms, 60-Hz power line. What is the rms inductor current? (b) Repeat if the same inductor is connected across the 230-V rms, 50-Hz power line commonly used in Europe.
19. A 50-mH inductor is connected across a 10-V rms AC generator, and an rms current of 2.0 mA flows. What is the generator frequency?
20. A 2.0-μF capacitor has a capacitive reactance of 1.0 kΩ. (a) What is the frequency of the applied voltage? (b) What inductance would give the same value for inductive reactance at this frequency? (c) How would the two reactances compare if the frequency were doubled?

21. A 1.2-μF capacitor is connected across a generator whose output is given by $V = V_p \sin 2\pi ft$, where $V_p = 22$ V, $f = 60$ Hz, and t is in seconds. (a) What is the peak current? (b) What are the magnitudes of the voltage and (c) the current at $t = 6.5$ ms?

22. A voltage $V = V_p \sin \omega t$ is applied across a capacitor. What is the minimum frequency for which the current will be zero at time $t = 20$ μs?

23. What is the maximum charge on the plates of a 16-μF capacitor connected across the 120-V rms, 60-Hz AC power line?

24. At 10 kHz an inductor has 10 times the reactance of a capacitor. At what frequency will their reactances be equal?

25. A 0.75-H inductor is in series with a fluorescent lamp, and the series combination is across the 120-V rms, 60-Hz power line. If the rms inductor voltage is 90 V, what is the rms lamp current?

26. A 2.2-nF capacitor and a capacitor of unknown capacitance are connected in parallel across a 10-V rms sine-wave generator. At 1.0 kHz, the generator supplies a total current of 3.4 mA rms. The generator frequency is then decreased until the rms current has dropped to 1.2 mA. Find (a) the unknown capacitance and (b) the lower frequency.

Section 33-3 LC Circuits

27. Find the resonant frequency of an LC circuit consisting of a 0.22-μF capacitor and a 1.7-mH inductor.

28. An LC circuit with $C = 18$ mF undergoes LC oscillations with period 2.4 s. What is the inductance?

29. You have a 2.0-mH inductor and wish to make an LC circuit whose resonant frequency spans the AM radio band (550 kHz to 1600 kHz). What range of capacitance should your variable capacitor cover?

30. The FM radio band covers the frequency range from 88 MHz to 108 MHz. If the variable capacitor in an FM receiver ranges from 10.9 pF to 16.4 pF, what inductor should be used to make an LC circuit whose resonant frequency spans the FM band?

31. You want to use an LC circuit in a timing application. The circuit is to start with the capacitor fully charged, and the voltage should drop to zero in 15 s. You have available a 25-H inductor. What capacitance should you use?

32. An LC circuit includes a 20-μF capacitor and has a period of 5.0 ms. The peak current is 25 mA. Find (a) the inductance and (b) the peak voltage.

33. An LC circuit includes a 0.025-μF capacitor and a 340-μH inductor. (a) If the peak voltage on the capacitor is 190 V, what is the peak current in the inductor? (b) How long after the voltage peak does the current peak occur?

34. If the capacitor in the preceding problem is rated at 600 V, what is the maximum inductor current that will keep the capacitor within its rating?

35. At the instant when the electric and magnetic energies are equal in the LC circuit of Problem 33, the current is 540 mA. (a) What is the instantaneous voltage? Find (b) the peak voltage, (c) the peak current, and (d) the total energy.

36. In an LC circuit, what fraction of a cycle passes before the energy in the capacitor falls to one-fourth of its peak value?

37. One-eighth of a cycle after the capacitor in an LC circuit is fully charged, what are each of the following as fractions of their peak values: (a) capacitor charge, (b) energy in the capacitor, (c) inductor current, (d) energy in the inductor?

38. Show from conservation of energy that the peak voltage and current in an LC circuit are related by $I_p = V_p \sqrt{\dfrac{C}{L}}$.

39. The 2000-μF capacitor in Fig. 33-30 is initially charged to 200 V. (a) Describe how you would manipulate switches A and B to transfer all the energy from the 2000-μF capacitor to the 500-μF capacitor. Include the times you would throw the switches. (b) What will be the voltage across the 500-μF capacitor once you've finished?

FIGURE 33-30 Problem 39.

40. A damped LC circuit consists of a 0.15-μF capacitor and a 20-mH inductor with resistance 1.6 Ω. How many cycles will the circuit oscillate before the peak voltage on the capacitor drops to half its initial value?

41. A damped RLC circuit includes a 5.0-Ω resistor and a 100-mH inductor. If half the initial energy is lost after 15 cycles, what is the capacitance?

Section 33-4 Driven RLC Circuits and Resonance

42. A series RLC circuit has $R = 75$ Ω, $L = 20$ mH, and a resonant frequency of 4.0 kHz. (a) What is the capacitance? (b) What is the impedance of the circuit at resonance? (c) What is the impedance at 3.0 kHz?

43. If the speaker system of Example 33-4 is driven by a 10-V peak, 1.0-kHz sine wave, what will be the peak voltage across the capacitor?

44. An RLC circuit includes a 1.5-H inductor and a 250-μF capacitor rated at 400 V. The circuit is connected across a sine-wave generator whose peak voltage is 32 V. What minimum resistance must the circuit have to ensure that the capacitor voltage does not exceed its rated value when the generator is at the resonant frequency?

45. TV channel 2 occupies the frequency range from 54 MHz to 60 MHz. A series *RLC* tuning circuit in a TV receiver includes an 18-pF capacitor and resonates in the middle of the channel 2 band. (a) What is the inductance? (b) To let the whole signal in, the resonance curve must be broad enough that the current throughout the band be no less than 70% of the current at the resonant frequency. What constraint does this place on the circuit resistance?

46. An *RLC* circuit includes a 10-Ω resistor, 1.5-μF capacitor, and 50-mH inductor. The capacitor is rated at 1200 V. The circuit is driven by an AC source whose peak voltage is 100 V. (a) What would be the peak capacitor voltage at resonance? (b) Make a graph of the peak capacitor voltage as a function of frequency, and from it determine the frequency range that should be avoided for the capacitor to stay within its voltage rating.

47. A 2.0-H inductor and a 3.5-μF capacitor are connected in series with a 50-Ω resistor, and the combination is connected to an AC generator supplying 24 V peak at 60 Hz. (a) At the instant the generator voltage is at its peak, what is the instantaneous voltage across each circuit element? Show explicitly that these sum to the generator voltage. (b) If rms voltmeters are connected across each of the three components, what will they read? Do their readings sum to the rms generator voltage? Does this contradict the loop law?

48. Show that the impedance of an *RLC* circuit driven at frequency ω_d can be written

$$Z = \sqrt{R^2 + \omega_d^2 L^2 (1 - \omega_0^2/\omega_d^2)^2} \, ,$$

where ω_0 is the resonant frequency.

49. Figure 33-31 shows the phasor diagram for an *RLC* circuit. (a) Is the driving frequency above or below resonance? (b) Complete the diagram by adding the applied voltage phasor, and from your diagram determine the phase difference between applied voltage and current.

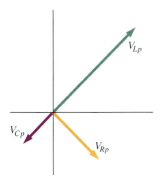

FIGURE 33-31 Problem 49.

50. An AC voltage of fixed amplitude is applied across a series *RLC* circuit. The component values are such that the cur-

rent at half the resonant frequency is half the current at resonance. (a) Show that the current at twice the resonant frequency is also half that at resonance. (b) Sketch phasor diagrams for both off-resonance cases.

51. For the circuit of Problem 46, find the phase relation between applied voltage and current at frequencies of (a) 550 Hz and (b) 700 Hz.

52. For the circuit of Problem 46, find two frequencies at which the voltage and current will be 60° out of phase. Which leads in each case?

Section 33-5 Power in AC Circuits

53. An electric drill draws 4.6 A rms at 120 V rms. If the current lags the voltage by 25°, what is the drill's power consumption?

54. A series *RLC* circuit has resistance 100 Ω and impedance 300 Ω. (a) What is the power factor? (b) If the rms current is 200 mA, what is the power dissipation?

55. A series *RLC* circuit has power factor 0.80 and impedance 100 Ω at 60 Hz. (a) What is the circuit resistance? (b) If the inductance is 0.10 H, what is the resonant frequency?

56. An *RLC* circuit with $R = 10$ Ω, $C = 2.0$ μF, and $L = 500$ mH is connected to an AC generator supplying 80 V rms. (a) Find the power factor when the generator frequency is half the resonant frequency. Find the power dissipation (b) at half the resonant frequency and (c) at the resonant frequency.

57. A power plant produces 60-Hz power at 365 kV rms and 200 A rms. The plant is connected to a small city by a transmission line with total resistance 100 Ω. What fraction of the power is lost in transmission if the city's power factor is (a) 1.0 or (b) 0.60? (c) Is it more economical for the power company if the load has a large power factor or a small one? Explain.

Section 33-6 Transformers and Power Supplies

58. A rural power line carries 2.3 A rms at 4000 V. A step-down transformer reduces this to 235 V rms to supply a house. Find (a) the turns ratio of the transformer and (b) the current in the 235-V line to the house.

59. A transformer steps up the 120-V rms AC power line voltage to 23 kV rms for a TV picture tube. If the rms current in the primary is 1.0 A, and the transformer is 95% efficient, what is the secondary current?

60. A car battery charger runs off the 120-V rms AC power line, and supplies 10 A DC at 14 V. (a) If the charger is 80% efficient in converting the line power to the DC power it supplies to the battery, how much current does it draw from the AC line? (b) If electricity costs 9.5¢/kWh, how much does it cost to run the charger for 10 hours? Assume the power factor is 1.

61. The transformer in the power supply of Fig. 33-26a has an output voltage of 6.3 V rms at 60 Hz, and the capacitance is 1200 μF. (a) With an infinite load resistance, what would be the output voltage of the power supply? (b) What is the minimum load resistance for which the output would not drop more than 1% from this value? Assume that the discharge time in Fig. 33-26b is essentially a full cycle.

62. A power supply like that in Fig. 33-26a is supposed to deliver 22 V DC at a maximum current of 150 mA. The transformer's peak output voltage is appropriate to charge the capacitor to a full 22 V, and the primary is supplied with 60 Hz AC. What value of capacitance will ensure that the output voltage stays within 3% of the rated 22 V?

Paired Problems

(Both problems in a pair involve the same principles and techniques. If you can get the first problem, you should be able to solve the second one.)

63. A sine-wave generator delivers a signal whose peak voltage is independent of frequency. Two identical capacitors are connected in parallel across the generator, and the generator supplies a peak current I_p at frequency f_1. The capacitors are then connected in series across the generator. To what frequency should the generator be tuned to bring the current back to I_p?

64. A 1.0-μF capacitor and a 2.0-μF capacitor are connected in parallel across a sine-wave generator, and the generator supplies a total rms current of 25 mA at 1.0 kHz. Assuming the generator voltage is independent of frequency, at what frequency will it supply the same current when the capacitors are in series?

65. The peak current in an oscillating LC circuit is 850 mA. If $L = 1.2$ mH and $C = 5.0$ μF, what is the peak voltage?

66. An LC circuit with $C = 470$ pF is oscillating at 7.3 MHz. If the peak voltage is 95 V, what is the peak current?

67. An RLC circuit includes a 3.3-μF capacitor and a 27-mH inductor. The capacitor is charged to 35 V, and the circuit begins oscillating. Ten full cycles later the capacitor voltage peaks at 28 V. What is the resistance?

68. An RLC circuit with $R = 1.2$ Ω and $C = 10$ μF loses 2% of its initial energy in one oscillation cycle. What is its inductance?

69. A series RLC circuit with $R = 5.5$ Ω, $L = 180$ mH, and $C = 0.12$ μF is connected across a sine-wave generator. If the inductor can handle a maximum current of 1.5 A, what is the maximum safe value for the generator's peak output voltage when it is tuned to resonance?

70. A series RLC circuit with $R = 1.3$ Ω, $L = 27$ mH, and $C = 0.33$ μF is connected across a sine-wave generator. If the capacitor's peak voltage rating is 600 V, what is the maximum safe value for the generator's peak output voltage when it is tuned to resonance?

Supplementary Problems

71. Two capacitors are connected in parallel across a 10-V rms, 10-kHz sine-wave generator, and the generator supplies a total rms current of 30 mA. When the capacitors are rewired in series, the rms generator current drops to 5.5 mA. Find the values of the two capacitances.

72. An LC circuit starts at $t = 0$ with its 2000-μF capacitor at its peak voltage of 14 V. At $t = 35$ ms the voltage has dropped to 8.5 V. (a) What will be the peak current? (b) When will the peak current occur?

73. An undriven RLC circuit with inductance L and resistance R starts oscillating with total energy U_0. After N cycles the energy is U_1. Find an expression for the capacitance, assuming the circuit is not heavily damped.

74. Figure 33-32 shows a **low-pass filter**. When an alternating voltage is applied at the V_{in} terminals, the output voltage V_{out} depends on frequency. (a) Show that $V_{out} = V_{in}/\sqrt{1 + (RC\omega)^2}$, where the voltages are either peak or rms values (there is also a phase difference). (b) At what frequency is the output voltage down from the input voltage by a factor of $1/\sqrt{2}$? (This is called the *half-power point* since the power—proportional to V^2—is down by a factor of $\frac{1}{2}$.) *Hint:* You can repeat the phasor analysis of Section 33-4, but without the inductor. Or you can start from Equation 33-14, with X_L set to zero.

FIGURE 33-32 Problem 74.

75. You wish to make a "black box" with two input connections and two output connections, as shown in Fig. 33-33. When you put a 12-V rms, 60-Hz sine wave across the input, a 6.0-V, 60-Hz signal should appear at the output, with the output voltage leading the input voltage by 45°. Design a circuit that could be used in the "black box."

FIGURE 33-33 Problem 75.

76. A series RLC circuit with $R = 47$ Ω, $L = 250$ mH, and $C = 4.0$ μF is connected across a sine-wave generator whose peak output voltage is independent of frequency.

Find the frequency range over which the peak current will exceed half its value at resonance. *Hint:* You can solve this problem graphically or, with appropriate algebraic manipulations, using quadratic equations.

77. A sine-wave generator with peak output voltage of 20 V is applied across a series *RLC* circuit. At the resonant frequency of 2.0 kHz the peak current is 50 mA, while at 1.0 kHz it is 15 mA. Find *R*, *L*, and *C*.

78. Use phasor analysis to show that the parallel *RLC* circuit of Fig. 33-34 has impedance $Z = \left[\dfrac{1}{R^2} + \left(\dfrac{1}{X_L} - \dfrac{1}{X_C} \right)^2 \right]^{-1/2}$.

FIGURE 33-34 Problem 78.

79. A 2.5-H inductor is connected across a 1500-μF capacitor. A 5.0-kg mass is connected to a spring. What should be the spring constant if the mechanical and electrical systems have the same resonant frequency?

80. Figure 33-35 shows a diode circuit called a *full-wave bridge,* whose output requires less filtering than the single-diode circuit of Fig. 33-25. (a) Sketch a graph of the resis-

FIGURE 33-35 A full-wave diode bridge (Problem 80).

tor current as a function of time, covering two full cycles of the AC generator, and (b) explain why less filtering is needed.

81. For *RLC* circuits in which the resistance is not too large, the *Q* factor may be defined as the ratio of the resonant frequency to the difference between the two frequencies where the power dissipated in the circuit is half that dissipated at resonance. Show, using suitable approximations, that this definition leads to the expression $Q = \omega_0 L / R$, with ω_0 the resonant frequency.

82. Consider a series circuit containing an AC generator, a resistor, and a capacitor. Construct a phasor diagram, and derive expressions for the circuit impedance and the phase angle between the applied voltage and the current. Show that the current always leads the voltage.

83. Consider a series circuit containing an AC generator, a resistor, and an inductor. Construct a phasor diagram, and derive expressions for the circuit impedance and the phase angle between the applied voltage and the current. Show that the voltage always leads the current.

34 Maxwell's Equations and Electromagnetic Waves

Electromagnetic waves include light and the radio waves essential to modern communications. This antenna communicates with orbiting satellites.

At this point we have introduced the four fundamental laws of electromagnetism—Gauss's law for electricity, Gauss's law for magnetism, Ampère's law, and Faraday's law—that govern the behavior of electric and magnetic fields throughout the universe. We have seen how these laws describe the electric and magnetic interactions that make matter act as it does and have explored many practical devices that exploit the laws of electromagnetism. Here we extend the fundamental laws to their most general form and show how they predict the existence of electromagnetic waves. Those waves include the light, radio, TV, microwaves, X-rays, ultraviolet, and infrared with which we see, communicate, cook our food, diagnose our diseases, learn about the universe beyond Earth, and perform a myriad of other tasks from the mundane to the profound.

Electromagnetic waves are certainly among the most important manifesta-tions of electromagnetism. After showing how electromagnetic waves arise from fundamental principles, we'll take a brief look at some of their properties. The next three chapters, on optics, then examine in detail the behavior of the electro-magnetic waves we call visible light.

34-1 THE FOUR LAWS OF ELECTROMAGNETISM

Table 34-1 summarizes the four laws as we introduced them in earlier chapters. As you look at these four laws together, you can't help noticing some strong similarities. On the left-hand sides of the equations, the two laws of Gauss are identical but for the interchanging of **E** and **B**. Similarly, the laws of Ampère and Faraday have left-hand sides that differ only in the interchange of **E** and **B**.

On the right-hand sides, things are more different. Gauss's law for electricity involves the charge enclosed by the surface of integration, while Gauss's law for magnetism has zero on the right-hand side. Actually, though, these laws are similar. Since we have no experimental evidence for the existence of isolated magnetic charge, the enclosed magnetic charge on the right-hand side of Gauss's law for magnetism is zero. If and when magnetic monopoles are discovered, then the right-hand side of Gauss's law for magnetism would be nonzero for any surface enclosing net magnetic charge.

The right-hand sides of Ampère's and Faraday's laws are distinctly different. In Ampère's law we find the current—the flow of electric charge—as a source of magnetic field. We can understand the absence of a similar term in Faraday's law because we have never observed a flow of magnetic monopoles. If we had such a flow, then we would expect this magnetic current to produce an electric field.

Two of the differences among the laws of electromagnetism would be resolved if we knew for sure that magnetic monopoles exist. That current theories of elementary particles suggest the existence of monopoles is a tantalizing hint that there may be a fuller symmetry between electric and magnetic phenomena. The search for symmetry, based not on logic or experimental evidence but on an intuitive sense that nature should be simple, has motivated some of the most important discoveries in physics. We'll see next how symmetry considerations help lead us, finally, to the complete set of fundamental laws of electromagnetism.

TABLE 34-1 *Four Laws of Electromagnetism (still incomplete)*

LAW	MATHEMATICAL STATEMENT	WHAT IT SAYS
Gauss for **E**	$\oint \mathbf{E} \cdot d\mathbf{A} = \dfrac{q}{\varepsilon_0}$	How charges produce electric field; field lines begin and end on charges
Gauss for **B**	$\oint \mathbf{B} \cdot d\mathbf{A} = 0$	No magnetic charge; magnetic field lines do not begin or end
Faraday	$\oint \mathbf{E} \cdot d\boldsymbol{\ell} = -\dfrac{d\phi_B}{dt}$	Changing magnetic flux produces electric field
Ampère (steady currents only)	$\oint \mathbf{B} \cdot d\boldsymbol{\ell} = \mu_0 I$	Electric current produces magnetic field

34-2 AMBIGUITY IN AMPÈRE'S LAW

There remains one difference between the equations of electricity and magnetism that would not be resolved by the discovery of magnetic monopoles. On the right-hand side of Faraday's law we find the term $d\phi_B/dt$ that describes changing magnetic flux as a source of electric field. We find no comparable term in Ampère's law. Are we missing something? Is it possible that a changing electric flux produces a magnetic field? So far, we've given no experimental evidence for such a conjecture. It's suggested only by our sense that the near symmetry between electricity and magnetism is not a coincidence. If a changing electric flux did produce a magnetic field, just as a changing magnetic flux produces an electric field, then we would expect a term $d\phi_E/dt$ on the right-hand side of Ampère's law.

When we first stated Ampère's law in Chapter 30, we emphasized that it applied only to *steady* currents. Why that restriction? Figure 34-1 shows a situation in which current is *not* steady, namely the *RC* circuit we discussed in Chapter 28. Initially current flows in this circuit to carry charge onto the plates of the capacitor. But the current gradually decreases to zero as the capacitor becomes fully charged. While it's flowing, the current should produce a magnetic field. Let's try to use Ampère's law to calculate that field.

Ampère's law says that the line integral of the magnetic field around any closed loop is proportional to the encircled current:

$$\oint \mathbf{B} \cdot d\boldsymbol{\ell} = \mu_0 I.$$

By the encircled current, we mean the current through *any open surface* bounded by the loop. Figure 34-2 shows four such surfaces. The same current flows through surfaces 1, 2, and 4, because each of them is pierced by a current-carrying wire. But no current pierces surface 3, because the right end of that surface lies in the insulating gap between the capacitor plates. Charge flows onto the plates of the capacitor, but it doesn't flow through that gap. So for surfaces 1, 2, and 4, the right-hand side of Ampère's law is $\mu_0 I$, but for surface 3 it's zero. Thus Ampère's law is ambiguous in this case of a changing current.

This ambiguity does not arise with steady currents. In an *RC* circuit the steady-state current is everywhere zero, and thus the right-hand side of Ampère's law is zero for *any* surface. It's only when currents are changing with time that there may be situations like that of Fig. 34-2 where Ampère's law becomes ambiguous. That's why the form of Ampère's law we have used until now is strictly valid only for steady currents.

FIGURE 34-1 A charging *RC* circuit, showing some magnetic field lines surrounding the current-carrying wire.

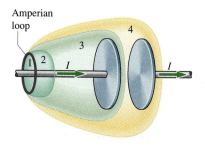

Amperian loop

FIGURE 34-2 Ampère's law relates the line integral around an amperian loop to the current through *any open surface* bounded by that loop. Figure 34-2 shows four such surfaces, all bounded by the same circular loop. Surface 1 is the flat, circular disk bounded by the loop. The others are all like soap bubbles in the process of being blown after dipping the loop into a soap solution; they're open at the left end, so if current does pass through a surface, it does so at the right end only. Current in the wires passes through surfaces 1, 2, and 4, but not 3, so Ampère's law is ambiguous.

Can we salvage Ampère's law, extending it to cover unsteady currents without affecting its validity in the steady case? Symmetry between Ampère's and Faraday's laws has already suggested that a changing electric flux might produce a magnetic field. Between the plates of a charging capacitor there is an electric field whose magnitude is increasing (Fig. 34-3). That means there is a changing electric flux through surface 3 of Fig. 34-2.

It was the Scottish physicist James Clerk Maxwell who, about 1860, suggested that a changing electric flux should give rise to a magnetic field. Since that time many experiments, including direct measurement of the magnetic field inside a charging capacitor, have confirmed Maxwell's remarkable insight. Maxwell quantified his idea by introducing a new term into Ampère's law:

FIGURE 34-3 There is a changing electric field in the charging capacitor and, therefore, a changing electric flux through surface 3 of Fig. 34-2.

$$\oint \mathbf{B} \cdot d\boldsymbol{\ell} = \mu_0 I + \mu_0 \varepsilon_0 \frac{d\phi_E}{dt}. \qquad (34\text{-}1)$$

Now there's no ambiguity. The integral is taken around any loop, I is the current through *any* surface bounded by the loop, and ϕ_E is the electric flux through that surface. With our charging capacitor, Equation 34-1 gives the same magnetic field no matter which surface we choose. For surfaces 1, 2, and 4 of Fig. 34-2, the current I makes all the contribution to the right-hand side of the equation. For surface 3, through which no current flows, the right-hand side of Equation 34-1 comes entirely from the changing electric flux. You can readily verify that the term $\varepsilon_0 d\phi_E/dt$ has the units of current, and that, for the charging capacitor, this term is numerically equal to the current I (see Problem 3).

Although changing electric flux is not the same thing as electric current, it has the same effect as a current in producing a magnetic field. For this reason Maxwell called the term $\varepsilon_0 d\phi_E/dt$ the **displacement current**. The word "displacement" has historical roots that don't provide much physical insight. But the word "current" is meaningful in that the effect of displacement current is indistinguishable from that of real current in producing magnetic fields. Although we developed the idea of displacement current using the specific example of a charging capacitor, we emphasize that Ampère's law in its now complete form (Equation 34-1) is truly universal: *any* changing electric flux results in a magnetic field. That fact will prove crucial in establishing the existence of electromagnetic waves.

EXAMPLE 34-1	*Displacement Current Produces Magnetic Field*

A parallel-plate capacitor with circular plates a distance d apart is charged through long, straight wires as shown in Fig. 34-4. The potential difference between the plates is increasing at the rate dV/dt. Find an expression for the magnetic field as a function of position between the plates.

Solution

With long, straight feed wires, the situation has cylindrical symmetry. The only magnetic field with this symmetry has

FIGURE 34-4 A circular capacitor (Example 34-1).

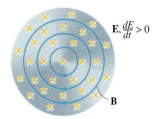

FIGURE 34-5 Electric and magnetic fields between the circular capacitor plates. The electric field strength is increasing, so the displacement current is in the same direction as the electric field. Pointing the right thumb in this direction then shows that the magnetic field circles clockwise.

circular field lines and a magnitude that depends only on the radial distance r from the symmetry axis, as shown in Fig. 34-5. A magnetic field line within the capacitor encircles no conduction current—no flow of charge—but it does encircle a changing electric field and therefore a displacement current. If the field line has radius r, the encircled electric flux is

$$\phi_E = \int \mathbf{E} \cdot d\mathbf{A} = \pi r^2 E = \pi r^2 \frac{V}{d},$$

where the uniformity of the field allows us to calculate the field as the ratio of potential difference to plate spacing and the flux as a simple product of field and area. Then the displacement current is

$$I_D = \varepsilon_0 \frac{d\phi_E}{dt} = \frac{\varepsilon_0 \pi r^2}{d} \frac{dV}{dt}.$$

With cylindrical symmetry, the line integral on the left-hand side of Ampère's law becomes

$$\oint \mathbf{B} \cdot d\boldsymbol{\ell} = 2\pi r B.$$

Equating this quantity to μ_0 times the encircled displacement current gives

$$2\pi r B = \frac{\mu_0 \varepsilon_0 \pi r^2}{d} \frac{dV}{dt},$$

so

$$B = \frac{\mu_0 \varepsilon_0 r}{2d} \frac{dV}{dt}.$$

This field, with its magnitude increasing linearly with r, should remind you of the magnetic field inside a cylindrical wire (see Example 30-4). Problem 4 extends this calculation to the field outside the capacitor.

We can find the direction of the induced magnetic field just as we did for the fields of ordinary conduction currents: Point your right thumb in the direction of the current and your right fingers curl in the direction of the magnetic field. But which way does the displacement current go? In this example the electric field strength is increasing, so $d\phi_E/dt$ is positive, and the displacement current is in the direction of the electric field (see Fig. 34-5). If the electric field strength were decreasing, the displacement current would be opposite the field.

The induced magnetic field in a practical capacitor is minuscule, as the following exercise illustrates. We'll soon see, however, that the significance of displacement-current-induced magnetic fields is vastly greater than in this simple example.

EXERCISE In 1984 D. F. Bartlett and T. R. Corle of the University of Colorado first measured the magnetic field inside a charging capacitor using a sensitive magnetometer called a superconducting quantum interference detector (SQUID). They used a capacitor with circular plates spaced 1.22 cm, connected across a 340-V peak sine-wave generator operating at 1.25 kHz. What was the peak magnetic field strength 3.0 cm from the capacitor axis?

Answer: 3.65×10^{-11} T, less than one millionth of Earth's magnetic field

Some problems similar to Example 34-1: 4–6

34-3 MAXWELL'S EQUATIONS

It was Maxwell's genius to recognize that Ampère's law should be modified to reflect the symmetry suggested by Faraday's law. The consequences of Maxwell's discovery go far beyond anything he could have imagined. To honor Maxwell, the four complete laws of electromagnetism are given the collective name **Maxwell's equations**. This full and complete set of equations, first published in 1864, governs the behavior of electric and magnetic fields everywhere. Table 34-2 summarizes Maxwell's equations.

These four simple, compact statements are all it takes to describe classical electromagnetic phenomena. Everything electric or magnetic that we have considered and will consider—from polar molecules to electric current; resistors, capacitors, inductors, and transistors; solar flares and cell membranes; electric generators and thunderstorms; computers and TV sets; the northern lights and fusion reactors—all these can be described using Maxwell's

TABLE 34-2 *Maxwell's Equations*

LAW	MATHEMATICAL STATEMENT	WHAT IT SAYS	EQUATION NUMBER
Gauss for **E**	$\oint \mathbf{E} \cdot d\mathbf{A} = \dfrac{q}{\varepsilon_0}$	How charges produce electric field; field lines begin and end on charges	(34-2)
Gauss for **B**	$\oint \mathbf{B} \cdot d\mathbf{A} = 0$	No magnetic charge; magnetic field lines do not begin or end	(34-3)
Faraday	$\oint \mathbf{E} \cdot d\boldsymbol{\ell} = -\dfrac{d\phi_B}{dt}$	Changing magnetic flux produces electric field	(34-4)
Ampère	$\oint \mathbf{B} \cdot d\boldsymbol{\ell} = \mu_0 I + \mu_0 \varepsilon_0 \dfrac{d\phi_E}{dt}$	Electric current and changing electric flux produce magnetic field	(34-5)

equations. And despite this wealth of phenomena, we have yet to discuss a most important manifestation of electromagnetism, namely electromagnetic waves. We've put off waves until now because they, unlike electromagnetic phenomena we've already introduced, depend crucially on Maxwell's extension of Ampère's law. It's easiest to understand electromagnetic waves when they propagate through empty space, so before beginning our study of waves we'll first simplify Maxwell's equations for the case of a vacuum.

Maxwell's Equations in Vacuum

Consider Maxwell's equations in a region free of any matter—in vacuum. We've learned enough about electromagnetism to anticipate that the fields themselves will still be able to interact, change, and carry energy even in the absence of matter. To express Maxwell's equations in vacuum, we simply remove all reference to matter—that is, to electric charge:

$$\oint \mathbf{E} \cdot d\mathbf{A} = 0 \qquad (\text{Gauss, } \mathbf{E}) \tag{34-6}$$

$$\oint \mathbf{B} \cdot d\mathbf{A} = 0 \qquad (\text{Gauss, } \mathbf{B}) \tag{34-7}$$

$$\oint \mathbf{E} \cdot d\boldsymbol{\ell} = -\frac{d\phi_B}{dt} \qquad (\text{Faraday}) \tag{34-8}$$

$$\oint \mathbf{B} \cdot d\boldsymbol{\ell} = \mu_0 \varepsilon_0 \frac{d\phi_E}{dt}. \qquad (\text{Ampère}) \tag{34-9}$$

In vacuum the symmetry is complete, with electric and magnetic fields appearing in the equations on an equal footing. With charge and current absent in a vacuum, the only source of either field is a change in the other field—as shown by the time derivatives on the right-hand sides of Faraday's and Ampère's laws.

34-4 ELECTROMAGNETIC WAVES

Faraday's law shows that a changing magnetic field induces an electric field. Ampère's law shows that a changing electric field induces a magnetic field. Together, the two laws suggest the possibility of **electromagnetic waves**, in which each type of field continually induces the other, resulting in an electromagnetic disturbance that propagates through space as a wave. We'll now confirm this qualitative suggestion with a rigorous demonstration, directly from Maxwell's equations, that electromagnetic waves are indeed possible. In the process we'll discover the properties of electromagnetic waves and will come to a deep understanding of the nature of light.

A Plane Electromagnetic Wave

Here we describe the simplest type of electromagnetic wave—a plane wave in vacuum. Recall from Chapter 16 that a plane wave is one whose properties don't vary in directions perpendicular to the wave propagation, so its wavefronts are planes (see Fig. 16-18). A plane wave is an approximation to the more realistic case of a spherical wave expanding from a localized source, but it's a good approximation at distances from the wave source that are large compared with the wavelength. Light waves reaching Earth from the Sun, for example, or radio waves miles from the transmitter, are essentially plane waves.

In vacuum, it turns out that the electric and magnetic fields of an electromagnetic wave are perpendicular to each other. They're both also perpendicular to the direction of wave propagation—making the electromagnetic wave a transverse wave, as defined in Chapter 16. To be concrete, we'll take the x direction to be the direction of propagation, the y direction that of the electric field, and the z direction that of the magnetic field (Fig. 34-6). We won't prove that this configuration of three mutually perpendicular directions is the only

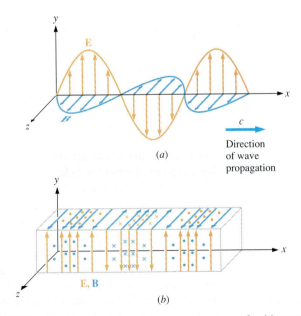

FIGURE 34-6 Fields of a plane electromagnetic wave, shown at a fixed instant of time. (*a*) Field vectors for points on the x axis show the sinusoidal variation in the fields. The electric and magnetic fields are perpendicular but in phase; they're also perpendicular to the propagation direction. (*b*) A partial representation of the field lines, which actually extend forever in both directions. Here the lines are pictured only in a finite rectangular slab. Lines on the facing surfaces of the slab are shown as arrows; lines going through the slab appear as dots or crosses depending on whether they're emerging from or going into the slab. Spacing of the field lines reflects the sinusoidal variation shown in (*a*).

one possible for an electromagnetic wave (although in vacuum it is; see Problem 11). What we will do, though, is prove that this configuration satisfies Maxwell's equations—thus showing that such electromagnetic waves are indeed possible. Before we can do that, we need a mathematical description of our plane electromagnetic wave.

In Chapter 16 we found that a sinusoidal wave propagating in the x direction is represented by a function of the form $A \sin(kx - \omega t)$, where A is the wave amplitude, k the wave number, and ω the angular frequency. For the mechanical waves of Chapters 16 and 17, the function $A \sin(kx - \omega t)$ described some physical quantity such as the height of a water wave or pressure variation in a sound wave. In an electromagnetic wave, the corresponding physical quantities are the electric and magnetic fields—which are vector quantities. It turns out that these two wave fields, although perpendicular, are in phase—meaning that their peaks and troughs coincide, as shown in Fig. 34-6. Having chosen the y direction for the electric field and the z direction for the magnetic field, we can then write the fields of our plane electromagnetic wave as

$$\mathbf{E}(x,\ t) = E_p \sin(kx - \omega t)\hat{\mathbf{j}} \qquad (34\text{-}10)$$

and

$$\mathbf{B}(x,\ t) = B_p \sin(kx - \omega t)\hat{\mathbf{k}}, \qquad (34\text{-}11)$$

where the peak amplitudes E_p and B_p are constants and where $\hat{\mathbf{j}}$ and $\hat{\mathbf{k}}$ are unit vectors in the y and z directions. Figure 34-6a is a "snapshot" of some field vectors of this wave at points on the x axis, shown at a fixed instant of time. That $\mathbf{E}$ and $\mathbf{B}$ are perpendicular is obvious from the figure, as is the fact that they're perpendicular to the propagation direction, in this case the x direction. You can also see the sinusoidal variation, as the field vectors get alternately longer, then shorter, then reverse direction, and so on. And you can see that $\mathbf{E}$ and $\mathbf{B}$ are in phase: they peak at the same points, and are zero at the same points. We emphasize that Fig. 34-6a shows field *vectors* for points on the x axis only; the fields extend forever throughout space, and because this is a plane wave, a picture of field vectors along any line parallel to the x axis would look just the same.

We can also draw field *lines* for our wave, in contrast to the field vectors of Fig. 34-6a. We can't draw complete field lines, because they extend forever in both directions. So in Fig. 34-6b we've shown the field lines only in a rectangular slab; that's enough to give a picture of what the fields look like everywhere. You should convince yourself that Figs. 34-6a and 34-6b show exactly the same thing, namely a plane electromagnetic wave described by Equations 34-10 and 34-11. In one case we use field *vectors,* whose lengths are proportional to the field magnitudes, and in the other we use field *lines,* which extend forever and whose spacing indicates the field magnitudes.

We'll now use Maxwell's equations to show that the electric and magnetic fields pictured in Fig. 34-6 and described by Equations 34-10 and 34-11 really do satisfy Maxwell's equations. We've chosen a sinusoidal waveform for our wave fields because of its mathematical simplicity. But the superposition principle holds for electric and magnetic fields, and we know from Section 16-6 that by superposition we can represent *any* waveform in terms of sinusoidal waveforms. So our proof that electromagnetic waves can exist actually holds for any wave shape (see Problem 74 here and Problem 54 in Chapter 16). That means we can use electromagnetic waves to communicate the complex waveforms of music, TV images, or computer data encoded as pulses of light.

We have four Maxwell equations to satisfy: the two Gauss's laws, and the laws of Faraday and Ampère.

Gauss's Laws

In vacuum, Gauss's laws for the electric and magnetic fields both have zero on the right-hand side (Equations 34-6 and 34-7), reflecting the absence of charge. That means, as we've seen many times before, that the field lines can't begin or end; they either form closed loops or extend to infinity. Our electromagnetic wave is a plane wave, meaning that no wave property varies in directions perpendicular to the wave propagation. Therefore the field lines shown partially in Fig. 34-6b must extend, straight, forever in both directions. So they don't begin or end, and thus the two Gauss laws are satisfied.

Faraday's Law

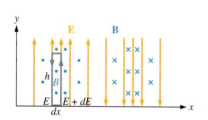

FIGURE 34-7 Cross section of Fig. 34-6 in the x-y plane. Also shown is a rectangular loop for evaluating the line integral in Faraday's law.

To see that Faraday's law is satisfied, consider an observer looking directly toward the x-y plane in Fig. 34-6. Such an observer would see electric field lines going up and down and magnetic field lines coming straight in and out, as shown in Fig. 34-7. Consider the small rectangular loop of height h and infinitesimal width dx shown in the figure. Evaluating the line integral of the electric field **E** around this loop, we get no contribution from the short ends because they are at right angles to the field. Going around counterclockwise, we get a contribution $-Eh$ as we go down the left side against the field direction. Then we get a positive contribution going up the right side. Because of the variation in field strength with position, the field strength on the right side of the loop is different from that on the left. Let the change in field be dE, so the field on the right side of the loop is $E + dE$, giving a contribution of $(E + dE)h$ to the line integral. Then the line integral of **E** around the loop is

$$\oint \mathbf{E} \cdot d\boldsymbol{\ell} = -Eh + (E + dE)h = h \, dE .$$

Physically, this nonzero line integral implies an induced electric field. Induced by what? By a changing magnetic flux through the loop. The electric field of the wave arises because of the changing magnetic field of the wave. The area of the loop is $h \, dx$, and the magnetic field **B** is at right angles to this area, so the magnetic flux through the loop is just

$$\phi_B = Bh \, dx .$$

The rate of change of flux through the loop is then

$$\frac{d\phi_B}{dt} = h \, dx \, \frac{dB}{dt} .$$

Faraday's law relates the line integral of the electric field to the rate of change of flux:

$$\oint \mathbf{E} \cdot d\boldsymbol{\ell} = -\frac{d\phi_B}{dt} ,$$

or, using our expressions for the line integral and the rate of change of flux,

$$h \, dE = -h \, dx \, \frac{dB}{dt} .$$

Dividing through by $h\, dx$, we have

$$\frac{dE}{dx} = -\frac{dB}{dt}. \qquad (34\text{-}12\text{a})$$

In deriving this equation, we considered changes in E with position at a fixed instant of time, as pictured in Fig. 34-7, so our derivative dE/dx means the rate of change of E with position while time is held fixed. Similarly, in evaluating the derivative of magnetic flux, we were concerned only with the time rate of change at the fixed position of our loop. Both our derivatives represent rates of change with respect to one variable while the other variable is held fixed, and are therefore partial derivatives (see Math Toolbox on p. 400 if you're not familiar with partial derivatives). Equation 34-12a should then be written more properly:

$$\frac{\partial E}{\partial x} = -\frac{\partial B}{\partial t}. \qquad (34\text{-}12\text{b})$$

Equation 34-12b—which is just Faraday's law applied to our electromagnetic wave—tells us that the rate at which the electric field changes with *position* is related to the rate at which the magnetic field changes with *time*.

Ampère's Law

Now imagine an observer looking down on Fig. 34-6 from above. This observer sees the magnetic field lines lying in the x-z plane, and electric field lines emerging perpendicular to the x-z plane as shown in Fig. 34-8. We can apply Ampère's law (Equation 34-9) to the infinitesimal rectangle shown, just as we applied Faraday's law to a similar rectangle in the x-y plane. Going counterclockwise around the rectangle, we get no contribution to the line integral of the magnetic field on the short sides, since they lie perpendicular to the field. Going down the left side, we get a contribution Bh to the line integral. Going up the right side, against the field, we get a negative contribution $-(B + dB)h$, where dB is the change in B from one side of the rectangle to the other. So the line integral in Ampère's law is

$$\oint \mathbf{B} \cdot d\boldsymbol{\ell} = Bh - (B + dB)h = -h\, dB.$$

The electric flux through the rectangle is simply $Eh\, dx$, so the rate of change of electric flux is

$$\frac{d\phi_E}{dt} = h\, dx\, \frac{dE}{dt}.$$

Ampère's law relates the line integral of the magnetic field to this time derivative of the electric flux, giving

$$-h\, dB = \varepsilon_0 \mu_0 h\, dx\, \frac{dE}{dt}.$$

Dividing through by $h\, dx$ and noting again that we are really dealing with partial derivatives, we have

$$\frac{\partial B}{\partial x} = -\varepsilon_0 \mu_0 \frac{\partial E}{\partial t}. \qquad (34\text{-}13)$$

FIGURE 34-8 Cross section of Fig. 34-6 in the x-z plane, showing a rectangular loop for evaluating the line integral in Ampère's law.

Equations 34-12 and 34-13—derived from Faraday's and Ampère's laws—express fully the requirements that Maxwell's universal laws of electromagnetism pose on the field structure of Fig. 34-6. The two equations are remarkable in that each describes an induced field that arises from the changing of the other field. That other field, in turn, arises from the changing of the first field. Thus we have a self-perpetuating electromagnetic structure, whose fields exist and change without the need for charged matter. If Equations 34-10 and 34-11, which describe the fields in Fig. 34-6, can be made consistent with Equations 34-12 and 34-13, then we will have demonstrated that our electromagnetic wave does indeed satisfy Maxwell's equations and is thus a possible configuration of electric and magnetic fields.

Faraday, Ampère, and the Wave Fields

To see that Equation 34-12 is satisfied, we differentiate the electric field of Equation 34-10 with respect to x, and the magnetic field of Equation 34-11 with respect to t:

$$\frac{\partial E}{\partial x} = \frac{\partial}{\partial x}[E_p \sin(kx - \omega t)] = kE_p \cos(kx - \omega t)$$

and

$$\frac{\partial B}{\partial t} = \frac{\partial}{\partial t}[B_p \sin(kx - \omega t)] = -\omega B_p \cos(kx - \omega t).$$

Putting these expressions in for the derivatives in Equation 34-12 gives

$$kE_p \cos(kx - \omega t) = -[-\omega B_p \cos(kx - \omega t)].$$

The cosine term cancels from this equation, showing that the equation holds if

$$kE_p = \omega B_p. \tag{34-14}$$

To see that Equation 34-13 is also satisfied, we differentiate the magnetic field of Equation 34-11 with respect to x and the electric field of Equation 34-10 with respect to t:

$$\frac{\partial B}{\partial x} = kB_p \cos(kx - \omega t)$$

and

$$\frac{\partial E}{\partial t} = -\omega E_p \cos(kx - \omega t).$$

Using these expressions in Equation 34-13 then gives

$$kB_p \cos(kx - \omega t) = -\varepsilon_0 \mu_0 [-\omega E_p \cos(kx - \omega t)].$$

Again, the cosine term cancels, showing that this equation is satisfied if

$$kB_p = \varepsilon_0 \mu_0 \omega E_p. \tag{34-15}$$

Our analysis has shown that electromagnetic waves whose form is given by Fig. 34-6 and Equations 34-10 and 34-11 can exist, provided that the amplitudes E_p and B_p, and the frequency ω and wave number k, are related by Equations 34-14 and 34-15. Physically, the existence of these waves is possible because a change in either kind of field—electric or magnetic—induces the other kind of field, giving rise to a self-perpetuating electromagnetic field structure. Maxwell's theory thus leads to the prediction of an entirely new phenomenon—the electromagnetic wave. We will now explore some properties of these waves.

34-5 THE SPEED OF ELECTROMAGNETIC WAVES

In Chapter 16 we found that the speed of a sinusoidal wave is given by the ratio of the angular frequency and wave number:

$$\text{wave speed} = \frac{\omega}{k}.$$

To determine the speed of our electromagnetic wave, we solve Equation 34-14 for E_p:

$$E_p = \frac{\omega B_p}{k},$$

and use this expression in Equation 34-15:

$$kB_p = \varepsilon_0 \mu_0 \omega E_p = \frac{\varepsilon_0 \mu_0 \omega^2 B_p}{k}.$$

Solving for the wave speed ω/k then gives

$$\text{wave speed} = \frac{\omega}{k} = \frac{1}{\sqrt{\varepsilon_0 \mu_0}}. \qquad (34\text{-}16)$$

This remarkably simple result shows that the speed of an electromagnetic wave in vacuum depends only on the electric and magnetic constants ε_0 and μ_0. All electromagnetic waves in vacuum, regardless of frequency or amplitude, share this speed. Although we derived this result for sinusoidal waves, the superposition principle ensures that it holds for any wave shape.

We can easily calculate the speed given in Equation 34-16:

$$\frac{1}{\sqrt{\varepsilon_0 \mu_0}} = \frac{1}{[(8.85 \times 10^{-12} \text{ F/m})(4\pi \times 10^{-7} \text{ H/m})]^{1/2}} = 3.00 \times 10^8 \text{ m/s}.$$

But this is precisely the speed of light!

As early as 1600, Galileo had tried to measure the speed of light by uncovering lanterns on different mountaintops. He was able to conclude only that "If not instantaneous, it is extraordinarily rapid." The first evidence for a finite speed of light came in the 1670s from observations by the Danish astronomer Ole Römer. He noted that eclipses of Jupiter's moons occurred at different times than predicted as Jupiter's distance from Earth changed. Römer interpreted the changes as being due to the different times for light traveling at a finite speed from Jupiter to Earth. Römer's data implied a speed of 2.3×10^8 m/s, about three quarters of the actual value. In 1728, James Bradley used changes in the apparent positions of stars resulting from Earth's orbital motion to calculate a value of 2.95×10^8 m/s for the speed of light—in error by less than 2%. As we saw in Chapter 1, the exact value $c = 2.99792458 \times 10^8$ m/s was adopted in

FIGURE 34-9 This image of Venus was made using data that include surface altitude determined by very accurate measurements of the travel time for radar signals reflected from Venus' surface. Radar, like all electromagnetic waves, travels at the speed of light.

1983 to define the meter. So we no longer measure the speed of light; instead, that speed provides an accurate way to measure distances (Fig. 34-9).

Do other properties of light besides its speed fit our picture of electromagnetic waves? In 1678—some 200 years before Maxwell—the Dutch physicist Christian Huygens had suggested that light is a wave. In 1801, Thomas Young experimented with a 2-slit system to show that light undergoes interference, giving conclusive evidence for the wave nature of light (see Fig. 16-25). But neither experiment nor theory could say what kind of wave light might be. Then, in the 1860s, came Maxwell. Using a theory developed from laboratory experiments involving electricity and magnetism, with no reference whatever to optics or light, Maxwell showed how the interplay of electric and magnetic fields could result in electromagnetic waves. The speed of those waves—calculated from the quantities ε_0 and μ_0 that were determined in laboratory experiments having nothing to do with light—was precisely the known speed of light. Maxwell was led inescapably to the conclusion that light is an electromagnetic wave.

Maxwell's identification of light as an electromagnetic phenomenon is a classic example of the unification of knowledge toward which science is ever striving. With one simple calculation, Maxwell brought the entire science of optics under the umbrella of electromagnetism. Maxwell's work stands as a crowning intellectual triumph, an achievement whose implications are still expanding our view of the universe.

34-6 PROPERTIES OF ELECTROMAGNETIC WAVES

Our demonstration that electromagnetic waves satisfy Maxwell's equations places definite constraints on the properties of those waves. The wave frequency ω and wave number k are not both arbitrary, but must be related through

$$\frac{\omega}{k} = c, \tag{34-17a}$$

where $c = 1/\sqrt{\varepsilon_0\mu_0}$ is the speed of light. In Chapter 16 we related the angular frequency ω and wave number k to the more familiar frequency f and wavelength λ through the equations $\omega = 2\pi f$ and $k = 2\pi/\lambda$. Therefore we can also write Equation 34-17a in the form

$$f\lambda = c. \tag{34-17b}$$

Furthermore, Equation 34-14 shows that

$$E = \frac{\omega}{k}B = cB. \tag{34-18}$$

Thus, the field magnitudes in the wave are not independent but are in the ratio of the speed of light. Also, Fig. 34-6 and Equations 34-10 and 34-11 have the electric and magnetic fields perpendicular to each other and to the direction of wave propagation, with the electric and magnetic fields in phase. It is in fact the case that only waves with this form—**E** and **B** in phase and with **E**, **B**, and the propagation direction all perpendicular—can satisfy Maxwell's equations in vacuum (see Problem 11).

EXAMPLE 34-2	*Laser Light*

A laser beam with wavelength 633 nm is propagating in the $+z$ direction. Its electric field is parallel to the x axis and has amplitude 6.0 kV/m. Find the wave frequency, and the direction and amplitude of the magnetic field.

Solution

Equation 34-17b relates the wavelength and frequency to the speed of light. Solving for f gives

$$f = \frac{c}{\lambda} = \frac{3.00 \times 10^8 \text{ m/s}}{633 \times 10^{-9} \text{ m}} = 4.74 \times 10^{14} \text{ Hz}.$$

If we imagine reorienting the wave of Fig. 34-6 so it propagates along the z direction, then rotate it about the z direction so the electric field is parallel to the x axis, we find that the magnetic field is parallel to the y axis. The magnetic field amplitude follows from Equation 34-18:

$$B_p = \frac{E_p}{c} = \frac{6.0 \times 10^3 \text{ V/m}}{3.00 \times 10^8 \text{ m/s}} = 2.0 \times 10^{-5} \text{ T}.$$

EXERCISE An electromagnetic wave is propagating in the $-y$ direction, with its magnetic field parallel to the x axis. The magnetic field amplitude is 8.0 μT. Write an expression for the wave's electric field vector at the point where the magnetic field points in the $+x$ direction and is at its peak value.

Answer: $\mathbf{E} = -2.4\hat{\mathbf{k}}$ kV/m

Some problems similar to Example 34-2: 24–27

Got It!

Light and radio waves are both electromagnetic waves; of the two, light has a much higher frequency. Does that mean light waves travel faster than radio waves? Regardless of your answer, are any other properties of these waves different?

34-7 THE ELECTROMAGNETIC SPECTRUM

Although an electromagnetic wave's frequency and wavelength must be related by Equation 34-17b, one or the other of these quantities is completely arbitrary. That means we can have electromagnetic waves of any frequency, or, equivalently, any wavelength. Direct measurement shows that visible light occupies a wavelength range from about 400 nm to 700 nm, corresponding to frequencies from 7.5×10^{14} Hz to 4.3×10^{14} Hz. The different wavelengths or frequencies correspond to different colors, with red at the long-wavelength, low-frequency end of the visible region and blue at the short-wavelength, high-frequency end (see the enlargement in Fig. 34-10).

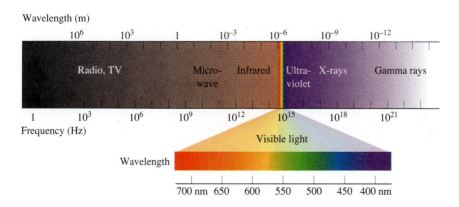

FIGURE 34-10 The electromagnetic spectrum ranges from radio waves to gamma rays, with visible light occupying only a narrow range of wavelengths and frequencies. Note the logarithmic scale, in which intervals between numbered tick marks correspond to factors-of-1000 changes in frequency and wavelength.

FIGURE 34-11 Subtle variations in body temperature are color coded in this infrared image of a human face. Regions at different temperatures emit different frequencies of infrared; these are coded into the image's visible colors according to the temperature scale at the top.

FIGURE 34-12 X rays are high-frequency, short wavelength electromagnetic waves that readily penetrate soft tissues but not bone. Here, an X-ray image reveals rheumatoid arthritis in a human knee joint.

Figure 34-10 shows the entire **electromagnetic spectrum**, including frequencies and wavelengths that differ by many orders of magnitude either way from those of visible light. The invisible electromagnetic waves beyond the narrow visible range were unknown in Maxwell's time. A brilliant confirmation of Maxwell's theory came in 1888, when the German physicist Heinrich Hertz succeeded in generating and detecting electromagnetic waves of much lower frequency than visible light. Hertz intended his work only to verify Maxwell's modification of Ampère's law, but the practical consequences have proven enormous. In 1896, the Italian scientist Guglielmo Marconi demonstrated that he could generate and detect the so-called Hertzian waves. In 1901, he transmitted electromagnetic waves across the Atlantic Ocean, creating a public sensation. From the pioneering work of Hertz and Marconi, spurred by the theoretical efforts of Maxwell, came the entire technology of radio, television, and microwaves that so dominates modern society. We now consider all electromagnetic waves in the frequency range from a few Hz to about 3×10^{11} Hz as radio waves, with ordinary AM radio at about 10^6 Hz, FM radio at 10^8 Hz, and microwaves used for radar, cooking, and satellite communications at 10^9 Hz and above.

Between radio waves and visible light lies the infrared frequency range. Electromagnetic waves in this region are emitted by warm objects, even when they are not hot enough to glow visibly. For this reason, infrared cameras are used to determine subtle body temperature differences in medical diagnosis, to examine buildings for heat loss, and to study the birth of stars in clouds of interstellar gas and dust (Fig. 34-11).

Beyond the visible region are the ultraviolet rays responsible for sunburn, then the highly penetrating X rays (Fig. 34-12), and finally the gamma rays whose primary terrestrial source is radioactive decay. All these phenomena, from radio to gamma rays, are fundamentally the same: They are all electromagnetic waves, differing only in frequency and wavelength. All travel with speed c, and all consist of electric and magnetic fields produced from each other through the induction processes described by Faraday's and Ampère's laws. Naming the different types of electromagnetic waves is just a matter of convenience; there are no gaps in the continuous range of allowed frequencies and wavelengths. Practical differences arise because waves of different wavelengths interact differently with matter; in particular, shorter wavelengths tend to be generated and absorbed most efficiently by smaller systems.

APPLICATION	*The New Astronomy*

Figure 34-10 shows that visible light occupies only a small part of the electromagnetic spectrum. For centuries our only information about the universe beyond Earth—except for an occasional meteorite—came from visible light. Processes like those occurring on the visible surface of our Sun and many other stars produce predominantly visible light. Optical astronomy, utilizing visible light, gave a good picture of the universe to the extent that it consists of objects not too different from the visible part of the Sun. The restriction to optical astronomy was in part imposed by Earth's atmosphere. Transparent to visible light, the atmosphere is largely opaque to other forms of electromagnetic radiation, although "windows" of relative transparency exist in parts of the radio and infrared bands. The

discovery by Bell Telephone Laboratories electrical engineer Karl Jansky in 1931 that radio waves from outer space can be detected on Earth led to the development of radio astronomy. For decades, radio astronomy has given a picture of the universe that complements the optical view, showing phenomena that are simply not detectable by optical means (Fig. 34-13).

The onset of the space age in the late 1950s finally opened the rest of the electromagnetic spectrum to astronomers. Before this time there were surprisingly few suggestions that anything interesting might be found beyond the visible range. But satellites carrying infrared, ultraviolet, X-ray, and gamma-ray detectors have literally revolutionized our view of the universe

(a)

(b)

FIGURE 34-13 (a) Some of the 27 dish antennas that comprise the Very Large Array (VLA) radio telescope in New Mexico. Each dish is 25 m in diameter, and the array can be configured to occupy an area larger than metropolitan Washington, DC. (b) The galaxy Centaurus A, a powerful radio emitter, imaged with the VLA. The two lobes are jets of material ejected from the galaxy's central core. The VLA was tuned to a wavelength of 20 cm for this observation.

FIGURE 34-14 This false-color infrared image of the Andromeda galaxy was taken with the Infrared Astronomical Satellite. Yellow indicates regions of brightest infrared emission, corresponding to places where new stars are probably forming.

(Fig. 34-14). Exotic objects such as neutron stars and black holes are now objects of astronomical study. The opening of the entire electromagnetic spectrum has brought a new richness to astronomy, showing that our universe contains some of the most unusual objects that the laws of physics permit. Phenom-

ena that were once bizarre conjectures of theoreticians are now observed regularly. For example, astronomers are convinced that massive black holes—with the mass of a million Suns—lurk at the centers of galaxies, including our own. Closer to home, observations of the Sun with ultraviolet and X-ray instruments have brought new understandings of the star that sustains us. And by turning space-borne infrared detectors toward Earth, we have learned much about the structure and resources of our own planet (Fig. 34-15).

FIGURE 34-15 This satellite image documents destruction of the Brazilian rainforest by human activities. False colors enhance the distinction between healthy forest (dark green) and cleared areas (light green, pink).

34-8 POLARIZATION

The fields of an electromagnetic wave in vacuum (and in common materials such as air and glass) are perpendicular to the propagation direction, but within the plane perpendicular to the wave propagation the orientation of one field is still arbitrary. **Polarization** is a wave property that specifies the electric field

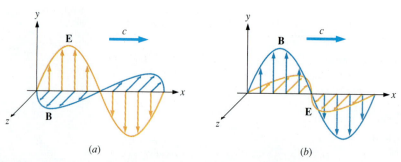

FIGURE 34-16 Field vectors for two electromagnetic waves. Both are propagating in the $+x$ direction, but have different polarizations. The polarization direction is that of the electric field, so the wave in (a) is vertically polarized (i.e., its electric field is in the y direction), while the wave in (b) is horizontally polarized (i.e., in the z direction). Unpolarized light would be a mix of such waves with their electric fields oriented at random in many different directions.

16.4
Polarizer

direction; since the two fields are perpendicular, polarization also determines the magnetic field direction (Fig. 34-16).

Electromagnetic waves used in radio, TV, and radar originate from antennas whose configuration gives the waves a definite polarization. The light waves produced by most lasers are also polarized. In contrast, visible light from hot sources such as the Sun or a light bulb is **unpolarized**, consisting of a mixture of electromagnetic waves with random field orientations.

Unpolarized light may be polarized either by reflection off surfaces or when it passes through substances whose molecular or crystal structure has a preferred direction called the **transmission axis**. Many crystals and synthetic materials such as the plastic Polaroid have this property. For example, sunlight reflecting off the hood of a car becomes partially polarized in the horizontal direction. Polaroid sunglasses, with their transmission axis vertical, block this reflected glare with only a modest reduction in overall light intensity.

A polarizing material passes unattenuated only that component of the wave's electric field that lies along its preferred direction. If θ is the angle between the field and the polarizer's preferred direction, then the field component in the preferred direction is $E\cos\theta$. As we will show shortly, the intensity S of an electromagnetic wave is proportional to the square of the field strength; as a result a wave of intensity S_0 incident on a polarizer emerges with intensity given by the so-called **Law of Malus**:

$$S = S_0 \cos^2\theta. \tag{34-19}$$

This equation shows that electromagnetic waves will be blocked completely if $\theta = 90°$, a situation that occurs when unpolarized light passes through one polarizer to give it a definite polarization, then through another oriented at $90°$ to the first (Fig. 34-17).

When unpolarized light passes through a polarizer its intensity is cut in half. You can see this from Equation 34-19 because the unpolarized light includes a mix of waves with random polarization angles θ. Averaging over all possible angles in Equation 34-19 amounts to taking the average of $\cos^2\theta$ over a full cycle. We've seen on several occasions that the average of the square of a sinusoidal function is $\frac{1}{2}$ (recall Fig. 16-16), so a polarizer does indeed cut the intensity of unpolarized light in half.

FIGURE 34-17 Two pairs of Polaroid sunglasses with their transmission axes at right angles. Where they overlap, no light can get through.

| **EXAMPLE 34-3** | *Multiple Polarizers* |

Unpolarized light with intensity S_0 is incident on a "stack" of three polarizers. The first has its polarization axis vertical, the second is at 25° to the vertical, and the third is at 70° to the vertical (Fig. 34-18). What is the intensity of light emerging from this stack?

Solution

We've just seen that the first polarizer cuts the unpolarized intensity in half, giving $\frac{1}{2}S_0$ for the intensity incident on the second polarizer. Equation 34-19 shows that the second and third polarizers each reduce the intensity by a factor $\cos^2\theta$, where θ is the angle between the incident polarization direction—established by one polarizer—and the next polarizer's axis. For the second polarizer this angle is 25°; for the third it is 70° − 25° = 45°. Thus light emerges from the stack with intensity

$$S = (\tfrac{1}{2})(\cos^2 25°)(\cos^2 45°)S_0 = 0.205S_0 .$$

Interestingly, this is greater than the intensity we would get passing light through a vertical polarizer followed by a single polarizer at 70°. And, as the exercise below shows, it is much

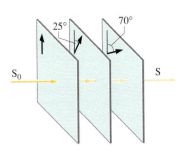

FIGURE 34-18 A stack of polarizers. Arrows on the sheets indicate directions of the polarization axes.

greater than what we would get by interchanging the second and third polarizers. Can you see why?

EXERCISE Rework Example 34-3 with the second and third polarizers interchanged.

Answer: $S = 0.029S_0$

Some problems similar to Example 34-3: 35, 36, 72

Polarization can tell us much about sources of electromagnetic waves or about materials through which the waves travel. Many astrophysical processes produce polarized waves; measuring the polarization then gives clues to the mechanisms operating in distant objects. Polarization of light as it passes through materials helps geologists to understand the composition and formation of rocks (Fig. 34-19) and helps engineers to locate stresses in structures (Fig. 34-20).

FIGURE 34-19 Photomicrograph of a thin section of rock placed between crossed polarizers. Individual mineral crystals, here a few mm in size, rotate the light's electric field, altering the transmitted light intensity.

FIGURE 34-20 Plastic model of a Gothic cathedral, photographed between polarizing sheets. The resulting patterns reveal stresses, helping architects and engineers understand the response of the building to wind and weight loading—topics related to our study of static equilibrium in Chapter 14.

They're everywhere, from watches, calculators, and gas pumps to laptop computers—the **liquid-crystal displays** (LCDs) that convert electrical signals into letters, numbers, pictures, and graphs that we can read. Fundamental to their operation is the polarization of light.

In Fig. 34-17 we saw that two polarizers oriented at right angles block all light from getting through the pair. But if we could rotate the light's polarization direction through 90° while it's between the polarizers, then light from the first polarizer would reach the second aligned with the latter's preferred direction, and so would pass through. That's just what happens in an LCD—but it happens selectively, under control of an electrical signal, allowing the transmission of light to be turned on or off.

In Chapter 23 we introduced liquid crystals as systems of long dipole-like molecules that align with an applied electric field. Figure 34-21 shows how this property is used to make a display. The liquid crystal is contained between two transpar-

ent striated plates that cause the molecules to align with their striations. The two plates' striations are mutually perpendicular, so the molecules' alignment gradually changes through the device. The electric field of a light wave interacts with the molecules, with the result that the polarization direction of the light rotates through 90° as it passes through the liquid crystal. The whole system is between crossed polarizers and so, because of the 90° rotation of the polarization, light incident on the system gets through (Fig. 34-21a).

Now suppose a voltage is applied between the plates confining the liquid crystal. This results in an electric field that aligns the molecules as shown in Fig. 34-21b. In this new orientation the liquid crystal no longer rotates the polarization of the light, so the situation is just like that of Fig. 34-17, and the light is blocked. There's one such system for each of the segments that make up the numbers and letters of a liquid crystal display, and each segment can be turned on or off to make the desired symbol

FIGURE 34-21 Polarization plays a central role in the operation of a liquid-crystal display.

(a)

Vertical polarizer passes only light with its electric field vertical

Horizontal polarizer passes the now horizontally polarized light.

Light

Electric field of incident light points in all directions perpendicular to the light's propagation

Liquid-crystal molecules align with striated plates and rotate the light's polarization

Since light gets through, this segment isn't visible

Since no light gets through, this segment is darkened, hence visible

(b)

Applying a voltage aligns the liquid crystals horizontally. They no longer rotate the light's polarization

Horizontal polarizer now blocks the still vertically polarized light

In Fig. 34-21 we show light incident from the back of the display and emerging from the front for viewing. In many LCDs the light at the back is replaced by a mirror that reflects ambient light. Then there's no power needed to provide light, and the LCD operates at minimal electrical power. Low power consumption is one of the key advantages of liquid-crystal displays.

Liquid crystals are rather slow in their response, so they aren't good for rapid switching of light. But some solid crystals have much the same property as the liquid-crystal system of Fig. 34-21, in that they selectively rotate the polarization of light depending on the presence or absence of an electric field (in this case, it takes a field to produce the rotation). This is known as the **electro-optic effect**.

Placing an electro-optic crystal between crossed polarizers makes an **electro-optic modulator** (EOM) that can switch light on timescales as short as 10^{-10} s. Such devices, used as electronic shutters to interrupt laser beams and thus produce very short pulses of light, have been used to make some of the most accurate measurements of the speed of light. Applying a varying voltage to the EOM causes the light transmission to vary continuously. Voice or music, for example, can be transmitted on a laser beam by applying the amplified signal from a microphone to an EOM. EOMs are used in a wide variety of scientific and commercial applications. An especially important use is the conversion of electrical signals to light pulses on the highest-speed fiber optic communications systems.

34-9 PRODUCING ELECTROMAGNETIC WAVES

We have shown that electromagnetic waves can exist, and have explored some of their properties. But how do these waves originate?

All that's necessary is to produce a changing electric or magnetic field. Once a changing field of either type exists, Faraday's and Ampère's laws ensure the production of the other type—and so on, to give a propagating electromagnetic wave. Ultimately, changing fields of either type occur when we alter the motion of electric charge. Therefore:

> *Accelerated* electric charge is the source of electromagnetic waves.

In a radio transmitter, the accelerated charges are electrons moving back and forth in an antenna, driven by an alternating voltage from an *LC* circuit (Fig. 34-22). In an X-ray tube, high-energy electrons decelerate rapidly as they

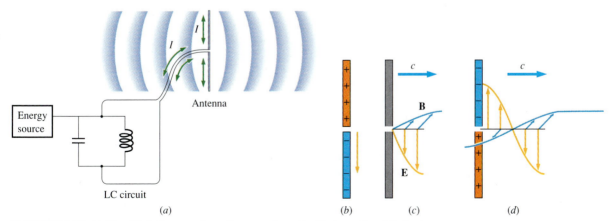

FIGURE 34-22 (*a*) Simplified diagram of a radio transmitter. Oscillations of an *LC* circuit drive alternating current (green arrows) in the antenna, while a power source replenishes energy carried away in electromagnetic waves. (*b*)–(*d*) A changing electric field arises from the changing charge distribution in the antenna. The changing electric field induces a changing magnetic field, and the field structure propagates away from the antenna at the speed of light. Frames (*b*) and (*d*) are half a wave period apart in time, at times when charge separation in the antenna is a maximum.

slam into a target; their deceleration is the source of the electromagnetic waves, now in the X-ray region of the spectrum. In the magnetron tube of a microwave oven, electrons circle in a magnetic field; their centripetal acceleration is the source of the microwaves that cook your food. And the altered movement of electrons in atoms—although described accurately only by quantum mechanics—is the source of most visible light. If the motion of the accelerated charges is periodic, then the wave frequency is that of the motion; more generally, systems are most efficient at producing (and receiving) electromagnetic waves whose wavelength is comparable to the size of the system. That's why TV antennas are on the order of 1 m in size, while nuclei—some 10^{-15} m in diameter—produce gamma rays.

Calculation of electromagnetic waves emitted by accelerated charges presents challenging but important problems for physicists and communications engineers. Figure 34-23a shows a "snapshot" of the electric field produced by a single point charge undergoing simple harmonic motion, while Fig. 34-23b shows the field of an oscillating dipole—a configuration approximated by many systems from antennas to atoms and molecules. Both figures show that the waves are strongest in the direction at right angles to the acceleration of the charge distribution and that there is no radiation in the direction of the acceleration. This accounts for, among other phenomena, the directionality of radio and TV antennas, which transmit and receive most effectively perpendicular to the long direction of the antenna.

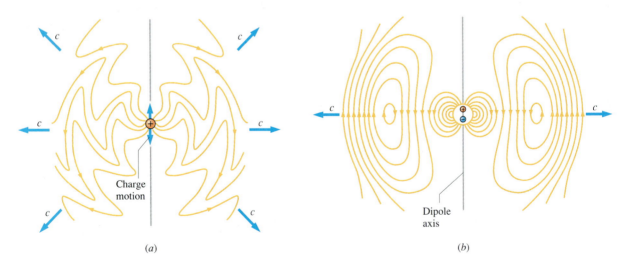

(a)   (b)

FIGURE 34-23 "Snapshots" showing the electric fields of oscillating charge distributions. (a) A single point charge executing simple harmonic motion in the horizontal plane. Note that the field close to the charge approximates the radial field of a stationary point charge, but that farther out the "kinks" in the field—resulting from the accelerated motion—are more prominent and become essentially perpendicular to the radial direction. These transverse kinks move outward at the speed of light, and constitute the wave fields. (b) The electric field of an oscillating dipole. Note that the field forms closed loops, detached from the dipole. These are the outward propagating wave fields. The larger field loops shown were formed when the oscillating dipole had the opposite orientation. Not shown in either figure are the equally important magnetic fields.

The fields shown in Fig. 34-23 seem to bear little resemblance to the plane-wave fields of Fig. 34-7 that we used to demonstrate the possibility of electromagnetic waves. We could produce true plane waves only with an infinite sheet of accelerated charge—an obvious impossibility. But far from the source, the curved field lines evident in Fig. 34-23b, for example, would appear straight, and the wave would begin to approximate a plane wave. So our plane-wave analysis is a valid approximation at great distances—typically many wavelengths—from a localized wave source. Closer to the source more complicated expressions for the wave fields apply, but these, too, satisfy Maxwell's equations.

34-10 ENERGY IN ELECTROMAGNETIC WAVES

We showed in previous chapters that electric and magnetic fields contain energy. Here we have considered electromagnetic waves, in which a combination of electric and magnetic fields propagates through space. As the wave moves, it must transport the energy contained in those fields.

We define **intensity**, S, as the rate at which an electromagnetic wave transports energy across a unit area. This is the same definition we used for wave intensity in Chapter 16, and the units are also the same: power per unit area, or W/m^2. We can calculate the intensity of a plane electromagnetic wave by considering a rectangular box of thickness dx and cross-sectional area A with its face perpendicular to the wave propagation (Fig. 34-24). Within this box are wave fields **E** and **B** whose energy densities are given by Equations 26-3 and 32-11:

FIGURE 34-24 A box of length dx and cross-sectional area A at right angles to the propagation of an electromagnetic wave.

$$u_E = \tfrac{1}{2}\varepsilon_0 E^2$$

$$u_B = \frac{B^2}{2\mu_0}.$$

If dx is sufficiently small, the fields don't change much over the box, so the total energy in the box is just the sum of the electric and magnetic energy densities multiplied by the box volume $A\,dx$:

$$dU = (u_E + u_B)\,A\,dx = \frac{1}{2}\!\left(\varepsilon_0 E^2 + \frac{B^2}{\mu_0}\right) A\,dx.$$

This energy moves with speed c, so all the energy contained in the box length dx moves out of the box in a time $dt = dx/c$. The rate at which energy moves through the cross-sectional area A is then

$$\frac{dU}{dt} = \frac{1}{2}\!\left(\varepsilon_0 E^2 + \frac{B^2}{\mu_0}\right)\frac{A\,dx}{dx/c} = \frac{c}{2}\!\left(\varepsilon_0 E^2 + \frac{B^2}{\mu_0}\right) A.$$

So the intensity S, or rate of energy flow per unit area, is

$$S = \frac{c}{2}\!\left(\varepsilon_0 E^2 + \frac{B^2}{\mu_0}\right).$$

We can recast this equation in simpler form by noting that, for an electromagnetic wave, $E = cB$ and $B = E/c$. Using these expressions to replace one of

(a)

(b)

FIGURE 34-25 (a) The intensity of candle light is only a few W/m². (b) This laser produces a modest 3W of power, but because its beam diameter is less than 0.5 mm, its intensity is some 20 MW/m²—2000 times that of bright sunlight.

the E's in the term E^2 with B and similarly one of the B's in the term B^2 with E, we have

$$S = \frac{c}{2}\left(\varepsilon_0 c E B + \frac{EB}{\mu_0 c}\right) = \frac{1}{2\mu_0}(\varepsilon_0 \mu_0 c^2 + 1)\,EB.$$

But $c = 1/\sqrt{\varepsilon_0 \mu_0}$, so $\varepsilon_0 \mu_0 c^2 = 1$, giving

$$S = \frac{EB}{\mu_0}. \tag{34-20a}$$

Although we derived Equation 34-20a for an electromagnetic wave, it is in fact a special case of the more general result that nonparallel electric and magnetic fields are accompanied by a flow of electromagnetic energy. In general, the rate of energy flow per unit area is given by

$$\mathbf{S} = \frac{\mathbf{E} \times \mathbf{B}}{\mu_0}. \tag{34-20b}$$

Here a vector **S** is used to signify not only the magnitude of the energy flow, but also its direction. For an electromagnetic wave in vacuum, in which **E** and **B** must be at right angles, Equation 34-20b reduces to Equation 34-20a, with the direction of energy flow the same as the direction of wave travel. The vector intensity **S** is called the **Poynting vector** after the English physicist J. H. Poynting, who suggested it in 1884. Poynting's name is especially fortuitous, for the Poynting vector points in the direction of energy flow. Problem 76 explores an important application of the Poynting vector to fields that do not constitute an electromagnetic wave.

Equations 34-20 give the intensity at the instant when the fields have magnitudes E and B. In an electromagnetic wave the fields oscillate, and so does the intensity. We're usually not interested in this rapid oscillation. For example, an engineer designing a solar collector doesn't care that sunlight intensity oscillates at about 10^{14} Hz. What she really wants is the *average* intensity, $\bar{S}$. Because the instantaneous intensity of Equation 34-20a contains a product of sinusoidally varying terms, which are in phase, the average intensity is just half the peak intensity:

$$\bar{S} = \frac{\overline{EB}}{\mu_0} = \frac{E_p B_p}{2\mu_0} \quad \text{(average intensity)} \tag{34-21a}$$

(This follows because, as we've seen on several occasions, the average of $\sin^2 \omega t$ over one cycle is $\frac{1}{2}$.) Typical values for $\bar{S}$ in visible light range from a few W/m² in the faint light of a candle to many MW/m² in the most intense laser beams (Fig. 34-25).

We wrote Equation 34-21a in terms of both the electric and magnetic fields, but we can use the wave condition $E = cB$ to eliminate either field in terms of the other:

$$\bar{S} = \frac{E_p^{\,2}}{2\mu_0 c} \tag{34-21b}$$

and

$$\bar{S} = \frac{cB_p^{\,2}}{2\mu_0}. \tag{34-21c}$$

Got It!

Lasers 1 and 2 emit light of the same color, and the electric field in the beam from laser 1 is twice as strong as that in laser 2's beam. How do their (a) magnetic fields, (b) intensities, and (c) wavelengths compare?

EXAMPLE 34-4	*Solar Energy*

The average intensity of sunlight on a clear day at noon is about 1 kW/m^2 (Fig. 34-26). What are the electric and magnetic fields in sunlight? How many solar collectors would you need to replace a 4.8-kW electric water heater in noonday sun, if each collector has an area of 2.0 m^2 and converts 40% of the incident sunlight to heat?

Solution

Solving Equation 34-21b for the electric field gives

$$E_p = \sqrt{2\mu_0 c \bar{S}}$$

$$= [(2)(4\pi \times 10^{-7} \text{ H/m})(3.0 \times 10^8 \text{ m/s})(1 \times 10^3 \text{ W/m}^2)]^{1/2}$$

$$= 0.87 \text{ kV/m}.$$

The peak magnetic field is then given by $B_p = E_p/c$, so

$$B_p = \frac{E_p}{c} = \frac{870 \text{ V/m}}{3.0 \times 10^8 \text{ m/s}} = 3 \times 10^{-6} \text{ T}.$$

At 1 kW/m^2, we would then need 4.8 m^2 of collector area if the collectors were 100% efficient. At 40% efficiency, we therefore need 4.8 m^2/0.40 = 12 m^2, for a total of 6 collectors.

FIGURE 34-26 In bright sunlight, energy is incident on each square meter of these solar collectors at the rate of about 1000 watts.

EXERCISE A laser produces an average power of 7.0 W in a light beam 1.0 mm in diameter. Find (a) the average intensity and (b) the peak electric field of the laser light.

Answers: (a) 8.9 MW/m^2; (b) 82 kV/m

Some problems similar to Example 34-4: 38–41, 43

Waves from Localized Sources

As an electromagnetic wave propagates through empty space, its total energy does not change. With plane waves the intensity—power per unit area—does not change either. But when a wave originates in a localized source such as an atom, a radio transmitting antenna, a light bulb, or a star, its wavefronts are not planes but expanding spheres (recall Fig. 16-18). The wave's total energy remains the same, but as it expands that energy is spread over the area of an ever larger sphere—whose area increases as the square of the distance from the source. Therefore, as we found in Chapter 16, the power per unit area—the intensity—decreases as the inverse square of the distance:

$$S = \frac{P}{4\pi r^2}. \tag{34-22}$$

Here S and P can be either the peak or average intensity and power, respectively, and r is the distance from a localized source. This intensity decrease occurs not because electromagnetic waves "weaken" and lose energy but because that energy gets spread ever more thinly.

Because the intensity of an electromagnetic wave is proportional to the *square* of the field strengths (Equations 34-21), Equation 34-22 shows that the *fields* of a spherical wave decrease as $1/r$. Contrast that with the $1/r^2$ decrease in the electric field of a stationary point charge, and you can see why the electromagnetic wave fields associated with an accelerated charge dominate in all but the immediate vicinity of the charge (see Fig. 34-23a).

EXAMPLE 34-5	*A Garage-Door Opener*

A radio-activated garage-door opener responds to signals with average intensity as weak as 20 μW/m^2. If the transmitter unit produces a 240-mW signal, broadcast in all directions, what is the maximum distance at which the transmitter will activate the door opener? What is the minimum value for the peak electric field to which the unit responds?

Solution

Since the waves spread out in all the directions, Equation 34-22 applies. Solving for r gives

$$r = \sqrt{\frac{P}{4\pi S}} = \sqrt{\frac{240\times10^{-3}\text{ W}}{(4\pi)(20\times10^{-6}\text{ W/m}^2)}} = 31 \text{ m}.$$

Solving Equation 34-21b gives the electric field corresponding to the unit's 20-μW/m^2 sensitivity:

$$E_p = \sqrt{2\mu_0 c\overline{S}}$$

$$= \sqrt{(2)(4\pi\times10^{-7}\text{ H/m})(3.00\times10^8\text{ m/s})(20\times10^{-6}\text{ W/m}^2)}$$

$$= 0.12 \text{ V/m}.$$

The sensitivity of radio receiving equipment is often expressed in terms of the minimum electric field strength.

EXERCISE A stereo receiver's AM tuner section has a rated sensitivity of 2.1 mV/m. What is the maximum distance at which this unit can receive broadcasts from a radio station's 5.0-kW transmitter, assuming the signal is broadcast in all directions?

Answer: 261 km

Some problems similar to Example 34-5: 49, 51, 52, 61, 62

34-11 WAVE MOMENTUM AND RADIATION PRESSURE

We know from mechanics that moving objects carry both energy and momentum. The same is true for electromagnetic waves. Maxwell showed that the wave energy U and momentum p are related by

$$p = \frac{U}{c}. \tag{34-23}$$

If an electromagnetic wave is incident on an object and the object absorbs the wave energy (as, for example, a black object exposed to sunlight), then the object also absorbs the momentum given by Equation 34-23. If the wave's average intensity is $\overline{S}$, then it carries energy per unit area at the average rate $\overline{S}$ J/s/m^2. According to Equation 34-23 it therefore carries momentum per unit area at the rate $\overline{S}/c$. Newton's law in its general form $\mathbf{F} = d\mathbf{p}/dt$ tells us that the rate of change of an object's momentum is equal to the net force on the object. Therefore, if an object absorbs electromagnetic wave momentum $\overline{S}/c$ per unit area per unit time, it experiences a force per unit area of this magnitude. Since force per unit area is pressure, we call this quantity the **radiation pressure**:

$$P_{\text{rad}} = \frac{\overline{S}}{c}. \tag{34-24}$$

FIGURE 34-27 The bright dot at the center of this picture is a 20-micron particle levitated by a laser beam reflected upward by the prism shown at the bottom.

FIGURE 34-28 Two-stage sailing spacecraft proposed for interstellar travel. At the target star, laser light beamed all the way from the solar system would reflect from the large sail to the smaller one, bringing the latter to a stop. The diameter of the large sail is 1000 km.

The radiation pressure is doubled if an object reflects electromagnetic waves, in the same way that bouncing a basketball off a backboard changes the ball's momentum by $2mv$ and, therefore, delivers momentum $2mv$ to the backboard.

The pressure exerted by ordinary light is very small, but Dartmouth College physicists E. F. Nichols and G. F. Hull demonstrated its existence in a sensitive experiment performed in 1903. With high-energy laser light or with objects of low mass and large area, radiation pressure can be appreciable. Lasers exert enough light pressure to levitate small particles (Fig. 34-27), and the pressure of light has been suggested as a means of driving interstellar "sailing ships" (Fig. 34-28). Finally, the idea that electromagnetic waves carry momentum played a crucial role in Einstein's development of his famous equation $E = mc^2$.

EXAMPLE 34-6	*Star Wars*

A proposed ballistic missile defense system calls for a laser that can focus 25 MW of light on an attacking warhead. The weapon works by heating the warhead to the point of destruction, but it also delivers momentum that alters the warhead's trajectory. If the beam dwells on a 200-kg warhead for 15 s, what velocity change does it impart to the warhead? Estimate the distance by which the warhead will be knocked off course over its remaining 30 minutes of flight.

Solution

The energy delivered in a 25-MW beam acting for 15 s is (25 MW)(15 s) = 375 MJ. According to Equation 34-23, the associated momentum is

$$p = \frac{U}{c} = \frac{375 \times 10^6 \text{ J}}{3.00 \times 10^8 \text{ m/s}} = 1.25 \text{ kg·m/s} .$$

The change in the warhead's velocity is given by $m\Delta v = \Delta p$, where Δp is the change in its momentum. Assuming the warhead absorbs all the beam's momentum, we then have

$$\Delta v = \frac{\Delta p}{m} = \frac{1.25 \text{ kg·m/s}}{200 \text{ kg}} = 0.00625 \text{ m/s} .$$

This is insignificant compared with a typical warhead speed of 7 km/s. Even though we don't know the direction of the velocity change, we can estimate crudely the error Δx in the impact point by multiplying this change by the flight time:

$$\Delta x = \Delta v\, t = (0.00625 \text{ m/s})(30 \text{ min})(60 \text{ s/min}) = 11 \text{ m} .$$

This is totally negligible, especially for a nuclear warhead. Even with this enormously powerful laser, radiation pressure has an insignificant effect. It's the energy delivered, not the momentum, that matters here.

EXERCISE A laser delivers 5.0 MW/m². If the beam is directed upward, what is the maximum mass for a 100-μm-diameter particle to be suspended in the beam?

Answer: 1.3×10^{-11} kg

Some problems similar to Example 34-6: 56–59

CHAPTER SYNOPSIS

Summary

1. Maxwell's modification of Ampère's law adds a **displacement current** term $\varepsilon_0 d\phi_E/dt$, showing that changing electric flux is a source of magnetic field. This modified law completes the set of **Maxwell's equations**—the four equations that govern the behavior of electromagnetic fields.

2. The interplay of electric and magnetic fields described by Faraday's and Ampère's laws gives rise to **electromagnetic waves**. When they propagate through vacuum, these waves

   a. Travel at the speed of light, $c = 1/\sqrt{\varepsilon_0\mu_0} = 3.00\times10^8$ m/s.

   b. Have their electric and magnetic fields at right angles to each other and to the direction of wave propagation.

   c. Have their fields in phase, with magnitudes related by $E = cB$.

   d. Can have any frequency or wavelength, provided the two are related by the equivalent expressions $f\lambda = c$ or $\omega/k = c$.

3. Radio waves, television, microwaves, infrared, visible light, ultraviolet, X rays, and gamma rays are all forms of electromagnetic radiation. They differ only in frequency and wavelength, and together comprise the **electromagnetic spectrum**.

4. **Polarization** describes the orientation of a wave's electric field in the plane perpendicular to the propagation direction. When a polarized wave passes through a polarizing material, its intensity is reduced by a factor $\cos^2\theta$, where θ is the angle between the wave polarization and the preferred axis of the material.

5. Electromagnetic waves are produced by accelerated electric charges, as in the alternating current of a radio antenna.

6. Electromagnetic waves carry energy. The rate at which energy is transported per unit area is the wave **intensity**. The **Poynting vector**,

$$\mathbf{S} = \frac{\mathbf{E} \times \mathbf{B}}{\mu_0},$$

describes this energy transport for any configuration of electromagnetic fields. The average intensity has half the peak value, or

$$\bar{S} = \frac{E_p B_p}{2\mu_0}.$$

The intensity of a plane wave remains constant, while the intensity from a localized source decreases as the inverse square of the distance from the source.

7. An electromagnetic wave with energy U also carries momentum $p = U/c$. As a result, it exerts a **radiation pressure** $P_{rad} = \bar{S}/c$ on an object that absorbs the wave and twice this pressure on a reflecting object.

Terms You Should Understand

(Pairs are closely related terms whose distinction is important; number in parentheses is chapter section where term first appears.)

displacement current (34-2)
Maxwell's equations (34-3)
electromagnetic wave (34-4)
electromagnetic spectrum (34-7)
polarization (34-8)
intensity, Poynting vector (34-10)
radiation pressure (34-11)

Symbols You Should Recognize

$\varepsilon_0 d\phi_E/dt$ (34-2)
S, $\mathbf{S}$, $\bar{S}$ (34-10)
c (34-5)
P_{rad} (34-11)

Problems You Should Be Able to Solve

evaluating induced magnetic fields in symmetric situations (34-2)
relating frequency and wavelength of electromagnetic waves (34-6)
relating electric and magnetic field strengths in electromagnetic waves (34-6)
calculating light intensity emerging from one or more polarizers (34-8)
relating wave intensity and fields (34-10)
evaluating wave intensity and fields as a function of distance from localized sources (34-10)
calculating radiation pressure and its effects (34-11)

Limitations to Keep in Mind

The description of electromagnetic waves developed in this chapter applies strictly only in vacuum.

QUESTIONS

1. Why is Maxwell's modification of Ampère's law essential to the existence of electromagnetic waves?
2. The presence of magnetic monopoles would require modification of Gauss's law for magnetism. Which of the other Maxwell equations would also need modification?
3. There is displacement current between the plates of a charging capacitor, yet no charge is moving between the plates. In what sense is the word "current" appropriate here?
4. Is there displacement current in an electromagnetic wave? Is there ordinary conduction current?
5. List some similarities and differences between electromagnetic waves and sound waves.
6. What aspect of the electromagnetic wave considered in Section 34-4 ensures that Gauss's laws for electricity and magnetism are satisfied?
7. Explain why parallel electric and magnetic fields in vacuum could not constitute an electromagnetic wave.
8. The speed of an electromagnetic wave is given by $c = \lambda f$. How does the speed depend on frequency? On wavelength?
9. When astronomers observe a supernova explosion in a distant galaxy, they see a sudden, simultaneous rise in visible light and other forms of electromagnetic radiation. How is this evidence that the speed of light is independent of frequency?
10. Turning a TV antenna so its rods point vertically may change the quality of your TV reception. Why? Think about polarization.
11. Unpolarized light is incident on two sheets of Polaroid with their polarization directions at right angles, and no light

gets through. A third sheet is inserted between the other two, and now some light gets through. How can this be?
12. Why is it not possible to define exactly where the visible region of the spectrum ends?
13. Why did the field of X-ray astronomy flourish only after the advent of space flight?
14. The Sun emits most of its electromagnetic wave energy in the visible region of the spectrum, with the peak in the yellow-green. Our eyes are sensitive to the same range, with peak sensitivity in the yellow-green. Is this a coincidence?
15. Suppose your eyes were sensitive to radio waves rather than light. What things would look bright?
16. An LC circuit is made entirely from superconducting materials, yet its oscillations eventually damp out. Why?
17. If you double the field strength in an electromagnetic wave, what happens to the intensity?
18. The intensity of light falls off as the inverse square of the distance from the source. Does this mean that electromagnetic wave energy is lost? Explain.
19. When your picture is taken with a flash camera, why doesn't the momentum of the light flash knock you over?
20. Some long-distance power transmission lines use DC rather than AC, despite the need to convert between DC and AC at either end. Why might this be? What energy loss mechanism occurs with AC but not DC?
21. Electromagnetic waves do not readily penetrate metals. Why might this be?

PROBLEMS

Section 34-2 Ambiguity in Ampère's Law

1. A uniform electric field is increasing at the rate of 1.5 V/m·μs. What is the displacement current through an area of 1.0 cm^2 at right angles to the field?
2. A parallel-plate capacitor has square plates 10 cm on a side and 0.50 cm apart. If the voltage across the plates is increasing at the rate of 220 V/ms, what is the displacement current in the capacitor?
3. A parallel-plate capacitor of plate area A and spacing d is charging at the rate dV/dt. Show that the displacement current in the capacitor is equal to the conduction current flowing in the wires feeding the capacitor.
4. A capacitor with circular plates is fed with long, straight wires along the axis of the plates. Show that the magnetic field *outside* the capacitor, in a plane that passes through the interior of the capacitor and is perpendicular to the

axis, is given by $B = \dfrac{\mu_0 \varepsilon_0 R^2}{2rd} \dfrac{dV}{dt}$. Here R is the plate radius, d the spacing, dV/dt the rate of change of the capacitor voltage, and r the distance from the axis.
5. A parallel-plate capacitor has circular plates with radius 50 cm and spacing 1.0 mm. A uniform electric field between the plates is changing at the rate 1.0 MV/m·s. What is the magnetic field between the plates (a) on the symmetry axis, (b) 15 cm from the axis, and (c) 150 cm from the axis?
6. An electric field points into the page and occupies a circular region of radius 1.0 m, as shown in Fig. 34-29. There are no electric charges in the region, but there is a magnetic field forming closed loops pointing clockwise, as shown. The magnetic field strength 50 cm from the center of the

FIGURE 34-29 Problem 6.

time $= 50\mu s$

FIGURE 34-30 Problem 14.

region is 2.0 μT. (a) What is the rate of change of the electric field? (b) Is the electric field increasing or decreasing?

Section 34-4 Electromagnetic Waves

7. At a particular point the instantaneous electric field of an electromagnetic wave points in the $+y$ direction, while the magnetic field points in the $-z$ direction. In what direction is the wave propagating?

8. The fields of an electromagnetic wave are $\mathbf{E} = E_p \sin(kz + \omega t)\hat{\mathbf{j}}$ and $\mathbf{B} = B_p \sin(kz + \omega t)\hat{\mathbf{i}}$. Give a unit vector in the direction of propagation.

9. The electric field of a radio wave is given by $\mathbf{E} = E\sin(kz - \omega t)(\hat{\mathbf{i}} + \hat{\mathbf{j}})$. (a) What is the peak amplitude of the electric field? (b) Give a unit vector in the direction of the magnetic field at a place and time where $\sin(kz - \omega t)$ is positive.

10. Show by differentiation and substitution that Equations 34-12b and 34-13 can be satisfied by fields of the form $E(x, t) = E_p f(kx \pm \omega t)$ and $B(x, t) = B_p f(kx \pm \omega t)$, where f is any function of the argument $kx \pm \omega t$.

11. Show that it is impossible for an electromagnetic wave in vacuum to have a time-varying component of its electric field in the direction of its magnetic field. *Hint:* Assume $\mathbf{E}$ does have such a component, and show that you cannot satisfy both Gauss and Faraday.

Section 34-5 The Speed of Electromagnetic Waves

12. A light-minute is the distance light travels in one minute. Show that the Sun is about 8 light-minutes from Earth.

13. Your intercontinental telephone call is carried by electromagnetic waves routed via a satellite in geosynchronous orbit at an altitude of 36,000 km. Approximately how long does it take before your voice is heard at the other end?

14. An airplane's radar altimeter works by bouncing radio waves off the ground and measuring the round-trip travel time (Fig. 34-30). If that time is 50 μs, what is the altitude?

15. Roughly how long does it take light to go 1 foot?

16. If you speak via radio from Earth to an astronaut on the moon, how long is it before you can get a reply?

17. "Ghosts" on a TV screen occur when part of the signal goes directly from transmitter to receiver, while part takes a longer route, reflecting off mountains or buildings (Fig. 34-31). The electron beam in a 50-cm-wide TV tube "paints" the picture by scanning the beam from left to right across the screen in about 10^{-4} s. If a "ghost" image appears displaced about 1 cm from the main image, what is the difference in path lengths of the direct and indirect signals?

FIGURE 34-31 Ghost images of highways appear on this TV traffic report (Problem 17).

18. A computer can fetch information from its memory in 3.0 ns, a process that involves sending a signal from the central processing unit (CPU) to memory and awaiting the return of the information. If signals in the computer's wiring travel at $0.60c$, what is the maximum distance between the CPU and the memory? Your answer shows why high-speed computers are necessarily compact.

19. Problem 69 shows that the speed of electromagnetic waves in a transparent dielectric is given by $1/\sqrt{\kappa \varepsilon_0 \mu_0}$, where κ is the dielectric constant described in Chapter 26. An experimental measurement gives 1.97×10^8 m/s for the speed of light in a piece of glass. What is the dielectric constant of this glass at optical frequencies?

Section 34-6 Properties of Electromagnetic Waves

20. What are the wavelengths of (a) a 100-MHz FM radio wave, (b) a 3.0-GHz radar wave, (c) a 6.0×10^{14}-Hz light wave, and (d) a 1.0×10^{18}-Hz X ray?

21. A 60-Hz power line emits electromagnetic radiation. What is the wavelength?

22. Antennas for transmitting and receiving electromagnetic radiation usually have typical dimensions on the order of half a wavelength. Look at a TV antenna, and estimate the wavelength and frequency of a TV signal.

23. A CB radio antenna is a vertical rod 2.75 m high. If this length is one-fourth of the CB wavelength, what is the CB frequency?

24. A microwave oven operates at 2.4 GHz. What is the distance between wave crests in the oven?

25. What would be the electric field strength in an electromagnetic wave whose magnetic field equalled that of Earth, about 50 μT?

26. Dielectric breakdown in air occurs at an electric field strength of about 3×10^6 V/m. What would be the peak magnetic field in an electromagnetic wave with this value for its peak electric field?

27. A radio receiver can detect signals with electric fields as low as 320 μV/m. What is the corresponding magnetic field?

Section 34-8 Polarization

28. An electromagnetic wave is propagating in the z direction. What is its polarization direction, if its magnetic field is in the y direction?

29. Polarized light is incident on a sheet of polarizing material, and only 20% of the light gets through. What is the angle between the electric field and the polarization axis of the material?

30. Vertically polarized light passes through a polarizer whose polarization axis is oriented at 70° to the vertical. What fraction of the incident intensity emerges from the polarizer?

31. A polarizer blocks 75% of a polarized light beam. What is the angle between the beam's polarization and the polarizer's axis?

32. An electro-optic modulator is supposed to switch a laser beam between fully off and fully on, as its crystal rotates the beam polarization by 90° when a voltage is applied. But a power-supply failure results in only enough voltage for a 72° beam rotation. What fraction of the laser light is transmitted when it is supposed to be fully on?

33. Unpolarized light of intensity S_0 passes first through a polarizer with its polarization axis vertical, then through one with its axis at 35° to the vertical. What is the light intensity after the second polarizer?

34. Vertically polarized light passes through two polarizers, the first at 60° to the vertical and the second at 90° to the vertical. What fraction of the light gets through?

35. Unpolarized light with intensity S_0 passes through a stack of five polarizing sheets, each with its axis rotated 20° with respect to the previous one. What is the intensity of the light emerging from the stack?

36. Unpolarized light of intensity S_0 is incident on a "sandwich" of three polarizers. The outer two have their transmission axes perpendicular, while the middle one has its axis at 45° to the others. What is the light intensity emerging from this "sandwich?"

37. Polarized light with average intensity S_0 passes through a sheet of polarizing material which is rotating at 10 rev/s. At time $t = 0$ the polarization axis is aligned with the incident polarization. Write an expression for the transmitted intensity as a function of time.

Section 34-10 Energy in Electromagnetic Waves

38. A typical laboratory electric field is 1000 V/m. What is the average intensity of an electromagnetic wave with this value for its peak field?

39. What would be the average intensity of a laser beam so strong that its electric field produced dielectric breakdown of air (which requires $E_p = 3 \times 10^6$ V/m)?

40. Estimate the peak electric field inside a 625-W microwave oven under the simplifying approximation that the microwaves propagate as a plane wave through the oven's 750-cm^2 cross-sectional area.

41. A radio receiver can pick up signals with peak electric fields as low as 450 μV/m. What is the average intensity of such a signal?

42. Show that the electric and magnetic energy densities in an electromagnetic wave are equal.

43. A laser blackboard pointer delivers 0.10 mW average power in a beam 0.90 mm in diameter. Find (a) the average intensity, (b) the peak electric field, and (c) the peak magnetic field.

44. The laser of Example 34-6 produces a spot 80 cm in diameter at its target. What are the rms electric and magnetic fields at the target?

45. The United States' safety standard for continuous exposure to microwave radiation is 10 mW/cm^2. The glass door of a microwave oven measures 40 cm by 17 cm and is covered with a metal screen that blocks microwaves. What fraction of the oven's 625-W microwave power can leak through the door window without exceeding the safe exposure to someone right outside the door? Assume the power leaks uniformly through the window area.

46. A 1.0-kW radio transmitter broadcasts uniformly in all directions. What is the intensity of its signal at a distance of 5.0 km from the transmitter?

47. Use the fact that sunlight intensity at Earth's orbit is 1368 W/m^2 to calculate the Sun's total power output.

48. About two-thirds of the solar energy at Earth's orbit reaches the planet's surface. At what rate is solar energy incident on the entire Earth? See the previous problem,

and compare your result with the roughly 10^{13} W rate at which humanity consumes energy.

49. During its 1989 encounter with Neptune, the Voyager 2 spacecraft was 4.5×10^9 km from Earth (Fig. 34-32). Its images of Neptune were broadcast by a radio transmitter with a mere 21-W average power output. What would be (a) the average intensity and (b) the peak electric field received at Earth if the transmitter broadcast equally in all directions? (The received signal was actually somewhat stronger because Voyager used a directional antenna.)

FIGURE 34-32 Neptune, photographed by the Voyager II spacecraft when it was 4.5×10^9 km from Earth. How long did it take the radio signal carrying this image to reach Earth? (Problem 49)

50. A quasar 10 billion light-years from Earth appears the same brightness as a star 50,000 light-years away. How does the power output of the quasar compare with that of the star?

51. At 1.5 km from the transmitter, the peak electric field of a radio wave is 350 mV/m. (a) What is the transmitter's power output, assuming it broadcasts uniformly in all directions? (b) What is the peak electric field 10 km from the transmitter?

52. The peak electric field at a point 25 m from a point source of electromagnetic waves is 4.2 kV/m. What is the peak magnetic field 1.0 m from the source?

53. A typical fluorescent lamp is a little over 1 m long and a few cm in diameter. How do you expect the light intensity to vary with distance (a) near the lamp but not near either end and (b) far from the lamp?

Section 34-11 Wave Momentum and Radiation Pressure

54. A camera flash delivers 2.5 kW of light power for 1.0 ms (Fig. 34-33). Find (a) the total energy and (b) the total momentum carried by the flash.

55. What is the radiation pressure exerted on a light-absorbing surface by a laser beam whose intensity is 180 W/cm²?

56. A laser beam shines vertically upward. What laser power is necessary for this beam to support a flat piece of aluminum foil with mass 30 μg and diameter equal to that of the beam? Assume the foil reflects all the light.

FIGURE 34-33 How much energy and momentum are in light from the camera flash? (Problem 54)

57. The average intensity of noonday sunlight is about 1 kW/m². What is the radiation force on a solar collector measuring 60 cm by 2.5 m if it is oriented at right angles to the incident light and absorbs all the light?

58. Serious proposals have been made to "sail" spacecraft to the outer solar system using the pressure of sunlight. How much sail area must a 1000-kg spacecraft have if its acceleration at Earth's orbit is to be 1 m/s²? Assume the sails are made from reflecting material. You can neglect the Sun's gravity. (Why?)

59. A 65-kg astronaut is floating in empty space. If the astronaut shines a 1.0-W flashlight in a fixed direction, how long will it take the astronaut to accelerate to a speed of 10 m/s?

60. A "photon rocket" emits a beam of light instead of the hot gas of an ordinary rocket. How powerful a light source would be needed for a photon rocket with thrust equal to that of a space shuttle (35 MN)? Compare your answer with humanity's total electric power-generating capability, about 10^{12} W.

Paired Problems

(Both problems in a pair involve the same principles and techniques. If you can get the first problem, you should be able to solve the second one.)

61. Find the peak electric and magnetic fields 1.5 m from a 60-W light bulb that radiates equally in all directions.

62. At 4.6 km from a radio transmitter, the peak electric field in the radio wave measures 380 mV/m. What is the transmitter's power, assuming it broadcasts equally in all directions?

63. Unpolarized light is incident on two polarizers with their axes at 45°. What fraction of the incident light gets through?

64. Find the angle between two polarizers if unpolarized light incident on the pair emerges with 10% of its incident intensity.

65. What is the radiation force on the door of a microwave oven if 625 W of microwave power hits the door at right angles and is reflected?

66. What is the power output of a laser whose beam exerts a 55-mN force on an absorbing object oriented at right angles to the beam? The object is larger than the beam's cross section.

67. A 60-W light bulb is 6.0 cm in diameter. What is the radiation pressure on an opaque object at the bulb's surface?

68. A white dwarf star is approximately the size of Earth but radiates about as much energy as the Sun. Estimate the radiation pressure on an absorbing object at the white dwarf's surface.

Supplementary Problems

69. Maxwell's equations in a dielectric resemble those in vacuum (Equations 34-6 through 34-9), but with ϕ_E in Ampère's law replaced by $\kappa\phi_E$, where κ is the dielectric constant introduced in Chapter 26. Show that the speed of electromagnetic waves in such a dielectric is $c/\sqrt{\kappa}$.

70. Use appropriate data from Appendix E to calculate the radiation pressure on a light-absorbing object at the Sun's surface.

71. A radar system produces pulses consisting of 100 full cycles of a sinusoidal 70-GHz electromagnetic wave. The average power while the transmitter is on is 45 MW, and the waves are confined to a beam 20 cm in diameter. Find (a) the peak electric field, (b) the wavelength, (c) the total energy in a pulse, and (d) the total momentum in a pulse. (e) If the transmitter produces 1000 pulses per second, what is its average power output?

72. In a stack of polarizing sheets, each sheet has its polarization axis rotated 14° with respect to the preceding sheet. If the stack passes 37% of the incident, unpolarized light, how many sheets does it contain?

73. The peak electric field measured at 8.0 cm from a light source is 150 W/m², while at 12 cm it measures 122 W/m². Describe the shape of the source.

74. Show that Equations 34-12b and 34-13 may be combined to yield a wave equation like Equation 16-13. *Hint:* Take the partial derivative of one equation with respect to x and of the other with respect to t, and use the fact that

$$\frac{\partial}{\partial x}\left(\frac{\partial f}{\partial t}\right) = \frac{\partial}{\partial t}\left(\frac{\partial f}{\partial x}\right)$$

for any well-behaved function $f(x, t)$.

75. Studies of the origin of the solar system suggest that sufficiently small particles might be blown out of the solar system by the force of sunlight. To see how small such particles must be, compare the force of sunlight with the force of gravity, and solve for the particle radius at which the two are equal. Assume the particles are spherical and have density 2 g/cm³. Why do you not need to worry about the distance from the Sun?

76. A cylindrical resistor of length ℓ, radius a, and resistance R carries a current I. Calculate the electric and magnetic fields at the surface of the resistor, assuming the electric field is uniform throughout, including at the surface. Calculate the Poynting vector, and show that it points into the resistor. Calculate the flux of the Poynting vector (that is, $\int \mathbf{S} \cdot d\mathbf{A}$) over the surface of the resistor to get the rate of electromagnetic energy flow into the resistor, and show that the result is just I^2R. Your result shows that the energy heating the resistor comes from the fields surrounding it. These fields are sustained by the source of electrical energy that drives the current.

PART 4 *Cumulative Problems*

These problems combine material from chapters throughout the entire part or, in addition, from chapters in earlier parts, or they present special challenges.

1. An air-insulated parallel-plate capacitor has plate area 100 cm² and spacing 0.50 cm. The capacitor is charged and then disconnected from the charging battery. A thin-walled, nonconducting box of the same dimensions as the capacitor is filled with water at 20.00°C. The box is released at the edge of the capacitor and moves without friction into the capacitor (Fig. 1). When it reaches equilibrium the water temperature is 21.50°. What was the original voltage on the capacitor?

FIGURE 1 Cumulative Problem 1.

2. A wire of length ℓ and resistance R is formed into a closed rectangular loop twice as long as it is wide. It is mounted on a nonconducting horizontal axle parallel to its longer dimension, as shown in Fig. 2. A uniform magnetic field **B** points into the page, as shown. A long string of negligible mass is wrapped many times around a drum of radius a attached to the axle, and a mass m is attached to the string. When the mass is released it falls and eventually reaches a speed that, averaged over one cycle of the loop's rotation, is constant from one rotation to the next. Find an expression for that average terminal speed.

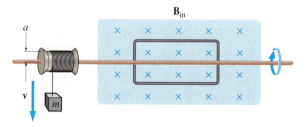

FIGURE 2 Cumulative Problem 2.

3. Five wires of equal length 25 cm and resistance 10 Ω are connected as shown in Fig. 3. Two solenoids, each 10 cm in diameter, extend a long way perpendicular to the page. The magnetic fields of both solenoids point out of the page; the field strength in the left-hand solenoid is increasing at

50 T/s while that in the right-hand solenoid is decreasing at 30 T/s. Find the current in the resistance wire shared by both triangles. Which way does the current flow?

FIGURE 3 Cumulative Problem 3.

4. A long solenoid of length ℓ and radius R has a total of N turns. The solenoid current is increasing linearly with time: $I(t) = bt$, where b is a constant. (a) Find an expression for the rate at which the magnetic energy in the solenoid is increasing. (b) Find an expression for the induced electric field at the inner edge of the solenoid coils. (c) Evaluate the Poynting vector at the inner edge of the coils, and show by integration that electromagnetic energy is flowing into the solenoid at a rate equal to the buildup of magnetic energy.

5. A coaxial cable consists of an inner conductor of radius a and an outer conductor of radius b; the space between the conductors is filled with insulation of dielectric constant κ (Fig. 4). The cable's axis is the z axis. The cable is used to carry electromagnetic energy from a radio transmitter to a broadcasting antenna. The electric field between the conductors points radially from the axis, and is given by $E = E_0(a/r) \cos(kz - \omega t)$. The magnetic field encircles the axis, and is given by $B = B_0(a/r) \cos(kz - \omega t)$. Here E_0, B_0, k, and ω are constants. Show, using appropriate closed surfaces and loops, that these fields satisfy Maxwell's equations. Your result shows that the cable acts as a "waveguide," confining an electromagnetic wave to the space between the conductors.

(a) (b)

FIGURE 4 Cumulative Problem 5. (*a*) A coaxial cable. (*b*) Cross section, showing the electric and magnetic fields. The fields also vary with position z along the cable axis, according to the equations given.

Part Five — Optics

In "Prismatic Abstract," multiple light beams converge on a prism to create a dazzlingly colorful effect. Photographic artist Pete Saloutous exploited the principles of optics in creating this work.

Imagine a world without light. We see because light reflects off objects; our eyes form images because light refracts in our corneas and lenses; and the more subtle effect of interference lets us make some of the most precise measurements possible and is behind the operation of everyday technologies like compact discs. Although the behavior of light is ultimately grounded in Maxwell's equations of electromagnetism, we can learn much about light from the simpler perspective of optics. The next three chapters explore the behavior of light, images and optical instruments, and the phenomena of interference.

35 Reflection and Refraction

Reflection and refraction guide light in a wide range of natural and technological applications. Here the image of a bee's head appears in a large-scale version of the optical fibers that are essential to modern communications.

Maxwell's brilliant work shows that the phenomena of **optics**—that is, the behavior of light—are manifestations of the laws of electromagnetism. Except in the atomic realm, where it is necessary to use quantum mechanics, all optical phenomena can be understood in terms of electromagnetic wave fields as described by Maxwell's equations. But often we need not resort to the full electromagnetic or even wave description of light to understand optics.

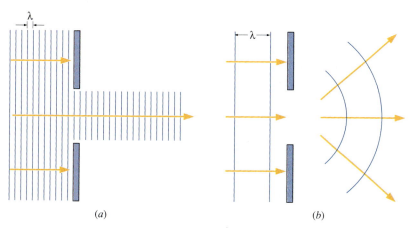

FIGURE 35-1 Light waves incident on an opaque barrier with a hole in it. (*a*) When the hole diameter is much greater than the wavelength λ, light emerges from the hole in essentially a straight line. In this case it is appropriate to treat the light as traveling in straight rays except where it actually hits something. (*b*) When the hole diameter is comparable to or smaller than the wavelength, then interference causes the wavefronts to bend, and the ray approximation is no longer adequate.

When the objects with which light—or, for that matter, any other wave—interacts are much larger than the wavelength, then to a good approximation the light travels in straight lines called rays (Fig. 35-1). Geometrical optics is the study of light under conditions when the ray approximation is valid. In this chapter we show how geometrical optics describes the behavior of light at interfaces between two different materials. In the next chapter we will show how geometrical optics explains optical systems including mirrors, lenses, the human eye, and many optical instruments.

35-1 REFLECTION AND TRANSMISSION

When a light ray propagating in one medium strikes the interface with a second medium, some light may be **reflected** back into the original medium and some **transmitted** into the new medium. Properties of the two materials, and the propagation direction of the incident light, determine the details of the reflection and transmission.

Some materials—notably metals—reflect nearly all the light incident on them. It's no coincidence that these materials are also good electrical conductors. The oscillating electric field of a light wave drives the metal's free electrons into oscillatory motion, and this accelerated motion, in turn, produces electromagnetic waves. The effect of all the oscillating electrons together is simply to reradiate the wave back into the original medium. Ultimately, that's why metals appear shiny.

In other materials, the atomic and molecular configurations are such that the material absorbs most of the incident light energy. Such materials therefore appear dark and opaque. Since an opaque material basically destroys light that's transmitted into it by converting the light to other forms of energy, these materials play little role in our exploration of optics.

FIGURE 35-2 A laser beam incident on a glass prism shows partial reflection and partial transmission at the interfaces between air and glass. Can you tell which is the incident beam?

Still other materials are essentially transparent, allowing light to propagate with little energy loss. These materials are generally insulators whose electrons, bound to individual atoms, cannot respond freely to the fields of an incident wave. The electrons do respond in a more limited way, however, effectively producing oscillating molecular dipoles. Although a microscopic description of this process is complicated, the net effect in most simple dielectric materials is a reduction in the propagation speed of electromagnetic waves from the speed in a vacuum c, as wave energy is absorbed and reradiated by the molecular dipoles.

In this chapter we explore the processes that occur at the interfaces between transparent and reflective materials and between different transparent materials. Reflection is the significant process in the former case, while in the latter both reflection and transmission generally occur (Fig. 35-2).

35-2 REFLECTION

Reflection returns some or all of the light incident on an interface to its original medium. Whether the reflection is essentially complete, as from a metal, or partial, as from a transparent material, it satisfies the same geometrical condition. Experiment—as well as analysis based on Maxwell's equations—shows that the incident ray, the reflected ray, and the normal to the interface between the two materials all lie in the same plane, and that the angle θ_1' that the reflected ray makes with the normal is equal to the angle θ_1 made by the incident ray (Fig. 35-3a). That is,

$$\theta_1' = \theta_1, \tag{35-1}$$

where the subscript 1 designates angles in the first medium. These angles are designated the **angle of reflection** and **angle of incidence**, respectively.

When a beam of parallel light rays reflects off a smooth surface, each ray in the beam reflects at the same angle, and the entire beam is thus reflected without distortion (Fig. 35-3b). This process is called **specular reflection**. But if the surface is rough, then individual rays, while still obeying Equation 35-1, reflect from differently oriented pieces of the surface. As a result the reflection is **diffuse**, with the original beam spreading in all directions (Fig. 35-3c). White wall paint is a good example of a diffuse reflector, while the aluminum or silver coating of a mirror is an excellent specular reflector. When we speak of reflection we generally mean specular reflection.

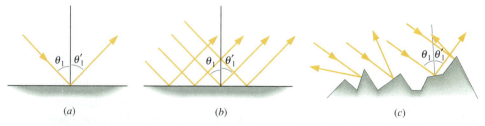

(a) (b) (c)

FIGURE 35-3 (a) The angles of reflection and incidence are equal. (b) In specular reflection, a smooth surface reflects a light beam undistorted. (c) A rough surface results in diffuse reflection. The law of reflection still holds for each individual ray.

EXAMPLE 35-1	*The Corner Reflector*

Two mirrors are joined at right angles, as shown in Fig. 35-4. Show that any light ray incident in the plane of the page will return antiparallel to its incident direction.

Solution

The law of reflection ensures that the two angles marked θ in Fig. 35-4 are equal, as are the two marked ϕ. But the mirrors make a 90° angle, and therefore $\phi = 90° - \theta$. The incident and first reflected ray make an angle 2θ, while the first reflected ray and the outgoing ray make an angle $2\phi = 180° - 2\theta$. Thus these two angles sum to 180°, which shows that the incident and outgoing rays are antiparallel. This result holds regardless of the actual value of the incidence angle θ.

Adding a third mirror at right angles to the other two makes a corner reflector that returns any beam in the direction from which it came—regardless of the orientation of the beam or the reflector (Fig. 35-5b). Corner reflectors, often made with prisms rather than mirrors, are widely used in optics. A corner

(a)   *(b)*

FIGURE 35-5 (*a*) Astronauts left this array of corner reflectors on the moon. Reflecting pulses of laser light off the array allows determination of the moon's position to within 15 cm. (*b*) Each reflector is functionally equivalent to three mutually perpendicular mirrors, although the reflectors are actually made from partial cubes of glass and work by the mechanism of total internal reflection that we'll explore in Section 35-4.

reflector left on the moon allows laser-based measurements of the moon's distance to within about 15 cm (Fig. 35-5a).

EXERCISE Two mirrors make an angle of 135°. A light ray is incident on the first mirror at an angle of 60° to the mirror's normal. Find (a) the angle of incidence on the second mirror and (b) the angle between the original incident beam and the final outgoing beam.

Answers: (a) 75°; (b) 90°

Some problems similar to Example 35-1: 2, 4, 5

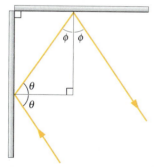

FIGURE 35-4 Two-dimensional corner reflector, made from two mirrors at right angles. Any ray incident in the horizontal plane returns parallel to its original direction.

35-3 REFRACTION

Figures 35-2 and 35-6 show that light passing between two transparent media is partially reflected and partially transmitted at their interface. In addition, the transmitted beam changes direction at the interface—a phenomenon known as **refraction**.

Physically, refraction occurs because the wave speeds in the two media are different. That difference results from delays introduced by the interaction of the electromagnetic wave fields with atomic electrons. But the wave frequency

FIGURE 35-6 Reflection and refraction at an interface. This case, where the refracted ray is bent *toward* the normal, occurs when medium 2 has a higher refractive index and therefore a lower wave speed. Angles θ_1, θ_1', and θ_2 are, respectively, the angles of incidence, reflection, and refraction.

(a)   (b)

FIGURE 35-7 (a) Waves refract at an interface because wave speeds—and therefore the wavelengths—are different in the two media. Two shaded triangles have a common hypotenuse, whose length is $vT/\sin\theta$, where v and θ are taken on either side of the interface. (b) Water waves refract as they pass over a triangular patch of shallower water. Note the decreased wavelength and different orientations of the waves within the shallow region. Reflection at the interfaces has resulted in waves propagating in several directions. (Wave speed in shallow water depends on depth, so a change in depth corresponds to a change in medium for light waves.)

ActivPhysics

15.1, 15.2

Reflection and Refraction

f—and thus the wave period $T = 1/f$—must be the same on both sides of the interface; otherwise, on one side of the interface more wave crests would pass in a given time than on the other side, implying the creation or destruction of waves at the interface. In Fig. 35-7a waves in medium 1 travel at speed v_1, and the wavelength—the distance between wave crests—is therefore $v_1 T$. We'll assume that in medium 2 the speed has some lower value v_2, so the wavelength $v_2 T$ is correspondingly shorter. The shaded triangles in Fig. 35-7a are right triangles with a common hypotenuse, and the ratio of the opposite side to the length of this hypotenuse defines the sines of the angles θ_1 and θ_2. Equating expressions for the hypotenuse length (opposite side divided by sine) in terms of these two angles gives

$$\frac{v_1 T}{\sin\theta_1} = \frac{v_2 T}{\sin\theta_2},$$

or

$$\frac{\sin\theta_2}{\sin\theta_1} = \frac{v_2}{v_1}.$$

We characterize the effect of a transparent medium on light through its **index of refraction**, n, defined as the ratio of the speed c of light in vacuum to the speed v of light in the medium:

$$n = \frac{c}{v}. \qquad \text{(index of refraction)} \qquad (35\text{-}2)$$

(Again there's an electromagnetic connection: the index of refraction is just the square root of the dielectric constant that we introduced in Chapter 26. But don't try to calculate refractive indices from the dielectric constants of

Table 26-1; the dielectric constant is frequency dependent, and its value at optical frequencies is significantly different from the DC values of Table 26-1.) Table 35-1 lists some indices of refraction. Note that for gases the index of refraction is essentially 1, the same as that of vacuum.

Using the definition 35-2 in our ratio of the sines of the angles of refraction and incidence, and then cross multiplying, gives **Snell's law**:

$$n_1 \sin \theta_1 = n_2 \sin \theta_2. \quad \text{(Snell's law)} \tag{35-3}$$

This law was developed geometrically in 1621 by Willebrord van Roijen Snell of the Netherlands and described analytically in the 1630s by René Descartes of France, where it is known to this day as Descartes' law. It allows us to predict what will happen to light at an interface, provided we know the refractive indices of the two media. As a special case, note that when $n_1 = n_2$ there's no change in angle; in general, the more different the refractive indices of the two media, the greater the change in angle.

Snell's law applies whether light goes from a medium of lower to higher refractive index or the reverse, as you can see by reversing the path of the light in Fig. 35-7. In the former case the refracted ray bends *toward* the normal, while in the latter case it bends *away* from the normal. Example 35-2 treats both cases.

TABLE 35-1 *Indices of Refraction**

SUBSTANCE	INDEX OF REFRACTION, n
Gases	
Air	1.000293
Carbon dioxide	1.00045
Liquids	
Water	1.333
Ethyl alcohol	1.361
Glycerine	1.473
Benzene	1.501
Diiodomethane	1.738
Solids	
Ice (H_2O)	1.309
Polystyrene	1.49
Glass	1.5–1.9
Sodium chloride (NaCl)	1.544
Diamond (C)	2.419
Rutile (TiO_2)	2.62

*At 1 atm pressure and temperatures ranging from 0°C to 20°C, measured at a wavelength of 589 nm (the yellow line of sodium).

EXAMPLE 35-2	*In and Out: Parallel Rays*

In Fig. 35-8, a light ray propagating in air strikes a transparent slab of thickness d and refractive index n with incidence angle θ_1. Show that the ray emerges from the slab propagating parallel to its original direction.

Solution
Applying Snell's law to the upper interface gives

$$\sin \theta_2 = \frac{\sin \theta_1}{n},$$

where we've taken $n_1 = 1$ for air and $n_2 = n$ for the slab. At the lower interface, with the light going from the slab to air, we have $n_1 = n$ and $n_2 = 1$, so Snell's law gives

$$\sin \theta_4 = n \sin \theta_3.$$

But the slab faces are parallel so, as the figure suggests, $\theta_3 = \theta_2$. Combining our two versions of Snell's law then gives

$$\sin \theta_4 = n \left(\frac{\sin \theta_1}{n} \right) = \sin \theta_1,$$

showing that the incident and outgoing rays are indeed parallel. They are, however, displaced by the distance x shown in the figure. You can find that displacement in Problem 54.

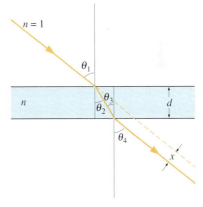

FIGURE 35-8 A light beam incident on a transparent slab emerges with its original direction, but is displaced from its original path.

EXERCISE A piece of glass with $n = 1.52$ is immersed in diiodomethane. A light ray strikes the glass with incidence angle 40°. Find the angle the refracted beam in the glass makes with the normal to the interface.

Answer: 47.3°

Some problems similar to Example 35-2: 11, 13, 54

EXAMPLE 35-3	CD Music

The laser beam that "reads" information from a compact disc is 0.737 mm wide at the point where it strikes the underside of the disc and forms a converging cone with half-angle 27°, as shown in Fig. 35-9. It then travels through a 1.2-mm-thick layer of transparent plastic with refractive index 1.55 before reaching the very thin, reflective information layer near the disc's top surface. What is the beam diameter (d in Fig. 35-9) at the information layer?

Solution

Figure 35-9 shows that $d = D - 2x$, where $D = 0.737$ mm is the beam diameter as it hits the disc. From the figure we also see that $x = t \tan\theta_2$, where $t = 1.2$ mm is the thickness of the plastic. Finally, Snell's law gives $\theta_2 = \sin^{-1}\left(\dfrac{\sin\theta_1}{n}\right)$, where we set the refractive index of air to 1. Putting these relations together gives

$$d = D - 2t \tan\left[\sin^{-1}\left(\frac{\sin\theta_1}{n}\right)\right]$$

$$= 737 \ \mu m - (2)(1200 \ \mu m) \tan\left[\sin^{-1}\left(\frac{\sin 27°}{1.55}\right)\right]$$

$$= 1.8 \ \mu m,$$

which is a little larger than the "pits" cut into the CD to store its information. This narrowing of the beam plays a crucial role in keeping CDs noise free. The tiniest dust speck would blot out information at the μm-scale information layer, but at the point where the laser beam actually enters the disc—the closest dust can get to the information layer—it would take mm-size dust to cause problems.

In Chapter 37 we'll see more on how optical phenomena are at the heart of CD technology.

EXERCISE Figure 35-10 shows a polystyrene cylinder whose height is equal to its diameter. What is the maximum incidence angle θ_1 at which a light ray striking the top center of the cylinder will emerge through the bottom without first striking the side? The medium surrounding the cylinder is air.

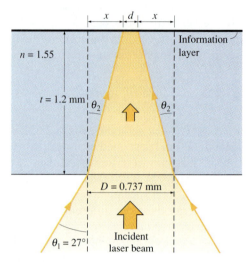

FIGURE 35-9 Section through a compact disc, showing convergence of the laser beam to a narrow spot at the information layer. All CDs share a common refractive index of 1.55 (Example 35-3).

FIGURE 35-10 What is the maximum θ_1 for which the beam will emerge through the bottom of the polystyrene cylinder?

Answer: 42°

Some problems similar to Example 35-3: 14, 15, 17, 18

We derived Snell's law using Fig. 35-7a, which shows the wavelength change that occurs as the wave speed changes between two media. There we argued that the frequencies in the two media must be the same. But wavelength, frequency, and wave speed are related by $\lambda f = v$; therefore, since wave speeds depend inversely on refractive index (Equation 35-2), so do the wavelengths. Thus the wavelengths in the two media are related by

$$\frac{\lambda_2}{\lambda_1} = \frac{n_1}{n_2}. \qquad (35\text{-}4)$$

EXAMPLE 35-4   *Light and Diamond*

Light with wavelength 589 nm in vacuum enters a diamond. Find the light speed and wavelength in the diamond.

Solution

Equation 35-2 gives

$$v = \frac{c}{n} = \frac{3.00 \times 10^8 \text{ m/s}}{2.419} = 1.24 \times 10^8 \text{ m/s}.$$

The refractive index of vacuum is 1, so Equation 35-4 gives

$$\lambda_{\text{diamond}} = \frac{\lambda_{\text{vacuum}}}{n} = \frac{589 \text{ nm}}{2.419} = 243 \text{ nm}.$$

The wavelength and speed are reduced by the same factor, as they must be to keep the wave frequency unchanged.

EXERCISE Microwaves propagate through glass at about 1.4×10^8 m/s. What is the refractive index of glass at microwave frequencies?

Answer: 2.14

Some problems similar to Example 35-4: 8, 9, 19

Got It!

Figure 35-11 shows the path of a light ray through three different media. Rank the media according to their indices of refraction.

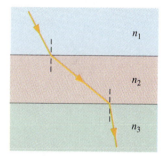

FIGURE 35-11 How do the refractive indices compare?

Multiple Refractions

Engineered optical systems often use several layers of refractive material to minimize reflective losses and certain types of distortion. To describe the path of a light ray in such a system, we need only apply Snell's law at each of the interfaces using the appropriate pair of refractive indices (Fig. 35-12a). When the layers are parallel the angular deflection of a light ray is the same as if it had gone through a single interface from the first medium to the last (see Problem 48). In many natural situations, including the human eye and Earth's atmosphere, the index of refraction is a continuously varying function of position (Fig. 35-12b). We can approximate such a case as a sequence of thin layers, each with a different refractive index. Going toward the limit of infinitely many infinitesimal layers gets us arbitrarily close to the exact solution, in which the

(a)   (b)

FIGURE 35-12 (a) Light propagating through a series of slabs with increasing refractive indices. At each interface the light bends more toward the normal. (b) Light follows a curved path in a medium with a continuously increasing refractive index.

(a)

FIGURE 35-13 (a) Mirages on a hot road. (b) The mirage occurs because hot air near the highway surface has a lower refractive index, resulting in a curved path for the light. The apparent position of the vehicle is not its actual position. Can you see why it appears upside down?

(b)

light follows a curved path. The mirage shown in Fig. 35-13 results from the fact that the refractive index of air is temperature dependent, causing the path of light rays to bend continuously.

35-4 TOTAL INTERNAL REFLECTION

Figure 35-14 shows light propagating inside a glass block and striking the interface with the surrounding air. Since air's refractive index is lower than that of glass, rays are bent *away* from the normal as they leave the glass. As the incidence angle increases, so does the angle of refraction—and Snell's law shows that the latter is always greater than the incidence angle. So at some incidence angle (see ray 3 in Fig. 35-14) the angle of refraction reaches 90°. What then?

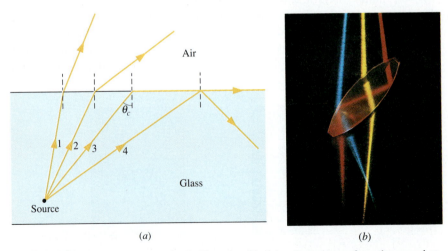

(a)   (b)

FIGURE 35-14 (a) Light propagating inside a glass block is refracted away from the normal at the glass-air interface. Ray 3, incident at the critical angle, just skims along the interface. At higher incidence angles, as with ray 4, the light undergoes total internal reflection at the interface. Not shown are weak reflected rays at angles less than the critical angle. (b) Three light beams strike a lens and are refracted at the air-glass interface. The red beam strikes the subsequent glass-air interface at an incidence angle greater than the critical angle and undergoes total internal reflection.

If the incidence angle is increased further, we find that the light is *totally* reflected at the interface. (There is always *some* reflection back into the glass, but now it's *all* reflected.) This phenomenon is called **total internal reflection**, and the incidence angle at which it first occurs is the **critical angle**, θ_c. We can find θ_c by setting $\theta_2 = 90°$ (i.e., $\sin\theta_2 = 1$) in Snell's law (Equation 35-3). The critical angle is then θ_1, and we have

$$\sin\theta_c = \frac{n_2}{n_1}. \qquad (35\text{-}5)$$

Since the sine of an angle cannot exceed 1, we must have $n_2 \leq n_1$ in order for this equation to have a solution. Thus, total internal reflection occurs only when light propagating in one medium strikes an interface with a medium of lower refractive index, and it occurs whenever the incidence angle exceeds the critical angle. You can simulate total internal reflection with ActivPhysics Activity 15.1, by clicking on the "Larger *n* region" button and varying the incidence angle until the refracted ray disappears.

Total internal reflection makes uncoated glass an excellent reflector when it's oriented appropriately (Fig. 35-15). Corner reflectors (Example 35-1) use total internal reflection in solid cubes of glass, rather than individual mirrors at right angles. For an observer inside a medium of higher refractive index, the existence of the critical angle affects the view of the outside world, as the example below shows. Finally, total internal reflection is the basis of the optical fibers now widely used in communications.

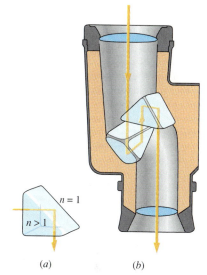

FIGURE 35-15 (*a*) A glass prism redirects light through total internal reflection. (*b*) Binoculars use a pair of prisms to "fold" the light path, allowing a more compact design.

EXAMPLE 35-5	*Whale Watch*

Planeloads of whale watchers fly above the ocean, as shown in Fig. 35-16. A whale looks upward, watching the planes. Within what range of viewing angles can the whale see the planes?

Solution

If the whale emitted light, that light would emerge from the ocean surface only for incidence angles less than the critical angle—that is, those angles within the cone shown in Fig. 35-16. Since the path of light is reversible, the whale can see objects above the surface only when it looks within this cone. For the water-air interface Equation 35-5 gives

$$\theta_c = \sin^{-1}\left(\frac{1}{1.333}\right) = 48.6°,$$

where we found water's refractive index in Table 35-1. The geometry of Fig. 35-16 then shows that this is also the half-angle of the cone, so the whale must look within 48.6° of the vertical to see out.

Can the whale see a plane only if it's *actually* within this angle? No. As the strongly refracted ray from the right-hand plane suggests, the entire outside world appears to the whale compressed into a cone of half-angle θ_c. If the whale looks beyond this cone, it will see instead reflections of objects below the surface.

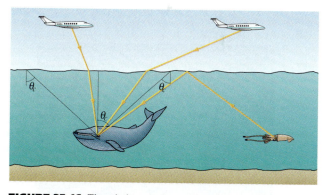

FIGURE 35-16 The whale sees the entire world above the surface in a cone of half-angle θ_c. Looking beyond this cone, it sees reflections of objects below the surface.

EXERCISE A diamond is submerged in water. What is the critical angle at the diamond-water interface?

Answer: 33.4°

Some problems similar to Example 35-5: 22, 23, 26, 28, 33

Refraction and total internal reflection are the basis for **optical fibers**, which revolutionized communications in the 1980s. Some three *billion* km of optical fiber were installed in the United States alone during that decade, and today they carry telephone conversations, television signals, computer data, and other information. Undersea fibers link the entire planet in a fiber-optic network.

A typical fiber consists of a glass core only 8 μm in diameter, surrounded by a so-called cladding consisting of glass with a lower refractive index than the core. The propagation of light in the fiber is a process whereby the core-cladding interface guides the light along the fiber. In some fibers this takes place by abrupt internal reflection at the interface (Fig. 35-17), while in others gradual refraction in the cladding guides the light. The glass used in optical fibers is so pure that a 1-km thick slab would appear as transparent as an ordinary window pane. Today's fibers use infrared light at wavelengths of 0.85 μm, 1.31 μm, and 1.55 μm. A recent development are optical fibers that actually regenerate signals as they travel long distances, extracting energy from an additional laser beam; these fibers are now used on some intercontinental and other ultra-long fiber communications systems.

FIGURE 35-18 The thin fiber-optic cable and the much bulkier cable of copper wires carry information at the same rate.

Optical fibers offer several advantages over copper wire or open-air transmission of electromagnetic waves. The main advantage is their very high **bandwidth**—the amount of information they carry per unit time. This large bandwidth results because the information carried on fiber is encoded on infrared radiation with a frequency on the order of 10^{14} Hz—much higher than the microwave frequencies used in conventional communication systems. A single fiber, for example, can carry tens of thousands of telephone conversations (Fig. 35-18).

Fibers are lighter and more rugged than copper cables and are less easy to "tap" illicitly. Because they are insulators, optical fibers are also less susceptible to electrical "noise" and are therefore used to carry information in electrically noisy environments like power plants or high-energy physics laboratories.

Optical fibers play a key role in the global Internet that links nearly all the world's computers. Computers on one floor or within a building may be connected in a small, relatively low-bandwidth network with copper wire. But connections between buildings are nearly always made with optical fibers, linking individual local networks into larger institution-wide networks. Entire institutions—corporations, universities, government laboratories, and the like—are then linked by very high speed fiber-optic "superhighways" that carry the Internet's burgeoning information "traffic."

Optical fiber technology requires more than just fiber: appropriate opto-electronic devices are needed at each end to convert information from light to electrical forms and vice versa. Such devices include miniature lasers made from semiconductors, and high-speed light-sensitive diodes. As the cost of these devices drops, high-speed optical fiber is becoming available to individual homes and offices, allowing nearly instant access to telecommunications, video resources, libraries, and databases.

(a)

(b)

FIGURE 35-17 (a) A beam of light undergoes a series of total internal reflections that guide it along an optical fiber. (b) A bundle of actual fibers.

35-5 DISPERSION

Refraction ultimately occurs because of the interaction of electromagnetic wave fields with atomic electrons. Although the details of that interaction require a quantum description, it should not be surprising that the index of refraction depends on frequency. After all, as we found in Chapter 15, the response of a system (here an atom) generally depends on the frequency of the driving force (here the oscillating fields of a wave).

Because the index of refraction depends on frequency, different frequencies—different colors for visible light—will refract through different angles. A light beam containing many colors will therefore spread into its constituent colors, a process called **dispersion** (Fig. 35-19). The classic example of dispersion is Newton's demonstration that white light is really a mixture of all the colors in the visible spectrum. Newton not only broke white light into its constituent colors, as in Fig. 35-19, but he also recombined the colors to produce the original white light.

In most materials in most frequency ranges, the index of refraction increases with increasing frequency and therefore decreases with increasing wavelength (Fig. 35-20). That means colors toward the violet end of the spectrum are refracted through the greatest angles, as is evident in Fig. 35-19.

Dispersion is the basis for the widely used technique of **spectral analysis** or **spectroscopy**, in which substances are identified and characterized by analyzing their **spectra**—meaning the range of wavelengths of electromagnetic radiation they emit, transmit, or absorb. Hot, dense objects, for example, emit a continuous spectrum of radiation, while diffuse gases radiate at only a few specific wavelengths (Fig. 35-21). The existence of those discrete spectra provided some of the strongest evidence for the nature of the atom, and today spectral analysis allows astronomers to identify and measure the abundances of elements in

FIGURE 35-19 Dispersion of white light by a glass prism. The refractive index of the glass is greater at higher frequencies—shorter wavelengths—and therefore results in greater refraction at the blue end of the spectrum. The incident beam comes in from the lower left edge, and a white reflected beam leaves the prism going straight downward. This beam has undergone an additional refraction that has again combined its colors.

FIGURE 35-20 Index of refraction as a function of wavelength for high-dispersion crown glass.

FIGURE 35-21 (Top) The solar spectrum is an essentially continuous band of wavelengths, produced by the hot, dense gases of the Sun's visible surface. Dark lines are discrete wavelengths absorbed by overlying gases in the solar atmosphere. (Bottom) Spectrum of a diffuse gas—in this case hydrogen—consists of light at discrete wavelengths. The pattern of lines allows identification of the emitting material.

distant astrophysical objects. Geologists use spectral analysis to identify minerals, and chemists use infrared spectra to study molecules. Spectral analysis is a powerful tool in nearly every branch of science. Although early spectroscopes used prisms, most modern instruments use instead diffraction gratings, whose operation we describe in Chapter 37.

Dispersion can be a nuisance in optical systems. Glass lenses, for example, focus different colors at different points, resulting in a distortion known as chromatic aberration. This effect can be minimized by making composite lenses of materials with different refractive indices.

EXAMPLE 35-6   *How Much Dispersion?*

White light strikes the prism in Fig. 35-22 normal to one surface. The prism is made of the glass whose refractive index is plotted in Fig. 35-20. Find the angle between outgoing red (700 nm) and violet (400 nm) light.

Solution

There is no refraction at the air-glass interface since the incident ray is normal to the surface. At the second interface medium 2 is air with $n_2 = 1$, and medium 1 is the glass whose indices at the two wavelengths we can read from Fig. 35-20: $n_{400} = 1.538, n_{700} = 1.516$. The geometry of Fig. 35-22 shows that the incidence angle at the second interface is the angle $\alpha = 40°$ at the top of the prism. The angles of refraction are then given by solving Snell's law for the two values of θ_2:

$$\theta_{400} = \sin^{-1}(n_{400}\sin\alpha) = \sin^{-1}[(1.538)(\sin 40°)] = 81.34°,$$

and

$$\theta_{700} = \sin^{-1}(n_{700}\sin\alpha) = \sin^{-1}[(1.516)(\sin 40°)] = 77.02°.$$

The angle between the two outgoing beams is therefore $\theta_{400} - \theta_{700} = 4.32°$, with the violet beam (400 nm) experienc-

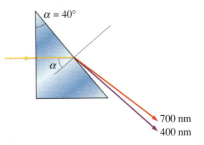

FIGURE 35-22 Example 35-6.

ing the greatest deflection. This 4.32° spread is called the *angular dispersion* of the beam.

EXERCISE If the angle α in Fig. 35-22 is increased, what is the maximum angular dispersion that can be achieved by refracting both the 400 nm and 700 nm beams? At what α does this occur?

Answer: $\Delta\theta = 9.7°$ at $\alpha = \sin^{-1}(1/n_{400}) = 40.556°$

Some problems similar to Example 35-6: 34-38

APPLICATION   *The Rainbow*

Nature provides a beautiful application of dispersion and internal reflection in the rainbow (Fig. 35-23), which occurs when sunlight strikes rain or other water droplets in the air. An observer standing between the Sun and the rain then sees the circular arc of colored bands. Figure 35-24 shows that the center of that arc lies on the line joining the Sun to the observer's eye. That means each observer sees a different rainbow! Furthermore, the rainbow's arc always subtends an angle of approximately 42°. How does the rainbow form, and why does it have this geometry?

Theories of the rainbow date back many centuries. By 1635 Descartes had produced a nearly complete explanation of the rainbow's shape and apparent location, but because he did not

FIGURE 35-23 Reflection, refraction, and dispersion all act to produce a rainbow.

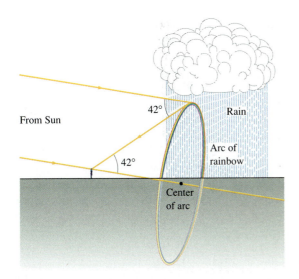

FIGURE 35-24 The rainbow is a circular arc located at 42° from the line that includes the Sun, the observer, and the center of the arc. The Sun is so far away that its rays are essentially parallel. Here part of the rainbow is blocked by the ground; however, observers in aircraft can sometimes see the entire circle.

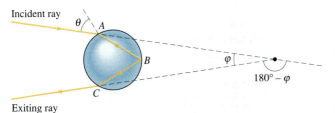

FIGURE 35-25 A light ray passing through a spherical raindrop undergoes refraction at each interface and internal reflection at the back of the drop. (Not shown are the reflected rays at interfaces A and C and the transmitted ray at interface B.) The ray undergoes an overall deflection of $180° - \phi$.

know about dispersion he could not account for the colors. A few years later Newton, in his *Optics*, produced a full explanation.

Figure 35-25 shows a light ray passing through a spherical raindrop. The incidence angle θ in Fig. 35-25 is arbitrary, and

FIGURE 35-26 Parallel rays striking a water drop. The minimum angle through which a ray is deflected is about 138°, corresponding to a maximum of about 42° in the angle ϕ of Fig. 35-25. Furthermore, rays tend to "bunch" at this angle, as suggested by the broad outgoing beam defined by three nearly parallel rays. This "bunching" causes an observer to see a bright arc at 42° from the antisolar direction in Fig. 35-24. The thicker ray undergoes the minimum deviation and has, correspondingly, the maximum ϕ.

parallel light rays striking the curved surface of the drop will experience a range of values for θ. There will, therefore, be a range of angles ϕ between the incident and outgoing rays. As Fig. 35-26 shows, however, there is a maximum angle ϕ_{max} of about 42° and more light is returned at angles close to ϕ_{max} than at other angles. That's why a bright band—the rainbow—appears in the sky at an angle of about 42° to the direction of the Sun's rays. Problems 58 and 59 show how to find ϕ_{max}.

The "bunching" of light rays near ϕ_{max} explains why a bright band should appear, but why should it be colored? Because the refractive index varies with wavelength, so does ϕ_{max}. Each color will therefore appear brightest at a slightly different angle. For water, the refractive index in the visible region ranges from $n_{red} = 1.330$ to $n_{violet} = 1.342$. Using these values with the results of Problems 58 and 59 yields $\phi_{red} = 42.53°$ and $\phi_{violet} = 40.78°$. Thus the rainbow is seen as a band, itself subtending an angle of about 1.75°, with red at the top.

One occasionally sees a fainter and larger arc above the primary rainbow. This secondary rainbow results from two internal reflections, and as a result the order of its colors is reversed. Problem 60 explores the secondary rainbow.

35-6 REFLECTION AND POLARIZATION

Geometrical optics describes the paths of light rays at interfaces between different media, but doesn't tell how much of the light is reflected and how much transmitted at an interface. Application of Ampère's and Faraday's laws to electromagnetic wave fields at an interface does give that information. We won't undertake the calculation here, but will instead describe briefly the results.

FIGURE 35-27 Reflection in a plate-glass window is especially prominent at oblique incidence angles.

When light is incident on an interface, some fraction of it is reflected. The ratio of the reflected to the incident intensity is called the **reflection coefficient**. In general, the least reflection occurs with normal incidence—i.e., with light incident perpendicular to the interface. For glass with refractive index $n = 1.5$, for example, only about 4 percent of normally incident light is reflected—meaning the reflection coefficient in this case is 0.04. You usually don't notice this faint reflection, except when you're inside a lighted room at night; then there's no light coming through the windows from outside to overwhelm the reflection.

The reflection coefficient generally increases at oblique angles, approaching 1 as the incidence angle approaches 90°. You've undoubtedly experienced this effect when standing in front of a plate-glass window; as you look along the window at an oblique angle, the reflection of objects on your side of the window becomes more prominent (Fig. 35-27).

The Polarizing Angle

Reflection ultimately involves an interaction of the electric field of an incident light wave with electrons near the surface of the reflecting medium. It's not surprising, therefore, that the reflection coefficient depends on the orientation of a light wave's electric field relative to the interface. In Chapter 34 we defined the polarization direction of an electromagnetic wave as the direction of the wave's electric field; thus, the reflection coefficient depends on polarization.

For all but normal incidence, the incident, reflected, and refracted rays are in different directions and together define a plane (see Fig. 35-28, where that plane is the plane of the page). The electric field of the incident light may lie in that plane, or be perpendicular to it, or be at some angle in between. When the field lies in the plane defined by the three rays, there's a special angle at which incident light does not undergo any reflection, and instead is transmitted 100 percent across the interface. This special angle is called the **Brewster angle** or the **polarizing angle**, and designated θ_p. The name "polarizing angle" is apt because if light incident at this angle has a mix of polarizations, only the component with electric field perpendicular to the plane of Fig. 35-28 will be reflected; thus the reflected beam becomes completely polarized.

Why is there no reflection of the preferred polarization at this special angle? In Chapter 34 we saw that electromagnetic waves result from accelerated charge; Fig. 34-23 showed, nevertheless, that no electromagnetic radiation is emitted in the direction of a charged particle's acceleration. Knowing that, we can use Fig. 35-28 to understand the reason for the polarizing angle. For glass with refractive index $n = 1.5$, the polarizing angle is 56.3°. At this incidence angle, Snell's law gives an angle of refraction $\theta_2 = \sin^{-1}(\sin\theta_p/n) = 33.7°$. Now $56.3° + 33.7° = 90°$ and that means, as Fig. 35-28 shows, that any reflected ray would be perpendicular to the refracted ray. But the reflected ray really arises from the acceleration of the electrons in the glass—acceleration

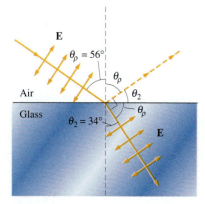

FIGURE 35-28 An electromagnetic wave polarized in the plane of the figure is incident on an interface. When the angles of incidence and refraction sum to 90°, the reflected ray would be in the direction of the electric field in the lower medium. Since there is no radiation in the direction of charged-particle acceleration, there is no reflected ray in this special case. Numbers shown are for an air-glass interface.

which, according to Newton's law of motion, is in the direction of the driving force. But here the driving force comes from the wave's electric field, and with polarization in the plane of Fig. 35-28, that field is itself parallel to the direction the reflected ray would take. But we've seen that there is no radiation in the direction of the acceleration, and hence for this special geometrical condition there is no reflected ray.

Figure 35-28 shows that the condition of no reflection will be met when the angles of incidence and refraction sum to 90°: $\theta_p + \theta_2 = 90°$, where we've set the incidence angle equal to the polarizing angle. This, in turn, implies that $\sin\theta_2 = \cos\theta_p$. But with the incidence angle $\theta_1 = \theta_p$, Snell's law gives $\sin\theta_2 = (n_1/n_2)\sin\theta_p$. Applying our condition $\sin\theta_2 = \cos\theta_p$, we then have $\cos\theta_p = (n_1/n_2)\sin\theta_p$. Multiplying both sides by $n_2/n_1\cos\theta_p$ then gives

$$\tan\theta_p = \frac{n_2}{n_1}. \tag{35-6}$$

For an air-glass interface with $n_1 = 1$ and $n_2 = 1.5$, this equation indeed gives $\theta_p = 56.3°$.

The polarizing angle is important in the construction of lasers, which require nearly loss-free transmission of light reflected from external mirrors back into the medium that generates the laser light. The common red-light helium-neon laser used in physics demonstrations and supermarket scanners, for example, includes a glass tube containing a helium-neon mixture; the ends of the tube are formed at the polarizing angle so that light with the correct polarization enters the tube without reflecting. Because zero reflection occurs only for light polarized in the plane of the incident and refracted rays, the laser itself produces light with this polarization. (We'll see more on how lasers work in Chapter 39 or, for extended-version readers, in Chapter 41).

A phenomenon similar to the polarizing angle occurs for reflection from metals and other surfaces, again because of the interaction of the electric field of the light wave with electrons. Somewhat similarly, scattering of sunlight by air molecules partially polarizes the light. Reduction of glare using Polaroid sunglasses or a camera's polarizing filter works by blocking the component of reflected or scattered light that has the enhanced polarization (Fig. 35-29).

(a)

(b)

FIGURE 35-29 Identical views of a storefront, photographed *(a)* without and *(b)* with a polarizing filter. Light reflecting obliquely from the glass is partially polarized. The polarizing filter eliminates this component, allowing the inside of the store to show much more clearly.

CHAPTER SYNOPSIS

Summary

1. **Geometrical optics** treats the behavior of light under the approximation that it travels in straight lines—**rays**—except at interfaces between different materials. This approximation is valid whenever waves interact with systems that are much larger than their wavelength.

2. **Reflection** occurs to some extent at nearly all interfaces. When a light ray reflects, the **angle of incidence** and **angle of reflection**—both measured from the normal to the interface—are equal. **Specular reflection** occurs from smooth surfaces, while rough surfaces produce **diffuse reflection**.

3. **Refraction** is the bending of light at an interface between transparent materials. The directions of the incident and refracted rays are related by **Snell's law**:

$$n_1\sin\theta_1 = n_2\sin\theta_2,$$

where θ_1 and θ_2 are the angles of incidence and refraction, respectively. The **indices of refraction** are n_1 and n_2, defined as the ratios of the speed of light in vacuum to the speed in a given medium.

4. **Total internal reflection** occurs when light propagating in a medium with refractive index n_1 is incident on an

interface at an angle greater than the **critical angle** θ_c given by

$$\sin \theta_c = \frac{n_2}{n_1}.$$

Total internal reflection is possible only when $n_2 < n_1$.

5. The index of refraction generally depends on frequency. This results in **dispersion** of the different colors as they refract through different angles. Dispersion is the basis of **spectroscopy**.

6. Some light is usually reflected at an interface, even with a transparent material. Generally, reflection increases as the angle of incidence becomes more oblique. But for the special case of light whose polarization is in the plane defined by incident and refracted rays, there's no reflection when the angle of incidence is equal to the **polarizing angle**, also called the **Brewster angle**. As a result, unpolarized light incident at this angle becomes completely polarized on reflection.

Terms You Should Understand

(Pairs are closely related terms whose distinction is important; number in parentheses is chapter section where term first appears.)

geometrical optics (introduction)
ray (introduction)
angles of incidence, reflection, refraction (35-2, 35-3)
specular reflection, diffuse reflection (35-2)
refraction, index of refraction (35-3)
Snell's law (35-3)

total internal reflection (35-4)
critical angle (35-4)
optical fiber (35-4)
dispersion (35-5)
spectroscopy (35-5)
reflection coefficient (35-6)
polarizing angle (35-6)

Symbols You Should Recognize

θ_1, θ_1', θ_2 (35-2, 35-3)
n (35-3)
θ_c (35-4)
θ_p (35-6)

Problems You Should Be Able to Solve

determining the directions of reflected and refracted rays at interfaces (35-2 and 35-3)
evaluating conditions for total internal reflection (35-4)
analyzing dispersion (35-5)
determining reflected and transmitted intensities at normal incidence (35-6)
evaluating the polarizing angle (35-6)

Limitations to Keep in Mind

Geometrical optics is an approximation valid only when light interacts with systems much larger than its wavelength.
Characterizing the optical properties of a material by a single number, the index of refraction, is a simplification. In many materials optical properties depend on direction, and include absorption as well as transmission.

QUESTIONS

1. Are light rays real? Discuss.
2. It's usually inappropriate to consider low-frequency sound waves as traveling in rays. Why? Why is it more appropriate for high-frequency sound and for light?
3. Describe why a spoon appears bent when it's in a glass of water.
4. Why do a diamond and an identically shaped piece of glass sparkle differently?
5. Specular reflection occurs with "smooth" surfaces. But on the microscopic scale all surfaces are rough. What do you suppose should be the criterion for "smoothness" in dealing with reflection?
6. White light goes from air through a glass slab with parallel surfaces. Will its colors be dispersed when it emerges from the glass?
7. Would light behave as in Fig. 35-15a if the refractive index of the prism were 1.25? Explain.

8. You send white light through two identical glass prisms, oriented as shown in Fig. 35-30. Describe the beam that emerges from the right-hand prism.

FIGURE 35-30 Question 8.

9. Why can optical fibers carry much more information than copper wires?
10. What would happen if you scratched the outside of the reflecting surface of a prism used for total internal reflection?

11. Lightning produces a sudden burst of static in a nearby radio receiver. The static comprises a broad band of radio frequencies. But in a very distant receiver the "noise" from the flash arrives over an extended time. What does this say about the frequency dependence of the refractive index of Earth's atmosphere for radio waves?

12. What does a fish see as it looks around in directions above the horizontal? Explain.

13. In glass, which end of the visible spectrum has the lowest critical angle for total internal reflection?

14. Looking out the window of a lighted room at night, you see clear reflections of the room's interior. In the daytime those reflections would be much less obvious, yet the reflection coefficient has not changed. Explain.

15. Why can't you walk to the end of the rainbow?

16. What is wrong with the painting in Fig. 35-31? *Hint:* The rainbow subtends a half-angle of 42°.

FIGURE 35-31 What's wrong with this painting (*Niagara,* by Harry Fenn)? (Question 16)

17. Suppose the refractive index of water were not frequency dependent. Would anything like the rainbow occur?

FIGURE 35-32 Question 18.

18. Figure 35-32 shows a ball inside a transparent sphere inside an aquarium tank. The transparent sphere and the tank can each be filled with water. Explain which combination is occurring in each frame.

19. Why are polarizing sunglasses better than glasses that simply cut down on the total amount of light?

20. Does the transmitted intensity always exceed the reflected intensity at an air-glass interface?

21. Under what conditions will the polarizing angle be less than 45°?

PROBLEMS

ActivPhysics can help with these problems:
Activities 15.1, 15.2

Section 35-2 Reflection

1. Through what angle should you rotate a mirror in order that a reflected ray rotate through 30°?

2. The mirrors in Fig. 35-33 make a 60° angle. A light ray enters parallel to the symmetry axis, as shown. (a) How many reflections does it make? (b) Where and in what direction does it exit the mirror system?

3. To what angular accuracy must two ostensibly perpendicular mirrors be aligned in order that an incident ray returns on a path within 1° of its incident direction?

4. If a light ray enters the mirror system of Fig. 35-33 propagating in the plane of the page and parallel to one mirror, through what angle will it be turned?

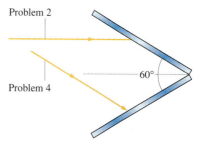

FIGURE 35-33 Problems 2, 4, 5.

5. Suppose the angle in Fig. 35-33 is changed to 75°. A ray enters the mirror system parallel to the axis. (a) How many reflections does it make? (b) Through what angle is it turned when it exits the system?

6. Two plane mirrors make an angle ϕ. For what value of ϕ will a light ray reflecting once off each mirror be turned through the same angle ϕ?

7. Two plane mirrors make an angle ϕ. A light ray enters the system and is reflected once off each mirror. Show that the ray is turned through an angle $360° - 2\phi$.

Section 35-3 Refraction

8. In which substance in Table 35-1 does the speed of light have the value 2.292×10^8 m/s?

9. Information in a compact disc is stored in "pits" whose depth is essentially one-fourth of the wavelength of the laser light used to "read" the information. That wavelength is 780 nm in air, but the wavelength on which the pit depth is based is measured in the $n = 1.55$ plastic that makes up most of the disc. Find the pit depth.

10. Light is incident on an air-glass interface, and the refracted light in the glass makes a 40° angle with the normal to the interface. The glass has refractive index 1.52. Find the incidence angle.

11. A light ray propagates in a transparent material at 15° to the normal to the surface. When it emerges into the surrounding air, it makes a 24° angle with the normal. What is the refractive index of the material?

12. Light propagating in the glass ($n = 1.52$) wall of an aquarium tank strikes the interior edge of the wall with incidence angle 12.4°. What is the angle of refraction in the water?

13. A block of glass with $n = 1.52$ is submerged in one of the liquids listed in Table 35-1. For a ray striking the glass with incidence angle 31.5°, the angle of refraction is 27.9°. What is the liquid?

14. A meter stick lies on the bottom of the rectangular trough in Fig. 35-34, with its zero mark at the left edge of the trough. You look into the long dimension of the trough at a 45° angle, with your line of sight just grazing the top edge of the tank, as shown. What mark on the meter stick do you see if the trough is (a) empty, (b) half full of water, and (c) full of water?

FIGURE 35-34 Problem 14.

15. You look at the center of one face of a solid cube of glass, on a line of sight making a 55° angle with the normal to the cube face. What is the minimum refractive index of the glass for which you will see through the opposite face of the cube?

16. The cylindrical tank in a public aquarium is 10 m deep, 11 m in diameter, and is full to the brim with water. If a flashlight shines on the tank from above, what is the minimum angle its beam can make with the horizontal if it is to illuminate part of the tank bottom?

17. You're standing 2.3 m horizontally from the edge of a 4.5-m-deep lake, with your eyes 1.7 m above the water surface. A diver holding a flashlight at the lake bottom shines the light so you can see it. If the light in the water makes a 42° angle with the vertical, at what horizontal distance is the diver from the edge of the lake?

18. You've dropped your car keys at night off the end of a dock into water 1.6 m deep. A flashlight held directly above the dock edge and 0.50 m above the water illuminates the keys when it's pointed at 40° to the vertical, as shown in Fig. 35-35. What is the horizontal distance x from the edge of the dock to the keys?

FIGURE 35-35 What is the horizontal distance x from the edge of the dock to the lost keys? (Problem 18)

19. A light ray is propagating in a crystal where its wavelength is 540 nm. It strikes the interior surface of the crystal with an incidence angle of 34° and emerges into the surrounding air at 76° to the surface normal. Find (a) the light's frequency and (b) its wavelength in air.

20. The prism in Fig. 35-36 has $n = 1.52$, $\alpha = 60°$, and is surrounded by air. A light beam is incident at $\theta_1 = 37°$. Find the angle δ through which the beam is deflected.

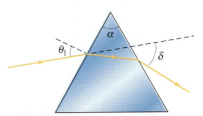

FIGURE 35-36 Problems 20, 51, 55.

Section 35-4 Total Internal Reflection

21. Find the critical angle for total internal reflection in (a) ice, (b) polystyrene, and (c) rutile. Assume the surrounding medium is air.

22. A drop of water is trapped in a block of ice. What is the critical angle for total internal reflection at the water-ice interface?

23. What is the critical angle for light propagating in glass with $n = 1.52$ when the glass is immersed in (a) water, (b) benzene, and (c) diiodomethane?

24. Total internal reflection occurs at an interface between a plastic and air at incidence angles greater than 37°. What is the refractive index of the plastic?

25. Light propagating in a medium with refractive index n_1 encounters a parallel-sided slab with index n_2. On the other side is a third medium with index $n_3 < n_1$. Show that the condition for avoiding internal reflection at *both* interfaces is that the incidence angle at the n_1-n_2 interface be less than the critical angle for an n_1-n_3 interface. In other words, the index of the intermediate material doesn't matter.

26. An aquarium measures 30 cm front to back, as shown in Fig. 35-37. It is made of glass with thickness much less than the size of the aquarium and is full of water with $n = 1.333$. You put your eye right up to the center of the aquarium's front wall and can still see the entire back wall. What is the maximum value of the aquarium's width w? *Hint:* You can ignore the glass; see the preceding problem.

FIGURE 35-37 Problem 26.

27. What is the minimum refractive index for which total internal reflection will occur as shown in Fig. 35-15a? Assume the surrounding medium is air and that the prism is an isosceles right triangle.

28. Where and in what direction would the main beam emerge if the prism in Fig. 35-15a were made of ice?

29. What is the speed of light in a material for which the critical angle at an interface with air is 61°?

30. The prism of Fig. 35-15a has $n = 1.52$. When it is immersed in a liquid, a beam incident as shown in the figure ceases to undergo total reflection. What is the minimum value for the liquid's refractive index?

31. A compound lens is made from crown glass ($n = 1.52$) bonded to flint glass ($n = 1.89$). What is the critical angle for light incident on the flint-crown interface?

32. Find a simple expression for the speed of light in a material in terms of the critical angle at an interface between the material and vacuum.

33. A scuba diver sets off a camera flash a distance h below the surface of water with refractive index n. Show that light emerges from the water surface through a circle of diameter $2h/\sqrt{n^2 - 1}$.

Section 35-5 Dispersion

34. Blue and red laser beams strike an air-glass interface with incidence angle 50°. If the glass has refractive indices of 1.680 and 1.621 for the blue and red light, respectively, what will be the angle between the two beams in the glass?

35. Suppose the red and blue beams of the preceding problem are now propagating in the same direction *inside* the glass. For what range of incidence angles on the glass-air interface will one beam be totally reflected and the other not?

36. White light propagating in air is incident at 45° on the equilateral prism of Fig. 35-38. Find the angular dispersion γ of the outgoing beam, if the prism has refractive indices $n_{red} = 1.582$, $n_{violet} = 1.633$.

FIGURE 35-38 Problem 36 (angles of dispersed rays are not accurate).

37. Two of the prominent spectral lines—discrete wavelengths of light—emitted by glowing hydrogen are hydrogen-α at 656.3 nm and hydrogen-β at 486.1 nm. Light from glowing hydrogen passes through a prism like that of Fig. 35-22, then falls on a screen 1.0 m from the prism. How far apart will these two spectral lines be? Use Fig. 35-20 for the refractive index.

38. Light from glowing sodium contains the two discrete wavelengths 589.0 nm and 589.6 nm. This light is passed through a prism like that of Fig. 35-22 and then allowed to fall on a screen 2.0 m distant. For wavelengths near 600 nm, the refractive index of the prism is $n = 1.546 - 4.47 \times 10^{-5}\lambda$, with λ the wavelength in nm. What must be the prism's apex angle α in order that the two sodium wavelengths be separated on the screen by 1.5 mm?

Section 35-6 Reflection and Polarization

39. Find the polarizing angle for diamond when light is incident from air.
40. What is the refractive index of a material for which the polarizing angle in air is 62°?
41. What is the polarizing angle for light incident from below on the surface of a pond?
42. For the interface between air (refractive index 1) and a material with refractive index n, show that the critical angle and the polarizing angle are related by $\sin\theta_c = \cot\theta_p$.

Paired Problems

(Both problems in a pair involve the same principles and techniques. If you can get the first problem, you should be able to solve the second one.)

43. Light propagating in air strikes a transparent crystal at incidence angle 35°. If the angle of refraction is 22°, what is the speed of light in the crystal?
44. A laser beam with wavelength 633 nm is propagating in air when it strikes a transparent material at incidence angle 50°. If the angle of refraction is 27°, what is the wavelength in the material?
45. A cylindrical tank 2.4 m deep is full to the brim with water. Sunlight first hits part of the tank bottom when the rising Sun makes a 22° angle with the horizon. Find the tank's diameter.
46. For what diameter tank in the preceding problem will sunlight strike some part of the tank bottom whenever the Sun is above the horizon?
47. Light is incident from air on the flat wall of a polystyrene water tank. If the incidence angle is 40°, what angle does the light make with the tank normal in the water?
48. A parallel-sided slab with refractive index n_2 separates two media with indices n_1 and n_3. Show that a light ray incident on the n_1-n_2 interface then enters the third medium with the same angle of refraction it would have had if the slab had not been present. (Assume total internal reflection does not occur at either interface.)
49. Light strikes a right-angled glass prism ($n = 1.52$) in a direction parallel to the prism's base, as shown in Fig. 35-39. The point of incidence is high enough that the refracted ray hits the opposite sloping side. (a) Through which side of the prism does the beam emerge? (b) Through what angle has it been deflected?

FIGURE 35-39 Problems 49, 50.

50. Repeat the preceding problem if the prism has refractive index 1.15.

51. Repeat Problem 20 for the case $n = 1.75$, $\alpha = 40°$, and $\theta_1 = 25°$.
52. The surfaces of a glass sheet are not quite parallel, but rather make an angle of 10°. The glass has refractive index $n = 1.52$. A light beam strikes one side of the sheet at incidence angle 35°, coming in on the thicker side of the normal. Through what angle is the beam direction changed when it emerges on the opposite side of the glass sheet?

Supplementary Problems

53. A cubical block is made from two equal-size slabs of materials with different refractive indices, as shown in Fig. 35-40. Find the index of the right-hand slab if a light ray is incident on the center of the left-hand slab and then describes the path shown.

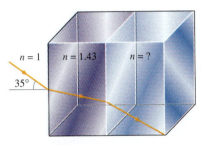

FIGURE 35-40 Problem 53.

54. Find an expression for the displacement x in Fig. 35-8, in terms of θ_1, d, and n.
55. Light is incident with incidence angle θ_1 on a prism with apex angle α and refractive index n, as shown in Fig. 35-36. Show that the angle δ through which the outgoing beam deviates from the incident beam is given by

$$\delta = \theta_1 - \alpha + \sin^{-1}\left\{n\sin\left[\alpha - \sin^{-1}\left(\frac{\sin\theta_1}{n}\right)\right]\right\}.$$

Assume the surrounding medium has $n = 1$.

56. Taking $n = 1.5$ and $\alpha = 60°$, plot the deviation δ of the preceding problem over the range $45° < \theta_1 < 50°$, and use your plot to find the incidence angle for minimum deviation. Trace the incident beam for this value of θ_1. Your result should be the symmetric path shown in Fig. 35-41; in fact, the minimum deviation always occurs with the incidence angle that gives this path, for any n and α.

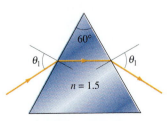

FIGURE 35-41 Minimum deviation through an equilateral prism occurs when the path is symmetric (Problem 56).

57. Show that a three-dimensional corner reflector (three mirrors in three mutually perpendicular planes, or a solid cube in which total internal reflection occurs) turns an incident light ray through 180°, so it returns in the direction from which it came. *Hint:* Let $\mathbf{q} = q_x\hat{\mathbf{i}} + q_y\hat{\mathbf{j}} + q_z\hat{\mathbf{k}}$ be a vector in the direction of propagation. How does this vector get changed on reflection by a mirror in a plane defined by two of the coordinate axes?

58. Show that the angle ϕ that appears in Fig. 35-25 is given by $\phi = 4\sin^{-1}\left(\dfrac{\sin\theta}{n}\right) - 2\theta$, where θ is the angle of incidence.

59. (a) Differentiate the result of the preceding problem to show that the maximum value of ϕ occurs when the incidence angle θ is given by $\cos^2\theta = \frac{1}{3}(n^2 - 1)$. (b) Use this result and that of the preceding problem to find ϕ_{max} in water with $n = 1.333$.

60. Figure 35-42 shows the approximate path of a light ray that undergoes internal reflection twice in a spherical water drop. Find the maximum angle ϕ for this case, taking $n = 1.333$. This is the angle at which the secondary rainbow appears.

61. *Fermat's principle* states that the path of a light ray between two points is such that the time to traverse that

FIGURE 35-42 Problem 60.

path is an extremum (either a minimum or a maximum) when compared with the times for nearby paths. Consider two points A and B on the same side of a reflecting surface, and show that a light ray traveling from A to B via a point on the reflecting surface will take the least time if its path obeys the law of reflection. Thus, the law of reflection (Equation 35-1) follows from Fermat's principle.

62. Use Fermat's principle (see preceding problem) to show that a light ray going from point A in one medium to point B in a second medium will take the least time if its path obeys Snell's law. Thus, Snell's law follows from Fermat's principle.

36 Image Formation and Optical Instruments

This mirror directs sunlight into the McMath–Pierce Solar Telescope in Arizona, which uses optical technology to form a detailed image of the Sun's surface.

Reflection and refraction alter the direction of light propagation, following laws we developed in the preceding chapter. Microscopes, telescopes, cameras, contact lenses, photocopiers, and your own eyes are among the many natural and technological systems that use reflection or refraction to form **images**—patterns of light that provide visual representations of reality. As you read this page, for example, refraction in your eye forms an image on the retina at the back of the eye. Your optic nerve conveys this image to your brain, which processes it to give you the conscience sense of seeing. In this chapter we study image formation using the approximation of geometrical optics—an approximation that remains valid as long as we consider only length scales much greater than the wavelength of light.

When we view an object with an optical system, we perceive light that seems to come straight from the object but whose path has actually been altered. As a result we see an image that may be different in size, orientation, or apparent position from the actual object. In some cases light actually comes from the image to our eyes; the image is then called a **real image**. In other cases light only apparently comes from the image location; the image is then called a **virtual image**.

36-1 PLANE MIRRORS

When you look at yourself in a flat mirror, you see an image that appears to be behind the mirror by the same distance that you are in front of it. The image is upright and the same size as you are, but appears reversed. Why?

Figure 36-1 shows how the image in a plane mirror comes about. In Fig. 36-1a we concentrate on a small object, in this case an arrowhead. (We'll frequently use arrows to represent objects in image-forming situations because they're both simple and sufficiently asymmetric that we can see whether images are inverted or upright.) We've drawn three light rays that leave the object, reflect off the mirror, and enter the observer's eye. The rays reflect at the mirror with equal angles of incidence and reflection. As Fig. 36-1a shows, light looks to the observer like it's coming from a point behind the mirror. That point is the location of the arrowhead's image. In this case the image is virtual because no light actually comes from behind the mirror.

Since two nonparallel lines define a point, we need only two rays to locate the arrowhead in Fig. 36-1a. We've repeated this image-location process in Fig. 36-1b, using as one of the rays the ray that reflects normally. The same procedure also locates the bottom of the arrow, and we could obviously fill in additional points to locate the entire arrow; the resulting image is shown in Fig. 36-1b.

Note that the triangles OPQ and $O'PQ$ in Fig. 36-1b share a common side and that the angles OPQ and $O'PQ$ are both right angles. And because the angles of incidence and reflection are equal, so are the angles OQP and $O'QP$. Therefore triangles OPQ and $O'PQ$ are congruent, showing that the distance PO' that the arrowhead's image lies behind the mirror is equal to the distance OP from the actual arrowhead to the mirror. A similar analysis applies to the rays from the bottom of the arrow, so we can conclude that the image appears as far behind the mirror as the object is in front. Furthermore, since extensions of the rays from the top and bottom of the arrow normal to the mirror pass through the top and bottom of the image, respectively, the image must be the same height as the object itself.

15.3
Plane Mirrors

(a)

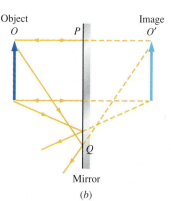

(b)

FIGURE 36-1 Image formation in a plane mirror. (a) Light reflected off the mirror seems to come from an image behind the mirror. Since there is really no light coming from behind the mirror, this is a virtual image. (b) Two rays from each point on an object serve to locate that point's image. Triangles OPQ and $O'PQ$ are congruent, showing that object and image are equidistant from the mirror.

EXAMPLE 36-1	*What Size Mirror to Buy?*

You want the smallest mirror that will show your full image. How tall must it be?

Solution

Figure 36-2 shows the situation. Because the angles of incidence and reflection are equal, light from your foot reflects from the mirror at a point that's vertically halfway between your eye and the floor. Similarly, light from the top of your head reflects midway between that point and your eye. The total distance from top to bottom of the mirror then needs to be half your eye-foot distance plus half the distance from your eye to the top of your head—for a total of half your height. Note that this result does not depend on how far from the mirror you stand. It does, however, require that you fix the mirror to the wall at just the right height.

EXERCISE You buy a mirror that's half your height, but you affix it to the wall 2 cm below its optimum location. How much of your image will be cut off?

FIGURE 36-2 A mirror half your height shows your entire image.

Answer: Top 4 cm

Some problems similar to Example 36-1: 1, 2

Image Reversal

Stand in front of a plane mirror and you appear reversed left to right; for example, your image's left hand is the image of your *right* hand (Fig. 36-3). It's not that the image of your left hand appears opposite your right hand, any more than the image of your head appears opposite your feet. A more accurate description is that the mirror reverses front to back. Figure 36-4 shows that the effect is to alter only one of the three coordinate axes, and that alters handedness, rotation, and all other phenomena connected with the right-hand rules we've been using.

Although image formation in a single plane mirror is straightforward, multiple reflections with more than one mirror can produce many—in some cases infinitely many—images; see Problem 2.

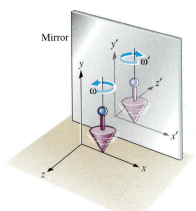

FIGURE 36-4 A plane mirror reverses front to back, reversing the direction of the *z* axis and making the image coordinate system a left-handed one. The rotation of the spinning top is reversed in the mirror, but its angular velocity vector still points upward because a left-hand rule applies in the "mirror world."

FIGURE 36-3 The image of a right hand is the image's left hand—but it's still the image of the *right* hand.

36-2 CURVED MIRRORS

In contrast to plane mirrors, curved mirrors form images that may be upright or inverted, virtual or real, and whose sizes need not be those of the original objects.

Parabolic Mirrors

A parabola—the curve generated by a quadratic function like $y = x^2$—has the property that a line drawn parallel to the parabola's axis makes the same angle to the normal as does a second line drawn to a special point called the **focus** or **focal point** (Fig. 36-5a). That means a concave mirror of parabolic shape will reflect rays parallel to the parabola's axis so they converge at the focus (Fig. 36-5b). This effect can be used to concentrate light to very high intensities (Fig. 36-6a). Conversely, a point source of light at the focus will emerge from the mirror in a beam of parallel rays (Fig. 36-6b).

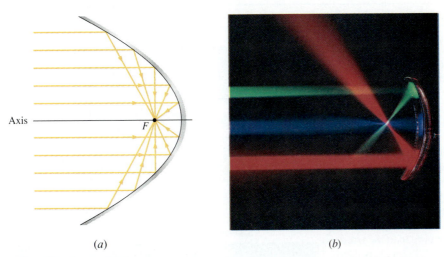

(a)   (b)

FIGURE 36-5 A parabolic mirror reflects rays parallel to its axis to a common focus. (a) Ray diagram. (b) Photo shows rays reflecting from an actual mirror.

(a)   (b)

FIGURE 36-6 (a) This solar furnace uses a huge parabolic reflector to concentrate sunlight. It's used to study properties of materials at high temperatures. (b) A flashlight has a light bulb near the focus of a parabolic mirror and thus produces a beam of nearly parallel light rays.

Spherical Mirrors

Near the apex of the parabolic mirror in Fig. 36-6, you can't tell whether the mirror's shape is parabolic or spherical; parabola and sphere are essentially the same over a limited range. Because a sphere is a more regular shape and thus easier to form, most mirrors used for focusing are, in fact, spherical. The slight distortion caused by the deviation from a perfect parabola—called **spherical aberration**—is minimized by making the actual mirror only a tiny fraction of the entire sphere. In that case the focal length is much larger than the size of the mirror, and light rays from distant objects strike the mirror only if they're close to and nearly parallel to the mirror axis. Such rays are called **paraxial rays**, and it's only for them that the approximation of a parabola by a sphere results in accurate focusing. We assume paraxial rays in what follows. For clarity, however, our diagrams show mirrors much more curved than they should be for distortion-free focusing, and consequently not all the rays we draw will seem paraxial.

APPLICATION	*Hubble Trouble*

The Hubble Space Telescope was launched in 1990 as the flagship of a new generation of space-based astronomical observatories. Although Hubble is smaller than many ground-based telescopes, its vantage point above the atmosphere was to make it optically superior in resolving astronomical objects. Furthermore, Hubble can observe in infrared, visible, and ultraviolet wavelengths.

In the months following Hubble's launch, engineers and scientists checking the telescope were frustrated by their inability to achieve a clear focus. They came reluctantly to the conclusion that Hubble's 2.4-m-diameter primary mirror was flawed. Subsequent investigation showed that an error of 1.3 mm in the placement of instruments used during manufacture of the mirror had resulted in its being ground to the wrong curvature. The mirror itself is off by only 2.3 μm at its edge, but this is an enormous flaw in an optical system designed to be accurate to a small fraction of the wavelength of light. Hubble specifications called for 70% of the light energy from a point source to fall within an angular diameter of 0.1 second of arc; because of its spherical aberration, at best 16% of the light fell in the prescribed zone.

Although the Hubble mirror could not be replaced or repaired, in 1993 astronauts managed to install corrective mirrors that restored Hubble's optical system to better than its original design specifications. The result is a superb astronomical instrument with image quality greatly superior to that of ground-based telescopes (Fig. 36-7).

FIGURE 36-7 (Top) An astronaut installing new optical equipment on the Hubble Space Telescope. (Bottom) Hubble images of M-100, a galaxy 50 million light-years from Earth, taken before and after the repair.

We can see how spherical mirrors form images by tracing two rays from each of several points on the object, just as we did for plane mirrors. Some special rays make this process simple; their properties all follow from the law of reflection and the special properties of a spherical mirror in the paraxial approximation:

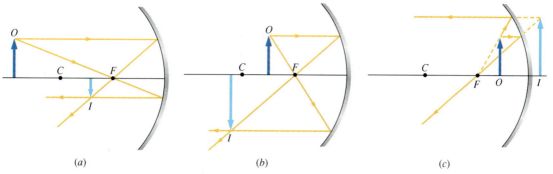

(a)   (b)   (c)

FIGURE 36-8 Image formation in a concave spherical mirror, using the fact that light passing through the focal point F reflects parallel to the mirror axis, and vice versa. O denotes the object and I its image. (a) With the object beyond the mirror's center of curvature C, the mirror forms a real image that is inverted and reduced in size. (b) With the object between the center of curvature and focus, the image is real, inverted, and magnified. (c) When the object is closer than the focus, the image is enlarged, upright, and virtual. Note, in this case, to get the ray including the object and the focus we had to extend the actual light path back toward the focus.

1. Any ray parallel to the mirror axis reflects through the focal point.
2. In the converse of (1), any ray that passes through the focal point reflects parallel to the axis.
3. Any ray that strikes the center of the mirror reflects symmetrically about the mirror axis.
4. Any ray through the center of curvature strikes the mirror normal to the mirror surface, and thus returns on itself.

Any two of these rays suffice to locate an image.

Figure 36-8 shows ray tracings, using our special rays (1) and (2) that go through the focal point, to find the image location in three cases. In all three cases symmetry ensures that the bottom of the image arrow will be on the axis, so we haven't bothered to trace it. In Fig. 36-8a we see that an object beyond the mirror's center of curvature (C) forms a smaller, inverted image. Light actually emerges from this image, so it's a *real* image. If you looked from the left in Fig. 36-8a you would actually see the image in space in front of the mirror (Fig. 36-9).

As the object moves closer to the mirror the real image grows; with the object between the center of curvature and the focus, the image is larger than the object, and farther from the mirror (Fig. 36-8b). As the object moves toward the focus the image grows larger and moves rapidly away from the mirror. With the object right at the focus the rays emerge in a parallel beam and there is no image. Finally, rays from an object closer to the mirror than the focus diverge after reflection. To an observer they appear to come from a point behind the mirror. Thus there is a virtual image, in this case upright and enlarged (Fig. 36-8c).

ActivPhysics Activity 15.4 provides a simulation of Fig. 36-8 in which you can move the object to any point.

FIGURE 36-9 A bear meets its real image, formed by the concave mirror at rear. The bear and its image are both in *front* of the mirror.

15.4
Spherical Mirrors

Got It!

Where would you place an object so its real image is the same size as the object?

Convex Mirrors

A convex mirror reflects on the outside of its spherical curvature, causing light to diverge rather than focus. Therefore, there is no possibility of forming a real image with a convex mirror. But Fig. 36-10 shows that the mirror can still form a virtual image. Although the focus has less obvious physical significance in this case, its location still controls the geometry of reflected rays. As Fig. 36-10 shows, we can still draw a ray parallel to the axis and another ray that would go through the focus if the mirror weren't in its way. By tracing these rays through the mirror we can see the directions in which they reflect. The reflected rays appear to diverge from a common point behind the mirror, showing that there is a virtual image, upright and reduced in size, behind the mirror. By considering different object positions, you can convince yourself that for a convex mirror the image always has these characteristics. Convex mirrors are widely used where an image of a broad region needs to be captured in a small space (Fig. 36-11).

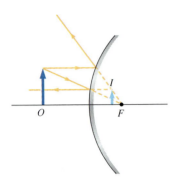

FIGURE 36-10 Image formation using a convex mirror. The image is always virtual, upright, and reduced in size.

The Mirror Equation

Drawing ray diagrams helps give an intuitive feel for image formation. More precise image locations and sizes follow from the **mirror equation**, which we now derive. This time we'll find the image using our special rays parallel to the axis and striking the mirror's center, as shown in Fig. 36-12a. The ray that strikes the center of the mirror reflects symmetrically about the axis; therefore, the two shaded triangles are similar. Then the **magnification**—the ratio image height h' to the object height h—is the same as the ratio of the image and object distances from the mirror. We'll consider the image height negative if the image is inverted; then from Fig. 36-12 we have

$$M = \frac{h'}{h} = -\frac{\ell'}{\ell}. \tag{36-1}$$

FIGURE 36-11 Reflecting spheres are convex mirrors, forming reduced, virtual, upright images.

Here object and image are both in front of the mirror, so we take object and image distances ℓ and ℓ' as positive quantities; the negative sign in Equation 36-1 then shows that in this case the image is inverted. Also, for the object

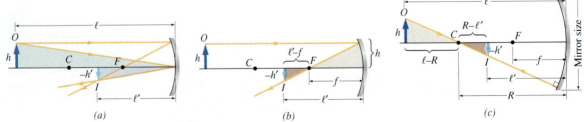

(a)   (b)   (c)

FIGURE 36-12 Finding the image I using the ray from the object O parallel to the axis, along with the ray that reflects from the center of the mirror. (*a*) Since the latter ray reflects symmetrically about the axis, the shaded triangles are similar, and allow us to relate the object and image heights h and h' to their distances ℓ and ℓ' from the mirror. (*b*) Another pair of similar triangles lets us relate the focal length f to the heights and distances. Length of the image arrow is marked $-h'$ because h' is considered negative for an inverted image. (*c*) The ray through the center of curvature strikes the mirror at 90°, so it reflects back on itself. Once again the shaded triangles are similar; now they let us relate the curvature radius to the heights and distances and thus, through the mirror equation, to the focal length. The curvature radius R proves to be twice the focal length f. The mirror size indicated should actually be considerably smaller than the curvature radius for the descriptions and equations of this section to be accurate.

location of Fig. 36-12, it's clear that $|M| < 1$, meaning the image is reduced rather than enlarged.

Figure 36-12*b* is the same as Fig. 36-12*a* except that now we show only the ray that reflects through the focus. We've also labeled the **focal length** *f*—i.e., the distance from the mirror to the focal point—and have shaded a different pair of similar triangles. From these triangles you can see that

$$\frac{-h'}{h} = \frac{\ell' - f}{f}.$$

Here we put the minus sign on h' because we've defined h' as a negative quantity for the inverted image, while comparing similar triangles requires a ratio of positive quantities. But Equation 36-1 shows that the ratio h'/h is the magnification $M = -\ell'/\ell$. So we have

$$-\frac{\ell'}{\ell} = \frac{\ell' - f}{f}$$

or, dividing both sides by ℓ' and doing a little algebra,

$$\frac{1}{\ell} + \frac{1}{\ell'} = \frac{1}{f}. \quad \text{(mirror equation)} \tag{36-2}$$

Equations 36-1 and 36-2 together give us all the information we would get from ray tracing.

Although we derived the mirror equation using a real image, the equation applies to virtual images with the convention that a *negative* image distance ℓ' means the image is *behind* the mirror—as are virtual images (recall Fig. 36-8*c*). And we can handle *convex* mirrors as well by taking the focal length to be a *negative* quantity. Table 36-1 summarizes these sign conventions.

We can extract one more useful piece of information by considering the ray that passes through the center of curvature, *C*. This point is the center of the sphere of which the mirror is a part; therefore, its distance from the mirror is the mirror's curvature radius, *R*. That's why a ray through *C* hits normal to the mirror; it's following a radius, which intersects the sphere at right angles. So a ray through *C* reflects back on itself. We show this ray in Fig. 36-12*c*, along with yet another pair of similar triangles. From them, you can see that

$$\frac{R - \ell'}{\ell - R} = \frac{-h'}{h} = \frac{\ell'}{\ell},$$

where again we write $-h'$ because the inverted image has negative height according to our sign conventions, and we need a ratio of positive distances. The

TABLE 36-1 *Sign Conventions for Mirrors*

FOCAL LENGTH f[1],	OBJECT DISTANCE, ℓ	IMAGE DISTANCE[2], ℓ'	TYPE OF IMAGE
+	+, $\ell > f$	+	Real, inverted, enlarged for $\ell < 2f$, reduced for $\ell > 2f$
+	+, $\ell < f$	−	Virtual, upright, enlarged
−	+	−	Virtual, upright, reduced

[1] + for concave mirror, − for convex.
[2] − means behind mirror.

last step in this equality follows from Equation 36-1. Solving the mirror equation for ℓ' and using the result in the equation above (see Problem 16) then yields

$$f = \frac{R}{2}. \qquad (36\text{-}3)$$

Thus the focal length of a spherical mirror is half its curvature radius.

15.7
Spherical Mirror Problems

We emphasize that the results derived in this section are approximations based on the assumption that the spherical mirror is a good approximation to a parabola. Equivalent ways of describing this approximation are (1) that the curvature radius is large compared with the mirror's size as indicated in Fig. 36-12c and (2) that all rays reflecting from the mirror are close to and nearly parallel to the mirror axis (the paraxial approximation). Again, our drawings can't accurately reflect these conditions while at the same time showing clearly the ray paths.

EXAMPLE 36-2	*Sizing Up Hubble: A Concave Mirror*

During assembly of the Hubble Space Telescope, a technician stood 3.85 m in front of the telescope's concave mirror and viewed his image (Fig. 36-13). Given the telescope's focal length of 5.52 m, find (a) the location and (b) the magnification of the technician's image. (c) Repeat for the case when the technician stands 15.0 m from the mirror.

Solution

Since the mirror is *concave,* the focal length f is *positive.*
(a) We can solve the mirror equation (Equation 36-2) to get

$$\frac{1}{\ell'} = \frac{1}{f} - \frac{1}{\ell} = \frac{\ell - f}{f\ell},$$

or

$$\ell' = \frac{f\ell}{\ell - f} = \frac{(5.52 \text{ m})(3.85 \text{ m})}{3.85 \text{ m} - 5.52 \text{ m}} = -12.7 \text{ m}.$$

Why the *negative* answer? Because the technician is closer to the mirror than the focal point, so this is a *virtual* image located *behind* the mirror.
(b) Equation 36-1 gives the magnification:

$$M = -\frac{\ell'}{\ell} = -\frac{(-12.7 \text{ m})}{3.85 \text{ m}} = 3.30.$$

This *positive* answer indicates an *upright* image, enlarged about three times as shown in Fig. 36-13.
(c) If the technician stands 15.0 m from the mirror, similar calculations give

$$\ell' = \frac{f\ell}{\ell - f} = \frac{(5.52 \text{ m})(15.0 \text{ m})}{15.0 \text{ m} - 5.52 \text{ m}} = 8.73 \text{ m}$$

and

$$M = -\frac{\ell'}{\ell} = -\frac{8.73 \text{ m}}{15.0 \text{ m}} = -0.582.$$

FIGURE 36-13 A technician standing in front of the Hubble Space Telescope mirror. Where and how big is the technician's image?

Now ℓ' is *positive,* so the image is *real* and in *front* of the mirror; the *negative* magnification shows that it's *inverted,* and it's reduced in size.

EXERCISE You're scrutinizing your nose using a handheld concave mirror with curvature radius 2.2 m. How far from your face should you hold the mirror to see your nose doubled in size?

Answer: 55 cm

Some problems similar to Example 36-2: 3–9, 11–14

EXAMPLE 36-3	*Jurassic Park: A Convex Mirror*

In the film *Jurassic Park,* horrified passengers in a car watch in the convex side-view mirror as a tyrannosaurus rex pursues them. Printed on the mirror is the warning "OBJECTS IN MIRROR ARE CLOSER THAN THEY SEEM." If the mirror's curvature radius is 12 m, and if the T-rex is actually 9.0 m from the mirror, by what factor does its image appear reduced in size?

Solution

This is a *convex* mirror, so its focal length is *negative.* Since the focal length is half the curvature radius, we have $f = -6.0$ m. Here we're asked for the magnification, given by Equation 36-1. For that we need the image distance ℓ'. We found an expression for ℓ' in the preceding example, and that expression holds here because the mirror equation from which it was derived works for both concave and convex mirrors. So Equation 36-1 becomes

$$M = -\frac{\ell'}{\ell} = -\frac{f\ell/(\ell - f)}{\ell} = -\frac{f}{\ell - f}$$

$$= -\frac{-6.0 \text{ m}}{9.0 \text{ m} - (-6.0 \text{ m})} = 0.40.$$

The T-rex in the mirror appears only 40 percent of its actual size, and thus it "seems" further away. Note that the mirror's warning isn't really a comparison of the image and object *distances,* but of the apparent versus actual *size* of objects. Image distances in a convex mirror are always *smaller* than object distances, so the images are always *reduced* and we therefore perceive objects viewed in a convex mirror as being farther away.

EXERCISE An object 30 cm from a convex mirror appears reduced to one-fourth of its actual size when viewed in a convex mirror. What is the mirror's curvature radius?

Answer: 20 cm

Some problems similar to Example 36-3: 10, 15, 62

APPLICATION	*Nonimaging Optics and the Quest for Solar Energy*

Sometimes we want to concentrate light energy without necessarily forming an image. In solar energy systems producing heat, for example, concentrated sunlight leads to higher temperature and thus to higher efficiency; with photovoltaic systems inexpensive reflectors can be used to concentrate solar energy onto more expensive photovoltaic cells, reducing the cell area needed.

Nonimaging optics is a new field, and the design of concentrators is an ongoing challenge for optical engineers. Figure 36-14 shows a popular concentrator design, called a compound parabolic concentrator. Unlike a parabolic mirror designed for image formation, this concentrator is made from parabolic segments that do not form a single complete parabola. As Fig. 36-14a shows, all light entering the concentrator

(a)   (b)

FIGURE 36-14 (a) A compound parabolic concentrator. Rays (blue) entering at the angle θ to the concentrator axis are reflected to the edge of the exit aperture. Rays incident at smaller angles (red) pass through the exit aperture after at most one reflection; thus all light entering over the angular range 2θ is concentrated at the exit. (b) A section of parabolic concentrators used to concentrate solar energy on a black tube carrying a heat-transfer fluid. A piece of pipe lies at the exit of one concentrator; since light paths are reversible, the fact that the entire concentrator appears black confirms that the path of an incident light ray ends up on the black tube.

from a broad range of angles ends up at the narrow exit end. The light doesn't converge to form an image, but its intensity has nevertheless been increased because its energy is spread over a smaller area. Thus, the concentrator acts as a "funnel" for light. Figure 36-14b shows a section of a compound parabolic reflector used to concentrate light onto a tube carrying heat-transfer fluid in a solar thermal power plant. Because the concentrator accepts light from a broad angular range, it works without the need for expensive tracking equipment that would keep it facing the Sun.

Nonimaging concentrators have other applications as well. The first compound parabolic concentrator, built in 1965, was designed to collect light from a high-energy physics experiment. Nonimaging optics in the infrared were used on the Cosmic Background Explorer satellite that has provided crucial evidence in support of the Big Bang theory of the origin of the universe. And under development are solar-powered lasers that use nonimaging concentrators as the "pump" that supplies energy to run the laser.

36-3 LENSES

A **lens** is a transparent piece of material that uses refraction of light to form images. As with mirrors, lenses can be either concave or convex. But light goes through a lens, while it reflects off a mirror, so the roles of the two types are reversed. A convex lens focuses parallel rays to a **focal point**, and is therefore called a **converging lens** (Fig. 36-15). As we'll soon see, a convex lens can form real and virtual images, depending on the object location. A concave lens, in contrast, is a **diverging lens**; it refracts parallel rays so they appear to be diverging from a common focus. Like a *convex* mirror, a *concave* lens can form only virtual images (Fig. 36-16).

(a)

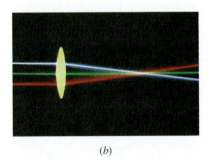

(b)

FIGURE 36-15 A convex lens brings parallel light rays to a focus F. The focal length f is the distance from the lens to the focal point. You can see in (a) that light is refracted at each surface of the lens, but as the lens is thin we can treat the two refractions as a single change of direction at the center plane of the lens. Because the lens surfaces are parallel at the center of the lens, any ray through the center passes undeflected.

(a)

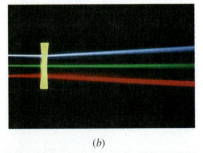

(b)

FIGURE 36-16 Parallel light rays passing through a concave lens diverge so it looks as though they are coming from a common focus. But light doesn't actually come from the focus, so this type of lens can produce only virtual images.

In Section 36-4 we'll examine the detailed behavior of light as it refracts at the interfaces between a lens and the surrounding medium. First, we explore the simpler situation of a **thin lens**—one whose thickness is small compared with the curvature radii of its two surfaces. Although light refracts once as it enters a lens and once as it exits, in the thin-lens approximation the two lens surfaces are so close that it suffices to consider that the light bends just once, as it crosses the center plane of the lens. Unlike a mirror, light can go either way through a lens; that means the lens has two focal points, one on either side. For a thin lens, the focal length proves to be the same in either direction, so it doesn't matter which way we orient the lens. We'll justify the thin-lens approximation mathematically in Section 36-4.

Lens Images by Ray Tracing

As with mirrors, two rays serve to fix the image formed by a lens. For lenses, two special rays make ray tracing easy:

15.8

Thin Lens Ray Diagrams

1. Any ray parallel to the lens axis refracts through the focal point.
2. Any ray through the center of the lens passes undeflected.

Figure 36-17 shows ray tracings for different object placements in relation to a converging lens. In Fig. 36-17a we see that an object farther out than two focal lengths produces a smaller, inverted real image on the other side of the lens.

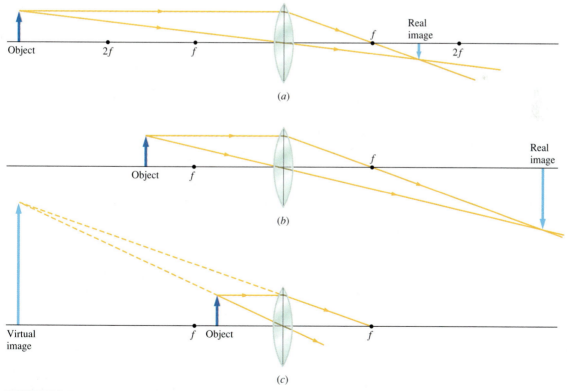

FIGURE 36-17 Image formation with a converging lens. Marks on axis are distances from the lens center, in units of the focal length f. In (a) and (b), an object distance greater than the focal length results in an inverted real image. The image is enlarged if the object distance is between one and two focal lengths, as shown in (b). In (c) a virtual image forms when the object is within the focal length. You can simulate these situations with ActivPhysics Activity 15.8.

FIGURE 36-18 Simplified diagram of a movie projector. The film lies just beyond the focal length, and thus the lens produces an enlarged real image on the distant screen. The audience normally views the image from the projector side of the screen. Note that the film is upside down.

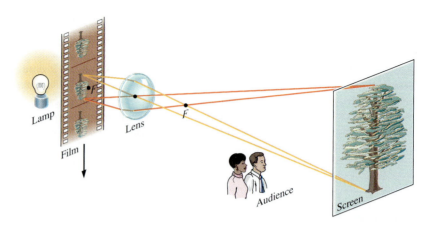

Since light really emanates from this image, you could see it without actually looking through the lens. As the object moves toward the lens, the image moves away and grows in size. When the object is between one and two focal lengths from the lens, the image has moved beyond $2f$, and is enlarged. The image on a movie screen is formed in this way (Fig. 36-18). Moving the object closer than the focal point produces an enlarged virtual image that can be seen only by an observer looking *through* the lens (Fig. 36-17c).

Figure 36-19 shows ray tracings for a diverging lens. Like a convex mirror, this lens produces only virtual images that are upright and reduced in size. Like the virtual image of Fig. 36-17c these virtual images are visible only through the lens. You should convince yourself that the basic geometry of Fig. 36-19 does not change even if the object moves within the focal length.

FIGURE 36-19 A diverging lens always forms a reduced, upright, virtual image, visible only through the lens.

Got It!

Before going on to the mathematics of lenses, try answering the following simple questions about the image shown in Fig. 36-20. (Remember that answers to GOT IT! boxes are in the back of the book.)
a. What would happen if the bottom half of the lens were covered?
b. What would happen if the lens were removed?
c. What would happen if the screen's distance from the lens were doubled?
d. Would there be an image in the absence of the screen?

FIGURE 36-20 A simple optical system, consisting of an object (the candle), a converging lens, and a white screen on which the image appears. This system is a realization of Fig. 36-17b.

A Lens Equation

We can locate lens images quantitatively by deriving an equation like we did for mirrors. Note in Fig. 36-21 that the two unshaded right triangles formed by

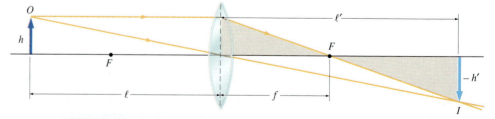

FIGURE 36-21 Ray diagram for deriving the lens equation. The unshaded pair of right triangles formed by the object and image arrows with their distances ℓ and ℓ' are similar, as are the pair of shaded triangles.

TABLE 36-2 *Sign Conventions for Lenses*

FOCAL LENGTH f^1,	OBJECT DISTANCE, ℓ	IMAGE DISTANCE^2, ℓ'	TYPE OF IMAGE
+	+, $\ell > f$	+	Real, inverted, enlarged for $\ell < 2f$, reduced for $\ell > 2f$
+	+, $\ell < f$	−	Virtual, upright, enlarged
−	+	−	Virtual, upright, reduced

^{1} + for convex lens, − for concave.
^{2} − means on same side of lens as object.

the object and image arrows with their distances ℓ and ℓ' are similar. Therefore, the magnification is

$$M = \frac{h'}{h} = -\frac{\ell'}{\ell},$$ (36-4)

where again we take a negative height to signify an inverted image. Thus, the magnitude of the magnification is the ratio of object to image distance, as it was with mirrors. The two shaded triangles in Fig. 36-21 are also similar, and therefore

$$\frac{-h'}{\ell' - f} = \frac{h}{f}.$$

Combining this result with Equation 36-4 and doing some algebra then gives

$$\frac{1}{\ell} + \frac{1}{\ell'} = \frac{1}{f}, \qquad \text{lens equation}$$ (36-5)

which is identical to the mirror equation 36-2. Note that putting the object at infinity ($\ell = \infty$) gives $\ell' = f$ and that putting the object at the focus ($\ell = f$) gives $\ell' = \infty$. Thus, Equation 36-5 reflects our ray-tracing diagrams that show parallel rays (such as those from an object at a great distance) converging at the focal point, and vice versa.

Although we derived Equation 36-5 for the case of a real image, the equation holds for virtual images if we consider the image distance negative; in that case the image is on the same side of the lens as is the object. And it holds for diverging lenses if we consider the focal length negative. Table 36-2 summarizes these sign conventions for lenses, while Fig. 36-22 describes graphically the sizes and types of images formed at different object distances.

Got It!

You look through a lens at this page and see the words magnified. Is the image you observe real or virtual? Is the lens concave or convex?

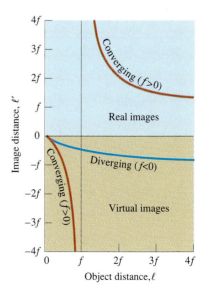

FIGURE 36-22 Image versus object distances for lenses. Real images correspond to positive image distances, virtual images to negative image distances. Red curves are for converging lenses, for which object distances below the focal length result in virtual images ($\ell' < 0$). The image moves toward infinity as the object approaches the focal point from either direction, and concurrently the image grows arbitrarily large. For diverging lenses (blue curve), images are always virtual and reduced in size.

EXAMPLE 36-4	Slide Show

You're projecting slides onto a wall 2.6 m from a slide projector whose single lens has focal length 12.0 cm. (a) How far should the slides be from the lens? (b) How big will be the image of a 35-mm slide?

Solution

We want the image focused on the screen, so the image distance ℓ' is 2.6 m. Solving Equation 36-5 for the object distance ℓ then gives

$$\ell = \left(\frac{1}{f} - \frac{1}{\ell'}\right)^{-1} = \left(\frac{1}{12 \text{ cm}} - \frac{1}{260 \text{ cm}}\right)^{-1} = 12.58 \text{ cm}.$$

This is just beyond the focal length, as Figs. 36-17 and 36-22 suggest it should be to get an enlarged, distant, real image.

Equation 36-4 then gives the height h' of the image formed of a 35-mm slide:

$$h' = -h\frac{\ell'}{\ell} = -(3.5 \text{ cm})\left(\frac{260 \text{ cm}}{12.58 \text{ cm}}\right) = -72 \text{ cm}.$$

The minus sign indicates inversion, showing that the slide must go in the projector upside down to get an upright image.

EXERCISE If the slide in Example 36-4 moves 1 mm farther from the lens, what will happen to the position of the image?

Answer: moves 36 cm toward projector

Some problems similar to Example 36-4: 18–30

EXAMPLE 36-5	Fine Print

You're using a magnifying glass (a converging lens) with 30 cm focal length to read a telephone book (Fig. 36-23). How far from the page should you hold the lens in order to see the print enlarged 3 times?

Solution

Here the image is virtual, so ℓ' is negative and $3\times$ magnification then corresponds to $\ell' = -3\ell$. So Equation 36-5 becomes

$$\frac{1}{\ell} - \frac{1}{3\ell} = \frac{2}{3\ell} = \frac{1}{f} = \frac{1}{30 \text{ cm}},$$

whence $\ell = (2)(30 \text{ cm})/3 = 20 \text{ cm}$. Figure 36-23 confirms that the image appears further from the lens than the actual page.

EXERCISE A magnifying glass enlarges print by 50% when it's held 9.0 cm from a page. What is its focal length?

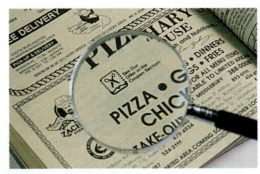

FIGURE 36-23 A magnifying glass is a converging lens used in its virtual-image mode.

Answer: 27 cm

Some problems similar to Example 36-5: 18–30

36-4 REFRACTION IN LENSES: THE DETAILS

We now examine in detail the refraction effects that cause lenses to form images. Every lens has two refracting surfaces, at least one of which is curved. We therefore look first at image formation due to refraction at a *single* curved interface. To understand the behavior of a lens we will then consider two such interfaces, using the image formed by the first as the object for the second.

Refraction at a Curved Surface

Figure 36-24 shows part of a spherically curved piece of transparent material with curvature radius R and refractive index n_2, surrounded by a medium with

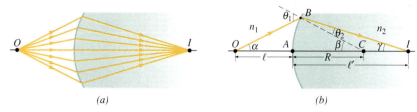

FIGURE 36-24 Refraction at an interface with a curved surface. (*a*) Rays from an object at *O* are refracted at the interface and converge to form an image at *I*. (*b*) Geometry for relating the object and image distances ℓ and ℓ'. All the labeled angles are considered small, even though the drawing doesn't show them as such.

index n_1 (typically air). A point-like object *O* lies on an axis through the center of curvature of the refracting surface. As we will now show, light rays diverging from this object at small angles to the optic axis are refracted to a common image point (Fig. 36-24*a*). The restriction to small angles is the same paraxial approximation we applied for spherical mirrors; again, our drawings don't always show the angles as being small.

In Fig. 36-24*b* we show a single ray in detail. Under the paraxial approximation the labeled angles in this figure are all small, and we can use the approximation $\sin x \simeq \tan x \simeq x$, where $x \ll 1$ with x an angle measured in radians. Then Snell's law—$n_1 \sin \theta_1 = n_2 \sin \theta_2$—becomes simply

$$n_1 \theta_1 = n_2 \theta_2 \,.$$

From triangles *BCI* and *OBC*, we see that $\theta_2 = \beta - \gamma$ and $\theta_1 = \alpha + \beta$. Using these results in our small-angle version of Snell's law gives

$$n_1(\alpha + \beta) = n_2(\beta - \gamma) \,.$$

Furthermore, in the small-angle approximation the arc *BA* is so close to a straight line that we can write $\alpha \simeq \tan \alpha \simeq BA/\ell$, with $\ell = OA$ the object's distance from the refracting surface. Similarly, $\beta \simeq BA/R$, and $\gamma \simeq BA/\ell'$. Thus, our expression of Snell's law becomes

$$n_1\left(\frac{BA}{\ell} + \frac{BA}{R}\right) = n_2\left(\frac{BA}{R} - \frac{BA}{\ell'}\right)$$

or, on canceling the arc length *BA* and rearranging,

$$\frac{n_1}{\ell} + \frac{n_2}{\ell'} = \frac{n_2 - n_1}{R} \,. \tag{36-6}$$

Notice that the angle α does not appear in this equation. Therefore, this relation between the object and image distances holds for *all* rays as long as they satisfy the small-angle approximation. That means all such rays come to a common focus at *I*, as in Fig. 36-24*a*, so an image must appear at this point.

Although we derived Equation 36-6 for a case of real image formation, as usual it holds for virtual images as well if we consider the image distance negative. It also works for surfaces that are concave toward the object—the opposite of Fig. 36-24—if we take *R* as a negative number. And it even works for flat surfaces, with $R = \infty$, as the exercise following Example 36-6 shows.

EXAMPLE 36-6	*A Cylindrical Aquarium*

An aquarium is made from a thin-walled tube of transparent plastic 70 cm in diameter (Fig. 36-25a). For a cat looking directly into the aquarium, what is the apparent distance to a fish 15 cm from the aquarium wall?

Solution

We can neglect the aquarium wall; since it's thin and has essentially parallel faces, light suffers no net deflection in passing through the wall. The surface is concave toward the object, so $R = -35$ cm. With $\ell = 15$ cm, $n_1 = 1.333$ for water, and $n_2 = 1$ for air, we can solve Equation 36-6 for the image distance ℓ':

$$\ell' = \frac{n_2}{\left(\dfrac{n_2 - n_1}{R} - \dfrac{n_1}{\ell}\right)} = \frac{1}{\left(\dfrac{1 - 1.333}{-35 \text{ cm}} - \dfrac{1.333}{15 \text{ cm}}\right)}$$

$$= -12.6 \text{ cm}.$$

The negative answer indicates that we have a virtual image, as shown in Fig. 36-25b.

A special case of Equation 36-6 is a flat surface, for which $R = \infty$. The right-hand side is then zero, but the equation still relates object and image distances. Looking down into a swimming pool from above, for example, you see virtual images of objects in the pool. The objects appear closer than they actually are, as Fig. 36-26 and the following exercise illustrate.

EXERCISE The bottom of a swimming pool looks to be 1.5 m below the surface. What is the pool's actual depth?

Answer: 2.0 m

Some problems similar to Example 36-6: 30, 31, 32, 34–36

(a)   *(b)*

FIGURE 36-25 (*a*) A cylindrical aquarium. (*b*) Top view, showing formation of a virtual image of a fish that is actually 15 cm from the aquarium wall.

FIGURE 36-26 Refraction at a flat surface produces an image *I* that appears closer than the object *O*. Objects at the bottom of a swimming pool, for example, appear closer than they really are.

Lenses, Thick and Thin

Figure 36-27 shows a lens of arbitrary thickness *t* made from material with refractive index *n*. For simplicity we will consider the lens surrounded by air or

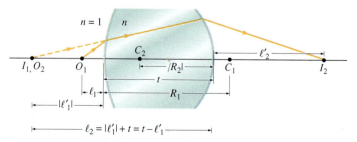

FIGURE 36-27 A thick lens. The left-hand surface forms the virtual image I_1, which is also labelled O_2 because it forms the object for the right-hand surface. Together, the two surfaces then produce the final real image I_2. Absolute value signs are used on distances whose algebraic signs in Equation 36-6 are negative—i.e., the distance ℓ'_1 to the virtual image and the curvature radius R_2 of the right-hand surface, which is concave toward the incident light.

vacuum, with refractive index equal to 1. An object O_1 lies a distance ℓ_1 to the left of the left-hand surface. This surface focuses light from O_1 to form image I_1. Light from this image impinges on the right-hand surface, forming a second image I_2. We want to relate the original object O_1 and final image I_2.

We developed Equation 36-6, our description of refraction at a single curved surface, using Fig. 36-24. In that figure we considered formation of a real image, but we quickly noted that Equation 36-6 applies to virtual and real images alike. In considering a two-surface lens it proves more convenient to place the object where its image in the first surface is a virtual one, as in Fig. 36-27. Again, our final result will apply whatever the object placement.

At the left-hand surface in Fig. 36-27, the quantities in Equation 36-6 are $\ell = \ell_1$, $\ell' = \ell_1'$, $n_1 = 1$, $n_2 = n$, and $R = R_1$, so Equation 36-6 becomes

$$\frac{1}{\ell_1} + \frac{n}{\ell_1'} = \frac{n-1}{R_1}. \qquad \text{(left-hand surface)}$$

The "object" O_2 for the right-hand surface is the image I_1 since light incident on that surface looks like it's coming from I_1. The distance ℓ in Equation 36-6 for this "object" is $\ell = \ell_2 = t - \ell_1'$, with t the lens thickness. Why minus? Because I_1 is a *virtual* image, so, according to our sign conventions, ℓ_1' is a *negative* quantity. The physical distance between the image and the lens is then the positive quantity $-\ell_1'$, and that quantity adds to the lens thickness to give the distance from this intermediate image to the right-hand surface. Also at the right-hand surface, $\ell' = \ell_2'$, $n_1 = n$, $n_2 = 1$, and $R = R_2$. Thus, at the right-hand surface Equation 36-6 reads

$$\frac{n}{t - \ell_1'} + \frac{1}{\ell_2'} = \frac{1-n}{R_2}. \qquad \text{(right-hand surface)}$$

Now we'll let the lens become arbitrarily thin, taking the limit $t \to 0$. Then the first term in our right-surface equation becomes $-n/\ell_1'$. But the term n/ℓ_1' also occurs in the left-surface equation. So we can add the two equations to eliminate the intermediate-image distance ℓ_1'. Since we'll be left with only one object distance, ℓ_1, and one image distance, ℓ_2', we can drop the subscripts 1 and 2 on these quantities. The result is

$$\frac{1}{\ell} + \frac{1}{\ell'} = (n-1)\left(\frac{1}{R_1} - \frac{1}{R_2}\right). \qquad (36\text{-}7)$$

The left-hand side of this equation is identical to the left-hand side of Equation 36-5. So we can equate the right-hand sides of the two equations to get an expression for the focal length of our lens:

$$\frac{1}{f} = (n-1)\left(\frac{1}{R_1} - \frac{1}{R_2}\right). \qquad \text{(lensmaker's formula)} \qquad (36\text{-}8)$$

We emphasize that the radii R_1 and R_2 in Equation 36-8 may be positive or negative, depending on the lens curvature. In Fig. 36-27, for example, R_1 is positive because the left-hand surface is convex toward the incident light but R_2 is negative because the right-hand surface is concave toward the light. One of the radii can also be infinite if the corresponding surface is flat.

Lenses are made in a variety of shapes, as shown in Fig. 36-28. Those that are thicker at the center are converging lenses, for which Equation 36-8 gives a positive focal length. Those that are thinner at the center are diverging lenses, with negative focal length. These characterizations of lens behavior reverse if

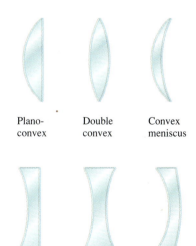

Plano-convex Double convex Convex meniscus

Plano-concave Double concave Concave meniscus

FIGURE 36-28 Common lens types.

the medium surrounding the lens has a higher refractive index than the lens itself (see Problem 73, which generalizes Equation 36-8 for an arbitrary refractive index in the surrounding medium).

EXAMPLE 36-7 — A Plano-Convex Lens

The plano-convex lens in Fig. 36-28 is made from material with refractive index n. Given that the curved surface has curvature radius R, find an expression for the focal length of the lens. Show that the focal length is the same whether light is incident on the lens from right or left.

Solution

With light incident from the left in Fig. 36-28, $R_1 = R$. A flat surface has infinite curvature, so $R_2 = \infty$. Then Equation 36-18 gives

$$f = \left[(n - 1)\left(\frac{1}{R} - \frac{1}{\infty}\right) \right]^{-1} = \frac{R}{n - 1},$$

since $1/\infty = 0$. If light is incident from the right, then $R_1 = \infty$ and, since the curved surface is now concave toward the light,

$R_2 = -R$. Then

$$f = \left[(n - 1)\left(\frac{1}{\infty} - \frac{1}{-R}\right) \right]^{-1} = \frac{R}{n - 1},$$

showing that the two focal points are indeed equidistant from the lens.

EXERCISE A double-convex lens (see Fig. 36-28) is made of glass with $n = 1.75$. If the curvature radii of the two sides are equal, what should that radius be in order to give the lens a 25-cm focal length?

Answer: 37.5 cm

Some problems similar to Example 36-7: 38–47

Lens Aberrations

Lenses exhibit several types of optical defects. We've already described **spherical aberration** in connection with mirrors; this defect occurs because a spherical mirror only approximates the ideally focusing shape of a parabola. Lenses with spherical surfaces also exhibit spherical aberration (Fig. 36-29a). In our analysis of image formation by a curved refracting surface we had to make the small-angle approximation; otherwise, we would not have reached the conclusion that all rays from an object come to a common focus. Spherical aberration can be minimized by ensuring that incident rays are as close and as parallel as possible to the lens axis. That's easy for distant objects but harder with objects close to the lens. Using only the central portion of the lens eliminates those rays at larger angles (Fig. 36-29b), leading to a sharper focus. That's why a camera focuses over a wider range when it is "stopped down," the outer part of its lens

(a)   (b)

FIGURE 36-29 (a) Spherical aberration occurs because rays striking the lens farther from the axis and at greater angles focus closer to the lens than do near-axial rays. The result is a "smearing" of the image. (b) This defect can be minimized by using only the central portion of the lens, at the expense of a dimmer image.

FIGURE 36-30 Chromatic aberration occurs because the refractive index varies with wavelength, causing different colors to focus at different points.

FIGURE 36-31 This magnifying lens shows both spherical aberration (distortion of the lines) and chromatic aberration (colors).

covered by an adjustable diaphragm. The trade-off, of course, is that there is less light available.

Another optical defect is **chromatic aberration** (Fig. 36-30), which occurs because the refractive index varies with wavelength. High-quality optical systems minimize this defect by using composite lenses made from different materials whose differing refractive indices allow several colors to focus at the same point. Chromatic aberration is unique to lenses since mirrors reflect light of all colors in exactly the same way. Figure 36-31 shows both spherical and chromatic aberration in a simple magnifying lens.

APPLICATION	*Fresnel Lenses*

Large-diameter lenses are impracticably thick. Lighthouses, in particular, cannot use single lenses to concentrate their intense beams because too much light would be absorbed in the glass. To solve this problem the French scientist Augustin Fresnel, in 1822, devised a way of making large lenses thin. A Fresnel lens consists of concentric rings shaped to approximate segments of an ordinary lens surface, with steplike jumps to keep the overall structure thin (Fig. 36-32a). Fresnel lenses are still used in lighthouses (Fig. 36-32b), while Fresnel lenses made from plastic sheets appear in home, office, and car windows to provide magnification or wide-angle views (Fig. 36-32c). They are also used in some overhead projectors.

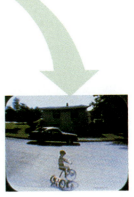

(a) (b) (c)

FIGURE 36-32 (a) A Fresnel lens approximates a normal curved lens by a series of short segments. (b) A giant Fresnel lens from a nineteenth-century lighthouse. (c) Fresnel lens made from sheet plastic mounted on the rear window of a van provides a wide-angle view of what's behind the van.

36-5 OPTICAL INSTRUMENTS

Numerous optical instruments make use of mirrors and/or lenses. We've already considered some simple applications using a single lens or mirror, including film projectors, magnifying glasses, and side-view mirrors. More complicated systems use several optical elements (lenses or mirrors), but the principles we have developed still apply. In particular, we trace light through a sequence of optical elements by using the image formed by one element as the object for the next.

The Eye

15.3

The Eye

Our eyes are our primary optical instruments. Each eye is a complex optical system with several refracting surfaces and mechanisms to vary both the focal length and the amount of light admitted. Figure 36-33*a* shows that the eye is essentially a fluid-filled ball about 2.3 cm in diameter. Light enters through the hard, transparent cornea and passes through a fluid called the aqueous humor before entering the lens. On exiting the lens, light traverses the vitreous humor that fills the main body of the eyeball and finally strikes the retina. The retina is covered with light-sensitive cells of two types (Fig. 36-33*b*). Cells called cones are sensitive to different colors but require moderate amounts of light, while rod cells function at low intensity but lack color discrimination. Both types of cells produce electrochemical signals that carry information to the brain.

A properly functioning eye produces a well-focused real image on the retina. Contrary to general belief, most of the refraction is provided not by the lens but by the cornea. The lens, however, is the adjustable element. Muscles pulling on the lens alter its focal length, allowing fine adjustment of the eye's focus—a process known as accommodation. Other muscles automatically adjust the iris, enlarging or contracting the pupil opening to compensate for different light levels.

When the muscles are relaxed, the lens is relatively flat, with focal length about 1.7 cm. But for nearsighted (myopic) people, the image still forms in front

(*a*)

(*b*)

FIGURE 36-33 (*a*) The human eye. (*b*) Scanning-electron-microscope image showing rods and a cone (blue structure) in a human retina.

(a) (b)

FIGURE 36-34 (a) A myopic eye focuses light from distant objects in front of the retina. (b) A diverging lens corrects the problem, creating a virtual image closer to the eye. The eye's image of this virtual image then falls on the retina.

of the retina, causing distant objects to appear blurred (Fig. 36-34a). Diverging corrective lenses produce closer intermediate images that the myopic eye can then focus (Fig. 36-34). In farsighted (hyperopic) eyes, the image of nearby objects would focus behind the retina, and converging corrective lenses are used (Fig. 36-35). Actually, everyone is farsighted, in the sense that there is a minimum distance, called the **near point**, below which the eye cannot focus sharply. In the typical human the near point is at about 25 cm, and this value is taken as a standard. By the time one is 50, however, the typical near point is at about 40 cm, and it may be several meters.

ActivPhysics Activity 15.13 simulates both near- and farsighted eyes.

Prescriptions for corrective lenses usually specify the corrective power, P, in **diopters**, where the diopter measure of a lens is the inverse of its focal length in meters. Thus, a 1-diopter lens has $f = 1$ m, while a 2-diopter lens has $f = 0.5$ m and is more powerful in that it refracts light more sharply.

Since even the closest objects we view are many centimeters from the eye, it doesn't matter whether a corrective lens is a few cm away from the eye, as with glasses, or right on the cornea, as with a contact lens. Today's soft contact lenses are more than 50 percent water and provide a natural-seeming addition to the cornea that corrects simple vision defects. Contact lenses can be quite thin because, as Equation 36-8 shows, it's the curvature radii rather than the lens thickness that establishes the focal length. On the other hand, glasses remain somewhat more versatile, with variable-focus lenses available that can compensate for defects in both near and far vision. A more radical approach is laser surgery to reshape the cornea; when successful, it can eliminate the need for corrective lenses.

The human eye is a complex biological system, in many ways a direct extension of the brain. Although we understand its optical behavior, we understand much less clearly how visual perception actually occurs. Recently biologists and computer scientists have teamed to produce an electronic "silicon retina" whose behavior mimics many subtle aspects of the natural eye and may therefore shed light on the process of perception.

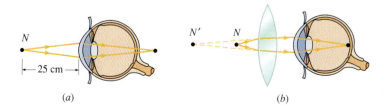

(a) (b)

FIGURE 36-35 (a) A farsighted eye cannot focus light from the standard 25-cm near point at N. (b) A converging corrective lens makes light from an object at the near point appear to come from the point N' which is at the minimum distance where this eye can focus.

EXAMPLE 36-8	*Lost Your Glasses!*

You're on vacation and have lost your reading glasses; without them, your eyes can't focus closer than 70 cm. Fortunately you can buy nonprescription reading glasses in a pharmacy, where they come in increments of 0.25 diopter. Which glasses should you buy?

Solution

Correcting your vision problem means bringing the range for clear focus to the standard 25-cm near point. According to Fig. 36-35*b*, that means you want a lens that will produce a virtual image at 70 cm of an object at 25 cm. The required power follows directly from Equation 36-5:

$$P = \frac{1}{f} = \frac{1}{\ell} + \frac{1}{\ell'} = \frac{1}{0.25 \text{ m}} + \frac{1}{-0.70 \text{ m}} = 2.57 \text{ diopters},$$

where the image distance is negative because the image is virtual. You'll do fine with 2.5-diopter glasses.

EXERCISE A nearsighted person cannot see clearly beyond 80 cm. Prescribe a lens power that will image the most distant objects at 80 cm, giving clear vision at all distances.

Answer: −1.25 diopters, the minus sign signifying a diverging lens

Some problems similar to Example 36-8: 48–50, 69

Got It!

You and your roommate have gotten your boxes of disposable contact lenses mixed up. One box is marked "−1.75 diopter," the other "+2.25 diopter." You're farsighted and your roommate is nearsighted. Which contact lenses are yours?

Cameras

A camera is much like the eye, except that in place of the eye's retina it focuses its image on film or a light-sensitive electronic device (Fig. 36-36). Most still cameras use the long-established technology of film based on light-sensitive chemicals, but light-sensitive silicon chips known as charge-coupled devices (CCDs) have already made film obsolete in astronomical imaging and, with the proliferation of digital cameras, are rapidly challenging conventional photography.

All but the simplest cameras have movable lenses that adjust, either manually or automatically, for optimum focus with different distances to the subject. Most

FIGURE 36-36 Optical system of a simple camera.

(a)   (b)

FIGURE 36-37 Photos taken from the same point with (a) short and (b) long focal length settings of an adjustable zoom lens.

cameras also have an adjustable diaphragm that covers part of the lens to regulate the amount of incoming light; "stopping down" the lens by closing the diaphragm admits less light but permits a broader range of distances to be in reasonably clear focus. Many cameras have zoom lenses whose focal lengths can be altered to provide different views of the same subject (Fig. 36-37).

Magnifiers and Microscopes

We wouldn't need optical instruments to examine small objects if we could bring our eyes arbitrarily close to the objects. But we've seen that the average human eye can't focus much closer than about 25 cm. We therefore use lenses to put enlarged images of small objects at distances where our eyes can focus.

What matters is not so much the actual size of the image, but how much of our field of view it occupies. Consequently we define the **angular magnification** m as the ratio of the angle subtended by an object seen through a lens to the angle subtended as seen by the naked eye when the object is at the standard 25-cm near point. Figure 36-38a shows that the former angle, α, is given

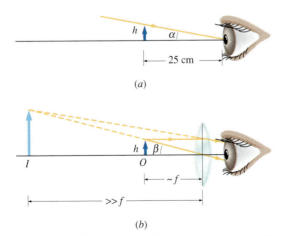

(a)

(b)

FIGURE 36-38 (a) An object of height h subtends a small angle $\alpha \simeq h/25$ cm at the standard 25-cm near point. (b) Putting the object near the focus of a converging lens gives an image that subtends an angle $\beta \simeq h/f$. The angular magnification is the ratio $m = \beta/\alpha$.

15.11
Two-Lens Systems

15.14
Microscope

by $\alpha = h/25$ cm, where h is the object height and α is in radians. The maximum magnification would occur with the image itself at the near point (see Problem 53), but it's more comfortable to view a very distant image. We therefore place the object at just inside the focal length, forming an enlarged virtual image at a great distance. Figure 36-38b shows this geometry, from which we see that the angle β subtended by the image is essentially h/f. Then the magnification is

$$m = \frac{\beta}{\alpha} = \frac{h/f}{h/25 \text{ cm}} = \frac{25 \text{ cm}}{f} \qquad \text{(simple magnifier)}. \qquad (36\text{-}9)$$

This angular magnification is achieved only with the eye very close to the lens, which is not the way we normally hold an ordinary magnifying glass. But it is the way we place our eyes on instruments such as microscopes and telescopes that use simple magnifying lenses for their eyepieces.

Single lenses can produce angular magnifications of about 4 before aberrations compromise the image quality. Higher power magnification therefore requires more than one lens. A **compound microscope** is a two-lens system in which a lens of short focal length called the **objective** forms a magnified real image. This image is then viewed with a second lens, the **eyepiece**, positioned as a simple magnifier (Fig. 36-39). The object being viewed is positioned just beyond the focal length of the objective lens, and its image falls just inside the focal length of the eyepiece. If both focal lengths are small compared with the distance between the lenses, then the object distance for the objective lens is approximately the objective focal length f_o, and the resulting image distance is approximately the lens spacing L. The real image formed by the objective lens is larger than the object by the ratio of the image to object distance, or $-L/f_o$. The eyepiece enlarges the image further, by a factor of its angular magnification 25 cm$/f_e$. Then the overall magnification of the microscope is

$$M = M_o m_e = -\frac{L}{f_o}\left(\frac{25 \text{ cm}}{f_e}\right), \qquad \text{(compound microscope)} \qquad (36\text{-}10)$$

where, as usual, the minus sign signifies an inverted image.

Optical microscopes work well as long as the approximation of geometrical optics holds—that is, when the object being viewed is much larger than the wavelength of light. Viewing smaller objects requires waves of shorter wavelength than visible light. In the widely used electron microscope, those "waves" are electrons, whose wavelike nature we will examine in Chapter 39.

FIGURE 36-39 Image formation in a compound microscope. Figure is not to scale; distance L should be much greater than either focal length, and the image I_1 should be very near the eyepiece's focus, resulting in greater magnification.

You can "build" and experiment with 2-lens optical systems, such as the microscope, using ActivPhysics Activity 15.11.

Telescopes

A telescope collects light from distant objects, either forming an image or supplying light to instruments for analysis. Telescopes are classified as **refracting** or **reflecting**, depending on whether the main light-gathering element is a lens or mirror. Small hand-held telescopes and binoculars are refracting instruments, as are telephoto camera lenses and some older astronomical telescopes. Modern astronomical telescopes are invariably reflectors.

The simplest refracting telescope consists of a single lens that images distant objects at essentially its focal point. Film or a CCD placed at that point captures the image, or an eyepiece is used to view the image. The world's largest refracting telescope, at Yerkes Observatory in Wisconsin, has a 1-m-diameter lens with 12-m focal length. Photographers can think of it as a 12,000-mm telephoto lens. Figure 36-40 shows the imaging process in an astronomical refracting telescope. The focal points of the objective and eyepiece lenses are nearly coincident, so the real image of a distant object that forms at the objective's focus is then seen through the eyepiece as a greatly enlarged virtual image. The angular magnification is the ratio of the angle β subtended by the final image to the angle α subtended by the actual object; Fig. 36-40 shows that this ratio is

15.12
The Telescope

$$m = \frac{\beta}{\alpha} = \frac{f_o}{f_e}. \qquad \text{(refracting telescope)} \qquad (36\text{-}11)$$

Since a real image is inverted and a virtual image is upright, a two-lens refracting telescope gives an inverted image. This is fine for astronomical work, but telescopes designed for terrestrial use have an extra lens, a diverging eyepiece (see Problem 72) or a set of reflecting prisms (as in binoculars; see Fig. 35-15) to produce an upright image.

Reflecting telescopes offer many advantages over refractors. Mirrors have reflective coatings on their front surfaces, eliminating chromatic aberration because light need not pass through glass. Having only one optically active

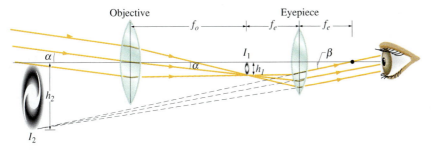

FIGURE 36-40 Image formation in a refracting telescope. A distant object, in this case a galaxy, is imaged first at the focus of the objective lens (image I_1). An eyepiece with its focus at nearly the same point then gives an enlarged virtual image (I_2). The angles α and β are given by $\alpha = h_1/f_o$ and $\beta = h_1/f_e$ in the small-angle approximation, leading to Equation 36-11 for the angular magnification.

FIGURE 36-41 One of the two identical Keck telescopes that occupy adjacent observatory domes atop Hawaii's Mauna Kea. Each telescope has a hexagonal mirror 10 m across, consisting of 36 individually adjustable segments; here the entire mirror is visible through the slit in the dome. The two Keck telescopes are being joined optically with four smaller telescopes to form an instrument with the resolving power of an 85-m telescope. (More on how this works in the next chapter.)

surface allows much larger reflectors to be built since the mirrors can be supported across their entire back surfaces—unlike lenses, which can be supported only at the edges. Where the largest refracting telescope ever built has a 1-m-diameter lens, the newest reflectors boast diameters in the 10-m range (Fig. 36-41). These designs incorporate segmented and/or flexible mirrors whose shape can be adjusted under computer control for optimum focusing; with so-called adaptive optics, such systems may adjust rapidly enough to compensate for the atmospheric turbulence that has traditionally limited the resolution of ground-based telescopes.

The simplest reflecting telescope is a curved mirror with a CCD or film at its focus. Superb image quality results, in principle limited only by wave effects we will discuss in the next chapter. More often the telescope is used as a "light bucket," collecting light from stars or other distant sources too small to image even with today's large optical telescopes. Then a secondary mirror sends light to a focus at a point that's convenient for telescope-mounted instrumentation. Optical fibers may also be used to bring light collected by the primary mirror to fixed instruments. Alternatively, an eyepiece can be mounted to examine the image visually. Figure 36-42 shows several common designs for reflecting telescopes.

Magnification is not a particularly important quantity in astronomical telescopes, which are used more for spectral and other analysis than for direct imaging. More important is the light-gathering power of the instrument, which is determined simply by the area of its objective lens or primary mirror. The 10-m Keck telescope, for instance, has 100 times the light-gathering power of the 1-m Yerkes refractor and more than 17 times the power of the 2.4-m Hubble Space Telescope.

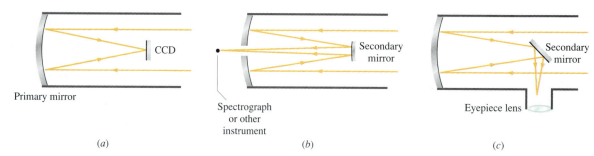

Primary mirror

CCD

Spectrograph or other instrument

Secondary mirror

Secondary mirror

Eyepiece lens

(a)

(b)

(c)

FIGURE 36-42 Common arrangements for reflecting telescopes. (a) Placing a CCD or film at the prime focus gives the best image quality. (b) In the Cassegrain design light reflects from a secondary mirror and passes through a hole in the primary. The secondary may be either plane or convex. This design is widely used in large telescopes, with the added option of placing detectors directly at the prime focus as in (a). (c) The Newtonian design, used primarily in small telescopes, has an angled secondary mirror to direct light to the eyepiece.

CHAPTER SYNOPSIS

Summary

1. Reflection and refraction can result in **images**, which are **real** or **virtual** depending on whether light actually comes from the image location.

2. Plane mirrors form only virtual images, equal in size to the object being imaged. Concave curved mirrors have a **focal point** at which parallel rays converge after reflection. Concave mirrors form either real or virtual images, depending on the object location. For convex mirrors, parallel rays reflect as though diverging from the focal point; such mirrors can form only virtual images. The **mirror equation** quantifies the relation between object and image distances ℓ and ℓ':

$$\frac{1}{\ell} + \frac{1}{\ell'} = \frac{1}{f},$$

where the **focal length** f is the distance from the mirror's apex to its focus. The **magnification** is the ratio $M = -\ell'/\ell$, where a negative ℓ' corresponds to a virtual image and therefore to a positive M and so to an upright image.

3. **Lenses**, made from transparent materials, refract light to a focus. In the **thin-lens** approximation, the curvature radii of the lens surfaces are much greater than the thickness of the lens. Such a lens has two foci, located equal distances f on either side of the lens. The object and image distances and magnification then obey equations identical to those for mirrors. The focal length of a thin lens is given by the **lensmaker's equation**:

$$\frac{1}{f} = (n-1)\left(\frac{1}{R_1} - \frac{1}{R_2}\right),$$

where R_1 and R_2 are the curvature radii of the lens surfaces, taken as positive when the surface is convex toward the incident light. A positive focal length f corresponds to a **converging lens** and a negative f to a **diverging lens**. Lens **aberrations** are focusing defects resulting from imperfect lens shapes and the variation of refractive index with wavelength.

4. Optical instruments use lenses and/or mirrors to form useful images. The power of instrument lenses is often given in **diopters**—the inverse of the focal length in meters.

Terms You Should Understand

(Pairs are closely related terms whose distinction is important; number in parentheses is chapter section where term first appears.)

real image, virtual image (introduction)
focal point, focal length (36-2)
magnification (36-2)
thin lens (36-3)
converging lens, diverging lens (36-3)
spherical aberration, chromatic aberration (36-2, 36-3)
near point (36-5)
diopter (36-5)
angular magnification (36-5)
compound microscope (36-5)
reflecting telescope, refracting telescope (36-5)

Symbols You Should Recognize

ℓ, ℓ' (36-2, 36-3)
f (36-2, 36-3)
M, m (36-2–36-4)

Problems You Should be Able to Solve

finding mirror images and their sizes using ray tracing and algebraic techniques (36-2)
finding lens images and their sizes using ray tracing and algebraic techniques (36-3)
analyzing image formation at a single refracting surface (36-4)
designing lenses and analyzing their focal properties (36-4)
designing and analyzing simple optical instruments (36-5)

Limitations to Keep in Mind

Our description of imaging is based on the approximation of geometrical optics, valid only when objects and optical components are much larger than the wavelength of light.
Formulas for image formation in spherical mirrors and lenses are approximations, valid under the conditions that the curved surfaces used form only a small portion of a full sphere, and that all light rays are nearly parallel to the mirror or lens axis.

QUESTIONS

1. How can you see a virtual image, when it really "isn't there"?

2. You're trying to photograph yourself in a mirror, using an autofocus camera that sets its focus by bouncing ultrasound waves off the subject at which the camera is pointed. Why might the photo come out blurred?

3. You lay a magnifying glass (which is just a converging lens) on a printed page. Looking toward the glass, you move it away from the page. Explain the changes in what you see, especially as you move the lens beyond its focal length.

4. Under what circumstances will the image in a concave mirror be the same size as the object?

5. Describe the shapes of the mirrors making the images in Fig. 36-43.

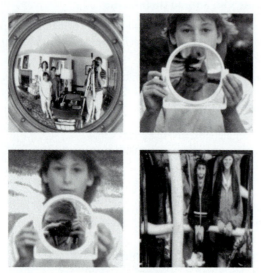

FIGURE 36-43 Question 5.

6. If you're handed a converging lens, what can you do to estimate quickly its focal length?
7. What is the meaning of a negative object distance? Of a negative focal length?
8. A diverging lens always makes a reduced image. Could you use such a lens to start a fire by focusing sunlight? Explain.
9. Is there any limit to the temperature you can achieve by focusing sunlight? Think about the second law of thermodynamics.

10. Can a concave mirror make a reduced real image? A reduced virtual image? An enlarged real image? An enlarged virtual image? Give conditions for each image that is possible.
11. If you placed a screen at the location of a virtual image, would you see the image on the screen? Why or why not?
12. Where must the object be placed to form a reduced real image with a concave mirror or converging lens?
13. Where should you place a flashlight bulb in relation to the focus of its reflector?
14. Is the image on a movie screen real or virtual? How do you know?
15. Does a fish in a spherical bowl appear larger or smaller than it actually is?
16. A block of ice contains a hollow, air-filled space in the shape of a double-convex lens. Describe the optical behavior of this space.
17. The refractive index of the human cornea is about 1.38. If you can see clearly in air, why can't you see clearly underwater? Why do goggles help?
18. The compound microscope and the refracting telescope are both two-lens optical systems. How do their designs reflect their different uses?
19. Cheap binoculars sometimes show blurred images with different colors evident across the blurred region. Why?
20. Do you want a long or short focal length for the objective lens of a telescope? Of a microscope?
21. Give several reasons reflecting telescopes are superior to refractors.
22. Given that star images cannot be resolved even with telescopes, why are large telescopes superior to ordinary cameras for studying stars?

PROBLEMS

ActivPhysics can help with these problems: All activities in Section 15

Sections 36-1 and 36-2 Plane and Curved Mirrors

1. A shoe store uses small floor-level mirrors to let customers view prospective purchases. At what angle should such a mirror be inclined so that a person standing 50 cm from the mirror with eyes 140 cm off the floor can see her feet?
2. Two plane mirrors occupy the first four meters of the positive x and y axes, as shown in Fig. 36-44. Find the locations of all images of an object at $x = 2$ m, $y = 1$ m.
3. (a) What is the focal length of a concave mirror if an object placed 50 cm in front of the mirror has a real image 75 cm from the mirror? (b) Where and what type will the image be if the object is moved to a point 20 cm from the mirror?

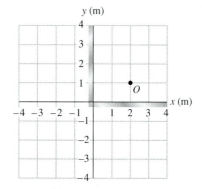

FIGURE 36-44 Problem 2.

4. A candle is 36 cm from a concave mirror with focal length 15 cm and on the mirror axis. (a) Where is its image? (b) How do the image and object sizes compare? (c) Is the image real or virtual?

5. An object is five focal lengths from a concave mirror. (a) How do the object and image heights compare? (b) Is the image upright or inverted?

6. The McMath-Pierce solar telescope at Kitt Peak National Observatory (Fig. 36-45) uses a single concave mirror to produce a real solar image 80 cm in diameter. (a) What is the focal length of the mirror? (b) How far is the image from the mirror? *Hint:* Consult Appendix E.

FIGURE 36-45 The McMath-Pierce solar telescope (Problem 6).

7. A virtual image is located 40 cm behind a concave mirror with focal length 18 cm. (a) Where is the object? (b) By how much is the image magnified?

8. (a) Where on the axis of a concave mirror would you place an object in order to produce a full-size image? (b) Will the image be real or virtual?

9. A 12-mm-high object is 10 cm from a concave mirror with focal length 17 cm. (a) Where, (b) how high, and (c) what type is its image?

10. Repeat the preceding problem for a convex mirror, assuming all numbers stay the same.

11. An object's image in a 27-cm-focal-length concave mirror is upright and magnified by a factor of 3. Where is the object?

12. What is the curvature radius of a concave mirror that produces a 9.5-cm-high virtual image of a 5.7-cm-high object, when the object is located 22 cm from the mirror?

13. When viewed from Earth, the moon subtends an angle of 0.5° in the sky. How large an image of the moon will be formed by the 3.6-m-diameter mirror of the Canada-France-Hawaii telescope, which has a focal length of 8.5 m?

14. At what two distances could you place an object from a 45-cm-focal-length concave mirror in order to get an image 1.5 times the object's size?

15. You look into a reflecting sphere 80 cm in diameter and you see an image of your face at one-third its normal size (Fig. 36-46). How far are you from the sphere's surface?

FIGURE 36-46 Problem 15.

16. Carry out the algebraic steps described just before Equation 36-3 to complete the proof that the focal length of a spherical mirror is half its curvature radius.

Section 36-3 Lenses

17. A light bulb is 56 cm from a convex lens, and its image appears on a screen located 31 cm on the other side of the lens. (a) What is the focal length of the lens? (b) By how much is the image enlarged or reduced?

18. By what factor is the image magnified when an object is placed 1.5 focal lengths from a converging lens? Is the image upright or inverted?

19. A lens with 50-cm focal length produces a real image the same size as the object. How far from the lens are image and object?

20. By holding a magnifying glass 25 cm from my desk lamp, I find I can focus an image of the lamp's bulb on a wall 1.6 m from the lamp. What is the focal length of my magnifying glass?

21. A simple camera uses a single converging lens to focus an image on its film. If the focal length of the lens is 45 mm, what should be the lens-to-film distance for the camera to focus on an object 80 cm from the lens?

22. A real image is 4 times as far from a lens as is the object. What is the object distance, measured in focal lengths?

23. How far from a page should you hold a lens with 32-cm focal length in order to see the print magnified 1.6 times?

24. A converging lens has a focal length of 4.0 cm. A 1.0-cm-high arrow is located 7.0 cm from the lens with its lowest point 5.0 mm above the lens axis. Make a full-scale drawing of the situation, and use ray tracing to locate the image. Confirm using the lens equation.

25. The largest refracting telescope in the world, at Yerkes Observatory, has a 1-m-diameter lens with focal length 12 m (Fig. 36-47). If an airplane flew 1 km above the telescope, where would its image occur in relation to the images of the very distant stars?

FIGURE 36-47 The Yerkes Observatory boasts the world's largest refracting telescope (Problem 25).

26. A small magnifying glass can focus sunlight sufficiently to ignite paper. Calculate the actual size of the solar image produced by a magnifying glass consisting of an optically perfect lens with 25-cm focal length. *Hint:* You'll need to consult Appendix E.

27. A lens has focal length $f = 35$ cm. Find the type and height of the image produced when a 2.2-cm-high object is placed at distances (a) $f + 10$ cm and (b) $f - 10$ cm.

28. How far apart are object and image produced by a converging lens with 35-cm focal length when the object is (a) 40 cm and (b) 30 cm from the lens?

29. A candle and a screen are 70 cm apart. Find two points between candle and screen where you could put a convex lens with 17 cm focal length to give a sharp image of the candle on the screen.

30. An object is placed two focal lengths from a diverging lens. (a) What type of image forms, (b) what is the magnification, and (c) where is the image?

Section 36-4 Refraction in Lenses: The Details

31. You're standing in a wading pool and your feet appear to be 30 cm below the surface. How deep is the pool?

32. A tiny insect is trapped 1.0 mm from the center of a spherical dew drop 4.0 mm in diameter. As you look straight into the drop at the insect, what is its apparent distance from the edge of the drop?

33. Use Equation 36-6 to show that an object at the center of a glass sphere will appear to be its actual distance—one radius—from the edge. Draw a ray diagram showing why this result makes sense.

34. You're underwater, looking through a spherical air bubble (Fig. 36-48). What is its actual diameter if it appears, along your line of sight, to be 1.5 cm in diameter?

FIGURE 36-48 Problem 34.

35. Rework Example 36-6 for a fish 15 cm from the *far* wall of the tank.

36. Consider the inverse of Example 36-6: You're inside a 70-cm-diameter hollow tube containing air, and the tip of your nose is 15 cm from the wall of the tube. The tube is immersed in water, and a fish looks in. To the fish, what is the apparent distance from your nose to the tube wall?

37. Two specks of dirt are trapped in a crystal ball, one at the center and the other halfway to the surface. If you peer into the ball on a line joining the two specks, the outer one appears to be only one-third of the way to the other. What is the refractive index of the ball?

38. My magnifying glass is a double convex lens with equal curvature radii of 32 cm. If the lens glass has $n = 1.52$, what is its focal length?

39. A contact lens is in the shape of a convex meniscus (see Fig. 36-28); the inner surface is curved to fit the eye, with a curvature radius of 7.80 mm. The lens is made from plastic with refractive index $n = 1.56$. If it's to have a focal length of 44.4 cm, what should be the curvature radius of its outer surface?

40. For what refractive index would the focal length of a plano-convex lens be equal to the curvature radius of its one curved surface?

41. An object is 28 cm from a double convex lens with $n = 1.5$ and curvature radii 35 cm and 55 cm. Where and what type is the image?

42. A double convex lens has equal curvature radii of 35 cm. An object placed 30 cm from the lens forms a real image at 128 cm. What is the refractive index of the lens?

43. A plano-convex lens has curvature radius 20 cm and is made from glass with $n = 1.5$. Use the generalized lens-maker's formula given in Problem 73 to find the focal length when the lens is (a) in air, (b) submerged in water ($n = 1.333$), and (c) embedded in glass with $n = 1.7$. Comment on the sign of your answer to (c).

44. A slide projector has a double convex lens with equal curvature radii, and is made from glass with $n = 1.58$. (a) What should be the curvature radius to give a focal length of 104 mm? (b) With this focal length, how far from the focal point should the slide be placed to focus its image on a screen 3.1 m distant from the lens?

45. Two plano-convex lenses are geometrically identical, but one is made from crown glass ($n = 1.52$), the other from flint glass. An object at 45 cm from the lens focuses to a real image at 85 cm with the crown-glass lens and at 53 cm with the flint-glass lens. Find (a) the curvature radius (common to both lenses) and (b) the refractive index of the flint glass.

46. A double convex lens with equal 38-cm curvature radii is made from glass with refractive indices $n_{red} = 1.51$, $n_{blue} = 1.54$ at the edges of the visible spectrum. If a point source of white light is placed on the lens axis at 95 cm from the lens, over what range will its visible image be smeared?

47. An object placed 15 cm from a plano-convex lens made of crown glass focuses to a virtual image twice the size of the object. If the lens is replaced with an identically shaped one made from diamond, what type of image will appear and what will be its magnification? See Table 35-1.

Section 36-5 Optical Instruments

48. You find that you have to hold a book 55 cm from your eyes for the print to be in sharp focus (Fig. 36-49). What power lens is needed to correct your farsightedness?

55 cm

FIGURE 36-49 Problem 48.

49. Grandma's new reading glasses have 3.8-diopter lenses to provide full correction of her farsightedness. Her old glasses were 2.5 diopters. (a) Where is the near point for her unaided eyes? (b) Where will be the near point if she wears her old glasses?

50. A particular eye has a focal length of 2.0 cm instead of the 2.2 cm that would be required for a sharply focused image on the retina. (a) Is this eye nearsighted or farsighted? (b) What power of corrective lens is needed?

51. A camera's zoom lens covers the focal length range from 38 mm to 110 mm. You point the camera at a distant object and photograph it first at 38 mm and then with the camera zoomed out to 110 mm. Compare the sizes of its images on the two photos.

52. A camera can normally focus as close as 60 cm, but it has provisions for mounting additional lenses at the outer end of the main lens to provide closeup capability. What type and power of auxiliary lens will allow the camera to focus as close as 20 cm? The distance between the two lenses is negligible.

53. The maximum magnification of a simple magnifier occurs with the image at the 25-cm near point. Show that the angular magnification is then given by $m = 1 + \dfrac{25 \text{ cm}}{f}$, where f is the focal length.

54. A compound microscope has objective and eyepiece focal lengths of 6.1 mm and 1.7 cm, respectively. If the lenses are 8.3 cm apart, what is the magnification of the instrument?

55. A 300-power compound microscope has a 4.5-mm-focal-length objective lens. If the distance from objective to eyepiece is 10 cm, what should be the focal length of the eyepiece?

56. To the unaided eye, the planet Jupiter has an angular diameter of 50 arc seconds. What will be its angular size when viewed through a 1-m-focal-length refracting telescope with an eyepiece whose focal length is 40 mm?

57. A Cassegrain telescope like that shown in Fig. 36-42b has 1.0-m focal length, and the convex secondary mirror is located 0.85 m from the primary. What should be the focal length of the secondary in order to put the final image 0.12 m behind the front surface of the primary mirror?

58. The Hubble Space Telescope is essentially a Cassegrain reflector like that shown in Fig. 36-42b. The focal lengths of the concave primary and convex secondary mirrors are 5520.00 mm and −679.00 mm, respectively. The secondary is located at 4906.071 mm from the apex of the primary. Draw a ray diagram showing the path of initially parallel incident rays through the telescope, and use appropriate equations to determine where in Fig. 36-42b such rays are finally focused.

Paired Problems

(Both problems in a pair involve the same principles and techniques. If you can get the first problem, you should be able to solve the second one.)

59. (a) How far from a 1.2-m-focal length concave mirror should you place an object in order to get an inverted image 1.5 times the size of the object? (b) Where will the image be?

60. (a) How far from a 48-cm-focal length concave mirror should you place an object in order to get an upright image 1.5 times the size of the object? (b) Where will the image be?

61. Find the focal length of a concave mirror if an object 15 cm from the mirror has a virtual image 2.5 times the object's actual size.

62. An object is held 6.0 cm from the surface of a reflecting ball, and its image appears three-quarters full size. What is the ball's diameter?

63. How far from a 1.6-m focal length concave mirror should you place an object to get an upright image magnified by a factor of 2.5?

64. How far from a 25-cm-focal-length lens should you place an object to get an upright image magnified by a factor of 1.8?

65. An object and its lens-produced real image are 2.4 m apart. If the lens has 55-cm focal length, what are the possible values for the object distance and magnification?

66. An object and its converging-lens-produced virtual image are 2.4 m apart. If the lens has 55-cm focal length, what are the possible values for the object distance and magnification?

67. An object is 68 cm from a plano-convex lens whose curved side has curvature radius 26 cm. The refractive index of the lens is 1.62. Where and of what type is the image?

68. Both surfaces of a double concave lens have curvature radii of 18 cm, and the refractive index is 1.5. If a virtual image appears 14 cm from the lens, where is the object?

Supplementary Problems

69. My contact lens prescription calls for +2.25-diopter lenses with an inner curvature radius of 8.6 mm to fit my cornea. (a) If the lenses are made from plastic with $n = 1.56$, what should be the outer curvature radius? (b) Wearing these lenses, I hold a newspaper 30 cm from my eyes. Where is its image as viewed through the lenses?

70. Show that the powers of closely spaced lenses add; that is, placing a 1-diopter lens in front of a 2-diopter lens gives the equivalent of a single 3-diopter lens.

71. Show that identical objects placed equal distances on either side of the focal point of a concave mirror or converging lens produce images of equal size. Are the images of the same type?

72. Galileo's first telescope used the arrangement shown in Fig. 36-50, with a double convex eyepiece placed slightly before the focus of the objective lens. Use ray tracing to show that this system gives an upright image, which makes the design useful for terrestrial observing.

73. Generalize the derivation of the lensmaker's formula (Equation 36-8) to show a lens of refractive index n_{lens} in an external medium with index n_{ext} has focal length given

FIGURE 36-50 Problem 72.

by

$$\frac{1}{f} = \left(\frac{n_{lens}}{n_{ext}} - 1 \right) \left(\frac{1}{R_1} - \frac{1}{R_2} \right).$$

74. An object is located 40 cm from a lens made from glass with $n = 1.5$. In air, the resulting image is real and is located 32 cm from the lens. When the entire system is immersed in a liquid, the image becomes virtual and is reduced to half the object's size. Use the result given in the preceding problem to find the refractive index of the liquid.

75. A Newtonian telescope like that of Fig. 36-42c has a primary mirror with 20-cm diameter and 1.2-m focal length. (a) Where should the flat diagonal mirror be placed to put the focus at the edge of the telescope tube? (b) What shape should the flat mirror have to minimize blockage of light to the primary?

76. A parabola is described by the equation $y = x^2/4f$, where f is the distance from vertex to focus. (a) Find the equation for the circle (which would be a sphere in three dimensions) that closely approximates the parabola $y = x^2$. *Hint:* How are the focal length and curvature radius of a spherical mirror related? (b) Solve the circle's equation for y, and use the binomial theorem to show that the equation reduces to that of the parabola for $x \ll 1$.

77. Just before Equation 36-7 are two equations describing refraction at the two surfaces of a lens with thickness t. Combine these equations to show that the object distance ℓ and image distance ℓ' for such a lens are related by

$$\frac{1}{\ell} + \frac{1}{\ell'} - \frac{[(n-1)\ell - R_1]^2 t}{\ell R_1 [t(\ell + R_1) + n\ell(R_1 - t)]}$$
$$= (n-1)\left(\frac{1}{R_1} - \frac{1}{R_2} \right).$$

78. Use the result of the preceding problem to find an expression for the focal length of a transparent sphere with radius R and refractive index n, as measured from the exit surface.

Interference and Diffraction   37

Interference of light plays an important role in extracting information from compact discs. Here adjacent tracks of the microscopic "pits" that code the CD's information produce interference that results in a rainbow of colors. This chapter explores many applications of wave interference and diffraction, including the operation of CDs and the newer DVDs.

T he preceding chapters considered reflection and refraction, and their application in image formation, from the approximation of geometrical optics—an approximation valid when we can ignore the wave nature of light. We now turn to **physical optics**, which treats optical phenomena for which the wave nature of light plays an essential role. Two related phenomena, interference and diffraction, are central to much of physical optics.

37-1 COHERENCE AND INTERFERENCE

We introduced wave **interference** in Chapter 16, showing how wave displacements add in a manner that may be constructive or destructive depending on the relative phases of the waves. Interference of electromagnetic waves—including light—occurs in the same way; since the electric and magnetic fields separately obey the superposition principle, the net electric and magnetic fields at any point are the vector sums of the fields of individual waves. The superposition of those fields may result in an increase (constructive interference) or decrease (destructive interference) in the field strength.

Coherence

Although interference occurs any time two waves interact, we get steady interference patterns only when the interacting waves are **coherent**, meaning that they maintain a constant phase relation. Ordinary sources such as light bulbs or the Sun produce light that is coherent only over very short distances. That's because light from these sources consists of short wavetrains emitted with random phases (Fig. 37-1a). Lasers, in contrast, produce relatively long wavetrains that maintain coherence over many wavelengths (Fig. 37-1b). The typical length of a wavetrain is the **coherence length** for a given light source.

Regardless of the source, it takes two or more waves to interfere. It's virtually impossible for two different light sources to maintain coherence, so such interference usually results only when light from a single source splits, travels different paths, and then recombines. Even light from an ordinary light bulb will produce interference patterns provided the light in the two recombining light beams originated at nearly the same place and time. With the more coherent light of a laser, interference occurs over a wider range of path differences.

Coherence requires that the interfering light beams have exactly the same frequency and therefore wavelength or color. With a white-light source such as sunlight, interference occurs separately for each different color. Again, lasers make things easier: their light is very nearly **monochromatic**, consisting of a narrow band of wavelengths. Very slight deviations from exactly equal

(a) (b)

FIGURE 37-1 (a) Light bulbs emit many short wavetrains whose phases are related in random ways. Coherent interference can occur only with light originating from a spatially limited region, so that a single wavetrain interferes with itself. The coherence length is defined as the average length of a wavetrain, here about 3 wavelengths. (b) Lasers produce light with much greater coherence length, making it easier to produce coherent interference with laser light.

FIGURE 37-2 Two waves that started out in phase but have traveled different paths before coming together. (*a*) Here the lower wave travels half a wavelength farther, so the two come together 180° out of phase, and their superposition results in destructive interference. (*b*) When the lower wave travels a full wavelength farther, the two come together in phase and the interference is constructive.

frequency and wavelength may still permit observable interference, and yield the optical equivalent of the beats we introduced in Section 16-5.

Destructive and Constructive Interference

Consider light waves that originate together at a single source, travel two different paths, and then come together again. Suppose one wave's path is exactly half a wavelength longer. Then when the waves recombine they will be out of phase by half a wavelength (Fig. 37-2*a*), and thus their superposition will have lower amplitude (zero, if the two interfering waves have exactly the same amplitude). If, on the other hand, the path lengths don't differ, or differ by a full wavelength, then the two waves recombine in phase (Fig. 37-2*b*) and their superposition has greater amplitude. These two cases correspond, respectively, to **destructive interference** and **constructive interference**. It doesn't really matter whether path lengths for the waves in Fig. 37-2*a* differ by half a wavelength, or $1\frac{1}{2}$ wavelengths, or $2\frac{1}{2}$ wavelengths—as long as the difference is an odd multiple of a half wavelength, the waves recombine out of phase and destructive interference results. Thus:

> **Destructive interference results when light paths differ by an odd integer multiple of a half wavelength.**

Similarly, it doesn't matter whether the path lengths in Fig. 37-2*b* are the same, or differ by 1, 2, 3, or any other integer number of wavelengths. Thus

> **Constructive interference results when light paths differ by an integer multiple of the wavelength.**

We'll use these two statements to build an understanding of interference in both simple and complicated situations.

There's one caveat to our statements: the path difference can't be greater than the coherence length that we defined in connection with Fig. 37-1. Otherwise the interfering waves will be from different wavetrains, and won't be coherent. Once again, laser light has the advantage here, because of its greater coherence length.

Of course, light paths don't have to differ by half or full multiples of the wavelength. In intermediate cases interfering waves superpose to make a composite wave whose amplitude may be enhanced or diminished, depending on the relative phase as determined by the path-length difference.

Example 35-3, "CD Music," showed how refraction in a compact disc (CD) helps focus the laser beam that "reads" information from the disc. Interference, too, plays a crucial role in "reading" a CD.

Information on a CD—whether an audio signal or computer data—is stored digitally in a sequence of "pits"—depressions stamped into a reflective metallic "information layer" (Fig. 37-3). The pits vary in length, but their depth is the same—very nearly one-quarter wavelength of the laser light used to "read" the CD. From the transparent underside of the disc, where the laser beam enters, each pit appears as an elevated bump. Since the bumps stick down one-quarter

FIGURE 37-4 Structure of a CD, showing that pits appear as bumps to the laser beam shining from below the disc. Path lengths for the laser beam differ by a half wavelength depending on whether the light reflects off a bump, resulting in destructive interference when the beam strikes a bump and the surrounding disc surface.

FIGURE 37-3 Information on a standard CD is stored in "pits" stamped into a metallic "information layer." The pits form a continuous spiral track that winds around the disc. Adjacent turns of the spiral are 1.6 μm apart, and the minimum pit length is 0.83 μm. Depth of the pits is approximately a quarter wavelength of the laser light used to "read" the CD.

wavelength, light reflecting off a bump follows a round-trip path that's shorter by half a wavelength compared with the path of light reflecting off the undisturbed information layer (Fig. 37-4). The laser beam that "reads" the disc is somewhat wider than the pit, so the reflected beam includes light both from the undisturbed disc as well as from the bump. The two interfere destructively, just as we showed in Fig. 37-2, making a much less intense reflected beam when a bump is present. As the disc spins, the result is a pattern of fluctuating light intensity conveying the information associated with the pattern of pits on the CD. A photodetector converts that pattern to electrical signals for processing by the electronic circuitry of the CD player or computer.

The new DVD discs introduced in the late 1990s work in exactly the same way, except—as we'll see later in this chapter—they can store much more information.

37-2 DOUBLE-SLIT INTERFERENCE

In Chapter 16 we looked briefly at interference patterns produced by a pair of coherent sources. With light, such a pair can be made by passing light from a single source through two narrow slits. In 1801 Thomas Young used this approach in a historic experiment that confirmed the wave nature of light. Young first admitted sunlight to his laboratory through a hole small enough to ensure coherence of the incoming light. The light then passed through a pair of narrow, closely spaced slits, after which it illuminated a screen. Each slit acts as a source of cylindrical wavefronts that interfere in the region between slits and screen (Fig. 37-5a). Constructive and destructive interference result in alternating regions of light and dark on the screen, as shown in Fig. 37-5b for laser light passed through double slits. The light and dark regions in Fig. 37-5b are called **interference fringes**.

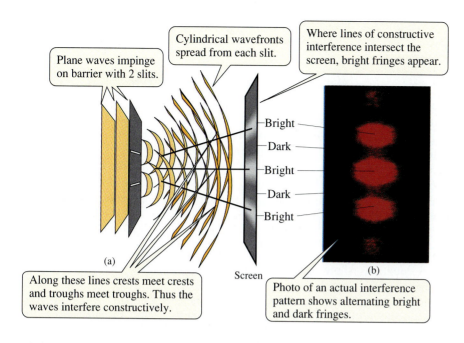

Plane waves impinge on barrier with 2 slits.

Cylindrical wavefronts spread from each slit.

Where lines of constructive interference intersect the screen, bright fringes appear.

Bright
Dark
Bright
Dark
Bright

(a)

Screen

Along these lines crests meet crests and troughs meet troughs. Thus the waves interfere constructively.

(b)

Photo of an actual interference pattern shows alternating bright and dark fringes.

FIGURE 37-5 Double-slit interference results when light from a single source passes through a pair of closely spaced slits. Photo in (b) was made by replacing the screen with film in an actual double-slit apparatus using laser light.

We can understand the occurrence and location of fringes in double-slit interference by applying our criteria for constructive and destructive interference. The bright fringes represent constructive interference, and therefore they occur where the difference in the path length for light traveling from the two different slits is a multiple of the wavelength. When the distance L from slits to screen is much larger than the slit spacing d, Fig. 37-6 then shows that the path difference from the two slits to a point on the screen is $d \sin \theta$, where θ is the angular position of a point on the screen, measured from an axis perpendicular to slits and screen. So our criterion for constructive interference—that this difference be an integer number of wavelengths—becomes

$$d \sin \theta = m\lambda. \quad \text{(bright fringes)} \quad (37\text{-}1a)$$

The integer m is the **order** of the fringe, with the central bright fringe being the zeroth order fringe and with higher order fringes on either side.

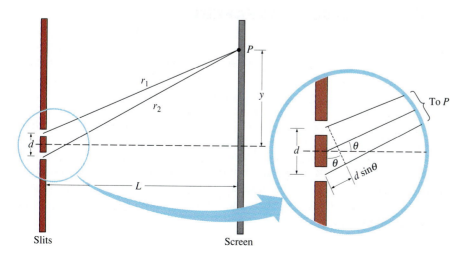

P
r_1
r_2
y
d
L
Slits
Screen
θ
d
θ
$d \sin\theta$
To P

FIGURE 37-6 Geometry for finding locations of the interference fringes. A bright fringe occurs when the path-length difference $r_2 - r_1$ is an integer multiple of the wavelength. In the blowup you can see that for $L \gg d$ the paths to P are nearly parallel, and the difference in their lengths is $d \sin \theta$. Can you find similar triangles to prove that the angles labeled θ are indeed the same?

FIGURE 37-7 Interference patterns made with the same double-slit system, using two different wavelengths of light. The different fringe spacings reflect the wavelength dependence in Equations 37-2.

Waves interfere destructively when they arrive at the screen 180° out of phase, which occurs when their path lengths differ by an odd integer multiple of a half wavelength:

$$d \sin \theta = (m + \tfrac{1}{2})\lambda, \qquad \text{(dark fringes)} \qquad (37\text{-}1\text{b})$$

where m is any integer.

In a typical double-slit experiment, L may be on the order of 1 m, d a fraction of 1 mm, and λ the sub-μm wavelength of visible light. Then we have the additional condition that $\lambda \ll d$. This makes the fringes very closely spaced on the screen, so the angle θ in Fig. 37-6 is small even for large orders m. Then $\sin \theta \simeq \tan \theta = y/L$, and Equations 37-1 and the geometry of Fig. 37-6 show that a fringe's position y on the screen, measured from the central maximum, is given by

$$y_{\text{bright}} = m \frac{\lambda L}{d} \qquad \text{and} \qquad y_{\text{dark}} = (m + \tfrac{1}{2}) \frac{\lambda L}{d}. \qquad (37\text{-}2\text{a, b})$$

16.5
Two-Source Interference

These equations show that the fringe spacing depends on wavelength, as confirmed experimentally in Fig. 37-7. Measurement of fringe spacing enabled Young to determine the wavelength of light. You can simulate two-slit interference—including the effect of varying wavelength—with ActivPhysics Activity 16.5.

Got It!

If you increase the slit separation in a 2-slit system, do the interference fringes become closer together or farther apart?

EXAMPLE 37-1	*Laser Wavelength*

A pair of narrow slits are 0.075 mm apart and are located 1.5 m from a screen. Laser light shining through the slits produces an interference pattern whose third-order bright fringe is 3.8 cm from the screen center. Find the wavelength of the light.

Solution
Here we have $m = 3$, $L = 1.5$ m, and $d = 0.075$ mm, so we can solve Equation 37-3a for the wavelength λ:

$$\lambda = \frac{y_{\text{bright}} d}{mL} = \frac{(0.038 \text{ m})(0.075 \times 10^{-3} \text{ m})}{(3)(1.5 \text{ m})} = 633 \text{ nm}.$$

This is in fact the wavelength of the red light from low-power helium-neon lasers commonly used in physics demonstrations.

EXERCISE What slit spacing will produce bright fringes 1.8 cm apart on a screen 85 cm from the slits, if the slits are illuminated with 589-nm light?

Answer: 27.8 μm

Some problems similar to Example 37-1: 2–5, 10

Intensity in the Interference Pattern

Geometric arguments allowed us to find the positions of the maxima and minima of a two-slit interference pattern. We can find the actual intensity variation by algebraically superposing the interfering waves. You might think this could be done by adding the wave intensities. But no! It's the electric and magnetic fields that obey the superposition principle, not the wave intensities. Intensity is proportional to the *square* of either field; if we added intensities we could never get the cancellation that occurs in destructive interference.

Consider again a point P on the screen of a double-slit apparatus (Fig. 37-8). Since light from the two slits reaches P over paths of different lengths, we expect that the waves will have different intensities when they reach P. In the approximation $d \ll L$, however, the path-length difference $d \sin \theta$ is so small that we can neglect this effect. So we consider that the two waves arriving at P have electric fields of equal amplitude, given by expressions like Equation 34-10. Since we're considering a fixed point P, it's convenient to take the origin at P to eliminate the kx term in Equation 34-10. Then we can express the electric fields of the two waves at P in the form

$$E_1 = E_p \sin \omega t \quad \text{and} \quad E_2 = E_p \sin(\omega t + \phi),$$

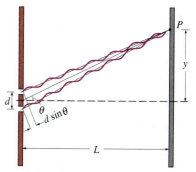

FIGURE 37-8 Waves leaving the slits with the same phase arrive at P displaced by the path-length difference $d \sin \theta$. This corresponds to phase difference $\phi = d \sin \theta (2\pi/\lambda)$.

where E_p is the common amplitude, ω the common frequency, and ϕ the phase difference that occurs because of the different path lengths. We don't bother with vector notation because both waves, since they originate in the same source, are polarized in the same direction and thus their electric fields will simply add algebraically. Then net electric field at P is

$$E = E_1 + E_2 = E_p[\sin \omega t + \sin(\omega t + \phi)].$$

In Appendix A we find the trigonometric identity $\sin \alpha + \sin \beta = 2 \sin[(\alpha + \beta)/2] \cos[(\alpha - \beta)/2]$, which, with $\alpha = \omega t$ and $\beta = \omega t + \phi$, transforms our expression for E into

$$E = 2E_p \sin\left(\omega t + \frac{\phi}{2}\right) \cos\left(\frac{\phi}{2}\right).$$

We also used $\cos(-x) = \cos x$ to eliminate a minus sign in the argument of the cosine. Thus, the electric field at P oscillates with the wave frequency ω, and its overall amplitude is scaled by the factor $\cos(\phi/2)$.

What is the phase difference ϕ? We've already seen that the path-length difference is $d \sin \theta$, with d the slit spacing and θ the angle subtended at the slits between P and the slit centerline. If this difference is one-half wavelength λ, then we have a phase difference of $180°$ or π radians. More generally, the phase difference in radians is whatever fraction of the full cycle (2π radians) the path difference $d \sin \theta$ is of the wavelength:

$$\phi = 2\pi \frac{d \sin \theta}{\lambda}.$$

Using this result in our expression for the electric field at P gives

$$E = 2E_p \sin\left(\omega t + \frac{\phi}{2}\right) \cos\left(\frac{\pi d \sin \theta}{\lambda}\right).$$

This equation describes a field whose peak amplitude is not E_p but $2E_p \cos(\pi d \sin \theta / \lambda)$. The average intensity then follows from Equation 34-20b:

$$\bar{S} = \frac{[2E_p \cos(\pi d \sin \theta/\lambda)]^2}{2\mu_0 c} = 4\bar{S}_0 \cos^2\left(\frac{\pi d \sin \theta}{\lambda}\right), \qquad (37\text{-}3)$$

where $\bar{S}_0 = E_p^2/2\mu_0 c$ is the average intensity of either wave alone. Equation 37-3 shows that the intensity varies between zero and $4\bar{S}_0$ as the angular position changes. We can also write Equation 37-3 in terms of position y on the screen. Under the approximation $d \gg \lambda$ even high-order fringes will occur at

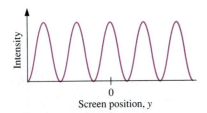

FIGURE 37-9 Intensity as a function of position y on the screen of a double-slit system. This intensity variation is reflected in Fig. 37-7, although saturation effects of the bright laser light on the film prevents the photo from showing accurately the sinusoidal dependence.

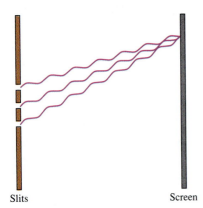

FIGURE 37-10 Waves from three evenly spaced slits interfere constructively when they arrive at the screen in phase.

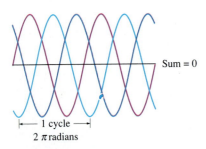

FIGURE 37-11 Waves from three slits must be out of phase by one-third of a cycle in order to interfere destructively. With this phase relationship the three waves sum to zero at every point.

small angles θ, so we can write $\sin\theta \simeq \tan\theta \simeq y/L$, giving

$$\bar{S} = 4\bar{S}_0 \cos^2\left(\frac{\pi d}{\lambda L}y\right). \tag{37-4}$$

Now, $\cos^2\alpha$ has its maximum value, 1, when its argument is an integer multiple of π. Thus, the maxima of Equation 37-4 occur when $dy/\lambda L$ is an integer m, or when $y = m\lambda L/d$. This is just the condition of Equation 37-2a, showing that our intensity calculation is fully consistent with the simpler geometrical analysis. But the intensity calculation tells us more: it gives not only the positions of bright and dark fringes, but also the intensity variation in between, as shown in Fig. 37-9.

37-3 MULTIPLE-SLIT INTERFERENCE AND DIFFRACTION GRATINGS

Systems with multiple slits play a crucial role in optical instrumentation and in the analysis of materials. As we will soon see, gratings manufactured with several thousand slits per centimeter make possible high-resolution spectroscopic analysis. At a much smaller scale the regularly spaced rows of atoms in a crystal act much like a multiple-slit system for X rays, and the resulting X-ray patterns reveal the crystal structure.

Figure 37-10 shows waves from three evenly spaced slits interfering at a screen. Maximum intensity requires that all three waves either be in phase, or differ in phase by an integer number of wavelengths. Our criterion for the maximum in a two-slit pattern, $d\sin\theta = m\lambda$, ensures that waves from two adjacent slits will add constructively. Since the slits are evenly spaced with distance d between each pair, waves coming through a third slit will be in phase with the other two if this criterion is met. So the criterion for a maximum in an N-slit system is still Equation 37-1a:

$$d\sin\theta = m\lambda. \quad \text{(maxima in multi-slit interference)}$$

With more than two waves, however, the criterion for destructive interference is more complicated. Somehow all the waves need to sum to zero. Figure 37-11 shows that this happens for three waves when each is out of phase with the others by one-third of a cycle. Thus, the path-length difference $d\sin\theta$ must be either $(m + \frac{1}{3})\lambda$ or $(m + \frac{2}{3})\lambda$, where m is an integer. The case $(m + \frac{3}{3})\lambda$ is excluded because then the path lengths differ by a full wavelength, giving constructive interference and thus a maximum in the interference pattern. More generally we can write

$$d\sin\theta = \frac{m}{N}\lambda, \tag{37-5}$$

for destructive interference in an N-slit system, where m is an integer *but not an integer multiple of N*. The reason for the exclusion is that when m is an integer multiple of N then m/N is an integer; then the path-length difference is an integer number of wavelengths, resulting in constructive rather than destructive interference. Mathematically, when m/N is an integer, Equation 37-5 becomes equivalent to Equation 37-1a that gives the condition for constructive interference.

FIGURE 37-12 Interference patterns for multiple slit systems with the same slit spacing. The bright fringes stay in the same place, but become narrower and brighter as the number of slits increases. Intensity plots do not have the same vertical scale; peak intensity in fact scales as the *square* of the number of slits.

Figure 37-12 shows interference patterns and intensity plots from some multiple-slit systems. Note that the bright, or *primary,* maxima are separated by several minima and fainter, or *secondary,* maxima. Why this complex pattern? Our analysis of the three-slit system shows two minima between every pair of primary maxima; for example, we considered the minima at $d \sin \theta$ equal to $(m + \frac{1}{3})\lambda$ or $(m + \frac{2}{3})\lambda$, which lie between the maxima at $d \sin \theta$ equal to $m\lambda$ and $(m + 1)\lambda$. More generally, Equation 37-5 shows that there are $N - 1$ minima between each pair of primary maxima given by Equation 37-2a. The secondary maxima that lie between these minima result from interference that is neither fully destructive nor fully constructive. The figure shows that the primary maxima become much brighter and narrower as the number of slits increases, while the secondary maxima become relatively less bright. With a large number N of slits, then, we should expect a pattern of bright but narrow primary maxima, with broad, essentially dark regions in between.

Diffraction Gratings

A set of many very closely spaced slits is called a **diffraction grating** and proves very useful in the spectroscopic analysis of light. Diffraction gratings commonly measure several cm across and have several thousand slits—usually called lines—per cm. Gratings are made by photoreducing images of parallel lines or by ruling with a diamond stylus on aluminum-plated glass (Fig. 37-13). Gratings like the slit systems we have been discussing are **transmission gratings** since light passes through the slits. **Reflection gratings** produce similar interference effects by reflecting incident light.

We've seen that the maxima of the multi-slit interference pattern are given by the same criterion, $d \sin \theta = m\lambda$, that applies to a two-slit system. For $m = 0$

FIGURE 37-13 A diffraction grating disperses white light into its constituent colors. The enlarged spectrum at rear results from reflecting the diffracted beam off a concave mirror.

2nd-order spectrum   1st-order spectrum

Screen

Grating

Entrance slit

Light source

FIGURE 37-14 Essential elements of a grating spectrometer. The entrance slit regulates the amount of light entering the instrument. The grating disperses the light into its component wavelengths, which reach the screen to produce spectra of the different orders. An electronic detector would normally be used in place of the screen.

this equation implies that all wavelengths peak together at the central maximum, but for larger values of m the angular position of the maximum depends on wavelength. Thus, a diffraction grating can be used in place of a prism to disperse light into its component wavelengths, and the integer m is therefore called the **order** of the dispersion. Figure 37-14 shows a grating spectrometer working on this principle. Because the maxima in N-slit interference are very sharp for large N (recall Fig. 37-12), a grating with many slits diffracts individual wavelengths to very precise locations. Incidentally, the rainbow of colors produced by the compact disc in this chapter's opening photo results because adjacent "tracks" of CD pits (see Fig. 37-3) act as a diffraction grating.

EXAMPLE 37-2	*A Grating Spectrometer*

Light from glowing hydrogen contains discrete wavelengths ("spectral lines") called hydrogen-α and hydrogen-β, at 656.3 nm and 486.1 nm, respectively. Find the angular separation between these two wavelengths in a spectrometer using a grating with 6000 slits per cm. Consider both the first-order ($m = 1$) and second order ($m = 2$) dispersion.

Solution

With 6000 slits/cm, the slit spacing is $d = (1/6000)$ cm $= 1.667$ μm. Applying the criterion $d \sin\theta = m\lambda$ for the first-order spectrum, we then have

$$\theta_{1\alpha} = \sin^{-1}\left(\frac{\lambda}{d}\right) = \sin^{-1}\left(\frac{0.6563\ \mu\text{m}}{1.667\ \mu\text{m}}\right) = 23.2°$$

and

$$\theta_{1\beta} = \sin^{-1}\left(\frac{\lambda}{d}\right) = \sin^{-1}\left(\frac{0.4861\ \mu\text{m}}{1.667\ \mu\text{m}}\right) = 17.0°.$$

Thus, the angular separation is 6.2°. Repeating the same calculation with $m = 2$ gives $\theta_{2\alpha} = 51.9°$ and $\theta_{2\beta} = 35.7°$, for an angular spread of 16.2°. This wider spacing is characteristic of higher-order dispersion.

EXERCISE The bright yellow light emitted by glowing sodium vapor actually consists of two spectral lines at 589.0 nm and 589.6 nm. Find the angular separation of these lines in a second-order spectrum taken with a 4800-slit/cm grating.

Answer: 0.04°

Some problems similar to Example 37-2: 17–19

16.3
Multiple Slits Diffraction

In Example 37-2 the two lines are near the ends of the visible spectrum, and the values calculated for the angular positions show that there is no overlap between the first- and second-order visible spectra. But higher-order spectra do overlap, a fact that astronomers use in high-resolution spectroscopy when they wish to observe two different spectral lines simultaneously. Problem 21 explores this situation, while Fig. 37-15 shows the relative positions of the different orders.

Resolving Power

The detailed shapes and wavelengths of spectral lines contain a wealth of information about the systems in which light originates. Studying these details requires a high dispersion in order to separate nearby spectral lines or to analyze the intensity versus wavelength profile of a single line. Suppose we pass light

FIGURE 37-15 Positions of the different orders in a grating spectrum. The vertical separation between orders has been introduced for clarity; in actuality they would overlap. The central line of each spectrum is at 550 nm. Note the increased dispersion of the higher orders.

containing two spectral lines of nearly equal wavelengths λ and λ' through a grating. Figure 37-16 shows that we will just be able to distinguish two spectral lines if the peak of one line corresponds to the first minimum of the other; any closer and the lines will blur together. Suppose wavelength λ has its mth-order maximum at angular position θ. The criterion for this maximum is, as usual, $d\sin\theta_{max} = m\lambda$. We can equally well write this as $d\sin\theta_{max} = \dfrac{mN}{N}\lambda$, with N the number of slits in the grating. Equation 37-5 then shows that we get an adjacent minimum if we add 1 to the numerator mN. Thus, there is an adjacent minimum whose position satisfies

$$d\sin\theta_{min} = \frac{mN + 1}{N}\lambda .$$

Our criterion that the two wavelengths λ and λ' be just distinguishable is that the maximum for λ' fall at the location of this minimum for λ. But the maximum for λ' satisfies $d\sin\theta'_{max} = m\lambda' = \dfrac{mN}{N}\lambda'$, so for $\theta'_{max} = \theta_{min}$ we must have

$$(mN + 1)\lambda = mN\lambda' .$$

It's convenient to express this result in terms of the wavelength difference $\Delta\lambda = \lambda' - \lambda$. Solving our equation relating λ and λ' for λ' and using the result to write $\Delta\lambda$ in terms of λ alone then gives

$$\frac{\lambda}{\Delta\lambda} = mN. \qquad \text{(resolving power)} \qquad (37\text{-}6)$$

The quantity $\lambda/\Delta\lambda$ is the **resolving power** of the grating, a measure of its ability to distinguish closely spaced wavelengths. The higher the resolving power, the smaller the wavelength difference $\Delta\lambda$ that can be distinguished in the spectrum. Equation 37-6 shows that the resolving power increases with the number of lines, N, on the grating, and also with the order, m, of the spectrum we observe. Both these points make sense. We saw in Fig. 37-12 that the intensity of the maxima increases and their width decreases with increasing N, making different wavelengths easier to distinguish, while Fig. 37-15 shows that higher-order spectra are more dispersed and thus, again, make it easier to distinguish different wavelengths.

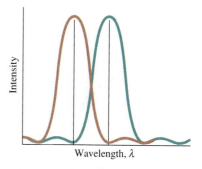

FIGURE 37-16 A plot of intensity versus wavelength for spectral lines of slightly different wavelengths, as observed with a spectrometer. The lines are just distinguishable if the maximum of one falls on the first minimum of the other; any closer and they blur together.

EXAMPLE 37-3	"Seeing" a Double Star

A certain double star system consists of a massive star essentially at rest, with a smaller companion in circular orbit. The stars are far too close to each other, and the system far too distant from Earth, for the pair to appear as anything but a single point in even the largest telescopes. Yet astronomers can "see" the companion star through the Doppler shift in the wavelengths of its spectral lines that occurs because of the star's motion. In the system under observation the hydrogen-α line from the companion star, at 656.272 nm when the source is at rest, is shifted to 656.215 nm (this corresponds to an orbital speed of about 26 km/s) when the companion is moving toward Earth. If the telescope's spectrometer grating has 2000 lines/cm and measures 2.5 cm across, what order spectrum will resolve the hydrogen-α lines from the stationary star and its orbiting companion?

Solution

Here $N = (2000 \text{ lines/cm})(2.5 \text{ cm}) = 5000$ lines. Solving Equation 37-6 for m then gives

$$m = \frac{\lambda}{N \, \Delta\lambda} = \frac{656.272 \text{ nm}}{(5,000)(656.272 \text{ nm} - 656.215 \text{ nm})} = 2.3 \, .$$

Since the order number must be an integer, the observation must be made in third order.

EXERCISE Putting atoms in a magnetic field causes what are normally single spectral lines to split, as the atoms produce light of two slightly different wavelengths. In a particular case, a spectral line of mercury at 435.8 nm splits into two lines separated in wavelength by 0.027 nm. To the nearest thousand, how many lines must a grating have to resolve these wavelengths in first order?

Answer: 16,000

Some problems similar to Example 37-3: 26–29

X-Ray Diffraction

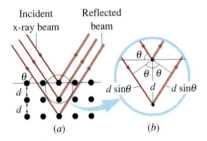

The wavelengths of X rays, around 0.1 nm, are far too short to be dispersed with diffraction gratings produced mechanically or photographically. The regular spacing of atoms in a crystal, however, provides a "grating" of the appropriate scale. In the classical electromagnetic description, the reflection of electromagnetic waves occurs as electrons in each atom are set into oscillation by the electric field of the incident X-ray beam. The oscillating electrons then reradiate the energy they have absorbed, and the combined beam from all the atoms obeys the law of reflection. When the atomic spacing is regular, and comparable to the wavelength, however, interference enhances the reflected radiation at certain angles. Figure 37-17 shows an X-ray beam interacting with the layers of atoms in a crystal. In Fig. 37-17b we see that waves reflecting at one layer travel a total distance $2d \sin \theta$ farther than those reflecting at the layer above, where θ is the angle between the incident beams and the atomic planes. The outgoing beams will interfere constructively when this difference is an integer multiple of the wavelength:

$$2d \sin \theta = m\lambda \, . \quad \text{(Bragg condition)} \qquad (37\text{-}7)$$

FIGURE 37-17 (a) X rays reflecting off the planes of atoms in a crystal. (b) X rays striking a lower plane travel an extra distance $2d \sin \theta$. The outgoing beam is enhanced by constructive interference when this distance is an integer multiple of the X-ray wavelength.

First derived by W. L. Bragg, this **Bragg condition** allows one to use a crystal with known spacing as a diffraction grating at X-ray wavelengths. More important is the converse: much of what we know about crystal structure comes from probing crystals with X rays and using the resulting patterns to deduce the positions of their atoms (Fig. 37-18).

FIGURE 37-18 This X-ray diffraction image of DNA, made by the British scientist Rosalind Franklin in 1952, was crucial in establishing the structure of the DNA molecule.

Anything containing regularly spaced structures—like the lines in a diffraction grating or the atoms in a crystal—can act as a diffraction grating for waves of suitable wavelength. A very useful technological development, the **acousto-optic modulator** (AOM), uses diffraction from the periodic variations in the structure of a quartz crystal caused by the presence of a sound wave in the crystal.

Figure 37-19 shows a diagram of an AOM. Attached to the crystal is a transducer—a loudspeaker-like device that converts an alternating voltage into sound waves that propagate through the quartz. The regular spacing of the acoustic wavefronts constitutes a diffraction grating whose spacing may be varied by changing the driving frequency. Light incident on the quartz is diffracted at preferred angles given by Equation 37-7, just as are X rays by regularly spaced atomic planes. Changing the sound frequency allows the diffracted beam to be scanned in direction; turning the sound on and off switches the diffracted beam on and off. These effects are widely used in lightwave communication and other optical technologies; most laser printers, for example, use AOMs to control the laser beam that "paints" a picture of the printed page on a light-sensitive surface.

AOMs are also used to encode audio and video signals onto light, allowing transmission of these signals by light beams. Setting up the AOM's "diffraction grating" requires propagating sound waves into the crystal. Since this takes time, the AOM is not as fast a lightwave modulator as is the electro-optic modulator discussed in Chapter 34. The AOM is, however, much less expensive and less demanding of the associated electronic circuitry.

(a)

(b)

FIGURE 37-19 (*a*) Schematic diagram of an acousto-optic modulator. The transducer drives sound waves into the crystal, and the acoustic wavefronts act like a moving diffraction grating to incident light. (*b*) An acousto-optic modulator. A laser beam enters the transparent crystal while electrical signals supplied by the cable in the foreground generate sound waves that act as a diffraction grating to modify the beam's propagation direction and frequency. Such modulators are used in laser printers and many other applications.

37-4 THIN FILMS AND INTERFEROMETERS

We treated the double-slit system first because it's one of the most straightforward examples of interference. Then we turned to the more complicated case of multiple-slit interference. But there are many ways to produce interfering light waves besides passing light through slits. All have in common the separation of light into two or more beams that travel on different paths, then recombine. Here we examine a few such examples.

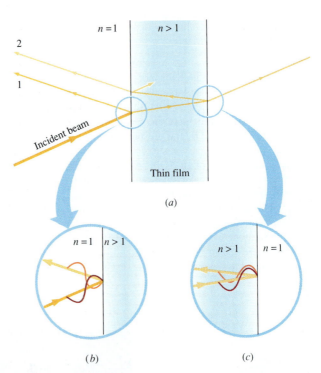

FIGURE 37-20 (*a*) Reflection and refraction at a thin layer of transparent material. (*b*) The reflected and incident beams are 180° out of phase when they reflect at an interface that goes from a lower to a higher refractive index. (*c*) There is no phase difference on reflection when the incident medium has a higher refractive index.

Interference in Thin Films

We saw in Section 35-6 that light is partially reflected and partially transmitted at an interface between two transparent media. Figure 37-20 shows what happens when light propagating in air strikes a thin film of transparent material. Partial reflection at both surfaces results in two beams propagating back into the air. Since these beams derive from the same source they're coherent, and therefore they interfere. (Additional reflections actually result in multiple beams, but they're successively fainter and we neglect them.)

In Section 17-5 we saw how waves on a string reflect when the end of the string is fixed, free, or tied to another string. Light incident from air on a medium with higher refractive index is like a wave on a string that's fixed or tied to a heavier string; the reflected wave undergoes a 180° phase change, as we showed in Figs. 17-5*a* and 17-6. Going the other way, from the medium with the higher refractive index to air, there's no phase change on reflection; here the situation is more like Fig. 17-5*b* or a string tied to a lighter string. So the incident light from air onto the film reflects with a 180° phase change, while light incident from inside the film on its rear surface reflects with no phase change. Figures 37-20*b* and *c* show these phase relations.

If the film in Fig. 37-20 were negligibly thin compared with the wavelength of the light, then the reflected beams 1 and 2 would be 180° out of phase because there's a 180° phase change at the first surface but none at the second. But if the film has thickness d, then there will be an additional phase difference due to the additional distance that beam 2 travels. We'll consider the case when light is incident on the film at nearly normal incidence, so that extra distance is essentially $2d$. In Section 37-1 we established that a path difference equal to an integer number of wavelengths results in constructive interference (recall Fig. 37-2), while an odd integer number of half wavelengths gives destructive interference. Here, though, we have an extra 180° phase change due to the reflections at the different surfaces of the film. Therefore a phase change of 180° due to the path length difference will combine with the reflection-caused 180° phase change to put the waves back in phase—giving constructive interference. Thus our usual criteria for constructive and destructive interference are reversed; for example, the condition for constructive interference is that the path difference be an integer multiple of a half wavelength, or

$$2d = (m + \tfrac{1}{2})\lambda_n,$$

where λ_n is the wavelength in the film, whose refractive index is n.

In Chapter 35 we saw that the wavelength in a material with refractive index n is reduced by a factor $1/n$ from its value λ in air or vacuum; thus $\lambda_n = \lambda/n$, and our criterion for constructive interference can be written

$$2nd = (m + \tfrac{1}{2})\lambda. \qquad \text{(constructive interference, thin film)} \qquad \text{(37-8a)}$$

Conversely, destructive interference occurs when

$$2nd = m\lambda. \qquad \text{(destructive interference, thin film)} \qquad \text{(37-8b)}$$

The destructive interference is not complete, however, since the two beams do not have the same intensity.

Suppose a film is illuminated with light of a single color—that is, a single wavelength λ. If the thickness of a film varies with position, then constructive interference described by Equation 37-8a will occur at different places. Thus there will be bright bands separated by darker areas in which destructive interference occurs. If, on the other hand, the film is illuminated with white light, then the interference conditions will be satisfied at different places for the different wavelengths of the colors that comprise white light. The bands of color you see in a soap bubble or oil slick result from such thin-film interference (Fig. 37-21). If part of the film is too thin to meet the constructive interference condition of Equation 37-8a for *any* visible wavelength, then that part of the film will appear dark. You can see this effect at the top of the soap film in Fig. 37-21.

FIGURE 37-21 Interference patterns formed in a soap film illuminated with white light. The film's thickness increases toward the bottom, resulting in constructive interference for a given wavelength occurring at several different vertical positions. The film is too thin at the top for constructive interference at any visible wavelength, so it appears dark.

EXAMPLE 37-4	*A Soap Film*

A rectangular wire loop 20 cm high is dipped into a soap solution and then held vertically, producing a soap film whose thickness varies linearly from essentially zero at the top to 1.0 μm at the bottom (Fig. 37-22). (a) If the film is illuminated with 650-nm light, how many bright bands (as shown in Fig. 37-21) will appear? (b) What region of the film would be dark if it were illuminated with white light? The refractive index of the film is that of water, $n = 1.33$.

Solution

The film thickness at the position of a bright band is given by Equation 37-8a. To find the number of bright bands, we can solve this equation for the value of m at which the thickness d would equal the maximum film thickness:

$$m = \frac{2nd}{\lambda} - \frac{1}{2} = \frac{(2)(1.33)(1.0\ \mu m)}{0.65\ \mu m} - \frac{1}{2} = 3.6 .$$

Since m must be an integer, the largest m corresponding to a thickness within the 1.0-μm maximum is 3. Since m ranges from zero to 3, there are a total of 4 bright bands.

At a given wavelength the minimum thickness for constructive interference occurs at $m = 0$. Taking the minimum wavelength for visible light at 400 nm = 0.40 μm, Equation 37-8a with $m = 0$ then gives

$$d = \frac{\lambda}{4n} = \frac{0.40\ \mu m}{(4)(1.33)} = 0.0752\ \mu m .$$

Since the film goes linearly from zero thickness to a maximum of 1.0 μm over its 20-cm height, this thickness occurs 0.0752

FIGURE 37-22 Cross section through a vertical soap film. The angle between the surfaces is greatly exaggerated.

of the way from the top edge, or at (0.0752)(20 cm) = 1.5 cm. Above this level the film is too thin for constructive interference in visible light, so the top 1.5 cm of film appears darker.

EXERCISE At what distances from the top of the film will bright bands appear if the film in Example 37-4 is illuminated with 450-nm light?

Answer: 1.69 cm, 5.08 cm, 8.46 cm, 11.8 cm, 15.2 cm, 18.6 cm

Some problems similar to Example 37-4: 31–33, 35

We derived Equations 37-8 on the assumption that our thin film was surrounded by air. Frequently, though, a thin film is sandwiched between two different media—as when an oil film floats on water. If the intermediate medium has a higher refractive index than the medium at its rear (i.e., at the right in Fig. 37-20), then our results still apply. But if the rear medium has a greater refractive index than the thin film, then there will be an additional 180° phase change at the rear interface, and therefore, our interference conditions will reverse (see the application below, as well as Problems 67 and 68).

APPLICATION	*Antireflection Coatings*

Partial reflection limits the amount of light that can be transmitted from one transparent material into another, reducing the light-gathering power of cameras, binoculars, and other lens-based instruments and of nonimaging devices such as windows and solar collectors.

Coating lenses, photovoltaic cells, and other critical light-gathering components with thin layers of appropriate materials can reduce reflection through the use of destructive interfer-

ence. Normally such **antireflection coatings** have refractive indices between those of air and glass; consequently, there is a 180° phase change at *each* interface, and thus, Equation 37-8a rather than 37-8b gives the condition for *destructive* interference. Thus, the minimum thickness for an antireflection coating, given by Equation 37-8a with $m = 0$, is $d = \lambda/4n$. Since this result depends on wavelength, antireflection coatings are not equally effective for all colors. With composite lenses and multiple layers, however, reduced reflection is possible over the visible spectrum.

A perfect antireflection coating might seem impossible, even in principle, since the reflected rays 1 and 2 in Fig. 37-20 do not have the same intensity. But the situation is actually more complicated. There are additional rays resulting from multiple reflections inside the transparent material, and these also interfere. A full solution of the problem involving the application of Maxwell's equations at both interfaces shows that the reflection becomes exactly zero when the antireflection layer has not only the right thickness but also refractive index $n_2 = \sqrt{n_1 n_3}$, where n_1 and n_3 are the indices of the two media separated by the antireflection coating. A widely used antireflection coating, magnesium fluoride (MgF_2), has $n = 1.38$, a value that approximates the zero-reflection condition for high-index flint glasses in air.

(a)

(b)

FIGURE 37-23 (a) Portion of a lens sitting on a flat glass plate. Newton's rings arise from the difference in path lengths between rays like 1 and 2. (b) Ring pattern produced in a test of a telescope's optical system.

Interference in thin layers is the basis of some very sensitive optical measuring techniques. The shape of a lens, for example, can be checked for accuracy to within a fraction of the wavelength of light using **Newton's rings**—interference patterns formed by interference of light reflected between the lens and a perfectly flat glass plate (Fig. 37-23; see also Problems 73–74).

The Michelson Interferometer

A number of optical instruments use interference for precise measurement of small distances. Among the simplest and most important of these is the **Michelson interferometer**, invented by the American physicist Albert Michelson and used in the 1880s by Michelson and his colleague Edward W. Morley in a famous experiment that paved the way for the theory of relativity. We discuss the Michelson-Morley experiment in the next chapter; here we describe the interferometer, which is still used for precision measurements.

Figure 37-24 shows the basic design of the Michelson interferometer. The key idea is that light from a monochromatic source is split into two beams by a half-silvered mirror called a **beam splitter**. The beam splitter is set at a 45° angle, so the reflected and transmitted beams travel perpendicular paths. Each then reflects off a flat mirror and returns to the beam splitter. The beam splitter again transmits and reflects half the light incident on it, with the result that some light from the originally separated beams is recombined. The recombined beams interfere, and the interference pattern is observed with a viewing lens at the bottom of Fig. 37-24.

(a)

(b)

FIGURE 37-24 (a) Schematic diagram of a Michelson interferometer. The beam splitter splits incident light into reflected and transmitted beams of equal intensity. (b) The observer looking through the viewer sees interference fringes arising from differing optical path lengths.

Suppose the path lengths in the two perpendicular arms of the interferometer were exactly the same or differed by a multiple of the wavelength. When the beams recombined they would then undergo fully constructive interference. If the path-length difference were a multiple of a half wavelength, on the other hand, the beams would interfere destructively. In reality, however, the mirrors are never exactly perpendicular, and therefore light reflecting from different parts of the mirrors experiences slightly different path lengths and thus recombines with different phase lags. To the observer, the result is a series of alternating light and dark fringes corresponding to constructive and destructive interference.

Now suppose one mirror is moved slightly. The path-length differences change and therefore, the interference pattern shifts. Moving the mirror a mere quarter wavelength adds an extra half wavelength to the round-trip path. That results in an additional 180° phase shift, moving dark fringes to where light ones were, and vice versa. An observer looking through the viewer as the mirror moves sees the fringes shift to their new positions. Shifts of a fraction of the distance between fringes are readily detected, allowing measurement of mirror displacements to within a small fraction of the wavelength.

A similar fringe shift occurs if a transparent material is placed in one path, retarding the beam because of its refractive index. This approach allows accurate measurements of the refractive indices of gases, which are so close to one that conventional methods would not be useful (see Problem 46).

Measurements with the Michelson interferometer depend not on the interference pattern itself but on *changes* in that pattern. Therefore, it doesn't really matter whether the path lengths are exactly equal. Whatever those lengths, there will be an interference pattern, and changes in that pattern will reflect changes in the relative optical paths.

EXAMPLE 37-5	*Sandstorm!*

A sandstorm has pitted the aluminum mirrors of a desert solar energy installation, and engineers want to know the depths of these pits so they can estimate the mirrors' useful lifetimes. They construct a Michelson interferometer with a sample from one of the pitted mirrors in place of one of the flat mirrors. With a 633-nm laser as the light source, the interference pattern shown in Fig. 37-25 results. What is the approximate depth of the pit?

Solution

The "bumps" in the interference pattern correspond to light that has traveled the extra distance into the bottom of the pit and back. A shift of one full cycle in the interference pattern would correspond to a full wavelength change in the path. As Fig. 37-25 shows, the pit causes a fringe shift corresponding to about 0.2 wavelengths. Since light makes a round trip through the pit, its actual depth is therefore 0.1λ, or 63 nm. Try measuring that with a meter stick!

EXERCISE A Michelson interferometer uses sodium light with wavelength 589.6 nm. As one mirror is moved, a photocell

FIGURE 37-25 Fringe pattern resulting from a pitted mirror. The size of the bump is a measure of the pit depth.

connected to a counter "watches" a fixed point through the viewer. If the counter records 4878 fringes passing that point, how far did the mirror move?

Answer: 1.438 mm

Some problems similar to Example 37-5: 44–46

37-5 HUYGENS' PRINCIPLE AND DIFFRACTION

The interference we've been studying in this chapter isn't the only optical phenomenon where the wave nature of light is important. There's also **diffraction**—the bending of light or other waves as they pass by objects. Interference and diffraction are closely related, and the double- and multiple-slit interference we've studied actually involves diffraction as well; hence the term "diffraction grating."

Diffraction, like other optical phenomena, is ultimately governed by Maxwell's equations of electromagnetism. But we can understand diffraction of light and other waves more readily using **Huygens' principle**, articulated in 1678 by the Dutch scientist Christian Huygens, who was first to suggest that light might be a wave. Huygens' principle states that

> All points on a wavefront act as point sources of spherically propagating "wavelets" that travel at the speed of light appropriate to the medium. At a short time Δt later, the new wavefront is the unique surface tangent to all the forward-propagating wavelets.

Figure 37-26 shows how Huygens' principle accounts for the propagation of plane and spherical (or cylindrical) waves. It is also possible to derive the laws of reflection and refraction from Huygens' principle.

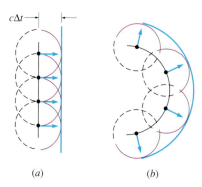

(a)   (b)

FIGURE 37-26 Application of Huygens' principle to (a) plane and (b) spherical waves. In each case the wavefront acts like a set of point sources that emit circular waves. A short time Δt later the wavelets have expanded to radius $c\Delta t$, and the new wavefront is the surface tangent to the wavelets. To follow the propagation further one could draw new wavelets originating on the new wavefront.

Diffraction

Figure 37-27 shows plane waves incident on an opaque barrier containing a hole. Since the waves are blocked by the barrier, Huygens' wavelets produced near each barrier edge cause the wavefronts to bend at the barrier (see blowups in Fig. 37-27). When the width of the hole is much greater than the wavelength, as in Fig. 37-27a, this diffraction is of little consequence, and the waves effectively propagate straight through the hole in a beam defined by the hole size. But when

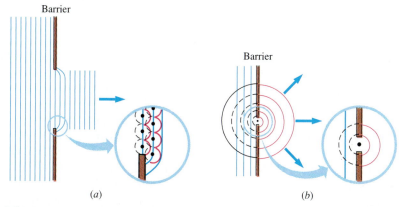

(a)   (b)

FIGURE 37-27 Plane waves incident on an opaque barrier with a hole in it are diffracted at the edges of the hole, as shown by Huygens' wavelet constructions. (a) When the hole size is much larger than the wavelength this diffraction is negligible, and the waves essentially propagate in a straight beam defined by the hole. (b) When the hole size and wavelength are comparable, the emerging wavefronts spread in a broad beam, approaching circular wavefronts as the hole size becomes negligibly small.

the hole size and wavelength are comparable, then wavefronts emerging from the hole spread in a broad pattern (Fig. 37-27b). Here diffraction is the dominant effect on the propagation. Thus diffraction, although it always occurs when waves pass an object, is significant only on length scales comparable to or smaller than the wavelength. That's why we could ignore diffraction and assume that light always travels through a single medium in straight lines, when we considered optical systems with dimensions much larger than the wavelength of light.

Diffraction ultimately limits our ability to image small objects and to focus light with arbitrary precision. Next, we'll see why this is so by examining quantitatively the behavior of light as it passes through a single slit. The result will help us understand optical challenges ranging from telescopic imaging of distant astrophysical objects, to "star wars" antimissile systems, to the development of the new digital video discs (DVDs) that hold a full-length movie on a disc identical in size to a standard audio CD.

37-6 SINGLE-SLIT DIFFRACTION

In treating double-slit and multiple-slit interference in Section 37-2, we assumed that plane waves passing through a slit emerged with circular wavefronts. According to Fig. 37-27, that assumption is vaild only if the width of the slits is very small compared with the wavelength, so the slit can be treated as a single, localized source of new waves. When the slit width is not small, Huygens' principle implies that we have to consider each point in the slit as a separate source—and then we can expect interference from waves originating at different points in the same slit. Thus a single wide slit is really like a multiple-slit system with infinitely many slits!

Figure 37-28 shows light incident on a slit of width a. Each point in the slit acts as a source of spherical wavelets propagating in all directions to the right of the slit. In Fig. 37-28 we focus on a particular direction described by the angle θ and will look at interference of light from the five points shown. Figure 37-28b concentrates on the points from which rays 1, 2, and 3 originate and shows that the path lengths for rays 1 and 3 differ by $\frac{1}{2}a \sin\theta$. These two beams will interfere destructively if this distance is half the wavelength; that is, if $\frac{1}{2}a \sin\theta = \frac{1}{2}\lambda$ or $a \sin\theta = \lambda$. But if rays 1 and 3 interfere destructively, so do rays 3 and 5, which have the same geometry, and so do rays 2 and 4, for the same reason. In fact, a ray leaving *any* point in the lower half of the slit will interfere destructively with the point located a distance $a/2$ above it. Therefore, an observer viewing the slit system at the angle θ satisfying $a \sin\theta = \lambda$ will see no light.

Similarly, the sources for rays 1 and 2 are $a/4$ apart and will therefore interfere destructively if $\frac{1}{4}a \sin\theta = \frac{1}{2}\lambda$, or $a \sin\theta = 2\lambda$. But then so will rays 2 and 3, and rays 3 and 4; in fact, any ray from a point in the lower three quarters of the slit will interfere destructively with a ray from the point $a/4$ above it, and therefore, an observer looking at an angle satisfying $a \sin\theta = 2\lambda$ will see no light.

We could equally well have divided the slit into six sections with seven evenly spaced points; we would then have found destructive interference if $\frac{1}{6}a \sin\theta = \frac{1}{2}\lambda$, or $a \sin\theta = 3\lambda$. We could obviously continue this process for any number of points in the slit, and therefore, we conclude that destructive

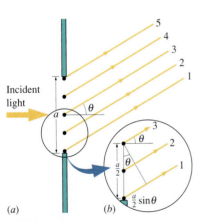

FIGURE 37-28 Each point in a slit acts as a source of Huygens' wavelets, which interfere in the region to the right of the slit. (a) Here we consider 5 points within the slit, and the relative phases of their light as viewed at an angle θ. (b) The path-length difference for two beams is their separation times $\sin\theta$.

interference occurs for all angles satisfying

$$a \sin \theta = m\lambda, \quad \text{(destructive interference, single-slit diffraction)} \quad (37\text{-}9)$$

16.1
Diffraction

with m any nonzero integer and a the slit width. Note that the case $m = 0$ is excluded; it produces not destructive interference but a central maximum in which all waves are in phase.

Tip

Interference and Diffraction Equation 37-9 for the *minima* of a single-slit diffraction pattern looks just like Equation 37-1a for the *maxima* of a multi-slit interference pattern, except that the slit width a replaces the slit spacing d. What's going on? Why does the same equation give the minima in one case and the maxima in another? Because we're dealing with two distinct but related phenomena. In the multi-slit case leading to Equation 37-1a, we considered each slit to be so narrow that it could be considered a single source, thus neglecting the interference of waves originating within the same slit. In the single-slit case leading to Equation 37-9, the diffraction pattern occurs precisely because of the interference of waves from different points within the same slit.

EXAMPLE 37-6	*Diffraction: A Narrow Slit*

For what slit width, in terms of wavelength, will the first minimum lie at an angular position of 45°?

Solution
With $m = 1$, Equation 37-9 gives

$$a = \frac{\lambda}{\sin \theta} = \frac{\lambda}{\sin 45°} = \sqrt{2}\lambda.$$

Here, with the slit width nearly equal to the wavelength, diffraction dominates the wave propagation. The incident light is therefore spread over a wide angular range. The exercise below shows that the beam spreading decreases as the slit width grows.

EXERCISE Light is incident on a slit whose width is 20 times its wavelength. Find the angular spread of the beam, taken as the angle between the first minima on either side of the central maximum.

Answer: 5.7°

Some problems similar to Example 37-6: 49–51

Intensity in Single-Slit Diffraction

We can find the intensity of the single-slit diffraction pattern by adding the electric fields of the individual beams, as we did for two-slit interference. Since there are infinitely many points along the slit, each constituting a point source of light, we might set up and evaluate a complicated integral. Instead we use the graphical method of phasors, introduced in Chapter 33 to deal with alternating currents and voltages of different phases. We have a similar situation here, as we want to combine waves with different phases that arise from different points on the slit. The phasor method is entirely equivalent to integrating over the electric field contributions from the individual sources in the slit.

We use phasors to represent the electric fields of the individual waves originating from points in the slit when they arrive at the screen. The length of a phasor gives the field amplitude E, and its direction gives its phase. Consider N such points, spaced evenly across a slit of width a, like the five points in Fig. 37-28.

These divide the slit into $N - 1$ sections, each of width $a/(N - 1)$. At some angle θ, the phase difference, in radians, of light coming from two adjacent points will be the ratio of their path-length difference to the wavelength, times the 2π radians that comprise a complete cycle. As usual, the path-length difference is the point spacing times $\sin\theta$ (see Fig. 37-28b). Here the point spacing is $a/(N - 1)$, so we have

$$\Delta\phi = \left(\frac{a}{N - 1}\sin\theta\right)\left(\frac{2\pi}{\lambda}\right) \qquad (37\text{-}10)$$

for the phase difference between waves from adjacent points. All the waves have essentially the same amplitude, so we now need to add N equal-length phasors each of which differs in phase by $\Delta\phi$ from its nearest neighbors.

Consider first the case $\theta = 0$. Then Equation 37-10 gives $\Delta\phi = 0$ so, as Fig. 37-29a shows, the phasors are all in the same direction and sum to give a large total amplitude. This is the central maximum of the diffraction pattern. If, on the other hand, $\Delta\phi$ is such that the N phasors sum to a closed path, then the total amplitude—the net displacement from the beginning to the end of the phasor diagram—is zero (Fig. 37-29b). Here we have a point of zero intensity in the interference pattern. More generally, the phasors sum to give an amplitude E_θ that is neither zero nor as great as a simple sum of the individual amplitudes, as shown in Fig. 37-29c.

Now each point in the slit differs in phase by $\Delta\phi$ from its immediate neighbors. Thus, the second point differs by $\Delta\phi$ from the first point, the third point by $2\Delta\phi$ from the first point, and so forth until the Nth point differs in phase by $(N - 1)\Delta\phi$ from the first point. But this last quantity $(N - 1)\Delta\phi$ is just the total phase difference ϕ from one end of the slit to the other. Using Equation 37-10, we can write this phase difference as

$$\phi = (N - 1)\left(\frac{a}{N - 1}\sin\theta\right)\left(\frac{2\pi}{\lambda}\right) = \frac{2\pi}{\lambda}a\sin\theta. \qquad (37\text{-}11)$$

To consider all points in the slit, we take the limit as $N \to \infty$; then the end-to-end chain of phasors in Fig. 37-29c becomes a circular arc of radius R, as shown in

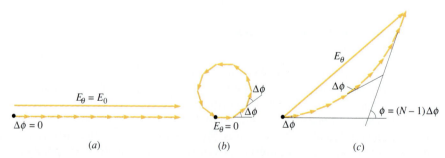

$E_\theta = E_0$

$\Delta\phi = 0$

(a)

$E_\theta = 0$

$\Delta\phi$

$\Delta\phi$

(b)

E_θ

$\Delta\phi$

$\phi = (N - 1)\Delta\phi$

$\Delta\phi$

(c)

FIGURE 37-29 Phasor addition to find the amplitude in single-slit diffraction. (a) When $\theta = 0$ in Fig. 37-28 all waves have the same phase, and their amplitudes add to produce the central maximum. (b) When the phasor sum is a closed loop, the net phasor displacement is zero and so is the wave amplitude. (c) In general, the phasors add to produce an amplitude that is neither zero nor as great as in the central maximum. The angle between the first and last phasor is $N\Delta\phi$. Here $N = 10$ in all three frames, and in general we designate the resultant amplitude by E_θ. When the phasors all have the same phase, E_0 is the resultant amplitude.

Fig. 37-30. If we stretched this arc into a line, its length would be the electric field amplitude E_0 of Fig. 37-29a; therefore, E_0 is also the length of the arc. From the geometry of Fig. 37-30 we see that

$$\sin(\phi/2) = \frac{E_\theta/2}{R}.$$

We can also write the angle $\phi/2$ using the definition of an angle in radians as the ratio of arc length to radius. Here $\phi/2$ subtends an arc of length $E_0/2$, so we have

$$\phi/2 = \frac{E_0/2}{R}.$$

Dividing these two equations gives the ratio of the amplitudes:

$$\frac{E_\theta}{E_0} = \frac{\sin(\phi/2)}{\phi/2}.$$

But the wave intensity $\bar{S}$ is proportional to the square of the amplitude, so

$$\bar{S}_\theta = \bar{S}_0 \left[\frac{\sin(\phi/2)}{\phi/2} \right]^2, \tag{37-12}$$

where ϕ is given by Equation 37-11.

Figure 37-31 shows plots of Equation 37-12 for several values of the slit width a in relation to the wavelength λ. Note that for wide slits—slit width a large compared with the wavelength λ—the central peak is very narrow and the secondary peaks are much smaller. Here diffraction is negligible, and the beam essentially propagates through the slit in the ray approximation of geometrical optics. But as the slit narrows the diffracted beam spreads, until, with $a = \lambda$, it covers an angular width of some 120°.

The intensity given by Equation 37-12 will be zero when the numerator on the right-hand side is zero—that is, when the argument of the sine function is an integer multiple of π. That occurs when $\dfrac{\phi}{2} = \dfrac{\pi a}{\lambda} \sin\theta = m\pi$, or when $a \sin\theta = m\lambda$. Thus, we recover our earlier result of Equation 37-9 for the angular positions where destructive interference gives zero intensity.

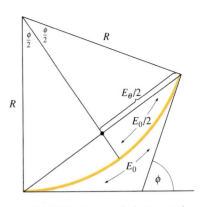

FIGURE 37-30 In the limit $N \to \infty$ the chain of phasors becomes a circular arc of length E_0.

FIGURE 37-31 Intensity in single-slit diffraction, as a function of the angle θ from the centerline, for three values of slit width a, expressed in units of wavelength λ. When the slit is much wider than the wavelength, most of the light is concentrated in a narrow central peak. But as the slit width approaches the wavelength, the diffracted beam becomes very wide.

| EXAMPLE 37-7 | *Other Peaks* |

Secondary maxima lie approximately midway between the minima of the diffraction pattern. Use this fact to find the intensity at the first of these secondary maxima, in terms of the central-peak intensity $\bar{S}_0$.

Solution

The first and second minima are at positions given by $a \sin\theta_1 = \lambda$ and $a \sin\theta_2 = 2\lambda$, respectively. With the first of the secondary maxima midway between them, its angular position is given by $a \sin\theta = \frac{3}{2}\lambda$. (Here we assume θ is small, so $\sin\theta \simeq \theta$, and midway in angular position θ is therefore also midway in $\sin\theta$.) Then $\frac{a}{\lambda}\sin\theta = \frac{3}{2}$, so Equation 37-11 gives $\frac{\phi}{2} = \frac{\pi a}{\lambda}\sin\theta = \frac{3\pi}{2}$. Using this result in Equation 37-12, we

have

$$\bar{S} = \bar{S}_0 \left[\frac{\sin(\phi/2)}{\phi/2}\right]^2 = \bar{S}_0 \left[\frac{\sin(3\pi/2)}{3\pi/2}\right]^2 = \frac{4\bar{S}_0}{9\pi^2} = 0.045\bar{S}_0.$$

Thus, the intensity at the first secondary maximum is only about 4.5% of the central-peak intensity. Note that this result is independent of the slit width, provided the secondary peak exists (which it may not; see Fig. 37-31c).

EXERCISE Show that the intensity in single-slit diffraction has half its maximum value when $\sin\theta = 1.3916\dfrac{\lambda}{\pi a}$.

Some problems similar to Example 37-7: 49–53

In analyzing single-slit diffraction we considered only parallel rays in the diffraction region. To make the diffraction pattern actually appear on a screen, we have to focus those rays with a lens between slit and screen (Fig. 37-32). Diffraction associated with parallel rays is called **Fraunhofer diffraction**. In general, Fraunhofer diffraction occurs when the distance from the diffracting system is large compared with the wavelength. Fraunhofer diffraction is an approximation to the more general case of **Fresnel diffraction**, whose analysis is more complicated because it also accounts for nonparallel rays that exist near a diffracting system.

Multiple Slits and Other Diffracting Systems

In treating multiple-slit systems in Section 37-2, we assumed the slits were so narrow compared with the wavelength that the central diffraction peak spread into the entire space beyond the slit system. When the slit width is not negligible, then the waves from each slit produce a single-slit diffraction pattern. The result is a pattern that combines single-slit diffraction with multiple-slit interference (Fig. 37-33).

FIGURE 37-32 Single-slit diffraction pattern produced by focusing light from a single slit onto a screen. Note the bright central peak and secondary maxima separated by regions of destructive interference.

FIGURE 37-33 When the slit width is not negligible, the double-slit pattern shows the regular variations of double-slit interference within a single-slit diffraction pattern.

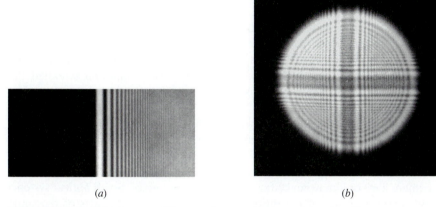

(a)   (b)

FIGURE 37-34 (a) Light waves diffract as they pass by the straight edge of an opaque barrier. Photo shows the resulting interference pattern on a screen some distance beyond the barrier, whose shadow is the black region at left. (b) Diffraction of monochromatic light by a pair of crosshairs in a circular aperture. Diffraction effects from both the crosshairs (straight fringes) and the aperture itself (circular fringes) are evident.

Diffraction occurs any time light passes a sharp, opaque edge like the edges of the slits we've been considering. Close examination of the shadow produced by a sharp edge shows parallel fringes resulting from interference of the diffracting wavefronts (Fig. 37-34a). More complex diffraction patterns result from objects of different shape (Fig. 37-34b). The presence of such diffraction patterns limits our ability to form sharp optical images, as we show in the next section.

37-7 THE DIFFRACTION LIMIT

Diffraction imposes a fundamental limit on the ability of optical systems to distinguish closely spaced objects. Consider two point sources of light illuminating a slit. The sources are so far from the slit that waves reaching the slit are essentially plane waves, but the different source positions mean the waves reach the slit at different angles. We assume the sources are incoherent, so they don't

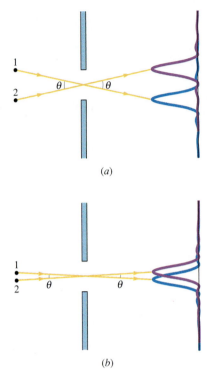

(a)

(b)

produce a regular interference pattern. Then light diffracting at the slit produces two single-slit diffraction patterns, one for each source. Because the sources are at different angular positions, the central maxima of these patterns don't coincide, as shown in Fig. 37-35.

If the angular separation between the sources is great enough, then the central maxima of the two diffraction patterns will be entirely distinct. In that case the eye or any other optical system can clearly distinguish the two sources (Fig. 37-35a). But as the sources get closer the central maxima begin to overlap (Fig. 37-35b). The two sources remain distinguishable as long as the total intensity pattern shows two peaks. Since the sources are incoherent the total intensity is just the sum of the individual intensities. Figure 37-36 shows how that sum loses its two-peak structure as the diffraction patterns merge. In general, two peaks are barely distinguishable if the central maximum of one coincides with the first minimum of the other. This condition is called the **Rayleigh criterion**, and when it is met we say that the two sources are just barely **resolved**.

What does all this have to do with optical instruments and images? Simply this: All optical systems are analogous to the single slit we've been considering. Every system has an aperture of finite size through which light enters the system. That aperture may be an actual slit or hole, like the diaphragm that "stops down" a camera lens, or it may be the full size of a lens or mirror. So all optical systems ultimately suffer loss of resolution if two sources—or two parts of the same extended object—have too small an angular separation. Thus, diffraction fundamentally limits our ability to probe the structure of objects that are either very small or very distant.

Figure 37-35 shows that the angular separation between the diffraction peaks is equal to the angular separation between the sources themselves. Then the Rayleigh criterion is just met if the angular separation between the two sources is equal to the angular separation between a central peak and the first minimum. We found earlier that the first minimum in single-slit diffraction occurs at angular position given by

$$\sin \theta = \frac{\lambda}{a},$$

with a the slit width and with θ measured from the central peak. In most optical systems the wavelength is much less than the size of any apertures, so we can use the small-angle approximation $\sin \theta \simeq \theta$ with θ in radians. Then the Rayleigh criterion—the condition that two sources be just resolvable—for single-slit diffraction becomes

$$\theta_{\min} = \frac{\lambda}{a}. \qquad \text{(Rayleigh criterion, slit)} \qquad (37\text{-}13\text{a})$$

(a)

(b)

(c)

FIGURE 37-38 Diffraction patterns produced by a pair of point sources imaged through a circular hole. The angular separation of the sources decreases going from left to right, and when the sources are too close they cannot be resolved.

Most optical systems have circular apertures rather than slits. The diffraction pattern from such an aperture is a series of concentric rings (Fig. 37-37). A more involved mathematical analysis shows that the angular position of the first ring relative to the central peak, and therefore, the minimum resolvable source separation for a circular aperture, is

$$\theta_{min} = \frac{1.22\lambda}{D}, \qquad \text{(Rayleigh criterion, circular aperture)} \quad (37\text{-}13b)$$

with D the aperture diameter. In most optical systems the angle θ is very small, and Equations 37-13a and b hold for this case. For larger angles, θ_{min} in both equations should be replaced with $\sin\theta_{min}$. Figure 37-38 shows the loss of resolution as two nearby sources are imaged through a circular aperture. You can simulate this effect using ActivPhysics Activity 16.6.

Equations 37-13 show that increasing the aperture size allows smaller angular differences to be resolved. In optical instrument design, that means larger mirrors, lenses, and other components. An alternative is to decrease the wavelength used, which may or may not be an option depending on the source. In high-quality optical systems diffraction is often the limiting factor preventing perfectly sharp image formation; such systems are said to be **diffraction limited**. For example, the diffraction limit sets a minimum size for objects resolvable with optical microscopes; that's why electron microscopes—with shorter effective wavelength—are used to image the smallest biological structures. Large ground-based telescopes are an exception to the diffraction limit; their image quality is limited by atmospheric turbulence, although this can be reduced with adaptive optics that we mentioned in Chapter 36. From its vantage point above the atmosphere, the Hubble Space Telescope is the first large diffraction-limited astronomical telescope.

(a)

(b)

FIGURE 37-37 (a) Diffraction pattern produced by a circular aperture. (b) Three-dimensional plot of intensity versus position.

16.6
Resolving Power

Got It!

You're a biologist trying to resolve details of structures within a cell, but they look fuzzy even at the highest power of your microscope. Why won't it help to substitute a new eyepiece with shorter focal length, as suggested by Equation 36-10?

EXAMPLE 37-8	*Asteroid Alert!*

An asteroid appears on a collision course with Earth, at a distance of 20×10^6 km. What is the minimum size asteroid that the 2.4-m-diameter diffraction-limited Hubble Space Telescope could resolve at this distance, using 550-nm reflected sunlight?

Solution

Resolving the asteroid means being able to distinguish its opposite edges in the telescope image and therefore to assess its size. Suppose the asteroid's long dimension (it might not be spherical) is ℓ. Then at a distance $L \gg \ell$ it subtends an angle given very nearly by $\theta = \ell/L$. Using this result in Equation 37-13b with the mirror diameter and wavelength given, we have

$$\frac{\ell}{L} = \frac{1.22\lambda}{D},$$

or

$$\ell = \frac{1.22\lambda L}{D} = \frac{(1.22)(550\times10^{-9}\ \text{m})(20\times10^9\ \text{m})}{2.4\ \text{m}} = 5.6\ \text{km}.$$

This is a potentially dangerous object, comparable in size to the asteroid that scientists believe caused the extinction of the dinosaurs, and somewhat larger than the comet fragments that slammed into Jupiter in 1994, causing Earth-sized disturbances on the giant planet.

EXERCISE Two ants stand 1 cm apart. Assuming diffraction limited vision, at what distance could a human eye, with an iris aperture of 4 mm, tell that two are indeed separate creatures? Assume a wavelength of 550 nm, near the middle of the visible spectrum. (Other limitations of the human eye prevent its realizing this diffraction limit.)

Answer: 60 m

Some problems similar to Example 37-8: 55–59

APPLICATION	*Movies on Disc: From CD to DVD*

Standard audio CDs have a maximum playing time of 74 minutes—a value that's set by the optical diffraction limit. In the Application "CD Music, Continued" earlier in this chapter, we showed how a CD encodes information in "pits" 1.6 μm apart and as short as 0.83 μm in length. Standard CDs are read with 780-nm infrared laser light and the pit size and separation are chosen to ensure that diffraction effects at this wavelength don't cause the CD player's optical system to confuse adjacent pits. Ultimately, therefore, the 74-minute playing time is limited by the laser wavelength.

When CDs were first developed, inexpensive semiconductor lasers were available only in the infrared. But today's semiconductor lasers produce light well into the visible—with significantly shorter wavelengths than the infrared light used in CD players and CD-ROM drives. The new DVDs introduced in the late 1990s (read either "digital video disc" or "digital versatile disc") exploit these shorter-wavelength lasers.

Using laser wavelengths of 635 and 650 nm, DVDs can function with significantly lower pit sizes and spacings because of the lower diffraction limit at these shorter wavelengths (Fig. 37-39). Coupled with a two-layer structure (as opposed to the standard CD's single information layer) and more sophisticated data-compression schemes, the smaller pits and pit spacing give DVDs more than 12 times the information-storage capacity of standard CDs. That translates into more than two hours of high quality video and audio, as opposed to the CD's 74 minutes of audio alone. In computer use, it means a DVD can hold some 8.5 gigabytes of information as opposed to a CD's 680 megabytes (by comparison, a 3.5″ floppy disc holds only 1.44 MB). And DVDs can be made in two-sided versions, providing another doubling in capacity. Despite their high capacity, DVDs are physically the same size as CDs, and DVD players are compatible with standard CDs as well.

FIGURE 37-39 A comparison of a standard CD and a DVD. The smaller pit size and closer pit spacing of the DVD result in a much higher information storage capacity, and are made possible by the lower diffraction limit associated with the DVD player's shorter wavelength laser light. Both images are microphotographs of the same size region, about 8 μm on a side. The pits lie on a single spiral track that covers most of the disc.

(a)

(b)

APPLICATION	*Interferometry*

At a given wavelength, Equations 37-13 show that resolving small angular separations requires a large aperture. To see detail in distant astronomical objects, in particular, requires impractically large apertures. A technique called **interferometry** provides a way around this problem. Used most commonly at radio wavelengths, interferometry employs two or more individual apertures (i.e., radio telescopes), usually separated by a considerable distance. Signals from each are combined with their phases intact, so that they interfere. A two-telescope interferometer works like a two-slit system in reverse: the

system is most sensitive to radiation from angular positions that produce constructive interference (Fig. 37-40). The resolution of an interferometer is approximately that of a single slit-like aperture whose width is the spacing between the telescopes.

Today's interferometers include installations with many radio telescopes at a single site (Fig. 37-41), as well as coordinated instruments spread across the globe. The first interferometric arrays of optical telescopes began operation in the 1990s, and astronomers look forward to radio interferometers using the Earth-moon distance as their "aperture."

FIGURE 37-40 A radio interferometer consists of two or more radio telescopes at different locations. The interferometer can detect very slight changes in phase of the incoming wavefronts and can therefore resolve very small differences in angular position of objects in the sky.

FIGURE 37-41 Radio images of the active galaxy M87 show a jet of material emerging from the galactic core. (*top*) Image made with the Very Large Array (VLA) in New Mexico. The VLA consists of 27 radio telescopes whose separation gives an effective aperture of 27 km. (*bottom two images*) Much higher resolution is obtained with the Very Long Baseline Array (VLBA), whose radio telescopes extend from Hawaii to Puerto Rico. The resulting effective aperture of 8,000 km has a much lower diffraction limit, hence the higher resolution.

CHAPTER SYNOPSIS

Summary

1. **Interference** and **diffraction** are wave phenomena that constitute the subject of physical optics. Interference effects require two or more beams of **coherent** light, which maintain a fixed phase relation. Such coherent beams can be produced by allowing light from a single source to travel two different paths. If the path lengths differ by an integer multiple of the wavelength, **constructive interference** results when the beams recombine. If the path lengths differ by an integer multiple of a half wavelength, the result is **destructive interference**.

2. When coherent light of wavelength λ passes through a pair of narrow slits with spacing d, the resulting interference pattern shows bright fringes at maxima given by

$$d \sin \theta = m\lambda,$$

where m is an integer. The average intensity in the interference pattern is given by

$$\bar{S} = 4\bar{S}_0 \cos^2\left(\frac{\pi d \sin \theta}{\lambda}\right),$$

where $\bar{S}_0$ is the average intensity incident on the slits.

3. A multiple-slit system has primary interference maxima in the same position as a double-slit system, with multiple minima and secondary maxima in between. For large numbers of slits the primary maxima are narrow and bright and the region between them relatively dark. A system with many slits constitutes a **diffraction grating**, which disperses light into its component wavelengths. A grating produces spectra of many **orders**, corresponding to the integer m in the equation that locates the interference maxima. The **resolving power** of an N-slit grating is given by

$$\frac{\lambda}{\Delta\lambda} = mN,$$

where $\Delta\lambda$ is the minimum separation between wavelengths that can be distinguished in the mth-order spectrum. Other periodic systems, like the layers of atoms in a crystal, can serve as diffraction gratings for appropriate wavelengths.

4. Interference occurs in thin transparent films when light reflected from the front and back surfaces of the film recombines. For a film whose refractive index is larger than that of its surroundings, the interference is constructive when the film thickness d, refractive index n, and the light wavelength λ are related by $2nd = (m + \frac{1}{2})\lambda$, where m is an integer.

5. The **Michelson interferometer** utilizes the interference of light traveling on two perpendicular paths to make precise distance measurements.

6. **Huygens' principle** treats each point on a wavefront as a source of expanding spherical wavelets. Superposition of the wavelets describes the propagation of the wavefront and shows that waves undergo **diffraction** when passing by an opaque edge.

7. When the width of a single slit is not negligible compared with the wavelength, interference of light passing through different parts of the slit produces a **diffraction pattern** with a central maximum surrounded by lesser maxima separated by points of zero intensity.

8. The **diffraction limit** in optical systems arises because diffraction effects merge the images of two objects when their angular separation is sufficiently small. The **Rayleigh criterion** gives the minimum angular separation that can

be resolved by a given aperture. For a circular aperture of diameter D, the Rayleigh criterion is

$$\theta_{\min} = \frac{1.22\lambda}{D},$$

where $\theta_{\min}$ is in radians. Large apertures are therefore necessary to resolve objects with small angular separation.

Terms You Should Understand

(Pairs are closely related terms whose distinction is important; number in parentheses is chapter section where term first appears.)

physical optics, geometrical optics (introduction and preceding chapters)
interference (37-1)
coherence (37-1)
monochromatic light (37-1)
interference fringe (37-2)
order (37-2, 37-3)
diffraction grating (37-3)
resolving power (37-3)
Bragg condition (37-3)
Michelson interferometer (37-4)
diffraction (37-5)
Huygens' principle (37-5)
diffraction limit (37-7)
Rayleigh criterion (37-7)

Symbols You Should Recognize

m (37-1, 37-2, 37-3) $\theta_{\min}$ (37-7)

Problems You Should Be Able to Solve

analyzing double-slit interference patterns (37-2)
finding locations of maxima and minima in multiple-slit interference (37-3)
analyzing dispersion of light with diffraction gratings (37-3)
determining conditions for constructive and destructive interference in thin films (37-4)
analyzing experiments using Michelson interferometers (37-4)
finding minima and beam widths in single-slit diffraction (37-6)
finding the diffraction limit in optical systems (37-7)

Limitations to Keep in Mind

This chapter's analysis of double-slit interference assumes slit widths much smaller than the wavelength; otherwise the pattern combines diffraction and interference.

Our analysis of diffraction applies only in the Fraunhofer limit, in which the incident light is essentially parallel and the pattern is formed at large distances from the diffracting aperture.

QUESTIONS

1. A prism bends blue light more than red. Is the same true of a diffraction grating?
2. Why does an oil slick show colored bands?
3. Would a Michelson interferometer work even if its two arms were not exactly the same length?
4. Why does a soap bubble turn colorless just before it dries up and breaks?
5. Why don't you see interference effects between the front and back of your eyeglasses?
6. Hold two fingers very close together while looking through them at a source of light. Explain what you see.
7. Figure 37-42 shows the shadow cast by a ball bearing on the end of a needle, under monochromatic laser light.

FIGURE 37-42 Question 7.

Explain the existence of the fringes shown and of the white spot at the center of the ball bearing's shadow.
8. You can hear around corners but you can't see around corners. Why the difference?
9. In deriving the intensity in double-slit interference, we could not simply add the intensities from the two slits. Why not?
10. In sketching the intensity pattern for two incoherent sources imaged through a single slit, we could simply add the intensities from the two sources. Why?
11. The primary maxima in multiple-slit interference are in the same angular positions as those in double-slit interference. Why, then, do diffraction gratings have thousands of slits instead of just two?
12. In what way is a widely separated pair of small radio telescopes superior to a single large one? In what way is it inferior?
13. Describe the change in the diffraction pattern of a single slit as the slit is narrowed.
14. What pattern would result from passing red and blue light simultaneously through a double-slit system?
15. When the moon passes in front of a star, the intensity of the starlight fluctuates instead of dropping abruptly. Explain.
16. In analyzing crystal structure using X-ray diffraction, it is necessary to take data with the crystal in several different orientations. Why?
17. A double-slit system has one slit much narrower than the wavelength of the incident light, the other much wider. Describe the resulting intensity pattern.
18. Sketch roughly the diffraction pattern you would expect for light passing through a square hole a few wavelengths wide.

PROBLEMS

ActivPhysics can help with these problems:
Activities in Section 16, Physical Optics

Section 37-2 Double-Slit Interference

1. A double-slit system is used to measure the wavelength of light. The system has slit spacing $d = 15$ μm and slit-to-screen distance $L = 2.2$ m. If the $m = 1$ maximum in the interference pattern occurs 7.1 cm from screen center, what is the wavelength?
2. A double-slit experiment with $d = 0.025$ mm and $L = 75$ cm uses 550-nm light. What is the spacing between adjacent bright fringes?
3. A double-slit experiment has slit spacing 0.12 mm. (a) What should be the slit-to-screen distance L if the bright fringes are to be 5.0 mm apart when the slits are

illuminated with 633-nm laser light? (b) What will be the fringe spacing with 480-nm light?
4. With two slits separated by 0.37 mm, the interference pattern has bright fringes with angular spacing 0.065°. What is the wavelength of the light illuminating the slits?
5. The green line of gaseous mercury at 546 nm falls on a double-slit apparatus. If the fifth dark fringe is at 0.113° from the centerline, what is the slit separation?
6. What is the angular position θ of the second-order bright fringe in a double-slit system with 1.5-μm slit spacing if the light has wavelength (a) 400 nm or (b) 700 nm?
7. Light shines on a pair of slits whose spacing is three times the wavelength. Find the locations of the first- and second-order bright fringes on a screen 50 cm from the slits. *Hint:* Do Equations 37-2 apply?

8. A double-slit experiment has slit spacing 0.035 mm, slit-to-screen distance 1.5 m, and wavelength 500 nm. What is the phase difference between two waves arriving at a point 0.56 cm from the center line?

9. For a double-slit experiment with slit spacing 0.25 mm and wavelength 600 nm, at what angular position is the path difference equal to one-fourth of the wavelength?

10. A screen 1.0 m wide is located 2.0 m from a pair of slits illuminated by 633-nm laser light, with its center on the centerline of the slits. Find the highest-order bright fringe that will appear on the screen if the slit spacing is (a) 0.10 mm; (b) 10 μm.

11. Laser light at 633 nm falls on a double-slit apparatus with slit separation 6.5 μm. Find the separation between (a) the first and second and (b) the third and fourth bright fringes, as seen on a screen 1.7 m from the slits.

12. A tube of glowing gas emits light at 550 nm and 400 nm. In a double-slit apparatus, what is the lowest-order 550-nm bright fringe that will fall on a 400-nm dark fringe, and what are the corresponding orders?

Section 37-3 Multiple-Slit Interference and Diffraction Gratings

13. In a 5-slit system, how many minima lie between the zeroth-order and first-order maxima?

14. In a 3-slit system the first minimum occurs at an angular position of 5°. Where is the first maximum?

15. A 5-slit system with 7.5-μm slit spacing is illuminated with 633-nm light. Find the angular positions of (a) the first 2 maxima and (b) the 3rd and 6th minima.

16. On the screen of a multiple-slit system, the interference pattern shows bright maxima separated by 0.86° and 7 minima between each bright maximum. (a) How many slits are there? (b) What is the slit separation if the incident light has wavelength 656.3 nm?

17. Green light at 520 nm is diffracted by a grating with 3000 lines per cm. Through what angle is the light diffracted in (a) first and (b) fifth order?

18. Find the angular separation between the red hydrogen-α spectral line at 656 nm and the yellow sodium line at 589 nm if the two are observed in 3rd order with a 3500 line/cm grating spectrometer.

19. Light is incident normally on a grating with 10,000 lines per cm. What is the maximum order in which (a) 450-nm and (b) 650-nm light will be visible?

20. Visible light has wavelengths between 400 nm and 700 nm. What is the lowest pair of consecutive orders for which there will be some overlap between the visible spectra as dispersed by a grating?

21. A solar astronomer is studying the Sun's 589-nm sodium spectral line with a 2500 line/cm grating spectrometer whose fourth order dispersion puts the wavelength range from 575 nm to 625 nm on a detector. The astronomer is interested in observing simultaneously the so-called calcium-K line, at 393 nm. What order dispersion will put this line also on the detector?

22. (a) What portions of the 4th and 5th order visible spectra overlap in a 3000 lines/cm grating spectrometer? (b) How would your answer change for a 1000 lines/cm grating? (c) For a 10,000 lines/cm grating?

23. Estimate the number of lines per cm in the grating used to produce Fig. 37-15.

24. A grating spectrometer's detector covers an angular range of 10° and can be swung at any angle within ±75° of the normal to the grating. If the grating has 1200 lines/cm, in what orders can the hydrogen-α spectral line at 656 nm and the calcium-K line at 393 nm both fall on the detector? (b) What will be the angular position of the K line under these conditions?

25. When viewed in 6th order, the 486.1-nm hydrogen-β spectral line is flanked by another line that appears at the position of 484.3 nm in the 6th order spectrum. Actually the line is from a different order of the spectrum. What are the possible visible wavelengths of this line?

26. (a) Find the resolving power of a grating needed to separate the sodium-D spectral lines, which are at 589.0 nm and 589.6 nm. (b) How many lines must the grating have to achieve this resolution in first order? (This is very low resolution by present-day spectroscopic standards.)

27. Echelle spectroscopy uses relatively coarse gratings in high order. Compare the resolving power of an 80 line/mm echelle grating used in 12th order with a 600 line/mm grating used in 1st order, assuming the two have the same width.

28. The International Ultraviolet Explorer satellite carries a spectrometer with a 2.0-cm-wide grating ruled at 102 lines/mm. What is the minimum wavelength difference it can resolve in 12th order when observing in the ultraviolet at 155 nm?

29. You wish to resolve the calcium-H line at 396.85 nm from the hydrogen-ε line at 397.05 nm in a 1st-order spectrum. To the nearest hundred, how many lines should your grating have?

30. X-ray diffraction in potassium chloride (KCl) results in a first-order maximum when the X rays graze the crystal plane at 8.5°. If the X-ray wavelength is 97 pm, what is the spacing between crystal planes?

Section 37-4 Thin Films and Interferometers

31. Find the minimum thickness of a soap film ($n = 1.33$) in which 550-nm light will undergo constructive interference.

32. Light of unknown wavelength shines on a precisely machined wedge of glass with refractive index 1.52. The

closest point to the apex of the wedge where reflection is enhanced occurs where the wedge is 98 nm thick. Find the wavelength.

33. Monochromatic light shines on a glass wedge with refractive index 1.65, and enhanced reflection occurs where the wedge is 450 nm thick. Find all possible values for the wavelength in the visible range.

34. White light shines on a 100-nm-thick sliver of fluorite ($n = 1.43$). What wavelength is most strongly reflected?

35. As a soap bubble ($n = 1.33$) evaporates and thins, the reflected colors gradually disappear. (a) What is its thickness just as the last vestige of color vanishes? (b) What is the last color seen?

36. An oil film ($n = 1.25$) floats on water, and a soap film ($n = 1.33$) is suspended in air. Find the minimum thickness for each that will result in constructive interference with 500-nm green light.

37. Light reflected from a thin film of acetone ($n = 1.36$) on a glass plate ($n = 1.5$) shows maximum reflection at 500 nm and minimum at 400 nm. Find the minimum possible film thickness.

38. What minimum thickness of a coating with refractive index 1.35 should you use on a glass lens to minimize reflection at 500 nm, the approximate center of the visible spectrum?

39. An oil film with refractive index 1.25 floats on water. The film thickness varies from 0.80 μm to 2.1 μm. If 630-nm light is incident normally on the film, at how many locations will it undergo enhanced reflection?

40. Microwave ovens operate at a frequency of 2.4 GHz. What is the minimum thickness for a plastic tray with refractive index 1.45 that will cause enhanced reflection of microwaves incident normal to the plate?

41. Two perfectly flat glass plates are separated at one end by a piece of paper 0.065 mm thick. A source of 550-nm light illuminates the plates from above, as shown in Fig. 37-43. How many bright bands appear to an observer looking down on the plates?

FIGURE 37-43 An air wedge (Problems 41, 42, 43, 72).

42. An air wedge like that shown in Fig. 37-43 shows N bright bands when illuminated from above. Find an expression for the number of bands that will appear if the air is replaced by a liquid of refractive index n different from that of the glass.

43. You apply a slight pressure with your finger to the upper of a pair of glass plates forming an air wedge as in Fig. 37-43. The wedge is illuminated from above with 500-nm light, and you place your finger where, initially, there is a dark band. If you push gently so the band becomes light, then dark, then light again, by how much have you deflected the plate?

44. A Michelson interferometer uses light from glowing hydrogen at 486.1 nm. As you move one mirror, 530 bright fringes pass a fixed point in the viewer. How far did the mirror move?

45. What is the wavelength of light used in a Michelson interferometer if 550 bright fringes go by a fixed point when the mirror moves 0.150 mm?

46. One arm of a Michelson interferometer is 42.5 cm long and is enclosed in a box that can be evacuated. The box initially contains air, which is gradually pumped out to create a vacuum. In the process, 388 bright fringes pass a fixed point in the viewer. If the interferometer uses light with wavelength 641.6 nm, what is the refractive index of the air?

47. The evacuated box of the previous problem is filled with chlorine gas, whose refractive index is 1.000772. How many bright fringes pass a fixed point as the tube fills?

48. Your personal stereo is in a dead spot caused by direct reception from an FM radio station at 89.5 MHz interfering with the signal reflecting off a wall behind you. How much farther from the wall should you move in order that the interference be fully constructive?

Sections 37-6 and 37-7 Single-Slit Diffraction and the Diffraction Limit

49. For what ratio of slit width to wavelength will the first minima of a single-slit diffraction pattern occur at $\pm 90°$?

50. Light with wavelength 633 nm is incident on a 2.5 μm wide slit. Find the angular width of the central peak in the diffraction pattern, taken as the angular separation between the first minima.

51. A beam of parallel rays from a 29-MHz citizen's band radio transmitter passes between two electrically conducting (hence opaque to radio waves) buildings located 45 m apart. What is the angular width of the beam when it emerges from between the buildings?

52. Use trial-and-error with a calculator, or a more sophisticated root-finding method, to verify the number 1.3916 in the exercise following Example 37-7.

53. Find the intensity as a fraction of the central peak intensity for the second secondary maximum in single-slit

diffraction, assuming the peak lies midway between the second and third minima.

54. A proposed "star wars" antimissile laser is to focus 2.8-μm wavelength infrared light to a 50-cm-diameter spot on a missile 2500 km distant. Find the minimum diameter for a concave mirror that can achieve this spot size, given the diffraction limit. Your answer suggests one of the many technical difficulties faced by antimissile defense systems.

55. The movie *Patriot Games* has a scene in which CIA agents use spy satellites to identify individuals in a terrorist camp (Fig. 37-44). Suppose that a minimum resolution for distinguishing human features is about 5 cm. If the spy satellite's optical system is diffraction limited, what diameter mirror or lens is needed to achieve this resolution from an altitude of 100 km? Assume a wavelength of 550 nm.

FIGURE 37-44 CIA agents using satellite imaging to identify terrorists in the film *Patriot Games*. How big a mirror or lens must the satellite's optical system have? (Problem 55)

56. Suppose one of the 10-m-diameter Keck telescopes in Hawaii could be trained on San Francisco, 3400 km away. Would it be possible to read (a) newspaper headlines or (b) a billboard sign at this distance? Justify your answers by giving the minimum separation resolvable with Keck at 3400 km, assuming 550-nm light. (c) Repeat for the case of the Keck optical interferometer, formed from the two 10-m Keck telescopes and several smaller ones, with an effective aperture of 50 m.

57. A camera has an $f/1.4$ lens, meaning that the ratio of focal length to lens diameter is 1.4. Find the smallest spot diameter (defined as the diameter of the first diffraction minimum) to which this lens can focus parallel light with 580-nm wavelength.

58. The distance from the center of a circular diffraction pattern to the first minimum on a screen 0.85 m distant from the diffracting aperture is 15,000 wavelengths. What is the aperture diameter?

59. While driving at night, your eyes' irises have dilated to 3.1-mm diameter. If your vision were diffraction limited, what would be the greatest distance at which you could see as distinct the two headlights of an oncoming car, which are spaced 1.5 m apart? Take $\lambda = 550$ nm.

60. Two stars are 4.0 light-years apart, in a galaxy 20×10^6 light-years from Earth. What minimum separation of two radio telescopes, acting together as an interferometer, is needed to resolve them? The telescopes operate at 2.1 GHz and are pointing straight upward; the stars are directly overhead.

61. Under the best conditions, atmospheric turbulence limits the resolution of ground-based telescopes to about 1 arc second (1/3600 of a degree) as shown in Fig. 37-45. For what aperture sizes is this limitation more severe than that of diffraction at 550 nm? Your answer shows why large ground-based telescopes do not produce better images than small ones, although they do gather more light.

FIGURE 37-45 Jupiter, photographed with a ground-based telescope (left) and from space (right). Atmospheric turbulence limits the ground-based image quality while diffraction limits the space-based image (Problem 61).

62. Two objects are separated by approximately one wavelength of the light with which an observer is attempting to resolve them. Show that the Rayleigh criterion then requires that the distance to the objects be less than the diameter of the observing aperture, and thus the Fraunhofer diffraction approximation is violated. It is in fact impossible to resolve two objects as close as one wavelength.

Paired Problems

(Both problems in a pair involve the same principles and techniques. If you can get the first problem, you should be able to solve the second one.)

63. Find the total number of lines in a 2.5-cm-wide diffraction grating whose third-order spectrum has the 656-nm hydrogen-α spectral line at an angular position of 37°.

64. Light is diffracted by a 5000 line/cm grating, and a detector sensitive only to visible light finds a maximum intensity at 28° from the central maximum. (a) What is the wavelength of the light? (b) In what order is it seen at the 28° position?

65. A 400 line/mm diffraction grating is 3.5 cm wide. Two spectral lines whose wavelengths average to 560 nm are just barely resolved in the 4th-order spectrum of this grating. What is the difference between their wavelengths?

66. What order is necessary to resolve wavelengths of 647.98 nm and 648.07 nm using a 4500-line grating?

67. A thin film of toluene ($n = 1.49$) floats on water. What is the minimum film thickness if the most strongly reflected light has wavelength 460 nm?

68. Oil with refractive index 1.38 forms a 210-nm-thick film on a piece of glass. What color of visible light is most strongly reflected?

69. What diameter optical telescope would be needed to resolve a Sun-sized star 10 light-years from Earth? Take $\lambda = 550$ nm. Your answer shows why stars appear as point sources in optical astronomy.

70. Could the 305-m radio telescope at Arecibo in Puerto Rico resolve the star in the preceding problem, if it were observing at a wavelength of 1.0 cm?

Supplementary Problems

71. White light shines on a 250-nm-thick layer of diamond ($n = 2.42$). What wavelength *of visible light* is most strongly reflected?

72. An air wedge like that of Fig. 37-43 displays 10,003 bright bands when illuminated from above. If the region between the plates is then evacuated, the number of bands drops to 10,000. Calculate the refractive index of the air.

73. In Fig. 37-23 the mth Newton's ring appears a distance r from the center of the lens. Show that the curvature radius of the lens is given approximately by $R = r^2/(m + \frac{1}{2})\lambda$, where the approximation holds when the thickness of the air space is much less than the curvature radius.

74. Given the result of the preceding problem, how many bright Newton's rings would be seen with a 2.5-cm-diameter glass lens with curvature radius 7.5 cm, when illuminated with 500-nm light?

75. How many rings would be seen if the system of the preceding problem were immersed in water ($n = 1.33$)?

76. A thin-walled glass tube of length L containing a gas of unknown refractive index is placed in one arm of a Michelson interferometer using light of wavelength λ. The tube is then evacuated, and during the process m bright fringes pass a fixed point as seen in the viewer. Find an expression for the refractive index of the gas.

77. The signal from a 103.9-MHz FM radio station reflects off a building 400 m away, effectively producing two sources of the same signal. You're driving at 60 km/h along a road parallel to a line between the station's antenna and the building and located a perpendicular distance of 6.5 km from them. How often does the signal appear to fade when you're driving roughly opposite the transmitter and building?

78. A satellite dish antenna 45 cm in diameter receives TV broadcasts at a frequency of about 12 GHz. (a) What is the angular size of its beam, defined as the full width of the central diffraction peak? (b) How many communications satellites could fit in geosynchronous orbit above Earth's equator if antennas like this one were not to pick up signals from more than one satellite? Your answer shows why geosynchronous orbit is such valuable "real estate."

79. The component of a star's velocity in the radial direction relative to Earth is to be measured using the doppler shift in the hydrogen-β spectral line, which appears at 486.1 nm when the source is stationary relative to the observer. What is the minimum speed that can be detected by observing in 1st order with a 10,000 line/cm grating 5.0 cm across? *Hint:* See Equation 17-9.

80. Light is incident on a diffraction grating at an angle α to the normal. Show that the condition for maximum light intensity becomes $d(\sin\theta \pm \sin\alpha) = m\lambda$.

81. In a double-slit experiment, a thin glass plate with refractive index 1.56 is placed over one of the slits. The fifth bright fringe now appears where the second dark fringe previously appeared. How thick is the plate if the incident light has wavelength 480 nm?

82. An arrangement known as Lloyd's mirror (Fig. 37-46) allows interference between a direct and a reflected beam from the same source. Find an expression for the separation of bright fringes on the screen, given the distances d and D in Fig. 37-46, and the wavelength λ of the light. *Hint:* Think of two sources, one the virtual image of the other.

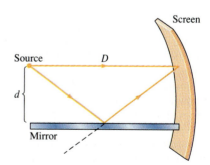

FIGURE 37-46 Lloyd's mirror (Problem 82).

PART 5 *Cumulative Problems*

These problems combine material from chapters throughout the entire part or, in addition, from chapters in earlier parts, or they present special challenges.

1. A *grism* is a grating ruled onto a prism, as shown in Fig. 1. The grism is designed to transmit undeviated one wavelength of the spectrum in a given order, as refraction in the prism compensates for the deviation at the grating. Find an equation relating the separation d of the grooves that constitute the grating, the wedge angle α of the prism, the refractive index n, the undeviated wavelength λ_0, and order m_0.

FIGURE 1 A grism (Cumulative Problem 1).

2. A double-slit system consists of two slits each of width a, with separation d between the slit centers ($d > a$). Light of intensity S_0 and wavelength λ is incident on the system, perpendicular to the plane containing the slits. Find an expression for the outgoing intensity as a function of angular position θ, taking into account both the slit width and the separation. Plot your result for the case $d = 4a$, and compare with Fig. 37-33.

3. A closed cylindrical tube whose glass walls have negligible thickness measures 5.0 cm long by 5.0 mm in diameter. It is filled with water, initially at 15°C, and placed with its long dimension in one arm of a Michelson interferometer. The water is not perfectly transparent, and it absorbs 3.2% of the light energy incident on it. The laser power incident on the water is 50 mW, and the wavelength is 633 nm. The refractive index of water in the vicinity of 15°C is given approximately by $n = 1.335 - 8.4 \times 10^{-5} T$, where T is the temperature in °C. As the water absorbs light energy, how long does it take the interference pattern to shift by one whole fringe?

4. A radio antenna broadcasts a 6.5-MHz signal in all directions. The antenna is on top of a tower 300 m above sea level, and the tower is located 2.0 km from the shore. An airplane is flying toward the tower, at twice the altitude of the tower top, as shown in Fig. 2. Radio waves from the tower reflect off the ocean surface with a 180° phase change, but there is no significant reflection off the land. As the plane heads toward the tower, at what horizontal distance or distances from the tower will its radio equipment detect a minimum in the radio signal amplitude due to destructive interference of the direct and reflected radio waves?

5. In one type of optical fiber, called a *graded-index fiber*, the refractive index varies in a way that results in light rays

FIGURE 2 Cumulative Problem 4 (figure is not to scale).

being guided along the fiber on curved trajectories, rather than undergoing abrupt reflections. Figure 3 shows a simple model that demonstrates this effect; it also describes the basic optical effect in mirages. A slab of transparent material has refractive index $n(y)$ that varies with position y perpendicular to the slab face. A light ray enters the slab at $x = 0$, $y = 0$, making an angle θ_0 with the normal just inside the slab. The refractive index at this point is $n(y = 0) = n_0$. (a) By writing $\sin\theta$ in Snell's law in terms of the components dx and dy of the ray path, show that that path (written in the form of x as a function of y) is given by

$$x = \int_0^y \frac{n_0 \sin\theta_0}{\sqrt{[n(y)]^2 - n_0^2 \sin^2\theta_0}}\, dy\,.$$

(b) Suppose $n(y) = n_0(1 - ay)$, where $n_0 = 1.5$ and $a = 1.0\ \text{mm}^{-1}$. If $\theta_0 = 60°$, find an explicit expression for x as a function of y, and plot your result to give the actual ray path. Explain the shape of your curve in terms of what happens when the ray reaches a point where $n(y) = n_0 \sin\theta_0$. What happens beyond this point?

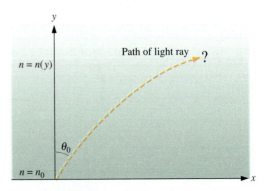

FIGURE 3 Cumulative Problem 5.

Part Six

Modern Physics

A "quantum corral" of 48 iron atoms on a copper surface encloses circular ripples associated with the wave-like nature of electrons on the surface. The image was taken with a scanning-tunneling microscope, which utilizes the principles of quantum mechanics. The ideas of modern physics allow scientists to not only understand but also, increasingly, to image and even manipulate matter at the atomic scale.

How big is the universe? What are the fundamental constituents of matter? What holds atoms together, and why do they emit only certain colors of light? Is nature fundamentally predictable, or does uncertainty rule in the microscopic world? How do we know that the universe began in a "big bang"? How will it end? All these are questions for relativity and quantum physics—collectively called "modern physics" because they were developed after the year 1900. In Part 6 we give a brief account of Einstein's relativity, followed by a glimpse at quantum physics and its applications. We end with an overview of the latest developments in fundamental physics, from the nature of elementary particles to the origin and ultimate fate of the entire universe.

Readers of the extended version of this text will find an expanded Part 6 with much more on quantum physics and its applications.

38 Relativity

Albert Einstein's relativity revolutionized our understanding of space and time. Here Einstein explains his theory at a 1931 lecture in California.

By the last quarter of the nineteenth century, the basic laws of electromagnetism had been formulated. Maxwell's theory had demonstrated the electromagnetic nature of light, whose practical consequences we explored in the three preceding chapters. In the same era the work of Samuel Morse (telegraph), Alexander Graham Bell (telephone), Hertz and Marconi (radio), Thomas A. Edison (electric light, phonograph), and many others laid the foundation of electromagnetic technology. Yet at the same time the insights of Maxwell led to baffling questions and contradictions that shook the roots of physical understanding and even of common sense.

From the resolution of these contradictions arose relativity, a theory that radically altered the philosophical basis for our understanding of the physical world, and whose influence spilled over into all areas of twentieth-century thought. The theory of relativity stands as a monument of human intellect and imagination. It transcends the everyday world of common sense, and shows us a universe whose richness is almost beyond imagination. We'll approach relativity from a historical perspective, building on our understandings of electromagnetism through the work of Maxwell. From this, you'll gain a sense of the baffling nature of the questions that electromagnetism raised in the minds of nineteenth-century physicists, and how Einstein's resolution of those questions was at once profoundly bold and sweepingly simple.

38-1 SPEED c RELATIVE TO WHAT?

Maxwell's equations show that electromagnetic waves can exist, and that all such waves travel with speed c. Speed c relative to what? When we described the mechanics of a taut string in Chapter 16, we showed that waves could propagate along the string with a certain speed. A certain speed relative to what? Clearly, to the string. Similarly, sound waves propagate through the air with a certain speed relative to the air. If you move through the air, the speed of sound *relative to you* won't be the same as its speed relative to the air (Fig. 38-1).

The Ether Concept

Each type of wave has a characteristic speed *relative to the medium in which it propagates*. What about light? What is the medium through which light propagates? Light reaches us from the most distant galaxies, traveling through seemingly empty space. Yet all our other experience with waves suggests that there should be a medium—and that the speed c in Maxwell's equations should be the speed relative to that medium. Nineteenth-century scientists, supposing that light waves were like mechanical waves, believed that light propagated through a tenuous substance called the **ether** that permeated the entire universe. Electric and magnetic fields were visualized as stresses and strains in the ether. This

FIGURE 38-1 A plane moves at speed V through air, in which the sound speed is v_{sound}. Sound waves approaching the plane from the front move at $v_{sound} + V$ relative to the plane, while those approaching from behind move at $v_{sound} - V$ relative to the plane.

mechanical view—that electromagnetic phenomena, including light, were dis-turbances of some substance—was deeply ingrained in the nineteenth-century scientists because of their previous experience that Newton's laws explained all known physical phenomena.

The ether had to have some unusual properties. It must offer no resistance to the motion of material bodies, or the planets would soon lose their energy and spiral into the Sun. At the same time the ether must be very stiff, for the speed of light is large. (If you make a spring stiffer, waves travel more quickly along it.) Indeed, the constants ε_0 and μ_0 must describe the mechanical properties of the ether that account for the high speed of light. These and other mechanical requirements make the ether a rather improbable substance, but without the ether we'd be left floundering for an answer to the question "speed c relative to what?"

The existence of electromagnetic waves traveling at speed c follows from Maxwell's equations. But this result could be true only in a frame of reference fixed with respect to the ether, for if we move relative to the ether then light should move at a speed other than c relative to us. Therefore Maxwell's equa-tions—that is, our description of electromagnetism—were presumably correct only in the ether's frame of reference.

This situation put electromagnetism in a rather different position from me-chanics. In mechanics, the concept of absolute motion is meaningless. You can eat your dinner, or throw a ball, or do any mechanical experiment as well on an airplane moving steadily at 1000 km/h as you can when the airplane is standing still on the ground. You need not take the uniform motion of the plane into account. This is the principle of **Galilean relativity**, which states that the laws of mechanics are valid in all inertial reference frames—i.e., frames of reference in uniform motion (see Section 3-5). But the laws of electromagnetism could be valid only in the ether's frame of reference, for it seemed that only in this frame could the prediction of electromagnetic waves moving at speed c be correct.

So the nineteenth-century physicists faced an unsatisfactory situation, in which the laws for one branch of physics (mechanics) seemed to work in all inertial frames, while those of another branch (electromagnetism) could not. But physicists had great faith in mechanical models and in the ether concept, for without ether the question "speed c relative to what?" seemed impossible to answer. Thus the late nineteenth century saw a flurry of activity as physicists sought to detect the ether. Ultimately they failed, paving the way for the new world view of relativity that, in Einstein's own words, "arose from necessity, from serious and deep contradictions in the old theory from which there seemed no escape."

38-2 MATTER, MOTION, AND THE ETHER

It was natural for nineteenth-century physicists to ask about Earth's motion relative to the ether. If Earth is moving through the ether, then the speed of light should be different in different directions, just as is the case for sound in Fig. 38-1. On the other hand, Earth might be at rest relative to the ether. Because other planets, stars, and galaxies move with respect to Earth, it's hard to imagine that ether is everywhere fixed with respect to Earth alone, for this violates the Copernican view that Earth does not occupy a privileged spot in the universe. But maybe Earth drags with it the ether in its immediate vicinity. If this "ether drag" occurs, then the speed of light must be independent of direction, but if ether drag does not occur then the speed of light measured on Earth must depend on direction. Through observation and experiment, nineteenth-century physicists sought to resolve the question of Earth's motion through the ether.

Aberration of Starlight

Imagine standing in a rainstorm with rain falling vertically. To keep dry, you hold your umbrella with its shaft straight up, as shown in Fig. 38-2*a*. But if you run, as in Fig. 38-2*b*, you'll keep driest if you tilt your umbrella forward. Why? Because then the direction of rainfall *relative to you* is not straight down but at an angle, as shown in Fig. 38-2*c*. This argument presupposes that you do not drag with you a large volume of air. If such an "air drag" occurred, raindrops entering the region around you would be accelerated quickly in the horizontal direction by the air moving with you, so they would now fall vertically relative to you, as in Fig. 38-2*d*. No matter which way you ran, as long as you dragged air with you, you would point your umbrella vertically upward to stay dry.

This umbrella example is exactly analogous to the observation of light from stars, with the rain being starlight and the umbrella a telescope. If Earth does not drag ether with it, the direction from which starlight comes will depend on the motion of Earth relative to the ether. But if "ether drag" occurs in analogy with Fig. 38-2*d*, then light from a particular star will always come from the same direction.

In fact we do observe a tiny change in the direction of starlight. As Earth swings around in its orbit, we must first point a telescope one way to see a particular star. Then, six months later, Earth's orbital motion is in exactly the opposite direction, and we must point the telescope in a slightly different direction. This phenomenon is called **aberration of starlight** and shows that *Earth does not drag the ether.*

The Michelson-Morley Experiment

If we reject the pre-Copernican notion that Earth alone is at rest relative to the ether, then aberration of starlight forces us to conclude that Earth moves through the ether. Furthermore, the relative velocity of the motion must change throughout the year, as Earth orbits the Sun.

In a series of experiments done in 1881–1887, the American scientists Albert A. Michelson and Edward W. Morley attempted to determine Earth's velocity

(a)

(b)

(c)

(d)

FIGURE 38-2 (*a*) Standing still in vertically falling rain, you hold your umbrella overhead to keep dry. (*b*) Running, you tilt the umbrella to compensate for the rain's motion relative to you. (*c*) The situation of (*b*) seen from the runner's frame of reference. (*d*) If you dragged a volume of air with you, you would hold the umbrella overhead whatever your state of motion.

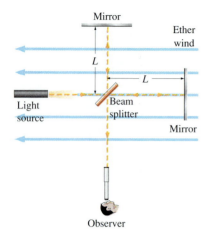

FIGURE 38-3 Simplified diagram of a Michelson interferometer. An "ether wind" blowing in the direction shown should result in a longer time for the light beam on the horizontal arm.

FIGURE 38-4 Vector diagram showing resultant velocity **u** of light moving at right angles to an ether wind with speed v. The speed of light relative to the ether is c.

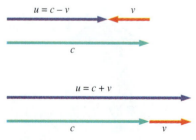

FIGURE 38-5 Vector diagrams showing the resultant velocities **u** for light moving with and against an ether wind whose speed is v.

relative to the ether. They used Michelson's interferometer (Fig. 38-3), whose operation we described in the preceding chapter. Recall that the interferometer produces a pattern of interference fringes that shifts if the round-trip travel time for light on one of its two perpendicular arms changes. The interference pattern reflects, among other things, possible differences in travel times that arise from differences in the speed of light in different directions—differences that should result from Earth's motion through the ether. Rotating the apparatus through 90° would interchange the directions of the arms and should therefore shift the interference pattern.

Now suppose that Earth moves at speed v relative to the ether. Then from the viewpoint of an observer on Earth, there is an "ether wind" blowing past Earth. Suppose that the Michelson-Morley apparatus is oriented with one light path parallel to the wind, the other perpendicular. Consider a light beam moving the distance L at right angles to the ether wind. The beam must be aimed slightly upwind, in order that it will actually move perpendicular to the wind. The light moves in this direction at speed c relative to the ether, but the ether wind sweeps it back so its path in the Michelson-Morley apparatus is at right angles to the wind. From Fig. 38-4, we see that its speed relative to the apparatus is

$$u = \sqrt{c^2 - v^2},$$

so the round-trip travel time is

$$t_{\text{perpendicular}} = \frac{2L}{u} = \frac{2L}{\sqrt{c^2 - v^2}}. \tag{38-1}$$

Light sent a distance L "upstream"—against the ether wind—travels at speed c relative to the ether but at speed $c - v$ relative to Earth. It therefore takes a time

$$t_{\text{upstream}} = \frac{L}{c - v}.$$

Returning, the light moves at $c + v$ relative to Earth, taking

$$t_{\text{downstream}} = \frac{L}{c + v}$$

(Fig. 38-5). So the round-trip time parallel to the wind is

$$t_{\text{parallel}} = \frac{L}{c - v} + \frac{L}{c + v} = \frac{2cL}{c^2 - v^2}. \tag{38-2}$$

The two round-trip travel times differ, with the trip parallel to the ether wind always taking longer (see Problems 1, 2, and 4). Light on the parallel trip is slowed when it moves against the ether wind, then speeds up when it moves with the wind. But slowing always dominates, because the light spends more time moving against the wind than with it.

The Michelson-Morley experiment of 1887 was sensitive enough to detect differences in the speed of light at least an order of magnitude smaller than Earth's orbital speed. The experiment was repeated with the apparatus oriented in different directions, and at different times throughout the year, and the same simple but striking result always emerged: there was never any difference in the travel times for the two light beams. In terms of the ether concept, the Michelson-Morley experiment showed that *Earth does not move relative to the ether.*

A Contradiction in Physics

Aberration of starlight shows that Earth does not drag ether with it. Earth must therefore move relative to the ether. But the Michelson-Morley experiment shows that it does not. This contradiction is a deep one, rooted in the fundamental laws of electromagnetism and in the analogy between mechanical waves and electromagnetic waves. The contradiction arises directly in trying to answer the simple question "with respect to what does light move at speed c?"

Physicists at the end of the nineteenth century made many ingenious attempts to resolve the dilemma of light and the ether, but their explanations were either inconsistent with experiment or lacked sound conceptual bases.

38-3 SPECIAL RELATIVITY

In 1905, at the age of 26, Albert Einstein (Fig. 38-6) proposed a theory that resolved the dilemma and at the same time altered the very foundation of physical thought. Einstein declared simply that the ether is a fiction. But then with respect to what does light move at speed c? With respect, Einstein declared, to anyone who cares to observe it. This statement is at once simple, radical, and conservative. Simple, because its meaning is clear and obvious. Anyone who measures the speed of light will get the value $c = 3.0 \times 10^8$ m/s. Radical, because it alters our commonsense notions of space and time. Conservative, because it asserts for electromagnetism what had long been true in mechanics: that the laws of physics do not depend on the motion of the observer. Einstein summarized his new ideas in the **special theory of relativity**, which is expressed in this simple sentence:

| **The laws of physics are the same in all inertial reference frames.**

Recall that inertial frames are those which are not accelerated—i.e., those in which the laws of *mechanics* were already valid. Einstein's statement encompasses *all* laws of physics, including mechanics and electromagnetism. The prediction that electromagnetic waves move at speed c must, then, be a universal prediction that holds in *all* inertial frames of reference. The *special* theory of relativity is special because it is valid only for the special case of inertial frames. Later we'll discuss the general theory of relativity, which removes this restriction.

Einstein's relativity readily explains the result of the Michelson-Morley experiment, for no matter what the speed of Earth relative to anything, an observer on Earth should measure the same speed for light in all directions. But at the same time, we will see that relativity flagrantly violates our common-sense notions of space and time.

38-4 SPACE AND TIME IN RELATIVITY

Consider a car driving past a pedestrian standing by the roadside (Fig. 38-7). Driver and pedestrian each measure the speed of the light from a blinking traffic signal. Relativity says they will get the same answer, $c = 3.0 \times 10^8$ m/s, even though the car is moving toward the source of light. How can this be? Consider how each observer might make the measurement. Let each be equipped with a

FIGURE 38-6 Albert Einstein was just 26 when he formulated the special theory of relativity.

FIGURE 38-7 As the car passes the pedestrian, a light pulse goes by. Both driver and pedestrian measure the same speed c for the light, even though they are in relative motion.

meter stick and an accurate, high-speed electronic stopwatch. Suppose that a light pulse passes the front ends of both meter sticks just as they coincide. Each observer measures the time it takes the light pulse to cross the meter stick, then divides the distance (one meter) by the measured time to get the speed of light. Since the stick on the car is moving toward the light source, common sense suggests that the light will pass the far end of this stick first, and therefore that the time on the car's stopwatch will be shorter. But this violates relativity, for if both observers use the same path length for their speed-of-light measurement, and if they get different times, then they will have measured different speeds for light. In fact, both stopwatches will read the same time, even though common sense tells us that the light passes the end of the "moving" meter stick "earlier."

How can this be? It follows logically from the statement of special relativity, which in turn is consistent with physical experiments. But how can it be? Something must be "wrong" with someone's meter stick or stopwatch. Maybe the motion of the car somehow affects the stopwatch on the car. But no: this suggestion violates the spirit of relativity, which says that steady, uniform motion is undetectable—that it makes no more sense to say that the car is moving and the pedestrian is at rest than to say the opposite. That's the whole point of relativity—any inertial reference frame is as good as any other for doing physics. So there can be nothing wrong with the clocks and meter sticks.

The only things left to go "wrong" are time and space. Time and space—the seemingly passive, universal backgrounds in which all physical events take place—must themselves depend on the observer. Two observers in different frames of reference, moving uniformly relative to each other, are measuring different quantities when they use clocks to record the passage of time and meter sticks to determine distances in space. In relativity it is the laws of physics—not measures of time and space—that must be the same for everyone. Time and space are altered in ways that allow the laws of physics, including Maxwell's theory and its prediction that light waves travel at speed c, to be the same for all observers in uniform motion.

In exploring space and time in relativity, we'll often speak of events. An **event** is an occurrence specified by giving its position—three spatial coordinates—and its time. Your birth, for example, is an event: it occurred at a certain place and a certain time, and both are needed to specify it fully.

Time Dilation

17.1
Relativity of Time

To understand how time gets altered, we'll consider the simple device shown in Fig. 38-8 (also simulated in ActivPhysics Activity 17.1), which we'll call a "light box." It consists of a box of length L with a light source at one end and a mirror at the other. A light flash leaves the source, reflects off the mirror, and returns to the source. We want to know the time interval between two distinct events: the light flash leaving the source and the flash returning to the source.

For concreteness, we'll imagine that the light box is in a spaceship moving past Earth at a uniform velocity. But don't think there's something special about space or spaceships going on here: the whole point of relativity is that all inertial frames are equivalent places for doing physics, so our spaceship is just one more inertial reference frame. We'll call that frame S'. There's also an accurate clock, C, in the spaceship, near the light source of the light box. Clock C reads zero just as the light flash is emitted.

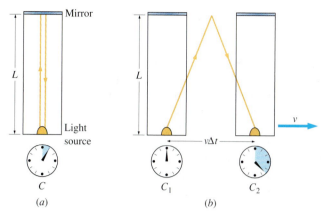

FIGURE 38-8 A "light box" provides a comparison of time intervals as measured in two different frames of reference. A light flash leaves the source, reflects off the mirror, and returns to the source. What's the time interval between emission and return of the flash? (*a*) In the reference frame in which the box is at rest—here the spaceship frame S'—the light travels a distance $2L$ at speed c. (*b*) In Earth's frame S, in which the box moves past with speed v, the light travels a greater distance. But its speed c is the same in *all* inertial frames, so the time interval is longer in this frame. Part (*b*) shows the box both when the light is emitted and again when it returns to the source.

In Fig. 38-8*a* we consider the light-box experiment viewed in the spaceship's frame of reference. Since the light box is at rest in this frame, the light travels a round-trip distance $2L$ from source to mirror and back, giving a round-trip travel time of

$$\Delta t' = \frac{2L}{c}.$$

Clearly, this is the time read on the spaceship's clock C.

Now consider the situation as viewed in Earth's frame of reference, which we'll call S. In this frame, spaceship and light clock are moving to the right with speed v, as shown in Fig. 38-8*b*. Suppose there are two clocks in Earth's frame, positioned so the light box passes clock C_1 just as the flash is emitted, and passes C_2 just as the flash returns to the source. The clocks are synchronized, and C_1 is set so it reads zero just as the light flash is emitted. What will C_2 read just as the light box passes it and the flash returns to the source? Whatever C_2 reads, that will be the time Δt between the emission and return of the light flash, as measured in the Earth frame S.

We can calculate the time interval in the Earth frame S, just as we did in the ship frame S', by figuring the total distance the light travels and dividing by its speed. Figure 38-8*b*—the situation viewed in the Earth frame S—shows that the box moves to the right a distance $v\Delta t$ in the time Δt between emission and return of the light flash. Meanwhile the light takes a diagonal path up to the mirror of the moving box, then back down to the source. The total length of this path is twice the diagonal from source to mirror, or, using the Pythagorean theorem, $2\sqrt{L^2 + (v\Delta t/2)^2}$. The time required for light to go this distance is just the distance divided by the speed of light, or

$$\Delta t = \frac{2\sqrt{L^2 + (v\Delta t/2)^2}}{c}. \tag{38-3}$$

Notice that we explicitly used relativity in writing Equation 38-3. We did not vectorially add the horizontal speed of the box to the vertical speed of light to get a new speed of light in frame S, for relativity says that the speed of light is the same in all frames of reference. Had we altered the speed, we would have had an increased path length in S, but an increased speed of light as well, and would have found that the time intervals in both frames were the same. But no! Relativity requires that we use the same speed c in both frames, even though the path lengths differ. That's why we get different answers for the time.

The unknown time Δt appears on both sides of Equation 38-3. Multiplying through by c and squaring gives

$$c^2(\Delta t)^2 = 4L^2 + v^2(\Delta t)^2.$$

We then solve for $(\Delta t)^2$ to get

$$(\Delta t)^2 = \frac{4L^2}{c^2 - v^2} = \frac{4L^2}{c^2}\left(\frac{1}{1 - v^2/c^2}\right).$$

Taking the square root of both sides, and noting that $2L/c$ is just the time $\Delta t'$ measured in the frame S' at rest with respect to the box, we have

$$\Delta t = \frac{\Delta t'}{\sqrt{1 - v^2/c^2}} \qquad \text{or} \qquad \Delta t' = \Delta t\sqrt{1 - v^2/c^2}. \qquad (38\text{-}4)$$

Equation 38-4 describes the phenomenon of **time dilation**, in which the time interval between two events is always shortest in a frame of reference in which the two events occur at the same place. In our example, the two events are the emission and return of the light flash, and they occur at the same place in the spaceship frame S', namely at the bottom of the box, which is at rest relative to the spaceship. They don't occur at the same place in the Earth frame S because the box moves relative to this frame, so the bottom of the box isn't in the same place when the light flash returns as it was when the flash was emitted. Thus $\Delta t'$—the time interval measured in the spaceship frame S', where the events occur at the same place—is shorter than Δt, as you can see from Equation 38-4 and as illustrated in Fig. 38-9.

The shorter time measured by a single clock present at two events is called a **proper time**. Here the word "proper" doesn't mean "correct" or "right"—that would violate relativity, since a time measurement in any inertial frame has equal claim to being valid. Rather, "proper" is used in the sense of "proprietary," in that proper time is the time that *belongs* to this one particular clock. In the Earth frame S there is no single clock present at both the emission and return of the light flash, so the time measurement in this frame doesn't "belong" to any one clock.

Time dilation is sometimes characterized as saying that "moving clocks run slow," but this statement violates the spirit of relativity because it suggests that some frames are "really" moving and others not. The whole point of relativity is that all inertial frames are equally good for describing physical reality, so none can claim to be "at rest" while others are "moving." What the statement "moving clocks run slow" is trying to convey is what we've just seen: that the time interval between two events is shortest in a reference frame where the two

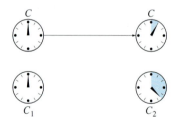

FIGURE 38-9 Clock C moves between clocks C_1 and C_2, which are at rest relative to each other and synchronized in their rest frame. Time between the event of C passing C_1 and the event of C passing C_2 is shorter in C's frame of reference.

occur at the same place. There's no significance whatever to our putting the light clock in a "moving" spaceship and comparing its time with Earth time. We could equally well have put the light box and its clock on Earth, and two separate clocks in the ship frame. Then Earth with its light box would be moving past the ship at speed v—so the Earth clock would measure the time $\Delta t'$ in Equation 38-4, and the two clocks in the ship frame would measure the longer time Δt. (That may sound like a contradiction, but it can't be because *there's nothing special about any inertial frame, including Earth's*. We'll return to this point in a few pages.)

We used a special "light box" to illustrate time dilation. But time dilation isn't something that happens only when we use light to determine time intervals. It's something that happens to time itself. Take away the light box in Fig. 38-8, and the clocks will show the same discrepancy. There's no use looking for a physical mechanism that slows things down. All manifestations of time—the oscillations of the quartz crystal in a digital watch, the swing of a pendulum clock, the period of vibration of atoms in an atomic clock, biological rhythms, and human lifetimes—all are affected in the same way.

EXAMPLE 38-1	*Star Trek*

A spaceship leaves Earth on a one-way trip that Earthbound observers judge will take 25 years. If the ship travels at $0.95c$ relative to Earth, how long is the journey as measured by a clock on board the ship?

Solution

The spaceship is like the light box we used in deriving Equation 38-4 for time dilation, in that in its frame the beginning and end of the journey occur at the same place—namely, on the ship. So the time interval on the ship clock is the $\Delta t'$ of Equation 38-4. For the observers on Earth, the beginning and end of the journey occur at different places, so their 25-year time interval is Δt. Applying Equation 38-4 then gives

$$\Delta t' = \Delta t \sqrt{1 - v^2/c^2} = (25 \text{ y})(\sqrt{1 - (0.95c)^2/c^2})$$

$$= 7.8 \text{ y}.$$

Thus at this high relative speed, the ship's time is considerably shorter. We'll soon explore what happens if the ship turns around and returns to Earth.

EXERCISE An extraterrestrial spacecraft whizzes through the solar system at $0.80c$. How long does it take to go the 8.3 light-minute distance from Earth to the Sun (a) according to an observer on Earth and (b) according to an alien aboard the ship?

Answers: (a) 10.4 min; (b) 6.23 min

Some problems similar to Example 38-1: 7, 8, 16

Why don't we notice time dilation as we travel about in our everyday lives? Because the factor v^2/c^2 in Equation 38-4 is so small for any velocities we have relative to Earth. Even in a jet airplane, we're moving at 1000 km/h or only about $10^{-6} c$. Then time in the airplane is different from that on Earth by only about 1 part in $(10^6)^2$, which amounts to a few milliseconds per century. This illustrates an important point: any results predicted by relativity should agree with our common sense, Newtonian ideas when relative velocities are small compared with the speed of light. Only at substantial fractions of c do relativistic effects become obvious. Since our intuitions and common sense are built on experience at low relative velocities, it's not surprising that effects at high velocities seem counter to common sense.

Time dilation is dramatically obvious in experiments with sub-atomic particles moving, relative to us, at speeds near that of light. In a classic experiment, the "clocks" are the lifetimes of unstable particles called muons, which are created by the inter-action of cosmic rays with Earth's upper atmosphere. The experiment consists in counting the number of muons incident each hour on the top of a mountain—Mt. Washington in New Hampshire, about 2000 m above sea level. The measurement is then repeated at sea level (Fig. 38-10).

Using a detector that records only those muons moving at about 0.994c at the mountaintop altitude, the experiment shows an average of about 560 muons with this speed are incident on the mountaintop each hour. If the mountain weren't there, the muons would travel from the mountaintop altitude to sea level in a time given by

$$\Delta t = \frac{2000 \text{ m}}{(0.994)(3.0 \times 10^8 \text{ m/s})} = 6.7 \ \mu\text{s} .$$

The muon's decay rate is such that one should expect only about 25 of the original 560 muons to remain after this 6.7-μs interval, so that's approximately the number we might expect to detect each hour at sea level. More muons would survive a short-er time interval; in particular, we should expect 414 muons surviving 0.73 μs after passing the mountaintop altitude.

Why the value 0.73 μs? Because the muons are moving at 0.994c, and the 6.7-μs interval from mountaintop to sea level is measured in Earth's frame of reference—not in the muons' frame. In the muons' frame, time dilation should reduce that interval to

$$\Delta t' = \Delta t \sqrt{1 - v^2/c^2} = (6.7 \ \mu\text{s})(\sqrt{1 - 0.994^2})$$
$$= 0.73 \ \mu\text{s} .$$

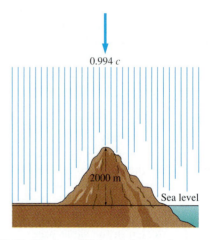

FIGURE 38-10 The flux of high-speed muons is measured on a mountaintop and again at sea level. The muons decay at such a rate that only a small fraction of those incident at the mountaintop altitude should survive to reach sea level. But the number measured at sea level is much larger, showing the effect of time dilation on muon lifetimes.

Since the muons' decay is determined by *their* measure of time, we should therefore expect 414 muons surviving at sea level.

So what happens? When the experiment is done, muon counts of just over 400 per hour are observed at sea level. This is no subtle effect! The difference between 25 and 414 is dra-matic. At 0.994c, the nonrelativistic description is hopelessly inadequate. At this speed, the factor $\sqrt{1 - v^2/c^2}$ is one-ninth, and time dilation is obvious.

The Twin Paradox

The phenomenon of time dilation has startling consequences, for it allows us to travel into the future! The famous "twin paradox" illustrates this possibility. One of two twins boards a fast spaceship for a journey to a distant star (Fig. 38-11). The other stays behind on Earth. Imagine that there are clocks at Earth and star, like the two clocks in frame *S* of our light-box experiment (Fig. 38-12a). There is a clock on the spaceship, like the one clock in our light-box frame *S'*. When the ship arrives at the distant star, less time will have elapsed on the ship clock than on the Earth and star clocks (Fig. 38-12b). Now the ship turns around and comes home. Again, the situation is identical to our light-box example, so again

FIGURE 38-11 At departure, the twins are the same age.

FIGURE 38-12 The traveling twin journeys to a distant star, then returns. Earth and star are at rest with respect to each other, and their clocks are synchronized. The figure is drawn from the Earth-star frame of reference. (*a*) Ship and Earth clocks agree as the ship leaves Earth. (*b*) When the ship reaches the star, less time has elapsed on its clock. (*c*) When the ship returns to Earth, its clock and Earth's no longer agree.

less time elapses on the ship clock, and the traveling twin arrives home younger than the earthbound twin (Fig. 38-13)! Depending on how far and how fast the traveling twin goes, the difference in ages could be arbitrarily large. The traveling twin could even return to Earth millions of years in the future, even though only hours had elapsed on the ship. But this is a one-way trip to the future! If the traveler doesn't like what he or she finds in the future, there's no going back!

FIGURE 38-13 It's not only clock readings, but all manifestations of time that differ. The traveling twin really has aged less!

EXAMPLE 38-2	*The Twin Paradox*

Earth and a star are 10 light-years (ly) apart, measured in a frame at rest with respect to Earth and star. Twin A boards a space ship and travels at 0.80*c* to the star, then immediately turns around and returns to Earth at 0.80*c*. Twin B remains behind. Determine the round-trip travel time in the Earth-star frame of reference and in the ship frame. By how much will the twins' ages differ when they get back together?

Solution

At 0.80*c*, the time to go 10 ly in the Earth-star frame is just

$$\Delta t = \frac{10 \text{ ly}}{0.80 \text{ ly/y}} = 12.5 \text{ y}.$$

The round-trip time is then 25 y. Equation 38-4 for $\Delta t'$ then gives the one-way travel time in the ship frame:

$$\Delta t' = \Delta t \sqrt{1 - v^2/c^2} = (12.5 \text{ y})(\sqrt{1 - 0.80^2}) = 7.5 \text{ y}.$$

Then the round-trip time in the ship frame is 15 y, so the twins' ages differ by 10 y when twin A returns.

Tip

Years, Light-Years, and the Speed of Light A light-year (ly) is the distance light travels in one year. By definition, therefore, the speed of light is 1 ly/y. It's often easiest in relativity to work in units where the speed of light is 1, whether those units be light-years and years, light-seconds and seconds, or whatever.

EXERCISE A spacecraft makes a round trip to a point a distance ℓ from Earth, as measured in Earth's frame of reference. The ship travels at 60% of the speed of light. If the round trip takes 1 hour by the ship's clock, (a) what is the distance ℓ and (b) how much time elapses on Earth between the ship's departure and its return?

Answers: (a) 0.375 light-hours (4×10^{11} m); (b) 1.25 h

Some problems similar to Example 38-2: 7, 9, 14, 15

This example of the twins is certainly unusual—but why is it a paradox? Consider the situation from the spaceship's reference frame. Doesn't the ship see Earth recede into the distance, turn around, and come back? And then shouldn't the earthbound twin be younger? This is the paradox. It's resolved by recognizing what's *special* about special relativity—namely that it applies only in inertial reference frames. The traveling twin must accelerate in order to return to Earth, and is therefore briefly in a noninertial reference frame. Although relativity precludes us saying that one twin is moving and the other is not, we can say that one twin's motion *changes* and the other's doesn't. This is obvious to the traveling twin, who experiences forces when the ship accelerates in turning around. But, of course, the earthbound twin doesn't feel anything unusual when the ship turns around. It isn't that all the unusual effects are crowded into the brief time during which the ship turns around; rather, it's that the ship on its round-trip journey occupies two distinct inertial reference frames, separated by that brief acceleration, while Earth remains in just one inertial frame. There's an asymmetry between the two twins, so there's no paradox.

Could it really happen? It could, and it has. Atomic clocks are now so accurate that experiments have been done to detect the minuscule time difference between a clock flown around the Earth and one left behind.

What if the traveling twin did not turn around? We could still argue that the ship clock runs slower than clocks on Earth and the star. But then isn't the situation symmetric? Couldn't the traveling twin argue that a clock on Earth should run slower than clocks on the ship? Yes—and we would find this to be true if we set up a series of clocks in the ship frame and measured time intervals on the Earth clock as Earth passed first one, then another of the ship clocks. But there's no contradiction. Unless the twins get together again, there is no way they can directly compare their clocks or their ages at the same place. Instead, they must compare one clock with a sequence of clocks that are all synchronized. And as we will soon see, clocks that are synchronized in one frame of reference are not synchronized in another frame! Only if the twins get back together can they compare just two clocks without having to worry about synchronization of distant clocks. And they can get back together only if at least one of them accelerates.

Got It!

Twins board their spaceships and head away from Earth in different directions, each traveling at the same high speed for the same distance. They turn around and head back, again at the same speed, and arrive at Earth together. How do their ages compare? Reconsider for the case where one twin travels twice as far, but goes twice as fast so that they still arrive home together.

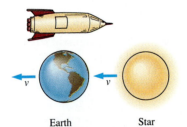

FIGURE 38-14 Earth-star trip viewed from the spaceship's frame of reference. Note that Earth-star distance is contracted, and the ship lengthened, relative to Fig. 38-12, which is drawn from the Earth-star frame.

Length Contraction

In Example 38-2 the spaceship moved 10 ly in 12.5 y at speed $0.80c$. These quantities are related by the simple expression $\Delta x = v \Delta t$, where Δx is the distance between Earth and star *measured in the Earth-star frame of reference S*. Now an observer in the ship frame of reference S' sees Earth and star moving past at speed v. First Earth passes the ship, then the star passes (Fig. 38-14). We found that the time interval between these two events, measured in the ship frame, is $\Delta t' = \Delta t \sqrt{1 - v^2/c^2} = 7.5$ y. Since Earth and star are moving past at $v = 0.80\,c$, the distance between Earth and star as measured in the ship frame must be

17.2
Relativity of Length

$$\Delta x' = v\,\Delta t' = v\,\Delta t\,\sqrt{1 - v^2/c^2} = \Delta x\,\sqrt{1 - v^2/c^2}, \qquad (38\text{-}5)$$

or 6.0 ly in our example. This equation shows that the distance between two points is always greatest in a frame (the Earth-star frame S, in this example) fixed with respect to those points. In any other frame the distance is smaller. This phenomenon of **length contraction** is also called **Lorentz contraction**, or Lorentz-Fitzgerald contraction, after the Dutch physicist H. A. Lorentz and the Irish physicist George F. Fitzgerald. In the 1890s, each independently proposed it as an ad hoc way of explaining the Michelson-Morley experiment. Only through Einstein's theory did the contraction acquire a solid conceptual basis.

Although we developed the Lorentz contraction using the distance between separate objects—Earth and a distant star—the effect occurs for any observer moving with respect to two fixed points. In particular, a rigid object like a meter stick or spaceship is shorter when measured by an observer with respect to whom it's moving. An object's length measured in a frame in which it's at rest is called its **proper length**; again, as with proper time, the word "proper" is used in the sense of being proprietary to that object. Proper length isn't the "right" or "real" length because a measurement made in any inertial frame has equal claim to be valid—and as length contraction shows, measurements made in different inertial frames yield different values for length.

As with time dilation, don't look for some physical mechanism that squashes moving objects. Rather, it is space itself that's different for different observers. In order to accept the simple fact that absolute motion is meaningless, we must alter our common-sense notions of time and space. Lorentz contraction and time dilation are manifestations of that alteration.

| **EXAMPLE 38-3** | *A Stanford Electron* |

At the Stanford Linear Accelerator Center (SLAC) (Fig. 38-15), subatomic particles are accelerated to high energies over a straight path whose proper length is 3.2 km. During a particular experiment, electrons are accelerated to 0.9999995 of the speed of light. In the SLAC frame, how long would it take electrons with this speed to travel the full length of the device? How long would the trip take in the rest frame of the electrons? How long would the accelerator be in the rest frame of the electrons?

Solution

The electron speed is so close to that of light that the travel time is, to a very good approximation,

$$\Delta t = \frac{\Delta x}{c} = \frac{3.2 \times 10^3 \text{ m}}{3.0 \times 10^8 \text{ m/s}} = 1.1 \times 10^{-5} \text{ s}.$$

FIGURE 38-15 The Stanford Linear Accelerator is 3.2 km (2 miles) long. But to electrons moving through it at $0.999\,999\,5c$, the accelerator is only 3.2 m long.

In the rest frame of the electrons, the time to traverse the accelerator is given by Equation 38-4, or

$$\Delta t' = \Delta t \sqrt{1 - v^2/c^2} = (1.1 \times 10^{-5} \text{ s})\sqrt{1 - 0.9999995^2}$$

$$= (1.1 \times 10^{-5} \text{ s})(1.0 \times 10^{-3}) = 1.1 \times 10^{-8} \text{ s} .$$

Our time calculation shows that the relativistic factor $\sqrt{1 - v^2/c^2}$ is 10^{-3}, so in the electron frame of reference the accelerator length is

$$\Delta x' = \Delta x \sqrt{1 - v^2/c^2} = 3.2 \times 10^{-3} \text{ km} = 3.2 \text{ m} .$$

EXAMPLE 38-4	*A Stanford Student*

A physics student from New York flies to San Francisco to do an experiment at SLAC. She travels a distance of 4800 km on a plane going at 1000 km/h. How long does the trip take in a frame at rest with respect to Earth? How long does it take according to the student's watch? How far is it from New York to San Francisco in the airplane's frame of reference?

Solution

At 1000 km/h, the 4800-km trip takes

$$\Delta t = \frac{\Delta x}{v} = \frac{4800 \text{ km}}{1000 \text{ km/h}} = 4.8 \text{ hours} .$$

In the frame of the moving airplane, time and distance are altered by the relativistic factor $\sqrt{1 - v^2/c^2}$. The speed of the plane is 1000 km/h, or 278 m/s, so

$$\sqrt{1 - v^2/c^2} = \left[1 - \frac{(278 \text{ m/s})^2}{(3.0 \times 10^8 \text{ m/s})^2} \right]^{1/2}$$

$$\simeq 1 - (\tfrac{1}{2})(8.6 \times 10^{-13}) = 0.99999999999957 .$$

Here we used the binomial theorem, $(1 + x)^n \simeq 1 + nx$ for $|nx| \ll 1$ because most calculators don't carry enough significant figures to distinguish the result from 1 (see Appendix A). We really need not carry the calculation further. The time on the student's watch is the same as the time on the ground to about five parts in 10^{13}, and the distance in the plane's frame is the same as the ground distance to within this same factor. The student need take no account of time dilation and Lorentz contraction, except in a physics exam or high-energy experiment!

EXERCISE Our Milky Way galaxy is about 100,000 light-years in diameter. What is its diameter as measured by an intergalactic spacecraft traveling at 0.96c?

Answer: 28,000 ly

Some problems similar to Examples 38-3 and 38-4: 6, 11, 12

Examples 38-3 and 38-4 show that relativistic effects are significant only at high relative velocities—so high that the quantity v^2/c^2 is comparable with 1. In our daily lives we have no experience with such velocities. It is for this reason that relativity so offends our common-sense notions of space and time. Those notions are built on a groundwork of limited experience that does not include high velocities. If we did move regularly with respect to our surroundings at speeds near that of light, the relativity of space and time would be as obvious as our common-sense notions now seem.

For physicists working with high-energy elementary particles, relativistic effects *are* obvious. Unstable particles moving through the laboratory at high speeds live longer than they would at rest in the lab. And high-energy particle accelerators would not work if their design did not take relativity into account.

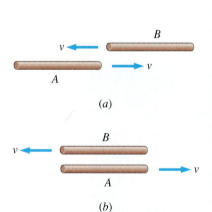

FIGURE 38-16 (*a*) In frame *S*, both sticks have the same speed *v* and both are contracted by the same amount. (*b*) Therefore their ends coincide at the same time.

Events and Simultaneity

Consider two identical sticks *A* and *B*, each of proper length *L*. Suppose these sticks are moving toward each other. For a frame of reference *S* in which both sticks are moving at the same speed *v*, the situation is shown in Fig. 38-16. Both sticks are Lorentz contracted, but since both are moving at the same speed *v* relative to the frame *S*, both are contracted by the same amount and therefore have the same length. What happens as the sticks pass each other? First, the

FIGURE 38-17 The passing sticks viewed in a frame S' at rest with respect to stick A. Relative speed is greater than the speed of either stick with respect to frame S. (a) First the left end of stick B passes the right end of A. (b) A while later, the right end of B passes the right end of A. This is event E_1. (c) Still later, the left end of B passes the left end of A. This is event E_2. Events E_1 and E_2 are not simultaneous in frame S'.

FIGURE 38-18 The passing sticks viewed in a frame of reference S'' at rest with respect to stick B. (a) First the right end of stick A passes the left end of B. (b) A while later, the left end of A passes the left end of B. This is event E_2. (c) Still later, the right end of A passes the right end of B. This is event E_1. The events E_1 and E_2 are not simultaneous in S'', and their time order is opposite what it was in S'.

right end of stick A and the left end of stick B pass (Fig. 38-16a). A little while later, the right end of A passes the right end of B. At the same time, *because the sticks have the same length in S*, the left end of A passes the left end of B (Fig. 38-16b). The passing of the two right ends of the sticks is an event that we designate E_1. Similarly, the passing of the two left ends we designate E_2. We have shown that, in the frame S, the two events E_1 and E_2 are **simultaneous**—they occur at the same time.

Now look at the situation from a frame of reference S' in which stick A is at rest. In this frame, stick B moves toward stick A. Since we are in S', we are at rest relative to stick A, and it has its proper length L. But stick B is contracted more than in frame S because of its higher relative velocity. The situation is shown in Fig. 38-17. As the figure indicates, the event E_1 occurs before E_2; the two events are not simultaneous in the frame S'. What happens in a frame S'' at rest with stick B? As Fig. 38-18 shows, the events E_1 and E_2 are again not simultaneous, and this time event E_2 occurs first.

Isn't this all just an illusion arising from the apparent length differences due to motion of the sticks? Isn't the picture in frame S (Fig. 38-16) "really" the right one? No! Relativity assures us that all inertial frames—including the frames S, S', and S'' of Figs. 38-16 through 38-18—are equally valid for describing physical reality. The length differences and the changes in time ordering of events E_1 and E_2 are not "apparent" and they are not "illusions." They arise from valid descriptions in different frames of reference, and each has equal claim to "reality." If you insist that one of the frames—say S—somehow has more validity, then you're reasserting the nineteenth-century notion that there is one favored reference frame in which alone the laws of physics are valid.

But how can observers disagree on the time order of events? Doesn't that violate causality? After all, if one event is a cause of another, we certainly expect the cause to precede the effect. It would be disturbing if some observer, with valid claim on "reality," found that cause and effect occurred in the reverse order. But there's no violation of causality. As we will soon show, the only events that can have their time order reversed are those that are so far apart in space, and so close in time, that not even light can travel fast enough to be at both events. There is no way that such events can influence each other, and therefore they can't be causally related. In a very real sense it doesn't matter which event occurs first, and indeed different observers will disagree on their relative time order. For example, an event on Earth now and another occurring five minutes from now on the Sun can't be causally related, since it takes light from the Sun eight minutes to reach Earth. For observers moving at high enough speeds relative to Earth and Sun, the solar event occurs first.

Only when events are close enough in space and separated enough in time so that light can travel from one to the other can the two be causally related. In that case, all observers will agree about their time order, although they may disagree about the actual time interval between the events. For example, an event on Earth now and another occurring fifteen minutes from now on the Sun could be causally related, and therefore all observers will agree that the terrestrial event occurs first. We'll explore these notions more quantitatively in the next section.

The Lorentz Transformations

Our demonstration that the time order of events may be relative deals implicitly with the coordinates—position and time—of specific events, and suggests that those coordinates may differ for different observers. Similarly, time dilation and length contraction arise as specific instances of the way positions and times in one frame of reference are related to their values in another frame. We now seek more general expressions—called **Lorentz transformations**—relating the space and time coordinates of an event in two frames of reference in relative motion. Consider coordinate axes in a frame of reference S and in another frame S' moving in the x direction with speed v relative to S. Suppose that the origins of the two coordinate systems coincide at time $t = t' = 0$. If an event has coordinates x, y, z, and t in S, what are its coordinates x', y', z', and t' in S'? Were it not for relativity, we would expect the coordinates y, z, and the time t to remain unchanged from one coordinate system to the other. For an event occurring at time $t = 0$, when the two origins coincide, we would expect the x coordinates to be the same too. But as S' moves in the positive x direction relative to S, a given x value in S would correspond to a value $x' = x - vt$ in S' (Fig. 38-19).

FIGURE 38-19 Nonrelativistic picture of two coordinate axes in relative motion. The x axis of frame S' moves to the right with speed v relative to S. At time $t = 0$ the two axes coincided. At a later time the x coordinates are related by $x' = x - vt$. Here $v = 1$ m/s, and the figure shows the two axes at $t = 2$ s.

How does relativity alter this coordinate transformation? Because of length contraction, we expect that the simple expression $x' = x - vt$ will need modification to be consistent with relativity. Any new expression we develop, however, must reduce to the nonrelativistic expression $x' = x - vt$ in the limit when $v \ll c$. A simple form that has this property is

$$x' = \gamma(x - vt), \tag{38-6}$$

where γ depends on the relative speed v. We could also transform the other way. The only difference is the direction of relative motion; frame S' is moving in the positive x direction relative to S, while S is moving in the negative x direction relative to S'. Therefore, the transformation from x' and t' to x should look like Equation 38-6 except with v replaced by $-v$:

$$x = \gamma(x' + vt'). \tag{38-7}$$

To see if we can make Equations 38-6 and 38-7 consistent with relativity, we impose the requirement that the speed of light be the same in both frames of reference. Suppose that a light flash goes off at the origin $x = 0$ at time $t = 0$. Since the origins of our frames coincide at this time, and since clocks at the origin in S and S' both read zero when the origins coincide, the light flash also occurs at $x' = 0$ and $t' = 0$ in frame S'. Call this event—the emission of the light flash—event E_1. Some time later, an observer at some position x in S observes the light flash. Call this event E_2. When does E_2 occur? Since light travels at speed c, we must have $x = ct$. Now in frame S' event E_2 has some coordinates x' and t'. But relativity requires that the speed of light in S' also be c, so we must have $x' = ct'$. Substituting $x = ct$ and $x' = ct'$ into Equations 38-6 and 38-7 gives

$$ct' = \gamma(ct - vt) = \gamma t(c - v)$$

and
$$ct = \gamma(ct' + vt') = \gamma t'(c + v).$$

Multiplying together the left-hand sides of these equations, and then the right-hand sides, and equating the results gives

$$c^2 t't = \gamma^2 tt'(c - v)(c + v),$$

so
$$c^2 = \gamma^2(c^2 - v^2),$$

or
$$\gamma = \frac{1}{\sqrt{1 - v^2/c^2}}. \tag{38-8}$$

That we could find a value of γ depending on the relative velocity but not on the coordinates shows that our guess for the form of the transformation equations was correct. Equations 38-6 and 38-7, with γ given by Equation 38-8, are the relativistically correct transformations for the coordinates x and x'. Taking $v \ll c$ in Equation 38-8 shows that $\gamma \to 1$ in this limit, so our transformation equations correctly reduce to the nonrelativistic result at low relative velocities.

What about the y and z coordinates? They're measured at right angles to the relative motion, so there's no length contraction involved, and thus we have

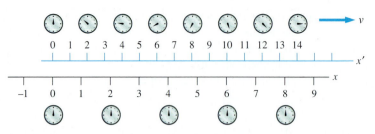

FIGURE 38-20 As measured in frame S, lengths in S' are contracted and the clocks in S' are not synchronized.

simply $y' = y$ and $z' = z$. But the fourth coordinate—time—*does* transform. You can find the time transformation by solving Equations 38-6 and 38-7 simultaneously for t' and t (see Problem 25). The result is

$$t' = \gamma\left(t - \frac{vx}{c^2}\right) \tag{38-9}$$

and

$$t = \gamma\left(t' + \frac{vx'}{c^2}\right). \tag{38-10}$$

Because we know about time dilation, we should not be too surprised to find that measures of time differ between the two frames of reference. But why should the time in one frame depend not only on the time in the other frame but also on location in space? Because, as we have found, events that are simultaneous in one frame of reference are not simultaneous in a frame of reference moving relative to the first. In this case, our simultaneous events are the pointing of all clock hands to the same time. For the clocks in S', these events are simultaneous in S'. But they are not simultaneous in S. In fact, as Equation 38-9 shows, clocks that are farther to the right in S' read successively earlier times (Fig. 38-20). The term vx/c^2 in Equation 38-9 and its analog in Equation 38-10 account for this nonsynchronism of clocks in one frame as measured from the other frame.

Our earlier qualitative discussion of simultaneity can be made quantitative using the Lorentz transformations, as Example 38-5 and Problems 22 to 24 illustrate. Similarly, applying the Lorentz transformations to the coordinates describing the emission and return of the light flash in our light-box example results in a derivation of time dilation (see Problem 26). Table 38-1 summarizes the Lorentz transformations between coordinates in frames S and S', where S' is moving at speed v in the positive x direction relative to S.

TABLE 38-1 *The Lorentz Transformations*

S TO S'	**S' TO S**
$y' = y$	$y = y'$
$z' = z$	$z = z'$
$x' = \gamma(x - vt)$	$x = \gamma(x' + vt')$
$t' = \gamma(t - vx/c^2)$	$t = \gamma(t' + vx'/c^2)$

$$\text{where } \gamma = \frac{1}{\sqrt{1 - v^2/c^2}}$$

EXAMPLE 38-5	*Galactic Fireworks*

Solution

Our Milky Way galaxy and the Andromeda galaxy are approximately at rest with respect to each other and are 2.0×10^6 light-years apart. At time $t = 0$ in the reference frame of these two galaxies, supernova explosions occur in both galaxies. Are these explosions simultaneous to the pilot of a spacecraft traveling at $0.80c$ from the Milky Way toward Andromeda? If not, what is the time interval between them, as measured in the spacecraft frame? Find also the spatial interval between the two explosions in the spacecraft frame.

The supernova explosions constitute two distinct events, and we're interested in their coordinates in the spaceship's frame of reference. Let the origin of the galaxy frame S be at the supernova in the Milky Way, and let the x axes of the galaxy frame S and spacecraft frame S' lie on the line connecting the two supernovae. Let the two frames coincide at time $t = t' = 0$. Then the space and time coordinates in S of the two supernova explosions are $x_1 = 0, t_1 = 0, x_2 = 2.0 \text{ Mly}, t_2 = 0$. Similarly, the coordinates of the Milky Way explosion in the spacecraft frame S' are $x_1' = 0, t_1' = 0$. We seek the coordinates x_2' and t_2' of the Andromeda explosion in S'.

Referring to Table 38-1, we first calculate the relativistic factor γ:

$$\gamma = \frac{1}{\sqrt{1 - v^2/c^2}} = \frac{1}{\sqrt{1 - 0.80^2}} = 1.67.$$

Then using the Lorentz transformations, we have
$$t_2' = \gamma(t_2 - vx_2/c^2)$$
$$= (1.67)\left[0 \text{ y} - \frac{(0.80 \text{ ly/y})(2.0 \text{ Mly})}{(1 \text{ ly/y})^2}\right] = -2.7 \text{ My}.$$
and $x_2' = \gamma(x_2 - vt_2) = (1.67)[2.0 \text{ Mly} - (0.80 \text{ ly/y})(0 \text{ ly})]$
$$= 3.3 \text{ Mly}.$$

Do these results make sense? In the spacecraft frame, the Andromeda supernova occurs nearly three million years before the Milky Way supernova! (The minus sign tells us that t_2' is earlier than the time $t_1' = 0$ of the Milky Way supernova.) Here is an example of events that are simultaneous in one frame but not in another. To make matters worse, consider an observer moving at $0.80c$ from Andromeda toward the Milky Way. For an observer in this frame, we reverse the sign of v in the transformation equations, obtaining a time of $+2.7$ million years. For this observer, the Milky Way supernova occurs first! How can this be? There's no contradiction, and no violation of cause and effect. In the spaceship's frame S' the two supernova events occur 3.3 Mly apart in space but only 2.7 My apart in time. Light from the "earlier" event cannot travel to the "later" event, so there can't be any causal influence between the two. It really doesn't matter which occurs first, and indeed which does depends on the observer.

Had we considered supernova events occurring not simultaneously but a long time apart—longer than 2 million years—in the galaxy frame of reference, we would find that all observers would agree on the time order of the two events, although not necessarily on the actual value of the time interval (see Problems 22 to 24).

EXERCISE Coordinate system S' is moving along the x axis of system S at $0.90c$. The two origins coincide when clocks in both systems read noon. An event occurs at $x = 5.0$ light-hours, $t = 3$ P.M. in frame S. Find the position and time of this event in S'.

Answers: 5.28 lh, 8:34 A.M.

Some problems similar to Example 38-5: 21–23, 53, 54

Relativistic Velocity Addition

If you're in an airplane moving at 1000 km/h relative to the ground and you walk toward the front of the plane at 5 km/h, common sense suggests that you move at 1005 km/h relative to the ground. But relativity implies that measures of time and distance vary among frames of reference in relative motion. For this reason the velocity of an object with respect to one frame does not simply add to the relative velocity between frames to give the object's velocity with respect to another frame. In the airplane your speed with respect to the ground is actually a little less than 1005 km/h as you stroll down the aisle of the plane, though the difference is insignificant at such a low speed.

The correct expression for **relativistic velocity addition** follows from the Lorentz transformations. Consider a frame of reference S and another frame S' moving in the positive x direction with speed v relative to S. Let their origins coincide at time $t = t' = 0$, so the Lorentz transformations of Table 38-1 apply.

Suppose an object moves with velocity u' along the x' axis in S'. In our airplane example, S' would be the airplane frame of reference, u' the velocity at which you walk through the plane, and v the velocity of the plane relative to the ground, or S frame. We seek the velocity u of the object relative to the frame S (that is, your velocity relative to the ground as you walk in the plane).

In either frame, velocity is the ratio of change in position to change in time, or

$$u = \frac{\Delta x}{\Delta t}.$$

Designating the beginning of the interval Δt by the subscript 1 and the end by 2, we can use Equations 38-7 and 38-10 to write

$$\Delta x = x_2 - x_1 = \gamma[(x_2' - x_1') + v(t_2' - t_1')] = \gamma(\Delta x' + v\,\Delta t')$$

and

$$\Delta t = t_2 - t_1 = \gamma[(t_2' - t_1') + v(x_2' - x_1')/c^2] = \gamma(\Delta t' + v\,\Delta x'/c^2).$$

Forming the ratio of these quantities, we have

$$\frac{\Delta x}{\Delta t} = \frac{\Delta x' + v\,\Delta t'}{\Delta t' + v\,\Delta x'/c^2} = \frac{(\Delta x'/\Delta t') + v}{1 + v(\Delta x'/\Delta t')/c^2}.$$

But $\Delta x'/\Delta t'$ is the velocity u' of the object in frame S', and $\Delta x/\Delta t$ is the velocity u, so

$$u = \frac{u' + v}{1 + u'v/c^2}. \tag{38-11}$$

The numerator of this expression is just what we would expect from common sense. But this simple sum of two velocities is altered by the second term in the denominator, which is significant only when both the object's velocity u' and the relative velocity v between frames are comparable with c. Solving Equation 38-11 for u' in terms of u, v, and c gives the inverse transformation:

$$u' = \frac{u - v}{1 - uv/c^2}. \tag{38-12}$$

EXAMPLE 38-6	*Collision Course!*

Two spacecraft approach Earth from opposite directions, each moving at $0.80c$ relative to Earth, as shown in Fig. 38-21. How fast do the spacecraft move relative to each other?

Solution

Call the Earth frame of reference S', and let S be the frame of spacecraft A. Then S' is moving at speed $v = 0.80c$ relative to S, while spacecraft B is moving at $u' = 0.80c$ relative to S'. Then the velocity of B relative to A is given by Equation 38-11:

$$u = \frac{u' + v}{1 + u'v/c^2} = \frac{0.80c + 0.80c}{1 + (0.80c)(0.80c)/c^2} = \frac{1.6c}{1.64} = 0.98c.$$

The relative speed remains less than the speed of light. This result is quite general: Equations 38-11 and 38-12 imply that as long as an object moves at a speed $v < c$ relative to some frame of reference, its speed relative to any other frame of reference will also be less than c (see Problem 20).

FIGURE 38-21 (a) Two spaceships approaching Earth at $0.80c$. (b) The situation in the frame of reference of the left-hand spaceship. Note changes in lengths of the ships and Earth.

EXAMPLE 38-7	*Catch That Light*

A light wave moves past Earth at the speed of light c. You try to chase the light wave by hopping on a fast spacecraft, moving at $0.95c$ relative to Earth. What is the speed of the light relative to the spacecraft?

Solution

Call the Earth frame S, so $u = c$, and the spacecraft frame S', so $v = 0.95c$. Then u', the speed of light relative to the spacecraft, is given by Equation 38-12:

$$u' = \frac{u - v}{1 - uv/c^2} = \frac{c - 0.95c}{1 - 0.95c^2/c^2} = \frac{0.05c}{0.05} = c.$$

We really didn't need to calculate this result, since a fundamental premise of relativity is that the speed of light is the same for all observers. The equations of relativistic velocity addition reflect this basic fact. No matter what the relative velocity v between two frames, light moving at c in one frame moves at c in any other frame. You cannot even begin to catch up with light!

EXERCISE A spacecraft whizzes by Planet X at $0.75c$, in excess of the Galactic Federation speed limit. A space cop takes off from Planet X at $0.90c$ relative to the planet. Find the relative speed of cop and speeder.

Answer: $0.46c$

Some problems similar to Examples 38-6 and 38-7: 17–19

Got It!

You're driving down the highway, and your speedometer reads exactly 30 km/h. A car passes you, going in the same direction at exactly 20 km/h relative to you. Does its speedometer—which measures the car's speed relative to the road—read more or less than 50 km/h?

38-5 ENERGY AND MOMENTUM IN RELATIVITY

Conservation of momentum and conservation of energy are cornerstones of Newtonian mechanics, where they hold in any inertial—i.e., uniformly moving—frame of reference. But both the momentum and energy of a particle are functions of its velocity, and we've just seen that relativity alters the Newtonian picture of how velocities transform from one reference frame to another. How, then, can momentum and energy be conserved in all frames of reference?

Momentum

Conservation of momentum is a cornerstone of mechanics, and, for consistency with relativity, we should hope that momentum conservation would hold in all inertial reference frames. In Newtonian mechanics the momentum of a particle with mass m and velocity $\mathbf{u}$ is $m\mathbf{u}$. (Here we use $\mathbf{u}$ for particle velocities, reserving $\mathbf{v}$ for the relative velocity between two reference frames.) But if a system's momentum—the sum of its individual particles' momenta $m\mathbf{u}$—is conserved in one frame of reference, then relativistic velocity addition suggests that it won't be conserved in another. The problem here lies not with momentum conservation but with the Newtonian expression for momentum. The expression $m\mathbf{u}$ is actually an approximation valid only for speeds u much less than c. The measure of momentum valid at any speed is

$$\mathbf{p} = \frac{m\mathbf{u}}{\sqrt{1 - u^2/c^2}} = \gamma m\mathbf{u}, \qquad (38\text{-}13)$$

FIGURE 38-22 The ratio of the relativistic momentum to the Newtonian expression mu. Curve is a plot based on Equation 38-13, while crosses and circles represent measurements from three different experiments done with electrons. The relativistic momentum goes asymptotically to infinity as $u \rightarrow c$.

where γ is the familiar relativistic factor. The momentum given in expression 38-13 is conserved in all reference frames, and at low velocities it reduces to the Newtonian expression $\mathbf{p} = m\mathbf{u}$.

As $u \rightarrow c$ the factor γ grows arbitrarily large, and so does the relativistic momentum (Fig. 38-22). Since force is the rate of change of momentum, that means a very large force is required to produce even the slightest change in the velocity of a rapidly moving particle. This effect shows one answer to a common question about relativity: Why is it impossible to accelerate an object to the speed of light? The answer is that the object's momentum would approach infinity, and no matter how close to c it was moving it would still require infinite force to give it the last bit of speed needed to reach c.

EXAMPLE 38-8	*Pushing Toward c*

Compare the momentum changes required to accelerate an electron (a) from rest to $0.01c$ and (b) from $0.98c$ to $0.99c$.

Solution
The momentum at each speed is given by Equation 38-13:

$$p(0) = \frac{mu}{\sqrt{1 - u^2/c^2}} = 0,$$

$$p(0.01c) = \frac{m(0.01c)}{\sqrt{1 - 0.01^2}} = 0.010 \ mc,$$

$$p(0.98c) = \frac{m(0.98c)}{\sqrt{1 - 0.98^2}} = 4.92 \ mc,$$

and $\quad p(0.99c) = \dfrac{m(0.99c)}{\sqrt{1 - 0.99^2}} = 7.02 \ mc.$

In both cases the speed has increased by the same $0.01c$, but the momentum changes are very different: Going from rest to $0.01c$ gives $\Delta p = 0.010mc$, while from $0.98c$ to $0.99c$ the momentum change is $\Delta p = (7.02mc - 4.92mc) = 2.1mc$—a factor of 210 greater than the slow-speed case. To accomplish the second velocity change in the same time would therefore require a force 210 times greater. Note, incidentally, that we would have had sufficient accuracy using the Newtonian expression $p = mu$ in the low-speed case.

EXERCISE An electron is moving at $0.35c$. If its speed is doubled, by what factor does its momentum increase?

Answer: 2.62

Some problems similar to Example 38-8: 28, 30–32

Energy and Mass

The most widely known result of relativity is the famous equation $E = mc^2$. Here we develop a general expression for relativistic energy and show just what $E = mc^2$ means. In the process we'll gain new insights into energy, momentum, and mass.

In Chapter 7 we derived the work-energy theorem, and thus developed the concept of kinetic energy, by calculating the work needed to accelerate a mass m from rest to some final speed. We did that by integrating force over distance, using Newton's law $F = dp/dt$ to write force in terms of momentum. We'll do the same thing here, now using our relativistic expression for momentum. So we have

$$\frac{dp}{dt} = \frac{d}{dt}\left[\frac{mu}{\sqrt{1 - u^2/c^2}}\right] = \frac{m(du/dt)}{(1 - u^2/c^2)^{3/2}}.$$

Then the kinetic energy gained as a particle accelerates from rest in our reference frame to a final speed u is

$$K = \int \frac{dp}{dt}\, dx = \int \frac{dp}{dt}\, u\, dt = \int \frac{m(du/dt)}{(1 - u^2/c^2)^{3/2}}\, u\, dt = \int_0^u \frac{mu}{(1 - u^2/c^2)^{3/2}}\, du,$$

where we used $u = dx/dt$ to replace dx with $u\, dt$. The integral is readily evaluated using the fact that $u\, du = \frac{1}{2}d(u^2)$, giving

$$K = \frac{mc^2}{\sqrt{1 - u^2/c^2}} - mc^2 = \gamma mc^2 - mc^2 \qquad (38\text{-}14)$$

for a particle's kinetic energy in a reference frame where the particle has speed u. Once again, γ here is the relativistic factor $1/\sqrt{1 - u^2/c^2}$.

For speeds low compared with c, Equation 38-14 should reduce to the familiar Newtonian expression $K = \frac{1}{2}mu^2$. And it does, as you can show in Problem 43. But Equation 38-14 suggests, more generally, that kinetic energy is the difference of two energies—the velocity-dependent quantity γmc^2 and the term mc^2 that depends only on mass but not velocity. Pursuing this interpretation, we identify γmc^2 as the particle's **total energy** and mc^2 as its **rest energy**. Rearranging Equation 38-14 lets us write the total energy as the sum of the kinetic energy and the rest energy:

$$E = K + mc^2$$

or, more simply

$$E = \gamma mc^2 = \frac{mc^2}{\sqrt{1 - u^2/c^2}} \quad \text{(total energy)}. \qquad (38\text{-}15)$$

What does all this mean? Put $u = 0$ in Equation 38-15 and $E = mc^2$—showing that the total energy of a stationary particle is not zero but is directly proportional to its mass. That means a particle has energy simply by virtue of having mass, or, as Einstein first recognized, that *mass and energy are equivalent*. The proportionality between mass and energy is a whopping big c^2—about 9×10^{16} J/kg in SI units.

Although we developed Equation 38-15 by considering kinetic energy, the mass-energy equivalence expressed in $E = mc^2$ is universal. Energy, like mass, exhibits inertia. A hot object is slightly harder to accelerate than a cold one because of the inertia of its thermal energy. A stretched spring is more massive than an unstretched one, because of its extra potential energy. When a system loses energy, it loses mass as well.

To the general public, $E = mc^2$ is synonymous with nuclear energy. This equation does describe mass changes that occur in nuclear reactions, but it applies equally well to chemical reactions and all other occurrences in which energy enters or leaves a system. If you weigh a nuclear power plant just after it's been refueled, then weigh again a month later, you will find it weighs slightly less. If you weigh a coal-burning power plant and all the coal and oxygen that go into it for a month, and then weigh all the carbon dioxide and other combustion products that come out, you will find a discrepancy between the mass of what goes in and what comes out. If both plants produce the same amount of energy, the mass discrepancy will be the same for both. The only difference lies in the amount of mass released as energy in each individual reaction. The

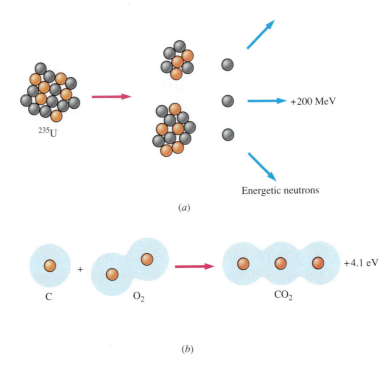

(a)

(b)

FIGURE 38-23 Energy release in (a) nuclear and (b) chemical reactions. A mass change occurs in both cases, but is more than 10^7 times greater in the nuclear reaction.

FIGURE 38-24 Pair creation events observed in a bubble chamber at Brookhaven National Laboratory. Each pair of curved paths represent the trajectories of a particle-antiparticle pair, bending in opposite directions in a magnetic field. The energy required to create the particles—mc^2 per particle—ultimately came from a single high-energy proton that collided with a stationary proton.

fissioning of a single uranium nucleus involves about 50 million times as much energy, and therefore mass, as the reaction of a single carbon atom with oxygen to make carbon dioxide (Fig. 38-23). That's why a coal-burning power plant consumes many hundred-car trainloads of coal each week, while a nuclear plant is refueled every 18 months with a few truckloads of uranium. Incidentally, neither process converts very much of the fuel mass to energy; if we could convert *all* the mass in a given object to energy, ordinary matter would be an almost limitless source of energy. Such conversion is in fact possible, but only in the annihilation of matter and antimatter. The opposite conversion also occurs, with a particle-antiparticle pair appearing where before there had been only energy (Fig. 38-24).

EXAMPLE 38-9	*Annihilation*

A positron is an antimatter particle with the same mass as the electron but the opposite electric charge. When an electron and a positron meet, they annihilate and produce a pair of gamma rays (bundles of electromagnetic wave energy) of equal energy. Find the energy of each gamma ray.

Solution

Here two electron masses annihilate to give two gamma rays. So the energy of each gamma ray is the energy equivalent of one electron mass, or

$$E = mc^2 = (9.11 \times 10^{-31} \text{ kg})(3.00 \times 10^8 \text{ m/s})^2$$
$$= 8.20 \times 10^{-14} \text{ J},$$

or 511 keV. The detection of 511-keV gamma rays from laboratory or astrophysical sources is a sure indication that electron-positron annihilation is occurring.

EXERCISE The Sun radiates energy at the rate of 3.85×10^{26} W. Find the rate at which it loses mass.

Answer: 4.28×10^9 kg/s

Some problems similar to Example 38-9: 38, 39

Given the fame of $E = mc^2$, it's easy to overlook the fact that the rest energy mc^2 is generally only part of a particle's total energy. Only when a particle is at rest does mc^2 equal its total energy. For a particle moving at velocity u that's small compared with c, the total energy is only slightly greater than mc^2; the extra is very nearly the Newtonian kinetic energy, $\frac{1}{2}mu^2$. (Here "at rest" and "moving" are, of course, relative to some inertial reference frame.) But when a particle moves with nearly the speed of light, the relativistic factor $\gamma = 1/\sqrt{1 - u^2/c^2}$ becomes much greater than 1, and the total energy γmc^2 is many times the rest energy. Such a particle is termed **relativistic**.

| **EXAMPLE 38-10** | *A Relativistic Electron* |

An electron has a total energy of 2.50 MeV. Find (a) its kinetic energy and (b) its speed.

Solution

In Example 38-9 we found that the rest energy of an electron is 511 keV, or 0.511 MeV. The electron's kinetic energy is the difference between its total energy and its rest energy, or

$$K = E - mc^2 = 2.5 \text{ MeV} - 0.511 \text{ MeV} = 1.99 \text{ MeV}.$$

Equation 38-15 shows that the total energy is just γ times the rest energy. Thus we have

$$\gamma = \frac{1}{\sqrt{1 - u^2/c^2}} = \frac{E}{mc^2} = \frac{2.5 \text{ MeV}}{0.511 \text{ MeV}} = 4.89.$$

Solving for u then gives

$$u = c\sqrt{1 - \frac{1}{4.89^2}} = 0.979c = 2.94 \times 10^8 \text{ m/s}.$$

EXERCISE Find (a) the rest energy of a proton, and (b) its kinetic energy when moving at $0.98c$.

Answers: (a) 938 Mev; (b) 3.78 GeV

Some problems similar to Example 38-10: 40–42

Got It!

The rest energy of a proton is 938 MeV. Without doing any calculations, give a quick estimate of the speed of a proton with total energy 1 TeV ($= 10^{12}$ eV).

The Energy-Momentum Relation

In Newtonian physics the equations $p = mu$ and $K = \frac{1}{2}mu^2$ yield the relation $p^2 = 2K/m$. Similarly, Problem 44 shows that in relativity we can combine the equations $p = \gamma mu$ and $E = \gamma mc^2$ to get

$$E^2 = p^2c^2 + (mc^2)^2, \qquad (38\text{-}16)$$

where now the energy-momentum relation involves E rather than K because in relativity the energy includes both kinetic and rest energies. For a particle at rest, $p = 0$ and Equation 38-16 shows that the total energy is just the rest energy. For highly relativistic particles the rest energy is negligible and the total energy becomes very nearly $E = pc$. Some "particles"—like the photons that, in quantum physics, are "bundles" of electromagnetic energy, have no mass. These particles exist only in motion at the speed of light, and for them Equation 38-16 gives the exact relation $E = pc$.

38-6 WHAT IS NOT RELATIVE

In relativity, space and time are not absolute but depend on the reference frame of the observer. But the speed of light c remains the same for all observers. Are there other such **relativistic invariants**? Yes—and these invariants, not the shifting measures of space and time, are at the basis of relativity's objective description of physical reality.

One invariant is mass. Rearranging Equation 38-16 gives

$$m = \frac{\sqrt{E^2 - p^2 c^2}}{c^2}. \tag{38-17}$$

If you look at a particle in a frame in which it's at rest, its total energy E is its rest energy mc^2, and Equation 38-17 obviously gives m for its mass. If you go to a frame in which the particle is moving, it now has kinetic energy and momentum as well. But Equation 38-16 shows that E and p change together in a way that keeps the mass m the same. Thus a particle's mass is invariant—it's a quantity that observers in different frames of reference will agree on.

We've been talking about the mass, energy, and momentum of a single particle. But the same concepts apply to systems of particles. In the case of a multiparticle system, Equation 38-17 can be taken as a definition of the system's mass in terms of its energy and momentum. The system's energy and momenta are the sums of the energies and momenta of its constituent particles—but, remarkably, Equation 38-17 then shows that the system's mass isn't just the sum of the masses of its constituent particles. That's because any relative motion between the system particles, or any potential energy associated with internal forces, also contributes to the system's mass.

In Newtonian physics the distance between two points is the same no matter who measures it. In relativity, distance depends on the observer. So does time. But there is a quantity, analogous to distance but incorporating time as well, that remains invariant. Called the **spacetime interval**, it is a kind of "four-dimensional distance," not between two points in space but between two events in space and time. The spacetime interval Δs is given by an expression that looks like a modified Pythagorean theorem:

$$(\Delta s)^2 = c^2 (\Delta t)^2 - [(\Delta x)^2 + (\Delta y)^2 + (\Delta z)^2], \tag{38-18}$$

where the Δ quantities describe the differences between the space and time coordinates of two events. The invariance of Equation 38-18 follows directly from the Lorentz transformations (see Problem 45).

The invariance of the spacetime interval suggests that something absolute underlies the shifting sands of relativistic space and time. That absolute is **spacetime**—a four-dimensional framework linking space and time. The points in spacetime are events, specified by four coordinates. The time interval or space interval between two events depends on the particular frame of reference of the observer, but the spacetime interval—a four-dimensional "distance" that takes all four coordinates into account—is the same for all observers.

In more advanced treatments of relativity, it is convenient to consider four-dimensional vectors called **four-vectors**. The displacement between two events in spacetime—specified by the four quantities Δx, Δy, Δz, and Δt—is a four-vector, with "length" given by Equation 38-18. Similarly, the three quantities $p_x c$, $p_y c$, $p_z c$, and E form a four-vector called the energy-momentum four vector or, more imaginatively, the momenergy vector. Either of Equations 38-16 or 38-17 shows that the "length" of this four-vector is just the rest energy mc^2.

It's possible to break an ordinary 2- or 3-dimensional vector into components in many different ways. Although the values of the individual components depend on your choice of coordinate system, the length or magnitude of the vector does not (Fig. 38-25). Similarly, the individual space and time components of a four-vector depend on your choice of reference frame—that is, on your velocity. But the "length" of a four-vector—for example, the spacetime interval between two events or the rest energy (equivalently, the mass) of a system—does not. Be careful, though, with the analogy in Fig. 38-25. The "length" of a vector in ordinary 2- or 3-dimensional space is given by the Pythagorean theorem. But the "length" of a four-vector involves a modified Pythagorean theorem, in which the Pythagorean sum of squares of the three spatial components is *subtracted* from the square of the time component. That's obvious in Equation 38-18, and you can also see it with Equations 38-16 or 38-17 if you isolate the rest energy term $(mc^2)^2$ on one side and recognize p^2 as the sum $p_x^2 + p_y^2 + p_z^2$. This unusual way of forming a vector's "length" reflects the fact that the underlying geometry of spacetime is not the Euclidean geometry you learned in high school.

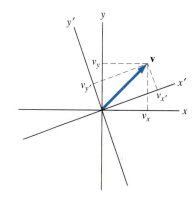

FIGURE 38-25 Although the x and y components of an ordinary vector depend on the choice of coordinate system, the length of the vector does not.

38-7 ELECTROMAGNETISM AND RELATIVITY

Historically, relativity arose from deep questions regarding the propagation of electromagnetic waves. We've seen that relativity alters concepts such as space, time, energy, and momentum, that are fundamental to Newtonian physics. For that reason, Newtonian physics becomes an approximation valid at small speeds. But relativity is built on the premise that Maxwell's equations of electromagnetism are correct in all reference frames—including the prediction of electromagnetic waves propagating at speed c. Even the title of Einstein's famous 1905 paper shows how intimately related are electromagnetism and relativity. The title isn't "The Theory of Relativity"—it's "On the Electrodynamics of Moving Bodies." Maxwell's equations are relativistically correct, and require no modification.

Although electric and magnetic fields in any frame of reference obey the same Maxwell equations, this doesn't mean the fields themselves are invariants. If, for example, you sit in the rest frame of a point charge, you see a spherically symmetric point-charge field. If you move relative to the charge, you see a magnetic field as well, associated with the moving charge. So electric and magnetic fields aren't absolutes; what one observer sees as a purely electric field another may see as a mix of electric and magnetic fields, and vice versa. You can think of the electric and magnetic fields as components of a more fundamental electromagnetic field; how that electromagnetic field breaks out into electric and magnetic fields depends on your frame of reference (see Problem 65). Although the fields are different in different reference frames, there is one important electromagnetic quantity that's invariant, namely electric charge.

We'll illustrate the deep relationship that relativity imposes on electricity and magnetism by considering the force on a charged particle near a current-carrying wire. For simplicity, we assume the wire contains equal line charge densities of positive and negative charge, and that both lines of charge are moving

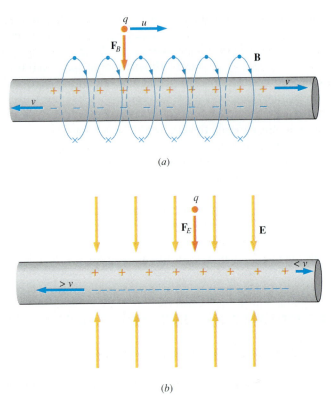

(a)

(b)

FIGURE 38-26 (a) A current-carrying wire with equal densities of positive and negative charge moving in opposite directions. A magnetic field surrounds the wire, so a charge q moving parallel to the wire experiences a magnetic force toward the wire. (b) The same situation, viewed in the rest frame of the charged particle. The line of negative charges is Lorentz contracted more, and therefore the positively charged particle "sees" a net negative charge on the wire. Thus the particle experiences an electric force toward the wire. There's still a magnetic field, but we don't show it since the stationary particle doesn't experience a magnetic force.

in opposite directions with the same speed v relative to the wire (Fig. 38-26a). The resulting current produces a magnetic field that encircles the wire, and the charged particle moving with velocity **u** as shown in Fig. 38-26a experiences a *magnetic* force $\mathbf{F} = q\mathbf{u} \times \mathbf{B}$ toward the wire. Because the positive and negative line charge densities are equal the wire is neutral, so there's no *electric* force on the charged particle.

Now look at the situation in the reference frame of the charged particle. The positive charges in the wire have a lower speed relative to the particle than do the negative charges, so in the particle's frame the distances between negative charges are contracted *more* than the distances between positive charges, as shown in Fig. 38-26b. But charge is invariant, so that means the charge per unit length is *greater* for the negative charges. So in the frame of the charged particle, *the wire carries a net negative charge!* That results in an *electric* field pointing toward the wire, and therefore the charged particle experiences an *electric* force toward the wire (see Fig. 38-26b). Of course there's still a magnetic field as well, but since the particle is at rest in its own frame, the magnetic force $q\mathbf{u} \times \mathbf{B}$ is zero.

We've given two quite different descriptions of the force on the charged particle. In the wire's frame, the particle experienced a purely magnetic force that we could determine knowing the magnetic force $q\mathbf{u}\times\mathbf{B}$ and how magnetic fields arise from currents. In contrast, describing the force in the particle's reference frame required no knowledge of magnetism whatever. We only needed to know the electric force $q\mathbf{E}$, and how electric fields arise from electric charges. This illustrates a profound point: that electricity and magnetism aren't independent phenomena that happen to be related. Rather, they're two aspects of a single phenomenon—electromagnetism. Given the relativity principle, it's not even logically possible to have electricity without magnetism, or vice versa. Relativity provides the complete unification of electromagnetism that we've hinted at throughout our study of these phenomena.

38-8 GENERAL RELATIVITY

The *special* theory of relativity is special because it's restricted to uniform motion. Following the development of special relativity, Einstein attempted to formulate a theory that would express the laws of physics in the same form in all frames of reference, including those in accelerated motion. But Einstein recognized that it is impossible to distinguish the effects of uniform acceleration from those of a uniform gravitational field (Fig. 38-27). Consequently, Einstein's general theory became a theory of gravity. Building on the notion of four-dimensional spacetime, Einstein introduced geometrical curvature of spacetime to account for gravity, and the result, published in 1916, is his **general theory of relativity**. The theory's predictions differ substantially from those of Newton's theory of gravity only in regions of very strong gravitational fields—far stronger than those found anywhere in our solar system. For that reason general relativity has become a cornerstone of modern astrophysics, describing the physics of such bizarre objects as neutron stars, black holes, and so-called gravitational lenses (Fig. 38-28). General relativity also addresses cosmological questions of the origin and ultimate fate of the universe. But we're not without terrestrial uses for general relativity; the satellite-based Global Positioning System (GPS), which can locate objects to within a few meters anywhere on Earth, would be off by several kilometers if the effects of general relativity weren't included in GPS calculations.

FIGURE 38-28 In general relativity, gravitation is synonymous with the curved geometry of spacetime. As a result, even light follows curved paths. This Hubble Space Telescope image shows the "Einstein Cross," whose four bright spots are images of the same distant quasar. The four images result from different light paths through the curved spacetime associated with a massive galaxy between the quasar and Earth. This process is called gravitational lensing.

9.8 m/s² 9.8 m/s²

Earth

(a) (b)

FIGURE 38-27 Why general relativity is a theory of gravity. (a) In a spaceship at rest on Earth, objects accelerate downward at $g = 9.8$ m/s². (b) Far from any gravitating body, a spaceship accelerates at 9.8 m/s². Relative to the accelerating reference frame of the spaceship, objects accelerate toward the back of the ship at 9.8 m/s². Situations (a) and (b) are impossible to distinguish, so a theory dealing with nonuniform motion must also consider gravity.

CHAPTER SYNOPSIS

Summary

1. The **ether** was a hypothetical medium whose properties were supposed to explain the propagation of electromagnetic waves. In particular, such waves were supposed to have speed c relative to the ether.

2. The **Michelson-Morley experiment** and the observation of the aberration of starlight led to a contradiction in physics: Earth's motion through the ether could not be detected, yet Earth did not drag ether with it.

3. Einstein's **special theory of relativity** (1905) resolved the contradiction by asserting that uniform motion is undetectable by any experiment, mechanical or electromagnetic. Einstein did away with the ether, declaring simply that **the laws of physics are the same in all inertial frames of reference**. Mechanics and electromagnetism alike are included in Einstein's theory, so Maxwell's prediction of electromagnetic waves moving at speed c is correct in all frames of reference.

4. The simple statement that the laws of physics are the same in all frames of reference requires profound changes in our common-sense notions of space and time. These changes are described by the **Lorentz transformations**, which relate space and time measurements made in different frames of reference:

$$y' = y$$
$$z' = z$$
$$x' = \gamma(x - vt)$$
$$t' = \gamma(t - vx/c^2),$$

where

$$\gamma = \frac{1}{\sqrt{1 - v^2/c^2}}.$$

Particular manifestations of these transformations include **time dilation**, **Lorentz contraction**, and the relativistic velocity addition formulas.

5. Relativistic transformations result in new expressions for momentum:

$$\mathbf{p} = \frac{m\mathbf{u}}{\sqrt{1 - u^2/c^2}} = \gamma m\mathbf{u}$$

and total energy:

$$E = \frac{mc^2}{\sqrt{1 - u^2/c^2}} = \gamma mc^2,$$

for a particle of mass m moving with velocity $\mathbf{u}$. Kinetic energy is the difference between the total energy E and the **rest energy** mc^2. The existence of rest energy shows that matter and energy may be converted into each other.

6. Relativity links space and time into a four-dimensional framework called **spacetime**. Although individual space and time measurements depend on one's frame of reference, the **spacetime interval** between two events does not.

7. Maxwell's equations of electromagnetism are fully consistent with relativity. But the fields themselves are different in different frames of reference; what appears as a magnetic field in one frame may be partially electric in another, and vice versa. Relativity imposes a logical relationship between electricity and magnetism, in that neither phenomenon is possible without the other.

8. The **general theory of relativity** is Einstein's generalization of relativity to include accelerated reference frames. Because the effects of acceleration mimic those of gravity, general relativity is a theory of gravity.

Terms You Should Understand

(Pairs are closely related terms whose distinction is important; number in parentheses is chapter section where term first appears.)

ether (38-1)
Michelson-Morley experiment (38-2)
special relativity, general relativity (38-2, 38-8)
time dilation, length contraction (38-4)
proper time, proper length (38-4)
Lorentz transformations (38-4)
rest energy (38-5)
spacetime (38-6)
spacetime interval (38-6)

Symbols You Should Recognize

γ (38-4)

Problems You Should Be Able to Solve

finding times and distances for different observers in relative motion (38-4)
transforming space and time coordinates among coordinate systems in relative motion (38-4)
transforming velocities (38-4)
applying mass-energy equivalence (38-5)
evaluating relativistic energy and momentum (38-5)

Limitations to Keep in Mind

The special theory of relativity applies only to inertial frames of reference—i.e., those that are not accelerated.

QUESTIONS

1. Why was the Michelson-Morley experiment a more sensitive test of motion through the ether than independent measurements of the speed of light in two perpendicular directions?

2. Why was it necessary to repeat the Michelson-Morley experiment at different times throughout the year?

3. Why do we reject the idea that the ether frame of reference is the Earth frame?

4. What is special about the special theory of relativity?

5. Does relativity require that the speed of sound be the same for all observers? Why or why not?

6. How would the world be different if the speed of light were 160 km/h (100 miles per hour)? Would our "common-sense" notions change?

7. A friend argues that the speed of light cannot be the same for all observers, for if one of them is moving toward a light source then that one will clearly measure a higher speed. How would you refute this argument?

8. Time dilation is sometimes described by saying that "moving clocks run slow." In what sense is this true? In what sense does the statement violate the spirit of relativity?

9. If you're in a spaceship moving at $0.95c$ relative to Earth, do you perceive time to be passing more slowly than it would on Earth? Think! Is your answer consistent with the principle of relativity?

10. In our light-box example for time dilation, we found that a time interval between two events measured in frame S' was shorter than in frame S. But you could equally well say that frame S is moving relative to frame S', so clocks in S should "run slow" compared with those in S'. An observer in each frame should judge the clocks in the other frame to "run slow." Is this a contradiction?

11. To try to circumvent the difficulty of accelerating an object to the speed of light, you build a series of conveyor belts, all running in the same direction, and each moving 10 m/s relative to the one next to it (Fig. 38-29). You step from the ground onto the first conveyor belt, then to the next, and so

forth. By the time you reach the 3×10^7th conveyor belt, you should be moving at c relative to the ground. Why doesn't this scheme work?

FIGURE 38-29 A series of conveyor belts, each moving at 10 m/s relative to its neighbors (Question 11).

12. If you took your pulse while traveling in a high-speed spacecraft, would it be faster, slower, or the same as on Earth?

13. The Andromeda galaxy is 2 million light-years from our Milky Way. Although nothing can go faster than light, it would still be possible to travel to Andromeda in much less than 2 million years. How is this possible?

14. Is matter converted to energy in a nuclear reactor? In a burning candle? In your body?

15. An unstretched rubber band is weighed on an extraordinarily sensitive scale. It is then stretched and weighed again. Is there a difference in the weight? Why or why not?

16. The rest energy of an electron is 511 keV. What is the approximate speed of an electron whose total energy is 1 GeV ($= 10^9$ eV)? You need not do any calculations!

17. An atom in an excited state emits a burst of light. What happens to the mass of the atom?

18. In some of the hottest parts of the universe, the thermal energy of particles may be many millions of electron volts. At such temperatures, the number of particles within a closed volume may vary. How is this possible? *Hint:* The mass of the electron is equivalent to about 0.5 MeV.

19. The quantity $\mathbf{E} \cdot \mathbf{B}$ is invariant. What does this say about how different observers will measure the angle between $\mathbf{E}$ and $\mathbf{B}$ in a light wave?

PROBLEMS

Section 38-2 Matter, Motion, and the Ether

1. Consider an airplane flying at 800 km/h airspeed between two points 1800 km apart. What is the round-trip travel time for the plane (a) if there is no wind? (b) if there is a wind blowing at 130 km/h perpendicular to a line joining the two points? (c) if there is a wind blowing at 130 km/h along a line joining the two points? Ignore relativistic effects. (Why are you justified in doing so?)

2. What would be the difference in light travel times on the two legs of the Michelson-Morley experiment if the ether existed and if Earth moved relative to it at (a) its orbital speed relative to the Sun (Appendix E)? (b) $10^{-2}c$? (c) $0.5c$? (d) $0.99c$? Assume each light path is exactly 11 m in length, and that the paths are oriented parallel and perpendicular to the ether wind.

3. Figure 38-30 shows a plot of James Bradley's data on the aberration of light from the star γ Draconis, taken in 1727–1728. (a) From the data, determine the magnitude of Earth's orbital velocity. (b) The data very nearly fit a perfect sine curve. What does this say about the shape of Earth's orbit?

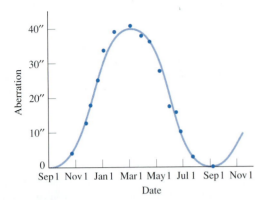

FIGURE 38-30 Bradley's data on the aberration of starlight (Problem 3). Aberration is measured in seconds of arc ($1'' = 1/3600°$).

4. Show that the time of Equation 38-2 is larger than that of Equation 38-1 as long as $0 < v < c$.

5. Suppose the speed of light differed by 100 m/s in two perpendicular directions. How long should the arms be in a Michelson interferometer if this difference is to cause the interference pattern to shift one-half cycle (i.e., a light fringe shifts to where a dark one was) relative to the pattern if there were no speed difference? Assume 550-nm light.

Section 38-4 Space and Time in Relativity

6. Two stars are 50 ly apart, measured in their common rest frame. How far apart are they to a spaceship moving between them at $0.75c$?

7. How long would it take a spacecraft traveling at 65% of the speed of light to make the 5.8×10^9 km journey from Earth to Pluto according to clocks (a) on Earth and (b) on the spacecraft?

8. A spaceship goes by at half the speed of light, and you determine that it is 35 m long. What is its length as measured in its rest frame?

9. Earth and Sun are 8.3 light-minutes apart, as measured in their rest frame. (a) What is the speed of a spacecraft that makes the trip in 5.0 min according to its on-board clocks? (b) What is the trip time as measured by clocks in the Earth-Sun frame?

10. The Andromeda galaxy is two million light-years from Earth, measured in the common rest frame of Earth and Andromeda. Suppose you took a fast spaceship to Andromeda, so it got you there in 50 years as measured on the ship. If you sent a radio message home as soon as you reached Andromeda, how long after you left Earth would it arrive, according to timekeepers on Earth?

11. How fast would you have to move relative to a meter stick for its length to measure 99 cm in your frame of reference?

12. Electrons in a TV tube move through the tube at 30% of the speed of light. By what factor is the tube foreshortened in the electrons' frame of reference, relative to its length at rest?

13. You wish to travel to a star N light-years from Earth. How fast must you go if the one-way journey is to occupy N years of your life?

14. The nearest star beyond our solar system is about 4 light-years away. If a spaceship can get to the star in 5 years, as measured on Earth, (a) how long would the ship's pilot judge the journey to take? (b) How far from Earth would the pilot find the star to be?

15. Twins A and B live on Earth. On their 20th birthday, Twin B climbs into a spaceship and makes a round-trip journey at $0.95c$ to a star 30 light-years distant, as measured in the Earth-star frame of reference. What are their ages when the twins are reunited?

16. Radioactive oxygen-15 decays at such a rate that half the atoms in a given sample decay every two minutes. If a tube containing 1000 O-15 atoms is moved at $0.80c$ relative to Earth for 6.67 minutes according to clocks at rest with respect to Earth, how many atoms will be left at the end of that time?

17. Two distant galaxies are receding from Earth at $0.75c$, in opposite directions. How fast does an observer in one galaxy measure the other to be moving?

18. Two spaceships are having a race. The "slower" one moves past Earth at $0.70c$, and the "faster" one moves at $0.40c$ relative to the slower one. How fast does the faster ship move relative to Earth?

19. Muons traveling vertically downward at $0.994c$ relative to Earth are observed from a rocket traveling upward at $0.25c$. What speed does the rocket's crew measure for the muons?

20. Use relativistic velocity addition to show that if an object moves at speed $v < c$ relative to some uniformly moving frame of reference, then its speed relative to any other uniformly moving frame must also be less than c.

21. Earth and Sun are 8.33 light-minutes apart. Event A occurs on Earth at time $t = 0$, and event B on the Sun at time $t = 2.45$ min, as measured in the Earth-Sun frame. Find the time order and time difference between A and B for observers (a) moving on a line from Earth to Sun at $0.750c$,

(b) moving on a line from Sun to Earth at 0.750c, and (c) moving on a line from Earth to Sun at 0.294c.

22. Two civilizations are evolving on opposite sides of a galaxy, whose diameter is 10^5 light-years (Fig. 38-31). At time $t = 0$ in the galaxy frame of reference, civilization A launches its first interstellar spacecraft. Civilization B launches its first spacecraft 50,000 years later. A being from a more advanced civilization C is traveling through the galaxy at 0.99c, on a line from A to B. Which civilization does C judge to have first achieved interstellar travel, and how much in advance of the other?

(a)

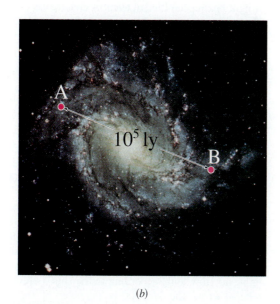

(b)

FIGURE 38-31 Civilizations A and B are on opposite sides of a galaxy, a distance of 10^5 light-years in the galaxy frame of reference (Problems 22, 23, 24).

23. Repeat the preceding problem, now assuming that civilization B lags A by 1 million years in the galaxy frame of reference.

24. Could there be observers who would judge the events in the two preceding problems to be simultaneous? If so, how must each be moving relative to the galaxy?

25. Derive the Lorentz transformations for time, Equations 38-9 and 38-10, from the transformations for space.

26. In the light box of Fig. 38-8, let event A be the emission of the light flash and event B its return to the source. Assign suitable space and time coordinates to these events in the frame in which the box moves with speed v. Apply the Lorentz transformations to show that the time $\Delta t'$ between the two events in the box frame is given by Equation 38-4.

27. Two spaceships are each 25 m long, as measured in their rest frames (Fig. 38-32). Ship A is approaching Earth at 0.65c. Ship B is approaching Earth from the opposite direction at 0.50c. Find the length of ship B as measured (a) in Earth's frame of reference and (b) in ship A's frame of reference.

FIGURE 38-32 Problem 27 (the drawing is in Earth's frame of reference).

Section 38-5 Energy and Momentum in Relativity

28. By what factor does the momentum of an object change if you double its speed when its original speed is (a) 25 m/s and (b) 1.0×10^8 m/s?

29. At what speed will the momentum of a proton (mass 1 u) equal that of an alpha particle (mass 4 u) moving at 0.5c?

30. At what speed will the Newtonian expression for momentum be in error by 1%?

31. A particle is moving at 0.90c. If its speed increases by 10%, by what factor does its momentum increase?

32. Compare the momentum changes needed to boost a spacecraft (a) from 0.1c to 0.2c and (b) from 0.8c to 0.9c.

33. Find (a) the total energy and (b) the kinetic energy of an electron moving at 0.97c.

34. A TV tube accelerates electrons from rest through a potential difference of 30 kV. Find their final speed.

35. At what speed will the relativistic and Newtonian expressions for kinetic energy differ by 10%?

36. Find (a) the speed and (b) the momentum of a proton whose kinetic energy is 500 MeV.

37. Among the most energetic cosmic rays ever detected are protons with energies around 10^{20} eV. Find the momentum of such a proton, and compare with that of a 25-mg insect crawling at 2 mm/s (Fig. 38-33).

(a)   (b)

FIGURE 38-33 (a) A cosmic ray proton slams into the upper atmosphere, creating a shower of elementary particles. How does the proton's energy compare with that of (b) a crawling bug? (Problem 37)

38. A large city consumes electrical energy at the rate of 10^9 W. If you converted all the rest mass in a 1-g raisin to electrical energy, for how long could it power the city?

39. In a nuclear fusion reaction, two deuterium nuclei (^{2}H) combine to give a helium nucleus (^{3}He) plus a neutron. The energy released in the process is 3.3 MeV. By how much do the combined masses of the helium nucleus and neutron differ from the combined masses of the original deuterium nuclei?

40. Find the kinetic energy of an electron moving at (a) 0.0010c, (b) 0.60c, and (c) 0.99c. Use suitable approximations where possible.

41. Find the speed of an electron with kinetic energy (a) 100 eV, (b) 100 keV, (c) 1 MeV, (d) 1 GeV. Use suitable approximations where possible.

42. How much energy would it take to accelerate a proton (a) from rest to 0.10c, (b) from 0.50c to 0.55c, (c) from 0.95c to 0.99c, and (d) from 0.99c to c?

43. Use the binomial approximation (Appendix A) to show that Equation 38-14 reduces to the Newtonian expression for kinetic energy in the limit $u \ll c$.

44. Show that Equation 38-16 follows from the expressions for relativistic momentum and total energy.

Section 38-6 What Is Not Relative

45. Show from the Lorentz transformations that the spacetime interval of Equation 38-18 has the same value in all frames of reference.

46. A spaceship travels at 0.80c from Earth to a star 10 light-years distant, as measured in the Earth-star frame (Fig. 38-34). Let event A be the ship's departure from Earth and event B its arrival at the star. (a) Find the distance and time between the two events in the Earth-star

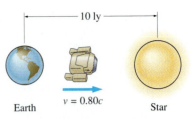

FIGURE 38-34 Problem 46.

frame. (b) Find the distance and time between the two events in the ship frame. *Hint:* The distance in the ship frame is the distance an observer has to move *with respect to that frame* to be at both events—not the same as the Lorentz-contracted distance between Earth and star. (c) Compute the square of the spacetime interval in both frames to show explicitly that it is invariant.

47. Use Equation 38-18 to calculate the square of the spacetime interval between the events (a) of Problem 22 and (b) of Problem 23. Comment on the signs of your answers in relation to the possibility of a causal relation between the events.

48. A light beam is emitted at event A and arrives at event B. Show that the spacetime interval between the two events is zero.

Paired Problems

(Both problems in a pair involve the same principles and techniques. If you can get the first problem, you should be able to solve the second one.)

49. An extraterrestrial spacecraft passes Earth and 4.5 s later, according to its clocks, it passes the moon. Find its speed.

50. How fast would you have to go to reach a star 200 light-years distant in a 75-year human lifetime?

51. An electron moves down a 1.2-km-long particle accelerator at 0.999992c. In the electron's frame, (a) how much time does the trip take and (b) how long is the accelerator?

52. An advanced civilization has developed a spaceship that goes, with respect to the galaxy, only 50 km/s slower than light. (a) How long, according to the ship's crew, does it take to cross the 100,000-ly diameter of the galaxy? (b) What is the galactic diameter as measured in the ship's frame of reference?

53. Event A occurs at $x = 0$ and $t = 0$ in a frame of reference S. Event B occurs at $x = 3.8$ light-years, $t = 1.6$ years in S. Find (a) the distance and (b) the time between A and B in a frame S' moving at 0.80c along the x axis of S.

54. Two nuclear reactions occur in a particle accelerator, at points 45 cm apart and separated by 6.8 ns in time, as measured in the accelerator's frame of reference. Find (a) the distance and (b) the time between the events as measured in the reference frame of a proton moving at 0.92c on a line between the two.

55. When a particle's speed doubles, its momentum increases by a factor of 3. What was the original speed?
56. Find the speed of an electron whose momentum is 50% greater than the value given by the Newtonian expression $p = mu$.

Supplementary Problems

57. How fast would you have to travel to reach the Crab Nebula, 6500 light-years from Earth, in 20 years? Give your answer to 7 significant figures.
58. At what speed are a particle's kinetic and rest energies equal?
59. A cosmic ray proton with energy 20 TeV is heading toward Earth. What is Earth's diameter measured in the proton's frame of reference?
60. Plot the ratio of relativistic to Newtonian kinetic energy as a function of speed, and from your graph find the speed where the relativistic kinetic energy is 50% greater than the Newtonian value.
61. When the speed of an object increases by 5%, its momentum goes up by a factor of 5. What was the original speed?
62. Use the Lorentz transformations to show that if two events are separated in space and time so that a light signal leaving one event could not reach the other, then there is an observer for whom the two events are simultaneous. Show that the converse is true as well: that if a light signal could get from one event to the other, then no observer will find them simultaneous.

63. A source emitting light with frequency f moves toward you at speed u. By considering both time dilation and the effect of wavefronts "piling up" as shown in Fig. 17-20, show that you measure a Doppler shifted frequency given by

$$f' = f\sqrt{\frac{c + u}{c - u}}.$$

Use the binomial approximation to show that this result can be written in the form of Equation 17-10 for $u \ll c$.
64. Use Equation 9-7 to estimate the size to which you would have to squeeze each of the following before the escape speed at its surface approximated the speed of light: (a) Earth; (b) the Sun; (c) the Milky Way galaxy, containing about 10^{11} solar masses. Your answers show why general relativity is not needed for most astronomical calculations.
65. Consider a line of positive charge with line charge density λ, as measured in a frame S at rest with respect to the charges. (a) Show that the electric field a distance r from this charged line has magnitude $E = \lambda/2\pi\varepsilon_0 r$, and that there is no magnetic field (no relativity needed here). Now consider the situation in a frame S' moving at speed v parallel to the line of charge. (b) Show that the line charge density as measured in S' is given by $\lambda' = \gamma\lambda$, with $\gamma = 1/\sqrt{1 - v^2/c^2}$. (c) Use the result of (b) to find the electric field in S'. Since the line of charge is moving with respect to S', there is a current in S'. (d) Find an expression for this current and (e) for the magnetic field it produces. Show that the quantities (f) $\mathbf{E} \cdot \mathbf{B}$ and (g) $E^2 - c^2B^2$ are the same in both frames of reference. (In fact, these quantities are always invariant.)

39 Inside Atoms and Nuclei

A high-energy cosmic ray (red) slams into an atomic nucleus, producing a spray of particles. By studying such interactions, physicists learn about the fundamental structure of matter.

Newtonian mechanics and Maxwell's electromagnetism constitute the core of **classical physics**, providing a rich and deep understanding of physical reality. Application of classical physics has led to many of the technological developments essential to modern civilization. Although these theories were firmly established by the middle of the nineteenth century, they remain central to the work of many contemporary scientists and engineers today.

Nevertheless, at the end of the nineteenth century a few seemingly minor phenomena defied classical explanation. Most physicists felt that it was only a matter of time before these, too, came under the classical umbrella. But that was not to be. We've already seen how questions about the speed of light led to a radical restructuring of our fundamental notions of space and time. Other questions, especially those concerning the behavior of matter at the atomic scale, were to bring an even more radical transformation of physical thought.

The essence of the new physics lies in the ideas of **quantum mechanics**, developed first to explain the workings of the atom and subsequently pushed into the nuclear realm and then to the subnuclear world of elementary particles. In this chapter we give a very brief introduction to quantum mechanics, to the structure of atoms and nuclei, and to current theories of the fundamental nature of matter. Today's physics has come full circle, linking questions about the smallest physical entities with those about the origin and evolution of the entire universe, and we conclude with a brief look at the connections between elementary particle physics and cosmology.

This chapter is not as comprehensive as those that precede it, nor will it give you a great deal of problem-solving skill. Rather, it's intended to whet your appetite for modern physics. Interested readers should consult the extended version of this text, whose additional chapters explore further the ideas and applications of quantum physics. ActivPhysics can also help you explore this material more quantitatively; watch for the ActivPhysics icons.

39-1 TOWARD THE QUANTUM THEORY

Are matter and energy continuously divisible? The essential difference between classical and quantum physics is that the former answers this question "in general, yes," while the latter says definitively "no." Instead, most physical quantities in quantum physics are **quantized**, meaning that they come only in certain discrete values.

The idea that physical quantities might come in discrete "chunks" is not new to modern quantum theory. Some 2400 years ago the Greek philosopher Democritus proposed that all matter consists of indivisible atoms of different types. By the start of the twentieth century a more scientifically grounded atomic theory was widely accepted. J. J. Thomson's discovery of the electron in 1897 showed that atoms might be divisible after all, but at the same time it revealed a finer division of matter into discrete "chunks." Millikan's 1909 oil-drop experiment (Section 23-2) showed that electric charge is similarly quantized, seemingly available only in integer multiples of the elementary charge e. Discovery of the proton and later the neutron further solidified the notion that matter is comprised of fundamental building blocks with definite values for their various physical properties.

Quantization of matter into particles with discrete properties is not incompatible with classical physics as long as those particles behave according to classical laws—in particular, that they move continuously through space and can have *any* amount of energy. Add electromagnetism to the picture and the classical viewpoint requires that the fields be continuous, exerting forces on charged particles and sometimes changing, in a gradual and continuous way, the particles' energies.

The startling fact of quantum physics is that this classical behavior does not occur at the atomic scale; instead, energy itself is in many instances quantized. Reconciling the implications of that fact with our commonsense notions of matter and motion has proved impossible; instead, the quantum world speaks a different language, one in which deeply ingrained ideas about causality and the solid reality of matter seem no longer to apply. Here we look at three distinct phenomena that force us to accept that energy can be quantized.

FIGURE 39-1 As the temperature of an electrically heated coil increases, it emits increasing amounts of radiation, with the maximum emission occurring at ever shorter wavelengths. The color, correspondingly, changes from a dull red to a bright yellow-white.

Blackbody Radiation

Heat a solid object hot enough and it begins to glow, emitting electromagnetic radiation in the form of light. As we saw in Section 19-6, the total power radiated is proportional to the fourth power of the temperature. There's also a change in wavelength with increasing temperature: The first visible glow is a dull red, changing with higher temperatures to orange and then yellow colors corresponding to ever shorter wavelengths. A familiar example is an incandescent lamp with a dimmer, which allows you to take the lamp filament from the faintest red glow through the yellow-white at full brightness (Fig. 39-1).

The radiation emitted by a dense, glowing substance that is a good absorber of radiation is **blackbody radiation**, so called because the substance appears black when viewed in reflected light only. Blackbody radiation covers a range of wavelengths, and experiment shows that the wavelength of greatest emission is inversely proportional to the temperature. Microscopically, blackbody radiation is associated with the thermal motions of atoms and molecules, so it's not surprising that the radiation increases with temperature. In the late 1800s physicists tried to apply the laws of electromagnetism and statistical mechanics to explain the experimental observations of blackbody radiation. They met with some success in describing the overall intensity and peak wavelength of the radiation, but could not reproduce completely the observed distribution of wavelengths.

In 1900 the German physicist Max Planck formulated an equation that fit the observed intensity-versus-wavelength curves of blackbody radiation at all wavelengths. Planck's equation, like its classical predecessors, describes blackbody radiation as arising from the thermally induced vibration of individual molecules. But where classical physics allows a vibrating molecule to have *any* amount of energy, Planck's equation has a startling implication:

The energy of a vibrating molecule can take on only certain discrete values.

If f is a molecule's vibration frequency, Planck's equation requires that its energy be an integer multiple of the quantity hf, where h is a constant whose value Planck determined by fitting his equation to the observed blackbody radiation curves. Today we know h as one of the fundamental constants of nature, and call it **Planck's constant**. Its value is approximately 6.63×10^{-34} J·s, and it is precisely because h is so small that quantum phenomena usually become obvious only when we delve into the atomic and molecular realm. Planck's quantization of the energy of vibrating molecules implies further that a molecule can absorb or emit energy only in discrete "bundles" of size hf, and

FIGURE 39-2 Energy-level diagrams are used frequently in quantum physics to indicate allowed energies. Usually, as here, the horizontal axis has no physical significance. (*a*) In classical physics, a vibrating molecule can have any energy, and its energy can change through absorption or emission of any amount of energy. (*b*) Allowed energies in Planck's theory are integer multiples of hf and can change only through absorption or emission of discrete energy "bundles" of size hf. Two-headed arrows indicate these allowed transitions.

that in doing so it jumps abruptly from one of its allowed energy levels to another (Fig. 39-2).

Planck's equation was simply a way of fitting observed data and had no deep theoretical justification. Thus, Planck could not say why energy should be quantized, nor could he answer questions such as, "What happens during the jump from one energy level to another?" Planck himself was reluctant to accept or elaborate on his theory's evident disagreement with classical physics; nevertheless, his revolutionary work won him the 1918 Nobel Prize. Other physicists emphasized the contrast between Planck's work and the classical treatment of blackbody radiation. That treatment was based on the assumption that all vibrational energy levels are equally likely, and led to the absurd conclusion that every glowing object should emit electromagnetic energy at an infinite rate, with that energy concentrated at the shortest wavelengths (Fig. 39-3). Since the shortest wavelength radiation known at the time was ultraviolet, this phenomenon was called the **ultraviolet catastrophe**.

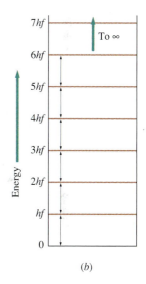

The Photoelectric Effect

In experiments that seem at first to have nothing whatsoever to do with Planck's work, physicists, beginning with Hertz in 1887, showed that some metals emit electrons when illuminated with light. This **photoelectric effect** is studied by putting a metal surface in an evacuated glass container that also contains a

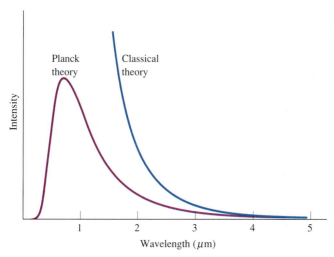

FIGURE 39-3 Intensity versus wavelength for blackbody radiation from an object at 4000 K. Classical and Planck theories agree at the longer wavelengths, but the classical theory predicts an excess of radiation at short wavelengths.

FIGURE 39-4 Apparatus for studying the photoelectric effect. An adjustable filter determines the wavelength of light incident on the apparatus. Light passes through a hole in a metal electrode and strikes a metal surface, where it ejects electrons. Varying the magnitude and polarity of the voltage between the electrode and the metal surface allows measurement of the number and energy of the ejected electrons.

17.3

Photoelectric Effect

second conducting electrode (Fig. 39-4). Making the second electrode positive with respect to the emitting surface attracts the electrons, and the resulting current provides a measure of the number of electrons ejected. Making the second electrode sufficiently negative with respect to the emitting surface, on the other hand, produces an electric field so strong that the emitted electrons do not have enough energy to reach the electrode. The value of this so-called stopping potential thus provides a measure of the ejected electrons' maximum kinetic energy.

Classical physics suggests that the photoelectric effect should occur because an electron in a metal experiences a force in the oscillating electric field of a light wave. As the wave continues past an electron, the amplitude of the electron's oscillatory motion should grow until eventually it has enough energy to escape from the metal. Because the energy in a wave is spread throughout the entire wave, it might take a while for a single tiny electron to absorb enough energy to escape. Increasing the light intensity should increase the electric field in the light wave, so should result in the electron being ejected sooner and with more energy. Changing the wave frequency should have little effect on the behavior of the free electrons in the metal.

The photoelectric effect does occur, but not in the way classical physics suggests. The major disagreements are

1. Electrons are ejected almost immediately, even in dim light.
2. The maximum electron energy is independent of the light intensity.
3. Below a certain cutoff frequency *no* electrons are emitted, no matter how intense the light. Above the cutoff frequency electrons are emitted with a maximum energy that increases in proportion to the light-wave frequency.

In 1905, the same year in which he formulated the special theory of relativity, Albert Einstein offered an explanation for the photoelectric effect. Einstein suggested that the energy of an electromagnetic wave is not spread throughout the wave, but is instead concentrated in "bundles" called **photons**. Einstein applied to these photons the same energy-quantization condition Planck had already proposed for molecular vibrations: that photons in light with frequency f have energy hf, where again h is Planck's constant:

$$E = hf. \quad \text{(energy of a photon)} \quad (39\text{-}1)$$

The more intense the light, the more photons—but the energy of each photon is unrelated to the light intensity.

Einstein's idea readily explains the nonclassical aspects of the photoelectric effect. Since the minimum amount of energy in light of frequency f is the energy hf of a single photon, the photons in low-frequency light will not have enough energy to eject electrons—no matter how many photons there are. At the cutoff frequency the photons have just enough energy to eject electrons, and as the frequency increases still further the electrons emerge with kinetic energy equal to the difference between the photon energy and that needed for electron ejection. That excess energy depends only on the photon energy—that is, on the light frequency but not on its intensity. Finally, the immediate ejection of electrons follows because an individual photon delivers its entire bundle of energy to an electron all at once. Einstein received the 1921 Nobel Prize for his explanation of the photoelectric effect; his special and general theories of relativity were at that time sufficiently controversial that they bore no mention in the Nobel citation.

The work of Planck and Einstein applies quantization of energy to two quite different systems, in Planck's case vibrating molecules and in Einstein's case electromagnetic waves. We now turn to the energies of atoms themselves.

Atomic Spectra and the Bohr Atom

In Chapter 34 we found that accelerated charges are the source of electromagnetic radiation. By 1900 it was known that atoms contain negative electrons as well as regions of positive charge; by 1911 experiments by Ernest Rutherford and his colleague Hans Geiger and student Ernest Marsden had localized the positive charge in the tiny but massive nucleus. According to classical physics, electrons should orbit the nucleus under the influence of the electric force, radiating electromagnetic wave energy as they accelerate in their orbits. In fact, a classical calculation shows that atomic electrons will quickly radiate away all their energy and spiral into the nucleus. Thus, the very existence of atoms seems at odds with classical physics.

A more subtle problem involving radiation from atoms dates to 1804, when William Wollastan noticed apparent lines of demarcation between some of the colors dispersed by a prism. Ten years later the German optician Josef von Fraunhofer dispersed the solar spectrum sufficiently that he could see hundreds of narrow, dark lines against the otherwise continuous spectrum of colors (Fig. 39-5a). Studies of light emitted by diffuse gases excited by electric discharges show similar **spectral lines**, these being bright lines against an otherwise

(a)

(b)

FIGURE 39-5 (a) The solar spectrum is a continuous band of colors overlain by dark lines where specific colors have been absorbed in the solar atmosphere. Prominent line in the red is hydrogen-alpha, and the pair in the yellow are the 589-nm sodium doublet. (b) Spectral lines emitted by a diffuse sample of hydrogen gas. This is the Balmer series of lines, with Hα the bright line in the red.

dark background (Fig. 39-5b). We now know that bright-line spectra—called **emission spectra**—are produced when atoms emit light of discrete frequencies. **Absorption spectra**, in contrast, arise when atoms in a diffuse gas absorb certain discrete frequencies of light from a continuous source. What Fraunhofer saw in sunlight were absorption lines arising from the diffuse gas overlying the bright visible surface of the Sun. We emphasize the word *diffuse:* Discrete spectra generally occur only when a gas is sufficiently diffuse that light from one atom stands a strong chance of escaping the gas before it interacts with other atoms. In dense gases, or in solids and liquids, multiple interactions result in the continuous spectrum characteristic of blackbody radiation.

But why should atoms emit and absorb light of discrete frequencies? In 1884, several decades before a satisfactory answer was given, a Swiss schoolteacher named Johann Balmer realized that the wavelengths of the lines in the visible spectrum of hydrogen (Fig. 39-5b) were related by the equation

18.1
Bohr Model

$$\frac{1}{\lambda} = R_H\left(\frac{1}{2^2} - \frac{1}{n^2}\right), \tag{39-2}$$

where $n = 3, 4, 5, 6 \dots$ and R_H is a constant called the **Rydberg constant** for hydrogen, with value approximately 1.097×10^7 m^{-1}.

In 1913 the great Danish physicist Niels Bohr (Fig. 39-6) proposed an atomic theory that accounted for the spectral lines of hydrogen. In the **Bohr atom** the electron moves in a circular orbit about the nucleus, held in orbit by the electric force. Classically, any orbital radius and, correspondingly, any energy and any angular momentum should be possible. But Bohr introduced quantization to the atom, stating that only certain orbits were possible—namely, those whose angular momentum is an integer multiple of Planck's constant divided by 2π. Angular momentum quantization implies energy quantization, and Bohr showed that the energy of an atomic electron should be proportional to $-1/n^2$, with n an integer (see Problem 42). The zero of potential energy is taken when the electron and proton are infinitely far apart, and Bohr's negative energy values thus imply that the electron in the atom is bound to the proton.

FIGURE 39-6 Niels Bohr (left) with Max Planck. Bohr was a powerful influence on many of the twentieth century's greatest physicists. In his later years he was also active in humanitarian causes, especially the effort to control nuclear weapons.

Bohr's theory asserted that an electron in any of the allowed orbits does not radiate energy, in direct contradiction to the predictions of classical electromagnetism. But an electron can jump from one orbit to another, emitting or absorbing a photon whose energy is equal to the energy difference between the two orbital levels. That difference, translated into wavelength through Equation 39-1 with $f = c/\lambda$ for the photon, leads directly to Balmer's formula for the spectral-line wavelengths. In fact, Bohr's model covers other series of spectral lines (see Fig. 39-7) in which the 2 in Balmer's formula is replaced with other integers:

$$\frac{1}{\lambda} = R_H\left(\frac{1}{n_2^2} - \frac{1}{n_1^2}\right). \tag{39-3}$$

Here λ is the wavelength of light emitted when an atomic electron jumps from the n_1th energy level to the n_2th level. Thus, the Balmer series arises in jumps from the $n = 3, 4, 5, \dots$ levels to the $n = 2$ level. Jumps to the lowest level, $n = 1$, give the ultraviolet lines of the Lyman series, while jumps to $n = 3$ give the infrared Paschen series. Figure 39-7 shows an energy level diagram for hydrogen in the Bohr theory.

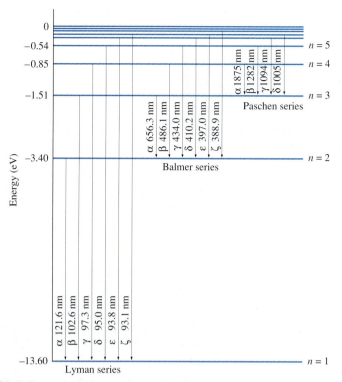

FIGURE 39-7 Energy-level diagram for the Bohr model of the hydrogen atom, showing transitions responsible for the first three series of spectral lines. Each series arises from jumps to a common final state; $n = 2$ gives the visible and ultraviolet lines of the Balmer series. The zero of energy corresponds to a widely separated electron-proton pair with no kinetic energy.

EXAMPLE 39-1	*Big Atoms*

The Bohr theory predicts that the lowest energy electron orbit in the hydrogen atom—the state with $n = 1$—should have radius 0.0529 nm, consistent with measurements of the "size" of the atom. But in the diffuse hydrogen gas of interstellar space, atoms can be found in highly excited states with sizes approaching a fraction of a millimeter. Transitions between adjacent energy levels of these so-called Rydberg atoms result in emission of photons at radio frequencies, and therefore, radio astronomers can study these enormous atoms. One of the longest wavelengths observed is the so-called 272α, corresponding to a transition from $n = 273$ to $n = 272$. At what wavelength and frequency should a radio telescope be set to observe this transition?

Solution

We use Equation 39-3 with $n_1 = 273$ and $n_2 = 272$:

$$\lambda = \left[R_H \left(\frac{1}{n_2^2} - \frac{1}{n_1^2} \right) \right]^{-1}$$

$$= \left[(1.097 \times 10^7 \text{ m}^{-1}) \left(\frac{1}{272^2} - \frac{1}{273^2} \right) \right]^{-1} = 92 \text{ cm}.$$

Using $f = c/\lambda$ gives the corresponding frequency of 325 MHz, which happens to lie in a gap between the VHF and UHF bands used for television broadcasting.

EXERCISE Find the wavelength of the spectral line $H\alpha$, corresponding to the transition from $n = 3$ to $n = 2$.

Answer: 656.3 nm

Some problems similar to Example 39-1: 6–9

Bohr's theory was astoundingly successful in describing the hydrogen atom but proved less suitable for more complicated atoms. Furthermore, like Planck's original quantum hypothesis, Bohr's quantization of atomic energy levels lacked a convincing theoretical basis.

APPLICATION	*The Laser*

Scientists and engineers have developed an astonishing array of devices based on quantum principles, and we can hardly begin to do them justice here. But we will describe briefly one quantum system that surely ranks among the important inventions of the twentieth century: the laser.

Bohr knew that an atomic electron could absorb a photon and jump to one of its higher quantized energy levels. In 1917 Einstein suggested that it could be induced to jump downward by the nearby passage of a photon with energy equal to the energy difference between the two levels. This phenomenon of **stimulated emission** is the basis of the laser. In a laser, energy is supplied to a solid, liquid, or gaseous medium in a way that causes a great many atoms to jump into higher energy excited states (Fig. 39-8). When one of these atoms drops back to the lower state, the photon it emits stimulates others to drop as well. The result is a burst of photons, all with the same energy and phase, that gives the laser its bright, coherent light output. In some lasers the "pumping" of the atoms to their higher states is done first, followed by a burst of light; in others the pumping and emission occur all the time, and the laser shines continuously. ActivPhysics Activity 18.4 simulates the laser.

Today, lasers are employed wherever bright, coherent, monochromatic light is needed. Applications range from the commonplace, such as scanning bar codes at supermarket checkouts, to technological feats, such as focusing billions of watts of power on tiny pellets in an attempt to harness the energy of nuclear fusion (Fig. 39-9).

(a)

(b)

FIGURE 39-8 (a) Normally, atomic electrons are in their lowest possible energy states. Each pair of lines represents an atom with two energy levels shown; blue dots are electrons. (b) In a laser, an external energy source "pumps" the electrons into a higher state. (c) When one electron drops back it emits a photon that stimulates the other electrons to drop as well. The result is a burst of photons that comprise a beam of coherent, monochromatic light. Here, the fourth electron is about to drop as it's stimulated by passage of the photons.

FIGURE 39-9 Laser applications. (a) Scanning bar codes in a supermarket checkout. (b) Cutting steel.

Matter Waves

ActivPhysics

18.4
Atomic Physics: The Laser

In classical physics, light is purely a wave phenomenon. Einstein's introduction of energy "bundles"—photons—gave light a particle-like quality as well. In

1923, ten years after Bohr published his atomic theory, the French prince Louis de Broglie (pronounced "de Broy") set forth a remarkable hypothesis in his doctoral thesis. If light has both wave-like and particle-like properties, he reasoned, why shouldn't matter also exhibit both properties?

We saw in Chapter 34 that light with energy E also carries momentum $p = E/c$. Combined with Equation 39-1, that means a photon of light with frequency f has momentum $p = hf/c$. Since $f\lambda = c$, the photon's momentum and wavelength are therefore related by

$$\lambda = \frac{h}{p}. \quad \text{(de Broglie wavelength)} \qquad (39\text{-}4)$$

De Broglie proposed that this same relation should hold for particles of matter; at nonrelativistic speed, for example, an electron should have associated with it a "wavelength" given by h/mv. De Broglie's startling new idea was verified experimentally in 1927, with the demonstration that electrons passing through a narrow aperture exhibit a diffraction pattern that we know must be associated with waves (Fig. 39-10).

De Broglie used his matter-wave hypothesis to explain why atomic electron orbits should be quantized. He showed that Bohr's allowed orbits were those in which standing waves could exist (Fig. 39-11), in much the same way that a violin string can support only certain frequencies of standing waves.

If matter has wave-like properties, why don't we notice them all the time? As in optics, wave effects become important only in systems whose size is comparable to or smaller than a wavelength. For macroscopic objects, and even for electrons moving at substantial speed in, say, a TV tube, the electron wavelength is so small that wave properties are unnoticeable. In the electron microscope, we choose the electron energy—and, therefore, momentum and wavelength—so the wavelength will be smaller than the system we want to observe (Fig. 39-12). But when an electron is confined to the smaller orbits of the Bohr atom, its wave properties are dominant.

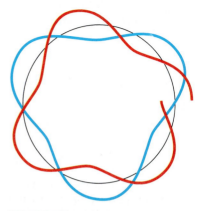

FIGURE 39-11 The allowed electron orbits in the Bohr atom are those that can fit an integral number of de Broglie wavelengths around the circular Bohr orbit. Blue curve represents the de Broglie standing wave for the $n = 3$ level; red curve does not satisfy the Bohr condition. See ActivPhysics Activity 18.3 for a simulation of this figure.

17.4
Electron Interference

18.3
Atomic Physics: Standing Electron Waves

FIGURE 39-12 Diffraction limits the resolution of an optical microscope to approximately the wavelength of light. The electron microscope circumvents this limitation by using electrons whose wavelength, given by Equation 39-4, can be made much smaller than that of light. Here we see a scanning electron microscope photo of sperm fertilizing a sea-urchin egg.

FIGURE 39-10 Diffraction pattern produced by passing an electron beam through a circular aperture shows that electrons have a wave-like character.

EXAMPLE 39-2	*Baseballs and Electrons*

Find the de Broglie wavelength of (a) a 150-g baseball pitched at 45 m/s and (b) an electron moving at 1.0×10^6 m/s. Compare with the sizes of home plate and an atom, respectively.

Solution

Equation 39-4 gives the wavelengths:

$$\lambda_{baseball} = \frac{h}{p} = \frac{h}{mv} = \frac{6.63 \times 10^{-34} \text{ J·s}}{(0.15 \text{ kg})(45 \text{ m/s})} = 9.8 \times 10^{-35} \text{ m}.$$

This is about 34 orders of magnitude smaller than home plate, showing that the baseball's wave properties are totally negligible in the systems with which it interacts. For the electron, on the other hand,

$$\lambda_{electron} = \frac{h}{mv} = \frac{6.63 \times 10^{-34} \text{ J·s}}{(9.11 \times 10^{-31} \text{ kg})(1.0 \times 10^6 \text{ m/s})} = 0.73 \text{ nm},$$

several times the size of an atom. Thus, we should expect wave effects to be prominent when electrons with this speed interact with atoms.

EXERCISE At what speed would a proton's de Broglie wavelength equal the approximately 0.1-nm diameter of the hydrogen atom?

Answer: 4 km/s

Some problems similar to Example 39-2: 10–13

39-2 QUANTUM MECHANICS

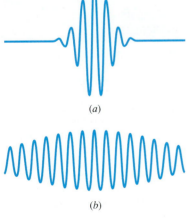

FIGURE 39-13 Erwin Schrödinger.

Planck's quantized vibrations, Einstein's photons, Bohr's atom, de Broglie's matter waves, and several refinements of these ideas comprise what is known as the **old quantum theory**. Together they provided a reasonably accurate first try at modeling the strange world at the atomic scale. But the old quantum theory could not handle atoms with more than one electron, nor could it predict the rates at which jumps among energy levels should occur. It clung to a mixture of classical ideas—like well-defined electron orbits—constrained by the strange new ideas of energy quantization and matter waves. It left the physical interpretation of matter waves vague. Most importantly, the old quantum theory lacked the intellectual coherence of a single guiding principle.

In 1926, the Austrian physicist Erwin Schrödinger (Fig. 39-13) succeeded in giving a mathematical theory, called **wave mechanics**, that did for de Broglie's electron waves what Maxwell's electromagnetic theory had done for light. The **Schrödinger equation** describes the spatial and temporal behavior of a **wave function**, usually designated ψ, that embodies de Broglie's matter-wave idea.

The interpretation of the wave function is at the heart of the profound philosophical difference between classical and quantum physics. Where the equations of classical physics predict a definite outcome in a given physical situation, the wave function determines only the probabilities of different outcomes. This probabilistic interpretation means that even the language of our macroscopic world is ill-suited to the quantum realm. An electron, for example, is neither here nor there; rather, it might have a greater probability of being here than there (Fig. 39-14). The discrete atomic orbits of the old Bohr atom make little sense in wave mechanics; they correspond instead to regions of higher probability. The

FIGURE 39-14 In quantum mechanics, the probability of finding a particle is proportional to the square of the wave function. (a) Here the wave function has significant amplitude only in a small region, and the particle is localized. (b) The particle described by this wave function has a nearly equal probability of being found anywhere in a broad region.

hydrogen atom is not a miniature solar system, but a fuzzy, statistical object with its single electron spread out in a kind of "probability cloud."

Philosophical debate about the interpretation of quantum theory continues to this day, despite the theory's stunning success in describing the universe at the atomic scale. Einstein himself was among the most persistent critics of the probabilistic interpretation, writing: "The theory says a lot, but does not really bring us any closer to the secret of the Old One. I, in any case, am convinced that He does not throw dice." This quotation is often paraphrased as "I cannot believe that God plays dice with the universe." But neither Einstein nor anyone else has yet found a consistent theory of the atomic realm that does not require a probabilistic interpretation.

17.6 Uncertainty Principle

17.7 Wave Packets

The Uncertainty Principle

Shortly before Schrödinger proposed his wave mechanics, the German physicist Werner Heisenberg developed a mathematical description of the atom based on the algebra of matrices. The two theories looked very different but were soon proved equivalent.

Heisenberg's formulation concentrated on what he called **observables**— quantities that could actually be measured in laboratory experiments. (Schrödinger's wave function, in contrast, could not be measured directly and, therefore, is not an observable). In 1927 Heisenberg presented his famous **uncertainty principle**, which states that certain pairs of observables cannot be measured simultaneously with arbitrary precision. Position and momentum constitute one such pair; if we measure a particle's position to within an uncertainty Δx, then its momentum must be uncertain by an amount Δp given by

$$\Delta x \, \Delta p \geq \frac{h}{2\pi}, \tag{39-5}$$

where h is Planck's constant. Similarly, if Δt is the time it takes to measure an energy to an accuracy ΔE, then

$$\Delta E \, \Delta t \geq \frac{h}{2\pi}. \tag{39-6}$$

Why this limitation on the accuracy of measurements? The fundamental reason is quantization. To measure some property of a system requires interacting with that system—for example, shining light on it. That interaction invariably involves energy, and the interaction energy disturbs the system slightly. As a result of this disturbance, values inferred from the measurement are no longer quite the right ones. In classical physics the energy can be made as small as possible, resulting in an arbitrarily small disturbance. But in quantum theory the minimum energy is a single quantum, like a photon of light, and thus, the disturbance cannot be made arbitrarily small.

So why not use lower-frequency light, whose photon energy hf is smaller? Because lower frequency means longer wavelength and, as we found in the preceding chapter, precise imaging requires light whose wavelength is much shorter than the system being imaged. Heisenberg summarized this dilemma with the "thought experiment" shown in Fig. 39-15. He imagined a

FIGURE 39-15 Heisenberg's "quantum microscope." (*a*) A short-wavelength, high-energy photon interacts with an electron. Diffraction is minimal, and the electron's position is accurately determined. But the high-energy photon disturbs the electron's trajectory, leaving its momentum very uncertain. (*b*) Using a long-wavelength, low-energy photon minimizes the disturbance and allows accurate determination of the electron's momentum. But now diffraction is significant, and the measurement does not give an accurate position.

"quantum microscope" observing a single photon interacting with an electron. Using a short-wavelength photon allows precise localization of the electron (Fig. 39-15a). But short wavelength means high frequency and, thus, through Equation 39-1, high photon energy. The high-energy photon imparts considerable momentum to the electron, and thus, any knowledge we had of the electron's momentum is seriously degraded by the very act that determines its position. We might instead choose a long-wavelength, low-energy photon, as in Fig. 39-15b. Then there's little disturbance, and we can get an accurate assessment of the electron's momentum. But now the photon wavelength is so long that diffraction effects severely limit our ability to tell just where the electron was. So we can measure the electron's position accurately, but only at the expense of our knowledge of its momentum. Or we can measure its momentum accurately, but then we'll know very little about its position. With a photon of intermediate wavelength we could measure both quantities, but neither with perfect accuracy. Equation 39-5 establishes the minimum uncertainties possible.

The uncertainty principle moves the observer from a passive onlooker to an active participant in physical events. To observe is necessarily to disturb, and quantum theory is therefore very much concerned with the role of the observer and the process of measurement. The uncertainty principle is fundamentally a statement about what can and cannot be learned through measurement.

So position and momentum cannot be measured simultaneously with arbitrary precision. Surely, though, an electron has well-defined values of both, even though we cannot know them? The answer seems to be no. The standard interpretation of quantum mechanics suggests that it makes no sense to talk about what cannot be measured, and recent experiments have ruled out "hidden variables" that might be active at a lower level to guide the electron in a deterministic path. We are left with uncertainty—or indeterminacy, as Heisenberg's word also translates—as a fundamental fact of our universe.

EXAMPLE 39-3	*Microelectronics*

A beam of aluminum atoms is used to "dope" a semiconductor chip to give it the proper electrical characteristics. If the atoms' velocity is required to be $(4.50000 \pm 0.00001) \times 10^4$ m/s, how accurately can the atoms be localized?

Solution

With a velocity spread of $\pm 0.00001 \times 10^4$ m/s, the maximum tolerable uncertainty in the atoms' velocity is $\Delta v = 0.00002 \times 10^4$ m/s, or 0.20 m/s. Then corresponding momentum uncertainty is

$$\Delta p = m \Delta v = (26.98 \text{ u})(1.66 \times 10^{-27} \text{ kg/u})(0.20 \text{ m/s})$$

$$= 8.96 \times 10^{-27} \text{ kg·m/s},$$

where we found the atomic weight of aluminum in Appendix D. Equation 39-5 then gives the uncertainty in position:

$$\Delta x \geq \frac{h}{2\pi \Delta p} = \left(\frac{6.63 \times 10^{-34} \text{ J·s}}{(2\pi)(8.96 \times 10^{-27} \text{ kg·m/s})} \right)$$

$$= 1.2 \times 10^{-8} \text{ m}.$$

This is about 100 atomic diameters and shows that the uncertainty principle ultimately limits our ability to manufacture very small microelectronic structures by the means now used.

EXERCISE You measure the velocity of a 3.0-g ping-pong ball to an accuracy of ± 0.01 mm/s. Find the minimum uncertainty in its position, and compare with the size of the ball.

Answer: 1.8×10^{-27} m, totally negligible compared with the ball

Some problems similar to Example 39-3: 14–20

Electron Spin and the Exclusion Principle

We have seen how different electron energy states in the hydrogen atom are distinguished by values of the integer n, which is called a **quantum number**. The theories of Schrödinger and Heisenberg use two additional quantum numbers that describe also the electron's orbital angular momentum. But detailed observation of the hydrogen spectrum shows that spectral lines are actually "doublets" of two closely spaced lines. In 1925, Wolfgang Pauli (Fig. 39-16) proposed a fourth quantum number to account for the doublet lines. At the end of the same year, Samuel Goudsmit and George Uhlenbeck realized that the line splitting could be explained if the electron possessed an intrinsic angular momentum, called **spin**. Although it's tempting to think of the electron as a little spinning ball, that classical analogy is grossly inadequate. Spin is an entirely quantum mechanical property, and its behavior is far from classical; in particular, the spin angular momentum of an electron can take on only two possible orientations, loosely called "spin up" and "spin down."

Earlier, Pauli had stated his famous **exclusion principle**, saying that no two electrons in an atom can have the same set of quantum numbers—i.e., the four numbers that describe the electron's energy, orbital angular momentum, and spin. In the Schrödinger theory with electron spin added, the Pauli exclusion principle means that at most two electrons—one with spin "up" and the other with spin "down"—can share the first three quantum numbers. In multielectron atoms, the exclusion principle governs the distribution of electrons among the different quantum states, often called shells and subshells. It is thus the basis for the chemical properties of the elements and explains the groupings of the periodic table (inside back cover).

FIGURE 39-16 Wolfgang Pauli and Niels Bohr watching a spinning top whose motion provides a classical analog of electron spin.

Relativistic Quantum Mechanics

Schrödinger's theory of quantum mechanics was based on the nonrelativistic relation between momentum and kinetic energy. In 1927, Paul A. M. Dirac developed a quantum-mechanical wave equation consistent with Equation 38-16 linking energy and momentum in special relativity: $E^2 = p^2c^2 + (mc^2)^2$. Dirac faced mathematical difficulties in dealing with the fact that energy appears squared in this equation. Two remarkable results followed from his handling of this problem: First, he found that consistency with relativity required that the electron have intrinsic angular momentum. Here was a fundamental justification for electron spin, proposed earlier on an *ad hoc* basis to account for spectral features that Schrödinger's theory left unexplained. Second, Dirac explored the fact that the relativistic equation for energy, like any quadratic equation, has two solutions. Rather than discarding the solution corresponding to negative energy, Dirac showed how it led to the concept of **antimatter**—in this case a particle with the mass of the electron but with opposite charge and other properties. The discovery of this particle—the **positron**—in 1932 was a remarkable vindication of Dirac's vision (Fig. 39-17). We know today that every particle has a corresponding antiparticle.

FIGURE 39-17 Cloud chamber photograph on which Carl Anderson of the California Institute of Technology discovered the positron in 1932. Anderson's discovery resulted in his sharing the 1936 Nobel Prize in physics.

Quantum Electrodynamics

Another high point in the development of quantum mechanics was the theory of **quantum electrodynamics (QED)**, set forth in 1948 by Sin-Itiro Tomonaga, Julian Schwinger, and Richard P. Feynman (Fig. 39-18). The theory of QED deals with the quantum-mechanical interaction between matter and electromagnetic radiation. In QED the electromagnetic interaction is visualized as an exchange of so-called **virtual photons** that exist only for the brief duration of the interaction and are never seen. Figure 39-19 shows a **Feynman diagram** for the quantum electrodynamical interaction of an electron and proton. Experiments have verified quantum electrodynamics to extremely high accuracy, and today it is our best-verified theory of physical reality.

The Wave-Particle Duality and Complementarity

One of the most disturbing aspects of quantum theory is the **wave-particle duality**—the seemingly contradictory fact that matter and light have both wave-like and particle-like properties. Bohr dealt with this conundrum through his **principle of complementarity**. The wave and particle pictures, he said, are complementary aspects of the same reality. If we do an experiment to measure a wave-like property—for example, the diffraction of electrons—then we find wave properties but not particle properties. If we do an experiment to measure a particle-like property—for example, localizing an electron—then we will not find wave properties. The two measurements require different experiments, and we can't perform both simultaneously on the same entity. So we will never catch wave and particle in an outright contradiction, and we can never definitively answer the question "Which is it, wave or particle?"

FIGURE 39-19 A Feynman diagram, showing electron-proton scattering as mediated by the exchange of a virtual photon. All electromagnetic interactions among particles can be described with such diagrams.

39-3 NUCLEAR PHYSICS

J. J. Thomson discovered the electron in 1897, but at that time it was not known how electrons and the equivalent positive charge were distributed in atoms. Thomson himself favored the **plum-pudding model**, with electrons embedded throughout a "pudding" of positive charge. In a 1909 to 1911 series of experiments suggested by Ernest Rutherford, Rutherford's colleague Hans Geiger and undergraduate student Ernest Marsden shot positively charged alpha particles (helium nuclei) from a radioactive source into thin gold foils. They expected the particles to pass straight through the gold or at most to be deflected very slightly. Most of them behaved as expected, but a few bounced back in nearly the direction they had come from (Fig. 39-20). It was, to paraphrase Rutherford, as though you shot a cannonball at a piece of tissue paper and the ball bounced back. Rutherford realized that a rebounding alpha particle had collided with a small but massive object exerting a large repulsive force. He therefore concluded that all the atom's positive charge and nearly all its mass must be concentrated in a small, massive core: the **nucleus**. A new atomic model emerged, with the

FIGURE 39-20 In the Rutherford-Geiger-Marsden experiment, alpha particles recoiling from a gold foil (red trajectory) revealed the existence of the massive atomic nucleus. Most alphas went right through the foil (green trajectories), showing that the nucleus, although it contains nearly all the mass of an atom, occupies only a tiny fraction of its volume.

tiny, positively charged nucleus at the center, surrounded by electrons in distant orbits (Fig. 39-21).

But the mutual electrical repulsion of all the positive charges in the nucleus would be strong, so what holds the nucleus together? There must be another force—the **nuclear force**—acting attractively between the constituents of the nucleus. By 1920 Rutherford had also proposed the existence of a neutral particle in the nucleus to "dilute" the repulsive effect of the nuclear protons. In 1932 James Chadwick discovered such a particle, the **neutron**. Together the protons and neutrons making up a nucleus are called **nucleons**.

The number of electrons in an atom determines its chemical properties, and that number is in turn equal to the number of protons in the nucleus. But the number of neutrons can vary, giving rise to **isotopes** of a given element. Different isotopes have the same number of protons but different numbers of neutrons. Their chemical properties are essentially the same but their nuclear properties may be very different.

Fission, Fusion, and the Curve of Binding Energy

In the nucleus protons and neutrons alike experience the attractive nuclear force, but only the charged protons feel the electrical repulsion. The nuclear force is very strong, but, unlike the $1/r^2$ electrical force, it drops rapidly—exponentially, in fact—with distance. Thus, electrical repulsion is the dominant effect on distant protons, but the attractive nuclear force can nevertheless bind together a cluster of closely spaced protons and neutrons.

The energy it would take to disassemble the nucleus—the so-called **binding energy**—is a measure of how tightly bound a given nucleus is. Comparing different nuclei makes more sense if we consider the binding energy per nucleon. As the number of nucleons grows, so does the binding energy per nucleon, because a given nucleon experiences attractive forces from more neighboring nucleons. But with larger nuclei the short-range nature of the nuclear force causes this effect to diminish. And with still larger nuclei the repulsion of relatively distant protons actually decreases the binding energy. The result is a **curve of binding energy** (Fig. 39-22) that has a broad peak in the vicinity of

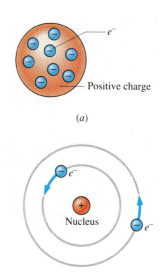

FIGURE 39-21 (*a*) Thomson's "plum-pudding" model of the atom had electrons immersed in a "pudding" of positive charge. (*b*) In Rutherford's nuclear model, electrons orbit the tiny but massive nucleus. Figure is not to scale; the nucleus is actually about 10^{-5} times the size of the atom.

19.2
Nuclear Binding Energy

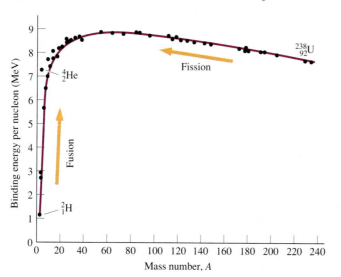

FIGURE 39-22 The curve of binding energy. Nuclei lighter than those at the peak of the curve can release energy by fusing to produce heavier nuclei. Nuclei heavier than those at the peak of the curve can release energy by fissioning into two smaller nuclei.

FIGURE 39-23 The awesome destructive power of a nuclear weapon is a testament to the strength of the nuclear force and the concomitant factor of 10 million difference between nuclear and chemical energy.

60 nucleons. Among the most tightly bound nuclei near this peak is the common iron isotope $^{56}_{26}$Fe. (Here the lower number is the **atomic number**, signifying 26 protons, while the upper number is the **mass number** A, the total number of protons and neutrons.)

The binding energy is the energy it takes to disassemble the nucleus, so it's also the energy released when a nucleus is formed. Any reaction among nucleons that increases the binding energy therefore results in net energy release. As Fig. 39-21 shows, the two possibilities are **fusion** and **fission**. Fusion reactions release energy when lighter nuclei fuse to make heavier ones; fission reactions release energy when more massive nuclei break apart. The great strength of the nuclear force means that nuclear reactions are about 10^7 times more energetic than the electrical interactions among atoms that constitute chemical reactions, and that difference accounts for the concentrated power of nuclear energy sources (Fig. 39-23).

The Austrian physicist Lise Meitner and her nephew Otto Frisch first recognized the phenomenon of fission in 1939 (Fig. 39-24). From the safety of Norway, where Meitner had fled to avoid Hitler's persecution, they interpreted the results of experiments by their German colleagues Otto Hahn and Fritz Strassmann as indicating that uranium nuclei had indeed split, each releasing some 200 MeV of energy in the process. It was the eve of World War II, and a race for military applications of nuclear energy began at once. That race culminated in the devastation of the Japanese cities Hiroshima and Nagasaki in 1945 and continued for 45 more years largely as a nuclear competition between the United States and the former Soviet Union. Nuclear fission has also found a more benign use, in the nuclear reactors that produce 20% of the United States' electric power and more in many other countries.

Fusion of hydrogen powers the Sun and other stars and is the basis of thermonuclear weapons—"hydrogen bombs"—that afford the almost unlimited destructive power of today's nuclear arsenals. Harnessing fusion for electric power generation remains a more elusive goal. To overcome their electrical repulsion, the fusing nuclei must have energies corresponding to temperatures in the 100 million kelvin range. Achieving such temperatures and containing the hot material while it undergoes fusion have proved enormous challenges. After decades of research, it appears that fusion reactors might become commercially viable sometime in the first half of the twenty-first century. If they do, we will have in each gallon of ordinary water the fuel equivalent of about 400 gallons of gasoline.

FIGURE 39-24 Lise Meitner and Otto Hahn. Meitner and her nephew Otto Frisch interpreted the experiments of Hahn and Strassman as evidence for uranium fission. In the 1920s Meitner, an Austrian, had braved sexist policies that denied her access to laboratories when men were present; by the 1930s she had become one of the world's most respected nuclear physicists.

Radioactivity

Not all combinations of nucleons are stable. If a nucleus has too many protons or gets too big, electrical repulsion can cause it to eject particles or even to fission spontaneously. It will also eject particles if it has too many neutrons. This phenomenon of **radioactivity** was first noticed by Henri Becquerel in 1896, when particles emitted by uranium compounds caused fogging of a nearby photographic plate. In the early 1900s his student Marie Curie and her husband Pierre Curie did pioneering experiments in the study of natural radioactivity

(Fig. 39-25); later, in 1934, their daughter Irène and her husband Frédérick Joliot-Curie were the first to produce radioactive isotopes in the laboratory.

We distinguish three common types of radioactivity. In **alpha emission**, a nucleus with too many protons ejects an alpha particle—a helium-4 nucleus, consisting of two protons and two neutrons—and drops by two in atomic number and four in mass number. In **beta emission** a nucleus emits an electron or a positron, changing its atomic number by ± 1, respectively, but not changing its mass number. Also emitted is a **neutrino**, an elusive, neutral particle whose mass was long thought to be zero but, as a result of experiments done in 1998, is now believed to be small but nonzero. Neutrinos interact with matter through the so-called **weak force** and, because this interaction is so weak, they can pass through solid bodies like Earth with very little probability of stopping. Finally nuclei, like atoms, can be excited to higher energy states. Dropping back, they undergo **gamma emission**, emitting a high-energy photon called a gamma ray.

Radioactive nuclei are characterized not only by the kind and energy of radiation they emit, but also by their **half-life**, meaning the time it takes half of the nuclei in a given sample to decay. Half-lives range from fractions of a second to billions of years.

Byproducts of nuclear fission and materials bombarded with high-energy particle beams contain a host of radioactive isotopes that are both dangerous and extremely useful. Common uses of radioactivity include medical diagnosis and cancer treatment, dating of ancient artifacts, geological dating, food preservation, tracing material flows in biological and other systems, and detecting bombs in airline luggage. Figure 39-26 is a chart showing all the known nuclei, both stable and unstable.

FIGURE 39-25 Marie Curie and Pierre Curie in their laboratory.

19.4
Radioactivity

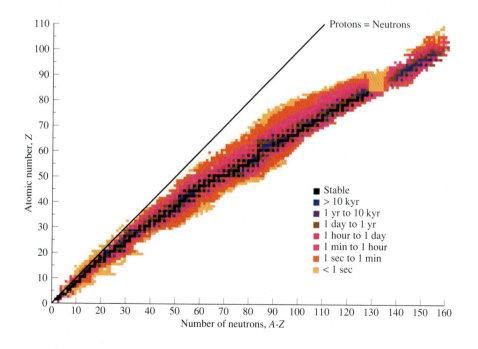

FIGURE 39-26 A chart of the nuclides, plotting all known nuclei according to the number of protons (atomic number Z) versus number of neutrons ($A-Z$). The nuclei are color coded by half-life. Note that the more massive nuclei are richer in neutrons; this is necessary to counter the electrical repulsion of the protons.

EXAMPLE 39-4	*Fallout From Chernobyl*

The 1986 accident at the Chernobyl nuclear power plant in the then-Soviet Ukraine spread radioactive fallout over eastern Europe and Scandinavia. A particularly dangerous isotope released was iodine-131, which is absorbed by the thyroid gland and can cause thyroid cancer. The half-life of I-131 is 8.0 days. Following the accident, I-131 levels in milk in Romania rose to 15 times the Romanian government's safety standard. How long did Romanians have to wait until their milk was safe to drink?

Solution

In one half-life, the number of radioactive nuclei and, therefore, also the level of radioactivity drop to half their original value; in two half-lives they drop to $1/2^2$, or one-fourth of their original value. And in n half-lives they drop to $1/2^n$ of their original value. Thus, we want

$$\frac{1}{2^n} = \frac{1}{15}$$

or, inverting and taking logarithms of both sides,

$$\ln(2^n) = \ln 15.$$

But $\ln(2^n) = n \ln 2$, so

$$n = \frac{\ln 15}{\ln 2} = 3.9 \text{ half-lives}.$$

Since I-131's half-life is 8 days, Romanians had to wait 31 days before their milk was considered safe.

EXERCISE A patient undergoing a PET scan is given a dose of radioactive oxygen-15 (half-life 2 minutes). How long will it take for the activity of the dose to decline to one one-millionth of its original level?

Answer: about 40 min (20 half-lives)

Some problems similar to Example 39-4: 21–24

Nuclear Structure

The proton and neutron both obey the Pauli exclusion principle, and thus, we might expect nucleons to arrange themselves into shells like the electrons in atoms. In the 1940s, Marie Goeppert Mayer (Fig. 39-27) and J. Hans Jensen independently developed such a **shell model**, which has proved reasonably successful in explaining nuclear properties. But the strength of the nuclear force and the close packing of nucleons makes it harder to model nuclei than it is to model atoms. As a result an alternative theory, the **liquid-drop model**, is also used to interpret nuclear experiments.

39-4 ELEMENTARY PARTICLES

By 1932 there were four "elementary" particles known: the electron, the proton, the neutron, and the neutrino. These, along with the photon of electromagnetic radiation, could explain the interactions of everyday matter. But as physicists began looking at higher energies, a host of new particles appeared, until there were soon more than 100 "elementary" particles. These fell into several categories. There were electrons and heavier electron-like particles called **muons**. There were three types of neutrinos. There were **mesons**, thought to be the "carriers" of the nuclear force in the way photons are the "carriers" of the electromagnetic force in quantum electrodynamics. There were a host of **baryons**, or heavy particles including protons and neutrons. And for each particle there was, as Dirac had foreseen, a corresponding antiparticle. Most of these particles—including the neutron when it's not in a stable nucleus—are unstable and quickly decay.

FIGURE 39-27 Maria Goeppert Mayer, shown with her daughter. She won the 1963 Nobel Prize for developing the shell model of nuclear structure.

Quarks

In 1964 Murray Gell-Mann and, independently, George Zweig suggested a set of three particles that could be combined in different ways to form many of the known particles. Gell-Mann called these particles **quarks**, a word used in James Joyce's novel *Finnegan's Wake*. One surprising thing about quarks is that they carry fractional electric charges. The two least massive quarks, called the **up quark** (u) and the **down quark** (d) carry $+\frac{2}{3}e$ and $-\frac{1}{3}e$, respectively; their antiparticles have the opposite charges. Baryons, like the proton and the neutron, consist of three quarks (Fig. 39-28). Mesons, in constrast, contain a quark and an antiquark (Fig. 39-29).

The Pauli exclusion principle precludes three quarks having the same quantum numbers, and therefore, there must be an additional property distinguishing quarks. Called **color**, this property is a kind of "charge"—not to be confused with electric charge—that can take on any of three values called red, green, and blue. (The word "color" as used here has an entirely new meaning and has nothing to do with light.) The force binding quarks of different colors is called the **color force**, and the quark theory is therefore known as **quantum chromodynamics (QCD)**. In QCD, particles called **gluons** play the role of photons in quantum electrodynamics, binding particles subject to the color force. The nuclear force, once thought to be fundamental, is actually a residual manifestation of the color force between quarks—in much the same way that the van der Waals force between gas molecules is a "residue" of the stronger electric force among the particles comprising the molecules.

A second surprising aspect of quarks is that the color force binding them into composite particles does not decrease with separation (Fig. 39-30). For that reason it appears impossible to isolate a single quark. As a result we never see individual particles with fractional electric charge.

Today the quark model is universally accepted, so we now know that many of the previously "elementary" particles—including protons and neutrons—are in fact composites of the simpler quarks. Electrons and their relatives seem, on the other hand, to be truly elementary.

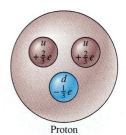

FIGURE 39-28 Protons and neutrons consist of the quark combinations *uud* and *udd,* respectively.

FIGURE 39-29 Mesons consist of quark-antiquark pairs. The meson shown here is the π^+ meson, consisting of an up quark and a down antiquark. (The bar over the d signifies an antiparticle.)

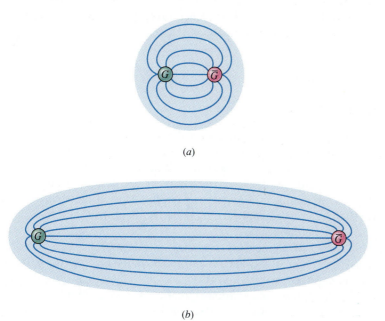

(a)

(b)

FIGURE 39-30 (a) A green and an antigreen quark form a meson. The quarks are bound by the color force, here depicted by field lines analogous to those of the electric field. (b) The field strength remains approximately constant even if the quarks move apart. Thus it would take infinite energy to separate them fully.

FIGURE 39-31 This image from a particle detector at Fermilab provided experimental evidence for the existence of the top quark.

FIGURE 39-32 Photo showing the location of the Super Proton Synchrotron of CERN, the European Laboratory for Particle Physics, in Geneva, Switzerland. The accelerator's main ring, buried beneath farmland, is 7 km in circumference and produces proton-antiproton collisions with total energy 640 GeV.

The up and down quarks proved insufficient to account for all the observed particles. A third quark, the **strange quark**, was introduced to account for the "strange" properties—in particular, slower-than-expected decay rates—of some particles. But by 1970 the theorist Sheldon Glashow was arguing for a fourth quark, which he called the **charmed quark**. Ten years later, following intensive searches, experimental teams at Brookhaven National Laboratory and Stanford University announced the discovery of a particle that implies the existence of the charmed quark. The Brookhaven group called the new particle J and the Stanford group called it ψ; to this day it is often called the J/ψ.

Since the J/ψ discovery yet another pair of quarks has been proposed. A 1977 experiment confirmed the existence of the **bottom quark**, and in 1994 experiments at Fermilab gave the first evidence for the **top quark** (Fig. 39-31). The more exotic quarks are more massive and therefore, through mass-energy equivalence, it takes more energy to produce particles containing them. This need for higher energy is what drives the push for ever more powerful and expensive particle accelerators (Fig. 39-32).

The Standard Model

We now have six **flavors** of quarks—up, down, strange, charmed, top, bottom—which seem to be truly elementary constituents of matter. As we've seen, quarks join to form baryons or mesons; together, these quark-based particles are called **hadrons**. But there are other particles, namely, the neutrinos, and the electron and its relatives, that are not made from quarks. Most of these particles are less massive than hadrons and collectively are called **leptons**. They, like the quarks, are believed to be indivisible.

In this "zoo" of elementary particles, physicists recognize three distinct "families" (see Table 39-1). The up and the down quarks comprise the neutron and proton; together with the electron and its related neutrino, these quarks account for the properties of ordinary matter. A second family consists of the strange and charmed quarks, the electron-like muon, and the muon neutrino. The quarks of this family are more massive than the up and down quarks, and the muon is more massive than the electron. More massive still are the particles of the third family, consisting of the top and bottom quarks, the electron-like tau particle, and the tau neutrino.

TABLE 39-1 *Standard Model of Quarks and Leptons*

QUARK NAME	SYMBOL	CHARGE	CORRESPONDING LEPTONS
Down	d	$-\frac{1}{3}e$	electron (e), electron neutrino (ν_e)
Up	u	$+\frac{2}{3}e$	
Strange	s	$-\frac{1}{3}e$	muon (μ), muon neutrino (ν_μ)
Charmed	c	$+\frac{2}{3}e$	
Bottom	b	$-\frac{1}{3}e$	tau (τ), tau neutrino (ν_τ)
Top	t	$+\frac{2}{3}e$	

You may be expecting that future editions of this book will tell of additional quarks and, therefore, of additional families of matter. Whether such additional families exist was an open question until 1991, when physicists at the Large Electron Positron Collider in Geneva, Switzerland, examined over half a million particle decay events to conclude that the number of different types of neutrinos that can exist is 2.99 ± 0.06. Since there is presumably a neutrino type for each family, this result seems to preclude the existence of additional families.

The current theory that describes elementary particles and their interactions is called the **standard model**. In addition to the constituent particles of matter shown in Table 39-1, the standard model includes the photons that mediate the electromagnetic interaction, the gluons of the color force, particles called the W and Z that mediate the weak force that couples leptons and hadrons, and the as yet undetected Higgs boson believed responsible for other particles' masses. The standard model is very successful in explaining the phenomena of particle physics, but it leaves many fundamental questions unanswered. Why, for example, do the quarks and leptons have the particular masses they do? Why are there only three families of elementary particles? Why are leptons and quarks distinct? Continuing theoretical work and experiments at ever higher energies may someday answer these questions.

39-5 UNIFICATION AND COSMOLOGY

We first introduced the fundamental forces of nature in Chapter 5, indicating that today physicists recognize just three such forces: gravity, the electroweak force, and the strong or color force. It was not always that simple, though. In Chapters 23 through 34 we studied the electric and magnetic forces, first separately but then with the realization that they fell under the single umbrella of electromagnetism. The unification of electricity and magnetism was a major step forward in our understanding of physical reality.

Electroweak Unification

In the 1960s and early 1970s, a century after Maxwell formalized the unification of electromagnetism, physicists Steven Weinberg, Abdus Salam, and Sheldon Glashow proposed that the electromagnetic force and the weak force are really aspects of the same thing. Their theory predicted the existence of a family of particles called W^+, Z^0, and W^-, which would join the photon as "carriers" of the unified electroweak force. In 1983 a huge international consortium headed by Carlo Rubbia discovered the W and Z particles, using advances in accelerator technology developed by Simon van der Meer (Fig. 39-33). That discovery

(a)

(b)

FIGURE 39-33 (a) Carlo Rubbia and Simon von der Meer headed the experimental efforts that led to the confirmation of electroweak unification. (b) This particle-track image led to the experimental discovery of the Z particle.

TABLE 39-2 *Nobel Prizes for Interpreting the Structure of Matter*

PRIZE YEAR	PRIZE RECIPIENT	RESEARCH CONTRIBUTION[†]
1903	Antoine H. Becquerel	Discovery of radioactivity (1896)
	Marie and Pierre Curie	Studies of radioactivity (1896–1903)
1906	J. J. Thomson	Discovery of the electron and other studies (1897)
1908	Ernest Rutherford*	Disintegration of elements using alpha particles (1902)
1935	James Chadwick	Discovery of the neutron (1932)
	Irène and Frédéric Joliot-Curie	Synthesizing new radioactive elements (1934)
1936	Victor F. Hess	Discovery of cosmic rays (1911)
	Carl D. Anderson	Discovery of the positron (1932)
1938	Enrico Fermi	Production of new radioactive elements (1934–37)
1949	Hideki Yukawa	Theoretical prediction of mesons (1934)
1951	John D. Cockcroft and Ernest T. S. Walton	Transmutation of nuclei (1932)
1957	C. N. Yang and T. D. Lee	Theoretical prediction of parity violation (1956)
1959	Emilio G. Segrè and Owen Chamberlain	Production of the antiproton (1955)
1963	Maria Goeppert Mayer and J. Hans Jensen	Nuclear shell model (1949)
	Eugene P. Wigner	Application of symmetry to elementary particle theories
1968	Luis Alvarez	Contributions to particle accelerators (1946)
1969	Murray Gell-Mann	Theory classifying elementary particles (1964)
1975	Aage Bohr, Ben Mottelson, and James Rainwater	Studies of nuclear structure and dynamics (1950s)
1976	Burton Richter and Samuel C. C. Ting	Discovery of the J/ψ particle, the first charmed particle (1973–74)
1979	Sheldon L. Glashow, Abdus Salam, and Steven Weinberg	Unification of the electromagnetic and weak force (1961–72)
1980	Val L. Fitch and James W. Cronin	Experimental proof of violation of conservation of charge-parity (1964)
1984	Carlo Rubbia and Simon van der Meer	Discovery of W particles, predicted by the electroweak unification (1983); stochastic cooling for focusing particle beams (1968)
1988	Leon M. Lederman, Melvin Schwartz, and Jack Steinberger	Production of neutrino beams and discovery of the μ neutrino (1960–62)
1990	Jerome Friedman, Henry Kendall, and Richard Taylor	Using scattering of electrons from protons and neutrons to explore the quark model.
1992	Georges Charpak	Developing electronic detectors for detecting subatomic particles in accelerators.
1995	Martin L. Perl	Discovery of the tau particle (1974–77)
	Frederick Reines	Pioneering work with neutrinos (1950s)

† Note: Number in parentheses is the year discovery was made.
* Rutherford and Joliot-Curie prizes in chemistry; all others in physics.

confirmed the electroweak unification, and Rubbia and van der Meer joined a long list of physicists who had won the Nobel Prize for contributions to our understanding of the structure of matter (Table 39-2).

Further Unification

Electroweak unification led to the present situation in physics, which has gravity, electroweak, and strong forces as the fundamental interactions of matter. A further step, **grand unification theory** (GUT), attempts to merge the electroweak and color forces. Some versions of the GUT predict that the proton is not stable, but should decay on the very long timescale of some 10^{31} years. We can't wait that long, but we can put 10^{34} protons together in the form of tens of thousands of tons of water and watch for proton decay (Fig. 39-34). Such experiments have not found the predicted decays, but another GUT prediction— that neutrinos have mass—was tentatively verified in 1998, also in the device of Fig. 39-34. Many physicists believe that some form of grand unification will soon be achieved.

Even grand unification would still leave two forces, one of them gravity. Attempts to reconcile our current theory of gravity—Einstein's general relativity—with quantum mechanics have so far made little progress. Yet such a reconciliation is a necessary prerequisite for a final unification of all known forces. In the 1980s a flurry of interest developed in so-called **superstring theories**, which picture elementary particles as fundamental vibration modes on string-like structures that may be as short as 10^{-35} m. This model is set not in the four-dimensional spacetime to which we have become accustomed, but in a ten-dimensional spacetime with six of its dimensions "compactified" in a way that makes them undetectable in normal interactions. To some physicists, string theories hold the promise of a "theory of everything," explaining all our observations about the behavior of the universe. To others they are another in a long list of unsuccessful attempts at a comprehensive explanation of physical phenomena. Time will tell.

FIGURE 39-34 The Super Kamiokande experiment in Japan consists of 50,000 tons of pure water in a deep underground chamber, surrounded by 11,200 photomultiplier tubes that detect light flashes from rare nuclear reactions. The device functions as a neutrino detector, and can also search for evidence of proton decay. Experiments with Super Kamiokande show that the proton has a lifetime of at least 10^{33} years, and that neutrinos probably have nonzero mass.

Symmetry Breaking

Unification theories predict that phenomena that appear distinct under normal conditions will be clearly seen as one at sufficiently high energies. The observed unification represents a kind of symmetry that is "broken" as the energy level drops. A crude mechanical analog for such **symmetry breaking** is a ball rolling around the rim of a bowl. As long as the ball keeps rolling, there is no preferred angular direction. But if the ball stops, it drops into the bowl in a particular direction. The symmetry of the original situation has been broken. Analogously, at energies above 100 GeV, what we call the electromagnetic and weak forces are one and the same. But at lower energies the symmetry is broken, and we see two distinct forces. Particle accelerators now in construction will exceed the energy of electroweak symmetry breaking, allowing us to explore that interaction in its fundamental simplicity. But the energy at which symmetry breaking occurs increases to some 10^{15} GeV as we move from electroweak to grand unification, making it unlikely that we will achieve that energy in the foreseeable future. And the energy at which gravity, too, would join a single unified force is an even more remote 10^{19} GeV.

The Origin of the Universe

Although the energy above which the electroweak and strong forces would appear unified seems out of reach of our terrestrial laboratories and even of processes in the most bizarre astrophysical systems known, there is one "place" we can look for phenomena at such enormous energies. That "place" is, rather, a time—the very earliest instants after the universe began.

A host of evidence points to a universe that has evolved to its present state from a hot, explosive beginning called the **big bang**. In 1929 the American

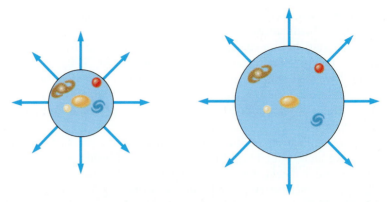

FIGURE 39-35 Expansion of a finite universe. Einstein's general relativity suggests that the universe could be a closed structure in four dimensions, analogous to the surface of a sphere in two dimensions. Such a surface has no boundary, and as it expands each point on the surface sees the other points moving away at speeds proportional to their distances.

astronomer Edwin Hubble (after whom the Space Telescope was named) found that spectral lines from distant galaxies were shifted toward the red end of the spectrum, with the shift proportional to a galaxy's distance from Earth. Interpreting the shift as akin to the Doppler effect, astronomers concluded that the distant galaxies are rushing away from each other at speeds proportional to their distances. This is exactly what one would expect if a colossal explosion had flung them apart. Although Hubble's observation might suggest that Earth is at the center, that is not the case. In a universe infinite in extent, every observer would see the same universal expansion, and the same would be true in a finite universe subject to Einstein's general theory of relativity (Fig. 39-35).

In 1965 Arno Penzias and Robert Wilson at Bell Laboratories in New Jersey found a faint "noise" of microwave radiation in a satellite communications antenna they were testing. They could not eliminate the noise, which seemed to come from all directions. Theorists at Princeton concluded that Penzias and Wilson had detected radiation emitted during the formation of the first atoms, some 10^5 years after the universe began. This **cosmic microwave background radiation** is some of the strongest evidence for the big bang theory. That evidence was further strengthened in 1992 with the discovery that the microwave background contains very faint "ripples" that led to the formation of galaxies.

With the microwave background, we can "see" the universe as it was about 10^5 years after its beginning. We may soon be able to look further back by studying a similar "background" of neutrinos believed to date from about 1 second after the big bang began. Evidence for still earlier times comes indirectly from applying elementary particle physics to the behavior of matter at extreme temperatures and seeing if the result suggests an evolution to conditions we do observe. Today's accelerators achieve conditions that existed only 10^{-9} s from the beginning of the universe, and the Large Hadron Collider at CERN will push that time back to 10^{-12} s when it begins operation around the year 2005. Thus, these early times provide a test of elementary particle physics, and particle physics in turn helps us to understand how the universe began and how it evolved

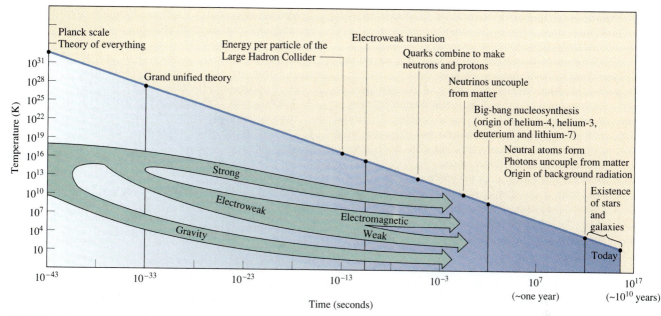

FIGURE 39-36 The evolution of the universe from the earliest times to the present. Note the highly logarithmic scale. As the universe has expanded, its average temperature and energy have fallen, giving rise to epochs in which different physical processes dominated. At first the fundamental forces were all one, but symmetry breaking caused them to separate as the energy dropped. Present-day physics cannot address times before 10^{-43} s, which requires a merging of quantum theory and general relativity.

to its present state. Figure 39-36 summarizes our understanding of the evolution of the universe, showing that the phenomena of particle physics and unification are inextricably tied with cosmic questions.

CHAPTER SYNOPSIS

Summary

1. **Quantum physics** describes matter and energy on the small scale. The essential difference between quantum and classical physics is that some physical quantities in quantum physics come only in certain discrete values, or quanta.

   a. Studies of blackbody radiation led Planck to the quantization of molecular vibration energies.

   b. The photoelectric effect led Einstein to propose quantization of electromagnetic wave energy in "bundles" called **photons**; each photon carries energy $E = hf$.

   c. Bohr was able to explain the spectrum of hydrogen by assuming quantized electron orbits in the atom. The wavelength of a photon emitted or absorbed when an atom jumps between two levels is given by

   $$\frac{1}{\lambda} = R_H\left(\frac{1}{n_2^2} - \frac{1}{n_1^2}\right),$$

   where R_H is the Rydberg constant for hydrogen. In all three cases quantization involved **Planck's constant**, $h = 6.63 \times 10^{-34}$ J·s.

2. Louis de Broglie proposed that matter, like light, has both particle and wave properties. If a particle has momentum p, then the associated wavelength is

   $$\lambda = \frac{h}{p}.$$

3. **Quantum mechanics**, developed by Schrödinger, Heisenberg, and others, provides a nearly complete theory of atomic-scale phenomena. In Schrödinger's version, a particle's behavior is governed statistically by a **wave function** that satisfies Schrödinger's equation.

   a. It is necessary to add the concept of electron **spin**, or intrinsic angular momentum, to Schrödinger's theory in order to account fully for atomic spectra. The **Pauli exclusion principle** says that no two electrons in an atom can be in the same state, where states with opposite spins count as distinct states.

   b. Heisenberg's **uncertainty principle** says that the act of observing a quantum-mechanical system necessarily disturbs the system. As a result, it is impossible to measure simultaneously a particle's exact position and momentum; instead, the uncertainties Δx and Δp must satisfy the inequality

   $$\Delta x \, \Delta p \geq \frac{h}{2\pi}.$$

   c. Relativistic quantum mechanics, developed by Dirac, shows that spin arises naturally as a consequence of relativity. Dirac's theory also predicts the existence of antimatter.

   d. **Quantum electrodynamics** describes the quantum-mechanical interaction of matter and electromagnetic radiation.

   e. The principle of **complementarity** resolves the contradiction seemingly inherent in the **wave-particle duality** by showing that it is impossible simultaneously to observe both aspects of either matter or light in the same experiment.

4. The atomic nucleus consists of protons and neutrons bound by the **nuclear force**.

   a. **Binding energy** measures how tightly bound a given nucleus is. Light nuclei undergoing **fusion** increase the binding energy per nucleon, releasing energy in the process. Heavier nuclei undergoing **fission** similarly release energy.

   b. **Radioactivity** is the emission of particles—typically alpha particles (helium nuclei), beta particles (electrons or positrons), or gamma rays (high-energy photons)—by unstable nuclei.

   c. Nuclear structure can be described using the shell and liquid-drop models.

5. Elementary particles consist of **quarks** and **leptons**. Quarks come in six flavors and three colors, and combine through the **strong** or **color force** to make **hadrons**. Hadrons with three quarks are **baryons** and include the proton and neutron. Hadrons with a quark and an antiquark are **mesons**. Leptons include electrons and the electron-like **muon** and **tau**, along with three types of **neutrino**. The **standard model** organizes the quarks and leptons into three families.

6. The fundamental forces of nature—gravity, electromagnetism, the weak force, and the strong force—may very well be aspects of a single fundamental interaction. Already **electroweak unification** has demonstrated that electromagnetism and the weak force are essentially one. **Grand unification** theories seek to unify the electroweak and strong interactions. Further off are theories that would unite gravity with the other forces.

7. Astronomical evidence, including the red shift of light from distant galaxies and the existence of the cosmic microwave background radiation, strongly suggests that the universe began with a hot, dense explosion called the **big bang**. Very early in the big bang event, particle energies would have been high enough that exotic phenomena predicted by elementary particle theories would have been commonplace. Today, cosmology and elementary-particle physics interact to push our understanding of the universe's evolution back toward the earliest times.

Terms You Should Understand

(Pairs are closely related terms whose distinction is important; number in parentheses is chapter section where term first appears.)

classical physics, quantum physics (introduction)
Planck's constant (39-1)
photon (39-1)
Bohr atom (39-1)
wave function (39-2)
exclusion principle (39-2)
spin (39-2)
uncertainty principle (39-2)
wave-particle duality (39-2)
principle of complementarity (39-2)
binding energy (39-3)
fission, fusion (39-3)
radioactivity (39-3)
quark (39-4)
hadron, baryon, meson, lepton (39-4)
unification (39-5)

Symbols You Should Recognize

h (39-1)
$^{56}_{26}$Fe and similar nuclear symbols (39-3)

Problems You Should Be Able to Solve

finding wavelengths emitted as electrons jump among energy levels in hydrogen (39-1)
evaluating de Broglie wavelengths (39-1)
applying the uncertainty principle (39-2)
working with radioactive half-lives (39-3)
distinguishing baryons and mesons given their quark composition (39-4)

Limitations to Keep in Mind

This chapter deals with the frontiers of physics, and therefore, especially in the later sections, the information given may well change.

QUESTIONS

1. Can you explain the workings of the telephone using classical physics? What about the laser? Why or why not?
2. Why does classical physics predict that atoms should collapse?
3. Imagine an atom that, unlike hydrogen, had only three energy levels. If these levels were evenly spaced, how many spectral lines would result? How would their wavelengths compare?
4. How many spectral lines are in the entire Balmer series?
5. Why are the lines of the Lyman series in the ultraviolet while some Balmer lines are visible (see Fig. 39-7)?
6. Why does the photoelectric effect suggest that light has particle-like properties?
7. Equation 39-4 suggests that a particle that's not moving should have infinite wavelength. Speculate on what this might mean.
8. If you measure a particle's position with perfect accuracy, what do you know about its momentum?
9. How might our everyday experience be different if Planck's constant had the value 1 J·s?
10. Name the most fundamental particles that make up ordinary matter.
11. The electric force between charged particles drops as $1/r^2$. The stronger nuclear force between two nucleons drops exponentially with distance. Use these properties to explain why smaller nuclei are stable but very large ones, like uranium, are not.
12. Can you get energy from fissioning helium nuclei? From fusing lead nuclei? Explain.
13. Can you get energy from fission of iron-56 nuclei? From fusion? Explain.
14. Use Fig. 39-22 to tell which is greater: the energy release per nucleon in the fusion of deuterium ($^2_1$H) to helium ($^4_2$He) or in the fission of uranium into nuclei with mass number around 100.
15. Are electrons and protons both elementary particles?
16. Why are physicists always pushing for accelerators of ever higher energy?
17. If quarks carry fractional charges, why don't we ever detect particles with fractional charge?

PROBLEMS

Section 39-1 Toward the Quantum Theory

1. Find the energy in electron-volts of (a) a 1.0-MHz radio photon, (b) a 5.0×10^{14}-Hz optical photon, and (c) a 3.0×10^{18}-Hz X-ray photon.
2. What is the wavelength of a 6.5-eV photon? In what spectral region is this?
3. A microwave oven uses electromagnetic radiation at 2.4 GHz. (a) What is the energy of each microwave photon? (b) At what rate does a 625-W oven produce photons?
4. A red laser at 650 nm and a blue laser at 450 nm emit photons at the same rate. How do their total power outputs compare?
5. Find the rate of photon production by (a) a radio antenna broadcasting 1.0 kW at 89.5 MHz, (b) a laser producing 1.0 mW of 633-nm light, and (c) an X-ray machine producing 0.10-nm X rays with a total power of 2.5 kW.
6. Calculate the wavelengths of the first three lines in the Lyman series for hydrogen.
7. Which spectral line of the hydrogen Paschen series ($n_2 = 3$) has wavelength 1282 nm?
8. The wavelengths of a spectral line series tend to a limit as $n_1 \rightarrow \infty$. Evaluate the series limit for (a) the Lyman series and (b) the Balmer series in hydrogen.
9. A Rydberg hydrogen atom makes a downward transition to the $n = 225$ state. If the photon emitted has energy 9.32 μeV, what was the original state?
10. Find the de Broglie wavelength of (a) Earth, in its 30 km/s orbital motion, and (b) an electron moving at 10 km/s.
11. How slowly must an electron be moving for its de Broglie wavelength to equal 1 mm?

12. A proton and an electron have the same de Broglie wavelength. How do their speeds compare, assuming both are much less than that of light?
13. Electron microscopes can usually resolve smaller objects than optical microscopes because they illuminate their subjects with electrons whose de Broglie wavelengths are much smaller than that of light (Fig. 39-37). What is the minimum electron speed that would make an electron microscope superior to an optical microscope using 450-nm light?

FIGURE 39-37 An image of skin tissue shows on the screen of this electron microscope (Problem 13).

Section 39-2 Quantum Mechanics

14. A proton is confined to a space 1 fm wide (about the size of the atomic nucleus). What is the minimum uncertainty in its velocity?

15. Is it possible to measure an electron's velocity to an accuracy of ± 1.0 m/s while simultaneously finding its position to an accuracy of ± 1.0 μm? What about a proton?

16. A proton has velocity $\mathbf{v} = (1500 \pm 0.25)\hat{\imath}$ m/s. What is the minimum uncertainty in its position?

17. An electron is moving in the $+x$ direction with speed measured at 5.0×10^7 m/s, to an accuracy of $\pm 10\%$. What is the minimum uncertainty in its position?

18. A proton is moving along the x axis with speed $v = (1500 \pm 0.25)$ m/s, but its direction ($+$ or $-x$) is unknown. Find the uncertainty in its position. *Hint:* What is the difference between the two extreme possibilities for the *velocity?*

19. An electron beam is accelerated at the back of a TV tube and then heads toward the center of the screen with a horizontal velocity of 2.2×10^7 m/s. As the electrons leave the acceleration region, their vertical position is known to within ± 45 nm. Find the minimum angular spread in the beam, as set by the uncertainty principle.

20. An electron has momentum of magnitude p, but the direction is unknown. (a) Argue that the uncertainty in its momentum is therefore $2p$. (b) Compare the minimum uncertainty in its position with its de Broglie wavelength. Why might the two be related?

Section 39-3 Nuclear Physics

21. What is the half-life of a radioactive material if 75% of it decays in 5.0 hours?

22. Iodine-131 has a half-life of 8 days. How many whole days after a nuclear power plant accidentally releases I-131 to the atmosphere will the number of I-131 nuclei be less than 1% of its original value?

23. Oxygen-15 is a radioactive isotope with a 2-minute half-life, widely used in medical studies because its short half-life ensures relative safety. Approximately how long will it take for 99.9% of the nuclei in a sample of O-15 to decay?

24. Carbon-14, widely used in archaeological dating, has a half-life of 5730 years (Fig. 39-38). How old is a bone sample if the amount of carbon-14 it contains has dropped to 15% of its value when the bone was in a living creature?

FIGURE 39-38 How old is the bone? Radiocarbon dating can tell (Problem 24).

25. The energy released in the fission of a single uranium-235 nucleus is about 200 MeV. Estimate the mass of uranium that fissioned in the Hiroshima bomb, shown in Fig. 39-39, whose explosive yield was 12.5 kilotons (see Appendix C for a useful conversion factor).

FIGURE 39-39 On August 6, 1945, the Japanese city of Hiroshima was devastated by a nuclear fission bomb. How much uranium fissioned to produce this blast? (Problem 25)

26. The dominant process powering the Sun is a sequence of fusion reactions that fuse four protons to make helium-4 along with neutrinos and positrons. The net energy released is about 27 MeV. At what rate must the Sun consume protons to produce its power output of about 4×10^{26} W?

Section 39-4 Elementary Particles

27. The lambda particle (Λ) consists of an up quark, a down quark, and a strange quark. What is its charge?

28. Find the charge of the omega minus particle (Ω^-), which consists of three strange quarks.

29. What is the quark composition of the antiproton?

30. Find all the baryons that can be made from the up and down quarks, and give the total charge of each.

31. One of two charged mesons called pions is formed from an up quark and a down antiquark. What is this meson's charge?

32. (a) Is the particle with quark composition $\overline{u}s$ a baryon or a meson? (b) What is its charge?

Paired Problems

(Both problems in a pair involve the same principles and techniques. If you can get the first problem, you should be able to solve the second one.)

33. (a) Find the energy of the highest energy photon that can be emitted as the electron jumps between two adjacent energy

levels in the Bohr hydrogen atom. (b) Which energy levels are involved?

34. Find (a) the wavelength and (b) the energy in eV of the photon emitted as a Rydberg hydrogen atom drops from the $n = 180$ level to the $n = 179$ level.

35. In which of the following will wave properties be more evident: an electron moving at 10 Mm/s or a proton moving at 1 km/s?

36. Give the ratio of de Broglie wavelength to diameter for (a) a 100-g ball, 10 cm in diameter, moving at 5 m/s; (b) a 4-u alpha particle, 3.4 fm in diameter, moving at 20 Mm/s; and (c) a 238-u uranium nucleus, 13 fm in diameter, moving at 1.4 km/s. (d) For which will wave properties be negligible, and for which will they be completely dominant?

37. An electron is known to be within ±0.05 nm of the nucleus of an atom. What is the uncertainty in its velocity?

38. Typically, an atom remains in an excited state for about 10^{-8} s before it drops to a lower energy state, emitting a photon in the process. What is the uncertainty in the energy of this transition?

Supplementary Problems

39. An electron is accelerated from rest through a 4.5-kV potential difference. What is its de Broglie wavelength?

40. Consider an electron confined in one dimension to a region of width Δx. The uncertainty principle can still be satisfied if the magnitude p of the electron's momentum is known, provided we don't know which way it's moving; then the uncertainty in momentum is the magnitude of the difference of the two possible oppositely directed momentum vectors, or $2p$. Show under these conditions that the mini-

mum possible value for p consistent with the uncertainty principle is $p = h/4\pi\Delta x$.

41. Use the result of the preceding problem to estimate the minimum possible kinetic energy for (a) an electron confined to a region of atomic dimensions, about 0.1 nm and (b) a proton confined to a region of nuclear dimensions, about 1 fm. Your answers show the order of magnitude of the energies to be expected in atomic and nuclear reactions, respectively.

42. Quantization in the Bohr model requires that the angular momentum mvr of an electron orbit be an integer multiple of Planck's constant divided by 2π. By adapting Section 9-4's discussion of energy in circular orbits to an electron orbiting a proton and applying Bohr's quantization condition, show that the total energies allowed are given by

$$E_n = -\frac{ke^2}{2a_0}\left(\frac{1}{n^2}\right),$$

where n is an integer, k is the constant in Coulomb's law and $a_0 = h^2/4\pi^2 m_e ke^2$. (Called the Bohr radius, a_0 is the radius of the lowest energy orbit in the Bohr model.)

43. The expansion of the universe is described by the so-called Hubble relation, $v = H_0 d$, where v is the recession speed of two galaxies a distance d apart, and where H_0 is called the Hubble constant. Estimates for the value of H_0 range from 50 km/s/megaparsec to 100 km/s/megaparsec. (See Appendix C for the distance unit parsec). If the expansion rate had been the same from the beginning, how long ago would two galaxies have been together? Give two answers, derived from the two extreme values for H_0. Your answers are estimates for the age of the universe.

APPENDIX A
Mathematics

A-1 ALGEBRA AND TRIGONOMETRY

Quadratic Formula

If $ax^2 + bx + c = 0$ then $x = \dfrac{-b \pm \sqrt{b^2 - 4ac}}{2a}$

Circumference, Area, Volume

Where $\pi \simeq 3.14159\ldots$

circumference of circle	$2\pi r$
area of circle	πr^2
surface area of sphere	$4\pi r^2$
volume of sphere	$\frac{4}{3}\pi r^3$
area of triangle	$\frac{1}{2}bh$
volume of cylinder	$\pi r^2 \ell$

Trigonometry

definition of angle (in radians): $\theta = \dfrac{s}{r}$

2π radians in complete circle
1 radian $\simeq 57.3°$

Trigonometric Functions

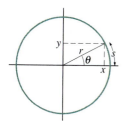

$$\sin \theta = \frac{y}{r}$$

$$\cos \theta = \frac{x}{r}$$

$$\tan \theta = \frac{\sin \theta}{\cos \theta} = \frac{y}{x}$$

Values at Selected Angles

$\theta \rightarrow$	0	$\dfrac{\pi}{6}$ (30°)	$\dfrac{\pi}{4}$ (45°)	$\dfrac{\pi}{3}$ (60°)	$\dfrac{\pi}{2}$ (90°)
$\sin\theta$	0	$\dfrac{1}{2}$	$\dfrac{\sqrt{2}}{2}$	$\dfrac{\sqrt{3}}{2}$	1
$\cos\theta$	1	$\dfrac{\sqrt{3}}{2}$	$\dfrac{\sqrt{2}}{2}$	$\dfrac{1}{2}$	0
$\tan\theta$	0	$\dfrac{\sqrt{3}}{3}$	1	$\sqrt{3}$	∞

Graphs of Trigonometric Functions

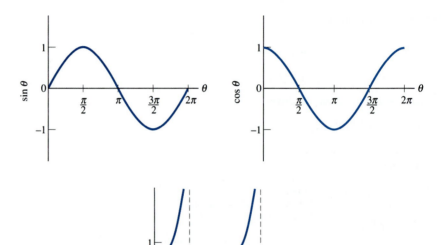

Trigonometric Identities

$\sin(-\theta) = -\sin\theta$

$\cos(-\theta) = \cos\theta$

$\sin\left(\theta \pm \dfrac{\pi}{2}\right) = \pm\cos\theta$

$\cos\left(\theta \pm \dfrac{\pi}{2}\right) = \mp\sin\theta$

$\sin^2\theta + \cos^2\theta = 1$

$\sin 2\theta = 2\sin\theta\cos\theta$

$$\cos 2\theta = \cos^2\theta - \sin^2\theta = 1 - 2\sin^2\theta = 2\cos^2\theta - 1$$

$$\sin(\alpha \pm \beta) = \sin\alpha\cos\beta \pm \cos\alpha\sin\beta$$

$$\cos(\alpha \pm \beta) = \cos\alpha\cos\beta \mp \sin\alpha\sin\beta$$

$$\sin\alpha \pm \sin\beta = 2\sin[\tfrac{1}{2}(\alpha \pm \beta)]\cos[\tfrac{1}{2}(\alpha \mp \beta)]$$

$$\cos\alpha + \cos\beta = 2\cos[\tfrac{1}{2}(\alpha + \beta)]\cos[\tfrac{1}{2}(\alpha - \beta)]$$

$$\cos\alpha - \cos\beta = -2\sin[\tfrac{1}{2}(\alpha + \beta)]\sin[\tfrac{1}{2}(\alpha - \beta)]$$

Laws of Cosines and Sines

Where A, B, C are the sides of an arbitrary triangle and α, β, γ the angles opposite those sides:

Law of cosines

$$C^2 = A^2 + B^2 - 2AB\cos\gamma$$

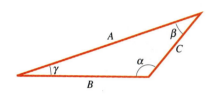

Law of sines

$$\frac{\sin\alpha}{A} = \frac{\sin\beta}{B} = \frac{\sin\gamma}{C}$$

Exponentials and Logarithms

Graphs

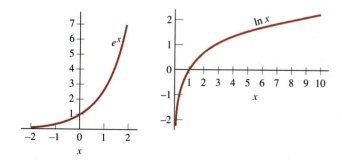

Exponential and Natural Logarithms Are Inverse Functions

$$e^{\ln x} = x, \quad \ln e^x = x \quad e = 2.71828\ldots.$$

Exponential and Logarithmic Identities

$$a^x = e^{x \ln a} \qquad \ln(xy) = \ln x + \ln y$$

$$a^x a^y = a^{x+y} \qquad \ln\left(\frac{x}{y}\right) = \ln x - \ln y$$

$$(a^x)^y = a^{xy} \qquad \ln\left(\frac{1}{x}\right) = -\ln x$$

$$\log x \equiv \log_{10} x = \ln(10)\ln x \approx 2.3\ln x$$

Expansions and Approximations

Series Expansions of Functions

Note: $n! = n(n-1)(n-2)(n-3)\cdots(3)(2)(1)$

$$e^x = 1 + x + \frac{x^2}{2!} + \frac{x^3}{3!} + \cdots \quad \text{(exponential)}$$

$$\sin x = x - \frac{x^3}{3!} + \frac{x^5}{5!} - \cdots \quad \text{(sine)}$$

$$\cos x = 1 - \frac{x^2}{2!} + \frac{x^4}{4!} - \cdots \quad \text{(cosine)}$$

$\left. \right\}$ (x in radians)

$$\ln(1 + x) = x - \frac{x^2}{2} + \frac{x^3}{3} - \cdots \quad \text{(natural logarithm)}$$

$$(1 + x)^p = 1 + px + \frac{p(p-1)}{2!}x^2 + \frac{p(p-1)(p-2)}{3!}x^3 + \cdots$$

(binomial, valid for $|x| < 1$)

Approximations

For $|x| \ll 1$, the first few terms in the series provide a good approximation; that is,

$$e^x \approx 1 + x$$
$$\sin x \approx x$$
$$\cos x \approx 1 - \tfrac{1}{2}x^2$$
$$\ln(1 + x) \approx x$$
$$(1 + x)^p \approx 1 + px$$

$\left. \right\}$ for $|x| \ll 1$

Expressions that do not have the forms shown may often be put in the appropriate form. For example:

$$\frac{1}{\sqrt{a^2 + y^2}} = \frac{1}{a\sqrt{1 + \dfrac{y^2}{a^2}}} = \frac{1}{a}\left(1 + \frac{y^2}{a^2}\right)^{-1/2}$$

For $y^2 \ll a^2$, this may be approximated using the binomial expansion $(1 + x)^p \simeq 1 + px$, with $p = -\frac{1}{2}$ and $x = y^2/a^2$:

$$\frac{1}{a}\left(1 + \frac{y^2}{a^2}\right)^{-1/2} \simeq \frac{1}{a}\left(1 - \frac{1}{2}\frac{y^2}{a^2}\right).$$

Vector Algebra

Vector Products

$\mathbf{A} \cdot \mathbf{B} = AB\cos\theta$

$|\mathbf{A} \times \mathbf{B}| = AB\sin\theta$, with direction of $\mathbf{A} \times \mathbf{B}$ given by right-hand rule:

Unit Vector Notation

An arbitrary vector $\mathbf{A}$ may be written in terms of its components A_x, A_y, A_z and the unit vectors $\hat{\mathbf{i}}$, $\hat{\mathbf{j}}$, $\hat{\mathbf{k}}$ that have length 1 and lie along the x, y, z axes:

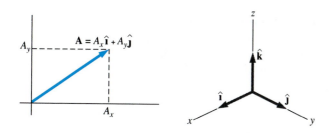

In unit vector notation, vector products become

$\mathbf{A} \cdot \mathbf{B} = A_x B_x + A_y B_y + A_z B_z$

$\mathbf{A} \times \mathbf{B} = (A_y B_z - A_z B_y)\hat{\mathbf{i}} + (A_z B_x - A_x B_z)\hat{\mathbf{j}} + (A_x B_y - A_y B_x)\hat{\mathbf{k}}$

Vector Identities

$\mathbf{A} \cdot \mathbf{B} = \mathbf{B} \cdot \mathbf{A}$

$\mathbf{A} \times \mathbf{B} = -\mathbf{B} \times \mathbf{A}$

$\mathbf{A} \cdot (\mathbf{B} \times \mathbf{C}) = \mathbf{B} \cdot (\mathbf{C} \times \mathbf{A}) = \mathbf{C} \cdot (\mathbf{A} \times \mathbf{B})$

$\mathbf{A} \times (\mathbf{B} \times \mathbf{C}) = (\mathbf{A} \cdot \mathbf{C})\mathbf{B} - (\mathbf{A} \cdot \mathbf{B})\mathbf{C}$

A-2 CALCULUS

Derivatives

Definition of the Derivative

If y is a function of x $[y = f(x)]$, then the **derivative of y with respect to x** is the ratio of the change Δy in y to the corresponding change Δx in x, in the limit of arbitrarily small Δx:

$$\frac{dy}{dx} = \lim_{\Delta x \to 0} \frac{\Delta y}{\Delta x}.$$

Algebraically, the derivative is the rate of change of y with respect to x; geometrically, it is the slope of the y versus x graph—that is, of the tangent line to the graph at a given point:

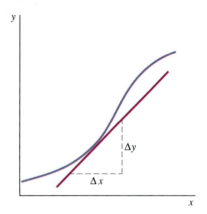

Derivatives of Common Functions

Although the derivative of a function can be evaluated directly using the limiting process that defines the derivative, standard formulas are available for common functions:

$$\frac{da}{dx} = 0 \quad (a \text{ is a constant}) \qquad\qquad \frac{d}{dx}\tan x = \frac{1}{\cos^2 x}$$

$$\frac{dx^n}{dx} = nx^{n-1} \quad (n \text{ need not be an integer}) \qquad \frac{de^x}{dx} = e^x$$

$$\frac{d}{dx}\sin x = \cos x \qquad\qquad\qquad\qquad \frac{d}{dx}\ln x = \frac{1}{x}$$

$$\frac{d}{dx}\cos x = -\sin x$$

Derivatives of Sums, Products, and Functions of Functions

1. Derivative of a constant times a function

$$\frac{d}{dx}[af(x)] = a\frac{df}{dx} \qquad (a \text{ is a constant})$$

2. Derivative of a sum

$$\frac{d}{dx}[f(x) + g(x)] = \frac{df}{dx} + \frac{dg}{dx}$$

3. Derivative of a product

$$\frac{d}{dx}[f(x)g(x)] = g\frac{df}{dx} + f\frac{dg}{dx}$$

Examples

$$\frac{d}{dx}(x^2\cos x) = \cos x\frac{dx^2}{dx} + x^2\frac{d}{dx}\cos x = 2x\cos x - x^2\sin x$$

$$\frac{d}{dx}(x\ln x) = \ln x\frac{dx}{dx} + x\frac{d}{dx}\ln x = (\ln x)(1) + x\left(\frac{1}{x}\right) = \ln x + 1$$

4. Derivative of a quotient

$$\frac{d}{dx}\left[\frac{f(x)}{g(x)}\right] = \frac{1}{g^2}\left(g\frac{df}{dx} - f\frac{dg}{dx}\right)$$

Example

$$\frac{d}{dx}\left(\frac{\sin x}{x^2}\right) = \frac{1}{x^4}\left(x^2\frac{d}{dx}\sin x - \sin x\frac{dx^2}{dx}\right) = \frac{\cos x}{x^2} - \frac{2\sin x}{x^3}$$

5. Chain rule for derivatives

If f is a function of u and u is a function of x, then

$$\frac{df}{dx} = \frac{df}{du}\frac{du}{dx}.$$

Examples

a. Evaluate $\dfrac{d}{dx}\sin(x^2)$. Here $u = x^2$ and $f(u) = \sin u$, so

$$\frac{d}{dx}\sin(x^2) = \frac{d}{du}\sin u\frac{du}{dx} = (\cos u)\frac{dx^2}{dx} = 2x\cos(x^2).$$

b. $\dfrac{d}{dt}\sin\omega t = \dfrac{d}{d\omega t}\sin\omega t\dfrac{d}{dt}\omega t = \omega\cos\omega t.$ (ω a constant)

c. Evaluate $\dfrac{d}{dx}\sin^2 5x$. Here $u = \sin 5x$ and $f(u) = u^2$, so

$$\frac{d}{dx}\sin^2 5x = \frac{d}{du}u^2\frac{du}{dx} = 2u\frac{du}{dx} = 2\sin 5x\frac{d}{dx}\sin 5x$$

$$= (2)(\sin 5x)(5)(\cos 5x) = 10\sin 5x\cos 5x = 5\sin 2x.$$

Second Derivative

The second derivative of y with respect to x is defined as the derivative of the derivative:

$$\frac{d^2y}{dx^2} = \frac{d}{dx}\left(\frac{dy}{dx}\right).$$

Example

If $y = ax^3$, then $dy/dx = 3ax^2$, so

$$\frac{d^2y}{dx^2} = \frac{d}{dx}3ax^2 = 6ax.$$

Partial Derivatives

When a function depends on more than one variable, then the partial derivatives of that function are the derivatives with respect to each variable, taken with all other variables held constant. If f is a function of x and y, then the partial derivatives are written

$$\frac{\partial f}{\partial x} \quad \text{and} \quad \frac{\partial f}{\partial y}.$$

Example

If $f(x, y) = x^3\sin y$, then

$$\frac{\partial f}{\partial x} = 3x^2\sin y \quad \text{and} \quad \frac{\partial f}{\partial y} = x^3\cos y.$$

Integrals

Indefinite Integrals

Integration is the inverse of differentiation. The **indefinite integral**, $\int f(x)\,dx$, is defined as a function whose derivative is $f(x)$:

$$\frac{d}{dx}\left[\int f(x)\,dx\right] = f(x).$$

If $A(x)$ is an indefinite integral of $f(x)$, then because the derivative of a constant is zero, the function $A(x) + C$ is also an indefinite integral of $f(x)$, where C is any constant. Inverting the derivatives of common functions listed in the preceding section gives the integrals on the next page (a more extensive table appears at the end of this appendix).

$$\int a\,dx = ax + C \qquad\qquad \int \cos x\,dx = \sin x + C$$

$$\int x^n\,dx = \frac{x^{n+1}}{n+1} + C, \quad n \neq -1 \qquad \int e^x\,dx = e^x + C$$

$$\int \sin x\,dx = -\cos x + C \qquad\qquad \int x^{-1}\,dx = \ln x + C$$

Definite Integrals

In physics we are most often interested in the **definite integral**, defined as the sum of a large number of very small quantities, in the limit as the number of quantities grows arbitrarily large and the size of each arbitrarily small:

$$\int_{x_1}^{x_2} f(x)\,dx \equiv \lim_{\substack{\Delta x \to 0 \\ N \to \infty}} \sum_{i=1}^{N} f(x_i)\,\Delta x,$$

where the terms in the sum are evaluated at values x_i between the limits of integration x_1 and x_2; in the limit $\Delta x \to 0$, the sum is over all values of x in the interval.

The definite integral is used whenever we need to sum over a quantity that is changing—for example, to calculate the work done by a variable force (Chapter 7), the entropy change in a system whose temperature varies (Chapter 22), or the flux of an electric field that varies with position (Chapter 24).

The key to evaluating the definite integral is provided by the **fundamental theorem of calculus**. The theorem states that, if $A(x)$ is an *indefinite* integral of $f(x)$, then the *definite integral* is given by

$$\int_{x_1}^{x_2} f(x)\,dx = A(x_2) - A(x_1) \equiv A(x)\Big|_{x_1}^{x_2}.$$

Geometrically, the definite integral is the area under the graph of $f(x)$ between the limits x_1 and x_2:

Evaluating Integrals

The first step in evaluating an integral is to express all varying quantities within the integral in terms of a single variable. For example, in evaluating $\int E\,dr$ to calculate an electric potential (Chapter 25), it is necessary first to express E as a function of r. This procedure is illustrated in many examples throughout this text; Example 23-7 provides a typical case.

Once an integral is written in terms of a single variable, it is necessary to manipulate the integrand—the function being integrated—into a form whose integral you know or can look up in tables of integrals. Two common techniques are especially useful:

1. **Change of variables**
   An unfamiliar integral can often be put into familiar form by defining a new variable. For example, it is not obvious how to integrate the expression

   $$\int \frac{x\,dx}{\sqrt{a^2 + x^2}}.$$

   where a is a constant. But let $z = a^2 + x^2$. Then

   $$\frac{dz}{dx} = \frac{da^2}{dx} + \frac{dx^2}{dx} = 0 + 2x = 2x,$$

   so $dz = 2x\,dx$. Then the quantity $x\,dx$ in our unfamiliar integral is just $\frac{1}{2}dz$, while the quantity $\sqrt{a^2 + x^2}$ is just $z^{1/2}$. So the integral becomes

   $$\int \tfrac{1}{2}z^{-1/2}\,dz = \frac{\frac{1}{2}z^{1/2}}{(1/2)} = \sqrt{z},$$

   where we have used the standard form for the integral of a power of the independent variable. Substituting back $z = a^2 + x^2$ gives

   $$\int \frac{x\,dx}{\sqrt{a^2 + x^2}} = \sqrt{a^2 + x^2}.$$

2. **Integration by parts**
   The quantity $\int u\,dv$ is the area under the curve of u as a function of v between specified limits. In the figure below, that area can also be expressed as the area of the rectangle shown minus the area under the curve of v as a function of u. Mathematically, this relation among areas may be expressed as a relation among integrals:

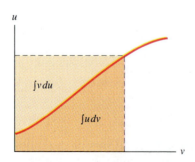

$$\int u\,dv = uv - \int v\,du. \qquad \text{(integration by parts)}$$

This expression may often be used to transform complicated integrals into simpler ones.

Example

Evaluate $\int x \cos x \, dx$. Here let $u = x$, so $du = dx$. Then $dv = \cos x \, dx$, so $v = \int dv = \int \cos x \, dx = \sin x$. Integrating by parts then gives

$$\int x \cos x \, dx = (x)(\sin x) - \int \sin x \, dx = x \sin x + \cos x,$$

where the $+$ sign arises because $\int \sin x \, dx = -\cos x$.

Table of Integrals

[More extensive tables are available in many mathematical and scientific handbooks; see, for example, ***Handbook of Chemistry and Physics*** (Chemical Rubber Co.) or Dwight, ***Tables of Integrals and Other Mathematical Data*** (Macmillan).] Increasingly, sophisticated computer software is used instead of tables for the symbolic evaluation of integrals; among the most widely used are *Maple*, *Mathematica*, and *Derive*.

In the expressions below, a and b are constants. An arbitrary constant of integration may be added to the right-hand side.

$$\int e^{ax} \, dx = \frac{e^{ax}}{a}$$

$$\int \sin ax \, dx = -\frac{\cos ax}{a}$$

$$\int \cos ax \, dx = \frac{\sin ax}{a}$$

$$\int \tan ax \, dx = -\frac{1}{a}\ln(\cos ax)$$

$$\int \sin^2 ax \, dx = \frac{x}{2} - \frac{\sin 2ax}{4a}$$

$$\int \cos^2 ax \, dx = \frac{x}{2} + \frac{\sin 2ax}{4a}$$

$$\int x \sin ax \, dx = \frac{1}{a^2}\sin ax - \frac{1}{a}x \cos ax$$

$$\int x \cos ax \, dx = \frac{1}{a^2}\cos ax + \frac{1}{a}x \sin ax$$

$$\int \frac{dx}{\sqrt{a^2 - x^2}} = \sin^{-1}\left(\frac{x}{a}\right)$$

$$\int \frac{dx}{\sqrt{x^2 \pm a^2}} = \ln(x + \sqrt{x^2 \pm a^2})$$

$$\int \frac{dx}{x^2 + a^2} = \frac{1}{a}\tan^{-1}\left(\frac{x}{a}\right)$$

$$\int \frac{x \, dx}{\sqrt{a^2 - x^2}} = -\sqrt{a^2 - x^2}$$

$$\int \frac{x \, dx}{\sqrt{x^2 \pm a^2}} = \sqrt{x^2 \pm a^2}$$

$$\int \frac{dx}{(x^2 \pm a^2)^{3/2}} = \frac{\pm x}{a^2\sqrt{x^2 \pm a^2}}$$

$$\int xe^{ax} \, dx = \frac{e^{ax}}{a^2}(ax - 1)$$

$$\int x^2 e^{ax} \, dx = \frac{x^2 e^{ax}}{a} - \frac{2}{a}\left[\frac{e^{ax}}{a^2}(ax - 1)\right]$$

$$\int \frac{dx}{a + bx} = \frac{1}{b}\ln(a + bx)$$

$$\int \frac{dx}{(a + bx)^2} = -\frac{1}{b(a + bx)}$$

$$\int \ln ax \, dx = x \ln ax - x$$

The International System of Units (SI)

This material is from the United States edition of the English translation of the sixth edition of "Le Système International d'Unités (SI)," the definitive publication in the French language issued in 1991 by the International Bureau of Weights and Measures (BIPM). The year the definition was adopted is given in parentheses.

unit of length (meter): The meter is the length of the path traveled by light in vacuum during a time interval of 1/299 792 458 of a second. (1983)

unit of mass (kilogram): The kilogram is the unit of mass; it is equal to the mass of the international prototype of the kilogram. (1889)

unit of time (second): The second is the duration of 9 192 631 770 periods of the radiation corresponding to the transition between the two hyperfine levels of the ground state of the cesium-133 atom. (1967)

unit of electric current (ampere): The ampere is that constant current which, if maintained in two straight parallel conductors of infinite length, of negligible circular cross section, and placed 1 meter apart in vacuum, would produce between these conductors a force equal to 2×10^{-7} newton per meter of length. (1948)

unit of thermodynamic temperature (kelvin): The kelvin, unit of thermodynamic temperature, is the fraction 1/273.16 of the thermodynamic temperature of the triple point of water. (1957) Also, the unit kelvin and its symbol K should be used to express an interval or a difference of temperature.

unit of amount of substance (mole): (1) The mole is the amount of substance of a system that contains as many elementary entities as there are atoms in 0.012 kilogram of carbon 12. (1971) (2) When the mole is used, the elementary entities must be specified and may be atoms, molecules, ions, electrons, other particles, or specified groups of such particles.

unit of luminous intensity (candela): The candela is the luminous intensity, in a given direction, of a source that emits monochromatic radiation of frequency 540×10^{12} hertz and that has a radiant intensity in that direction of (1/683) watt per steradian. (1979)

▲ *SI Base and Supplementary Units*

QUANTITY	SI UNIT NAME	SI UNIT SYMBOL
Base Unit		
Length	meter	m
Mass	kilogram	kg
Time	second	s
Electric current	ampere	A
Thermodynamic temperature	kelvin	K
Amount of substance	mole	mol
Luminous intensity	candela	cd
Supplementary Units		
Plane angle	radian	rad
Solid angle	steradian	sr

▲ *SI Prefixes*

FACTOR	PREFIX	SYMBOL
10^{24}	yotta	Y
10^{21}	zetta	Z
10^{18}	exa	E
10^{15}	peta	P
10^{12}	tera	T
10^{9}	giga	G
10^{6}	mega	M
10^{3}	kilo	k
10^{2}	hecto	h
10^{1}	deka	da
10^{0}	—	—
10^{-1}	deci	d
10^{-2}	centi	c
10^{-3}	milli	m
10^{-6}	micro	μ
10^{-9}	nano	n
10^{-12}	pico	p
10^{-15}	femto	f
10^{-18}	atto	a
10^{-21}	zepto	z
10^{-24}	yocto	y

▲ *Some SI Derived Units with Special Names*

QUANTITY	NAME	SYMBOL	SI UNIT EXPRESSION IN TERMS OF OTHER UNITS	SI UNIT EXPRESSION IN TERMS OF SI BASE UNITS
Frequency	hertz	Hz		s^{-1}
Force	newton	N		$m \cdot kg \cdot s^{-2}$
Pressure, stress	pascal	Pa	N/m^2	$m^{-1} \cdot kg \cdot s^{-2}$
Energy, work, heat	joule	J	$N \cdot m$	$m^2 \cdot kg \cdot s^{-2}$
Power	watt	W	J/s	$m^2 \cdot kg \cdot s^{-3}$
Electric charge	coulomb	C		$s \cdot A$
Electric potential, potential difference, electromotive force	volt	V	J/C	$m^2 \cdot kg \cdot s^{-3} \cdot A^{-1}$
Capacitance	farad	F	C/V	$m^{-2} \cdot kg^{-1} \cdot s^4 \cdot A^2$
Electric resistance	ohm	Ω	V/A	$m^2 \cdot kg \cdot s^{-3} \cdot A^{-2}$
Magnetic flux	weber	Wb	$V \cdot s$	$m^2 \cdot kg \cdot s^{-2} \cdot A^{-1}$
Magnetic field	tesla	T	Wb/m^2	$kg \cdot s^{-2} \cdot A^{-1}$
Inductance	henry	H	Wb/A	$m^2 \cdot kg \cdot s^{-2} \cdot A^{-2}$
Radioactivity	becquerel	Bq	1 decay/s	s^{-1}
Absorbed radiation dose	gray	Gy	J/kg, 100 rad	$m^2 \cdot s^{-2}$
Radiation dose equivalent	sievert	Sv	J/kg, 100 rem	$m^2 \cdot s^{-2}$

Conversion Factors

The listings below give the SI equivalents of non-SI units. To convert from the units shown to SI, multiply by the factor given; to convert the other way, divide. For conversions within the SI system see table of SI prefixes in Appendix B, Chapter 1, or inside front cover. Conversions that are not exact by definition are given to, at most, 4 significant figures.

Length

1 inch (in.) = 0.0254 m

1 foot (ft) = 0.3048 m

1 yard (yd) = 0.9144 m

1 mile (mi) = 1609 m

1 nautical mile = 1852 m

1 angstrom (Å) = 10^{-10} m

1 light-year (ly) = 9.46×10^{15} m

1 astronomical unit (AU) = 1.5×10^{11} m

1 parsec = 3.09×10^{16} m

1 fermi = 10^{-15} m = 1 fm

Mass

1 slug = 14.59 kg

1 metric ton (tonne; T) = 1000 kg

1 unified mass unit (u) = 1.660×10^{-27} kg

Force units in the English system are sometimes used (incorrectly) for mass. The units given below are actually equal to the number of kilograms multiplied by *g*, the acceleration of gravity.

1 pound (lb) = weight of 0.454 kg

1 ton = 2000 lb = weight of 908 kg

1 ounce (oz) = weight of 0.02835 kg

Time

1 minute (min) = 60 s

1 hour (h) = 60 min = 3600 s

1 day (d) = 24 h = 86 400 s

1 year (y) = 365.2422 d* = 3.156×10^7 s

*The length of the year changes very slowly with changes in Earth's orbital period.

Area

1 hectare (ha) $= 10^4$ m^2 1 acre $= 4047$ m^2
1 square inch (in.^{2}) $= 6.452 \times 10^{-4}$ m^2 1 barn $= 10^{-28}$ m^2
1 square foot (ft^2) $= 9.290 \times 10^{-2}$ m^2 1 shed $= 10^{-30}$ m^2

Volume

1 liter (L) $= 1000$ cm^3 $= 10^{-3}$ m^3 1 gallon (U.S.; gal) $= 3.785 \times 10^{-3}$ m^3
1 cubic foot (ft^3) $= 2.832 \times 10^{-2}$ m^3 1 gallon (British) $= 4.546 \times 10^{-3}$ m^3
1 cubic inch (in.^{3}) $= 1.639 \times 10^{-5}$ m^3
1 fluid ounce $= 1/128$ gal $= 2.957 \times 10^{-5}$ m^3
1 barrel $= 42$ gal $= 0.1590$ m^3

Angle, Phase

1 degree (°) $= \pi/180$ rad $= 1.745 \times 10^{-2}$ rad
1 revolution (rev) $= 360° = 2\pi$ rad
1 cycle $= 360° = 2\pi$ rad

Speed, Velocity

1 km/h $= (1/3.6)$ m/s $= 0.2778$ m/s   1 ft/s $= 0.3048$ m/s
1 mi/h (mph) $= 0.4470$ m/s   1 ly/y $= 3.00 \times 10^8$ m/s

Angular Speed, Angular Velocity, Frequency, and Angular Frequency

1 rev/s $= 2\pi$ rad/s $= 6.283$ rad/s (s^{-1})   1 rev/min (rpm) $= 0.1047$ rad/s (s^{-1})
1 Hz $= 1$ cycle/s $= 2\pi$ s^{-1}

Force

1 dyne $= 10^{-5}$ N   1 pound (lb) $= 4.448$ N

Pressure

1 dyne/cm^2 $= 0.10$ Pa   1 lb/in.^{2} (psi) $= 6.895 \times 10^3$ Pa
1 atmosphere (atm) $= 1.013 \times 10^5$ Pa   1 in. H$_2$O (60°F) $= 248.8$ Pa
1 torr $= 1$ mm Hg at 0°C $= 133.3$ Pa   1 in. Hg (60°F) $= 3.377 \times 10^3$ Pa
1 bar $= 10^5$ Pa $= 0.987$ atm

Energy, Work, Heat

1 erg $= 10^{-7}$ J   1 Btu* $= 1.054 \times 10^3$ J
1 calorie* (cal) $= 4.184$ J   1 kWh $= 3.6 \times 10^6$ J
1 electron-volt (eV) $= 1.602 \times 10^{-19}$ J   1 megaton (explosive yield; Mt)
1 foot-pound (ft·lb) $= 1.356$ J $= 4.18 \times 10^{15}$ J

---

* Values based on the thermochemical calorie; other definitions vary slightly.

Power

$$1 \text{ erg/s} = 10^{-7} \text{ W}$$
$$1 \text{ horsepower (hp)} = 746 \text{ W}$$

$$1 \text{ Btu/h (Btuh)} = 0.293 \text{ W}$$
$$1 \text{ ft·lb/s} = 1.356 \text{ W}$$

Magnetic Field

$$1 \text{ gauss (G)} = 10^{-4} \text{ T}$$

$$1 \text{ gamma } (\gamma) = 10^{-9} \text{ T}$$

Radiation

$$1 \text{ curie (ci)} = 3.7 \times 10^{10} \text{ Bq}$$

$$1 \text{ rad} = 10^{-2} \text{ Gy}$$
$$1 \text{ rem} = 10^{-2} \text{ Sv}$$

▲ *Energy Content of Fuels*

ENERGY SOURCE	ENERGY CONTENT
Coal	2.9×10^7 J/kg $= 7300$ kWh/ton $= 25 \times 10^6$ Btu/ton
Oil	43×10^6 J/kg $= 39$ kWh/gal $= 1.3 \times 10^5$ Btu/gal
Gasoline	44×10^6 J/kg $= 36$ kWh/gal $= 1.2 \times 10^5$ Btu/gal
Natural gas	55×10^6 J/kg $= 30$ kWh/100 ft^3 $= 1000$ Btu/ft^3
Uranium (fission)	
Normal abundance	5.8×10^{11} J/kg $= 1.6 \times 10^5$ kWh/kg
Pure U-235	8.2×10^{13} J/kg $= 2.3 \times 10^7$ kWh/kg
Hydrogen (fusion)	
Normal abundance	7×10^{11} J/kg $= 3.0 \times 10^4$ kWh/kg
Pure deuterium	3.3×10^{14} J/kg $= 9.2 \times 10^7$ kWh/kg
Water	1.2×10^{10} J/kg $= 1.3 \times 10^4$ kWh/gal $= 340$ gal gasoline/gal
H_2O	
100% conversion, matter to energy	9.0×10^{16} J/kg $= 931$ MeV/u $= 2.5 \times 10^{10}$ kWh/kg

The Elements

The atomic weights of stable elements reflect the abundances of different isotopes; values given here apply to elements as they exist naturally on Earth. For stable elements, parentheses express uncertainties in the last decimal place given. For elements with no stable isotopes (indicated in boldface), sets of most important isotopes are given. (Exceptions are the unstable elements thorium, protactinium, and uranium, for which atomic weights reflect natural abundances of long-lived isotopes.) See also periodic table inside back cover.

ATOMIC NUMBER	NAMES	SYMBOL	ATOMIC WEIGHT
1	Hydrogen	H	1.00794 (7)
2	Helium	He	4.002602 (2)
3	Lithium	Li	6.941 (2)
4	Beryllium	Be	9.012182 (3)
5	Boron	B	10.811 (5)
6	Carbon	C	12.011 (1)
7	Nitrogen	N	14.00674 (7)
8	Oxygen	O	15.9994 (3)
9	Fluorine	F	18.9984032 (9)
10	Neon	Ne	20.1797 (6)
11	Sodium (Natrium)	Na	22.989768 (6)
12	Magnesium	Mg	24.3050 (6)
13	Aluminum	Al	26.981539 (5)
14	Silicon	Si	28.0855 (3)
15	Phosphorus	P	30.973762 (4)
16	Sulfur	S	32.066 (6)
17	Chlorine	Cl	35.4527 (9)
18	Argon	Ar	39.948 (1)
19	Potassium (Kalium)	K	39.0983 (1)
20	Calcium	Ca	40.078 (4)
21	Scandium	Sc	44.955910 (9)
22	Titanium	Ti	47.88 (3)
23	Vanadium	V	50.9415 (1)
24	Chromium	Cr	51.9961 (6)
25	Manganese	Mn	54.93805 (1)
26	Iron	Fe	55.847 (3)
27	Cobalt	Co	58.93320 (1)

ATOMIC NUMBER	NAMES	SYMBOL	ATOMIC WEIGHT
28	Nickel	Ni	58.69 (1)
29	Copper	Cu	63.546 (3)
30	Zinc	Zn	65.39 (2)
31	Gallium	Ga	69.723 (1)
32	Germanium	Ge	72.61 (2)
33	Arsenic	As	74.92159 (2)
34	Selenium	Se	78.96 (3)
35	Bromine	Br	79.904 (1)
36	Krypton	Kr	83.80 (1)
37	Rubidium	Rb	85.4678 (3)
38	Strontium	Sr	87.62 (1)
39	Yttrium	Y	88.90585 (2)
40	Zirconium	Zr	91.224 (2)
41	Niobium	Nb	92.90638 (2)
42	Molybdenum	Mo	95.94 (1)
43	**Technetium**	**Tc**	**97, 98, 99**
44	Ruthenium	Ru	101.07 (2)
45	Rhodium	Rh	102.90550 (3)
46	Palladium	Pd	106.42 (1)
47	Silver	Ag	107.8682 (2)
48	Cadmium	Cd	112.411 (8)
49	Indium	In	114.82 (1)
50	Tin	Sn	118.710 (7)
51	Antimony (Stibium)	Sb	121.75 (3)
52	Tellurium	Te	127.60 (3)
53	Iodine	I	126.90447 (3)
54	Xenon	Xe	131.29 (2)
55	Cesium	Cs	132.90543 (5)
56	Barium	Ba	137.327 (7)
57	Lanthanum	La	138.9055 (2)
58	Cerium	Ce	140.115 (4)
59	Praseodymium	Pr	140.90765 (3)
60	Neodymium	Nd	144.24 (3)
61	**Promethium**	**Pm**	**145, 147**
62	Samarium	Sm	150.36 (3)
63	Europium	Eu	151.965 (9)
64	Gadolinium	Gd	157.25 (3)
65	Terbium	Tb	158.92534 (3)
66	Dysprosium	Dy	162.50 (3)
67	Holmium	Ho	164.93032 (3)
68	Erbium	Er	167.26 (3)
69	Thulium	Tm	168.93421 (3)
70	Ytterbium	Yb	173.04 (3)
71	Lutetium	Lu	174.967 (1)
72	Hafnium	Hf	178.49 (2)
73	Tantalum	Ta	180.9479 (1)
74	Tungsten (Wolfram)	W	183.85 (3)
75	Rhenium	Re	186.207 (1)
76	Osmium	Os	190.2 (1)
77	Iridium	Ir	192.22 (3)
78	Platinum	Pt	195.08 (3)
79	Gold	Au	196.96654 (3)
80	Mercury	Hg	200.59 (3)
81	Thallium	Tl	204.3833 (2)
82	Lead	Pb	207.2 (1)
83	Bismuth	Bi	208.98037 (3)

ATOMIC NUMBER	NAMES	SYMBOL	ATOMIC WEIGHT
84	Polonium	Po	209, 210
85	Astatine	At	210, 211
86	Radon	Rn	211, 220, 222
87	Francium	Fr	223
88	Radium	Ra	223, 224, 226, 228
89	Actinium	Ac	227
90	Thorium	Th	232.0381 (1)
91	Protactinium	Pa	231.03588 (2)
92	Uranium	U	238.0289 (1)
93	Neptunium	Np	237, 239
94	Plutonium	Pu	238, 239, 240, 241, 242, 244
95	Americium	Am	241, 243
96	Curium	Cm	243, 244, 245, 246, 247, 248
97	Berkelium	Bk	247, 249
98	Californium	Cf	249, 250, 251, 252
99	Einsteinium	Es	252
100	Fermium	Fm	257
101	Mendelevium	Md	255, 256, 258, 260
102	Nobelium	No	253, 254, 255, 259
103	Lawrencium	Lr	256, 258, 259, 261
104	Rutherfordium	Rf	257, 259, 260, 261
105	Dubnium	Db	260, 261, 262
106	Seaborgium	Sg	259, 260, 261, 263
107	Bohrium	Bh	261, 262
108	Hassium	Hs	264, 265
109	Meitnerium	Mt	266
110	—	—	269
111	—	—	272
112	—	—	277

Astrophysical Data

SUN, PLANETS, PRINCIPAL SATELLITES

BODY	MASS (10^{24} kg)	MEAN RADIUS (10^6 m EXCEPT AS NOTED)	SURFACE GRAVITY (m/s²)	ESCAPE SPEED (km/s)	SIDEREAL ROTATION PERIOD* (days)	MEAN DISTANCE FROM CENTRAL BODY† (10^6 km)	ORBITAL PERIOD	ORBITAL SPEED (km/s)
Sun	1.99×10^6	696	274	618	36 at poles 27 at equator	2.6×10^{11}	200 My	250
Mercury	0.330	2.44	3.70	4.25	58.6	57.6	88.0 d	48
Venus	4.87	6.05	8.87	10.4	−243	108	225 d	35
Earth	5.97	6.37	9.81	11.2	0.997	150	365.3 d	30
Moon	0.0735	1.74	1.62	2.38	27.3	0.385	27.3 d	1.0
Mars	0.642	3.38	3.74	5.03	1.03	228	1.88 y	24.1
Phobos	9.6×10^{-9}	9-13 km	0.001	0.008	0.32	9.4×10^{-3}	0.32 d	2.1
Deimos	2×10^{-9}	5-8 km	0.001	0.005	1.3	23×10^{-3}	1.3 d	1.3
Jupiter	1.90×10^3	69.1	26.5	60.6	0.414	778	11.9 y	13.0
Io	0.0889	1.82	1.8	2.6	1.77	0.422	1.77 d	17
Europa	0.478	1.57	1.3	2.0	3.55	0.671	3.55 d	14
Ganymede	0.148	2.63	1.4	2.7	7.15	1.07	7.15 d	11
Callisto	0.107	2.40	1.2	2.4	16.7	1.88	16.7 d	8.2
and 13 smaller satellites								
Saturn	569	56.8	11.8	36.6	0.438	1.43×10^3	29.5 y	9.65
Tethys	0.0007	0.53	0.2	0.4	1.89	0.294	1.89 d	11.3
Dione	0.00015	0.56	0.3	0.6	2.74	0.377	2.74 d	10.0
Rhea	0.0025	0.77	0.3	0.5	4.52	0.527	4.52 d	8.5
Titan	0.135	2.58	1.4	2.6	15.9	1.22	15.9 d	5.6
Iapetus	0.0019	0.73	0.2	0.6	79.3	3.56	79.3 d	3.3
and 12 smaller satellites								
Uranus	86.6	25.0	9.23	21.5	−0.65	2.87×10^3	84.1 y	6.79
Ariel	0.0013	0.58	0.3	0.4	2.52	0.19	2.52 d	5.5
Umbriel	0.0013	0.59	0.3	0.4	4.14	0.27	4.14 d	4.7
Titania	0.0018	0.81	0.2	0.5	8.70	0.44	8.70 d	3.7
Oberon	0.0017	0.78	0.2	0.5	13.5	0.58	13.5 d	3.1
and 11 smaller satellites								
Neptune	103	24.0	11.9	23.9	0.768	4.50×10^3	165 y	5.43
Triton	0.134	1.9	2.5	3.1	5.88	0.354	5.88 d	4.4
and 7 smaller satellites								
Pluto	0.015	1.2	0.4	1.2	−6.39	5.91×10^3	249 y	4.7
Charon	0.001	0.6			−6.39	0.02	6.39 d	0.2

*Negative rotation period indicates retrograde motion, in opposite sense from orbital motion. Periods are sidereal, meaning the time for the body to return to the same orientation relative to the distant stars rather than the Sun.

†Central body is galactic center for Sun, Sun for planets, and planet for satellites.

Got It! Answers

Chapter 2

p. 24 Average speed and average velocity are the same for direct and Kansas City stop flights; average speed is greater for Minneapolis stop flight

p. 27 (b) has constant speed; (a) reverses direction; (d) speeds up

Chapter 3

p. 52 (c)

Chapter 4

p. 70 None are true

Chapter 5

p. 95 The straight line

p. 99 $T > F_g$ for upward a; $T < F_g$ for downward a; $T = F_g$ for constant speed in either direction

p. 102 No; for example, a car slowing down is moving in the direction opposite the force that's slowing it

p. 107 The statement is nonsense. If there were no gravity in space, spacecraft, astronauts, and the moon would all move in straight lines and we would never see them again!

p. 109 Upward acceleration does not imply upward velocity; cable tension exceeds weight in (a) and (d)

p. 111 No, the force on the larger block is 1.5 N

Chapter 6

p. 134 Both 1 N

p. 139 Because the gravitational force is just enough to keep them accelerating in a circular path

p. 144 Because the objects were on sloping surfaces, and therefore the normal force was not equal to the weight

p. 153 The larger one; it has a greater ratio of mass to surface area

Chapter 7

p. 172 No, it's only 5 J, as the spring hasn't exerted 2 N the whole way

p. 177 Both do the same work; the faster hiker produces more power

Chapter 8

p. 200 Because an *increase* in potential energy (positive dU/dx) means one is doing work moving *against* a force

Chapter 10

p. 244 Second one from the top

p. 247 $30\hat{\jmath}$ kg·m/s

p. 249 Both skaters' momenta increase; the basketball's momentum reverses sign; system momentum is unchanged

Chapter 11

p. 264 The first two

p. 271 The object initially at rest

Chapter 12

p. 290 12-6*b*

p. 297 Because its mass is farther from the rotation axis

p. 304 The solid ball

Chapter 13

p. 323 The boy brings no additional angular momentum to the system, while the girl does

p. 327 Upward

Chapter 14

p. 339 The diagonal pair

Chapter 15

p. 369 Frequency and period are the same; amplitude and phase constants are different

p. 375 (a) no change; (b) doubles; (c) doubles

Chapter 17

p. 422 No, it drops by 20 dB

Chapter 18

p. 450 No, the water level stays the same

p. 451 Because you'll put the center of gravity over the center of buoyancy, making the canoe unstable as in Fig. 18-17*b*

p. 458 Lower

Chapter 19

p. 480 The rock

p. 486 Radiation; (a) conduction; (b) convection

Chapter 20

p. 504 100°C

Chapter 21

p. 526 In an isothermal process T is constant so pressure and volume are inversely proportional. But temperature changes in an adiabatic process, so P and V are not inversely proportional. Thus there's no contradiction between the two equations

Chapter 23
p. 576 (a) $-\hat{\mathbf{i}}$; (b) $\sqrt{2}/2(-\hat{\mathbf{i}} + \hat{\mathbf{j}})$
p. 583 (a) 200 N/C; (b) 100 N/C
p. 585 Because P isn't the same distance from **all** parts of the rod

Chapter 24
p. 606 (a) $\phi = 0$ for A, B; $\phi = Es^2$ for C; (b) $\phi = 0$ for A, $\phi = s^2 E\cos 45° = \sqrt{2}s^2 E/2$ for B, C
p. 608 ϕ doesn't change; $\mathbf{E}$ generally does
p. 611 (a) remains zero; (b) doubles
p. 617 (a) $E = \dfrac{Q}{-(2)(1\ m)^2(\varepsilon_0)}$ (b) $E = \dfrac{kQ}{(1000\ m)^2}$
p. 619 No

Chapter 25
p. 633 (a) doubles; (b) doubles; (c) becomes zero; (d) changes sign
p. 633 $W_\alpha = 2W_p$
p. 635 Proton: toward negative ΔV; electron: toward positive ΔV
p. 636 b, a, c
p. 637 More
p. 644 (a)
p. 645 Yes to both

Chapter 26
p. 666 They're the same
p. 670 Twice the working voltage
p. 673 (a) parallel; (b) series; (c) the series combination $1/2\ C$

Chapter 27
p. 686 (a) current to left; (b) upward current; (c) current to left; (d) no current; (e) no current
p. 700 (a) (2); (b) (1)

Chapter 28
p. 713 (a) 3 V; (b) 0 V; (c) 6 V
p. 716 (a) 2R; (b) 1/2 R
p. 718 A will be brightest; with C disconnected both A and B will have equal brightness
p. 732 (a) 6 mA; (b) 2 mA

Chapter 29
p. 746 Greatest force in (a); least (0) in (c); direction in (a) and (b) is into page
p. 749 Counterclockwise
p. 755 Upward

Chapter 30
p. 777 (a) into the page at P, out of the page at Q; (b) stronger at P
p. 778 Tighten, independent of the current direction
p. 780 Into the page
p. 782 (b) only

Chapter 31
p. 811 Same direction as in Fig. 31-11; you still do work
p. 812 Counterclockwise
p. 814 Harder
p. 817 (a) clockwise; (b) counterclockwise

Chapter 32
p. 838 Increasing
p. 843 Only when it's opened

Chapter 33
p. 857 The capacitor
p. 864 Smaller, by a factor of 10^{-4}
p. 866 Above

Chapter 34
p. 895 Both have the same speed; light has a much smaller wavelength
p. 905 (a) $B_1 = 2B_2$; (b) $S_1 = 4S_2$; (c) $\lambda_1 = \lambda_2$

Chapter 35
p. 923 $n_3 > n_1 > n_2$

Chapter 36
p. 943 At the mirror's center of curvature
p. 950 (a) The intensity diminishes, but the full image remains (b) there would be no image (c) there would be no image, or it would be very out of focus (d) yes, but not obviously visible except when looking straight toward lens
p. 951 Virtual, convex
p. 960 +2.25 diopter

Chapter 37
p. 976 Closer together

Chapter 38
p. 1020 When the twins move at the same speed they are the same age; the twin making the longer trip is younger
p. 1029 Less, although insignificantly so at these low relative speeds
p. 1033 Very nearly c

Answers to Odd-Numbered Problems

Chapter 1

3. 100,000 times bigger
   5.0.108 782 775 7 ns
7. 10^8
9. 0.79 rad
11. 28 g
13. 10^6
15. 7%
17. Less by about 3 mi/h
19. 30 AU
21. 143 m^2/kg
23. Approximately 0.0175 rad
25. L/T^2
27. (c) Actually, the speed is given by
   $v = \sqrt{\lambda g / 2\pi}$
29. 2.5×10^6 m
31. 7.4×10^6 m/s^2
33. (a) 2.5×10^{-11} m^2; (b) 5.0 μm
35. 280 K
37. 41 m
39. 7
43. $\sim 1.3 \times 10^6$
45. About 0.1%
47. (a) $\sim 1.4 \times 10^{18}$ m^3; (b) $\sim 1.3 \times 10^{12}$
49. ~ 10 times as much in stars
51. $\sim 10^4$
53. $d_{Sun}/d_{moon} = 380$;
   $R_{Sun} \sim 7 \times 10^5$ km
   (a) 4 μm; (b) 7500
55. (a) $\sim 10^{28}$; (b) $\sim 10^{14}$
59. $\sqrt{F_0/\mu}$; this is in fact the equation
   for the wave speed

Chapter 2

1. 10.16 m/s
3. 5.30 m/s
5. (a) 24 km north; (b) 9.6 km/h;
   (c) 16 km/h; (d) 0; (e) 0
7. 28.5 km/h
9. 48 mi/h
11. 1 m/s = 2.24 mi/h
13. 51 ft/s = 35 mi/h
15. (a) 84 km/h; (b) 55 h
17. 2.6 h later; 1800 km from New
   York
21. (a) 2.0 m/s; (b) 0; (c) -5.0 m/s; (d)
   1.2 m/s; (e) 0.17 m/s
23. (a) $b - 2ct$; (b) 8.4 s after launch
25. (a) $t = 0$ s, 0.13 s, 2.5 s;
   (b) $v = 3bt^2 - 2ct + d$;
   (c) $v_0 = 1.0$ m/s;
   (d) $t = 0.065$ s, 1.7 s
27. 125 m/s^2
29. 15 m/s^2
31. 31 s
33. (a) 126 m/s; (b) 0.46 m/s^2
35. $a = 6bt - 2c$
37. 100 m by both methods
41. (a) 46 m/s^2; (b) 61 s
43. (a) 2.0 m/s^2; (b) 150 m
45. 5×10^{-12} m
47. 12 km/s
49. (a) 0.014 s; (b) 0.51 m
51. 886 m
53. Yes, $a = 370$ m/s^2
55. No collision; 10 m apart
57. 4.6×10^{-3} m/s^2
59. Collide at 12 km/h
61. 11.3 m/s
63. (a) 27 m; (b) 4.7 s
65. Mars
67. 273 m
69. 2.0 m/s
71. 2.4 s
73. (a) 25 km/h; (b) 13 km/h
75. (a) 4.6 s; (b) 8.7 m/s
77. 0.196 s
79. 5.0 s; 17 km/h
81. (a) 7.0 m/s; (b) in 2.3 s
83. 83.113 m
85. (b) 3.8 s; (c) 19 m; (d) 100 m
87. (a) $v = \omega x_0 \cos \omega t$,
   $a = -\omega^2 x_0 \sin \omega t$;
   (b) $v_{max} = \omega x_0$, $a_{max} = \omega^2 x_0$
89. (a) 20 cm
91. 1.19 m

Chapter 3

1. 266 m, 34° N of W
3. 702 km, 21.3° E of N
5. $C = 5.0$ m; 127° clockwise from $\mathbf{A}$
7. (a) 0.68A vertically upward;
   (b) 1.88A, to the right
9. (a) L, $-x$ direction; (b) $\sqrt{3}L$,
   $+y$ direction; (c) 0; (d) $2L$,
   $-x$ direction
11. $\mathbf{V} = 105\hat{\mathbf{i}} + 58\hat{\mathbf{j}}$ km
13. $\mathbf{A} = 8.19\hat{\mathbf{i}} + 5.74\hat{\mathbf{j}}$;
   $\mathbf{B} = -3.44\hat{\mathbf{i}} - 4.91\hat{\mathbf{j}}$;
   $\mathbf{C} = -3.38\hat{\mathbf{i}} + 7.25\hat{\mathbf{j}}$
15. $\mathbf{A} + \mathbf{B} = 4.8\hat{\mathbf{i}} + 0.82\hat{\mathbf{j}}$;
   $\mathbf{A} - \mathbf{B} = 12\hat{\mathbf{i}} + 11\hat{\mathbf{j}}$;
   $\mathbf{A} + \mathbf{C} = 4.8\hat{\mathbf{i}} + 13\hat{\mathbf{j}}$;
   $\mathbf{A} + \mathbf{B} + \mathbf{C} = 1.4\hat{\mathbf{i}} + 8.1\hat{\mathbf{j}}$
17. $\mathbf{C} = -15\hat{\mathbf{i}} + 9\hat{\mathbf{j}} - 18\hat{\mathbf{k}}$
19. (a) $1.37\hat{\mathbf{i}} + 8.07\hat{\mathbf{j}}$;
   (b) $8.25\hat{\mathbf{i}} + 17.9\hat{\mathbf{j}}$; (c) $10.5\hat{\mathbf{i}} - 17.6\hat{\mathbf{j}}$
21. $0.19\hat{\mathbf{i}} + 0.88\hat{\mathbf{j}}$ km;
   (b) 1.0 km at 79° N of E
23. (a) $A_x = 5.9$, $A_y = 8.1$; $A_x' = 5.4$,
   $A_y' = 8.4$ units
25. $\hat{\mathbf{i}} + \hat{\mathbf{j}} + \hat{\mathbf{k}}$; magnitude = $\sqrt{3}$
27. (a) in x-y system $\Delta\mathbf{r} = 5.0\hat{\mathbf{i}} + 3.5\hat{\mathbf{j}}$ km; in x'-y' system
   $\Delta\mathbf{r} = 6.1\hat{\mathbf{i}} + 0.50\hat{\mathbf{j}}$ km;
   (b) $\Delta r = 6.1$ km
29. (a) 5.4 mi at 32° E of N;
   (b) 15 mi/h at 32° E of N
31. (a) 264 km/h, 29° west of north;
   (b) $-128\hat{\mathbf{i}} + 231\hat{\mathbf{j}}$ km/h

33. $19\hat{\imath} + 4.5\hat{\jmath} + 0.26\hat{k}$ km/h
35. (a) $24\hat{\imath} + 10\hat{\jmath}$ m;
    (b) $12\hat{\imath} + 5.0\hat{\jmath}$ m/s;
    (c) $12\hat{\imath} - 5.0\hat{\jmath}$ m/s
37. 5.12 m/s^2, 41° S of W (221° from x axis)
39. (a) $\bar{v} = -0.8\hat{\jmath}$ cm/h;
    (b) $\bar{a} = -0.42\hat{\imath}$ cm/h^2
41. (a) $10\hat{\imath} - 21\hat{\jmath}$ m/s; (b) 13.0 m/s;
    (c) 89.0°
43. $6.7\hat{\imath}$ m/s; (b) 1.66 s; (c) 8.24 m/s
45. (a) 18 km/h, 14 km/h, 10 km/h, 14 km/h; (b) 21 km/h, 17 km/h, 13 km/h, 17 km/h
47. $30\hat{\imath} + 64\hat{\jmath}$ km/s
49. (a) 1.6 m, 2.8 m/s, both vertically downward; (b) 2.03 m, 3.57 m/s, both at 38.1° to the vertical; (c) 9.8 m/s^2, vertically downward in both frames of reference
51. 16.2 m
53. (a) 1.8 km/h/s = 0.50 m/s^2;
    (b) 142°
55. (a) 0.32 cm/s; (b) 0.034 cm/s^2;
    (c) 90°
57. 25° upstream
59. (a) 1.30×10^6 m; (b) 7.78 km/s;
    (c) 9.19 m/s^2, almost g
61. $-b\hat{\imath} + a\hat{\jmath}$, $b\hat{\imath} - a\hat{\jmath}$
63. $\frac{\sqrt{2}}{2}\hat{\imath} + \frac{\sqrt{2}}{2}\hat{\jmath}$
67. 53.8°, 13.9 km/h

Chapter 4
1. 0°
3. $1.3\hat{\imath} + 2.3\hat{\jmath}$ m/s
5. 6.0 m/s at 53° below x axis
7. (a) 23°; (b) 5.4×10^3 km
9. 1.83 m
11. (a) $t = 18$ s; (b) 300 m; (c) 22 m/s, at 120° to x axis
13. (a) 2.6×10^{17} cm/s^2, upward;
    (b) parabolic
15. (a) 1.34 s; (b) 14.7 m
17. 5.7 m/s
19. 34 nm
21. 8.3 m/s at 61°
23. Yes
25. -14.6 m/s
27. (a) 6.64 km/s; (b) 16.0 min;
    (c) 8.28 km/s
29. 1.1 s
31. 1090 m

35. (a) 8.8 m; (b) 0.53 m
37. 11.2 m/s
41. 31.2° or 65.7°
43. 2.8×10^{-3} m/s^2
45. 54 min
47. 2.27 km
59. 5.07×10^3 s
51. $a_r = 0.947$ m/s^2;
    $a_t = 6.28 \times 10^{-2}$ m/s^2
53. $t = \sqrt{r/a_t}$
55. 89 m/s
57. 32 m
59. 19 m
61. 300 m, 119 m
63. $v_0 = 6.36\hat{\imath} + 10.3\hat{\jmath}$ m/s,
    or 12.1 m/s at 58.3°
65. 83°
71. 7.2 m/s at 77° to horizontal
75. 38°
77. $2v_0 \sin\theta_0/g$
79. 892 m/s^2
81. 364 m

83. (a) $\tan^{-1}\left(\tan\theta_0 - \dfrac{gt}{v_0\cos\theta_0}\right)$;

(b) $\tan^{-1}\left(\tan\theta_0 - \dfrac{gx}{v_0^2\cos^2\theta_0}\right)$

Chapter 5
1. 3.8 MN
3. 1.5×10^3 kN
5. 10^{-4} N
7. (a) $m_B = 3.0m_A$; (b) 2.0 m/s^2
9. Quadruples
11. (a) 11 m; (b) 24 m; (c) 43 m;
    (d) 53 m
13. $F_{\text{driver}} = 5.7$ kN; $F_{\text{passenger}} = 125$ kN, 22 times greater
15. 5.77 N at 72.2° to the x axis
17. Venus
19. (a) 3.3 N; (b) 12 oz
21. 9.1×10^3 kg
23. 7.7×10^{12} m/s^2
25. 4.26 m/s^2
27. 385 N
29. 2.9 m/s^2, downward
31. (a) 3.1×10^7 N; (b) 9.4×10^2 N
33. 0.53 s
35. 55 kN
37. 2.0 N
39. 1.3×10^{-21} cm

41. (a) 5.26 kN; (b) 1.08 kN;
    (c) 494 N; (d) 589 N
43. 130 N
45. 33 cm
47. 1.9 m/s^2
49. 830 g
51. (a) 132 cm; (b) 127 cm;
    (c) 120 cm; (d) 40 m/s^2
53. 30.7 kN
55. 4.1 cm
57. Apparent weight is 55% of actual weight
59. 240 N
61. 4.3 cm
63. 7.2 m
65. (a) $0.40mg$; (b) $2.40mg$; (c) $1.40mg$
67. (a) 16 kN; (b) 1.5 kN
69. (a) $a = \dfrac{m_f - m_s}{m_s}g$;

    (b) $y = \dfrac{m_f a_s h}{(m_f - m_s)(g + a_s)}$
71. $\ell + nm(a + g)/k$, where n is the spring number measured from the bottom
75. 900 N

Chapter 6
1. $2.7\hat{\imath} + 5.5\hat{\jmath}$ N, or 6.1 N at 64° to the x axis
3. (a) 2.0 kN; (b) 1.4 kN
7. 43 cm
9. 530 N; 3.6 times the weight
11. 98 N in horizontal string; $98\sqrt{2}$ N in vertical string
13. 230 N in short rope; 84 N in long rope
15. (a) 6.3 m/s^2; (b) 0.44 s
17. Right-hand mass 2.5 times left-hand mass
19. (a) 7.1 kg; (b) 3.9 kg
21. Left to right, 56.9 N, 34.4 N, 89.2 N
23. 8.18×10^{-8} N
27. (a) 13 m/s; (b) 4.4°
29. 132 m
31. (a) 310 N; (b) 0; (c) nothing
33. (a) 35°; (b) 22°
35. 24 m/s = 86 km/h
37. 17 m/s
39. 579 N
41. 5.43 kN
43. 0.21

45. 25.3 s
47. 11.4 m/s^2
49. 133 m
51. 2.7 cm
53. (a) 1.6 m/s^2; (b) 3.3 N
55. 4.2 m/s^2
57. 95 km/h
61. 0.72
63. 2.6 N
65. 4.7 m/s
67. 0.70 m/s^2, upward
69. 7.75 m/s
71. 1.40 s
73. (a) 0.12; (b) toward the inside of the turn
75. 2.0 rpm
79. (a) lower at equator, where a net downward force is needed to keep you accelerating with Earth's rotation; (b) 0.34%
85. 28 cm

Chapter 7

1. 900 J
3. 0.15 NJ
5. 9.6 MJ
7. (a) 400 J; (b) 31 kg
9. 4.4 MN
13. (a) 86.9 units^2; (b) 20.3 units^2
15. (a) 0; (b) 90°
19. 169 J
21. 622 J
23. (a) 60 kJ; (b) 20 kJ
25. (a) 360 J; (b) 350 J; (c) 357.5 J; (d) 359.375 J
27. $k_B = 8k_A$
29. 190 J
31. (a) 33 J; (b) 60 J; (c) 78 J
33. $F_0\left(x + \dfrac{x^2}{2\ell_0} + \dfrac{\ell_0^2}{\ell_0 + x} - \ell_0\right)$
35. (a) 0; (b) $2FR$; (c) πFR
37. 135 J
41. 2.56×10^{-15} J $= 16.0$ keV
43. 116 km/h
45. $1:2$
47. 113 m/s
49. 2.82 kN $= 635$ lbs
51. (a) 83.6 MJ; (b) 256 km/h; (c) 2.14 s; (d) 33.3 m/s^2
53. (a) 60 kW; (b) 1 kW; (c) 40 W
55. 9.4 MJ
57. (a) 36 MW; (b) 1.1 MW

61. 2.7 h
63. 430 million gal/day
65. 2.1 MJ
67. 7.7°
69. 1.9 m
71. $\frac{1}{2}F_0 x_0$
73. 70.5°
75. (a) 28 kJ; (b) 18 kJ
77. (a) 450 W; (b) 8.0 kJ
79. (a) $W = \frac{1}{2}bt^2$; (b) $a = \sqrt{b/m}$
81. (a) 71 kW·y; (b) 93 kW·y
83. About 450 J
85. (a) 33 J; (b) 167 J

Chapter 8

1. (a) $-2\mu mg\,\ell$; (b) $-\sqrt{2}\mu mg\,\ell$
3. (a) 0; (b) $F_0 a$
5. (a) 1.3 MJ; (b) 59 kJ
9. (a) 1.07 J; (b) 1.12 J
11. 5.2 J
13. 55 cm
15. 2.9 J
17. $U = -\frac{1}{3}ax^3 - bx$
19. $U = F_0\left(x + \dfrac{x^2}{2\ell} + \dfrac{\ell^2}{\ell + x} - \ell\right)$
21. 50 m/s (180 km/h)
23. 92 m
27. (a) 16 m/s; (b) 29%
29. 26 MN/m
31. 3.6 m/s $= 13$ km/h
35. 2.6 m/s
39. ± 2.0 m
43. (a) $U = -\dfrac{a}{2}x^2 + \dfrac{b}{4}x^4$; (b) $x = 0.66$ m, $x = 2.1$ m
45. (a) -6.7 N; (b) 0; (c) 4.5 N
49. (a) 30 cm; (b) 10.4 N/m
51. 35%
53. 19%
55. 0.36
57. 2.6 m/s
59. 0.036
61. 62 cm from left end of frictional zone
63. 1000 MW, twice that of the coal plant
65. $x = 2(h_1 - h_2)$
69. (a) $v = \sqrt{\sqrt{2}\,g\,\ell}$; (b) $T = \dfrac{3}{\sqrt{2}}mg$
71. ± 25 cm

73. 14 m
75. (a) 2.53×10^5 m/s; (b) 2.91×10^5 m/s; (c) 2.93×10^5 m/s
77. 54.6 mJ
79. 75 cm
81. (a) 1.74 cm; (b) 0.78 cm; (c) 7.4×10^7 m/s
83. (a) $v = \left[\dfrac{x^2}{m}(a - \frac{1}{2}bx^2)\right]^{1/2}$; (c) $v_{max} = a/\sqrt{2mb}$
85. $v = [2ax^{|b+1|}/m\,|b + 1|]^{1/2}$
87. 14.5 m

Chapter 9

1. $R_E/\sqrt{2}$
3. 58%
5. 8.6 kg
7. 46 nN
9. $(\sqrt{2} - 1)R_{planet} \simeq 0.41 R_{planet}$
11. 1.2×10^{-7}
13. 3.1 km/s
15. 1.8 days
17. 1.0 hour
19. 2.6×10^{41} kg, about 10^{11} solar masses
21. 6.3×10^{10} m
23. 2.64×10^{10} m
25. 2.47 times Earth's orbital radius
27. No
29. 3.2×10^9 J
31. 530 km
33. 58 MJ
35. $R_E/99 = 64$ km; underestimate
37. 3%
39. $\sqrt{2}$
41. 7.7 Mm
43. (a) 11.2 km/s; (b) 9.74 km/s; (c) no
47. $v = \sqrt{2GM\left(\dfrac{3}{R} + \dfrac{1}{r}\right)}$
49. 8.1×10^{11} m, just beyond Jupiter
53. 109 min
55. 15 km/s, 23 km/s
57. 7.95 km/s
59. 8.85×10^5 m
61. (a) 9.0×10^{10} m; (b) 5.3×10^{11} J; (c) 38 km/s
63. 4.60×10^{10} m
65. (b) 8.8 mm; (c) 2.9 km
67. 1400 km lower

Chapter 10

1. 0.75 m from the center
3. 14 m to the right, 4.5 m upward in Fig. 10-23
5. $\ell/2\sqrt{3}$ along the perpendicular bisector of any side
7. $X = 44$ cm, $Y = 55$ cm, with origin at lower left
9. $0.115a$ above the vertex of the missing triangle
11. 6.5 pm from the oxygen
13. $\mathbf{R} = (t^2 + \frac{10}{3}t + \frac{7}{3})\hat{\imath} + (\frac{2}{3}t + \frac{8}{3})\hat{\jmath}$; $\mathbf{V} = (2t + \frac{10}{3})\hat{\imath} + \frac{2}{3}\hat{\jmath}$; $\mathbf{A} = 2\hat{\imath}$
15. $\sim 10^{-10}$ m, the diameter of a hydrogen atom
17. $m_{\text{mouse}} = \frac{1}{4}m_{\text{bowl}}$
19. Moves in the opposite direction at 67 cm/s
21. 21 g, $-x$ direction
23. 498 m/s
25. 8.4 km/h
27. (a) 0.14 N/m²; (b) 0.014 mm
29. (a) 0.99 m; (b) 3.9 m/s
31. 3.9 km/h
33. $26\hat{\imath} + 16\hat{\jmath}$ m/s
35. 1100 kg
37. (a) 3.3×10^6 N (b) 3.4×10^5 kg
39. 0.22
41. $K_{\text{cm}} = 1.1 \times 10^{-14}$ J before and after; $K_{\text{int}} = 0$ before, $K_{\text{int}} = 1.3 \times 10^{-14}$ J after
43. before: $K_{\text{cm}} = 1.6$ MJ, $K_{\text{int}} = 21$ kJ; after: $K_{\text{cm}} = 1.6$ MJ, $K_{\text{int}} = 0$
45. (a) 1.7 cm above the bottom; (b) 2.7 cm above the bottom
47. 20 m
49. $-47\hat{\imath} - 68\hat{\jmath}$ m/s
51. (a) 3.5 m; (b) 1.3 m/s; (c) 0
53. (a) 0.096 m/s²; (b) 6.2 m/s
55. 9.3 m/s
57. (a) $m = \dfrac{\pi\rho h^2}{2a}$; (b) $Z = \frac{2}{3}h$
59. 3.0 mN
61. (a) 37.7°; (b) 0.657 m/s
63. 5.8 s after explosion
65. (a) thrust $= m\dfrac{dv}{dt} =$
$$\left[(1 + f)V_{\text{ex}} - V\right]\dfrac{dM_{\text{in}}}{dt};$$
(b) 1504 lb

67. $v_1 = \left(\dfrac{m_2 k x^2}{m_1^2 + m_1 m_2}\right)^{1/2}$;

$v_2 = \left(\dfrac{m_1 k x^2}{m_2^2 + m_1 m_2}\right)^{1/2}$

Chapter 11

1. 52 N·s
3. 4.3×10^3 N, $7.1mg$
5. (a) $-2.6\hat{\imath} + 0.74\hat{\jmath}$ N·s; (b) $-51\hat{\imath} + 14\hat{\jmath}$ N
7. 0.46 s
9. (a) 7.3 MN·s; (b) 5.6 MN
11. (a) 6.8×10^{-3} N·s; (b) 2.3 N
13. $\Delta P/P = 2\%$
15. 12 ms
17. (a) 5.4 mi/h; (b) 13%
19. 19 kg
23. 10^{21} kg
25. $4.0\hat{\imath} + 21.5\hat{\jmath}$ Mm/s
29. 1.3 μJ
31. 120°
33. 46 m/s
35. $v_{1f} = -11$ Mm/s; $v_{2f} = 6.9$ Mm/s
37. $3 + 2\sqrt{2} \approx 5.8$; it doesn't matter which is more massive
39. $v_A = -\frac{1}{3}v$; $v_B = \frac{2}{9}v$; $v_C = \frac{8}{9}v$
45. 22°
47. $(v_{1i} = 0.833$ m/s, $v_{2i} = 1.22$ m/s, $\theta_{2i} = 28.3°)$; $(v_{1i} = 1.20$ m/s, $v_{2i} = 1.12$ m/s, $\theta_{2i} = 31.2°)$
49. 13 m/s at 27° to horizontal
51. $v_A = -\frac{1}{5}v_0\hat{\imath}$; $v_B = \frac{3}{5}v_0\hat{\imath} + \frac{1}{5}\sqrt{3}v_0\hat{\jmath}$ $v_C = \frac{3}{5}v_0\hat{\imath} - \frac{1}{5}\sqrt{3}v_0\hat{\jmath}$
53. 350 N
55. 52 km/h at 33° north of east
57. $m_{\text{truck}} = 7.6m_{\text{car}}$
59. (a) $m_1 = 3m_2$; (b) $v_{2f} = 2v$
61. $v_{1f} = 1.66$ m/s; $v_{2f} = 0.703$ m/s; $\theta_{2f} = 67°$ clockwise from initial velocity of the first ball
63. (a) 12.0 m; (b) 15.4 m/s
65. 0.88
69. $v_{1\,\text{kg}} = 4.0$ m/s; $v_{4\,\text{kg}} = 1.0$ m/s at 50° clockwise from the x axis
71. $v_{1200} = 2.2$ km/h, $v_{1800} = 18$ km/h
73. (a) $v_1 = 0.28v_0$, $v_2 = 0.48v_0$; (b) 3, $0.26v_0$, $0.31v_0$

Chapter 12

1. (a) 7.27×10^{-5} rad/s; (b) 1.75×10^{-3} rad/s; (c) 1.45×10^{-4} rad/s; (d) 31.4 rad/s

3. (a) 75.4 rad/s; (b) 0.24 mrad/s; (c) 6283 rad/s; (d) 2.0×10^{-7} rad/s
5. (a) 66 rpm; (b) 3.7 s
7. (a) 21.7 rad/s, 207 rpm; (b) 34.7 rad/s, 331 rpm
9. (a) 0.068 rpm/s; (b) 7.1×10^{-3} rad/s²
11. (a) 12 min; (b) 2.2×10^4
13. 1.3 rad/s²
15. (a) 2.0 s; (b) 1.0 rev
17. 1.2 m
19. 0.079 N·m
21. 0.15 N·m
23. (a) 0.70 N·m, counterclockwise; (b) $\mathbf{F}_1$ and $\mathbf{F}_5$
25. 614 kg·m²
27. (a) $\frac{2}{3}m\ell^2$; (b) $\frac{2}{3}m\ell^2$; (c) $\frac{4}{3}m\ell^2$
29. 45 kg·m²
33. (a) 1×10^{38} kg·m²; (b) 2.6×10^{19} N·m
35. (a) 1.29×10^{38} kg·m²; (b) 6.45×10^{33} N·m
39. (a) 430 min; (b) 1900 rev
41. 1900 N·m
43. 170 rpm
45. $m_{\text{pulley}} = 0.49$ kg; $m_1 = 0.41$ kg; $m_2 = 0.58$ kg
47. (a) 450 J; (b) 140 W
49. 0.089%
51. 12.2 rad/s
53. 7.0 m/s
55. $v = \sqrt{\dfrac{2gh}{\alpha + 1}}$
57. 17%
59. hollow
61. (a) 0.156; (b) 0.070 rad/s
63. $\dfrac{253}{512}MR^2 = 0.494MR^2$
65. (a) 310 N; (b) 165 kg
67. (a) 3.5 m/s; (b) 24%
69. $\frac{27}{10}R$
71. $\omega = \sqrt{2A/I}$
73. $I = \frac{1}{2}Mb^2$
75. $2\sqrt{2g/3R}$
77. $\frac{1}{2}Mg\ell \cos\phi$

Chapter 13

1. 63 rad/s, west
3. 0.52 rad/s², $-37°$
5. 16.6 rad/s

7. (a) $-z$; (b) z; (c) in the x-y plane, 45° clockwise from the x axis

9. (a) $-12\hat{\mathbf{k}}$ N·m; (b) $36\hat{\mathbf{k}}$ N·m; (c) $12\hat{\mathbf{i}} - 36\hat{\mathbf{j}}$ N·m

11. $-9.0\hat{\mathbf{k}}$ N·m

13. Parallel to the x axis or 120° clockwise from x axis

17. $F_x = 1.33F_y - 3.13$ N

19. 414 kg·m²/s

21. 7.6 rad/s

23. 0.017 kg·m²/s

25. 37 kg·m²/s

27. 2.7×10^5 kg·m²/s, out of page in Fig. 13-30

29. 0.21 kg·m²

31. (a) 0.17 rev/s; (b) 386 J

33. (a) 142 rpm; (b) 21%

35. 2.5 days

37. (a) 23.7 rpm; (b) 3.49 mJ

39. (a) $\dfrac{2M\omega_0}{2M + 3m}$; (b) $\dfrac{M\omega_0}{M + 6m}$; (c) same as (b)

41. (a) 0.537 rad/s; (b) 6.44 m/s; (c) 207 N

43. 6.0 cm

45. $I = \dfrac{mgd}{2\omega\Omega}$

47. $\tan^{-1}(\frac{1}{2}) = 26.6°$

49. 0.37 rev/s

51. 22 g

53. $\dfrac{I}{I + mR^2}$

55. (a) 1.61; (b) 2.22

59. Sun's rotation 2.8%; Jupiter's orbital motion 60%

61. $v = \left[\dfrac{8(m + M)g\ell}{m^2}\left(\frac{1}{4}m + \frac{1}{3}M\right)\right]^{1/2}$

63. (a) $\dfrac{m\sqrt{2gh}}{(\frac{1}{2}M + m)R}$; (b) $\dfrac{\sqrt{2gm[hm - (\frac{1}{2}M + m)R]}}{(\frac{1}{2}M + m)R}$; (c) $h = \dfrac{(\frac{1}{2}M + m)R}{m}$

65. (a) $\frac{2}{7}\omega_0$; (b) $2\omega_0R/7\mu_k g$

Chapter 14

1. (a) $\frac{1}{3}\ell F_3 - \frac{2}{3}\ell F_2 + \ell F_1 = 0$; (b) $\frac{1}{2}\ell F_1 - \frac{1}{6}\ell F_2 - \frac{1}{6}\ell F_3 + \frac{1}{2}\ell F_4 - \frac{1}{2}\ell F_5 = 0$

3. (b) $\boldsymbol{\tau}_{\text{origin}} = -7\hat{\mathbf{k}}$ N·m

5. (a) A vector of length $\sqrt{2}\,F$, oriented 45° clockwise from the negative y axis, applied at the point $x = 0$ m, $y = +1$ m or anywhere on the line $y = (1 + x)$ m. (b) Not possible; the first two vectors sum to zero but produce a nonzero torque, so any other vector applied to balance torques will upset force balance.

7. Both sets have $-F_1 + F_2 \sin\phi + F_3 = 0$, $-F_2 \cos\phi + F_4 = 0$; torque equations are (a) $\ell_2 F_4 \cos\phi - \ell_2 F_3 \sin\phi - \ell_1 F_2 = 0$; (b) $(\ell_2 - \ell_1)F_2 - \ell_2 F_1 \sin\phi = 0$.

9. (a) $\tau_A = \frac{1}{2}\ell mg$; (b) $\tau_B = 0$; (c) $\tau_C = \frac{1}{2}\ell mg$

11. $\frac{1}{6}L$

13. (a) 61 cm from left end; (b) 1.4 m from left end

15. 120 N

17. 11.7 kN

19. (a) 40 N·m; (b) 1300 N

21. Vertical forces both 73.5 N, downward, horizontal forces both 33.6 N, away from door jamb at top, toward jamb at bottom

23. 5.0 kN; tension

25. 0.87

27. 500 N

29. 7.3°

31. 50 kN

33. 6.05 kN

35. $\frac{1}{8}$

37. Maximum height of CM is at sphere center; lower for clown (b)

39. Two equilibria for $|a| > 2\sqrt{3}$; one metastable, other unstable

41. 1.2 m

43. 170 N

45. 74 kg

47. $\frac{1}{2}(\sqrt{3} - 1)mgs$

49. $\mu = \dfrac{\sin 2\theta}{3 + \cos 2\theta}$

51. $mg/2k$

53. 28°

55. Left scale 16.3 N; right scale 22.9 N

57. Tip

59. Slide

61. (a) $0.44mg$, at 12° to Earth's polar axis; (b) $0.036mgR_E$, out of the plane of Fig. 14-57

Part 1 Cumulative Problems

1. 16.5 m from the post

3. $a = \dfrac{2g[(m_1 + m_2)\sin\theta - \mu m_1 \cos\theta]}{2m_1 + 3m_2}$

5. (a) $v = \frac{2}{7}\omega R$; (b) $\Delta x = \dfrac{2\omega^2 R^2}{49\mu g}$

Chapter 15

1. $T = 0.780$ s; $f = 1.28$ Hz

3. 11.5 fs

5. $A = 20$ cm, $\omega = \pi/2$ s^{-1}, $\phi = 0$; $A = 30$ cm, $\omega = 2.0$ s^{-1}, $\phi = -\pi/2$; $A = 40$ cm, $\omega = \pi/2$ s^{-1}, $\phi = \pi/4$

7. 63.3 kg

9. 1.7 kN/m

11. 0.69 s

13. (a) $\pi\sqrt{m/k}$; (b) $v_0\sqrt{m/k}$

17. (a) 1.0 cm; (b) 6.2 m; (c) 3.6 km

19. 0.11 N·m/rad

21. (a) $2\pi\sqrt{\ell/g}$; (b) $2\pi\sqrt{2\ell/3g}$; (c) $2\pi\sqrt{2\ell/g}$; (d) infinite

23. 0.34 s

25. $R = \sqrt{2\kappa/k}$

27. Within 1 μm

33. 5.0 g

35. $\omega^2 = \dfrac{k_1 k_2}{m(k_1 + k_2)}$

37. a and b are the amplitudes in the x and y directions, respectively

39. 400 J, or 1.4×10^{-3} of the total KE

41. $t = (0.14 + n)$ s, $t = (0.53 + n)$ s, n an integer; $x = \pm37$ cm

45. $\omega = \sqrt{2k/3M}$

47. 34

49. 77% at $0.90\,\omega$; 66% at 1.1ω

53. (a) 19 s^{-1}; (b) 0.33 s; (c) 92 m/s²

55. (a) 6.5 cm; (b) 0.51 s

57. 1.64 s

59. 300 g

61. (a) $E_2 = \frac{1}{4}E_1$; (b) $a_{2\,\text{max}} = \frac{1}{4}a_{1\,\text{max}}$

63. 2.1 m/s²

65. 0.44

67. $2\pi\sqrt{7/10ga}$

69. $f = 0.54$ Hz; $A = 22$ cm; $\phi = -0.11$ rad

71. $T = 2\pi\sqrt{R/g}$

73. $T = 2\pi\sqrt{mL/2F_0}$

Chapter 16

1. 3.4 s
3. 3.38 m
5. 1.81×10^8 m/s $= 0.604c$
7. (a) 400 nm; (b) 0.3 mm
9. 11 m
11. (a) 0.58 m^{-1}; (b) 1.53 s^{-1}
13. (a) 13.7 s^{-1}; (b) 0.393 cm^{-1};
    (c) $y = 2.5\cos(0.393x + 13.7t)$
15. (a) 25 cm; (b) 0.37 Hz; (c) 12 m;
    (d) 4.4 m/s
17. $y = \dfrac{2}{(x - 3t)^4 + 1}$
19. (a) 3.0 m; (b) 1.5 s; (c) 2.0 m/s;
    (d) $+x$
21. 250 m/s
23. (a) 7.6 N; (b) 1.7 m/s
25. 364 m/s
27. 94 N
29. 7.64 g/cm^3
31. 585 m/s
33. 9.9 W
35. 35 cm
37. $4\pi^2 A^2 F / \lambda$
39. 12 mW/m^2
41. (a) 9.1 kW/m^2; (b) 0.88 W/m^2
43. (a) 6.4 kW/m^2; (b) 4.9 W/m^2
45. 5.1 m
47. (a) 2 cm; (b) pulse 1 at $x = 0$,
    direction $+x$, pulse 2 at $x = 5$,
    direction $-x$; (c) $t = 2.5$ s
49. Every 6 s
51. 5.34 m
53. $\sqrt{gh}$
55. (a) 1.5 cm; (b) 63 cm; (c) 11 ms;
    (d) 56 m/s;
    (e) 18 W
57. $v = \sqrt{k\ell(\ell - \ell_0)/m}$
59. 10 m
61. Every 30 s
63. $u < 0.063v$
67. 5.2 km
69. 67 m

Chapter 17

3. $\lambda = 34$ cm; $T = 1.0$ ms;
    $\omega = 6.3 \times 10^3$ s^{-1};
    $k = 0.18$ cm^{-1}
5. 0.29 s
7. 0.14 kg/m^3
9. monatomic
11. 739 m/s
13. 190 m/s

15. 4.4 nm
17. (a) 3.8 mW/m^2; (b) 96 dB;
    (c) 1.8 N/m^2; (d) 1.6 μm
19. 1 kHz to 6.5 kHz
21. (a) 3.2 μW/m^2, 0.051 N/m^2;
    (b) 3.2×10^{-13} W/m^2;
    1.6×10^{-5} N/m^2
23. (a) 20 dB; (b) approximately
    250 Hz
27. 6.3 m
29. 1
31. 3.2 km/s
33. 0.75 mm
35. 39 μs
37. no; $F = 31$ kN
39. (a) 280 Hz; (b) 70 Hz; (c) 210 Hz
45. (a) 16.6 cm; (b) 424–457 Hz
47. 0.33 Hz
49. 91 Hz
51. 253 m/s
53. 400 Hz
55. 43 m/s $= 154$ km/h
57. (a) 2800 Hz; (b) 933 Hz
59. 25 m/s
63. $u/v = 1/\sin 45° = 1.4$
65. (a) 5.5×10^{-4} W/m^2; (b) 87 dB
67. (a) 112 m/s; (b) 4, 5
69. 960 m/s
71. 0.445 s
73. (a) $\lambda = 5.0$ m, $f = 0.56$ Hz;
    (b) $\lambda = 2.5$ m; $f = 0.79$ Hz
75. 1.36
77. $\Delta f = 2uf/(v - u)$
79. 16 kHz

Chapter 18

1. 1.2 kg
3. 10^{-14}
5. (a) 81 N; (b) 65 N
7. 1 in. H$_2$O $= 249$ Pa
9. 2×10^7 N, or 2000 tons
11. 21 N
13. 0.25 m^2
15. No; $F = 2.3 \times 10^4$ N, or 2.5 tons
17. 1700 kg/m^3
19. ~90 m
21. 890 Pa gauge
23. 8.1×10^{10} N
25. 3.6 mm
27. 93 cm higher in the eye
29. 8.11×10^3 kg
31. 44 kg
33. 0.75 %
35. 59 g

37. 27 m
39. (a) 49 kg; (b) 2500 kg
43. (a) 1.8×10^4 m^3/s; (b) 1.5 m/s
45. 1.75 m/s
47. (a) $h_2 = h_1$; (b) $h_2 = h_1 - \dfrac{3v^2}{2g}$
49. 14.3 m
51. 7.2 cm^3/s
53. (a) no; (b) yes
55. 13
57. 70%
59. $A\sqrt{2gh}$
61. (a) 14 m/s; (b) 2.2 m
65. (a) 25 L/s; (b) 55 m/s; (c) 1.8 kPa
67. $t = \dfrac{A_0}{A_1}\sqrt{\dfrac{2h}{g}}$
69. $P = P_a + \rho g h_0 + \frac{1}{2}\rho\omega^2 r^2$;
    (b) $h = h_0 + \dfrac{\omega^2 r^2}{2g}$
71. (a) $\rho(h) = \dfrac{P_0}{h_0 g} e^{-h/h_0}$; (b) 5.7 km

Part 2 Cumulative Problems

1. (a) $\ell = \dfrac{4M}{\pi d^2 \rho}$; (b) $T = 4\sqrt{\dfrac{\pi M}{d^2 \rho g}}$
5. 17.2 cm

Chapter 19

1. 720
3. 20°C
5. -40
7. -196°C, -321°F
9. (a) 138 kPa; (b) 33.4 kPa;
    (c) 233 kPa
11. 1.37 L
13. 586 mm
15. 240 kcal
17. 0.36 kg
19. 24 days
21. (a) 23 kJ; (b) 337 kJ; (c) 65 kJ
23. 7.5 kW
25. 2.4 kg
27. (a) 560 g; (b) 0.27 K/s
29. 1.8 kg
31. 0.70 K
33. 1.6 K/s
35. 197 g
37. 56.2°C
39. 55 kW
41. 0.293 W
43. 25 ft^2·°F·h/Btu
45. 200 W

47. (a) 12.3 ft^2·°F·h/Btu;
 (b) 715 Btu/h
49. Will save 10 gallons/month
51. 23°C
53. 80%
55. −25°C
57. Drop by 5.9 K
59. 24°C
61. 480 W
63. 1151 K
65. −2.5°C
67. (a) $87; (b) $10
69. 4.65%
71. $\Delta T_{\mathrm{copper}} = 0.16$ K; $\Delta T_{\mathrm{iron}} = 2.1$ K
73. 2.9 J
77. 10 hours

Chapter 20
1. 2.6 m^3
3. 1.8 MPa
5. (a) 27 L; (b) 330 K
7. 2.7×10^7
9. 11 L
11. 515 kPa
13. (a) 1.27 atm; (b) 0.0268 mol;
 (c) 0.786 atm
15. H$_2$
17. 268 K, compared with ideal gas
 292 K
19. 1.76 MPa
21. (a) 9.1×10^{20}; (b) 2.0×10^{20}
23. 22 kJ
25. 3.9 kg
27. 5.96 MJ
29. 1.3×10^{10} kg
31. 564 W
33. 44 minutes
35. 48 min
37. (a) 117 s
39. 3.55 MJ
41. 64°C
43. 177 g
45. 135 g solid in 865 g liquid, at 234 K
47. 5.0 kg
49. 4.9°C
51. 1.00021 cm
53. 3.9 km
55. 43.6 mm^3
57. 307 K
59. $d = \frac{1}{2}L_0\sqrt{2\alpha\,\Delta T + (\alpha\,\Delta T)^2}$
61. 120 mol/m^3
63. 19 kW
65. 79 g
67. 1.2 kg ice, 0.80 kg water, all at 0°C

69. 50 min
71. (a) 61 h; (b) 52 h
77. 34 km

Chapter 21
1. 29 kJ
3. Increases by 250 J
5. (a) 310 MW; (b) 54%
7. 0.02°C
9. $2P_1V_1$
11. 1.2 kJ
13. 4.3 kJ
15. 190 K
17. 1.99 kJ
19. (a) 399 J; (b) 264 kPa
21. (a) 571 kPa; (b) 438 J
23. 440°C
25. $V = 0.18V_0$
27. (b) Gas does 13 J of work;
 (c) 22 J heat lost from gas
29. (a) 300 K, 1.5 kJ; (b) 336 K, 0 J;
 (c) 326 K, 429 J
31. (a) 39.9 kPa; (b) 83.3 kPa;
 (c) 80.2 kJ
33. 928 J
35. (a) 211 J; (b) 12.9 L
37. 75°C
39. 128 J
41. (a) −9.0°C; (b) stable
43. 57.7%
45. 79%
47. 20 mol
49. Drops 23.1 K
51. 343 K
53. 28 kPa
55. (a) 598 J; (b) 2500 J flows in
57. 25 m
59. $\frac{4}{3}P_1V_1$
63. (a) 2.5 kJ; (b) 447 K
69. (a) $M = \dfrac{P_0A}{g}\left[\dfrac{h_1}{h_2} - 1\right];$

 (b) $M = \dfrac{P_0A}{g}\left[\left(\dfrac{h_1}{h_2}\right)^{\gamma} - 1\right]$

Chapter 22
1. (a) 12!/6!, or 6.7×10^5 states;
 (b) about 1 in 1000
3. 5×10^{24} J, assuming oceans cover
 75% of Earth to an average depth
 of 3 km; this is about 20,000 times
 annual use
5. (a) 27%; (b) 7.0%; (c) 77%
7. 0.95 K
9. 52% winter, 48% summer
11. (a) 1.75 GW; (b) 43%; (c) 505 K
13. 2×10^7 kg/s, slightly more than the
 Mississippi's flow
15. (a) 39%; (b) 550 J; (c) 190°C
17. 53.3 kJ
19. (a) 4.3; (b) maximum COP = 11
23. (a) COP$_{\mathrm{summer}}$ = 13, COP$_{\mathrm{winter}}$ = 3.5;
 (b) 0.076 J; (c) 0.22 J
25. (a) 561.7 J; (b) 464.1 J;
 (c) 97.66 J; (d) 17.4%;
 (e) $T_c = 403$ K, $T_h = 487$ K
29. 718 K
31. 1.22 kJ/K
33. 8.9°C
35. 1.36×10^8 J/K
39. (a) 53 J/K; (b) 74 J/K; (c) 0
41. (a) −109 J/K; (b) 122 J/K;
 (c) 13 J/K
43. $\Delta S_{AB} = 68.5$ J/K, $\Delta S_{BC} = 45.7$ J/K,
 $\Delta S_{CA} = -114.2$ J/K
45. 470 kPa
47. (a) 69%; (b) 967 K
49. Decrease in T_{minimum}
51. $58
53. (a) $W = Q = 345$ J; (b) $e = 24\%$
55. 598 J/K
57. About 30 km for 200 kg of water
 and a 60 kg bather
59. 166 MW
61. (a) $1 - 5^{1-\gamma}$; (b) $3T_{\mathrm{min}}(5^{\gamma-1})$;
 (c) $e_{\mathrm{Carnot}} = 1 - \frac{1}{3}(5^{1-\gamma})$
63. (a) 7.94; (b) 5.26; (c) $P_n = 2.96P_s$
65. (a) $T_h = T_{h0}e^{-P_0t/mc(T_{h0}-T_c)}$;
 (b) $P = 0$ at
 $t = \dfrac{mc(T_{h0} - T_c)}{P_0}\ln\!\left(\dfrac{T_{h0}}{T_c}\right)$
67.

	P	V	T	U − U$_A$	S − S$_A$
A					
B			3.4 T_0	6.0 P_0V_0	3.1 P_0V_0/T_0
C	1.5 P_0	2.2 V_0	3.4 T_0	6.0 P_0V_0	3.8 P_0V_0/T_0
D			3.0 T_0	5.0 P_0V_0	3.8 P_0V_0/T_0

Part 3 Cumulative Problems

1. $e = 1 - r^{1-\gamma}\left[\dfrac{r_c^{\gamma} - 1}{\gamma(r_c - 1)}\right]$

3. $W = an^2\left(\dfrac{1}{V_2} - \dfrac{1}{V_1}\right) +$

   $nRT \ln\left(\dfrac{V_2 - bn}{V_1 - bn}\right)$

5. (a) $t_1 = \dfrac{L_f \dot{M} T_h}{P_h T_0}$;

   (b) $P = P_h\left[1 - \dfrac{T_0}{T_h}e^{P_h(t - t_1)/McT_h}\right]$,

   (c) $t_2 = t_1 + \dfrac{McT_h}{P_h}\ln\dfrac{T_h}{T_0}$, with L_f

   the heat of fusion of ice and c the specific heat of water.

Chapter 23

1. Several coulombs
3. (a) uud; (b) udd
5. About 10^9 N; about 10^6 times typical human weight
7. 8.2×10^{-8} N
9. $21.8\ \mu$C
11. $-0.18\hat{\imath} + 0.64\hat{\jmath}$ nN
13. (a) $\hat{\jmath}$; (b) $-\hat{\imath}$; (c) $(\hat{\imath} + 3\hat{\jmath})/$
    $\sqrt{10} \approx 0.032\hat{\imath} + 0.95\hat{\jmath}$
15. $14\hat{\imath} - 7.4\hat{\jmath}$ N
17. $15\ \mu$C
19. $1.6\hat{\imath} - 0.33\hat{\jmath}$ N
21. $\dfrac{kq^2}{a^2}(\sqrt{2} + \tfrac{1}{2})$
23. $q_2 = 143\ \mu$C; $q_3 = 116\ \mu$C
25. 3.8×10^9 N/C
27. (a) 2.2 MN/C; (b) 77 N
29. 5.15×10^{11} N/C
31. (a) $26\hat{\jmath}$ MN/C; (b) $-5.15\hat{\jmath}$ MN/C;
    (c) $-58\hat{\jmath}$ MN/C
33. $-4e$
35. (a) $\mathbf{E} = \dfrac{2kqy}{(a^2 + y^2)^{3/2}}\hat{\jmath}$;
    (b) $y = \pm a/\sqrt{2}$
37. (a) $8.0\hat{\jmath}$ GN/C; (b) $190\hat{\jmath}$ MN/C;
    (c) $216\hat{\jmath}$ kN/C
39. 39 pm
41. (a) $\mathbf{E} = 2\sqrt{3}\,kqa/x^3\hat{\imath}$;
    (b) $p = \sqrt{3}\,qa$
43. 2.1 MN/C
45. $-\dfrac{2k\lambda_0}{\pi\ell}\hat{\imath}$

47. -137 nC
51. 1.1 kN/C
53. (a) $2.5\ \mu$C/m; (b) 3.0×10^5 N/C;
    (c) 1.8 N/C
55. 3.3×10^{-12} kg
57. (a) 1.35 cm; (b) reverses direction, accelerates and exits field region at 3.8×10^5 m/s
59. $v > \ell\sqrt{qE/md}$
61. 2.8 Mm/s
63. $-14\ \mu$C/m
65. (a) 3.0 mN·m; (b) 11 mJ
67. (b) Attractive
69. $x = -8.09$ nm
71. $\dfrac{k\lambda_0}{\ell}\hat{\imath}$
73. $2\sqrt{2}kQ/\pi a^2$
75. 1.4 cm
77. 33.3 μC
79. $-4q$, a distance $3a$ to the right of $-q$
81. 50.7 kN/C, downward
83. 7.0 cm; 0.54 μC
85. (a) $(2kep/r^3)\hat{\imath}$; (b) $(-2kep/r^3)\hat{\imath}$, with the $+x$ direction to the right

Chapter 24

1. $+3\ \mu$C
5. (a) 1.7 kN·m^2/C; (b) 1.2 kN·m^2/C;
   (c) 0
7. 490 N·m^2/C
9. $\pi R^2 E$
11. (a) $-q/\varepsilon_0$; (b) $-2q/\varepsilon_0$; (c) 0; (d) 0
13. 4.9×10^4 N·m^2/C
15. (a) 0.69 MN·m^2/C
    (b) -0.69 MN·m^2/C (c) 0
17. 10 kN/C
19. 1.8×10^{12} N/C
21. (a) 2.2×10^5 N/C, outward;
    (b) 2.5×10^4 N/C, outward;
    (c) 4.0×10^3 N/C, inward
23. (a) $8kQ/R^2$, inward; (b) $kQ/4R^2$, inward; (c) (a) would not change, (b) would become 0
25. (a) 3.6 MN/C; (b) 3.8 MN/C;
    (c) (a) would not change, (b) would nearly double
27. as $1/r$
29. 6.3 μC/m^3
33. 3.6 mC/m^3
35. 58 nC/m^2
37. $E_1 = \sigma/2\varepsilon_0$, left; $E_2 = \sigma/2\varepsilon_0$,
    right; $E_3 = 3\sigma/2\varepsilon_0$, right;
    $E_4 = \sigma/2\varepsilon_0$, right

39. 18 N/C
41. (a) $x < 1.83$ cm; (b) $x > 54.5$ cm
43. 1.6×10^5 N/C
45. (a) $\rho = 0$; (b) $\sigma = 4.0$ mC/m^2;
    (c) other charges would destroy the symmetry, making σ nonuniform
47. (a) $0.50\ \mu$C/m^2; (b) 56 kN/C
49. (b) $-Q$
51. 1.8 MN/C
53. (a) 0; (b) 180 kN/C; (c) 0;
    (d) 20 kN/C
57. (a) $4kq/R^2$; (b) $3kq/4R^2$
59. (a) 0; (b) 1.3 MN/C; (c) 0
61. (a) 1.9×10^{11} N/C;
    (b) 3.6×10^{10} N/C
63. $\dfrac{\rho r}{3\varepsilon_0} - \dfrac{\rho a^3}{3\varepsilon_0 r^2}$
65. $\tfrac{1}{3}E_0 a^2$
67. 0.39 μs
69. $E_{in} = \rho_0 x^2/2\varepsilon_0 d$; $E_{out} = \rho_0 d/8\varepsilon_0$
73. (a) 0; (b) $(ac/\varepsilon_0 r^2)(e^{-1} - e^{-r/a})$;
    (c) $(ac/\varepsilon_0 r^2)(e^{-1} - e^{-b/a})$
77. $+10.6\ \mu$C/m^2 on both outer faces,
    $\pm36.9\ \mu$C/m^2 on inner faces

Chapter 25

1. 600 μJ
3. 3.0 kV
5. 910 V
7. 5.6 kV/m
9. Proton and He$^+$ both gain
   100 eV $= 1.6\times10^{-17}$ J; α gains
   200 eV $= 3.2\times10^{-17}$ J
11. 4.5 V
13. 0.23 MC
17. 6.1 μC
19. 27.2 V
21. $Q = 5.4$ nC, $r = 17$ cm
23. (a) 442 kV; (b) 9.2 Mm/s
25. kQ/R.
27. $V(x) = -\tfrac{1}{2}ax^2$
29. 52 nC/m
31. $x = -a/2$, $x = a/4$
33. (a) 2.6 kV; (b) 1.8 kV; (c) 0
35. $kQ\left(\dfrac{2}{c} + \dfrac{1}{b} - \dfrac{1}{a}\right)$
37. $2kQ/R$
39. $2\pi k\sigma(\sqrt{x^2 + b^2} - \sqrt{x^2 + a^2})$
41. (a) $V(x, y) = -E_0(x + y) =$
    $-150(x + y)$ V/m; (b) 150V
45. (a) $\mathbf{E} = -ay\hat{\imath} - ax\hat{\jmath}$
47. (a) 4 V; (b) $E_x = 1$ V/m,
    $E_y = -12$ V/m, $E_z = 3$ V/m

49. $E = \dfrac{kQx}{(x^2 + a^2)^{3/2}}\hat{\mathbf{i}}$

51. $E = V_0/R$, radially outward

53. 3 kV

55. (a) 34 kV, -9.0 kV; (b) 12.6 kV on each; (c) 24 nC

57. (a) 43 kV; (b) 1.7 MV/m; (c) 540 V; (d) 0

59. 1.55 keV $= 2.47 \times 10^{-16}$ J

61. (a) $\dfrac{2kqx}{x^2 - a^2}$; (b) $\dfrac{2kq}{x}$

63. (a) 27 kV; (b) no change

65. -7.5 V

67. (a) $x = -3$ m, 0 m, 1 m; (b) $\mathbf{E} = (3x^2 + 4x - 3)\hat{\mathbf{i}}$; (c) $x = -1.87$ m, 0.535 m

69. (a) 7.2 kV; (b) 14.4 kV

71. 14 cm, 1.7 nC

73. 23 nC/m

75. (a) $V(x) = \dfrac{k\lambda_0 x}{\ell^2}\left[x \ln\left(\dfrac{2x + \ell}{2x - \ell}\right) - \ell\right]$; (b) $\frac{1}{12}\lambda_0 \ell$; (c) $\dfrac{k\lambda_0 \ell}{12x}$

77. $y^2 + (x - \frac{5}{3}a)^2 = (\frac{4}{3}a)^2$; i.e., a circle

79. $\dfrac{kq}{2a}\ln\left(\dfrac{\sqrt{2} + 1}{\sqrt{2} - 1}\right) \simeq \dfrac{0.881\,kq}{a}$

Chapter 26

1. $3kq^2/\ell$

3. 4.88 kJ

5. $v = 2q\sqrt{\dfrac{k}{m\ell}}$

7. $6kq^2/a$

9. (a) 2.0 MV/m; (b) 9.9 kV; (c) 5.5 mJ

11. (a) 0.74 μC; (b) 40 kV

13. $\frac{1}{2}kQ^2\left(\dfrac{1}{a} - \dfrac{1}{b}\right)$

15. (b) $dW = 2kq\,dq/a$; (c) $W = kQ^2/a$

17. 1 km^3

19. 9×10^{30} J/m^3

21. 24 μJ

25. $(kQ^2/R)(2^{2/3} - 1) = 0.60$ mJ

27. $U/\ell = \pi a^4 \rho^2/16\varepsilon_0$

29. ± 14 C

31. 6.5 mF

33. 0.74 nF

35. 55 pF

39. 70 nF

41. 1 μF stores 15 times as much energy

43. (a) 30 μF; (b) 0.1 μF; (c) 0.01 μF

45. (a) 5.0 kW; (b) 250 μF; (c) 0.50 W

47. (a) Increases by factor of 2.5; (b) drops to 40% of its original value

51. Equal

53. (a) 6.0 μF; (b) 0.55 μF; (c) 0.83 μF, 1.3 μF, 1.5 μF, 2.2 μF, 2.8 μF, 3.7 μF

55. (a) 2 series pairs in parallel or two parallel pairs in series; (b) 4 in series

57. 0.86 μF

61. $\pm 1\%$

63. (a) 64 V; (b) drops from 16 mJ to 14 mJ

65. (a) 3.5 mm; (b) 87 kV

67. 126 pF

69. (a) 50 nC, 170 nC; (b) 23 μJ, 77 μJ

71. 1.4 mm

73. (a) 0.90 J; (b) 1.8 J; energy comes from work done by agent separating the plates

75. (a) 1.2 μF; (b) 24 μC

77. 13 min

79. $\dfrac{kq^2}{a}(2\sqrt{3} - \frac{15}{2}) \simeq -4.04\dfrac{kq^2}{a}$

81. (a) $C = \frac{1}{2}(\kappa + 1)C_0$; (b) $U = \dfrac{C_0 V_0^2}{\kappa + 1}$; (c) $F = \dfrac{2C_0 V_0^2(\kappa - 1)}{L(\kappa + 1)^2}$, into capacitor

83. (a) 75 mF; (b) 1.4×10^{12} J

85. (a) $Q^2/2\varepsilon_0 a$; (b) $Q^2/\varepsilon_0 a$; (a) is right since (b) includes the fields of *both* plates, and a plate doesn't experience a force from its own field

87. $31 d^2 kp^2/1280\ell^5$

89. 7.2 pF/m

Chapter 27

1. 9.4×10^{18}

3. 2.9×10^5 C

5. 1.9×10^{11}

7. 7.65 MA/m^2

9. 1.23 cm/s

11. 0.31 mA

13. (a) 37 A/m^2; (b) 86%

15. 9.71 μC

17. 0.17 V/m

19. 2.2×10^{-6} $\Omega \cdot$m

21. (a) 5.95×10^7 $(\Omega \cdot$m$)^{-1}$; (b) 4.5 $(\Omega \cdot$m$)^{-1}$

23. 6.4×10^{-15} s

25. 253°C

27. 25 Ω

29. 2.34 mA

31. 25 mA

33. 1.5 kA

35. (a) 17 mΩ; (b) 86 A; (c) 18 MA/m^2; (d) 1.7 V/m

37. $d_{Al} = 1.26\,d_{Cu}$

39. (a) 2.07 cm; (b) 2.60 cm; (c) aluminum

41. 34 mΩ

43. 1.38 kW

45. 160 μA

47. 240 Ω

49. 48 W

51. 960 W$\cdot$h $= 3.5$ MJ

53. Resistor with more power has $\sqrt{2}$ times greater diameter

55. (a) 150 A; (b) 3.4 km

57. 0.54 mA

59. 0.94 Ω

61. (a) 8.7 kA; (b) 15%

63. 2.9 A

65. 2.5 A

67. 120 A

69. 17 J/K

Chapter 28

5. 1.4 hours

7. 6.0 V

9. 229 kΩ

11. 1.5 A

13. 0.02 Ω

15. 45 Ω

17. 30 A

19. R_1 for each

21. 24

23. (a) 162 Ω; (b) 125 mW

25. (a) $\dfrac{R_1 \mathcal{E}}{R + 2R_1}$; (c) $\frac{1}{2}\mathcal{E}$

27. 2.45 W

29. $(\mathcal{E}_2 R_1 - \mathcal{E}_1 R_2)/(R_1 + R_2)$

31. $\frac{7}{5}R$

33. $I_1 = 2.79$ A, $I_2 = 2.36$ A,
    $I_3 = 0.429$ A
35. $\mathscr{E}_2 > 5.49$ V
37. 8.5 nA, downward
39. 1.6% low
41. 1.2 kW41.24.99 kΩ
43. (a) 20 V; (b) 3.0 mA
49. (a) 9.0 V; (b) 1.5 ms; (c) 0.32 μF
51. (a) 0.35 s; (b) 0.17 s
53. 3.4 μF
55. (a) $I_1 = 25$ mA, $I_2 = 0$, $V_C = 0$;
    (b) $I_1 = I_2 = 10$ mA, $V_C = 60$ V;
    (c) $I_1 = 0$, $I_2 = 10$ mA,
    $V_C = 60$ V; (d) $I_1 = I_2 = 0$,
    $V_C = 0$
57. (a) $3\mathscr{E}/4R$; (b) $2\mathscr{E}/3R$
59. 3.4 kΩ
61. (a) 4.51 V; (b) 35.2 Ω
63. 1.07 A, left to right
65. (a) 13.0 V; (b) 2.23 mA
67. 15.9 ms
69. 83 μs
71. (a) 0; (b) 1.0 A; (c) 0.75 A; (d) 0;
    (e) 1.0 A; (f) 3.0 A; (g) 3.0 A;
    (h) 1.0 A
73. (b) 22 hours

Chapter 29

1. (a) 1.6 mT; (b) 2.3 mT
3. (a) 2.0×10^{-14} N; (b) 1.0×10^{-14} N;
   (c) 0
5. (a) $-1.1\hat{\imath} +1.5\hat{\jmath} + 1.7\hat{k}$ mN
7. $\mathbf{B} = 0.13\hat{k}$ T; $\mathbf{v}_2 = -14\hat{\imath}$ km/s
9. $-24.9\hat{\imath} - 40.1\hat{\jmath} - 87.3\hat{k}$ fN
11. 40.1° or 140°
13. (a) $1.2\hat{\imath} + 0.45\hat{\jmath}$ fN;
    (b) $-1.2\hat{\imath} + 35\hat{\jmath} - 15\hat{k}$ fN
15. 3.9 mm
17. 1.5 mT
19. $r_{proton} = 43 \, r_{electron}$
21. (a) 86 mT; (b) 1.01 keV
23. 1.3 μs
25. (a) 15 MHz; (b) 19 MeV; (c) 6467
29. 0.43%
31. 1.1 mm, 2.6 mm
33. 0.38 N
35. (a) 49 mT; (b) 0.73 N/m
37. 43 kN
39. 0.12 T
41. 21 mN, diagonally toward the
    upper right
45. 76 mT
47. (a) 1.1 mA·m^2; (b) 1.0 mN·m

49. 0.15 A·m^2
51. (a) 0.35 A·m^2; (b) 4.2×10^{-2} N·m
53. 1.97×10^{-25} J $= 1.23 \, \mu$e V
55. $42\hat{\imath} + 88\hat{\jmath} - 25\hat{k}$ fN
57. 30 km
59. 0.27 N, to right
61. 0.010 T
63. 6.8 mm
65. (a) 12.8 N/m; (b) 24.9 cm
67. $I = Mg/2Bd$
69. 77 mT
73. $\mu = 9.25\times10^{-24}$ A·m^2

Chapter 30

1. 12 cm
3. 1.23 mT
5. 3.8 GA
7. 0.875 cm^2
9. 732
11. Between the wires, 2.0 cm from
    center of 5.0-A wire
13. 23° west of magnetic north
15. $\mu_0 I/4a$, into page
17. $\dfrac{\mu_0 I}{4ab}(b - a)$, out of the page
19. 5 μN
21. 3.8 mm
23. 13.2 μN/m, at 71.6° below
    right-pointing horizontal
25. 23.5 mN
27. 7.0 A
29. 24 A
31. 123 mA
33. (a) 0; (b) 0.36 mT; (c) 1.9 mT;
    (d) 0.50 mT
35. (a) $\mu_0 J_0 r^2/3R$; (b) $\mu_0 J_0 R^2/3r$
37. (a) 5.3 mm; (b) maximum;
    (c) 130 A
41. (a) 0; (b) $\dfrac{\mu_0 I(r^2 - a^2)}{2\pi r(b^2 - a^2)}$; (c) $\dfrac{\mu_0 I}{2\pi r}$
43. 17 T
45. (a) 38 mT; (b) 5.9 μT
47. 3.3 m
49. $1/2\pi nR$
51. $\chi_M = -1.6\times10^{-3}$; diamagnetic
53. 7.2×10^3
55. $I_{outer} = 2I_{inner}$, in opposite direction
57. Out of page
59. 1 km
61. (a) 8.0 μT; (b) 4.0 μT; (c) 0
63. (a) 0.40 mT; (b) 1.0 nT
65. $B = \mu_0 I/\ell$ inside, $B = 0$ outside
67. 55A

Chapter 31

3. 1.4×10^{-4} T·m^2
5. 160 T/s
7. (a) 0.30 A; (b) 0.20 A
9. $B^2\ell^3 v/R$
11. 39 V
13. 0.32 V
15. 9.0 μA, counterclockwise in
    Fig. 31-5
17. (a) $I = -25$ mA for $0 < t < 2$ s;
    $I = 0$ for 2 s $< t < 3$ s;
    $I = +25$ mA for 3 s $< t < 5$ s;
    (b) $P = 3.1$ mW for $0 < t < 2$ s
    and 3 s $< t < 5$ s; otherwise 0
19. (a) Left to right; (b) 140 μA;
    (c) 28 μA
21. (a) $I_R = -I_{peak} \cos \omega t$, where
    (b) $I_{peak} = 110$ m A; (c) 0
23. 0.16 s
25. 7.1 mV
27. (a) Downward; (b) $(B\ell v)^2/R$
29. $v_{final} = \mathscr{E}/B\ell$; R affects time to
    reach final speed
31. (a), (b) Both 6.7 m A,
    counterclockwise; (c) 0.44 mW in
    both cases
33. (a) 25 m A; (b) 1.25 mN;
    (c) 2.5 mW; (d) 2.5 mW
35. (a) 77 mV; (b) 94 mV
37. 1.57 μN
39. $dB/dt = 10$ T/s
41. $E = \frac{1}{2}bh$, to the left above the field
    region and to the right below
43. $\frac{16}{3}B_0 x_0^2$
45. 42 mA, clockwise
47. $mgR/B^2\ell^2$
49. $\frac{1}{2}BR^2\omega$
51. 58 T/ms
53. $I = at^2$, with $a = 0.81$ A/s^2
57. (a) 2.4 km; (b) 2.89 kW; (c) $6.94;
    (d) their generators get harder to
    turn, so they use more fuel
59. (a) $J = rb/2\rho$; (b) $P = \pi b^2 a^4 h/8\rho$

Chapter 32

1. 120 V
3. 12 V
5. (a) $-2\pi fMI_p \cos 2\pi ft$; (b) 133 mH
7. $\mu_0 n^2 \pi R^2 \ell$
9. $\dfrac{\mu_0 \ell}{2\pi} \ln\left(\dfrac{a + w}{a}\right)$
11. 3.2 mH

13. 40 kV

15. 1350

17. (a) 2.1 A; (b) −1.5 A (minus indicates direction reversal)

19. 26 A/ms

21. 11 A

25. 130 Ω

27. 15 s

29. (a) 0.11 H; (b) 20 mA

31. (a) 76 mA; (b) 4.4 V (c) 7.6 V; (d) 2.2 A/s; (e) 0.58 W

33. 400 Ω

35. 50 Ω

37. (a) 2.0 A; (b) 6.0 A; (c) 60 V

39. 100 mA

41. (a) 52 J; (b) 1.8 s

43. (a) 2.5 kW; (b) no

45. 15 W

47. (a) 5.7 MJ; (b) 31 mΩ; (c) 39 s

49. 9.9×10^8 J/m^3

51. 10^{11} times that of gasoline; 2600 times that of U-235

53. Smaller by factor $1/4n^2R^2$

55. 10^{18} J

57. $|\mathscr{E}| = 2Mbt$

59. 48 H

61. (a) 18.4 V; (b) 0; (c) 70 V

63. $(\mu_0 I^2 \ln 100)/4\pi$

65. (a) $L = \dfrac{\mu_0 N^2 \ell}{2\pi} \ln\left(\dfrac{R + \ell}{R}\right)$

67. (a) $P = I_0^2 R e^{-2Rt/L}$

69. $E/B = 1/\sqrt{\mu_0 \varepsilon_0} = 3.0 \times 10^8$ m/s $= c$

Chapter 33

1. $V = 325 \sin(314t)$, with V in volts and t in seconds.

3. 9.9 V

5. (a) 350 mA; (b) 1.50 kHz

9. $V_{\text{rms}} = V_p/\sqrt{3}$

11. $I_1 = I_p \cos\phi$, $I_2 = I_p \sin\phi$

13. 45 mA

15. (a) 804 Ω; (b) 48.2 Ω; (c) 2.41 Ω

17. 1.47 μF

19. 15.9 kHz

21. (a) 10 mA; (b) 14 V; (c) 7.7 mA

23. 2.7 mC

25. 0.32 A

27. 8.23 kHz or 5.17×10^4 s^{-1}

29. 4.9 pF to 42 pF

31. 3.65 F

33. (a) 1.63 A; (b) 4.58 μs

35. (a) 63 V; (b) 89 V; (c) 764 mA; (d) 99 μJ

37. (a) $1/\sqrt{2}$; (b) 1/2; (c) $-1/\sqrt{2}$; (d) 1/2

39. Close switch B for 702 ms, then simultaneously close A and open B. After 351 ms, open A; (b) 400 V

41. 0.22 μF

43. 16.2 V

45. (a) 0.43 μH; (b) $R > 16$ Ω

47. (a) $V_{Rp} = 23.86$ V, $V_{Cp} = 28.19$ V, $V_{Lp} = -28.05$ V; (b) $V_{R\text{rms}} = 16.9$ V, $V_{C\text{rms}} = 256$ V, $V_{L\text{rms}} = 255$ V

49. (a) above; (b) current lags by approximately 49°

51. (a) I leads V by 63.6°; (b) I lags V by 81.7°

53. 500 W

55. (a) 80 Ω; (b) 97 Hz

57. (a) 5.5%; (b) 9.1%; (c) large

59. 5.0 mA

61. (a) 8.91 V; (b) 1.38 kΩ

63. $4f_1$

65. 13.2 V

67. 0.64 Ω

69. 8.25 V

71. 36.2 nF, 11.5 nF

73. $C = \dfrac{L[\ln(U_0/U_1)]^2}{4\pi^2 N^2 R^2}$

77. $R = 400$ Ω, $L = 67$ mH, $C = 0.094$ μF

79. 1.3 kN/m

Chapter 34

1. 1.3 nA

5. (a) 0; (b) 8.33×10^{-13} T; (c) 9.26×10^{-13} T

7. $-x$

9. (a) $\sqrt{2}E$; (b) $(\hat{\jmath} - \hat{\imath})/\sqrt{2}$

13. 0.24 s

15. 1 ns

17. 600 m

19. 2.32

21. 5000 km

23. 27.3 MHz

25. 15 kV/m

27. 1.1 pT

29. 63°

31. 30°

33. $0.34S_0$

35. $0.304S_0$

37. $S = S_0 \cos^2 \omega t$, with $\omega = 20\pi$ s^{-1}

39. 12 GW/m^2

41. 2.7×10^{-10} W/m^2

43. (a) 157 W/m^2; (b) 344 V/m; (c) 1.15 μT

45. 1.1%

47. 3.9×10^{26} W

49. (a) 8.3×10^{-26} W/m^2; (b) 7.9×10^{-12} V/m

51. (a) 4.6 kW; (b) 52.5 mV/m

53. (a) as $1/r$; (b) as $1/r^2$

55. 6.0 mPa

57. 5.0 μN

59. 6.18×10^3 years

61. $E_p = 40$ V/m, $B_p = 0.13$ μT

63. 1/4

65. 4.2 μN

67. 17.7 μPa

71. (a) 1.0 MV/m; (b) 4.3 mm; (c) 64 mJ; (d) 2.1×10^{-10} kg·m/s; (e) 64 W

73. Long, with cylindrical symmetry

75. 0.3 μm

Part 4   Cumulative Problems

1. 6.0 MV

3. 15.7 mA, top to bottom

5. (b) $c/\sqrt{\kappa}$

Chapter 35

1. 15°

3. ±0.5°

5. (a) 2; (b) 210°

9. 126 nm

11. 1.57

13. Ethyl alcohol

15. 1.83

17. 5.1 m

19. (a) 3.20×10^{14} Hz; (b) 937 nm

21. (a) 49.8°; (b) 42.2°; (c) 22.4°

23. (a) 61.3°; (b) 80.9°; (c) there is none

27. $\sqrt{2}$

29. 2.62×10^8 m/s

31. 53.5°

35. 36.5° to 38.1°

37. About 3.4 cm

39. 67.5°

41. 36.9°

43. 1.96×10^8 m/s

45. 2.32 m

47. 28.8°

49. (a) base; (b) 63.2°

51. 35.2°

53. $n = 1.17$

59. (b) 42.1°

Chapter 36

1. Mirror surface 55° to horizontal
3. (a) 30 cm; (b) virtual, 60 cm behind mirror
5. (a) Image height is 1/4 object height; (b) inverted
7. (a) 12.4 cm in front of mirror; (b) 3.22 times
9. (a) 24.3 cm behind the mirror; (b) 29 mm; (c) virtual
11. 18 cm in front of mirror
13. 7.42 cm
15. 40 cm
17. (a) 20 cm; (b) reduced to 55% actual size
19. 12 cm
21. 47.7 mm
23. 2.3 mm
27. (a) Real, inverted, 7.7 cm high; (b) virtual, upright, 7.7 cm high
29. 29 cm or 41 cm from the candle
31. 40 cm
35. $\ell' = -67.9$ cm
37. 2
39. 7.56 mm
41. Virtual image, 81 cm from lens on same side as object
43. (a) 40 cm; (b) 160 cm; (c) −170 cm (the lens becomes a diverging lens)
45. (a) 15.3 cm; (b) 1.63
47. Real image, magnified 2.74 times
49. (a) 5.0 m; (b) 37 cm
51. (a) Enlarged 2.9 times at 110 mm
55. 1.85 cm
57. −17.7 cm
59. (a) 2.0 m; (b) 3.0 m in front of the mirror
61. 25 cm
63. 96 cm
65. ($\ell = 85.4$ cm, $m = -1.81$); ($\ell = 155$ cm, $m = -0.552$)
67. Real image, 109 cm on other side of lens
69. (a) 8.31 mm; (b) 92 cm from my eye
71. No, one is virtual, the other real
75. (a) 1.1 m from primary; (b) elliptical

Chapter 37

1. 484 nm
3. (a) 95 cm; (b) 3.8 mm
5. 1.25 mm
7. 17.7 cm, 44.7 cm
9. 0.034°

11. (a) 17.1 cm; (b) 20.0 cm
13. 4
15. (a) 4.8°, 9.7°; (b) 2.9°, 6.8°
17. (a) 8.97°; (b) 51.3°
19. (a) 2nd; (b) 1st
21. 6th order
23. 3200
25. 415 nm, 581 nm
27. Echelle grating has 60% greater resolving power
29. 2000
31. 103 nm
33. 424 nm, 594 nm
35. (a) 75.2 nm; (b) violet
37. 368 nm
39. 5
41. 236
43. 375 nm (i.e., $\frac{3}{4}\lambda$)
45. 545 nm
47. 1022
49. $a/\lambda = 1$
51. 26.6°
53. 0.0162
55. 1.3 m
57. 2.0 μm
59. 6.9 km
61. For diameters greater than 14 cm
63. 7645
65. 0.01 nm
67. 77.2 nm
69. 46 m
71. 484 nm
75. 5542
77. Every 2.8 s
79. 6.0 km/s
81. 3.0 μm

Part 5 Cumulative Problems

1. $m_0 = (n - 1)d(\sin\alpha)/\lambda_0$
3. 3.2 min
5. (b) $x = \dfrac{\sqrt{3}}{2a}\ln\left[2(1 - ay - \sqrt{\tfrac{1}{4} - 2ay + a^2y^2})\right]$

Chapter 38

1. (a) 4.50 h; (b) 4.56 h; (c) 4.62 h
3. (a) $v/c = \tan\theta$, with θ the amplitude of the sine curve. Here $\theta = 20''$ (20/3600 degree), giving $v = 29$ km/s; (b) the orbit is nearly circular
5. 41 cm
7. (a) 8.26 h; (b) 6.28 h
9. (a) 0.857c; (b) 9.69 min
11. 0.14c

13. $c/\sqrt{2}$
15. Twin A: 83 years; twin B: 40 years
17. 0.96c
19. 0.996c
21. (a) B first, by 5.74 min; (b) A first, by 13.1 min; (c) essentially simultaneous
23. A, by 6.4 My
27. (a) 21.7 m; (b) 12.4 m
29. 0.918c
31. 3.4
33. (a) 2.1 MeV; (b) 1.6 MeV
35. 0.36c
37. 5.3×10^{-8} kg·m/s, about the same as the insect
39. 5.9×10^{-30} kg
41. (a) 0.020c; (b) 0.55c; (c) 0.94c; (d) essentially c
47. (a) -0.75×10^{10} ly²; (b) 99×10^{10} ly²; events can be causally related only if $(\Delta s)^2 > 0$
49. 0.274c
51. (a) 16 ns; (b) 4.8 m
53. (a) 4.2 ly; (b) −2.4 years (i.e., B occurs earlier)
55. 0.395c
57. 0.9999953c
59. 598 m
61. 0.95c

Chapter 39

1. (a) 4.1 neV; (b) 2.1 eV; (c) 12.4 keV
3. (a) 1.6×10^{-24} J; (b) 3.9×10^{26} photons/s
5. (a) 1.7×10^{28} s⁻¹; (b) 3.2×10^{15} s⁻¹; (c) 1.3×10^{18} s⁻¹
7. β ($n_1 = 5$)
9. $n = 229$
11. 73 cm/s
13. 1.6 km/s
15. Electron: no; proton: yes
17. 12 pm
19. 0.0034°
21. 2.5 h
23. 20 minutes
25. 0.64 kg
27. 0
29. $\bar{u}\,\bar{u}\,\bar{d}$
31. $+e$
33. (a) 10.2 eV; (b) $n_1 = 2$, $n_2 = 1$
35. The proton
37. 1.16×10^6 m/s
39. 18 pm
41. (a) 1 eV; (b) 5 MeV
43. 10−20 billion years

Index

Page numbers in *italics* refer to illustrations; page numbers followed by t refer to tables.

F

GEOPHYSICAL AND ASTROPHYSICAL DATA

EARTH

Mass	5.97×10^{24} kg
Mean radius	6.37×10^{6} m
Orbital period	3.16×10^{7} s (365.3 days)
Mean distance from Sun	1.50×10^{11} m
Mean density	5.5×10^{3} kg/m^3
Surface gravity	9.81 m/s^2
Surface pressure	1.013×10^{5} Pa
Magnetic moment	8.0×10^{22} A·m^2

SUN

Mass	1.99×10^{30} kg
Mean radius	6.96×10^{8} m
Orbital period (about galactic center)	6×10^{15} s (200 My)
Mean distance from galactic center	2.6×10^{20} m
Power output (luminosity)	3.85×10^{26} W
Mean density	1.4×10^{3} kg/m^3
Surface gravity	274 m/s^2
Surface temperature	5.8×10^{3} K

MOON

Mass	7.35×10^{22} kg
Mean radius	1.74×10^{6} m
Orbital period	2.36×10^{6} s (27.3 days)
Mean distance from Earth	3.85×10^{8} m
Mean density	3.3×10^{3} kg/m^3
Surface gravity	1.62 m/s^2

COMPARATIVE ENERGIES

Supernova explosion	10^{46} J	World per capita energy use, per second	2×10^{3} J
Sun's output, per second	4×10^{26} J	Food energy used by human body,	
Solar energy incident on Earth, per second	2×10^{17} J	per second	10^{2} J
Explosive yield of MX missile		Energy to lift this book 1 foot	8 J
(10 350-kiloton nuclear warheads)	1×10^{16} J	Particle energy in Superconducting	3.2×10^{-6} J
Human energy use, per second	10^{13} J	Super Collider	(20 TeV)
1 ounce uranium-235	2.3×10^{12} J	Energy release in U-235 fission (200 MeV)	3.2×10^{-11} J
1 gallon seawater		Energy release in deuterium-tritium fusion	2.8×10^{-12} J
(with deuterium content as fusion fuel)	4.7×10^{10} J		(17.6 MeV)
1 ton of coal	2.6×10^{10} J	Energy release in forming hydrogen atom	2.2×10^{-18} J
Electrical output of large power plant,			(13.6 eV)
per second	10^{9} J	Thermal energy kT at room temperature	4×10^{-21} J
1 gallon of gasoline	1.3×10^{8} J		(0.025 eV)
1500-kg car going 60 mph	6.3×10^{5} J	Thermal energy kT associated with cosmic	4×10^{-23} J
U.S. per capita energy use, per second	10^{4} J	background radiation	(0.23 meV)